Houghton Mifflin Math

fraction

radius

angle

HOUGHTON MIFFLIN

BOSTON

Printed in the U.S.A.

ISBN: 978-0-618-27722-3 ISBN: 0-618-27722-6

13 14-0868-14 13 12 11
4500329064

Program Authors & Consultants

Authors

Dr. Carole Greenes

Professor of Mathematics Education

Boston University
Boston, MA

Dr. Matt Larson

Curriculum Specialist for Mathematics

Lincoln Public Schools
Lincoln, NE

Dr. Miriam A. Leiva

Distinguished Professor of Mathematics Emerita

University of North Carolina
Charlotte, NC

Dr. Jean M. Shaw

Professor Emerita of Curriculum and Instruction

University of Mississippi
Oxford, MS

Dr. Lee Stiff

Professor of Mathematics Education

North Carolina State University
Raleigh, NC

Dr. Bruce R. Vogeli

Clifford Brewster Upton Professor of Mathematics

Teachers College, Columbia University
New York, NY

Karol Yeatts

Associate Professor

Barry University
Miami, FL

Consultants

Strategic Consultant

Dr. Liping Ma

Senior Scholar

Carnegie Foundation for the Advancement of Technology
Palo Alto, CA

Language and Vocabulary Consultant

Dr. David Chard

Professor of Reading

University of Oregon
Eugene, OR

Reviewers

Grade K

Hilda Kendrick
W E Wilson
Elementary School
Jefferson, IN

Debby Nagel
Assumption
Elementary School
Cincinnati, OH

Jen Payet
Lake Ave. Elementary School
Saratoga Springs, NY

Karen Sue Hinton
Washington Elementary
School
Ponca City, OK

Grade 1

Karen Wood
Clay Elementary School
Clay, AL

Paula Rowland
Bixby North Elementary
School
Bixby, OK

Stephanie McDaniel
B. Everett Jordan
Elementary School
Graham, NC

Juan Melgar
Lowrie Elementary School
Elgin, IL

Sharon O'Brien
Echo Mountain School
Phoenix, AZ

Grade 2

Sally Bales
Akron Elementary School
Akron, IN

Rose Marie Bruno
Mawbey Street Elementary
School
Woodbridge, NJ

Kiesha Doster
Berry Elementary School
Detroit, MI

Marci Galazkiewicz
North Elementary School
Waukegan, IL

Ana Gaspar
Lowrie Elementary School
Elgin, IL

Elana Heinoren
Beechfield Elementary
School
Baltimore, MD

Kim Terry
Woodland Elementary School
West
Gages Lake, IL

Megan Burton
Valley Elementary School
Pelham, AL

Kristy Ford
Eisenhower Elementary
School
Norman, OK

Grade 3

Jenny Chang
North Elementary School
Waukegan, IL

Patricia Heintz
Harry T. Stewart
Elementary School
Corona, NY

Shannon Hopper
White Lick Elementary School
Brownsburg, IN

Allison White
Kingsley Elementary School
Naperville, IL

Amy Simpson
Broadmoore Elementary
School
Moore, OK

Reviewers

Grade 4

Barbara O'Hanlon
Maurice & Everett Haines Elementary School
Medford, NJ

Connie Rapp
Oakland Elementary School
Bloomington, IL

Pam Rettig
Solheim Elementary School
Bismarck, ND

Tracy Smith
Blanche Kelso Bruce Academy
Detroit, MI

Brenda Hancock
Clay Elementary School
Clay, AL

Karen Scroggins
Rock Quarry Elementary School
Tuscaloosa, AL

Lynn Fox
Kendall-Whittier Elementary School
Tulsa, OK

Grade 5

Jim Archer
Maplewood Elementary School
Indianapolis, IN

Maggie Dunning
Horizon Elementary School
Hanover Park, IL

Mike Intoccia
McNichols Plaza
Scranton, PA

Jennifer LaBelle
Washington Elementary School
Waukegan, IL

Anne McDonald
St. Luke The Evangelist School
Glenside, PA

Ellen O'Rourke
Bower Elementary School
Warrenville, IL

Gary Smith
Thomas H. Ford Elementary School
Reading, PA

Linda Carlson
Van Buren Elementary School
Oklahoma City, OK

Grade 6

Robin Akers
Sonoran Sky Elementary School
Scottsdale, AZ

Ellen Greenman
Daniel Webster Middle School
Waukegan, IL

Angela McCray
Abbott Middle School
West Bloomfield, MI

Mary Popovich
Horizon Elementary School
Hanover Park, IL

Debbie Taylor
Sonoran Sky Elementary School
Scottsdale, AZ

Across Grades

Jacqueline Lampley
Hewitt Elementary School
Trussville, AL

Rose Smith
Five Points Elementary School
Orrville, AL

Winnie Tepper
Morgan County Schools
Decatur, AL

Place Value/Addition and Subtraction

1 Place Value of Whole Numbers and Decimals

Algebra Indicates lessons that include algebra instruction.

2 Add and Subtract Whole Numbers

FINISHING THE UNIT

Unit 1
Literature Connection
The Most Amazing Sights in Nature
page 638

WR Indicates WEEKLY WR READER Connection

Multiplication, Division, and Algebra

Algebra Indicates lessons that include algebra instruction.

Divide by Two-Digit Numbers

FINISHING THE UNIT

Unit 2
Literature Connection
Ready for Anything
page 640

WR Indicates 

Measurement/Data and Graphing

6 Units of Measure

7 Graph Data

Algebra Indicates lessons that include algebra instruction.

8 Data and Statistics

FINISHING THE UNIT

Unit 3
Literature Connection
Ships of the Desert
pages 641

WR Indicates WEEKLY WR READER® Connection

Addition and Subtraction of Fractions and Decimals

9 Number Theory and Fraction Concepts

Algebra Indicates lessons that include algebra instruction.

10 Add and Subtract Fractions

11 Add and Subtract Decimals

FINISHING THE UNIT

Unit 4
Literature Connection
The Fruitomatic
page 642

 Indicates 

Multiplication and Division of Fractions and Decimals

12 Multiply and Divide Fractions

13 Multiply Decimals

Algebra Indicates lessons that include algebra instruction.

14 Divide Decimals

FINISHING THE UNIT

Unit 5
Literature Connection
The World's Largest Trees
page 644

WR Indicates  WEEKLY WR READER Connection

Geometry and Measurement

15 Plane Figures and Geometric Concepts

16 Perimeter, Area, and Circumference

Algebra Indicates lessons that include algebra instruction.

17 Solid Figures, Surface Area, and Volume

FINISHING THE UNIT

Unit 6
Literature Connection
No Place to Go
page 646

WR Indicates  WEEKLY WR READER® Connection

Ratio, Proportion, Percent, and Probability

18 Ratio and Proportion

19 Percent

UNIT 7 Ratio, proportion, Percent, and Probability

Algebra Indicates lessons that include algebra instruction.

20 Probability

FINISHING THE UNIT

Unit 7
Literature Connection
Numbers
page 647

WR Indicates  WEEKLY WR READER® Connection

Algebra, Integers, and Coordinate Graphing

21 Equations and Functions

22 Integers

Algebra Indicates lessons that include algebra instruction.

23 Coordinate Graphing

Unit 8
Literature Connection
Treasure Hunt
page 648

FINISHING THE UNIT

BOOK RESOURCES

WR Indicates WEEKLY WR READER Connection

Test-Taking Tips

You can do well on a math test if you know how to think about the math and how to take a test.

Your book helps you learn the math and practice the strategies you need to take tests. Look for these special signs on the pages.

are ways you can think about math when you take a test or solve any problem.

provides practice for answering the kinds of questions you will find on tests.

Cumulative Test Prep Practice

has practice in answering multiple-choice, open-response, and other test questions.

Two Important Things You Can Do Before A Test

- *Get plenty of sleep the night before.*
- *Eat a good breakfast in the morning.*

Use Reading Strategies to Think About Math

What you learn during reading class can help you understand how to solve word problems.

Understand What the Question Is

Read the problem once to be sure it makes sense to you. Ask yourself the question in your own words. Picture the situation and make a drawing if it helps.

Think About the Words

As you read, pay attention to the vocabulary words. If you don't understand a word, try to decide what it means by looking at the words around it.

Be Sure You Have Enough Information

Identify the information. Look at tables or graphs as well as the words. Think about what you already know that may help.

Plan What You Will Do

Think about the problem-solving plan and strategies. Decide what computation method is needed. Then make a plan and follow it.

Evaluate Your Work

Look back at what the question asked, and check that your answer really answers that question. Be sure you have labeled your answer.

Strategies for Taking Tests

You need to think differently about how to answer various kinds of questions.

All Questions

If you can't answer a question, go on to the next question. You can return to it if there is time.

Always check your computation.

Multiple-Choice Questions

Estimate the answer. This can help eliminate any unreasonable choices.

On bubble sheets, be sure you mark the bubble for the right question and for the right letter.

Short-Answer Questions

Follow the directions carefully. You may need to show your work, write an explanation, or make a drawing.

If you can't give a complete answer, show what you do know. You may get credit for part of an answer.

Long-Answer Questions

Take time to think about these questions because you often need to explain your answer.

When you finish, reread the question and answer to be sure you have answered the question correctly.

Student Scoring Rubric

Your teacher may use a scoring rubric to evaluate your work. An example is on the next page. Not all rubrics are the same, so your teacher may use a different one.

Scoring Rubric

Rating	My work on this problem
Exemplary (full credit)	• has no errors, has the correct answer, and shows that I checked my answer • is explained carefully and completely • shows all needed diagrams, tables, or graphs
Proficient (some credit)	• has small errors, has a close answer, and shows that I checked only the math • is explained but may have missing parts • shows most needed diagrams, tables, or graphs
Acceptable (little credit)	• has some errors, has an answer, and shows that I did not check my answer • is not explained carefully and completely • shows few needed diagrams, tables, or graphs
Limited (very little credit)	• has many errors and may not have an answer • is not explained at all • shows no needed diagrams, tables, or graphs

More Test Prep Help in Your Book

help you think about the math and how to answer a question.

gives you practice with questions like those that will be on tests.

Daily Review | Test Prep 

helps you review key concepts and practice the lesson skill the way you will see it on a test.

helps you review problem-solving strategies as you learn what tests are like.

gives you more test practice as you review the math that may be on the test.

Test Prep on the Net is another way to practice test-taking skills. Go to **eduplace.com/math/kids/mw/**.

Your Plan For Problem Solving!

Follow this four-part plan and you'll become a problem solving superstar!

Plan

Solve

Look Back

Remember!

Always START at the "Understand" step and move on. But if you can't get an answer, don't give up. Just go back and start again.

Always be sure you know what the question means! Here are some hints to help you:

- Read the problem twice.
- Replace any hard names you can't read with easier ones.
- Ignore extra information you don't need to solve the problem.
- Look for words that help you decide whether to add, subtract, multiply, or divide.
- Identify what the question is asking.

Start by making a plan!
Ask yourself:

- Do I have too much or too little information?
- Should I do more than one step?
- Which operation should I use?
- Should I use paper and pencil, mental math, or a calculator?
- What strategy should I use?

PROBLEM-SOLVING
Strategies
Draw a Picture
Find a Pattern
Guess and Check
Make an Organized List
Make a Table
Solve a Simpler Problem
Use Logical Reasoning
Work Backward
Write an Equation

Finally! Now you're ready to solve the problem!

- Carry out your plan.
- Test your method and strategy.
- Adjust your plan if needed.
- Check your calculations.

Congratulations! You've solved the problem. But is it correct? Once you have an answer, ask:

- Is my answer reasonable?
- Is my answer labeled correctly?
- Did I answer the question that was asked?
- Do I need to explain how I found the answer?

Study Skills

Knowing how to study math will help you do well in math class.

To be a good math student, you need to learn

- ★ **How to listen when your teacher is teaching**
- ★ **How to work alone and with others**
- ★ **How to plan your time**

Listen carefully when your teacher is showing the class how to do something new. Try to understand what is being taught as well as how to do each step.

If you don't understand what your teacher is showing the class, ask a question. Try to let your teacher know what you don't understand.

Listening carefully will also help you be ready to answer any questions your teacher may ask. Or you may be able to help another student.

Working Alone and With Others

When you work alone, try to connect the math you are learning to math you already know. Knowing how parts of math fit together helps you remember and understand the math.

When you work with others, help as much as you can. Cooperating is another word for working together. When people cooperate, they often learn more because they share ideas.

Planning Your Time

Doing your homework on time is part of being a good math student. Make sure that you take the assignment home with you.

Have a place at home to do your homework—it could be in your room or at the kitchen table or anywhere that works for your family.

Get extra help if you are having trouble. Write questions about what you don't understand. This will help your teacher give you the extra help you need.

Building Vocabulary

Reviewing Vocabulary

Here are some math vocabulary words that you should know.

place value	the position of a digit in a number that determines the value of the digit
rounding	to find about how many or about how much by expressing a number to the nearest ten, hundred, thousand, and so on
sum	the answer in addition
difference	the answer in subtraction

Reading Words and Symbols

In mathematics, numbers and computation with numbers can be read and written in different ways.

All these statements represent the same number:

- One thousand, two hundred thirty-four
- $(1 \times 1{,}000) + (2 \times 100) + (3 \times 10) + (4 \times 1)$
- 1,234

Different ways to read and write addition:

- The *sum of* 4,385 and 1,729 *is* 6,114.
- 4,385 *plus* 1,729 *equals* 6,114.

Different ways to read and write subtraction:

- The *difference between* 6,025 and 574 *is* 5,451.
- 6,025 *minus* 574 *equals* 5,451.

Write each of the following in a different way.

1. two thousand, eight hundred ninety-six
2. The sum of 3,333 and 197 is 3,530.
3. 26,257
4. $2{,}463 - 1{,}087 = 1{,}376$

Reading Test Questions

Choose the correct answer for each.

7. Which number represents the sum of these sets of blocks?

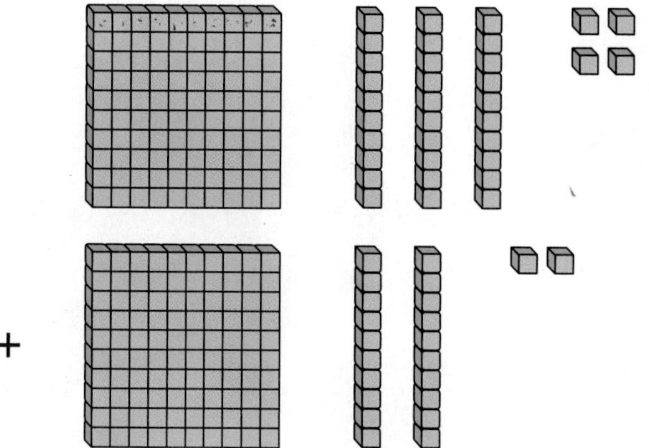

   a. 652

   b. 625

   c. 265

   d. 256

Represents means "stands for," or "shows," or "names."

8. Find the approximate difference between 3,867 and 2,124.

   a. 5,991

   b. 2,000

   c. 1,743

   d. 1,300

Approximate means to use estimation to find the answer.

9. Calculate the sum of 626 and 321.

   a. 305

   b. 947

   c. 957

   d. 1,057

To **calculate** you use a mathematical operation to find an exact answer.

Learning Vocabulary

Watch for these new words in this unit. Write their definitions in your journal.

base

exponent

power of ten

variable

expression

evaluate

Vocabulary

e • **Glossary**

e • **WordGame**

Literature Connection

Read "The Most Amazing Sights in Nature" on pages 638–639. Then work with a partner to answer questions about the story.

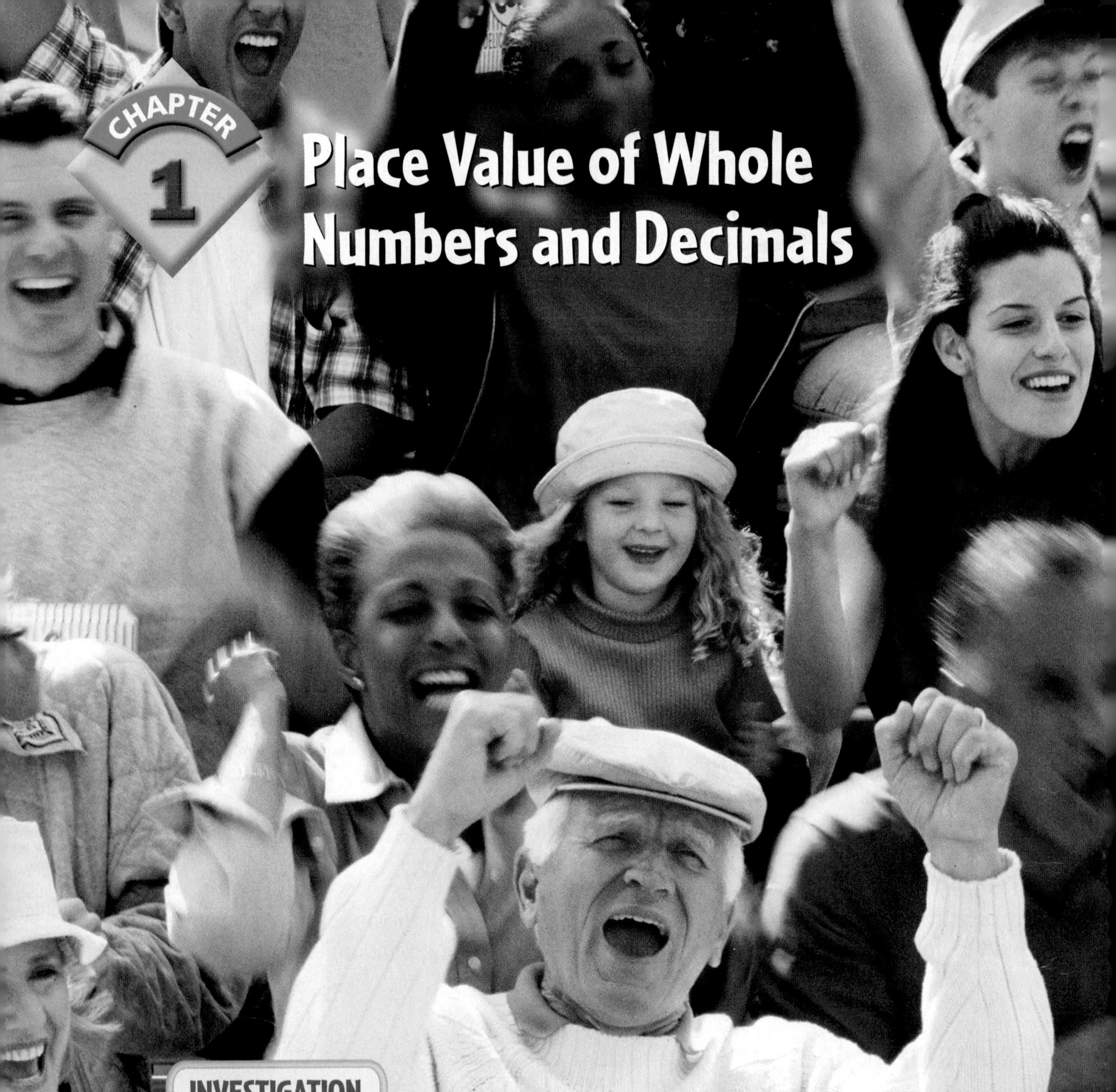

CHAPTER 1

Place Value of Whole Numbers and Decimals

INVESTIGATION

Use Data

Children and senior citizens are important parts of the American population. The graph shows estimates for 2020. Out of every 100 people in the United States in 2020, about how many will be either under 18 or over 64?

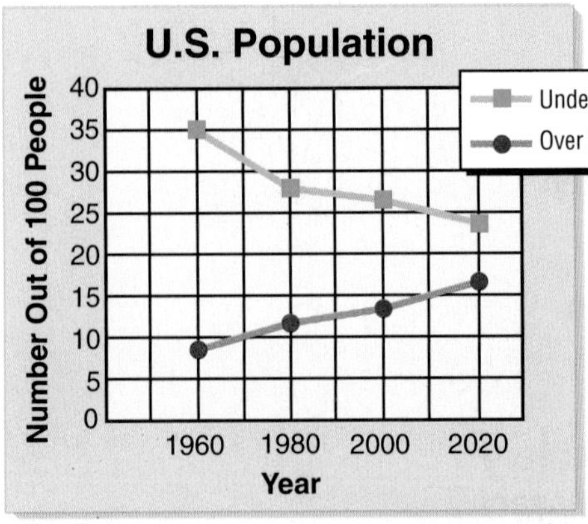

U.S. Population

Under 18
Over 64
Number Out of 100 People
0 5 10 15 20 25 30 35 40
1960 1980 2000 2020
Year

Chapter Pretest

Use this page to review and remember what you need to know for this chapter.

VOCABULARY

Choose the best word to complete each sentence.

1. In a number, each group of 3 digits separated by a comma is called a ____.
2. A ____ is a number with one or more digits to the right of a decimal point.
3. The ____ of "two hundred seventeen" is 217.

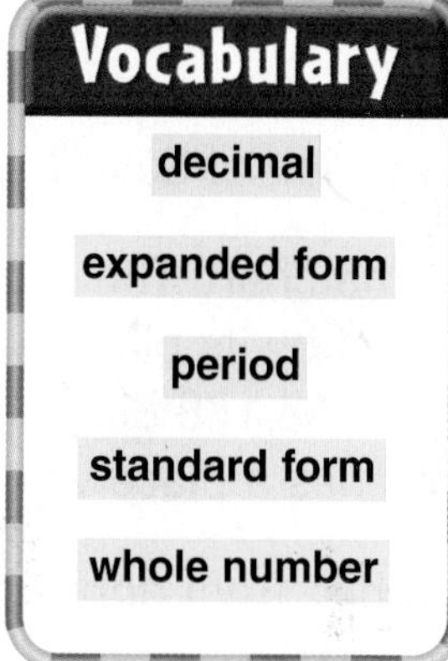

CONCEPTS AND SKILLS

Write the place value of the 7 in each number.

4. 374,928
5. 32,794
6. 87,312
7. 196,217

Write the number that is 10 more, 1,000 more, and 100,000 more.

8. 88,402
9. 197,651
10. 368,990
11. 71,161

Match each item in Column A with an item in Column B.

Column A	Column B
12. 50,892	**a.** $(5 \times 10{,}000) + (8 \times 100) + (9 \times 10) + (2 \times 1)$
13. 58,920	**b.** 58 hundredths
14. 5.89	**c.** five and eighty-nine hundredths
15. 0.58	**d.** 58 thousand, 920

Write the number that is greater.

16. 426,719
426,900
17. 2.20
0.87
18. 41,997
41,987
19. 5.51
5.49

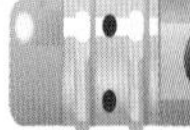

20. Why are the zeros important in 206,905?

Test Prep on the Net

Visit *Education Place* at **eduplace.com/kids/mw/** for more review.

Lesson 1

Place Value Through Hundred Thousands

Objective Read and write numbers through hundred thousands in standard and expanded form.

e Glossary

Vocabulary
- place value
- period
- standard form
- expanded form

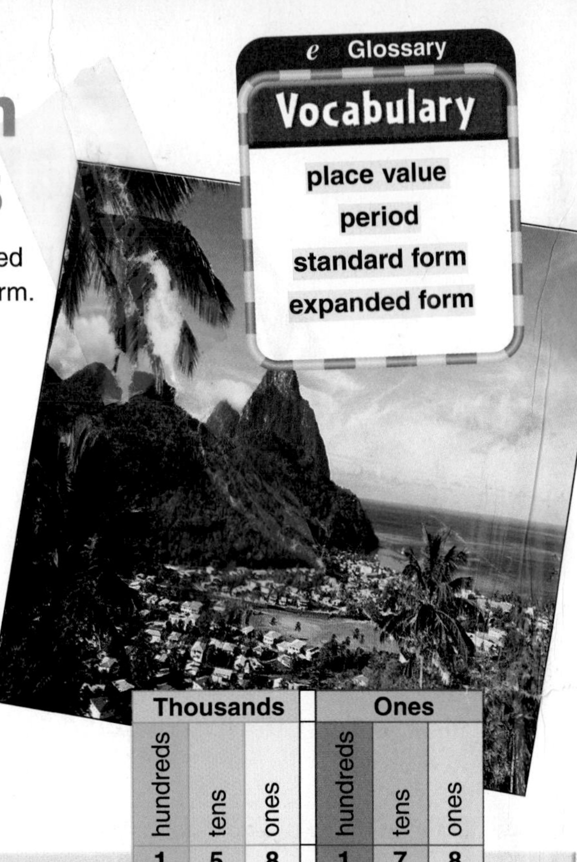

Learn About It

Saint Lucia is located in the Caribbean Sea. In 2001, the population of Saint Lucia was 158,178.

Look at the chart. The value of a digit in a number is determined by its place. For example, the first 8 from the left in 158,178 has a **place value** of 8,000. The second 8 has a place value of 8.

In a number, from right to left each group of 3 digits, called a **period**, is separated by a comma.

Thousands				Ones		
hundreds	tens	ones		hundreds	tens	ones
1	5	8	,	1	7	8

Different Ways to Read and Write Numbers

Way 1 You can use **standard form**.

158,178

Way 2 You can use **expanded form**.

$100{,}000 + 50{,}000 + 8{,}000 + 100 + 70 + 8$
$= (1 \times 100{,}000) + (5 \times 10{,}000)$
$+ (8 \times 1{,}000) + (1 \times 100) + (7 \times 10)$
$+ (8 \times 1)$

Way 3 You can use word form.

one hundred fifty-eight thousand,
one hundred seventy-eight

Way 4 You can use short word form.

158 thousand, 178

Guided Practice

Write each number in standard form.

1. 45 thousand, 79
2. three hundred sixty thousand, nine hundred eight
3. $400{,}000 + 8{,}000 + 600 + 20$

Ask Yourself
- What is the greatest place value in the number?
- What is the value for each place?

Explain Your Thinking ▶ In Exercise 1, how did you decide in which places to write the digits 4 and 5?

Practice and Problem Solving

Write each number in standard form.

4. 8 thousand, 752 **5.** 240 thousand, 357 **6.** 872 thousand, 12

7. one hundred forty thousand, four

8. eight hundred thirty thousand, three hundred four

9. 300,000 + 5,000 + 30 + 1 **10.** 900,000 + 10,000 + 4,000 + 60

11. 60,000 + 5 **12.** 800,000 + 800 + 8

Write the value of the underlined digit.

13. 2,346 **14.** 34,501 **15.** 257,824 **16.** 649,192

Write each number in word form, short word form, and expanded form.

17. 25,064 **18.** 693,412 **19.** 231,940 **20.** 60,080

Data **Use the table for Problems 21–25.**

21. What was the population of Nauru in 2001? Write the word name for the number.

22. Analyze Write the population of San Marino in expanded form. Is this greater or less than 20,000? Use expanded form to explain your answer.

23. Explain Suppose the population of Palau increases by 100. What would be the new population? Use place value to explain your answer.

24. Explain Suppose the population of Tuvalu decreased by 1,000. What would be the new population? Use place value to explain your answer.

Least Populated Countries in 2001

Name	Population
Vatican City	880
Tuvalu	10,991
Nauru	12,088
Palau	19,092
San Marino	27,336

25. Create and Solve Write your own problem involving information from the table. Solve your problem. Then have a partner solve the problem.

Daily Review Test Prep

Multiply or divide. (Grade 4)

26. 7 × 8 **27.** 48 ÷ 8

28. 54 ÷ 9 **29.** 12 × 12

30. 6 × 7 **31.** 63 ÷ 9

32. What is the value of the digit 7 in 379,548?

A 70 **C** 70,000

B 7,000 **D** 700,000

Extra Practice See page 25, Set A.

Lesson 2

Place Value and Exponents

Objective Read and write numbers through hundred thousands with exponents.

exponent ▼

10^5

▲ base

Learn About It

A short way to write the product 10 × 10 × 10 × 10 × 10 is 10^5. To read 10^5, say "ten to the fifth power." The 10 is the base. The small raised 5 is the exponent. The **base** is the factor that is repeated in the product. The **exponent** shows the number of times the base is used as a factor.

Thousands			Ones		
hundreds	tens	ones	hundreds	tens	ones
100,000	10,000	1,000	100	10	1
10×10×10×10×10	10×10×10×10	10×10×10	10×10	10	1
10^5	10^4	10^3	10^2	10^1	10^0

Think

Note the pattern

$1{,}000 = 10^3$

$100 = 10^2$

$10 = 10^1$

$1 = 10^0$

The place-value chart above shows each place as a **power of ten**. You can use powers of ten to write numbers in expanded form.

Different Ways to Write 473,826

Way 1 You can use expanded form.

(4 × 100,000) + (7 × 10,000) + (3 × 1,000) + (8 × 100) + (2 × 10) + (6 × 1)

Way 2 You can use expanded form with exponents.

$(4 \times 10^5) + (7 \times 10^4) + (3 \times 10^3) + (8 \times 10^2) + (2 \times 10^1) + (6 \times 10^0)$

Other Examples

A. 2 as the Base

$2^4 = 2 \times 2 \times 2 \times 2$

Read: "two to the fourth power"

Standard form: 16

B. 6 as the Base

$6^3 = 6 \times 6 \times 6$

Read: "six to the third power"

Standard form: 216

Guided Practice

Use exponents to write each number in expanded form.

1. 47,052 **2.** 712,943 **3.** 823,930

Ask Yourself

- What power of ten represents the greatest place value?

TEST TIPS

Explain Your Thinking ▶ In Exercise 2, how did you decide how to represent the value of the digit 7 in expanded form?

Practice and Problem Solving

Use exponents to write each number in expanded form.

4. 6,507 **5.** 980,062 **6.** 107,914 **7.** 728,050 **8.** 43,207

Write each number in standard form.

9. $(7 \times 10^4) + (5 \times 10^3) + (3 \times 10^2) + (2 \times 10^1) + (8 \times 10^0)$

10. The base is five, and the exponent is two.

11.
$2^5 = 32$
$2^4 = 16$
$2^3 = 8$
$2^2 = 4$
$2^1 = \blacksquare$
$2^0 = \blacksquare$

12.
$3^5 = 243$
$3^4 = 81$
$3^3 = 27$
$3^2 = \blacksquare$
$3^1 = \blacksquare$
$3^0 = \blacksquare$

13.
$4^5 = 1{,}024$
$4^4 = 256$
$4^3 = 64$
$4^2 = \blacksquare$
$4^1 = \blacksquare$
$4^0 = \blacksquare$

14.
$5^5 = 3{,}125$
$5^4 = \blacksquare$
$5^3 = 125$
$5^2 = 25$
$5^1 = \blacksquare$
$5^0 = \blacksquare$

Algebra • Equations **What is the value of *n* in each equation?**

15. $n = 6 \times 2^3$ **16.** $300 = n \times 10^2$ **17.** $2{,}000 = 2 \times 10^n$ **18.** $50{,}000 = 5 \times 10^n$

Solve.

19. What's Wrong? The paper shows Celine's work. What did Celine do wrong?

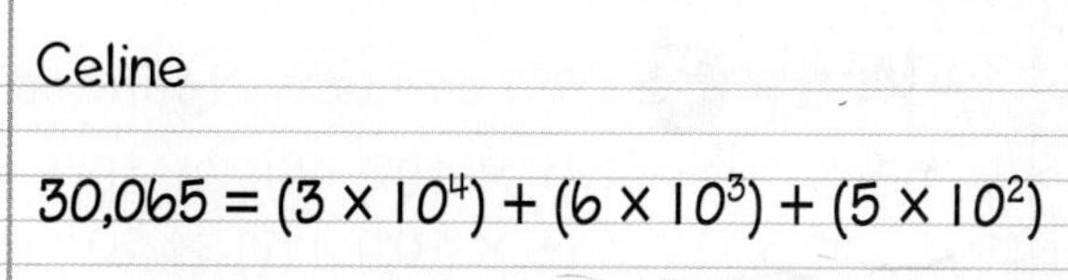

Celine
$30{,}065 = (3 \times 10^4) + (6 \times 10^3) + (5 \times 10^2)$

20. Write About It Without calculating, how can you tell which number is greater, 5×10^4 or 7×10^3?

Daily Review **Test Prep**

Subtract. (Grade 4)

21. 16 − 9 **22.** 17 − 8 **23.** 15 − 7

24. Free Respons
to write the nu
expanded form

Extra Practice See page 25, Set B.

Lesson 3

Place Value Through Hundred Billions

Objective Read and write numbers through hundred billions in standard and expanded forms.

Learn About It

In 2001, the population of China reached 1,273,111,290. What are some different ways to write this number?

Billions			Millions			Thousands			Ones		
hundreds	tens	ones	hundreds	tens	ones	hundreds	tens	ones	hundreds	tens	ones
0	0	1,	2	7	3,	1	1	1,	2	9	0

Different Ways to Read and Write Numbers

Way 1 **You can use standard form.**

1,273,111,290

Way 2 **You can use expanded form.**

$(1 \times 1{,}000{,}000{,}000) + (2 \times 100{,}000{,}000) + (7 \times 10{,}000{,}000) +$
$(3 \times 1{,}000{,}000) + (1 \times 100{,}000) + (1 \times 10{,}000) + (1 \times 1{,}000) +$
$(2 \times 100) + (9 \times 10)$

Way 3 **You can use expanded form with exponents.**

$(1 \times 10^9) + (2 \times 10^8) + (7 \times 10^7) + (3 \times 10^6) + (1 \times 10^5) +$
$(1 \times 10^4) + (1 \times 10^3) + (2 \times 10^2) + (9 \times 10^1)$

Way 4 **You can use word form.**

one billion, two hundred seventy-three million, one hundred eleven thousand, two hundred ninety

You can use the short word form.

1 billion, 273 million, 111 thousand, 290

Guided Practice

Ask Yourself

- What place comes before each comma?

Write each number in standard form.

1. 8 million, 345 thousand, 752
2. one hundred nine million, three hundred forty-two
3. $(8 \times 10^{10}) + (3 \times 10^{8}) + (4 \times 10^{6}) + (6 \times 10^{5}) + (7 \times 10^{3})$

 **Explain Your Thinking** ▶ In Exercise 2, how did you decide in which place the digit 9 should be written?

Practice and Problem Solving

Write each number in standard form.

4. 24 million, 79 thousand, 129
5. 392 billion, 34 million, 25
6. three billion, fourteen million, five hundred eighty-nine
7. four hundred two billion, three million, one hundred seventeen
8. $(4 \times 10^{10}) + (6 \times 10^{8}) + (9 \times 10^{7}) + (6 \times 10^{4}) + (1 \times 10^{3}) + (2 \times 10^{0})$

Write the value of the underlined digit in short word form.

9. 45,<u>8</u>76,541
10. 2,<u>3</u>46,780,102
11. 4<u>5</u>6,073,969,208

Write each number in expanded form using exponents.

12. 78,056,432,941
13. 245,087,705
14. 19,650,120

Solve.

15. **Measurement** Russia has a land area of 17,075,400 square kilometers. The United States has a land area of about 9 million square kilometers. Write each measurement in expanded form using exponents.

16. In 2000 the population of the United States was two hundred eighty-one million, four hundred twenty-one thousand, nine hundred six. Write that number in standard form.

Daily Review | Test Prep

Add or subtract. (Grade 4)

17. 99 − 96
18. 32 + 45
19. 57 − 32
20. 71 + 28
21. 12 + 23 + 34
22. 96 − 81

23. What is the value of the digit 4 in 12,648,067,905?

A 40,000　**B** 400,000　**C** 4,000,000　**D** 40,000,000

Extra Practice See page 25, Set C.

Lesson 4

Compare, Order, and Round Whole Numbers

Objective Compare, order, and round whole numbers through hundred billions.

Learn About It

The map shows the populations of some of the world's largest metropolitan areas in the year 2000. Which metropolitan area had a greater population, Bombay, India or Mexico City, Mexico?

New York City, U.S. 16,640,000

Tokyo, Japan 26,444,000

Mexico City, Mexico 18,131,000

São Paulo, Brazil 17,755,000

Bombay (Mumbai), India 18,066,000

Compare 18,066,000 and 18,131,000.

STEP 1 Line up the numbers by place value.

18,066,000
18,131,000

STEP 2 Start from the left. Compare the digits until they are different.

18,066,000
18,131,000

The hundred thousands digits are different. 1 is greater than 0, so 18,131,000 > 18,066,000.

Solution: Mexico City, Mexico had the greater population.

You can use the same method to order three or more numbers.

List the cities—New York City, Tokyo, and São Paulo—in order from greatest population to least population.

STEP 1 Line up the numbers by place value.

16,640,000
26,444,000
17,755,000

STEP 2 Start at the left. Compare digits.

16,640,000
26,444,000 2 > 1
17,755,000

26,444,000 is the greatest number.

STEP 3 Continue comparing.

16,640,000 7 > 6
17,755,000

17,755,000 > 16,640,000

So, 26,444,000 > 17,755,000 > 16,640,000.

Solution: The cities, in order from greatest population to least population, are Tokyo, São Paulo, and New York City.

The populations on the map on page 10 were rounded to the nearest thousand. Round the population of Tokyo to the nearest million.

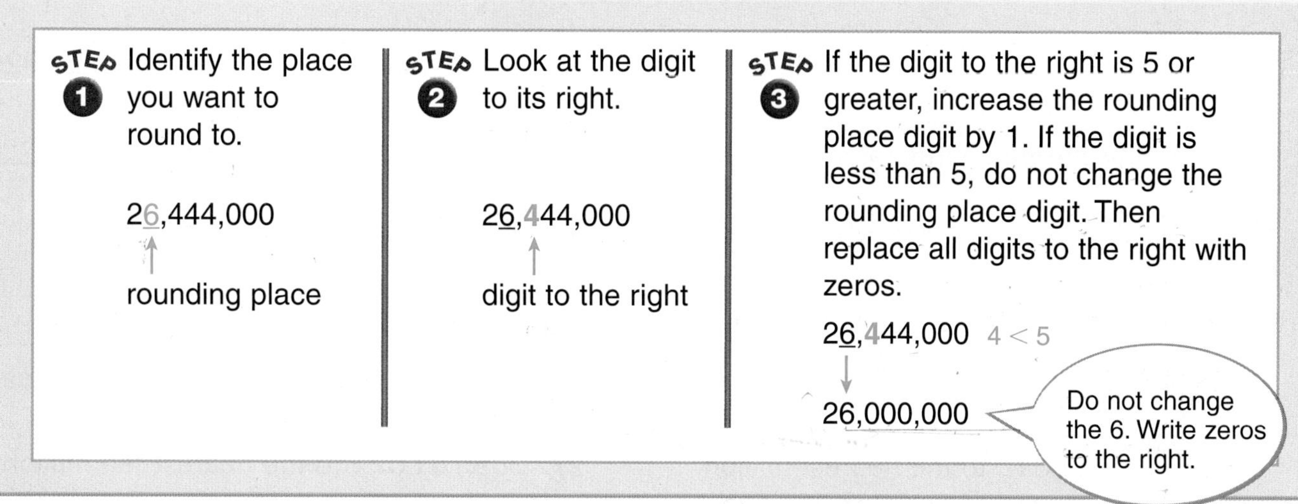

STEP 1 Identify the place you want to round to.
2<u>6</u>,444,000
rounding place
STEP 2 Look at the digit to its right.
2<u>6</u>,444,000
digit to the right
STEP 3 If the digit to the right is 5 or greater, increase the rounding place digit by 1. If the digit is less than 5, do not change the rounding place digit. Then replace all digits to the right with zeros.
2<u>6</u>,444,000 4 < 5
26,000,000
Do not change the 6. Write zeros to the right.

Solution: 26,444,000 rounded to the nearest million is 26,000,000.

Guided Practice

Ask Yourself

- Are the numbers lined up by place value?
- Where are the digits different?
- What is the digit to the right of the place I am rounding to?

TEST TIPS

Compare. Write >, <, or = for each ●.

1. 25,431 ● 25,661
2. 4,569,102 ● 4,570,000
3. 73,000 ● 9,995
4. 37,329,410 ● 38,000,116

Order each set of numbers from greatest to least.

5. 43,055; 422,007; 42,007
6. 812,661; 82,811,121; 82,935,661

Round to the place indicated by the underlined digit.

7. <u>5</u>45
8. 78<u>3</u>,256
9. 2<u>4</u>,592,124
10. 674,12<u>9</u>,811

Explain Your Thinking ▶ Why is the digit in the hundreds place used to round a number to the nearest thousand?

Practice and Problem Solving

Compare. Write >, <, or = for each ●.

11. 1,652 ● 1,709
12. 38,459 ● 38,459
13. 9,302,124 ● 9,298,116
14. 164,275,808 ● 167,001,005
15. 90,456,292 ● 89,509,765

Go On

Order each set of numbers from greatest to least.

16. 8,714; 8,764; 8,734

17. 541,536; 511,394; 601,345

18. 3,906,211; 4,031,232; 4,029,306

19. 265,616,845; 99,678,784; 257,724,925

Round to the place indicated by the underlined digit.

20. $5,\underline{2}61$

21. $57\underline{4},238$

22. $3,\underline{4}89,112$

23. $65\underline{9},324,721$

Round each number.

24. 28,652 to the nearest thousand

25. 624,314 to the nearest hundred thousand

26. 421,062,312 to the nearest million

27. 385,781,521 to the nearest ten million

Algebra • Equations Find the correct value of *n*.

28. $n + 100 = 1,000,000$

29. $n - 1,000 = 9,990,000$

30. $n + 100 = 100,000,000$

31. $100,000 + n = 1,000,000$

32. $n + 100 = 1,000$

33. $9,000,000,000 - n = 100$

Write a number for the missing digit that will make the inequality true.

34. 17,7■5 > 17,786

35. 32■,494 < 324,210

36. 765,789 < 7■5,789

Data Use the table to solve Problems 37–40.

37. Which city is projected to have the greatest population in 2015? Which city will have the least population?

38. Arrange the cities in order from least population to greatest population based on the projected populations in 2015.

39. Which two cities will have populations that round to the same number when rounded to the nearest million?

40. **Explain** In 2015, which city will have the closest population to 20,000,000? Explain your thinking.

Metropolitan Area	Projected Population for the Year 2015
Bombay	26,138,000
Mexico City	19,180,000
New York City	17,432,000
São Paulo	20,397,000
Tokyo	26,444,000

Extra Practice See page 25, Set D.

Quick Check

Check your understanding of Lessons 1–4.

Write each number in standard form. (Lessons 1 and 3)

1. 96 thousand 18

2. 700,000 + 60,000 + 400 + 8

3. two hundred four billion, eight hundred seventy-nine thousand, sixty

Write each number in expanded form with exponents. (Lesson 2)

4. 5,956

5. 734,508

6. 95,096

Order each set of numbers from greatest to least. (Lesson 4)

7. 27,509; 27,590; 29,705

8. 324,678; 315,798; 324,778

Digit Challenge

2 players

What you'll need • two copies of Learning Tool 6, one copy of Learning Tool 29 for each player

How to Play

1. Cut out the cards and game board for each player. Shuffle all cards together and place them in a stack.
2. Each player draws a card and places it on his or her game board. Once placed, the card cannot be moved.
3. Repeat Step 2 until each player has placed 6 cards. The player with the greater number scores a point.

Repeat Steps 2–3. The first player to score a total of 10 points is the winner.

4. Return all cards to the deck and reshuffle.

Lesson 5

Place Value Through Thousandths

Objective Read and write decimals through thousandths.

e Glossary

Vocabulary

decimal

decimal point

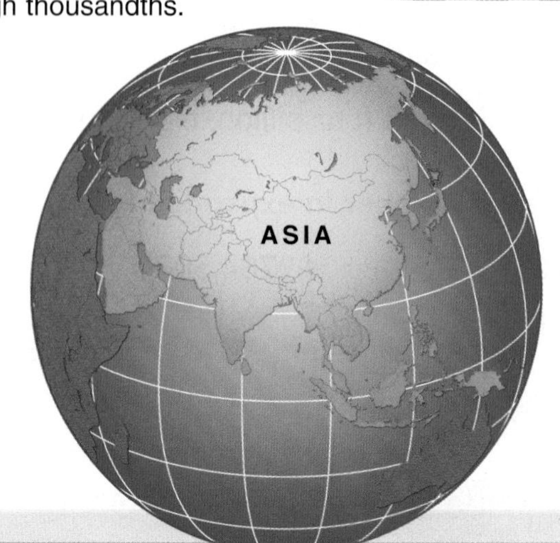

Learn About It

In comparing the land areas of the world, area can be shown as **decimals**. The land area of Asia is 0.214 of the land area on Earth.

Express 0.214 in words.

Use the place-value chart to understand decimals.

The value of the digits to the right of the **decimal point** is less than 1.

Whole Numbers				Decimals		
hundreds	tens	ones		tenths	hundredths	thousandths
		0	.	2	1	4

decimal point

Standard form: 0.214

Word form: two hundred fourteen thousandths

Short word form: 214 thousandths

The last digit after the decimal point tells how to name the decimal parts.

Another Example

Decimals Greater Than 1

Write 4.035 in word form.

four and thirty-five thousandths.

Notice that the decimal point is indicated by the word "and."

Guided Practice

Ask Yourself

- How can I use the word name to find the last place in the decimal?
- What word do I write for the decimal point?

Write each in standard form.

1. five tenths
2. four and sixteen thousandths

Write each decimal in word form.

3. 2.7
4. 0.15
5. 0.094

Explain Your Thinking ▶ How does the value of the last digit help you read a decimal?

Practice and Problem Solving

Write each in standard form.

6. nine hundredths
7. one hundred thirty-eight thousandths
8. twenty-five thousandths
9. five and forty-six hundredths
10. eleven and seven tenths
11. seventy-nine thousandths
12. eighteen and nine thousandths
13. ten and twenty-four hundredths

Write each decimal in words.

14. 0.019
15. 0.3
16. 0.34
17. 25.4
18. 0.789
19. 4.306
20. 0.082
21. 3.17

Write the value of the underlined digit in words.

22. $5.7\underline{7}$
23. $6.\underline{2}45$
24. $7.8\underline{8}$
25. $8.37\underline{4}$
26. $8.10\underline{9}$
27. $4.\underline{7}3$
28. $\underline{3}.99$
29. $0.2\underline{0}4$

Use the graph for Problems 30–33.

30. What part of the Earth's land area does North America cover? Write the decimal in words.

31. Which continent covers one hundred twenty-one thousandths of Earth's land area?

32. **Analyze** Which continent or region covers the smallest part of Earth's land area?

33. **Represent** Which continents each cover more than two tenths of Earth's land area? Use a place-value chart to explain your answer.

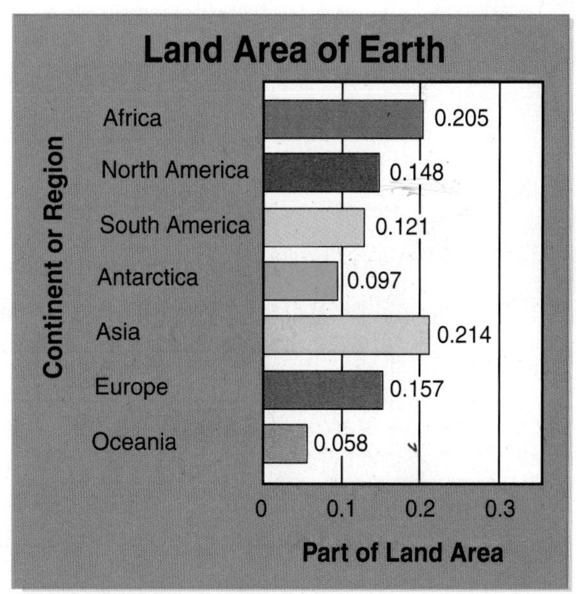

Daily Review | Test Prep

Multiply or divide. (Grade 4)

34. 7×11
35. $36 \div 4$
36. $16 \div 8$
37. 12×4

38. **Free Response** Write the decimal 30.068 in word form and in short word form.

Extra Practice See page 25, Set E.

Lesson 6

Problem-Solving Strategy

Find a Pattern

Objective Look for a pattern to solve a problem.

Problem Postage stamps are collected around the world. Some rare stamps are worth over $100,000. In 1980, the 1¢ British Guiana stamp was sold for $935,000.

Lani collects stamps. In 1998, a particular stamp was worth $1,520. The value in 2000 was $1,620. The value in 2002 was $1,720. The value in 2004 was $1,820. If the trend continues, what is the value of the stamp likely to be in 2008?

UNDERSTAND

This is what you know:

- In 1998, a particular stamp was worth $1,520.
- The value in 2000 was $1,620.
- The value in 2002 was $1,720.
- The value in 2004 was $1,820.

PLAN

You can look for a pattern to solve the problem.

SOLVE

Make a table to organize the data.
Then study the table to find a pattern.

Year	1998	2000	2002	2004	2006	2008
Value of Stamp	$1,520	$1,620	$1,720	$1,820	?	?

The value of the stamp increases by $100 every two years.
Use the pattern to complete the table.

$1,820 + 100 = $1,920 $1,920 + 100 = $2,020

Solution: The value of the stamp in 2008 is likely to be $2,020.

LOOK BACK

Look back at the problem. How can I check the answer?

MathTracks 1/3
Listen and Understand

Guided Practice

Use the Ask Yourself questions to help you solve each problem.

1. The value of a rare stamp from Thailand is \$130 in 1990, \$150 in 1995, \$170 in 2000, and \$190 in 2005. Predict the value of the stamp in 2010.

2. Michelle writes the following series of numbers.

   0.014, 0.034, _?_, 0.074, 0.094

   What is the missing number in the pattern?

   Hint Think about the numbers just before and just after the missing number.

Ask Yourself

UNDERSTAND What facts do I know? Can I find a pattern?

PLAN Did I describe the pattern?

SOLVE Did I continue the pattern?

LOOK BACK Did I solve the problem?

Independent Practice

Find a pattern to solve each problem.

3. People are bidding for a rare stamp from China. The first bid is \$120,000. The next three bids are \$150,000; \$180,000; and \$210,000. The seventh bid is the final bid. If the pattern continues, what is the final bid?

4. Eileen visits her family in Ireland every year. During one visit, she planted a 3-meter tree. The tree was 3.4 meters tall after one year, 3.8 meters tall after two years, and 4.2 meters tall after three years. How tall will the tree likely be after five years?

5. **Estimate** One city had a population of 18,649 in 1970, 18,446 in 1980, 18,233 in 1990, and 18,021 in 2000. Round each total to the nearest hundred. Then estimate the population of this city in 2010.

6. Carla writes the following series of numbers:

   0.496, 0.796, _?_, 1.396, 1.696

   What is the missing number in the pattern?

Choose a Strategy

Solve. Show your work.
Tell what strategy you used.

7. Peter has 7 United States coins worth 53¢. What are the 7 coins?

8. Katya buys a Greek coin, an Egyptian coin, and a Japanese coin. The Greek coin costs $4 less than the Egyptian coin and $6 more than the Japanese coin. The Japanese coin costs $25. How much does the Egyptian coin cost?

9. Kareem received $15 in change from a stamp dealer. The stamps he bought were $6, $8, and $21. How much money did Kareem give the stamp dealer?

PROBLEM-SOLVING Strategies

- Use Models
- Draw a Diagram
- Find a Pattern
- Guess and Check
- Make an Organized List
- Make a Table
- Solve a Simpler Problem
- Use Logical Reasoning
- Work Backward
- Write an Equation

Data **Use the graph to solve Problems 10–13.**

The graph shows Blue Globe Air's round-trip airfares for trips between New York City and selected foreign cities.

10. Mr. Tanner goes to Egypt. Including his airfare from New York City to Cairo, Egypt, Mr. Tanner spends a total of $2,500 on his trip. How much does Mr. Tanner spend on expenses other than airfare?

11. Jose buys a round-trip ticket between New York City and Athens, Greece. Helen buys a round-trip ticket to a different city that costs the same amount. To which city is Helen flying?

12. Souvir buys a round-trip ticket between New York City and Bombay, India. Souvir pays $600 towards his ticket. His parents pay the rest. How much do his parents pay?

13. **What's Wrong?** Lisa estimates that a round-trip ticket to each city shown on the graph would cost a total of about $5,000. Explain why Lisa's estimate is not reasonable.

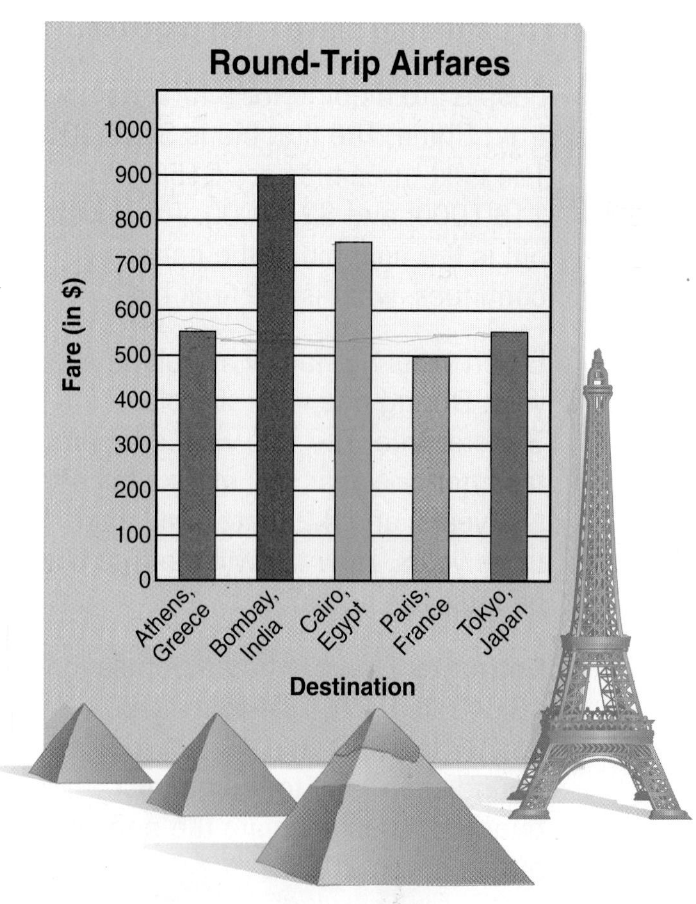

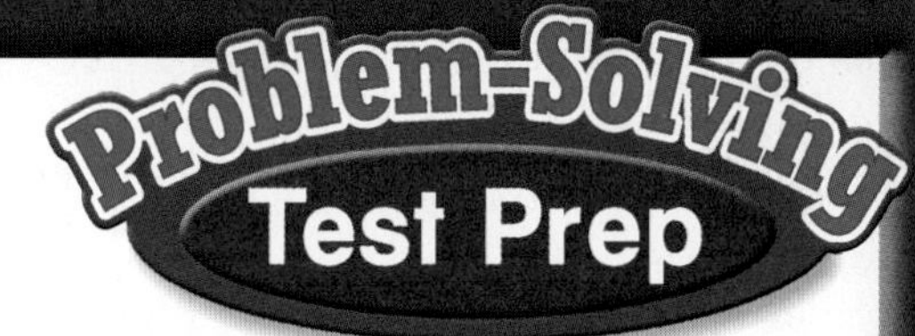

Choose the letter of the correct answer.
If a correct answer is not here, choose NH.

1. What will likely be the next picture in this pattern?

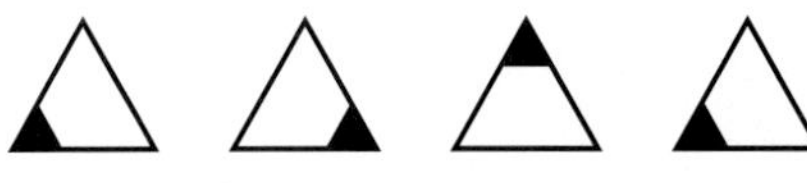

A 

B 

C

D

(Grade 4)

2. Measurement At a museum, a short film starts every 45 minutes. On Saturday the first film starts at 10:00 A.M. What time does the fifth movie start?

F 10:45 A.M. **H** 1:00 P.M.

G 12:00 P.M. **J** 1:45 P.M.

(Grade 4)

3. Nina bought 8 stamps and gave away 3 stamps. Then she bought 4 more stamps and sold 2 stamps. After buying 3 more stamps, Nina had 47 stamps. How many stamps did Nina start with?

A 27 **C** 37

B 32 **D** NH

(Grade 4)

4. Seventy people buy tickets to the Franklin School Teacher Awards Dinner. Each table seats 6 people. What is the minimum number of tables required?

F 4 **H** 11

G 10 **J** NH

(Grade 4)

5. The swim team has 20 trophies. Ginny wants to put the trophies on shelves. If she puts 5 trophies on each shelf, which equation can be used to find the number of shelves she will need?

A $20 \div 5 = n$ **C** $20 + 5 = n$

B $20 \times 5 = n$ **D** $20 - 5 = n$

(Grade 4)

6. How many will balance ?

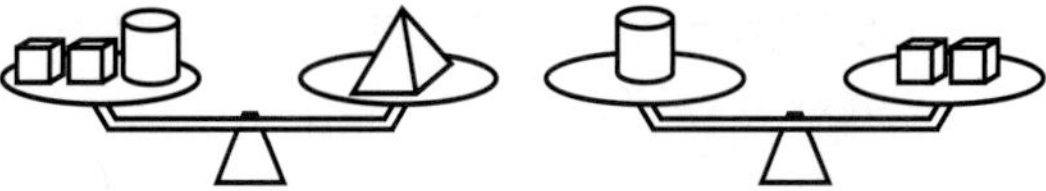

Explain How can you use logical reasoning to solve the problem?

(Grade 4)

7. The Drama Club voted to decide which play to produce. One fourth of the club voted for *The Music Man*. The club has 24 members. How many members voted for *The Music Man*?

Represent Support your solution with a picture.

(Grade 4)

Test Prep on the Net

Check out *Education Place* at **eduplace.com/kids/mw/** for test prep practice.

Lesson 7

Compare, Order, and Round Decimals

Objective Compare, order, and round decimals.

Learn About It

Which of the numbers at the right is greater?

0.25

0.5

Compare 0.5 and 0.25.

Different Ways to Compare 0.5 and 0.25

Way 1 You can use a number line.

0.5 is to the right of 0.25, so 0.5 > 0.25.

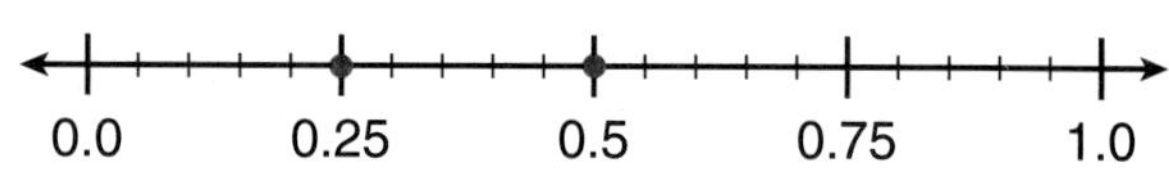

Way 2 You can compare digits.

STEP 1 Align the decimal points.

0.50
0.25

STEP 2 Start from the left. Compare the digits until they are different.

0.50
0.25 Since 5 > 2, 0.5 > 0.25.

Solution: 0.5 is greater than 0.25.

You can use what you know to order three or more decimals.

Order 4, 4.32, and 4.317 from greatest to least.

STEP 1 Align the decimal points. Write zeros if necessary.

4.000
4.320
4.317

STEP 2 Start from the left. Compare the digits.

4.000
4.320 0 < 3
4.317

4.000 is the least number.

STEP 3 Continue comparing.

4.320 2 > 1
4.317

4.320 > 4.317

So, 4.320 > 4.317 > 4.000.

Solution: Ordered from greatest to least, the numbers are 4.32, 4.317, 4.

Round 0.607 to the nearest hundredth.

Different Ways to Round 0.607 to the Nearest Hundredth

Way 1 **You can use a number line.**

0.607 is closer to 0.61 than to 0.60.

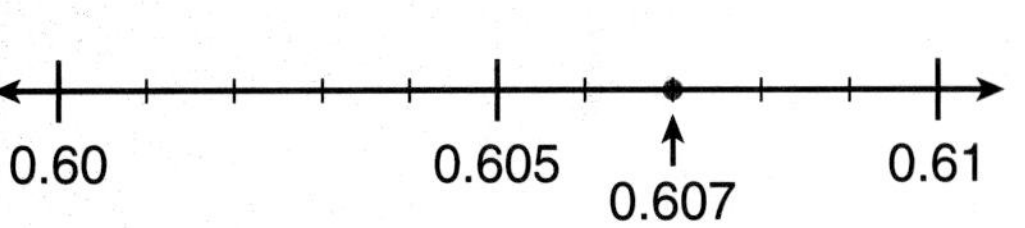

Way 2 **You can use rules for rounding decimals.**

STEP 1 Identify the place you want to round to.

0.607

↑

rounding place

STEP 2 Look at the digit to its right.

0.607

↑

digit to the right

STEP 3 If that digit is 5 or greater, increase the rounding-place digit by 1. If that digit is less than 5, do not change the rounding-place digit. Then drop all digits to the right.

0.607

↓

0.61

$7 > 5$ Change 0 to 1.

Solution: 0.607 rounded to the nearest hundredth is 0.61.

Other Examples

A. Round to the Nearest Tenth

0.418

$1 < 5$ 0.418 rounds to 0.4.

B. Round to the Nearest Whole Number

2.798

7 is greater than 5. 2.798 rounds to 3.

Guided Practice

Ask Yourself

- Did I align the decimal points?
- Where are the digits different?
- What is the digit to the right of the rounding place?

Compare. Write >, <, or = for each ●.

1. 0.45 ● 0.88 **2.** 0.6 ● 0.006 **3.** 4.153 ● 4.2

Order the numbers from greatest to least.

4. 0.0825; 0.56; 0.8 **5.** 1.3; 1.52; 2.08

Round to the place of the underlined digit.

6. 0.085 **7.** 0.572 **8.** 0.145 **9.** 3.957

Explain Your Thinking How does aligning the decimal points help you compare decimals?

Practice and Problem Solving

Compare. Write >, <, or = for each ●.

10. 0.09 ● 0.11 **11.** 0.945 ● 0.941 **12.** 0.3 ● 0.300 **13.** 0.023 ● 0.23

14. 17 ● 16.882 **15.** 2.454 ● 2.462 **16.** 3.631 ● 3.7 **17.** 9.9 ● 10.1

Order the numbers from greatest to least.

18. 4; 0.425; 4.25 **19.** 0.6; 0.68; 68 **20.** 2.544; 2.545; 25.43

21. 0.34; 0.4; 3 **22.** 3.55; 3.472; 4.14 **23.** 0.72; 7.2; 7

Round to the place of the underlined digit.

24. $0.\underline{4}57$ **25.** $\underline{6}.459$ **26.** $7.5\underline{3}8$ **27.** $28.\underline{7}26$

28. $3.2\underline{1}9$ **29.** $\underline{4}.09$ **30.** $6.\underline{4}63$ **31.** $27.3\underline{5}3$

Algebra • **Properties Compare. Write >, <, or = for each ●, given $a = 0.895$, $b = 0.75$, $c = 0.075$, and $d = 0.1$.**

32. b ● c **33.** a ● d **34.** c ● d **35.** b ● a

Find the missing digit that will make the inequality true.

36. 0.■5 > 0.37 **37.** 0.4■6 < 0.468 **38.** 2.396 < 2.39■

Solve.

39. Australia has 2.5 persons per square kilometer, Mongolia has 1.7 persons per square kilometer, and Namibia has 2.2 persons per square kilometer. Order the countries from least to most crowded.

40. **Represent** Suppose a 10 × 10 grid represents the number 1. Use 10 × 10 grids to represent the numbers 1.24 and 1.05. Explain how you can use the grids to compare the two numbers.

41. During a regular week, Robin works 35 hours and is paid $525. On holidays, Robin is paid an hourly rate that is twice as much as her rate during a regular week. What is Robin's hourly pay on holidays?

42. Many libraries use the Dewey Decimal System to classify and order books. Books are shelved from lowest numbers to highest numbers. Three books are numbered 0.971, 0.978, and 0.97. Which book should be first on the shelf?

Extra Practice See page 25, Set F.

Quick Check

Check your understanding of Lessons 5–7.

Write each decimal in words. (Lesson 5)

1. 0.17 **2.** 0.9 **3.** 62.103 **4.** 716.039

Order each set of numbers from greatest to least. (Lesson 7)

5. 306.905, 36.999, 306.91 **6.** 0.378, 0.42, 0.424

Round each number. (Lesson 7)

7. 40.845 to the nearest tenth **8.** 7.179 to the nearest whole number

Solve. (Lesson 6)

9. What is the missing number in the pattern?

0.176, 0.286, __?__, 0.506, 0.616

WEEKLY WR READER® eduplace.com/kids/mw/

ROMAN NUMERALS

Our number system is just one way to write numbers. The Romans created a number system using symbols called Roman numerals:

I (1)
V (5)
X (10)
L (50)
C (100)
D (500)

To read Roman numerals, follow these rules:

- Add the numerals from left to right.

VI = 5 + 1 = 6 XI = 10 + 1 = 11
XX = 10 + 10 = 20 DC = 500 + 100 = 600

- If a numeral has a value that is less than the numeral on its right, subtract those numerals. Then continue to add.

XIV = 10 + (5 − 1) = 14 CXLV = 100 + (50 − 10) + 5 = 145

What is each number below?

1. II **2.** XII **3.** LXXIX **4.** DXLIII **5.** DXCVII

6. Explain the similarities and differences between our decimal system and Roman numerals.

Chapter Review/Test

VOCABULARY

1. In the number 10^5, the 5 tells how many times 10 is used as the factor. It is called the ____.
2. In the number 10^5, the 10 is called the ____.
3. A number written in ____ shows the value of each digit.

Vocabulary

- base
- expanded form
- exponent
- place value
- power of ten

CONCEPTS AND SKILLS

Write each number in standard form. (Lessons 1–3, pp. 4–9, Lesson 5, pp. 14–15)

4. two million, four hundred three thousand, seventy-six
5. $(4 \times 10{,}000{,}000) + (7 \times 1{,}000{,}000) + (9 \times 10{,}000) + (1 \times 1{,}000) + (5 \times 100)$
6. two hundred two and twenty-two hundredths

Use exponents to write each number in expanded form. (Lessons 2–3, pp. 6–9)

7. 71,983,203,438 **8.** 1,203,487,386 **9.** 38 **10.** 3,402

Round each number to the place of the underlined digit. (Lesson 1, pp. 4–5, Lesson 4, pp. 10–13, Lesson 7, pp. 20–23)

11. 12.<u>0</u>43 **12.** 126,<u>9</u>53 **13.** 12<u>6</u>.925 **14.** 37.6<u>2</u>8 **15.** 37<u>6</u>.255

Order the numbers from greatest to least. (Lesson 4, pp. 10–13, Lesson 7, pp. 20–23)

16. 37,483; 37,493; 39,473
17. 0.02; 0.021; 0.201
18. 459,321,002; 49,321,001; 458,399,999
19. 5,034,966; 5,350,955; 5,034,965

PROBLEM SOLVING

Find a pattern to solve the problem.
(Lesson 6, pp. 16–19)

20. The membership of the local stamp collectors' club increased steadily in past years. In 2000, there were 21 members; in 2001, 29 members; in 2002, 37 members. How many members is it likely to have in 2005?

Show You Understand

Explain the difference in value of each digit in the number 1,111,111.

Extra Practice

Set A (Lesson 1, pp. 4–5)

Write each number in word form, short word form, and expanded form.

1. 16,362
2. 279,018
3. 36,109
4. 148,300
5. 567,255
6. 100,002

Set B (Lesson 2, pp. 6–7)

Use exponents to write each number in expanded form.

1. 7,094
2. 43,729
3. 309,309
4. 873,209

Set C (Lesson 3, pp. 8–9)

Write each number in standard form.

1. six hundred fifty-three million, seventy-five thousand, one hundred forty-nine
2. $(3 \times 10^9) + (2 \times 10^5) + (9 \times 10^4) + (6 \times 10^3) + (5 \times 10^2) + (5 \times 10^1) + (6 \times 10^0)$

Write each number in expanded form using exponents.

3. 34,503,598
4. 81,094,389,002
5. 430,398,278,021

Set D (Lesson 4, pp. 10–13)

Order the numbers from greatest to least.

1. 84,392; 804,381; 84,492
2. 2,394,309; 239,410; 2,395,301

Round each number.

3. 108,273 to the nearest ten thousand
4. 489,560,711 to the nearest million

Set E (Lesson 5, pp. 14–15)

Write each decimal in words.

1. 0.069
2. 1.14
3. 0.056
4. 0.049
5. 2.901
6. 0.03

Set F (Lesson 7, pp. 20–23)

Order the numbers from least to greatest.

1. 0.149, 0.073, 0.72
2. 10.002, 0.103, 1.03
3. 0.009, 0.15, 0.8

Round to the place of the underlined digit.

4. $0.\underline{4}7$
5. $\underline{7}.12$
6. $8.5\underline{3}9$
7. $32.\underline{8}09$

Add and Subtract Whole Numbers

INVESTIGATION

Use Data

Roller coasters did not appear in the United States until 1873. How many years later did the first suspended roller coaster appear?

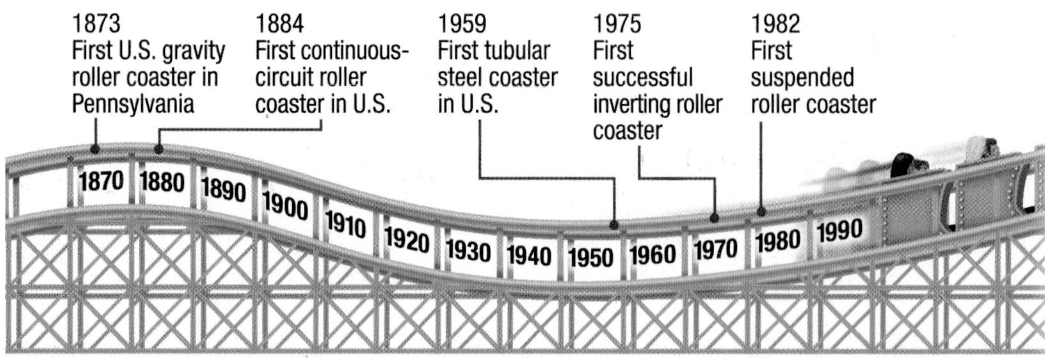

Use this page to review and remember what you need to know for this chapter.

VOCABULARY

Choose the best word to complete each sentence.

1. The answer to a subtraction problem is the ____.
2. A ____ is the answer to an addition problem.
3. Two or more numbers added together are called ____.

CONCEPTS AND SKILLS

Write an expression for each word phrase.

4. 8 reduced by 4
5. 7 more than 6
6. take 12 from 15

Round each number to the greatest place.

7. 46
8. 308
9. 5,555

Use mental math to find the answers.

10. $60 − $20
11. 1,400 − 800
12. 5,000 + 2,000 + 4,000

Regroup.

13. 462 as 3 hundreds, ■ tens, 2 ones
14. 57 as ■ tens and 17 ones
15. 13 hundreds as ■ thousand ■ hundreds
16. 24 tens as 1 ten ■ ones

Substitute a 6 for each ■. Find each expression's value.

17. ■ + ■
18. ■ + 2
19. ■ − 6

Write About It

20. You buy two items. One costs $12, and the other costs $4. Explain how to find how much change you get from a $20 bill.

Algebra

Expressions and Addition Properties

Objective Read, write, and evaluate expressions containing variables and apply addition properties.

e Glossary

Vocabulary

variable
expression
evaluate
Commutative Property
Associative Property
Identity Property

Learn About It

Steve has 4 more ride tickets than Lily has. Since you do not know how many tickets Lily has, you can use a **variable**, a letter such as x or n, to stand for the number of tickets Lily has.

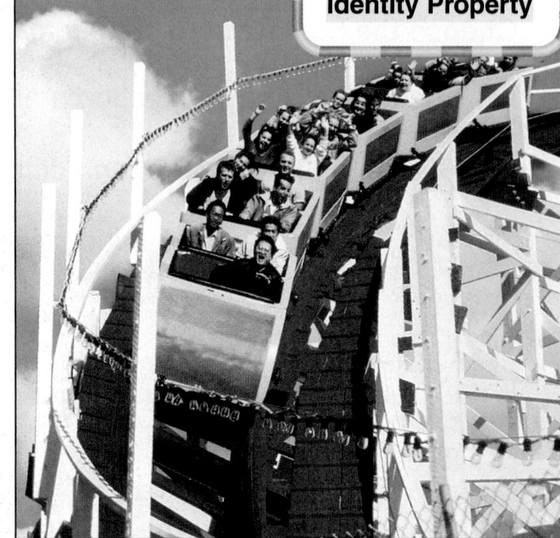

You can compare the number of tickets Steve has with the number of tickets Lily has by using a mathematical **expression** that uses a variable. Mathematical expressions that use variables are called algebraic expressions.

Write an expression.

What if Lily has 1 ticket?	**What if Lily has 10 tickets?**	**What if Lily has *n* tickets?**
Then $1 + 4$ shows how many tickets Steve has.	Then $10 + 4$ shows how many tickets Steve has.	Then $n + 4$ shows how many tickets Steve has.
The expression means 4 more than 1.	The expression means 4 more than 10.	The expression means 4 more than n.

Algebraic expressions allow you to replace variables with different numbers.

To **evaluate** an expression, substitute a number for the variable.

Matt has 2 fewer tickets than Lily.

Write the expression for the number of tickets Matt has.	Substitute a number for n. If Lily has 5 tickets,	Simplify.
$n - 2$ ↑ number of tickets Lily has	then $n - 2$ becomes $5 - 2$.	$5 - 2 = 3$

Solution: If Lily has 5 tickets, then Matt has 3 tickets.

There are three properties that make adding easier.

Addition Properties		
Commutative Property When you add two numbers or variables, you can change the order without changing the sum. $a + b = b + a$	**Associative Property** When you add numbers or variables, you can group them in different ways without changing the sum. $(a + b) + c = a + (b + c)$	**Identity Property** When you add 0 to a number or variable, the result is the same number or sum. $a + 0 = 0 + a = a$
Example: How many tickets do Lily and Steve have in all? $5 + 4 = 4 + 5$ $9 = 9$	Example: How many tickets do Lily, Steve, and Matt have? $(5 + 9) + 2 = 5 + (9 + 2)$ $14 + 2 = 5 + 11$ $16 = 16$	Example: Matt has 5 tickets and Steve has no tickets. How many do they have together? $5 + 0 = 5$ same number

Another Example

Write an Algebraic Expression in Words

Translate $n - 3$ into words.

$n - 3$

The expression $n - 3$ means to subtract three from some number.

Other Possible Answers

Often there is more than one way to write an algebraic expression in words. Other possible ways include:

- three less than some number
- take three away from some number
- a number minus three

Guided Practice

Write an algebraic expression for each word phrase.

1. some number plus 6
2. 8 less than a number

Translate each algebraic expression into words. Then evaluate when $n = 4$.

3. $n + 9$
4. $11 - n$
5. $14 + n$
6. $n - 4$

Ask Yourself

- Do the words describe an addition expression or a subtraction expression?
- What words did I use for the variables?

Is the Commutative Property true for subtraction? Why or why not? Support your answers with examples.

Go On

Practice and Problem Solving

Write an algebraic expression for each word phrase.

7. subtract 10 from a number
8. 9 plus a number
9. 3 more than a number
10. take 15 from a number
11. add 5 to a number
12. 6 is decreased by a number

Translate each algebraic expression into words.

13. $n + 8$
14. $8 + n$
15. $x - 12$
16. $12 - x$
17. $a + 0$
18. $k - 5$
19. $5 + y$
20. $h + 9$
21. $16 - t$
22. $x - y$

Evaluate each expression when $a = 15$. Then write >, <, or = to compare the expressions.

23. $a + 9$ ⬤ $9 + a$
24. $a + 0$ ⬤ $a - 2$
25. $a - 14$ ⬤ $20 - a$
26. $(a + 4) + 6$ ⬤ $a + (4 + 6)$

Solve.

27. At 310 feet, the Millennium Force roller coaster once was the tallest coaster in the world. Write an expression to show the height of the current record holder. Explain what the variable represents.

28. **Analyze** To ride on the Millennium Force, passengers must be at least 48 inches tall. Al is taller than that. Write an expression to show how tall Al is. Explain what the variable represents.

29. **Represent** Draw a diagram and write an expression to show how many are in the group.

A group of friends went on the roller coaster.
- first car: 3 friends
- second car: 4 friends
- third car: ? friends

How many are in the group if 2 friends are in the third car?

30. **What's Wrong?** Alma wrote the associative property this way.

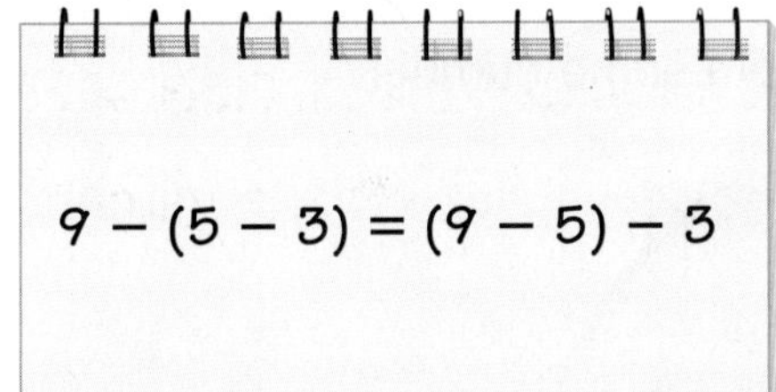

Explain how you know what Alma did wrong.

Daily Review | Test Prep

Write >, <, or = to compare. (Grade 4)

31. \$3.06 ⬤ 3 dollars + 1 dime
32. \$0.55 ⬤ 1 quarter + 1 nickel
33. 2 dollars ⬤ 8 quarters.

34. Ben has \$6 less than Emily. If n stands for Emily's money, which expression shows Ben's money?

A $n + \$6$ **B** $\$6 + n$
C $n - \$6$ **D** $\$6 - n$

Extra Practice See page 45, Set A.

Miniature Numbers

Engineers design larger structures like roller coasters, but they also design extremely small things, too.

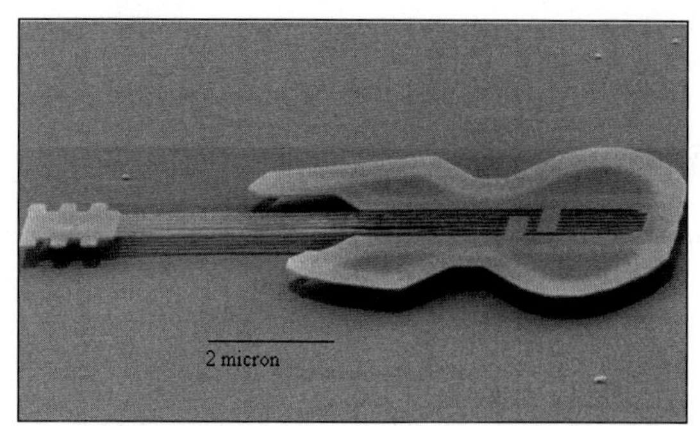

This nanoguitar is about the size of 1 blood cell. It measures 10 micrometers long. One micrometer is 1 millionth of a meter. The width of each string on the guitar is about 50 nanometers, which is 50 billionths of a meter; about the size of 100 atoms!

ones		tenths	hundredths	thousandths	ten thousandths	hundred thousandths	millionths	ten millionths	hundred millionths	billionths
0	.	0	0	0	0	0	1	0	0	0
0	.	0	0	0	0	0	0	0	5	0

You can round, compare, and order these very small numbers the same way you round, compare, and order other decimals.

Round each number to the nearest millionth.

Then order from *greatest* to *least*.

1. 0.0006723; 0.0010257; 0.0004925
2. 0.0089437; 0.0089586; 0.0089564
3. 0.0000078; 0.0000072; 0.0000086
4. 0.0004624; 0.000480; 0.00046343

Digit Prices

The price, in cents, of a souvenir pencil at an amusement park is a two-digit number. The ones digit is 3 less than the tens digit. The sum of the digits is 15. How much does a souvenir pencil cost?

Brain Teaser

Use only the digits 0, 1, and 9 to write a decimal in billionths. Use each digit at least once.

Your decimal should be the least possible decimal that rounds up to the nearest millionth.

Technology

Visit *Education Place* at **eduplace.com/kids/mw/** to try more brain teasers.

Lesson 2

Estimate Sums and Differences

Objective Estimate sums and differences.

Learn About It

MathTracks 1/6
Listen and Understand

One flume ride is 3,610 feet long. Another flume ride is 1,315 feet long. About how many feet different are these lengths?

You can round to estimate sums or differences.

Different Ways to round.

Way 1 **Rounding to the greatest place gives an estimate.**

$$\begin{array}{r} 3{,}610 \\ -\ 1{,}315 \\ \hline \end{array} \rightarrow \begin{array}{r} 4{,}000 \\ -\ 1{,}000 \\ \hline 3{,}000 \end{array}$$

Solution: The difference is about 3,000 ft.

Way 2 **Rounding to a lesser place is more precise. This gives a better estimate.**

$$\begin{array}{r} 3{,}610 \\ -\ 1{,}315 \\ \hline \end{array} \rightarrow \begin{array}{r} 3{,}600 \\ -\ 1{,}300 \\ \hline 2{,}300 \end{array}$$

Solution: The difference is about 2,300 ft.

Way 3 **Rounding both numbers up and down gives an estimated range of answers.**

Round down

$$\begin{array}{r} 3{,}000 \\ +\ 1{,}000 \\ \hline 4{,}000 \end{array} \leftarrow \begin{array}{r} 3{,}610 \\ +\ 1{,}315 \\ \hline \end{array} \rightarrow \begin{array}{r} 4{,}000 \\ +\ 2{,}000 \\ \hline 6{,}000 \end{array}$$

Round up

Solution: The sum of 3,610 and 1,315 is between 4,000 and 6,000.

Other Examples

A. Front-End Estimation

Use the front digits.

$$\begin{array}{r} 3{,}458 \\ +\ 1{,}555 \\ \hline \end{array}$$

$$\begin{array}{r} 3{,}000 \\ +\ 1{,}000 \\ \hline 4{,}000 \end{array}$$

$3{,}458 + 1{,}555 \approx 4{,}000$

B. Clustering

$54 + 49 + 41 + 62 + 39 + 46 = ?$

The numbers *cluster* around 50.
There are 6 numbers.
Use multiplication to estimate the sum.
$6 \times 50 = 300$

$54 + 49 + 41 + 62 + 39 + 46 \approx 300$

Guided Practice

Estimate. Tell which method you used.

1. 746 + 746
2. 30,909 − 18,850
3. 7,749 − 1,654

Ask Yourself

- Did I use the rounding rules correctly?
- Did I add or subtract the rounded numbers correctly?

TEST TIPS **Explain Your Thinking ▶** If you are estimating a sum and you round both numbers up, will your sum be greater than or less than the actual sum? Explain.

Practice and Problem Solving

Estimate. Tell which method you used.

4. 595 + 820
5. 828 − 371
6. 7,502 + 2,875
7. 3,199 + 2,539
8. 3,392 − 2,800
9. 9,839 + 8,000
10. 3,567 − 2,249
11. 9,003 − 1,654
12. 29,678 − 12,854
13. \$29 + \$54
14. 3,498 + 2,909 + 2,701

Solve.

15. **Estimate** In one hour, 1,076 riders rode a coaster. In the next hour, 1,423 riders rode the coaster. About how many riders rode the coaster in those two hours?

16. Some coasters can go more than 100 miles per hour. The new X coaster goes 76 miles per hour. About how much less than 100 miles per hour is that?

17. **Analyze** Each hour 1,800 people can ride one roller coaster. In another 1,600 people ride per hour. If both rides are filled for 8 hours, find the difference in the number of riders.

18. **Create and Solve** Write your own problem about roller coasters that requires estimating a sum or a difference. Solve your problem and give it to a partner to solve.

Daily Review | Test Prep

Write the value of the underlined digit.
(Ch. 1, Lesson 1)

19. 2$\underline{8}$1,475
20. 35$\underline{5}$,072
21. 907,3$\underline{1}$1
22. $\underline{1}$12,111

23. **Free Response** Sandy spent \$164 on tickets, \$45 on food, and \$38 on souvenirs. What is a reasonable estimate of the amount she spent?

Explain.

Extra Practice See page 45, Set B.

Add and Subtract Whole Numbers

Objective Add and subtract whole numbers with up to five digits.

Learn About It

On Monday 6,395 people rode on a roller coaster. On Tuesday 2,768 people rode. How many people rode the roller coaster on those two days?

Find 6,395 + 2,768.

STEP 1 Add the ones.

Regroup 10 ones as 1 ten whenever possible.

13 ones = 1 ten 3 ones

$$\begin{array}{r} \scriptstyle 1 \\ 6,395 \\ +\ 2,768 \\ \hline 3 \end{array}$$

STEP 2 Add the tens.

Regroup 10 tens as 1 hundred whenever possible.

16 tens = 1 hundred 6 tens

$$\begin{array}{r} \scriptstyle 1\ 1 \\ 6,395 \\ +\ 2,768 \\ \hline 63 \end{array}$$

STEP 3 Add the hundreds.

Regroup 10 hundreds as 1 thousand whenever possible.

11 hundreds = 1 thousand 1 hundred

$$\begin{array}{r} \scriptstyle 1\ 1\ 1 \\ 6,395 \\ +\ 2,768 \\ \hline 163 \end{array}$$

STEP 4 Add the thousands.

$$\begin{array}{r} \scriptstyle 1\ 1\ 1 \\ 6,395 \\ +\ 2,768 \\ \hline 9,163 \end{array}$$

Solution: The total is 9,163 people.

You should check your work.

Use estimation to check.

6,395	rounds to	6,000
+ 2,768	rounds to	+ 3,000
		9,000

The sum is close to 9,000.

Use a calculator to check.

The sum is 9,163.

Solution: The total is 9,163 people.

How many more riders were there on Monday than on Tuesday?

You can draw a model to show the information.

Monday: 6,395 riders	
Tuesday: 2,768 riders	Difference: ? riders

Now you can use the model to solve the problem.

Find 6,395 − 2,768.

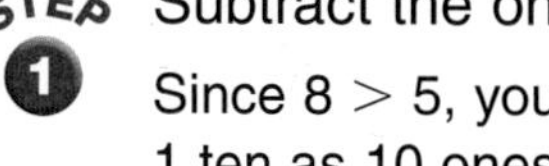

STEP 1 Subtract the ones.

Since 8 > 5, you must regroup 1 ten as 10 ones.

```
      8 15
  6, 3 9 5
− 2, 7 6 8
        7
```

STEP 2 Subtract the tens.

```
      8 15
  6, 3 9 5
− 2, 7 6 8
      2 7
```

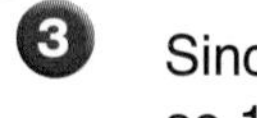

STEP 3 Subtract the hundreds.

Since 7 > 3, regroup 1 thousand as 10 hundreds.

```
  5  13 8 15
  6,  3 9 5
− 2,  7 6 8
      6 2 7
```

STEP 4 Subtract the thousands.

```
  5  13 8 15
  6,  3 9 5
− 2,  7 6 8
  3,  6 2 7
```

Add to check.

```
  3, 6 2 7
+ 2, 7 6 8
  6, 3 9 5
```

Solution: The difference is 3,627 riders.

You can also use a calculator to check.

The difference is 3,627.

Another Example

Zeros in Subtraction

30,058 − 17,874 = *n*

```
  2 9  9 15
  3 0, 0 5 8
− 1 7, 8 7 4
  1 2, 1 8 4
```

← You cannot subtract 7 tens from 5 tens. There are no hundreds or thousands to regroup, so rename 3 ten thousands.

Think
300 hundreds equals 299 hundreds plus 10 tens.

Go On

Guided Practice

Add or subtract. Check that your answer is reasonable.

1. 457 + 285
2. 6,701 + 3,495
3. 54,187 + 12,579
4. 829 − 287
5. 3,402 − 1,689
6. 42,317 − 19,675
7. 7,814 + 543
8. 34,516 + 478 + 2,347
9. 867 − 328
10. 68,615 − 3,786

Ask Yourself

- Do I need to regroup?
- Where should I write the regrouped numbers?

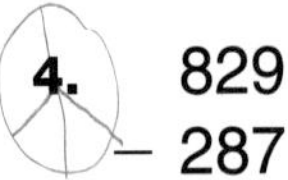

Explain Your Thinking When subtracting, how do you regroup tens when there is a zero in the hundreds place?

Practice and Problem Solving

Add or subtract. Check that your answer is reasonable.

11. 746 + 459
12. 952 + 374
13. 843 + 199
14. 587 + 96
15. 2,874 + 1,568
16. 746 − 199
17. 752 − 97
18. 500 − 354
19. 3,958 − 498
20. 34,440 − 5,485
21. 3,985 + 439
22. 56,583 − 9,407
23. 67,109 − 15,407
24. 4,782 + 561
25. 80,412 − 667
26. 567 + 4,986 + 6,998
27. 5,050 − 3,328
28. 7,685 − 3,858

Algebra • Patterns Find each sum or difference when $n = 1{,}000{,}000$ and $s = 499$.

29. $n + 9$
30. $n + 9{,}000$
31. $n + 9{,}000{,}000$
32. $1{,}000 - s$
33. $10{,}000 - s$

Data Use the table to solve Problems 34–37.

34. **Mental Math** How much longer is Shock Wave™ than Flashback?
35. **Reasoning** A mile is 5,280 feet. If you ride Titan twice, how much more or less than 2 miles have you ridden?
36. How much higher is Mr. Freeze™ than Flashback?
37. What is the range of heights of these roller coasters?

Roller Coaster	Length (in feet)	Height (in feet)
Flashback	1,876	125
Mr. Freeze™	1,480	238
Shock Wave™	3,500	116
Titan	5,312	255

Extra Practice See page 45, Set C.

Quick Check

Check your understanding of Lessons 1–3.

Evaluate each expression for $n = 8$. (Lesson 1)

1. $n + 14$
2. $12 - n$
3. $n - n$

Estimate each sum or difference. (Lesson 2)

4. 432 + 675
5. 9,240 − 582
6. 647 + 290 + 36

Add or subtract. Check your answer. (Lesson 3)

7. 548 + 397
8. 1,462 − 841
9. 3,290 + 1,876
10. 7,005 − 1,527

WEEKLY WR READER® eduplace.com/kids/mw/

Social Studies Connection

TIME ZONES

Each time you cross into a new time zone while traveling from east to west, you need to set your watch 1 hour earlier. Portland, Oregon is located three time zones west of Portland, Maine.

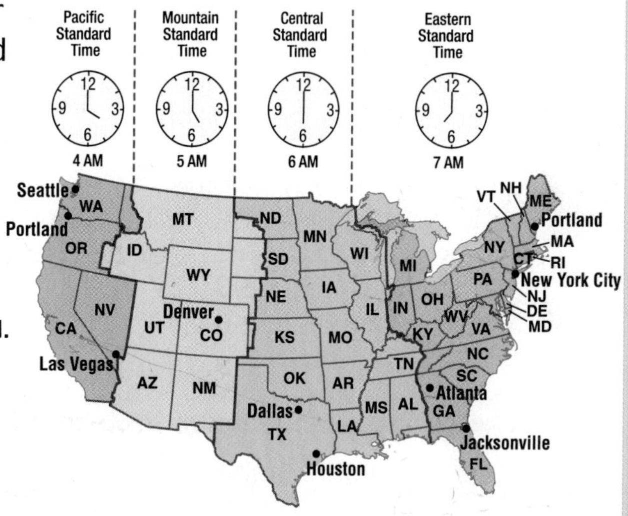

It is 1:30 P.M. in Portland, Maine. What time is it in Portland, Oregon?

Count back 3 hours from 1:30 P.M.

1:30 P.M. 12:30 P.M. 11:30 A.M. 10:30 A.M.

When it is 1:30 P.M. in Portland, Maine, it is 10:30 A.M. in Portland, Oregon.

Identify each missing time.

1. 3:10 P.M. in Atlanta, Georgia is ___ in Houston, Texas.
2. 1:15 P.M. in Dallas, Texas is ___ in Las Vegas, Nevada.
3. 9:00 A.M. in Denver, Colorado is ___ in New York City, New York.
4. 8:30 A.M. in Seattle, Washington is ___ in Jacksonville, Florida.

Add and Subtract Greater Numbers

Objective Use mental math, pencil and paper, estimation, or technology to add and subtract greater numbers.

Learn About It

When you add or subtract greater numbers, you need to choose the most appropriate method for solving the problem. You can use mental math, pencil and paper, estimation, a calculator, or a computer.

One amusement park had 2,349,783 visitors in one year. Another park had 2,185,326 visitors. How many visitors did both parks together have that year?

Add. **2,349,783 + 2,185,326 = *n***

Estimate before you add. Round to the greatest place.

2,349,783	→	2,000,000
+ 2,185,326	→	+ 2,000,000
		4,000,000

The sum should be about 4,000,000.
Then complete the addition.

STEP 1 Add the digits in the ones period.

$$\begin{array}{r} \scriptstyle 1\ 1 \quad \\ 2,349,783 \\ +\ 2,185,326 \\ \hline 109 \end{array}$$

STEP 2 Add the digits in the thousands period.

$$\begin{array}{r} \scriptstyle 1\ 1\ 1\ \ 1 \qquad \\ 2,349,783 \\ +\ 2,185,326 \\ \hline 535,109 \end{array}$$

STEP 3 Add the digits in the millions place.

$$\begin{array}{r} \scriptstyle 1\ 1\ 1\ \ 1 \qquad \\ 2,349,783 \\ +\ 2,185,326 \\ \hline 4,535,109 \end{array}$$

Solution: The total number of visitors is 4,535,109.

Another Example

You can use a calculator to find the difference in attendance at the two parks.

Subtract. 2,349,783 − 2,185,326

2 3 4 9 7 8 3 − 2 1 8 5 3 2 6 Enter = 164457

Guided Practice

- Did I regroup in the correct places?
- Did I choose a method that makes sense?

Add or subtract. Tell which method you used.

1. 247,625 + 53,218

2. 746,000 − 156,923

3. 2,386,940 − 1,000,000

Explain Your Thinking ▶ When is a computer a good choice for adding greater numbers? When is it not a good choice? Explain.

Practice and Problem Solving

Add or subtract. Tell which method you used.

4. 612,956 + 423,890

5. 2,345,976 − 254,500

6. 617,700 + 82,430

7. 5,321,908 + 4,600,000

8. 234,809 − 150,000

9. 7,210,658 − 6,800,321

10. 547,987 − 476,000

11. 475,000 + 125,000

12. 400,000 − 73,300

13. 1,754,867 − 1,235,800

Choose a Computation Method

Mental Math • Estimation • Paper and Pencil • Calculator

Use the table for Problems 14–16.

14. How many fewer than 40,000,000 riders have been on the most popular ride listed in the table?

15. Reasoning All together, have these four roller coasters had 1 billion riders? How can you tell?

16. Explain How many more than 2,750,000 riders have been on Flight of Fear? Show how you got the answer.

Roller Coaster	Total Number of Riders Since Opened (to 2002)
Flight of Fear	2,768,065
The Beast	32,904,365
The Racer	39,963,282
Top Gun	9,239,507

Daily Review | Test Prep

Multiply. (Grade 4)

17. 2 × 4

18. 5 × 2

19. 4 × 4

20. 9 × 2

21. 5 × 5

22. 7 × 6

23. In one week 213,360 people rode on a roller coaster. How much less than 250,000 riders is that?

A 36,640 **B** 43,360

C 47,740 **D** 463,360

Extra Practice See page 45, Set D.

Algebra

Addition and Subtraction Equations

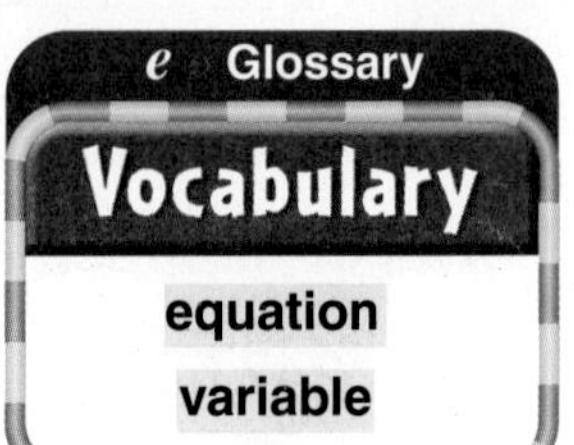

Objective Use mental math to solve addition and subtraction equations.

Learn About It

At a rafting ride at the water park, the blue rafts have three more seats than the yellow rafts. The blue rafts have 7 seats. How many seats do the yellow rafts have?

You can make a model of the information.

Blue raft seats: 7	
Yellow raft seats: n	Difference: 3

Use the model to write an equation.

An **equation** is a mathematical statement indicating that the quantities on either side of the equal sign (=) have the same value.

- Write the equation in words. → yellow raft seats + difference = blue raft seats
- Replace the words with values from the model. → $n + 3 = 7$
- Solve the equation using mental math. → $n + 3 = 7$
  Replace the **variable** n with 4. $4 + 3 = 7$

What number plus 3 equals 7? Try 4.

Solution: The yellow rafts have 4 seats.

Another Example

Write the equation shown by the model. Use mental math to solve the equation.

46	
n	18

You can write an addition equation.

$46 = n + 18$
$n = 28$

You can write a subtraction equation.

$46 - n = 18$
$n = 28$

Guided Practice

Write the equation shown by the model. Use mental math to solve the equation.

1.

Cars on the first coaster: 15	
Cars on the second coaster: *n*	Difference: 4

2.

12	
8	*x*

Ask Yourself

- Does my equation match the information in the model?
- Did I check my solution by substituting it into the equation?

Explain Your Thinking ▶ What model could you draw to show $49 + c = 74$?

Practice and Problem Solving

Write the equation shown by the model. Then solve the equation.

3.

Total minutes: 25	
Time waiting: 23	Time on ride: *a*

4.

18	
n	13

Use mental math to solve the equations. Use models if necessary.

5. $n + 4 = 9$
6. $17 - k = 12$
7. $50 - n = 20$
8. $93 + s = 100$
9. $15 + x = 25$
10. $v + 34 = 36$
11. $p - 6 = 70$
12. $17 - n = 10$
13. $m - 5 = 71$
14. $x + 24 = 40$
15. $\$2 + n = \$20$
16. $x - 87 = 0$

Solve.

17. **Represent** Henry had 8 rides more than Davey did. If Henry had 15 rides, how many rides did Davey have? Draw a model to represent the problem and solve.

18. Two rides have a 5-mile per hour difference in top speed. The faster ride has a top speed of 21 miles per hour. What is the top speed of the other ride?

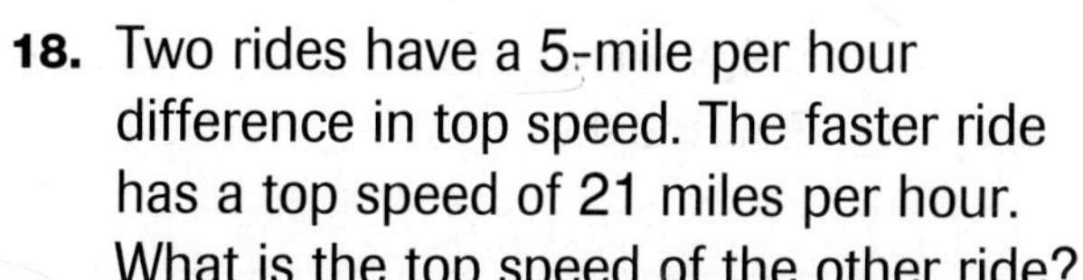

19. **Measurement** Draw a line that is 12 centimeters long. How much longer must you draw the line to make it 20 centimeters long?

20. **What If?** Suppose the line you drew in Problem 19 were half as long. How much longer must you draw it to be 20 centimeters long?

Daily Review | Test Prep

Identify the value of the underlined digit in each number. (Ch. 1, Lesson 1)

21. <u>7</u>5,000,000

22. 3,7<u>6</u>8,099

23. **Free Response** Explain how to find the value of *n* in this equation.

$34 - n = 20$

Extra Practice See page 45, Set E.

Lesson 6

Problem-Solving Decision

Relevant Information

Objective Find the information needed to solve a problem.

When a problem has too much information, you must decide which information is important. When a problem does not give enough information, you must decide what is missing.

Problem At an amusement park 9,576 tickets were sold on Saturday. Ticket sales included adults and senior citizens, and children. There were 3,085 senior citizen tickets sold. There were 1,027 more tickets sold for adults than senior citizens. How many tickets for adults were sold on Saturday?

Ask Yourself

What is the question?	What do you need to know?	What do you not need to know?
• How many tickets for adults were sold on Saturday?	• 3,085 tickets for senior citizens were sold on Saturday. • 1,027 more tickets for adults were sold on Saturday than for senior citizens.	• 9,576 tickets were sold on Saturday. • The number of tickets sold for children.

Draw the model to solve.

Total adult tickets: n	
Senior citizen tickets: 3,085	Difference: 1,027

Write an equation to represent the problem. $n = 3{,}085 + 1{,}027$ $n = 4{,}112$

Solution: On Saturday, 4,112 adult tickets were sold.

Try These

Draw a model to solve. If there is not enough information, tell what information is needed.

1. Last week, the park had 10,687 visitors. This week the park had 94,612 visitors. Normally, it has about 85,000 visitors per week. How many visitors less than normal did it have last week?

2. You have to be at least 48 inches tall to ride on most thrill rides. Casey cannot ride the roller coaster because she is too short. By how much does she miss the cut-off height?

Quick Check

Check your understanding of Lessons 4–6.

Add or subtract. (Lesson 4)

1. $657{,}912 + 12{,}819$

2. $4{,}319{,}007 - 3{,}287{,}650$

3. $239{,}456 - 98{,}724$

4. $2{,}823{,}065 + 423{,}889$

Use mental math to solve each equation. Use models if necessary. (Lesson 5)

5. $n + 17 = 24$

6. $36 - x = 18$

7. $n - 75 = 15$

8. $220 + x = 230$

Draw a model to solve. If there is not enough information, tell what information is needed. (Lesson 6)

9. A ride can take up to 1,800 riders each hour. There were 1,143 riders the first hour. There were 1,456 and 1,723 riders the next two hours. How many riders were there in the first 2 hours?

Visual Thinking

Math Reasoning

Cubing Dates

You can make a calendar using three cubes. One cube shows the day of the week. Since a cube has only 6 faces, Saturday and Sunday are on the same face.

This cube calendar shows the date for Monday the 15th.

Arrange the numbers of the faces of the other two cubes. Each face should only have one number.

Hint Do any numbers need to be on both cubes?

Chapter Review/Test

VOCABULARY

Vocabulary
Associative Property
Commutative Property
Identity Property
evaluate
variable

1. The ____ states that the order of addends does not change the sum.
2. A(n) ____ is a letter or symbol that represents a number in an algebraic expression.
3. The ____ states that the sum of any number and 0 is that number.
4. To ____ a mathematical expression is to substitute the value given for each variable and then compute the answer.

CONCEPTS AND SKILLS

Evaluate each expression for $a = 18$. Then write >, <, or = to compare the expressions. (Lesson 1, pp. 28–31)

5. $a + 0$ ● $a - 0$
6. $(a + 7) + 9$ ● $a + (7 + 9)$
7. $50 + a$ ● $a + 50$

Estimate. (Lesson 2, pp. 32–33)

8. 679 + 291
9. 423 − 201
10. 63,947 − 12,508
11. 47,031 + 58,098

Add or subtract. (Lessons 3–4, pp. 34–39)

12. 4,608 − 379
13. 28,347 + 16,017
14. 947 + 258
15. 3,694 + 2,613

Use mental math to solve. (Lesson 5, pp. 40–41)

16. $n + 12 = 25$
17. $81 - p = 80$
18. $b - 52 = 17$
19. $75 - t = 70$

PROBLEM SOLVING (Lesson 6, pp. 42–43)

Solve. If there is not enough information, tell what information is needed.

20. The amusement park stops admitting people at 5:00 P.M. Between 5:00 and 5:30, 427 cars left the parking lot. By 6:00, an additional 216 cars had left. How many cars were still parked in the lot at 6:00?

Show You Understand

Look at these examples. Explain how regrouping in addition is different from regrouping in subtraction.

$$\begin{array}{r} 4{,}072 \\ +\ 3{,}180 \\ \hline \end{array} \qquad \begin{array}{r} 4{,}072 \\ -\ 3{,}180 \\ \hline \end{array}$$

Extra Practice

Set A (Lesson 1, pp. 28–31)

Write an algebraic expression for each word phrase.

1. take 2 from a number **2.** 5 increased by a number **3.** 20 is reduced by a number

Translate each algebraic expression into words.

4. $n - 25$ **5.** $17 + a$ **6.** $100 - c$ **7.** $k + 12$ **8.** $m + n$

Evaluate each expression for a = 12. Then write >, <, or =.

9. $a + 1$ ● $a - 1$ **10.** $100 + a$ ● $a + 100$ **11.** $a - 5$ ● $18 - a$

Set B (Lesson 2, pp. 32–33)

Estimate. Tell which method you used.

1. $686 + 231$ **2.** $346 - 188$ **3.** $706 + 197$ **4.** $4,673 - 3,927$ **5.** $9,706 + 3,048$ **6.** $92,545 - 36,789$

Set C (Lesson 3, pp. 34–37)

Add or subtract. Check that your answer is reasonable.

1. $276 + 412$ **2.** $8,603 + 587$ **3.** $9,706 - 3,048$ **4.** $5,308 - 3,591$ **5.** $72,314 + 17,921$ **6.** $95,678 - 89,679$

Set D (Lesson 4, pp. 38–39)

Add or subtract. Tell which method you used.

1. $342,617 + 629,313$ **2.** $580,604 - 450,000$ **3.** $628,589 + 223,000$ **4.** $781,130 - 674,086$ **5.** $4,453,299 + 3,958,214$ **6.** $6,624,120 - 5,921,532$

Set E (Lesson 5, pp. 40–41)

Use mental math to solve the equations.

1. $4 + z = 10$ **2.** $14 - g = 8$ **3.** $5 + p = 12$ **4.** $d - 17 = 50$

5. $61 + w = 72$ **6.** $r - \$14 = \$35$ **7.** $23 - b = 19$ **8.** $n + \$9 = \$20$

WEEKLY WR READER®

Science Connection

SWARM!

Imagine thousands of bees flying overhead or hundreds of thousands of grasshoppers leaping from one field to another.

Swarming is actually a natural behavior of some animals. When honeybees outgrow their hive, the swarm separates to form a new hive. When ants or grasshoppers need food, large numbers of individuals band together to solve the group's problem. As scientists study this "swarm intelligence,"they may find ways to solve human problems, such as traffic congestion and ocean pollution.

Problem Solving

Use the data from the chart about the honeybee swarm to solve Problems 1–3.

Honeybee Swarm		
Type of Bee	**Number**	**Average Length**
Queen	1	1.8 cm
Drone	250	1.55 cm
Worker	12,800	1.2 cm

1. What is the total number of honeybees in this swarm?

2. Compare the lengths of the different types of honeybees. What digit is in the tenths place of each of the lengths?

3. When too many honeybees live in a hive, a swarm of half the bees and one queen look for a new home. If this swarm represents half the original hive, how many more than 25,000 bees were in the original hive?

Technology
Visit *Education Place* at
eduplace.com/kids/mw/
to learn more about this topic.

Unit 1 Test

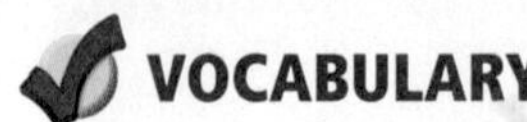

VOCABULARY

Write *true* or *false* for each statement. If a statement is false, rewrite it to make it true.

Vocabulary

- base
- period
- variable
- evaluate
- exponent
- expression
- power of ten

1. A variable is a letter that stands for a number.
2. A period shows the number of times a base is used as a factor.
3. You evaluate an expression when you substitute values for the variables to find the value of the expression.

CONCEPTS AND SKILLS

Write each number in standard form. (Chapter 1)

4. 28 thousand, 28
5. 600,000 + 70,000 + 300 + 9
6. $(8 \times 10^9) + (7 \times 10^7) + (7 \times 10^6) + (9 \times 10^5) + (4 \times 10^2) + (1 \times 10^0)$
7. One hundred eight billion, three hundred million, ninety-eight

Write in expanded form using exponents. (Chapter 1)

8. 520,106
9. 1,084,756

Order each set of numbers from greatest to least. (Chapter 1)

10. 9,825; 9,875; 9,845
11. 2,805,110; 3,020,121; 3,022,407
12. 6; 0.625; 6.25
13. 3.655; 3.656; 36.53; 36.35

Write each decimal in words. (Chapter 1)

14. 0.19
15. 0.6
16. 219.042

Round each number. (Chapter 1)

17. 4.328 to the nearest hundredth
18. 3.526 to the nearest tenth

Evaluate each expression for $n = 6$. (Chapter 2)

19. $n + 17$
20. $18 - n$
21. $n + n$

Estimate each sum or difference. (Chapter 2)

22. 523 + 684
23. 8,140 − 793
24. 752 + 580 + 39

Add or subtract. (Chapter 2)

25. $768{,}923 + 14{,}918$

26. $5{,}428{,}003 - 2{,}472{,}460$

27. $439{,}654 - 97{,}835$

Use mental math to solve each equation. (Chapter 2)

28. $n + 19 = 27$

29. $25 - x = 16$

PROBLEM SOLVING

30. The value of a rare coin was $7,800 in 1998. In 2000 the value rose to $8,300, in 2002 it rose to $8,800, and in 2004 it rose to $9,300. If the pattern continues what is the value of the coin likely to be in 2008?

31. In April, Chris had $1,360 in his bank account. In May, the amount was $1,320, in June it was $1,280, and in July it was $1,240. If the pattern continues, how much will he have in his account in September?

Draw a model to solve. If there is not enough information, tell what information is needed.

32. Last year $12,350 was spent on new math books. This year, $15,690 was spent on math books. Usually $17,000 per year is spent on math books. How much less than usual was spent on math books this year?

33. Tickets for a circus were priced at $18 for adults and $10 for students. At last week's performance, 1,432 student tickets were sold. What was the total number of tickets sold for last week's performance?

Decision Making

Extended Response

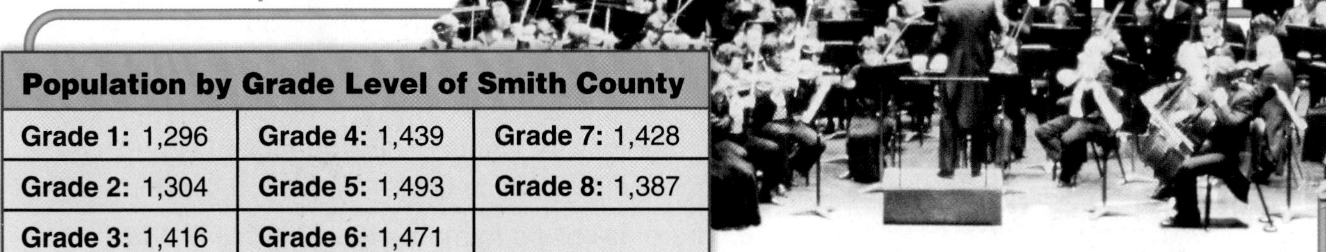

Population by Grade Level of Smith County		
Grade 1: 1,296	**Grade 4:** 1,439	**Grade 7:** 1,428
Grade 2: 1,304	**Grade 5:** 1,493	**Grade 8:** 1,387
Grade 3: 1,416	**Grade 6:** 1,471	

Task A symphony orchestra is offering free concerts for students in Smith County.

Use the population figures above and the information to the right. In what combinations should the superintendent of schools send the grades to hear the concerts? How many concerts will be needed? How many students will be at each concert? Explain your thinking.

Information You Need

- The entire population of a grade must attend a concert together.
- The concert hall has 2,900 seats.
- At least 2,750 seats must be filled for each performance.
- Students in Grades 1 and 2 will not go to the concerts.

Performance Assessment

TASK 1

Lights! Camera! Action! (Chapters 1, 2)

You are the new head of a movie studio! Your first picture will cost $25,000,000. The director's salary must be less than the combined salaries of all the actors. Costumes and scenery will cost more than the director's salary but less than the combined salaries of all the actors. You must keep $2,500,000 aside in case of emergencies. You must spend the entire $25,000,000.

a. Decide how much money the actors will make.

b. How much money will the director make?

c. How much will the costumes and scenery cost?

d. After you complete your budget, you learn that the actors want the total of their salaries to be twice the director's salary. Revise your budget to keep the actors happy.

TASK 2

Happy Trails to You (Chapter 1)

Hiking Trail	Length (in miles)
Grassy Gait	0.75
Fir Mountain	2.60
Rabbit Hill	1.28
Dear Run	2.59
Cliff Challenge	1.78
Rocks and Streams	2.07

You are a ranger at a state park. You have made the list shown at the left.

a. A park visitor wants to hike a trail that is at least 1.5 miles long. Which trail(s) would you recommend?

b. Another visitor wants to hike a trail that is no longer than 2 miles. Which trail(s) would you recommend?

c. There are plans to mark off a new trail that is longer than Dear Run but shorter than Fir Mountain. What are three possible lengths for the new trail?

Self Check

- Did I answer the questions for each task?
- Did I check all my work?

Enrichment

Fibonacci Numbers

About 800 years ago a mathematician named Leonardo Fibonacci noticed a sequence of numbers that appears throughout nature.

1, 1, 2, 3, 5, 8, 13, 21, 34, 55,...

When Fibonacci analyzed the sequence, he found that each number beginning with 2 is the sum of the two numbers that come before it:

$1 + 1 = 2$, $2 + 1 = 3$, $3 + 2 = 5$, and so on.

Look at this pine cone. It has 8 righthand spirals and 13 lefthand spirals. Both numbers are in the Fibonacci sequence.

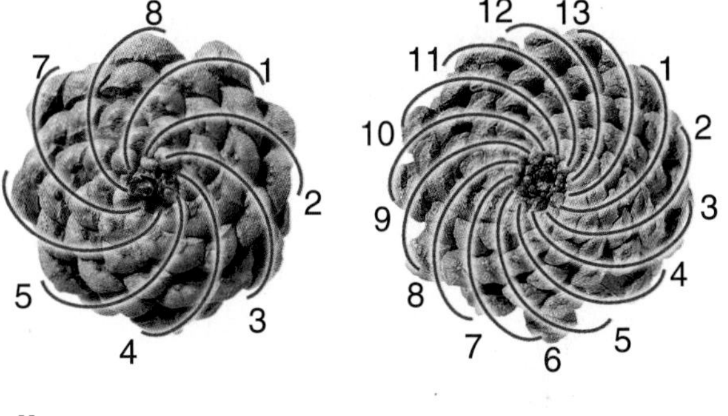

Try These!

Use grid paper to show how the Fibonnaci sequence appears in the spiral of a Nautilus shell.

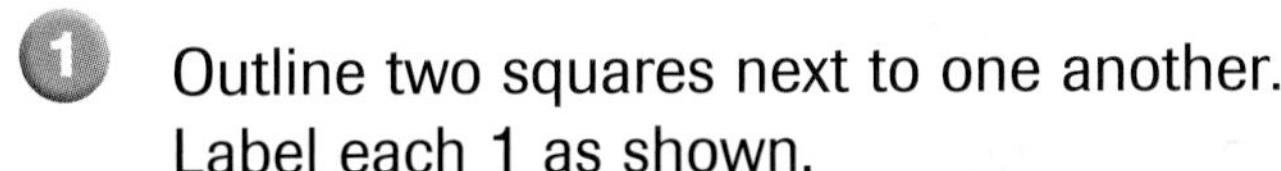

1. Outline two squares next to one another. Label each 1 as shown.

2. The next square in your drawing must have sides whose length is the sum of the lengths of the first two squares. Outline this square alongside the first two. Label it 2.

3. Continue adding squares. The length of the sides of each new square must be the sum of the lengths of the previous two squares' sides. Label each square. Repeat until you cannot fit any more squares on your paper.

4. If you continued to use this sequence, would you eventually draw a square with sides 1,000 centimeters long? Explain.

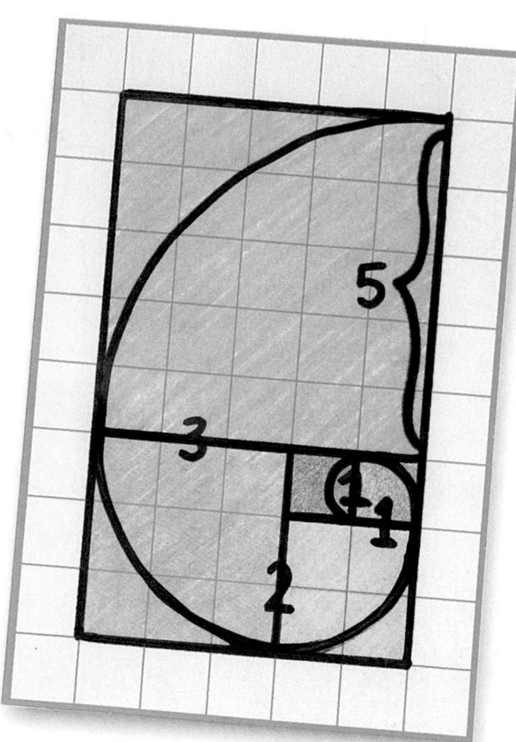

Cumulative Test Prep Practice

Solve Problems 1–10.

Test-Taking Tip

Sometimes when you take a multiple choice test, you can eliminate answer choices that are clearly wrong.

Look at the example below.

Gary jogged 5 fewer kilometers this week than he jogged last week. If n stands for the distance he jogged last week, which expression shows the distance he jogged this week?

A $n + 5$ **C** $5 - n$

B $5 + n$ **D** $n - 5$

THINK

Look at the first two choices, $n + 5$ and $5 + n$. You know from the Commutative Property of Addition that these two expressions represent the same amount. Therefore, you can eliminate choices A and B.

Multiple Choice

1. There are 12 fewer students in Marie's class than there are in Adele's class. If a stands for the number of students in Adele's class, which expression shows the number of students in Marie's class?

A $a + 12$ **C** $12 - a$

B $a - 12$ **D** $12 + a$

(Chapter 2, Lesson 1)

2. What is the value of n in this equation?

$$46 - n = 20$$

F 66 **H** 26

G 46 **J** 16

(Chapter 2, Lesson 5)

3. What is the value of the digit 3 in 354,968?

A 300 **C** 30,000

B 3,000 **D** 300,000

(Chapter 1, Lesson 1)

4. Tyler spent \$32 on clothing, \$19 on records, and \$28 on food. Which is the best estimate of the total amount he spent?

F \$50 **H** \$90

G \$80 **J** \$170

(Chapter 2, Lesson 2)

 For more Test-Taking Tips, see pages xxii–xxv.

Free Response

5. What is the value of the underlined digit?

16,2̲08

(Chapter 1, Lesson 5)

6. A city plans to spend $1,953,631 on schools. What is the digit in the ten thousands place of the number that represents the money spent on schools?

(Chapter 1, Lesson 3)

7. In 1810, the land area of the United States was 1,681,828 square miles. By 1820 the land area was 1,749,462 square miles. By how many square miles had the land area of the United States increased?

(Chapter 2, Lesson 4)

8. Each month, Dale recorded the height of his tomato plant in centimeters. If the heights form a pattern, what is the missing height?

Month	Height (in centimeters)
May	25
June	38
July	?
August	64
September	77

(Chapter 1, Lesson 6)

9. This expression shows the greatest distance from the Earth to the Sun:

$$(9 \times 10^7) + (4 \times 10^6) + (5 \times 10^5)$$

How many times does the digit 0 appear in this number when written in standard form?

(Chapter 1, Lesson 2)

Extended Response

10. This chart shows the 1990 and 2000 populations of the largest counties in Florida.

County	Population	
	1990	**2000**
Miami-Dade	1,937,094	2,253,362
Broward	1,255,488	1,623,018
Palm Beach	863,518	1,131,184
Hillsborough	834,054	998,948
Orange	677,491	896,344

A What was the total population of the two largest counties in 2000?

B In 1990, which two counties had a combined population that was about the same as the population of Miami-Dade County?

C Which county had the greatest population growth from 1990 to 2000? Explain how you found your answer.

D In 1990, which county had a population closest to 1 million?

E Suppose the population of Miami-Dade County eventually doubles from the 2000 figure. Write this population figure in expanded form using exponents.

(Chapter 2, Lesson 4)

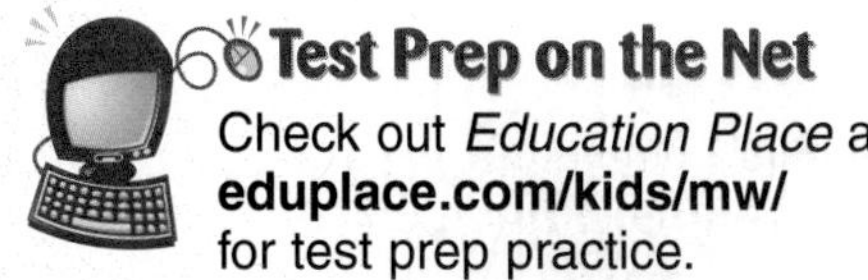

Test Prep on the Net
Check out *Education Place* at **eduplace.com/kids/mw/** for test prep practice.

Cross-Calculations

Copy the puzzles onto grid paper.
Use a calculator to help you solve each problem.

Across

Row A: 152,609 + 24,247 = ■

Row B: 975,621 − 102,290 = ■

Row C: 838,620 + ■ = 991,460

Down

Column D: 963,221 − ■ = 205,371

Column E: 900,632 − 57,347 = ■

Column F: ■ − 412,809 = 258,196

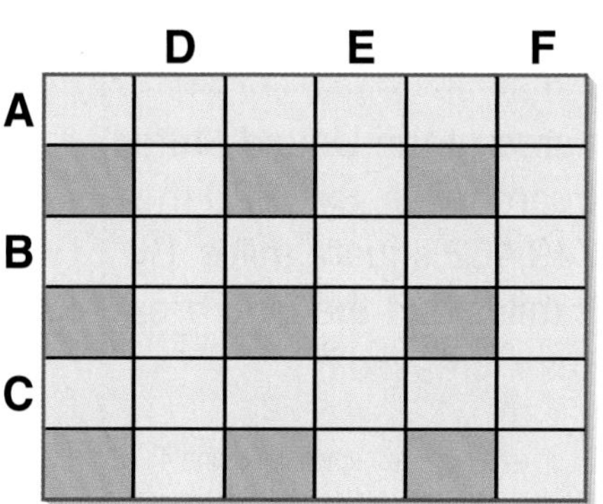

Across

Row G: 546,309 − ■ = 228,453

Row H: 411,256 − 187,388 = ■

Row I: ■ − 175,612 = 61,042

Down

Column J: 685,311 − ■ = 492,381

Column K: 668,321 + 150,139 = ■

Column L: ■ + 334,200 = 962,940

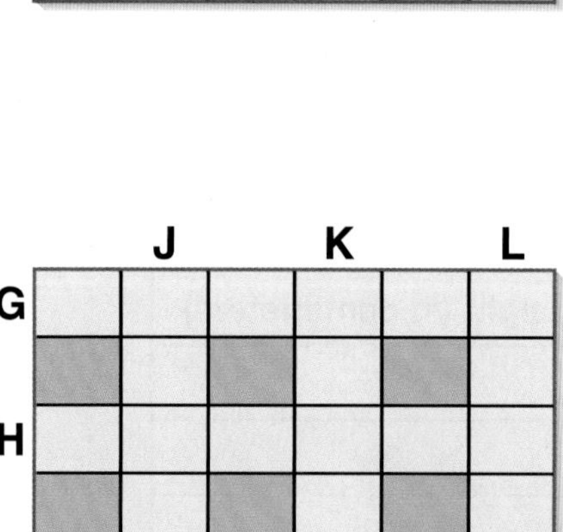

Challenge **Write clues to go along with the cross number puzzle shown at the right.**

		D		E		F
A	3	6	7	2	1	5
		8		1		3
B	7	8	2	1	0	1
		0		8		1
C	3	6	5	7	9	2
		7		1		7

Vocabulary Wrap-Up for Unit 1

WEEKLY WR READER Activity Almanac
See page 678 for the activity for this unit.

Look back at the big ideas and vocabulary in this unit.

Big Ideas

A number can be expressed in different ways.

Compare numbers by aligning them according to place value and, starting from the left, comparing digits until they are different.

You can estimate a sum or difference of whole numbers before you compute to help you judge the reasonableness of a computed sum or difference.

e Glossary

Key Vocabulary

number
estimate
sum
difference

Math Conversations

Use your new vocabulary to discuss these big ideas.

1. Explain how to write 3,050,710,380 in expanded form with exponents.
2. Explain how to estimate the sum 84,924 + 121,499.
3. Explain how to order these numbers: 8; 0.89; 8.19
4. Explain how you would find the next number in this pattern: 1,283; 1,498; 1,713; ?
5. **Write About It** Every ten years, there is a census in which the people of the United States are counted. Find census information about your state. Has the population been increasing? How many people do you think will live in your state when the next census is taken? Explain your thinking.

I need to compare these two numbers.
Don't forget to line up the numbers according to place value before comparing.

Building Vocabulary

Reviewing Vocabulary

Here are some math vocabulary words that you should know.

factors	numbers that are multiplied to get a product
product	the answer in a multiplication problem
dividend	the number that is divided in division
divisor	the number by which a number is being divided
quotient	the answer in division
estimate	a number close to an exact amount that tells about how much or about how many

Reading Words and Symbols

You can use words, symbols, or words and symbols to express multiplication and division in different ways.

All these statements represent the same multiplication problem:

three groups of four

- 3 times 4
- 3×4
- 4×3
- $\begin{array}{r} 4 \\ \times\ 3 \\ \hline \end{array}$

All these statements represent the same division problem:

twelve divided by three

- 12 divided by 3
- $12 \div 3$
- $3\overline{)12}$

Write whether the symbol *n* represents a factor or a product. Then find the value of *n*.

1. $8 \times n = 40$ **2.** $n = 8 \times 4$

Tell if the ■ symbol represents the divisor, the dividend, or the quotient. Then find the value of ■.

3.  $4\overline{)36}$ **4.** $35 \div$ ■ $= 5$ 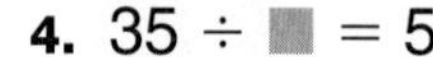 **5.** ■ $\div 7 = 8$

Reading Test Questions

Choose the correct answer for each.

9. Which multiplication statement is modeled by the array of dots at the right?

a. $1 \times 24 = 24$

b. $2 \times 12 = 24$

c. $3 \times 8 = 24$

d. $4 \times 6 = 24$

An **array** is an arrangement of objects, pictures, or numbers in columns and rows.

10. Which of these statements about $48 \div 6 = 8$ is false?

a. The dividend is greater than the divisor.

b. The quotient is greater than the divisor.

c. The divisor is greater than the quotient.

d. The quotient is less than the dividend.

False means "wrong" or "not true."

11. Which of the following has a quotient that is at least 7?

a. $48 \div 12$

b. $56 \div 7$

c. $35 \div 7$

d. $30 \div 5$

At least means "equal to or greater than."

Learning Vocabulary

Watch for these new words in this unit. Write their definitions in your journal.

compatible numbers

divisible

Distributive Property

front-end estimation

order of operations

partial products

Vocabulary

e • **Glossary**

e • **WordGame**

Literature Connection

Read "Ready for Anything" on page 640. Then work with a partner to answer the questions about the story.

CHAPTER 3

Multiply Whole Numbers

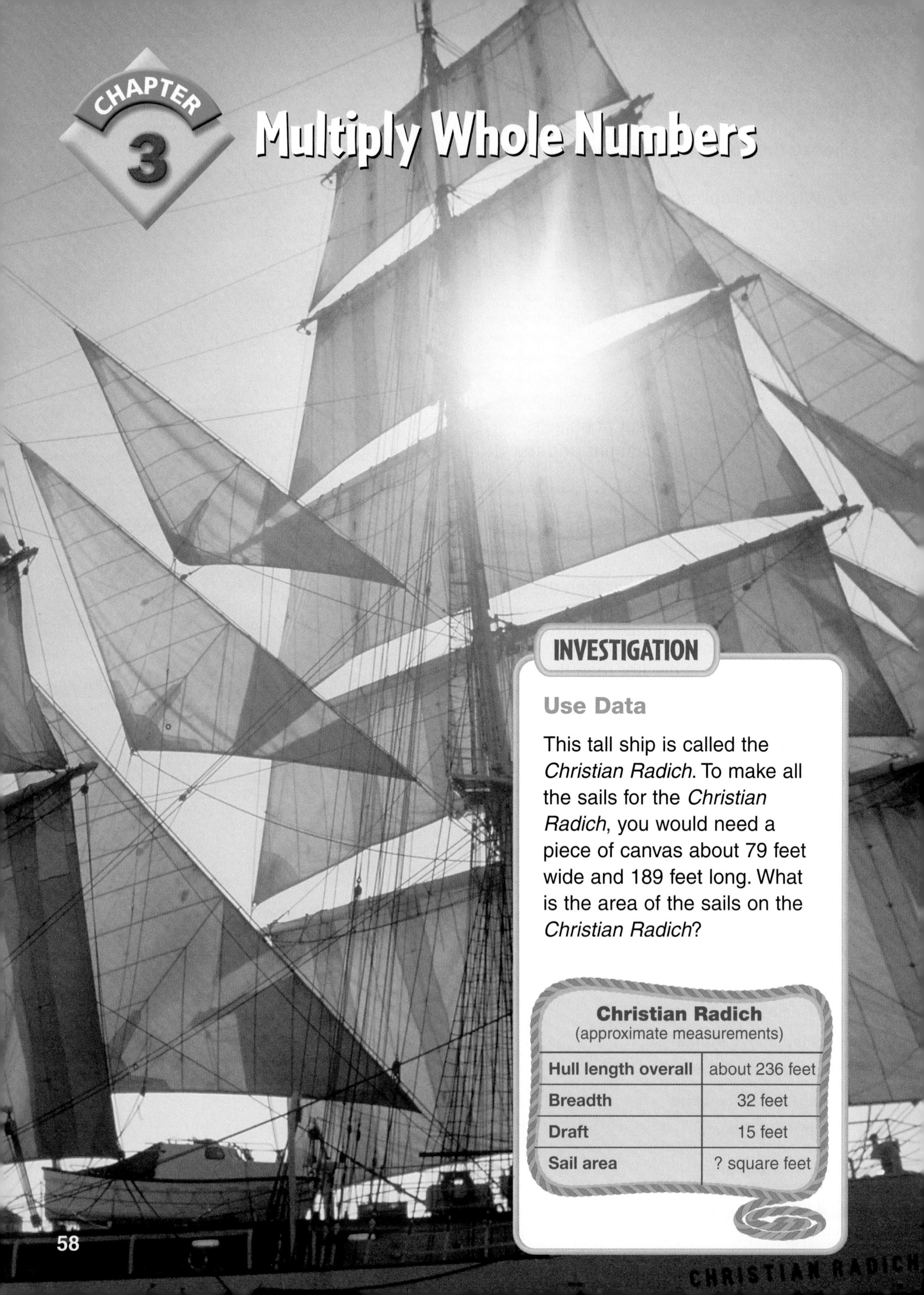

INVESTIGATION

Use Data

This tall ship is called the *Christian Radich*. To make all the sails for the *Christian Radich*, you would need a piece of canvas about 79 feet wide and 189 feet long. What is the area of the sails on the *Christian Radich*?

Christian Radich
(approximate measurements)

Hull length overall	about 236 feet
Breadth	32 feet
Draft	15 feet
Sail area	? square feet

CHRISTIAN RADICH

Chapter Pretest

Use this page to review and remember what you need to know for this chapter.

VOCABULARY

Choose the best word to complete each sentence.

1. In $5 \times 3 = 15$, the number 15 is called the ■.
2. A(n) ____ can help you tell whether an answer is reasonable.
3. If you know the number of equal sets and the number in each equal set, you can ____ to find the total.
4. An example of the ____ of Addition is $7 + 0 = 7$.

CONCEPTS AND SKILLS

Use basic facts and patterns to find each product.

5. 8×7
8×70
8×700
$8 \times 7{,}000$
6. 6×9
6×90
6×900
$6 \times 9{,}000$
7. 5×7
5×70
5×700
$5 \times 7{,}000$

Find a value for *n* that makes each equation true.

8. $n + 4 = 4 + 5$
9. $(n + 9) + 2 = 6 + (9 + 2)$
10. $8 + n = 8$

Estimate using front-end estimation. Then estimate by rounding.

11. 845 + 656 + 312
12. 267 + 458 + 522
13. 789 + 362 + 163
14. 584 + 471 + 110
15. \$30.95 + \$63.20
16. \$1.38 + \$5.76

Estimate by clustering.

17. 32 + 27 + 36 + 29
18. 76 + 79 + 84 + 81
19. 302 + 315 + 279

20. How can the Associative Property of Addition help you add mentally?

Test Prep on the Net

Visit *Education Place* at **eduplace.com/kids/mw/** for more review.

Algebra

Expressions and Multiplication Properties

Objective Evaluate algebraic expressions and use the properties of multiplication.

e Glossary

Vocabulary

Commutative Property
Associative Property
Identity Property
Zero Property

Learn About It

MathTracks 1/7
Listen and Understand

A minivan holds 6 passengers. Write an expression to find the number of passengers that n minivans can hold. Then find how many passengers 5 minivans will hold.

Write and evaluate an algebraic expression.

STEP 1 Write an expression.

2 minivans hold 2×6 passengers.

n minivans hold $n \times 6$ passengers.

STEP 2 Evaluate $n \times 6$ when $n = 5$.

Substitute 5 for n to see how many passengers 5 minivans will hold.

$$6 \times n = 6 \times 5 = 30$$

Solution: Five minivans will hold 30 passengers.

Different ways to express multiplication.
$n \times 6$ $n \bullet 6$ $n(6)$ $6n$

You can use multiplication properties to evaluate expressions.

Properties of Multiplication

Commutative Property

Changing the order of factors does not change the product.

$$a \times b = b \times a$$

Example: $5 \times 10 = 10 \times 5$

Identity Property

The product of any number and 1 is that number.

$$m \times 1 = m$$

Example: $72 \times 1 = 72$

Associative Property

Changing the grouping of factors does not change the product.

$$a \times (b \times c) = (a \times b) \times c$$

Example: $3 \times (5 \times 4) = (3 \times 5) \times 4$

Zero Property

The product of any number and 0 is 0.

$$z \times 0 = 0$$

Example: $36 \times 0 = 0$

Guided Practice

Write an expression for each.

1. a number multiplied by 5
2. 7 more than a number

Evaluate. Tell which property you used.

3. $27 \times 0 \times 3$
4. (38)(25)(4)
5. $20(34 \times p)$, given $p = 5$
6. $a \bullet 15 \bullet 3$, given $a = 1$

Ask Yourself

- What mathematical symbols can I substitute for words?
- Which property can I use to help me evaluate the expression?

TEST TIPS

TEST TIPS **Explain Your Thinking** ▶ How can knowing multiplication properties help you evaluate $(96 \times 20) \times 5$?

Practice and Problem Solving

Write an expression for each.

7. the product of 5 and a number
8. 125 decreased by a number
9. a number divided by 18
10. 96 added to a number

Evaluate. Tell which property you used.

11. $1 \times 17 \times 2$
12. $(49 \bullet 500) \bullet 2$
13. $36 \times 0 \times 8$
14. $5 \bullet 27 \bullet 2$

Evaluate each expression, given $n = 4$, $t = 7$, and $v = 5$.

15. $5 \bullet t$
16. $(n \bullet 8) \bullet v$
17. $t \bullet (n + v)$
18. $200 \div v$
19. $n + t + v$

Solve.

20. A plane flies 600 miles per hour. Write an expression for the distance traveled in m hours. Then find the number of miles the plane flies in 3 hours.
21. Larry spent $25 on books and $32 on CDs. Then Sarah gave him $10. Larry now has $31. How much did he have before he bought the books and CDs?
22. **What's Wrong?** Ted says that $2 \times (3 \times d)$ gives twice the sum of 3 and a number d. What's wrong?
23. **Analyze** Muriel has $26. She wants to buy 3 books for $7 each and 2 magazines for $3 each. Does she have enough money?

Daily Review | Test Prep

Write in expanded form. (Ch. 1, Lesson 5)

24. 734
25. 8,965
26. 26,421

27. **Free Response** Which property helps you find the product 26×0?

Explain how you got your answer.

Extra Practice See page 83, Set A.

Model the Distributive Property

Objective Use the Distributive Property to multiply.

Materials
grid paper
straightedge
colored pencils

Work Together

You can draw a rectangle to show how to find a product.

A rectangle is 5 units wide and 16 units long. You can use simple multiplication facts to find the area of the rectangle.

Work with a partner to use models to multiply.

STEP 1 With a straightedge, draw a rectangle 5 units wide and 16 units long.

- Would it be easier to find the area of the rectangle if you divided it into two parts? Explain.

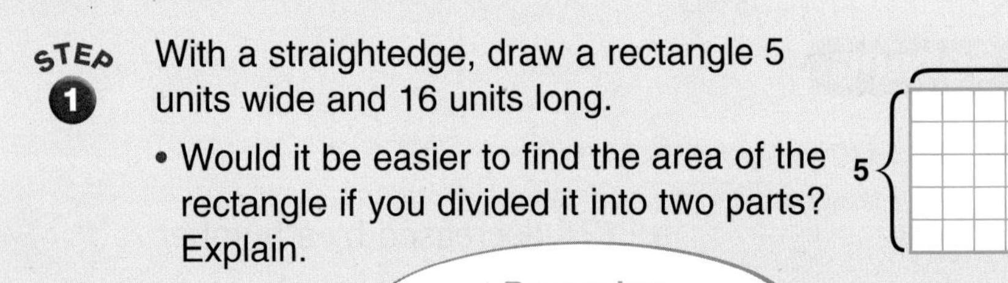

Remember
Area = length × width

STEP 2 The diagram shows one way to divide the rectangle. Divide your rectangle. Shade and label each part.

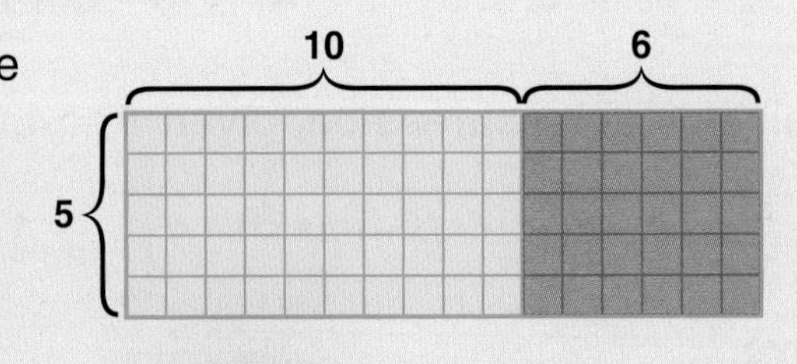

Find the area of the rectangle.

Use the **Distributive Property** to complete the number sentences shown below.

Area = 5 × 16
= 5 × (10 + 6)
= (5 × 10) + (5 × 6)
= ? + ? ← **partial products**
= ?

Distributive Property

When you multiply the sum of two or more addends by a factor, the product is the same as if you multiplied each addend by the factor and then added the products.

$a(b + c) = (a \times b) + (a \times c)$

On Your Own

Use the Distributive Property to multiply. Show the partial products for each and find the sum. Then write a multiplication sentence for each.

1. 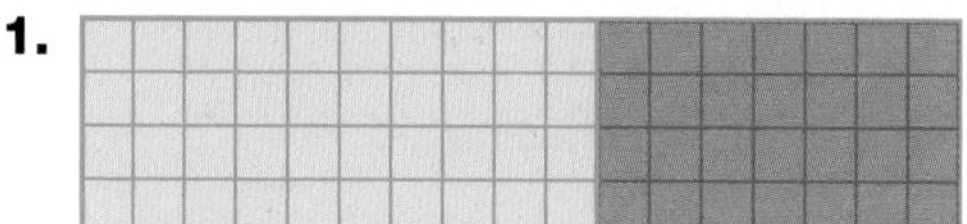

2. 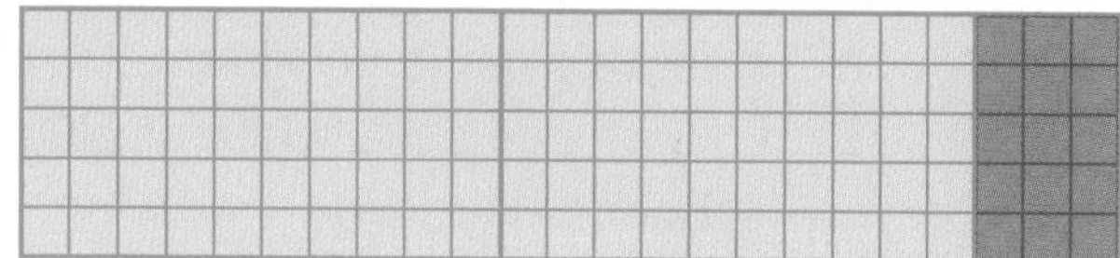

3. 

4. 

Draw and divide a rectangle to show each product. Use the Distributive Property to find the product.

5. 6 × 18
6. 7 × 25
7. 8 × 34
8. 9 × 42
9. 7 × 36
10. 3 × 41
11. 3 × 54
12. 8 × 23

Talk About It • Write About It

You learned how to use the Distributive Property to multiply.

13. Explain how you can use the Distributive Property to find the product of 6 × 27.

14. When you use the Distributive Property to find areas of rectangles, why does it make sense to separate the rectangles so you get groups of 10?

Lesson 3

Problem-Solving Strategy

Use Logical Reasoning

Objective Use logical reasoning to solve problems.

Problem Laura, Rita, Ty, and Mike each have one car. Each car is a different color. Laura's car is not green. Rita's car is not white or blue. Ty's car is red. Mike's car is not blue. What color is each person's car?

UNDERSTAND

This is what you know:

- Each car is a different color.
- Laura's car is not green.
- Rita's car is not white or blue.
- Ty's car is red.
- Mike's car is not blue.

PLAN

You can use logical reasoning to help solve the problem.

SOLVE

- Ty's car is red, so no other car can be red.
- Rita's car is not red, because Ty's car is red. It is also not white or blue. So, Rita's car must be green.
- Since Ty's car is red and Rita's car is green, Mike and Laura must have blue and white cars.
- Mike's car is not blue. So, it must be white.
- Laura's car is blue because that is the only remaining color.

Solution: Ty's car is red, Rita's car is green, Mike's car is white, and Laura's car is blue.

LOOK BACK

Look back at the problem. Does the solution make sense?

Guided Practice

Use the Ask Yourself questions to help you solve each problem.

1. Neil, Karen and Tonya sit together in an airplane. There are three seats in a row–aisle, middle, and window. Neither Karen nor Tonya sits next to the window. Tonya sits next to Neil. In which seat is each person?

2. Four planes are waiting to take off. They will fly to four cities: Atlanta, Charlotte, Miami, and Houston. The plane to Atlanta is not the first or the last. The plane to Charlotte is second. The plane to Miami is not the first. In what order will the planes take off?

Hint Start with a list of what you know.

Ask Yourself

What facts do I know?

PLAN

Did I make a table?

SOLVE

- Does my table show all possibilities?
- How can I use each fact to write yes or no in the table?

LOOK BACK

Does the solution make sense?

Independent Practice

Use logical reasoning to solve each problem.

3. Ned, Martin, Astrid, and Nasser each arrive on a different flight shown at the right. Astrid arrives after 3:30 P.M. Ned arrives between 3:10 P.M. and 3:50 P.M. Nasser arrives after Astrid. At what time does each person arrive?

Flight Number	Arriving From	Arrival Time	Gate Number
104	Atlanta	3:05 P.M.	E14
078	San Francisco	3:20 P.M.	E22
3456	Portland	3:45 P.M.	E16
7092	Minneapolis	4:00 P.M.	E31

4. Ken, Lisa, and Barry buy a different kind of ticket shown to the right. Barry does not buy the most expensive ticket. Ken's ticket is less expensive than Barry's. Which kind of ticket does each person buy?

Round Trip Boston to San Francisco

Ticket Class	Price
First Class	$1,605
Business	$1,100
Coach	$ 479

5. Fawn, Bill, Celine, and Suki each use a different kind of transportation: boat, car, bus, or airplane. Bill's transportation has no wheels. Fawn flies. Suki does not use a car. Which kind of transportation does each person use?

Choose a Strategy

Solve. Show your work. Tell what strategy you used.

6. The price of a car is $16,000 in 2001, $17,500 in 2002, $19,000 in 2003, and $22,000 in 2005. Based on this information, what, most likely, is the price of the car in 2004?

7. Jerry is thinking of two numbers that have a difference of 8 and a product of 48. What are the two numbers?

8. Janelle thinks of a number, doubles it, and then adds 15. The result is 39. What equation could you use to find the number? Of what number was Janelle thinking?

PROBLEM-SOLVING Strategies

- Use Models
- Draw a Diagram
- Find a Pattern
- Guess and Check
- Make an Organized List
- Make a Table
- Solve a Simpler Problem
- Use Logical Reasoning
- Work Backward
- Write an Equation

Data **Use the advertisement to solve Problems 9–12.**

9. Willow buys a three time-zone watch, a computer case, and an appointment book. How much did she spend?

10. **Explain** Maxwell has $90. He needs to buy a daypack and an insulated water bottle for his trip. He would also like to get a portable disc player. Does he have enough money for all three? Explain why or why not.

11. Kaya is going to buy 4 insulated water bottles and a magnetic chess set. Use b to represent the cost of the water bottles and c to represent the cost of the chess set. What expression could you write to show the cost of all 5 items?

12. **Create and Solve** Write and solve a problem about 3 students going on a hike. Use the data from the advertisement.

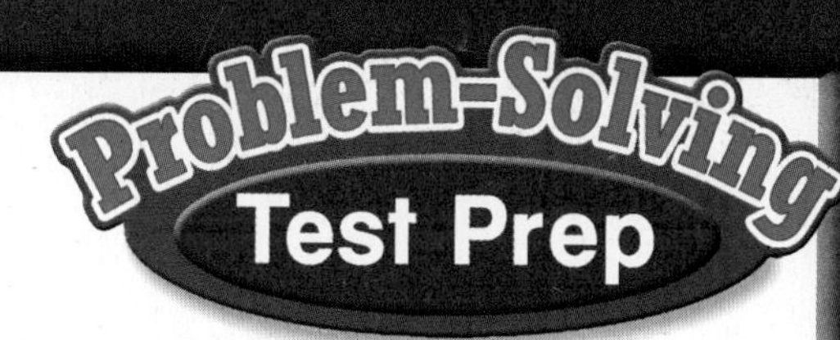

Choose the letter of the correct answer.
If a correct answer is not here, choose NH.

1. A package holds 12 pencils. Which of the following expressions gives the number of pencils you have if you buy *n* packages of pencils and 3 single pencils?

A $n + 3$ **C** $12n + 3$

B $12n$ **D** $12n + 3n$

(Chapter 3, Lesson 1)

2. Joel works a total of 16 hours on Friday, Saturday, and Sunday. He works twice as many hours on Saturday as on Friday. Joel works 4 hours on Sunday. How many hours does Joel work on Saturday?

F 3 hours **H** 6 hours

G 4 hours **J** NH

(Grade 4, Chapter 18, Lesson 1)

3. The table shows how many passengers use an airport each year.

Year	Passengers
1980	1,450,000
1990	1,520,000
2000	1,590,000

If the pattern continues, how many passengers will use the airport in 2020?

A 1,620,000 **C** 1,720,000

B 1,660,000 **D** 1,730,000

(Chapter 1, Lesson 6)

4. Hamburger buns come in packs of eight. Which of the following is *not* needed in order to find out how much you will spend on hamburger buns for a picnic?

F the cost of a pack of buns

G the number of buns you need

H the cost per pound of hamburger

J all of the information in A, B, and C is needed.

(Chapter 2, Lesson 6)

5. Regina's kitchen is 8 feet long and 10 feet wide. Regina wants to cover the floor with tiles that are 1 foot long and 1 foot wide. How many tiles will Regina need?

Represent Support your solution with a picture.

(Grade 4, Chapter 18, Lesson 1)

6. Find the value of each symbol:

■, ●, ▲

■ + ■ = 80

■ + ● = 140

● − ▲ = ▲

Explain How did you find the value of each symbol?

(Chapter 2, Lesson 5)

Test Prep on the Net

Check out *Education Place* at **eduplace.com/kids/mw/** for test prep practice.

Lesson 4

Multiply by One-Digit Numbers

Objective Multiply by one-digit numbers.

Learn About It

A plane flies at an average speed of 528 miles an hour. How far does it fly in 6 hours?

Multiply to solve the problem.

Find 6 × 528.

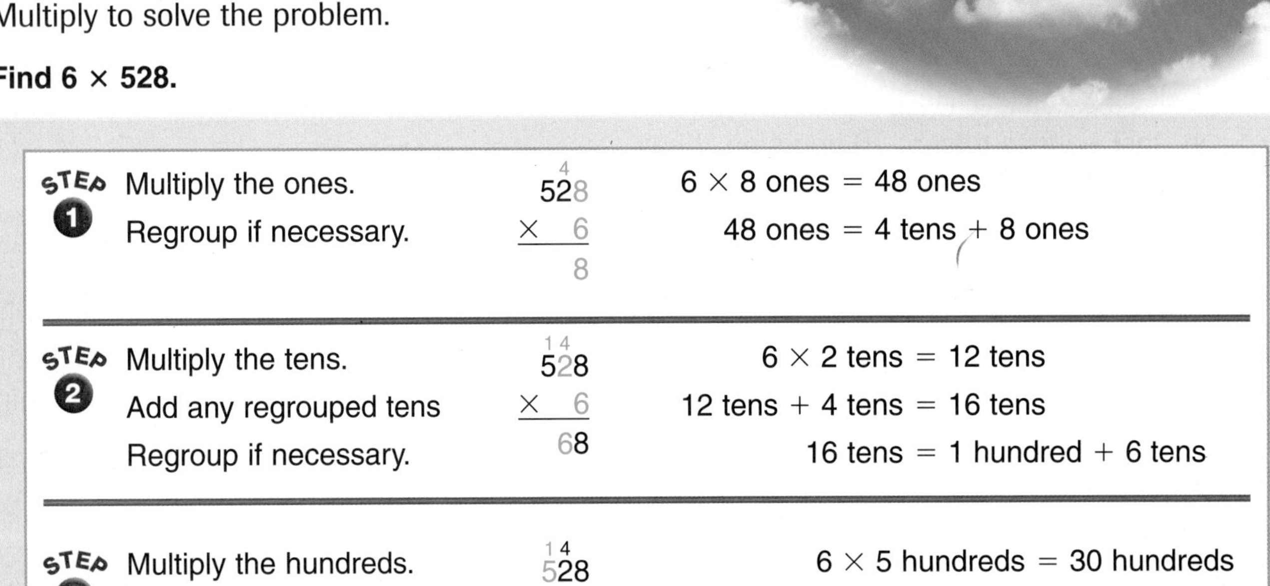

STEP 1	Multiply the ones. Regroup if necessary.	$\begin{array}{r} \scriptstyle 4 \\ 528 \\ \times\ 6 \\ \hline 8 \end{array}$	6×8 ones $=$ 48 ones 48 ones $=$ 4 tens $+$ 8 ones
STEP 2	Multiply the tens. Add any regrouped tens Regroup if necessary.	$\begin{array}{r} \scriptstyle 1\,4 \\ 528 \\ \times\ 6 \\ \hline 68 \end{array}$	6×2 tens $=$ 12 tens 12 tens $+$ 4 tens $=$ 16 tens 16 tens $=$ 1 hundred $+$ 6 tens
STEP 3	Multiply the hundreds. Add any regrouped hundreds.	$\begin{array}{r} \scriptstyle 1\,4 \\ 528 \\ \times\ 6 \\ \hline 3{,}168 \end{array}$	6×5 hundreds $=$ 30 hundreds 30 hundreds $+$ 1 hundred $=$ 31 hundreds

Solution: In 6 hours, the plane flies 3,168 miles.

To help you understand how multiplication works, you can use the Distributive Property.

Find the value of 6*n*, when *n* = 528.

6×528 ⟵ Substitute 528 for *n*.

$6 \times 528 = 6 \times (500 + 20 + 8)$ ⟵ Write one factor as a sum of numbers.

$= (6 \times 500) + (6 \times 20) + (6 \times 8)$ ⟵ Use the Distributive Property.

$= 3{,}000 + 120 + 48$

$= 3{,}168$

Guided Practice

Ask Yourself

- Do I need to regroup?
- Did I remember to add the regrouped numbers?

Find the product.

1. 51×6
2. 673×4
3. $24{,}087 \times 4$
4. 3×84
5. 809×7
6. $6 \times 4{,}582$

TEST TIPS **Explain Your Thinking** ▶ How can you use the Distributive Property to find the product in Exercise 6?

Practice and Problem Solving

Find the product.

7. 84×7
8. 38×9
9. 41×5
10. 96×2
11. 746×3
12. 314×8
13. 859×4
14. 738×6
15. 773×3
16. 246×7
17. 507×5
18. 487×8
19. $4{,}251 \times 8$
20. $7{,}645 \times 9$
21. $57{,}962 \times 6$
22. $15{,}794 \times 9$
23. $14{,}676 \times 4$
24. $314{,}796 \times 2$
25. $4{,}775 \times 2$
26. $7{,}689 \times 5$
27. $93{,}007 \times 7$
28. $3{,}785{,}092 \times 2$
29. $90{,}608{,}374 \times 3$
30. $76{,}524 \times 6$
31. $7 \times 8{,}741{,}218$
32. $92{,}144{,}000 \times 4$

Algebra • Functions Copy and complete each function table.

33.

Rule: $y = 5x$				
x	478	392	5,206	1,821
y				

34.

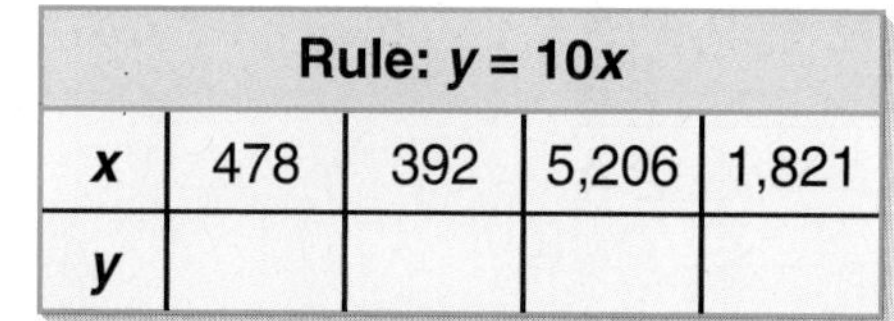

Rule: $y = 10x$				
x	478	392	5,206	1,821
y				

35.

Rule: $y = 3x$				
x	478	392	5,206	1,821
y				

36.

Rule: $y = 6x$				
x	478	392	5,206	1,821
y				

37. Explain how you could use the answers from number 35 to find the answers for number 36.

Use the Distributive Property to rewrite each expression. Then solve.

38. 5×76 **39.** 902×6 **40.** $7 \times 8{,}041$ **41.** $92{,}100 \times 4$

42. 8×925 **43.** 9×430 **44.** $8 \times 82{,}752$ **45.** $92{,}751 \times 4$

Algebra • Expressions Evaluate each expression, when $a = 3$, $b = 67$, $c = 489$, and $d = 9{,}570$.

46. $7c$ **47.** $4 \cdot d$ **48.** $3a \times b$ **49.** $(a \times b) \times 8$

50. $9(2 \times d)$ **51.** $427 \cdot a$ **52.** $a \cdot c$ **53.** $a \times d$

Solve.

54. Cleveland, Ohio, is about 2,550 miles from Los Angeles, California. If a train makes 4 round trips from Cleveland to Los Angeles, how far does it travel?

55. Peter averages 5 miles an hour on his scooter. At that rate, how many miles would he travel if he rode the scooter for an entire day?

56. **Explain** It is approximately 400 miles from The Everglades in southern Florida to the Florida/Georgia border. If a hot air balloon is traveling 86 mi/h, could it cover that distance in 4 hours? Explain how you got your answer.

57. One train car can carry a maximum of 108 passengers. How many passengers can a train carry with 6 completely full cars? If, in one day, that train makes 8 trips while completely full, how many passengers did it carry that day?

58. Hot air balloons can travel at speeds of up to 200 mi/h. At that rate, how many miles can a hot air balloon travel in 7 hours?

59. **Analyze** Look at the problem below. Find digits that make the multiplication true. Can you find two different answers?

$$\begin{array}{r} \blacksquare\,\blacksquare{,}8\,\blacksquare\,4 \\ \times \quad\quad 6 \\ \hline \blacksquare\,4{,}\,\blacksquare\,2\,4 \end{array}$$

Extra Practice See page 83 Set B.

Quick Check

Check your understanding of Lessons 1–4.

Evaluate each expression. Tell which property you used. (Lesson 1)

1. $(32 \times n) \times 25$, given $n = 4$

2. $2 \times 20 \times a$, given $a = 1$

Draw and divide a rectangle to show each product. Use the Distributive Property to find the product. (Lesson 2)

3. 5×13

4. 9×24

5. 3×35

Find the product. (Lesson 4)

6. $\begin{array}{r} 69 \\ \times\ 7 \\ \hline \end{array}$

7. $\begin{array}{r} 342 \\ \times\ \ 9 \\ \hline \end{array}$

8. $\begin{array}{r} 274 \\ \times\ \ 4 \\ \hline \end{array}$

Solve. Tell what strategy you used. (Lesson 3)

9. Barbara, Elmo, Zachary, and Alejandro are in line to buy tickets to ride on a hot air balloon. Barbara is third. Zachary is not first or second. Alejandro is not first. In what position is each person?

Calculator Connection

Product Patterns

Use a calculator to find the products below.

1. $37 \times 3 = ?$
$37 \times 6 = ?$
$37 \times 9 = ?$

2. $99 \times 11 = ?$
$99 \times 22 = ?$
$99 \times 33 = ?$

3. $143 \times 7 = ?$
$143 \times 14 = ?$
$143 \times 21 = ?$

For each set:

- Describe the pattern in the factors.
- Describe the pattern in the products.
- Predict the next two equations. Use your calculator to check your predictions.

Challenge **Now use your calculator to make your own pattern. Write the first three equations. Then give them to a classmate and have them predict the next 2 equations.**

Algebra

Patterns in Multiples of 10

Objective Use mental math to multiply a number by a multiple of 10.

Learn About It

Some large ships can carry about 2,000 passengers per trip. About how many passengers could such a ship carry in 8 trips?

Multiply. $8 \times 2,000 = n$

Different Ways to Multiply by Multiples of 10

Way 1 You can use patterns.

$8 \times 2 = 16$
$8 \times 20 = 160$
$8 \times 200 = 1,600$
$8 \times 2,000 = 16,000$

Way 2 You can use mental math.

$8 \times 2,000 = 8 \times 2 \times 1,000$
$= 16 \times 1,000$
$= 16,000$

Solution: It could carry about 16,000 passengers in 8 trips.

Multiplying 24 × 40 is the same as doing one-digit multiplication and then multiplying by 10.

Find 24 × 40

Think
$24 \times 40 = 24 \times 4 \times 10$

STEP 1 Find 24 × 4.

$$\begin{array}{r} 24 \\ \times\ 4 \\ \hline 96 \end{array}$$

STEP 2 Then multiply the result by 10.

$96 \times 10 = 960$

Other Examples

A. First Product Ends in Zero

Find 6 × 50,000.

$6 \times 5 = 30$
$6 \times 5,000 = 30,000$
$6 \times 50,000 = 300,000$

B. Both Factors Are Multiples of 10

Find 8,000 × 4,000.

$8,000 \times 4,000 = 8 \times 1,000 \times 4 \times 1,000$
$= 8 \times 4 \times 1,000 \times 1,000$
$= 32,000,000$

Guided Practice

Ask Yourself

- How many places in the product will contain zeros?
- Have I multiplied correctly?

Use a pattern or mental math to find each product.

1. 4×90
2. 7×500
3. 5×700
4. 800×50
5. 40×60
6. $60 \times 4{,}000$

Multiply.

7. 59×10
8. 32×40
9. 265×30
10. $3{,}970 \times 80$

Explain Your Thinking ▶ How many zeros will be in the product of $40 \times 3{,}000$? How do you know?

Practice and Problem Solving

Use a pattern or mental math to find each product.

11. 80×4
12. 50×9
13. 400×3
14. 700×7
15. 40×5
16. 60×6
17. $9{,}000 \times 2$
18. $7{,}000 \times 8$
19. $7{,}000 \times 30$
20. $6{,}000 \times 30$
21. 20×500
22. 70×900

Multiply.

23. 28×10
24. 74×30
25. 88×60
26. 42×70
27. 376×20
28. 66×60
29. 675×70
30. 812×60

Solve.

31. A round-trip plane ticket from Raleigh to Chicago costs $300. How much would it cost a family of 4 to fly round trip from Raleigh to Chicago?
32. **Reasoning** Maureen and Sally drove 8 hours a day for 6 days. Their average speed was about 50 miles an hour. How many miles did they drive?

Daily Review | Test Prep

Round to the place of the underlined digit.
(Ch. 1, Lesson 3)

33. <u>6</u>7
34. 7<u>4</u>,498
35. <u>3</u>52
36. <u>8</u>,624

37. **Free Response** How can you use mental math to find the product of $50 \times 9{,}000$?

Explain how you got your answer.

Extra Practice See page 83, Set C.

Estimate Products

Objective Estimate products using front-end estimation and rounding.

e Glossary
Vocabulary
front-end estimation

MathTracks 1/9
Listen and Understand

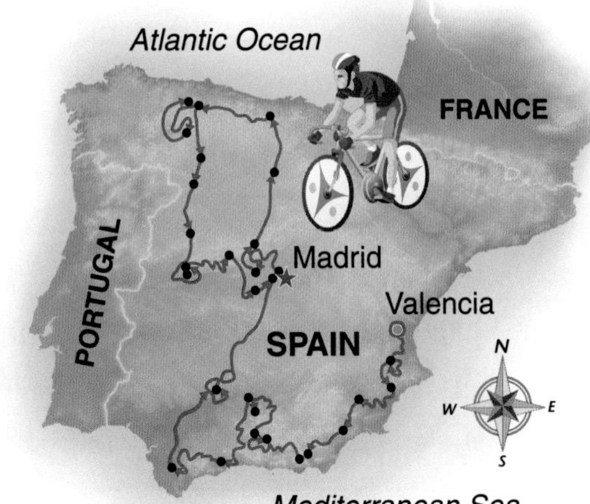

The Tour of Spain bicycle race is held every year. The map shows a recent race course of 3,144 kilometers. If you cycle an average of 75 kilometers a day, can you finish this course in 8 weeks?

8 weeks = 56 days

Since you only need to know if 56 days is enough time to complete the course, use **front-end estimation**.

Estimate: **56 × 75.**

To use front-end estimation, multiply the digits in the greatest place.

$$\begin{array}{r} 75 \\ \times\ 56 \\ \hline \end{array}$$

Front-end estimate: 50 × 70 = 3,500

Since you are rounding both numbers down, a front-end estimate is less than the actual answer.

Solution: Yes. Since 3,500 > 3,144, eight weeks is enough time.

If you cycle an average of 75 km a day for 56 days, about how many kilometers can you cycle?

You can use rounding to estimate.

STEP 1 Round each factor.

75 rounds to 80

56 rounds to 60

STEP 2 Multiply the rounded factors.

$$\begin{aligned} 80 \times 60 &= 8 \times 10 \times 6 \times 10 \\ &= (8 \times 6) \times 10 \times 10 \\ &= 48 \times 100 \\ &= 4{,}800 \end{aligned}$$

Solution: You can cycle about 4,800 kilometers.

You can find a range for the actual product by rounding both factors down and rounding both factors up.

Round both down.	Round both up.
70	80
× 50	× 60
3,500	4,800

Solution: The actual product will fall between 3,500 and 4,800.

Guided Practice

Estimate by using front-end estimation. Then estimate by rounding.

1. 48×86
2. 73×34
3. 62×871

Estimate. Give a range for the actual product.

4. 25×47
5. 31×87
6. 88×491

Ask Yourself

- How do I round each number?
- How do I use front-end estimation and rounding to find a range in which the actual product may fall?

TEST TIPS **Explain Your Thinking** ▶ How do you know that the actual product of 69×58 is between 3,000 and 4,200?

Practice and Problem Solving

Estimate by using front-end estimation. Then estimate by rounding.

7. 65×84
8. 28×67
9. 33×54
10. 17×96
11. 76×521
12. 975×76
13. 709×71
14. 13×555

Estimate. Give a range that includes the actual product.

15. 16×39
16. 45×22
17. 58×67
18. 37×51
19. 76×473
20. 507×45
21. 87×712
22. 364×39

Solve.

23. Ken cycles an average of 12 kilometers per day. About how many kilometers does Ken cycle in 4 weeks?
24. Nicolas had 6 coins that are worth a total of 32¢. What are the coins that he has?
25. **Write About It** Suppose you estimate 49×28. Which method will give you a more accurate estimate, front-end estimation or rounding? Explain.
26. **Explain** Nina made 27 prints that she sells for $29 a piece. Does Nina have enough prints to earn $1,000? Use estimation to explain your answer.

Daily Review | Test Prep

Add. (Ch. 2, Lesson 3)

27. $29 + 5$
28. $36 + 8$
29. $57 + 7$
30. $43 + 4$
31. $13 + 3$
32. $60 + 9$

33. Which is the best estimate of 447×68?

A 24,000 **C** 30,000

B 28,000 **D** 35,000

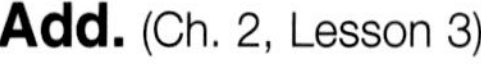
Extra Practice See page 83, Set D.

Lesson 7

Multiply by Two-Digit Numbers

Objective Multiply by a two-digit number.

Learn About It

One train engineer makes a weekly salary of $986. How much does that train engineer earn in a year?

There are 52 weeks in a year.

Find 986 × 52.

Different Ways to Use the Distributive Property to Find 52 × 986

Way 1 Use an equation.

$$986 \times 52 = n$$
$$\begin{aligned}986 \times 52 &= 986 \times (50 + 2)\\ &= (986 \times 50) + (986 \times 2)\\ &= 49{,}300 + 1{,}972\\ &= 51{,}272\end{aligned}$$

Way 2

STEP 1 Multiply by the ones digit.

$$\begin{array}{r} \scriptstyle 11 \\ 986 \\ \times\ 52 \\ \hline 1972 \end{array} \leftarrow 2 \times 986$$

STEP 2 Multiply by the tens digit.

$$\begin{array}{r} \scriptstyle 43 \\ \scriptstyle 11 \\ 986 \\ \times\ 52 \\ \hline 1972 \\ 49300 \end{array} \leftarrow 50 \times 986$$

STEP 3 Add the partial products.

$$\begin{array}{r} \scriptstyle 43 \\ \scriptstyle 11 \\ 986 \\ \times\ 52 \\ \hline 1972 \\ +\ 49300 \\ \hline 51{,}272 \end{array}$$

Solution: The engineer earns $51,272 a year.

Other Examples

A.

$$\begin{array}{r} \scriptstyle 2 \\ \scriptstyle 5 \\ 47 \\ \times\ 38 \\ \hline 376 \\ +\ 1410 \\ \hline 1{,}786 \end{array} \quad \begin{array}{l} \\ \\ \\ \\ \leftarrow 8 \times 47 \\ \leftarrow 30 \times 47 \\ \\ \end{array}$$

B.

$$\begin{array}{r} \scriptstyle 1 \\ \scriptstyle 1\,1 \\ 2{,}231 \\ \times\ \ 54 \\ \hline 8924 \\ +\ 111550 \\ \hline 120{,}474 \end{array} \quad \begin{array}{l} \\ \\ \\ \\ \leftarrow 4 \times 2{,}231 \\ \leftarrow 50 \times 2{,}231 \\ \\ \end{array}$$

Guided Practice

Find each product. Estimate or use a calculator to check.

1. $\begin{array}{r} 57 \\ \times 26 \\ \hline \end{array}$

2. $\begin{array}{r} 71 \\ \times 34 \\ \hline \end{array}$

3. $\begin{array}{r} 406 \\ \times 25 \\ \hline \end{array}$

4. $\begin{array}{r} 236 \\ \times 78 \\ \hline \end{array}$

Ask Yourself

- Did I align the digits correctly to add the partial products?

Explain Your Thinking ▶ How can you use the Distributive Property to find the product in Exercise 2?

Practice and Problem Solving

Find each product. Estimate or use a calculator to check.

5. $\begin{array}{r} 59 \\ \times 15 \\ \hline \end{array}$

6. $\begin{array}{r} 36 \\ \times 19 \\ \hline \end{array}$

7. $\begin{array}{r} 74 \\ \times 24 \\ \hline \end{array}$

8. $\begin{array}{r} 249 \\ \times 33 \\ \hline \end{array}$

9. $\begin{array}{r} 405 \\ \times 69 \\ \hline \end{array}$

10. $\begin{array}{r} 82 \\ \times 57 \\ \hline \end{array}$

11. $\begin{array}{r} 178 \\ \times 16 \\ \hline \end{array}$

12. $\begin{array}{r} 840 \\ \times 35 \\ \hline \end{array}$

13. $\begin{array}{r} 98 \\ \times 89 \\ \hline \end{array}$

14. $\begin{array}{r} 234 \\ \times 63 \\ \hline \end{array}$

15. 25×98
16. 37×85
17. 54×73
18. 918×87
19. 605×52
20. 62×63
21. 758×76
22. 57×70
23. 308×68
24. 54×495
25. 48×72
26. 79×678

Use the Distributive Property to rewrite each expression. Then evaluate.

27. 28×76
28. 57×14
29. 29×206
30. 38×532

Algebra • Expressions Evaluate each expression, when $f = 10$, $g = 50$, and $h = 100$.

31. $39h$
32. $375f$
33. $35g$
34. $30(f \cdot g)$
35. $(7 \cdot h) \cdot 21$

Evaluate each expression.

36. $52m$, when $m = 105$
37. $74 \cdot z$, when $z = 708$
38. $8 \cdot 4 \cdot p$, when $p = 62$
39. $2 \cdot x \cdot y$, when $x = 7$ and $y = 32$
40. $3b \cdot b$, when $b = 17$
41. $(d \cdot e) \cdot f$, when $d = 5$, $e = 29$, and $f = 46$

Go On

Choose a Computation Method

Mental Math • Estimation • Paper and Pencil • Calculator

Data Use the tables to solve Problems 42–47.

Passengers who fly on Europa Air between the cities shown in the Air Distances table earn one frequent flier mile for each mile they fly. They can use frequent flier miles to buy the awards shown in the frequent flier award table.

Frequent Flier Awards	
Award	**Miles Required for Award**
Upgrade ticket from Coach to First-Class, one-way	10,000
Free Round-Trip Coach Ticket	25,000
Free Round-Trip First-Class Ticket	40,000

42. Mr. Himmel flies round trip between Berlin and Rome once a month. How many frequent flier miles does he earn from these trips in a year?

43. Ingrid has enough frequent flier miles to get 10 free round-trip coach tickets. What is the minimum number of frequent flier miles that Ingrid must have?

44. Ms. Nolan makes 21 round trips between Madrid and London and 4 round trips between Madrid and Stockholm. How many miles does she fly?

Air Distances		
From \ To	Berlin	Madrid
London	583 mi	785 mi
Moscow	1,006 mi	2,147 mi
Paris	548 mi	655 mi
Rome	737 mi	851 mi
Stockholm	528 mi	1,653 mi

45. **Explain** Joel makes 10 round trips between Moscow and Madrid. About how many miles does he fly? Does he earn enough frequent flier miles for a free round-trip first-class ticket? Explain your answer.

46. **Estimate** About how many round trips do you need to make between Stockholm and Berlin to earn enough miles for a ticket upgrade?

47. **You Decide** Suppose you are living in Berlin. You have 120,000 frequent flier miles. How would you use your miles? Explain your thinking.

Daily Review | Test Prep

How many minutes and hours are there between these times?
(Grade 4)

48. 3:15 A.M. to 11:05 A.M.

49. 10:20 P.M. to 2:53 A.M.

50. A plane carries 425 passengers. How many passengers can the plane carry in 24 trips?

A 1,700 **C** 10,200

B 8,500 **D** 12,000

Extra Practice See page 83, Set F.

"Don't Get Caught Short"

Different situations require different types of estimation.

In a store, you should always round up. Remember that there may be a sales tax on certain items. Depending on the state in which you shop, the average sales tax is 5 to 10 cents for every dollar that you spend.

- Allie has $50. She wants to buy 3 DVDs. Each one costs $16. The total tax is $3. Does she have enough money? Explain how you got your answer.

Transportation Estimation

The number of air travelers is expected to triple over the next 20 years. In 1997, Los Angeles International Airport was the fourth busiest in the world, with 60,143,000 passengers. If the number of travelers triples as expected, about how many passengers will use that airport in 2017?

Brain Teaser

What are the next 3 letters in each pattern?

S S M T W _ _ _

O T T F F _ _ _

J F M A M _ _ _

Technology

Visit *Education Place* at **eduplace.com/kids/mw/** to try more brain teasers.

Lesson 8

Problem-Solving Decision

Explain Your Solution

Objective Decide whether an exact answer or a range of estimates is needed to explain the solution.

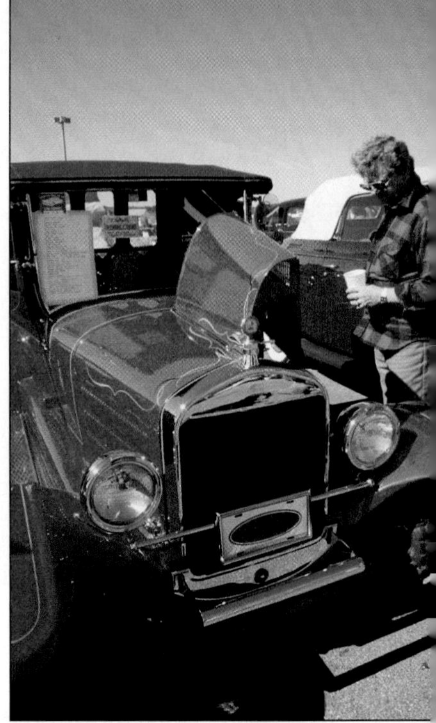

When you solve a problem, you may need an exact computation to explain your solution. At other times, an estimate may be sufficient.

Problem For the past 3 years, the Antique Automobile Club's show has averaged 880 tickets sold per year. Ticket sales are expected to be about the same this year. If the show costs $30,000 to put on, will a ticket price of $35 be enough to cover costs? Explain your answer.

Ask Yourself

- **Do I need an exact answer or is a range of estimates good enough?**

Estimate first.

800 × $30 = $24,000

900 × $40 = $36,000

I can't tell if $35 will work.

Find the exact answer.

880 × $35 = $30,800

Solution: Since $30,800 > $30,000, a ticket price of $35 will be enough to cover costs. In this case an estimate did not give the needed information to solve the problem.

Try These

Solve. Explain your answer.

1. Zida and Sarah are driving from New York to San Francisco. The trip is 2,934 miles. If they travel a maximum of 385 miles per day, will they complete the trip in a week?
2. There are 36 antique cars on display at the antique auto show. A photographer wants to take 16 shots of each car. If he has rolls of film with 24 pictures each, will 24 rolls of film be enough?
3. Alfred bought an antique car for $24,495. Alfred spent $6,000 restoring the car. He sold the car for $60,000. Did Alfred receive double the amount of money he spent buying and restoring the car?
4. **Create and Solve** Write and solve a problem that requires an exact answer. Then, write and solve a problem in which a range of estimates will be sufficient.

Quick Check

Check your understanding of Lessons 5–8.

Estimate by using front-end estimation. Then estimate by rounding. (Lesson 6)

1. 29 × 36

2. 207 × 25

3. 52 × 74

4. 6 × 15,612

Multiply. (Lesson 5)

5. 37 × 20

6. 964 × 30

Find the product. Estimate to check that your answer is reasonable. (Lessons 6 and 7)

7. 18 × 37

8. 96 × 57

Solve. Explain your answer. (Lesson 8)

9. Tickets for the boat show are $24. The cost of putting on the boat show is $12,000. If 600 people come to the boat show, will this be enough to cover costs?

10. Marni has $125. She spends $49 on pants and $58 on sandals. Does she have enough money to buy a $25 tee shirt?

WEEKLY WR READER® eduplace.com/kids/mw/

"In 1,500 Words or Less. . ."

In school, you may be asked to write a book report that is a certain number of words or a certain number of pages in length.

If you double space, you can fit about 250 words on each page.

You can use that estimate, 250 words per page, to determine how many words a paper will be without counting each individual word.

- If you are asked to write a 10-page paper, how many words is that?
- Suppose you are to write an essay in "1,500 words or less". If you use all 1,500 words, how many pages will that be?

Chapter Review/Test

VOCABULARY

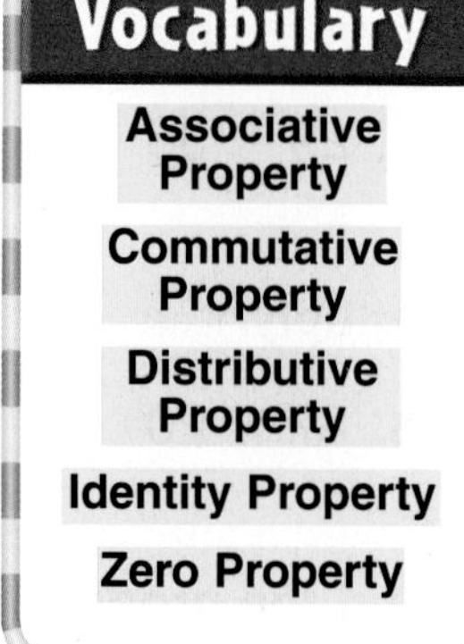

Vocabulary
Associative Property
Commutative Property
Distributive Property
Identity Property
Zero Property

1. The equation $5 \times 24 = 5 \times 20 + 5 \times 4$ illustrates the ____.
2. The ____ of Multiplication states that the product of any number and 0 is 0.
3. An example of the ____ is $3 \times 4 = 4 \times 3$.
4. $12 \times (2 \times 5) = (12 \times 2) \times 5$ illustrates the ____.

CONCEPTS AND SKILLS

Evaluate. Tell which property or properties you used.
(Lessons 1–2, pp. 60–63)

5. $2 \times 7 \times 5$
6. 5×15
7. $9 \times 0 \times 8$
8. 2×93
9. $6 \times 1 \times 1$
10. $25 \times 3 \times 4$

Find the product. (Lessons 4–5, 7, pp. 68–70, 72–73, 76–78)

11. 65×9
12. 347×5
13. $21{,}407 \times 4$
14. 5×700
15. 50×900
16. 87×44
17. 571×83
18. 605×76

Estimate using front-end estimation. Then estimate by rounding. (Lesson 6, pp. 74–75)

19. 25×42
20. 91×74
21. 37×629
22. 88×456
23. 75×29

PROBLEM SOLVING

Solve. Tell whether you estimated or found an exact answer for Problem 25.
(Lesson 3, pp. 64–66, Lesson 8, p. 80)

24. Luis, Sy, Dov, and Rey went to music camp for 4, 5, 6, and 8 weeks. Luis did not stay at camp for 4 weeks. Sy was away the longest. Rey was at camp longer than Luis. How much time did each spend at camp?
25. If Amy sells items worth \$500 or more during the school fundraiser, she will receive a prize. Amy sells to 47 households at an average price of \$11.95 per sale. Will Amy receive a prize?

Show You Understand

How are the identity properties of addition and multiplication alike? How are they different?

Extra Practice

Set A (Lesson 1, pp. 60–61)

Write an expression for each.

1. 12 more than a number **2.** the product of a number and 20 **3.** a number divided by 5

Evaluate. Tell which property you used.

4. $(50 \cdot 16) \cdot 2$ **5.** $57 \times 0 \times 9$ **6.** $250 \cdot (9 \cdot 4)$ **7.** $3 \cdot 1 \cdot 9$

Evaluate each expression, given $n = 2$, $t = 12$, $v = 9$.

8. $8 \cdot n$ **9.** $3 \cdot (t - v)$ **10.** $v \cdot (t - n)$ **11.** $50 - v$

Set B (Lesson 4, pp. 68–71)

Find the product.

1. 67×4 **2.** 382×6 **3.** $92{,}093 \times 7$ **4.** $471{,}526 \times 9$ **5.** $1{,}378{,}602 \times 8$

Set C (Lesson 5, pp. 72–73)

Use a pattern or mental math to find each product.

1. 70×5 **2.** 30×9 **3.** 400×5 **4.** $2{,}000 \times 9$

5. 90×50 **6.** 20×80 **7.** $6{,}000 \times 60$ **8.** $70 \times 7{,}000$

Set D (Lesson 6, pp. 74–75)

Estimate by using front-end estimation. Then estimate by rounding.

1. 45×76 **2.** 33×29 **3.** 81×45 **4.** 86×76

5. 37×891 **6.** 495×62 **7.** 98×663 **8.** 278×48

Set E (Lesson 7, pp. 76–79)

Find each product. Estimate to check.

1. 84×29 **2.** 136×23 **3.** 619×97 **4.** 680×72 **5.** 456×25

6. 82×43 **7.** 96×17 **8.** 902×65 **9.** 740×79 **10.** 807×92

CHAPTER 4

Divide by One-Digit Numbers

INVESTIGATION

Use Data

Jennifer has a collection of stamps. She wants to put her stamps in an album. She does not want to mix different categories of stamps. She has decided to put 8 stamps on each page of her album. How many pages will she need for each category of stamp?

Category	Number
President stamps	8
State stamps	24
Animal stamps	20
Flower stamps	44
Foreign stamps	29

Chapter Pretest

Use this page to review and remember what you need to know for this chapter.

VOCABULARY

Choose the best word to complete each sentence.

1. In 16 ÷ 2, 16 is the ____.
2. If the quotient is not a factor of the dividend, there is a ____.
3. In 16 ÷ 2, 2 is the ____.

CONCEPTS AND SKILLS

Write the fact family for each set of numbers.

4. 7, 9, 63 **5.** 3, 8, 24 **6.** 6, 7, 42 **7.** 8, 7, 56 **8.** 3, 5, 15

Complete.

9. $4\overline{)8 \text{ hundreds}}$ with quotient ■ hundreds

10. $5\overline{)15 \text{ hundreds}}$ with quotient ■ hundreds

11. $7\overline{)\blacksquare \text{ hundreds}}$ with quotient 6 hundreds

12. $9\overline{)\blacksquare \text{ thousands}}$ with quotient 5 thousands

Divide.

13. 640 ÷ 80 **14.** 484 ÷ 4 **15.** $4\overline{)73}$ **16.** $2\overline{)55}$ **17.** $6\overline{)73}$

Tell whether each statement is true or false. If false, correct the statement to make it true.

18. The quotient and the divisor can sometimes be equal.

19. The dividend and the divisor can never be equal.

20. Why is the remainder always less than the divisor?

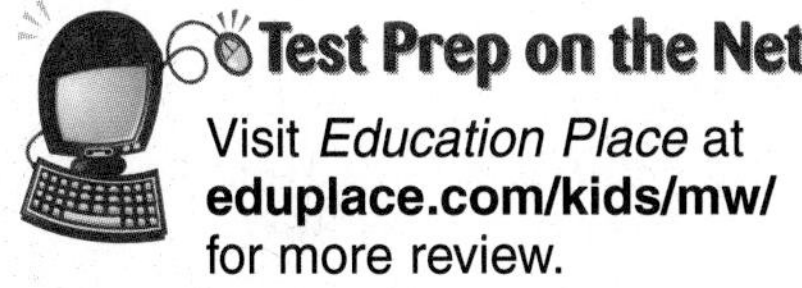

Test Prep on the Net

Visit *Education Place* at **eduplace.com/kids/mw/** for more review.

Lesson 1

Estimate Quotients

Objective Estimate quotients using basic multiplication facts.

Learn About It

Mary wants to organize her 2,340 baseball cards in album pages that each hold 8 cards. About how many pages will she need?

If a dividend is a multiple of a divisor, the dividend and divisor are **compatible numbers.** You can use compatible numbers to estimate a quotient.

Remember

$$\text{divisor}\,\overline{)\text{dividend}}^{\ \text{quotient}}$$

Estimate 2,340 ÷ 8.

Decide where to place the first digit of the quotient. Use a basic fact to find the first digit.

$$8\overline{)2,340}$$? hundreds

Which numbers are compatible with 8?

What value of n makes $8 \times n$ close to 23?

$8 \times 3 = 24$

24 is close to 23, so 3 is the first digit.

Rewrite the dividend so that it is a multiple of the divisor.

$$\begin{array}{r} 300 \\ 8\overline{)2,400} \end{array}$$

2,400 is close to the dividend.
The estimated quotient is 300.

Check.
Multiplication and division are inverse operations. Use multiplication to check your division.

$8 \times 300 = 2,400$

Solution: Mary will need about 300 album pages.

Other Examples

A. Three-Digit Dividend

$5\overline{)347}$

$34 \div 5 \approx 35 \div 5$

347 is close to 350.

$$\begin{array}{r} 70 \\ 5\overline{)350} \end{array}$$

$347 \div 5$ is about 70.

B. Five-Digit Dividend

$4\overline{)91,654}$

$9 \div 4 \approx 8 \div 4$

91,654 is close to 80,000.

$$\begin{array}{r} 20,000 \\ 4\overline{)80,000} \end{array}$$

$91,654 \div 4$ is about 20,000.

Guided Practice

Estimate the quotient.

1. $8\overline{)658}$
2. $5\overline{)2{,}674}$
3. $4\overline{)17{,}987}$
4. 7,274 ÷ 3
5. 36,149 ÷ 7
6. 563,217 ÷ 9

Ask Yourself

- What multiplication fact will help me find compatible numbers?
- How many digits should be in the estimated quotient?

Without dividing, how do you know how many digits there will be in a quotient?

Practice and Problem Solving

Estimate the quotient.

7. $7\overline{)223}$
8. $8\overline{)334}$
9. $9\overline{)713}$
10. $5\overline{)4{,}456}$
11. $7\overline{)1{,}498}$
12. $8\overline{)4{,}129}$
13. $9\overline{)45{,}212}$
14. $9\overline{)42{,}825}$
15. $8\overline{)39{,}541}$
16. $6\overline{)162{,}432}$
17. $9\overline{)342{,}785}$
18. $4\overline{)294{,}563}$
19. 248 ÷ 5
20. 813 ÷ 3
21. 2,514 ÷ 6
22. 3,512 ÷ 4
23. 16,945 ÷ 7
24. 46,127 ÷ 8
25. 648,792 ÷ 9
26. 791,342 ÷ 8

Solve.

27. A new box of baseball cards contains 718 cards. If the pages for an album hold 9 cards each, about how many pages are needed to hold all the cards in the set?

28. **You Decide** A box of 100 album pages costs $14.95. Each page holds 6 cards. Album folders with 10 pages, which hold 9 cards each, sell for $14.95. Which would you buy if you had 50 cards? 100 cards? Explain.

29. **Create and Solve** Write your own problem about a baseball card collection. Your problem should require estimating a quotient. Solve your problem, then give it to a partner to solve.

Daily Review | Test Prep

Fill in each ■. (Grade 4)

30. 9 yd = ■ ft
31. 3 yd = ■ in.
32. 6 ft = ■ in.
33. 12 ft = ■ yd
34. 2 mi = ■ ft
35. 36 in. = ■ yd

36. Grant put 356 baseball cards in pages that hold 9 cards each. Which is a reasonable estimate of the number of pages he used?

A 4 pages **B** 40 pages
C 400 pages **D** 3,600 pages

Extra Practice See page 107, Set A.

Lesson 2

One-Digit Divisors

Objective Use compatible numbers and place value to divide.

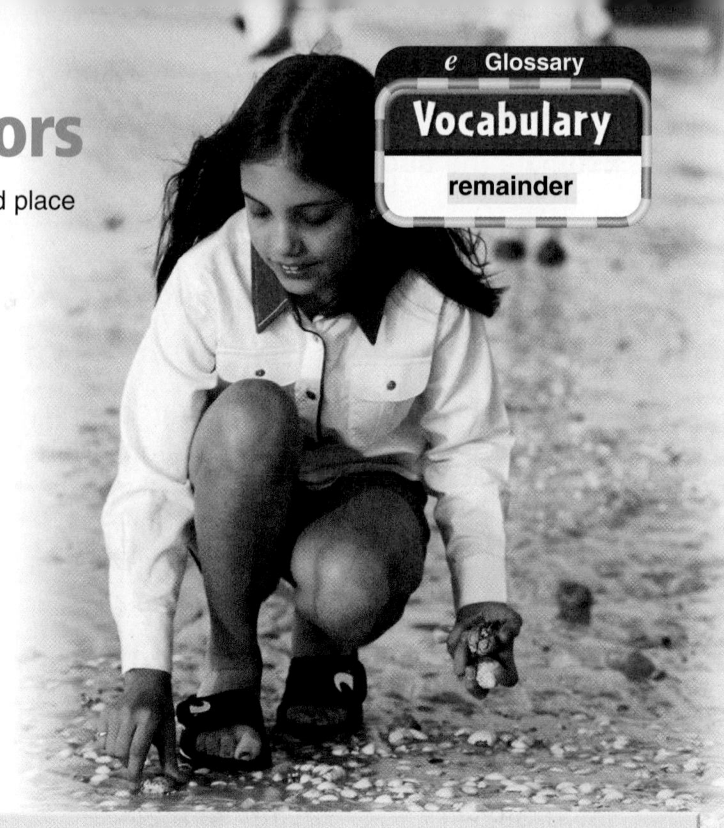

e Glossary

Vocabulary

remainder

Learn About It

A group of fifth-grade students collected 378 seashells. When they got back to class, they put an equal number of shells into 4 piles to study. How many shells are in each pile? How many are left over?

If the divisor is not a factor of the dividend then the answer will include a **remainder**.

Find 378 ÷ 4.

STEP 1 Use basic facts, rounding, and compatible numbers to decide where to place the first digit of the quotient.

Think

$4\overline{)3 \text{ hundreds}}$? hundreds

$\mathbf{3 < 4}$ There are not enough hundreds to divide. $378 \div 4 < 100$

$\mathbf{37 > 4}$ Place the first digit in the tens place.

STEP 2 Divide the tens.

Think

$4\overline{)37 \text{ tens}}$? tens

```
   9
4)378    Multiply. 9 × 4
 - 36    Subtract. 37 − 36
    1    Compare. 1 < 4
```

STEP 3 Bring down the ones. Divide the ones. Write the **remainder**.

Think

$4\overline{)18 \text{ ones}}$? ones

```
   94 R2
4)378
 - 36
    18   Bring down the 8 ones.
  - 16   Multiply. 4 × 4
     2   Subtract. 18 − 16
         Compare. 2 < 4
         The remainder is 2.
```

Check.
Multiply the quotient by the divisor. Then add the remainder. The result should be equal to the dividend.

$(94 \times 4) + 2 = 378$

Solution: There are 94 shells in each group and 2 shells left over.

Guided Practice

Divide.

1. $6\overline{)582}$
2. $8\overline{)9{,}814}$
3. $5\overline{)4{,}217}$
4. $2{,}616 \div 4$
5. $8{,}129 \div 7$
6. $469{,}642 \div 9$

Ask Yourself

- Can I divide the first digit in the dividend?
- Where should I write the first digit?

Explain Your Thinking ▶ Why must the remainder always be less than the divisor?

Practice and Problem Solving

Divide and check.

7. $6\overline{)556}$
8. $5\overline{)285}$
9. $3\overline{)732}$
10. $7\overline{)6{,}387}$
11. $4\overline{)5{,}824}$
12. $8\overline{)5{,}975}$
13. $9\overline{)38{,}217}$
14. $3\overline{)45{,}849}$
15. $9\overline{)58{,}239}$
16. $6\overline{)793{,}481}$
17. $9\overline{)867{,}142}$
18. $7\overline{)412{,}447}$
19. $894 \div 4$
20. $763 \div 2$
21. $4{,}873 \div 3$
22. $8{,}767 \div 5$

Algebra • **Equations The division statement $13 \div 2 = 6$ R1 can be written as $(2 \times 6) + 1 = 13$. Write and solve a division statement for each equation.**

23. $3a + r = 20$
24. $4a + r = 11$
25. $5a + r = 16$
26. $6a + r = 25$

Solve.

27. A shop sells shadow boxes for displaying shells. If each box holds 8 shells, how many boxes are needed to display 456 shells?

28. Mavis has 512 shells. She has 3 times as many small shells as large shells. How many of each size does she have?

Divide. (Grade 4)

29. $36 \div 3$
30. $56 \div 7$
31. $48 \div 8$
32. $54 \div 6$
33. $55 \div 5$
34. $14 \div 2$

35. **Free Response** Midge arranges her collection of 762 seashells into trays with 8 shells in each tray. Show how to find the number of trays she needs.

Extra Practice See page 107, Set B.

Lesson 3

Problem-Solving Application

Use Operations

Objective Choose operations to solve a problem.

You need to decide which operations to use to solve word problems.

Problem The Ryans have been collecting snowdomes for years. Now they want to organize their collection onto shelves. They will put 8 snowdomes on each shelf.

How many shelves will they need for their entire collection?

OUR SNOWDOMES

KIND	NUMBER
United States	96
World	48
Assorted	72

UNDERSTAND

What is the question?

How many shelves will they need for their entire collection?

What do you know?

- There are 96 snowdomes from the United States, 48 snowdomes from the world, and 72 assorted snowdomes.
- Each shelf will have 8 snowdomes.

PLAN

Add to find the total number of snowdomes.

Then divide by 8 to find the number of shelves needed.

SOLVE

- Find the total number of snowdomes. $96 + 48 + 72 = 216$
- Then divide. $216 \div 8 = 27$

Solution: The Ryans will need 27 shelves.

LOOK BACK

How can I check my answer?

Guided Practice

Use the table on page 90 to solve each problem. Name the operation(s) you used.

1. Suppose the Ryans decide to put 8 snowdomes of only one kind on each shelf. How many shelves will they need for their collection?

   Hint How many shelves do they need for each kind of snowdome?

2. The Ryans bought a box of snowdomes from the United States. They now have 32 shelves of snowdomes with 8 on each shelf and 1 more shelf with 6 snowdomes. How many snowdomes were in the box?

Ask Yourself

UNDERSTAND What does the question ask me to find?

PLAN Did I use the correct information from the table?

SOLVE
- Did I decide which operation(s) to use?
- Did I use the operations in the correct order?

LOOK BACK Did I check my answer?

Independent Practice

Data **Use the table for Problems 3–6. Name the operation(s) you used.**

3. Sue Ann paid $6 each for her Remember the Alamo snowdomes. How much profit will she make if she sells all of her Remember the Alamo snowdomes?

4. Sue Ann put all the snowdomes in layers in a carton. She put 8 snowdomes in a layer. How many layers in the carton did she make with her snowdomes?

5. **Estimate** Since Sue Ann posted her snowdomes on her Web site, she has sold half of her collection. About how much money has she made?

6. **Explain** Robert spent $19 on 3 snowdomes. He bought The Windy City, Remember the Alamo, and one other. Which other snowdome did he buy? Explain the steps you took to find your answer.

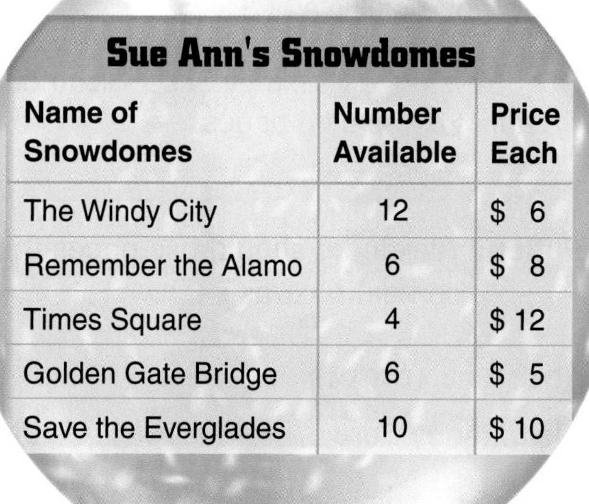

Sue Ann's Snowdomes

Name of Snowdomes	Number Available	Price Each
The Windy City	12	$ 6
Remember the Alamo	6	$ 8
Times Square	4	$ 12
Golden Gate Bridge	6	$ 5
Save the Everglades	10	$ 10

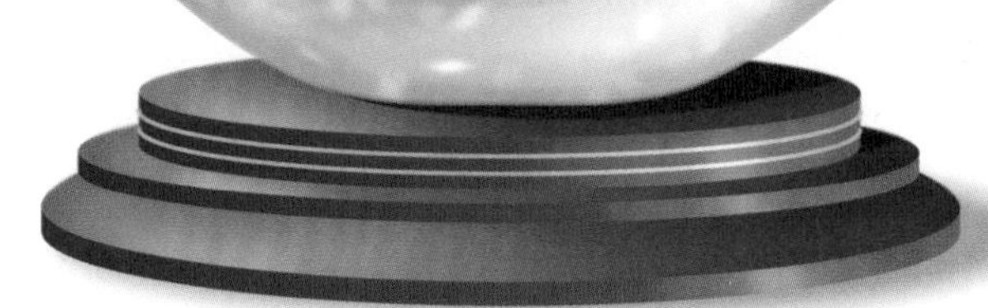

Lesson 4

Divisibility

Objective Determine when 2, 3, 4, 5, 6, 9, or 10 is a factor of a number.

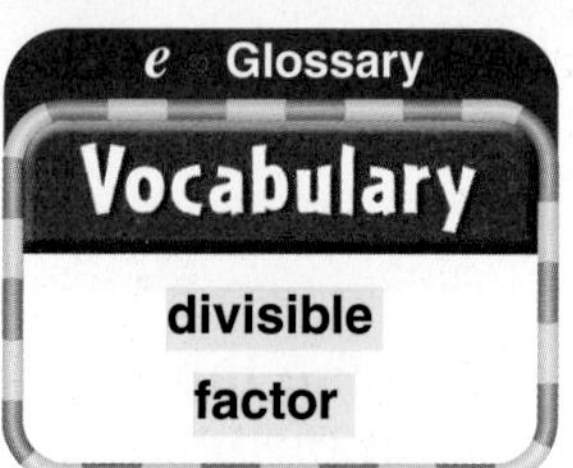

Learn About It

A number is **divisible** by another number when the quotient is a whole number and there is no remainder. Any **factor** of a given number divides into that number with no remainder.

Alexander has collected 2,032 picture postcards from around the world. He wants to organize the collection into 3-ring binders, and he wants each page filled, with no cards left over. Should he use pages that can contain 3 cards each or 4 cards each?

Is 2,032 divisible by 3 or 4?

Decide whether 2,032 is divisible by 3.

If 2,032 is divisible by 3, then the sum of the digits of 2,032 is equal to a multiple of 3.

$$2 + 0 + 3 + 2 = 7$$

7 is not a multiple of 3.

2,032 is not divisible by 3, so Alexander cannot use 3-card pages.

Decide whether 2,032 is divisible by 4.

If 2,032 is divisible by 4, then the last 2 digits make up a multiple of 4.

The last 2 digits are 3 and 2, and 32 is a multiple of 4.

2,032 is divisible by 4, so Alexander can use 4-card pages.

Solution: Alexander should use pages that can contain 4 cards each.

Another Example

Divisibility by Zero

There are no numbers divisible by 0.

If $5 \div 0 = n$, then $n \times 0 = 5$.

There is no value for n that makes $n \times 0 = 5$ true. This means that the equivalent division sentence, $5 \div 0 = n$, has no solution.

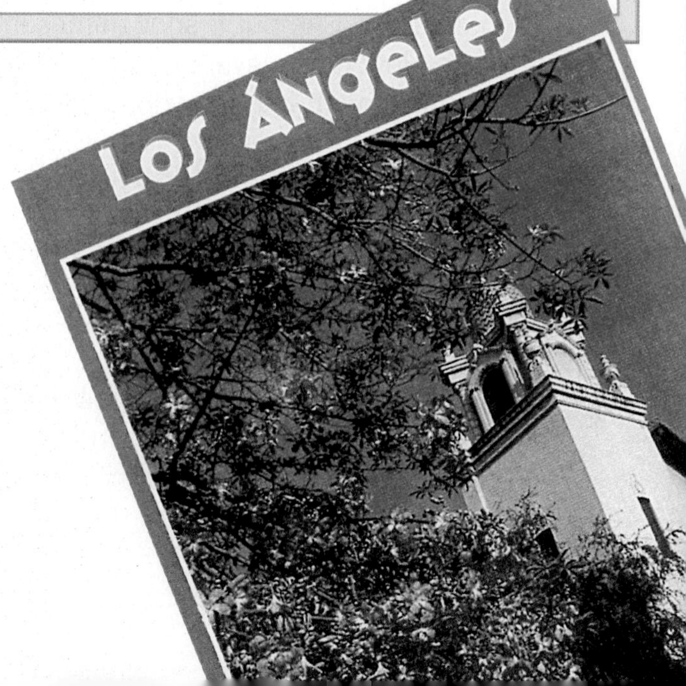

Use divisibility rules to decide which of the numbers at right is divisible by 2, 3, 4, 5, 6, 9, and 10.

725 240 536
360 382 590

Eliminate the numbers that are not divisible by 2, 3, 4, 5, 6, 9, and 10.

STEP 1 Check for divisibility by 2. The number must end with 0, 2, 4, 6, or 8.

~~725~~ 240 536
360 382 590

STEP 2 Check for divisibility by 5. The number must end with 0 or 5.

240 ~~536~~ 360
~~382~~ 590

STEP 3 Check for divisibility by 10. The number must end in 0.

240 360 590

All of the remaining numbers are divisible by 10.

STEP 4 Check for divisibility by 4. The last two digits make up a number divisible by 4.

240 360 ~~590~~

STEP 5 Check for divisibility by 3. The sum of the digits must be divisible by 3.

240 360

Both are divisible by 3.

STEP 6 Check for divisibility by 6. The number must be divisible by both 2 and 3.

240 360

Both are divisible by 6.

STEP 7 Check for divisibility by 9. The sum of the digits must be divisible by 9.

~~240~~ 360

Think
$2 + 4 + 0 = 6$
$3 + 6 + 0 = 9$

Solution: The number 360 is divisible by 2, 3, 4, 5, 6, 9, and 10.

Guided Practice

Tell whether each number is divisible by 2, 3, 4, 5, 6, 9, or 10.

1. 325 **2.** 540 **3.** 393 **4.** 632

5. 315 **6.** 990 **7.** 323 **8.** 3,012

Ask Yourself

- Did I check the final digits for divisibility by 2, 4, 5, and 10?
- Did I check for divisibility by 3, 6, and 9?

If a number is divisible by 9, must it be divisible by 3? Explain why or why not.

Go On

Practice and Problem Solving

Tell whether each number is divisible by 2, 3, 4, 5, 6, 9, or 10.

9. 110 **10.** 29 **11.** 177 **12.** 531 **13.** 455

14. 7,100 **15.** 1,278 **16.** 1,123 **17.** 6,765 **18.** 1,107

Algebra • **Expressions Find a value of n that makes the expression divisible by 2, 3, and 5.**

19. $18n$ **20.** $n + 7$ **21.** $10n$ **22.** $20 + n$

23. $9n + 3$ **24.** $n - 5$ **25.** $5n$ **26.** $2n - 4$

Data **The table below shows the number of stamps in various stamp sets. Use the table for Problems 27–30.**

Stamp Sets

Country	Number Per Set
Mexico	245
Canada	144
Brazil	270
United States	210

27. Analyze Dwayne bought a set of stamps whose number of stamps is divisible by 2, 3, 5, 6, 9, and 10. Which set is it?

28. Mental Math One set of stamps is divisible only by 5. Which set is it? How can you tell?

29. Berta puts all the stamps from a set in an album. She puts 9 stamps on each page because that is the greatest number by which the number of stamps is divisible. Which set did Berta use?

30. Calculator Shelly bought one of each set. Use divisibility rules to see if 2, 3, 4, 5, 6, 9, or 10 stamps will fit on a page so that the same number of stamps are on each page.

31. Reasoning Is a multiple of 2 always a multiple of 4? Is a multiple of 4 always a multiple of 2? Explain why or why not.

32. Write About It Tony says that if a number is divisible by 3 and 9, it must also be divisible by 6. Using examples, explain whether or not his rule works.

Extra Practice See page 107, Set C.

Quick Check

Check your understanding of Lessons 1–4.

Estimate each quotient. Then divide. (Lessons 1–2)

1. 634 ÷ 8 **2.** 8,256 ÷ 7 **3.** 523 ÷ 6 **4.** 7,294 ÷ 3

Tell whether each number is divisible by 2, 3, 4, 5, 6, 9, or 10. (Lesson 4)

5. 332 **6.** 540 **7.** 945

Solve. Name the operation(s) you used. (Lesson 3)

8. Aunt Karen bought one set of 236 stamps and another set of 149 stamps. She gave the same number of stamps to each of her 5 nieces. How many stamps did each girl get?

Finding Patterns

You can use your calculator to find division patterns.

STEP 1 Enter 1 followed by as many zeros as your display will show.

STEP 2 Now divide by 9. Drop the numbers after the decimal point.

100000000 ÷ 9 → 11111111

STEP 3 Repeat Steps 1 and 2 but enter a 2 first in Step 1.

200000000 ÷ 9 → 22222222

What do you predict you will see when you divide 300000000 by 9? Try it. What pattern do you notice? Use the pattern to predict what you will see when you divide 800000000 by 9.

Use the same steps as above but this time divide by 99. How is the pattern the same? How is it different?

Lesson 5

Zeros in the Quotient

Objective Determine when to put zeros in the quotient.

Learn About It

Ramón has 2,515 marbles. He has bought 5 plastic boxes for storing his marbles. If Ramón puts the same number of marbles in each box, how many marbles will be in each box?

Solve 2,515 ÷ 5 = *n*.

STEP 1 Decide where to place the first digit of the quotient. Then divide.

Think $\frac{?\text{ thousands}}{5)\overline{2\text{ thousands}}}$

There are not enough thousands to divide.

Think $\frac{?\text{ hundreds}}{5)\overline{25\text{ hundreds}}}$

```
   5
5)2515    Multiply 5 × 5
 - 25  ←  Subtract. 25 − 25
    0     Compare. 0 < 5
```

STEP 2 Bring down the tens. Divide the tens.

Think $\frac{?\text{ ten}}{5)\overline{1\text{ ten}}}$

There are not enough tens to divide.

```
   50  ←  Write 0 in the tens
5)2515    place to show that
 -25↓     the quotient has 0
   01     tens.
```

STEP 3 Bring down the ones. Divide the ones.

Think $\frac{?\text{ ones}}{5)\overline{15\text{ ones}}}$

```
   503
5)2,515
 - 25 ↓
    015  ←  Multiply. 3 × 5
   - 15     Subtract. 15 − 15
      0     There is no
            remainder.
```

Check.
Multiply.
503 × 5 = 2,515

Solution: There will be 503 marbles in each of the 5 boxes.

Other Examples

A. Zero In The Dividend

```
  2,265 R3
4)9,063
 - 8↓
   10  ←  Bring down the zero from
  - 8     the hundreds place.
   26
  - 24
    23
  - 20
     3
```

B. More Than One Zero

```
   700 R4
7)4,904
 - 49
    00  ←  The result is 0, but there
   - 0     are more places to divide.
    04     Write 0 in the quotient,
   - 0     because 0 tens ÷ 7 = 0
     4     tens. Then continue.
```

Guided Practice

Divide and check.

1. $7\overline{)284}$ **2.** $4\overline{)3{,}602}$ **3.** $8\overline{)34{,}421}$

4. 301 ÷ 5 **5.** 2,801 ÷ 3 **6.** 240,120 ÷ 6

Ask Yourself

- Where do I write the first digit?
- How do I know when the division is done?

Explain Your Thinking ▶ In Exercise 5, what would happen if you did not bring down the zero?

Practice and Problem Solving

Divide and check.

7. $7\overline{)568}$ **8.** $3\overline{)624}$ **9.** $2\overline{)801}$ **10.** $8\overline{)5{,}632}$

11. $4\overline{)3{,}603}$ **12.** $5\overline{)43{,}004}$ **13.** $6\overline{)300{,}056}$ **14.** $2\overline{)121{,}481}$

15. 613 ÷ 3 **16.** 5,522 ÷ 6 **17.** 8,208 ÷ 8 **18.** 18,006 ÷ 5

19. 70,200 ÷ 9 **20.** 63,564 ÷ 7 **21.** 627,153 ÷ 3 **22.** 457,287 ÷ 9

Solve.

23. A company made 52,250 of one kind of marble in 5 days. Each day, it made the same amount of marbles. How many marbles are made each day?

24. Reasoning Fill in the missing numbers in the division.

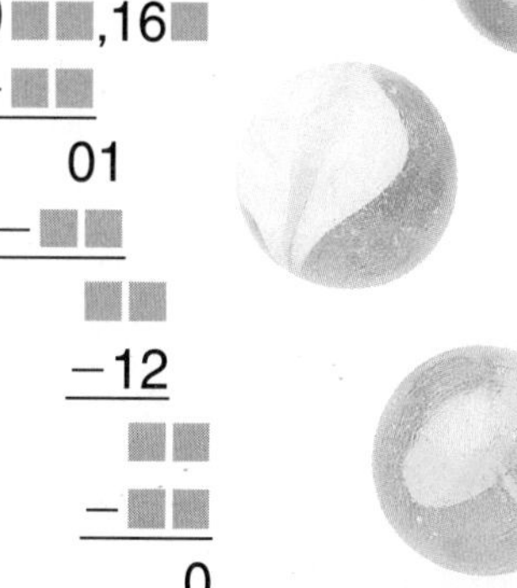

25. Analyze A toy show ran for two days. Tickets cost \$3. On the first day, ticket sales were \$3,213. On the second day, sales were \$2,949. How many tickets were sold?

26. Mental Math A collector of antique marbles paid \$1,000 for 4 marbles. What is the average price paid per marble?

Daily Review Test Prep

Round each number to the underlined place. (Ch. 1, Lessons 4 and 7)

27. 1.06$\underline{7}$4 **28.** $\underline{2}$45,324,936,316

29. 2.$\underline{5}$4 **30.** 22$\underline{4}$,809,302

31. 0.0$\underline{3}$5 **32.** 71$\underline{9}$,805

33. A marble collector has 1,230 marbles. If she displays them in trays that hold 6 marbles each, how many trays does she need?

A 25 trays **B** 200 trays

C 205 trays **D** 230 trays

Extra Practice See page 107, Set D.

Lesson 6

Problem-Solving Strategy

Guess and Check

Objective Use guess and check to solve a problem.

Problem Glen collects 3 different kinds of salt and pepper shakers. The number of his sets with food is 3 times the number that show characters. The number of sets that show animals is divisible by 2 and 3. Glen has 24 sets. How many of each kind does he have?

This is what you know:

- Glen has 24 sets of salt and pepper shakers.
- The number of food sets is 3 times the number of character sets.
- The number of animal sets is divisible by 2 and 3.

PLAN

You can use a Guess-and-Check strategy to solve the problem.

SOLVE

Use what you know. Organize your guesses in a table.

3 times C = F

A is divisible by 2 and 3.

F + C + A = 24

Continue guessing and checking until you know you have the correct answer.

Solution: Glen has 3 character, 12 animal, and 9 food sets.

Characters (C)	Food (F)	Animals (A)	Correct?
Think: If C is 1, then F must be 3 and A is 24 − (1 + 3), or 20.			
1	3	20	No. 20 is not divisible by 3.
2	6	16	No.
3	9	12	Yes.
4	12	8	No.
5	15	4	No.
6	18	0	No. He has 3 kinds of shakers.

LOOK BACK

Look back at the problem.

Is my answer reasonable? How do I know?

Guided Practice

Use the Ask Yourself questions to help you solve each problem.

1. Ella has 18 cuckoo clocks. Each clock is made of wood or plastic. She has twice as many wood cuckoo clocks as plastic ones. How many of each kind does she have?

2. Gene spent $25 for an unusual set of salt and pepper shakers. He paid for the set using $10, $5, and $1 bills. If he gave the clerk 8 bills in all, how many of each bill did he use?

   Hint What is the maximum number of $10 bills he could have used?

Ask Yourself

UNDERSTAND **What facts do I know?**

PLAN **Can I use Guess and Check?**

SOLVE
- **Did I make a reasonable first guess?**
- **Did I use the results from the guess to make a better guess?**

LOOK BACK **Did I solve the problem?**

Independent Practice

Use Guess and Check to solve each problem.

3. The fifth grade made $25 on a hobby show. They received only $5 and $1 bills and collected a total of 9 bills. What combination of bills did they receive?

4. Claudio has 6 more trees in his front yard than Flora. If they have 20 trees together, how many trees does each person have?

5. Scott has 13 music boxes that play either patriotic songs or holiday tunes. He has 5 more music boxes that play patriotic tunes than music boxes that play holiday tunes. How many of each kind does he have?

6. Ashley has 9 lawn ornaments. She has cat, dog, and bird lawn ornaments. If there are 30 legs in all on her lawn ornaments, how many bird ornaments does she have?

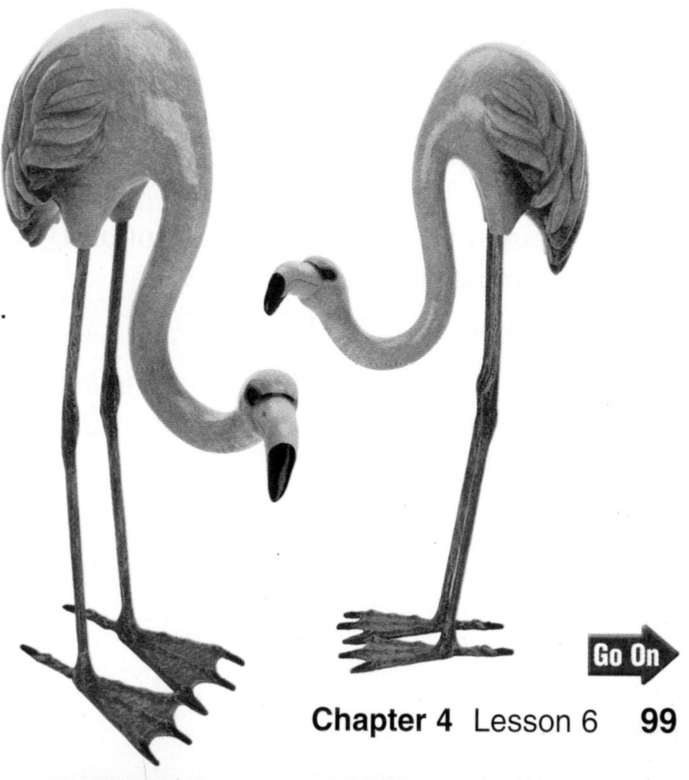

Go On

Choose a Strategy

Solve. Show your work. Tell what strategy you used.

Strategies

- Use Models
- Draw a Diagram
- Find a Pattern
- Guess and Check
- Make an Organized List
- Make a Table
- Solve a Simpler Problem
- Use Logical Reasoning
- Work Backward
- Write an Equation

7. At the first stop, 3 people got off and 7 people got on a bus. At the next stop, 8 people got off and 12 got on. Now the bus has 30 passengers. How many people did the bus have on it in the beginning of its route?

8. Pranee bought three shirts: one white, one blue, and one yellow. She bought a pair of tan shorts and a pair of green slacks. How many outfits can she make with these clothes?

9. **Measurement** Draw a rectangle whose length is 2 centimeters less than twice its width of 10 centimeters.

10. In the pet store, Kim counted 16 birds and cats. She also counted 46 legs. How many of each kind of animal are there?

Data Use the graph to solve Problems 11–15.

Angie has an auction Web site for collectors of dolls and action figures. The graph shows the number of bids she got on her Web site at four times during one day.

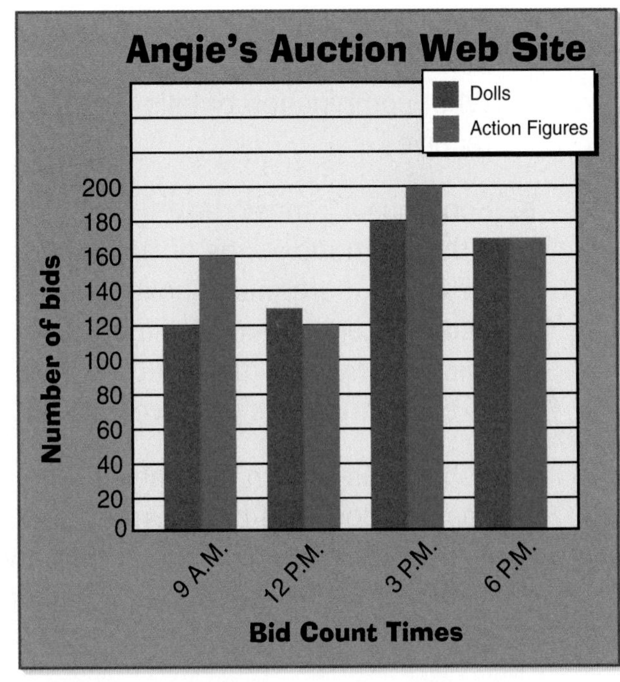

11. At 9:00 P.M., the number of bids on dolls was double the number at 9:00 A.M. How many bids on dolls were there at 9:00 P.M.?

12. **Calculator** Of the total number of bids, were more bids placed on dolls or action figures? How many more?

13. How many more bids for dolls came in at 3:00 P.M. and 6:00 P.M. than at 9:00 A.M. and 12:00 P.M.?

14. **Analyze** At which time was the combined number of bids on dolls and action figures between 300 and 350?

15. **Create and Solve** From the information given in the graph above, write your own problem and solve it.

Problem-Solving Test Prep

Choose the letter of the correct answer. If a correct answer is not here, choose NH.

1. In May, 42,872 people visited a Web site. In June, 18,305 people visited the same Web site. About how many more visitors were there in May than in June?

A 25,000 **C** 43,000

B 35,000 **D** 60,000

(Chapter 1, Lesson 1)

2. Alex, Sue, and Jo sold tickets for a show. Alex sold fifty-two tickets. Sue sold ten more than Alex. Jo sold ten more than Sue. How many tickets did Alex, Jo, and Sue sell in all?

F 32 tickets **H** 124 tickets

G 72 tickets **J** 186 tickets

(Chapter 2, Lesson 6)

3. You exercise 10 minutes each day of Week 1. Each week you double your daily exercise time from the week before. How many minutes per day will you exercise in Week 5?

A 50 minutes **C** 160 minutes

B 80 minutes **D** 320 minutes

(Chapter 1, Lesson 6)

4. Which of the following equations best represents this model?

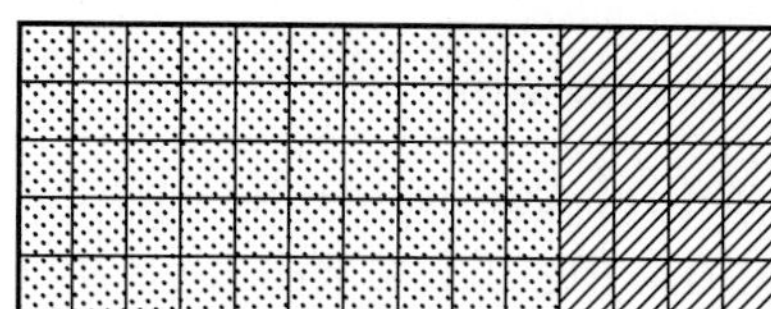

F $5 \times 14 = (5 \times 10) \times (5 \times 4)$

G $5 \times 14 = (5 + 10) \times (5 + 4)$

H $5 \times 14 = (5 \times 10) + (5 \times 4)$

J NH

(Chapter 1, Lesson 6)

5. Which point on the number line represents a number that is divisible by both 2 and 6?

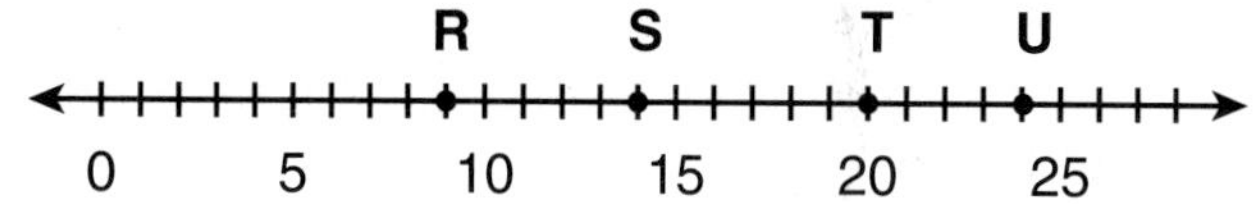

(Chapter 3, Lesson 2)

6. Manny packed 8 boxes. The small boxes contain 4 bowls each, and the big boxes have 6 bowls each. If Manny packed 40 bowls, how many of each size box did he pack?

Represent Support your solution by drawing a picture or making a table.

(Chapter 4, Lesson 6)

Test Prep on the Net

Check out *Education Place* at **eduplace.com/kids/mw/** for test prep practice.

Lesson 7

Algebra

Solve Equations

Objective Use mental math to solve multiplication and division equations.

Learn About It

MathTracks 1/13
Listen and Understand

Alvin brought his comic book collection to school to show the class. He gave n comic books to each of 4 small groups. If he had 12 comic books, how many did each group get?

You can make a model of the information and write an equation.

Total number of comic books: 12			
n	n	n	n

Solve $4n = 12$.

Remember
$4n$ means $4 \times n$

You can use mental math to solve the equation.

$$4n = 12$$
$$n = 3$$

What number times 4 equals 12?
Try 3.

Solution: Each group got 3 comic books.

Other Examples

A. Use Mental Math.

$28 \div n = 7$

28						
n	n	n	n	n	n	n

$28 \div 4 = 7$

$n = 4$

What number times 7 equals 28?
Try 4.

B. Find the Unknown Dividend.

$n \div 7 = 9$

n						
9	9	9	9	9	9	9

$63 \div 7 = 9$

$n = 63$

Since $n \div 7 = 9$, $n = 7 \times 9$.
Try 63.

Guided Practice

Ask Yourself

- What multiplication or division fact can help me solve this equation?
- Did I check my solution?

Solve each problem.

1. Jonah has 30 comic books. He wants to read them over the next 5 days. If he reads the same number each day, how many will he read a day?

   Solve $5n = 30$.

Total number of comic books: 30				
n each day	n each day	n each day	n each day	n each day

2. Marion gave each of her 7 friends 7 comic books. How many comic books did she give out?

   Solve $7 \times 7 = n$.

Total number of comic books: n						
7 to each friend	7 to each friend	7 to each friend	7 to each friend	7 to each friend	7 to each friend	7 to each friend

How does knowing multiplication and division facts help you solve equations mentally?

Practice and Problem Solving

Solve each problem.

3. Sharon has 36 comic books. She has 4 of each type of comic book. How many types does she have?

   Solve $4n = 36$.

36			
n	n	n	n

4. At the comic book convention, Nelson sold comic books for \$3 apiece. He sold \$27 worth. How many did he sell?

   Solve $27 \div n = 3$.

27		
n	n	n

5. Seven issues of a certain comic book cost \$42. How much does one issue cost?

   Solve $7n = 42$.

42						
n	n	n	n	n	n	n

6. Five friends shared some comic books. Each friend got 8 comic books. How many did they share?

   Solve $n \div 5 = 8$.

n				
8	8	8	8	8

Go On

Use mental math to solve the equations.

7. $6n = 48$ **8.** $4x = 8$ **9.** $9y = 81$ **10.** $5s = 20$

11. $18 \div y = 6$ **12.** $49 \div n = 7$ **13.** $45 \div n = 5$ **14.** $12 \div n = 2$

15. $8t = 32$ **16.** $18 \div s = 9$ **17.** $36 \div n = 6$ **18.** $7t = 21$

19. $4y = 24$ **20.** $n \div 4 = 5$ **21.** $72 \div x = 8$ **22.** $t \div 4 = 8$

Algebra • Equations Replace *n* with 4. Is the equation true? Write *yes* or *no*.

23. $3n = 12$ **24.** $n \div 4 = 8$ **25.** $8 \div n = 2$ **26.** $6n = 24$

27. $20 \div n = 5$ **28.** $7n = 74$ **29.** $n \div 2 = 2$ **30.** $n \times n = 16$

Use the function rule to find each value of y.

31.

Rule: $y = 3x$				
x	2	4	6	8
y				

32.

Rule: $x = 36 \div y$				
x	3	4	6	9
y				

Solve.

33. Savannah organizes her collection of 28 comic books in bags. If she puts n books in each of 7 bags, how many books are in each bag?

34. Represent Draw a model or use algebra tiles to show $6n = 24$. Solve the equation and explain how your model helped you.

35. Debbie saves $5 each week for n weeks from her babysitting money. If she spends $18 of her savings on comic books and has $2 left, how many weeks did she save her money?

36. Kevin has 3 times as many comic books as Jen. Serena has twice as many comic books as Jen. If Serena has 6 comic books, how many comic books do the three friends have in all?

37. What If? Look back at Problem 36. What if Serena had 30 comic books? How many comic books would Kevin, Serena, and Jen have in all?

38. Create and Solve Choose an equation. Then write a word problem for it and solve it.

$5x = 35$ $r \div 4 = 9$ $12y = 3$

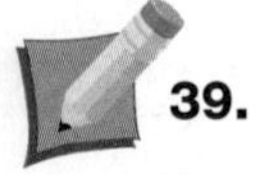

39. Write About It Write a fact family for $3n = 18$. How can writing a fact family help you solve this equation?

40. What's Wrong? Jason said that to solve $6n = 12$, you multiply 6 and 12. What is wrong with Jason's answer?

Extra Practice See page 107, Set E.

Quick Check

Quick Check

Check your understanding of Lessons 5–7.

Divide. (Lesson 5)

1. $820 \div 4$
2. $1{,}808 \div 3$
3. $9{,}625 \div 3$
4. $30{,}262 \div 5$

Use mental math to solve each equation. (Lesson 7)

5. $8n = 24$
6. $2n = 14$
7. $35 \div n = 7$
8. $n \div 8 = 9$

Solve. (Lesson 6)

9. Yolanda has $35 in 10 bills in her wallet. She has $1, $5, and $10 bills. How many of each kind of bill does she have?
10. Matthew is thinking of a number between 20 and 40 that is divisible by 4 and 6 but not by 9. Which number is he thinking of?

Algebraic Thinking

Math Reasoning

Patterns on a Hundred Chart

You can use a hundred chart to find divisibility patterns.

This pattern shows the numbers that are divisible by 10.

If you draw a triangle around each number that is divisible by 5, how will that pattern be the same or different from the pattern for divisibility by 10?

Copy the hundred chart on another sheet of paper.

1. Draw an X on each number in the chart that is divisible by 2. What pattern do you notice?
2. If you draw a square around all the numbers that are divisible by 4 and put a star on the numbers that are divisible by 8, what patterns do you notice?
3. Use a different color to draw a horizontal line through the numbers that are divisible by 3. Next, draw a vertical line through numbers that are divisible by 6. What new patterns do you notice?

1	2	3	4	5	6	7	8	9	10
11	12	13	14	15	16	17	18	19	20
21	22	23	24	25	26	27	28	29	30
31	32	33	34	35	36	37	38	39	40
41	42	43	44	45	46	47	48	49	50
51	52	53	54	55	56	57	58	59	60
61	62	63	64	65	66	67	68	69	70
71	72	73	74	75	76	77	78	79	80
81	82	83	84	85	86	87	88	89	90
91	92	93	94	95	96	97	98	99	100

Chapter Review/Test

VOCABULARY

1. A number is ____ by another number if the quotient has no remainder.
2. A ____ of a number divides into that number with no remainder.
3. If a dividend is a multiple of a divisor, the dividend and the divisor are ____.

Vocabulary

compatible numbers
divisible
factor
quotient
remainder

CONCEPTS AND SKILLS

Estimate the quotient. (Lesson 1, pp. 86–87)

4. $598 \div 3$
5. $18{,}320 \div 9$
6. $173{,}462 \div 4$
7. $21{,}568 \div 7$

Divide. (Lesson 2, pp. 88–89, Lesson 5, pp. 96–97)

8. $2{,}014 \div 6$
9. $672{,}461 \div 7$
10. $16{,}715 \div 5$
11. $9\overline{)18{,}207}$
12. $7\overline{)2{,}906}$
13. $7\overline{)49{,}079}$

Test each number to see whether it is divisible by 2, 3, 4, 5, 6, 9, or 10. (Lesson 4, pp. 92–95)

14. 315
15. 600
16. 720
17. 317

Use mental math to solve each equation. (Lesson 7, 102–105)

18. $8b = 64$
19. $16 \div c = 4$
20. $c \div 7 = 7$
21. $9b = 18$
22. $72 \div n = 24$
23. $6y = 54$

PROBLEM SOLVING

Name the operation(s) you used to solve the problem. (Lesson 3, pp. 90–91)

24. Ralph buys a used collection of 105 snowdomes for $50. If only 8 can ship in a box, how many boxes will he receive?

Solve. (Lesson 6, pp. 98–101)

25. Toni has a collection of 24 angel figurines. She has 5 times the number of crystal angels as hand-painted ones. How many of each kind does she have?

Show You Understand

If a number is divisible by 6, what other numbers is it divisible by? Explain.

Extra Practice

Set A (Lesson 1, pp. 86–87)

Estimate the quotient.

1. $9\overline{)355}$
2. $4\overline{)118}$
3. $7\overline{)2{,}906}$
4. $6\overline{)5{,}280}$
5. $42{,}426 \div 8$
6. $290{,}000 \div 9$
7. $322{,}164 \div 8$
8. $375{,}166 \div 4$

Set B (Lesson 2, pp. 88–89)

Divide.

1. $6\overline{)547}$
2. $9\overline{)6{,}642}$
3. $5\overline{)70{,}655}$
4. $8\overline{)490{,}826}$
5. $160 \div 7$
6. $6{,}444 \div 4$
7. $57{,}699 \div 9$
8. $684{,}996 \div 7$

Set C (Lesson 4, pp. 92–95)

Tell whether each number is divisible by 2, 3, 4, 5, 6, 9, or 10.

1. 174
2. 630
3. 725
4. 164
5. 279
6. 204
7. 432
8. 1,080
9. 4,096
10. 1,188

Set D (Lesson 5, pp. 96–97)

Divide.

1. $8\overline{)810}$
2. $5\overline{)7{,}050}$
3. $6\overline{)36{,}094}$
4. $9\overline{)630{,}728}$
5. $413 \div 4$
6. $15{,}514 \div 3$
7. $60{,}432 \div 6$
8. $738{,}264 \div 7$

Set E (Lesson 7, pp. 102–105)

Solve each problem.

1. Laura has collected 81 stamps. If 9 stamps fit on one page of her album, how many pages will she need?
2. There are 54 people waiting in line for a roller coaster ride. If each car holds 6 people, how many cars will be needed?

Use mental math to solve the equations.

3. $5x = 25$
4. $64 = 8k$
5. $72 = 9p$
6. $10g = 110$
7. $4x = 48$
8. $w \div 3 = 9$
9. $21 \div z = 7$
10. $42b = 84$

CHAPTER
5

Divide by Two-Digit Numbers

INVESTIGATION

Use Data

Amelia Earhart's first solo flight across the Atlantic lasted about 15 hours. She flew about 2,025 miles. Find her average speed in miles per hour.

1911
Harriet Quimby
First American woman to earn pilot's license
1932
Amelia Earhart
First woman to solo across Atlantic Ocean
1953
Jacqueline Cochran
First woman to fly at the speed of sound
1983
Sally Ride
First American woman in space
2001
Susan Helms
First woman to live on the International Space Station

Chapter Pretest

Use this page to review and remember what you need to know for this chapter.

VOCABULARY

Choose the best word to complete each sentence.

1. If one number can be evenly divided by another, the first number is ____ by the second number.
2. To check division, ____ the divisor by the quotient.
3. The number to be divided in division is called the ____.
4. The ____ is the number by which another number is to be divided.

CONCEPTS AND SKILLS

Multiply.

5. 4×71
6. 8×34
7. 7×216
8. 9×147
9. 131×5
10. 10×13
11. 911×6
12. 3×222

Tell whether each number is divisible by 2, 3, 4, 5, 6, 9, or 10.

13. 432
14. 3,000
15. 735
16. 690
17. 582
18. 600

Divide. Then check.

19. $2\overline{)83}$
20. $9\overline{)724}$
21. $6\overline{)468}$
22. $75 \div 8$
23. $127 \div 5$
24. $549 \div 7$

25. Explain or demonstrate why there are no numbers divisible by 0.

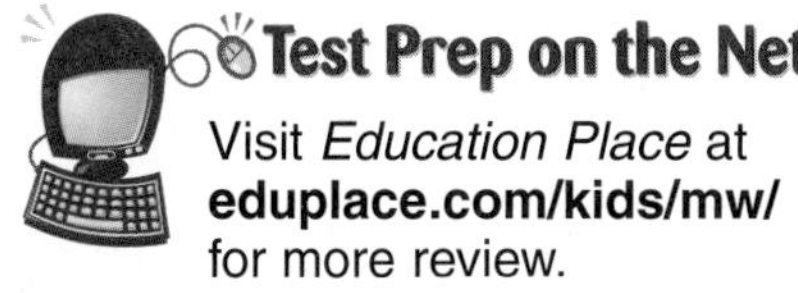

Visit *Education Place* at **eduplace.com/kids/mw/** for more review.

Lesson 1

Divide by Multiples of 10, 100, and 1,000

Objective Use patterns and mental math to divide by multiples of 10, 100, and 1,000.

Learn About It

In 1998, John Glenn was the oldest astronaut to orbit Earth. As the first American to orbit Earth in 1962, part of his orbit was 99 miles above Earth. It is about 240,000 miles to the Moon. About how many times farther would a trip to the Moon be than the height of Glenn's orbit?

Estimate. 240,000 ÷ 99 ≈ 240,000 ÷ 100

Find 240,000 ÷ 100.

240,000 ÷ 1 = 240,000
240,000 ÷ 10 = 24,000
240,000 ÷ 100 = 2,400
240,000 ÷ 1,000 = 240

What do you notice about the pattern?

Solution: The distance to the Moon is about 2,400 times farther.

Other Examples

A. Use Basic Facts

Find 16,000 ÷ 8.

16 ÷ 8 = 2
160 ÷ 8 = 20
1,600 ÷ 8 = 200
16,000 ÷ 8 = 2,000

B. Use Multiples of 10

Find 28,000 ÷ 7,000.

28 ÷ 7 = 4
280 ÷ 70 = 4
2,800 ÷ 700 = 4
28,000 ÷ 7,000 = 4

C. Use Compatible Numbers

Estimate 26,000 ÷400.

28 ÷ 4 = 7;
28,000 ÷ 400 = 70

24 ÷ 4 = 6;
24,000 ÷ 400 = 60

The quotient is between 60 and 70.

Guided Practice

Divide. Use mental math.

1. 800 ÷ 4
2. 6,000 ÷ 20
3. 4,000 ÷ 500
4. $80\overline{)6,400}$
5. $900\overline{)36,000}$
6. $4,000\overline{)200,000}$

Ask Yourself

- Which basic division fact should I use?
- Did I write the correct number of zeros?

What pattern do you notice in the quotients when you divide multiples of 10 by multiples of 10?

Practice and Problem Solving

Divide. Use mental math.

7. 280 ÷ 7
8. 540 ÷ 90
9. 18,000 ÷ 600
10. 4,800 ÷ 800
11. 24,000 ÷ 8,000
12. 32,000 ÷ 40
13. 180,000 ÷ 2,000
14. 56,000 ÷ 8,000
15. 36,000 ÷ 600
16. $80\overline{)64{,}000}$
17. $300\overline{)900{,}000}$
18. $1{,}000\overline{)700{,}000}$
19. $700\overline{)140{,}000}$
20. $50\overline{)25{,}000}$
21. $4{,}000\overline{)120{,}000}$

Use compatible numbers and multiples of 10 to estimate each quotient.

22. 7,240 ÷ 80
23. 8,500 ÷ 40
24. 624,000 ÷ 900
25. 23,900 ÷ 46
26. 623,000 ÷ 270
27. 938,000 ÷ 526

Data **Use the table to solve Problems 28–31.**

28. How long did one orbit last?
29. **Estimate** About how many miles did Glenn travel each minute in orbit?
30. At what time did John Glenn's flight end?
31. What was the difference between Glenn's closest and farthest points from Earth during his orbits?
32. **Create and Solve** Use the data in the table to write and solve your own problem.

John Glenn's Earth Orbits

Blast off time	9:47 A.M. (EST)
Number of orbits	3
Time in orbit	90 minutes
Total orbit length	80,966 miles
Orbit altitudes	99-163 miles
Flight duration	4 hours 55 minutes

Daily Review | Test Prep

Fill in each blank. (Grade 4)

33. 3,000 centimeters = ■ meters
34. 8,000 milliliters = ■ liters
35. 56,000 grams = ■ kilograms
36. 227,000 meters = ■ kilometers
37. 49,000 millimeters = ■ meters

38. The distance from Earth to the Moon is about 240,000 miles. The *Ulysses* spacecraft can travel about 30,000 miles in one hour. How long would it take *Ulysses* to travel 240,000 miles?

A 8 hours **C** 800 hours
B 80 hours **D** 8,000 hours

Extra Practice See page 133, Set A.

Lesson 2

Two-Digit Divisors

Objective Divide by a two-digit divisor and estimate to place the first digit in the quotient.

e Glossary

Vocabulary

estimate

quotient

Learn About It

From 1841 to 1866, more than a half million people moved west. The Oregon Trail was a popular route for wagon trains to take. A wagon train left Independence and arrived in Fort Laramie 45 days later. About how many miles did the wagon train travel daily?

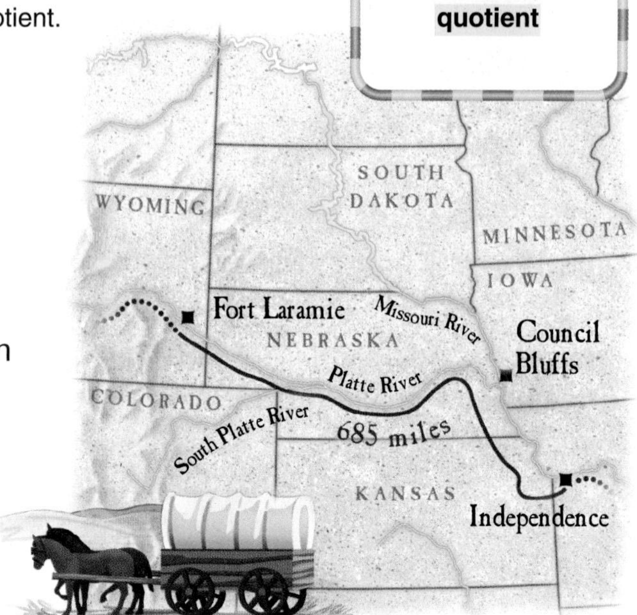

Find 685 ÷ 45.

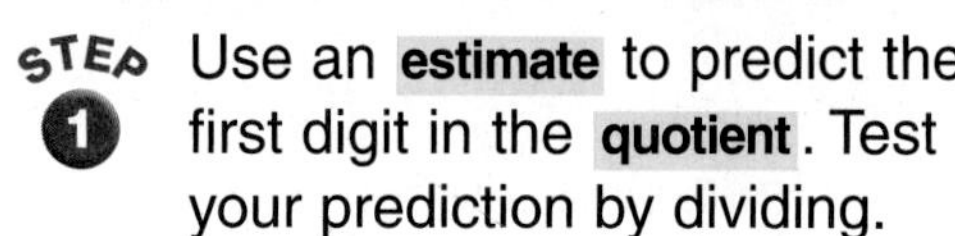

STEP 1 Use an **estimate** to predict the first digit in the **quotient**. Test your prediction by dividing.

What compatible numbers will help you place the first digit?

$45\overline{)685} \rightarrow 50\overline{)500}$ (quotient 10)

```
     1
45)685     Multiply. 1 × 45 = 45
  - 45  ←  Subtract. 68 − 45 = 23
    23     Compare. 23 < 45
```

STEP 2 Bring down the ones. Divide and record the remainder.

What compatible numbers will help you place the next digit?

$45\overline{)235} \rightarrow 50\overline{)250}$ (quotient 5)

```
     15 R10
45)685
  - 45↓
    235      Multiply. 5 × 45 = 225
  - 225  ←   Subtract. 235 − 225 = 10
     10      Compare. 10 < 45
```

Solution: The wagon train traveled about 15 miles daily.

Check.
Multiply the quotient by the divisor and add the remainder.

$(15 \times 45) + 10 = 685$

The result equals the dividend, so the quotient is correct.

Another Example

Zeros in the Quotient

Find 852 ÷ 42.

Estimate

$42\overline{)852} \rightarrow 40\overline{)800}$ (quotient 20)

```
     20 R12
42)852
  - 84
     12
    - 0
     12
```

Guided Practice

Divide. Check your answer.

1. 11)89
2. 45)905
3. 19)798
4. 91 ÷ 27
5. 68 ÷ 31
6. 663 ÷ 82

Ask Yourself

- What basic fact can I use to estimate the first digit of the quotient?

Explain Your Thinking In Exercise 6, how did you know where to place the first digit in the quotient?

Practice and Problem Solving

Divide. Check your answer.

7. 20)87
8. 26)84
9. 31)93
10. 27)56
11. 32)74
12. 43)86
13. 21)66
14. 32)98
15. 31)930
16. 15)724
17. 41)825
18. 41)945
19. 11)568
20. 61)860
21. 42)882
22. 81)415
23. 47 ÷ 22
24. 88 ÷ 44
25. 99 ÷ 32
26. 60 ÷ 29
27. 390 ÷ 75
28. 544 ÷ 32
29. 378 ÷ 62
30. 519 ÷ 51

Solve.

31. A family spent $260 for oxen to pull their wagon along the Oregon Trail. If each ox cost $65, how many oxen did they buy?

32. A family saved the same amount each month for two years to get $792 they needed for oxen and supplies for their trip west. How much did they save each month?

33. **Measurement** A wagon train left Missouri on April 15. It arrived in Oregon 138 days later. On what date did they arrive?

34. **What If?** Suppose the family in Problem 32 only had 18 months to save the money they needed. How much money would they need to save each month?

Daily Review | Test Prep

Evaluate each expression. Write >, <, or = for each ●. (Ch. 2, Lesson 1; Ch. 3, Lesson 1)

35. (24 − 8) × (82 − 82) ● 77 − 13
36. (9 × 8) × 1 ● (4 × 5) × 2
37. 32 × 6 ● 240 ÷ 10

38. **Free Response** A wagon train with 90 wagons uses 8 wagons for supplies. The remaining wagons contain 574 travelers with the same number of people in each wagon. How many people are in each wagon? Explain.

Extra Practice See page 133, Set B.

Lesson 3

Problem-Solving Strategy

Work Backward

Objective Solve problems by working backward.

Problem One fourth of the total number of signers of the Declaration of Independence were from Pennsylvania and Massachusetts. There were 4 fewer signers from Massachusetts than from Pennsylvania. If there were 9 signers from Pennsylvania, how many signers were there in all?

UNDERSTAND

This is what you know:

- One fourth of the total number of signers were from Massachusetts and Pennsylvania.
- Four fewer signers were from Massachusetts than from Pennsylvania.
- Nine signers were from Pennsylvania.

PLAN

You can use Working Backward to solve the problem.

You can draw a model.

Total number of signers			
PA + *MA*	*PA* + *MA*	*PA* + *MA*	*PA* + *MA*

Think
$PA = 9$;
$MA = 9 - 4$;
$PA + MA = 9 + (9 - 4)$

SOLVE

Start at the end of the problem with facts you know and work backward through the problem. $PA = 9$

- Find the number of signers from Massachusetts. $9 - 4 = 5$ $MA = 5$
- Find the number of signers from Massachusetts and Pennsylvania. $9 + 5 = 14$ $PA + MA = 14$
- Find the total number of signers. $14 \times 4 = 56$

Solution: There were 56 signers of the Declaration of Independence.

LOOK BACK

Look back at the problem.

Does the answer seem reasonable and make sense?

MathTracks 1/16
Listen and Understand

Guided Practice

Use the Ask Yourself questions to help you solve each problem.

1. Thomas Jefferson, the third President of the United States, was in office for 8 years. He began his term 25 years after he drafted the Declaration of Independence in 1776. During what years was Thomas Jefferson President?

   Hint: Should you start with the number of years he was in office or the year he drafted the Declaration of Independence?

2. Most delegates signed the Declaration of Independence 1 month and 1 day after the Continental Congress first met to discuss it. They began discussing it 3 days before adopting it on July 4, 1776. When was it signed?

Ask Yourself

UNDERSTAND: **What facts do I know?**

PLAN: **Did I plan the operations to use at each step by drawing a model?**

SOLVE:
- **Did I start with facts I learned from the end of the problem?**
- **Which operations did I need to use?**
- **Did I work backward through the facts in the problem?**

LOOK BACK: **Did I solve the problem?**

Independent Practice

Work backward to solve each problem.

3. To find out how old John Adams was when he signed the Declaration of Independence, divide the sum of 24 and the year he signed it by 45. How old was John Adams, our second President, in 1776 when he signed?

4. Ben Franklin was the oldest signer of the Declaration of Independence. To find his age when he signed it, divide the product of 50 and Franklin's age when he died by 60. Franklin died at age 84. How old was he when he signed?

5. Of all the signers of the Declaration of Independence, Carter Braxton had the most children. He had twice as many children as Arthur Middleton, who had 3 times as many as Ben Franklin. Franklin had 3 children. How many did Braxton have?

6. Samuel Adams, cousin of John Adams, was a delegate to the Continental Congress for 7 years. He became Massachusetts' governor 13 years after that. His 3 years as governor ended in 1797. When did Samuel Adams begin work in the Continental Congress?

IN CONGRESS, JULY 4, 1776.

The unanimous Declaration of the thirteen united States of America,

Choose a Strategy 

Solve. Show your work.
Tell what strategy you used.

Strategies

- Use Models
- Draw a Diagram
- Find a Pattern
- Guess and Check
- Make an Organized List
- Make a Table
- Solve a Simpler Problem
- Use Logical Reasoning
- Work Backward
- Write an Equation

7. Of the 56 signers of the Declaration of Independence, only William Ellery was a lawyer and a merchant. Of the rest, 39 were either lawyers or merchants. There were 9 more lawyers than merchants. The product of the numbers of these careers is 360. How many lawyers were there?

8. When Dr. Benjamin Rush signed the Declaration of Independence, he was half as old as his fellow delegate George Taylor, who was seven years older than Samuel Adams at the time. If Samuel Adams was fifty-three, how old was Dr. Rush?

Data **Use the table to solve Problems 9–14.**

District 12 Middle School Students	
Grade	**Number of Students**
5	336
6	312
7	288
8	306

9. **Analyze** One middle school grade orders buses for their field trip to the National Archives. If the buses each seat 48 students, and this grade just fits in 7 buses, which grade is it?

10. Three of the 10 classes in one grade have 2 more students than the other classes have. If this is eighth grade, how many students are in each of the other classes?

11. Of the students in the spring play, 1 less than half have speaking parts. A third of all the fifth-graders in the school are involved in the play. How many fifth-graders have speaking parts?

12. All of the students in two grades went on a ski trip for the weekend. There was one adult for every 10 students. There were exactly 60 adults. Which two grades went on the ski trip?

13. **Calculator** For a school assembly, Mr. Lang sets up chairs with 24 chairs per row. How many rows will each grade need?

14. **Create and Solve** Write a division problem using data from the chart. Solve your problem.

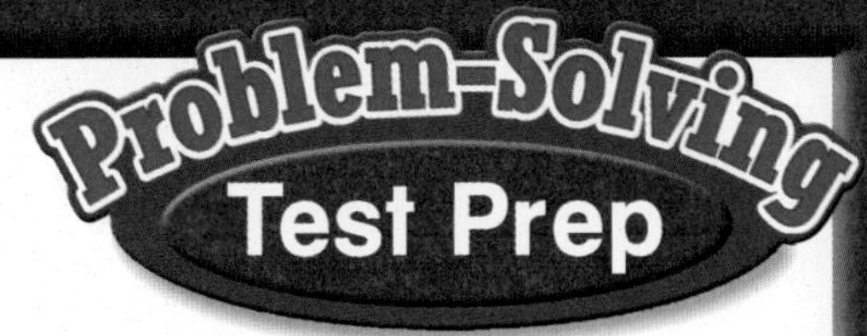

Choose the letter of the correct answer.
If a correct answer is not here, choose NH.

1. If this pattern continues, how many shaded squares will be in the seventh term of this pattern?

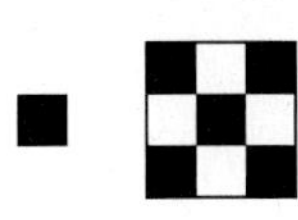  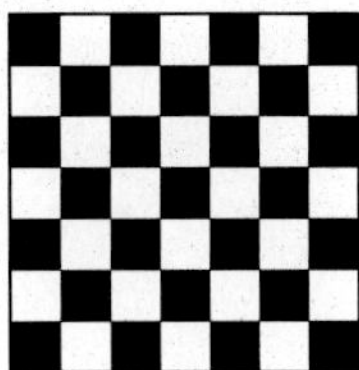

A 61 squares **C** 73 squares

B 71 squares **D** 85 squares

(Chapter 1, Lesson 6)

2. Juán has 42 autographs in his book. Marta has x more than Juán has. If Marta has 51 autographs, how many more autographs does Marta have?

$$42 + x = 51$$

F 9 autographs **H** 11 autographs

G 93 autographs **J** NH

(Chapter 2, Lesson 5)

3. Tanya has dolls on 5 shelves. Some shelves have 3 dolls. Some have 5 dolls, and some have 8 dolls. If Tanya has 24 dolls, how many of each kind of shelf is it possible for her to have?

A 1 shelf of 3; 1 shelf of 5; 1 shelf of 8

B 1 shelf of 3; 2 shelves of 5; 3 shelves of 8

C 2 shelves of 3; 2 shelves of 5; 1 shelf of 8

D NH

(Chapter 1, Lessons 6 and 7)

4. This decimal model shows 0.06. Which of these statements about 0.06 is true?

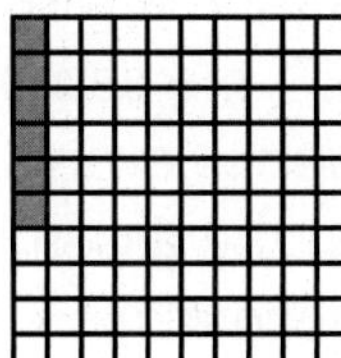

F $0.06 > 0.0$ **H** 0.06 rounds to 1.0

G $0.06 = 0.6$ **J** $0.06 < 0.01$

(Chapter 1, Lesson 7)

5. Which of these expressions has the *greatest* value?

A 2^5 **B** 3^4 **C** 4^3 **D** 5^2

(Chapter 1, Lesson 2)

6. By which of the following numbers is 4,680 divisible?

2, 3, 4, 5, 6, 9, 10

Explain Use divisibility rules to explain how to find the answer.

(Chapter 4, Lesson 4)

7. This year's field trip to Washington, D.C., costs each student \$5.50 for the bus, \$18.75 for food, and \$29.95 for the hotel room. Last year the trip cost \$49.65 per student. By how much has the trip's price gone up?

Represent Draw a model to show how to find the answer.

(Chapter 4, Lesson 4)

Test Prep on the Net

Check out *Education Place* at **eduplace.com/kids/mw/** for test prep practice.

Lesson 4

Adjusting Quotients

Objective Adjust the estimate of the quotient.

Learn About It

MathTracks 1/17
Listen and Understand

Henry Ford invented a way to make automobiles quickly. By 1927, the assembly line completed one Model T automobile every 24 seconds. How many Model T's could the assembly line complete in 15 minutes (900 seconds)?

Find 24)900. Estimate first. 24)900 → 800 ÷ 20 = 40

Estimate Too Large

STEP 1 Place the first digit in the quotient. Try 4.

```
    4
24)900
  - 96
```

96 > 90
4 is too large.

STEP 2 Adjust. Try 3.

```
    3
24)900
 - 72
   18
```

18 < 24
3 is correct.

STEP 3 Try 8.

```
    38
24)900
 - 96↓
   180
 - 192
```

192 > 180
8 is too large.

STEP 4 Adjust.

```
    37 R 12
24)900
 - 96↓
   180
 - 168
    12
```

12 < 24
7 is correct.

Solution: They could make 37 Model T's in 15 minutes.

Remember
In division the remainder must be less than the divisor.

Find 16)849. Estimate first. 16)849 → 800 ÷ 20 = 40

Estimate Too Small

STEP 1 Place the first digit. Try 4.

```
    4
16)849
 - 64
   20
```

20 > 16
4 is too small.

STEP 2 Adjust. Try 5.

```
    5
16)849
 - 80
    4
```

4 < 16
5 is correct.

STEP 3 Try 2.

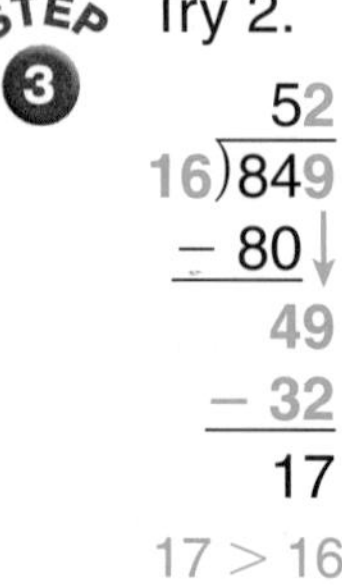

```
    52
16)849
 - 80↓
    49
  - 32
    17
```

17 > 16
2 is too small.

STEP 4 Adjust. Try 3.

```
    53 R1
16)849
 - 80↓
    49
  - 48
     1
```

1 < 16
3 is correct.

Solution: 849 ÷ 16 = 53 R1.

Guided Practice

Divide. Check your answers.

1. $64\overline{)558}$
2. $64\overline{)316}$
3. $27\overline{)139}$
4. 420 ÷ 46
5. 782 ÷ 16
6. 650 ÷ 24

Ask Yourself

- Did I estimate the first digit of the quotient?
- Is the remainder less than the divisor?

TEST TIPS **Explain Your Thinking** What should you do if your estimated quotient is too large? too small?

Practice and Problem Solving

Divide. Check your answers.

7. $45\overline{)230}$
8. $75\overline{)626}$
9. $23\overline{)823}$
10. $24\overline{)620}$
11. $64\overline{)439}$
12. $18\overline{)176}$
13. $73\overline{)431}$
14. $67\overline{)408}$
15. $16\overline{)120}$
16. $93\overline{)362}$
17. $29\overline{)203}$
18. $43\overline{)808}$
19. 618 ÷ 32
20. 314 ÷ 63
21. 816 ÷ 27
22. 629 ÷ 17

Algebra • Functions Copy and complete.

23. Rule: Divide by 12.

Input	Output
24	■
48	■
144	■
192	■

24. Rule: Divide by 25.

Input	Output
50	■
■	3
■	5
200	■

25. Rule: ■

Input	Output
200	10
240	12
360	18
480	24

Solve.

26. A Model T could travel at a maximum speed of 45 miles per hour. At that rate, how long would it take for a Model T to travel a distance of 315 miles?

27. **Estimate** Ford's 1914 assembly line could turn out a Model T in 93 minutes. About how many times faster than the normal 728 minutes is that?

Daily Review | Test Prep

Name the place value of the digit 6 in each number. (Ch. 1, Lesson 5)

28. 2.067
29. 0.624
30. 1.376
31. 0.6
32. 6.041
33. 0.060

34. A Model T could go 19 miles on a gallon of gas. How much gas would it use to go 475 miles?

A 25 gallons
B 26 gallons
C 35 gallons
D 250 gallons

Extra Practice See page 133, Set C.

Lesson 5

Division With Greater Numbers

Objective Divide a two-digit number into a dividend with up to six digits.

Learn About It

In the 1850s, stagecoaches delivered letters and packages out West. Suppose a stagecoach traveled from Missouri to California and back in 42 days. If it traveled 5,416 miles, about how many miles did the stagecoach travel each day?

Find 5,416 ÷ 42.

STEP 1 Estimate the first digit of the quotient. Then divide the hundreds.

Try 1 hundred.

$$\begin{array}{r} 1 \\ 42\overline{)5,416} \\ -\,4\,2 \\ \hline 1\,2 \end{array}$$

Multiply. 1×42
Subtract. $54 - 42$
Compare. $12 < 42$

Think
$40\overline{)4,000}$ = 100

STEP 2 Bring down the tens. Divide the tens.

Try 3 tens.

$$\begin{array}{r} 13 \\ 42\overline{)5,416} \\ -\,4\,2\downarrow \\ \hline 1\,21 \\ -\,1\,26 \end{array}$$

Estimate is too large. Try 2 tens.

$$\begin{array}{r} 12 \\ 42\overline{)5,416} \\ -\,4\,2\downarrow \\ \hline 121 \\ -\,84 \\ \hline 37 \end{array}$$

Multiply. 2×42
Subtract. $121 - 84$
Compare. $37 < 42$

Think
$40\overline{)1,200}$ = 30

STEP 3 Bring down the ones. Divide the ones.

Try 9 ones.

$$\begin{array}{r} 129 \\ 42\overline{)5,416} \\ -\,4\,2 \\ \hline 1\,21 \\ -\,84 \\ \hline 376 \\ -\,378 \\ \hline \end{array}$$

Estimate is too large. Try 8 ones.

$$\begin{array}{r} 128 \text{ R40} \\ 42\overline{)5,416} \\ -\,4\,2 \\ \hline 121 \\ -\,84 \\ \hline 376 \\ -\,336 \\ \hline 40 \end{array}$$

Multiply. 8×42
Subtract. $376 - 336$
Compare. $40 < 42$

Think
$40\overline{)360}$ = 9

Solution: The stagecoach traveled between 128 and 129 miles each day.

Other Examples

A. Zeros in the Quotient

Find 72,096 ÷ 24.

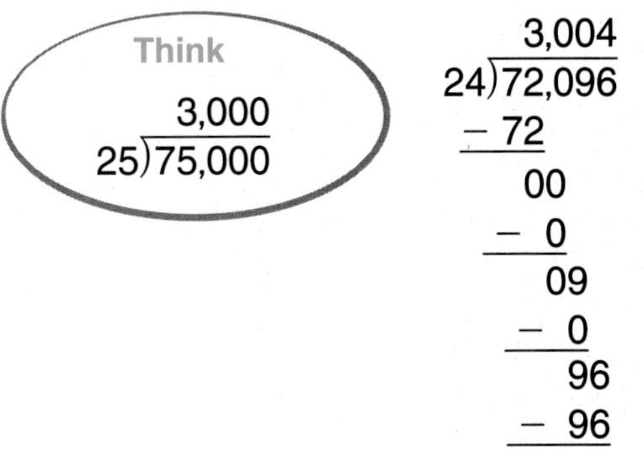

B. Three-Digit Divisor

Find 74,530 ÷ 256.

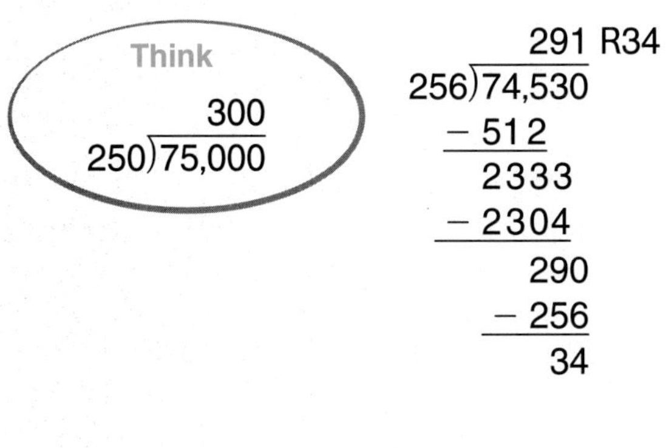

Guided Practice

Ask Yourself

- Where should I place the first digit?
- Is the estimated digit too large or too small?

TEST TIPS

Divide.

1. 14)5,634
2. 38)6,375
3. 42)5,425
4. 29,622 ÷ 12
5. 485,215 ÷ 25
6. 91,233 ÷ 731

Explain Your Thinking ▶ Explain how to use multiplication and addition to check your answer in Exercise 6.

Practice and Problem Solving

Divide.

7. 17)5,185
8. 48)2,400
9. 73)7,408
10. 36)7,239
11. 35)11,144
12. 59)35,424
13. 91)27,636
14. 62)26,935
15. 9,427 ÷ 31
16. 9,454 ÷ 47
17. 7,664 ÷ 58
18. 4,800 ÷ 24
19. 493,438 ÷ 16
20. 682,675 ÷ 25
21. 75,223 ÷ 729
22. 20,702 ÷ 298

Algebra • Equations If q is the quotient and r is the remainder, write and solve a division problem for each equation.

23. $20q + r = 3{,}221$
24. $35q + r = 7{,}805$
25. $29q + r = 16{,}258$
26. $52q + r = 89{,}162$
27. $11q + r = 1{,}090$
28. $15q + r = 3{,}333$

Go On

Solve.

29. **Measurement** June wants to place a border along the top of her bedroom. She needs 576 inches. How many packages will she need to buy if each package contains 10 feet of border?

30. **Analyze** The variables *a*, *b*, and *c* in the division problem shown below represent 3 different digits. The division has been started for you. Complete the division.

$$\begin{array}{r} a \\ ab\overline{)a,ccb} \\ -ab \\ \hline a \end{array}$$

31. **Analyze** What is the maximum number of digits there could be in the quotient of a five-digit dividend divided by a three-digit divisor? Give examples to show your reasoning.

Choose a Computation Method

Mental Math • Estimation • Paper and Pencil • Calculator

The table shows information about the Butterfield Overland Stage Company. Use the table for Problems 32–34. Then explain which method you chose.

Stagecoach Routes	
Total length	2,812 miles
Number of stations	139
One-way fare	$200
Average time to travel the total length of the route	22 days

32. If each of the stations on the route was the same distance apart, about how far is the distance between stations?

33. **Reasoning** If the fare is based on the length of a trip, about how much would it cost to travel 700 miles?

34. **Analyze** When the Pony Express began delivering mail in 1860, its riders took an average of 12 days to cover 1,866 miles. On average, who covered more miles in a day, Pony Express riders or stagecoach drivers? How did you decide?

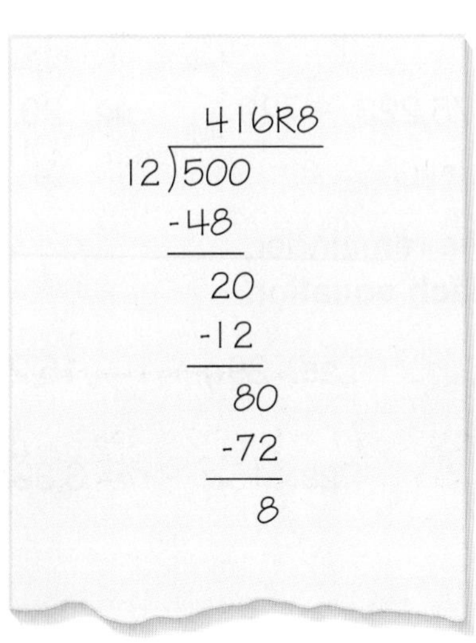

35. **What's Wrong?** Stagecoach horses might be changed every 12 miles. To find the number of changes made in 500 miles, Jared divided 500 by 12. Jared's work is shown at the left. What did he do wrong?

36. **Create and Solve** Do some research about transportation in the 1800s. Write a problem based on your research. Trade problems with a classmate and solve.

Quick Check

Check your understanding for Lessons 1–5.

Divide. Check your answer. (Lessons 1, 2, 4, and 5)

1. $600 \div 60$ **2.** $25{,}000 \div 500$ **3.** $420{,}000 \div 7{,}000$ **4.** $32\overline{)672}$

5. $15\overline{)107}$ **6.** $34\overline{)884}$ **7.** $4{,}290 \div 56$ **8.** $36{,}247 \div 29$

Work backward to solve each problem. (Lesson 3)

9. Maggie rides her horse 3 more miles than Tasha. Emmaline rides 5 more miles than Tasha. Catherine rides 2 fewer miles than Emmaline. Emmaline rides 6 miles. How many miles does each girl ride?

10. At one shop, there are 2 fewer jackets with beads than jackets with fringe. There are 3 fewer plain jackets than jackets with beads. How many jackets with fringe are there if there are 15 plain jackets?

Quotient Quest

2 Players

What You'll Need
- four sets of number cards (Learning Tool 6)
- division frames (Learning Tool 30)

How to Play

1. Shuffle the cards and give five cards to each player.

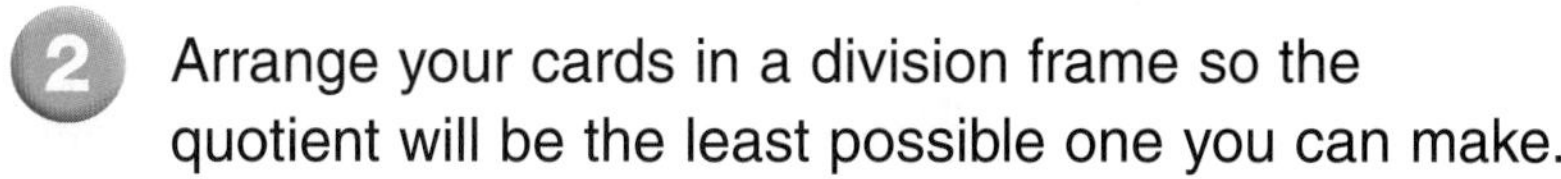

2. Arrange your cards in a division frame so the quotient will be the least possible one you can make.

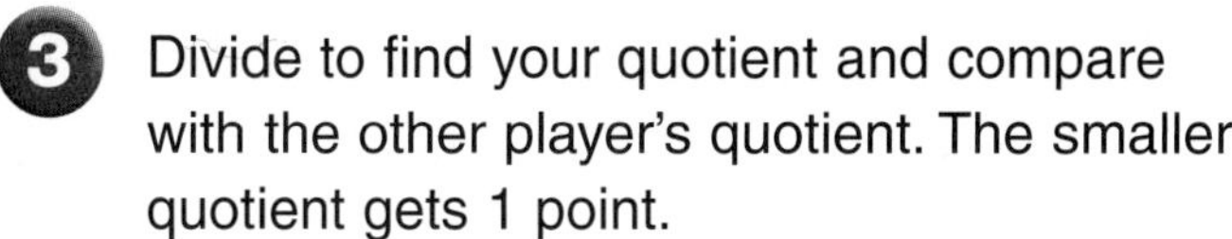

3. Divide to find your quotient and compare with the other player's quotient. The smaller quotient gets 1 point.

Take turns dealing the cards, repeating Steps 1 to 3. The first player to get a total of 10 points wins.

Algebra

Order of Operations

Objective Use the order of operations to simplify expressions.

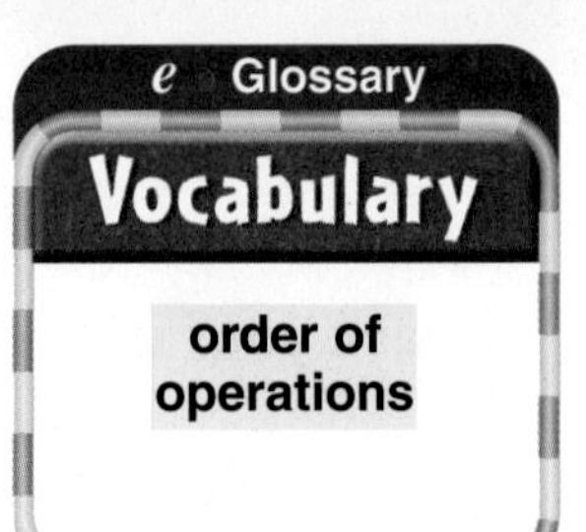

Learn About It

MathTracks 1/18
Listen and Understand

Simplify. 8 + (4 × 24) ÷ 32

To simplify an expression when there are more than two terms in the expression, you must use a set of rules called the **order of operations**. The order of operations tells you in which order to perform the operations when simplifying.

Some people use this sentence as a memory device to help them remember the order of operations: **P**lease **e**xcuse **m**y **d**ear **A**unt **S**ally.

Order of Operations

1. Simplify the terms within **parentheses**.
2. Simplify the terms with **exponents**.
3. **Multiply** and **divide** from left to right.
4. **Add** and **subtract** from left to right.

Find 8 + (4 × 24) ÷ 32.

STEP 1 Simplify within the parentheses.

(4×24) $\quad \begin{array}{r} 24 \\ \times\ 4 \\ \hline 96 \end{array}$

STEP 2 Divide 96 by 32.

$\begin{array}{r} 3 \\ 32\overline{)96} \\ -\,96 \\ \hline 0 \end{array}$

STEP 3 Add 8.

$\begin{array}{r} 3 \\ +\,8 \\ \hline 11 \end{array}$

Solution: $8 + (4 \times 24) \div 32 = 11$

Using the order of operations to simplify an expression ensures that the expression has the same value.

Here are the ways two students simplified $14 - (5 + 2) \times 2$.

Problem: Who used the order of operations correctly?

Solution: Delia used the correct order of operations. After simplifying the terms within the parentheses, she multiplied 7 and 2 before subtracting.

Janet	Delia
14 − (5 + 2) X 2	14 − (5 + 2) X 2
= 14 − 7 X 2	= 14 − 7 X 2
= 7 X 2	= 14 − 14
= 14	= 0

You can use the order of operations in an algebraic expression to help you predict whether the value will change if you change the parentheses.

In these three cases, the value of the expression *does not* change when the parentheses are changed.

Addition Only	**Addition Then Subtraction**	**Multiplication Only**
$(a + b) + c \;=\; a + (b + c)$	$(a + b) - c \;=\; a + (b - c)$	$(a \times b) \times c \;=\; a \times (b \times c)$
$(5 + 4) + 6 \bigcirc 5 + (4 + 6)$	$(7 + 6) - 5 \bigcirc 7 + (6 - 5)$	$(2 \times 3) \times 4 \bigcirc 2 \times (3 \times 4)$
$9 + 6 \bigcirc 5 + 10$	$13 - 5 \bigcirc 7 + 1$	$6 \times 4 \bigcirc 2 \times 12$
$15 = 15$	$8 = 8$	$24 = 24$

In the cases below, changing the parentheses *does* change the value of the expression.

Subtraction Only	**Subtraction Then Addition**	**Division Only**
$(a - b) - c \neq a - (b - c)$	$(a - b) + c \neq a - (b + c)$	$(a \div b) \div c \neq a \div (b \div c)$
$(12 - 4) - 3 \bigcirc 12 - (4 - 3)$	$(10 - 2) + 3 \bigcirc 10 - (2 + 3)$	$(12 \div 6) \div 2 \bigcirc 12 \div (6 \div 2)$
$8 - 3 \bigcirc 12 - 1$	$8 + 3 \bigcirc 10 - 5$	$2 \div 2 \bigcirc 12 \div 3$
$5 \neq 11$	$11 \neq 5$	$1 \neq 4$

Another Example

Parentheses and Exponents

$(12 \div 4)^2 \times (4 \times 5) - (8 - 4) + 5^2$

$= 3^2 \times 20 - 4 + 5^2$ ← Simplify within parentheses.

$= 9 \times 20 - 4 + 25$ ← Simplify exponents.

$= 180 - 4 + 25$ ← Multiply.

$= 176 + 25 = 201$ ← Add and subtract from left to right.

Guided Practice

Ask Yourself

- Which operation should I start with?
- Have I simplified the expression completely?

Simplify.

1. $5 + (8 - 6)$

2. $(14 \div 2) \times 5$

3. $25 + (2 + 20) - 40$

4. $(12 + 13) \times (8 \div 4)$

How would you solve Exercise 2 if you did not have parentheses to show which operations go together?

Go On

Practice and Problem Solving

Simplify.

5. $(12 + 6) - 3$
6. $9 + (18 \div 9) \times 6$
7. $(8 \times 2) \div 4^2$
8. $(27 - 2) - (20 \div 5)^2$
9. $(21 - 3) \div (4 + 5) + (3 \times 5)$
10. $(8^2 + 6) \div (10 - 3)$
11. $5 + (124 - 2) + 32$
12. $1{,}295 - (49 - 42) \times 14$
13. $(65 \div 5) + 4^2$

Write >, <, or = for each ●.

14. $11 + (32 - 7)$ ● $(11 + 32) - 7$
15. $26 - (18 \div 6)$ ● $(24 \div 3) + 2^2$
16. $(36 \div 3^2) \times 8$ ● $(24 \times 2) - 42$
17. $1{,}822 - (153 + 22)$ ● $(1{,}822 - 153) + 22$

Mental Math Use mental math to simplify.

18. $(7 + 2) - 9 + 8$
19. $(4 + 2) + (3 + 3) + (7 - 1)$
20. $(5 \times 5) \times 2 \times (2 \times 2)$
21. $(4 \div 4) \times 4 \div (2 \times 2)$

Algebra • Expressions Evaluate the expression, given $x = 2$ and $y = 6$.

22. $x^2 + (y - x)$
23. $(y^2 - 4) \div x$
24. $3x + y^2$
25. $2(x + y) - x^2$
26. $(x \cdot y)^2$
27. $(4x + 3) - y$

Solve.

28. A steamboat has 112 passengers. At one stop, 2 groups of 8 passengers get off the boat to sightsee and 24 more passengers go shopping. How many passengers are left on the boat?

29. **Write About It** Use parentheses to write two different expressions with equal values.

30. **What's Wrong?** When Alexander simplified the expression $5^2 + 8 \times 3 - 4$, he said the result was 95. Did he follow the order of operations? If he did not, which rule did he fail to follow, and what should the result have been?

31. **You Decide** Copy this expression on paper and decide where you want the parentheses to go. Simplify.

    $4 \times 5 + 6 - 8 \div 2 + 2^2$

    Tell a partner the value of your expression. Have your partner find where the parentheses belong.

Daily Review **Test Prep**

Add or subtract. (Ch. 2, Lesson 3)

32. 34,229 + 6,183

33. 72,405 + 8,924 + 16,308

34. 2,419 − 1,728

35. Free Response Explain the steps you would take to simplify this expression. Then simplify. Show your work.

$(4 + 3) \times 8 - (18 \div 2) + 3^2$

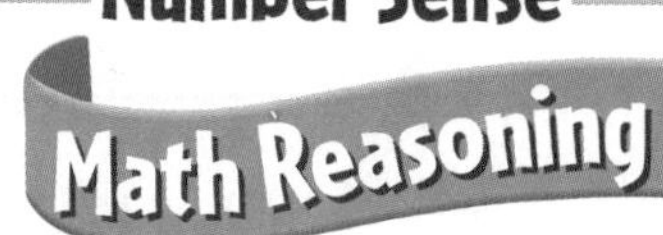

Other Ways to Divide

Find 7,473 ÷ 8.

Way 1 Short Division

STEP 1 Divide 74 hundreds by 8. Write the remainder in the dividend.

Think
74 ÷ 8 = 9 R2

Write: $8\overline{)74^{2}73}$ with quotient 9

STEP 2 Divide 27 tens by 8. Write the remainder in the dividend.

Think
27 ÷ 8 = 3 R3

Write: $8\overline{)74^{2}7^{3}3}$ with quotient 9 3

STEP 3 Divide 33 by 8. Write the last remainder in the quotient.

Think
33 ÷ 8 = 4 R1

Write: $8\overline{)74^{2}7^{3}3}$ with quotient 9 3 4 R1

Way 2 Repeated Subtraction

Find 224 ÷ 56.

STEP 1 Start with 224. Subtract 56 repeatedly.

Think
How many groups of 56 are there in 224?

```
 224
− 56
 168
− 56
 112
− 56
  56
− 56
   0
```

STEP 2 Count how many times you subtracted 56.

You subtracted 56 four times, so there are 4 groups of 56 in 224.

$56 + 56 + 56 + 56 = 224$

$4 \times 56 = 224$

$224 \div 56 = 4$

Divide. Show your work. Use short division or repeated subtraction.

1. 5622 ÷ 9 **2.** $7\overline{)23,401}$ **3.** $28\overline{)10,634}$ **4.** 78,435 ÷ 567

Extra Practice See page 133, Set D.

Problem-Solving Application

Interpret Remainders

Objective Solve problems involving remainders.

When you solve a problem with a remainder, you need to decide how to interpret the remainder.

Problem One summer 103 hikers signed up to hike part of Lewis and Clark's route. If a maximum of 8 people could be in a group, how many groups were there?

What is the question?

How many groups of hikers were there?

What do you know?

- There were 103 hikers.
- A maximum of 8 people were in a group.

PLAN

Divide 103 by 8. Decide how you will interpret the remainder.

- **Will you increase the quotient?** Increase the quotient when you must include the remainder.
- **Will you drop the remainder?** Drop the remainder when you do not need to include it.
- **Will your remainder be the answer?** Use the remainder as the answer when you want to know how many are left over.

SOLVE

- Find the number of full groups of hikers.
- Decide how to use the remainder.

$$8\overline{)103} = 12 \text{ R}7$$

The 7 remaining people made their own group.
Add 1 more group to your answer. $12 + 1 = 13$

Solution: There were 13 groups on the hike.

Look back at the problem.

Does the answer make sense?

Guided Practice

Use the Ask Yourself questions to help you solve each problem.

1. To keep hikers away from delicate plants on the Lewis and Clark trail, park rangers set up rope barriers. If they cut rope into 7-foot strips, how many strips of rope can they make from 85 feet of rope?

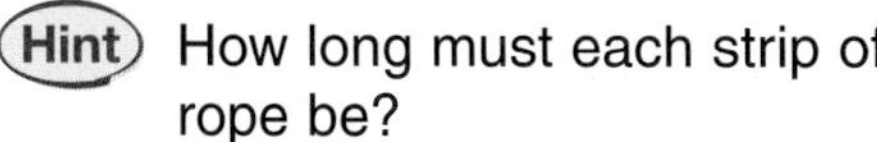

Hint How long must each strip of rope be?

2. A group of 300 hikers will stay in cabins. Each cabin, except one, holds 8 hikers. How many hikers are in the smaller cabin?

Ask Yourself

UNDERSTAND What facts do I know?

PLAN What question must I answer?

SOLVE
- Did I use the remainder to add to the quotient?
- Did I drop the remainder?
- Did I use the remainder as the answer?

LOOK BACK Did I interpret the remainder correctly so that the answer makes sense?

Independent Practice

Solve. Explain how you decided to interpret each remainder.

3. From April 8 to April 11, 1805, suppose the Lewis and Clark expedition traveled 93 miles up the Missouri River. Captain Lewis hoped to average 23 miles per day. Did he reach his goal?

4. A white-water rafting company gets 57 life jackets ready for a trip along a river where Lewis and Clark explored. Each raft must have 8 life jackets. How many spare life jackets are there?

5. After hiking all day, a group of tourists ordered pizzas for dinner. If they ate 309 slices of pizza and each pizza was cut into 6 slices, how many whole pizzas did they eat?

6. A group of 39 people go on a rafting trip. If 7 people can go on each raft, how many rafts must they rent?

2003–2006 marks the 200-year anniversary of the Lewis and Clark expedition. Lewis and Clark with their Shoshone guide, Sacagawea, mapped the West for then-President Thomas Jefferson.

Choose a Strategy

Solve. Show your work.
Tell what strategy you used.

PROBLEM-SOLVING Strategies

- Use Models
- Draw a Diagram
- Find a Pattern
- Guess and Check
- Make an Organized List
- Make a Table
- Solve a Simpler Problem
- Use Logical Reasoning
- Work Backward
- Write an Equation

7. Janell took 71 photographs. She wants to put them in an album. If each page holds 6 pictures, how many pages will Janell need for her photographs?

8. Miguel made 40 sandwiches for his hiking group. He made half as many with peanut butter as with jam. The rest are cheese sandwiches. If he made 10 cheese sandwiches, how many peanut butter sandwiches did he make?

9. Don bought shirts for the Lewis and Clark bicentennial. Sweatshirts cost $16, and T-shirts cost $10. If he spent $46, how many of each did Don buy?

Data **The Water Sports Center on the river has many different kinds of boats to rent. Use the table to solve Problems 10–13.**

10. The Water Sports Center has reservations for 4 groups of 4 and 1 group of 8 people who want to go kayaking. If they only rent 2-person kayaks, how many are left for others?

11. **Analyze** A group of 40 students wants to go kayaking. Are there enough kayaks for them? If so, what is the fewest number they can rent?

12. **Calculator** What is the greatest number of people that can be in the Water Sports Company's boats at the same time?

13. **Create and Solve** Use the data in the table to write your own problem. Solve it and give it to a partner to solve.

Water Sports Center Rentals

Type of Boat	Number Available
2-person kayak	16
1-person kayak	12
3-person canoe	8
4-person row-boat	8
10-person raft	8
6-person raft	8

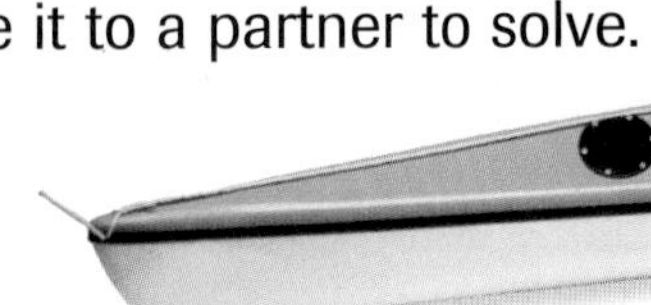

Quick Check

Check your understanding for Lessons 6–7.

Simplify. (Lesson 6)

1. $4 + (3 \times 2) - 1$
2. $(8 \times 3) - (9 \times 2) + 4$
3. $(6 \times 4) - 3^2 + (2 \times 5)$
4. $(8 + 4) \times 5 - 8$
5. $(2 + 4)^2 - (5 \times 4)$
6. $8 + (8 \times 2) \div 4$

Solve. Explain how you decided to interpret each remainder. (Lesson 7)

7. The 246 sixth-graders are going to see a play in the school's auditorium. If each row seats 14, what is the fewest number of rows the students need?
8. At the start of a game, Kendra divides 40 marbles evenly among 3 players. She puts the extra marbles in a jar. How many marbles does each player get?
9. Mrs. Palmer buys 70 apples for making pies. Each pie uses 11 apples. The rest will be used for applesauce. How many apples will go into the applesauce?
10. Matt saves \$15 each week towards a bike. The bike he wants costs \$112. How many weeks must he save to have enough money for the bike?

Calculator Connection

Order of Operations

Not all calculators have the algebraic logic required to perform the order of operations. Try entering $3 + (4 \times 6) - 8$ into your calculator in order from left to right.

If your answer is 19, then your calculator does order of operations for you. If your answer is 34, then your calculator doesn't use order of operations. *You* have to enter the keys in the correct order according to the order of operations.

Press:          

You need to press the equals sign after each operation in order to get the correct result.

Use your calculator to find each value.

1. $7 \times (8 - 3) + 12$
2. $(16 \times 4) \div (2 + 6)$
3. $(15 - 8) \times (4 + 7)$

Chapter Review/Test

VOCABULARY

Vocabulary

estimate
multiple
order of operations
quotient

1. The ____ is a set of rules that tells the order in which you perform the operations when simplifying.
2. A ____ is the product of a given number and any other number.

CONCEPTS AND SKILLS

Divide. Check your answer. (Lessons 1–2, pp. 110–113, Lesson 4, pp. 118–119, Lesson 5, pp. 120–122)

3. $20\overline{)4{,}000}$
4. $27\overline{)198}$
5. $81\overline{)476}$
6. $785 \div 12$
7. $928 \div 32$
8. $596 \div 34$
9. $19\overline{)2{,}834}$
10. $80\overline{)8{,}000}$
11. $87\overline{)21{,}484}$
12. $45\overline{)30{,}655}$
13. $55\overline{)55{,}055}$
14. $34\overline{)12{,}062}$

Simplify. (Lesson 6, pp. 124–127)

15. $(76 - 14) - (48 \div 8)^2$
16. $(63 - 7) \div (7 - 5)^3 + 8$
17. $(24 + 6) \div (30 \div 6)$
18. $(6 \times 9) \div 3^3$
19. $2{,}000 - (95 - 45) \times 20$
20. $72 + 24 - 16$
21. $12 + 11 \times 7 - 20$
22. $121 \div 11 + 3^2$
23. $44 + (63 \div 9) \times 8$

PROBLEM SOLVING

Solve. (Lesson 3, pp. 114–116, Lesson 7, pp. 128–130)

24. At the age of 54, Hattie Caraway became the first woman elected to the United States Senate. She served in the Senate until 1945, thirteen years after she was elected. In what year was Hattie Caraway born?
25. Park rangers are cutting 7-foot lengths of rope. How many lengths can they make from 85 feet of rope?

Show You Understand

Why must the remainder always be less than the divisor?

Extra Practice

Set A (Lesson 1, pp. 110–111)

Divide. Use mental math.

1. $240 \div 4$
2. $560 \div 80$
3. $9{,}000 \div 10$
4. $2{,}100 \div 30$
5. $16{,}000 \div 200$
6. $64{,}000 \div 800$
7. $720{,}000 \div 800$
8. $450{,}000 \div 500$
9. $49{,}000 \div 7{,}000$

Set B (Lesson 2, pp. 112–113)

Divide. Check your answer.

1. $22\overline{)53}$
2. $32\overline{)98}$
3. $24\overline{)72}$
4. $41\overline{)89}$
5. $840 \div 42$
6. $727 \div 42$
7. $496 \div 61$
8. $245 \div 22$

Set C (Lesson 4, pp. 118–119)

Divide. Check your answer.

1. $68\overline{)201}$
2. $74\overline{)294}$
3. $47\overline{)338}$
4. $89\overline{)566}$
5. $58\overline{)264}$
6. $38\overline{)183}$
7. $22\overline{)433}$
8. $39\overline{)707}$
9. $26\overline{)514}$
10. $42\overline{)803}$
11. $27\overline{)628}$
12. $29\overline{)415}$

Set D (Lesson 5, pp. 120–121)

Divide.

1. $24\overline{)7{,}252}$
2. $46\overline{)1{,}286}$
3. $62\overline{)1{,}406}$
4. $19\overline{)7{,}365}$
5. $63\overline{)25{,}864}$
6. $26\overline{)14{,}610}$
7. $82\overline{)46{,}613}$
8. $65\overline{)23{,}486}$

Set E (Lesson 6, pp. 124–126)

Simplify.

1. $(15 + 6) - 8$
2. $7 + (24 \div 6) \times 8$
3. $(7 \times 4) \div 2^2$
4. $(72 - 3) - (16 \div 4)^3$
5. $(36 - 9) - (9 - 4)^2 + (6 \times 7)$
6. $(3^2 + 7) \div (20 \div 5)$
7. $8 + (11 - 7) + 42$
8. $2{,}550 - (69 - 64) \times 500$
9. $(108 \div 12) + 3^3$

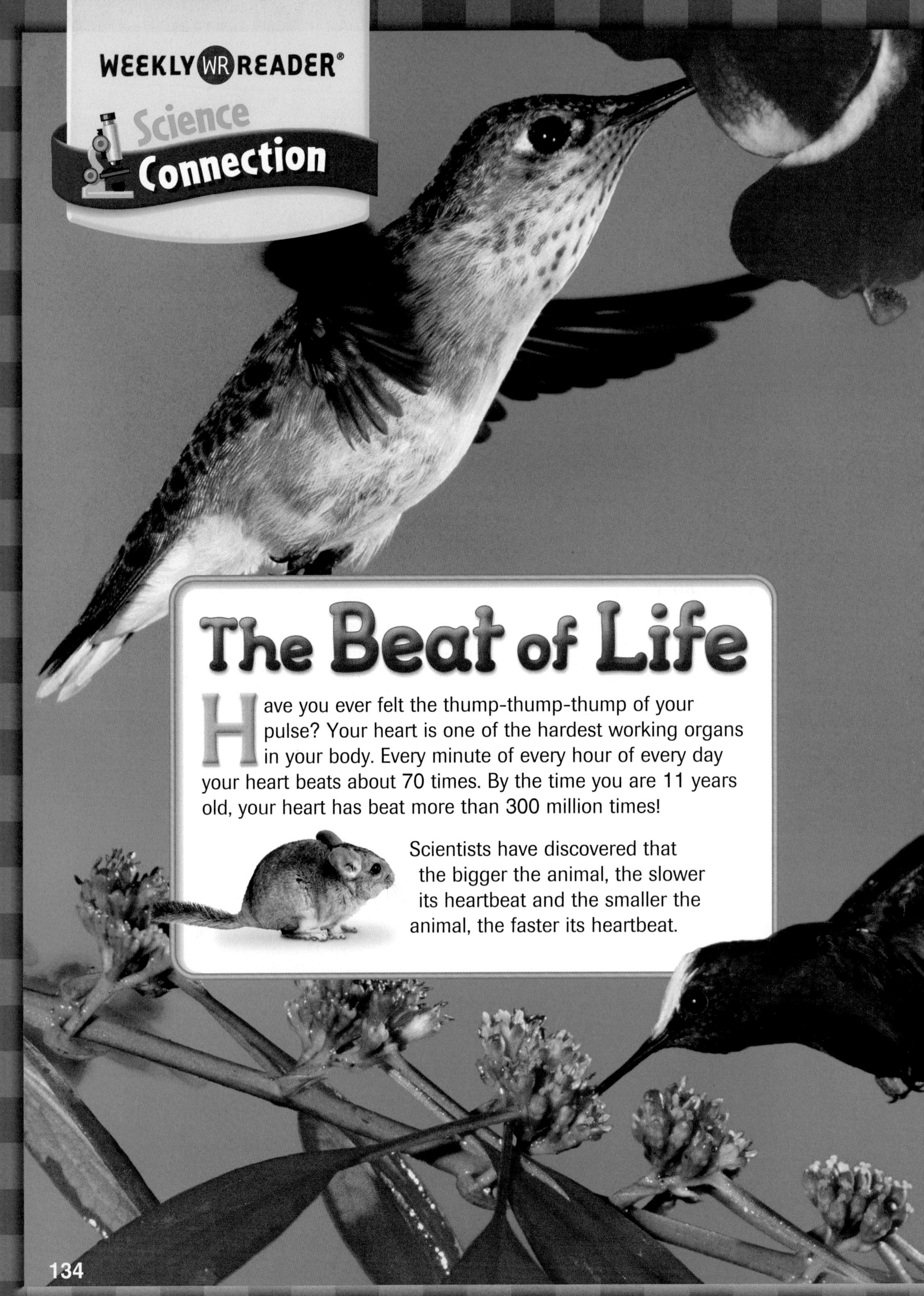

The Beat of Life

Have you ever felt the thump-thump-thump of your pulse? Your heart is one of the hardest working organs in your body. Every minute of every hour of every day your heart beats about 70 times. By the time you are 11 years old, your heart has beat more than 300 million times!

Scientists have discovered that the bigger the animal, the slower its heartbeat and the smaller the animal, the faster its heartbeat.

Heartbeats per Minute (at rest)			
Whale	8	Ground Squirrel	150
Polar Bear	46	Hummingbird	480
Human	70	Mouse	650

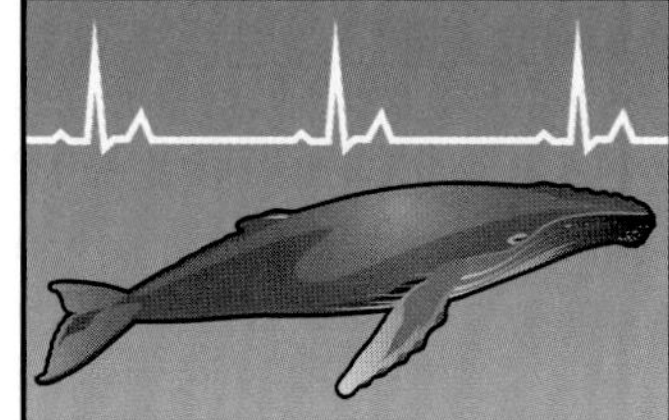

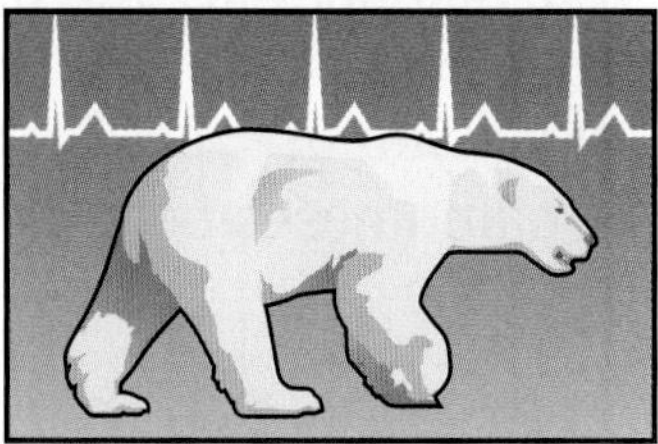

Problem Solving

Use the data in the chart to solve Problems 1–5.

1. How many times does a ground squirrel's heart beat in 1 hour? (Hint: 60 minutes = 1 hour)

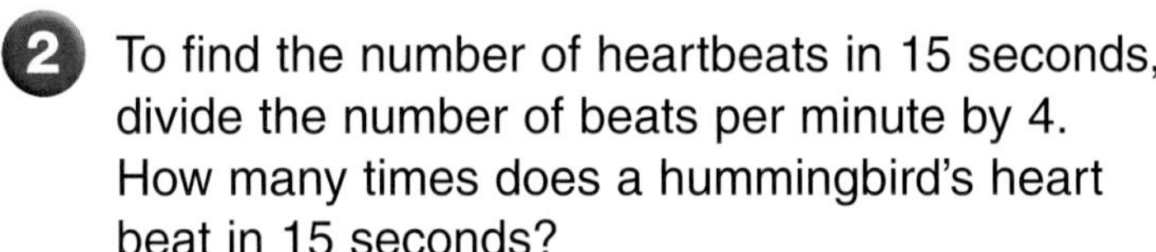

2. To find the number of heartbeats in 15 seconds, divide the number of beats per minute by 4. How many times does a hummingbird's heart beat in 15 seconds?

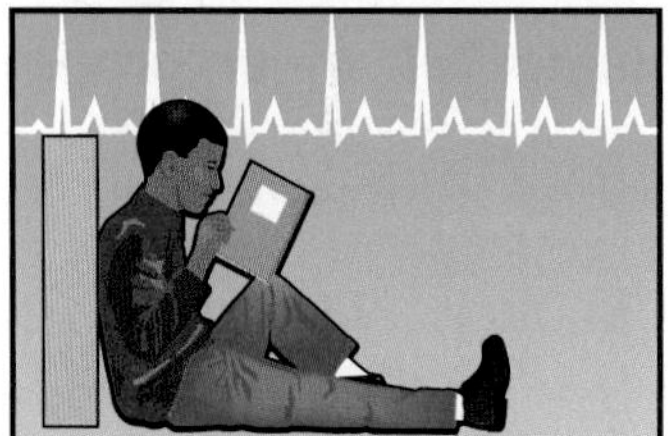

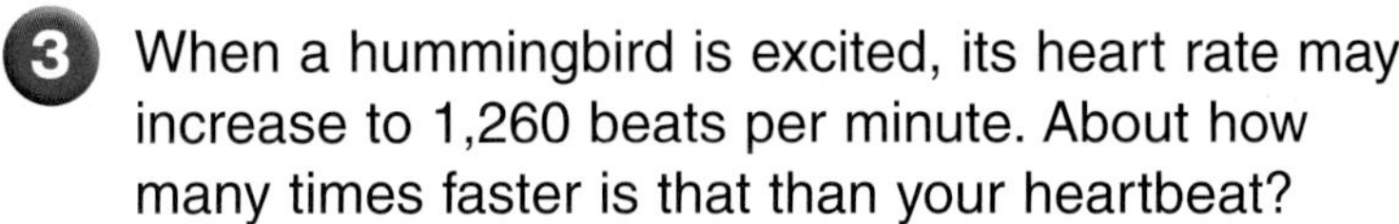

3. When a hummingbird is excited, its heart rate may increase to 1,260 beats per minute. About how many times faster is that than your heartbeat?

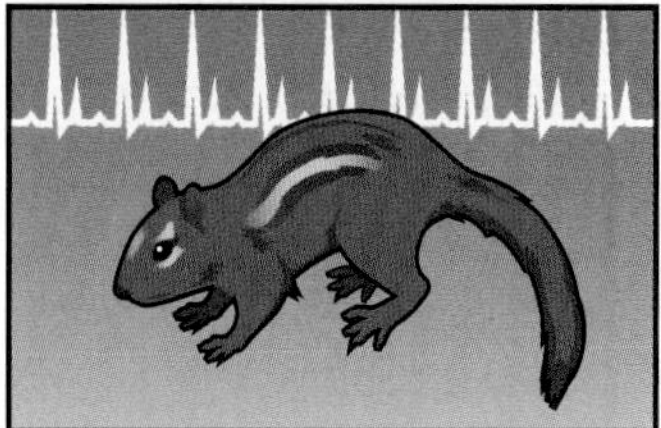

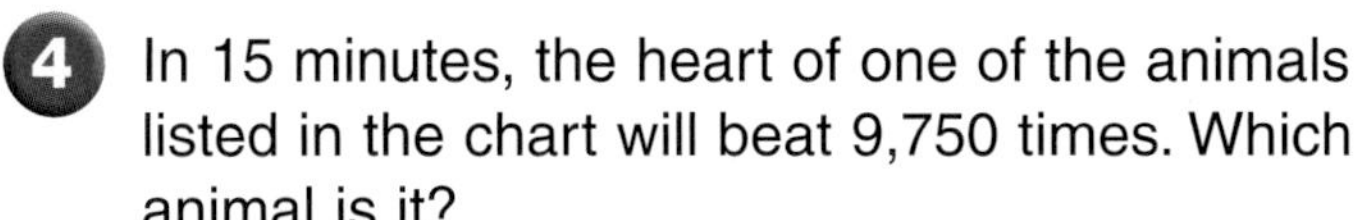

4. In 15 minutes, the heart of one of the animals listed in the chart will beat 9,750 times. Which animal is it?

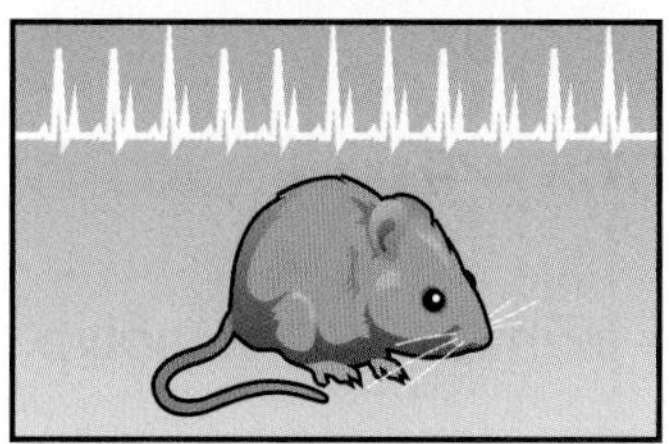

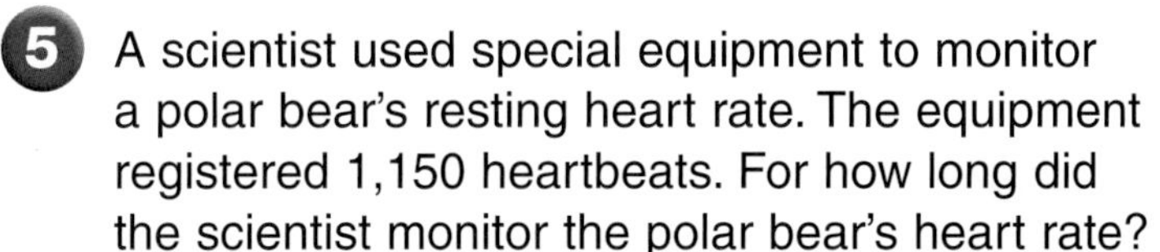

5. A scientist used special equipment to monitor a polar bear's resting heart rate. The equipment registered 1,150 heartbeats. For how long did the scientist monitor the polar bear's heart rate?

Technology

Visit Education Place at **eduplace.com/kids/mw/** to learn more about this topic.

Unit 2 Test

VOCABULARY

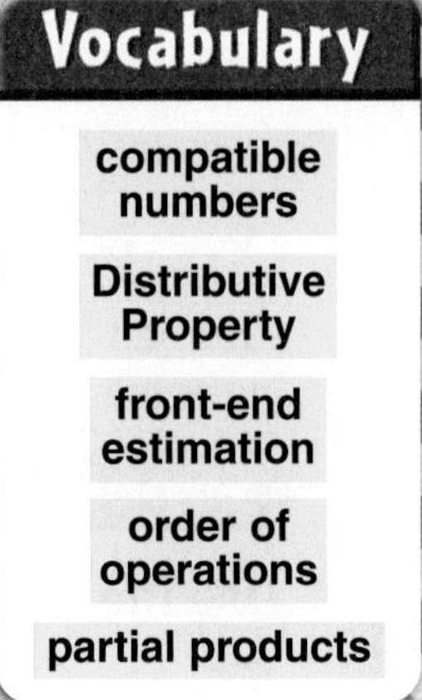

Vocabulary
compatible numbers
Distributive Property
front-end estimation
order of operations
partial products

1. When you multiply 25×28, you get the ■ 200 and 50, which you then add to find the product.
2. If one number divides into another with a remainder of 0, the numbers are called ■.
3. When you use the ■, you simplify expressions in parentheses before you simplify exponents.

CONCEPTS AND SKILLS

Evaluate. Tell which property you used. (Chapter 3)

4. $(57 \times n) \times 25$, given $n = 4$
5. $4 \times 40 \times a$, given $a = 1$
6. Show how to use the Distributive Property to find the product 8×53. Show your work.

Find the product. (Chapter 3)

7. 432×7
8. 86×67

Estimate. (Chapters 3–4)

9. 69×83
10. 79×318
11. $705 \div 9$
12. $1{,}452 \div 7$

Use mental math to solve each equation. (Chapter 4)

13. $7n = 56$
14. $64 \div n = 8$

Divide. Check your answer. (Chapters 4–5)

15. $1{,}705 \div 3$
16. $1{,}080 \div 16$

Divide. Use mental math. (Chapter 5)

17. $4{,}900 \div 70$
18. $64{,}000 \div 800$

Simplify. (Chapter 5)

19. $9 \times 9 - 6 \div 2 + 1$
20. $(7 \times 5) - 4^2 - (11 + 8)$
21. $(3 + 4)^2 - (4 + 3)$

PROBLEM SOLVING

22. Eric, Fran, Greg, and Hannah each have a different color pencil: red, yellow, gray, or brown. Fran's pencil is not red or yellow. Greg's pencil is brown. Hannah's pencil is not yellow. What color is each student's pencil?

23. Theresa spent $45 on refreshments for the fifth-grade class party. She paid for the refreshments using $10, $5, and $1 bills. She received no change. If Theresa gave the cashier 10 bills in all, how many of each bill did she use?

24. A group of 59 students signed up to go on a field trip. Each mini-van holds 1 driver and 7 student passengers. How many mini-vans will be needed?

25. A shipment of 300 math books came in boxes. Each box, except one, held 24 books. How many books were in the carton that did not hold 24 books?

Decision Making

Extended Response

Task Mitchell has saved $400. He would like to use some of the money to buy clothes while they are on sale.

Use the advertisement above and the information at the right. What can Mitchell buy? Explain your thinking.

Information You Need

- Mitchell wants to spend only half of the money he's saved at the clothing sale.
- He wants to buy at least one of each type of clothing that is on sale.
- He wants no more than $5 in change for the entire purchase.

Performance Assessment

TASK 1

Let's Go On With the Show (Chapter 3)

You are the producer of a variety show.

a. If you want to hire 5 of each kind of performer, how much will you pay in all?

b. Suppose you hire the same number of singers and dancers, and pay $160 more for the singers. How many singers and dancers did you hire?

c. Your budget for performers is $4,400. You want to spend at least $4,200, and must have at least 2 of each kind of performer. How many of each kind could you hire?

Performers	Fee
Dancers	$125
Actors	$ 90
Singers	$145
Magicians	$110

TASK 2

Many Marbles (Chapters 4–5)

You decide to give away your collection of 1,800 marbles. Your friends Lena and Mel have agreed to help you. You divide the marbles equally among the three of you.

a. You give away your share to 24 different children. Each child gets an equal number. How many marbles will each child get?

b. Lena gives away her share to 30 different children. How many marbles will each child get if she divides her share evenly?

c. Mel decides to keep half the marbles you gave him. He gives away the other half. He wants to give fewer than 100 marbles to each child. Find three different numbers of children who could get an equal number of marbles from Mel.

Self Check

- Did I answer the questions for each task?
- Did I check all my work?

Enrichment

Your school is celebrating its 25th anniversary. Using 365 days per year, you find that 9,131 days have passed since your school first opened. How can you use the Distributive Property to check your multiplication?

```
  365     There have been 6 leap
×  25     years, so add 6 days.
-----
 1825       9,125
 730      +     6
-----     -------
9,125       9,131
```

You can use a special table, called a diagram.

Write each factor in expanded form and multiply:

$25 \times 365 = (20 + 5) \times (300 + 60 + 5).$

	300	**60**	**5**	
20	20 × 300 = 6,000	20 × 60 = 1,200	20 × 5 = 100	
5	5 × 300 = 1,500	5 × 60 = 300	5 × 5 = 25	

Now add all the partial products.

	300	**60**	**5**	
20	20 × 300 = 6,000	20 × 60 = 1,200	20 × 5 = 100	7,300
5	5 × 300 = 1,500	5 × 60 = 300	5 × 5 = 25	+ 1,825
	7,500 +	1,500 +	125 =	**9,125**

Notice that by adding across and then down you get the same sum as when you add down and then across.

Show how to use the Distributive Property to solve each problem.

1. Daniel's father earns $28 per hour. He works 35 hours each week. Find how much Daniel's father earns in one week.

2. Heather's mother is 38 years old. Find how many days old she is. There have been 9 leap years since she was born.

Cumulative Test Prep Practice

Solve Problems 1–10.

Test-Taking Tip

Some answer choices are word statements. Translate the word statements into number statements to help you decide whether the statements are *true* or *false*.

Look at the example below.

Which of the following statements is false?

A The product of two different even counting numbers is always greater than either of the factors.

B If the dividend is greater than the divisor, then the quotient of two counting numbers is always less than the dividend.

C The product of two counting numbers is always greater than either of the factors.

D If the product of two counting numbers is odd, then the factors are both odd.

THINK

Translate Statement **A** to $2 \times 4 = 8$.
Translate Statement **B** to $12 \div 6 = 2$.
Translate Statement **C** to $1 \times 2 = 2$.
Translate Statement **D** to $15 = 3 \times 5$.

Because of the Identity Property of multiplication, you know that if a factor is 1, the product is equal to the other factor. So Statement **C** is false.

Multiple Choice

1. Which of the following statements is true?

A A number divisible by 6 is also divisible by 3.

B A number divisible by 3 is also divisible by 9.

C A number divisible by 5 is also divisible by 10.

D A number divisible by 3 is also divisible by 6.

(Chapter 4, Lesson 4)

2. Which of the following statements is true about whole numbers?

F The third place from the right is the thousands place.

G The tens place is to the left of the hundreds place.

H The ones place is to the right of the tens place.

J The hundreds place is to the right of the tens place.

(Chapter 1, Lesson 1)

3. Which of the following statements is false?

A The hundredths place is to the right of the tenths place.

B The tenths place is to the right of the hundredths place.

C The ones place is to the left of the tenths place.

D The hundredths place is to the left of the thousandths place.

(Chapter 1, Lesson 7)

 For more Test-Taking Tips, see pages xxii–xxv.

Free Response

4. The population of the city where Matt lives increased from 126,780 to 135,017. How much did the population increase?

(Chapter 2, Lesson 4)

5. Tyler consumed an average of 620 calories for breakfast each day for two weeks. How many total calories did he consume for all breakfasts during those two weeks?

(Chapter 3, Lesson 7)

6. Carrie jogs every day. Last week she jogged a total of 105 kilometers. On average, how many kilometers did she jog each day?

(Chapter 4, Lesson 2)

7. A can of paint covers 500 square feet. How many cans of paint will Ellen need to buy to cover 3,000 square feet?

(Chapter 5, Lesson 1)

8. During a 32-day recycling campaign, a group of fifth-graders collected 3,360 pounds of newspaper. On average, how many pounds did they collect per day?

(Chapter 5, Lesson 5)

9.

VACATION PACKAGE SPECIALS	
Adults	$349
Senior Citizens	$289
Children	$250

What would the total cost be for a group of 8 adults, 4 senior citizens, and 12 children?

(Chapter 3, Lesson 7)

Extended Response

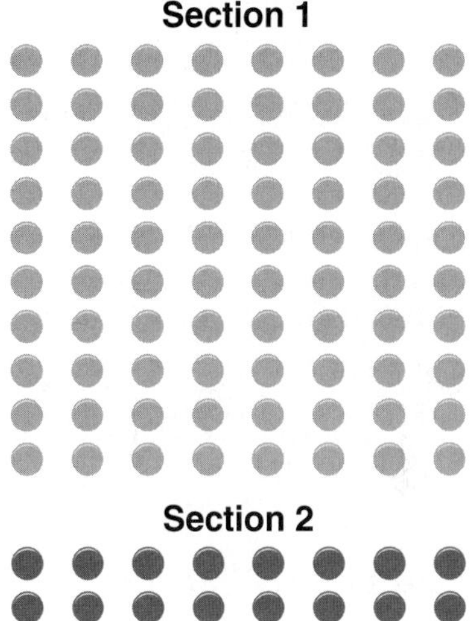

10. This diagram represents a marching band. There is a section with 8 rows of 10 marchers and a section of 8 rows of 2 marchers.

A How many marchers are in each section? How many marchers are there in all? How do you know?

B Suppose 1 row of marchers were added to each section. How many marchers would be in each section? How many would there be in all?

C Suppose one more row per section were added to the original formation and then one more marcher in each row. How many marchers would be in each section? How many marchers would there be in all? Make a drawing to explain your answer.

(Chapter 5, Lesson 2)

Test Prep on the Net

Check out *Education Place* at **eduplace.com/kids/mw/** for test prep practice.

Tic-Tac-Toe

Work with a partner and try to be the first to get 4 in a row!

How to Play:

1. Copy the game board shown below.

Multiplication Tic-Tac-Toe				
	29	51	12	68
327				
479				
512				
716				

2. Decide who will be X's and who will be O's.
3. The first player chooses a number from the top and a number from the side and estimates their product. The player then finds the actual product using a calculator.
4. If the difference between the estimate and the actual product is less than 500, the first player marks their letter in the box where the column and row meet. If the difference is greater than 500, the second player marks their letter in the box.
5. Players take turns until one player gets 4 in a row horizontally, vertically, or diagonally.

Now, try Division Tic-Tac-Toe. Estimate the quotient, then use the Int÷ key to check.

Division Tic-Tac-Toe				
	39,502	52,438	88,692	69,730
22				
39				
32				
11				

Vocabulary Wrap-Up for Unit 2

WEEKLY WR READER Activity Almanac
See page 679 for the activity for this unit.

Look back at the big ideas and vocabulary in this unit.

Big Ideas

You can estimate a product to help you decide if a computed product is reasonable.

When you simplify expressions, use the order of operations: parentheses, exponents, multiplication, division, addition, subtraction.

e Glossary

Key Vocabulary

product

simplify

expression

Math Conversations

Use your new vocabulary to discuss these big ideas.

1. Explain how you evaluate the following expression.
   $3 \times (5 - 1)^2 + (28 \div 4)$
2. Explain how you can tell that 75,834 is divisible by 6 without doing the division.
3. Explain how to find the product mentally.
   $80{,}000 \times 9{,}000$
4. Explain how to find the quotient of $6{,}553 \div 47$.
5. **Write About It** Find data on how much money is spent on schools in your area. How could you estimate the amount spent on the fifth grade? How could you estimate the amount spent on each student?

I multiplied 19 by 62 and got 1,178. Is that reasonable?
Try multiplying 20 by 60 to check.

Building Vocabulary

Reviewing Vocabulary

Here are some math vocabulary words that you should know.

mass	a measure of the amount of matter in an object
metric system	a system of measures in which all units are formed by multiplying or dividing a standard unit by a power of 10.
meter	the standard unit of length in the metric system
liter	the standard unit of capacity in the metric system
gram	the standard unit of mass in the metric system

Reading Words and Symbols

Units of measure are often abbreviated to save space.

Examples: *3 in.* is read as *three inches.*
12 cm is read as *twelve centimeters.*

In the table below, write the word or abbreviation for each ■. The first one is done for you.

Customary Units of Measure	Metric Units of Measure
1. 1 yard (yd) = 3 feet (■)	**4.** 1 kilometer (■) = 1,000 ■ (m)
2. 1 ■ (qt) = 2 pints (■)	**5.** 1 ■ (L) = 1,000 ■ (mL)
3. 1 pound (■) = 16 ■ (oz)	**6.** 1 ■ (kg) = 1,000 grams (■)

Reading Test Questions

Choose the correct answer for each.

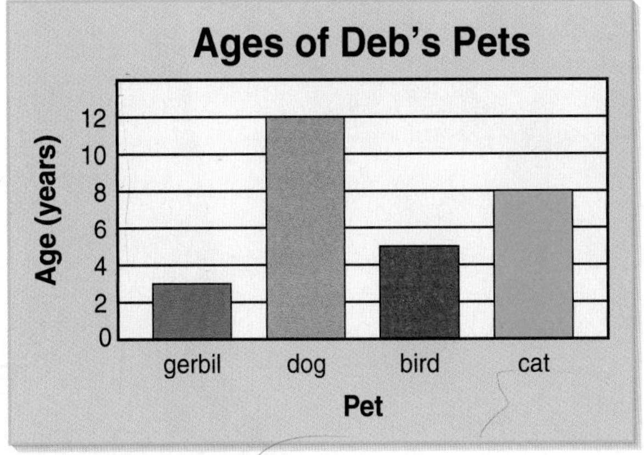

7. Which unit would you use to measure the ages of Deb's pets?

a. inches **c.** years

b. gallons **d.** miles

A **unit** is any standard amount that is used to measure something.

8. Which interval is used on the graph to show the pets' ages?

a. 2 years

b. 4 years

c. 5 years

d. 12 years

Intervals are the equal spaces between marks on the numerical scale of a graph. Intervals show how the data are measured.

9. Based on the data in the graph, which of these statements is **not** true?

a. The bird is older than the gerbil.

b. The cat is less than 10 years old.

c. The dog is 12 years old.

d. The cat is younger than the bird.

Data are pieces of information.

Learning Vocabulary

Watch for these new words in this unit. Write their definitions in your journal.

metric ton
milligram
double bar graph
histogram
double line graph
stem-and-leaf plot

Vocabulary
e • **Glossary**
e • **WordGame**

Literature Connection

Read "Ships of the Desert" on page 641. Then work with a partner to answer the questions about the story.

CHAPTER 6

Units of Measure

INVESTIGATION

Use Data

This black-browed albatross chick will grow to be a large bird that lives most of its life at sea. The table shows some information about this kind of albatross. Find your height in centimeters. What is the difference between your height and the head and body length of an adult black-browed albatross?

Size Range for Adult Black-Browed Albatross

Mass	3–5 kg
Head and Body Length	80–95 cm
Wingspan	210–250 cm

Chapter Pretest

Use this page to review and remember what you need to know for this chapter.

VOCABULARY

Choose the best word to complete each sentence.

1. There are three ____ in a yard.
2. If the wheels on a bicycle are 26 ____ wide, they would be a little wider than 2 feet.
3. To find the number of inches in 2 feet, you would ____ by 12.

CONCEPTS AND SKILLS

Which unit would you use to measure each? Write *inch, foot, yard,* or *mile*.

4. a pencil
5. the distance from school to your home

Choose the most reasonable measure for each.

6. width of a lion's cage
   4 cm   4 m   4 km
7. weight of a zebra
   270 mg   270 g   270 kg

Compute.

8. $5,280 \times 3 + 4$
9. $4,004 \div 2$

10. Which would serve more people at a party, 1 gallon of ice cream or 7 pints of ice cream? Use pictures, symbols, or words to explain your answer.

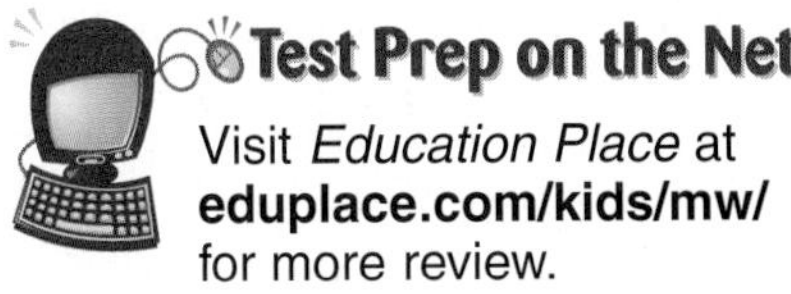

Visit *Education Place* at **eduplace.com/kids/mw/** for more review.

Measurement Concepts

Objective Measure to a given degree of precision using appropriate tools and units of measure.

e Glossary
Vocabulary
precision

Materials
tape measure
ruler
Learning Tool 31

Work Together

The **precision** of a measurement is determined by the unit of measure that you use. A smaller unit produces a more precise measurement than a larger unit.

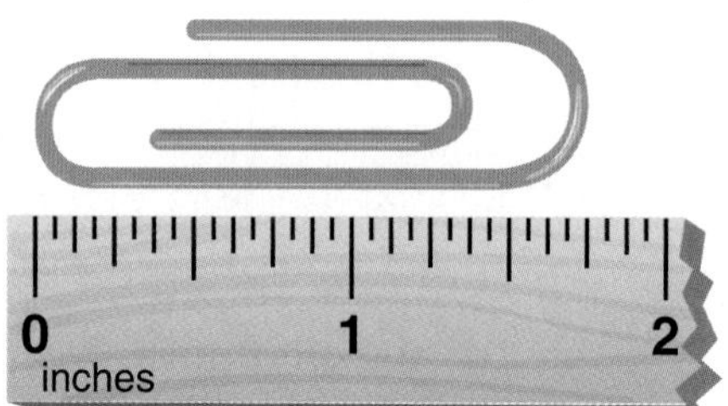

To the nearest inch, this paper clip is 2 inches long. To the nearest quarter inch, the paper clip is $1\frac{3}{4}$ inches long. The measurement $1\frac{3}{4}$ inches is a more precise measurement than 2 inches.

Work with a partner to estimate and measure lengths to the nearest yard, foot, inch, half inch, and quarter inch.

STEP 1 Estimate the length of your classroom in yards. Record your estimate.

Use a tape measure. Measure the length to the nearest yard, the nearest foot, and the nearest inch. Record your measurements.

Measurement and Precision

Object	Estimate	Measurements
Length of room		

STEP 2 Estimate the width of your desk in feet. Record your estimate.

Use a ruler. Measure the width to the nearest foot, the nearest inch, and the nearest half inch. Record your measurements.

STEP 3 Estimate the width of your hand in inches. Record your estimate.

Use a ruler. Measure the width to the nearest inch, the nearest half inch, and the nearest quarter inch. Record your measurements.

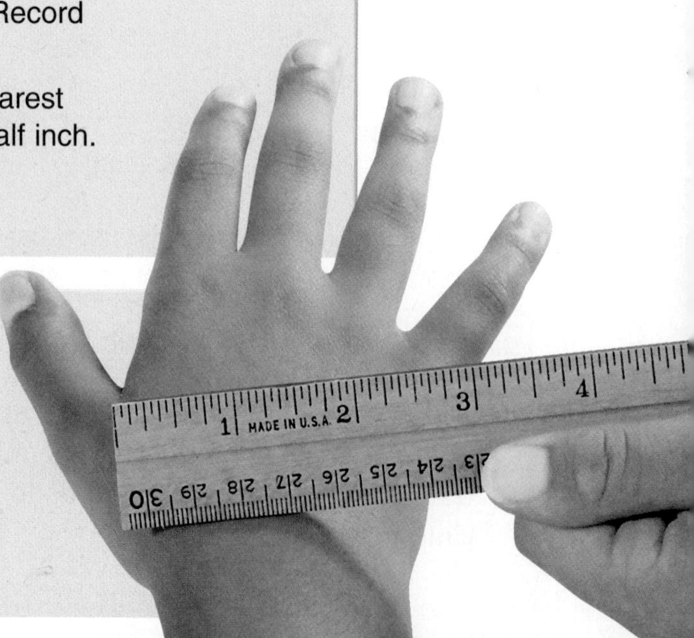

On Your Own

Estimate. Then use a tape measure, yardstick, or ruler to measure.

1. the length of the chalkboard
2. the length of a pencil
3. the height of your desk
4. the width of an eraser
5. the width of your foot
6. the length of your arm

Tell whether a measurement is needed or if an estimate is sufficient. Explain your answer.

7. finding the length and width of a picture that you want to frame
8. finding the distance between Chicago, Illinois, and Jacksonville, Florida
9. finding the height of a twenty-five-story building
10. finding the lengths of wood boards for a bookcase

Make a list of 3 objects that you think have about the given measurement. Check your estimates and record the actual measurement of each object.

11. 1 inch
12. 6 inches
13. 1 foot
14. 1 yard

Choose an object that is between one foot and one yard long. Measure its length to the nearest

15. foot
16. yard
17. inch
18. half inch

You learned how to estimate and measure using different customary units of length.

19. When you measure an object, can you ever get an exact measurement? Explain your answer.
20. How do you choose which measuring tool to use for an object? For what objects would you use the least precise units of measure?
21. The length of a pencil measured to the nearest inch, half inch, and quarter inch is 2 inches. Use a drawing to explain how this is possible.

Lesson 2

Customary Units of Length

Objective Estimate, compare, and convert customary units of length.

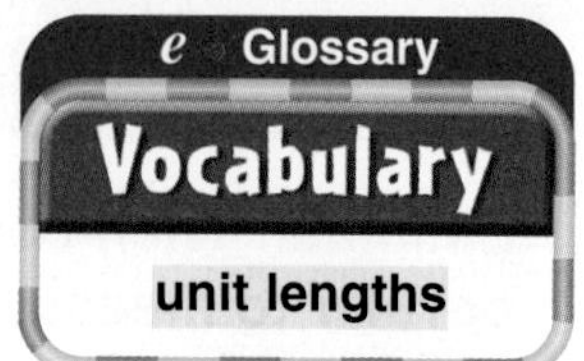

Learn About It

The system of measurement used in the United States is called the customary system of measurement. Standard **unit lengths** in this system include mile (mi), yard (yd), foot (ft), and inch (in.).

The snake shown at the right is an anaconda. Anaconda snakes are some of the largest snakes in the world and can be up to 360 inches long. How many feet is this?

360 in. = ■ ft

Changing Customary Units of Length

STEP 1 Use the table to find the relationship between inches and feet.

Customary Units of Length
12 inches (in.) = 1 foot (ft)
3 feet = 1 yard (yd)
5,280 feet = 1 mile (mi)
1,760 yards = 1 mile

STEP 2 Divide by 12 to find the number of feet.

$360 \div 12 = 30$

360 in. = 30 ft

Solution: Since 360 inches is equal to 30 feet, an anaconda can be up to 30 feet long.

Other Examples

A. Feet and Inches

54 in. = ■ ft ■ in.

Since 12 in. = 1 ft, divide 54 by 12.

$54 \div 12 = 4$ R6

54 in. = 4 ft 6 in.

B. Yards and Feet

5 yd 2 ft = ■ ft

Since 1 yd = 3 ft, multiply 5 by 3.

$5 \times 3 = 15$; then add the 2 feet.

15 ft + 2 ft = 17 ft

5 yd 2 ft = 17 ft

Guided Practice

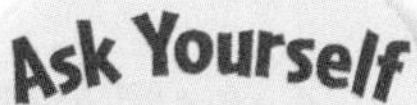

- How do I decide whether to multiply or divide to change units?

Complete.

1. 2 mi = ■ ft
2. 70 in. = ■ ft ■ in.
3. 3 ft = ■ in.
4. 12 yd 2 ft = ■ ft

Explain Your Thinking ▶ Do you multiply or divide to change from a smaller unit to a larger unit? Explain your choice.

Practice and Problem Solving

Complete.

5. 7 ft = ■ in.
6. 15 yd = ■ ft
7. ■ ft = 3 yd 1 ft
8. 18 in. = ■ ft ■ in.
9. ■ in. = 2 ft 6 in.
10. 125 in. = ■ ft ■ in.
11. 5 mi = ■ yd
12. 6,000 ft = ■ mi ■ ft
13. ■ in. = 3 yd 2 ft

Compare. Write >, <, or = for each ●.

14. 4 ft ● 46 in.
15. 6 yd 2 ft ● 20 ft
16. 4 mi ● 24,000 ft
17. 200 in. ● 20 ft
18. 5 mi ● 10,000 yd
19. 3 yd 2 ft ● 100 in.

Which unit would you use to measure each? Write *inch, foot, yard,* or *mile*.

20. the height of a giraffe
21. the width of a monkey's foot
22. the distance a migrating bird travels
23. the length of an alligator

Solve.

24. One elephant seal is 21 feet long. A ringed seal is 48 inches long. How many feet longer is the elephant seal?
25. One fully grown lion is 107 inches long, and another is 8 feet 2 inches long. Which lion is longer? Explain.
26. **Write About It** Explain how to change 112 inches to feet and inches, then to yards, feet, and inches.
27. **Estimate** About how many inches are there in a mile? Explain how you got your estimate.

Daily Review | Test Prep

Use mental math to solve the equation.
(Ch. 2, Lesson 5)

28. $m + 3 = 12$
29. $16 - n = 2$
30. $p - 3 = 15$
31. $b + 5 = 5$

32. Choose the best unit of measure to find the distance from Utah to Texas.

A inch
B foot
C yard
D mile

Extra Practice See page 169, Set A.

Lesson 3

Customary Units of Weight and Capacity

e Glossary

Vocabulary

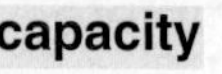

capacity

Objective Change one customary unit of weight or capacity to another.

Learn About It

An African elephant weighs about 14,000 pounds. What is the weight of an African elephant in tons?

14,000 lb = ■ T

Changing Customary Units of Weight

- Use the table to find the relationship between pounds and tons.
- Divide by 2,000 to find the number of tons.

  14,000 ÷ 2,000 = 7
  14,000 lb = 7 T

Customary Units of Weight
16 ounces (oz) = 1 pound (lb)
2,000 pounds = 1 ton (T)

Solution: An African elephant weighs about 7 tons.

▶ **Capacity** is the amount that a container can hold. Gallons, quarts, and pints are all units of capacity.

An African elephant can take $1\frac{1}{2}$ gallons of water into its trunk for a drink. How many quarts are in $1\frac{1}{2}$ gallons?

$1\frac{1}{2}$ gal = ■ qt

Changing Customary Units of Capacity

- Use the table to find the relationship between gallons and quarts.
- Each gallon is 4 quarts. So $\frac{1}{2}$ gallon is 2 quarts.

  $1\frac{1}{2}$ gal = 4 qt + 2 qt = 6 qt

Customary Units of Capacity
8 fluid ounces (fl oz) = 1 cup (c)
2 cups = 1 pint (pt)
2 pints = 1 quart (qt)
4 quarts = 1 gal (gal)

Solution: There are 6 quarts in $1\frac{1}{2}$ gallons.

Guided Practice

Ask Yourself

- Do I multiply or divide to change units?

Complete.

1. 32 oz = ■ lb

2. ■ lb = 2 T

3. ■ c = 2 pt

4. 8 qt = ■ gal

5. 6 pt = ■ qt

6. ■ pt = 64 fl oz

TEST TIPS **Explain Your Thinking** ▶ How many fluid ounces are in $1\frac{1}{2}$ pints? How do you know?

Practice and Problem Solving

Complete.

7. 5 T = ■ lb

8. ■ lb = 48 oz

9. 19 pt = ■ qt ■ pt

10. $16\frac{1}{2}$ T = ■ lb

11. 80 oz = ■ lb

12. 17,500 lb = ■ T ■ lb

13. 12 c = ■ pt

14. ■ gal = 24 pt

15. $8\frac{1}{2}$ gal = ■ qt

16. 15 pt = ■ c

17. ■ oz = 7 lb

18. 26 qt = ■ gal ■ qt

Compare. Write >, <, or = for each ●.

19. 52 oz ● 3 lb

20. 2 lb 3 oz ● 35 oz

21. 4,200 lb ● 2 T 300 lb

22. 13 c ● 7 pt

23. 6 gal 3 qt ● 27 qt

24. 62 pt ● 7 gal 2 qt

Which unit would you use to measure each?
Write *oz, lb, T, fl oz, c, pt, qt,* or *gal.*

25. A gorilla weighs about 220 ■.

26. A dozen apples weigh about 5 ■.

27. A swimming pool holds 10,000 ■ of water.

28. The capacity of a drinking glass is about 10 ■.

29. A single-serving container of yogurt has a capacity of 8 ■.

30. A car's fuel tank can hold about 20 ■ of gasoline.

31. A picture postcard from your favorite state weighs about $\frac{1}{2}$ ■.

32. The heaviest turtle in the world weighs about $\frac{3}{4}$ ■.

The table at the right shows the weights of some sea creatures. Use the table for Problems 33–36.

33. **Estimate** About how many pounds does an Olive Ridley turtle weigh?

34. What is the weight of a Baird's whale in tons?

35. **Analyze** Alexander said that 25,990 lb was the difference in weight between the heaviest and the lightest sea creatures. What error did he make? What answer should he have given?

36. List the sea creatures in order from lightest to heaviest.

37. **Represent** Draw a bar graph that compares the weights of the 3 heaviest sea creatures.

38. **Explain** A baby African elephant can weigh as much as 3,600 ounces at birth. Is that more than or less than one-half ton? Explain how you found your answer.

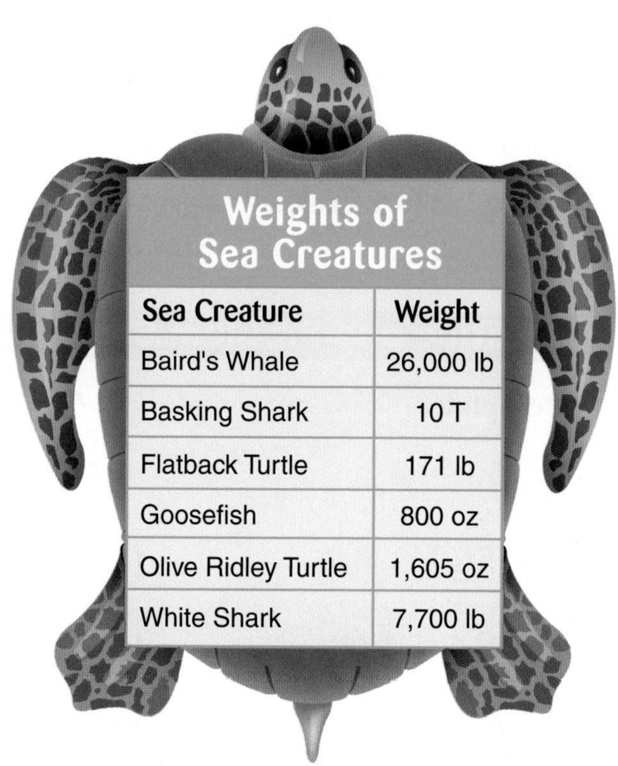

Weights of Sea Creatures

Sea Creature	Weight
Baird's Whale	26,000 lb
Basking Shark	10 T
Flatback Turtle	171 lb
Goosefish	800 oz
Olive Ridley Turtle	1,605 oz
White Shark	7,700 lb

39. **What's Wrong?** Look at the notebook below. It shows how Kyle changed fluid ounces to pints. Explain what Kyle did wrong. Then show how to complete the problem correctly.

> 32 fl oz = ? pt
>
> Since 1 pt = 8 fl oz, multiply 32 × 8 to find the number of pints.
>
> 32 × 8 = 256
>
> 32 fl oz = 256 pt

40. Sandra bought 2 gallons of orange juice for a party. The juice came in quart containers. The total cost of the juice was $24. What was the cost of each quart?

41. **Calculator** There are 240 people weighing an average of 150 pounds each on a plane. What is the weight, in tons, of the people on that plane?

42. Marla took 168 pictures in a rainforest. She took 3 times as many pictures of plants as pictures of animals. How many pictures of plants did she take?

43. **Create and Solve** Write your own problem about animals. Draw a picture to go with your problem. Then solve.

Extra Practice See page 169, Set B.

Quick Check

Check your understanding of Lessons 1–3.

Estimate. Then use a tape measure, yardstick, or ruler to measure. (Lesson 1)

1. the width of your chair
2. the length of your thumb

Which unit would you use to measure each? Write *c, ft, gal, lb, mi,* or *T*. (Lessons 2–3)

3. A bowling ball weighs about 10 ■.
4. A door is about 3 ■ wide.
5. At breakfast, you might drink 2 ■ of milk.
6. A beluga whale might weigh about 2 ■.

Complete. (Lessons 2–3)

7. 48 in. = ■ ft
8. 3 lb = ■ oz
9. ■ qt = 16 pt
10. 84 in. = ■ yd ■ ft

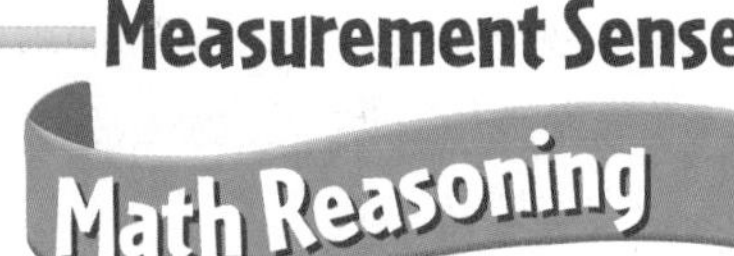

How Tall Is It?

Materials: tape measure or yardstick, ruler

Work with your partner to find the height of your classroom.

To find a way to solve this problem, discuss the following questions with your partner.

- Is the classroom wall made of cinderblocks? If so, find the height of a cinderblock. How can you use this measurement to estimate the height of the classroom?
- Choose an object with a height that is easy to measure. How can you use the height of this object to help you estimate the height of the classroom?

Metric Units of Length

Objective Measure lengths in metric units and change from one unit of metric length to another.

e Glossary

Vocabulary

decimeter (dm)
centimeter (cm)
millimeter (mm)

Learn About It

The metric system is used in many countries. It is a system of measurement based on powers of 10. Scientists use the metric system for their measurements, including the measurement of animals. This Siberian tiger is about 3.3 meters long.

Measure the length of the line segment below using metric units.

Measuring With Metric Units of Length

Measure the length to the nearest decimeter.

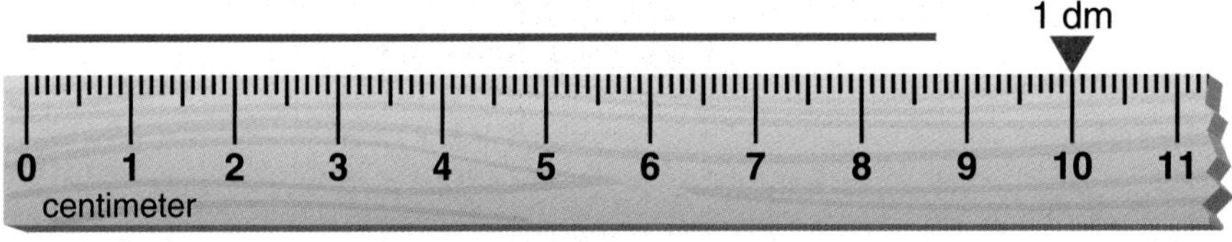

- 1 **decimeter** (1 dm) = 10 **centimeters** (cm)
- Between which two decimeter marks is the end of the purple line segment?
- What is the length of the segment to the nearest decimeter?

Measure the length to the nearest centimeter.

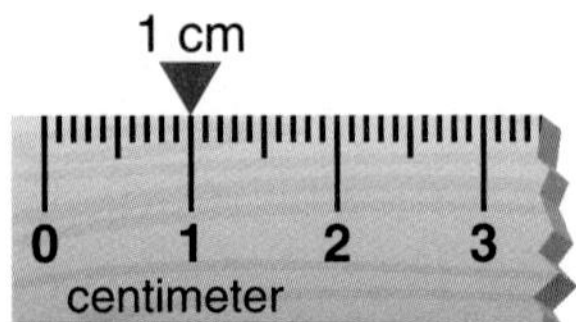

- Is the length of the purple line segment closer to 8 cm or to 9 cm? How can you tell?
- What is the length of that segment to the nearest centimeter?

Measure the length to the nearest millimeter.

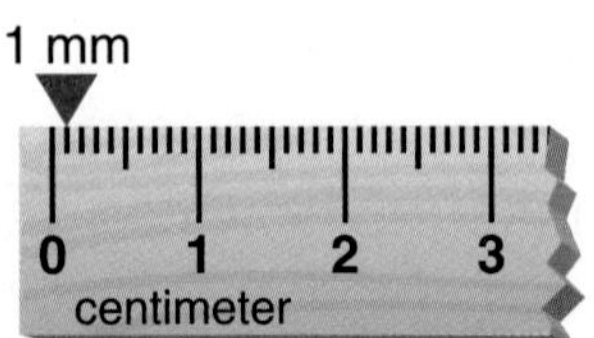

- 1 **millimeter** (mm) = 0.1 cm
- How many millimeters are in 1 cm?
- What is the length of the purple line segment to the nearest millimeter?

Changing Metric Units of Length

To change from one metric unit of length to another, multiply or divide by a power of 10. Powers of 10 include 10, 100, and 1,000.

Metric Units of Length
10 millimeters (mm) = 1 centimeter (cm)
10 centimeters = 1 decimeter (dm)
10 decimeters = 1 meter (m)
1,000 meters = 1 kilometer (km)

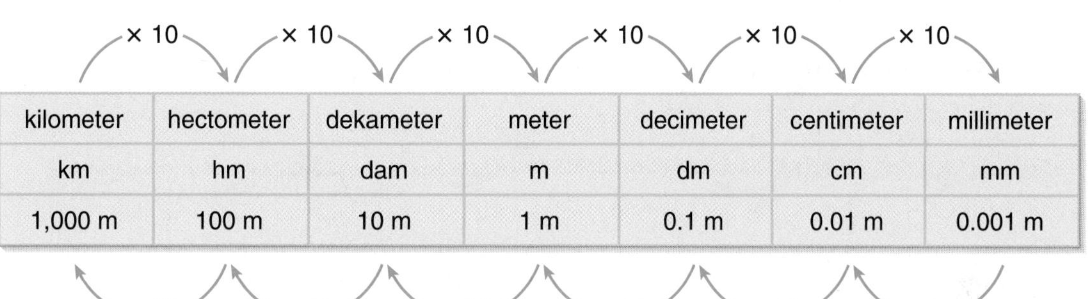

kilometer	hectometer	dekameter	meter	decimeter	centimeter	millimeter
km	hm	dam	m	dm	cm	mm
1,000 m	100 m	10 m	1 m	0.1 m	0.01 m	0.001 m

Multiply to change from a larger unit to a smaller unit.

2 cm = ■ mm

2 × 10 = 20

2 cm = 20 mm

Think
1 cm = 10 mm

Divide to change from a smaller unit to a larger unit.

5,000 m = ■ km

5,000 ÷ 1,000 = 5

5,000 m = 5 km

Think
1,000 m = 1 km

Guided Practice

Use a ruler. Measure each line segment to the nearest decimeter, centimeter, and millimeter.

1. ———

2. ————————————————

3. ————————————————————————————

Ask Yourself

- Which unit of measure am I using?
- Which marks on the ruler show that unit of measure?

Complete.

4. 3 km = ■ m **5.** ■ m = 20 dm **6.** 120 mm = ■ cm

TEST TIPS **Explain Your Thinking** ▶ What is the relationship between multiplying and dividing by powers of 10 and moving the decimal point? Use an example to explain your answer.

Practice and Problem Solving

Grass and twigs are part of an African elephant's diet. Measure each twig below to the nearest decimeter, centimeter, and millimeter.

7.

8. 

9. 

10. 

11. Draw a blade of grass that is 2 decimeters long. How many millimeters long is your blade of grass?

12. **Estimate** What is the length of the longest blade of grass you can draw on your paper? It must be a single straight blade.

Complete.

13. 3 m = ■ cm

14. ■ dm = 10 m

15. 600 mm = ■ dm

16. 3,000 cm = ■ m

17. 500 cm = ■ dm

18. ■ mm = 25 cm

19. 2 km = ■ m

20. 750 dm = ■ cm

21. 30 m = ■ dm

Compare. Write >, <, or = for each ●.

22. 300 cm ● 30 m

23. 250 mm ● 25 cm

24. 5 dm ● 60 cm

25. 7 km ● 700 m

26. 3,600 cm ● 4 m

27. 9,000 mm ● 10 m

28. 410 cm ● 4 m

29. 8,400 mm ● 84 dm

30. 95 m ● 906 dm

For Exercises 31–34, write the metric unit of length that is reasonable.

31.

32. 

33. 

34.

Solve.

35. An Arabian camel is 35 decimeters long. A hippopotamus is 4 meters long. Which animal has the greater length?

36. The Brookfield Zoo is 27,000 meters from the Lincoln Park Zoo. How many kilometers apart are the two zoos?

37. Robert has $27 in his wallet. He has $10, $5, and $1 bills. Robert has 10 bills in all. How many of each bill does he have?

38. **Reasoning** Will a book that is 278 millimeters stand up straight in a bookcase with shelves that are 27 centimeters apart? Explain.

39. **Estimate** Look at the giraffe at the right. Which is a better estimate of its height in meters, 5 meters or 6 meters? Explain.

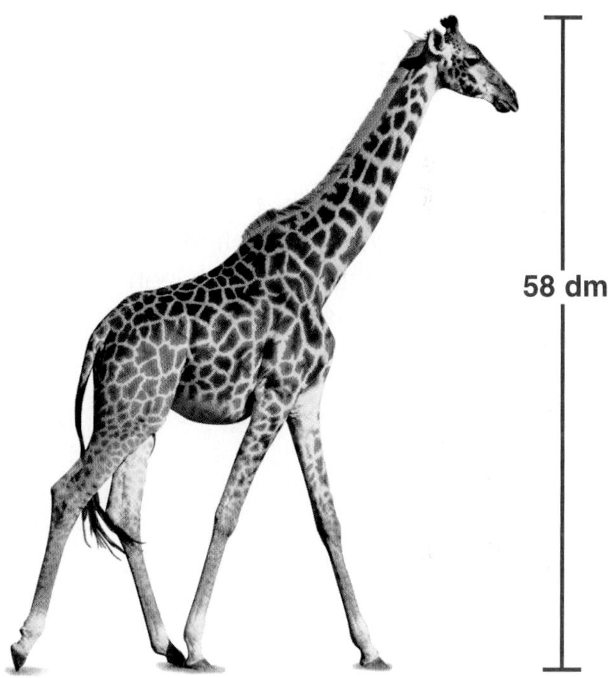

40. **Analyze** How is changing from one metric unit to another like changing from one customary unit to another? How is it different?

41. In the line for the dolphin show, Josh was ahead of Anne, and Barbara was ahead of David. Mary was in the middle. Anne was second. Tell the order of the 5 people in line.

42. **Write About It** Choose an object from your classroom and measure its length to the nearest millimeter, centimeter, and decimeter. Which measure best describes the object's length? Tell why.

Daily Review | Test Prep

Multiply. (Ch.3, Lesson 5)

43. 223×20

44. 17×300

45. 9×40

46. 24×600

47. 158×200

48. 460×600

49. 999×900

50. **Free Response** Use the data in the table to find how many decimeters taller Francisco is than Bethany.

Name	Height
Andrew	100 cm
Bethany	120 cm
Danita	140 cm
Francisco	160 cm

Extra Practice See page 169, Set C.

Lesson 5

Metric Units of Mass and Capacity

Objective Change from one metric unit of mass or capacity to another.

e Glossary

Vocabulary

metric ton (t)

Learn About It

If a hippopotamus has a mass of 2,000 kilograms, what is its mass in **metric tons** (t)?

2,000 kg = ■ t

Changing Metric Units of Mass

STEP 1 Use the table to find the relationship between kilograms and metric tons.

1,000 kg = 1 t

STEP 2 Divide by 1,000 to find the number of metric tons.

2,000 ÷ 1,000 = 2

2,000 kg = 2 t

Metric Units of Mass
1,000 milligrams (mg) = 1 gram (g)
1,000 grams = 1 kilogram (kg)
1,000 kilograms = 1 metric ton (t)

Solution: A hippopotamus with a mass of 2,000 kilograms has a mass of 2 metric tons.

There are 35 liters of water in a bucket. How many milliliters of water are in the bucket?

35 L = ■ mL

Changing Metric Units of Capacity

STEP 1 Use the table to find the relationship between liters and milliliters.

1 L = 1,000 mL

STEP 2 Multiply by 1,000 to find the number of milliliters.

35 × 1,000 = 35,000

35 L = 35,000 mL

Metric Units of Capacity
1,000 milliliters (mL) = 1 liter (L)
10 deciliters (dL) = 1 liter (L)

Solution: There are 35,000 milliliters of water in the bucket.

Guided Practice

Ask Yourself

- Which power of 10 do I use?
- Do I multiply or divide?

Complete.

1. 2 L = ■ mL
2. 3,000 dL = ■ L
3. 8,000 kg = ■ t
4. 6 g = ■ mg
5. 31,000 mg = ■ g
6. 5 t = ■ kg

TEST TIPS **Explain Your Thinking ▶** What power of 10 would you use to change liters to milliliters? Would you multiply or would you divide?

Practice and Problem Solving

Complete.

7. 4 kg = ■ g
8. 7 L = ■ mL
9. 7,000 g = ■ kg
10. 10 t = ■ kg
11. 2 L = ■ dL
12. 13 g = ■ mg
13. 5,000 kg = ■ t
14. 25,000 mg = ■ g
15. 250 dL = ■ L

Choose the most reasonable measure for each.

16. 

a. 65 g
b. 65 mg
c. 6 kg

17. 

a. 3 mL
b. 35 mL
c. 350 mL

18. 

a. 120 t
b. 120 kg
c. 1,200 g

Compare. Write >, <, or = for each ●.

19. 2 t ● 20,000 kg
20. 2,000 g ● 3 kg
21. 12 kg ● 10,000 g
22. 4,000 mL ● 40 L
23. 8 L ● 8,000 mL
24. 400 kg ● 4 t
25. 5,000 mL ● 60 dL
26. 9,005 g ● 9 kg
27. 50 t ● 5,100 kg

For Exercises 28–31, tell which metric unit you would use to measure each. Explain your choice.

28. the amount of water in a glass
29. the amount of medicine in an eye dropper
30. the mass of a hummingbird
31. the mass of an elephant

Go On

Data Use the table for Problems 32–34.

The table at the right shows sizes and prices of bottled water available at a store.

Bottled Water

Container Size	Price
350 mL	$0.69
1 L	$1.29
1.5 L	$1.79
2 L	$2.39

32. Erica buys three 350-milliliter containers of water. Does she buy more or less than 1 liter of water?

33. What is the least expensive way to buy 3 liters of bottled water? Explain your answer.

34. A store has six-packs of 350-milliliter containers of bottled water on sale for $2.39 each. Is this a better buy than a 2-liter container of water that is selling for the price shown in the table? Explain.

35. A penny has a mass of 2,500 milligrams. What is the mass in grams, of a roll of 50 pennies?

36. **Explain** A sink holds 1,500 deciliters of water. Explain how you can find its capacity in liters.

37. A moose has a mass of about 550 kg. An American bison has a mass of one metric ton. The mass of a bison is how many kilograms greater than the mass of a moose?

38. **Estimate** Are there less than one million, exactly one million, or more than one million milligrams in one kilogram?

39. **What's Wrong?** On her visit to the zoo, Kaya saw the sign at the right. What's wrong with this sign?

Daily Review Test Prep

Estimate the product. (Ch. 3, Lesson 6)

40. 22×387

41. $38 \times 4{,}224$

42. 94×671

43. $39 \times 7{,}003$

44. 27×875

45. $31 \times 8{,}661$

46. Hector drank 2 liters of water. Tanya drank 2,500 milliliters of water. How much more water did Tanya drink than Hector?

A 2,500 mL

B 2,000 mL

C 1,500 mL

D 500 mL

Extra Practice See page 169, Set D.

Estimating Measures

2–4 Players

What You'll Need
- customary measurement tools (inch ruler, yardstick, tape measure, measuring cups, scale)
- metric measurement tools (centimeter ruler, meter stick, tape measure, measuring cups, scale)
- Learning Tool 32

How to Play

1. Pick one player to be the "measure master." This player thinks of a distance or an object that can be measured with the tools provided. This player also chooses the type of measurement (length, capacity, or weight/mass) to be made.
2. In a table like the one shown, each player records what will be measured and the kind of measurement that will be made. Players then estimate the measurement in both customary and metric units and record the estimates.
3. The "measure master" uses a customary tool to make the measurement. He or she then uses a metric tool to make the measurement.
4. Players compare their estimates to the actual measurement. The player who has the estimate that is closest to the actual measurement is the "measure master" for the next round.

Learning Tool 32

Name ______________________

Estimating Measures

Object	Type of Measure (circle one.)	Tool	Costumary Units		Metric Units	
			Estimate	Measurement	Estimate	Measurement
	Length Capacity Weight Mass					
	Length Capacity Weight Mass					
	Length Capacity Weight Mass					
	Length Capacity Weight Mass					
	Length Capacity Weight Mass					
	Length Capacity Weight Mass					

Learning Tool 32

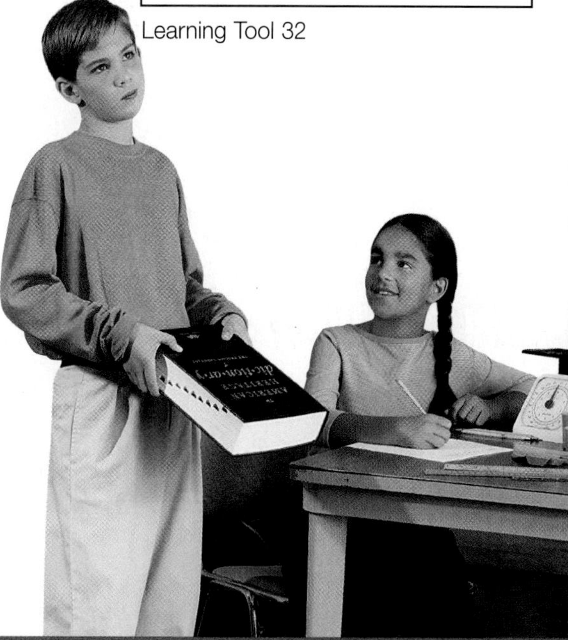

Lesson 6

Add and Subtract Measurements

Objective Add and subtract measurements.

Learn About It

The picture shows a giraffe that is 13 feet 3 inches tall and a boy who is 4 feet 8 inches tall. How much taller is the giraffe than the boy?

Find 13 ft 3 in. – 4 ft 8 in.

STEP 1 Subtract inches. Since 3 < 8, regroup 1 ft as 12 in.

$$\begin{array}{r} \overset{12}{\cancel{13}} \text{ ft } \overset{15}{\cancel{3}} \text{ in.} \\ -\ 4 \text{ ft } 8 \text{ in.} \\ \hline 7 \text{ in.} \end{array}$$

Think
1 ft = 12 in.
3 + 12 = 15; so
13 ft 3 in. = 12 ft 15 in.

STEP 2 Subtract feet.

$$\begin{array}{r} \overset{12}{\cancel{13}} \text{ ft } \overset{15}{\cancel{3}} \text{ in.} \\ -\ 4 \text{ ft } 8 \text{ in.} \\ \hline 8 \text{ ft } 7 \text{ in.} \end{array}$$

Solution: The giraffe is 8 feet 7 inches taller than the boy.

Other Examples

A. Metric Units

1 m – 35 cm = 65 cm

1 m = 100 cm
100 – 35 = 65

B. Time

$$\begin{array}{r} 3 \text{ h } 35 \text{ min} \\ +\ 5 \text{ h } 46 \text{ min} \\ \hline 8 \text{ h } 81 \text{ min} \end{array}$$

8 h 81 min = 8 h + 1 h + 21 min
= 9 h 21 min

81 min = 60 min + 21 min

Guided Practice

Add or subtract.

1. 6 ft 7 in. + 4 ft 9 in.
2. 7 h 12 min – 4 h 32 min
3. 5 m 7 dm + 1 m 3 dm

Ask Yourself

- Are the units the same?
- Do I need to regroup or simplify?

Explain Your Thinking When you add or subtract feet and inches, when do inches need to be regrouped as feet?

Practice and Problem Solving

Add or subtract.

4. 7 ft 3 in. − 4 ft 2 in.

5. 3 lb 5 oz + 2 lb 14 oz

6. 12 h 29 min + 6 h 43 min

7. 5 yd 1 ft + 1 yd 2 ft

8. 5 T 112 lb + 2 T 400 lb

9. 9 gal 1 qt − 5 gal 2 qt

10. 9 g 600 mg + 8 g 900 mg

11. 8 km 500 m − 1 km 900 m

12. 4 L 5 dL + 5 L 7 dL

13. 9 t 900 kg + 5 t 300 kg

14. 10 yd 1 ft − 4 yd 2 ft

15. 5 h 18 min − 2 h 39 min

16. 9 ft − 7 in.

17. 5 h 15 min + 51 min

18. 1 gal − 1 pt

19. 3 m + 42 cm

20. 9 kg − 240 g

21. 4 L − 49 mL

22. 59 cm − 122 mm

23. 1 L − 17 mL

24. 3 m − 41 cm

Algebra • Equations **Find the height represented by *h*.**

025. 7 ft − h = 6 ft 4 in.

26. h − 34 mm = 66 mm

27. 4 yd − h = 3 yd 1 ft

28. h − 3 cm = 1 dm 7 cm

Solve.

29. A gorilla weighs 192 pounds 4 ounces. Another gorilla weighs 186 pounds 9 ounces. How much more does the heavier gorilla weigh?

30. Chef Jourdan put a 13-pound turkey in the oven at 11:20 A.M. He removed it from the oven at 4:30 P.M. How long did the turkey cook?

31. Joel bought a computer for $978. This price included a tax of $28 and a discount of $139. Find the original price before the tax and discount.

32. **Create and Solve** Write a problem in which a unit of measure must be regrouped in order to solve the problem. Then solve your problem.

Daily Review | Test Prep

Find the product. (Ch. 3, Lesson 7)

33. 66 × 34

34. 82 × 50

35. 76 × 24

36. 89 × 43

37. **Free Response** Subtract.

6 lb 4 oz − 2 lb 10 oz

Extra Practice See page 169, Set E.

Lesson 7

Problem-Solving Decision

Multistep Problems

Objective Decide how to solve problems that involve more than one step.

To solve some problems, you need to complete more than one step.

Problem Ellen takes Train 409 from Summit to Center Station. She needs about 15 minutes to drive from her house to Summit Station. About how long does it take Ellen to get from her house to Center Station?

Train Number	409	545	1008
Station	**A.M.**	**A.M.**	**A.M.**
Summit	**6:38**	**7:05**	**7:35**
Smoke Rise	....	7:12	....
Melrose	....	7:22	....
Newburgh	....	7:31	....
Steen's Mountain	**7:00**	**7:39**	**7:58**
Oakwood	....	7:50	8:09
Great Hills	....	8:01	8:21
Fort Tyron	....	8:13	8:34
Ithaca	**7:26**	**8:22**	**8:43**
Center Station	**7:51**	**8:50**	**9:09**

Ask Yourself

What data do I need to use to solve the problem?	Which operation or operations do I need to use to solve the problem?	How do I find the solution?
• 15 minutes to drive • Train 409 from Summit to Center Station takes from 6:38 to 7:51.	• Subtract to find how long the train trip is. • Add 15 min to find how long the total trip is.	7:51 − 6:38 = 1:13 1 hr 13 min + 15 min = 1 hr 28 min

Solution: It takes Ellen about 1 hour 28 minutes to get from her house to Center Station.

Try These

Use the schedule to solve. Show all your steps.

1. Mr. Parker gets on Train 1008 at Steen's Mountain. The train reaches Center Station 12 minutes late. How long does it take Mr. Parker to get from Steen's Mountain to Center Station?

2. Judy takes Train 545 from Melrose to Fort Tyron. She needs about 10 minutes to drive from her house to Melrose. About how long does it take Judy to get from her house to Fort Tyron?

3. Lucy takes Train 409 from Steen's Mountain to Ithaca. Eric takes Train 545 from Oakwood to Ithaca. Whose trip takes less time? How much less?

4. Charles takes Train 1008 from Great Hills to Center Station. Linda takes Train 545 from Newburgh to Center Station. Whose trip takes longer? How much longer?

Quick Check

Check your understanding of Lessons 4–7.

Complete. (Lessons 4–6)

1. 4 m = ■ cm **2.** 70 dL = ■ L **3.** 2,000 cm = ■ m

4. ■ mL = 4 L **5.** ■ kg = 94 t **6.** 6000 mg = ■ g

7. 6 ft 3 in. − 2 ft 10 in. = ■ ft ■ in. **8.** 20 mm + 10 cm = ■ mm

Solve. (Lessons 6–7)

9. Naomi has 2 pounds of cream cheese. She uses 14 ounces to bake a cake. How many pounds and ounces of cream cheese does she have left?

10. If there are 8 commercials shown during a 30-minute television show, how many commercials might be shown in 90 minutes?

WEEKLY WR READER® eduplace.com/kids/mw/

Science Connection

TIME AND TIDE

The table shows the times of high tides for three days at the beach.

How much time passed between high tides on Tuesday?

To find the elapsed time from 8:51 A.M. to 9:34 P.M., answer these questions:

- How much time passed between 8:51 A.M. and 12:00 noon?
- How much time passed between 12:00 noon and 9:34 P.M.?

Now solve the problem.

High Tides

Tuesday	Wednesday	Thursday
8:51 A.M.	9:43 A.M.	10:39 A.M.
9:34 P.M.	10:29 P.M.	11:27 P.M.

Explain how you found your answer.

1. How much time passed between high tides on Wednesday?

2. The morning high tide on Friday is at 11:37 A.M. The next high tide is 12 h 47 min later. When is the next high tide?

Chapter Review/Test

VOCABULARY

Vocabulary
capacity
centimeter (cm)
milligram
millimeter (mm)
precision

1. A(n) ____ is the smallest metric unit typically used to measure length.

2. A liter is a measure of ____.

3. A(n) ____ is a metric unit of mass.

CONCEPTS AND SKILLS

Complete. (Lessons 1–5, pp. 148–162)

4. 22 in. = ■ ft ■ in.
5. 2 T 826 lb = ■ lb
6. 250 dm = ■ cm
7. 3,680 mL = ■ L ■ mL
8. 14,000 mg = ■ g
9. 38 qt = ■ gal ■ qt

Compare. Write >, <, or = for each ●. (Lessons 1–5, pp. 148–162)

10. 40 ft ● 400 in.
11. 3 lb 7 oz ● 56 oz
12. 17 fl oz ● 2 c
13. 2 yd 2 ft ● 96 in.
14. 22 L ● 2,200 mL
15. 3 km ● 3,000 m

Add or subtract. (Lesson 6, p. 166)

16. 4 lb 8 oz
+ 3 lb 9 oz
17. 6 ft 4 in.
− 3 ft 8 in.
18. 3 L 6 dL
+ 9 L 7 dL

PROBLEM SOLVING

Solve. (Lesson 7, p. 166)

19. Paul's train ride takes 56 minutes. From there he has a 20-minute walk to his office. If he allows himself $1\frac{1}{2}$ hours from the time he gets on the train, how much extra time is left when he reaches the office?

20. Sandra buys $1\frac{1}{2}$ pounds of grated cheese. She uses 13 ounces of it for a recipe. How much more cheese does she need to make another dish that calls for 14 ounces of cheese?

Show You Understand

Sheree wants to make a paper cover for her math book. Does she need an exact measurement of how large a sheet of paper she needs, or can she use an estimate? Explain.

Extra Practice

Set A (Lesson 2, pp. 150–151)

Complete.

1. ■ in. = 10 ft
2. 2 mi = ■ yd
3. 8 ft = ■ in.

Compare. Write >, <, or = for each ●.

4. 1 mi ● 5,000 ft
5. 2 yd 2 ft ● 10 ft
6. 9 yd ● 28 ft

Set B (Lesson 3, pp. 152–155)

Complete.

1. 9 c = ■ fl oz
2. 20 oz = ■ lb
3. 5,280 lb = ■ T ■ lb

Compare. Write >, <, or = for each ●.

4. 30 fl oz ● 2 pt
5. 4 lb ● 64 oz
6. 2 pt 7 fl oz ● 40 fl oz

Set C (Lesson 4, pp. 156–159)

Complete.

1. 92 km = ■ m
2. 860 cm = ■ dm
3. 40 m = ■ dm
4. ■ cm = 420 dm
5. ■ cm = 780 mm
6. 400 mm = ■ dm

Compare. Write >, <, or = for each ●.

7. 45 km ● 4,500 m
8. 33 cm ● 330 mm
9. 550 m ● 5 dm

Set D (Lesson 5, pp. 160–163)

Complete.

1. 400 kg = ■ g
2. ■ g = 6,000 mg
3. 20 dL = ■ mL
4. ■ t = 1,500 kg
5. ■ mL = 25 L
6. ■ L = 1250 dL

Compare. Write >, <, or = for each ●.

7. 89 g ● 89,000 mg
8. 70 L ● 67,000 mL
9. 10,001 g ● 10 kg

Set E (Lesson 6, pp. 164–165)

Find each sum or difference.

1. 6 ft 2 in. − 3 ft 8 in.
2. 6 lb 3 oz + 3 lb 13 oz
3. 8 gal 2 qt − 6 gal 3 qt
4. 6 h 20 min + 45 min
5. 5 L − 839 mL
6. 8 kg − 160 g

CHAPTER 7 Graph Data

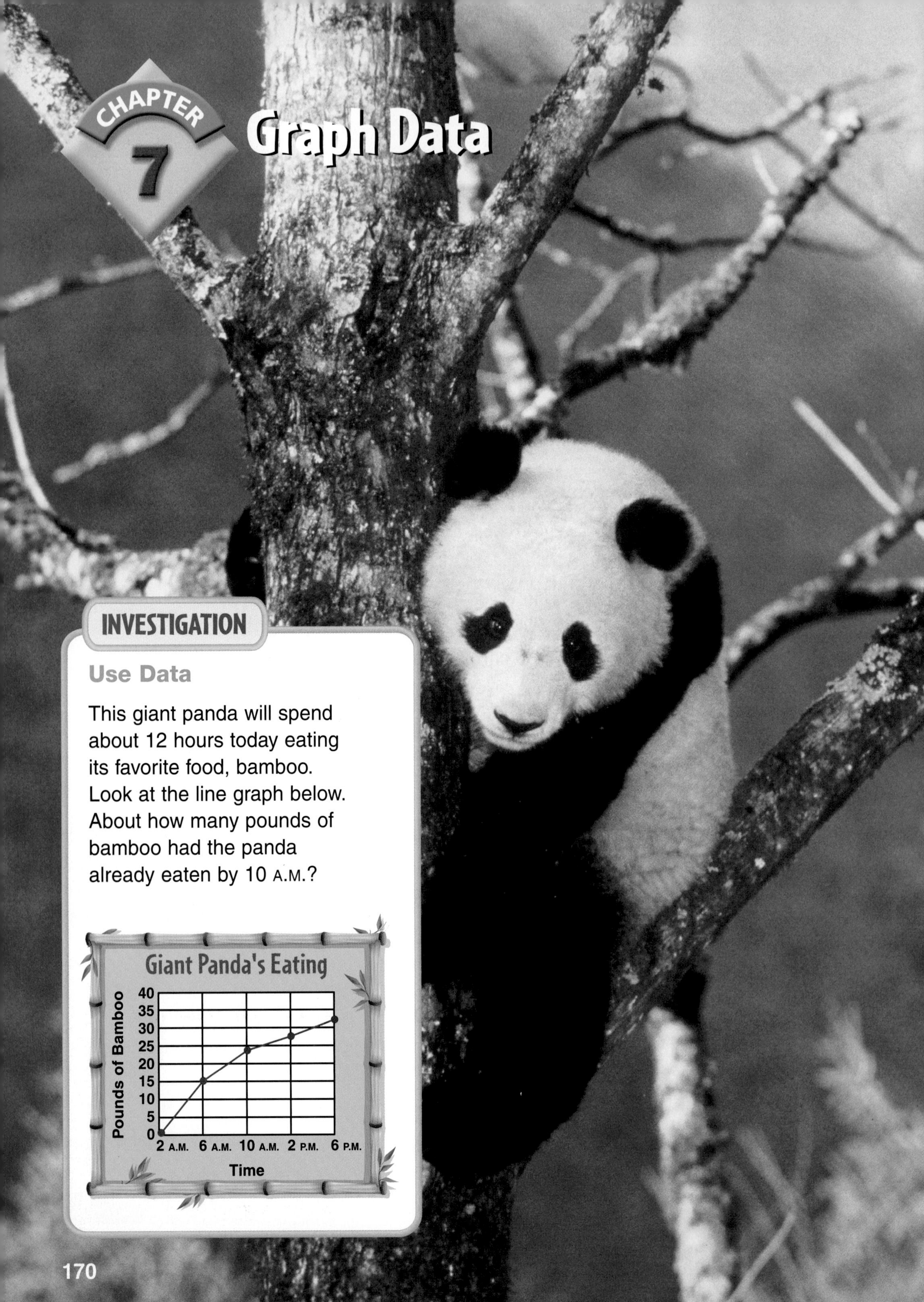

INVESTIGATION

Use Data

This giant panda will spend about 12 hours today eating its favorite food, bamboo. Look at the line graph below. About how many pounds of bamboo had the panda already eaten by 10 A.M.?

Chapter Pretest

Use this page to review and remember what you need to know for this chapter.

VOCABULARY

Choose the best word to complete each sentence.

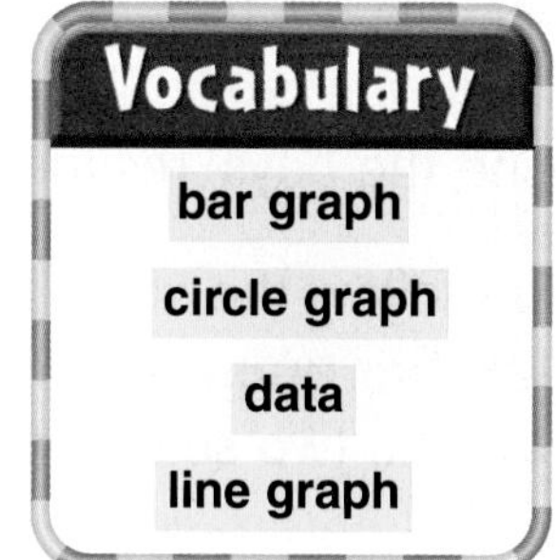

1. A ____ would be the best graph to show how many inches of rain fell on five different days.

2. When you collect information, you have ____ that you can use to make a graph.

CONCEPTS AND SKILLS

Copy and complete the frequency table to tally how many times each letter occurs in the data set.

A	C	D	C	Q	A
D	A	A	A	C	D
Q	C	D	C	C	C

	Letter	Tally Marks	Frequency
3.	A		
4.	C		
5.	D		
6.	Q		

Use the bar graph for Problems 7–10.

7. On which three days were more vegetarian meals sold than on Wednesday?

8. On which day were the most vegetarian meals sold?

9. How many more meals were sold on Tuesday than on Monday?

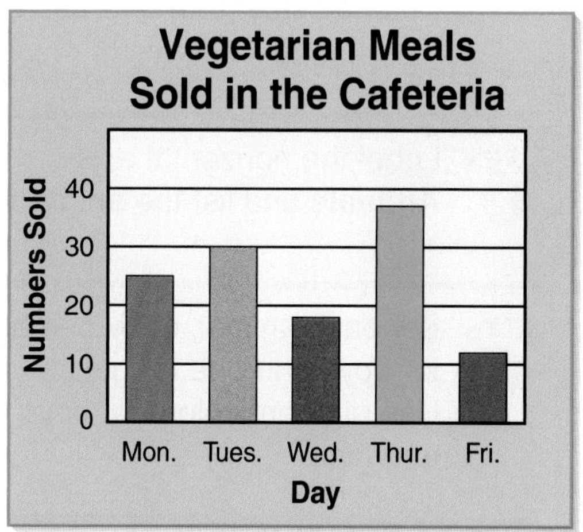

Write About It

10. Look at the bar graph. Tell how many vegetarian meals were sold during the week shown on the graph. Explain how you found your answer.

Test Prep on the Net

Visit *Education Place* at **eduplace.com/kids/mw/** for more review.

Double Bar Graphs

Objective Use a double bar graph to compare sets of data.

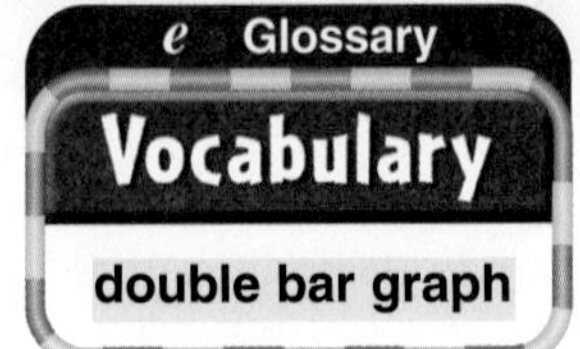

Learn About It

Linda took a survey to find out which wild animals the boys and girls in her class liked the most. She recorded the girls' and the boys' responses separately.

You can follow the steps below to make a **double bar graph** in order to visually compare the two sets of data.

Favorite Wild Animals

Animal	Boys	Girls
Giraffe	8	24
Cheetah	6	6
Tiger	36	10
Gorilla	6	2

Making a Double Bar Graph

STEP 1 Draw the axes.

STEP 2
- Label the vertical axis **Number of Students**.
- Choose an appropriate scale and mark equal intervals.
- For this double bar graph, use a scale from 0 to 36. Use equal intervals of 4.

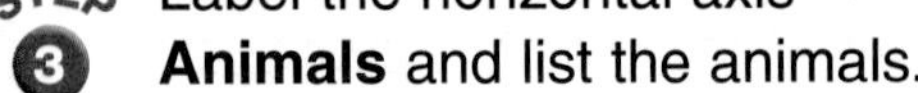

STEP 3 Label the horizontal axis **Animals** and list the animals.

STEP 4 For each animal, draw one bar for boys and one for girls. Use different colors for boys and girls.

STEP 5 Make a key to show what each color represents. Then give the graph a title.

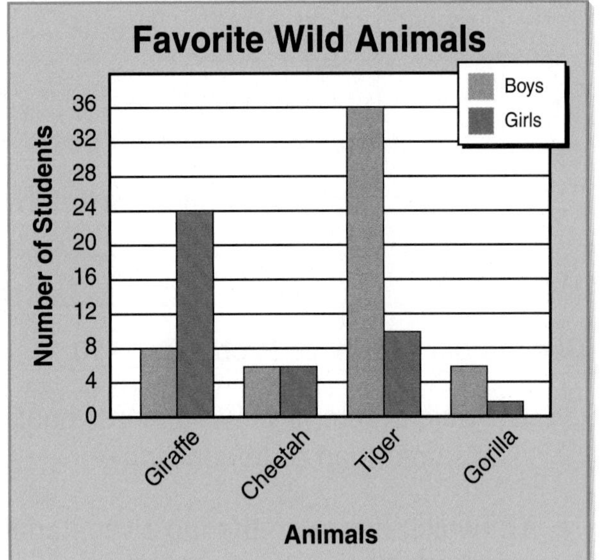

Try this activity with a partner to compare two sets of data by using a double bar graph.

Materials Learning Tools 33 and 34, grid paper, 10 pennies, ruler

STEP 1 Make a target like the one shown or use Learning Tool 33.

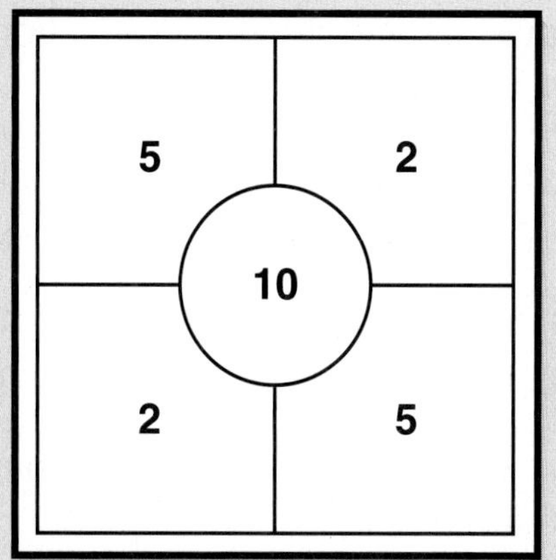

Learning Tool 33

STEP 2 Players take turns dropping 5 pennies onto the target. The score for each turn is determined by where the penny lands. A penny landing on the border of two regions scores the lesser of the two values.

STEP 3 Repeat Step 2 four more times. Use Learning Tool 34 to record the scores.

STEP 4 Use a ruler and grid paper to make a double bar graph to compare your score in each round with your partner's score in each round.

- What scale should you use? What equal intervals should you use?
- How will you label the horizontal axis? the vertical axis?
- What title will you choose for the graph?

Round Number	Round Score	Total Score

Learning Tool 34

Use the graph on page 172 for Problems 1–3.

1. How many more girls than boys liked giraffes the most?

2. For which wild animal is there the greatest difference between boys and girls?

3. Which animal was chosen equally by boys and girls?

Ask Yourself

- Do I need to see the numbers survey or could I answer by looking at the bar lengths?
- Did I read the graph correctly?

TEST TIPS **Explain Your Thinking** ▶ Why is it important to choose an appropriate scale for a graph? Use an example to support your thinking.

Go On

Practice and Problem Solving

Use the graph for Problems 4–7.

Five hundred zoologists were surveyed in 1992 and 2002 about which animals they thought were at risk of extinction.

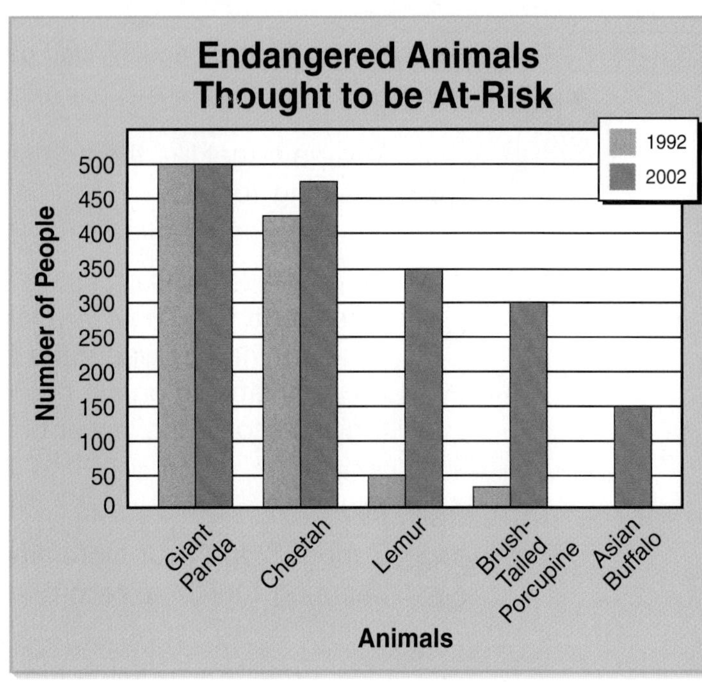

4. Which endangered animal did most zoologists think was at risk in both 1992 and 2002?

5. How many more zoologists thought the lemur was at risk in 2002 than in 1992?

6. **Explain** Why is there no bar to represent the Asian Buffalo in 1992?

7. **Analyze** If only 500 zoologists were surveyed, how could 500 zoologists choose Giant Panda and 300 zoologists choose Brush-Tailed Porcupine in 2002?

Choices of T-Shirt Colors for the Ecology Club

	Purple	Orange	Blue	Green	Red
Like	12	6	18	14	10
Dislike	6	16	6	10	4

8. **Represent** Use the table of students' T-shirt color preferences to make a double bar graph.

9. **Write About It** If you were designing a T-shirt for other students, which color would you choose? Explain your thinking.

10. Make up your own survey about T-shirt color preferences. Give your survey to your classmates. Present your results in a tally chart.

11. Use your results in Exercise 10 to create a double bar graph.

12. **Create and Solve** Write a problem based on the graph in Exercise 11. Exchange problems with a classmate and solve.

Use the double bar graph for Problems 13–17.

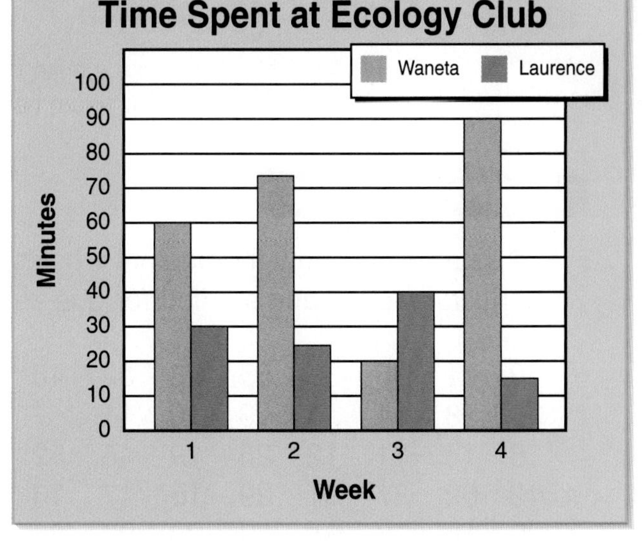

13. During which week did Laurence spend more time at the Ecology Club than Waneta?

14. During which week did Waneta and Laurence together spend the least amount of time at the Ecology Club?

15. During week 4, about how much longer did Waneta spend at the Ecology Club than Laurence spent?

16. **Estimate** About how many hours total did Laurence spend at the Ecology Club that month?

17. How much more time did Waneta spend than Laurence at the Ecology Club that month?

18. **Represent** Five teachers surveyed their students to see how many went to the WildLife Zoo. Make a double bar graph showing the data from the table.

Did You Visit the Wildlife Zoo?					
Class	Mrs. Smith	Mr. Kaufman	Mr. Ross	Ms. Brown	Ms. Cruz
Yes	12	10	9	20	5
No	12	15	14	4	19

Daily Review Test Prep

1 foot = 12 inches
1 yard = 3 feet
1 mile = 5,280 feet
1 mile = 1,760 yards

Complete. (Ch. 6, Lesson 2)

19. 16 inches = ■ feet ■ inches

20. 2 miles = ■ feet

21. 6 yards 2 feet = ■ inches

22. 110 inches = ■ yard ■ inches

23. How many more boys than girls want to work in forestry?

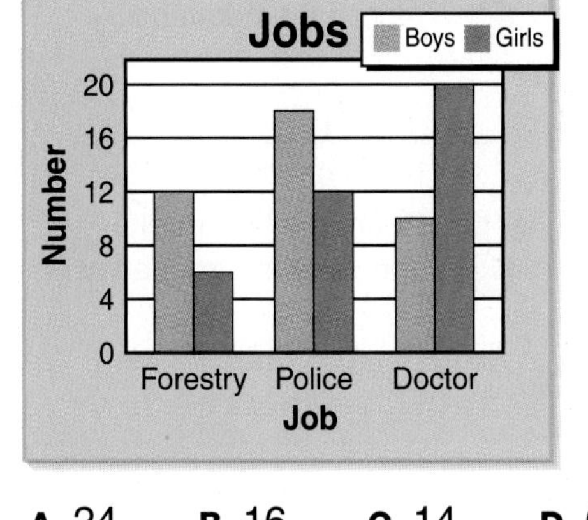

A 24 **B** 16 **C** 14 **D** 6

Extra Practice See page 189, Set A.

Lesson 2

Histograms

Objective Make and use a histogram and understand the differences between bar graphs and histograms.

e Glossary

Vocabulary

histogram
frequency table

Learn About It

The data below show the ages of whales that scientists tracked and studied for one year.

10	11	35	36	55	28	32	46	57
69	58	14	8	9	10	11	7	12
8	13	11	12	25	19	45	52	35
42	62	27	31	29	15	17	16	18
20	19	22	34	29	30	20	25	13
14	15	16	15	17				

How did the number of whales in the 20–29 age group compare with that in the 10–19 age group?

You can use a histogram to display and compare the data. A **histogram** is a bar graph that displays how frequently data occur within equal intervals.

Follow these steps to make a histogram. Start by making a **frequency table** to organize the data in equal intervals.

Making a Frequency Table

STEP 1 Look at the data to decide what intervals to use.

STEP 2 Use tally marks to record the frequency.

STEP 3 Count the tally marks and write the frequency.

Intervals	Tally Marks	Frequency
0–9	||||	4
10–19	~~||||~~ ~~||||~~ ~~||||~~ ~~||||~~ |	21
20–29	~~||||~~ ||||	9
30–39	~~||||~~ ||	7
40–49	|||	3
50–59	||||	4
60–69	||	2

Then use the frequency table to make a histogram.

Making a Histogram

STEP 1 Draw the axes. Label the vertical axis. Choose an appropriate scale and mark equal intervals.

STEP 2 Label the horizontal axis and list the age intervals.

STEP 3 Draw a bar for each age interval. Do not leave spaces between the bars.

STEP 4 Give the graph a title.

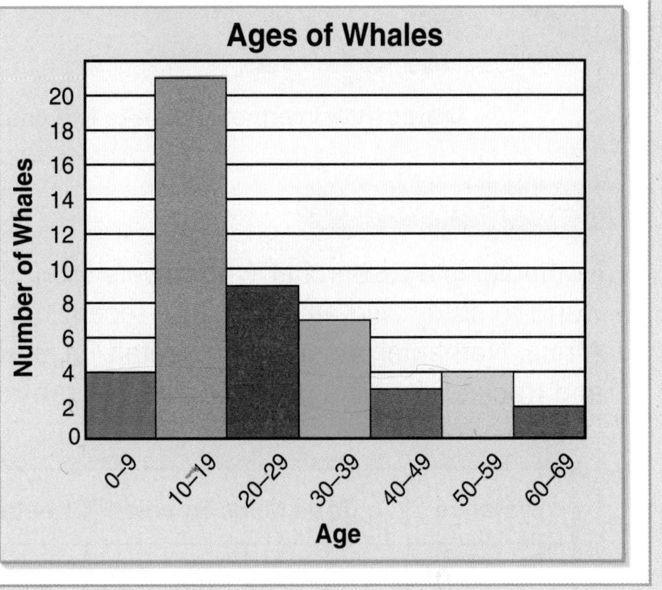

Solution: There were more than twice as many whales in the 10–19 age group as there were in the 20–29 age group.

Guided Practice

Use the histogram above for Problems 1–2.

1. How many whales were in the 20–29 age group?

2. How many more whales were there in the 20–29 age group than in the 50–59 age group?

Ask Yourself

- Do I need to know the exact number the bar shows?

When would you use a histogram instead of a bar graph to display data? Explain your thinking.

Practice and Problem Solving

Use the histogram at the right for Problems 3 and 4.

3. How many whales have been studied from 4 to 15 years?

4. How many more whales have been studied from 8 to 11 years than from 0 to 3 years?

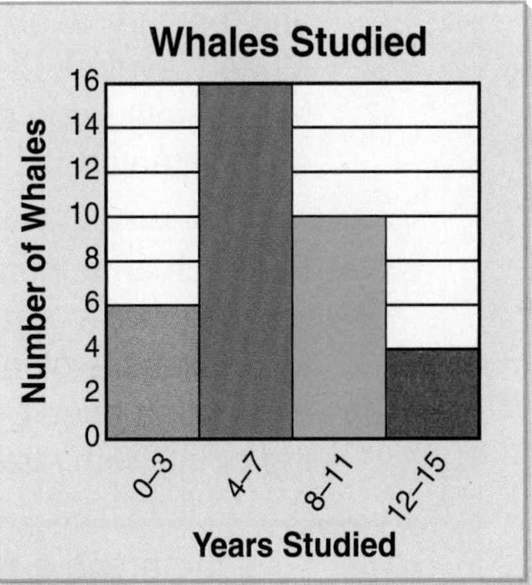

Daily Review | Test Prep

Estimate. (Ch. 3, Lesson 6)

5. 299 × 8

6. 2,763 × 5

7. 708 × 9

8. 8,950 × 6

9. **Free Response** What intervals would you use to graph these data?

7, 9, 12, 10, 7, 8, 15, 7, 11

Extra Practice See page 189, Set B.

Lesson 3

Line and Double Line Graphs

e Glossary

Vocabulary

ordered pair
double line graph

Objective Interpret and make line graphs and double line graphs.

Learn About It

Nathaniel is a researcher who travels around the world to study wild animals. On a recent trip to Africa, Nathaniel observed a cheetah for 6 hours and tracked the total distance the cheetah roamed.

Distance	Total Miles Traveled (Cheetah)					
Time (hours)	1	2	3	4	5	6
Total Miles	30	42	48	71	94	127

Make a line graph to show the data Nathaniel collected.

Making a Line Graph

STEP 1 Draw the axes. Label the horizontal axis **Time (hours)** and the vertical axis **Total Miles Traveled**. Choose an appropriate scale and mark equal intervals.

STEP 2 For each amount of time, draw a point to show the total miles traveled at the end of that hour. Connect the points with straight lines.

STEP 3 Give the graph a title.

The point on the grid that corresponds to 1 hour on the horizontal axis and 30 miles on the vertical axis is represented by the **ordered pair** (1, 30).

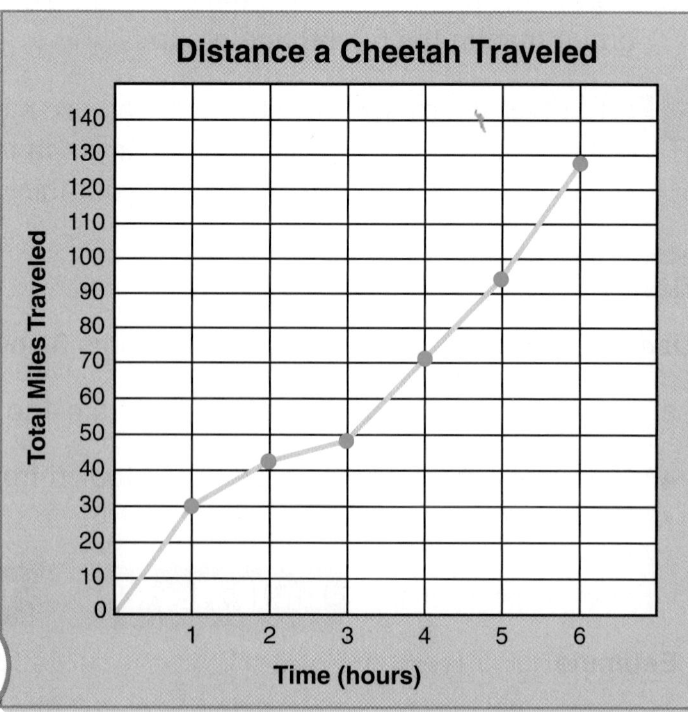

While on a trip to India, Nathaniel also observed how far a tiger roamed in 6 hours. Make a **double line graph** to compare the data for the cheetah and the tiger.

Distance	Total Miles Traveled (Tiger)					
Time (hours)	1	2	3	4	5	6
Total Miles	6	21	27	33	42	49

Note: The table at the left gives the *total* miles traveled. During the first hour, the tiger traveled 6 miles. During the second hour, the tiger traveled 15 miles.

Making a Double Line Graph

STEP 1 Draw the axes. Label the horizontal axis **Time (hours)** and the vertical axis **Total Miles Traveled**. Choose an appropriate scale and mark equal intervals.

STEP 2 Plot the ordered pairs and draw the line graph for the cheetah data.

STEP 3 Repeat Step 2 for the tiger data. Use a different color for the points and the line.

STEP 4 Make a key to show what each line represents. Then write a title for the graph.

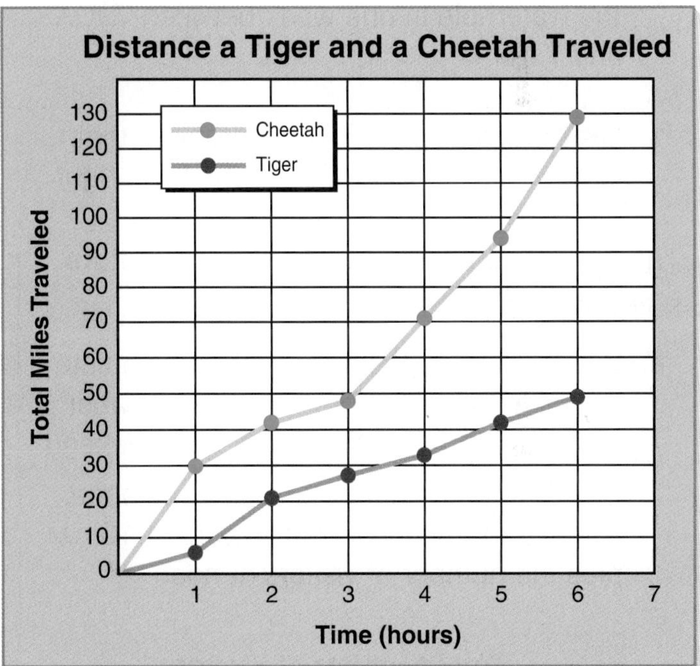

Guided Practice

Use the graph above for Problems 1 and 2.

1. How much farther had the cheetah traveled than the tiger at the end of 6 hours?

2. Between which two hours did the cheetah travel the farthest? the least?

Ask Yourself

- What scale is used?
- What does the key tell me?
- Is the information I need on the horizontal or the vertical axis?

Explain Your Thinking ▶ Why are line graphs useful for showing data over time?

Practice and Problem Solving

Use the graph at the right for Exercises 3–7.

3. As of 10 A.M., how many more wildebeest than elephants had visited the waterhole?

4. During which 3-hour time period did no elephants visit the waterhole?

5. During which 3-hour time period did the most animals visit the waterhole?

6. **Predict** If the graph shows the results for a typical day at the waterhole, how many elephants would you expect to visit the waterhole in one week between 7 A.M. and 7 P.M.?

7. **Create and Solve** Write a problem that can be solved using the graph at the right.

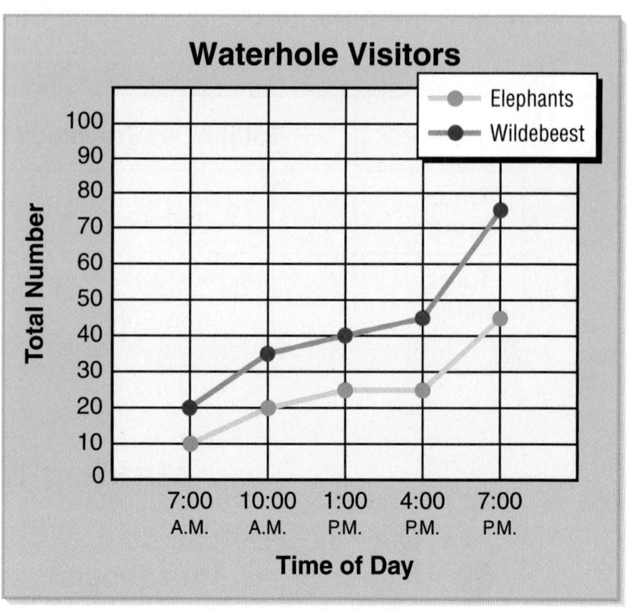

The bar graph shows the number of visitors entering Safari Fun Land one weekend.

8. Use the data in the bar graph to complete the table below to show the total number of visitors to Safari Fun Land that weekend.

   Hint: The total number of visitors at noon is equal to the number of visitors at 10 A.M. plus the number of visitors at noon.

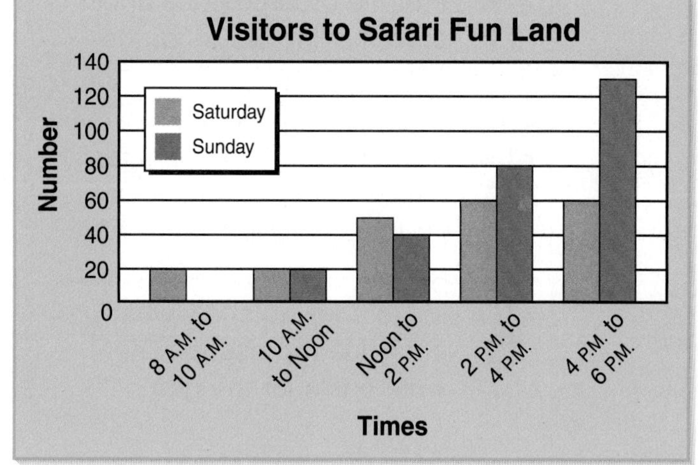

Total Number of Visitors to Safari Fun Land

	10 A.M.	Noon	2 P.M.	4 P.M.	6 P.M.
Sat.	20	40			
Sun.					

9. Use the data in your table from Exercise 8 to make a double line graph.

10. **You Decide** Describe a situation in which you could use a double line graph to display data.

Extra Practice See page 189, Set C.

Quick Check

Check your understanding of Lessons 1–3.

Use the double bar graph for Questions 1–4.
(Lessons 1 and 2)

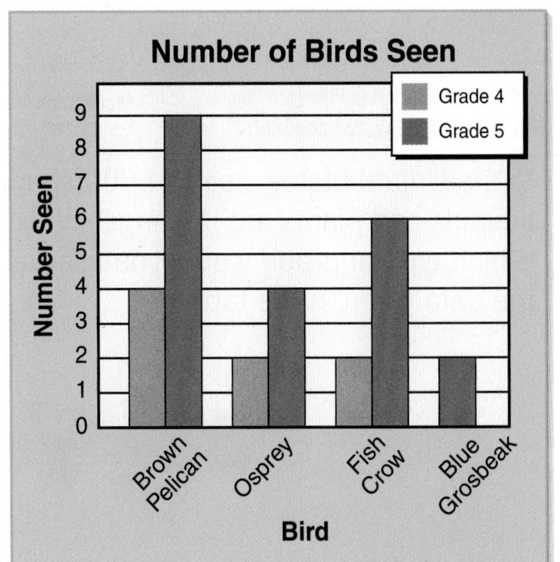

1. How many more ospreys were seen by grade 5 students than by grade 4 students?
2. How many of these four kinds of birds did the grade 5 students see?
3. For which bird is there the greatest difference in the number seen between the two grades?
4. Overall, which bird did the students see the least? How many of these birds did they see?
5. Create a double line graph of the information in the table. (Lesson 3)

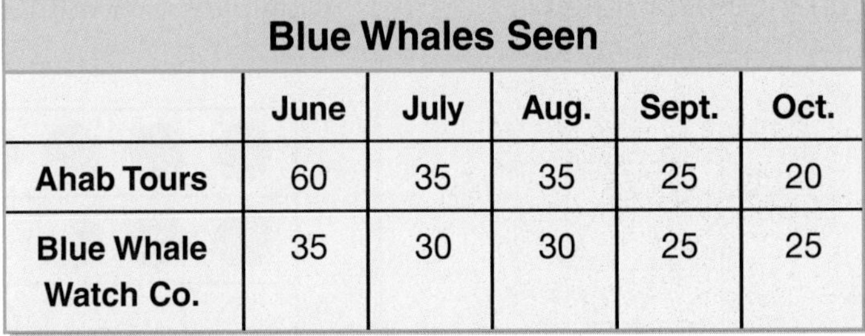

Blue Whales Seen					
	June	**July**	**Aug.**	**Sept.**	**Oct.**
Ahab Tours	60	35	35	25	20
Blue Whale Watch Co.	35	30	30	25	25

Math Challenge

Without Numbers

Even though the graph at the right has no numbers, you can still find information from it.

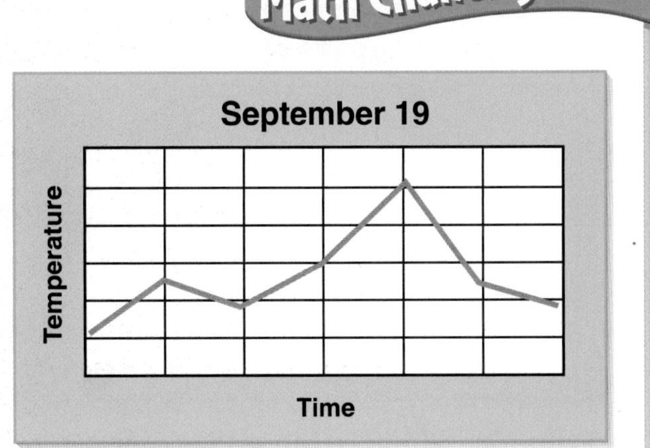

1. Was it colder at the start of the day or at the end of the day?
2. Estimate the time of day when the highest temperature occurred.

Lesson 4

Choose an Appropriate Graph

Objective Choose an appropriate graph to display data.

Learn About It

MathTracks 1/20
Listen and Understand

In the United States, nearly 1,000 species of animals and plants are in danger of extinction. Which type of graph would you use to show the data given in the table?

Endangered Species

Group	Number of Species
Mammals	61
Birds	74
Reptiles	14
Amphibians	9
Fish	69
Total	227

Different Types of Graphs

A bar graph is a good choice when the data can be counted and you want to make comparisons.

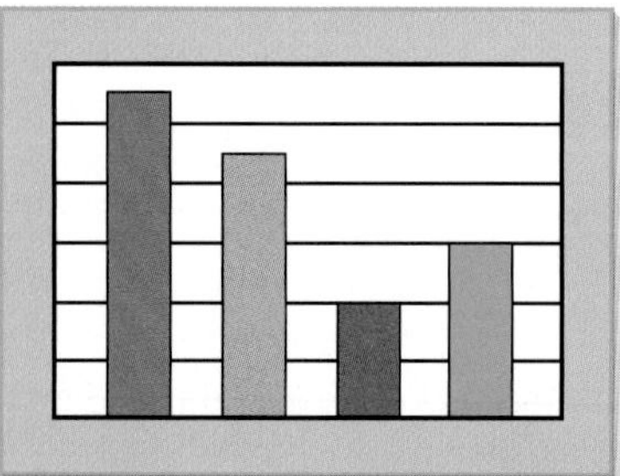

A line graph is appropriate when you want to show change over time.

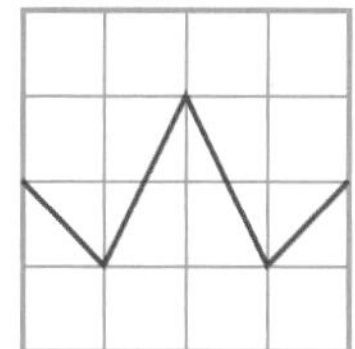

A pictograph is a good choice when the data are multiples of a number.

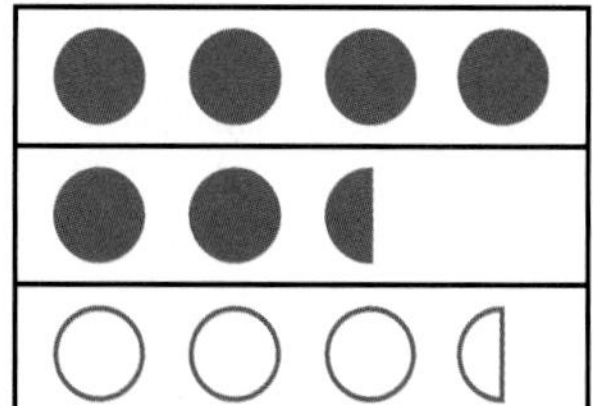

A circle graph is a good choice when the data are parts of a whole.

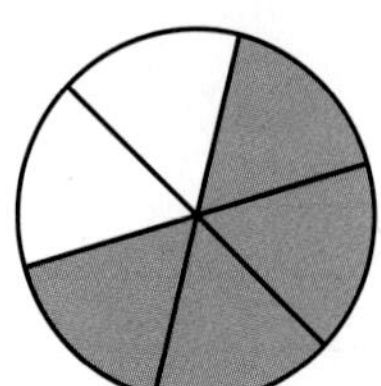

A histogram is a good choice to show how frequently data occur within equal intervals.

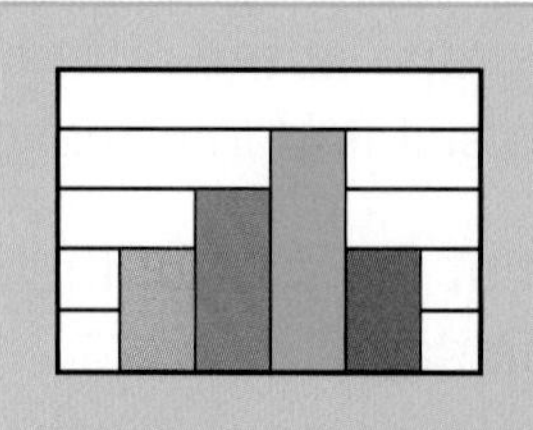

Solution: A bar graph or circle graph would be an appropriate choice.

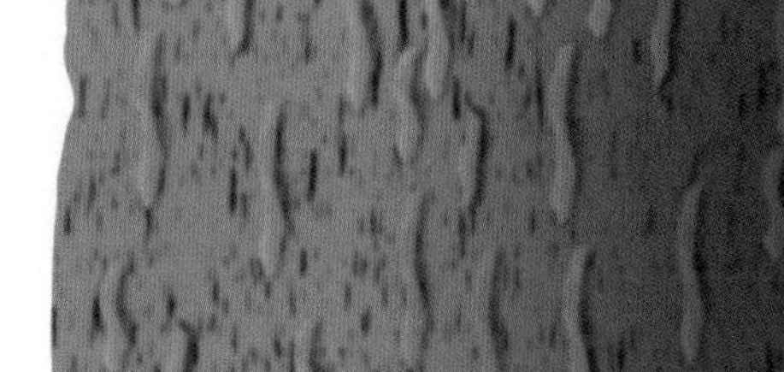

Guided Practice

- Do I arrange the data in intervals?
- Do I show separate data, parts of a whole, or change over time?

Choose an appropriate graph for the data described.

1. Wingspans of these endangered or threatened birds: bobwhite, California condor, Mariana mallard, whooping crane, and Hawaiian hawk.
2. The number of species of birds sighted, organized in the intervals 0–2, 3–5, 6–8, 9–11, and 12–14.

Give an example of data that could be shown in a line graph.

Practice and Problem Solving

Choose and make an appropriate graph for the data.

3.

Amount Collected to Save the Manatees	
Day	**Amount ($)**
Monday	200
Tuesday	250
Wednesday	300
Thursday	225
Friday	450

4.

Life Expectancy of Endangered Animals	
Animal	**Average (years)**
Bison	15
Chimpanzee	20
Kangaroo	7
Zebra	15
Leopard	12

5.

Fish Hatchery Weight Check	
Weight (oz)	**Fish**
0–3.99	6
4–7.99	3
8–11.99	2
12–15.99	3
16–19.99	2

Data **Use the table at the right for Problems 6 and 7.**

6. **Estimate** By about how many pairs did the bald eagle population increase from 1981 to 1998?
7. **Reasoning** What type of graph would be appropriate to represent the data? Explain. Draw and label the graph you chose.

Bald Eagle Population	
Year	**Adult Pairs**
1981	1,188
1986	1,875
1990	3,020
1998	5,748

Daily Review | Test Prep

Write each number in word form.
(Ch. 1, Lesson 1)

8. 6,780
9. 48,309
10. 586,147
11. 2,346
12. 34,501
13. 257,824

14. Which would be the best choice to display data about the mass of an owl from birth to 18 months?

A circle graph
B line graph
C pictograph
D histogram

Extra Practice See page 189, Set D.

Lesson 5

Misleading Graphs

Objective Recognize when and explain why data on graphs are displayed in misleading ways.

Learn About It

The two line graphs at the right both show the number of visitors to the Wildlife Zoo for 4 months. What differences do you notice?

Look at the scale on each graph. The intervals you choose for a scale can affect the appearance of the graph.

Which graph would you use if you wanted to say that this zoo's popularity has not changed much in six months?

- The scale on Graph A shows equal intervals of 1,000. The scale also does not begin intervals at zero. The scale gives the appearance that the number of visitors to the Wildlife Zoo increased greatly between May and August.
- The scale on Graph B shows equal intervals of 6,000. What appearance does the scale give to Graph B?

Graph A

Graph B

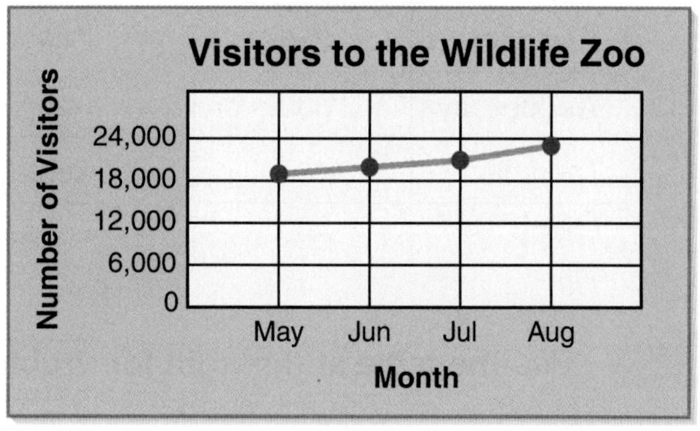

Another Example

Many newspapers show data in circle graphs. One way to make these graphs misleading is to tilt the graph. Which graph looks like it shows more foreign visitors?

Visitors to the State Capital

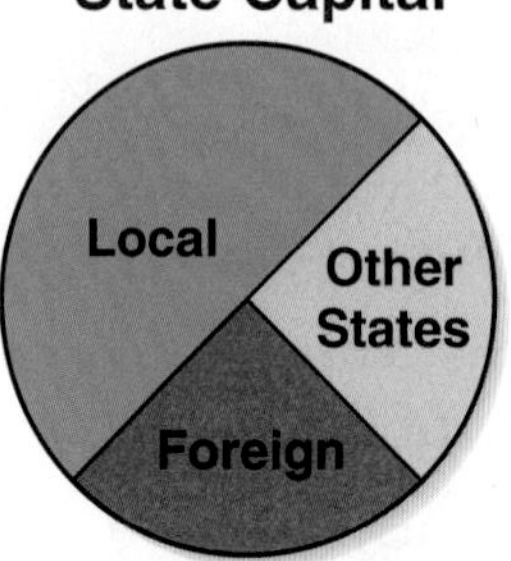

Visitors to the State Capital

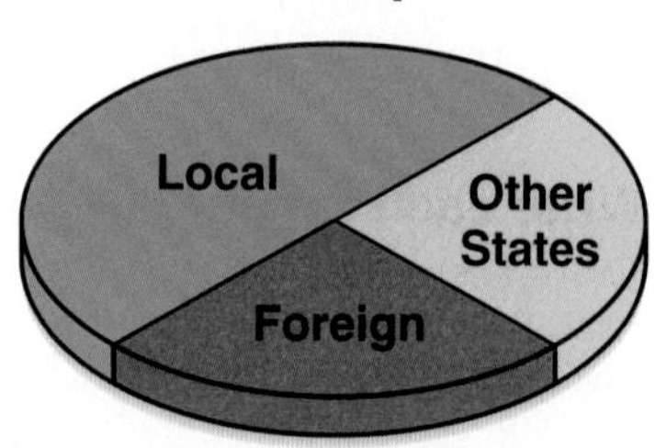

Guided Practice

Ask Yourself

- Did I read the graph carefully?

TEST TIPS

Use the graph below for Exercises 1–3.

1. What was the zoo attendance in 2005?
2. What was the zoo attendance in 2000?
3. What is misleading about the graph?

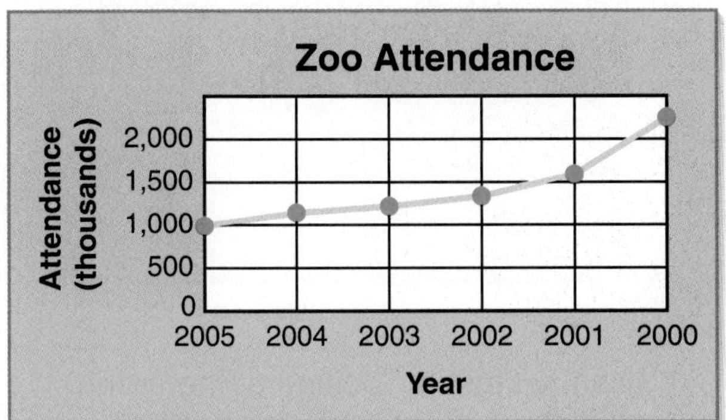

TEST TIPS **Explain Your Thinking ▶** How does a change in the scale affect the appearance of a graph?

Practice and Problem Solving

Use the graph at the right for Problems 4–5.

4. **Explain** Tell why it seems as if the walrus is more than two times as popular as the polar bear.
5. **Represent** Make a new bar graph, using a scale that represents the data on the graph more accurately.
6. **What's Wrong?** Suppose Jack graphed the the data from a survey and used the following scale intervals for the vertical axis of the bar graph: 10, 15, 19, 25, 27, 29, and 30. What would be wrong with his graph?

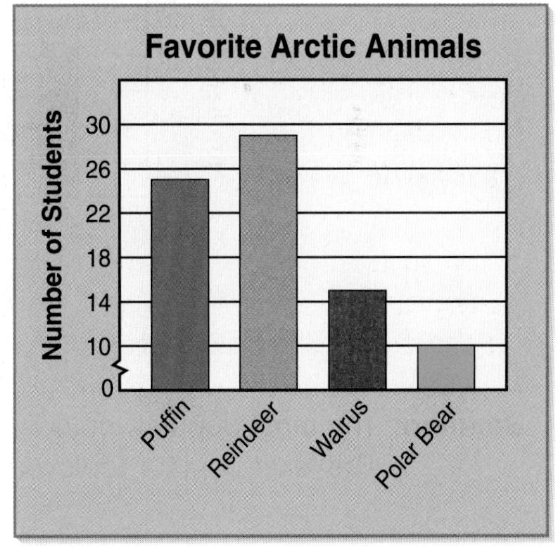

Daily Review | Test Prep

Evaluate. (Ch. 5, Lesson 6)

7. $5 \times 3 - 12 \div 4$
8. $4 \times 6 - 8 \div 2$
9. $3 + 6 \div 3 + 8$
10. $5 \times 5 \div 5 + 7$

11. **Free Response** A graph used intervals of 0, 100, 200, 700, 800, 1,000. Explain how the graph is misleading.

Extra Practice See page 189, Set E.

Lesson 6

Problem-Solving Decision

Relevant Information

Objective Decide which information on a graph is relevant.

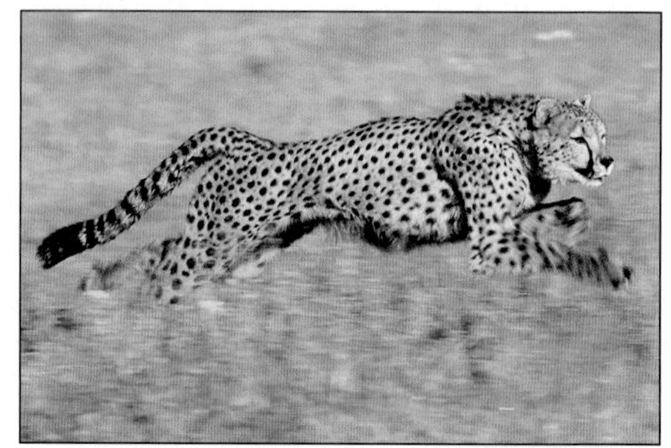

Problem The students in grades 5 and 6 were given their choice of animals to research for a project. The results of their choices are organized in the double bar graph. Which topic was the most popular? Which was the least popular?

When you look at the information on a graph, you need to determine what information is relevant.

To find the most popular topic, use the scale to find the totals for each topic.

You can tell just by looking at the graph that the least popular topic was Elephants.

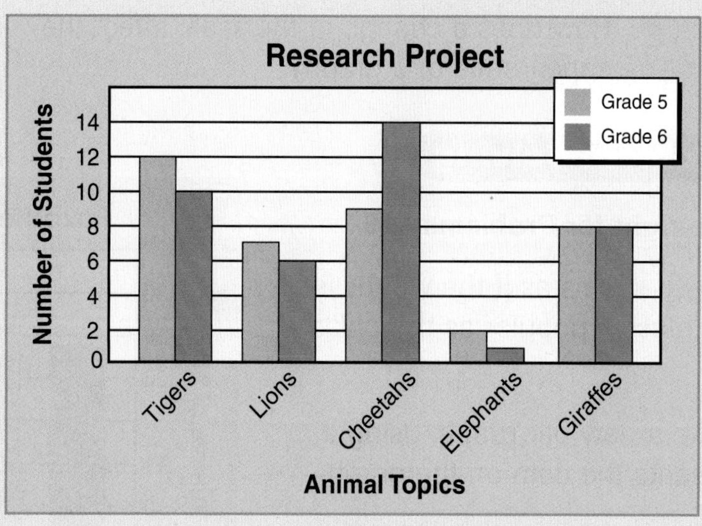

Solution: The most popular topic was Cheetahs.
The least popular topic was Elephants.

Try These

Use the relevant information in the graph above to solve.

1. The number of students who chose Lions and Elephants is equal to the number of students who chose what other topic?
2. For which topic is there the greatest difference in popularity between fifth-graders and sixth-graders? What is this difference?
3. Which grade has the greater number of students–grade 5 or grade 6? Explain how you know.
4. Six times as many fifth-graders chose this topic over another. What topics were they?

Quick Check

Check your understanding of Lessons 4–6.

1. José surveyed his classmates about their favorite ice cream flavors. Which kinds of graphs would be good choices to display the results? (Lesson 4)

2. How would the appearance of the data change if you used a bar graph to display the data in the Socks Sales graph? Explain. (Lesson 4)

3. How would the appearance of the graph about sock sales change if intervals of 5,000 were used? (Lesson 5)

4. The graph shows the cooking times for pasta. Does it take longer to cook fresh pasta or packaged pasta? (Lesson 6)

5. How much longer does it take to cook packaged lasagna than packaged fettucine? (Lesson 6)

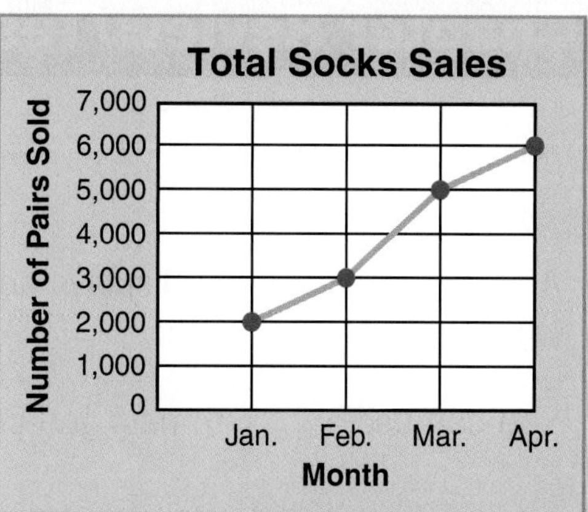

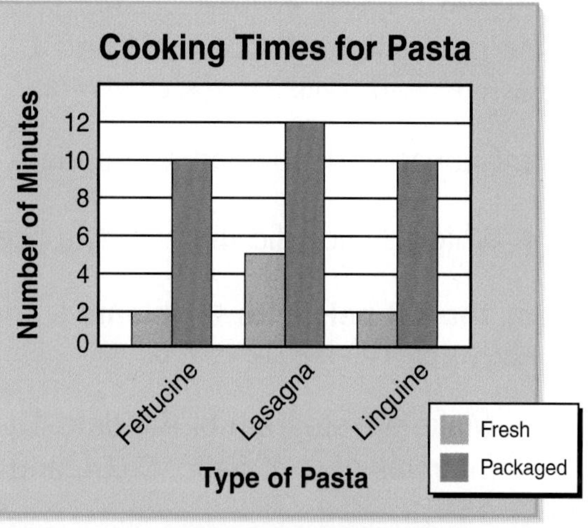

Graph It

You can use a spreadsheet like the one below to create a graph.

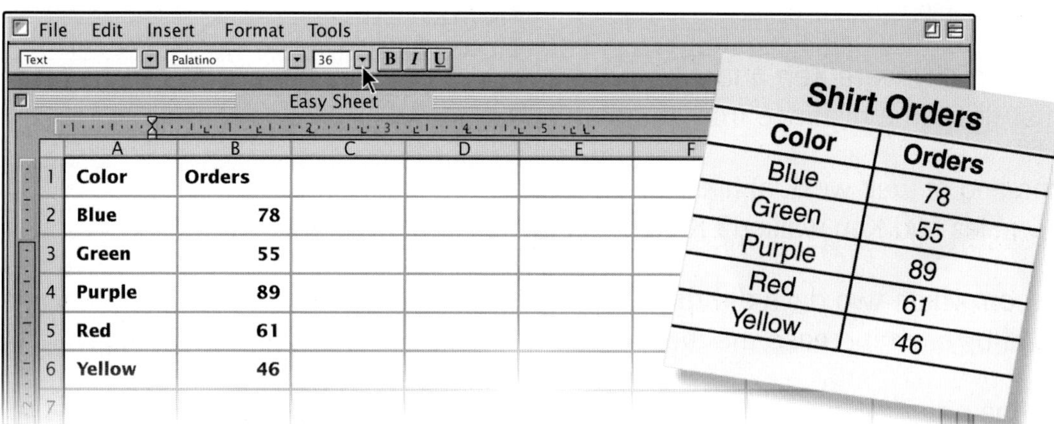

	A	B	C	D	E	F
1	Color	Orders				
2	Blue	78				
3	Green	55				
4	Purple	89				
5	Red	61				
6	Yellow	46				
7						

Shirt Orders

Color	Orders
Blue	78
Green	55
Purple	89
Red	61
Yellow	46

1. Enter the data shown in a spreadsheet program.

2. Use the help menu from the spreadsheet program to create a bar graph that displays the data.

Chapter Review/Test

VOCABULARY

Vocabulary
double line graph
frequency table
histogram

1. A ____ is a graph that displays how often data occur within equal intervals.
2. You can use a ____ to help you count and organize data.

CONCEPTS AND SKILLS

Use the table for Problems 3 and 4.
(Lesson 1, pp. 172–175; Lesson 4, pp. 182–183)

3. Choose and make an appropriate graph for the data.
4. Which choice did most people like? dislike?

Transportation Choice

	Like	Dislike
Car	16	6
Bus	7	15
Train	18	3
Plane	14	9

Use the list below for Problems 5 and 6.
(Lesson 2, pp. 176–177; Lesson 6, p. 186)

5. Make a histogram of the data. Use intervals of 0–4, 5–9, 10–14, and 15–19.
6. Did most of the students read more than or fewer than 10 books during the summer?

Number of Books Read

5	10	2	7	3	9	8	10	3	0	5	19
11	7	15	6	10	12	9	13	8	17	12	7

PROBLEM SOLVING

Use the line graph for Problems 7–9.
(Lesson 3, pp. 178–180; Lesson 6, p. 186)

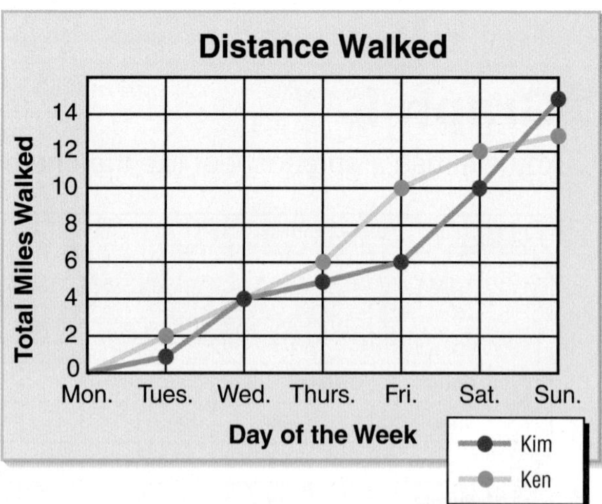

7. On which day were Ken and Kim at the same distance from the start?
8. By the end of their week of hiking, how many miles had Ken walked? Kim?
9. Between which two days did the distance walked by each increase the most?
10. Describe one way in which a graph can be misleading. (Lesson 5, pp. 184–185)

Write About It

Show You Understand

Why is it important to look at the scale when interpreting a graph?

Extra Practice

Set A (Lesson 1, pp. 172–175)

Use the graph for Problems 1–3.

1. Which activity was more popular with girls than boys?
2. How many times more do boys use computers for games than for Web searches?

How Computers Are Used

Boys
Girls
Number of Students
0 4 8 12 16 20 24 28 32 36
E-mail Web Search Games Word Processing
Computer Use

Set B (Lesson 2, pp. 176–177)

The data show the distances of bright stars from the Earth in light-years.

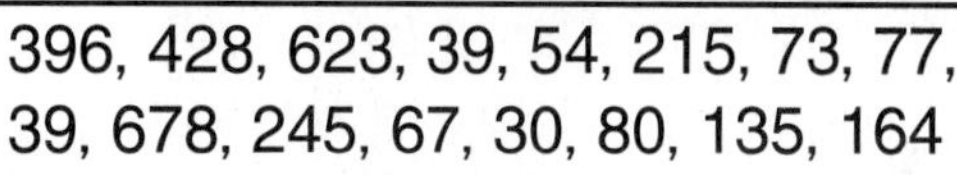

396, 428, 623, 39, 54, 215, 73, 77,
39, 678, 245, 67, 30, 80, 135, 164

1. Make a histogram of the data using intervals of 100 light-years.
2. How many more stars are between 0 and 99 light-years away than are between 100 and 199 light-years away?

Set C (Lesson 3, pp. 178–180)

The tables show the use of gas and electric power for heating in new homes from 1970 to 2000.

1. Make a double line graph to compare the data.
2. In 1990, how many new homes out of 100 were heated with electricity? with natural gas?

Number of New Homes Out of 100

Electricity			
1970	1980	1990	2000
30	50	30	25

Natural Gas			
1970	1980	1990	2000
60	40	60	70

Set D (Lesson 4, pp. 182–183)

Choose an appropriate graph for the data.

1. the parts in 100 of nitrogen, oxygen, water vapor, and other gases in air
2. the amounts of snow in two cities, over a one-year span
3. the weight of a baby from birth to 18 months

Set E (Lesson 5, pp. 184–185)

Use the graph at the right for the following questions.

1. Explain what is misleading in the graph at the right.
2. Draw a graph that is not misleading.

Data and Statistics

INVESTIGATION

Use Data

In order to improve his shooting skills, William practiced every day for two weeks. He took 25 shots during each practice. The results are shown on the line plot. What was the average number of shots William made?

Chapter Pretest

Use this page to review and remember what you need to know for this chapter.

VOCABULARY

Choose the best word to complete each sentence.

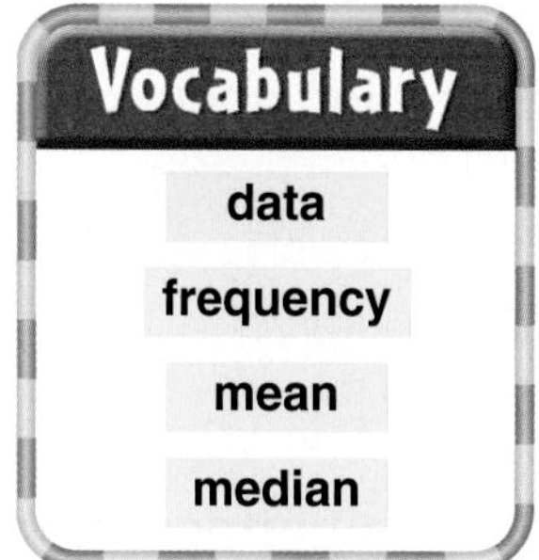

1. The ____ of an item of data is the number of times it occurs.
2. The ____ of a set of data is sometimes called the average.

CONCEPTS AND SKILLS

Order these numbers from least to greatest.

3. 4, 9, 7, 7, 5, 6, 8, 2, 3
4. 36, 48, 16, 93, 21, 73, 4

Match each definition with a word.

5. The number that occurs most often in a data set
6. The middle number in a set of numbers ordered from least to greatest
7. The difference between the greatest number and the least number in a set of data

a. mean
b. median
c. mode
d. range

Decide whether each statement is always, sometimes, or never true.

8. A set of data has a mode.
9. A line plot uses bars to represent data.

10. A survey is done to find out your class's favorite snacks. What graph would best display the results? Explain your choice.

Test Prep on the Net

Visit *Education Place* at **eduplace.com/kids/mw/** for more review.

Collect and Organize Data

Objective Collect, organize, and interpret data from a survey.

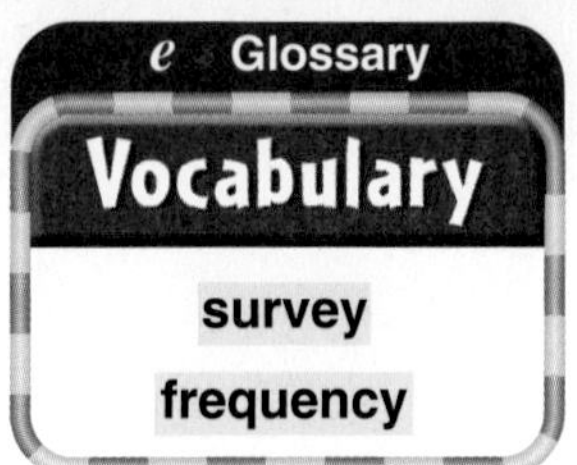

Materials
Learning Tool 35

Work Together

▶ A **survey** is a method of collecting information about a group of people.

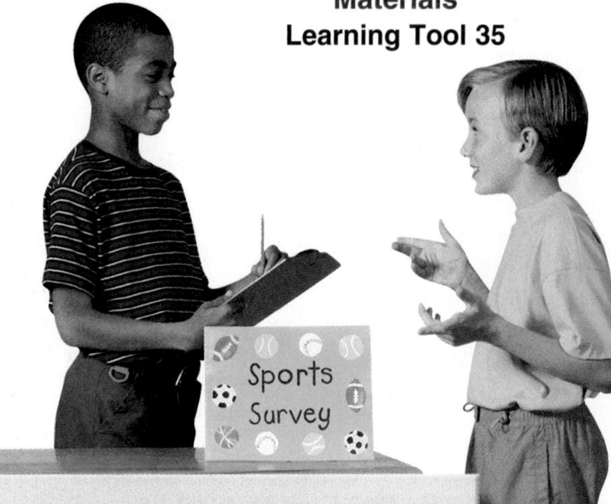

Work with a partner to conduct a survey and interpret the results.

STEP 1 Make up a survey question like "What is your favorite sport?" or "What is your favorite color?" Write your question on the record sheet.

Survey Results	
Survey Question: What is your favorite sport?	
Answer Choice	**Tally Marks**

STEP 2 List five or six likely answer choices for the survey question on the record sheet.

Survey Results	
Survey Question: What is your favorite sport?	
Answer Choice	**Tally Marks**
Baseball	
Basketball	
Football	
Soccer	
Tennis	
Other	

STEP 3 Ask each of your classmates the survey question.

- Use a tally mark to record each answer.
- Count the tally marks for each answer and write the number in the Frequency column. The **frequency** of each answer is the number of times it is chosen.

Survey Results		
Survey Question: What is your favorite sport?		
Answer Choice	**Tally Marks**	**Frequency**
Baseball	𝍸	5
Basketball	𝍸 I	6
Football	𝍸	5
Soccer	𝍸 III	8
Tennis	II	2
Other	III	3

Discuss your results.

- Which choice was the most popular? the least popular?
- Was that choice picked by less than one half, one half, or more than one half of the class?
- Use the information you collected to write a short summary of your survey results.

On Your Own

The table shows the results of a survey of a fifth-grade class. Use the table for Problems 1–4.

1. Copy and complete the table.
2. How many of those surveyed had 2 brothers and sisters?
3. How many students were in the survey?
4. **Analyze** Can you tell how many students surveyed had 5 brothers and sisters? Explain your answer.

Number of Brothers and Sisters	Tally	Frequency
0	|	
1	|||	
2	~~||||~~	
3	||||	
4	|||	
More than 4	||	

Follow Steps 1–3 on page 192 to survey your classmates about their favorite kinds of music. Then use your results for Problems 5–8.

5. Which answer choice was the most popular? Which answer choice was the least popular?
6. Did any of your answer choices have the same frequency? Which ones?
7. What is the difference in frequency between the most popular choice and the least popular choice?
8. Write a short summary of your survey results. Did any of your results surprise you? Explain.

Talk About It • Write About It

You learned how to conduct a survey and interpret the results.

9. Look at your results from the activity on pages 192–193. Do you think your results would be different if you surveyed adults? Explain why or why not.
10. How might a store owner use a survey to decide what games to sell in the store?

Lesson 2

Mean, Median, Mode, and Range

Objective Make and use a line plot to find the mean, median, mode, and range of a set of data.

e Glossary

Vocabulary

line plot
cluster
gap
mean
median
mode
range

Learn About It

Kenny's class had a bowling party. Their scores in the first game are shown at the right.

▶ You can organize the data in a **line plot** to make the data easier to describe.

10th Frame	Final Score
3 4 84	84
1 8 72	72
8 1 83	83
7 - 84	84
X 2 4 92	92
6 3 85	85
9 - 80	80
7 1 83	83
6 / 4 84	84

Make a line plot.

STEP 1 List the data in order.
72, 80, 83, 83, 84, 84, 84, 85, 92

STEP 2 Create a number line that covers all the numbers in your list.

STEP 3 Put an *X* above each number as many times as the number appears in the list. For example, the score 84 appears 3 times in the list, so put 3 *X*'s above 84.

A **cluster** is an isolated group of data. There is a cluster from 83 to 85.

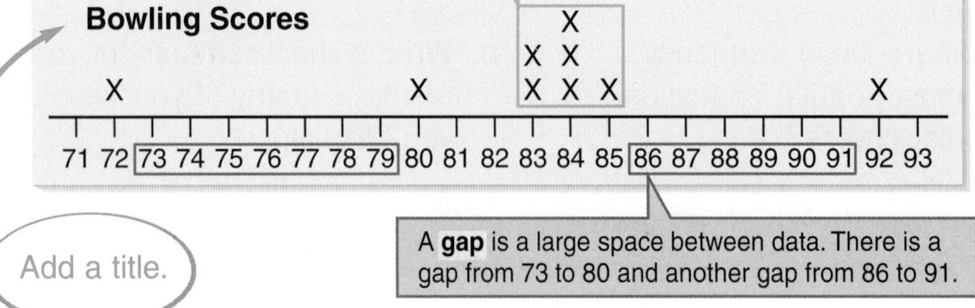

Add a title.

A **gap** is a large space between data. There is a gap from 73 to 80 and another gap from 86 to 91.

- Can you tell just by looking at the line plot what the typical scores of the group were? Were there any scores that were not typical?
- How do the gaps and clusters help you see this?

▶ **To describe a set of data, you can use the mean, median, and mode. You can use the range to tell how far the data are spread out.**

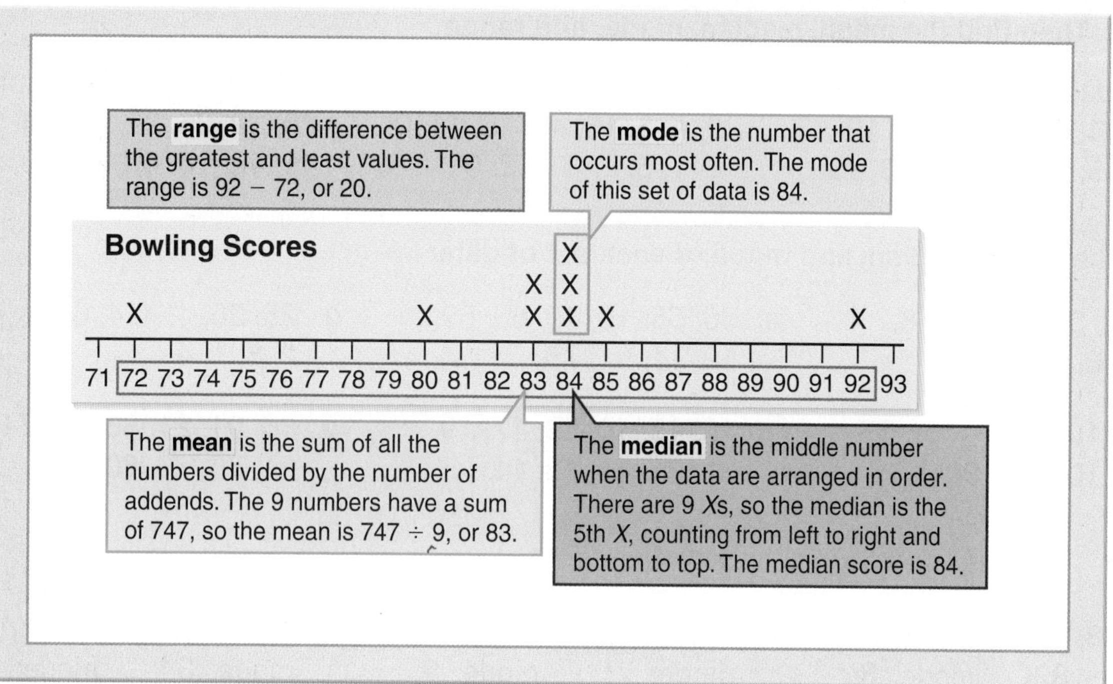

The **range** is the difference between the greatest and least values. The range is 92 − 72, or 20.
The **mode** is the number that occurs most often. The mode of this set of data is 84.
Bowling Scores
71 72 73 74 75 76 77 78 79 80 81 82 83 84 85 86 87 88 89 90 91 92 93
The **mean** is the sum of all the numbers divided by the number of addends. The 9 numbers have a sum of 747, so the mean is 747 ÷ 9, or 83.
The **median** is the middle number when the data are arranged in order. There are 9 *X*s, so the median is the 5th *X*, counting from left to right and bottom to top. The median score is 84.

Other Examples

A. Even Number of Data

For an even number of data, the median is the average of the middle two numbers.

Find the median of 6, 10, 11, 13, 13, and 13.

$\frac{11 + 13}{2} = 12$ The median is 12.

B. More Than One Mode

Find the mode of 1, 1, 2, 2, 2, 3, 3, 4, 4, 4, and 7.

1 1 2 2 2 3 3 4 4 4 7

The numbers 2 and 4 both occur three times, so both numbers are modes.

Guided Practice

Make a line plot for the data in Exercise 1. Then use the line plot to complete Exercises 2–3.

1. Miniature golf scores
69, 72, 74, 73, 73, 72, 75, 73, 70, 71, 90, 72, 91
2. Describe the data. Where do these data cluster? Are there any gaps? Where?
3. Find the mean, median, mode, and range of the data.

Ask Yourself

- Did I arrange the numbers in order?
- Did I include all the data on the line plot?

TEST TIPS **Explain Your Thinking ▶** Why is it helpful to describe the miniature golf scores above by using the mean, median, mode, and range?

Go On

Practice and Problem Solving

Make a line plot for each set of data. Identify clusters and gaps. Then find the mean, median, mode, and range.

4. number of miles biked
15, 14, 8, 27, 15, 20, 19, 13, 19, 15, 20, 14, 15, 13, 13

5. trips to the zoo
2, 4, 5, 16, 4, 5, 5, 11, 0, 2, 1, 5, 2, 3, 1, 2, 0

6. dollars in bank account
28, 32, 36, 22, 12, 40, 32, 46, 42, 18, 42, 32, 28, 24

Find the mean, median, and mode of each set of data.

7. 13, 2, 3, 6, 9, 8, 4, 8, 10, 10, 6, 5

8. 66, 55, 15, 49, 60, 59, 59, 11, 91, 75

9. 25, 26, 1, 4, 4, 6, 11, 4, 2, 8, 1, 4

10. 103, 104, 101, 102, 75, 100, 100, 89, 90

11. 16, 15, 10, 43, 17, 19, 31, 31, 14, 13, 11

12. 86, 91, 21, 86, 83, 74, 61, 75, 76, 80, 81

• Equations Find n.

13. 3, 4, 8, 8, 10, 12, 16, n
range: 32 mode: 8
median: 9 mean: 12

14. 5, 6, 7, 9, 12, n
range: 7 mode: 9
median: 8 mean: 8

15. 4, 8, 10, 16, 20, 38, n
range: 34 mode: n
median: n mean: n

Data **Use the line plot below for Problems 16–19.**

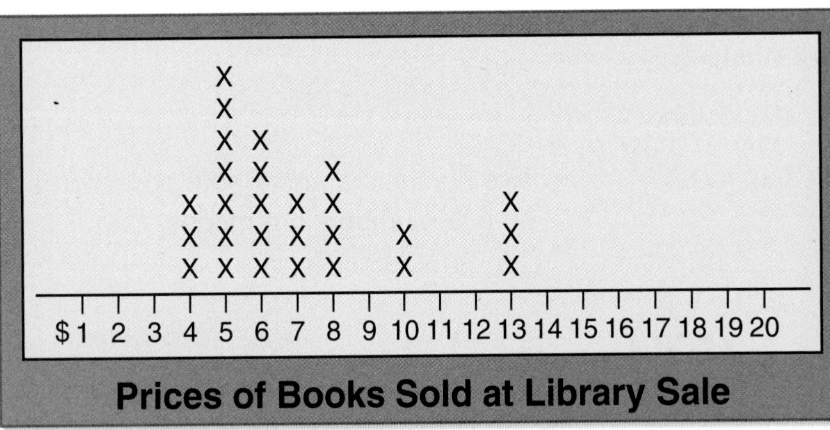

Prices of Books Sold at Library Sale

16. How many books are represented in the line plot?

17. Find the range, mean, median, and mode of the data.

18. Write About It Use your results from Problem 17 to write a short summary of the data.

19. How many books cost less than $7? How many books cost more than $7?

Test Prep

Complete. (Ch. 6, Lessons 4–5)

20. 5 m = ■ cm

21. 7,000 mg = ■ g

22. 96 dm = ■ m

23. 3,500 mL = ■ L

24. Nathan's math grades are 85, 70, 84, 91, 88, and 92. Find the mean of his grades.

A 85 **B** 87 **C** 88 **D** 90

Extra Practice See page 209, Set A.

Bell Building

Materials
number cubes

Have you ever seen the shape shown below?

It is called a *bell curve.*

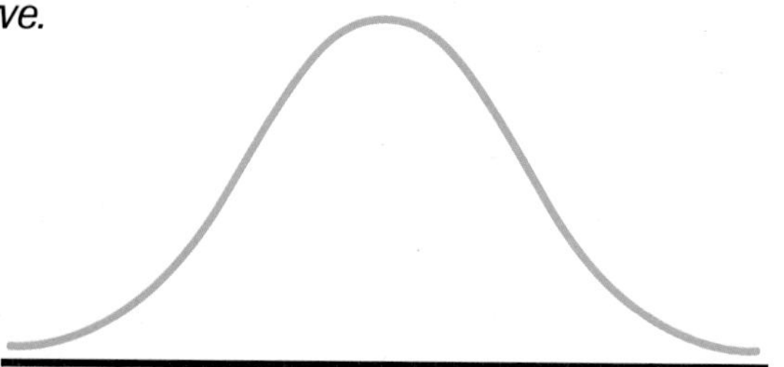

Follow the steps below. See if your results look like the bell curve.

STEP 1 Roll a pair of number cubes. Record the sum of the numbers showing. Repeat this step 24 times.

STEP 2 Make a line plot to show your results. Does your line plot look at all like a bell curve?

STEP 3 Combine your results with 4 other students'. Make a new line plot. Does this new line look like a bell curve?

Raise It Up

You have a mean of 78 for five quizzes. Each quiz has a possible score of 100.

- Can you raise your mean to 80 after six quizzes?
- Can you raise your mean to 82 after six quizzes?
- If there will be 10 quizzes in all, can you ever raise your mean to 90?

Explain each of your answers.

Brain Teaser

The numbers below are ordered from least to greatest. The mean of the numbers is 5, the median is 6, and the mode is 2. What are the numbers?

Ask Yourself
How do I find the median?

Lesson 3

Make and Use a Stem-and-Leaf Plot

Objective Use a stem-and-leaf plot to display data.

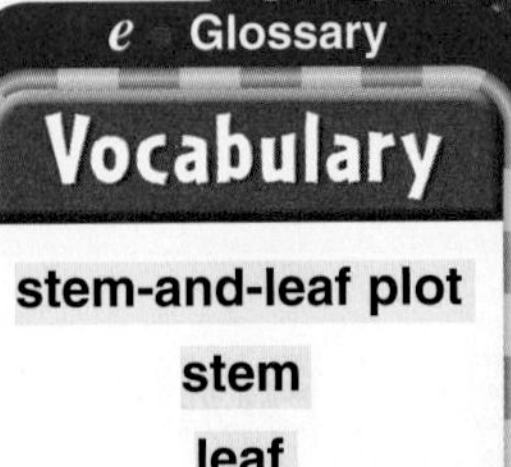

Learn About It

Have you ever ridden on an inverted roller coaster, where your feet hang free? The list below shows the speeds, in miles per hour, of some inverted roller coasters.

25, 45, 46, 50, 50, 50, 55, 55, 55, 55,
55, 57, 58, 58, 60, 60, 62, 65, 67, 72

One way to display these data is to make a **stem-and-leaf plot.**

Making a Stem-and-Leaf Plot

STEP 1 Write a title.

STEP 2 Write the tens digits needed to represent the data in order from least to greatest. Each of these numbers is a **stem.**

STEP 3 For each piece of data, write the ones digit, or **leaf**, next to its tens digit. Arrange the leaves in order from least to greatest. Write a key.

Roller Coaster Speeds (miles per hour)

Stem	Leaf
2	5
3	
4	5 6
5	0 0 0 5 5 5 5 5 7 8 8
6	0 0 2 5 7
7	2

7 | 2 means 72.

Guided Practice

Use the stem-and-leaf plot above for Problems 1–4.

1. What does 4 | 6 mean in the stem-and-leaf plot above?
2. How many roller coasters are represented in the data?
3. How many of the inverted roller coasters reach speeds of more than 55 miles per hour?
4. Find the mean, median, mode, and range of the data.

- What do the stems represent?
- What do the leaves represent?

How did you use the stem-and-leaf plot to find the mean, median, mode, and range of the data?

Practice and Problem Solving

Use the stem-and-leaf plot for Problems 5–8.

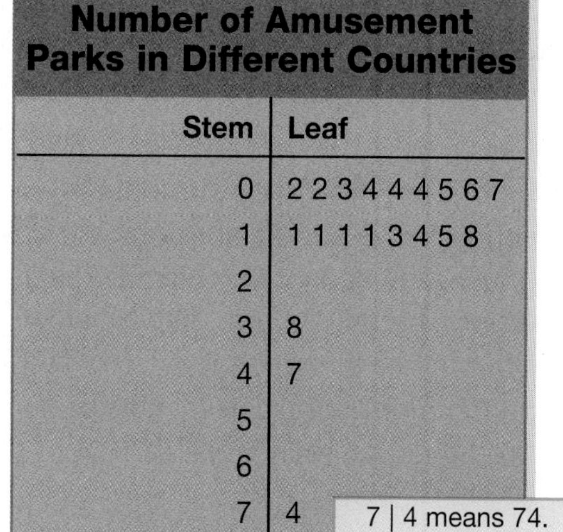

Number of Amusement Parks in Different Countries

Stem	Leaf
0	2 2 3 4 4 4 5 6 7
1	1 1 1 1 3 4 5 8
2	
3	8
4	7
5	
6	
7	4

7 | 4 means 74.

5. What does 0 | 7 mean in this line plot?

6. How many countries are represented in the data?

7. **Write About It** Identify any clusters and gaps you see. What do these tell you about the data?

8. Find the mean, median, mode, and range of the data.

9. Suppose you had these scores on a computer game: 123, 123, 123, 123, 123. What is true about the mean score, the median score, and the mode?

Make a stem-and-leaf plot for the data at the right. Each "ring" of a peg scores 2 points. Then solve Problems 10–15.

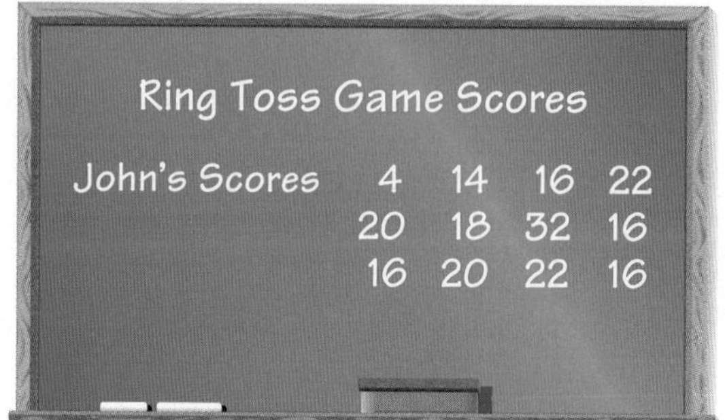

Ring Toss Game Scores
John's Scores 4 14 16 22
20 18 32 16
16 20 22 16

10. How many times did John play the game?

11. What was John's highest score?

12. What was John's lowest score?

13. Find the mean, median, mode, and range of the data.

14. **What's Wrong?** Ana and John will compete in the Ring Toss Game. Ana says that she needs to score about 10 points to have a good chance of beating John's score. What's wrong with Ana's prediction?

15. **Analyze** Tell why the median of John's scores is not the best statistic to use to describe John's typical score. Explain your thinking.

Daily Review Test Prep

Evaluate each expression when $n = 7$.
(Ch. 2, Lesson 3)

16. $n + 3$

17. $4 + n$

18. $2 + n - 5$

19. $13 - n$

20. $25 - (n + 5)$

21. $(n + n) - 1$

22. **Free Response** List the data below in order from greatest to least.

Stem	Leaf
1	0 1 1 2
2	2
3	4 4 5 7 9

3 | 4 means 34.

Lesson 4

Problem-Solving Strategy

Make a Table

Objective Make a table to solve problems.

Problem Fifth-grade students conducted a survey about how many hours they spend watching TV each week. The results are shown below. Do most of the students watch TV 0–4 hours, 5–9 hours, 10–14 hours, or 15–19 hours each week?

Survey Results

0	5	7	11	13	10
5	3	9	1	15	7
16	8	0	9	4	8
13	4	8	2	15	5

UNDERSTAND

This is what you know:

The number of hours each student watches TV each week.

PLAN

You can make a table to help you solve the problem.

SOLVE

- Make a table with the intervals stated in the problem: 0–4 hours, 5–9 hours, 10–14 hours, and 15–19 hours.
- Write a tally mark next to the correct interval for each number in the list. Then count the tally marks and write the frequencies.
- Compare the frequencies.

$10 > 7 > 4 > 3$

Hours	Tally	Frequency
0–4	𝍸 ||	7
5–9	𝍸 𝍸	10
10–14	||||	4
15–19	|||	3

Solution: Most of the students surveyed watch TV 5–9 hours each week.

LOOK BACK

Look back at the problem. Is your answer reasonable? How can you check the answer?

MathTracks 1/23
Listen and Understand

Guided Practice

Use the Ask Yourself questions to help you solve each problem.

1. Kami and Brady played a word game. The scores for each word are shown below. Are most of the scores from 1–10, 11–20, 21–30, or over 30 points?

   12, 17, 42, 16, 22, 14, 22, 38, 9, 14, 20, 8, 7, 27, 19, 13, 18, 25, 6, 29, 17, 24, 7, 18, 16, 50, 9, 22, 27, 18, 15, 42, 6, 12, 30, 8, 4

Ask Yourself

What facts do I know?

Did I make a table with the correct headings and intervals?

- **Did I tally the data?**
- **Did I find the frequency for each interval?**

Did I check my answer?

2. Use the data above. Are more of the scores from 11–15 points or 16–20 points?

   Hint Make a new table. The sum of these frequencies should equal the frequency for 11–20 above.

Independent Practice

Make a table to solve each problem.

3. The students in Shayna's class recorded the number of minutes they spent on the Internet during one night. The results are shown at the right. Did most of the students spend 0–20 minutes, 21–41 minutes, 42–62 minutes, 63–83 minutes, or over 83 minutes?

0	18	12	48	64	12	32	52
20	45	58	84	26	34	100	0
46	8	42	0	18	42	53	4

4. Use the data above. How many students in Shayna's class spent 0–10 minutes on the Internet? How many spent 11–20 minutes?

5. Taylor collects coins. The dates of the coins are shown at the right. Are most of Taylor's coins from before 1940, between 1940 and 1960, or after 1960?

1944	1957	1955	1953	1960
1931	1949	1985	1966	1943
1982	1947	1922	1978	1964
1970	1974	1941	1976	1980
1936	1952	1980	1932	1995

6. **Create and Solve** Find out in which month each of your classmates was born. Were most of them born from January–March, April–June, July–September, or October–December? Make a table to solve the problem.

7. Could you solve Problem 6 by using a line plot? Explain.

Go On

Choose a Strategy

Solve. Show your work. Tell what strategy you used.

8. Brett bought a T-shirt and a baseball cap for $40. The T-shirt was $8 less than the baseball cap. What was the cost of the T-shirt? What was the cost of the baseball cap?

9. In a basketball game, Amber scored 5 more points than Tonya and 4 fewer points than Juanita. Juanita scored 22 points. How many points did Tonya score?

10. The price for two people to play a round of miniature golf is $11 in 2000, $13 in 2002, $15 in 2004, and $17 in 2006. If the pattern continues, what will the price be in 2010?

11. Paige is thinking of two numbers that have a product of 180 and a difference of 3. What are the two numbers?

PROBLEM-SOLVING Strategies

- Use Models
- Draw a Diagram
- Find a Pattern
- Guess and Check
- Make an Organized List
- Make a Table
- Solve a Simpler Problem
- Use Logical Reasoning
- Work Backward
- Write an Equation

Data **Use the graph to solve Problems 12–15.**

Ed and Sal earn money by giving tennis lessons to younger children. The graph shows how much money Ed and Sal earned in three months.

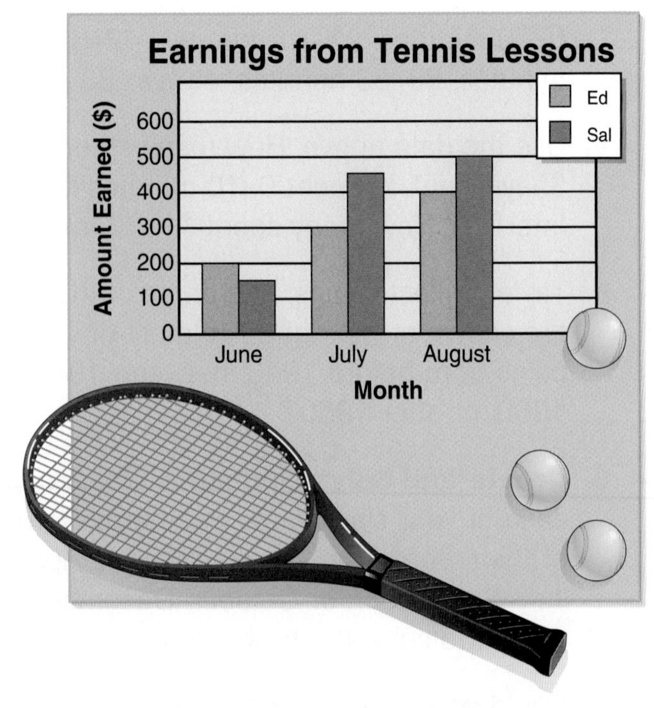

12. In which month was the difference between Ed and Sal's earnings the greatest?

13. **Estimate** Who has more total earnings over the three months shown on the graph? About how much more?

14. Sal saves half of his total earnings. About how much money did he save from June to August?

15. **Create and Solve** Write and solve a problem that uses data from the graph.

Problem-Solving Test Prep

Choose the letter of the correct answer. If a correct answer is not here, choose NH.

1. In what order should the operations be performed?

$5 \times (6 - 2) + 8$

A multiplication, subtraction, addition

B subtraction, multiplication, addition

C addition, subtraction, multiplication

D subtraction, addition, multiplication

(Chapter 5, Lesson 6)

2. Naomi paid $36 for the notebook and T-shirt. Which equation could you use to find the cost of the T-shirt?

F $\$36 + \$6 = c$

G $\$6 + c = \$36$

H $\$6 \times c = \$36$

J NH

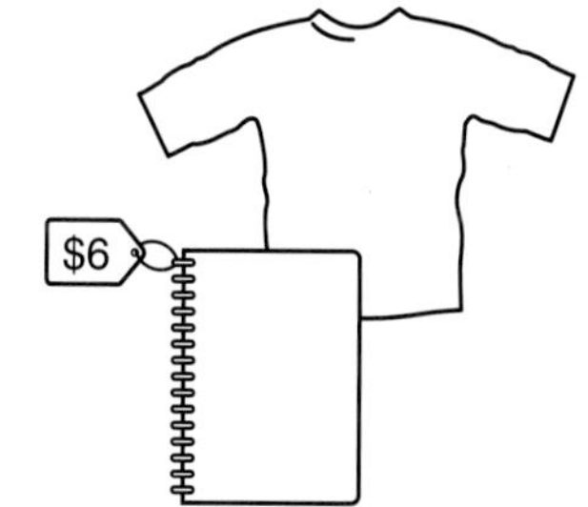

(Chapter 6, Lesson 3)

3. Look at the histogram. How many people surveyed saw fewer than 11 plays this year?

A 18

B 10

C 8

D 2

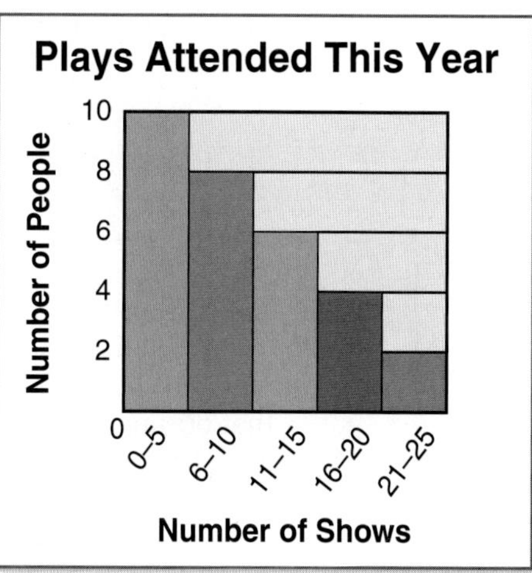

(Chapter 5, Lesson 7)

4. Measurement Norbert brought 3 quarts and 2 cups of water on a hike. How many cups of water did he bring?

F 8 cups

G 12 cups

H 14 cups

J 26 cups

(Chapter 7, Lesson 2)

5. Eighty people buy tickets to a dinner. They will sit at tables with 6 seats each. What is the least number of tables needed?

A 12 tables

B 13 tables

C 14 tables

D NH

(Chapter 4, Lesson 6)

6. Allan made model cars and motorcycles. He made 12 models that used a total of 40 wheels. How many model motorcycles did Allan make?

Represent Support your solution with a picture or a table.

(Chapter 1, Lesson 6)

7. A Web site lists the number of hits since it was started. Shari checks the site each Friday and records these totals: 57,600; 61,600; 65,600; 69,600. If the pattern continues, what will be the total number of hits shown the next time Shari checks?

Write About It How did you find the pattern? How did you use the pattern to solve the problem?

(Chapter 1, Lesson 6)

Test Prep on the Net

Check out *Education Place* at **eduplace.com/kids/mw/** for test prep practice.

Lesson 5

Draw Conclusions and Make Predictions

Objective Draw conclusions based on data and make predictions based on those conclusions.

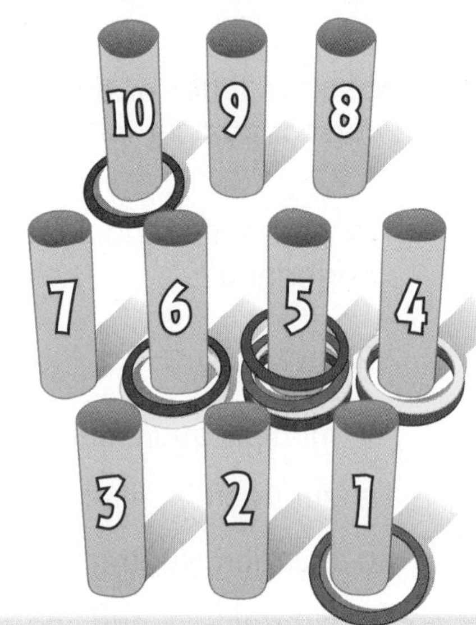

Learn About It

MathTracks 1/24
Listen and Understand

Chase, Kimiko, and Jared each threw 10 rings in a ring-toss game. The line plots below show their scores.

You can use the mean, median, and mode to describe each student's typical score.

Jared

Mean = **5.1**
Median = **5**
Mode = **5**

```
            X
            X
        X   X   X
X       X   X   X           X
----------------------------------
1   2   3   4   5   6   7   8   9   10
```

Since the mean, median, and mode are all about 5, Jared's typical score is 5.

Kimiko

Mean = **8**
Median = **9.5**
Mode = **10**

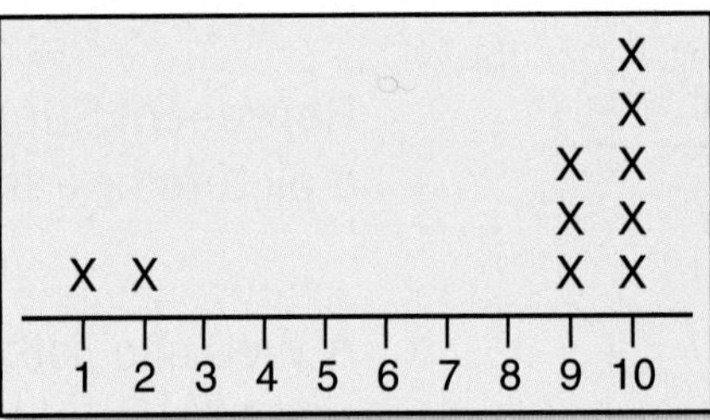

The two low scores "pull" the mean away from the rest of the data. Use the median and the mode. Kimoko's typical score is 9 or 10.

Chase

Mean = **4**
Median = **3**
Mode = **1**

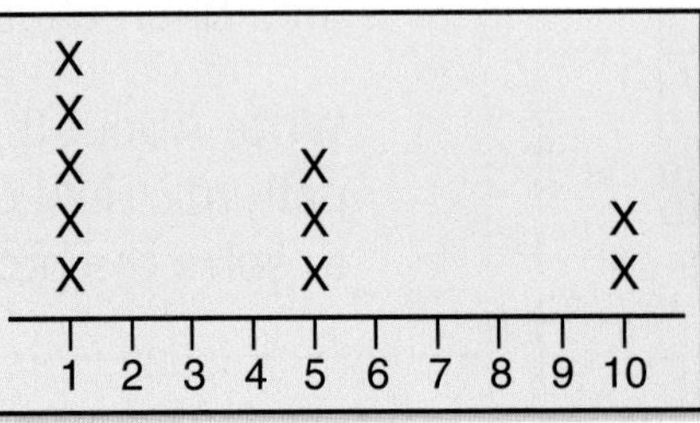

These data do not center around any score. So the score that occurs most often, the mode, best describes Chase's typical score.

Guided Practice

Ask Yourself

- Do most of the data center around one or a few numbers?
- Is the mean "pulled" away from the rest of the data?

The line plot shows the ticket prices for movie theaters in Metropole. Use the line plot below for Problems 1–3.

1. Find the mean, median, and mode of the data.

2. Suppose you are going to a movie in Metropole. How much money should you expect to pay for a ticket? Use the mean, median, and mode to explain your answer.

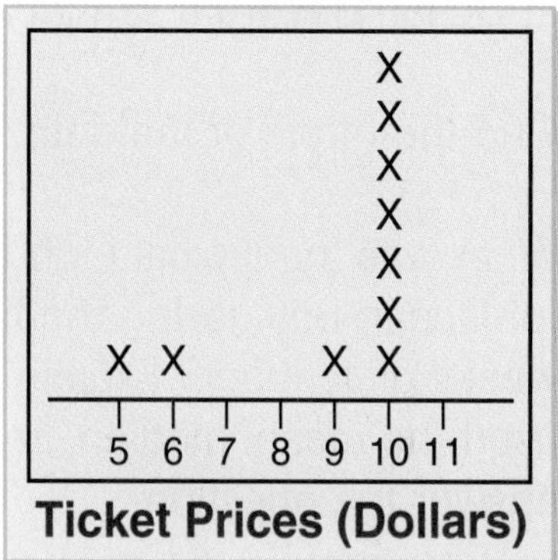

Ticket Prices (Dollars)

For the summer, the two movie theaters with the lowest-priced tickets doubled their ticket prices. Two of the movie theaters with $10 ticket prices cut their ticket prices in half.

3. Make a new line plot to show the summer ticket prices for the ten theaters.

4. Using the new data, how much would you expect to pay for a theater ticket? Explain your reasoning.

Explain Your Thinking When looking at data, why is it important to know all three statistics–the mean, median, and mode?

Practice and Problem Solving

Use the data from the line plot for Problems 4–6.

The line plot shows attendance at seven softball games that were played at the home field.

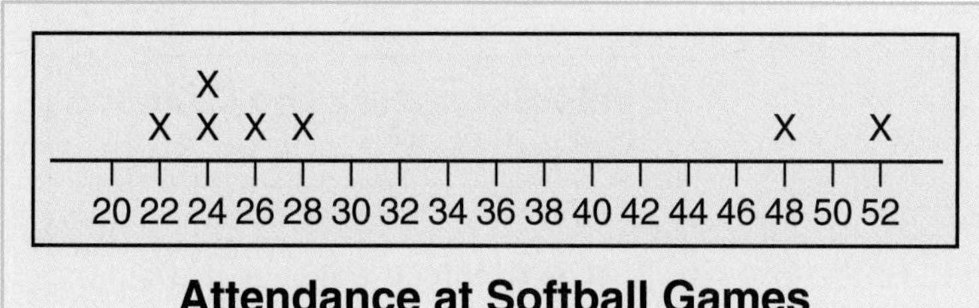

Attendance at Softball Games

5. Find the mean, median, and mode of the data.

6. Use the mean, median, or mode to describe the typical number of people who attended the games. Explain your answer.

7. Suppose the eighth, ninth, and tenth home games get crowds of 52 each. How would that affect your answer in Problem 5. Explain your thinking.

Go On

Data **Use the stem-and-leaf plot for Problems 8–13.**

8. What are the highest and lowest temperatures shown in the plot?

9. What is the range of the data?

10. Find the mean of the data.

11. What was the median high temperature at Ocean Bay from January 1–14?

12. Find the mode of the data.

13. What was the typical high temperature for Ocean Bay during the first two weeks of January? Explain how you used the mean, median, or mode to answer the question.

High Temperatures (°F) at Ocean Bay, January 1–14

Stem	Leaf
7	9
8	0 0 0 3 6 8
9	0 0 1 1 3 3 4

9 | 0 means 90.

14. **Analyze** The page to the right is from a travel brochure for Ocean Bay. Do you think the brochure's description of Ocean Bay's weather is accurate? How do you think the brochure's writer used the data to create the description?

The table shows the goals scored by a field hockey team in thirteen regular-season games. Use the data from the table for Problems 15–18.

15. **Represent** Show the data on a line plot.

16. **Calculator** Find the mean of the data.

17. Find the median, mode and range of the data.

18. **Write About It** Which would you use to best describe the typical number of goals scored by the team—the mean, median, or mode? Explain why you chose this statistic.

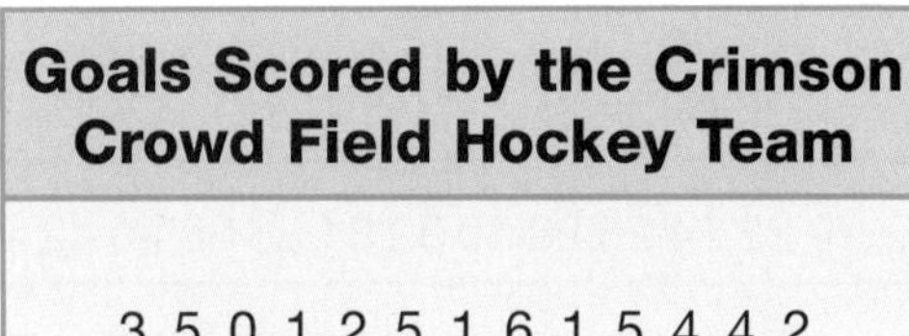

Goals Scored by the Crimson Crowd Field Hockey Team
3 5 0 1 2 5 1 6 1 5 4 4 2

19. **Explain** The team scored the same number of goals in the next two games and brought their mean goals up to 3.4. How many goals did they score in their next two games?

Extra Practice See page 209, Set C.

Quick Check

Check your understanding of Lessons 1–5.

Use the table to complete Problems 1–3.
(Lessons 1–3)

1. Make a tally sheet for the data in the table. Write the frequency for each answer choice.
2. Make a line plot for the data in the table.
3. Find the mean, median, mode, and range.

Number of Years Each Student Has Lived in Town

4	10	4	7	8	8	9	10	9	8
6	8	10	10	9	8	6	7	9	10
5	6	9	9	10	9	7	8	8	9

Use the stem-and-leaf plot for Problems 4 and 5.
(Lessons 4–5)

4. Find the mean, median, and mode of the data.
5. Suppose you want to describe Randi's typical quiz score. Which statistic would be the better one to use, the mean or the median? Explain your answer.

Randi's Quiz Scores

Stem	Leaf
6	1
7	9
8	1 2 2

8 | 1 means 81.

WEEKLY WR READER® eduplace.com/kids/mw/

Social Studies Connection

Slippery Samples

Surveys were conducted at a water park to find which water slide was the most popular. Group 1 surveyed students between the ages of 6 and 10. Group 2 randomly surveyed adults and children at the park. Why are their results different?

To collect data about a large group of people, researchers must choose a **representative sample** of the group. Group 2 chose a representative sample because they randomly interviewed children and adults at the water park.

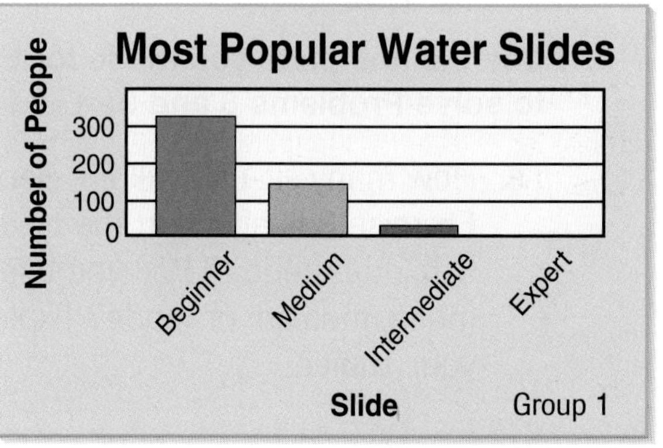

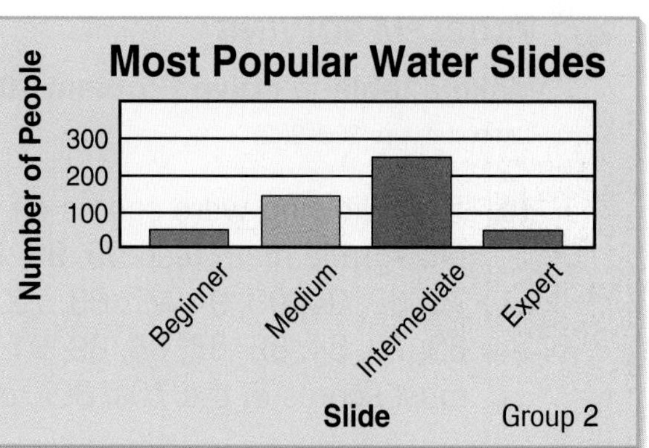

Discuss how you would choose a representative sample to answer each question.

1. Which sport do the students at your school like the most?
2. Which type of music is the most popular in your state?

Chapter Review/Test

VOCABULARY

Vocabulary
cluster
gap
line plot
stem-and-leaf plot
survey

1. In a data display, a large space between data is called a ____.
2. A ____ is a group of data that are close together.

CONCEPTS AND SKILLS

Make a line plot for each set of data. Identify any clusters or gaps. Then find the mean, median, mode, and range. (Lessons 1–2, pp. 192–196)

3. number of sit-ups in 5 minutes: 35, 31, 40, 35, 35, 35, 35, 34, 35, 31
4. number of points scored: 59, 60, 60, 59, 51, 60, 59, 52, 53, 60

Use the stem-and-leaf plot at the right for Problems 5–7. (Lesson 3, pp. 198–199)

5. What were the highest and lowest admission charges?
6. How many admission charges were higher than $25?
7. Find the mean, median, mode, and range of the data.

Admission Charges

Stem	Leaf
5	0
4	5 2 2 2 0
3	9 7 6 0
2	9 8 4 0

Use the line plots you made for Exercises 3 and 4 to solve Problems 8 and 9. (Lesson 5, pp. 204–206)

8. How many sit-ups will the person in Exercise 3 likely do in the next 5-minute period? Will you use the mean, median, or mode? Explain your choice.
9. How many points will the person in Exercise 4 likely score in the next turn? Will you use the mean, median, or mode? Explain your choice.

PROBLEM SOLVING

Make a table to solve Problem 10. (Lesson 4, pp. 200–202)

10. The following were scores on a fifth-grade math test: 99, 98, 89, 87, 75, 69, 94, 93, 94, 97, 83, 73, 74, 84, 83, 73, 84, 85, 87, 88, 89, 91. Were most scores in the 70s, 80s, or 90s?

Show You Understand

How does a line plot make it easier to find the mode and median?

Extra Practice

Set A (Lesson 2, pp. 194–197)

Make a line plot for each set of data. Identify any clusters or gaps. Then find the mean, median, mode, and range.

1. number of CD's owned
   15, 22, 5, 10, 23, 18, 24, 14, 19, 4, 22
2. class attendance
   28, 24, 23, 26, 14, 29, 20, 18, 25, 29, 26, 14
3. test scores
   101, 98, 100, 97, 100, 87, 103, 98, 99, 100

Find the mean, median, and mode of each set of data.

4. 45, 46, 39, 47, 49, 42, 38, 46, 49, 43
5. 68, 59, 67, 66, 54, 67, 68, 70, 63, 66, 61
6. 120, 118, 117, 107, 123, 121, 119, 120, 120, 118

Set B (Lesson 3, pp. 198–199)

Use the stem-and-leaf plot for Problems 1–4.

1. How many amusement parks are represented in the data?
2. How many parks had fewer than 20 rides?
3. What is the greatest number of rides at any amusement park?
4. Find the mean, median, mode, and range of the data.

Kinds of Rides in Amusement Parks

Stem	Leaf
0	9
1	2 4 5 5 6 8 9
2	0 0 0 1 2 4 4 5 5 6 6 7 7 8 8 9
3	0

1 | 2 means 12 rides.

Set C (Lesson 5, pp. 204–209)

Use the data from the line plot for Problems 1–5.

1. How many days had a low temperature below 5°?
2. How long was the winter break?
3. Which low temperatures occurred more than once?
4. Find the mean, median, mode, and range of the data.
5. Use the mean, median, or mode to predict the normal low temperature for Green Bay in February. Explain your answer.

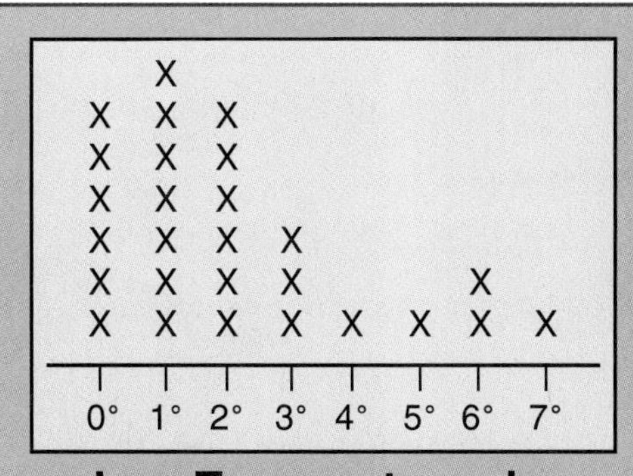

Low Temperatures in Green Bay During February

What a Kick!

The largest international soccer tournament is the World Cup. Thirty-two countries from 6 different continents send their national teams to compete once every four years.

The first World Cup soccer tournament was held in Uruguay in 1930. Over the next 60 years the tournament was played only by men's teams. In 1991, however, the first Women's World Cup was held in China. The U.S. women's team achieved stardom by winning the World Cup in 1999.

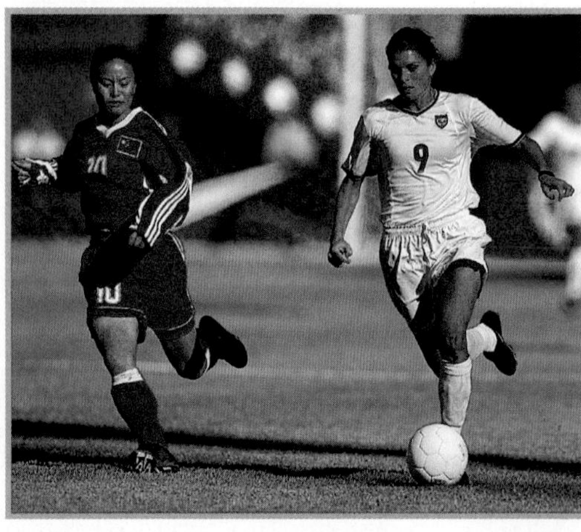

Problem Solving

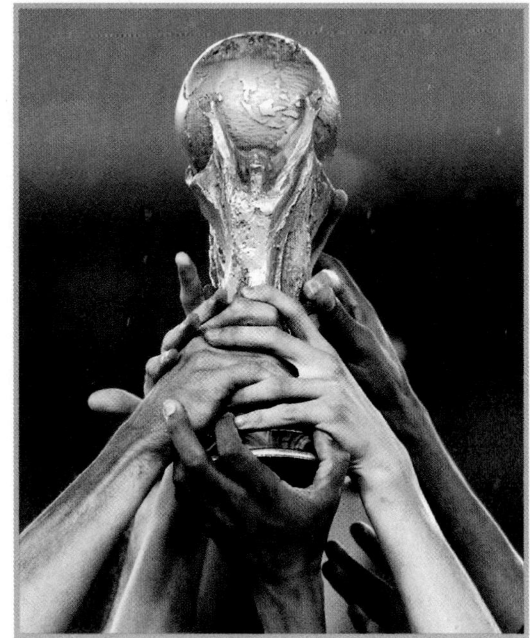

1 The men's World Cup trophy is made of solid gold and a green semi-precious mineral called malachite. The trophy has a mass of 5,000 grams and stands 0.36 meter tall. What is the trophy's mass in kilograms? What is its height in centimeters?

2 Nearly 1,400,000 people attended the 1999 Women's World Cup games. The mean for the number of people attending these games was 40,000. How many games were played?

Use the bar graph for Problems 3–5.

3 If you combined the number of goals scored by the men's and women's World Cup teams for each country, which country would have the most goals?

4 Find the range of the number of goals scored by the men's teams.

5 Find the difference between the median number of goals for the men's and women's teams.

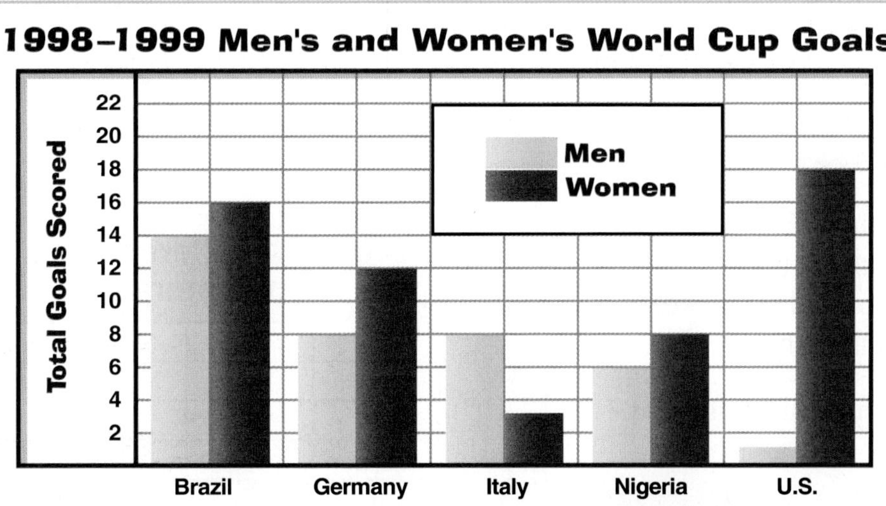

Technology

Visit *Education Place* at **eduplace.com/kids/mw/** to learn more about this topic.

Unit 3 Test

VOCABULARY

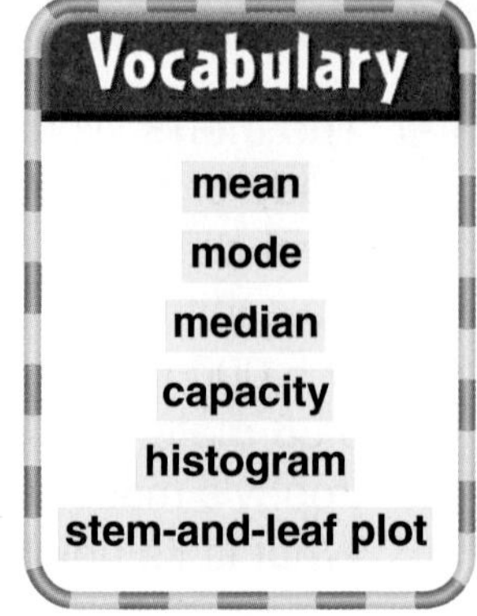

Match the definitions below with the correct vocabulary word.

1. A way to display data in which the size of the bars shows how frequently the data occur in equal intervals.
2. The amount a container can hold.
3. The number found by dividing the sum of a group of addends by the number of addends.
4. A display that uses place value to show frequencies of data.

CONCEPTS AND SKILLS

Measure the line segment according to the directions given below. (Chapter 6)

5. to the nearest $\frac{1}{8}$ inch
6. to the nearest decimeter
7. to the nearest centimeter

Compare. Write >, <, or = . (Chapter 6)

8. 1 g ⬬ 750 mg
9. 1,000 mL ⬬ 1 L
10. 3 qts ⬬ 7 pts

Use the graph to answer Problems 11–12. (Chapter 7)

11. Tyrell collected some data and made the graph at the right. What kind of graph did he make? What does the graph show?
12. What was the temperature at 3 P.M.?

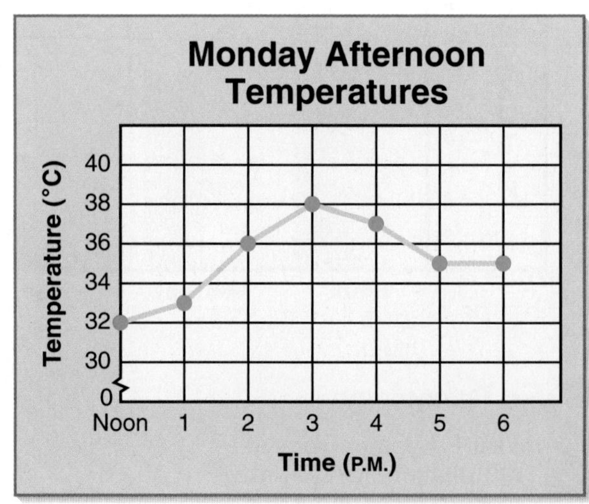

Use the line plot to find the data described below. (Chapter 8)

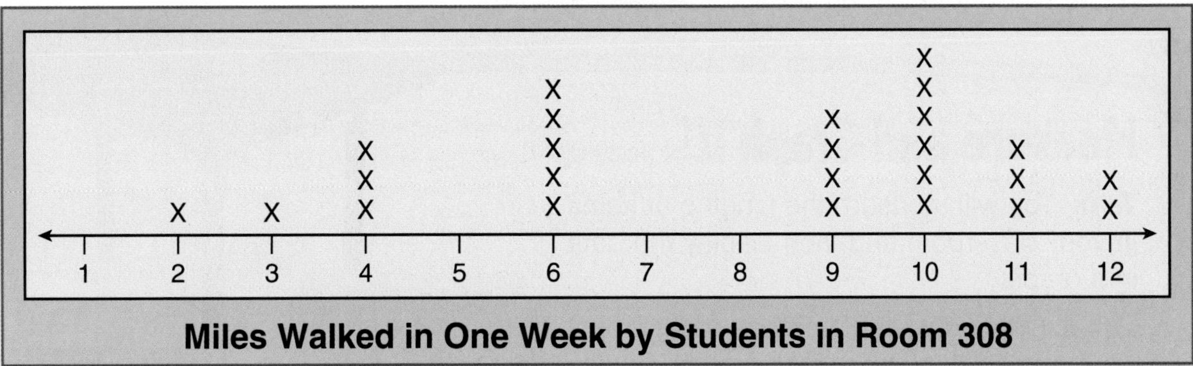

Miles Walked in One Week by Students in Room 308

13. mean **14.** median **15.** mode **16.** range

PROBLEM SOLVING

Use the line graph on page 212 to solve Problems 17–18.

17. Use Data Between which two times did the temperature change the most? not change at all?

18. Use Data Tina says that Tyrell's graph is misleading. Is she correct? Explain your answer.

19. You Decide Suppose you survey 50 people who can respond *yes*, *no*, or *not sure*. Decide whether the data are best displayed in a line graph, a bar graph, or a histogram. Explain your choice.

20. Write About It You are to make a line plot showing the sizes of shoes worn by students in your class. Describe how to make the line plot and how to find the mean, median, and mode.

Decision Making

Extended Response

Task Four students were in a race. The chart at the right shows the results of the race.

Choose the best way to display the data. Consider a bar graph, line graph, pictograph, circle graph, or histogram. Make a graph to display the data. What affected the type of graph you chose? Explain your thinking.

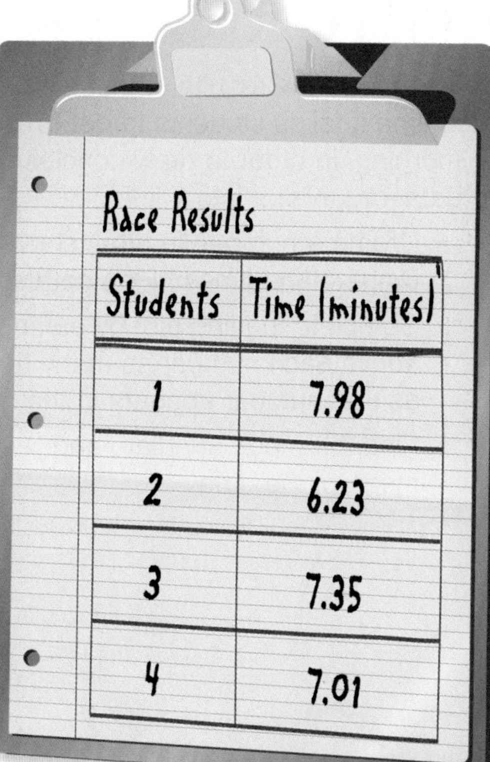
Race Results

Students	Time (minutes)
1	7.98
2	6.23
3	7.35
4	7.01

Performance Assessment

TASK 1

Measure and Graph It! (Chapters 6–7)

Task You will measure the lengths of items in your classroom and then display the data in a graph.

a. Choose several items to measure, such as pencils, erasers, notebooks, or bulletin boards. They must be of different lengths, and you must have at least four items.

b. Decide on the unit of measure you will use, such as centimeters, inches, or feet.

c. Measure the length of each item to the nearest whole unit and record each on paper.

d. Make a bar graph to compare lengths.

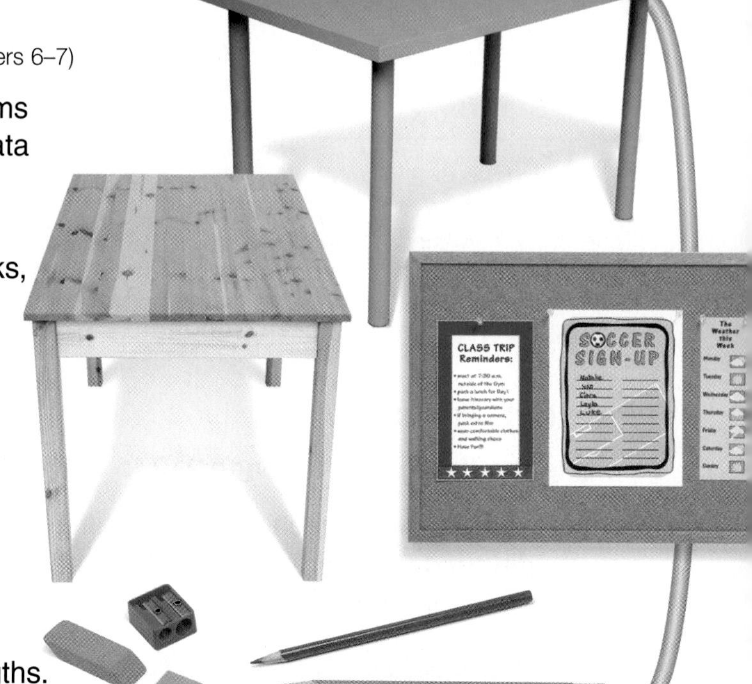

TASK 2

Getting to School (Chapter 8)

The list shows the results of a survey about how much time it takes students to get to school in the morning. In order to draw conclusions about the data, organize it into a line plot.

a. Create a number line that shows the range of the times in the data set.

b. Complete the line plot by putting an X above each number as many times as that number appears in the list.

c. Find the mode, median, and mean of the data.

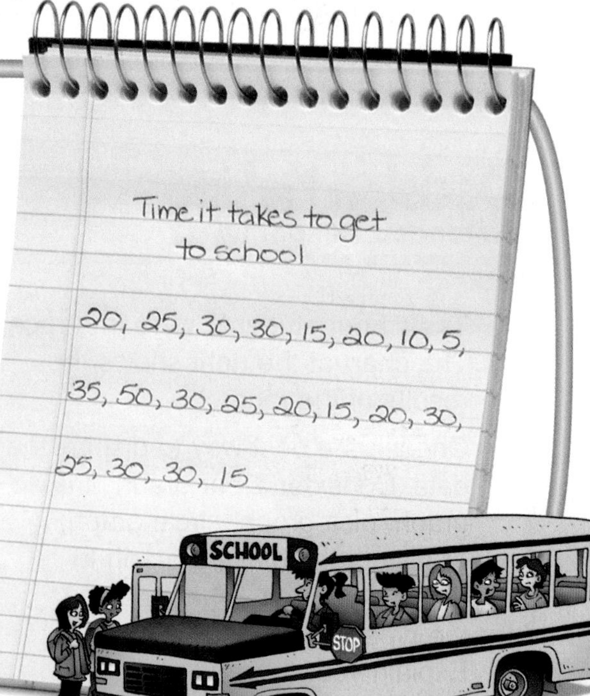

Time it takes to get
to school
20, 25, 30, 30, 15, 20, 10, 5,
35, 50, 30, 25, 20, 15, 20, 30,
25, 30, 30, 15
SCHOOL
STOP

Self Check

- Did I answer the questions for each task?
- Did I check all my work?

Enrichment: Graphs in Everyday Life

Whether you are watching TV, reading a newspaper or magazine, or doing your homework, you will find graphs to read and interpret. Why? Because a picture is worth a thousand words.

The graph at the right supports the headline that says that from 2001 to 2002, gas prices dropped.

You can read specific data from this graph. For example, notice how, even before the decrease in prices, the $1.380 cost of gas per gallon in Texas was less than the other states' 2002 prices.

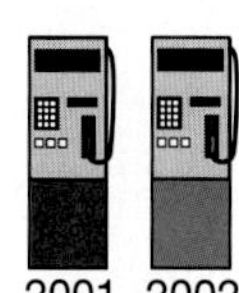

Gas Prices Drop!

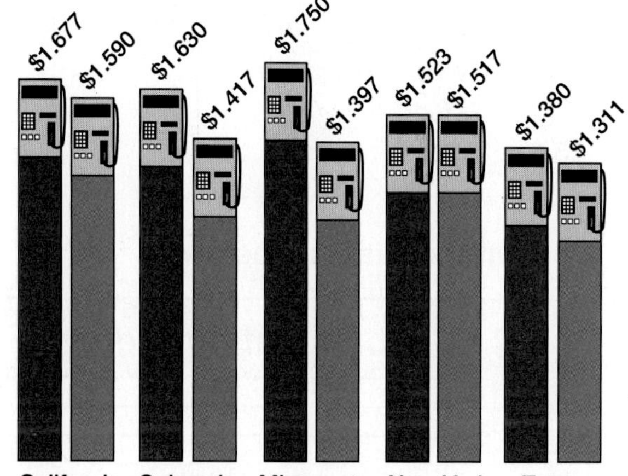

Try These!

Use the graph at the right for Problems 1–4.

1. In 1970, the Clean Air Act required the reduction of lead in gasoline. About how many fewer tons of lead were emitted in 1980 than in 1970?

2. During which five-year period did lead emissions drop the most between 1970 and 1990?

3. In 1990, lead emissions were 1,197,000 tons. By 1999, the amount of lead emitted was 661,000 tons less than 1990. How many tons of lead were put into the air in 1999?

4. Explain why it would be hard to show data for years after 1990 on the graph.

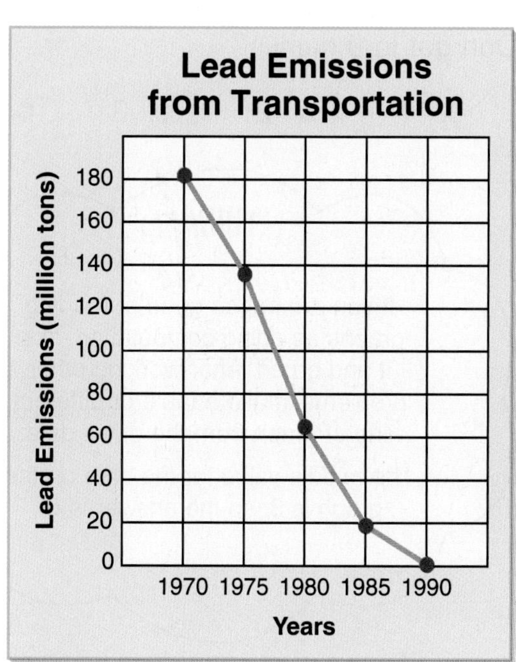

Cumulative Test Prep Practice

Solve Problems 1–10.

Test-Taking Tip

If you get stuck on a problem, skip it and go on. Then go back to it, if you have time, and try again to work the problem.

Look at the example below.

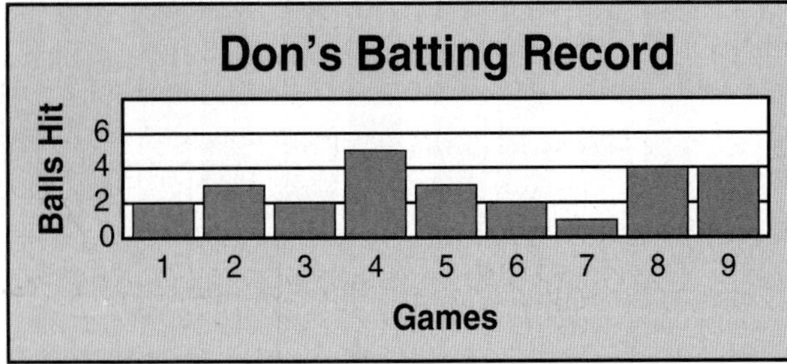

What is the median of the number of hits Don got in 9 games?

A 1 **B** 2 **C** 3 **D** 4

THINK

If you are not as good at reading graphs as doing computation, skip it and go on. After working other problems, make a table or different kind of graph from the given data.

The middle value for the data on the graph is 3, so the answer is **C**.

Multiple Choice

1. Which numeral is in the thousandths place?

40,321.978

A 0 **C** 7

B 4 **D** 8

(Chapter 1, Lesson 5)

2. Which distance traveled by fifth-grade students last summer is the greatest?

F 7×10^3 miles **H** 5 hundred miles

G 8.432 miles **J** 900 + 50 miles

(Chapter 1, Lesson 4)

3. Marty has kept track of how he has spent his money during the past year. He wants to display the data on a graph. Which type of graph is the best choice?

A circle graph **C** double line graph

B double bar graph **D** frequency table

(Chapter 7, Lesson 1)

4. Sally wants to make a graph that shows how much her grades have improved over the past few months. Which kind of graph is her best choice?

F circle graph **H** line graph

G bar graph **J** histogram

(Chapter 7, Lesson 3)

 For more Test-Taking Tips, see pages xxii–xxv.

Free Response

5. Exactly 5,092 fans came to the school's first football game. There are 4,887 fans at the second game. How many fewer fans came to the second game than the first game?

(Chapter 2, Lesson 3)

6. Otis and Ellen mixed batter for a pancake breakfast. If they mixed 20 batches and each batch makes 12 pancakes, how many pancakes can they make in all?

(Chapter 3, Lesson 6)

7. Sarah has $135.75, and she wants to buy 5 outfits that are about the same price for school. Find out how much she can spend on each outfit to the nearest dollar.

(Chapter 4, Lesson 1)

8. Bala and her sisters used 3,000 beads to make 150 necklaces. Each necklace has the same number of beads. How many beads are in each necklace?

(Chapter 5, Lesson 1)

9. A mini-bus can carry a maximum weight of one ton. If the average weight of each of the 27 students going on a field trip is 105 pounds. The bus driver weighs 150 pounds. What is the greatest number of students who can ride the bus? (Hint: 1 ton = 2,000 pounds)

(Chapter 6, Lesson 3)

Extended Response

Ring Toss Results

Stem	Leaf
0	9 9
1	0 0 1 3 4 4 5 8
2	2 3 3 7
3	0

Key: 3 | 0 means 30.

10. The stem-and-leaf plot above shows how many times 15 ring toss players were able to ring a bottle in 50 tries.

A Explain the meaning of the numbers in the two columns.

B What is the greatest cluster you find in these data? What gaps, if any, do you find?

C Explain why a stem-and-leaf plot is a good way to organize this kind of data.

(Chapter 8, Lesson 3)

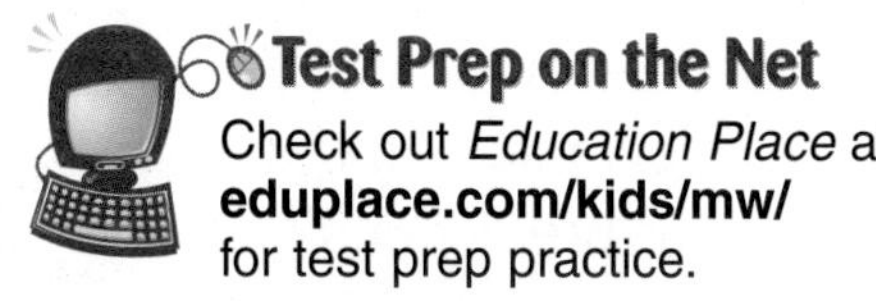
Test Prep on the Net
Check out *Education Place* at **eduplace.com/kids/mw/** for test prep practice.

What's It All Mean?

How much does a pair of sneakers cost? Use the Internet to find the prices of 8 different pairs of sneakers. Then use Easy Sheet to graph your data and find the mean and median.

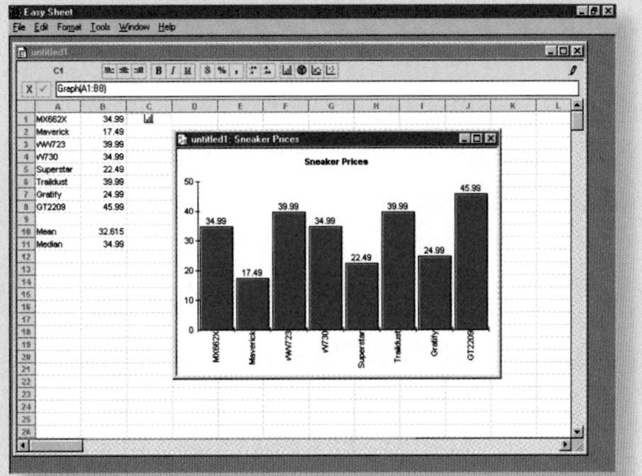

- Enter the shoe names in Column A.
- Enter the shoe prices in Column B. Do not include dollar signs.
- Click on cell A1 and drag to cell B8 to highlight the data.
- Click . Double click on the graph.
- Click on the tab marked **Labels**. Enter a title for your graph. Click the box next to **Label Data**. Click **OK**.
- Type "Mean" in cell A10 and "Median" in A11.
- Click **Window**. Choose **Function List**.
- Click on cell B10. Double click **Avg(range)**. Click on cell B1 and drag to cell B8. Press **Enter**. Click on cell B11. Double click **Median(range).** Click on cell B1 and drag to cell B8. Press **Enter**.

Solve.

1. What are the mean and median of the sneaker prices?
2. How can you use the graph to find the mode and range of the data?
3. **Challenge** Add 1 more sneaker price to your graph. Predict how your mean and median will change. Follow the steps above to find the new mean and median, this time dragging from cell B1 to cell B9. How do your new mean and median compare to your predictions?

Vocabulary Wrap-Up for Unit 3

WEEKLY WR READER
Activity Almanac
See page 680 for the activity for this unit.

Look back at the big ideas and vocabulary in this unit.

Big Ideas

Measurements can be added and subtracted. First, write the measurements to the same unit of measure.

Double bar graphs and double line graphs compare two sets of data. Predictions can be made from data displays.

e Glossary

Key Vocabulary

measurement

data

prediction

Math Conversations

Use your new vocabulary to discuss these big ideas.

1. Explain the relationship between decimeters and centimeters.
2. Explain how you can change a measurement of 7 yards into feet.
3. Explain how to read a double bar graph.
4. Explain how to make a line plot.
5. **Write About It** Search for graphs in books, newspapers, and magazines. List the kinds of graphs you find and tell what you can learn from the way the data are displayed.

Let's compare how many inches we have grown in the last year.
That's 2 sets of data. We should use a double line graph to compare.

Building Vocabulary

Reviewing Vocabulary

Here are some math vocabulary words that you should know.

fraction	a number that describes part of a whole or part of a group
numerator	the number above the bar in a fraction that tells how many equal parts of the whole have been counted
denominator	the number below the bar in a fraction that tells how many equal parts are in the whole
decimal	a number with one or more digits to the right of a decimal point
decimal point	a symbol used to separate the ones and tenths places in a decimal

Reading Words and Symbols

Sometimes the same number can be expressed in more than one way. Here is an example:

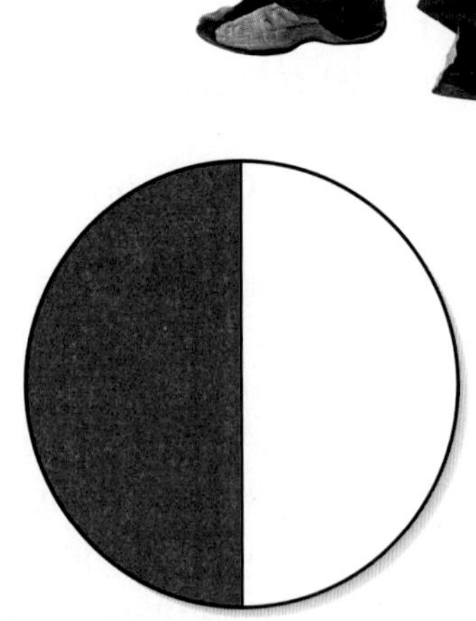

Write in words: one half

Write as a fraction: $\frac{1}{2}$

Write as a decimal: 0.5

Write as a division expression: $1 \div 2$

Use words and symbols to answer the questions.

1. In the fraction $\frac{4}{8}$, which number is the denominator? What does the number mean?
2. How do you express the decimal 0.5 in words?

Reading Test Questions

Use the diagram at the right for Exercises 3–5. Choose the correct answer for each.

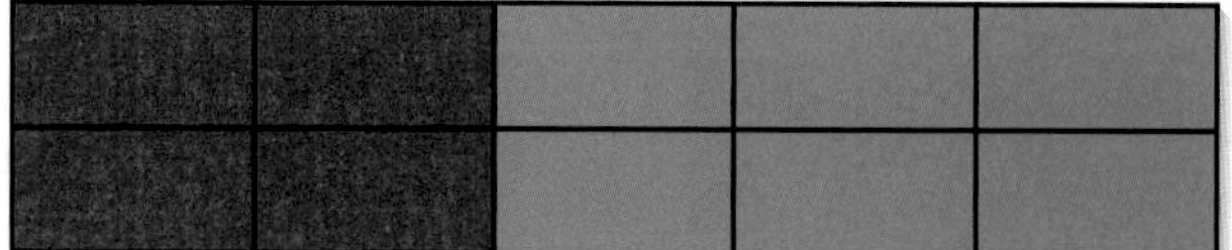

3. Which of these statements is unreasonable?

a. Part of the rectangle is red.

b. Most of the rectangle is red.

c. Some of the rectangle is red.

d. Some of the rectangle is blue.

Unreasonable means not reasonable or not possible.

4. Which fraction represents the red part of the rectangle?

a. $\frac{1}{5}$ **c.** $\frac{2}{4}$

b. $\frac{1}{4}$ **d.** $\frac{2}{5}$

Represents means stands for, or shows, or names.

5. Which decimal represents the blue part of the model?

a. 0.3 **c.** 0.5

b. 0.4 **d.** 0.6

A **model** is something that represents, or shows, an idea.

Learning Vocabulary

Watch for these new words in this unit. Write their definitions in your journal.

prime number

composite number

prime factorization

greatest common factor (GCF)

least common multiple (LCM)

least common denominator (LCD)

Vocabulary
e • **Glossary**
e • **WordGame**

Literature Connection

Read "Fruitomatic" on pages 642–643. Then work with a partner to answer the questions about the story.

CHAPTER 9

Number Theory and Fraction Concepts

INVESTIGATION

Use Data

This T-Rex skeleton is named Sue. It is the most complete skeleton of a T-Rex ever found. The African elephant is the largest living land mammal today. It is about 21 feet less in length than Sue was. About how many yards long is an African elephant?

A T-Rex Named Sue

Length	about 41 feet
Weight of skull	about 1 ton
Full weight	about 7 tons
Number of teeth	58

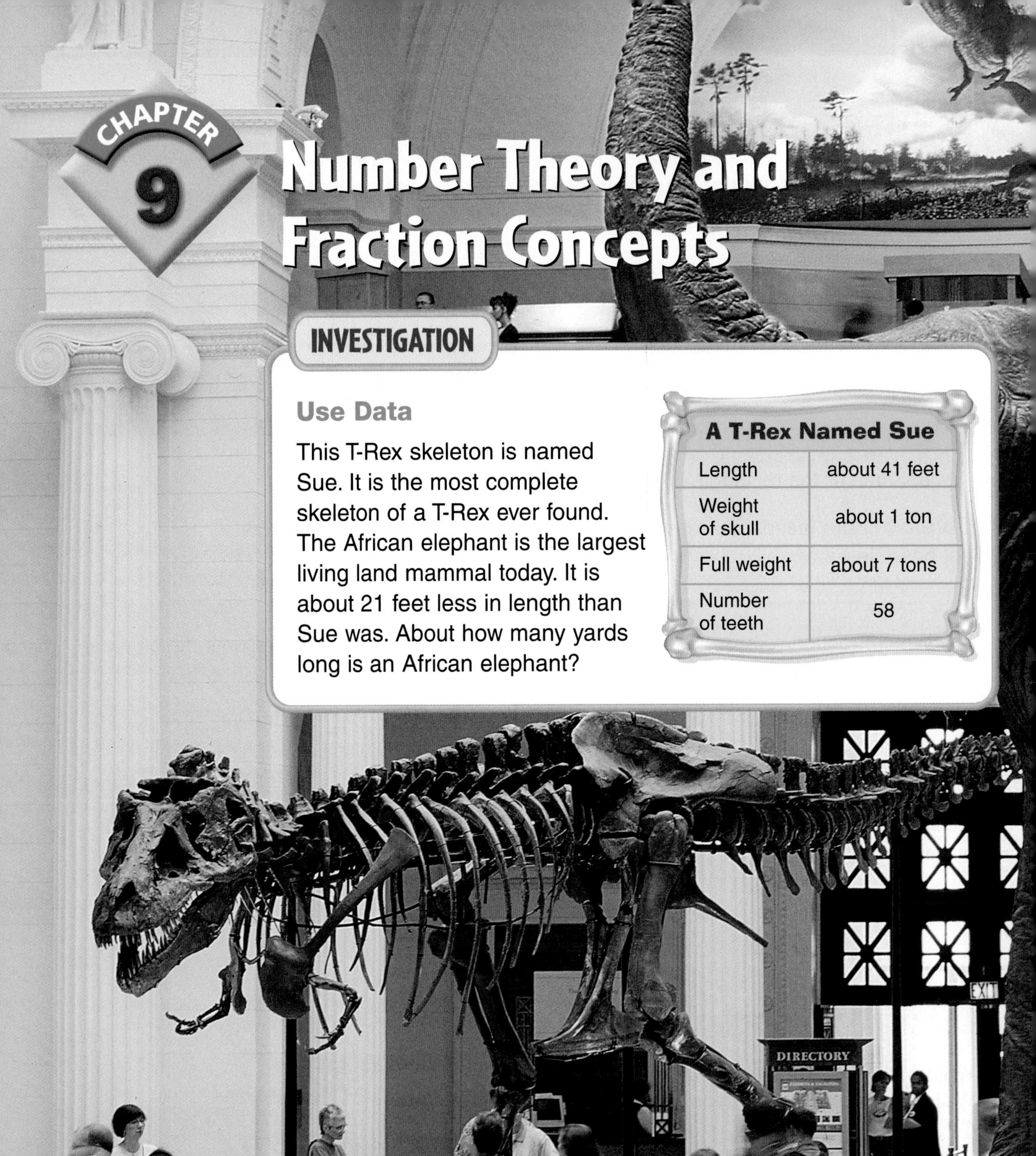

Chapter Pretest

Use this page to review and remember what you need to know for this chapter.

VOCABULARY

Choose the best word to complete each sentence.

1. A number that is a factor of two or more numbers is a(n) ____ of those numbers.
2. A number that is a multiple of two or more numbers is a(n) ____ of those numbers.
3. A(n) ____ is a fraction that has a numerator that is greater than or equal to its denominator.

Vocabulary

- common factor
- common multiple
- improper fraction
- mixed number

CONCEPTS AND SKILLS

Write the factors of each number. Then list the first three multiples of each.

4. 2 **5.** 4 **6.** 10 **7.** 20

8. 12 **9.** 21 **10.** 11 **11.** 30

Draw a picture to represent each fraction or mixed number.

12. $\frac{1}{4}$ **13.** $\frac{3}{7}$ **14.** $\frac{5}{5}$ **15.** $1\frac{1}{2}$ **16.** $2\frac{1}{4}$

Order the decimals from least to greatest.

17. 0.4, 0.20, 0.02 **18.** 1.54, 5.51, 5.45 **19.** 1.0, 0.100, 0.01

Write About It

20. Do pictures A and B below show the same fraction? Explain.

A. 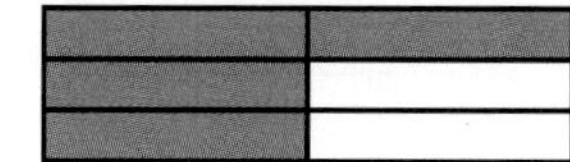

B.     

Test Prep on the Net

Visit *Education Place* at **eduplace.com/kids/mw/** for more review.

Prime and Composite Numbers

Objective Identify prime and composite numbers.

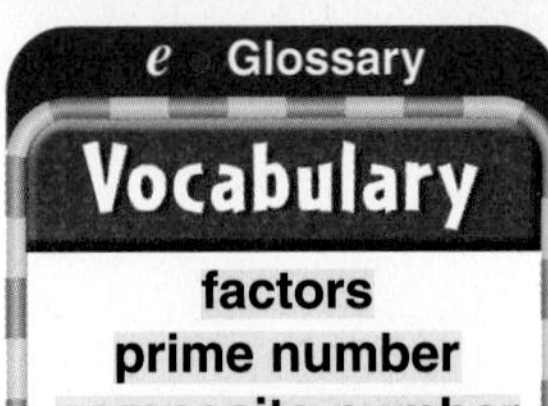

Materials
grid paper

Work Together

Henry is arranging 8 photographs for a museum exhibit. He has been told that each row must contain the same number of photographs. Henry sketched two possible arrangements by drawing squares on grid paper.

How many ways can he arrange the photographs in equal rows?

Work with a partner to solve the problem.

STEP 1 Copy the table below.

Number of Photographs	Arrangements Possible	Factors
1	1 × 1	1
2	1 × 2, 2 × 1	1, 2
3	■	■
4	■	■
5	■	■
6	1 × 6, 6 × 1, 2 × 3, 3 × 2	1, 2, 3, 6
7	■	■
8	■	■

When a number is written as a product of counting numbers, those counting numbers are called **factors**.

STEP 2 Draw squares on grid paper to help you complete the table.

Solution: Henry can arrange the photographs 4 different ways: 1 row of 8, 8 rows of 1, 2 rows of 4, or 4 rows of 2.

▶A **prime number** is a counting number greater than 1 with exactly two different factors—1 and the number itself.

Which of the numbers from 1 to 8 are prime numbers?

▶A **composite number** is a counting number that has more than two different factors.

Which of the numbers from 1 to 8 are composite numbers?

On Your Own

Write all the factors of each number. Then identify the number as prime or composite.

1. 17	**2.** 18	**3.** 20	**4.** 23	**5.** 24
6. 26	**7.** 27	**8.** 28	**9.** 29	**10.** 30

Solve.

11. At a science museum, visitors were handed numbered tickets. Tickets with prime numbers won free posters. Which tickets at the right would win posters?

13 75 15 2
52 37 19 7

12. Look back at page 224. How many different ways could Henry have arranged 20 photographs? Use factors to explain your answer.

13. Melina has 45 photographs. She wants to arrange them in equal rows. In how many ways can she arrange them?

14. The science museum has 80 stones available for display in equal rows. How many different arrangements of these stones can be made if each row must contain at least 8 stones?

15. The director of the art museum has between 45 and 55 paintings to display. She wishes to display an equal number on each of two walls. How many paintings could the museum display? Give as many answers as possible.

Talk About It • Write About It

16. Use the definitions of *prime number* and *composite number* above to explain why the number 1 is neither prime nor composite.

17. There is only one prime number that is not an odd number. Which number is it? Tell how you know.

Lesson 2

Prime Factorization

Objective Write the prime factorization of a number.

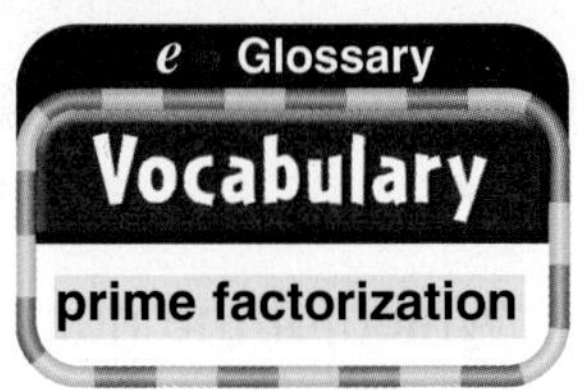

Learn About It

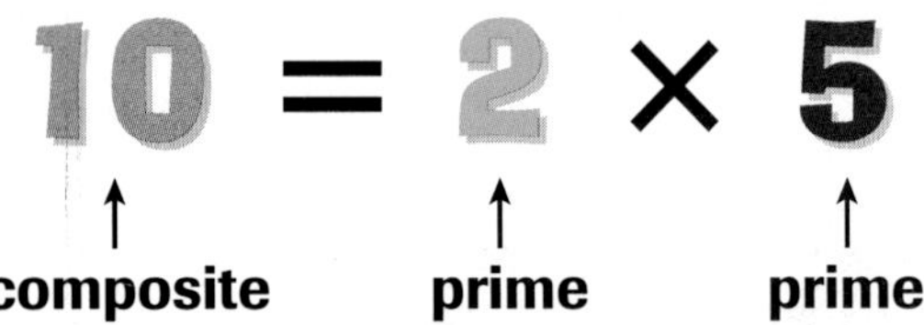

Any composite number can be written as a product of prime numbers. An expression written as a product of prime factors is called the **prime factorization** of the number.

You can use a factor tree to find the prime factorization of a number.

Write the prime factorization of 45.

STEP 1 Write 45 as the product of two numbers.

45

5 × 9

STEP 2 Write each composite factor as a product of two numbers until only prime numbers are obtained.

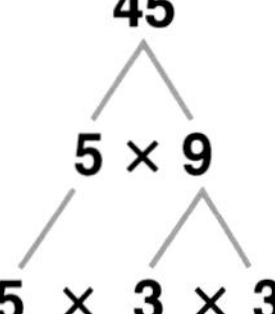

STEP 3 Write the prime factors from the bottom row of the factor tree in order. Use exponents to write the prime factorization.

$45 = 3 \times 3 \times 5$

$= 3^2 \times 5$

Solution: The prime factorization of 45 is $3^2 \times 5$.

Guided Practice

Complete each factor tree. Then write the prime factorization. Use exponents if possible.

1. 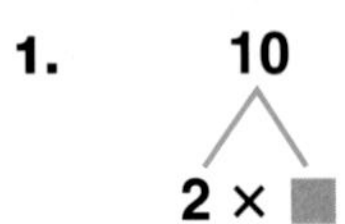

2. 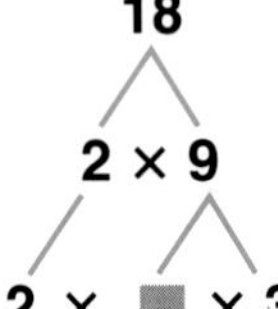

3. 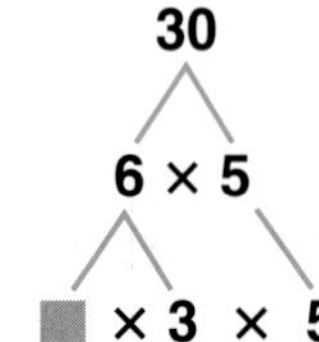

Ask Yourself

- What basic multiplication fact do I use?
- Can I use exponents to write the prime factorization?

TEST TIPS

Look back at Exercise 2. If you used 3 and 6 for the first factor pair, would the prime factorization be the same? Why or why not?

Practice and Problem Solving

Complete the factor tree. Then write the prime factorization.

4. 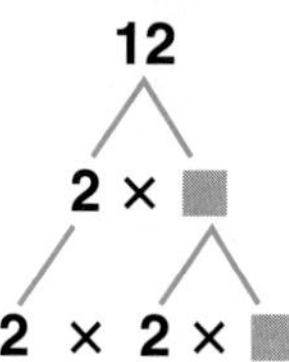

5. 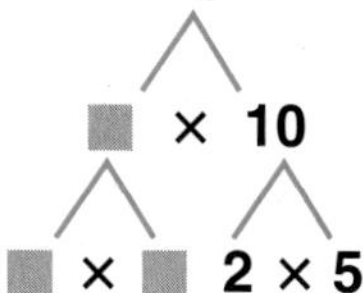

6. 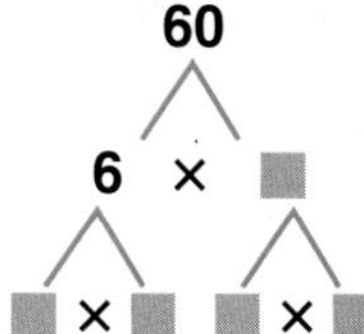

Write the prime factorization of each number. Use exponents if possible. If the number is prime, write prime.

7. 2 **8.** 3 **9.** 4 **10.** 5 **11.** 6 **12.** 7

13. 8 **14.** 9 **15.** 10 **16.** 11 **17.** 12 **18.** 13

19. 14 **20.** 15 **21.** 16 **22.** 17 **23.** 18 **24.** 19

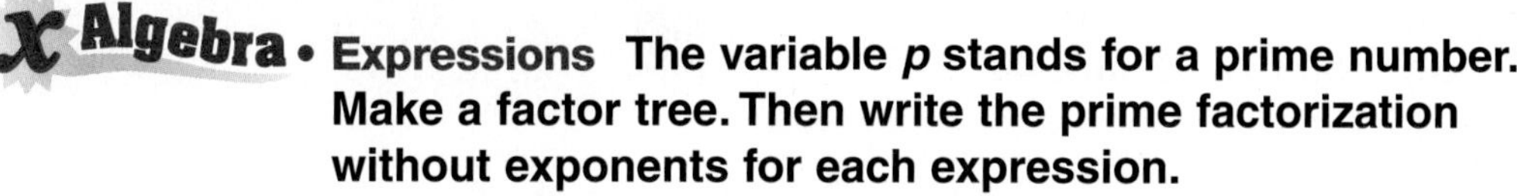

Algebra • Expressions **The variable p stands for a prime number. Make a factor tree. Then write the prime factorization without exponents for each expression.**

25. $6p$ **26.** $50p$ **27.** p^2 **28.** $2p^2$ **29.** $13p^2$ **30.** $12p^3$

Solve.

31. You are told that the prime factorization of a number is $2 \times 3^2 \times 5 \times 7 \times 13$. What is the number?

32. **Explain** For any composite number, why does the last row of its factor tree contain only prime numbers?

33. The price of a painting was $12,000 in 1980, $36,000 in 1990, and $108,000 in 2000. If the pattern continues, what is the price likely to be in 2010?

34. Each of two composite numbers has 2, 3, and 5 in its prime factorization, but one of the numbers is twice as large as the other. What might the numbers be?

35. **Write About It** What does the factor tree of a prime number look like? Use an example to explain.

36. Takala designs a box for paint cans. The box is 2 cans high, 6 cans long, and 3 cans wide. How many cans fit in the box?

Daily Review Test Prep

Write each number in expanded form with exponents. (Ch. 1, Lesson 2)

37. 36,519 **38.** 602,708 **39.** 562,412

40. **Free Response** Write the prime factorization of 140.

Show how you got your answer.

Extra Practice See page 253, Set A.

Lesson 3

Greatest Common Factor

Objective Find common factors and the greatest common factor of two numbers.

e Glossary

Vocabulary

common factor
greatest common factor (GCF)
greatest common divisor (GCD)

Learn About It

If a number is a factor of two or more counting numbers, it is called a **common factor** of those numbers. The **greatest common factor (GCF)** of two or more numbers is the common factor that is greater than any other common factor.

You are to arrange 32 Egyptian statues and 40 Chinese statues in groups. Each group must have the same number of statues, and all be from one country. What is the greatest number of statues you can put in each group?

Since $32 = 2 \times 16$ and $40 = 2 \times 20$, I could put 2 statues in each group. Can the groups be larger?

Find the greatest common factor of 32 and 40.

Different Ways to Find the GCF of 32 and 40

Think about factor pairs.
$32 = 1 \times 32$
$32 = 2 \times 16$
$32 = 4 \times 8$

Way 1 You can make a list.

STEP 1 List all the factors of each number.
Factors of 32: 1, 2, 4, 8, 16, 32
Factors of 40: 1, 2, 4, 5, 8, 10, 20, 40

STEP 2 Identify common factors.
The common factors are 1, 2, 4, and 8.

STEP 3 Compare to find the greatest common factor.
The greatest common factor of 32 and 40 is 8.

Way 2 You can use prime factorization.

STEP 1 Make factor trees for 32 and 40.

STEP 2 Identify all the common prime factors.

STEP 3 The product of the common prime factors is the GCF. The GCF is 8.

32
4×8
$2 \times 2 \times 4 \times 2$
$2 \times 2 \times 2 \times 2 \times 2$

40
2×20
$2 \times 2 \times 10$
$2 \times 2 \times 2 \times 5$

$32 = \boxed{2} \times \boxed{2} \times \boxed{2} \times 2 \times 2$
$40 = \boxed{2} \times \boxed{2} \times \boxed{2} \times 5$

The GCF is $2 \times 2 \times 2 = 2^3 = 8$.

Solution: You can put 8 statues at most in each group.

Since each common factor of two or more numbers is a divisor of each number, the GCF often is called the **greatest common divisor (GCD)**.

Other Examples

A. GCF of Greater Numbers

Find the GCF of 160 and 200.

Write each prime factorization.

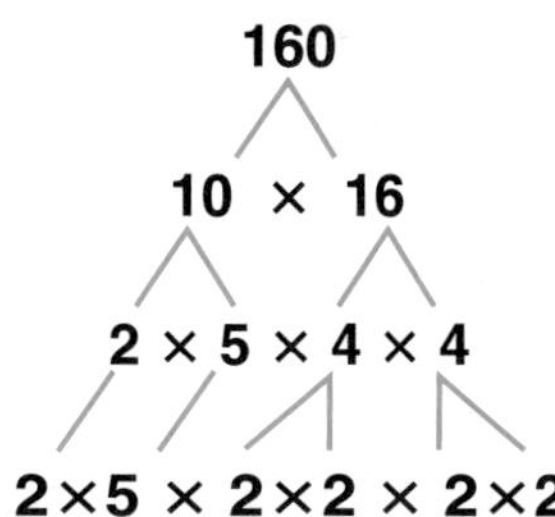

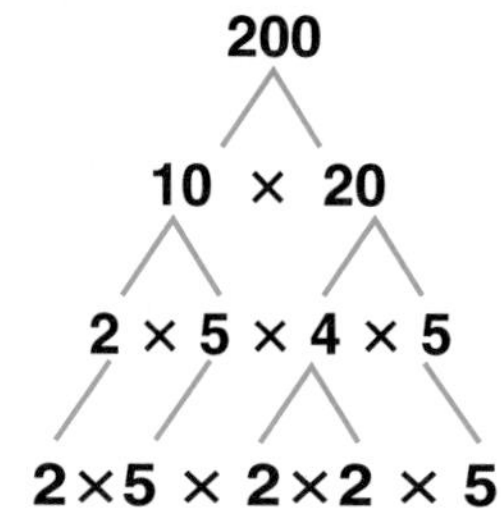

Ring common factors

160 = 2 × 2 × 2 × 2 × 2 × 5

200 = 2 × 2 × 2 × 5 × 5

The GCF of 160 and 200 is $2^3 \times 5$, or 40.

B. GCF is 1

Find the GCF of 21 and 26.

List the factors of each number.

Factors of 21: 1, 3, 7, 21
Factors of 26: 1, 2, 13, 26

1 is the only common factor.

The GCF is 1.

Guided Practice

Ask Yourself

- What are the factors of each number?
- Did I find all the common factors?

List the factors of each number. Then find the greatest common factor (GCF) of the numbers.

1. 9, 27 **2.** 15, 22 **3.** 20, 28

Write the prime factorization of each number using exponents. Then find the greatest common factor (GCF) of the numbers.

4. 10, 45 **5.** 45, 100 **6.** 16, 100

Explain Your Thinking ▶ Why is the prime factorization a good way to find the GCF of two large numbers?

Practice and Problem Solving

List the factors of each number. Then find the GCF of the numbers.

7. 14, 22 **8.** 30, 55 **9.** 10, 12 **10.** 9, 25 **11.** 15, 17

12. 20, 38 **13.** 26, 34 **14.** 13, 19 **15.** 12, 24 **16.** 36, 45

Write the prime factorization of each number using exponents. Then find the GCF of the numbers.

17. 10, 24 **18.** 6, 15 **19.** 9, 28 **20.** 10, 55 **21.** 12, 42

22. 75, 120 **23.** 20, 125 **24.** 35, 105 **25.** 10, 240 **26.** 30, 150

Algebra • **Variables** **Give three possible values for *n*.**

	Numbers	GCF
27.	9, *n*	3
28.	16, *n*	4
29.	20, *n*	5

	Numbers	GCF
30.	36, *n*	12
31.	50, *n*	10
32.	72, *n*	18

Solve.

33. A display shows five paintings. "Red River" is immediately to the right of "Blue Bayou." "Green Grass" is not first. "Pink Plateaus" is in the middle. "Orange Outback" is at the far right. List the paintings in order from left to right.

34. An artist made copies of a sculpture. She had 45 pieces of turquoise and 60 cat's eye marbles. Each sculpture had the same number of turquoise pieces and marbles. What is the greatest number of sculptures the artist could have made?

35. **Measurement** Computers in the research room of the history museum are 30 inches wide, 30 inches apart, and, at either end of a row, 30 inches from the wall. How many computers can fit across a room that is 25 feet wide?

36. The museum is arranging 42 plates from the 1800s and 64 plates from the 1900s in equal groups. All plates in each group must be from the same century. What is the greatest number of plates they can put in each group?

37. **Analyze** The GCF of an odd number and an even number is 17. The greater number is 51. Find the other number.

38. **Write About It** If two numbers are prime, is their GCF always 1? Support your answer with examples.

Daily Review **Test Prep**

Divide. (Ch. 5, Lesson 5)

39. 6,229 ÷ 27 **40.** 54,907 ÷ 69

41. 39,524 ÷ 82 **42.** 62,424 ÷ 47

43. Find the GCF of 24 and 36.

A 6 **C** 12

B 8 **D** 18

Extra Practice See page 253, Set B.

The Sieve of Eratosthenes

In the third century B.C., Eratosthenes, a Greek mathematician, developed a method for finding prime numbers.

Follow these steps to find the prime numbers from 1 to 100.

- Copy the table at the right.
- Cross out 1, since 1 is not a prime.
- Circle 2 because 2 is a prime. Cross out all the multiples of 2.
- Go to the next number that is not crossed out. Circle it. Then cross out its multiples.
- Repeat the previous step until all the numbers are either circled or crossed out.

Explain how you know that the circled numbers are prime numbers.

Sieve of Eratosthenes

1	2	3	4	5	6	7	8	9	10
11	12	13	14	15	16	17	18	19	20
21	22	23	24	25	26	27	28	29	30
31	32	33	34	35	36	37	38	39	40
41	42	43	44	45	46	47	48	49	50
51	52	53	54	55	56	57	58	59	60
61	62	63	64	65	66	67	68	69	70
71	72	73	74	75	76	77	78	79	80
81	82	83	84	85	86	87	88	89	90
91	92	93	94	95	96	97	98	99	100

Twin Primes

Prime numbers with a difference of 2 are called twin primes. The numbers 3 and 5 are twin primes. List all pairs of twin primes between 1 and 99.

Brain Teaser

A three-digit number greater than 500 has five consecutive numbers among its factors. What could the three-digit number be?

Technology

Visit *Education Place* at **eduplace.com/kids/mw/** to try more brain teasers.

Least Common Multiple

Objective Find common multiples and the least common multiple of two or more numbers.

Learn About It

A **multiple** of a number is the product of the number and any counting number. If a number is a multiple of two or more numbers, it is called a **common multiple** of the numbers.

The **least common multiple (LCM)** of two or more numbers is the common multiple that is less than all other common multiples.

In a museum, the sculpture garden has a new show every 9 months. The sculpture gallery has a new show every 12 months. Suppose the garden and the gallery have new shows that begin today. How long will it be until they have new shows that begin on the same day again?

Find the LCM of 9 and 12.

When do new shows begin in the sculpture garden?
List some multiples of 9. — 9: 9, 18, 27, 36, 45, 54, 63, 72

When do new shows begin in the sculpture gallery?
List some multiples of 12. — 12: 12, 24, 36, 48, 60, 72

When do new shows begin in both sculpture areas?
List the common multiples. — 36, 72

How long will it be until both sculpture areas have new shows on the same day again? — The LCM is 36.

Solution: The sculpture garden and the sculpture gallery will have new shows begin on the same day in 36 months.

Other Examples

A. LCM is One of the Numbers Itself

Find the LCM of 2 and 6.

Multiples of 2: 2, 4, **6,** 8, 10, **12,** 14,...

Multiples of 6: **6, 12,** 18, 24, 30...

The LCM of 2 and 6 is 6.

B. LCM of Greater Numbers

Find the LCM of 10 and 25.

Multiples of 10: 10, 20, 30, 40, **50,**...

Multiples of 25: 25, **50,** 75, **100,**...

The LCM of 10 and 25 is 50.

You can use prime factorization to find the LCM.

Find the LCM of 45 and 55.

STEP 1 Use factor trees to find the prime factorizations of the two numbers.

45 55

STEP 2 List all the prime factors of the two numbers. Be sure to include repeated factors.

45: 3, 3, 5

common factor

55: 5, 11

The number 5 is a common factor of 45 and 55.

STEP 3 Determine the LCM. Find the product of all the factors. *Use each common factor only once.*

The LCM of 45 and 55 is $3 \times 3 \times 5 \times 11$, or 495.

Solution: The LCM of 45 and 55 is 495.

Other Examples

A. No Common Prime Factors

Find the LCM of 6 and 49.

Prime factors of 6: 2, 3

Prime factors of 49: 7, 7

$\text{LCM} = 2 \times 3 \times 7 \times 7 = 294$

The LCM of 6 and 49 is 294.

B. LCM of Greater Numbers

Find the LCM of 84 and 120.

$84 = 2 \times 2 \times 3 \times 7$

$120 = 2 \times 2 \times 2 \times 3 \times 5$

$\text{LCM} = 2 \times 2 \times 2 \times 3 \times 5 \times 7 = 840$

The LCM of 84 and 120 is 840.

Guided Practice

Ask Yourself

- Did I list enough multiples of both numbers?
- Is my answer a multiple of both numbers?

List multiples to find the LCM.

1. 5, 20 **2.** 18, 24 **3.** 12, 30 **4.** 21, 28

Use prime factorization to find the LCM.

5. 20, 25 **6.** 17, 51 **7.** 100, 288 **8.** 30, 45

TEST TIPS **Explain Your Thinking** How can you use division to check if a number is a common multiple of two numbers?

Go On

Practice and Problem Solving

Write the first five multiples of each number.

9. 8 **10.** 14 **11.** 7 **12.** 25 **13.** 15

14. 12 **15.** 11 **16.** 30 **17.** 18 **18.** 24

Write the prime factorization of each number.

19. 9 **20.** 6 **21.** 4 **22.** 8 **23.** 10

24. 15 **25.** 20 **26.** 12 **27.** 25 **28.** 16

Find the LCM of the numbers in each pair.

29. 5, 9 **30.** 4, 10 **31.** 2, 11 **32.** 3, 15 **33.** 10, 12

34. 15, 20 **35.** 16, 32 **36.** 12, 18 **37.** 18, 27 **38.** 7, 13

39. 16, 18 **40.** 24, 72 **41.** 36, 48 **42.** 16, 80 **43.** 40, 50

Solve.

44. The museum has tours every 75 minutes. A video about mobiles begins every 45 minutes. The tour and the video both start at 10:00 A.M. When will they start at the same time again?

45. A sculpture has a gong that strikes every 6 minutes, a whistle that blows every 8 minutes, and a bell that rings every 12 minutes. How often will you hear all three sounds at the same time?

Use the following information to solve Problems 46–48.

A museum is building a brick wall on one side of an exhibit. The wall is made of 8-inch and 10-inch bricks. Whenever the ends of the bricks align, a vertical decorative divider is placed in the wall.

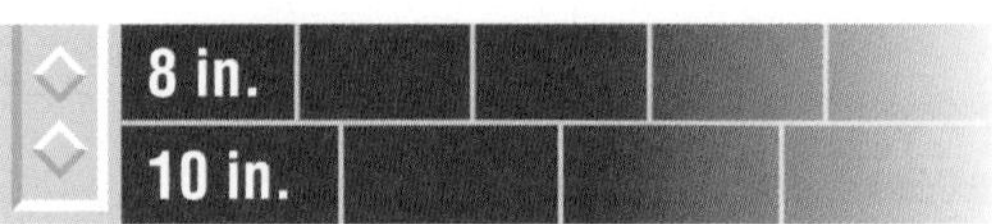

46. There is a decorative divider used at the beginning of the wall. How far from that first divider will the next divider be placed?

47. The brick part of the wall is 10 feet long. There is a decorative divider at the beginning and at the end of the wall. How many decorative dividers will be used in all?

48. **What If?** Suppose 8-inch, 10-inch, and 12-inch bricks are used as shown at the right. Then how far from that first divider will the next divider be?

Extra Practice See page 253, Set C.

Daily Review | Test Prep 

Write each number in standard form.
(Ch. 1, Lesson 2)

49. $(5 \times 10^4) + (2 \times 10^3) + (8 \times 10^1)$

50. $(7 \times 10^5) + (4 \times 10^2) + (9 \times 10^0)$

51. $(6 \times 10^4) + (8 \times 10^3) + (5 \times 10^2)$

52. $(4 \times 10^4) + (3 \times 10^3) + (5 \times 10^1)$

53. Free Response Films about three artists are shown each day. The films all begin at 10:00 A.M. The film on Maya Lin is 45 minutes, the one on Frida Kahlo is 60 minutes, and the one on Grandma Moses is 30 minutes. When will the films begin again at the same time?

Math Challenge

Riddle Me This

What is the easiest way to make a bandstand?

Copy the table at the right. Find the least common multiple for each pair of numbers. Then use the key to decode the puzzle. Read down the last column to find the answer to the riddle.

Decoding Key:

LCM	Letter
8	R
10	I
12	Y
15	K
16	W
18	T
20	E

LCM	Letter
22	D
24	A
26	S
28	X
30	H
40	C
48	M

Numbers	LCM	Letter
6, 9	18	T
12, 8	■	■
3, 5	■	■
4, 10	■	■
3, 18	■	■
2, 15	■	■
5, 4	■	■
10, 8	■	■
6, 10	■	■
24, 4	■	■
5, 2	■	■
8, 4	■	■
13, 2	■	■
6, 8	■	■
16, 4	■	■
8, 24	■	■
6, 4	■	■

Lesson 5

Fractions and Mixed Numbers

Objective Write fractions and mixed numbers.

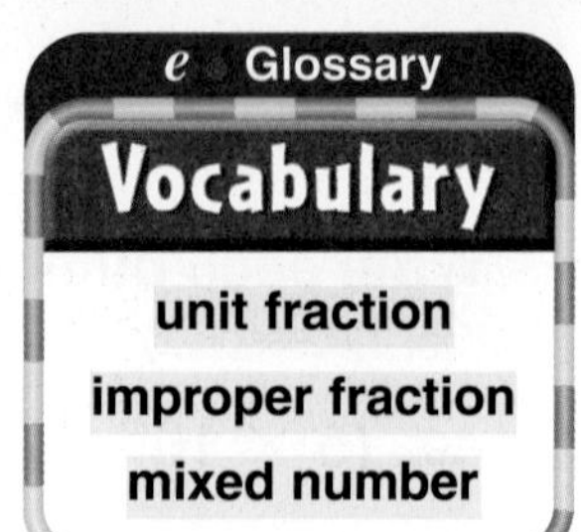

Learn About It

Some museums and other historic buildings have beautiful stained glass windows.

A fraction can represent part of a set.

$\frac{1}{3}$ of the glass panels are blue.

A fraction can represent part of a whole.

$\frac{3}{4}$ of the center panel is orange.

A unit fraction has a numerator of 1.

$\frac{1}{3}$ is a unit fraction. $\frac{3}{4}$ is not a unit fraction.

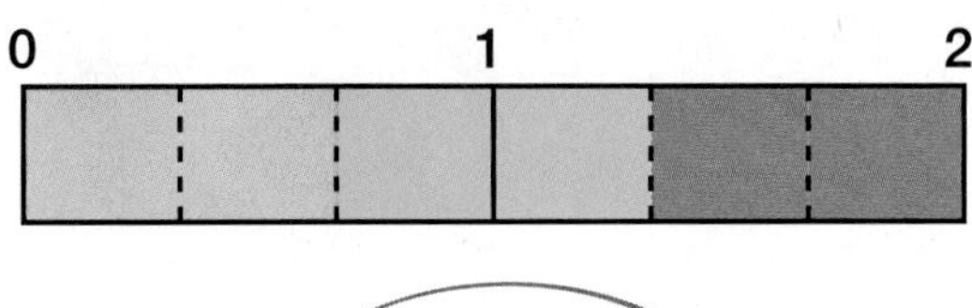

Any fraction can be thought of as a division problem. For example, when 2 units are separated into 3 equal parts, each is $\frac{2}{3}$ of 1 unit.

$\frac{2}{3}$ can be written as $2 \div 3$ or $3\overline{)2}$

You can represent fractions on a number line.

If intervals of length 1 on the number line are separated into 3 equal pieces, the length of any one of the pieces represents $\frac{1}{3}$.

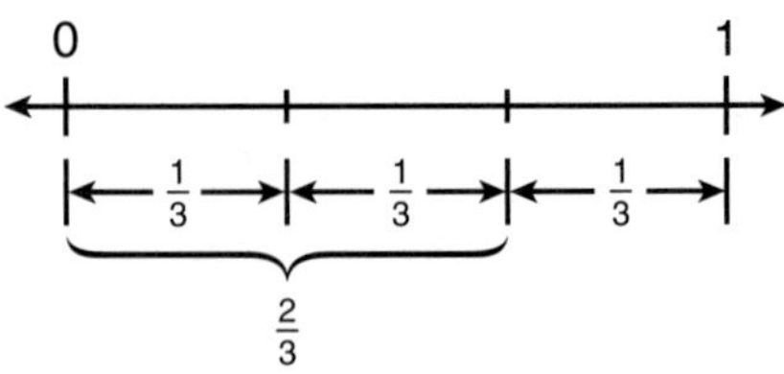

A fraction is written $\frac{a}{b}$ where a and b are whole numbers and $b \neq 0$. The fraction $\frac{2}{3}$ means 2 unit fractions of $\frac{1}{3}$.

Fractions can be used to label many points on a number line.

This number line is labeled with $\frac{0}{3}, \frac{1}{3}, \frac{2}{3}, \ldots$.

The number line shows that $\frac{0}{3} = 0$, $\frac{3}{3} = 1$, $\frac{6}{3} = 2$, and $\frac{9}{3} = 3$.

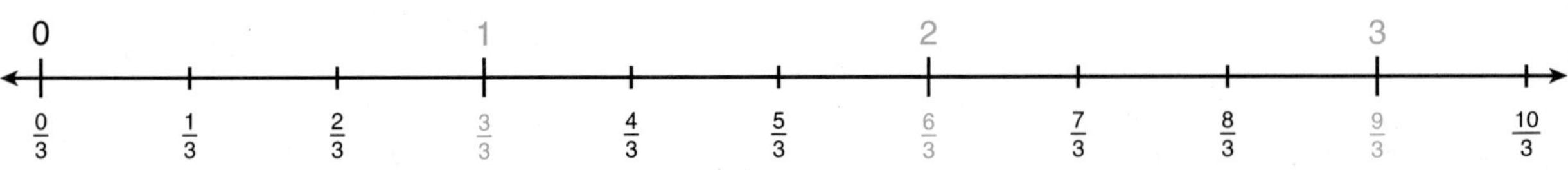

An **improper fraction** has a numerator that is greater than or equal to its denominator. Numbers like $\frac{3}{3}$ and $\frac{4}{3}$ are improper fractions.

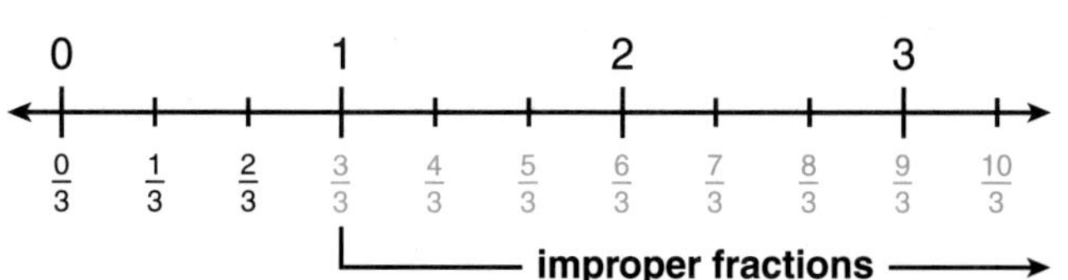

Improper fractions can be written as whole numbers or **mixed numbers**. A mixed number is the sum of a whole number and a fraction.

Here's how to change from one to another.

To change an improper fraction to a mixed number, you can divide.

The fraction bar stands for "divided by." So $\frac{9}{4}$ means "9 divided by 4."

$$\begin{array}{r} 2 \\ 4\overline{)9} \\ -8 \\ \hline 1 \end{array}$$

2 ← number of wholes

1 ← number of fourths

So $\frac{9}{4}$ is equal to $2\frac{1}{4}$.

To change a mixed number to an improper fraction, you can multiply and add.

$2\frac{1}{4} = \frac{9}{4}$ ← $(4 \times 2) + 1$; ← denominator stays the same

The shortcut shows $2\frac{1}{4}$ means $2 + \frac{1}{4} = \frac{8}{4} + \frac{1}{4} = \frac{9}{4}$. So $2\frac{1}{4} = \frac{9}{4}$.

Guided Practice

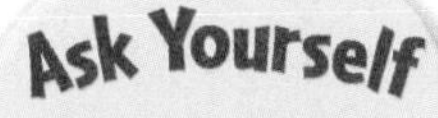

Ask Yourself

- How can I use division to find or check my answers?

1. Study the number line below. Write each missing fraction. Then draw a picture to represent each missing fraction.

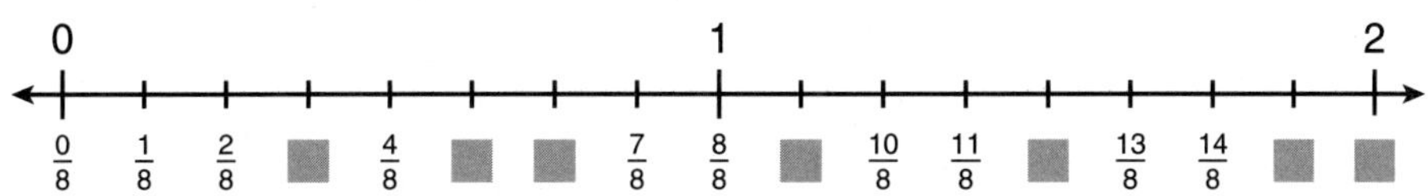

Write each improper fraction as a mixed number or a whole number.

2. $\frac{7}{2}$ 3. $\frac{3}{2}$ 4. $\frac{8}{2}$ 5. $\frac{5}{2}$ 6. $\frac{10}{2}$

Write each mixed number as an improper fraction.

7. $4\frac{1}{2}$ 8. $7\frac{1}{2}$ 9. $3\frac{1}{8}$ 10. $6\frac{5}{7}$ 11. $4\frac{2}{3}$

TEST TIPS **Explain Your Thinking** ▶ How can you tell whether a fraction can be written as a mixed number or a whole number?

Go On

Practice and Problem Solving

12. Study the number line below. Write each missing fraction. Then draw different models to represent each fraction you wrote.

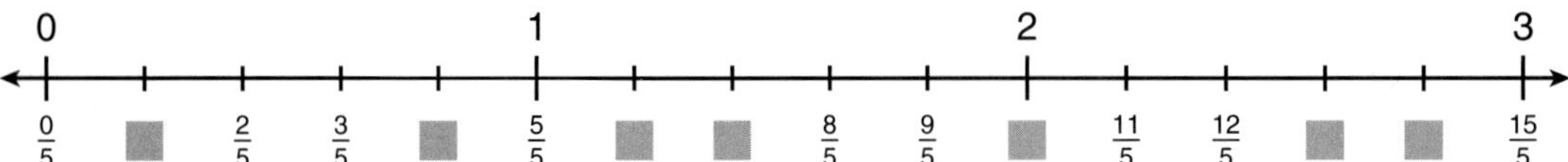

Write each improper fraction as a mixed number or a whole number.

13. $\frac{10}{5}$ **14.** $\frac{8}{5}$ **15.** $\frac{15}{7}$ **16.** $\frac{9}{4}$ **17.** $\frac{12}{5}$

Write each mixed number as an improper fraction.

18. $2\frac{3}{4}$ **19.** $2\frac{3}{5}$ **20.** $5\frac{2}{3}$ **21.** $4\frac{2}{7}$ **22.** $6\frac{1}{6}$

Algebra • Expressions If *m* and *n* are whole numbers not equal to zero, explain how *m* and *n* are related in each case.

23. $\frac{m}{n}$ is a fraction between 0 and 1.

24. $\frac{m}{n}$ is a fraction between 1 and 2.

25. $\frac{m}{n}$ is equal to a whole number.

Solve.

26. A totem pole is made of 8 equal sections. Three sections have been painted. Write a fraction to show the part of the totem pole that is not painted.

27. The total value of paintings by Pablo Picasso sold at auctions is over 1.3 billion dollars. Is this number an exact figure or an estimate? How do you know?

28. **Analyze** What division expression is equivalent to the fraction $\frac{37}{4}$? How can you use this expression to write a mixed number for $\frac{37}{4}$?

29. **Represent** Show each mixed number on the same number line. Then write each as an improper fraction.

a. $2\frac{2}{3}$ **b.** $4\frac{1}{3}$ **c.** $1\frac{2}{3}$

30. **Measurement** Each year Roberto makes 12 quarts of strawberry jam to give equally to his 3 friends. How many cups of jam does each friend get?

31. **Create and Solve** Write a problem that uses mixed numbers and improper fractions. Solve your problem. Then give it to a partner to solve.

Extra Practice See page 253, Set D.

Quick Check

Check your understanding of Lessons 1–5.

Write all the factors of each number. Then identify the number as prime or composite. (Lesson 1)

1. 19 **2.** 48 **3.** 41

Write the prime factorization of each number. Then find the greatest common factor (GCF) of the numbers. (Lessons 2–3)

4. 20, 32 **5.** 21, 24 **6.** 36, 54

Find the LCM of the numbers. (Lesson 4)

7. 18, 30 **8.** 12, 16 **9.** 15, 60

Use the number line for Exercise 10. (Lesson 5)

10. Write each missing fraction.

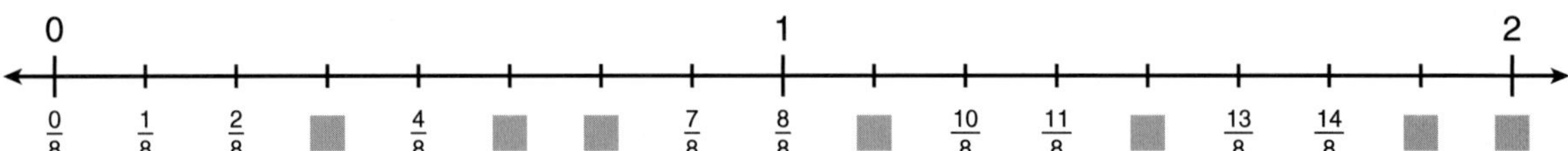

Visual Thinking

Math Reasoning

Are Halves Always the Same?

The pictures show three pizzas.

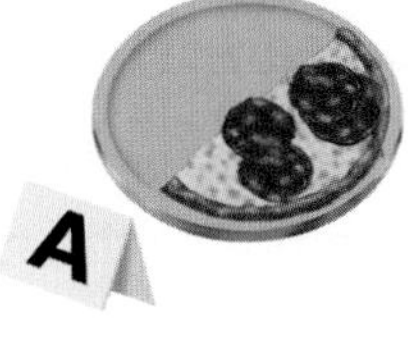

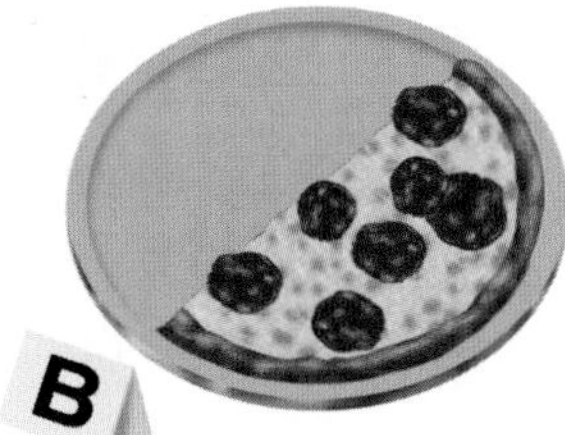

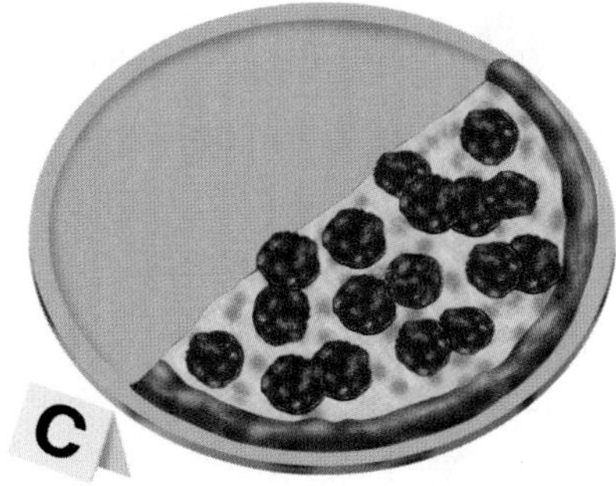

1. What fraction of each pizza is left?

2. Compare the amount of pizza that is left in each pan. Is $\frac{1}{2}$ of pizza A the same amount as $\frac{1}{2}$ of pizza C? Explain.

3. How does the value of a fraction depend on the size of the region or set that it describes?

Lesson 6

Equivalent Fractions and Simplest Form

Objective Find equivalent fractions and write fractions in simplest form.

e Glossary

Vocabulary

equivalent fractions

simplest form

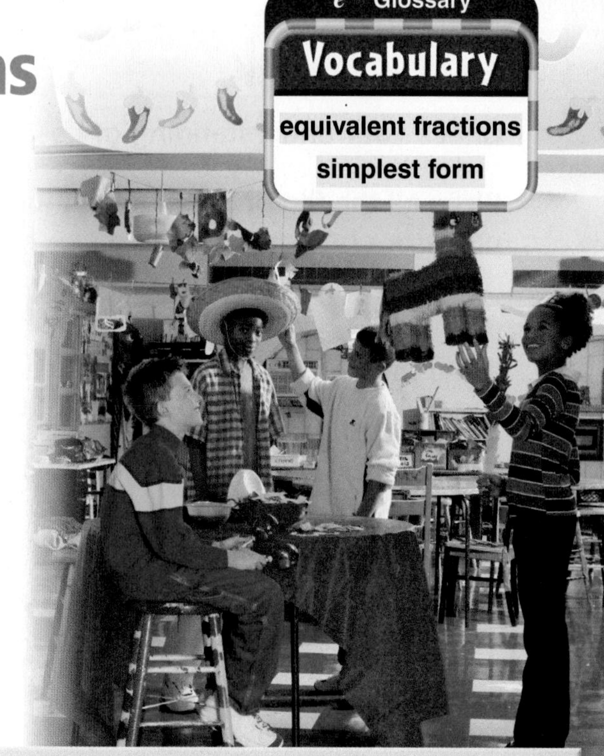

Learn About It

Equivalent fractions name the same number.

Four sixths of the 12 art club members helped decorate for a Cinco de Mayo party. Did two thirds of the members help? How many members helped?

Find two equivalent fractions for $\frac{2}{3}$.

Different Ways to Find Equivalent Fractions

Way 1 You can use number lines.

$\frac{4}{6}$, $\frac{8}{12}$, and $\frac{2}{3}$ are equivalent fractions.

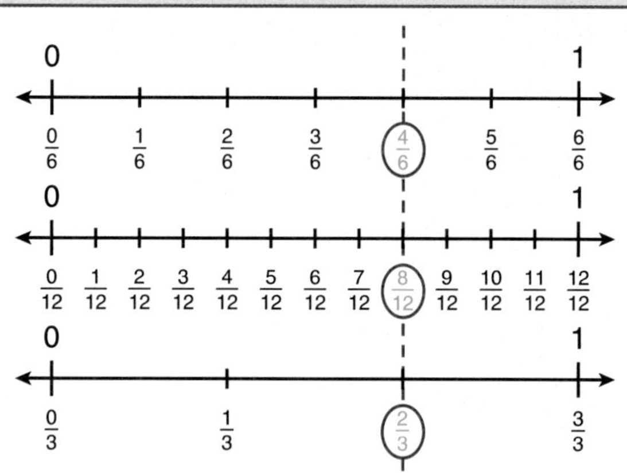

Way 2 You can multiply.

Find the number to multiply the denominator by to obtain the new denominator. Multiply by that number.

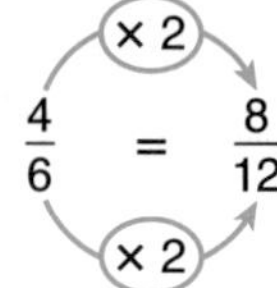

$\frac{4}{6}$ and $\frac{8}{12}$ are equivalent fractions.

Way 3 You can divide.

Find the number to divide the denominator by to obtain the new denominator. Divide by that number.

$$\frac{4 \div 2}{6 \div 2} = \frac{2}{3}$$

$\frac{4}{6}$ and $\frac{2}{3}$ are equivalent fractions.

Solution: Two thirds of the art club (eight members) volunteered to decorate the cafeteria.

▶ A fraction is in **simplest form** when the GCF of its numerator and denominator is 1.

Different Ways to Find Simplest Form

Way 1 **You can divide the numerator and the denominator by the GCF of the numbers.**

$12 = 2 \times 2 \times 3$
$18 = 2 \times 3 \times 3$

The GCF of 12 and 18 is 2×3, or 6.

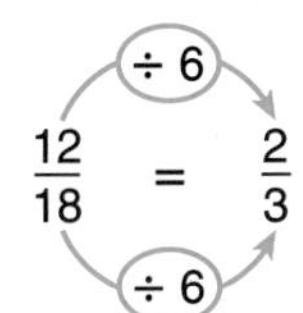

$\frac{12}{18} = \frac{2}{3}$ (÷ 6)

Way 2 **You can cancel common factors.**

Write the prime factorization of the numerator and the denominator. Then cancel common factors.

$\frac{12}{18} = \frac{\not{2} \times 2 \times \not{3}}{\not{2} \times \not{3} \times 3} = \frac{2}{3}$

Think $\frac{2}{2} = 1$, $\frac{3}{3} = 1$

Guided Practice

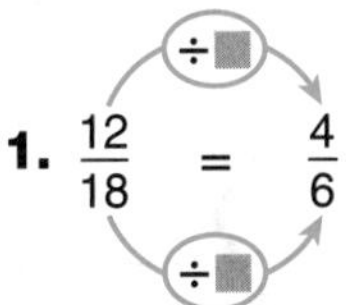

Complete.

1. $\frac{12}{18} = \frac{4}{6}$ (÷■)
2. $\frac{21}{12} = \frac{■}{4}$ (÷■)
3. $\frac{4}{9} = \frac{■}{54}$

Ask Yourself

- Did I multiply or divide the numerator and denominator by the same number?

TEST TIPS **Explain Your Thinking** ▶ In Exercise 3, how did you decide whether to multiply or divide to find the missing numerator?

Practice and Problem Solving

Complete.

4. $\frac{1}{3} = \frac{■}{9}$
5. $\frac{15}{35} = \frac{■}{7}$
6. $\frac{3}{10} = \frac{9}{■}$
7. $1\frac{3}{12} = \frac{■}{4}$
8. $4 = \frac{■}{6}$

Simplify each fraction.

9. $\frac{5}{10}$
10. $\frac{39}{15}$
11. $\frac{15}{18}$
12. $\frac{26}{18}$
13. $\frac{28}{42}$
14. $\frac{22}{30}$

15. **Write About It** How many equivalent fractions can be written for any given fraction? Explain.

16. The art club has 6 girls. If $\frac{3}{5}$ of the members are girls, how many members does the club have? How many are boys?

Daily Review | Test Prep

Find the mean, median, mode, and range.
(Ch. 8, Lesson 2)

17. 24, 28, 24, 32
18. 8, 20, 6, 20, 101

19. Simplify $\frac{30}{42}$.

A $\frac{5}{8}$ B $\frac{5}{7}$ C $\frac{3}{4}$ D $\frac{6}{7}$

Extra Practice See page 253, Set E.

Problem-Solving Strategy

Use Logical Reasoning

Objective Use logical reasoning to solve a problem.

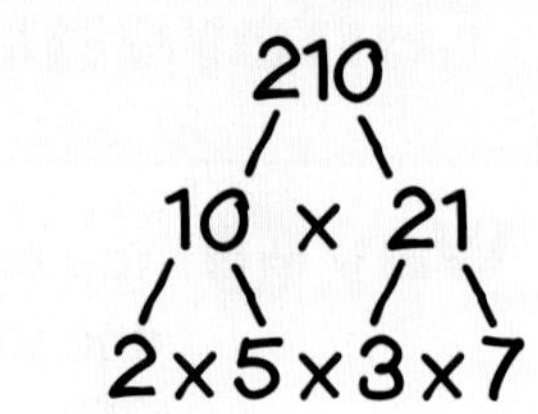

Problem The LCM of two numbers, x and y, is 210. Their GCF is 3. The numbers differ by 9. What are the numbers?

UNDERSTAND

This is what you know:

- The LCM is 210.
- The GCF is 3.
- The numbers differ by 9.

Remember The GCF must be a factor of both numbers. The LCM must contain all the prime factors of both numbers.

PLAN

You can use logic to analyze the information you have.

SOLVE

Make a Venn diagram to represent the factors of the two numbers, x and y.

- Write the common factor 3 in both circles.

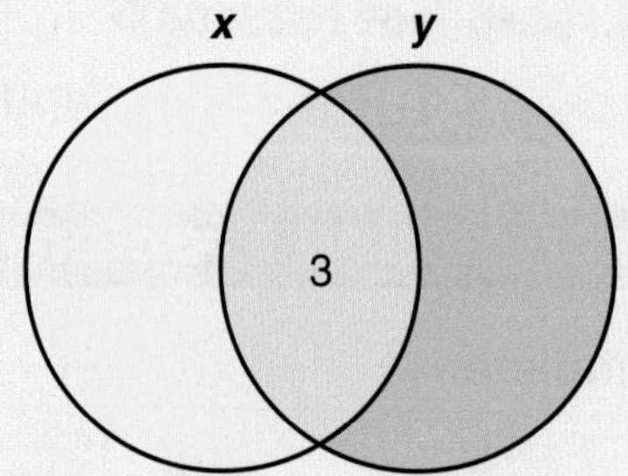

- Factor the LCM to find all the factors of both numbers, x and y.

$$210 = 2 \times 3 \times 5 \times 7$$

If 3 is the GCF, then 2, 5, and 7 cannot be common factors.

- Try different arrangements of factors.

Look for the pair of numbers with a difference of 9.

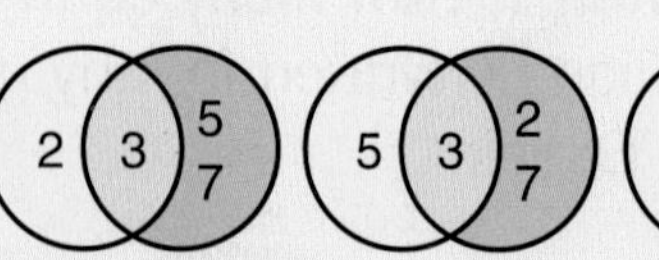

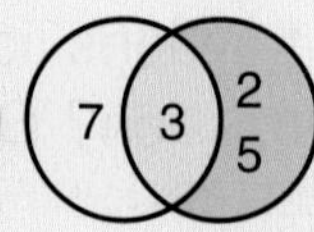

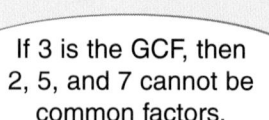

Solution: The numbers are 21 and 30.

LOOK BACK

Look back at the problem. Does your answer meet all the given conditions?

MathTracks 1/28
Listen and Understand

Guided Practice

Use the Ask Yourself questions to help you solve each problem.

1. The LCM of two numbers is 60. One of the numbers is 20. The other number is even and has only two prime factors. What is the other number?

2. The GCF of two numbers is 12. Both of these numbers are greater than 12 and both are less than 40. What are the numbers?

Think about how you can use the GCF to find possible answers. Check those answers to see if they fit with the other information in the problem.

Ask Yourself

What facts do I know?

How can I organize what I know so that I can use logical thinking?

- **Can I draw a Venn diagram?**
- **Did I label the parts of my diagram?**
- **Did I find the factors of the two numbers?**

How can I check the answer?

Independent Practice

Use logical reasoning to solve each problem.

3. The LCM of two numbers is 120. The GCF of the same two numbers is 4. The sum of the numbers is 44. What are the numbers?

4. The LCM of two numbers is 360. The GCF of two numbers is 8. The numbers differ by 32. What are the numbers?

5. A number is called "perfect" if it equals the sum all of its factors except the number itself. Factors of 6: 1, 2, 3, 6; $1 + 2 + 3 = 6$. Find all the perfect numbers greater than 0 and less than 40.

6. **Explain** For fraction $\frac{a}{b}$, $b - a = 9$ and $a \times b = 90$. Find the fraction. Explain how you can use a factor tree and a Venn diagram to help you solve the problem.

7. Fraction $\frac{c}{d}$ is equivalent to $\frac{4}{14}$, and $c + d = 27$. Find fraction $\frac{c}{d}$.

8. Fraction $\frac{e}{f}$ is equivalent to $\frac{5}{6}$, and $f - e = 7$. Find fraction $\frac{e}{f}$.

9. **Write About It** The GCF of two numbers is 30. The LCM is 420. One of the numbers is 210. What is the other number? Tell how you found your answer.

10. Numbers are relatively prime if their GCF is 1. Find a pair of composite numbers greater than 1 and less than 10 that are relatively prime.

Go On

Choose a Strategy

Solve. Show your work. Tell what strategy you used.

PROBLEM-SOLVING Strategies

- Use Models
- Draw a Diagram
- Find a Pattern
- Guess and Check
- Make an Organized List
- Make a Table
- Solve a Simpler Problem
- Use Logical Reasoning
- Work Backward
- Write an Equation

11. In his first month at an art gallery, Ken sells $10,000 worth of art. Ken's goal is to increase his sales by $1,500 each month. If Ken meets his goal, what will his sales be in the sixth month?

12. Mr. Sammler bought a group of 12 prints for his collection. Then Mr. Sammler sold 3 prints. Mr. Sammler now has 38 prints. How many prints did Mr. Sammler have before he bought the group of 12 prints?

13. Marina bought a set of paintbrushes and a set of oil paints for $90. The oil paints cost $42 more than the paintbrushes. What was the cost of the oil paints? What was the cost of the paintbrushes?

Data **Use the stem-and-leaf plot to solve Problems 14–17.**

Paul is selling photos at an art fair. The stem-and-leaf plot shows the sale prices for the photos that Paul has sold so far.

Sale Prices of Paul's Photos

Stem	Leaf
0	
1	9
2	5 9
3	0 5 5
4	9 9 9 9
5	0 0 5 5
6	
7	
8	8 9 9 9 9 9
9	8

9 | 8 means $98.

14. How many photos has Paul sold so far?

15. Calculator Find the mean, median, mode, and range of the data. Round your answers to the nearest cent.

16. Analyze Would you use the mean or the median to describe the typical sale price? Explain your choice.

17. The next photo Paul sells raises the mean sale price of his photos to $59. What is the sale price of the photo?

18. In Clare's painting of a farm, there are 36 sheep and geese. She has painted all of their 118 legs. How many of each kind of animal are in Clare's painting?

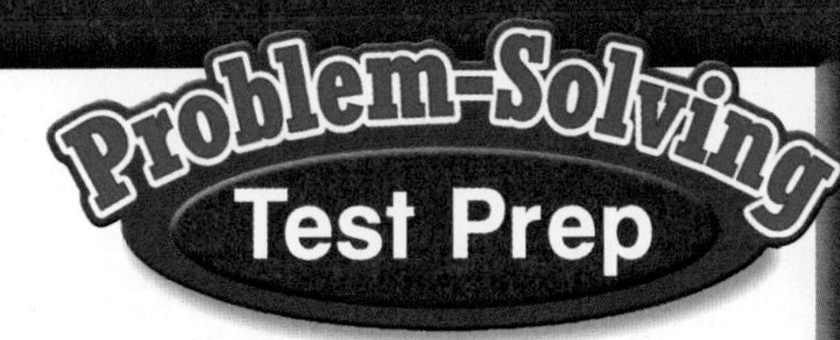

Choose the letter of the correct answer.
If a correct answer is not here, choose NH.

1. The Owls play 30 games per season. Below are the results for three seasons. If the pattern continues, what will be the record for the fifth season?

Season	Wins	Losses
1st	13	17
2nd	15	15
3rd	17	13

A 19-11 **C** 21-9

B 20-10 **D** NH

(Chapter 1, Lesson 6)

2. A high school wants to find out how many minutes per day students use computers. Which of the following choices would give results that best represent the entire school?

F Survey the entire computer club.
G Survey 30 students in each grade.
H Survey the advanced math classes.
J Survey 75 tenth graders.

(Chapter 8, Lesson 1)

3. The first movie at The Three Moon Cinema starts at 11:45 A.M. There is another showing every 1 hour and 50 minutes. When is the third showing?

A 1:35 P.M. **C** 2:35 P.M.
B 1:40 P.M. **D** NH

(Chapter 6, Lesson 7)

4. Jerry thinks of a number. He then doubles the number and adds 5. The result is 39. Which equation could you use to find Jerry's number?

F $2 \times n = 39$
G $2 \times (n + 5) = 39$
H $(2 \times n) + 5 = 39$
J $2 \times (n - 5) = 39$

(Chapter 5, Lesson 6)

5. What is the next picture likely to be in this pattern?

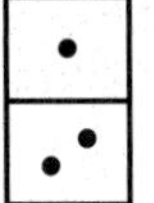 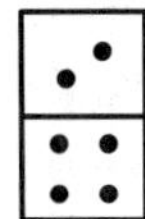 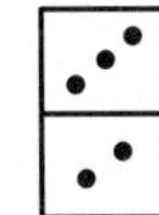 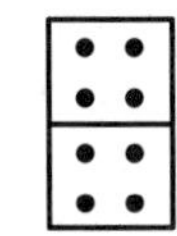

A 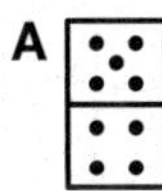 **B** 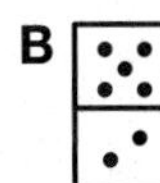 **C** 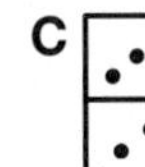 **D** 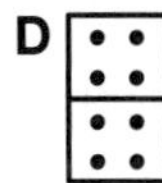

(Chapter 2, Lesson 3)

6. Forty-five students and 12 adults are going on a trip. They are traveling in minivans that hold 8 students and 2 adults. How many minivans will be needed for the trip?

Represent Support your **solution** with a picture or a table.

(Chapter 5, Lesson 7)

7. Maria has test scores of 75, 76, 81, and 84. What score does Maria need on her fifth test in order to raise her mean to 80?

Explain How did you **find** your answer?

(Chapter 8, Lesson 2)

Test Prep on the Net

Visit *Education Place* at **eduplace.com/kids/mw/** for test prep practice.

Relate Fractions, Mixed Numbers, and Decimals

Objective Change decimals to fractions and mixed numbers, and change mixed numbers and fractions to decimals.

Work Together

A survey found that 0.2 of the visitors to an art museum stopped at the gift store. A survey five years later finds that $\frac{2}{5}$ of the museum's visitors go to the gift store. Did the two surveys produce the same result?

Work with a partner to decide whether 0.2 and $\frac{2}{5}$ represent the same number.

Way 1 **Write the decimal as a fraction in simplest form.**

$0.2 = \frac{2}{10} = \frac{1}{5}$

Locate the fractions on a number line.

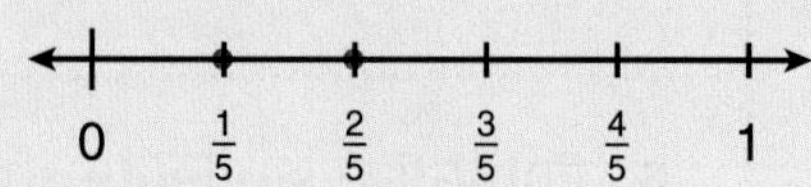

- Are the results the same?

Way 2 **Write the fraction as a decimal.**

$\frac{2}{5} = \frac{4}{10}$

$\frac{4}{10} = 0.4$

Think
To write a fraction as a decimal, the denominator needs to be a power of 10.

Locate the decimals on a number line.

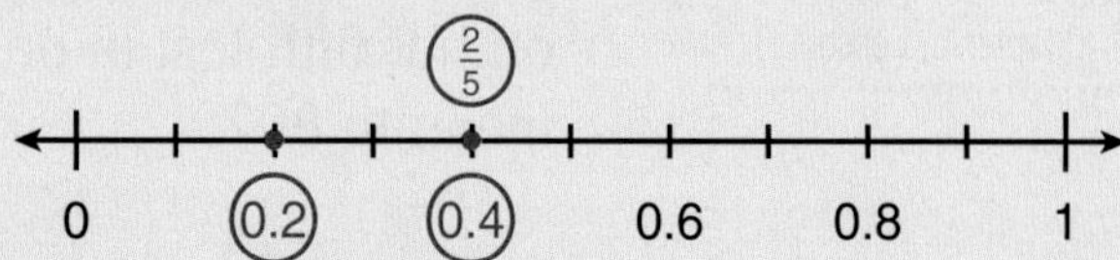

- Are the results the same?

Now decide whether 1.25 and $1\frac{1}{4}$ represent the same number.

STEP 1 Write the decimal as a mixed number in simplest form.

$1.25 = 1\frac{25}{100} = 1\frac{1}{4}$

$1\frac{1}{4} = 1\frac{1}{4}$

STEP 2 Write the mixed number as a decimal.

$1\frac{1}{4} = 1\frac{25}{100}$

$1\frac{25}{100} = 1.25$

$1.25 = 1.25$

$\frac{1}{4} = \frac{?}{100}$

On Your Own

Write each decimal as a fraction or mixed number in simplest form.

1. 0.8
2. 0.13
3. 0.75
4. 3.6
5. 4.5
6. 7.25

Write each fraction or mixed number as a decimal.

7. $\frac{1}{5}$
8. $\frac{7}{10}$
9. $\frac{3}{25}$
10. $2\frac{7}{10}$
11. $3\frac{3}{4}$
12. $5\frac{3}{100}$

Use the number line to complete Exercises 13–16.

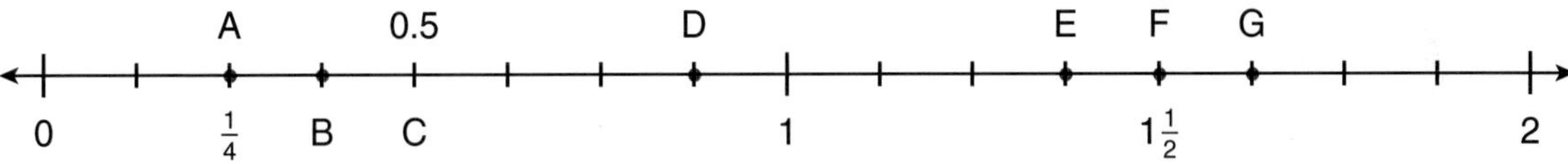

13. Write the decimal represented by point *A*.
14. Write the fraction represented by point *C*.
15. Write the fraction and the decimal represented by point *D*.
16. Which point represents 1.375? Explain your answer.
17. **What's Wrong?** Each flat represents one whole. Marnie says the shaded parts of the flats show that $2.3 = 2\frac{3}{100}$. Do you agree? Explain your reasoning.

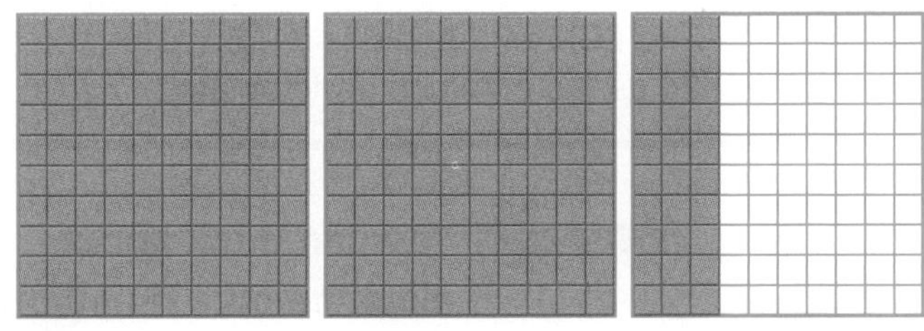

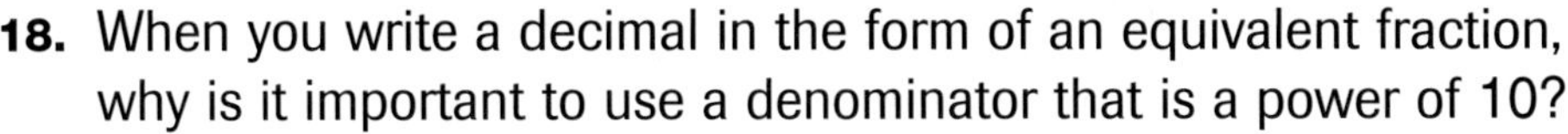

18. When you write a decimal in the form of an equivalent fraction, why is it important to use a denominator that is a power of 10?
19. How do you know what power of 10 to use as a denominator, when writing a decimal as an equivalent fraction?

Lesson 9

Compare and Order Fractions and Decimals

Objective Compare and order fractions and decimals.

Learn About It

Jeff made a clay animal that is $\frac{3}{8}$ foot tall. Andrea made a clay animal that is $\frac{5}{8}$ foot tall. Who made the taller animal?

Two fractions with the same, or like, denominators are said to have a **common denominator**. You can compare them by comparing the numerators.

$5 > 3$, so $\frac{5}{8} > \frac{3}{8}$. Andrea made the taller animal.

Fractions with different, or unlike, denominators can also be compared.

Compare $\frac{5}{6}$ and $\frac{5}{8}$.

Different Ways to Compare $\frac{5}{6}$ and $\frac{5}{8}$

Way 1 You can find equivalent fractions with a common denominator.

STEP 1 Find the LCM of the denominators of the fractions.

Multiples of 6: 6, 12, 18, 24, 30, ...

Multiples of 8: 8, 16, 24, 32, ...

The LCM of 6 and 8 is 24. So, use 24 as the common denominator.

STEP 2 Use the common denominator to find equivalent fractions.

$\frac{5 \times 4}{6 \times 4} = \frac{20}{24}$ $\qquad$ $\frac{5 \times 3}{8 \times 3} = \frac{15}{24}$

STEP 3 To compare the fractions, compare the numerators.

Since $20 > 15$, $\frac{20}{24} > \frac{15}{24}$.

So, $\frac{5}{6} > \frac{5}{8}$.

Way 2 You can think about distance on a number line.

When the numerators are the same, the fraction with the greater denominator is less than the other fraction.

$\frac{5}{6} > \frac{5}{8}$

Way 3 You can relate fractions to benchmarks.

$\frac{5}{6}$ is close to 1 on the number line.

$\frac{5}{8}$ is closer to $\frac{1}{2}$ than it is to 1.

$1 > \frac{1}{2}$, so $\frac{5}{6} > \frac{5}{8}$.

Solution: $\frac{5}{6} > \frac{5}{8}$

You can use what you know about comparing fractions to order fractions and decimals.

To order fractions, you can find equivalent fractions, then compare.

Order $\frac{3}{5}$, $\frac{3}{4}$, and $\frac{7}{10}$ from least to greatest.

- Use the LCM of the denominators to find a common denominator.
- Find equivalent fractions with that common denominator.

$\frac{3}{5} = \frac{12}{20}$ (× 4) $\frac{3}{4} = \frac{15}{20}$ (× 5) $\frac{7}{10} = \frac{14}{20}$ (× 2)

- Order the fractions.

$\frac{12}{20} < \frac{14}{20} < \frac{15}{20}$, so $\frac{3}{5} < \frac{7}{10} < \frac{3}{4}$

To order fractions and decimals, write them in the same form.

Order 1.5, $1\frac{9}{20}$, and 1.42 from least to greatest.

- Write the mixed number as a decimal.

$1\frac{9}{20} = 1 + \frac{9}{20}$

$= 1 + \frac{45}{100}$

$= 1.45$

Think
$\frac{9}{20} = \frac{45}{100}$

- Order the numbers.

$1.42 < 1.45 < 1.5$,

so $1.42 < 1\frac{9}{20} < 1.5$

Work with a partner.

Materials fraction strips

Complete the steps to order decimals and fractions.

STEP 1 Write the following numbers on a sheet of paper: 0.6, $\frac{3}{8}$, and $\frac{2}{3}$.

- Guess the order of the values, from least to greatest.
- Discuss your guess with your partner.

STEP 2 Use fraction strips to show each of the three numbers. Line up the fraction strips so that they align on one end.

- Order the numbers from least to greatest.
- Is the order the same as your guesses?

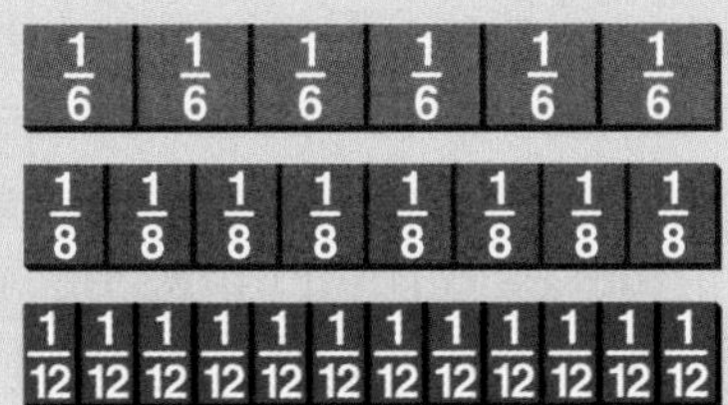

STEP 3 Use equivalent fractions to check your answer.

Go On

Guided Practice

> **Ask Yourself**
> - Did I find a common denominator?
> - Did I write the numbers in the same form to compare them?
>
> 
>

Compare. Write >, <, or = for each ●.

1. $\frac{7}{9}$ ● $\frac{5}{9}$
2. $\frac{5}{9}$ ● $\frac{5}{8}$
3. $\frac{2}{3}$ ● $\frac{7}{12}$
4. $3\frac{1}{4}$ ● $3\frac{2}{5}$
5. 0.25 ● $\frac{1}{5}$
6. $1\frac{1}{2}$ ● 1.5

Explain Your Thinking ▶ How can you compare $\frac{4}{9}$ and $\frac{4}{11}$ without using a common denominator?

Practice and Problem Solving

Compare. Write >, <, or = for each ●.

7. $\frac{3}{8}$ ● $\frac{5}{12}$
8. $\frac{9}{10}$ ● $\frac{5}{6}$
9. $3\frac{8}{15}$ ● $3\frac{3}{5}$
10. $2\frac{3}{10}$ ● $2\frac{1}{3}$
11. $\frac{5}{8}$ ● 0.6
12. 0.75 ● $\frac{3}{4}$
13. 1.4 ● $1\frac{2}{5}$
14. $4\frac{1}{8}$ ● 4.2

Order each set of numbers from least to greatest.

15. $\frac{17}{24}, \frac{7}{12}, \frac{5}{8}$
16. $2\frac{17}{20}$, 2.75, $2\frac{4}{5}$, 0.9
17. $\frac{7}{20}, 1\frac{1}{8}, \frac{11}{15}$, 0.5

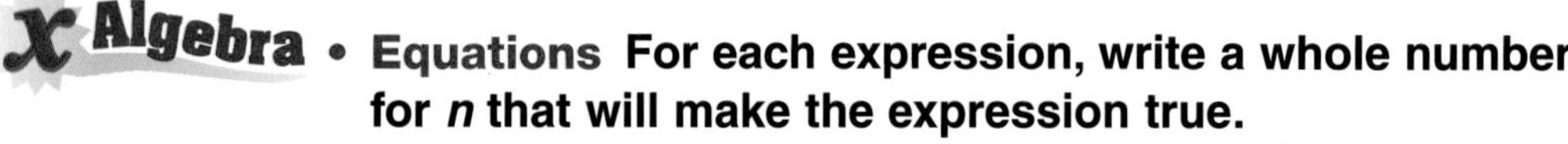

Algebra • Equations For each expression, write a whole number for *n* that will make the expression true.

18. $\frac{n}{4} = 0.25$
19. $0.3 = \frac{n}{10}$
20. $\frac{5}{6} < \frac{n}{7}$
21. $\frac{1}{2} > \frac{n}{10}$

Solve.

22. Some students made clay sculptures. Juan used $\frac{3}{4}$ pound of clay. Arleta used $\frac{1}{2}$ pound of clay. Maureen used $\frac{5}{6}$ pound of clay. Who used the most clay? Who used the least clay?

23. **Represent** Penny cuts three lengths of ribbons. The ribbons are $1\frac{3}{4}$ ft, $1\frac{7}{12}$ ft, and 1.5 ft. Show all three of these lengths on a number line. Then list the lengths from shortest to longest.

24. **Use Data** The table at the right shows prices of train tickets from Eastport to Central City. During two weeks, Max makes 8 round trips between the towns. He spends $71. Does he make the same number of trips each week? Explain.

25. **You Decide** During the month of January, you make the round trip between Eastport and Central City 3 times per week. What tickets would you buy? Explain your thinking.

Type of Ticket	Price
Single Trip	$6.50
Round Trip	$11.00
10-Trip Pass	$55
Weekly Pass	$60
Monthly Pass	$225

Extra Practice See page 253, Set F.

Quick Check

Check your understanding of Lessons 6–9.

Simplify each fraction. (Lesson 6)

1. $\frac{11}{22}$ **2.** $\frac{12}{20}$ **3.** $\frac{21}{25}$

Write each decimal as a fraction or mixed number in simplest form. (Lesson 8)

4. 0.3 **5.** 0.16 **6.** 1.15

Compare. Write >, <, or = for each ●. (Lesson 9)

7. $\frac{7}{15}$ ● $\frac{9}{20}$ **8.** 0.4 ● $\frac{7}{15}$ **9.** 2.5 ● $2\frac{3}{8}$

Solve. (Lesson 7)

10. The LCM of two numbers is 36. The GCF of the same two numbers is 3. The sum of the numbers is 21. What are the numbers?

WEEKLY WR READER® eduplace.com/kids/mw/

Mangled Money

Each day the United States Bureau of Engraving and Printing produces **thirty-seven million** pieces of paper money. This money has a face value of approximately **six hundred ninety-six million dollars**.

If a piece of paper money is torn apart and more than half of it remains, the U.S. Treasury Department will issue a check for the face value of the bill. The U.S. Treasury handles about **thirty thousand** claims every year for torn or mutilated currency, worth over **thirty million dollars**.

1. Write the four numbers shown above in bold print in standard form.

Write *yes* or *no* to indicate if the U.S. Treasury would issue a check for that part of the dollar bill.

2. $\frac{2}{3}$ **3.** $\frac{3}{8}$ **4.** $\frac{5}{12}$ **5.** $\frac{5}{10}$

Chapter Review/Test

VOCABULARY

Vocabulary

- composite number
- greatest common factor (GCF)
- least common multiple (LCM)
- prime factorization
- prime number

1. A ____ is a number greater than 1 with exactly two different factors–itself and 1.
2. A ____ is the greatest whole number that is a common factor of two or more numbers.
3. A whole number that has more than two factors is called a ____.

CONCEPTS AND SKILLS

Write the prime factorization of each number. Use exponents if possible. If the number is prime, write *prime*. (Lessons 1–2, pp. 224–227)

4. 7
5. 12
6. 19
7. 20
8. 16
9. 30

Find the GFC of the numbers. (Lesson 3, pp. 228–230)

10. 36, 81
11. 18, 45
12. 35, 77
13. 24, 96

Find the LCM of the numbers. (Lesson 4, pp. 232–235)

14. 6, 18
15. 20, 48
16. 15, 55
17. 12, 32

Simplify if possible. Then write each as a decimal.
(Lessons 5–6, pp. 236–241; Lesson 8, pp. 246–247)

18. $\frac{18}{36}$
19. $\frac{3}{2}$
20. $\frac{4}{10}$
21. $\frac{32}{20}$
22. $\frac{15}{4}$
23. $\frac{3}{10}$
24. $\frac{2}{5}$
25. $2\frac{23}{100}$
26. $\frac{11}{50}$
27. $1\frac{3}{25}$

Compare. Write >, <, or = for each ●.
(Lesson 9, pp. 248–251)

28. $\frac{5}{7}$ ● $\frac{5}{8}$
29. 1.2 ● $1\frac{2}{5}$
30. $\frac{3}{25}$ ● 0.12
31. $\frac{3}{10}$ ● 0.15
32. 3.25 ● $\frac{7}{2}$

PROBLEM SOLVING

Solve. (Lesson 7, pp. 242–245)

33. The LCM of two numbers is 200. The GCF is 10. The sum of the numbers is 90. What are the numbers?

Show You Understand

How does knowing that $\frac{1}{9} < \frac{1}{8}$ help you know that $\frac{7}{8} < \frac{8}{9}$ without using a common denominator?

Extra Practice

Set A (Lesson 2, pp. 226–227)

Write the prime factorization of each number. Use exponents if possible. If the number is prime, write *prime*.

1. 23 2. 41 3. 48 4. 50 5. 51

Set B (Lesson 3, pp. 228–231)

Find the greatest common factor of the numbers.

1. 16, 36 2. 27, 54 3. 48, 72 4. 56, 120 5. 99, 121
6. 24, 56 7. 12, 48 8. 39, 51 9. 15, 60 10. 36, 54

Set C (Lesson 4, pp. 232–234)

Find the least common multiple of the numbers.

1. 7, 42 2. 16, 36 3. 13, 52 4. 8, 28 5. 12, 32
6. 9, 45 7. 6, 20 8. 20, 30 9. 7, 9 10. 12, 40

Set D (Lesson 5, pp. 236–239)

Write each improper fraction as a mixed number or a whole number. Write each mixed number as an improper fraction.

1. $\frac{11}{3}$ 2. $\frac{16}{5}$ 3. $\frac{12}{6}$ 4. $\frac{17}{8}$ 5. $\frac{30}{7}$
6. $5\frac{1}{7}$ 7. $7\frac{1}{3}$ 8. $3\frac{5}{8}$ 9. $10\frac{2}{3}$ 10. $6\frac{3}{10}$

Set E (Lesson 6, pp. 240–241)

Simplify each fraction.

1. $\frac{16}{36}$ 2. $\frac{33}{54}$ 3. $\frac{6}{27}$ 4. $\frac{18}{48}$ 5. $\frac{55}{77}$

Set F (Lesson 9, pp. 248–251)

Compare. Write >, <, or = for each ⬬.

1. $\frac{3}{14}$ ⬬ $\frac{3}{28}$ 2. $2\frac{5}{6}$ ⬬ $2\frac{1}{12}$ 3. 5.2 ⬬ $5\frac{5}{25}$ 4. 1.8 ⬬ $1\frac{23}{25}$
5. $\frac{1}{5}$ ⬬ 0.08 6. $\frac{1}{4}$ ⬬ 0.25 7. $\frac{11}{12}$ ⬬ $\frac{5}{12}$ 8. 1.75 ⬬ $1\frac{3}{4}$

Add and Subtract Fractions

INVESTIGATION

Use Data

In-line skating is a good way to keep fit. What is the difference, in calories burned per minute while in-line skating, between a 150 lb person at 10 mi/h and a 120 lb person at 12 mi/h?

Calories Burned (per minute) In-Line Skating					
Skater's Weight (pounds)	Speed of Skater (miles per hour)				
	8	9	10	11	12
120	$4\frac{1}{5}$	$5\frac{4}{5}$	$7\frac{2}{5}$	$8\frac{9}{10}$	$10\frac{1}{2}$
150	$5\frac{3}{5}$	$7\frac{1}{5}$	$8\frac{4}{5}$	$10\frac{2}{5}$	$11\frac{9}{10}$

Chapter Pretest

Use this page to review and remember what you need to know for this chapter.

VOCABULARY

Choose the best word to complete each sentence.

1. The fractions $\frac{1}{3}$ and $\frac{1}{4}$ have ____.
2. The fractions $\frac{2}{5}$ and $\frac{3}{5}$ have ____.
3. Fractions that represent the same number are called ____.

equivalent fractions

like denominators

unlike denominators

CONCEPTS AND SKILLS

Write each fraction in simplest form.

4. $\frac{2}{6}$
5. $\frac{8}{10}$
6. $\frac{3}{12}$
7. $\frac{3}{18}$

Write each improper fraction as a mixed number or whole number.

8. $\frac{25}{8}$
9. $\frac{18}{3}$
10. $\frac{19}{5}$
11. $\frac{4}{4}$

Complete.

12. $\frac{1}{3} = \frac{3}{\blacksquare}$
13. $\frac{5}{20} = \frac{\blacksquare}{4}$
14. $1\frac{1}{5} = \frac{\blacksquare}{5} = \frac{\blacksquare}{10}$
15. $4\frac{2}{3} = \frac{\blacksquare}{3} = \frac{\blacksquare}{6}$

Find the least common multiple of these numbers.

16. 6, 36
17. 4, 10
18. 3, 11
19. 3, 25

20. Is $\frac{3}{8}$ closer to 0, $\frac{1}{2}$, or 1? Use a number line or words to explain your thinking.

Visit *Education Place* at **eduplace.com/kids/mw/** for more review.

Lesson 1

Estimate With Fractions

Objective Estimate fraction sums and differences.

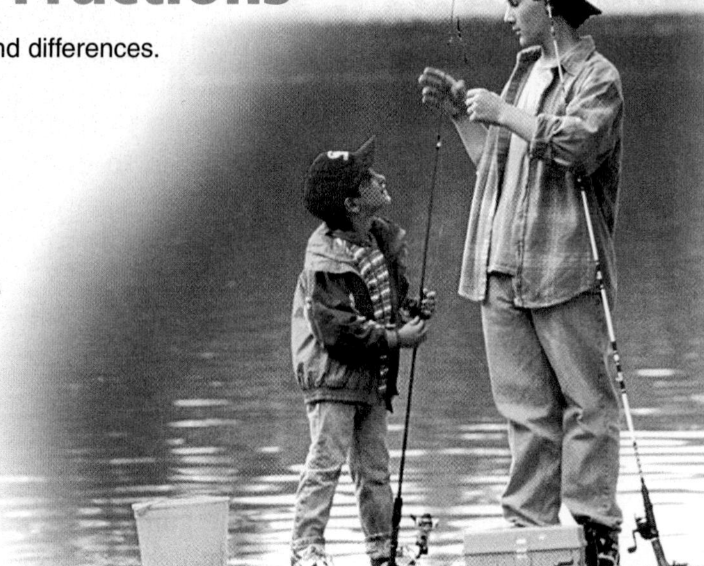

Learn About It

Dan is $53\frac{1}{8}$ inches tall. His older brother is $72\frac{3}{4}$ inches tall. About how many more inches would Dan need to grow to match his brother's height?

Estimate the difference $72\frac{3}{4} - 53\frac{1}{8}$.

You can use front-end estimation.

STEP 1 Identify the greatest place in each number.

$$\begin{array}{r} 72\frac{3}{4} \\ -\ 53\frac{1}{8} \\ \hline \end{array}$$

STEP 2 Subtract. Write zeros in the other whole-number places.

$$\begin{array}{r} 72\frac{3}{4} \\ -\ 53\frac{1}{8} \\ \hline \end{array} \Rightarrow \begin{array}{r} 70 \\ -\ 50 \\ \hline 20 \end{array}$$

Solution: Dan would need to grow about 20 inches to match his brother's height.

You can also use rounding to estimate with fractions.

Estimate the sum $\frac{5}{6} + \frac{7}{12} + \frac{1}{6}$.

You can round fractions to 0, $\frac{1}{2}$, or 1 in order to estimate.

STEP 1 Decide if each fraction is closest to 0, $\frac{1}{2}$, or 1. A number line can help you decide.

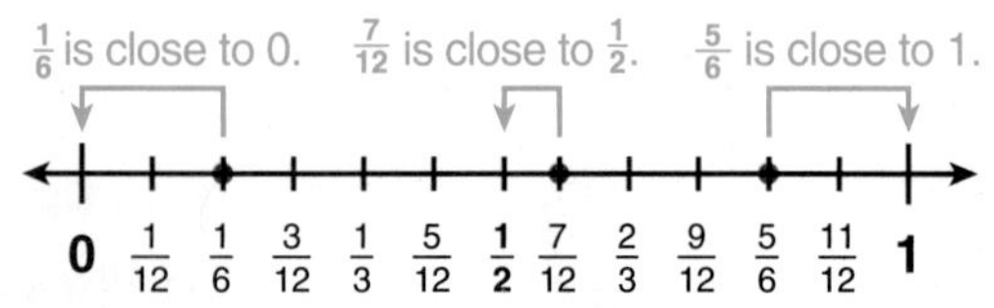

STEP 2 Round up or down. Then add the rounded numbers.

$$\frac{5}{6} + \frac{7}{12} + \frac{1}{6}$$
$$\downarrow \quad \downarrow \quad \downarrow$$
$$1 + \frac{1}{2} + 0 \approx 1\frac{1}{2}$$

$\approx$ means "is approximately equal to."

Solution: The sum of $\frac{5}{6}$, $\frac{7}{12}$, and $\frac{1}{6}$ is about $1\frac{1}{2}$.

Guided Practice

Estimate the sum or difference. Name the method you used to estimate.

1. $\frac{5}{8} - \frac{3}{8}$
2. $15\frac{3}{4} + 12\frac{7}{8}$
3. $\frac{7}{8} + \frac{1}{12}$
4. $22\frac{9}{10} - 18\frac{2}{5}$

Ask Yourself

- Is the fraction close to 0, $\frac{1}{2}$, or 1?
- Can I use front-end estimation?

TEST TIPS **Explain Your Thinking** ▶ Explain how you could use rounding to find the difference in Exercise 4 above.

Practice and Problem Solving

Estimate the sum or difference.
Name the method you used to estimate.

5. $\frac{1}{4} + \frac{7}{10}$
6. $\frac{3}{5} + \frac{2}{3}$
7. $16\frac{1}{8} + 12\frac{1}{12}$
8. $\frac{4}{5} + \frac{1}{8} + \frac{3}{4} + \frac{1}{2}$
9. $\frac{7}{8} - \frac{1}{12}$
10. $\frac{5}{8} - \frac{1}{10}$
11. $9\frac{1}{8} - 3\frac{3}{4}$
12. $19\frac{5}{12} + 14\frac{1}{2}$
13. $\frac{4}{5} - \frac{1}{6}$
14. $\frac{1}{2} - \frac{3}{8}$
15. $37\frac{5}{8} + 26\frac{3}{5}$
16. $87\frac{1}{3} - 24\frac{4}{5}$
17. $16\frac{2}{3} - \frac{7}{8}$
18. $58 - 46\frac{1}{3}$
19. $6\frac{7}{8} + \frac{2}{3} + 4\frac{9}{10} + 5\frac{1}{10} + \frac{4}{5}$

Solve.

20. **Represent** Show why this statement is true: $1\frac{1}{8} - \frac{3}{4} \approx 0$. Use a number line or draw a picture to explain your reasoning.

21. **Estimate** Melba is $60\frac{3}{4}$ inches tall. When she puts on her new shoes, she grows $3\frac{1}{2}$ inches. About how tall is Melba in her new shoes?

Daily Review | Test Prep

Complete. (Grade 4)

22. 3 hours = ■ seconds
23. 300 minutes = ■ hours
24. 1 day = ■ minutes
25. 2 years = ■ days

26. Last year Robin was $50\frac{1}{4}$ inches tall. Now Robin is $54\frac{7}{8}$ inches tall. Which is the best estimate of the change in height?

A 1 inch
B 2 inches
C 3 inches
D 5 inches

Extra Practice See page 279, Set A.

Lesson 2

Add With Like Denominators

Objective Add fractions and mixed numbers with like denominators.

TRAIL MIX

$\frac{1}{4}$ cup yogurt-covered peanuts

$\frac{1}{4}$ cup mini–chocolate chips

$\frac{2}{4}$ cup dried cherries

$\frac{3}{4}$ cup granola

$\frac{3}{4}$ cup dried apricots

Learn About It

Delia chooses foods that will help keep her body healthy. At the right is her recipe for trail mix.

How much fruit is in the trail mix?

Add. $\frac{2}{4} + \frac{3}{4} = n$

The sum of 2 unit fractions of $\frac{1}{4}$ and 3 unit fractions of $\frac{1}{4}$ is 5 unit fractions of $\frac{1}{4}$.

Add. Then simplify the sum.

$\frac{2}{4} + \frac{3}{4} = \frac{5}{4} = \frac{4}{4} + \frac{1}{4} = 1\frac{1}{4}$

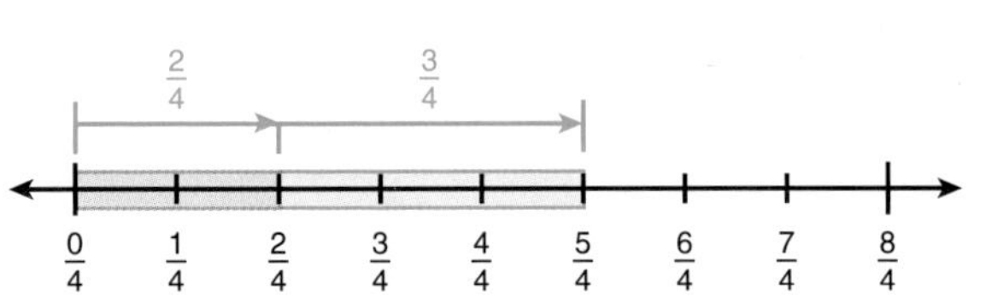

To add fractions with like denominators, add the numerators and keep the same denominator.

Solution: The trail mix has $1\frac{1}{4}$ cups of fruit.

Mike also likes to make healthy snacks. His recipe mixes $1\frac{5}{8}$ cups of mini-pretzels with $1\frac{7}{8}$ cups of yogurt-covered cranberries. How much snack does this recipe make?

Find $1\frac{5}{8} + 1\frac{7}{8}$.

STEP 1 Add the fractions.

$$\begin{array}{r} 1\frac{5}{8} \\ +\ 1\frac{7}{8} \\ \hline \frac{12}{8} \end{array}$$

STEP 2 Add the whole numbers.

$$\begin{array}{r} 1\frac{5}{8} \\ +\ 1\frac{7}{8} \\ \hline 2\frac{12}{8} \end{array}$$

STEP 3 Simplify the sum, if possible.

$$\begin{array}{r} 1\frac{5}{8} \\ +\ 1\frac{7}{8} \\ \hline 2\frac{12}{8} \end{array} = 3\frac{1}{2}$$

Think

$\frac{12}{8} = 1\frac{4}{8} = 1\frac{1}{2}$

$2 + 1\frac{1}{2} = 3\frac{1}{2}$

Solution: Mike's recipe makes $3\frac{1}{2}$ cups of his healthy snack.

Guided Practice

Add. Write each sum in simplest form.

1. $\frac{2}{5} + \frac{2}{5}$
2. $\frac{5}{6} + \frac{1}{6}$
3. $\frac{3}{4} + \frac{2}{4}$
4. $2\frac{4}{5} + 4\frac{3}{5}$
5. $3\frac{2}{3} + 3\frac{2}{3}$
6. $1\frac{5}{8} + \frac{7}{8}$

Ask Yourself

- Did I add the numerators?
- Did I add the whole numbers?
- Is the sum in simplest form?

Explain Your Thinking ▶ When you add fractions with like denominators, why do you only add the numerators?

Practice and Problem Solving

Add. Write each sum in simplest form.

7. $\frac{3}{10} + \frac{4}{10}$
8. $\frac{5}{8} + \frac{7}{8}$
9. $2\frac{5}{12} + 1\frac{1}{12}$
10. $3\frac{2}{3} + 4\frac{1}{3}$
11. $\frac{2}{6} + \frac{2}{6}$
12. $\frac{4}{9} + \frac{3}{9}$
13. $3\frac{5}{6} + 1\frac{1}{6}$
14. $2\frac{5}{6} + 3\frac{5}{6}$
15. $6\frac{7}{10} + 3\frac{9}{10}$

Mental Math **Use mental math to add. Write each sum in simplest form.**

16. $\frac{7}{16} + \frac{9}{16}$
17. $\frac{3}{8} + \frac{5}{8}$
18. $2\frac{3}{4} + \frac{1}{4}$
19. $1\frac{1}{2} + 4\frac{1}{2}$

Solve.

20. To stay healthy, about $\frac{1}{5}$ of the foods that you eat should be vegetables, and about $\frac{2}{5}$ should be grains. What fraction of the foods that you eat should be vegetables and grains?

21. Sonja and Adam need $1\frac{3}{4}$ cups of cucumbers, $\frac{1}{4}$ cup of onions, and $\frac{1}{2}$ cup of cheese to make a snack. Find how many cups of vegetables they need to make their snack.

Daily Review | Test Prep

Add or subtract. (Ch. 2, Lesson 3)

22. 362 + 517
23. 1,376 − 429
24. 24,522 − 7,165

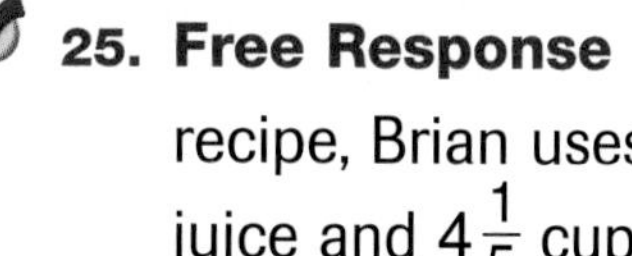

25. **Free Response** For a punch recipe, Brian uses $2\frac{2}{5}$ cups of fruit juice and $4\frac{1}{5}$ cups of ginger ale. How much punch is he making?

Extra Practice See page 279, Set B.

Lesson 3

Add Fractions With Unlike Denominators

Objective Add fractions with unlike denominators.

e Glossary

Vocabulary

equivalent fractions

least common denominator (LCD)

Learn About It

About $\frac{1}{5}$ of the bones in your body are in your hands and $\frac{1}{4}$ of your bones are in your feet. What fraction of the bones in your body are in your hands and feet?

Add. $\frac{1}{5} + \frac{1}{4} = n$

STEP 1 To add the fractions, you need to find a common denominator.

Use the product of the denominators to write **equivalent fractions** with like denominators.

$5 \times 4 = 20$ ← common denominator

$\frac{1}{5} = \frac{4}{20}$ (× 4) $\frac{1}{4} = \frac{5}{20}$ (× 5)

STEP 2 Rewrite the problem. Then add.

$$\frac{1}{5} + \frac{1}{4} = \frac{4}{20} + \frac{5}{20}$$
$$= \frac{9}{20}$$

Solution: About $\frac{9}{20}$ of the bones in your body are in your hands and feet.

To add fractions, find the **least common denominator (LCD)**.

Find $\frac{7}{8} + \frac{5}{12}$.

STEP 1 Find the least common multiple (LCM) of the denominators. This is the LCD.

8: 8, 16, **24**, 32

12: 12, **24**, 36

The LCD of the fractions is 24.

STEP 2 Use the LCD to find equivalent fractions.

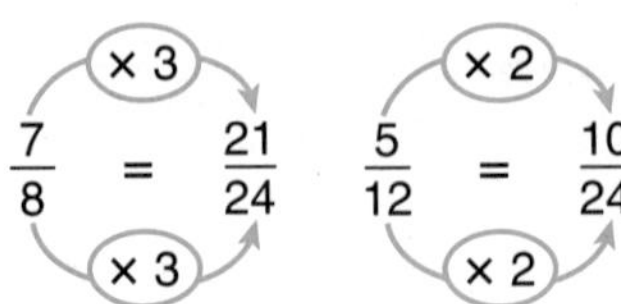

STEP 3 Add the fractions. Write the sum in simplest form.

$$\frac{21}{24} + \frac{10}{24} = \frac{31}{24}$$

$$\frac{31}{24} = \frac{24}{24} + \frac{7}{24} = 1\frac{7}{24}$$

Solution: $\frac{7}{8} + \frac{5}{12} = 1\frac{7}{24}$

Guided Practice

Ask Yourself

- Did I use equivalent fractions?
- Is each sum in simplest form?

TEST TIPS

Add. Write each sum in simplest form.

1. $\frac{1}{6} + \frac{1}{3}$ **2.** $\frac{2}{3} + \frac{5}{6}$ **3.** $\frac{1}{8} + \frac{1}{4}$ **4.** $\frac{1}{3} + \frac{2}{5}$

5. $\frac{2}{3} + \frac{5}{9}$ **6.** $\frac{7}{8} + \frac{1}{12}$ **7.** $\frac{2}{5} + \frac{1}{10}$ **8.** $\frac{5}{6} + \frac{5}{8}$

TEST TIPS **Explain Your Thinking** ▶ How can you use estimation to check your answer in Exercise 8?

Practice and Problem Solving

Add. Write each sum in simplest form.

9. $\frac{1}{6} + \frac{1}{4}$ **10.** $\frac{1}{10} + \frac{3}{4}$ **11.** $\frac{2}{3} + \frac{3}{4}$ **12.** $\frac{9}{16} + \frac{1}{12}$ **13.** $\frac{1}{2} + \frac{9}{10}$

14. $\frac{1}{2} + \frac{1}{4}$ **15.** $\frac{3}{8} + \frac{9}{16}$ **16.** $\frac{11}{12} + \frac{5}{6}$ **17.** $\frac{7}{16} + \frac{7}{8}$ **18.** $\frac{5}{8} + \frac{7}{12}$

Solve.

19. Anna mixed $\frac{3}{4}$ cup peanuts with $\frac{3}{8}$ cup almonds. How many cups of nuts did she have?

20. Estimate Rob added $\frac{5}{8}$ cup of water to $\frac{1}{3}$ cup of juice concentrate. About how much juice did Rob make?

21. Write About It Without adding, decide if each sum is greater than or less than $\frac{1}{2}$. Explain your decision.

a. $\frac{1}{3} + \frac{1}{4}$ **b.** $\frac{3}{8} + \frac{1}{5}$

22. What's Wrong? Rob found that 9 was the LCD of $\frac{1}{3}$ and $\frac{1}{6}$ this way:

$\frac{1}{3} + \frac{1}{6}$ $3 \times 6 = 18$ $18 \div 2 = 9$

Explain why Rob's way is wrong.

Daily Review | Test Prep

Write *prime* or *composite* to classify each number. (Ch. 9, Lesson 1)

23. 10 **24.** 7 **25.** 4

26. 9 **27.** 15 **28.** 5

29. 13 **30.** 21 **31.** 12

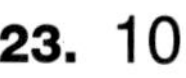

32. In simplest form, what is the sum of $\frac{3}{4}$ and $\frac{5}{8}$?

A $\frac{2}{3}$ **C** $1\frac{3}{8}$

B $1\frac{1}{8}$ **D** 2

Extra Practice See page 279, Set C.

Add Mixed Numbers With Unlike Denominators

Objective Add mixed numbers with unlike denominators.

Learn About It

As you walk, swim, or bike, your heart pumps oxygen-rich blood through your circulatory system.

Evelyn walks each day to keep her heart healthy. Her journal shows the number of miles she walked on Monday and Tuesday. How far did she walk in those two days?

Walking Journal	
Monday	$3\frac{1}{2}$
Tuesday	$2\frac{4}{5}$

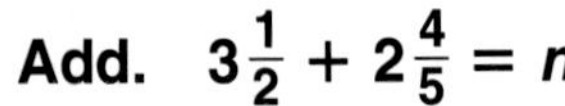

Add. $3\frac{1}{2} + 2\frac{4}{5} = n$

STEP 1 Write equivalent fractions for $\frac{1}{2}$ and $\frac{4}{5}$ by using the LCD, which is 10.

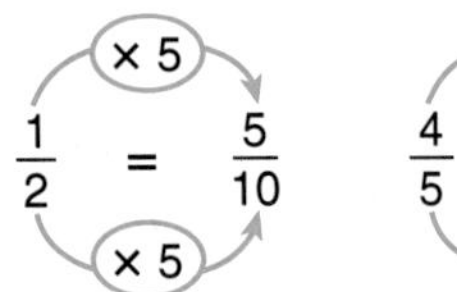

$$\frac{1}{2} = \frac{5}{10} \qquad \frac{4}{5} = \frac{8}{10}$$

STEP 2 Add. Simplify the sum if possible.

$$\begin{array}{rcr} 3\frac{1}{2} & = & 3\frac{5}{10} \\ +\,2\frac{4}{5} & = & +\,2\frac{8}{10} \\ \hline & & 5\frac{13}{10} \end{array}$$

$$5\frac{13}{10} = 5 + 1 + \frac{3}{10}$$
$$= 6\frac{3}{10}$$

$$\frac{13}{10} = \frac{10}{10} + \frac{3}{10}$$

Solution: Evelyn walked $6\frac{3}{10}$ miles on Monday and Tuesday.

Check your work.

Estimate to check that your answer is reasonable.

Round $\frac{1}{2}$ and $\frac{4}{5}$ to 0, $\frac{1}{2}$, or 1. $\quad 3\frac{1}{2} = 3\frac{1}{2} \qquad 2\frac{4}{5} \approx 3$

Add the rounded numbers. $\quad 3\frac{1}{2} + 3 = 6\frac{1}{2}$

$$6\frac{1}{2} \approx 6\frac{3}{10}$$

Guided Practice

Add. Write each sum in simplest form.

1. $1\frac{1}{2} + 1\frac{1}{4}$

2. $2\frac{1}{4} + 3\frac{1}{6}$

3. $2\frac{4}{5} + 4\frac{1}{2}$

4. $3\frac{5}{12} + 7\frac{5}{6}$

5. $8\frac{9}{16} + 5\frac{1}{2}$

6. $1\frac{3}{4} + 6\frac{1}{3}$

7. Jeremiah jogged $3\frac{1}{4}$ miles on Saturday and $4\frac{2}{5}$ miles on Sunday. Find the total distance he jogged on those two days.

Ask Yourself

- Did I write equivalent fractions?
- Is each sum in simplest form?

Why is it easy to find the LCD when one denominator is a multiple of the other?

Practice and Problem Solving

Add. Write each sum in simplest form.

8. $3\frac{5}{6} + 1\frac{1}{6}$

9. $2\frac{1}{4} + 8\frac{3}{8}$

10. $1\frac{1}{2} + 2\frac{3}{4}$

11. $4\frac{3}{5} + 5\frac{7}{10}$

12. $2\frac{5}{6} + 3\frac{1}{3}$

13. $4\frac{3}{5} + 2\frac{1}{2}$

14. $3\frac{1}{3} + 7\frac{5}{6}$

15. $9\frac{11}{12} + 6\frac{2}{3}$

16. $2\frac{5}{8} + 6\frac{2}{3}$

17. $5\frac{3}{4} + 4\frac{1}{3}$

18. $8\frac{1}{2} + 9\frac{3}{5}$

19. $10\frac{7}{8} + 2\frac{3}{4}$

20. $4\frac{1}{6} + 7\frac{1}{12}$

21. $3\frac{1}{2} + 1\frac{7}{8}$

22. $6\frac{2}{5} + 3\frac{1}{6}$

23. $7\frac{1}{3} + 4\frac{7}{12}$

24. $5\frac{3}{10} + 2\frac{1}{2}$

25. $5\frac{2}{3} + 3\frac{4}{5}$

26. $8\frac{2}{3} + 10\frac{11}{16}$

27. $2\frac{9}{16} + 12\frac{1}{4}$

28. $2\frac{2}{5} + 2\frac{5}{6}$

29. $1\frac{1}{2} + 9\frac{5}{8}$

X Algebra • Expressions Evaluate. Let $x = \frac{1}{2}$, $y = 3\frac{1}{3}$, and $z = 1\frac{3}{4}$.

30. $y + z$

31. $z + x$

32. $y + x$

33. $z + z$

Go On

Add. Write each sum in simplest form.

34. $1\frac{3}{8} + 2\frac{5}{6} + 1\frac{1}{6}$

35. $2\frac{1}{10} + 1\frac{3}{4} + 4\frac{7}{10}$

36. $5\frac{1}{2} + 2\frac{1}{2} + 6\frac{3}{4}$

37. $8\frac{1}{10} + 5\frac{7}{8} + 2\frac{1}{8}$

38. $1\frac{1}{3} + 3\frac{5}{6} + 4\frac{1}{6}$

Solve.

39. Manuel runs the same route each day. It's $1\frac{3}{4}$ miles on River Road, $1\frac{7}{10}$ miles on Back Street, and $2\frac{1}{4}$ miles on Elm Street. How far does Manuel run each day?

40. Lily practices for a swim meet by warming up for $\frac{1}{4}$ hour, swimming slow laps for $1\frac{2}{3}$ hours, and doing sprints for $\frac{1}{6}$ hour. How long is her practice?

41. Mental Math Emma figured out that her heart beats about 80 times each minute. How many times does her heart beat in an hour? Explain how you got your answer.

42. Analyze What mixed number, when added to itself three times, equals 10?

$$n + n + n = 10$$

Data Use the table for Problems 43–48.

43. On Saturday, Jerome played basketball for the same amount of time he exercised on Monday and Tuesday. How long did he play basketball?

44. Explain Jeff's goal was to exercise at least 5 hours by the end of the day on Wednesday. Did he reach his goal? Explain.

45. Analyze What pattern do you notice in the amount of time Jerome exercised during the week?

46. Mental Math On which day did Jerome and Jeff together spend exactly 4 hours exercising?

47. Calculator How many hours did each athlete spend exercising this week?

48. Create and Solve Write your own problem that uses data from the table. Solve your problem.

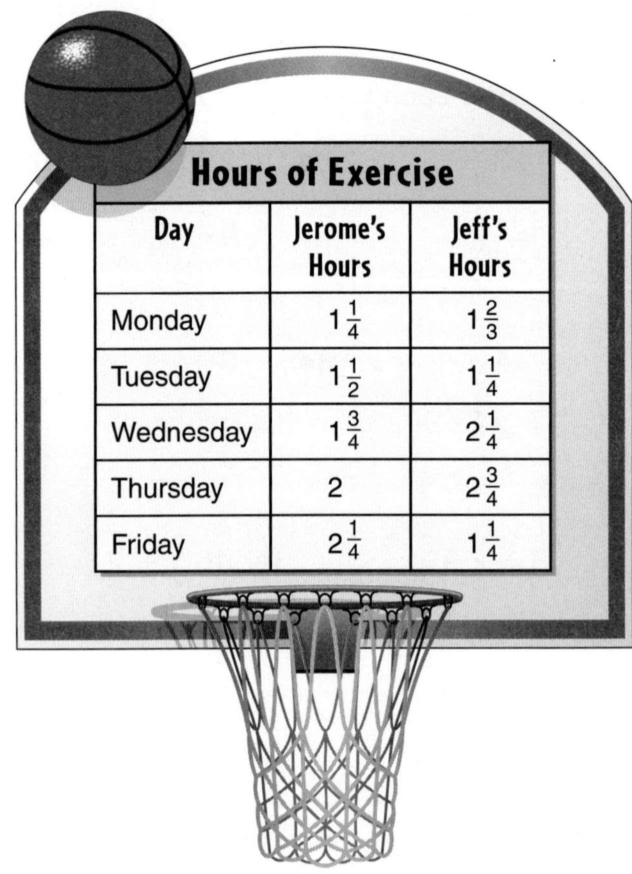

Hours of Exercise

Day	Jerome's Hours	Jeff's Hours
Monday	$1\frac{1}{4}$	$1\frac{2}{3}$
Tuesday	$1\frac{1}{2}$	$1\frac{1}{4}$
Wednesday	$1\frac{3}{4}$	$2\frac{1}{4}$
Thursday	2	$2\frac{3}{4}$
Friday	$2\frac{1}{4}$	$1\frac{1}{4}$

Extra Practice See page 279, Set D.

Quick Check

Check your understanding of Lessons 1–4.

Estimate the sum or difference. (Lesson 1)

1. $\frac{1}{10} + \frac{1}{16}$

2. $14\frac{7}{8} + 10\frac{3}{5}$

3. $\frac{9}{10} - \frac{5}{8}$

4. $83\frac{4}{8} - 12\frac{5}{6}$

Add. Write each sum in simplest form. (Lessons 2–4)

5. $\frac{5}{8} + \frac{7}{8}$

6. $\frac{2}{3} + \frac{1}{2}$

7. $\frac{9}{10} + \frac{4}{5}$

8. $4\frac{5}{6} + 2\frac{1}{6}$

9. $7\frac{3}{4} + 4\frac{5}{8}$

10. $3\frac{1}{5} + 4\frac{1}{2}$

Number Sense

Math Reasoning

Magic Squares

In a magic square, each row, column, and diagonal has the same sum.

In the magic square at the right, each row, column, and diagonal should have a sum of $1\frac{1}{2}$, and each missing numerator is a different number from 1 to 9.

Copy and complete this fraction magic square.

Can you find another way to complete the fraction magic square?

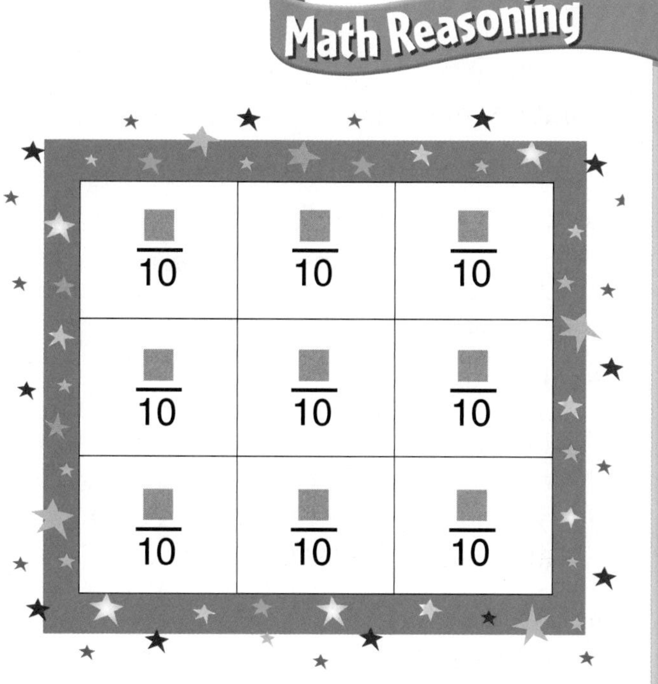

Lesson 5

Subtract With Like Denominators

Objective Subtract fractions and mixed numbers with like denominators.

Learn About It

Did you know that your brain grows? When you were born, your brain's mass was about $\frac{4}{10}$ kilogram. By age $1\frac{1}{2}$ its mass was about $\frac{7}{10}$ kilogram. How much mass does your brain gain in those $1\frac{1}{2}$ years?

Subtract. $\frac{7}{10} - \frac{4}{10} = n$

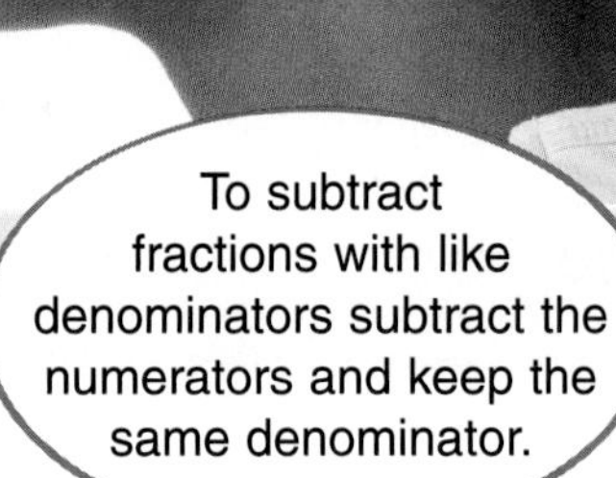

To subtract fractions with like denominators subtract the numerators and keep the same denominator.

The difference between 7 unit fractions of $\frac{1}{10}$ and 4 unit fractions of $\frac{1}{10}$ is 3 unit fractions of $\frac{1}{10}$.

$$\frac{7}{10} - \frac{4}{10} = \frac{3}{10}$$

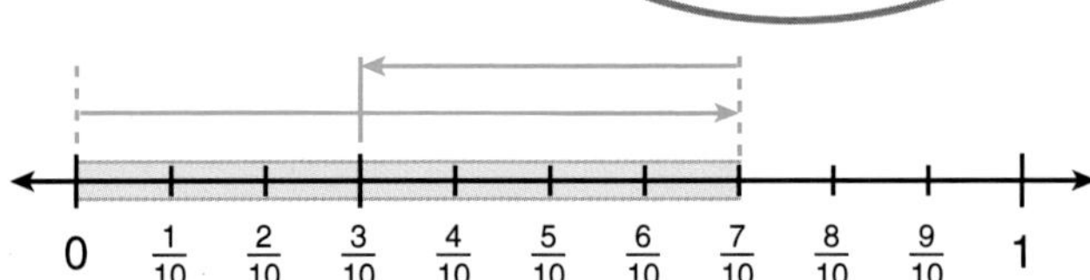

Add to check.
$\frac{3}{10} + \frac{4}{10} = \frac{7}{10}$

Solution: In the first $1\frac{1}{2}$ years, your brain gains about $\frac{3}{10}$ kilogram.

Any fraction with the same numerator and denominator is equivalent to 1.

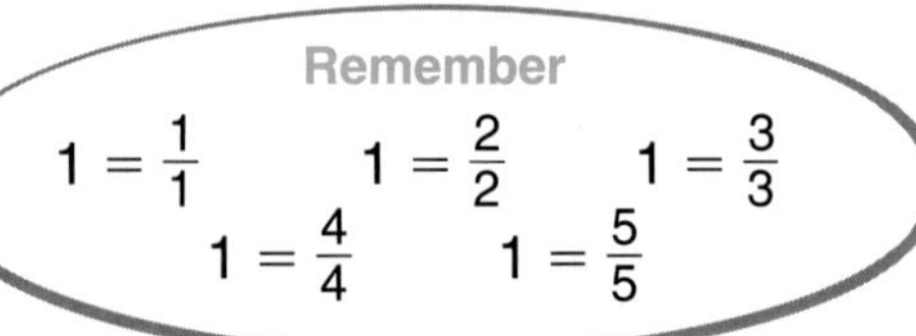

Remember
$1 = \frac{1}{1}$ $1 = \frac{2}{2}$ $1 = \frac{3}{3}$
$1 = \frac{4}{4}$ $1 = \frac{5}{5}$

Find $5 - 1\frac{2}{3}$.

STEP 1 Rename 5 as 4 + 1. Then rename 1, using 3 for the denominator.

$5 = 4 + 1$

$4 + \frac{3}{3} = 4\frac{3}{3}$

STEP 2 Subtract the fractions.

$$\begin{array}{rcr} 5 & = & 4\frac{3}{3} \\ -1\frac{2}{3} & = & -1\frac{2}{3} \\ \hline & & \frac{1}{3} \end{array}$$

STEP 3 Subtract the whole numbers.

$$\begin{array}{rcr} 5 & = & 4\frac{3}{3} \\ -1\frac{2}{3} & = & -1\frac{2}{3} \\ \hline & & 3\frac{1}{3} \end{array}$$

Solution: $5 - 1\frac{2}{3} = 3\frac{1}{3}$

Find $7\frac{1}{4} - 1\frac{3}{4}$.

STEP 1 Rename $7\frac{1}{4}$.

$$7\frac{1}{4} = 7 + \frac{1}{4}$$
$$= 6 + \frac{4}{4} + \frac{1}{4}$$
$$= 6 + \frac{5}{4} = 6\frac{5}{4}$$

STEP 2 Subtract the fractions.

$$\begin{array}{rcr} 7\frac{1}{4} & = & 6\frac{5}{4} \\ -\,1\frac{3}{4} & = & -\,1\frac{3}{4} \\ \hline & & \frac{2}{4} \end{array}$$

STEP 3 Subtract the whole numbers. Simplify.

$$\begin{array}{rcr} 7\frac{1}{4} & = & 6\frac{5}{4} \\ -\,1\frac{3}{4} & = & -\,1\frac{3}{4} \\ \hline & & 5\frac{2}{4} = 5\frac{1}{2} \end{array}$$

Solution: $7\frac{1}{4} - 1\frac{3}{4} = 5\frac{1}{2}$

Guided Practice

Ask Yourself
- Do I need to rename?
- Did I simplify my answer?
- Did I check my work?

Subtract. Write each difference in simplest form.

1. $\frac{3}{10} - \frac{1}{10}$
2. $2 - 1\frac{1}{3}$
3. $10\frac{1}{9} - 9\frac{4}{9}$

TEST TIPS **Explain Your Thinking** ▶ Show how to check your answer in Exercise 3.

Practice and Problem Solving

Subtract. Write each answer in simplest form.

4. $\frac{11}{12} - \frac{5}{12}$
5. $2 - 1\frac{5}{8}$
6. $8 - 4\frac{1}{5}$
7. $5\frac{2}{9} - 3\frac{8}{9}$
8. $\frac{8}{9} - \frac{5}{9}$
9. $\frac{3}{4} - \frac{1}{4}$
10. $3 - 2\frac{4}{6}$
11. $27 - 11\frac{3}{10}$
12. $14\frac{5}{9} - 12\frac{7}{9}$
13. $32\frac{1}{5} - 21\frac{4}{5}$
14. $2\frac{2}{8} - 1\frac{5}{8}$
15. $2\frac{1}{6} - 1\frac{5}{6}$

16. At birth, a person's brain weighs about $\frac{9}{10}$ pound. An adult's brain weighs about 3 pounds. By how much does the weight of your brain increase from birth to adulthood?

Daily Review | Test Prep

Write the LCM of the numbers.
(Ch. 9, Lessons 3–4)

17. 15, 18
18. 12, 30
19. 10, 12

20. **Free Response** Find $2\frac{5}{8} - 1\frac{7}{8}$. Be sure to write your answer in simplest form.

Extra Practice See page 279, Set E.

Lesson 6

Subtract With Unlike Denominators

Objective Subtract fractions with unlike denominators.

e Glossary

Vocabulary

common denominator

simplest form

Learn About It

When you are in a dark room, the pupil of your eye opens to let in as much light as possible. The diameter of your pupil then may be $\frac{3}{10}$ inch.

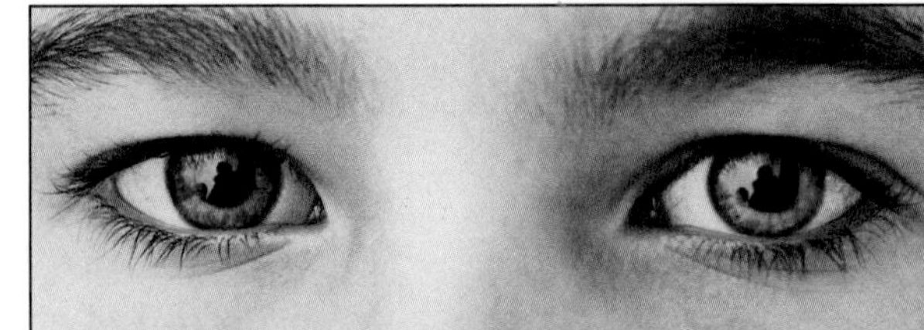

When in bright light, your pupil will contract or get smaller to let in less light. If the diameter of your pupil contracts to $\frac{3}{20}$ inch, how much does it contract?

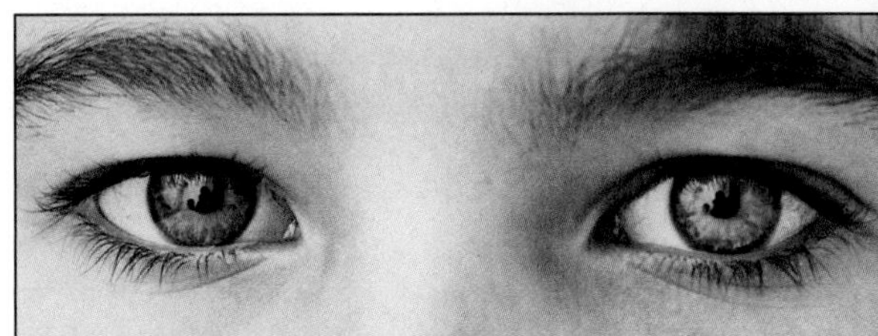

Subtract. $\frac{3}{10} - \frac{3}{20} = n$

Different Ways to Find $\frac{3}{10} - \frac{3}{20}$

Way 1 You can use any common denominator.

The product of the denominators, 10×20, can be used to write equivalent fractions with a common denominator.

$\frac{3}{10} = \frac{60}{200}$ (× 20)　　$\frac{3}{20} = \frac{30}{200}$ (× 10)

$\frac{60}{200} - \frac{30}{200} = \frac{30}{200}$

$\frac{30}{200} = \frac{3}{20}$ in **simplest form**.

Way 2 You can use the least common denominator.

The LCM of 10 and 20 is 20.
So the LCD of the fractions is 20.

$\frac{3}{10} = \frac{6}{20}$ (× 2)　　$\frac{3}{20} = \frac{3}{20}$ (× 1)

$\frac{6}{20} - \frac{3}{20} = \frac{3}{20}$

The difference already is in simplest form.

Solution: Your pupil contracts $\frac{3}{20}$ inch.

Check your answer.
Use addition.

$\frac{3}{20} + \frac{3}{20} = \frac{6}{20}$

$\frac{6}{20} = \frac{3}{10}$ in **simplest form**.

Guided Practice

Ask Yourself

- Can I find the LCD?
- Is my answer in simplest form?

TEST TIPS

Subtract. Write the difference in simplest form.

1. $\frac{1}{2} - \frac{1}{6}$
2. $\frac{2}{3} - \frac{1}{9}$
3. $\frac{2}{3} - \frac{1}{6}$
4. $\frac{5}{12} - \frac{3}{8}$
5. $\frac{4}{5} - \frac{1}{4}$
6. $\frac{1}{2} - \frac{2}{5}$

TEST TIPS **Explain Your Thinking** ▶ Why does multiplying the numerator and the denominator of a fraction by the same number produce an equivalent fraction?

Practice and Problem Solving

Subtract. Write the difference in simplest form.

7. $\frac{7}{8} - \frac{1}{2}$
8. $\frac{3}{4} - \frac{1}{2}$
9. $\frac{11}{12} - \frac{1}{3}$
10. $\frac{7}{10} - \frac{2}{5}$
11. $\frac{11}{12} - \frac{2}{3}$
12. $\frac{1}{2} - \frac{2}{5}$
13. $\frac{1}{3} - \frac{1}{8}$
14. $\frac{3}{4} - \frac{2}{5}$
15. $\frac{2}{3} - \frac{2}{10}$
16. $\frac{1}{4} - \frac{1}{10}$
17. $\frac{4}{5} - \frac{3}{4}$
18. $\frac{9}{18} - \frac{3}{6}$
19. $\frac{3}{4} - \frac{1}{10}$
20. $\frac{3}{8} - \frac{1}{16}$

Solve.

21. In soft light, your pupil contracts from about $\frac{3}{10}$ inch to about $\frac{1}{5}$ inch. How much does your pupil contract in soft light?

22. In one class, $\frac{3}{8}$ of the students have brown eyes, and $\frac{1}{3}$ of the students have blue eyes. What fraction of the students do not have brown or blue eyes?

23. **Predict** Write the three fractions that will likely come next in the pattern. Explain your answer.

$\frac{1}{2}$ $\frac{2}{3}$ $\frac{3}{4}$ $\frac{4}{5}$ ■ ■ ■

Daily Review | Test Prep

Multiply or divide.
(Ch. 3, Lessons 2–3; Ch. 4, Lesson 1)

24. 673×4
25. $894 \div 4$
26. 202×3
27. $612 \div 9$

✔ 28. If you spend $50, you can win a discount of $\frac{1}{5}$ off or $\frac{1}{2}$ off. What is the difference in the two discounts?

A $\frac{1}{3}$ **B** $\frac{1}{7}$ **C** $\frac{3}{5}$ **D** $\frac{3}{10}$

Extra Practice See page 279, Set F.

Lesson 7

Problem-Solving Strategy

Draw a Diagram

Objective Use a diagram to solve problems.

Problem Miguel and Heather are building a model of human lungs for the science fair. Together they have worked $\frac{3}{4}$ hour. Miguel has worked twice as long as Heather has. How long has each student worked?

This is what you know:

- Together they have worked $\frac{3}{4}$ hour.
- Miguel has worked twice as long as Heather has.

PLAN

You can draw a diagram to help you solve the problem.

SOLVE

- Draw 2 strips. Make one strip twice the length of the other.

Miguel

Heather

$\frac{3}{4}$ hour

- There are 3 small strips that make $\frac{3}{4}$. So each small strip is $\frac{1}{4}$, because 3 unit fractions of $\frac{1}{4}$ make $\frac{3}{4}$.
- Miguel has worked 2 unit fractions of $\frac{1}{4}$, or $\frac{1}{2}$ hour.

$$\frac{1}{4} + \frac{1}{4} = \frac{2}{4} = \frac{1}{2}$$

- Heather has worked 1 unit fraction of $\frac{1}{4}$, or $\frac{1}{4}$ hour.

Miguel has worked $\frac{1}{2}$ hour, and Heather has worked $\frac{1}{4}$ hour.

LOOK BACK

Look back at the problem. Is the answer reasonable? How do you know?

Guided Practice

Use the Ask Yourself questions to help you solve the problem.

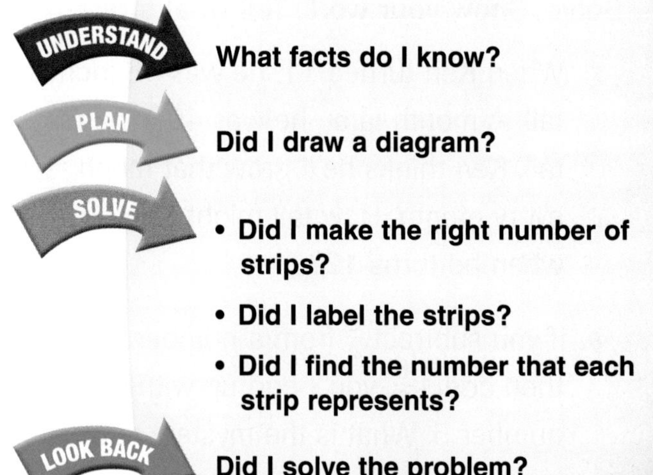

1. Josh worked $\frac{3}{4}$ hour on a science fair project. That's three times as long as Chester worked. How many hours did they work in all?

   Hint Think about the fraction each rectangle represents.

   Josh [| |]

   Chester [ ]

2. Sarah and Flora won the science fair. Sarah worked $2\frac{1}{3}$ hours on their project, and Flora worked $\frac{1}{2}$ hour more than Sarah. How much time did they work altogether?

   Sarah [$2\frac{1}{3}$ hours]

   Flora [| $\frac{1}{2}$ hour]

Independent Practice

Draw a diagram to solve each problem.

3. Three fifths of Miss Kwon's and Mr. Taylor's students are boys. Miss Kwon's class has twice as many boys as Mr. Taylor's class. If the classes have the same number of students, what part of each class is boys?

4. Catherine and Alexandria studied together for a history test for $1\frac{1}{2}$ hours. Afterwards Catherine studied for $\frac{2}{3}$ of that time by herself. Alexandria studied for $\frac{1}{2}$ of the time they studied together. How much time did each girl study?

5. A total of 135 students entered the science fair. There were 15 more girls than boys who entered. How many boys and how many girls entered the science fair?

6. A school has 40 classrooms. Three times as many classrooms are used for grades 4 and 5 together as for grade 6 alone. How many classrooms does grade 6 use?

Choose a Strategy

Solve. Show your work. Tell what strategy you used.

PROBLEM-SOLVING Strategies

- Use Models
- Draw a Diagram
- Find a Pattern
- Guess and Check
- Make an Organized List
- Make a Table
- Solve a Simpler Problem
- Use Logical Reasoning
- Work Backward
- Write an Equation

7. When Ken turned 11, he was 48 inches tall. A month later, he was $49\frac{1}{4}$ inches tall. Ken thinks he'll grow that much every month. How tall might Ken be when he turns 12?

8. If you subtract $\frac{3}{4}$ from a number and then add $1\frac{6}{8}$, you'll end up with the number 5. What is the mystery number?

9. Use your inch ruler. Measure each line segment to the nearest eighth of an inch. What will the length of the tenth line segment likely be?

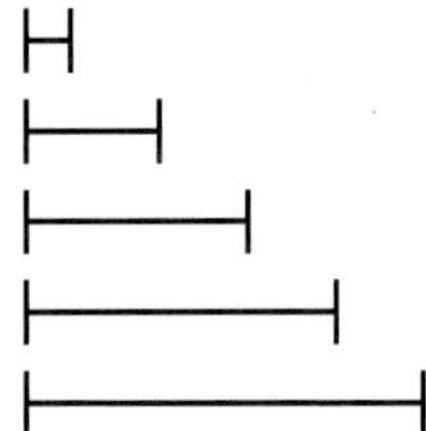

10. A science museum has 60 hands-on exhibits. For every 2 exhibits for young children, there are 3 exhibits for older children. How many exhibits are for each group?

Exhibits for Young Children
Exhibits for Older Children
60

Choose a Computation Method

Mental Math • Estimation • Paper and Pencil • Calculator

Data **Use the graph to solve Problems 11–14. Then explain which method you used.**

The graph shows survey results about breakfasts of fifth-grade students.

11. How many fifth-grade students responded to the survey?

12. How many more fifth-graders ate cold cereal than hot cereal on Saturday?

13. What fraction of the students surveyed ate a cold cereal on Saturday?

14. What fraction of the students surveyed did not eat hot cereal on Saturday?

Problem-Solving Test Prep

Choose the letter of the correct answer. If the correct answer is not here, choose NH.

1. Sally is $5\frac{1}{2}$ years old. Hal is $1\frac{1}{2}$ years older than that. Angie is $3\frac{1}{4}$ years older than Hal. How old is Angie?

A $6\frac{1}{2}$ yr **C** 10 yr

B 7 yr **D** $10\frac{1}{4}$ yr

(Chapter 10, Lesson 4)

2. Which shows equivalent fractions?

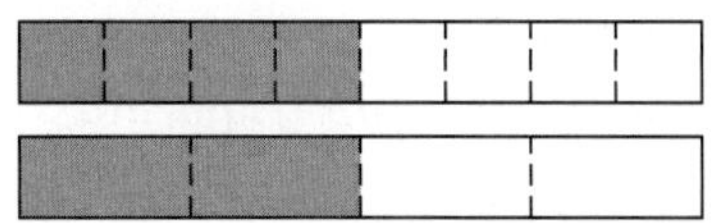

F $\frac{1}{2} = \frac{3}{4}$ **H** $\frac{3}{8} = \frac{2}{4}$

G $\frac{1}{2} = \frac{1}{4}$ **J** $\frac{4}{8} = \frac{2}{4}$

(Chapter 9, Lesson 6)

3. Which statements are true about the data set 16, 24, 25, 30, and 35?

A The range is 25. The mean is 30.

B The median is 25. The mean is 26.

C The median and the mode are 25.

D The mean is 25. There is no mode.

(Chapter 8, Lesson 5)

4. What is the least possible whole number you can make that uses the digits 9, 6, 8, and 3 only once and has a 9 in the tens place?

F 3,896 **H** 3,698

G 3,986 **J** NH

(Chapter 9, Lesson 7)

5. A recipe calls for $1\frac{1}{2}$ cups of flour. You are supposed to set $\frac{1}{4}$ cup aside and put the rest in a bowl. How much do you put in the bowl?

A $1\frac{1}{4}$ cups **C** $1\frac{1}{2}$ cups

B $1\frac{1}{3}$ cups **D** $1\frac{3}{4}$ cups

(Chapter 10, Lesson 6)

6. This Venn diagram shows factors of 24 and 36.

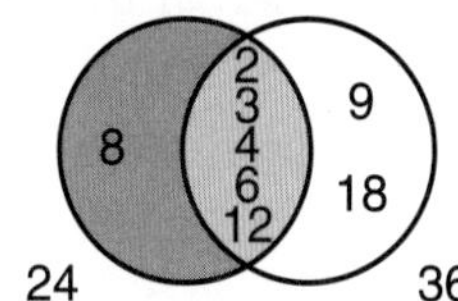

What is the GCF of 24 and 36?

Explain How does a Venn diagram help you identify the GCF?

(Chapter 9, Lesson 3)

7. Sal has a collection of stamps. He has 30 stamps in all. For every stamp from another country, Sal has two from the United States. How many United States stamps does Sal have?

Represent Support your solution with a diagram.

(Chapter 10, Lesson 7)

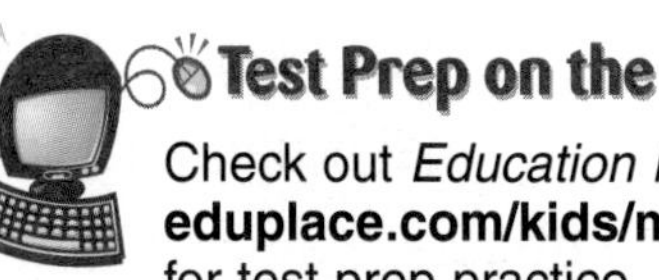

Test Prep on the Net

Check out *Education Place* at **eduplace.com/kids/mw/** for test prep practice.

Lesson 8

Subtract Mixed Numbers With Unlike Denominators

Objective Subtract mixed numbers with unlike denominators.

Learn About It

MathTracks 1/33
Listen and Understand

Last night, Tyler slept $8\frac{1}{2}$ hours, and Vanessa slept $9\frac{1}{4}$ hours. How much longer did Vanessa sleep than Tyler?

Subtract. $9\frac{1}{4} - 8\frac{1}{2} = n$

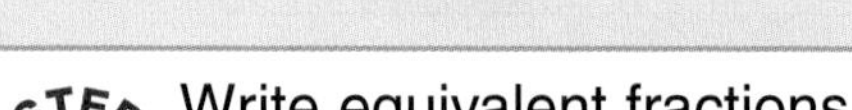

STEP 1 Find the LCD of the fractions.

$$\begin{array}{rcrl} 9\frac{1}{4} & = & 9\frac{\blacksquare}{4} & \leftarrow \\ -\,8\frac{1}{2} & = & -\,8\frac{\blacksquare}{4} & \leftarrow \text{ LCD} \\ \hline \end{array}$$

STEP 2 Write equivalent fractions.

$$\begin{array}{rcr} 9\frac{1}{4} & = & 9\frac{1}{4} \\ -\,8\frac{1}{2} & = & -\,8\frac{2}{4} \\ \hline \end{array}$$

STEP 3 Rename mixed numbers if necessary.

$$\begin{array}{rcr} 9\frac{1}{4} & = & 8\frac{5}{4} \\ -\,8\frac{2}{4} & = & -\,8\frac{2}{4} \\ \hline \end{array}$$

STEP 4 Subtract and simplify.

$$\begin{array}{rcr} 9\frac{1}{4} & = & 8\frac{5}{4} \\ -\,8\frac{2}{4} & = & -\,8\frac{2}{4} \\ \hline & & \frac{3}{4} \end{array}$$

Solution: Vanessa slept $\frac{3}{4}$ hour longer than Tyler.

Guided Practice

Subtract. Write each difference in simplest form.

1. $4\frac{1}{3} - 2\frac{1}{5}$
2. $9\frac{9}{10} - 4\frac{2}{5}$
3. $4\frac{1}{2} - 2\frac{7}{10}$
4. $8\frac{5}{12} - 6\frac{7}{8}$

Ask Yourself

- Did I rename when necessary?
- Did I simplify each difference?

Explain Your Thinking The value of a number does not change when it is renamed correctly. Explain why.

Practice and Problem Solving

Subtract. Write each difference in simplest form.

5. $9\frac{6}{8} - 2\frac{1}{2}$

6. $7\frac{1}{2} - 3$

7. $7\frac{3}{16} - 6\frac{1}{8}$

8. $3\frac{1}{5} - 1\frac{4}{20}$

9. $7\frac{4}{9} - 1\frac{2}{3}$

10. $4\frac{1}{5} - 3\frac{3}{10}$

11. $4\frac{7}{10} - 1\frac{7}{15}$

12. $2\frac{1}{2} - 1\frac{2}{3}$

13. $4\frac{1}{3} - 1\frac{3}{4}$

14. $8\frac{1}{6} - 5\frac{2}{3}$

15. $6\frac{3}{4} - 3\frac{5}{8}$

16. $9\frac{1}{4} - 6\frac{5}{6}$

17. $2\frac{5}{12} - 1\frac{4}{5}$

18. $7\frac{2}{3} - 5\frac{3}{4}$

Write >, <, or = for each ●.

19. $3\frac{3}{8} - 1\frac{1}{4}$ ● $4 - 2\frac{2}{3}$

20. $8\frac{1}{4} - 3\frac{1}{2}$ ● $6\frac{3}{4} - 2$

21. $5 - 1\frac{1}{8}$ ● $7\frac{1}{5} - 3\frac{1}{2}$

22. $6\frac{1}{3} - 2\frac{4}{5}$ ● $9\frac{1}{8} - 4\frac{5}{12}$

23. $6\frac{1}{4} - 4\frac{5}{8}$ ● $10 - 7\frac{1}{8}$

24. $3\frac{3}{5} - 1\frac{1}{10}$ ● $5\frac{1}{3} - 2\frac{5}{6}$

Mental Math Use mental math to subtract.

25. $5\frac{5}{8} - 3\frac{5}{8}$

26. $9\frac{2}{3} - 1\frac{1}{3}$

27. $6\frac{3}{4} - 4$

28. $7 - 3\frac{1}{2}$

29. $1\frac{1}{2} - 1\frac{1}{2}$

30. $15 - 7\frac{1}{2}$

31. $10\frac{1}{11} - 9$

32. $12\frac{1}{4} - 6\frac{1}{4}$

Algebra • **Expressions** Evaluate each expression when $a = 3\frac{3}{4}$, $b = 5\frac{1}{8}$, and $c = 1\frac{2}{3}$.

33. $a - c$

34. $b - a$

35. $b - c$

36. $(a + c) - b$

Copy and complete each function table.

37.

Rule: $y = x - 2$.	
x	y
$3\frac{1}{4}$	■
$5\frac{7}{8}$	■
$9\frac{3}{5}$	■

38.

Rule: $y = x + 1\frac{1}{2}$.	
x	y
$1\frac{2}{3}$	■
$4\frac{1}{2}$	■
$6\frac{5}{8}$	■

39.

Rule: $y = x - 1\frac{3}{4}$.	
x	y
4	■
$5\frac{3}{4}$	■
$7\frac{1}{4}$	■

Go On

Solve.

40. On Friday night, Lim slept for $10\frac{1}{3}$ hours. That was $2\frac{1}{2}$ hours more than he slept the night before. How many hours did Lim sleep on Thursday night?

41. Frances used to get 8 hours sleep each night. Now she takes a $1\frac{1}{2}$ hour nap and sleeps 5 hours at night. How much has her total sleep time changed?

42. Leon's goal is to sleep at least $8\frac{1}{2}$ hours each night. He goes to bed at 10:30 and wakes up at 6:45. Does Leon get the sleep he wants? If not, by how much does he miss his goal?

43. **Analyze** An infant sleeps about 16 hours each day. On Tuesday, her longest nap was $2\frac{2}{3}$ hours long, and her shortest nap was $\frac{3}{10}$ of an hour long. What is the range of her nap times?

44. **Measurement** With your math book closed, measure the length and width of its pages to the nearest eighth of an inch. What is the difference in these measures?

45. **You Decide** Teenagers should get $9\frac{1}{4}$ hours sleep each night. A middle school starts at 7:30 A.M. What do you think might be a better starting time? Explain your reasoning.

Choose a Computation Method

Mental Math • Estimation • Paper and Pencil • Calculator

Use the table for Problems 46–50. Then explain which method you chose.

46. How much more time does Judy spend getting ready for school than Rob does?

47. On which activity does Judy spend $\frac{1}{4}$ hour more than Rob does?

48. From the time he leaves school to the time he goes to bed, how much time does Rob spend on homework and other activities?

49. **Mental Math** How much time is Judy awake during the day?

50. **Create and Solve** Write your own problem that uses data from the table. Solve your problem. Then give your problem to a partner to solve.

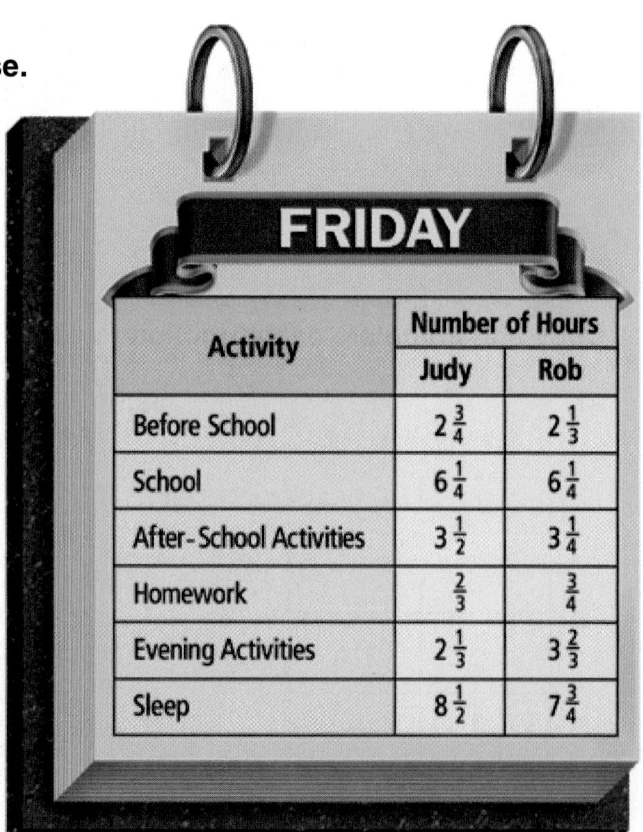

FRIDAY

Activity	Number of Hours	
	Judy	Rob
Before School	$2\frac{3}{4}$	$2\frac{1}{3}$
School	$6\frac{1}{4}$	$6\frac{1}{4}$
After-School Activities	$3\frac{1}{2}$	$3\frac{1}{4}$
Homework	$\frac{2}{3}$	$\frac{3}{4}$
Evening Activities	$2\frac{1}{3}$	$3\frac{2}{3}$
Sleep	$8\frac{1}{2}$	$7\frac{3}{4}$

Extra Practice See page 279, Set G.

Quick Check

Check your understanding for Lessons 5–8.

Subtract. Write each difference in simplest form. (Lessons 5, 6, and 8)

1. $\frac{9}{10} - \frac{1}{10}$
2. $6\frac{7}{8} - 3\frac{5}{8}$
3. $3\frac{1}{4} - 2\frac{3}{8}$
4. $\frac{3}{4} - \frac{2}{5}$
5. $9 - 3\frac{2}{3}$
6. $\frac{4}{5} - \frac{1}{3}$
7. $4\frac{3}{5} - 3\frac{1}{2}$
8. $6\frac{1}{8} - 2\frac{1}{2}$

Draw a diagram to solve each problem. (Lesson 7)

9. On Saturday and Sunday, John jogged for a total of $4\frac{1}{2}$ hours. On Saturday, he jogged twice as long as on Sunday. How long did he jog each day?
10. For every $2\frac{1}{4}$ hour shift Cam worked last week, Al worked 3 shifts. How many hours in all did Cam and Al work last week if Cam only worked 2 shifts?

What's the Rule?

You can use your calculator to show fractions as decimals by dividing the numerator by the denominator.

For each exercise, complete the following:

- Describe the pattern in the numerators and denominators.
- Use your calculator to convert the fractions to decimals.
- Describe the pattern in the decimals.
- Predict the next 2 fractions and decimals in the pattern.

1. $\frac{1}{50}$ $\frac{2}{50}$ $\frac{3}{50}$ $\frac{4}{50}$
2. $\frac{2}{5}$ $\frac{2}{10}$ $\frac{2}{20}$ $\frac{2}{40}$
3. $\frac{1}{25}$ $\frac{2}{50}$ $\frac{3}{75}$

Chapter Review/Test

VOCABULARY

1. The ____ of two or more denominators is the least common denominator.
2. $\frac{3}{4}$ and $\frac{6}{8}$ are ____.
3. The ____ of $\frac{7}{8}$ and $\frac{3}{4}$ is 8.

Vocabulary

equivalent fractions
least common denominator
least common multiple
simplest form

CONCEPTS AND SKILLS

Estimate each sum or difference.
Name the method you used to estimate. (Lesson 1, pp. 256–257)

4. $\frac{7}{8} - \frac{1}{6}$
5. $3\frac{3}{4} + \frac{5}{8}$
6. $23\frac{1}{8} + 14\frac{1}{4}$
7. $\frac{7}{9} - \frac{9}{16}$
8. $\frac{5}{8} - \frac{11}{20}$
9. $\frac{3}{8} + \frac{5}{6}$

Add. Write each sum in simplest form. (Lessons 2–4, pp. 258–265)

10. $\frac{7}{8} + \frac{5}{12}$
11. $\frac{2}{5} + \frac{2}{3}$
12. $4\frac{1}{2} + 8\frac{3}{8}$
13. $3\frac{3}{4} + 6\frac{3}{8}$
14. $\frac{5}{16} + \frac{7}{8}$
15. $\frac{5}{11} + \frac{7}{11}$
16. $6\frac{2}{5} + 9\frac{4}{5}$
17. $3\frac{1}{5} + 5\frac{1}{2}$

Subtract. Write each answer in simplest form. (Lessons 5–6, pp. 266–269; Lesson 8, pp. 274–277)

18. $\frac{6}{7} - \frac{2}{7}$
19. $21\frac{1}{8} - 18\frac{6}{8}$
20. $13\frac{2}{5} - 4\frac{1}{4}$
21. $\frac{13}{15} - \frac{2}{3}$
22. $\frac{2}{3} - \frac{3}{8}$
23. $10 - 4\frac{3}{4}$

PROBLEM SOLVING

Draw a diagram to solve each problem.
(Lesson 7, pp. 270–273)

24. Roger walks $6\frac{1}{2}$ blocks to school. Juanita walks $2\frac{3}{4}$ blocks to school. How much farther does Roger walk than Juanita?

25. Jorge worked $2\frac{1}{3}$ hours on his exhibit for the science fair. Juan worked $\frac{3}{4}$ hour more than Jorge. How long did the boys work altogether?

Show You Understand

Mandy added $\frac{3}{5}$ and $\frac{12}{15}$. Did she do it correctly? If not, explain.

$$\frac{3}{5} + \frac{12}{15} = \frac{3 + 12}{5 + 15} = \frac{15}{20} = \frac{3}{4}$$

Extra Practice

Set A (Lesson 1, pp. 256–257)

Estimate each sum or difference. Name the method you used to estimate.

1. $\frac{5}{6} + \frac{7}{8}$
2. $75\frac{1}{4} - 36\frac{1}{8}$
3. $7\frac{9}{10} - \frac{5}{8}$
4. $43\frac{2}{3} + 22\frac{5}{8}$
5. $3\frac{3}{4} - \frac{4}{7}$
6. $\frac{1}{9} + \frac{4}{5} + \frac{1}{3} + \frac{1}{15}$
7. $\frac{1}{5} + 1\frac{2}{3} + 2\frac{1}{3} + 3\frac{1}{6} + \frac{2}{10}$

Set B (Lesson 2, pp. 258–259)

Add. Write each sum in simplest form.

1. $2\frac{1}{5} + 3\frac{2}{5}$
2. $3\frac{5}{8} + 2\frac{3}{8}$
3. $4\frac{3}{4} + 5\frac{3}{4}$
4. $2\frac{1}{6} + 3\frac{1}{6}$

Set C (Lesson 3, pp. 260–261)

Add. Write each sum in simplest form.

1. $\frac{1}{4} + \frac{1}{8}$
2. $\frac{2}{3} + \frac{2}{9}$
3. $\frac{3}{5} + \frac{3}{10}$
4. $\frac{1}{5} + \frac{3}{10}$
5. $\frac{5}{12} + \frac{1}{3}$
6. $\frac{7}{8} + \frac{1}{16}$
7. $\frac{11}{12} + \frac{2}{3}$
8. $\frac{3}{8} + \frac{7}{12}$
9. $\frac{1}{4} + \frac{2}{5}$
10. $\frac{1}{6} + \frac{2}{3}$

Set D (Lesson 4, pp. 262–265)

Add. Write each sum in simplest form.

1. $4\frac{2}{3} + 5\frac{3}{4}$
2. $4\frac{1}{2} + 3\frac{3}{4}$
3. $3\frac{3}{4} + 3\frac{7}{8}$
4. $6\frac{3}{4} + 7\frac{5}{6}$
5. $2\frac{1}{2} + 3\frac{3}{4}$
6. $8\frac{1}{16} + 9\frac{1}{3}$
7. $6\frac{5}{12} + 3\frac{2}{3}$
8. $5\frac{1}{5} + 3\frac{1}{2}$

Set E (Lesson 5, pp. 266–267)

Subtract. Write each difference in simplest form.

1. $\frac{7}{8} - \frac{5}{8}$
2. $\frac{4}{5} - \frac{1}{5}$
3. $\frac{9}{10} - \frac{3}{10}$
4. $\frac{6}{7} - \frac{3}{7}$
5. $7 - 3\frac{1}{6}$

Set F (Lesson 6, pp. 268–269)

Subtract. Write each difference in simplest form.

1. $\frac{3}{4} - \frac{1}{8}$
2. $\frac{5}{12} - \frac{1}{6}$
3. $\frac{11}{12} - \frac{5}{8}$
4. $\frac{5}{6} - \frac{1}{2}$
5. $\frac{3}{4} - \frac{3}{5}$
6. $\frac{6}{8} - \frac{5}{16}$
7. $\frac{19}{24} - \frac{1}{6}$
8. $\frac{9}{10} - \frac{2}{5}$

Set G (Lesson 8, pp. 274–277)

Subtract. Write each answer in simplest form.

1. $3\frac{3}{4} - 2\frac{2}{3}$
2. $8\frac{1}{2} - 4\frac{3}{4}$
3. $6\frac{5}{6} - 3\frac{2}{3}$
4. $2\frac{3}{8} - 1\frac{1}{4}$
5. $4\frac{3}{12} - 2\frac{3}{4}$
6. $9\frac{1}{4} - 6\frac{3}{8}$
7. $7 - 1\frac{4}{5}$
8. $5\frac{1}{6} - 2\frac{1}{4}$

Add and Subtract Decimals

INVESTIGATION

Use Data

The table shows some of the winning times of race cars in the Indy 500. What is the difference between the fastest winning time and the slowest?

Indy 500 Winning Times

Year	Approx. Time (hours)
1970	3.210
1980	3.500
1990	2.688
2000	2.983

Chapter Pretest

Use this page to review and remember what you need to know for this chapter.

VOCABULARY

Choose the best word to complete each sentence.

1. In the number 3.25, the 2 is in the ____ place.
2. The decimals 5.6 and 5.60 are ____.
3. When comparing numbers, you compare the ____ that are in the same place.
4. In the number 5.20, the 0 is in the ____ place.

CONCEPTS AND SKILLS

Write a fraction and a decimal for the shaded part.

5. 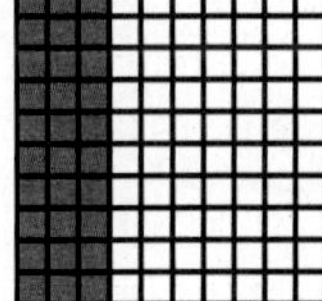

6. 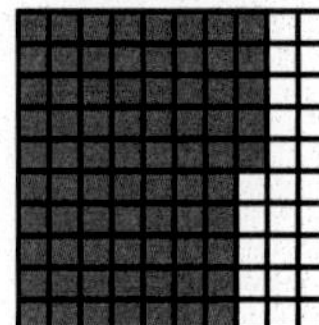

7. 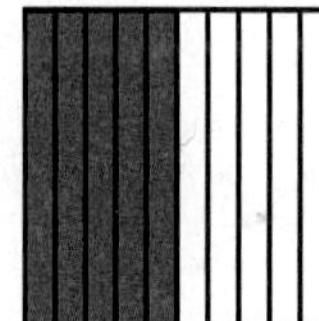

Order the numbers from greatest to least.

8. 4.06, 3.14, 3.7, 4.08
9. 235.03, 194.3, 235.3, 194.03
10. 11.52, 12.07, 12.8, 12.5
11. 4.05, 4.5, 4.005, 45
12. 2.2, 22.02, 2.22, 2.02
13. 0.3, 0.081, 0.2, 0.02

Round to the place of the underlined digit.

14. 2.324
15. 3.259
16. 0.265
17. 83.351
18. 0.672
19. 13.559

20. The Rivoli Theater sold 12,217 tickets, and the Capital Theater sold 2,250. About how many more tickets did the Rivoli sell? Explain how you found your answer.

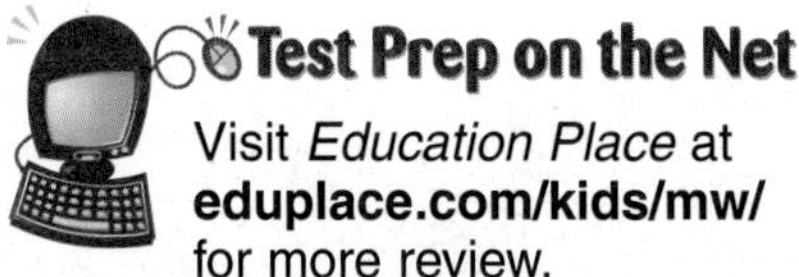

Lesson 1

Explore Addition and Subtraction With Decimals

Objective Add and subtract decimals.

Learn About It

A car dealer sells used sports cars. Of all the cars she has on her lot, 0.89 are red. Only 0.03 are green. What part of the cars on her lot are red or green?

Solve 0.89 + 0.03 = *n*.

You can use models and what you know about fractions to find 0.89 + 0.03. Try changing the decimals to fractions and then modeling the addition.

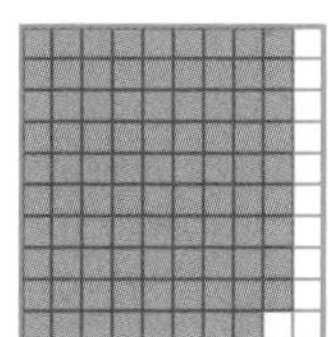
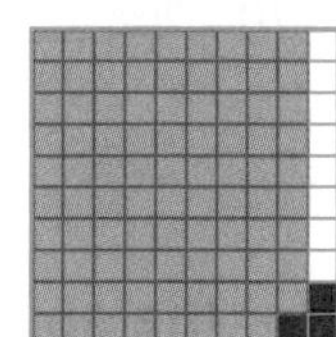

- What fractions are equivalent to 0.89 and 0.03? $0.89 = \frac{89}{100}$ $0.03 = \frac{3}{100}$
- How can you model $\frac{89}{100}$?
- How can you show $\frac{3}{100}$ more than $\frac{89}{100}$?
- Think about what you are to find.

  How much is 0.89 + 0.03?

  How much is $\frac{89}{100}$ plus $\frac{3}{100}$?
- How do you add fractions with like denominators? $\frac{89}{100} + \frac{3}{100} = \frac{92}{100}$
- How can you write your answer as a decimal? $\frac{92}{100} = 0.92$

Solution: Of the cars on the dealer's lot, 0.92 are red or green.

Another Example

Subtract Decimals

Subtract. 2.14 − 1.12 = *n*

$2.14 = 2\frac{14}{100}$ $1.12 = 1\frac{12}{100}$

$2\frac{14}{100} - 1\frac{12}{100} = 1\frac{2}{100}$

So 2.14 − 1.12 = 1.02

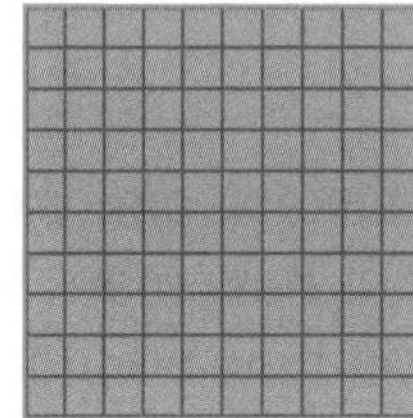
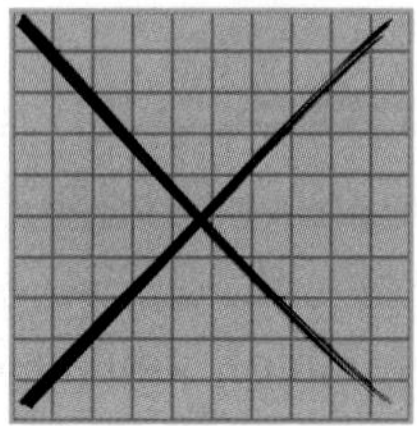
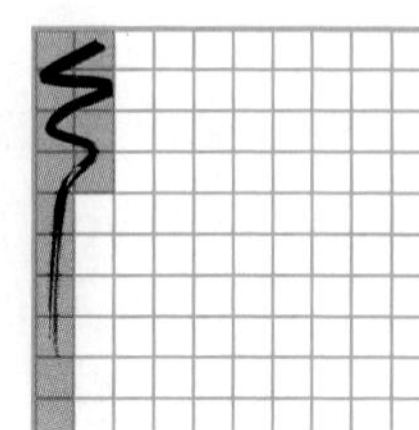

Guided Practice

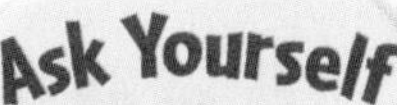

- Did I change the decimals to fractions?
- Did I write my answer as a decimal?

Change each decimal to a fraction. Model each addition and subtraction. Write each sum as a decimal.

1. 0.3 + 0.5 **2.** 0.25 + 0.15 **3.** 1.2 + 1.8

4. 0.9 − 0.1 **5.** 0.67 − 0.22 **6.** 2.08 − 1.15

Explain Your Thinking Why is it easy to change a decimal to a fraction and then change it back again? Give examples to support your thinking.

Practice and Problem Solving

Change each decimal to a fraction. Model each addition and subtraction. Write each sum as a decimal.

7. 0.7 + 0.7 **8.** 0.76 + 0.15 **9.** 0.34 + 0.98 **10.** 1.25 + 2.37

11. 0.4 − 0.3 **12.** 0.25 − 0.12 **13.** 1.26 − 1.05 **14.** 2.8 − 1.4

15. 0.56 + 0.3 **16.** 0.92 + 0.8 **17.** 0.93 − 0.5 **18.** 0.6 − 0.15

Solve.

19. **Represent** Of the cars the dealer sold two years ago, 0.4 were blue. Last year 0.09 of the cars she sold were blue. In which year did she sell a greater fraction of blue cars? Draw a model to explain.

20. A car dealer noted that an older sports car model was 167.3 inches long and a newer model was 12.4 inches longer than that. How long was the newer model?

21. In her first year a dealer sold 300 cars. Last year she sold 3,230 cars. How many more cars did she sell last year than during her first year?

22. **Estimate** Of the 3,460 sports cars sold this year, only 4 were gold. Is that about 0.1, 0.01, or 0.001 sports cars? Explain how you know.

Daily Review | Test Prep

Draw the next two figures in each pattern.
(Grade 4)

23.    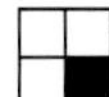    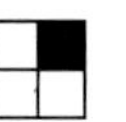 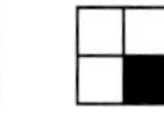

24.      

 **25.** **Free Response** Dave spent 4.5 hours cleaning his car. He spent 3.5 hours polishing it. Write a fraction equation and draw a model to show how much longer it took Dave to clean his car than to polish it.

Extra Practice See page 295, Set A.

Lesson 2

Add Decimals

Objective Add decimals through thousandths.

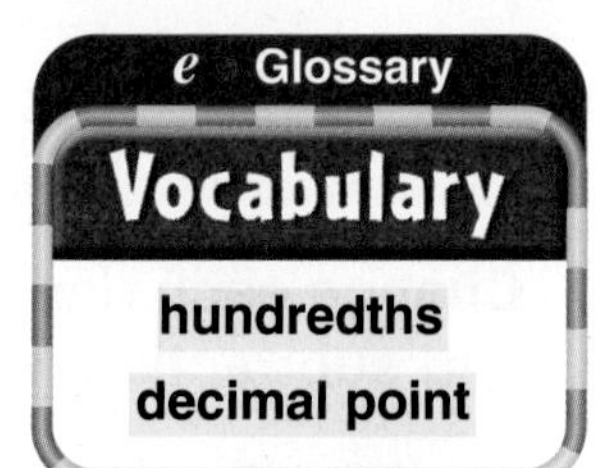

Learn About It

California has some of the strictest vehicle air pollution standards in the country. The chart shows the maximum amount of three pollutants a light-duty truck may emit per mile. How many grams of pollution is that per mile?

Light-Duty Truck Pollutants

Non-methane organic gas (NMOG)	Carbon monoxide (CO)	Nitrogen oxides (NO_X)
0.07 gram/mile	2.8 grams/mile	0.5 gram/mile

Add. $0.07 + 2.8 + 0.5 = n$

STEP 1 Align the digits in the addends. Use the decimal points as guides. Then add the **hundredths**.

$$\begin{array}{r} 0.07 \\ 2.80 \\ +\ 0.50 \\ \hline 7 \end{array}$$

Write zeros as needed.

STEP 2 Add the tenths.

$$\begin{array}{r} \overset{1}{0}.07 \\ 2.80 \\ +\ 0.50 \\ \hline 37 \end{array}$$

STEP 3 Add the ones.

$$\begin{array}{r} \overset{1}{0}.07 \\ 2.80 \\ +\ 0.50 \\ \hline 3.37 \end{array}$$

Align the decimal point in the sum with the **decimal point** in the addends.

Use a calculator to check.

0 . 0 7 + 2 . 8 + 0 . 5 Enter =

Solution: A light-duty truck may emit a maximum of 3.37 grams of pollutants per mile.

Guided Practice

Add. Use a calculator to check.

1. $\begin{array}{r} 4.517 \\ +\ 2.824 \\ \hline \end{array}$

2. $\begin{array}{r} \$57.99 \\ +\ \ 4.23 \\ \hline \end{array}$

3. $\begin{array}{r} 54.1 \\ 8.376 \\ +\ 12 \\ \hline \end{array}$

4. 78.94 + 5.57

5. 19.07 + 1.23

6. 8 + 4.794 + 2.3

Ask Yourself

- Did I line up the digits in the addends?
- Did I remember to write the decimal point in the answer?

Explain Your Thinking ▶ Why is it important to align the decimal points in the addends?

Practice and Problem Solving

Add. Use a calculator to check.

7. $8.49 + 4.59
8. 9.527 + 3.75
9. 178.03 + 8.4
10. 1.699 + 90.5
11. $10.00 + 8.05
12. $51.70 + 83.62
13. 78.427 + 27.309
14. 85.076 + 7.925
15. 5.76 + 28.569
16. 41.75 + 9.863
17. 31.85 + 5.8 + 53.85
18. $8.03 + 9.80 + 24.57
19. 7.9 + 5.662 + 14.038
20. 4.887 + 46.2 + 7.09
21. 4.47 + 4.46 + 6.592
22. 28.5 + 85.7
23. 2.06 + 46.99
24. 0.007 + 0.925
25. 7.48 + 0.351
26. 11.2 + 16.801
27. 5.05 + 1.3
28. 2.089 + 5 + 4.8
29. 20.49 + 17.5

Use the table below to solve Problems 30–32.

The table shows the California emissions standards for light-duty trucks that are expected to last 100,000 miles.

30. **Mental Math** How many grams of CO and NO_x may a low-emission vehicle (LEV) emit per mile?

31. **Analyze** For which type of truck will the maximum emissions of NMOG, CO, and NO_x be between 6.0 and 6.2 grams per mile?

32. **Write About It** Write a problem that uses the information in the table. Exchange with a classmate and solve.

Light-Duty Truck Emissions Standards

Class	Pollutant (in grams/mile)		
	NMOG	CO	NO_x
TLEV	0.2	5.5	0.9
LEV	0.13	5.5	0.5
ULEV	0.07	2.8	0.5

Daily Review Test Prep

Estimate the sums and differences.
(Ch. 2, Lesson 4)

33. 324 + 456 + 535
34. 9,220 + 984
35. 13,562 − 9,480
36. 10,100 − 750

37. **Free Response** A car emitted 0.750 grams more of a pollutant than the 0.09 grams allowed. How many grams of this pollutant did the car emit? Explain how you found your answer.

Extra Practice See page 295, Set B.

Lesson 3

Subtract Decimals

Objective Subtract decimals through thousandths with and without regrouping.

Learn About It

On the highway, John's car can travel 31.42 miles on one gallon of gas. When he is driving in the city, his car gets 26.98 miles per gallon. How many more miles per gallon does John's car get on the highway than in the city?

You can draw a model to help you solve the problem.

Highway miles per gallon	
City miles per gallon	Difference: ?

Highway: 31.42 miles per gallon	
City: 26.98 miles per gallon	Difference: ?

Subtract. 31.42 − 26.98 = *n*

STEP 1 Write the addends so the digits are aligned. Subtract the hundredths.

```
      3 12
  3 1.4 2
− 2 6.9 8
        4
```

STEP 2 Subtract the tenths.

```
    0 13 12
  3 1. 4 2
− 2 6. 9 8
       4 4
```

STEP 3 Subtract the ones. Write the decimal point in the answer.

```
  2 10 13 12
  3 1.  4 2
− 2 6.  9 8
    4.  4 4
```

STEP 4 Subtract the tens.

```
  2 10 13 12
  3 1.  4 2
− 2 6.  9 8
    4.  4 4
```

Add to check.

```
  1 1  1
  2 6. 9 8
+   4. 4 4
  3 1. 4 2
```

Solution: John's car gets 4.44 more miles per gallon on the highway than in the city.

Other Examples

A. Zeros as Placeholders

Find 27.5 − 2.71.

```
   6 1410
 2 7̸.5̸0̸
−  2.71
 24.79
```

B. Money

Find $28 − $9.76.

```
    17  9
   1 1̸8̸ 1̸0̸10
 $2̸8̸.0̸0̸
−   9.76
 $18.24
```

Guided Practice

Ask Yourself

- Have I aligned the digits correctly?
- Do I need to write zeros to help me subtract?

Subtract. Add or use a calculator to check your answer.

1. 4.5 − 3.7
2. 7.0 − 4.37
3. $4.18 − 2.99
4. 7.514 − 5.439
5. 2 − 0.065
6. $84.01 − $47.86

Use the model to solve the problem.

7. A car gets 4.6 more miles per gallon on the highway than it does in the city. If the car gets 26.25 miles per gallon on the highway, how many miles per gallon does it get in the city?

Highway: 26.25 miles per gallon	
City: ?	Difference: 4.6 miles per gallon

Explain Your Thinking How is subtraction with decimals like subtraction with whole numbers? How is it different?

Practice and Problem Solving

Subtract. Add or use a calculator to check your answer.

8. 5.6 − 4.9
9. 9.2 − 3.7
10. 12.5 − 9.8
11. $28.09 − 17.99
12. $43.72 − 27.65
13. $3.45 − 0.79
14. 72.325 − 5.61
15. 57.681 − 24.925
16. 8.42 − 3.693
17. 13.0 − 8.429
18. 6.74 − 5.89
19. $34.56 − $13.67
20. 65.23 − 37.68
21. 0.7 − 0.067
22. 4.056 − 2.345
23. 29.547 − 18.918
24. 0.523 − 0.097
25. $5 − $1.87

Go On

Mental Math Add or subtract using mental math.

26. 0.8 + 0.1
27. 4.5 + 1.5
28. 0.9 − 0.2
29. \$3 − \$0.50
30. 0.006 + 0.027
31. 0.09 + 0.01
32. 0.5 − 0.3
33. 2.6 − 2.1
34. 0.042 − 0.03
35. 9.08 − 9.03
36. \$5.85 + \$1.15
37. 3.065 − 2.05
38. 0.004 + 0.076
39. 4.34 − 0.28
40. \$7.05 + \$2.15
41. 5.709 + 0.001

Algebra • Variables Find the value of *x*.

42. $x + 1.4 = 2$
43. $x - 1.4 = 2$
44. $2.8 - x = 2.3$
45. $0.5 + x = 1.0$
46. $3.2 + x = 4.3$
47. $2.65 - x = 2.5$

Data Use the table below to solve Problems 48–50.

Roberta drives her car to her job. The table shows her gas log for the month of April.

48. What is the range for the gas mileage (miles per gallon) that Roberta gets on her car?

49. Roberta budgets \$100 per month for gasoline for her job. How much over or under her budget was Roberta during April?

50. In May, Roberta bought 56.8 gallons of gas. How many more or fewer gallons of gas did Roberta buy during April?

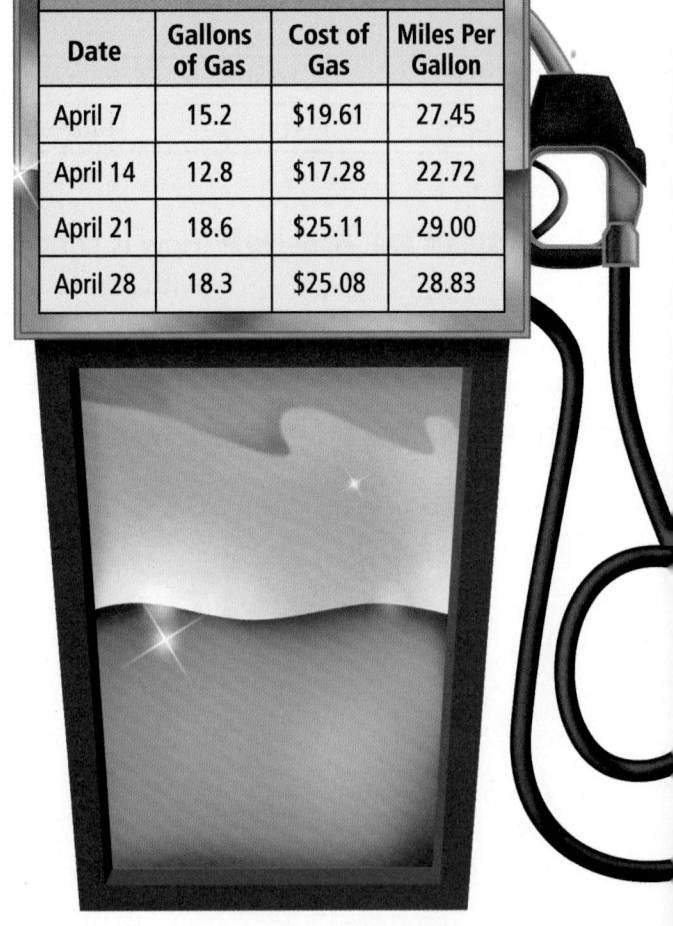

Gas Log: April

Date	Gallons of Gas	Cost of Gas	Miles Per Gallon
April 7	15.2	\$19.61	27.45
April 14	12.8	\$17.28	22.72
April 21	18.6	\$25.11	29.00
April 28	18.3	\$25.08	28.83

51. **Analyze** Write the missing digits.

```
  4.■3■
− ■.684
  2.5■1
```

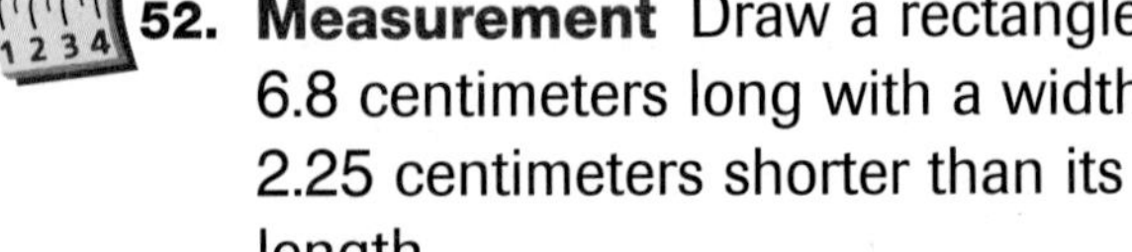

52. **Measurement** Draw a rectangle 6.8 centimeters long with a width 2.25 centimeters shorter than its length.

53. **Analyze** The sum of two numbers is 16.4. Their difference is 0.8. What are the two numbers?

Extra Practice See page 295, Set C.

Daily Review **Test Prep** 

Add or subtract. Write your answers in simplest form. (Ch. 10, Lessons 2 and 5)

54. $\frac{3}{4} + \frac{3}{4}$

55. $2\frac{5}{8} + 1\frac{3}{8}$

56. $6\frac{2}{3} - 4\frac{1}{3}$

57. $7\frac{1}{10} - 4\frac{9}{10}$

58. $12\frac{5}{6} + 2\frac{1}{6}$

59. $20\frac{3}{5} - 2\frac{4}{5}$

60. $15\frac{1}{4} + 7\frac{3}{4}$

61. $19\frac{5}{8} - 7\frac{3}{8}$

 **62.** A car gets 38.6 miles per gallon on the highway. It gets 5.75 miles per gallon less when it is in the city. How many miles per gallon does the car get in the city?

A 32.85 miles per gallon

B 32.95 miles per gallon

C 33.15 miles per gallon

D 33.95 miles per gallon

Zero Sum-thing

If you subtract 2 − 2, you know the answer is zero. If you add 4 and then subtract 1 and then subtract 3, the answer is also zero. These are zero sums. Adding and subtracting the same amount is the same as adding 0. Do you think this also works with decimals? Check It Out.

 Write your birthday or another date as a decimal. For example July 19 becomes 7.19.

- Add 2.06.
- Subtract 1.32.
- Subtract 0.08.
- Add 3.5.
- Subtract 2.16.
- Subtract 2.

$$\begin{array}{r} 7.19 \\ +\,2.06 \\ \hline 9.25 \\ -\,1.32 \\ \hline 7.93 \\ -\,0.08 \\ \hline 7.85 \\ +\,3.5 \\ \hline 11.35 \\ -\,2.16 \\ \hline 9.19 \\ -\,2.00 \\ \hline 7.19 \end{array}$$

2 What do you notice about your answer?

3 Why did this work?

4 Use decimals to make up your own zero sum challenge for a friend to try.

Lesson 4

Estimate Decimal Sums and Differences

Objective Estimate decimal sums and differences.

e Glossary
Vocabulary
round

Learn About It

MathTracks 1/36
Listen and Understand

In a race, the second-place finisher was about 0.038 seconds behind the winner. The third-place car was about 0.139 seconds behind the winner. About how many seconds behind the second-place car was the third-place car?

Estimate 0.139 − 0.038.

You can use what you know about rounding decimals to estimate the difference. For decimals less than one, **round** to the nearest tenth. For decimals greater than 1, round to the nearest whole number.

STEP 1 Round each number to the nearest hundredth.

0.139 ≈ 0.14
↑
9 > 5, so round up.

0.038 ≈ 0.04
↑
8 > 5, so round up.

STEP 2 Subtract.

$$\begin{array}{r} 0.14 \\ -\ 0.04 \\ \hline 0.10 \text{ or } 0.1 \end{array}$$

Solution: The third-place car was about 0.1 second behind the second-place car.

Other Examples

A. Nearest Whole Number

Estimate 23.27 − 15.64.

Round each decimal to the nearest whole number.

23.27 ≈ 23
15.64 ≈ 16

23 − 16 = 7
23.27 − 15.64 ≈ 7

B. Front-End Estimation

Estimate 4.14 + 5.22.

Add the leading digits.

4.14 → 4
5.22 → 5

4 + 5 = 9
4.14 + 5.22 ≈ 9

Since both decimals are rounded down, the estimated sum will be a little less than the actual sum.

C. Clustering

Estimate.

$$\begin{array}{r} 0.46 \\ 0.54 \\ 0.76 \\ +\ 0.28 \\ \hline \end{array}$$

0.46 and 0.54: about 1 whole
0.76 and 0.28: about 1 whole

The sum is about 2.

Guided Practice

Ask Yourself

- Did I follow the rounding rules?
- Did I estimate to the given place?
- Is my estimate reasonable?

Estimate each sum or difference to the place indicated.

1. 0.45 + 0.37 (tenths)
2. 0.389 − 0.258 (tenths)
3. 24.346 + 36.789 (ones)
4. 75.44 − 32.98 (ones)

Explain Your Thinking Why wouldn't rounding to the nearest tenth make sense if you want to estimate the sum of 14,302.85 and 9,394.83?

Practice and Problem Solving

Estimate each sum or difference to the nearest tenth.

5. 0.237 + 0.129
6. 0.545 + 0.435
7. 0.321 + 0.434
8. 0.854 + 0.649
9. 0.298 − 0.154
10. 0.934 − 0.856
11. 0.487 − 0.265
12. 0.912 − 0.544

Estimate each sum or difference to the nearest whole number.

13. 1.56 + 4.58
14. 12.87 + 6.7
15. 64.97 + 31.9
16. 43.983 + 8.6
17. 76.84 − 52.19
18. 27.8 − 15.99
19. 87.4 − 74.18
20. 7.824 − 0.516

Solve.

21. The average winning speed at the first Indy 500 was 74.602 miles per hour. The 2002 average winning speed was 166.499 miles per hour. Estimate the difference in those two speeds.

22. **Create and Solve** Write a problem about racing times and speeds that requires estimating a decimal sum or difference. Solve your problem and give it to a partner to solve.

23. **Estimate** The track for the Indy 500 has two straightaways. Each is 0.625 mile long. Together, about how long are the straightaways?

24. **What's Wrong?** Gina estimated the sum of 0.925 and 0.674 as 0.16. Why is Gina's estimate unreasonable? What did she do wrong?

Daily Review | Test Prep

Write the numbers in order from least to greatest. (Ch. 1, Lessons 4 and 7)

25. 19	18.76	18.903	19.09
26. 5.609	5.702	5.92	5.6
27. 7.04	7.082	7	7.45

28. **Free Response** During one pit-stop, the first-place car took 8.555 seconds. The second-place car took 1.5 to 2 seconds more than that. What is a reasonable estimate of the second-place car's time? Explain.

Extra Practice See page 295, Set D.

Lesson 5

Problem-Solving Decision

Choose a Method

Objective Choose a computation method to solve a problem.

Before you solve a problem with decimals, you need to decide what is the best computation method to use.

Problem Last year at the Auto Show, a car company rented a booth that covered 453.75 square meters of floor space. This year they are cutting back to a booth that is 378.5 square meters. How much less floor space do they have this year than last year?

Ask Yourself

Should I use mental math?

Think

453.75 − 378.5 = 75.25

Do I need to use pencil and paper?

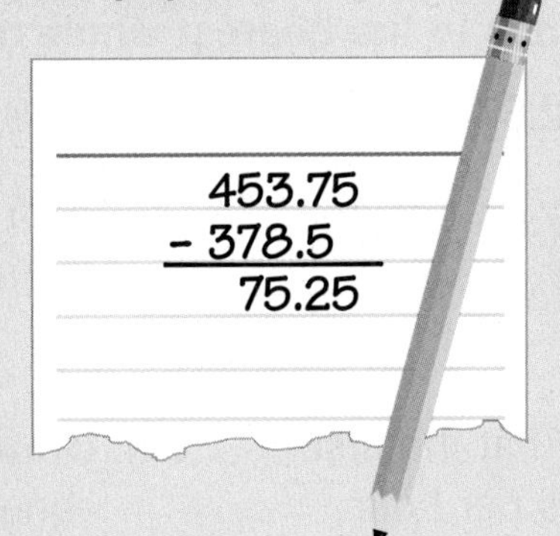

Does it make sense to use a calculator?

Which method would you choose?

Solution: This year's booth is 75.25 square meters smaller than last year's booth.

Try These

Solve. Explain which method you chose.

1. Ben worked at the Auto Show for 3.5 hours on Friday and 8.25 hours on Saturday. How many more hours did he work on Saturday than Friday?
2. During the show, Deanna sold two cars. One sold for $22,156.94 and the other sold for $19,209.38. What is the total of her two sales?
3. A speaker gave a 1.5-hour presentation followed by a 2.5-hour documentary film on experimental electric cars. How long were the two presentations?
4. Jill's car averages 18.65 miles per gallon of gasoline. The car she likes at the Auto Show averages 22 miles per gallon. How much better mileage does the new car get?

Quick Check

Check your understanding of Lessons 1–5.

Add or subtract. (Lessons 1–4)

1. $0.9 - 0.2$
2. $\$53.24 + \$16.82$
3. $4.9 + 3.75 + 0.84$
4. $9 - 0.87$
5. $0.025 - 0.006$
6. $\$20 - \$5.29$

Estimate each sum and difference to the nearest tenth. (Lesson 4)

7. $0.296 + 0.324 + 0.74$
8. $1.732 - 0.585$

Solve. (Lesson 5)

9. Amy's average on spelling tests is 4.2 points lower than her average on math tests. If her math test average is 88, what is her spelling test average?

Estimation Destination

2 players

What You'll Need • a number cube labeled 1 to 6 • pennies • 4 sets of number cards labeled 0 to 9 or Learning Tool 6.

How to Play

1. One player rolls the number cube twice and writes the numbers rolled in order. The other player uses a penny as a decimal point and places it before, after, or between the numbers. This is the target number.

2. Each player then draws 4 number cards. Players use the cards to make two decimal numbers, whose sum or difference is as close as possible to the target number.

3. The sum or difference closest to the target number scores two points. Repeat. The first player with 10 points wins.

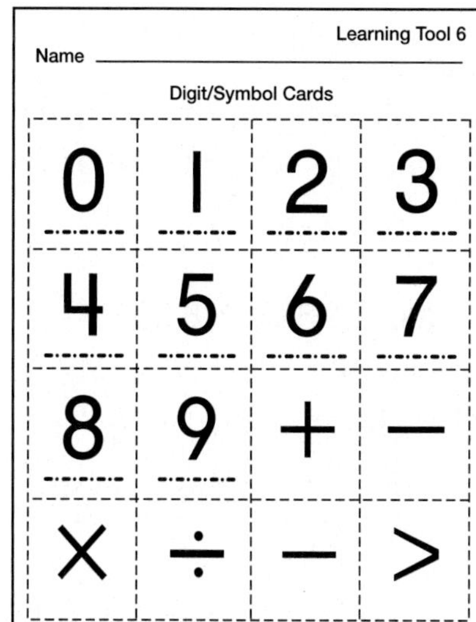

Learning Tool 6

Chapter Review/Test

VOCABULARY

Vocabulary

decimal point
fraction
hundredths
tenths
thousandths

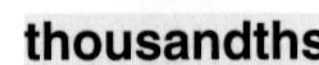

1. The ____ separates the ones and tenths places in a decimal.
2. The decimal 0.04 is read as "four ____."
3. The 6 in the decimal 2.416 is in the ____ place.
4. Any decimal can be written as a ____ or mixed number.

CONCEPTS AND SKILLS

Change each decimal to a fraction. Write each sum or difference as a decimal. (Lesson 1, pp. 282–283)

5. 0.6 + 0.5
6. 0.46 + 3.76
7. 2.3 + 1.2
8. 0.82 + 1.19

Add or subtract. (Lessons 2–3, pp. 284–289)

9. 8.3 + 4.73 + 38.407
10. \$37.05 + 95.89 + 6.81
11. 3.668 + 52.75 + 5.14
12. 4.076 + 7 + 5.3
13. 5.7 − 3.9
14. \$95.09 − 67.57
15. 16.08 − 7.657
16. 0.8 − 0.059

Estimate each sum or difference to the nearest tenth.
(Lesson 4, pp. 290–291)

17. 0.539 + 0.283
18. 0.679 − 0.261
19. 0.935 + 0.364
20. 0.825 − 0.177

Estimate each sum or difference to the nearest whole number. (Lesson 4, pp. 290–291)

21. 4.068 − 0.375
22. 77.26 − 41.82
23. 34.612 + 8.09
24. 7.159 + 3.123

PROBLEM SOLVING

Solve. Write the computation method you used. (Lesson 5, pp. 292–293)

25. Mustafa worked at a store for 4.5 hours on Monday and 1.75 hours on Tuesday. How many more hours did he work on Monday?

Show You Understand

Antonio estimated the sum of 0.825 and 0.415 as 12. Was his estimate reasonable? Explain.

Extra Practice

Set A (Lesson 1, pp. 282–283)

Change each decimal to a fraction. Write each answer as a decimal.

1. 0.3 + 0.5
2. 5.3 + 6.4
3. 0.31 + 0.52
4. 0.12 + 0.63
5. 0.83 − 0.6
6. 0.65 − 0.27
7. 1.82 − 1.36
8. 1.91 − 0.04
9. 0.85 + 0.9
10. 0.7 + 0.23
11. 2.1 − 0.06
12. 1.76 − 0.17

Set B (Lesson 2, pp. 284–285)

Add.

1. $\begin{array}{r} 7.42 \\ +\ 22.58 \\ \hline \end{array}$
2. $\begin{array}{r} 2.09 \\ +\ 56.43 \\ \hline \end{array}$
3. $\begin{array}{r} \$\ 8.65 \\ +\ 40.25 \\ \hline \end{array}$
4. $\begin{array}{r} \$27.45 \\ +\ 53.75 \\ \hline \end{array}$
5. $\begin{array}{r} 46.3 \\ 5 \\ +\ 3.821 \\ \hline \end{array}$
6. $\begin{array}{r} 18.07 \\ 7.3 \\ +\ 5.682 \\ \hline \end{array}$
7. $\begin{array}{r} 93.14 \\ 5.78 \\ +\ 235.309 \\ \hline \end{array}$
8. $\begin{array}{r} 23.06 \\ 15.7 \\ 3.28 \\ +\ 71.697 \\ \hline \end{array}$
9. 51.6 + 3.7 + 5
10. 27.06 + 0.97 + 0.002
11. 5.825 + 3.45
12. 17.067 + 5.643

Set C (Lesson 3, pp. 286–291)

Subtract. Add to check your answer.

1. $\begin{array}{r} 4.4 \\ -\ 3.5 \\ \hline \end{array}$
2. $\begin{array}{r} 7.3 \\ -\ 5.6 \\ \hline \end{array}$
3. $\begin{array}{r} 5.87 \\ -\ 1.09 \\ \hline \end{array}$
4. $\begin{array}{r} \$47.75 \\ -\ 12.99 \\ \hline \end{array}$
5. $\begin{array}{r} 43.634 \\ -\ 10.81 \\ \hline \end{array}$
6. $\begin{array}{r} 5.650 \\ -\ 0.789 \\ \hline \end{array}$
7. $\begin{array}{r} 66.9 \\ -\ 36.782 \\ \hline \end{array}$
8. $\begin{array}{r} 47.0 \\ -\ 46.071 \\ \hline \end{array}$
9. 5.038 − 1.429
10. 92.745 − 81.819
11. 78.49 − 57.565
12. 24.63 − 15.44

Set D (Lesson 4, pp. 290–291)

Estimate each sum or difference to the nearest tenth.

1. 0.623 + 0.192
2. 0.924 + 0.817
3. 0.869 + 0.032
4. 0.524 + 0.238
5. 0.843 − 0.316
6. 0.549 − 0.273
7. 0.741 − 0.692
8. 0.485 − 0.214

WEEKLY WR READER®

Real World Connection

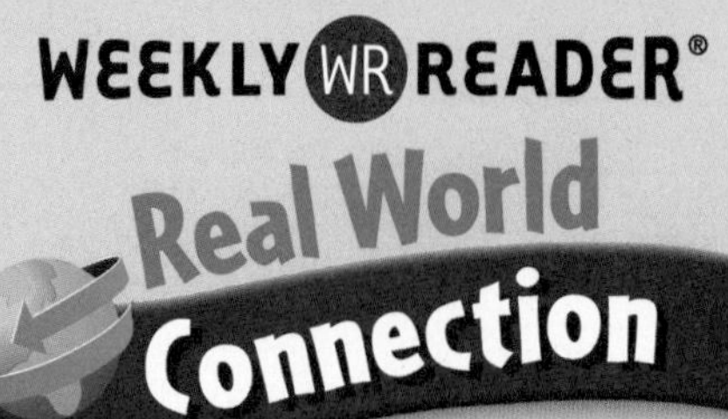

Speed Story

The roller coaster craze probably began in Russia where giant ice slides over 27 meters high were built in the 1600s. Riders would climb all the way to the top, then speed down the icy slope on sleds at 50 miles per hour. It took only a few seconds to cover several city blocks but, oh, what a ride!

Over the centuries, inventors have improved upon the idea of these Russian "Flying Mountains." They have added wheels to the sleds, tracks for the cars, and cables to pull riders to the top of each hill. Today roller coasters all over the world give riders a thrill.

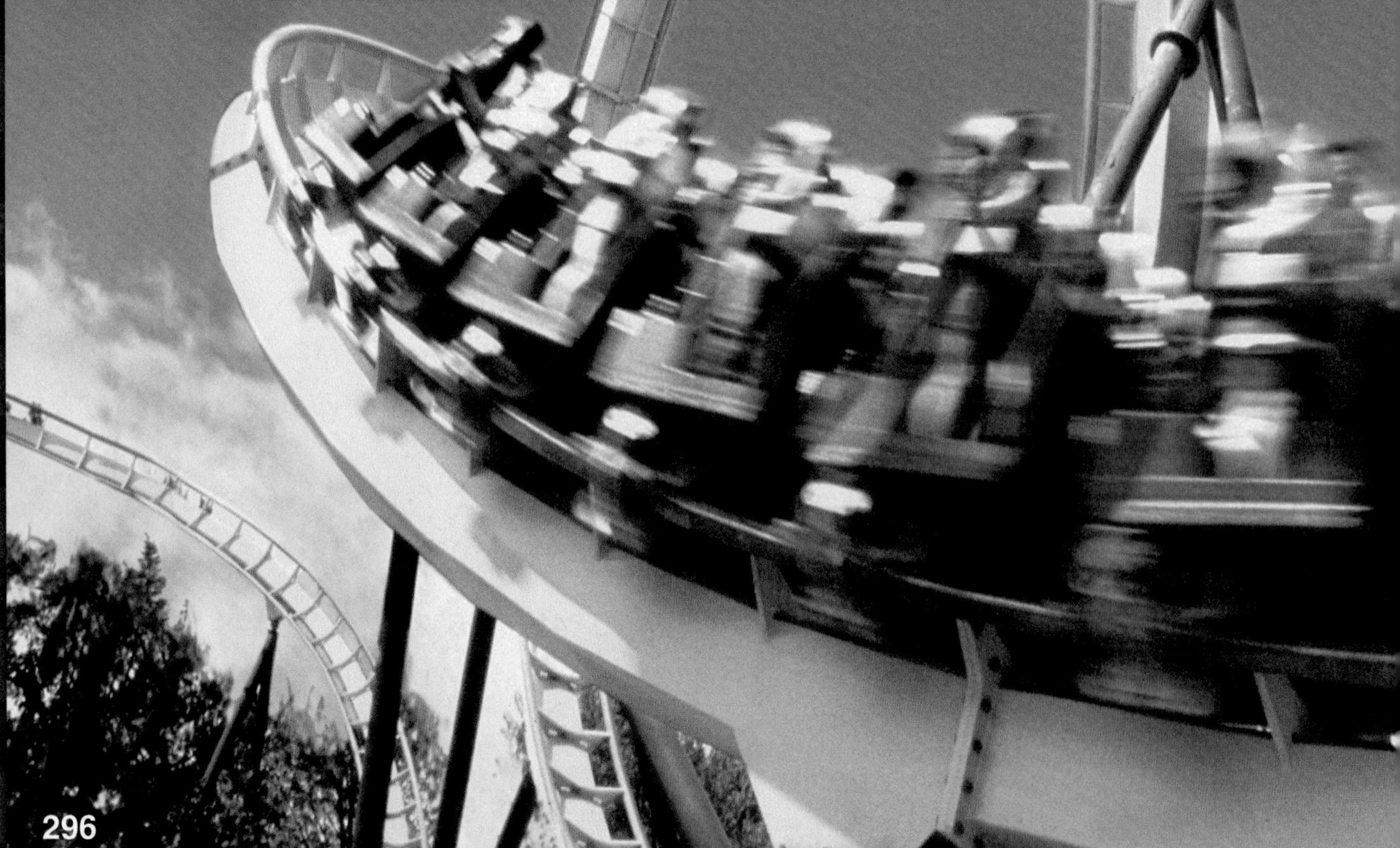

Problem Solving

Many wooden roller coasters built in the 1920s and 1930s are still in operation. Use the data in the graph to solve Problems 1–4.

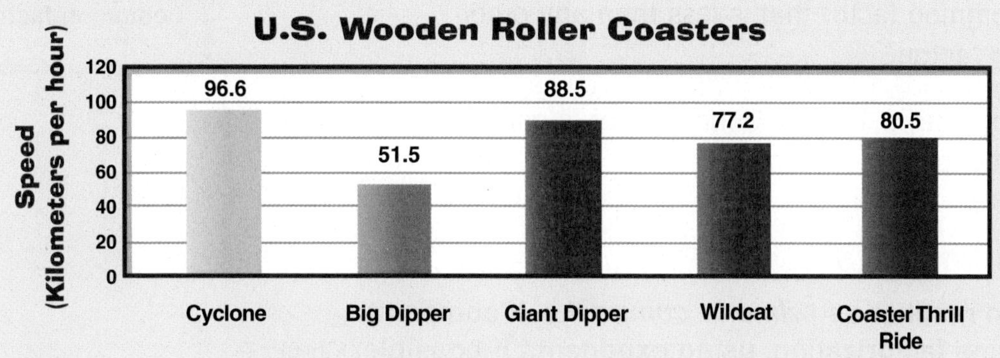

1. How much faster is the fastest coaster shown than the second fastest?

2. What is the range of speeds of the coasters shown?

3. The fastest wooden roller coaster in 2002 had a top speed of 29.6 kilometers per hour faster than the Cyclone. How fast was that?

4. A ride on the Wildcat is $\frac{1}{2}$ minute shorter than a ride on the Big Dipper. A ride on the Cyclone is $\frac{1}{12}$ minute longer than the Big Dipper's ride. The ride on the Wildcat is $1\frac{1}{4}$ minutes long. How long does a ride on the Cyclone last?

5. The Mauch Chunk Switchback Railway was the earliest U.S. roller coaster ride. This coal train ride down a mountain was 29 kilometers long. Today's longest wooden coaster is 2,255.5 meters long. How many meters longer was the Mauch Chunk Railway?

Technology

Visit *Education Place* at
eduplace.com/kids/mw/
to learn more about this topic.

Unit 4 Test

VOCABULARY

Write *true* or *false* for each statement. Rewrite each false sentence to make it true.

1. A prime number is a counting number greater than 1 whose only factors are 1 and the number itself.
2. The greatest common factor of two or more numbers is the common factor that is less than any other common factor.
3. A fraction with a 1 in the denominator is called a unit fraction.

Vocabulary

equivalent fractions
unit fraction
prime number
least common multiple
greatest common factor

CONCEPTS AND SKILLS

Identify each number as *prime* or *composite*. If composite, write the prime factorization, using exponents if possible. (Chapter 9)

4. 9
5. 17
6. 20

Find the greatest common factor (GCF) and the least common multiple (LCM) of each pair. (Chapter 9)

7. 6 and 15
8. 2 and 3

Write each as a whole number or mixed number in simplest form. (Chapter 9)

9. 4.2
10. $\frac{24}{12}$
11. $\frac{17}{6}$
12. 25.75

Compare. Write >, <, or =. (Chapter 9)

13. $\frac{1}{3}$ ⬭ $\frac{1}{2}$
14. 2 ⬭ $\frac{6}{3}$
15. $\frac{7}{3}$ ⬭ $2\frac{3}{4}$

Estimate. Then add or subtract. Write your answers in simplest form. (Chapter 10)

16. $\frac{5}{8} + \frac{1}{16}$
17. $3\frac{1}{2} + 2\frac{2}{3}$
18. $\frac{7}{10} - \frac{3}{5}$
19. $7\frac{1}{4} - 3\frac{5}{6}$

Estimate. Then add or subtract. (Chapter 11)

20. $\begin{array}{r} 3.479 \\ -\ 2.581 \\ \hline \end{array}$
21. $\begin{array}{r} 68.2 \\ 345.301 \\ +\ 18 \\ \hline \end{array}$
22. $\begin{array}{r} \$2.68 \\ -\ 0.81 \\ \hline \end{array}$

PROBLEM SOLVING

23. Connie is making a 9-foot long path through her garden. If each square stone is $\frac{3}{4}$ foot long, how many stones should she buy?

24. Hong is planting a garden. In one row he plants $4\frac{1}{2}$ feet of lettuce and $5\frac{3}{4}$ feet of carrots. How long is that row of lettuce and carrots?

25. At his father's vegetable stand, Abdul made a list of his sales for three days. What was the value of the vegetables he sold on all three days? Tell which computation method you used and why.

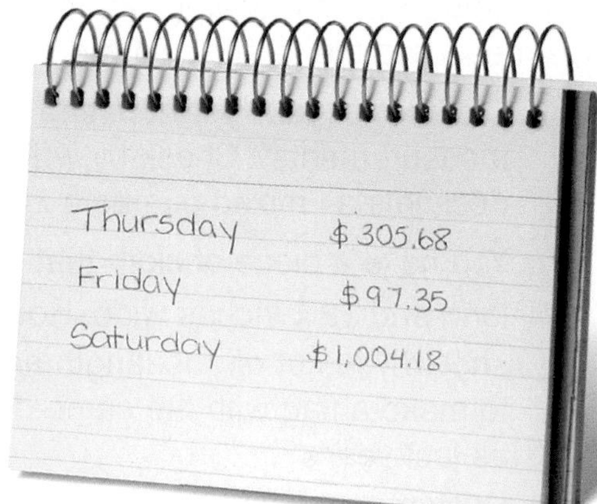

Decision Making

Extended Response

Task David and Angie have only 2 hours to ride their bicycles in the park. They bike at a speed of 8 miles per hour.

Plan a route for David and Angie that will allow them to bike as many of the trails as possible and yet get them back to the park entrance within 2 hours. Explain why your route is the best route for them to take.

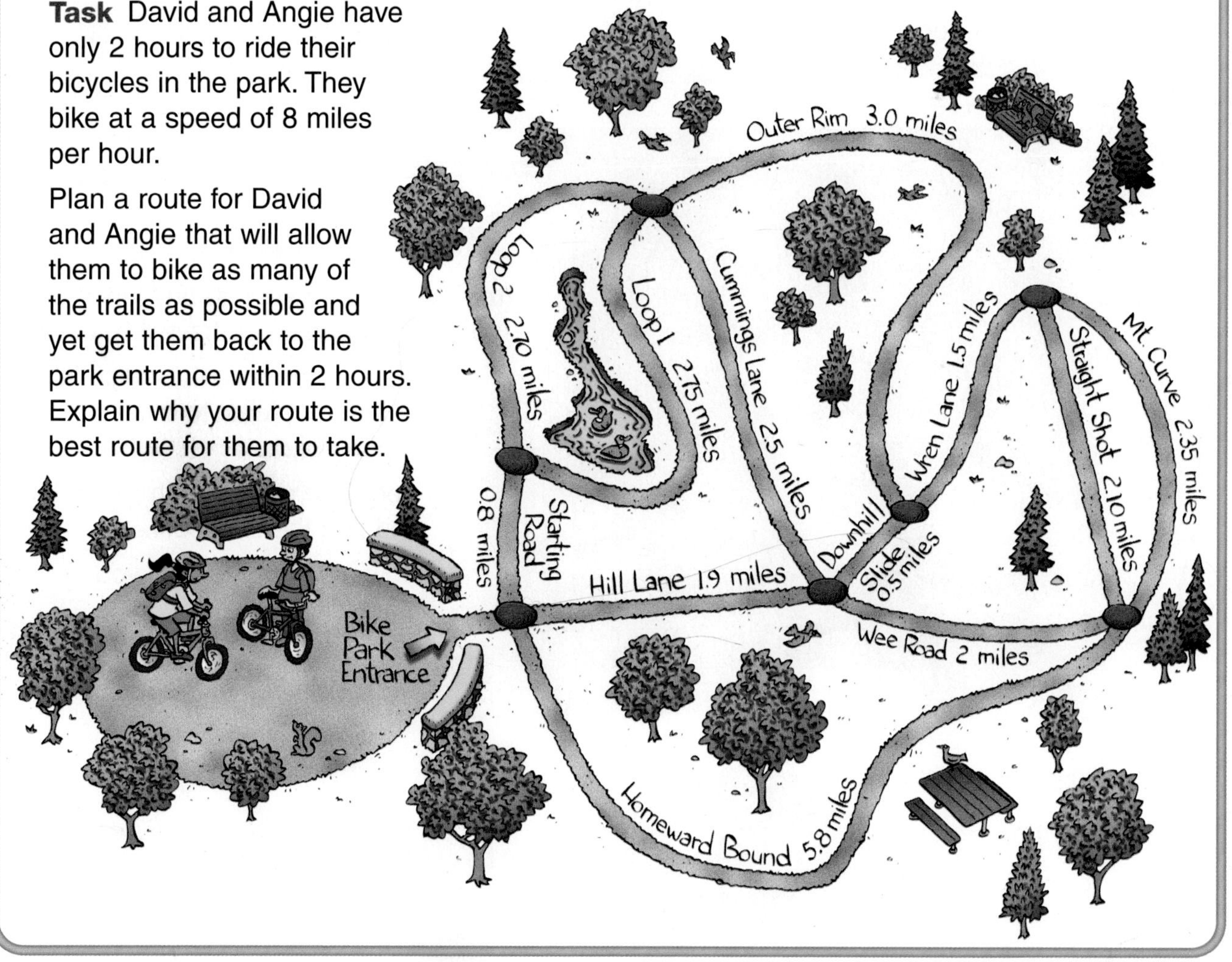

Outer Rim 3.0 miles
Loop 2 2.70 miles
Loop 1 2.75 miles
Cummings Lane 2.5 miles
Wren Lane 1.5 miles
Mt. Curve 2.35 miles
Straight Shot 2.10 miles
Starting Road 0.8 miles
Hill Lane 1.9 miles
Downhill
Slide 0.5 miles
Wee Road 2 miles
Homeward Bound 5.8 miles
Bike Park Entrance

Performance Assessment

TASK 1

Making a Classroom Flag (Chapters 9–10)

You and two classmates want to make a classroom flag the same size as last year's flag. Your two partners have measured the length and width of last year's flag.

a. Did both of your partners find the same measurements? Check by writing the decimals as mixed numbers in simplest form.

b. You have a piece of cloth that is $24\frac{1}{8}$ inches long and $12\frac{1}{2}$ inches wide. How much should you cut off the length and the width to make a flag with the same dimensions as last year's?

c. Design a new flag that is wider but shorter in length. Using mixed numbers, tell the dimensions of your new flag. Remember to use fractions of an inch that can be measured on a ruler.

TASK 2

MARTA'S FOOD STAND

JUICE	PIZZA	SALAD
$1.20	$3.65	$4.09
MILK	HOTDOG	FRUIT
$0.85	$2.49	$1.50
	TACO	
	$1.88	

Saturday Lunch (Chapters 9, 11)

You and a friend want to buy lunch at the mall. Together, you have $16.80.

a. List the items on the menu in order, from least to most expensive.

b. Decide what you both will order, and find the total cost.

c. How much money will you have left?

Self Check

- Did I answer the questions for each task?
- Did I check all my work?

Enrichment: Adding and Subtracting Decimals

Keeping a Checkbook

You can use a checkbook to keep a record of how much money you put into and take out of a bank account. See how each of the following transactions are recorded in a checkbook register.

Recording a Deposit

A deposit is an amount of money added to the account. Enter the amount in the deposit column and add it to the previous balance.

You deposit a gift check from your aunt.

$$\begin{array}{r} \$75.65 \\ +\ 15.50 \\ \hline \$91.15 \end{array}$$

Recording a Withdrawal

A withdrawal is an amount of money subtracted from the account. Enter the amount of the money in the withdrawal column and subtract it from the previous balance.

You withdraw $10.00 from your account.

$$\begin{array}{r} \$91.15 \\ -\ 10.00 \\ \hline \$81.15 \end{array}$$

Fees

Some banks charge a fee if you use an ATM card. Be sure to record these fees, so your checkbook balance is accurate. Other banks may charge a monthly fee for maintaining your account.

You get $20.00 from the ATM. There is a fee of $1.50.

$$\begin{array}{r} \$81.15 \\ -\ 20.00 \\ \hline \$61.15 \\ -\ \ 1.50 \\ \hline \$59.65 \end{array}$$

NUMBER	DATE	TRANSACTION	DEPOSIT	FEE	WITHDRAWAL	BALANCE
	1/4	Balance from last page				$75 65
	1/15	Check from Aunt Joan	15 50			91 15
919	1/17	Lincoln School/Lunch			10 00	81 15
	1/24	ATM - Money for shopping		1.50	20 00	59 65

If you write a check, the number goes here.

It is always a good idea to check your computations.

Try These!

Make your own checkbook record sheet. Use the current date for all transactions.

1. Start with the balance of $59.65 as shown above.
2. You deposit $18.50 from dog walking in your checking account.
3. You write a check, numbered 920, for $8.75 for a hat.
4. You withdraw $30.00 at the ATM. There is a $1.50 fee.

Cumulative Test Prep Practice

Solve Problems 1–10.

Test-Taking Tip

As time permits, check your answers. You can check computation by using the inverse, or opposite, operation.

Look at the example below.

Sheldon wants to buy a 3-piece snorkel set for $17.88. He has $9.89. How much more money does Sheldon need?

A $7.99 **C** $12.01

B $8.01 **D** $25.77

THINK

When computing with decimals, remember to align the decimal points.

Use the inverse operation, addition, to check subtraction.

$17.88	same	$ 7.99	
− 9.89		+ 9.89	
$ 7.99		$17.88	It checks.

Since the answer checks, mark **A** as the answer.

Multiple Choice

1. Florida has an area of 65,755 square miles. Texas has an area of 268,581 square miles. How much greater is the area of Texas than the area of Florida?

   A 202,826 **C** 212,213

   B 208,213 **D** 325,555

   (Chapter 2, Lesson 3)

2. String cheese costs $2.99 per package. If Selma buys 15 packages, how much will she spend altogether?

   F $42.45 **H** $44.45

   G $42.85 **J** $44.85

   (Chapter 3, Lesson 7)

3. Which is the prime factorization of 24?

   A 2×3 **C** $2^2 \times 3$

   B 2×4 **D** $2^3 \times 3$

   (Chapter 9, Lesson 2)

4. Brian is making a friendship bracelet. On Tuesday it was $3\frac{3}{8}$ inches long. He added $4\frac{1}{4}$ inches on Wednesday. How much more must he add for the bracelet to be 8 inches long?

   F $\frac{1}{4}$ inch **H** $\frac{1}{2}$ inch

   G $\frac{3}{8}$ inch **J** 1 inch

   (Chapter 10, Lesson 4)

 For more Test-Taking Tips, see pages xxii–xxv.

Free Response

5. Write the names of the states in the chart in order from the greatest to the least area.

State	Area (square miles)
Nebraska	77,358
North Dakota	70,704
South Dakota	77,121
Washington	71,300

(Chapter 1, Lesson 4)

6. Mr. Broeker purchased three mountain bikes for his daughters at a total cost of $357. If each bike costs the same amount, how much did each bike cost?

(Chapter 5, Lesson 2)

7. The Kendalls' car broke down $\frac{1}{3}$ mile from home. How many feet from home did the car break down? (Hint: 1 mi = 5,280 ft)

(Chapter 6, Lesson 2)

8. Karin wants to glue a $4\frac{1}{2}$-inch piece of ribbon onto her hat. The ribbon she has is $8\frac{5}{8}$ inches long. How much of the ribbon should she cut off?

(Chapter 10, Lesson 8)

9. A January snowstorm left 12.2 inches of snow on Rapid City, South Dakota, and 6.5 inches on Minneapolis, Minnesota. How much more snow did Rapid City get?

(Chapter 11, Lesson 8)

Extended Response

Activity	Time (minutes)
Swimming	45
Reading	35
Lunch	30
Crafts	45
Canoeing	55
Bow and arrow	45
Camping skills	60
Cooking	55

10. The chart above shows the amount of time that each summer camp activity takes.

A Make a line plot of the amounts of time the activities take.

B What is the range of the data?

C Find the mode, median, and mean of the data.

D Which of the activities would you say take an average amount of time? Explain your thinking.

(Chapter 8, Lesson 2)

Test Prep on the Net
Check out *Education Place* at **eduplace.com/kids/mw/** for test prep practice.

Fraction Finesse

You can add and subtract fractions on your calculator.

Find the sum of $3\frac{5}{6}$ and $2\frac{1}{2}$.

• Enter the first addend.	3 Unit 5 n 6 d	$3\frac{5}{6}$
• Enter the operation, the second addend and the equals sign.	+ 2 Unit 1 n 2 d Enter =	$3\frac{5}{6}+2\frac{1}{2}=$ $6\frac{2}{6}$
• Change the answer to simplest form.	Simp Enter =	$6\frac{2}{6}$ ▸S $6\frac{1}{3}$

Use a calculator. Write each sum or difference in simplest form. Then match the answers to a letter to solve the riddle below.

1. $1\frac{3}{4} + \frac{1}{5}$

2. $3\frac{6}{8} - 1\frac{1}{4}$

3. $8\frac{1}{4} - 3\frac{5}{6}$

4. $6\frac{6}{16} - 3\frac{1}{5}$

5. $2\frac{4}{7} + 3\frac{2}{8}$

6. $5\frac{3}{9} - 2\frac{1}{3}$

7. $4\frac{3}{6} + \frac{2}{5}$

8. $1\frac{9}{15} - 1\frac{1}{4}$

9. $3\frac{8}{12} + 4\frac{2}{4}$

10. $3\frac{1}{8} + 5\frac{1}{6}$

11. $2\frac{6}{9} - 1\frac{1}{3}$

12. $4\frac{12}{13} - 3\frac{1}{7}$

RIDDLE: What do you get when you cross a dog with a calculator?

____ (8)   ____ (2) ____ (3) ____ (6) ____ (12) ____ (4) ____ (1)   ____ (10) ____ (7) ____ (9)

____ (11) ____ (8) ____ (4)   ____ (11) ____ (7) ____ (9) ____ (4) ____ (5)   ____ (7) ____ (4) !

KEY:

$\frac{7}{20}$	$1\frac{1}{3}$	$1\frac{19}{20}$	$1\frac{71}{91}$	$2\frac{1}{2}$	$2\frac{2}{3}$	3	$3\frac{7}{40}$	$4\frac{9}{10}$	$4\frac{5}{12}$	$4\frac{19}{20}$	$5\frac{23}{28}$	$8\frac{1}{6}$	$8\frac{7}{24}$
A	C	D	E	F	G	I	N	O	R	S	T	U	Y

Vocabulary Wrap-Up for Unit 4

WEEKLY WR READER Activity Almanac
See page 681 for the activity for this unit.

Look back at the big ideas and vocabulary in this unit.

Big Ideas

A factor tree can be used to find the prime factorization of a number.

You can estimate sums and differences of fractions by rounding to 0, $\frac{1}{2}$, or 1.

e Glossary

Key Vocabulary

factor
prime
composite

Math Conversations

Use your new vocabulary to discuss these big ideas.

1. Explain how you can decide whether a number is prime or composite.
2. Explain how to write decimals as fractions and fractions as decimals.
3. Explain how to write answers in simplest form.
4. Explain how to subtract \$5.17 from \$10.00.
5. **Write About It** Measuring cups and measuring spoons are used to measure ingredients when cooking or baking. Describe different ways you might go about measuring these ingredients: $5\frac{1}{3}$ cups flour; $2\frac{2}{3}$ cups milk; $1\frac{3}{4}$ teaspoons baking powder.

15 is divisible by 5 and 3, so it can't be prime.
Is 15 a prime number?

Building Vocabulary

Reviewing Vocabulary

Here are some math vocabulary words that you should know.

factor	one of two or more numbers that are multiplied to give a product
common factor	a factor of two or more numbers
prime factor	a prime number that is a factor of a composite number
unit fraction	a fraction that has 1 as the numerator
simplest form	a fraction whose numerator and denominator have 1 as their only common factor

Reading Words and Symbols

Sometimes a model can be used to illustrate more than one idea in mathematics.

The model at the right can be used to show that each of the following statements is true:

Words and Symbols	Symbols Only
The sum of $\frac{3}{4}$ and $\frac{1}{4}$ is 1.	$\frac{3}{4} + \frac{1}{4} = 1$
Subtracting $\frac{3}{4}$ from 1 leaves $\frac{1}{4}$.	$1 - \frac{3}{4} = \frac{1}{4}$

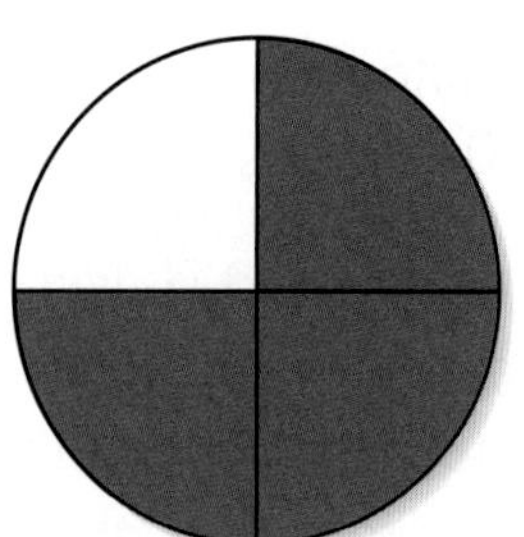

Use words and symbols to answer the questions.

1. How many equal sections are in the model above? What fraction represents each section?
2. What decimal represents the purple portion of the model? What decimal represents $\frac{1}{3}$ of the purple portion?

Reading Test Questions

Choose the correct answer for each.

3. Using the fraction strips, find the number of eighths there are in $\frac{3}{4}$.

   a. 5 c. 7

   b. 6 d. 8

$\frac{1}{4}$	$\frac{1}{4}$	$\frac{1}{4}$	$\frac{1}{4}$

$\frac{1}{8}$	$\frac{1}{8}$	$\frac{1}{8}$	$\frac{1}{8}$	$\frac{1}{8}$	$\frac{1}{8}$	$\frac{1}{8}$	$\frac{1}{8}$

Fraction strips are models used to show fraction equivalents. These are sometimes called fraction bars.

4. What is the sum of $\frac{5}{8}$ and $\frac{1}{8}$? Express your answer in lowest terms.

   a. $\frac{6}{16}$ c. $\frac{6}{8}$

   b. $\frac{4}{8}$ d. $\frac{3}{4}$

When you express a fraction in **lowest terms**, you express it in simplest form.

5. Find $\frac{7}{8} - \frac{5}{8}$. Be sure to reduce your answer.

   a. $\frac{1}{4}$ c. $1\frac{1}{2}$

   b. $\frac{2}{8}$ d. 2

To **reduce** an answer means to express it in lowest terms or in simplest form.

Learning Vocabulary

Watch for these new words in this unit. Write their definitions in your journal.

- **reciprocal**
- **compatible numbers**
- **power of 10**
- **exponent**
- **repeating decimal**

Vocabulary
e • **Glossary**
e • **WordGame**

Literature Connection

Read "The World's Largest Trees" on pages 644–645. Then work with a partner to answer the questions about the story.

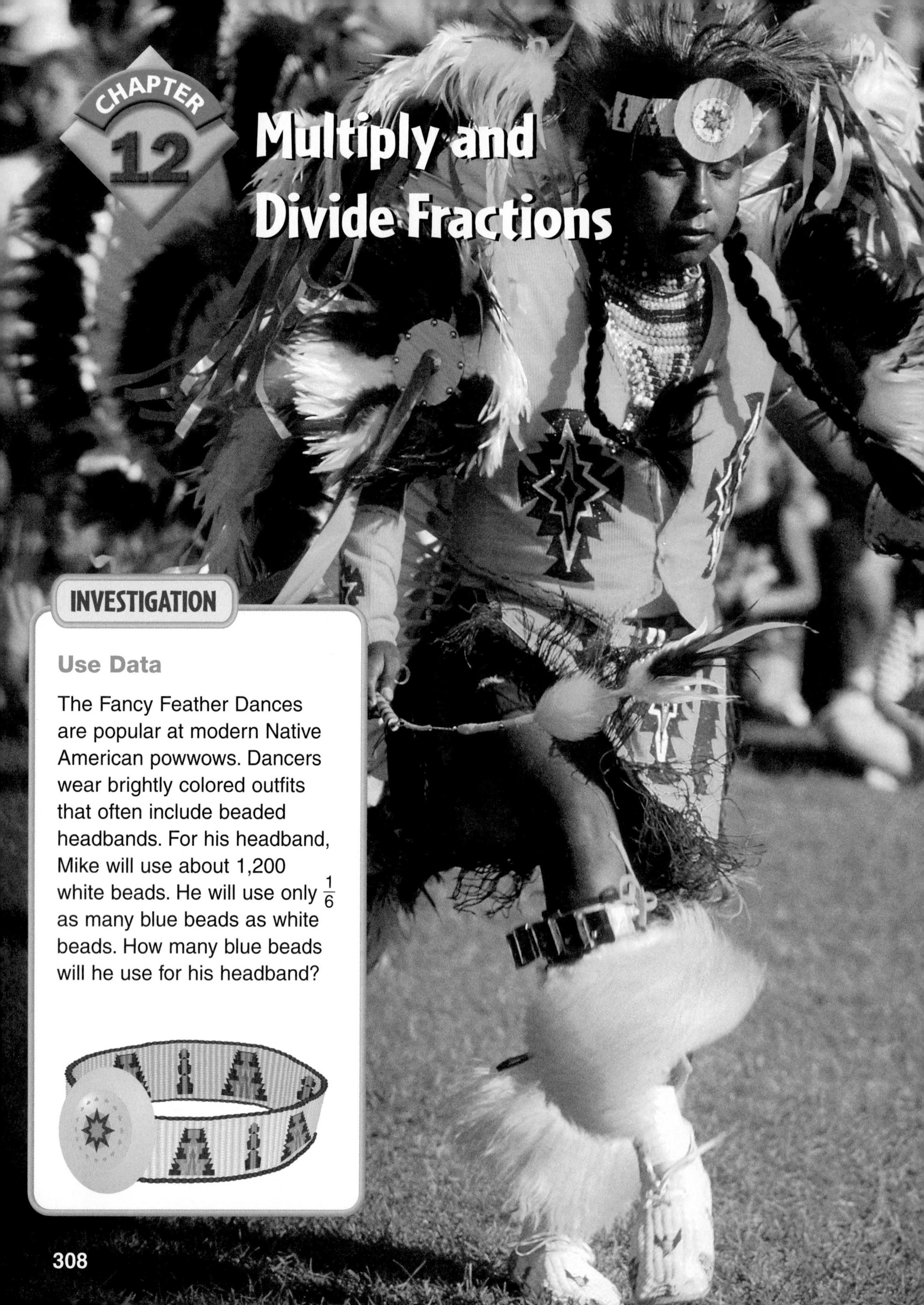

CHAPTER 12 Multiply and Divide Fractions

INVESTIGATION

Use Data

The Fancy Feather Dances are popular at modern Native American powwows. Dancers wear brightly colored outfits that often include beaded headbands. For his headband, Mike will use about 1,200 white beads. He will use only $\frac{1}{6}$ as many blue beads as white beads. How many blue beads will he use for his headband?

Chapter Pretest

Use this page to review and remember what you need to know for this chapter.

VOCABULARY

Choose the best word to complete each sentence.

1. You can always rename a mixed number as a(n) ____.
2. A(n) ____ is the largest number that divides evenly into two or more numbers.
3. You can use the greatest common factor of the numerator and denominator to find the ____ of a fraction.

CONCEPTS AND SKILLS

Use the numbers listed to answer each question.

$\frac{1}{3}$ $\frac{4}{2}$ 2 $\frac{1}{6}$ $\frac{4}{10}$

4. Which two name the same number?
5. Which two fractions have an LCD of 6?
6. Which fractions are not in simplest form?
7. Which is a counting number?

Rename each mixed number as an improper fraction.

8. $6\frac{2}{9}$
9. $11\frac{4}{5}$
10. $4\frac{3}{7}$

Rename each improper fraction as a mixed number.

11. $\frac{301}{3}$
12. $\frac{23}{8}$
13. $\frac{38}{5}$

Find the GCF of each pair.

14. 15, 27
15. 12, 32
16. 10, 25
17. 14, 35
18. 72, 144
19. 81, 108

Write About It

20. How can you use multiplication to find an equivalent fraction for $\frac{2}{5}$?

Test Prep on the Net

Visit *Education Place* at **eduplace.com/kids/mw/** for more review.

Model Multiplication

Objective Use area to find the product of two fractions.

You can use an area model to multiply two fractions.

Find $\frac{2}{3} \times \frac{4}{5}$.

STEP 1

Draw a 5×3 square.

Use horizontal lines to separate the square into thirds. Label each third.

Use vertical lines to separate the square into fifths. Label each fifth.

- How many rectangles have you separated the large square into?
- What fraction of the square does each rectangle represent?

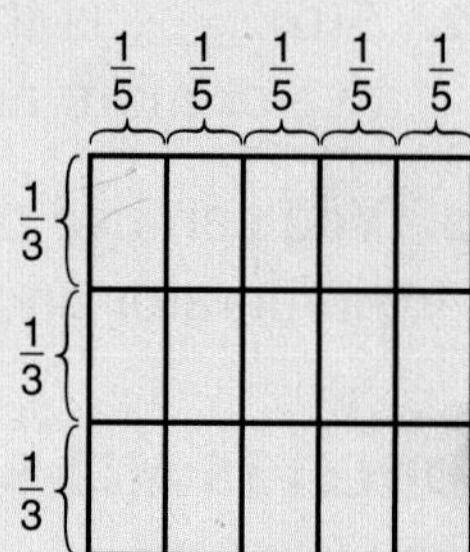

Shade part of the square to show $\frac{2}{3} \times \frac{4}{5}$ by doing the following:

Shade $\frac{2}{3}$ of the square red.

Shade $\frac{4}{5}$ of the square blue.

- Identify the part that is shaded twice. That part shows $\frac{2}{3} \times \frac{4}{5}$.
- Complete: $\frac{2}{3} \times \frac{4}{5} = \frac{\blacksquare}{\blacksquare}$ ← number of rectangles shaded twice / ← total number of rectangles

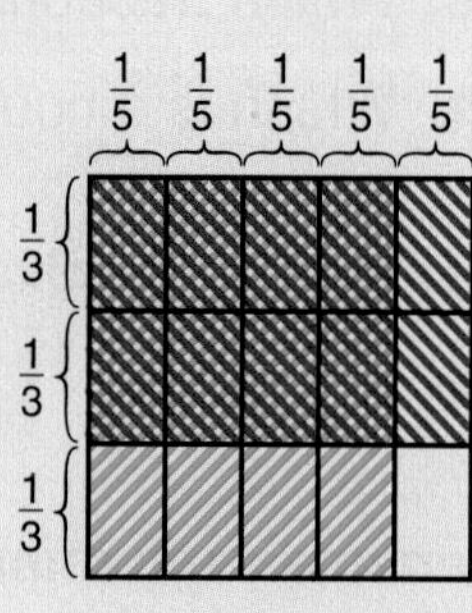

Check your answer.

You are multiplying $\frac{2}{3}$ and $\frac{4}{5}$.

You know that you can multiply any number by 1 to get the same number again.
$\frac{2}{3} \times 1 = \frac{2}{3}$, so $\frac{2}{3} \times \frac{4}{5} < \frac{2}{3}$ and $\frac{4}{5} \times \frac{2}{3} < \frac{4}{5}$.

Is your answer less than either factor?

▶ You can use models to multiply a fraction and a counting number.

Find $2 \times \frac{3}{4}$.

STEP 1 Draw two squares.
Shade the two squares blue.

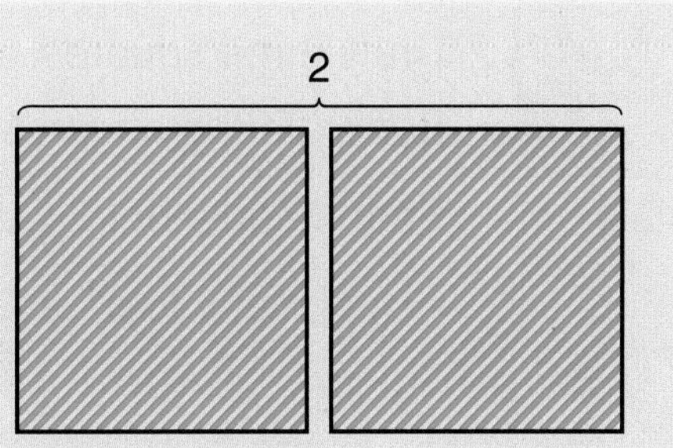

STEP 2 Separate both squares into fourths.
Shade $\frac{3}{4}$ of each square red.

- How many fourths are shaded twice?

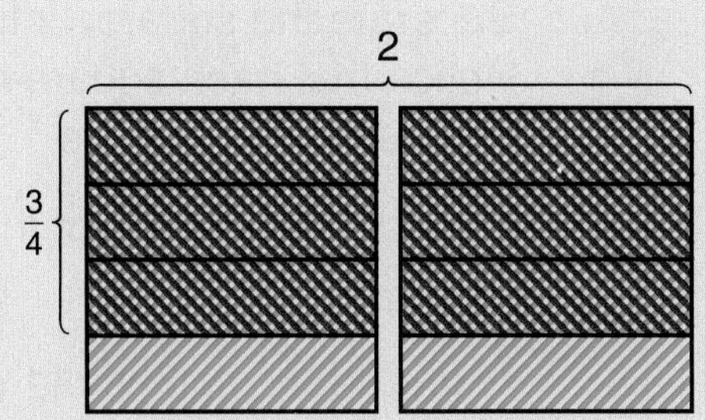

- Complete: $2 \times \frac{3}{4} = \frac{\blacksquare}{4}$ ← number of fourths shaded twice / ← number of fourths in 1 square
- Write your answer in simplest form.

Check your answer.
You are multiplying 2 and $\frac{3}{4}$. You know that if you multiply any number *n* by 1, the product is that number.

$2 \times 1 = 2$, so $2 \times \frac{3}{4} < 2$.

Is your answer less than the counting number?

Go On

▶ You can use models to multiply with mixed numbers.

Find $\frac{1}{2} \times 2\frac{1}{4}$.

STEP 1 Draw three squares.

Separate the squares into fourths.

Shade and label $2\frac{1}{4}$ of the three squares.

- How many fourths are in $2\frac{1}{4}$?

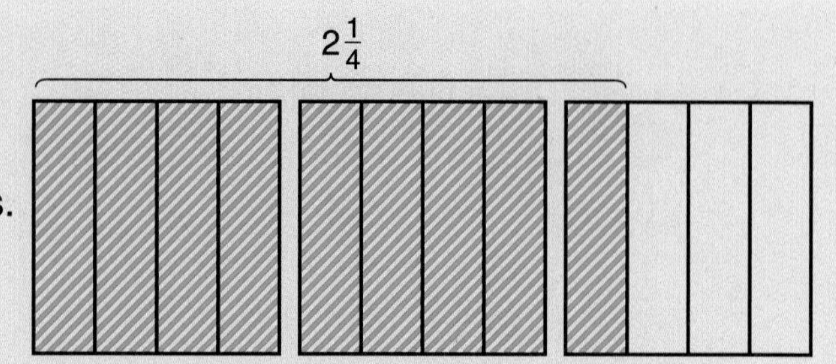

STEP 2 Separate the squares into halves. Notice that each square is now separated into eighths.

- Shade and label $\frac{1}{2}$ of the three squares.
- How many eighths did you shade twice?
- Complete: $\frac{1}{2} \times 2\frac{1}{4} = \frac{■}{8}$ ← number of eighths shaded twice / ← number of eighths in 1 square
- Write your answer in simplest form.

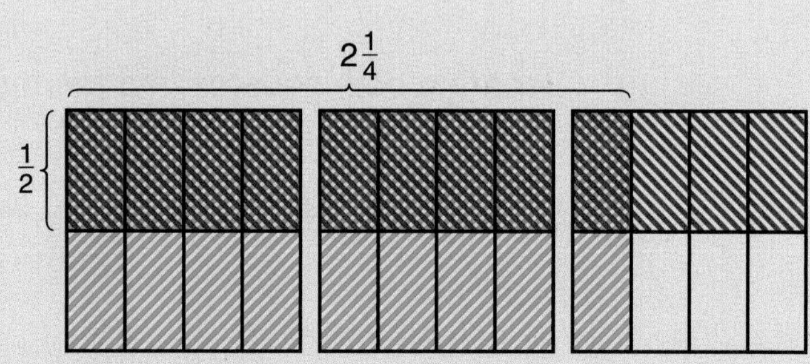

Check your answer.

Another way to estimate products is to round fractions to 0, $\frac{1}{2}$, or 1.

$\frac{1}{2}$ rounds to $\frac{1}{2}$ and $2\frac{1}{4}$ rounds to 2.

$\frac{1}{2} \times 2\frac{1}{4} \approx \frac{1}{2} \times 2$

$\frac{1}{2} \times 2 = 1$

The product of $\frac{1}{2}$ and $2\frac{1}{4}$ is about 1.

On Your Own

1. Use area to model multiplication of $\frac{2}{5}$ and $\frac{3}{4}$. Draw a unit square. Use horizontal lines to separate the square into fifths. Use vertical lines to separate the square into fourths.

   a. What fraction of the square does each small rectangle represent?

   b. Shade and label $\frac{2}{5} \times \frac{3}{4}$.

   c. Write your answer in simplest form. $\frac{2}{5} \times \frac{3}{4} = ■$

Complete the equation represented by each model.
Write each answer in simplest form.

2. 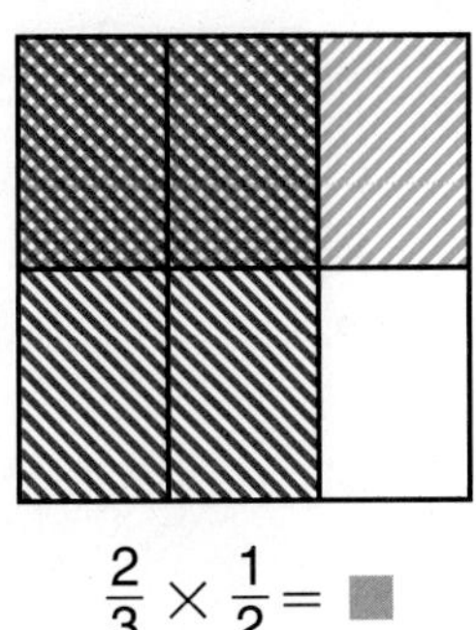

$\frac{2}{3} \times \frac{1}{2} = \blacksquare$

3. 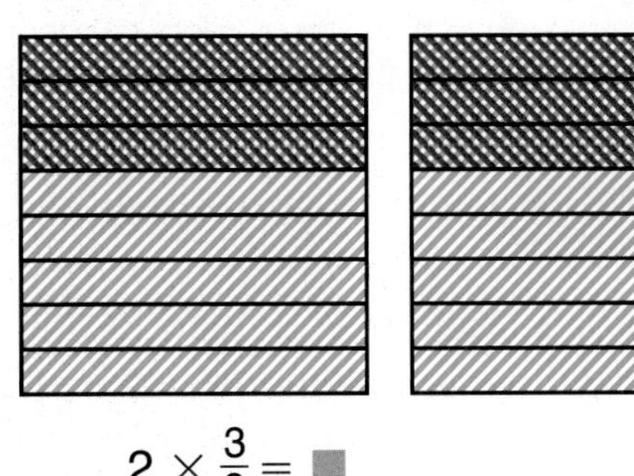

$2 \times \frac{3}{8} = \blacksquare$

4. 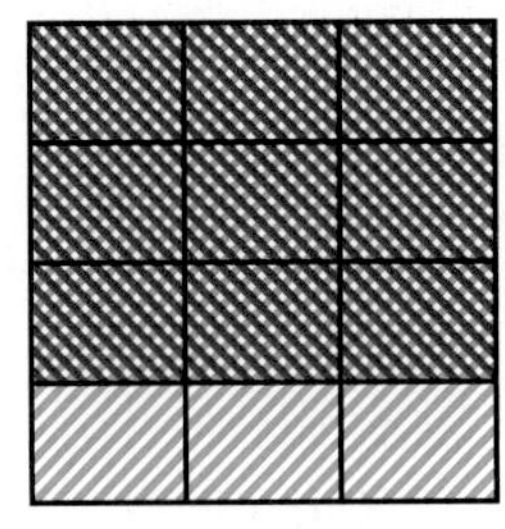 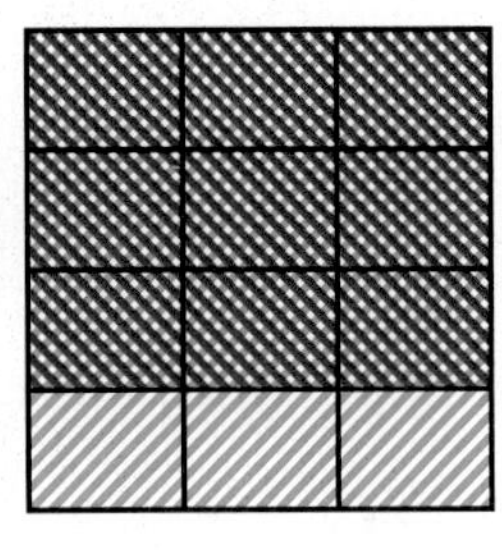

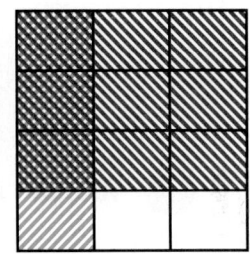

$\frac{3}{4} \times 3\frac{1}{3} = \blacksquare$

Use models to find each product.
Write each product in simplest form.

5. $\frac{1}{2} \times \frac{1}{3} = \blacksquare$
6. $\frac{1}{3} \times \frac{3}{4} = \blacksquare$
7. $4 \times \frac{1}{2} = \blacksquare$
8. $\frac{3}{4} \times \frac{4}{5} = \blacksquare$
9. $3 \times \frac{2}{3} = \blacksquare$
10. $5 \times \frac{3}{5} = \blacksquare$
11. $\frac{3}{4} \times 4\frac{1}{2} = \blacksquare$
12. $1\frac{2}{5} \times 2\frac{1}{2} = \blacksquare$
13. $2 \times \frac{1}{6} = \blacksquare$
14. $\frac{1}{4} \times \frac{3}{5} = \blacksquare$
15. $\frac{2}{3} \times 1\frac{2}{3} = \blacksquare$
16. $3\frac{1}{3} \times 2\frac{1}{8} = \blacksquare$

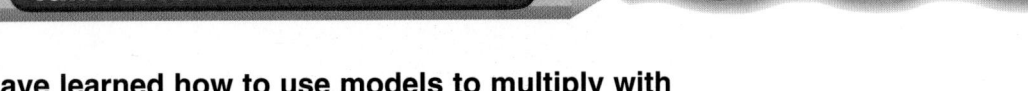

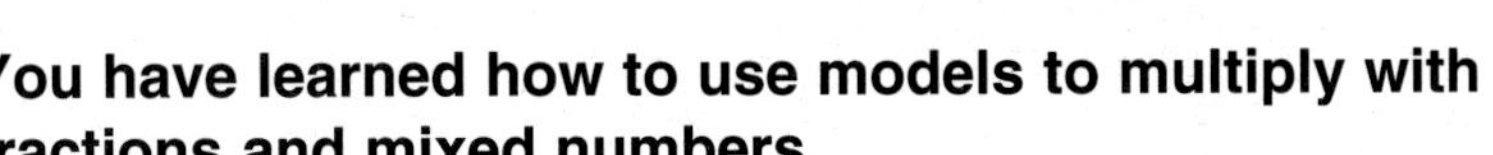

TEST PREP

You have learned how to use models to multiply with fractions and mixed numbers.

17. When you multiply two fractions that are both less than one, will the product be less than or greater than either factor? Use words, pictures, and numbers to justify your answer.

18. When you multiply a counting number by a fraction less than one, will the product be a counting number all of the time, some of the time, or none of the time? Explain how you know.

Lesson 2

Multiply Fractions

Objective Find the product of two fractions.

Learn About It

To find a fraction of a fraction, you need to find the product of the fractions. You know how to use models to multiply fractions. Here are some other ways to find products of fractions.

$\frac{3}{4}$

$\frac{5}{6}$

Find $\frac{5}{6}$ of $\frac{3}{4}$.

Different Ways to Find $\frac{5}{6}$ of $\frac{3}{4}$

Way 1 You can multiply first, then simplify.

STEP 1 Multiply the numerators. Multiply the denominators.

$$\frac{5}{6} \times \frac{3}{4} = \frac{5 \times 3}{6 \times 4} = \frac{15}{24}$$

STEP 2 Simplify the product if necessary.

$$\frac{15}{24} = \frac{5}{8}$$

÷ 3

÷ 3

Way 2 You can simplify first, then multiply.

STEP 1 Rewrite using factors.

$$\frac{5}{6} \times \frac{3}{4} = \frac{5 \times 3}{2 \times 3 \times 4}$$

STEP 2 Divide by common factors.

$$\frac{5}{6} \times \frac{3}{4} = \frac{5 \times \cancel{3}^{1}}{2 \times \cancel{3}_{1} \times 4}$$

STEP 3 Multiply.

$$\frac{5 \times 1}{1 \times 2 \times 4} = \frac{5}{8}$$

Solution: $\frac{5}{6}$ of $\frac{3}{4}$ is $\frac{5}{8}$.

Other Examples

A. Prime Factorization

$$\frac{9}{10} \times \frac{2}{3} = \frac{9 \times 2}{10 \times 3}$$

$$= \frac{3 \times 3 \times 2}{2 \times 5 \times 3}$$

$$= \frac{3}{5} \times \frac{3}{3} \times \frac{2}{2}$$

$$= \frac{3}{5}$$

Notice that $\frac{2}{2} = 1$ and $\frac{3}{3} = 1$. The product of 1 and any number is that number.

B. Fraction and Whole Number

$$\frac{1}{5} \times 4 = \frac{1}{5} \times \frac{4}{1}$$

$$= \frac{1 \times 4}{5 \times 1}$$

$$= \frac{4}{5}$$

Guided Practice

Multiply. Write your answer in simplest form.

1. $\frac{2}{3} \times \frac{3}{5}$ **2.** $\frac{3}{8} \times \frac{4}{5}$ **3.** $\frac{5}{6} \times \frac{3}{10}$

4. $8 \times \frac{3}{4}$ **5.** $6 \times \frac{2}{5}$ **6.** $\frac{4}{7} \times 4$

Ask Yourself

- Can I use prime factorization?
- Did I write my answer in simplest form?

Explain Your Thinking ▶ Why can you divide by common factors in the numerator and denominator to simplify a fraction?

Practice and Problem Solving

Multiply. Write your answer in simplest form.

7. $\frac{1}{5} \times \frac{5}{8}$ **8.** $\frac{2}{5} \times \frac{5}{8}$ **9.** $\frac{3}{5} \times \frac{5}{9}$ **10.** $\frac{4}{5} \times \frac{5}{12}$ **11.** $\frac{1}{6} \times \frac{2}{3}$

12. $\frac{1}{8} \times 6$ **13.** $\frac{3}{8} \times 4$ **14.** $9 \times \frac{5}{8}$ **15.** $8 \times \frac{1}{6}$ **16.** $2 \times \frac{3}{4}$

Algebra • Expressions **Multiply. Write each answer in simplest form.**

17. $\frac{a}{6} \cdot \frac{2}{b}$ **18.** $2 \cdot \frac{2}{n}$ **19.** $\frac{p}{q} \cdot \frac{q}{p}$

20. $3 \cdot \frac{6}{y}$ **21.** $\frac{x}{8} \cdot \frac{2}{y}$ **22.** $\frac{a}{x} \cdot \frac{b}{y}$

The multiplication dot is used to avoid confusion between the multiplication symbol *(x)* and the variable *x*.

Solve.

23. Two fifths of a class is in the drama club. Only $\frac{1}{4}$ of them have parts in a play. What fraction of that class has parts in the play?

24. The middle school has 135 students. Two thirds of them are girls. How many of the students are girls? How many are boys?

25. Write About It How could you use two-color counters or coins to model $\frac{3}{4} \times \frac{1}{2}$?

26. Explain A bottle of water contains $\frac{7}{8}$ liter. Annette buys 12 bottles. How many liters does she buy? Explain.

Daily Review | Test Prep

Find the product. (Ch.3, Lesson 7)

27. 24×32 **28.** 18×43

29. 15×16 **30.** 92×87

31. 42×27 **32.** 83×13

33. John memorized $\frac{2}{3}$ of his lines for the school play. Then he memorized $\frac{1}{3}$ of what was left on Sunday. What fraction of his lines did he memorize on Sunday?

A $\frac{1}{9}$ **B** $\frac{1}{3}$ **C** $\frac{1}{2}$ **D** 1

Extra Practice See page 331, Set A.

Lesson 3

Multiply With Mixed Numbers

Objective Find products of fractions and mixed numbers.

Learn About It

You can multiply with a **mixed number**, like $2\frac{3}{4}$, or an **improper fraction**, like $\frac{11}{4}$.

Max is a clown who juggles and does yo-yo tricks for parties. He has been hired for a party that will last $1\frac{3}{4}$ hours. Max plans to spend $\frac{2}{3}$ of that time juggling. How long will Max's juggling last?

Multiply. $\frac{2}{3} \times 1\frac{3}{4} = n$

You can write the mixed number as an improper fraction and multiply.

STEP 1 Write the mixed number as an improper fraction.

$1\frac{3}{4} = \frac{4}{4} + \frac{3}{4} = \frac{7}{4}$

$\frac{2}{3} \times 1\frac{3}{4} = \frac{2}{3} \times \frac{7}{4}$

STEP 2 Use common factors to simplify. Then multiply.

$\frac{2}{3} \times \frac{7}{4} = \frac{\overset{1}{\cancel{2}} \times 7}{3 \times 2 \times \underset{1}{\cancel{2}}}$

$= \frac{1 \times 7}{3 \times 2}$

$= \frac{7}{6}$

STEP 3 Simplify. Write the fraction as a mixed number if necessary.

$\frac{7}{6} = \frac{6}{6} + \frac{1}{6} = 1\frac{1}{6}$

$\frac{2}{3} \times 1\frac{3}{4} = 1\frac{1}{6}$

Solution: Max will juggle for $1\frac{1}{6}$ hours.

Other Examples

A. Two Mixed Numbers

$1\frac{2}{3} \times 3\frac{1}{4} = \frac{5}{3} \times \frac{13}{4}$

$= \frac{5 \times 13}{3 \times 4}$

$= \frac{65}{12}$ (65 ÷ 12 = ■)

$= 5\frac{5}{12}$

B. Mixed Number and Whole Number

$2\frac{1}{8} \times 4 = \frac{17}{8} \times \frac{4}{1}$

$= \frac{17 \times \overset{1}{\cancel{2}} \times \overset{1}{\cancel{2}}}{2 \times \underset{1}{\cancel{2}} \times \underset{1}{\cancel{2}}}$

$= \frac{17}{2}$

$= 8\frac{1}{2}$

Guided Practice

Ask Yourself

- Did I use improper fractions?
- Did I write my answer in simplest form?

Multiply. Write each product in simplest form.

1. $\frac{4}{5} \times 1\frac{2}{3}$ **2.** $2\frac{3}{4} \times 1\frac{1}{2}$ **3.** $1\frac{3}{8} \times 4$

4. $6 \times 2\frac{3}{4}$ **5.** $1\frac{2}{3} \times \frac{2}{5}$ **6.** $1\frac{1}{4} \times 3\frac{2}{5}$

TEST TIPS **Explain Your Thinking** ▶ How is multiplying with mixed numbers similar to multiplying with fractions?

Practice and Problem Solving

Multiply. Write each product in simplest form.

7. $1\frac{5}{6} \times \frac{1}{3}$ **8.** $\frac{3}{4} \times 2\frac{1}{3}$ **9.** $1\frac{7}{9} \times 2$ **10.** $5 \times 4\frac{1}{5}$

11. $2\frac{1}{3} \times 3\frac{3}{4}$ **12.** $3\frac{1}{2} \times \frac{2}{5}$ **13.** $3 \times 4\frac{1}{6}$ **14.** $2\frac{5}{6} \times 2\frac{1}{4}$

15. $\frac{3}{8} \times 1\frac{1}{4}$ **16.** $3\frac{5}{8} \times 2\frac{1}{2}$ **17.** $1\frac{7}{9} \times \frac{1}{12}$ **18.** $2\frac{3}{4} \times \frac{5}{6}$

19. $3\frac{1}{8} \times 4$ **20.** $2\frac{1}{5} \times \frac{2}{3}$ **21.** $3 \times 2\frac{2}{3}$ **22.** $4\frac{5}{8} \times 2\frac{2}{3}$

23. $9 \times 2\frac{1}{3}$ **24.** $\frac{5}{8} \times 1\frac{3}{5}$ **25.** $2\frac{1}{4} \times 3\frac{1}{9}$ **26.** $3\frac{5}{6} \times 2\frac{3}{8}$

Complete each multiplication equation.

27. $\frac{1}{6} \times ■ = \frac{5}{6}$ **28.** $■ \times 32 = 8$ **29.** $■ \times 4 = 3$ **30.** $\frac{2}{3} \times ■ = 10$

31. $\frac{3}{4} \times ■ = 6$ **32.** $■ \times 24 = 3$ **33.** $■ \times \frac{6}{7} = 36$ **34.** $45 \times ■ = 10$

Algebra • **Functions** Complete each function table. Write each answer in simplest form.

35.

Rule: $y = \frac{1}{4}x$				
x	$2\frac{1}{8}$	$2\frac{1}{4}$	$2\frac{3}{8}$	$2\frac{1}{2}$
y				

36.

Rule: $y = 8x$				
x	$3\frac{3}{4}$	4	$4\frac{1}{4}$	$4\frac{1}{2}$
y				

37.

Rule: $y = 1\frac{1}{4}x$				
x	$\frac{4}{5}$	$1\frac{3}{5}$	$3\frac{1}{3}$	$6\frac{2}{3}$
y				

38.

Rule: $y = 3\frac{1}{3}x$				
x	$1\frac{1}{8}$	$2\frac{1}{8}$	$3\frac{1}{8}$	$4\frac{1}{8}$
y				

Go On

Solve.

39. For the yo-yo trick "Rock the Baby," Max places his fingers halfway down the string. The string is $2\frac{3}{4}$ feet long. How long is each half?

40. Vicki bought a yo-yo with a string that was $\frac{5}{8}$ of her height. How long was the string on Vicki's yo-yo?

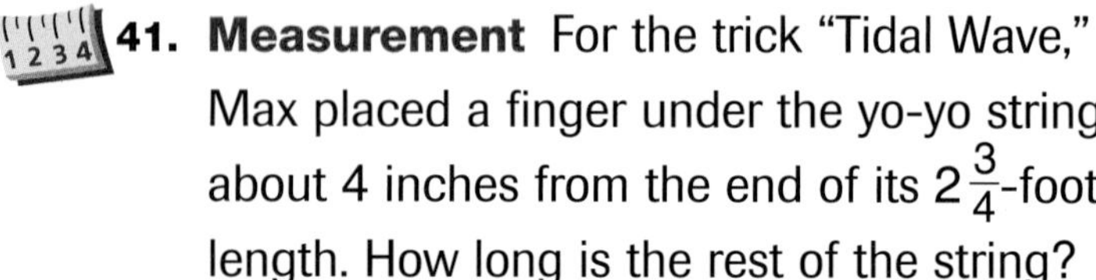

41. **Measurement** For the trick "Tidal Wave," Max placed a finger under the yo-yo string about 4 inches from the end of its $2\frac{3}{4}$-foot length. How long is the rest of the string?

42. **Mental Math** For one job, Max earned \$8 for each hour he worked. How much did he earn if he worked $1\frac{1}{2}$ hours?

43. Of the 40 jobs Max has worked so far this year, $\frac{5}{8}$ of them were from repeat customers. How many of his jobs were from new customers?

Use the table for Problems 44–47.

The table shows the number of hours Max worked at various jobs this week and the amount he was paid for each job.

Jobs

Event	Hours Worked	Amount Earned
Mall Opening	$6\frac{1}{2}$	\$65
Rosa's Party	$3\frac{3}{4}$	\$40
Graduation	$1\frac{1}{3}$	\$15
Josh's Party	$2\frac{1}{4}$	\$20
Town Picnic	$5\frac{2}{3}$	\$60

44. Max sets aside $\frac{1}{4}$ of his earnings to put into savings. How much did he save from the five jobs shown in the table?

45. Max spent half of his time at Rosa's party putting on a magic show. How long was the magic show?

46. **Analyze** Find the mean, median, mode, and range of the amounts Max earned at his jobs this week.

47. **Create and Solve** Write your own problem that uses data from the table. Solve your problem.

Extra Practice See page 331, Set B.

Quick Check

Check your understanding for Lessons 1–3.

Multiply. Write your answer in simplest form. (Lessons 1 and 2)

1. 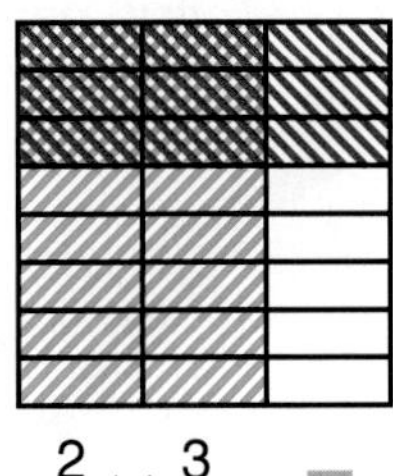

$\frac{2}{3} \times \frac{3}{8} = \blacksquare$

2. 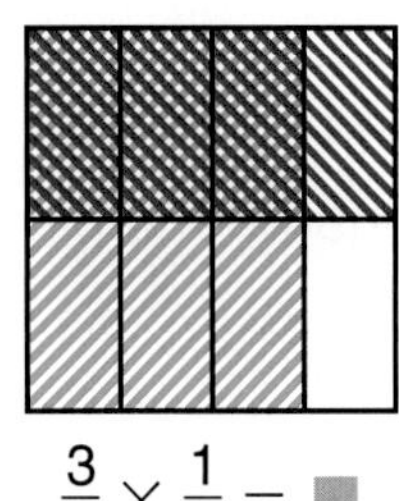

$\frac{3}{4} \times \frac{1}{2} = \blacksquare$

3. $\frac{4}{5} \times \frac{5}{6}$
4. $\frac{1}{3} \times \frac{5}{8}$
5. $\frac{7}{8} \times 6$
6. $8 \times \frac{3}{4}$

Multiply. Write each product in simplest form. (Lesson 3)

7. $2\frac{7}{8} \times 8$
8. $1\frac{3}{5} \times 2\frac{1}{2}$
9. $4 \times 5\frac{3}{4}$
10. $2\frac{1}{3} \times 5\frac{1}{7}$

WEEKLY WR READER® eduplace.com/kids/mw/

How Hot Is It?

If a recipe shows a temperature in °C, you can convert that temperature to °F using this formula: $F = \frac{9}{5}C + 32$.

Here's how to change 200°C to °F.

STEP 1 Substitute values in the formula.

$$F = \frac{9}{5}C + 32$$
$$= \left(\frac{9}{5} \times 200\right) + 32$$

STEP 2 Multiply first.

$$F = \left(\frac{9}{5} \times 200\right) + 32$$
$$= \left(\frac{9}{\cancel{5}_1} \times \frac{\cancel{200}^{40}}{1}\right) + 32$$
$$= 360 + 32$$

STEP 3 Then add.

$$F = 360 + 32$$
$$F = 392$$

The temperature 200°C is the same as the temperature 392°F.

Change these temperatures to °F.

1. 190°C
2. 150°C
3. 235°C
4. 100°C

Model Division

Objective Use models to divide with fractions.

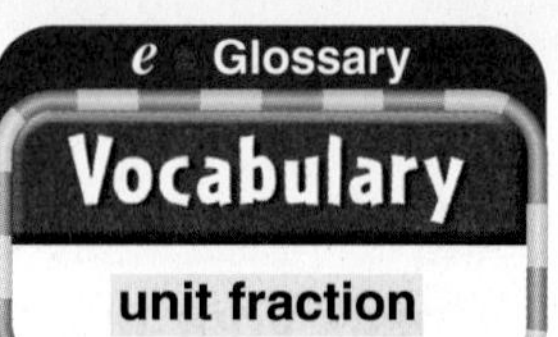

Materials
grid paper
fraction strips

Work Together

A **unit fraction** is a fraction in which the numerator is 1. You can use models to divide a counting number by a unit fraction.

Work with a partner to find $6 \div \frac{1}{2}$.

STEP 1 Draw 6 whole circles.

Separate each circle in half.

Dividing 6 by $\frac{1}{2}$ is the same as finding how many halves are in 6.

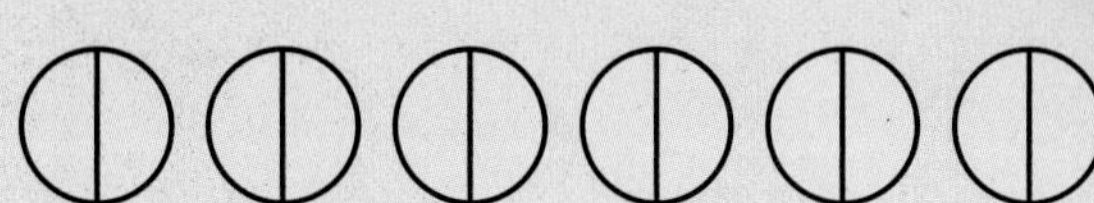

STEP 2 Count to find how many halves are in 6 circles.

- What is $6 \div \frac{1}{2}$?

There are 12 halves in 6 circles, so $6 \div \frac{1}{2} = 12$.

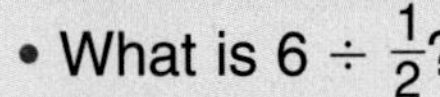

Check your answer using multiplication.

$12 \times \frac{1}{2} = 6$

You can use models to divide a fraction by a fraction.

Work with a partner to find $\frac{4}{5} \div \frac{2}{5}$.

STEP 1 Model $\frac{4}{5}$.

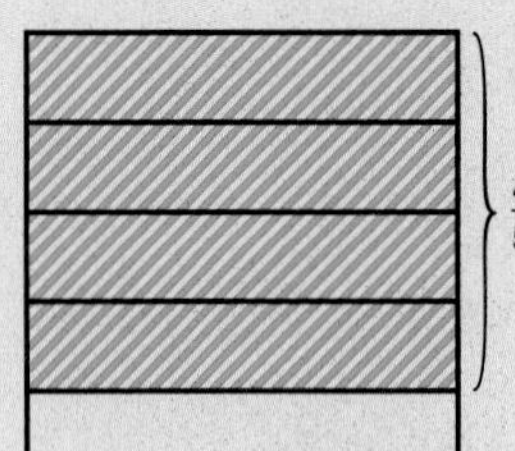

STEP 2 Find how many 2 fifths are in 4 fifths.

- What is $\frac{4}{5} \div \frac{2}{5}$?

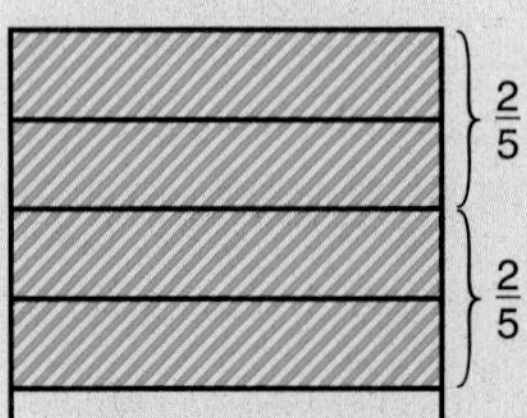

Check.

$2 \times \frac{2}{5} = \frac{4}{5}$

On Your Own

Match each question with the correct model. Then complete the division sentence.

1. What is 3 divided by $\frac{1}{4}$?
   $3 \div \frac{1}{4} = ■$

2. What is 3 divided by $\frac{1}{2}$?
   $3 \div \frac{1}{2} = ■$

3. What is 3 divided by $\frac{1}{6}$?
   $3 \div \frac{1}{6} = ■$

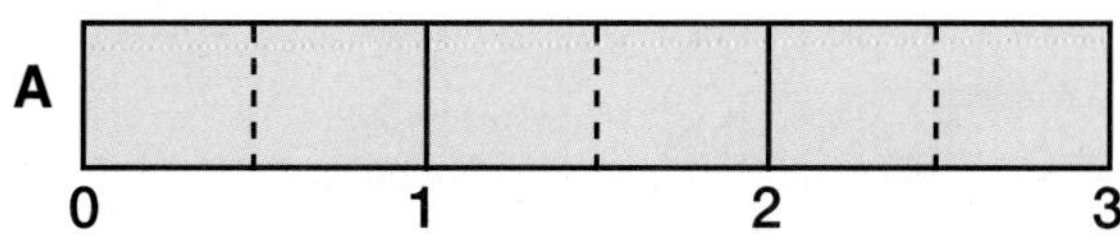

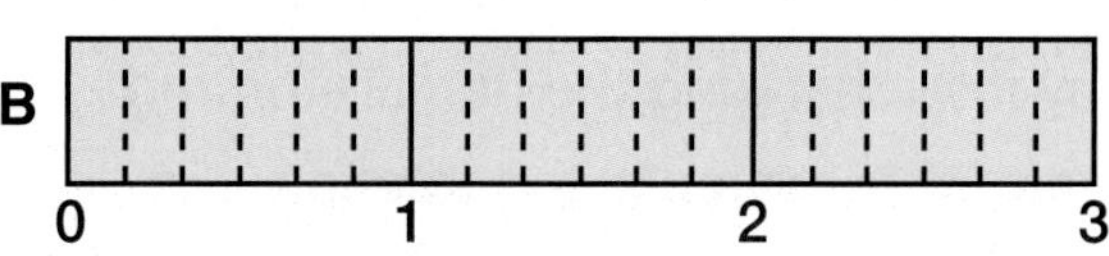

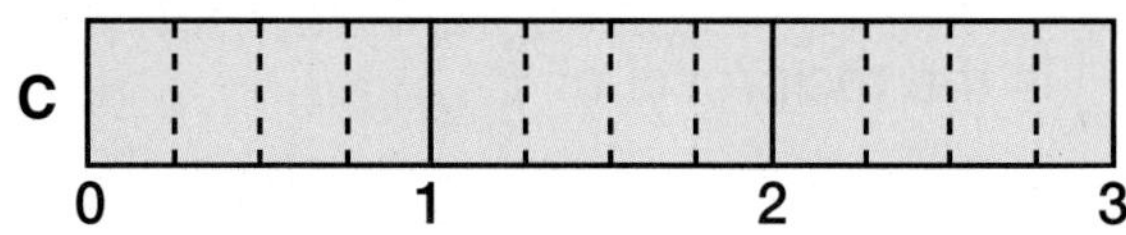

Complete each division and multiplication to find *a* and *b*. Use fraction strips or grid paper for help.

4. $4 \div \frac{1}{2} = a \quad 4 \times 2 = b$
5. $5 \div \frac{1}{3} = a \quad 5 \times 3 = b$
6. $6 \div \frac{1}{5} = a \quad 6 \times 5 = b$
7. $9 \div \frac{1}{2} = a \quad 9 \times 2 = b$

Use your answers from Exercises 4–7 to answer Exercises 8–9.

8. What is true about *a* and *b* in each exercise?

9. To divide a whole number by a unit fraction, by what can you multiply the whole number?

Divide. Check your answers.

10. $\frac{3}{4} \div \frac{1}{4}$
11. $\frac{2}{3} \div \frac{1}{3}$
12. $\frac{4}{5} \div \frac{1}{5}$
13. $\frac{4}{9} \div \frac{2}{9}$
14. $\frac{6}{8} \div \frac{2}{8}$
15. $\frac{9}{12} \div \frac{3}{12}$
16. $\frac{8}{10} \div \frac{2}{10}$
17. $\frac{4}{6} \div \frac{2}{6}$

Talk About It • Write About It

You have learned how to use models to divide fractions.

18. How would you explain to another student how to divide a fraction by a unit fraction?

19. Explain how you found the answers to Exercises 16 and 17.

Lesson 5

Divide Fractions

Objective Use the reciprocal to divide fractions.

Learn About It

If a fraction is not equal to 0, then its **reciprocal** is obtained by interchanging the numerator and the denominator. For example, the fraction $\frac{4}{3}$ is the reciprocal of $\frac{3}{4}$. If neither *a* nor *b* is zero, then the fraction $\frac{b}{a}$ is the reciprocal of $\frac{a}{b}$.

The product of a fraction and its reciprocal is always 1.

$$\frac{3}{4} \times \frac{4}{3} = \frac{\overset{1}{\cancel{3}} \times \overset{1}{\cancel{4}}}{\underset{1}{\cancel{4}} \times \underset{1}{\cancel{3}}} = \frac{a}{b} \times \frac{b}{a} = 1$$

A concert lasted for 4 hours. The concert was divided into acts. Each act was different and lasted $\frac{2}{5}$ hour. How many acts performed at the concert?

Find $4 \div \frac{2}{5}$.

STEP 1 Rewrite the division as a multiplication by the reciprocal of the divisor.

$$4 \div \frac{2}{5} = \frac{4}{1} \times \frac{5}{2}$$

STEP 2 Look for common factors to cancel.

$$= \frac{\overset{2}{\cancel{4}} \times 5}{1 \times \underset{1}{\cancel{2}}} = 10$$

Check your work.

$$10 \times \frac{2}{5} = \frac{\overset{2}{\cancel{10}} \times 2}{\underset{1}{\cancel{5}}} = 2 \times 2 = 4$$

Solution: Ten acts performed.

Other Examples

A. Divide by Counting Number

Find $\frac{9}{10} \div 3$.

$$\frac{9}{10} \div 3 = \frac{9}{10} \times \frac{1}{3}$$
$$= \frac{9}{30}$$
$$= \frac{3}{10}$$

B. Divide Counting Numbers

Find $3 \div 6$.

$$3 \div 6 = 3 \times \frac{1}{6}$$
$$= \frac{3}{6}$$
$$= \frac{1}{2}$$

C. Divide Fractions

Find $\frac{3}{4} \div \frac{5}{8}$.

$$\frac{3}{4} \div \frac{5}{8} = \frac{3}{4} \times \frac{8}{5}$$
$$= \frac{3 \times \overset{2}{\cancel{8}}}{\underset{1}{\cancel{4}} \times 5} = \frac{6}{5}$$
$$= 1\frac{1}{5}$$

Guided Practice

Divide. Write each answer in simplest form.

1. $3 \div \frac{1}{2}$ **2.** $\frac{1}{2} \div \frac{7}{12}$ **3.** $\frac{1}{2} \div 7$

4. $6 \div 8$ **5.** $\frac{2}{3} \div 12$ **6.** $\frac{5}{12} \div \frac{1}{4}$

Ask Yourself

- Did I multiply by the reciprocal of the divisor?
- Did I divide by common factors to simplify?

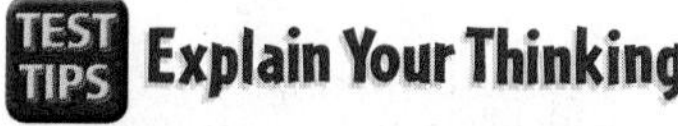

Why does multiplying by 2 give the same result as dividing by $\frac{1}{2}$?

Practice and Problem Solving

Divide. Write each answer in simplest form.

7. $8 \div \frac{1}{4}$ **8.** $\frac{4}{5} \div 8$ **9.** $\frac{1}{4} \div \frac{2}{3}$ **10.** $\frac{5}{6} \div \frac{5}{12}$ **11.** $12 \div \frac{2}{3}$

12. $\frac{3}{4} \div \frac{1}{3}$ **13.** $\frac{3}{8} \div 2$ **14.** $\frac{1}{3} \div 6$ **15.** $5 \div 15$ **16.** $\frac{4}{7} \div 2$

17. $9 \div 12$ **18.** $12 \div 9$ **19.** $\frac{9}{10} \div \frac{7}{10}$ **20.** $\frac{7}{8} \div \frac{3}{4}$ **21.** $\frac{3}{10} \div \frac{4}{5}$

Algebra • Functions **Complete each function table. Write each answer in simplest form.**

22.

Rule: $y = x \div 8$				
x	$1\frac{1}{4}$	2	$2\frac{3}{4}$	$3\frac{1}{2}$
y				

23.

Rule: $y = x \div \frac{4}{5}$				
x	$\frac{4}{5}$	$1\frac{3}{5}$	$2\frac{2}{5}$	$3\frac{1}{5}$
y				

Solve.

24. A band played for $\frac{1}{2}$ hour on stage. Each song lasted $\frac{1}{10}$ hour. How many songs did they perform?

25. One band played 4 audience requests in 15 minutes. What was the average length of each song they played?

26. A band took 3 breaks during a 4-hour concert. Each break was $\frac{1}{6}$ hour. How many minutes of breaks were there?

27. During a $\frac{1}{4}$-hour act, the band performs 3 songs. Each song is the same length. How long is each song?

Daily Review | Test Prep

Divide. (Ch. 4, Lesson 2)

28. $674 \div 3$ **29.** $984 \div 8$

30. $742 \div 9$ **31.** $102 \div 5$

32. **Free Response** During a 2 hour meeting, each person spoke for $\frac{1}{6}$ hour. How many speakers were there? Explain how you got your answer.

Extra Practice See page 331, Set C.

Lesson 6

Divide Mixed Numbers

Objective Divide with mixed numbers.

e Glossary
Vocabulary
mixed number

Learn About It

A dance teacher has scheduled $3\frac{1}{2}$ hours of practice before the spring recital. Today's practice lasted $1\frac{1}{4}$ hours. What fraction of the practice time is that? You can write each **mixed number** as an improper fraction to divide.

Divide. $1\frac{1}{4} \div 3\frac{1}{2} = n$

STEP 1 Write the mixed numbers as improper fractions.

$$1\frac{1}{4} \div 3\frac{1}{2} = \frac{5}{4} \div \frac{7}{2}$$

STEP 2 Rewrite as a multiplication problem using the reciprocal of the divisor.

$$\frac{5}{4} \div \frac{7}{2} = \frac{5}{4} \times \frac{2}{7}$$

STEP 3 Look for common factors.

$$\frac{5}{4} \times \frac{2}{7} = \frac{5 \times 2}{4 \times 7}$$

$$= \frac{5 \times \overset{1}{\cancel{2}}}{2 \times \underset{1}{\cancel{2}} \times 7}$$

STEP 4 Multiply. Be sure the answer is in simplest form.

$$\frac{5 \times 1}{2 \times 1 \times 7} = \frac{5}{14}$$

Check your work.

$$\frac{5}{14} \times 3\frac{1}{2} = \frac{5}{14} \times \frac{7}{2}$$

$$= \frac{5 \times \overset{1}{\cancel{7}}}{2 \times \underset{1}{\cancel{7}} \times 2}$$

$$= \frac{5}{4}, \text{ or } 1\frac{1}{4}$$

Solution: $1\frac{1}{4} \div 3\frac{1}{2} = \frac{5}{14}$

Other Examples

A. Dividend is Counting Number

Find $9 \div 2\frac{1}{4}$.

$$9 \div 2\frac{1}{4} = \frac{9}{1} \div \frac{9}{4}$$

$$= \frac{9}{1} \times \frac{4}{9}$$

$$= \frac{\overset{1}{\cancel{9}} \times 4}{1 \times \underset{1}{\cancel{9}}}$$

$$= \frac{4}{1} = 4$$

B. Divisor is Fraction

Find $2\frac{1}{4} \div \frac{3}{4}$.

$$2\frac{1}{4} \div \frac{3}{4} = 2\frac{1}{4} \times \frac{4}{3}$$

$$= \frac{9}{4} \times \frac{4}{3}$$

$$= \frac{9 \times \overset{1}{\cancel{4}}}{\underset{1}{\cancel{4}} \times 3}$$

$$= \frac{9}{3} = 3$$

C. Dividend is Fraction

Find $\frac{5}{8} \div 1\frac{2}{3}$.

$$\frac{5}{8} \div 1\frac{2}{3} = \frac{5}{8} \div \frac{5}{3}$$

$$= \frac{5}{8} \times \frac{3}{5}$$

$$= \frac{\overset{1}{\cancel{5}} \times 3}{8 \times \underset{1}{\cancel{5}}}$$

$$= \frac{3}{8}$$

Guided Practice

Ask Yourself

- Did I invert the divisor to form the reciprocal?
- Did I cancel common factors?
- Did I write the quotient in simplest form?

Rewrite each division as a multiplication. Write all mixed numbers as improper fractions.

1. $\frac{2}{3} \div 4\frac{2}{5}$ **2.** $11 \div 1\frac{1}{2}$ **3.** $8\frac{2}{3} \div 12\frac{1}{2}$

4. $2\frac{1}{3} \div 4$ **5.** $1\frac{3}{4} \div \frac{1}{2}$ **6.** $5\frac{3}{8} \div 1\frac{3}{4}$

Write each quotient in simplest form.

7. $\frac{1}{4} \div 1\frac{1}{4}$ **8.** $4\frac{7}{8} \div 2$ **9.** $8\frac{5}{8} \div 2\frac{7}{8}$ **10.** $6 \div 1\frac{1}{2}$

Explain Your Thinking ▶ How are the reciprocals of unit fractions and counting numbers related?

Practice and Problem Solving

Rewrite each each division as a multiplication.

11. $\frac{3}{4} \div 1\frac{2}{3}$ **12.** $10 \div 3\frac{1}{5}$ **13.** $7\frac{3}{4} \div 4$ **14.** $1\frac{1}{5} \div 3\frac{7}{8}$

Write each quotient in simplest form.

15. $\frac{4}{5} \div 1\frac{1}{2}$ **16.** $4\frac{1}{4} \div 3$ **17.** $\frac{2}{3} \div 1\frac{1}{3}$ **18.** $3\frac{2}{3} \div \frac{1}{3}$

19. $2\frac{1}{8} \div \frac{1}{2}$ **20.** $4\frac{1}{2} \div \frac{3}{8}$ **21.** $3 \div 1\frac{1}{2}$ **22.** $6 \div 3\frac{1}{3}$

23. $3\frac{1}{4} \div \frac{2}{3}$ **24.** $\frac{3}{4} \div 2\frac{1}{2}$ **25.** $1\frac{1}{4} \div 2\frac{1}{2}$ **26.** $4 \div 1\frac{3}{4}$

27. $6 \div 1\frac{3}{4}$ **28.** $6\frac{1}{2} \div \frac{3}{4}$ **29.** $5\frac{1}{8} \div 3$ **30.** $\frac{2}{3} \div 2\frac{2}{3}$

Algebra • Expressions **Rewrite each expression as a fraction in simplest form. No variable equals 0.**

31. $n \div 2$ **32.** $2 \div n$ **33.** $4a \div \frac{4}{b}$ **34.** $b \div a$

35. $3n \div 3m$ **36.** $6xy \div 3x$ **37.** $\frac{1}{a} \div \frac{1}{a}$ **38.** $5ab \div \frac{a}{2}$

Compare **Write >, <, or = for each ⬬.**

39. $6\frac{3}{4} \div 2\frac{1}{4}$ ⬬ $6\frac{1}{3} \div 2$ **40.** $5 \div 1\frac{1}{2}$ ⬬ $2 \div \frac{1}{2}$

41. $\frac{1}{2} \div \frac{1}{3}$ ⬬ $\frac{5}{8} \div \frac{2}{3}$ **42.** $3\frac{3}{4} \div \frac{1}{2}$ ⬬ $1\frac{7}{8} \div \frac{1}{4}$

Go On

Choose a Computation Method

Mental Math • Estimation • Paper and Pencil • Calculator

Use the schedule for Problems 43–46.

Beth is studying at a ballet school. The schedule at the right shows her Monday classes and their times.

Beth's Monday Schedule	
Class	**Number of Hours**
Modern Dance	2
Ballet	$2\frac{1}{2}$
Jazz	$1\frac{1}{4}$
Character	$1\frac{1}{2}$
Strength Training	$\frac{3}{4}$

43. What fraction of Beth's Monday class schedule does ballet represent?

44. Last Monday, Beth was late for her Jazz class. She missed $\frac{1}{3}$ of the class. How much time is that?

45. Analyze One of Beth's teachers divides each hour of class into thirds. She uses those six sessions to work with different groups. Which class is this?

46. Reasoning Beth's Tuesday schedule is like Monday's, except ballet class is half as long, and jazz class is twice as long. Does her total time change?

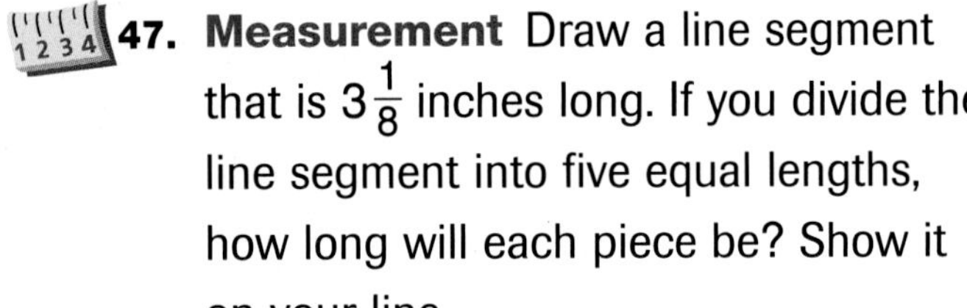

47. Measurement Draw a line segment that is $3\frac{1}{8}$ inches long. If you divide the line segment into five equal lengths, how long will each piece be? Show it on your line.

48. Glennis drew a line segment that was $9\frac{3}{5}$ inches long. Then she divided it into line segments that were each $1\frac{1}{5}$ inches long. How many line segments did she make?

49. Write About It When dividing by a fraction greater than one, is the quotient less than or greater than the dividend? Support your conclusion.

50. Patrick plans to study for $3\frac{3}{4}$ hours. He wants to spend $\frac{3}{4}$ hour on each subject. How many subjects will Patrick be able to study?

Daily Review | Test Prep

Write the prime factorization. Use exponents if possible. (Ch. 9, Lesson 2)

51. 36 **52.** 42

53. 25 **54.** 9

55. 56 **56.** 72

57. Lance did homework for $2\frac{1}{4}$ hours. He spent the same amount of time on each of 3 subjects. How long did he spend on each subject?

A $\frac{1}{4}$ hour **C** $1\frac{1}{3}$ hours

B $\frac{3}{4}$ hour **D** $6\frac{3}{4}$ hours

Extra Practice See page 331, Set D.

Division Scramble

2 players

What You'll Need • two copies of Learning Tool 42 or 2 game boards; 4 sets of number cards, numbered 1 to 10

How to Play

1. Shuffle the number cards and place them on the table facedown in a stack. Give each player a game board. The goal of the game is to create a division example that will have a greater quotient than your opponent's example has.

2. In turn each player takes one card from the stack and places that card face up on his or her game board. Once placed, a card cannot be moved.

3. The game continues until each player has four cards showing on his or her game board.

4. Each player then divides the fractions displayed on the game board. The player whose example has the greater quotient wins.

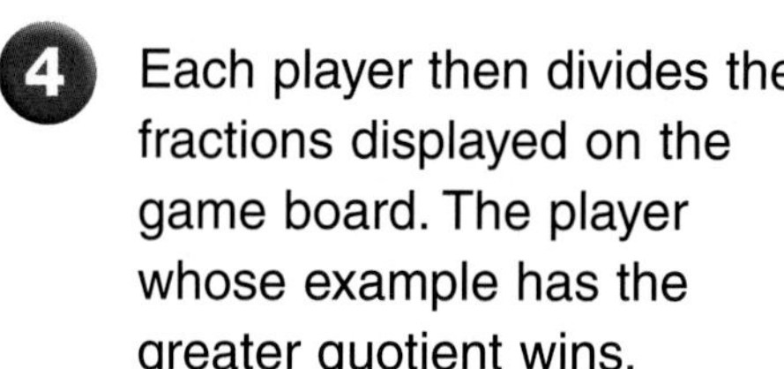

5. Shuffle the number cards and play again. This time the player whose example has the lesser quotient wins.

Lesson 7

Problem-Solving Decision
Choose the Operation

Objective Review how to choose the operation that will help you solve a problem.

When solving problems you must decide which operation to use.

Problem The area of the gym floor is 610 square feet. Five eighths of the floor will be used as the stage for a "battle of the bands" concert. The stage will be separated equally into four sections–one for each of the four bands. How much space is given to each band?

Find the area of the gym floor to be used as the stage.	**Find how much of the stage each band will have.**
Multiply to find a fraction of a number.	**Divide to separate a number equally.**
$610 \times \frac{5}{8} = 381\frac{1}{4}$	$381\frac{1}{4} \div 4 = 95\frac{5}{16}$

Solution: Each band is given $95\frac{5}{16}$ square feet of space.

Try These

Solve.

1. Look back at the problem above. The remaining $\frac{3}{8}$ of the gym floor was separated equally into 5 sections for seating. How large was each section?

2. Tickets for the concert cost \$5.00 at the door. Students could buy tickets in advance for $\frac{3}{4}$ of the door price. How much did advance tickets cost?

3. The drummer needs $29\frac{1}{4}$ square feet. The bassist needs $10\frac{1}{2}$ square feet of space. How much more space does the drummer need? How much space do they need combined?

4. The 320 people in the audience each cast one vote for their favorite band. If $\frac{5}{16}$ of the audience voted for Band 1, $\frac{1}{8}$ for Band 2, $\frac{3}{16}$ for Band 3, and $\frac{3}{8}$ for Band 4, how many votes did each band get?

Quick Check

Check your understanding for Lessons 4–7.

Use the models to divide. Write each quotient in simplest form. (Lessons 4–6)

1. 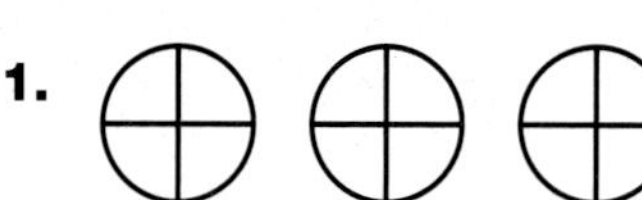

$3 \div \frac{1}{4} = \frac{\blacksquare}{\blacksquare}$

2. $\frac{9}{10} \div \frac{3}{10} = \frac{\blacksquare}{\blacksquare}$

3. $6 \div \frac{3}{5}$ **4.** $\frac{7}{9} \div \frac{5}{6}$ **5.** $8 \div 3$ **6.** $\frac{7}{12} \div \frac{3}{4}$ 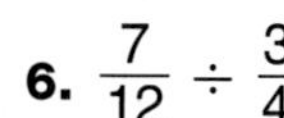 **7.** $2\frac{2}{3} \div 1\frac{1}{3}$ **8.** $2\frac{1}{2} \div \frac{3}{5}$

Name the operation(s) you chose to solve. Write each answer in simplest form. (Lesson 7)

9. A recipe makes two and one half dozen cookies. How many dozen cookies can Sarah make if she used three times the original recipe?

10. Rachael's garden has 134 square feet. She wants to separate the space equally into 6 parts. What will be the size of each part?

WEEKLY WR READER® eduplace.com/kids/mw/

United States Congress

The United States Congress is made up of the House of Representatives and the Senate. The House of Representatives has 435 members and the Senate has 100 members. To pass a bill, a majority of the members (one half of the members plus 1) of each house must vote to pass the bill.

Problem To pass a bill, how many members of the Senate must vote for the bill?

Now solve the problem. Look back. Does your answer make sense?

1. How many members of the House of Representatives are needed for a majority?

2. It takes $\frac{2}{3}$ of the House of Representatives and $\frac{2}{3}$ of the Senate to vote to override a veto. How many members of each house is that?

Chapter Review/Test

VOCABULARY

Vocabulary
improper fraction
mixed number
reciprocal
unit fraction

1. The product of a number and its ____ is always 1.
2. A(n) ____ is a fraction in which the numerator is 1.
3. A(n) ____ has a numerator that is greater than or equal to the denominator.

CONCEPTS AND SKILLS

Draw a model to show how you find each product. Write your answer in simplest form. (Lesson 1, pp. 310–313)

4. $\frac{1}{2} \times \frac{2}{3}$
5. $\frac{1}{6} \times 3$

Multiply. Write your answers in simplest form. (Lessons 2–3, pp. 314–319)

6. $\frac{3}{7} \times 21$
7. $\frac{5}{8} \times \frac{1}{3}$
8. $\frac{5}{8} \times \frac{4}{25}$
9. $6 \times 2\frac{5}{6}$
10. $\frac{3}{8} \times \frac{4}{7}$
11. $2\frac{3}{5} \times 5$
12. $9\frac{1}{5} \times 1\frac{1}{2}$
13. $2\frac{1}{4} \times 3\frac{1}{3}$

Use the models to divide. Write each answer in simplest form. (Lesson 4, pp. 320–321)

14. 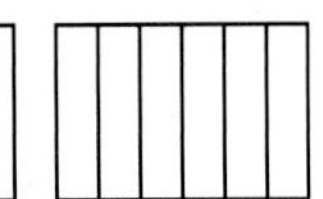 $2 \div \frac{1}{6} = ■$
15.  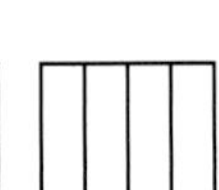 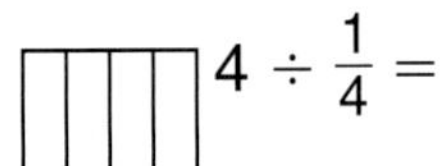 $4 \div \frac{1}{4} = ■$

Divide. Write each answer in simplest form. (Lessons 5–6, pp. 322–327)

16. $\frac{3}{4} \div \frac{1}{2}$
17. $\frac{7}{9} \div \frac{2}{3}$
18. $\frac{5}{8} \div \frac{5}{6}$
19. $8 \div 20$
20. $\frac{3}{5} \div 9$
21. $9 \div \frac{3}{5}$
22. $2\frac{1}{4} \div 1\frac{1}{2}$
23. $3\frac{3}{5} \div 1\frac{2}{7}$

PROBLEM SOLVING

Solve and name the operation(s) you chose. (Lesson 7, pp. 328–329)

24. The string section is $\frac{3}{5}$ of the school orchestra. 50 students are in the orchestra. How many of them are string players?

25. Marianne practices her violin $7\frac{1}{2}$ hours each week. If she practices $1\frac{1}{4}$ hours each day, how many days does she practice each week?

Write About It

Show You Understand

Why is $3 \div 6$ equal to $\frac{1}{2}$ and not 2? Explain, using pictures, symbols, or words.

Extra Practice

Set A (Lessons 1–2, pp. 310–315)

Multiply. Write your answer in simplest form.

1. $\frac{1}{3} \times \frac{1}{6}$ **2.** $8 \times \frac{3}{5}$ **3.** $\frac{5}{9} \times \frac{2}{3}$ **4.** $\frac{3}{4} \times 4$

5. $\frac{2}{5} \times 3$ **6.** $\frac{5}{8} \times \frac{1}{3}$ **7.** $5 \times \frac{3}{4}$ **8.** $\frac{5}{6} \times 6$

9. $\frac{1}{4} \times \frac{8}{9}$ **10.** $\frac{7}{8} \times \frac{6}{7}$ **11.** $\frac{5}{6} \times \frac{9}{10}$ **12.** $\frac{4}{7} \times \frac{5}{2}$

13. $\frac{2}{3} \times \frac{1}{12}$ **14.** $\frac{10}{13} \times \frac{1}{10}$ **15.** $\frac{3}{10} \times \frac{7}{9}$ **16.** $\frac{1}{5} \times \frac{10}{11}$

Set B (Lesson 3, pp. 316–319)

Multiply. Write each product in simplest form.

1. $1\frac{4}{5} \times \frac{5}{6}$ **2.** $\frac{1}{3} \times 1\frac{1}{3}$ **3.** $3\frac{1}{4} \times \frac{4}{9}$ **4.** $\frac{4}{9} \times 1\frac{3}{4}$

5. $1\frac{1}{8} \times \frac{4}{7}$ **6.** $2\frac{2}{5} \times \frac{5}{7}$ **7.** $2\frac{1}{4} \times \frac{8}{9}$ **8.** $4 \times 3\frac{1}{8}$

9. $1\frac{2}{3} \times 3\frac{6}{7}$ **10.** $2\frac{7}{8} \times 2$ **11.** $1\frac{12}{13} \times \frac{1}{5}$ **12.** $2\frac{4}{7} \times \frac{5}{9}$

13. $3\frac{3}{8} \times \frac{7}{9}$ **14.** $\frac{3}{4} \times 4\frac{3}{5}$ **15.** $3\frac{1}{5} \times 2\frac{5}{8}$ **16.** $2\frac{1}{2} \times 1\frac{3}{5}$

Set C (Lessons 4–5, pp. 320–323)

Divide. Write each answer in simplest form.

1. $4 \div \frac{1}{5}$ **2.** $\frac{5}{6} \div \frac{3}{4}$ **3.** $\frac{1}{6} \div 2$ **4.** $10 \div \frac{1}{10}$

5. $3 \div \frac{1}{4}$ **6.** $\frac{4}{5} \div \frac{2}{3}$ **7.** $4 \div 6$ **8.** $\frac{1}{2} \div 16$

9. $\frac{1}{4} \div \frac{7}{8}$ **10.** $5 \div \frac{1}{3}$ **11.** $\frac{1}{6} \div \frac{1}{2}$ **12.** $\frac{2}{5} \div 10$

13. $\frac{7}{8} \div \frac{5}{9}$ **14.** $12 \div 8$ **15.** $\frac{5}{7} \div \frac{1}{4}$ **16.** $\frac{6}{7} \div \frac{1}{4}$

Set D (Lesson 6, pp. 324–327)

Write each quotient in simplest form.

1. $\frac{2}{5} \div 1\frac{1}{5}$ **2.** $\frac{2}{3} \div 6$ **3.** $2\frac{1}{4} \div \frac{3}{8}$ **4.** $\frac{3}{4} \div 2\frac{5}{8}$

5. $2\frac{5}{6} \div 1\frac{7}{9}$ **6.** $\frac{5}{9} \div 3$ **7.** $\frac{5}{8} \div 2\frac{3}{4}$ **8.** $1\frac{3}{4} \div \frac{1}{8}$

9. $10 \div 3\frac{1}{5}$ **10.** $2\frac{4}{5} \div 1\frac{2}{3}$ **11.** $1\frac{3}{4} \div 1\frac{3}{8}$ **12.** $\frac{2}{5} \div 1\frac{3}{5}$

13. $4 \div 2\frac{1}{4}$ **14.** $11 \div 3\frac{2}{3}$ **15.** $1\frac{1}{8} \div 4$ **16.** $3\frac{1}{3} \div \frac{2}{9}$

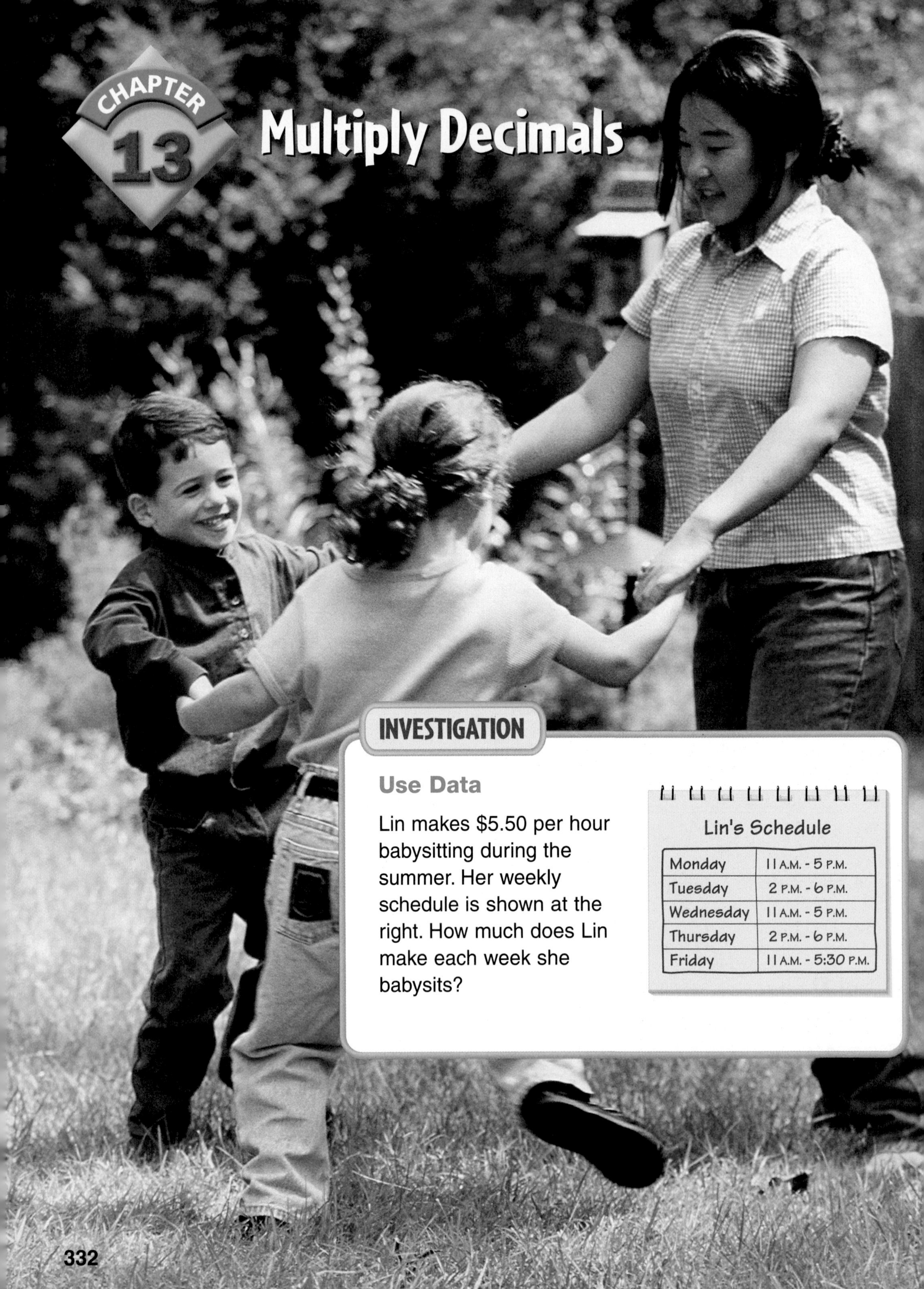

Multiply Decimals

INVESTIGATION

Use Data

Lin makes $5.50 per hour babysitting during the summer. Her weekly schedule is shown at the right. How much does Lin make each week she babysits?

Lin's Schedule

Monday	11 A.M. - 5 P.M.
Tuesday	2 P.M. - 6 P.M.
Wednesday	11 A.M. - 5 P.M.
Thursday	2 P.M. - 6 P.M.
Friday	11 A.M. - 5:30 P.M.

Chapter Pretest

Use this page to review and remember what you need to know for this chapter.

VOCABULARY

Choose the best word to complete each sentence.

1. In the decimal 0.095, the 9 is in the ____ place.
2. The six in the decimal 0.62 is in the ____ place.
3. The decimal 0.002 is read as “two ____.”
4. The decimal 10.02 is read as ____ and two hundredths.

CONCEPTS AND SKILLS

Write each fraction as a decimal.

5. $\frac{8}{10}$ 6. $\frac{32}{100}$ 7. $\frac{1}{4}$ 8. $\frac{1}{2}$

Write these numbers from least to greatest.

9. 60.05, 6.5, 6.005
10. 74.3, 79.02, 54.85, 54.58
11. 1.1, 9.11, 3.4, 1.101

Write >, <, or = for each ⬬.

12. 27.1 ⬬ 27.01
13. 6.102 ⬬ 6.021
14. 13.20 ⬬ 13.2

Multiply.

15. 31×23
16. 49×17
17. 52×36
18. 22×45
19. 93×90

Write About It

20. Adventure videos cost $7.49, and comedies are on sale at 3 for $20. If you could afford to buy three videos, which kind of movie would cost you less? Explain.

Visit *Education Place* at **eduplace.com/kids/mw/** for more review.

Lesson 1

Explore Multiplication

Objective Use models to explore multiplication with decimals.

Learn About It

How many more liters of juice does the larger container of Just Juice hold?

Materials
grid paper
(Learning Tool 1)
Decimal/Percent Models
(Learning Tool 4)

You need to find $\frac{1}{5}$ of 1.5.

Different Ways to Find $\frac{1}{5}$ of 1.5

Way 1 You can use models to find $\frac{1}{5}$ of 1.5.

STEP 1 Use 10×10 grids. Shade 1.5 in blue.

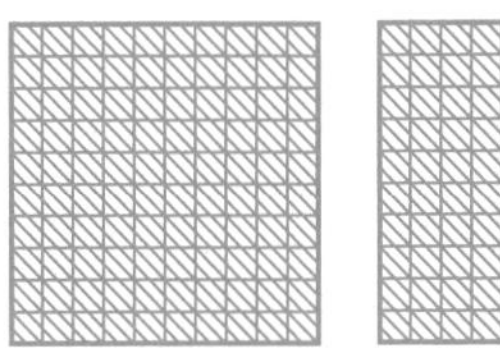

STEP 2 Shade $\frac{1}{5}$ of 1.5 in red.

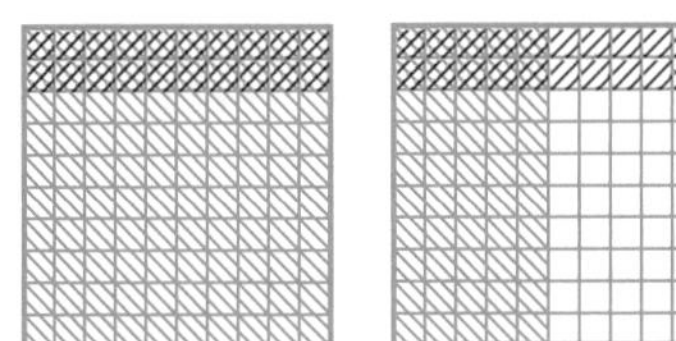

STEP 3 Count the purple squares.

$\frac{1}{5}$ of 1.5 is $\frac{30}{100}$, or 0.30, or 0.3.

Way 2 You can use what you know about multiplication of fractions and mixed numbers to find $\frac{1}{5}$ of 1.5.

STEP 1 Change 1.5 to a mixed number.

$1.5 = 1\frac{5}{10}$, or $1\frac{1}{2}$

STEP 2 Multiply.

$$1\frac{1}{2} \times \frac{1}{5} = \frac{3}{2} \times \frac{1}{5}$$
$$= \frac{3}{10}, \text{ or } 0.3$$

Solution: The larger container of Just Juice holds 0.3 liter more.

Another Example **Find 0.18 × 3.**

Use fractions.

$$\frac{18}{100} \times \frac{3}{1} = \frac{54}{100}$$
$$= 0.54$$

Use models.

54 of 100 squares, or 0.54 is shaded.

$$\frac{18}{100} + \frac{18}{100} + \frac{18}{100} = \frac{54}{100}$$

Guided Practice

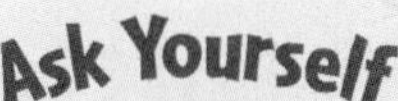

Ask Yourself

- Did I model the multiplication correctly?
- Did I multiply correctly?
- Did I write the product as a decimal?

Use models or fractions to multiply. Write each product as a decimal.

1. 0.6×0.2 **2.** 0.5×0.8 **3.** 0.7×2.6

4. 1.5×0.4 **5.** 0.8×0.9 **6.** 0.6×1.4

TEST TIPS **Explain Your Thinking** ▶ Is $\frac{1}{2} \times 0.4$ equal to $\frac{2}{5} \times 0.5$? Explain why or why not.

Practice and Problem Solving

Use models or fractions to multiply. Write each product as a decimal.

7. 0.6×0.5 **8.** 0.4×0.8 **9.** 1.5×0.5 **10.** 0.5×2.8 **11.** 2.1×0.5

12. 1.7×0.3 **13.** 0.9×0.9 **14.** 0.3×0.3 **15.** 1.3×0.8 **16.** 1.2×0.2

Solve.

17. Miguel works at a juice bar 8.5 hours each week. Kim works half as many hours. How many hours does Kim work in a week?

18. Mental Math A manufacturer puts a bonus coupon on 0.1 of its juice bottles. In a case with 20 bottles, how many juice bottles will have the coupon?

19. Create and Solve Write a problem that can be solved using the model at the right. Solve your problem. Then give it to a partner to solve.

20. Analyze Look back at page 334. Suppose the advertisement read, "New size holds 0.2 liter more!" How many liters would the new container hold?

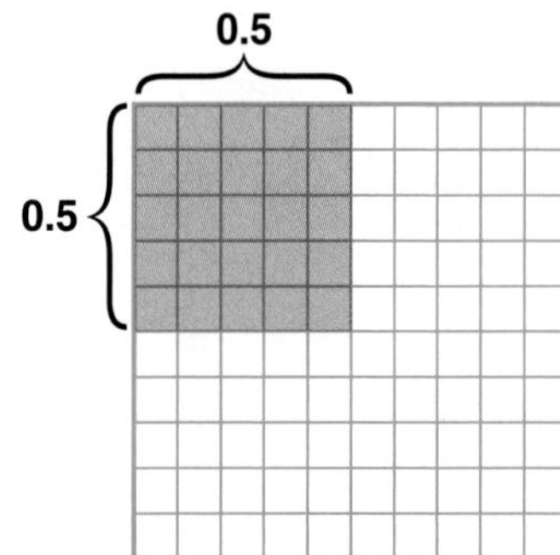

Daily Review | Test Prep

Subtract. (Ch. 11, Lesson 3)

21. $23.2 - 7.5$ **22.** $107.26 - 27.05$

23. $222.22 - 78.51$ **24.** $79.305 - 12.047$

25. Use models or fractions to find $\frac{2}{3}$ of 0.6.

A 0.2 **C** 0.4

B 0.5 **D** 0.9

Extra Practice See page 349, Set A.

Lesson 2

Multiply Whole Numbers and Decimals

Objective Find the product of a whole number and a decimal.

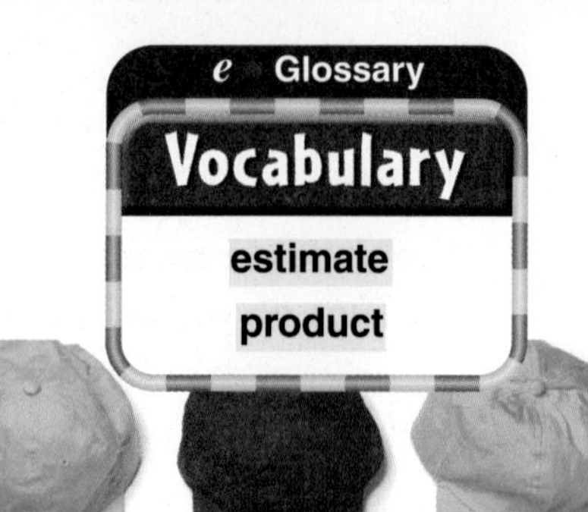

Learn About It

Lian bought 3 caps that were on sale. How much did Lian pay for the caps?

Multiply. $3 \times \$5.68 = c$

STEP 1 **Estimate** before solving by rounding to the nearest whole number.

$3 \times \$6 = \$18$

Your answer should be close to $18.

STEP 2 Multiply. Ignore the decimal point.

$$\begin{array}{r} 5.68 \\ \times \quad 3 \\ \hline 1704 \end{array}$$

STEP 3 Place the decimal point in the **product.**

The number of decimal places in the product must equal the total number of decimal places in the factors.

$$\begin{array}{rcr} 5.68 & \leftarrow & \text{2 decimal places} \\ \times \quad 3 & \leftarrow & + \text{ 0 decimal places} \\ \hline 17.04 & \leftarrow & \text{2 decimal places} \end{array}$$

Compare your answer with your estimate.

$18 is close to $17.04.

An answer of $17.04 is a reasonable answer.

Solution: Lian paid $17.04 for the caps.

Another Example

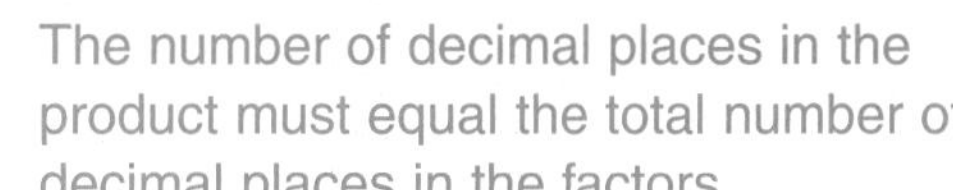

Find 14 × 0.45.

$$\begin{array}{rcr} 0.45 & \leftarrow & \text{2 decimal places} \\ \times \quad 14 & \leftarrow & + \text{ 0 decimal places} \\ \hline 180 & & \\ \underline{450} & & \\ 6.30 & \leftarrow & \text{2 decimal places} \end{array}$$

Guided Practice

Find each product.

1. 4×1.3 **2.** 2.6×5 **3.** 0.59×8

4. 6×1.82 **5.** 3.25×16 **6.** 0.515×7

Ask Yourself

- Did I estimate first?
- Did I use the correct number of decimal places in my answer?

Explain Your Thinking ▶ Why does it help to estimate before you find the exact answer?

Practice and Problem Solving

Find each product.

7. 6×2.4
8. 3.8×2
9. 9.6×8
10. 9×5.6
11. 0.13×5
12. 3×3.4
13. 9×0.18
14. 0.1×13
15. 8×10.8
16. 3×31.44
17. 7×7.7
18. 20.5×4
19. 0.9×11
20. 50.2×6
21. 4.412×8
22. 6×9.8
23. 12×0.56
24. 23×2.1
25. 16×9.5
26. 35×0.86

Algebra • Expressions Find a value of *n* to make each statement true.

27. $13 \times n$ is between 55 and 65.
28. $n \times 138$ is between 200 and 250.
29. $n \times 11$ is between 135 and 140.
30. $n \times 25$ is between 40 and 45.

Solve.

31. Kayla works 8 hours one week and earns $48. If 0.08 of that amount is for taxes, how much money does Kayla have to spend that week?

32. John's cost for a sweater is $21 after his discount of 0.7. Is the price of the sweater before the discount more or less than $42? Explain.

33. Sierra worked 3.5 hours on Saturday morning and 2.5 hours on Sunday afternoon. If Sierra earns $9.80 per hour, how much did she earn on Saturday and Sunday?

34. **Analyze** Because his father works at the store, Gavin pays only 0.7 of the marked price on clothing. Wayne has a coupon for $5 off any jacket. Who will pay the least for the jacket at the right? Explain how you decided.

Daily Review Test Prep

Add. (Ch. 11, Lesson 2)

35. $1.8 + 3.246$
36. $4.01 + 5.07$
37. $3.02 + 4.08$
38. $5.02 + 2.88$
39. $8.6 + 3.4$
40. $3.21 + 3.22$
41. $6.90 + 1.1$
42. $0.35 + 0.07$

43. **Free Response** Grant's purchases at the grocery store come to $130. He saves 0.2 of this by using coupons. How much does Grant pay after using the coupons?

Explain how you got your answer.

Extra Practice See page 349, Set B.

Lesson 3

Estimate Products

Objective Use rounding to estimate products of decimals.

Learn About It

When Isaac's father makes a call on his cell phone, it costs 11 cents for each minute the call lasts. About how much did it cost Isaac to talk on his father's cell phone for 86 minutes after school?

Estimate the product. 86 × $0.11

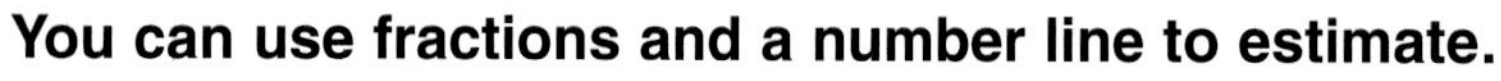

You can use fractions and a number line to estimate.

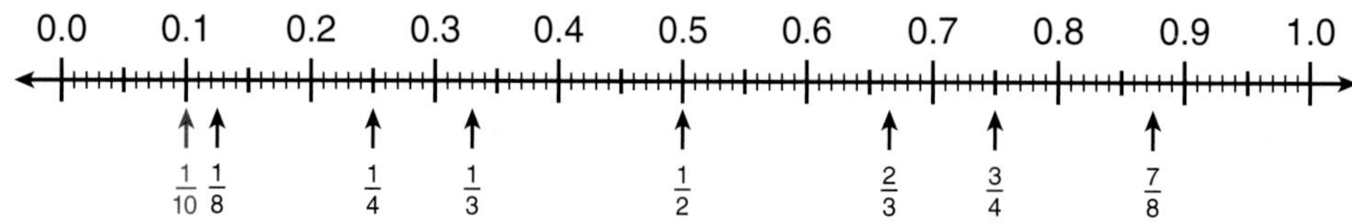

STEP 1 Round the numbers.

86 rounds to 90.

0.11 is about $\frac{1}{10}$.

STEP 2 Multiply.

$90 \times \frac{1}{10} = \frac{90}{10}$, or 9

Solution: It cost about $9 for Isaac's phone call.

You can round each factor to a greater or lesser number, depending on whether you want a high or a low estimate.

Other Examples

A. Lesser Numbers

Estimate 328 × 0.62.

$$\begin{array}{r} 328 \\ \times\ 0.62 \\ \hline \end{array} \rightarrow \begin{array}{r} 300 \\ \times\ 0.6 \\ \hline 180 \end{array}$$

Since both factors were rounded to a lesser number, the actual product must be greater than 180.

B. Greater and Lesser Numbers

Estimate 0.34 × 359.

$0.34 \approx \frac{1}{3}$

$359 \approx 360$

$\frac{1}{\cancel{3}_1} \times \cancel{360}^{120} \approx 120$

Guided Practice

Ask Yourself

- How can I round each number?
- Can I easily use fractions?

TEST TIPS

Estimate each product.

1. $\begin{array}{r} 6.572 \\ \times\ 18 \\ \hline \end{array}$

2. $\begin{array}{r} 122 \\ \times\ 0.24 \\ \hline \end{array}$

3. $\begin{array}{r} 532 \\ \times\ 1.7 \\ \hline \end{array}$

4. 87×3.12

5. 32×0.48

6. 2.5×351

Explain Your Thinking ▶ How does your estimated product in Exercise 6 compare with the actual product? Explain.

Practice and Problem Solving

Estimate each product.

7. 0.23×41
8. 8×0.119
9. 12.7×32
10. 209×0.467
11. 6.6×27
12. 0.45×80
13. 3.5×58
14. 25×7.92

Data
Use the table for Problems 15–19.

The table shows the current cellular phone plan Mr. Henry uses and two alternate plans to which he may consider switching.

Plan	Peak Minute Cost	Off-Peak Minute Cost
Current Plan	$0.350	$0.055
Alternate 1	$0.700	Free
Alternate 2	$0.125	$0.125

15. **Estimate** Last month, Mr. Henry's cellular phone bill included 135 peak minutes and 240 off-peak minutes. About how much was this bill?

16. **Explain** If a person uses 100 peak and 100 off-peak minutes each month, which plan is least expensive to use?

17. Which calling plan has the greatest difference between peak and off-peak charges? How much is the difference?

18. **Calculator** A customer with Alternate 1 plan has a bill of $35. The customer used the same number of peak and off-peak minutes. How many minutes each was that?

19. Mr. Henry's average bill includes 98 peak minutes and 516 off-peak minutes. Should he switch plans or stay with the one he has? Explain your reasoning.

Daily Review | Test Prep

Write each sum or difference in simplest form. (Ch. 10, Lessons 2 and 5)

20. $\frac{1}{4} + \frac{1}{4}$
21. $\frac{3}{7} + \frac{2}{7}$
22. $\frac{7}{8} - \frac{3}{8}$
23. $\frac{5}{9} - \frac{2}{9}$
24. $\frac{3}{5} + \frac{7}{5}$
25. $\frac{6}{3} - \frac{3}{3}$

26. A box of crackers costs $0.296 per ounce. Which is a reasonable estimate for the cost of a 12-ounce box of those crackers?

A $2.00
B $6.00
C $4.00
D $12.00

Extra Practice See page 349, Set C.

Lesson 4

Multiply Decimals

Objective Find the product of two decimals.

Learn About It

The parking lot at the shopping mall covers 0.9 acre. Three tenths of the parking lot is reserved for compact cars. How large is the area reserved for compact cars?

You can multiply 0.9 and 0.3 to solve the problem.

Before you multiply, estimate to get a sense of where the decimal point belongs in your answer.

$0.9 \approx 1$
$1 \times 0.3 = 0.3$

Remember $\approx$ means "about equal to."

The answer should be a little less than 0.3.

Multiply. $0.9 \times 0.3 = n$

Multiply and then place the decimal point.

STEP 1 Multiply. Ignore the decimal points.

$$\begin{array}{r} 3 \\ \times 9 \\ \hline 27 \end{array}$$

STEP 2 Place the decimal point in the product.

0.3	←	1 decimal place
× 0.9	←	+ 1 decimal place
0.27	←	2 decimal places

Use fractions to check.

$$\frac{3}{10} \times \frac{9}{10} = \frac{3 \times 9}{10 \times 10}$$
$$= \frac{27}{100}, \text{ or } 0.27$$

Solution: In the parking lot, 0.27 acre is reserved for compact cars.

Other Examples

A. Factor in Hundredths

0.71	←	2 decimal places
× 0.9	←	+ 1 decimal place
0.639	←	3 decimal places

B. Factors Greater Than 1

1.43	←	2 decimal places
× 3.2	←	+ 1 decimal place
286		
4290		
4.576	←	3 decimal places

Guided Practice

Multiply.

1. $\begin{array}{r} 0.6 \\ \times\ 0.4 \\ \hline \end{array}$

2. $\begin{array}{r} 0.6 \\ \times\ \ 5 \\ \hline \end{array}$

3. $\begin{array}{r} 0.46 \\ \times\ \ \ 2 \\ \hline \end{array}$

4. 0.8×0.34

5. 4.28×1.2

6. 0.23×0.7

Ask Yourself

- Did I count the number of decimal places in the product correctly?

TEST TIPS

TEST TIPS **Explain Your Thinking** ▶ Look back at Exercise 1. Why would 24 be an unreasonable answer to 0.6×0.4?

Practice and Problem Solving

Multiply.

7. $\begin{array}{r} 0.5 \\ \times\ 0.5 \\ \hline \end{array}$

8. $\begin{array}{r} 0.9 \\ \times\ 0.2 \\ \hline \end{array}$

9. $\begin{array}{r} 0.4 \\ \times\ 0.7 \\ \hline \end{array}$

10. $\begin{array}{r} 0.7 \\ \times\ 0.3 \\ \hline \end{array}$

11. $\begin{array}{r} 0.6 \\ \times\ 0.9 \\ \hline \end{array}$

12. $\begin{array}{r} 1.6 \\ \times\ 0.8 \\ \hline \end{array}$

13. $\begin{array}{r} 4.5 \\ \times\ 0.7 \\ \hline \end{array}$

14. $\begin{array}{r} 0.47 \\ \times\ \ 0.3 \\ \hline \end{array}$

15. $\begin{array}{r} 1.34 \\ \times\ \ 0.2 \\ \hline \end{array}$

16. $\begin{array}{r} 9.53 \\ \times\ \ 0.6 \\ \hline \end{array}$

17. 0.8×0.22

18. 0.68×0.5

19. 0.4×0.44

20. 0.8×0.62

21. 0.92×0.3

22. 8.34×4.7

23. 12.3×5.4

24. 1.66×2.2

X Algebra • **Expressions Choose the value for the variables from the box that makes each equation true.**

25. $n \times 4 = 0.08$

26. $n \times 0.1 = 0.2$

27. $16 \times n = 35.2$

28. $n^2 = 4.84$

29. $n \times 8 = 1.6$

30. $n \times 0.5 = 0.1$

31. $a \times b = 4.4$

32. $a \times b = 0.4$

2 | 2.2 | 0.02 | 0.2

Compare. Write >, <, or =.

33. 0.4×0.5 ⬤ 0.2×0.6

34. 0.8×0.4 ⬤ 0.7×0.5

35. 4×0.9 ⬤ 6×0.6

36. 0.2×7 ⬤ 0.7×2

37. 6×0.05 ⬤ 0.7×0.6

38. 8×0.1 ⬤ 0.4×2

Go On

Solve.

39. A new parking lot at the city swimming pool will cover 0.7 acre. The planners want to use two tenths of the parking lot for handicapped parking. How large is the handicapped parking area?

40. At a bookstore, *The World Almanac for Kids* costs \$11.95. If you bought that book at the school book sale, you would pay 0.4 of that amount. How much does the book cost at the book sale?

41. Shane walks 1.2 miles to school. Michael's home is 0.6 of the way between Shane's home and school. How far has Shane walked when he reaches Michael's on the way to school?

42. Look back at Problem 41. Emma's home is 0.4 of the way between Shane's home and Michael's home. How far is Emma's from Shane's? How far is Emma's from school?

Choose a Computation Method

Mental Math • Estimation • Paper and Pencil • Calculator

Data **Use the table for Problems 43–46.**

43. Last year, Ursula's allowance was \$10 a week. The table shows how she spent her money. How much did she spend each week on clothing?

44. Ursula earned \$24.50 from doing yard work. According to her budget, how much of that should she save?

Ursula is keeping the same budget this year. Her allowance is now \$17.50 a week.

45. This year, how much should Ursula save in 4 weeks?

46. How much more will she spend each week on clothes than on food?

Ursula's Budget From Last Year	
Food	$\frac{2}{10}$
Entertainment	$\frac{4}{10}$
Savings	$\frac{1}{10}$
Clothing	$\frac{3}{10}$

47. Measurement Draw a line that is 8.6 cm long. Draw a second line that is 0.5 of that length. Draw a third line that is 0.5 the length of the second line. How long is the third line?

48. Write About It Jennifer multiplied two decimals less than one and got an answer greater than one. Explain to Jennifer why her answer cannot be correct. Use words, examples, and drawings to explain.

Extra Practice See page 349, Set D.

Quick Check

Check your understanding of Lessons 1–4.

Use models or fractions to multiply. Write each product as a decimal. (Lesson 1)

1. 0.5×0.8
2. 0.2×0.3

Estimate each product. (Lesson 3)

3. 0.83×6
4. 5.22×4.79

Find each product. (Lessons 2 and 4)

5. 7×0.2
6. 0.4×5
7. 5.28×7
8. 1.6×0.05
9. 0.9×0.6
10. 0.7×0.7

Number Sense

Math Reasoning

Far, Far Away

You can use scientific notation to write very large numbers.
The mean distance from the Sun to Pluto is about 5 billion, 900 million km.

Pluto

5,900,000,000 km

In scientific notation: $\mathbf{5.9 \times 10^9}$

A number between 1 and 10 — A power of 10

Earth is only about 150,000,000 km from the Sun. Try writing that number in scientific notation.

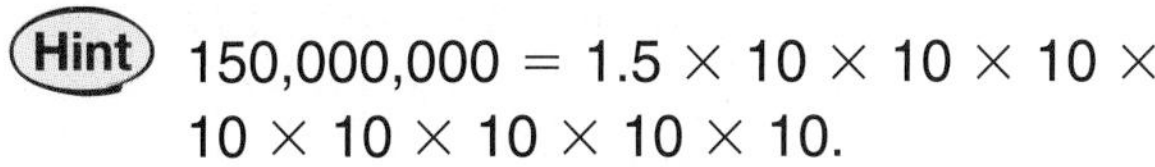

Hint $150{,}000{,}000 = 1.5 \times 10 \times 10 \times 10 \times 10 \times 10 \times 10 \times 10 \times 10.$

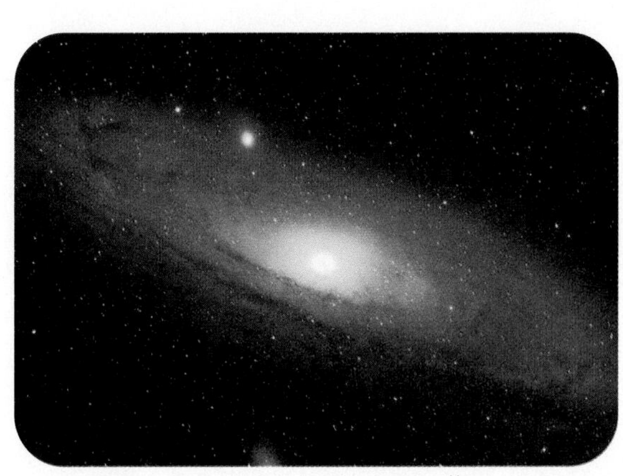

The Andromeda Galaxy is the nearest spiral galaxy to our own galaxy. It is about 21 quintillion km away. That is 21,000,000,000,000,000,000 km. How would you write that distance in scientific notation?

Lesson 5

Zeros in the Product

Objective Decide when to write zeros in the products of decimal factors.

e Glossary
Vocabulary
factor

Learn About It

Sylvia bought a pencil for \$0.40. Where Sylvia lives, a sales tax of \$0.05 for every dollar spent is added to all purchases. How much will the sales tax be on the pencil Sylvia bought?

Find 0.4 × 0.05.

STEP 1 Multiply as you would with whole numbers. Ignore the decimal points.

$$\begin{array}{r} 0.05 \\ \times\ 0.4 \\ \hline 20 \end{array}$$

STEP 2 Count the number of decimal places needed for the product.

$$\begin{array}{rl} 0.05 & \leftarrow \text{2 decimal places} \\ \times\ 0.4 & \leftarrow +\ \text{1 decimal place} \\ \hline 20 & \leftarrow \text{3 decimal places} \end{array}$$

STEP 3 Write zeros in front of the whole number to place the decimal point correctly.

$$\begin{array}{r} 0.05 \\ \times\ 0.4 \\ \hline 0.020 \end{array}$$

Solution: The sales tax on the pencil will be \$0.02.

Other Examples

A. Factors in Tenths and Hundredths

$$\begin{array}{rl} 0.17 & \leftarrow \text{2 decimal places} \\ \times\ 0.5 & \leftarrow +\ \text{1 decimal place} \\ \hline 0.085 & \leftarrow \text{3 decimal places} \end{array}$$

B. Factor in Thousandths

$$\begin{array}{rl} 0.001 & \leftarrow \text{3 decimal places} \\ \times\ \ \ 9 & \leftarrow +\ \text{0 decimal place} \\ \hline 0.009 & \leftarrow \text{3 decimal places} \end{array}$$

Guided Practice

Multiply.

1. $\begin{array}{r} 0.1 \\ \times\ 0.7 \\ \hline \end{array}$
2. $\begin{array}{r} 0.04 \\ \times\ 2 \\ \hline \end{array}$
3. $\begin{array}{r} 0.34 \\ \times\ 0.1 \\ \hline \end{array}$
4. 0.06 × 1.3
5. 0.3 × 0.02
6. 0.004 × 3

Ask Yourself

- Did I multiply the factors as if they were whole numbers?
- Do I have the correct number of decimal places in my answer?

Explain Your Thinking ▶ Why can 0.020 be written as 0.02?

Practice and Problem Solving

Multiply.

7. $\begin{array}{r} 3 \\ \times\ 0.3 \\ \hline \end{array}$

8. $\begin{array}{r} 0.3 \\ \times\ 0.3 \\ \hline \end{array}$

9. $\begin{array}{r} 0.03 \\ \times\ 0.3 \\ \hline \end{array}$

10. $\begin{array}{r} 0.03 \\ \times\ 3 \\ \hline \end{array}$

11. $\begin{array}{r} 7 \\ \times\ 0.2 \\ \hline \end{array}$

12. $\begin{array}{r} 0.7 \\ \times\ 0.2 \\ \hline \end{array}$

13. $\begin{array}{r} 0.7 \\ \times\ 0.02 \\ \hline \end{array}$

14. $\begin{array}{r} 0.07 \\ \times\ 0.2 \\ \hline \end{array}$

15. $\begin{array}{r} 0.2 \\ \times\ 0.06 \\ \hline \end{array}$

16. $\begin{array}{r} 0.5 \\ \times\ 0.06 \\ \hline \end{array}$

17. 0.04 × 0.6 **18.** 0.6 × 0.25 **19.** 0.8 × 0.1 **20.** 0.03 × 0.7

21. 0.5 × 0.3 **22.** 0.01 × 0.9 **23.** 0.09 × 0.5 **24.** 0.7 × 0.06

25. 0.02 × 0.4 **26.** 0.04 × 0.04 **27.** 0.05 × 0.8 **28.** 0.002 × 6

Use the table for Problems 29–34.

The table shows sales tax per dollar for some states in 2002.

State	Sales Tax per Dollar (2002)
Texas	0.0625
New Jersey	0.06
Maryland	0.05
Georgia	0.04
Colorado	0.029

29. A shirt is priced at $11.95. With sales tax, what will that shirt cost in Colorado? in Texas?

30. A jacket costs $25. How much will the sales tax be on this jacket if it is sold in Maryland?

31. Calculator You are in Georgia and you buy items that cost $4.79, $5.99, and $9 before tax. All you have in your wallet is $20. Do you have enough money? Explain.

32. Suppose a city government in Maryland decides to add on a local sales tax that is 0.5 of the state sales tax. What would the combined sales tax be in that city?

33. What is the mean, median, and range of the sales taxes for the states listed in the table?

34. Create and Solve Use the information in the table to write and solve a problem.

Daily Review | Test Prep

Find the mean, median, mode, and range of each set of data. (Ch. 8, Lesson 2)

35. 78°F, 74°F, 75°F, 68°F, 75°F

36. 6°C, 8°C, 8°C, 8°C, 4°C, 6°C, 7°C, 9°C

37. 85, 85, 85, 80, 84, 85

38. Free Response What is the sales tax on $5, if a state charges 6.5¢ sales tax on every dollar you spend? Explain how you found your answer.

Extra Practice See page 349, Set E.

Lesson 6

Problem-Solving Decision

Reasonable Answers

Objective Review how to decide if the answer to a problem is reasonable.

After you have solved a problem, look back at the problem and decide if the answer is reasonable.

Problem Ishana's dad tells her she must save 0.6 of the money she earns. Ishana earns \$15 one week. She figures that her savings must be \$6. Is this reasonable?

Here are the responses from three students:

Hannah	Antonio	Sora
No, Ishana's answer should be \$15.60. \$15 + \$0.60 is \$15.60 **The problem may be misinterpreted.** To find the amount Ishana must save, you have to multiply, not add. $0.6 \times \$15$	No, Ishana's answer should be \$15. $0.6 \approx 1 \quad 1 \times \$15 = \$15$ **An answer may not make sense.** \$15 is the total amount Ishana earned. She is only saving part of her money, not all of it.	No, Ishana needs to multiply. $0.6 \times \$15 = \$0.90$ **The calculations may be incorrect.** Check that you have the correct number of decimal places in the product. 15 ← 0 decimal places × 0.6 ← + 1 decimal place 9.0 ← 1 decimal place

Solution: Ishana's answer is not reasonable. Ishana should save $0.6 \times \$15$, or \$9.

Try These

Solve. Explain why the answer is reasonable or unreasonable.

1. Each month Dan's savings account pays 0.03 of the balance as interest. Dan says that the interest on his \$200 will be \$0.03. Is he correct?

2. Ella's credit card balance is \$325. Interest charges are 0.06 of the balance. Ella thinks the interest would be \$1.95. Is Ella correct?

3. Linda earns \$40. She plans to put 0.5 of that money into savings and 0.5 of what is left toward a new bike. She says she'll have \$10 left. Is she correct?

4. Clarice has \$2 and she wants to buy a fruit drink for \$1.80. The sales tax on the drink is 0.05. Clarice says she has enough money. Is she right?

MathTracks 2/5
Listen and Understand

Quick Check

Check your understanding of Lessons 5–6.

Multiply. (Lesson 5)

1. $\begin{array}{r} 0.04 \\ \times\ 0.6 \\ \hline \end{array}$

2. $\begin{array}{r} 0.008 \\ \times\ \ \ 4 \\ \hline \end{array}$

3. $\begin{array}{r} 0.3 \\ \times\ 0.1 \\ \hline \end{array}$

4. $\begin{array}{r} 0.009 \\ \times\ \ \ 4 \\ \hline \end{array}$

5. 0.003×7

6. 2.1×0.05

7. 4×0.016

8. 0.02×0.8

Solve. Explain why the answer is reasonable or unreasonable. (Lesson 6)

9. Jason plans to save 0.25 of his earnings for a gift for his mom. He earns $50 this week. He thinks he needs to put $25 of that money away toward his mom's gift. Is this reasonable?

10. In one district, 0.8 of the students ride a bus to school. Of those students, 0.03 of them need wheelchair vans. Terry says that 1.1 of the students need wheelchair vans. Is he right?

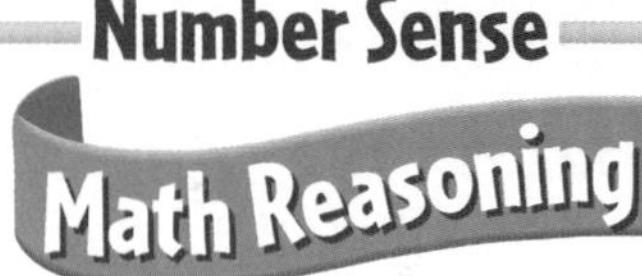

It Goes On and On and On—or Does It?

Start with a sheet of paper that is 10 inches by 10 inches. Think about folding the paper exactly in half. Then folding it in half again and then again.

1. **Calculator** Copy and complete the table to show mathematically what will happen to the area that the folded paper covers. Round answers to the nearest tenth.

2. Try the experiment. Measure to check your results with your table. What happened?

3. Try the experiment again with a piece of paper that is 2 or 4 times as big as the 10 by 10 square. What happened this time?

Number of Folds	Area Covered	
1	50 in.^{2}	← 100×0.5
2	25 in.^{2}	← 50×0.5
3	12.5 in.^{2}	← 25×0.5
4	■	
5	■	
6	■	
7	■	
8	■	
9	■	
10	■	

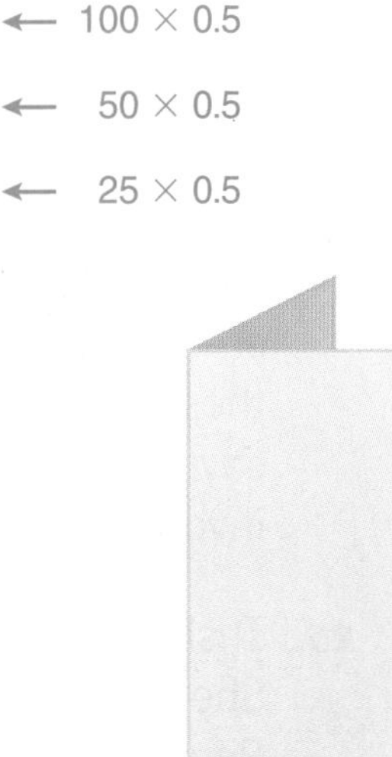

Chapter Review/Test

VOCABULARY

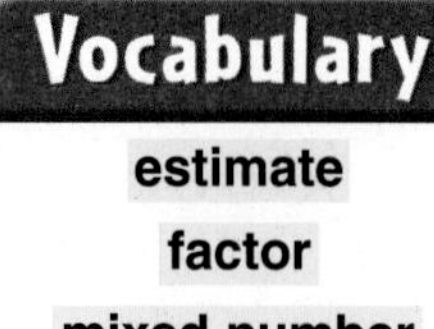

Vocabulary
estimate
factor
mixed number
product
round

1. To ____ is to find an approximate rather than an exact answer.
2. When you ____ a number, you express it to the nearest hundredth, tenth, and so on.
3. A ____ is made up of a whole number and a fraction.

CONCEPTS AND SKILLS

Use models or fractions to multiply. Write each product as a decimal. (Lesson 1, pp. 334–335)

4. 0.9×0.5
5. 0.3×1.7
6. 0.2×2.4
7. 1.9×0.6

Estimate each product. (Lesson 3, pp. 338–339)

8. 0.85×7
9. 3.82×5
10. 8.36×61
11. 4.72×4.9

Multiply. (Lessons 2, 4, pp. 336–337, 340–343)

12. 7×6.2
13. 7.25×0.4
14. 8.3×6.5
15. 2.6×4
16. 9.12×4.7
17. 0.96×0.8
18. 3.15×7.4
19. 0.7×0.77

Multiply. Write zeros in front of the whole number to place the decimal point correctly. (Lesson 5, pp. 344–345)

20. 0.8×0.007
21. 0.4×0.012
22. 0.06×0.4
23. 4×0.0008

PROBLEM SOLVING

Solve. (Lesson 6, pp. 346–347)

24. At Franklin Middle School, 0.24 of the students are involved in a school sport. Of these students, 0.4 of them are girls. Janet says this means about 0.1 of girls are involved in sports. Is she correct?
25. Trisha makes $65 dollars a month babysitting. She makes $40 of this babysitting for Mrs. Ramirez. She thinks this is about 0.33 of her income. Is this reasonable?

Write About It

Show You Understand

Look at how Sasha multiplied.

$$\begin{array}{r} 0.2 \\ \times\ 0.007 \\ \hline 0.014 \end{array}$$

Explain what Sasha did wrong.

Extra Practice

Set A (Lesson 1, pp. 334–335)

Use models or fractions to multiply. Write each product as a decimal.

1. 0.7×0.3
2. 0.6×0.9
3. 0.4×1.3
4. 0.3×0.6
5. 1.7×0.5
6. 0.5×1.8
7. 0.9×2.1
8. 1.2×0.8
9. 0.7×0.9
10. 3.2×0.2

Set B (Lesson 2, pp. 336–337)

Find each product.

1. 6×0.2
2. 9×0.5
3. 8×0.61
4. 5×0.82
5. 2×5.47
6. 8×4.17
7. 6×7.08
8. 3×4.98
9. 6.5×4.2
10. 7.4×17

Set C (Lesson 3, pp. 338–339)

Estimate each product.

1. 0.17×4
2. 3.97×6
3. 7.22×7
4. 11.79×3
5. 82×0.58
6. 21×4.07
7. 48×9.39
8. 4×10.77
9. 0.42×300
10. 4.25×6

Set D (Lesson 4, pp. 340–343)

Multiply.

1. 0.6×0.3
2. 0.5×0.7
3. 0.8×0.8
4. 0.5×0.8
5. 0.18×0.8
6. 5.75×0.5
7. 3.6×1.3
8. 6.14×3.5
9. 0.83×0.7
10. 5.16×6.1

Compare. Write >, <, or =.

11. 0.3×0.5 ⬬ 0.4×0.4
12. 0.9×0.3 ⬬ 0.7×0.4
13. 0.7×0.7 ⬬ 0.6×0.8

Set E (Lesson 5, pp. 344–345)

Multiply. Write zeros in front of the whole number to place the decimal point correctly.

1. $\begin{array}{r} 0.6 \\ \times\ 4 \\ \hline \end{array}$
2. $\begin{array}{r} 0.4 \\ \times\ 0.6 \\ \hline \end{array}$
3. $\begin{array}{r} 0.4 \\ \times\ 0.06 \\ \hline \end{array}$
4. $\begin{array}{r} 0.9 \\ \times\ 0.09 \\ \hline \end{array}$
5. $\begin{array}{r} 0.09 \\ \times\ 0.08 \\ \hline \end{array}$
6. 0.5×7
7. 0.5×0.7
8. 0.5×0.07
9. 0.05×0.07
10. 0.5×0.04

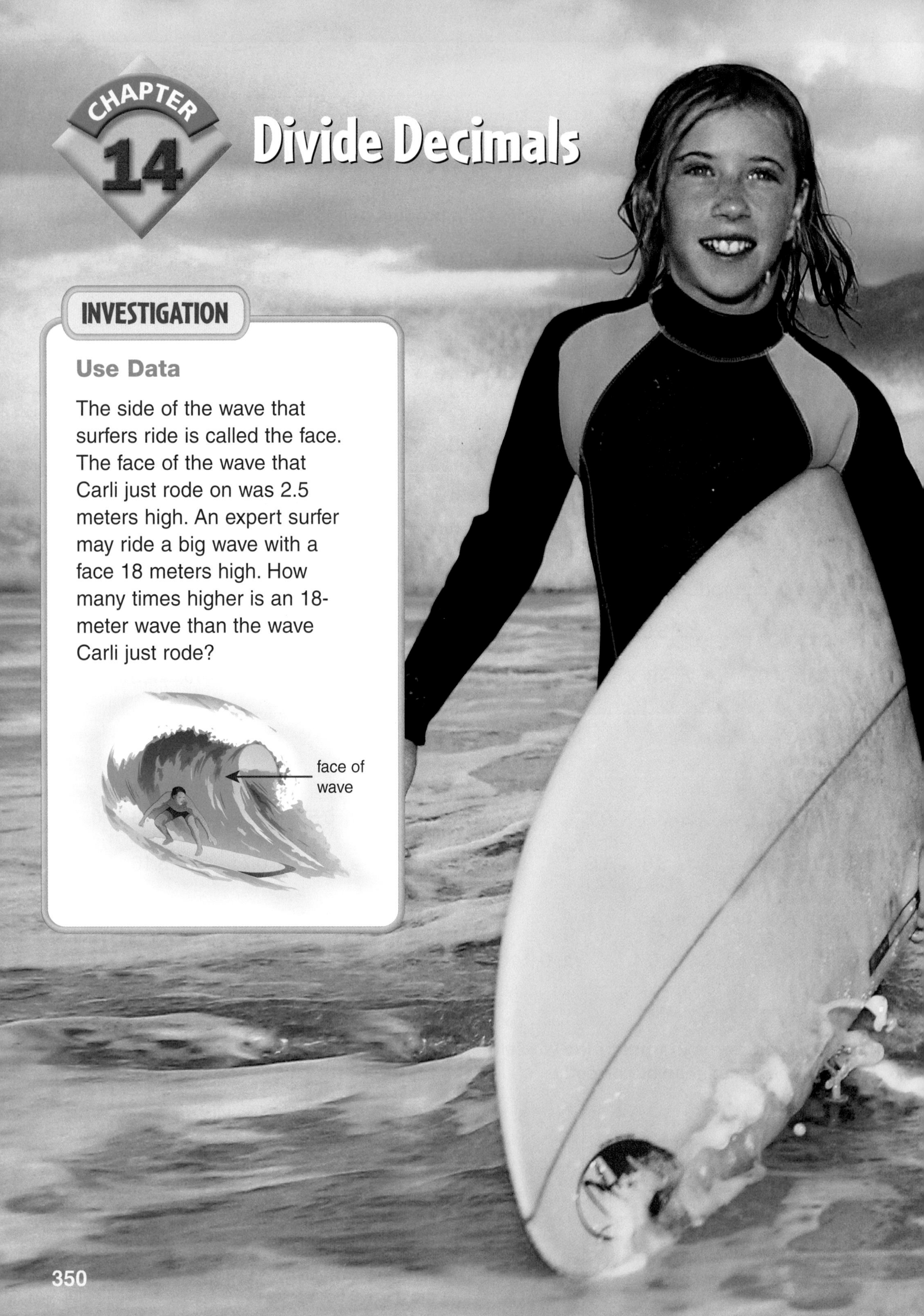

CHAPTER 14 Divide Decimals

INVESTIGATION

Use Data

The side of the wave that surfers ride is called the face. The face of the wave that Carli just rode on was 2.5 meters high. An expert surfer may ride a big wave with a face 18 meters high. How many times higher is an 18-meter wave than the wave Carli just rode?

Chapter Pretest

Use this page to review and remember what you need to know for this chapter.

VOCABULARY

Choose the best word to complete each sentence.

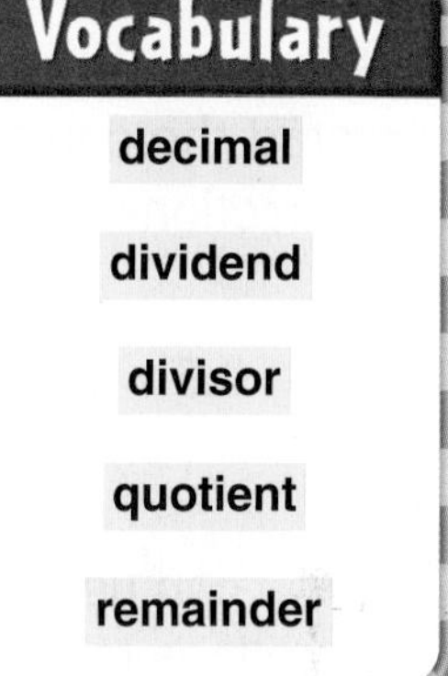

1. The ____ is the result of dividing one number by another.
2. In the expression 24 ÷ 6, 24 is the ____.
3. In the expression 63 ÷ 9, the ____ is 9.

CONCEPTS AND SKILLS

Write a fraction in simplest form for each decimal.

4. 0.2
5. 0.5
6. 0.75
7. 0.6

Estimate using compatible numbers.

8. 92 ÷ 28
9. 403 ÷ 17
10. 2,361 ÷ 74
11. 589 ÷ 28

Multiply.

12. $\frac{8}{10} \times \frac{1}{6}$
13. $\frac{45}{10} \times \frac{1}{5}$
14. $\frac{36}{10} \times \frac{1}{4}$
15. $\frac{16}{10} \times \frac{1}{9}$

Divide.

16. $22\overline{)451}$
17. 738 ÷ 17
18. $65 ÷ 13
19. 9,802 ÷ 34

Write About It

20. Amelia computed 237 ÷ 18 and got a quotient of 13 R3. Explain how you could check to see whether her answer is correct.

Test Prep on the Net

Visit *Education Place* at **eduplace.com/kids/mw/** for more review.

Lesson 1

Explore Division With Decimals

Objective Use models to show the relationship between dividing fractions and decimals.

Learn About It

Melissa is training for a 5-kilometer race. Her coach has separated the course into 0.5-kilometer sections. How many sections is that for a 5-kilometer course?

Find $5 \div 0.5 = n$.

You can use models and what you know about fractions to find $5 \div 0.5$. Try changing the decimals to fractions and then modeling the division.

STEP 1 Write 5 and 0.5 as fractions.

$5 = \frac{5}{1}$

$0.5 = \frac{5}{10} = \frac{1}{2}$

STEP 2 Model 5 wholes.

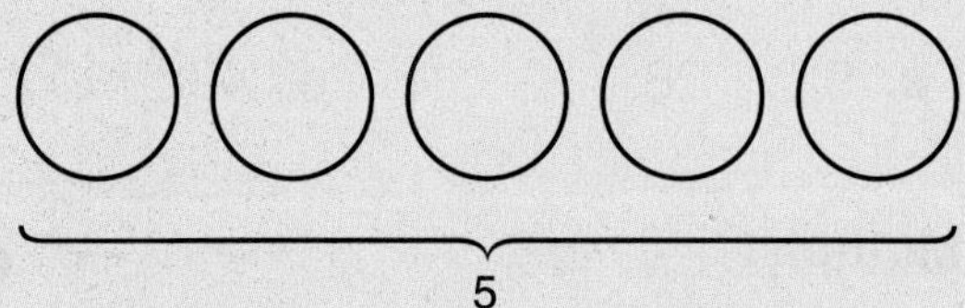

STEP 3 Separate the 5 wholes into halves.

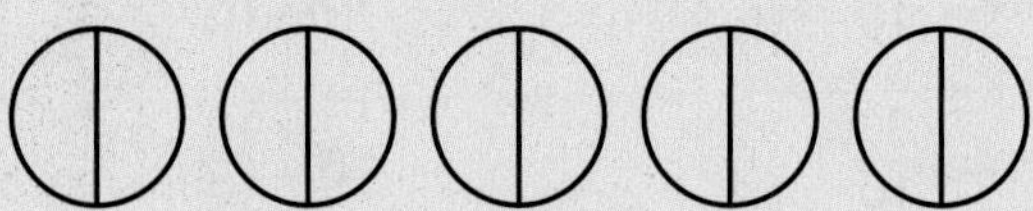

STEP 4 Think about what you are asked to find.

- How many 0.5s are in 5?
- How many $\frac{1}{2}$s are in 5?

STEP 5 Count to find the number of $\frac{1}{2}$s in 5?

There are 10 halves in 5 wholes.

Write a multiplication sentence that shows the answer to $5 \div \frac{1}{2}$.

$5 \div \frac{1}{2} = 5 \times 2 = 10$.

There are two $\frac{1}{2}$s in each whole. Multiplying 2 times 5 shows that there are 10 halves in 5 wholes.

Solution: Since $5 \div \frac{1}{2} = 10$, then $5 \div 0.5 = 10$.

Other Examples

A. Use a Model

Find $2 \div 0.4$.

You can use models to show how many groups of 4 tenths there are in 2.

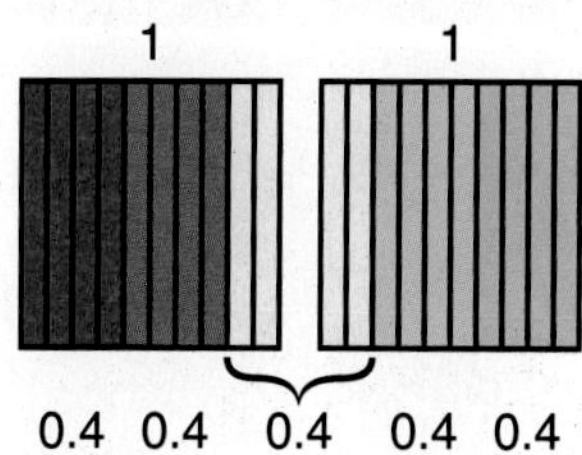

There are 5 groups of 4 tenths in 2, $2 \div 0.4 = 5$

B. Use Number Sense

Find $6 \div 0.2$.

Think
Since $0.2 = \frac{1}{5}$, then there are 5 fifths in each whole.

So, in 6 wholes, there are 6×5, or 30 fifths.

$6 \div 0.2 = 30$

Guided Practice

Ask Yourself
- Did I change the decimal to a fraction?
- Did I think about the number of parts in each whole?

Model the division. Write the quotient in decimal form.

1. $6 \div 0.5$ **2.** $4 \div 0.4$ **3.** $12 \div 0.25$

4. $10 \div 0.25$ **5.** $8 \div 0.5$ **6.** $9 \div 0.2$

Explain Your Thinking Explain how you could use number sense to find the quotient for Exercise 6.

Practice and Problem Solving

Model the division and write the quotient in decimal form.

7. $3 \div 0.5$ **8.** $4 \div 0.5$ **9.** $8 \div 0.4$ **10.** $2 \div 0.25$ **11.** $3 \div 0.25$

12. $4 \div 0.25$ **13.** $3 \div 0.6$ **14.** $4 \div 0.8$ **15.** $5 \div 0.2$ **16.** $10 \div 0.2$

17. Mental Math As Melita trains, she checks her heart rate every 0.25 kilometer. How many times does she check it in 1 kilometer?

18. Represent Cameron speed walks 2 miles in 0.5 hour. At this pace, how far can he speed walk in 1 hour? Draw a model to show your solution.

Daily Review | Test Prep

Compare. Write <, >, or = for each ●.
(Ch. 9, Lessons 8 and 9)

19. 0.5 ● $\frac{1}{3}$ **20.** $1\frac{3}{4}$ ● 1.6

21. 2.6 ● $2\frac{3}{5}$ **22.** 0.125 ● $\frac{1}{8}$

23. Each runner's number bib uses 0.2 meter of cloth. How many bibs can be made from 3 meters of cloth?

A 0.2 **C** 6

B 1.5 **D** 15

Extra Practice See page 375, Set A.

Lesson 2

Estimate Quotients

Objective Estimate decimal quotients using compatible numbers.

Learn About It

During its history, one team's win ratio has been 0.23. They have won 38 games. To find about how many games they have played in all, divide 38 by 0.23.

You can use fractions, rounded decimals, and compatible numbers to estimate a quotient. Using equivalent unit fractions for decimals makes estimation easier.

$0.1 = \frac{1}{10}$	$0.25 = \frac{1}{4}$
$0.125 = \frac{1}{8}$	$0.33... = \frac{1}{3}$
$0.2 = \frac{1}{5}$	$0.5 = \frac{1}{2}$

Estimate. $38 \div 0.23 = n$

STEP 1 Change the decimal to an equivalent unit fraction.

$0.23 \approx 0.25$

$0.25 = \frac{1}{4}$

STEP 2 Change the dividend to a compatible number.

$38 \approx 40$

40 is easy to work with.

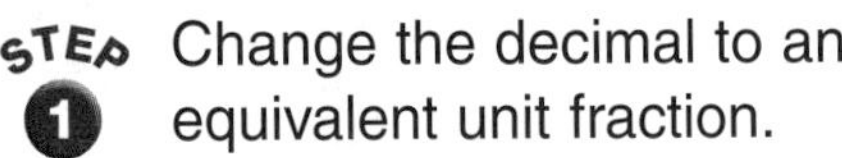

STEP 3 Estimate the number of fourths in 40.

There are 160 fourths in 40.
The quotient will be about 160.

$38 \div 0.23 \approx 160$

Think
There are 4 fourths in 1. 40 has 4 × 40 fourths, or 160 fourths.

Solution: The team has played about 160 games.

Another Example

Dividend and Divisor Are Decimals

Estimate. $54.8 \div 0.13 = n$

$54.8 \approx 50$, $0.13 \approx 0.125$ and $0.125 = \frac{1}{8}$

$54.8 \div 0.13 \approx 50 \div \frac{1}{8}$

$54.8 \div 0.13 \approx 400$

Think
There are 8 eighths in 1, so there are 50 × 8 or 400 eighths in 50.

Guided Practice

Estimate each quotient.

1. 127 ÷ 0.19 **2.** 57 ÷ 0.32 **3.** 190 ÷ 0.49

4. 17.6 ÷ 0.09 **5.** 48.4 ÷ 0.27 **6.** 57.6 ÷ 0.11

Ask Yourself

- Did I change the decimal to an equivalent unit fraction?
- Is my new dividend easy to work with?

Explain Your Thinking ▶ Explain how you chose the numbers you used to estimate the quotient in Exercise 1.

Practice and Problem Solving

Estimate each quotient.

7. 47 ÷ 0.53 **8.** 152 ÷ 0.29 **9.** 408 ÷ 0.18 **10.** 36 ÷ 0.54

11. 8 ÷ 0.236 **12.** 19 ÷ 0.179 **13.** 5 ÷ 0.475 **14.** 47 ÷ 0.345

15. 8.38 ÷ 0.24 **16.** 6.97 ÷ 0.341 **17.** 52.1 ÷ 0.18 **18.** 17.6 ÷ 0.26

Solve.

19. Estimate A newspaper finds the field hockey team's winning ratio by dividing the number of games won by the number of games played. The team has won 6 games and has a winning ratio of 0.33. About how many games has the team played?

Field Hockey Team Gets 6TH Win

In the last ten minutes of hectic play and two turn-arounds, our team surprised the fans with the final goal against the Panthers.

The Rockets are becoming dominant in local girls field hockey as they defeated the Panthers for their sixth consecutive win.

The Rock Falls Rockets started the season as defending state champion. The team has bounced back from a loss in the opening game of the season with a 4-2 victory last night over the Afton Panthers.

Rockets' coach Jill Williams knows it may be a challenge for the team to maintain the focus, but she also has the benefit of experienced on-field leadership. Seven starters from the team were on last year's state championship team.

"We have clear leaders who lead by example and are very supportive other players," said coach Williams.

"We're excited to get out there and prove we can win it all again," senior Glenda Bruns said.

20. You Decide Decide on a win ratio for a team and the number of games it has won. Use the data you create to figure out the number of games the team has lost.

21. Write About It How does thinking about an equivalent fraction for a decimal help you estimate quotients?

22. In field hockey the goal cage takes up $\frac{1}{5}$ of the 60-yard goal line. How many feet long is the goal cage?

Daily Review | Test Prep

Add or subtract. Write your answer in simplest form. (Ch. 10, Lessons 4 and 8)

23. $2\frac{3}{5} + 1\frac{7}{10}$ **24.** $5\frac{3}{4} + 2\frac{1}{3}$

25. $4\frac{2}{3} - 3\frac{5}{6}$ **26.** $7\frac{1}{8} - \frac{9}{10}$

27. Free Response For fifth-graders, field hockey games last an average of 0.55 hour. About how many games can be played during a 4-hour tournament?

Extra Practice See page 375, Set B.

Mental Math

Multiply and Divide by Powers of 10

Objective Use patterns to multiply and divide by powers of 10.

Learn About It

When you multiply a number by 10^n, or a **power of 10**, you are using 10 as a factor n times. In 10^n, n is called the **exponent.**

A researcher might need to examine blood cells. The diameter of a red blood cell is 0.008 millimeter. Microscopes can make objects appear 10^1 times, 10^2 times, or 10^3 times larger.

How large would a red blood cell appear at each magnification level?

Remember
Multiplying a number by 10 moves the decimal point one place to the right.

Multiply 0.008 mm by 10^1, 10^2, and 10^3.

10^1 level	10^2 level	10^3 level
0.008×10^1	0.008×10^2	0.008×10^3
$\begin{array}{r} 0.008 \\ \times\ 10 \\ \hline 0.080 \text{ or } 0.08 \end{array}$	$\begin{array}{r} 0.008 \\ \times\ 100 \\ \hline 0.800 \text{ or } 0.8 \end{array}$	$\begin{array}{r} 0.008 \\ \times\ 1{,}000 \\ \hline 8.000 \text{ or } 8 \end{array}$
The diameter of the cell appears to be 0.08 mm.	The diameter of the cell appears to be 0.8 mm.	The diameter of the cell appears to be 8 mm.

Solution: A red blood cell can be enlarged so its diameter appears to be 0.08 millimeter, 0.8 millimeter, or 8 millimeters.

Remember
Dividing a number by 10 moves the decimal point one place to the left.

Other Examples

A. Use Patterns

$6.5 \div 10^1 = 0.65$

The decimal point moves one place to the left.

B. Divide by 10^2

$6.5 \div 10^2 = 0.065$

The decimal point moves two places to the left.

Guided Practice

Multiply or divide by using patterns.

1. 0.5×10^2
2. $0.2 \div 10$
3. 3.8×100
4. $159 \div 10^3$
5. 0.04×10^3
6. $6.1 \div 10^2$

Ask Yourself

- Do I move the decimal point to the right or to the left?

TEST TIPS **Explain Your Thinking** ▶ Why is the expression 4.2×10^3 equal to the expression 42×10^2?

Practice and Problem Solving

Multiply or divide by using patterns.

7. 5.34×10^1
8. 5.34×10^2
9. $5.34 \div 10^1$
10. $5.34 \div 10^2$
11. 2.0×10^3
12. $75 \div 10^2$
13. 0.68×10^3
14. $4.72 \div 10^1$

Algebra • **Equations** **Solve for *a*.**

15. $100 = 10^a$
16. $1{,}000 = 10^a$
17. $10 = 10^a$
18. $10{,}000 = 10^a$
19. $0.01a = 12$
20. $0.001a = 12$
21. $\frac{a}{10} = 15$
22. $\frac{a}{100} = 15$

Solve.

23. One type of cell is 0.005 mm across. It is put under a microscope so it appears to be 10^3 larger. How large would that cell seem under that microscope?

24. **Represent** Draw a line segment to show how large the cell in Problem 23 would appear under the microscope.

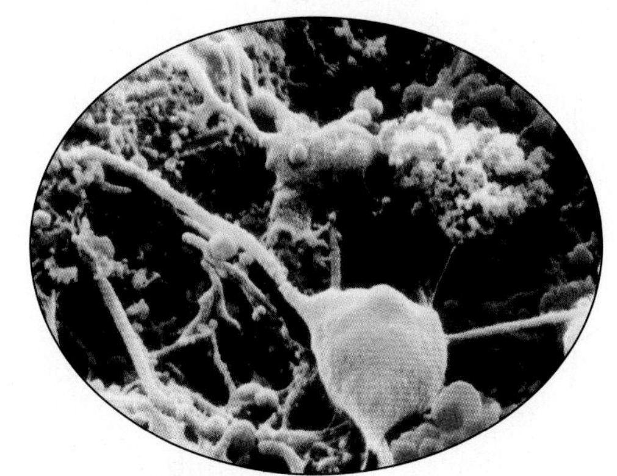

Daily Review | Test Prep

Multiply. Write each product in simplest form. (Ch. 12, Lessons 2 and 3)

25. $\frac{4}{5} \times \frac{1}{3}$
26. $3\frac{1}{2} \times \frac{5}{7}$
27. $\frac{3}{4} \times 1\frac{5}{9}$
28. $5\frac{1}{3} \times 1\frac{1}{2}$

29. A sports photographer's telephoto lens keeps the shutter open for only $1.0 \div 10^3$ seconds. Which fraction shows how long that is?

A $\frac{10}{1}$ B $\frac{1}{10}$ C $\frac{1}{100}$ D $\frac{1}{1{,}000}$

Extra Practice See page 375, Set C.

Lesson 4

Divide a Decimal by a Whole Number

Objective Divide a decimal by a whole number.

Learn About It

The starting section for a BMX race is 7.2 meters wide. It is divided into equal-width lanes for 8 riders. How wide is each rider's lane?

Divide. $7.2 \div 8 = n$

Different Ways to Divide 7.2 by 8

Way 1 You can use fractions.

STEP 1 Write the dividend and the divisor as fractions.

$$\frac{72}{10} \div \frac{8}{1}$$

$$7.2 = 7\frac{2}{10} = \frac{72}{10}$$

STEP 2 Multiply the dividend by the reciprocal of the divisor.

$$\frac{72}{10} \times \frac{1}{8} = \frac{72}{80}$$

STEP 3 Write the quotient as a decimal.

$$\frac{72}{80} = \frac{9}{10} = 0.9$$

Way 2 You can divide and place the decimal point in the quotient.

STEP 1 Divide as though the dividend were a whole number.

$$\begin{array}{r} 9 \\ 8\overline{)72} \\ -\,72 \\ \hline 0 \end{array}$$

STEP 2 Place a decimal point in the quotient directly above the decimal point in the dividend.

$$\begin{array}{r} 0.9 \\ 8\overline{)7.2} \\ -\,7\;2 \\ \hline 0 \end{array}$$

Estimate to check.

Since 7.2 m is a little less than 8 m, each of the 8 lanes would be a little less than 1 m wide. So 0.9 m is a reasonable answer.

Solution: Each lane is 0.9 meter wide.

Other Examples

A. Quotient Less Than 1

$$\begin{array}{r} 0.92 \\ 7\overline{)6.44} \\ -6\,3 \\ \hline 14 \\ -14 \\ \hline 0 \end{array}$$

Estimate to check.

$6.44 \approx 7$
$7 \div 7 = 1$
$0.92 \approx 1$

B. Quotient Is in Dollars and Cents

$$\begin{array}{r} \$0.15 \\ 5\overline{)\$0.75} \\ -5\downarrow \\ \hline 25 \\ -25 \\ \hline 0 \end{array}$$

Multiply to check.

$$\begin{array}{r} \$0.15 \\ \times 5 \\ \hline \$0.75 \end{array}$$

Guided Practice

Ask Yourself

- Would it help me to use fractions?
- Did I place the decimal point correctly?

Divide and check.

1. $2\overline{)16.2}$ **2.** $5\overline{)9.75}$ **3.** $6\overline{)5.4}$

4. $22.8 \div 4$ **5.** $58.1 \div 7$ **6.** $0.03 \div 3$

TEST TIPS **Explain Your Thinking** ▶ Why is it important to align the quotient and the dividend correctly when you divide with decimals?

Practice and Problem Solving

Divide and check.

7. $6\overline{)7.2}$ **8.** $7\overline{)41.3}$ **9.** $3\overline{)16.2}$ **10.** $7\overline{)11.9}$ **11.** $4\overline{)0.08}$

12. $5.5 \div 5$ **13.** $8.4 \div 4$ **14.** $0.8 \div 2$ **15.** $20.7 \div 3$ **16.** $75.6 \div 9$

17. $8\overline{)2.80}$ **18.** $2\overline{)3.46}$ **19.** $6\overline{)1.44}$ **20.** $7\overline{)26.25}$ **21.** $9\overline{)45.27}$

22. $42.8 \div 4$ **23.** $3.87 \div 9$ **24.** $9.75 \div 3$ **25.** $6.32 \div 8$ **26.** $0.84 \div 2$

Insert a decimal point in each dividend to make each quotient correct.

27. $24 \div 6 = 0.4$ **28.** $35 \div 7 = 0.5$ **29.** $129 \div 3 = 0.43$

30. $196 \div 4 = 4.9$ **31.** $3252 \div 4 = 0.813$ **32.** $5327 \div 7 = 7.61$

X Algebra • Expressions Evaluate each expression for $a = 3.2$, $b = 0.08$, $c = 2$, and $d = 8$.

33. $a \div c$ **34.** $\frac{b}{c}$ **35.** $a \div d$ **36.** $b \div d$

Go On

Write the missing values in each table.

37.

Rule: $b = a \div 3$				
a	0.96	1.29	6.33	6.78
b				

38.

Rule: $b = a \div 5$				
a	0.65	1.5	2.25	2.75
b				

39.

Rule: $b = a \div 6$				
a	0.72			0.90
b		0.13	0.14	

40.

Rule: $b = a \div 9$				
a		6.3	4.68	
b	0.75			0.91

Solve.

41. One third of the entry fee for each rider in the BMX race shown at the right goes to pay taxes and other fees. If 150 riders enter a race, how much goes for taxes and other fees?

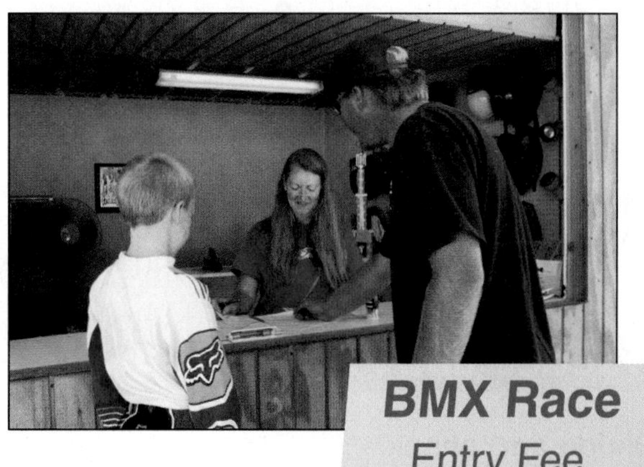

42. A BMX track is made up of 0.8 part clay and 0.2 part sand for every 1 part of soil. There are 3,500 cubic yards of soil on the track. How many cubic yards of clay are there? of sand?

43. **Estimate** The maximum length of a BMX track is 454 meters. The minimum length is 0.66 of that. Estimate the minimum length.

44. **Analyze** Tony and Jan are training for a bike race. Tony rode his bike 4.5 km in 9 minutes. Jan rode her bike 3.6 km in 6 minutes. Who rides farther in 1 minute? How much farther?

45. **Explain** Which will be greater: the quotient $6.56 \div 8$, or the quotient $656 \div 80$? Explain how you can tell without dividing.

46. **Represent** A city bought a 20-acre section of land for recreational use. The land was split into 0.5-acre pieces. Draw a model to show the number of 0.5-acre pieces that can be made from that 20 acres.

47. **What's Wrong?** Darlene divided 1.2 by 6. Her work is shown below. Explain why Darlene's method is not correct.

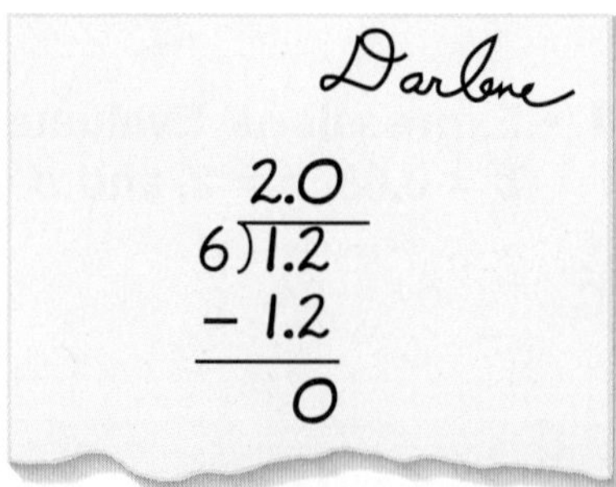

48. **Write About It** How is dividing a decimal by a whole number the same or different from dividing a whole number by a whole number?

Extra Practice See page 375, Set D.

Quick Check

Check your understanding of Lessons 1–4.

Use models to divide. Write the quotients. (Lesson 1)

1. 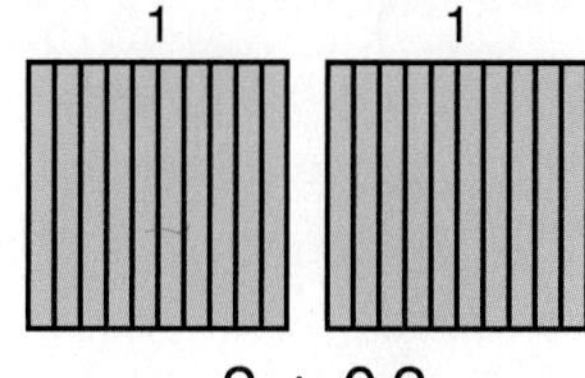

$2 \div 0.2$

2. 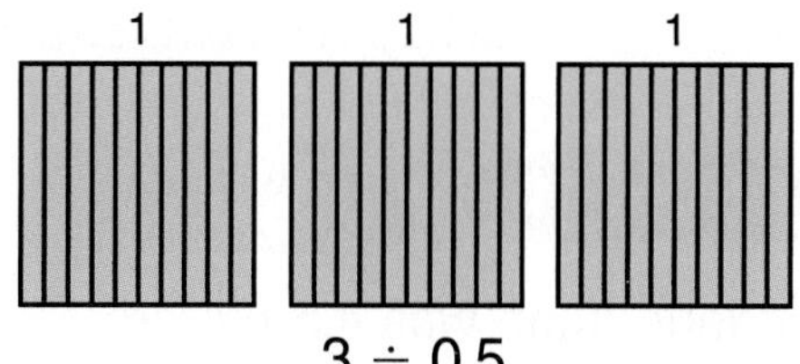

$3 \div 0.5$

3. $5 \div 0.2$ **4.** $2 \div 0.5$

Estimate each quotient. (Lesson 2)

5. $28 \div 0.34$ **6.** $57.9 \div 0.46$

Multiply or divide. (Lessons 3 and 4)

7. 52.3×10^2 **8.** $53.2 \div 10^2$ **9.** $0.84 \div 7$ **10.** $16.05 \div 3$

Math Challenge

Use What You Know

You know how to divide whole numbers with two-digit divisors. You also know how to divide decimals with one-digit divisors. You can use what you know to divide decimals by two-digit divisors.

STEP 1 Divide the dividend by the divisor as if both are whole numbers.

```
      604
24)14.496
 - 14 4↓↓
      096
     - 96
        0
```

STEP 2 Place a decimal point in the quotient directly above the decimal point in the dividend.

```
    0.604
24)14.496
 - 14 4↓↓
      096
     - 96
        0
```

Divide. Show your work.

1. $37.5 \div 15$ **2.** $157.44 \div 32$ **3.** $64.05 \div 21$ **4.** $0.406 \div 14$

Lesson 5

Write Zeros in the Dividend

Objective Write one or more zeros in the dividend to help solve division problems.

Learn About It

Billie's first long jump was 4.5 meters. Her second long jump was 6 meters. What part of her second long jump was Billie's first attempt?

Divide. $4.5 \div 6 = n$

Different Ways to Divide 4.5 by 6

Way 1 You can use the pencil-and-paper method.

STEP 1 Divide as though the dividend were a whole number.

$$\begin{array}{r} 7 \\ 6\overline{)4.5} \\ -4\,2 \\ \hline 3 \end{array}$$

Think: $45 \div 6$ is about 7.

STEP 2 To continue, write a 0 in the hundredths place.

$$\begin{array}{r} 75 \\ 6\overline{)4.50} \\ -4\,2\downarrow \\ \hline 30 \\ -30 \\ \hline 0 \end{array}$$

Bring down the 0. Continue dividing.

STEP 3 Place the decimal point in the quotient above the decimal point in the dividend.

$$\begin{array}{r} 0.75 \\ 6\overline{)4.50} \\ -4\,2\downarrow \\ \hline 30 \\ -30 \\ \hline 0 \end{array}$$

Write 0 in the ones place.

Way 2 You can divide decimals using a calculator.

STEP 1 Press the calculator keys to enter the division. Press the equals sign to calculate the quotient.

0.75

Solution: Billie's first long jump was 0.75 of her second long jump.

Check that the quotient is reasonable.

Think How many 6s are in 4.5?

$6 \times 1 = 6$

There is less than one 6 in 4.5.

0.75 is a reasonable answer.

Another Example

Divide Whole Numbers

When dividing whole numbers, you can add zeros after the decimal point to get a decimal answer.

Find 42 ÷ 8.

$$\begin{array}{r} 5.25 \\ 8\overline{)42.00} \\ -\,40 \\ 2\,0 \\ -\,1\,6 \\ 40 \\ -\,40 \\ 0 \end{array}$$

Guided Practice

Ask Yourself

- Did I place the first digit of the quotient correctly?
- Did I write zeros in the dividend until there was no remainder?

TEST TIPS

Divide. Check using a calculator or estimation.

1. $5\overline{)2.7}$ **2.** $5\overline{)24}$ **3.** $4\overline{)3.5}$

4. $6\overline{)0.75}$ **5.** $8\overline{)51}$ **6.** $2\overline{)39.77}$

7. 6.11 ÷ 2 **8.** 9.6 ÷ 5 **9.** 2.7 ÷ 4

Explain Your Thinking ▶ Why does writing zeros to the right of the least-place digit in a decimal not change the value of that number?

Practice and Problem Solving

Divide. Check using a calculator or estimation.

10. $2\overline{)9}$ **11.** $8\overline{)5.2}$ **12.** $4\overline{)19}$ **13.** $16\overline{)12.4}$ **14.** $18\overline{)0.9}$

15. $46\overline{)16.1}$ **16.** $10\overline{)6.24}$ **17.** $5\overline{)24.72}$ **18.** $6\overline{)106.5}$ **19.** $8\overline{)474.8}$

20. $8\overline{)19}$ **21.** $24\overline{)15}$ **22.** $12\overline{)4.2}$ **23.** $6\overline{)8.67}$ **24.** $4\overline{)28.18}$

25. 33 ÷ 22 **26.** 9 ÷ 5 **27.** 15 ÷ 8 **28.** 32.6 ÷ 4 **29.** 37 ÷ 10

Compare. Write >, <, or = for each ⬬.

30. 2.5 ÷ 4 ⬬ 5 ÷ 8 **31.** 3.6 ÷ 8 ⬬ 1 ÷ 4 **32.** 12 ÷ 5 ⬬ 9 ÷ 4

33. 2 ÷ 4 ⬬ 0.8 ÷ 2 **34.** 0.4 ÷ 2 ⬬ 0.2 ÷ 4 **35.** 0.35 ÷ 7 ⬬ 3 ÷ 12

36. 3.2 ÷ 8 ⬬ 8 ÷ 2 **37.** 0.4 ÷ 4 ⬬ 0.2 ÷ 2 **38.** 5.25 ÷ 3 ⬬ 14 ÷ 8

Go On

Algebra • **Equations Find each missing value for *n*.**

39. $19 \div n = 4.75$ **40.** $n \div 4 = 0.525$ **41.** $n \div 5 = 3.44$ **42.** $15 \div n = 7.5$

Data Use the chart below to solve Problems 43–47.

The chart shows two jumps each member of a track team made during a recent meet.

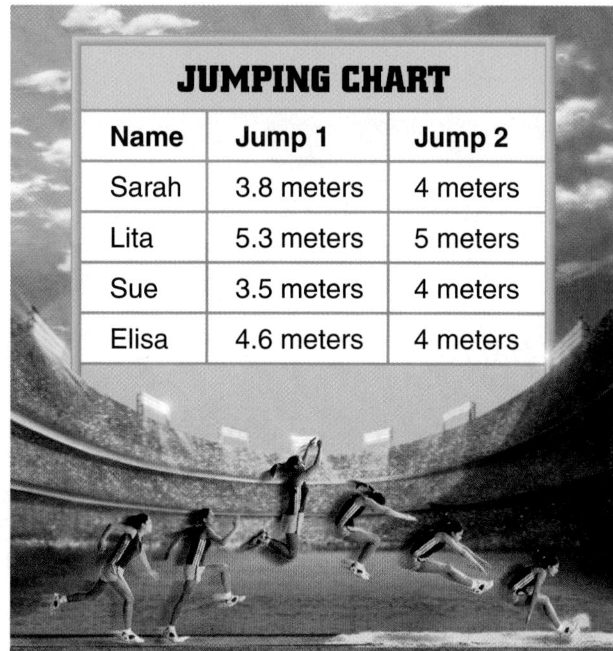

JUMPING CHART		
Name	**Jump 1**	**Jump 2**
Sarah	3.8 meters	4 meters
Lita	5.3 meters	5 meters
Sue	3.5 meters	4 meters
Elisa	4.6 meters	4 meters

43. What part of her second jump is Sarah's first jump?

44. What is the mean of the distances of Lita's jumps? Remember, to find the mean, you divide the sum of the distances by the number of jumps.

45. Calculator What is the mean distance of the jumps made by this team?

46. Which team member had the greatest range in her jumps? How much difference was there between her longest and shortest jumps?

47. Measurement To convert from meters to feet, multiply the number of meters by 3.281. Who had a first jump of about 15 feet?

48. Write About It When you are dividing 63 by 4, how can you tell whether or not you need to write zeros in the dividend?

49. In the 2000 Olympics, second place in the long jump was a jump of 6.92 m. The winning jump was 7 cm longer. How long was the winning jump?

Daily Review Test Prep

Multiply. Write your answer in simplest form. (Ch. 12, Lessons 2 and 3)

50. $\frac{2}{3} \times \frac{3}{5}$

51. $\frac{3}{4} \times \frac{8}{9}$

52. $1\frac{5}{6} \times 2\frac{3}{4}$

53. $4\frac{2}{5} \times 3\frac{1}{4}$

54. $1\frac{2}{3} \times 1\frac{3}{5}$

55. $7\frac{1}{5} \times 3\frac{2}{3}$

56. Free Response The following temperatures were recorded in Antarctica: 27.2°F, 24.6°F, 29°F, 22.1°F, and 28.1°F. What was the mean daily temperature for these five days?

Explain your thinking.

Extra Practice See page 375, Set E.

Flying Measures

In the 1920s, the Frisbie Baking Company sold pies to students at Yale University. The students discovered that the empty pie tins made great flying discs. Adding a spin to their toss kept the pie tins aloft for great distances.

In 1948, a California building inspector and carpenter made the first plastic flying disc. Since that time, these discs have gained in popularity.

Four results for outdoor distance throwing are shown below. Convert the results to feet using 1 m $\approx$ 3.281 ft. Round your answer to the nearest hundredth.

1. Boys under 11: 82.3 m
2. Girls under 11: 70.2 m
3. Boys under 12: 101.5 m
4. Girls under 12: 97.74 m

Money Power

Businesses circulate coupons on the Internet. One Web site offers a coupon worth $3.25. If the value of the coupons that have been downloaded so far totals $32,500, how many coupons have been downloaded so far?

Brain Teaser

1 2 3 4 5

Use each of these digits once to create a decimal division expression whose quotient is about 2.

Technology

Visit *Education Place* at **eduplace.com/kids/mw/** to try more brain teasers.

Lesson 6

Repeating Decimals

Objective Change a fraction to a decimal using division.

e Glossary

Vocabulary

repeating decimal

Learn About It

Mack had 5 hits out of 11 times at bat. His batting average is $\frac{5}{11}$. What is his batting average in decimal form?

To change a fraction to a decimal, divide the numerator by the denominator. Sometimes the remainder is not 0. If the division continues indefinitely, the quotient will be a **repeating decimal.**

Find 5 ÷ 11.

STEP 1 Divide until the quotient ends or repeats.

```
      0.4545
 11)5.0000...
   − 4 4
       60
     − 55
       50   ← The division pattern
     − 44     begins to repeat each
       60     time the remainder is 5.
     − 55
        5
```

The three dots (...) means that pattern continues.

STEP 2 Write a bar over the part of the quotient that repeats.

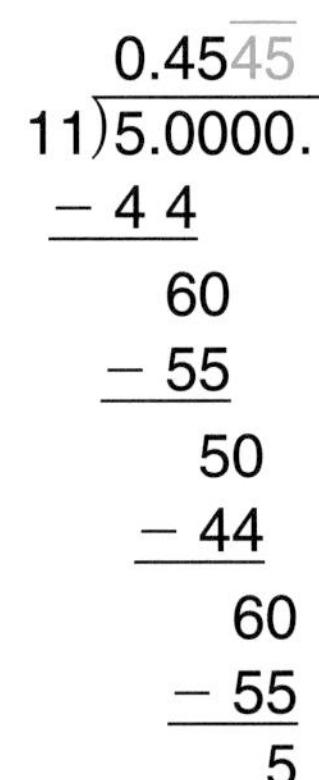

$$
\begin{array}{r}
0.45\overline{45} \\
11\overline{)5.0000\ldots} \\
-\,4\,4 \\
\hline
60 \\
-\,55 \\
\hline
50 \\
-\,44 \\
\hline
60 \\
-\,55 \\
\hline
5
\end{array}
$$

The bar over the digits 4 and 5 show that they are the digits that repeat.

Solution: Mack's batting average is $0.\overline{45}$.

Other Examples

A. Single Repeating Digit

Change $\frac{1}{3}$ to decimal form.

$$
\begin{array}{r}
0.33\ldots \\
3\overline{)1.0\ldots} \\
-\,9 \\
\hline
10 \\
-\,0 \\
\hline
1
\end{array}
$$

The decimal form of $\frac{1}{3}$ is $0.\overline{3}$.

B. Calculator

Some calculators round the last digit of a repeating decimal. Check how your calculator displays repeating decimals.

5 ÷ 9 =
0.5555555556

Guided Practice

Ask Yourself

- Does the decimal terminate or not?
- Do one or more digits repeat?

Change each fraction to decimal form.

1. $\frac{1}{6}$
2. $\frac{2}{6}$
3. $\frac{5}{6}$
4. $\frac{7}{15}$
5. $\frac{4}{9}$
6. $\frac{1}{11}$

TEST TIPS **Explain Your Thinking** ▶ If you know the decimal for $\frac{1}{3}$, how can you find the decimal for $\frac{2}{3}$?

Practice and Problem Solving

Change each fraction to decimal form.

7. $\frac{1}{12}$
8. $\frac{2}{12}$
9. $\frac{3}{12}$
10. $\frac{4}{12}$
11. $\frac{5}{12}$
12. $\frac{2}{11}$
13. $\frac{3}{11}$
14. $\frac{4}{11}$
15. $\frac{5}{11}$
16. $\frac{6}{11}$
17. $\frac{10}{4}$
18. $\frac{10}{11}$
19. $\frac{1}{5}$
20. $\frac{1}{15}$
21. $\frac{1}{30}$

Solve.

22. **Calculator** Compare the quotients of $\frac{8}{7}$ and $\frac{22}{7}$. How are they alike? How are they different?

23. Ed has had 5 hits in his last 8 at bats. How much more or less than a 0.500 batting average does he have?

24. **Analyze** Look at the denominators of the fractions below. Which denominators always result in a repeating decimal? Give examples.

$$\frac{\blacksquare}{5} \quad \frac{\blacksquare}{6} \quad \frac{\blacksquare}{9} \quad \frac{\blacksquare}{10} \quad \frac{\blacksquare}{11}$$

25. **Predict** Look at the decimal values for the fractions below.

$$\frac{1}{9} = 0.\overline{1} \quad \frac{2}{9} = 0.\overline{2} \quad \frac{3}{9} = 0.\overline{3}$$

Without dividing, predict the quotients of $\frac{5}{9}$, $\frac{7}{9}$, and $\frac{8}{9}$.

Daily Review | Test Prep

Write each pair of numbers as fractions with common denominators. Then write >, <, or = for each ⬬. (Ch. 9, Lessons 8 and 9)

26. $\frac{8}{5}$ ⬬ 1.3
27. $\frac{16}{7}$ ⬬ $\frac{7}{3}$
28. $5\frac{1}{4}$ ⬬ 5.25
29. 3.02 ⬬ $\frac{16}{5}$

30. Lionel's batting average is $\frac{7}{11}$. Which of the following best represents his batting average in decimal form?

A 0.6 **C** $0.\overline{63}$
B 0.63 **D** 0.636

Lesson 7

Divide a Decimal by a Decimal

Objective Divide one decimal by another.

Learn About It

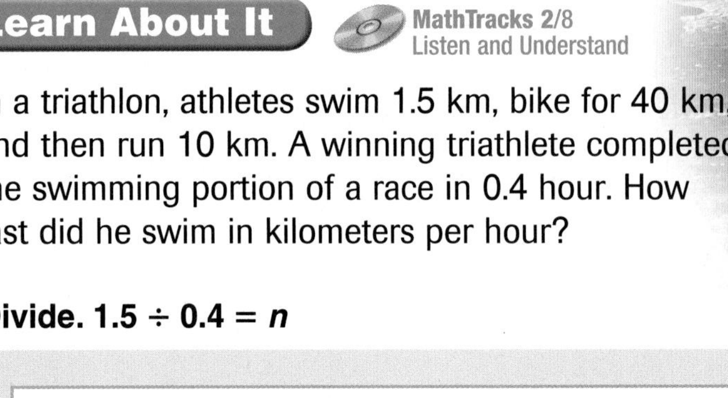

In a triathlon, athletes swim 1.5 km, bike for 40 km, and then run 10 km. A winning triathlete completed the swimming portion of a race in 0.4 hour. How fast did he swim in kilometers per hour?

Divide. $1.5 \div 0.4 = n$

STEP 1 Multiply the divisor and dividend by the same power of 10.

$0.4\overline{)1.5}$

$\frac{1.5}{0.4} \overset{\times 10}{=} \frac{15}{4}$ (numerator × 10, denominator × 10)

When dividing by a decimal, use multiplication to change the divisor to a whole number. Remember to multiply the dividend by the same number.

STEP 2 Write a decimal point and zeros after the final digit to continue dividing.

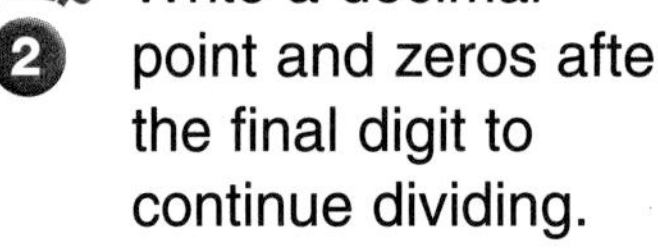

```
   3 75
4)15.00
 - 12
    30
  - 28
    20
  - 20
     0
```

STEP 3 Place a decimal point in the quotient over the decimal point in the dividend.

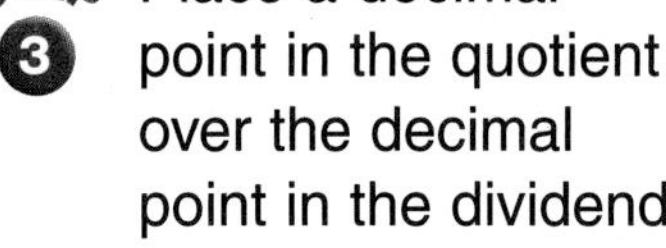

```
   3.75
4)15.00
 - 12
    30
  - 28
    20
  - 20
     0
```

Estimate to check.
$0.4 \approx 0.5$ and $1.5 \approx 2$.
$2 \div 0.5 = 4$
A quotient of 3.75 is reasonable.

Solution: The triathlete swam at an average speed of 3.75 kilometers per hour.

Another Example

Divide to a Specified Place

Divide $1.5 \div 0.45$ to the nearest hundredth.

To find a quotient to the nearest hundredth, divide to the nearest thousandth and round the quotient to the nearest hundredth.

```
        3.333
0.45)1.50000
    - 1 35
        150
      - 135
         150
       - 135
          150
        - 135
           15
```

3 < 5 so round down.
$1.5 \div 0.45 = 3.33$ to the nearest hundredth

Guided Practice

Divide. Check that your answer is reasonable.

1. $0.8\overline{)1.6}$
2. $0.4\overline{)1.84}$
3. $0.2\overline{)0.101}$
4. $9 \div 0.8$
5. $30 \div 1.5$
6. $1.44 \div 1.2$

Ask Yourself

- Do I need to write any zeros after the dividend?
- Did I place the decimal point correctly?

Explain Your Thinking ▶ How do you decide which power of 10 to use for multiplying when simplifying division by a decimal?

Practice and Problem Solving

Divide. Round to the nearest hundredth if necessary. Check that your answer is reasonable.

7. $0.3\overline{)1.8}$
8. $0.3\overline{)0.18}$
9. $0.5\overline{)38.5}$
10. $0.5\overline{)3.85}$
11. $0.05\overline{)0.385}$
12. $6.1\overline{)32}$
13. $3.5\overline{)17.5}$
14. $0.35\overline{)17.5}$
15. $0.8\overline{)1.12}$
16. $0.08\overline{)11.2}$
17. $0.7\overline{)42}$
18. $4.5\overline{)387}$
19. $0.23\overline{)54.3}$
20. $0.04\overline{)4.3}$
21. $1.4\overline{)0.342}$

Solve.

22. A triathlete averaged 33.3 kilometers per hour for a 40-kilometer portion of a bike race. To the nearest tenth, how long did this portion of the race take?

24. Catherine ran the 10-kilometer race portion of a triathlon in 0.91 hour. To the nearest tenth, what was her average speed in kilometers per hour?

23. **Explain** You know that $4 \div 8 = 0.5$. Use patterns below to explain how to complete divisions involving small numbers. Then complete the next division problem in each pattern.

a.
$4 \div 8 = 0.5$
$4 \div 0.8 = 5$
$4 \div 0.08 = 50$
$4 \div 0.008 = ■$

b.
$4 \div 8 = 0.5$
$0.4 \div 8 = 0.05$
$0.04 \div 8 = 0.005$
$0.004 \div 8 = ■$

Daily Review | Test Prep 

Add or subtract. Write your answers in simplest form. (Chapter 10, Lessons 4 and 8)

25. $3\frac{3}{4} + 2\frac{5}{8}$
26. $7\frac{1}{6} + 1\frac{1}{5}$
27. $4\frac{3}{4} - 2\frac{1}{8}$
28. $6\frac{1}{4} - 4\frac{2}{3}$

29. **Free Response** A triathlete swims the 1.5-kilometer course in 0.5 hour. What is the athlete's average speed in kilometers per hour?

Extra Practice See page 375, Set G.

Lesson 8

Problem-Solving Application

Decide How to Write the Quotient

Objective Decide how to write the quotient to solve a problem.

Learn About It

When you solve a division problem, sometimes you need to decide how to interpret the remainder.

▶ **Sometimes you use the remainder to decide on the answer.**

A store received boxes containing 19 jackets. Only 5 jackets fit in each box. How many boxes did they receive?

$$\begin{array}{r} 3 \text{ R4} \\ 5\overline{)19} \\ -\,15 \\ \hline 4 \end{array}$$

There are 3 full boxes. Another box is needed for the extra 4 jackets.

Solution: They received 4 boxes in all.

▶ **Sometimes you write the remainder as a fraction.**

A group makes sweatshirts. They use 18 feet of material to make 4 sweatshirts. How much material does each sweatshirt require?

$$\begin{array}{r} 4 \text{ R2} = 4\frac{2}{4} = 4\frac{1}{2} \\ 4\overline{)18} \\ -\,16 \\ \hline 2 \end{array}$$

Solution: Each sweatshirt requires $4\frac{1}{2}$ feet of material.

▶ **Sometimes you write the quotient as a decimal.**

Liang buys 8 identical T-shirts at the sports center store. If he spends $30 in all, how much does each shirt cost?

$$\begin{array}{r} 3.75 \\ 8\overline{)30.00} \\ -\,24 \\ \hline 60 \\ -\,56 \\ \hline 40 \\ -\,40 \\ \hline 0 \end{array}$$

Solution: Each T-shirt costs $3.75.

Look Back How does thinking about the question in each situation help you decide what to do with the remainder?

Guided Practice

Ask Yourself

- What does the question ask me to find?
- What does the remainder represent?
- Does my answer make sense?

Use the Ask Yourself questions to help you solve each problem.

1. Each pair of sweatpants requires 2 yards of fabric. How many pairs of sweatpants can be made with 7 yards of fabric?

   Hint Can you make part of a pair of sweatpants?

2. It cost 8 runners a total of $42.00 to enter a local race. How much was each runner's entry fee?

Independent Practice

Solve. Explain how you used each remainder.

3. During a parade, 46 award winners from the Youth Sports Center rode in automobiles. If only 6 winners could fit in each automobile, how many automobiles did they need for all the winners?

4. At the car wash shown in the picture below, $434 was raised for the Youth Sports Center. Of that, $107 was from donations. The rest was from washing cars. How many cars did they wash?

5. Pedro is making a 7-foot banner for Awards Night. Pedro needs to find the center of the banner so he can space the lettering correctly. How far from the end of the banner is its center?

6. The Youth Sports Center will have pizzas at their Awards Night. Each pizza is cut into 8 slices. If 150 people plan to attend and each eats 3 slices of pizza, what is the fewest number of pizzas they should order?

7. **Write Your Own** Write a word problem in which the quotient must be used to decide the answer.

8. **Create and Solve** Write a word problem in which the quotient must be written as a decimal.

Go On

Choose a Computation Method 

Mental Math • Estimation • Paper and Pencil • Calculator

Solve each problem. Name the computation method you used.

8. The room for the Youth Sports Center's Awards Night has tables that seat 4 people. If 146 people attend the Awards Night, how many tables are needed?

9. Val donated four times as much money to the equipment fund as Gary did. Together they donated $150. How much did each person donate?

10. The board at the Youth Sports Center got an estimate of $15,450 to redo the basketball courts. They've raised $\frac{2}{3}$ of the amount they need. About how much do they still have to raise?

11. To decorate for a party, a youth group needed 750 feet of ribbon. The ribbon is sold on rolls of 8 yards each. No partial rolls are sold. How many rolls of ribbon will they need?

12. The sports club members made refrigerator magnets for a fundraiser. On Monday they made 20 magnets, 2 more than on Sunday. On Sunday they made 4 fewer than on Saturday. On Saturday they made twice as many as on Friday. How many did they make in all?

Data Use the table for Problems 13–16.

Program	Number of Participants
Basketball	128
Soccer	142
Swimming	95
Tennis	48
Weight Lifting	18

13. Each soccer team has 11 players. What is the greatest number of soccer games that these players could have going on at the same time?

14. About 0.6 of the people who participate in swimming also take part in another sport at the Sports Center. About how many people is that?

15. Each morning at 8:00 A.M. all the people signed up for weight lifting show up. They each sign up for a $\frac{1}{2}$-hour session on one of the four weight benches. At what time does the last of those people finish?

16. It costs the Youth Sports Center $250 to rent each 48-person bus. If they hire enough buses to take all the people signed up for basketball to a local tournament, how much do they spend on buses?

Quick Check

Check your understanding of Lessons 5–8.

Divide. (Lesson 5)

1. $2\overline{)3}$
2. $5\overline{)6.4}$
3. $22\overline{)5.5}$

Change each fraction to decimal form. (Lesson 6)

4. $\frac{4}{5}$
5. $\frac{6}{11}$
6. $\frac{5}{6}$

Divide. Round each quotient to the nearest hundredth. (Lesson 7)

7. $0.3\overline{)1.4}$
8. $1.8\overline{)5}$
9. $2.4\overline{)9.25}$

Solve. (Lesson 8)

10. The Sports Center is having a soup label drive. They put rubber bands on packs of 100 labels. How many packs with rubber bands are there for the 23,285 labels they have so far?

Calculator Connection

Garden Math

What kind of flower do you get if you plant a crazy pickle?

Copy the chart at the right.

Use a calculator to find each quotient. Then use the key to decode the puzzle. Read down the last column to find the answer to the riddle.

Quotient	Letter
0.24	A
0.36	D
0.58	F
0.71	G
0.82	I
0.95	L
1.26	N
1.32	O
1.67	T
1.75	Y

Problem	Quotient	Letter
0.192 ÷ 0.8	■	■
0.9 ÷ 2.5	■	■
0.84 ÷ 3.5	■	■
0.232 ÷ 0.4	■	■
5.394 ÷ 9.3	■	■
0.665 ÷ 0.38	■	■
0.09 ÷ 0.25	■	■
0.656 ÷ 0.8	■	■
4.275 ÷ 4.5	■	■
0.931 ÷ 0.98	■	■

Chapter Review/Test

VOCABULARY

Vocabulary
compatible numbers
exponent
power of 10
repeating decimal

1. In the expression 83×10^r, 10^r is a(n) ____.
2. ____ can be used to estimate a quotient.
3. When a denominator does not divide into a numerator without a remainder, the result may be a(n) ____.

CONCEPTS AND SKILLS

Model the division and write the quotient in decimal form. (Lesson 1, pp. 352–353)

4. $7 \div 0.5$
5. $9 \div 0.9$
6. $9 \div 0.3$
7. $6 \div 0.4$
8. $8 \div 0.25$

Estimate each quotient. (Lesson 2, pp. 354–355)

9. $4 \div 0.19$
10. $82 \div 0.26$
11. $16 \div 0.147$

Divide. (Lessons 4–5, pp. 358–365)

12. $0.8 \div 101$
13. $4.2 \div 7$
14. $4\overline{)6.5}$
15. $1{,}593.65 \div 104$
16. $8.8 \div 5$
17. $8\overline{)56.36}$

Change each fraction to decimal form. (Lesson 6, pp. 366–367)

18. $\frac{3}{5}$
19. $\frac{7}{12}$
20. $\frac{2}{9}$

Divide to the greatest place or the nearest hundredth. (Lesson 7, pp. 368–369)

21. $0.4\overline{)6.4}$
22. $6.2\overline{)31.62}$
23. $4.1\overline{)33.62}$

PROBLEM SOLVING

Solve. Explain how you used each remainder. (Lesson 8, pp. 370–373)

24. Each pep squad uniform requires 2.5 yards of fabric. How many uniforms can be made from 22 yards of fabric?
25. There are 27 people going to a soccer game. If each car can hold 5 people, how many cars will be needed?

Show You Understand

Josh divides these two decimals incorrectly. Explain what he did wrong. Show how to find the correct quotient.

$$\begin{array}{r} 5.45 \\ 0.5\overline{)27.25} \\ -25 \\ \hline 2.2 \\ -2.0 \\ \hline 25 \\ -25 \\ \hline 0 \end{array}$$

Extra Practice

Set A (Lesson 1, pp. 352–353)

Model the division and write the quotient in decimal form.

1. $6 \div 0.2$
2. $9 \div 0.5$
3. $5 \div 0.25$
4. $12 \div 0.6$

Set B (Lesson 2, pp. 354–355)

Estimate each quotient.

1. $79 \div 0.77$
2. $309 \div 0.33$
3. $26 \div 0.492$
4. $54.7 \div 0.89$
5. $5.63 \div 0.621$
6. $9 \div 0.258$
7. $16.2 \div 0.41$
8. $22 \div 0.108$

Set C (Lesson 3, pp. 356–357)

Multiply or divide by using patterns.

1. 6.12×10^1
2. 8.34×10^2
3. $2{,}745.64 \div 10^2$
4. $7.25 \div 10^1$
5. $8.67 \div 10^2$
6. $6.534 \div 10^3$
7. 0.054×10^2
8. 0.19×10^3

Set D (Lesson 4, pp. 358–361)

Divide and check.

1. $6\overline{)4.8}$
2. $2\overline{)2.36}$
3. $4\overline{)21.84}$
4. $7\overline{)\$61.95}$
5. $7.2 \div 6$
6. $\$24.75 \div 3$
7. $1.44 \div 6$
8. $0.87 \div 3$

Set E (Lesson 5, pp. 362–365)

Divide and check using estimation.

1. $4\overline{)4.2}$
2. $5\overline{)6.7}$
3. $10\overline{)7.74}$
4. $8\overline{)24.6}$
5. $8\overline{)4}$
6. $4\overline{)15}$
7. $63 \div 15$
8. $36.8 \div 5$

Set F (Lesson 6, pp. 366–367)

Change each fraction to decimal form.

1. $\frac{1}{15}$
2. $\frac{7}{12}$
3. $\frac{7}{11}$
4. $\frac{4}{15}$
5. $\frac{15}{4}$
6. $\frac{5}{9}$

Set G (Lesson 7, pp. 368–369)

Divide to the greatest place or the nearest hundredth.
Check that your answer is reasonable.

1. $0.5\overline{)1.5}$
2. $0.15\overline{)55.5}$
3. $0.6\overline{)3.6}$
4. $0.52\overline{)13}$
5. $0.8\overline{)5.84}$
6. $3.7\overline{)22.2}$
7. $0.9\overline{)5.04}$
8. $0.8\overline{)0.584}$

WEEKLY WR READER®

Social Studies Connection

Philatelic Fun

Are you a philatelist? If you collect or study postage stamps, you are. Some people collect stamps for the pure pleasure of it. Others collect stamps because some historic stamps are worth a lot of money.

The very first postage stamps were used on May 6, 1840, in England. The "1 Penny Black" and "2 Pence Blue" were so named because of their purchase price and color. Before long, most countries in the world were using postage stamps.

New stamps are being issued all the time. Recently, the U.S. Postal Service even released a series of stamps called *Stampin' the Future* that used drawings made by children between the ages of 8 and 12.

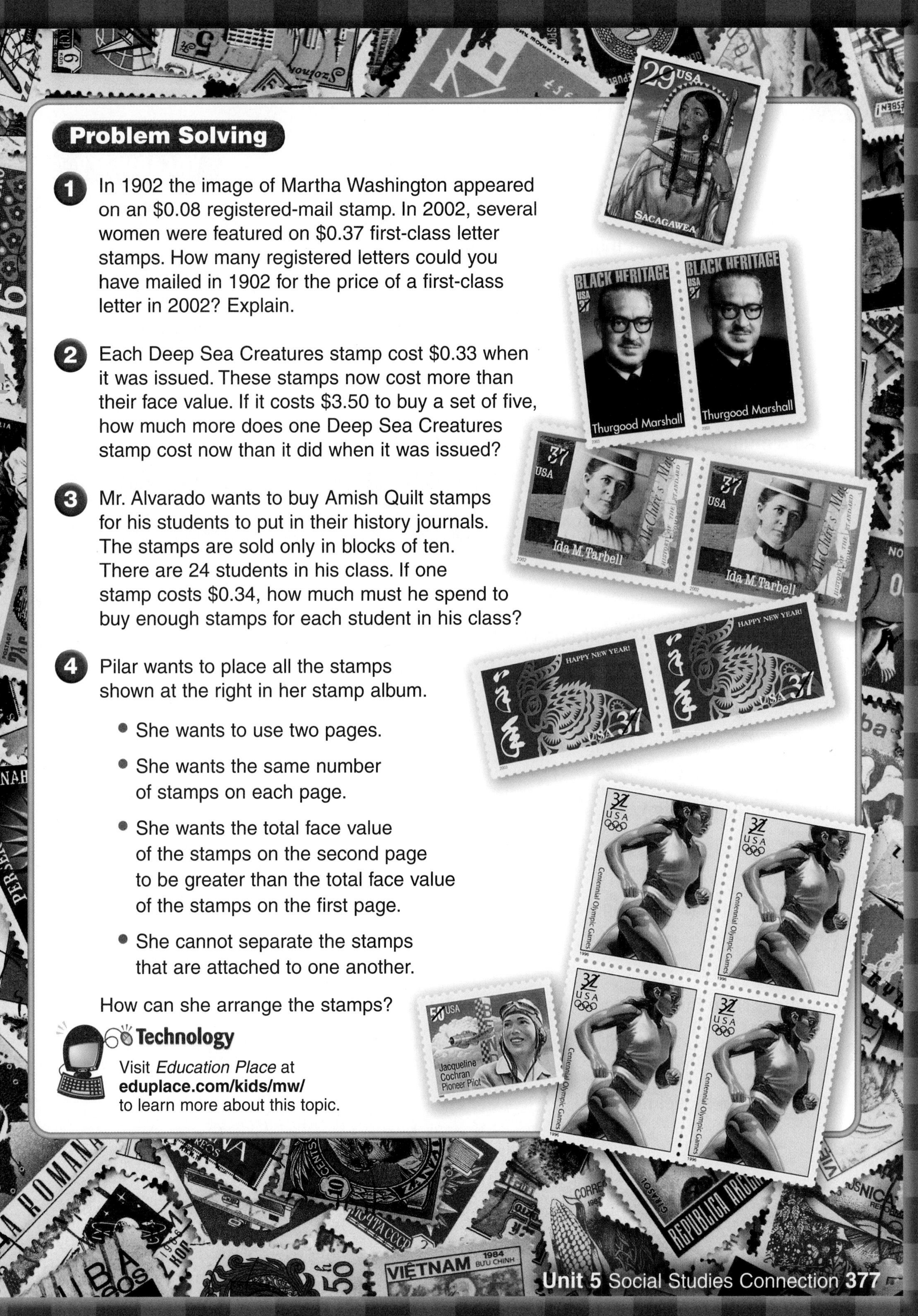

Problem Solving

1. In 1902 the image of Martha Washington appeared on an $0.08 registered-mail stamp. In 2002, several women were featured on $0.37 first-class letter stamps. How many registered letters could you have mailed in 1902 for the price of a first-class letter in 2002? Explain.

2. Each Deep Sea Creatures stamp cost $0.33 when it was issued. These stamps now cost more than their face value. If it costs $3.50 to buy a set of five, how much more does one Deep Sea Creatures stamp cost now than it did when it was issued?

3. Mr. Alvarado wants to buy Amish Quilt stamps for his students to put in their history journals. The stamps are sold only in blocks of ten. There are 24 students in his class. If one stamp costs $0.34, how much must he spend to buy enough stamps for each student in his class?

4. Pilar wants to place all the stamps shown at the right in her stamp album.
   - She wants to use two pages.
   - She wants the same number of stamps on each page.
   - She wants the total face value of the stamps on the second page to be greater than the total face value of the stamps on the first page.
   - She cannot separate the stamps that are attached to one another.

   How can she arrange the stamps?

Technology

Visit *Education Place* at **eduplace.com/kids/mw/** to learn more about this topic.

Unit 5 Test

VOCABULARY

1. The product of a number and its ■ is 1.
2. A(n) ■ is a quotient that repeats digits an unlimited number of times.
3. A(n) ■ is a number that tells how many times the base is used as a factor.

Vocabulary

- exponent
- reciprocal
- compatible numbers
- mixed number
- repeating decimal

CONCEPTS AND SKILLS

Write a multiplication sentence for each model. (Chapter 12)

4. 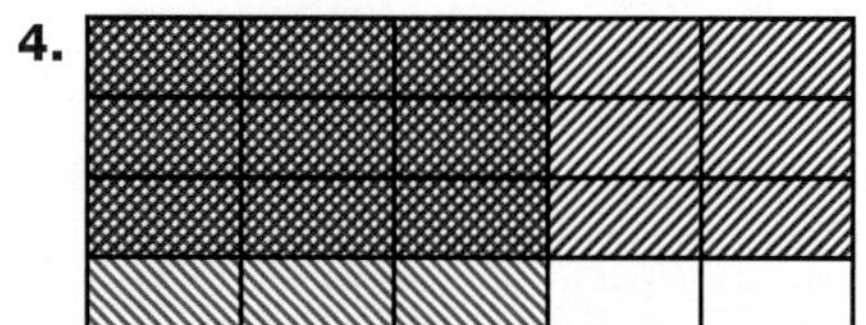

5. 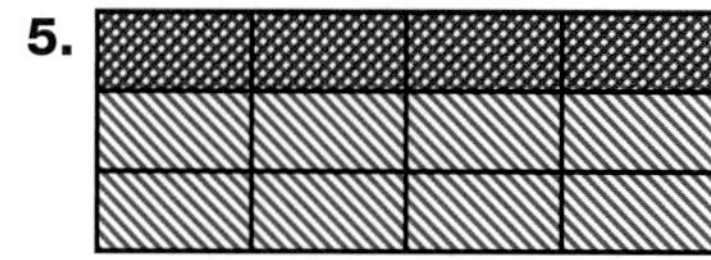 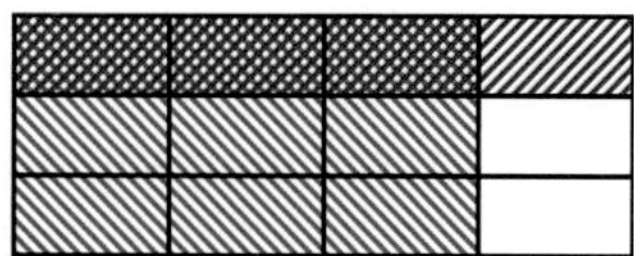

Multiply or divide. Write your answer in simplest form. (Chapter 12)

6. $\frac{2}{3} \times \frac{3}{9}$
7. $5\frac{1}{6} \times \frac{2}{7}$
8. $7 \times \frac{1}{3}$
9. $2 \div \frac{5}{6}$
10. $2\frac{3}{4} \div \frac{5}{8}$
11. $3\frac{1}{6} \times 1\frac{1}{3}$
12. $\frac{3}{4} \div 2\frac{1}{2}$
13. $4\frac{1}{3} \div \frac{1}{2}$

Estimate. Then multiply. (Chapter 13)

14. 7×6.2
15. 1.02×0.6
16. 204×7.81
17. 17.24×52

Multiply or divide by using patterns. (Chapter 14)

18. 6.23×10^3
19. $8.6 \div 10^1$
20. 5.348×10^2
21. $267.9 \div 10^3$

Estimate. Then find each quotient and check your answer. (Chapter 14)

22. $8\overline{)20.8}$
23. $4\overline{)5.3}$
24. $426 \div 0.8$
25. $50.84 \div 6.2$

Write each as a decimal. (Chapter 14)

26. $\frac{3}{10}$
27. $\frac{2}{3}$
28. $\frac{4}{11}$
29. $\frac{1}{7}$

PROBLEM SOLVING

30. The Reading-For-All group raised \$308 for new library books. Each book costs \$5. How many new library books can they buy?

31. The temperature during the day on Mercury is 450°C. What is Mercury's temperature during the day in degrees Fahrenheit? Hint: $F = \frac{9}{5}C + 32$.

32. Earth makes a complete revolution around the sun in about 365 days. Mercury revolves around the sun in 0.24 of an Earth year. How many days does it take for Mercury to revolve around the sun?

33. Lil deposited \$1 in her savings account after the first week of summer, \$2.50 after the second week, \$4 after the third week, and \$5.50 after the fourth week. If she continues this pattern, how much will Lil deposit after the tenth week?

Decision Making

Extended Response

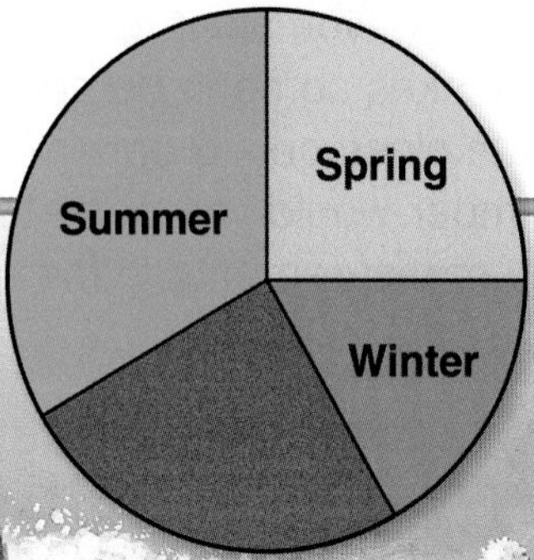

Summer

Spring

Winter

Task Tamara surveyed 48 fifth-grade students about their favorite season. Before she could finish a circle graph of the data, she lost the survey data.

Show what Tamara's finished graph should look like. Find how many students said they prefer each of the seasons. Explain how you found your answers. Show the fraction for each of the seasons on the completed circle graph of the data.

What Tamara remembers:

- One third of the students prefer summer, and half that many prefer winter.
- Spring and fall are preferred by the same number of students.

Performance Assessment

TASK 1

Pancakes for Twelve (Chapter 12)

You need to make 12 pancakes for a special birthday breakfast.

a. Identify the number by which to multiply the measurements in the recipe to make 12 pancakes.

b. Rewrite the pancake recipe so it will make 12 pancakes. Write fractions in simplest form.

c. Suppose you want to make enough pancakes so each person in your math class gets 2 pancakes. By what number would you need to multiply the measurements in the recipe?

d. How much flour will you need for the pancakes in part **c**?

Pancakes
MAPLE SYRUP
Recipe
$1\frac{2}{3}$ cups flour
$\frac{1}{2}$ teaspoon baking powder
$\frac{2}{3}$ cup milk
$2\frac{1}{2}$ tablespoons oil
1 egg
Makes 4 pancakes

TASK 2

School Shopping Spree (Chapters 13–14)

You are shopping for school clothes.

a. Decide how to combine the items on sale to create about a week's worth of outfits. How many T-shirts, belts, and jeans will you buy? Buy at least two of each item.

b. Multiply to find the total cost of each type of item. Then find the total cost of your purchase.

c. Suppose you bought the same number of each item. If you spent a total of $134.68, how many of each item did you buy?

Self Check

- Did I answer the questions for each task?
- Did I check all my work?

Enrichment: Estimating With Mixed Numbers

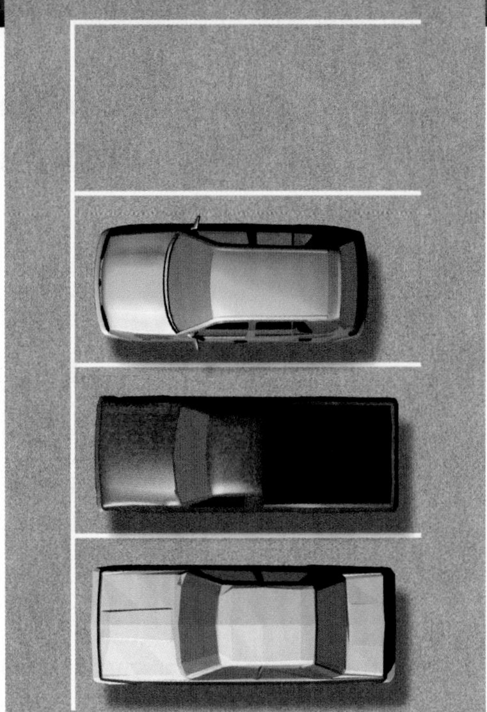

The width of a parking lot is $78\frac{1}{3}$ feet, and each space is to be the same width. For compact cars, each parking space must be at least $7\frac{3}{4}$ feet wide. What is the greatest number of compact-car parking spaces that will fit in one row? How wide will each space be?

First, you need to estimate how many parking spaces will fit. Then you can divide to find how wide to make each parking space.

Rules for Rounding Mixed Numbers

To estimate with mixed numbers, round to the nearest whole number:

- If the fraction part of the mixed number is equal to $\frac{1}{2}$ or greater, round up.
- If the fraction part of the mixed number is less than $\frac{1}{2}$, round down.

Estimate: $78\frac{1}{3} \div 7\frac{3}{4} = ?$

Round down for fractions less than $\frac{1}{2}$. $78\frac{1}{3} \rightarrow 78$

Round up for fractions $\frac{1}{2}$ or greater. $7\frac{3}{4} \rightarrow 8$

$78 \div 8 = 9$ R6 or $9\frac{3}{4}$.

There will be 9 or 10 parking spaces in the lot.

Solve: Check whether 9 spaces will fit. $78\frac{1}{3} \div 9 \approx 9$; 9 feet is too wide.

Check whether 10 spaces will fit. $78\frac{1}{3} \div 10 = 7\frac{5}{6}$

$\frac{5}{6} > \frac{3}{4}$, so $7\frac{5}{6}$ feet wide works.

Solution: There will be 10 spaces, each $7\frac{5}{6}$ feet wide.

Find the greatest number of spaces that will fit in one row. Then find the width of each space.

1. The width of a compact-car parking lot is $47\frac{1}{4}$ feet. Each parking space must be at least $7\frac{3}{4}$ feet wide. Each space is to be the same width.

2. The width of a full-size car parking lot is 70 feet. Each parking space must be at least $8\frac{1}{2}$ feet wide. Each space is to be the same width.

Cumulative Test Prep Practice

Solve Problems 1–10.

Test-Taking Tip

Compute the answer *before* you read the answer choices. Then check whether your answer is reasonable. If you find an answer choice that matches your answer, you will feel more confident that your answer choice is correct.

Look at the example below.

It rained $\frac{3}{4}$ inch on Saturday and $1\frac{3}{4}$ inches on Sunday. How much did it rain over the weekend?

A $2\frac{1}{4}$ **C** $2\frac{3}{4}$

B $2\frac{1}{2}$ **D** 3

THINK

I must add the fractions to get the answer and show the answer in simplified form:

$$\frac{3}{4} + 1\frac{3}{4} = 1\frac{6}{4} = 1 + \frac{4}{4} + \frac{2}{4} = 2\frac{1}{2}$$

My answer, $2\frac{1}{2}$, is answer choice **B**.

Multiple Choice

1. Subtract $\frac{1}{5}$ from $\frac{3}{4}$.

A $\frac{7}{20}$ **B** $\frac{7}{10}$ **C** $\frac{11}{20}$ **D** $\frac{11}{10}$

(Chapter 4, Lesson 6)

2. Mario wants to extend a shelf that is 7 feet 10 inches long by 2 feet 3 inches. What is the length of the new shelf?

F 5 feet 7 inches **H** 10 feet 1 inch

G 9 feet 7 inches **J** 10 feet 3 inches

(Chapter 3, Lesson 6)

3. In May, Roberto was $59\frac{7}{8}$ inches tall. By the end of October, he had grown $\frac{3}{4}$ inch. How tall was Roberto at the end of October?

A $59\frac{1}{8}$ inches **C** $60\frac{5}{8}$ inches

B $59\frac{1}{4}$ inches **D** $60\frac{8}{13}$ inches

(Chapter 4, Lesson 4)

4. On a camping trip, $5\frac{1}{2}$ cups of oatmeal were made for breakfast. The oatmeal is divided equally among 4 campers. How much does each camper get?

F $1\frac{3}{8}$ cups **H** $1\frac{5}{6}$ cups

G $1\frac{1}{2}$ cups **J** $2\frac{1}{3}$ cups

(Chapter 5, Lesson 6)

 For more Test-Taking Tips, see pages xxii–xxv.

Free Response

5. Every Monday for 3 weeks, a truck brought 1.5 tons of crushed stone to a construction site. How many tons of stone did the truck bring in all?

(Chapter 13, Lesson 3)

6.

Metric Units of Capacity
1,000 milliliters (mL) = 1 liter (L)
10 deciliters (dL) = 1 liter (L)

Hamid wants to pour equal amounts from a pitcher holding 2 liters of apple juice into several glasses. How many deciliters should he pour into each of 5 glasses?

(Chapter 6, Lesson 5)

7. The school board budget is $7,000,000. What is the largest exponent you would use to write this number in expanded form?

(Chapter 1, Lesson 2)

8. A city school district has 1,701 students in 9 elementary schools. If the same number of students go to each school, how many students are in each school?

(Chapter 4, Lesson 5)

9. A hummingbird flaps its wings once every 0.074 second. How much time does it take a hummingbird to flap its wings 12 times?

(Chapter 13, Lesson 4)

Extended Response

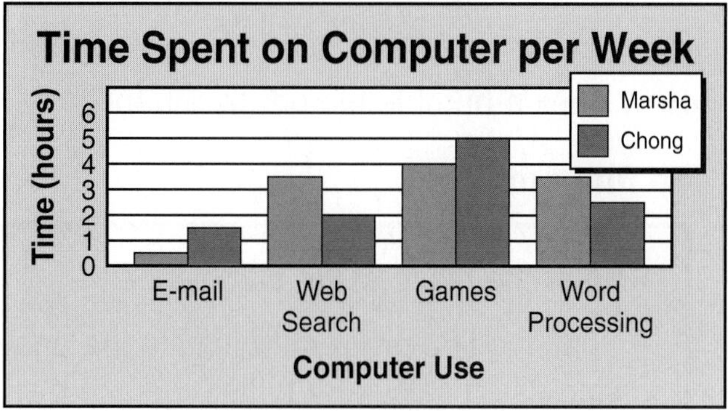

10. The double bar graph shows how many hours Chong and Marsha spend on different computer activities each week.

   A On which computer activity does each student spend the most time?

   B Who spends more time using a word processing application?

   C What is the total time that Marsha spends using a computer each week? Chong?

   D How much more time does Chong spend playing computer games than Marsha?

   E Write two to three sentences to compare Chong and Marsha's computer use.

(Chapter 7, Lesson 1)

Test Prep on the Net
Check out *Education Place* at **eduplace.com/kids/mw/** for test prep practice.

It's A-maze-ing!

How does a bumblebee get to school?

To find out:

- Enter the maze at the bumblebee.
- Copy the first problem. Estimate the answer and then use a calculator to find the exact answer.
- Find the answer in the maze and write the letter found below it.
- Follow the correct answer to the next problem.
- Continue until you reach the schoolhouse at the end of the maze and have found the answer to the riddle.

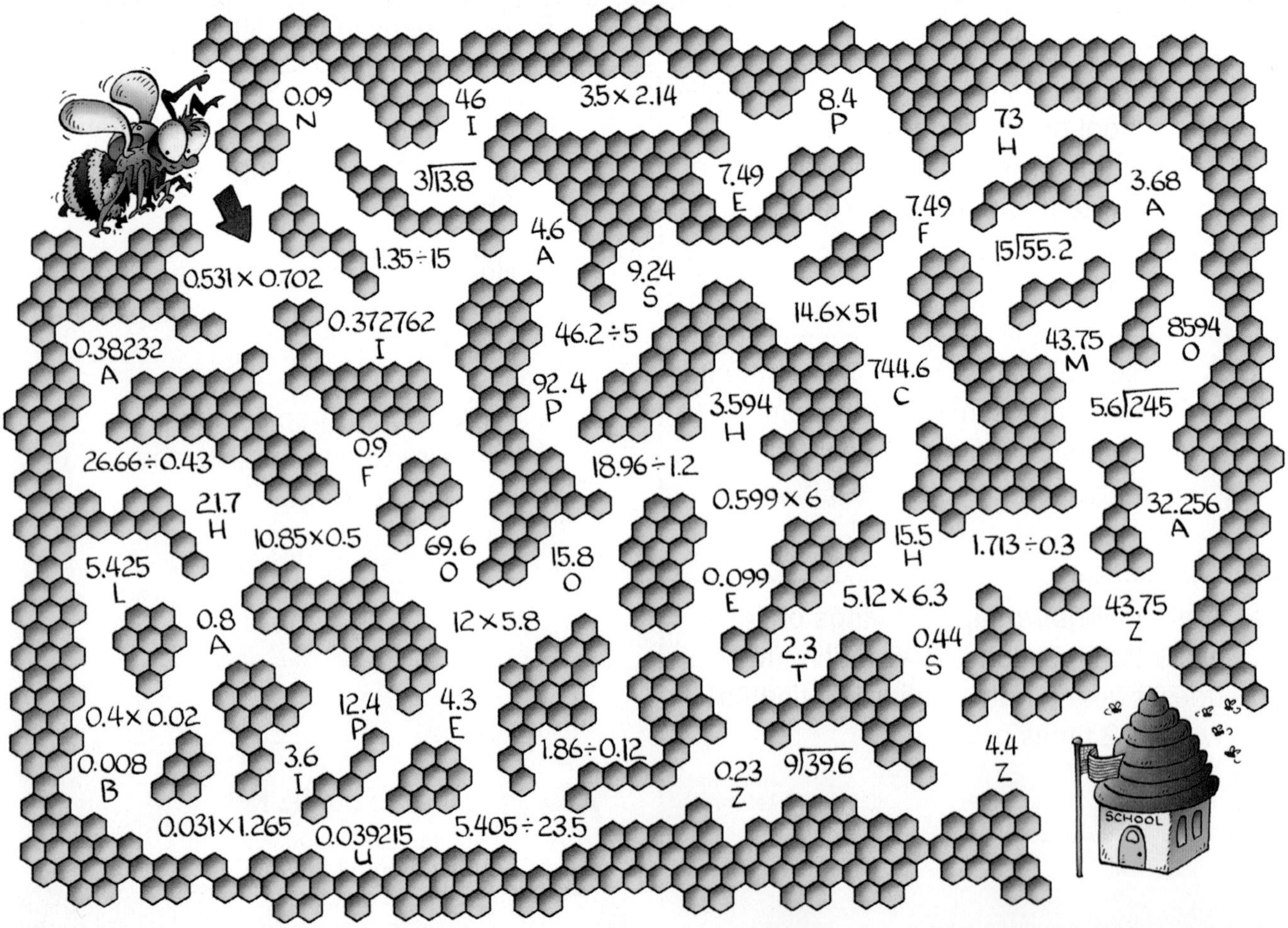

0.09 N
46 I
3.5 × 2.14
8.4 P
73 H
$3\overline{)13.8}$
7.49 E
7.49 F
3.68 A
$15\overline{)55.2}$
4.6 A
1.35 ÷ 15
9.24 S
0.531 × 0.702
0.372762 I
46.2 ÷ 5
14.6 × 51
43.75 M
8594 O
0.38232 A
744.6 C
92.4 P
3.594 H
$5.6\overline{)245}$
0.9 F
26.66 ÷ 0.43
18.96 ÷ 1.2
0.599 × 6
21.7 H
32.256 A
10.85 × 0.5
69.6 O
15.8 O
15.5 H
1.713 ÷ 0.3
5.425 L
0.099 E
5.12 × 6.3
0.8 A
12 × 5.8
43.75 Z
2.3 T
0.44 S
0.4 × 0.02
12.4 P
4.3 E
3.6 I
0.008 B
1.86 ÷ 0.12
0.23 Z
$9\overline{)39.6}$
4.4 Z
0.031 × 1.265
0.039215 U
5.405 ÷ 23.5
SCHOOL

Vocabulary Wrap-Up for Unit 5

WEEKLY WR READER Activity Almanac
See page 682 for the activity for this unit.

Look back at the big ideas and vocabulary in this unit.

Big Ideas

To divide a fraction by a fraction, multiply by the reciprocal of the divisor.

The product of two decimals will have the same number of decimal places as the sum of the decimal places in each factor.

e Glossary

Key Vocabulary

reciprocal
product
quotient

Math Conversations

Use your new vocabulary to discuss these big ideas.

1. Explain what the written form of this decimal means: $1.\overline{2}$
2. Explain how the numbers $\frac{3}{5}$, $\frac{6}{10}$, and 0.6 are related.
3. Explain how you would locate the decimal point in this product.

   $0.02 \times 0.4 = 0008$

   Why are zeros used in the answer?
4. **Write About It** Meteorologists often write daily amounts of rainfall in decimal form, even when the rainfall is measured in inches. With a partner, discuss and then explain in writing some reasons why scientists might use decimals instead of fractions when measuring rainfall.

To find the reciprocal of a fraction, I exchange the numerator and denominator.
Right. So the reciprocal of $\frac{1}{10}$ is $\frac{10}{1}$.

Building Vocabulary

Reviewing Vocabulary

Here are some math vocabulary words that you should know.

ray	part of a line that begins at an endpoint and goes on forever in one direction
angle	a figure formed by two rays with the same endpoint
line segment	part of a line that has two endpoints
polygon	a simple closed plane figure made up of three or more line segments
circle	a closed figure in which every point is the same distance from a given point called the center

Reading Words and Symbols

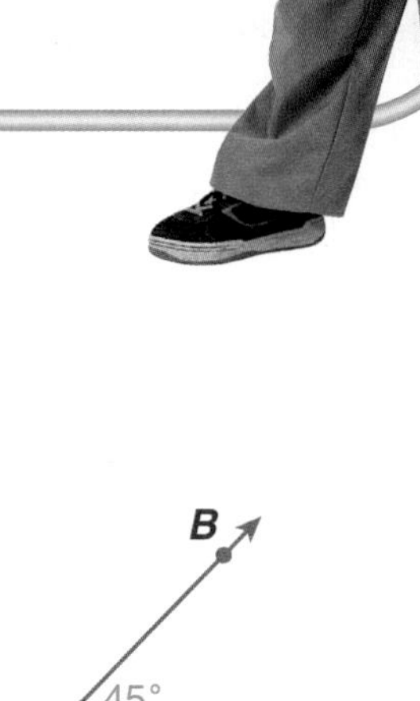

The two rays that make up the angle have a common endpoint, which is called the vertex.

One way you can name angles is to name three points on the angle—a point on each ray and the vertex. The vertex must always be in the middle.

Another way you can name angles is by using only the vertex letter. In $\angle BAC$, A is the vertex. For $\angle BAC$ (read "angle BAC") you can also write $\angle A$ (read "angle A").

The measure of angles is given in degrees. The symbol for degrees is °. This angle has a measure of forty-five degrees or 45°.

Use words and symbols to answer these questions.

1. What are two other names for $\angle BAC$? Explain.
2. What is the measure of an angle that has twice the measure of $\angle BAC$? three times the measure of $\angle BAC$?

Reading Test Questions

Choose the correct answer for each.

3. Which figure is shown on the grid paper?

a. square

b. rectangle

c. parallelogram

d. all of the above

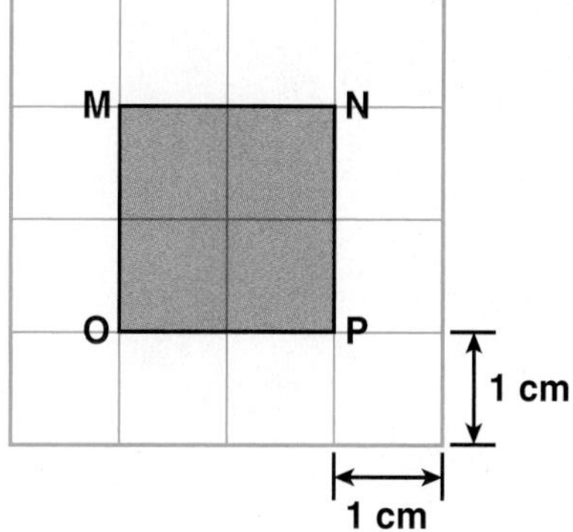

A **grid** is an arrangement of lines intersecting at right angles and dividing a plane into congruent squares.

4. As part of which group would you classify the figure?

a. circles

b. quadrilaterals

c. triangles

d. pentagons

To **classify** in geometry means to identify the type of figure.

5. How many square centimeters do you count inside the figure?

a. 4

b. 8

c. 12

d. 16

A **square centimeter** is a metric unit used for measuring the area of a figure. The symbol for square centimeter is cm^2. Each cm^2 has a measure of 1 cm $\times$ 1 cm.

Learning Vocabulary

Watch for these new words in this unit. Write their definitions in your journal.

- **diagonal**
- **transformation**
- **tessellation**
- **circumference**
- **π (pi)**
- **net**

Vocabulary

e • **Glossary**

e • **WordGame**

Literature Connection

Read "No Place to Go" on page 646. Then work with a partner to answer the questions about the story.

CHAPTER 15

Plane Figures and Geometric Concepts

INVESTIGATION

Use Data

A geodesic dome is a type of structure that uses triangles to approximate the shape of a sphere. Richard Buckminster Fuller (1895–1983) created the geodesic dome in the early 1950s.

Can you find these shapes in the picture?

a rectangle

a parallelogram

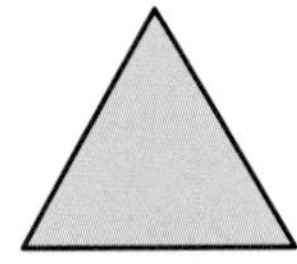
an equilateral triangle

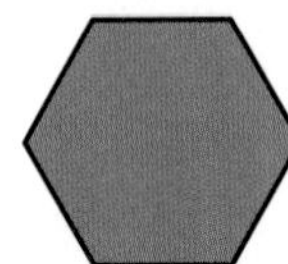
a hexagon

Chapter Pretest

Use this page to review and remember what you need to know for this chapter.

VOCABULARY

Choose the best word to complete each sentence.

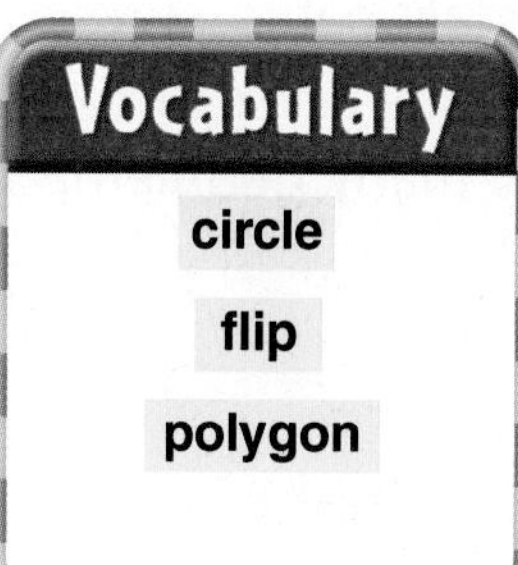

1. A _____ is a closed, flat figure made up of line segments.
2. A _____ is a figure made up of points that are all the same distance from the center point.

CONCEPTS AND SKILLS

Is each figure a polygon? Write *yes* or *no*.

3. 
4. 
5. 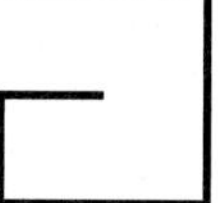

Match. Write the letter of the figure with the same size and shape.

6. 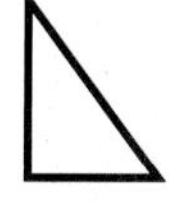
7. 
8. 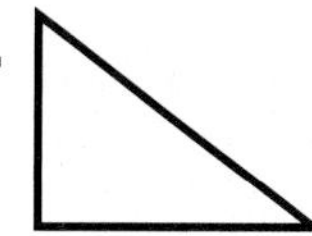
9. 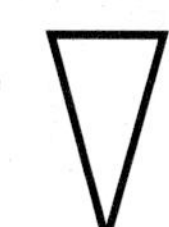

a. 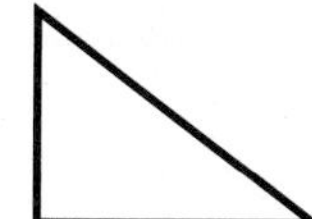

b. 

c. 

d. 

Write About It

10. Is a circle a polygon? Explain your answer.

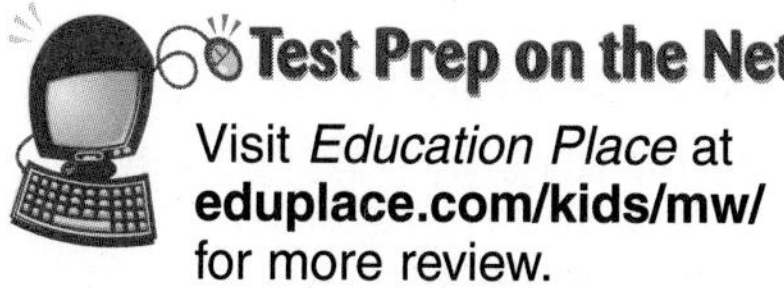

Test Prep on the Net

Visit *Education Place* at **eduplace.com/kids/mw/** for more review.

Lesson 1

Points, Lines, and Rays

Objective Identify and label points, lines, line segments, and rays.

Learn About It

The widest cable-stayed bridge in the world spans the Charles River in Boston. In the picture you can identify many geometric features.

Leonard P. Zakim Bunker Hill Bridge

- A **point** is an exact location in space.

  C

  Read: point *C* **Write:** *C*

- A **line** is an endless straight path made up of a continuous collection of points.

  C D

  Read: line *CD* or line *DC*
  Write: $\overleftrightarrow{CD}$ or $\overleftrightarrow{DC}$

- A **line segment** is a part of a line and has two endpoints.

  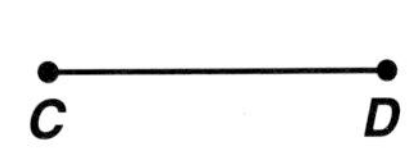

  Read: line segment *CD* or line segment *DC*
  Write: $\overline{CD}$ or $\overline{DC}$

- A **ray** has one endpoint and extends without end in one direction.

  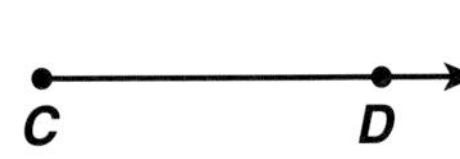

  Read: ray *CD*
  Write: $\overrightarrow{CD}$ (The endpoint is always the first letter.)

- A **plane** is a collection of points that forms a flat, continuous, and unending surface.

  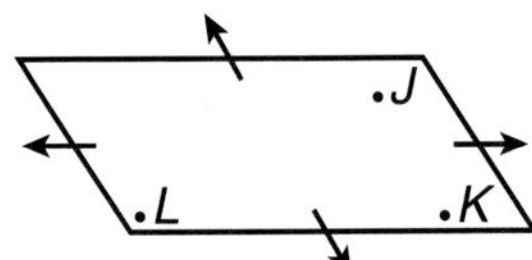

  Read: plane *JKL*
  (The 3 letters can be in any order.)

- **Intersecting lines** have one point in common.

  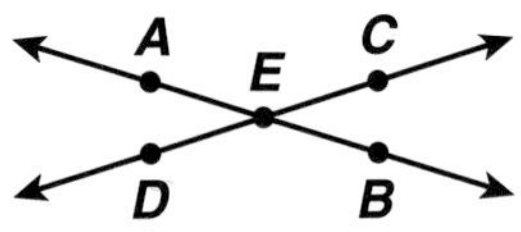

  Read: Line *AB* intersects line *CD* at point *E*.

- **Perpendicular lines** intersect at right angles.

  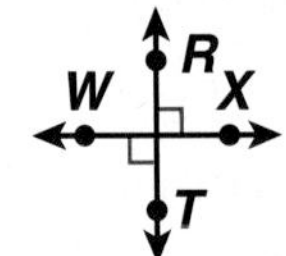

  Read: Line *RT* is perpendicular to line *WX*.
  Write: $\overleftrightarrow{RT} \perp \overleftrightarrow{WX}$

- **Parallel lines** lie in the same plane and do not intersect.

  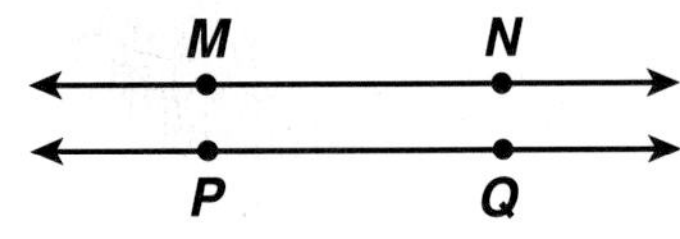

  Read: Line *MN* is parallel to line *PQ*.
  Write: $\overleftrightarrow{MN} \parallel \overleftrightarrow{PQ}$

Guided Practice

Ask Yourself

- Which letters do I use to name each figure?
- Do I need to write the letters in a certain order?

Name each figure.

1. T

2. F E

3. S T

4. C M

Explain Your Thinking ▶ Why do $\overrightarrow{CD}$ and $\overrightarrow{DC}$ name different rays?

Practice and Problem Solving

Name each figure.

5. Y Z

6. 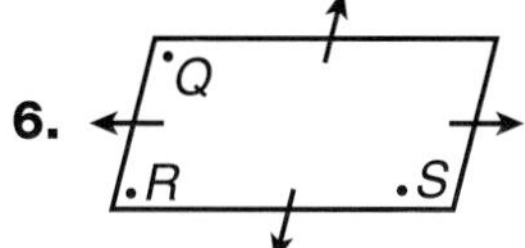

7. U T

Describe each pair of lines. Use symbols if possible.

8. 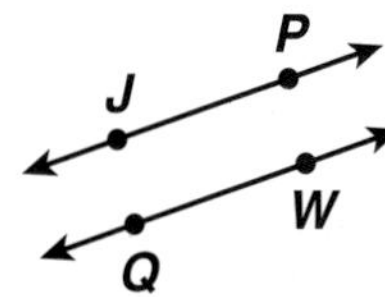

9. 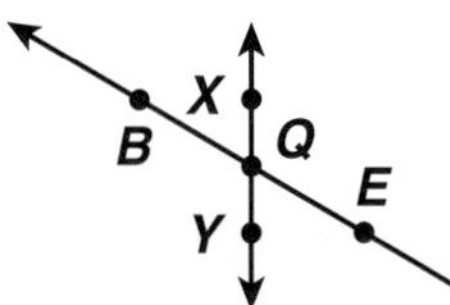

10. 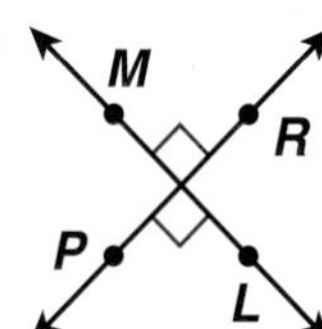

Draw and label each figure.

11. $\overrightarrow{DR}$

12. $\overleftrightarrow{DF} \perp \overleftrightarrow{LN}$

13. $\overleftrightarrow{CQ} \parallel \overleftrightarrow{DX}$

14. plane *EBT*

Solve.

15. **Analyze** Four parallel lines are perpendicular to two other lines. At how many points do the lines intersect?

16. Which of these—a line, a line segment, or a ray—can contain the other two?

17. **Write About It** Explain how perpendicular lines are similar to intersecting lines.

18. **Explain** How many lines can intersect at a point? Use a diagram to explain your thinking.

Daily Review | Test Prep

For each exercise, write the fractions that are equivalent. Then circle the fraction in the pair that is in simplest form. (Ch. 9, Lesson 6)

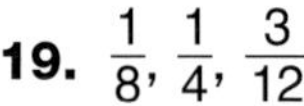

19. $\frac{1}{8}, \frac{1}{4}, \frac{3}{12}$

20. $\frac{1}{8}, \frac{8}{16}, \frac{2}{16}$

21. $\frac{9}{18}, \frac{2}{6}, \frac{1}{2}$

22. $\frac{1}{6}, \frac{1}{3}, \frac{5}{15}$

23. Identify this figure.

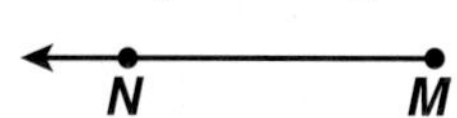

A line *MN*

B point *MN*

C plane *MN*

D ray *MN*

Extra Practice See page 419, Set A.

Measure, Draw, and Classify Angles

Objective Measure, draw, and classify angles.

e Glossary

Vocabulary

degrees
right angle
acute angle
obtuse angle
straight angle

Materials
protractor or Learning Tool 12

Angles are formed by two rays with a common endpoint. The common endpoint of the rays is called the vertex of the angle. A small arc is used to identify the inside, or interior, of an angle.

To name an angle, you can name three points on the angle–a point on each ray and the vertex in the middle. You can also name an angle just by naming its vertex.

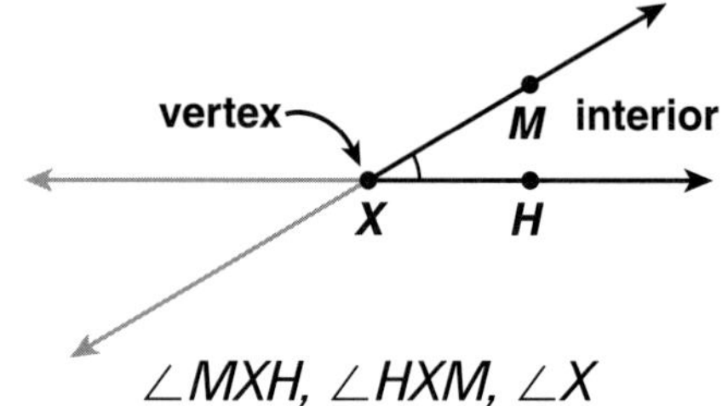

The symbol ∠ is used to identify an angle.

∠*MXH*, ∠*HXM*, ∠*X*

A protractor is a tool used to measure angles in **degrees**. Follow the steps below to measure ∠*FDE* and ∠*BDC*.

Measuring Angles

Place the center mark of the protractor on the vertex, *D*. Align the 0° mark of one of the protractor scales with one ray of the angle.

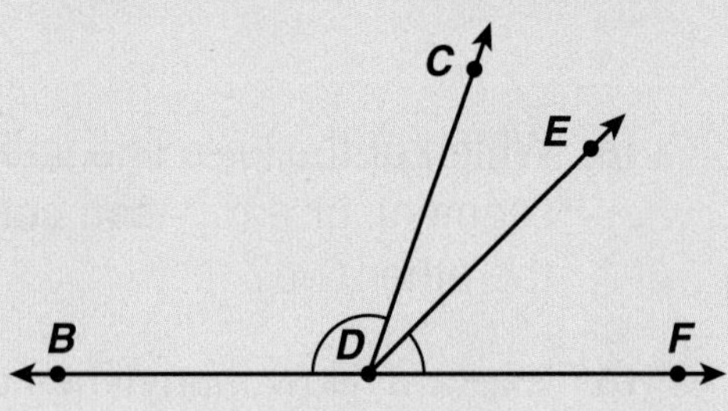

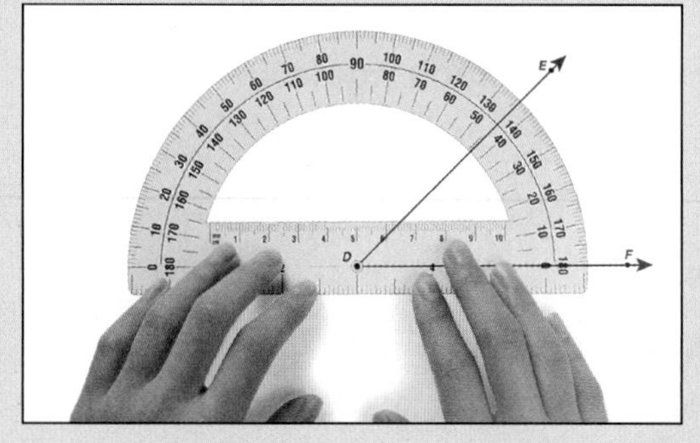

Find where the other ray passes through the same scale. Read the measure of the angle on that scale.

- What is the measure of ∠*FDE*? ∠*BDC*?
- How can you tell when to use the inside scale and when to use the outside scale of the protractor?

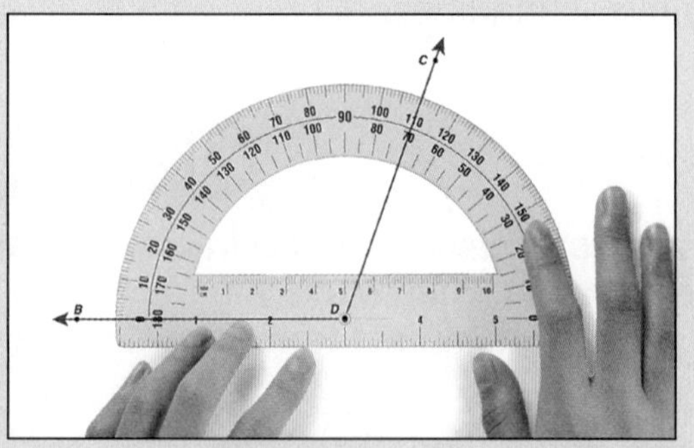

You can also use a protractor to draw an angle of a given measure.

Draw an angle that measures 75°.

Drawing Angles

STEP 1 On a sheet of paper, draw and label a ray.

STEP 2 Place the center mark of the protractor on the endpoint of the ray. Align the ray with the 0° mark of one of the protractor scales. The endpoint of the ray will be the vertex of the angle.

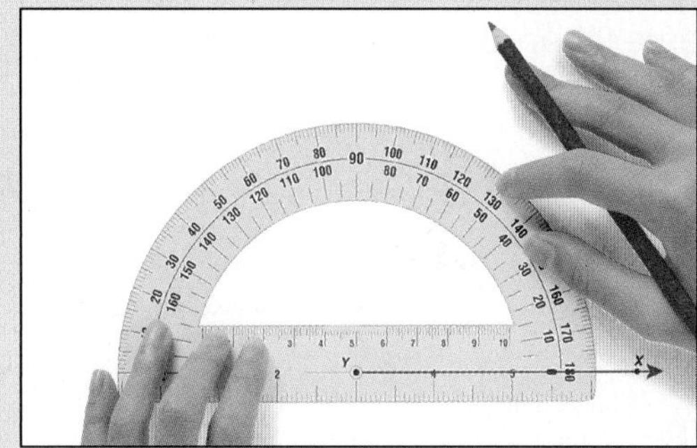

STEP 3 Using the scale on which the ray aligns with 0°, mark the point at 75°. Label the point.

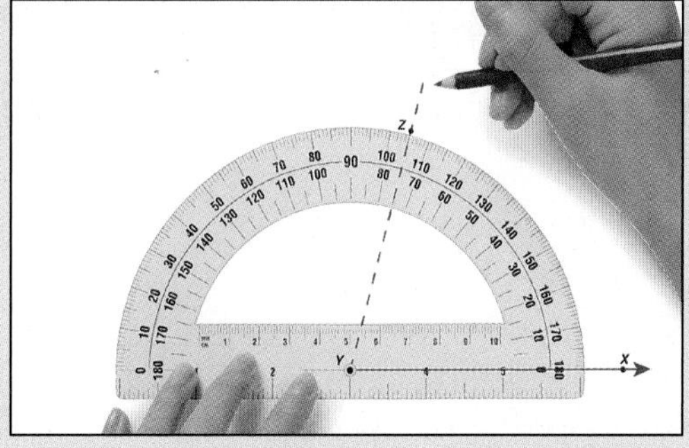

STEP 4 Draw a ray from the vertex through the point you labeled. Write the name of the angle.

- What is the measure of the angle?
- Which point is the vertex of the angle?

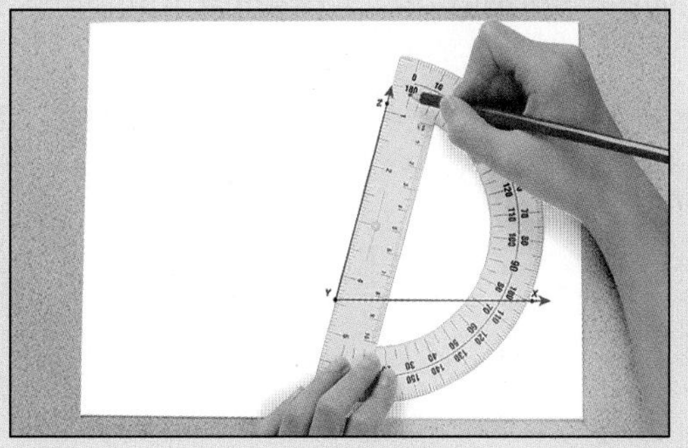

Go On

You can classify an angle by its measure.

Classifying Angles

The measure of a **right angle** is equal to 90°.

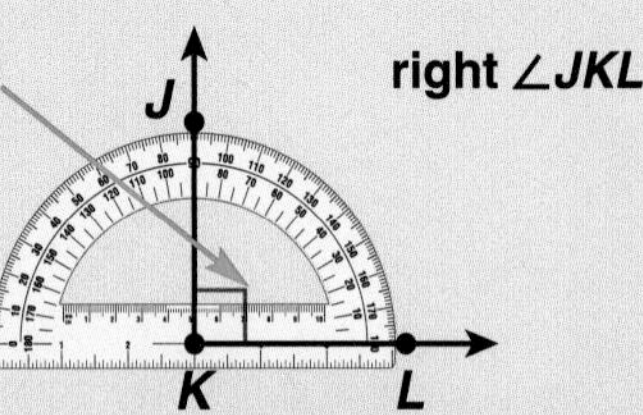

The measure of an **acute angle** is greater than 0° and less than 90°.

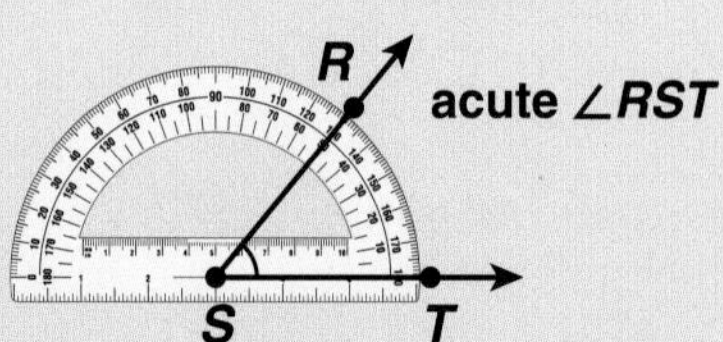

The measure of an **obtuse angle** is greater than 90° and less than 180°.

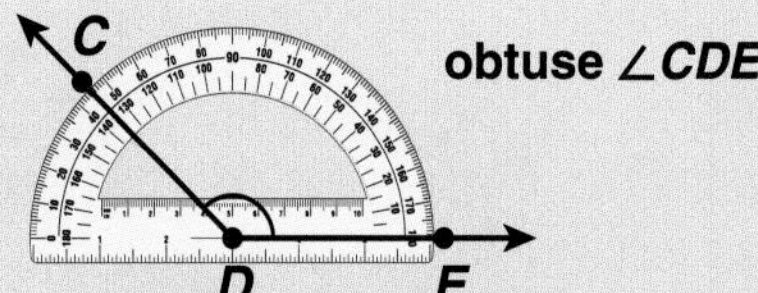

The measure of a **straight angle** is equal to 180°.

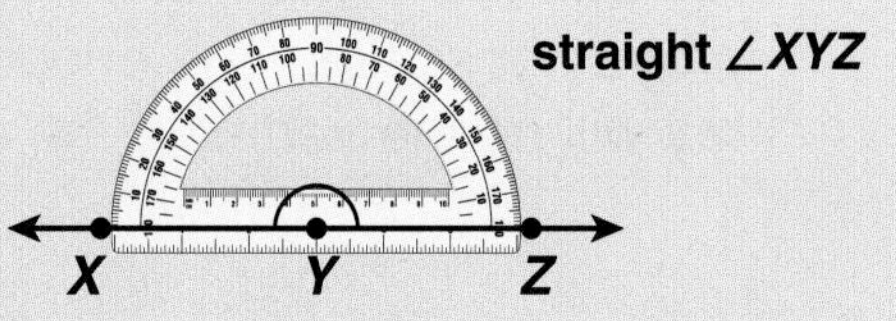

On Your Own

In Exercises 1–4, use symbols to name each angle three different ways.

1. 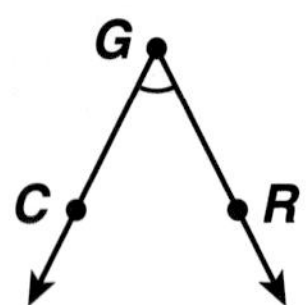

2. 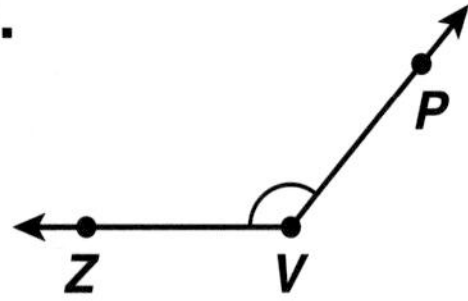

3. 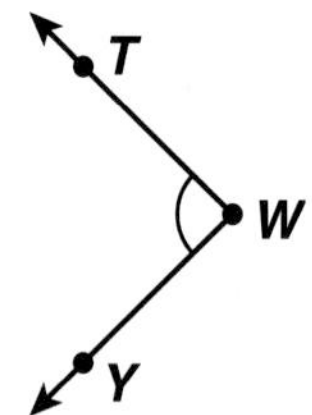

4. 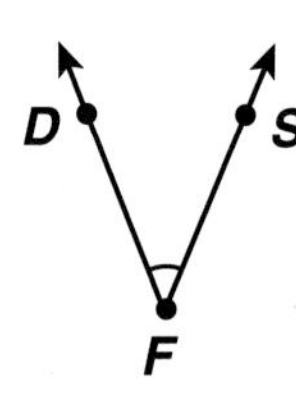

5. Which angle has a greater measure, $\angle CGR$ or $\angle ZVP$?

Classify each angle as acute, obtuse, straight, or right.

6. 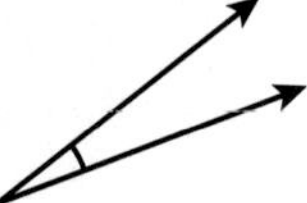

7. 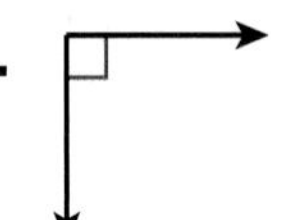

8. 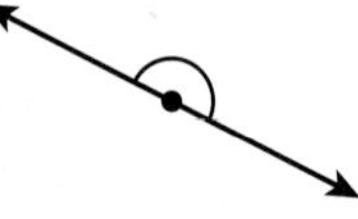

9. 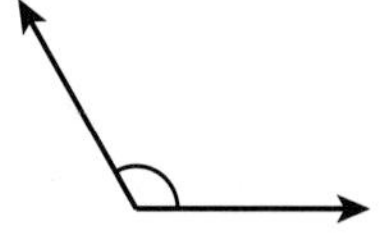

10. 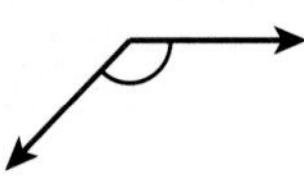

11. 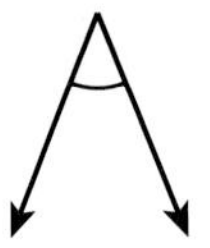

12. 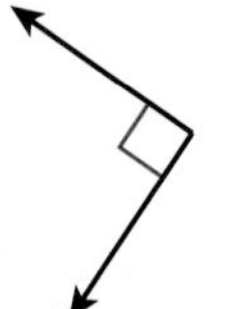

13. 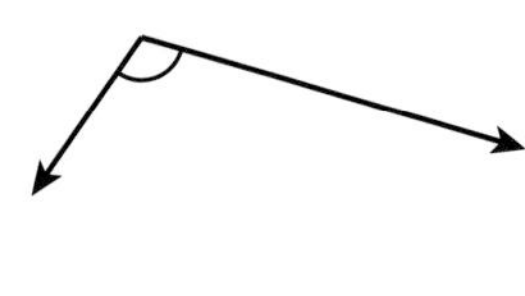

Use a protractor to draw an angle having each measure. Classify each angle as right, acute, obtuse, or straight.

14. 165°
15. 90°
16. 20°
17. 85°
18. 50°
19. 115°
20. 10°
21. 135°

Talk About It • Write About It

You have learned how to classify, draw, and measure angles.

22. **Analyze** Is the sum of the measures of two acute angles always less than 90°? Explain why or why not.

23. How could you list the kinds of angles you know–right, straight, acute, and obtuse–in order from least to greatest measure? Explain.

Visual Thinking

Math Reasoning

Construct Perpendicular Lines

You can use a compass and a straightedge to construct perpendicular lines.

Follow these steps to construct perpendicular lines.

STEP 1 Draw line *c* and point *W* as shown at the right. Put the compass point on *W*. Draw an arc that intersects line *c* at two points. Label these points *X* and *Y*.

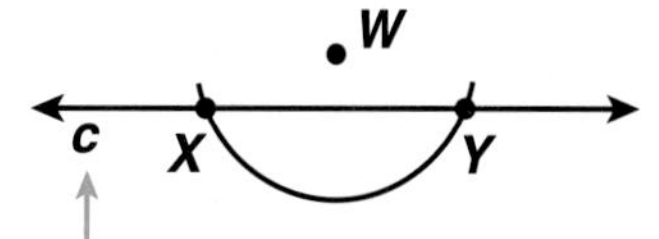

Lines can be named using lowercase letters.

STEP 2 Place the point of the compass at *X* and draw an arc below line *c*. From point *Y*, use the same compass measure and draw an arc below line *c*. Label the intersection point *V*.

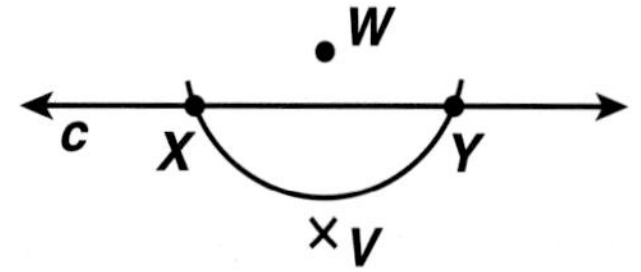

STEP 3 Draw line *WV* and label it *d*. Line *d* is perpendicular to line *c*.

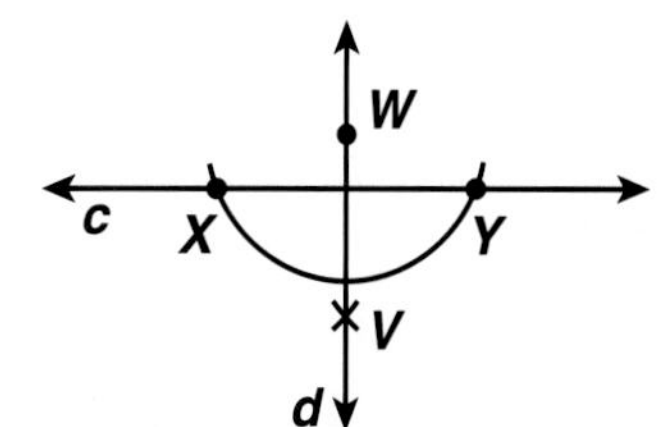

Lesson 3

Triangles

Objective Classify triangles and find missing angle measures.

Learn About It

A triangle is made up of 3 line segments called sides. Each pair of sides has a common endpoint, or vertex, and forms an angle.

You can classify triangles by the lengths of their sides.

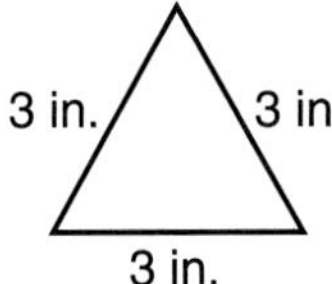

equilateral triangle
All sides are the same length.

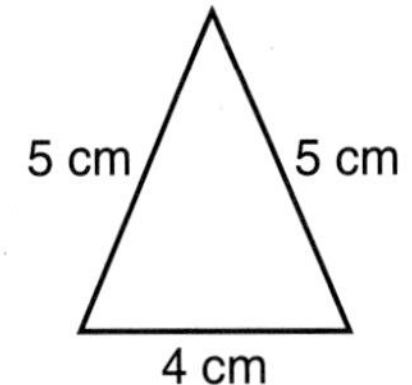

isosceles triangle
At least two sides are the same length.

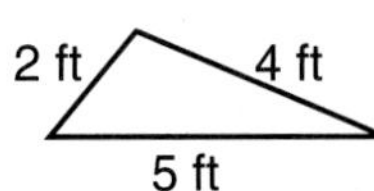

scalene triangle
No sides are the same length.

You can classify triangles by their angle measures.

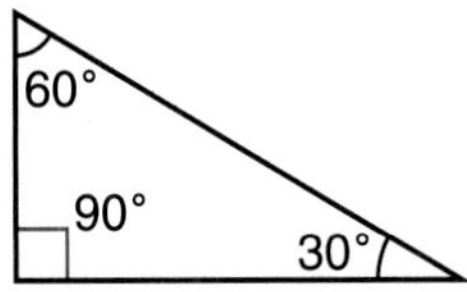

right triangle
one right angle

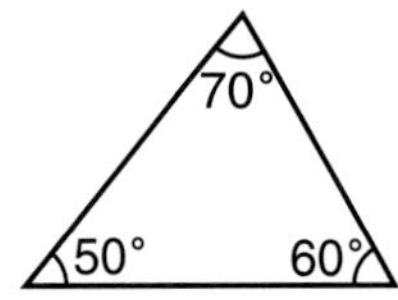

acute triangle
all acute angles

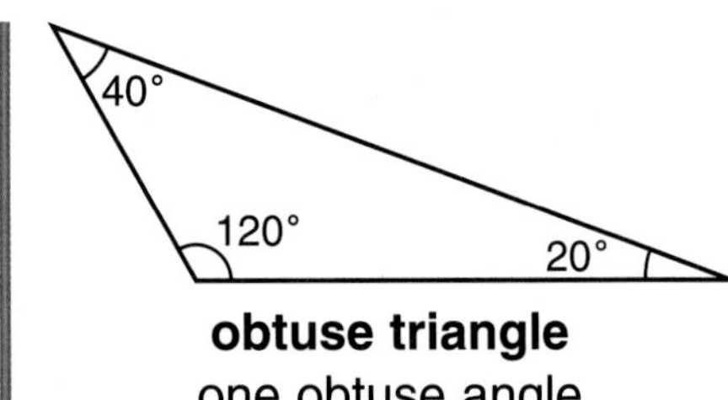

obtuse triangle
one obtuse angle

Try this activity with a partner to learn about angle measures in a triangle.

Materials straightedge

STEP 1 Use a straightedge to draw a triangle. Cut it out. Label the angles *a*, *b*, and *c*.

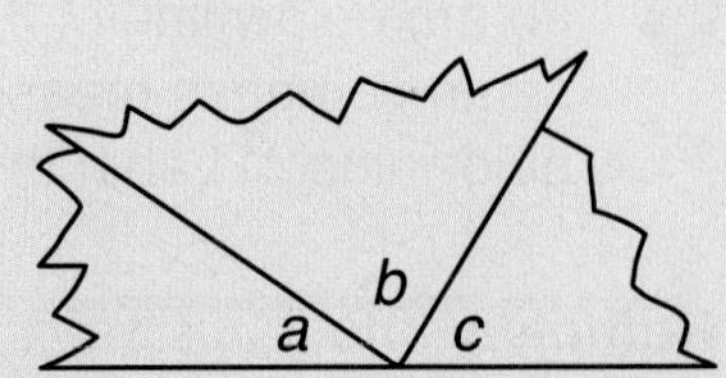

STEP 2 Tear off the three angles of the triangle.

STEP 3 Arrange the angles to make a straight angle.

- What is the measure of a straight angle?
- What is the sum of the angle measures in a triangle?
- Does this work for any triangle? Explain.

Guided Practice

Classify each triangle in two ways. Then find the missing angle measures.

1. 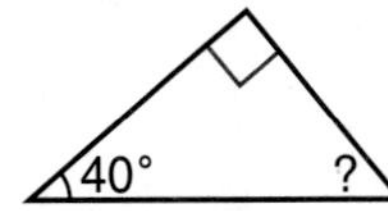

2. 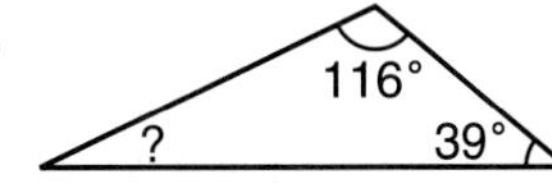

Ask Yourself

- Are the angles acute? obtuse? right?
- What is the sum of the angle measures in a triangle?

TEST TIPS **Explain Your Thinking ▶** Is an equilateral triangle also an isosceles triangle? Explain why or why not.

Practice and Problem Solving

Classify each triangle in two ways.

3. 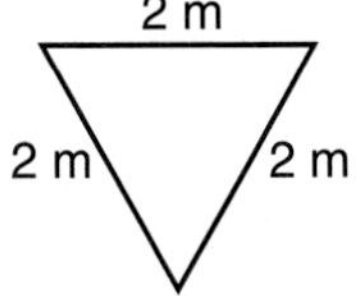

4. 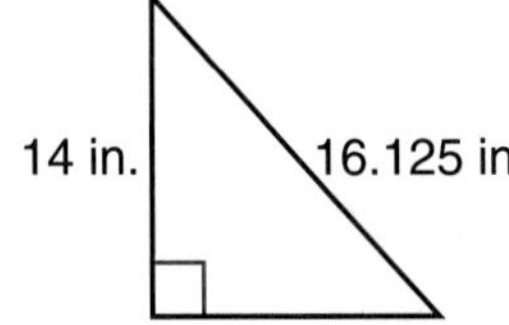

5. 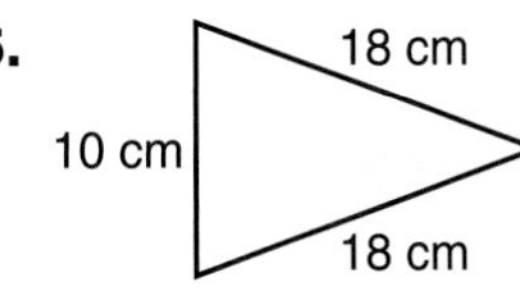

6. 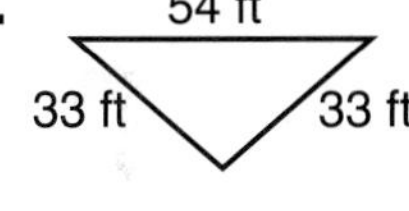

Algebra • Expressions **Write an expression to represent *a*. Then find the value of *a*.**

7. 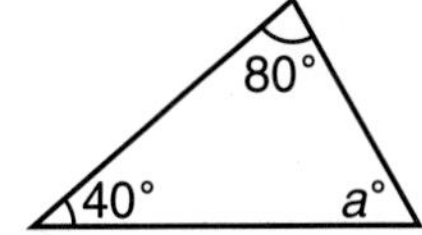

8. 

9. 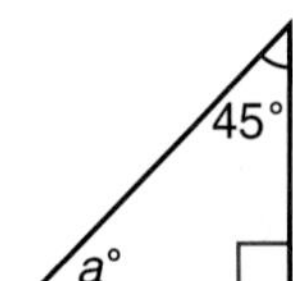

10. 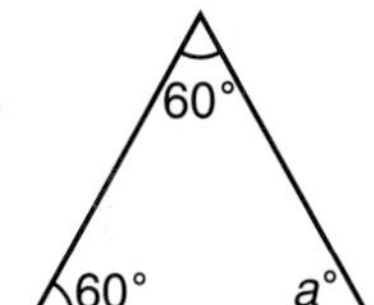

11. What's Wrong? Ari says that an isosceles triangle can also be obtuse. Is Ari right or wrong? Draw triangles to help you explain.

13. Create and Solve Use the sum of the angle measures in a triangle to write and solve your own triangle problem.

12. Represent Try to draw each of the following. If a figure cannot be drawn, explain why.

- a scalene acute triangle
- an equilateral right triangle
- a scalene right triangle

Multiply. Write each product in simplest form. (Ch. 12, Lesson 2)

14. $\frac{2}{3} \times \frac{3}{5}$ **15.** $\frac{3}{8} \times \frac{4}{5}$ **16.** $\frac{5}{6} \times \frac{3}{10}$

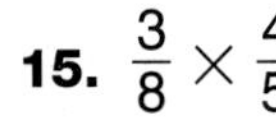

17. $\frac{4}{9} \times \frac{3}{4}$ **18.** $\frac{2}{25} \times \frac{2}{5}$ **19.** $\frac{3}{8} \times \frac{4}{11}$

20. Free Response Find *p*. Explain how you found your answer.

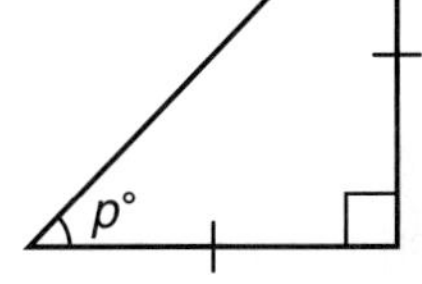

Extra Practice See page 419, Set B.

Congruence

Objective Identify congruent figures and congruent parts of figures.

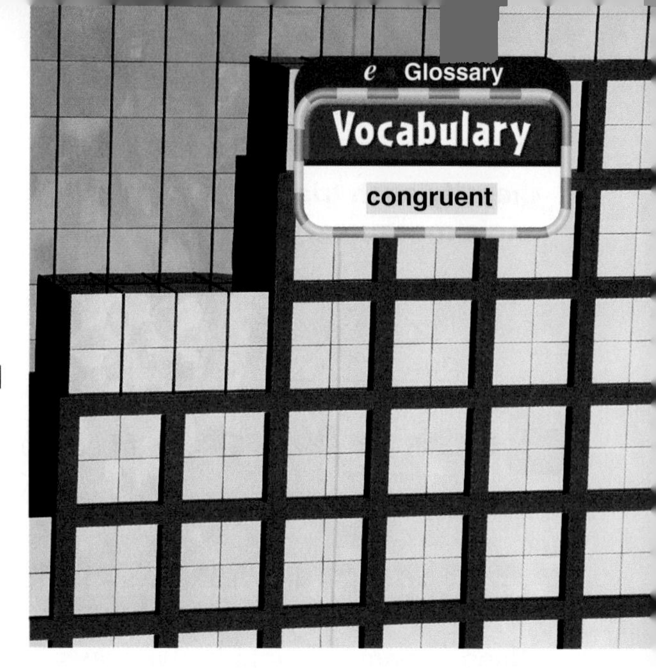

Learn About It

Figures that are the same size and shape are called **congruent** figures. The symbol ≅ is used to indicate congruence.

Which figures in the photograph appear to be congruent?

Different Ways to Check for Congruence

Way 1 You can use tracing.

If you trace triangle *ABC* and place the tracing on top of triangle *DEF*, you will find that the triangles are congruent.

The symbol △ is used to identify a triangle.

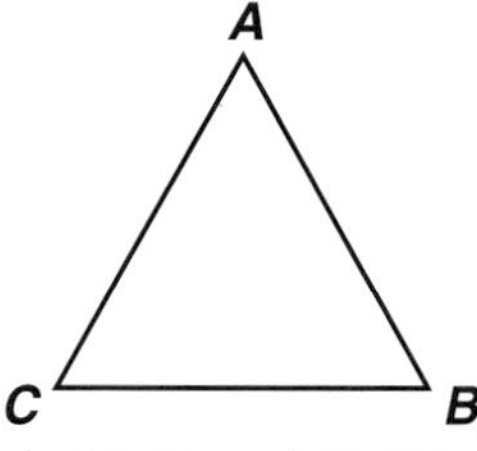

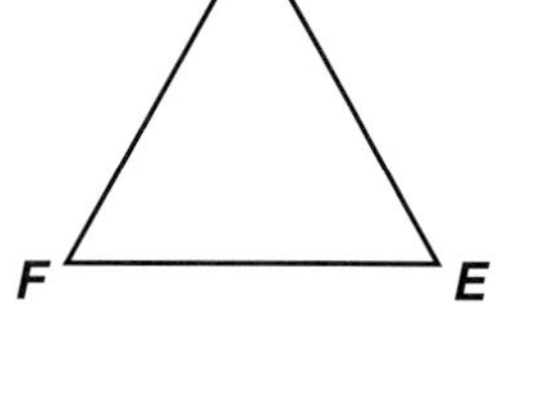

$\triangle ABC \cong \triangle DEF$

So, $\overline{AB} \cong \overline{DE}$, $\overline{BC} \cong \overline{EF}$, $\overline{CA} \cong \overline{FD}$.

Also, $\angle A \cong \angle D$, $\angle B \cong \angle E$, and $\angle C \cong \angle F$.

Way 2 You can use a ruler and a protractor.

In an equilateral triangle, the three sides are congruent and the three angles are congruent. Small lines indicate congruent sides and congruent angles.

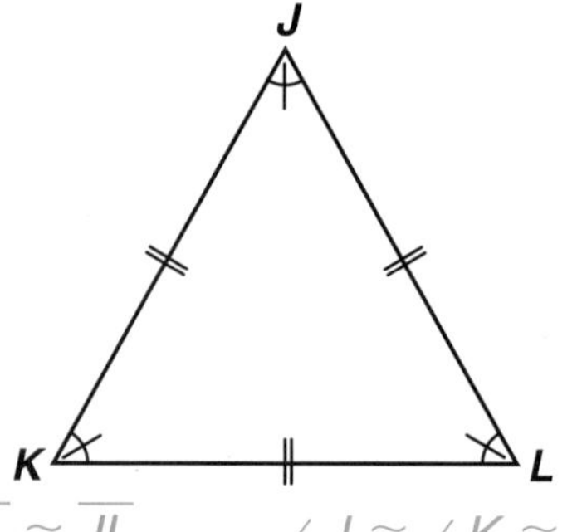

$\overline{JK} \cong \overline{KL} \cong \overline{JL}$ $\angle J \cong \angle K \cong \angle L$

Another Example

Squares

These squares are not congruent. They have the same shape, but they are not the same size.

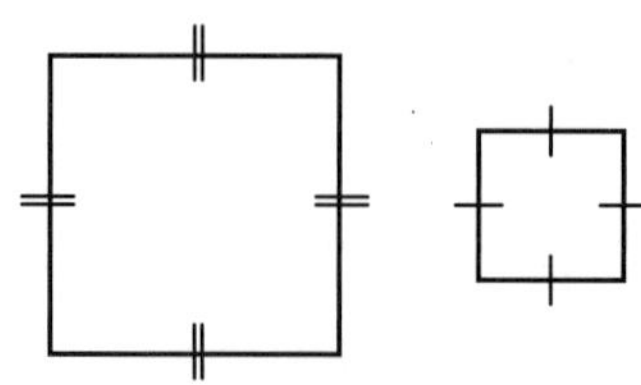

Guided Practice

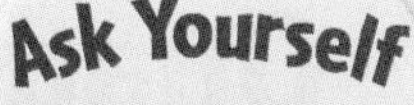

- Which sides are the same length?
- Which angles have the same measure?

Trace each figure. Mark the congruent sides and the congruent angles.

1. 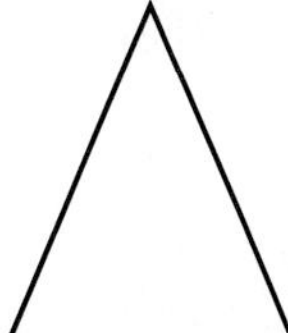

2. 

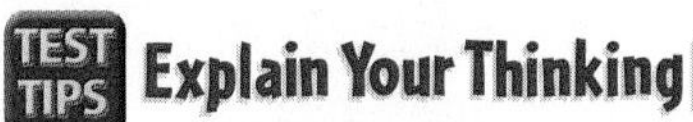

Draw three squares on a piece of paper. Can you divide each square differently into four congruent parts? Show your work.

Practice and Problem Solving

Trace each figure. Use a ruler to measure the sides and a protractor to measure the angles of each figure. Mark the congruent sides and angles.

3. 

4. 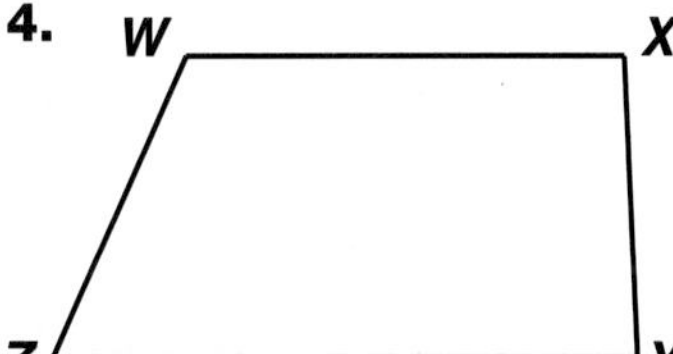

5. 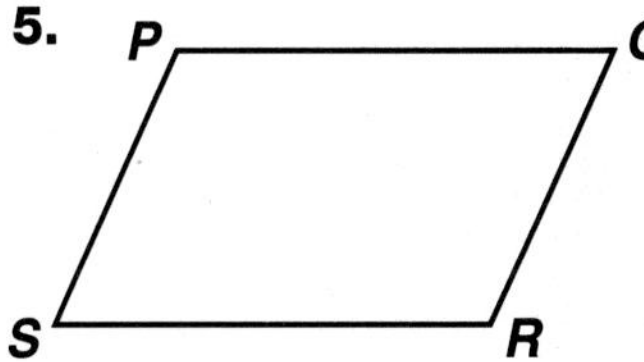

Use the diagram to answer the questions. Explain your reasoning.

6. What is the length of $\overline{DE}$?
7. What is the measure of $\angle A$?
8. What is the measure of $\angle F$?
9. What is the length of $\overline{DF}$?
10. What is the measure of $\angle D$?

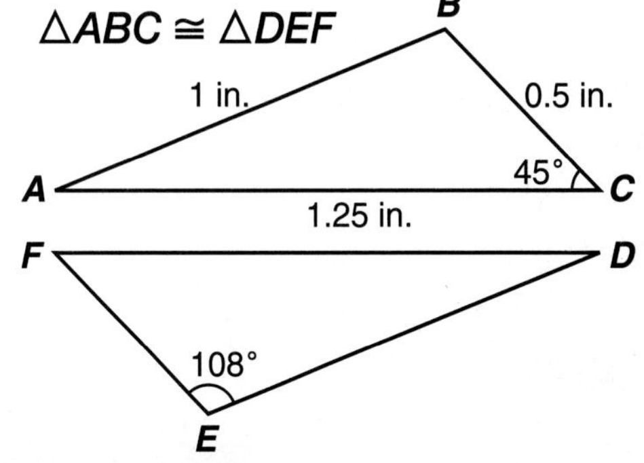

Daily Review | Test Prep

Find each statistic for the data below.
(Ch. 8, Lesson 2)

90, 75, 80, 80, 80

11. mean
12. range
13. mode
14. median

15. Which of the following statements is true?

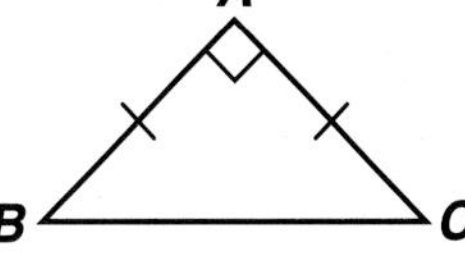

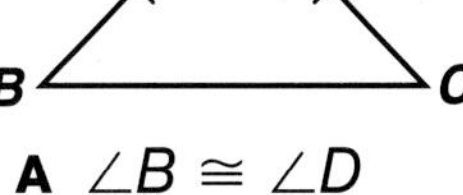

A $\angle B \cong \angle D$
B $\overline{AC} \cong \overline{DF}$
C $\overline{EF} \cong \overline{BC}$
D $\angle A \cong \angle D$

Extra Practice See page 419, Set C.

Lesson 5

Quadrilaterals and Other Polygons

Objective Identify, classify, and compare polygons.

e Glossary

Vocabulary

quadrilateral
polygon
regular polygon
diagonal

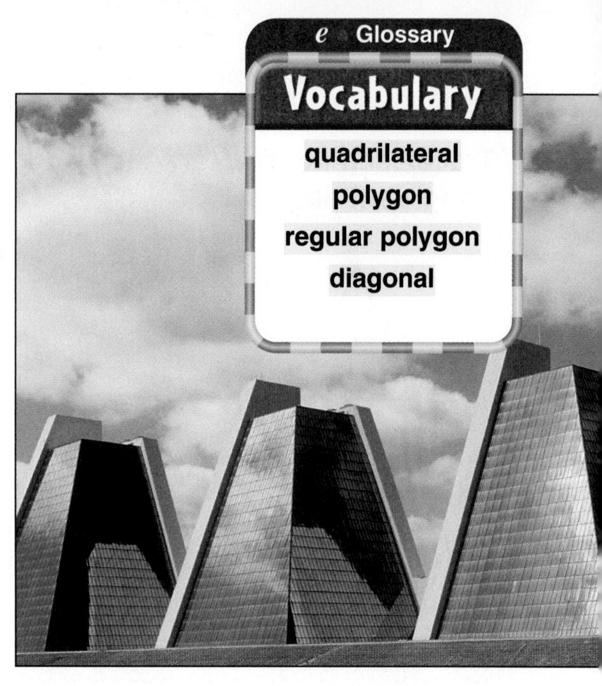

Learn About It

A **quadrilateral** is a four-sided figure. The sum of the angle measures in any quadrilateral is 360°. In a city you will see many things that are like quadrilaterals.

There are many different kinds of quadrilaterals. You can use sides and angles to classify them.

Classifying Quadrilaterals

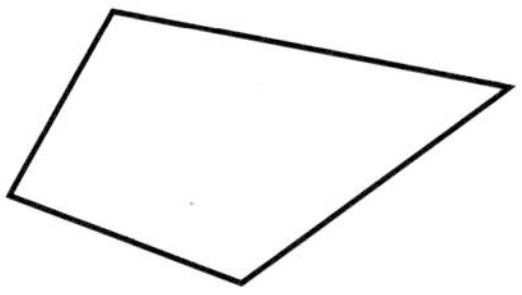

quadrilateral
four sides
four angles

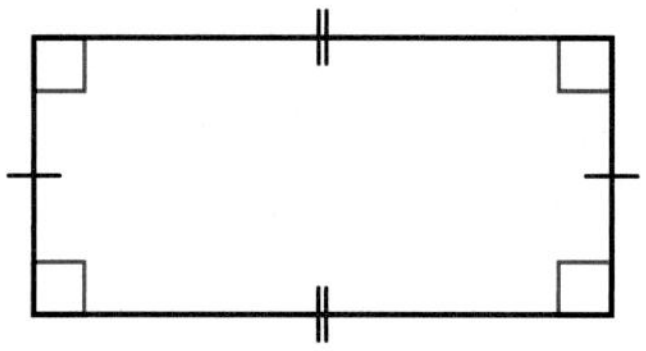

rectangle
opposite sides congruent
four right angles

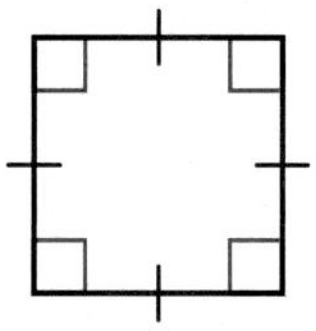

square
four congruent sides
four right angles

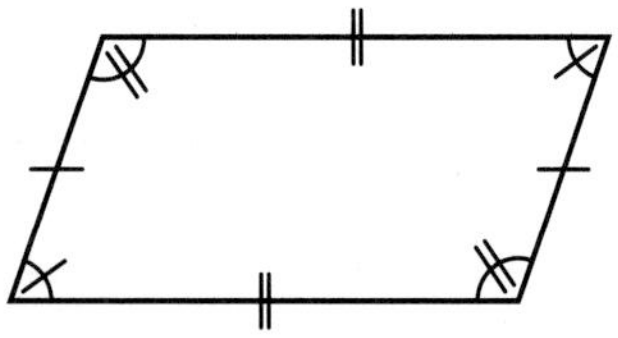

parallelogram
opposite sides congruent and parallel

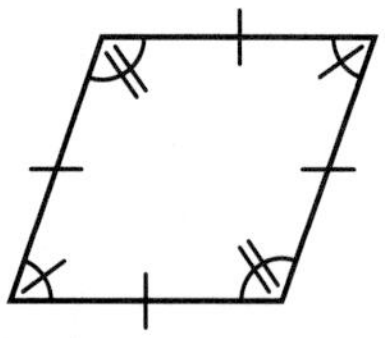

rhombus
four congruent sides
opposite sides parallel

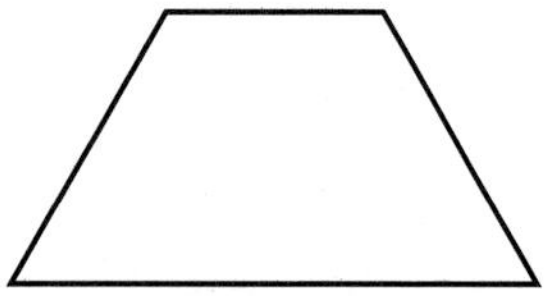

trapezoid
only one pair of parallel sides

A quadrilateral is one type of **polygon**. A polygon is a closed figure that has three or more sides. Each side is a line segment, and the sides meet only at their endpoints.

Polygons

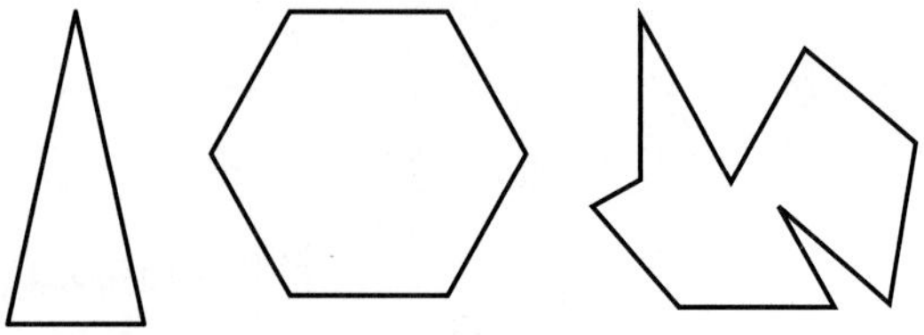

Not Polygons

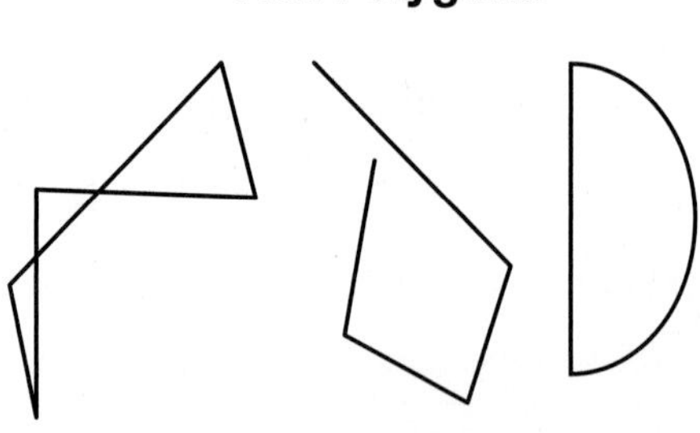

▶ A **regular polygon** is a polygon with all sides congruent and all angles congruent.

Polygons			
Name	**Examples**	**Name**	**Examples**
Triangle 3 sides		**Octagon** 8 sides	
Quadrilateral 4 sides		**Nonagon** 9 sides	
Pentagon 5 sides		**Decagon** 10 sides	
Hexagon 6 sides		**Undecagon** 11 sides	
Heptagon 7 sides		**Dodecagon** 12 sides	

▶ A **diagonal** of a polygon is a segment that joins two vertices of a polygon but is not a side.

$\overline{AD}$ and $\overline{BE}$ are two diagonals of this hexagon.

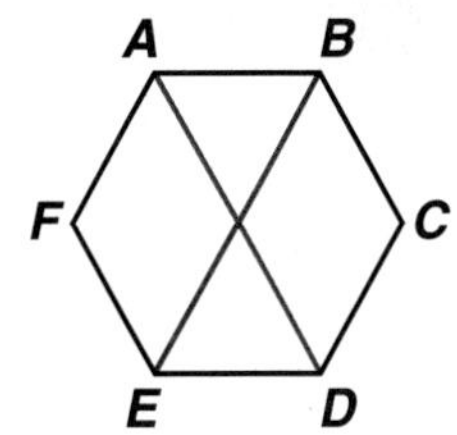

Go On

Guided Practice

Classify each polygon in as many ways as you can.

1. 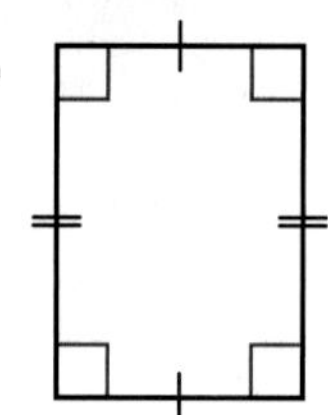

2. 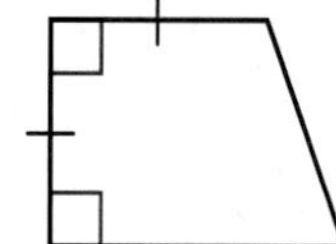

3. 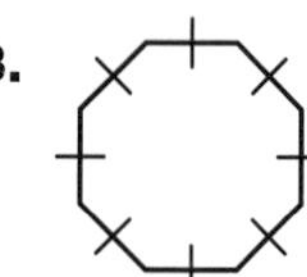

Ask Yourself

- How many sides does the polygon have?
- Are any sides parallel?
- Are any sides congruent?
- Are any angles congruent?

TEST TIPS **Explain Your Thinking** ▶ Use the drawing at the right to explain why the sum of the angle measures in a quadrilateral is 360°.

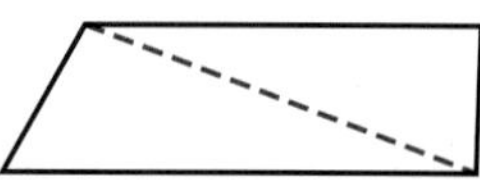

Practice and Problem Solving

Classify each polygon in as many ways as you can.

4. 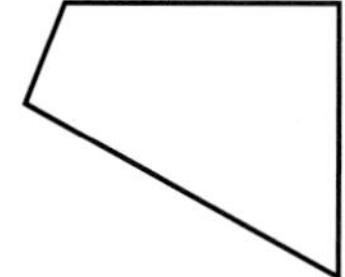

5. 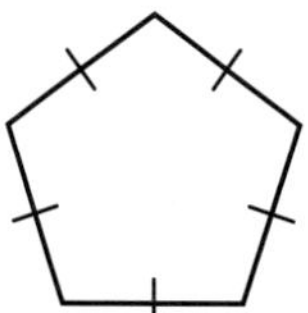

6. 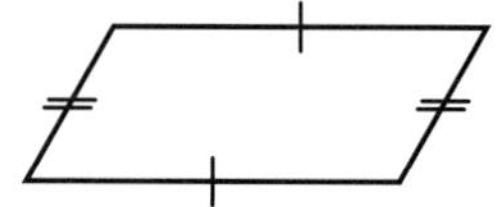

7. 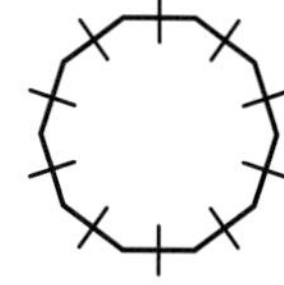

Write *polygon* or *not a polygon* to classify each figure. If possible, find the measure of each missing angle.

8. 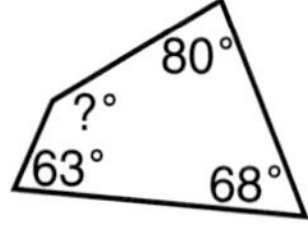

9. 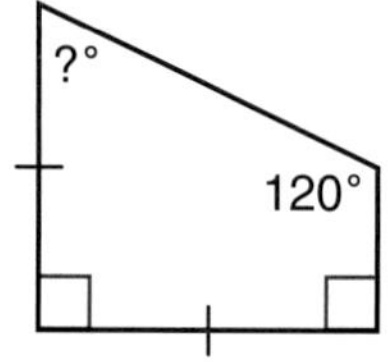

10. 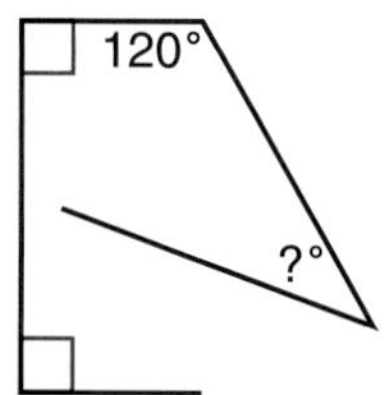

11. 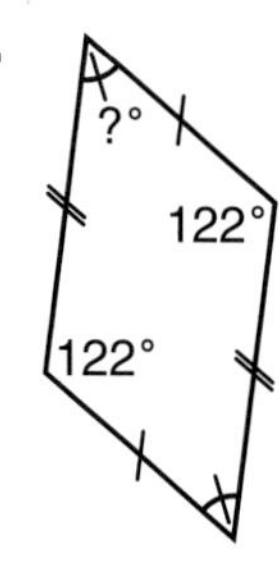

12. 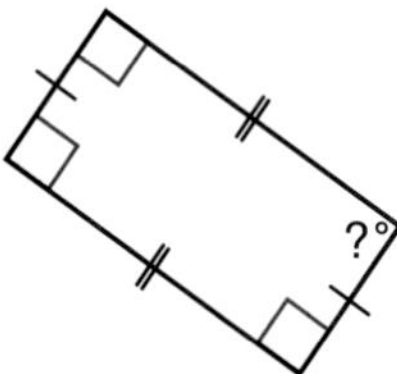

13. 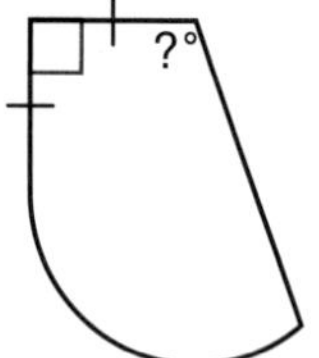

14. 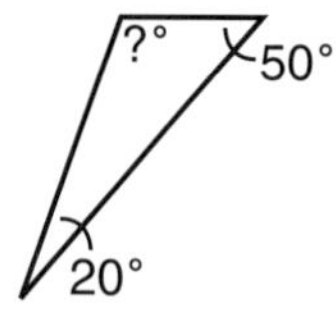

15. 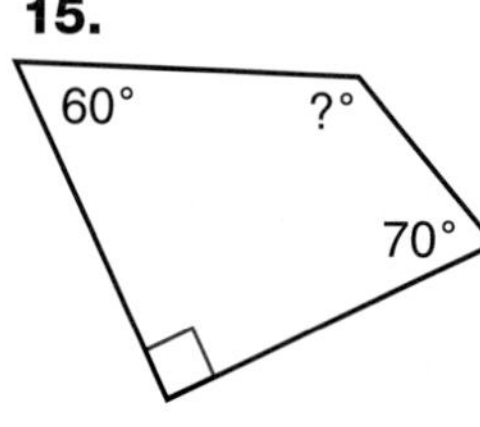

Solve.

16. **Represent** Draw a quadrilateral that is not a parallelogram and has two pairs of congruent sides.

18. **Analyze** Is every square a rhombus? Is every rhombus a square? Explain.

17. Draw several parallelograms, including special cases–squares, rectangles, and rhombi. For each figure draw the diagonals. In which kind of parallelogram are the diagonals perpendicular? congruent?

Extra Practice See page 419, Set D.

Quick Check

Check your understanding of Lessons 1–5.

Classify each figure in as many ways as possible. (Lessons 1–2)

1. 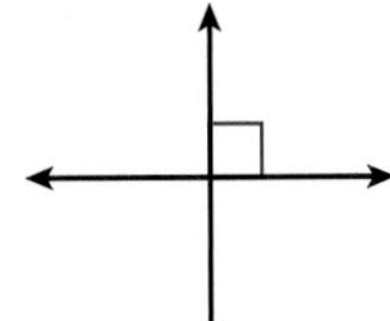

2. 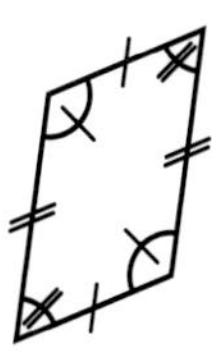

3. 

4. 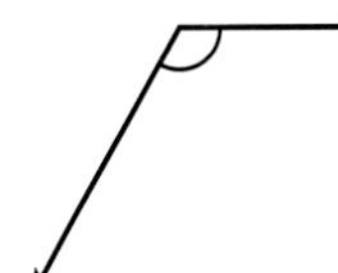

5. 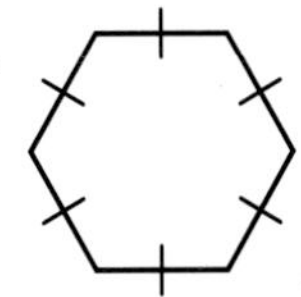

Find the missing angle measures. (Lessons 3–4)

6. 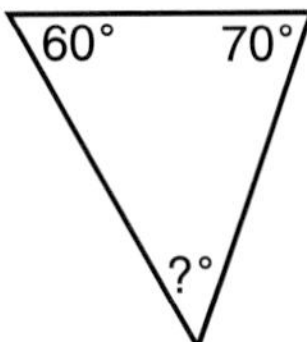

7. 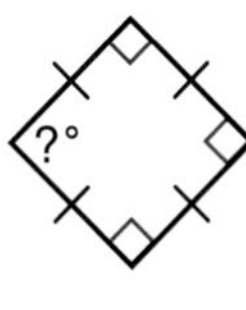

8. 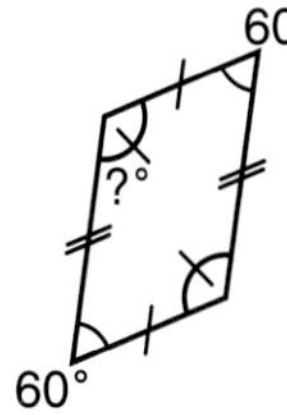

9. 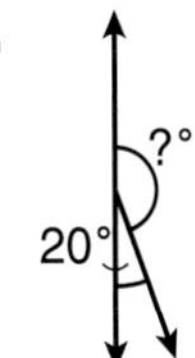

10. Are the figures in Exercises 2 and 8 congruent? Explain how you know. (Lesson 5)

Algebraic Thinking

Math Reasoning

Sum It Up

These figures show how to use triangles to determine the sum of the angle measures of a polygon.

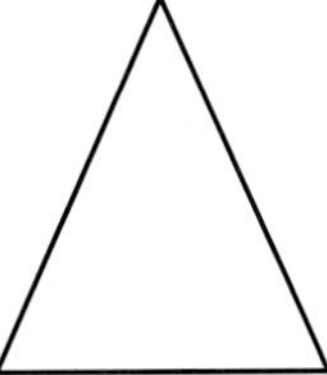

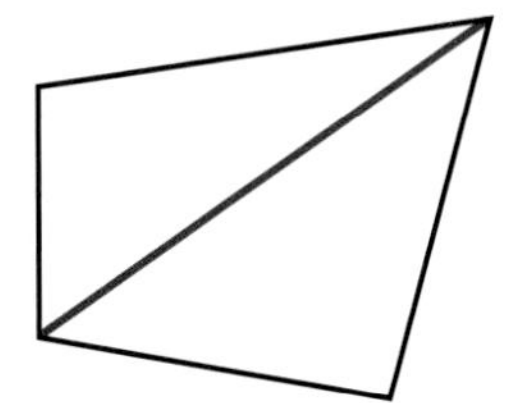

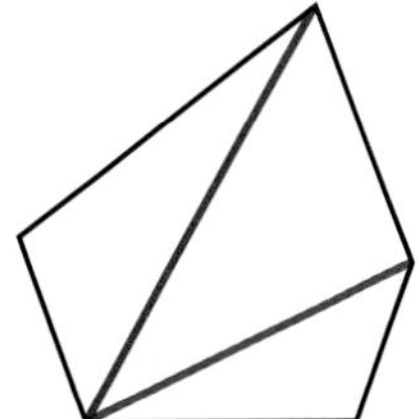

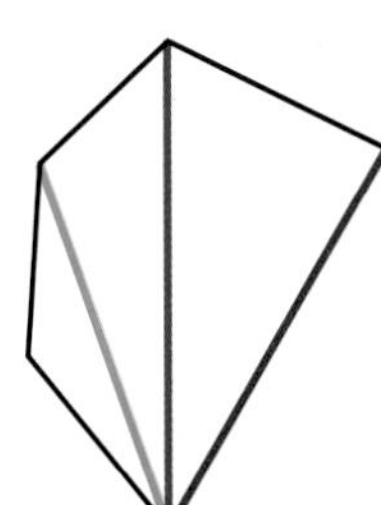

Use a table like the one shown to organize the information above.

1. Use the table to help you write a formula for finding the sum of the angle measures in any polygon.

2. Use your formula to find the number of degrees in an octagon.

Number of Sides	Number of Diagonals Drawn from One Vertex	Sum of Angles	180° × ?
3	0	180°	180° × ■
4	1	360°	180° × ■
5	2	540°	180° × ■
6	3	720°	180° × ■

Rotations, Reflections, and Translations

Objective Identify and model translations, rotations, and reflections.

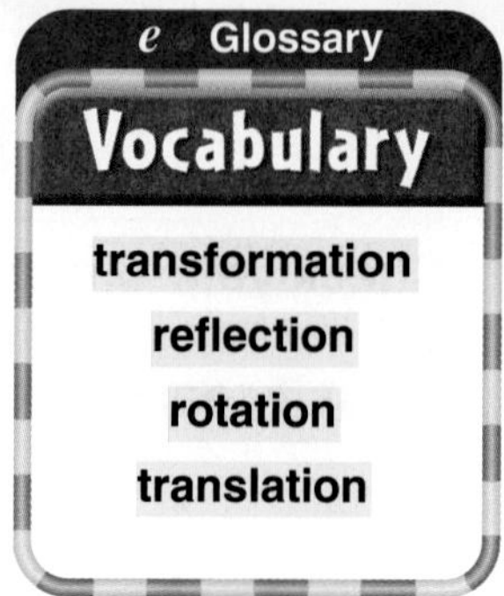

Work Together

Materials
grid paper
ruler

A **transformation** changes the position, but not the shape, of a plane figure. Reflections, rotations, and translations are three kinds of transformations.

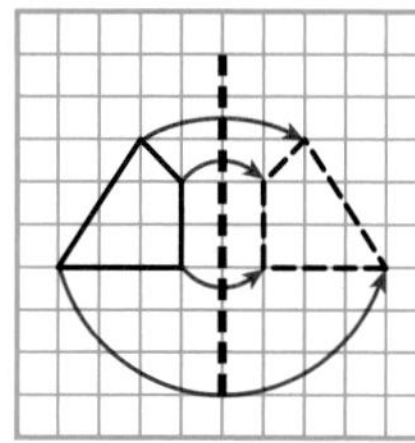

reflection
figure flips over a line

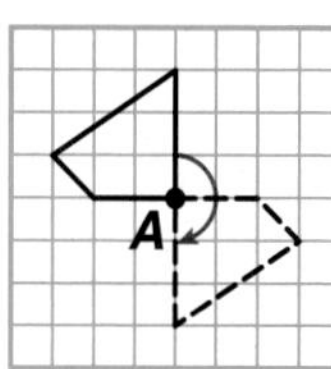

rotation
figure turns about a point

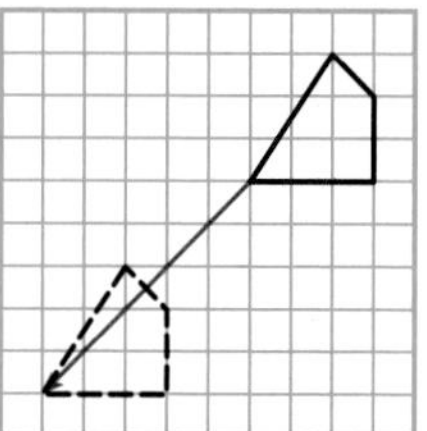

translation
figure slides a given distance in a given direction

You can describe a rotation using the 360° of a circle.

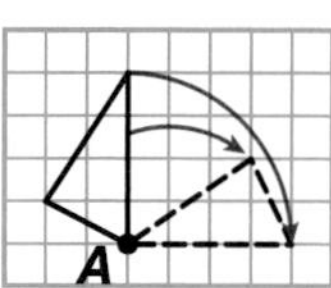

90°
a quarter turn clockwise about point *A*

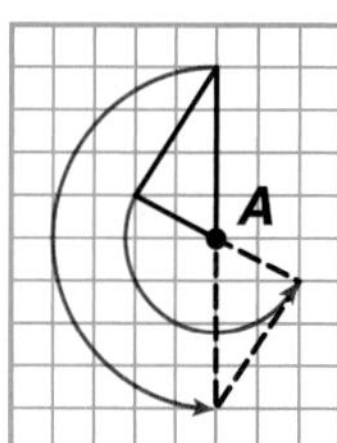

180°
a half turn counterclockwise about point *A*

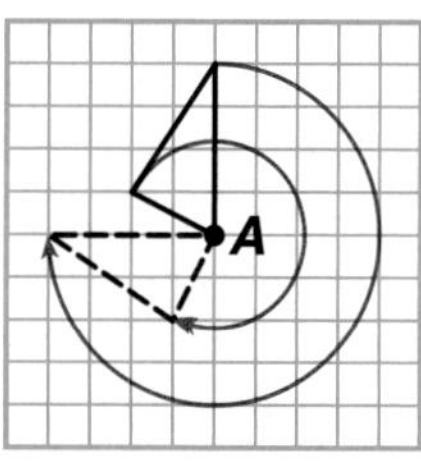

270°
a three-quarter turn clockwise about point *A*

Work with a partner to model transformations.

STEP 1 Use a ruler to draw a right triangle on grid paper. Shade and cut out the triangle.

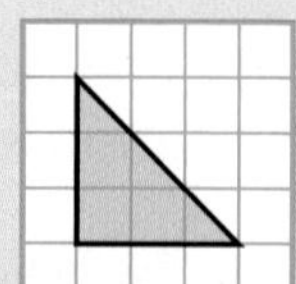

STEP 2 Outline the cut-out triangle on a new sheet of grid paper. Label the triangle with *A*. Then draw and label point *O* on the grid paper as shown.

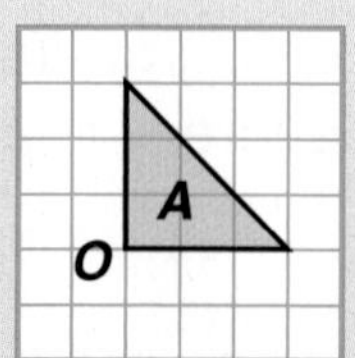

Rotate triangle *A* a half turn counterclockwise about point *O*. Outline the triangle. Label the triangle with *B*.

- What transformation did you perform?
- How many degrees did you rotate the triangle?

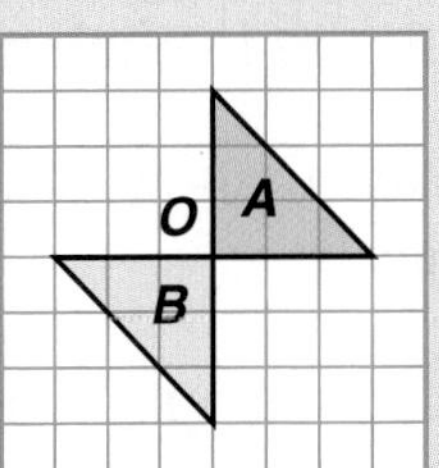

STEP 4

Now reflect triangle *B* across a vertical line through point *O*. Outline the triangle. Label the triangle with *C*.

- What transformation did you perform?

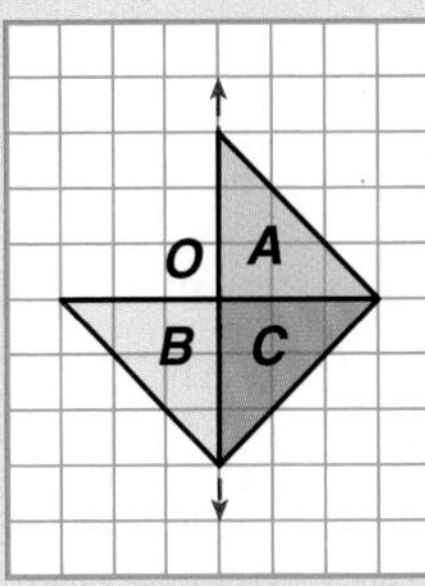

STEP 5

Rotate triangle *C* a half turn clockwise about point *O* as shown. Outline the triangle. Label the triangle with *D*.

- Is triangle *D* congruent to triangle *A*? Use a transformation to find out.
- Show another way to use reflections, rotations, or translations to transform triangle *A* into triangle *D*.

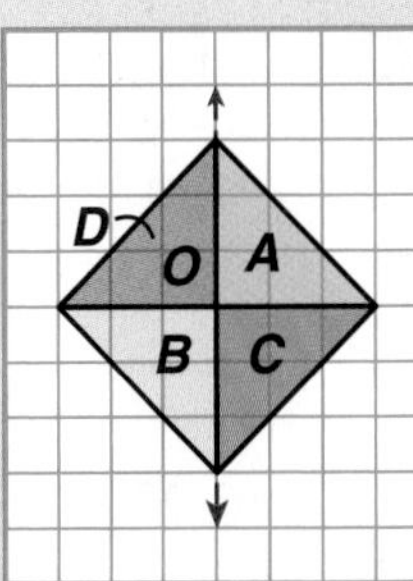

On Your Own

Tell whether each figure shows a translation, reflection, or rotation. If a figure shows a rotation, name the number of degrees of rotation.

1.

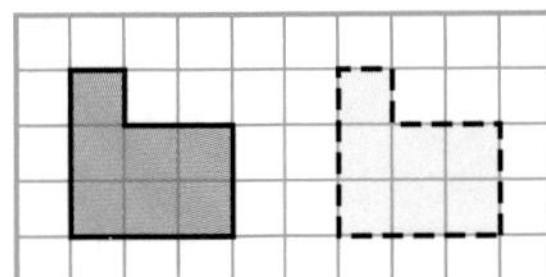

2.

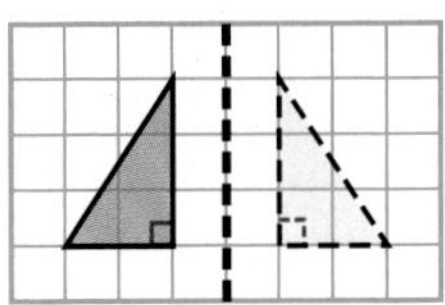

3.

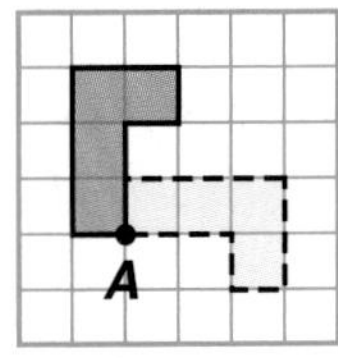

Copy each figure onto grid paper. Then complete the given transformation.

4.

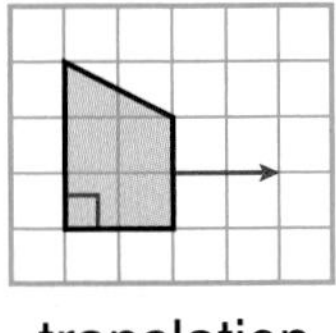

translation

5.

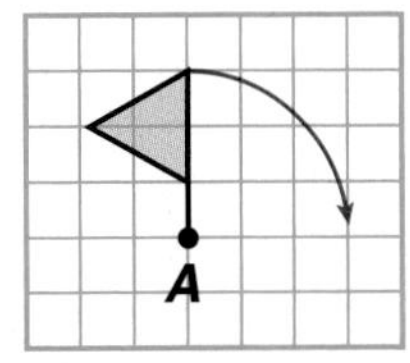

rotation of 90° clockwise

6.

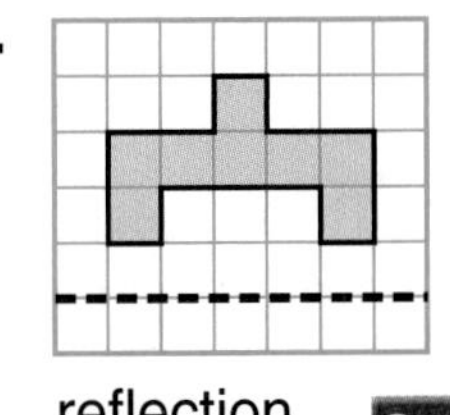

reflection

On grid paper, copy triangle *A*. Label point *O*. Draw and label the figure in each new position for Exercises 7–11.

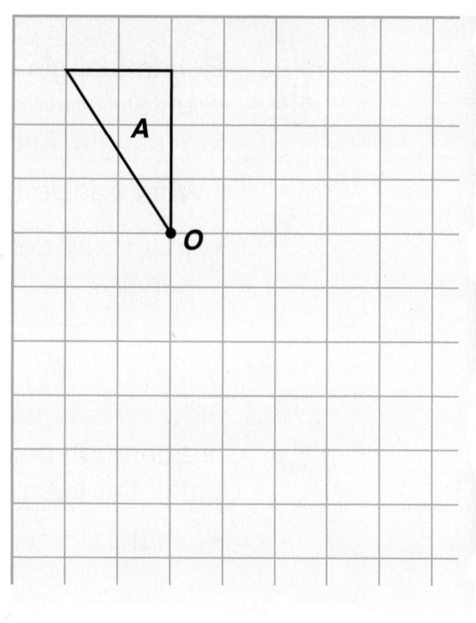

7. Translate triangle *A* 2 units to the right. Label the new triangle *B*.
8. Translate triangle *A* 5 units down. Label the new triangle *C*.
9. Rotate triangle *A* 90° counterclockwise about point *O*. Label the new triangle *D*.
10. Reflect triangle D across a vertical line through point *O*. Label the new triangle *E*.
11. What one transformation can be used to move triangle *A* to the position shown by triangle *E*?

12. Which picture shows a reflection of the shaded figure?

a. 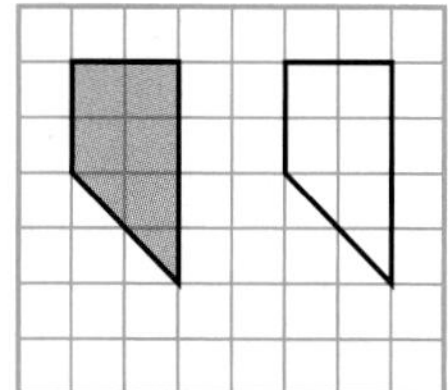

b. 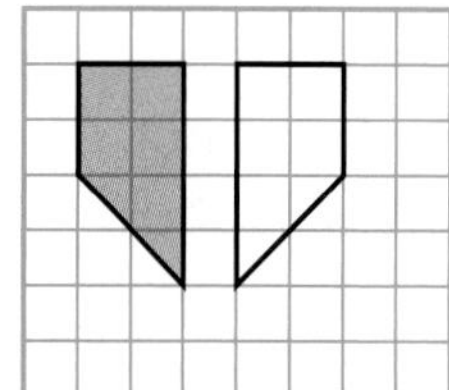

c. 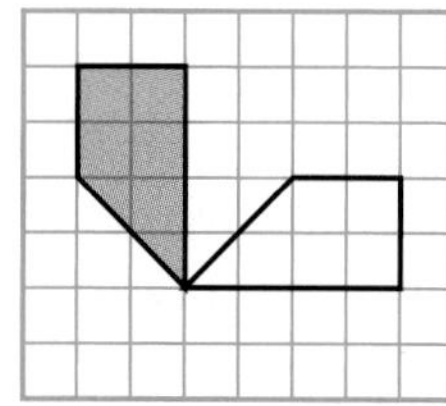

d. 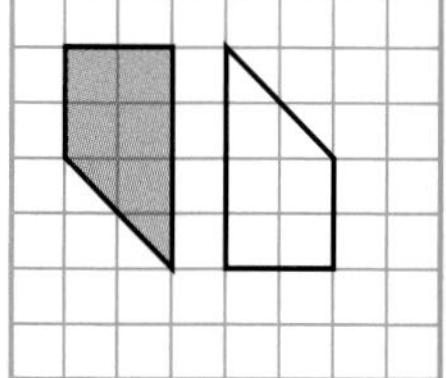

13. Which picture shows a rotation of the shaded figure?

a. 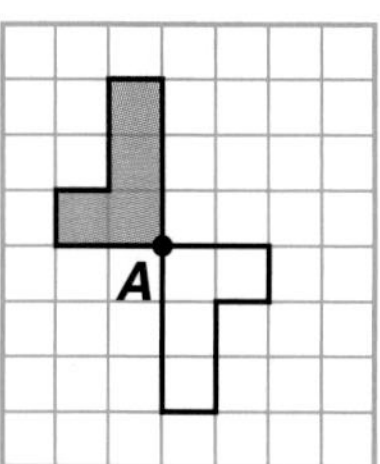

b. 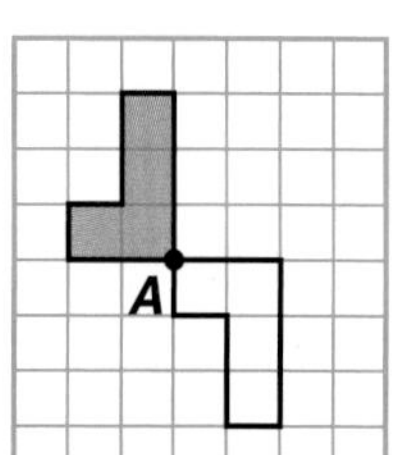

c. 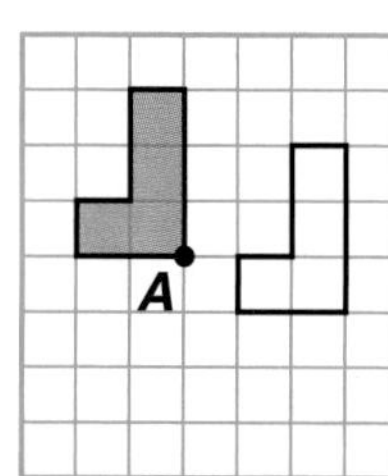

d. 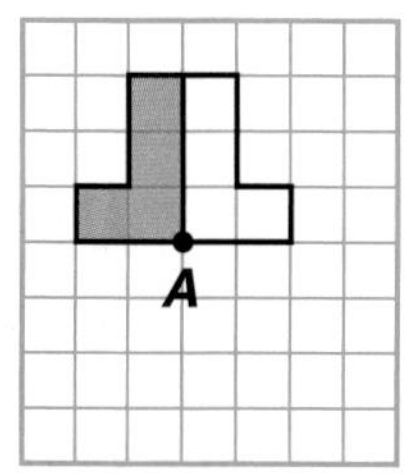

14. Which picture shows a translation of the shaded figure?

a. 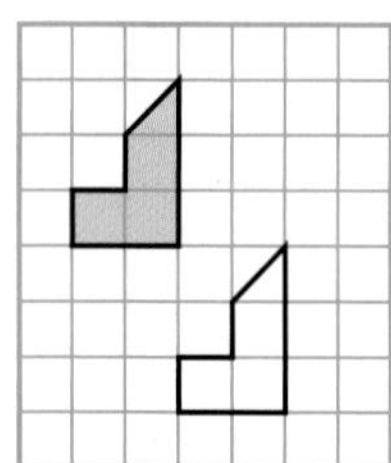

b. 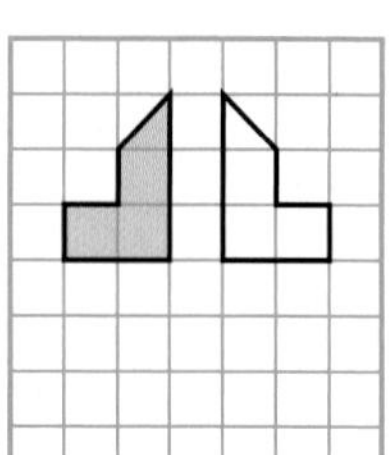

c. 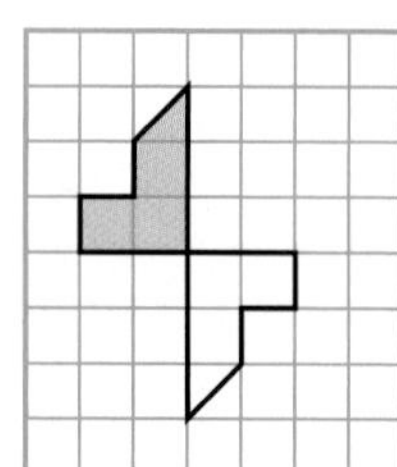

d. 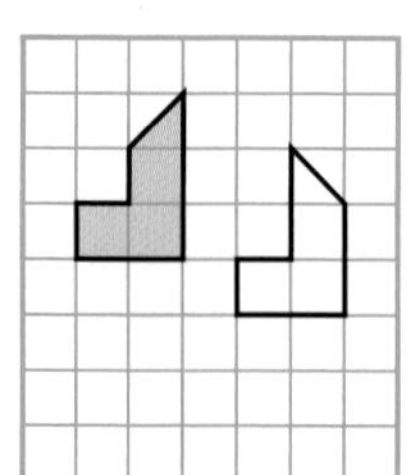

15. **Represent** Donya says that reflecting a right triangle across its base is the same as rotating it 180° about its right angle. Is she right? Draw a diagram to explain.

16. **Create and Solve** Draw a design on grid paper. Write steps to change the design using rotations, reflections, and translations. Draw the solution.

Talk About It • Write About It

You learned how to identify and model reflections, rotations, and translations.

17. Explain how reflections and rotations are alike and different. Use words or a diagram.

18. Explain how rotations, reflections, and translations can help you decide if two figures are congruent.

Tangrams

2 players

What You'll Need • Learning Tool 52 or a set of tangram pieces like the ones shown.

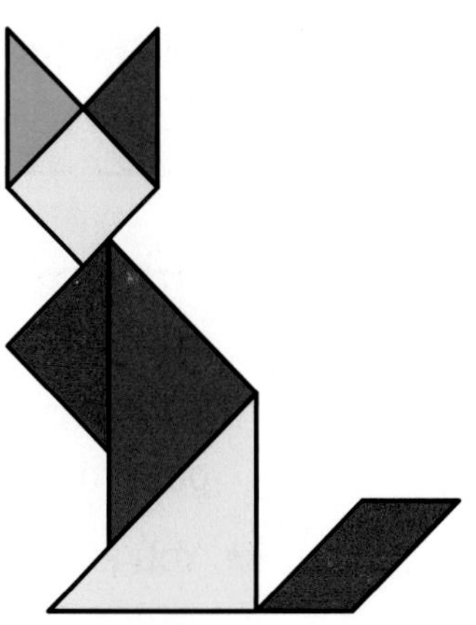

How to Play

1. If you don't have tangrams or Learning Tool 9, you can make your own pieces by tracing the ones on this page and cutting them out.
2. The first player makes a shape with the tangram pieces and traces its outline. The pieces should not overlap. At least some of them should be placed edge to edge.
3. The pieces are removed and mixed up. The second player must decide how to arrange the pieces within the outline, without any overlapping pieces.
4. Take turns repeating Steps 2 and 3.

You may want to make a sketch of your design to help you remember it if your partner can't solve the puzzle.

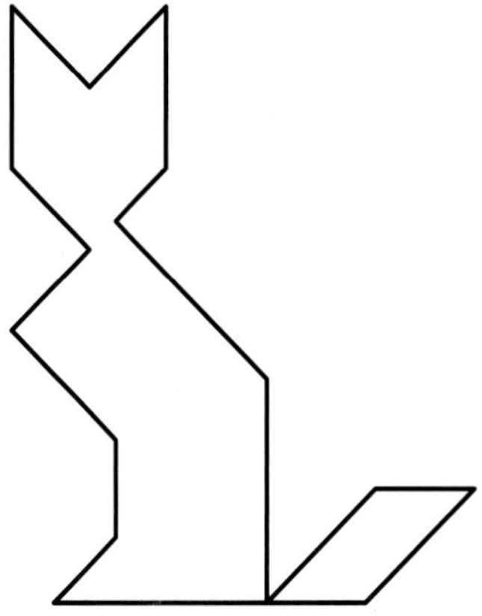

Problem-Solving Strategy

Make a Model

Objective Make models to solve tessellation problems.

Problem In social studies class, Vi and her classmates have been studying tessellation patterns from a dome on a building. A tessellation is a repeating pattern that covers a plane without gaps or overlaps. Vi made a tile using four trapezoid pattern blocks. Will Vi's pattern tessellate?

UNDERSTAND

This is what you know:

- A tessellation is a repeating pattern that covers a plane without gaps or overlaps.
- There are four trapezoids in the pattern.

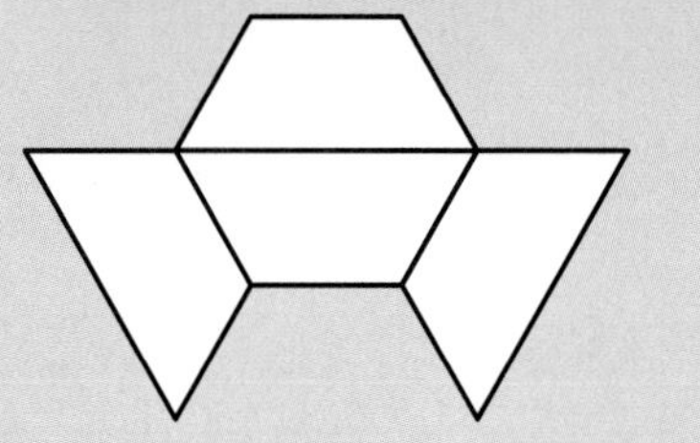

PLAN

You can make a model to help you solve the problem.

SOLVE

- Use pattern blocks to make a model of Vi's pattern. Trace the pattern and cut it out.
- You know that a translation moves a figure a given distance in a given direction. So you can translate the pattern to begin the tessellation.
- You know that you can rotate figures 180°. So use rotation to fill in the gaps.

Solution: Vi's pattern tessellates.

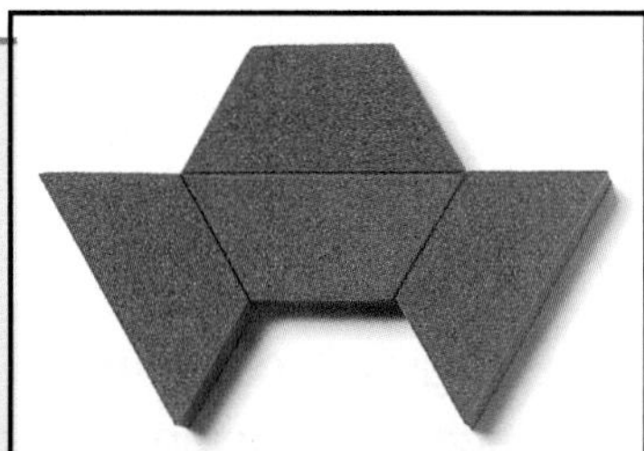

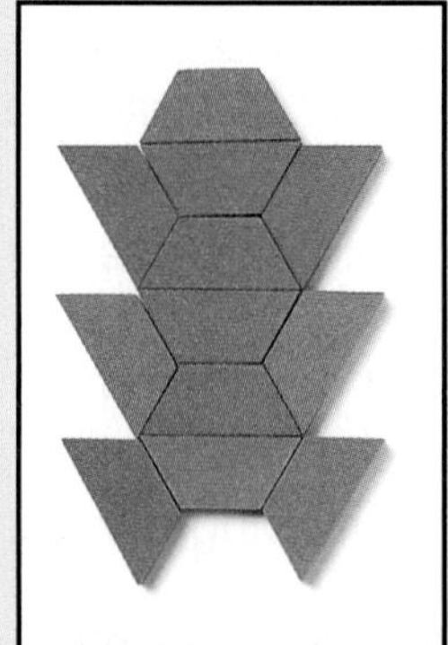

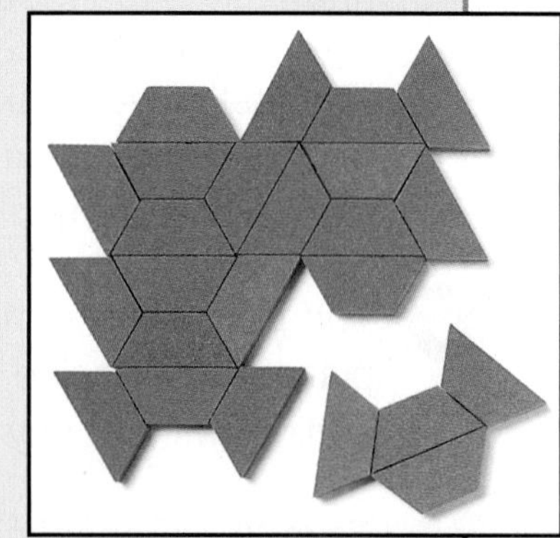

LOOK BACK

Look back at the problem. Can you use a different strategy to check the answer?

MathTracks 2/11
Listen and Understand

Guided Practice

Use the Ask Yourself questions to help you solve each problem.

1. Hamid cut a small square from one side of a large square and translated it to the other side of the square. Will Hamid's pattern tessellate?

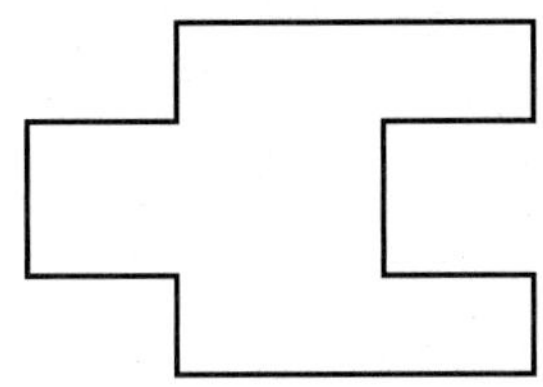

2. Jan cut out two pentagons. Only one pentagon tessellates. Which one is it?

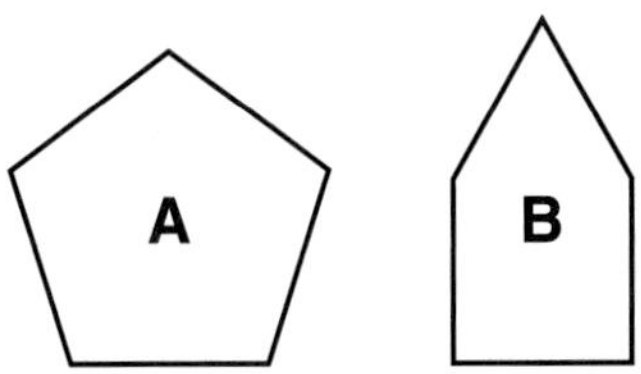

Hint To tessellate, the sum of the angles that meet must be 360°.

UNDERSTAND **What facts do I know?**

PLAN **Did I make a model?**

Did I use transformations to test if the patterns fit together?

SOLVE
- **Did I repeat the pattern enough so I could see if it tessellated?**
- **Did I tile the plane without gaps or overlaps?**

LOOK BACK **Did I solve the problem?**

TEST TIPS

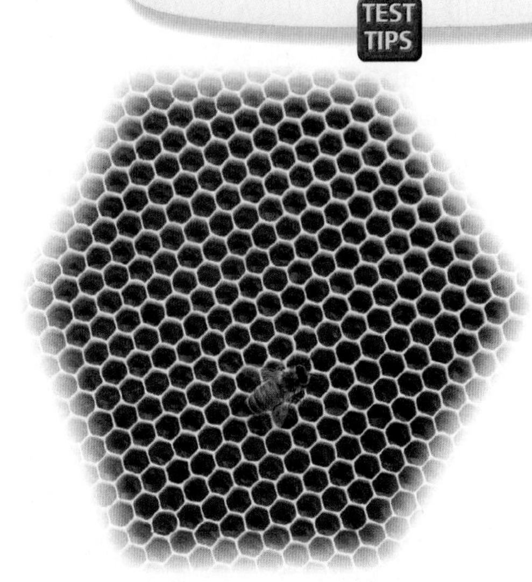

Independent Practice

Make a model to solve each problem.

3. **Explain** Brittany designed this pattern. Will it tessellate? Explain why or why not.

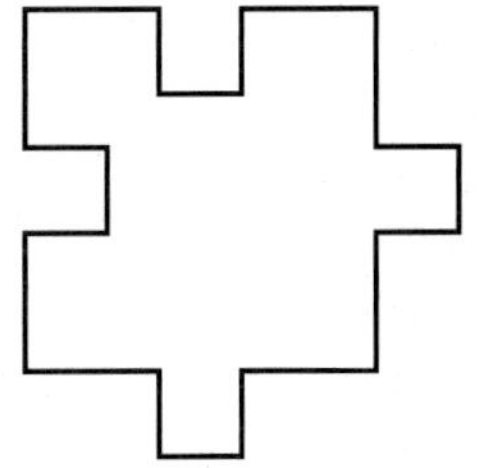

4. **What's Wrong?** Ricky said that a regular octagon will tessellate. Is he right or wrong? How do you know?

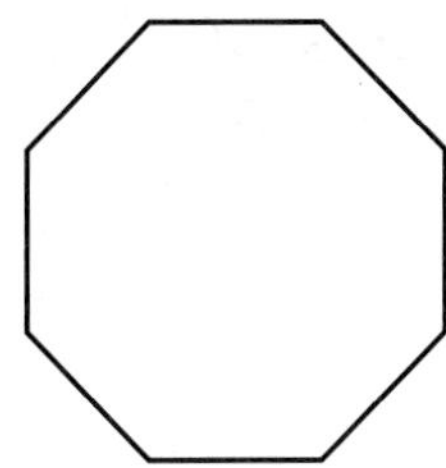

5. **Create and Solve** Start with a rectangle. Create a pattern that will tessellate. Then create a different pattern that will not tessellate. Trade patterns with a classmate. Then tell which of the two patterns will tessellate.

Choose a Strategy

Solve. Show your work. Tell what strategy you used.

PROBLEM-SOLVING Strategies

- Use Models
- Draw a Diagram
- Find a Pattern
- Guess and Check
- Make an Organized List
- Make a Table
- Solve a Simpler Problem
- Use Logical Reasoning
- Work Backward
- Write an Equation

6. A panel of 5 architects sit in a row. Juan is to the right of Mike. Mavis is to the left of Tara. Mike is on Yuki's right. Juan is on one end. Name their order from left to right.

7. What's Wrong? Bob says that any triangle will tessellate. Is Bob right or wrong? Explain why.

8. A building has 264 windows. There are three times as many rectangular windows as circular windows. How many of each kind of window are there?

9. Lita uses cubes to design a building. For the top four layers she uses 1, 2, 4, and 8 cubes. If she continues this way, which layer will use more than 100 cubes?

The graph at the right shows the tolls to be paid for crossing the George Washington Bridge going into New York. Use the graph for Problems 10–13.

10. Sue drives her car into New York each Saturday afternoon. How much will she save in 4 weeks if she gets an E-Z Pass instead of paying cash?

11. Bena just got her E-Z Pass bill. She made 5 trips into the city for a cost of $21. How many peak and off-peak trips was that?

12. A car with an E-Z pass has 4 passengers. They travel into New York during peak hours 5 weekdays each week. If they share the cost of the tolls equally, how much do they each pay at the end of each week?

13. Max does not have an E-Z Pass for his 2-axle dual rear-wheel truck, but he does have one for his car. He went to New York twice in off-peak hours with each vehicle. How much more did it cost to drive the truck in?

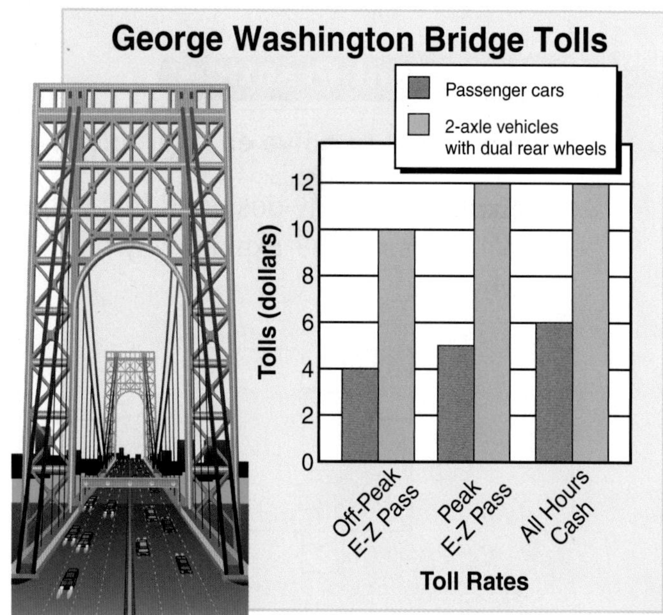

Peak hours: 6–9 A.M. and 4–7 P.M. on weekdays; 12 noon–8 P.M. on weekends

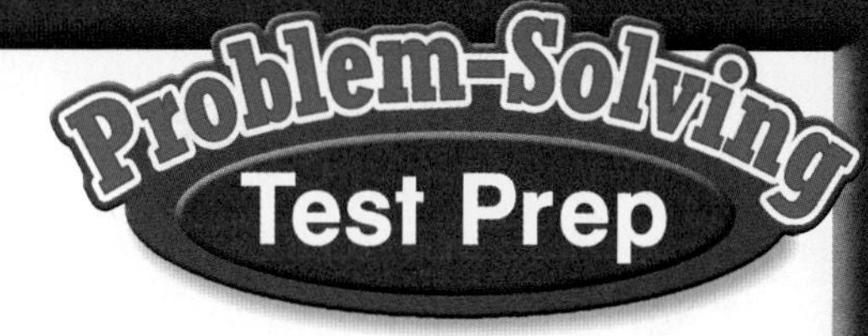

Choose the letter of the correct answer.
If a correct answer is not here, choose NH.

1. Use your ruler to measure the length of the segment to the nearest centimeter. How many centimeters less than a meter is this?

A 1 centimeter
B 6 centimeters
C 94 centimeters
D NH

(Chapter 6, Lesson 4)

2. In a skyscraper, the first floor is 20 feet tall. All the other floors are 12.5 feet. On which floor is the ceiling 70 feet off the ground?

F 3rd **G** 4th **H** 5th **J** 6th

(Chapter 1, Lesson 6)

3. A new building has 3 offices for rent. It has $\frac{1}{3}$ more offices than that already rented. It has twice as many offices under construction than already rented. How many offices are under construction?

A 1 office
B 3 offices
C 5 offices
D 8 offices

(Chapter 5, Lesson 3)

4.

Ann's office is 2 doors down from Ed's. Jill's office is 1 door to the left of Ed's and 2 doors to the right of Jim's. Who has Office 2?

F Ann
G Ed
H Jill
J Jim

(Chapter 3, Lesson 3)

5. A toll bridge charges $1.50 for a vehicle with 4 tires. It charges $0.25 more for each extra tire. Which expression shows how to find the toll for an 18-wheel truck?

A $(\$1.50 + \$0.25) \times 18$
B $(\$1.50 \times 18) + \$0.25$
C $(4 \times \$1.50) + (\$0.25 \times 18)$
D NH

(Chapter 3, Lesson 1)

6. The greatest common factor of two numbers is 4. Their least common multiple is 120. Their sum is 52. What are the numbers?

Explain Show how to use a Venn diagram to solve the problem.

(Chapter 9, Lesson 7)

7. Angie said that all quadrilaterals tessellate. She drew these quadrilaterals to prove she is correct.

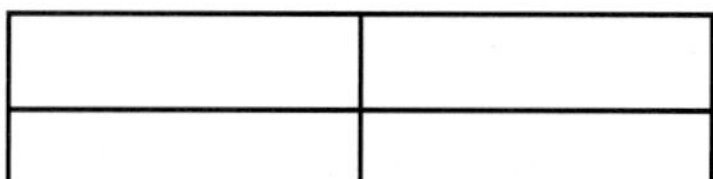

Do all quadrilaterals tessellate?

Represent Support your solution by making a model or drawing a picture.

(Chapter 15, Lesson 7)

Test Prep on the Net
Check Out *Education Place* at **eduplace.com/kids/mw/** for test prep practice.

Circles

Objective Draw circles and construct and identify parts of a circle.

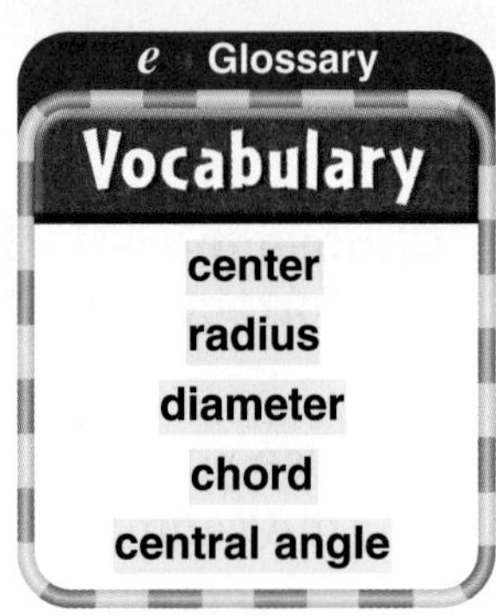

Materials
safe drawing compass
straightedge

Work Together

A circle is the set of all points in a plane that are the same distance from a given point called the **center**. A safe drawing compass and straightedge can be used to draw a circle and the parts of that circle.

Follow these steps to draw a circle with center *A* and to measure and identify parts of a circle.

- Draw a point and label it *A*. This is the center of the circle.
- Place the pivot point of your compass on point *A* and move the slider to any measure.
- Insert your pencil in one of the holes in the slider and draw a circle.

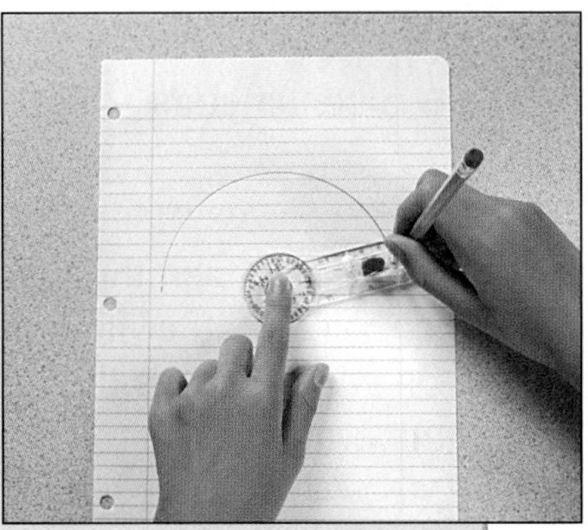

A **radius** is a segment that connects the center of a circle to any point on the circle. To draw a radius,

- Label point *B* on the circle.
- Connect *A* and *B* to draw radius $\overline{AB}$.

The plural of *radius* is *radii.* How many radii can a circle have?

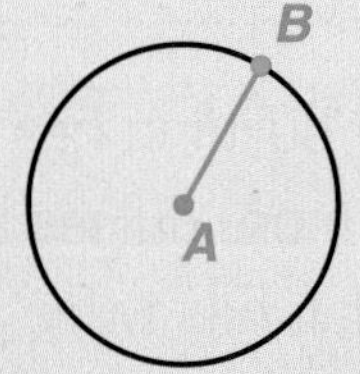

A **diameter** is a segment that connects two points on the circle and passes through the center of the circle. To draw a diameter,

- Draw point *C*. Connect *C* to *A* and extend the segment until it intersects the circle. Label that point *D*.
- $\overline{CD}$ is a diameter.

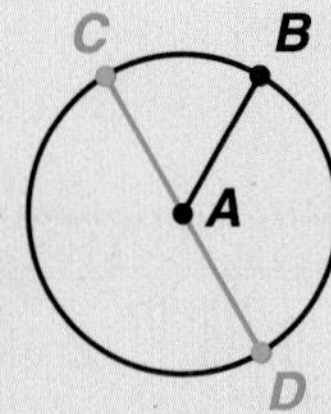

A **chord** is any segment that connects two points on the circle. To draw a chord,

- Draw points *E* and *F* on the circle.
- Draw chord $\overline{EF}$.

Is a diameter of a circle also a chord of that circle?

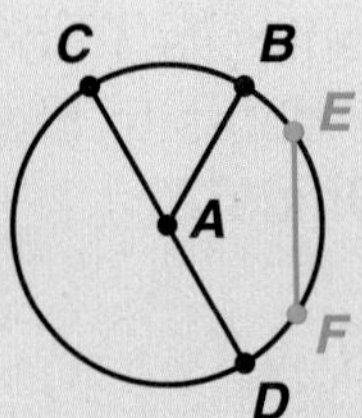

A **central angle** is an angle with its vertex at the center of the circle. To identify a central angle,

- Look for an angle whose vertex is the center point of the circle.
- ∠CAB is a central angle.

Name another central angle of the circle.

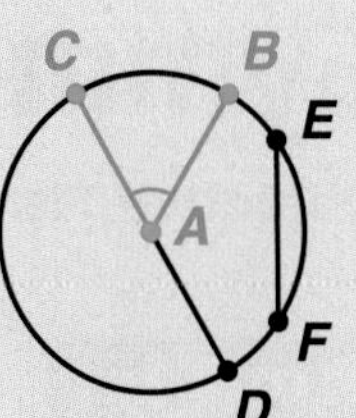

On Your Own

Use symbols to identify the following parts of this circle.

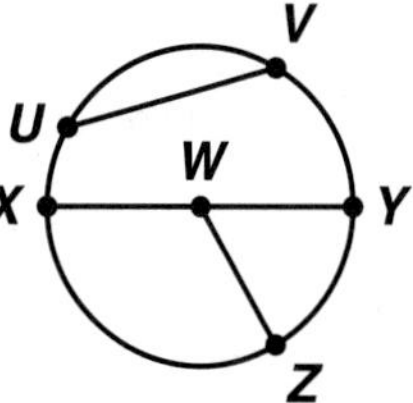

1. radii
2. chords
3. diameter
4. central angles

Classify each figure as a radius, diameter, chord, or central angle. Indicate if more than one term applies.

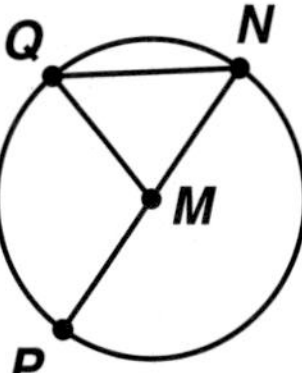

5. $\overline{MP}$
6. $\overline{MQ}$
7. ∠*NMQ*
8. $\overline{QN}$
9. $\overline{NP}$
10. ∠*QMP*

On a separate sheet of paper, construct a circle that contains all of the following.

11. center *B*
12. radius $\overline{BC}$
13. diameter $\overline{RL}$
14. central angle *RBH*
15. chord $\overline{CL}$
16. chord $\overline{RH}$
17. For the circle at the right, write a number sentence that can be used to find the missing angle measures. Then solve.

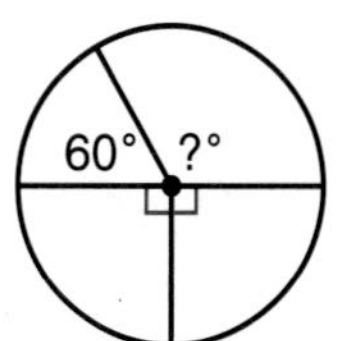

Talk About It • Write About It

18. How are a radius and a diameter of a circle related?
19. **Analyze** A diameter forms two central angles of a circle. What is the sum of the measures of these central angles?

Lesson 9

Symmetry

Objective Identify rotational and line symmetry.

e Glossary

Vocabulary

rotational symmetry

line symmetry

Learn About It

MathTracks 2/12
Listen and Understand

Suppose the blades of this windmill make a half turn (180°). How will the appearance of the windmill compare to the way it looks in this picture?

If you can turn a figure less than a full turn about a fixed point and the figure looks exactly the way it did before the turn, that figure has **rotational symmetry.**

Try this activity to explore rotational symmetry.

Remember

full turn = 360°

$\frac{1}{2}$ turn = 180°

$\frac{1}{4}$ turn = 90°

Materials: ruler, unlined paper, compass, scissors

STEP 1 Trace the hexagon at the right and cut it out.

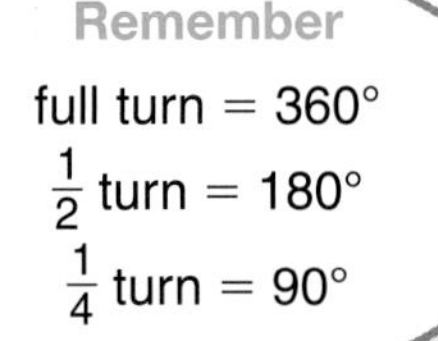

STEP 2 Use a ruler and a compass to draw a circle as shown at the right. Label the circle as shown.

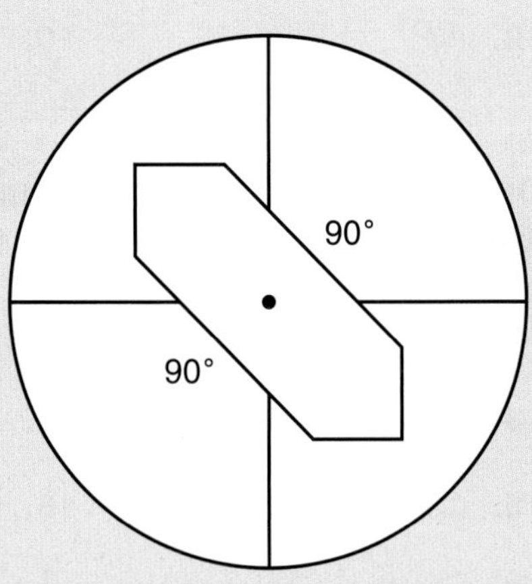

STEP 3 Place the point in the hexagon on the center of the circle. With the point of your pencil, hold the figure at the center point. With your other hand, slowly rotate the figure.

STEP 4 Continue turning until the figure matches the original image.

- What kind of turn resulted in a figure that matched the original image? How many degrees is this?
- Does the hexagon have rotational symmetry?

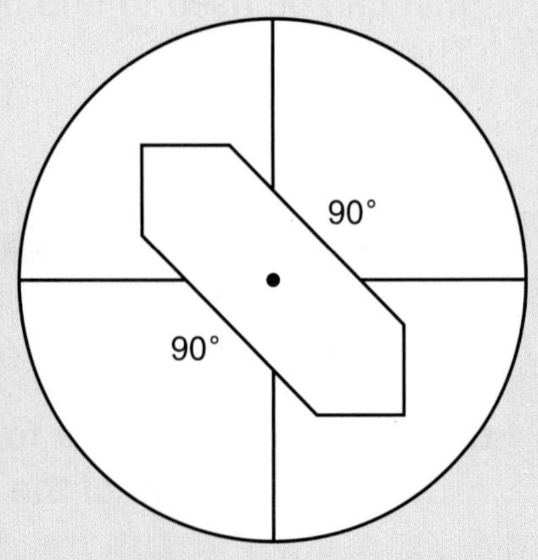

If a figure can be folded in half, and the two halves are congruent, the figure has **line symmetry**. The fold is called a line of symmetry.

Try this activity to explore line symmetry.

STEP 1 Use a sheet of rectangular paper.

STEP 2 Try to fold the rectangle in as many ways as possible so that both halves are congruent.

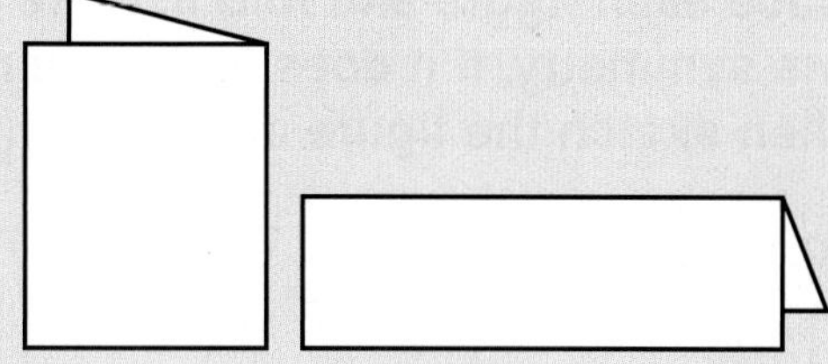

Your rectangle has two lines of symmetry. Draw dashed lines to show the lines of symmetry.

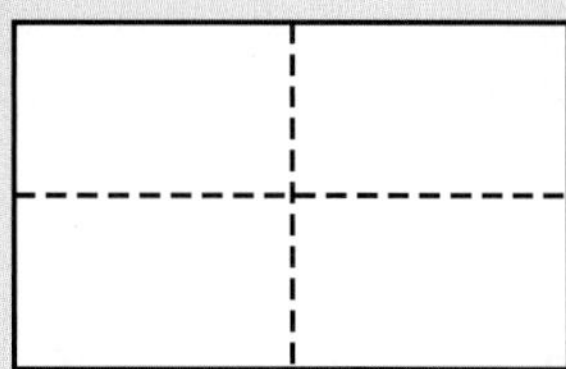

- Can a figure have more than one line of symmetry?
- Try this activity with a square. How many lines of symmetry does a square have?

Guided Practice

Ask Yourself

- Does this figure look exactly the way it did before the turn?
- How many degrees are in a full turn? a half turn? a quarter turn?

Trace each figure and turn it. Write *yes* or *no* to tell if it has rotational symmetry. If it does, tell how many degrees you turned it.

1. 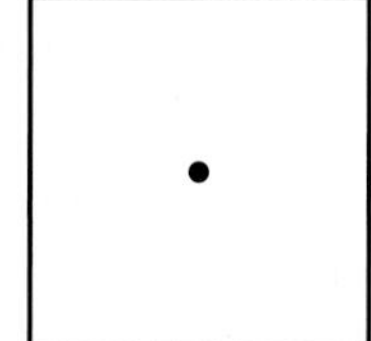

2. 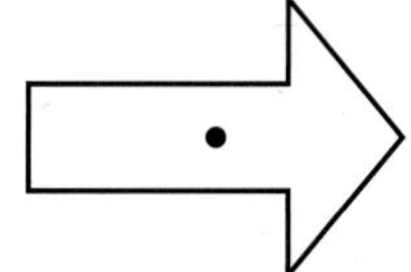

Trace each figure and fold it. Write *yes* or *no* to tell if it has line symmetry. If it does, write the number of lines of symmetry it has.

3. 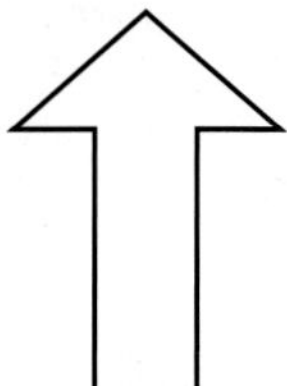

4. 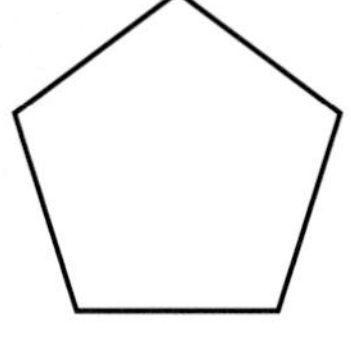

5. 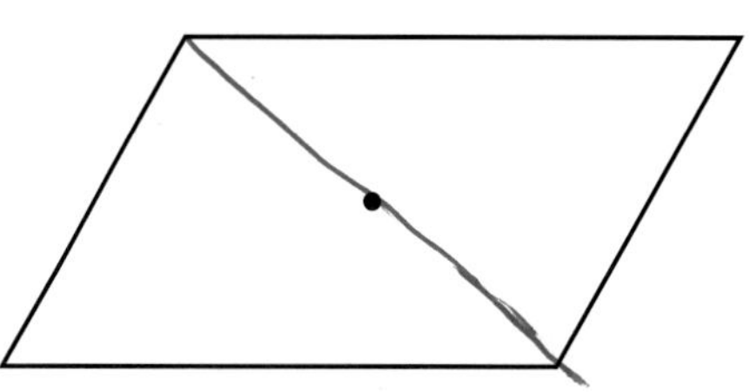

Can a figure have both line and rotational symmetry? Give an example to support your thinking.

Practice and Problem Solving

Trace each figure and turn it. Write *yes* or *no* to tell if it has rotational symmetry. If it does, tell how many degrees you turned it.

6. 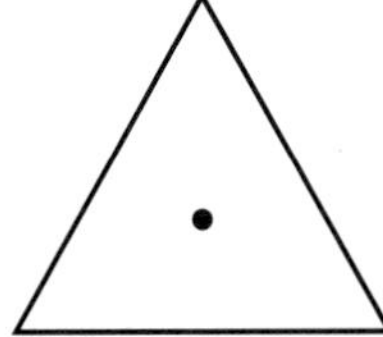

7. 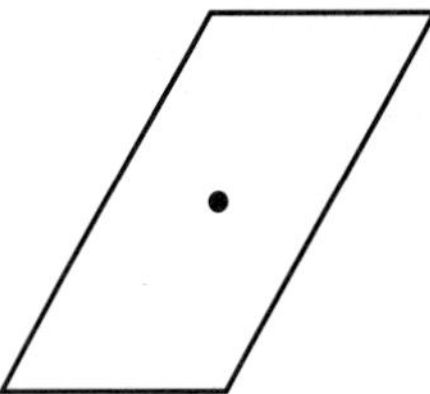

8. 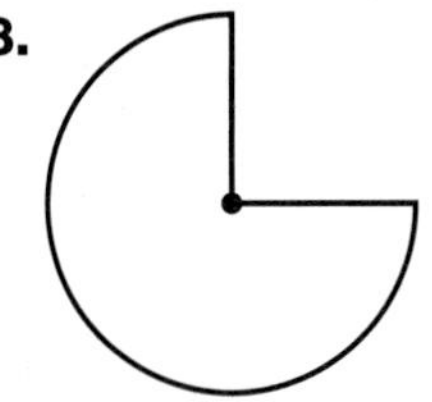

9. 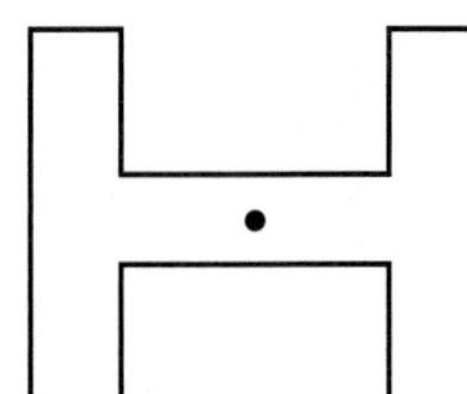

Trace each figure and fold it. Write *yes* or *no* to tell if it has line symmetry. If it does, write the number of lines of symmetry it has. Then sketch the figure and its line(s) of symmetry.

10. 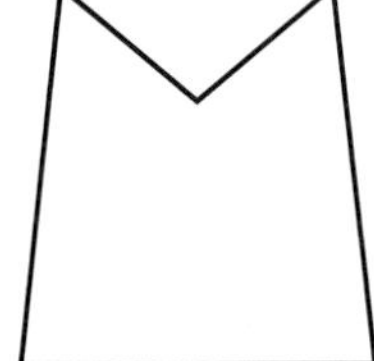

11. 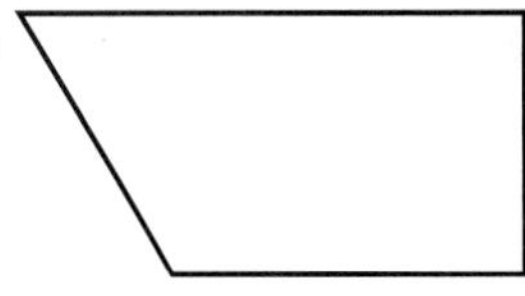

12. 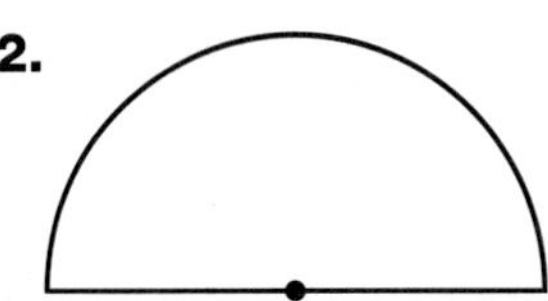

13. 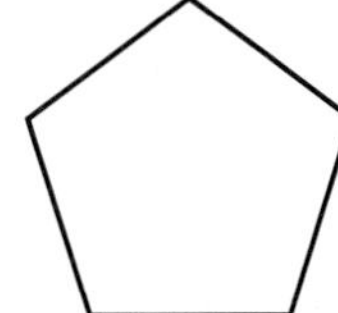

14. 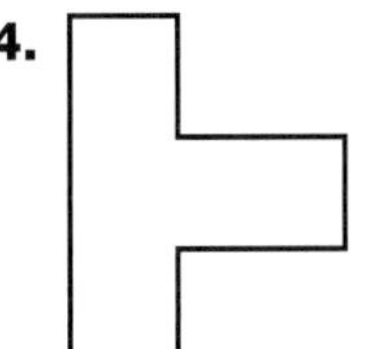

15. 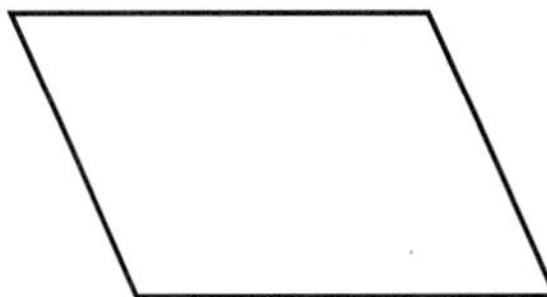

16. 

17. 

Use a compass and a protractor to draw these figures.

18. a figure that has line symmetry but not rotational symmetry

19. a figure that has rotational symmetry but not line symmetry

Use the photograph at the right for Problems 20–22.

20. Analyze Make a list of the geometric shapes you see.

21. Write About It Write a paragraph about the kinds of symmetry you see.

22. You Decide Windows can be squares, rectangles, circles, or semicircles. Draw the front or side of a house that has at least one line of symmetry. Decide on the shape of the house and its windows. Explain how you made it symmetrical.

Quick Check

Check your understanding for Lessons 6–9.

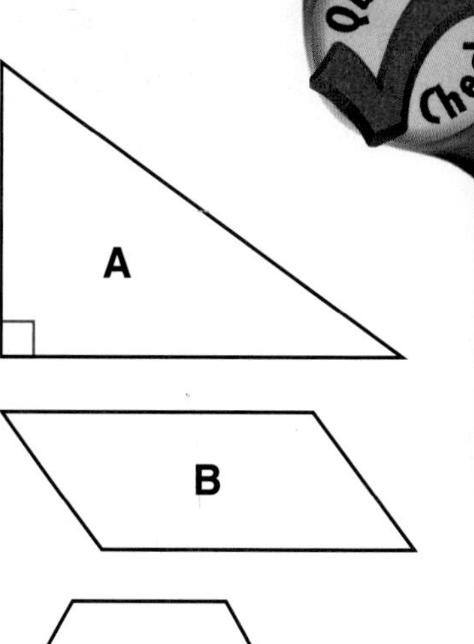

Use Figures A, B, and C for Exercises 1–8. (Lessons 6–7, 9)

1. Trace Figure A on grid paper and then show a translation.
2. Trace Figure B on grid paper and then show a reflection.
3. Which figure will tessellate?
4. Which figure has rotational symmetry?
5. Which figure has line symmetry?
6. How many lines of symmetry does the figure you named in Exercise 5 have?

B

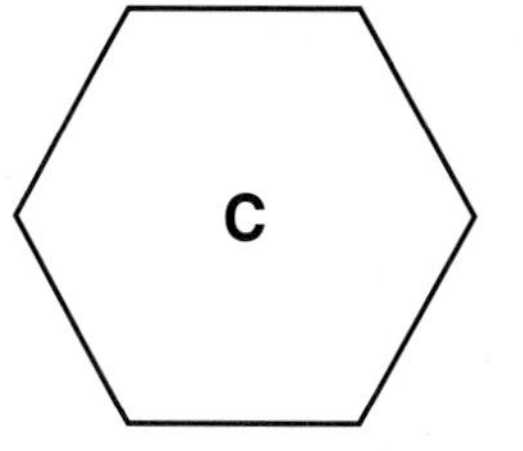

Use symbols to identify the following parts of the circle at the right. (Lesson 8)

7. radius 8. center 9. diameter 10. chords

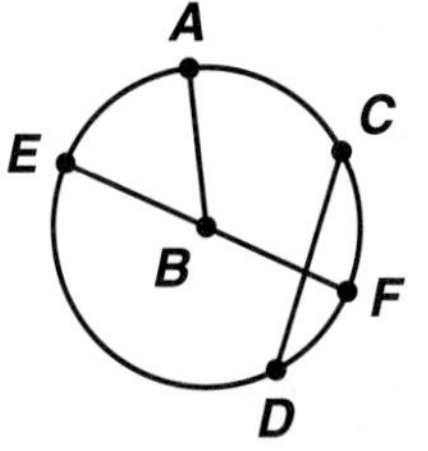

WEEKLY WR READER® eduplace.com/kids/mw/

Escher-esque

M. C. Escher was a famous Dutch artist who used transformations to make unusual tessellation patterns.

Use what you learned about tessellations in Lesson 7 to make an Escher-like tessellation of your own.

Extra Practice See page 419, Set E.

Chapter Review/Test

VOCABULARY

1. Two lines that intersect at right angles are said to be ____.
2. A ____ occurs when you flip a figure over a line.

Vocabulary

diagonal
perpendicular
reflection
rotation

CONCEPTS AND SKILLS

3. Identify this figure.

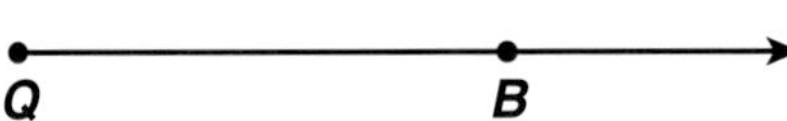

Use the figures at right for Exercises 4–7.

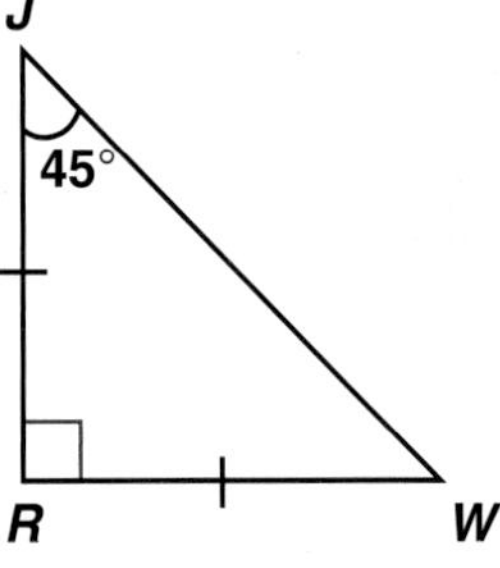

4. Find the missing angle measure in $\triangle RJW$. Then classify the triangle in two ways. (Lessons 2–3, pp. 292–297)
5. Trace each figure. Use a ruler to measure the sides of each figure to the nearest $\frac{1}{16}$ inch. Mark congruent sides. (Lesson 4, pp. 398–399)

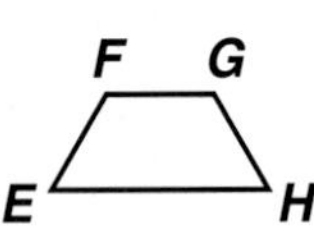

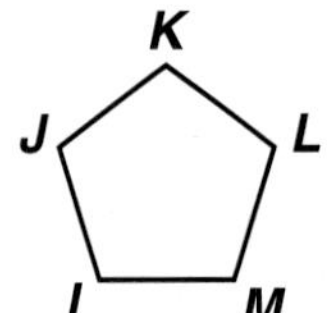

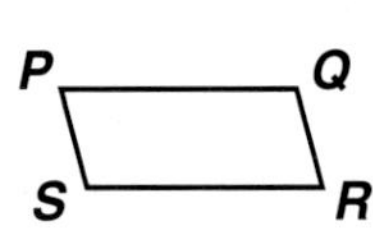

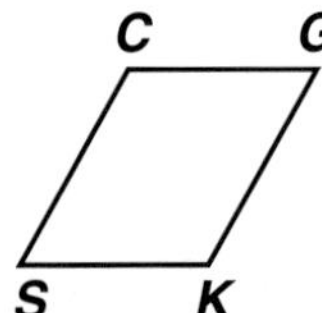

6. Classify *CGKS* in as many ways as possible. (Lesson 5, pp. 400–402)

7. Tell whether *CGKS* has rotational and/or line symmetry. (Lesson 9, pp. 414–417)
8. Sketch a triangle and its reflection. (Lesson 6, pp. 404–407)
9. In the circle at the right, name each of the following: a radius, a diameter, and a chord. (Lesson 8, pp. 412–413)

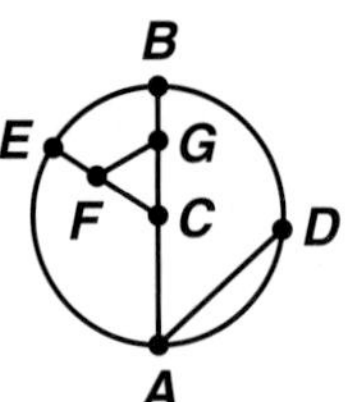

PROBLEM SOLVING

Make a model to solve. (Lesson 7, pp. 408–411)

10. Does the figure to the right tessellate? Explain why or why not.

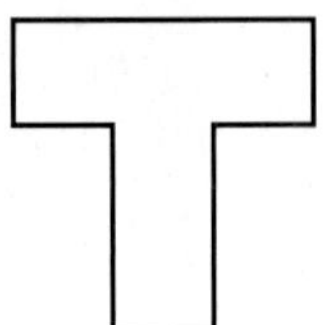

Write About It

Show You Understand

You know that $\triangle JBW$ has line symmetry. Can $\triangle JBW$ be a scalene triangle? Explain how you know.

Extra Practice

Set A (Lesson 1, pp. 390–391)

Name each figure.

1. 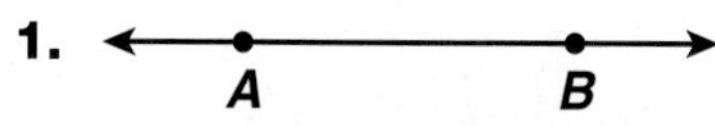

2. S L

3. H G

Set B (Lesson 3, pp. 396–397)

Classify each triangle in two ways. Then find the missing angle measures.

1. 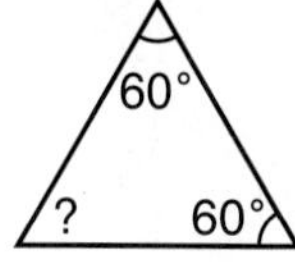

2. 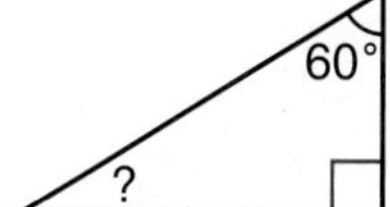

3. 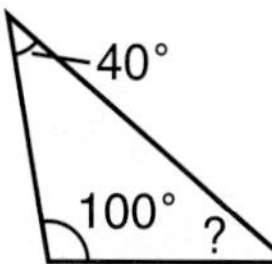

4. 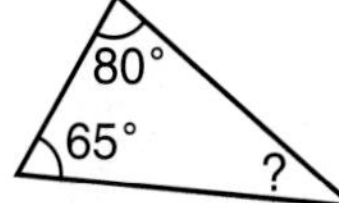

Set C (Lesson 4, pp. 398–399)

Trace each figure. Mark the congruent sides and congruent angles.

1. 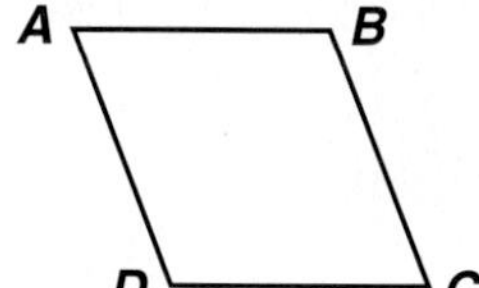

2. 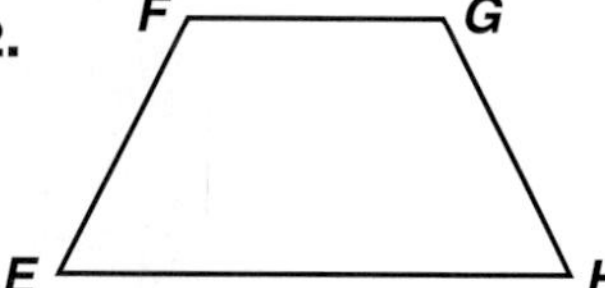

3. 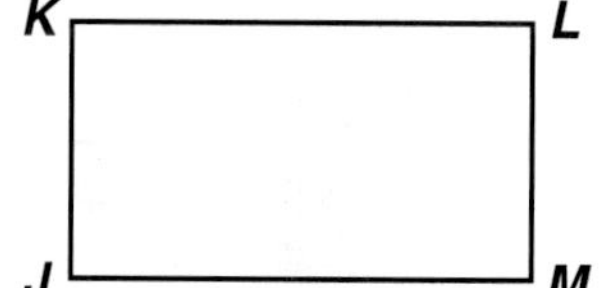

Set D (Lesson 5, pp. 400–403)

Classify each polygon in as many ways as possible.

1. 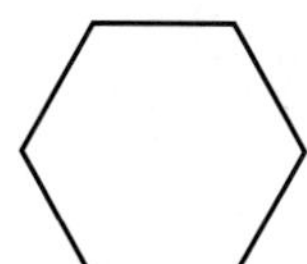

2. 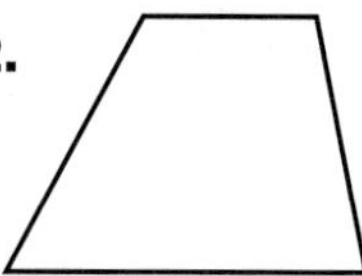

3. 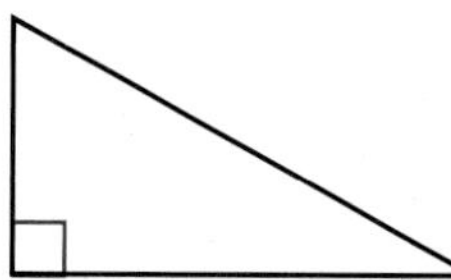

4. 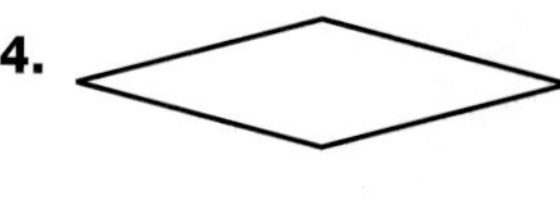

Set E (Lesson 9, pp. 414–417)

Tell whether each figure has rotational symmetry and/or line symmetry.

1. 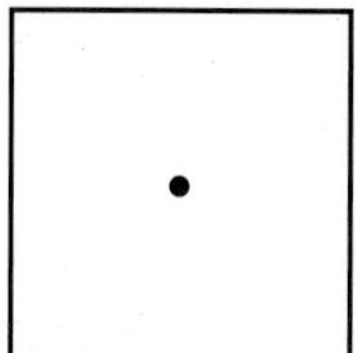

2. 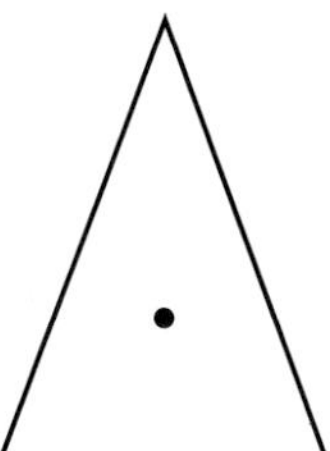

3. 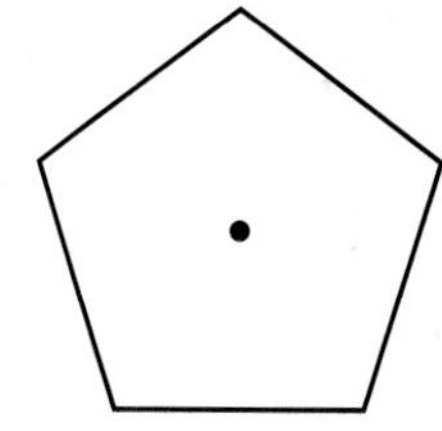

CHAPTER 16

Perimeter, Area, and Circumference

INVESTIGATION

Use Data

Marcy is making a quilt for her bed. It will be 21 inches wider than her bed and 9 inches longer. Find the perimeter and area of the quilt she plans to make.

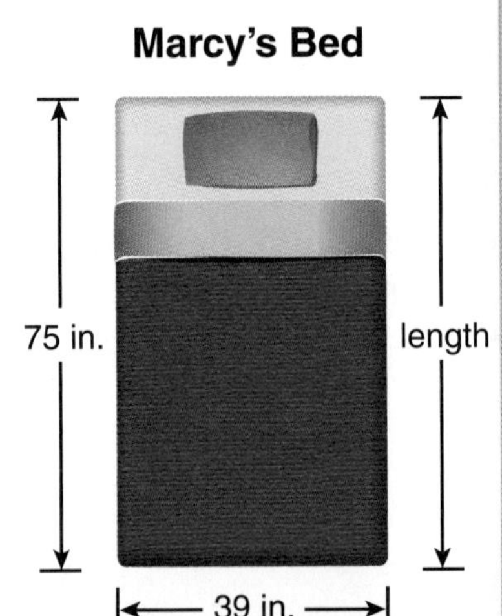

Chapter Pretest

Use this page to review and remember what you need to know for this chapter.

VOCABULARY

Choose the best word to complete each sentence.

1. Two sides of a polygon meet at a point called the ____.
2. A polygon made up of three line segments is called a ____.
3. A quadrilateral with four right angles and four congruent sides is a ____.

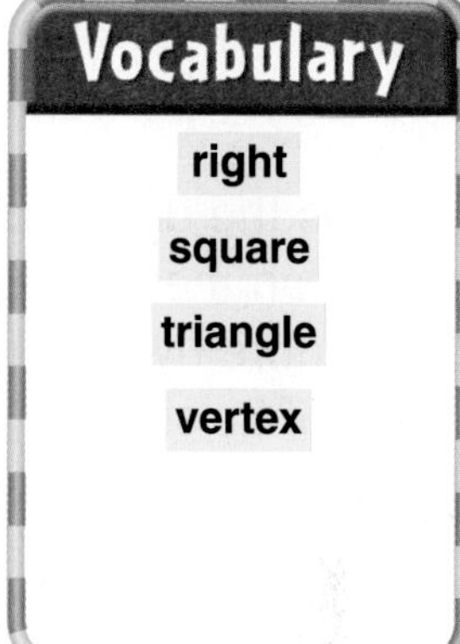

CONCEPTS AND SKILLS

Add.

4. $7 + 3\frac{1}{2} + 4\frac{1}{2} + 10$
5. $2.45 + 6.7 + 8.05$
6. $6.2 + 3.91 + 3.91 + 6.2$
7. $3\frac{1}{4} + 5\frac{1}{2} + 1\frac{1}{2} + 6\frac{1}{4}$

Multiply.

8. $3\frac{1}{2} \times 6$
9. 3.14×25

Write About It

10. Copy the figures shown below. Then explain how to separate the figure into one rectangle and two triangles.

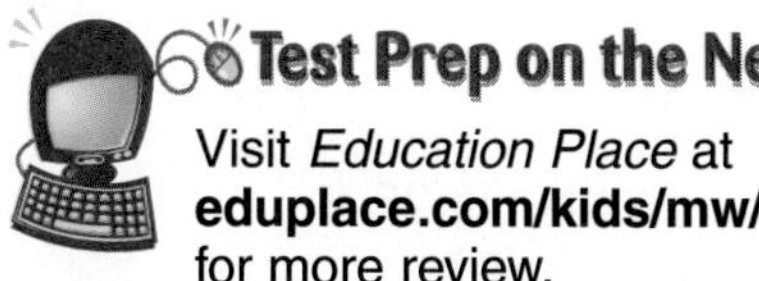

Test Prep on the Net

Visit *Education Place* at **eduplace.com/kids/mw/** for more review.

Lesson 1

Algebra

Perimeter

Objective Find the perimeter of plane figures.

Learn About It

Lance is putting braid around a picture that is 16 inches long and 14 inches wide for a gift. He needs to find the perimeter of the picture.

Perimeter is the distance around a plane figure. You can measure the perimeter of a plane figure by finding the sum of the lengths of its sides.

Materials: centimeter grid paper

STEP 1 On a piece of centimeter grid paper, draw this rectangle.

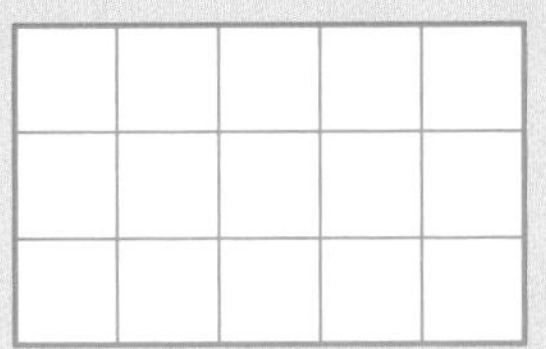

STEP 2 Copy and complete the addition sentence to find the perimeter of the rectangle.

5 + 3 + ■ + ■ = ____

You can also use a formula to find the perimeter of a rectangle. If P represents perimeter, l represents length, and w represents width, then:

$$P = l + w + l + w$$
$$= 2 \times l + 2 \times w$$
or
$$2l + 2w$$

You can use formulas to find the perimeter of any square or rectangle.

Using Formulas for Perimeter

Perimeter of a rectangle.

Length is 8 ft and width is 5 ft.

$P = 2l + 2w$

$= (2 \times 8) + (2 \times 5)$

$= 16 + 10$

$= 26$ ft

The perimeter is 26 ft.

Perimeter of a square.

Each side is 5 mm long.

$P = 4s$

$= 4(5)$

$= 20$ mm

The perimeter is 20 mm.

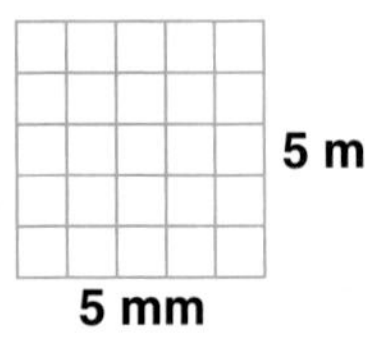

Guided Practice

Ask Yourself

- Can I use $P = 2l + 2w$?
- Can I use $P = 4s$?

Find the perimeter of each rectangle.

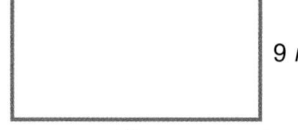

1. 3 in. by 4 in.

2. 5 ft by 5 ft

TEST TIPS **Explain Your Thinking** ▶ How much braid does Lance need for the picture shown on page 422? Explain how you know.

Practice and Problem Solving

Find the perimeter or the missing measurement for each rectangle.

3.

4.

5.
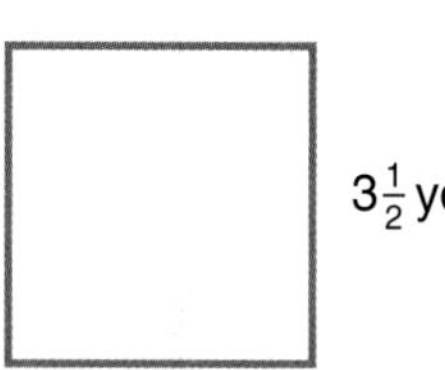

6.
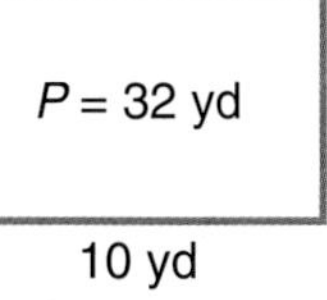

7. *P* = 80 ft; 20 ft

8. *P* = 21.6 m; 4.1 m

Copy and complete the chart below. Each figure in the chart is a regular figure with sides of 3 centimeters.

	Regular Figure	Addition Expression	Multiplication Expression	Perimeter
9.	pentagon	3 + 3 + 3 + 3 + 3	5 × 3	
10.	hexagon			
11.	octagon			

Solve.

12. Analyze A border will be put at the top of the walls in a 12 ft by 16 ft room. What is the maximum length of border that should be bought? Why might less be needed?

13. Explain A rectangular room has sides of 15 feet and 18 feet. You want to use the formula $P = 2l + 2w$. What values would you use for l and w? Does it matter if you switch the values? Explain.

Daily Review | Test Prep

Complete. (Ch. 6, Lessons 2–3)

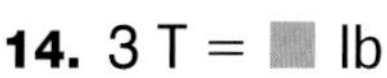

14. 3 T = ■ lb

15. 6 ft = ■ in.

16. 2 gal = ■ qt

17. 3 lb = ■ oz

18. Find the perimeter of a rectangle with a length of 6 cm and width of 8 cm.

A 14 cm

B 24 cm

C 28 cm

D 32 cm

Extra Practice See page 443, Set A.

Lesson 2

Problem-Solving Strategy

Find a Pattern

Objective Use a pattern to solve a problem.

Problem Jenny uses triangular tiles to make the shapes on the right. If the pattern continues, how many tiles will be in the sixth figure in the pattern?

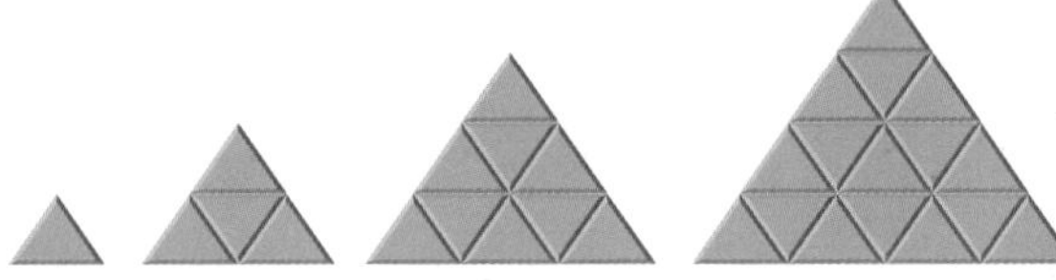

This is what you know:

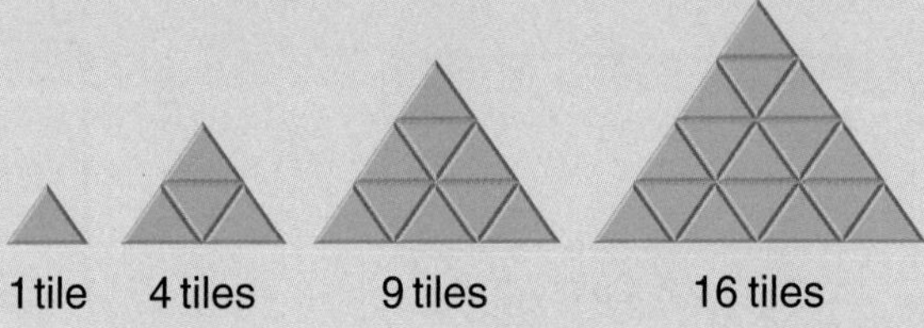

PLAN

You can find a pattern to solve the problem.

SOLVE

Make a table to organize the data. Then study the table to find a pattern.

Shape in Pattern	1st	2nd	3rd	4th	5th	6th
Tiles	1	4	9	16	?	?

One Pattern

The number of additional tiles needed to make the next figure increases by 2 each time. Use the pattern to complete the table.

$16 + 9 = 25$

$25 + 11 = 36$

Another Pattern

The table shows square numbers:

$1 = 1 \times 1$ $4 = 2 \times 2$

$9 = 3 \times 3$ $16 = 4 \times 4$

Find the next two square numbers:

$5 \times 5 = 25$ $6 \times 6 = 36$

Solution: There will be 36 tiles in the sixth figure.

Look back at the problem.
How can I check the answer?

Guided Practice

Use the Ask Yourself questions to help you solve each problem.

1. Look at the figures below. If the pattern continues, how many small squares will be in the fifth figure?

2. Find the seventh figure in the pattern shown below.

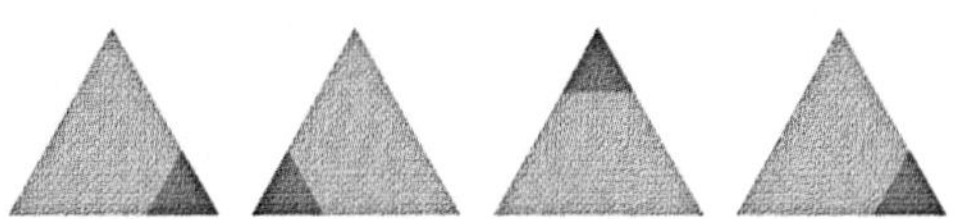

Hint Think about how the shape moves.

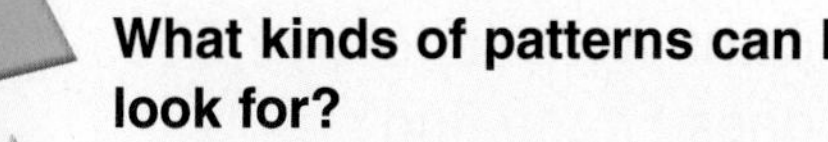

UNDERSTAND What facts do I know?

PLAN What kinds of patterns can I look for?

SOLVE
- Did I figure out how each shape in the pattern was different from the shape before it?
- Did I describe the pattern?
- Did I continue the pattern?

LOOK BACK How can I check the answer?

Independent Practice

Find a pattern to solve each problem.

3. Howard uses triangular tiles to make the figure at the right. If the finished figure has 7 rows, and the pattern continues, how many white tiles are in the figure?

row 1
row 2
row 3
row 4

4. Look at these grids. How many squares of any size are there in a 5×5 grid?

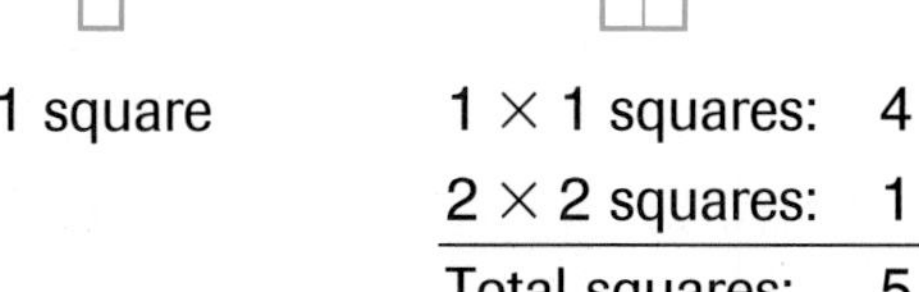
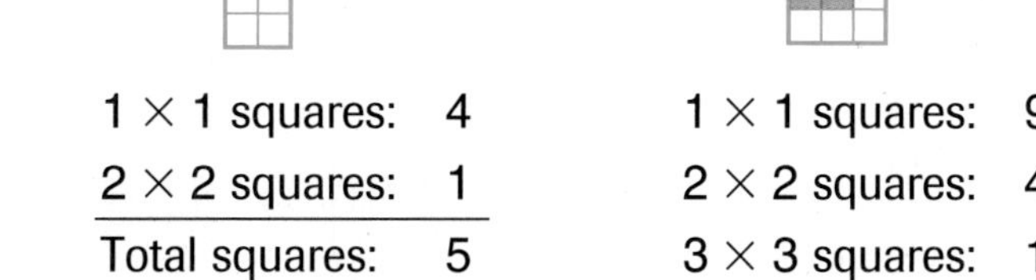

1 square

1×1 squares:	4
2×2 squares:	1
Total squares:	5

1×1 squares:	9
2×2 squares:	4
3×3 squares:	1
Total squares:	?

5. **Reasoning** Find the next three times in the pattern that the shaded triangle will be in the same position as it was in the first shape in the pattern. Explain.

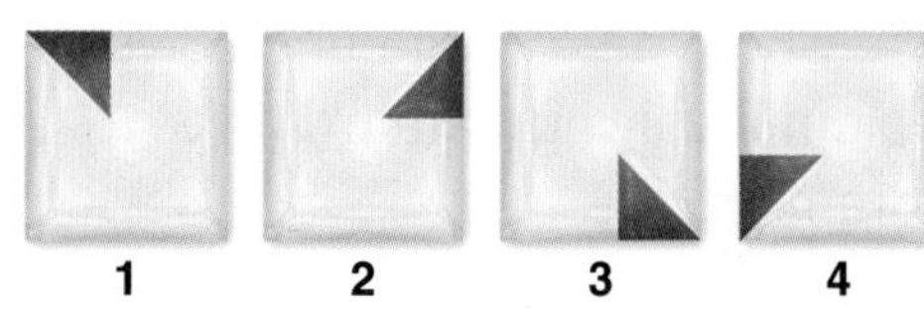

Go On

Choose a Strategy

Solve. Show your work. Tell what strategy you used.

PROBLEM-SOLVING Strategies

Use Models
Draw a Diagram
Find a Pattern
Guess and Check
Make an Organized List
Make a Table
Solve a Simpler Problem
Use Logical Reasoning
Work Backward
Write an Equation

6. Emma cleans her couch. She finds 8 coins worth a total of 58¢. What coins does Emma find?

7. Ken cuts a 10-foot long speaker wire into two pieces. The first piece is three times as long as the second piece. How long is each piece of speaker wire?

8. Yossi used blocks to build a pattern. How many blocks will be in the next figure in the pattern?

Data **Use the histogram to solve Problems 9–13.**

The histogram shows how old the houses on Wyoming Avenue were in the year 2000.

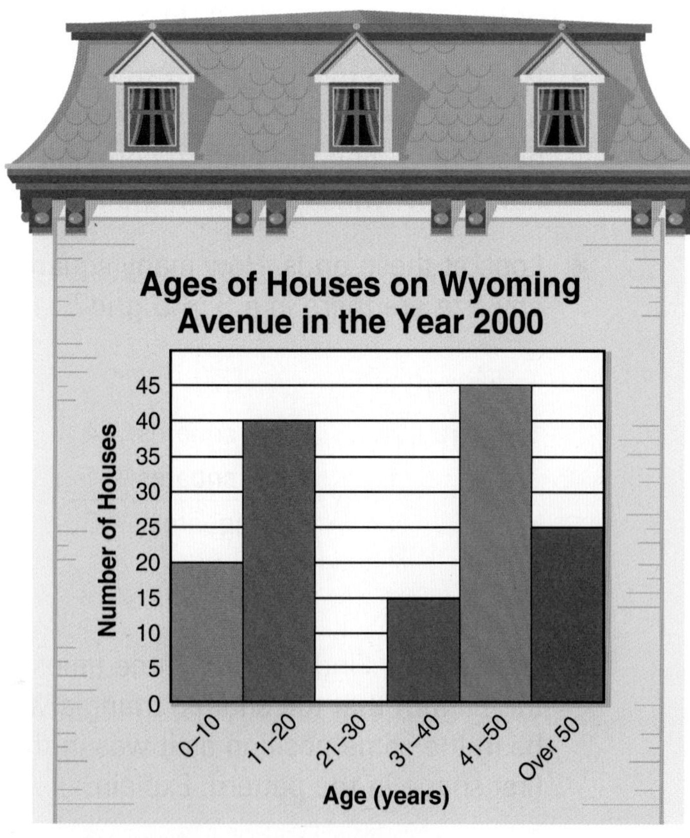

9. How many houses are on Wyoming Avenue?

10. How many houses were built more than 30 years before 2000?

11. How many houses were built less than 30 years before 2000?

12. How many houses were built within 10 years before 2000?

13. What years are represented by Age (years) labeled 21–30?

14. **Create and Solve** Write and solve a problem involving data from the histogram.

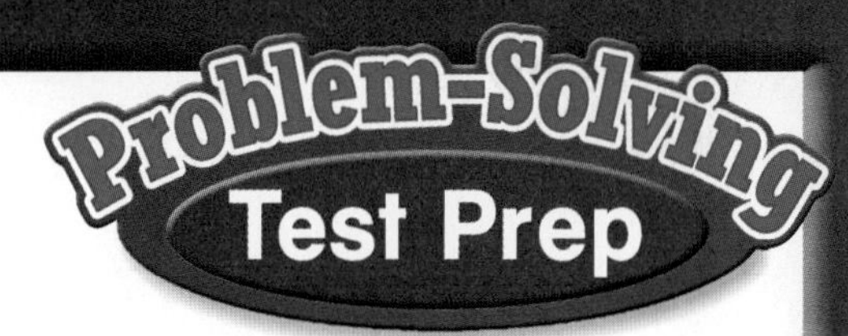

Choose the letter of the correct answer.
If a correct answer is not here, choose NH.

1. Helen is packing her collection of 250 books. Each carton can hold 75 books. How many cartons does Helen need?

   A 2 **B** 3 **C** 4 **D** NH

   (Chapter 14, Lesson 8)

2. What is the order of operations to solve this equation?

   $500 - (6 + 2) \times 8$

   F subtraction, addition, multiplication

   G multiplication, subtraction, addition

   H addition, subtraction, multiplication

   J addition, multiplication, subtraction

   (Chapter 5, Lesson 6)

3. What angle measure is missing?

   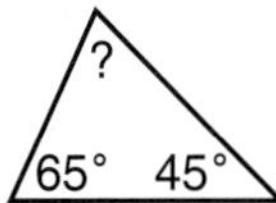

   A 45° **C** 115°

   B 70° **D** NH

   (Chapter 15, Lesson 3)

4. At Sentry Avenue, 10 people leave a bus and 6 people get on. At Whitman Street, 8 people get on and 4 people leave. There are now 40 people on the bus. How many people were on the bus when it arrived at Sentry Avenue?

   F 26 **G** 32 **H** 40 **J** 48

   (Chapter 5, Lesson 3)

5. Awilda buys 16 pounds of oranges. If the average weight of each orange is 8 ounces, how many oranges does Awilda buy?

   A 16 **B** 24 **C** 32 **D** 64

   (Chapter 6, Lesson 3)

6. Two fifths of Mr. Wilson's class of 20 students are in after-school clubs. One third of Ms. Judd's class of 24 students are in after-school clubs. In which class are more students in after-school clubs?

   Represent Support your solution with a picture.

   (Chapter 12, Lesson 2)

7. The table shows the population growth of Marion Falls. If the pattern continues, what will be the population in 2010?

Marion Falls Population			
Year	**1980**	**1990**	**2000**
Population	**4500**	**4150**	**3800**

   Explain How did you find the pattern? How did you use the pattern to solve the problem?

   (Chapter 1, Lesson 6)

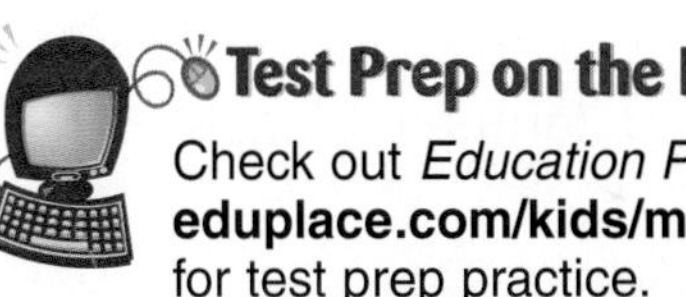

Test Prep on the Net
Check out *Education Place* at **eduplace.com/kids/mw/** for test prep practice.

Algebra

Area of a Parallelogram

Objective Use a formula for the area of parallelograms.

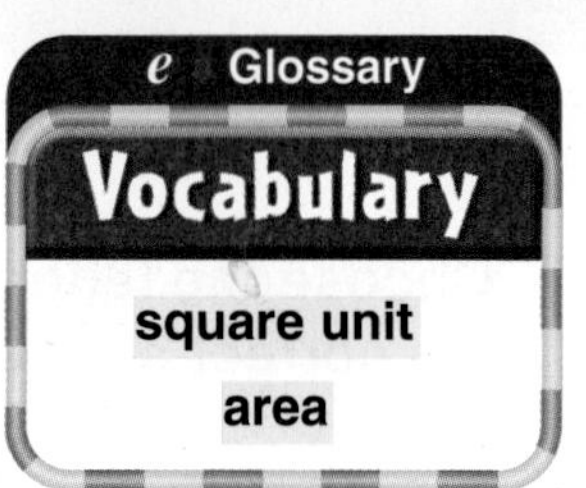

Learn About It

A hallway is 9 feet × 5 feet. How much carpeting do you need to cover the floor in the hallway completely?
To solve the problem, you need to find the area of the hallway.

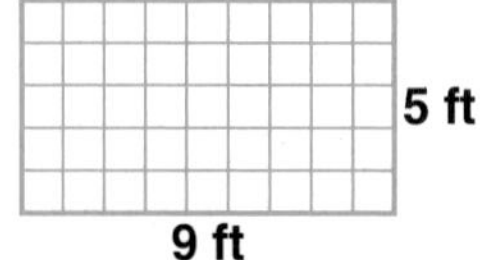

A **square unit** is a square with sides one unit long. You can measure **area** (A) by finding the number of square units that cover a surface with no overlap.

To find the area of a rectangle, you can count square units, or you can multiply its length by its width.

$$A \text{ (rectangle)} = l \times w$$
$$= 9 \times 5$$
$$= 45 \text{ square feet, or } 45 \text{ ft}^2$$

Remember
Area is expressed in square units. For example, if the length and width are measured in feet, the area will be written in square feet, or ft^2.

Solution: You need 45 square feet of carpeting.

Since the length and width of a square are the same, you can write the formula for area of a square as $A = s \times s$, or $A = s^2$.

$A = s^2$
$A = 3^2$
$A = 9$ square meters, or 9 m^2

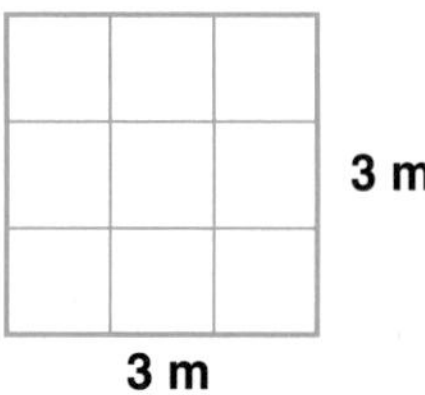

You can use what you know about the area of a rectangle to find the formula for the area of any parallelogram.

Materials: centimeter grid paper, ruler, scissors

STEP 1 On a sheet of centimeter grid paper, copy the parallelogram shown at the right. The red dotted line is perpendicular to the base, b, and represents the height, h.

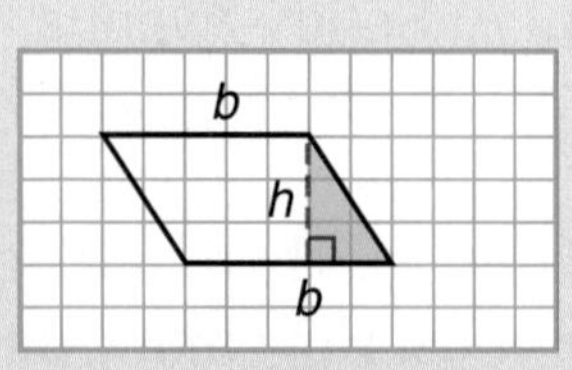

STEP 2 Cut along the red dotted line. Move the right triangle to the other side of the parallelogram to form a rectangle.

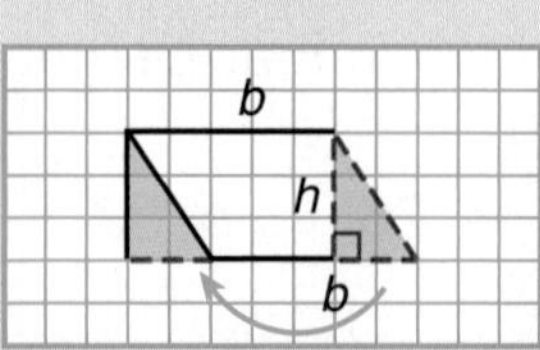

Write a multiplication sentence for the area of the rectangle. You can also use the formula for the area of a rectangle to find the formula for the area of a parallelogram.

You can use a formula to find the area of any parallelogram.

Using the Formula for Area of a Parallelogram

$A = bh$
$= 6.2 \times 3$
$= 18.6$

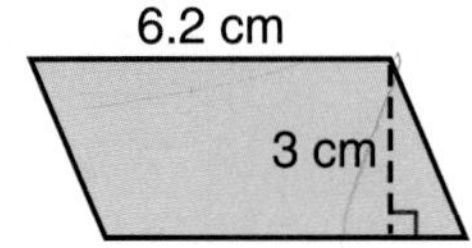

The area is 18.6 square centimeters, or 18.6 cm².

$A = bh$
$= 7 \times 5\frac{1}{2}$
$= 38\frac{1}{2}$

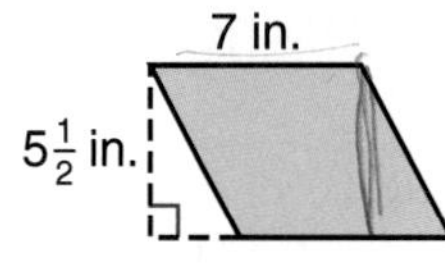

The area is $38\frac{1}{2}$ square inches, or $38\frac{1}{2}$ in.².

Guided Practice

Ask Yourself

- Which measure is the height?
- Which measures do I multiply?

Find the area of each figure.

1. 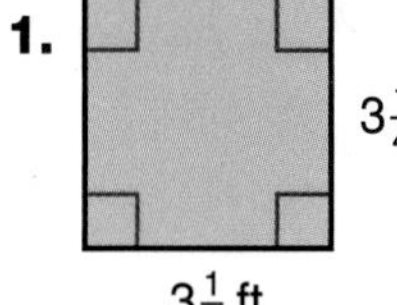

2.  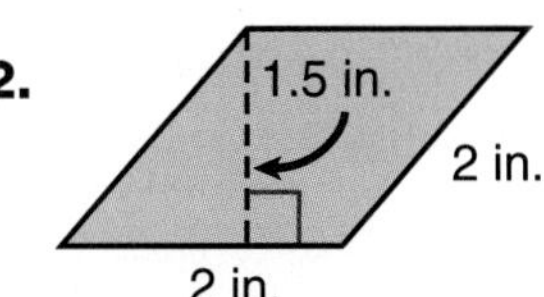

TEST TIPS **Explain Your Thinking** ▶ Can the formula $A = bh$ be used to find the area of any rectangle? Explain.

Practice and Problem Solving

Find the area of each figure.

3. 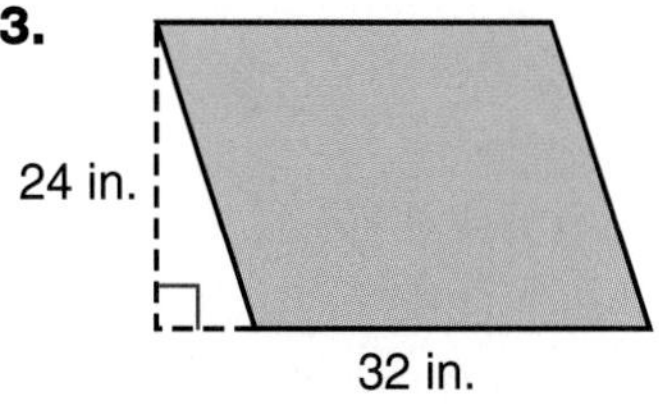

4. 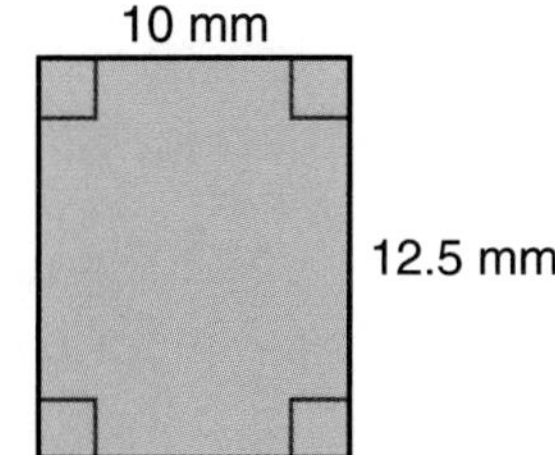

5. 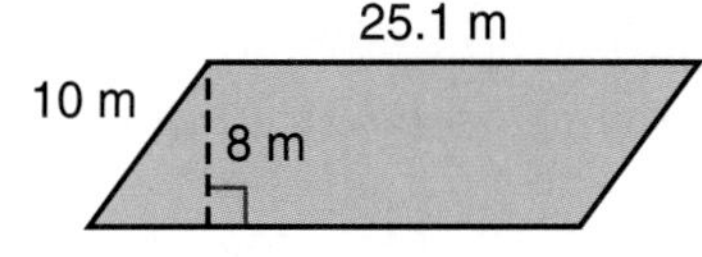

6. 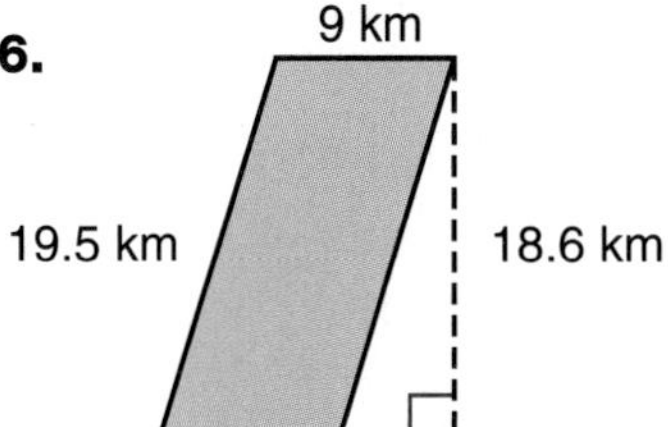

7. 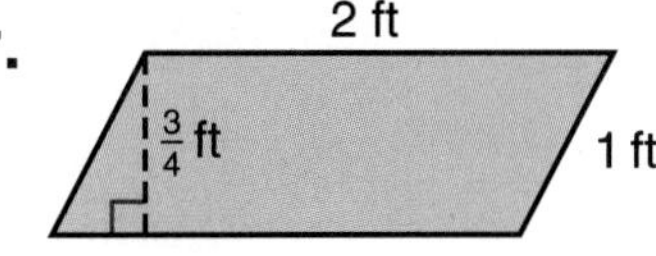

8. 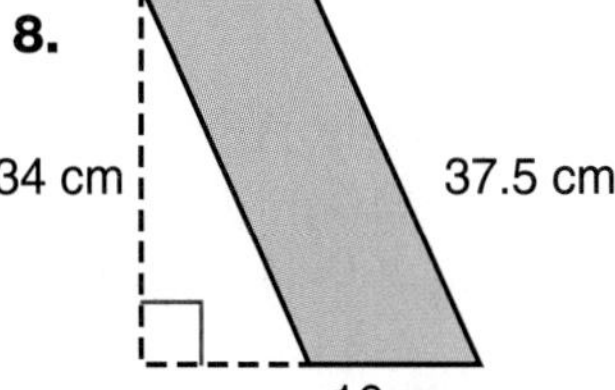

Go On

Practice and Problem Solving

Use Figures A, B, and C for Exercises 9–14.

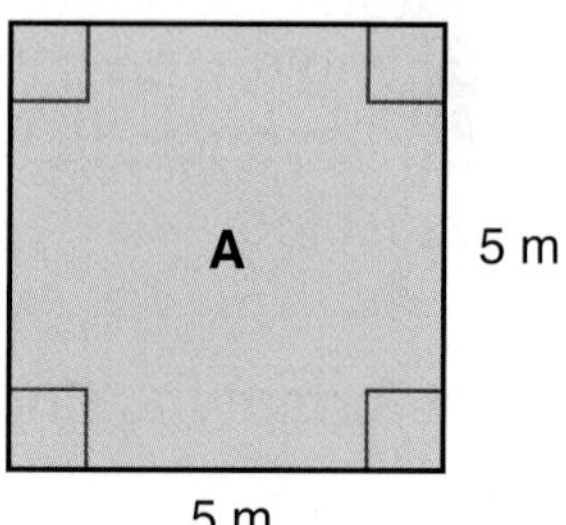

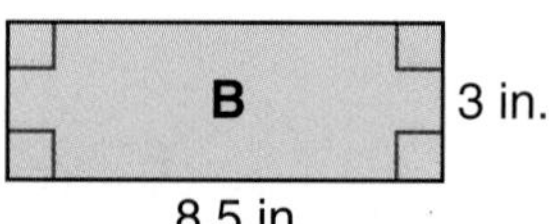

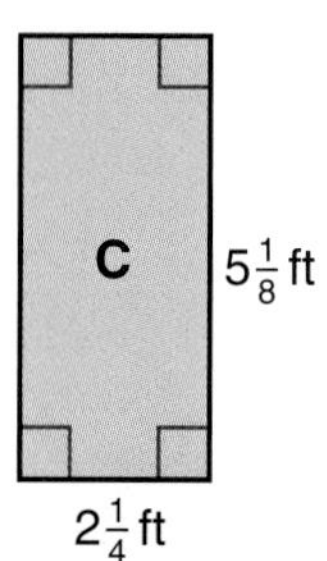

9. Find the perimeter of each figure.

10. Find the perimeter of a rectangle that has twice the length and twice the width as Figure A. Repeat for Figure B and Figure C.

11. **Analyze** What is the relationship between the perimeter of a figure and the perimeter of a figure when the length and width are doubled.

12. Find the area of each figure.

13. Find the area of a rectangle that has twice the length and twice the width as the Figure A. Repeat for Figure B and Figure C.

14. **Analyze** What is the relationship between the area of a figure and the area of a figure with twice the length and width?

Copy and complete the table so that it shows the length, width, and perimeter for different rectangles with an area of 36 square inches.

	Area of Rectangle	Length	Width	Perimeter
15.	36 in.^{2}	1 in.		
16.	36 in.^{2}	2 in.		
17.	36 in.^{2}	3 in.		
18.	36 in.^{2}	4 in.		
19.	36 in.^{2}	6 in.		

20. **Analyze** Look at the results of Exercises 15–19. What is the relationship between the length and the width of rectangles with the same area? How does that relationship affect the perimeter?

21. **Represent** Joe drew a parallelogram with a height of 2 centimeters and an area of 14.7 square centimeters. Draw Joe's parallelogram. How long is its base?

22. **Reasoning** Nan used 64 feet of fencing to make a rectangular space for her dog. Find the dimensions of the space if she made the largest possible area for the dog?

23. **Write About It** A square and a non-square rhombus each have 3-centimeter sides. Which has the greater area? Use a diagram to explain.

24. A garden is planted in the shape of a rhombus and fenced with 40 feet of fencing. The height of the rhombus is 3 feet. What is the area of the garden?

Extra Practice See page 443, Set B.

Quick Check

Check your understanding of Lessons 1–3.

Find the perimeter and area. (Lessons 1 and 3)

1.

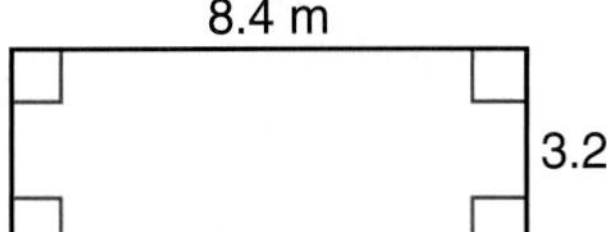

2.

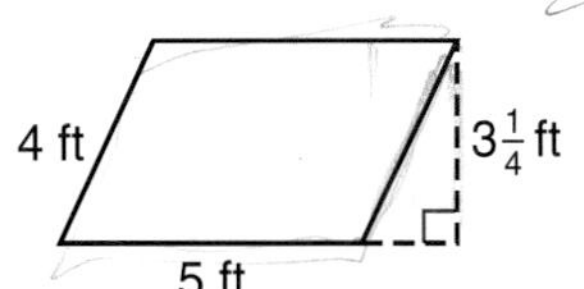

3.

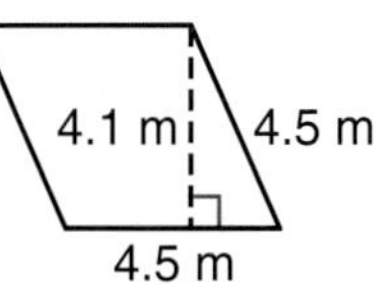

Solve. (Lesson 2)

4. Look at the figures below. If the pattern continues, how many small squares will be in the fifth figure?

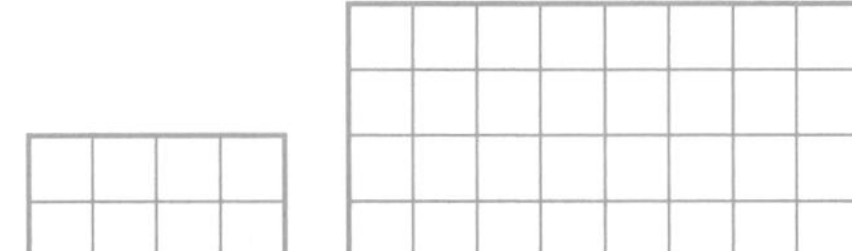

5. The first four figures in a pattern are shown below. When will the dot be in the same position as it was in the first figure in the pattern?

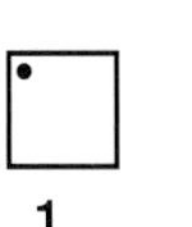
1

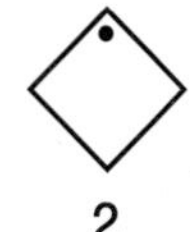
2

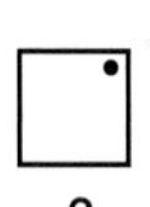
3

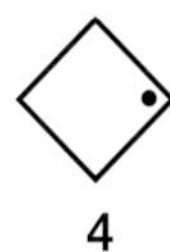
4

WEEKLY WR READER® eduplace.com/kids/mw/

Social Studies Connection

On The Farm

1 square inch (in.^{2})

1 in.

1 in.

1 square foot (ft^2)

12 in.

12 in.

144 square inches

1 square yard (yd^2)

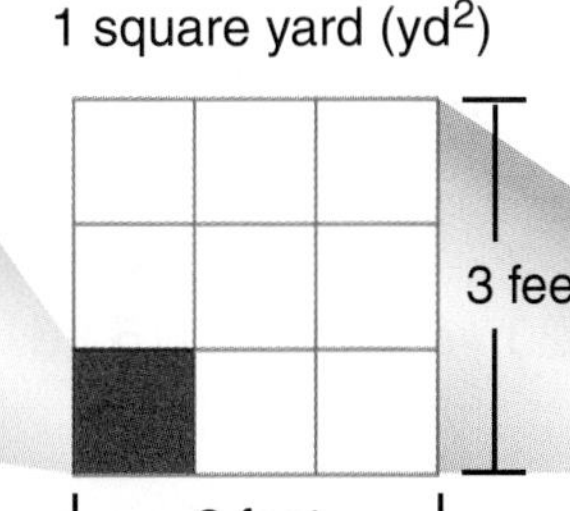

9 square feet

1 acre

43,560 square feet

The area of a farm is measured in acres.

1. How large is an acre in square yards?

2. Calculator How many square feet are in 1 square mile?

3. Calculator How many acres are there in 1 square mile?

4. Guess and Check A rectangular piece of land is almost a square, and is 2 acres in area. Find its dimensions in feet, rounded to the nearest ten feet.

Algebra

Area of a Triangle

Objective Find and use the formula to find the area of a triangle.

Learn About It

A surveyor lays out building lots along a river. Some lots are parallelograms and some are triangles. How can the surveyor find the area of a triangular lot?

Use what you know about the formula for the area of a parallelogram to write a formula for the area of the triangle.

STEP 1 Trace and cut out this triangle.

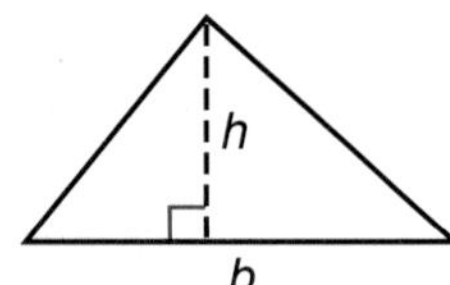

STEP 2 Place the triangle you traced next to the one shown to make the parallelogram.

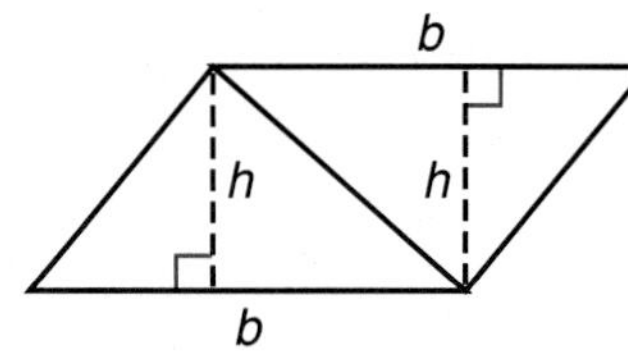

Remember
The formula for the area of a parallelogram is $b \times h$.

STEP 3

- The triangles are congruent so each triangle represents one half of the area of the parallelogram.
- The area of the triangle is $\frac{1}{2} \times b \times h$.

  So, $A = \frac{1}{2} \times b \times h$ or $A = \frac{1}{2}bh$

- In the building lot, $b = 20$ yd and $h = 15$ yd. $A = \frac{1}{2} \times 20 \text{ yd} \times 15 \text{ yd} = 150 \text{ yd}^2$

15 yd
20 yd

Solution: The area of the building lot is 150 yd^2.

Guided Practice

Find the area of each triangle.

1.

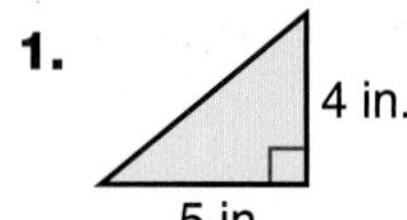

2.

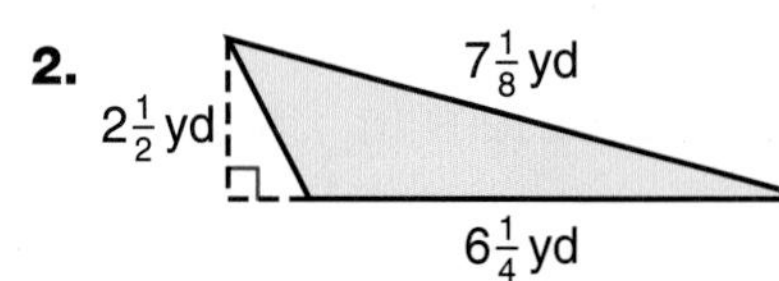

Ask Yourself

- What formula do I use?
- Did I use the right numbers?

Explain Your Thinking If you know the lengths of the sides of a right triangle, can you find its area? Use a diagram to explain.

Practice and Problem Solving

Find the area of each triangle.

3. 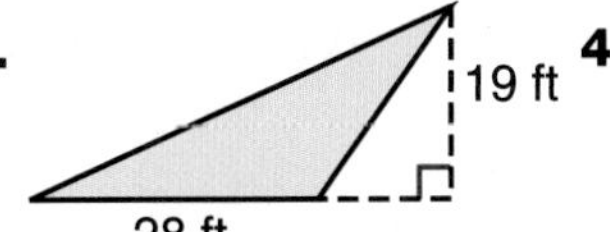

4. 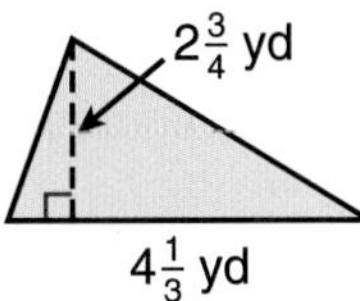

5. 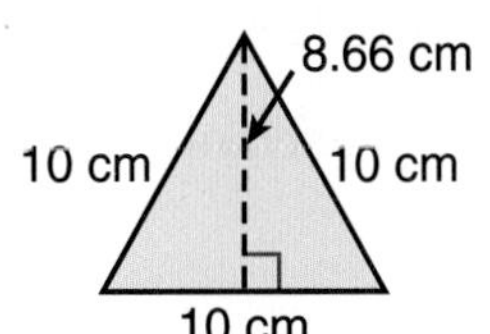

6. 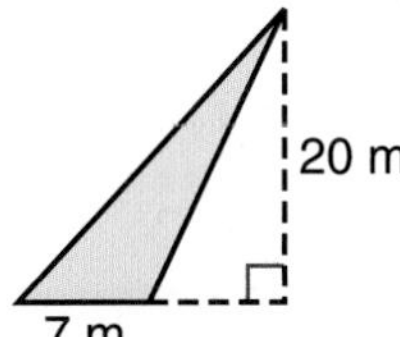

Solve.

7. The corners of the yellow pane of glass at the right meet at the midpoints of each side of the window. What is the area of each purple pane? What is the area of the yellow pane? (Hint: The midpoint of a side is the center point, or middle of that side.)

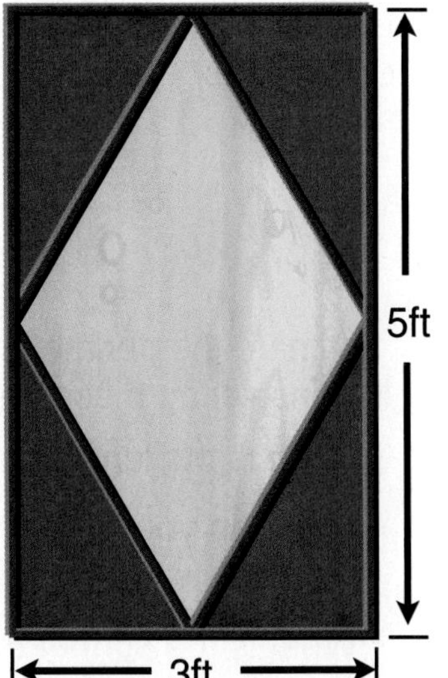

8. A triangle has a height of 6 inches and an area of 24 in.^{2}. What is the length of the base of that triangle?

9. A triangle has a base of 4.5 cm and an area of 27 cm^2. Find its height.

10. **Represent** A triangle has a height of *m* inches and a base of *p* inches. Write an expression to represent the area of that triangle.

11. **What's Wrong?** The notebook at the right shows how Alan found the area of a triangle. Explain what Alan did wrong.

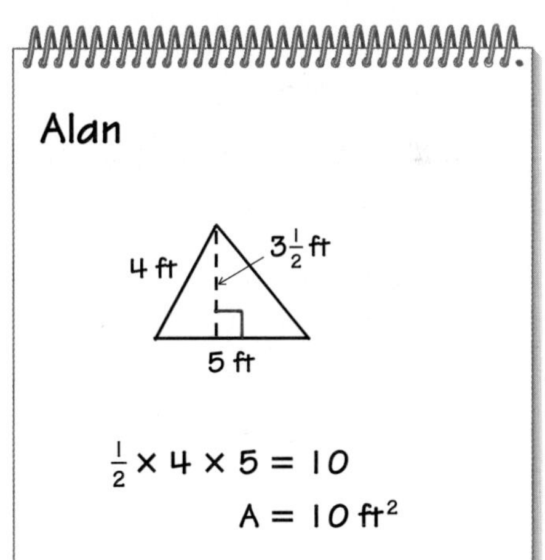

12. **You Decide** You need $1\frac{1}{2}$ pounds of peanuts to make trail mix. A 6-oz jar of peanuts costs $1.99. A 10-oz can of peanuts costs $2.89. How will you buy the peanuts? Explain.

Daily Review Test Prep

For each figure, name the number of lines of symmetry it has. (Ch. 15, Lesson 9)

13. 

14. 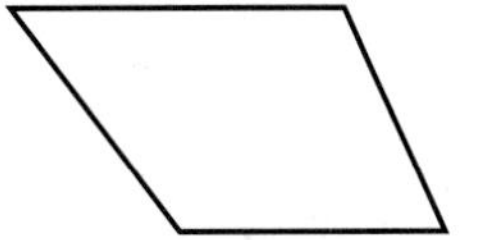

15. Find the area of a triangle with a height of 8 inches and base of $6\frac{1}{4}$ inches.

A $14\frac{1}{4}$ in.^{2}

B 25 in.^{2}

C $28\frac{1}{2}$ in.^{2}

D 52 in.^{2}

Extra Practice See page 443, Set C.

Perimeter and Area of Irregular Figures

Objective Find the perimeters and areas of irregular figures.

Materials
centimeter grid paper
inch grid paper
(Learning Tool 13)
(Learning Tool 15)

Work Together

Some figures are irregular and have curved sides. You can estimate the perimeter and area of these figures.

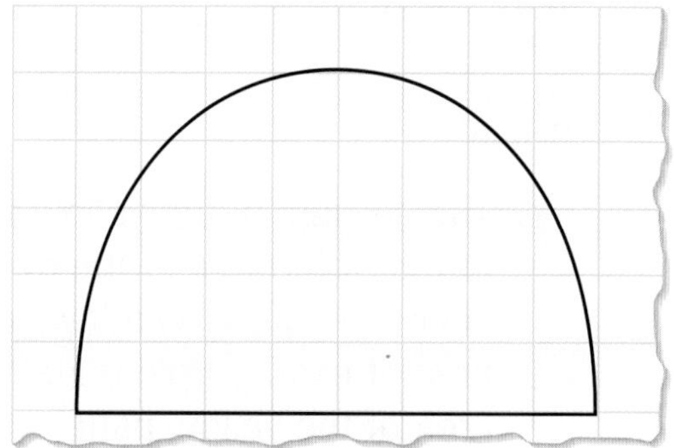

STEP 1 Estimate the perimeter of the figure above by answering these questions.

- What is the length of each straight line in the figure?
- How can you estimate the length of the curved side? About how long is the curved side?
- What is the sum of the sides?
- What is your estimate of the perimeter?

STEP 2 Estimate the area by answering these questions.

- How many whole squares are in the figure?
- How many partial squares are in the figure?
- What is your estimate of the area?

STEP 3 Now trace the same figure on a piece of grid paper that has squares of a smaller size. Estimate the perimeter and area.

- How does changing the size of the squares affect the perimeter and the area of the figure?

Some shapes are complex figures that are made of smaller polygons. You can use what you know about finding the perimeter and area of simple figures to find the perimeter and area of these shapes.

STEP 1 Find any missing lengths.

15 ft − 6 ft = 9 ft

18 ft − 9 ft = 9 ft

Add the lengths of the sides to find the perimeter of the figure.

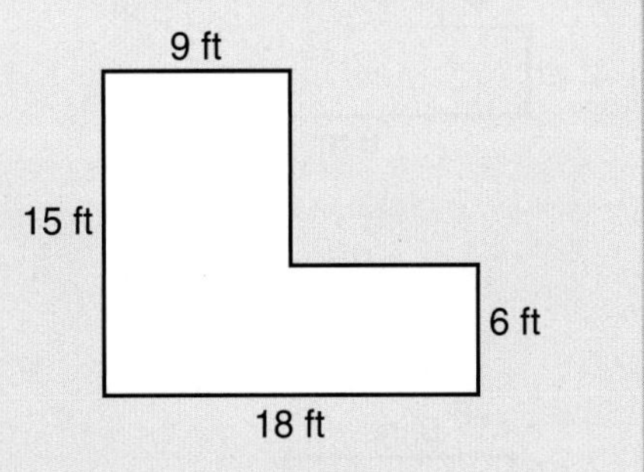

STEP 2 Find the area by separating the figure into simple figures.

Draw a line that separates the figure into a square and a rectangle.

Use formulas to find the area of each figure.

- What is the area of the square?
- What is the area of the rectangle?
- What is the sum of the areas?
- Can you think of another way to find the area of this figure?

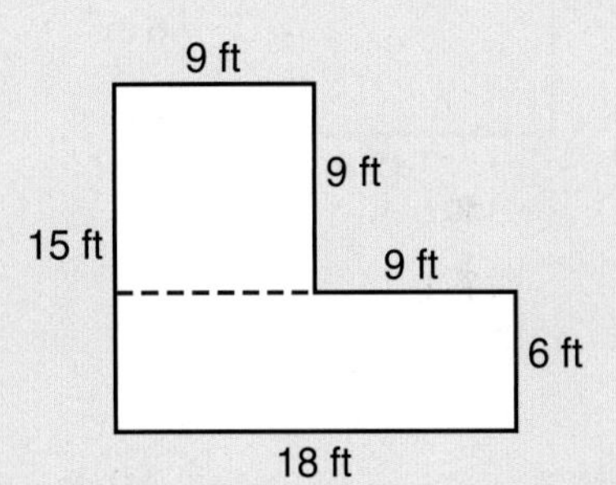

Hint
Think of the figure as a large rectangle with a small rectangle cut from one corner.

On Your Own

Estimate the perimeter and area of each figure. Each square is 1 cm².

1. 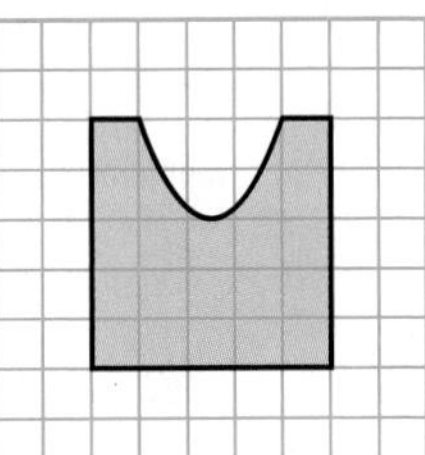

2. 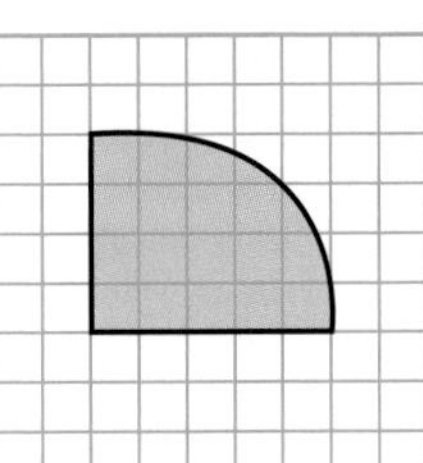

3. 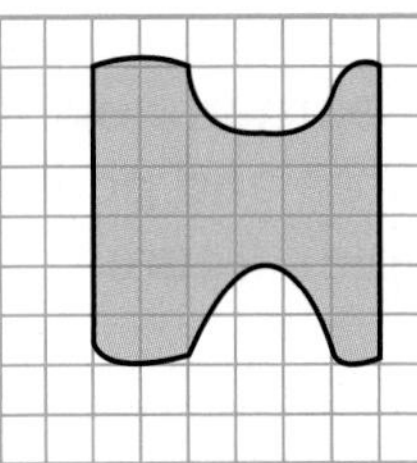

4. 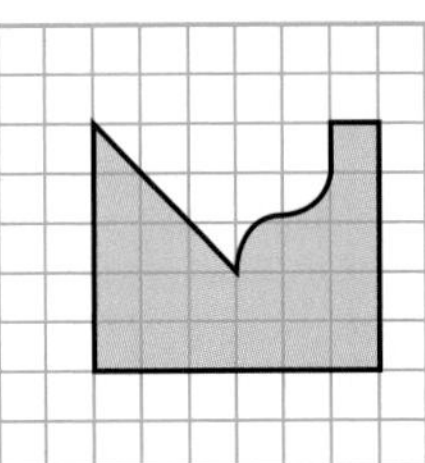

5. 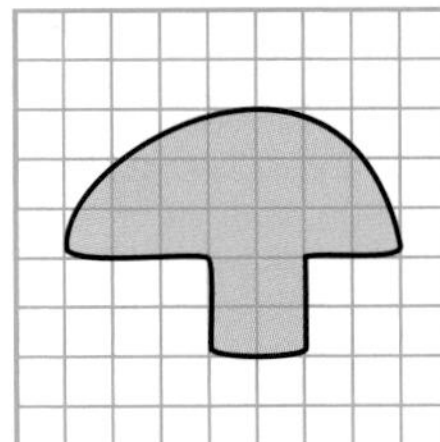

6. 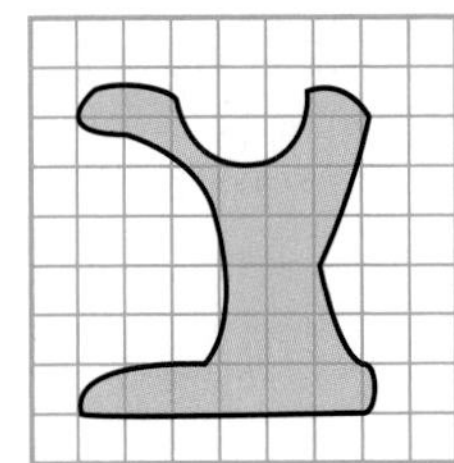

Go On

Find the perimeter and area of each figure. All intersecting sides meet at right angles.

7. 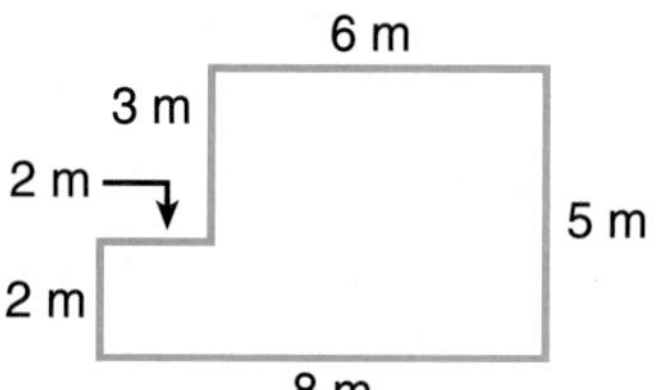

8. 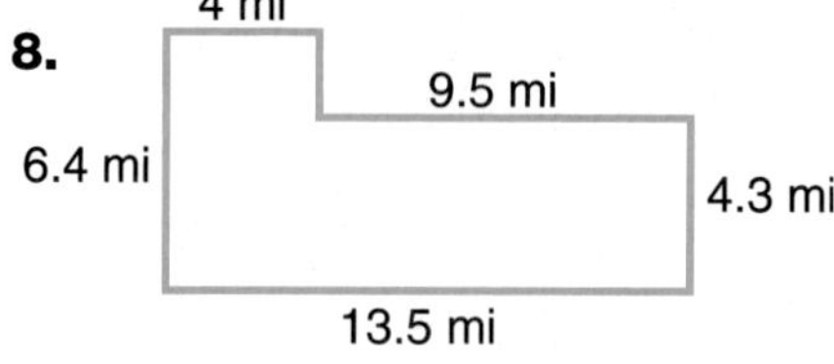

9. 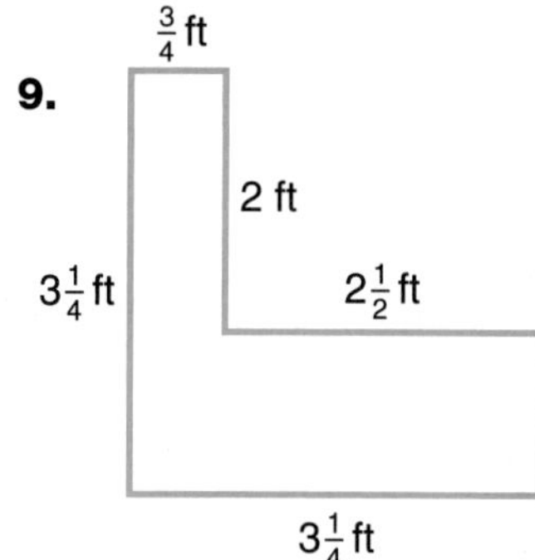

10. 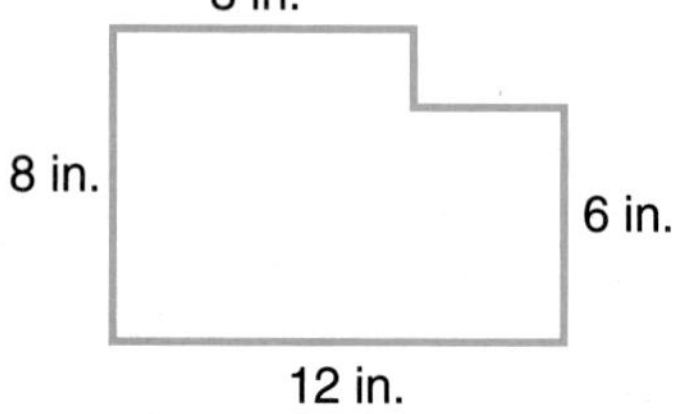

11. 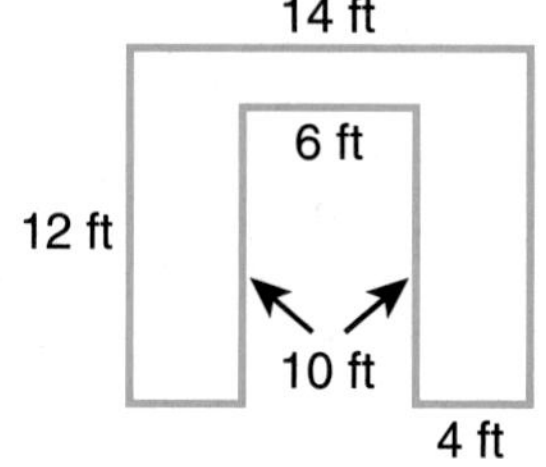

12. 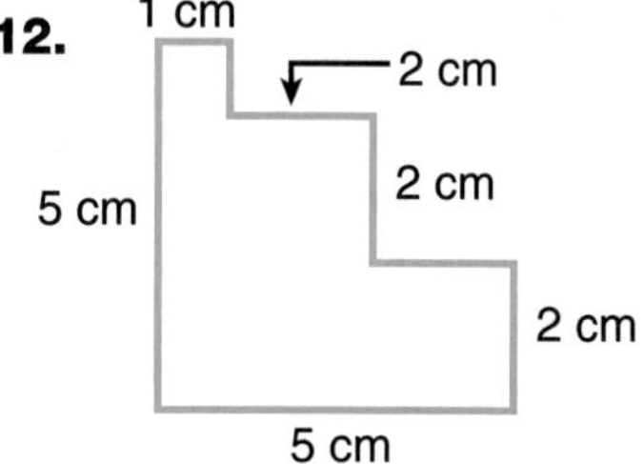

Algebra • Expressions Write an expression to represent the perimeter of each figure. Then write an expression to represent the area of each figure.

13. 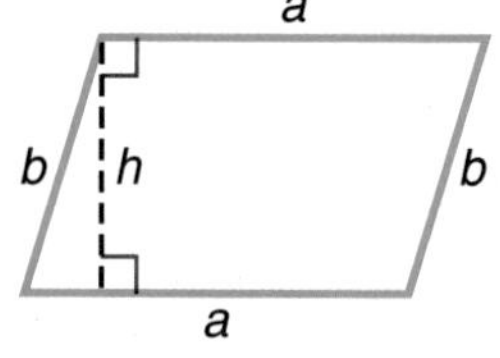

14. 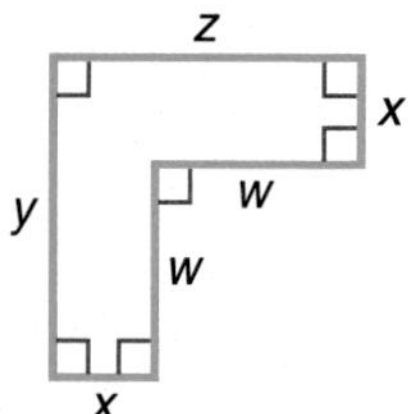

15. 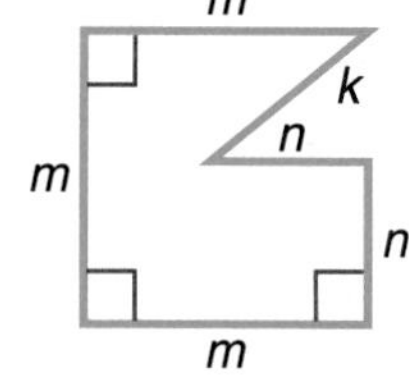

Talk About It • Write About It

TEST PREP

You learned how to estimate and find the area and perimeter of irregular and complex figures.

16. Explain how to estimate the perimeter and area of Shape A.

17. Explain how to find the area of Shape B.

A

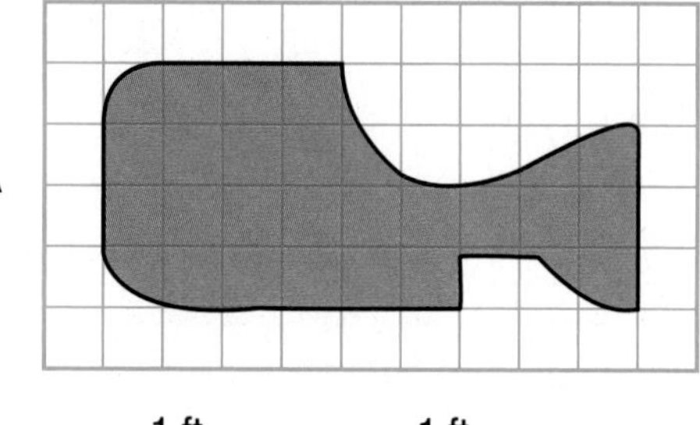

B

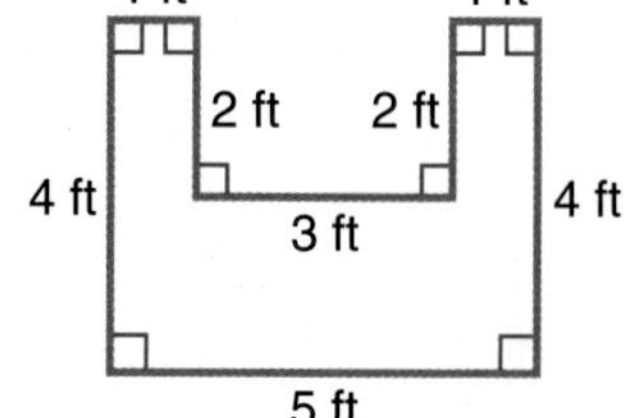

Historical Blueprints

Thomas Jefferson was an author of the Declaration of Independence and was the third President of the United States (1801–1809). Jefferson was also one of the leading architects of his time.

Besides designing the Virginia Capitol and the University of Virginia, Jefferson designed his home, called Monticello. The diagram at the right shows floor plans for the tea room and the dining room in Monticello.

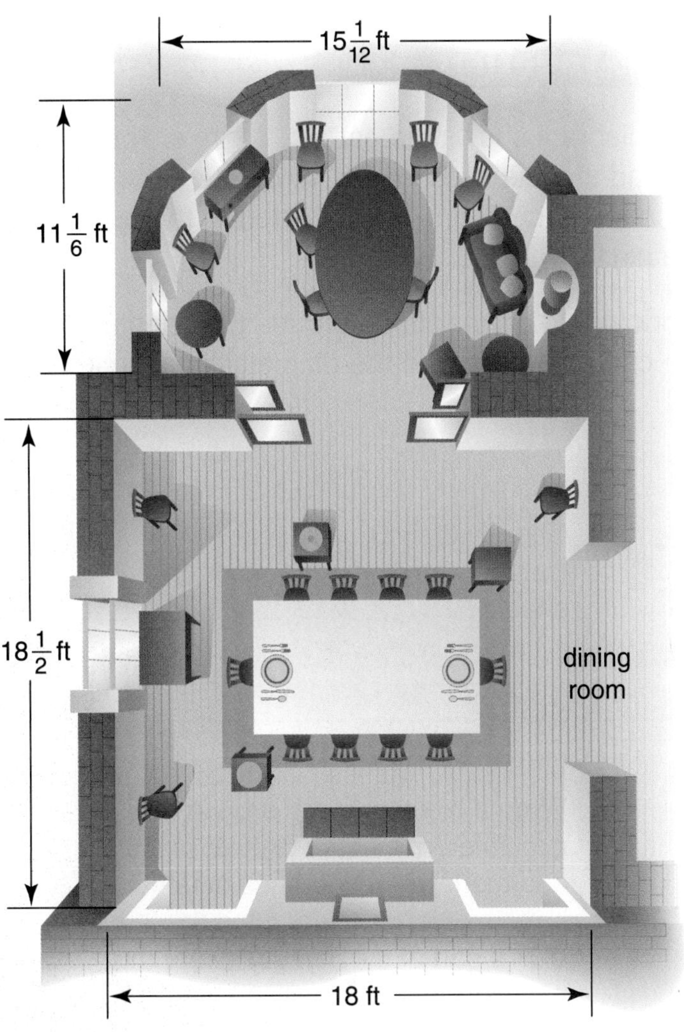

Study the floor plan.

- Estimate the area of the tea room. You may wish to trace the diagram on a piece of grid paper to help you.
- About how much smaller is the tea room than the dining room?
- About how much of the tea room's area does the large table in the center cover?
- Would the rug from the dining room fit in the tea room? Explain.

Tetrominoes

A tetromino is a design made of 4 squares. Each square has at least one side in common with another.

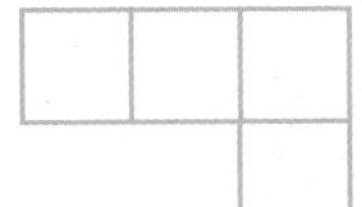

Two tetrominoes are shown. How many different tetrominoes can you make?

Brain Teaser

Square Deal

The area of one square is 16 times the area of another square. How are the side lengths of the two squares related? How are the perimeters of the two squares related?

Technology

Visit *Education Place* at **eduplace.com/kids/mw/** to try more brain teasers.

Algebra

Circumference of a Circle

Objective Find and use the formula to find the circumference of a circle.

e Glossary

Vocabulary

circumference

pi (π)

Materials
Learning Tool 53
string
circular objects
calculator
ruler or meter stick

Work Together

The diagram shows the parts of a circle. The distance around a circle is called the **circumference** *(C)* The circumference of a circle is related to the diameter of the circle.

Work with a partner to determine the relationship of the circumference and the diameter of a circle.

diameter (*d*)
radius (*r*)
center
circumference (*C*)

STEP 1 Choose 3 circular objects. List the objects on the recording sheet.

Circumference and Diameter			
Object	Circumference (*C*)	Diameter (*d*)	$C \div d$
Can			

STEP 2 Wrap a piece of string around the circumference of the circular object and mark where the ends meet. Use a meter stick or ruler to find the length of this part of the string. Record this measurement.

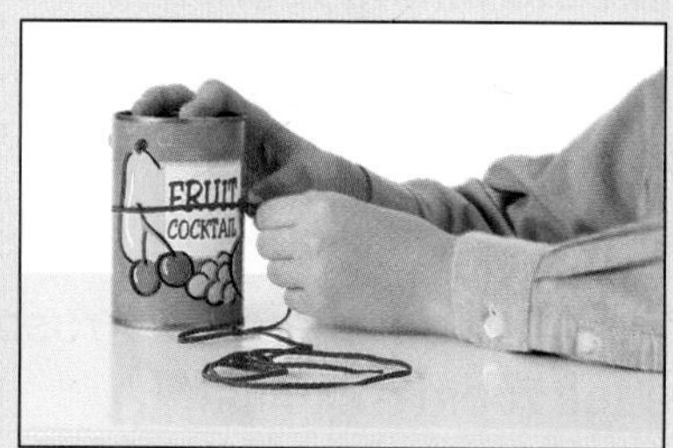

STEP 3 Measure the diameter of the circular object. Record this measurement.

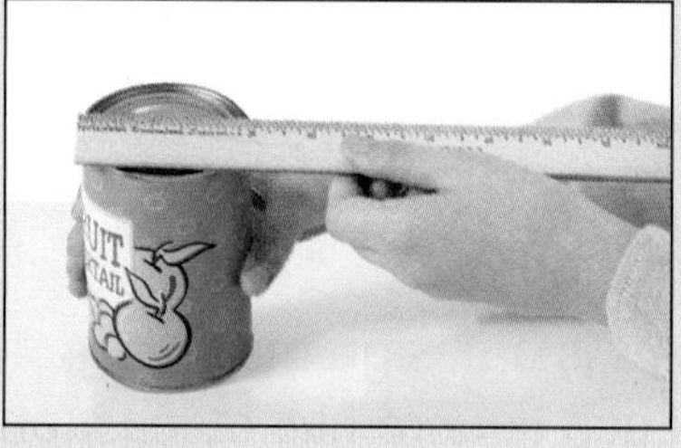

STEP 4 Use a calculator to complete the last column of the recording sheet. Round each quotient ($C \div d$) to the nearest hundredth.

- What patterns do you see?
- How is the circumference of a circle related to its diameter?

In the activity, you found that the circumference of a circle is always a little more than three times its diameter. The quotient for $C \div d$ is represented by the Greek letter **π**. The name for that letter is **pi**.

As a decimal, $\pi \approx 3.14$
As a fraction, $\pi \approx \frac{22}{7}$

≈ means "is approximately equal to"

If you know the diameter of a circle, you can use π to find the circumference.

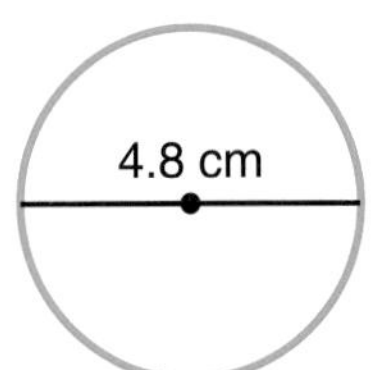

$$C = \pi d$$
$$\approx 3.14 \times 4.8$$
$$\approx 15.072$$

Rounded to the nearest tenth of a centimeter, the circumference is about 15.1 centimeters.

The diameter of a circle is twice as long as the radius, $d = 2r$. If you know the radius of a circle, you can use π to find the circumference.

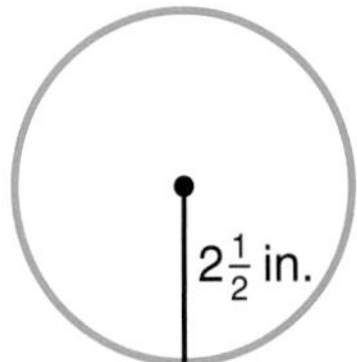

$$C = 2\pi r$$
$$\approx 2 \times \frac{22}{7} \times 2\frac{1}{2}$$
$$\approx 15\frac{5}{7}$$

The circumference of the circle is about $15\frac{5}{7}$ inches.

You can check your answer by using the value of π rounded to a whole number, 3.
$$C \approx 2 \times 3 \times 2\frac{1}{2}$$
$$\approx 15$$

Sometimes you should round your answers when working with measurements.

You can use the π key to find the circumference of the circle at the right.

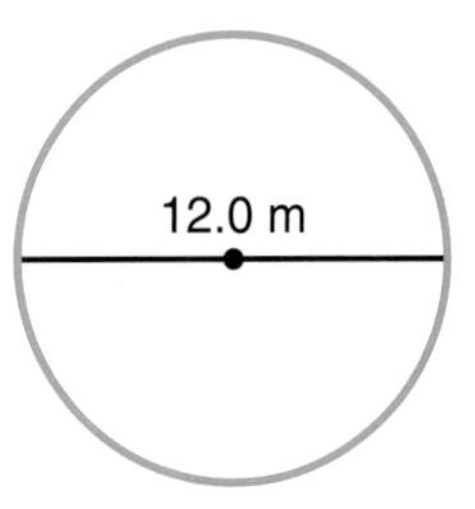

The result will be:

An answer of 37.699112 meters indicates that the answer is accurate to six decimal places. A more sensible answer would be 37.7 meters. The diameter of the circle is given in tenths, so the answer should also be given in tenths.

When working with measurements, round the answer to the same degree of precision as the least precise of the measurements in the problem.

The circumference of the circle is 37.7 m.

Go On

On Your Own

Find the circumference. Use 3.14 for π. Round your answer to the same degree of precision as given in the diameter.

1.

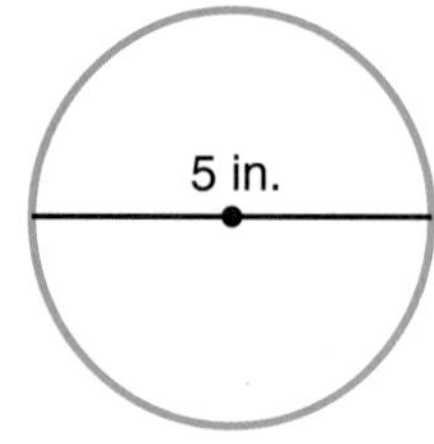

2.

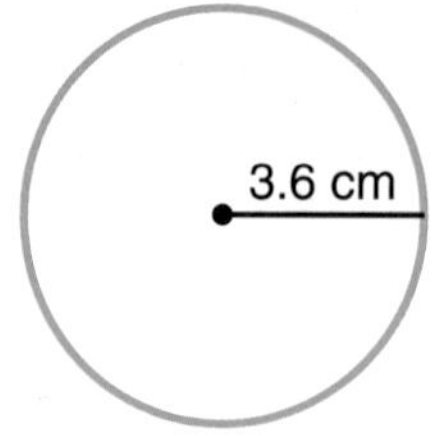

3.

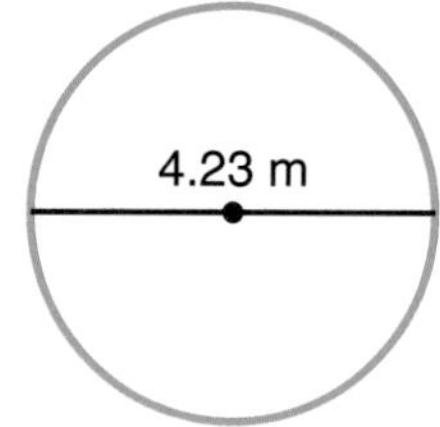

4. diameter = 10 yd

5. radius = 10 m

6. diameter = 24.362 m

Express each circumference as a fraction or mixed number in simplest form. Use $\frac{22}{7}$ for π.

7.

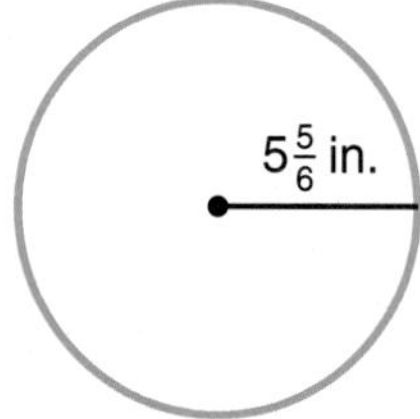

8.

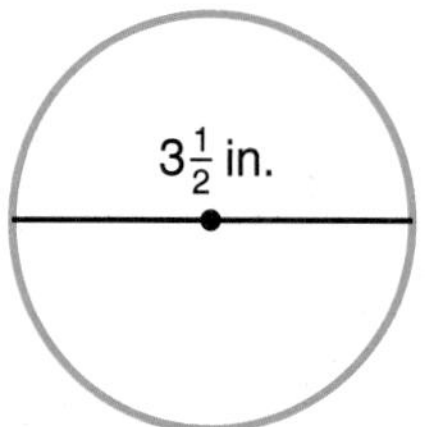

9.

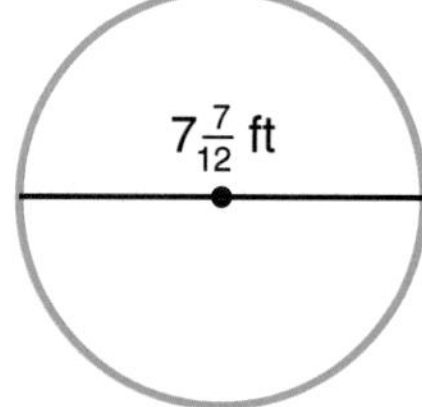

10. diameter = 7 ft

11. radius = 7 in.

12. diameter = $22\frac{3}{4}$ ft

Data **Use the table for Problems 13 and 14.**

13. Calculate the length of the label around each can. Use 3.14 for π.

14. If the height of the label of the tomato can is 11 cm, what is the approximate area of the label?

15. Suppose the cans of fruit cocktail and peas are both 10 cm tall. Find the difference between the areas of the labels.

Can	Diameter
tomatoes	10 cm
fruit cocktail	7.5 cm
soup	2.5 in.
peas	85 mm

Talk About It • Write About It

TEST PREP

You learned how to use a formula to find the circumference of a circle, and how to round your answer.

16. Explain how you can find the circumference of the circle at the right.

17. To which digit should you round your answer? Explain.

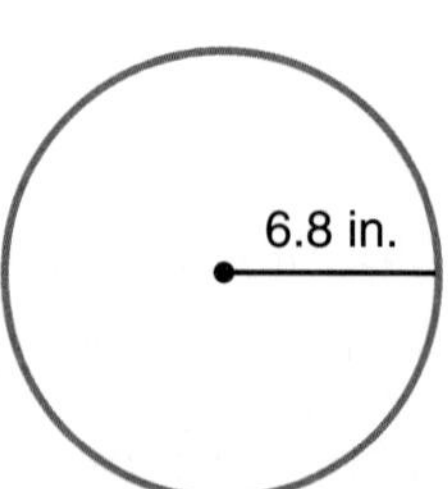

Quick Check

Check your understanding of Lessons 4–6. (Lessons 4, 5)

1. Find the perimeter of Figure A.

2. Find the area of Figure A.

3. Find the perimeter of Figure B.

4. Find the area of Figure B.

A. $3\frac{1}{2}$ in. $4\frac{1}{4}$ in. 10 in. 7 in.

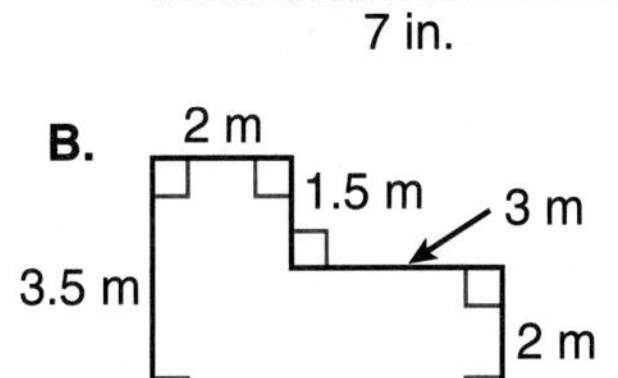

In Exercises 5 and 6, each square represents 1 cm². (Lesson 5)

5. Estimate the perimeter of Figure C.

6. Estimate the area of Figure C.

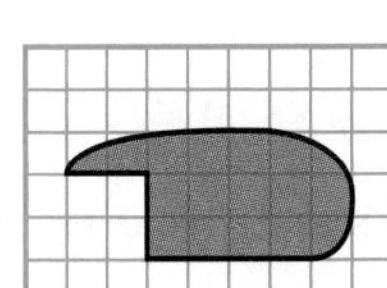

Find the circumference of each circle. Use 3.14 or $\frac{22}{7}$. (Lesson 6)

7. diameter = 3.2 cm **8.** radius = $1\frac{3}{4}$ in. **9.** diameter = $\frac{7}{8}$ ft **10.** radius = 10.5 m

Measurement Sense

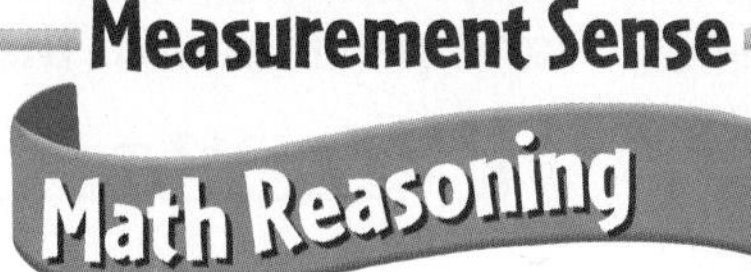

Cut-Ups

Materials: paper plate, scissors

Use this activity to find the formula for the area of a circle.

STEP 1 Fold a paper plate into eighths. Unfold the plate. Shade $\frac{1}{2}$ of the circle red. Cut along the folds.

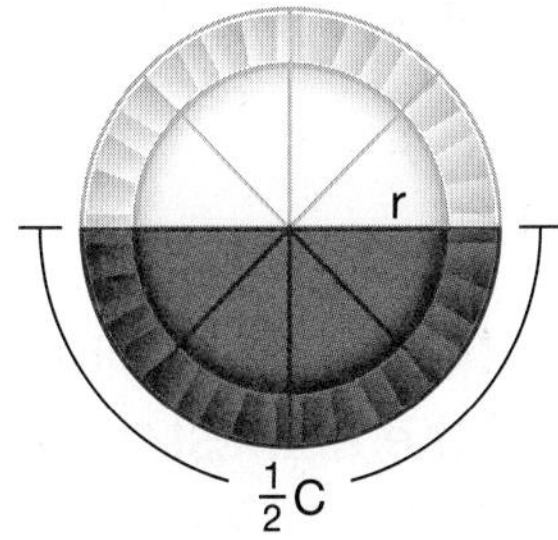

STEP 2 Rearrange the pieces to form a shape somewhat like a parallelogram, as shown at right.

- What part of the circle could be used as the height of the "parallelogram?"
- How is the circumference of the circle related to the base of the parallelogram?
- How would you find the approximate area of the parallelogram? Express your answer using parts of the circle.

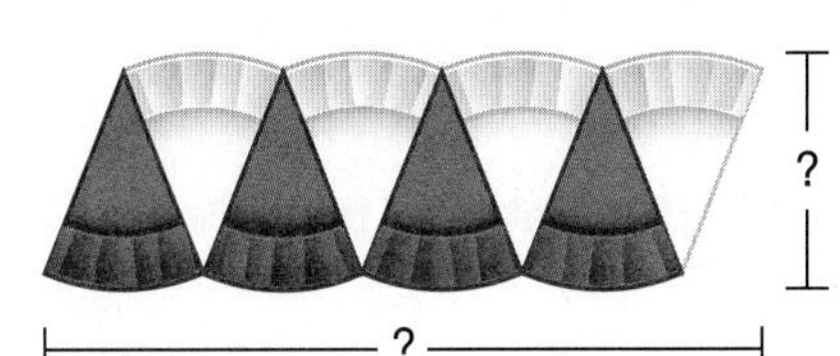

STEP 3 Write the formula for area of a circle. Express the area in terms of π and the radius (r).

Find each area to the nearest whole number.

a. radius = 4 cm **b.** diameter = 6 m

Chapter Review/Test

VOCABULARY

1. The distance around a circle is called the ____.
2. The quotient of $C \div d$ is called ____.
3. ____ is the number of square units needed to cover a region.

Vocabulary
area
circumference
perimeter
pi
square units

CONCEPTS AND SKILLS

Find the perimeter and area of each figure. (Lessons 1, 3, 4; pp. 422–423, 428–433)

4. 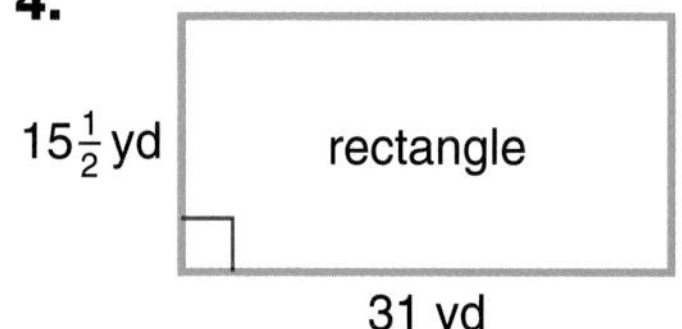

5. 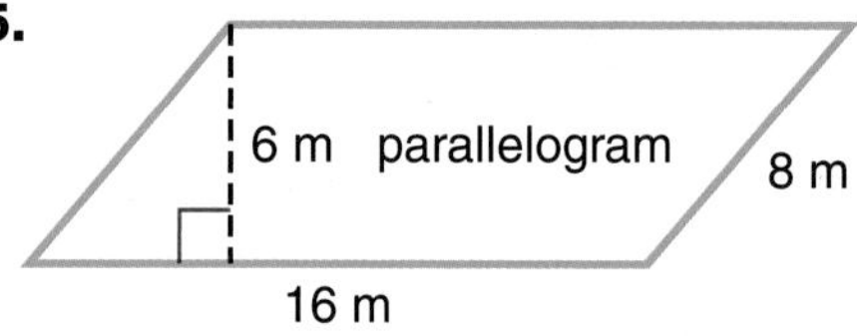

6. 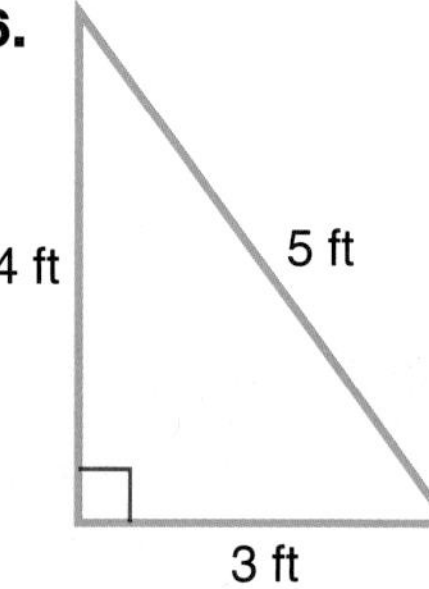

Estimate the area of each figure. Then find the area and perimeter of the figures. (Lesson 5, 434–437)

7. 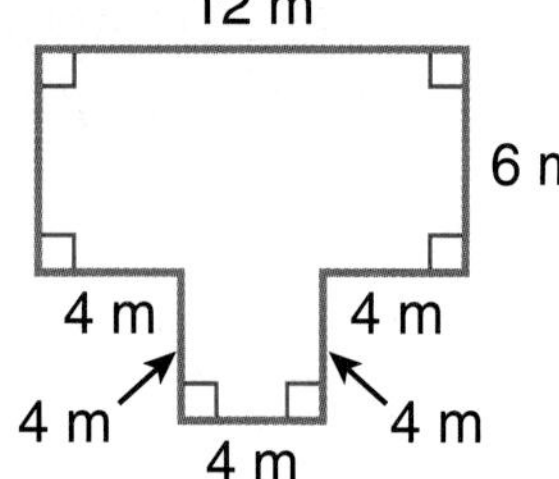

8. 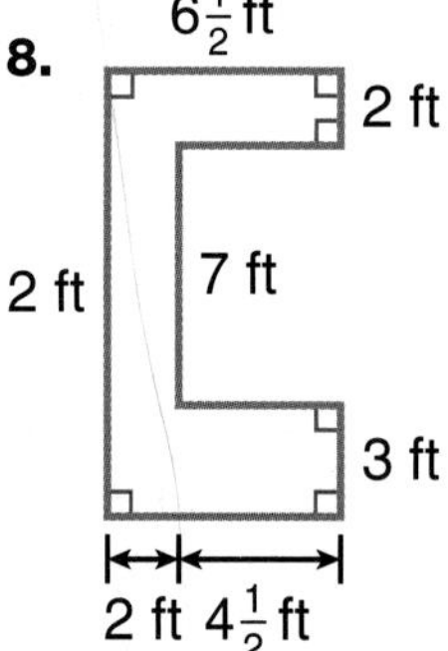

9. Find the circumference of the circle at right to the nearest tenth. Use 3.14 for π. (Lesson 6, pp. 438–441)

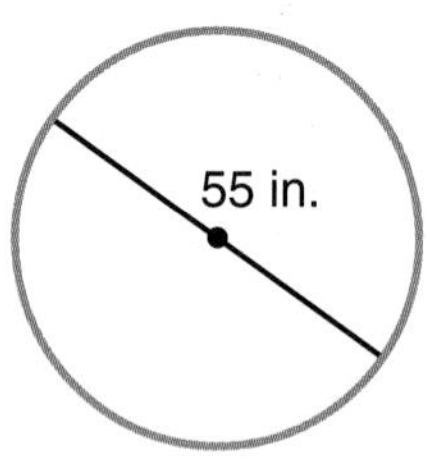

PROBLEM SOLVING

Find a pattern to solve. (Lesson 2, pp. 424–427)

10. If the pattern continues, draw the ninth figure.

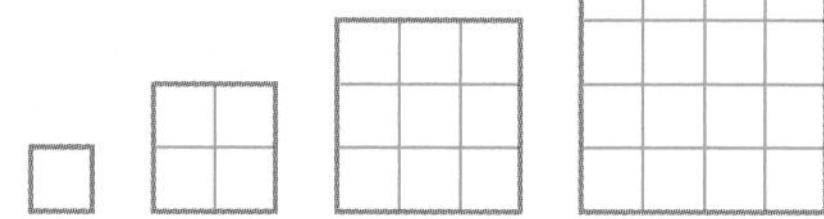

Write About It

Show You Understand

How are perimeter and circumference alike? How are they different?

Extra Practice

Set A (Lesson 1, pp. 422–423)

Find the perimeter or missing length for each rectangle.

1. 4 ft, 9 ft

2. 11 yd, 11 yd

3.

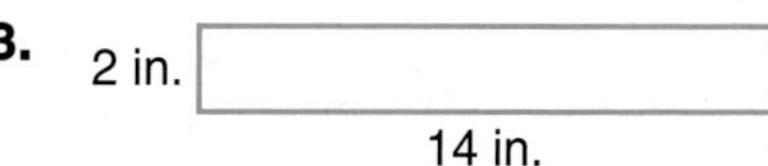

4. 10 m, 22 m

5.

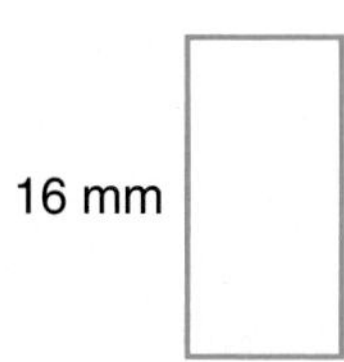

P = 48 mm

6. 6 ft

P = 42 ft

Set B (Lesson 3, pp. 428–431)

Find the area of each figure.

1.

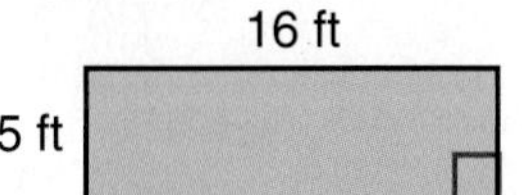

2.

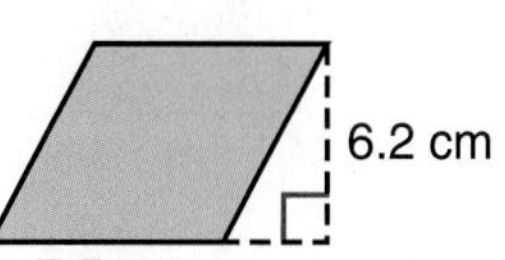

3.

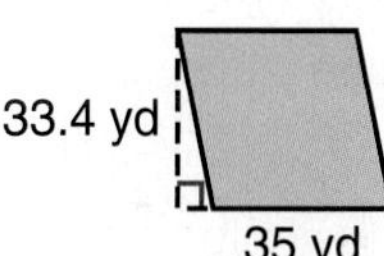

4.

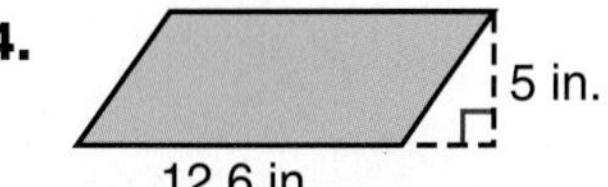

5.

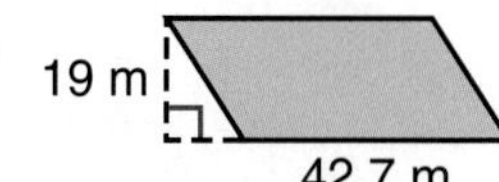

6.

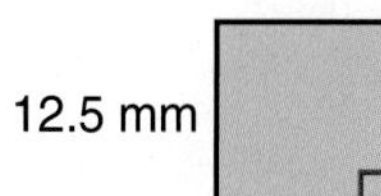

Set C (Lesson 4, pp. 432–433)

Find the area of each triangle.

1.

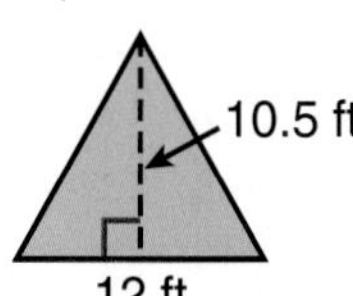

2.

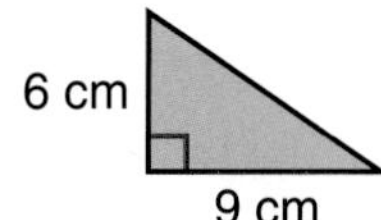

3.

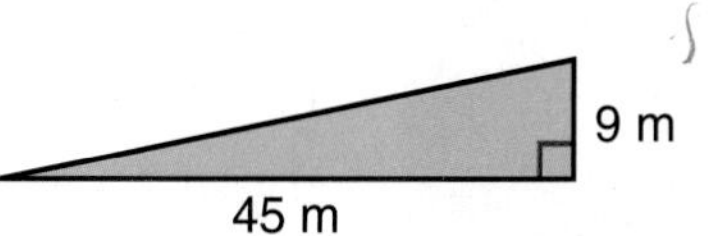

4.

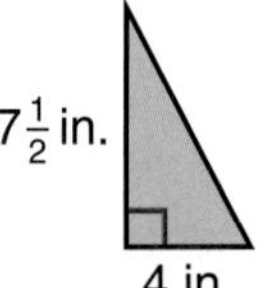

5.

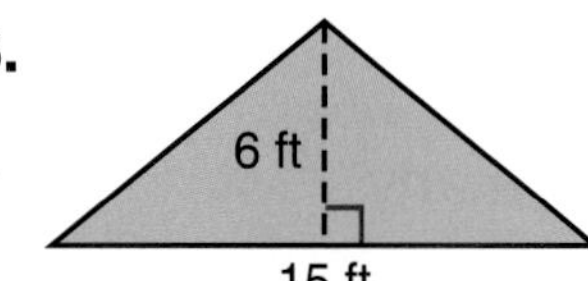

6.

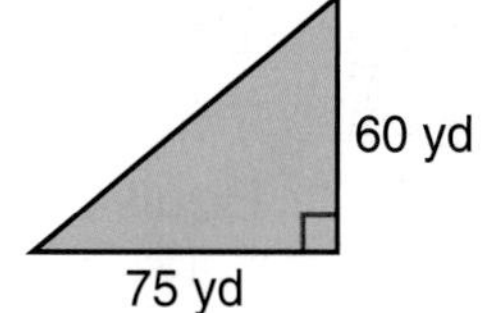

CHAPTER 17

Solid Figures, Surface Area, and Volume

INVESTIGATION

Use Data

Container ships carry thousands of boxes, all the same sizes. At the right is a drawing of a twenty-foot container that holds 1 TEU. The abbreviation TEU means Twenty-feet Equivalent Units. How many cubic feet are in 1 TEU?

Chapter Pretest

Use this page to review and remember what you need to know for this chapter.

VOCABULARY

Choose the best word to complete each sentence.

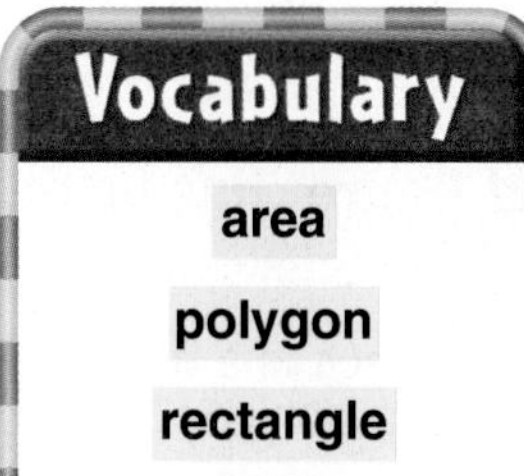

1. A ____ is a simple closed plane figure made up of three or more line segments.
2. The ____ of a solid figure is the number of cubic units that make up a solid figure.
3. The number of square units in a region is called the ____ of the region.

CONCEPTS AND SKILLS

Identify each figure.

4. 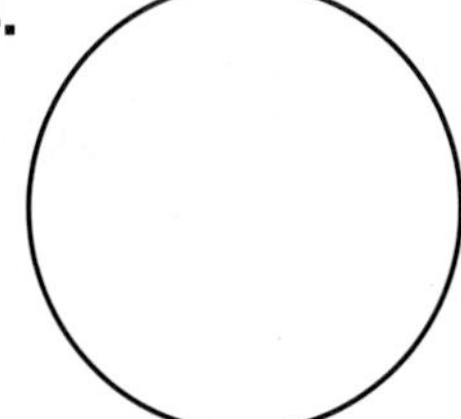

5. 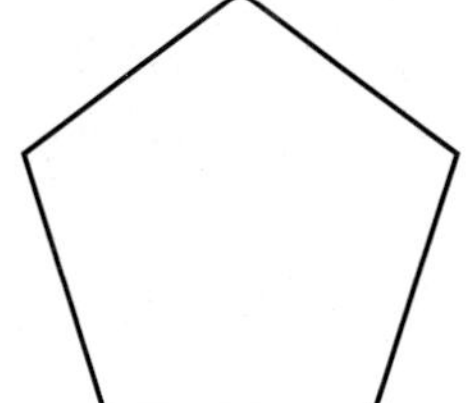

6. 

Find the perimeter and area of each figure.

7. 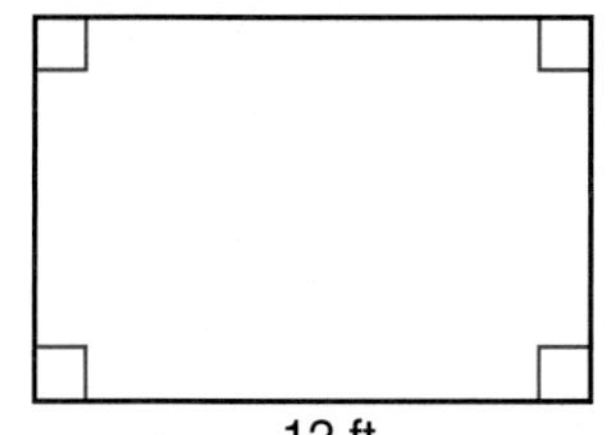

8. 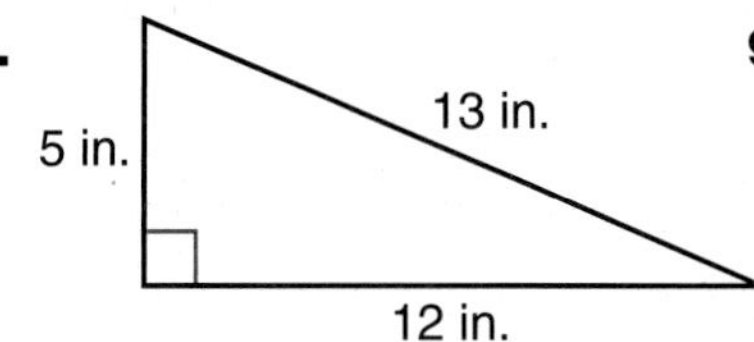

9. 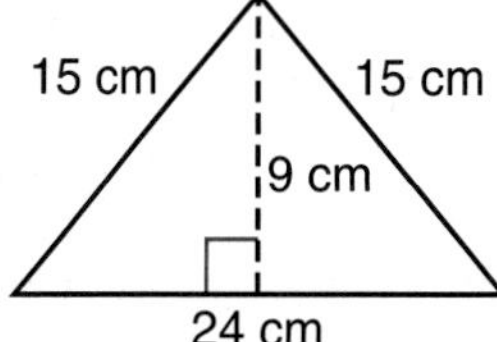

Write About It

10. Suppose you know the area of a parallelogram. Can you find the area of a triangle that has the same base and height as the parallelogram? Explain.

Test Prep on the Net

Visit *Education Place* at **eduplace.com/kids/mw/** for more review.

Lesson 1

Solid Figures

Objective Identify solid figures.

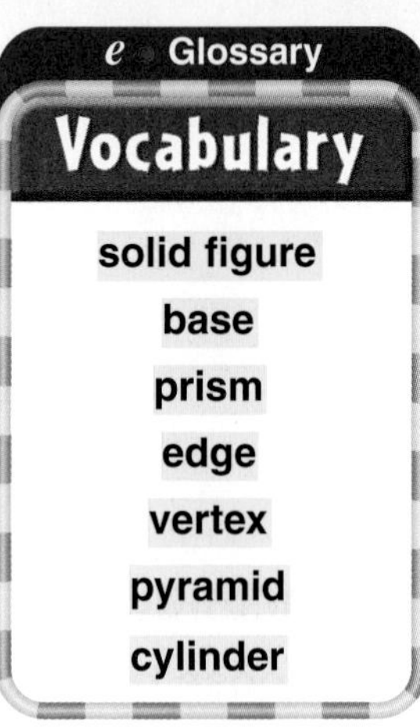
e Glossary
Vocabulary
solid figure
base
prism
edge
vertex
pyramid
cylinder

Learn About It

MathTracks 2/16
Listen and Understand

Most of the objects that you see every day are solid figures. Boxes, cups, cans, and other containers are all examples of solid figures.

▶A **solid figure** has length, width, height, and takes up space.

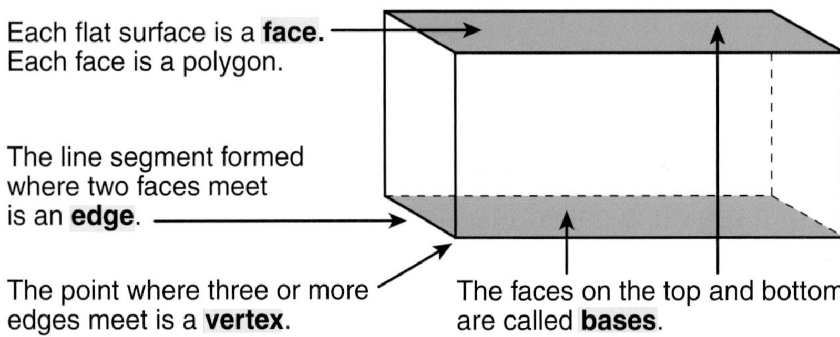
Each flat surface is a **face.**
Each face is a polygon.
The line segment formed where two faces meet is an **edge**.
The point where three or more edges meet is a **vertex**.
The faces on the top and bottom are called **bases**.

▶A **prism** is a solid figure that has two parallel congruent bases joined by rectangular faces. Each prism is named by the shape of its base. The pasta box to the right is a rectangular prism since its bases are rectangles.

SOUP
CHICKEN NOODLE
Pasta

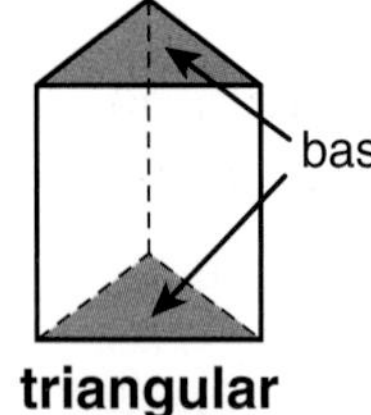
bases

triangular prism

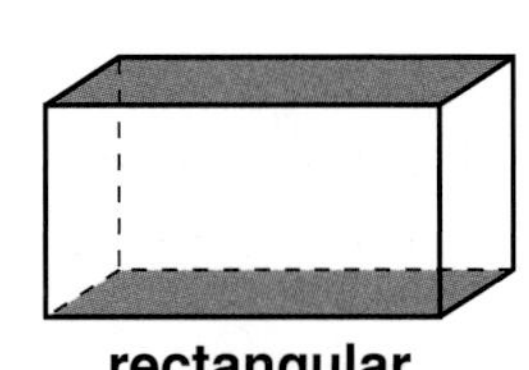

rectangular prism

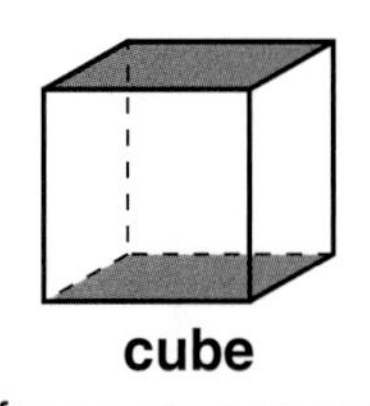

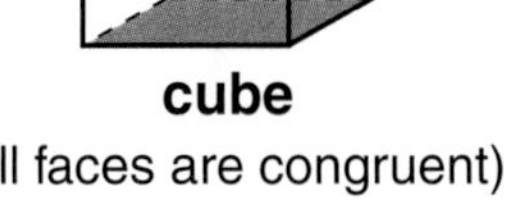

cube
(all faces are congruent)

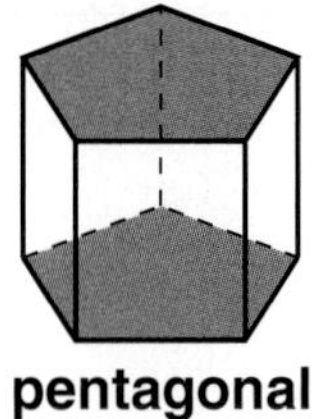

pentagonal prism

▶A **pyramid** has one base that can be any polygon. All of the other faces are triangles that share a vertex.

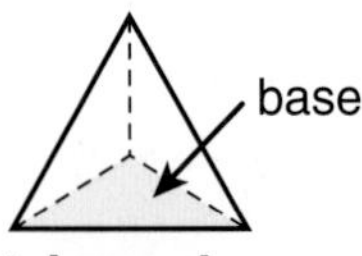
base

triangular pyramid

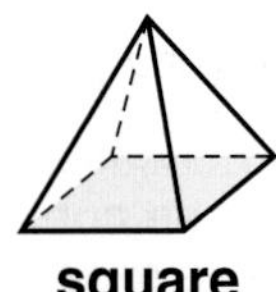

square pyramid

pentagonal pyramid

Some solid figures have curved surfaces.

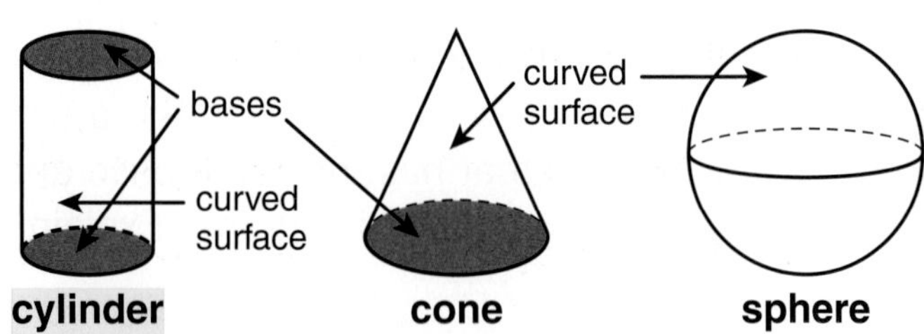
bases
curved surface
curved surface

cylinder **cone** **sphere**

Guided Practice

Ask Yourself

- How many bases are there?
- What shape is the base?

Classify each solid figure. Then write the number of faces, vertices, and edges.

1. 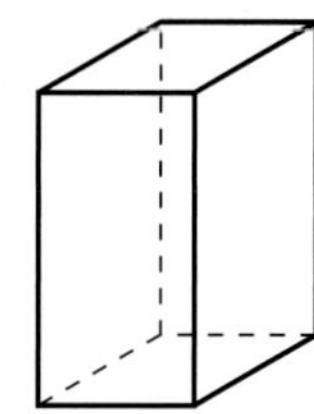
2. 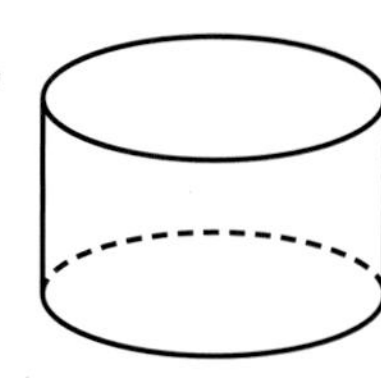
3. 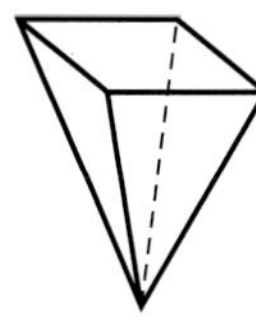

Explain Your Thinking ▶ What is the difference between a rectangular pyramid and a rectangular prism?

Practice and Problem Solving

Name each solid figure. Then write the number of faces, vertices, and edges.

4. 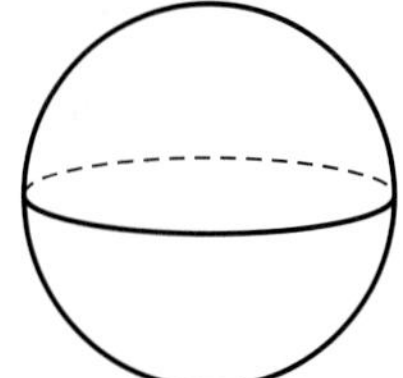
5. 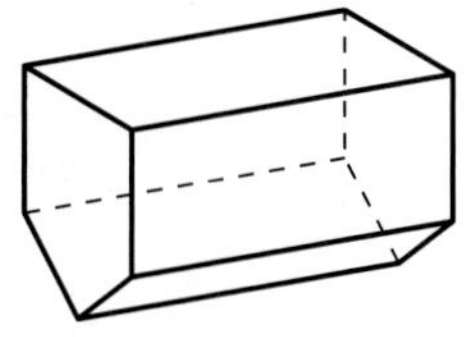
6. 
7. 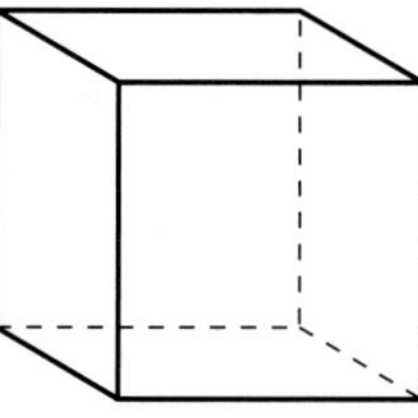
8. 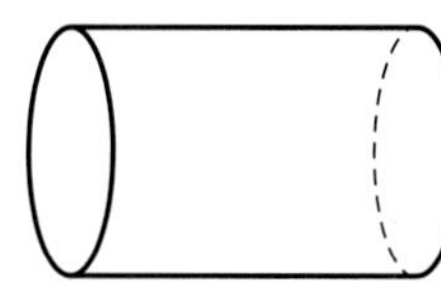
9. 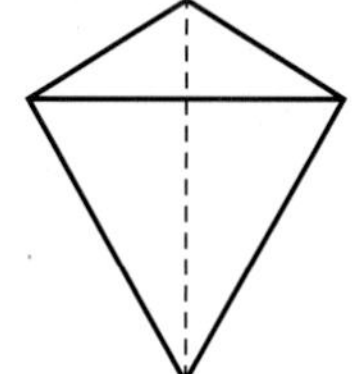
10. 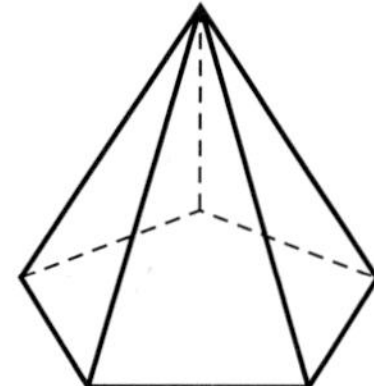
11. 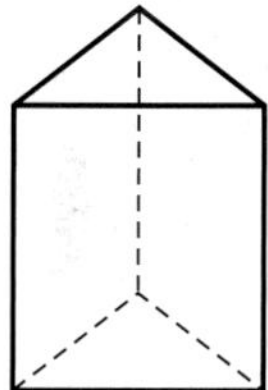

Solve.

12. **Model** Use 24 cubes to build a rectangular prism. Then sketch it on a sheet of graph paper.

13. **Represent** Sketch a figure with one square base and four triangular faces. Then name the figure.

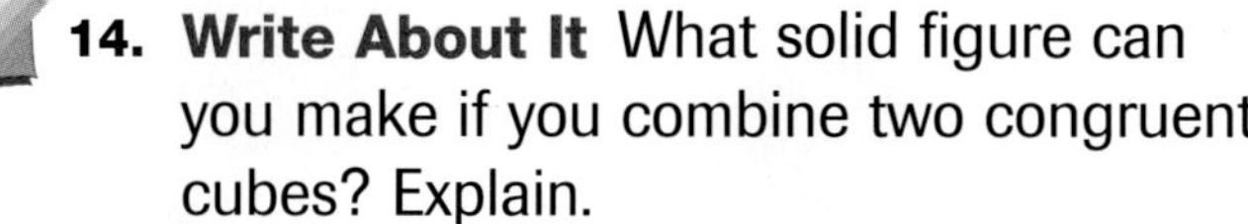

14. **Write About It** What solid figure can you make if you combine two congruent cubes? Explain.

15. **Reasoning** A pyramid has six faces, including the base. What type of pyramid must it be? Explain.

Daily Review Test Prep

Estimate. Then add or subtract.
(Ch. 11, Lessons 2–3)

16. $4.73 + 6.8$
17. $23.81 - 5.64$
18. $0.69 + 0.45$
19. $0.9 - 0.44$

20. Which solid figure has exactly one circular base?

A cone
B cylinder
C pyramid
D sphere

Extra Practice See page 469, Set A.

Two-Dimensional Views of Solid Figures

Objective Identify different two-dimensional views of a solid figure.

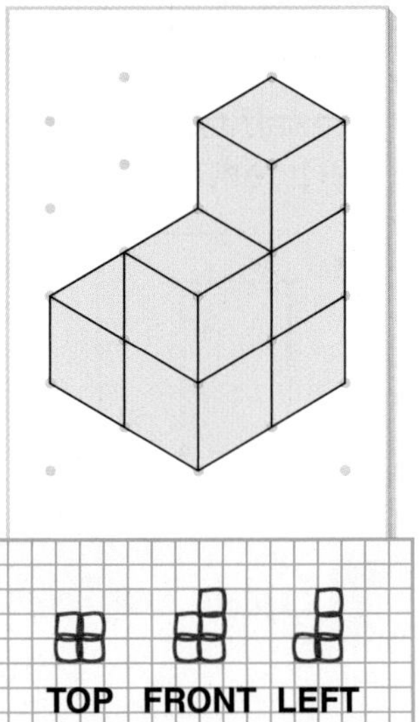

Work Together

To make a two-dimensional drawing of the solid figure, you can use triangular dot paper and grid paper as shown at the right. You can also use two-dimensional drawings to show what solid figures look like from different views.

Materials: cubes, grid paper **(Learning Tool 14)**

Try this activity to identify different two-dimensional views of the figure shown below.

STEP 1 Use cubes to build the figure.

STEP 2 Draw these views on grid paper:
- the top view
- the view from the right side
- the front view

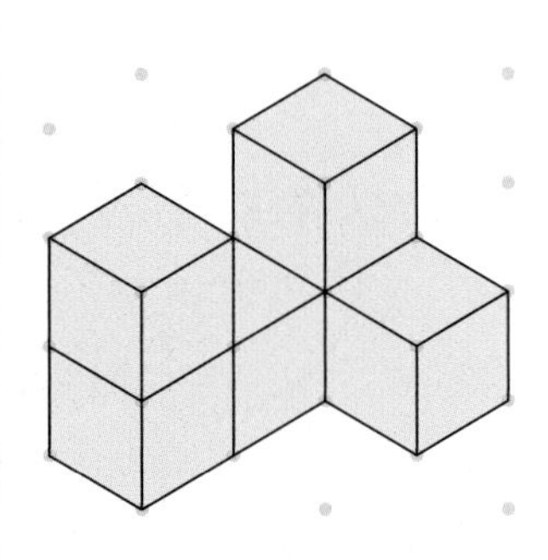

You can use two-dimensional views to build and draw a three-dimensional figure.

Materials: cubes, triangular dot paper **(Learning Tool 17)**

Try this activty to create a solid figure that looks like this:

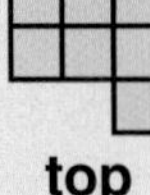

top

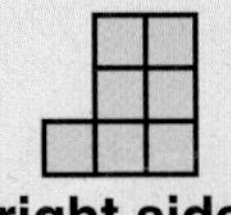

right side

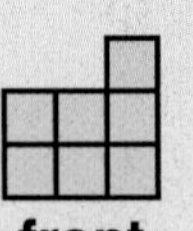

front

STEP 1 Look at the top view. What can you say about the bottom of the figure? Use cubes to build the bottom layer of the figure.

STEP 2 Use the side and front views to visualize the middle layer and then the top layer of the figure. Build each layer.

STEP 3 Draw the figure on triangular dot paper. Could you draw another figure? Explain.

On Your Own

Use cubes to build each figure. On graph paper, draw each figure from the top, from the side, and from the front.

1.

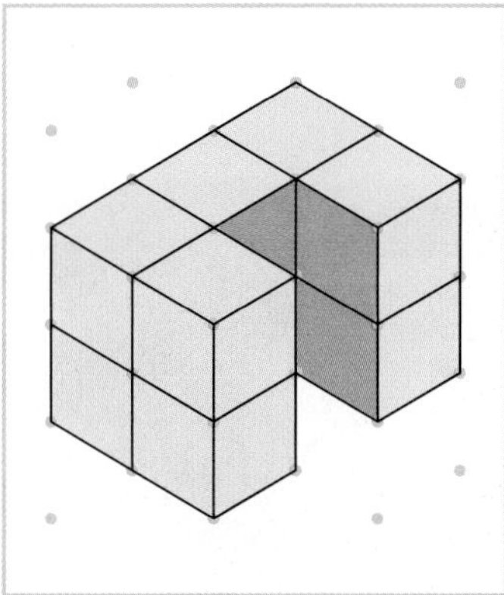

2.

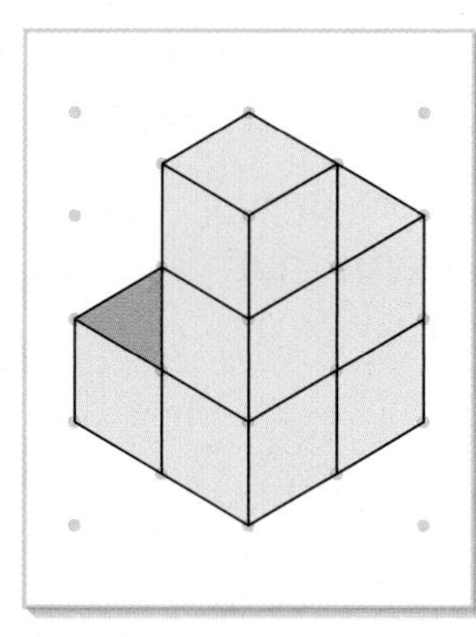

3.

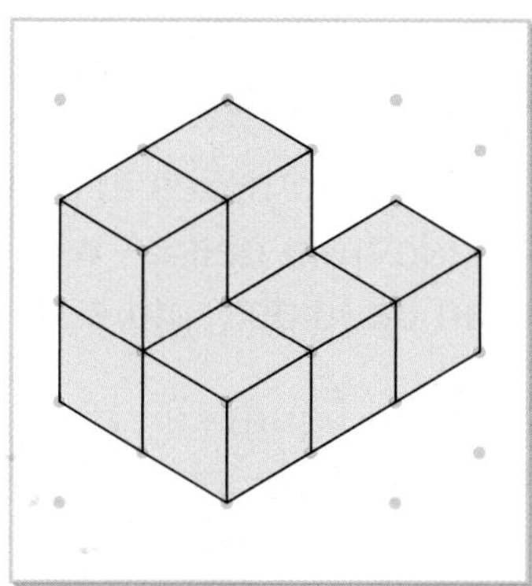

Use cubes to build a three-dimensional figure with these views. Then draw the figure on triangular dot paper.

4.

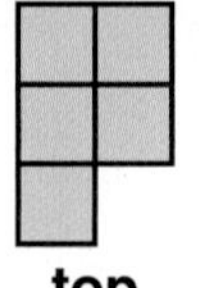

top **side** **front**

5.

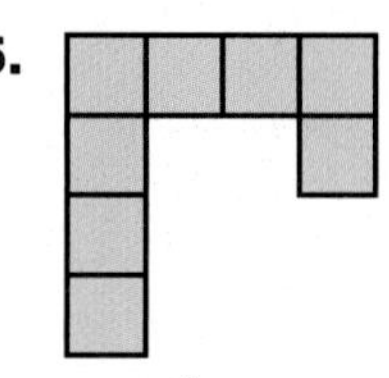

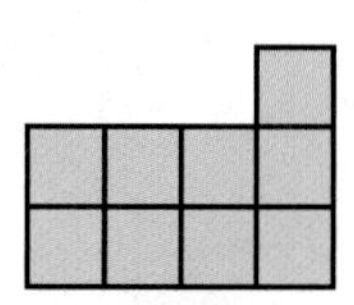

top **side** **front**

6. **Reasoning** Could the three views shown below be views of a rectangular prism? Explain.

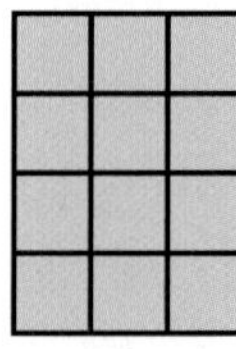

top

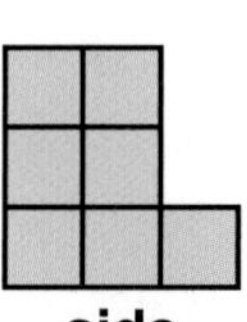

side

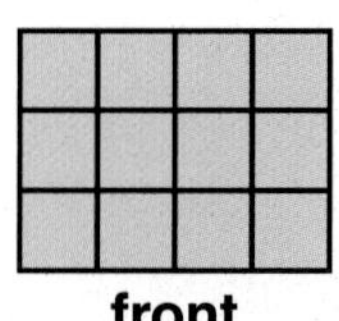

front

7. Name a solid figure that is a triangle from the top view and has congruent rectangles from the side views.

8. Sketch the top, side, and front views of each solid figure.

 a. cube **b.** cylinder

 c. cone **d.** sphere

Talk About It • Write About It

Use what you have learned about modeling and drawing solid figures to answer these questions.

9. Why does the top view tell you how the bottom layer of cubes must be arranged?

10. A figure has a top view and side view that are identical. What type solid figure might this be? Explain how you know.

Lesson 3

Nets

Objective Identify the nets of solid figures.

Learn About It

Cardboard boxes and other containers are made from nets. A **net** is a flat pattern that can be folded into a solid figure.

A solid figure can have more than one net. For example, both nets below can be folded to make a triangular prism.

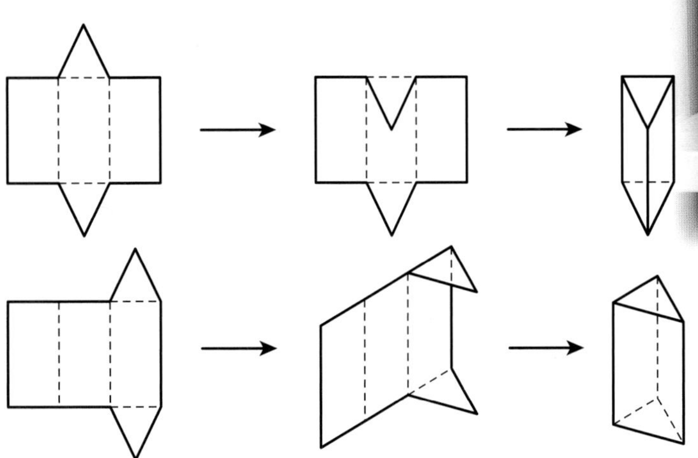

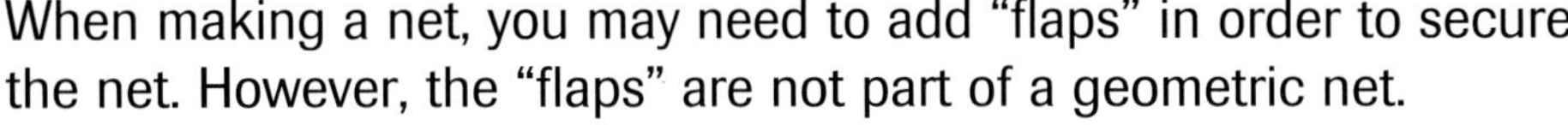

When making a net, you may need to add "flaps" in order to secure the net. However, the "flaps" are not part of a geometric net.

Try this activity to make nets.

Materials: inch grid paper **(Learning Tool 15)**, scissors, tape

STEP 1 On a sheet of grid paper, draw the net shown at the right. Then cut it out.

- Predict what solid figure the net will make.

STEP 2 Fold the net on the dotted lines. Tape the edges together.

- Was your prediction correct?

STEP 3 Repeat Step 1 and Step 2 using the net at the right.

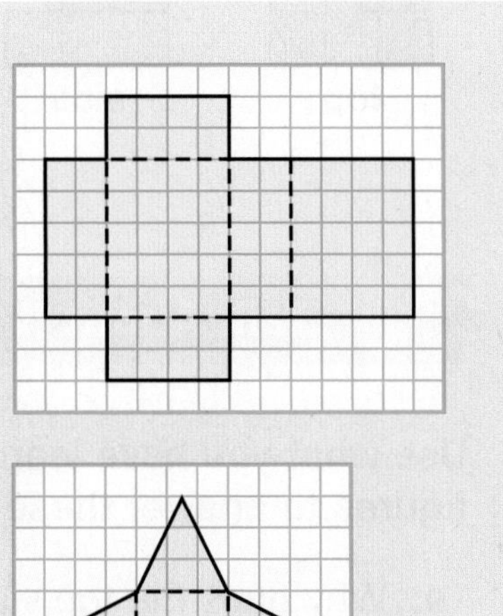

Guided Practice

Ask Yourself

- Which side of the net is the base? What shape does it have?
- How many faces will the shape have?

Predict what shape each net will make.

1. 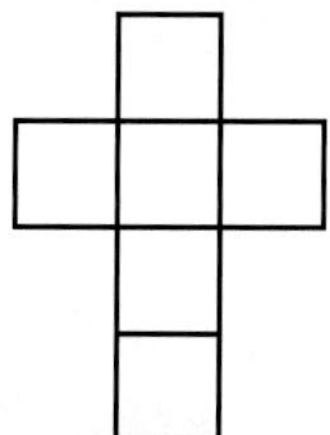

2. 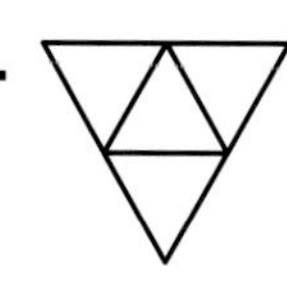

3. 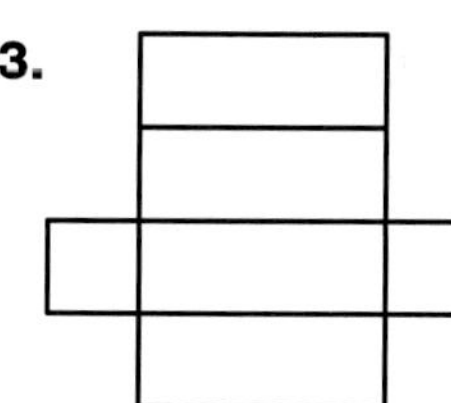

Explain Your Thinking ▶ How did you make your prediction for Exercise 2?

Practice and Problem Solving

Predict what shape each net will make.

4. 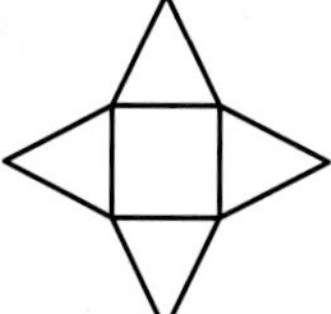

5. 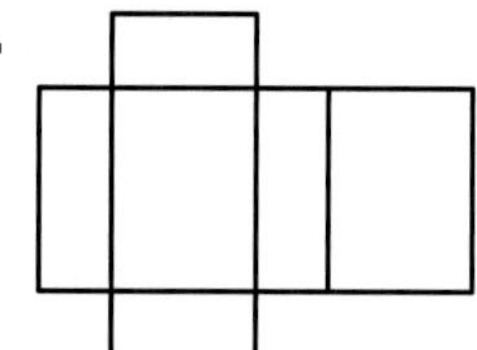

6. 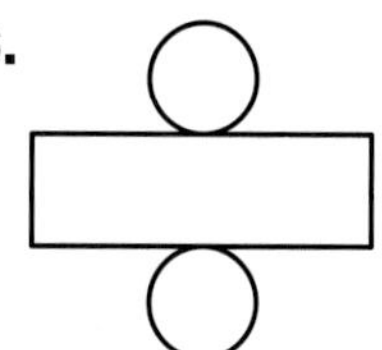

7. 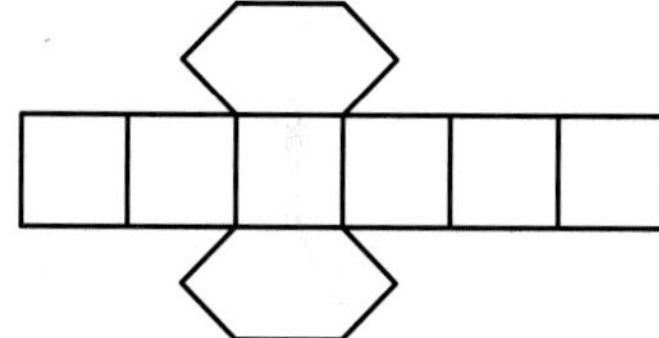

Draw a net for each solid figure.

8. 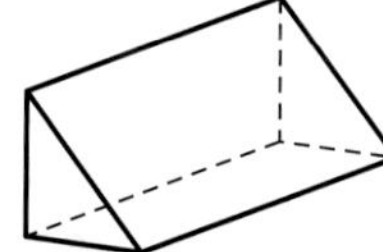

9. 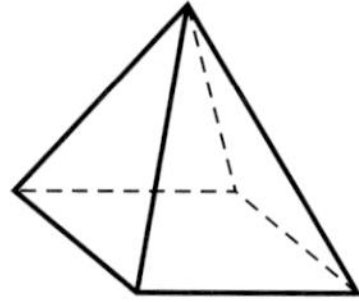

10. 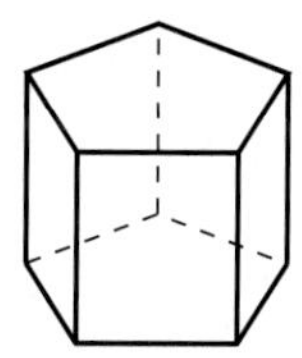

11. 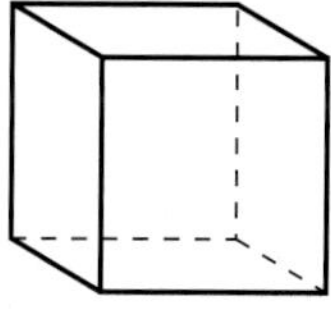

Solve.

12. **Predict** Which of the nets to the right will not form a cube? Explain your answer.

13. **Represent** Draw another net that will form a cube.

14. **Calculator** A rectangular room is 15 feet by 17 feet. How much will it cost to cover the floor with carpet that costs $8.99 per square foot?

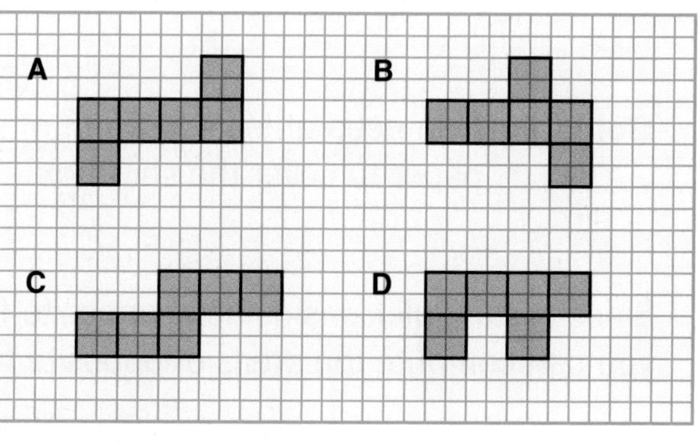

Daily Review | Test Prep

Find the area. (Ch. 16, Lessons 3–4)

15. 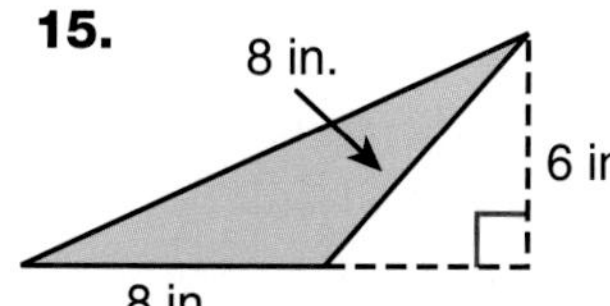

16. 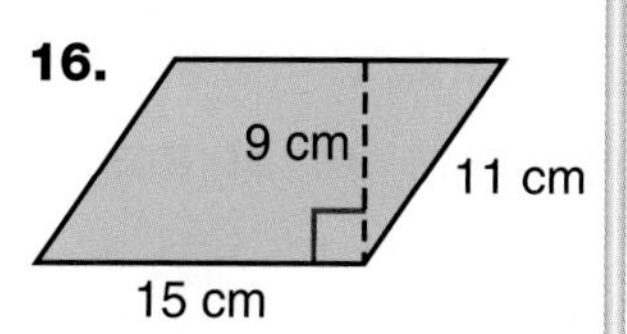

17. **Free Response** Describe the solid that could be made from this net. Explain your thinking.

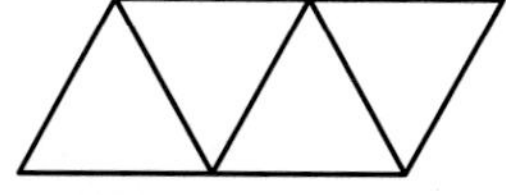

Extra Practice See page 469, Set B.

Lesson 4

Surface Area

Objective Use nets to find the surface area of solid figures.

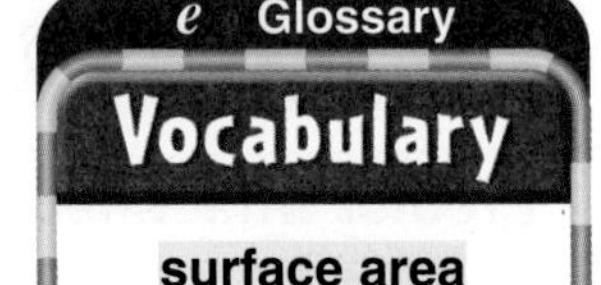

Learn About It

A department store stocks wrapping paper that can be folded to wrap shirt boxes. What is the least amount of wrapping paper you need to cover this shirt box?

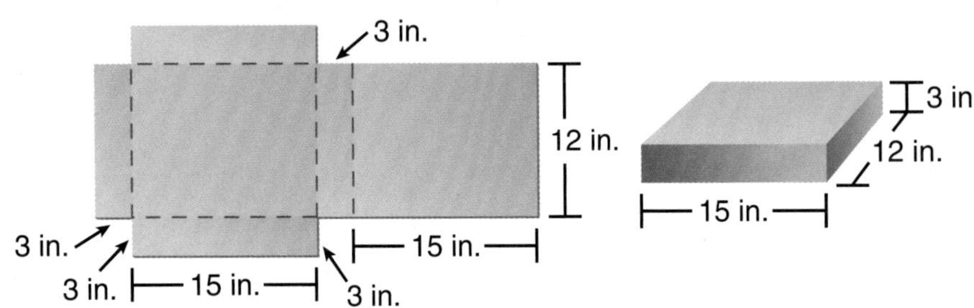

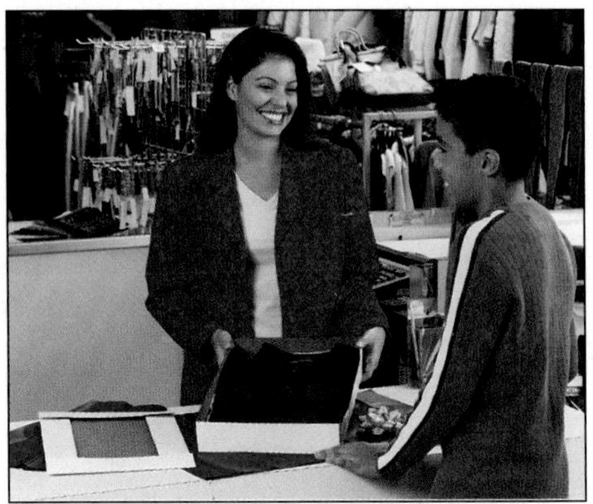

To solve the problem, find the surface area of the box. The **surface area** of a solid figure is the sum of the areas of all its faces and is measured in square units.

You can use a table to list the area of each face.

Face	Length	Width	Area
top	15 in.	12 in.	180 in.^{2}
bottom	15 in.	12 in.	180 in.^{2}
front	3 in.	12 in.	36 in.^{2}
back	3 in.	12 in.	36 in.^{2}
left side	3 in.	15 in.	45 in.^{2}
right side	3 in.	15 in.	45 in.^{2}
		sum:	522 in.^{2}

Solution: You need at least 522 in.^{2} of wrapping paper to cover the shirt box.

Think
However, you will probably need more paper, because the paper will have to overlap.

Since rectangular prisms have opposite faces that are congruent, you can compute the areas of opposite faces to find surface area.

Determine the surface area of the solid figure.

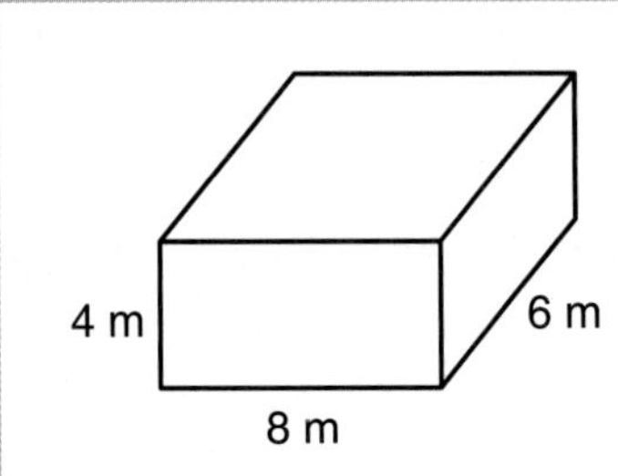

Area of Faces:

top and bottom: $2 \times (8 \times 6) = 96$
front and back: $2 \times (8 \times 4) = 64$
right and left sides: $2 \times (6 \times 4) = 48$

The sum of the areas is: $96 + 64 + 48 = 208$

Solution: The surface area is 208 m^2.

Another Example

Surface Area of a Triangular Prism

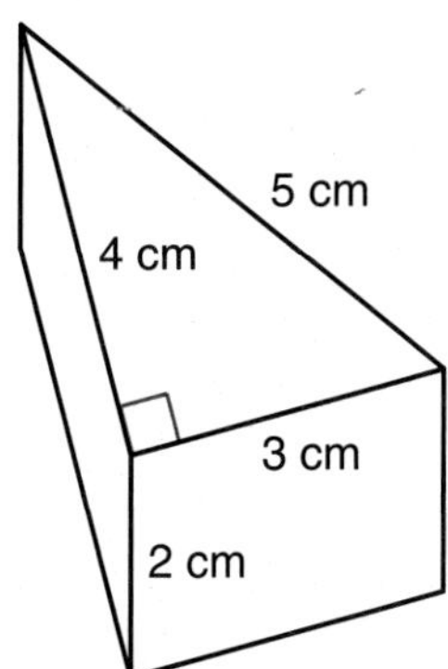

Think
The top and the bottom are congruent triangles. The front, left side, and right side are rectangles that are not congruent.

Area of Faces:

top and bottom: $2 \times (\frac{1}{2} \times 3 \times 4) = 12$

front: $3 \times 2 = 6$

left side: $2 \times 4 = 8$

right side: $2 \times 5 = 10$

The sum of the area is: $12 + 6 + 8 + 10 = 36$

Solution: The surface area is 36 cm^2.

Guided Practice

Ask Yourself

- Which numbers do I multiply to find the surface area of each face?
- Which numbers do I add to find the surface area of the solid?

Predict what solid each net will make. Then determine the surface area of the solid figure. Each square is 1 cm^2.

1.

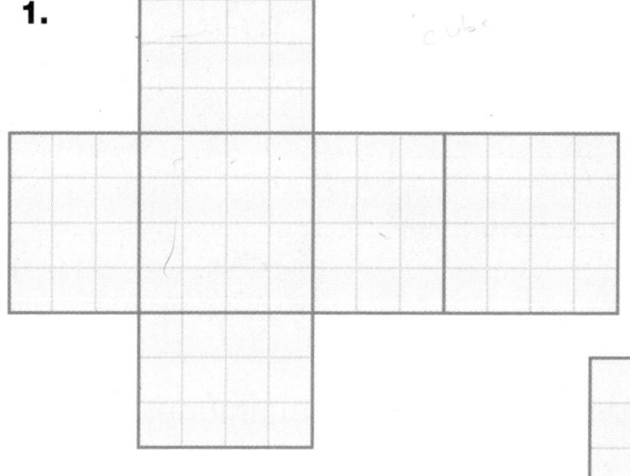

2.

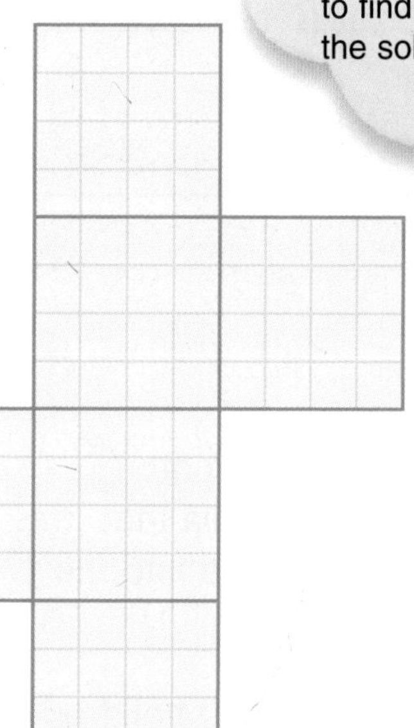

Determine the surface area of each solid figure.

3.

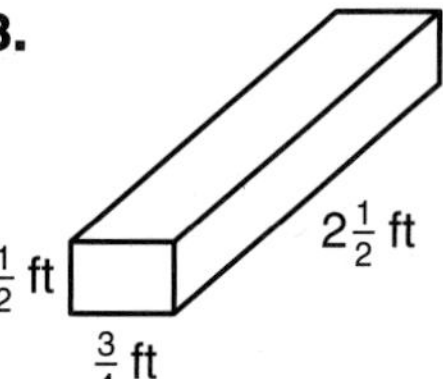

4.

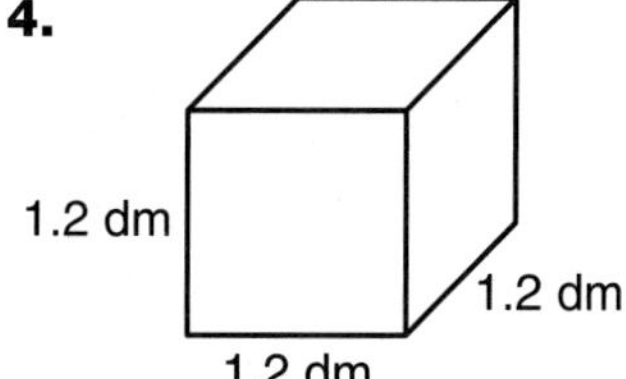

5.

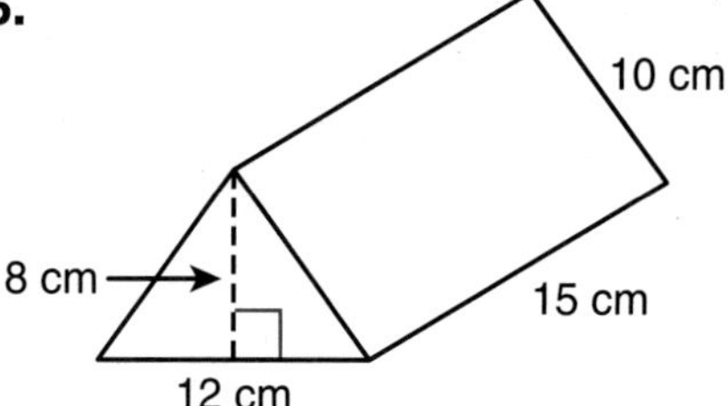

Explain Your Thinking ▶ Explain how you found the surface area in Exercise 5.

Practice and Problem Solving

Determine the surface area of each solid figure.

6. 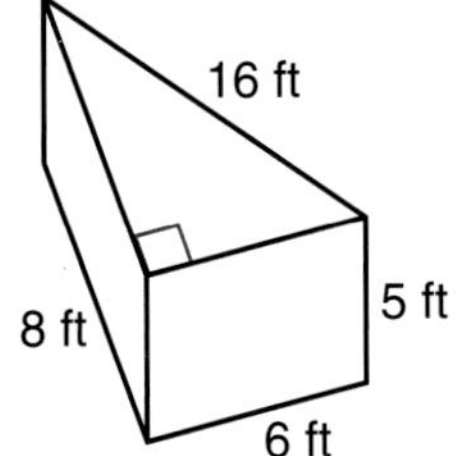

7. 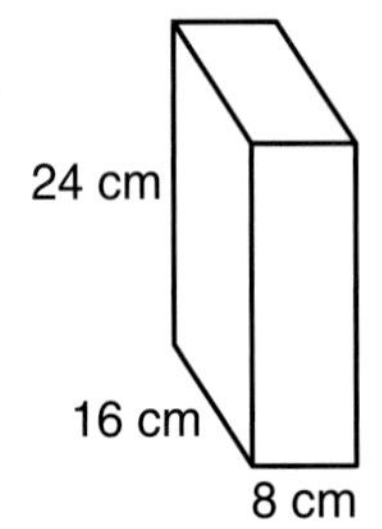

8. 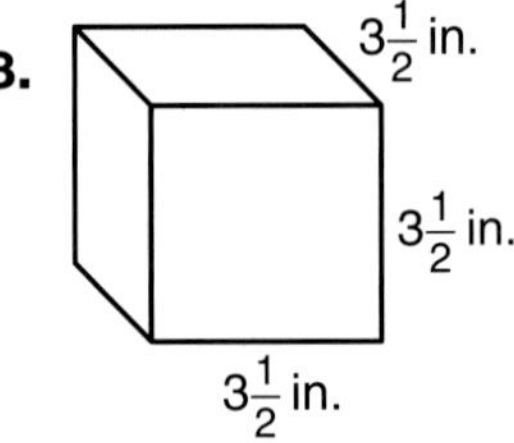

Copy and complete the table.

	Length of One Side (*s*) of cube	Area of One Face (*f*)	Surface Area of Cube (*SA*)
9.	3 cm		
10.	4 cm		
11.	15 cm		
12.	6 cm		
13.	7 cm		
14.	8 cm		

Solve.

15. **Analyze** Study your results from Exercises 9–14. Write a formula that uses the length of a side (*s*) to find the surface area of a cube (*SA*).

16. What is the minimum amount of wrapping paper needed to wrap a box that has a length of 6 inches, a height of 4 inches, and a width of 5 inches?

17. The Graysons are sending 140 holiday cards. The cards come in boxes of 25. How many boxes of cards do the Graysons need?

18. **Predict** A box that is 10 inches long, 3 inches deep, and 4 inches high holds 6 pounds of snack mix. What size box will hold 12 pounds?

19. A fish tank is $2\frac{2}{3}$ feet long, $1\frac{1}{3}$ feet wide, and $1\frac{1}{2}$ feet high. The tank is open on top. How many square feet of glass were used to make the tank?

20. Find the volume of the tank in Exercise 19. Suppose it is $\frac{3}{4}$ full of water. What is the volume of the water in that tank?

21. **Write About It** How does the surface area of a box change if you double each dimension of the box? Give examples to support your conclusion.

22. **Explain** A box is 10 cm long, 12 cm wide, and 14 cm high. Does doubling the height double the surface area of the figure? Explain.

Extra Practice See page 469, Set C.

Quick Check

Check your understanding of Lessons 1–4.

Name each solid figure. Then write the number of faces, vertices, and edges. (Lesson 1)

1. 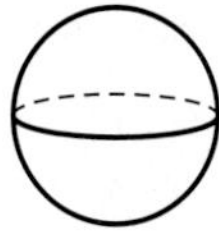

2. 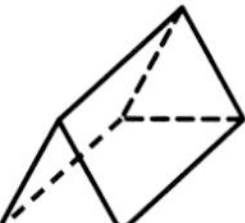

Predict what solid figure the net will make. Then determine the surface area. Each square is 1 cm^2. (Lessons 3–4)

3. 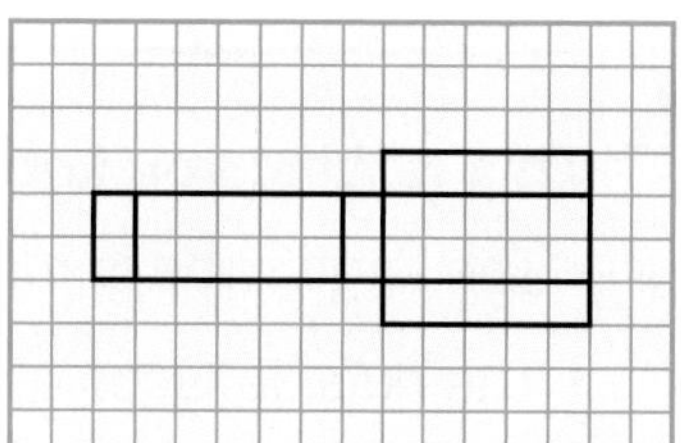

Use cubes to build each figure. Then draw the top view, the side view, and the front view of each figure. (Lesson 2)

4. 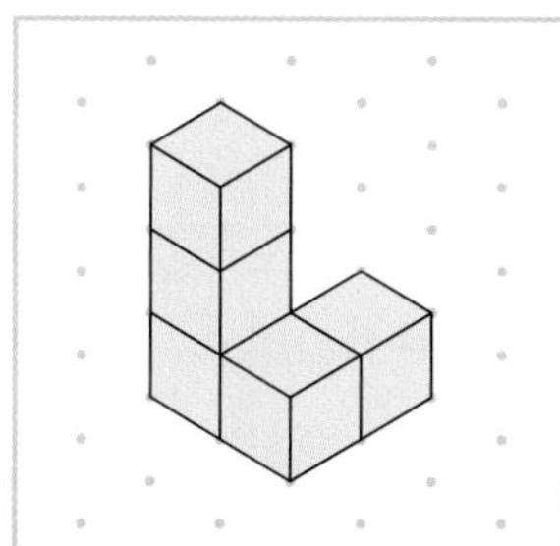

5. 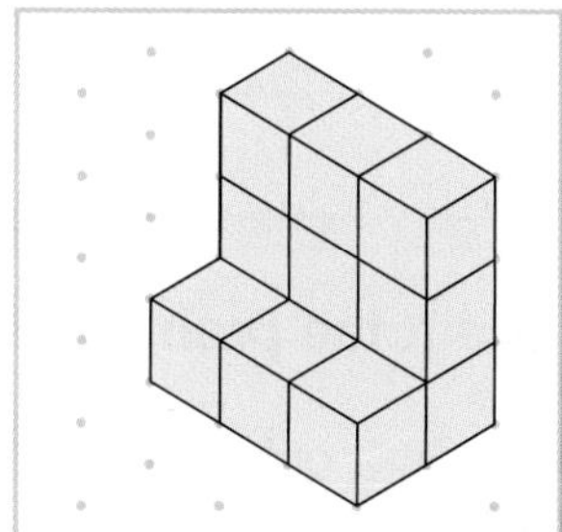

Visual Thinking

Math Reasoning

Wrap It Up

Find the approximate length and width of a single rectangular sheet of wrapping paper that will completely wrap each gift below. Explain how you found your answers.

Remember when you wrap a gift, some of the paper usually overlaps. Note the overlap allowed for each.

1. 25 cm, 25 cm, 25 cm

2. 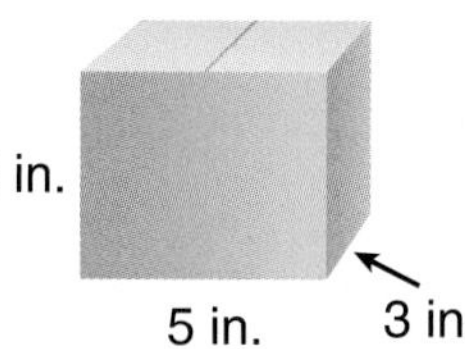

3. 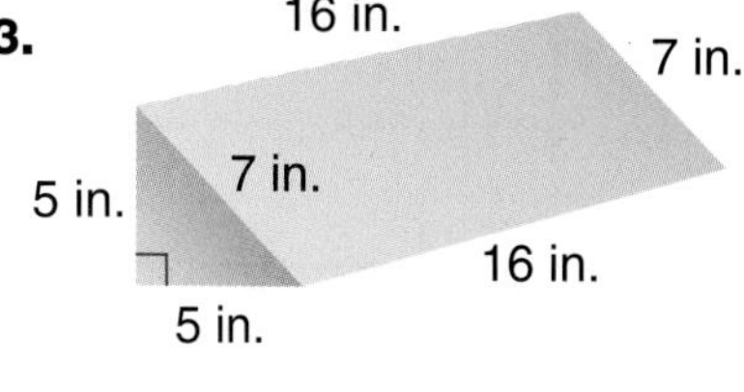

Problem-Solving Strategy

Solve a Simpler Problem

Objective Solve problems by first solving simpler problems.

Problem José makes a solid figure that is 6 cubes long, 6 cubes high, and 6 cubes wide. José paints the outside of the figure orange. Suppose José takes the figure apart. How many of the cubes will have no orange paint on them?

This is what you know:

- The large cube is made of $6 \times 6 \times 6$ small cubes.
- The outside faces of the small cubes are painted orange.

You can solve a simpler problem.

SOLVE

Use models to represent the problem for smaller solid figures.

- Build a large cube that is 2 cubes long, 2 cubes wide, and 2 cubes high.
- Put a sticker or small piece of tape on the outside of each small cube.
- Take the large cube apart. Count the number of cubes with no stickers. Record that number in a table.
- Repeat the steps above.
- Look for a pattern in your results. Use the pattern to find the answer.

Solution: The pattern shows that there will be 4^3, or 64 cubes with no orange paint.

Dimensions of Large Cube	Cubes With No Orange Paint	Pattern
$2 \times 2 \times 2$	0	0^3
$3 \times 3 \times 3$	1	1^3
$4 \times 4 \times 4$	8	2^3
$5 \times 5 \times 5$	27	3^3
$6 \times 6 \times 6$	?	?

Visualize the cubes without paint as a solid figure within the larger cube. What are the dimensions of the figure without paint?

Look back at the problem. Does the solution answer the question? Is the answer reasonable?

Guided Practice

Use the Ask Yourself questions to help you solve each problem.

1. Suppose 7 friends meet for dinner. Each friend shakes hands with every other friend. How many handshakes will there be?

 Draw pictures of simpler problems with fewer handshakes.

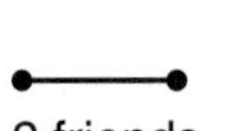

2 friends
1 handshake

3 friends
3 handshakes

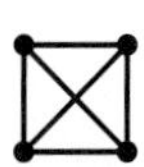

4 friends
6 handshakes

2. Pilar makes a figure 6 cubes long, 6 cubes high, and 6 cubes wide. She paints the outside of the figure red. How many of the cubes have 2 or more red faces?

Ask Yourself

UNDERSTAND What facts do I know?

PLAN Did I use all the needed information?

SOLVE Did I solve a simpler problem first?

- Did I find the pattern?
- Did I continue the pattern to find the number of handshakes for 7 friends?

LOOK BACK Did I solve the problem?

Independent Practice

Solve each problem by solving a simpler problem.

3. A warehouse has 10 security guards. A team of 2 guards must be present at any given time. How many different teams of 2 guards are possible?

4. **Explain** Mark builds a brick wall that is 10 bricks long and 3 bricks high. He paints the front, back, top, and sides of the wall. How many of the sides of individual bricks are painted? Explain the pattern you used to find the answer.

5. Janelle's Restaurant has 12 square tables. Each table can seat one person on each side. If the tables are pushed together to make one long table, how many people can sit at the long table?

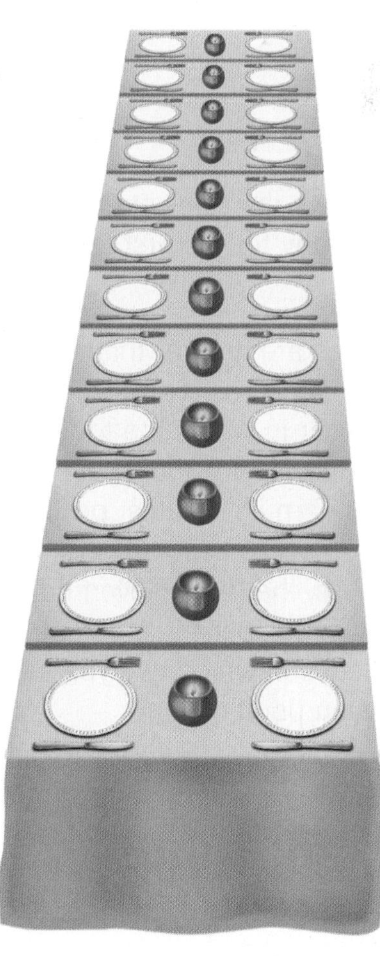

6. An industrial park has 8 storage centers. Each storage center has a direct road to each of the other storage centers. How many roads are in the industrial park?

Go On

Choose a Strategy

Solve each problem. Tell what strategy you used.

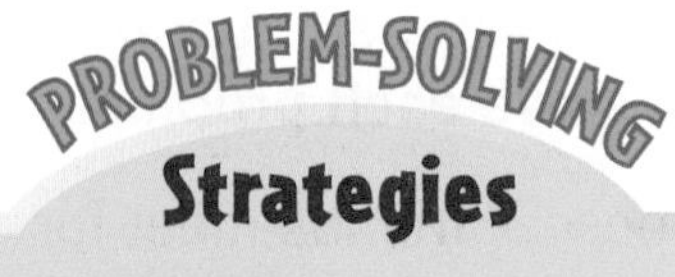

- Use Models
- Draw a Diagram
- Find a Pattern
- Guess and Check
- Make an Organized List
- Make a Table
- Solve a Simpler Problem
- Use Logical Reasoning
- Work Backward
- Write an Equation

7. Find the seventh figure in the pattern shown below.

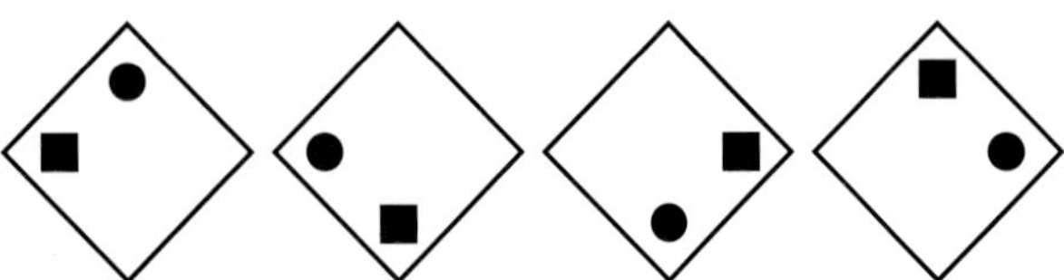

8. The LCM of two numbers is 60. The GCF of the same two numbers is 4. The sum of the numbers is 32. What are the numbers?

9. A solid figure is made up of blue cubes and white cubes. It is 4 cubes wide, 4 cubes long, and 4 cubes high. There are 3 times as many blue cubes as white cubes. How many blue cubes are there?

10. A supply store sells 10 boxes of glasses. Then it receives 24 boxes of glasses. The store now has 40 boxes of glasses. How many boxes of glasses did the store have before it sold the 10 boxes?

Data **Use the graph to solve Problems 11–14.**

The graph shows the sales and expenses for a toy company for the first five years in business.

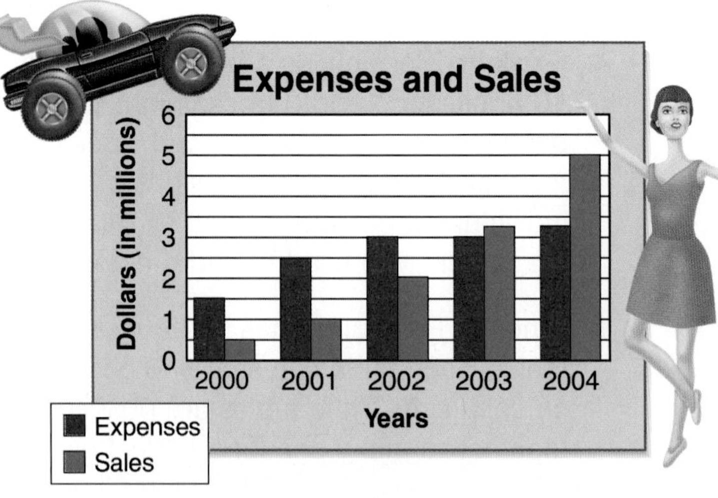

11. When sales are greater than expenses, the company earns a profit. What was the first year in which the toy company earned a profit? In which year did the company earn its greatest profit?

12. In business, the "break-even point" occurs when expenses are equal to sales. Between which two years did the break-even point occur?

13. When expenses are greater than sales, the company has a loss. During which years was there a loss? In which year did the company have its greatest loss?

14. **Predict** Do you think the company will have a profit or loss in 2005? About how great do you think that profit or loss will be? Explain your answer.

Problem-Solving Test Prep

Choose the letter of the correct answer. If a correct answer is not here, choose NH.

1. Nick buys 5 packs of baseball cards. When he adds these cards to the 64 cards he already has, he has a total of 124 cards. Which equation could you use to find the number of cards in each pack?

A $64 + n = 124$ **C** $124 - 64 = n$

B $124 = 5n$ **D** NH

(Chapter 4, Lesson 7)

2. The area of the triangle is 30 square centimeters. What is the measure of side A?

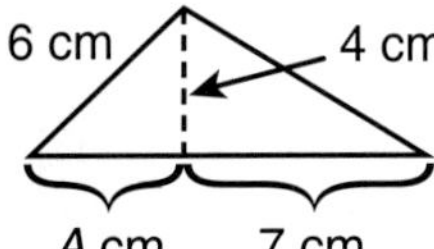

F 3 cm **H** 8 cm

G 7.5 cm **J** 15 cm

(Chapter 16, Lesson 4)

3. This month, Gary has read twice as many books as Erin. Li has read three times as many books as Gary. Li has read 18 books. How many books has Erin read?

A 3 **C** 6

B 4 **D** 9

(Chapter 5, Lesson 3)

4. **Measurement** Gracie feeds her dog an average of 8 ounces of dog food per day. About how many pounds of dog food does Gracie feed her dog per month?

F 15 lb **H** 60 lb

G 20 lb **J** NH

(Chapter 6, Lesson 3)

5. **Measurement** The diagram shows how Kerri painted the door to her room. How many square feet were painted gray?

A 10 ft^2

B 11 ft^2

C 21 ft^2

D 31 ft^2

(Chapter 16, Lesson 3)

6. Melanie uses 6-inch blocks to build a tower that is 24 inches high. Jack uses 8-inch blocks to build a tower of the same height. Who uses more blocks? How many more?

Represent Support your solution with a picture.

(Chapter 10, Lesson 7)

7. In the first six games of a seven-game tournament, a basketball player has these point totals: 18, 24, 22, 12, 15, and 24. The player's score in the seventh game does not change her median score. What does the player score in the seventh game?

Explain How did you find your answer?

(Chapter 8, Lesson 2)

Test Prep on the Net

Check out *Education Place* at **eduplace.com/kids/mw/** for test prep practice.

Algebra

Volume

Objective Use a formula to find the volume of a cube, a rectangular prism, and a triangular prism.

Learn About It

Cedric's collection of CDs is growing. Each case is a rectangular prism, and when he stacks the cases, they form an even larger prism. Soon the "prism" of CDs will be too large for Cedric's shelf!

The **volume** of a solid figure is the amount of space the figure occupies. Volume is measured using **cubic units**. A cube measuring 1 unit on each edge has a volume of 1 cubic unit.

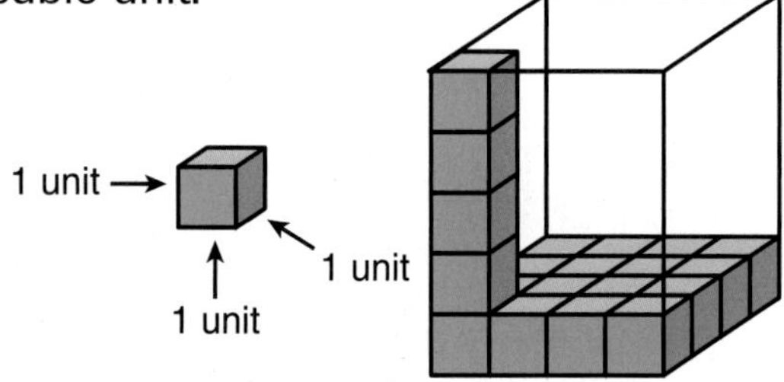

Try this activity to find the volume of a solid figure.

Materials: cubes

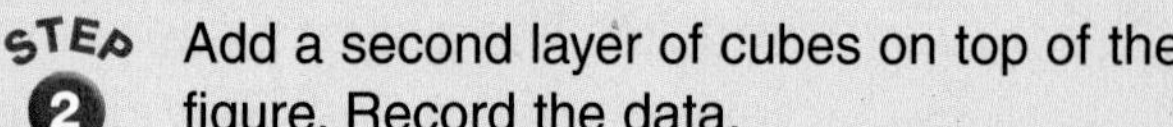

STEP 1 Create a rectangular prism that is 2 cubes long, 3 cubes wide, and 1 cube high. Count the number of cubes. Record the data on the recording sheet.

STEP 2 Add a second layer of cubes on top of the figure. Record the data.

STEP 3 Add a third layer of cubes on top of the figure. Record the data.

STEP 4 Write a multiplication sentence that shows how to find the volume of each of the following:

a. one layer of cubes

b. two layers of cubes

c. three layers of cubes

What multiplication equation could you use to find the volume (V) of any rectangular prism with length l, width w, and height h? Explain.

In a cube, the length, width, and height are equal and are represented by the variable s. What equation could you use to find the volume of any cube?

You can use a formula to find the volume of any prism.

Using Formulas for Volume

Volume of a Cube

$V = s^3$

$= 4 \times 4 \times 4$

$= 64$ cubic units

Volume of a Rectangular Prism

$V = l \times w \times h$

$= 3 \times 5 \times 8$

$= 120 \text{ in.}^3$

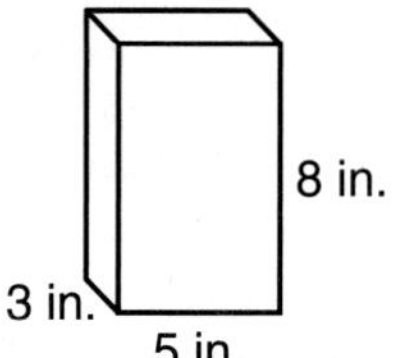

Volume of a Triangular Prism

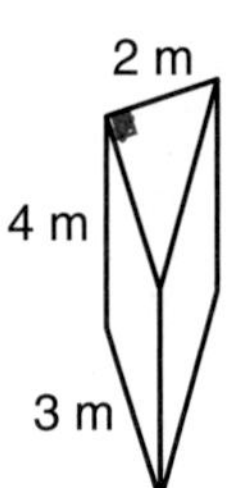

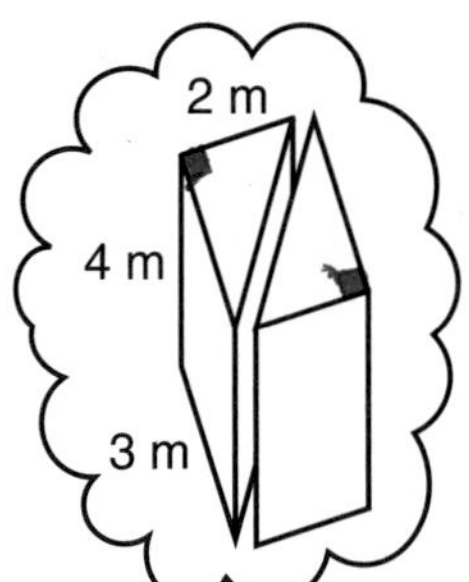

Think
The volume of the triangular prism at the left is one half of the volume of a rectangular prism with the same length, width, and height.

$V = B \times h$

$= \frac{1}{2} \times l \times w \times h$

$= \frac{1}{2} \times 3 \times 2 \times 4$

$= 12 \text{ m}^3$

B means "area of base"
Area of base $= \frac{1}{2}lw$

Remember
how to write abbreviations
cubic inches: in.^{3}
cubic centimeters: cm^3
cubic meters: m^3

Some solid figures are complex figures that are made of smaller prisms. You can use what you know about finding the volume of prisms to find the volume for these figures.

Determine the volume of the solid figure.

STEP 1 Separate the figure into simpler solid figures. Find the volume of each figure.

Volume of A $= 1 \times 3 \times 2$

$= 6 \text{ cm}^3$

Volume of B $= 2 \times 3 \times 3$

$= 18 \text{ cm}^3$

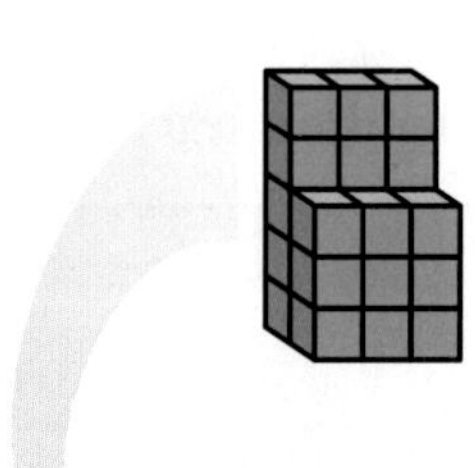

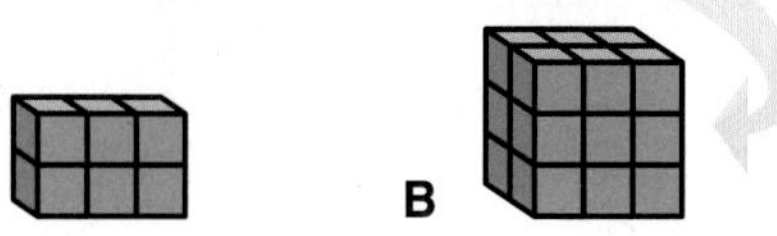

STEP 2 Add the volumes of the simpler solid figures to find the volume of the complex solid.

$V = 6 \text{ cm}^3 + 18 \text{ cm}^3$

$= 24 \text{ cm}^3$

Solution: The volume of the solid figure is 24 cm^3.

Guided Practice

Ask Yourself

- Which numbers do I multiply?
- Which unit symbol do I use?
- Is the answer in cubic units?

Determine the volume of each solid figure.

1. 

2. 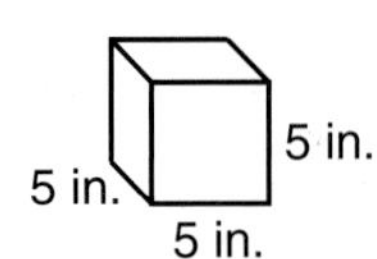

3. 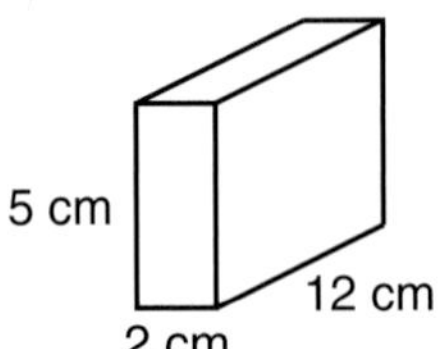

4. 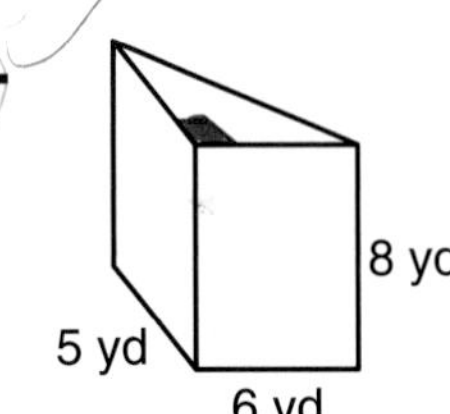

5. 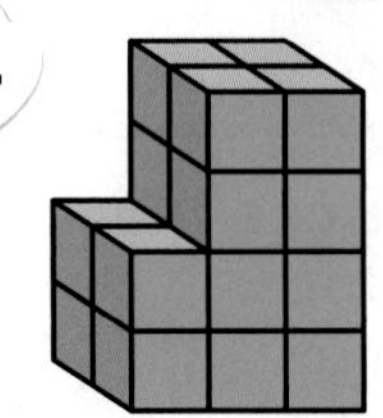

TEST TIPS **Explain Your Thinking** ▶ How can you use multiplication and addition to find the volume of the figure in Exercise 5?

Practice and Problem Solving

Determine the volume of each solid figure.

6. 

7. 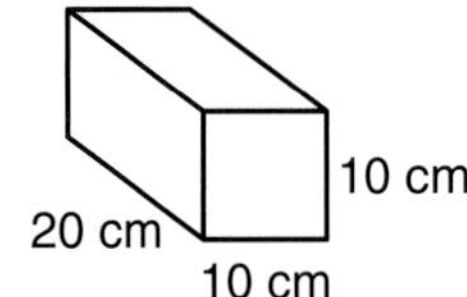

8. 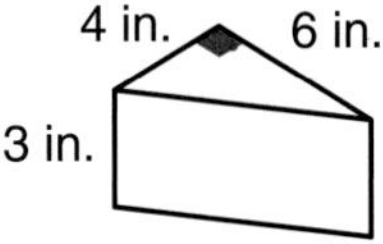

9. 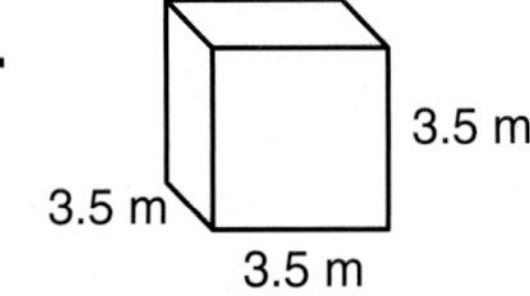

10. 

11. 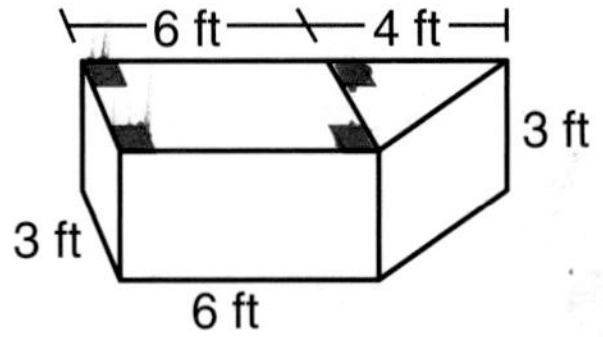

Copy and complete the chart below.

	Measurements of Rectangular Prisms					
	length	width	height	perimeter of base	area of base	volume
12.	3 cm	5 cm		16 cm	15 cm^2	30 cm^3
13.	4 cm	5 cm	2 cm			
14.	5 cm		4 cm	20 cm	25 cm^2	
15.	8 cm	3 cm				72 cm^3
16.		6 cm	10 cm			180 cm^3
17.	7 cm		4 cm	30 cm	56 cm^2	

Choose the most appropriate measure. Write *perimeter, area,* or *volume*.

18. the distance around a baseball diamond

19. the amount of sand needed to fill a box

20. the amount of carpeting to cover a floor

21. the amount of space in a car's trunk

22. the amount of fencing to enclose a rectangular garden

23. the amount of wall space one gallon of paint will cover

Data **Use the picture to solve Problems 24–28.**

Cynthia builds the cedar chest shown on the right. The bottom and each side is 1 inch thick.

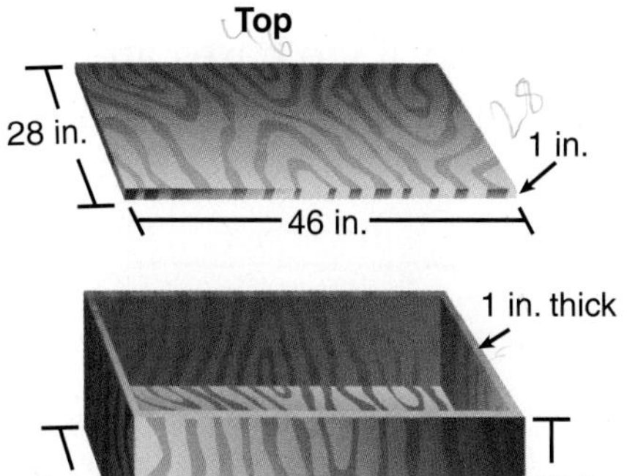

24. She lines the bottom of the inside with felt. How much felt does she need? Explain how you found your answer.

25. Cynthia puts a strip of copper around the top of the chest. How much copper does she need?

26. Analyze What is the volume of the cedar chest? Explain how you decided what dimensions should be used to find the volume. [*Hint:* The volume is not 21,896 in.^{3}.]

27. Cynthia packs the chest with sweater bags that are 12 inches wide, 13 inches long, and 2 inches high. How many sweater bags can Cynthia fit in the chest?

28. What If? Suppose that Cynthia increases the height of the chest by 2 inches. How would that increased height change the volume of the chest? How many more sweater bags would Cynthia be able to put in the chest?

29. You Decide Think of something you might need to store, such as books or clothing. Design a container for storing that item. Include the dimensions and an explanation of why that container would be suited for storing that item.

Daily Review Test Prep

Divide (Ch. 5, Lesson 1)

30. 10,000 ÷ 2

31. 18,000 ÷ 600

32. 2,500 ÷ 50

33. 81,000 ÷ 900

34. 80)64,000

35. 1,000)70,000

36. 60)540,000

37. 50)600,000

38. Free Response The box below has a volume of 80 cm^3. Find the height of the box. Explain how you got your answer.

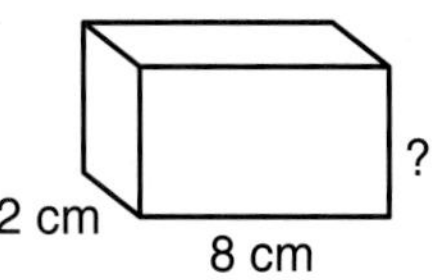

Extra Practice See page 469, Set D.

Lesson 7

Problem-Solving Application

Use Formulas

Objective Use a formula to solve a problem.

You can use formulas to solve problems.

Problem The manager of a warehouse wants to know how much space he will need to stack a shipment of boxes. Each edge of each box is 3 feet long. The total shipment will take up 3,240 cubic feet of space. If the boxes are stacked 6 high and 4 deep, how many feet wide will the stack of boxes be?

UNDERSTAND

What is the question?

- How many feet wide will the stack of boxes be?

What do you know?

- Each edge of each box is 3 feet long.
- The entire shipment is 3,240 cubic feet.
- The boxes can be stacked 6 high and 4 deep.

PLAN

Find the height of 6 boxes and the length of 4 boxes. Then divide the volume by the product of the height and length.

Volume of a rectangular prism = length × width × height = $l \times w \times h$

SOLVE

- Find the height of 6 boxes.

  $h = 3 \text{ ft} \times 6 = 18 \text{ ft}$

- Find the length of 4 boxes.

  $l = 3 \text{ ft} \times 4 = 12 \text{ ft}$

- Multiply $l \times h$.

  $18 \times 12 = 216$

- Then divide.

  $3{,}240 \div 216 = 15$

Solution: The stack of boxes will be 15 ft wide.

LOOK BACK

Look back at the problem.
Does the solution make sense?

Guided Practice

Use the formulas for area and volume to solve Problems 1 and 2.

1. Warren builds a flower planter that is 4 feet long, 3 feet wide, and 2 feet high. He paints the outside of the planter, but not the bottom. What area did Warren paint?

2. A tank is 5 meters long and 3 meters wide. The tank holds 30 cubic meters of water. How deep is the tank?

What measurements do you know?
What measurement do you need to find?

Ask Yourself

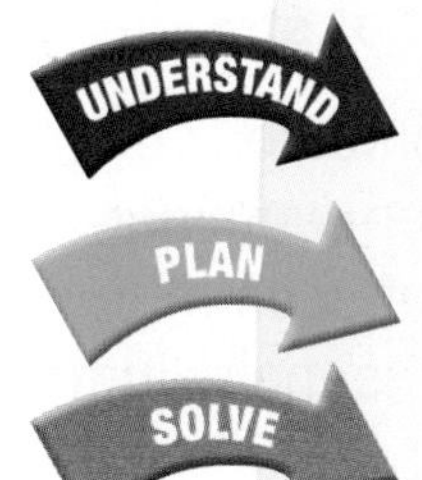

UNDERSTAND What does the question ask me to find?

PLAN Which formulas do I need to use?

SOLVE
- Did I choose the correct formulas?
- Did I substitute the correct numbers for the variables?

LOOK BACK Is the answer reasonable?

Independent Practice

Use the formulas for perimeter, area, and volume to solve Problems 3–7.

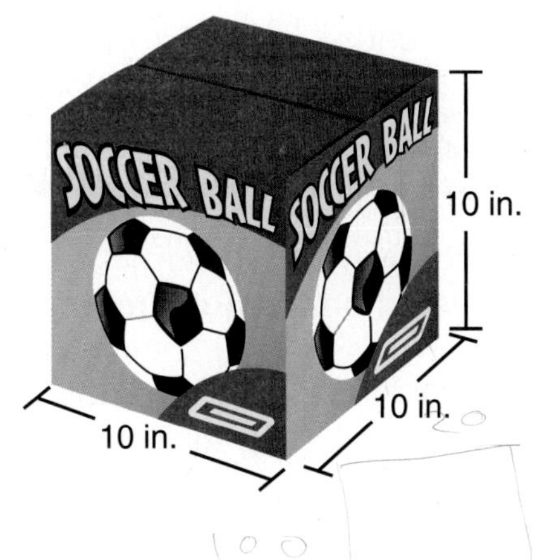

3. A manufacturer packages soccer balls in 10-inch cubes. How many boxes of soccer balls can fit in a cardboard container that is 30 in. by 40 in. by 20 in.?

4. What is the minimum amount of cardboard that is needed to make one soccer-ball box as shown at the right?

5. Kevin covers the rectangular floor of his room with 240 square feet of carpet. The length of the room is 20 feet. What is the width of the room? What is the perimeter of the room?

6. **Calculator** A restaurant buys the freezer shown at the right. What is the volume of the freezer in cubic inches?

7. **Reasoning** There are 1,728 cubic inches in one cubic foot. What is a reasonable estimate for the volume of the freezer in cubic feet? Explain how you made your estimate.

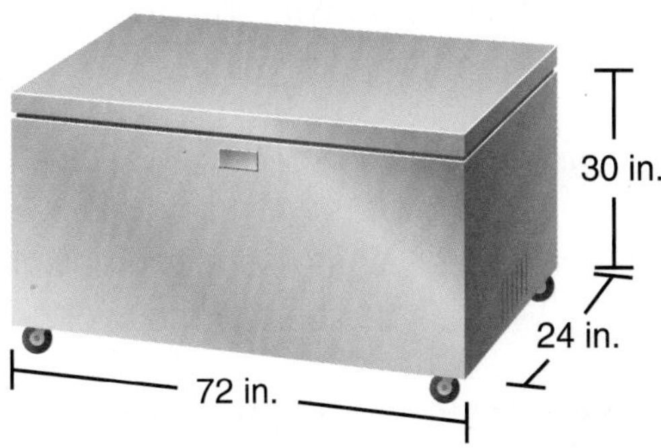

Choose a Strategy

Solve. Show your work. Tell what strategy you used.

8. Three containers have a combined volume of 144 cubic feet. The larger container has two times the volume of each of the other two containers. What is the volume of each container?

9. At the end of its first month, a health club had 240 members. The manager's goal is to sign up at least 25 new members per month. If the manager meets her goal, how many members will there be at the end of the first year?

10. Sarah, Michael, Fred, and Tawana are waiting in line. Neither Sarah nor Michael is first. Tawana is behind Sarah. Fred is ahead of Michael. The two girls are not next to each other. In what order are the four friends?

PROBLEM-SOLVING Strategies

- Use Models
- Draw a Diagram
- Find a Pattern
- Guess and Check
- Make an Organized List
- Make a Table
- Solve a Simpler Problem
- Use Logical Reasoning
- Work Backward
- Write an Equation

Choose a Computation Method

Mental Math • Estimation • Paper and Pencil • Calculator

Data **Use the table for Problems 11–15.**

11. The backpack with the least volume is recommended for kindergartners and first-graders. Which backpack is this? What is the volume of this backpack?

12. **What If?** Suppose the company makes a wheeled version of the Alpha Backpack that is 2 inches wider than the version without wheels. What will be the change in volume?

13. **What's Wrong?** Martin says that the volume of the Gym Bag is 1,200 square inches. What mistake did Martin make? What is the correct answer?

14. Donna has a Mars Backpack. The backpack is about half full. About how many cubic inches of it are filled?

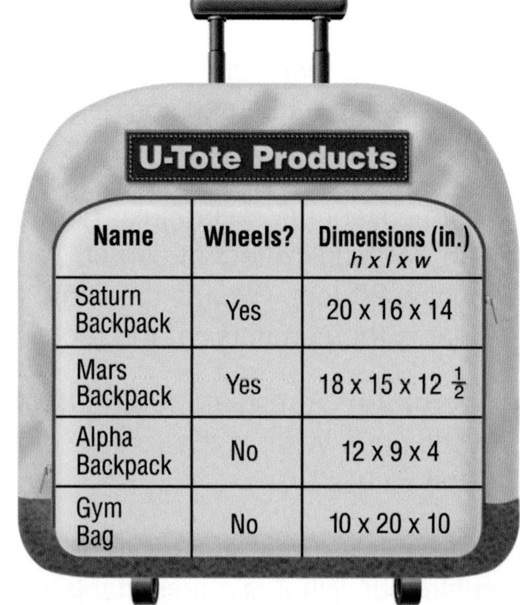

U-Tote Products

Name	Wheels?	Dimensions (in.) $h \times l \times w$
Saturn Backpack	Yes	20 x 16 x 14
Mars Backpack	Yes	18 x 15 x 12 $\frac{1}{2}$
Alpha Backpack	No	12 x 9 x 4
Gym Bag	No	10 x 20 x 10

15. **Create and Solve** Use the data from the table to create and solve your own problem.

Quick Check

Check your understanding of Lessons 5–7.

Determine the volume of each solid figure. (Lesson 6)

1. 

2. 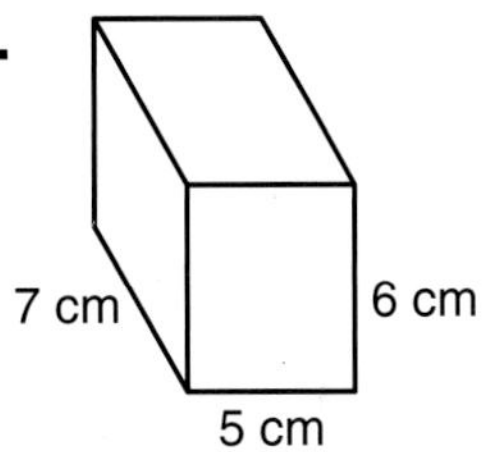

3. 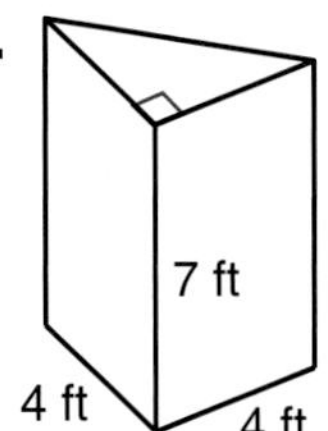

Solve. (Lessons 5 and 7)

4. Eleven friends play in a chess match. After the match, each player shakes hands with every other player. How many handshakes will there be?

5. A small rectangular playground is 2,250 square feet. The width of the playground is 45 feet. What is the length of the playground?

WEEKLY WR READER® eduplace.com/kids/mw/

Science Connection

Fish for an Aquarium

To choose fish for an aquarium, you need to know the size of the aquarium and the size of the fish.

Fish	Length (in inches)
Neon Tetra	1.5
Tiger Barb	2.75
Marble Angelfish	6
Goldfish	5

1. Find the volume of the aquarium at the right.

2. The volume of 1 gallon of water is about 231 cubic inches. About how many gallons will the aquarium hold?

3. Many aquarium owners follow this rule: 1 inch of fish per gallon of tank space. According to this rule, about how many 2-inch fish can fit in the aquarium?

4. **You Decide** Suppose you stock your aquarium with the fish shown in the table. How many of each type of fish will you put in your tank?

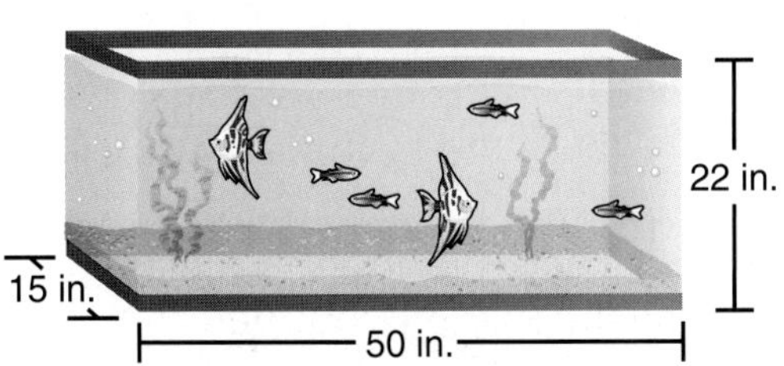

Chapter Review/Test

VOCABULARY

1. A ____ is a solid figure that has two parallel congruent bases and rectangles and parallelograms for faces.

2. A solid figure whose base can be a polygon and whose faces are triangles is called a ____.

CONCEPTS AND SKILLS

Use Figures A, B, and C for Exercises 3–8.

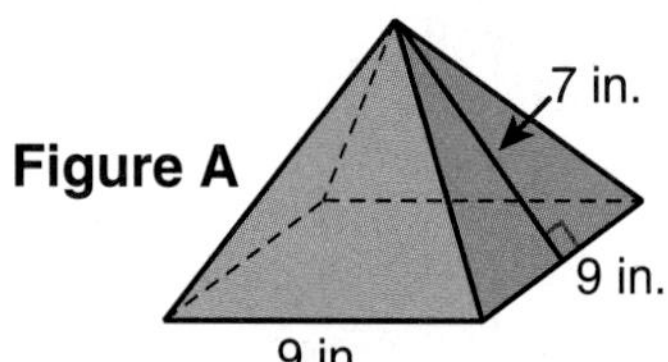

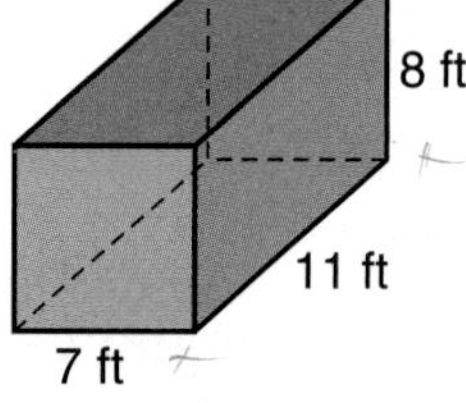

Figure C
14 m
15 m
16 m
10 m

3. Name each solid figure. (Lesson 1, pp. 446–447)

4. Determine the number of faces, vertices, and edges for each figure. (Lesson 1, pp. 446–447)

5. Draw a net for Figure A. (Lessons 2–3, pp. 448–451)

6. Draw a net for Figure C. (Lessons 2–3, pp. 448–451)

7. Determine the surface area for each figure. (Lesson 4, pp. 452–455)

8. Find the volume for Figures B and C. (Lesson 6, pp. 460–463)

PROBLEM SOLVING

Solve. (Lessons 5, 7, pp. 456–458, 464–466)

9. Elyse plans to cover the triangular prism below with gold foil. How much gold foil will she need?

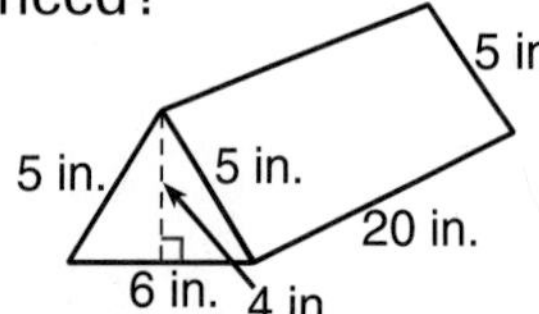

10. A box shaped like a rectangular prism is 24 cm wide and 8 cm high. Its volume is 1,920 cm^3. How long is the box?

Write About It

Show You Understand

If you know the number of sides of the base of a pyramid, can you determine the number of its faces and vertices with or without counting? Explain.

Extra Practice

Set A (Lesson 1, pp. 446–447)

Name each solid figure. Then write the number of faces, vertices, and edges.

1. 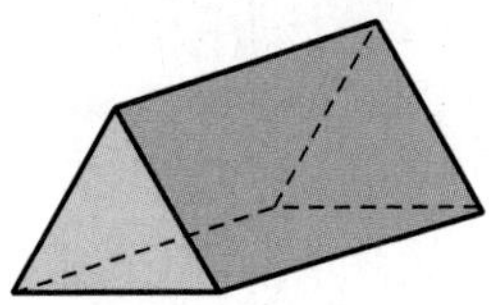

2. 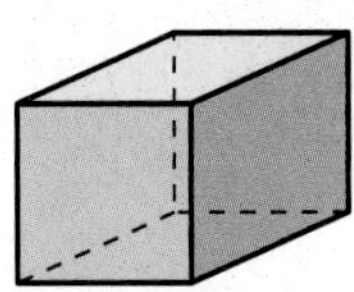

3. 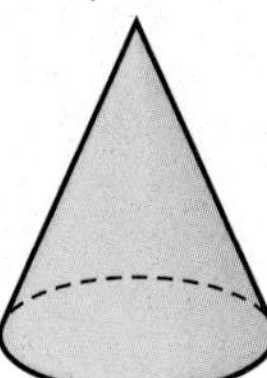

4. 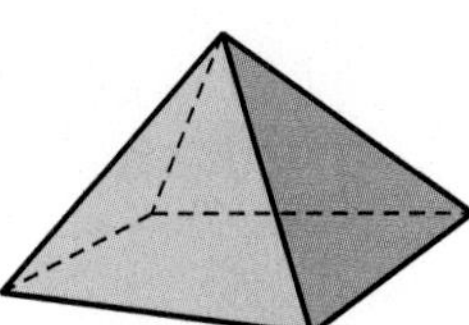

Set B (Lesson 3, pp. 450–451)

Draw a net for each solid figure.

1. 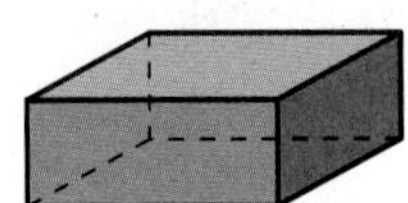

2. 

3. 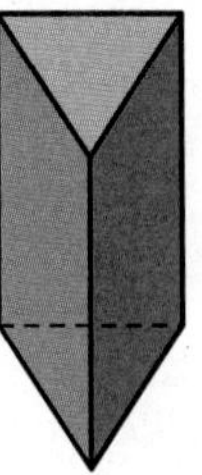

Set C (Lesson 4, pp. 452–455)

Determine the surface area of each solid figure.

1. 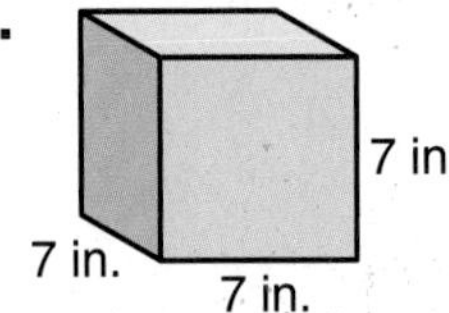

2. 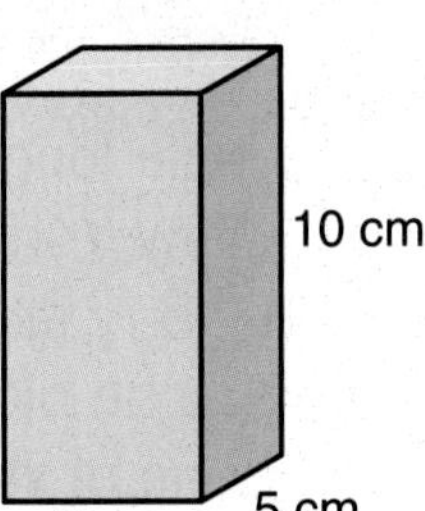

3. 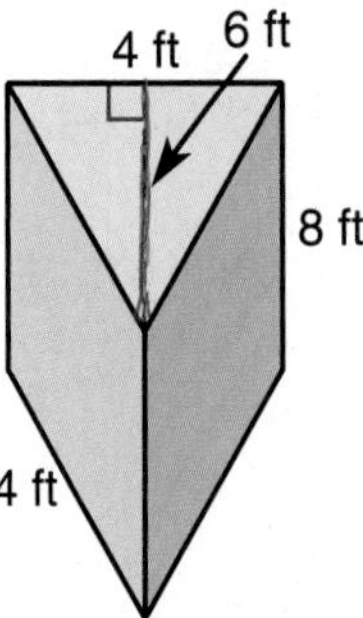

Set D (Lesson 6, pp. 460–463)

Determine the volume of each solid figure.

1. 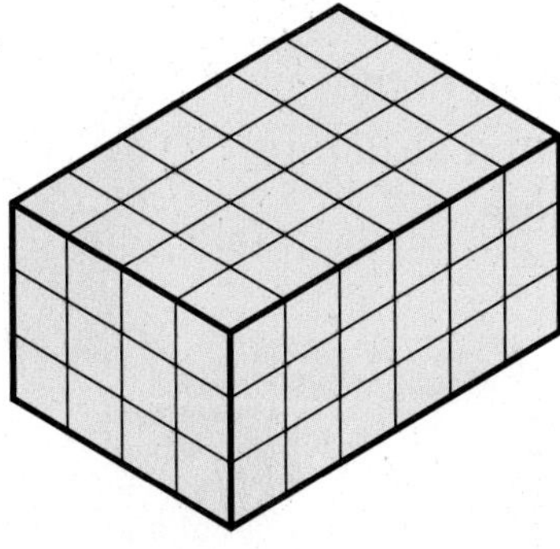

2. 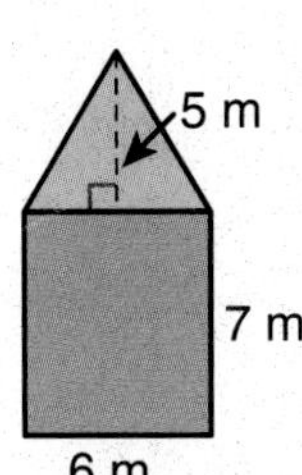

3. 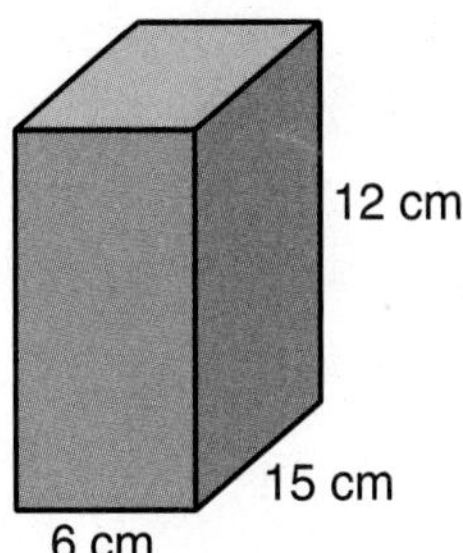

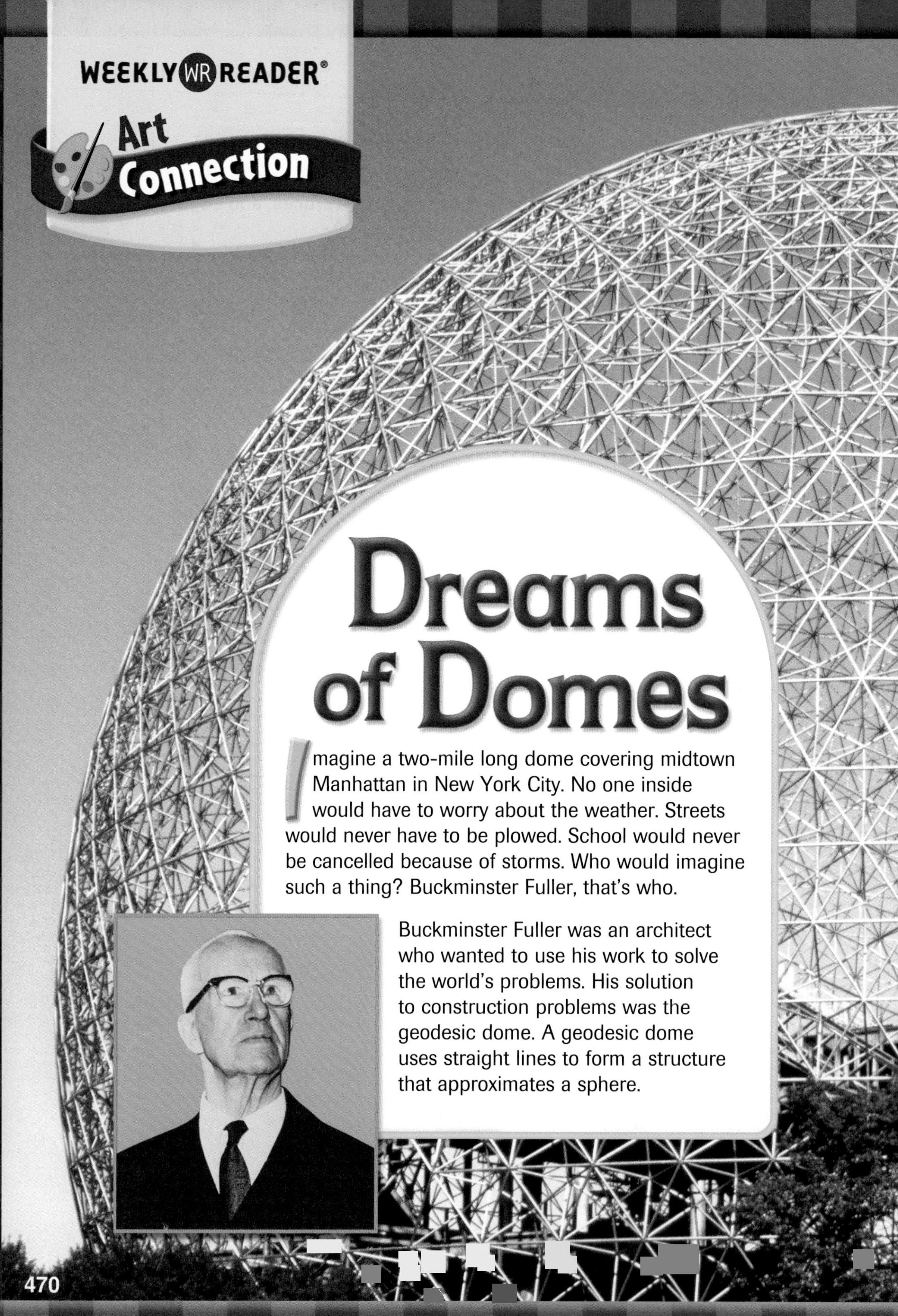

Dreams of Domes

Imagine a two-mile long dome covering midtown Manhattan in New York City. No one inside would have to worry about the weather. Streets would never have to be plowed. School would never be cancelled because of storms. Who would imagine such a thing? Buckminster Fuller, that's who.

Buckminster Fuller was an architect who wanted to use his work to solve the world's problems. His solution to construction problems was the geodesic dome. A geodesic dome uses straight lines to form a structure that approximates a sphere.

Problem Solving

Use the data in the chart to solve Problems 1–6. Use $\pi = 3.14$.

U.S. Pavilion	
Height	206 ft
Diameter of outer dome	250 ft
Side length of outer dome triangle	8 ft
Side length of inner dome hexagon	5 ft

1. Classify the kind of triangle Fuller used to make the outer part of the dome. Explain how you decided.

2. If the height of an outer dome triangle of the U.S. pavilion is about 7 feet, estimate the area of a hexagon made from six of these triangles.

Since a geodesic dome approximates a sphere, you can use the formula for the circumference of a circle to find the circumference of the dome.

3. What is the circumference of the outer dome of the U.S. Pavilion?

4. The outer dome of the U.S. Pavilion is made of triangles, and the inner dome is made of hexagons. If the surface of the inner dome is 3 feet inside the outer dome, what is the circumference of the inner dome? Explain your thinking.

5. What about the triangles and hexagons that Fuller used make them excellent choices for building the geodesic dome?

6. The U.S. Pavilion is not a complete sphere. Draw a top and front view of the dome. How are the views different?

Technology
Visit *Education Place* at
eduplace.com/kids/mw/
to learn more about this topic.

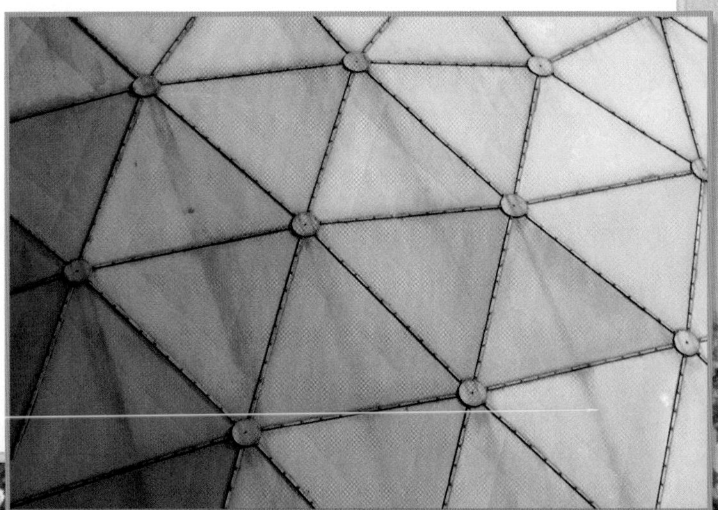

Unit 6 Test

VOCABULARY

Match each definition with the correct vocabulary word.

Vocabulary

- pi
- net
- radius
- diameter
- circumference
- obtuse angle

1. The distance around a circle is called its ■.
2. A(n) ■ is a flat pattern that can be folded to represent a solid figure.
3. A segment that connects the center of a circle to any point on the circle is called a(n) ■.
4. A(n) ■ has a measure greater than that of a right angle and less than 180°.

CONCEPTS AND SKILLS

Classify each polygon in as many ways as you can. (Chapter 15)

5. 

6. 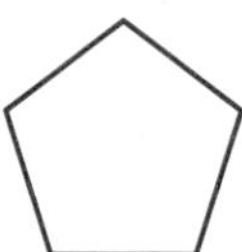

7. 

8. 

Identify each transformation. (Chapter 15)

9. 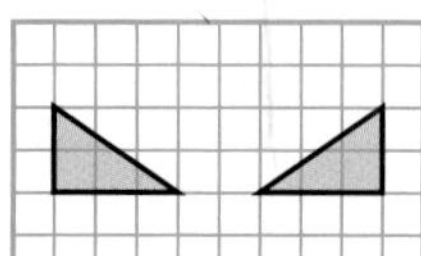

10. 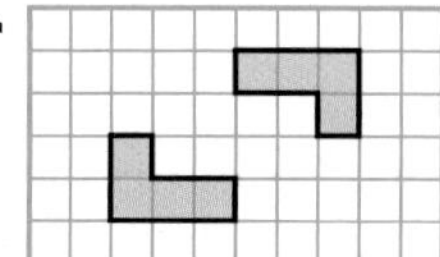

11. 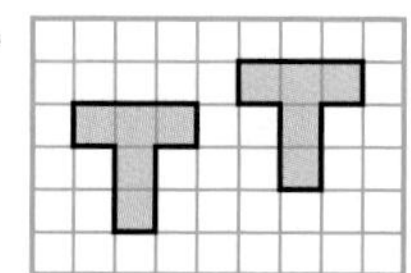

Find the perimeter and area of each figure. (Chapter 16)

12. 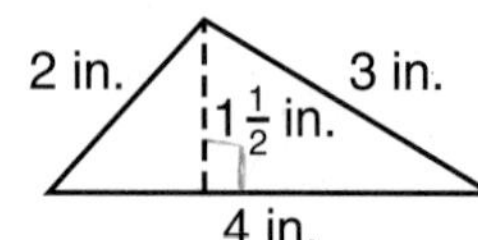

13. 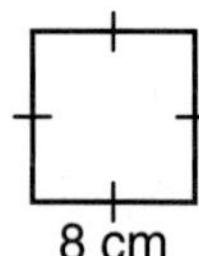

14. 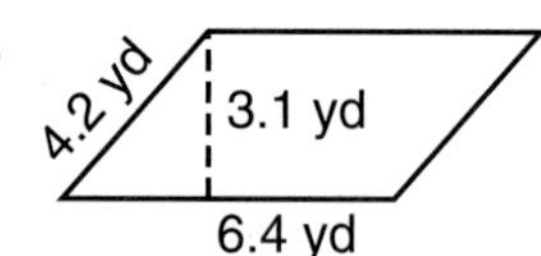

15. 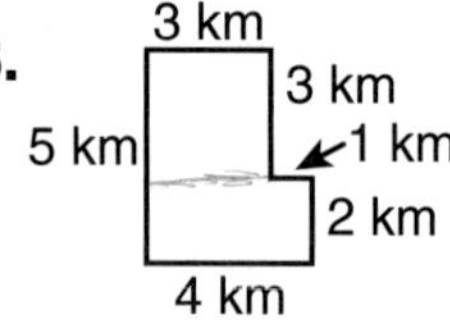

Name the figure. Then find the information for each. (Chapter 17)

16. 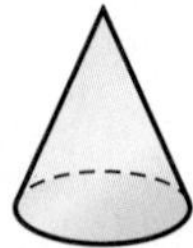
2-dimensional view of base: ■

17. 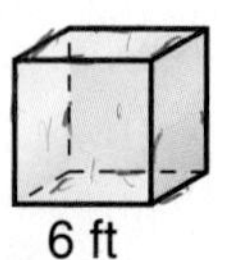

surface area: ■

18. 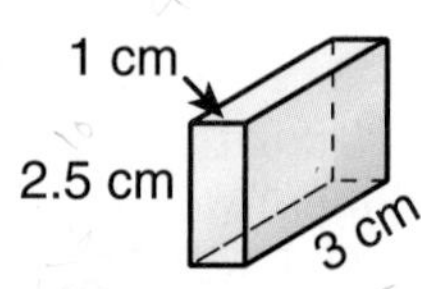

volume: ■

19. 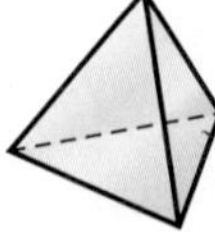
number of faces: ■

PROBLEM SOLVING

20. Gaby is designing a tessellation using a right triangle that measures 3 inches by 4 inches by 5 inches. To fill in an area that is 8 inches by 9 inches, how many triangles must she use?

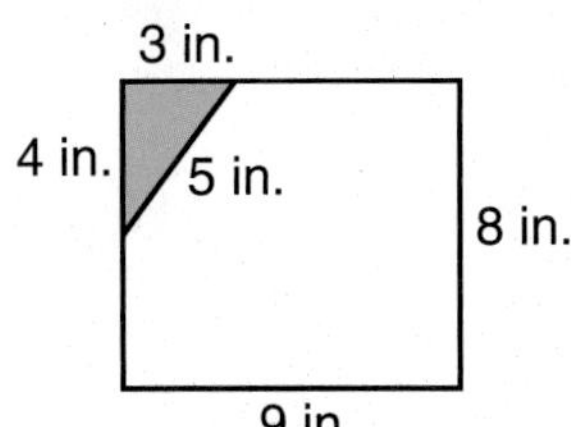

21. **Represent** Jennifer is tracing pattern blocks to draw a five-pointed star like the one below. Will she be able to use the same triangle pattern block to draw the entire star? Explain.

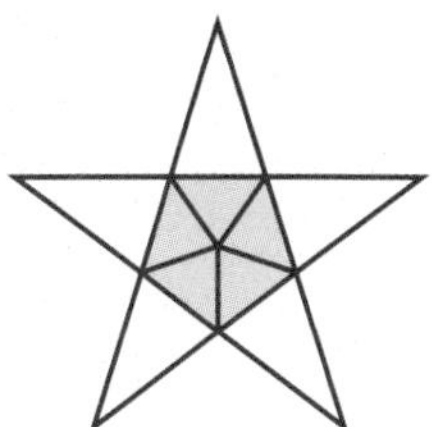

22. **Reasoning** Sandra is measuring the angles in a parallelogram. One of the angles has a measure of 60°. What are the measures of the other three angles?

23. **Measurement** Hamid builds a sandbox that is 4 feet long, 2 feet wide, and 1.5 feet high. How many cubic feet of sand does he need to fill it completely?

24. **Measurement** Robert draws a rectangle that is 8 inches long and 5 inches wide. If he decides to double the dimensions, what will the area of the new rectangle be?

25. **Algebra** Franklin is digging a circular flower bed. He wants to place flexible edging around the entire bed. If the radius is 5 feet, how many feet of edging will he need? (Use $\pi = 3.14$.)

Decision Making

Extended Response

The students in Mrs. Pierce's art class are painting a mural on the wall near the cafeteria. The mural will show various school activities. Copy the diagram of the wall at the right to plan your mural. You may use grid paper or dot paper to help you. Find the wall's perimeter and area. Decide how much of the area you will use for each image of an activity. Explain your thinking.

Information You Need

- You can't paint on the doors.
- Activities to show include: after-school sports, chorus, school clean-up day, science fair, art fair, local history day.

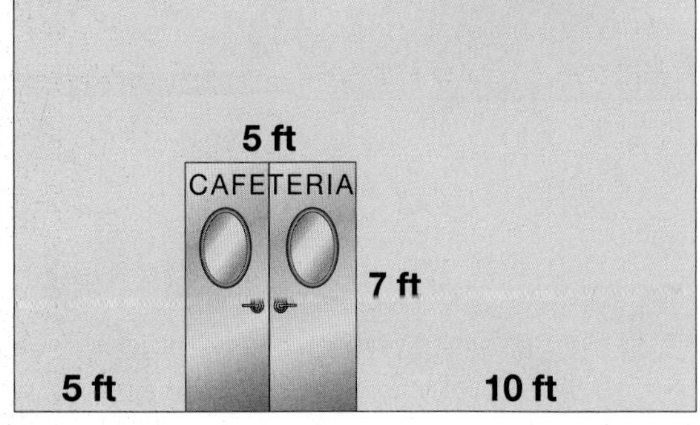

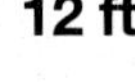

Performance Assessment

TASK 1

Cover all the Bases (Chapters 15, 16)

You want to make a diagram of a baseball diamond.

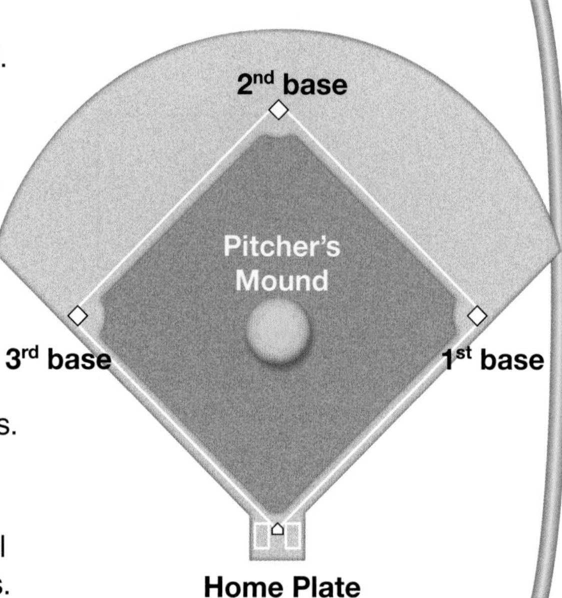

a. Use grid paper. Choose the length of the line segment you will draw to represent the baseline between home plate and first base.

b. Draw a line segment of the same length to represent the baseline between first base and second base. What is the measure of the angle whose vertex is first base?

c. To complete the diamond, draw a reflection of the angle formed by the two line segments. Label the bases and mark the location of the pitcher's mound with a circle.

d. Give the perimeter and area of your baseball diamond. Show how you found your answers.

TASK 2

A Net of Your Classroom (Chapter 17)

You want to make a net of your classroom.

a. Measure and record your classroom's length, width, and height. How do these measurements compare to one another?

b. Draw polygons to represent the floor, the ceiling, and each wall.

c. Decide how to arrange the parts of your net so that they fold up into the shape of your classroom. What solid figure does your classroom most resemble?

Self Check

- Did I answer the questions for each task?
- Did I check all my work?

Enrichment: Fractals

INFINITE SIMILARITY

Have you ever noticed that each small piece of broccoli is similar to the shape of the whole head? This type of pattern occurs often in nature and is called **self-similarity**. In mathematics, self-similar patterns are called **fractals**.

You can make a self-similar pattern using an equilateral triangle. This pattern was invented by the mathematician Waclaw Sierpinski. It is called the Sierpinski Triangle.

STEP 1 Draw a large equilateral triangle. **Remember:** Each angle of an equilateral triangle measures 60°.

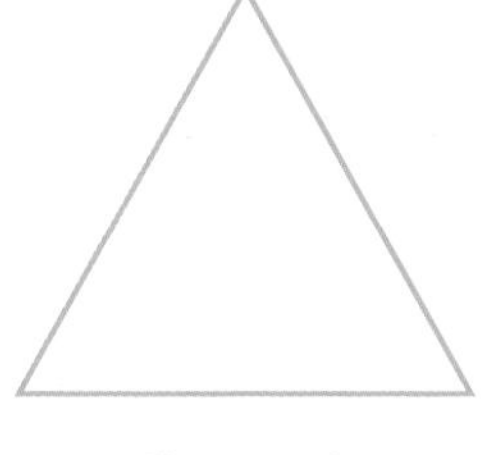

Stage 0

STEP 2 Find the midpoint of each side, and connect them to form 4 similar triangles. "Remove" the middle triangle by shading it.

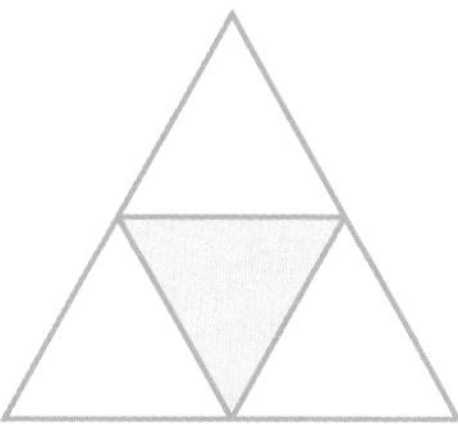

Stage 1

STEP 3 Connect the midpoints to make more similar triangles. Shade the middle triangle in each to continue the pattern.

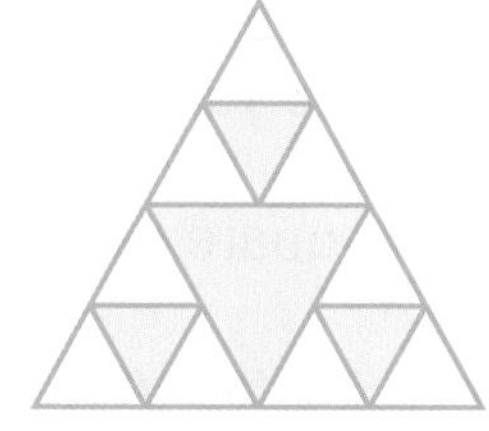

Stage 2

Try These!

Use the Sierpinski Triangle above for Problems 1–2.

1. Draw Stage 3 of the Sierpinski Triangle. How many shaded triangles are in your drawing?

2. If you continue the Sierpinski Triangle from Problem 1, how many stages are possible? Explain how you decided.

3. At the right is Stage 1 of a fractal pattern that divides each side of the triangle into thirds. Draw Stage 2.

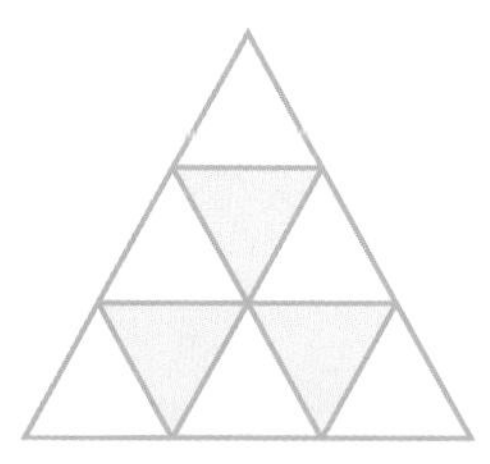

Cumulative Test Prep Practice

Solve Problems 1–10.

Test-Taking Tip

If one of the answer choices is *none of the above*, compute to see if your solution is one of the other choices.

Look at the example below.

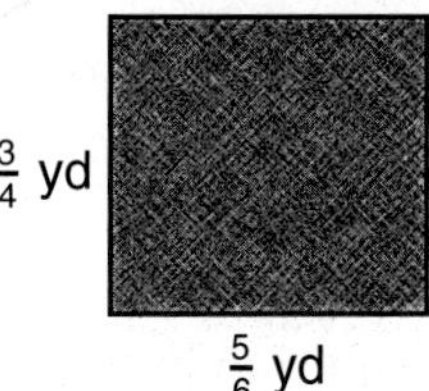

If a cloth measures $\frac{5}{6}$ yard by $\frac{3}{4}$ yard, how many square yards of fabric do you have?

A $\frac{3}{8}$ square yard **C** $1\frac{1}{8}$ square yards

B $\frac{5}{8}$ square yard **D** none of the above

THINK

First solve the problem.

$$\frac{5}{6} \times \frac{3}{4} = \frac{5}{\not{6}_2} \times \frac{\not{3}^1}{4} = \frac{5}{8}$$

After you compute, look to see if your solution is one of the choices. Choice B matches the solution, so the answer is **B**. Choice D, *none of the above*, cannot be the answer.

Multiple Choice

1. About 60,000 people live in Albertville. How would you express this estimate using expanded form with exponents?

A 6×10^3 **C** 6×10^5

B 6×10^4 **D** none of the above

(Chapter 1, Lesson 2)

2. Millie takes 2,000 milligrams of Vitamin C each day. How many grams of Vitamin C does she take?

F 1 gram **H** 5 grams

G 2 grams **J** none of the above

(Chapter 6, Lesson 5)

3. One fourth of the students in Mr. Roger's class were absent on Wednesday. If there are 24 students in the class, how many were present on Wednesday?

A 16 **C** 22

B 20 **D** none of the above

(Chapter 12, Lesson 3)

4. Name the figure.

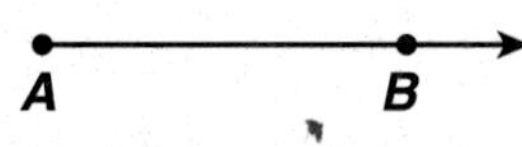

F ray **H** segment

G line **J** none of the above

(Chapter 15, Lesson 1)

 For more Test-Taking Tips, see pages xxii–xxv.

Free Response

5. A stadium can seat 52,320 people. If there are 24 seating sections of equal capacity, how many people does each section seat?

(Chapter 5, Lesson 5)

6. Katrina made this stem-and-leaf plot to show scores for a card game. What is the mean of the scores?

Card Game Scores

Stem	Leaf
0	7 8
1	2 4 9
2	0 1 6 6

Key: 2|0 means 20.

(Chapter 8, Lesson 3)

7. Ms. Johnson ordered 5 jumbo pizzas for a class party. If each pizza cost \$14.59, how much did she pay for the pizzas?

(Chapter 13, Lesson 3)

8. This net is for a prism. What is the volume of the prism in cubic centimeters?

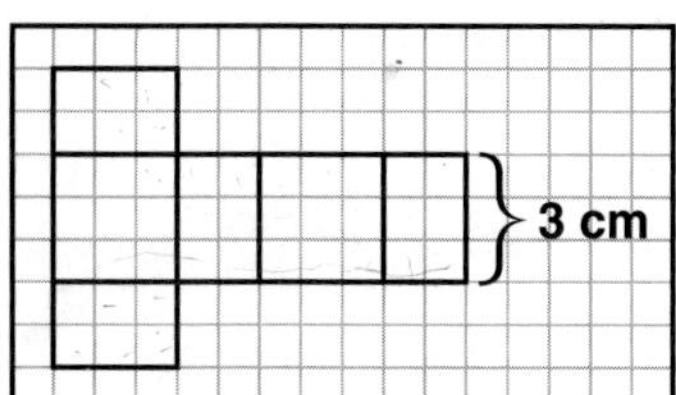

(Chapter 17, Lesson 1)

Extended Response

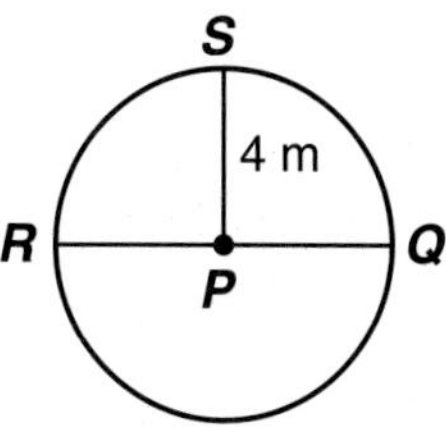

9. In the circle above, $\overline{RQ}$ passes through the center, *P*.

A You have a friend visiting from a foreign country. Use the proper vocabulary to talk about the line segments in circle *P*. Assume your friend knows about circles, but does not know the English words to name each line segment.

B If $\overline{SP}$ is perpendicular to $\overline{RQ}$, what are each of the measures of $\angle RPS$ and $\angle SPQ$?

(Chapter 15, Lesson 8)

10. You can use a formula to find the circumference of circle *P*.

A Use the formula $C = \pi d$ to find the circumference of circle *P*. Round your answer to the nearest whole number. (Use $\pi = 3.14$)

B The radius of the circle is given in meters. If the radius had been given in centimeters, would your computation of the circle's circumference be more exact? Explain.

(Chapter 16, Lesson 6)

Test Prep on the Net

Check out *Education Place* at **eduplace.com/kids/mw/** for test prep practice.

Is it Right?

The Pythagorean Theorem states that, in a right triangle, if the lengths of the two shorter sides are squared then added, the sum equals to the square of the longest side. The equation $a^2 + b^2 = c^2$ is used to represent the Pythagorean Theorem.

In the equation $a^2 + b^2 = c^2$:

- a and b are always the lengths of the shorter sides
- c is always the length of the longest side

The [^] key on a calculator is the exponent key.

For 3^2, enter:

[3] [^] [2] [Enter =]

For 12^2, enter:

$3^2 + 4^2 = 5^2$

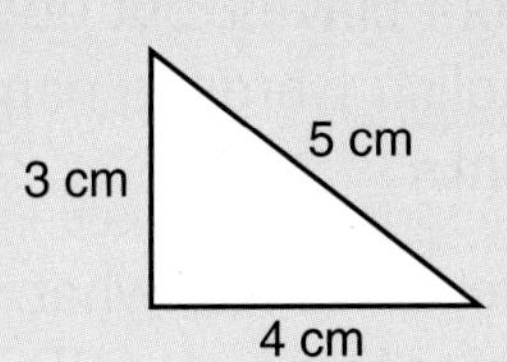

A right triangle

Press: [3] [^] [2] [+] [4] [^] [2] [Enter =] → 25

Press: [5] [^] [2] [Enter =] → 25

25 is equal to 25

$7^2 + 12^2 \neq 13^2$

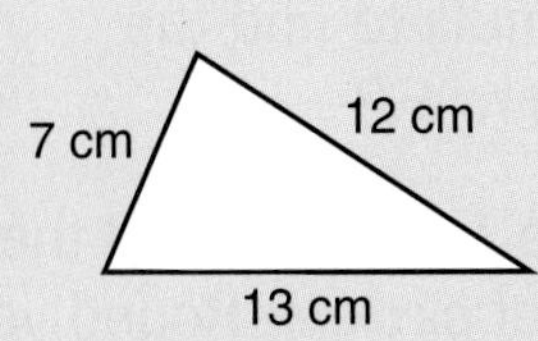

Not a right triangle

Press: [7] [^] [2] [+] [1] [2] [^] [2] [Enter =] → 193

Press: [1] [3] [^] [2] [Enter =] → 169

193 is not equal to 169

Use your calculator to determine if the lengths of sides given below will form right triangles.

1. 28, 45, and 53

2. 16, 18, and 28

3. 20, 21, and 29

4. 20, 25, and 36

5. 23, 264, and 265

6. 15, 112, and 113

7. 8, 12, and 120

8. 16, 63, and 65

9. 62, 67, and 114

Vocabulary Wrap-Up for Unit 6

WEEKLY WR READER Activity Almanac

See page 683 for the activity for this unit.

Look back at the big ideas and vocabulary in this unit.

Big Ideas

A geometric figure may have line symmetry or rotational symmetry, or both.

You can use formulas to find the area of a polygon, the circumference of a circle, and the volume of a solid figure.

e Glossary

Key Vocabulary

symmetry

area

circumference

volume

Math Conversations

Use your new vocabulary to discuss these big ideas.

1. Explain how these pairs of lines are similar and different: intersecting lines, perpendicular lines, and parallel lines.
2. Explain how congruent figures are used to determine whether or not a figure has symmetry.
3. Explain how you find the perimeter of a regular polygon. Then explain how circumference is related to perimeter and tell how to find the circumference of a circle.
4. **Write About It** Look around to find examples of geometric figures in buildings, bridges, furniture, and other objects. Describe how some of these figures serve a particular purpose.

How can I find the volume of a box?
Use the formula length × width × height.

Building Vocabulary

Reviewing Vocabulary

Here are some math vocabulary words that you should know.

fraction	a number that describes part of a whole or part of a group
unit fraction	a fraction in which the numerator is 1, such as $\frac{1}{3}$
decimal	a number with one or more digits to the right of a decimal point
circle graph	a circular graph that shows data as part of a whole

Reading Words and Symbols

A fraction or a decimal can represent parts of a whole or part of a group. Statements about parts of a whole or part of a group can be written with words, a combination of words and symbols, or only symbols.

All these statements represent the same situation:

- Three out of the ten crayons are yellow.
- Of the ten crayons, there are three yellow crayons.
- The part of the group that is yellow is three tenths.
- $\frac{3}{10}$ of the crayons are yellow.
- 0.3 of the crayons are yellow.

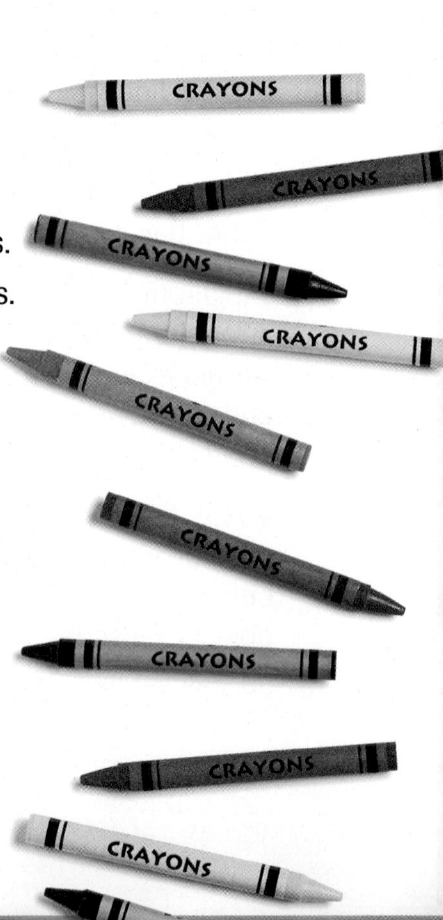

Use the picture of the crayons. Write a statement for each situation. Use words, words and symbols, or just symbols.

1. The part of the crayons that is green
2. The part of the crayons that is red

Use the picture of the crayons. For each fraction or decimal, write a word statement.

3. 0.2 **4.** $\frac{1}{10}$ **5.** 0.4

Reading Test Questions

Choose the correct answer for each.

6. Write a fraction to tell how much of the pizza has been eaten. Then write an equivalent fraction.

a. $\frac{2}{6}, \frac{1}{4}$ **c.** $\frac{2}{8}, \frac{1}{5}$

b. $\frac{2}{6}, \frac{1}{3}$ **d.** $\frac{2}{8}, \frac{1}{4}$

Equivalent means "the same value" or "equal to."

7. Nancy has $100 in savings. Petra has saved one quarter of that amount. How much does Petra have in savings?

a. $4 **c.** $40

b. $25 **d.** $2,500

One quarter in this problem means $\frac{1}{4}$. So to find one quarter of an amount, you multiply by $\frac{1}{4}$ or divide by 4. Find $\frac{1}{4} \times 100$.

8. Martha should leave for school at quarter to eight. At which time should she leave for school?

a. 8:45 **c.** 8:15

b. 8:25 **d.** 7:45

Quarter to in this problem refers to $\frac{1}{4}$ hour before eight. Since 1 hour = 60 minutes, find one fourth of 60. $\frac{1}{4} \times 60 = 15$.

Learning Vocabulary

Watch for these new words in this unit. Write their definitions in your journal.

ratio
rate
proportion
similar figures
percent
probability

Vocabulary
e • **Glossary**
e • **WordGame**

Literature Connection

Read "Numbers" on page 647. Then work with a partner to answer the questions about this story.

CHAPTER 18

Ratio and Proportion

INVESTIGATION

Use Data

Ray plays with and collects marbles. He has 64 marbles in a cloth sack and another 80 marbles in a box. What is the ratio of the marbles in the cloth sack to the total number of marbles Ray has collected?

Chapter Pretest

Use this page to review and remember what you need to know for this chapter.

VOCABULARY

Choose the best word to complete each sentence.

1. When the numerator and denominator have 1 as their only common factor, the fraction is in ____.
2. ____ are two or more fractions that have the same value.
3. The fractions $\frac{2}{4}$ and $\frac{3}{4}$ have a(n) ____.

Vocabulary

common denominator

equivalent fractions

estimate

simplest form

CONCEPTS AND SKILLS

Write three equivalent fractions for each.

4. 

5.

6.

7.

Write each fraction in simplest form.

8. $\frac{8}{10}$
9. $\frac{32}{36}$
10. $\frac{75}{100}$
11. $\frac{56}{84}$

Complete.

12. $\frac{1}{2} = \frac{■}{10}$
13. $\frac{2}{3} = \frac{■}{24}$
14. $\frac{8}{48} = \frac{1}{■}$
15. $\frac{20}{55} = \frac{■}{11}$
16. $\frac{■}{8} = \frac{24}{32}$
17. $\frac{3}{■} = \frac{18}{24}$
18. $\frac{7}{100} = \frac{■}{900}$
19. $\frac{■}{5} = \frac{48}{60}$

20. Are the fractions $\frac{3}{5}$ and $\frac{60}{100}$ equivalent? Explain how you know.

Test Prep on the Net

Visit *Education Place* at **eduplace.com/kids/mw/** for more review.

Ratios

Objective Read, write, and simplify ratios.

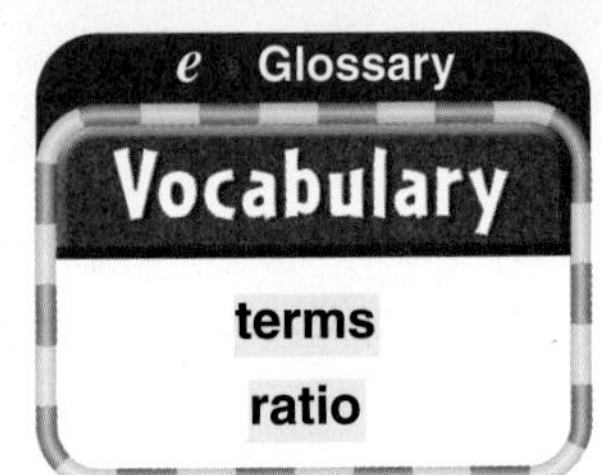

Learn About It

Olga finds 7 wooden tangram pieces in a box. Two shapes are quadrilaterals and 5 are triangles. One way to compare the number of quadrilaterals with the number of triangles is to write a ratio.

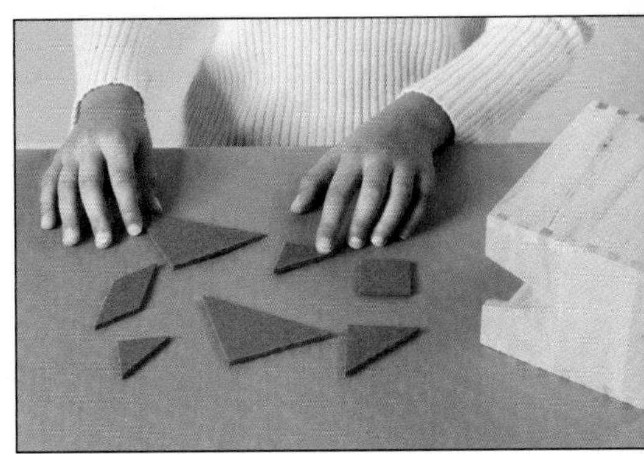

The **terms** of a ratio are the numbers you are comparing. You can write a **ratio** in fraction form, with the first term above the bar and the second term below the bar.

What is the ratio of quadrilaterals to triangles?

STEP 1 Identify the terms of the ratio.

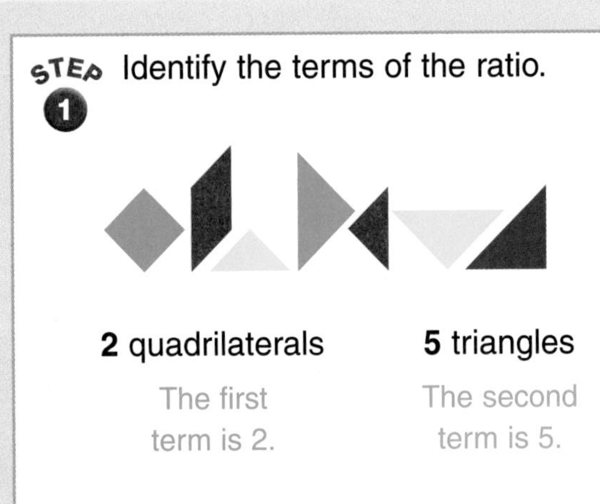

2 quadrilaterals — The first term is 2.

5 triangles — The second term is 5.

STEP 2 Write the ratio of quadrilaterals to triangles.

The ratio can be written 3 ways.

Word form: **2 to 5**

Ratio form: **2:5**

Fraction form: $\frac{2}{5}$

To read all three forms, say, "2 to 5."

Solution: The ratio of quadrilaterals to triangles is 2 to 5, 2:5, or $\frac{2}{5}$.

Guided Practice

Write each ratio three different ways.

1. 5 cars to 6 trucks
2. 16 cats to 3 dogs
3. 2 balls to 3 bats
4. 4 caps to 5 coats
5. 7 squares to 2 triangles
6. 9 paints to 4 brushes

Ask Yourself

- Did I write the terms in the correct order?
- Did I write each ratio three different ways?

Explain Your Thinking In Exercise 6, if you write the ratio of brushes to paints, why write 4:9 instead of 9:4?

Practice and Problem Solving

Use the triangles, squares, and circles below to write each ratio three different ways.

7. squares to triangles
8. circles to squares
9. circles to triangles
10. squares to circles
11. triangles to squares
12. triangles to circles
13. circles to all figures
14. triangles to squares and circles

Use the table and the completed tangram to answer Problems 15–19.

Tangram Pieces	Number of Each Shape
triangles	15
squares	3
parallelograms	3

15. Olivia emptied a box of wooden tangram pieces onto the desk. She counted the number of each shape and organized her findings in a table. What is the ratio of triangles to squares?

16. **Analyze** A tangram is made from 5 triangles, 1 square, and 1 parallelogram. If all the pieces are the right size, how many complete tangrams can be made from the shapes Olivia has?

17. Write the ratio of the number of yellow pieces to the number of blue pieces.

18. Write the ratio of the number of blue pieces to the number of yellow pieces.

19. **Write About It** Explain why the answers to Problems 17 and 18 are not the same.

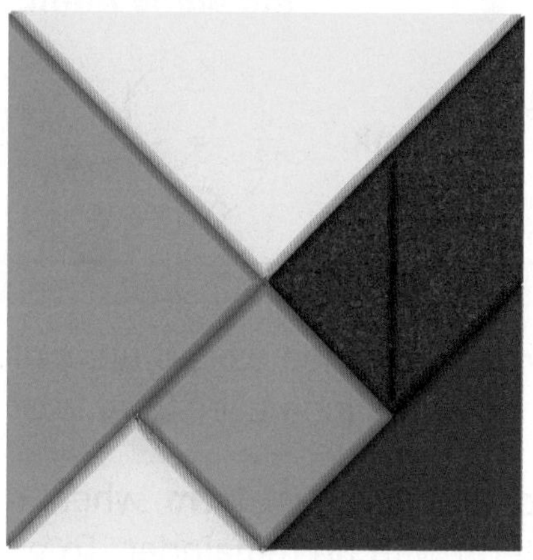

Daily Review | Test Prep

Write two equivalent fractions. Use multiplication and division. (Ch. 9, Lesson 6)

20. $\frac{4}{6}$
21. $\frac{5}{20}$
22. $\frac{7}{14}$
23. $\frac{8}{20}$

24. **Free Response** Write the ratio of triangles to figures that are not triangles. Explain.

Extra Practice See page 503, Set A.

Lesson 2

Equivalent Ratios

Objective Use multiplication and division to find equivalent ratios.

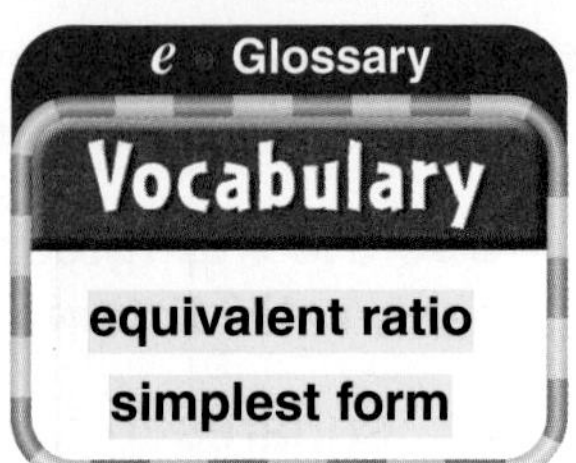

Learn About It

Melinda wants to paint her little sister's dollhouse. She has chosen a color that requires 4 parts of red for every 12 parts of yellow. The ratio of red to yellow is $\frac{4}{12}$.

If Melinda uses 8 parts of red, how many parts of yellow will she need? If Melinda uses 2 parts of red, how many parts of yellow will she need?

You can find an **equivalent ratio** for $\frac{4}{12}$ that has 8 as its first term. Then you can find an equivalent ratio for $\frac{4}{12}$ that has 2 as its first term.

Different Ways to Find Equivalent Ratios

Way 1 **Multiply each term by the same number.**

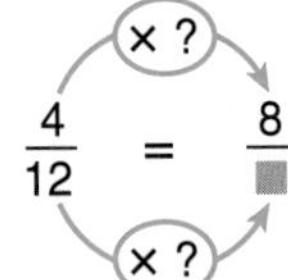

Think: $\frac{4}{12} = \frac{8}{■}$ (× ?) $\qquad \frac{4}{12} = \frac{8}{24}$ (× 2)

Way 2 **Divide each term by the same number.**

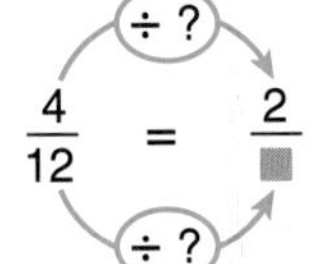

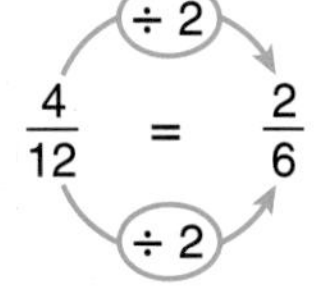

Think: $\frac{4}{12} = \frac{2}{■}$ (÷ ?) $\qquad \frac{4}{12} = \frac{2}{6}$ (÷ 2)

Solution: If Melinda uses 8 units of red, she will need 24 units of yellow.
If Melinda uses 2 units of red, she will need 6 units of yellow.

▶ A ratio is in **simplest form** when 1 is the only number that divides each term with no remainder. To write a ratio in simplest form, divide each term by its greatest common factor (GCF).

Write $\frac{12}{16}$ in simplest form.

$\frac{12}{16} = \frac{3}{4}$ (÷ 4)

Think
$12 = (2 \times 2) \times 3$
$16 = (2 \times 2) \times 2 \times 2$
2×2, or 4, is the GCF.

The simplest form of $\frac{12}{16}$ is $\frac{3}{4}$.

Complete the equivalent ratio: $\frac{4}{6} = \frac{■}{9}$.

STEP 1 Write the ratio in simplest form.

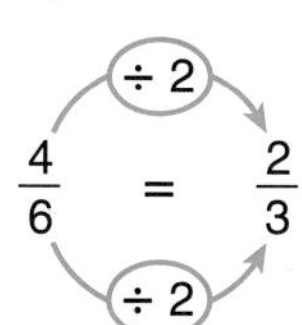

STEP 2 Multiply by a number so 9 is the new second term.

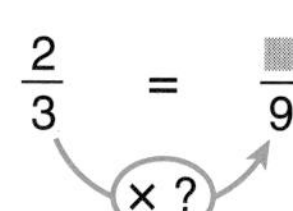

STEP 3 Multiply each term by the same number.

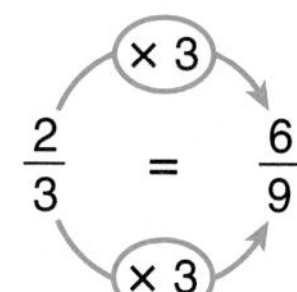

Solution: $\frac{4}{6} = \frac{6}{9}$.

Guided Practice

Ask Yourself

- Did I multiply or divide both terms by the same number?

Write four equivalent ratios for each.

1. $\frac{4}{8}$
2. 8 to 12
3. 6:15
4. $\frac{20}{25}$

TEST TIPS **Explain Your Thinking** ▶ How would you write 6:15 in simplest form? How did you get your answer?

Practice and Problem Solving

Write four equivalent ratios for each.

5. $\frac{1}{3}$
6. 5 to 6
7. 1:5
8. 10 to 4
9. 10:16
10. $\frac{6}{3}$

Write each ratio in simplest form.

11. $\frac{10}{40}$
12. 6:18
13. 24 to 42
14. 12:60
15. $\frac{16}{36}$
16. 28:32

Algebra • Equations Complete each set of equivalent ratios.

17. $\frac{1}{4} = \frac{■}{12}$
18. $\frac{8}{24} = \frac{■}{6}$
19. $\frac{15}{25} = \frac{9}{■}$
20. $\frac{6}{9} = \frac{■}{12}$

Daily Review | Test Prep

Multiply. (Ch. 13, Lessons 4–5)

21. 0.09×0.8
22. 3.2×0.6
23. 0.21×0.9
24. 8.34×4.7
25. 0.002×0.6
26. 0.03×0.03

27. Complete the equivalent ratio: $\frac{20}{24} = \frac{■}{6}$.

A 4 **C** 80

B 5 **D** 120

Extra Practice See page 503, Set B.

Lesson 3

Rates

Objective Compare two quantities with different units.

e Glossary

Vocabulary

rate
unit rate
per
speed

Learn About It

A **rate** is a ratio that compares numbers expressed in different units. A rate in which the second term is 1 is called a **unit rate**.

A toy factory produces 120 robots in 5 days. At this rate, how many robots will it produce in 20 days?

Different Ways to Solve Problems With Rates

Way 1 **Use equivalent ratios.**

$\frac{120 \text{ robots}}{5 \text{ days}} = \frac{■ \text{ robots}}{20 \text{ days}}$

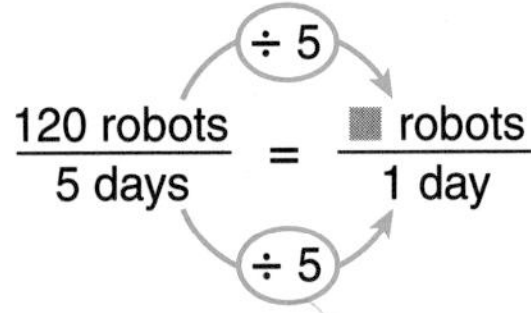

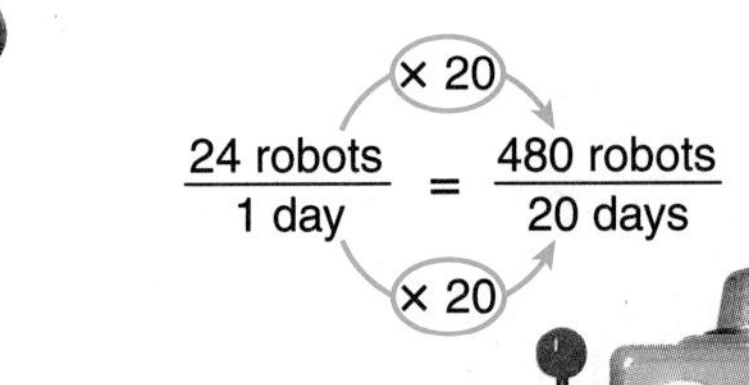

Way 2 **Find the unit rate and multiply.**

STEP 1 Divide to find the unit rate in robots per day. **Per** means "for each."

$\frac{120 \text{ robots}}{5 \text{ days}} = \frac{■ \text{ robots}}{1 \text{ day}}$ (÷ 5 on top and bottom)

The rate is 24 robots per day.

STEP 2 Multiply by the number of days.

$\frac{24 \text{ robots}}{1 \text{ day}} = \frac{480 \text{ robots}}{20 \text{ days}}$ (× 20 on top and bottom)

Solution: The factory will produce 480 robots in 20 days.

Other Examples

A. Speed as a Unit Rate

A car travels 220 miles in 4 hours.
Find the unit rate in miles per hour.

$\frac{220 \text{ mi}}{4 \text{ h}} = \frac{55 \text{ mi}}{1 \text{ h}}$ (÷ 4 on top and bottom)

A rate that shows distance per unit of time is called **speed**. A slash, /, is often used for the word *per*.

The rate is 55 miles per hour, or 55 mi/h.

B. Use Speed to Find Time

How long will it take to travel 450 km at a rate of 90 km/h?

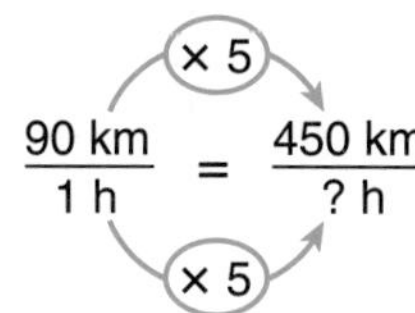

It will take 5 hours.

C. Rates With Money

A worker receives $75 for 6 hours of work. What is the rate of pay per hour?

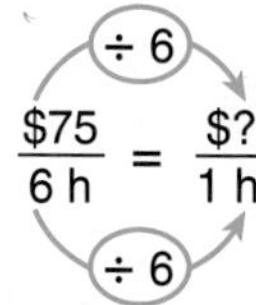

The rate is $12.50 per hour.

Guided Practice

Ask Yourself

- Did I write the units?
- Is my answer reasonable?

Find the unit rate.

1. 30 toys in 10 days
2. $20 in 4 hours
3. 60 meters in 5 seconds
4. $1,000 in 5 days
5. 100 miles in 4 hours
6. 50 km in 5 hours

TEST TIPS **Explain Your Thinking** ▶ How can you use division to find any unit rate?

Practice and Problem Solving

Find the unit rate.

7. 80 miles in 16 min
8. 72 ft in 9 seconds
9. 108 meters in 18 min
10. 160 pages in 8 days
11. $100 in 5 hours
12. $56 in 7 hours

Complete the unit rate.

13. 400 mi:16 gal = ■ mi:1 gal
14. 84¢:12 copies = ■ ¢:1 copy
15. $6:2 oz = $■:1 oz
16. 437 mi:23 gal = ■ mi:1 gal
17. 1,394 people:34 square miles = ■ people:1 square mile
18. 288 photos:12 rolls of film = ■ photos:1 roll of film

Find the distance traveled in the given amount of time.

19. 5 hours at 50 mi/h
20. 3 min at 9 m/min
21. 12 seconds at 16 ft/s
22. 0.5 hour at 30 mi/h
23. 7 days at 25 mi/day
24. 2.5 hours at 40 km/h

Go On

Find the length of time for each trip.

25. 200 mi at 50 mi/h
26. 75 km at 25 km/h
27. 1,500 ft at 30 ft/s
28. 225 mi at 45 mi/h
29. 252 ft at 12 ft/sec
30. 175 m at 35 m/min

• Variables

Use the rate of 140 toy robots produced in 5 days to complete each rate.

31. *n* robots in 8 days
32. *n* robots in 2 days
33. *n* robots in 0.5 days
34. 420 robots in *n* days
35. 350 robots in *n* days
36. 490 robots in *n* days

Use the advertisement for Problems 37–40.

37. To the nearest cent, what is the unit price of an action figure?

38. Which has a greater price per game, the Action Games package or the Software 5-Game package? What is the difference between the two unit prices?

39. Which package of building blocks has a greater price per block, the 75-block pack or the 125-block bucket? To the nearest cent, what is the difference between the two unit prices?

40. **You Decide** Suppose you play a game in which you need at least 50 Can-Do Canned Zoo animals. How would you buy the animals? To the nearest cent, what is the unit rate per animal?

41. **What's Wrong?** Hal's car travels 450 miles on 15 gallons of gas. Hal calculated that he would need 63,000 gallons for a 2,100-mile trip. What did Hal do wrong?

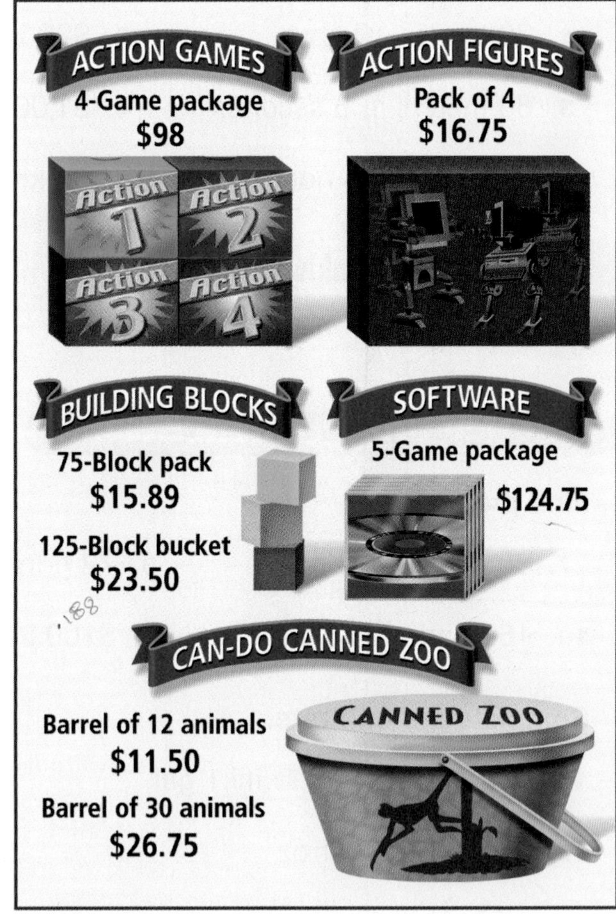

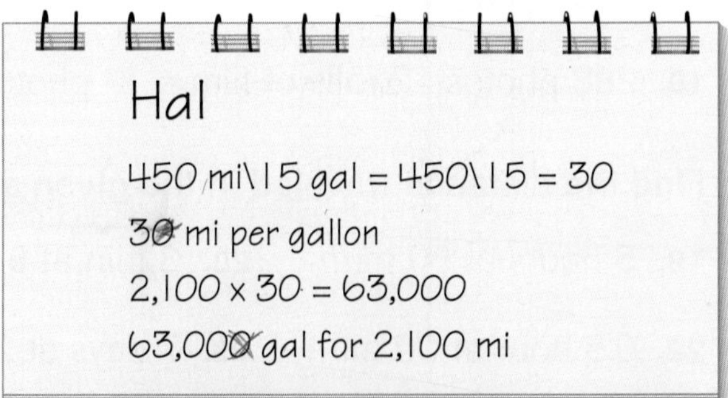

Hal
450 mi\15 gal = 450\15 = 30
30 mi per gallon
2,100 x 30 = 63,000
63,000 gal for 2,100 mi

Extra Practice See page 503, Set C.

Quick Check

Check your understanding for Lessons 1–3.

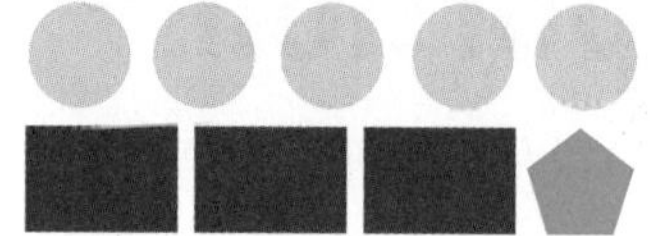

Write each ratio three different ways. (Lesson 1)

1. circles to rectangles
2. rectangles to circles
3. pentagons to circles
4. pentagons to other shapes

Write four equivalent ratios for each. (Lesson 2)

5. $\frac{2}{7}$
6. 8 to 10
7. 6:2
8. 12 to 9

Complete the unit rate. (Lesson 3)

9. 252 mi:9 gal = ■ mi:1 gal
10. \$3.48:6 cans = \$■:1 can

Math Challenge

Heart Smart

Complete the following activity in order to determine your heart rate for a minute, an hour, a day, and a week.

The easiest place to find your pulse is on the side of your neck.

STEP 1 Make the following table.

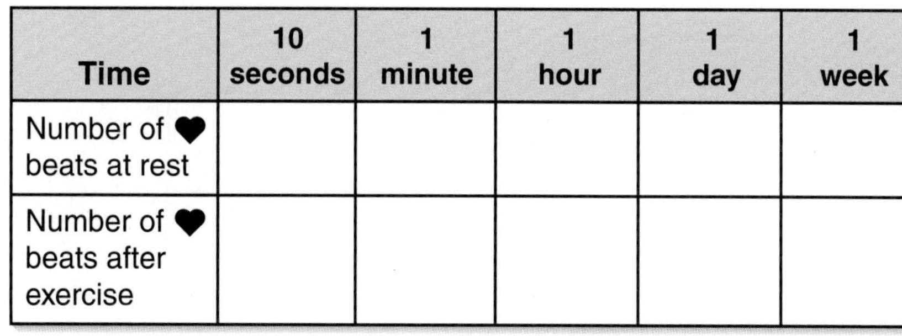

Time	10 seconds	1 minute	1 hour	1 day	1 week
Number of ♥ beats at rest					
Number of ♥ beats after exercise					

STEP 2 Take your pulse for 10 seconds. Based on your 10-second heart rate, fill in the first row of your table.

STEP 3 *Let's exercise!!* Do as many jumping jacks as you can in 1 minute.

STEP 4 Take your pulse for 10 seconds. Based on your 10-second heart rate after exercising, fill in the second row of your table.

Lesson 4

Algebra

Proportions

Objective Learn what a proportion is and how to find cross products.

e Glossary

Vocabulary

proportion

cross product

Learn About It

Martin and Tina are playing a word game. In Martin's group of tiles, the ratio of vowel tiles to his total tiles is 5 to 9. This is the same as the ratio of vowel tiles to the total tiles in the game. The game has a total of 81 tiles. How many vowel tiles does the game have?

To solve the problem, you can write a proportion. A **proportion** is a statement that two ratios are equivalent.

Martin's vowel tiles → $\frac{5}{9} = \frac{n}{81}$ ← vowel tiles in the game
Martin's total tiles → ← total tiles in the game

Solve for n. $\frac{5}{9} = \frac{n}{81}$

Different Ways to Solve $\frac{5}{9} = \frac{n}{81}$

Way 1 Use equivalent ratios.

$\frac{5}{9} = \frac{■}{81}$

$9 \times ? = 81$

$\frac{5}{9} = \frac{■}{81}$ (× ?, × ?)

$\frac{5}{9} = \frac{45}{81}$ (× 9, × 9)

Way 2 Use cross products.

STEP 1 Write the proportion.

$\frac{5}{9} = \frac{n}{81}$

STEP 2 Identify the terms to be multiplied. These are the **cross products.**

$\frac{5}{9} \; \frac{n}{81}$ → $9 \times n$, → 5×81

STEP 3 Write an equation that shows cross products are equal. Solve for n.

$5 \times 81 = 9 \times n$

$\frac{405}{9} = \frac{9 \times n}{9}$

$45 = n$

Solution: The game has 45 vowel tiles.

Dina says that you can use $\frac{18}{48}$ and $\frac{3}{8}$ to form a proportion. Is she correct? You can use cross multiplication to find out if two ratios form a proportion.

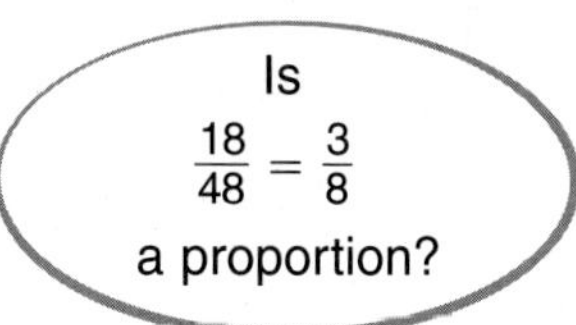

Do $\frac{18}{48}$ and $\frac{3}{8}$ form a proportion?

STEP 1 Write the two ratios.

$$\frac{18}{48} \stackrel{?}{=} \frac{3}{8}$$

STEP  Write the cross products.

$\frac{18}{48} \times \frac{3}{8}$ → 48×3, 18×8

$$48 \times 3 \stackrel{?}{=} 18 \times 8$$

STEP 3 Whenever the cross products are equal, the ratios are equivalent.

$$144 = 144$$

The cross products are equal.

Solution: Since the cross products are equal, the ratios are equivalent, and therefore, form a proportion.

Another Example

Find Another Term

$\frac{15}{18} = \frac{10}{t}$ Cross multiply. $\frac{15}{18} \times \frac{10}{t}$ → 18×10, $15 \times t$

Cross products are equal. $15 \times t = 180$

Solve for t. $\frac{15 \times t}{15} = \frac{180}{15}$ $t = 12$

Guided Practice

Solve each proportion.

1. $\frac{18}{24} = \frac{a}{8}$
2. $\frac{t}{20} = \frac{9}{15}$
3. $\frac{6}{30} = \frac{2}{b}$

Ask Yourself

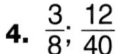

- Did I write the cross products correctly?
- Are the cross products equal?

TEST TIPS

Write the cross products for each pair of ratios. Do the two ratios form a proportion? Write *yes* or *no*.

4. $\frac{3}{8}; \frac{12}{40}$
5. $\frac{12}{8}; \frac{3}{2}$
6. $\frac{5}{6}; \frac{10}{18}$

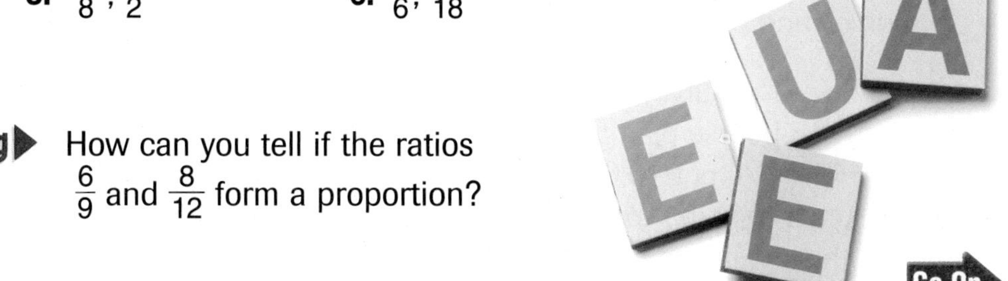

TEST TIPS **Explain Your Thinking** ▶ How can you tell if the ratios $\frac{6}{9}$ and $\frac{8}{12}$ form a proportion?

Go On

Practice and Problem Solving

Solve each proportion.

7. $\frac{5}{15} = \frac{h}{3}$
8. $\frac{4}{9} = \frac{12}{n}$
9. $\frac{k}{16} = \frac{4}{8}$
10. $\frac{12}{j} = \frac{6}{2}$
11. $\frac{32}{24} = \frac{8}{f}$
12. $\frac{w}{7} = \frac{8}{8}$
13. $\frac{14}{20} = \frac{a}{30}$
14. $\frac{16}{y} = \frac{14}{35}$
15. $\frac{9}{20} = \frac{m}{100}$
16. $\frac{36}{48} = \frac{21}{v}$
17. $\frac{q}{12} = \frac{14}{24}$
18. $\frac{s}{90} = \frac{16}{60}$

Write the cross products for each pair of ratios. Do the two ratios form a proportion? Write *yes* or *no*.

19. $\frac{3}{5}; \frac{9}{15}$
20. $\frac{6}{18}; \frac{1}{3}$
21. $\frac{3}{8}; \frac{9}{32}$
22. $\frac{15}{20}; \frac{3}{5}$
23. $\frac{8}{24}; \frac{3}{9}$
24. $\frac{10}{12}; \frac{24}{30}$
25. $\frac{3}{12}; \frac{9}{36}$
26. $\frac{12}{3}; \frac{6}{2}$
27. $\frac{32}{40}; \frac{6}{10}$
28. $\frac{15}{27}; \frac{25}{45}$
29. $\frac{42}{28}; \frac{12}{8}$
30. $\frac{4}{7}; \frac{16}{21}$
31. $\frac{20}{5}; \frac{16}{4}$
32. $\frac{40}{48}; \frac{12}{16}$
33. $\frac{9}{6}; \frac{15}{10}$
34. $\frac{10}{8}; \frac{25}{16}$

Data Use the table for Problems 35–37.

At the right are the results of a survey of two fifth grade classes. Six students did not respond to the survey.

Favorite Computer Game

Name of Game	Chosen by
City Builder	15 of 50 students
Gem Star 5	9 of 50 students
Good Knight	12 of 50 students
Final Race	8 of 50 students

35. **Predict** Suppose 350 students are in your school. Based on the survey, about how many of those students would you expect to choose Gem Star 5?

36. Suppose there are 500 students in a school. Predict how many more students would choose Good Knight than Final Race.

37. **Create and Solve** Write and solve a problem in which the data from the survey and proportions are used.

38. **Estimate** A survey of 239 voters shows that 148 people plan to vote for McAllen for Mayor. About 10,000 people are expected to vote. About how many do you think will vote for McAllen?

39. **Represent** Nick draws 4 green squares and 5 red squares. Draw a group of 27 squares in which the ratio of green squares to red squares is equivalent to the ratio shown in Nick's drawing.

Extra Practice See page 503, Set D.

Daily Review | Test Prep

Estimate. Then add or subtract. (Ch. 10, Lessons 1, 4, and 8)

40. $12\frac{7}{8} - 5\frac{1}{8}$

41. $9\frac{1}{2} + 8\frac{3}{10}$

42. $20\frac{1}{10} - 7\frac{4}{5}$

43. $6\frac{3}{4} + 9\frac{7}{8}$

44. Find the value of x to make the proportion true. $\frac{6}{8} = \frac{x}{32}$

A $x = 18$

B $x = 20$

C $x = 22$

D $x = 24$

Proportion Pushups

Practice making proportions by playing this game with a partner or several friends. Two to six can play. Try to be the first person to score 10 points.

2 Players

What You'll Need • 2 proportion cards (Learning Tool 55)
• 4 sets of number cards, numbered 1–9 (Learning Tool 6)

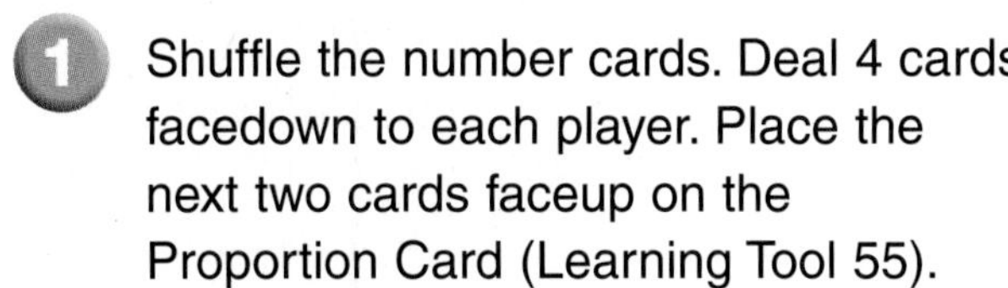

Here's What to Do

1. Shuffle the number cards. Deal 4 cards facedown to each player. Place the next two cards faceup on the Proportion Card (Learning Tool 55).

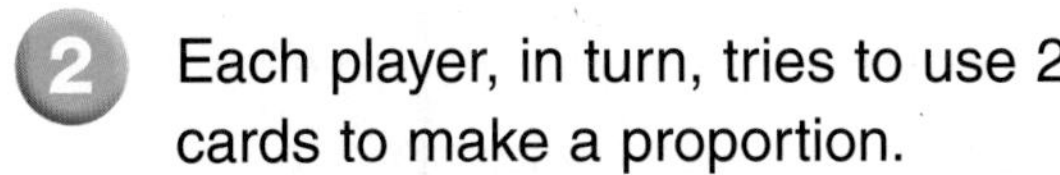

2. Each player, in turn, tries to use 2 cards to make a proportion.
   - If a correct proportion is made, that player scores 2 points.
   - If an incorrect proportion is made, the other players score 1 point.
   - If no proportion is made, the player scores 0 points.

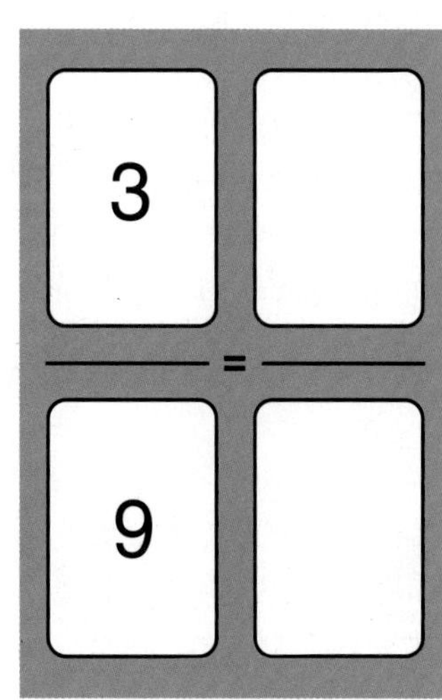

Reshuffle all cards and repeat Steps 1 and 2. The first player to score 10 points wins.

Lesson 5

Similar Figures and Scale Drawings

Objective Use equivalent ratios to interpret scale drawings.

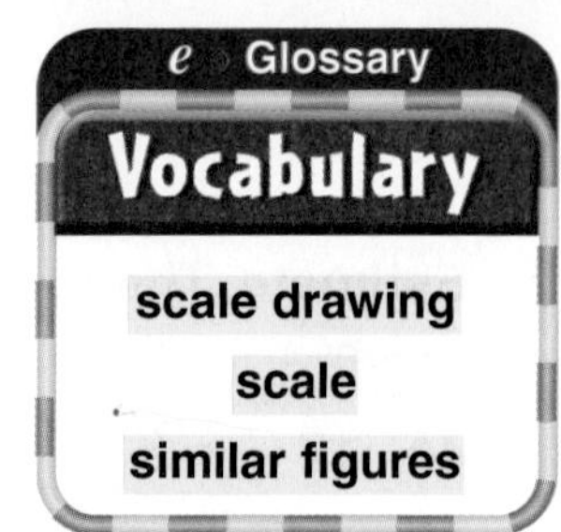

Learn About It

A **scale** is a ratio of the measurements in a drawing of an object to the corresponding measurements of the actual object. When a drawing is created using a scale, it is called a **scale drawing.**

You can create a scale drawing by enlarging or reducing all of the actual measurements by the same factor.

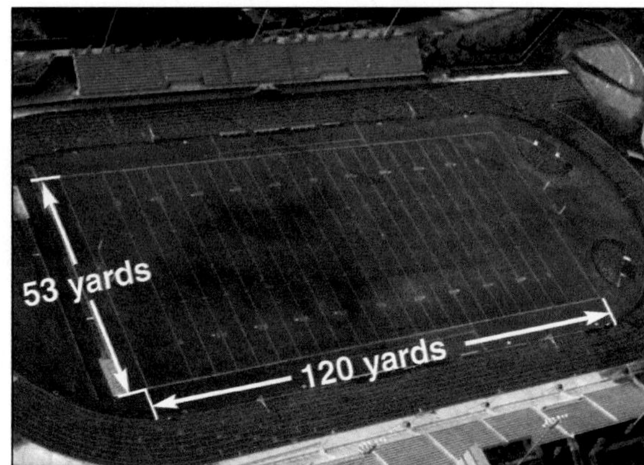

Make a scale drawing of a football field using the scale 1 cm:10 yd.

STEP 1 Write the scale as the first half of a proportion.

distance on drawing → 1 cm
actual distance → 10 yd

$\frac{1 \text{ cm}}{10 \text{ yd}}$

STEP 2 Write and solve a proportion that shows the scale is equivalent to the length of the field in the drawing to the actual length.

length in drawing / actual length

$\frac{1 \text{ cm}}{10 \text{ yd}} = \frac{\blacksquare \text{ cm}}{120 \text{ yd}}$ (× 12)

scale length = 12 cm

STEP 3 Repeat these steps to find the scale width of the field.

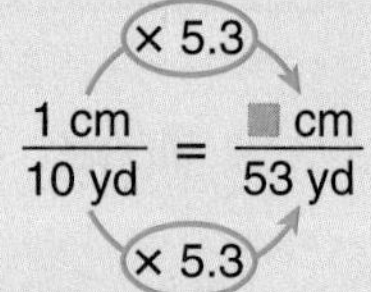

$\frac{1 \text{ cm}}{10 \text{ yd}} = \frac{\blacksquare \text{ cm}}{53 \text{ yd}}$ (× 5.3)

scale width = 5.3 cm

STEP 4 Use the answers you found in Steps 2 and 3 to create your scale drawing.

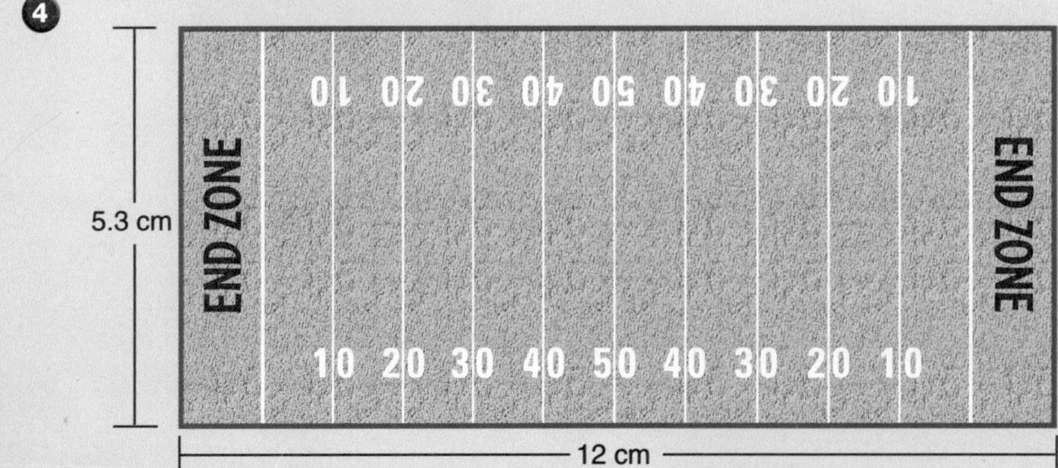

Scale drawings and the actual figures they represent are similar figures. **Similar figures** have the same shape, but they do not have to be the same size.

If figures are similar, the lengths of their corresponding sides are proportional and the measures of their corresponding angles are equal.

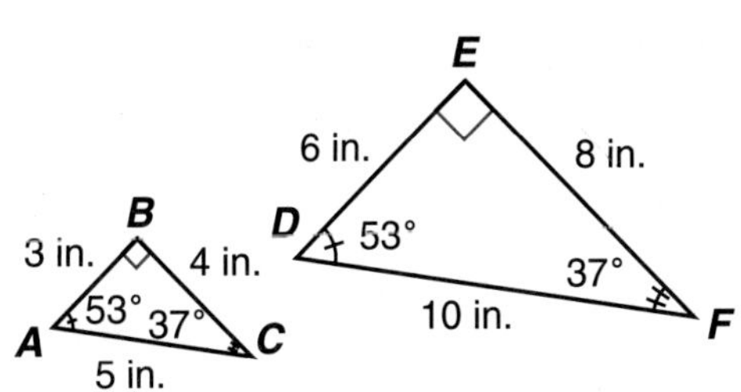

The symbol ~ is read as "is similar to."

Determine whether or not the given triangles are similar.

STEP 1 Make sure all corresponding angles have equal measures.

$\angle A \cong \angle D$

$\angle B \cong \angle E$

$\angle C \cong \angle F$

STEP 2 Write a proportion to represent the relationship between the pairs of corresponding sides.

$$\frac{3}{6} = \frac{4}{8} = \frac{5}{10}$$

STEP 3 Write each ratio in simplest form. If they are equivalent, the figures are similar.

$$\frac{3}{6} = \frac{4}{8} = \frac{5}{10}$$

$$\frac{1}{2} = \frac{1}{2} = \frac{1}{2}$$

Solution: $\triangle ABC \sim \triangle DEF$

Guided Practice

Ask Yourself

- Did I write a proportion?
- Did I use the correct units in my answers?

Use the scale 1 in.:5 ft to find *n*.

1. 4 in. in the drawing represents *n* ft.

   Hint: in drawing → $\frac{1 \text{ in.}}{5 \text{ ft}} = \frac{4 \text{ in.}}{n \text{ ft}}$ ← in drawing; actual → ← actual

2. 6 in. in the drawing represents *n* ft.
3. *n* in. in the drawing represents 45 ft.

Use the figures to the right to answer each question.

In the triangles, $\angle J \cong \angle P$ and $\angle K \cong \angle Q$. The measure of $\angle J$ is 53°.

4. What is the measure of $\angle P$?
5. What is the measure of $\angle K$?
6. What is the measure of $\angle Q$?

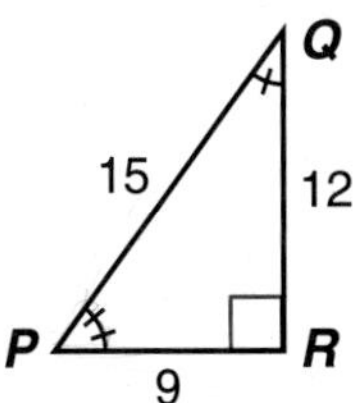

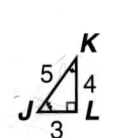

7. Write a proportion to represent the relationship between the pairs of corresponding sides. Are the ratios equivalent? Explain how you know.
8. Are the two triangles similar? How do you know?

TEST TIPS **Explain Your Thinking** ▶ Can you determine if two figures are similar just by looking at them? Explain why or why not.

Go On

Practice and Problem Solving

Use the scale 1 cm:4 m to find *n*.

9. 2 cm in the drawing represents *n* m.
10. 7 cm in the drawing represents *n* m.
11. *n* cm in the drawing represents 100 m.
12. *n* cm in the drawing represents 60 m.
13. 6 cm in the drawing represents *n* m.
14. *n* cm in the drawing represents 80 m.

A blueprint is made with a scale of $\frac{1}{8}$ in.:1 ft. Find *n*.

15. *n* in. represents 5 ft.
16. $\frac{1}{4}$ in. represents *n* ft.
17. $\frac{3}{4}$ in. represents *n* ft.
18. *n* in. represents 12 ft.
19. *n* in. represents 1.5 ft.
20. $\frac{5}{16}$ in. represents *n* ft.

Tell whether the rectangles in each pair are similar. Explain your answers.

21. rectangle ABCD and rectangle EFGH
22. rectangle EFGH and rectangle WXYZ
23. rectangle STUV and rectangle ABCD

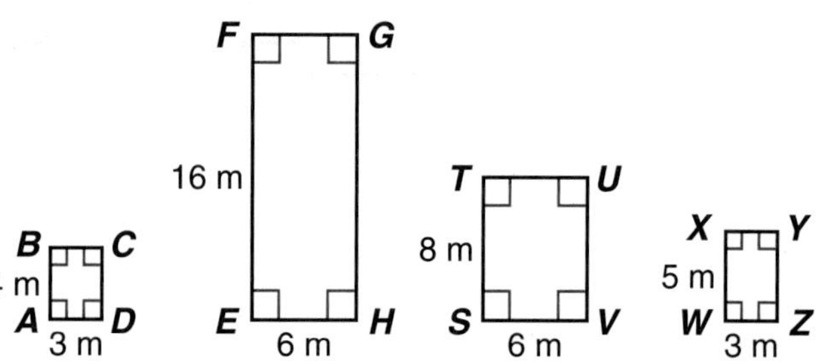

Solve.

24. An architect is making a scale drawing of a room that is 12 ft by 18 ft. He is using a scale of 1 in.:2 ft. What are the measurements of the drawing?

25. An architect's drawing of a room has a scale of 1 in.:2 ft. What are the measurements of the actual room if it is 30 in. by 16 in. in the drawing?

26. Name something that would require a scale enlargement in order for the human eye to see what the actual object looks like.

27. The official measurements of an NBA basketball court are 94 ft by 50 ft. Make a scale drawing of an NBA basketball court using the scale 1cm:10 ft.

Daily Review | Test Prep

Write each quotient in simplest form.
(Ch.12, Lessons 5-6)

28. $6 \div 1\frac{1}{5}$
29. $1\frac{1}{3} \div 3$
30. $\frac{5}{8} \div 1\frac{1}{4}$
31. $2\frac{3}{4} \div 3$
32. $\frac{5}{6} \div 3\frac{2}{3}$
33. $2\frac{1}{4} \div 1\frac{3}{4}$

34. **Free Response** Are these two triangles similar? Explain.

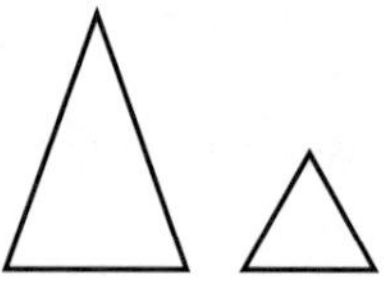

Extra Practice See page 503, Set E.

Social Studies Connection

Map Skills

A standard orienteering course consists of a start, a series of control sites marked on the map, and a finish. The person who visits all of the control sites in the fastest time wins.

At the right, there is an example of an orienteering map. The standard scale on an orienteering map is 1 cm:15,000 cm, which is the same as 1 cm:150 m.

The map's scale is used to compare the distance on the map with the actual distance.

On the map, the distance between the start of the course and the first control site is 2 cm. What is the actual distance? Use the scale 1 cm:150 m.

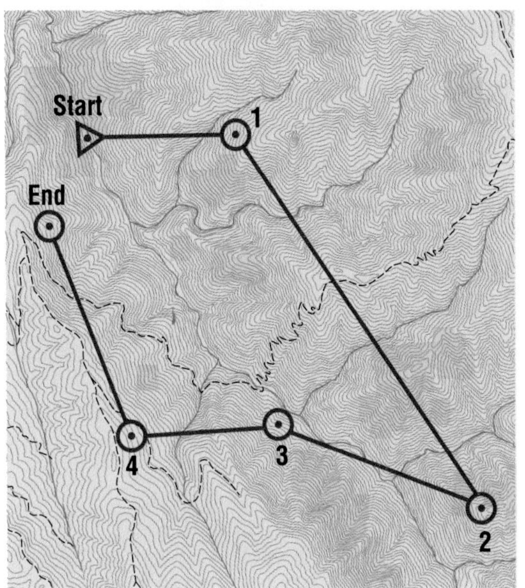

STEP 1 Write the scale as the first half of a proportion.

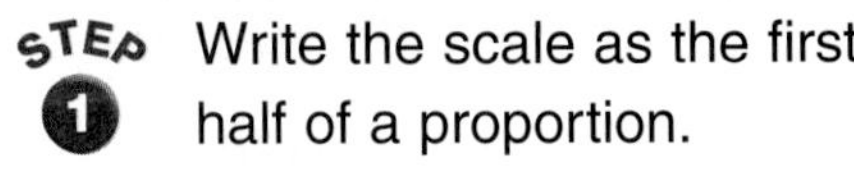

STEP 2 Write and solve a proportion that shows the scale is equivalent to the ratio of the distance on the map to the actual distance.

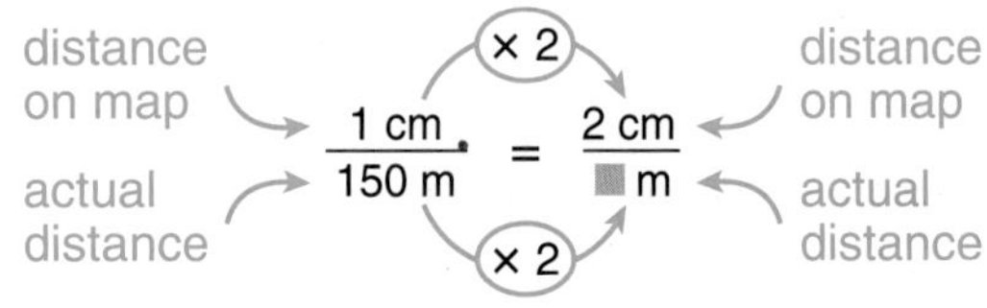

Solution: The actual distance between the start of the course and the first control site is 300 meters.

Use the map above and a centimeter ruler to answer each question.

1. What is the distance between control site 2 and control site 3?

2. What is the distance along the course from control site 3 to the end of the course?

3. How much longer is it from site 4 to the end of the course than it is from the beginning of the course to site 1?

4. **Create and Solve** Create your own problem based on the map above. Ask a partner to solve your problem.

Problem-Solving Decision

Estimate or Exact Answer?

Objective Decide when to estimate or calculate an exact answer.

When you solve a problem, you can sometimes use an estimate. An estimate is often easier. At other times, you need an exact answer. An exact answer gives you more precise information.

Problem Look at the ads for table tennis balls shown at the right. Which is the better buy?

Ask Yourself

Can I use an estimate?

If I use compatible numbers to estimate the unit prices:

$\frac{\$4.49}{5} \approx \frac{\$4.50}{5} = \$0.90$

$\frac{\$7.09}{8} \approx \frac{\$7.20}{8} = \$0.90$

$\$0.90 = \$0.90$

The estimated unit prices are equal.

Do I need to find the exact answer?

$\frac{\$4.49}{5} = \$0.898 \approx \$0.90$

$\frac{\$7.09}{8} = \$0.886 \approx \$0.89$

$\$0.89 < \$0.90$

The exact unit prices are slightly different.

Solution: The exact answer shows that $7.09 for 8 table tennis balls is a better buy than $4.49 for 5 table tennis balls. The estimate did not show a difference. Therefore, I would need an exact answer.

Try These

Solve. Tell whether you used an estimate or an exact answer, and explain why.

1. At Ted's Toys, a bag of 20 marbles costs $3.99. At Toy Club, a bag of 30 marbles costs $7.49. Which is the better buy?
2. A package of 6 miniature flags costs $11.95. A package of 10 miniature flags costs $19.79. Which is the better buy?
3. The Balloon Stop sells 200 balloons for $99. The Fun Factory sells 500 balloons for $299. Which is the better buy?
4. A barrel of 50 Tough Tiles costs $15.99. A barrel of 75 Tough Tiles costs $22.49. Which is the better buy?

Quick Check

Check your understanding for Lessons 4–6.

Solve each proportion. (Lesson 4)

1. $\frac{4}{7} = \frac{y}{21}$
2. $\frac{15}{18} = \frac{5}{t}$
3. $\frac{w}{16} = \frac{5}{20}$
4. $\frac{12}{j} = \frac{30}{5}$
5. $\frac{8}{12} = \frac{12}{p}$
6. $\frac{g}{8} = \frac{21}{24}$

Use the scale 1 in.:8 ft to find *n*. (Lesson 5)

7. *n* in. in the drawing represents 240 ft.
8. *n* in. in the drawing represents 112 ft.

Solve. Tell whether you used an estimate or an exact answer, and explain why. (Lesson 6)

9. A 6-oz tube of toothpaste costs $2.98. A 10-oz tube of toothpaste costs $3.99. Which one is the better buy?
10. At Mel's Office Supplies, a package of 6 pens costs $4.09. At Office King, a package of 8 pens costs $5.55. Which is the better buy?

WEEKLY WR READER® eduplace.com/kids/mw/

Model Railroads

Model railroad designs have many of the features of an actual railroad system. They include such items as trains, stations, signals, and bridges.

Model railroad cars are exact scale replicas of real trains. Many model trains use the HO scale, which is 1 in.:87 in. Another popular scale is the *N* scale, which is 1 in.:160 in.

1. The length of a model boxcar done in HO scale is 6.07 in. What is the actual length of the boxcar in inches?
2. The length of a model engine done in *N* scale is 4.8 in. What is the actual length of the engine in inches?

Chapter Review/Test

VOCABULARY

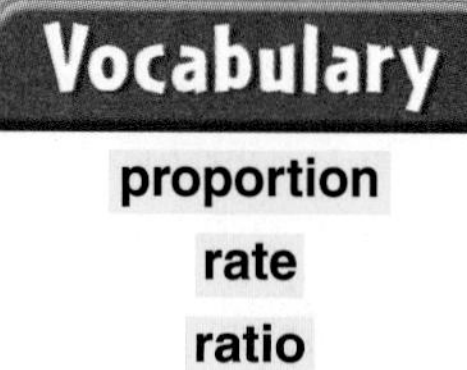

1. Two figures that have the same shape but are not the same size are ____.
2. A ratio that compares different units is called a ____.
3. A ____ is a ratio of the measurements in a scale drawing of an object to the corresponding measurements of the actual object.
4. A statement that two ratios are equivalent is a ____.

CONCEPTS AND SKILLS

Write each ratio three different ways. (Lesson 1, pp. 484–485)

5. 7 drums to 14 drumsticks
6. 11 forks to 8 knives

Write 4 equivalent ratios for each. (Lesson 2, pp. 486–487)

7. $\frac{2}{3}$
8. 1 to 7
9. 12:9
10. $\frac{10}{6}$

Find the rate per unit of time. (Lesson 3, pp. 488–491)

11. $240 in 6 days
12. 455 km in 7 h
13. 360 beats in 5 min

Do the two ratios form a proportion? Write *yes* or *no*. (Lesson 4, pp. 492–495)

14. $\frac{3}{4}$ $\frac{39}{52}$
15. $\frac{5}{6}$ $\frac{4}{5}$
16. $\frac{77}{132}$ $\frac{7}{12}$

Use the scale $\frac{1}{2}$ in.:5 mi to find *n*. (Lesson 5, pp. 496–499)

17. *n* in. represents 20 mi
18. 3 in. represents *n* mi
19. *n* in. represents 45 mi

PROBLEM SOLVING

Solve. Tell whether you used an estimate or an exact answer, and explain why.
(Lesson 6, pp. 500–501)

20. A box of 30 diskettes costs $15.99. A box of 50 diskettes costs $26.00. Which is the better buy?

Show You Understand

Alan says that the ratios $\frac{3}{5}$ and $\frac{4}{6}$ form a proportion. Is he correct? Explain your thinking.

Extra Practice

Set A (Lesson 1, pp. 484–485)

Write each ratio three different ways.

1. 5 cups to 8 saucers
2. 3 windows to 2 doors
3. 6 girls to 7 boys
4. 9 red to 4 blue
5. 1 car to 5 buses
6. 13 horses to 6 sheep

Set B (Lesson 2, pp. 486–487)

Write each ratio in simplest form.

1. 6 to 10
2. 9:24
3. $\frac{25}{100}$
4. 14:56
5. $\frac{8}{12}$
6. 30:72

Write four equivalent ratios for each.

7. $\frac{1}{3}$
8. $\frac{2}{5}$
9. $\frac{3}{7}$
10. $\frac{1}{2}$
11. $\frac{1}{4}$
12. $\frac{5}{6}$

Set C (Lesson 3, pp. 488–491)

Find the rate per unit of time.

1. 96 meters in 12 seconds
2. 360 words in 3 min
3. $420 in 35 hours

Complete the unit rate.

4. $4:5 lb = $■:1 lb
5. 275 mi:11 gal = ■ mi:1 gal

Set D (Lesson 4, pp. 492–495)

Solve each proportion.

1. $\frac{6}{30} = \frac{u}{5}$
2. $\frac{5}{75} = \frac{1}{v}$
3. $\frac{24}{w} = \frac{8}{2}$
4. $\frac{x}{100} = \frac{4}{25}$

Do the ratios form a proportion? Write *yes* or *no*.

5. $\frac{2}{3}$ $\frac{9}{12}$
6. $\frac{5}{8}$ $\frac{30}{48}$
7. $\frac{32}{80}$ $\frac{2}{5}$
8. $\frac{10}{4}$ $\frac{15}{5}$

Set E (Lesson 5, pp. 496–499)

Use the scale $\frac{1}{4}$ in.:1 ft to find *n*.

1. *n* in. represents 8 ft
2. 3 in. represents *n* ft

Use the figure at the right to answer each question.

3. What is the measure of $\angle G$?
4. Are the triangles similar? How do you know?

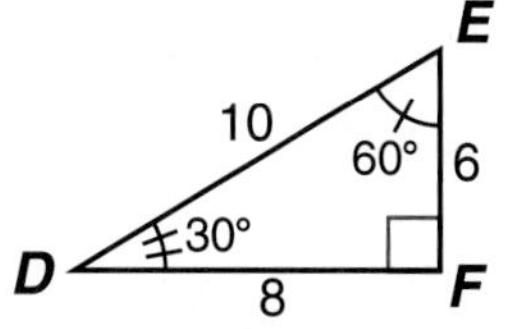

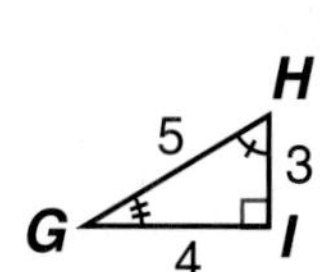

CHAPTER 19

Percent

INVESTIGATION

Use Data

Eva's family made the budget shown by the circle graph. The family income is $3,000 per month. How much does Eva's family spend on food each month? How much do they save each month?

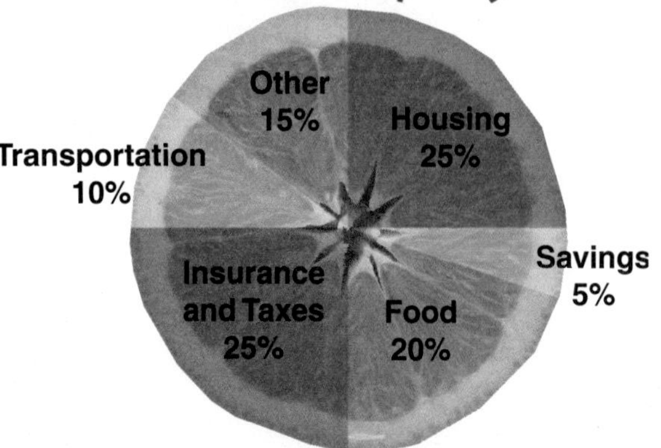

Chapter Pretest

Use this page to review and remember what you need to know for this chapter.

VOCABULARY

Choose the best word to complete each sentence.

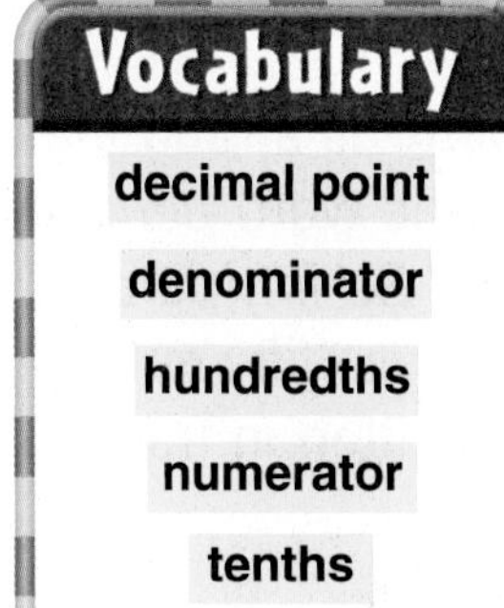

1. In the decimal 3.45, the 5 is in the ____ place.
2. The ____ of a fraction tells the number of equal parts in the whole.
3. In writing money amounts, the dollars and cents are separated by a ____ .

CONCEPTS AND SKILLS

Write a decimal and a fraction to represent the shaded part of each model.

4. 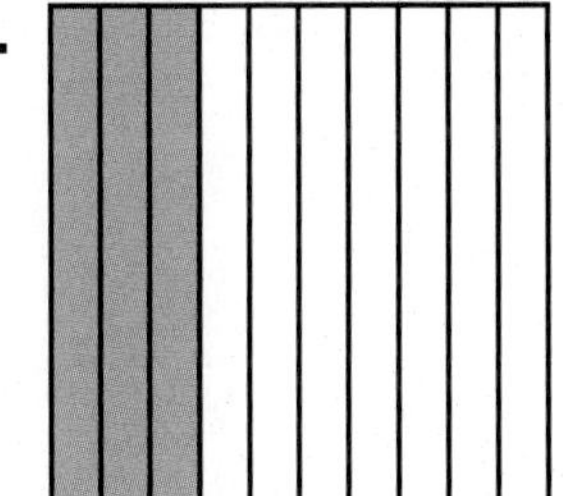

5. 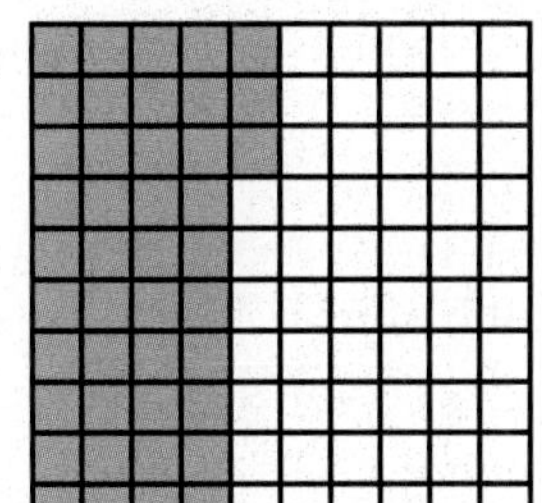

6. 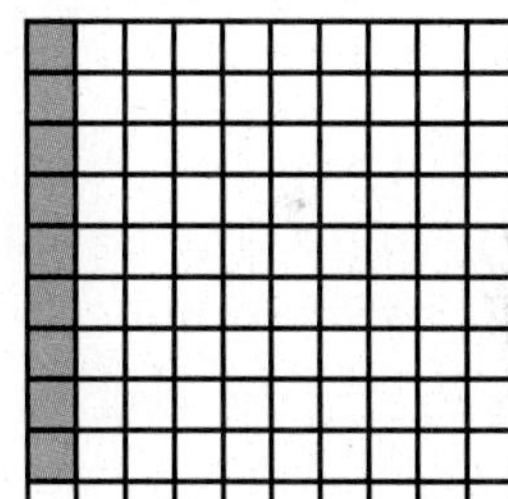

Write each decimal as a fraction in simplest form.

7. 0.4
8. 0.75
9. 0.35
10. 0.66

Find each product.

11. 0.5×21
12. 0.26×300
13. 0.34×192
14. 0.62×475
15. $\frac{3}{4} \times 80$
16. $\frac{1}{2} \times 644$
17. $\frac{4}{5}$ of 135
18. $\frac{3}{8}$ of 96
19. $\frac{1}{5}$ of 200

20. Would you prefer to multiply 0.25×84 or $\frac{1}{4} \times 84$? Explain.

Test Prep on the Net

Visit *Education Place* at **eduplace.com/kids/mw/** for more review.

Understand Percent

Objective Understand percents as ratios.

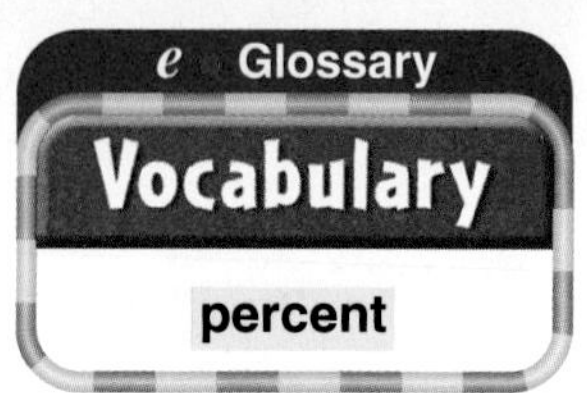

Materials
grid paper
ruler
colored pencils

Work Together

Work with a partner to write percents.

A **percent** is a ratio that compares a number to 100. The word *percent* means "per hundred." So *fifty percent* means "fifty per hundred," or "fifty out of 100." Percents can also be written in fraction or decimal form.

The symbol for percent is %.

Fifty percent is written 50%.

$50\% = 50{:}100 = \frac{50}{100} = 0.50$ or 0.5

STEP 1 On a sheet of grid paper, use a ruler to outline an area that measures 10 units by 10 units.

- How many square units are in the figure?

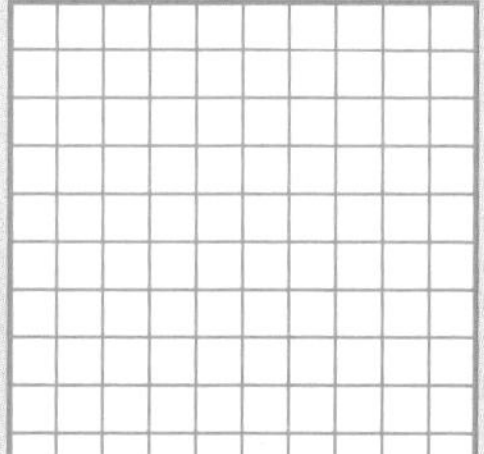

STEP 2 Shade 40 square units blue, 25 square units yellow, and 15 square units green.

- What is the ratio of blue squares to the total number of squares?
- What is the ratio of yellow squares to the total number of squares?
- What is the ratio of shaded squares to the total number of squares?

STEP 3 Use the percent symbol to write each percent. What percent of the figure is

- blue?
- yellow?
- green?
- shaded?
- unshaded?

On Your Own

Write the percent of each grid that is shaded.

1. 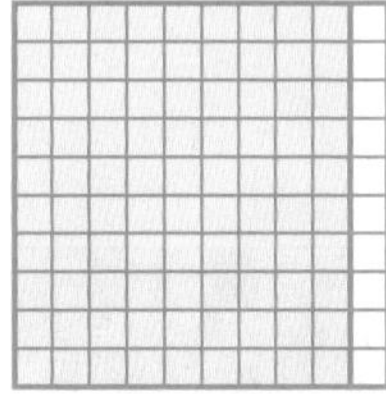

2. 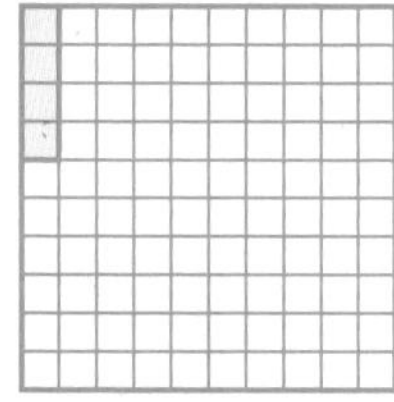

3. 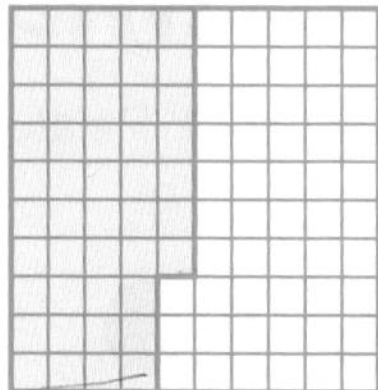

4. 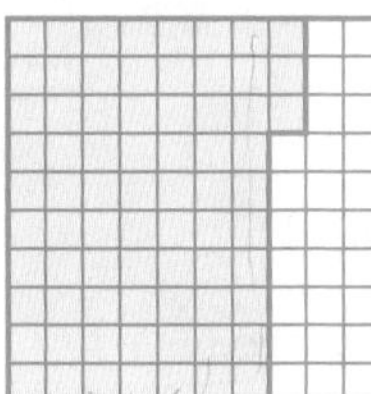

5. 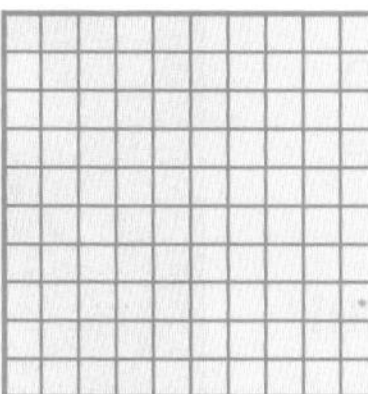

6. 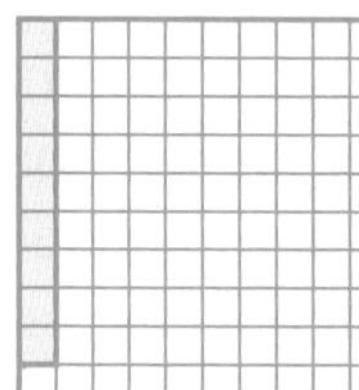

Write each ratio as a percent.

7. $\frac{55}{100}$
8. $\frac{2}{100}$
9. $\frac{31}{100}$
10. $\frac{79}{100}$
11. $\frac{90}{100}$
12. 48:100
13. 16:100
14. 91:100
15. 63:100
16. 8:100
17. 35 parts out of 100
18. 6 parts out of 100
19. 15 parts out of 100
20. 1 part out of 100
21. 0 parts out of 100
22. 50 parts out of 100

Write each percent as a ratio in simplest form.

23. 10%
24. 28%
25. 81%
26. 12%
27. 39%
28. 53%
29. 62%
30. 98%
31. 70%
32. 23%
33. 40%
34. 75%
35. 65%
36. 17%
37. 99%
38. 100%

You learned about percents as ratios and how to write percents.

39. How would you show 10% on a 10 × 10 grid? How would you show 100%?

40. Use models to show how 9% and 90% are different. Which model shows the decimal 0.9? Which model shows the decimal 0.09?

Lesson 2

Relate Fractions, Decimals, and Percents

Objective Relate fractions, decimals, and percents.

Learn About It

On Saturday, 50% of the people who visited a department store bought only one item and one out of four people bought more than one item. The rest of the people did not buy anything. What decimal represents the percent of people who bought nothing?

You can write percents in fraction form or in decimal form.

Try this activity to relate fractions, decimals, and percents.

Materials grid paper, ruler, colored pencils

STEP 1 Fifty percent of the people bought only one item. Outline a 10 × 10 grid on grid paper. Shade 50% of the grid red.

- How many square units do you need to shade?
- What decimal can you write for 50%?
- What fraction of the grid is shaded?

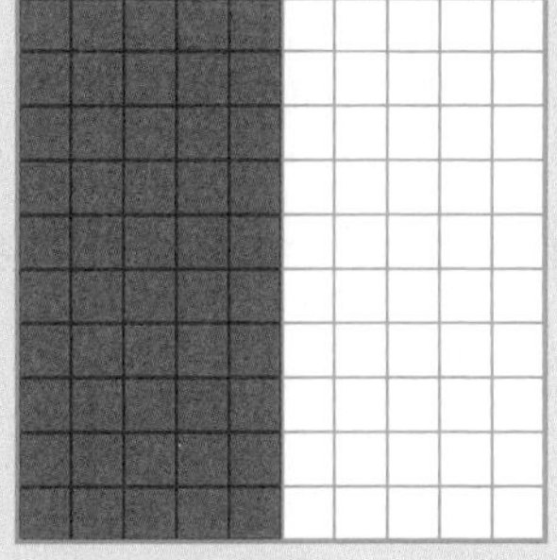

STEP 2 One out of four people who visited the store bought more than one item. Shade $\frac{1}{4}$ of the grid blue.

- How many square units did you shade blue?
- What percent of the grid is shaded blue?
- What decimal can you write for that percent?

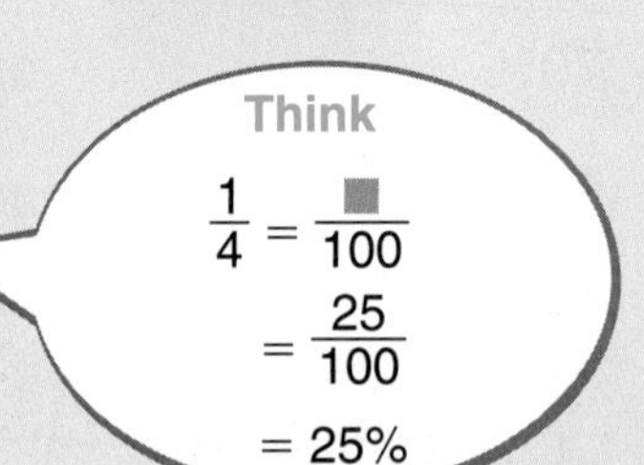

Think

$$\frac{1}{4} = \frac{■}{100}$$
$$= \frac{25}{100}$$
$$= 25\%$$

STEP 3 The part of the grid that is unshaded represents the percent of the people who bought nothing on Saturday.

- What percent of the grid is unshaded?
- What decimal can you write for that percent?

Solution: 25% of the people bought nothing at the store on Saturday. The decimal form of this percent is 0.25.

Guided Practice

Copy and complete the table. Write each fraction in simplest form.

	Fraction Form	Decimal Form	Percent
1.	$\frac{1}{10}$	■	10%
2.	■	0.2	■
3.	■	■	65%

Ask Yourself

- Did I write each percent or decimal as a ratio with a second term of 100?
- Did I write each fraction in simplest form?

Explain Your Thinking ▶ Explain why $\frac{5}{100}$ and 5% represent the same ratio.

Practice and Problem Solving

Copy and complete the table. Write each fraction in simplest form.

	Fraction Form	Decimal Form	Percent
4.	■	■	50%
5.	■	0.6	■
6.	$\frac{3}{4}$	■	■

	Fraction Form	Decimal Form	Percent
7.	■	■	80%
8.	■	0.9	■
9.	■	0.4	■

Algebra • Equations **Solve each equation for *n*.**

10. $\frac{25}{100} = \frac{1}{n}$ **11.** $\frac{36}{n} = \frac{9}{25}$ **12.** $12\% = \frac{n}{25}$ **13.** $18\% = \frac{36}{n}$

14. $n\% = \frac{7}{20}$ **15.** $n\% = \frac{23}{50}$ **16.** $0.94 = n\%$ **17.** $0.72 = n\%$

Solve.

18. Three fifths of the items in a grocery store are marked down from their original prices. What percent of the items in the store are marked down?

19. There are 25 students practicing soccer. Nine of them are girls. What percent of the students are girls? What percent of the students are boys?

Daily Review Test Prep

Estimate. Then add or subtract.
(Ch. 11, Lessons 2-4)

20. 5.691 + 0.78 **21.** 0.932 − 0.64

22. Free Response A goalie blocked 95% of the shots during a soccer game. How many shots out of 20 did the goalie block? Explain.

Extra Practice See page 525, Set A.

Lesson 3

Compare Fractions, Decimals, and Percents

Objective Use fractions, decimals, and percents to compare numbers.

Learn About It

On the first of the month, The Beach Shop received a shipment of shorts in 3 colors—red, blue, and green. There were equal numbers of each color.

By the end of the month, $\frac{2}{5}$ of the red shorts, 78% of the blue shorts, and 0.55 of the green shorts had been sold. Which color of shorts was the most popular that month?

Try this activity to represent and compare $\frac{2}{5}$, 78%, and 0.55.

Materials grid paper, ruler, colored pencils

STEP 1 Outline a 10 × 10 grid on grid paper.
Shade 2 of every 5 squares red.

- How did you find $\frac{2}{5}$ of the grid?
- What decimal does the grid show?

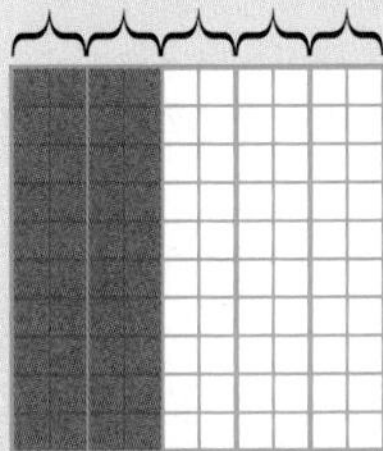

STEP 2 Outline another 10 × 10 grid and shade 78% blue.

- How did you know how to show 78%?
- What decimal does the grid show?

STEP 3 Outline a third 10 × 10 grid and shade 0.55 green.

- How did you know how to show 0.55?

STEP 4 Compare the three grids.

- Which color had the greatest number of squares shaded?
  Which percent is greatest?

Solution: Blue shorts were the most popular that month.

Compare $\frac{4}{5}$, 27%, and 0.7.

Different Ways to Compare $\frac{4}{5}$, 27%, and 0.7

Way 1 You can use a number line.

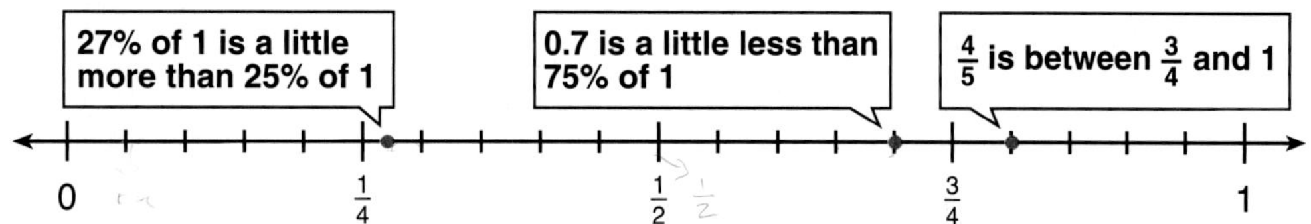

27% of 1 is a little more than 25% of 1
0.7 is a little less than 75% of 1
$\frac{4}{5}$ is between $\frac{3}{4}$ and 1
0
$\frac{1}{4}$
$\frac{1}{2}$
$\frac{3}{4}$
1

$\frac{4}{5}$ is farthest to the right. $\frac{4}{5}$ is greater than 0.7 which is greater than 27%.

Way 2 You can rewrite each in decimal form.

Step 1 To rewrite the fraction, divide the numerator by the denominator.

$$5\overline{)4.0} = 0.8$$

$$\frac{4}{5} = 0.8$$

Step 2 Think of the percent as a number of hundredths.

$$27\% = \frac{27}{100} = 0.27$$

Step 3 Compare 0.8, 0.27, and 0.7.

$$0.8 > 0.7 > 0.27$$

so, $\frac{4}{5} > 0.7 > 27\%$

Solution: $\frac{4}{5} > 0.7 > 27\%$

Another Example

Order $\frac{9}{25}$, 38%, and 0.313 from the greatest to the least.

$9 \div 25 = 0.36$, so $\frac{9}{25} = 0.36$. 38% can be written in decimal form as 0.38.

$0.38 > 0.36 > 0.313$, so $38\% > \frac{9}{25} > 0.313$.

Guided Practice

Which is greatest?

1. 0.4 $\frac{1}{2}$ 30%

2. $\frac{1}{5}$ 30% 0.25

3. $\frac{1}{8}$ 0.2 40%

4. $\frac{9}{20}$ 44% $\frac{3}{8}$

Ask Yourself

- Did I write the numbers in the same form?
- Did I check the order to see if it's reasonable?

TEST TIPS

TEST TIPS **Explain Your Thinking** ▶ How could you write $\frac{9}{20}$ in decimal form by first writing it as a percent in ratio form?

Go On

Practice and Problem Solving

Which is greatest?

5. $\frac{3}{5}$ 59% 0.62

6. $\frac{3}{8}$ 9% 0.8

7. $\frac{11}{25}$ 0.4 43%

8. $\frac{5}{8}$ 0.56 59%

9. $\frac{17}{25}$ 70% 0.69

10. $\frac{1}{10}$ 8% 0.09

Which is least?

11. $\frac{4}{5}$ 0.2 60%

12. $\frac{3}{5}$ 0.4 80%

13. $\frac{4}{5}$ 0.9 85%

14. $\frac{1}{5}$ 0.1 25%

15. $\frac{3}{20}$ 4% 0.06

16. $\frac{7}{10}$ 0.6 30%

Order each set from greatest to least.

17. $\frac{3}{10}$ 0.25 20%

18. $\frac{9}{10}$ 0.75 80%

19. $\frac{7}{20}$ 0.3 40%

20. $\frac{12}{25}$ 0.3 50%

21. $\frac{13}{20}$ 0.7 67%

22. $\frac{3}{50}$ 0.6 3%

23. $\frac{19}{20}$ 0.99 98%

24. $\frac{1}{3}$ 0.25 30%

25. $\frac{3}{8}$ 0.43 52%

Algebra • **Inequalities Write a number that will make the number sentence true.**

26. $\frac{2}{5} < \blacksquare < 45\%$

27. $62\% < \blacksquare < \frac{2}{3}$

28. $\frac{12}{25} < \blacksquare < 50\%$

29. $0.82 < \blacksquare\% < \frac{17}{20}$

30. $\frac{5}{8} < \blacksquare < 63\%$

31. $0.03 < \blacksquare\% < \frac{1}{16}$

Solve.

32. Analyze In Ben's Books, 0.3 of the shelves have adult fiction, 25% have adult nonfiction, and $\frac{9}{20}$ of the shelves have children's books. Which kinds of books take up the most shelves in the bookstore?

33. What's Wrong? Sam ordered the numbers $\frac{7}{20}$, 4%, and 0.34 from least to greatest. What did Sam do wrong?

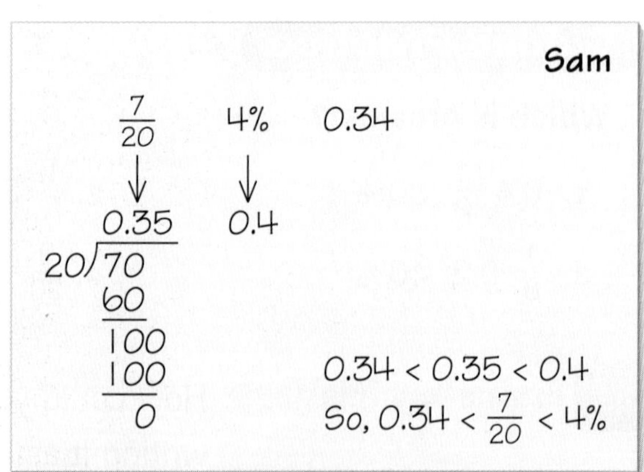

34. Orange juice and lemonade were sold during a concert intermission. Three fifths of the sales were orange juice and 40% were lemonade. Which drink was less popular?

Extra Practice See page 525, Set B.

Quick Check

Check your understanding of Lessons 1–3.

Write each ratio as a percent. (Lesson 1)

1. $\frac{27}{100}$
2. 6:100
3. 41 out of 100

Write a decimal, a percent, and a fraction in simplest form for each ratio. (Lesson 2)

4. $\frac{12}{50}$
5. $\frac{29}{100}$
6. $\frac{40}{100}$
7. $\frac{112}{200}$

Order each set from the greatest to the least. (Lesson 3)

8. $\frac{13}{40}$ 0.3 25%
9. 0.65 $\frac{21}{25}$ 70%
10. 5% 0.1 $\frac{1}{8}$

WEEKLY WR READER® eduplace.com/kids/mw/

LOOKING AROUND

You have learned about percent.

Look around your school, your home, and your shopping mall. Make a display of all the places where you see percents!

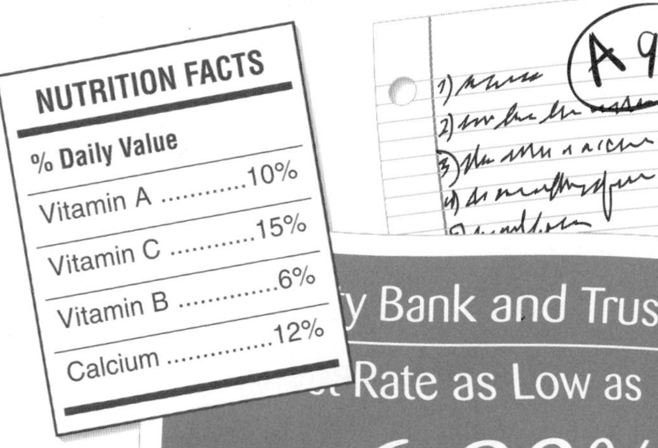

NUTRITION FACTS
% Daily Value
Vitamin A 10%
Vitamin C 15%
Vitamin B 6%
Calcium 12%
A 95%
y Bank and Trust
Rate as Low as
6.99%

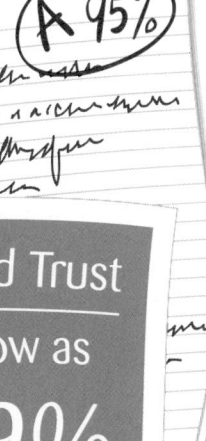

Lesson 4

Find 10% of a Number

Objective Use mental math to find 10% and multiples of 10% of a number.

Learn About It

A skateboard regularly sells for \$60. The skateboard is on sale for 10% off the regular price. How much money would you save if you bought the skateboard on sale?

10% of 60 = *n*

Different Ways to Find 10% of 60

Way 1 You can use a model.

To find n, divide \$60 by 10.

$60 \div 10 = \$6$

100% of \$60 = \$60

10%									

n

Way 2 You can multiply by $\frac{1}{10}$.

Finding 10% of a number is the same as finding $\frac{1}{10}$ of that number.

$$10\% \times 60 = \frac{1}{10} \times 60$$

$$\frac{1}{10} \times \frac{60}{1} = \frac{60}{10} = 6$$

Way 3 You can divide by 10 by moving the decimal point to the left.

An easy way to find 10% of any number is to move the decimal point one place to the left to divide the number by 10.

$60 \div 10 = 6.0$

Solution: You would save \$6.

Other Examples

A. Find 20% of a Number

Find 20% of 42.

$20\% \text{ of } 42 = 42 \div 5$

$= 8.4$

100% of 42 = 42

20%	20%	20%	20%	20%

20% of 42

B. Estimate a Percent of a Number

Estimate 11% of 47.

11% of 47 is about 10% of 50

$10\% \times 50 = \frac{1}{10} \times 50 = 5$

$11\% \text{ of } 47 \approx 5$

Guided Practice

Ask Yourself

- Did I move the decimal point one place to the left to find 10%?

Find 10% of each number.

1. 75 **2.** 19 **3.** 3.8 **4.** 0.4

Find 20% of each number.

5. 40 **6.** 120 **7.** 26 **8.** 8.2

Explain Your Thinking ▶ What decimal would you multiply by to find 10% of a number? Explain.

Practice and Problem Solving

Find 10% of each number.

9. 42 **10.** 25 **11.** 9 **12.** 3 **13.** 1

14. 783 **15.** 4,012 **16.** 7.8 **17.** 100.5 **18.** 4.41

Find 20% of each number.

19. 20 **20.** 46 **21.** 1,020 **22.** 8.4 **23.** 0.6

Estimate each percent of a number.

24. 12% of 73 **25.** 48% of 69 **26.** 18% of 503 **27.** 9% of 397

Find the number.

28. 10% of a number is 32.

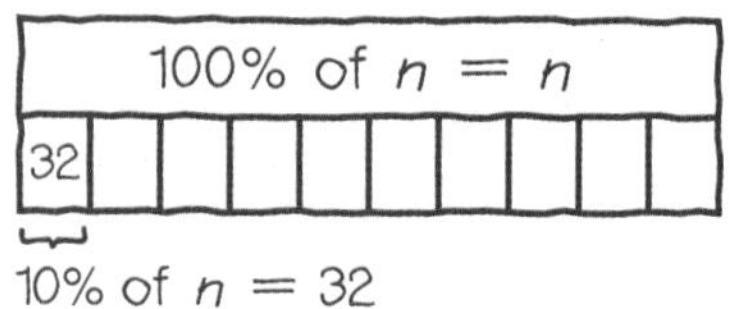

29. 20% of a number is 27.

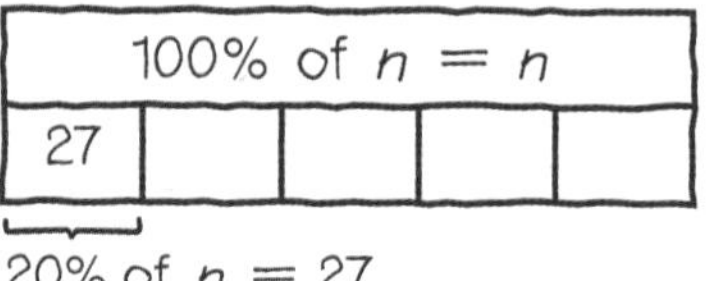

Solve.

30. Mel's bill comes to $31. He leaves 20% of the bill as a tip. How much is the tip?

31. The sum of two numbers is 17. Their product is 60. Find the two numbers.

32. **What's Wrong?** Monique says that 13% of 152 is about 50. Is her estimate reasonable? Tell how you know.

33. **Explain** How can you find 50% of a number? How can you find 100% of a number?

Daily Review Test Prep

Divide. (Ch. 14, Lessons 4–5)

34. 2.1 ÷ 6 **35.** 28.63 ÷ 7

36. Find 20% of 140.

A 28 **B** 14 **C** 7 **D** 1.4

Extra Practice See page 525, Set C.

Lesson 5

Algebra

Percent of a Number

Objective Use different ways to find a percent of a number.

Learn About It

On display in a store window are 20 kites. If 75 percent of the kites are red, how many kites are red?

75% of 20 = *n*

Different Ways to Find 75% of 20

Way 1 You can use a model.

To find n, divide 20 by 4. Then multiply by 3.

$20 \div 4 = 5 \qquad 5 \times 3 = 15$

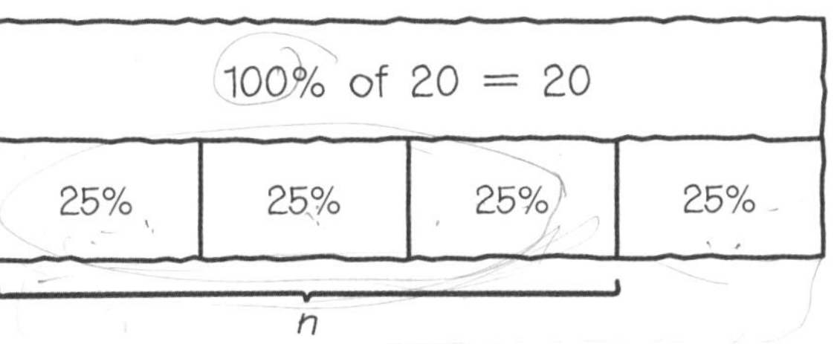

Way 2 You can write the percent as a fraction and multiply.

STEP 1 Write the percent as a ratio.

$$75\% = \frac{75}{100} = \frac{3}{4}$$

STEP 2 Multiply.

$$\frac{3}{4} \times \frac{20}{1} = \frac{60}{4} = 15$$

Way 3 You can write the percent in decimal form and multiply.

STEP 1 Write the percent in decimal form.

75% = 75 hundredths
= 0.75

STEP 2 Multiply.

```
   20
× 0.75   ← 2 decimal places in the factors
  1 00
 14 00
 15.00   ← 2 decimal places in the product
```

Solution: There are 15 red kites.

Guided Practice

Ask Yourself

- Do I write the percent as a fraction?
- Do I write the percent as a decimal?

Solve by using a model.

1. 50% of 80
2. 75% of 28

Solve by writing the percent as a fraction.

3. 70% of 90
4. 5% of 80

Solve by writing the percent as a decimal.

5. 16% of 40
6. 80% of 150

Explain Your Thinking ▶ Which method would you use to find 28% of 66? Why?

Practice and Problem Solving

Solve by writing the percent as a fraction.

7. 90% of 30
8. 35% of 300
9. 20% of 45
10. 40% of 25
11. 75% of 80
12. 15% of 40
13. 50% of 36
14. 30% of 1,000

Solve by writing the percent as a decimal.

15. 25% of 44
16. 33% of 30
17. 16% of 15
18. 90% of 50
19. 7% of 20
20. 60% of 12
21. 37% of 20
22. 14% of 300

Solve. Use any method.

23. 25% of 232
24. 20% of 20
25. 1% of 100
26. 65% of 40
27. 7% of 30
28. 19% of 200
29. 75% of 4
30. 49% of 300

Algebra • **Functions** **Use the rule to complete each function table.**

31. $y = x\%$ of 200

x	y
5	■
10	■
15	■
20	■

32. $y = 25\%$ of x

x	y
10	■
20	■
30	■
40	■

33. $y = x\%$ of 200

x	y
■	50
■	100
■	150
■	200

Go On

Choose a Computation Method

Mental Math • Estimation • Paper and Pencil • Calculator

Data Use the table for Problems 34–36.

34. A *discount* is the amount of money deducted from the price of an item. Use a calculator to find the price of a box kite after the discount indicated in the table has been subtracted.

35. **Analyze** Elena has saved $15. Does she have enough money to buy a dragon kite after the discount? Explain how you know.

36. **You Decide** You are in charge of buying kites for the kite club. You have $100 to spend, and want to buy a few different kinds of kites. Which kites will you buy? What is the total cost?

37. **Estimate** At the Flying Kite Festival, 7,958 children's tickets were sold. The total number of tickets sold was about 20,608. About what percent were children's tickets?

38. **Create and Solve** A newspaper reported that the attendance at this year's kite festival was 20% less than the year before. This year's attendance was 12,000. Use this information to write your own problem. Then solve the problem.

Kite	Price	Discount
Parafoil	$50.00	10%
Dragon	$25.00	20%
Box	$20.00	30%
Delta	$40.00	50%

Daily Review | Test Prep

Find the area and perimeter.
(Ch. 16, Lessons 1 and 3)

39. Rectangle: 5 in. by 2.5 in.

40. Triangle: sides $\frac{1}{2}$ yd, $\frac{1}{2}$ yd, $\frac{1}{2}$ yd; height $\frac{3}{8}$ yd

41. **Free Response** Helena has $25. She wants to buy a disc player that has a regular price of $39. The player is on sale with a 30% discount. Does Helena have enough money? Explain how you found your answer.

Extra Practice See page 525, Set D.

Ratios and Percents

You buy a sweatshirt that is on sale. How much will you save? When you estimate or calculate a percent of a number, it helps to think of ratios and their related percents. Here are some relationships you should know.

Ratio	$\frac{1}{20}$	$\frac{1}{10}$	$\frac{1}{8}$	$\frac{1}{6}$	$\frac{1}{5}$	$\frac{1}{4}$	$\frac{1}{3}$	$\frac{1}{2}$
Percent	5%	10%	12.5%	$16\frac{2}{3}$%	20%	25%	$33\frac{1}{3}$%	50%

Estimate 35% of 48.

If you only need an estimate, you can find a ratio that converts to a percent close to 35%.

Estimate

$33\frac{1}{3}\% = \frac{1}{3}$, so 35% of 48 is about $\frac{1}{3}$ of 48.

$48 \div 3 = 16$

So 35% of 48 must be slightly more than 16.

You will save about $16.

Find 35% of 48.

If you need an exact calculation, you can find ratios whose corresponding percents have a sum or difference of 35%.

Think: Add 25% of 48 and 10% of 48 to get 35% of 48.

$25\% + 10\% = 35\%$

25% of 48 $= \frac{1}{4}$ of 48 $= 48 \div 4 = 12$

10% of 48 $= \frac{1}{10}$ of 48 $= 48 \div 10 = 4.8$

So, 35% of 48 $= 12 + 4.8 = 16.8$.

You will save $16.80

1. Why are ratios and their related percents helpful if you want to find the percent of a number using mental math?
2. How could you use ratios to find 20% of 60? to find 45% of 90?

Lesson 6

Problem-Solving Application

Use Circle Graphs

Objective Interpret data to make circle graphs to solve problems.

Making a circle graph is a good way to display data expressed as percents.

Problem The table at the right shows the results of a survey of 240 customers at a department store. How can you show the data from the table as percents in a circle graph?

PAYMENT FOR PURCHASES

Method of Payment	Number of Customers
Cash	60
Check	30
Credit Card	120
Debit Card	30

UNDERSTAND

What is the question?

How can you show the data from the table as percents in a circle graph?

What do you know?

- 60 customers used cash.
- 120 customers used credit cards.
- 240 customers were in the survey.
- 30 customers used checks.
- 30 customers used debit cards.

PLAN

Find the ratio of the data represented by each method of payment to total sales. Write each ratio as a percent. Then divide a circle so that it shows the percent.

SOLVE

- Find the ratio for each method.
- Write the ratio in simplest form and as a percent.

Cash $= \frac{60}{240} = \frac{1}{4} = 25\%$

Check $= \frac{30}{240} = \frac{1}{8} = 12.5\%$

Credit card $= \frac{120}{240} = \frac{1}{2} = 50\%$

Debit card $= \frac{30}{240} = \frac{1}{8} = 12.5\%$

- Use the ratios to make a circle graph.
- Label each section.

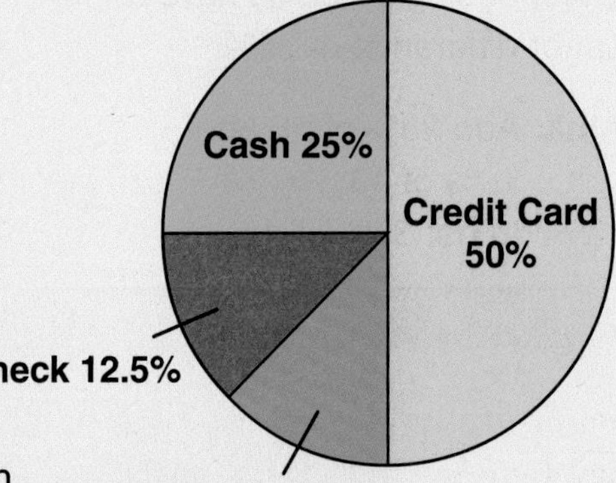

LOOK BACK

Look back at the data. Does the graph seem reasonable?

Guided Practice

Use the circle graph on page 520 to solve each problem.

1. Predict the number of customers out of 1,000 that would use a method other than cash.

   Hint What part of the circle represents other payment methods?

2. Suppose 120 more customers are surveyed. Of these customers, 60 use credit cards, 30 use checks, and 30 use debit cards. If that data is added to the existing data, how will the circle graph change?

Ask Yourself

UNDERSTAND — **What does the question ask me to find?**

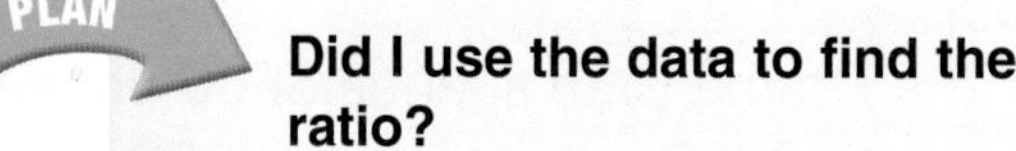

PLAN — **Did I use the data to find the ratio?**

SOLVE — **Did I write each ratio as a percent?**

LOOK BACK — **Does my answer make sense?**

Independent Practice

Use the circle graph for Problems 3 and 4.

3. The circle graph at the right shows how Ted budgets his money. If his total budget is $3,000, how much money does Ted spend on his rent?

4. **You Decide** Ted wants to increase his savings to $600 per month. Suggest a way that Ted can change his spending to increase his savings.

Ted's Budget

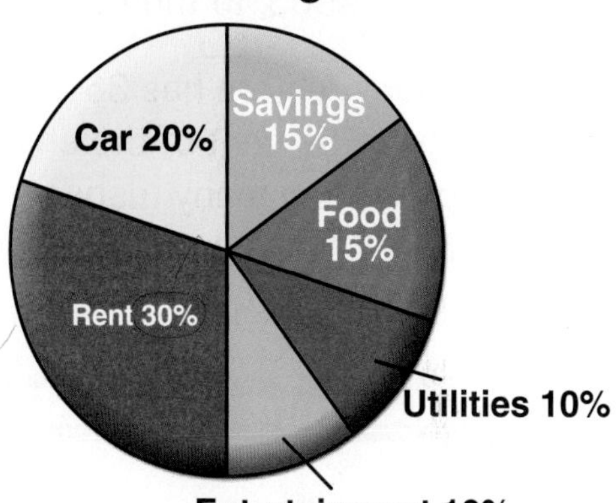

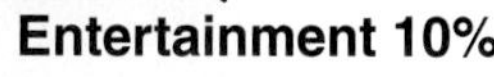

Use the table at the right for Problems 5–7.

5. The table at the right shows the results of a survey of 560 people who bought sneakers at 4 kinds of stores. Make a circle graph to display the data as percents.

6. Use the circle graph that you made in Problem 5. What percent of the people bought their sneakers in a store other than a sneaker store?

7. **Predict** Based on the survey results, how many people out of 1,600 would you expect to buy sneakers from a sneaker store?

Buying Sneakers

Type of Store	Number of People
Sporting Goods	140
Department or Discount	280
Sneaker	70
Other	70

Go On

Choose a Strategy

Solve. Show your work. Tell what strategy you used.

8. **Measurement** A rectangle has a perimeter of 26 cm and an area of 36 cm^2. What are the dimensions of the rectangle?

9. The Drama Club spends \$600 on sets and props, \$500 on costumes, \$250 on tickets and programs, and \$200 on a cast party. After spending this money, the club is left with \$325. How much did the club start with?

10. The monthly rent on an apartment was \$1,000 in 2000, \$1,050 in 2001, and \$1,103 in 2002. What was the rent increase each year? What percent is each increase? Predict the rent in 2003, to the nearest dollar.

11. **Represent** A store has 36 employees. Twenty-five percent of the employees are managers. How many managers does the store have? Draw a picture that supports your solution.

PROBLEM-SOLVING Strategies

- Use Models
- Draw a Diagram
- Find a Pattern
- Guess and Check
- Make an Organized List
- Make a Table
- Solve a Simpler Problem
- Use Logical Reasoning
- Work Backward
- Write an Equation

Choose a Computation Method

Mental Math • Estimation • Paper and Pencil • Calculator

Use the diagram for Problems 12–14.

The diagram shows the floor plan of a home supplies store. The labels show the different departments within the store.

12. **Measurement** How many square feet of space does the store have?

13. Find the percent of each department's space in the store. Round your answers to the nearest tenth of a percent.

14. The store has total sales of \$10,000,000. The ratio of the Kitchen Wares Department's sales to total sales is equal to the ratio of its floor area to the total floor area. Find the Kitchen Wares Department's sales.

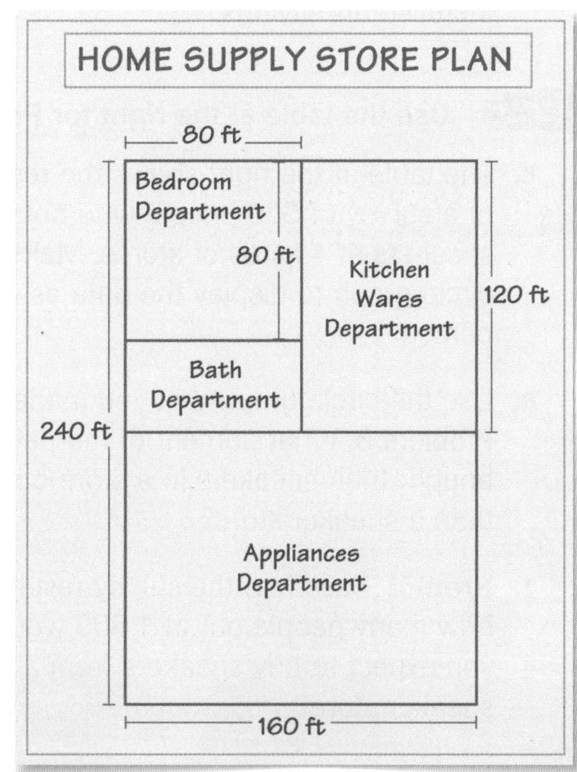

Quick Check

Check your understanding of Lessons 4–6.

Find each percent. (Lessons 4 and 5)

1. 10% of 98
2. 10% of 0.94
3. 20% of 200
4. 20% of 413
5. 25% of 120
6. 47% of 20
7. 58% of 300
8. 45% of 40

Solve. (Lesson 6)

9. At Sandy's Subs, 120 customers bought sandwiches—90 Sandy's Specials, 15 roast beef sandwiches, and 15 subs. Create a circle graph to display these data as percents.
10. Use the circle graph that you made in Problem 9. What percent of lunch customers bought sandwiches that were not Sandy's Specials?

Line 'Em Up

You can use a calculator to convert ratios and percents to decimal form.

To find the decimal equivalent for $\frac{4}{5}$ press: 4 ÷ 5 Enter =

To find the decimal equivalent for 75% press: 7 5 ÷ 1 0 0 Enter =

Use a calculator to rewrite each set in order from least to greatest. Then match each one to a word to solve the riddle below.

1. $\frac{3}{20}$ 0.2 18%

   ____ ____ ____

2. $\frac{5}{7}$ 0.688 74%

   ____ ____ ____

3. $\frac{7}{16}$ 45% 0.4499

   ____ ____ ____

Riddle: Why didn't the fraction slurp his soup?

Key:

$\frac{3}{20}$	$\frac{7}{16}$	$\frac{5}{7}$	0.2	0.4499	0.688	18%	45%	74%
He	he	would	afraid	was	someone	was	improper	think

Chapter Review/Test

VOCABULARY

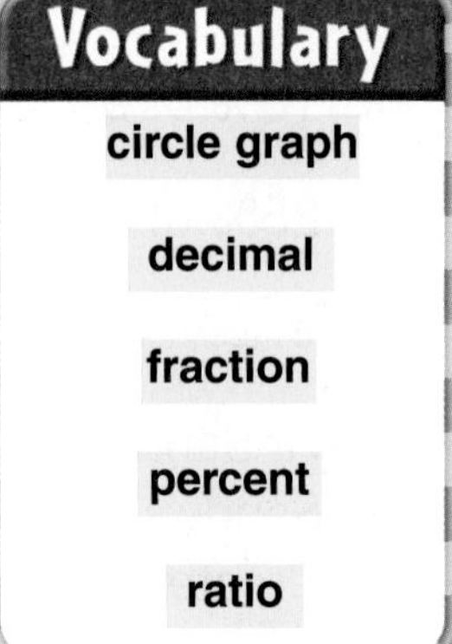

1. A ____ is a ratio of a number to 100.
2. You can show how parts of a whole are related in a ____.
3. A ____ is a number that shows tenths, hundredths, thousandths, and so on.

CONCEPTS AND SKILLS

Copy and complete each table. Write each fraction in simplest form. (Lessons 1–2, pp. 506–509)

	Fraction	Decimal	Percent
4.	$\frac{1}{2}$	■	■
5.	■	0.08	■

	Fraction	Decimal	Percent
6.	$\frac{1}{5}$	■	■
7.	■	■	15%

Order each set from the greatest to the least part of a unit. (Lesson 3, pp. 510–513)

8. $\frac{17}{40}$ 35% 0.4 **9.** $\frac{7}{20}$ 68% 0.37 **10.** $\frac{8}{10}$ 75% 0.95

Find 10% of each number. Then find 20% of each number. (Lesson 4, pp. 514–515)

11. 95 **12.** 3,780 **13.** 54.7 **14.** 0.14

Solve. Use any method. (Lesson 5, pp. 516–519)

15. 25% of 96 **16.** 70% of 120 **17.** 60% of 60 **18.** 30% of 40

PROBLEM SOLVING

Use the circle graph to solve.
(Lesson 6, pp. 520–523)

19. How many students play soccer and baseball?

20. What fraction of the students surveyed play football?

500 Students' Activities

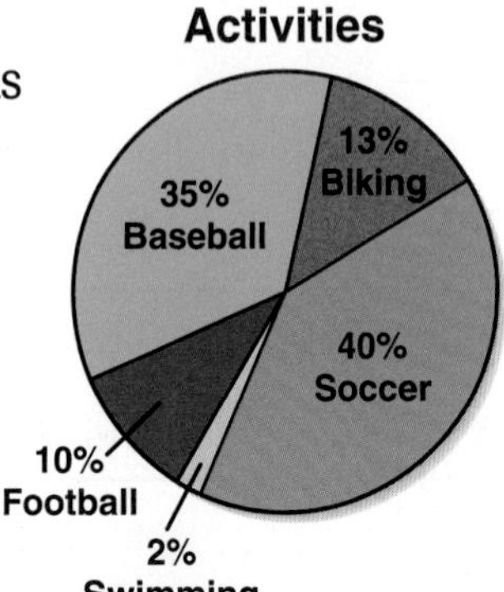

Write About It

Show You Understand

Sue says that $\frac{15}{20}$ is equal to 60%. Is this reasonable? Explain.

Extra Practice

Set A (Lesson 2, pp. 508–509)

Copy and complete each table. Write each fraction in simplest form.

	Fraction	Decimal	Percent
1.	$\frac{3}{10}$	0.3	■
3.	$\frac{7}{10}$	■	■
5.	■	0.09	■
7.	■	0.45	■

	Fraction	Decimal	Percent
2.	$\frac{21}{100}$	■	■
4.	■	■	40%
6.	■	■	84%
8.	$\frac{3}{5}$	■	■

Set B (Lesson 3, pp. 510–513)

Order each set from the greatest to the least part of a unit.

1. $\frac{7}{10}$ 0.5 80%
2. $\frac{2}{5}$ 0.35 27%
3. $\frac{13}{20}$ 0.92 30%
4. $\frac{5}{8}$ 50% 0.61
5. $\frac{12}{25}$ 78% 0.4
6. $\frac{7}{8}$ $\frac{37}{50}$ 86%
7. 0.47 $\frac{3}{8}$ 39%
8. 28% 0.27 $\frac{7}{20}$
9. 0.6 59% $\frac{8}{10}$

Set C (Lesson 4, pp. 514–515)

Find 10% of each number. Then find 20% of each number.

1. 72
2. 2,410
3. 5
4. 700
5. 12,305
6. 39.5
7. 8.31
8. 2
9. 514.74
10. 6.3502

Set D (Lesson 5, pp. 516–519)

Solve by writing the percent as a fraction.

1. 30% of 70
2. 75% of 96
3. 60% of 85
4. 50% of 64
5. 25% of 40
6. 20% of 10
7. 45% of 200
8. 55% of 800

Solve by writing the percent as a decimal.

9. 25% of 88
10. 37% of 90
11. 15% of 70
12. 85% of 200
13. 40% of 20
14. 75% of 400
15. 8% of 64
16. 1% of 6

Probability

INVESTIGATION

Use Data

These athletes have come from all over the world to compete for a medal in table tennis. The table shows the games currently being played. If each of these 8 athletes plays each other athlete once, how many games will be played?

Table Tennis Tournament

(Round 2)

Player versus Player	
H ⟷ C	
D ⟷ A	
F ⟷ E	
B ⟷ G	

Chapter Pretest

Use this page to review and remember what you need to know for this chapter.

VOCABULARY

Choose the best word to complete each sentence.

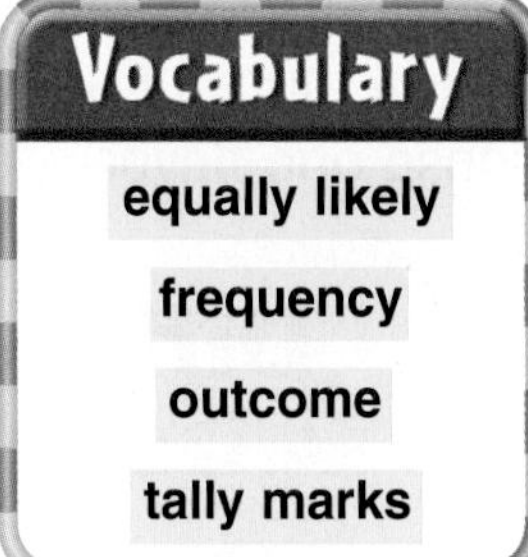

1. Groups of five ____ help you keep a running count of how often an object appears or something occurs.
2. A(n) ____ is a possible result of a probability experiment.
3. In a table, the number that tells how often something happens is called the ____.

CONCEPTS AND SKILLS

Write the fraction for the shaded part in simplest form.

4. 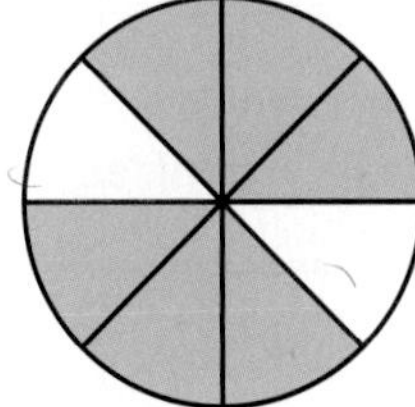

5.

Write each ratio in simplest form.

6. 2 to 6
7. $\frac{4}{10}$
8. 30:72
9. $\frac{8}{48}$

Write About It

10. How do you write a fraction in simplest form?

Test Prep on the Net

Visit *Education Place* at **eduplace.com/kids/mw/** for more review.

Lesson 1

Make Choices

Objective Use organized lists, tree diagrams, and multiplication to find all the possible combinations of given items.

Learn About It

At the school fair frozen yogurt is sold in two flavors–vanilla and peach. You can choose one of three toppings for your yogurt–fruit, nuts, or sprinkles. How many different ways can you choose one flavor and one topping?

Different Ways to Find the Number of Choices

Way 1 **You can make an organized list.**

peach, fruit
peach, nuts
peach, sprinkles
vanilla, fruit
vanilla, nuts
vanilla, sprinkles

Way 2 **You can make a tree diagram.**

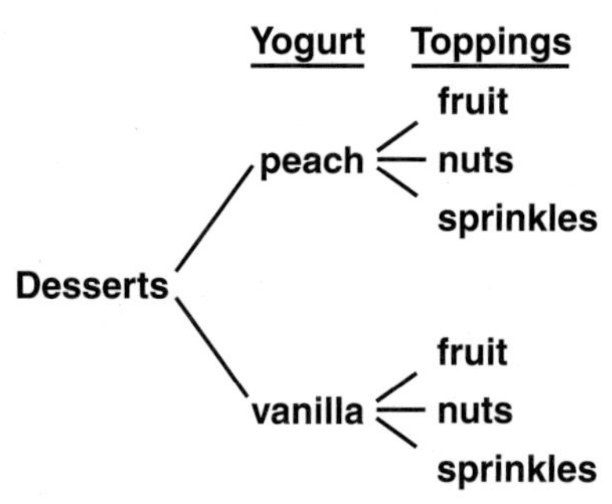

Way 3 **You can multiply to find the number of possible choices.**

flavor choices × topping choices = number of choices

$2 \times 3 = 6$

Solution: You can choose one flavor and one topping in 6 different ways.

Guided Practice

You have one choice from each category.
Make an organized list to show all the possible choices.

1. 3 flavors, 4 toppings

2. 4 styles, 5 colors

3. 7 colors, 3 designs

Ask Yourself

- How do I organize the list so I don't miss any choices?

How can you be sure that an organized list of choices is complete?

Practice and Problem Solving

You have one choice from each column. Make an organized list and a tree diagram to show all the possible choices.

4.

T-Shirts	
Style	**Color**
V-neck	blue
crew neck	yellow
sleeveless	black
	red

5.

School Ring	
Metal	**Stone**
silver	turquoise
gold	amber
	agate
	lapis

6.

Games	
3:00 Game	**3:45 Game**
Ring Toss	Frisbee Golf
Darts	Sack Race
Spelling	Brain Teasers
Horseshoes	Extreme Math

You have one choice from each category. Multiply to find the number of choices possible.

7. 5 styles, 3 sizes

8. 4 colors, 12 designs

9. 8 flavors, 4 toppings

10. 7 cars, 4 colors

11. 8 dinners, 7 desserts

12. 3 drinks, 1 flavor

Data **Use the menu to solve Problems 13–15.**

13. How many choices are there if you want to order a hot sandwich and a large drink?

14. How many choices are there if you want to order a salad and a small drink?

15. Reasoning How could you find the number of choices for a hot sandwich, a salad, and a small drink?

16. Write About It Does the order in which the choices are listed on a tree diagram affect the number of possible choices? Explain your thinking.

Daily Review Test Prep

Name each shape. (Ch. 15, Lesson 4)

17. 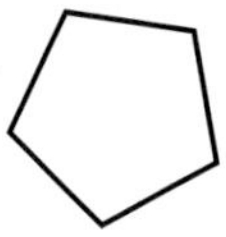 [pentagon figure]

18. 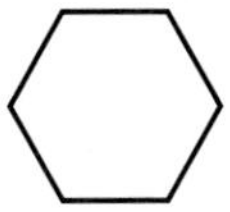 [hexagon figure]

19.  [parallelogram figure]

20. Free Response Nell packs blue pants, white pants, a striped shirt, a gray shirt, and a yellow shirt. How many different ways can she choose a pair of pants and a shirt?

Explain how you got your answer.

Extra Practice See page 551, Set A.

Lesson 2

Probability Concepts

Objective Describe the probability of an event.

Learn About It

Look at this game spinner. It has four congruent sectors.

- If the spinner lands on green, Player *A* wins.
- If the spinner lands on purple, Player *B* wins.
- If the spinner lands on yellow, no one wins.

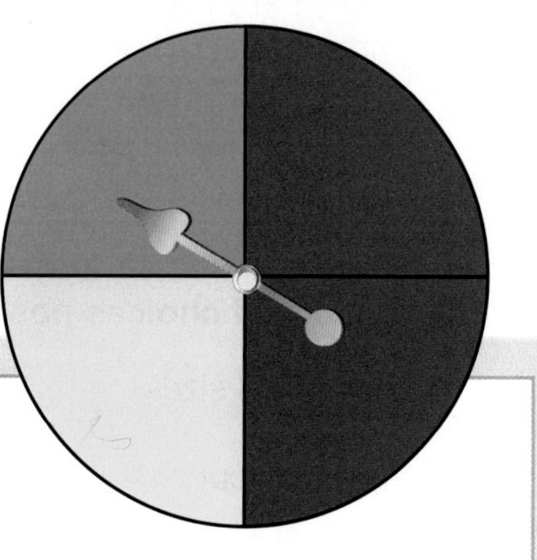

Is this a fair game?

When a player spins the spinner, there are three possible results, or outcomes. The spinner can land on a green, yellow, or purple sector. Why is the spinner more likely to land on purple than on green or yellow?

Solution: There are more purple sectors than green sectors. The game is not fair, because Player *B* has a greater chance of winning than Player *A*.

The **probability** of an **event** describes the likelihood that the event will occur. When an event has a probability of 0, it is called an **impossible event**. An event that has a probability of 1 is a **certain event**. The sum of all the experimental probabilities of an event must equal 1.

impossible	less likely ← - - - - → more likely	**certain**
The probability of spinning red is 0.	0 ———————— 1	The probability of landing on a colored section is 1.

Look at the diagram above. As the probability of an event gets closer to 1, it becomes more likely. As it gets closer to 0, the event becomes less likely.

If Event *A* is more likely than Event *B*, Event *A* has a greater probability than Event *B*. If Event *A* is less likely than Event *B*, Event *A* has a lesser probability than Event *B*. In the spinner at the top of the page, having the spinner land on purple is more likely than it landing on yellow.

Guided Practice

You spin once on a spinner that has six congruent sectors labeled 2, 2, 3, 4, 5, and 5. Tell which event is more likely. If possible, describe an event that is impossible or certain.

Ask Yourself

- How many sectors of the spinner are labeled with each number?

1. a 2 or a 6

2. a 3 or a 5

3. a composite number or a prime number

4. a number greater than 5 or a number less than 5

Explain Your Thinking ▶ Why is the second event in Exercise 2 more likely?

Practice and Problem Solving

You spin once on the spinner at the right. Tell which event is less likely. If possible, describe an event as impossible or certain.

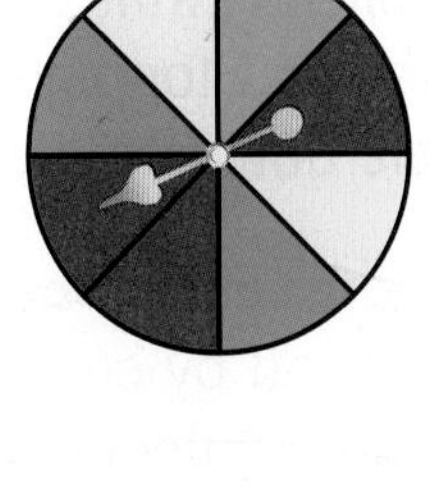

5. yellow or green

6. orange or green

7. green or blue

8. red or blue

9. purple or any other color on the spinner

Use the spinner at the right for Problems 10 and 11.

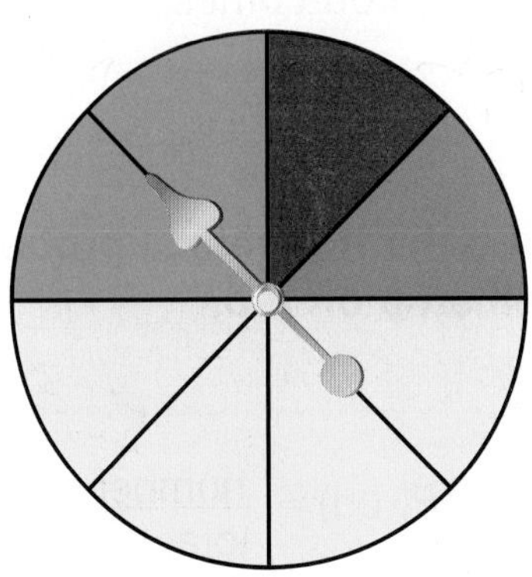

10. Explain Shari and Sam play a game. If the spinner lands on red or blue, Shari wins. If the spinner lands on green, Sam wins. Is the game fair? Explain.

11. Create and Solve Use the spinner to create a fair game and an unfair game that are different from the game in Problem 10. Explain why each game is fair or unfair.

12. Analyze Survey your classmates to find out what board games they play. If you chose someone from your class at random, which games would he or she be likely to play?

Daily Review | Test Prep

Write 4 equivalent ratios for each.
(Ch. 18, Lesson 2)

13. 1 to 4

14. 10 to 12

15. 2:3

16. 20 to 25

17. 3:8

18. 6:10

19. 5 to 1

20. 14:6

21. A spinner has congruent sectors labeled 1, 3, 5, 7, 9, and 11. What is the probability of spinning an odd number?

A 0

B $\frac{1}{6}$

C $\frac{1}{2}$

D 1

Extra Practice See page 551, Set B.

Lesson 3

Theoretical Probability

Objective Use fractions to find theoretical probability.

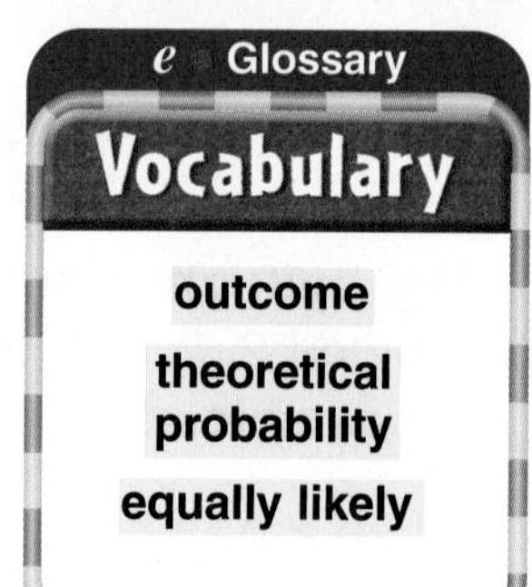

Learn About It

If the wheel stops on a red sector, Tamara wins a prize. What is the probability that the wheel will stop on red?

Since the wheel has 16 sectors of equal size, there are 16 possible **outcomes.**

To solve the problem, you want to find out how likely it is that the wheel will stop on a red sector. Stopping on red is called a favorable outcome.

The **theoretical probability** of an event can be found by comparing the number of favorable outcomes with the number of possible outcomes.

Find the theoretical probability that the wheel will stop on red.

$$P(\text{red}) = \frac{\text{number of red sectors}}{\text{total number of sectors}}$$

$$= \frac{8}{16}$$

$$= \frac{1}{2}$$

There are 8 red sectors and 8 other sectors. It is **equally likely** that the wheel will stop on red as on a different colored sector.

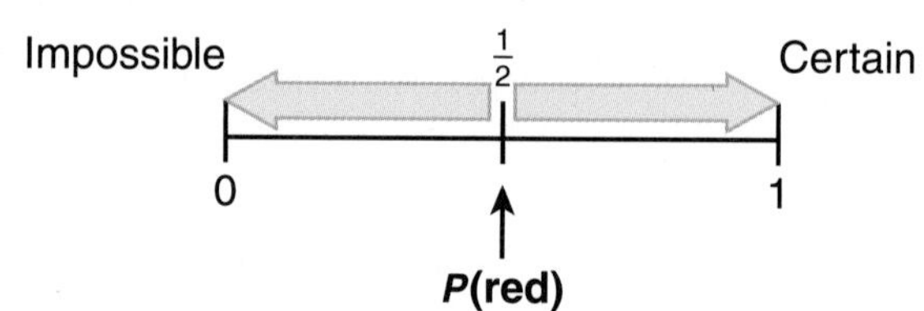

When you express probability as a fraction, write the fraction in simplest form.

Solution: The theoretical probability that the wheel will stop on red is $\frac{1}{2}$.

Guided Practice

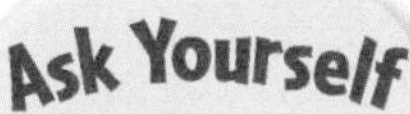

- How many outcomes are there?
- How many outcomes are favorable?

Look at the wheel on page 532. Express the theoretical probability of each event as a fraction in simplest form.

1. yellow
2. green
3. blue
4. not yellow
5. orange
6. blue or yellow

Explain Your Thinking ▶ In Exercise 6, how did you find the theoretical probability?

Practice and Problem Solving

Use the spinner for Problems 7–14. Express the theoretical probability of each event as a fraction in simplest form.

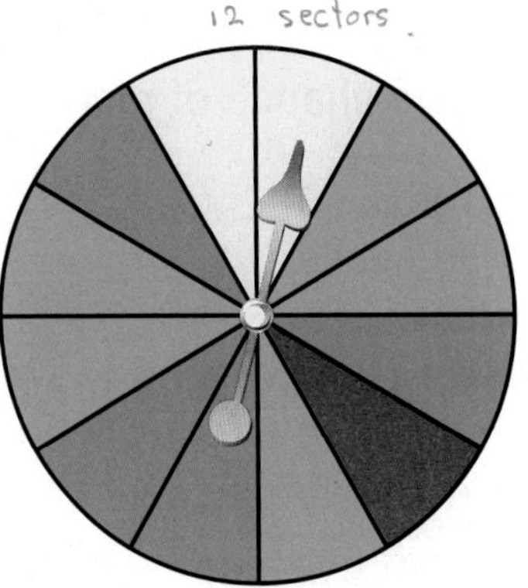

7. yellow
8. red
9. green
10. blue
11. blue or yellow
12. not red
13. not yellow
14. not green or blue

Use the bag of marbles for Problems 15–26. You pick one marble from the bag without looking. Find the theoretical probability of each event. Express the probability as a fraction in simplest form.

15. a black marble
16. a marble that is not black
17. a yellow marble
18. a marble that is not yellow
19. a green marble
20. a marble that is not green
21. a purple marble
22. a marble that is not purple
23. a red or black marble
24. a white marble
25. a marble that is not green or red or black
26. a marble that is green or yellow

Suppose you toss a number cube that has sides labeled 1–6. Find the theoretical probability of each event.

27. a 6
28. an even number
29. a number that is not 2 or 4
30. a number greater than 1 and less than 6

Go On

Use the bag of cubes for Problems 31–35.

The bag of cubes is used for a game in which you pick one cube without looking. Tell how you would add or remove cubes in order to create the given situation.

31. The probability of picking a red cube is $\frac{1}{3}$.

32. The chances of picking any color cube are equally likely.

33. The chance of picking a black cube is 1 out of 10.

34. The probability of picking a blue cube is $\frac{1}{6}$.

35. The chance of picking a purple cube is 1 out of 4.

Use the pictograph for Problems 36–40.

Toy ducks are picked without looking and replaced in the pond after each pick.

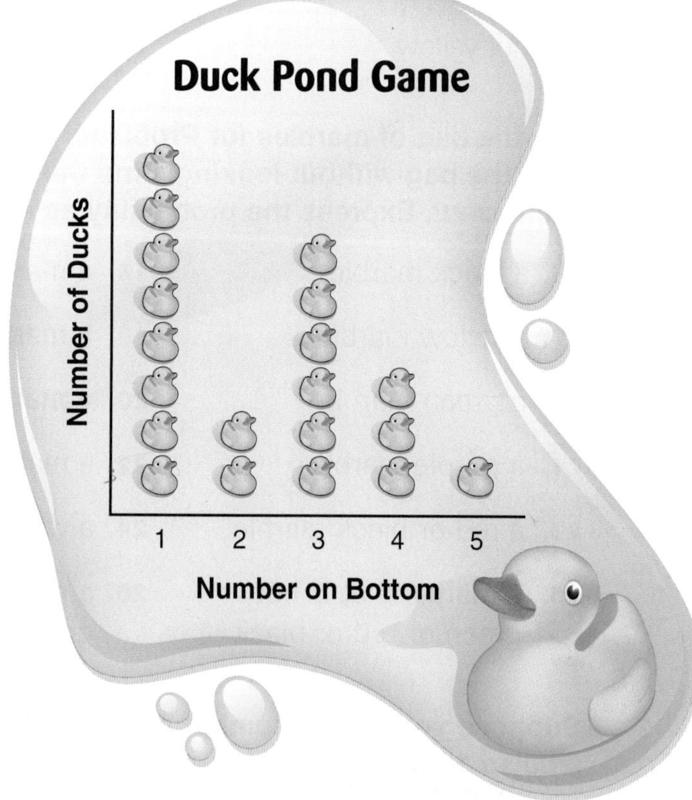

36. How many ducks are in the pond if each duck symbol represents 1 duck?

37. What is the probability of picking a yellow duck with a number 5 on the bottom?

38. Analyze Which two numbers are the most likely to be picked?

39. The probability of picking a duck with one of two numbers is $\frac{9}{20}$. What could those two numbers be?

40. Reasoning Suppose each duck symbol represented 3 ducks instead of 1 duck. Would the probability of picking each number change? Explain.

41. Write About It If the theoretical probability of winning a game is $\frac{1}{2}$, does this mean that if you play that game twice, you are certain to win one of the games? Explain your reasoning.

Extra Practice See page 551, Set C.

Quick Check

Check your understanding of Lessons 1–3.

Make an organized list and a tree diagram to show all the possible choices. Then multiply to find the number of possible choices. (Lesson 1)

1.

Footwear	Color
sneakers	brown
slippers	red
boots	black
	white

2.

Snack	Size
peanuts	small
cashews	large
walnuts	
almonds	

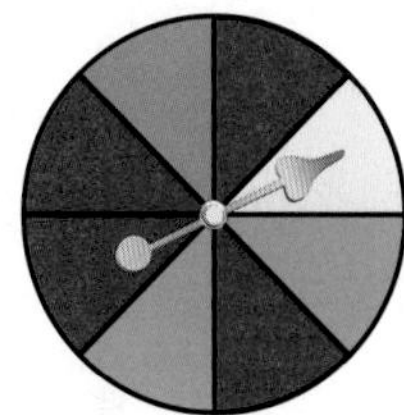

Use the spinner for Problems 3–6. Tell which event is more likely. If possible, describe an event as impossible or certain. (Lesson 2)

3. yellow or blue **4.** red or green **5.** blue or green **6.** red or orange

Suppose you toss a number cube that has sides labeled 2, 2, 2, 4, 8, and 10. Find the theoretical probability of each event. (Lesson 3)

7. a 4 **8.** an even number **9.** a number that is not a 2

Logical Thinking

Math Reasoning

NOT a Chance

Look at the spinner. The probability of spinning blue is $\frac{5}{12}$. What is the probability of NOT spinning blue? To find the probability of NOT spinning blue, you can subtract $\frac{5}{12}$ from 1.

$$1 - \frac{5}{12} = \frac{12}{12} - \frac{5}{12} = \frac{7}{12}$$

Solution: The probability of NOT spinning blue is $\frac{7}{12}$.

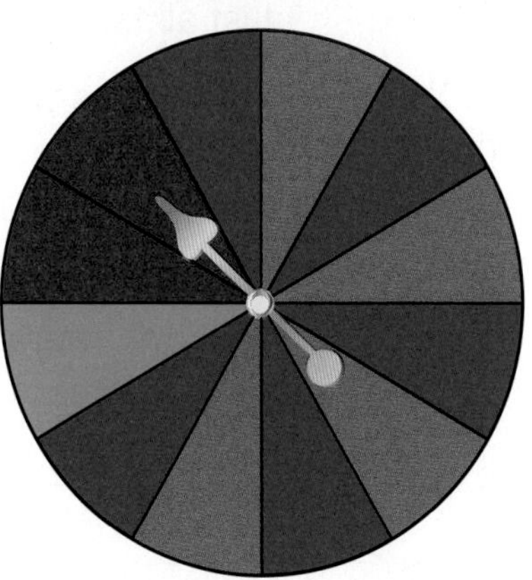

Use the spinner above. Subtract to find each probability.

1. not spinning green **2.** not spinning red **3.** not spinning purple

4. Explain Use what you know about probability to explain why this method works.

Problem-Solving Strategy

Make an Organized List

Objective: Solve a problem by making an organized list.

There is room for one more team of 2 players in the three-legged race. Sal, Ed, Juan, and Mia are willing to be on the team. How many different ways can you choose a team of 2 players from these 4 children?

This is what you know:

Sal, Ed, Juan, and Mia are willing to be on the team.

Each team has 2 players.

PLAN

You can make an organized list to show all of the possible ways to select the team.

SOLVE

Make an organized list. Use letters to stand for each player's name.

- List all teams of 2 that include Sal (S).
- List all teams of 2 that include Ed (E).
- List all teams of 2 that include Juan (J).
- List all teams of 2 that include Mia (M).
- Ring teams with the same 2 players. Then count the rings. The order of the players does not matter. The team of Sal and Ed is the same as the team of Ed and Sal.

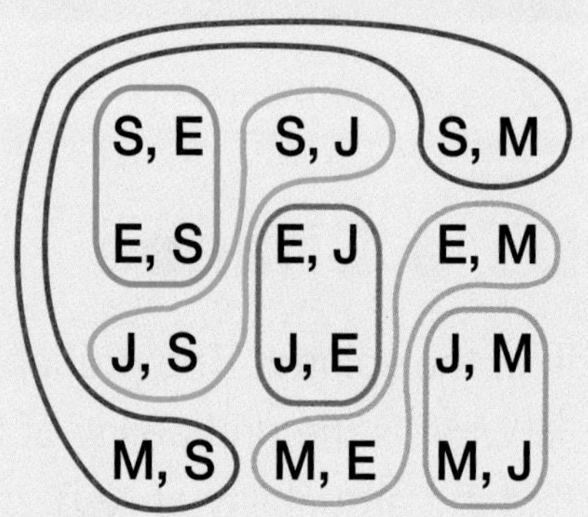

Solution: There are 6 different ways to choose a team of 2 players.

LOOK BACK

Look back at the problem.

Does the solution make sense?

MathTracks 2/26
Listen and Understand

Guided Practice

Use the Ask Yourself questions to help you solve each problem.

1. Billy wins enough points to choose 3 prizes. The available prizes are a puzzle, a goldfish, a pack of cards, a toy monkey, and a model car. How many different ways can Billy choose 3 different prizes?

2. Benjamin, Erin, Chun, Julia, Amanda, and Elizabeth are in a race. First place receives a gold medal and second place receives a silver medal. How many different ways can the medals be given out?

Since the order of the racers matters, there are no duplicates in a list of possible first and second place winners.

UNDERSTAND **What facts do I know?**

PLAN **Did I make an organized list?**

Does the order of the possibilities matter?

SOLVE
- **How can I show all of the possibilities?**
- **Do I need to cross out duplicates?**

LOOK BACK **Did I solve the problem?**

Independent Practice

Make an organized list to solve each problem.

3. A team of 4 players is needed for tug of war. How many different teams of 4 players can be chosen from a group of 5 children?

4. The 4 finalists in a history quiz game are Jessica, Brian, Evan, and Grace. The top 2 finalists win first prize and second prize. In how many different ways can these prizes be given out to the 4 finalists?

5. The school fair has a hall of mirrors, a carousel, a horse ride, and a maze. You buy a ticket that allows you to do 3 of these activities. In how many different ways can you go to 3 of these activities?

6. Shawn, Scott, Rip, Trish, and Yoshi are finalists in a drawing for a trip to Water World. Two winners will be picked at random. How many different pairs could go to Water World?

Choose a Strategy

TEST PREP

Solve. Show your work. Tell what strategy you used.

7. Wendy, Barbara, Howard, and Marvin are the top four finishers in a race. Barbara is not first or second. Marvin finishes after Barbara. Howard finishes before Wendy. Who is in each of the top four places?

8. Number cards for the numbers 3, 4, 5, 6, 7, 8, 9, and 10 are placed facedown on a table. Suppose you turn up two cards. How many different pairs of numbers are possible?

9. Mr. Willard has 8 bills in his wallet. The bills are \$10, \$5, and \$1. If Mr. Willard has \$29, what bills does he have in his wallet?

- Use Models
- Draw a Diagram
- Find a Pattern
- Guess and Check
- Make an Organized List
- Make a Table
- Solve a Simpler Problem
- Use Logical Reasoning
- Work Backward
- Write an Equation

Data **Use the graph to solve Problems 10–13.**

The graph shows the number of game tickets that each of four students sold.

Game Tickets Sold

	Number of Tickets
George	
Myra	
Evan	
Daisy	

= 20 Tickets

10. How many more tickets did Daisy sell than Evan?

11. **Estimate** A game ticket sells for \$2.95. About how many dollars worth of game tickets did Myra sell?

12. **Calculator** How many game tickets did the four students sell in all? How many dollars worth of tickets is this?

13. Last year, George's ticket sales were 20% greater than his total shown in the graph. How many tickets did George sell last year?

14. **Explain** Sierra, Gavin, Kayla, John, and Catherine can tutor some third-grade students in math. Only 2 tutors are needed. How many different pairs of tutors can there be? Explain how you found your answer.

Problem-Solving Test Prep

Choose the letter of the correct answer. If a correct answer is not here, choose NH.

1. What is the next picture in this pattern?

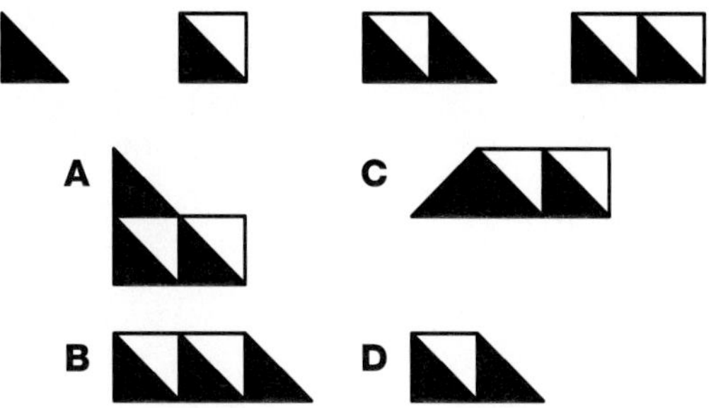

(Chapter 16, Lesson 2)

2. Howard is 4 feet 11 inches tall. Howard's father is 17 inches taller than Howard. How tall is Howard's father?

   F 5 feet 6 inches

   G 6 feet

   H 6 feet 4 inches

   J 6 feet 6 inches

(Chapter 6, Lesson 6)

3. Daniel has bowling scores of 192, 180, 212, 214, and 177. What score does Daniel need in his sixth game to have a mean score of 200?

   A 195 **C** 225

   B 202 **D** 250

(Chapter 8, Lesson 2)

4. In a survey of 200 students at Warren High School, 88 say they favor year-round schools. Warren High School has a total of 950 students. Based on the survey, how many students are likely to favor year-round schools?

   F 418 **H** 880

   G 440 **J** 936

(Chapter 18, Lesson 4)

5. What is the missing angle measure?

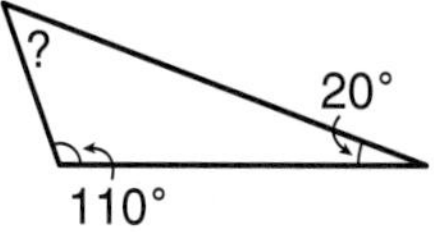

   A 60° **C** 160°

   B 70° **D** NH

(Chapter 15, Lesson 3)

6. A restaurant has 3 tables. Each table can seat 1 person on each end and 3 people along each of the other sides. The ends of the tables are pushed together to make one long table. How many people can sit at the long table?

   Represent Support your solution with a picture.

(Chapter 10, Lesson 7)

7. **Measurement** A rug that measures 2 yards by 3 yards costs $540. Another rug that measures 5 feet by 8 feet costs $360. Which rug has a higher price per square foot of area?

   Explain How did you find your answer?

(Chapter 16, Lesson 3)

Test Prep on the Net

Check out *Education Place* at **eduplace.com/kids/mw/** for test prep practice.

Experimental Probability

Objective Determine the experimental probability for a given set of data.

e Glossary

Vocabulary

experimental probability

Materials
number cube
Learning Tool 56
red, blue, and yellow connecting cubes

Work Together

When you perform an experiment, you may get results that differ from the results predicted by theoretical probability.

To find the **experimental probability** of an event, compare the number of favorable outcomes with the total number of completed trials or experiments.

Work with a partner to find experimental probability of tossing each number on a number cube.

STEP 1 On the recording sheet, list all the possible outcomes for tossing a number cube once. Then write the theoretical probability for each outcome.

- How many possible outcomes are there?
- How can you find the theoretical probability of each outcome?

Event	Theoretical Probability	Prediction ? times in ? trials
1	$\frac{1}{6}$	$\frac{1}{6} = \frac{x}{30}$
2		
3		

STEP 2 Use theoretical probability to predict the number of times each outcome should occur in an experiment with 30 trials. Write your predictions on the recording sheet.

- How did you make your predictions?

Perform the experiment. Toss the number cube 30 times. Record each outcome. Then find the total number of times each outcome occurred.

- Find the experimental probability of each outcome and record it in the last column on the sheet.
- How close are the experimental probabilities to the theoretical probabilities?

Event	Number of Favorable Outcomes	Experimental Probability
	RIMENT RESULTS	
1	7	$\frac{7}{30}$
2	5	$\frac{5}{30} = \frac{1}{6}$
3	4	$\frac{4}{30} = \frac{2}{15}$
4	5	$\frac{5}{30} = \frac{1}{6}$
5	4	$\frac{4}{30} = \frac{2}{15}$
6	5	$\frac{5}{30} = \frac{1}{6}$

Repeat the experiment. Toss the cube another 30 times. Combine your results with the results of the original experiment.

- How did including the additional 30 trials affect the results of the entire experiment?

On Your Own

Use the recording sheet to complete each probability experiment. Record each probability as a fraction in simplest form.

1. Toss a number cube and get an even number. Complete 20 tosses.

Event	Theoretical Probability	Prediction ? times in ? trials	EXPERIMENT RESULTS		
			Tally of Favorable Outcomes	Number of Favorable Outcomes	Experimental Probability
Even (2, 4, 6)	$\frac{3}{6} = \frac{1}{2}$	$\frac{1}{2} = \frac{x}{20}$			

Go On

For Problems 2–5, select 2 blue cubes, 5 yellow cubes, and 3 red cubes—a total of 10 cubes. Place them in a bag. Then use the recording sheet to complete each probability experiment.

2. Find the theoretical probability of selecting a blue cube. Then pick a cube, tally the result, and return the cube to the bag. Repeat 20 times. Then find the experimental probablility.

3. Find the theoretical probability of selecting a yellow cube. Then pick a cube, tally the result, and return the cube to the bag. Repeat 20 times. Then find the experimental probablility.

4. Find the theoretical probability of selecting a red cube. Then pick a cube, tally the result, and return the cube to the bag. Repeat 20 times. Then find the experimental probablility.

5. Do the experiment in Problem 4 of selecting a red cube, but repeat 50 times. Then find the experimental probablility.

Event	Theoretical Probability	Prediction ? times in ? trials	EXPERIMENT RESULTS		
			Tally of Favorable Outcomes	Number of Favorable Outcomes	Experimental Probability
Blue	$\frac{2}{10} = \frac{1}{5}$	$\frac{1}{5} = \frac{X}{20}$			
Yellow					$\frac{?}{20}$
Red					

Talk About It • Write About It

TEST PREP

You learned the difference between experimental probability and theoretical probability.

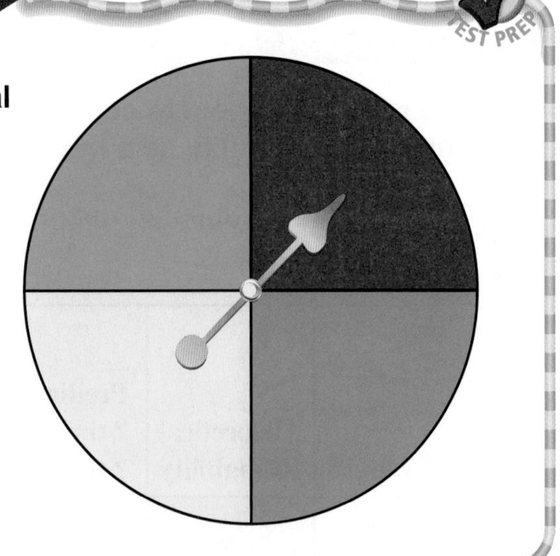

6. Suppose you spin this spinner 20 times and find the experimental probability of spinning red is $\frac{1}{5}$. Is this close to what you would have predicted? Explain.

7. Use your results from Problems 4 and 5. Does the experimental probability get closer to or farther from the theoretical probability as the number of trials increases?

The 50 States

Suppose you choose one of the 50 states at random.

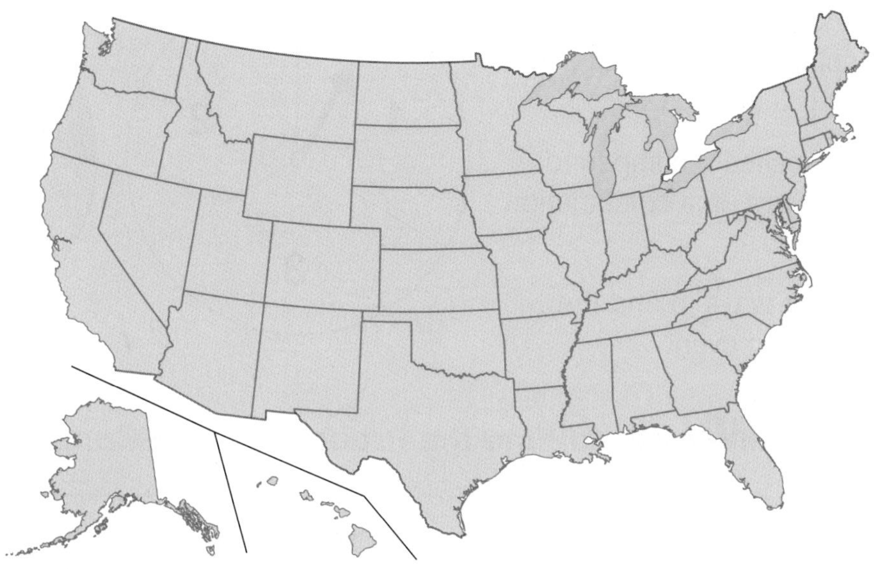

1. What is the probability of choosing a state name that begins with the letter F? the letter N?

2. Is there a greater chance of choosing a state east of the Mississippi River or west of it? Explain.

3. Write 5 probability problems about the 50 states. Solve your problems and then give them to a partner to solve.

Common Sense

Describe each event as *likely, unlikely, impossible,* or *certain*.

- It will snow tomorrow.
- You will read a book today.
- Your school will grow legs and walk.
- The sun will set tonight.
- You will finish reading this sentence.

Brain Teaser

The cards shown are numbered 1 to 4. One card has been set aside. What is the probability that the next card is a 2?

Ask Yourself
What is the probability if 3 cards are set aside?

Technology
Visit *Education Place* at **eduplace.com/kids/mw/** to try more brain teasers.

Compound Events

Objective Find the probability of compound events.

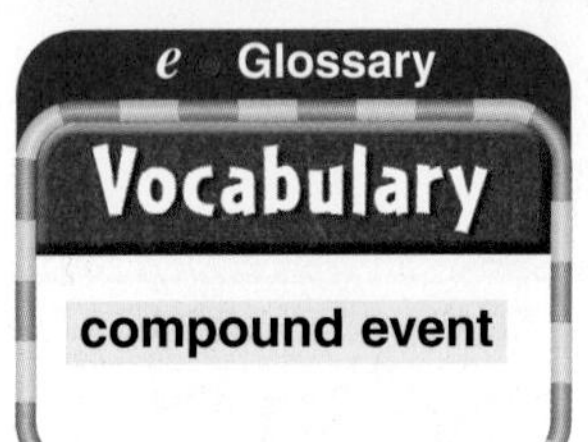

Learn About It

Lara and Will play a game using two spinners. If Lara spins both spinners once, what is the probability of spinning 3 and red?

Spinning 3 and red is called a compound event. A **compound event** is a combination of two or more events.

Here are some different ways to find the probability of a compound event.

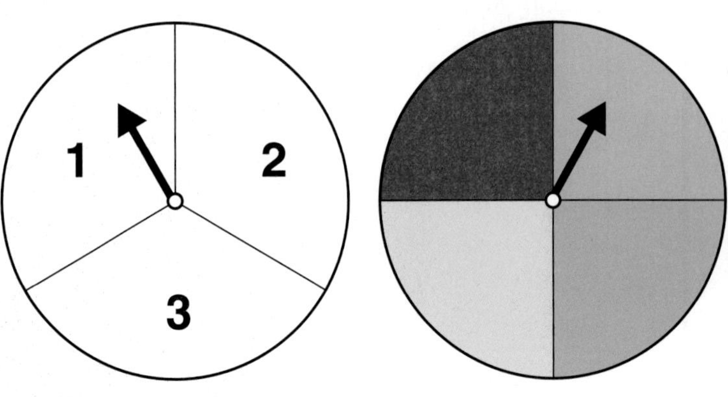

Different Ways to Find the Probability of a Compound Event

Way 1 You can make a tree diagram.

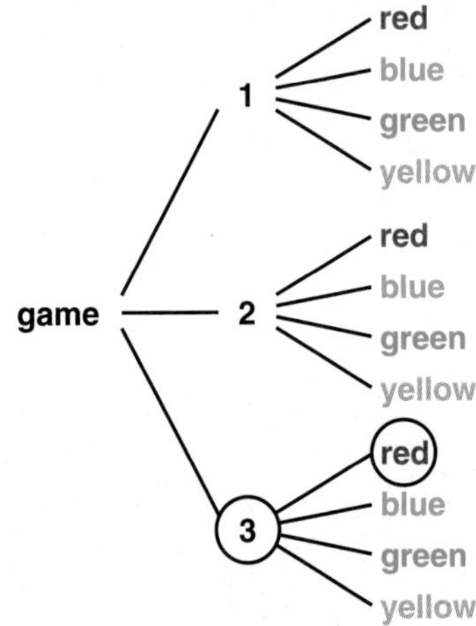

There are 12 possible outcomes and 1 favorable outcome.

Way 2 You can make an organized list.

1 red	2 red	(3 red)
1 blue	2 blue	3 blue
1 green	2 green	3 green
1 yellow	2 yellow	3 yellow

There are 12 possible outcomes and 1 favorable outcome.

Solution: The probability of spinning red and 3 can be expressed as $\frac{1}{12}$.

Guided Practice

Suppose you toss a nickel and roll a number cube labeled 1–6. Find the probability of each compound event.

1. heads and 3
2. tails and an odd number

Ask Yourself

- Did I find all of the possible outcomes?
- What is the favorable outcome?

Explain Your Thinking ▶ In Exercise 2, how did you find the probability?

Practice and Problem Solving

Suppose you spin each spinner once. Find the probability of each compound event.

3. purple and 5

4. yellow and 3

5. red and even

6. yellow and odd

7. blue or purple, and 4

8. purple, and 2 or 3

9. red or purple, and even

10. yellow or red, and odd

Use a penny and the spinners to solve Problems 11–15.

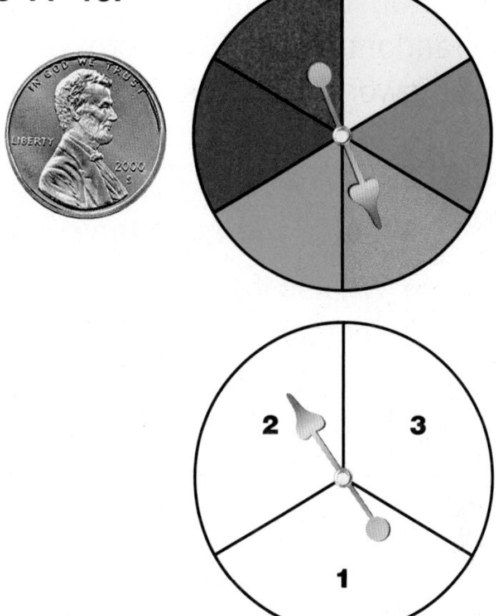

11. Use a tree diagram to show all the possible outcomes of the compound event of tossing a penny and spinning the color spinner. Then find the probability of tossing tails and spinning green.

12. Find the probability of tossing heads with the penny. Then find the probability of spinning the color red on the color spinner. How can you use the first two probabilities to find the probability of tossing heads and spinning red?

13. Make an organized list to show all the possible outcomes of spinning the number and color spinners. What is the probability of spinning 2 and purple?

14. Explain Decide which is more likely: to spin red and toss heads or to spin purple and 2? Explain how you made your decision.

15. Write Your Own Write and solve a probability problem of your own involving the penny, the number spinner, and/or the color spinner.

16. Analyze Suppose you toss the penny and spin both spinners above. What is the probability of getting heads, the number 2, and red?

Daily Review | Test Prep

Find the product. (Ch. 13, Lessons 3–5)

16. 0.7×0.4

17. 5×1.49

18. 0.68×0.3

19. 0.9×0.2

20. 1.63×2.5

21. 4.29×1.3

22. Free Response You toss a coin and roll a number cube labeled 1–6. Find the probability of getting heads and an even number.

Explain how you got your answer.

Extra Practice See page 551, Set D.

Problem-Solving Application

Make Predictions

Objective Use data to make predictions.

Sometimes you can use data to make predictions about outcomes.

Problem At the Tuscan Middle School Fair some students conducted a homework survey. The table shows the results.

What is the probability that a student chosen at random does 15 or more hours of homework per week?

Homework Survey Results

Hours of Home Work per Week	Tally of Students	Frequency
0 – 4.9	|||	3
5 – 9.9	~~||||~~ |||	8
10 – 14.9	~~||||~~ ~~||||~~ ~~||||~~ ~~||||~~ ||	22
15 – 19.9	~~||||~~ |	6
20 – 24.9	|	1

What is the question?

- What is the probability that a student chosen at random does 15 or more hours of homework per week?

What do you know?

- A total of 40 students were surveyed.
- 6 students did between 15 and 19.9 hours of homework.
- 1 student did between 20 and 24.9 hours of homework.

PLAN

Use the formula for probability. $P = \frac{\text{number of favorable outcomes}}{\text{number of possible outcomes}}$

SOLVE

- Use the number of students who were surveyed as the number of possible outcomes.
- Use the number of students who did 15 or more hours of homework per week as the number of favorable outcomes.

$P = \frac{6 + 1}{40} = \frac{7}{40}$

Solution: The probability that a randomly chosen student does 15 or more hours of homework per week is $\frac{7}{40}$.

Look back at the problem.

Is the answer reasonable?

Guided Practice

Use the table on page 546 to solve each problem.

1. What is the probability of a student doing less than 10 hours of homework per week?

2. Tuscan Middle School has 600 students. How many students would you expect to do between 5 and 15 hours of homework per week?

   Hint What part of the students surveyed did between 5 and 15 hours of homework per week?

UNDERSTAND **What does the question ask me to find?**

PLAN **Did I use the formula for probability?**

SOLVE
- **Did I use the correct information from the table?**
- **Did I find the probability of the event?**
- **Did I use the probability to make a prediction?**

LOOK BACK **Does my answer make sense?**

Use the table to solve Problems 3–7.

Each ticket to the Tuscan Middle School Fair gives you a chance to win a prize. The table shows the prizes won by the first 50 people who came to the fair.

Prizes Won at Middle School Fair

Prize Won	Number of Ticket Holders
No prize	38
Flashlight	6
School cap	4
Pizza party	2

3. What is the probability of winning no prize?

4. Suppose 400 people come to the fair. How many people would you expect to win a prize?

5. Suppose 500 people come to the fair. About how many more people would you expect to win flashlights than school caps?

6. **What's Wrong?** Marina found the probability of winning a school cap. What did Marina do wrong?

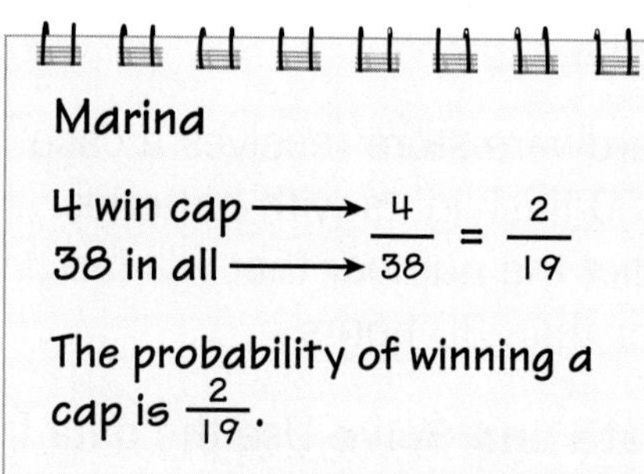

Marina

4 win cap ⟶ $\frac{4}{38} = \frac{2}{19}$
38 in all ⟶

The probability of winning a cap is $\frac{2}{19}$.

7. Of 800 tickets, 8 have a code that shows that the owner wins a pizza party. Is the number of winners in the first 50 tickets less than, greater than, or the same as you would expect? Explain your answer.

Go On

Choose a Strategy

Solve. Show your work. Tell what strategy you used.

PROBLEM-SOLVING Strategies

- Use Models
- Draw a Diagram
- Find a Pattern
- Guess and Check
- Make an Organized List
- Make a Table
- Solve a Simpler Problem
- Use Logical Reasoning
- Work Backward
- Write an Equation

8. Norma spends \$7 on playing games, \$5.95 on a sandwich, \$2.50 on drinks, and \$19.95 on a sweatshirt. She has \$25 left. How much money did she start with?

9. Two numbers have a sum of 54 and a quotient of 5. What are the numbers?

10. Sabrina, Paul, Nina, Fred, and Tyrone are the last players left in the Math Challenge contest. The last two players will win first prize and second prize. How many different ways can the prizes be given out?

Choose a Computation Method

Mental Math • Estimation • Paper and Pencil • Calculator

Use the histogram to solve Problems 11–14. Then explain which method you chose.

A hardware store donated flashlights with new batteries to the Tuscan Middle School Fair. The flashlights were given out as prizes. The histogram shows the results of the number of hours that the flashlight batteries last.

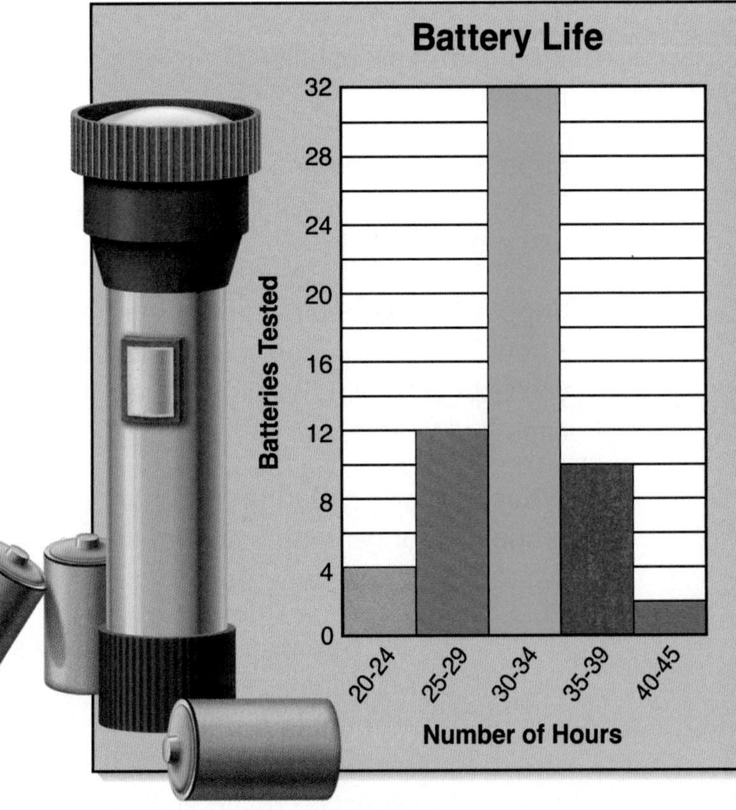

11. About what percent of flashlight batteries last between 30 and 34 hours?

12. **Explain** Is it reasonable to expect one of these flashlights to last 35 hours or more? Use probability to explain your answer.

13. A hardware store receives a case of 120 flashlights with batteries. Predict the number that will last fewer than 30 hours.

14. **Create and Solve** Use the data from the histogram to create and solve your own problem.

Quick Check

Check your understanding of Lessons 4–7.

Use the recording sheet to complete the probability experiment. Record each probability as a fraction in simplest form. (Lesson 5)

1. Toss a number cube and get a number greater than 1. Complete 30 tosses.

Event	Theoretical Probability	Prediction ? times in ? trials
$n > 1$		

Suppose you spin each spinner once. Find the theoretical probability of each compound event. (Lesson 6)

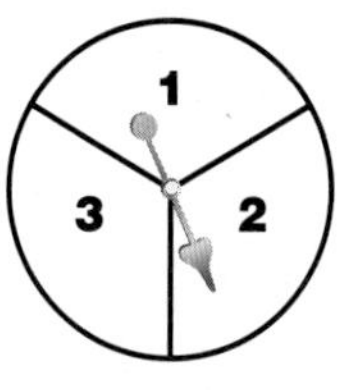

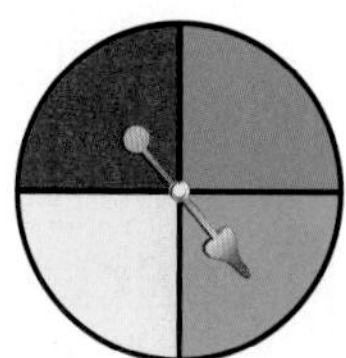

2. red and 1
3. blue and odd

Solve each problem. (Lessons 4 and 7)

4. There are 2 seats left on an airplane. There are 5 people who want to fly on the airplane. In how many different ways can these 2 seats be filled?

5. A spinner has five congruent sectors labeled 1, 2, 3, 2, and 4. Suppose you spin the spinner 100 times. How many times would you expect to spin 2?

WEEKLY WR READER® eduplace.com/kids/mw/

Likely Letters

The letter E is the most frequently occurring letter in the English language. When you read, you probably will see the letter E more often than any other letter.

Count 100 letters in a newspaper, magazine, or a favorite book. Record how many times each of the letters in the list occurs.

- Use your data to predict how many times out of 500 letters you will see each letter in the list. Then test your predictions.
- Repeat this activity for other letters of the alphabet.

Chapter Review/Test

VOCABULARY

1. The chance that an event will occur is called the ____ of the event.

2. Rolling a 9 on a 1-6 number cube is a(n) ____.

3. If there are 12 different letters on each equal section of a spinner, each letter is a(n) ____.

Vocabulary

certain event
impossible event
outcome
probability

CONCEPTS AND SKILLS

You have one choice from each category.
Multiply to find the number of choices possible. (Lesson 1, pp. 528–529)

4. 3 sizes, 5 flavors
5. 6 colors, 5 styles
6. 4 salads, 9 soups

Use the bag of balls to tell which event is more likely.
Then find the probability of that event. (Lessons 2–3, pp. 530–535)

7. 0 or 5
8. 3 or 4
9. 1 or 3
10. 1 or 5
11. 2 or 3
12. not 4 or not 5

Suppose you toss a 1–6 number cube and spin the spinner once.
Find the probability of each compound event. (Lessons 5–6, pp. 540–545)

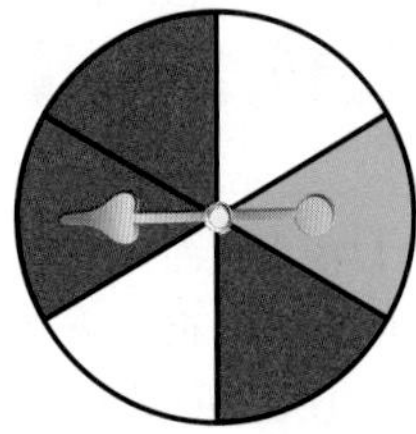

13. 1 and white
14. 6 and blue
15. 4 or 5 and white
16. 5 and red
17. odd and red
18. even and white

PROBLEM SOLVING

Solve. (Lessons 4, 7, pp. 536–537, 547–549)

19. Shannon wants to enter 3 pies in the 4-H fair. The pie categories are apple, squash, pecan, lemon meringue, and banana cream. How many different sets of 3 pies can she bake?

20. A wheel is divided into 20 equal sections. Each section is labeled differently. Suppose you spin 100 times. How many times would you expect to land on any one of the sections?

Show You Understand

What is the difference between theoretical probability and experimental probability?

Describe a situation for each to show this difference.

Extra Practice

Set A (Lesson 1, pp. 528–529)

You have one choice from each column. Make an organized list and a tree diagram to show all the possible choices.

1. Sweaters

Style	Color
crew neck	red
V-neck	blue
	black
	yellow

2. Pizzas

Size	Topping
small	green peppers
medium	mushrooms
large	onions

3. Book Reports

Type	Subject
fiction	people
non-fiction	animals
	places

Set B (Lesson 2, pp. 530–531)

You spin once on the spinner at the right. Tell which event is more likely. If possible, describe an event as impossible or certain.

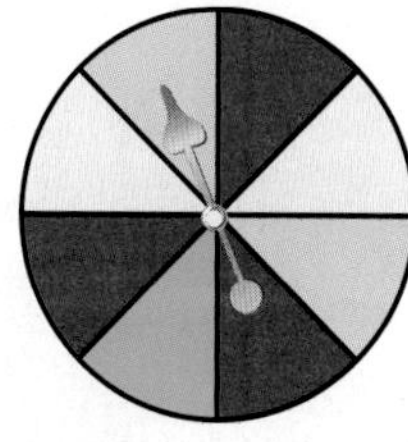

1. red or blue **2.** green or yellow **3.** blue or green

4. green or red **5.** black or red **6.** yellow or red

Set C (Lesson 3, pp. 532–535)

Use the spinner at the right. Express the probability of each event as a fraction in simplest form.

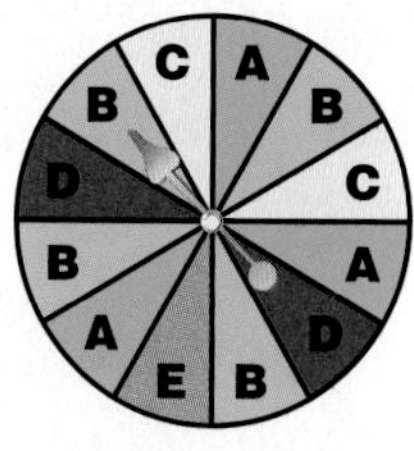

1. A **2.** C **3.** D **4.** B

5. A or B **6.** A or C **7.** D or E **8.** not F

9. not E **10.** not A or C **11.** not D or E **12.** not A or E

Set D (Lesson 6, pp. 544–545)

Suppose you spin each spinner once. Find the probability of each compound event.

1. A and 3 **2.** C and odd

3. B and 1 **4.** A and even

5. C or B, and 3 **6.** A or C, and 4

7. not B, and 3 **8.** B or C, and not 4

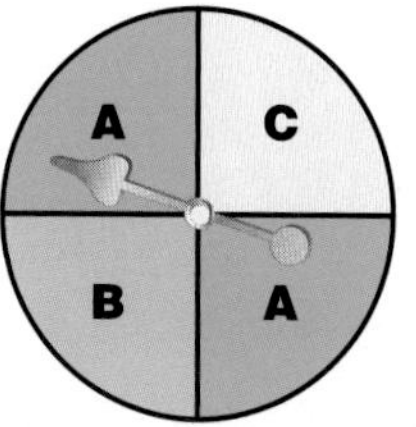

All in the Family

When a family is about to have a baby, everyone wonders, "Will the baby be a boy or a girl?" In humans and other mammals, the X- and Y-chromosomes determine a baby's gender. Babies who get two X-chromosomes are female. Babies getting one X-chromosome and one Y-chromosome are males.

Scientists can use special tests to determine whether a baby will be male or female, but many people still rely on probability. Since there are only two outcomes, it is equally likely that a couple will have a boy or a girl. In probability notation, P(boy) $= \frac{1}{2}$ and P(girl) $= \frac{1}{2}$.

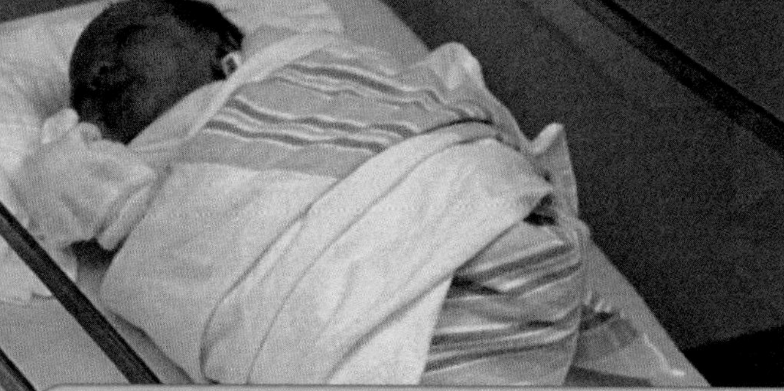

Problem Solving

A couple wants to have 4 children. They hope to have 2 boys and 2 girls. To find the probability that the couple will get their wish, work with a partner to solve the problems.

1. Find the theoretical probability that the 4 children will be 2 boys and 2 girls. Draw a tree diagram as your sample space.

2. Create a simulation to find the experimental probability.
   - Use a coin or a two-color counter. Decide which side of the coin or counter stands for girls and which side stands for boys.
   - Flip the coin 4 times to simulate the birth of each of the 4 children in one family.
   - Repeat the experiment until you have completed 24 trials. Record the results on a recording sheet to show the number of girls and the number of boys in each "family."
   - Use your results to find the experimental probability P(2 girls and 2 boys).

***P* (2 girls and 2 boys)**		
Trial "Family"	**Girls**	**Boys**
1		
2		
3		

3. Compare the results of your experiment with the theoretical probability. Describe any differences.

4. Conduct a survey with a large number of students in your school. Ask for the number of boys and girls in each family, and record each as a trial in a probability experiment. Compare the survey results with results from your coin-tossing experiment.

Technology

Visit *Education Place* at **eduplace.com/kids/mw/** to learn more about this topic.

Unit 7 Test

VOCABULARY

Write *true* or *false* for each. Rewrite each false statement to make it true.

1. A rate is a ratio that compares different units.

2. A probability shows that two ratios are equal.

3. Similar figures have the same shape.

4. An event that has a probability of 0 is a certain event.

Vocabulary

ratio
rate
percent
proportion
probability
certain event
similar figures
impossible event

CONCEPTS AND SKILLS

Write each ratio three different ways. (Chapter 18)

5. 2 trucks to 5 cars

6. 9 rectangles to 5 triangles

Find the unit rate. (Chapter 18)

7. 90 miles in 15 minutes

8. $105 in 7 hours

Find the missing term in each proportion. (Chapter 18)

9. $\frac{n}{5} = \frac{6}{30}$

10. $\frac{4}{6} = \frac{6}{n}$

11. $\frac{10}{8} = \frac{n}{12}$

A blueprint has a scale of $\frac{1}{4}$ inch:1 foot. Find *n*. (Chapter 18)

12. *n* inches represent 7 feet

13. $\frac{1}{2}$ inch represents *n* feet

Copy and complete the table. Write each fraction in simplest form. (Chapter 19)

	Fraction	Decimal	Percent
14.	■	■	30%
15.	■	0.8	■
16.	$\frac{9}{20}$	■	■

Order each set from the greatest to the least part of a unit. (Chapter 19)

17. $\frac{1}{3}$, 0.25, 13%

18. $\frac{5}{8}$, 0.65, 63%

Estimate each percent of a number. (Chapter 19)

19. 11% of 59

20. 48% of 81

Solve by writing each percent as a fraction or as a decimal. (Chapter 19)

21. 15% of 80

22. 75% of 64

23. 2% of 300

You have one choice from each category. Find the total number of possible combinations. (Chapter 20)

24. 3 styles, 4 colors

25. 7 flavors, 3 toppings

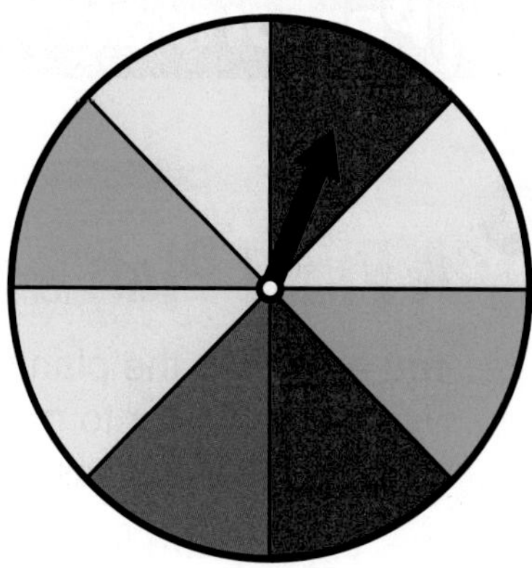

Use the spinner. Express the probability of each event in simplest form. (Chapter 20)

26. red

27. not yellow or green

Suppose you flip a penny and roll a 1–6 number cube. Find the probability of each compound event. (Chapter 20)

28. heads and 5

29. tails and an even number

PROBLEM SOLVING

30. At Produce Patch market, a bag of 20 large green apples sells for $5.99. At Fruit Fresh market a bag of 30 large green apples sells for $7.59. Which is the better buy?

31. Tad wants to buy 3 T-shirts in different colors. The available colors are blue, red, yellow, brown, and black. How many different ways can he choose 3 different colors of T-shirts?

32. The school cafeteria surveyed 160 students about favorite lunches. There were 40 votes for salad, 80 votes for pizza, and 40 votes for sandwiches. Create a circle graph to display these data as percents.

33. Use the data from Problem 32. Suppose you interviewed a student from the school in which the favorite lunch survey was conducted. What is the probability that the student prefers sandwiches for lunch?

Decision Making

Extended Response

Which sport is most important in our school sports program?
Please check only one choice.

☐ Baseball ☐ Basketball ☐ Volleyball ☐ Soccer ☐ Football

Task Students used the survey form above to collect data. They plan to present the results to the school athletic committee.

Use the information at the right. Arrange the sports in order from first to last choice. Explain your thinking.

Information You Need

- $\frac{1}{5}$ chose baseball.
- The probability that a student voted for basketball was $\frac{1}{8}$.
- 0.12 chose football.
- 18% chose volleyball.
- The remaining students chose soccer.

Performance Assessment

TASK 1

A Plant Plan (Chapters 18–19)

You are using the plan at the right to design a garden. Use an inch ruler to measure the scale drawing and help you complete this task.

a. What are the actual dimensions of the garden?

b. You need to include a square planting area whose actual sides measure 30 feet. What will be the dimensions of the square in the drawing?

c. Suppose you have to design a new garden whose dimensions are 75% of the length and 75% of the width of the garden pictured on the right. What will be the actual dimensions of the new garden?

d. Will the polygon defining the shape of the new garden (in part **c**) and that of the original garden be similar? Explain.

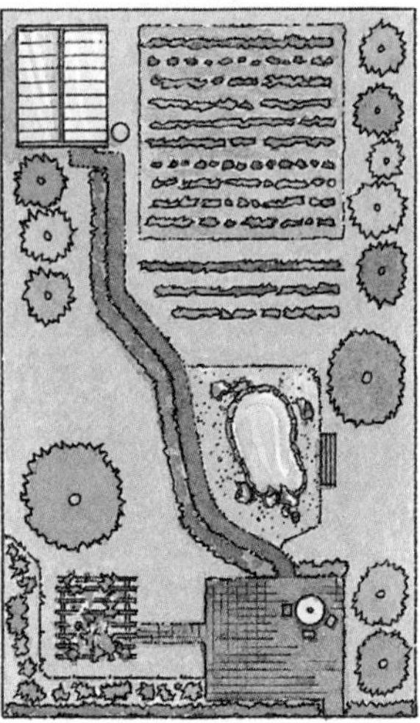

Scale: $\frac{1}{4}$ inch = 10 feet

TASK 2

Game Playing (Chapter 20)

You are playing a game with the spinner shown.

a. Name two outcomes that are equally likely.

b. Name the outcome that is least likely.

c. Name an event that has a probability of $\frac{1}{2}$.

d. Name an event that has a probability of 0. Then name an event that has a probability of 1.

e. Another game also has a number cube labeled 1–6. Name a compound event of tossing the cube and flipping a coin that has a probability of $\frac{1}{12}$.

Self Check

- Did I answer the questions for each task?
- Did I check all my work?

Enrichment: Circle Graphs and Percents

The 20 students in a fifth-grade class wanted to decide on the kind of booth they would have at the school fair. The sections of the circle graph show the percent of the class that voted for each kind of booth.

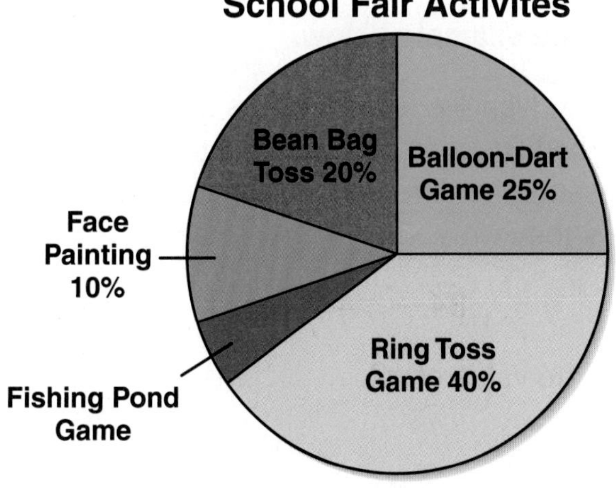

The graph shows that 25% of the students voted for the Balloon-Dart Game. The figure 25% means $\frac{25}{100}$. You can write 25% as a fraction or as a decimal.

$$25\% = \frac{25}{100} = \frac{1}{4}$$

$$25\% = 0.25$$

Try These!

Use the circle graph to solve the problems.

1. Write a fraction for the part of the class that voted for the Ring-Toss Game. How many students does that represent?
2. Write a decimal for the part of the class that voted for the Face Painting booth. How many students does that represent?
3. Which activity received 4 votes? Explain how you found your answer.
4. Arrange all the games in order from greatest to least number of votes.
5. **Represent** Find the number of students who voted for the Fishing Pond Game. Explain how you found your answer.
6. **Write Your Own** Create and solve a problem using the data in the graph. The problem should involve working with percents.

Cumulative Test Prep Practice

Solve Problems 1–10.

Test-Taking Tip

When a test question involves an equation with variables, you can check your answer by substituting answer choices for the variable in the given equation.

Look at the example below.

Last week, Ivan worked 21 hours and Jeff worked 34 hours. In this equation, h represents the difference in the number of hours they worked.

$$34 - h = 21$$

What is the value of h?

A 3 **C** 17

B 13 **D** 23

THINK

Substitute each value in the left side of the equation:

A $34 - 3$
B $34 - 13$
C $34 - 17$
D $34 - 23$

Then simplify, and compare the result with 21. The difference between 34 and 13 is 21, so the answer is **B**.

Multiple Choice

1. Kendra earned \$40 and Lenny earned \$19. In this equation, n represents the number of dollars more than Lenny that Kendra earned.

$$19 + n = 40$$

What is the value of n?

A 11 **B** 21 **C** 31 **D** 59

(Chapter 2, Lesson 5)

2. Twenty-four ride tickets were shared equally by some students. Each student received 4 tickets. In this equation, s represents the number of students.

$$24 \div s = 4$$

What is the value of s?

F 2 **G** 6 **H** 20 **J** 28

(Chapter 4, Lesson 7)

3. Mona drove 120 miles at a speed of 40 miles per hour. In this equation, t represents the number of hours she drove.

$$120 = 40 \times t$$

What is the value of t?

A 3 **B** 30 **C** 80 **D** 160

(Chapter 4, Lesson 7)

4. Nina completed 12 more laps than Otis. Otis completed 9 laps. In this equation, n represents the number of laps Nina completed.

$$n - 12 = 9$$

What is the value of n?

F 3 **G** 21 **H** 31 **J** 41

(Chapter 2, Lesson 5)

 For more Test-Taking Tips, see pages xxii–xxv.

Free Response

5. Tracey collected these data on the number of calories consumed by classmates at lunch.

640, 570, 710, 640, 720, 690, 700

What is the median of her data?

(Chapter 8, Lesson 2)

6. Stuart has a piece of wood that is 135 inches long. How many blocks, each 1.5 inches long, can he cut from the wood?

(Chapter 14, Lesson 7)

7. Paolo wants to fence in a square patch of basil plants. The patch measures 500 centimeters on a side. How many meters of fencing will he need?

(Chapter 16, Lesson 1)

8. Rosa wants to cover this gift box with wrapping paper. What is the least number of square inches of wrapping paper she'll need?

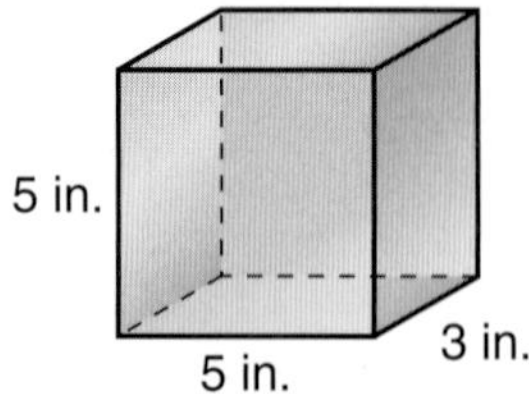

(Chapter 17, Lesson 4)

9. The original price of a DVD was $50. Hugo bought the DVD on sale and paid 75% of the original price. How much did Hugo pay for the DVD?

(Chapter 19, Lesson 5)

Extended Response

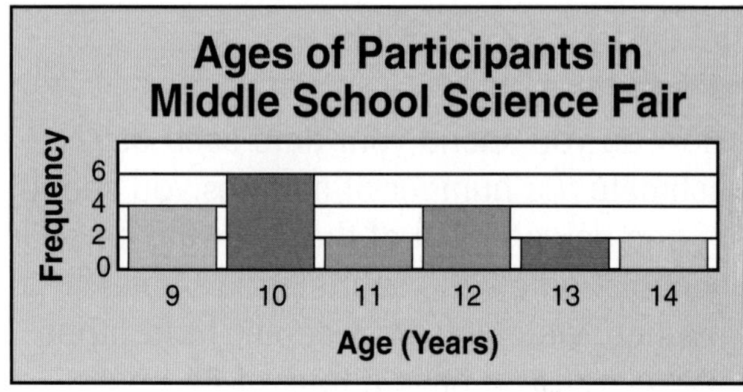

10. Use the bar graph above to answer the following questions.

A How many students were at least 11 years old?

B How many students were under 12 years old?

C What is the mode of the data?

D What is the median of the data? Explain how you found the answer.

E Find the mean of the data to the nearest whole number. Explain how you found the answer.

(Chapter 7, Lesson 2 and Chapter 8, Lesson 2)

Test Prep on the Net

Check out *Education Place* at **eduplace.com/kids/mw/** for test prep practice.

It Takes Time!

How do you spend your time each day? Estimate the number of minutes you spend in one day on each of the following categories: school, homework, sports and hobbies, reading, watching TV, sleeping, and other. Make sure you have a total of 24 hours.

You can make a circle graph of your data using Easy Sheet.

- Enter the categories in column A.
- Enter the number of minutes you spend on each category in column B.
- Click on cell A1 and drag to cell B7 to highlight all the cells with data.
- Click .
- Double click anywhere on the graph.
- Click on the tab marked **Labels**. Enter a title. Click the box next to **Label Data**. Click **OK**.

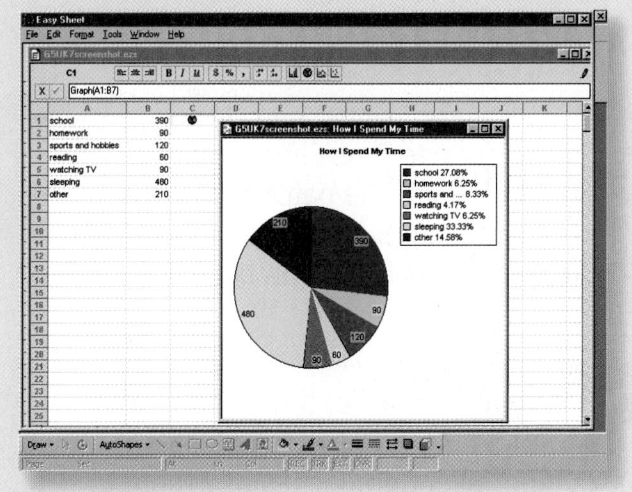

Use the graph you created to answer Problems 1–5.

1. On which activity do you spend the most amount of time? the least amount of time?
2. What percentage of your day is spent on things other than school and homework?
3. Suppose you added eating as another category. How would it affect your graph?
4. Look at the legend. Round each percent to the nearest whole number and then write as a ratio in simplest form.
5. Write the ratio of the number of minutes spent on each activity to 1,440, the number of minutes in a day. Use a calculator to simplify each ratio. Do these ratios match the ones from Problem 4?

Vocabulary Wrap-Up for Unit 7

WEEKLY WR READER Activity Almanac
See page 684 for the activity for this unit.

Look back at the big ideas and vocabulary in this unit.

Big Ideas

You can use equivalent fractions or cross products to find the missing term in a proportion.

The theoretical probability of an event is the ratio of the number of favorable outcomes to the total number of outcomes.

e Glossary

Key Vocabulary

proportion
ratio
probability

Math Conversations

Use your new vocabulary to discuss these big ideas.

1. Explain what it means when an event has a probability of 1.
2. Explain how to find 25% of 60 in two different ways.
3. Explain how to find the missing term in this proportion. $\frac{10}{n} = \frac{15}{9}$.
4. Explain how to find the probability of this compound event: tails when tossing a coin and rolling a number less than 5 on a 1–6 number cube.
5. **Write About It** Look for examples of percents in newspapers, magazines, and on television. Make a list of the kinds of articles that use percents. Tell why percents are used in these articles.

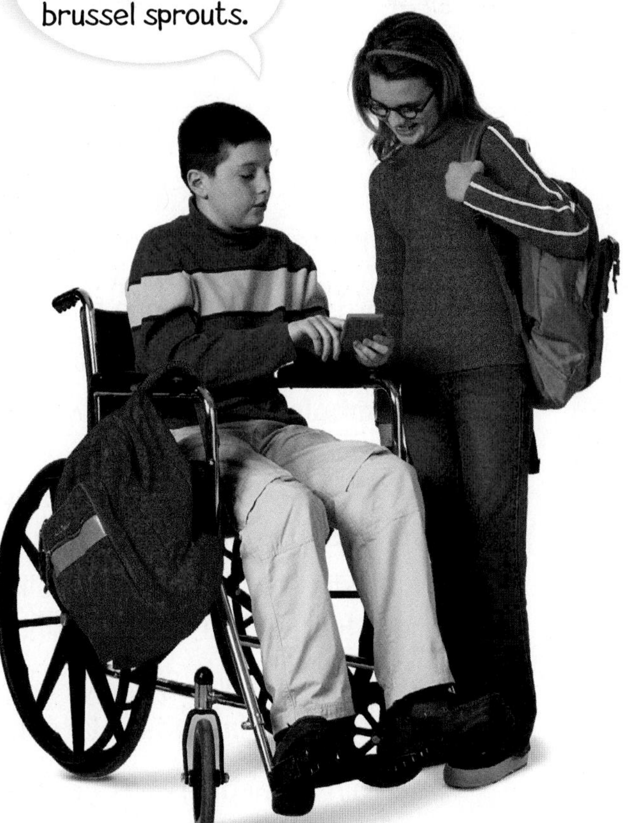

8 percent of the class likes brussel sprouts.
You can also write that as $\frac{8}{100}$ or 0.08

Building Vocabulary

Reviewing Vocabulary

Here are some math vocabulary words that you should know.

function	a rule that pairs each input value *x* with exactly one output value *y*
function table	a table that shows the *x* and corresponding *y* values for a function rule
equation	a mathematical sentence with an equals sign
negative number	a number that is less than zero
inverse operations	a pair of operations that have opposite effects, such as addition and subtraction or multiplication and division
ordered pair	a pair of numbers in which one number is considered to be first and the other number second

Reading Words and Symbols

You can use words, a combination of words and symbols, or symbols to describe relationships between numbers.

Words: Carola, who is fifteen, is three times as old as Donald.

Words and symbols: Carola's age $=$ 3 $\times$ Donald's age

Symbols: $15 = 3 \times d$ (with *d* representing Donald's age)

Use words and symbols or only symbols to describe each situation.

1. Eddie saved seventeen dollars, which is four dollars more than Frieda saved.
2. Ginny completed twelve laps, which is five fewer laps than Hal completed.
3. Thirty-six apples were divided into equal shares. There were four apples in each share.

Reading Test Questions

Choose the correct answer for each.

4. Which ordered pair shows the location of the library?

   a. (2, 3)

   b. (3, 2)

   c. (2, 5)

   d. (3, 5)

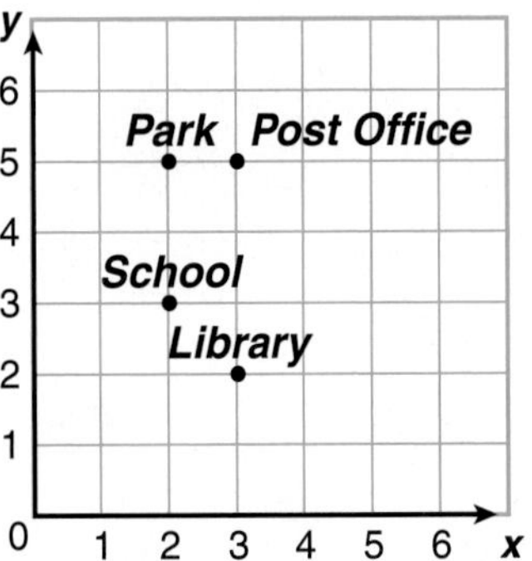

Location means "position" or "place."

5. Which number is the solution of this equation?

$$m - 34 = 19$$

   a. 15 c. 45

   b. 43 d. 53

To find the **solution** of an equation means to find "a number that can be substituted for the variable to make the equation true."

6. Al, Ben, Cara, and Donna scored $^-4$, 3, 2, and $^-3$ points respectively. Who scored the fewest points?

   a. Al c. Cara

   b. Ben d. Donna

Respectively means the scores are in the same order as the names. So, Al scored $^-4$, Ben scored 3, Cara scored 2, and Donna scored $^-3$.

Learning Vocabulary

Watch for these new words in this unit. Write their definitions in your journal.

integer

coordinates

origin

translation

reflection

rotation

Vocabulary

e • **Glossary**

e • **WordGame**

Literature Connection

Read "Treasure Hunt" on pages 648–649. Then work with a partner to answer the questions about the story.

CHAPTER 21

Equations and Functions

INVESTIGATION

Use Data

Artists often use scale drawings and grids to plan large pieces of art. Each square contains a simple part of the total form. Part of one of the stained-glass pieces in the picture has been copied onto a grid. To enlarge this, use 1 in. × 1 in. graph paper to reproduce this part of the picture, square by square.

Use this page to review and remember what you need to know for this chapter.

VOCABULARY

Choose the best word to complete each sentence.

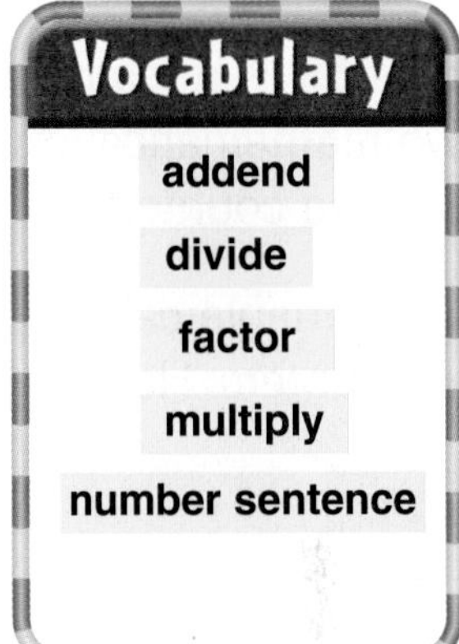

1. In the expression $4 + x = 5$, the 4 is a(n) ____.
2. The equation $36 \div 9 = 4$ asks that you ____ 36 by 9.
3. To check division, you ____ the quotient and the divisor.

CONCEPTS AND SKILLS

Find the missing addend.

4. $5 + ■ = 13$
5. $■ + 11 = 31$
6. $22 + ■ = 61$
7. $■ + 49 = 74$

Find the missing factor.

8. $7 \times ■ = 42$
9. $■ \times 9 = 99$
10. $■ \times 8 = 56$
11. $■ \times 15 = 60$

Match. Write the letter of the correct missing number.

12. $42 - ■ = 33$ **a.** 8
13. $■ \div 9 = 7$ **b.** 9
14. $■ - 16 = 40$ **c.** 56
15. $96 \div ■ = 12$ **d.** 63

Write the next two numbers in each pattern.

16. 2, 9, 16, 23, 30, …
17. 2, 10, 18, 26, 34, …
18. 5, 20, 35, 50, 65, …
19. 79, 67, 55, 43, 31, …

Write About It

20. Describe this pattern in words. Then name the next two numbers.

    79, 85, 75, 81, 71

Algebra

Model Equations

Objective Determine what happens when you perform the same operation on both sides of an equation.

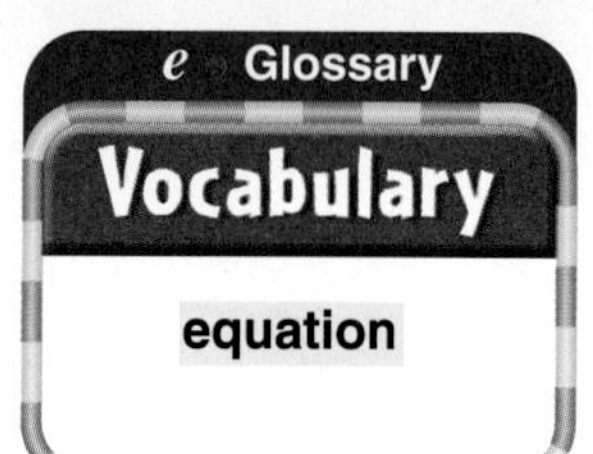

Materials
counters
variable cards
plus sign cards
equal sign cards

Work Together

An **equation** is a mathematical sentence showing that two mathematical expressions are equal. You can use counters to model equations.

The blue variable card represents the number of hidden counters. How many counters are hidden?

$x + 3 = 7$

What number plus 3 equals 7? Since $4 + 3 = 7$, then $x = 4$. There are 4 hidden counters.

Work with a partner to see what happens when you perform the same operation on both sides of an equation.

STEP 1 Use the variable card, counters, and an equal sign card to model the equation $x + 3 = 7$.

- Add 2 counters to each side of the equal sign. What equation does your model represent now?
- How many counters does the blue card represent? Did adding 2 counters to each side change the value of x?

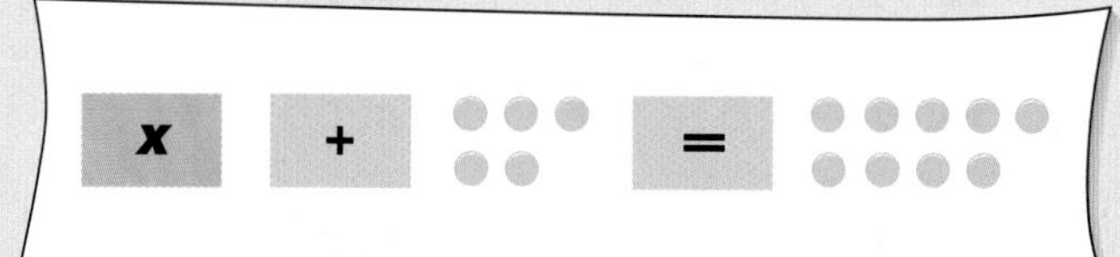

STEP 2 Model the equation $x + 3 = 7$ again.

- Subtract 2 counters from each side of the equal sign. What equation does your model represent now?
- How many counters does the blue card represent? Did taking away 2 counters from each side change the value of x?

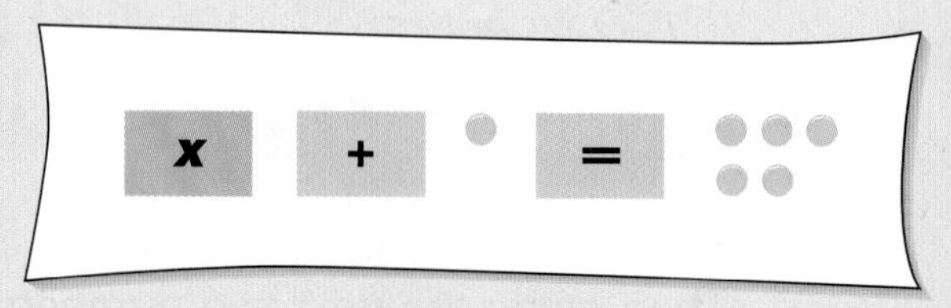

STEP 3 Model the equation $x = 2$ with 1 variable card and 2 counters.

- Use variable cards and counters to show multiplying both sides of the equation by 5. What equation does your model represent now?
- How many counters does the blue card represent? Did multiplying each side by 5 change the value of x?

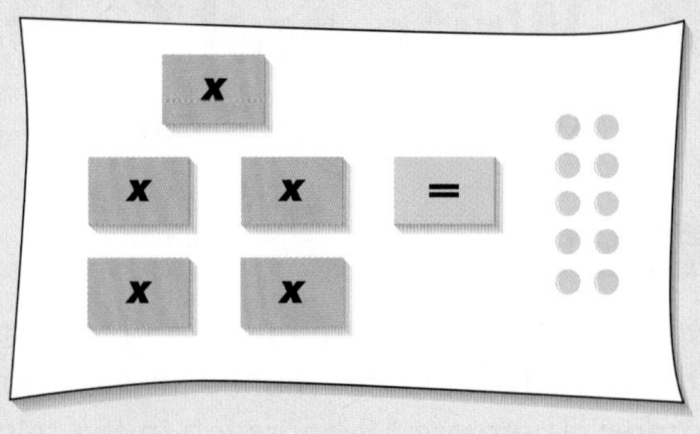

On Your Own

1. In $x + 3 = 5$, what value does x represent?
2. Add 2 to both sides of $x + 3 = 5$. What value does x represent?
3. Subtract 1 from both sides of $x + 3 = 5$. What value does x represent?

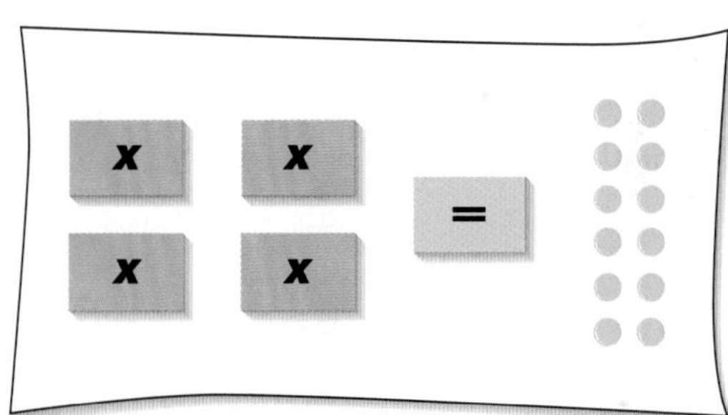

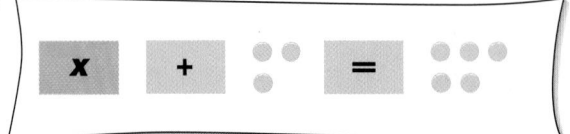

4. In $4x = 12$, what value does x represent?
5. Multiply both sides of $4x = 12$ by 2. What value does x represent?
6. Divide both sides of $4x = 12$ by 2. What value does x represent?

Talk About It • Write About It

TEST PREP

You learned that the two sides of an equation are always balanced.

7. What happens to the value of the variable when you add or subtract the same number from both sides of the equation?
8. What happens to the value of the variable when you multiply or divide both sides of the equation by the same counting number?

Lesson 2

Algebra

Write and Solve Equations

Objective Write and solve equations.

e Glossary

Vocabulary

inverse operations

Learn About It

MathTracks 2/28
Listen and Understand

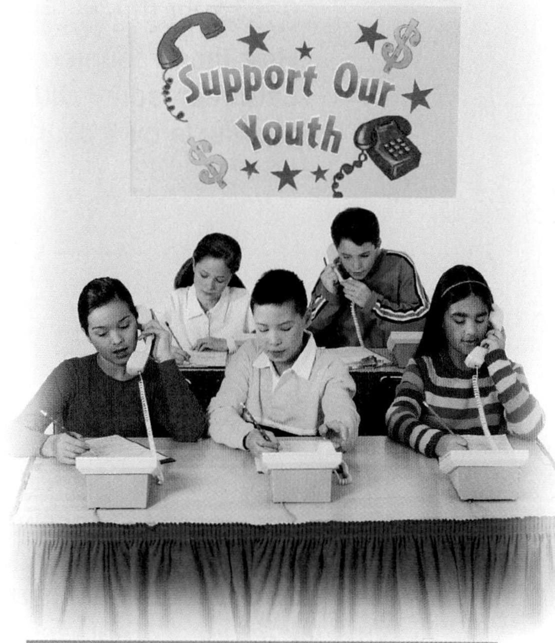

Wayne and his friends are answering telephones at a 24-hour telethon to raise money for local youth programs. There are 18 hours left in the telethon. How many hours has the telethon been on?

Write and solve an equation to solve the problem.

Let n represent the number of hours the telethon has been on.

Equation: $n + 18 = 24$ ← total number of hours in telethon

n: hours telethon has been on

18: number of hours left

▶ You can use inverse operations to solve equations. **Inverse operations** are two operations that have opposite effects.

Addition and subtraction are inverse operations.

Inverse Operations	
addition ⟷	subtraction
multiplication ⟷	division

Solve Addition and Subtraction Equations

Solve: $n + 18 = 24$

$$n + 18 = 24$$
$$n + 18 - 18 = 24 - 18$$
$$n + 0 = 6$$
$$n = 6$$

Think
18 is added to n.
Addition and subtraction are inverse operations. So subtract 18 from both sides.

Solve: $x - 8 = 27$

$$x - 8 = 27$$
$$x - 8 + 8 = 27 + 8$$
$$x + 0 = 35$$
$$x = 35$$

Think
8 is subtracted from x.
Addition and subtraction are inverse operations. So add 8 to both sides.

Multiplication and division are inverse operations.

Multiplication and Division Equations

Solve: $4m = 36$

$4m = 36$

$4m \div 4 = 36 \div 4$

$1 \cdot m = 9$

$m = 9$

Think
m is multiplied by 4. Multiplication and division are inverses. So divide by 4 on both sides.

Remember
$4m$ means $4 \bullet m$, or four times m. The multiplication sign, $\times$, is not used to avoid confusion with the variable x.

Solve: $t \div 6 = 12$

$t \div 6 = 12$

$(t \div 6) \cdot 6 = 12 \cdot 6$

$t \div 1 = 72$

$t = 72$

Think
t is divided by 6. Multiplication and division are inverse operations. So multiply by 6 on both sides.

Guided Practice

Solve using inverse operations.

1. $7d = 28$
2. $c \div 9 = 3$
3. $h + 26.5 = 51.3$
4. $j - 14 = 13$
5. $f \div 8 = 12$
6. $y - 48.2 = 98.6$

Use words to describe each equation.

7. $15 + x = 20$
8. $3c = 16$
9. $y \div 6 = 8$

Ask Yourself

- Which operation can I use to undo the operation in the equation?

Explain Your Thinking Describe how you can write and solve an equation that shows increasing the number of hours worked by 7 hours equals 32 hours in all.

Practice and Problem Solving

Solve using inverse operations.

10. $6k = 42$
11. $c + 108 = 242$
12. $g \div 6 = 90$
13. $n + 484 = 911$
14. $h \div 14 = 84$
15. $n \cdot 29 = 319$
16. $a - 174 = 308$
17. $333 = 9f$
18. $u \div 12 = 70$
19. $92 \cdot k = 2{,}208$
20. $r \div 8 = 18$
21. $49 + w = 102$

Go On

Use words to describe each equation.

22. $m + 14 = 20$ **23.** $p \div 3 = 12$ **24.** $w - 6 = 18$

25. $31 + b = 72$ **26.** $5 \cdot x = 50$ **27.** $24 - r = 17$

In Problems 28–31, write and solve an equation for each problem.

28. Matt raised \$18 on Saturday morning. He raised more money Saturday afternoon. In all, he raised \$43 on Saturday. How much did he raise Saturday afternoon?

29. Marcus had 28 ride tickets. Each ride took the same number of tickets. Marcus rode 7 rides and used all his tickets. How many tickets did it take for each ride?

30. Margarita had some money. She spent \$28 on jewelry. Then she had \$29. How much did she have before buying jewelry?

31. Each floor of a hotel has an equal number of rooms. The total number of rooms on 12 floors is 240 rooms. How many rooms are on each floor?

32. What's Wrong? Jonah solved the equation $n \div 6 = 18$. What did Jonah do wrong? What is the value of n?

Jonah

$n \div 6 = 18$

$(n \div 6) \div 6 = 18 \div 6$

$n = 3$

33. Create and Solve Write a problem that could be described by the equation $5r = 125$. Then solve the problem.

34. Janice, Ellen, Roberto, Heather, and Christopher are finalists in a contest. The contest has prizes for first and second place. How many different ways can the prizes be awarded?

Daily Review Test Prep

Divide. (Ch. 12, Lessons 5–6)

35. $\frac{15}{32} \div \frac{3}{4}$ **36.** $2\frac{2}{3} \div \frac{5}{6}$

37. $7 \div \frac{4}{5}$ **38.** $4\frac{1}{2} \div 2\frac{3}{4}$

39. $3\frac{5}{8} \div 4$ **40.** $\frac{6}{7} \div 3$

41. $12 \div \frac{3}{4}$ **42.** $\frac{3}{4} \div 12$

43. $12 \div 1\frac{1}{3}$ **44.** $1\frac{1}{3} \div 12$

45. In a crew of 32 workers, each member works the same number of hours. They work a total of 1,600 hours in a week. Choose the equation for this situation.

A $32h = 1{,}600$

B $1{,}600h = 32$

C $32 \div h = 1{,}600$

D $h \div 1{,}600 = 32$

Extra Practice See page 583, Set A.

Square Numbers and Exponents

You can use your calculator to work with square numbers and exponents. The product of a number multiplied by itself is a **square number**. For example, 9 is a square number because it is the product of 3 × 3.

To show that a number has been squared, write the number and then the exponent 2.

3^2 ← exponent
↑
base

The exponent tells you how many times the base is a factor in the product. So, $3^2 = 3 \times 3$.

To find the square of 3, press 3    9

Sometimes you need to multiply a number by itself more than once. This means you are raising it to a power greater than 2.

To show 5 × 5 × 5, write 5^3. The exponent 3 tells you that the base, 5, is a factor 3 times. So, $5 \times 5 \times 5 = 5^3$.

To find 5^3 on your calculator, press     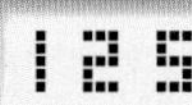

1. **a.** Multiply to square the numbers 1 through 8.
   b. Write an equation in the form of $a^2 = a \times a$ to represent each square number.
   c. Complete the table at the right. Describe the patterns you notice.

1	1
2	4
3	9
4	
5	
6	
7	49
8	

Use the ^ key to simplify the expressions below.

2. $4^3 + 5^2 - 2^2$ **3.** $5^3 - 3 \times 2^4$ **4.** $6^2 \div 3^2 + 5^3$

5. $30 \times (40 - 3^2)$ **6.** $a^2 + 9$, if $a = 5$ **7.** $b^3 - b^2 \times 2$, if $b = 3$

Lesson 3

Problem-Solving Strategy

Write an Equation

Objective Write an equation to solve a problem.

You can often use an equation to help you find an unknown amount.

Problem Nate is paid by the hour. He works 6 hours and earns $48. How much does Nate earn each hour?

UNDERSTAND

This is what you know:

- Nate is paid by the hour.
- He works 6 hours and earns $48.

PLAN

You can write an equation to describe the situation. First you have to decide which operation to use. Then you can write and solve the equation.

SOLVE

Think: Why write a multiplication equation?

- Write the equation.

  Let d represent the amount that Nate is paid each hour.

  6 hours times d dollars per hour equals $48.

- Solve the equation using inverse operations.

$$6d = 48$$

$$6d \div 6 = 48 \div 6$$

$$d = 8$$

Solution: Nate earns $8 per hour.

LOOK BACK

Look back at the problem.

How can you check your answer?

MathTracks 2/29
Listen and Understand

Guided Practice

Use the Ask Yourself questions to help you solve each problem.

1. Last week, Terri worked 9.5 hours. This was 3.5 hours less than the number of hours that Brad worked. How many hours did Brad work?

2. A company has 160 employees. This is 4 times the number of employees that it had ten years ago. How many employees did the company have ten years ago?

Hint What will the variable represent?

Ask Yourself

What facts do I know?

Did I write an equation?

- **Did I use a variable to represent what I need to know?**
- **Did I use the correct operation to solve the equation?**

LOOK BACK
Does my answer make sense?

Independent Practice

Write an equation to solve each problem.

3. Benita gets a raise of $315 per month. Her new monthly salary is $3,425. What was Benita's monthly salary before she got a raise?

4. In one restaurant, the waiter gives the dishwasher $\frac{1}{4}$ of his tips. On Friday night, the waiter receives $88 in tips. How much does the waiter give to the dishwasher?

5. **You Decide** Find how much each job listed to the right pays per hour. Decide which job you would prefer. Give reasons for your decision.

6. Tom has a weekly salary of $750. This is $95 less than Carol's weekly salary. What is Carol's weekly salary?

7. One department has 4 employees. Each employee works the same number of hours per week. The employees in that department worked a total of 150 hours in one week. How many hours did each employee work?

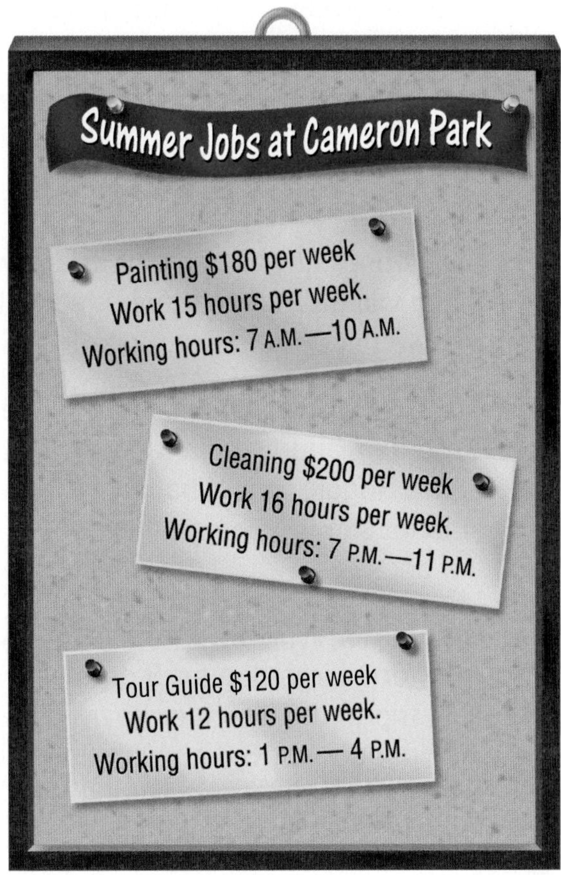

Summer Jobs at Cameron Park
Painting $180 per week
Work 15 hours per week.
Working hours: 7 A.M.—10 A.M.
Cleaning $200 per week
Work 16 hours per week.
Working hours: 7 P.M.—11 P.M.
Tour Guide $120 per week
Work 12 hours per week.
Working hours: 1 P.M.— 4 P.M.

Choose a Strategy

Solve. Show your work. Tell what strategy you used.

PROBLEM-SOLVING Strategies

- Use Models
- Draw a Diagram
- Find a Pattern
- Guess and Check
- Make an Organized List
- Make a Table
- Solve a Simpler Problem
- Use Logical Reasoning
- Work Backward
- Write an Equation

8. In a blizzard, a technician monitors the snowfall each hour. The total snowfall is 2.8 cm after 2 hours, 4.2 after 3 hours, and 5.6 cm after 4 hours. If the pattern continues, what will be the total snowfall after 5 hours?

9. Fran makes a set of 49 prints. If all 49 prints sell for a total of $9,800, how much does Fran charge for one print?

10. A jewelry store has 7 clerks. Two clerks must be working at the store at any time that it is open. How many different combinations of 2 clerks are possible?

11. Julianna earned $344 last week working at a local print shop. She earned $8 per hour. How many hours did Julianna work last week at the print shop?

Data **Use the table to solve Problems 12–15.**

The Dog Bone Inn offers the services to dog owners shown in the table.

12. Mari's dog, Jiffy, weighs 32 lbs. How much will it be to board and feed Jiffy for two days at the Dog Bone Inn?

13. Ms. Owens has two small dogs, one large dog, and two giant dogs to groom at the Doggie Spa. What is the total amount she will charge the owners of the dogs?

14. **Calculator** Which will cost less: day care for a large dog for 5 days with a field trip to the beach or boarding a medium dog for 6 days with 3 field trips to the lake, and a grooming at the Doggie Spa? How much less?

15. **Create and Solve** Use the data from the table to create and solve a problem.

DOG BONE INN

Daily Charges

	Small	Medium	Large	Giant
Day Care	$11	$14	$17	$30
Boarding	$16	$22	$27	$50
Doggie Spa	$15	$20	$35	$60
Feeding	$1.75	$3.50	$3.50	$3.50

Field Trips To:		
	Tail-wagging Bakery	$15
	Lake	$25
	Beach	$100

Small dogs: Up to 25 pounds **Large dogs:** 61 to 110 pounds
Medium dogs: 26 to 60 pounds **Giant dogs:** Over 110 pounds

Problem-Solving Test Prep

Choose the letter of the correct answer.
If a correct answer is not here, choose NH.

1. Yuri makes a scale model of his house. The scale model is shown below. What is the actual height of Yuri's house?

Scale: 1 in. = 6 ft

A 24 ft **B** 27 ft **C** 30 ft **D** 42 ft

(Chapter 18, Lesson 5)

2. A telephone pole that is 45 feet high falls into the street. A worker cuts the pole into logs. What is the greatest number of 18-inch logs that can be made from the telephone pole?

F 25 **G** 29 **H** 30 **J** 45

(Chapter 6, Lesson 2)

3. A sound system is on sale for 10% off list price. Including a sales tax of $9, Jeremy pays $189 for the sound system. Which equation could you use to find the list price (P)?

A $0.9 \times P = \$189$

B $(0.9 \times P) - \$9 = \$189$

C $(0.9 \times P) + \$9 = \$189$

D $(0.1 \times P) - (\$9) = \$189$

(Chapter 19, Lesson 5)

4. Which set of numbers is equivalent?

F $\frac{1}{3}$, 0.3, 3% **G** $\frac{1}{5}$, 0.25, 25%

H $\frac{3}{10}$, 0.03, 3% **J** $\frac{3}{5}$, 0.6, 60%

(Chapter 19, Lesson 3)

5. The area of the parallelogram is 72 square centimeters. What is the measure of side A?

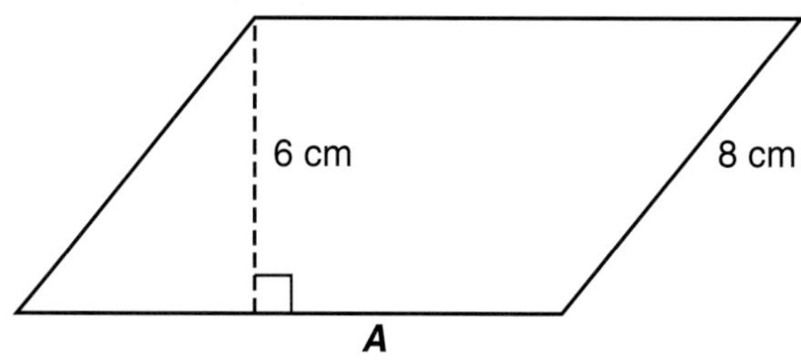

A 6 cm **C** 9 cm

B 8 cm **D** 12 cm

(Chapter 16, Lesson 3)

6. A park has 6 entrance gates. A direct path connects each gate to every other gate. How many paths are there in all?

Represent Support your solution with a picture.

(Chapter 17, Lesson 5)

7. Bill has twice as many stickers as Amy. Together they have 24 stickers. Let *a* represent the number of stickers that Amy has. Write an equation that you can use to find how many stickers Amy has.

Explain How does your equation represent the situation?

(Chapter 21, Lesson 3)

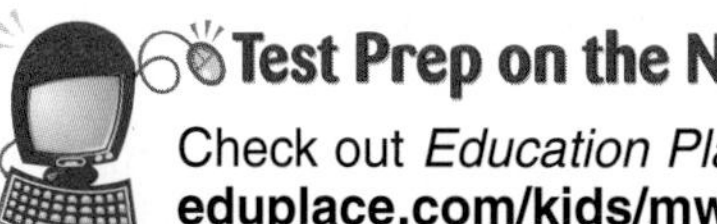

Test Prep on the Net
Check out *Education Place* at **eduplace.com/kids/mw/** for test prep practice.

Algebra

Variables and Functions

Objective Use a function table to solve equations.

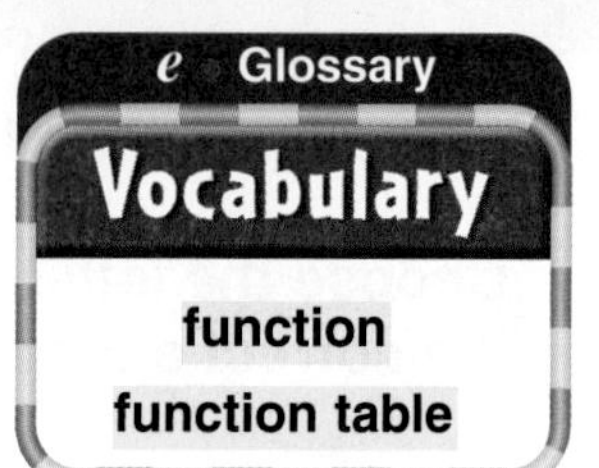

MathTracks 2/30
Listen and Understand

A **function** is a rule that relates pairs of variables, such as x and y. For each value of x, there is exactly one related value of y. A function is often written as an equation.

Look at the pattern. How many squares will there be in Shape 10?

1 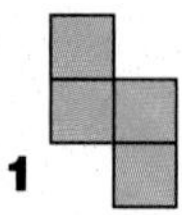 2 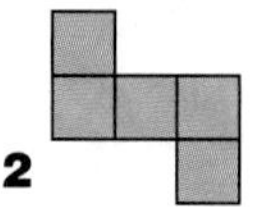 3 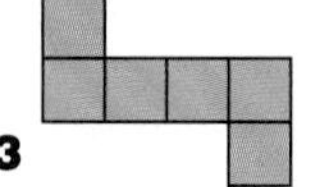 4 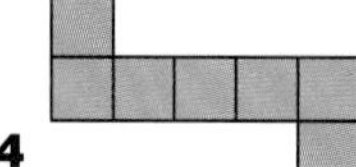

STEP 1 Organize the information in a table. Write the shape number in the first column. Write the number of squares in the second column.

The table of values is called a **function table** because there is exactly one entry in the second column for each shape number.

Shape Number	Number of Squares
1	4
2	5
3	6
4	7

STEP 2 Write the equation that describes the relationship between x and y.

The number of squares is always equal to 3 more than the shape number.

$$y = x + 3$$

y ↑ number of squares x ↑ shape number

STEP 3 To find the number of squares in Shape 10, substitute 10 for x and simplify.

$$y = x + 3$$
$$y = 10 + 3$$
$$y = 13$$

Solution: There will be 13 squares in Shape 10.

Another Example

Find the Value

The rule $y = 9x$ describes a function. What is the value of y when $x = 4$?

$y = 9x$ Substitute 4 for x in the equation.

$y = 9(4)$
$y = 36$

Guided Practice

Ask Yourself

- What value did I use for x?
- How did I get the value of y?
- Did a pattern help me find the missing values?

Copy and complete each function table.

1. $y = 5 + x$

x	y
4	■
3	■
2	■

2. $y = x - 5$

x	y
10	■
7	■
6	■

3. $y = 7x$

x	y
12	■
■	14
8	■

Explain Your Thinking ▶ What are some other pairs of values that would fit in the function table in Exercise 2?

Practice and Problem Solving

Copy and complete each function table.

4. $y = 12 \div x$

x	y
1	■
2	■
3	■

5. $y = 4 - x$

x	y
0	■
3	■
4	■

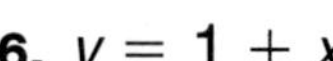

6. $y = 1 + x$

x	y
0	■
6	■
9	■

7. $y = 9x$

x	y
0	■
■	9
2	■

Use the figures for Problems 8–10.

8. Make a function table to show how the number of circles in each figure is related to the figure number.

Figure 1

9. Make a function table to show how the number of triangles in each figure is related to the figure number.

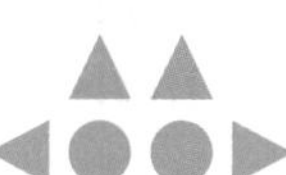

Figure 2

10. Analyze Write an expression for the number of circles and for the number of triangles in the nth figure. Use the expressions to find how many circles and triangles are in the nth figure.

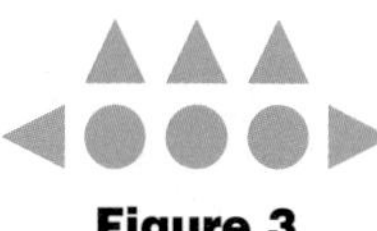

Figure 3

Daily Review | Test Prep

Find the missing term.
(Ch. 18, Lesson 4)

11. $\frac{6}{9} = \frac{g}{3}$ **12.** $\frac{8}{10} = \frac{20}{a}$ **13.** $\frac{3}{z} = \frac{9}{21}$

14. Free Response Ron's earnings (y) for a number of hours (x) are given by the rule $y = 10x$. Make a function table for five values of x.

Extra Practice See page 583, Set B.

Lesson 5

Algebra

Patterns and Functions

Objective Use function tables and equations to describe and extend patterns.

Learn About It

Some functions involve more than one operation.

Theo opened a savings account at the local bank with a deposit of \$250. Theo intends to deposit \$5 each week. How much will Theo have in his savings account after 7 weeks?

Different Ways to Represent Functions

Way 1 You can use a function table.

The function table for the first \$250 shows that each week after the first deposit adds \$5 to the bank account.

Use that pattern to extend the function table so that it shows the amount for 7 weeks.

Number of weeks(x)	Amount in Savings(y)
0	\$250
1	\$255
2	\$260
3	\$265
4	\$270
5	\$275
6	\$280
7	\$285

Way 2 You can use an equation that represents the values in the function table.

STEP 1 Write an equation that represents the relationship between x and y.

The function table shows that the initial deposit is \$250 and each week adds \$5 to the account.

amount deposited each week

$$y = 250 + 5x$$

← number of weeks

total amount; beginning deposit

STEP 2 To find the amount, substitute the number of weeks after the initial deposit for x and simplify.

Think
7 weeks in all.
$x = 7$

$y = 250 + 5(7)$

$y = 250 + 35$

$y = 285$

Solution: Theo will have \$285 in his bank account in 7 weeks.

Guided Practice

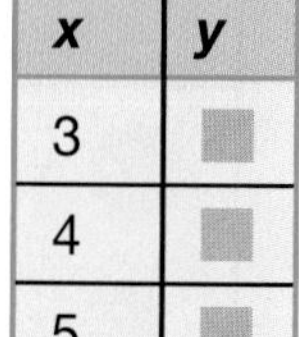

Ask Yourself

- What pattern does the function table show?

Copy and complete each function table.

1. $y = 2x - 3$

x	y
3	■
4	■
5	■

2. $y = 5 + 5x$

x	y
1	■
2	■
3	■

3. $y = (x \div 2) - 4$

x	y
26	■
24	■
22	■

Use the function table. Find the value of *y* for the given value of *x*.

4. If $x = 6$, $y =$ ■.

x	y
0	4
1	7
2	10
3	13

5. If $x = 8$, $y =$ ■.

x	y
0	5
1	10
2	15
3	20

6. If $x = 10$, $y =$ ■.

x	y
0	7
1	11
2	15
3	19

7. If $x = 25$, $y =$ ■.

x	y
3	8
5	14
7	20
9	26

Explain Your Thinking ▶ What equation describes the relationship between *x* and *y* in Exercise 6?

Practice and Problem Solving

Copy and complete each function table.

8. $y = 10x + 2$

x	y
0	■
1	■
2	■

9. $y = 65 + 2x$

x	y
0	■
3	■
6	■

10. $y = 20 - 4x$

x	y
0	■
2	■
■	8

11. $y = 9 + 4x$

x	y
0	■
■	13
■	25

Use the function table. Find the value of *y* for the given value of *x*. Then write the equation.

12. If $x = 5$, $y =$ ■.

x	y
0	1
1	7
2	13
3	19

13. If $x = 9$, $y =$ ■.

x	y
0	9
3	12
5	14
7	16

14. If $x = 8$, $y =$ ■.

x	y
0	8
2	18
4	28
6	38

15. If $x = 6$, $y =$ ■.

x	y
0	10
1	14
2	18
3	22

Go On

Problems 16–20. Julio's grandfather designed the gardens shown in the diagram below.

16. **Analyze** Look at the trees and flowers of the gardens. What patterns do you see?

17. **Reasoning** Write an equation that relates the number of trees of a garden (x) to the number of flowers of the garden (y).

18. **Represent** Draw diagrams to show three more gardens in which the relationship between the number of trees and the number of flowers is the same as in the gardens shown at the right.

19. Create a function table that shows the values for the number of trees (x) and the number of flowers (y) for the gardens shown at the right. Then extend the function table to show the next five gardens in the pattern.

20. Suppose Julio's grandfather creates another garden that fits this pattern. The number of flowers is 84. What is the number of trees?

Garden 1

Garden 2

Garden 3

Key
— tree
— flower

Use the function table to solve Problems 21–23.

Aftershock Studios Rental Rates

Number of Hours (x)	Total Costs (y)
1	$250
2	$300
3	$350
4	$400

21. Cindy records a CD at Aftershock Studios. She rents a studio for 8 hours. How much does Cindy pay?

22. **Write About It** Write an equation that represents the function in the function table. Explain why the equation represents the function.

23. **You Decide** Echo Studios charges a flat fee of $100 plus a charge of $75 per hour. Describe a situation in which you would record at Echo Studios, and one in which you would record at Aftershock Recording. Explain your examples.

24. Two numbers have a greatest common factor of 3 and a least common multiple of 45. What are the numbers?

Extra Practice See page 583, Set C.

Quick Check

Check your understanding of Lessons 1–5.

Solve. (Lessons 1 and 2)

1. $5t = 80$

2. $j - 7 = 46$

3. $a \div 4 = 32$

4. $v + 84 = 152$

Copy and complete each function table. (Lessons 4 and 5)

5. $y = x \div 2$

x	y
2	■
4	■
6	■

6. $y = 5 - x$

x	y
0	■
1	■
2	■

7. $y = 2x + 15$

x	y
3	■
5	■
7	■

8. $y = 3x + 2$

x	y
1	■
5	■
7	■

Write an equation to solve each problem. (Lesson 3)

9. Greg works 35 hours and earns $525. How much does Greg earn each hour?

WEEKLY WR READER® eduplace.com/kids/mw/

Science Connection

Nutrition Facts

Nutritionists study the way a body uses the nutrients that are in food. Three of the main kinds of nutrients are:

- **Carbohydrates** come from starch and sugar in food.
- **Fats** are contained in eggs, fish, meat, nuts, butter, and shortening.
- **Proteins** come from cheese, eggs, meat, fish, milk, beans, grains, nuts, and vegetables.

You might see the information about nutrients at the right on a yogurt container.

Amount per serving	
Total Fat	2 g
Total Carbohydrate	40 g
Protein	9 g

Use the label and an equation to solve.

1. How many times more carbohydrates are there than fats?

2. **Estimate** About how many times more proteins are there than fats?

3. How many times more carbohydrates are there than proteins?

Chapter Review/Test

VOCABULARY

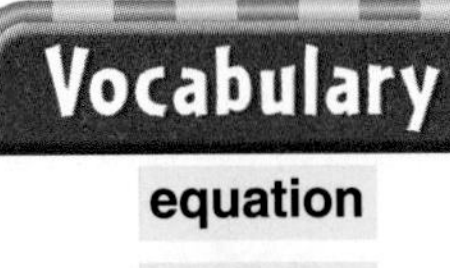

equation

function

inverse operations

variable

1. A letter that stands for a number in an algebraic expression is called a(n) ____ .
2. ____ are two operations that have opposite effects.

CONCEPTS AND SKILLS

Solve using inverse operations. (Lessons 1–2, pp. 566–571)

3. $w - 95 = 890$
4. $231 = x + 67$
5. $9y = 135$

Copy and complete each function table. (Lesson 4, pp. 576–577)

6. $y = 9 - x$

x	*y*
4	■
5	■
6	■

7. $y = 8 + x$

x	*y*
10	■
12	■
14	■

8. $y = 36 \div x$

x	*y*
3	■
6	■
9	■

Use the function table. Find the value of *y* for the given value of *x*. (Lesson 5, pp. 578–579)

9. If $x = 9$, $y =$ ■.

x	*y*
3	7
4	9
5	11

PROBLEM SOLVING

Solve. (Lesson 3, pp. 572–573)

10. Last week, each of 5 students spent the same amount of time on homework. They spent a total of 68 hours on homework. How many hours did each student spend on homework?

Show You Understand

Write an equation and then make a function table for the equation. Explain how a function table works.

Extra Practice

Set A (Lesson 2, pp. 568–571)

Solve using inverse operations.

1. $15 + d = 27$
2. $e - 118 = 110$
3. $6f = 48$
4. $12 = g \div 9$
5. $h + 76 = 201$
6. $12 \cdot j = 132$
7. $145 = k - 423$
8. $m \div 8 = 23$
9. $15n = 1{,}275$
10. $p + 167 = 903$
11. $q \div 13 = 9$
12. $r - 619 = 586$

Set B (Lesson 4, pp. 576–578)

Copy and complete each function table.

1. $y = 2 + x$

x	y
6	■
8	■
10	■
12	■

2. $y = 8 - x$

x	y
0	■
1	■
2	■
3	■

3. $y = 5x$

x	y
2	■
4	■
6	■
8	■

4. $y = 24 \div x$

x	y
1	■
2	■
3	■
4	■

Set C (Lesson 5, pp. 579–581)

Copy and complete each function table.

1. $y = 3x + 4$

x	y
0	■
2	■
4	■
6	■

2. $y = 7x - 5$

x	y
2	■
3	■
4	■
5	■

3. $y = (x \div 2) + 6$

x	y
4	■
6	■
8	■
10	■

4. $y = 10x - 8$

x	y
3	■
6	■
■	82
■	112

Use the function table. Find the value of y for the given value of x.

5. If $x = 6$, $y = n$.

x	y
1	7
2	8
3	9
4	10

6. If $x = 8$, $y = n$.

x	y
0	2
1	5
2	8
3	11

7. If $x = 10$, $y = n$.

x	y
0	10
2	30
4	50
6	70

8. If $x = 12$, $y = n$.

x	y
2	4
4	16
6	36
8	64

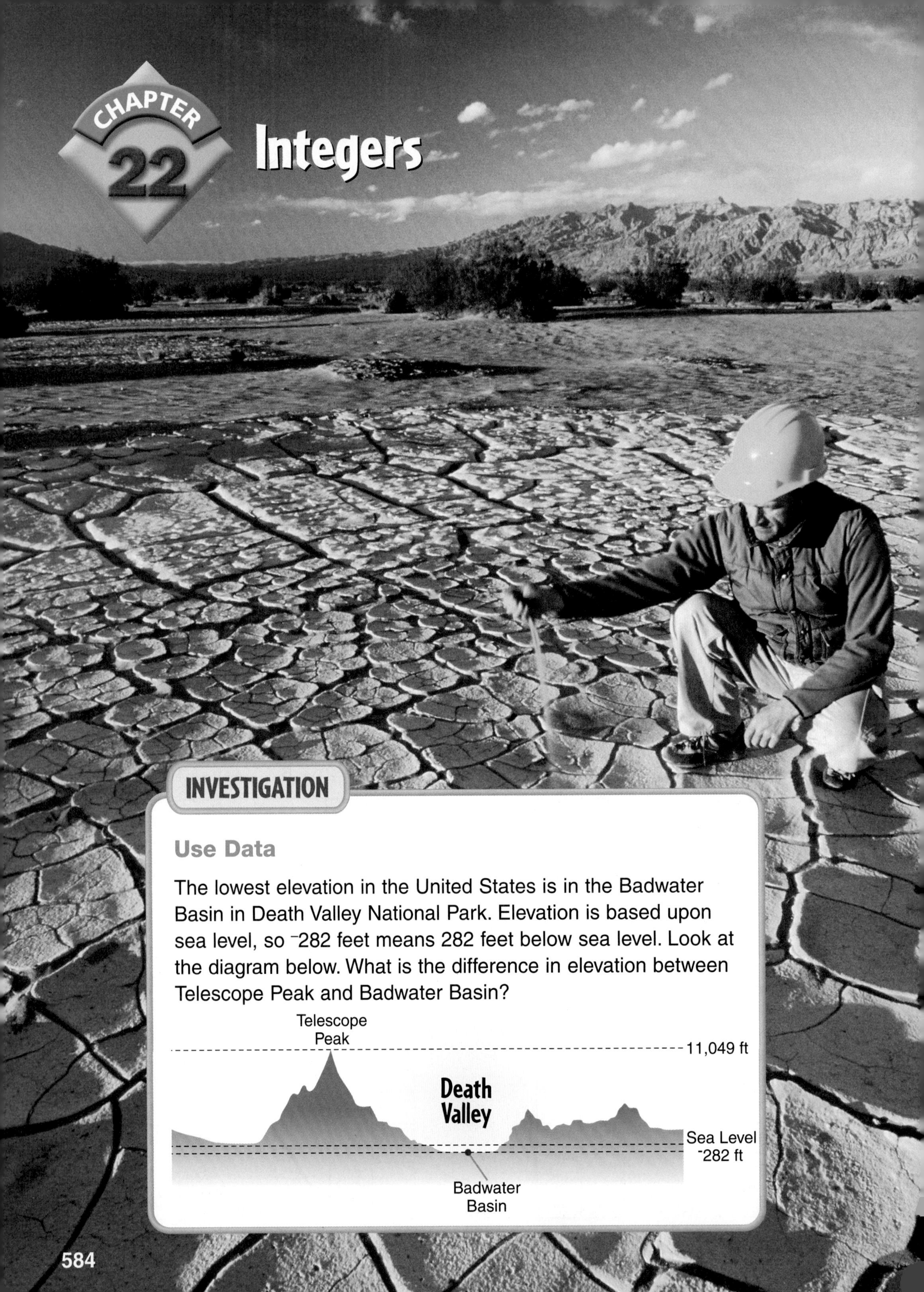

CHAPTER 22 Integers

INVESTIGATION

Use Data

The lowest elevation in the United States is in the Badwater Basin in Death Valley National Park. Elevation is based upon sea level, so $^-282$ feet means 282 feet below sea level. Look at the diagram below. What is the difference in elevation between Telescope Peak and Badwater Basin?

Chapter Pretest

Use this page to review and remember what you need to know for this chapter.

VOCABULARY

Choose the best word to complete each sentence.

1. Use a ____ to measure temperature.
2. On a ____, numbers are assigned to equally spaced points.
3. The temperature ⁻5°C is read as "five degrees ____ zero Celsius."

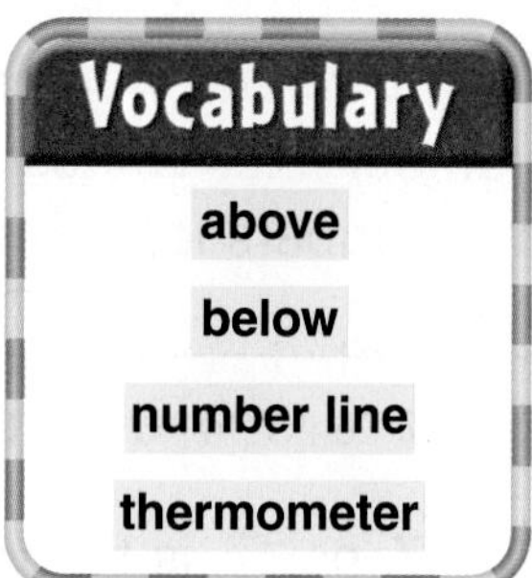

CONCEPTS AND SKILLS

Compare. Write >, <, or = for each ⬭.

4. 357 ⬭ 375
5. 89 ⬭ 98
6. 0.7 ⬭ 0.70
7. 2 ⬭ 0.2

Add or subtract.

8. 156 + 10
9. 459 − 250
10. 348 + 121
11. 627 − 227

Write each missing number.

12. 75, ■, 85, 90, ■, 100, 105
13. 75, 100, ■, ■, 175, 200, ■
14. 47, 51, ■, 59, ■, 67, 71
15. 200, ■, 450, 575, ■, 825, ■

Write each temperature in °F.

16. 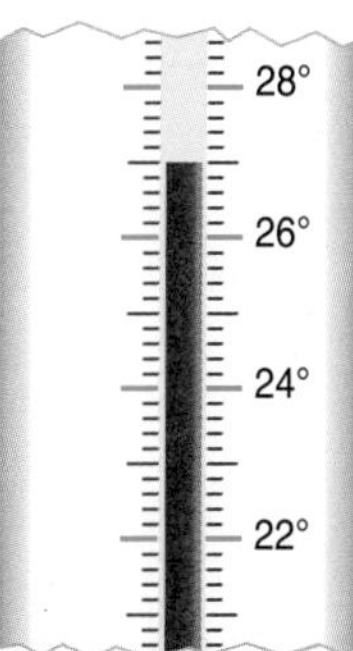

17. 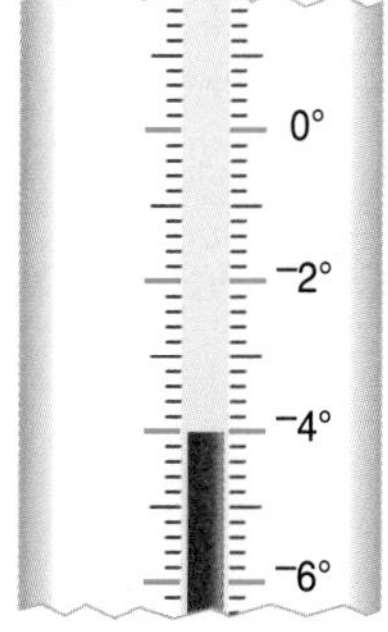

18. 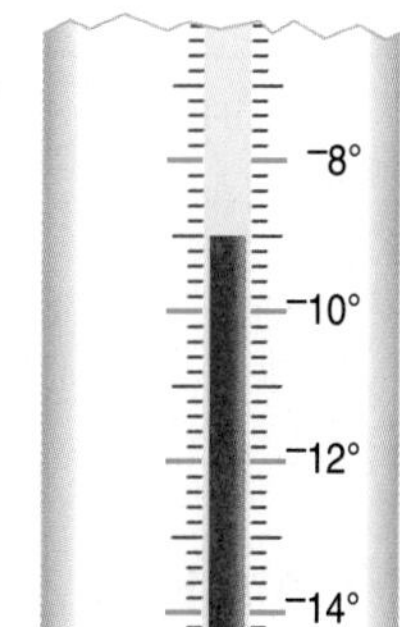

19. 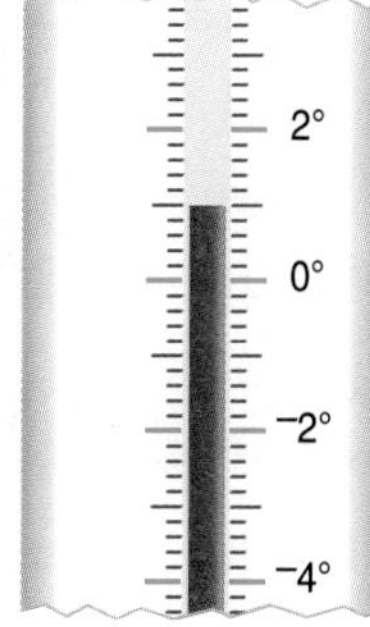

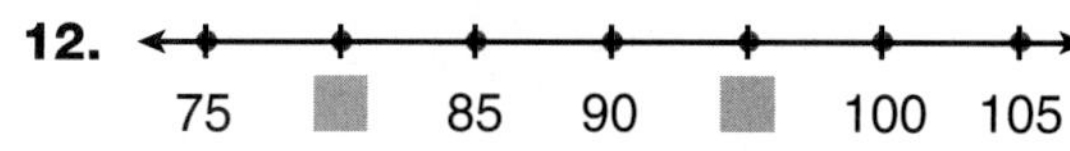

20. Suppose the temperature at 8:00 A.M. is 6°F and at 8:00 P.M. is ⁻2°F. How many degrees did the temperature drop? Use pictures or words to explain your answer.

Test Prep on the Net

Visit *Education Place* at **eduplace.com/kids/mw/** for more review.

Lesson 1

Integers and Absolute Value

Objective Identify integers and find the absolute value of an integer.

e Glossary

Vocabulary

positive numbers
opposite
integers
absolute value

Learn About It

Positive numbers, numbers greater than zero, can be shown on a number line. You can extend the number line from zero to show numbers less than zero, called the *negative numbers*.

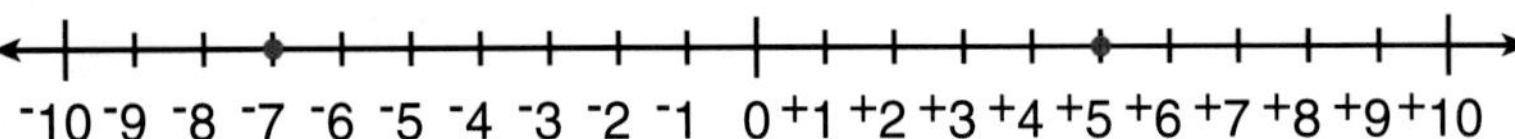

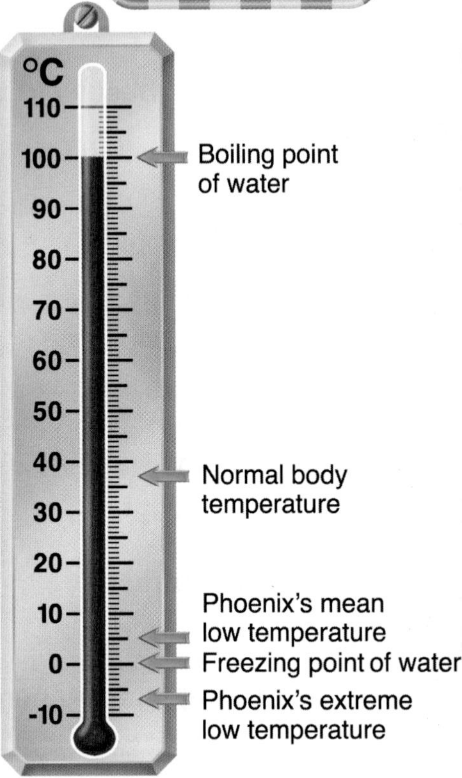

Negative 7, or $^-7$, is the **opposite** of positive 7, or $^+7$. The set of **integers** includes zero, the counting numbers, and their opposites.

To write the opposite of an integer, change its sign.

The opposite of $^+8$ is $^-8$. The opposite of $^-15$ is $^+15$.

Opposite numbers are the same distance from zero on the number line. A number's distance from zero is called its **absolute value.** The absolute value of $^-3$ and $^+3$ is 3 because both are 3 units from zero.

Finding Absolute Value

What is the absolute value of $^+5$?

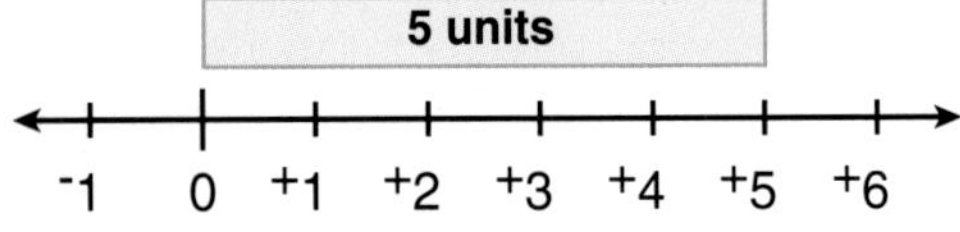

What is the absolute value of $^-4$?

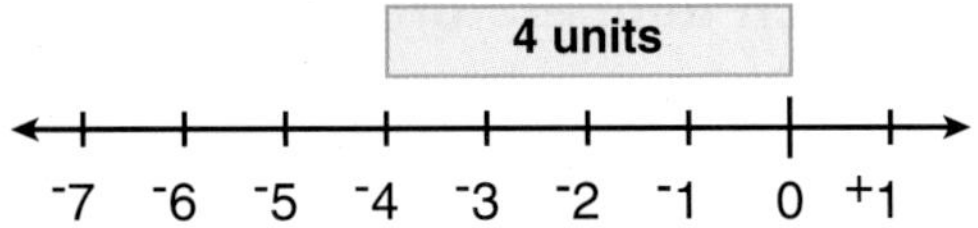

Solution: The absolute value of $^+5$ is 5. The absolute value of $^-4$ is 4.

Guided Practice

Write the opposite of each integer.

1. $^-9$ **2.** $^+6$ **3.** $^-4$ **4.** $^-45$ **5.** $^+134$ **6.** $^+87$

Write the absolute value of each integer.

7. $^+3$ **8.** $^-1$ **9.** $^-8$ **10.** 0 **11.** $^+11$ **12.** $^-23$

Explain Your Thinking ▶ Is the absolute value of an integer the same as the opposite of that integer? Explain.

Practice and Problem Solving

Write the opposite of each integer.

13. $^{-}17$	**14.** $^{-}30$	**15.** $^{+}6$	**16.** $^{-}12$	**17.** $^{+}28$	**18.** $^{+}106$
19. $^{+}82$	**20.** $^{+}184$	**21.** $^{+}19$	**22.** $^{-}44$	**23.** $^{+}102$	**24.** $^{-}59$

Write the absolute value of each integer.

25. $^{+}7$	**26.** $^{-}6$	**27.** $^{+}1$	**28.** $^{-}7$	**29.** $^{-}16$	**30.** $^{-}9$
31. $^{-}10$	**32.** $^{+}15$	**33.** $^{+}6$	**34.** $^{-}3$	**35.** $^{+}8$	**36.** $^{+}10$

Data **Use the graph to solve Problems 37–40.**

37. Which city had an extreme low temperature of $^{-}16$°C?

38. Mental Math Which two temperatures shown on the graph are opposites?

39. Estimate Which city does not have about a 20°C difference between its mean and extreme low temperatures?

40. Charleston, South Carolina, has an extreme low temperature of $^{-}14$°C. Which city from the graph has that same extreme low temperature?

41. Represent Mobile, Alabama, is about 8 feet above sea level. New Orleans, Louisiana, is about 5 feet below sea level. Draw a graph to show the elevations of these two cities.

42. Explain Zero is not positive or negative. What is the opposite of 0?

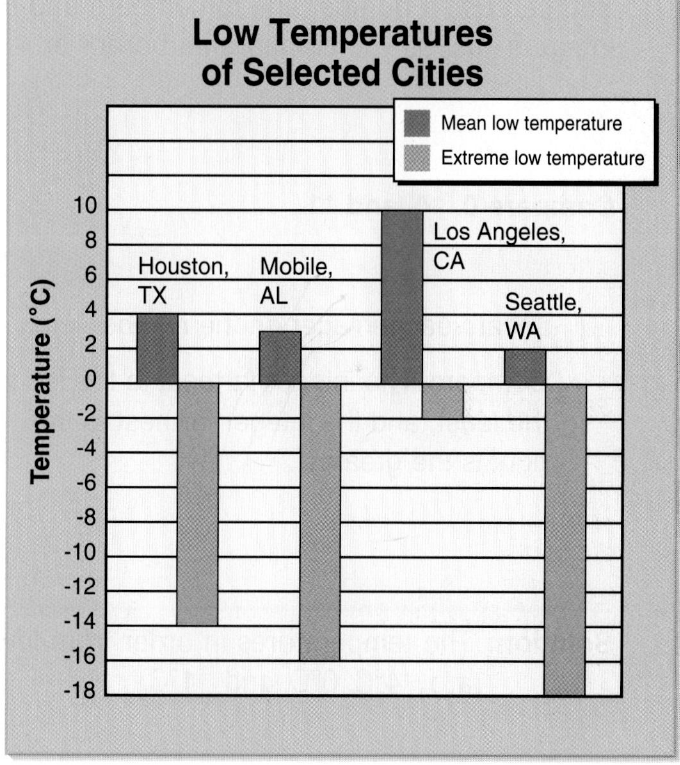

Daily Review | Test Prep

Solve each equation. (Ch. 21, Lesson 2)

43. $55 = 11y$ **44.** $n \div 6 = 5$

45. $x \div 8 = 2$ **46.** $6c = 18$

47. $c \div 9 = 45$ **48.** $3x = 33$

49. The lowest point in the United States is in Death Valley, California. Its elevation is $^{-}282$ feet. What is the absolute value of this elevation?

A $^{-}2$ **B** $^{-}282$ **C** 2 **D** 282

Extra Practice See page 607, Set A.

Lesson 2

Compare and Order Integers

Objective Use a number line to compare integers.

Learn About It

People in northern climates expect snow in the winter. Snow crystals have different shapes depending on the temperature at which they are formed.

At 0°C, water begins to freeze, and ice crystals shaped like thin plates begin to form. At $^{-}4$°C, the crystals look like needles. At $^{+}1$°C, the ice crystals begin to melt. Order the temperatures from lowest to highest.

You can use a number line to compare and order integers, just as you compare and order other numbers.

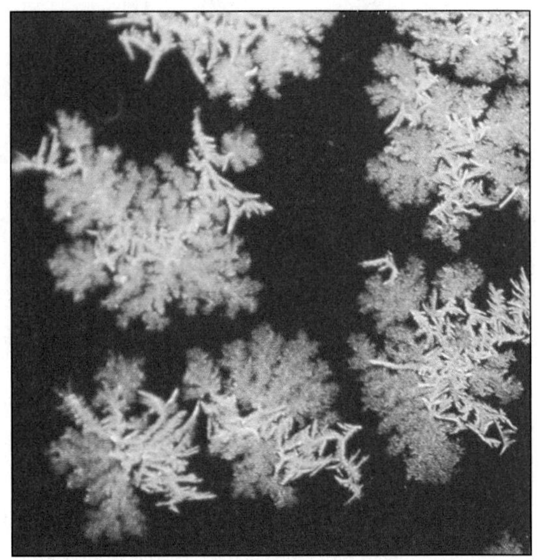

Compare 0, $^{-}4$, and $^{+}1$.

Locate each integer on the number line.

Compare. The integer farthest to the left is the least, and the integer farthest to the right is the greatest.

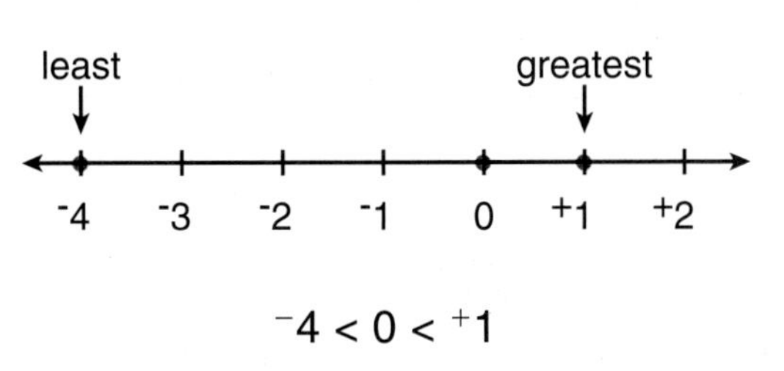

$^{-}4 < 0 < {}^{+}1$

Solution: The temperatures in order from lowest to highest are $^{-}4$°C, 0°C, and $^{+}1$°C.

Guided Practice

Compare. Draw a number line from $^{-}4$ to $^{+}4$ and label each integer. Write >, <, or = for each ●.

1. $^{+}1$ ● $^{+}2$
2. $^{+}1$ ● $^{-}1$
3. $^{-}3$ ● 0
4. $^{-}3$ ● $^{-}1$
5. $^{-}3$ ● $^{+}2$
6. $^{-}3$ ● $^{-}4$

Ask Yourself

- Did I check on the number line that the integer to the left is less than the integer to the right?

If you are comparing two negative integers, how can you tell which one is greater?

Practice and Problem Solving

Compare. Draw a number line from $^{-}5$ to $^{+}5$ and label each integer. Write $>$, $<$, or $=$ for each ●.

7. $^{+}2$ ● $^{-}1$ **8.** $^{-}5$ ● $^{-}2$ **9.** $^{+}5$ ● $^{-}3$ **10.** $^{+}1$ ● 0

11. $^{-}5$ ● $^{+}3$ **12.** $^{-}5$ ● $^{+}5$ **13.** $^{-}1$ ● $^{+}1$ **14.** 0 ● $^{+}2$

15. $^{-}4$ ● $^{-}2$ **16.** 0 ● $^{-}1$ **17.** $^{-}3$ ● $^{-}4$ **18.** $^{-}2$ ● $^{+}1$

Use your number line from Exercises 7–18. Write an integer to make the statement true.

19. ■ $< ^{-}1$ **20.** ■ > 0 **21.** $^{-}2 >$ ■ **22.** $^{-}5 <$ ■

23. $^{-}1 >$ ■ **24.** ■ $< ^{-}3$ **25.** $^{-}4 >$ ■ **26.** ■ $< ^{+}2$

Write the integer that belongs at each point.

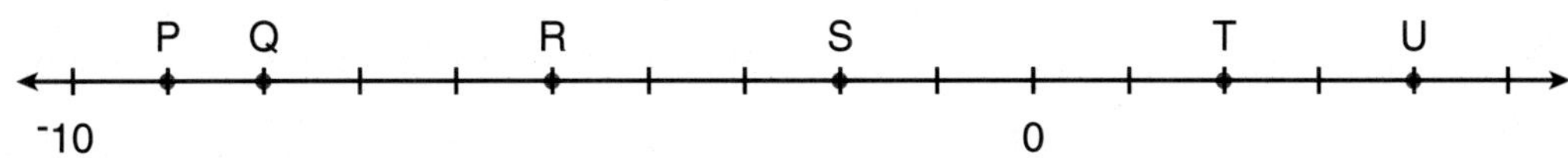

27. point P **28.** point Q **29.** point R

30. point S **31.** point T **32.** point U

Use the number line below. Write *true* or *false* to describe each statement.

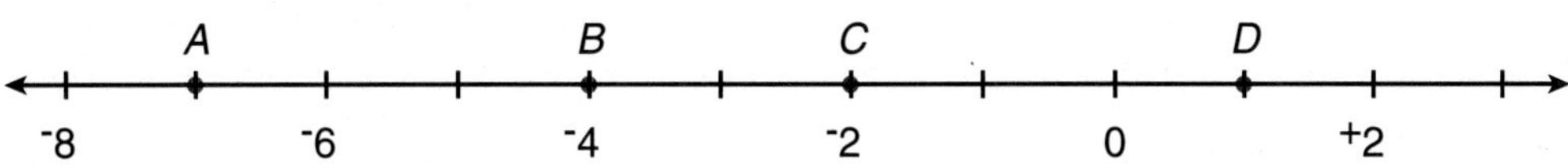

33. $D > C$ **34.** $C < B$ **35.** $D < A$

36. $A > B$ **37.** $C > A$ **38.** $B > D$

Write the integers in order from least to greatest. Draw a number line if you wish.

39. $0, ^{-}4, ^{-}2, ^{+}3$ **40.** $^{+}2, ^{-}2, ^{+}4, ^{-}5$ **41.** $^{-}7, ^{-}10, ^{-}6, ^{-}4$

42. $^{-}9, 0, ^{-}10, ^{-}5$ **43.** $^{-}3, ^{-}8, ^{-}7, ^{-}2$ **44.** $^{+}5, ^{-}2, ^{-}6, ^{+}6$

Go On

Solve. Draw number lines if you wish.

45. Ice crystals that look like hollow columns first form at $^{-}6$°C. Ice crystals called sector plates look like flowers. Sector plates begin to form at $^{-}10$°C. Which kind of ice crystal forms at the lower temperature?

46. Reasoning Hollow column ice crystals first form between $^{-}6$°C and $^{-}10$°C. They also form at temperatures lower than $^{-}22$°C. Name three temperatures lower than $^{-}22$°C at which hollow column crystals form.

47. Ice crystals called dendrites look like tree branches. This kind of ice crystal forms between $^{-}12$°C and $^{-}16$°C. Write the integers that are in this temperature range.

48. Represent Use the information in Problems 45–47 to draw and label a number line showing the temperatures at which different kinds of ice crystals begin to form.

49. Create and Solve Use the data given in Problems 45–47 to create your own problem. Solve your problem. Give your problem to a classmate to solve.

50. Explain In January in Barrow, Alaska, normal temperatures range from $^{-}22$°C to $^{-}28$°C. Which is the higher temperature?

51. What's Wrong? Debra drew and labeled the number line at the right. Why is it incorrect? How should she have labeled the number line?

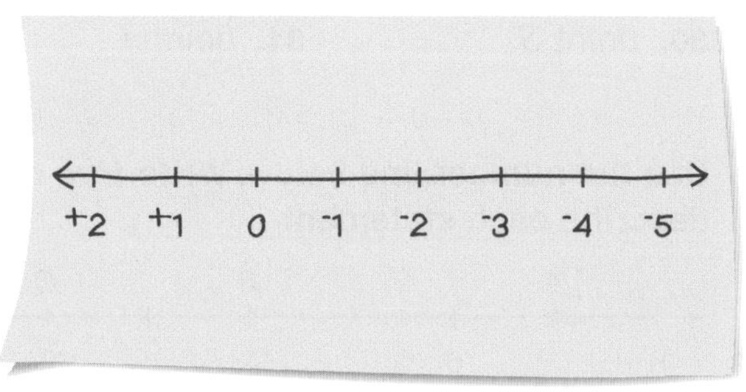

52. Write About It How can drawing a number line help you compare and order integers?

Daily Review Test Prep

Find the percent of the number. Use mental math if you can. (Ch. 19, Lessons 4–5)

53. 10% of 50

54. 5% of $10

55. 50% of 60

56. 20% of 200

57. 15% of 20

58. 35% of $60

59. 24% of 90

60. 18% of 7

61. Free Response At $^{-}15$°C, water molecules form snowflakes. From $^{-}6$°C to $^{-}4$°C, water molecules make hollow columns. Is the water temperature lower when they form snowflakes or when they form hollow columns? Explain.

Extra Practice See page 607, Set B.

Compare and Order Rational Numbers

Rational numbers are numbers that can be expressed in the form $\frac{a}{b}$, where *a* and *b* are integers, and *b* is not zero. Integers, fractions, improper fractions, mixed numbers, and repeating or terminating decimals are all rational numbers.

A number line can be used to order rational numbers just as it is used to order and compare integers and other numbers.

$-\frac{6}{2}$ $-\frac{5}{2}$ $-\frac{4}{2}$ $-\frac{3}{2}$ $-\frac{2}{2}$ $-\frac{1}{2}$ 0 $+\frac{1}{2}$ $+\frac{2}{2}$ $+\frac{3}{2}$ $+\frac{4}{2}$ $+\frac{5}{2}$ $+\frac{6}{2}$

$^-3$ $^-2.5$ $^-2$ $^-1.5$ $^-1$ $^-0.5$ 0 $^+0.5$ $^+1$ $^+1.5$ $^+2$ $^+2.5$ $^+3$

$^-2\frac{1}{2} = \frac{^-5}{2}$

Order $^-1.5$, $\frac{^+1}{2}$, and $^-2\frac{1}{2}$ from least to greatest.

STEP 1 Locate each number on a number line.

$-\frac{5}{2}$ $-\frac{4}{2}$ $-\frac{3}{2}$ $-\frac{2}{2}$ $-\frac{1}{2}$ 0 $+\frac{1}{2}$ $+\frac{2}{2}$

$^-2.5$ $^-2$ $^-1.5$ $^-1$ $^-0.5$ 0 $^+0.5$ $^+1$

STEP 2 Compare the numbers. Use > and <.

- Since $\frac{^-5}{2}$ is farthest to the left, $\frac{^-5}{2}$ is the least number.
- Since $\frac{^+1}{2}$ is farthest to the right, $\frac{^+1}{2}$ is the greatest number.

$$\frac{^-5}{2} < {^-1.5} < \frac{^-1}{2}$$

STEP 3 Write the numbers in order from least to greatest.

$$^-2\frac{1}{2},\ {^-1.5},\ \frac{^+1}{2}$$

Order the rational numbers from least to greatest.

1. $\frac{^-3}{2}$, $^+0.5$, $^-1$
2. $\frac{^+4}{2}$, $\frac{^-4}{2}$, 0
3. $\frac{^-2}{2}$, $^+1\frac{1}{2}$, $\frac{^-1}{2}$
4. $\frac{^+1}{2}$, $\frac{^-6}{2}$, $^-2.5$
5. $^+1.5$, $^-3$, $^-0.5$
6. $\frac{^-4}{2}$, $^-1$, $^-1\frac{1}{2}$

Model Addition of Integers

Materials
For each group:
10 yellow counters
10 red counters

Objective Use counters to model addition of integers.

Work Together

You can use two-color counters to model the addition of integers.

Find $^{-}3 + {}^{+}5$.

STEP 1 Use red counters to represent negative integers.

- Let 3 red counters represent $^{-}3$.

STEP 2 Use yellow counters to represent positive integers.

- Let 5 yellow counters represent $^{+}5$.

STEP 3 Match each red counter to a yellow counter.

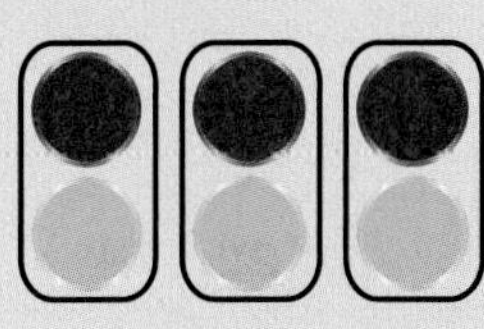

Think
A red (negative) counter and a yellow (positive) counter are a pair of opposite counters. Each pair of opposite counters has a sum of 0.

- How many pairs are there?

STEP 4 The counters that remain represent the sum $^{-}3 + {}^{+}5$.

- How many counters remain?

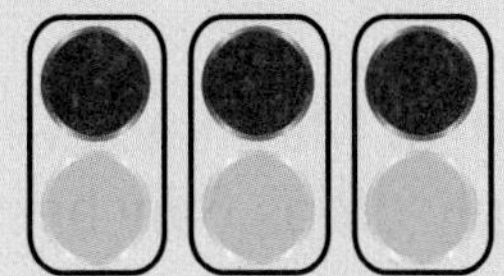

- What color are the remaining counters?

Since 2 yellow counters remain, the sum is positive 2.

$^{-}3 + {}^{+}5 = {}^{+}2$

On Your Own

Write the addition expression shown by the counters and then find the sum.

1.

2.

3.

4.

5.

6.

7.

8.

9.

10.

Go On

Use two-color counters to find each sum.

11. $^{+}7 + ^{+}3$ **12.** $^{-}6 + ^{-}2$ **13.** $^{-}9 + ^{-}1$ **14.** $^{-}4 + ^{-}9$

15. $^{-}7 + ^{+}4$ **16.** $^{-}2 + ^{+}5$ **17.** $^{+}3 + ^{-}8$ **18.** $^{-}5 + ^{+}10$

19. $^{-}5 + ^{+}3$ **20.** $^{+}7 + ^{-}6$ **21.** $^{+}8 + ^{-}8$ **22.** $^{-}4 + ^{+}5$

Use two-color counters to find each sum. Then compare. Write >, <, or =.

23. $^{-}5 + ^{+}5$ ● $^{-}4 + ^{+}2$ **24.** $^{-}6 + ^{+}5$ ● $^{+}3 + ^{-}4$ **25.** $^{+}9 + ^{-}3$ ● $^{-}2 + ^{+}4$

26. $^{-}6 + ^{-}1$ ● $^{+}3 + ^{-}4$ **27.** $^{-}5 + ^{-}5$ ● $^{-}8 + ^{+}2$ **28.** $^{-}4 + ^{+}6$ ● $^{+}4 + ^{-}6$

Solve.

29. A farmer plants 8 fewer acres of corn than normal. He plants 3 more acres of soybeans instead. Write an integer to represent the change in the number of acres the farmer typically plants.

30. **Represent** In May, the level of a town's water supply drops 6 inches below normal. In June, it rises 2 inches. At the end of June, how much above or below normal is the water level?

31. **What If?** Suppose in Problem 30 the water level drops 2 inches in July. What integer would represent the number of inches above or below normal the water level is at the end of July?

32. For 6 months, rainfall in an area was 5 inches below normal. During the next 6 months, rainfall was another 3 inches below normal. How many inches below normal is the rainfall in that year?

Talk About It • Write About It

TEST PREP

You learned how to use counters to model addition of integers.

33. If you were to combine two sets of yellow counters, what color counter would represent the answer? What does that tell you about the sum of two positive integers?

34. If you were to combine two sets of red counters, what color counter represents the answer? What does that tell you about the sum of two negative integers?

35. When you combine a set of yellow counters and a set of red counters, how can you tell what color counters will represent the answer? What does that tell you about the sum of a positive and a negative integer?

Quick Check

Check your understanding for Lessons 1–3.

Write the absolute value of each integer. (Lesson 1)

1. $^{-}5$ **2.** $^{+}4$ **3.** $^{-}6$

Compare. Write >, <, or = for each ⬬. (Lesson 2)

4. $^{-}3$ ⬬ $^{+}3$ **5.** 0 ⬬ $^{-}1$ **6.** $^{-}4$ ⬬ $^{+}5$

Use red and yellow counters to add. (Lesson 3)

7. $^{+}4 + ^{-}6$ **8.** $^{-}8 + ^{-}1$ **9.** $^{-}5 + ^{+}8$

Solve. (Lesson 3)

10. The water level in a well fell 3 inches from last year to the beginning of this year. Now the water level is up 5 inches from the beginning of the year. Write an integer to represent the water level now as compared to the beginning of last year.

Math Challenge

Target Practice

Choose one beanbag from each basket so the sum of the three numbers is equal to the number on the target.

Use counters to help you.

Model Subtraction of Integers

Materials
For each group:
10 yellow counters
10 red counters

Objective Use counters to model subtraction of integers.

Work Together

You can use two-color counters to model the subtraction of integers.

Find $^-6 - ^-4$.

Use red counters to represent $^-6$.

- What does each counter represent?
- How many counters will you use?

Take away counters to subtract $^-4$.

- How many red counters will you take away?
- What is $^-6 - ^-4$? How do you know?

Sometimes you may not have enough counters to subtract.

Find $^-5 - ^+2$.

Use red counters to represent $^-5$.

- How many counters will you place down?

You need to subtract $^+2$ but there are no yellow counters to take away.

Add pairs of red and yellow counters. Each pair represents 0. Adding zero does not change the answer.

- How many pairs do you need to add in order to be able to remove 2 yellow counters?

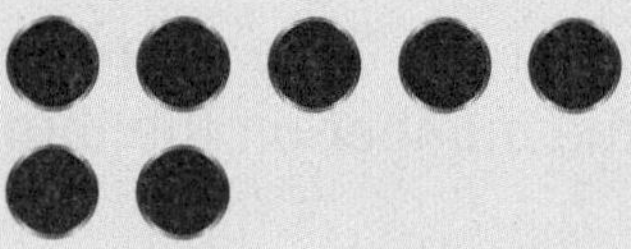

Take away counters to subtract $^+2$.

- How many counters will you take away? What color will they be?

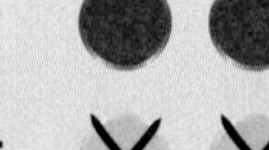

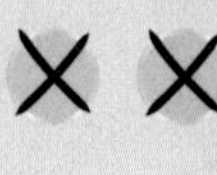

The counters that remain represent the answer.

- How many counters are left?
- What color are they?
- What is $^-5 - ^+2$?

On Your Own

Write a subtraction expression for each. Then find the difference.

1. Take away 4 reds.

2. Take away 3 yellows.

3. Take away 5 reds.

4. Take away 6 yellows.

5. Take away 2 yellows.

6. Take away 3 reds.

7. Take away 5 reds.

8. Take away 3 yellows.

9. Take away 3 yellows.

10. Take away 5 reds.

Use two-color counters to find each difference.

11. $^{+}3 - {}^{-}6$

12. $^{+}2 - {}^{-}8$

13. $^{-}2 - {}^{-}6$

14. $^{-}8 - {}^{-}3$

15. $^{-}8 - {}^{-}8$

16. $^{+}8 - {}^{+}4$

17. $^{+}8 - {}^{+}8$

18. $^{-}8 - {}^{+}8$

19. $^{-}4 - {}^{-}4$

20. $^{-}3 - {}^{-}7$

21. $^{+}5 - {}^{-}4$

22. $^{+}2 - {}^{+}7$

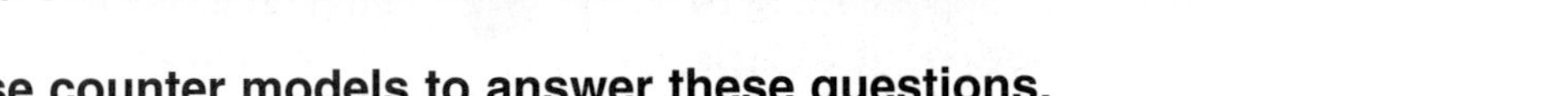

TEST PREP

Use counter models to answer these questions.

23. Find $^{-}3 - {}^{+}4$ and $^{-}3 + {}^{-}4$. Did you get the same result adding the opposite of an integer instead of subtracting?

24. How can you tell if one integer is greater than another integer?

25. If a greater integer is being subtracted from a lesser integer, is the answer positive or is it negative?

26. If a lesser integer is being subtracted from a greater integer, is the answer positive or is it negative?

Lesson 5

Add and Subtract Integers

Objective Use a number line to add and subtract integers.

e Glossary
Vocabulary
integers
opposite

Learn About It

Two winters with above-average temperatures caused a decrease in snow cover on a mountain. The snow cover was down 6 inches from normal in one year and down another 3 inches the next year. By how much did the snow cover change during those two years?

You can use a number line to add **integers**.

Find $^{-}6 + {}^{-}3$.

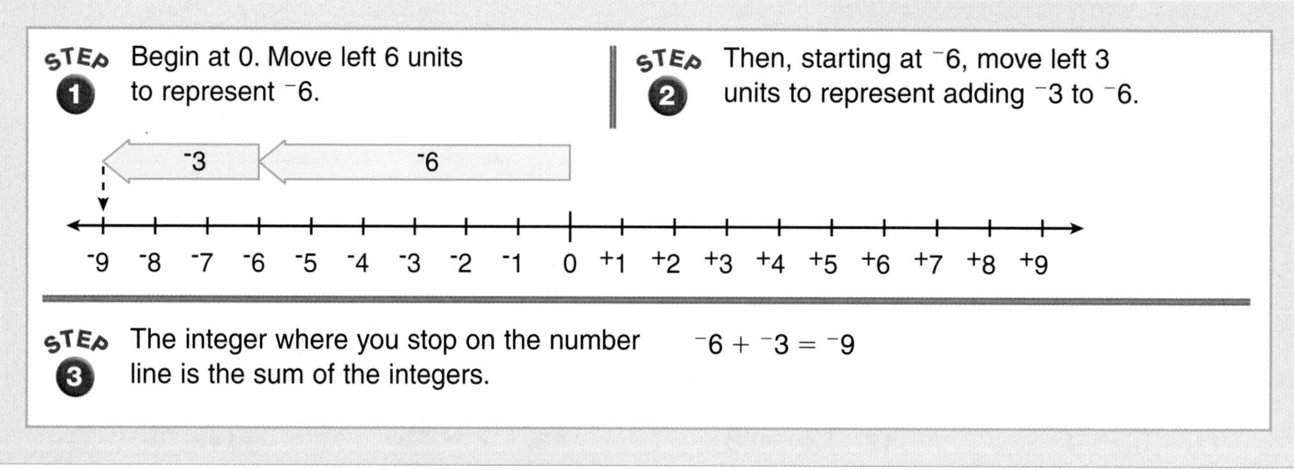

STEP 1 Begin at 0. Move left 6 units to represent $^{-}6$.
STEP 2 Then, starting at $^{-}6$, move left 3 units to represent adding $^{-}3$ to $^{-}6$.
$^{-}3$
$^{-}6$
$^{-}9$ $^{-}8$ $^{-}7$ $^{-}6$ $^{-}5$ $^{-}4$ $^{-}3$ $^{-}2$ $^{-}1$ 0 $^{+}1$ $^{+}2$ $^{+}3$ $^{+}4$ $^{+}5$ $^{+}6$ $^{+}7$ $^{+}8$ $^{+}9$
STEP 3 The integer where you stop on the number line is the sum of the integers.
$^{-}6 + {}^{-}3 = {}^{-}9$

Solution: The snow cover changed $^{-}9$ inches.

You can also use a number line to subtract integers.

Find $^{-}7 - {}^{-}5$.

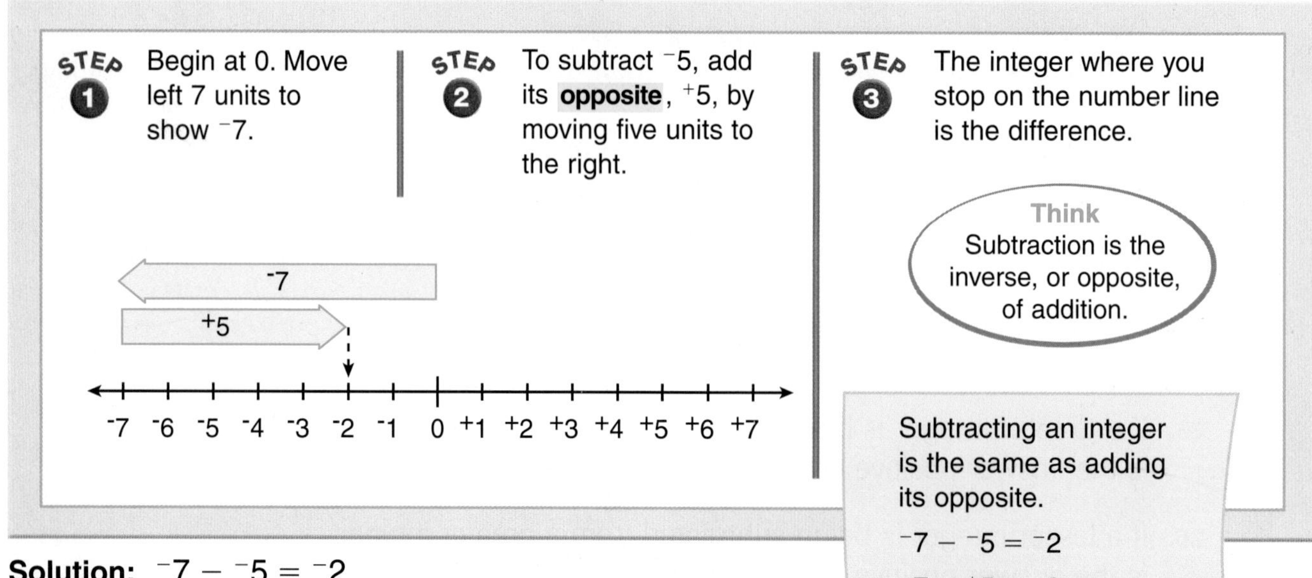

STEP 1 Begin at 0. Move left 7 units to show $^{-}7$.
STEP 2 To subtract $^{-}5$, add its **opposite**, $^{+}5$, by moving five units to the right.
STEP 3 The integer where you stop on the number line is the difference.
$^{-}7$
$^{+}5$
$^{-}7$ $^{-}6$ $^{-}5$ $^{-}4$ $^{-}3$ $^{-}2$ $^{-}1$ 0 $^{+}1$ $^{+}2$ $^{+}3$ $^{+}4$ $^{+}5$ $^{+}6$ $^{+}7$
Think
Subtraction is the inverse, or opposite, of addition.

Subtracting an integer is the same as adding its opposite.

$^{-}7 - {}^{-}5 = {}^{-}2$

$^{-}7 + {}^{+}5 = {}^{-}2$

Solution: $^{-}7 - {}^{-}5 = {}^{-}2$

Before adding or subtracting, you can use these rules to decide whether the sum of two integers will be positive or negative.

The sum of two positive integers is positive.	$^{+}3 - {}^{-}5 = {}^{+}8$ $\mathbf{^{+}3 + {}^{+}5 = {}^{+}8}$
The sum of two negative numbers is negative.	$^{-}3 - {}^{+}5 = {}^{-}8$ $\mathbf{^{-}3 + {}^{-}5 = {}^{-}8}$
The sum of a positive integer and a negative integer will have the same sign as the integer with the greater absolute value.	$^{+}3 - {}^{+}5 = {}^{-}2$ $\mathbf{^{+}3 + {}^{-}5 = {}^{-}2}$ $^{-}3 - {}^{-}5 = {}^{+}2$ $\mathbf{^{-}3 + {}^{+}5 = {}^{+}2}$

Remember
You can change any subtraction expression to addition by adding the opposite.

Other Examples

A. Sum of a Positive and a Negative Integer

Find $^{-}5 + {}^{+}2$.

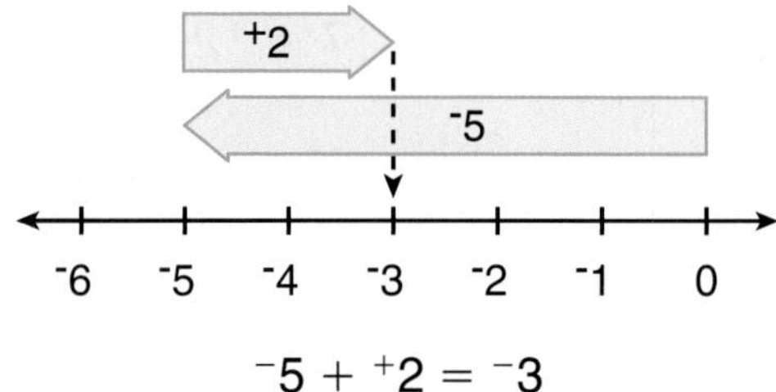

$^{-}5 + {}^{+}2 = {}^{-}3$

B. Sum of Two Negative Integers

Find $^{-}3 + {}^{-}1$.

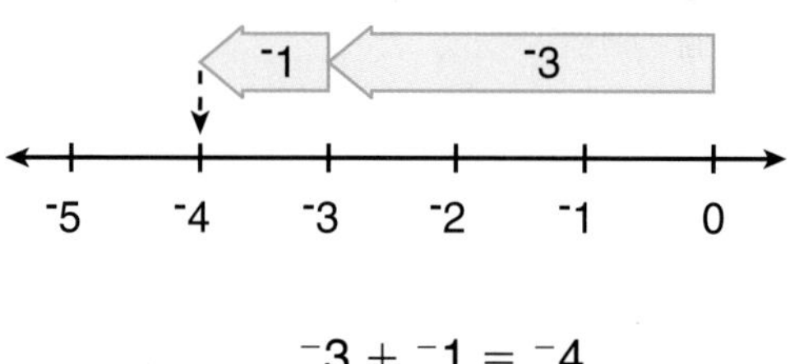

$^{-}3 + {}^{-}1 = {}^{-}4$

C. Difference of Two Negative Integers

Find $^{-}4 - {}^{-}5$.
Write a related addition expression: $^{-}4 + {}^{+}5$.

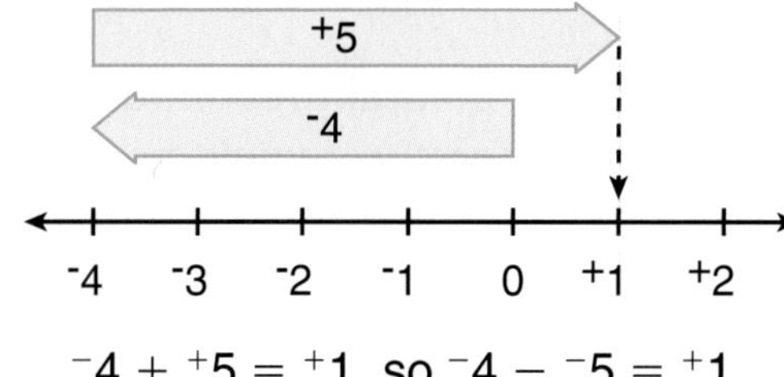

$^{-}4 + {}^{+}5 = {}^{+}1$, so $^{-}4 - {}^{-}5 = {}^{+}1$

D. Difference of Two Positive Integers

Find $^{+}3 - {}^{+}5$.
Write a related addition expression: $^{+}3 + {}^{-}5$.

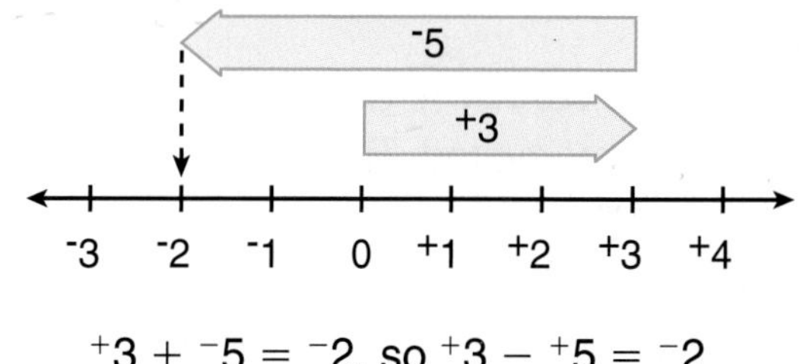

$^{+}3 + {}^{-}5 = {}^{-}2$, so $^{+}3 - {}^{+}5 = {}^{-}2$

Guided Practice

Decide whether the answer will be positive or negative. Then use a number line to add or subtract.

$^{-}7$ $^{-}6$ $^{-}5$ $^{-}4$ $^{-}3$ $^{-}2$ $^{-}1$ 0 $^{+}1$ $^{+}2$ $^{+}3$ $^{+}4$ $^{+}5$ $^{+}6$ $^{+}7$

1. $^{+}1 + {}^{+}3$ **2.** $^{-}4 + {}^{+}2$ **3.** $^{-}2 + {}^{-}5$

4. $^{-}2 - {}^{-}5$ **5.** $^{+}3 - {}^{-}4$ **6.** $^{-}7 - {}^{-}5$

Ask Yourself

- Do I move left or right from 0 for the first integer?
- Can I add the opposite?
- What is the sign of the integer with the greater absolute value?

TEST TIPS **Explain Your Thinking** ▶ Why is subtracting an integer the same as adding its opposite?

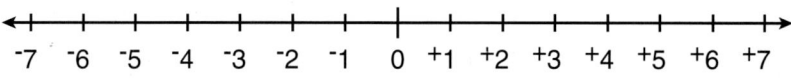

Practice and Problem Solving

Decide whether the answer will be positive or negative. Then use the number line to add or subtract.

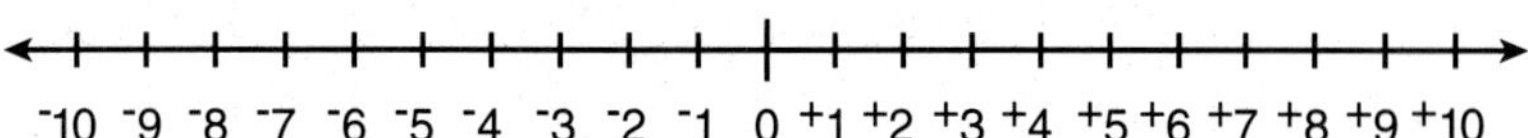

7. ${}^{+}9 + {}^{-}2$ **8.** ${}^{+}5 + {}^{+}1$ **9.** ${}^{-}3 + {}^{+}4$ **10.** ${}^{+}6 + {}^{-}10$

11. ${}^{-}1 + 3$ **12.** ${}^{+}6 - {}^{+}6$ **13.** ${}^{-}7 + {}^{+}9$ **14.** ${}^{+}2 - {}^{-}5$

15. ${}^{-}7 - {}^{-}2$ **16.** ${}^{-}10 - {}^{-}6$ **17.** ${}^{-}1 - 0$ **18.** ${}^{-}9 - {}^{-}9$

Algebra • Equations **Solve each equation. Use a number line to help you.**

19. ${}^{-}4 - {}^{-}4 = ■$
${}^{-}4 + {}^{+}4 = ■$

20. ${}^{+}8 - {}^{+}3 = ■$
${}^{+}8 + {}^{-}3 = ■$

21. ${}^{+}7 - {}^{-}2 = ■$
${}^{+}7 + {}^{+}2 = ■$

22. ${}^{+}10 - {}^{-}3 = ■$
${}^{+}10 + {}^{+}3 = ■$

23. ${}^{-}9 - {}^{+}4 = ■$
${}^{-}9 + {}^{-}4 = ■$

24. ${}^{-}12 - {}^{-}5 = ■$
${}^{-}12 + {}^{+}5 = ■$

25. ${}^{-}11 + x = {}^{-}13$ **26.** $x + {}^{+}4 = {}^{-}8$ **27.** ${}^{+}8 + x = {}^{+}14$

28. $x + {}^{-}2 = {}^{-}4$ **29.** $x + {}^{-}2 = {}^{+}4$ **30.** $x - {}^{-}2 = {}^{-}4$

Solve.

31. **Write About It** On a warm day, 5 inches of snow melted. That night a storm brought 10 inches of snow. If there is now 20 inches of snow, how much snow was there in the beginning? Explain.

32. Without the natural greenhouse effect, Earth's temperature would be a frigid ${}^{-}18$°C. Instead, the global temperature is 33° higher than ${}^{-}18$°C. What is Earth's temperature?

Daily Review | Test Prep

Use the GCF to write each ratio in simplest form. (Ch. 18, Lesson 2)

33. $\frac{16}{48}$ **34.** 20:30

35. 15 to 5 **36.** $\frac{19}{26}$

37. 7:31 **38.** $\frac{81}{9}$

39. 60:6 **40.** 3:300

41. You earn \$6 and spend \$5. Then you earn \$4 more and spend \$5. Which of these does NOT tell you how much you have?

A $({}^{+}6 - {}^{+}5) + ({}^{+}4 - {}^{+}5)$

B $({}^{+}6 - {}^{-}5) + ({}^{+}4 - {}^{-}5)$

C $({}^{+}6 + {}^{-}5) + ({}^{+}4 + {}^{-}5)$

D $({}^{+}6 + {}^{+}4) - ({}^{+}5 + {}^{+}5)$

Extra Practice See page 607, Set C.

Back Track

Start with $^{+}1$. Add as you move to each number. Find a path that leads to each sum. Can you find different solutions?

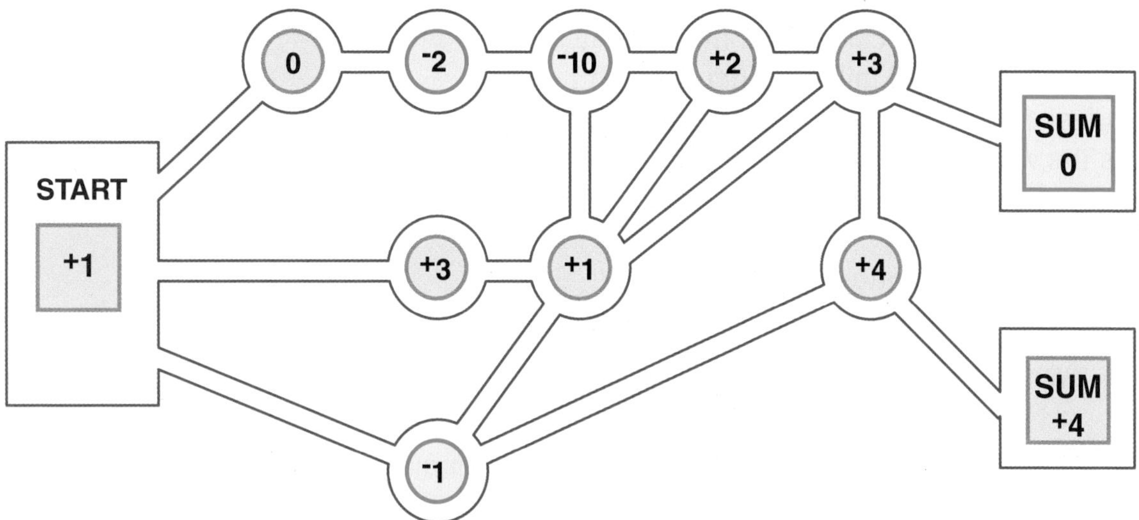

Funny Forecast

"This is the hottest day of the year, folks! It's nine degrees warmer than on the same day last year, which was fifteen degrees warmer than yesterday. Get out your swimsuits and sunscreen! This isn't going to last long. Rain is moving in tomorrow, bringing the temperature down about five degrees to 85°F."

What was the temperature yesterday?

Write your own funny forecast for a partner to solve.

Brain Teaser

Find the missing signs to make the number sentence true.

$$\blacksquare 1 - \blacksquare 2 + \blacksquare 3 < {}^{-}4$$

Ask Yourself

How can I find all the possible choices?

Technology

Visit *Education Place* at **eduplace.com/kids/mw/** to try more brain teasers.

Lesson 6

Problem-Solving Application

Use Integers

Objective Solve problems that include integers.

*The wind cools your skin and you feel colder than the actual temperature. This is called **wind chill.***

You can use integers to solve problems.

Problem When Alma stepped outside, the wind was blowing at 5 miles per hour, which made the actual temperature of 10°F feel 9° colder. Ten minutes later, the wind was blowing at 20 miles per hour, which made Alma feel 10° colder than when she first stepped out. What is the wind chill temperature now?

UNDERSTAND

What is the question?
What is the wind chill temperature that Alma feels now?

What do you know?

- The actual temperature is 10°F.
- At first, the wind chill was 9° less than the actual temperature.
- Now the wind chill is 10° less than when Alma first went outside.

PLAN

Record actual temperatures above 0°F as positive integers. Record temperature drops as negative integers. Then find the total change in temperature.

SOLVE

- Find the temperature after the first change of $^{-}9°$.

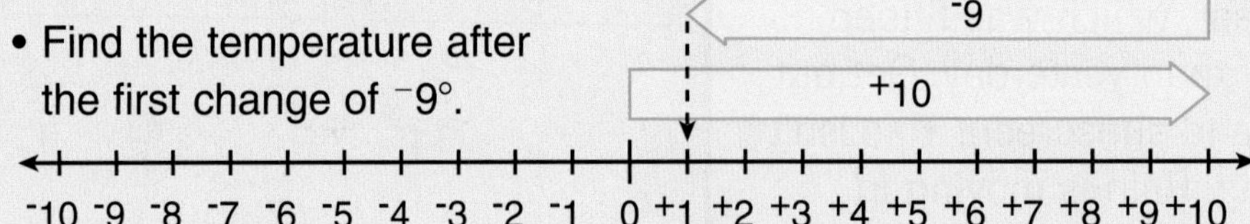

$^{+}10 + {}^{-}9 = {}^{+}1$

- Find the wind chill now.

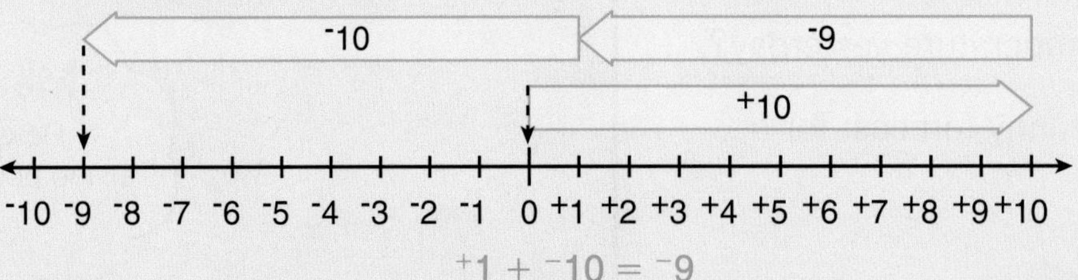

$^{+}1 + {}^{-}10 = {}^{-}9$

Solution: The wind chill temperature now is $^{-}9$°F.

LOOK BACK

Look back at the problem. How can you check your answer?

Guided Practice

Use the Ask Yourself questions to help you solve each problem.

1. Use an integer to describe the rise and fall of temperatures, in degrees Fahrenheit, represented by the set of integers ($^-3$, $^+4$, 0).

2. One day the temperature went up 8° and then down 12°. If the final temperature is $^-31$°F, what was the temperature at first?

   Hint How do you record temperatures that go up and those that go down?

Ask Yourself

UNDERSTAND What does the question ask me to find?

PLAN Did I record the correct information?

SOLVE
- Did I use positive and negative integers?
- Did I use a number line or counters to solve?

LOOK BACK Did I check my answer by working through the problem?

Independent Practice

Solve. Use a number line to help you.

3. At halftime, the temperature was 17° lower than at the start of the game. By the end, the temperature was 6° higher than at halftime. The temperature at the end was $^-16$°F. Find the temperature at the start of the game.

4. At a certain temperature, unprotected skin will get frostbitten in 30 minutes. If the temperature drops 26° to $^-48$°F, that will cause frostbite in 5 minutes. At what temperature will unprotected skin get frostbitten in 30 minutes?

5. At 6:00 A.M., the temperature was $^-5$°F. By noon of the same day, the temperature was 6°F. How many degrees did the temperature change in 6 hours?

6. At the beginning of the day, the temperature was $^+2$°F. During the day, the temperature rose 4° and then dropped 10°. What was the temperature at the end of the day?

7. **What's Wrong?** Roberta left the note below for her father. What did Roberta do wrong? What should she have written?

Dad,
Temperature now: $^-3$°
Going down to $^-12$° tonight.
That's 15° colder than now.
Roberta

Go On

Choose a Strategy

Solve. Show your work. Tell what strategy you used.

8. Estimate Antarctica's climate is the harshest on Earth. The record low temperature there was about 70°F lower than the mean temperature of $^{-}58$°F. Is $^{-}130$°F a reasonable estimate for the record temperature? Explain.

9. Calculator A liquid lake lies miles below Antarctica's ice sheet. Lake Vostok is 250 kilometers long, 40 kilometers wide, and 0.4 kilometers deep. What is the lake's volume?

10. Jacqui, Ajay, Terri, and Mason are having a race. Jacqui is not riding a bike or roller-skating. Terri is on a skateboard. Mason will not roller-skate or use a scooter. Match each person with the correct mode of transportation.

PROBLEM-SOLVING Strategies

- Use Models
- Draw a Diagram
- Find a Pattern
- Guess and Check
- Make an Organized List
- Make a Table
- Solve a Simpler Problem
- Use Logical Reasoning
- Work Backward
- Write an Equation

Choose a Computation Method

Mental Math • Estimation • Paper and Pencil • Calculator

The table below shows wind chill temperatures for actual temperatures from $^{+}15$ to $^{-}10$°F. Use the table to solve Problems 11–14. Then explain which method you chose.

11. Analyze At which actual temperature does the wind chill temperature drop 11°F, then drops 5°, 3°, 3°, and 2° as the winds change from 0 miles per hour to 25 miles per hour?

12. Predict What would be a reasonable prediction for the wind chill temperature at 10°F if the wind speed is 60 miles per hour?

13. You Decide A school in the Northeast has outdoor recess if the temperature is not too low. Use the data in the table to create guidelines for the school to decide when to cancel outdoor recess.

Wind Chill Index

Wind (mi/h)	Temperature (°F)					
0	+15	+10	+5	0	$^{-}5$	$^{-}10$
5	7	1	$^{-}5$	$^{-}11$	$^{-}16$	$^{-}22$
10	3	$^{-}4$	$^{-}10$	$^{-}16$	$^{-}22$	$^{-}28$
15	0	$^{-}7$	$^{-}13$	$^{-}19$	$^{-}26$	$^{-}32$
20	$^{-}2$	$^{-}9$	$^{-}15$	$^{-}22$	$^{-}29$	$^{-}35$
25	$^{-}4$	$^{-}11$	$^{-}17$	$^{-}24$	$^{-}31$	$^{-}37$
30	$^{-}5$	$^{-}12$	$^{-}19$	$^{-}26$	$^{-}33$	$^{-}39$
35	$^{-}7$	$^{-}14$	$^{-}21$	$^{-}27$	$^{-}34$	$^{-}41$
40	$^{-}8$	$^{-}15$	$^{-}22$	$^{-}29$	$^{-}36$	$^{-}43$

14. An old wind chill formula gave a wind chill index for $^{+}5$°F and a 5 mi/h wind that was about 5° higher than in this table. What was that wind chill index?

Quick Check

Check your understanding for Lessons 4–6.

Use counters to subtract. (Lesson 4)

1. Take away 2 yellow counters.

2.   

   Take away 7 red counters.

Decide whether the answer will be positive or negative. Then add or subtract. (Lesson 5)

3. $^{+}7 + {}^{-}3$
4. $^{-}19 + {}^{-}5$
5. $^{+}27 - {}^{-}16$

Solve. (Lesson 6)

6. On three consecutive plays, a football team gains 1 yard, gains 7 yards, and then loses 5 yards. Use integers to find the total number of yards lost or gained.

Algebraic Thinking

Math Reasoning

Patterns With Integers

You can find and use patterns with integers.

Find the rule and the missing term for this pattern: $^{-}19, {}^{-}15, {}^{-}11, {}^{-}7, {}^{-}3,$ ■

STEP 1 Decide whether the numbers increase or decrease.

The integers in this pattern increase.

STEP 2 Find a rule for the pattern.

$^{-}19 +$ what integer $= {}^{-}15$?

$^{-}19 + {}^{+}4 = {}^{-}15$

Try adding $^{+}4$ to each term.

$^{-}15 + {}^{+}4 = {}^{-}11$

$^{-}11 + {}^{+}4 = {}^{-}7$

$^{-}7 + {}^{+}4 = {}^{-}3$

STEP 3 Apply the rule to find terms in the pattern.

$^{-}3 + {}^{+}4 = {}^{+}1$

Solution: The rule is to add $^{+}4$. The missing term is $^{+}1$.

Write the rule and name the missing term in the pattern.

1. 0, ■, $^{-}10, {}^{-}15, {}^{-}20, {}^{-}25$
2. $^{+}12, {}^{+}8, {}^{+}4, 0, {}^{-}4, {}^{-}8, {}^{-}12,$ ■
3. $\frac{11}{2}, \frac{9}{2}, \frac{7}{2}, \frac{5}{2}, \frac{3}{2}, \frac{1}{2},$ ■
4. $^{-}4.5, {}^{-}3, {}^{-}1.5,$ ■, $^{+}1.5, {}^{+}3$

VOCABULARY

1. Counting numbers, their opposites, and zero are called ____.

2. Numbers to the left of 0 on a number line are called ____.

3. The distance of a number from 0 on a number line is the ____ of that number.

Vocabulary

- absolute value
- integers
- negative numbers
- opposite
- positive numbers

CONCEPTS AND SKILLS

Write the opposite of each integer. Then write the absolute value of each integer. (Lesson 1, pp. 586–587)

4. $^{-}98$	**5.** $^{+}75$	**6.** $^{+}629$	**7.** $^{-}52$
8. $^{-}31$	**9.** $^{-}163$	**10.** $^{+}312$	**11.** $^{+}98$

Draw a number line from $^{-}10$ to $^{+}10$ and label each integer. Write >, <, or = for each ●. (Lesson 2, pp. 588–591)

12. $^{-}9$ ● $^{-}4$	**13.** $^{+}3$ ● $^{-}1$	**14.** $^{-}6$ ● $^{+}4$	**15.** $^{+}2$ ● $^{-}10$

Decide whether the answer will be positive or negative. Then use the number line to add or subtract. (Lessons 3–5, pp. 592–601)

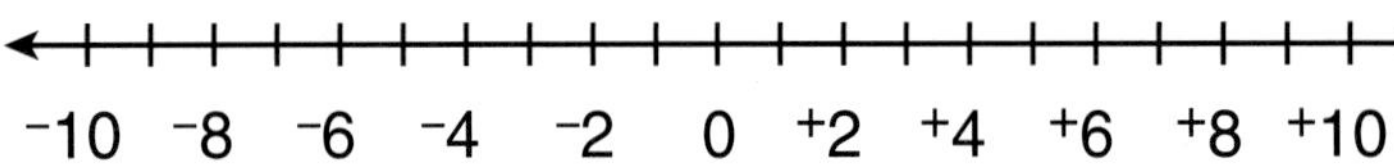

16. $^{-}9 + {}^{+}6$	**17.** $^{+}7 - {}^{-}2$	**18.** $^{-}8 - {}^{+}1$	**19.** $^{-}3 - {}^{-}1$

PROBLEM SOLVING

Solve. Use a number line to help you.
(Lesson 6, pp. 602–605)

20. At noon on Monday, the temperature was $^{-}2$°F. By 6:00 P.M., the temperature had risen 10°. By midnight, the temperature had fallen 8°. What was the temperature at midnight?

Show You Understand

From looking at the absolute value of an integer, can you tell whether that integer is positive or negative? Explain.

Extra Practice

Set A (Lesson 1, pp. 586–587)

Write the opposite of each integer. Then write the absolute value of each integer.

1. $^{+}5$	**2.** $^{-}7$	**3.** $^{+}17$	**4.** $^{+}89$	**5.** $^{-}45$
6. $^{-}72$	**7.** $^{+}100$	**8.** $^{-}36$	**9.** $^{-}29$	**10.** $^{+}55$
11. $^{-}10$	**12.** $^{+}31$	**13.** $^{-}127$	**14.** $^{+}66$	**15.** $^{-}64$

Set B (Lesson 2, pp. 588–591)

Draw a number line from $^{-}8$ to $^{+}8$ and label each integer. Write >, <, or = for each ●.

1. $^{+}4$ ● 0	**2.** $^{+}3$ ● $^{+}5$	**3.** $^{-}2$ ● $^{-}5$	**4.** $^{-}6$ ● 0
5. $^{-}8$ ● $^{+}8$	**6.** $^{-}5$ ● $^{-}4$	**7.** $^{+}1$ ● $^{-}2$	**8.** $^{+}6$ ● $^{+}7$

Write the integers in order from least to greatest.

9. 0, $^{+}7$, $^{-}5$, $^{-}3$	**10.** $^{+}5$, $^{+}8$, $^{-}4$, $^{-}5$	**11.** $^{-}2$, 0, $^{+}6$, $^{-}1$
12. $^{-}4$, $^{-}8$, $^{+}5$, $^{+}2$	**13.** $^{-}5$, 0, $^{+}5$, $^{-}7$	**14.** $^{+}3$, $^{-}1$, $^{-}3$, $^{+}1$

Set C (Lesson 5, pp. 598–601)

Decide whether the answer will be positive or negative. Then use the number line to add or subtract.

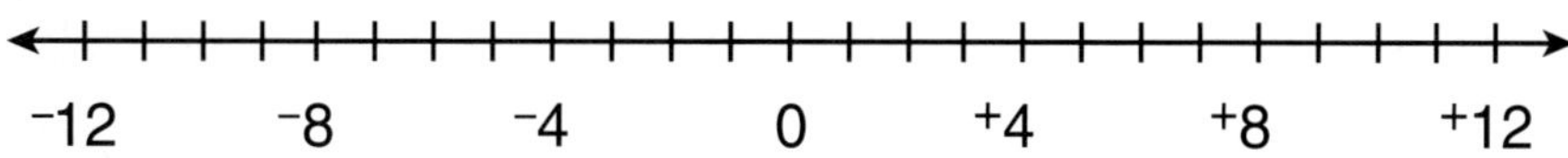

1. $^{+}4 + {}^{+}5$	**2.** $^{+}6 + {}^{-}8$	**3.** $^{-}11 + {}^{+}7$	**4.** $^{-}6 + {}^{-}2$
5. $^{+}9 - {}^{+}6$	**6.** $^{-}4 - {}^{-}2$	**7.** $^{+}5 - {}^{-}3$	**8.** $^{-}7 - {}^{+}5$
9. $^{+}10 - {}^{-}2$	**10.** $^{-}8 + {}^{+}3$	**11.** $^{+}6 + {}^{-}5$	**12.** $^{-}4 - {}^{+}4$
13. $^{+}9 + {}^{-}9$	**14.** $^{+}2 - {}^{+}8$	**15.** $^{-}7 - {}^{-}5$	**16.** $^{-}8 + {}^{+}9$

Coordinate Graphing

INVESTIGATION

Use Data

The constellation Cassiopeia looks like a giant "W" or "M". The coordinate graph shows the locations of the major stars in Cassiopeia. Which star is located ($^+2$, $^-1$)?

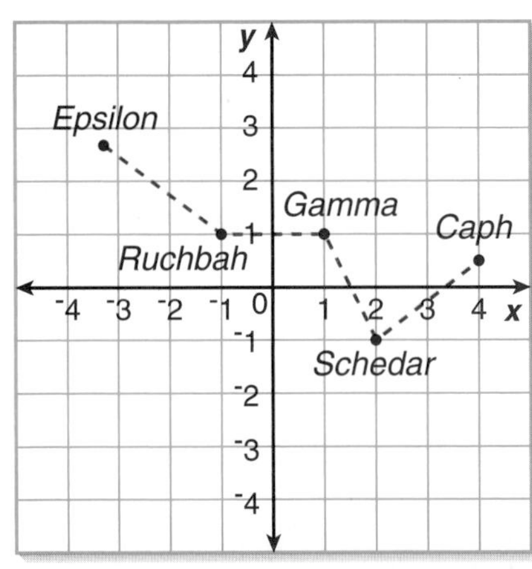

Chapter Pretest

Use this page to review and remember what you need to know for this chapter.

VOCABULARY

Choose the best word to complete each sentence.

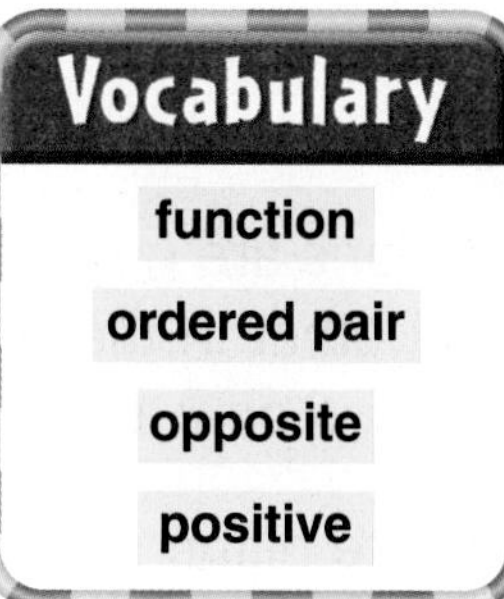

1. The number $^{+}5$ is a ____ number.
2. A(n) ____ is a rule that gives exactly one value of y for each value of x.

CONCEPTS AND SKILLS

Compare. Use the number line. Write >, <, or = for each ●.

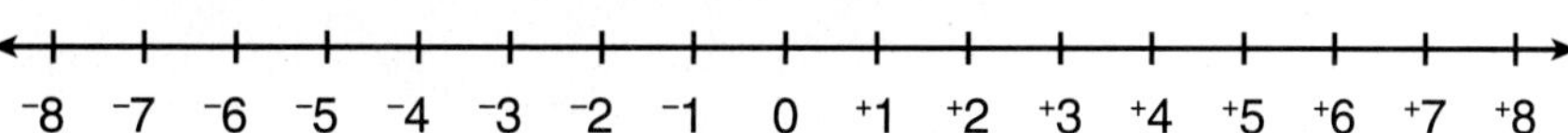

3. $^{-}8$ ● $^{-}6$
4. 0 ● $^{-}5$
5. $^{+}3$ ● $^{-}7$

Add or subtract. You may use the number line above if you wish.

6. $^{+}4 + {}^{-}8$
7. $^{+}1 - {}^{-}3$
8. $^{-}5 + {}^{+}5$
9. $^{-}2 - {}^{+}6$

Write About It

10. Describe the pattern in the values of x and y in the function table below.

X	Y
4	18
5	15
6	12
7	9

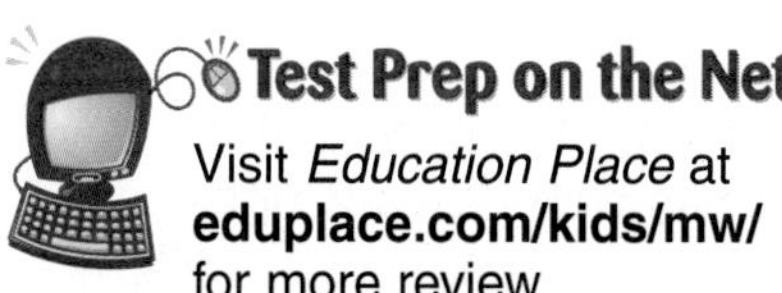

Visit *Education Place* at **eduplace.com/kids/mw/** for more review.

Integers and the Coordinate Plane

Objective Graph ordered pairs in the four quadrants of the coordinate plane.

Learn About It

Constellations are groups of stars that appear together in the sky. You can portray constellations on a **coordinate plane**.

A coordinate plane is formed by two perpendicular lines called axes, that lie in the plane. The horizontal axis is called the ***x*-axis**. The vertical axis is called the ***y*-axis**. These axes divide the plane into 4 **quadrants**, numbered I, II, III, and IV.

Some of the stars for the constellation Hercules are mapped on the coordinate plane at the right.

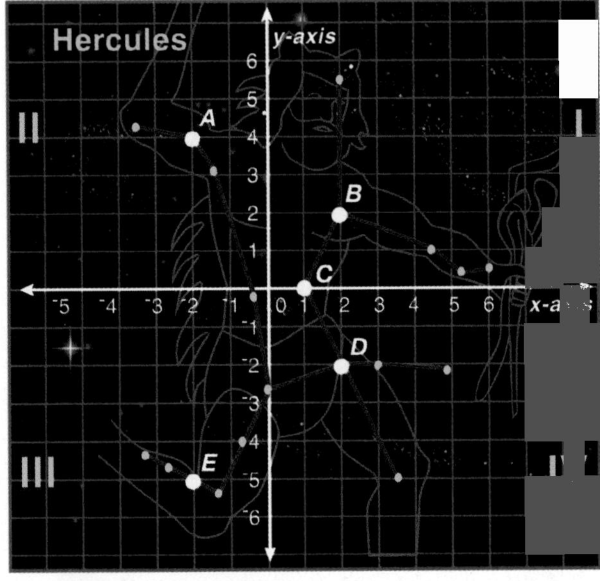

Constellation Hercules

What is another way to describe the location of the star at point *A*?

You can describe any location on the plane by using an **ordered pair** (x, y). The point named by the ordered pair (0, 0) is the **origin**.

- To reach point *A*, move left from the origin to $^{-}2$ and up to $^{+}4$.
- The numbers $^{-}2$ and $^{+}4$ are the **coordinates** of point *A*.

Solution: The location of the star at *A* is given as ($^{-}2$, $^{+}4$) in Quadrant II.

Other Examples

A. Point in Quadrant IV

- Point *D* is in Quadrant IV.
- To reach point *D*, start at the origin. Move right 2 units and down 2 units.
- Point *D* is at ($^{+}2$, $^{-}2$).

B. Distance Between Points

- Point A is at ($^{-}2$, 4) and point E is at ($^{-}2$, $^{-}5$).
- For two points, if the *x*-coordinates or the *y*-coordinates are the same, you can count to find the distance between those two points.
- The distance between *A* and *E* is 9 units.

Materials: grid paper

Here is how to use ordered pairs to represent the major stars in the constellation Volans, or the Flying Fish.

Plot the star located at point V ($^-8$, $^+3$).

- Start at the origin (0, 0).
- Go left to $^-8$ and up to $^+3$.
- Mark a point at ($^-8$, $^+3$). Label it V.

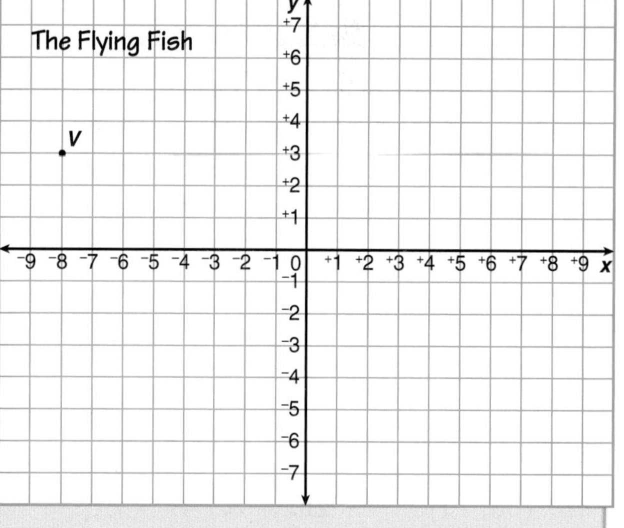

To plot the other stars in Volans, copy the graph and use these ordered pairs.

($^+3$, $^-3$) → (right 3, down 3) → point A
($^+6$, $^+3$) → (right 6, up 3) → point N
(0, $^+2$) → (no move, up 2) → point L
($^-3$, $^+4$) → (left 3, up 4) → point O
($^+7$, $^-1$) → (right 7, down 1) → point S

Remember
Always start at the origin. Move left or right along the *x*-axis first. Then up or down along the *y*-axis.

Guided Practice

Ask Yourself
- Do I move left or right from 0 to find the *x* coordinate?

TEST TIPS

Use the coordinate plane below for Exercises 1–6.

Write the ordered pair for each point.

1. L **2.** M **3.** N

Write the letter name of each point.

4. ($^+4$, $^+5$) **5.** ($^-3$, 0) **6.** ($^-4$, $^-2$)

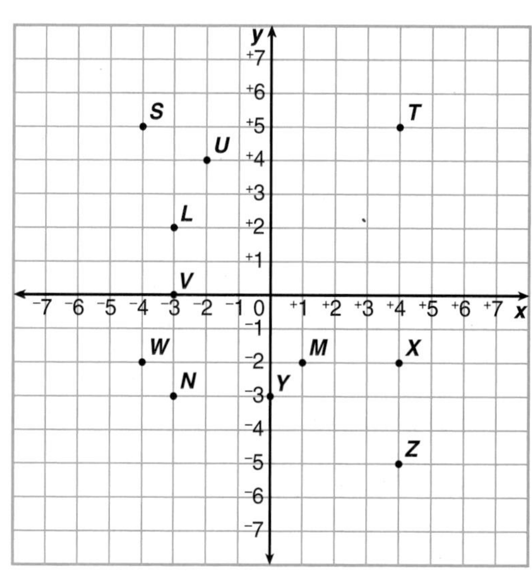

Use the coordinates to plot each point. Label each point with its letter.

7. A ($^-2$, $^+3$) **8.** B ($^+2$, $^+2$)

9. C ($^-1$, $^+1$) **10.** D ($^-4$, $^-1$)

Find the distance between each pair of points.

11. X and Z **12.** W and M

TEST TIPS **Explain Your Thinking ▶** Is the location ($^-2$, $^+3$) the same as ($^+3$, $^-2$)? Why or why not?

Go On

Practice and Problem Solving

Use the graph of the Big Dipper and Little Dipper asterisms for Exercises 13–24. Write the ordered pair for each point.

13. *B* **14.** *D*

15. *F* **16.** *I*

17. *K* **18.** *L*

Write the letter name of each point.

19. $(^-8, ^-1)$ **20.** $(^-3, ^-4)$

21. $(^-2, ^-7)$ **22.** $(^+3, ^-6)$

Find the distance between each pair of points.

23. *G* and *H* **24.** *Z* and *F*

Use grid paper. Plot points using the coordinates for stars in the constellation called the Whale, or the Sea Monster. Label each point with its letter.

25. $A\ (^-12, ^+5)$ **26.** $B\ (^-11, ^+8)$ **27.** $C\ (^-9, ^+8)$ **28.** $D\ (^-9, ^+4)$ **29.** $E\ (^-8, ^+2)$

30. $F\ (^-4, 0)$ **31.** $G\ (0, ^-4)$ **32.** $H\ (^+4, ^-4)$ **33.** $I\ (^+10, ^-5)$ **34.** $J\ (^+7, ^-9)$

35. $K\ (^-2, ^-10)$ **36.** $L\ (^-11, ^-4)$ **37.** $M\ (^+1, ^-7)$ **38.** $N\ (^+6, ^-5)$

39. Connect points *A–L* in order. Then connect *L* to *E* and *M* to *J*. Can you see the whale? Which point represents the eye of the whale?

Algebra • Expressions Use grid paper. Plot each point when $m = 2$ and $n = 3$.

40. $P\ (m + 1, n - 2)$ **41.** $Q\ (m - 5, n + 6)$ **42.** $R\ (m - 8, n - 3)$ **43.** $S\ (m + 7; n + 5)$

Solve.

44. Write About It Draw your own constellation on grid paper. List the ordered pairs. Write instructions for drawing your constellation.

45. Analyze What pattern can you find in this group of ordered pairs: (0, 0), $(^+1, ^+2)$, $(^+2, ^+4)$, $(^+3, ^+6)$, $(^+4, ^+8)$, $(^+5, ^+10)$?

46. Reasoning The constellations Taurus, Cygnus, and Draco look like a swan, a dragon, and a bull. Cygnus is not a bull or a dragon. Taurus is not a dragon. Match each constellation to its animal.

47. Explain The coordinates of each point in Quadrant I are always positive: (+, +). Write rules for the coordinates in Quadrants II, III, and IV. Explain why your rules work.

Extra Practice See page 627, Set A.

Daily Review | Test Prep 

Evaluate each expression, when $a = 2$, $b = 4$, and $c = 3$. Write >, <, or = to compare. (Ch. 5, Lesson 6)

48. $2 \times (b - a)$ ⬬ $(a + b) \div c$

49. $(b \times c) \div a$ ⬬ $(10 \div a) + a$

50. In which quadrant would the ordered pair ($^-3$, $^+2$) appear?

A I

B III

C II

D IV

Where's the Spaceship?

2 Players

What You'll Need • grid paper • colored pencils

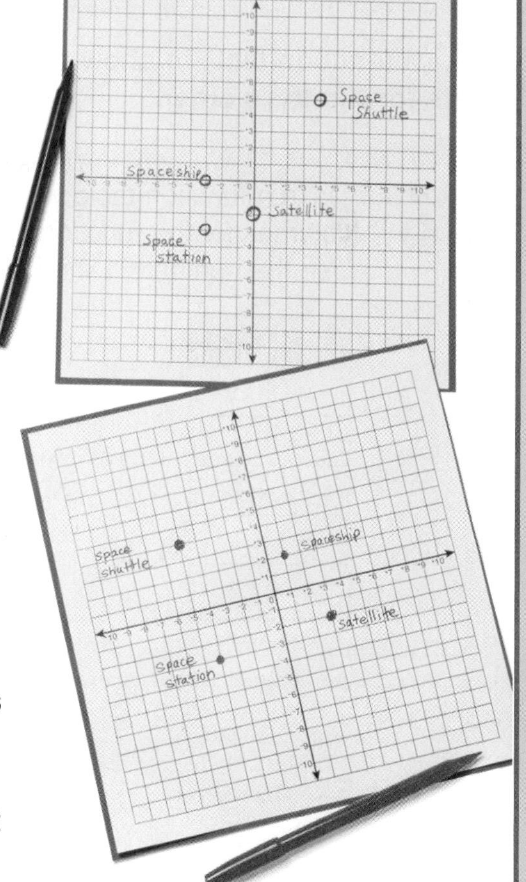

How to Play

1. Each player draws a coordinate plane on a sheet of grid paper and labels the *x*-axis from $^-10$ to $^+10$ and the *y*-axis from $^-10$ to $^+10$.

2. Each player marks the location of 4 spacecraft on the graph without showing the other player. Each spacecraft should be located at a different pair of coordinates.
   - Satellite
   - Spaceship
   - Space shuttle
   - Space station

3. The object of the game is to find each other's spacecraft. Players take turns naming coordinates to try to locate the other player's spacecraft.

4. After each attempt, tell the player if the spacecraft was located or give a hint by telling whether the spacecraft is above, below, to the left of, or to the right of the named point.

The first player to find all the other player's spacecraft wins the game.

Lesson 2

Algebra

Integers and Functions

Objective Use a function rule to find the value of ordered pairs.

Learn About It

You learned that a **function** relates the value of two variables, such as x and y. For each value of x, there is exactly one related value of y.

Kirsten ordered some space posters. Each poster cost \$2, and there was a shipping charge of \$3 per order.

The total cost of Kirsten's order is a function of the number of posters she orders. She can use the equation $y = 2x + 3$, where x is the number of posters ordered.

$$y = 2x + 3$$

total cost (y) — number of posters ordered (x) — shipping cost (3)

Make a function table to show the possible total costs for Kirsten's order.

STEP 1 Make a function table with x and y columns for the function $y = 2x + 3$. Use the numbers 1 through 4 for x.

$y = 2x + 3$	
x	y
1	
2	
3	
4	

STEP 2 Substitute each value of x into the function to find the value of y.

$y = 2x + 3$		
x	y	
1	5	$(2 \times 1) + 3 = 2 + 3$
2	7	$(2 \times 2) + 3 = 4 + 3$
3	9	$(2 \times 3) + 3 = 6 + 3$
4	11	$(2 \times 4) + 3 = 8 + 3$

Positive 5 can be written as $^{+}5$ or 5

Another Example

Integers as values

In a function, the values for x and y also can be negative.

Substitute to find y.

$y = x - 6$		
x	y	
10	4	$10 - 6$
6	0	$6 - 6$
2	$^{-}4$	$2 - 6$
$^{-}2$	$^{-}8$	$^{-}2 - 6$

Think
$2 + {}^{-}6$
$^{-}2 + {}^{-}6$

Guided Practice

Ask Yourself

- Did I substitute the correct value for the variable?
- Can I see a pattern that will help me find the rule?

Complete the function table.

1. Function: $y = 3 - x$

x	y
$^{-}2$	5
$^{-}1$	■
0	■

2. Function: $y = 2x$

x	y
3	6
5	■
10	■

Explain Your Thinking ▶ Why is it helpful to organize the x- and y-values in a function table?

Practice and Problem Solving

Complete the function table.

3. $y = x + 5$

x	y
$^{-}2$	■
$^{-}1$	■
0	■
1	■

4. $y = x - 5$

x	y
3	■
4	■
5	■
6	■

5. $y = 5x$

x	y
3	■
2	■
1	■
0	■

Solve.

6. The cost for souvenir star charts is $12 each plus $5 shipping per order. Make a table to show the total cost for ordering 1, 2, 3, 4, or 5 charts.

7. Reasoning Together Bob and Deb scored 28 points. Bob scored 4 more points than Deb. How many points did each person score?

8. Kirk puts money in his savings account each month and his father then adds $5. Write a function to describe how much money is put in the account each month.

9. Analyze Who will win the game? Jodi started with 17 points, lost 6, and gained 4. Sara started with 11 points, gained 8, and lost 2?

Daily Review | Test Prep

Multiply or divide. (Ch. 12, Lessons 2–3, 5–6)

10. $\frac{2}{3} \times \frac{1}{2}$

11. $10\frac{4}{5} \times \frac{3}{4}$

12. $6 \div \frac{2}{3}$

13. $2\frac{1}{4} \div \frac{3}{4}$

14. Free Response The function $a = e + {}^{-}4$ expresses Anne's age (a) in terms of Earl's age (e). How old will Anne be when Earl is 27? Explain how you found your answer.

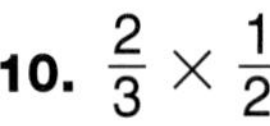

Extra Practice See page 627, Set B.

Algebra

Use Functions and Graphs

Objective Graph an equation on a coordinate plane.

Learn About It

You can use both a function table and a graph to show the corresponding *x*- and *y*-values of a function rule.

In the last lesson, you saw that $y = 2x + 3$ shows the total cost (y) for the number of posters (x) that Kirsten ordered.

You can graph $y = 2x + 3$ to show the possible total costs for different orders.

$y = 2x + 3$

x	y	Ordered Pair
1	5	(1, 5)
2	7	(2, 7)
3	9	(3, 9)

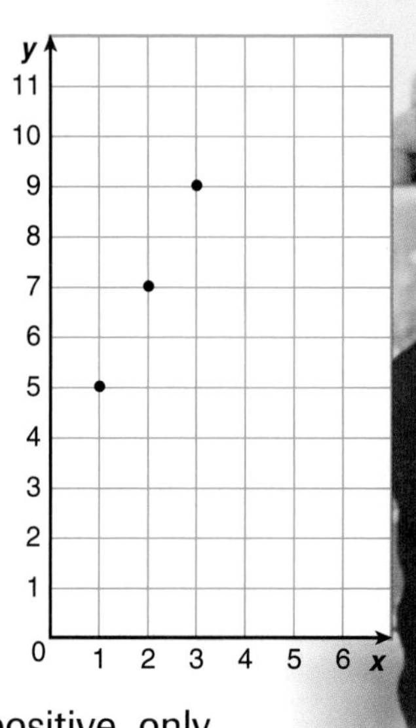

Notice that since all values for *x* and *y* are positive, only the first quadrant of the coordinate plane is shown.

Since you can only buy a whole number of posters, *x* must be a whole number. So only points are graphed.

You can also graph functions that involve negative numbers. To do that, you need to show all quadrants of the coordinate plane.

Graph the equation $y = x - 2$ on a coordinate plane.

STEP 1 Make a function table.

Rule: $y = x - 2$	
x	y
$^{-}3$	$^{-}5$
$^{-}2$	$^{-}4$
$^{-}1$	$^{-}3$
0	$^{-}2$
1	$^{-}1$

STEP 2 Graph each ordered pair.

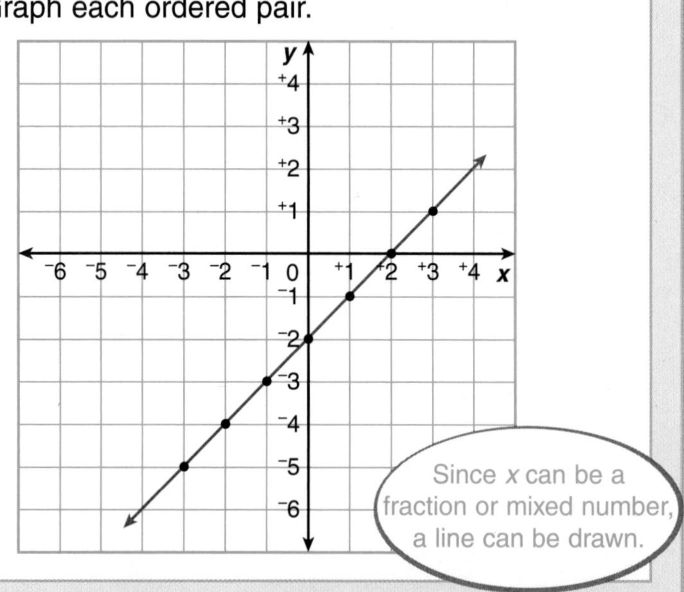

You can also use the graph of a function to predict what other pairs may be included in the function.

Graph the equation $y = x - 2$ on a coordinate plane, using the values $^-2$ to 2 for x. Use the graph to predict the value of y when $x = 5$.

STEP 1 Make a function table.

Rule: $y = x - 2$	
x	y
$^-2$	$^-4$
$^-1$	$^-3$
0	$^-2$
1	$^-1$
2	0

STEP 2 Graph each ordered pair.

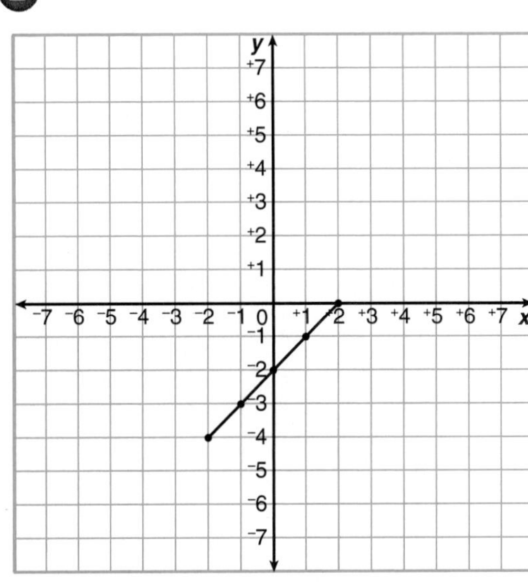

STEP 3 Extend the line. Read the y value where the line crosses the x value 5.

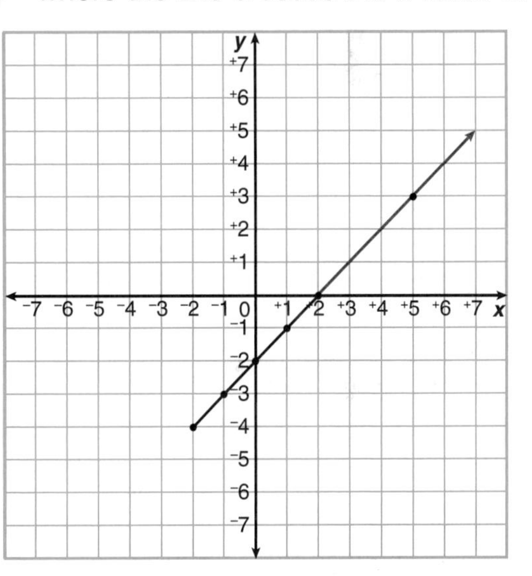

Solution: For $y = x - 2$, when x is 5, y is 3.

Guided Practice

Find values of y to complete each function table. Then graph each function on grid paper.

1. $y = x - 2$

x	y
$^-1$	■
0	■
3	■

2. $y = x + 3$

x	y
$^-1$	■
0	■
1	■

3. $y = 2x - 1$

x	y
0	■
1	■
2	■

Ask Yourself

- Did I substitute each value for x in the equation to find y?
- Did I graph the equation as a straight line?

TEST TIPS **Explain Your Thinking** ▶ How could extending the graph in Exercise 3 help you find the value for y when $x = {}^-2$?

Practice and Problem Solving

Find values of *y* to complete each function table. Then graph each equation as a straight line on grid paper.

4. $y = x - 1$

x	y
⁻2	■
⁻1	■
0	■
1	■

5. $y = x + 4$

x	y
⁻3	■
⁻2	■
⁻1	■
0	■

6. $y = 3x - 2$

x	y
0	■
1	■
2	■
3	■

7. $y = 3x + 1$

x	y
0	■
1	■
2	■
3	■

Find three ordered pairs for each function. Then use them to graph the function as a straight line.

8. $y = x + 1$ **9.** $y = x - 4$ **10.** $y = x + 6$ **11.** $x - 5 = y$

12. $y = 2x$ **13.** $y = 4x$ **14.** $y = 3x - 1$ **15.** $y = 2x + 2$

Solve.

16. Explain Graph $y = 2x$ and $y = 4x$ as straight lines on the same coordinate plane. How are the graphs alike? How are they different?

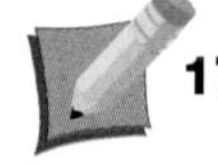

17. Write About It Graph $y = x - 2$ and $y = x + 2$ as straight lines on the same coordinate plane. How are the graphs alike? How are they different?

18. Reasoning Explain how you can use the graph at the beginning of this lesson to find how much it would cost Kirsten for 8 posters.

19. Plot 3 or more points in a straight line on a coordinate plane. Find an equation for the line. Ask a partner to check the equation.

Daily Review Test Prep

Multiply or divide. (Ch. 13, Lessons 2–5; Ch. 14, Lessons 4–7)

20. 8×0.8 **21.** 0.4×0.05

22. $4 \div 0.8$ **23.** $2.8 \div 0.07$

24. Which of these ordered pairs is not a solution for $y = 4x + 2$?

A (1, 4) **B** (⁻1, ⁻2)

C (0, 2) **D** (1, 6)

Extra Practice See page 627, Set C.

Where in the U.S.A.?

Mapmakers use a system very similar to a coordinate grid to identify positions of places on Earth. Latitude 0° is at the equator. Latitudes are North (N) or South (S) of the equator.

Longitude 0° passes through Greenwich, England. Longitudes are either West (W) or East (E) of 0°.

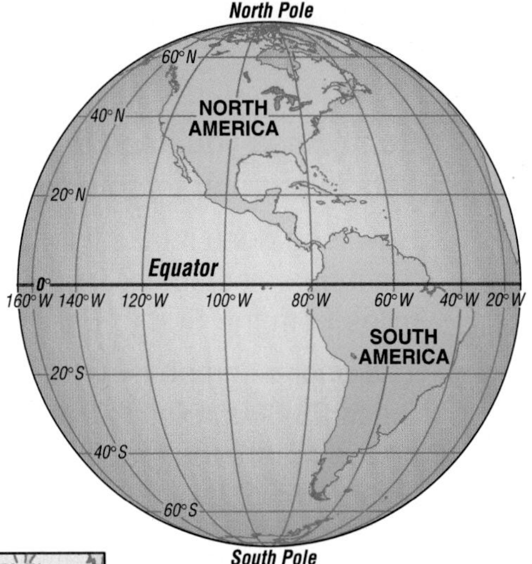

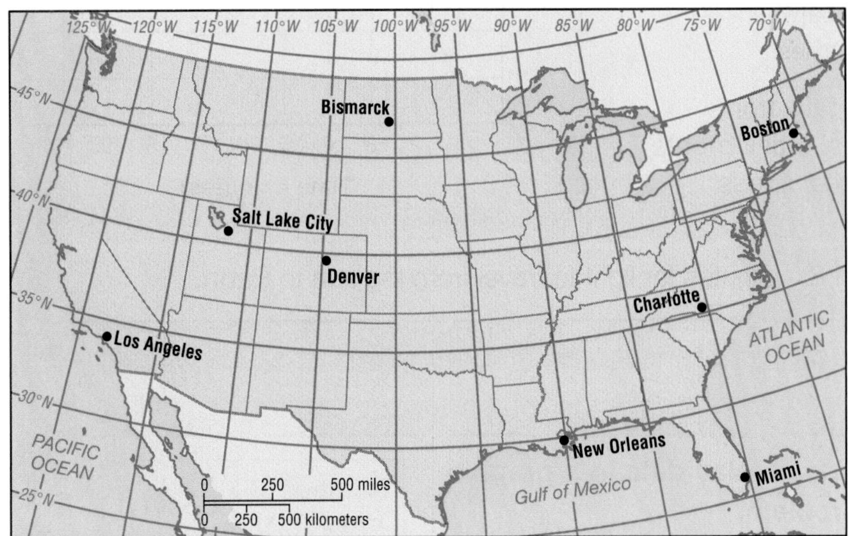

Estimate the latitude and longitude for each city.

1. Boston, MA
2. New Orleans, LA
3. Denver, CO
4. Los Angeles, CA

Use a map or an atlas.

5. Find the latitude and longitude for where you live.

Find what city is nearest each location.

6. 25°N, 80°W
7. 45°N, 100°W
8. 40°N, 110°W
9. 35°N, 80°W

10. Explain the differences and similarities of locating and labeling a point on the coordinate plane and locating and labeling a city on a map.

Problem-Solving Application

Use a Graph

Objective Use graphs to solve problems.

Sometimes you need to read the data in a graph to solve a problem.

How long does it take light to travel the mean distance of 93,000,000 miles from the Sun to Earth?

The original graph is shown in black. Since 93,000,000 miles is not shown on the graph, the graph was extended as shown in red.

Think: 93 million miles is between 90 million and 100 million miles.

A line is drawn horizontally from about 93,000,000 miles until it meets the graph. Then a vertical line is drawn to find the time.

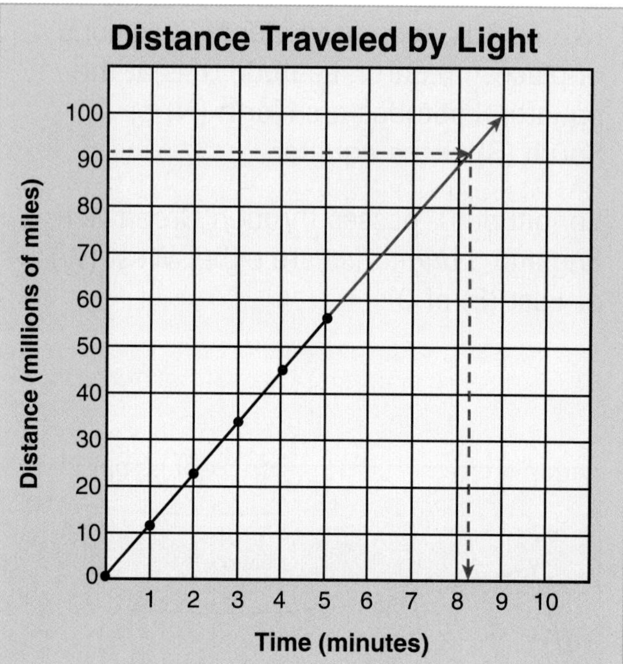

Solution: It takes about $8\frac{1}{2}$ minutes for light to travel from the sun to Earth.

Sometimes you need to display data in a graph to help you solve a problem.

One planetarium uses the table at the right to determine the cost for a group to see a show. How much would it cost for a group of 9 people?

Number of People (*x*)	Cost (*y*)
2	$7
3	$9
4	$11

STEP 1 Use the table to write ordered pairs. (2, 7); (3, 9); (4, 11)

STEP 2 Graph the given coordinates.

STEP 3 Extend the graph with coordinates for 5 through 9 people, as shown in red.

Solution: The cost for 9 people is $21.

Since you cannot have part of a person, only the points are graphed for counting numbers 2 through 9.

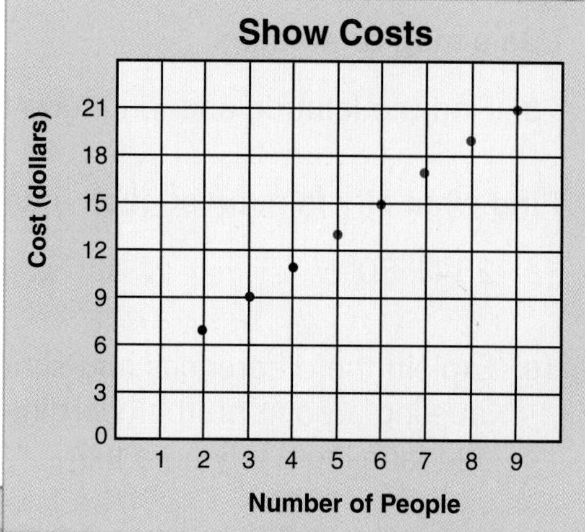

Guided Practice

Use the graphs and the table on page 620 for Problems 1–2.

Ask Yourself

- What do I need to find?
- What patterns do I see?

1. It takes light about 6 minutes to reach Venus from the sun. About how far from the Sun is Venus?

2. Using the data from table and its graph, write an equation that relates the number of people to the total cost of admission for the group.

   Hint The equation is $y = (■ \cdot x) + ■$. Look at the graph. If you extend the graph to the y-axis, what is the value of y for $x = 0$?

Independent Practice

Solve.

3. The gift shop at the planetarium marks up the cost of model solar systems as shown in the table. Write an equation to show how to find the store price (y) of any model solar system at cost x.

Cost	Store Price
\$20	\$40
\$25	\$50
\$30	\$60
\$35	\$70

4. Solve the equation you wrote in Problem 3 to find the store price for a model that costs \$120.

Comparing Weights on Earth and Mars

Weight on Earth (pounds): 0, 20, 40, 60, 80, 100, 120

Weight on Mars (pounds): 10, 20, 30, 40, 50, 60

5. **Estimate** The graph at the left shows the relationship between an object's weight on Earth and its weight on Mars. Suppose a rock weighs 15 pounds on Mars. About how much would that same rock weigh on Earth?

6. On Earth an astronaut weighs 118 pounds. About how much would that astronaut weigh if she landed on Mars?

7. **Explain** Martha says that the equation representing the data in the graph is $y = 4x$. If y is the weight on Earth and x is the weight on Mars, is Martha correct? Explain your reasoning.

Transformations in the Coordinate Plane

Objective Identify and describe transformations in the coordinate plane.

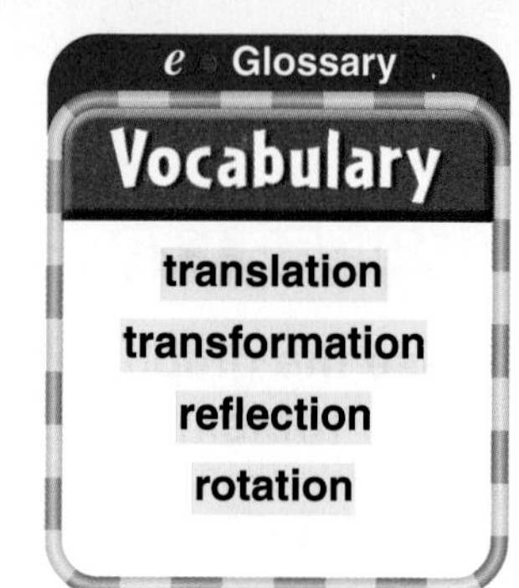

Learn About It

On Miranda's map, her home is at point (0, 0). She leaves home and walks west 3 blocks and north 5 blocks. Where is she? What **translations** take her to this point? Remember that a translation slides a point or figure a given distance in a given direction.

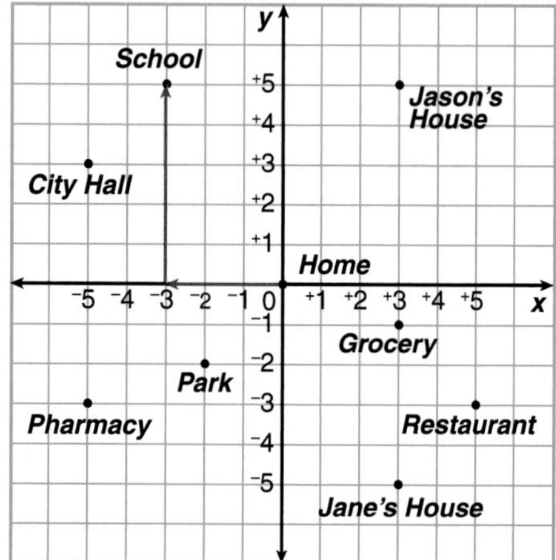

Find Miranda's location after moving 3 blocks west and 5 blocks north.

After walking 3 blocks west, Miranda is at point ($^-3$, 0). Walking 5 blocks north puts her at ($^-3$, $^+5$).

Solution: Miranda is at her school.

Try this activity to translate figures and points on a coordinate plane.

Materials: coordinate grid, scissors

STEP 1 Draw a rectangle in Quadrant I.

STEP 2 Trace the rectangle on another sheet of paper and cut it out.

STEP 3 Translate the rectangle and trace it.

STEP 4 Record the coordinates for each vertex.

STEP 5 Describe the translation you made.

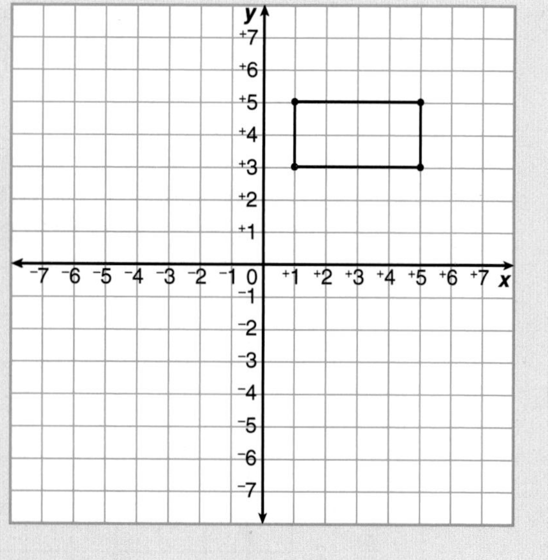

A **transformation** is a change in the position of a figure on a graph. Transformations include translations, **reflections**, and **rotations**.

Reflections and Line Symmetry

▶ A **reflection** is a flip of a figure that results in a mirror image.

Name the coordinates of points *A* and *B* after a reflection across the *y*-axis.

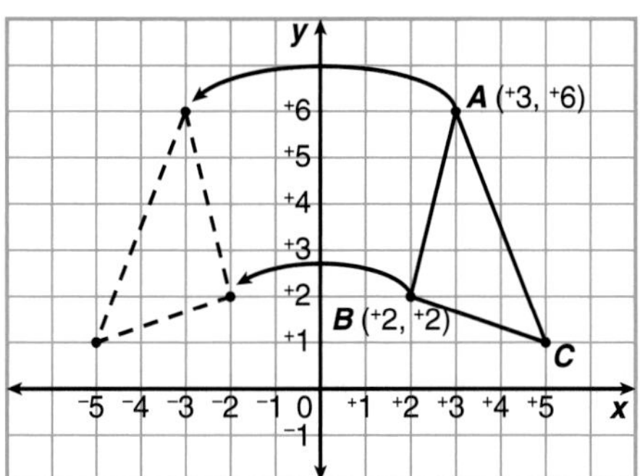

Reflect each vertex across the *y*-axis. The new points will be the same distance to the left of the *y*-axis as *A* and *B* are to its right.

The new points will be (⁻3, 6) and (⁻2, 2).

Use a reflection to decide whether the figure has line symmetry.

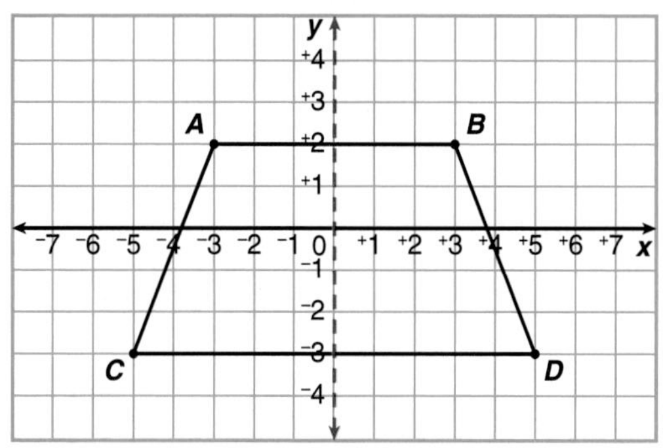

If an axis is a line of symmetry, then either its *x* or *y* coordinates will be opposites.

Point *A* (⁻**3**, 2) is opposite Point *B* (**3**, 2).

Point *C* (⁻**5**, ⁻3) is opposite Point *D* (**5**, ⁻3).

Rotations and Rotational Symmetry

▶ A **rotation** is a turn around a given point.

Name the coordinates of point *A* after a half-turn around the origin.

$\frac{1}{4}$ turn = 90° $\frac{1}{2}$ turn = 180°

$\frac{3}{4}$ turn = 270° 1 turn = 360°

Trace the axes, mark point *A*, and turn the tracing 180°.

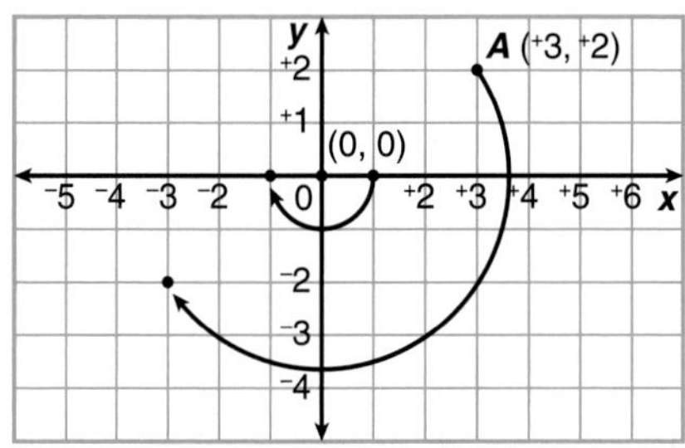

After the rotation, the new point is (⁻3, ⁻2.)

A figure has rotational symmetry if it looks exactly the same after being rotated less than 360° around a center point. When the figure turns 90°, it looks the same. The figure has rotational symmetry.

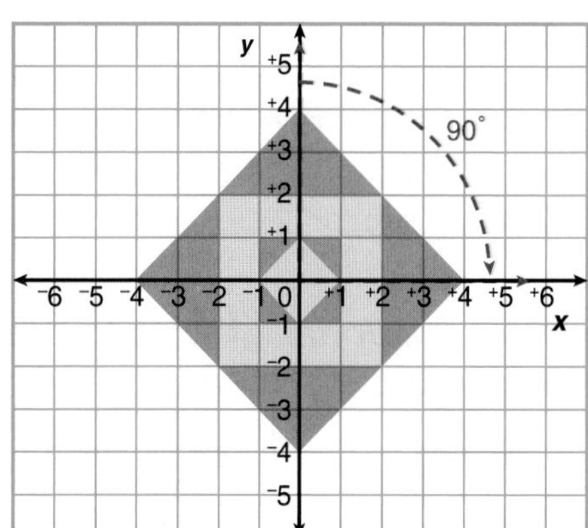

Go On

Guided Practice

Ask Yourself

- Did I move each point in the correct direction?

Use the diagram. Name the coordinates of triangle *LMN* after the transformations.

1. Translate the triangle left 3 units, then down 1 unit.
2. Reflect the triangle over the *x*-axis.
3. Rotate the triangle a $\frac{3}{4}$ turn about (0, 0).

Write *line, rotational,* or *both* to describe the symmetry of the figure.

4. 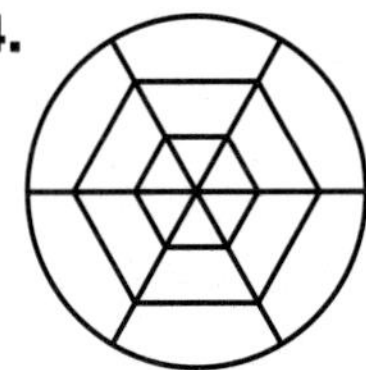

5. 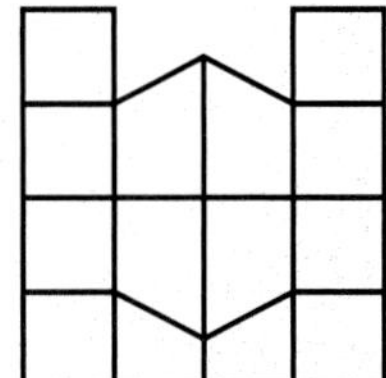

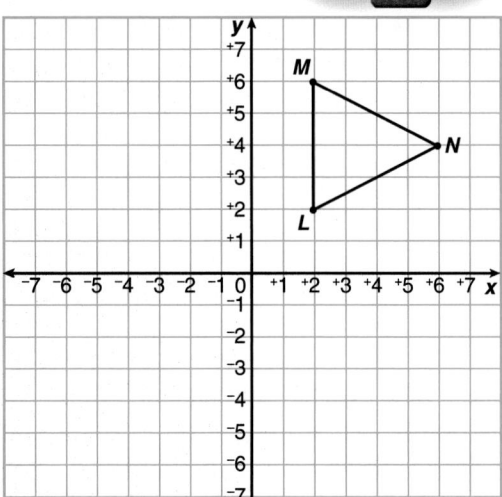

TEST TIPS **Explain Your Thinking** ▶ Does a transformation change the shape of the original figure? Explain.

Practice and Problem Solving

Use the diagram. Name the coordinates of triangle *RST* after each transformation.

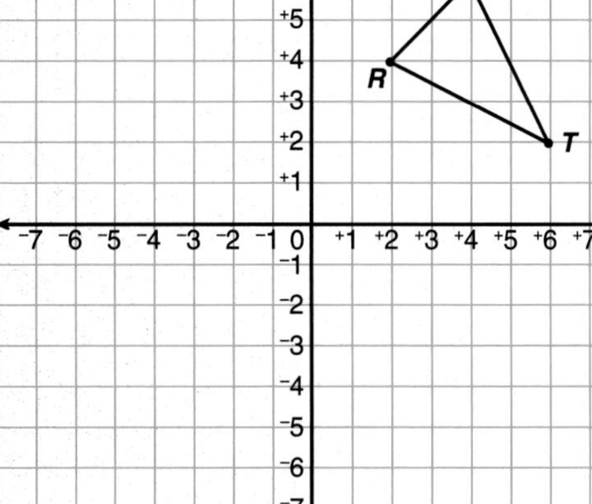

6. Translate right 4, then down 1.
7. Reflect over the *y*-axis.
8. Rotate a $\frac{1}{4}$ turn clockwise about (0, 0).
9. Reflect over the *y*-axis. Then rotate counterclockwise a quarter turn around (0, 0).

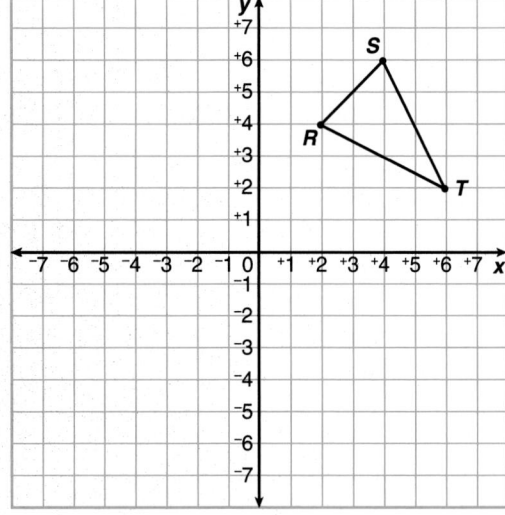

Write *line, rotational,* or *both* to describe the symmetry of each figure.

10. 

11. 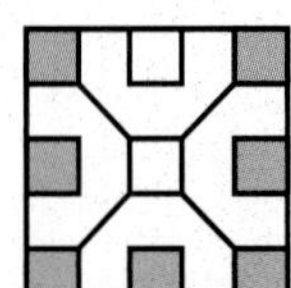

12. 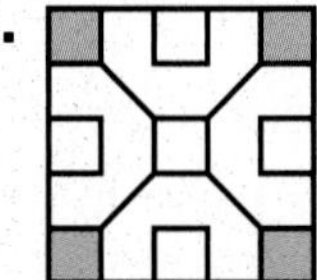

13. Triangle *ABC* was translated left 3 units and up 1 unit. It ended up at *A*(2, 4), *B*(2, 6), and *C* (6, 6). What were the original coordinates?

Extra Practice See page 627, Set D.

Quick Check

Check your understanding of Lessons 1–5.

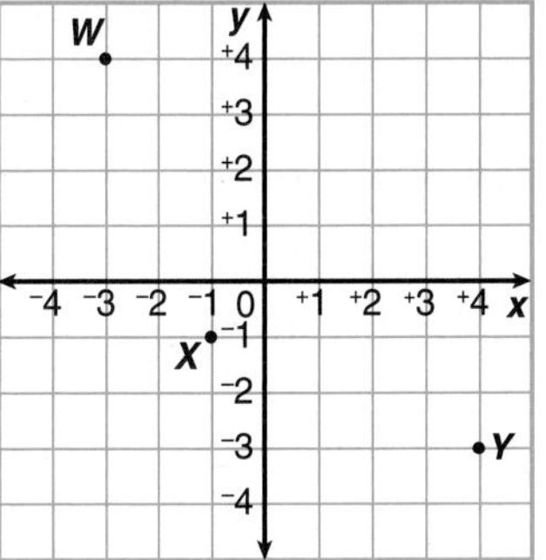

Write the ordered pair for each point. (Lesson 1)

1. W **2.** X **3.** Y

Make a table for each function. Use $x = 0, 1, 2$, and 3. Write the ordered pairs and then graph the function.
(Lessons 2 and 3)

4. $y = x - 4$ **5.** $y = 2x$ **6.** $y = 2x + 1$

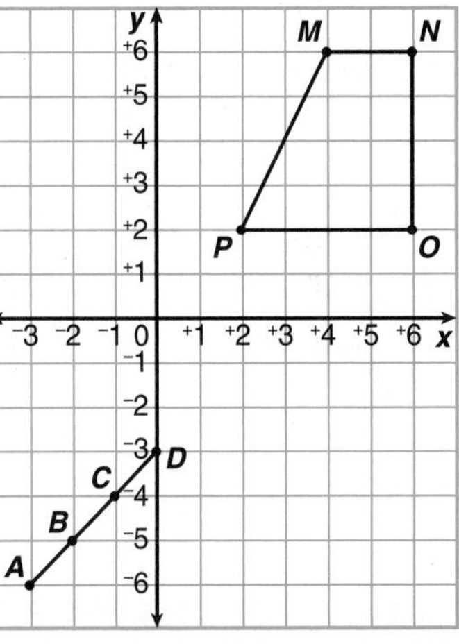

Use the coordinate plane to solve Problems 7–9. (Lessons 4-5)

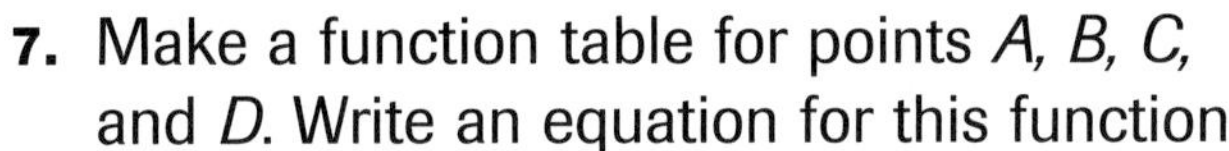

7. Make a function table for points A, B, C, and D. Write an equation for this function.

8. If you translate point A right 3 and up 2, what are the new coordinates for point A?

9. If you rotate trapezoid $MNOP$ 180° counterclockwise, what would be its new coordinates?

Trans Sym Club

Visual Thinking

Math Reasoning

Can you discover the names of the members of Trans Sym Club?

How do you think the members decided on a name for their club?

Chapter Review/Test

VOCABULARY

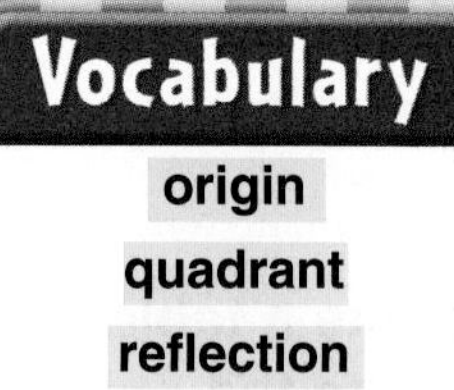

1. One of the four regions in a coordinate plane formed by the coordinate axes is called a(n) ____.
2. A figure that is flipped over a line shows a(n) ____.
3. The ____ is the point at which the *x*-axis and *y*-axis of a coordinate plane intersect.
4. A(n) ____ is a figure that is turned about a given point.

CONCEPTS AND SKILLS

Use the coordinates to plot each point on grid paper. Label. (Lesson 1, pp. 610–613)

5. $R\,(^-3, {}^+3)$
6. $M\,(^+2, {}^-2)$
7. $P\,(^-2, {}^-4)$
8. $N\,(^-5, 0)$
9. $O\,(^+4, {}^+4)$
10. $Q\,(0, {}^+3)$
11. $T\,(^+4, {}^-3)$
12. $S\,(^-3, {}^-2)$

Find 4 ordered pairs for each function. Then use them to graph each function. (Lessons 2–3, pp. 614–619)

13. $y = x + 4$
14. $y = x - 5$
15. $y = 2x + 1$
16. $y = 2x - 6$

Use the diagram. Name the coordinates of triangle *DEF* after the transformations. (Lesson 5, pp. 622–625)

17. Translate right 4 units.
18. Rotate a $\frac{1}{4}$ turn clockwise about (0, 0).
19. Reflect over the *y*-axis.

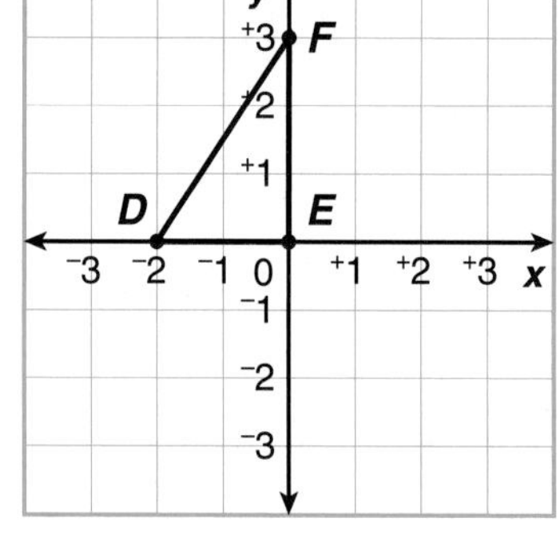

PROBLEM SOLVING

Use the table to solve. (Lesson 4, pp. 620–621)

20. Write an equation to show how to find the retail price of an item.

Wholesale Cost (*x*)	Retail Price (*y*)
\$2	\$5
\$4	\$9
\$6	\$13
\$8	\$17

Show You Understand

Does a parallelogram have rotational symmetry? Explain.

Extra Practice

Set A (Lesson 1, pp. 610–613)

Use the coordinate plane at the right for Exercises 1–6. Write the ordered pair for each point.

1. *J* **2.** *E* **3.** *M* **4.** *B*

Write the letter name of each point.

5. $(^{+}1, ^{+}1)$ **6.** $(^{-}3, ^{-}2)$ **7.** $(^{-}2, 0)$

Use grid paper. Use the coordinates to plot and label each point.

8. $W(^{+}3, ^{+}5)$ **9.** $X(^{-}2, ^{-}4)$ **10.** $Y(^{+}4, ^{-}4)$ **11.** $Z(^{-}5, ^{+}1)$

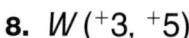

Set B (Lesson 2, pp. 614–615)

Make a function table for each of the following using 0, 4, 8, 12 for *x*.

1. $y = x + 4$ **2.** $y = 4x$ **3.** $y = x - 4$ **4.** $y = 10 - x$

Set C (Lesson 3, pp. 616–619)

Find 4 sets of coordinates for each function. Then graph the functions on grid paper.

1. $y = x - 6$ **2.** $y = x + 5$ **3.** $y = 2x + 2$ **4.** $y = 3x - 5$

Set D (Lesson 5, pp. 622–625)

Use the diagram. Name the coordinates of triangle *ABC* after the transformations.

1. Translate left 5 units.

2. Reflect over the *x*-axis.

3. Rotate a half turn about (0, 0).

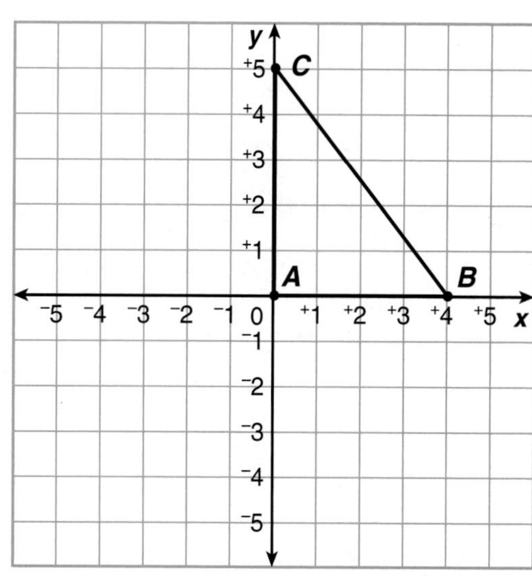

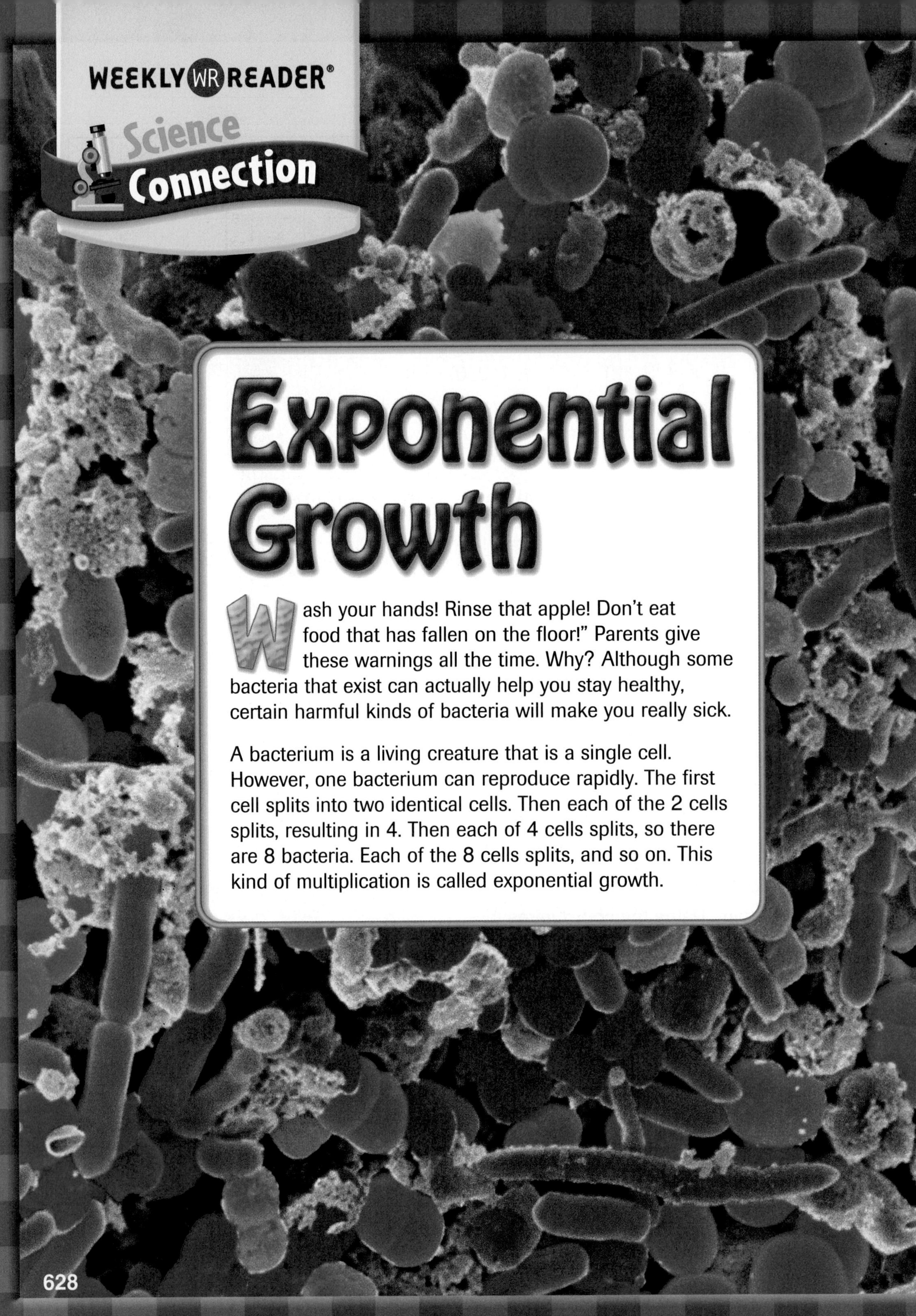

Exponential Growth

"Wash your hands! Rinse that apple! Don't eat food that has fallen on the floor!" Parents give these warnings all the time. Why? Although some bacteria that exist can actually help you stay healthy, certain harmful kinds of bacteria will make you really sick.

A bacterium is a living creature that is a single cell. However, one bacterium can reproduce rapidly. The first cell splits into two identical cells. Then each of the 2 cells splits, resulting in 4. Then each of 4 cells splits, so there are 8 bacteria. Each of the 8 cells splits, and so on. This kind of multiplication is called exponential growth.

Problem Solving

Each bacterium in the table divides into 2 cells every 20 minutes. Use these data to solve Problems 1–6.

Bacterial Growth	
Time	**Number of Bacteria**
0:00	1
0:20	2
0:40	4

1. Create a function table to show the exponential growth of the bacteria in 2 hours.

2. Use your function table from Problem 1 to graph the function of the bacteria's growth. Graph only points. Why should you not connect the points?

3. Describe the shape of your graph. Why do you think the graph has this shape?

4. A school day lasts 6 hours. You start with 1 bacterium at the beginning of the day. How many bacteria are there by the end of the day?

5. How many 20-minute intervals are needed for one bacterium to become at least one million bacteria?

6. If you start with one bacterium, how many bacteria will there be at the beginning of the tenth hour?

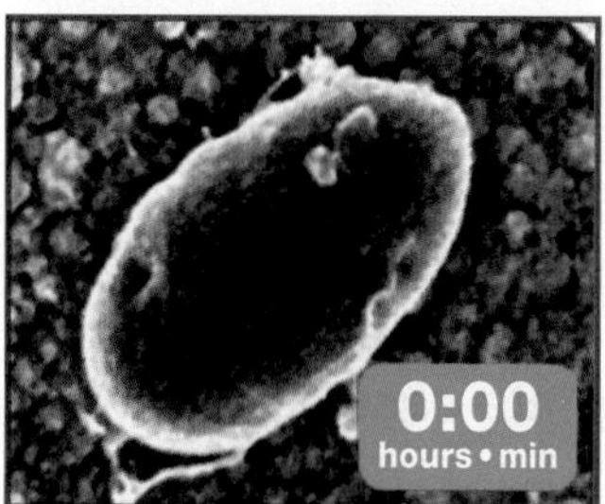

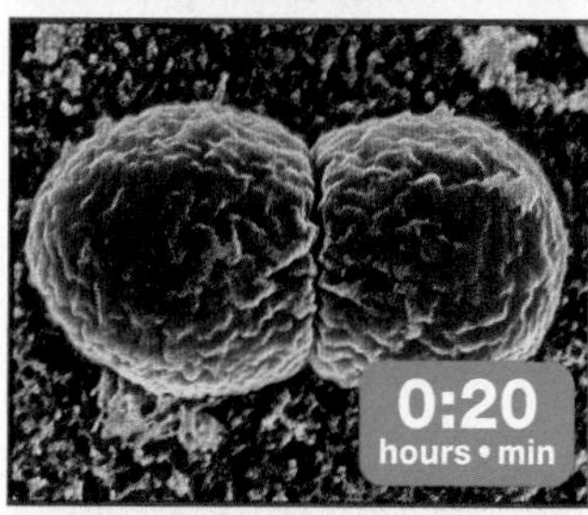

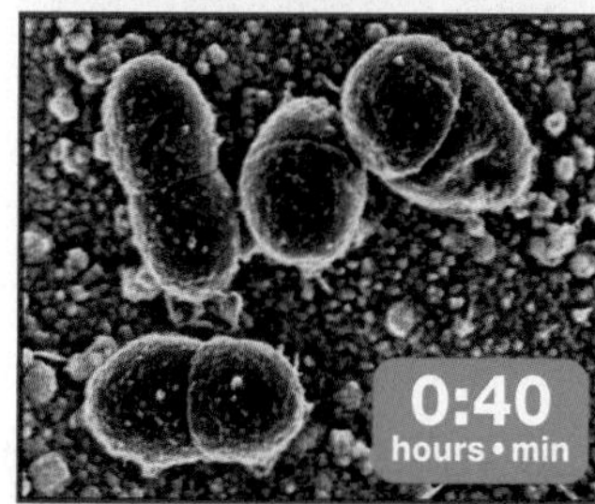

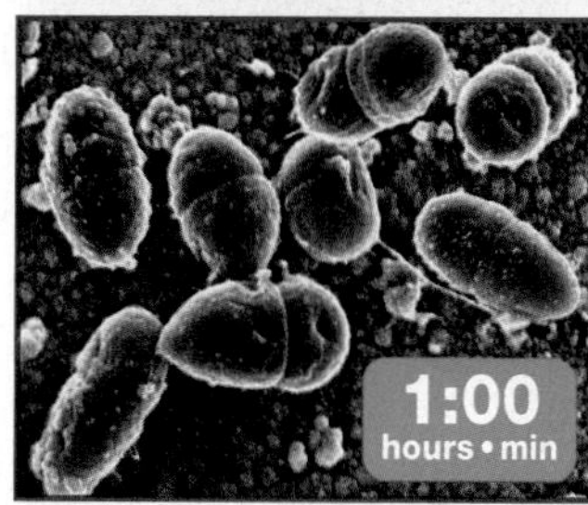

Technology
Visit *Education Place* at
eduplace.com/kids/mw/
to learn more about this topic.

Unit 8 Test

VOCABULARY

1. Opposite numbers have the same ■, or distance from zero.

2. A(n) ■ is a flip of a figure that results in a mirror image.

3. The point named by the ordered pair (0, 0) is the ■ .

Vocabulary

origin
rotation
integers
reflection
translation
coordinates
absolute value

CONCEPTS AND SKILLS

Solve using inverse operations. (Chapter 21)

4. $9n = 495$
5. $m \div 8 = 43$
6. $372 = k - 138$
7. $68 + a = 172$

Copy and complete each function table. (Chapter 21)

8. $y = 36 \div x$

x	y
1	■
2	■
3	■
4	■

9. $y = 21 - x$

x	y
0	■
1	■
2	■
3	■

10. $y = 7x - 3$

x	y
0	■
2	■
■	32
■	53

11. $y = 32 - 5x$

x	y
0	■
■	17
■	12
6	■

Write the opposite of each integer. (Chapter 22)

12. $^{+}37$
13. $^{-}3$
14. $^{-}19$

Write the absolute value of each integer. (Chapter 22)

15. $^{-}22$
16. 0
17. $^{+}19$

Write these integers in order from least to greatest. (Chapter 22)

18. 0, $^{-}5$, $^{-}3$, $^{+}4$
19. $^{-}8$, $^{-}11$, $^{-}7$, $^{+}7$
20. $^{-}6$, $^{+}7$, $^{-}8$, $^{+}9$

Add or subtract. (Chapter 22)

21. $^{+}8 + {}^{-}3$
22. $^{-}7 + {}^{-}8$
23. $^{+}7 - {}^{-}5$
24. $^{-}9 - {}^{-}5$

Use the coordinate plane for Exercises 25–29. Name the coordinates for each. (Chapter 23)

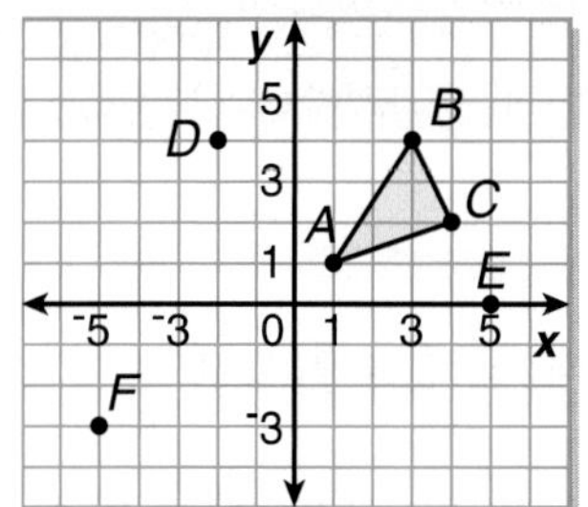

25. point *D**26.** point *C**27.** point *E*

28. triangle *ABC* after a translation 3 units left

29. triangle *ABC* after a reflection over the *x*-axis

PROBLEM SOLVING

30. At sunrise, the temperature outdoors was $^{-}4$°C. By the time school started, the temperature had risen 6°. What was the temperature when school started?

31. A carpenter made \$124 for building a bookcase. She paid $\frac{1}{4}$ of that amount to her assistant. Write and solve an equation to find how much she paid her helper.

Use the graph for Problems 32–33. Alice charges a fee of \$30 plus \$5 per hour. Beth charges \$10 per hour.

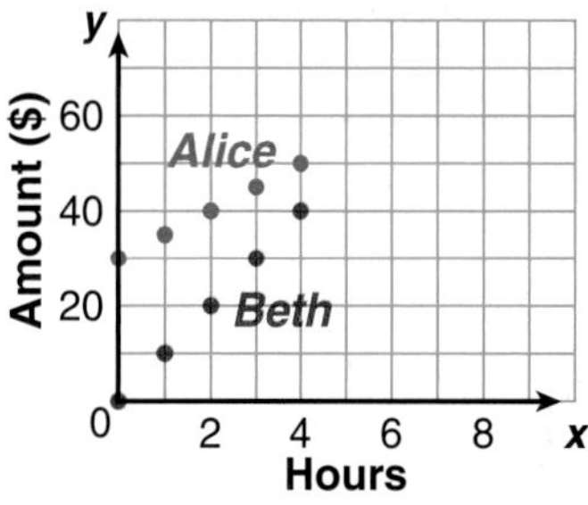

32. How many hours must Alice work to make \$70?

33. After how many hours will they make the same amount of money? After that, who will make more?

Decision Making

Extended Response

Task Laura, Mitch, and Natalie played a game using the spinner base shown. Each student spun a different set of numbers, but each got a score of 0. What numbers did each student spin? Is it more likely that a person playing this game would get a positive score or a negative score? Explain your thinking.

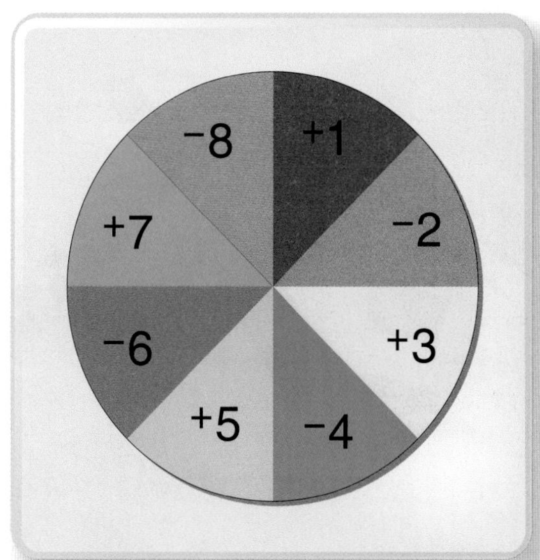

Information You Need

- Each student got three spins.
- Each student's score was the sum of his or her three spins.
- One of the numbers Laura spun was $^{-}8$.
- One of the numbers Mitch spun was $^{+}5$.

Performance Assessment

TASK 1

A Cool Activity (Chapters 21, 22)

Karen's class recorded the 10:00 A.M. temperatures for one week during January. The table on the right shows the results.

10:00 A.M.	Temperatures
Monday	2°C
Tuesday	⁻3°C
Wednesday	1°C
Thursday	⁻4°C
Friday	3°C

a. What is the range of the recorded temperatures?

b. Which temperature has the greatest absolute value? Explain.

c. Write an expression to find the difference between the Wednesday temperature and the Thursday temperature. Then find the difference.

TASK 2

A Moment of Reflection? (Chapter 23)

You are working as a wallpaper designer. Your job is to use transformations of a given triangle to make a design. Copy the coordinate grid on the left.

a. What are the coordinates of the vertices of $\triangle ABC$?

b. Reflect $\triangle ABC$ over the y-axis. What coordinates do vertices of the new triangle have? Which quadrant contains the triangle?

c. Reflect the triangle you found in **b** over the x-axis. What coordinates do the vertices of this new triangle have? Which quadrant contains the triangle?

d. Compare the original triangle with the triangle you found in **c**. What transformation could be used to change the position of one to the other? Explain.

Self Check

- Did I answer the questions for each task?
- Did I check all my work?

Enrichment: Picture Graphing

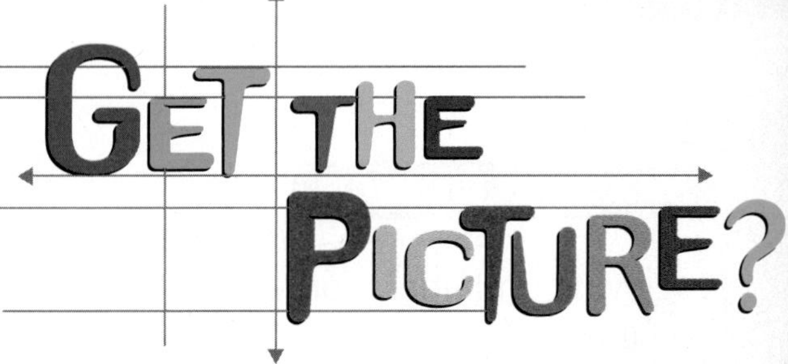

Computer programmers and designers use a grid system to draw the shapes that appear on your monitor's screen. You can use a similar process to create pictures on a coordinate grid.

Follow these steps to draw the rectangular prism on a coordinate grid.

STEP 1 Draw a square whose bottom left corner is at (1, 2) and whose top right corner is at (3, 4).

STEP 2 Draw a square whose bottom left corner is at $(^-3, ^-1)$ and whose top right corner is at $(^-1, 1)$.

STEP 3 Draw three lines: from $(^-3, 1)$ to (1, 4); from $(^-1, 1)$ to (3, 4); and from $(^-1, ^-1)$ to (1, 2).

STEP 4 Draw a dashed line from $(^-3, ^-1)$ to $(^-1, 1)$.

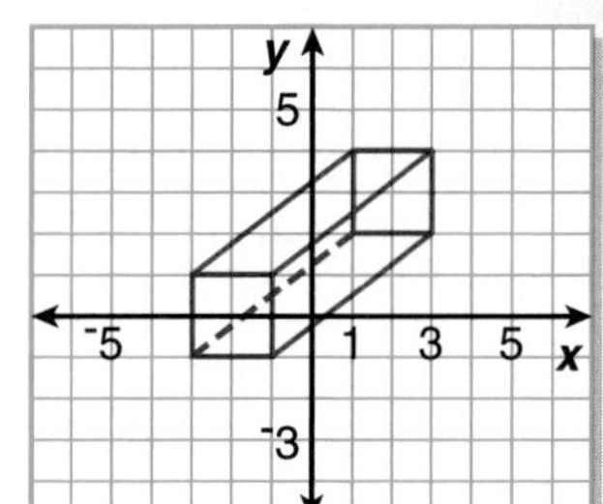

Try These

1. On a coordinate grid, connect the following points in the order given. Name the object you drew.

$(1, ^-6)$	(1, 0)	(2, 0)	(3, 1)	(3, 4)
(2, 4)	(2, 2)	(1, 2)	(1, 5)	(0, 6)
$(^-1, 6)$	$(^-2, 5)$	$(^-2, 0)$	$(^-3, 0)$	$(^-3, 2)$
$(^-4, 2)$	$(^-4, ^-1)$	$(^-3, ^-2)$	$(^-2, ^-2)$	$(^-2, ^-6)$
$(1, ^-6)$				

2. **Create Your Own** Write your own set of directions for drawing a picture on a coordinate grid. Give your directions to a partner to follow.

Cumulative Test Prep Practice

Solve Problems 1–10.

Test-Taking Tip

Sometimes when you take a test, you can circle important words that will help you understand what the question is asking.

Look at the example below.

Yuri collected these data on the weights, in pounds, of members of the basketball team:

$122.8, 129\frac{1}{2}, 122.75, 129\frac{1}{4}, 128$

He decided to list the weights from greatest to least. Which weight will be second on his list?

A 122.75 **C** $129\frac{1}{4}$

B 122.8 **D** $129\frac{1}{2}$

THINK

First circle the words "greatest to least," which mean that you have to order the given numbers. Another important word is "second," which indicates that you are looking for the second greatest weight, not the greatest.

The correct order is $129\frac{1}{2}$, $129\frac{1}{4}$, 128, 122.8, 122.75. So the correct answer is **C** $129\frac{1}{4}$.

Multiple Choice

1. Which numbers for *n* make this inequality true? $n > {}^{-}5$

A $^{-}5, {}^{-}6, {}^{-}7$ **C** $^{-}5, {}^{-}4, {}^{-}3$

B $^{-}6, {}^{-}7, {}^{-}8$ **D** $^{-}4, {}^{-}3, {}^{-}2$

(Chapter 22, Lesson 2)

2. The average temperature for January in Fairbanks, Alaska, is $^{-}10$°F. The average temperature for June is 60°F. What is the difference between these temperatures?

F 50° **H** 70°

G 60° **J** 80°

(Chapter 22, Lesson 5)

3. A hallway measures 3 feet by 9 feet. How many square yards of carpeting are needed to cover the floor of this hallway?

A 3 **C** 12

B 9 **D** 27

(Chapter 16, Lesson 3)

4. In a class of 30 fifth-graders, 20% of the students participated in the science fair. How many of the fifth-graders did not participate in the science fair?

F 6 **H** 14

G 10 **J** 24

(Chapter 19, Lesson 5)

 For more Test-Taking Tips, see pages xxii–xxv.

Free Response

5. A car service uses this formula to determine the cost of a ride. The variable n represents the number of miles.

Cost = $\$8 + \$3 \times (n - 1)$

What is the cost of a 5-mile trip?

(Chapter 5, Lesson 6)

6. Use the stem-and-leaf plot to identify the median of this set of data.

Hours Spent Training for Track Meet

Stem	Leaf
1	2 3 4 5 5 9
2	0 1 6 6 6 9
3	0

Key: 3 | 0 means 30.

(Chapter 8, Lesson 3)

7. In a survey of 36 students, $\frac{1}{3}$ of the students said that their one favorite subject was math and $\frac{1}{4}$ said that their favorite subject was history. How many students in all reported that their favorite subject was either math or history?

(Chapter 12, Lesson 2)

8. A scale drawing has the scale $\frac{1}{4}$ inch: 1 foot. What is the actual length of a room that is $2\frac{3}{4}$ inches long in the drawing?

(Chapter 18, Lesson 5)

9. Ethan bought a sweater that had a price of \$25. The sales tax was an additional 8% of the price of the sweater. How much did Ethan pay in all?

(Chapter 19, Lesson 5)

Extended Response

10. The rectangular prism in the drawing above represents the box design for a new breakfast cereal.

A What is the least number of square inches of cardboard needed to build the box? Explain.

B The cereal company plans to produce a jumbo-sized box with dimensions that are twice those shown. Would twice as much cardboard be needed? Explain.

C Find the volume of the original cereal box and the volume of the jumbo-sized box.

D Suppose you are hired to design a new cereal box in the shape of a rectangular prism. The box must have a volume that is greater than 600 cubic inches but less than 700 cubic inches. What dimensions can you use? Explain how you decided.

(Chapter 17, Lessons 4 and 6)

Test Prep on the Net

Check out *Education Place* at **eduplace.com/kids/mw/** for test prep practice.

Graph It

You can use Easy Sheet to create and compare the graphs of equations in Quadrant I.

- Enter and complete the table shown at the right, starting in cell A1.
- Click on cell A1 and drag to cell C6.
- Click on [chart icon].

	A	B	C
1	x	y = x + 1	y = x + 2
2	1	2	
3	2		
4	3		
5	4		
6	5		

Use Easy Sheet to answer the questions below.

1. How is the graph transformed each time you increase x by 1?
2. Predict what the graph for $y = x + 3$ will look like. Enter the values in column D and graph the line.
3. Based on the graphs you made above, predict what the lines will look like for the equations $y = 2x$ and $y = \frac{1}{2}x$.
4. Enter and complete the table shown at the right, starting in cell E1. Make a line graph of the data in cells A1 to F6.
5. How is the graph transformed when you multiply by 2? By $\frac{1}{2}$? How do the graphs compare to your predictions?
6. **Challenge** Predict what the graphs of $y = 2x + 1$ and $y = 2x + 2$ will look like based on the lines you have already graphed. Enter the equations and the first 5 values for each, in columns H and I. Make a new line graph of the data in cells H1 to I6.

E	F
$y = 2x$	$y = \frac{1}{2}x$
2	0.5

Vocabulary Wrap-Up for Unit 8

WEEKLY WR READER
Activity Almanac
See page 685 for the activity for this unit.

Look back at the big ideas and vocabulary in this unit.

Big Ideas

You can use inverse operations to solve equations.

A function written in the form of an equation relates two variables, such as *x* and *y*.

You can add and subtract integers using counters or a number line.

e Glossary

Key Vocabulary

inverse operations

function

integer

Math Conversations

Use your new vocabulary to discuss these big ideas.

1. Explain how to solve this equation:

   $a - 47 = 47$

2. Explain how to find values for *y* for the function $y = x - 9$.

3. Explain how to find this difference:

   $^-18 - 7$

4. Explain how to locate the point $(5, {}^-3)$ on a coordinate plane.

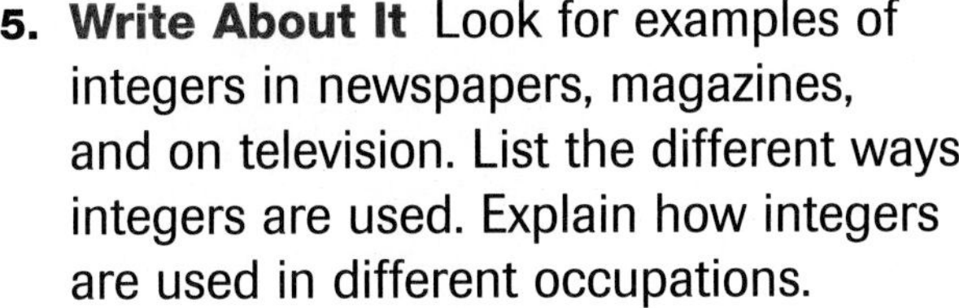

5. **Write About It** Look for examples of integers in newspapers, magazines, and on television. List the different ways integers are used. Explain how integers are used in different occupations.

I need to add ⁻6 and 4.
You could use a number line to show your work.

THE MOST AMAZING Sights in Nature

SOURCE OF INFORMATION: THE WORLD ALMANAC AND BOOK OF FACTS

Topping the list of amazing natural sights is Mt. Everest. It sits on the border between Tibet and Nepal in Asia. Mt. Everest is the highest mountain in the world. However, nobody agrees about just how high it is. Edmund Hillary and Tenzing Norgay first climbed the mountain in 1953. They believed it was 29,002 feet high. Later, the Indian government measured it at 29,028 feet. Satellites have been used to measure the mountain. They suggest that Mount Everest could be more than 29,800 feet high.

Victoria Falls in Africa is no small wonder, either. It is the world's largest waterfall. At its widest point, Victoria Falls is more than a mile across. Its height ranges from 256 feet to about 400 feet at its center.

Arizona's Grand Canyon was slowly carved out of the earth by the Colorado River over the past million years. This wonder is both steep and deep — more than a mile deep, in fact. It runs some 217 miles long and up to 18 miles wide. It is one of the most popular places to visit in the United States.

The length of the Grand Canyon is small compared to the length of the Great Barrier Reef. It is the world's largest coral reef. It stretches 1,250 miles along the northeastern coast of Australia. What is a coral reef? It is formed by the bodies of tiny sea creatures called corals. The Great Barrier Reef is home to 1,500 kinds of fish and 215 types of birds. It also has 500 kinds of seaweed. Whales visit in the winter. You won't find many sharks, however, because they prefer the open sea.

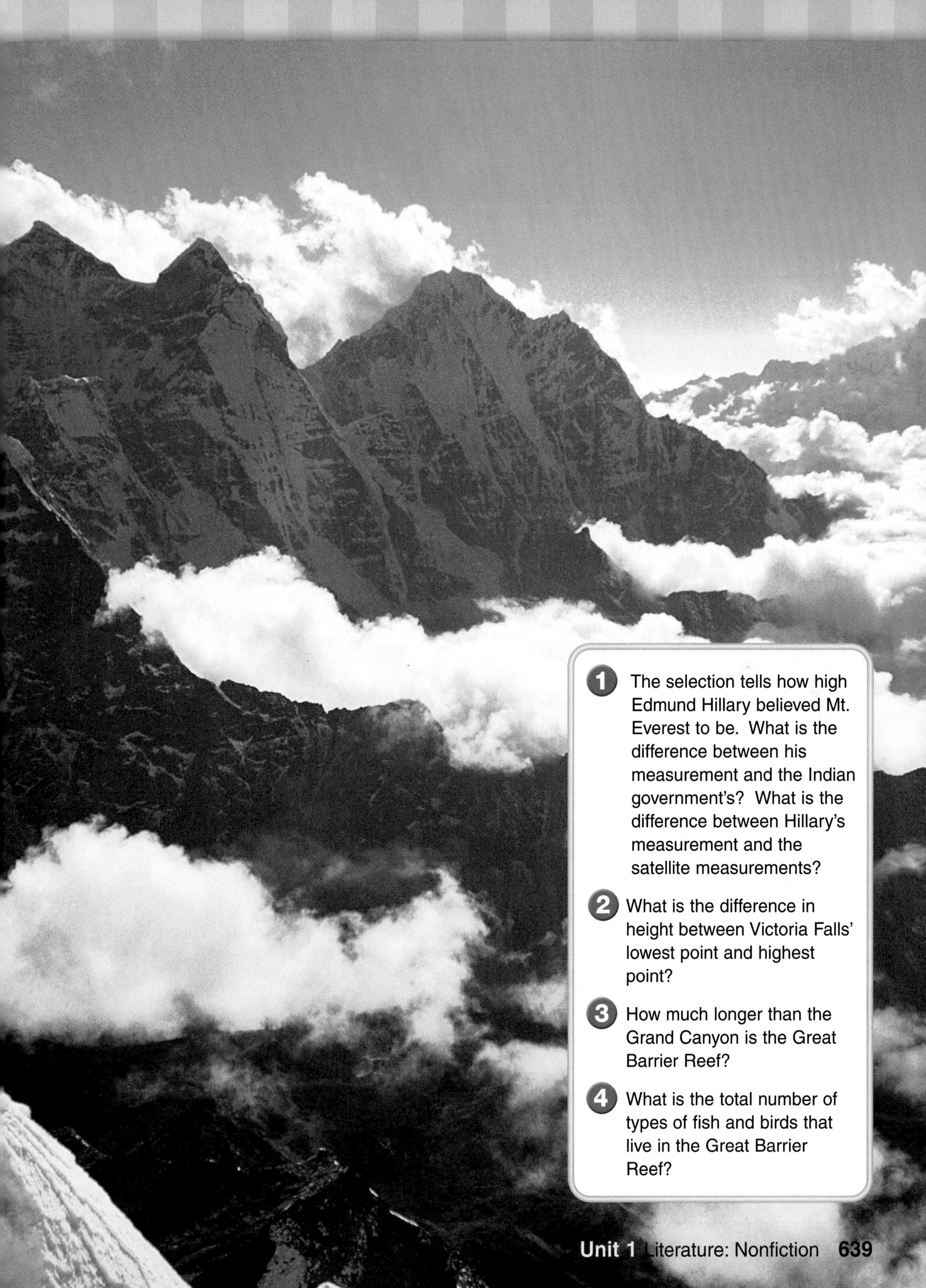

1. The selection tells how high Edmund Hillary believed Mt. Everest to be. What is the difference between his measurement and the Indian government's? What is the difference between Hillary's measurement and the satellite measurements?
2. What is the difference in height between Victoria Falls' lowest point and highest point?
3. How much longer than the Grand Canyon is the Great Barrier Reef?
4. What is the total number of types of fish and birds that live in the Great Barrier Reef?

Ready for Anything

Ryan Shaw

My name is Jedediah, but people call me Jed. My story begins on March 5, 1849. That day, my family and I set out from St. Louis for California.

Our covered wagon, pulled by five yoke of oxen, was loaded with supplies. For you city folk, a yoke is a wood frame that fastens together two animals to pull a wagon or plow. We joined a train of 20 other wagons.

We thought we were ready for anything — huge deserts, fast rivers, and even bandits. Little did we know what was really in store for us.

It started one morning in May. The early sun gave way to dark skies, then a dead calm. Suddenly, a twister was spotted about 10 miles off. It looked like a long, dirty finger. And it was heading straight for us.

As luck would have it, the twister changed direction. We lost most of our belongings but we were alive. Some weren't as lucky. Two families had unknowingly headed right in the path of the twister.

1. In all, how many oxen pulled Jed's family's covered wagon? Write a multiplication sentence to solve.
2. Why, do you think, did Jed explain the meaning of the word *yoke* for "city folk"?

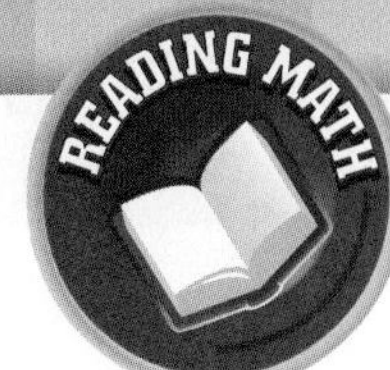

Ships of the Desert

Source of Information: The Information Please Almanac

Camels are made for the desert. They have broad, flat, leathery pads on each foot. As the camel walks, the pads spread, keeping the foot from sinking into the sand. Camels move both feet on one side of their body and then the feet on the other side. This makes them look as if they are rolling, the way a ship does in the ocean, and explains the nickname "ship of the desert."

How Fast Can Animals Run?

Animals	Speed (in Miles per Hour)
Cheetah	70
Zebra	40
Elephant	25
Grizzly bear	30
Lion	50
Camel	12

Camels can go from 5 to 7 days on little or no food and water. They can also travel great distances, carrying loads ranging from 400 to almost 1,000 pounds. Their usual speed is about 3 miles per hour. However, when they gallop, they can go as fast as 12 miles per hour. Depending on their load, camels can travel between 25 and 50 miles a day.

1. What's the mean, median, and range of the speed of the animals listed in the table?
2. How does the camel's speed affect the mean of the speeds shown in the table?

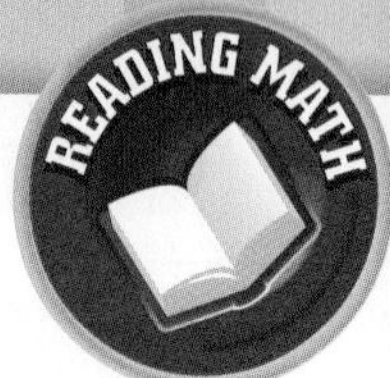

The Fruitomatic

HELEN STAKENICH

Darcy Devine was bored. Her parents had left for a day trip to Mars to celebrate her dad's birthday. Cousin Mindy was "babysitting" 12-year-old Darcy, as if Darcy wasn't old enough to take care of herself. Sixteen-year-old Mindy was no fun. All she wanted to do was talk on the disto-phone with her friends from the Andromeda Galaxy.

Darcy decided to check out Dad's latest kitchen invention, the Fruitomatic. Dad was always inventing cool, new gadgets for the kitchen — or at least Darcy thought they were cool.

The Fruitomatic could zap any fruit — well, just about any fruit. Watermelons and pineapples were too big to fit into the machine, and raspberries and blueberries were too small. Darcy pulled the Fruitomatic from under the sink, where Mom kept it. The Fruitomatic had two side-by-side chambers. You put the fruit into the chamber on the left, and you could get ice cream, juice, sliced fruit, fruit salad, and even cooked fruit in the chamber on the right.

"That's it," thought Darcy. "I'll make fruit salad." Watching her dad fiddle with the Fruitomatic always eased her boredom. Now she would try the machine herself. But there was a problem; the fruit bowl was empty.

Darcy was about to give up all hope of improving her boring day when she spied lemons on the kitchen counter. She decided to make lemonade instead. She slipped the lemons into the left chamber of the Fruitomatic. Then she entered the number 4 and pressed the Enter button. Darcy looked into the right chamber. It was empty! She entered the number 6 and pressed Enter again. Still nothing. Then she remembered that Dad had said the machine could only make juice using prime numbers. She knew that 3 was a prime number. She entered three and — bingo! Out came more juice than she had ever seen. She entered 5, 7, and 9. Two of the three numbers worked!

By now, the lemon juice was pouring from the machine and Darcy was filling all the pitchers she could find. But she was having too much fun to stop. Darcy entered the number 12 and something strange happened. Out came a lemon cut into two halves. Then she entered 14 and got a lemon sliced into quarters. For some reason, the number 15 created a lemon cut into fifths. Darcy wasn't sure what was going on, but she was having a real blast. Before long, she had every pitcher in the kitchen filled with juice, and every bowl filled with lemon slices.

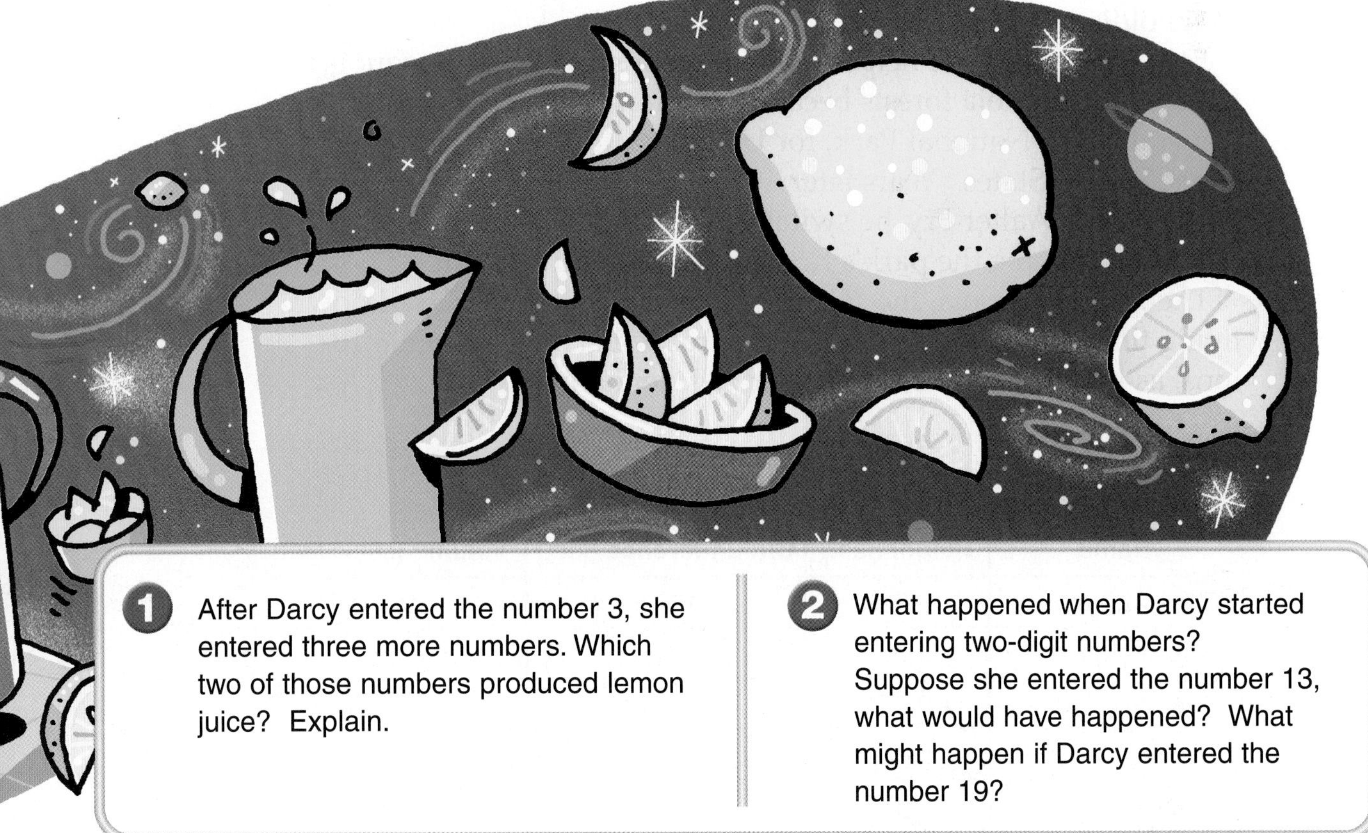

1. After Darcy entered the number 3, she entered three more numbers. Which two of those numbers produced lemon juice? Explain.

2. What happened when Darcy started entering two-digit numbers? Suppose she entered the number 13, what would have happened? What might happen if Darcy entered the number 19?

READING MATH

The World's Largest Trees

Source of Information: The National Park Service

The largest trees in the world are the giant sequoias. They grow on the western side of the Sierra Nevada Mountains in California. The tallest sequoias are as large as a 26-story building. At their base, they are wider than a city street. Sequoias are very old trees. Experts believe the largest of these trees may be as much as 2,700 years old.

In 1888, six loggers spent five days cutting down a giant sequoia. Walter Fry, one of the loggers, counted the growth rings on the tree stump. He knew that most trees add a ring to their circumference about once a year. When Fry finished counting, he was shocked and saddened. The tree they had just cut down was more than 3,000 years old!

Fry quit his job. He helped start a petition to save the sequoias. In 1890, the sequoia forests became a national park. It was named General Grant National Park, for Ulysses S. Grant, the 18th President of the United States. Years later, it was renamed Sequoia National Park. As for Walter Fry, he switched jobs and became a park ranger. Later, Fry became the park's first civilian superintendent.

The largest sequoia, the "General Sherman" is the largest known living thing on earth. The Sherman Tree weighs more than 6,167 tons, as much as 41 blue whales or 740 elephants.

The Five Largest Sequoias

Name	**Height** (feet)	**Circumference** (feet)	**Volume** (cubic feet)
General Sherman	274.9	102.6	52,508
Washington	254.7	101.1	47,850
General Grant	268.1	107.6	46,608
Lincoln	255.8	98.3	45,148
President	240.9	93.0	44,471

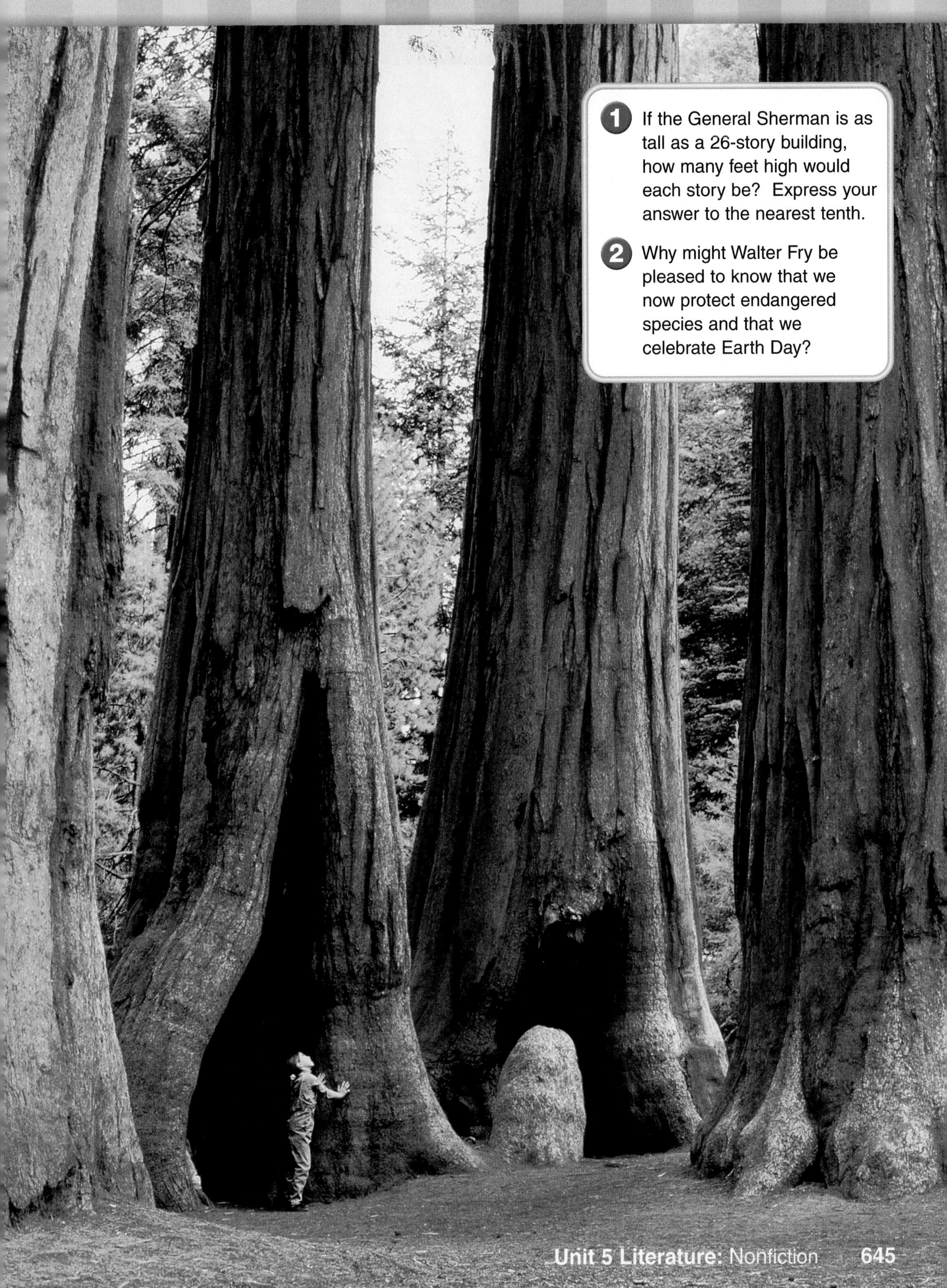

1. If the General Sherman is as tall as a 26-story building, how many feet high would each story be? Express your answer to the nearest tenth.
2. Why might Walter Fry be pleased to know that we now protect endangered species and that we celebrate Earth Day?

READING MATH

No Place to Go

HELENA SERPA

Vanessa, Jen, Megan, and Natasha were 11 years old and friends. They had been looking forward to a summer of fun. Now their vacation was only a week old, and they were already bored.

"We need a place to play," Vanessa said.

"What, like a clubhouse?" Natasha asked.

Suddenly, the same idea struck the four girls. "The shed!" they shouted.

A wooden shed sat unused in the farthest corner of Natasha's back yard. With its triangle-shaped roof, it looked like a real cabin, only lots smaller. Was it too small for a clubhouse? Vanessa ran home and grabbed the tape measure from the toolbox. Minutes later, she was holding one end as Megan pulled the tape and measured the shed's outside dimensions. It was 10 feet long, and much to their surprise, 12 feet wide. And its walls were 7 feet tall.

The shed needed to be patched up and painted. But it was nothing the girls couldn't handle. That night, Natasha's parents quickly agreed to the deal.

Five days later, Natasha held open the freshly-painted door of the new clubhouse.

"Ladies first," she joked, as she waved her friends in.

1. Make a drawing of the clubhouse. Label the measurements of each dimension.

2. Calculate the area of a longer wall of the clubhouse. Then find the area of the clubhouse floor.

READING MATH

NUMBERS

BY MARY CORNISH
from Sing a Song of Popcorn

I like the generosity of numbers.
The way, for example,
they are willing to count
anything or anyone:
two pickles, one door to the room,
eight dancers dressed as swans.

I like the domesticity of addition —
add two cups of milk and stir —
the sense of plenty: six plums
on the ground, three more
falling from the tree.

And multiplication's school
of fish times fish,
whose silver bodies breed
beneath the shadow
of a boat.

Even subtraction is never loss,
just addition somewhere else:
five sparrows take away two,
the two in someone else's
garden now.

There's an amplitude to long division,
as it opens Chinese take-out
box by paper box,
inside every folded cookie
a new fortune.

And I never fail to be surprised
by the gift of an odd remainder,
footloose at the end:
forty-seven divided by eleven equals four,
with three remaining.

Three boys beyond their mothers' call,
two Italians off to the sea,
one sock that isn't anywhere you look.

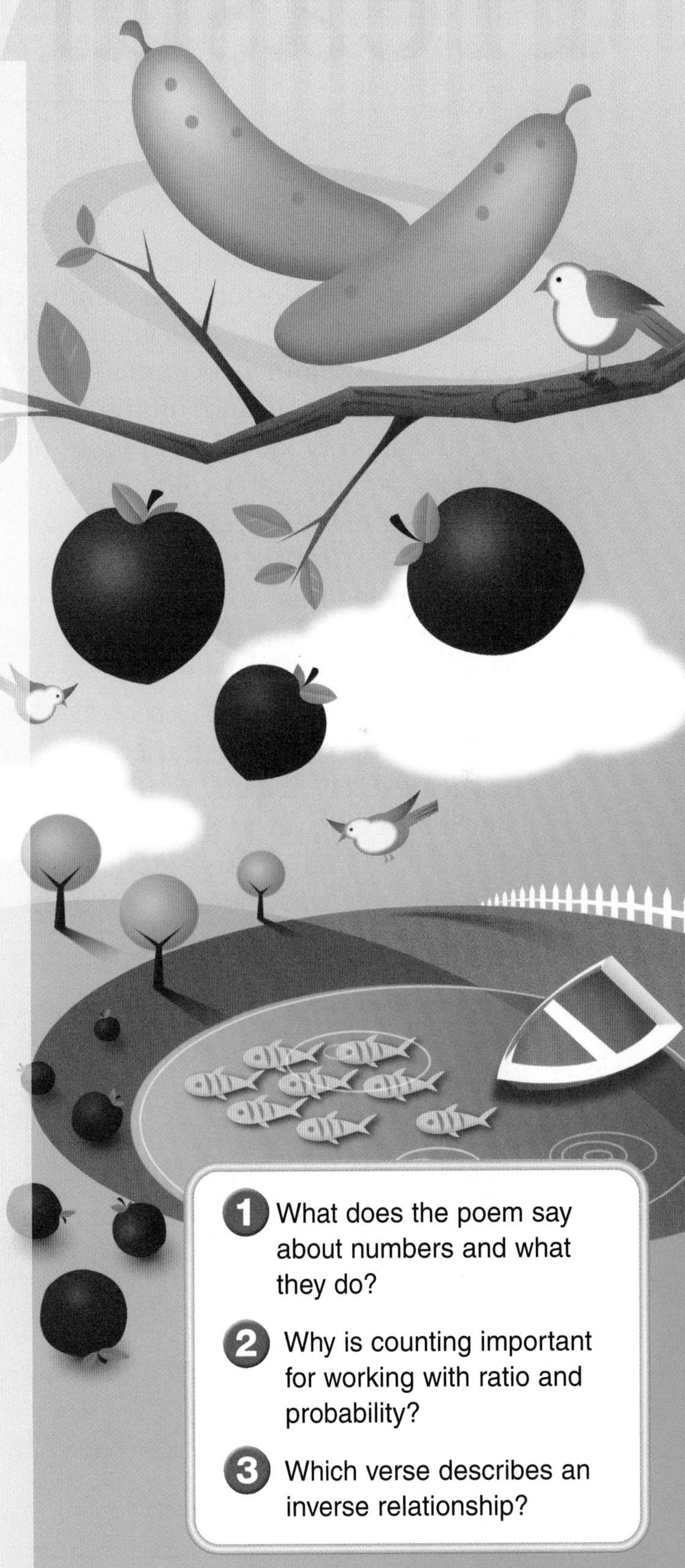

1. What does the poem say about numbers and what they do?
2. Why is counting important for working with ratio and probability?
3. Which verse describes an inverse relationship?

READING MATH

Treasure Hunt

DOUGLAS COBLEIGH

The treasure hunt was Jack's bright idea. He and I had grown up near Boston. We went to different colleges but stayed close friends. After college, we decided to have some fun. So in December, we joined a company that was digging for treasure. Our destination: Oak Island, off the eastern coast of Nova Scotia, Canada.

Oak Island is 350 nautical miles northeast of Boston. Now, Boston winters can get pretty cold. But we soon discovered they were nothing compared to the damp cold of Nova Scotia. At first, we didn't mind it too much. After all, we were here to search for buried treasure.

We learned this search had been going on since 1795, when a Nova Scotia teenager had come across a sunken spot shaped like a circle. The boy had heard plenty of tales about pirates who had used the islands off Nova Scotia as secret hideouts. Legend had it that Captain Kidd and his crew had buried their treasure on one of these islands.

The next day, the boy returned to the spot with some friends. They started digging. And they continued to dig over the next year until they found a rather large stone with mysterious writing on it. By that time the hole was about 90 feet deep. When they returned the

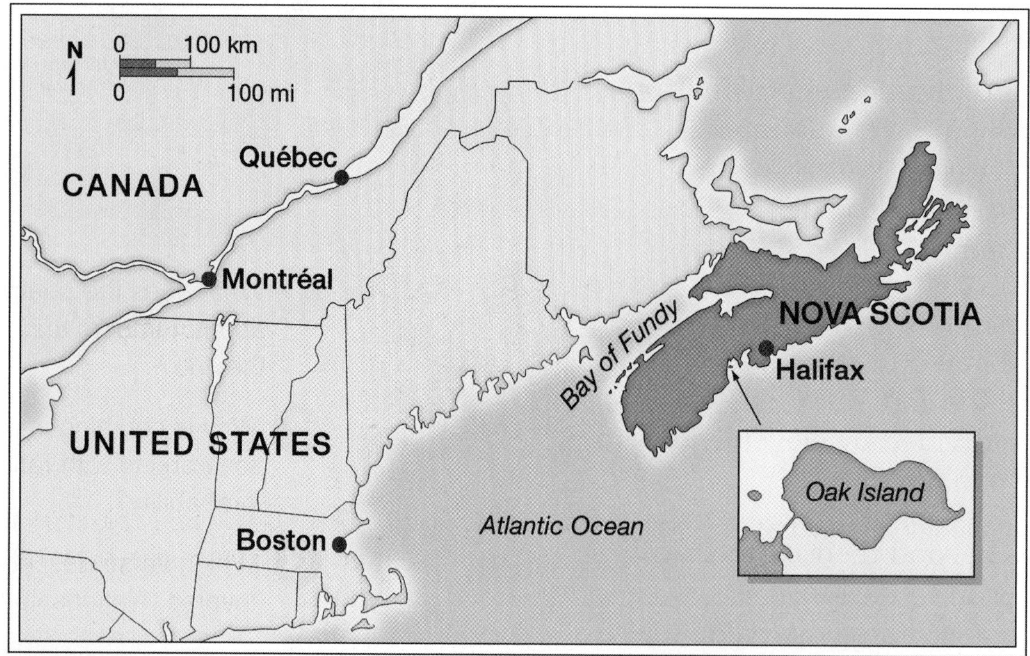

following day, the hole was filled with water. When they removed the stone, they accidentally set off a trap that flooded the hole.

Over the years, various people have taken turns digging out the Money Pit, as the spot came to be called. Several were killed. But treasure hunters continued digging. Eventually, they dug down almost 190 feet. But they failed to find any treasure.

The company Jack and I worked for had a new idea. About 180 feet northeast of the Money Pit, engineers sank a steel tube more than 230 feet into the ground. Then they lowered a specially-made video camera. We could see what looked like three treasure chests and various tools.

The company decided to sink a second shaft close to where the cameras showed the three chests and tools. When we raised the chests, we found old china and glass in one, old bottles in another, and the remnants of what had been clothing in the third.

So much for the Money Pit!

1. What story information does each of the following integers stand for?
   A. $^{-}190$; B. $^{+}350$; C. $^{-}230$

2. List three details from the story that are facts. Explain why you think they are facts.

Table Of Measures

Customary Units of Measure / Metric Units of Measure

Length

Customary			Metric		
1 foot (ft)	=	12 inches (in.)	1 centimeter (cm)	=	10 millimeters (mm)
1 yard (yd)	=	36 inches	1 decimeter (dm)	=	10 centimeters
1 yard	=	3 feet	1 meter (m)	=	1,000 millimeters
1 mile (mi)	=	5,280 feet	1 meter	=	100 centimeters
1 mile	=	1,760 yards	1 meter	=	10 decimeters
			1 kilometer (km)	=	1,000 meters

Area

Customary			Metric		
144 square inches (in.^{2})	=	1 square foot (ft^2)	1 square centimeter (cm^2)	=	100 square millimeters (mm^2)
9 square feet	=	1 square yard (yd^2)	1 square decimeter (dm^2)	=	100 square centimeters
			1 square meter (m^2)	=	100 square decimeters

Volume

Customary			Metric		
1,728 cubic inches (in.^{3})	=	1 cubic foot (ft^3)	1 cubic centimeter (cm^3)	=	1,000 cubic millimeters (mm^3)
27 cubic feet	=	1 cubic yard (yd^3)	1 cubic decimeter (dm^3)	=	1,000 cubic centimeters
			1 cubic meter (m^3)	=	1,000 cubic decimeters

Capacity

Customary			Metric		
1 tablespoon (tbsp)	=	3 teaspoons (tsp)	1 liter (L)	=	1,000 milliliters (mL)
1 fluid ounce (fl oz)	=	2 tablespoons	1 liter	=	10 deciliters (dL)
1 cup (c)	=	8 fluid ounces	1 liter	=	1 cubic decimeter (dm^3)
1 pint (pt)	=	2 cups	1,000 liters	=	1 cubic meter (m^3)
1 quart (qt)	=	2 pints			
1 quart	=	4 cups			
1 gallon (gal)	=	4 quarts			
1 gallon	=	8 pints			

Weight/Mass

Customary			Metric		
1 pound (lb)	=	16 ounces (oz)	1 gram (g)	=	1,000 milligrams (mg)
1 ton (T)	=	2,000 pounds (lb)	1 kilogram (kg)	=	1,000 grams
			1 metric ton (t)	=	1,000 kilograms

Units of Time

1 minute (min)	=	60 seconds (s)	1 year	=	365 days
1 hour (h)	=	60 minutes	1 leap year	=	366 days
1 day	=	24 hours	1 decade	=	10 years
1 week (wk)	=	7 days	1 century	=	100 years
1 year (yr)	=	12 months (mo)	1 millennium	=	1,000 years

Glossary

absolute value The distance a number is from zero on a number line.

acute angle An angle with a measure less than that of a right angle.

acute triangle A triangle in which each of the three angles is acute.

addend A number to be added in an addition expression. In $7 + 4 + 8$, the numbers 7, 4, and 8 are addends.

algebraic expression An expression that consists of one or more variables. It could contain some constants and some operations.

Example: $2x + 3y + 6$.

angle An angle is formed by two rays with a common endpoint.

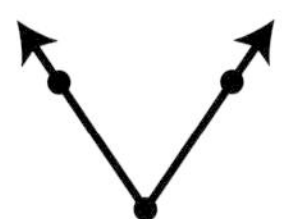

area The number of square units that cover a surface with no overlap.

array An arrangement of objects, pictures, or numbers in columns and rows.

Associative Property of Addition Changing the grouping of addends does not change their sum. It is also called the *Grouping Property of Addition.*

Example: For all numbers a, b and c, $a + (b + c) = (a + b) + c$.

Associative Property of Multiplication Changing the grouping of factors does not change their product. It is also called the *Grouping Property of Multiplication.*

Example: For all numbers a, b and c, $a \times (b \times c) = (a \times b) \times c$.

average The number found by dividing the sum of a group of numbers by the number of addends. Also known as the *mean.*

bar graph A graph in which information is shown by means of rectangular bars.

base of a geometric figure A bottom side or face of a geometric figure.

base of a power A number used as a repeated factor in a product. *Example:* 10^3. 10 is the base of the power

capacity The amount a container can hold.

Celsius The metric temperature scale with the freezing point of water set to 0 degrees, and the boiling point set to 100 degrees.

center of a circle A point that is the same distance from all points on a circle.

central angle An angle with a vertex at the center of a circle.

certain event An event that has a probability of 1.

chord Any segment within a circle that connects two points on the circle.

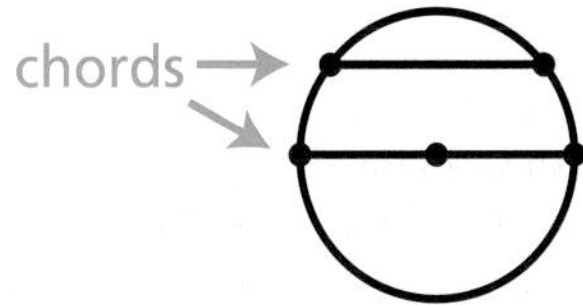

circle A closed figure in which every point is the same distance from a given point called the center of the circle.

circle graph A graph used for data that are parts of a whole.

circumference The distance around a circle.

cluster In a data display, a group of data points that are close to each other.

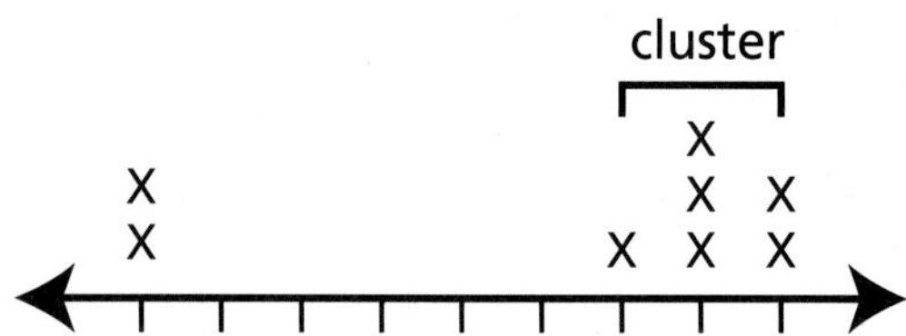

common denominator Any common multiple of the denominators of two or more fractions.

common factor A number that is a factor of two or more numbers.

common multiple A number that is shared as a multiple of two or more numbers.

Commutative Property of Addition Changing the order of addends does not change their sum. It is also called the *Order Property of Addition.*

Example: For all numbers a and b, $a + b = b + a$.

Commutative Property of Multiplication Changing the order of factors does not change their product. It is also called the *Order Property of Multiplication.*

Example: For all numbers a and b, $a \times b = b \times a$.

compatible numbers Numbers that are close to the original numbers and are easy to divide.

composite number A whole number that has more than two factors.

compound event In probability, a combination of two or more events.

cone A solid that has a circular base and a surface from a boundary of the base to the vertex.

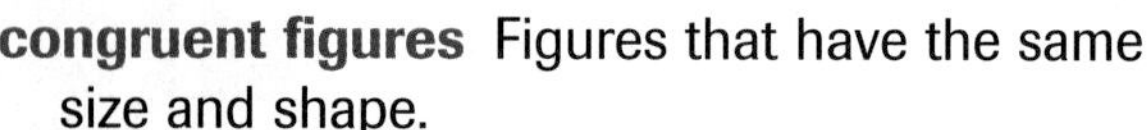

congruent figures Figures that have the same size and shape.

coordinate plane A plane formed by two perpendicular number lines in which every point is assigned an ordered pair of numbers.

coordinates An ordered pair of numbers that locates a point in the coordinate plane with reference to the x-axis and y-axis.

cross product A product obtained by multiplying the second term of one ratio by the first term of another.

cube A solid figure that has six square faces of equal size.

cubic unit A unit for measuring volume. A cube with sides one unit long.

customary system The measurement system that uses foot, quart, pound, and degrees Fahrenheit.

cylinder A solid with two circular faces that are congruent and a cylindrical surface connecting the two faces.

D

data A set of numbers or pieces of information.

data set A collection of numbers or pieces of information.

decimal A number with one or more digits to the right of a decimal point.

decimal point A symbol used to separate the ones and tenths places in a decimal.

degrees A unit used to describe angle measures and also temperature. Its symbol is °.

denominator The number below the bar in a fraction.

diagonal A segment that joins two vertices of a polygon but is not a side.

diameter A chord that connects two points on the circle and passes through the center.

difference The result of subtraction.

discount A decrease in the price of an item.

Distributive Property When two addends are multiplied by a factor, the product is the same as if each addend was multiplied by the factor and those products were added.

Example: $a \times (b + c) = (a \times b) + (a \times c)$

dividend The number that is divided in a division problem.

divisible One number is divisible by another if the quotient is a whole number and there is a remainder of 0.

divisor The number by which a number is being divided.

double bar graph A graph in which data are compared by means of pairs of rectangular bars drawn next to each other.

double line graph A graph that is used to compare two or more sets of data over time.

edge The segment where two faces of a solid figure meet.

endpoint The point at either end of a line segment. The beginning point of a ray.

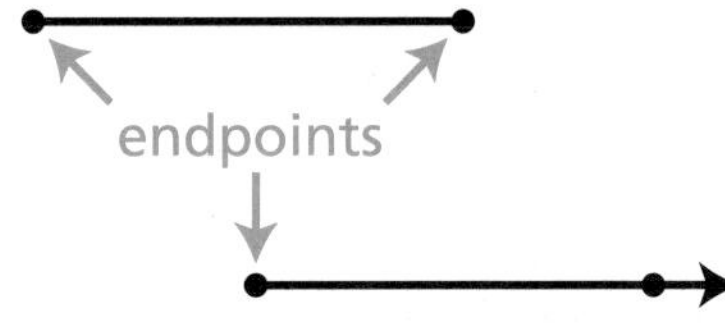

equally likely Events which have the same chance of occurring.

equation A mathematical sentence that shows that two expressions are the same value.

equilateral triangle A triangle that has three congruent sides.

equivalent fractions Fractions that show different numbers with the same value.

equivalent ratios Ratios that show the same comparison.

estimate A number close to an exact amount. An estimate tells about how much or about how many.

evaluate To substitute the values given for the variables and perform the operations to find the value of the expression.

evaluating an expression For a numerical expression, performing the operations to find the value of the expression. For an algebraic expression, substituting number(s) for the variable(s) and then performing the operations to find the value of the expressions.

even number A whole number that is a multiple of 2. The ones digit in an even number is 0, 2, 4, 6, or 8. The numbers 56 and 48 are examples of even numbers.

event In probability, a result of an experiment that can be classified as certain, likely, unlikely, or impossible.

expanded form A way of writing a number as the sum of the values of its digits.

experimental probability The number of favorable outcomes in an event divided by the total number of completed trials of an experiment.

exponent The number in a power that tells the number of times the base is used as a factor.

base → 5^3 ← exponent

expression A number, variable, or any combination of numbers, variables, and operation signs.

face A flat surface of a solid figure.

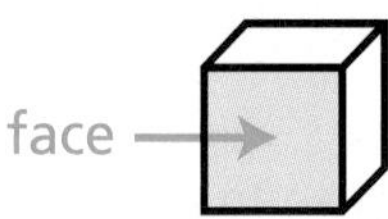

fact family Facts that are related, using the same numbers.

Examples: $1 + 4 = 5$ $\quad 4 + 1 = 5$

$5 - 1 = 4$ $\quad 5 - 4 = 1$

$3 \times 5 = 15$ $\quad 5 \times 3 = 15$

$15 \div 3 = 5$ $\quad 15 \div 5 = 3$

factor One of two or more numbers that are multiplied to give a product.

factor tree A diagram that is used to show the prime factorization of a number.

factorization A number written as a product of its factors.

Fahrenheit The customary temperature scale.

fraction A number that names a part of a whole, a part of a collection, or a part of a region.

frequency In surveys, the number of times a response is chosen.

frequency table A table used to record the number of times a response is chosen.

front-end estimation Estimation by looking at the digits in the greatest place of each number.

function A rule that gives exactly one value of *y* for every value of *x*.

function table A table that matches each input value with one output value.

gap In a data display, a large space between data points.

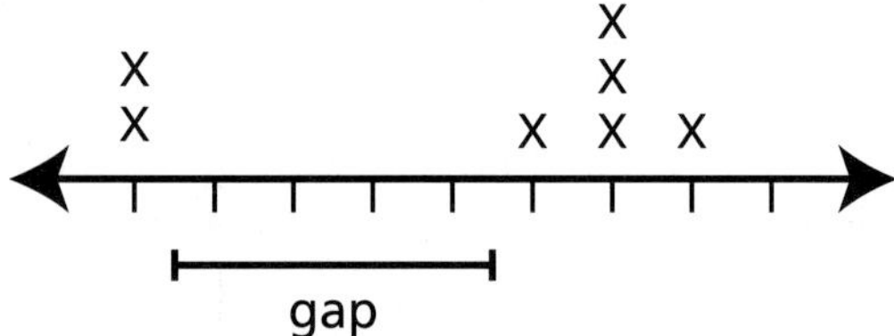

greatest common divisor (GCD) The greatest whole number that is a common factor of two or more numbers. It is also called the *greatest common factor.*

greatest common factor (GCF) The greatest whole number that is a common factor of two or more numbers. It is also called the *greatest common divisor.*

histogram A graph in which bars are used to display how frequently data occurs within equal intervals.

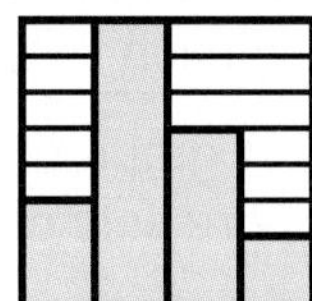

horizontal axis The x-axis in a coordinate system. It is a number line that is used to locate points to the left or to the right of the origin.

Identity Property of Addition The property which states that the sum of any number and 0 is that number.

Example: $x + 0 = x$

Identity Property of Multiplication The property which states that the product of any number and 1 is that number.

Example: $a \times 1 = a$

impossible event An event that has a probability of 0.

improper fraction A fraction which has a numerator that is greater than or equal to its denominator.

inequality A relation that is expressed by placing an inequality symbol between two expressions.

Examples: $8 > 2$, $2 < 8$, $5 + 7 \neq 6 + 4$

integers The set of positive whole numbers, their opposites (negative numbers), and 0.

intersecting lines Lines that meet or cross at a common point.

interval A measure of space between two or more numbers.

inverse operations Operations that have opposite effects. Subtraction is the inverse operation of addition. Division is the inverse operation of multiplication.

invert To interchange the numerator and the denominator.

irregular polygon A polygon with at least one side or angle that is not congruent to the others.

isosceles triangle A triangle that has at least two congruent sides.

leaf The last digit of a number in a stem-and-leaf plot.

least common denominator (LCD) The least common multiple of two or more denominators.

least common multiple (LCM) The least number that is a multiple of two or more numbers.

line A straight, continuous, and unending set of points in a plane.

line graph A graph that uses a broken line to show changes in data. A line graph is often used to display data that vary with time.

line of symmetry The line along which a figure can be folded so that the two halves match exactly.

line plot A diagram that organizes data using a number line.

line segment A part of a line that has two endpoints.

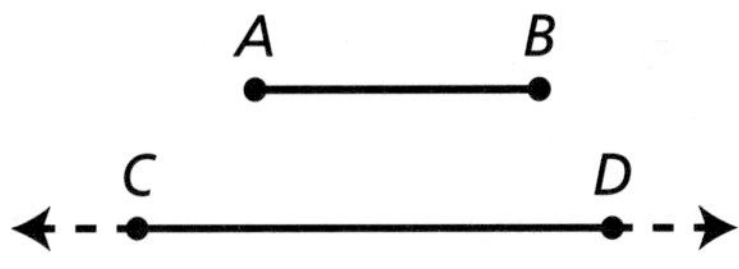

line segments *AB* and *CD*

line symmetry A figure has line symmetry if it can be folded in half and the two halves are congruent.

mass The amount of matter in an object.

mean The number found by dividing the sum of the numbers in a group by the number of addends. Also known as the *average*.

measures of central tendency The mean, median, and mode.

median The middle number when data are arranged in order.

metric system A system of measurement in which the basic units of length, mass and capacity are the meter, gram and liter.

midpoint The point that divides the segment into two congruent parts.

mixed number A number made up of a whole number and a fraction.

whole number → $5\frac{2}{3}$ ← fraction

↑

mixed number

mode The number or numbers that occur most often in a set of data.

multiple A number that is the product of the given number and a counting number.

negative numbers Numbers that are less than 0.

net A flat pattern that can be folded to make a solid figure.

number line a line on which numbers are assigned points.

numerator The number above the bar in a fraction.

obtuse angle An angle with a measure greater than that of a right angle and less than 180°.

obtuse triangle A triangle that has one obtuse angle.

odd number A whole number that is not a multiple of 2. The ones digit in an odd number is 1, 3, 5, 7, or 9.

Examples: 67 and 493 are odd numbers.

opposite of a number The same number but of opposite sign. Also called the *additive inverse*.

order of operations Rules for performing operations in order to simplify expressions.

ordered pair A pair of numbers (x, y) indicating the x-coordinate and y-coordinates of a point on a graph.

origin The point where the x- and y-axis intersect in a coordinate plane.

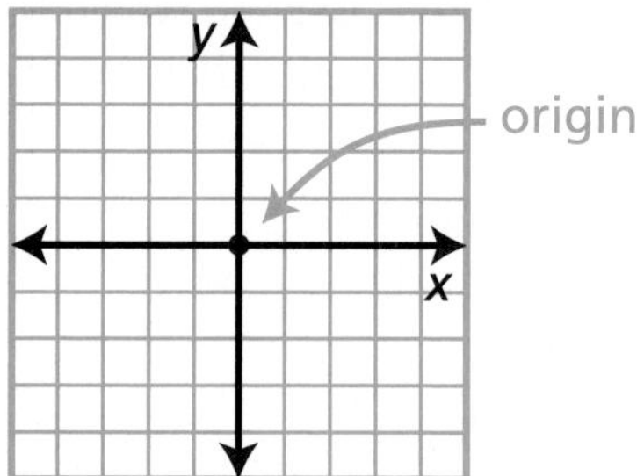

outcome A single result in a probability experiment.

outlier A number or numbers whose values are much less or much greater than the other numbers in the data set.

parallel lines Lines that lie in the same plane and do not intersect. They are everywhere the same distance apart.

parallelogram A quadrilateral in which both pairs of opposite sides are parallel.

partial product In multiplication of numbers with two or more digits, the product of each digit in one factor and the other number.

$$\begin{array}{r} 48 \\ \times\ 23 \\ \hline 144 \\ +\ 960 \\ \hline 1{,}104 \end{array}$$

← partial products (144 and 960)

per Used in talking about rates. *Per* means "to each" or "for each."

percent Per hundred. A ratio of a number to 100.

period In a number, each group of three digits separated by a comma.

perimeter The distance around a plane figure.

perpendicular Two lines or line segments that cross or meet to form right angles.

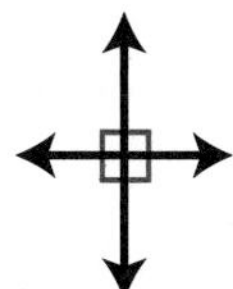

pi (π) A number defined by the ratio of the circumference of any circle to its diameter. Two common approximations used for pi are $\frac{22}{7}$ and 3.14.

pictograph A graph that uses pictures or symbols to represent data.

place value The value of a digit determined by its place in a number.

plane A flat surface made up of a continuous and unending collection of points that are not all in the same line.

point An exact location in space, represented by a dot.

polygon A simple closed plane figure made up of three or more line segments.

positive number A number that is greater than 0.

power of ten A power with a base of 10.

precision A term used to refer to the accuracy of a measurement. A smaller unit produces a more precise measurement than a larger unit.

prime factorization Writing a number as the product of prime factors.

prime number A whole number greater than 1 that has exactly two factors.

prism A solid figure that has two parallel congruent bases and parallelograms for faces.

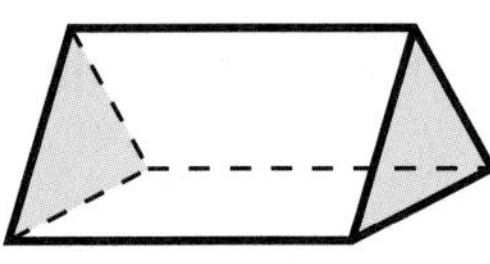

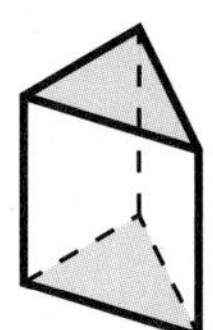

probability The chance of an event occurring. A probability can be any number from 0 through 1.

product The result in multiplication.

proper fraction A fraction in which the numerator is less than the denominator.

Example: $\frac{4}{7}$

proportion A statement that two ratios are equivalent.

pyramid A solid figure whose base can be any polygon and whose faces are triangles.

quadrant Each of the four parts into which a plane is separated by the *x*-axis and the *y*-axis. The axes are not parts of the quadrant.

quadrilateral A polygon with four sides.

quotient The result in division.

radius A segment that connects the center of a circle to any point on the circle.

range The difference between the greatest and least numbers in a set of data.

rate A ratio of two quantities using different units.

ratio A comparison of two numbers by division.

ray Part of a line that starts at an endpoint and goes on infinitely in one direction.

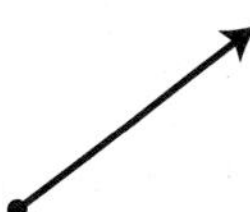

reciprocal The product of a number and its reciprocal is 1.

rectangle A polygon with opposite sides parallel and four right angles.

rectangular prism A solid figure with six faces that are rectangles.

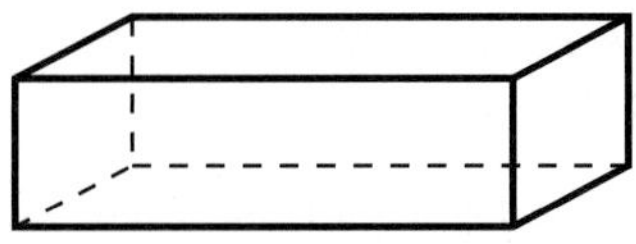

rectangular pyramid A solid figure whose base is a rectangle and whose faces are triangles.

reflection A transformation that flips a figure over a line.

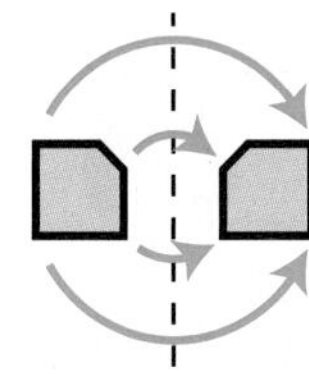

regular polygon A polygon with all sides congruent and all angles congruent.

remainder The number that is left over after one whole number is divided by another.

repeating decimal A decimal quotient that contains a repeating block of digits.

rhombus A parallelogram with all four sides congruent.

right angle An angle that measures 90°.

right triangle A triangle that has one right angle.

rotation A transformation that turns a figure about a given point.

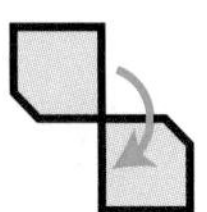

rotational symmetry If a figure can be turned less than a full turn about a given point and the figure looks exactly the way it did before the turn, that figure has rotational symmetry.

sale price The price of an item after the discount is subtracted.

sample space A list of all possible outcomes.

scale A ratio of the measurements in a drawing to actual measurements.

scale drawing A drawing created using a scale.

scalene triangle A triangle with no congruent sides.

sequence An ordered set of numbers.

side One of the line segments that make up a polygon.

similar figures Figures that have the same shape but not necessarily the same size.

simplest form A fraction is in simplest form when the GCF of the numerator and denominator is 1.

solid figure A three-dimensional figure in space.

speed A rate that shows distance per unit of time.

sphere A solid figure that is shaped like a round ball.

square A polygon with four right angles and four congruent sides.

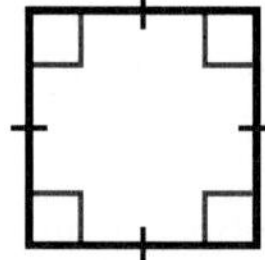

square unit A square with sides one unit long.

standard form A way of writing a number using only digits.

stem The digit or digits to the left of the leaves in a stem-and-leaf plot.

stem-and-leaf plot A frequency distribution that arranges data in order of place value.

straight angle An angle that measures 180°.

sum The result in addition.

surface area The total area of the surface of a solid.

survey A method of collecting information about a group of people.

symmetric figure A figure that has line or rotational symmetry.

T

terms of a ratio The numerator and denominator of a ratio expressed as a fraction. The numerator is the first term, and the denominator is the second term.

tessellation A repeating pattern that covers a plane without gaps or overlaps.

theoretical probability For a single event, the probability calculated by dividing the number of favorable outcomes in the event by the total number of possible outcomes.

tip A percentage portion of a total bill, customarily left after service.

transformation A transformation changes the position of a plane figure.

translation A transformation that slides a figure a given distance in a given direction.

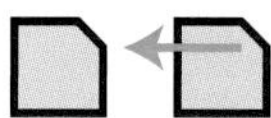

trapezoid A quadrilateral with exactly one pair of parallel sides.

tree diagram A diagram that shows combinations of outcomes of an event.

triangle A polygon with three sides.

triangular prism A prism whose bases are triangles.

triangular pyramid A pyramid whose base is a triangle.

U

unit cost The cost of a single item.

unit cube A cube with an edge length of 1.

unit fraction A fraction in which the numerator is 1.

unit lengths Standard lengths in the customary and metric systems of measurement.

unit rate A rate in which the second term is 1.

V

variable A letter that represents a number in an algebraic expression.

variable

$6 + (r \div 2)$

vertex of an angle A point common to the two sides of an angle.

vertical axis The y-axis in the coordinate system. It is a number line used to locate points above or below the origin.

volume The number of cubic units that make up a solid figure.

weight The measure of how heavy an object is.

***x*-axis** The horizontal number line in a coordinate plane.

***y*-axis** The vertical number line in a coordinate plane.

Zero Property of Multiplication The property which states that the product of any number and 0 is 0.

Example: $a \times 0 = 0$

Index

N

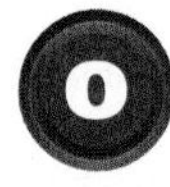
O

T

U

V

W

X

Y

Z

Credits

PERMISSIONS ACKNOWLEDGMENTS
Houghton Mifflin Mathematics © 2005, Grade 5 PE/TE

"Numbers," by Mary Cornish. Copyright © 2000 by the Modern Poetry Association. Reprinted by permission of the editor of *Poetry* and the author.

Cover © HMCo./Bruton Stroube Studios.

PHOTOGRAPHY

vi © Leonard de Selva/CORBIS. **vii** © Karl Weatherly/CORBIS. **2** © Tom & Dee Ann McCarthy/CORBIS. **4** © Angelo Cavalli/Imagebank /Getty Images. **8** Omni Photo Communications, Inc./Index Stock. **12** © Chabruken/ Getty Images. **16** Courtesy Robert A. Siegel Auction Galleries, Inc. **17** © Leonard de Selva/CORBIS. **22** Spectrum/Robertstock.com. **26** Harold M. Lambert/SuperStock. **28** Camerique/Robertstock.com. **31** Cornell University. **32** © Karl Weatherly/CORBIS. **34** © Richard Cummins/CORBIS. **38** SuperStock. **40** Jim Corwin/Stock Boston. **42** Lars Howlett/AURORA. **46-7** © Gallo Images/CORBIS. **47** © Ralph A. Clevenger/CORBIS. **49** (br) Mark Tomalty/Masterfile. **50** (tr) Gail Mooney/Masterfile. **58** © Morton Beebe, S.F./CORBIS. **60** Guy Spangenberg/Transtock. **66** © Joe Cornish/Stone/Getty Images. **68** © Felix Clouzot/Imagebank/Getty Images. **70** © Frans Lemmens/Imagebank/Getty Images. **72** Robin Hill/Index Stock. **76** Joe Sohm/The Image Works. **79** Danilo Boschung/eStock Photo. **80** Margot Granitsis/The Image Works. **88** © Photomondo/Taxi/Getty Images. **84** Spencer Grant/PhotoEdit. **96** Roger Allyn Lee/SuperStock. **97** Comstock KLIPS. **99** Classic PIO Collection. **108** © Bettman/CORBIS. **110** NASA. **114** © Bettman/CORBIS. **118** Topham/The Image Works. **120** © Otto Herschan/Hulton Archive/Getty Images. **126** Deborah Davis/PhotoEdit. **128** Marilyn "Angel" Wynn/nativestock.com. **129** Courtesy of The Montana Historical Society. **130** PhotoDisc/Getty Images. **134-5** (b) © Michael & Patricia Fogden/CORBIS. **134** (t) Tom Ulrich/Getty Images. **146** Frans Lanting/Minden Pictures. **147** PhotoDisc/Getty Images. **152** Reinhard/Mauritius/Robertstock.com. **153** Look GMBH/eStock Photo. **156** Tom Brakefield/SuperStock. **159** IT Stock Int'l/Index Stock. **160** Mark Newman/SuperStock. **162** © Dennis Gottlieb /FoodPix/Getty Images. **170** Look GMBH/eStock Photo. **172** Kenneth W. Fink/Photo Researchers, Inc. **176** © Art Wolfe/Stone/Getty Images. **178** Tim Davis/Photo Researchers, Inc. **186** James Urbach/SuperStock. **190** © Lawrence Migdale/Stone/Getty Images. **198** AP/Wide World Photos. **205** © Carl Schneider/Taxi/Getty Images. **210-1** Bob Thomas/Getty Images. **210** (b) Al Bello/Allsport/Getty Images. **211** Ben Radford/Getty Images. **222** The Field Museum, Neg# GN89717, John Weinstein. **224** © Julie Toy/Taxi/Getty Images. **228** Targa/agefotostock. **229** Targa/agefotostock. **230** © Gail Mooney/CORBIS. **231** (t) Ronald Sheridan@Ancient Art & Architecture Collection. (b) Jaume Gual/agefotostock. **232** courtesy Jeff Koons. **235** Rudi Von Briel/PhotoEdit. **246** Susan Van Etten/PhotoEdit. **254** Mark Thayer/Index Stock. **256** Richard Hutchings/PhotoEdit. **260** David Young-Wolff/PhotoEdit. **268** BSIP Agency/Index Stock. **270** Syracuse Newspapers/The Image Works. **272** ComstockKLIPS. **274** Myrleen Cate/PhotoEdit. **280** © Mike Powell/Allsport Concepts/Getty Images. **290** © Neil Rabinowitz/CORBIS. **292** Fujifotos/The Image Works. **296-7** © Lester Lefkowitz/CORBIS. **308** © Owen Franken/CORBIS. **316** Benelux Press/ Index Stock/Picture Quest. **322** © Bruce Forster/Stone/Getty Images. **324** © David Hanson/Stone/Getty Images. **328** © Paul A. Souders/CORBIS. **329** Paul Conklin/PhotoEdit. **332** NOVASTOCK/PhotoEdit. **342** © SW Productions/PhotoDisc/Getty Images. **343** Bill Schoening, Vanessa Harvey/REU program/NOAO/AURA/NSF. **346** David Young-Wolff/PhotoEdit. **350** © Christoph Wilhelm/Taxi/Getty Images. **352** Jose Galvez/PhotoEdit. **354** Scott Barrow/ImageState. **355** Royalty-Free/CORBIS. **356** (l) SuperStock. (r) Stephens B Myers/ImageState. **357** PROF. P. MOTTA / DEPT. OF ANATOMY / UNIVERSITY, "LA SAPIENZA", ROME / SPI/Custom Medical Stock Photo. **358**Novastock/PhotoEdit. **360**Tony Freeman/PhotoEdit. **362**Daemmrich/Stock Boston. **364** © Globus,Holway & Lobel/CORBIS. **365**© AFP/CORBIS. **366**Table Mesa Productions/IndexStock. **368**© Royalty-Free/CORBIS. **372** (t) (l) Comstock KLIPS. **376-7** © H.D. Thoreau/CORBIS. **376** (m) USPS. **377** (r) USPS. **388** © Gunter Marx/CORBIS. **390** Frank Siteman/agefotostock. **398** R.O. Photosure.com/agefotostock. **400** R. Krubner/Robertstock.com. **401** Herb Levart/SuperStock. **408** S. Piumatti/Robertstock.com. **409** © Ralph A. Clevenger/CORBIS. **414** © George Hunter/Stone/Getty Images. **416** SuperStock. **417** Bill Aron/PhotoEdit. **420** The Newark Museum/Art Resource, NY. **422** Art Resource, NY. **444** © Greg Pease/CORBIS. **464** © Lester Lefkowitz/CORBIS. **470-1** © Lee Snider; Lee Snider/CORBIS. **470** (b) © Bettmann/CORBIS. **471** (b) © Bob Rowan; Progressive Image/CORBIS. **473** (br) PhotoDisc/Getty Images. **482** © Kelley-Mooney Photography/CORBIS. **488** © Garry Gay/Imagebank/Getty Images. **496** Tony Freeman/PhotoEdit. **501** © Robert Holmes/CORBIS. **504** Tomas del Amo/Index Stock. (b) ComstockKLIPS. **508** Jeff Greenberg/PhotoEdit. **514** Davis Barber/PhotoEdit. **516** Bob Burch/Index Stock. **518** © Guy Grenier/Masterfile. **526** © Duomo/CORBIS. **537** © Richard Cummins/CORBIS. **552-3** © Blaine Harrington III/CORBIS. **553** (t) RON CHAPPLE/Getty Images. **584** Alan Kearney/agefotostock. **588** © Michael Keller/CORBIS. **590** Barry Runk/Stan/Grant Heilman Photography, Inc. **594** © Bob Krist/CORBIS. **598** Walter Geiesperger/agefotostock. **602** Tom Rosenthal/SuperStock. **603** © Duomo/CORBIS. **608** Tony & Daphne Hallas/Astrophoto.com. **618** © George Hall/CORBIS. **628-9** Gary D. Gaugler/Photo Researchers, Inc. **629** (t) Gary D. Gaugler/Photo Researchers, Inc. **629** (tm)(bm)(b) Gary D. Gaugler/Visuals Unlimited. **636** (tr) Mark Tomalty/Masterfile. **638-9** © Chris Noble/Getty Images. **641** © Ark/Alamy. **645** © Ken Biggs/Getty Images.

WEEKLY READER PHOTOGRAPHY

676 © Richard T. Nowitz/CORBIS.
677 (tl) © Richard T. Nowitz/CORBIS. (tr) © Randy Wells/Stone/Getty Images. (b) © Eastcott Momatiuk/Stone/Getty Images.
678 (t) AP/Wide World Photos. (b) The Henry Ford Museum.
679 (t) AP/Wide World Photos. (b) © CORBIS.
680 © Stone/Getty Images.
681 (l) © Imagebank/GettyImages.
(r) © Scott T. Smith/CORBIS.

Credits continued

682-3 (bkgd) Bon Secour NWR.
682 (inset) AP/Wide World Photos.
683 (inset) AP/Wide World Photos.
684 (t, br) Courtesy of the City of Hopewell and the William and Mary Center for Archaeological Research. (bl) Archivo Iconpgrafico, SA/CORBIS. (bc) Frank Lane Picture Agency/CORBIS.
685 Courtesy of the City of Hopewell and the William and Mary Center for Archaeological Research.

ASSIGNMENT PHOTOGRAPHY

xxii, xxviii, xxix © HMCo./Joel Benjamin.

632 (bl) © HMCo./Ray Boudreau.

2 (t), **56, 144, 220, 306, 386, 480, 562** © HMCo./Dave Bradley.

55, 62, 81, 90, 92, 102, 143, 148, 155, 163, 164, 174, 192, 200, 219, 240, 248, 262, 266, 282, 286, 305, 311, 318, 327, 338, 344, 371,385, 392, 393, 412, 434, 438, 448, 450, 452, 456, 460, 479, 484, 486, 491, 492, 506, 510, 532, 536, 540, 561, 564, 566, 568, 572, 578, 580, 581, 592, 613, 614, 616, 637 © HMCo./Angela Coppola.

xxiii, xxiv, xxv, © HMCo./Allan Landau.

51, 54, 138, 142 (tr), **214, 299** (tr), **300** (bl), **301** (bc), **478** (tr), **478** (br) © HMCo./Dave Starrett.

2 (cr), **51, 380** (bl), **475** (tr), **633** (r) © HMCo./Ron Tanaka.

ILLUSTRATION

18, 58, 91, 111, 122, 166, 167 (b), **170, 190, 202, 204, 222, 264, 284, 308, 326, 342 , 410, 426, 496, 521, 526, 534** (b), **547, 580** (b), **595, 604,** Argosy. **137, 214** (br), **299** (b), **384, 557** (tr) Steve Attoe. **64, 350, 420, 431** (l), **437, 444, 455** (b), **452, 463, 465** (b) Kenneth Batelman. **50** (br), **139** (tr), **481** (tr) Gary Bullock. **43** Estelle Carol. **417** (r), **432** John Edwards, Inc. **79** Ruth Flanigan. **647** Jim Gordon. **197, 337, 519** Mike Gordan. **215** (tr,) **381** (tr), **473** (br), **474** (tr), **555** (b) Jeff Grunewald. **163, 167, 207, 231, 251, 319, 407, 417** Ken Hansen. **150** Robert Hynes. **300** (tr), **304** (r) Kelly Kennedy. **642-43** Dave Klug. **379** (c) Bernadette Lau. **213** (br) **556** (bl)Dave McKay. **556** (tr) Jack McMaster. **154** Martucci Designs. **380** (tr), **632** (tr) Dirk Michiels. **112. 648-49** Karen Minot. **10,14, 37,499, 619** Ortelius Design, Inc. **379** (cr), **474** (bl), **562** (br) Jun Park. **158** (t), Precision Graphics. **158** (bl), **158** (br), **161**, **266** Precision Graphics. **26, 65, 66, 94, 108, 182, 194, 206, 239, 254, 276, 288, 340, 409, 457, 458, 466, 500, 520, 529, 533, 534** (t), **548, 550** (t), **573, 574, 586, 610,** Rob Schuster. **218** (tr), **560** (tr) Paul Watson. **640** Rob Wood.

WEEKLY READER ILLUSTRATION

678 Peter Amis.
685 Leigh Haeger.

All tech art by Pronk & Associates.

WEEKLY WR READER®

Activity Almanac

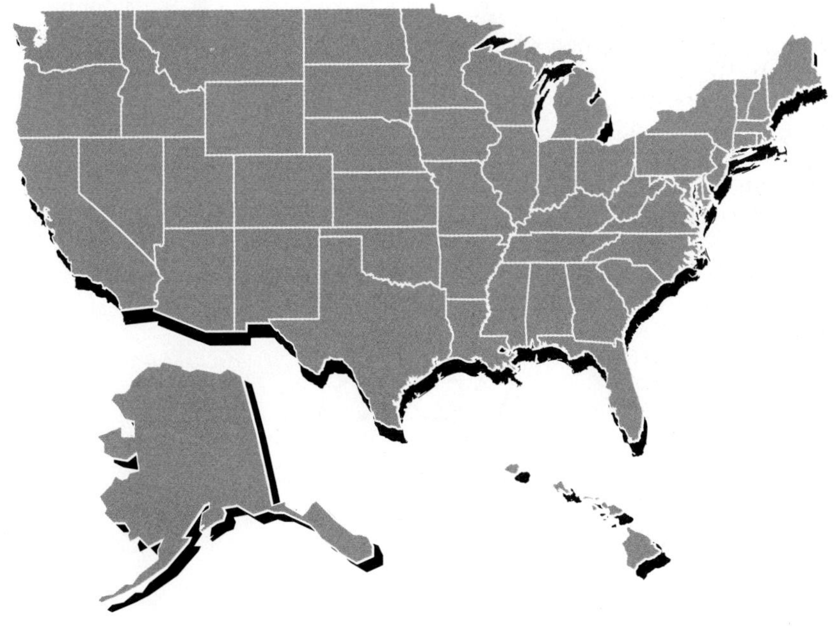

Weekly Reader Web Link
Visit *Education Place* at
eduplace.com/math/kids/mw/ to learn more.

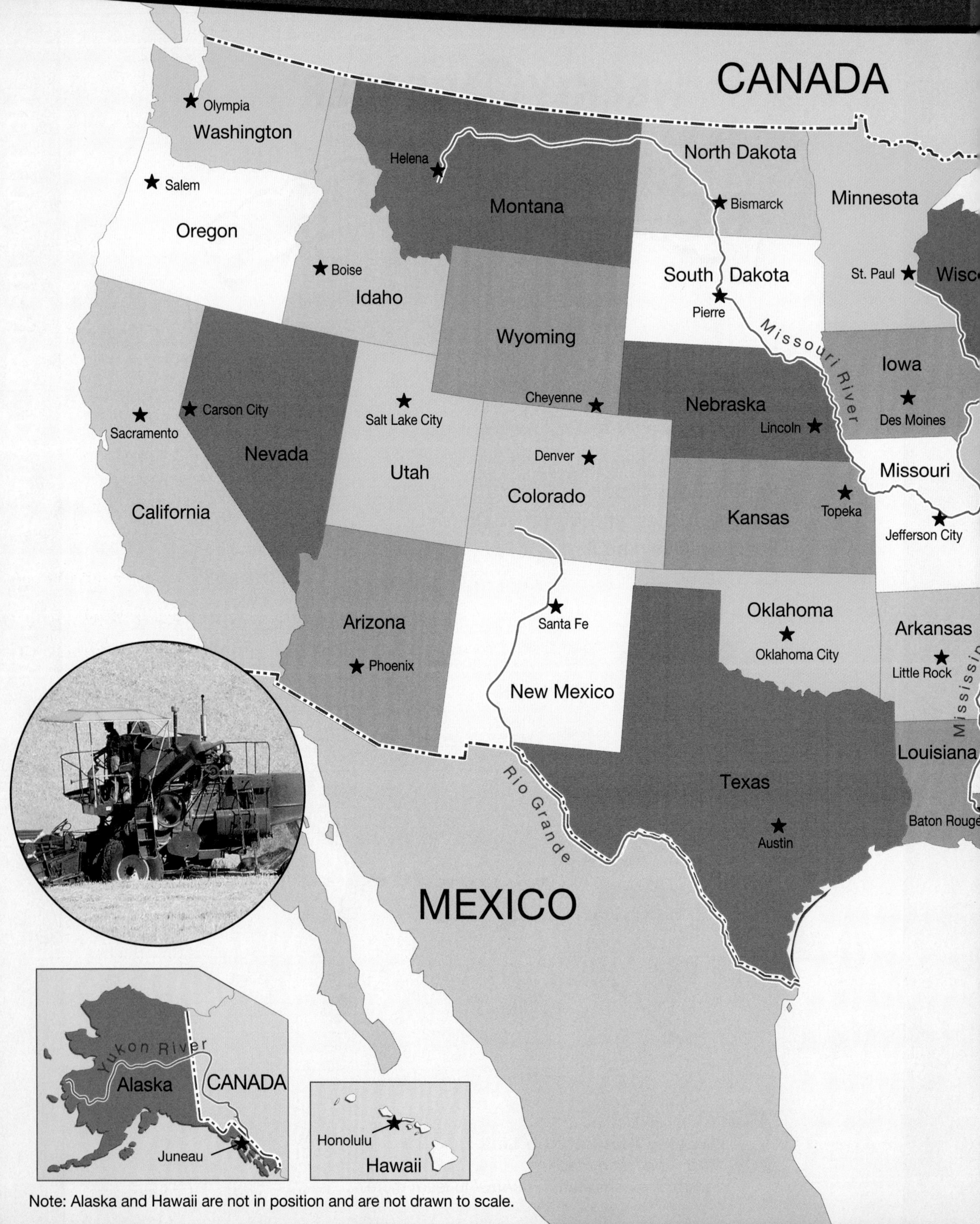

Note: Alaska and Hawaii are not in position and are not drawn to scale.

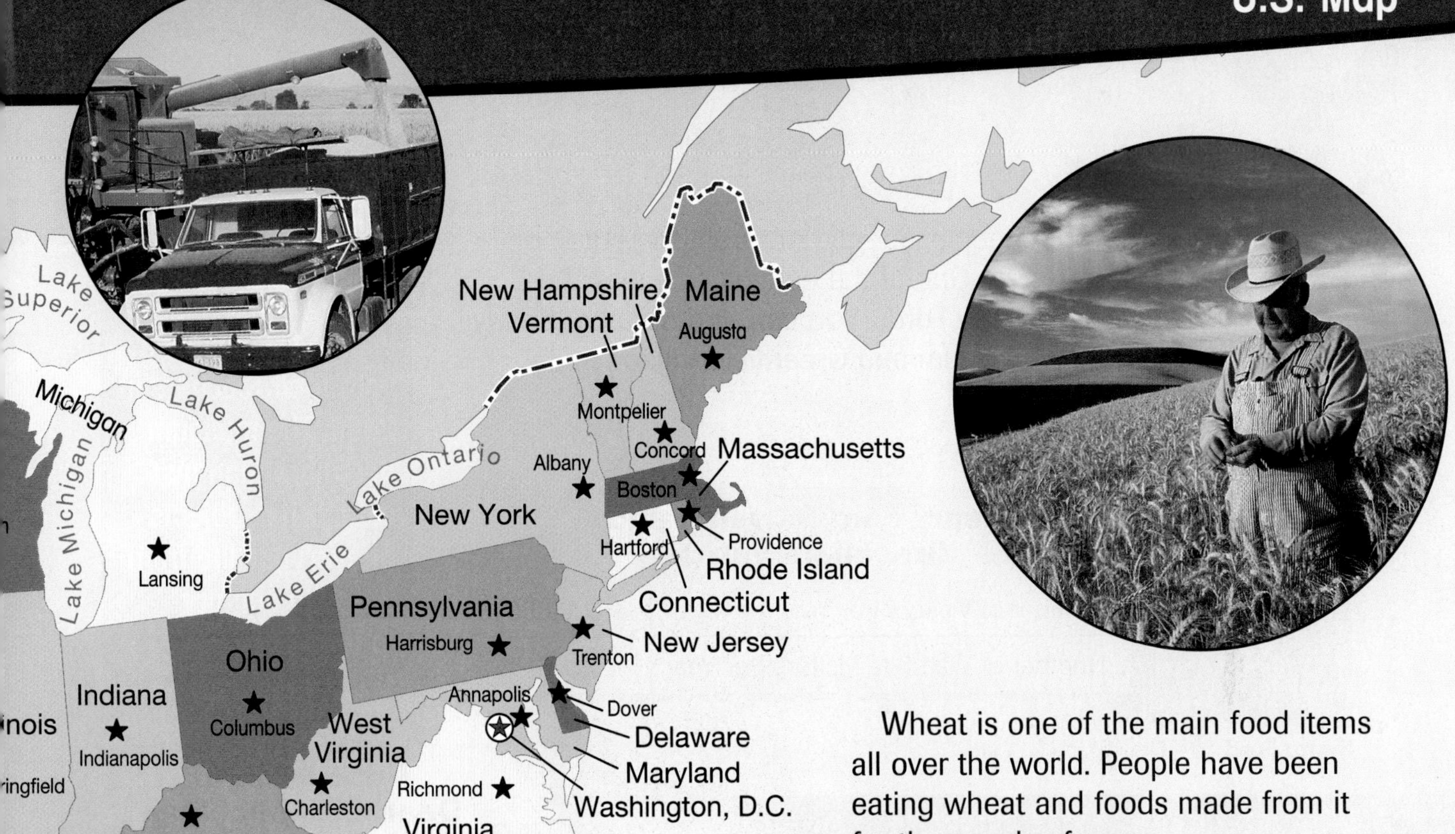

Wheat is one of the main food items all over the world. People have been eating wheat and foods made from it for thousands of years.

Choose a state from the table below.

How many thousands of acres of wheat were harvested in 2002? How many were harvested in 2001?

Wheat Harvested in 2002

State	Number of Acres (thousands)	Change from Previous Year
Alabama	60	⁻10
Idaho	1,200	0
Illinois	655	⁻70
Michigan	177	⁺10
New Jersey	32	⁺5
New York	128	⁺8
Tennessee	300	⁻40
Virginia	170	0
West Virginia	7	⁻1

A New Car

Get a horse! That's what people who did not trust the automobile said when it was first invented. One of the earliest cars was the Model T Ford, invented by Henry Ford. You can find out about early vehicles at the Henry Ford Museum and Greenfield Village in Dearborn, Michigan.

FAST FACTS

300,000 students visited the museum with their teachers in 2000. The museum has more than just cars. It has objects of everyday life from the 17th century to today.

Henry Ford

Henry Ford Museum and Greenfield Village	
Number of Visitors Per Year	1,600,000
Number of Web Site Visitors Per Year	69,991,614

Population of Dearborn, Michigan	
Year	Number of People
1900	844
2000	97,775

Henry Ford Museum and Greenfield Village

At the museum, you can see...

- more than 10,000 toys and games
- more than 600 musical instruments
- more than 400 posters from World War I
- farm tools from the 1800s
- mechanical calculators from the 1940s
- swim trunks from the 1880s

Data Hunt

Imagine you are a tour guide at the museum. Think about what facts you would tell visitors. Use the data on this page to write a script for your tour.

- Use comparisons of data in your script, including population comparisons.
- Include these comparisons as facts to tell to your tour group. For example, "The population of Dearborn grew by about 97,000 in 100 years."

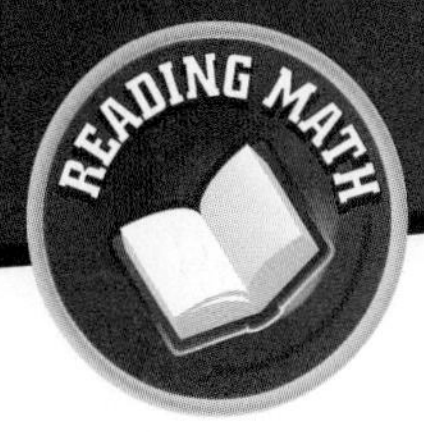

Car Facts

The number of cars, the price of cars, and the weight of cars have all increased. Only the advertising has stayed the same. Early advertising sheets urged consumers to buy the best at the lowest price. Sound familiar?

The Ford Model T 1908–1909

1908–1909 Model T Facts	
Number Built 1908–1927	15,000,000
Weight	1,200 pounds
Price	$850

1912 Model T Facts	
Number Built in 1912	75,000
Touring Car Price	$690
Commercial Roadster Price	$590
Town Car Price	$900
Delivery Car Price	$700

The Ford Model T 1912

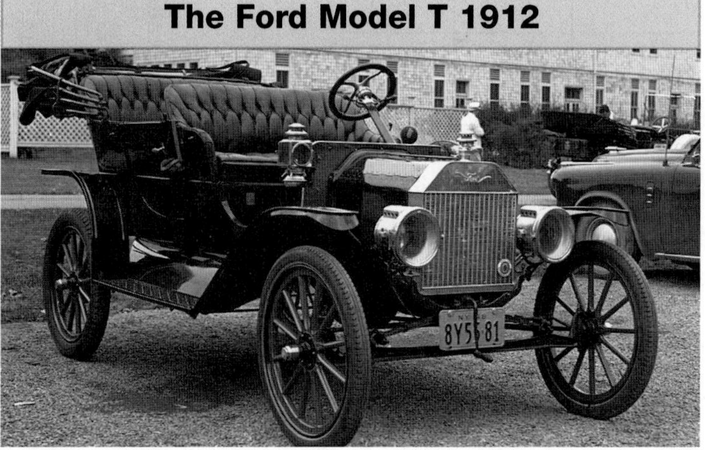

Data Hunt

You have been asked to create math riddles for a booth at a school math fair. Use the data on these pages to prepare your questions.

- Your answers will be the data about the Model T cars or the museum.
- At least two riddles must involve multiplication and at least two riddles must involve division.

  Example: *You must divide my cost by 2 to get $425. Which car am I?*
  Answer: The 1909 Ford Model T.

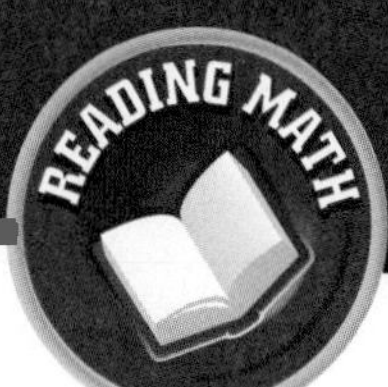

Falls Favorite

Imagine 35 million gallons each minute cascading 180 feet down! It happens at Niagara Falls in New York, one of the most popular tourist destinations in the world.

The falls are open year-round, but some outdoor activities depend on the weather.

Record High and Low Temperatures Niagara Falls, NY

Month	High	Low
January	72°F	⁻16°F
February	70°F	⁻20°F
March	81°F	⁻7°F
April	94°F	12°F
May	90°F	26°F
June	96°F	35°F
July	97°F	43°F
August	99°F	38°F
September	98°F	32°F
October	87°F	20°F
November	80°F	9°F
December	74°F	⁻10°F

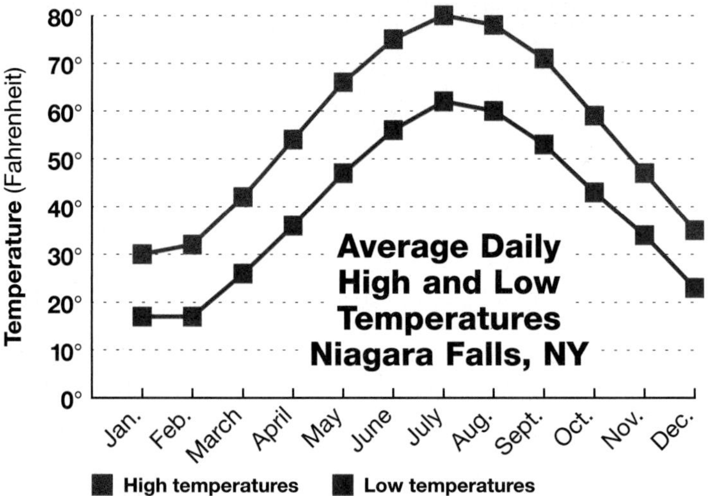

Ways to See Niagara Falls

Ways to See Niagara Falls
You can ride to an observation tower to see the 180-foot-high falls from above.
You can ride an elevator 175 feet down to see part of the falls close up—just 20 feet away!
You can take a 30-minute boat ride in the waters below.

Data Hunt

Imagine you are planning a campaign to encourage people to visit Niagara Falls.

- Write an announcement with information about the weather and attractions.
- Use the data on this page to create a bar graph or line graph that you think would encourage people to visit.
- Surround your graph with fun facts about Niagara Falls.

Winter Wonderland

Snow in the Niagara Falls–Buffalo (New York) area? Of course! This Great Lakes region gets lots of snow. The result is a variety of winter activities, including snowboarding, ice-skating, and snowshoeing.

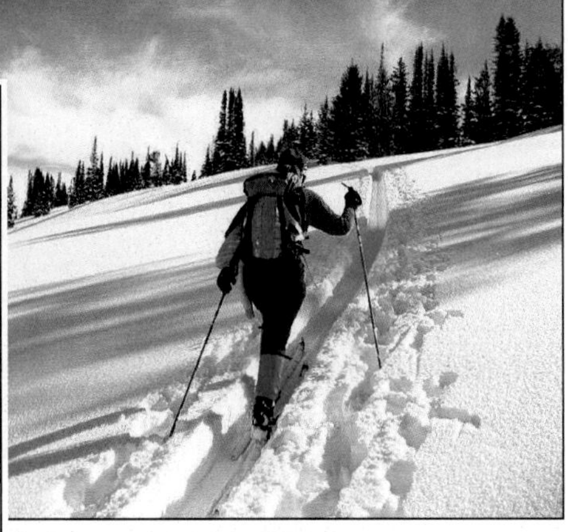

FAST FACTS

In November 2001, no snowfall was recorded in Buffalo, New York. It was the first November in 122 years with absolutely no snow!

But in late December 2001, Buffalo had record snowfalls. The monthly snowfall of 83.5 inches was a new record for any month.

Average Monthly Snowfall (Inches)

City	November	December	January	February	March
Buffalo, NY	11.4	24.1	24.2	17.7	12.4
Albany, NY	4.2	14.3	16.6	13.9	11.7
Newark, NJ	0.6	5.4	7.7	8.3	4.9
Columbus, OH	2.2	5.4	8.9	6.0	4.5
Richmond, VA	0.4	2.0	4.9	3.9	2.4

Data Hunt

Imagine you are a weather reporter for a TV station.

- Create a special report on winter weather in the Buffalo–Niagara Falls region.
- Include comparisons between cities. Use snowfall data to highlight differences.
- Include information about total amounts of snowfall and records set.

Reptile Roundup

How do you study alligators? By going where the gators go! Field biologists study alligators in swampy areas like the Choctawatchee River in southeastern Alabama. The 170-mile long river teems with alligators, beavers, deer, muskrats, raccoons, and water birds.

FAST FACTS

An alligator's tail is half of its total length.

American Alligator Facts	
Largest Found in the U.S.	5.8 meters
Number of Teeth	about 80
Alabama Alligator Population	35,000
Weight of Adult Male	180 kilograms to 228 kilograms
Number of Eggs in a Nest	20–50

Lengths of Some Large Alligators

Female	Male
3.1 meters	4.3 meters
3.0 meters	4.1 meters
2.9 meters	3.8 meters

The number of male and female alligator hatchlings depends on the temperature of their nest. If the temperature is 89.6°F, about $\frac{3}{4}$ of the hatchlings will be female. The rest will be male.

Data Hunt

Imagine you are a wildlife scientist in Alabama. You are going to visit a school and talk about alligators. Use the data to write a report for your talk.

- Include the tail lengths of the large alligators in your report. Prepare questions that ask students to find tail lengths of different-sized alligators. Include answers.
- Include information about how many female hatchlings there would be in a nest of 48 eggs with a temperature of 89.6°F.

Gators, Turtles, and Birds... Oh My!

On a summer afternoon in Alabama, volunteers are keeping watch as just-hatched sea turtles crawl into the Gulf of Mexico. They are helping the Kemp's Ridley sea turtle survive. At Bon Secour National Wildlife Refuge, you can see rare turtles, alligators, migrating birds, and more.

FAST FACTS

10 to 15 Kemp's Ridley turtles nest each year on Alabama's Gulf Coast.

The sea turtles nest 2 times a year and lay about 110 eggs in each nest.

Bon Secour National Wildlife Refuge High and Low Tides—May 2002

Date	High Tide	Time	Low Tide	Time
May 5	1.7 feet	5:57 P.M.	0.2 feet	5:19 A.M.
May 12	1.9 feet	11:39 A.M.	0.1 feet	10:18 P.M.
May 23	1.4 feet	11:04 A.M.	0.5 feet	8:35 P.M.

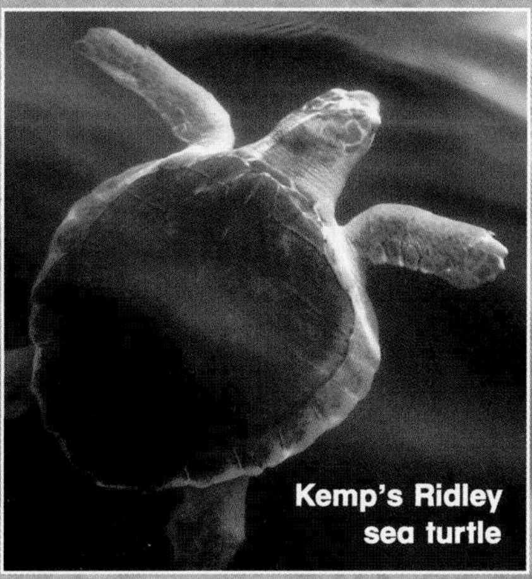
Kemp's Ridley sea turtle

Bon Secour National Wildlife Refuge Average High Temperatures

Month	May	June	July	August
Temperature	83.2°F	88.5°F	89.9°F	89.4°F

Data Hunt

Imagine you are a product designer asked to create a souvenir to sell to visitors at the refuge. Think about a box that will hold the souvenir. The box can be a rectangular prism or a triangular prism.

- Make a net of the solid figure you choose for your box.
- Write the dimensions of the cardboard you will need for the box. Calculate the surface area of the box.
- Use the data on these pages to create a fact sheet to put inside the box. Include animal facts and suggest the best times to visit the refuge.

Puzzling Over the Past

It's like a puzzle—finding pieces of the past and figuring out what the pieces mean. Archeologists are finding clues about Native Americans, settlers, merchants, soldiers, and factory workers as they dig up the past of the City Point region of Hopewell, Virginia.

Workers lay out a grid for a test dig.

Quartz
16 pieces

Jasper
4 pieces

Points
(whole or fragments)
18 pieces

FAST FACTS

The population of early settlers in 1600 was about half of the population in 1840.

HOPEWELL TIMELINE

1600 | 1700 | 1800 | 1900 | 2000

Early 1600s
English settlers

1830–1840
One of the first U.S. railroads built

Town population: 300

1860s
Civil War skirmishes

President Lincoln visits.

1914–1920s
Factories built.

Town grows.

1980
Population: about 23,000

2000
Population: about 22,000

Data Hunt

Imagine that you are working to promote Hopewell's archaeology project. Your job is to design a poster.

- Use any of the data on these two pages.
- Highlight interesting facts about the pieces found and Hopewell's history.
- Be sure to present at least two facts that use ratios or proportions.

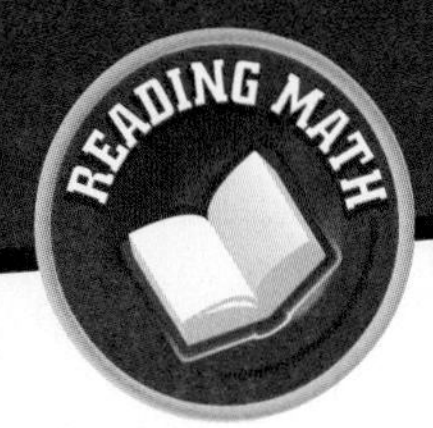

Grid Game

Archeologists find pieces of pottery, tool fragments, and other items made or used by people from the past. These items are called artifacts. The archeologists mark points on the grid by pounding nails into the ground. Then they use the coordinate grid to identify the places where artifacts are found.

Distribution of Artifacts

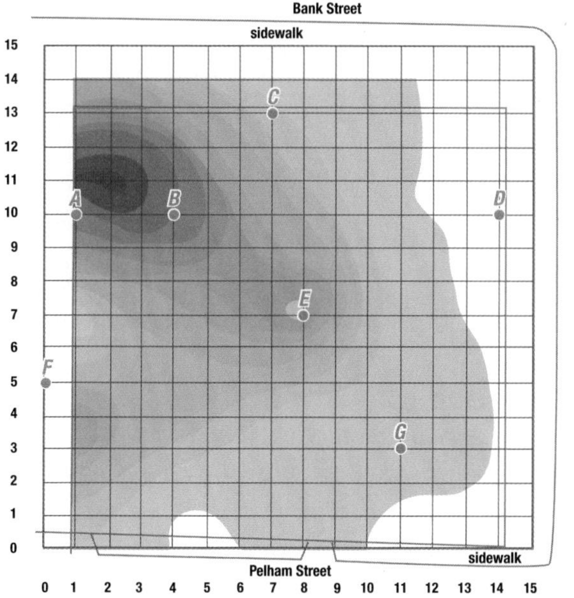

FAST FACTS

A computer created the map on the left to show the distribution of the artifacts found in City Point. The darker the blue, the more artifacts found.

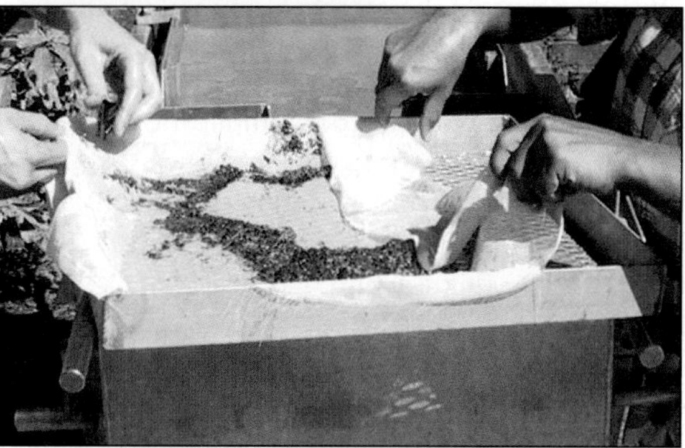

Workers sift through soil in search of artifacts.

Data Hunt

Imagine that a toy company has asked you to design a board game about archaeology.

- Use a coordinate grid and the data on these pages to create a game about the City Point region in Hopewell.
- Think about how you use the grid to find where things are.
- Be sure to include coordinates for places where more, fewer, or no objects were found!
- After you create the game, try playing it with a friend.

NCTM Standards for Grades 3–5

Number and Operations Standards • Expectations	Houghton Mifflin Math Grade 5 Correlation*
Understand numbers, ways of representing numbers, relationships among numbers, and number systems	
• understand the place-value structure of the base-ten number system and be able to represent and compare whole numbers and decimals;	• Ch. 1, L. 4, 5, 7
• recognize equivalent representations for the same number and generate them by decomposing and composing numbers;	• Ch. 1, L. 1–3; Ch. 9, L. 6
• develop understanding of fractions as parts of unit wholes, as parts of a collection, as locations on number lines, and as divisions of whole numbers;	• Ch. 9, L. 5
• use models, benchmarks, and equivalent forms to judge the size of fractions;	• Ch. 9, L. 8, 9
• recognize and generate equivalent forms of commonly used fractions, decimals, and percents;	• Ch. 11, L. 1; Ch. 19, L. 1–3
• explore numbers less than 0 by extending the number line and through familiar applications;	• Ch. 22, L. 1–4, 6
• describe classes of numbers according to characteristics such as the nature of their factors.	• Ch. 9, L. 1–5
Understand meanings of operations and how they relate to one another	
• understand various meanings of multiplication and division;	• Ch. 3, L. 4
• understand the effects of multiplying and dividing whole numbers;	• Ch. 4, L. 2; Ch. 5, L. 2
• identify and use relationships between operations, such as division as the inverse of multiplication, to solve problems;	• Ch. 21, L. 2; Ch. 22, L. 5
• understand and use properties of operations, such as the distributivity of multiplication over addition.	• Ch. 3, L. 1, 2
Compute fluently and make reasonable estimates	
• develop fluency with basic number combinations for multiplication and division and use these combinations to mentally compute related problems, such as 30×50;	• Ch. 3, L. 5; Ch. 5, L. 1
• develop fluency in adding, subtracting, multiplying, and dividing whole numbers;	• Ch. 2, L. 3, 4; Ch. 3, L. 7; Ch. 4, L. 4, 5, 7; Ch. 5, L. 5
• develop and use strategies to estimate the results of whole-number computations and to judge the reasonableness of such results;	• Ch. 2, L. 2; Ch. 3, L. 6, 8; Ch. 4, L. 1; Ch. 5, L. 5, 7
• develop and use strategies to estimate computations involving fractions and decimals in situations relevant to students' experience;	• Ch. 10, L. 1; Ch. 11, L. 4; Ch. 13, L. 3; Ch. 14, L. 2
• use visual models, benchmarks, and equivalent forms to add and subtract commonly used fractions and decimals;	• Ch. 10, L. 2–7; Ch. 11, L. 2, 3
• select appropriate methods and tools for computing with whole numbers from among mental computation, estimation, calculators, and paper and pencil according to the context and nature of the computation and use the selected method or tools.	• See **Calculator Connection** in Ch. 21, L. 2

* For each lesson, the key content and process standards have been identified.

Algebra Standards • Expectations	Houghton Mifflin Math Grade 5 Correlation
Understand patterns, relations, and functions	
• describe, extend, and make generalizations about geometric and numeric patterns;	• Ch. 1, L. 6; Ch. 16, L. 2
• represent and analyze patterns and functions, using words, tables, and graphs.	• Ch. 1, L. 6; Ch. 19, L. 5; Ch. 23, L. 2
Represent and analyze mathematical situations and structures using algebraic symbols	
• identify such properties as commutativity, associativity, and distributivity and use them to compute with whole numbers;	• Ch. 5, L. 6
• represent the idea of a variable as an unknown quantity using a letter or a symbol;	• Ch. 2, L. 1; Ch. 21, L. 3
• express mathematical relationships using equations.	• Ch. 2, L. 5; Ch. 21, L. 2, 3
Use mathematical models to represent and understand quantitative relationships	
• model problem situations with objects and use representations such as graphs, tables, and equations to draw conclusions.	• Ch. 21, L. 1
Analyze change in various contexts	
• investigate how a change in one variable relates to a change in a second variable;	• Ch. 21, L. 4
• identify and describe situations with constant or varying rates of change and compare them.	• Ch. 21, L. 5

Geometry Standards • Expectations	Houghton Mifflin Math Grade 5 Correlation
Analyze characteristics and properties of two- and three-dimensional geometric shapes and develop mathematical arguments about geometric relationships	
• identify, compare, and analyze attributes of two- and three-dimensional shapes and develop vocabulary to describe the attributes;	• Ch. 15, L. 1, 2, 9
• classify two- and three-dimensional shapes according to their properties and develop definitions of classes of shapes such as triangles and pyramids;	• Ch. 15, L. 3, 5, 8
• investigate, describe, and reason about the results of subdividing, combining, and transforming shapes;	• Ch. 15, L. 6; Ch. 23, L. 5
• explore congruence and similarity;	• Ch. 15, L. 4; Ch. 18, L. 5
• make and test conjectures about geometric properties and relationships and develop logical arguments to justify conclusions.	• Ch. 17, L. 3
Specify locations and describe spatial relationships using coordinate geometry and other representational systems	
• describe location and movement using common language and geometric vocabulary;	• Ch. 23, L. 1
• make and use coordinate systems to specify locations and to describe paths;	• Ch. 23, L. 3, 4

Geometry Standards (continued) • Expectations	Houghton Mifflin Math Grade 5 Correlation*
• find the distance between points along horizontal and vertical lines of a coordinate system.	• Ch. 23, L. 1
Apply transformations and use symmetry to analyze mathematical situations	
• predict and describe the results of sliding, flipping, and turning two-dimensional shapes;	• Ch. 15, L. 6; Ch. 23, L. 5
• describe a motion or a series of motions that will show that two shapes are congruent;	• Ch. 15, L. 6
• identify and describe line and rotational symmetry in two- and three-dimensional shapes and designs.	• Ch. 15, L. 9
Use visualization, spatial reasoning, and geometric modeling to solve problems	
• build and draw geometric objects;	• Ch. 15, L. 1, 2
• create and describe mental images of objects, patterns, and paths;	• Ch. 17, L. 3, 5
• identify and build a three-dimensional object from two-dimensional representations of that object;	• Ch. 15, L. 7
• identify and draw a two-dimensional representation of a three-dimensional object;	• Ch. 17, L. 1, 2
• use geometric models to solve problems in other areas of mathematics, such as number and measurement;	• Ch. 3, L. 2; Ch. 9, L. 1; Ch. 11, L. 1; Ch. 12, L. 1, 2, 4; Ch. 13, L. 1; Ch. 14, L. 1
• recognize geometric ideas and relationships and apply them to other disciplines and to problems that arise in the classroom or in everyday life.	• Ch. 16, L. 3; Ch. 17, L. 4, 7

Measurement Standards • Expectations	Houghton Mifflin Math Grade 5 Correlation
Understand measurable attributes of objects and the units, systems, and processes of measurement	
• understand such attributes as length, area, weight, volume, and size of angle and select the appropriate type of unit for measuring each attribute;	• Ch. 16, L. 1, 3–5; Ch. 17, L. 4, 6
• understand the need for measuring with standard units and become familiar with standard units in the customary and metric systems;	• Ch. 6, L. 2–5
• carry out simple unit conversions, such as from centimeters to meters, within a system of measurement;	• Ch. 6, L. 3–5
• understand that measurements are approximations and how differences in units affect precision;	• Ch. 6, L. 1
• explore what happens to measurements of a two-dimensional shape such as its perimeter and area when the shape is changed in some way.	• Ch. 16, L. 2, 3
Apply appropriate techniques, tools, and formulas to determine measurements	
• develop strategies for estimating the perimeters, areas, and volumes of irregular shapes;	• Ch. 16, L. 5

* For each lesson, the key content and process standards have been identified.

Measurement Standards (continued) • Expectations	Houghton Mifflin Math Grade 5 Correlation
• select and apply appropriate standard units and tools to measure length, area, volume, weight, time, temperature, and the size of angles;	• Ch. 6, L. 7
• select and use benchmarks to estimate measurements;	• See **Practice Game** in Ch. 6, L. 5
• develop, understand, and use formulas to find the area of rectangles and related triangles and parallelograms;	• Ch. 16, L. 2–4
• develop strategies to determine the surface areas and volumes of rectangular solids.	• Ch. 17, L. 1, 4, 6, 7

Data Analysis and Probability Standards • Expectations	Houghton Mifflin Math Grade 5 Correlation
Formulate questions that can be addressed with data and collect, organize, and display relevant data to answer them	
• design investigations to address a question and consider how data-collection methods affect the nature of the data set;	• Ch. 8, L. 1
• collect data using observations, surveys, and experiments;	• Ch. 8, L. 1
• represent data using tables and graphs such as line plots, bar graphs, and line graphs;	• Ch. 7, L. 1–3; Ch. 8, L. 3, 4
• recognize the differences in representing categorical and numerical data.	• Ch. 7, L. 4, 5
Select and use appropriate statistical methods to analyze data	
• describe the shape and important features of a set of data and compare related data sets, with an emphasis on how the data are distributed;	• Ch. 8, L. 2
• use measures of center, focusing on the median, and understand what each does and does not indicate about the data set;	• Ch. 8, L. 2
• compare different representations of the same data and evaluate how well each representation shows important aspects of the data.	• Ch. 7, L. 4
Develop and evaluate inferences and predictions that are based on data	
• propose and justify conclusions and predictions that are based on data and design studies to further investigate the conclusions or predictions.	• Ch. 8, L. 5; Ch. 20, L. 7
Understand and apply basic concepts of probability	
• describe events as likely or unlikely and discuss the degree of likelihood using such words as certain, equally likely, and impossible;	• Ch. 20, L. 2, 3
• predict the probability of outcomes of simple experiments and test the predictions;	• Ch. 21, L. 3, 5
• understand that the measure of the likelihood of an event can be represented by a number from 0 to 1.	• Ch. 20, L. 2, 3

Problem Solving Standards	Houghton Mifflin Math Grade 5 Correlation*
• build new mathematical knowledge through problem solving;	• See **Problem-Solving Application** lessons, such as Ch. 1, L. 6; Ch. 11, L. 3; and Ch. 23, L. 4
• solve problems that arise in mathematics and in other contexts;	• See Science, Social Studies, and Art Connections at the end of each unit. Also see **Connection** features, such as Ch. 4, L. 3 and Ch. 17, L. 5.
• apply and adapt a variety of appropriate strategies to solve problems;	• See **Problem-Solving Strategy** lessons, such as Ch. 4, L. 3; Ch. 10, L. 7; and Ch. 17, L. 5
• monitor and reflect on the process of mathematical problem solving.	• See **Problem-Solving Decision** lessons, such as Ch. 5, L. 3; Ch. 12, L. 7; and Ch. 18, L. 6.

Reasoning and Proof Standards	Houghton Mifflin Math Grade 5 Correlation
• recognize reasoning and proof as fundamental aspects of mathematics;	• Ch. 3, L. 3; Ch. 9, L. 7
• make and investigate mathematical conjectures;	• Ch. 4, L. 1, 6; Ch. 10, L. 4
• develop and evaluate mathematical arguments and proofs;	• Ch. 5, L. 6; Ch. 13, L. 6
• select and use various types of reasoning and methods of proof.	• Ch. 3, L. 3; Ch. 4, L. 7; Ch. 9, L. 5

Communication Standards	Houghton Mifflin Math Grade 5 Correlation
• organize and consolidate their mathematical thinking through communication;	• See **Math Conversations** in **Vocabulary Wrap-Up** at the end of each unit. Also see **Write About It** questions, such as those in Ch. 3, L. 2 and Ch. 9, L. 8.
• communicate their mathematical thinking coherently and clearly to peers, teachers, and others;	• See **Hands-On** lessons such as Ch. 3, L. 8; Ch. 15, L. 2; and Ch. 20, L. 5.
• analyze and evaluate the mathematical thinking and strategies of others; use the language of mathematics to express mathematical ideas precisely.	• See **What's Wrong** questions, such as those in Ch. 3, L. 1; Ch. 4, L. 7; and Ch. 5, L. 6.
• use the language of mathematics to express mathematical ideas precisely.	• See **Explain Your Thinking** questions, such as those in Ch. 3, L. 8; Ch. 5, L. 1; Ch. 7, L. 1.

Connections Standards	Houghton Mifflin Math Grade 5 Correlation
• recognize and use connections among mathematical ideas;	• Ch. 1, L. 4
• understand how mathematical ideas interconnect and build on one another to produce a coherent whole;	• Ch. 3, L. 4
• recognize and apply mathematics in contexts outside of mathematics.	• Ch. 1, L. 7; Ch. 2, L. 3; Ch. 6, L. 7; Ch. 7, L. 6; Ch. 8, L. 5; Ch. 9, L. 9; Ch. 12, L. 3, 7

Representation Standards	Houghton Mifflin Math Grade 5 Correlation
• create and use representations to organize, record, and communicate mathematical ideas;	• Ch. 1, L. 5; Ch. 7, L. 3; Ch. 8, L. 2, 3; Ch. 9, L. 5
• select, apply, and translate among mathematical representations to solve problems;	• See **Different Ways** in Ch. 1, L. 1–3, 7; Ch. 3, L. 5–7; Ch. 7, L. 4; Ch. 9, L. 3, 6; Ch. 12, L. 2; Ch. 13, L. 1, 5; Ch. 14, L. 5; Ch. 18, L. 2–4; Ch. 19, L. 3–5; Ch. 20, L. 1; Ch. 21, L. 1
• use representations to model and interpret physical, social, and mathematical phenomena.	• Ch. 2, L. 5–7; Ch. 10, L. 7; Ch. 11, L. 3; Ch. 15, L. 7

* For each lesson, the key content and process standards have been identified.

LE GUIDE 2011 DE L'AUTO

Rédacteur en chef
Denis Duquet
Coordination éditoriale
Alain Morin
Coordination de production
Marie-France Rock, Kim Malczewski
Journalistes et photographes
Gabriel Gélinas, Sylvain Raymond, Gilles Olivier, Marc Lachapelle, Nadine Filion, Bill Petro
Fiches techniques
Alain Morin, Frédéric Mercier, Kevin Davignon
Liste de prix
Guy Desjardins
Conception et production
LC Média Inc., Lexis Média Inc., Groupe Librex
Retouche photo
NumérArt
Révision et correction
Hélène Paraire, Julie Lapierre, Isabelle Dowd, Danielle Assaad, Julie Thibault
Administration et ventes
Simon Fortin, Jean Lemieux
Fondateur du Guide de l'auto
Jacques Duval

1895 boul de l'industrie, suite 200
St-Mathieu-de-Belœil QC J3G 4S5
Tél. : 450-464-1479
Fax : 450-464-8271

Site Internet : www.guideautoweb.com

Catalogage avant publication de Bibliothèque et Archives nationales du Québec et Bibliothèque et Archives Canada

Vedette principale au titre :

Le guide de l'auto
ISSN 0315-9205
ISBN 978-2-89568-450-3

1. Automobiles - Achat - Guides, manuels, etc.
2. Automobiles - Spécifications - Guides, manuels, etc.

HD9710.A2D8 629.222029 C2010-300224-3

Remerciements
Les Éditions du Trécarré reconnaissent l'aide financière du gouvernement du Canada par l'entremise du Fonds du livre du Canada pour leurs activités d'édition. Nous remercions la Société de développement des entreprises culturelles du Québec (SODEC) du soutien accordé à notre programme de publication.
Gouvernement du Québec – Programme de crédit d'impôt pour l'édition de livres – gestion SODEC.

Les Éditions du Trécarré
Groupe Librex inc.
Une compagnie de Quebecor Media
La Tourelle
1055, boul. René-Lévesque Est
Bureau 800
Montréal (Québec) H2L 4S5
Tél. : 514 849-5259
Téléc. : 514 849-1388
www.edtrecarre.com

Dépôt légal – Bibliothèque et Archives nationales du Québec et Bibliothèque et Archives Canada, 2010

ISBN : 978-2-89568-450-3

Imprimé au Canada

Distribution au Canada
Messageries ADP
2315, rue de la Province
Longueuil (Québec) J4G 1G4
Téléphone : 450 640-1234
Sans frais : 1 800 771-3022
www.messageries.adp.com

Diffusion hors Canada
Interforum

Denis **DUQUET**

Nadine **FILION**

Gabriel **GÉLINAS**

Marc **LACHAPELLE**

Alain **MORIN**

Gilles **OLIVIER**

Sylvain **RAYMOND**

LE GUIDE 2011 DE L'AUTO

TRÉCARRÉ
Une compagnie de Quebecor Media

Le Guide de l'auto tient à remercier les personnes et les organisations dont les noms suivent et qui ont apporté leur précieuse collaboration à la réalisation de l'édition 2011.

Martine Bélanger
François Dubois
Nadia Duchesneau
Vanessa Geoffroy
Robert Hétu
Philippe Leblanc
Kim Malczewski
François Ménard
Karine Phaneuf
Marie-France Rock

Participants aux matchs comparatifs:
Théo De Guire-Lachapelle, Daniel Duquet, David Duquet, Yvan Fournier, Robert Gariepy, Marc Girardin, Franck Kirchhoff, André Lalanne, Alexandre Langlois, Gilles Olivier, Bertrand Plouffe.

Pour leur collaboration, merci à:
Jacquie Adams (Mitsubishi), Bob Austin (Rolls-Royce), Amyot Bachand (Subaru), Barbara Barrett (Jaquar \ Land Rover), Caroline Bastien (Kia), André Beaucage (Suzuki), Denis Bellemare (Mercedes-Benz), Joanne Bon (BMW), Umberto Bonfa (Ferrari Québec), Gisèle Bradley (Honda), Lara Brown (Mitsubishi), Rick Bye (Porsche), JoAnne Caza (Mercedes-Benz), Nicole Chambers (Subaru), Josée Chaumont (Audi Lauzon), Marie-Michèle Crevier (Cohn & Wolfe), Sabrina Damico (Ferrari Québec), Alain Desrochers (Mazda), Rob Dexter (BMW), Sandy DiFelice (Toyota / Lexus / Scion), Bernard Durand (Lotus John Scotti), Woods Dustin (General Motors), Erin Farquharson (Volvo), Christine Flynn (Volvo Laval), Ian Forsythe (Nissan / Infiniti), Mathieu Fournier (Mazda), Jochen Frey (BMW), Jen Giler (Subaru), Gérald Godin (Hyundai), Terry Grant (BMW Laval), Nicole Grant (Toyota / Lexus / Scion), François Gravel (Volkswagen Arbour), Elaine Griffin (Subaru), Jacques Guertin (Sanair), Carole Guindon (Mazda), Rania Guirguis (Mazda), Cristina Guizzardi (Lamborghini), Rose Hasham (Toyota / Lexus / Scion), Chad Heard (Hyundai), Christine Hollander (Ford), Richard Jacobs (Honda), Frank Kirchhoff (Mécaglisse), Daniel Labre (Chrysler / Dodge / Jeep), Alain Laforêt (BMW), Tony LaRocca (General Motors), Cathy Laroche (Kia), Ghyslain Lavallée (Roch Lavallée et fils), Maiti Leinss (Pneus Continental), Rebecca Lucas (Nissan / Infiniti), Robert Lupien (Cohn & Wolfe), Patrice Marchesseault (L.A. Detail), Josée Marin (Hyundai), Richard Marsan (Subaru), Didier Marsaud (Nissan / Infiniti), Heather Meehan (Nissan / Infiniti), Nadia Mereb (Honda / Acura), Michael Minielli (Mercedes-Benz), Arden Nerling (Mercedes-Benz), Cort Nielsen (Audi), Roberto Oruna (Audi), Robert Pagé (General Motors), Luc Paquette (Hyundai), Anthony Paulozza (Pneus Pirelli), Barbara Pitblado (BMW), Louis Renaud (Mitsubishi Gabriel), Jacynthe Rioux (Volkswagen Arbour), Sophie St-Germain (Plaza Chevrolet), George Saratlic (General Motors), John Scotti (John Scotti Auto), Frédéric Senay (ICAR), Joel Siegal (Décarie Motors), Marie-Claude Simard (Audi), Steve Spence (Services Spenco), Rob Tabacs (Mercedes-Benz), Derrick Tan (Toyota / Lexus / Scion), Thomas Tetzlaff (Volkswagen), Paul Vaillancourt (Torchia Communications), John Vernile (Hyundai), Stéphanie Viger (Des Sources Chrysler), Peter Viney (Volkswagen), John White (Volkswagen), Laurance Yap (Porsche), Greg Young (Mazda), Karen Zlatin (Mercedes-Benz)

UN TÉMOIN PRIVILÉGIÉ

Le *Guide de l'auto* célèbre ses 45 ans, ce qui est un fait unique en soi. Cet ouvrage, qui a été le premier du genre en Amérique, a réussi à demeurer pendant quatre décennies et demie non seulement le meilleur vendeur de la catégorie, mais il est toujours l'ouvrage de référence. Beaucoup de choses ont évolué pendant toutes ces années. Les dimensions physiques du bouquin lui-même ont connu une croissance exponentielle. La première édition ne comportait que 158 pages, faisait l'essai de seize voitures et ne comportait aucune photo couleur. La présente édition comprend 672 pages et pas moins de 2 500 photos, toutes en couleur !

Bien entendu, en 1967, l'Internet était une notion inexistante. Tout comme le site Web portant le nom de notre publication. Sans oublier l'émission télévisée Le Guide de l'auto qui est diffusée au Canal Vox de Vidéotron depuis plus de 10 ans. Vous avouerez que notre ouvrage a bien évolué avec son époque. Et toujours dans cette vague, la première version électronique iPad du *Guide de l'auto* sera commercialisée dans le cadre du 45e anniversaire de la première édition.

Tout au long de ces années, le *Guide* a été un témoin de l'évolution des automobiles et de leur marché. Il y a 45 ans, une voiture dont le moteur possédait un ou deux arbres à cames en tête était une grande sportive ou une voiture de luxe. Il en était de même des suspensions arrière indépendantes. Mieux encore, les freins à disques aux roues avant étaient la plupart du temps optionnels. Même les appuie-tête étaient offerts en option sur plusieurs voitures. Et, en 1967, c'était l'époque des *muscle cars* avec leurs gros moteurs V8, leur carrosserie du tonnerre et leurs accélérations… musclées.

De cette époque à nos jours, il y a eu la crise du pétrole au milieu des années 70, l'arrivée des systèmes antipollution, la crise économique du début des années 80 et la popularité sans cesse croissante des marques japonaises. Qui se souvient qu'à une certaine époque le constructeur Mazda a été sauvé de la débandade financière par Ford et que Toyota, dans les années 70, voulait quitter le marché américain faute de résultats? À la même époque, la Volkswagen Coccinelle était remplacée par la Golf dessinée par Giugiaro et concoctée par l'ingénieur Ferdinand Piech, le petit-fils de Ferdinand Porsche, le créateur de la Beetle. Au cours des années 80, il y avait des voitures nord-américaines propulsées par un gros V8 qui produisait à peine 150 chevaux quand ce n'était pas moins. C'est au cours de cette décennie que les constructeurs ont commencé à incorporer l'électronique pour mieux gérer la mécanique et le comportement routier. Et j'allais oublier, grâce au bagout de Lee Iaccoca, Chrysler a été sauvé de la faillite par le gouvernement américain

Dans les années 90, l'injection électronique de carburant, les freins ABS, les suspensions à amortisseurs à contrôle électronique et des boîtes automatiques plus efficaces à gestion électronique sont quelques-unes des nouveautés qui ont rendu les voitures plus performantes et réduit leur consommation de carburant. Par la même occasion, les camionnettes intermédiaires ont fait leur apparition. Cette décennie a également été marquée par l'arrivée des marques de luxe japonaises Lexus et Infiniti tandis que Mazda abandonnait son projet de faire de même. Il ne faut pas oublier au cours de ces années la prolifération des pneus à taille basse après l'utilisation des pneus à carcasse radiale sur la majorité des voitures dans les années 70-80. Enfin, l'industrie automobile britannique était en pleine déroute alors que les Américains et les Allemands se partageaient les restes.

Le nouveau siècle s'est amorcé sous le signe de l'écologie, des voitures hybrides et d'une plus grande sensibilisation du public à l'égard de voitures plus propres. Les balbutiements des voitures électriques permettent aux écologistes purs et durs de rouler sans produire aucune émission nocive. Enfin, avec la HTT Pléthore, le Québec et même le Canada possèdent la première super voiture de fabrication nationale. Il s'agit de la seule voiture de conception et fabrication québécoise depuis la légendaire Manic.

Que nous réserve l'avenir? Nous en aurons un aperçu plus clair lorsque *Le Guide de l'auto* célèbrera ses 50 ans de parution en 2016. En attendant, bonne lecture de cette 45e édition.

Denis Duquet

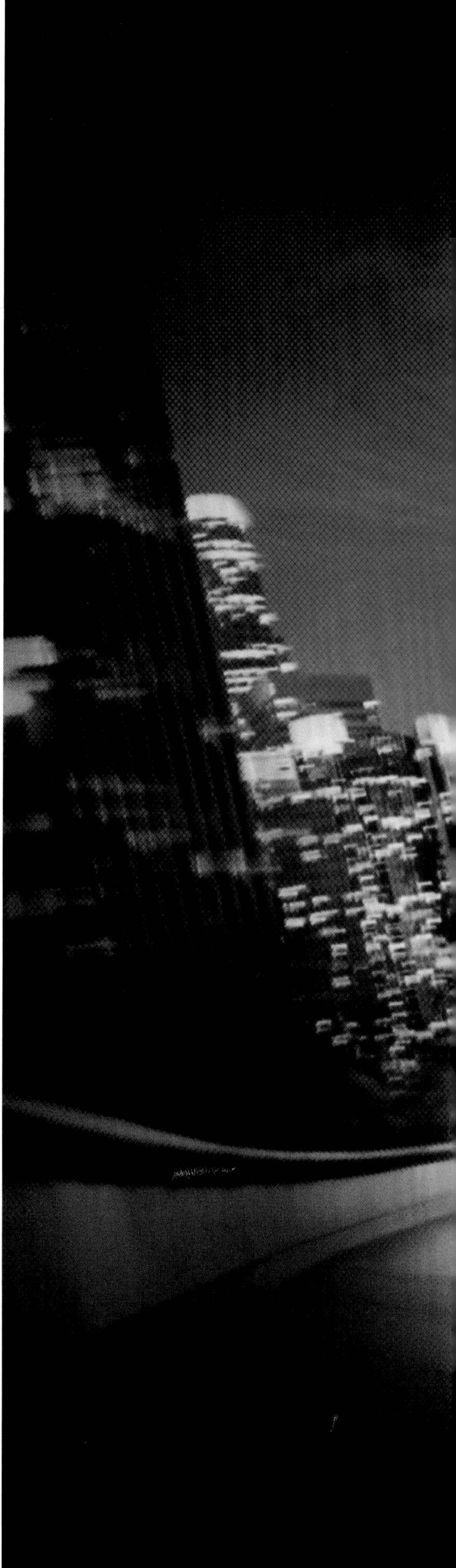

SOMMAIRE

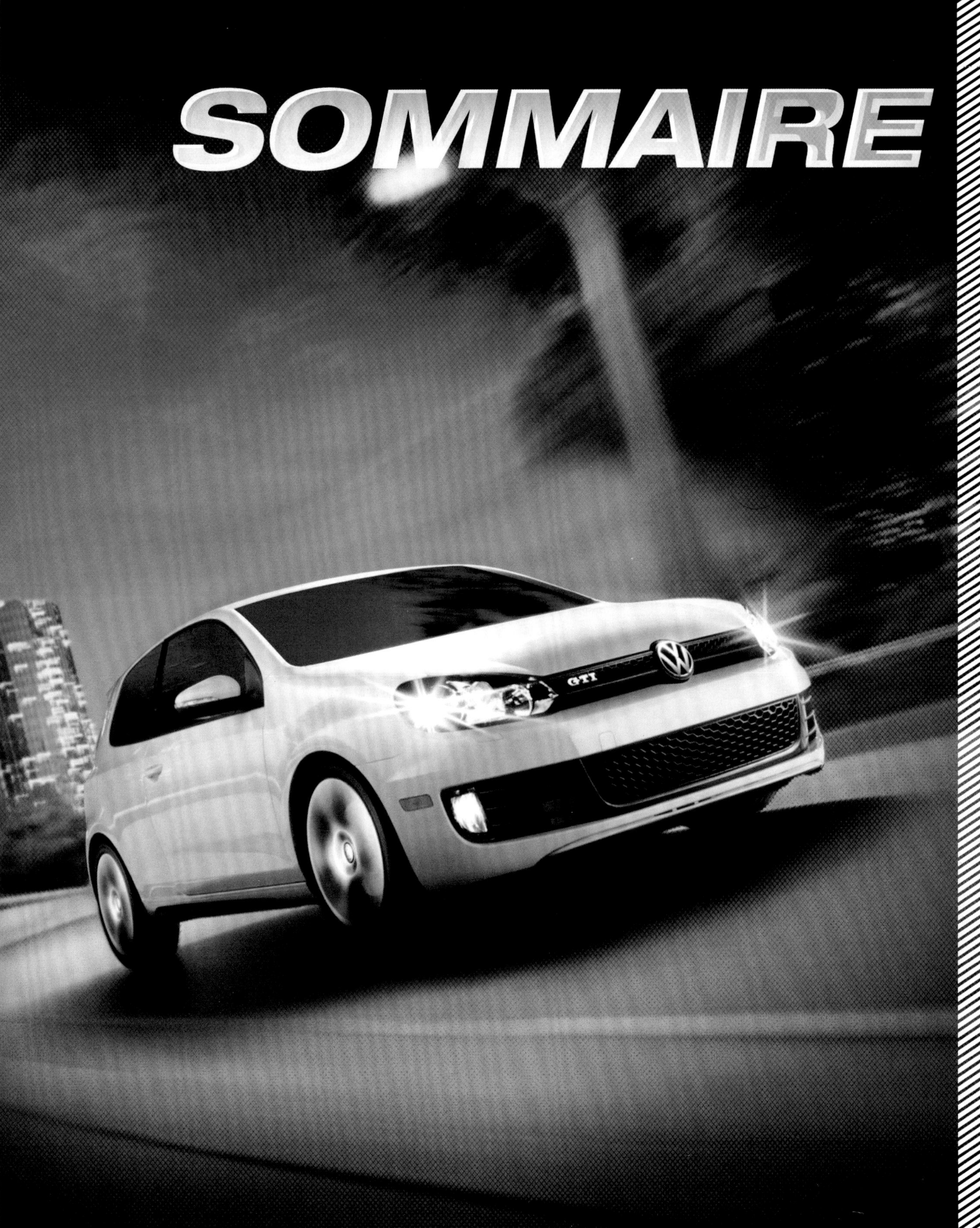

INDEX

CONCEPTS

Aston Martin / Audi / Bertone / Bugatti / BMW / Cadillac / Chevrolet / Citroën / Fiat / GMC
Honda / Hyundai / Kia / Lexus / Mazda / Mercedes-Benz / Mini / Mitsubishi / Peugeot
Pininfarina / Porsche / Renault / Rinspeed / Sbarro / Subaru / Toyota / Volkswagen

CYGNET CONCEPT (GENÈVE 2010)

Cette voiture conceptuelle est rapidement devenue un modèle de série à tirage très limité et réservée à la clientèle de la marque britannique. Elle a été concoctée en partenariat avec Toyota sur la base du modèle iQ. Ainsi, on passe d'une voiture d'entrée de gamme à un modèle très cossu afin d'être digne de porter le nom Aston Martin. Son petit moteur de 1,3 litre est accouplé à une boîte CVT et développe 98 chevaux.

E-TRON DETROIT SHOW CAR (DETROIT 2010)

Malgré son nom, ce concept est nettement plus sérieux qu'il n'y paraît. Il annonce la venue d'ici une couple d'années du coupé Audi R4. De format compact et de catégorie compacte, son moteur sera tout électrique. Selon toute probabilité, la puissance avoisinera les 204 chevaux répartis aux roues arrière. Les marques Volkswagen et Porsche pourraient également utiliser ce concept comme base au développement de futurs modèles plus compacts et à propulsion électrique.

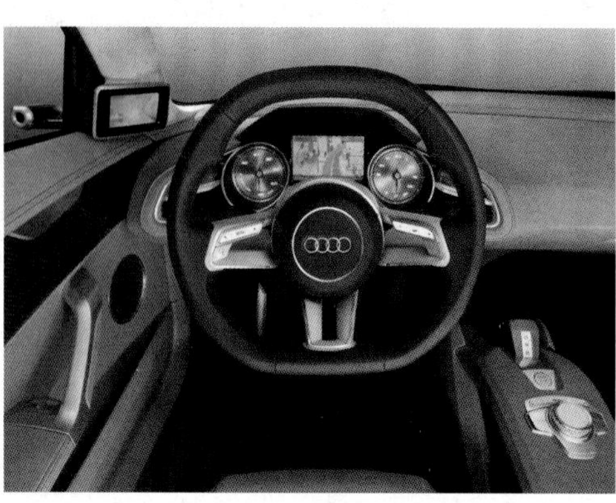

AUDI

E-TRON CONCEPT (FRANCFORT 2009)

L'indicatif « e-Tron » utilisé par Audi signifie que nous aurons affaire à un véhicule à motorisation entièrement électrique. L'Audi e-Tron Concept conçue sur la base de la très séduisante R8 deviendra dès 2012 un modèle de série. Elle sera à la fois plus légère et de dimensions réduites par rapport à la R8. Elle utilise quatre moteurs électriques placés derrière les roues. Au total, la puissance est de 313 chevaux et son couple de 3272 lb-pi est hallucinant. Elle abat le 0 à 100 km/h en seulement 4,8 secondes. Sa vitesse de pointe est de 200 km/h et son autonomie annoncée est de 250 km.

BERTONE
PANDION CONCEPT (GENÈVE 2010)

Pour commémorer les 100 ans d'histoire de l'italienne Alfa Romeo, le célèbre carrossier Bertone a conçu son modèle Pandion. Développé autour des principaux éléments mécaniques de la séduisante Alfa 8C Competizione, le concept Pandion avec ses portes en élytre est une réussite esthétique de très haut niveau. Son design évoque à la fois le passé et surtout un avenir plus prometteur pour la marque italienne. Son poids de seulement 1 000 kg est dû à l'utilisation de matériaux ultralégers.

BUGATTI
16C GALIBIER CONCEPT

Elle n'est pas sans évoquer la berline Bugatti 57 Galibier de 1934. C'est aussi un concept annonciateur du retour prochain d'une berline dans la petite famille de voitures griffées de la célèbre marque britannique. Ici, le foudroyant moteur W16 de la Veyron est associé à un compresseur à deux étages plutôt que les quatre turbos utilisés sur les autres modèles. La 16C Galibier serait un peu moins puissante que les coupés, mais elle pourra s'abreuver à l'éthanol.

BMW

VISION EFFICIENT DYNAMICS CONCEPT (FRANCFORT 2009)

Les voitures hybrides de BMW sont identifiées par l'indicatif « Efficient Dynamics » et ce nouveau concept ne fait nullement exception à cette règle, bien au contraire. Ainsi, son moteur trois cylindres turbo diesel de 1,5 litre développe 163 chevaux et est accouplé à deux moteurs électriques. Pour celui qui est placé à l'avant, ajoutez 141 chevaux tandis que le moteur placé sur l'essieu arrière en annonce 52 supplémentaires. Le véhicule abat le 0 à 100 km/h en seulement 4,8 secondes. À la fois économe et écolo, sa consommation d'essence est limitée à 3,76 L/100 km et ses émanations de CO^2 ne dépassent pas 99 g/km.

CONCEPT GRAN COUPE (BEIJING 2010)

Cette grande berline conceptuelle donnera bientôt vie à la toute nouvelle mouture des BMW de Série6 laquelle devrait comprendre un séduisant coupé à quatre portières dont la mission sera de freiner les ventes de la Mercedes-Benz de Classe CLS. À l'instar des nouvelles BMW de Série5, la Grand Coupé a été concoctée à partir du châssis de la Série7. Ce futur coupé quatre portes bénéficiera des éléments les plus musclés des BMW des Série5 et Série7.

XTS PLATINUM (DETROIT 2010)

Les Audi A8, BMW de Série7, Lexus LS460 et Mercedes-Benz de ClasseS pourraient bientôt devoir affronter une berline américaine de classe mondiale, dérivée du concept XTS Platinum de Cadillac. Cette limousine très haut de gamme qui mesure 5170 mm, cache sous son long capot une motorisation hybride rechargeable. Ce système hybride à technologie Voltec se compose d'un moteur V6 à injection directe et électrique délivrant une puissance de 354 chevaux.

CHEVROLET

VOLT MPV5 CONCEPT (BEIJING 2010)

Après les berlines Chevrolet Volt et Opel Ampera toutes deux propulsées par une motorisation hybride innovante, il se peut que cette approche exclusive à GM se retrouve sous le capot d'un véhicule de type multisegment. Ainsi, le concept Volt MPV5 utilise la technologie Voltec par laquelle le moteur thermique agit comme générateur d'électricité. Ceci permet au véhicule de bénéficier d'une autonomie de 480 kilomètres et de pouvoir rouler jusqu'à 50 kilomètres en mode tout électrique.

CITROËN

SURVOLT CONCEPT (GENÈVE 2010)

Après le Revolte Concept de Francfort, voici un coupé sport au style très agressif mu par un moteur électrique dont les données techniques demeurent un secret d'État. De par ses dimensions et surtout sa hauteur de seulement 1 200 mm on peut aisément considérer ce concept comme un exercice de style qui pourrait être éventuellement utilisé dans le développement de futurs modèles. Ce généreux coupé deux places présente un intérieur à caractère ultrasportif.

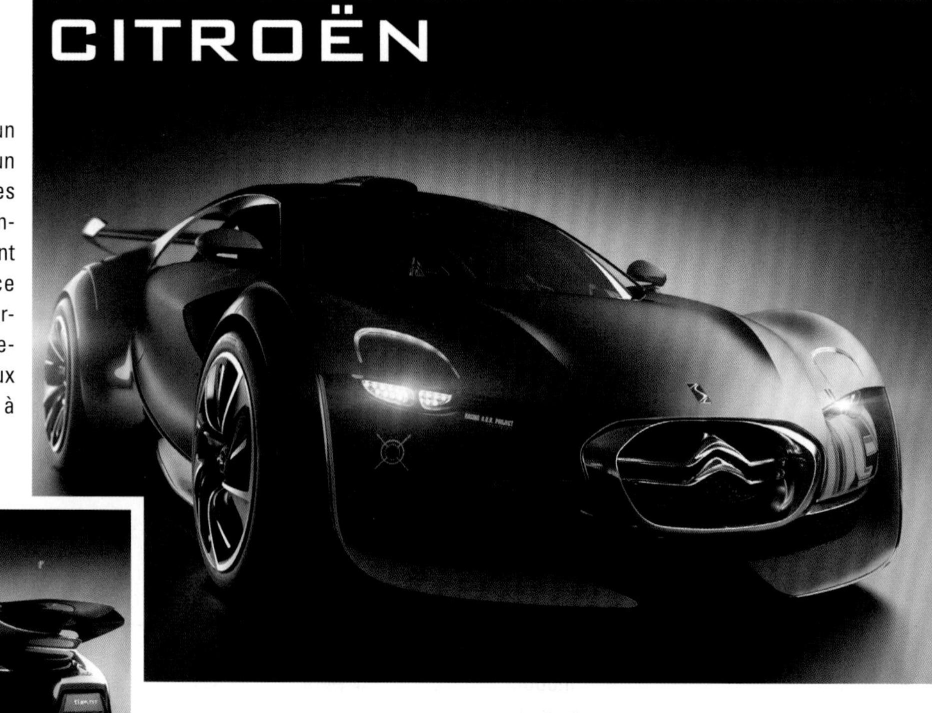

FIAT

500 EV CONCEPT (DETROIT 2010)

Après la sortie nord-américaine prévue pour le début de l'année 2011 de la petite Fiat 500 à moteur thermique, Chrysler compte offrir la p'tite italienne avec un moteur électrique dès l'année suivante. Dans un premier temps, la Fiat 500 EV sera vendue exclusivement sur l'échiquier automobile nord-américain. Les ingénieurs de Chrysler LLC utiliseront un moteur électrique à haut rendement associé à des batteries au lithium-ion et géré par un module conçu et développé par l'entreprise américaine.

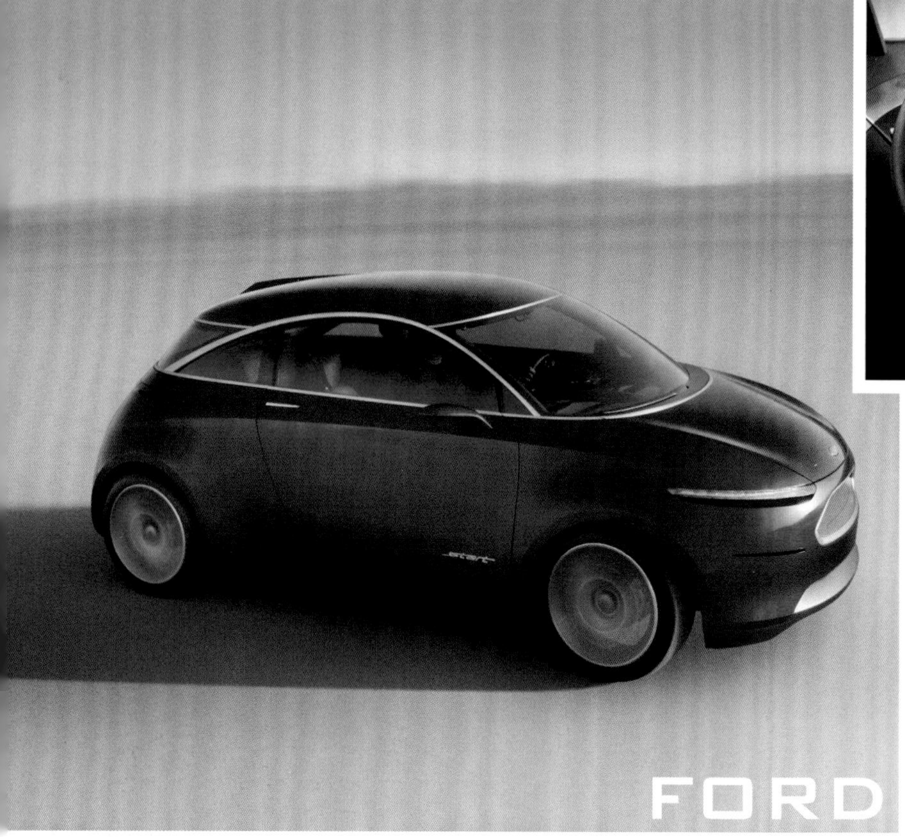

START CONCEPT (BEIJING 2010)

Drôle de marmotte que ce concept signé Ford. Tous les constructeurs cherchent actuellement à concevoir la citadine idéale et chez Ford c'est cette petite coquine qui semble servir de plateforme au développement rapide d'un modèle de série à venir. Parmi ses principales caractéristiques, on note l'utilisation d'un châssis entièrement fait d'aluminium et de sections de la carrosserie en matières composites recyclables.

GRANITE CONCEPT (DETROIT 2010)

La division GMC de General Motors est à la recherche d'un véhicule de type multisegment ultracompact dont la mission sera d'affronter les Kia Soul, Nissan cube et Scion xB de ce monde. Ainsi, le concept Granite présente tous les attributs qui devraient lui permettre d'affronter lesdits véhicules. De plus, ses créateurs pourraient offrir des versions de type Panel à vocation commerciale, lesquelles pourraient servir de véhicules de livraison ou à usages spécifiques.

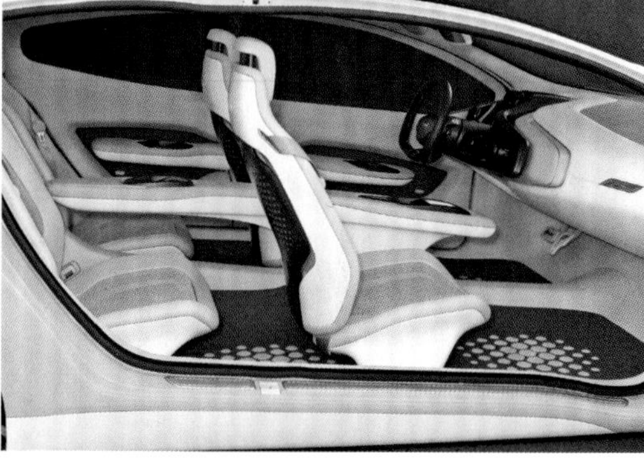

RAY CONCEPT (CHICAGO 2010)

Ce séduisant coupé quatre portes propose sous son capot une motorisation hybride rechargeable qui en étonnera plus d'un. Ainsi, on retrouve un petit moteur à essence de 1,4 litre à injection directe (GDI) de 153 chevaux. Le moteur électrique qui l'accompagne vient ajouter 104 chevaux à sa cavalerie. Ce dernier s'alimente par le biais de batteries au lithium-ion polymère rechargeables, tandis qu'une boîte CVT complète le tout.

LF-CH CONCEPT (FRANCFORT 2009)

Bien que cette voiture conceptuelle bénéficie d'une motorisation hybride, l'important à retenir à son sujet concerne la venue prochaine de la première compacte griffée du nom de Lexus. D'ailleurs, elle va donner naissance à un modèle de série appelé CT200h lequel devra affronter les populaires Audi A3 et BMW de Série1. Son moteur hybride n'est pas sans rappeler celui de la très populaire Toyota Prius. Elle sera la seule voiture de sa catégorie mue par un moteur hybride.

MERCEDES-BENZ

F800 STYLE CONCEPT (GENÈVE 2010)

C'est un imposant laboratoire tout plein de technologies de pointe qui se retrouve sous cette carrosserie. À titre d'exemple, son système Distronic Plus, qui peut carrément prendre le contrôle de la voiture sous les 40 km/h, le tout avec corrections du volant, accélérations et freinages contrôlés. Une approche qui pourrait s'avérer des plus intéressantes, notamment lorsque nous sommes coincés dans un embouteillage. Côté hybridation, il regroupe un moteur V6 atmosphérique à injection directe qui développe 300 chevaux, associé à un moteur électrique qui vient ajouter 109 chevaux à cette cavalerie, déjà bien armée.

COUPÉ CONCEPT (FRANCFORT 2009)

Tout récemment, la direction de la marque Mini a pris la sage décision de produire un coupé aux lignes relativement trapues lequel empruntera le style du Coupé Concept. Son pavillon extrêmement bas, le pare-brise coupé et son toit en aluminium très court ont pour mission de rendre hommage à la Mini Marcos produite au milieu des années '60. Malgré les apparences, ce petit coupé au style « Red Baron » a de bons espaces de chargement équivalent à 250 litres. Afin de nous en mettre plein la vue, le Mini Coupé Concept reçoit le moteur John Cooper Works délivrant 211 chevaux.

MINI

ROADSTER CONCEPT (FRANCFORT 2009)

Cette année, Mini nous a présenté deux voitures-concepts des plus intéressantes. À savoir un coupé et surtout un séduisant roadster qui va éventuellement devenir un modèle de série. Ce modèle découvrable à deux places dispose d'une capote à déploiement manuel. Son système *Allways Open* a pour fonctionnalité de comptabiliser le temps écoulé à rouler à découvert. Derrière les sièges, on a aménagé une petite trappe qui donne accès à l'espace de chargement.

I-MIEV ET HYDRO-QUÉBEC (MONTRÉAL 2010)

Thierry Vandal, président d'Hydro-Québec, est arrivé au Salon de l'auto de Montréal au volant d'une Mitsubishi i-MiEV mue par un moteur électrique. Ce fut une belle occasion pour Vandal d'officialiser un accord entre la société d'État et le constructeur Mitsubishi. Ainsi, en collaboration avec la ville de Boucherville, la société d'État pourra évaluer une cinquantaine de voitures électriques i-MiEV dans différentes situations, notamment concernant leur fiabilité en saison hivernale. Son moteur électrique délivre 63 chevaux.

PX-MIEV CONCEPT (TOKYO 2009)

Ce concept aux lignes des plus réalistes attend son heure pour entrer en service. Ce grand VUS est animé par un moteur à essence de 1,6 litre jumelé à deux moteurs électriques placés respectivement sur les trains avant et arrière. Le moteur thermique peut être utilisé comme source motrice ou en tant que générateur d'énergie. La batterie au lithium-ion peut être rechargée par le biais de prises de 110 ou 220 volts, et même par des bornes de recharge ultrarapide.

FLEXTREME GT/E (GENÈVE 2010)

C'est la Chevrolet Volt qui a servie de base au développement de la berline européenne Opel Ampera, sa p'tite cousine, et voilà que cette dernière en a fait de même lorsque les ingénieurs de la marque allemande ont planchés sur le concept Flextreme GT/E. Ce long coupé à cinq portières peut se déplacer en mode tout électrique sur une distance de 60 kilomètres lui permettant ainsi de répondre aisément aux besoins journaliers d'un pourcentage élevé de citoyens.

PEUGEOT

BB1 CONCEPT (FRANCFORT 2009)

Cette petite voiture ultra urbaine aux formes très inusitées utilise deux moteurs électriques, chacun placé dans une roue avant. Chacun délivre une puissance de 15 kW (environ 20 ch), mais surtout un couple absolument phénoménal de 320 Nm (236 lb-pi) sur chaque roue. Des plaques solaires assurent une énergie constante à la batterie au lithium-ion. Conçue conjointement par les divisions auto et moto de Peugeot, elle voit son volant traditionnel être remplacé par un guidon.

PININFARINA

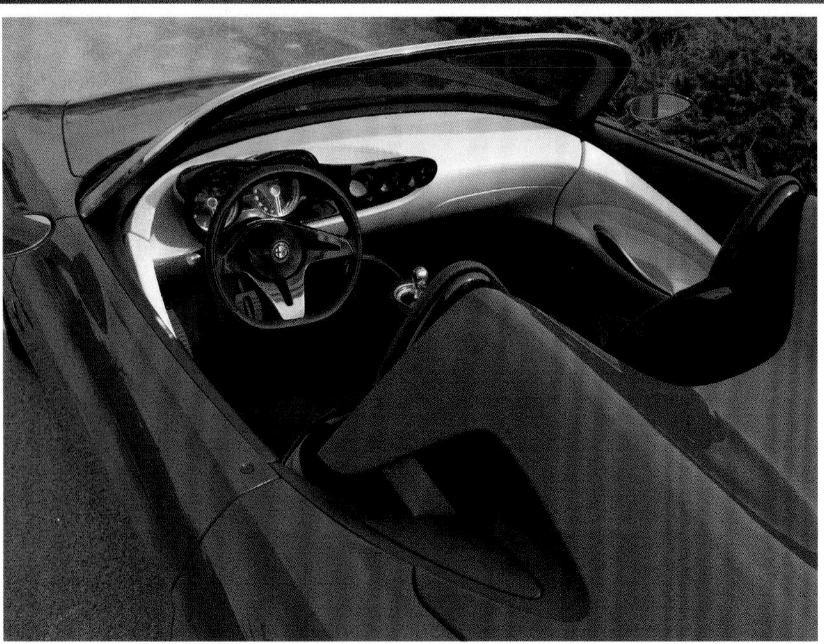

2UETTOTTANTA CONCEPT (GENÈVE 2010)

Le célèbre carrossier italien Pininfarina fête ses 80 ans d'existence et Alfa Romeo en fait de même pour son centenaire. Et la séduisante 2Uettottanta rend hommage aux deux jubilaires. Ce nom avait été utilisé en 1986 pour identifier l'Alfa Romeo Spider carrossée par Pininfarina. Ce concept qui nous est aujourd'hui présenté est annonciateur de la venue prochaine d'un modèle de série qui prendra la place de l'actuelle Alfa Spider.

PORSCHE

918 SPYDER CONCEPT (GENÈVE 2010)

La vedette incontestée de la 80e édition du Salon international de l'automobile de Genève serait actuellement convoitée par au moins 900 personnes prêtes à ouvrir leur chéquier pour l'acquérir. Outre son style des plus séduisants, ce bolide a surtout la particularité de bénéficier d'une motorisation hybride impressionnante laquelle regroupe un moteur atmosphérique de 3,4 litres de 493 chevaux associé à un moteur électrique qui vient y ajouter 215 chevaux. Elle rejoint les 100 km/h en seulement 3,2 secondes. Malgré cette puissante cavalerie, sa consommation d'essence ne serait que de 3,0 L/100 km tandis que ses émanations de CO_2 ne dépasseraient pas les 70 g/km.

TWIZY Z.E. CONCEPT (FRANCFORT 2009)

Fred Caillou aurait pu concevoir ce petit concept à mobilité urbaine, sans problème. Toutefois, ce véhicule bizarroïde est de conception beaucoup plus sérieuse qu'il n'y paraît. Ainsi, la Twizy fait partie d'une flotte de véhicules concepts qui donneront naissance à compter de 2012 à des modèles de série à motorisation tout électrique. À vocation ultra-urbaine, la minuscule Renault peut accueillir deux passagers assis en tandem, compte tenu de sa largeur limitée à seulement 1 130 mm.

UC CONCEPT (GENÈVE 2010)

Le génial préparateur suisse a conçu une micro-voiture à mobilité extrême dont le volant et les pédales ont été remplacés par un manche de type *joystick*, très contrôlant. Sa principale caractéristique consiste en la possibilité de monter à bord d'un train, bien sûr à l'intérieur de compartiments qui lui sont réservés. De plus, ces espaces bénéficient de prises électriques performantes afin de permettre la recharge des batteries au lithium-ion, pendant que la voiture est immobilisée.

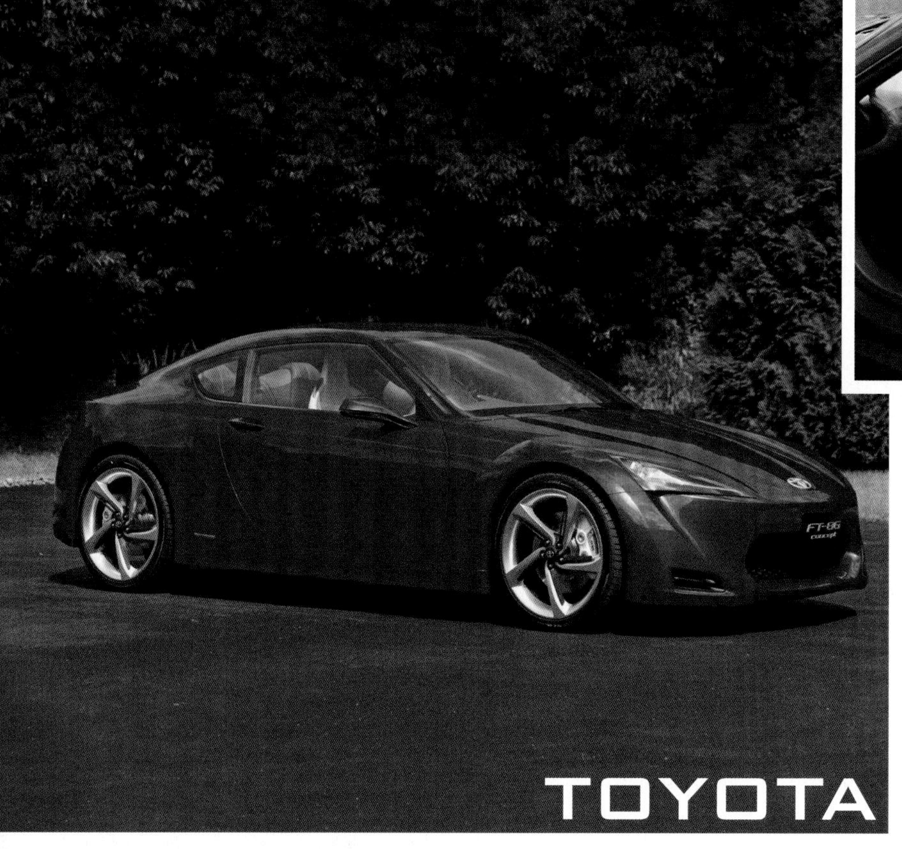

FT-86 CONCEPT (TOKYO 2009)

Les Japonais Toyota et Subaru travaillent conjointement au développement d'un coupé sport compact qui pourrait devenir un modèle de série en 2011. Conçu sur la base du concept FT-86, cet élégant coupé à propulsion héritera d'un moteur Subaru à plat de 2,0 litres dont la puissance minimale avoisinerait les 160 chevaux. Subaru commercialiserait lui aussi un coupé 2+2 sur la même base, sauf que son modèle serait offert avec une traction intégrale à prise constante.

FT-CH CONCEPT (DETROIT 2010)

Voici deux modèles à venir pour le prix d'un. C'est ce que représente cette voiture conceptuelle qui pourrait servir au développement de la prochaine Yaris, laquelle comprendra une version hybride destinée à venir affronter la compacte Honda Insight. Le « Future Toyota Compact Hybrid » a été conçu et développé par le Centre européen de design et de développement de Toyota, situé en France. Sous son capot, on retrouve une motorisation hybride dont les données demeurent confidentielles.

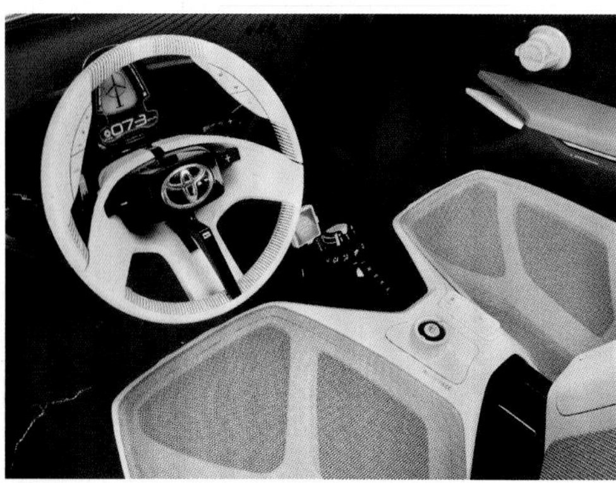

VOLKSWAGEN

NCC CONCEPT (DETROIT 2010)

Cette étude de style, bien qu'elle se présente sous la forme d'un élégant coupé, annonçait la venue de la 6e génération des populaires Volkswagen Jetta. Ce fut d'ailleurs officialisé à New York, en juin dernier, avec le dévoilement d'une toute nouvelle berline Jetta 2011, plus respectueuse des goûts et coutumes de l'automobiliste nord-américain. De son côté, l'élégant coupé conceptuel abritait une motorisation hybride pouvant offrir une consommation d'essence moyenne de seulement 4,2 L/100 km.

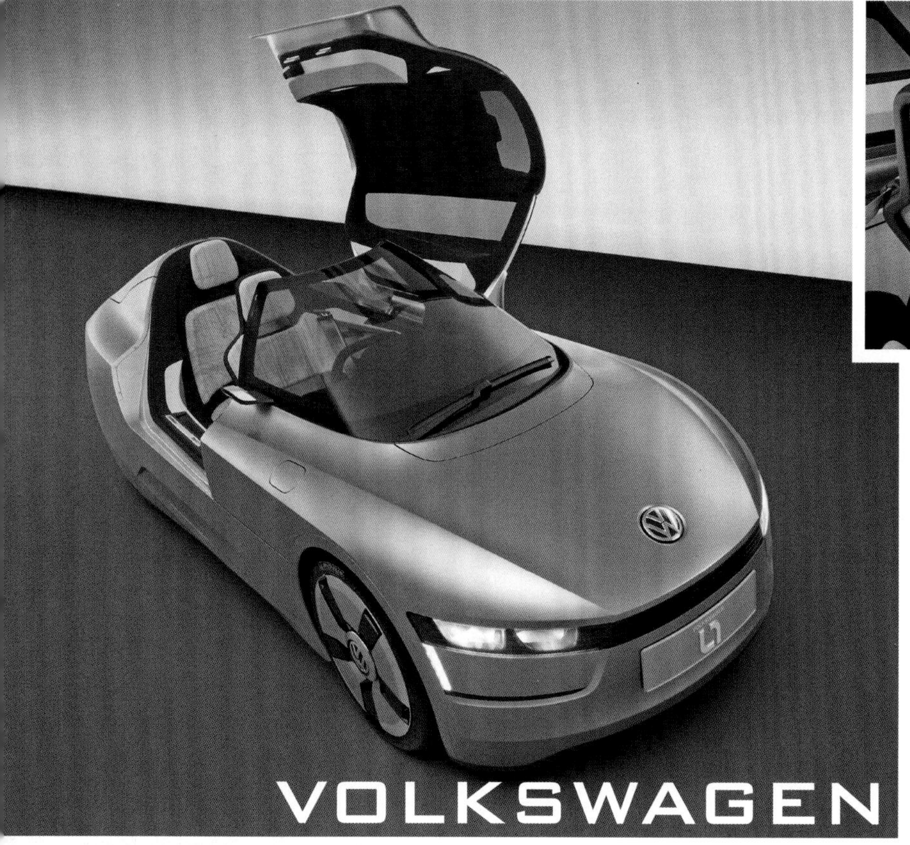

L1 CONCEPT (FRANCFORT 2009)

Après le concept « 1-Liter » de 2002, voici que les ingénieurs de Volkswagen reviennent en force en dévoilant le « L1 Concept ». Dans les deux cas, le but est de concevoir un véhicule extrêmement frugal. Grâce à l'utilisation de fibres de carbone, le plus récent concept ne pèse que 380 kg et annonce un coefficient de pénétration dans l'air de seulement 0,195. Très étroit, il accueille deux passagers assis en tandem. Sa motorisation TDI hybride compte 29 chevaux. La consommation annoncée n'est que de 1,38 L/100 km tandis que ses émanations de CO_2 sont limitées à 36 g/km.

UP! LITE CONCEPT (LOS ANGELES 2009)

Voici que se présente la déclinaison la plus réaliste des concepts Up! de Volkswagen, le Up! Lite. Ultraléger, il ne pèse que 695 kg et son Cx n'est que de 0,23. Bien que les dimensions de sa largeur soient très comptées, il peut tout de même accueillir quatre passagers. Sa motorisation hybride regroupe un moteur bicylindre TDI de seulement 0,8 litre qui développe 51 chevaux. Celui-ci est associé à un moteur électrique de 10 kW (14 ch) et accouplé à une boîte DSG à sept rapports. Sa consommation moyenne de carburant est impressionnante : 2,44 L/100 km (100 mi/gal).

VOLVO

C30 ELECTRIC (FRANCFORT 2009)

Ici, nous n'avons pas vraiment affaire à un concept, mais plutôt à un prototype qui sert de laboratoire roulant pour les ingénieurs de Volvo. La firme compte commercialiser dès 2012 ses premières voitures à propulsion entièrement électrique. Son moteur électrique est alimenté par des batteries au lithium-ion que l'on peut recharger par le biais de prises électriques domestiques. Avec son autonomie évaluée à 150 kilomètres, elle peut facilement répondre aux besoins journaliers de 90 % des Européens.

MATCHS COMPARATIFS

Ford / Honda / Mazda / Mitsubishi / Nissan / Toyota / Volkswagen

CINQ COMPACTES SPORTIVES
Pour le vrai monde

Texte et photos : **Marc Lachapelle**

Les pages du *Guide* regorgent d'exotiques qui font rêver, mais qu'une proportion infime d'entre nous peut s'offrir. De toute manière, on ne peut logiquement exploiter qu'une fraction des performances et de la tenue de route de ces voitures sur nos routes bosselées, encombrées et patrouillées sans risquer gros. C'est pourquoi, après les coupés sport abordables de l'an dernier, nous sommes allés plus loin en mettant cette fois à l'épreuve les meilleures compactes sportives.

Le prétexte était d'ailleurs tout trouvé puisque Volkswagen a lancé l'an dernier la sixième génération de la Golf GTI. Cette nouvelle venue décrocha aussitôt le titre de Voiture de l'année au pays décerné par l'AJAC après avoir été primée meilleure voiture de sport et performance de moins de 50000$ par le même groupe. Or, la première GTI fut la pionnière, en 1976, de ce que les Européens et nos voisins du Sud surnomment « hot hatches » parce qu'il s'agit de versions plus performantes de modestes compactes généralement dotées d'un hayon. Bref, ce sont la plupart du temps des « hatchbacks » comme on les appelle encore souvent chez nous.

UNE ALLEMANDE ET QUATRE JAPONAISES

Nous avons évidemment voulu confronter la nouvelle GTI à ses meilleures rivales actuelles en choisissant la version à deux portières équipée de la boîte de vitesses à double embrayage automatisé. Nous voulions savoir si la boîte DSG offre effectivement le meilleur des deux mondes sur une voiture qui ne renie surtout pas sa vocation pratique. La GTI est toujours munie du merveilleux quatre cylindres turbocompressé à injection directe de 200 chevaux.

Pour l'affronter, d'abord la Honda Civic Si, même si elle en est à sa sixième année dans sa forme actuelle. Le coupé Si avait lui aussi été primé par l'AJAC dans la catégorie des sportives à ses débuts en 2006. C'est vrai qu'il n'a pas de hayon, mais c'est quand même un rival sérieux qui est toujours dans le coup avec un quatre cylindres VTEC de 2,0 litres qui affectionne toujours les hauts régimes pour produire ses 197 chevaux.

Vient ensuite la Mazdaspeed3, deuxième génération de la plus performante des Mazda3. Elle a d'ailleurs eu droit, elle aussi, à un recarrossage et à une série de retouches et de modifications l'an dernier. Son moteur turbo de 2,3 litres, qui produit toujours 263 chevaux, a aussi été revu. Il est, de loin, le plus puissant du groupe et transmet toute cette cavalerie à ses seules roues avant.

Ce n'est pas le cas pour la Lancer Sportback Ralliart de Mitsubishi, la seule du groupe à bénéficier d'un rouage intégral. Le sien comporte un différentiel central électronique « actif » et des différentiels autobloquants aux deux essieux. La Sportback est la plus récente des Lancer et se distingue par le hayon qui lui taille une silhouette plus élancée. Son moteur turbo de 2,0 litres et 237 chevaux est le deuxième plus musclé du groupe, et il est jumelé exclusivement à une boîte de vitesses à double embrayage automatisé.

La cinquième de nos aspirantes a des airs d'invitée-surprise. Même son constructeur

n'était pas certain de vouloir l'inscrire à notre match. Il est vrai que la Nissan Sentra SE-R n'est habituellement pas perçue comme une rivale directe des GTI, Civic Si ou Mazdaspeed 3 chez les compactes sportives. Mais il s'agit de la version Spec V dont le prix est nettement plus bas malgré son équipement très complet. Elle se démarque de la SE-R par une série de modifications destinées à resserrer sa tenue de route et son freinage, mais aussi par sa boîte manuelle à 6 rapports. Son quatre cylindres atmosphérique de 2,5 litres et 200 chevaux est également le plus costaud du groupe en cylindrée. Chose certaine, sans la moindre prétention, la SE-R s'en est très bien tirée.

Nous avons également cherché à inclure dans ce groupe d'aspirantes la nouvelle Subaru Impreza WRX de même qu'une Mini Cooper S ou une Clubman Cooper S, mais aucune n'était disponible à la date de notre match. Même histoire pour le coupé BMW 128i, qui aurait pu défendre l'honneur des propulsions et le titre décroché par son frère, le coupé 135i, dans notre match des sportives de l'an dernier.

PARCOURS ET CIRCUIT TAILLÉS SUR MESURE

Pour évaluer nos cinq rivales, nous avons d'abord pointé leurs calandres vers le nord pour nous rendre à Notre-Dame-de-la-Merci, tout près de St-Donat et du Parc du Mont-Tremblant. C'est là que se trouve le complexe Mécaglisse, développé et géré par Franck Kirchhoff, son père Vincent et leur équipe. Nous nous y sommes rendus en empruntant surtout la route 125 et en nous échangeant les volants à quelques reprises en chemin, question de noter nos premières impressions et observations.

Mécaglisse comporte plus de 15 kilomètres de pistes en tous genres sur 700 acres. Nous venions surtout pour le circuit asphalté de 2,2 kilomètres formé de boucles qu'on peut combiner à souhait. Étroit, sinueux et ondulé, il est parfait pour ces cinq compactes vitaminées dont nos essayeurs ont pu explorer à fond la tenue de route, l'équilibre, les performances et le freinage.

À cette fin, Franck Kirchhoff, en instructeur aguerri, nous a tracé un parcours qui comportait un slalom, un changement de voie et une zone de freinage maximum. Chaque essayeur a bouclé quelques tours au volant de chacune des concurrentes. Parfaitement familier avec son circuit, Franck a également établi pour nous le chrono de référence pour chacune, tout en nous offrant ses impressions et commentaires sur son comportement en piste.

Pour le trajet de retour vers Montréal, nous avons emprunté les routes diaboliquement entortillées qui mènent vers Entrelacs et ensuite St-Hippolyte, avec une autre série de changements de voitures et de prises de notes. Puis ce fut le crochet par St-Jérôme et l'épreuve de la traversée de la ville à l'heure de pointe, qui nous apprend toujours quelque chose de plus sur nos candidates. Les mesures d'accélération et de freinage furent effectuées le surlendemain, par une température idéale, sur notre tracé rectiligne habituel.

Notre groupe d'essayeurs comptait d'abord Yvan Fournier, technicien en aéronautique et vétéran des matches du *Guide de l'auto* depuis plus de vingt-cinq ans. Bertrand Plouffe est un formateur et un expert en multimédia doublé d'un excellent pilote avec un solide bagage en course automobile. Et pour représenter le groupe cible des compactes sportives, nous avions deux gaillards de 22 ans qui font tous deux près de 1,90 m. Alexandre Langlois et mon fils Théo sont des amis d'enfance qui partagent le même intérêt pour la conduite et les voitures belles, performantes et bien faites, entre autres passions pour des jeunes de leur âge. Ce qui ne les empêche aucunement de jeter sur elles un regard frais, critique et sans complaisance.

L'auteur a lui aussi ajouté son grain de sel au fil des essais et des kilomètres, en plus d'ouvrir la route, d'effectuer les mesures de performance, de faire quelques photos et de payer le lunch. Voilà ce que nous avons découvert en comparant et en examinant de près ces cinq voitures.

1

Mazdaspeed3

Elle exagère avec talent

Le moins qu'on puisse dire est que la Mazdaspeed3 est généreuse. Elle est de loin la plus puissante du groupe avec son moteur turbo de 263 chevaux, mais également la mieux équipée et la plus spectaculaire. Après avoir jugé la prise d'air sur le capot « efficace mais peut-être un peu exagérée », Yvan suggère que Mazda recherchait peut-être « le *look* intimidant ». Nos essayeurs ont apprécié l'aménagement et la finition de l'habitacle, le dessin du tableau de bord, les commandes claires et le bon amalgame de confort et de maintien des sièges avant, mais aussi leurs réglages électriques avec mémoires. Alexandre a noté la chaîne audio Bose, le système de navigation simple à utiliser, le bon confort aux quatre places et la clé à puce. La puissance du turbo est par contre une arme à double tranchant. Tous ont goûté aux accélérations et aux reprises solides, même sur le 6e rapport. Combinées au mordant des pneus et à une tenue de route solide, elles ont permis à la Mazdaspeed3 de boucler le tour le plus rapide à Mécaglisse. Nos essayeurs n'ont cependant pas manqué de souligner les « accélérations brusques et sauvages », que Bertrand attribue à une forte réaction de couple et à une grande sensibilité aux contours du pavé. Théo en conclut « qu'aucun compromis n'a été fait pour la performance », et c'est une des raisons qui l'ont amené à faire de la Mazdaspeed3 sa préférée du groupe. Il fut toutefois le seul, même si ses camarades ont apprécié l'impression de contact direct avec la route et les bonnes sensations tactiles du volant, mais peut-être moins son côté plus brusque. Chose certaine, la Mazdaspeed3 offre beaucoup pour le prix et c'est ce qui lui a finalement valu cette victoire. Elle la mérite, mais pour l'apprécier pleinement, il faut reconnaître son côté excessif et savoir en doser et en maîtriser les effets.

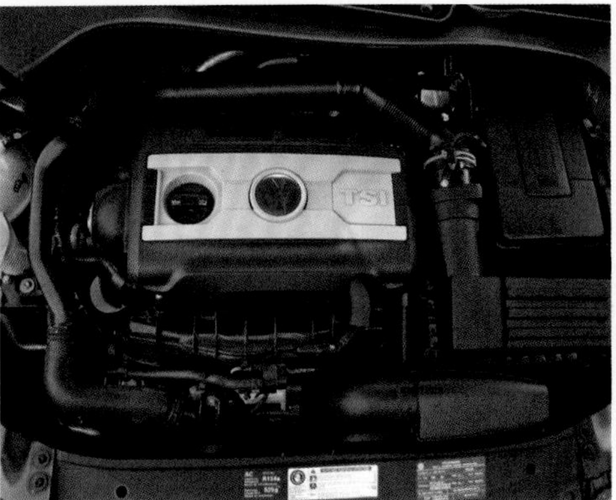

2

Volkswagen GTI
La plus raffinée

La GTI n'a jamais été la plus puissante de sa catégorie. Volkswagen a toujours cultivé plutôt l'équilibre entre performance et agilité. Or, cette GTI de sixième génération est sa plus belle réussite à ce jour. Bertrand aurait souhaité plus d'audace et d'originalité, mais les stylistes se sont plutôt inspirés de la première GTI, au nom de la tradition. Nos essayeurs ont d'ailleurs louangé la finition et le dessin de son habitacle, son équipement complet, le confort de ses sièges et son volant sport. Yvan apprécie les multiples réglages des sièges, mais note que l'accès aux places arrière est difficile sur ce modèle à deux portières. Alexandre souligne par contre que les places arrière sont spacieuses pour les personnes de grande taille. Nos jeunes essayeurs ont prisé la chaîne audio, qui intègre un lecteur numérique, et l'écran tactile complété d'un système de navigation qu'Alexandre juge excellent. Théo note par contre que les commandes qui ne se trouvent pas sur l'écran tactile sont trop petites. Tous ont aimé son moteur nerveux, souple et plein de caractère. Théo ajoute qu'il génère beaucoup de couple sans imposer d'attente comme les autres moteurs turbocompressés du match. La plupart ont jugé la boîte DSG rapide et efficace, mais Bertrand a été agacé par des changements de rapports non voulus sur le circuit, même en mode Sport. La GTI a également déçu notre pilote expert Franck Kirchhoff, qui l'a trouvée plus souple et moins précise que le modèle antérieur sur piste. Elle n'a d'ailleurs inscrit que le 4e chrono du groupe. Sans le groupe « cuir de luxe », une option de 2600$, la GTI l'aurait d'ailleurs emporté au classement final. Le plus ironique est de songer que le motif carrelé des sièges en tissu est plus fidèle à la tradition. De toute manière, cette deuxième place par un seul point est certainement une victoire morale pour une GTI véritablement exceptionnelle.

3

Honda Civic Si
Encore vive et dans le coup

Honda n'a pas hésité à nous confier un coupé Civic Si, même s'il allait être confronté à des rivales fraîches alors qu'il en est à sa sixième (et dernière) année dans sa forme actuelle. Il n'a pas eu tort puisque la Si s'en est très bien tirée. Nos essayeurs ont noté le confort et le maintien des sièges, l'excellente visibilité et la précision de la boîte de vitesses, la meilleure manuelle du groupe. Ils ont apprécié la clarté des commandes et des cadrans, la position de conduite et le pédalier. Alexandre aurait toutefois préféré des phares automatiques et un système de navigation. Bertrand, quant à lui, a jugé que la Si était la plus équilibrée du groupe sur le circuit, malgré une légère tendance à sous-virer. Théo a par contre trouvé ses freins moyens et c'est d'ailleurs la Honda qui a inscrit la plus longue distance en freinage d'urgence. Nos pilotes ont par ailleurs déploré l'accès plus ardu et l'espace limité aux places arrière, et pas seulement les plus grands. Ils ont cependant surtout souligné la nature très pointue du quatre cylindres à calage variable VTEC, qui ne s'anime sérieusement qu'à partir de 6000 tr/min. C'est d'autant plus criant par rapport au couple à bas régime des moteurs turbo. Or, le coupé Civic est tout à fait à l'aise en conduite normale où on goûte la docilité et la flexibilité de son moteur. La Civic Si s'est révélée être la déception du groupe pour Yvan, qui en attendait beaucoup plus, mais Bertrand en a fait son deuxième choix, malgré ses critiques à l'égard du moteur. Chose certaine, il fallait que le coupé Civic Si ait des qualités exceptionnelles dès son lancement pour être encore aussi frais et compétitif après six ans, sans retouche majeure. Le fait qu'il soit nettement moins cher que les deux rivales qui l'ont devancé dans notre match le rend encore plus intéressant.

Mitsubishi Lancer Sportback Ralliart

Le paradoxe intégral

La sœur de la bouillante Evo s'est présentée à notre match avec de solides arguments. La Sportback a d'abord fière allure avec son hayon et sa silhouette élancée. La version Ralliart lui vaut ensuite le seul rouage intégral du groupe, hérité de la génération précédente de l'Evo, et un moteur turbo de 237 chevaux pour bien l'exploiter. Elle n'y a pas manqué en réalisant le deuxième meilleur temps sur le circuit Mécaglisse et les meilleurs chronos en accélération. Elle aurait devancé ses rivales encore plus nettement avec un mode départ-canon. Ces démarrages lents ne sont qu'un des aspects qui ont valu à sa boîte de vitesse à double embrayage automatisé de vives critiques. Nos essayeurs ont déploré sa lenteur et le fait qu'elle change de rapports « inutilement en conduite normale », selon Bertrand, pour qui la Sportback Ralliart a été la déception du match, ce qui lui a valu une de ses trois dernières places au classement personnel des essayeurs. Ces derniers n'ont pas aimé non plus les manettes fixées à la colonne de direction, qui forcent à lâcher le volant d'une main pour passer les vitesses et le refus de rétrograder au freinage. La Mitsubishi a par contre reçu des compliments pour sa tenue de route et la polyvalence que lui procure son rouage intégral. On a également loué son confort et son silence de roulement sur l'autoroute. Théo a trouvé ses sièges Recaro « impeccables », mais Yvan a déploré, à juste titre, l'absence d'un réglage en hauteur parce que l'assise est vraiment trop basse. Alexandre a simplement décrété que son habitacle « n'est pas fait pour les grands ». De façon générale, malgré ses performances, sa silhouette et l'attrait unique de son rouage intégral, la Sportback Ralliart a déçu. Avec une boîte de vitesse beaucoup plus vive avec manettes au volant et des sièges à hauteur réglable, ce serait peut-être une toute autre histoire.

5

Nissan Sentra SE-R Spec V
Une transformation réussie

Loin d'être larguée, la petite berline Sentra SE-R Spec V a «talonné ses rivales» dans ce match, pour reprendre les mots d'Yvan Fournier. En piste, elle s'est même permis un chrono à seulement 32 centièmes de seconde de la GTI et a inscrit la distance la plus courte en freinage d'urgence. Sur les routes bosselées du retour, la SE-R affichait le roulement le plus confortable en échange d'un peu plus de roulis. Le moteur atmosphérique de 2,5 litres offre la plus forte cylindrée du groupe et de bonnes reprises, mais son embrayage à sec exige une adaptation. Nos essayeurs ont apprécié le système de navigation et la caméra de marche arrière qu'on ne s'attend pas à trouver dans une compacte abordable. Théo note que les sièges, bien que confortables, sont plus «de style sofa» et ne procurent pas le maintien des autres. Tandis qu'Alexandre constate que l'espace à l'arrière est limité pour les «grandes personnes», Yvan mentionne que les barres de renforcement en «V» fixées sur la paroi avant du coffre éliminent le dossier arrière repliable et, du même coup, une bonne part de commodité. Nos deux plus jeunes essayeurs déplorent l'absence de contrôles au volant, mais apprécient les prises pour lecteurs numériques et la clarté de l'écran et des cadrans. Ils n'ont pas aimé le pare-soleil gauche qui accroche le rétroviseur central et se sont joints à leurs collègues pour dénigrer le cadran qui mesure la force d'accélération en temps réel au sommet du tableau de bord. Avec une pointe de cynisme, Bertrand présente enfin la SE-R Spec V comme «une auto de matante» à laquelle on a greffé des accessoires pour lui donner «un *look* un peu sportif» en ajoutant toutefois aussitôt qu'en raison de son prix et de son comportement, cette petite voiture dont il n'attendait rien a été sa surprise du match. Tout est dit.

POINTAGE

		Honda Civic Si	Mazda Mazdaspeed3	Mitsubishi Lancer Ralliart	Nissan SE-R Spec V	Volkswagen GTI
Design / Style						
Extérieur *(silhouette, proportions, originalité, style, attrait visuel pur)*	/30	24,375	22,9	22,5	18	24,0
Intérieur *(design, couleurs, style, originalité, agencement des matériaux)*	/10	7,6	8,4	7,0	6,6	8,5
Total	/40	32,00	31,25	29,50	24,58	32,50
Carrosserie						
Finition intérieure + extérieure *(qualité de peinture, écarts, assemblage)*	/20	16,0	16,3	14,8	13,8	17,5
Qualité des matériaux *(texture, couleur, surface, odeur)*	/20	16,4	17,3	15,5	15,5	18,0
Tableau de bord *(clarté, lisibilité des cadrans, graphisme, disposition)*	/10	9,0	8,3	7,5	7,7	8,4
Équipement *(accessoires, innovations, gadgets, système audio, etc.)*	/10	7,1	7,9	7,0	8,6	8,6
Coffre *(accès, volume, commodité, modularité, polyvalence : passage)*	/10	7,7	8,4	8,0	6,8	7,7
Rangements *(accès, nombre, taille, commodité, efficacité)*	/10	8,0	7,8	7,6	7,1	7,5
Total	/80	64,18	65,80	60,33	59,40	67,60
Confort / Ergonomie						
Position de conduite *(volant, sièges avant, repose-pied, réglages)*	/20	16,7	17,8	13,4	14,3	16,8
Ergonomie *(facilité à atteindre les commandes, douceur, précision)*	/10	8,1	8,7	7,7	7,3	8,6
Places arrière *(nombre, accès, confort, espace, appuie-tête)*	/10	6,8	8,4	8,1	6,8	7,0
Silence de roulement *(sur chaussée lisse ou raboteuse, bruit de vent)*	/10	7,6	7,6	7,3	7,5	7,8
Total	/50	39,15	42,40	36,35	35,75	40,13
Conduite						
Tenue de route *(équilibre, agilité, adhérence, facilité, marge de sécurité)*	/50	40,0	39,4	35,6	33,1	40,6
Moteur *(rendement, puissance, couple à bas régime, réponse, agrément)*	/40	31,1	32,7	27,4	28,5	35,3
Direction *(précision, « feedback », résistance aux secousses, braquage)*	/20	16,5	16,5	10,8	14,0	15,9
Freins *(sensations, modulation, constance, performances, résistance)*	/20	17,0	15,3	14,0	13,3	16,0
Transmission *(précision, rapidité, étagement, douceur, embrayage)*	/10	7,9	7,5	7,1	7,2	8,1
Confort de roulement *(suspension, solidité structurelle)*	/10	7,7	7,9	7,1	7,4	8,1
Total	/150	120,18	119,18	101,88	103,43	124,00
Sécurité						
Visibilité *(surface vitrée, largeur des montants, angles morts)*	/10	7,9	7,4	6,7	6,9	8,0
Rétroviseurs *(taille, forme, emplacement, clarté - bloquent points de corde?)*	/5	4,0	3,9	3,8	3,5	3,8
Systèmes d'aide à la conduite *(efficacité, adaptabilité, rapidité)*	/5	3,9	3,8	3,3	3,4	3,9
Total	/20	15,85	14,98	13,70	13,81	15,66
Performances mesurées						
Parcours circuit Mécaglisse	/40	24	40	32	16	20
Accélération 0-100 km/h	/10	4	6	10	5	8
Accélération 1/4 de mille	/10	4	6	10	5	8
Freinage de 100 km/h	/20	8	16	10	20	12
Consommation réelle	/20	5,94	3,15	9,45	7,03	9,22
Total	/100	45,94	71,15	71,45	53,03	57,22
Autres classements						
Choix des essayeurs	/60	36,0	48,0	27,6	28,8	57,6
Total	/500	353,3	392,8	340,8	318,8	394.7
Pointage final*	/500	324,5	353,5	305,9	293,8	352,5
Rang		3	1	4	5	2

* Avec pondération pour le prix selon la courbe de valeur de l'AJAC

La meilleure note du groupe (cellule grisée)

Un quintette en trois temps

La nouvelle GTI se présentait à ce match en grande favorite. Elle a très bien fait, mais ce ne fut pas la domination qu'on attendait. Voilà le risque des attentes élevées. À l'inverse, la Sentra SE-R Spec V est arrivée sans claironner et nous a étonnés. Elle termine cinquième au pur pointage et quatrième au classement des essayeurs, mais c'est la belle surprise de ce match.

Quant à la Mazdaspeed3, avec une fiche technique, un équipement et une gueule comme la sienne, on pouvait s'attendre à ce qu'elle chauffe la GTI et c'est assurément ce qu'elle a fait. De son côté, le coupé Honda Civic Si n'avait rien à perdre, lui qui fait un dernier tour de piste cette année. Il nous a malgré tout rappelé sa finesse et son brio en terminant en milieu de peloton, à une encablure des meneuses, trahissant toutefois des faiblesses que Honda voudra sans nul doute corriger avec son successeur. La Mitsubishi Lancer Sportback Ralliart, enfin, avait beaucoup à offrir et autant à prouver. Elle a manqué la cible de peu cette fois-ci, mais il suffirait d'une poignée de changements judicieux pour qu'elle soit dans le coup.

Une victoire par la marge d'un seul point sur un total possible de 500 c'est infime, mais la Mazdaspeed3 mérite pleinement la sienne. Elle l'a effectivement ravie à la GTI grâce à son prix inférieur de plus de 2600$, malgré un équipement plus complet et cinq douzaines de chevaux en prime sous le capot. Pour être justes et rationnels, nous devons conclure que le choix doit se faire entre le raffinement, l'équilibre et la finesse de la GTI ou le muscle, le caractère fougueux et l'équipement généreux de la Mazda. Dans un camp comme dans l'autre, on ne risque ni d'être déçu, ni de s'ennuyer.

FRANCK KIRCHHOFF

MERCI À NOS ESSAYEURS;
Théo De Guire-Lachapelle, Yvan Fournier, Alexandre Langlois et Bertrand Plouffe.

Et des remerciements très spéciaux à Franck et Vincent Kirchhoff pour l'aide et l'accueil fantastiques chez eux, au complexe Mécaglisse.

Assurances : pilule amère

La question du coût des assurances est évidemment importante pour cette catégorie de voitures. Surtout pour des acheteurs comme nos deux essayeurs dans la jeune vingtaine. La note peut facilement devenir très salée si l'assuré est le premier conducteur et que la voiture est à son nom. Là encore, nos deux meneuses, la GTI et la Mazdaspeed3, nous ont surpris en exhibant les coûts d'assurance les plus faibles, selon les prix obtenus par Alexandre, un de nos deux essayeurs de 22 ans. Sa demande portait sur une couverture complète feu-vol-vandalisme avec une franchise de 500$ et la clause «valeur à neuf». Nous ne mentionnons ces prix au tableau de données qu'à titre indicatif, mais ils dépassent tous le cap des 2000$. C'est peut-être le seul coût exagéré qu'il faut redouter, surtout si on est jeune, pour un achat qui demeure très pragmatique pour le reste.

MÉCAGLISSE QUÉBEC
1253, chemin Dufresne,
Notre-Dame-de-la-Merci,
Québec, JOT 2A0
Téléphone: 819-424-3324
Courriel : info@mecaglisse.com
Site Web : www.mecaglisse.com

FICHES TECHNIQUES

	Mazda Mazdaspeed3	**Volkswagen** GTI
Empattement (mm)	2 640	2 578
Longueur (mm)	4 490	4 213
Largeur (mm)	1 765	1 779
Hauteur (mm)	1 465	1 469
Voie avant / arrière (mm)	1 535 / 1 525	1 533 / 1 514
Poids (kg)	1 461	1 376
Répartition poids avant / arrière (%)	62 / 38	60 / 40
Coefficient de traînée	0.32	0.32
Places	5	5
Boîte de vitesses / rapports	manuelle / 6	double embrayage auto / 6
Rouage	traction	traction
Moteur	4L DACT turbo	4L DACT turbo
Cylindrée	2,3 litres	2,0 litres
Cylindrée	2 260 cm³	1 984 cm³
Puissance maximale	263 ch à 5 500 tr/min	200 ch à 5 100 tr/min
Couple maximal	280 lb-pi à 3 000 tr/min	207 lb-pi à 1 700 tr/min
Essence recommandée / indice d'octane	super / 91 *	super / 91 **
Suspension avant	jambes de force	jambes de force
Suspension arrière	ind. / bras multiples	ind. / bras multiples
Freins avant / diamètre (mm) / pistons	disques / 320	disques / 312
Freins arrière / diamètre (mm) / piston(s)	disques / 280	disques / 285
Pneus	P225/40R18	P225/45R17
Direction	crémaillère assistée	crémaillère assistée
Diamètre de braquage (m)	11,00	10,91
Réservoir de carburant (litres)	60	55
Capacité coffre (litres)	481 à 1 213	419 à 1 311
Accélération 0-100 km/h (sec)	7,32	6,81
Accélération 1/4 de mille (sec / km/h)	15,33	15,01
Freinage de 100 km/h (mètres)	39,87	40,77
Parcours circuit Mécaglisse (minute / secondes)	1:03,11	1:04,37
Consommation réelle essai (L/100 km)	16,56	12,79
Consommation RNC (ville/route L/100 km)	11,5 / 8,0	10,0 / 6,6
Coût d'assurance ***	2 243 $	2 052 $
Prix de base	32 995 $	30 075 $
Prix essai	32 995 $	35 640 $
Lieu de fabrication	Hiroshima, Japon	Wolfsburg, Allemagne

* Essence super exigée
** Essence super recommandée
*** À titre indicatif seulement, conducteur de 22 ans résidant à Montréal

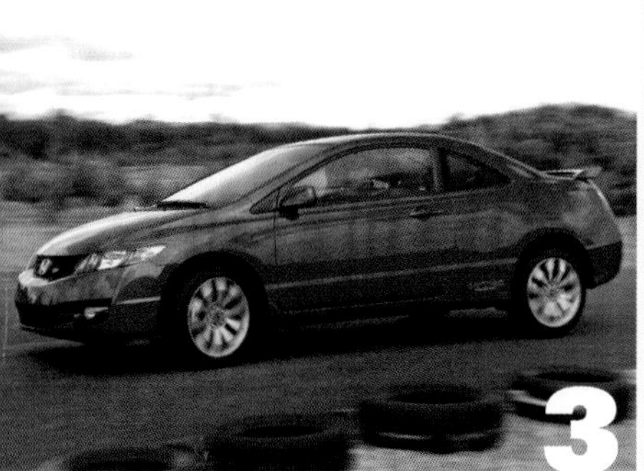

Honda Civic Si	**Mitsubishi Lancer** Sportback Ralliart	**Nissan Sentra** SE-R Spec V
2 650	2 635	2 685
4 457	4 585	4 575
1 751	1 760	1 790
1 396	1 515	1 501
1 499 / 1 526	1 530 / 1 530	1 511 / 1 534
1 314	1 620	1 387
61 / 39	58 / 42	62 / 38
n.d.	n.d.	0.34
5	5	5
manuelle / 6	double embrayage auto / 6	manuelle / 6
traction	intégral	traction
4L DACT	4L DACT turbo	4L DACT
2,0 litres	2,0 litres	2,5 litres
1 998 cm³	1 998 cm³	2 488 cm³
197 ch à 7 800 tr/min	237 ch à 6 000 tr/min	200 ch à 6 600 tr/min
139 lb-pi à 6 100 tr/min	253 lb-pi à 3 000 tr/min	180 lb-pi à 5 200 tr/min
super / 91 *	super / 91 *	super / 91 **
jambes de force	jambes de force	jambes de force
ind. / double triangle	ind. / bras multiples	semi ind. / barres torsion
disques / 300	disques / 295	disques / 320
disques / 259	disques / 302	disques / 292
P215/45R17	P215/45R18	P225/45R17
crémaillère assistée	crémaillère assistée	crémaillère assistée
10,85	10,00	10,79
50	55	55
327	390 à 1 492	340
8,21	6,18	8,20
16,30	14,52	16,09
43,06	41,33	38,90
1:04,17	1:03,86	1:04,69
14,90	12,04	14,30
10,2 / 6,8	12,2 / 8,0	9,8 / 7,0
2 880$	2 861$	2 318$
25 880$	33 498$	23 198$
25 880$	33 698$	24 033$
Alliston, Ontario	Mizushima, Japon	Aguascalientes, Mexique

UN MATCH INCONTOURNABLE

Confrontation vétérans vs recrues

Avec l'arrivée fort annoncée des nouvelles Ford Fiesta et Mazda2, il était devenu impératif de les comparer avec les autres modèles de cette catégorie. Notre dernière évaluation comparative des voitures sous-compactes s'est effectuée dans le cadre du *Guide de l'auto 2007* et les modèles suivants s'étaient affrontés : Honda Fit, Hyundai Accent, Kia Rio, Nissan Versa, Pontiac Wave, Suzuki Swift + et Toyota Yaris.

Pour effectuer la présente comparaison pour l'édition 2011, nous avons invité les trois premiers méritants de ce dernier match, soit la gagnante, la Honda Fit, son dauphin la Nissan Versa et finalement la troisième, la Toyota Yaris. Inutile d'inviter les autres qui sont soit en instance d'être remplacés ou ne sont plus de nature à se démarquer de façon positive. Ce trio affronte plutôt les deux nouvelles Darling de notre marché, la Ford Fiesta et la Mazda2, qui sont arrivées à grand renfort de publicité.

Notre intention était de confronter des modèles équipés de la transmission automatique, qu'elle soit traditionnelle ou à rapports continuellement variables. Malheureusement, le destin en a décidé autrement. En effet, si la nouvelle Mazda2 qui a participé à cette évaluation était dotée de la boîte automatique, la Ford Fiesta, elle, était dotée d'une transmission manuelle, parce que la version à boîte automatique a été endommagée dans le transport. De plus, comme si les choses n'étaient pas suffisamment compliquées, la seule Honda Fit disponible était également une version à boîte manuelle. Pour équilibrer les choses et ne pas comparer des pommes avec des oranges, nous avons pris une décision que certains vont contester, mais que nous jugeons la plus équitable possible pour les autres modèles inscrits à cet essai. Au chapitre des performances et des prix, nous avons donc utilisé les données des modèles équipés de boîte automatique. Par exemple, nous sommes partis du prix de la Ford Fiesta qui nous avait été confiée, puis nous avons tout simplement additionné le coût supplémentaire de sa boîte automatique. Nous avons fait de même pour la Fit. Nous avons également utilisé les temps d'accélération et de reprise des modèles à boîte automatique dans les deux cas. Cela était relativement facile, mais la question, alors, était d'évaluer le rendement de ces transmissions, alors que les autres modèles sont automatiques et que nos deux cas problèmes possèdent des transmissions manuelles. La solution est digne de celle du roi Salomon, du moins nous le croyons. Comme c'est le cas dans le cadre des essais annuels du prix de la Voiture de l'année de l'AJAC, nous n'avons attribué aucune note pour la transmission. Les 20 points qui y étaient alloués ont été divisés en deux : 10 points pour la tenue de route et autant pour l'agrément de conduite.

Une fois ce problème réglé, notre quintette d'essayeurs s'est donné rendez-vous devant les bureaux du *Guide de l'auto* pour procéder à une évaluation statique des modèles en lice avant de prendre la route. Nos essayeurs invités étaient André Lalanne et Marc Girardin, deux testeurs qui avaient connu leur baptême du feu lors de notre essai des véhicules hybrides l'an dernier, Robert Gariepy, un vétéran de nombreux tests, ainsi que David et Daniel

Duquet qui ont participé dans le passé à genre d'évaluation. Et oui, ce sont mes fils, pourquoi pas un peu de népotisme ? Nous avions réussi à trouver deux représentantes de la gent féminine, mais celles-ci ont préféré aller en vacances à la plage. Qui pourrait le leur reprocher ?

Une fois notre examen statique complété, la caravane prit la route et se dirigea vers la région des monts Rougemont et Saint-Grégoire où nous avons serpenté les routes pendant plusieurs heures, chaque essayeur roulant pendant plusieurs dizaines de kilomètres au volant de chaque véhicule.

Voici leur verdict.

Honda Fit

Mazda2

Ford Fiesta

Nissan Versa

Toyota Yaris

Ils ont dit :

Robert Gariepy

« La Fit se mérite cette première place surtout en raison de son habitabilité remarquable, de son comportement routier en général et de son ergonomie. Sans oublier son *look* superbe. »

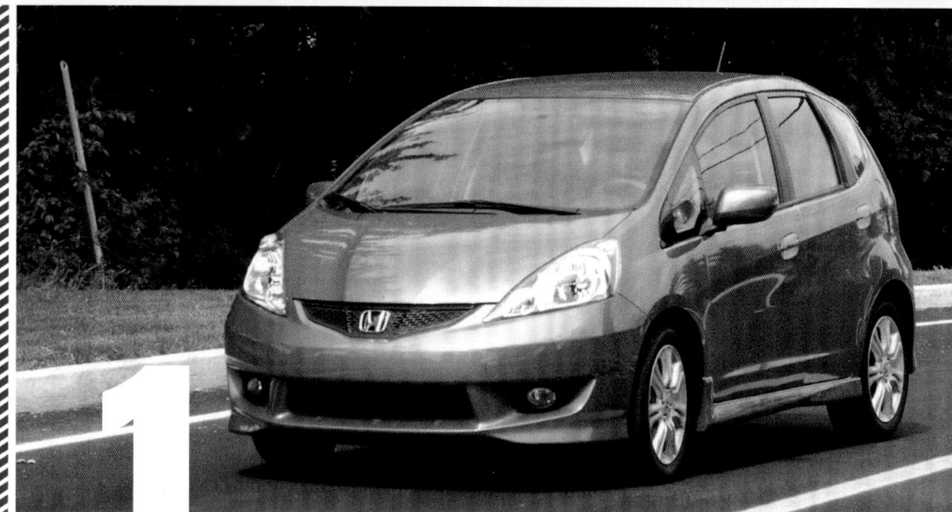

Honda Fit
Toujours en tête

Lors de notre match comparatif réalisé en 2007, cette Honda avait terminé première, surpassant la Nissan Versa. Cette fois, son dauphin a été relégué au troisième rang, pendant qu'elle continue à dominer la catégorie des sous-compactes. Et il ne s'agit pas d'une victoire de justesse, car comme le confirment nos chiffres, sa supériorité a été aisément démontrée. En fait, elle a remporté plus de catégories que tous les autres véhicules de ce match. C'est surtout au chapitre de la tenue de route et de l'agrément de conduite qu'elle a dominé, mais en plus, la Fit s'est avérée la voiture la plus pratique du groupe avec son incroyable système d'aménagement intérieur qui se démarque par son « siège magique ». Les ingénieurs ont astucieusement placé le réservoir de carburant sous les sièges avant (à l'extérieur de l'habitacle, bien entendu) et cela a permis de gagner de l'espace à l'arrière. En plus, l'ingénieux siège arrière se relève verticalement pour donner encore plus d'espace. Ensuite, une fois les sièges arrière complètement à plat, il est possible d'y loger des objets de taille vraiment impressionnante pour une voiture de cette grosseur.

Or, son succès ne tient pas uniquement à cet habitacle ingénieux. Il y a la qualité de fabrication, le tableau de bord moderne, un assemblage précis et surtout un moteur qui, malgré des performances peu étincelantes, ne faillit jamais à la tâche. Un détail cependant, notre modèle d'essai était une version Sport toute équipée proposant un niveau de confort plus élevé. Malgré tout, son prix demeure compétitif. De leur côté, les versions plus abordables, mais plus dépouillées, sont moins confortables et leur niveau sonore est plus élevé. D'ailleurs, s'il est vrai que la tenue de route, la précision de la direction et l'agrément de conduite viennent s'ajouter à la polyvalence de l'habitacle, force est d'admettre que l'insonorisation n'est pas nécessairement le point fort de ce véhicule. De plus, la suspension a tendance à sautiller sur mauvaise route, sans toutefois être pire que les autres versions, plus petites, qui sont également affectées par un empattement relativement court. À ce chapitre, seule la Nissan Versa la devance.

Il faut également ajouter que depuis notre première confrontation, qui a vu la Fit l'emporter, une nouvelle génération est arrivée. Ce qui explique qu'elle continue de dominer la catégorie. Il s'agit en effet d'une version plus élégante et plus raffinée, mais toujours aussi intéressante à piloter que celle de la première génération.

Ils ont dit:

David Duquet

«Cette voiture correspond vraiment au caractère *Vroom-Vroom* de la marque. Je l'aurais sans doute appréciée davantage avec une boîte manuelle, mais sa tenue de route et son agilité m'ont convaincu.»

2

Mazda2
La première des petites

Vous avez certainement constaté, à la lecture de notre fiche technique, que ce match comporte deux catégories de voitures: des sous-compactes qui sont vraiment des sous-compactes, et deux autres qui sont relativement hors normes bien que la Honda Fit soit entre les deux catégories. Par contre, la Nissan Versa est pratiquement une compacte déguisée en sous-compacte. Si on part de ces prémisses, la Mazda2 remporte la palme chez les petites. Il faut admettre que le défi était de taille puisque cette petite nipponne est dotée du moteur le moins puissant, alors que sa boîte automatique à quatre rapports laissait présager un jugement plutôt sévère. Au chapitre des performances, il n'y a pas à s'inquiéter puisque cette petite Mazda a réussi à se débrouiller et à nous offrir des temps d'accélération et des reprises dans la moyenne de cette catégorie. La seule ombre au tableau avec cette boîte automatique est le niveau sonore assez élevé dans l'habitacle car si on adopte une conduite pressée ou un tantinet sportive, le moteur est constamment sollicité et le niveau de bruit est amplifié.

Pour le reste, cette voiture s'est méritée d'excellentes notes en raison de sa silhouette, de sa finition et de la position de conduite, alors que son agrément de conduite a été jugé être parmi les meilleurs de notre essai. Il est certain que si vous roulez surtout en ville, ses dimensions compactes et son habilité à zigzaguer dans la circulation vont être appréciée. Et même si cela n'entre pas en ligne de compte dans le cadre de cet essai, Mazda propose également une décalcomanie exclusive ainsi qu'un modèle «pimpé», le Yozora, qui risque de devenir la coqueluche du marché.

Par contre, si elle est la meilleure des petites, certains vont trouver que c'est un peu étroit et vont se tourner vers la Nissan Versa qui s'incline de peu. En fait, c'est pratiquement un match égal. La Nissan possède un moteur nettement plus puissant et un habitacle plus spacieux. L'une se fait apprécier par son confort et son moteur tandis que la Mazda2 est plus petite, moins puissante, mais plus agréable à conduire.

Ils ont dit:

Marc Girardin

« C'est la voiture du gros bon sens. Elle est spacieuse, puissante, confortable et en plus son prix est plus que compétitif. Il est difficile de demander plus. »

3

Nissan Versa
La bourgeoise du groupe

Ce n'est pas que nous voulons atténuer le résultat de cette troisième place, mais force est d'admettre que la différence entre la seconde et la troisième place est l'affaire de quelques points seulement. Si cette Nissan avait été un tantinet plus agréable à conduire et avait offert une tenue de route légèrement supérieure, elle se serait méritée le second rang. Par contre, elle n'aurait jamais pu décrocher le premier rang, boulonné dans le ciment par la Honda Fit qui domine presque toutes les catégories d'évaluation.

Toutefois, si vous êtes à la recherche d'une voiture sous-compacte qui se vend à un prix d'aubaine, qui offre des sièges très confortables et dont l'habitabilité est supérieure à la moyenne de la catégorie, la Versa sera votre choix. Si ce sont vos critères de sélection, il n'est pas certain que vous allez apprécier la Mazda2, trop petite et trop directe de par sa conduite. Certains n'ont pas trouvé la silhouette de la Nissan très élégante, mais il faut croire qu'elle plaît à beaucoup de gens si l'on se fie aux nombreuses Versa qui circulent sur nos routes.

Les ingénieurs ont adopté une approche différente de celle utilisée par les autres constructeurs. Ils ont préféré opter pour un moteur de plus grosse cylindrée et plus puissant. Cela assure des accélérations intéressantes et en douceur. Par contre, il faut souligner une fois de plus que cette Nissan est en fait une compacte jouant dans la cour des sous-compactes.

Puisque ce modèle est avec nous depuis quelques années déjà, sa silhouette extérieure, de même que son habitacle, n'ont pas mérité de très bonnes notes face aux modèles récemment arrivés. C'est correct et sympathique, mais une fois de plus cela manque de piquant. Par contre, si vous devez transporter des passagers à l'arrière, le choix est facile, la Nissan l'emporte et de loin. Encore une fois, un autre des avantages de ce gabarit plus important que les autres de la catégorie.

Par contre, à force d'être pratique et spacieux, on devient parfois peu intéressant à conduire et c'est ce qui se produit, et causant la perte de plusieurs points précieux face à sa grande rivale dans ce match, soit la Mazda2 pourtant plus petite et beaucoup moins puissante.

Ses devancières ont des qualités que nos essayeurs ont jugées supérieures à cette Nissan, mais le fait que celle-ci jouisse d'une très grande popularité n'est pas le fruit du hasard non plus. Vendue à un prix d'aubaine, elle propose une combinaison unique de performances, d'habitabilité et de confort. Dommage que l'agrément de conduite ne soit pas au rendez-vous.

Ils ont dit:

Daniel Duquet

« Cette voiture m'a laissé sur mon appétit. Même en faisant abstraction du moteur et de la transmission, son comportement routier ne m'a pas impressionné, pas plus que son habitacle. »

Ford Fiesta
La surprise

Bien honnêtement, plusieurs s'attendaient à ce que cette nouvelle Ford balaie le match. En effet, sa silhouette moderne, son tableau de bord songé de même qu'une campagne publicitaire fort bien orchestrée, avait mis la table pour une domination du palmarès. Alors, comment s'est-elle retrouvée au quatrième rang? Peut-être parce que les gens s'attendaient à beaucoup mieux. Peut-être également du fait qu'elle était dotée d'une boîte manuelle. À ce propos, nous n'avons pas tenu compte des résultats obtenus avec cette transmission. En effet, les quatrième et cinquième rapports sont des surmultipliées, de sorte qu'en conduite normale on a l'impression que le moteur a oublié ses chevaux quelque part en cours de route. Nous avons tenu compte dans nos chiffres des performances d'une version dotée de la transmission à double embrayage qui assure d'excellentes accélérations et reprises. Malgré cette entourloupette, elle se classe tout de même quatrième.

La raison en est fort simple: bien qu'elle soit très élégante et conçue intelligemment, cette Ford possède certaines déficiences qui l'ont pénalisée. Par exemple, ses places arrière sont non seulement exiguës, mais y prendre place demeure difficile. Seule la Toyota était moins bien pourvue à ce chapitre. Et son moteur manque de vivacité, peu importe la transmission à laquelle il est associé. Soulignons au passage que la présentation du moteur nous a rappelé les années 70 avec ses couettes de fils un peu partout, des tuyaux omniprésents et une batterie qui est presque aussi grosse que le moteur.

L'agrément de conduite a été jugé acceptable, sans plus. Étant donné que cette voiture est supposée être plus moderne que certaines autres concurrentes, les évaluateurs sont restés sur leur appétit. Ils ont par ailleurs souligné la suspension, qu'ils ont jugé particulièrement ferme. Un détail en passant, les modèles européens importés l'an dernier pour être essayés par la presse automobile canadienne possédaient une suspension plus souple. Finalement, elle n'a pas réussi non plus à enthousiasmer nos essayeurs. Nous leur avons dit de faire fi du moteur et de la transmission dans leur évaluation, mais cela n'a pas suffi. Il semble manquer un petit brin d'homogénéité à cette voiture. Un essayeur souligne toutefois que cette Ford est disponible dans une palette de couleurs vraiment jeunes et dynamiques, un facteur qui en convaincra plusieurs.

Tout cela ne signifie pas qu'il faille l'ignorer pour autant, bien au contraire. Elle a été tout simplement devancée par des modèles qui sont plus pratiques, plus agréables à conduire ou encore, en ce qui concerne la Nissan Versa, plus puissant.

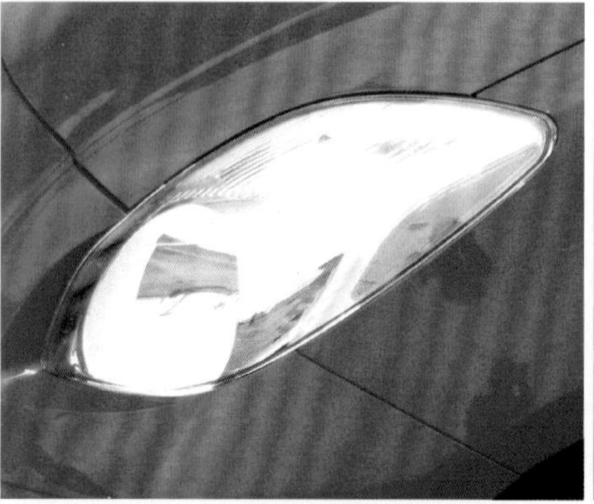

Ils ont dit:

André Lalanne

« Son style commence à dater tout comme son intérieur. Elle est également pénalisée par un moteur bruyant et un coffre à bagages petit. »

5

Toyota Yaris
Trahie par son âge et son prix

Malheureusement pour la plus petite des Toyota sur notre marché, elle a rétrogradé de deux rangs par rapport à notre dernière confrontation. Si elle avait été devancée à l'époque par la Honda et la Nissan, elle doit également s'incliner devant nos jeunes recrues que sont la Fiesta et la Mazda2. Non seulement celles-ci ont des lignes plus modernes, un équipement mieux adapté et un comportement supérieur, mais la Yaris est de surcroît la plus chère du lot. Alors que la majorité des autres concurrentes propose un prix entre 19 000 $ et 20 000 $, notre Toyota en exigeait au moins 1 300 $ de plus. Ce qui est assez élevé compte tenu des performances quelque peu ténues de son moteur et de sa boîte automatique à seulement quatre rapports.

Les essayeurs ont également critiqué la qualité de ses matériaux, l'exiguïté de son coffre tandis que son tableau de bord en a pris pour son rhume. Non seulement le positionnement central des instruments et des cadrans indicateurs n'a pas fait l'unanimité, mais les plastiques durs et bons marché ont également été sanctionnés. L'un des essayeurs, en prenant place à bord, s'est même exclamé : « Ils ont oublié la planche de bord ! ».

L'agrément de conduite de cette petite nipponne cinq portes n'a pas non plus emballé notre équipe. Elle s'est méritée la plus basse note du groupe. Par ailleurs, quant au choix personnel des essayeurs, elle se mérite la dernière place. Il faut souligner que nous avions une version RS, la plus huppée de la famille Yaris. Même l'élégant petit aileron arrière monté sur la partie supérieure du hayon n'a pas réussi à influencer nos essayeurs.

Heureusement pour Toyota, ce modèle sera renouvelé d'ici quelques mois et il est certain que cette version sera nettement plus compétitive. Si cette voiture se retrouve présentement en queue de peloton, c'est tout simplement qu'il s'agit d'un modèle qui a accompli son cycle et qui est devancé par des modèles soit plus gros, soit plus puissants ou encore récemment arrivés sur le marché. C'est la loi implacable du marché automobile, alors que les modèles les plus récents ont généralement l'avantage sur les autres. Toutefois, à la lecture des résultats, il y a des exceptions à cette règle.

POINTAGE

		Ford Fiesta	Honda Fit	Nissan Versa	Mazda Mazda2	Toyota Yaris
Style / 20 pts						
Extérieur	/10	7,6	8,2	6,4	8,8	8
Intérieur	/10	7,7	9	6,3	8	5,8
Carrosserie/ 120 pts						
Finition intérieure et extérieure.	/30	25	22	23	26,2	10
Qualité des matériaux	/30	24,5	21,5	26	26,5	20,5
Coffre *(accès/volume)*	/10	7,7	8,2	8	7,2	6,5
Espaces de rangement	/20	16,5	16	18,5	16,7	14,5
Astuces et originalité *(innovation intéressante, gadget hors série)*	/10	7	8,2	7,5	7,2	7
Équipement	/10	8,7	8,5	7	8	7
Tableau de bord	/10	7,5	9	6,5	7	6
Confort/ 40 pts						
Position conduite/volant/sièges av.	/10	7,7	9	6,8	9	7
Places arr. *(espace 2 ou 3 pers.)*	/10	6,5	7,7	9,2	7	6,7
Ergonomie *(facilité d'atteindre les commandes et lisibilité des instruments)*	/10	7,7	8,5	7	8	6,5
Silence de roulement	/10	7,5	7,2	8	7	6,7
Conduite/ 110 pts						
Moteur *(rendement, puissance, couple à bas régime, réponse. agrément)*	/20	12,2	14	17	13	13
Transmission *(passage des rapports, étagement, rétrocontact,levier, agrément)*	/0	0	0	0	0	0
Direction *(précision, « feedback », braquage)*	/20	17,5	18,5	15	16,5	16
Tenue de route	/30	23,2	28,5	21,7	26,7	24
Freins *(endurance, sensations, performances)*	/20	15	17	14	16	14
Confort de la suspension	/20	14,5	16	17	15,2	15
Sécurité/ 30 pts						
Visibilité	/10	8	9	8	7,5	7
Rétroviseurs	/10	9	8,5	8	9	8,2
Nombre de coussins de sécurité	/10	10	9	9	9	9
Performances mesurées /60 pts						
Reprises	/20	16	16	20	15	16
Accélération	/20	18	16	20	14	14
Freinage	/20	20	16	18	17	20
Rapport qualité/prix /120						
Agrément de conduite	/50	40	46,5	38,7	44	38,2
Choix des essayeurs	/50	44	50	46	48	42
Valeur pour le prix	/20	18	19	20	18	16
TOTAL	/500	407	427	412,6	415,5	364,6

La meilleure note du groupe

FICHES TECHNIQUES	Honda Fit	Mazda2
Empattement	2500 mm	2489 mm
Longueur	4105 mm	3950 mm
Largeur	1695 mm	1694 mm
Hauteur	1525 mm	1476 mm
Poids	1147 kg	1075 kg
Transmission	Manuelle	Auto
No. de rapports	5	4
Moteur	4L	4L
Cylindrée	1,5 litre	1,5 litre
Puissance	117 ch	100 ch
Suspension avant	indépendante	indépendante
Suspension arrière	demi indépendante	demi indépendante
Freins avant	disques	disques
Freins arrière	tambours	tambours
ABS	oui	oui
Pneus	P185/55R16	P185/55R15
Direction	à crémaillère, ass. él.	à crémaillère, ass. Var.
Diamètre de braquage	10,5 mètres	9,8 mètres
Coussin gonflable	frt/lat/rideaux	fdr/lat/rid
Réservoir de carburant	40 litres	43 litres
Capacité coffre	603 litres	382 litres
Accélération 0-100 km/h (automatique):	11,3 secondes	9,8 secondes
Vitesse de pointe	180 km/h	185 km/h
Consommation	7,1 litres/100 km	7,5 litres / 100 km
Prix (boîte automatique):	19998$	19 295$

Les temps ont changé

La catégorie des sous-compactes a évolué de façon spectaculaire au cours des dernières années. Les voitures communément appelées de Classe B ont progressé autant sur le plan esthétique et mécanique, qu'au niveau de l'agrément de conduite. Au début de la dernière décennie, il fallait gratter les fonds de tiroirs pour trouver quatre ou cinq véhicules au maximum pour pouvoir organiser une telle confrontation et les résultats étaient souvent biaisés car la plupart des modèles n'étaient pas à la hauteur. Il y a quatre ans, nous avions été agréablement surpris par la qualité des véhicules impliqués. Cette année, nous avons dû effectuer une sélection et limiter le nombre de participants.

Il est toujours possible d'interpréter les chiffres comme on le désire. Le plus important dans cette évaluation n'est pas de se contenter de choisir la voiture qui est arrivée en première ou seconde place, mais bien celle qui répond le plus à vos besoins. La Honda Fit l'emporte surtout en raison de son habitabilité et de sa conduite. Toutefois, certaines personnes n'apprécieront pas nécessairement sa silhouette ou encore une suspension à caractère sportif. Pour ces gens, une Nissan Versa sera plus susceptible de rencontrer leurs critères. Tel que mentionné précédemment, ce match comportait trois authentiques sous-compactes de configuration semblable. La Mazda2 a

Nissan Versa	**Ford** Fiesta	**Toyota** Yaris
2600 mm	2489 mm	2460 mm
4295 mm	4066 mm	3825 mm
1695 mm	1722 mm	1695 mm
1535 mm	1473 mm	1525 mm
1 141 kg	1 168 kg	1 000 kg
Auto	Manuelle	Auto
CVT	5	4
4L	4L	4L
1,8 litre	1,6 litre	1.5 litre
122 ch	120 ch	106 ch
indépendante	indépendante	indépendante
demi indépendante	demi indépendante	demi indépendante
disques	disques	disques
tambours	tambours	tambours
oui	oui	oui
P195/65R15	P185/50R16	P185/60R15
à crémaillère, ass. él.	à crémaillère	à crémaillère,
10,4 mètres	10,5 mètres	9,4 mètres
frt/lat/rideaux	frt/lat/rideaux/genoux	frontaux/latéraux
50 litres	45 litres	45 litres
504 litres	382 litres	228 litres
9,5 secondes	9,8 secondes	9,4 secondes
185 km/h	185 km/h	185 km/h
7,8 litres /100 km	7,2 litres/100 km	7,0 litres /100 km
17 733$	20 895$	21 985$

devancé sa grande rivale dans cette catégorie, la Ford Fiesta, car elle a semblé un peu plus homogène et un peu plus incisive sur la route. Par contre, il est important de souligner qu'il sera possible d'équiper une Fiesta d'un plus grand nombre d'accessoires et que celle-ci est un tantinet plus luxueuse. Elle est moins urbaine que la Mazda toutefois.

Finalement, la Yaris sera modernisée d'ici quelques mois, et cela ne sera pas superflu. C'est une honnête et vaillante petite voiture, mais elle a de la difficulté à se faire justice face à des modèles plus récents, plus puissants et aussi plus raffinés, tant au chapitre de la présentation que de la tenue de route. Par contre, la légendaire fiabilité et la durabilité des Toyota réussiront sans doute à en convaincre plusieurs. De plus, plusieurs de nos essayeurs ont bien aimé sa silhouette.

Cette catégorie ne demeurera toutefois pas stationnaire, car une Hyundai Accent complètement transformée devrait arriver d'ici peu et il en sera de même de la Kia Rio. Finalement, il ne faut pas oublier non plus la future Chevrolet Aveo RS qui n'a aucun lien en commun avec la version que nous connaissons actuellement. Il en est de même chez Suzuki, alors que la Swift européenne devrait faire son entrée sur notre marché. Comme chez Chevrolet, cette nouvelle venue fera rapidement oublier la Swift + actuelle.

Somme toute, la table est mise pour un autre match comparatif dans une prochaine édition.

Denis Duquet

MANIC GT

DOSSIER QUÉBEC

Allard Motor Works / Bombardier Produits Récréatifs inc
Campagna Motors / HTT Technologies Inc / Manic / Taylor /

L'hiver dernier, lorsque l'équipe du *Guide de l'auto* s'est réunie pour discuter du contenu du *Guide 2011*, plusieurs avenues s'offraient à nous. Encore une fois, la question d'insérer ou non les Can-Am Spyder et T-Rex est revenue sur le tapis. Ces véhicules ne sont pas vraiment des automobiles et nous ne voulions pas les insérer dans le *Guide* juste parce qu'ils sont fabriqués au Québec. En grattant un peu plus le dossier «Québec», nous nous sommes rendu compte que ce n'est pas parce que les GM (Boisbriand) et Hyundai (Bromont) nous avaient quittés que l'industrie automobile était morte. Même qu'il y avait, dans la région de St-Eustache une petite entreprise, HTT Technologies Inc, qui tentait, depuis déjà quelques années, de percer le marché de la voiture d'exception. Il s'agit, vous l'avez deviné, de la Pléthore qui orne la page couverture du *Guide* que vous tenez entre vos mains.

Au début de la seconde décennie du XXIième siècle, l'industrie automobile québécoise semble vouloir se brancher dans les marchés spécialisés. Une façon originale de percer ! Et comme le prouvent les prochaines pages, les Québécois sont suffisamment originaux pour être internationaux !

LE BOGHEI D'HENRY SETH TAYLOR

L'équipe éditoriale du présent Guide de l'auto avait prévu, dans cet hommage à la voiture québécoise, ne parler que des voitures construites en quantité suffisantes pour être qualifiées de production. Difficile, dans ce contexte, de justifier la présence du boghei d'Henry Seth Taylor, construit à un seul exemplaire. Mais comme il s'agit de la première voiture sans chevaux connue à avoir roulé au pays et qu'elle a été fabriquée à Stanstead, au Québec, son statut de doyenne l'autorise à certains égards...

Comme celui d'avoir été la première voiture à faire l'objet d'un timbre (1993) ou d'une pièce de monnaie de collection (2000) ou encore d'être la vedette de l'exposition « À la recherche de la voiture canadienne », actuellement tenue au Musée des Sciences et de la Technologie d'Ottawa.

En 1865, Taylor, bijoutier et inventeur (le divan-lit, c'est lui !) commence la fabrication d'une voiture sans chevaux. Il la présente au public à la foire agricole de Stanstead en 1867 mais l'engin tombe en panne. Ayant retapé son véhicule, Taylor se promène plusieurs fois dans le village et le présente même dans plusieurs expositions au Canada et aux États-Unis. Par exemple, on raconte qu'il s'était même rendu à la foire de Newport au Vermont.

Mais un jour, Taylor perd le contrôle de sa machine (qui n'a pas de freins !) et la première voiture de construction canadienne est victime du premier accident au Canada... Découragé, Taylor se lance plutôt dans la fabrication d'un bateau à vapeur et, pour ce faire, il prend la chaudière de sa voiture sans chevaux. Cette dernière, amochée, se retrouve au rancart dans une grange. Il faudra attendre la vente de la propriété, en 1959, pour qu'on découvre la « machine » sans son moteur. Le nouveau propriétaire, un Américain, Richard M. Stewart, président de l'Anaconda American Brass Cie du Connecticut, décide de la restaurer. L'entreprise prendra quatre ans ! Stewart doit partir du châssis, un des seuls morceaux qui n'a pas été mangé par la pourriture. Une photo de 1867 est aussi d'une précieuse aide. En 1967, la voiture revient au Canada, dans un musée de Toronto. Puis, en 1984, le Musée des Sciences et de la Technologie s'en porte acquéreur.

Cette « machine » fonctionnait grâce à un moteur bicylindre alimenté par la vapeur créée par une chaudière alimentée par un feu de bois. La réserve d'eau est placée à l'avant pour une meilleure distribution du poids. La chose pouvait atteindre 15 mph (24 km/h) mais ne possédait pas de freins ! La voiture pouvait avancer et reculer et tournait grâce à une tige, appelée tiller. Puisque le bois est un matériau plutôt léger, l'ensemble ne fait que 500 livres (227 kg).

Comme nous l'avons vu plutôt, le Steam Buggy d'Henry Seth Taylor actuel n'est pas parfaitement original. Cependant, le châssis en bois, les éléments mécaniques et la direction à crémaillère sont d'origine. La partie supérieure n'est pas très fidèle à la création d'antan. Quand à la chaudière originale, elle n'a jamais été retrouvée.

Le Boghei de Taylor n'est pas beau ni performant. Il n'a qu'une place et j'image que son confort est à l'image de celui d'une carriole, c'est-à-dire inexistant. Mais ce véhicule possède quelque chose d'extraordinairement émouvant. Il y a 143 ans, il a roulé, sans aucune aide extérieure. L'automobile est devenue, avec le temps, un objet de consommation banal. Le Buggy d'Henry Seth Taylor nous rappelle qu'il a fallu des pionniers, des visionnaires, pour créer un objet qui allait changer le cours de l'Histoire.

Alain Morin

PHOTO : ALAIN MORIN

PHOTO : ALAIN MORIN

PHOTO : AMYOT BACHAND

PHOTO : MUSÉE DES SCIENCES ET DE LA TECHNOLOGIE

MANIC GT 1971

C'était au début des années 70. La Belle Province passait de la Révolution Tranquille à une période très prospère. C'était l'époque des grandes réalisations. L'autoroute Métropolitaine et l'échangeur Turcot étaient tout neufs, les Jeux Olympiques autorisaient les rêves les plus fous et nos meilleurs ingénieurs érigeaient les plus imposants barrages hydro-électriques au monde.

Dans cet élan socio-économique, une petite voiture sport est apparue, porteuse d'avenir. La Manic. Un nom qui référait à l'immensité du territoire québécois, au prestige et à la solidité de l'œuvre.

Curieusement (peut-être pas tant que ça pourraient confirmer des sociologues !), c'est un Français qui est à l'origine de la Manic. Jacques About, coureur automobile et hommes d'affaires, est attiré par l'émergence du Québec là où il y a assurément de bonnes opportunités. Cependant, le Français n'a pas un sou vaillant en poche. Tout ce qu'il sait, c'est qu'il y construira une voiture qui s'appellera Manic!

L'histoire de la Manic commence par la course automobile. Pour financer sa future création, About se lance en compétition automobile. Soutenu par le cigarettier Gitanes (les temps ont changé…) et le constructeur français GRAC, notre homme d'affaires veut faire connaître le nom Manic. La monoplace de Formule B établit de nouveaux records aux circuits de St-Jovite et de Mosport, fournissant ainsi capital et crédibilité au projet de About.

Attisés par le feu ardent du profit, Bombardier, la Caisse de Dépôt, la famille Steinberg et le gouvernement du Canada ainsi que plusieurs autres bailleurs de fonds aux reins solides investissent un million et demi de dollars dans l'aventure. Les premières Manic GT sont montées à Terrebonne mais Jacques About voit grand. Une usine de 60 000 pieds carrés est déjà en construction à Granby (l'actuelle Velan pour ceux qui connaissent cette ville). Elle est inaugurée le 1er janvier 1971. Quarante emplois sont créés et il sera possible de produire trois Manic GT par jour. On prévoit déjà une production de plus de 2 000 voitures par année.

La Manic GT est étroitement dérivée de la Renault 8 dont elle reprend le châssis et la mécanique. La carrosserie est inédite même si le pare-brise et la vitre arrière proviennent encore de Renault. Son moteur arrière est un quatre cylindres de 1,3 litre et est proposé en trois versions 65, 80 et 105 chevaux. La transmission de base possède quatre rapports et une boîte optionnelle en propose cinq. Chose rare pour l'époque, les quatre freins sont à disque et les suspensions avant et arrière sont indépendantes. Selon le moteur choisi, la vitesse de pointe peut atteindre 169, 193 ou 217 km/h. Mais à de telles vitesses, la voiture d'à peine 658 kilos (1 450 livres) se soulève, victime de la mauvaise répartition du poids (tout à l'arrière) et de son aérodynamique, peu étudiée. À cette époque, la conception de la sécurité était bien différente… Puisqu'il s'agit d'une Renault carrossée différemment, l'entretien était assuré par les concessionnaires québécois de la marque française. Neuve, une Manic GT coûtait entre 2 200 et 3 400 $, une valeur assez élevée pour l'époque.

Une usine flambant neuve, du capital et une voiture bien née, selon le *Guide de l'auto 1970*. Pourtant, après seulement 100 voitures complétées, le 29 mai 1971, on met la clé dans l'usine. La Manic dépendait exclusivement de pièces Renault et comme l'entreprise française hésitait à s'embarquer à fond dans l'aventure, Jacques About dut rapidement mettre un terme à sa folle équipée.

Qui sait ce que serait devenue l'industrie automobile québécoise si la Manic GT avait connu le succès espéré…

Alain Morin

Photos : Brochure

CAMPAGNA T-REX
Unique en son genre

PHOTOS : CAMPAGNA INC.

C'est un fait connu, le Québec regorge de génies inventifs et de bricoleurs inspirés de toutes sortes. J. Armand Bombardier faisait partie de ce groupe sélect de personnes capables de développer un nouveau véhicule original et exclusif. Daniel Campagna est également membre de ce gotha des génies de la mécanique. Ce brillant mécanicien et technicien a développé un véhicule unique en son genre, le T-Rex. Cet ancien mécanicien de Gilles Villeneuve, à la dernière saison complète de celui-ci en motoneige, a concocté un véhicule hybride trois roues propulsé par un moteur de motocyclette actionnant la roue unique arrière par une transmission caténaire. L'aventure a débuté dans les années 80 et c'est Marc Lachapelle dans l'édition 1990 du *Guide de l'auto* qui a été le premier journaliste à faire un essai exclusif. Soulignons au passage que Daniel Campagna était un passionné des voitures de type Formule et qu'il a tenté de combiner les qualités de celles-ci avec les performances d'une motocyclette. C'est la lecture d'un article dans lequel le regretté Colin Chapman, le créateur des fabuleuses Lotus de l'époque, avait affirmé que s'il avait le temps de créer une remplaçante à sa légendaire Lotus 7, la voiture aurait trois roues et serait propulsée par un moteur de motocyclette. Il n'en fallait pas plus pour que Daniel Campagna se mette au travail.

Si le véhicule était relativement frustre à ses débuts, il a gagné en raffinement esthétique, technologique et mécanique au fil des années. Sa silhouette actuelle lui a été donné par le talentueux designer québécois Paul Deutchman qui a habillé ce châssis tubulaire pour lui donner la silhouette si typique qu'il a conservée jusqu'à ce jour. La partie avant stylisée n'est pas uniquement pour des fonctions esthétiques, elle permet également de protéger les

occupants des débris de la route, des projections des automobiles et bien entendu du vent et de la pluie. Quant à sa section arrière, ses ailettes contribuent à la stabilité longitudinale.

Le véhicule est devenu un objet culte surtout chez nos voisins du sud, car c'est là que l'on retrouve le plus de personnes ayant les ressources financières pour se payer le T-Rex dont le prix de vente a toujours été élevé. Cela s'explique en bonne partie par le fait qu'il s'agit d'un véhicule assemblé à la main doté d'un châssis tubulaire de haute qualité. En outre, au début de la fabrication, pour obtenir un moteur de motocyclette, il fallait acheter une moto au complet, enlever son moteur et l'installer dans la T-Rex. Voilà un mode de production qui n'est certainement pas économique. Et la fabrication en petite série, l'utilisation de matériaux de qualité et une attention portée aux composantes justifient également le prix.

Au fil des années, la compagnie a traversé plusieurs crises financières qui ont parfois interrompu la fabrication. Au gré des changements de propriétaires cependant, le véhicule n'a jamais perdu de ses qualités routières et de ses performances. Par exemple, une Campagna T-Rex 14R est capable de boucler le 0-100 km/h en quatre secondes tandis que sa vitesse de pointe est de 220 km/h. En outre, avec un poids de 472 kg et une puissance de 197 chevaux, le T-Rex propose l'un des meilleurs rapports poids puissance sur le marché. Il est propulsé de nos jours par un moteur Kawasaki de 1352 cc relié à une transmission manuelle à six rapports. Son unique pneu arrière se charge de la propulsion et il est de taille impressionnante: P 295/35ZR18. Soulignons qu'au tout début, la taille de ce pneu était P295/50R15.

Ce qui rend ce véhicule si exaltant à conduire est le fait que le pilote et son passager sont assis très près du sol tandis que les accélérations sont à couper le souffle. Il faut ajouter que la conduite d'un véhicule sans toit est une expérience appréciée de plusieurs. Et avec la capacité de réaliser 1.3 G en virage, c'est mieux que plusieurs voitures de course ou sportives de haut niveau.

Daniel Campagna n'est plus impliqué dans la compagnie qui porte son nom, mais celle-ci lui survit. Elle a été entièrement réorganisée en 2008 alors que deux passionnés, David Morissette et André Nault, ont unis leurs efforts afin de restructurer l'entreprise qui est dorénavant établie dans de nouveaux locaux situés sur la Rive-Sud de Montréal. Campagna possède plusieurs concessionnaires aux États-Unis et a récemment signé une entente avec un distributeur japonais.

Espérons que cette bête de la route unique en son genre et de fabrication québécoise continuera l'ouvre amorcée par son créateur.

Denis Duquet

ALLARD J2X MK II

Rarement vue, jamais oubliée !

PHOTOS : ALAIN MORIN

Imaginez la scène. Vous vous rendez en Angleterre pour faire l'achat d'un *roadster* des années '50. Vous en profitez pour trouver de la documentation sur ce modèle. En fouillant dans une pile de livres, vous tombez, tout à fait par hasard, sur une voiture datant des mêmes années… et qui porte votre nom !

C'est l'histoire qui est arrivée au Québécois Roger Allard. Il oublie aussitôt l'objet de son voyage et s'informe sur la marque éponyme dont il ignorait jusqu'alors l'existence. Fondée en 1936, par Sydney Allard, la Allard Motor Company a produit environ 1 900 voitures, dont plusieurs sont des sportives, son fondateur étant un pilote chevronné. Entre autres modèles, la J2X est construite à 83 exemplaires entre 1951 et 1954 et fut la plus couronnée des Allard en course. D'ailleurs, certains grands noms de l'automobile ont piloté, avec succès, des J2X : Zora-Arkus Duntov, le père de la Corvette, l'inimitable Carroll Shelby, John Fitch (1ière place GP Argentine) et l'acteur/pilote Steve McQueen. À cause de coûts de développement trop élevés, la Allard Motor Company cesse sa production en 1959. Sydney Allard demeure actif dans le domaine de la course automobile jusqu'à son décès en 1966.

Aujourd'hui, la marque Allard revit… et de belle façon ! Lors de son périple britannique, le Québecois apprend qu'un Californien fabrique des carrosseries de Allard J2X en fibre de verre et il va le rencontrer. Six mois plus tard, après bien des péripéties, Roger Allard devient, avec un ami, propriétaire des droits de la Allard et fonde Allard Motor Works.

La voiture actuelle, la MK II, est une telle réussite qu'elle est approuvée par le Répertoire Allard (*Allard Register*) comme étant une véritable J2X. À preuve, chaque MK II reçoit une plaque délivrée par cette autorité, confirmant son authenticité. Mais pour en

arriver là, il a fallu à Roger Allard créer une voiture moderne qui soit le plus près possible de l'originale. L'entrepreneur québécois devait, en plus, répondre aux normes actuelles, autant au chapitre de la mécanique, du confort que de la sécurité. Par exemple, la MK II est 4 pouces (10 cm) plus longue que l'originale, question de pouvoir aménager suffisamment d'espace pour les deux occupants. Il existe plusieurs autres petites différences mais les similarités sont étonnantes.

Tout comme les premières J2X, les MK II peuvent recevoir trois moteurs, un Chrysler (5,7 et le 6.1 Hemi) ou un GM (350 Ramjet). La transmission est une manuelle Tremec à cinq rapports. Pour avoir conduit la « numéro 7 » (rouge Ferrari et 5,7 litres) sur quelques kilomètres, l'auteur de ce texte peut vous confirmer que ses performances sont éblouissantes, rien de moins. Et quelle sonorité du V8 !

La J2K MKII est vouée à l'exportation et, jusqu'à présent, une dizaine de personnes s'en sont porté propriétaires, principalement aux États-Unis. Le prix unitaire de ce *roadster* est de $138500 US, ce qui peut sembler élevé. Cependant, il n'en n'est rien car la voiture est infiniment plus qu'un « kit car ». Quoique Allard Motor Works ne soit pas un constructeur, il réunit les talents de plusieurs artisans de la région pour faire revivre la légende Allard aux mains de leurs nouveaux propriétaires. Pour plus d'informations : www.allardj2x.com.

Alain Morin

Nos remerciements au Club de golf Le Parcours du Cerf de Longueuil pour la séance de photos.

BRP CAN-AM SPYDER ROADSTER

À l'image de son illustre fondateur

PHOTOS: BRP

Dans le cadre d'une spectaculaire réorganisation corporative, la compagnie Bombardier s'est départie de sa division des produits récréatifs qui a été vendue à de nouveaux actionnaires, incluant les membres de la famille Bombardier. Dorénavant, plus question que les ventes d'avions ou de trains viennent combler les pertes de cette division qui éprouvait certaines difficultés. D'ailleurs, cette nouvelle compagnie ne pouvait même plus utiliser le nom de Bombardier comme tel, d'où la boiteuse appellation BRP pour Bombardier Recreational Products. On a du même coup créé une nouvelle identification visuelle, combinant le célèbre engrenage de la compagnie originale avec les trois lettres BRP. Ceci étant dit, on a continué à produire des motoneiges Ski-Doo et des VTT Can-am qui connaissaient du succès sans oublier les fameuses embarcations Sea-Doo. Mais la direction trouvait qu'il fallait développer un produit original et unique en son genre, un peu comme la première motoneige Ski-Doo en 1959. Elle était la création du fondateur de la compagnie et d'un homme visionnaire, J. Armand Bombardier.

Les ingénieurs du centre de recherche et développement de BRP à Valcourt se sont mis au travail et ont concocté une machine pour le moins originale qui s'inspire en quelque sorte de la motoneige, l'âme et la raison d'être de cette compagnie, tout en étant un véhicule sur roues capable de circuler sur les routes et les autoroutes. Le spectaculaire Spyder Roadster était né. Il s'agit d'un véhicule à trois roues doté de deux roues à l'avant et d'une seule à l'arrière. Sa configuration ressemble quelque peu à une

motoneige sur trois roues. La propulsion est par courroie crantée et la puissance est fournie par un moteur Rotax à bicylindres en V de 998 cc produisant 106 chevaux et associé à une boîte manuelle à cinq rapports. Il est également possible de commander en option une boîte semi-automatique à cinq vitesses également actionnée par deux boutons.

Deux modèles sont au catalogue, le premier est la RS qui a été la première à être commercialisée en 2008. Il s'agit d'une version plus sportive que la RT, un modèle Touring doté d'un siège du passager plus confortable ainsi que des caisses de chargement de chaque côté. De plus, il est pourvu d'un déflecteur d'air avant beaucoup plus imposant et son équipement est davantage axé vers le confort. Soulignons que son moteur est de même cylindrée, mais développe six chevaux de moins que le RS.

L'arrivée du Can-Am Spyder sur le marché a eu l'effet d'une bombe. Les commandes se sont accumulées à un rythme effarant, un peu comme le Ski-Doo à ses débuts. Le public ciblé était celui des personnes qui appréciaient rouler en plein air, mais qui n'étaient pas nécessairement intéressées par une motocyclette. Le fait de proposer deux roues à l'avant fournit une excellente stabilité et donne confiance. Plusieurs spécialistes ont regretté toutefois que le véhicule ne penche pas dans les virages comme certains scooters à trois roues, mais chez BRP on est demeuré fidèle à la tradition de la motoneige puisque les patins avant de celle-ci ne s'inclinent pas eux non plus.

Naturellement, les premiers marchés ciblés ont été ceux des États-Unis et du Canada, mais le Can-Am Spyder Roadster est dorénavant commercialisé dans plusieurs pays européens. Au Québec, il n'est plus nécessaire de posséder un permis de motocycliste pour pouvoir le piloter. Il suffit de suivre un cours de quelques heures pour avoir la permission de rouler au guidon de ce véhicule pour le moins original.

Il est important de souligner que la présentation visuelle est nettement supérieure à la moyenne avec ses roues avant carénées, sa partie avant très originale et une qualité de fabrication digne des meilleures motos sur le marché. Curieusement, dans le cadre du développement de ce produit, les collègues Nadine Fillion, Gabriel Gélinas et Marc Lachapelle ont tous participé à des essais de préproduction afin d'émettre leur opinion d'expert. Selon eux, BRP avait en main un nouveau Goldwing à trois roues et c'est l'aspect Touring qui devait être poussé davantage. Si l'on considère la popularité de ce dernier modèle, nos collègues avaient raison.

Il s'agit pour l'instant du véhicule routier d'un constructeur québécois qui est produit en plus grand nombre dans l'histoire des véhicules moteurs au Québec. Une fois de plus, c'est à Valcourt qu'on a développé un produit exclusif et unique qui brille autant par son originalité que par sa conception technique intéressante. Et comme la première motoneige développée à cet endroit, l'engouement initial est également très fort.

Denis Duquet

PLÉTHORE LC-750

Le premier *supercar* québécois roule

PHOTOS : BILL PETRO

Luc Chartrand est fasciné depuis toujours par les exotiques, ces grandes sportives incroyablement longues, basses, rapides et racées. Celles qu'on appelle les *supercars*. Jusque là rien d'exceptionnel. L'histoire le devient lorsque ce constructeur autodidacte décide un jour de dessiner, développer et produire sa propre exotique. Au Québec.

Électronicien de métier, Luc a travaillé aussi dans le domaine de l'aéronautique et de l'avionique. Mais c'est un mordu d'automobile qui se fait une spécialité de fabriquer des répliques rigoureusement exactes de sportives italiennes. Des Ferrari et Lamborghini surtout.

PREMIÈRES MAQUETTES

Il est à la mi-trentaine lorsqu'il se met à imaginer sa super-sportive au milieu des années 90. Les croquis et les esquisses se succèdent et en 1998 il fabrique une première maquette à l'échelle « seulement pour m'amuser ». Le résultat est assez réussi pour qu'il trouve un premier client potentiel assez emballé pour lui verser un dépôt pour une première voiture.

Ce client c'est Carl Descoteaux un chirurgien-dentiste passionné de mécanique qui est venu de Grand-Mère voir les répliques que fabrique Luc Chartrand après avoir lu un article qui vantait leur qualité exceptionnelle. Ce premier client lui versera même un dépôt pour une deuxième de ses futures sportives et deviendra peu après un associé.

En 2000 le projet se concrétise. Luc met fin à ses autres activités pour se consacrer pleinement à la création de son *supercar*. Il fonde une entreprise qui se nomme alors Locus Technologies. Une première maquette grandeur nature est produite en 2002. Son idée était alors de construire la voiture sur des bases mécaniques connues et plus modestes mais il décide bientôt d'y aller à fond et de concevoir une véritable super-voiture, sans compromis.

PREMIER BAIN DE FOULE ET FINANCEMENT

La première Pléthore est dévoilée au Salon de l'auto de Montréal le 19 janvier 2007. Elle est noire et le V8 qui lui est destiné est exposé derrière elle. Les deux comparses qui font glisser le voile noir qui recouvrait la voiture sont Carl Descoteaux et Sébastien Forest. Ils se sont connus à l'école des HÉC avant que Carl ne se réoriente en médecine dentaire et que Sébastien ne complète des études de droit, spécialisé en gestion internationale. Il se joindra à HTT Technologies (pour High Tech Toys) à titre de président à l'automne 2008.

De gauche à droite : Carl Descoteaux, Luc Chartrand, Sébastien Forest

PHOTO : MARC LACHAPELLE

Carl Descoteaux continue d'investir dans la firme et d'y augmenter sa participation. Il y consacre 40 heures par semaine en plus de son travail de dentiste : « Ça ne me fait pas de longues nuits de sommeil mais les heures ne paraissent pas quand c'est une passion. »

HTT multiplie ses démarches auprès d'agences gouvernementales qui peuvent apporter une aide financière aux entreprises en recherche et développement. Elle reçoit notamment l'appui du Ministère du Développement économique, de l'Innovation et de l'Exportation du Québec et de l'Agence de développement économique du Canada. À ce jour, c'est environ 1,5$ million qui a été consacré au développement de la Pléthore et la plus grande portion de cette somme a été dépensée ces deux dernières années.

COUPS D'ÉCLAT AMÉRICAINS

Après le Salon de Montréal, Luc et John Dorrington, un carrossier chevronné qui est devenu son adjoint chez HTT, se lancent dans la fabrication d'une version plus raffinée de la super-voiture à moteur central. Luc lui apporte constamment des modifications et a toujours les prochaines en tête. Après une année de travail acharné, HTT dévoile une nouvelle Pléthore couleur orange, au gigantesque salon SEMA de Las Vegas, la Mecque des voitures d'exception et modifiées. La voiture fait sensation et suscite une série d'articles et de reportages dans des médias d'un peu partout.

Étape suivante : le célèbre encan Barrett-Jackson à Scottsdale en Arizona au cours du mois de janvier 2010 qui fait cependant rater à la Pléthore sa rentrée montréalaise. Elle se reprend au Salon de Toronto en février et traverse enfin l'Atlantique pour participer au salon Top Marques de Monaco à la mi-avril.

PROCHAINE ÉTAPE : LA PRODUCTION

Luc Chartrand a mis quinze ans pour arriver à la voiture qui est devant nous, immobile, imposante, dans les ateliers sans aucune prétention de HTT, aux abords de l'Autodrome St-Eustache. Son concepteur la regarde et dit d'abord « elle vaut quelques millions ». Il se ravise et ajoute « en fait elle n'a pas de prix ». Ce n'est d'ailleurs pas la voiture dont HTT compte amorcer bientôt la production. Trop large pour être transportée dans un conteneur sans risque de dommage. Puisque HTT compte vendre la Pléthore surtout à l'étranger, c'est un argument majeur.

La Pléthore de série sera plus étroite d'environ 8 cm mais également plus longue d'une dizaine de centimètres. C'est l'empattement qui y gagne mais Luc Chartrand assure que l'habitacle sera plus long de près de 30 cm pour accueillir les grandes tailles. HTT a entièrement numérisé la voiture avec l'aide de Creaform3d et amorcé le travail d'analyse d'éléments finis et de soufflerie virtuelle avec les gens de Lx, deux firmes québécoise à la fine pointe. Luc Chartrand est particulièrement fier du coefficient de traînée aérodynamique (Cx) de 0,37 de sa création. Pas mal pour un aérodynamicien empirique.

Si la carrosserie est l'âme d'une exotique, le moteur est certainement son cœur. HTT affirme que celui de la Pléthore sera une version du fabuleux V8 LS9 compressé de la Corvette ZR1 dont la puissance doit atteindre 750 chevaux (d'où l'appellation LC-750 avec les initiales du concepteur). Le moteur serait en préparation chez le spécialiste américain Pratt & Miller qui a mené l'équipe Corvette à des victoires aux grandes classiques des 24 Heures du Mans et de Daytona.

PHOTO : BILL PETRO

La course est un autre rêve de Luc Chartrand qui aimerait faire courir ses voitures en série American le Mans et aux 24 Heures du Mans, rien de moins. La Pléthore est d'ailleurs déjà équipée d'une cage de sécurité intégrée à la structure de fibre de carbone qui serait conforme aux normes de la FIA. Les acheteurs pourront se lancer sur les circuits ou en course sans devoir ajouter une cage par la suite comme ce fut le cas avec la McLaren F1, par exemple.

La suspension modulaire actuelle peut être remplacée en quelques heures par une pure suspension de course. Pour l'instant, la Pléthore roule sur des éléments de suspension de Corvette modifiés. Chartrand compte aussi l'équiper de ressorts pneumatiques qui permettront de modifier la garde au sol au besoin et assurer un bon confort de roulement.

L'objectif de HTT est de produire quatre ou cinq voitures par année et Luc Chartrand nous assure qu'il fera tout ce travail dans les ateliers actuels, avec John Dorrington. Et si le carnet des commandes grossit au delà de ce nombre, il a déjà imaginé un système de production où chaque voiture aurait son espace, comme dans les équipes de F1.

PREMIERS TOURS PRUDENTS ET PROMETTEURS

Nous sommes les premiers à conduire la Pléthore à l'extérieur de HTT. Il faut d'abord se glisser dans le poste de conduite central, une acrobatie qui rappelle l'accès à une voiture de course. La position de conduite est tout juste correcte pour mon gabarit moyen. L'habitable allongé est une nécessité pour les plus grands. Une poussée sur le bouton de démarrage, au plafond comme dans un avion, et le V8 rugit. La sonorité d'échappement est fantastique. Luc garde le secret de sa recette.

Embrayage enfoncé, je tire sur le très court levier du sélecteur électronique et c'est parti. Les vitesses passent très facilement. Ce n'est qu'un court galop d'essai, très prudent, mais la Pléthore impressionne surtout par sa solidité. C'est un prototype mais il est tout d'une pièce, sans le moindre craquement. Le confort de roulement sur la ligne droite bosselée du circuit de St-Eustache me rappelle la Audi R8, la meilleure référence.

La Pléthore LC-750 inspire confiance mais le premier essai véritable viendra plus tard. Le premier acheteur, un Américain arrive alors que nous partons. Il donnera des sueurs à Luc Chartrand, assis à ses côtés, en conduisant son précieux prototype beaucoup plus énergiquement mais il est emballé. Il affirme l'aimer déjà mieux que les Lamborghini et Ferrari qu'il a possédées.

Il reste beaucoup de travail pour voir les premières Pléthore sortir des ateliers de HTT Technologies. Mais la LC-750 est déjà étonnante, spectaculaire, bien conçue et elle roule vraiment. Prochaine version : la LC-1300 « Devil ». Vous avez deviné : 1300 chevaux. Un conseil : ne pariez pas contre Luc Chartrand et ses associés.

Marc Lachapelle

LE GUIDE DE L'AUTO
LE GUIDE DE L'AUTO

ESSAIS LONG TERME

Acura / BMW / Hyundai / Mazda / Nissan / Volkswagen

Élégance sportive

Acura TL

L'Acura TL s'est jointe à notre flotte d'essai à long terme sur six mois, et le choix du modèle à rouage intégral s'imposait de lui-même en raison de sa supériorité marquée au niveau de l'adhérence. De plus, la présence de ce système baptisé SH-AWD (Super Handling All-Wheel-Drive) a pour effet d'éliminer presque complètement l'effet de couple dans le volant, qui est très présent sur la TL à traction avant en accélération franche.

Précisons également que notre TL était le modèle le plus équipé de la gamme, soit le SH-AWD Tech équipé de l'ensemble Technologie. Au programme : système de navigation assisté par satellite, caméra de recul, un système audio de 440 watts et à 10 haut-parleurs capable de lire des DVD-Audio avec son ambiophonique, système de chauffage/climatisation automatique à deux zones, accès et démarrage sans clé, touches illuminées sur le volant et sièges en cuir perforé, entre autres. L'aspect le plus intéressant de ce modèle, c'est qu'une TL pleinement équipée soit proposée à un prix de 48 490 $, ce qui lui confère un rapport équipement/prix presque imbattable dans la catégorie des berlines sport, les rivales directes en provenance de BMW ou d'Audi étant beaucoup plus chères au départ en plus d'afficher des prix supérieurs pour les équipements offerts en option.

Au cours de nos six mois d'essai, la TL n'a connu aucun problème de nature mécanique ou électronique et son dossier de fiabilité est demeuré sans tache, ce qui est plutôt typique des véhicules de la marque Acura. Côté sécurité, la TL se mérite la note supérieure lors de tests de collision réalisés par l'IIHS (*Insurance Institute for Highway Safety*), dont les normes dépassent celles des organismes gouvernementaux canadiens et américains.

Pour ce qui est de la vie au quotidien, la TL souffre d'un défaut majeur, soit la très petite ouverture du coffre dont le seuil de chargement est élevé. Il suffit de jeter un coup d'œil à la partie arrière de la TL pour constater que la ligne de découpe du couvercle du coffre donne en effet un certain style à la voiture au détriment de la considération pratique qu'est l'accès à l'espace cargo. Toujours au chapitre de la vie au quotidien, la TL exige du carburant super et notre consommation moyenne s'est chiffrée à 12 litres aux 100 kilomètres, ce qui est un peu élevé et qui s'explique partiellement par le fait que la boîte automatique ne compte que cinq rapports plutôt que les boîtes à six rapports que l'on trouve chez certaines rivales sans parler de la présence du rouage intégral qui a une incidence directe sur la consommation.

Quant au comportement routier, la TL à rouage intégral offre une bonne tenue de route et s'accroche bien à l'asphalte en virages, étant donné que le rouage transmet graduellement plus de couple aux roues extérieures, ce qui vient gommer le sous-virage qui est parfois caractéristique des voitures à traction intégrale. Toutefois, la fermeté des suspensions fait en sorte que les inégalités de la route sont parfois trop bien senties dans l'habitacle et la direction manque de précision au centre.

La présence de tous les équipements compris dans l'ensemble Technologie proposé en option a pour effet de rendre la vie à bord très agréable, et le système audio est plus que réussi. Par contre, il faut prendre le temps d'apprivoiser la myriade de boutons présents sur la console de même que sur le volant ainsi que les fonctions contrôlées par le système de télématique intégré.

Ce n'est pas la plus performante de la catégorie, mais la TL à rouage intégral présente un excellent rapport équipement/prix et une fiabilité sans reproche, ce qui lui permet de marquer plusieurs points.

Gabriel Gélinas

La magie du diesel

BMW X5 xDrive35d

Après un essai prolongé de plus de 12000 kilomètres, la consommation moyenne de notre BMW X5d s'est chiffrée à 10,6 litres aux 100 kilomètres, ce qui est un véritable exploit étant donné qu'il s'agit d'un sport-utilitaire de plus de deux tonnes et demie. Cette consommation remarquable représente une économie d'environ 30 % par rapport aux X5 animés par des moteurs à essence. De plus, le X5d n'est pas en reste côté performances, car son moteur développe un couple de 425 livres-pied, ce qui est largement supérieur à celui du V8 de 4,8 litres qui ne développe que 350 livres-pied. Bref, avec le X5d on bénéficie à la fois d'excellentes performances en accélération (7,5 secondes pour le 0-100 km/h) et en reprises, mais également d'une cote de consommation qui est égale à celle d'une berline intermédiaire conventionnelle. Il faut juste apprendre à composer avec le léger délai qui survient avant l'entrée en action des turbocompresseurs en accélération franche, et on obtient le meilleur des deux mondes.

La supériorité de la motorisation diesel pour ce type de véhicule ne faisant aucun doute, il est encore surprenant de constater que certains automobilistes optent pour un véhicule sport-utilitaire propulsé par un moteur à essence lorsque le même véhicule est disponible avec le diesel. Ajoutez à cela que le carburant diesel coûte en ce moment moins cher que l'essence ordinaire et on est gagnant sur presque toute la ligne. Le seul bémol que l'on peut relever au sujet du moteur diesel qui équipe le X5 est le fait qu'il est un peu plus bruyant, mais c'est là son seul handicap qui est largement compensé par ses points forts.

Et puisqu'il est question de points forts, le dynamisme relevé d'un cran par rapport à la concurrence directe fait du X5 le plus performant des VUS en conduite sportive avec le Cayenne de Porsche, le ML de Mercedes-Benz et le Q7 d'Audi, ces deux derniers ayant un comportement plus axé sur la conduite souple et le confort. Prendre une bretelle d'accès ou de sortie d'une autoroute, presque les seuls endroits où l'on peut se faire plaisir aujourd'hui, est toujours agréable au volant du X5d dont le train avant s'inscrit rapidement en courbe alors que le véhicule suit la trajectoire parfaite, même si notre véhicule d'essai n'était doté que des jantes de 18 pouces de série. En fait, notre X5d s'est avéré extrêmement stable et très agile malgré son gabarit et son poids imposants.

Au volant, il est rapidement facile de trouver une position de conduite efficace et confortable, grâce aux sièges grand confort qui équipaient notre véhicule d'essai et qui assuraient un maintien exemplaire, même en conduite sportive. Précisons également que le volant, télescopique et inclinable, ainsi que la présence d'un repose-pied bien dimensionné ajoutent à l'ergonomie du X5. La qualité de la finition intérieure s'est révélée excellente et le coup d'œil est réussi avec la richesse de la sellerie de cuir Nevada de couleur Saddle Brown, sans parler de la qualité tactile de ce cuir, et le *look* également très riche des appliqués de bois en bambou foncé.

Le prix de base d'un X5d (au moment de notre essai) était de 62800$, mais celui avec lequel nous avons roulé comportait plusieurs ensembles d'options (Executive, Technology Package, Premium Package, Premium Sound Package), ce qui portait la facture à 74800$, mais rendait la vie à bord des plus agréables. Le toit ouvrant surdimensionné Panorama et les sièges chauffants, à l'avant comme à l'arrière, ont été particulièrement appréciés par les passagers. Par ailleurs, la cote de fiabilité s'est avérée parfaite, aucun problème ne s'étant manifesté lors de cet essai prolongé.

Gabriel Gélinas

Son élégance impressionne

Hyundai Sonata

Après un hiatus de quelques années, un véhicule Hyundai s'est à nouveau joint à notre flotte d'essais à long terme. Et notre patience a été récompensée, car nous avons pu mettre à l'épreuve la toute nouvelle Sonata. Cette berline est fort spectaculaire avec une silhouette qui fait tourner les têtes à coup sûr. Nous sommes loin des voitures de ce constructeur dont la carrosserie était d'un anonymat total quand elle n'était pas carrément laide ou rétro. Ce n'est certainement pas le cas avec ce modèle. Chaque fois que nous arrivions quelque part, les gens se tournaient vers notre voiture et venaient nous dire qu'ils appréciaient sa ligne et nous demandaient si la Sonata était à la hauteur de son image. Et notre réponse était immanquablement la même: «Elle est aussi agréable à conduire qu'elle est jolie.» En effet, en raison des ressources de recherche et de développement que ce constructeur a mises sur pied en Corée et aux États-Unis, les ingénieurs maison ont tout en main pour développer des voitures aussi modernes sinon meilleures que celles de la concurrence. Nous sommes loin des pâles copies plus ou moins bien assemblées qui sont arrivées sur notre marché il y a quelques décennies. L'élément visuel le plus spectaculaire de ce véhicule est sans conteste sa grille de calandre qui attire les regards et qui constitue son caractère. Et les gens qui prenaient place à bord se disaient impressionnés par le stylisme du tableau de bord et la qualité des matériaux. Si on veut trouver à redire, on peut souligner que les tissus des sièges pourraient être d'une texture améliorée tandis que les plastiques de la planche de bord étaient un tantinet durs. Mais tous ont fortement apprécié les commandes de contrôle de la climatisation ainsi que le confort des sièges.

Lorsqu'on voit cette voiture pour la première fois, elle a tellement l'air d'un véhicule de luxe, qu'on est persuadé qu'elle est propulsée par un moteur V6, tout au moins en option. Mais ces gens font fausse route, car le seul moteur offert est un quatre cylindres de 2,4 litres produisant 198 chevaux et un couple de 184 lb-pi. Il est de conception fort moderne avec l'injection directe d'essence qui améliore les performances et réduit la consommation. Notre voiture d'essai était équipée d'une boîte automatique à six rapports avec la possibilité de passer les vitesses en mode manuel. Tous les essayeurs se sont amusés à passer les rapports en mode manuel pour ensuite se contenter de laisser la transmission accomplir son travail. Et il est difficile de lui reprocher quoi que ce soit.

Quant au comportement routier, il surprend et déçoit à la fois. Je m'explique. La conduite de cette voiture est sans histoire. Le moteur propose de bonnes accélérations et des reprises adéquates. On peut lui reprocher sa direction à assistance électrique qui «assiste» trop. Mais la quasi-majorité des personnes qui ont pris le volant n'ont trouvé rien à redire à propos de cette assistance trop généreuse et d'un manque de rétroaction. Il faut croire que c'est correct et que je suis toujours trop difficile à ce chapitre. Que ce soit sur la grand route ou sur des routes secondaires, la voiture est stable, sans surprise et il faut vraiment prendre des risques calculés et dépasser les limites de vitesse de beaucoup pour trouver un survirage relativement prononcé. De plus, les pneumatiques offrent des prestations dans la bonne moyenne, même s'ils n'aiment pas se faire bousculer. Vous aurez doit alors à des crissements de pneus assez spectaculaires. Mais dans l'ensemble, c'est l'une des bonnes berlines de cette catégorie. Cependant, elle déçoit, car sa silhouette est tellement prometteuse qu'on s'attend à se trouver au volant d'une voiture dont les prestations seraient similaires à celles d'une automobile vendue au double du prix. Il s'agit d'une perception, car en réalité cette Hyundai est non seulement élégante et agréable à conduire, mais elle semble dotée d'une fiabilité de bon aloi si on se fie à la fiche vierge d'ennuis mécaniques dans le cadre de cet essai alors qu'on a bouclé 6000 km en trois mois.

Denis Duquet

Du solide !

Kia Sorento

Le Kia Sorento qui nous a été confié était une version passablement équipée, dotée du rouage intégral et du moteur V6 de 3,5 litres produisant 276 chevaux et un couple de 248 lb-pi. Ce moteur est de conception mécanique fort moderne et il ne craint pas les hauts régimes. Il s'est fait apprécier tout au long de cet essai qui a duré tout l'été. Il faut souligner que cette nouvelle version en remplace une autre qui était munie d'un châssis à échelle et nous nous sommes rapidement rendu compte que cette nouvelle génération est non seulement plus silencieuse, mais que son châssis monocoque est également plus rigide. Comme nous n'avons pas eu l'occasion d'effectuer du remorquage avec notre modèle d'essai, nous n'avons pu constater son efficacité dans cet exercice. Soulignons par ailleurs que la capacité de remorquage est passée de 5000 lb à 3500 lb, ce qui devrait être amplement suffisant pour la plupart des gens. Si vous voulez remorquer une charge plus lourde et demeurer dans la gamme Kia, le Borrego possède, quant à lui, une capacité de remorquage de 5000 lb.

Tous les essayeurs ont mentionné l'impression de solidité que procure la conduite de ce VUS. En outre, ils ont également été unanimes à indiquer que la suspension était relativement ferme. Pas assez pour se faire brasser la carcasse, mais suffisamment robuste pour être digne de mention. Par contre, comme la carrosserie est très rigide, l'effet est passablement atténué. Certaines personnes ont été quelque peu intimidées par les dimensions assez imposantes de cette Kia, surtout en conduite urbaine.

Comme notre modèle était équipé d'à peu près tous les accessoires offerts, le confort était au rendez-vous, et ce, malgré cette suspension parfois sèche. La position de conduite a été jugée bonne par des personnes de toutes tailles. Sur le plan de la conduite, le rendement du moteur est légèrement supérieur à la moyenne tout comme la boîte automatique à six rapports. À ce propos, c'est incroyable de constater qu'une version commercialisée récemment peut avoir un tel avantage par rapport à d'autres modèles qui sont sur le marché depuis deux ou trois ans.

À l'usage, les sièges avant ont été jugés confortables tandis que ceux de la seconde rangée se méritaient la note convenable pour des personnes de taille moyenne. Par contre, la troisième rangée a été assez peu utilisée, mais les gens qui y ont pris place n'ont formulé aucune plainte. Mais il ne s'agissait pas de joueurs de football ou de basket. Au fil des semaines, nous avons apprécié la facilité avec laquelle on pouvait relever ou rabattre les dossiers que ce soit ceux de la seconde ou de la troisième rangée. Mais une fois la troisième rangée déployée, l'espace de rangement disponible était assez mince. Au contraire, une fois tous les sièges arrière repliés, on a droit à beaucoup d'espace.

Nous n'avons pas été en mesure d'en faire l'essai durant l'hiver, mais le rouage intégral a démontré son efficacité au cours des nombreuses averses qui ont sévi au cours de l'été.

Il est vrai que notre essai s'est limité à environ 7000 km, mais aucun pépin mécanique n'est venu assombrir notre test. Et ce qui s'est avéré le plus intéressant dans tout cet exercice, c'est la sensation de confiance que nous avions chaque fois que nous lancions le moteur. À son volant, on se sentait en sécurité et nous n'appréhendions jamais un bris mécanique. Le Sorento est donc un véhicule intéressant, car il peut associer robustesse, confort et rouage intégral sophistiqué. Et même si sa capacité de remorquage a quelque peu diminué, elle demeure toujours respectable.

Denis Duquet

Un party de 10 000 km

Kia Soul

Notre essai de la Soul s'est terminé après plus ou moins 10 000 km de conduite. Puisque nous avons perdu certaines pages de notre carnet de route, il est impossible de vous indiquer quel était le kilométrage exact lorsque nous avons rendu la voiture à Kia. Je sais que cela s'est effectué avant le 15 décembre, car Kia ne voulait pas être obligé d'installer des pneus d'hiver sur notre véhicule d'essai. À chacun sa politique, mais nous aurions bien aimé pouvoir évaluer le comportement de ce véhicule en hiver et voir si les qualités notées par temps clément se seraient toujours manifestées dans la tempête.

Et c'est d'autant plus dommage, car toutes les personnes qui ont essayé cette voiture ont apprécié son caractère ludique. Souvent, les autos qui ont une silhouette très distinctive perdent rapidement de leur attrait. Dans le cas de la Soul, les gens la trouvaient toujours aussi « cool » en mai qu'au début du mois de décembre. Cette allure pas comme les autres a certainement contribué à ce que les gens l'apprécient. La plupart des essayeurs ont accordé de bonnes notes au contraste des couleurs du tableau de bord, à la console verticale séparant la planche de bord en plus de souligner l'élégance des boutons de contrôle qui sont également de bonnes dimensions. Même si le couvercle de l'espace de rangement situé dans la partie supérieure de cette console n'était pas toujours facile à ouvrir, on a apprécié son emplacement et son caractère pratique. De bonnes notes ont également été accordées au volant, tant sur le plan esthétique que pratique. Son gros moyeu raccordant trois rayons stylisés s'est mérité des commentaires positifs et c'est la même chose pour les diverses commandes qui y sont logées. Soulignons également la présence de deux prises de courant 12 volts encadrant une fiche USB et une prise accessoire dans la partie inférieure de cette même console. Par la même occasion, la qualité des matériaux a été jugée excellente pour une voiture de cette catégorie. Enfin, le système d'éclairage ambiant Mood faisait toujours son effet même après plusieurs mois d'utilisation.

Les sièges avant sont confortables et ils se sont avérés corrects même lors de longues randonnées tandis qu'il est facile de prendre place à bord, car ils sont à la hauteur des hanches et on se glisse dans l'habitacle. Quant aux places arrière, elles sont acceptables et devraient convenir à la plupart des gabarits. Lorsqu'elles ne sont pas utilisées, il est très facile de replier les deux sections du dossier arrière pour faire un espace réservé aux bagages de dimension intéressante. Ce tour de passe-passe permet de quasiment doubler l'espace de chargement qui est de 546 litres une fois les dossiers relevés et de 1 511 litres lorsque ceux-ci sont abaissés. Par contre, l'ouverture du hayon arrière est assez petite, mais heureusement le seuil de chargement est bas.

La caractéristique la moins impressionnante de cette voiture est son groupe propulseur. Il a été solide comme le roc, mais les performances du moteur 2,0 litres de 142 chevaux couplé à une boîte automatique à quatre rapports se sont révélées dans la bonne moyenne tout au plus. Le moteur est quelque peu rugueux et la majorité aurait apprécié un cinquième rapport, histoire de réduire la consommation de carburant.

Pour le reste, cette petite Coréenne se conduit au doigt et à l'œil. C'est une voiture citadine fort appréciée aussi bien en raison de ses dimensions que par son agilité à se stationner. Par contre, sa consommation de carburant est un peu plus élevée que certains autres modèles de sa catégorie. Et finalement, rien à redire en fait de fiabilité. Et nous avons une confession à faire, nous devons avouer une petite bosse sur la partie supérieure de la portière avant gauche, résultant d'un contact avec une boîte de commande d'un lave-auto ! C'est un sans-faute pour la voiture et un carton jaune pour un essayeur distrait.

Denis Duquet

La plus populaire

Mazda3 Sport

Comme le veut la coutume au Guide de l'auto, le véhicule qui se mérite le titre de Voiture de l'année fait l'objet d'un essai à long terme l'année suivante. Dans l'édition 2010, c'est la Mazda3 qui a décroché la palme. Pour la mettre à l'épreuve pendant plusieurs milliers de kilomètres, nous avons hérité d'une Mazda3 Sport GT dotée du nouveau moteur de 2,5 litres produisant 167 chevaux et associé à une boîte automatique à cinq rapports. Ce modèle était passablement équipé avec des sièges en cuir, la climatisation et un système audio de qualité. Parmi les omissions, on peut souligner le système de navigation par satellite et la caméra de recul, deux éléments dont nous nous sommes facilement passés.

La nouvelle silhouette a été jugée sophistiquée par tous les essayeurs et ils ont bien aimé ce petit air déjanté que ses flancs en relief lui donnent. La partie avant de la voiture avec sa grille de calandre en forme de sourire n'a été critiquée que par une seule personne. Par ailleurs, tous ont été ravis par la qualité des matériaux utilisés dans l'habitacle, l'ergonomie et la simplicité d'opération des commandes. Bien entendu, le moteur est suffisamment performant tandis que la boîte automatique de type manumatique s'est avéré excellente. De plus, les gens ont apprécié la configuration de petite familiale de cette Mazda, toujours très populaire au Québec. En effet, il suffisait d'abaisser les dossiers des bancs arrière pour pouvoir transporter des objets relativement encombrants. Parlant de places arrière, les gens de grande taille ont dû demander la collaboration des occupants des places avant qui ont avancé leur siège pour qu'ils puissent bénéficier d'un bon dégagement pour les jambes. Et lorsque tout le monde voulait collaborer, ce n'était pas mauvais du tout.

De toutes les voitures ayant fait l'objet d'essais à long terme au fil des années, cette Mazda a joui d'une incroyable popularité, tant et si bien que les kilomètres se sont accumulés au compteur. Au moment d'écrire ces lignes, la petite voiture avait franchi 18000 km en 10 mois ! Toutes les occasions étaient bonnes pour la conduire. Un petit voyage d'agrément, une tournée en ville ou tout simplement pour le simple plaisir de rouler dans ce véhicule. Les gens ont apprécié la rigidité de sa caisse, la précision de sa direction et son agrément de conduite. De plus, son excellente position de conduite figure aussi parmi les éléments positifs ainsi que les commandes des sièges chauffants qui sont placées juste devant le levier de vitesses. Elles sont non seulement faciles d'accès, mais comportent de nombreux réglages, ce qui permet de réchauffer votre popotin selon vos goûts. Dans le carnet de bord, la qualité de la finition et des matériaux a été mentionnée à plusieurs reprises; les gens se sont dits surpris que cette voiture en offre autant tout en se vendant à un prix tout de même fort compétitif compte tenu de la présentation intérieure.

Plusieurs avaient quelques craintes concernant la consommation de carburant, étant donné qu'il est de bon ton pour plusieurs de souligner qu'une Mazda consomme plus que la moyenne de la catégorie. Au fil de tous ces kilomètres, de toutes ces randonnées en ville et de toutes ces heures au ralenti dans les embouteillages, nous avons enregistré une moyenne globale de 9,1 litres aux 100 km. Ce qui est correct, étant donné que la conduite était parfois sportive et que notre modèle d'essai était doté d'une boîte automatique.

Au chapitre de la mécanique, le seul pépin est un pare-brise fissuré gracieuseté d'un camionneur qui avait oublié de mettre sa toile sur son chargement. Merci encore une fois!

Pour le reste, rien à signaler. Somme toute, c'est un essai concluant autant en fonction de la popularité de cette voiture auprès de nos essayeurs qu'en raison de son agrément de conduite et de sa polyvalence.

Denis Duquet

Un joyeux trio

Volkswagen Golf

Au cours de l'hiver, nous avons procédé à un essai assez inusité, trois Volkswagen en trois mois, une par mois, et toutes des Golf en plus ! Cet essai nous a permis, dans une certaine mesure, de vérifier leur fiabilité à court terme et surtout de les évaluer en hiver. La première a été la Golf cinq portes 2,5. Il s'agissait d'une version de milieu de gamme et elle s'est révélée pratique, agréable à conduire tout en étant assez sportive. Les prestations du moteur se sont avérées intéressantes de même que la consommation, qui a été d'environ 10,1 litres aux 100 km. Les essayeurs ont apprécié les sièges avant, la solidité de la caisse et la qualité de la finition. Mais tous ont pesté contre les boutons de commande de la climatisation qui sont à revoir. Et sur tous les modèles, il faut que les essuie-glaces soient en position hiver pour pouvoir soulever les balais pour nettoyer le pare-brise. Trop sophistiqué pour nous.

Puis nous nous sommes vraiment payé la traite avec la GTi. Nous avons donc roulé pendant tout le mois de février au volant d'une version trois portes dotée de la boîte manuelle. De plus, des pneus d'hiver Pirelli de 18 pouces avaient pour mission d'offrir adhérence et traction lorsque le temps hivernal ferait des siennes. Soulignons tout de suite que les chutes de neige dans la région métropolitaine ont été assez clairsemées. Nous avons pu circuler tout de même dans des régions du Québec qui étaient fortement enneigées et avons pu vérifier l'efficacité de ces pneumatiques.

Cette Golf survitaminée est dotée d'un moteur turbocompressé de 2,0 litres d'une puissance de 200 chevaux. Cette cavalerie est gérée par une boîte manuelle à six rapports. La plus huppée des Golf a fait preuve d'une grande fiabilité tout au long de ce mois. Je sais que quelques milliers de kilomètres ne constituent pas un indice quant à la fiabilité à long terme, mais c'est mieux que rien.

La GTi a été d'un agrément de conduite supérieur à la moyenne, et ce, à tous les points de vue. Les sièges offrent un excellent support latéral de même que pour les cuisses. Pour le reste, ce véhicule est confortable et pratique. Sa soute à bagages est d'assez bonnes dimensions tandis que les places arrière peuvent être jugées convenables.

À son volant, on a l'impression que c'est nous qui menons et non pas la voiture. Il était facile de la contrôler et de la guider dans les virages afin d'optimiser notre conduite. L'élément le plus fantastique de cette Golf est son magnifique moteur 2,0 litres turbocompressé qui n'a aucun équivalent sur le marché. Ses performances sont très bonnes avec un temps d'accélération d'environ 7,0 secondes pour boucler le 0-100 km/h, mais il est en plus toujours au bon régime lorsqu'on en a besoin. Le délai de réponse du turbo est quasiment inexistant. Cette voiture est donc à l'aise en ville, car lorsqu'on veut se faufiler dans la circulation, il suffit d'un p'tit coup d'accélérateur et voilà notre GTi qui répond instantanément. La consommation de carburant enregistrée a été d'environ 8,9 litres aux 100 km, ce qui est quand même raisonnable.

Finalement, la troisième Golf a été la version familiale avec moteur diesel TDI. Celle-ci offre toutes les caractéristiques des autres modèles en fait de qualité, de confort et de conduite. Comme il s'agit d'une familiale, sa capacité de charge est supérieure. Et son moteur diesel associé à la transmission automatique DSG à double embrayage rend la conduite plus agréable. Quant à la consommation enregistrée, elle a été de 8,3 litres aux 100 km, ce qui ajoute une autre note positive.

Ces Volkswagen sont jugées trop austères par certains, trop chères par d'autres, mais il est difficile de critiquer leur agrément de conduite et leur confort.

Denis Duquet

ARHL 955
SUBARU
S LS 6363

PREMIERS DE CLASSE

SOUS-COMPACTES

1 HONDA FIT

EN LICE - Chevrolet Aveo, Ford Fiesta, Hyundai Accent, Kia Rio / Rio 5, Smart Fortwo, Suzuki Swift+, Toyota Yaris

2 MAZDA2

3 NISSAN VERSA

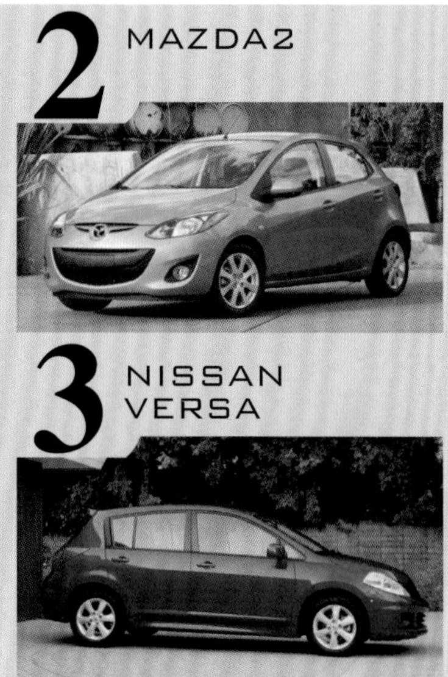

COMPACTES

1 MAZDA3

EN LICE - Acura CSX, Chevrolet Cruze, Chevrolet HHR, Dodge Caliber, Ford Focus, Honda Insight, Honda CRZ, Hyundai Elantra, Kia Forte / Koup, Kia Soul, Mini Cooper, Mitsubishi Lancer, Nissan Sentra, Nissan Cube, Subaru Impreza, Suzuki SX-4, Toyota Corolla, Toyota Matrix, Toyota Prius, Volkswagen Jetta

2 HONDA CIVIC

3 VOLKSWAGEN GOLF

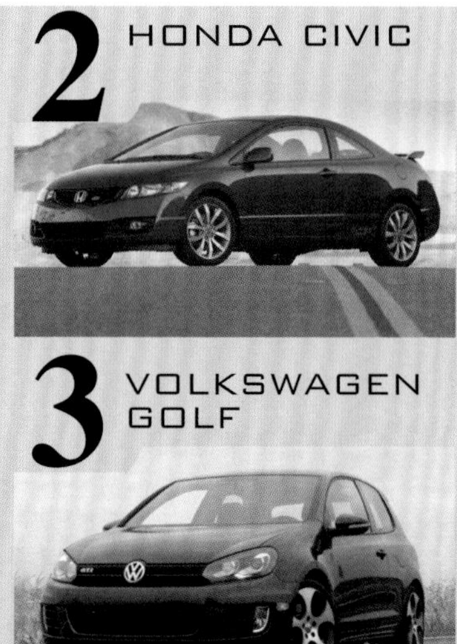

INTERMÉDIAIRES

1 BUICK REGAL

EN LICE - BuickLa Crosse, Chevrolet Malibu, Chrysler Sebring, Dodge Avenger, Honda Accord, Hyundai Sonata, Kia Optima, Mazda6, Nissan Altima, Suzuki Kizashi, Toyota Camry, Volkswagen Passat CC

2 FORD FUSION

3 SUBARU LEGACY

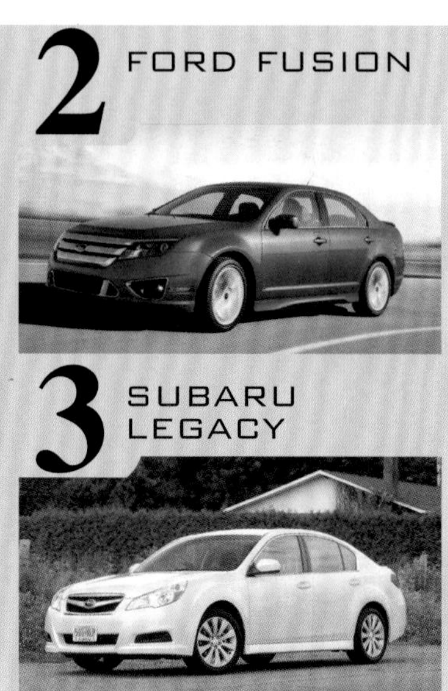

BERLINES MOINS DE 50 000 $

1 BMW SÉRIE 3

2 MERCEDES-BENZ CLASSE C

3 ACURA TL

EN LICE - Acura TSX, Audi A4, Audi A3, Cadillac CTS, Hyundai Genesis, Infiniti G, Lexus IS, Lexus ES, Lexus HS, Lincoln MKZ, Volvo S40

GRANDES BERLINES

1 FORD TAURUS

2 CHRYSLER 300

3 NISSAN MAXIMA

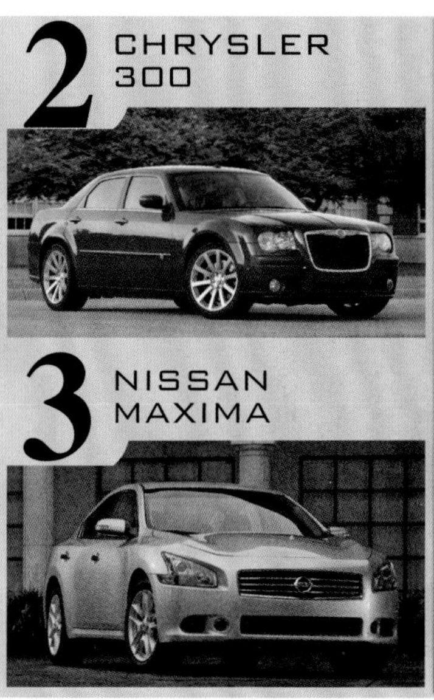

EN LICE - Buick Lucerne, Cadillac DTS, Chevrolet Impala, Dodge Charger, Toyota Avalon

COUPÉS SPORT MOINS DE 50 000 $

1 BMW SÉRIE 1

2 VOLKSWAGEN GTI

3 NISSAN 370Z

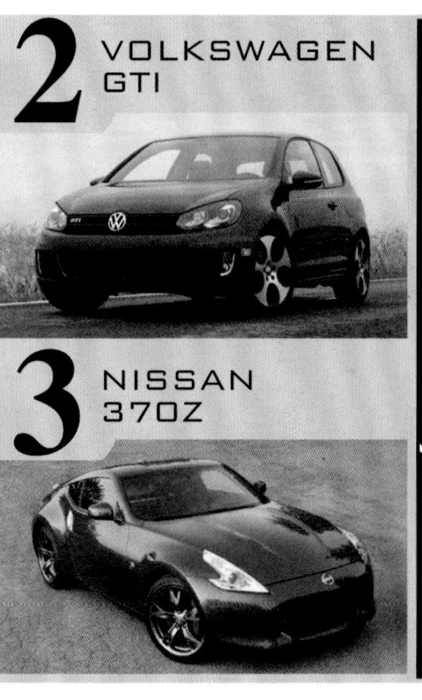

EN LICE - Chevrolet Camaro, Dodge Challenger, Ford Mustang, Honda Accord Coupé, Hyundai Genesis Coupé, Mazda RX-8, Mitsubishi Eclipse, Nissan Altima Coupé, Volvo C30

BERLINES ET COUPÉS SPORT 50 000 $ - 100 000 $

1 BMW SÉRIE 5

2 MERCEDES-BENZ CLASSE E

3 AUDI A6

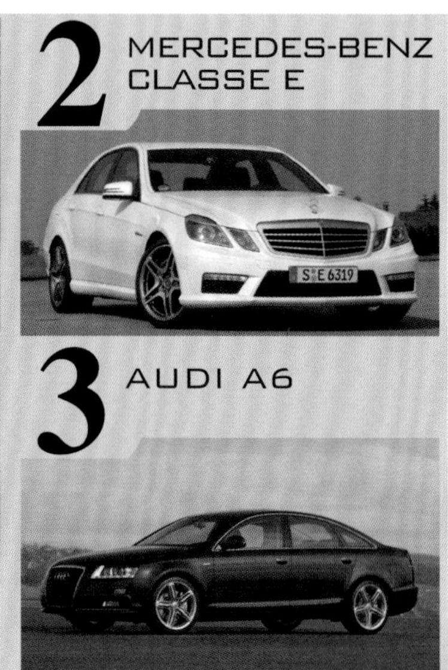

EN LICE - Acura RL, Audi A5, Audi A6, Cadillac STS, Hyundai Equus, Infiniti M, Jaguar XF, Lexus GS, Lincoln MKS, Lotus Evora, Mercedes-Benz Classe E Coupé, Volvo S80, Volvo S60

VOITURES DE PRESTIGE

1 PORSCHE PANAMERA

2 BMW SÉRIE 7

3 MERCEDES-BENZ CLASSE S

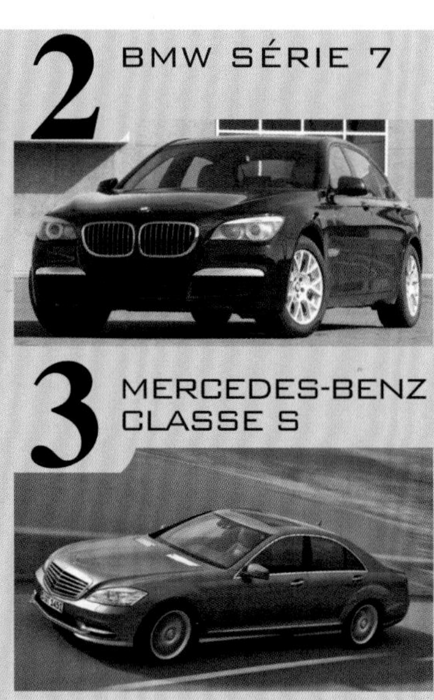

EN LICE - Audi A8, Aston Martin Rapide, Bentley Continental, Bentley Mulsanne, Jaguar XJ, Lexus LS, Maserati Quattroporte, Maybach 57-62, Mercedes-Benz Classe CL, Mercedes-Benz Classe CLS, Rolls-Royce Drophead Coupé, Rolls-Royce Phantom, Rolls-Royce Ghost

CABRIOLETS ET *ROADSTER* MOINS DE 50 000 $

1 MAZDA MX-5

2 BMW SÉRIE 1

3 VOLKSWAGEN EOS

EN LICE - Chrysler Sebring, Ford Mustang, Mitsubishi Eclipse

CABRIOLETS ET *ROADSTER* PLUS DE 50 000 $

1 PORSCHE BOXSTER

EN LICE - Audi A5, Audi TT, BMW Série 3, Infiniti G, Lexus IS, Lotus Elise, Mercedes-Benz Classe SLK, Mercedes-Benz Classe , Nissan 370Z, Volvo C70

2 BMW Z4

3 CHEVROLET CORVETTE

GT / SPORT PERFORMANCE

1 MERCEDES-BENZ SLS AMG

EN LICE - Aston Martin DB9/DBS/Vantage, BMW Série 6, Chevrolet Corvette ZR1, Dodge Viper, Ferrari 458 Italia/599 GTB Fiorano/612 Scaglietti/California, Jaguar XK, Lamborghini Gallardo/Murciélago, Lexus LF-A, Maserati Gran Turismo, Mercedes-Benz Classe SL, Nissan GT-R, Porsche Cayman, Tesla Roadster

2 AUDI R8

3 PORSCHE 911

MULTISEGMENTS MOINS DE 50 000 $

1 SUBARU OUTBACK

EN LICE - Chevrolet Traverse, Dodge Journey, Ford Edge, GMC Acadia, Honda Accord Crosstour, Hyundai Veracruz, Kia Rondo, Mazda CX-7, Mazda CX-9, Mercedes-Benz Classe B, Mercedes-Benz Classe R, Mitsubishi Endeavor, Nissan Murano, Subaru Tribeca, Toyota Highlander

2 FORD FLEX

3 TOYOTA VENZA

MULTISEGMENTS PLUS DE 50 000 $

1 CADILLAC SRX

2 LEXUS RX

3 LINCOLN MKX

EN LICE - Acura ZDX, BMW X6, Buick Enclave, Infiniti FX, Lincoln MKT, Volvo XC70, Volvo XC90

VUS COMPACTS MOINS DE 40 000 $

1 KIA SPORTAGE

2 HYUNDAI TUCSON

3 TOYOTA RAV4

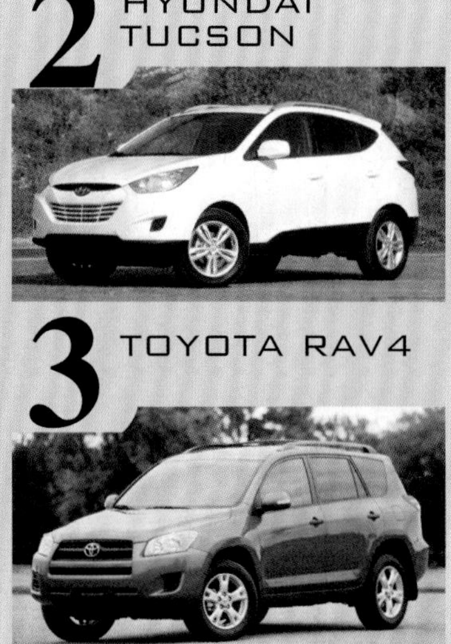

EN LICE - Chevrolet Equinox, Dodge Nitro, Ford Escape, Honda CR-V, Honda Element, Hyundai Santa Fe, Jeep Compass, Jeep Liberty, Jeep Patriot, Jeep Wrangler, Mazda Tribute, Mitsubishi Outlander, Nissan Rogue, Subaru Forester, Suzuki Grand Vitara, Volkswagen Tiguan

VUS COMPACTS PLUS DE 40 000 $

1 AUDI Q5

2 MERCEDES-BENZ CLASSE GLK

3 VOLVO XC60

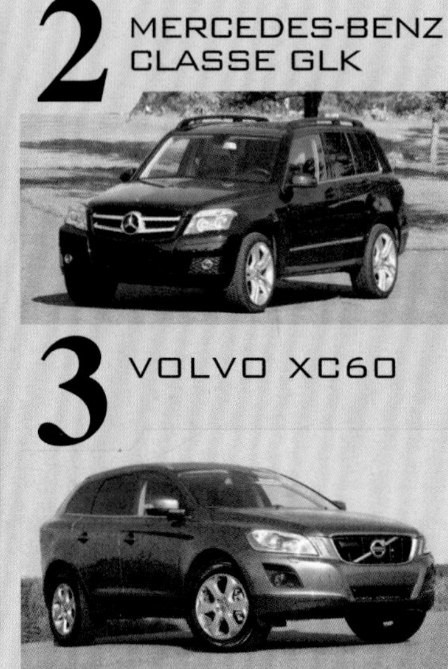

EN LICE - Acura RDX, BMW X3, Infiniti EX, Land Rover LR2

VUS INTERMÉDIAIRES MOINS DE 50 000 $

1 HONDA PILOT

2 FORD EXPLORER

3 JEEP GRAND CHEROKEE

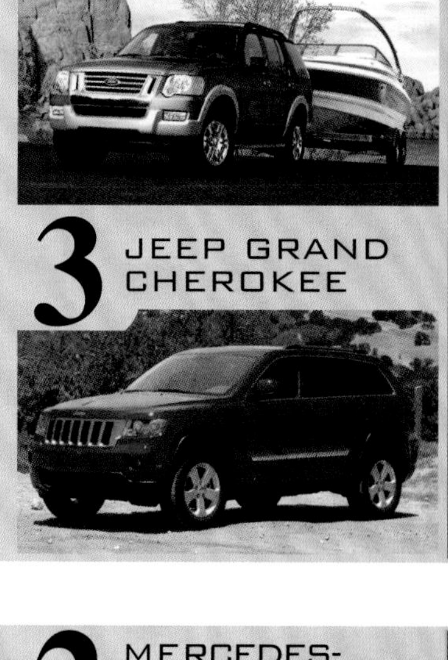

EN LICE - Jeep Commander, Kia Borrego, Kia Sorento, Nissan Pathfinder, Nissan Xterra, Toyota 4Runner, Toyota FJ Cruiser

VUS INTERMÉDIAIRES PLUS DE 50 000 $

1 EX-AEQUO VOLKSWAGEN TOUAREG / PORSCHE CAYENNE

2 MERCEDES-BENZ CLASSE M

3 AUDI Q7

EN LICE - Acura MDX, BMW X5, Land Rover LR4, Lexus GX

VUS GRAND FORMAT

1 CHEVROLET SUBURBAN

2 FORD EXPEDITION

3 MERCEDES-BENZ CLASSE GL

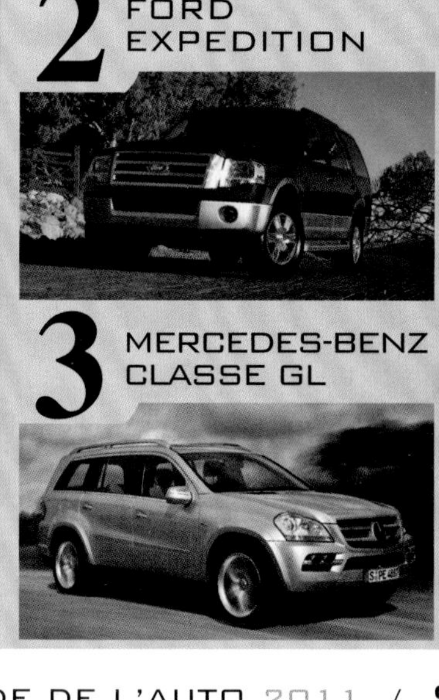

EN LICE - Cadillac Escalade, Chevrolet Tahoe, GMC Yukon, Infiniti QX, Land Rover Range Rover, Land Rover Range Rover Sport, Lexus LX, Lincoln Navigator, Mercedes-Benz Classe G, Nissan Armada, Toyota Sequoia

FOURGONNETTES

1 HONDA ODYSSEY

EN LICE - Dodge Grand Caravan, Ford Transit Connect, Kia Sedona, Mazda5, Nissan Quest, Volkswagen Routan

2 TOYOTA SIENNA

3 CHRYSLER TOWN & COUNTRY

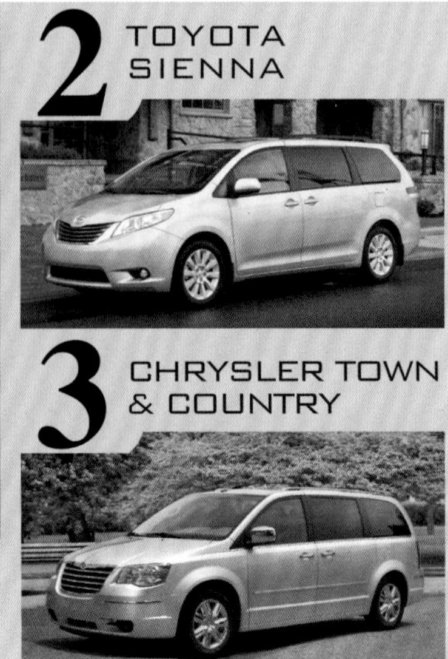

CAMIONNETTES COMPACTES / INTERMÉDIAIRES

1 HONDA RIDGELINE

EN LICE - Chevrolet Colorado, GMC Canyon, Nissan Frontier, RAM Dakota, Suzuki Equator

2 TOYOTA TACOMA

3 FORD RANGER

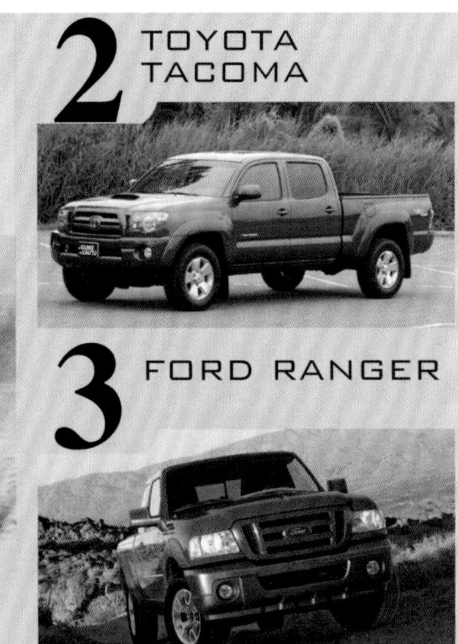

GRANDES CAMIONNETTES

1 FORD F-150

EN LICE - Cadillac Escalade EXT, Chevrolet Avalanche, Chevrolet Silverado, Nissan Titan, Toyota Tundra

2 GMC SIERRA

3 RAM 1500

MERCEDES-BENZ SLS AMG

MEILLEURE NOUVELLE VOITURE DE L'ANNÉE

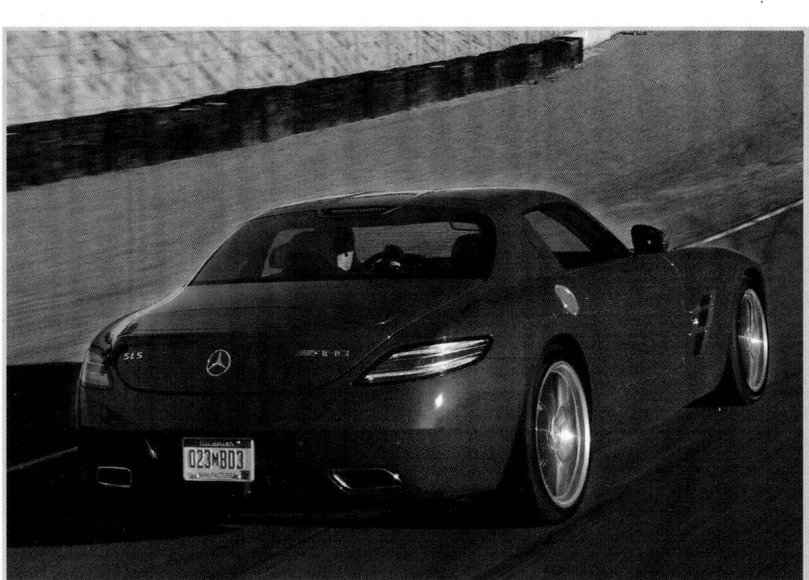

EN LICE

- Audi A8
- Audi R8 Spyder
- BMW Série 5
- BMW Série 7
- Buick Regal
- Cadillac CTS Coupe
- Chevrolet Cruze
- Ferrari 458 Italia
- Ford Fiesta
- Honda CR-Z
- Hyundai Sonata
- Hyundai Equus
- Jaguar XJ
- Kia Optima
- Infiniti M37/56
- Lotus Evora
- Mazda2
- Mercedes-Benz Cabriolet Classe-E
- Mercedes-Benz SLS AMG
- Mini Countryman
- Nissan Juke
- Nissan Leaf
- Porsche Boxster Spyder
- Rolls-Royce Ghost
- Scion tC
- Suzuki Kizashi
- Volkswagen Jetta
- Volvo S60

KIA SPORTAGE

MEILLEUR NOUVEL UTILITAIRE DE L'ANNÉE

EN LICE

Ford Edge
Ford Explorer
Honda Odyssey
Hyundai Tucson
Infiniti QX56
Jeep Grand Cherokee
Kia Sorento
Kia Sportage
Lexus GX460
Lincoln MKX
Porsche Cayenne
Toyota Sienna
Toyota 4Runner
Volkswagen Touareg

TECHNOLOGIES VERTES

Dans le but de démystifier les différentes technologies vertes qui sont de plus utilisées par les manufacturiers automobiles, le Guide de l'auto a demandé à un expert de monter un dossier sur le sujet.

Détenteur d'un baccalauréat en génie mécanique de l'Université de Sherbrooke et d'une maîtrise en génie automobile du University of Michigan à Ann Arbor, Maxime Ouellet est ingénieur au Centre National de Transport Avancé (cnta.ca), situé à St-Jérôme. Il a précédemment travaillé dans plusieurs entreprises dont 3 ans en Angleterre chez Renault F1 Team.

BMW Serie7 Active Hybrid

Dans les récentes années, l'augmentation du coût du pétrole et le désir de diminution des émissions de gaz à effet de serre ont amené l'apparition de plusieurs nouvelles technologies visant la réduction de la consommation de carburant. Le transport, responsable de 40 % des émissions totales au Québec, est le principal contributeur de gaz à effet de serre (CO_2) en Amérique du Nord. Des lois plus sévères sont graduellement appliquées, dont la fameuse norme CAFE (Corporate Average Fuel Economy) américaine, qui impose aux divers constructeurs une réduction majeure de la consommation sur l'ensemble de leur flotte, sous peine d'amende. Ainsi, les prérogatives commerciales forcent ces derniers à recourir à diverses technologies plus complexes mais plus efficaces pour réduire la consommation de leurs véhicules. Pour mieux comprendre ce qui en découle, voici un aperçu de certaines technologies actuelles et à venir.

HYBRIDE

Le concept de toute voiture hybride est d'utiliser deux modes d'énergie pour se mouvoir, soit le moteur thermique et le moteur électrique. Leur économie de carburant est principalement liée au freinage régénératif, qui contrairement à une idée répandue, ne provient pas des freins ou de la chaleur du freinage. En fait, c'est le moteur électrique qui ralentit le véhicule, les freins mécaniques n'étant utilisés que lorsque le freinage doit être puissant. L'énergie ainsi récupérée est emmagasinée dans des batteries et retransmise lorsque le véhicule accélère, réduisant le recours au moteur à essence ; ce dernier peut donc être plus petit et tourner à vitesse presque constante dans sa plage optimale, abaissant ainsi la consommation. L'arrêt du moteur thermique en période de ralenti, à une lumière rouge par exemple, ainsi que l'utilisation de systèmes auxiliaires électriques comme la direction assistée et la climatisation pouvant être démarrés ou arrêtés au besoin indépendamment du moteur, au lieu d'être constamment reliés à celui-ci par des poulies, réduisent davantage la consommation d'essence.

HYBRIDE SÉRIE

Dans un hybride série, uniquement le moteur électrique sert à déplacer le véhicule, un peu comme une voiture complètement électrique, le moteur à essence n'étant pas lié de façon mécanique aux roues. Ce dernier fonctionne indépendamment et sert à charger la batterie et à alimenter le moteur électrique via un générateur, un peu comme dans une locomotive. De cette façon, on utilise un moteur thermique plus petit qui fournit l'énergie moyenne consommée par le véhicule, puisque le moteur électrique est responsable des accélérations. Cette architecture s'adapte bien aux hybrides rechargeables, car le moteur électrique est puissant et le moteur thermique peut être complètement éteint durant plusieurs kilomètres. Le système a toutefois le désavantage d'être moins efficace à vitesse constante, lorsque la batterie est épuisée, car l'énergie du moteur à essence doit passer par un chemin plus complexe qu'un simple engrenage mécanique pour se rendre aux roues, et donc, plus il y a de transfert d'énergie, plus il y a de pertes et plus la consommation en souffre.

Véhicule : Chevrolet Volt

HYBRIDE PARALLÈLE

Dans le système parallèle, la transmission relie le moteur thermique au moteur électrique. Ce dernier remplace aussi le démarreur et il sert à récupérer l'énergie de freinage qui est envoyée dans les batteries. À l'accélération, il utilise cette énergie pour assister le moteur thermique, ce qui permet de réduire la consommation et les émissions polluantes. Cette architecture ne permet toutefois pas de circuler en mode tout électrique.

Quelques véhicules :

Honda Civic hybride, Honda Insight, Honda CR-Z, BMW ActiveHybrid 7, Mercedes S400 BlueHybrid

HYBRIDE SÉRIE-PARALLÈLE

Le système série-parallèle combine les deux systèmes précédents et possède deux ou trois moteurs électriques reliés entre eux et au moteur thermique par un ou plusieurs trains planétaires, une sorte d'engrenage qui permet de sélectionner la combinaison des divers moteurs ainsi que le transfert d'énergie désirée. Ainsi, le moteur à essence peut simultanément fournir de l'énergie à la batterie et propulser le véhicule. En accélération, le moteur thermique se combine à un des moteurs électriques pour propulser le véhicule, tandis qu'au freinage, les deux moteurs électriques sont appelés à contribution pour maximiser le freinage régénératif. Le système permet de circuler en mode complètement électrique et peut même améliorer le couple à bas régime, pour tirer une remorque par exemple, dans certains cas.

Véhicules :

- Toyota Prius, Camry hybride, Highlander hybride
- Lexus RX 450h, LS 600h, HS 250h et GS 450h
- Nissan Altima hybride
- Ford Fusion hybride et Escape hybride
- Chevrolet Tahoe Hybrid
- Mercedes ML 450 BlueHybrid
- BMW ActiveHybrid X6
- Porsche Cayenne S Hybrid

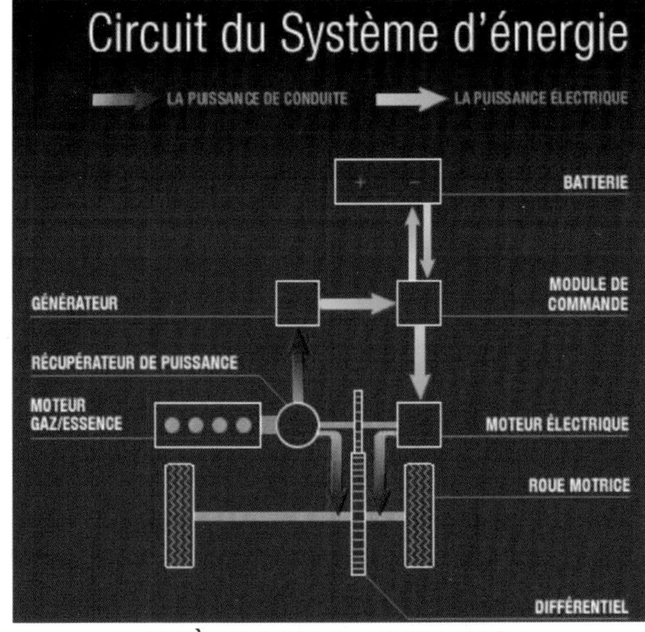

SYSTÈME HYBRIDE DE LA TOYOTA PRIUS

HYBRIDE RECHARGEABLE

L'avenir des voitures hybrides réside fort probablement dans la possibilité de recharger la batterie chez soi, et de rouler de façon totalement électrique pour un kilométrage limité. Ainsi, les trajets quotidiens peuvent être faits seulement sur l'électricité et les voyages plus longs, avec le moteur à essence, souvent appelé prolongateur d'autonomie. Les hybrides série ou série-parallèle peuvent théoriquement être rechargeables ou « plug-in », mais une batterie de plus grande capacité par rapport à l'hybride conventionnel est évidemment nécessaire pour permettre la plus grande autonomie. Les stratégies préconisées par les divers constructeurs varient et les distances en mode tout électrique annoncées se situent entre 15 à 70 km. Si plusieurs véhicules rechargeables sont à l'essai, seulement la Chevrolet Volt devrait être disponible dans un avenir rapproché.

Véhicules hybride rechargeable :

Chevrolet Volt, Toyota Prius Plug-In

VOITURE ÉLECTRIQUE

Lorsqu'une voiture possède seulement un moteur électrique, sans moteur auxiliaire à essence, elle est considérée comme une voiture complètement électrique. Ses batteries doivent être encore plus volumineuses pour offrir une autonomie respectable, puisqu'elle ne peut être rechargée que par un réseau électrique. La batterie constitue donc l'élément crucial du véhicule et comme leur commercialisation est récente, l'élément le plus coûteux aussi. Le véhicule complètement électrique apporte toutefois un changement important dans la conception du véhicule. Il n'y a pas de moteur thermique, plus besoin de système d'alimentation en carburant, d'échappement et d'antipollution, et les divers systèmes sont reliés par des fils, ce qui allège et simplifie grandement le véhicule. Il est à noter qu'un véhicule muni d'un prolongateur d'autonomie, « une génératrice », est considéré comme un véhicule hybride série rechargeable.

Véhicules électriques :

2011 - Tesla roadster, Nissan Leaf, Smart ED, Tesla S.
2012 - Ford Focus EV, Mitsubishi i-MiEV,

LES BATTERIES ET LA RECHARGE

Plusieurs chimies de batteries sont disponibles, mais la majorité des voitures électriques utilisent un composé incluant du lithium, tandis que les voitures hybrides actuelles se fient au nickel. La grande question reste quel est le temps de recharge, qui dépend autant de l'alimentation électrique fournie, que de la capacité de la batterie à accepter du courant. Il existe trois types de recharge. La plus simple, le niveau 1, utilise une prise électrique conventionnelle, à 120V et peut convenir aux hybrides rechargeables. La recharge rapide de niveau 2 utilise du 240V ou ce que l'on appelle communément une prise de sécheuse; cette méthode devrait être au moins deux fois plus rapide que le niveau 1 et est conseillée pour les voitures totalement électriques. Enfin, la recharge haute puissance, de niveau 3, nécessite un circuit triphasé qui convertit le tout en 400 à 480V à courant continu (DC) et s'adresse davantage aux bornes de recharge publiques, qui pourraient théoriquement recharger la voiture en quelques minutes. Toutefois, le temps de recharge dépend aussi de la batterie et de sa capacité à accepter toute cette énergie rapidement, sans chauffer ou se dégrader, ce qui n'est pas le lot de toutes !

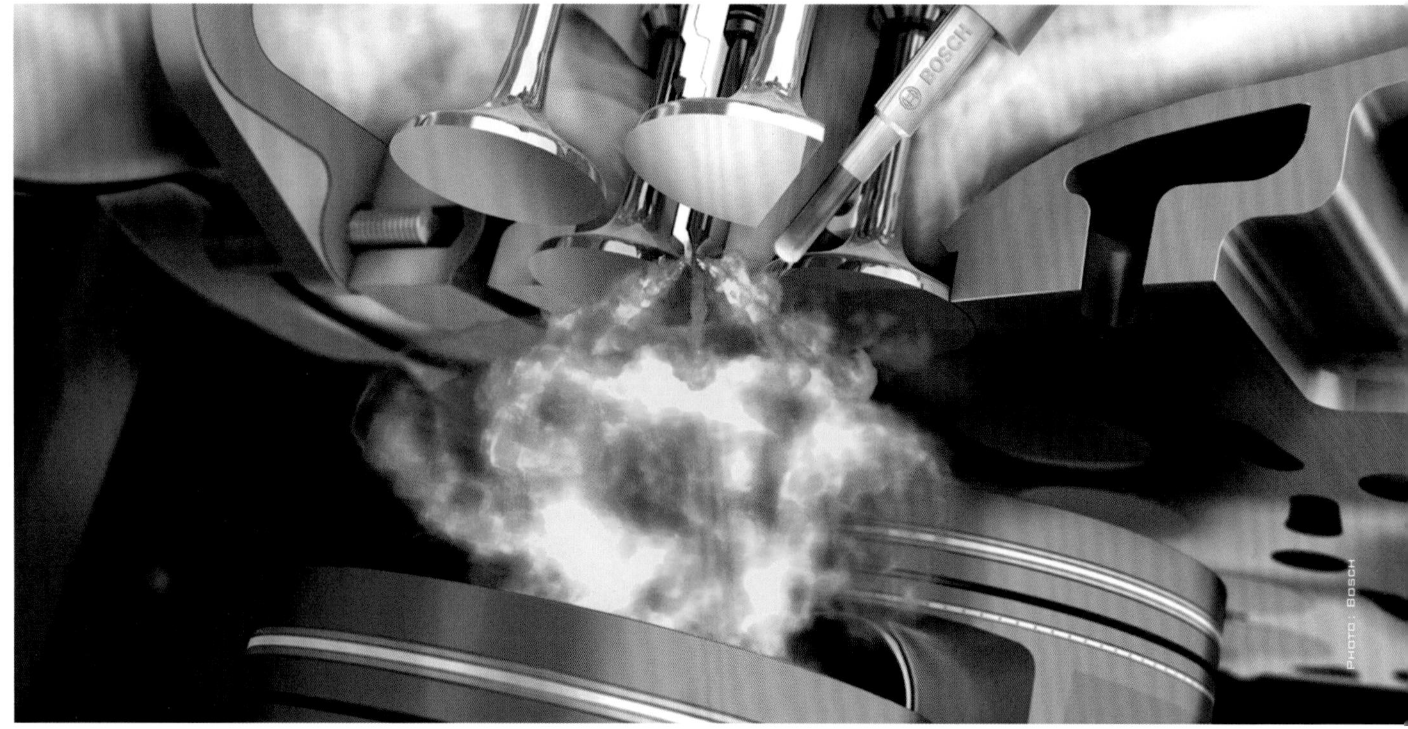

INJECTION DIRECTE

Si l'hybridation a la cote, le moteur à combustion n'est pas en reste. De plus en plus de constructeurs, autant dans les voitures haut de gamme que sur des modèles plus communs, ont recours à l'injection directe de l'essence. Les moteurs équipés de l'injection directe offrent près de 5 % plus de couple , et une économie de carburant pouvant atteindre 15 % , en plus d'accroître le gain d'un turbocompresseur si le véhicule en est équipé. La différence majeure de l'injection directe est la localisation de l'injecteur de carburant qui est dorénavant dans le cylindre, l'essence étant injectée directement dans la chambre de combustion, au lieu d'être dans le conduit d'admission, derrière la soupape. Cette approche permet de contrôler le moment de l'injection indépendamment de l'admission d'air dans le cylindre. L'injection peut se faire autant durant la phase d'admission, que dans la phase de compression du moteur ou même plusieurs fois par cycle, ce qui n'est pas possible avec l'injection traditionnelle, et requiert des injecteurs et une pompe haute pression pour injecter la quantité requise dans un court laps de temps. La haute pression de l'essence a aussi un effet refroidissant qui réduit la température à l'intérieur du cylindre, ce qui permet d'augmenter le taux de compression. Qui dit plus haut taux de compression dit plus de couple pour la même quantité d'essence, on obtient donc un moteur plus efficace et économe.

INJECTEUR TRADITIONNEL, DERRIÈRE LA SOUPAPE D'ADMISSION

INJECTEUR LOCALISÉ DANS LE CYLINDRE POUR L'INJECTION DIRECTE

En Europe et au Japon, certains constructeurs commencent à utiliser l'injection directe pour un procédé appelé stratification du mélange air-essence, qui consiste à injecter à haute pression un jet de carburant très fin et précis dirigé très près de la bougie, rendant cette zone inflammable. La tête du piston, en forme de bol, et de la tubulure d'admission sont conçues de façon à faire tourbillonner l'air pour optimiser la combustion très près de la bougie, le reste du cylindre ayant un excès d'air. Cette technique permet de n'utiliser qu'une très faible quantité d'essence lorsque la demande au moteur est faible, sans provoquer les ratés qui se produisent normalement lorsque la bougie ne parvient pas à enflammer un mélange trop pauvre en essence.

Quelques véhicules utilisant l'injection directe :

- Audi - toutes
- BMW 135, 335, séries 5, 7, X5, X6 et Z4
- Buick Enclave, LaCrosse et Regal
- Cadillac CTS (sauf CTS-V), SRX (3.0), STS (V6)
- Chevrolet Camaro (V6), Cobalt SS, Cruze, HHR SS, Equinox, Traverse
- Ferrari California et 458 Italia
- Ford (Ecoboost) Taurus SHO, Flex Ecoboost
- Hyundai Sonata
- Infiniti M56
- Lexus IS350, IS-F, GS450h, LS460 et LS600h
- Lincoln MKS Ecoboost, MKT Ecoboost
- Mazda CX-7 2.3, Mazdaspeed3
- Mercedes-Benz S63
- Mini Cooper S
- Nissan Juke
- Porsche (toutes sauf GT3 et GT2)
- VW Eos, GTI, Jetta 2.0T, Passat, Tiguan, Touareg

Mercedes-Benz F 700 DIESOTTO

Moteur à combustion interne de nouvelle technologie

Consommation	5,3 l/100 km
Émission CO_2	127 gr/km
Niveau d'émission	EU 6
Puissance	238 ch
Couple	400 Nm
Accélération	0-100 km/h en 7,5 secondes
Vitesse maximale	200 km/h

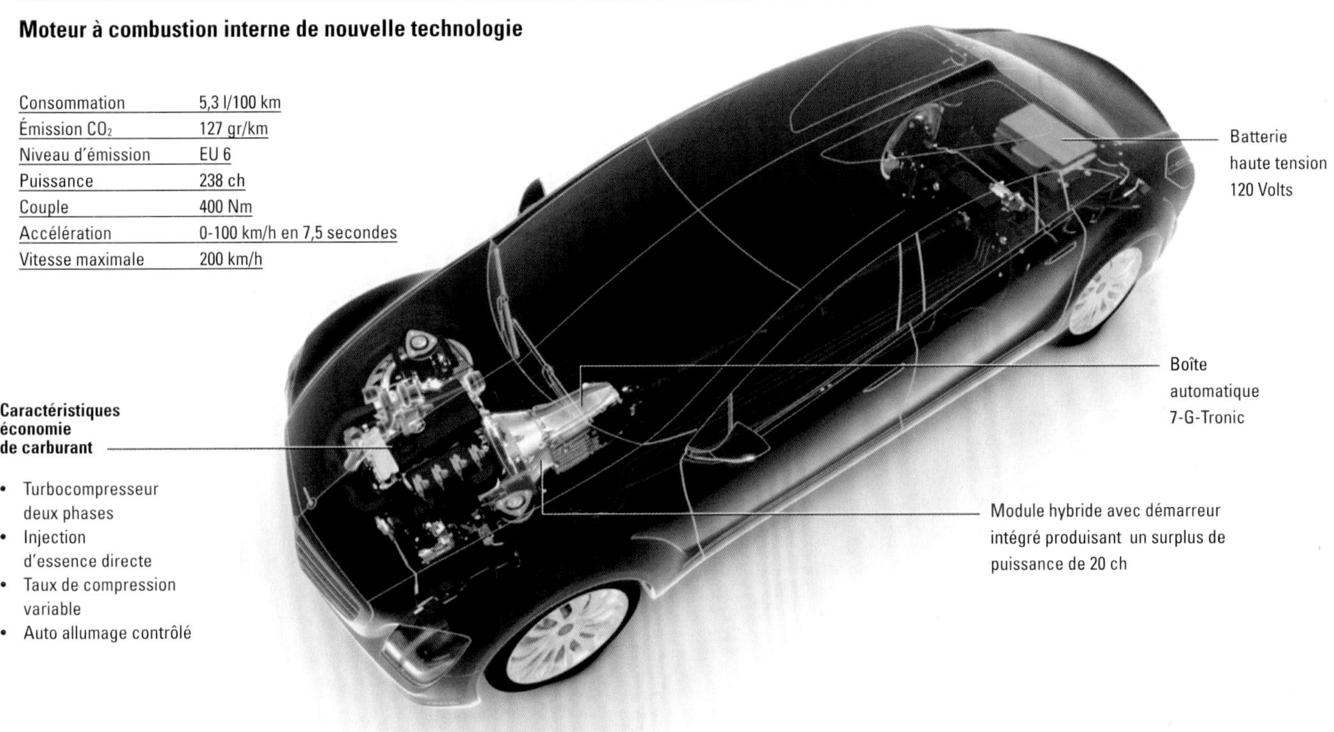

Caractéristiques économie de carburant

- Turbocompresseur deux phases
- Injection d'essence directe
- Taux de compression variable
- Auto allumage contrôlé

TECHNOLOGIE DIESOTTO OU HCCI

Traditionnellement, il y a deux principaux types de moteur à combustion, soit le cycle Otto (essence), fonctionnant à l'aide d'une bougie d'allumage, et le cycle Diesel, qui n'en a pas et accomplit son explosion grâce à la compression du mélange air-carburant. Le principe de combustion homogène (DiesOtto ou HCCI) combine les deux, car s'il utilise de l'essence, il la compresse comme un moteur diesel, pour l'enflammer sans bougie d'allumage.

L'avantage du moteur diesel est sa plus faible consommation, grâce à une meilleure efficacité. L'avantage du moteur à essence réside en de plus faibles émissions polluantes, principalement au niveau de l'oxyde d'azote (NOx), qui constitue le problème du diesel. D'ailleurs, les moteurs diesel modernes doivent recourir à toutes sortes d'artifices chers, complexes et lourds comme l'urée ou les filtres à particules pour s'ajuster aux normes anti-pollution de plus en plus sévères. Ainsi, l'objectif de la technologie DiesOtto/HCCI est de combiner l'efficacité du diesel aux faibles émissions du moteur à essence.

En effet, le défi est de compresser le mélange air-essence pour qu'il s'enflamme au bon moment sans l'intervention de la bougie. Un mélange air-essence qui explose trop rapidement cause une déflagration appelée cognement qui peut endommager de façon importante le moteur. D'ailleurs, les moteurs sont équipés de détecteurs pour les protéger contre ce phénomène. Par contre, si le mélange n'arrive pas à s'allumer, le moteur a donc des ratés. Ainsi, il faut donc contrôler l'allumage pour qu'il se produise exactement au bon moment, sans bougie. Grâce aux progrès récents dans le contrôle des moteurs, comme l'ouverture et le calage variable des soupapes, l'explosion peut être contrôlée. Dans les faits, comme le contrôle de ce moment est très complexe, le HCCI conserve sa bougie, qu'elle utilise pour les hauts régimes (plus de 3500 RPM), lors de fortes accélérations et pour l'allumage à froid. Mais dans les régimes de croisière et à faibles accélérations, le moteur se montre sobre comme un diesel, avec un potentiel de 10 à 15 % de diminution de la consommation par rapport à l'essence.

Aucun véhicule en production n'est actuellement équipé de cette technologie, mais plusieurs compagnies font de la recherche pour améliorer sa fiabilité, Mercedes et GM étant les plus actifs dans ce domaine. En effet, malgré les aspects alléchants, le moteur se doit d'être gros et solide comme un diesel pour résister à la force de l'explosion et d'être équipé des dernières technologies de contrôle. Ainsi, il demeure très complexe et relativement lourd, et son contrôle n'est pas tout à fait maîtrisé, donc sa fiabilité est à prouver. Le futur dira si cette technologie émergera.

Maxime Ouellet

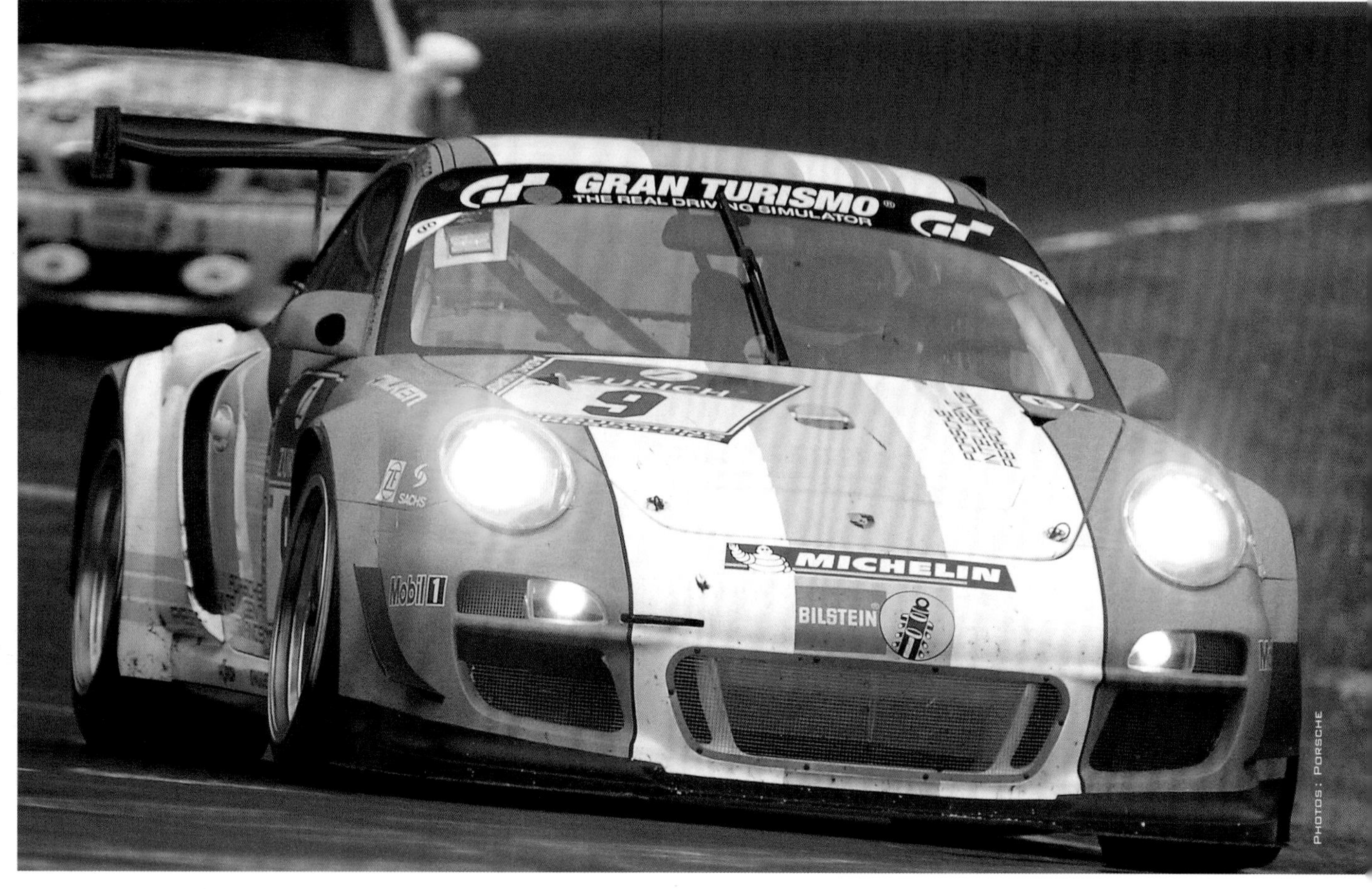

PHOTOS : PORSCHE

Voiture de course écolo au Nürburgring

Dans l'esprit de bien des gens, une voiture écologique s'adresse à des personnes désireuses de contribuer aux efforts afin de réduire la pollution causée par l'automobile. Mais depuis quelques années, on a également développé des technologies vertes pour les voitures de course. Cette utilisation peut sembler conflictuelle aux yeux de certains pour qui la course automobile ne fait que polluer, mais si on développe des technologies vertes pour les voitures de course, cela aura certainement pour effet d'améliorer la situation et de diminuer la pollution sur les circuits.

Porsche s'est intéressé à la chose et a concocté la 911 GT3 Hybrid. Et mieux encore, on ne s'est pas contenté de l'exhiber dans les salons automobiles, la voiture a été dévoilée au Salon automobile de Genève 2010, mais on l'a inscrite pour la course. Et pas sur n'importe quel circuit! Sur celui du Nürburgring, réputé pour être le plus long et le plus difficile au monde.

ÉCOLOGIE POUR LA COURSE

La quasi-majorité des voitures hybrides sur le marché sont équipées de batteries qui sont rechargées par la récupération d'énergie au freinage et le moteur thermique qui sert de génératrice. Ceci permet d'utiliser des batteries qui ont une certaine capacité de charge afin de pouvoir rouler à basse vitesse en mode purement électrique. Cette technologie permet de donc de rouler plus économiquement dans la circulation alors que le moteur thermique coupe à l'arrêt et que le moteur électrique permet de rouler à basse vitesse. Les besoins d'une voiture de course ne sont absolument pas les mêmes.

Il faut tout d'abord un système léger capable d'emmagasiner rapidement une certaine charge électrique et de fournir promptement une énergie électrique. Les ingénieurs de Porsche ont décidé d'utiliser un volant d'inertie mis au point par l'équipe de Formule Un Williams et sa filiale Williams Hybrid Power. Ce système comprend un volant moteur actionné électriquement et un moteur/générateur sur la boîte de vitesse. Pendant le freinage, le générateur monté dans la boîte de vitesse fait tourner le volant moteur à une vitesse allant jusqu'à 40 000 tr/min. Lorsque le pilote a besoin de plus de puissance, selon la nature de la course, le volant moteur transmet l'énergie à la boîte de vitesse. Dans le cas de la 911 GT3 Hybride, une paire de moteurs-générateurs reliés aux roues avant ajoutent un peu plus de vélocité.

Le volant moteur est fabriqué d'un matériau composite dans lequel sont intégrées des particules magnétiques au moulage. Ceci sert donc d'aimant permanent pour le moteur, ce qui permet de limiter le poids de cette unité. Il en résulte un système efficace et plus léger que si l'on utilisait des batteries.

En outre, l'énergie est absorbée plus vite, comme s'il s'agissait d'un super capaciteur. Par contre, les capacités de stockage d'énergie sont moindres qu'avec des batteries, mais l'énergie disponible est livrée rapidement, ce qui convient fort bien à une application en course.

Ce volant d'inertie est constitué d'une unité en matériau composite placée plus ou moins où se trouve le siège du passager dans la version de tourisme. Cette position permet d'équilibrer la voiture par la même occasion. Il est relié aux moteurs avant par un câble à haut voltage. C'est d'une conception simple alors qu'à part ces deux pièces électromécaniques, le reste est formé de systèmes de gestion électronique.

NÜRBURGRING : LA RÉFÉRENCE EN FAIT DE PISTE D'ESSAI

Les constructeurs automobiles sont de plus en plus nombreux à claironner que tel ou tel modèle a été mis au point sur le légendaire circuit du Nürburgring. Cette piste de course est située dans le village médiéval de Nürburg, à environ 70 kilomètres au sud de Cologne et 120 kilomètres au nord-ouest de Francfort. Sa construction a débuté dans les années 1920 et lors de son ouverture, cette piste est devenue la plus longue, la plus difficile et la plus dangereuse au monde. Originalement, ce circuit possédait quatre configurations: le Circuit Complet Gesamtstrecke d'une longueur de 28,2 kilomètres, la Boucle Nord Nordschleife longue de 22,8 km, la Boucle Sud Südschleife longue de 7,7 km. Finalement, la dernière section était une boucle servant à réchauffer les mécaniques des voitures. Elle était longue de 2,2 km et s'appelait le Zielschleife ou plus familièrement le Betonschleife car elle était autour de l'aire des puits.

Au fil des années, ce circuit a été utilisé pour toutes sortes d'épreuves locales et internationales. Puis, entre 1982 et 1983, de sérieuses modifications ont été apportées afin de réaliser un circuit moderne comprenant un passage dans le Stadium, alors que la piste serpente entre d'importantes estrades pour les spectateurs.

De nos jours, le Nordschleife est la section de l'ancien circuit qui est toujours utilisée pour des courses et des essais routiers de la

4

1. Contrôle électronique de la puissance
2. Arbres d'entraînement avec deux moteurs électriques
3. Câble de haute tension
4. Pile à volant d'inertie
5. Contrôle électronique de la puissance

part des constructeurs. Ce circuit est également ouvert au public certains jours de la semaine. D'une longueur de 22.8 km ce parcours comprend 33 virages à gauche et 40 virages à droite. Cependant, ce n'est pas tant le nombre de virages qui compte, mais bien leur difficulté. Parmi les plus mythiques, soulignons Flugplatz (Aéroport), Bergwerk (La Mine) — sans doute le plus célèbre — et finalement, l'infâme Caracciola Karussell (Le Carrousel) où a eu lieu le triste accident de Nicki Lauda lors du Grand Prix d'Allemagne en 1978. Et au moment d'écrire ces lignes, le record du tour en essai a été réalisé par une Pagani Zonda R en 6 min 47 s.

Enfin, un tour de piste pour les voitures de tourisme coûte 22 euros. Et si ce détail vous intéresse, un carnet de 25 tours coûte 390 euros.

NICO HULKENBERG IMPRESSIONNÉ

Puisque c'est l'écurie Williams de Formule 1 qui a développé le volant d'inertie utilisé par les ingénieurs de Porsche, il était plus que normal qu'on demande à Nico Hulkenberg, pilote de cette équipe, d'en faire l'essai. Bien entendu, son essai s'est déroulé sur le parcours Nordschleife du Nürburgring, l'endroit même où le développement de la voiture a eu lieu. Hulkenberg a effectué trois tours de piste en avril 2010 au volant de cette voiture hybride et ses commentaires ont été positifs.

« C'est tout d'abord une piste formidable aussi bien en raison des vitesses qu'on y atteint, mais également à cause des courbes techniques qui la parsèment. C'est vraiment le circuit de référence par excellence. Mais ce qui m'a le plus impressionné, c'est la facilité de conduite et les performances de la 911 GT3 Hybrid. Elle se conduit comme toute voiture Porsche de course et elle s'est révélée performante sur toutes les parties du parcours. Mais c'est encore plus épatant lorsqu'on fait appel à l'assistance des moteurs électriques. Il suffit d'appuyer sur un bouton placé sur le volant pour bénéficier d'un surplus de puissance aux roues avant pendant six à huit secondes. Chacune des roues est reliée à un moteur électrique de 82 chevaux. Lorsqu'ils travaillent de concert avec les 480 chevaux du moteur thermique six cylindres, la voiture est impressionnante. Finalement, j'ai été surpris de constater que l'adhérence dans les virages à basse vitesse est quasiment identique à ma voiture de Formule 1. »

Cet essai de Nico Hulkenberg avait pour but d'attirer les projecteurs sur la voiture et de sensibiliser le public sur les débuts en course de cette Porsche fort originale.

SPECTACULAIRE EN PISTE

Le test ultime pour une voiture est la compétition — et les courses d'endurance en particulier. Chez Porsche, on aurait pu faire tourner la 911 GT3 Hybrid sur des centaines de tours en essai, mais rien ne peut se comparer au stress mécanique d'une course. La voiture a donc

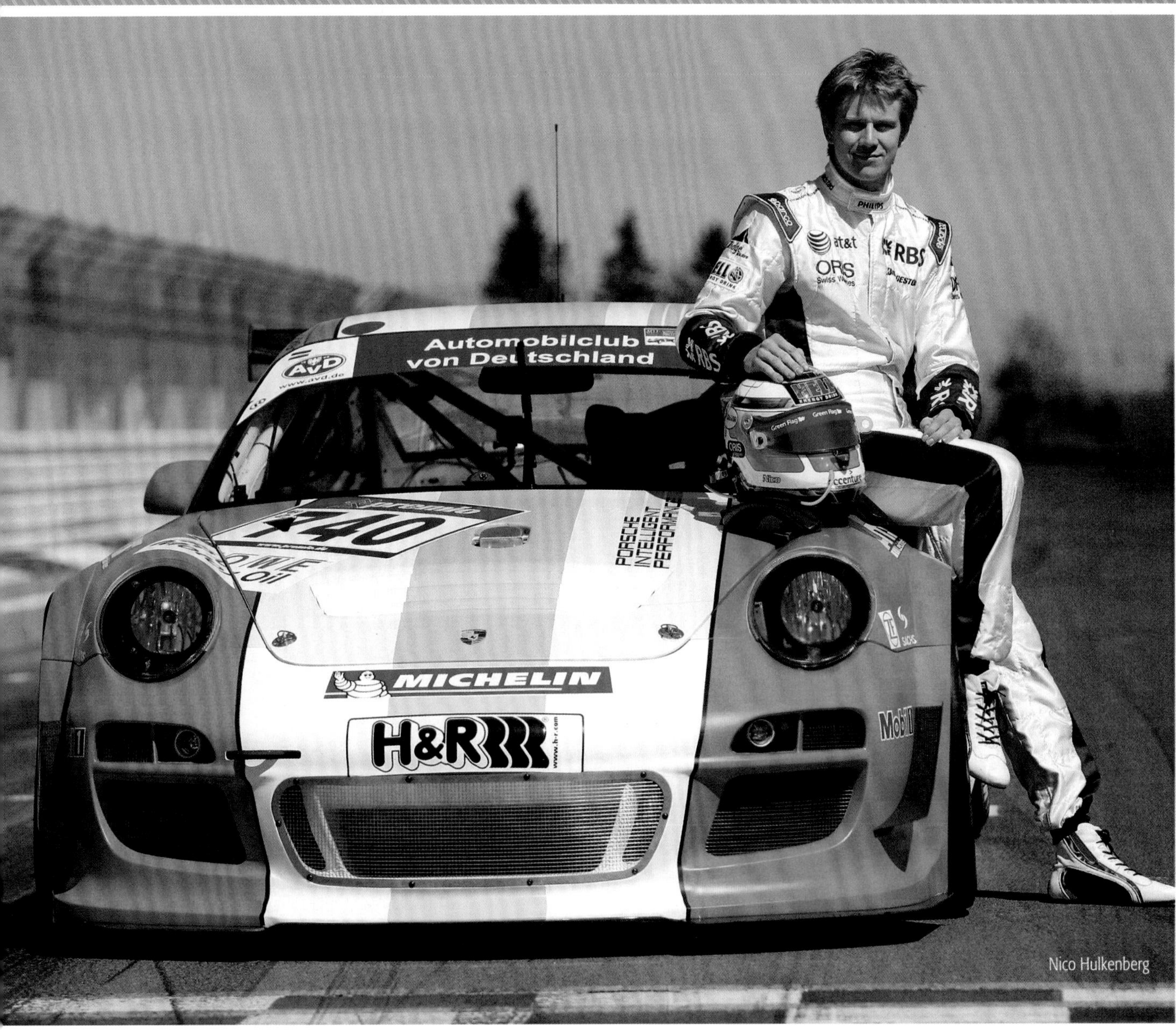

Nico Hulkenberg

effectué ses premiers tours de roue en course dans le cadre du Championnat de Longue Distance du Nürburgring le 30 mars dernier. Les pilotes allemands Joerg Bergmeister et Martin Ragginger ont lié leurs efforts à l'Autrichien Richard Lietz lors de la première épreuve de ce championnat. Leur but n'était pas nécessairement de remporter la course, mais de mettre la voiture à l'épreuve. Le trio s'est classé au sixième rang tandis que c'était la Porsche 911 GT3 pilotée par Timo Bernhard, Marc Lieb et Marcel Tieman qui a franchi la ligne en premier.

Mais la course qui allait mettre cet hybride en évidence a été celle des 24 Heures du Nürburgring, disputée à la mi-mai. Lors de la séance de qualification du 10 mai 2010, la 911 GT3 Hybrid s'est qualifiée au second rang. Les pilotes Richard Lietz, Marco Holzer et Martin Ragginger avaient ensuite la délicate tâche de ramener ce bolide d'exception à bon port sur le plus difficile circuit du monde des courses.

La compagnie Porsche voulait non seulement éprouver la durabilité de son système hybride mais voulait en même temps profiter d'une course d'endurance afin de recueillir des informations techniques. En fait, leurs espoirs ont été comblés car la 911 GT3 Hybrid a dominé la course et a même eu une avance de deux tours à un certain moment. Malheureusement, l'histoire n'a pas connu une fin heureuse. Car après 22 heures et 15 minutes de cette course de 24 heures, le moteur thermique a eu des ennuis graves qui ont forcé le retrait de la voiture.

Malgré tout, Porsche avait gagné son pari et démontré spectaculairement le potentiel en course de la technologie hybride. Et il est certain que le constructeur de Stuttgart a l'intention d'utiliser cette technique à l'avenir. Il a d'ailleurs fait faire des tours de démonstration à une 911 GT3 Hybrid lors de la plus récente épreuve des 24 Heures du Mans en juin 2010. Ce n'est qu'un début.

En terminant, si vous voulez rouler au volant d'une Porsche à moteur hybride, la nouvelle Cayenne Hybrid est commercialisée sur notre continent en tant que modèle 2011. C'est moins spectaculaire, mais plus écolo.

IN R 8101

Acura / Aston martin / Audi / Bentley / BMW / Buick / Cadillac / Chevrolet / Chrysler / Dodge
Ferrari / Fiat / Ford / Honda / Hyundai / Infiniti / Jaguar / Jeep / Kia / Lamborghini / Land Rover
Lexus / Lincoln / Lotus / Maserati / Maybach / Mazda / Mercedes-benz / Mini / Mitsubishi / Nissan
Porsche / RAM / Rolls Royce / Saab / Scion / Smart / Subaru / Suzuki / Tesla / Toyota / Volkswagen / Volvo

COMME UN NOUVEAU MILLIONNAIRE

Une personne possédant un travail honorable rémunéré à sa juste valeur gagne un jour plusieurs millions de dollars à la loterie. Cette personne ne devient pas plus intelligente, ni plus humaine, elle est juste plus riche. Prenez une voiture tout à fait banale et apportez-lui une foule de petites améliorations. Elle ne devient pas plus fiable (surtout si elle l'était déjà beaucoup), ni plus sportive, elle est juste plus luxueuse. Voici l'Acura CSX !

Ce n'est plus un secret pour personne. L'Acura CSX est, en fait, une Honda Civic de luxe distribuée uniquement sur le marché canadien. Aux États-Unis, Honda propose une EX-L dotée d'un GPS, une voiture équivalente à notre CSX. Au nord du 45ième parallèle, on a préféré séparer la gamme Civic pour donner une voiture abordable aux concessionnaires Acura. Mais il faut aussi savoir que les Canadiens aiment bien une voiture tout équipée dotée d'un logo prestigieux. La CSX est là pour les accommoder à peu de frais. Pour être assuré que les deux véhicules ne se chevauchent pas au niveau des accessoires et, surtout, dans l'esprit de gens, le GPS est réservé à la CSX. Cependant, si vous désirez un coupé, il faut alors lorgner du côté de Honda.

Physiquement, les deux voitures se ressemblent passablement mais les designers d'Acura ont réussi à donner à la CSX une allure plus racée. Ainsi, on retrouve la fameuse grille avant en forme de coin, beaucoup mieux intégrée à la voiture qu'à bien d'autres produits Acura. À l'arrière, les feux diffèrent et l'aileron sur le coffre de la CSX est plus imposant.

UNE CIVIC EN MIEUX

La CSX a droit à un quatre cylindres de 2,0 litres de 155 chevaux, passablement dégourdi et qui aime les hauts régimes, comme la plupart des produits Honda/Acura. Ce moteur est fort moderne avec son double arbre à cames en tête et sa technologie i-VTEC. On peut l'associer à deux transmissions, soit une manuelle à cinq rapports un peu flasque ou une automatique à cinq rapports aussi avec palettes derrière le volant. La conduite de cette voiture est à peu près celle d'une Honda Civic plus puissante, beaucoup mieux insonorisée (il aurait été difficile de faire une voiture qui l'était moins...) et au comportement routier plus affuté. Malgré tout, on ne parle aucunement d'une voiture sportive et sa conduite demeure beaucoup plus confortable qu'autre chose même si elle s'accroche avec détermination au bitume. Son moteur consomme environ 1 litre d'essence supplémentaire à tous les cent kilomètres, par rapport à une Civic. Ce qui est normal compte tenu que cette dernière est moins puissante avec son 1,8 litre.

Bien entendu, l'habitacle reflète le niveau de luxe propre à Acura, à défaut d'être plus originale que la roturière Civic. On retrouve donc le tableau de bord entièrement digital de la Honda que certains adorent alors que d'autres fustigent. Les sièges de cuir sont confortables, le petit volant de cuir se prend très bien

ACURA CSX

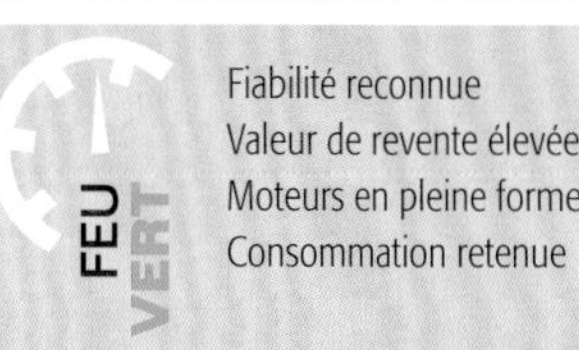

- Fiabilité reconnue
- Valeur de revente élevée
- Moteurs en pleine forme
- Consommation retenue

FEU ROUGE

- Image de la Civic trop évidente
- Abandon de la Type-S
- Pas de version coupé
- Boutons du système audio trop petits

en main et la plupart des matériaux sont de belle facture et bien assemblés. Comme on l'a déjà vu, le système GPS est livré d'office, avec ses petits boutons difficiles à manipuler l'été. Alors imaginez l'hiver avec des gants... Système audio de 160 watts incluant la radio satellite, technologie Bluetooth et colonne de direction télescopique sont au rendez-vous. L'habitacle s'avère très logeable et même les gens prenant place à l'arrière ne s'y sentiront pas trop à l'étroit. Bien entendu, l'équipement est plus relevé que dans une vulgaire Civic, prix et écusson obligent !

HURLEMENTS

Pour les gens désirant à la fois le prestige de l'écusson Acura et la sportivité, il y avait, jusqu'à l'année dernière, la CSX Type-S, l'équivalent de la Civic Si. Dotée du même moteur 2,0 litres de 197 chevaux et de la même transmission manuelle à six rapports, cette version s'avérait beaucoup plus enjouée que la CSX régulière. Cependant, il fallait être prêt à y mettre le prix, autant en termes de $$$$$ que de plaisir de conduire. Ce moteur n'aimait pas les hauts régimes, il les adorait. À preuve, la zone rouge du tachymètre débutait à 8000 tours/minute ! Le hurlement du quatre cylindres lorsqu'il était rendu près de cette limite pouvait être agréable pour les jeunes oreilles mais pour les miennes, il ne valait pas la sonorité profonde d'un bon vieux V8 américain. Cependant, il est fort possible que la Civic Si, disponible autant en version coupé que berline venait joyeusement ravager les ventes de la CSX Type-S, ce qui aurait incité les gens de chez Acura à se concentrer sur la version régulière.

Il est même de mise de se poser la question sur l'avenir de la CSX. Le fait qu'elle soit destinée uniquement au marché canadien et que les différences avec la Civic ne soient pas très évidentes pourraient nuire à son avenir. Il ne faut pas oublier non plus que la Civic devrait être complètement révisée l'an prochain. En extraira-t-on une CSX ? D'un autre côté, il faut donner aux concessionnaires Acura un produit accessible, question de faire tourner leur entreprise.

La CSX, Type-S ou pas, n'en demeure pas moins qu'une Civic de luxe. Est-ce que le luxe plus abondant, le logo d'Acura et un système GPS sont suffisant pour convaincre les gens de dépenser plus ?

Alain Morin

PHOTOS : ACURA

Catégorie	Berline
Échelle de prix	27 490 $ à 29 990 $ (2010)
Garanties	4 ans/80 000 km, 5 ans/100 000 km
Assemblage	Alliston, Ontario, Canada
Cote d'assurance	n.d.

CHÂSSIS - DONNÉES POUR I-TECH

Emp/lon/lar/haut	2 700/4 544/1 752/1 435 mm
Coffre	341 litres
Réservoir	50 litres
Nombre coussins sécurité	6
Antipatinage / contrôle stabilité	oui / oui
Suspension avant	indépendante, jambes de force
Suspension arrière	indépendante, double triangulation
Freins avant / arrière	disque (ABS) / disque (ABS)
Direction	à crémaillère, ass. variable
Diamètre de braquage	10,0 m
Pneus avant / arrière	P215/45R17 / P215/45R17
Poids	1 313 kg
Capacité de remorquage	n.d.

COMPOSANTES MÉCANIQUES

i-Tech

Cylindrée, soupapes, alim.	4L 2,0 litres 16 s atmos.
Puissance / Couple	155 chevaux / 139 lb-pi
Tr. base (opt) / rouage base (opt)	M5 (A5) / Tr
0-100 / 80-120 / 100-0 km/h	8,5 s / 7,5 s / 42,5 m
Type ess. / ville / autoroute	Ordinaire / 8,7 / 6,4 l/100 km

DANS LA MÊME CATÉGORIE

Chevrolet Cruze, Ford Focus, Honda Civic, Hyundai Elantra, Kia Forte, Mazda3, Mitsubishi Lancer, Nissan Sentra, Subaru Impreza, Toyota Corolla, Volkswagen Jetta

DU NOUVEAU EN 2011

Aucun changement majeur. Abandon de la version Type-S

NOS IMPRESSIONS

Agrément de conduite :	7/10
Fiabilité :	9/10
Sécurité :	8/10
Qualités hivernales :	7/10
Espace intérieur :	7/10
Confort :	8/10

www.acura.ca

Plus d'informations dans la section statistiques en dernière partie du Guide

ÉQUILIBRE ASSURÉ, ESTHÉTIQUE CONTESTÉE

Aussi bien se débarrasser de cet épineux sujet tout de suite, il y a maintenant plusieurs mois que le plus populaire des modèles Acura, le MDX a connu une refonte esthétique, notamment sa grille de calandre. Et vous pouvez être certain que l'unanimité ne s'est pas faite suite à ces changements. Il est vrai qu'on voulait chez cette division de Honda donner plus de caractère au gros VUS, mais nombreuses sont les personnes qui ont toujours de la difficulté à accepter ce museau différent. Il y en a même qui parlent de décapsuleur !

Bref, certains aiment, d'autres n'aiment pas. Mais il ne faut pas uniquement s'arrêter à cet appendice nasal, car le MDX a connu plusieurs changements sur le plan mécanique qui ont nettement amélioré l'agrément de conduite et le comportement routier.

MÉCANIQUE SOPHISTIQUÉE

On peut critiquer la compagnie Honda pour bien des choses, mais il est difficile de la prendre en défaut lorsque vient le temps de développer et produire des moteurs. En effet, ce constructeur s'est toujours targué de commercialiser des groupes propulseurs d'une cylindrée inférieure à la moyenne de la catégorie tout en offrant des performances de moteurs plus gros. Et cela, avec une consommation de carburant inférieure à la moyenne. L'an dernier, les ingénieurs se sont donnés pour mandat de réviser le moteur V6 de 3,7 litres afin d'améliorer son couple et sa plage de puissance à l'aide d'un système plus sophistiqué de calage variable des soupapes, d'un nouveau collecteur d'admission en plus d'apporter de nombreuses autres améliorations à divers niveaux. Il en résulte un moteur dont le rendement et les performances sont supérieurs à la moyenne de la catégorie tandis que la consommation de carburant demeure toujours raisonnable, du moins pour un moteur produisant 300 chevaux.

Toute cette cavalerie a été associée à une nouvelle transmission automatique à six rapports qui est venue remplacer une boîte un peu moins sophistiquée à cinq rapports. Cela peut sembler peu de choses, mais c'est pratiquement le jour et la nuit en raison d'un niveau sonore nettement diminué et de passages de rapport plus doux que précédemment. En fait, il faut noter que les cinq premiers rapports sont relativement courts tandis que le sixième a pour but de réduire la consommation de carburant.

En plus de ces améliorations mécaniques, la suspension a été recalibrée et on a profité de l'occasion pour réviser une foule d'autres éléments. Détail à souligner, depuis l'an dernier, les embouts des tuyaux d'échappement sont quasiment rectangulaires.

NETTEMENT PLUS HOMOGÈNE

Le MDX est un véhicule aux dimensions imposantes, ce qui lui permet d'accommoder trois rangées de sièges. Les places avant

FEU VERT
- Moteur performant
- Rouage intégral efficace
- Finition impeccable
- Équipement complet
- Prix compétitifs

FEU ROUGE
- Pédale de frein capricieuse
- Ergonomie du tableau de bord à revoir
- Troisième rangée peu pratique
- Grille de calandre controversée

sont spacieuses et confortables, le siège médian est relativement accueillant pour la majorité des gabarits tandis que la troisième rangée est plus ou moins limitée à des personnes de petite taille ou à des enfants. Mais mode, quand tu nous tiens ! Même si la logique n'est pas respectée, vu que les gens sont influencés par la possibilité d'avoir une troisième rangée de sièges, on leur en offre une, qu'elle soit pratique ou non…

C'est probablement l'une des rares critiques que l'on puisse faire à cet habitacle dont la finition est superbe et la qualité des matériaux supérieure. Les cadrans indicateurs sont de types électroluminescents et très faciles à consulter. Toutefois, il faut apporter un sérieux bémol à l'ergonomie des commandes audio et de climatisation. On a affaire à une mer de boutons, généralement petits, qui ne sont pas disposés logiquement, quoi qu'en disent les communiqués de presse de ce constructeur. Une personne qui n'est pas habituée doit pratiquement immobiliser le véhicule pour régler la radio ou la climatisation. Plusieurs constructeurs concurrents font beaucoup mieux à ce chapitre.

Toutes les modifications et améliorations apportées l'an dernier avaient pour but de raffiner la tenue de route et le confort dans l'habitacle avec une réduction des vibrations et une meilleure insonorisation. Ces objectifs ont été facilement atteints et la différence est vraiment remarquable. Il faut de plus mentionner l'homogénéité du comportement routier et des prestations du moteur. En effet, il existe une belle harmonie entre le rendement du moteur, la boîte automatique à six rapports et une suspension calibrée afin d'offrir un niveau de confort supérieur sur mauvaise route sans pour autant handicaper la tenue de route.

Un autre élément important à souligner est le rouage intégral de série. Appelé SH-AWD, ce mécanisme transfère le couple à la roue extérieure afin de compenser et prévenir tout dérapage dans un virage. Les résultats sont convaincants. D'ailleurs, plusieurs autres constructeurs ont modifié leur rouage intégral afin d'adopter plus ou moins cette technologie.

En raison de toutes ces qualités et d'un prix de détail suggéré fort impressionnant par rapport à la qualité du véhicule et son niveau d'équipement, le MDX est le succès de cette division.

Denis Duquet

PHOTOS : ALAIN MORIN

Catégorie	VUS
Échelle de prix	52 900 $ à 62 500 $ (2010)
Garanties	4 ans/80 000 km, 5 ans/100 000 km
Assemblage	Alliston, Ontario, Canada
Cote d'assurance	moyenne

CHÂSSIS - DONNÉES POUR ELITE

Emp/lon/lar/haut	2 750/4 867/1 994/1 733 mm
Coffre	425 à 2 364 litres
Réservoir	79 litres
Nombre coussins sécurité	6
Antipatinage / contrôle stabilité	oui / oui
Suspension avant	indépendante, jambes de force
Suspension arrière	indépendante, multibras
Freins avant / arrière	disque (ABS) / disque (ABS)
Direction	à crémaillère, ass. variable
Diamètre de braquage	11,4 m
Pneus avant / arrière	P255/50R19 / P255/50R19
Poids	2 088 kg
Capacité de remorquage	2 269 kg (5 002 lb)

COMPOSANTES MÉCANIQUES

Base, Technologie, Elite

Cylindrée, soupapes, alim.	V6 3,7 litres 24 s atmos.
Puissance / Couple	300 chevaux / 270 lb-pi
Tr. base (opt) / rouage base (opt)	A6 / Int
0-100 / 80-120 / 100-0 km/h	7,6 s / 5,7 s / 46,2 m
Type ess. / ville / autoroute	Super / 13,2 / 9,6 l/100km

DANS LA MÊME CATÉGORIE

Audi Q7, BMW X5, Buick Enclave, Cadillac SRX, Infiniti FX, Lexus RX, Lincoln MKX, Mercedes-Benz Classe M, Porsche Cayenne, Volkswagen Touareg, Volvo XC90

DU NOUVEAU EN 2011

Aucun changement majeur

NOS IMPRESSIONS

Agrément de conduite :	7/10
Fiabilité :	10/10
Sécurité :	8/10
Qualités hivernales :	9/10
Espace intérieur :	8/10
Confort :	8/10

www.acura.ca

Plus d'informations dans la section statistiques en dernière partie du Guide

VAISSEAU AMIRAL EN PERDITION

Si la RL était un cheval, on devrait abréger immédiatement ses souffrances. Voilà, hélas, où en est rendue cette grande berline à sa septième année sous sa forme actuelle, inchangée à quelques détails et une calandre près. Le supposé joyau de la famille Acura se retrouve plutôt largué par les ténors européens et bousculé par des rivales nipponnes affamées qui savent tenir le rythme et jouer le jeu dans cette catégorie impitoyable. Elle fait même pâle figure devant sa sœur la TL qui devrait pourtant se contenter de son ombre et de son sillage. Il est grand temps d'y voir chez Acura.

La RL n'est pas une mauvaise voiture, mais n'excelle en rien. Passons vite sur une silhouette qui la rend carrément invisible, malgré la calandre en ouvre-boîte dont sont affligées toutes les Acura. Les sièges avant sont confortables et la jante du volant, qui combine boiseries d'érable et cuir perforé, est bien taillée et de prise très agréable. La position de conduite est bonne, mais on se râpe trop facilement la cheville gauche sur la pédale du frein de stationnement en voulant profiter du repose-pied.

Les cadrans principaux sont grands et impeccablement clairs, tandis que la console est tapissée de boutons; deux traditions chez Acura, la première appréciée, l'autre pas. Le groupe Élite ajoute des phares orientables, un régulateur de vitesse automatique, des sièges avant climatisés et le freinage d'urgence assisté, mais gonfle également la facture d'un bon 5500$.

STABLE, CONFORTABLE ET . . . DÉCLASSÉE

La tenue de cap et la stabilité en virage sont sans reproche, grâce à la saine géométrie du train avant et à l'excellent rouage à couple variable. La direction est peu tactile, mais le braquage très court rend la RL très maniable pour sa taille. Le confort roulement est très correct, sauf pour une allergie prononcée aux gros nids-de-poules. Le V6 de 3,7 litres a le brio et le raffinement habituel des moteurs Honda, mais la RL s'arrache difficilement et paresseusement au démarrage.

C'est d'ailleurs face à sa propre sœur, la berline TL, que la RL paraît le plus mal. De taille presque égale, à quelques millimètres près, la première est pourtant plus légère de 180 kg, même avec l'excellent rouage intégral SH-AWD et le poids supplémentaire qu'il amène. Puisque les deux partagent un groupe propulseur quasi-identique, rien d'étonnant à ce que la TL atteigne 100 km/h en 6,47 secondes et franchisse le quart-de-mille en 14,78 secondes alors que la RL y met 8,12 et 16,08 secondes.

La TL est pratiquement aussi spacieuse à l'intérieur que la RL et ne lui concède qu'un léger avantage en volume de coffre. Ni l'une ni l'autre n'est exceptionnelle à cet égard de toute manière, avec des coffres de 371 et 354 litres, respectivement, soit moins que les 400 litres qui sont la norme officieuse pour ce type de véhicule.

FEU VERT
- Comportement routier très sûr
- Excellent rouage intégral
- Diamètre de braquage très court
- Sièges avant confortables
- Voiture fiable

FEU ROUGE
- Silhouette parfaitement banale
- Pédale de frein d'urgence encombrante
- Performances quelconques
- Équation équipement-prix à revoir
- Modèle en sursis

Il ne manque pratiquement à la TL qu'un volant à réglage électrique et des sièges avant climatisés pour égaler quasi-parfaitement la RL en matière de luxe. Pourtant, son modèle le mieux équipé coûte près de 20000$ de moins que la dernière RL Elite que nous avons conduite. Insensé, cet état de fait a été remarqué par le marché. Au premier trimestre de l'année, alors que les ventes de la TL étaient en hausse et celles de la TSX encore plus, Acura n'a pas vendu une seule RL au Québec. C'est plutôt gênant, en effet.

EN MANQUE DE LUXE ET D'AUDACE

En résumé, la RL n'a tout simplement pas le style, l'équipement, les performances et le panache pour avoir la moindre chance devant des étalons comme les Audi A6, BMW Série 5 et Mercedes-Benz Classe E dont le seul nom de famille est un atout majeur. Sans compter les A8, Série 7 et Classe S qui trônent au sommet des gammes du triumvirat germanique.

Honda n'aura pas eu la volonté ou les milliards de sa grande rivale pour attaquer de front les Européens avec une voiture comme la Lexus LS. De son côté, voilà que Hyundai s'y met avec ses berlines Equus et Genesis qui ont cette même audace, mais également les V8 qui ont toujours manqué à la championne d'Acura pour viser plus haut.

Quel que soit l'angle sous lequel on l'aborde, la RL se fait rosser à tout coup. Prenez simplement les boîtes de vitesses: alors que les autres roulent pratiquement toutes avec des boîtes à six rapports et que les plus récentes en affichent sept et même huit, la RL se contente encore d'une boîte à cinq rapports. C'était la norme lors de son lancement en 2005, mais ce n'est plus suffisant dans une catégorie où la fiche technique et les apparences sont au moins aussi importantes que les vraies performances.

Le modèle phare de la gamme Acura devrait démontrer toute la maîtrise et le brio technique de ce constructeur, tout en offrant un niveau d'équipement, de performance, de luxe et de comportement routier de premier ordre. C'est ce que réussit déjà la TL, à prix très compétitif. Tout est une question de volonté, mais également de moyens, bien entendu.

Marc Lachapelle

PHOTOS: MARC LACHAPELLE

Catégorie	Berline
Échelle de prix	63 900$ à 69 500$ (2010)
Garanties	4 ans/80 000 km, 5 ans/100 000 km
Assemblage	Saitama, Japon
Cote d'assurance	n.d.

CHÂSSIS - DONNÉES POUR ELITE

Emp/lon/lar/haut	2 800/4 973/1 847/1 455 mm
Coffre	371 litres
Réservoir	73 litres
Nombre coussins sécurité	6
Antipatinage / contrôle stabilité	oui / oui
Suspension avant	indépendante, double triangulation
Suspension arrière	indépendante, multibras
Freins avant / arrière	disque (ABS) / disque (ABS)
Direction	à crémaillère, assistée
Diamètre de braquage	12,1 m
Pneus avant / arrière	P245/45R18 / P245/45R18
Poids	1 863 kg
Capacité de remorquage	454 kg (1 000 lb)

COMPOSANTES MÉCANIQUES

Base, Elite

Cylindrée, soupapes, alim.	V6 3,7 litres 24 s atmos.
Puissance / Couple	300 chevaux / 271 lb-pi
Tr. base (opt) / rouage base (opt)	A5 / Int
0-100 / 80-120 / 100-0 km/h	7,2 s / 6,6 s / 40,2 m
Type ess. / ville / autoroute	Super / 13,1 / 9,0 l/100 km

DANS LA MÊME CATÉGORIE

Audi A6, BMW Série 5, Cadillac STS, Infiniti M, Jaguar XF, Lexus GS, Mercedes-Benz Classe E, Volvo S80

DU NOUVEAU EN 2011

Aucun changement majeur

NOS IMPRESSIONS

Agrément de conduite:	7/10
Fiabilité:	8/10
Sécurité:	10/10
Qualités hivernales:	9/10
Espace intérieur:	8/10
Confort:	9/10

www.acura.ca

Plus d'informations dans la section statistiques en dernière partie du Guide

QUOTIENT DE PLAISIR DE CONDUITE: ÉLEVÉ

Sur papier, le RDX commence à dater et une nouvelle génération sera la bienvenue. Mais sur route, le petit utilitaire d'Acura en donne encore suffisamment pour rester l'un des plus agréables à piloter.

Si l'on commençait par les mauvaises nouvelles, question de finir avec les bonnes? L'Acura RDX n'a toujours pas le démarrage sans clé, dommage. Sa transmission cinq rapports n'a plus la cote face aux concurrents qui en ont six, voire sept. On regrette que la banquette ne se rabatte pas tout à fait à plat – ça réduit l'espace de chargement, pourtant l'un des plus généreux du segment (1 716 litres). Cette banquette ne s'avance ni se recule, ce qui aurait accordé plus de place aux jambes et son dossier ne s'incline pas, ce qui aurait permis plus de confort lors des longs trajets. Aussi, le hayon est lourd à manipuler; de l'aluminium aurait retranché du poids au véhicule, mais ne chialons pas: l'Acura se targue déjà d'être un poids plume dans sa catégorie (1 783 kg).

LA *SWITCH À BITCH*

On continue le *bitching*? Les sièges avant sont enveloppants, mais le soutien lombaire est «trop»; les petits gabarits se fatiguent vite de la bosse qui leur enfonce le bas du dos. Sans système de navigation (une option), l'écran livre des écritures ennuyantes et d'ailleurs, la planche de bord n'a pas le panache des Mercedes GLK et Volvo XC60. La disposition des commandes ne permet pas une manipulation instinctive et c'est à se demander si Honda/Acura s'est donné le mot pour rater son ergonomie, côté climatisation: dans le RDX, comme dans l'Accord et l'Insight, la logique des contrôles est des plus discutables...

Découragés? Ben non, voyons, le meilleur s'en vient! Terminons juste avec les mauvaises nouvelles: avec son pavillon plus bas que la concurrence (mis à part le minus Infiniti EX), le RDX offre un petit dégagement aux têtes: 982 mm à l'avant, c'est limite. Le remorquage (tout juste 682 kg) est deux fois moindre que pour la compétition, mais il faut dire que l'Acura est le seul à proposer un moteur quatre cylindres, aussi turbo soit-il. Enfin, la mise à niveau esthétique de l'an dernier fait s'accrocher à la calandre cette traverse chromée qui s'inspire fort malencontreusement des *can openers*. Sinon, la silhouette vieillit bien et elle est encore jolie.

LES BONNES NOUVELLES, MAINTENANT

Voilà pour les mauvaises nouvelles, les bonnes, maintenant. Malgré son «vieil» âge – le RDX est avec nous depuis 2006 –, le petit Acura est l'un des plus intéressants utilitaires à piloter. Sa direction est sa plus grande qualité: précise et de parfaite résistance, elle fait corps avec le conducteur qui sent alors les petites dimensions du véhicule comme une extension de lui-même. On ne reproche qu'un large (et surprenant) rayon de braquage: 11,9 mètres pour un compact, ça frise presque le handicap en stationnement.

On a beau dire que le quatre cylindres (2,3 litres, 240 chevaux) ne livre pas la puissance des V6 offerts par la concurrence, reste

FEU VERT

Plaisir de conduite très élevé
Généreux espace de chargement
Passage des vitesses au volant
On aime le « super » AWD
Suspension de belle fermeté

FEU ROUGE

Pas de démarrage sans clé
Commandes peu instinctives
Capacité de remorquage réduite
Calandre en *can opener*
À quand le toit panoramique?

que c'est toujours agréable à faire frémir, un turbo. Techniquement moderne avec son i-Vtec et son Variable flow, ce moteur mériterait néanmoins l'injection directe, pour une mise en action plus rapide. Peut-être que ça lui donnerait aussi une linéarité et une douceur qui lui font actuellement défaut – on sent de la rugosité sous le pied droit, mais le tout est compensé par un beau zeste d'athlétisme qu'on ne manque pas d'exploiter. Et après, on se demande pourquoi le réservoir d'essence se vide plus vite qu'à son tour…

On a beau critiquer le fait que l'automatique n'ait que cinq rapports, reste que la boîte fait monter de série (*yes!*) des passages au volant fort agréables et instinctifs à manier. La suspension est indéniablement plus ferme qu'ailleurs, sauf peut-être pour le BMW X3. Certes, les journalistes automobiles adorent ces suspensions sèches, mais Monsieur et Madame Tout-le-Monde se fatiguent de ressentir toutes les aspérités de la route. Alors, un conseil: faites un essai ailleurs que sur l'autoroute avant de vous commettre.

Est-ce cette suspension ultraferme? L'empattement parmi les plus courts de la catégorie? La super traction intégrale qui fait varier le couple entre les essieux, mais aussi entre les roues arrière? Ou encore la basse garde au sol – à peine 159 mm? Toujours est-il que le RDX est une vraie jouissance à lancer en virage, où il se montre plus assuré que bon nombre d'utilitaires, mais aussi de voitures. Si, en pleine action, les yeux se risquent à quitter la route, ils aperçoivent en instantané, à même un (trop) petit écran, à quelle roue va le couple; c'est passionnant. Néanmoins, ne pensez pas « fond des bois » pour le RDX; sans plaque de protection ni de contrôle de descente, le véhicule mise plutôt sur son AWD pour le maintenir sur la route – et c'est là qu'il excelle.

On espère que la prochaine génération apportera le toit panoramique et le correctif à toutes les critiques ci-haut, sinon encensons l'actuelle géante console centrale, l'excellente finition intérieure et la caméra de recul qui retransmet les images au rétroviseur central (beaucoup plus logique qu'à l'écran de bord, placé plus bas). Enfin, on aime que les sièges chauffants, le (petit) toit ouvrant et la climatisation bizone soient de série. Bref, même s'il a vieilli, le RDX demeure l'un des utilitaires compacts de luxe les plus intéressants du marché, tant pour sa conduite que pour son niveau d'équipements.

Nadine Filion

PHOTOS : ACURA

Catégorie	VUS
Échelle de prix	39 990 $ à 42 990 $ (2010)
Garanties	4 ans/80 000 km, 5 ans/100 000 km
Assemblage	Marysville, Ohio, É-U
Cote d'assurance	n.d.

CHÂSSIS - DONNÉES POUR TECHNOLOGIE TI

Emp/lon/lar/haut	2 650/4 635/1 870/1 655 mm
Coffre	788 à 1 716 litres
Réservoir	68 litres
Nombre coussins sécurité	6
Antipatinage / contrôle stabilité	oui / oui
Suspension avant	indépendante, jambes de force
Suspension arrière	indépendante, multibras
Freins avant / arrière	disque (ABS) / disque (ABS)
Direction	à crémaillère, ass. variable
Diamètre de braquage	11,9 m
Pneus avant / arrière	P235/55R18 / P235/55R18
Poids	1 788 kg
Capacité de remorquage	681 kg (1 501 lb)

COMPOSANTES MÉCANIQUES

RDX

Cylindrée, soupapes, alim.	4L 2,3 litres 16 s turbocompressé
Puissance / Couple	240 chevaux / 260 lb-pi
Tr. base (opt) / rouage base (opt)	A5 / Int
0-100 / 80-120 / 100-0 km/h	8,5 s / 5,9 s / 40,3 m
Type ess. / ville / autoroute	Super / 13,8 / 10,7 l/100 km

DANS LA MÊME CATÉGORIE

Audi Q5, BMW X3, Infiniti EX, Land Rover LR2, Mercedes-Benz Classe GLK, Volvo XC60

DU NOUVEAU EN 2011

Aucun changement majeur

NOS IMPRESSIONS

Agrément de conduite :	■■■■■■■□□□	7/10
Fiabilité :	■■■■■■■■□□	8/10
Sécurité :	■■■■■■■■■□	9/10
Qualités hivernales :	■■■■■■■■□□	8/10
Espace intérieur :	■■■■■■■□□□	7/10
Confort :	■■■■■■■■□□	8/10

www.acura.ca

Plus d'informations dans la section statistiques en dernière partie du Guide

TAILLÉE AU COUTEAU

Le moins que l'on puisse dire c'est que le style de la TL est loin de faire l'unanimité. Dans la refonte vers le modèle actuel, les designers de la marque ont joué à fond la carte des lignes ciselées et ont donné à cette voiture une calandre que l'on peut presque comparer à un bon vieux décapsuleur. Bref, on aime ou on n'aime pas, mais on ne peut pas reprocher à la TL de manquer d'originalité, et ce look taillé au couteau marque un clivage évident avec le style plutôt anonyme du modèle de génération précédente.

Dans cette catégorie des berlines sport de luxe, la TL se démarque en raison de son gabarit supérieur à celui des BMW de Série 3, Audi A4 ou Infiniti G37, la TL étant l'une des plus longues voitures de cette catégorie. Cet élément fait en sorte que la voiture dispose d'un habitacle spacieux et confortable pour quatre personnes, la place médiane arrière étant nettement moins accueillante, ce qui permet à la TL de transporter les passagers en grand confort grâce à des sièges plutôt bien sculptés.

APPRENTISSAGE REQUIS

Prendre contact avec la TL signifie également prendre le temps d'examiner attentivement les fonctions associées à cet océan de boutons localisés sur la console centrale et sur le volant, où l'on en retrouve pas moins de onze. De plus, il est parfois difficile de s'y retrouver parmi les diverses fonctions du système de télématique pour identifier et programmer certains paramètres; le rendu visuel de la carte du système de navigation n'est pas des plus attrayants et l'écran lui-même est parfois difficile à lire dans certaines conditions d'ensoleillement. Et si l'on reste toujours dans la catégorie des éléments pratico-pratiques, précisons que l'ouverture du coffre est très restreinte, ce qui complique inutilement le chargement d'objets de grande taille comme un sac de golf ou une poussette de bébé, par exemple. Aussi, les dossiers des sièges arrière ne sont pas rabattables, seul un passage pour skis étant au programme. Les ingénieurs ont opté pour une rigidité accrue de la caisse et tant pis pour le côté pratique.

LE DYNAMISME APPRÉCIÉ DE L'INTÉGRALE

Le modèle le plus intéressant de la gamme TL est sans contredit celui qui est équipé du rouage intégral, appelé SH-AWD (Super Handling All-Wheel-Drive) par Honda et Acura, d'abord parce qu'il est jumelé à un V6 de 3,7 litres qui développe 305 chevaux, mais surtout parce que la présence de ce rouage a pour effet d'éliminer presque complètement l'effet de couple retrouvé sur le modèle à traction avant, qui est équipé d'un V6 de 3,5 litres dont la puissance est de 280 chevaux. En effet, en accélération franche, la TL à simple traction avant a tendance à louvoyer de gauche à droite en raison du fait que le couple est transmis à l'une des roues avant plus rapidement qu'à l'autre, ce qui est dû à la longueur inégale des demi-arbres de transmission reliant les roues avant au différentiel.

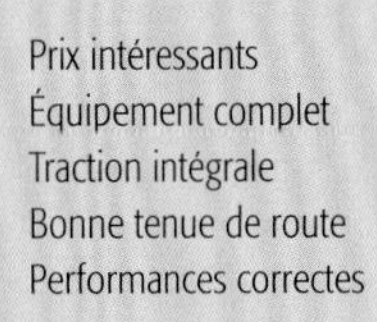

FEU VERT

Prix intéressants
Équipement complet
Traction intégrale
Bonne tenue de route
Performances correctes

FEU ROUGE

Style discutable
Accès étroit au coffre
Effet de couple (traction avant)
Trop de boutons au tableau de bord
Carbure au super

Le choix du modèle à traction intégrale s'impose donc de lui-même non seulement parce qu'il permet de disposer d'une voiture mieux adaptée à l'hiver québécois, mais également parce que le rouage intégral de Honda/Acura autorise une dynamique surprenante en virage, puisqu'il permet de répartir plus de couple aux roues extérieures. Le résultat, c'est que la tenue de route est très bonne en courbes, même si la direction ne donne pas beaucoup de feedback. Voilà qui nous amène également à parler plus en détail de la direction, qui présente un aspect moins intéressant, soit une vague imprécision au centre qui fait en sorte que la voiture a parfois tendance à suivre les inégalités de la route lorsqu'elle roule en ligne droite sur une chaussée creusée de dépressions causées par le passage des véhicules, ce qui requiert certains ajustements pour la tenue de cap et fait en sorte que le conducteur ne sent pas étroitement le contact avec la route. Sur le plan des qualités routières et du dynamisme, la TL à rouage intégral s'accroche donc très bien en virages, mais le comportement de la voiture n'est pas des plus homogènes et ses rivales allemandes que sont les BMW et Audi, de même que la G37 d'Infiniti, lui dament le pion en livrant une conduite plus directe et plus inspirée. La TL se qualifie donc comme une voiture compétente sur le plan de la dynamique, ce qui en fait un bon joueur de deuxième ou troisième trio, mais ce n'est pas le joueur vedette d'une équipe pour faire un parallèle avec une équipe de hockey.

Là où la TL marque des points, c'est au chapitre de la dotation d'équipement de série et sur le rapport qualité/prix qui lui est très favorable. En quelques mots, la TL propose de série certains équipements qui ne sont offerts qu'en option chez la concurrence, et les groupes d'options proposés sur la TL le sont à des prix plus abordables. Voilà une tactique de mise en marché qui a fait ses preuves par le passé.

En guise de conclusion, le choix du rouage intégral s'impose de lui-même et la TL affiche un bon rapport qualité/prix, même si elle ne figure pas dans le top trois de la catégorie pour ce qui est des qualités dynamiques. Reste à savoir si vous êtes d'accord ou non avec le style ciselé de la carrosserie.

Gabriel Gélinas

PHOTOS: MARC LACHAPELLE

ACURA TL

Catégorie	Berline
Échelle de prix	39 990 $ à 44 490 $ (2010)
Garanties	4 ans/80 000 km, 5 ans/100 000 km
Assemblage	Marysville, Ohio, É U
Cote d'assurance	pauvre

CHÂSSIS - DONNÉES POUR BASE AWD

Emp/lon/lar/haut	2 775/4 966/2 118/1 452 mm
Coffre	371 litres
Réservoir	70 litres
Nombre coussins sécurité	6
Antipatinage / contrôle stabilité	oui / oui
Suspension avant	indépendante, double triangulation
Suspension arrière	indépendante, multibras
Freins avant / arrière	disque (ABS) / disque (ABS)
Direction	à crémaillère, ass. variable
Diamètre de braquage	12,1 m
Pneus avant / arrière	P245/45R18 / P245/45R18
Poids	1 797 kg
Capacité de remorquage	n.d.

COMPOSANTES MÉCANIQUES

Base

Cylindrée, soupapes, alim.	V6 3,5 litres 24 s atmos.
Puissance / Couple	280 chevaux / 254 lb-pi
Tr. base (opt) / rouage base (opt)	A5 / Tr
0-100 / 80-120 / 100-0 km/h	7,1 s / 5,8 s / 39,8 m
Type ess. / ville / autoroute	Super / 11,6 / 7,5 l/100 km

Base AWD

Cylindrée, soupapes, alim.	V6 3,7 litres 24 s atmos.
Puissance / Couple	305 chevaux / 273 lb-pi
Tr. base (opt) / rouage base (opt)	A5 (M6) / Int
0-100 / 80-120 / 100-0 km/h	6,8 s / 6,0 s / 38,8 m
Type ess. / ville / autoroute	Super / 12,3 / 8,1 l/100 km

DANS LA MÊME CATÉGORIE

Audi A4, BMW Série 3, Cadillac CTS, Infiniti G, Lexus IS, Lincoln MKZ, Volvo S60

DU NOUVEAU EN 2011

Aucun changement majeur

NOS IMPRESSIONS

Agrément de conduite :	9/10
Fiabilité :	8/10
Sécurité :	10/10
Qualités hivernales :	9/10
Espace intérieur :	8/10
Confort :	8/10

www.acura.ca

Plus d'informations dans la section statistiques en dernière partie du Guide

MOINS, C'EST BIEN MIEUX

Décidément, la berline intermédiaire d'Acura, la TSX, a décidé de ne plus jouer les seconds violons. Non contente d'offrir un des meilleurs quatre cylindres de l'industrie, la concurrente des BMW Série 3, Audi A4, Cadillac CTS et de la Mercedes-Benz Classe C passe en mode attaque ! L'an dernier, elle adoptait un V6 et cette année, une version familiale. Offrir plusieurs modèles à partir d'une même plate-forme, une approche de plus en plus populaire, a le mérite de rejoindre un plus large public pour un coût de développement assez bas. Parlez-en à General Motors... Mais ça, c'est une autre histoire !

L'Acura TSX, cette Honda Accord européenne, a été entièrement revue en 2009. On ne peut pas dire que ses lignes ciselées et, surtout, sa grille de calandre, moins tape-à-l'œil que sur certains autres modèles Acura, sont passées inaperçues !

Si la carrosserie s'attire quelques remarques blessantes, l'habitacle n'a jamais semé le doute tant par ses dimensions généreuses et son équipement très complet, que par la qualité des matériaux et de leur finition. Certes, on retrouve beaucoup trop de boutons au tableau de bord et il s'agit d'une caractéristique qui afflige pratiquement toutes les Acura. Les sièges avant s'avèrent très confortables et la position de conduite se trouve en criant « ci » (même pas le temps de crier « ciseau » au complet !). Les places arrière sont difficiles d'accès à cause de l'ouverture très étroite des portières et les grands pieds se retrouvent invariablement coincés entre la base du siège et le montant de la porte. Quant au coffre, il est passablement grand et son ouverture est suffisamment importante.

LE QUATRE CYLINDRES AVANT LE V6

Jusqu'à l'an dernier, un seul moteur était proposé, soit un quatre cylindres de 2,4 litres associé à une transmission manuelle à six rapports ou à une automatique à cinq rapports. Ce moteur a du souffle et, comme tous les moteurs Honda/Acura, il apprécie les hauts régimes. Ses prestations sont tout à fait honnêtes, tout comme celles des deux boîtes. La manuelle est agréable à manier et la course du levier est précise, tandis que l'automatique passe les rapports au bon moment. Elle possède un mode Sport qui, lorsqu'il est engagé, fait passer les révolutions du moteur de 2 000 tours/minute (à 100 km/h) à 3 800, ce qui donne à peu près l'impression d'injecter une dose de nitro dans le moteur !

Depuis l'automne 2009, la TSX, sans doute pour attirer un public américain encore très entiché de pouces cubes, peut recevoir le V6 de 3,5 litres de sa grande sœur, la TL. Ce moteur est très puissant et il permet à la voiture d'afficher des chronos fort intéressants. Cependant, et malgré tout le respect que je dois au V6, le quatre cylindres demeure le meilleur choix pour la TSX.

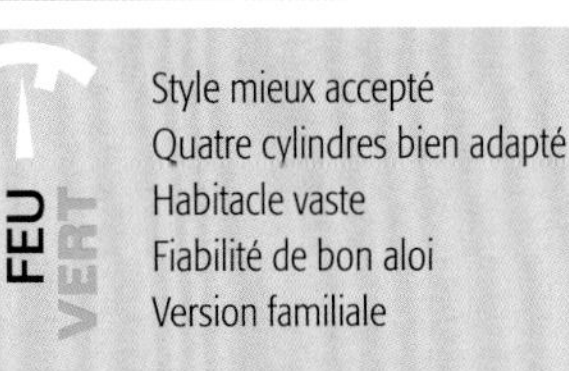

FEU VERT

Style mieux accepté
Quatre cylindres bien adapté
Habitacle vaste
Fiabilité de bon aloi
Version familiale

FEU ROUGE

Style encore «trop» pour certains
Moteur V6 plus ou moins utile
Coffre de la Sport Wagon peu grand
Places arrière difficiles d'accès
Confusion des modèles Acura/Honda

La TSX, peu importe la version, est une traction, ce qui implique que seules les roues avant sont motrices. Et les 280 chevaux du V6 représentent une écurie difficile à contenir pour une traction. Si les réactions de la voiture dotée du quatre cylindres sont bien équilibrées (on sent un peu de sous-virage, mais très peu d'effet de couple dans le volant en accélération), celles du V6 sont un peu plus brusques. Quand on pousse la bête, il faut se battre davantage avec le volant pour pouvoir contenir les chevaux récalcitrants. C'est ce qu'on appelle l'effet de couple. Par contre, ce n'est pas aussi marqué que sur une Nissan Maxima, par exemple, et les ingénieurs d'Acura ont quand même fait du bon boulot compte tenu des limites dictées par la traction. Ce V6 ne peut être jumelé qu'avec la transmission automatique à cinq rapports. Elle a beau fonctionner à merveille, un sixième rapport ne serait pas de refus.

UNE PETITE NOUVELLE

La grande nouvelle de 2011 est la version familiale, appelée Sport Wagon chez Acura. Cette Honda Accord Tourer européenne est passablement bien tournée et son côté utile en ravira sans doute plusieurs. Il est difficile de ne pas faire le rapprochement avec la Honda Accord Crosstour offerte en Amérique depuis quelques mois, mais il n'y aurait, semble-t-il, aucun lien. La TSX Sport Wagon, même si elle est appelée à transporter de plus lourdes charges que la berline, n'a droit qu'au quatre cylindres, du moins au début. Curieusement, lors de son lancement au Salon de l'auto de New York en mars dernier, Acura n'avait livré absolument aucun détail sur ses capacités de chargement, élément plutôt important pour une familiale! Vérification faite sur le site de Honda France, la version européenne peut engouffrer entre 406 et 1 183 litres selon que les dossiers soient relevés ou abaissés. Avec de tels chiffres, on comprend mieux le silence d'Acura... La Accord Crosstour, moins chère, engouffre entre 728 et 1 453 litres...

S'il est un domaine où le duo Honda/Acura devrait prendre des cours, c'est au niveau du marketing. La TSX ne reçoit peut-être pas le rouage intégral SH-AWD de sa grande sœur TL, mais elle en reçoit le V6 tout en commandant quelques milliers de dollars en moins. D'un autre côté, la Honda Accord Crosstour n'affiche pas d'écusson prestigieux sur sa calandre et s'avère moins agréable à conduire, mais son coffre est plus logeable et dans sa version à traction, elle coûte plusieurs milliers de dollars en moins...

Alain Morin

PHOTOS : ALAIN MORIN

Catégorie	Berline
Échelle de prix	32 900 $ à 42 790 $ (2010)
Garanties	4 ans/80 000 km, 5 ans/100 000 km
Assemblage	Saitama, Japon
Cote d'assurance	pauvre

CHÂSSIS - DONNÉES POUR V6 TECHNOLOGIE

Emp/lon/lar/haut	2 705/4 726/1 840/1 440 mm
Coffre	357 litres
Réservoir	70 litres
Nombre coussins sécurité	6
Antipatinage / contrôle stabilité	oui / oui
Suspension avant	indépendante, double triangulation
Suspension arrière	indépendante, double triangulation
Freins avant / arrière	disque (ABS) / disque (ABS)
Direction	à crémaillère, ass. variable
Diamètre de braquage	n.d.
Pneus avant / arrière	P235/45R18 / P235/45R18
Poids	1 669 kg
Capacité de remorquage	450 kg (992 lb)

COMPOSANTES MÉCANIQUES

TSX

Cylindrée, soupapes, alim.	4L 2,4 litres 16 s atmos.
Puissance / Couple	201 chevaux / 172 lb-pi
Tr. base (opt) / rouage base (opt)	M6 (A5) / Tr
0-100 / 80-120 / 100-0 km/h	8,0 s / 6,3 s / 43,8 m
Type ess. / ville / autoroute	Super / 10,5 / 7 l/100 km

TSX V6

Cylindrée, soupapes, alim.	V6 3,5 litres 24 s atmos.
Puissance / Couple	280 chevaux / 254 lb-pi
Tr. base (opt) / rouage base (opt)	A5 / Tr
0-100 / 80-120 / 100-0 km/h	7,2 s / 5,4 s / 43,8 m
Type ess. / ville / autoroute	Super / 11,3 / 7,4 l/100 km

DANS LA MÊME CATÉGORIE

Audi A3, Audi A4, BMW Série 3, Lexus IS, Mercedes-Benz Classe C, Volvo S40

DU NOUVEAU EN 2011

Version familiale Sport Wagon sera dévoilée en cours d'année

NOS IMPRESSIONS

Agrément de conduite:	■■■■■■□□□□	6/10
Fiabilité:	■■■■■■■■□□	8/10
Sécurité:	■■■■■■■■■■	10/10
Qualités hivernales:	■■■■■■■□□□	7/10
Espace intérieur:	■■■■■■■□□□	7/10
Confort:	■■■■■■■□□□	7/10

www.acura.ca

Plus d'informations dans la section statistiques en dernière partie du Guide

L'IMAGE AVANT TOUT

Acura a choisi de s'inspirer de BMW et de son X6 décliné du X5, pour créer le nouveau ZDX à partir du sport-utilitaire MDX. Présenté comme un coupé à quatre portes et comme le véhicule le plus stylé de la marque Acura à ce jour, le ZDX s'inscrit dans le créneau plus typé de ces véhicules qui veulent offrir le meilleur de deux mondes, soit le côté pratique et polyvalent d'un utilitaire ainsi que le style plus expressif et les performances plus relevées d'un coupé sport. La mission est-elle accomplie? Pas vraiment...

Côté style, il est clair que le ZDX se démarque complètement des autres modèles Acura, même si la calandre en forme de décapsuleur assure la filiation avec le reste de la gamme. Dessinée au nouveau studio de design américain d'Acura localisé à Los Angeles, la forme particulière du ZDX est l'œuvre de la designer Michelle Christensen qui a réalisé la première ébauche de ce véhicule à l'âge de 25 ans, tout juste après sa graduation du Art Center College of Design à Pasadena en Californie. Comparé au BMW X6, le ZDX affiche une silhouette nettement moins sportive et plus féminine. On aime ou on n'aime pas mais ce véhicule ne laisse assurément pas indifférent.

LES PASSAGERS ARRIÈRE EN TROISIÈME CLASSE

Le design de l'habitacle a été conçu afin de prioriser d'abord le confort du conducteur et du passager avant ainsi que l'aménagement de l'espace de chargement, les places arrière étant reléguées au troisième rang des priorités. Les occupants de la première rangée se retrouvent donc dans un environnement plutôt luxueux, comme en témoigne la longue bande en cuir qui ceinture le conducteur et le passager, ainsi que le toit panoramique entièrement réalisé en verre. Même l'espace de chargement a été aménagé avec un grand souci du détail, puisque le tapis est bouclé et que le compartiment de rangement dissimulé sous le plancher est équipé à la fois de tiges hydrauliques et d'une poignée en chrome ! Mais en dépit de ce luxe, cet espace est plutôt restreint, le volume de chargement du ZDX étant inférieur à celui de la Honda Fit et comme le seuil du coffre est très élevé cela vient compliquer quelque peu le chargement. Autre considération pratique, le pneu de secours est rangé sous le véhicule. Prévoyez donc de transporter une paire de gants de travail pour pouvoir le déloger de son emplacement en cas de besoin. L'accès aux places arrière est sérieusement compromis par l'étroitesse des portières ainsi que par la ligne de toit, aussi, les passagers doivent-ils prendre garde afin de ne pas se cogner la tête sur le toit en montant à bord et ne pas salir leurs vêtements sur le rebord de la portière. En quelques mots, le ZDX a d'abord été conçu pour deux personnes qui partent en escapade pour un long week-end, et non pas pour rivaliser avec un VUS typique.

UNE MÉCANIQUE IDENTIQUE AU MDX

Sur le plan mécanique, le ZDX est virtuellement identique au MDX avec le moteur V6 de 300 chevaux et 270 livres-pied de couple

FEU VERT

Style distinctif
Places avant confortables
Rouage intégral performant
Équipement complet

FEU ROUGE

Accès difficile et espace limité aux places arrière
Volume de chargement limité
Poids élevé
Carbure au super

jumelé à la nouvelle boîte automatique à six rapports qui comporte également des paliers de changement de vitesse au volant. En conduite normale, la motorisation s'acquitte raisonnablement bien de sa tâche, les changements de rapports étant à peine perceptibles et la sonorité du moteur demeurant feutrée. C'est lorsque l'on pousse le ZDX en conduite sportive que ses limites deviennent plus évidentes. D'abord, le véhicule pèse plus de 2000 kilos ce qui fait que les accélérations franches ne sont pas très satisfaisantes, le V6 ayant un peu de peine à déplacer toute cette masse avec aplomb. Ensuite, la boîte automatique réagit avec un certain délai lors du passage des rapports en mode manuel. Bref, il s'agit ici d'une puissance adéquate, mais sans plus. Pour ce qui est de la consommation, nous avons enregistré une moyenne frisant les 14 litres aux 100 kilomètres, et précisons que le ZDX demande du carburant super…

Pour ce qui est du comportement routier, il est clair que les concepteurs ont mis l'accent sur le confort et non sur les performances. La direction est surassistée et plutôt vague et la tenue de route est limitée par les pneus Michelin toutes saisons ainsi que par l'intervention hâtive du système de contrôle électronique de stabilité. Le système SH-AWD permet de contrer le sous-virage en conduite sportive, mais le ZDX est nettement moins sportif que le BMW X6 qui est dans une tout autre ligue. Acura a choisi de concevoir un véhicule pour ceux qui ne sont pas du tout intéressés par les performances, mais qui souhaitent disposer d'un véhicule confortable (pour deux) et capable de les mener à bon port, peu importe les conditions météorologiques, grâce à son rouage intégral.

Comme c'est souvent le cas pour les véhicules de la marque, l'équipement est complet et la sélection du groupe d'options Technologie permet d'obtenir d'une chaîne stéréo ambiophonique avec 10 haut-parleurs, de l'entrée sans clé, et d'un système de navigation qui n'est cependant pas particulièrement efficace puisque plusieurs rues de localités secondaires ne sont même pas affichées.

En résumé, le ZDX se veut un véhicule au style accrocheur qui plaira aux conducteurs souhaitant se démarquer et qui n'ont pas besoin du côté pratique normalement associé aux VUS. Il s'agit donc d'un autre de ces véhicules de niche qui s'adresse à un créneau très précis et très limité de la clientèle.

Gabriel Gélinas

PHOTOS : ALAIN MORIN

ACURA ZDX

Catégorie	Multisegment
Échelle de prix	55 990 $ à 59 590 $ (2010)
Garanties	4 ans/80 000 km, 5 ans/100 000 km
Assemblage	Alliston, Ontario, Canada
Cote d'assurance	n.d.

CHÂSSIS - DONNÉES POUR TECHNOLOGIE

Emp/lon/lar/haut	2 750/4 887/1 993/1 596 mm
Coffre	745 à 1 580 litres
Réservoir	80 litres
Nombre coussins sécurité	6
Antipatinage / contrôle stabilité	oui / oui
Suspension avant	indépendante, jambes de force
Suspension arrière	indépendante, multibras
Freins avant / arrière	disque (ABS) / disque (ABS)
Direction	à crémaillère, ass. variable
Diamètre de braquage	11,7 m
Pneus avant / arrière	P555/50R19 / P255/50R19
Poids	2 016 kg
Capacité de remorquage	680 kg (1 499 lb)

COMPOSANTES MÉCANIQUES

ZDX

Cylindrée, soupapes, alim.	V6 3,7 litres 24 s atmos.
Puissance / Couple	300 chevaux / 270 lb-pi
Tr. base (opt) / rouage base (opt)	A6 / Int
0-100 / 80-120 / 100-0 km/h	7,6 s / 5,9 s / 40,5 m
Type ess. / ville / autoroute	Super / 12,7 / 8,8 l/100 km

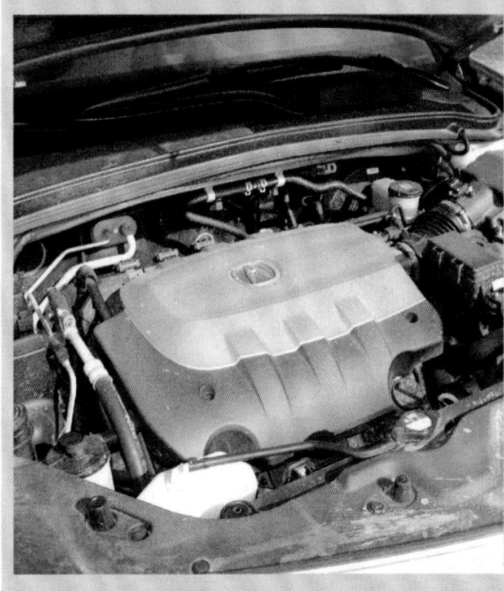

DANS LA MÊME CATÉGORIE

BMW X6, Cadillac SRX, Infiniti FX, Volvo XC70

DU NOUVEAU EN 2011

Aucun changement majeur

NOS IMPRESSIONS

Agrément de conduite :	7/10
Fiabilité :	Nouveau modèle
Sécurité :	10/10
Qualités hivernales :	9/10
Espace intérieur :	6/10
Confort :	9/10

www.acura.ca

Plus d'informations dans la section statistiques en dernière partie du Guide

L'ÉVOLUTION DU DESIGN

Lancée en 2003, la DB9 continue d'évoluer sur les plans du design et de la technique, comme en témoignent les subtiles retouches apportées à l'élégante GT britannique pour 2011. Pour l'occasion, la voiture reçoit un nouveau pare-choc avant, des bas de caisse reprofilés, de même qu'une calandre légèrement retouchée.

Ces changements relativement mineurs ne troublent pas l'élégance d'une grande qualité propre à la marque, mais il faut reconnaître qu'il est parfois difficile de différencier une DB9 d'une DBS ou même d'une Vantage, tellement toutes ces voitures en viennent à se ressembler. Voilà qui sera sans doute le lot d'Aston Martin pour les années à venir, car la marque anglaise n'a plus accès aux ressources de Ford pour développer de nouveaux modèles. Ceci obligera les concepteurs à peaufiner ce qui existe déjà, tant sur le plan du design que de la technologie, le développement de tous nouveaux modèles étant devenu une proposition très coûteuse.

UNE DYNAMIQUE REHAUSSÉE D'UN CRAN

Pour 2011, la DB9 reçoit une suspension pilotée électroniquement faisant appel à des amortisseurs Bilstein, soit la même configuration utilisée par la DBS, ainsi que par la plus récente Rapide, et qui permet la sélection des modes Sport ou Confort, histoire d'adapter le comportement routier de la voiture aux conditions routières ou à la volonté du conducteur.

La DB9 est beaucoup plus à l'aise sur les routes balisées que dans l'environnement plus éprouvant d'un autodrome, comme j'ai pu le constater en bouclant plusieurs tours du circuit Mont Tremblant. Comparativement à d'authentiques sportives mieux adaptées à la piste, la DB9 est plutôt lourde puisqu'elle

pèse 1 800 kilos, ce qui signifie que les freins sont très sollicités et que le roulis en virages devient souvent très marqué. De plus, la boîte automatique avec paliers de changement de vitesse au volant avait tendance à surchauffer, ce qui entravait alors la sélection des rapports inférieurs. Malgré ces impairs, c'est un véritable plaisir d'entendre le V12 tourner à haut régime et de contempler la somptuosité de l'habitacle. Le cuir est tout simplement magnifique, les appliques de bois sont de bon ton et l'effet produit est splendide. Fait à noter, la DB9 à boîte automatique est dépourvue d'un traditionnel levier de vitesse, la sélection du mode « Drive » ou de la marche arrière se faisant par la pression d'une touche sur la console centrale, alors que le passage des rapports en mode manuel se fait au moyen des commandes localisées sur le volant. Voilà qui donne une touche d'exotisme de plus à l'environnement princier de l'habitacle.

La DBS poursuit sa route en coupé et en cabriolet pour 2011 et continue de se distinguer, par rapport à la DB9, par son allure plus typée ainsi que par son V12 dont la puissance est chiffrée à 510 chevaux de même que par sa boîte manuelle à six vitesses. La DBS fait également usage d'éléments de carrosserie réalisés en

FEU VERT

- Puissance du V12
- Style intemporel
- Freins puissants (DBS)
- Performances relevées (DBS)

FEU ROUGE

- Fiabilité aléatoire
- Visibilité vers l'arrière
- Volume du coffre
- Diffusion limitée

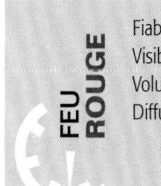

fibre de carbone, ce qui a permis à la marque de développer une certaine expertise dans la confection de pièces faites de ce matériau plus léger. Dans ce créneau très exclusif, la DBS se retrouve en concurrence directe avec la Maserati Gran Turismo, ainsi que la Ferrari GTB Fiorano qui dame sérieusement le pion à l'anglaise puisqu'elle est à la fois plus légère et plus puissante grâce à son V12 développant 612 chevaux.

LA ONE-77

Après avoir renoué avec la compétition aux 24 Heures du Mans, Aston Martin fait le pari de se lancer dans la production d'un modèle encore plus exclusif que ses Vantage ou autres DB9 et DBS, puisque seulement 77 de ces voitures seront construites sur une période de deux ans. D'autant plus qu'elles seront beaucoup plus chères, puisque le prix a été fixé à 1,2 millions de livres sterling... Voici donc la One-77, dont l'arrivée à été annoncée par la voiture concept qui a remporté les honneurs du concours d'élégance de Villa d'Este, une compétition de design qui est justement réservée exclusivement aux voitures concept et aux prototypes.

Stylisée par Marek Reichman, à qui l'on doit la refonte du Range Rover en 2003, la One-77 se distingue des autres modèles de cette marque par l'adoption de nouveaux éléments de design, notamment la présence d'ailes avant qui sont plus élevées que la ligne du capot ou encore, les « hanches » très prononcées et l'intégration d'un immense diffuseur à l'arrière qui fait presque toute la largeur de la voiture. Sur le plan technique, la One-77 se démarque par sa structure réalisée en fibre de carbone, ce qui permet à la voiture de ne peser que 1 500 kilos tout en étant une fois et demie plus rigide que les autres voitures de ce constructeur automobile. Aussi bien dire que la One-77 est presque une voiture de course déguisée en GT, puisque sa vitesse de pointe est chiffrée à 220 milles à l'heure (354 kilomètres/heure).

Davantage de type GT que sportives, les DB9 et DBS continuent de jouer la carte du style avec une élégance remarquable et un pedigree de renom. On aimerait seulement pouvoir compter sur une fiabilité plus relevée. Quant à la One-77, parions qu'Aston Martin réussira sans trop de problèmes à trouver 77 clients très fortunés qui voudront s'afficher dans la plus performante et la plus exclusive des voitures de cette marque.

Gabriel Gélinas

One-77

PHOTOS: ASTON MARTIN

Catégorie	Cabriolet, Coupé
Échelle de prix	206 765 $ à 327 195 $
Garanties	3 ans/illimité, 3 ans/illimité
Assemblage	Gaydon, Warwickshire, Angleterre
Cote d'assurance	n.d.

CHÂSSIS - DONNÉES POUR DBS COUPE

Emp/lon/lar/haut	2 740/4 721/1 905/1 280 mm
Coffre	186 litres
Réservoir	78 litres
Nombre coussins sécurité	4
Antipatinage / contrôle stabilité	oui / oui
Suspension avant	indépendante, double triangulation
Suspension arrière	indépendante, double triangulation
Freins avant / arrière	disque (ABS) / disque (ABS)
Direction	à crémaillère, assistée
Diamètre de braquage	11,5 m
Pneus avant / arrière	P245/35ZR20 / P295/30ZR20
Poids	1 695 kg
Capacité de remorquage	n.d.

COMPOSANTES MÉCANIQUES

DBS, DBS Volante

Cylindrée, soupapes, alim.	V12 6,0 litres 48 s atmos.
Puissance / Couple	510 chevaux / 420 lb-pi
Tr. base (opt) / rouage base (opt)	M6 (A6) / Prop
0-100 / 80-120 / 100-0 km/h	4,3 s / 4,0 s / 37,0 m
Type ess. / ville / autoroute	Super / 18,1 / 11,2 l/100 km

DB9, DB9 Volante

Cylindrée, soupapes, alim.	V12 6,0 litres 48 s atmos.
Puissance / Couple	470 chevaux / 443 lb-pi
Tr. base (opt) / rouage base (opt)	M6 (A6) / Prop
0-100 / 80-120 / 100-0 km/h	4,8 s / 4,3 s / 37,0 m
Type ess. / ville / autoroute	Super / 16,2 / 10,1 l/100 km

One-77

Cylindrée, soupapes, alim.	V12 7,3 litres 48 s atmos.
Puissance / Couple	environ 700 ch
Tr. base (opt) / rouage base (opt)	A6 / Prop
0-100 / 80-120 / 100-0 km/h	3,7 s / 3,0 s (est) / 34,0 m (est)
Type ess. / ville / autoroute	Super / n.d.

DANS LA MÊME CATÉGORIE

Audi R8, Bentley Continental, Ferrari 599, Ferrari 612 Scaglietti, Lamborghini Murciélago, Mercedes-Benz SLS

DU NOUVEAU EN 2011

Nouveau modèle One-77

NOS IMPRESSIONS

Agrément de conduite :	■■■■■■■□□□	7/10
Fiabilité :	■■■■■■□□□□	6/10
Sécurité :	■■■■■■■■□□	8/10
Qualités hivernales :	n.d.	
Espace intérieur :	■■■■■■□□□□	6/10
Confort :	■■■■■■■■□□	8/10

www.astonmartin.com

Plus d'informations dans la section statistiques en dernière partie du Guide

MINIMUM 420, MAXIMUM 510

C'est une intéressante proposition que fait Aston Martin pour la cadette de la marque, à savoir d'en offrir deux versions animées respectivement par le V8 de 420 chevaux, qui était précédemment le seul moteur offert pour la Vantage, ainsi que par le V12 de 510 chevaux emprunté à la DBS. Équipée de ce moteur plus puissant, la Vantage se permet même de porter ombrage aux DB9 et DBS.

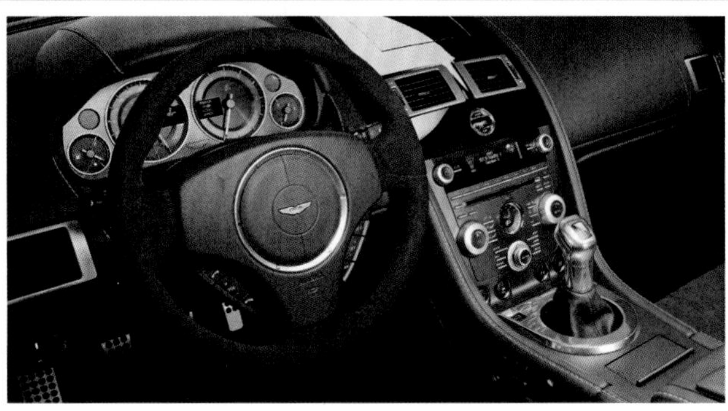

Pour 2011, Aston Martin remet la Vantage au goût du jour avec une édition spéciale appelée N420, qui a été créée afin de commémorer sa participation aux 24 Heures du Nürburgring. Le V8 demeure inchangé, mais son échappement a été modifié pour lui conférer une signature vocale encore plus frappante, et la voiture reçoit en dotation de série l'ensemble sport comprenant des suspensions plus fermes. La « plastique » de la N420 a également fait l'objet de subtiles retouches, puisqu'elle reçoit des bas de caisse ainsi qu'un bouclier avant reprofilés, de même que des roues exclusives à cette édition spéciale. De plus, l'ouverture de la calandre est cerclée d'une mince bande de couleur contrastante, tout comme sur les modèles de la marque, lorsque l'acheteur opte pour une peinture provenant du catalogue Race Collection.

L'ÉPREUVE DU CIRCUIT

Sur le Circuit Mont-Tremblant, la V8 Vantage n'est pas aussi rapide qu'une Porsche 911, l'Allemande étant plus légère, ce qui a une incidence directe sur les performances en piste, le poids plus élevé de la Britannique affectant les distances de freinage, la vitesse de passage en virage de même que les ré-accélérations en sortie de courbe. De plus, la boîte *Sportshift* avec paliers de commande au volant ne dispose que d'un seul embrayage, plutôt que deux comme c'est de plus en plus la norme, et cette boîte ne permet pas le passage au rapport supérieur si l'ordinateur détecte que l'angle du volant est encore trop prononcé en sortie de virage. Aussi, la V8 Vantage exige une bonne pression sur la pédale de frein avant que l'on ne ressente l'entrée en action des étriers de marque Brembo.

LA PLUS PETITE SPORTIVE À MOTEUR V12 AU MONDE

Singulière distinction que celle qui est accordée à la V12 Vantage, soit celle de la plus petite sportive à moteur V12 au monde en raison de ses dimensions compactes, puisque sa longueur n'est que de 4,38 mètres. C'est donc un véritable tour de force qui a été accompli par les ingénieurs qui ont réussi à loger le le moulin de la DBS dans le compartiment moteur de la Vantage, puisqu'ils ont dû revoir les systèmes de lubrification et de refroidissement du, tout en optant pour un alternateur plus compact afin de réussir cet exploit. Comme le rapport poids/puissance de la V12 Vantage est plus favorable que celui de la DBS, la cadette de la marque s'avère plus rapide, quoique de peu, en accélération, et la présence du V12 a pour effet de littéralement transformer le comportement de la Vantage, qui offre alors un dynamisme épatant, en raison du couple nettement supérieur du moteur plus puissant.

Catégorie	Coupé, *Roadster*
Échelle de prix	137 495 $ à 183 000 $
Garanties	3 ans/illimité, 3 ans/illimité
Assemblage	Newport Pagnell, Angleterre
Cote d'assurance	n.d.

FEU VERT
- Silhouette superbe
- Exclusivité assurée
- Sonorité envoûtante
- Disponibilité du V12

FEU ROUGE
- Fiabilité aléatoire
- Poids élevé
- Visibilité vers l'arrière
- Transmission peu concurrentielle

La boîte est une manuelle à six vitesses, développée par l'équipementier italien Graziano, dont l'engagement est rapide et précis, mais le pédalier de la Vantage n'est pas disposé de façon idéale pour le talon-pointe, ce qui pose problème en conduite sportive. Pour ce qui est des freins, les ingénieurs d'Aston Martin sont allés puiser dans le stock de pièces de la DBS pour équiper la V12 Vantage de freins en céramique de carbone.

Qu'il s'agisse de la Vantage à moteur V8 ou V12, l'ouverture des portières se fait de façon singulière puisqu'elles pivotent légèrement vers le haut, comme c'est le cas sur les autres modèles de la marque, et la cadette des Aston Martin partage aussi plusieurs éléments avec la DB9, dans le but de réduire les coûts de fabrication. Un modèle roadster à moteur V8 est également offert, mais la capacité de son coffre est réduite de moitié par rapport au coupé et ne se chiffre qu'à 144 litres. De plus, le modèle roadster doit composer avec un gain de poids de l'ordre de 80 kilos puisque certains éléments de structure ont dû être ajoutés à la voiture afin de la rigidifier en raison de la perte du toit.

Du côté de l'habitacle, on note la présentation soignée et le souci du détail, mais la présence d'un écran de navigation qui se soulève pour qu'on puisse l'utiliser détonne un peu dans cet environnement cossu. Aussi, les Aston Martin ne démarrent pas au moyen d'une simple clé, mais plutôt à l'aide d'une télécommande faite de verre ainsi que d'acier inoxydable, désignée par Aston Martin avec les termes plutôt ronflants de *Emotion Control Unit*, que l'on doit insérer dans la planche de bord puis pousser pour mettre le moteur en marche. Quand on vend ses voitures à un prix aussi élevé, même la clé se doit de faire son cinéma…

Superbement dessinée, la Vantage partage une filiation évidente avec les DB9 et DBS, ce qui en fait l'un des sportives les plus élégantes actuellement, et l'arrivée du moteur V12 lui permet de jouer le grand jeu avec un dynamisme plus relevé. Le choix d'une Aston Martin confère à l'acheteur une exclusivité assurée, en raison de la production très limitée de la marque britannique, et le style intemporel de ces voitures ne laisse personne indifférent. Mais comme toujours avec ces belles Anglaises, leur caractère à part et leur fiabilité n'est pas toujours au rendez-vous. Mais pour plusieurs, c'est ce qui fait leur charme.

Gabriel Gélinas

PHOTOS : ASTON MARTIN

CHÂSSIS - DONNÉES POUR V8 COUPÉ

Emp/lon/lar/haut	2 600/4 380/1 865/1 255 mm
Coffre	300 litres
Réservoir	80 litres
Nombre coussins sécurité	4
Antipatinage / contrôle stabilité	oui / oui
Suspension avant	indépendante, double triangulation
Suspension arrière	indépendante, double triangulation
Freins avant / arrière	disque (ABS) / disque (ABS)
Direction	à crémaillère, assistée
Diamètre de braquage	11,1 m
Pneus avant / arrière	P235/40ZR19 / P275/35ZR19
Poids	1 630 kg
Capacité de remorquage	n.d.

COMPOSANTES MÉCANIQUES

V8 Coupé , V8 Roadster

Cylindrée, soupapes, alim.	V8 4,3 litres 32 s atmos.
Puissance / Couple	420 chevaux / 346 lb-pi
Tr. base (opt) / rouage base (opt)	M6 (seq) / Prop
0-100 / 80-120 / 100-0 km/h	5,0 s / 4,5 s / 39,0 m
Type ess. / ville / autoroute	Super / 17,4 / 10,8 l/100 km

V12 Coupé

Cylindrée, soupapes, alim.	V12 6,0 litres 48 s atmos.
Puissance / Couple	510 chevaux / 420 lb-pi
Tr. base (opt) / rouage base (opt)	M6 / Prop
0-100 / 80-120 / 100-0 km/h	4,2 s / 3,8 s / 39,0 m
Type ess. / ville / autoroute	Super / 17,8 / n.d. l/100 km

DANS LA MÊME CATÉGORIE

Audi R8, BMW Série 6, Chevrolet Corvette, Dodge Viper, Ferrari California, Jaguar XK, Lamborghini Gallardo, Maserati Gran Turismo, Mercedes-Benz Classe SL, Nissan GT-R, Porsche 911

DU NOUVEAU EN 2011

Aucun changement majeur

NOS IMPRESSIONS

Agrément de conduite :	■■■■■■■□□□	7/10
Fiabilité :	■■■■■■□□□□	6/10
Sécurité :	■■■■■■■□□□	7/10
Qualités hivernales :	n.d.	
Espace intérieur :	■■■■■■□□□□	6/10
Confort :	■■■■■■□□□□	6/10

www.astonmartin.com

Plus d'informations dans la section statistiques en dernière partie du Guide

UNE BELLE ANGLAISE

On a beau écrire quoi que ce soit sur les voitures Aston Martin, le fait demeure qu'elles sont d'une grande élégance et que leur style est toujours unique. Le premier modèle cinq portes, quatre places produit par ce constructeur britannique a enfin été dévoilé au Salon de l'auto de Francfort en septembre 2009. Le kiosque Aston Martin était situé dans le même pavillon que celui de Ferrari, Lamborghini et autres ténors chez les grandes sportives. Malgré l'espace restreint, une foule de gens s'était agglutinée autour de la Rapide et son élégance a fait l'unanimité.

Comme il s'agissait de la première voiture lancée depuis l'entrée en fonction de la nouvelle administration de ce petit constructeur, la grande question n'était pas son élégance et les aménagements de l'habitacle, mais ses performances sur la route. Après tout, Porsche et sa Panamera se révélaient un obstacle de taille.

LA TRADITION RESPECTÉE

Ce n'est pas une mince tâche pour un constructeur qui n'a produit que des coupés de dessiner une version cinq portes d'une belle élégance. Force est d'admettre que c'est réussi et il semble que le verdict soit en faveur de la Britannique par rapport à la Porsche Panamera dont la silhouette est un peu moins affûtée. Mais si vous trouvez que la Porsche est plus jolie, à vous de choisir. Le secret de la Rapide réside dans sa grille de calandre traditionnelle et les phares en forme d'amande montés sur les ailes. On y trouve également des diodes électroluminescentes sur le long de ces optiques qui servent de phare de jour. De plus, une sortie d'air chromée coiffant la partie supérieure arrière des ailes avant se prolonge par une bande chromée sur la portière, ce qui donne beaucoup de dynamisme à la silhouette. Il faut également mentionner la présence de petits volets extracteurs d'air sur le capot.

Les constructeurs britanniques de voitures de luxe sont réputés pour leurs habitacles très cossus. Comme il se doit, la Rapide ne fait pas exception à la règle. Les cuirs les plus fins sont omniprésents, tandis que la console centrale est garnie de bois exotique, du noyer plus précisément. Et comme les Britanniques ne font rien comme les autres, le bouton de contact est placé en plein centre de la partie médiane de cette console. À sa gauche se trouve le bouton Park tandis que celui le plus près du contact est la marche arrière. Puis à droite du contact, il y a le Neutre et le bouton D des vitesses avant. Heureusement, il est possible de passer les rapports à l'aide des palets fixés non pas sur le volant, mais sur la colonne de direction. Le volant, cependant, pourrait avoir une présentation moins bourgeoise et un tantinet plus sportive.

Bien que cette voiture soit plus longue que la Porsche Panamera, l'habitabilité est inférieure à celle-ci. La console placée entre les sièges est très large de sorte que l'espace se veut assez limité, tandis que le dégagement pour les jambes est faible. Soulignons

FEU VERT
- Silhouette remarquable
- Moteur V12
- Bonnes performances
- Habitacle luxueux
- Bonne routière

FEU ROUGE
- Prix corsé
- Fiabilité inconnue
- Visibilité ¾ arrière
- Habitabilité limitée
- Boutons poussoirs de la transmission

au passage que les commandes des sièges avant sont situées de chaque côté de la console, ce qui ne plaira pas à tous. D'ailleurs en conduite rapide, le pilote verra sa cuisse droite frotter contre ces boutons et ce n'est pas tellement confortable. Je ne voudrais pas oublier les places arrière constituées de deux sièges baquets. Les occupants de ces sièges pourront visionner une vidéo sur un écran apposé sur la partie supérieure des sièges avant. Par contre, il est aussi difficile de s'y asseoir que de s'en extirper.

LA MAGIE DU V12

Lorsqu'on soulève le capot, on ne peut être qu'impressionné par ce gros moteur V12 de 6,0 litres qui occupe tout l'espace. Produisant 470 chevaux, il est associé à une boîte automatique à six rapports. À titre de comparaison, le moteur V8 turbo de la Porsche développe 30 chevaux de plus tandis que sa boîte automatique est à sept rapports et à double embrayage. Ces données techniques expliquent sans doute pourquoi la Panamera est plus rapide en accélération alors qu'elle ne met que 3,7 secondes pour effectuer le 0-100 km/h, tandis que la Rapide a besoin d'une seconde et trois dixièmes de plus. Les distances de freinage sont également plus courtes pour la Porsche et sa vitesse de pointe est supérieure.

Cela ne signifie pas que l'Aston Martin soit totalement déclassée. Sur un circuit, cette cinq portes fait preuve d'une extraordinaire stabilité dans les courbes et la voiture est d'une grande docilité. Il ne faut pas oublier non plus que ce n'est pas un coupé agile. La Rapide s'inspire de la DB9, dont elle emprunte également le moteur V12, et la méthode de construction à assemblage vertical.

La DB9 est considérée comme une Grande Sportive qui est plus à l'aise sur la route que sur une piste. Il est certain que la Rapide, plus grosse et plus lourde, n'a pas gagné en agilité, mais elle est quand même impressionnante à ce chapitre. Et en conduite de tous les jours, cette voiture est agréable, docile et moyennement confortable tandis que la visibilité arrière n'est pas le point fort de cette Aston Martin.

Il est certain que les personnes fortunées à la recherche d'une certaine exclusivité vont apprécier la Rapide.

Jean Léon

PHOTOS: ASTON MARTIN

ASTON MARTIN RAPIDE

Catégorie	Berline
Échelle de prix	215 000$
Garanties	3 ans/illimité, 3 ans/illimité
Assemblage	Gaydon, Warwickshire, Angleterre
Cote d'assurance	n.d.

CHÂSSIS - DONNÉES POUR BASE

Emp/lon/lar/haut	2 989/5 019/2 140/1 360 mm
Coffre	n.d.
Réservoir	90 litres
Nombre coussins sécurité	6
Antipatinage / contrôle stabilité	oui / oui
Suspension avant	indépendante, double triangulation
Suspension arrière	indépendante, double triangulation
Freins avant / arrière	disque (ABS) / disque (ABS)
Direction	à crémaillère, ass. variable
Diamètre de braquage	n.d.
Pneus avant / arrière	245/40ZR20 / 295/35ZR20
Poids	1 990 kg
Capacité de remorquage	n.d.

COMPOSANTES MÉCANIQUES

Base

Cylindrée, soupapes, alim.	V12 6,0 litres 48 s atmos.
Puissance / Couple	470 chevaux / 443 lb-pi
Tr. base (opt) / rouage base (opt)	seq (A6) / Prop
0-100 / 80-120 / 100-0 km/h	3,7 s / 3,2 s (est) / n.d.
Type ess. / ville / autoroute	Super / n.d.

DANS LA MÊME CATÉGORIE

Jaguar XJ, Maserati Quattroporte, Mercedes-Benz Classe CLS, Porsche Panamera

DU NOUVEAU EN 2011

Nouveau modèle

NOS IMPRESSIONS

Agrément de conduite :	■■■■■■■□□□ 7/10
Fiabilité :	Nouveau modèle
Sécurité :	■■■■■■■■□□ 8/10
Qualités hivernales :	■■■■■□□□□□ 5/10
Espace intérieur :	■■■■■■■□□□ 7/10
Confort :	■■■■■■■■□□ 8/10

www.astonmartin.com

Plus d'informations dans la section statistiques en dernière partie du Guide

QU'EST-CE QUE TU PRENDS POUR ÊTRE SI BELLE?

Du diesel, répond la jolie! En effet, alors que l'Audi A3 était déjà très attrayante, l'arrivée d'une motorisation diesel au courant de 2010 vient encore rehausser la donne. En réalité, il y a à peine quelques années, associer diesel et voiture de luxe en Amérique aurait gravement porté atteinte à la réputation de la marque. Plusieurs se souviennent douloureusement de leur expérience avec des Cadillac munies de diesels de pacotille, au début des années 80. En Europe, le diesel n'a jamais été préjudiciable à l'image d'une marque, bien au contraire.

Quoi qu'il en soit, les retouches apportées il y a quelques années à la A3 lui permettent d'être encore dans le coup, visuellement parlant, et on a peine à croire qu'elle partage son châssis avec la commune Volkswagen Golf. Mais comme Audi et Volkswagen font partie de la même famille, qui regroupe aussi Lamborghini, Bugatti, Bentley, SEAT, Skoda et maintenant Porsche, on ne s'en formalisera pas, d'autant plus que la A3 se démarque passablement de sa cousine.

Le style mais aussi l'habitacle est différent. Toujours sobre, voire austère comme la plupart des créations germaniques, le tableau de bord de la A3 est, à l'instar de celui des autres modèles de la marque, esthétiquement très réussi, en plus d'être ergonomique et superbement fini. Les sièges sont durs mais confortables et j'ajouterais, au risque de me répéter, comme la plupart des créations germaniques. Cette Audi, malgré son luxe, demeure une voiture compacte et ce sont surtout les places arrière qui écopent. Non pas qu'elles soient inconfortables, mais sur mauvaise route, les secousses sont plus senties à l'arrière qu'à l'avant. C'est juste que trois adultes de taille moyenne s'installant sur la banquette sont mieux d'avoir des atomes crochus... De plus, le coffre n'est pas le plus grand de sa catégorie. Au moins, les dossiers de la banquette s'abaissent en deux parties et il est même possible d'ouvrir une trappe pour y faire passer des objets très longs comme des skis. J'allais écrire « des 2x4 » mais des skis conviennent mieux à la A3 que des bouts de bois...

TOUT EST SOUS LA ROBE

Cependant, je soupçonne les gens qui se procurent une A3 de préférer la conduite aux questions pratiques. Et ils sont bien servis! Le moteur de base, un quatre cylindres de 2,0 litres à injection directe turbocompressé possède suffisamment de puissance et de couple pour assurer des performances enlevées. Il est accouplé d'office à une manuelle à six rapports très agréable à utiliser. Mais la plupart lui préfèrent désormais la boîte automatique S-Tronic à six rapports. Cette transmission à double embrayage relaie le couple aux quatre roues par l'intermédiaire du rouage quattro. La manuelle est réservée pour le modèle à traction.

L'autre moteur, on le devine, est un diesel de 2,0 litres (que les initiés appellent TDI) qui ne développe que 140 chevaux mais qui se

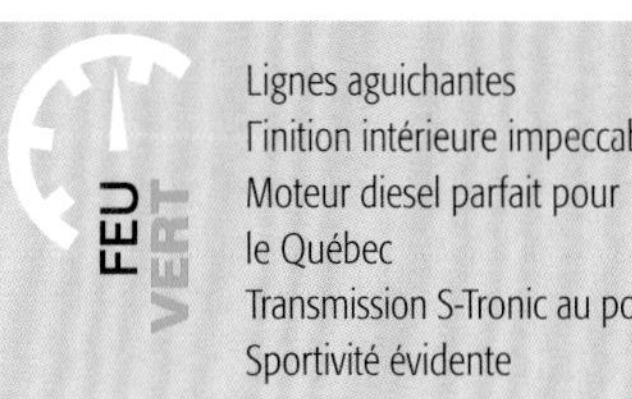

Lignes aguichantes
Finition intérieure impeccable
Moteur diesel parfait pour le Québec
Transmission S-Tronic au point
Sportivité évidente

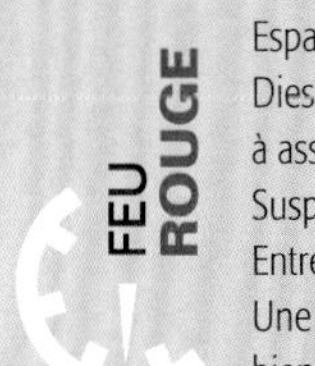

Espace habitable restreint
Diesel et quattro impossibles à associer
Suspensions assez dures
Entretien dispendieux
Une Volks GTi peut aussi bien faire...

reprend avec un couple phénoménal de 236 livres-pied disponibles dès les 1 750 tours/minute. Les départs ne sont peut-être pas canon mais les reprises, elles, en valent la peine. La consommation de carburant est retenue et, durant notre semaine d'essai, nous avons maintenu une moyenne de 7,0 litres/100 km pour une autonomie d'environ 1 000 km, ce qui n'est pas rien et qui nous fait oublier que ce moteur est un peu plus bruyant que celui à essence. En revanche, on s'y habitue rapidement. De toute façon, on est loin des anciens diesels de GM !

Ce moteur est invariablement assisté de la boîte automatique S-Tronic, toujours aussi efficace. Passer les rapports en mode manuel devient vite une drogue. Une drogue légale, faut-il préciser ! En plus du mode M (manuel), on retrouve aussi un mode S (sport). Encore une fois, il est possible de changer les rapports manuellement mais il vaut mieux laisser la voiture s'arranger avec cette activité. En mode Sport, elle passe les rapports plus tard mais au bon moment pour exploiter au maximum les capacités du moteur et du châssis, châssis d'une rigidité édifiante. Bémol : la version TDI n'a pas droit au rouage intégral... Seule la traction est offerte, ce qui lui enlève un peu de son attrait mais qui réduit le poids de la voiture.

BEAUCOUP DE PLAISIR...

Le volant se prend superbement bien en main, la direction est précise et rend très bien compte du travail du train avant. Quant aux suspensions, elles sont fermes, trop pour certains physiques plus sensibles mais c'est le prix à payer pour avoir droit à une tenue de route exceptionnelle, surtout dans la version quattro, quoique la traction ne démérite pas non plus. Notons que les pneus à taille basse, en plus d'être bruyants, sont plutôt durs. En cas de pépin majeur, les freins assurent des distances d'arrêt très correctes, les nombreux systèmes d'aide à la conduite s'uniront pour replacer la voiture et huit coussins gonflables veillent au grain si le pilote a plus d'hormones que de talent...

L'Audi A3 a beau être agile comme un singe, n'empêche que la S3, réservée aux Européens, ferait un tabac chez nous. Il y a aussi la version cabriolet qui ne serait pas déparée dans notre monde automobile. Par contre, la décision d'Audi Canada de ne pas importer la A3 trois portes est parfaitement justifiable. Il ne nous reste qu'à espérer une A3 munie du diesel ET du rouage quattro...

Alain Morin

PHOTOS : ALAIN MORIN

AUDI A3

Catégorie	Familiale
Échelle de prix	3 800 $ à 39 950 $ (2010)
Garanties	4 ans/80 000 km, 4 ans/80 000 km
Assemblage	Ingolstadt, Allemagne
Cote d'assurance	n.d.

CHÂSSIS - DONNÉES POUR 2.0 TDI PREMIUM

Emp/lon/lar/haut	2 578/4 292/1 765/1 423 mm
Coffre	370 à 1 546 litres
Réservoir	55 litres
Nombre coussins sécurité	6
Antipatinage / contrôle stabilité	oui / oui
Suspension avant	indépendante, jambes de force
Suspension arrière	indépendante, multibras
Freins avant / arrière	disque (ABS) / disque (ABS)
Direction	à crémaillère, ass. variable électronique
Diamètre de braquage	10,7 m
Pneus avant / arrière	P225/45R17 / P225/45R17
Poids	1 505 kg
Capacité de remorquage	n.d.

COMPOSANTES MÉCANIQUES

2,0 TDI

Cylindrée, soupapes, alim.	4L 2,0 litres 24 s turbocompressé
Puissance / Couple	140 chevaux / 236 lb-pi
Tr. base (opt) / rouage base (opt)	A6 / Tr
0-100 / 80-120 / 100-0 km/h	9,8 s / 7,2 s / 37,5 m
Type ess. / ville / autoroute	Diesel / 6,7 / 4,6 l/100 km

2,0T

Cylindrée, soupapes, alim.	4L 2,0 litres 16 s turbocompressé
Puissance / Couple	200 chevaux / 207 lb-pi
Tr. base (opt) / rouage base (opt)	M6 (A6) / Tr (Int)
0-100 / 80-120 / 100-0 km/h	7,0 s / 6,4 s / 37,5 m
Type ess. / ville / autoroute	Super / 9,6 / 7,5 l/100 km

DANS LA MÊME CATÉGORIE

Acura TSX, MINI Cooper, Mercedes-Benz Classe B, Volvo C30, Volvo S40, Volvo V50

DU NOUVEAU EN 2011

Moteur diesel proposé depuis début 2010

NOS IMPRESSIONS

Agrément de conduite :	8/10
Fiabilité :	6/10
Sécurité :	10/10
Qualités hivernales :	8/10
Espace intérieur :	7/10
Confort :	7/10

www.audi.ca

Plus d'informations dans la section statistiques en dernière partie du Guide

UNE BELLE RÉUSSITE

Entièrement redessinée il y a deux ans, la superbe A4 poursuit sa route en 2010 en proposant un look ravageur, une tenue de route devenue presque aussi sportive que celle d'une BMW et un confort aussi souverain que celui d'une Mercedes-Benz. Une réussite sur tous les plans? Presque...

Le moins que l'on puisse dire c'est que la A4 a de la gueule, particulièrement dans le cas du modèle de type familiale qui est, à mon avis, encore plus réussi que la berline. La qualité d'assemblage est de premier plan tout comme celle des matériaux utilisés pour l'intérieur et, de ce côté, Audi fait encore et toujours figure de leader dans l'industrie automobile. C'est toujours la référence en la matière aussi bien pour les modèles de prix plus abordable que pour la très luxueuse A8. Le châssis fait montre d'un bel équilibre, surtout lorsque la voiture est équipée de l'option Audi Drive Select permettant de «personnaliser» les paramètres de performance des suspensions, de la direction, de la boîte automatique, ainsi que de la réponse à l'accélérateur par la voie de l'électronique. Aussi, le moteur turbo de 2,0 litres s'est maintes fois mérité une place dans la liste très sélecte des dix meilleurs moteurs au monde selon le réputé magazine spécialisé Ward's Auto World. Évidemment, la présence du rouage intégral assure une parfaite maîtrise, peu importe les conditions routières. Il est difficile de trouver mieux.

DES PRIX CORSÉS

C'est du côté des prix que ça se gâte pour la belle d'Ingolstadt, et c'est la faute de la concurrence directe. Au Canada, une lutte de tous les instants s'est instaurée entre BMW et Mercedes-Benz pour atteindre la première position en ce qui a trait à la quantité de véhicules vendus par année, avec le résultat que ces deux marques proposent maintenant de nombreux incitatifs pour tenter de damer le pion à la marque rivale, ces deux constructeurs étant plus à la recherche de parts de marché que de profits record. Jusqu'à maintenant, Audi a refusé de se prêter à ce petit jeu, préférant vendre ses véhicules au mérite, ce qui signifie que les prix des véhicules, de leurs options, ou encore leurs taux de financement sont souvent plus élevés.

LA S4, UN VÉRITABLE «SLEEPER»...

L'histoire récente du modèle S4 nous présente tour à tour une voiture animée par un moteur V6 de 2,7 litres et deux turbos qui a été délaissé en 2003 au profit d'un V8 atmosphérique de 4,2 litres, afin d'opposer une concurrence plus relevée à la BMW M3 de l'époque. Aujourd'hui, la mission première de la S4 n'est plus de rivaliser avec la M3, mais bien de se mesurer aux BMW 335i et Mercedes-Benz C350, entre autres. Voilà ce qui explique en partie pourquoi le V8 est maintenant remplacé par un V6 de 3,0 litres avec compresseur volumétrique développant 333 chevaux, soit 15 de moins qu'auparavant. Cependant, le V6 suralimenté offre plus de couple, consomme moins et surtout permet à la S4 de retrouver un meilleur équilibre, le V6 étant moins lourd que le V8, ce qui

FEU VERT

Ligne élégante
Moteur performant et économe
Rouage intégral performant
Qualité des matériaux et de l'assemblage

FEU ROUGE

Prix élevés
Coût des options
Moteurs qui exigent du carburant super

autorise une meilleure répartition des masses et une réduction de la tendance marquée au sous-virage qui était le propre de la S4 de génération précédente.

Sur circuit, dès les premiers tours de piste, la S4 impressionne par son équilibre et par sa tenue de route grâce à son rouage intégral, mais surtout grâce à son différentiel arrière sport, qui est offert en option et qui achemine plus de couple à la roue arrière extérieure en virage, ce qui aide la voiture à mieux négocier les courbes en réduisant le sous-virage. De plus, ce différentiel autorise une légère glissade du train arrière en sortie de virage en accélération franche. Tout simplement génial. Pour les vrais amateurs de conduite sportive, voilà une option qui doit obligatoirement figurer sur la commande, tout comme le système « Audi Drive Select », qui permet non seulement au conducteur de calibrer la fermeté des suspensions et de la direction ainsi que la réponse du moteur à la commande des gaz, mais également de calibrer chacun de ces paramètres, indépendamment l'un de l'autre, afin de « personnaliser » la réponse du châssis. C'est alors un jeu d'enfant d'adopter le mode « confort » pour les routes balisées pour ensuite passer en mode « dynamique » sur le circuit ou simplement pour négocier une bretelle d'accès à l'autoroute en conduite de tous les jours.

Parmi les points faibles, on peut noter que la boîte manuelle à six vitesses n'enchante pas particulièrement en raison de la course un peu longue et « caoutchoutée » du levier. De plus, le V6 suralimenté exige que l'on soit toujours sur le bon rapport de boîte afin d'éviter le léger délai à l'accélération. La boîte à double embrayage S tronic est également au programme, et comme elle compte sept rapports plutôt que six et qu'elle les passe beaucoup plus rapidement que le conducteur ne pourrait le faire, il est facile de la recommander à l'acheteur.

Côté style, la S4 ne se démarque pas tellement de la simple A4, ce qui en fait un véritable « sleeper », et l'habitacle est presque en tous points conforme à celui de la A4, exception faite des sièges sport plus moulants et de certains détails de présentation. Comme toujours, Audi impressionne par le choix de matériaux de qualité pour la réalisation de l'habitacle, et la qualité d'assemblage demeure inégalée dans toute l'industrie automobile.

Gabriel Gélinas

PHOTOS : AUDI

Catégorie	Berline, Familiale
Échelle de prix	38 300 $ à 57 200 $ (2010)
Garanties	4 ans/80 000 km, 4 ans/80 000 km
Assemblage	Ingolstadt, Allemagne
Cote d'assurance	passable

CHÂSSIS - DONNÉES POUR S4 BERLINE QUATTRO

Emp/lon/lar/haut	2 808/4 703/1 826/1 427 mm
Coffre	480 litres
Réservoir	64 litres
Nombre coussins sécurité	6
Antipatinage / contrôle stabilité	oui / oui
Suspension avant	indépendante, multibras
Suspension arrière	indépendante, multibras
Freins avant / arrière	disque (ABS) / disque (ABS)
Direction	à crémaillère, assistée
Diamètre de braquage	11,1 m
Pneus avant / arrière	P245/40R18 / P245/40R18
Poids	1 700 kg
Capacité de remorquage	n.d.

COMPOSANTES MÉCANIQUES

2,0T

Cylindrée, soupapes, alim.	4L 2,0 litres 16 s turbocompressé
Puissance / Couple	211 chevaux / 258 lb-pi
Tr. base (opt) / rouage base (opt)	CVT (A6) / Tr (Int)
0-100 / 80-120 / 100-0 km/h	7,1 s / 5,4 s / 42,2 m
Type ess. / ville / autoroute	Super / 10,1 / 7,3 l/100 km

S4

Cylindrée, soupapes, alim.	V6 3,0 litres 16 s surcompressé
Puissance / Couple	333 chevaux / 325 lb-pi
Tr. base (opt) / rouage base (opt)	M6 (A7) / Int
0-100 / 80-120 / 100-0 km/h	5,2 s / 4,1 s / 38,7 m
Type ess. / ville / autoroute	Super / 12,1 / 7,9 l/100 km

DANS LA MÊME CATÉGORIE

Acura TL, Acura TSX, BMW Série 3, Cadillac CTS, Infiniti G, Lexus IS, Mercedes-Benz Classe C, Volvo S40, Volvo S60, Volvo V50

DU NOUVEAU EN 2011

Aucun changement majeur

NOS IMPRESSIONS

Agrément de conduite :	8/10
Fiabilité :	6/10
Sécurité :	10/10
Qualités hivernales :	8/10
Espace intérieur :	8/10
Confort :	8/10

www.audi.ca

Plus d'informations dans la section statistiques en dernière partie du Guide

D'UNE RARE BEAUTÉ

Walter de Silva, le designer italien œuvrant chez Audi, a dit que la A5 est la plus belle voiture qu'il ait créée à ce jour, et il suffit d'un simple coup d'œil porté vers le coupé ou le cabriolet A5 pour reconnaître que ce modèle se démarque beaucoup dans le paysage automobile, tout en intégrant les éléments de design typiques de la marque aux quatre anneaux.

Si les lignes superbes de la A5 ont capté l'attention de l'acheteur, celui-ci devra d'abord faire un choix entre un modèle coupé ou un cabriolet à toit souple, pour ensuite choisir le niveau de performance de la voiture. En effet, la gamme des A5 est composée du modèle de base mais également du modèle S5, lancé l'an dernier, et dont la vocation est nettement plus sportive, même si elle n'arrive toujours pas à égaler la BMW M3 au chapitre des performances. C'est maintenant chose faite avec la nouvelle RS5, dont le moteur V8 de 450 chevaux dame le pion à la BMW M3 dont le moulin n'en développe que 414, et qui se qualifie d'emblée comme un *über-sleeper*. Avec ses ailes élargies et leurs rebords au tracé horizontal qui rappelle celui d'une Audi classique et pionnière (l'Audi quattro de 1980), ses jantes en alliage de 19 pouces de série (des 20 pouces sont proposées en option), une garde au sol abaissée de 20 millimètres et un aileron intégré qui se déploie à 120 kilomètres/heure, la nouvelle RS5 réussit le pari d'allier élégance et sportivité avec brio.

LE MOTEUR DE LA R8 4.2

Sous le capot de la RS5 se trouve une version remaniée du V8 de 4,2 litres qui équipe la R8 4.2, les ingénieurs de quattro GmbH ayant réussi à extraire 30 chevaux de plus du V8 à hauts régimes, dont la limite de révolution est fixée à 8 250 tours/minute et qui est jumelé à la boîte S tronic à double embrayage et sept rapports, ainsi qu'au rouage intégral quattro. La vitesse maximale est fixée à 250 kilomètres/heure, mais elle peut être augmentée à 280 kilomètres/heure à la demande du propriétaire. Le sprint de 0 à 100 kilomètres/heure ne prend que 4,6 secondes et pourtant la voiture affiche une consommation moyenne de 10,8 litres aux 100 kilomètres selon Audi, grâce en partie à un septième rapport allongé en vue de réduire la consommation.

L'ÉPREUVE DU CIRCUIT

Quelques tours bouclés sur le fabuleux circuit Ascari de Ronda en Espagne, qui était en partie détrempé, ont suffi pour confirmer le potentiel de performance de la RS5 et l'efficacité de son groupe motopropulseur. Dès la sortie des puits, j'ai été impressionné par la sonorité évocatrice du V8, particulièrement lorsque les volets du système d'échappement s'ouvrent quand le moteur est à pleine charge. La livrée de la puissance est très linéaire, le couple maximal est atteint entre 4 000 et 6 000 tours/minute, et le passage des rapports se fait à la vitesse de l'éclair grâce aux paliers de commande localisés sur le volant. Le résultat, c'est qu'on est catapulté vers le prochain virage à haute vitesse, ce qui ne pose aucun problème au système de freinage ni à ses disques avant en

Ligne très élégante
Rouage intégral
quattro performant
Performances très relevées (RS5)
Excellent comportement routier
Qualité d'assemblage et
de finition

FEU ROUGE

Prix très élevés (S5 et RS5)
Visibilité vers l'arrière
Coût des options
Confort relatif sur
routes dégradées (S5 et RS5)

composite de céramique qui équipaient notre voiture d'essai. La réponse au volant en entrée de virage est précise et immédiate, grâce en partie aux pneus haute-performance de Pirelli, mais également grâce à la direction dynamique dont la démultiplication évolue en continu en fonction de la vitesse de la voiture, et qui peut même induire de légers contrebraquages si la vitesse est un peu trop élevée en entrée de courbe. Vers le milieu du virage, les différentiels central et arrière se mettent de la partie en conjonction avec le système Audi Drive Select, qui est de série sur la RS5, afin d'optimiser la répartition du couple et de livrer un maximum de puissance en sortie de virage. Le résultat, c'est que la RS5 est une voiture emballante à conduire à la limite et qu'elle s'est montrée très à l'aise sur le circuit, particulièrement lorsque celui-ci était encore détrempé et glissant. En fait, j'ai eu la très nette impression que je n'aurais pas réussi à rouler aussi vite sur le circuit cette journée-là au volant d'une M3, qui est une simple propulsion. L'un des as dans la manche de la RS5 est son nouveau différentiel interponts qui fait appel à deux pignons qui présentent une denture frontale, ainsi qu'à un embrayage multidisques afin d'augmenter la plage de modulation dans le transfert du couple moteur entre les trains avant et arrière. En situation normale, la répartition est de 60 pour cent sur l'arrière et de 40 pour cent sur l'avant, mais le nouveau différentiel interponts peut livrer jusqu'à 85 pour cent du couple aux roues arrière, ou jusqu'à 70 pour cent sur l'avant, permettant à la voiture de mieux composer avec les changements de condition d'adhérence.

Équipé des sièges sport proposés en option, l'habitacle de la RS5 se qualifie presque d'un cockpit avec ses appliques réalisées en fibre de carbone, ainsi que son pédalier et ses paliers de commande de passage des vitesses au volant au look d'aluminium. La qualité des matériaux utilisés ainsi que la finition sont de tout premier ordre, ce à quoi Audi nous a habitués depuis un certain temps déjà. L'attente sera longue avant que la RS5 ne débarque chez nous, mais elle en vaudra certainement la peine.

Gabriel Gélinas

PHOTOS : AUDI

Catégorie	Cabriolet, Coupé
Échelle de prix	46 200 $ à 68 300 $ (2010)
Garanties	4 ans/80 000 km, 4 ans/80 000 km
Assemblage	Ingolstadt, Allemagne
Cote d'assurance	n.d.

CHÂSSIS - DONNÉES POUR 2.0T QUATTRO CABRIOLET

Emp/lon/lar/haut	2 751/4 625/1 854/1 383 mm
Coffre	288 litres
Réservoir	64 litres
Nombre coussins sécurité	6
Antipatinage / contrôle stabilité	oui / oui
Suspension avant	indépendante, multibras
Suspension arrière	indépendante, multibras
Freins avant / arrière	disque (ABS) / disque (ABS)
Direction	à crémaillère, assistée
Diamètre de braquage	11,4 m
Pneus avant / arrière	P245/40R18 / P245/40R18
Poids	1 830 kg
Capacité de remorquage	n.d.

COMPOSANTES MÉCANIQUES

A5

Cylindrée, soupapes, alim.	4L 2,0 litres 16 s turbocompressé
Puissance / Couple	211 chevaux / 258 lb-pi
Tr. base (opt) / rouage base (opt)	M6 (A8) / Int
0-100 / 80-120 / 100-0 km/h	8,5 s / 6,2 s / 41,6 m
Type ess. / ville / autoroute	Super / 10,1 / 7,5 l/100 km

S5

Cylindrée, soupapes, alim.	V6 3,0 litres 24 s surcompressé
Puissance / Couple	333 chevaux / 325 lb-pi
Tr. base (opt) / rouage base (opt)	A7 / Int
0-100 / 80-120 / 100-0 km/h	5,6 s /4,2 s (est) / n.d.
Type ess. / ville / autoroute	Super / 12,9 / 8,1 l/100 km

A5 (option)

V6 3,2 l, 265 ch, 243 lb-pi - 0-100 : 6,6 s - 11,6 / 7,6 l/100 km

RS5

V8 4,2 l, 450 ch, 317 lb-pi - 0-100 : 4,6 s - l/100 km = n.d.

DANS LA MÊME CATÉGORIE

BMW Série 3, Infiniti G, Mercedes-Benz Classe E Coupe

DU NOUVEAU EN 2011

Aucun changement majeur. Modèle RS5 à venir (2012)

NOS IMPRESSIONS

Agrément de conduite :	10/10
Fiabilité :	6/10
Sécurité :	10/10
Qualités hivernales :	7/10
Espace intérieur :	7/10
Confort :	8/10

www.audi.ca

Plus d'informations dans la section statistiques en dernière partie du Guide

LE LUXE À LA CARTE

Au Québec, tout comme dans le reste du Canada, la A6 n'est pas nécessairement le modèle le plus en demande chez Audi. Pourtant, sur le continent européen, il est le plus populaire dans sa catégorie. Cette situation s'explique en bonne partie par le fait qu'il se vend à un prix relativement élevé et que notre marché est davantage orienté vers des modèles intermédiaires et moins coûteux, comme la A4 qui jouit d'une très grande popularité en sol canadien.

Lors du lancement de la nouvelle A6 en 2009, la présentation des changements esthétiques de cette voiture se fit assez rapidement, et pour cause: à peine avait-on apporté quelques légères modifications à la carrosserie afin que l'on puisse distinguer cette édition des précédentes. Étant donné la grande popularité de ce modèle, on a opté pour la continuité, en conservant sensiblement la même silhouette déjà connue et appréciée. Doit-on spécifier que cette voiture est toujours considérée comme l'une des plus élégantes de sa catégorie? Les quelques retouches apportées n'auront servi qu'à la mettre au goût du jour. Par contre, on s'est beaucoup attardé à la mécanique et tout particulièrement au moteur V6 avec compresseur.

PLUS PETIT, PLUS PUISSANT

De nos jours, la tendance actuelle n'est pas d'augmenter la cylindrée des moteurs, mais plutôt de la réduire, tout en augmentant l'efficacité du moteur en le rendant plus performant et plus économique en carburant. Lorsque Audi a annoncé qu'elle remplaçait son moteur V6 de 3,2 litres pour un autre V6 d'une cylindrée de 3,0 litres, la réaction fut mitigée. Pour plusieurs, c'était faire un pas en arrière.

Pourtant, le nouveau moteur est commercialisé depuis plusieurs mois maintenant et il faut bien admettre que la direction de Audi avait diablement raison. En effet, on a compensé la diminution de la cylindrée par l'utilisation d'un compresseur volumétrique qui permet d'offrir des accélérations et des reprises un peu plus musclées que son prédécesseur, tout en offrant une réduction notable de la consommation. Sa puissance est de 300 chevaux, c'est-à-dire 100 chevaux au litre, ce qui n'est pas négligeable. Sa sonorité est plus gutturale en raison de la présence du compresseur, mais personne ne s'en plaindra et il faut moins de six secondes pour effectuer le 0-100 km/h.

C'est décidément le groupe propulseur le plus utilisé sur ce type de modèle. Il est toutefois possible de commander une version toujours équipée du moteur V6 3,2 litres de 265 chevaux. Par contre, ce moteur n'est livré qu'avec la version à traction avant et il est couplé d'une transmission CVT. Soulignons au passage que Audi maîtrise à merveille la technologie de cette transmission à rapports continuellement variables. Il est également possible de commander une berline A6 propulsée par un moteur V8 de 4,2 litres produisant 350 chevaux. Tous les modèles, à l'exception

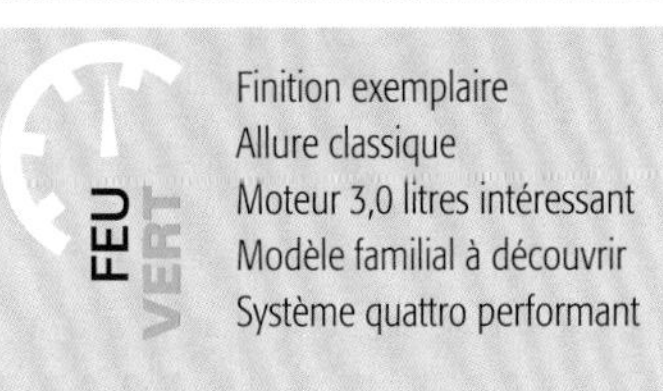

Finition exemplaire
Allure classique
Moteur 3,0 litres intéressant
Modèle familial à découvrir
Système quattro performant

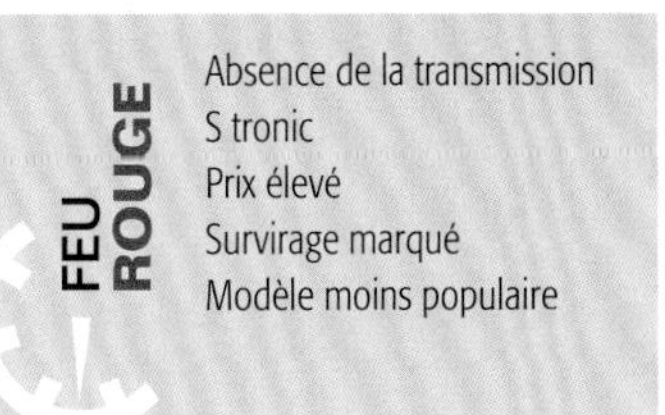

Absence de la transmission S tronic
Prix élevé
Survirage marqué
Modèle moins populaire

de celui équipé du moteur 3,2 litres, sont à rouage intégral *quattro* et dotés de la technologie *Tiptronic* à six rapports. Si vous priorisez la conduite d'une Audi dotée de la transmission *STronic* à double embrayage, vous devrez choisir un autre modèle. Ceci s'applique également au modèle Avant, une familiale fort élégante qui est à la fois agréable à conduire, confortable et très pratique. Malheureusement, elle ne semble pas jouir de la popularité qu'elle devrait avoir. D'ailleurs, à ce chapitre, peu importe de quel constructeur allemand il est question, les versions familiales de leurs modèles intermédiaires sont boudées.

ET LA S6?

Impossible de ne pas parler de ce modèle d'anthologie. La S6 est vraiment dans une classe à part si on la compare autres modèles A6 offerts sur notre marché. Avec son moteur V10 de 435 chevaux associé à une transmission intégrale *quattro*, cette berline permet de combiner performances impressionnantes, confort, luxe et conduite sportive. Pour ceux qui aiment afficher leurs goûts en matière de voiture d'exception, la S6 propose toute une gamme d'extérieurs raffinés qui la démarque des autres. Bien entendu, l'agrément de conduite de la S6 est équivalent à son prix de vente !

Bien qu'elle soit plus musclée et plus puissante que les autres modèles A6, elle possède tout comme eux un habitacle dont l'élégance en fait sa marque de commerce. Audi est reconnue pour ses postes de conduite raffinés et toutes les A6 sont à la hauteur de cette réputation. Bien conçu et bien réalisé, tout est en sobriété dans ces habitacles. Aucune lumière qui clignote ou gadget inutile qui encombrent l'espace et saturent le regard. La simplicité de l'aménagement met en évidence les matériaux qui sont d'une qualité exemplaire. De plus, les stylistes maison sont passés maîtres dans l'art de bien agencer les éléments en aluminium brossé avec les composantes en plastique et en cuir. Ajoutez à cela des sièges de grand confort, et vous obtenez un intérieur des plus agréables à fréquenter.

Sur la route, c'est une voiture douce, silencieuse et rassurante grâce à sa tenue de route impeccable. Par contre, lorsqu'elle est pilotée au-dessus des limites de vitesse sur une route sinueuse, un survirage accentué se fait sentir. Malgré cela, grâce à la technologie *quattro* et aux nombreux systèmes électroniques d'assistance au pilotage, la voiture demeure toujours prévisible.

Denis Duquet

PHOTOS : AUDI

Catégorie	Berline, Familiale
Échelle de prix	52 900 $ à 99 500 $ (2010)
Garanties	4 ans/80 000 km, 4 ans/80 000 km
Assemblage	Neckarsulm, Allemagne
Cote d'assurance	passable

CHÂSSIS - DONNÉES POUR 3.0T BERLINE PREMIUM QUATTRO

Emp/lon/lar/haut	2 843/4 927/1 855/1 459 mm
Coffre	450 litres
Réservoir	80 litres
Nombre coussins sécurité	8
Antipatinage / contrôle stabilité	oui / oui
Suspension avant	indépendante, multibras
Suspension arrière	indépendante, multibras
Freins avant / arrière	disque (ABS) / disque (ABS)
Direction	à crémaillère, ass. variable
Diamètre de braquage	11,9 m
Pneus avant / arrière	P245/40R18 / P245/40R18
Poids	1 870 kg
Capacité de remorquage	n.d.

COMPOSANTES MÉCANIQUES

3,0T

Cylindrée, soupapes, alim.	V6 3,0 litres 24 s surcompressé
Puissance / Couple	300 chevaux / 310 lb-pi
Tr. base (opt) / rouage base (opt)	A6 / Int
0-100 / 80-120 / 100-0 km/h	5,1 s / 5,1 s / n.d.
Type ess. / ville / autoroute	Super / 12,0 / 8,0 l/100 km

3,2

Cylindrée, soupapes, alim.	V6 3,2 litres 24 s atmos.
Puissance / Couple	265 chevaux / 243 lb-pi
Tr. base (opt) / rouage base (opt)	CVT / Tr
0-100 / 80-120 / 100-0 km/h	7,0 s (est) / 6,0 s (est) / n.d.
Type ess. / ville / autoroute	Super / 11,4 / 7,4 l/100 km

4,2

V8 4,2 l, 350 ch, 325 lb-pi - 0-100 : 5,8 s - 13,1 / 8,8 l/100 km

S6

V10 5,2 l, 435 ch, 398 lb-pi - 0-100 : 5,1 s - 15,2 / 10,4 l/100 km

DANS LA MÊME CATÉGORIE

Acura RL, BMW Série 5, Cadillac STS, Infiniti M, Jaguar XF, Lexus GS, Lincoln MKS, Mercedes-Benz Classe E, Volvo S80, Volvo V70

DU NOUVEAU EN 2011

Quelques changements mineurs à la carrosserie, V6 3,0 litres surcompressé

NOS IMPRESSIONS

Agrément de conduite :	8/10
Fiabilité :	6/10
Sécurité :	10/10
Qualités hivernales :	9/10
Espace intérieur :	8/10
Confort :	9/10

www.audi.ca

Plus d'informations dans la section statistiques en dernière partie du Guide

UNE VOCATION PLUS SPORTIVE

Dans le créneau des voitures de grand luxe, l'approche d'Audi a toujours été conservatrice avec un style moins typé, qui a permis à la A8 de voler « sous le radar » sans trop attirer l'attention, contrairement à la Série 7 de BMW ou la Classe S de Mercedes-Benz. En bref, la sobre A8 était la voiture de luxe de choix pour ceux qui ne voulaient pas attirer l'attention sur eux-mêmes ou sur leur portefeuille.

Sur le plan technique, Audi garde le cap en ce qui a trait à l'utilisation du *Space Frame* réalisé en alliage d'aluminium, qui est plus léger de 40 pour cent qu'un châssis conventionnel construit en acier, et celui de la nouvelle berline de luxe est également plus rigide que l'ancien dans une proportion de 25 pour cent. Avec le nouveau modèle 2011, Audi a cependant choisi de donner à la A8 une allure à la fois plus sportive et plus aérodynamique qui respecte la filiation avec les autres modèles de la marque.

À l'avant, la calandre a été revue avec l'ajout de huit bandes horizontales réalisées en chrome et des phares qui pivotent et « suivent » la route selon les informations transmises par le système de navigation. À l'arrière, la nouvelle A8 ressemble beaucoup à une A4 de grande taille et l'impression créée par cette berline de grand luxe est celle d'une voiture plus basse, ce qui est confirmé par son coefficient de traînée aérodynamique qui n'est que de 0,26, même si elle est plus longue et plus large que sa devancière ainsi que ses principales rivales en provenance d'Allemagne.

Sous le capot, la nouvelle A8 fait appel à une version remaniée du V8 de 4,2 litres qui développe 372 chevaux ainsi que 325 livres-pied de couple, mais qui ne permet pas à Audi de prétendre à la suprématie de la catégorie, la A8 accusant un léger recul par rapport à sa concurrence immédiate côté puissance. Cependant, Audi annonce une réduction de la consommation de carburant de l'ordre de 15% par rapport au modèle précédent, en raison du jumelage à la boîte ZF à huit rapports avec paliers de commande de passage des rapports au volant, ainsi qu'au rouage intégral quattro qui est maintenant synonyme de la marque d'Ingolstadt. Pour le marché européen, la A8 peut être équipée d'une paire de motorisations diesel turbocompressées, soit un V6 de 3,0 litres ainsi qu'un V8 de 4,2 litres, et ce dernier pourrait éventuellement être proposé en Amérique du Nord d'ici deux ans.

UN DIFFÉRENTIEL ARRIÈRE SPORT

Comme c'était le cas précédemment, le moteur est toujours localisé devant l'axe des roues avant, ce qui n'est pas idéal pour la répartition des masses et entraîne souvent une tendance naturelle pour le sous-virage en conduite sportive. Pour la nouvelle A8, Audi a cependant choisi d'emprunter le différentiel arrière sport actif développé pour la S4 et de la S5. Au braquage du volant ou en accélération en sortie de virage, le couple est transféré à la roue extérieure au virage avec pour effet de plaquer la berline dans le virage grâce à ce supplément d'appui. Le système contrecarre d'emblée toute tendance au survirage ou au sous-virage. Sur les routes montagneuses du Sud de l'Espagne, ce différentiel actif s'est avéré très efficace en rehaussant les qualités dynamiques de la A8, qui compte également sur le système Audi Drive Select permettant au conducteur de sélectionner le degré de fermeté des suspensions pneumatiques adaptives, le temps de réponse à la commande des gaz, les points de passage des rapports de boîte, ainsi que la rapidité de la direction.

Le passage du réglage « confort » à « dynamique » produit un effet immédiat, particulièrement du côté de la direction, qui passe de « légère » à « lourde » à la simple pression du contrôleur du système de télématique MMI. Le système Audi Drive Select permet ainsi au conducteur de « personnaliser » le comportement de la voiture afin d'attaquer les virages avec aplomb ou d'adopter une conduite plus relaxe sur autoroute. Tout cela fait en sorte que la nouvelle A8 est plus agile et plus apte à la conduite sportive que sa devancière, et que l'on a tendance à oublier qu'il s'agit d'une grande voiture de luxe à rouage intégral de plus de deux tonnes, sauf lorsque vient le temps de freiner fortement à l'approche d'un virage serré, où la A8 nous rappelle son pedigree.

CONNECTIVITÉ HIGH-TECH

Poursuivant sur sa lancée, Audi continue de réaliser les intérieurs les plus soignés de l'industrie tout en ajoutant de nouvelles fonctionnalités de haute technologie comme le système de vision nocturne proposé en option ou le régulateur de vitesse intelligent, qui sont maintenant de rigueur dans ce créneau, mais également avec sa nouvelle interface à pavé tactile qui permet au conducteur de tracer les lettres ou les chiffres avec son doigt lorsque vient le temps de programmer une destination dans le système de navigation, plutôt que de manier le contrôleur rotatif. Il suffit de quelques

secondes pour apprivoiser cette nouvelle interface et il est plus efficace de tracer les lettres en gros pour que le système les reproduise bien à l'écran. Évidemment, ce n'est pas idéal d'essayer d'écrire avec son doigt lorsque la voiture est en mouvement, c'est pourquoi le contrôleur MMI propose aussi la sélection des lettres et des chiffres par rotation, tout comme auparavant.

Par ailleurs, la Audi A8 est la première voiture au monde à être équipée de l'application Google Earth permettant de reproduire des cartes en trois dimensions avec relief des environs via la connectivité assurée par le dispositif Bluetooth et le jumelage à un téléphone portable. Cette connexion permet également au conducteur d'accéder à Internet via le système de télématique MMI. Le système de son de série compte 14 haut-parleurs et un amplificateur de 600 watts, alors qu'un exceptionnel système Bang & Olufsen avec 1 400 watts de puissance et 19 haut-parleurs est proposé en option. Deux de ces haut-parleurs « apparaissent » en montant de la planche de bord aux abords des piliers « A », un peu comme deux soucoupes volantes qui décollent.

LA VERSION ALLONGÉE...

Signe des temps, la version à empattement allongé de la nouvelle A8 n'a pas été dévoilée dans l'un ou l'autre des grands salons de l'automobile d'Europe ou d'Amérique du Nord, mais bien à celui de Beijing, la Chine étant en voie de déclasser tous les autres pays au chapitre des ventes de la marque. En effet, le marché chinois absorbe une quantité toujours plus grande de voitures de grand luxe et les clients choisissent toujours les versions les plus cossues et les plus équipées, ce qui contribue grandement aux profits de la marque allemande.

La nouvelle A8 fait plus de 5 mètres 30 en longueur et son moteur est un W12 de 500 chevaux qui est jumelé à la boîte automatique à huit rapports. Mais ce qui impressionne le plus est tout l'espace et le luxe accordés aux passagers prenant place à l'arrière, qui disposent d'une console centrale, de sièges chauffants et climatisés avec fonction de massage, et même d'un repose-pieds repliable à commande électrique.

... ET L'HYBRIDE

Audi a également procédé au dévoilement d'un concept d'une éventuelle version hybride de la A8 au printemps 2010 au Salon de l'Auto de Genève. Il s'agit d'un modèle à traction avant qui est animé par le 4 cylindres de 2,0 litres turbocompressé jumelé à un moteur

Catégorie	Berline
Échelle de prix	95 000 $ à 100 000 $ (2010)
Garanties	4 ans/80 000 km, 4 ans/80 000 km
Assemblage	Ingolstadt, Allemagne
Cote d'assurance	n.d.

CHÂSSIS - DONNÉES POUR 4.2 L QUATTRO

Emp/lon/lar/haut	3 073/5 081/1 880/1 422 mm
Coffre	396 litres
Réservoir	87 litres
Nombre coussins sécurité	7
Antipatinage / contrôle stabilité	oui / oui
Suspension avant	indépendante, multibras
Suspension arrière	indépendante, multibras
Freins avant / arrière	disque (ABS) / disque (ABS)
Direction	à crémaillère, assistée
Diamètre de braquage	12,5 m
Pneus avant / arrière	P255/45R18 / P255/45R18
Poids	2 000 kg
Capacité de remorquage	n.d.

COMPOSANTES MÉCANIQUES

4.2 L Quattro, 4.2 Quattro

Cylindrée, soupapes, alim.	V8 4,2 litres 32 s atmos.
Puissance / Couple	372 chevaux / 325 lb-pi
Tr. base (opt) / rouage base (opt)	A8 / Int
0-100 / 80-120 / 100-0 km/h	6,0 s (est) / 5,0 s (est) / n.d.
Type ess. / ville / autoroute	Super / 13,1 / 8,7 l/100 km

W12

Cylindrée, soupapes, alim.	V12 6,3 litres 48 s atmos.
Puissance / Couple	500 chevaux / 460 lb-pi
Tr. base (opt) / rouage base (opt)	A8 / Int
0-100 / 80-120 / 100-0 km/h	5,0 s (est) / n.d. / n.d.
Type ess. / ville / autoroute	Super / 16,8 / 11,2 l/100 km

DANS LA MÊME CATÉGORIE

BMW Série 7, Jaguar XJ, Lexus LS, Maserati Quattroporte, Mercedes-Benz Classe S

DU NOUVEAU EN 2011

Nouveau modèle

NOS IMPRESSIONS

Agrément de conduite :	■■■■■■■■■□	9/10
Fiabilité :	Nouveau modèle	
Sécurité :	■■■■■■■■■■	10/10
Qualités hivernales :	■■■■■■■■□□	8/10
Espace intérieur :	■■■■■■■■□□	8/10
Confort :	■■■■■■■■■□	9/10

www.audi.ca

Plus d'informations dans la section statistiques en dernière partie du Guide

FEU VERT

Rouage intégral performant
Boîte automatique à huit rapports
Qualité d'assemblage et de finition
Confort assuré

FEU ROUGE

Prix élevé
Coût des options
Châssis en aluminium coûteux à réparer en cas d'accident

électrique de 33 kilowatts (45 chevaux) pour une puissance totale chiffrée à 245 chevaux et un couple maximal de 354 livres-pied.

Selon Audi, ce concept est capable d'abattre le 0-100 kilomètres/heure en 7,6 secondes avec une consommation moyenne de 6,2 litres aux 100 kilomètres, tout ça pour une berline de grande taille et de grand luxe. Les récentes Lexus LS et Mercedes-Benz de Classe S à motorisation hybride sont donc résolument dans la mire d'Audi, alors que la BMW Série 7 Hybride doit être classée comme « hors catégorie », le constructeur bavarois ayant décidé de faire de son hybride de grand luxe à moteur V8 une voiture dont les performances égalent presque celles de la Série 7 à moteur V12 !

Avec son contenu high-tech et son allure plus typée, la nouvelle A8 devient plus dynamique et sportive tout en continuant de séduire par son grand luxe.

Gabriel Gélinas

PHOTOS : AUDI

LUXE COMPACT ET PLAISIR GARANTI

Dans l'édition 2010 du Guide de l'auto, le Q5 de Audi s'est vu décerner le titre amplement mérité de premier de classe dans la catégorie des VUS compacts de plus de quarante mille dollars. Un an plus tard, force est de constater que le Q5 poursuit sa route en conservant les attributs qui font sa force, mais qu'il devra également affronter une concurrence plus affûtée avec l'arrivée du BMW X3 de nouvelle génération.

Dans ce créneau en popularité croissante du marché, la concurrence est vive et les écarts sont minces entre les prétendants au titre, et pourtant, le Q5 réussit à se démarquer du lot en proposant un véhicule de luxe aux dimensions compactes qui fait preuve d'une remarquable homogénéité. Côté style, le Q5 s'inscrit aux antipodes du Mercedes-Benz GLK. En effet, autant ce dernier adopte des lignes carrées, autant le Q5 joue la carte des formes plus arrondies tout en conservant une certaine présence recherchée par les acheteurs de la catégorie. De ce côté, la calandre surdimensionnée y est pour beaucoup, mais il faut également considérer la ligne de toit qui s'abaisse à l'arrière et qui donne au Q5 une allure un brin sportive. Il faut également souligner les affinités de cette silhouette avec la Q7, histoire de conserver un air de famille.

ÉQUILIBRÉ ET HOMOGÈNE

Avec son moteur V6 de 3,2 litres et ses 270 chevaux, le Q5 a tout ce qu'il faut pour assurer des performances relevées en accélération, et son rouage intégral quattro lui confère une excellente stabilité peu importe les conditions routières. Si les véhicules concurrents proposent tous une fiche technique comparable, le Q5 marque des points par sa remarquable homogénéité et son comportement routier équilibré. Pour ce qui est des considérations pratiques, notons que le Q5 offre un habitacle à la finition très soignée qui fait beaucoup plus luxueux que l'intérieur du GLK de Mercedes-Benz, et que la marque Audi prend le plus grand soin pour ce qui est de l'utilisation de matériaux de qualité supérieure pour la réalisation de la planche de bord. De plus, le système de télématique MMI adopté par Audi est facile d'utilisation puisque son contrôleur rotatif est doublé de touches permettant l'accès direct aux diverses fonctionnalités du véhicule. C'est passablement intuitif à l'usage. Le Q5 est également légèrement supérieur au GLK pour ce qui est du dégagement pour les jambes aux places arrière, de même que pour ce qui est du volume du coffre.

UNE OPTION À RETENIR: AUDI DRIVE SELECT

Comme c'est souvent le cas avec la marque Audi et les marques allemandes en général, plusieurs équipements et accessoires ne sont proposés qu'en option ou en groupes d'options, alors que les modèles offerts dans ce créneau par Acura ou Infiniti sont souvent moins chers à contenu égal. Il faut donc faire preuve d'une certaine retenue en parcourant le catalogue d'options. Toutefois, il y en a une qui devrait absolument figurer sur la commande de l'acheteur de Q5 qui est désireux de retrouver l'excellent

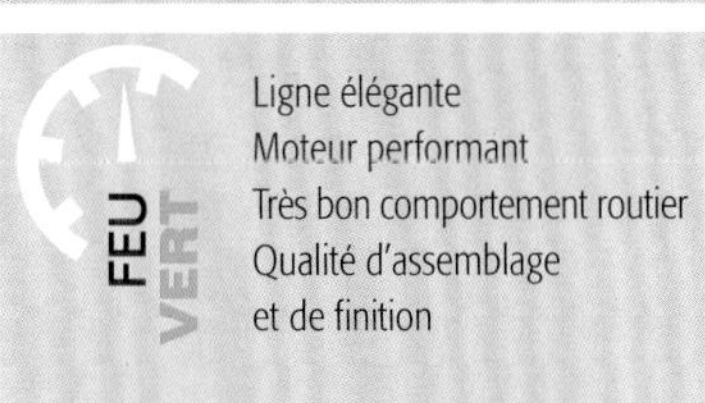

Ligne élégante
Moteur performant
Très bon comportement routier
Qualité d'assemblage
et de finition

Prix élevé
Coût des options
Poids un peu trop élevé

comportement routier d'une berline de luxe malgré le fait qu'il se trouve à choisir un VUS au centre de gravité plus élevé, et c'est l'option Audi Drive Select. En quelques mots, ce système s'avère capable de rehausser l'agrément de conduite en permettant de « personnaliser » les paramètres de performance des suspensions, de la direction, de la boîte automatique et de la réponse à l'accélérateur.

Contrairement à d'autres systèmes du genre qui ne proposent que deux ou trois modes, tels que « normal », « sport » ou « confort », le système Audi Drive Select permet également au conducteur de composer sa « recette personnelle », en choisissant lui-même le degré de réponse de chacun des systèmes indépendamment l'un de l'autre. Par exemple, si vous désirez une réponse rapide de la direction conjuguée à des calibrations plus souples pour les suspensions, il suffit de programmer vous-même ces paramètres en accédant au menu des réglages de la voiture au moyen du système MMI (Multi Media Interface). La beauté du Audi Drive Select réside donc dans le fait que le choix des calibrations les plus sportives (position « Dynamique ») permet d'obtenir une tenue de route phénoménale qui vous fera carrément oublier que vous n'êtes pas au volant d'une berline ou d'une familiale. Ou vous pouvez ensuite choisir le mode « Individuel » dans lequel se trouvent vos réglages personnalisés, ou encore le mode « Confort » si vous transportez la petite famille. Le système comporte également un mode « Automatique » qui adopte les réglages appropriés en fonction de la vitesse de la voiture et de votre style de conduite. Bref, le système Audi Drive Select est à ce point efficace et performant que vous aurez carrément l'impression d'être au volant d'une voiture différente selon les calibrations retenues. Dans le cas du Q5, cette option s'avère tout simplement géniale puisqu'elle permet d'émuler la très bonne tenue de route d'une berline sport et de compenser en partie pour le poids un peu trop élevé du VUS de luxe aux dimensions compactes de la marque aux quatre anneaux.

Les dimensions du Q5 sont compactes mais le facteur luxe répond présent partout, que ce soit dans la réalisation de l'habitacle ou dans la livrée linéaire de la puissance livrée par sa motorisation, sans parler du comportement routier très équilibré qui fait de ce VUS de luxe l'un des meilleurs choix de la catégorie. Si on l'équipait du moteur V6 diesel 3,0 litres, l'offre serait encore plus étoffée.

Gabriel Gélinas

PHOTOS : AUDI

Catégorie	VUS
Échelle de prix	43 500 $ à 48 600 $
Garanties	4 ans/80 000 km, 4 ans/80 000 km
Assemblage	n.d.
Cote d'assurance	n.d.

CHÂSSIS - DONNÉES POUR 3.2 PREMIUM QUATTRO

Emp/lon/lar/haut	2 807/4 629/1 880/1 653 mm
Coffre	540 à 1 560 litres
Réservoir	75 litres
Nombre coussins sécurité	8
Antipatinage / contrôle stabilité	oui / oui
Suspension avant	indépendante, multibras
Suspension arrière	indépendante, multibras
Freins avant / arrière	disque (ABS) / disque (ABS)
Direction	à crémaillère, ass. variable
Diamètre de braquage	n.d.
Pneus avant / arrière	P235/60R18 / P235/60R18
Poids	1 895 kg
Capacité de remorquage	2 000 kg (4 409 lb)

COMPOSANTES MÉCANIQUES

3.2 Quattro, 3.2 Premium Quattro

Cylindrée, soupapes, alim.	V6 3,2 litres 24 s atmos.
Puissance / Couple	270 chevaux / 243 lb-pi
Tr. base (opt) / rouage base (opt)	A6 / Int
0-100 / 80-120 / 100-0 km/h	7,8 s / 6,5 s / 41,8 m
Type ess. / ville / autoroute	Super / 11,5 / 9,0 l/100 km

DANS LA MÊME CATÉGORIE

Acura RDX, BMW X3, Infiniti EX, Land Rover LR2, Mercedes-Benz Classe GLK, Volvo XC60

DU NOUVEAU EN 2011

Aucun changement majeur

NOS IMPRESSIONS

Agrément de conduite :	8/10
Fiabilité :	10/10
Sécurité :	10/10
Qualités hivernales :	8/10
Espace intérieur :	8/10
Confort :	8/10

www.audi.ca

Plus d'informations dans la section statistiques en dernière partie du Guide

SURALIMENTATION INTÉGRALE AU MENU

La marque aux quatre anneaux a bien fait en ajoutant l'an dernier un premier diesel à la motorisation nord-américaine du Q7 en plus de rafraîchir sa carrosserie. À sa quatrième année, le grand utilitaire de luxe d'Audi pouvait enfin donner le change à ses rivaux allemands avec une équation consommation/performance nettement meilleure. Les ingénieurs d'Ingolstadt poursuivent leur besogne en remplaçant les moteurs à essence atmosphériques par une paire de V6 plus performants et moins gloutons, en plus de présenter un V6 diesel plus léger et puissant.

Audi est parfaitement dans le ton en mettant à la retraite le V8 de 4,2 litres et le V6 de 3,6 litres qui équipaient le Q7 depuis son lancement en 2007. Surtout en leur substituant des moteurs de plus faible cylindrée, lesquels sont plus écolos et performants grâce à la magie combinée de la suralimentation et de l'injection directe.

Ces deux V6, dont l'appellation officielle est 3.0 TFSI, portent leurs cylindres à un angle de 90 degrés. Entre les deux rangées se trouvent un compresseur de suralimentation et deux échangeurs thermiques qui refroidissent l'air d'admission pour produire du muscle avec plus de constance. La version la plus sage et la moins chère livre 272 chevaux et 295 lb-pi de couple. C'est huit chevaux de moins mais presque trente livres-pied de couple en plus que l'ancien V6 atmosphérique, avec 0,6 litre de cylindrée en moins. Le constructeur affirme que le Q7 équipé de ce moteur peut atteindre 100 km/h en 6,9 secondes, ce qui se compare plus qu'avantageusement aux 8,6 secondes du Q7 mû par l'ancien V6 à essence.

Le plus performant des deux nouveaux V6 compressés équipe le modèle Sport et ses cotes sont de 333 chevaux et 325 lb-pi de couple. Il s'agit essentiellement du même moteur que dans la berline S4, axé sur le couple et la souplesse plutôt que sur la performance pure. Audi promet quand même un 0-100 km/h de 6,9 secondes dans le Q7 Sport, ce qui serait nettement mieux que les 8,5 secondes que nous avions enregistrées avec l'ancien Q7 à V8 de 4,2 litres.

ÉLÉMENT-CLÉ : UNE NOUVELLE BOÎTE AUTOMATIQUE

Les gains en efficacité et en puissance de ces nouveaux moteurs seraient moins nets si tous les Q7 n'étaientdotés d'une nouvelle boîte de vitesse automatique à 8 rapports. Au tour d'Audi d'égaler Lexus dans cette course au nombre maximum de rapports que se livrent les marques de luxe en passant d'un coup de six à huit.

Grâce à cet étagement plus grand, la nouvelle boîte Tiptronic améliore les accélérations en minimisant les chutes de régime entre les rapports mais réduirait aussi la consommation de 5 %. Pour la créer, les ingénieurs ont ajouté un module de sélection à l'ancienne boîte à six rapports. Le carter est un peu plus gros mais

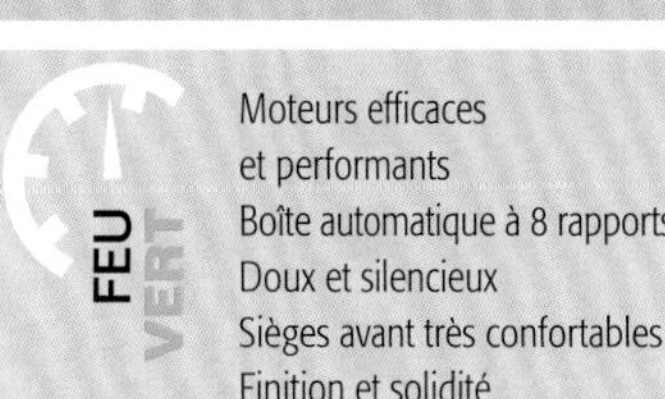

FEU VERT

- Moteurs efficaces et performants
- Boîte automatique à 8 rapports
- Doux et silencieux
- Sièges avant très confortables
- Finition et solidité sans reproche

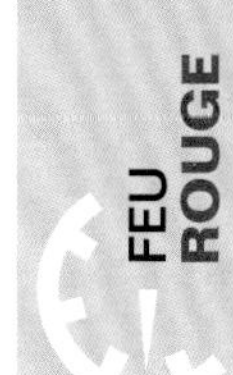

FEU ROUGE

- Fiabilité en retrait des meilleurs
- Rétroviseurs extérieurs encombrants
- Freinage difficile à doser
- Troisième banquette très limitée
- Trop lourds

l'ensemble est malgré tout un peu plus court, grâce à de nouveaux convertisseurs de couple plus étroits. Il est même plus léger de 11 kilos.

Toutes les autres fonctions et composantes ont été optimisées, entre autres pour que les convertisseurs de couple soient verrouillés le plus possible pour limiter les pertes par glissement. Chaque moteur dispose de sa propre version de la nouvelle boîte à 8 rapports, y compris le V6 diesel.

LE DIESEL PROGRESSE AUSSI

Les inconditionnels du diesel sont d'ailleurs gâtés puisque le Q7 profite désormais de la deuxième génération du V6 TDI de 3 litres. Ce nouveau moteur produit 240 chevaux, soit 15 de plus. Statu quo pour le couple à 405 lb-pi. Le nouveau TDI est également plus léger de 20 kg et respecte les nouvelles normes américaines d'émissions polluantes et la norme Euro 6 qui ne sera en vigueur qu'en 2014.

Les Européens gardent toutefois pour eux le V8 diesel de 4,2 litres qui fait 340 chevaux et 590 lb-pi de couple, ainsi que le V12 TDI de 500 chevaux et 590 lb-pi de couple (c'est quand même 1 000 Newtons-mètres), le diesel le plus puissant de l'industrie automobile. C'est d'ailleurs avec un moteur de cette configuration qu'Audi a occupé toutes les places du podium à la plus récente édition des 24 Heures du Mans avec un trio de ses barquettes R15.

LE BON ÉLÈVE

Les changements sont surtout d'ordre mécanique pour le Q7. Il n'a donc pas encore suivi la cure d'amaigrissement qui a permis à ses cousins, le Porsche Cayenne et le Volkswagen Touareg, de perdre quelque 100 et 200 kilos respectivement lors de leur dernier remodelage. Les trois partagent la même architecture de base, mais le Q7 a toujours la carrosserie et l'empattement les plus longs des trois. En fait, son rival le plus direct est le Mercedes-Benz GL qui le devance de seulement deux millimètres, plutôt que le ML du même constructeur.

Le Q7 est certes le plus spacieux de sa famille élargie. Le plus raffiné et le plus urbain aussi. Ce qui ne l'empêche pas d'être costaud. Il peut même tracter jusqu'à 3,5 tonnes avec le groupe de remorquage et l'attache qui sont offerts en option.

Marc Lachapelle

PHOTOS : MARC LACHAPELLE

Catégorie	VUS
Échelle de prix	55 550 $ à 62 800 $ (2010)
Garanties	4 ans/80 000 km, 4 ans/80 000 km
Assemblage	Bratislava, Slovaquie
Cote d'assurance	n.d.

CHÂSSIS - DONNÉES POUR TDI QUATTRO

Emp/lon/lar/haut	3 002/5 086/1 983/1 737 mm
Coffre	1 136 à 2 512 litres
Réservoir	100 litres
Nombre coussins sécurité	6
Antipatinage / contrôle stabilité	oui / oui
Suspension avant	indépendante, double triangulation
Suspension arrière	indépendante, double triangulation
Freins avant / arrière	disque (ABS) / disque (ABS)
Direction	à crémaillère, assistée
Diamètre de braquage	12,0 m
Pneus avant / arrière	P255/55R18 / P255/55R18
Poids	2 500 kg
Capacité de remorquage	2 495 kg (5 500 lb)

COMPOSANTES MÉCANIQUES

TDI quattro

Cylindrée, soupapes, alim.	V6 3,0 litres 24 s turbocompressé
Puissance / Couple	240 chevaux / 405 lb-pi
Tr. base (opt) / rouage base (opt)	A8 / Int
0-100 / 80-120 / 100-0 km/h	7,9 s / 7,0 s (est) / n.d.
Type ess. / ville / autoroute	Diesel / 13,2 / 8,3 l/100 km

3.0 quattro

Cylindrée, soupapes, alim.	V6 3,0 litres 24 s turbocompressé
Puissance / Couple	272 chevaux / 295 lb-pi
Tr. base (opt) / rouage base (opt)	A8 / Int
0-100 / 80-120 / 100-0 km/h	7,9 s / 6,9 s (est) / n.d.
Type ess. / ville / autoroute	Super / 16,1 / 11,2 l/100 km

3.0 quattro Premium

Cylindrée, soupapes, alim.	V6 3,0 litres 24 s surcompressé
Puissance / Couple	333 chevaux / 325 lb-pi
Tr. base (opt) / rouage base (opt)	A8 / Int
0-100 / 80-120 / 100-0 km/h	6,9 s / 6,0 s (est) / n.d.
Type ess. / ville / autoroute	Super / 14,9 / 10,3 l/100 km

DANS LA MÊME CATÉGORIE

Acura MDX, BMW X5, Cadillac SRX, Infiniti FX, Land Rover Range Rover Sport, Lexus RX, Mercedes-Benz Classe GL, Mercedes-Benz Classe M, Porsche Cayenne, Volkswagen Touareg, Volvo XC90

DU NOUVEAU EN 2011

Nouveau V6 3,0 litres remplace le V6 3,6 litres et le V8 4,2 litres, nouveau V6 3,0 litres diesel

NOS IMPRESSIONS

Agrément de conduite :	9/10
Fiabilité :	6/10
Sécurité :	10/10
Qualités hivernales :	9/10
Espace intérieur :	9/10
Confort :	8/10

www.audi.ca

Plus d'informations dans la section statistiques en dernière partie du Guide

LA DOMINATION SE POURSUIT

Lorsqu'Audi a commercialisé son spectaculaire coupé R8, ce véhicule est immédiatement devenu une voiture culte. Partout sur la planète, elle a glané tous les prix possibles, notamment le titre de voiture de l'année au Canada décerné par l'Association des journalistes automobiles du Canada (AJAC). À l'époque, ce titre avait fait jaser: une voiture de ce prix méritait-elle un tel titre? Plusieurs soutenaient qu'on aurait du la nommer la voiture la plus parfaite de l'année, la plus spectaculaire et j'en passe. Quoi qu'il en soit, son entrée en scène a été fortement remarquée.

Pourquoi? Tout simplement parce qu'elle excellait à tous les points de vue! Sa silhouette faisait tourner les têtes, son habitacle était confortable et d'une finition impeccable en plus d'un design très relevé, tandis que ses performances sur la route étaient supérieures. Non seulement son moteur V8 de 4,2 litres assurait des performances dignes de la catégorie, mais sa tenue de route était irréprochable et son freinage spectaculaire. Bref, cette Audi avait tout pour plaire. Mais, à Ingolstadt, on ne se repose pas sur ses lauriers. Tant et si bien que cette année, on nous propose un impressionnant cabriolet.

TOUJOURS LA PERFECTION

Vous croyez que je déjante? Très bien, je vous mets au défi de trouver un article relatant l'essai routier de la R8 Spyder qui soit négatif! En premier lieu, les stylistes ont réussi ce qui était pratiquement impossible, soit de préserver l'élégance de la silhouette du coupé. En effet, la plupart du temps, lorsqu'on enlève le toit rigide d'un coupé pour le remplacer par un toit souple, ce n'est pas toujours réussi. Prenons le cas de la Porsche 911 Cabrio qui est l'exemple type d'une conversion plus ou moins esthétique.

Concernant l'Audi R8, celle-ci est très jolie le toit remisé, mais elle est également fort élégante une fois le toit souple en place. Précisons qu'il faut moins de 20 secondes pour que ce toit se déploie ou s'escamote! Lorsqu'il se rétracte, c'est un ballet de pièces mobiles qui s'activent et ceci peut s'effectuer en roulant jusqu'à 50 km/h. Ce tour de magie élimine malheureusement la vitre qui, sur le coupé, nous permet d'admirer le moteur. Détail au passage, la bande noire en fibre de carbone placée derrière la portière a disparu, la carrosserie est maintenant monochrome.

Mais ce qui nous intéresse, c'est surtout la conduite de ce cabriolet. Une fois de plus, les ingénieurs de chez Audi ont réalisé un véritable miracle en trouvant le moyen de ne pas réduire la rigidité de la plate-forme tout en imposant un surplus de poids de moins de 100 kilos, ce qui est exceptionnel. La voiture demeure agile et nerveuse, mais il est certain que la version coupé enregistrera un temps plus rapide que le cabriolet propulsé par le même moteur V10 de 525 chevaux. Toujours au sujet des performances, la différence entre les deux versions est relativement mince. À titre d'exemple, le coupé effectue le 0-100 km/h en 3,9 secondes alors que la Spyder ne prend que 4,1 secondes! Il y a de quoi être impressionné.

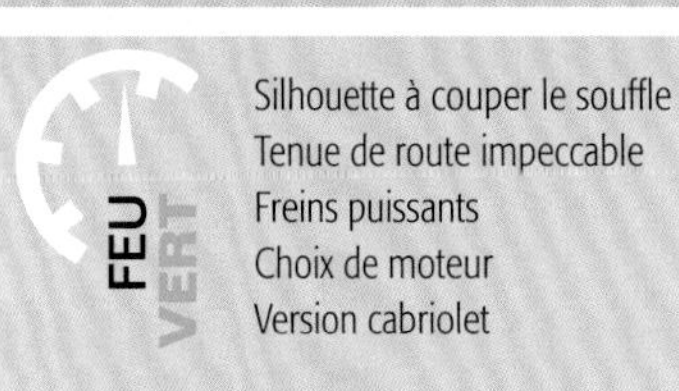

- Silhouette à couper le souffle
- Tenue de route impeccable
- Freins puissants
- Choix de moteur
- Version cabriolet

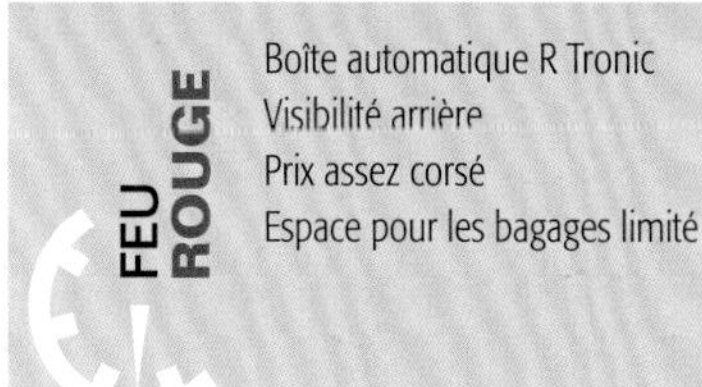

- Boîte automatique R Tronic
- Visibilité arrière
- Prix assez corsé
- Espace pour les bagages limité

Lors du lancement de ce modèle, nous avons été en mesure de franchir le mythique trajet empruntant la corniche de l'Esterel entre Cannes et Saint-Raphaël. C'est tout un plaisir que de piloter au fil des virages, de jouer du levier de vitesses de la boîte manuelle dont la grille en H assure un guidage parfait bien qu'il faille avoir de la poigne pour passer les rapports. Et quelle musique émanant du moteur ! En jouant des vitesses et en modulant l'accélérateur, la sonorité gutturale varie selon le régime du moteur. Les ingénieurs ont eu la bonne idée de placer une glace arrière escamotable qui permet d'entendre ce concert même lorsque la capote est déployée. Avis aux amateurs du genre.

Si parfois le rouage Quattro a tendance à sous-virer, ce n'est pas le cas dans la Spyder dont l'équilibre et la neutralité impressionnent. Bref, il est difficile de trouver à redire. Malgré tout, il faut souligner que la boîte automatique n'est pas à double embrayage et ses performances sont correctes, mais sans plus.

On ne doit pas cacher que l'habitacle est relativement étroit et que l'espace pour les bagages est limité, comme il faut s'y attendre sur une voiture de cette configuration. Par contre, la finition et la qualité des matériaux sont irréprochables. Donc, une note quasiment parfaite pour la Spyder.

ET LE V8?

Aussi bien le coupé que le cabriolet à moteur V10 sont des voitures spectaculaires et performantes. Mais après avoir conduit ces deux voitures, nous concluons que le modèle original à moteur V8 n'est certainement pas à dédaigner. S'il manque quelque peu de puissance par rapport aux deux autres, pour le reste c'est le même équilibre, la même finition impeccable, la même boîte de vitesse aux rapports bien étagés et la même puissance de freinage. Le tout à un prix très alléchant comparé à tout ce qui se trouve dans la catégorie. Et il ne faut pas nous oublier que toutes ces autos sont dotées du rouage Quattro, ce qui en fait une espèce à part.

Souvent, certaines nouvelles voitures dans la catégorie des grandes sportives arrivent sur la scène avec éclat pour ensuite perdre les faveurs du public en raison d'un manque de fiabilité ou d'une silhouette qui a rapidement perdu de son charme. Rien de tout cela dans ce trio de R8 qui continue de faire tourner les têtes.

Denis Duquet

PHOTOS : AUDI

Catégorie	Coupé, *Roadster*
Échelle de prix	141 000$ à 173 000$ (2010)
Garanties	4 ans/80 000 km, 4 ans/80 000 km
Assemblage	Neckarsulm, Allemagne
Cote d'assurance	n.d.

CHÂSSIS - DONNÉES POUR 5.2 SPYDER

Emp/lon/lar/haut	2 650/4 435/1 930/1 252 mm
Coffre	100 litres
Réservoir	90 litres
Nombre coussins sécurité	4
Antipatinage / contrôle stabilité	oui / oui
Suspension avant	indépendante, double triangulation
Suspension arrière	indépendante, double triangulation
Freins avant / arrière	disque (ABS) / disque (ABS)
Direction	à crémaillère, assistée
Diamètre de braquage	11,5 m
Pneus avant / arrière	P235/35R19 / P295/30R19
Poids	1 720 kg
Capacité de remorquage	non recommandé

COMPOSANTES MÉCANIQUES

4.2

Cylindrée, soupapes, alim.	V8 4,2 litres 32 s atmos.
Puissance / Couple	420 chevaux / 317 lb-pi
Tr. base (opt) / rouage base (opt)	M6 (A6) / Int
0-100 / 80-120 / 100-0 km/h	4,6 s / 3,2 s / 36,1 m
Type ess. / ville / autoroute	Super / 17,1 / 10,3 l/100 km

5.2 Spyder, 5.2

Cylindrée, soupapes, alim.	V10 5,2 litres 40 s atmos.
Puissance / Couple	525 chevaux / 390 lb-pi
Tr. base (opt) / rouage base (opt)	M6 (A6) / Int
0-100 / 80-120 / 100-0 km/h	3,9 s / 3,1 s / 37,7 m
Type ess. / ville / autoroute	Super / 19,1 / 11,6 l/100 km

DANS LA MÊME CATÉGORIE

Aston Martin Vantage, BMW Série 6, Dodge Viper, Ferrari 458 Italia, Jaguar XK, Lamborghini Gallardo, Mercedes-Benz Classe SL, Nissan GT-R, Porsche 911

DU NOUVEAU EN 2011

Modèle Spyder

NOS IMPRESSIONS

Agrément de conduite :	10/10
Fiabilité :	6/10
Sécurité :	10/10
Qualités hivernales :	7/10
Espace intérieur :	6/10
Confort :	8/10

www.audi.ca

Plus d'informations dans la section statistiques en dernière partie du Guide

L'EXCELLENCE PAR LA TECHNOLOGIE

L'an dernier, au cours de l'une des pires crises économiques de l'histoire, la compagnie Audi continuait d'enregistrer des hausses de ventes et des résultats financiers positifs pendant que plusieurs autres connaissaient les affres des bilans écrits à l'encre rouge les forçant à réduire leurs plans de développement et à sacrifier de nouveaux modèles.

Même si Audi avait été prise dans la tourmente, la survie de la TT n'aurait jamais été mise en doute car, selon son constructeur, elle est la plus populaire au monde dans la catégorie. Ceci dit, à Ingolstadt on ne se repose pas sur ses lauriers. La seconde génération de la TT a été dévoilée en 2006 alors qu'on avait amélioré la plate-forme et conçu une carrosserie partiellement en aluminium afin d'alléger la voiture tandis qu'un moteur V6 de 3,2 litres et un moteur quatre cylindres de 2,0 litres étaient disponibles. Puis, l'an dernier, le V6 a cédé sa place à une version turbocompressée du moteur 2,0 litres dont la puissance a été portée à 272 chevaux sur la TTS. Cette course à l'excellence se poursuit en 2011 avec un moteur 2,0 litres entièrement revu dans le but d'améliorer les performances et de réduire la consommation de carburant.

LA RS AU CANADA! YOUPPIE!

Les TT et TTS sont des voitures supérieures à la moyenne, mais elles se font damer le pion par la version RS qui n'était pas arrivée sur notre marché. Cette fois, ce sera chose faite et comme toutes les voitures d'exception, elle se démarque par son moteur.

Il s'agit d'un cinq cylindres de 2,5 litres produisant 340 chevaux grâce à son turbocompresseur et son injection directe d'essence FSI. Avec ça, le 0-100 km/h se boucle en 4,6 secondes. Et la boîte S Tronic à sept rapports et double embrayage est une merveille.

Elle permet de changer de vitesse en quelques centièmes de seconde et fonctionne en mode complètement automatique ou manuel, avec une commande par palettes sur le volant. Le programme de démarrage « Launch Control » permet d'effectuer des accélérations plus spectaculaires.

Sur le plan visuel, la RS se distingue par son aileron exclusif, ses freins plus puissants et une suspension abaissée de 10 mm. Dans l'habitacle, c'est similaire aux autres, mais ses sièges sport procurent un excellent support latéral qui se fait apprécier en conduite rapide sur des parcours sinueux. Bien entendu, la stabilité latérale et longitudinale est exceptionnelle. À son volant, on a vraiment l'impression d'être le maître à bord.

L'AUTRE BONNE NOUVELLE

La RS est une bonne nouvelle, mais Audi nous en réserve une autre avec l'arrivée d'un nouveau moteur 2,0 litres sous le capot de la version courante. Baptisé TFI, ce moulin produit 211 chevaux grâce à l'ajout d'un turbocompresseur et du système Audi Valvelift. Associé à la boîte manuelle à six rapports, il boucle le 0 à100 km/h en 6,1 secondes tandis que la vitesse de pointe atteint 245 km/h. La

- Arrivée de la RS
- Boîte S Tronic
- Rouage quattro
- Agrément de conduite
- Silhouette unique

- Visibilité perfectible
- Prix élevé
- Suspension ferme
- Accès à bord
- Places arrière (coupé)

boîte optionnelle S Tronic à six rapports réalise le 0-100 km/h en seulement 5,6 secondes. Avec la boîte manuelle, ce moteur permet une réduction de la consommation de 14 pour cent.

Par ailleurs, celui de la TTS nous revient pour 2011. Ce TFSI 2,0 litres, avec son turbocompresseur plus gros et de nombreuses autres modifications, fournit 272 chevaux. Avec sa boîte de vitesse S Tronic à six rapports (en option), le TTS Coupé est propulsé en 5,2 secondes de 0 à 100 km/h et sa vitesse de pointe limitée électroniquement est de 250 km/h.

Qu'il s'agisse de la version Coupé ou du Roadster, la TT est passablement inchangée sur le plan esthétique, à l'exception de modifications de détail pour raffiner sa silhouette et améliorer son aérodynamisme. À l'avant, le pare-chocs comporte des prises d'air agrandies tandis que les feux antibrouillards portent des anneaux en chrome. Les feux optionnels Xenon Plus sont dotés sous leur bord inférieur d'une ligne rectiligne comprenant douze diodes électroluminescentes blanches qui forment les feux de croisement de jour. L'aileron arrière est intégré dans les contours du couvercle du coffre et il sort automatiquement à une vitesse de 120 km/h et se rétracte à moins de 80 km/h. Le conducteur peut en outre l'activer à tout moment à l'aide d'un commutateur. L'habitacle a très peu changé et demeure la référence pour cette catégorie.

Sur la route, cette voiture est relativement neutre en virage et d'une grande agilité. Les changements de cap se font rapidement. Le nouveau moteur de base atteint son couple maximum à un régime moteur bas, ce qui rend la conduite urbaine beaucoup plus facile. Comme précédemment, la boîte manuelle est bien étagée et le passage des rapports s'effectue sans problème. Il faut souligner une fois de plus l'effarante efficacité de la transmission S Tronic à double embrayage disponible en option.

La TTS est un bon compromis entre la TT et la RS. Elle propose une suspension à réglage magnétique qui se règle automatiquement à la vitesse de l'éclair et qui semble toujours retrouver la solution à la condition de la chaussée. Son moteur fournit un bon rendement tandis que les accélérations et les reprises ont du mordant.

Denis Duquet

PHOTOS : DENIS DUQUET

Catégorie	Coupé, *Roadster*
Échelle de prix	49 350 $ à 61 900 $ (2010)
Garanties	4 ans/80 000 km, 4 ans/80 000 km
Assemblage	Gyor, Hongrie
Cote d'assurance	n.d.

CHÂSSIS - DONNÉES POUR 2.0T COUPE QUATTRO

Emp/lon/lar/haut	2 468/4 187/1 842/1 352 mm
Coffre	371 à 700 litres
Réservoir	55 litres
Nombre coussins sécurité	4
Antipatinage / contrôle stabilité	oui / oui
Suspension avant	indépendante, jambes de force
Suspension arrière	indépendante, multibras
Freins avant / arrière	disque (ABS) / disque (ABS)
Direction	à crémaillère, assistée
Diamètre de braquage	11,0 m
Pneus avant / arrière	P225/50R17 / P225/50R17
Poids	1 430 kg
Capacité de remorquage	n.d.

COMPOSANTES MÉCANIQUES

2.0 T

Cylindrée, soupapes, alim.	4L 2,0 litres 16 s turbocompressé
Puissance / Couple	211 chevaux / 258 lb-pi
Tr. base (opt) / rouage base (opt)	M6 (A6) / Int
0-100 / 80-120 / 100-0 km/h	6,1 s / 5,0 s (est) / n.d.
Type ess. / ville / autoroute	Super / 9,5 / 6,6 l/100 km

TTS

Cylindrée, soupapes, alim.	4L 2,0 litres 16 s turbocompressé
Puissance / Couple	272 chevaux / 258 lb-pi
Tr. base (opt) / rouage base (opt)	M6 (A6) / Int
0-100 / 80-120 / 100-0 km/h	5,2 s / 4,7 (est) / n.d.
Type ess. / ville / autoroute	Super / 10,0 / 7,7 l/100 km

TT RS

Cylindrée, soupapes, alim.	5L 2,5 litres 20 s turbocompressé
Puissance / Couple	340 chevaux / 332 lb-pi
Tr. base (opt) / rouage base (opt)	M6 (A7) / Int
0-100 / 80-120 / 100-0 km/h	4,6 s / 3,9 (est) / n.d.
Type ess. / ville / autoroute	Super / n.d.

DANS LA MÊME CATÉGORIE

Lotus Elise, Mazda RX-8, Mercedes-Benz Classe SLK, Nissan Z, Porsche Boxster, Porsche Cayman

DU NOUVEAU EN 2011

Nouveau 2,0 litres, version TT RS à venir

NOS IMPRESSIONS

Agrément de conduite :	9/10
Fiabilité :	8/10
Sécurité :	9/10
Qualités hivernales :	8/10
Espace intérieur :	7/10
Confort :	7/10

www.audi.ca

Plus d'informations dans la section statistiques en dernière partie du Guide

VOCATION TARDIVE

Pendant des décennies, la marque Bentley servait pratiquement de faire-valoir à sa grande sœur Rolls Royce qui la surpassait en prestige et en renommée. Les vieilles familles nobles, riches et célèbres du Royaume-Uni préféraient les voitures Bentley moins ostentatoires que les Rolls, mais ces dernières avaient plus de panache et leur réputation était nettement supérieure partout sur la planète. Il a fallu une acquisition ratée par le groupe Volkswagen pour que Bentley prenne son envol.

En effet, comme le groupe germanique n'a pu mettre la main sur la compagnie Rolls-Royce, il a jeté son dévolu sur sa filiale. Ce fut en quelque sorte une bénédiction puisque cela a permis à Volkswagen de ressusciter cette prestigieuse marque qui avait été dans l'ombre pendant des décennies.

Et puisque c'est l'incomparable Ferdinand Piech qui dirigeait Volkswagen à cette époque, il a trouvé des solutions techniques ingénieuses pour permettre à Bentley de revenir à l'avant-scène. L'arrivée de la Continental a été spectaculaire.

LOGIQUE ET EFFICACE

Étant donné que presque tous les modèles de cette marque étaient pratiquement caducs en 1998, date de leur arrivée dans le groupe VW, il fallait faire vite pour mettre Bentley à l'avant-plan et au goût du jour. Pour ce faire, les ingénieurs germaniques ont puisé dans leurs ressources et utilisé la plate-forme de leur super berline Phaeton pour développer une nouvelle catégorie de modèles de prix plus abordables chez Bentley, la Continental. Le Coupé GT a été le premier à être commercialisé et les résultats ont été spectaculaires. Mieux encore, pour donner à Bentley une image sportive et gagnante, on a concocté une voiture de course Bentley qui était en fait une Audi R10 déguisée et dont la cabine était fermée. Une victoire au Mans en 2003 a fait des merveilles pour l'image de marque.

Mieux encore, on a doté la GT d'un magnifique moteur W12 6,0 litres associé à une boîte automatique à six rapports. Comme il se doit, le rouage était intégral. En plus de cette mécanique fort songée, la silhouette de la voiture était et demeure toujours extraordinaire. En fait, cette belle britannique aurait été propulsée par un moteur de taxi londonien que les gens se seraient précipités pour l'acheter.

Dans l'habitacle, les stylistes ont réussi à concilier tradition et modernité. Il est vrai qu'on a conservé la présentation des berlines de grand luxe de fabrication britannique, mais c'est en même temps plus moderne et plus pratique. Il y a bien entendu des cuirs fins un peu partout et des boiseries réalisées à partir de matière ligneuse exotique, mais on ne se croit pas en 1930, plutôt au 21e siècle.

Le plus impressionnant dans tout cela est que la GT est agréable à conduire en offrant des performances dignes d'une sportive avec

FEU VERT

- Silhouettes réussies
- Luxe assuré
- Moteur fabuleux
- Versions Speed
- Surprenante tenue de route

FEU ROUGE

- Prix corsés
- Dimensions hors-norme
- Voitures lourdes
- Consommation élevée
- Places arrière étriquées (sauf Flying Spur)

un temps d'un peu plus de six secondes pour boucler l'habituel 0-100 km/h. Mais ce qui épate davantage, c'est la douceur de ce moteur dont les accélérations et les reprises sont fort linéaires. En plus, la tenue de route est très bonne malgré un soupçon de sous-virage dans les courbes un peu plus accentuées. Et si on ose rouler trop vite à son volant, de puissants freins et des systèmes d'aide électroniques au pilotage garderont votre bolide de plus de 200 000 $ dans le droit chemin.

Les ingénieurs ont utilisé la même mécanique et la même plate-forme pour décoiffer ce coupé et en faire un cabriolet. Souvent, ce genre d'exercice se traduit par une voiture dont la silhouette est bizarre, que le toit soit en place ou non. Cette fois, c'est élégant dans les deux cas. Ceci témoigne de l'excellence du design du Continental GT. On y trouve le même habitacle à quelques exceptions près tandis que la conduite est toute en douceur. C'est la voiture idéale pour aller faire un tour sur Rodeo Drive. Cependant, si son pilote ose pousser quelque peu la GTC, il se rendra compte assez vite que le châssis est moins rigide. Raison de plus pour aller se pavaner sur les grands boulevards et pas sur les circuits !

UNE ERREUR ET UNE TROUVAILLE

Depuis les débuts de cette gamme, tout est au beau fixe. Mais un jour, on a raté le coche; de peu, mais quand même. En effet, devant le succès de ce modèle, la direction a décidé de produire une berline dérivée du coupé avec une plate-forme allongée de 300 millimètres et les résultats sont moyens. La tenue de route n'en souffre pas ou du moins si peu. Par contre, ce manque de rigidité de la plate-forme a une incidence sur celle de la carrosserie. À ce prix, on s'attend à ce que ce soit plus rigide que la nouvelle Buick Regal. Et la voiture à l'essai souffrait d'une finition perfectible alors que plusieurs éléments étaient mal arrimés ou mal installés.

Devant cette popularité, on a également décidé d'ajouter une variante, plus exclusive... comme si les GT, GTC et Flying Spur n'étaient pas assez exotiques ! En tout cas, c'est une loi immuable du marketing : quand une auto se vend, c'est le temps d'offrir des variantes. Cette fois, il s'agit de l'édition Speed. Comme vous l'aurez deviné, avec une telle appellation, les performances sont au programme. Le moteur W12 produit 600 chevaux, la suspension a été abaissée et raffermie tandis que la direction est moins démultipliée. Enfin, des roues de 20 pouces s'ajoutent à l'ensemble.

Denis Duquet

PHOTOS : BENTLEY

Catégorie	Berline, Cabriolet, Coupé
Échelle de prix	199 300 $ à 308 400 $
Garanties	3 ans/illimité, 3 ans/illimité
Assemblage	Crew, Angleterre
Cote d'assurance	n.d.

CHÂSSIS - DONNÉES POUR GTC SPEED

Emp/lon/lar/haut	2 745/4 804/2 194/1 388 mm
Coffre	260 litres
Réservoir	90 litres
Nombre coussins sécurité	6
Antipatinage / contrôle stabilité	oui / oui
Suspension avant	indépendante, multibras
Suspension arrière	indépendante, multibras
Freins avant / arrière	disque (ABS) / disque (ABS)
Direction	à crémaillère, assistée
Diamètre de braquage	11,4 m
Pneus avant / arrière	P275/35ZR20 / P275/35ZR20
Poids	2 540 kg
Capacité de remorquage	non recommandé

COMPOSANTES MÉCANIQUES

Flying Spur, GT, GTC

Cylindrée, soupapes, alim.	W12 6,0 litres 48 s turbocompressé
Puissance / Couple	552 chevaux / 479 lb-pi
Tr. base (opt) / rouage base (opt)	A6 / Int
0-100 / 80-120 / 100-0 km/h	6,1 s / 4,7 s / 36,5 m
Type ess. / ville / autoroute	Super / 20,9 / 11,9 l/100 km

GT Speed, GTC Speed, Flying Spur Speed

Cylindrée, soupapes, alim.	W12 6,0 litres 48 s turbocompressé
Puissance / Couple	600 chevaux / 553 lb-pi
Tr. base (opt) / rouage base (opt)	A6 / Int
0-100 / 80-120 / 100-0 km/h	4,5 s / n.d. / n.d.
Type ess. / ville / autoroute	Super / 25,3 / 11,6 l/100 km

Supersports Convertible

Cylindrée, soupapes, alim.	W12 6,0 litres 32 s turbocompressé
Puissance / Couple	621 chevaux / 590 lb-pi
Tr. base (opt) / rouage base (opt)	A6 / Int
0-100 / 80-120 / 100-0 km/h	4,1 s / n.d. / n.d.
Type ess. / ville / autoroute	Super / 25,5 / 11,6 l/100 km

DANS LA MÊME CATÉGORIE

Aston Martin DB9, Audi A8, Ferrari 599, Ferrari 612 Scaglietti, Maserati Quattroporte, Mercedes-Benz Classe S

DU NOUVEAU EN 2011

Aucun changement majeur

NOS IMPRESSIONS

Agrément de conduite :	7/10
Fiabilité :	8/10
Sécurité :	9/10
Qualités hivernales :	6/10
Espace intérieur :	8/10
Confort :	8/10

www.bentleymotors.com

Plus d'informations dans la section statistiques en dernière partie du Guide

LE PRESTIGE, ÇA N'A PAS DE PRIX

Il y a quelques années, Bentley avait pris le monde automobile par surprise en dévoilant sa sublime Continental GT. S'ensuivirent une version décapotable GTC et une berline, la Flying Spur. Pour combler les plus blasés, il y eut ensuite les versions ultraperformantes Speed. Durant ce temps, la petite entreprise de Crewe en Angleterre, avec l'aide du consortium Volkswagen, trouvait le temps de peaufiner la future génération de son joyau qui allait succéder à la vétuste série Arnage.

C'est chose faite et la Mulsanne est désormais plus qu'une voiture de Salon ! Même si cette Mulsanne remplace un modèle qui datait de 1998 (aussi bien dire une éternité dans le domaine de l'automobile), on ne peut pas dire qu'elle diffère beaucoup de son aïeule. Le style général rappelle donc l'Arnage, autant par ses lignes que par ses dimensions des plus généreuses. Le Guide de l'auto vous le confirme en trois copies notariées, une Mulsanne, c'est gros, terriblement gros. Cependant, il faut savoir que dans ce marché, gros rime avec prestige, très gros avec très prestigieux. Et la Mulsanne, tout comme la Rolls-Royce Phantom et la Maybach, s'adresse à des gens qui adorent le super prestigieux...

UNE VOITURE PHARE

L'élément stylistique qui frappe le plus lorsqu'on voit la Mulsanne pour la première fois, c'est les immenses phares ceinturés de plusieurs petits feux à DEL qui trouvent place de chaque côté de l'imposante grille de radiateur. Certains adorent, d'autres tiquent mais nul doute qu'on reconnaîtra une Mulsanne deux kilomètres à la ronde, une jouissance pour son propriétaire. Après tout, quand on se promène dans une voiture dont la carrosserie a pris 125 heures/homme à fabriquer, on n'a pas à rougir !

Dans l'habitacle, Daniel Boone ne serait pas dépaysé tant le bois et les peaux d'animaux sont omniprésents. Quand vous aurez trouvé du plastique, prenez-le en photo et faites-nous parvenir cette dernière. On veut voir ça ! Inutile de préciser que la qualité de matériaux nobles est tout simplement renversante. On dit même que la Mulsanne contient 40 % plus de bois que l'Arnage qui, pourtant, n'était pas démunie à ce chapitre ! L'habitacle est immense, démesurément gigantesque serait plus approprié, et le propriétaire a le choix entre une infinité de couleurs, autant pour les boiseries, les tapis, les cuirs que pour les... ceintures de sécurité ! Le tableau de bord est massif et la petitesse des boutons, dans la plus pure tradition anglaise, contraste royalement. Mais ces boutons, ainsi que tout accessoire en acier inoxydable poli, sont fabriqués par une main cajoleuse et experte. Qu'ils soient difficiles à manipuler est le dernier des soucis d'une personne se procurant une Mulsanne. Même si la plupart des Bentley sont conduites par leur propriétaire, on n'a pas lésiné sur la qualité des places arrière. Juste manipuler les nombreux boutons qui permettent d'obtenir un confort parfait doit demander au minimum un doctorat en électronique. Le système audio Naim, offert en option et développé spécialement pour cette nouvelle Bentley, promet une sonorité exquise. Si ses

FEU VERT

Prestige visible de loin
Exclusivité assurée
40 % plus de bois !
Confort fantastique
Puissance démesurée

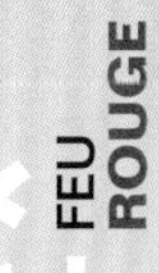

FEU ROUGE

Style controversé
Dimensions déraisonnables
Consommation d'une navette spatiale
Prix démentiel
Poids exagéré

2200 watts ne vous satisfont pas, de grâce, rencontrez un ORL le plus tôt possible. Au privé. Ça ira plus vite et vous n'aurez pas à côtoyer la populace. D'un autre côté, il se peut qu'une Mulsanne, comme proposée par Bentley, ne corresponde pas à vos désirs les plus basiques. À ce moment, il y a Mulliner, un spécialiste de la personnalisation associé à Bentley depuis plusieurs décennies, qui saura réaliser vos désirs les plus fous. Moyennant un léger supplément, s'entend…

PAS EXACTEMENT UNE MÉCANIQUE DE SMART…

Le nom Mulsanne provient d'un virage du réputé circuit du Mans et souligne le prestigieux passé de Bentley en course automobile. Même si nous n'avons pas encore pu faire l'essai de cette nouvelle voiture, il est presque certain que la sportivité ne devrait pas porter ombrage au confort même si la tenue de route, assurée par des suspensions pneumatiques indépendantes aux quatre roues et d'immenses roues de 20 pouces (21 pouces en option), devrait être très relevée. Les performances non plus ne devraient pas faire défaut. Comme toujours chez Bentley, la puissance du V8 double turbo est plus que suffisante tandis que le couple, lui, est tout simplement ahurissant. Au volant de l'Arnage, les accélérations et les dépassements étaient carrément impressionnants. La Mulsanne continuera dans la même veine puisque Bentley annonce un 0-100 km/h en 5,3 secondes pour une vitesse de pointe de 296 km/h. N'importe quelle Porsche peut en faire autant me direz-vous… mais aucune ne pèse 2585 kilos (5700 livres) ! Si la consommation d'essence de ce stade olympique mobile vous inquiète, c'est que vous n'avez pas les moyens de le posséder. Au Guide de l'auto, elle nous inquiète énormément… Il faut cependant savoir que la plupart de ces immeubles sur roues ne parcourent pas beaucoup de kilométrage annuellement. Les « greenpeaceux » peuvent dormir en paix !

Une transmission automatique ZF à huit rapports relaiera le couple aux roues arrière, avec toute la délicatesse requise. Les freins promettent des arrêts rapides tandis qu'une foule d'aides à la conduite feront constamment le guet. On retrouve seulement six coussins gonflables, une hérésie. Sauf que ceux pour la tête font partie du siège, question d'assurer un positionnement maximal en cas d'impact. Remarquez qu'à moins de frapper un 18 roues, on ne voit pas ce qui pourrait faire éclater les coussins…

Alain Morin

PHOTOS : BENTLEY

Catégorie	Berline
Échelle de prix	n.d.
Garanties	n.d.
Assemblage	n.d.
Cote d'assurance	n.d.

CHÂSSIS - DONNÉES POUR MULSANNE

Emp/lon/lar/haut	3266/5575/2208/1521 mm
Coffre	443 litres
Réservoir	96 litres
Nombre coussins sécurité	6
Antipatinage / contrôle stabilité	oui / oui
Suspension avant	indépendante, double triangulation
Suspension arrière	indépendante, multibras
Freins avant / arrière	disque (ABS) / disque (ABS)
Direction	à crémaillère, assistée
Diamètre de braquage	n.d.
Pneus avant / arrière	265/45ZR20 / 265/40ZR21
Poids	2585 kg
Capacité de remorquage	n.d.

COMPOSANTES MÉCANIQUES

Mulsanne

Cylindrée, soupapes, alim.	V8 6,8 litres 32 s turbocompressé
Puissance / Couple	505 chevaux / 752 lb-pi
Tr. base (opt) / rouage base (opt)	A8 / Prop
0-100 / 80-120 / 100-0 km/h	5,3 s (est) / n.d. / 40.0 m (est)
Type ess. / ville / autoroute	Super / 26,3 / 11,5 l/100 km

DANS LA MÊME CATÉGORIE

Maybach 57 - 62, Rolls-Royce Phantom

DU NOUVEAU EN 2011

Nouveau modèle

NOS IMPRESSIONS

Agrément de conduite :	Données insuffisantes
Fiabilité :	Données insuffisantes
Sécurité :	■■■■■■■□□□ 7/10
Qualités hivernales :	Données insuffisantes
Espace intérieur :	■■■■■■■■■□ 9/10
Confort :	■■■■■■■■■■ 10/10

www.bentleymotors.com

Plus d'informations dans la section statistiques en dernière partie du Guide

UN CARRÉ D'AS SANS PRÉTENTION

Le constructeur bavarois a bien joué ses cartes en nous offrant enfin ses modèles les plus abordables il y a déjà quatre ans. Les coupés et cabriolets de Série 1 permettent de s'initier aux vertus indéniables des BMW à prix moindre que les Série 3, pour peu qu'on y aille prudemment avec les options. Le coupé 135i nous a démontré son sérieux en survolant littéralement le match des sportives de notre dernière édition, mais ses sœurs sont tout aussi intéressantes, chacune à sa manière.

Avec leur silhouette plus ronde et trapue, un peu boursouflée même, les Série 1 se démarquent nettement de leurs grandes sœurs et grands frères au sein de la gamme actuelle de BMW. Elles ont un peu l'allure incertaine, encore mal définie d'un ado au milieu des berlines, coupés et décapotables racés qu'elles côtoient chez les concessionnaires de la marque. Même les camions et autres utilitaires qui portent le célèbre écusson bleu et blanc sont plus sexy !

PHYSIQUE ÉLÉMENTAIRE

Les Série 1 sont pourtant des voitures tout à fait abouties qui peuvent en remontrer à leurs frangines à certains égards. Elles sont par exemple un peu plus légères que les Série 3, ce qui leur permet de tirer des performances légèrement meilleures des groupes propulseurs qu'elles partagent avec ces dernières. Le coupé 135i à boîte manuelle qui a raflé les grands honneurs de notre match des sportives de l'an dernier a bouclé le 0-100 km/h en 5,14 secondes et franchi le quart de mille en 13,54 secondes, tandis qu'un coupé 335i s'exécute en 5,30 et 13,70 secondes.

L'avantage de poids de la 135i est d'environ 90 kg et son prix de base est inférieur de quelque 10 000$ à celui du coupé 335i. Par contre, les Série 1 ne sont pas offertes avec le rouage intégral xDrive des Série 3, sans parler d'une rivale comme l'Audi A3 quattro. Qu'à cela ne tienne puisqu'elles sont dotées de l'antidérapage DSC, superbement rapide et efficace, et surtout qu'elles profitent de la répartition des masses quasi parfaite et du comportement équilibré et précis qui font la réputation de BMW.

EN PLEIN CONTRÔLE AUX COMMANDES

Même constat pour l'ergonomie de conduite, qu'il s'agisse du confort et du maintien des sièges, du volant gainé de cuir, des commandes précises et bien disposées ou des cadrans superbement clairs. C'est encore mieux avec le Groupe sport M, option exclusive à la 135i, qui ajoute des roues d'alliage de 18 pouces, des sièges et un volant sport M en plus d'un pommeau de levier de vitesses gainé de cuir.

Le coupé 135i inscrit au match de l'an dernier était pourvu du Groupe sport M et de très peu d'autres options. Pas de sièges à

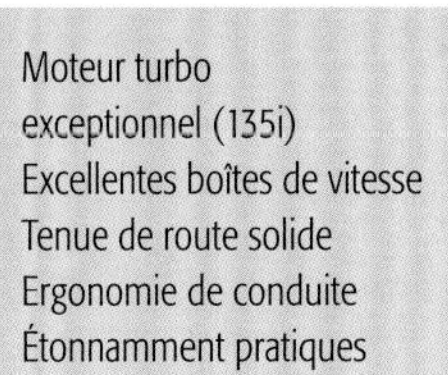

FEU VERT

Moteur turbo exceptionnel (135i)
Excellentes boîtes de vitesse
Tenue de route solide
Ergonomie de conduite
Étonnamment pratiques

FEU ROUGE

Silhouette rondouillarde
Pas de rouage intégral
Groupes optionnels chers
Porte-gobelet amovible rudimentaire
Visibilité arrière limitée (Cabriolet)

réglage électrique, ni de système de navigation, par exemple. Sa présentation était dépouillée, presque austère, mais la qualité et la texture des matériaux, leur assemblage serré et le dessin du tableau de bord n'appelaient aucun reproche. Ce coupé avait d'ailleurs mérité les meilleures notes pour tout ce qui touchait l'habitacle, l'ergonomie et le rangement, y compris le coffre.

La petite « BM » n'a cédé le premier rang qu'au chapitre des accessoires. Malgré son équipement raisonnable, elle était la plus chère du groupe. Il est donc sage de privilégier les options qui bonifient la conduite et de laisser le luxe à la clientèle des Série 3 et semblables. Lors du lancement nord-américain de la Série 1, BMW l'a comparée à sa mythique 2002. Or, cette dernière n'avait rien d'une berline de luxe. La Série 1 est parfaitement fidèle à cet esprit, si on s'en tient à l'essentiel.

On aurait d'ailleurs grand tort de croire qu'il faut s'offrir la 135i, le modèle le plus puissant et cher pour profiter pleinement de ses qualités. Rien n'est moins vrai. Le modèle 128i, propulsé par un autre des merveilleux six cylindres en ligne BMW de 3,0 litres, cette fois en version atmosphérique, est une perle. Le coupé 128i doté de la boîte manuelle de série est particulièrement réjouissant pour la précision de ses contrôles, la vivacité, la sonorité et la souplesse de son moteur, sa construction solide et son comportement. Seules fausses notes : une tenue de cap légèrement floue et les réactions parfois sèches de sa suspension.

LE PLUS NOUVEAU DES TURBOS

La 135i n'est certainement pas en reste cette année puisqu'elle a droit au premier six cylindres en ligne BMW à réunir l'injection directe, le calage variable des soupapes Valvetronic et un turbocompresseur. Au singulier, d'ailleurs, car on a remplacé les deux turbos du moteur N54 par un nouveau turbo à double chambre plus simple et plus efficace.

La crête de puissance du moteur N55 et identique, soit 300 chevaux à 5 800 tr/min, mais son couple maxi de 300 lb-pi est livré à un régime encore plus bas, soit 1 200 tr/min. Les cotes de consommation ville/route, avec la boîte manuelle, sont de 10,4 et 7,0 L/100 km contre 11,6 et 7,7 L/100 km pour le modèle précédent, une réduction appréciable. En prime, on peut maintenant doter les 135i de la boîte de vitesse à double embrayage automatisé à 7 rapports de BMW en guise d'automatique.

Marc Lachapelle

PHOTOS : BMW

Catégorie	Cabriolet, Coupé
Échelle de prix	35 800 $ à 48 500 $
Garanties	4 ans/80 000 km, 4 ans/80 000 km
Assemblage	Leipzig, Allemagne
Cote d'assurance	n.d.

CHÂSSIS - DONNÉES POUR 135I COUPE

Emp/lon/lar/haut	2 660/4 373/1 748/1 408 mm
Coffre	370 litres
Réservoir	53 litres
Nombre coussins sécurité	6
Antipatinage / contrôle stabilité	oui / oui
Suspension avant	indépendante, jambes de force
Suspension arrière	indépendante, multibras
Freins avant / arrière	disque (ABS) / disque (ABS)
Direction	à crémaillère, ass. variable
Diamètre de braquage	10,7 m
Pneus avant / arrière	215/40R18 / 215/40R18
Poids	1 530 kg
Capacité de remorquage	non recommandé

COMPOSANTES MÉCANIQUES

128i

Cylindrée, soupapes, alim.	6L 3,0 litres 24 s atmos.
Puissance / Couple	230 chevaux / 200 lb-pi
Tr. base (opt) / rouage base (opt)	M6 (A6) / Prop
0-100 / 80-120 / 100-0 km/h	6.4 s / 5,2 s / n.d.
Type ess. / ville / autoroute	Super / 10,8 / 6,9 l/100 km

135i

Cylindrée, soupapes, alim.	6L 3,0 litres 24 s turbocompressé
Puissance / Couple	300 chevaux / 300 lb-pi
Tr. base (opt) / rouage base (opt)	M6 (A6) / Prop
0-100 / 80-120 / 100-0 km/h	5,1 s / 4,6 s / 35,4 m
Type ess. / ville / autoroute	Super / 11,6 / 7,7 l/100km

DANS LA MÊME CATÉGORIE

Audi A3, MINI Cooper, Volkswagen Eos, Volvo C30

DU NOUVEAU EN 2011

Aucun changement majeur

NOS IMPRESSIONS

Agrément de conduite :	9/10
Fiabilité :	7/10
Sécurité :	8/10
Qualités hivernales :	7/10
Espace intérieur :	7/10
Confort :	7/10

www.bmw.ca

Plus d'informations dans la section statistiques en dernière partie du Guide

POUR LE LOGO OU POUR SES QUALITÉS?

Si vous magasinez pour une petite berline de luxe, il y a fort à parier que vous avez songé à la BMW de Série 3, surtout si vous êtes amateur de voitures à vocation plus sportive. Sinon, c'est sans doute le prestige et l'image associés au logo du constructeur bavarois qui vous attirent; éléments qui, avouons-le, s'avèrent quasi essentiel pour plusieurs acheteurs dans ce créneau. Quoi qu'il en soit, BMW demeure un joueur d'importance aux côtés de Mercedes-Benz, mais force est d'admettre qu'Audi leur chauffe sévèrement la couette depuis quelque temps...

Il y belle lurette que la BMW de Série 3 repousse les standards en matière de sportivité et de plaisir de conduite dans son segment. Difficile d'égaler la sensation que l'on éprouve au volant de cette voiture, que ce soit sur la route ou sur une piste, et ce, même à bord des versions de base. Ajoutez une gamme de modèles pratiquement aussi étendue qu'il y a de versions du Ford F-150 et vous obtenez des choix pour tous les goûts. Outre le prestige du logo, voilà sans doute l'élément qui explique le succès de plusieurs constructeurs dans ce créneau. Dans le cas de BMW, on ratisse large avec toutes ces versions.

UNE PANOPLIE DE MOTORISATIONS

Histoire d'attirer la clientèle, la berline 323i fait office de modèle d'entrée de gamme avec sous le capot un six cylindres en ligne de 200 chevaux. C'est une voiture qui en impose et dont les performances ne sont pas inintéressantes.

Probablement la plus populaire du lot, la 328i dispose d'un peu plus de puissance, soit 230 chevaux, grâce à son moteur six cylindres de 3,0 litres. Le fait qu'elle puisse revêtir les traits d'une berline, d'un coupé, d'un cabriolet et d'une familiale avec, dans certains cas, un rouage intégral, joue sans doute pour beaucoup dans sa grande popularité. Bref, la 328i offre un excellent compromis au chapitre de la puissance et du comportement, tout en demeurant relativement abordable.

Pour un budget un peu plus important, vous pourrez vous tourner vers la berline ou le coupé 335i, cette dernière proposant certainement l'un des meilleurs moteurs de cette catégorie, soit un six cylindres de 3,0 litres suralimenté déployant 300 chevaux. C'est en fait son couple étonnant de 300 lb-pi développé dès les 1 200 tr/min qui en fait tout un moteur et qui procure à ce bolide des performances aussi intéressantes que l'ancienne M3. La grande nouveauté cette année est l'arrivée de la 335is, une version poussant d'un cran les performances avec ses 20 chevaux supplémentaires, mais c'est surtout son aspect qui lui octroie son attitude distincte. Cette version, au chapitre du prix, permet de faire le pont entre la 335i et la M3 et rivalise un peu plus avec l'Audi S4. Il ne manque que le rouage intégral à cette 335is, élément non offert, malheureusement...

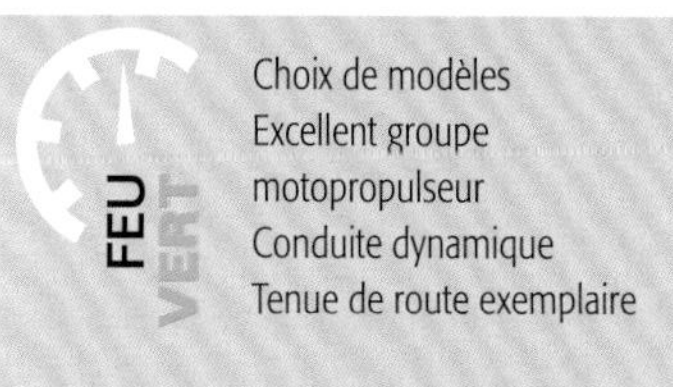

Choix de modèles
Excellent groupe motopropulseur
Conduite dynamique
Tenue de route exemplaire

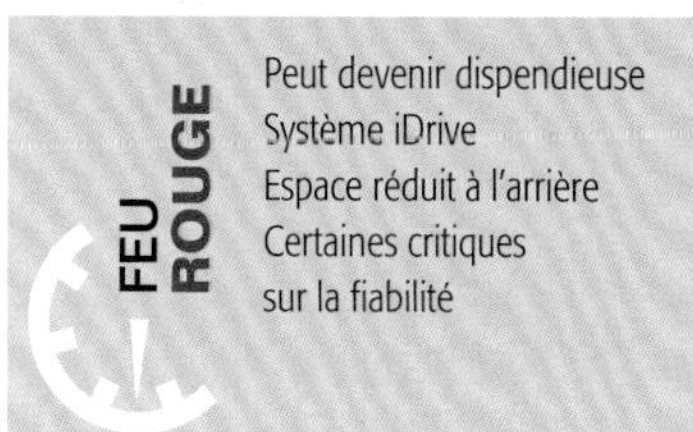

Peut devenir dispendieuse
Système iDrive
Espace réduit à l'arrière
Certaines critiques sur la fiabilité

Venons-en d'ailleurs à la M3 qui, cette année, ne subit aucun changement, mais qui demeure un emblème chez les berlines sport. Elle est propulsée par un moteur V8 de 4,0 litres produisant pas moins de 414 chevaux. Toute cette puissance est transmise aux roues arrière par le biais d'une boîte manuelle à six rapports ou séquentielle à sept rapports. Concernant la puissance, la M3 doit néanmoins concéder la victoire à la Mercedes C63 AMG dont le V8 de 6,2 litres commande 451 chevaux. Sachez que la C63 AMG se vend à un prix inférieur de plus de 6000$. Voilà une féroce concurrente pour la M3.

Et si tout cela n'est pas assez, les amateurs de motorisation diesel peuvent aussi se tourner vers la 335d, une version qui favorise l'économie de carburant sans compromettre la performance. Cependant, son prix assez corsé aura tôt fait d'en décourager plusieurs, mais il faut avouer que c'est tout de même une bonne voiture.

SPORTIVITÉ À L'AVANT-PLAN

Au chapitre du style, peu importe la version choisie, vous aurez une voiture agréable à l'œil dont les lignes accentuent la sportivité. Ce sont surtout les jantes qui mettent bien en valeur le véhicule et de ce côté, BMW sait y faire. Bien entendu, la nouvelle 335is tout comme la M3 dispose d'éléments les rendant uniques et drôlement réussies esthétiquement.

À bord de la Série 3, difficile de faire des reproches au sujet de la qualité et de la finition. On note un excellent souci du détail et une fois de plus, la sportivité est mise en évidence. Le tout débute par des sièges fournissant un support plus rigoureux, vous maintenant bien en place. Le volant se prend bien en main et vous donne l'impression de pouvoir contrôler la voiture du bout des doigts. Par contre, comme tout n'est pas parfait, il faut composer avec un espace à bord plus réduit, surtout pour les passagers arrière. Cet élément est encore plus vrai à bord des cabriolets. L'ergonomie à bord n'est pas mauvaise, mais on a toujours de la difficulté à s'habituer au système multifonction iDrive qui contrôle de nombreuses fonctions en rendant certaines simples, et d'autres, plus complexes !

Du reste, la Série 3 charme davantage lorsqu'on la conduit. Sa rigidité exemplaire, sa tenue de route et sa direction dont l'assistance variable est presque toujours bien dosée en font une voiture que l'on pilote, beaucoup plus que l'on conduit.

Sylvain Raymond

PHOTOS : MARC LACHAPELLE

Catégorie	Berline, Cabriolet, Coupé, Familiale
Échelle de prix	34 900 $ à 81 900 $
Garanties	4 ans/80 000 km, 4 ans/80 000 km
Assemblage	Dingolfing, Allemagne
Cote d'assurance	passable

CHÂSSIS - DONNÉES POUR 335I XDRIVE BERLINE

Emp/lon/lar/haut	2 760/4 531/2 013/1 421 mm
Coffre	460 litres
Réservoir	61 litres
Nombre coussins sécurité	6
Antipatinage / contrôle stabilité	oui / oui
Suspension avant	indépendante, jambes de force
Suspension arrière	indépendante, multibras
Freins avant / arrière	disque (ABS) / disque (ABS)
Direction	à crémaillère, ass. variable
Diamètre de braquage	11,0 m
Pneus avant / arrière	P225/45R17 / P225/45R17
Poids	1 730 kg
Capacité de remorquage	480 kg (1 058 lb)

COMPOSANTES MÉCANIQUES

335i, 335 xi

Cylindrée, soupapes, alim.	6L 3,0 litres 24 s turbocompressé
Puissance / Couple	300 chevaux / 300 lb-pi
Tr. base (opt) / rouage base (opt)	M6 (A6) / Prop (Int)
0-100 / 80-120 / 100-0 km/h	5,7 s / 4,9 s / 36,4 m
Type ess. / ville / autoroute	Super / 11,8 / 7,6 l/100km

M3

Cylindrée, soupapes, alim.	V8 4,0 litres 32 s atmos.
Puissance / Couple	414 chevaux / 295 lb-pi
Tr. base (opt) / rouage base (opt)	M6 (A7) / Prop
0-100 / 80-120 / 100-0 km/h	4,8 s / 3,9 s / 37,1 m
Type ess. / ville / autoroute	Super / 15,7 / 10,1 l/100km

323i

6L 2,5 l, 200 ch, 180 lb-pi - 0-100 : 9,0 s - 11,1 / 6,9 l/100 km

328i, 328xi

6L 3,0 l, 230 ch, 200 lb-pi - 0-100 : 6,6 s - 11,4 / 7,3 l/100 km

335d

6L 3,0l, 265 ch, 425 lb-pi - 0-100 : 6,3 s - 9,0 / 5,4 l/100 km

DANS LA MÊME CATÉGORIE

Acura TL, Acura TSX, Audi A4, Audi A5, Cadillac CTS, Infiniti G, Lexus IS, Mercedes-Benz Classe C, Volvo C70, Volvo S40, Volvo V50

DU NOUVEAU EN 2011

Aucun changement majeur

NOS IMPRESSIONS

Agrément de conduite :	■■■■■■■■■■	10/10
Fiabilité :	■■■■■■■■□□	8/10
Sécurité :	■■■■■■■■□□	8/10
Qualités hivernales :	■■■■■■■□□□	7/10
Espace intérieur :	■■■■■■■■□□	8/10
Confort :	■■■■■■■■□□	8/10

www.bmw.ca

Plus d'informations dans la section statistiques en dernière partie du Guide

COMME UNE GRANDE

L'année-modèle 2011 marque le début de la sixième génération pour la BMW Série 5 qui a fait son entrée au Canada au printemps 2010 avec les modèles 535i et 550i. Depuis l'arrivée de la Série 5 en 1972, BMW a vendu plus de 5,5 millions d'exemplaires de sa berline de milieu de gamme à travers le monde, ce qui en fait l'un des modèles les plus importants de la gamme du constructeur bavarois.

Au lancement mondial de cette nouvelle berline, nous avons eu l'occasion de prendre contact avec la 535i et son nouveau moteur 6 cylindres turbocompressé de 300 chevaux qui reçoit la désignation interne N55. Il remplace le six cylindres à double turbo, appelé N54, qui équipait précédemment la 535i. Ce nouveau moteur a été développé pour diminuer la consommation de carburant et les émissions polluantes et devient d'office le moteur «de base» de la Série 5 Le moteur précédent et le nouveau se différencient au niveau de la turbocompression, le nouveau moteur (N55) n'étant muni que d'un seul turbo. Ce dernier comporte cependant deux entrées distinctes (TwinScroll), ce qui permet de réduire la longueur des tubulures d'échappement jusqu'au convertisseur catalytique assurant ainsi des émissions moins polluantes, surtout immédiatement après le démarrage, cela améliore le bilan de la marque à cet égard. Au chapitre des performances, le nouveau moteur N55 à simple turbo affiche des statistiques identiques à celles du N54 à deux turbos avec ses 300 chevaux et 300 livres-pied de couple, la principale différence entre ces deux moulins étant que le nouveau atteint son couple maximal dès 1 200 tours/minute soit 200 tours plus rapidement que le moteur à doubles turbos, lequel ne sera pas délaissé pour autant puisqu'il a été revu afin d'offrir plus de puissance et qu'il sera destiné à des modèles à vocation plus sportive, comme la nouvelle BMW 335is conçue exclusivement pour le marché nord-américain. Notons également que la nouvelle 5 reçoit une boîte automatique à huit rapports, toujours en vue d'améliorer la consommation et de réduire les émissions, et qu'il est possible de la contrôler en mode manuel au moyen de paliers au volant.

LE SYSTÈME ADAPTIVE DRIVE : DES RÉGLAGES PERSONNALISÉS

Sur le circuit d'Estoril, la nouvelle 535i a fait preuve d'un aplomb remarquable et d'une agilité surprenante en conduite sportive même si ce n'est pas sa vocation première. La contribution du système Adaptive Drive, proposé en option, y est pour beaucoup puisqu'il est possible de sélectionner les modes Sport et Sport + pour bénéficier d'une réponse plus rapide à la commande des gaz ainsi qu'à la direction, d'un tarage plus ferme des suspensions et d'une intervention moins hâtive du système de contrôle électronique de la stabilité. Les modes Normal et Confort sont à privilégier pour une conduite plus décontractée ou lorsque l'on ne veut pas brusquer les passagers.

Ainsi, le comportement de la Série 5 s'adapte au souhait du conducteur à la seule pression d'un bouton, courtoisie de l'électronique avancée. À cela, on peut ajouter la direction active qui fait en sorte que les roues arrière pivotent dans la même direction que les roues avant jusqu'à 2,5 degrés quand la vitesse de la voiture est supérieure à 60 kilomètres/heure, assurant une bonne stabilité lors des changements de voie à haute vitesse. Si la voiture roule sous les 60 km/h, les roues arrière pivotent alors dans la direction opposée à celle des roues avant ce qui facilite les manœuvres de stationnement avec cette nouvelle berline qui mesure 40 millimètres de plus en longueur hors tout comparativement à l'ancien modèle. Contrairement au modèle de génération précédente, la nouvelle 5 fait appel à une suspension avant à doubles triangles obliques ainsi qu'à une nouvelle suspension arrière composée de l'essieu *Integral V*, ces deux éléments permettent de bonifier à la fois le confort et la tenue de route de la nouvelle 5.

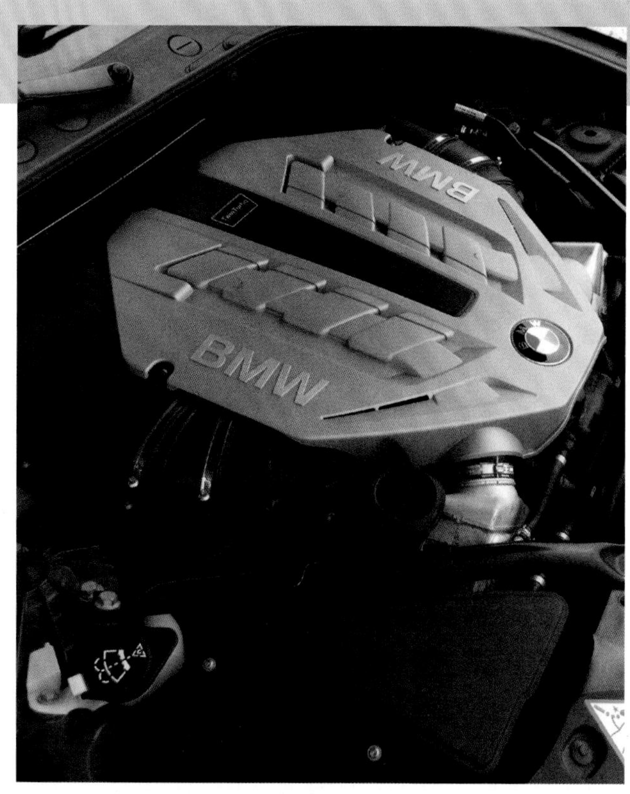

UNE ARCHITECTURE COMMUNE AVEC LA SÉRIE 7

Les dimensions accrues de la nouvelle 5 s'expliquent par le fait qu'elle partage sa plate-forme et ses suspensions avec la plus grande Série7. D'ailleurs, l'aspect le plus frappant de cette transformation est l'accroissement de l'empattement qui mesure 80 millimètres de plus que celui du modèle précédent. Sur la route, on sent vraiment que le comportement de la nouvelle 5 s'approche beaucoup de celui de la 7, surtout lorsque les modes Confort et Normal sont sélectionnés. La contribution de la direction active se fait également bien sentir quand on enchaîne les virages en lacet, typiques des routes montagnardes de l'Europe puisque le pivotement des roues arrière en virage nous donne l'impression de conduire une voiture plus courte et plus agile.

Côté style, la filiation avec la Série 7 est assurée par la ligne portant sur les poignées des portières, ligne qui commence cependant à la roue avant plutôt que dès la partie avant de la voiture, comme c'est le cas sur la 7. De plus, cette ligne prend davantage de volume vers l'arrière sur la 5 afin de souligner son caractère plus dynamique. À l'avant, la calandre à deux naseaux est à la fois plus basse et plus large. À l'intérieur, la console centrale asymétrique est tournée vers le conducteur sur un angle de 7 degrés cela définit le caractère plus actif de la 5.

LA SÉRIE 5 GRAN TURISMO ET LA M5

La Série 5 « classique » se double d'une nouvelle version appelée Gran Turismo qui se veut un croisement entre une berline conventionnelle et un sport-utilitaire. BMW ayant choisi de créer une nouvelle variante dont le style est loin de faire l'unanimité et de segmenter encore plus son offre dans ce créneau. L'un des éléments les plus frappants de cette nouvelle venue est sans contredit l'adoption d'un hayon arrière, ce qui représente une exception dans le créneau des voitures de luxe, exception toutefois partagée par la récente Porsche Panamera. Dans le cas de Série 5 Gran Turismo, les ingénieurs ont décidé d'innover en concevant un coffre bimode accessible par l'ouverture d'un couvercle conventionnel ou par l'ouverture complète du hayon. Pourquoi un tel concept d'ouverture bimode ? Les ingénieurs ont répondu que l'ouverture du coffre seulement permettait de charger des bagages sans déranger les passagers qui seraient déjà à bord, alors que l'ouverture complète du hayon facilite le chargement d'objets plus volumineux. Voilà pour le concept, mais au quotidien, on se trouve à utiliser le hayon la plupart du temps, l'accès au coffre étant plus étroit et moins commode avec la seule ouverture à la verticale du panneau de couvercle du coffre.

Sur la route, la Série 5 Gran Turismo maintient un bel équilibre mais n'est pas aussi sportive de caractère que les autres berlines de la

marque en raison d'un poids très élevé. De plus, au Canada, les premiers modèles n'étaient disponibles qu'avec la simple propulsion, ceux à traction intégrale n'arrivant que plus tard en cours d'année 2010. Compte tenu de la vocation de ce modèle, il est évident que la traction intégrale est de mise et qu'une Série 5 Gran Turismo de type propulsion est dénuée d'intérêt. C'est ce que m'a signalé un collègue resté embourbé dans seulement trois ou quatre centimètres de neige en stationnant en ville, malgré le fait que la voiture était chaussée de pneus d'hiver…

Les suspensions de la 5 GT sont ajustables et trois paliers sont proposés, soit « normal », « sport » et « sport plus ». Précisons tout de suite que le roulement est assez ferme même en mode normal,

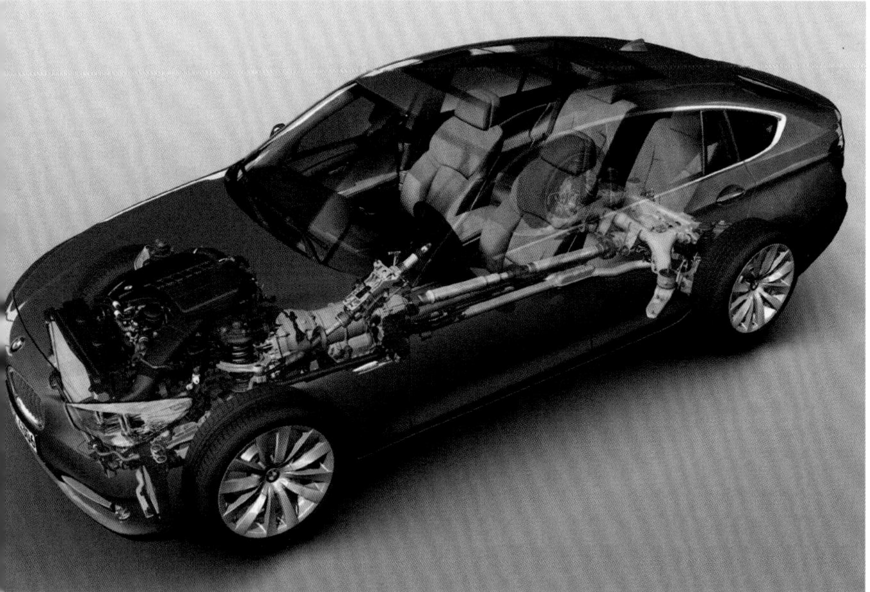

Catégorie	Berline
Échelle de prix	53 900 $ à 79 900 $
Garanties	4 ans/80 000 km, 4 ans/80 000 km
Assemblage	Dingolfing, Allemagne
Cote d'assurance	passable

CHÂSSIS - DONNÉES POUR 528I XDRIVE

Emp/lon/lar/haut	2 888/4 854/1 846/1 468 mm
Coffre	520 litres
Réservoir	70 litres
Nombre coussins sécurité	6
Antipatinage / contrôle stabilité	oui / oui
Suspension avant	indépendante, double triangulation
Suspension arrière	indépendante, multibras
Freins avant / arrière	disque (ABS) / disque (ABS)
Direction	à crémaillère, ass. variable
Diamètre de braquage	11,4 m
Pneus avant / arrière	P225/50R17 / P225/50R17
Poids	1 710 kg
Capacité de remorquage	n.d.

COMPOSANTES MÉCANIQUES

528i

Cylindrée, soupapes, alim.	6L 3,0 litre 24 s atmos
Puissance / Couple	240 chevaux / 230 lb-pi
Tr. base (opt) / rouage base (opt)	M6 (A6) / Prop (Int)
0-100 / 80-120 / 100-0 km/h	6,7 (est) / n.d. / n.d.
Type ess. / ville / autoroute	Super / 12,3 / 7,6 l/100 km

535i

Cylindrée, soupapes, alim.	6L 3,0 litres 24 s atmos
Puissance / Couple	300 chevaux / 300 lb-pi
Tr. base (opt) / rouage base (opt)	A6 (M6) / Prop
0-100 / 80-120 / 100-0 km/h	6,0 s (est) / 5,9 s (est) / n.d.
Type ess. / ville / autoroute	Super / 11,8 / 6,6 l/100 km

550i, 550i xDrive

Cylindrée, soupapes, alim.	V8 4,4 litres 24 s turbocompressé
Puissance / Couple	400 chevaux / 450 lb-pi
Tr. base (opt) / rouage base (opt)	A8 / Prop (Int)
0-100 / 80-120 / 100-0 km/h	n.d. / n.d. / n.d.
Type ess. / ville / autoroute	Super / 12,3 / 7,6 l/100 km

FEU VERT

- Bonne habitabilité
- Gamme étendue
- Comportement équilibré
- Boîte automatique à huit rapports
- Qualité de la finition

FEU ROUGE

- Prix élevés
- Coût des options
- Version propulsion de la 5 GT inintéressante
- Poids élevé (5 GT)

rendant par conséquent les autres réglages plutôt inutiles, à moins de décider d'attaquer une bretelle d'accès à l'autoroute, mais ça ne cadre pas vraiment avec la vocation première de cette voiture.

Au moment d'écrire ces lignes, tout porte à croire que BMW procédera au lancement de la nouvelle M5 au Mondial de l'Automobile de Paris et qu'elle sera commercialisée en cours d'année 2011. Comme le veut la récente tendance au downsizing des motorisations adoptées par l'ensemble des constructeurs, la nouvelle M5 délaisse le V10 de 5,0 litres au profit d'une version plus performante du V8 biturbo. Les ingénieurs de la division M évoquent une puissance annoncée à 570 chevaux et un couple de 530 livres-pied, une augmentation notoire par rapport au plus faible couple du moteur V10. Le changement d'un moteur atmosphérique pour un moteur suralimenté par turbocompression représentera également une première pour les voitures de la division M.

Gabriel Gélinas

PHOTOS : MARC LACHAPELLE

DANS LA MÊME CATÉGORIE

Acura RL, Audi A6, Cadillac STS, Infiniti M, Jaguar XF, Lexus GS, Lincoln MKS, Mercedes-Benz Classe E, Volvo S80

DU NOUVEAU EN 2011

Nouveau modèle, version M5 à venir

NOS IMPRESSIONS

Agrément de conduite :	8/10
Fiabilité :	Nouveau modèle
Sécurité :	10/10
Qualités hivernales :	8/10
Espace intérieur :	8/10
Confort :	9/10

www.bmw.ca

Plus d'informations dans la section statistiques en dernière partie du Guide

EN ATTENDANT LA RELÈVE

Pour BMW, la Série 6 désigne une voiture de niche, les ventes mondiales de ce modèle ne s'élevant qu'aux alentours de 20 000 unités par année. Mais la Série 6 représente également une très belle opportunité de réaliser des marges de profits plus qu'intéressantes pour le constructeur bavarois qui peut développer à peu de frais ce qui est essentiellement un modèle dérivé de la berline de Série 5 pour ensuite le vendre à un prix nettement supérieur.

La Série 6 est proposée en deux versions : rapide et très rapide... Nous faisons évidemment référence ici à la 650i dont le moteur déballe 360 chevaux et à la M6 qui en livre 500. Incidemment, ces deux versions sont livrables en coupé ou en cabriolet qui est cependant équipé d'un simple toit souple à commande électrique, plutôt que d'un toit rigide-rétractable, ce qui étonne un peu compte tenu du prix de plus de 105 000 dollars demandé pour la 650i Cabriolet, sans parler du prix supérieur à 133 000 de la M6 Cabriolet. De plus, le modèle Cabriolet avec le toit en place n'est pas aussi élégant que le Coupé, en plus de présenter une lacune très prononcée au niveau de la visibilité vers l'arrière. Ce qui est particulièrement frappant avec la Série 6, c'est de constater jusqu'à quel point le gabarit de la voiture est imposant et l'espace intérieur est limité, surtout aux places arrière où des adultes se retrouvent avec un dégagement très serré pour les jambes.

VOCATION GRAND TOURISME

Peu importe qu'il s'agisse de la 650i ou de la M6, la vocation première de la Série 6 est celle d'une voiture Grand Tourisme plutôt que d'une authentique sportive. Oui, les moteurs sont performants à souhait et les boîtes de vitesse sont bien adaptées, mais la Série 6 demeure une voiture au gabarit imposant et dont le poids est très élevé, et ces deux éléments doivent être pris en compte lors de la conduite sportive.

Lorsque la M6 est poussée à la limite sur circuit, il est relativement facile de la mettre en dérive et de faire s'évaporer en fumée les pneus Pirelli P Zero Corsa, grâce à la puissance élevée livrée par le V10 qui ne demande qu'à atteindre sa limite de révolutions de 8 250 tours-minute.

Sur circuit, la performance de toute voiture se réduit essentiellement à son rapport poids-puissance et, dans le cas de la M6, celui-ci est plus favorable que celui de la berline M5, le coupé étant plus léger de 45 kilogrammes. Cette réduction de poids s'explique notamment par le toit fixe en plastique renforcé de fibre de carbone qui permet également d'abaisser le centre de gravité de la voiture. Par ailleurs, le coupé M6 fait aussi un grand usage de matériaux légers comme l'aluminium pour la réalisation de la partie avant, du capot et des portières, ainsi que pour les suspensions. De plus, les panneaux de carrosserie latéraux et le couvercle du coffre sont en plastique renforcé de fibre de verre. Le résultat, c'est que la M6 dispose ainsi d'un rapport poids-

FEU VERT
- Version M6 très performante
- Style distinctif
- Confort relevé
- Offert aussi en version cabriolet
- Disponibilité de la boîte manuelle

FEU ROUGE
- Gabarit imposant
- Habitacle restreint
- Prix élevés
- Coût des options
- Visibilité réduite (cabriolet)

puissance phénoménal de 3,37 kilos par cheval-vapeur (3,5 pour la berline M5). Malgré tous ces efforts, il faut tenir compte des dimensions généreuses de la voiture dont le poids atteint tout de même les 1710 kilos, ce qui fait que la M6 a tendance à adopter un comportement sous-vireur lorsque ses limites sont atteintes sur circuit et lorsque le système de contrôle de la stabilité est désactivé.

INSPIRATION CONCEPT GRAN COUPE

Au moment d'écrire ces lignes, il appert que la nouvelle génération de la Série 6 sera présentée en grande première au Mondial de l'Automobile de Paris. 2011 marquera donc une transition importante pour ces coupés et cabriolets de prestige à quatre places qui arriveront au pays en cours d'année, possiblement en tant que modèles 2012. Dans le cas de la nouvelle génération de la Série 6, tout indique que BMW retiendra l'approche qui a fait ses preuves dans le passé, c'est-à-dire que le nouveau modèle empruntera plusieurs éléments importants à la berline de Série 5, et que la nouvelle Série 6 poursuivra la récente tradition en étant déclinée à la fois en coupé ainsi qu'en cabriolet à toit souple.

Par la suite, BMW pourrait poursuivre sur sa lancée et en décliner d'autres variantes comme un coupé à quatre portes, qui pourrait s'appeler Série 6 GT comme la récente variante Grand Turismo de la Série 5, et qui émulerait le style de la CLS de Mercedes-Benz ou la prochaine A7 d'Audi, un scénario évoqué par la présentation du Concept Gran Coupe de BMW au récent Salon de l'auto de Pékin.

À en juger par les photos de cette plus récente voiture-concept et celles prises sur le vif lors de tests de prototypes de la Série 6, il devient assez clair que l'ère Bangle est bel et bien révolue chez le constructeur bavarois puisque les lignes adoptées par ces modèles révèlent une nouvelle approche avec un style nettement plus typé. Ainsi, la partie arrière plutôt ronde de la Série 6 qui a vu le jour en 2005 sera remplacée par des lignes plus athlétiques, et le nouveau modèle sera également doté d'un empattement allongé (tout comme celui de la récente Série 5) et de porte-à-faux réduits par rapport au modèle antérieur. Il y a fort à parier qu'une nouvelle M6 fera son entrée suite à l'arrivée de la 6 de nouvelle génération.

Gabriel Gélinas

PHOTOS : BMW

Catégorie	Cabriolet, Coupé
Échelle de prix	95 500 $ à 131 300 $ (2010)
Garanties	4 ans/80 000 km, 4 ans/80 000 km
Assemblage	Dingolfing, Allemagne
Cote d'assurance	n.d.

CHÂSSIS - DONNÉES POUR 650I COUPE

Emp/lon/lar/haut	2 780/4 831/1 855/1 374 mm
Coffre	368 litres
Réservoir	70 litres
Nombre coussins sécurité	6
Antipatinage / contrôle stabilité	oui / oui
Suspension avant	indépendante, jambes de force
Suspension arrière	indépendante, multibras
Freins avant / arrière	disque (ABS) / disque (ABS)
Direction	à crémaillère, assistée
Diamètre de braquage	11,4 m
Pneus avant / arrière	P245/40R19 / P275/35R19
Poids	1 730 kg
Capacité de remorquage	n.d.

COMPOSANTES MÉCANIQUES

650i

Cylindrée, soupapes, alim.	V8 4,8 litres 32 s atmos.
Puissance / Couple	360 chevaux / 360 lb-pi
Tr. base (opt) / rouage base (opt)	M6 (A6) / Prop
0-100 / 80-120 / 100-0 km/h	6,7 s / 4,9 s / 38.5 m
Type ess. / ville / autoroute	Super / 13,9 / 9,6 l/100 km

M6

Cylindrée, soupapes, alim.	V10 5,0 litres 40 s atmos.
Puissance / Couple	500 chevaux / 383 lb-pi
Tr. base (opt) / rouage base (opt)	M6 (A7) / Prop
0-100 / 80-120 / 100-0 km/h	4,6 s / 3,9 s / 37,0 m
Type ess. / ville / autoroute	Super / 20,3 / 11,7 l/100 km

DANS LA MÊME CATÉGORIE

Aston Martin Vantage, Chevrolet Corvette, Dodge Viper, Jaguar XK, Maserati Gran Turismo, Mercedes-Benz Classe SL, Nissan GT-R, Porsche 911

DU NOUVEAU EN 2011

Nouveau modèle sera dévoilé en cours d'année

NOS IMPRESSIONS

Agrément de conduite :	7/10
Fiabilité :	8/10
Sécurité :	10/10
Qualités hivernales :	6/10
Espace intérieur :	6/10
Confort :	8/10

www.bmw.ca

Plus d'informations dans la section statistiques en dernière partie du Guide

L'ARRIVÉE DE L'HYBRIDE

Un an à peine après le lancement de l'actuelle génération de la Série 7, le constructeur bavarois propose maintenant une version à motorisation hybride de sa berline de grand luxe avec comme objectif de rattraper Lexus et sa LS600h L.

Dans un scénario classique des «voisins gonflables», BMW ne sera pas l'unique concurrent dans cette confrontation avec Lexus, car Mercedes-Benz a procédé, l'an dernier, au lancement d'une Classe S hybride, les deux constructeurs allemands ayant fait front commun pour développer ensemble l'ajout d'une motorisation électrique à leurs berlines de grand luxe.

Si rejoindre Lexus est l'un des enjeux dans cette course, il faut également reconnaître que le but premier qui est visé par l'ajout de ces deux nouvelles variantes de la Série 7 et de la Classe S est de réduire la marque des deux constructeurs allemands aux normes américaines CAFE (*Corporate Average Fuel Economy*) qui deviennent de plus en plus exigeantes.

UNE MOTORISATION HYBRIDE AUSSI PUISSANTE QU'UN V12

Dans le cas de BMW, le système hybride met d'abord l'emphase sur l'accroissement de la performance, accompagné d'une réduction de la consommation de 2 litres aux 100 kilomètres par rapport à la 750i conventionnelle et, par conséquent, d'une réduction des gaz à effets de serre. La Série 7 ActiveHybrid ajoute un moteur électrique de 15 kilowatts (environ 20 chevaux) au V8 biturbo, ce qui permet à la Série 7 hybride de développer une puissance combinée de 455 chevaux et de se qualifier comme «l'hybride aux accélérations les plus rapides au monde», selon BMW, avec un chrono de 4,9 secondes pour le 0-100 kilomètres/heure. La Série 7 ActiveHybrid ne se contente pas de faire jeu égal avec ses rivales directes au chapitre des performances, puisqu'elle est plus rapide d'une seconde et demie que la Lexus alors qu'elle devance la Mercedes-Benz par plus de deux secondes, ce dernier constructeur ayant décidé de jumeler le même moteur électrique de 15 kilowatts à un moteur thermique V6.

Au volant de cette Série 7 hybride, on sent instantanément le couple phénoménal de 516 livres-pied, dont 155 sont produites par le seul moteur électrique, et la voiture accélère avec le même aplomb que la Série 7 à moteur V12. Avoir autant de puissance et de couple sous le pied droit peut rapidement développer une certaine accoutumance aux accélérations à tout casser ainsi qu'aux reprises bien senties, la Série 7 ActiveHybrid éclipsant littéralement les voitures plus lentes lors de dépassements sur routes secondaires... À un point tel que l'on oublie complètement que l'on est au volant d'un véhicule hybride, du moins jusqu'à ce que l'indicateur de consommation nous rappelle à l'ordre. Parlant consommation, BMW annonce une moyenne de 9,4 litres aux 100 kilomètres pour sa nouvelle hybride, mais il faut obligatoirement adopter une conduite plus «civilisée» pour pouvoir espérer l'atteindre.

Disponibilité de la traction intégrale
Tenue de route surprenante
Technologie de pointe
Disponibilité d'un modèle hybride

Prix très élevés
Coût des options
Dimensions encombrantes
Certaines commandes peu intuitives

Dans la Série 7 ActiveHybrid, le moteur électrique est logé entre le V8 biturbo et la boîte de vitesse automatique à huit rapports développée par la firme ZF. Le moteur électrique agit également comme un alternateur lorsque le conducteur lève le pied de l'accélérateur ou quand il freine, ce qui recharge la batterie au lithium-ion qui pèse moins de 30 kilos et qui réside dans le coffre, dont elle réduit le volume de 500 à 460 litres par rapport à la Série 7 à motorisation conventionnelle.

UNE TECHNOLOGIE DE POINTE

La Série 7 hybride est aussi pourvue du système Start-Stop qui coupe automatiquement le contact au moteur à essence lors d'un arrêt afin de réduire la consommation et les émissions polluantes. Le moteur à essence est redémarré par le moteur électrique dès que le conducteur relâche la pédale de frein ou qu'il enfonce l'accélérateur, la Série 7 hybride ne disposant tout simplement pas d'un démarreur conventionnel, d'un alternateur ou d'une courroie entraînant le compresseur du système de climatisation, celui-ci étant alimenté directement par la batterie au lithium-ion. Le dispositif Start-Stop est disponible sur plusieurs modèles BMW et MINI vendus en Europe depuis quelque temps, mais fera sa première apparition en Amérique du Nord avec la Série 7 ActiveHybrid. Il est également important de noter que la nouvelle technologie hybride de BMW est entièrement compatible avec le rouage intégral développé par la marque allemande, et qu'il sera éventuellement possible de commander une Série 7 ActiveHybrid à rouage intégral.

Par ailleurs, les Série 7 à motorisation conventionnelle sont toujours au programme avec un choix entre le V8 biturbo de 400 chevaux et le très puissant V12 qui en livre 535 et dont le prix de base de 186000 dollars peut être qualifié de stratosphérique. Comme c'est invariablement le cas avec la marque bavaroise, toute une panoplie d'options et de groupes d'options figure au catalogue, ce qui a une incidence directe sur le degré de personnalisation du véhicule et du montant global de la facture. À titre d'exemple, précisons qu'il est relativement facile d'ajouter jusqu'à plus de 30000 dollars en équipements optionnels sur la Série 7...

Dans le créneau très exclusif des berlines de luxe de grande taille, la Série 7 se démarque comme étant la voiture la plus agréable à conduire.

Gabriel Gélinas

PHOTOS : MARC LACHAPELLE

BMW SÉRIE 7

Catégorie	Berline
Échelle de prix	108 600$ à 186 000$
Garanties	4 ans/80 000 km, 4 ans/80 000 km
Assemblage	n.d.
Cote d'assurance	n.d.

CHÂSSIS - DONNÉES POUR 750LI XDRIVE

Emp/lon/lar/haut	3 210/5 212/1 902/1 478 mm
Coffre	500 litres
Réservoir	82 litres
Nombre coussins sécurité	7
Antipatinage / contrôle stabilité	oui / oui
Suspension avant	indépendante, double triangulation
Suspension arrière	indépendante, multibras
Freins avant / arrière	disque (ABS) / disque (ABS)
Direction	à crémaillère, ass. variable
Diamètre de braquage	12,1 m
Pneus avant / arrière	P245/50R18 / P245/50R18
Poids	2 055 kg
Capacité de remorquage	n.d.

COMPOSANTES MÉCANIQUES

750i xDrive, 750Li xDrive

Cylindrée, soupapes, alim.	V8 4,4 litres 32 s turbocompressé
Puissance / Couple	400 chevaux / 450 lb-pi
Tr. base (opt) / rouage base (opt)	A6 / Prop
0-100 / 80-120 / 100-0 km/h	5,0 s (est) / 6,0 s (est) / 38,0 m
Type ess. / ville / autoroute	Super / 16,4 / 8,5 l/100 km

ActiveHybrid7

Cylindrée, soupapes, alim.	V8 4,4 litres atmos.
Puissance / Couple	455 chevaux / 515 lb-pi
Tr. base (opt) / rouage base (opt)	A8 / Prop (Int)
0-100 / 80-120 / 100-0 km/h	n.d. / n.d. / n.d.
Type ess. / ville / autoroute	Super / n.d. / n.d. l/100 km

760 Li

Cylindrée, soupapes, alim.	V12 6,0 litres turbocompressé
Puissance / Couple	535 chevaux / 550 lb-pi
Tr. base (opt) / rouage base (opt)	A8 / Prop
0-100 / 80-120 / 100-0 km/h	4,6 s / 5,0 s / n.d.
Type ess. / ville / autoroute	Super / 15,8 / 10,2 l/100 km

DANS LA MÊME CATÉGORIE

Audi A8, Jaguar XJ, Lexus LS, Maserati Quattroporte, Mercedes-Benz Classe S

DU NOUVEAU EN 2011

Nouvelle version hybride

NOS IMPRESSIONS

Agrément de conduite :	8/10
Fiabilité :	7/10
Sécurité :	10/10
Qualités hivernales :	8/10
Espace intérieur :	9/10
Confort :	9/10

www.bmw.ca

Plus d'informations dans la section statistiques en dernière partie du Guide

IL FAUDRA VOIR...

BMW aura mis sept ans avant de nous livrer une X3 de deuxième génération. Sept ans, dans l'industrie automobile, surtout dans le marché du luxe, c'est long. C'est même très long. Est-ce que l'attente aura valu la peine? C'est ce que nous saurons lorsque le petit utilitaire arrivera chez les concessionnaires au début de l'année prochaine.

Pour l'heure, on sait que deux motorisations seront offertes. (Quoi, pas de diesel? Eh non, pas encore.) Dans la livrée xDrive28i, on retrouvera l'actuel six cylindres en ligne de 3,0 litres, celui-là même qui a raflé tant de récompenses internationales. Sa puissance développée grimpe de 215 à 240 chevaux et on nous promet le 0-100 km/h en 7,1 secondes. Assurément que la vigueur sous le pied droit sera plus enivrante que pour la X3 de base qu'on nous a proposée l'automne dernier et qui, sincèrement, manquait de reprise.

En variante xDrive35i, on ajoute le turbo et, modernité oblige, l'injection directe. On dégage ainsi 300 chevaux et 300 lb-pi de couple, pour un 0-100 km/h en 5,8 secondes. Tant l'une que l'autre des versions héritent de la nouvelle boîte automatique huit rapports – soit deux de plus qu'actuellement. On s'attend évidemment à encore plus de douceur et une meilleure consommation en carburant. Le constructeur soutient que le dynamisme ne sera pas brimé puisqu'on pourra, en conduite dynamique, passer du 8e au 2e rapport sans rien faire grincer. Mais le passage des vitesses au volant n'est toujours pas offert – dites donc, qu'attend-on? Oh, et oubliez aussi la boîte manuelle; absente l'an dernier, elle ne reprendra pas plus de service avec cette 2e génération.

LA « PETITE » LA PLUS LONGUE

Qui dit passage générationnel, dit évidemment dimensions accrues

– d'autant plus que la X3 doit faire de la place à sa sœurette X1 qui arrivera l'an prochain. Les 83 mm additionnels qui viennent allonger la X3 (et 15 mm à l'empattement) seront encensés par les passagers arrière, qui devraient profiter d'un meilleur dégagement aux jambes. Sans surprise, le cargo pourra accueillir davantage (15 % plus de chargement) une fois la banquette relevée, de même que les 28 mm gagnés en largeur permettront de se desserrer les coudes à bord.

Du coup, la X3 devient la « petite la plus longue » – mais est-ce vraiment une bonne nouvelle, point de vue tenue de route? D'autant que la garde au sol est rehaussée de 12 mm; voilà qui facilitera les entrées et sorties à bord, mais en contrepartie, le centre de gravité s'en trouve relevé et il faudra voir si les aptitudes routières générales en seront affectées. Une chose est sûre: BMW soutient avoir réussi à retrancher le poids de l'ensemble de 40 kilos, ce qui ne peut être qu'une bonne nouvelle.

C'est la troisième génération de traction intégrale (xDrive) qui monte à bord de la X3 et le constructeur dit avoir revu le dispositif pour rehausser la flexibilité et aviver les réactions aux conditions

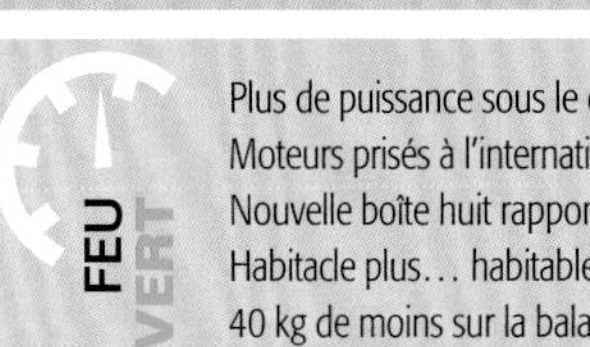

FEU VERT

- Plus de puissance sous le capot
- Moteurs prisés à l'international
- Nouvelle boîte huit rapports
- Habitacle plus… habitable
- 40 kg de moins sur la balance

FEU ROUGE

- Toujours pas de passage des vitesses au volant
- Pas de diesel pour l'instant
- Pas de boîte manuelle
- Pas de contrôle manuel des suspensions

changeantes de la route. En conditions normales, 60 % du couple gratifie les roues arrière, afin de conserver le comportement de type propulsion. Côté suspension, l'architecture à multibras à l'arrière demeure, mais est hautement révisée. Une nouveauté, mais qui sera offerte aux États-Unis et qui ne traversera malheureusement pas nos frontières (du moins, pour l'instant): le contrôle manuel des amortisseurs, question de donner plus de souplesse – ou de fermeté à la balade, selon ce qui est voulu. Le dispositif met également en scène le contrôle de performance, qui veille à ce que la traction intégrale se fasse encore plus sportive en laissant 80 % du couple aux roues arrière en situation normale. Mais bon, au Canada, on n'y aura pas droit non plus.

On se doute que la direction de la X3 gardera ses belles propriétés de résistance et de précision. Et on apprend que l'assistance variable selon la vitesse, jusqu'à présent optionnelle, sera désormais offerte de série, et ce, pour toutes les versions. Bravo, sincèrement bravo! Il ne reste plus qu'à souhaiter une révision du freinage. Car l'actuelle X3 souffre d'une pédale beaucoup trop réactive pour être agréable et les manœuvres difficiles à doser sont souvent trop brutales, malgré toute la douceur du monde qu'on peut employer.

PLUS DE CARACTÈRE

Côté style, la X3 de seconde génération s'affirme beaucoup plus, notamment avec ses lignes latérales au caractère plus prononcé. La monotone et peu élégante macédoine de stries en bas de caisse disparaît au profit d'une cambrure plus marquée, et la calandre se muscle d'une grille à la fois plus large et plus compacte. Le coup d'œil reste celui d'une X3, mais bien tamisé à la sauce de la nouvelle décennie et c'est nettement plus joli.

Par contre, si on se fie aux premiers clichés intérieurs de la X3, l'habitacle tombe trop près de l'arbre pour qu'on parle d'une révolution. Et c'est bien dommage parce qu'une telle révolution commence à être bien nécessaire, notamment avec cette planche de bord qui conserve sa terne sobriété, à la limite du rébarbatif. À quand les commandes plus engageantes, les inscriptions déchiffrables, bref un tableau de bord possédant une personnalité conviviale et une compétence digne de la marque ? Pas pour cette fois, semble-t-il.

Nadine Filion

PHOTOS: MARC LACHAPELLE

BMW X3

DONNÉES 2010

Catégorie	VUS
Échelle de prix	39 900 $ à 45 300 $ (2010)
Garanties	4 ans/80 000 km, 4 ans/80 000 km
Assemblage	Dingolfing, Allemagne
Cote d'assurance	bonne

CHÂSSIS - DONNÉES POUR XDRIVE 30I

Emp/lon/lar/haut	2 795/4 569/1 853/1 674 mm
Coffre	480 à 1 560 litres
Réservoir	67 litres
Nombre coussins sécurité	8
Antipatinage / contrôle stabilité	oui / oui
Suspension avant	indépendante, jambes de force
Suspension arrière	indépendante, multibras
Freins avant / arrière	disque (ABS) / disque (ABS)
Direction	à crémaillère, ass. variable électronique
Diamètre de braquage	11,7 m
Pneus avant / arrière	P235/55R17 / P235/55R17
Poids	1 845 kg
Capacité de remorquage	1 700 kg (3 747 lb)

COMPOSANTES MÉCANIQUES

xDrive 28i

Cylindrée, soupapes, alim.	6L 3,0 litres 24 s atmos.
Puissance / Couple	215 chevaux / 185 lb-pi
Tr. base (opt) / rouage base (opt)	A6 (M6) / Int
0-100 / 80-120 / 100-0 km/h	n.d. / n.d. / 43,0 m
Type ess. / ville / autoroute	Super / 12,2 / 8,3 l/100 km

xDrive 30i

Cylindrée, soupapes, alim.	6L 3,0 litres 24 s atmos.
Puissance / Couple	260 chevaux / 225 lb-pi
Tr. base (opt) / rouage base (opt)	A6 (M6) / Int
0-100 / 80-120 / 100-0 km/h	7,8 s / 7,0 s / 43,0 m
Type ess. / ville / autoroute	Super / 12,5 / 8,2 l/100 km

DANS LA MÊME CATÉGORIE

Acura RDX, Audi Q5, Infiniti EX, Land Rover LR2, Mercedes-Benz Classe GLK, Volvo XC60

DU NOUVEAU EN 2011

Nouveau modèle à venir

NOS IMPRESSIONS

Agrément de conduite :	8/10
Fiabilité :	6/10
Sécurité :	10/10
Qualités hivernales :	8/10
Espace intérieur :	8/10
Confort :	6/10

www.bmw.ca

Plus d'informations dans la section statistiques en dernière partie du Guide

RELATIVEMENT NOUVEAU

BMW présente son X5 2011 comme un tout nouveau véhicule, mais en réalité, il s'agit plutôt ici d'un léger restylage accompagné d'améliorations aux groupes motopropulseurs, ce qui fait que les X5 versions 2010 et 2011 se prêtent parfaitement bien au jeu des sept différences lorsque stationnés l'un à côté de l'autre…

Vu de profil, le X5 2011 est virtuellement identique au modèle 2010, et les changements apportés à la carrosserie du « nouveau » modèle sont très subtils. À l'avant, le bouclier a été redessiné et les feux antibrouillard ont été déplacés, alors que les feux arrière héritent d'un design similaire à ceux de la Série 5GT ou de la Série 7, en plus d'adopter la technologie DEL. Même constat pour ce qui est de l'habitacle, où le modèle 2011 se contente d'adopter le système de télématique iDrive de nouvelle génération et de proposer, parfois en option, des équipements comme le régulateur de vitesse intelligent ou le dispositif de visualisation tête haute, qui se retrouvaient déjà à bord d'autres modèles de la marque. Soulignons au passage que le catalogue des options est passablement complet.

BOÎTE À HUIT RAPPORTS ET NOUVEAUX MOTEURS

C'est sous la carrosserie légèrement remaniée que se dissimulent les plus importantes améliorations apportées au VUS bavarois, soit l'adoption de la boîte automatique à huit rapports développée pour les récentes Série 7 et Série 5 Gran Turismo, qui permet de bonifier la consommation du X5 d'environ 10 pour cent par rapport au modèle antérieur. Cette boîte est un modèle de souplesse et d'efficacité, les changements de rapport se faisant tout en douceur en conduite normale, alors qu'une conduite plus « inspirée » fait en sorte que la boîte réagit en rétrogradant très rapidement d'un ou même de plusieurs rapports lors d'une manoeuvre de

dépassement par exemple. De plus, deux des quatre moteurs proposés sont nouveaux pour le X5, puisque le six cylindres turbo diesel du X5d (voir notre compte-rendu détaillé de l'essai du X5 à motorisation diesel dans la section « Essais à long terme ») et le V8 biturbo de 555 chevaux du X5 M reprennent du service en 2011 en étant essentiellement inchangés. Les versions 35i et 50i du X5 reçoivent donc maintenant les moteurs de la nouvelle Série 5, soit le six cylindres à simple turbo qui développe 300 chevaux et le V8 biturbo de 400 chevaux.

UN COMPORTEMENT ROUTIER TRÈS SPORTIF

Peu importe la motorisation retenue, rouler en X5 c'est rouler avec le VUS le plus performant de la catégorie pour ce qui est de ses qualités dynamiques, que seul le Porsche Cayenne est en mesure de reproduire. Si les Q7 de Audi et ML de Mercedes-Benz sont d'abord axés sur le confort, le X5 est d'abord et avant tout conçu avec l'agrément de conduite en priorité, ce qui en fera le premier choix des conducteurs de berlines sport migrant vers les VUS pour des considérations pratiques et/ou familiales. Et comme si ce n'était pas assez, BMW en rajoute avec le X5 M, une véritable bombe de plus de deux tonnes qui se qualifie d'emblée comme

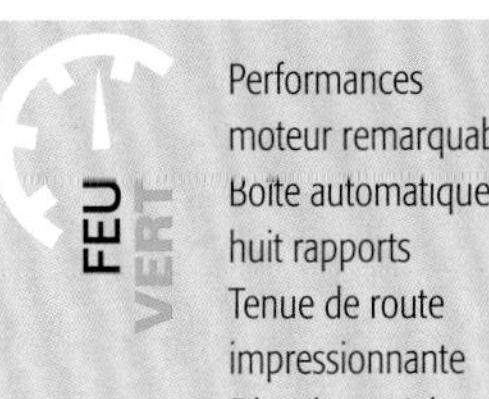

Performances moteur remarquables
Boîte automatique à huit rapports
Tenue de route impressionnante
Direction précise

Poids élevé
Consommation élevée (moteurs V8)
Pertinence d'un VUS de 555 chevaux
Dégagement pour la tête aux places arrière

le «über-sleeper» de la catégorie des VUS avec son moteur V8 biturbo de 555 chevaux et une tenue de route qui est exceptionnelle au point d'en faire pâlir d'envie plusieurs voitures sport. Ayant eu l'occasion de boucler quelques tours de circuit au volant du X5 M, je peux affirmer que le seul facteur limitatif en ce qui a trait à la vitesse de passage en virages s'est avéré son poids très élevé, ce qui avait une incidence sur les distances de freinage et sur la vitesse en entrée de courbe. Une fois inscrit sur la trajectoire idéale, le X5 M est resté très stable et ne présentait qu'un minime roulis facilement contrôlable. Dès la croisée du point de corde, il est possible de commander une réaccélération presque immédiate, en raison du fait que le délai de réponse des turbocompresseurs est minime. Aussi, il est relativement facile de provoquer une belle glissade du train arrière grâce à l'intervention du système DPC (Dynamic Performance Control), qui autorise des accélérations particulièrement dynamiques en sortie de virage, et au mode M Dynamic qui agit sur le rouage intégral xDrive et qui livre un plus grand pourcentage du couple aux roues arrière.

Le principal point faible noté pour la conduite sur circuit à été le relatif manque de performance des freins, qui se sont rapidement échauffés en conduite sportive, rendant la pédale spongieuse. Je n'ai jamais manqué de freins sur la piste, mais le fait que la pédale se rende beaucoup plus loin que la mi-course exigeait une certaine confiance. Encore une fois, le poids élevé du X5 M est en cause sur le circuit, mais en conduite normale sur routes balisées, les freins n'ont présenté aucun problème. Au fil des tours, je me suis vraiment dit que ce véhicule ne devrait pas être en mesure de rouler aussi rapidement, et pourtant il en est capable, ce qui en dit long sur les prouesses que les ingénieurs ont été capables de réaliser, courtoisie de la contribution massive des aides électroniques au pilotage.

En bout de ligne, le X5 se distingue par son comportement routier qui met l'accent sur l'agrément de conduite et la tenue de route. Il suffit simplement de choisir jusqu'à quel point on veut le transformer en émule d'une voiture sport par la sélection de sa motorisation.

Gabriel Gélinas

PHOTOS : DENIS DUQUET

Catégorie	VUS
Échelle de prix	59 900 $ à 97 900 $
Garanties	4 ans/80 000 km, 4 ans/80 000 km
Assemblage	Spartanburg, Caroline du Sud, É-U
Cote d'assurance	passable

CHÂSSIS - DONNÉES POUR XDRIVE 50I

Emp/lon/lar/haut	2 933/4 857/1 933/1 776 mm
Coffre	620 à 1 750 litres
Réservoir	85 litres
Nombre coussins sécurité	6
Antipatinage / contrôle stabilité	oui / oui
Suspension avant	indépendante, double triangulation
Suspension arrière	indépendante, multibras
Freins avant / arrière	disque (ABS) / disque (ABS)
Direction	à crémaillère, assistée
Diamètre de braquage	12,1 m
Pneus avant / arrière	P255/50R19 / P255/50R19
Poids	2 190 kg
Capacité de remorquage	3 500 kg (7 716 lb)

COMPOSANTES MÉCANIQUES

xDrive 35d

Cylindrée, soupapes, alim.	6L 3,0 litres 24 s turbocompressé
Puissance / Couple	265 chevaux / 425 lb-pi
Tr. base (opt) / rouage base (opt)	A6 / Int
0-100 / 80-120 / 100-0 km/h	7,4 s / n.d. / n.d.
Type ess. / ville / autoroute	Diesel / 10,7 / 7,5 l/100 km

xDrive 35i

Cylindrée, soupapes, alim.	6L 3,0 litres 24 s turbocompressé
Puissance / Couple	300 chevaux / 300 lb-pi
Tr. base (opt) / rouage base (opt)	A8 / Int
0-100 / 80-120 / 100-0 km/h	6,8 s / n.d. / n.d.
Type ess. / ville / autoroute	Super / 13,2 / 8,3 l/100 km

xDrive 50i

V8 4,4 l, 400 ch, 450 lb-pi - 0-100 : 5,5 s - 17,5 / 9,6 l/100 km

M

V8 4,4 l, 555 ch, 500 lb-pi - 0-100 : 4,7 s - 17,0 / 11,9 l/100 km

DANS LA MÊME CATÉGORIE

Acura MDX, Audi Q7, Buick Enclave, Cadillac SRX, Infiniti FX, Land Rover LR4, Lexus RX, Mercedes-Benz Classe M, Porsche Cayenne, Volkswagen Touareg, Volvo XC90

DU NOUVEAU EN 2011

Changements subtils à la carrosserie, nouvelle transmission huit rapports, nouveaux moteurs pour 35i et 50i

NOS IMPRESSIONS

Agrément de conduite :	8/10
Fiabilité :	4/10
Sécurité :	10/10
Qualités hivernales :	9/10
Espace intérieur :	8/10
Confort :	7/10

www.bmw.ca

Plus d'informations dans la section statistiques en dernière partie du Guide

MACHO, ÉCOLO OU EXCENTRIQUE?

Lorsque BMW a dévoilé son modèle X6, un journaliste américain présent a souligné que c'était la réponse à une question qui n'avait jamais été posée. En effet, ce *hatchback* cinq portes, dont la partie arrière très effilée ressemble à celle d'une berline, est vraiment iconoclaste. Pourtant, il a dû avoir un certain impact sur le marché, puisque la marque Acura a répliqué avec son modèle ZDX. Dans les deux cas, la silhouette est controversée.

Ce qui n'a pas empêché le constructeur bavarois de concocter une version M et une autre à propulsion hybride qui sont venues s'aligner dans les salles de démonstration à côté de la version originale.

RÉGULIER OU SUPER?

Avant de parler de motorisation, de rouage intégral et de puissance, un mot quant à la silhouette et l'habitacle qui sont plus ou moins communs à toutes les versions. En tout premier lieu, cette carrosserie aux allures sportives n'a pas que ses partisans. Les dénigreurs ne manquent pas de souligner le caractère futile d'une telle version. Non seulement il ne s'agit que d'un véhicule quatre places, mais son style rend la visibilité arrière quasiment nulle pour le conducteur tandis que la capacité de chargement est également réduite en raison du style fuyant de la partie arrière. En fait, la visibilité arrière est nulle lorsque les deux places arrière sont occupées, atroce quand les sièges sont libres mais le dossier arrière relevé, et presque bloquée une fois ce dernier rabattu ! Par contre, il est difficile de critiquer la qualité de la finition et la présentation du tableau de bord. Aussi, le système i-Drive visant à gérer la radio, la climatisation, le système de navigation et plusieurs autres fonctions s'est amélioré au fil des années, mais ce n'est toujours pas intuitif. Bien entendu, tous les accessoires de luxe et les systèmes d'aide au pilotage sont de la partie, que ce soit en équipement de série ou par l'intermédiaire du catalogue passablement étoffé des options.

L'unanimité se fait quant aux groupes propulseurs: que vous choisissiez le six cylindres en ligne ou le V8, les deux sont excellents. Le modèle de base est doté du moteur six cylindres en ligne turbocompressé produisant 300 chevaux. Il est associé à une boîte automatique à six rapports et à une transmission intégrale. Celle-ci dirige le couple d'une roue opposée à l'autre afin de réduire le sous-virage. Ce système est plus ou moins semblable au rouage intégral utilisé sur les Acura RL et autres véhicules équipés du SH-AWD. Les prestations de ce moteur sont plus qu'adéquates tandis que son poids inférieur a une influence positive sur la tenue de route.

Vous aimez les véhicules super dans le sens de supérieur à la moyenne? Vous pouvez commander la version renfermant le moteur V8 de 4,4 litres dont les 400 chevaux permettent de boucler le 0-100 km/h en moins de six secondes. Bien entendu, ce moteur est un perpétuel assoiffé et son poids plus élevé nuit à la tenue de route lorsque vient le temps de négocier des courbes.

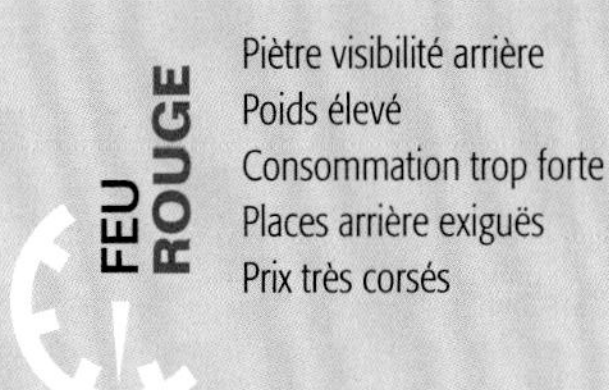

FEU VERT

- Choix de moteurs
- Performances remarquables
- Tenue de route impressionnante
- Équipement complet
- Finition impeccable

FEU ROUGE

- Piètre visibilité arrière
- Poids élevé
- Consommation trop forte
- Places arrière exiguës
- Prix très corsés

M POUR MUSCLÉ

Croyez le ou non, à notre époque où il est de bon ton d'être écolo, il est possible de commander la X6 M dont le moteur V8 à double turbo produit la bagatelle de 555 chevaux, ce qui est passablement déjanté. Comme il se doit, la tenue de route de ce bolide de course déguisé en VUS est excellente. Nous sommes dans le superflu avancé. On a beau parler de tenue supérieure sur un circuit routier, de capacité de boucler le 0-100 km/h en 4,7 secondes, il est certain que ce modèle est pour les gens qui habitent sur une autre planète. *Standing*, quand tu nous tiens !

POUR LES ÉCOLOS

Sans doute pour se faire pardonner les excès du X6M, BMW a dévoilé l'automne dernier le X6 ActiveHybrid. Il est presque en tout point similaire aux versions conventionnelles. En fait, c'est sous le capot que ça se passe. On y retrouve un V8 de 4,4 litres biturbo déployant 400 chevaux et un couple de 450 lb-pi. Il est relié à une paire de moteurs électriques pouvant générer 2,4 KW, ce qui porte la puissance totale à 480 chevaux et le couple à 575 lb-pi. Ce X6 est capable de boucler le 0-100 km/h en 5,6 secondes. De quoi donner des boutons aux écolos ! Si le rouage intégral est identique à celui monté sur les autres modèles, la transmission est une automatique à sept rapports à variation continue.

Comme tout hybride qui se respecte, il est possible de rouler en mode électrique seulement. Selon BMW, on peut rouler à une vitesse maximum de 60 km/h ou sur une distance d'environ 2,5 km en mode électrique. Voilà pour la théorie. Mais en pratique, il faut avoir le pied très léger, rouler avec précaution, ce qui a pour effet d'irriter au plus haut point les automobilistes derrière vous et qui vous font savoir leur mécontentement à grands coups de klaxon. Il faut souffrir pour être écolo !

Cette version ne transcende rien et il faut admettre que les ingénieurs de Porsche avec le Cayenne Hybride ont trouvé des solutions techniques plus intéressantes, comme le mode roue libre sur les autoroutes.

Mais peu importe le modèle choisi, le BMW X6 ne laisse personne indifférent aussi bien en raison de ses excès de style que de motorisation. Et si quelqu'un vous affirme avoir acheté ce modèle pour aller sur un circuit de course, frappez-le de ma part !

Denis Duquet

PHOTOS : SYLVAIN RAYMOND

Catégorie	Multisegment
Échelle de prix	65 700 $ à 99 900 $
Garanties	4 ans/80 000 km, 4 ans/80 000 km
Assemblage	n.d.
Cote d'assurance	n.d.

CHÂSSIS - DONNÉES POUR XDRIVE 50I

Emp/lon/lar/haut	2 933/4 877/1 983/1 690 mm
Coffre	570 à 1 450 litres
Réservoir	85 litres
Nombre coussins sécurité	6
Antipatinage / contrôle stabilité	oui / oui
Suspension avant	indépendante, leviers triangulés
Suspension arrière	indépendante, multibras
Freins avant / arrière	disque (ABS) / disque (ABS)
Direction	à crémaillère, ass. variable
Diamètre de braquage	n.d.
Pneus avant / arrière	255/50R19 / 255/50R19
Poids	2 390 kg
Capacité de remorquage	2 722 kg (6 000 lb)

COMPOSANTES MÉCANIQUES

xDrive 35i

Cylindrée, soupapes, alim.	6L 3,0 litres 24 s turbocompressé
Puissance / Couple	300 chevaux / 300 lb-pi
Tr. base (opt) / rouage base (opt)	A6 / Int
0-100 / 80-120 / 100-0 km/h	7,2 s / 6,0 s / 40,0 m
Type ess. / ville / autoroute	Super / 14,4 / 10 l/100 km

xDrive 50i

Cylindrée, soupapes, alim.	V8 4,4 litres 32 s turbocompressé
Puissance / Couple	400 chevaux / 450 lb-pi
Tr. base (opt) / rouage base (opt)	A6 / Int
0-100 / 80-120 / 100-0 km/h	5,8 s / 4,8 s / 37,6 m
Type ess. / ville / autoroute	Super /17,1 / 11,0 l/100 km

M6

V8 4,4 l, 555 ch, 500 lb -pi - 0-100 : 4,7 s - 19,3 / 10,8 l/100 km

ActiveHydrid

V8 4,4 l, 480 ch, 575 lb-pi - 0-100 : 5,6 s - 10,8 / 9,4 l/100 km

DANS LA MÊME CATÉGORIE

Infiniti FX, Land Rover Range Rover Sport, Mercedes-Benz Classe M, Porsche Cayenne

DU NOUVEAU EN 2011

Aucun changement majeur. Nouvelle version hybride.

NOS IMPRESSIONS

Agrément de conduite :	■■■■■■■□□□	7/10
Fiabilité :	■■■■■■□□□□	6/10
Sécurité :	n.d.	
Qualités hivernales :	■■■■■■■■□□	8/10
Espace intérieur :	■■■■■■□□□□	6/10
Confort :	■■■■■■□□□□	6/10

www.bmw.ca

Plus d'informations dans la section statistiques en dernière partie du Guide

À LA FOIS COUPÉ ET ROADSTER

Lorsque BMW a décidé de redessiner sa sportive à deux places, une nouvelle mission a été donnée aux designers, soit celle de remplacer les modèles cabriolet et coupé de la Z4 de génération antérieure par une seule et même voiture. C'est pourquoi la Z4 dévoilée l'an dernier fait donc usage d'un toit rigide rétractable, mais ce n'est pas son seul signe distinctif, puisque la nouvelle sportive se démarque également par l'adoption de lignes plus racées pour cette première BMW entièrement dessinée par un tandem de designers féminin.

Autrefois presque exclusivement la chasse gardée de la gent masculine, le design automobile s'est ouvert aux femmes. Il suffit de penser à la voiture concept YCC (Your Concept Car) de Volvo qui a été dessinée il y a quelques années par une équipe entièrement composée de femmes, au nouveau Acura ZDX qui est l'œuvre de Michelle Christensen, mais aussi à la récente Z4 conçue par les Allemandes Juliane Blasi et Nadya Arkaout. Comparée au modèle antérieur, force est d'admettre que la nouvelle Z4 a toute une gueule avec sa partie avant nettement plus agressive jumelée aux proportions classiques d'un roadster typique, avec son très long capot avant et sa partie arrière allongée par rapport au modèle de la génération antérieure. Même lorsque la voiture est immobile, on a cette très nette impression de vitesse et la Z4 paraît tout aussi bien avec le toit replié ou en place, ce qui n'est certainement pas le cas avec toutes les décapotables. Par ailleurs, le volume de chargement du coffre est de 310 litres avec le toit en place et de 180 litres avec le toit replié. On a gagné en élégance et en silence de roulement, mais on y perd en fait de capacité de coffre ; on ne peut tout avoir.

PAS JUSTE UNE AFFAIRE DE LOOK

C'est donc une belle réussite côté design, mais la Z4 ne mise pas que sur son look pour séduire, puisque ses performances sont très relevées. Dans cette catégorie, la Porsche Boxster fait figure de référence, elle est la voiture à battre, et la Z4 a toujours été un peu en retrait par rapport à la sportive de Stuttgart. Mais avec le nouveau modèle, l'écart entre la Boxster et la Z4 s'est considérablement rétréci.

Quelques tours de circuit ont suffi pour confirmer le potentiel de performance de la Z4 sDrive 35i, qui présente un très bel équilibre surtout lorsque le système DDC (Driving Dynamics Control) qui est offert de série sur tous les modèles est réglé en mode Sport. Avec ce réglage, les amortisseurs se raffermissent, le passage des rapports de la boîte à double embrayage se fait plus rapidement, la direction électromécanique gagne en fermeté, et le système DSC (Dynamic Stability Control) devient plus permissif, puisqu'il permet au conducteur de provoquer de légères glissades en sortie de courbe avant que n'intervienne l'antidérapage. Bref, la voiture a tout ce qu'il faut pour plaire, et le seul léger défaut que la torture

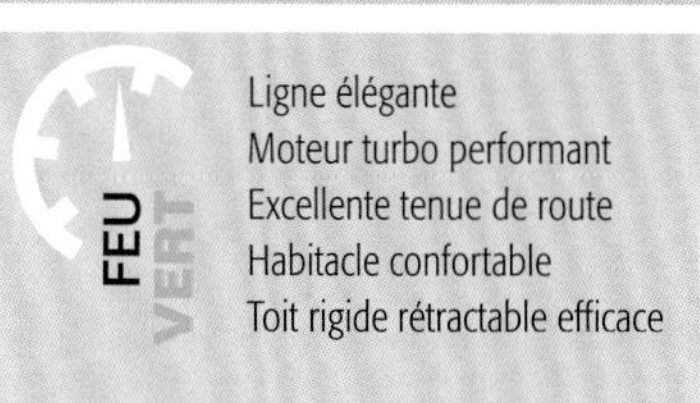

FEU VERT

- Ligne élégante
- Moteur turbo performant
- Excellente tenue de route
- Habitacle confortable
- Toit rigide rétractable efficace

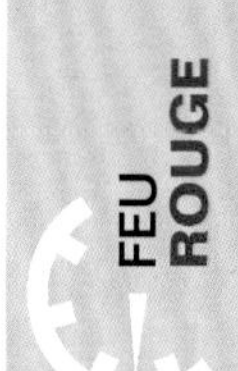

FEU ROUGE

- Prix élevés
- Coût des options
- Peu de rangements dans l'habitacle
- Un peu de flexion dans le châssis

Catégorie	*Roadster*
Échelle de prix	53 900 $ à 61 900 $
Garanties	4 ans/80 000 km, 4 ans/80 000 km
Assemblage	Allemagne
Cote d'assurance	n.d.

CHÂSSIS - DONNÉES POUR SDRIVE30I

Emp/lon/lar/haut	2 496/4 239/1 790/1 291 mm
Coffre	180 à 310 litres
Réservoir	55 litres
Nombre coussins sécurité	6
Antipatinage / contrôle stabilité	oui / oui
Suspension avant	indépendante, leviers triangulés
Suspension arrière	indépendante, multibras
Freins avant / arrière	disque (ABS) / disque (ABS)
Direction	à crémaillère, ass. variable
Diamètre de braquage	10,7 m
Pneus avant / arrière	P225/45R17 / P225/45R17
Poids	1 470 kg
Capacité de remorquage	non recommandé

COMPOSANTES MÉCANIQUES

sDrive30i

Cylindrée, soupapes, alim.	6L 3,0 litres 24 s atmos.
Puissance / Couple	255 chevaux / 220 lb-pi
Tr. base (opt) / rouage base (opt)	M6 (A6) / Prop
0-100 / 80-120 / 100-0 km/h	5,9 s / n.d. / n.d.
Type ess. / ville / autoroute	Super / 10,8 / 6,9 l/100 km

sDrive35i

Cylindrée, soupapes, alim.	6L 3,0 litres 24 s turbo
Puissance / Couple	300 chevaux / 300 lb-pi
Tr. base (opt) / rouage base (opt)	M6 (A7) / Prop
0-100 / 80-120 / 100-0 km/h	5,4 s / n.d. / n.d.
Type ess. / ville / autoroute	Super / 11,6 / 7,7 l/100 km

sDrive35is

Cylindrée, soupapes, alim.	6L 3,0 litres 24 s turbo
Puissance / Couple	335 chevaux / 332 lb-pi
Tr. base (opt) / rouage base (opt)	M6 (A7) / Prop
0-100 / 80-120 / 100-0 km/h	4,8 s / n.d. / n.d.
Type ess. / ville / autoroute	Super / 12,6 / 6,9 l/100 km

DANS LA MÊME CATÉGORIE

Audi TT, Lotus Elise, Mercedes-Benz Classe SLK, Nissan Z, Porsche Boxster

DU NOUVEAU EN 2011

Modèle sDrive35is

NOS IMPRESSIONS

Agrément de conduite :	■■■■■■■■□□ 8/10
Fiabilité :	■■■■■■■■□□ 8/10
Sécurité :	n.d.
Qualités hivernales :	■■■■■□□□□□ 5/10
Espace intérieur :	■■■■■■□□□□ 6/10
Confort :	■■■■■■□□□□ 6/10

www.bmw.ca

Plus d'informations dans la section statistiques en dernière partie du Guide

du circuit a pu mettre en lumière est une certaine flexion dans le châssis en conditions extrêmes.

Sur la route, la Z4 s'est révélée extrêmement stable et particulièrement silencieuse avec son toit rigide rétractable en place, ce qui lui permet de marquer des points côté confort, alors que la conduite avec le toit replié permet d'apprécier la sonorité plutôt basse de son moteur. On peut cependant émettre un bémol en ce qui a trait aux roues de 19 pouces proposées en option, qui ne sont malheureusement pas très bien adaptées à la mauvaise qualité de nos routes, ce qui affecte désagréablement le confort.

TROIS VARIANTES ET TROIS VOCATIONS

La gamme des Z4 est composée de trois variantes dont les appellations sont inutilement compliquées puisqu'elles sont présentées comme la Z4 sDrive30i, la Z4 sDrive35i et la toute nouvelle Z4 sDrive35is. Pour simplifier les choses pour le reste de ce texte, nous allons simplement oublier le très redondant « sDrive » pour utiliser les chiffres de la désignation technique des modèles. Ainsi la 30i devient d'office le modèle d'entrée de gamme avec son moteur atmosphérique de six cylindres en ligne et 255 chevaux, et sa vocation est celle d'un coupé-cabriolet; pour ceux qui aiment s'afficher au volant d'une très belle voiture, mais pour qui les performances ne sont pas au sommet des priorités. Les 35i et 35is ajoutent la double turbocompression pour afficher 300 et 335 chevaux respectivement, mais il ne s'agit pas du même moteur pour les deux variantes. Essentiellement, la 35i reçoit le nouveau moteur développé pour la nouvelle Série 5, soit le N55, qui n'est équipé que d'un seul turbo qui comporte cependant deux entrées distinctes (Twin Scroll), ce qui permet de réduire la longueur des tubulures d'échappement jusqu'au convertisseur catalytique, assurant ainsi des émissions moins polluantes, surtout immédiatement après le démarrage. La 35is reçoit le moteur N54 qui, lui, comporte véritablement deux turbocompresseurs, et dont la puissance a été augmentée par rapport aux années antérieures. On peut donc reprocher à BMW un certain manque de transparence ou encore de créer une certaine confusion dans l'esprit de l'acheteur, puisque les deux modèles sont présentés comme étant dotés de deux turbos « Twin Power » alors que ce n'est pas le cas et qu'ils sont différents sur le plan technique.

Plus racée et plus sportive que le modèle antérieur, la Z4 ne manque pas d'atouts pour plaire, mais, la Porsche Boxster demeure encore et toujours la référence.

Gabriel Gélinas

PHOTOS : BMW

GMC Acadia

LES TEMPS ONT CHANGÉ

Il est tout de même curieux de constater que ce General Motors ne propose pratiquement plus de VUS avec un châssis autonome et un rouage 4X4 à temps partiel. Pour le châssis autonome, il faut se tourner vers les grosses pointures que sont les Chevrolet Tahoe et GMC Yukon. Quant au rouage 4X4, il n'est tout simplement plus offert chez ce constructeur. Bref, on s'est finalement rendu compte que les besoins de la clientèle avaient changé. De plus, compte tenu de la restructuration massive qu'a connue ce constructeur au cours des derniers mois, il était plus simple de confier les modèles à vocation plus limitée à la concurrence.

Les acheteurs désirant se munir de véhicules multisegments sont normalement davantage intéressés par des versions modernes, dotées d'une plate-forme monocoque, proposant le même confort qu'une automobile et munies d'un rouage intégral ne nécessitant aucune intervention de la part du conducteur.

CHOIX MÉCANIQUE SIMPLIFIÉ

On a toujours reproché à GM d'utiliser une mécanique commune à plusieurs modèles. En réalité, ce n'est pas tellement le principe qui était en cause, mais son application. Proposer un excellent moteur pour plusieurs modèles n'est pas une mauvaise idée. Par contre, monter une mécanique ancienne et peu performante sur plusieurs modèles, c'est courir à la catastrophe. Il semble qu'on ait finalement compris chez GM. On continue toujours de proposer la même mécanique sur plusieurs modèles, mais cette mécanique figure parmi les meilleures de sa catégorie.

Le seul moteur disponible est donc à la hauteur de la tâche. Il s'agit d'unV6 de 3,6 litres dont la fiche technique souligne son caractère moderne. En effet, ce moteur est doté de l'injection d'essence à haute pression en plus du calage infiniment variable des soupapes. Sa puissance est de 288 chevaux et il est associé à une transmission automatique à six rapports qui est efficace et qui est une des plus douces de sa catégorie. L'acheteur pourra opter pour la traction ou encore un rouage intégral et ce, pour chacun de ces trois modèles.

TROIS VÉHICULES DISTINCTS

Un autre reproche que l'on adressait à ce constructeur était de produire des véhicules qui non seulement étaient dotés d'une mécanique médiocre, mais qui en plus ne se démarquaient pas spécifiquement les uns des autres. Nous avons mentionné que la mécanique est d'une qualité supérieure et force est d'admettre que chaque modèle possède une silhouette qui lui est propre, de même qu'une personnalité distinctive.

Le modèle le plus original est certainement le Buick Enclave. Avec son impressionnante grille de calandre chromée, ce modèle se

BUICK ENCLAVE / CHEVROLET TRAVERSE / GMC ACADIA

Catégorie	Multisegment
Échelle de prix	43 505 $ à 51 475 $ (2010)
Garanties	4 ans/80 000 km, 5 ans/160 000 km
Assemblage	Lansing, Michigan, É-U
Cote d'assurance	passable

FEU VERT

Plate-forme rigide
Moteur bien adapté
Consommation correcte
Troisième rangée de sièges presque confortables
Comportement routier sain

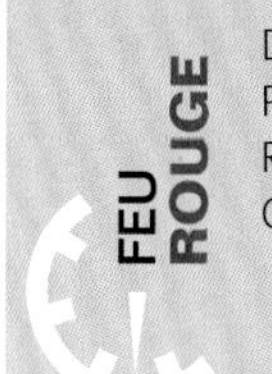

FEU ROUGE

Dimensions généreuses
Piètre visibilité arrière
Rouage intégral cher
Grand rayon de braquage

démarque aisément de tous les autres. Il en est de même pour l'habitacle, puisque le tableau de bord est fabriqué à partir de matériaux qui nous semblent de meilleure qualité. Cette Buick cible une clientèle qui recherche confort et polyvalence. Cela signifie que la suspension est légèrement plus souple que celle des deux autres modèles. Par contre, le roulis en virage est plus marqué. En outre, il semble que la direction offre moins de feed-back que sur les autres versions. La tenue de route est tout de même appréciable, mais on a privilégié le confort, ce qui explique sans doute pourquoi la capacité de remorquage du Buick (2 045 kg / 4 500 lb) est inférieure à celle du Chevrolet Traverse et du GMC Acadia (2 358 kg / 5 200 lb). Nous devons également souligner que ce trio propose une troisième rangée de sièges, portant sa capacité à huit occupants. Cette troisième rangée est relativement facile d'accès en raison du système *Smart Slide* qui fait coulisser la deuxième banquette.

Le Chevrolet Traverse est le plus sobre des trois et celui promettant d'offrir le meilleur rapport qualité-prix. Ce qui signifie que la présentation du tableau de bord est davantage épurée, mais pas nécessairement plus mauvaise. Il en est de même pour la qualité de tissu des sièges de la version de base qui, sans être luxueux, sont d'une qualité notable. Pour le reste, le Traverse est aussi pratique que les deux autres, tout en possédant, sans aucun doute, une meilleure tenue de route. De là à qualifier cette voiture de sportive, il y a un pas que nous ne franchirons pas: c'est un véhicule lourd doté d'un centre de gravité passablement élevé.

Si le Buick Enclave est le plus luxueux du lot et le Chevrolet Traverse le plus populiste, il semble bien que chez GM, on ait décidé de faire du GMC Acadia, le multisegment du juste milieu. En effet, sa présentation extérieure est moins spectaculaire que celle du Buick, mais elle a un peu plus de mordant que celle du Chevrolet. Il en est de même de la planche de bord qui est la plus réussie des trois, à notre humble avis. Des trois réglages de suspension essayés, celui de l'Acadia se situe à mi-chemin entre les deux autres modèles au niveau du confort. Par contre, tous les membres de ce trio offrent le même roulement silencieux.

Somme toute, GM a réussi le pari de créer trois modèles à partir d'une même mécanique et de leur donner une personnalité distincte. Les trois véhicules proposent une bonne tenue de route et offrent de bonnes performances.

Denis Duquet

Chevrolet Traverse

PHOTOS: BUICK

CHÂSSIS - DONNÉES POUR ENCLAVE CXL TI

Emp/lon/lar/haut	3 023/5 118/2 006/1 842 mm
Coffre	657 à 3 265 litres
Réservoir	83 litres
Nombre coussins sécurité	6
Antipatinage / contrôle stabilité	oui / oui
Suspension avant	indépendante, jambes de force
Suspension arrière	indépendante, multibras
Freins avant / arrière	disque (ABS) / disque (ABS)
Direction	à crémaillère, assistée
Diamètre de braquage	12,3 m
Pneus avant / arrière	P255/60R19 / P255/60R19
Poids	2 261 kg
Capacité de remorquage	2 045 kg (4 500 lb)

COMPOSANTES MÉCANIQUES

CX TA, CX TI, CXL TA, CXL TI

Cylindrée, soupapes, alim.	V6 3,6 litres 24 s atmos.
Puissance / Couple	288 chevaux / 270 lb-pi
Tr. base (opt) / rouage base (opt)	A6 / Tr (Int)
0-100 / 80-120 / 100-0 km/h	9,4 s / 8,5 s / 44,1 m
Type ess. / ville / autoroute	Ordinaire / 13,4 / 9,0 l/100 km

Buick Enclave

DANS LA MÊME CATÉGORIE

Acura MDX, Audi Q7, BMW X5, Cadillac SRX, Land Rover LR4, Lexus RX, Lincoln MKT, Mercedes-Benz Classe M, Volkswagen Touareg, Volvo XC90

DU NOUVEAU EN 2011

Aucun changement majeur

NOS IMPRESSIONS

Agrément de conduite:	7/10
Fiabilité:	5/10
Sécurité:	10/10
Qualités hivernales:	8/10
Espace intérieur:	8/10
Confort:	8/10

www.gm.ca

Plus d'informations dans la section statistiques en dernière partie du Guide

DRÔLE DE NOM MAIS VOITURE SÉRIEUSE

Même si elle a été lancée l'année dernière, ne cherchez pas de Buick LaCrosse dans le *Guide de l'auto 2010*. Elle s'appelait alors Allure ! À ce moment, cette nouvelle Buick n'avait pas encore fait son entrée chez les concessionnaires canadiens et comme elle remplaçait l'Allure, nous avions réglé le cas de son appellation, GM ne le faisant pas. Mais, dans une décision éclairée, GM du Canada décidait par la suite d'appeler sa berline intermédiaire LaCrosse comme partout ailleurs au monde. Au Québec, ce nom peut faire sourire, mais le coût des matrices d'un nom séparé, de la paperasse et de la gestion des stocks est beaucoup trop élevé pour plaire à quelques Québécois trop susceptibles.

Quoi qu'il en soit, la Buick Lacrosse fait partie de la nouvelle génération de Buick, une marque qui tente désespérément d'attirer le plus d'acheteurs possible. Même si la LaCrosse présente une ligne des plus modernes et très dynamique, les designers continuent d'utiliser les fameux *portholes*, ces petites ouvertures latérales qui ont marqué les Buick des années 50 et 60. Aujourd'hui, ces ouvertures (fictives) n'ont plus leur place et le fait de les avoir déplacées sur le capot n'apporte rien au design, bien au contraire.

TURQUOISE, C'EST BEAU

Dans l'habitacle, par contre, bien peu à redire. Le tableau de bord est superbe, surtout les jauges dont le centre est cerclé d'une bande turquoise. Aussi, la nuit venue, une jolie bande illuminée parcourt le tableau de bord de gauche à droite. La qualité des matériaux est relevée et leur assemblage très correct. On retrouve beaucoup de boutons, principalement dans la partie

centrale mais, en général, ils sont placés logiquement, ce qui aide à les manipuler sans quitter la route des yeux. Cependant, j'ai eu beaucoup de difficultés à m'habituer aux poignées de porte intérieures, difficiles à manipuler.

Les sièges sont confortables et la position de conduite se trouve rapidement. Par contre, la visibilité, autant vers l'arrière que vers l'avant, est obstruée par d'imposants piliers… Les places arrière offrent beaucoup d'espace mais je ne les ai pas trouvées trop confortables. Et qu'une voiture récente offre cinq places et seulement quatre appuie-têtes dépasse l'entendement ! Les dossiers s'abaissent pour agrandir le coffre mais, malheureusement, ils ne forment pas un fond plat. Et puis, l'ouverture du coffre est trop petite pour qu'il puisse accueillir de gros objets malgré ses dimensions très correctes.

EXIT LE 3,0, BIENVENUE AU 2,4

Déjà, un an après son lancement, la LaCrosse connaît des changements au niveau de sa motorisation. On retrouve maintenant un quatre cylindres Ecotec de 2,4 litres et un V6 de 3,6 litres. Exit le 3,0 litres. Autant le quatre cylindres que le V6 sont modernes avec

Lignes agréables
Tableau de bord réussi
Habitacle vaste
Tenue de route relevée
Moteurs bien adaptés

Portholes inutiles
Coffre plus ou moins réussi
Poignées de porte intérieures ratées
Visibilité réduite
Consommation assez élevée (3,6 litres)

leur injection directe. Au moment de mettre sous presse, nous n'avions pas pu mettre la main sur le modèle mu par un 2,4 litres mais ses données techniques laissent supposer un rendement économique et suffisamment performant. Quant au V6 de 3,6 litres, il trimballe les 1 800 kilos de la voiture sans aucun problème ! Si, bien entendu, « aucun problème » signifie pour vous un effet de couple en accélération vive des modèles à traction et une consommation d'essence qui peut facilement grimper à 13 litres/100 km en ville par temps froid. Le 3,0 litres souffrait d'une consommation à peu près identique pour bien moins de puissance, ce qui explique sans doute son retrait. Pour régler le problème de l'effet de couple en accélération, la LaCrosse peut recevoir un rouage intégral, disponible uniquement avec le V6. Ce rouage ajoute environ 80 kilos à la voiture mais la rend encore plus stable dans la neige. J'ai dit « encore » car une LaCrosse à traction l'est déjà passablement dans les mêmes conditions. La transmission est une automatique à six rapports, peu importe le moteur. Son fonctionnement est parfaitement transparent même si son mode manuel n'est pas tellement inspirant.

La marque Buick a beau avoir pris une nouvelle direction, il n'en demeure pas moins qu'on est encore loin du comportement routier d'une BMW ou d'une Audi. Cependant, la LaCrosse peut très bien satisfaire les « jeunes » de 50 ou 55 ans. Le châssis, comme c'est devenu la mode chez General Motors, affiche une solidité de bon augure. Les suspensions sont toujours plus portées vers le confort que vers le dynamisme, mais une conduite plus « hormonale » sur une route en lacets prouve que la tenue de route est plus que satisfaisante. On dénote bien un certain roulis en courbe mais ce n'est pas dramatique. En revanche, le V6 m'a paru suffisamment lourd pour affecter un peu la direction qui n'aime pas être brusquée. Il faut dire qu'à ce moment, notre voiture était chaussée de pneus d'hiver, ce qui est rarement un avantage. Au moins, la direction procure un bon retour d'informations, un petit bout de phrase peu souvent lu dans un texte sur une Buick... Il faut aussi souligner le silence de roulement troublé seulement par un « kok, kok, kok » occasionnel qui semblait venir de la suspension avant. Un simple ajustement, sans doute.

La nouvelle Buick LaCrosse est jolie, bien assemblée, bien motorisée et son comportement routier est au goût du jour. Elle n'est pas la moins dispendieuse de la catégorie mais elle en est assurément l'une des valeurs les plus sûres.

Alain Morin

PHOTOS : DENIS DUQUET

BUICK LACROSSE

Catégorie	Berline
Échelle de prix	31 645 $ à 40 795 $ (2010)
Garanties	4 ans/80 000 km, 5 ans/160 000 km
Assemblage	Oshawa, Ontario, Canada
Cote d'assurance	n.d.

CHÂSSIS - DONNÉES POUR CXL TI

Emp/lon/lar/haut	2 837/5 001/1 857/1 496 mm
Coffre	377 litres
Réservoir	72 litres
Nombre coussins sécurité	6
Antipatinage / contrôle stabilité	oui / oui
Suspension avant	indépendante, jambes de force
Suspension arrière	indépendante, multibras
Freins avant / arrière	disque (ABS) / disque (ABS)
Direction	à crémaillère, ass. variable
Diamètre de braquage	11,8 m
Pneus avant / arrière	P235/50R18 / P235/50R18
Poids	1 905 kg
Capacité de remorquage	454 kg (1 000 lb)

COMPOSANTES MÉCANIQUES

CX, CXL, CXL TI

Cylindrée, soupapes, alim.	4L 2,4 litres 16 s atmos.
Puissance / Couple	182 chevaux / 172 lb-pi
Tr. base (opt) / rouage base (opt)	A6 / Tr (Int)
0-100 / 80-120 / 100-0 km/h	n.d. / n.d. / n.d.
Type ess. / ville / autoroute	Ordinaire / 10,9 / 6,6 l/100 km

CXS

Cylindrée, soupapes, alim.	V6 3,6 litres 24 s atmos.
Puissance / Couple	280 chevaux / 259 lb-pi
Tr. base (opt) / rouage base (opt)	A6 / Tr
0-100 / 80-120 / 100-0 km/h	7,7 s / 5,3 s / 41,4 m
Type ess. / ville / autoroute	Ordinaire / 12,2 / 7,3 l/100 km

DANS LA MÊME CATÉGORIE

Chevrolet Impala, Chrysler 300, Ford Taurus, Honda Accord, Lexus ES, Lincoln MKZ, Toyota Camry

DU NOUVEAU EN 2011

Nouveau moteur Ecotec 2,4 litres, abandon du V6 de 3,0 litres

NOS IMPRESSIONS

Agrément de conduite :	7/10
Fiabilité :	7/10
Sécurité :	7/10
Qualités hivernales :	7/10
Espace intérieur :	8/10
Confort :	9/10

www.gm.ca

Plus d'informations dans la section statistiques en dernière partie du Guide

VESTIGES DU PASSÉ

À une exception près, tous les modèles de la gamme Buick ont été dévoilés récemment. Ils font appel à des plates-formes modernes et sont propulsés par des moteurs sophistiqués. Ce qui explique pourquoi le modèle le plus cher et le plus huppé de la marque, le Lucerne, est celui qui a recours à une technologie un peu en retrait par rapport aux nouvelles venues et dont les composantes mécaniques datent de quelques années.

En fait, cette grosse traction n'est rien d'autre qu'une Cadillac DTS déguisée en Buick puisque les deux se partagent la même plate-forme et la même mécanique sauf que la « Caddy » ne propose pas de moteur V6, question de *standing* et de marketing.

LES BONNES VIEILLES RECETTES

Il n'y a pas si longtemps, le centre de design de GM dessinait des carrosseries en fonction des catégories de modèles: très gros, gros, moyen et petit. Par la suite, ces carrosseries étaient attribuées aux différentes divisions qui tentaient alors d'en faire des Chevrolet, des Cadillac et des Buick sans oublier les autres marques. La Lucerne est inspirée de cette époque avec sa carrosserie aux lignes anonymes et passe-partout. Pour essayer de lui donner une identité, les stylistes de Buick ont fait appel à une calandre identitaire avec sa grille en forme de chute d'eau. Puis, pour renouer avec le passé jadis glorieux de cette marque, on a placé les légendaires *portholes* — ou prises d'air — sur le haut des ailes avant. Ajoutez quelques écussons ici et là, des jantes chromées et vous avez la Buick haut de gamme. Ceci dit, la voiture est tout de même élégante et ses lignes bien équilibrées. Par contre, il lui manque ce petit quelque chose qui permettrait d'obtenir une meilleure identification.

À une certaine époque, toutes les voitures produites par ce constructeur proposaient un tableau de bord d'une désolation quasiment totale. C'était hypersimplifié en fait de commandes tandis que l'instrumentation, réduite à sa plus simple expression, était abritée dans un réceptacle rectangulaire. C'est comme si on n'avait pas voulu intimider le pilote avec une instrumentation inutilement complexe. Heureusement, la qualité des matériaux et de l'assemblage est supérieure à la moyenne. La position de conduite est bizarre avec une colonne de direction impossible à régler correctement. L'assise du siège est trop plate et le support latéral est inexistant. On a sans doute voulu que les occupants des places avant se croient assis dans leur salon. Quant aux places arrière, l'assise du siège pourrait être un peu plus élevée, en revanche, l'habitabilité est excellente. Malheureusement, sans doute pour des questions de rigidité de la caisse, le dossier des sièges arrière ne s'abaisse pas. Par chance, le coffre est d'assez bonnes dimensions bien que son ouverture soit relativement petite.

Cette année encore, les modifications sur le plan esthétique sont quasiment nulles, un indice qui ne trompe pas. En effet, ce modèle vit sur du temps emprunté et il ne faudrait pas se surprendre qu'il

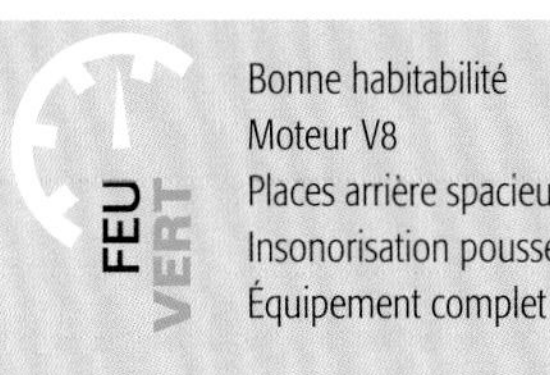

FEU VERT
- Bonne habitabilité
- Moteur V8
- Places arrière spacieuses
- Insonorisation poussée
- Équipement complet

FEU ROUGE
- Moteur V6 anémique
- Boîte à 4 rapports
- Roulis en virage
- Direction engourdie
- Effet de couple dans le volant

soit abandonné un jour — et ce, dans un avenir rapproché — ou encore complètement modifié.

CORRECTE SANS PLUS

La carrosserie de la Lucerne est sobre et discrète et en général, il en est de même pour la mécanique. En effet, pas de moteur ultrasophistiqué, pas de performances retentissantes, juste une mécanique adéquate encourageant une consommation de carburant raisonnable pour la taille du véhicule, et livrant des performances correctes. Ceci dit, nous avons une bonne idée de l'acheteur moyen de cette voiture. Il s'agit d'une personne recherchant une voiture spacieuse, arborant un écusson d'un certain prestige et dont le comportement routier s'apparente davantage au confort qu'aux performances. Les personnes à la recherche d'émotions fortes devraient certainement regarder ailleurs.

Le moteur propulsant les versions CX et CXL est un V6 de 3,9 litres produisant 227 chevaux, ce qui est assez modeste compte tenu du poids de ce véhicule qui est d'une tonne et demie ! Ce moteur est associé à une boîte automatique à quatre rapports qui n'est vraiment plus capable de soutenir la comparaison avec ce que la majorité des modèles concurrents propose. Cela dit, cette boîte automatique est fiable, robuste et les passages de rapport presque imperceptibles. Cette transmission est également celle qui équipe l'autre moteur disponible, un V8 de 4,6 litres d'une puissance de 292 chevaux qui est livré avec la version Super. C'est nettement mieux adapté à la voiture, mais il est important de souligner qu'en accélérations franches, un important effet de couple se fait sentir dans le volant.

Si vous conduisez raisonnablement, sans entrer dans les virages à toute vitesse et respectez en général les limites de vitesse affichées, le confort de cette Buick et sa docilité vous plairont. Par contre, ce n'est pas la plus agile des voitures et ses dimensions encombrantes la rendent plus ou moins agréable à conduire en ville. Cette année, il est rassurant de savoir que le système de stabilité latérale StabiliTrack est dorénavant de série sur tous les modèles. Il était plus que temps.

Malgré tout, la Lucerne est en sursis. Chez Buick on s'est affairé à développer des modèles ciblant une plus vaste clientèle en premier et on verra d'ici peu quel sera le sort réservé au « gros modèle ».

Denis Duquet

PHOTOS : BUICK

Catégorie	Berline
Échelle de prix	33 095 $ à 52 315 $ (2010)
Garanties	4 ans/80 000 km, 5 ans/160 000 km
Assemblage	Hamtrack, Michigan, É-U
Cote d'assurance	n.d.

CHÂSSIS - DONNÉES POUR CXL

Emp/lon/lar/haut	2 936/5 161/1 874/1 473 mm
Coffre	481 litres
Réservoir	70 litres
Nombre coussins sécurité	6
Antipatinage / contrôle stabilité	oui / oui
Suspension avant	indépendante, jambes de force
Suspension arrière	indépendante, multibras
Freins avant / arrière	disque (ABS) / disque (ABS)
Direction	à crémaillère, ass. variable
Diamètre de braquage	13,4 m
Pneus avant / arrière	P235/55R17 / P235/55R17
Poids	1 726 kg
Capacité de remorquage	454 kg (1 000 lb)

COMPOSANTES MÉCANIQUES

CX, CXL

Cylindrée, soupapes, alim.	V6 3,9 litres 24 s atmos.
Puissance / Couple	227 chevaux / 237 lb-pi
Tr. base (opt) / rouage base (opt)	A4 / Tr
0-100 / 80-120 / 100-0 km/h	10,8 s / 8,0 s / 42,4 m
Type ess. / ville / autoroute	Ordinaire / 12,0 / 7,4 l/100 km

Super

Cylindrée, soupapes, alim.	V8 4,6 litres 32 s atmos.
Puissance / Couple	292 chevaux / 288 lb-pi
Tr. base (opt) / rouage base (opt)	A4 / Tr
0-100 / 80-120 / 100-0 km/h	7,4 s / 6,1 s / 41,8 m
Type ess. / ville / autoroute	Ordinaire / 13,8 / 8,7 l/100 km

DANS LA MÊME CATÉGORIE

Chrysler 300, Ford Taurus, Hyundai Genesis, Lexus ES, Lincoln MKZ, Toyota Avalon

DU NOUVEAU EN 2011

StabiliTrak de série sur version Super

NOS IMPRESSIONS

Agrément de conduite :	7/10
Fiabilité :	8/10
Sécurité :	8/10
Qualités hivernales :	7/10
Espace intérieur :	9/10
Confort :	9/10

www.gm.ca

Plus d'informations dans la section statistiques en dernière partie du Guide

OUBLIEZ LE PASSÉ

Dans sa dernière mouture, la Regal était une intermédiaire propulsée par l'incontournable moteur V6 3,8 litres à soupapes en tête et associé à une boîte automatique à quatre rapports plus fiable que sophistiquée. La tenue de route était correcte, la présentation quelconque tandis que l'habitacle était doté de plastiques durs et d'une finition plus que moyenne. Bref, c'était à cette époque dans la bonne moyenne de General Motors.

Mais ce constructeur avait déjà entamé son programme d'amélioration de ses modèles et c'est dans cet esprit qu'on a abandonné la production de la Regal en 2004, dans l'attente d'une meilleure voiture. On connaît les péripéties commerciales et financières de GM de sorte qu'il aura fallu attendre sept ans avant de revoir ce modèle. Et cette fois, pas question de tergiverser sur la qualité mécanique et technique tandis que la qualité des matériaux est devenue monnaie courante aussi bien chez Buick que dans les autres divisions.

Mais il fallait redonner vie à cette division quasiment moribonde sur notre continent. La remontée s'est amorcée avec l'Enclave, il y a environ trois ans, suivi de la LaCrosse l'automne dernier qui était connue comme l'Allure précédemment au Canada. La Regal est le troisième nouveau modèle en autant d'années. Cette intermédiaire a été pendant longtemps le modèle le plus populaire chez Buick avant d'être abandonné.

Bien que la Regal utilise le même nom que le modèle délaissé en début de ce siècle, il n'y a aucune affiliation entre les deux. Pour bien l'évaluer, nous devons oublier complètement le passé et en faire l'essai pour ce qu'elle est et non pas pour ce qu'elle était.

OUBLIEZ VOS PRÉJUGÉS

Élégant mais ennuyant, voilà comment on aurait décrit le style des voitures Buick il y a quatre ou cinq ans. Mais ce n'est plus le cas de nos jours. La silhouette de style coupé quatre portes est moderne et distinguée. C'est juste ce qu'il faut, même si un peu plus de caractère visuel permettant d'identifier une Buick ne ferait pas de tort. Ce rôle revient à la traditionnelle grille de calandre en forme de chute d'eau qui est l'élément dominant de la partie avant. Les célèbres prises d'air sur les ailes — ou *portholes* — sont également propres aux voitures Buick mais n'ont pas été retenues sur ce modèle. La section avant est plutôt arrondie, les passages de roue sont légèrement en relief et le capot plongeant.

Les porte-à-faux sont passablement réduits ce qui améliore le style tout en offrant plus d'espace dans l'habitacle. Les flancs sculptés avec une partie arrondie en bas de caisse donnent un certain dynamisme lorsque la voiture est vue de côté. La section arrière est relativement courte afin d'accentuer l'effet de coupé. On note la présence d'un petit déflecteur sur le couvercle du coffre qui est traversé de part en part par une barre en chrome C'est celle-ci qui nous fait songer à l'Opel Insignia dont la Regal est dérivée. Quant au coffre à bagages, il est plutôt grand pour la catégorie.

Pendant longtemps, les voitures Buick proposaient des planches de bord d'un ennui mortel. Celle-ci est nettement plus dynamique et respecte la présentation en vigueur sur la majorité des voitures contemporaines. Les commandes sont regroupées au centre, dans un rectangle placé sous l'écran de navigation. Les stylistes ont choisi un plastique non texturé pour encercler ces touches de commande, ce qui a incité certaines personnes à conclure que les matériaux sont de qualité inférieure. Elles ont droit à leur opinion, mais ces plastiques sont pratiques tandis que le dessus de la planche de bord est recouvert d'un matériau souple. Un bouton de commande

placé sur la console horizontale permet de gérer le système audio, de navigation et la connexion Bluetooth. Cette commande est facile d'accès et son fonctionnement relativement simple. D'ailleurs, la disposition de toutes les commandes est très bonne.

Autant le conducteur que le passager sont assis dans des sièges confortables offrant un bon support latéral et pour les cuisses, alors que la position de conduite est bonne grâce à un volant réglable en hauteur et en profondeur. Ledit volant, doté d'un boudin moyennement gros, se prend bien en main et possède sur ses branches horizontales les commandes du régulateur de croisière et de la radio. Les deux principaux cadrans indicateurs sont cerclés de chrome et l'indicateur de vitesse est à droite, le compte-tours à gauche. On retrouve entre les deux un tableau d'information affichant le kilométrage parcouru, la consommation et autre information du genre.

MÊME PAS DE V6!

La tendance actuelle est aux moteurs quatre cylindres livrant une puissance adéquate et affichant une bonne consommation de carburant. Même chez Buick on adhère à cette nouvelle règle, utilisant la turbo compression au lieu de cylindrées plus importantes. La version CXL est équipée du quatre cylindres Ecotec de 2,4 litres produisant 182 chevaux et associé à une boîte automatique à six rapports de type manumatique. La CXL Turbo est propulsée par le moteur 2,0 litres turbo de 220 chevaux, lui aussi offert avec la même boîte automatique à six rapports. Par contre, une boîte manuelle à six vitesses sera disponible un peu plus tard mais uniquement avec le moteur Turbo. Ces deux moteurs sont techniquement sophistiqués et dotés de l'injection directe.

Mais il n'y a pas que les moteurs qui soient techniquement avancés, la plate-forme est parmi les meilleures. Il s'agit de celle de l'Opel Insignia qui a été nommée Voiture européenne de l'année. En plus de ça, ce modèle figure présentement parmi les plus populaires sur le marché européen, là où les clients sont très exigeants en fait d'agrément de conduite et de performances. Bien entendu, la suspension est indépendante aux quatre roues et il est également possible d'obtenir une suspension active — IDCS — en option sur le modèle Turbo. En fait, celle-ci possède trois modes de réglages qui influencent les passages des vitesses, la fermeté de la suspension ainsi que la direction. Il y a le mode Normal, le mode Touring et le mode de Sport. On les contrôle à l'aide de touches placées sous l'écran de navigation.

Selon le modèle choisi, cette voiture roule sur des pneus de 18 ou 19 pouces. Bien entendu, la version à moteur turbo hérite des 19 pouces. En plus, ce modèle a des freins un peu plus gros et un peu plus puissants afin de pouvoir être à la hauteur de la puissance accrue de ce moteur.

FINI LA GUIMAUVE

À une certaine époque, chez Buick, on ne parlait pas de tenue de route mais de confort de suspension. La plupart des modèles conduits donnaient l'impression d'avoir des amortisseurs remplis de guimauve. C'était hier. La nouvelle Regal possède une plate-forme très rigide ce qui a permis aux ingénieurs d'utiliser des amortisseurs moyennement fermes sans pour autant nuire au confort et à la tenue de route. Ajoutez à cela une direction précise dont l'assistance est fort bien dosée et vous vous retrouvez au volant d'une voiture proposant une bonne tenue de route et un bel agrément de conduite. Cette Buick n'affiche aucun roulis en virage et les freins sontprogressifs, puissants et résistants à l'échauffement.

FEU VERT

- Belle silhouette
- Plate-forme rigide
- Direction précise
- Bonne tenue de route
- Moteur turbo

FEU ROUGE

- Réglage énigmatique de la climatisation
- Certaines options onéreuses
- Réputation à refaire
- Fiabilité inconnue

Le quatre cylindres 2,4 litres de 182 chevaux offre des performances correctes et des accélérations dans la bonne moyenne. Par contre, lorsque nous avons conduit sur des routes relativement inclinées et à une certaine altitude, il a fallu jouer de la transmission manumatique et passer les rapports manuellement afin d'obtenir les performances désirées. Heureusement, cette transmission est excellente tandis que le passage des rapports est instantané et s'effectue en douceur. Le moteur turbo propose 38 chevaux de plus et c'est nettement mieux à tous les chapitres. Le temps de réponse du turbo est quasiment inexistant et la puissance très linéaire. Étant donné qu'il faut débourser un peu plus de 2 000 $ pour cette version, c'est à mon avis un excellent choix.

La nouvelle Regal est moderne, bien assemblée et agréable à conduire tout en étant de prix compétitif. La plus grosse difficulté pour la direction de GM sera de convaincre les acheteurs qu'elle n'a rien à voir avec les Buick des années 90.

Denis Duquet

PHOTOS : ALAIN MORIN

Catégorie	Berline
Échelle de prix	31 990 $ à 34 990 $
Garanties	3 ans/60 000 km, 5 ans/100 000 km
Assemblage	n.d.
Cote d'assurance	n.d.

CHÂSSIS - DONNÉES POUR CXL

Emp/lon/lar/haut	2 738/4 831/1 857/1 483 mm
Coffre	402 litres
Réservoir	68 litres
Nombre coussins sécurité	6
Antipatinage / contrôle stabilité	oui / oui
Suspension avant	indépendante, jambes de force
Suspension arrière	indépendante, multibras
Freins avant / arrière	disque (ABS) / disque (ABS)
Direction	à crémaillère, assistée
Diamètre de braquage	11,4 m
Pneus avant / arrière	P235/50R18 / P235/50R18
Poids	1 633 kg
Capacité de remorquage	454 kg (1 000 lb)

COMPOSANTES MÉCANIQUES

CXL

Cylindrée, soupapes, alim.	4L 2,4 litres 16 s atmos.
Puissance / Couple	182 chevaux / 172 lb-pi
Tr. base (opt) / rouage base (opt)	A6 / Tr
0-100 / 80-120 / 100-0 km/h	9,0 s (est) / 7,5 s (est) / n.d.
Type ess. / ville / autoroute	Ordinaire / 10,8 / 6,5 l/100 km

CXL Turbo

Cylindrée, soupapes, alim.	4L 2,0 litres 16 s turbo
Puissance / Couple	220 chevaux / 258 lb-pi
Tr. base (opt) / rouage base (opt)	A6 / Tr
0-100 / 80-120 / 100-0 km/h	7,8 s (est) / 6,5 s (est) / n.d.
Type ess. / ville / autoroute	Super / n.d. / n.d.

DANS LA MÊME CATÉGORIE

Acura TSX, Lexus ES, Mercedes-Benz Classe C, Volvo S60

DU NOUVEAU EN 2011

Nouveau modèle

NOS IMPRESSIONS

Agrément de conduite :	8/10
Fiabilité :	Nouveau modèle
Sécurité :	10/10
Qualités hivernales :	8/10
Espace intérieur :	8/10
Confort :	8/10

www.gm.ca

Plus d'informations dans la section statistiques en dernière partie du Guide

DE L'AUDACE...

S'il y a une voiture américaine qui se démarque totalement dans le paysage automobile actuel, c'est bien la CTS de Cadillac qui vient d'ajouter coup sur coup un modèle de type «familiale» ainsi qu'un coupé aux berlines CTS et CTS-V que l'on connaissait déjà. C'est donc une gamme complète qui est maintenant proposée par la division de General Motors, la plus avant-gardiste côté design.

Au sommet de la pyramide se trouve la CTS-V qui se qualifie d'emblée comme la Cadillac la plus puissante de l'histoire de la marque avec son V8 suralimenté de 556 chevaux et qui a comme mission d'en découdre avec la BMW M5 ou la Classe E de Mercedes-Benz en version AMG, rien de moins. Cette Cadillac gonflée aux stéroïdes ne se contente pas de livrer des accélérations et des reprises époustouflantes. Son comportement routier est bien équilibré, la voiture étant dotée d'une tenue de route surprenante conjuguée à un niveau de confort étonnant pour une berline sport, courtoisie de sa suspension assurée par des amortisseurs à variation magnétique semblables à ceux utilisés sur la Corvette ZR1.

UNE FAMILIALE EFFICACE... ET CHÈRE.

L'ajout d'une familiale représente aussi une première pour Cadillac, ce qui lui permet de rivaliser avec les marques européennes qui proposent également ce genre de voiture, plus populaire en Europe qu'en Amérique du Nord où les véhicules sport-utilitaire ou, depuis quelques années, les multisegements, sont plus en vogue. Alors que la berline offre un volume de chargement de 385 litres, celui de la familiale passe de 736 à 1642 litres avec les dossiers des sièges arrière rabattus. La familiale est également plus courte de 7 millimètres et plus haute de 30 millimètres que la berline CTS. Mentionnons

que cette dernière ne connaît aucun changement pour 2011, sauf deux nouvelles couleurs, le noir glacé et le vert évolution.

Mise à l'essai au cours de l'hiver, la CTS familiale équipée du rouage intégral et du moteur V6 de 3,6 litres s'est distinguée non seulement par sa polyvalence supérieure à la berline, mais aussi par son comportement routier qui était tout aussi impressionnant que celui de la CTS conventionnelle, et ce, malgré son poids plus élevé. On peut bien relever quelques bémols du côté de la direction légèrement trop assistée ou du côté des suspensions dont le calibrage autorise un peu trop de plongée vers l'avant lors de freinages intensifs, mais ça se limite essentiellement à ça pour ce qui est des points faibles associés à la dynamique de la voiture, ce qui indique que Cadillac a toujours du travail à faire avant de pouvoir faire jeu égal à BMW qui demeure la référence en la matière. Le V6 de 3,6 litres s'acquitte bien de sa tâche, tout en offrant des performances plus relevées que celles livrées par le V6 de 3,0 litres, mais il s'avère parfois rugueux en accélération franche. La présence du rouage intégral fait en sorte que la CTS ne rechigne pas à l'idée d'aller jouer dehors en hiver, où elle fait preuve d'un bel équilibre dans ces conditions particulières.

Catégorie	Berline, Coupé, Familiale
Échelle de prix	40650$ à 72045$ (2010)
Garanties	4 ans/80000 km, 5 ans/160000 km
Assemblage	Lansing, Michigan, États-Unis
Cote d'assurance	moyenne

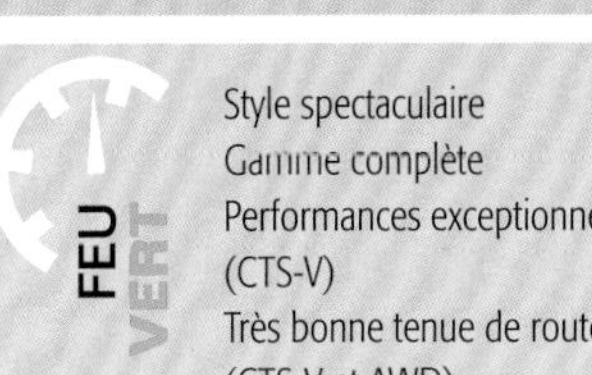

FEU VERT
Style spectaculaire
Gamme complète
Performances exceptionnelles (CTS-V)
Très bonne tenue de route (CTS-V et AWD)

FEU ROUGE
V6 de 3,6 litres parfois rugueux
Valeur de revente incertaine
Visibilité arrière limitée
Beaucoup de boutons au tableau de bord

Pour le reste, la CTS s'ouvre sur un habitacle confortable. La qualité des matériaux utilisés pour la planche de bord de même que la qualité de la finition intérieure a grandement progressé par rapport aux modèles de première génération de la CTS. On peut cependant déplorer que le tableau de bord comporte beaucoup de boutons, ce qui n'aide pas lors de la première prise en mains. Par contre, le système de navigation est très convivial et très facile d'utilisation. Par ailleurs, le prix de base de la CTS familiale est abordable, mais le prix de notre modèle d'essai, qui comprenait plusieurs options, était supérieur à 62000 dollars, ce qui est un peu moins alléchant…

LE STYLE RAVAGEUR DU COUPÉ

Le plus récent modèle de la gamme est le coupé qui n'est pas simplement une berline amputée de deux portières. Non, il est plus court, son pare-brise est plus incliné de 2 degrés, son toit est abaissé et sa voie arrière est élargie par rapport à la berline. De plus, le coupé se démarque de la berline par le remplacement des poignées de portières par deux boutons qui commandent l'ouverture des portes, tout comme sur la Corvette. Un autre élément unique au coupé est son échappement central, repris de la voiture-concept, qui permet également de mieux entendre la sonorité évocatrice du moteur. Les points d'ancrage des sièges sont localisés un peu plus bas d'environ un pouce, donnant ainsi l'impression que la ceinture de caisse de la voiture est plus élevée. Finalement, les liaisons à la route sont assurées par des suspensions dont les ressorts sont plus fermes et dont la barre antiroulis est d'un plus gros diamètre que sur la berline. Lors des premiers mois de commercialisation, seul le moteur V6 de 3,6 litres sera offert, mais une version V du modèle Coupé sera proposé peu après. Ce sera sans doute une combinaison gagnante.

Malgré les déboires de General Motors, Cadillac poursuit sur sa lancée non seulement avec la CTS, qui est de loin la meilleure voiture produite par la marque américaine, mais également avec l'arrivée prochaine de la ATS qui aura la Série 3 de BMW et les autres berlines sport de luxe allemandes dans son collimateur, et par la XTS qui remplacera les actuelles STS et DTS. La suite des choses promet d'être passionnante.

Gabriel Gélinas

Cadillac CTS coupé

PHOTOS : ALAIN MORIN

CHÂSSIS - DONNÉES POUR 3.6L SPORTWAGON

Emp/lon/lar/haut	2880/4859/1841/1502 mm
Coffre	736 à 1642 litres
Réservoir	68 litres
Nombre coussins sécurité	6
Antipatinage / contrôle stabilité	oui / oui
Suspension avant	indépendante, bras inégaux
Suspension arrière	indépendante, multibras
Freins avant / arrière	disque (ABS) / disque (ABS)
Direction	à crémaillère, ass. variable
Diamètre de braquage	11,0 m
Pneus avant / arrière	P235/50R18 / P235/50R18
Poids	n.d.
Capacité de remorquage	454 kg (1000 lb)

COMPOSANTES MÉCANIQUES

CTS, CTS Sportwagon

Cylindrée, soupapes, alim.	V6 3,0 litres 24 s atmos.
Puissance / Couple	270 chevaux / 223 lb-pi
Tr. base (opt) / rouage base (opt)	M6 (A6) / Prop (Int)
0-100 / 80-120 / 100-0 km/h	n.d. / n.d. / n.d.
Type ess. / ville / autoroute	Ordinaire / 11,9 / 7,7 l/100 km

CTS Coupe, CTS Sportwagon

Cylindrée, soupapes, alim.	V6 3,6 litres 24 s atmos.
Puissance / Couple	304 chevaux / 273 lb-pi
Tr. base (opt) / rouage base (opt)	A6 (M6) / Prop (Int)
0-100 / 80-120 / 100-0 km/h	7,4 s / 5,0 s / 41,7 m
Type ess. / ville / autoroute	Ordinaire / 11,7 / 7,4 l/100 km

CTS-V, CTS-V Coupe

Cylindrée, soupapes, alim.	V8 6,2 litres 16 s surcompressé
Puissance / Couple	556 chevaux / 551 lb-pi
Tr. base (opt) / rouage base (opt)	M6 (A6) / Prop
0-100 / 80-120 / 100-0 km/h	4,9 s / 3,9 s / 38,0 m
Type ess. / ville / autoroute	Super / 14,9 / 10,5 l/100 km

DANS LA MÊME CATÉGORIE

Acura TL, Audi A4, BMW Série 3, Infiniti G, Lexus IS, Lincoln MKZ, Mercedes-Benz Classe C, Volvo S60

DU NOUVEAU EN 2011

Ajout du modèle Coupe

NOS IMPRESSIONS

Agrément de conduite :	8/10
Fiabilité :	6/10
Sécurité :	10/10
Qualités hivernales :	8/10
Espace intérieur :	8/10
Confort :	8/10

www.gm.ca

Plus d'informations dans la section statistiques en dernière partie du Guide

LA FORD T DES TEMPS MODERNES

Non, la Cadillac DTS ne sera pas fabriquée par Ford ! Non plus qu'elle n'est proposée qu'en noir (en fait, il est faux de prétendre que tous les Modèle T de Ford étaient offerts en noir uniquement. Ce fut le cas seulement entre 1915 et 1925, mais je m'éloigne de la Cadillac DTS.) Si nous la comparons à la T, c'est parce qu'elle aurait dû quitter le monde automobile depuis quelques années et qu'elle s'accroche à la production avec l'énergie du désespoir tout comme sa vénérable ancêtre, produite entre 1908 et 1927.

La DTS est avec nous depuis 2006 en remplacement de la DeVille qui, elle, officiait depuis 2000. Or, cette dernière reprenait le châssis des Oldsmobile Aurora ainsi que des Buick LeSabre et Park Avenue. Allô le modernisme… Depuis les déboires de GM, on s'attend à ce que cette Caddy rétro nous quitte, mais le marché sans aucun doute fort lucratif des limousines et des corbillards a encore son mot à dire, d'autant plus que les matrices doivent être payées depuis des lunes. Personne ne sera donc surpris d'apprendre que les changements pour 2011 sont inexistants.

POURQUOI FAIRE SIMPLE…

Curieusement, pour une voiture aux chiffres de vente assurément bas, GM continue de proposer deux versions du V8 4,6 litres, une à 275 chevaux, l'autre à 292. Si, au moins, le couple de ce dernier moteur était supérieur. Mais non, il déballe 288 livres-pied de couple contre 295 pour le premier. Allez y comprendre quelque chose ! Dans la même veine, GM poursuit cette année encore avec la transmission automatique à quatre rapports, une boîte qui, semble-t-il, aurait été refusée par Cugnot pour son fardier, sa conception étant, en 1769, déjà dépassée. Enfin, c'est ce qu'on m'a dit… Remarquez que cette transmission fonctionne très bien, passant les rapports doucement et au bon moment. Mais deux, ou trois et même quatre rapports supplémentaires permettraient de faire baisser la consommation, surtout en ville. Cette boîte a pour mission de diriger le couple vers les roues avant, la DTS étant une traction. Eh, oui, elle date de l'époque où GM avait décidé du tout à l'avant, pour revenir à la propulsion pour ses voitures haut de gamme. La DTS n'en est que plus anachronique, ce qui la rend encore plus désirable aux yeux de certains !

Sauf que traction et 275 (ou 292) chevaux font rarement bon ménage et la DTS ne fait pas exception. En accélération vive, les roues avant veulent partir chacune de leur côté, ce qui n'est jamais très rassurant. D'autant plus que la direction, qui ne laisse passer aucune émotion, n'est pas un modèle de précision. Mais j'imagine qu'il s'agit là d'une qualité pour ce type de voitures… Les suspensions, on n'en sera pas surpris, sont axées vers le confort plutôt que vers la sportivité. La première courbe prise à une allure le moindrement élevée nous le rappelle sans équivoque ! Néanmoins, il faut noter que la version Platine, celle qui possède le moteur le plus puissant, reçoit une suspension *Magnetic*

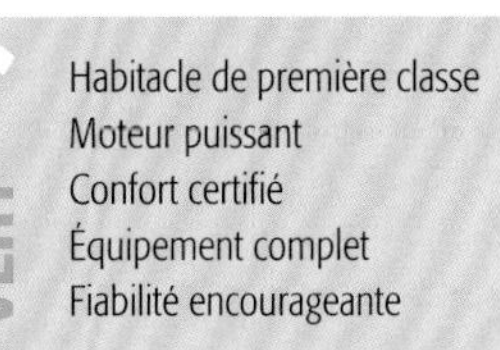

FEU VERT

- Habitacle de première classe
- Moteur puissant
- Confort certifié
- Équipement complet
- Fiabilité encourageante

FEU ROUGE

- Dimensions hors normes
- Comportement «bateau» en virage
- Transmission dépassée
- Effet de couple en accélération
- Modèle en fin de carrière

Ride Control qui, si elle ne fait pas de la DTS une Corvette, lui fait prendre les courbes de manière plus assurée. Il faut toutefois toujours se souvenir qu'en plus de ne pas être un modèle de sportivité, ces suspensions doivent contenir un poids de près de 1 900 kilos…

Mais sans doute que les propriétaires de DTS, qu'ils soient directeurs de funérailles ou non, se foutent passablement de ce qui se passe sous le capot. Ce qui importe, c'est le confort ! Et là, la DTS excelle. Son habitacle est vaste, les cuirs et les boiseries se marient avec bonheur et la finition, toute GM fait un peu plastique mais, dans l'ensemble, on a déjà vu bien pire. Le tableau de bord montre de plus en plus des signes de vieillissement mais toute l'information nécessaire est là, y compris la montre carrée. Les sièges sont distributeurs de ce confort tout moelleux que les gens ayant appris à conduire dans les années 50 apprécient à sa juste valeur. La DTS est d'ailleurs l'une des dernières voitures pouvant recevoir une banquette pleine largeur à l'avant lui permettant d'y asseoir trois personnes. Et croyez-moi, six adultes de bonne taille peuvent aisément monter à bord d'une DTS. Je dirais même que la voiture devient plus sportive à ce moment. Non, elle ne s'accroche pas davantage dans les courbes mais, au moins, les gens sont moins portés à glisser sur des sièges qui n'offrent aucun soutien latéral ! La promiscuité a de très bons côtés…

Si l'habitacle est caverneux, on peut presque en dire autant du coffre. Pourtant, une Ford Taurus, un peu plus petite, possède un coffre plus grand. D'un autre côté, celui d'une Chrysler 300 est plus petit. On ne sera pas étonné d'apprendre que les manœuvres de stationnement au volant d'une DTS ne sont pas qu'une petite affaire. Heureusement, les nombreux détecteurs d'objets à proximité sont là pour nous aider.

Les services spécialisés de GM proposent, via un catalogue assez complet, des Cadillac DTS à empattement allongé, limousines ou corbillards et je ne serais absolument pas surpris qu'il se vende plus de ces voitures à caractère officiel que de voitures personnelles. Cependant, quiconque recherche une grande berline confortable et logeable sera très bien servi par la DTS. Et pour rouler vite dans les courbes, il y a toujours la Corvette !

Alain Morin

PHOTOS : CADILLAC

Catégorie	Berline
Échelle de prix	56 535 $ à 74 675 $ (2010)
Garanties	4 ans/80 000 km, 5 ans/160 000 km
Assemblage	Hamtrack, Michigan, É-U
Cote d'assurance	n.d.

CHÂSSIS - DONNÉES POUR PLATINUM

Emp/lon/lar/haut	2 936/5 273/1 900/1 463 mm
Coffre	532 litres
Réservoir	68 litres
Nombre coussins sécurité	6
Antipatinage / contrôle stabilité	oui / oui
Suspension avant	indépendante, jambes de force
Suspension arrière	indépendante, multibras
Freins avant / arrière	disque (ABS) / disque (ABS)
Direction	à crémaillère, assistée
Diamètre de braquage	14,0 m
Pneus avant / arrière	P245/50R18 / P245/50R18
Poids	1 818 kg
Capacité de remorquage	454 kg (1 000 lb)

COMPOSANTES MÉCANIQUES

Base

Cylindrée, soupapes, alim.	V8 4,6 litres 32 s atmos.
Puissance / Couple	275 chevaux / 295 lb-pi
Tr. base (opt) / rouage base (opt)	A4 / Tr
0-100 / 80-120 / 100-0 km/h	7,8 s / 6,7 s / 42,4 m
Type ess. / ville / autoroute	Ordinaire / 13,8 / 8,7 l/100 km

Platinum

Cylindrée, soupapes, alim.	V8 4,6 litres 32 s atmos.
Puissance / Couple	292 chevaux / 288 lb-pi
Tr. base (opt) / rouage base (opt)	A4 / Tr
0-100 / 80-120 / 100-0 km/h	7,8 s / 6,7 s / 42,4 m
Type ess. / ville / autoroute	Ordinaire / 13,8 / 8,7 l/100 km

DANS LA MÊME CATÉGORIE

Buick Lucerne, Chrysler 300, Hyundai Genesis, Lexus GS, Lincoln MKS, Mercedes-Benz Classe E, Volvo S80

DU NOUVEAU EN 2011

Aucun changement majeur

NOS IMPRESSIONS

Agrément de conduite :	6/10
Fiabilité :	6/10
Sécurité :	8/10
Qualités hivernales :	7/10
Espace intérieur :	9/10
Confort :	9/10

www.gm.ca

Plus d'informations dans la section statistiques en dernière partie du Guide

SAGE MÉTAMORPHOSE RÉUSSIE

Le plus accessible des utilitaires de Cadillac a subi une transformation radicale l'an dernier. Délaissant le profil de familiale surélevée que promenait la première génération de cette série, le SRX est rentré dans le rang pour se lancer résolument dans la bataille des multisegments avec une silhouette plus haute et costaude sur une architecture offrant le choix de la traction ou des quatre roues motrices. Le pari a visiblement réussi.

Subaru continue de démontrer avec son Outback qu'une familiale bien conçue peut devenir un multisegment exceptionnel. Le premier SRX, produit de 2004 à 2009, était prometteur mais n'a jamais su s'imposer. Il faut dire que ses ennuis de fiabilité n'ont pas aidé. Rien d'étonnant à ce que GM ait donné un sérieux coup de barre en le remplaçant.

Ce deuxième génération du SRX adopte ainsi l'architecture Theta conçue pour des multisegments compacts ou intermédiaires à roues avant motrices. Le rouage à quatre roues motrices s'ajoute par la suite. Le nouveau SRX partage l'essentiel de la structure des Chevrolet Equinox et GMC Terrain. Il est cependant plus long, plus large, plus bas, plus lourd et posé sur un empattement un peu plus court que celui de ses cousins plus modestes.

Sa finition est évidemment plus riche et son équipement plus abondant. Le SRX est toutefois offert avec le choix de roues avant motrices ou d'un rouage à quatre roues motrices pour donner le change à ses concurrentes.

DOUBLE PERSONNALITÉ

Les modèles traction et les versions à quatre roues motrices les plus accessibles du SRX sont propulsées par le V6 à double arbre à cames en tête qui a d'abord animé la berline CTS. Ce groupe moderne, doté de l'injection directe et du calage variable des soupapes, est censé produire 265 chevaux à 6 950 tr/min mais on se demande parfois où ils sont passés. Nos mesures d'accélération, à bord d'un SRX à quatre roues motrices doté du V6 atmosphérique, ont produit un 0-100 km/h de 9,48 seconds et un chrono de 17,02 secondes pour le quart de mille départ-arrêté, ce qui n'a rien d'exceptionnel, même pour un utilitaire.

Les versions à quatre roues motrices équipées du V6 turbocompressé optionnel de 2,8 litres sont plus performantes et franchement plus réjouissantes à conduire. Avec une puissance de 300 chevaux à 5 500 tr/min et surtout un couple maxi de 295 lb-pi à seulement 2 000 tr/min, il procure au SRX un 0-100 km/h de 8,5 secondes et un chrono de 16,11 secondes sur un quart de mille à une vitesse de 146,8 km/h.

Le V6 atmosphérique se reprend un peu en consommation avec des cotes officielles de 12,2 L/100 km en ville, 8,8 L/100 km sur la route et une note combinée de 10,7 L/100 km tandis que le V6

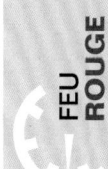

FEU VERT
- Silhouette moderne
- Moteur turbo optionnel plus animé
- Finition soignée
- Sièges avant confortables
- Volant cuir agréable

FEU ROUGE
- Le V6 de base dénué de caractère
- Présentation intérieure froide
- Fiabilité du moteur turbo à confirmer
- Version traction illogique
- Éclairage automatique frustrant

turbo est coté à 13,6 / 9,1 et 11,6 L/100 km. De surcroît, le premier se contente d'essence normale tandis que Cadillac recommande du super pour le turbo. Il sera intéressant de voir à quel point ce moteur turbo développé par Saab s'avèrera fiable et durable.

Les deux mêmes modèles se sont débrouillés correctement en freinage d'urgence simulé avec des distances moyennes de 42,59 et 44,06 mètres. La plongée est légère et la pédale est plutôt haute et dure, avec un effort assez élevé.

DU TRAVAIL BIEN FAIT

Le tableau de bord du SRX est bien dessiné et très bien fini, avec la froideur un peu clinique des Cadillac récentes. L'éclairage des commandes et cadrans n'est toutefois pas réglable lorsqu'on roule en plein jour. Il est lié plutôt à l'ensoleillement et à la lumière ambiante ce qui n'a rien de très commode.

Les sièges avant sont très bien sculptés, avec un coussin long qui maintient bien les cuisses. Le volant est très bien taillé, sa jante offrant une prise agréable sur son cuir lisse. L'espace est limité et plutôt étroit pour le pied gauche à la pointe du repose-pied. Il n'y a pas d'écran pour une caméra de marche arrière dans le SRX. Il y des sonars mais pas d'image. Dommage parce que le système qu'on trouve dans certains autres modèles de GM est très efficace.

La direction est très juste en conduite normale avec des réactions linéaires et un effort très bien dosé. La conduite est sans histoire et sans grand ravissement non plus. C'est évidemment un peu mieux avec le moteur turbo, dont le caractère, la sonorité et les performances sont plus conformes à ce qu'on attend encore d'un modèle de luxe.

Pour tout dire, malgré une silhouette moderne et plutôt réussie, un équipement complet, des prix compétitifs et plein d'autres qualités, les SRX laissent finalement un peu indifférent. Ils font leur boulot honnêtement, comme de bons élèves, mais ne ressortent pas vraiment du lot dans une catégorie où les modèles et les concurrents sérieux foisonnent. Comme les Equinox et Terrain qui partagent la même architecture, c'est un utilitaire intéressant, bien tourné et bien construit.

Marc Lachapelle

PHOTOS : ALAIN MORIN

Catégorie	Multisegment
Échelle de prix	41 575 $ à 62 770 $ (2010)
Garanties	4 ans/80 000 km, 5 ans/160 000 km
Assemblage	Ramos Aripze, Mexique
Cote d'assurance	n.d.

CHÂSSIS - DONNÉES POUR DE LUXE TI

Emp/lon/lar/haut	2 807/4 834/1 910/1 669 mm
Coffre	839 à 1 733 litres
Réservoir	80 litres
Nombre coussins sécurité	6
Antipatinage / contrôle stabilité	oui / oui
Suspension avant	indépendante, jambes de force
Suspension arrière	indépendante, multibras
Freins avant / arrière	disque (ABS) / disque (ABS)
Direction	à crémaillère, assistée
Diamètre de braquage	12,2 m
Pneus avant / arrière	P235/65R18 / P235/65R18
Poids	1 981 kg
Capacité de remorquage	1 136 kg (2 504 lb)

COMPOSANTES MÉCANIQUES

SRX TA, SRX TI

Cylindrée, soupapes, alim.	V6 3,0 litres 24 s atmos.
Puissance / Couple	265 chevaux / 223 lb-pi
Tr. base (opt) / rouage base (opt)	A6 / Tr (Int)
0-100 / 80-120 / 100-0 km/h	9,7 s / 8,1 s / 42,6 m
Type ess. / ville / autoroute	Ordinaire / 12,2 / 8,8 l/100 km

SRX TI

Cylindrée, soupapes, alim.	V6 2,8 litres 24 s turbo
Puissance / Couple	300 chevaux / 295 lb-pi
Tr. base (opt) / rouage base (opt)	A6 / Int
0-100 / 80-120 / 100-0 km/h	8,5 s / 4,8 s / 44,1 m
Type ess. / ville / autoroute	Super / 13,6 / 9,1 l/100 km

DANS LA MÊME CATÉGORIE

Acura MDX, Audi Q7, BMW X5, Infiniti FX, Lexus RX, Lincoln MKX, Mercedes-Benz Classe M, Porsche Cayenne, Volkswagen Touareg, Volvo XC90

DU NOUVEAU EN 2011

Aucun changement majeur

NOS IMPRESSIONS

Agrément de conduite :	8/10
Fiabilité :	7/10
Sécurité :	9/10
Qualités hivernales :	8/10
Espace intérieur :	8/10
Confort :	7/10

www.gm.ca

Plus d'informations dans la section statistiques en dernière partie du Guide

UN MODÈLE À DÉCOUVRIR

De nos jours, l'attention est portée sur la famille des modèles CTS qui est parmi l'une des plus complètes dans sa catégorie et bien entendu sur la nouvelle SRX qui a été dévoilée avec succès l'an dernier. Malheureusement, on oublie trop souvent la STS, une berline pleine grandeur qui n'est pas dépourvue de qualités. Pour une raison ou pour une autre, on l'associe à tort aux anciennes Cadillac avec leurs suspensions ultrasouples, leur intérieur désolant et un flagrant manque de personnalité. Pourtant, la STS n'est rien de tout cela.

Par ailleurs, l'un des problèmes de cette Cadillac, c'est qu'elle est dans la même catégorie que les grosses pointures parmi les voitures de luxe. Il suffit de mentionner les Mercedes-Benz de Classe E, les BMW de Série 5, les Audi A6, sans oublier la nouvelle Infiniti M et la Lincoln MKS. Bref, la concurrence est affûtée et cette Cadillac n'a pas bénéficié des derniers changements apportés à sa silhouette comme cela a été le cas avec la séduisante CTS. Chez Cadillac, on a préféré améliorer la cadette et on a quelque peu laissé la STS à elle-même.

ENTRE LES DEUX

C'est vrai que cette berline adopte le style de toutes les Cadillac modernes: phares avant verticaux, grille de calandre en cinq points et feux arrière verticaux; elle a la plupart des caractéristiques propres à toute Cadillac. Mais il y a un léger problème, c'est qu'il lui manque cette petite touche de modernité que possède la CTS. En effet, les angles de cette dernière sont plus aigus et plus incisifs. Bref, sa silhouette a plus de mordant tandis que la STS affiche un peu trop de rondeurs pour être au goût du jour. Par contre, l'assemblage de la carrosserie est au niveau des autres modèles concurrents. Mais comme c'est souvent la coutume chez ce constructeur, il y a toujours ce petit détail infime qui nous saute aux yeux et qui nous porte à croire qu'il y a encore beaucoup de progrès à réaliser au chapitre de la finition.

L'habitacle est une heureuse surprise. Il n'y a pas si longtemps, jeter un coup d'œil au tableau de bord d'une Cadillac vous donnait envie de prendre du Prozac tant s'était déprimant! Les stylistes avaient adopté la loi du rectangle et des cadrans indicateurs simplistes. On avait beau nous dire que les matériaux étaient de qualité et qu'on utilisait du bois authentique et des cuirs fins, l'effet était raté. Au moins, cette fois, c'est dans la moyenne des voitures modernes. La console verticale respecte les tendances du moment avec deux buses de ventilation encadrant l'écran de navigation qui surplombe les lecteurs CD et DVD. On retrouve ensuite les boutons de commandes de la climatisation et du système audio. Il faut souligner la qualité de la finition qui est presque à la hauteur de celle d'une Lexus. Vous pouvez m'accuser d'avoir la berlue, mais je persiste et signe! Et comme sur certaines marques japonaises fort bien cotées, les cadrans sont électroluminescents, tandis que le volant à trois branches se pare d'une partie supérieure en bois qui

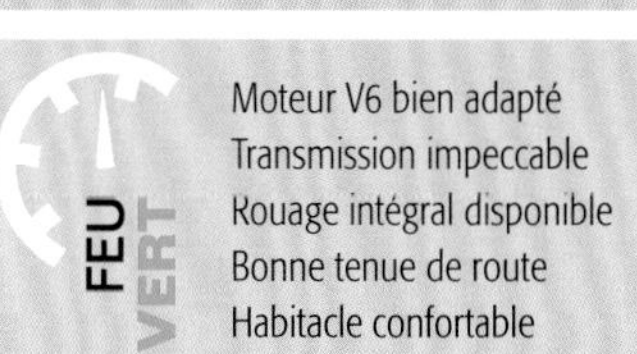

FEU VERT

Moteur V6 bien adapté
Transmission impeccable
Rouage intégral disponible
Bonne tenue de route
Habitacle confortable

FEU ROUGE

Dimensions encombrantes
Fiabilité moyenne
Moteur V8 abandonné
Valeur de revente problématique

est d'un bel effet. J'avoue par contre que ce n'est pas aussi créatif et exclusif que sur certaines allemandes, mais beaucoup mieux qu'auparavant.

Cette berline a abandonné les fauteuils de salon qui servaient de sièges avant. Ceux qui nous sont proposés offrent quand même un bon support latéral pour autant qu'on ne décide pas de jouer au cascadeur au volant de sa Cadillac. Compte tenu des dimensions de cette voiture, les places arrière sont spacieuses et confortables.

ADIEU V8

Au cours des trois dernières années, la gamme STS s'est rationalisée et pas à peu près. Tout d'abord, dans la tourmente financière qu'a connue ce constructeur, on a délesté le fantastique moteur V8 4,4 litres suralimenté qui était sans doute une merveille technologique mais qui cadrait mal dans le portrait étant donné que la compagnie était en faillite. On a coupé dans le gras et la STS-V avec ses 469 chevaux a pris le chemin de la retraite. Ce qui est d'autant plus logique puisque la CTS-V était — et est encore — propulsée par un tonitruant V8 de 556 chevaux ! Quand un modèle de plus petit gabarit et plus léger propose un moulin qui a un avantage de 107 chevaux, la décision est facile à prendre. On tentait de se consoler en soulignant que le moteur V8 de 4,6 litres produisait quand même 320 chevaux, ce qui n'était pas mal après tout.

Cette année, ce moteur nous tire sa révérence à son tour. Mais n'ayez crainte, il n'y a pas de quatre cylindres tournant sous le capot de cette Cadillac. On a préféré donner l'exclusivité au V6 de 3,6 litres qui était toujours là l'an dernier. Même s'il concède un peu moins de 20 chevaux par rapport au V8 qui n'est plus disponible, ses performances sont quasiment similaires et sa consommation de carburant est bien entendue inférieure à celle du moteur V8.

Terminons en disant que cette voiture a une excellente tenue de route. Elle est agile et agréable à conduire tandis que la boîte automatique à six rapports est sans reproche. Et si le moteur V6 est moins puissant que l'ancien V8, son poids plus léger assure un bel équilibre au chapitre de la tenue de route.

C'est vrai qu'il manque un peu de panache à cette grosse berline qu'est la Cadillac STS, mais force est d'admettre qu'elle possède d'intéressantes qualités.

Denis Duquet

PHOTOS : CADILLAC

Catégorie	Berline
Échelle de prix	61 085 $ à 73 910 $ (2010)
Garanties	4 ans/80 000 km, 6 ans/160 000 km
Assemblage	Lansing, Michigan, É-U
Cote d'assurance	n.d.

CHÂSSIS - DONNÉES POUR V6 TI

Emp/lon/lar/haut	2 957/4 985/1 845/1 464 mm
Coffre	391 litres
Réservoir	66 litres
Nombre coussins sécurité	6
Antipatinage / contrôle stabilité	oui / oui
Suspension avant	indépendante, bras inégaux
Suspension arrière	indépendante, multibras
Freins avant / arrière	disques (ABS) / disques (ABS)
Direction	à crémaillère, assistée
Diamètre de braquage	11,5 m
Pneus avant / arrière	P235/50R17 / P235/50R17
Poids	1 871 kg
Capacité de remorquage	454 kg (1 000 lb)

COMPOSANTES MÉCANIQUES

V6, V6 TI

Cylindrée, soupapes, alim.	V6 3,6 litres 24 s atmos.
Puissance / Couple	302 chevaux / 272 lb-pi
Tr. base (opt) / rouage base (opt)	A6 / Prop (Int)
0-100 / 80-120 / 100-0 km/h	7,0 s / 6,0 s (est) / 40,1 m
Type ess. / ville / autoroute	Ordinaire / 11,7 / 7,4 l/100 km

DANS LA MÊME CATÉGORIE

Acura RL, Audi A6, BMW Série 5, Infiniti M, Jaguar XF, Lexus GS, Lincoln MKS, Mercedes-Benz Classe E, Volvo S80

DU NOUVEAU EN 2011

Aucun changement majeur. Abandon du V8

NOS IMPRESSIONS

Agrément de conduite :	■■■■■■■■□□	8/10
Fiabilité :	■■■■■■□□□□	6/10
Sécurité :	■■■■■■■■□□	8/10
Qualités hivernales :	■■■■■■■■□□	8/10
Espace intérieur :	■■■■■■■■■□	9/10
Confort :	■■■■■■■■■□	9/10

www.gm.ca

Plus d'informations dans la section statistiques en dernière partie du Guide

CADILLAC STS

Chevrolet Aveo

DESIGN ALLÉCHANT, EXÉCUTION RATÉE

Lorsque General Motors a lancé l'Aveo et ses variantes au printemps 2004, ce fut un succès sur toute la ligne. En effet, cette voiture arborait une silhouette moderne et se vendait à des prix ridiculement bas. Les gens se sont précipités dans les salles de démonstration pour examiner cette nouvelle venue. Désireux de surfer sur la vague et afin de remplir les obligations de partenariat, Suzuki a adopté la petite coréenne qui est devenue la Swift+. Mais ce n'était que le début.

Il n'a pas fallu beaucoup de temps aux propriétaires de ces petites merveilles pour découvrir qu'ils étaient au volant de voitures manquant de puissance, ayant une tenue de route passable tout au plus et dont la fiabilité faisait fortement défaut. Les ventes ont rapidement décliné. Au fil des années, les améliorations se sont succédé, notamment avec l'arrivée d'un moteur plus puissant, d'une version berline et finalement, de la Pontiac Wave, maintenant disparue, afin d'équilibrer l'offre chez les deux marques. Quant à Suzuki, on s'est contenté de suivre les évolutions et de ne proposer qu'une version *hatchback*.

FIÈRE ALLURE

Force est d'admettre que le style de ces voitures est intéressant. Si la berline ne casse rien en fait de silhouette, la hatchback est beaucoup mieux réussie avec sa partie arrière dotée de feux de recul circulaires qui lui donnent une petite touche à part. Les designers ont également eu le coup de crayon inspiré lorsqu'est venu le temps de dessiner le tableau de bord. Certains vont souligner que le nombre de boutons et de commandes est minimaliste, mais encore fallait-il les agencer de belle façon. L'utilisation de certaines pièces en aluminium brossé relève le tout. De plus, le volant à quatre branches est tout de même assez inspiré tout en étant pratique avec ses commandes placées en périphérie du moyeu. Mais là s'arrêtent les choses positives que l'on a à dire à propos de cet habitacle.

Il n'y a aucune preuve réelle, mais les plastiques semblent être d'une grande fragilité et on a l'impression de pouvoir tout démolir uniquement à l'aide de ses deux mains. Les sièges avant ne paraissent pas plus solides et leur confort n'a rien pour écrire à sa mère. On peut rouler pendant quelques heures sans trop souffrir, mais il y a beaucoup mieux dans la catégorie. Quant aux places arrière, elles sont quasiment symboliques. En plus de manquer d'espace, lorsqu'on abaisse le dossier de la version *hatchback*, on est en mesure de contempler la structure de ce siège et de réaliser que ce n'est pas tellement solide là non plus... Et ne croyez pas que c'est mieux chez Suzuki. Peu importe la marque ou le modèle, l'apparence est agréable mais l'exécution décevante.

PIÈTRES ROUTIÈRES

Il arrive parfois que des voitures mal foutues en fait de qualité des matériaux et d'assemblage se fassent pardonner ces faiblesses par un agrément de conduite digne de mention et par une tenue de route supérieure à la moyenne. Certaines autres n'ont qu'à

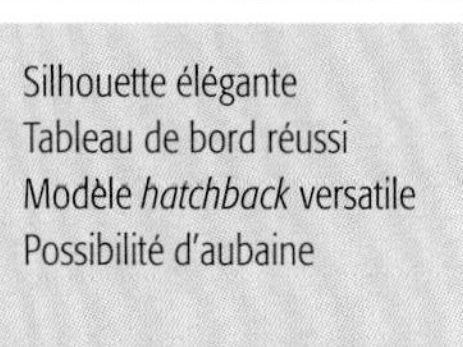

FEU VERT

Silhouette élégante
Tableau de bord réussi
Modèle *hatchback* versatile
Possibilité d'aubaine

FEU ROUGE

Performances décevantes
Consommation élevée
Transmission d'une autre époque
Fabrication peu convaincante

posséder un moteur performant qui fait baver les enthousiastes. Dans le cas qui nous concerne, rien de cela ne se matérialise...

Le faible moteur quatre cylindres de 1,6 litre est censé produire 108 chevaux, mais après avoir conduit cette voiture, je suis persuadé qu'il existe une différence entre les chevaux-vapeur coréens et les nôtres! En effet, le rendement du moteur est si décevant qu'on a l'impression qu'il manque au moins une vingtaine d'équidés sous le capot. On a beau boucler le 0-100 km/h en 12 secondes, il faut tellement faire hurler le moteur que c'est presque inapproprié de répéter l'exercice à plusieurs reprises. De plus, la pauvre petite boîte manuelle à cinq rapports ne facilite pas l'exercice. Le passage des rapports est saccadé tandis que le guidage du levier de vitesses est imprécis. Et ce n'est pas en commandant la boîte automatique que les choses vont se régler. Il s'agit d'une unité quasiment rétro avec quatre vitesses et des passages de rapport qui manquent définitivement de douceur. Parlant de performances, lors d'un essai comparatif réalisé pour le *Guide de l'auto 2007* par une journée de canicule, la Suzuki Swift+ qui participait à ce match avait de la difficulté à suivre le peloton qui roulait à des vitesses légales. Compte tenu de la chaleur, le conducteur avait mis le climatiseur en marche, ce qui avait ralenti la vitesse de la voiture. Que dire de plus?

Et c'est une bonne chose que le groupe propulseur ne soit pas plus puissant, car la plate-forme de toutes ces voitures n'est pas ce qui s'est fait de mieux au fil des ans. Le manque de rigidité est flagrant et la suspension mal calibrée a beaucoup de difficultés à négocier les routes en mauvais état, ce qui signifie la quasi-totalité des routes de notre province...

Il malheureux que l'exécution de ces voitures n'ait pas été meilleure. GM avait l'occasion de s'implanter avec vigueur dans un créneau du marché qui est appelé à s'accroître grandement au fil des années en raison des hausses certaines du prix de l'essence et des nouvelles lois visant les normes antipollution des voitures. Par contre, il y a de l'espoir. L'Aveo sera remplacée par un modèle plus gros, plus puissant et fabriqué dans une usine aux États-Unis, ce qui devrait permettre de produire un véhicule capable de soutenir la comparaison avec une concurrence de plus en plus pointue.

Denis Duquet

Chevrolet Aveo

PHOTOS : CHEVROLET

Catégorie	Berline, *Hatchback*
Échelle de prix	13 950 $ à 16 850 $ (2010)
Garanties	3 ans/60 000 km, 5 ans/160 000 km
Assemblage	Bupyong, Corée du Sud
Cote d'assurance	moyenne

CHÂSSIS - DONNÉES POUR AVEO 5 LT

Emp/lon/lar/haut	2 480/3 920/1 680/1 505 mm
Coffre	425 à 1 054 litres
Réservoir	45 litres
Nombre coussins sécurité	4
Antipatinage / contrôle stabilité	non / non
Suspension avant	indépendante, jambes de force
Suspension arrière	semi-indépendante, poutre de torsion
Freins avant / arrière	disque (ABS en option) / tambour (ABS en option)
Direction	à crémaillère, assistée
Diamètre de braquage	10,1 m
Pneus avant / arrière	P185/60R14 / P185/60R14
Poids	1 155 kg
Capacité de remorquage	non recommandé

COMPOSANTES MÉCANIQUES

5 LS, LS, 5 LT, LT

Cylindrée, soupapes, alim.	4L 1,6 litre 16 s atmos.
Puissance / Couple	108 chevaux / 105 lb-pi
Tr. base (opt) / rouage base (opt)	M5 (A4) / Tr
0-100 / 80-120 / 100-0 km/h	12,0 s / 11,1 s / 42,8 m
Type ess. / ville / autoroute	Ordinaire / 7,5 / 5,7 l/100 km

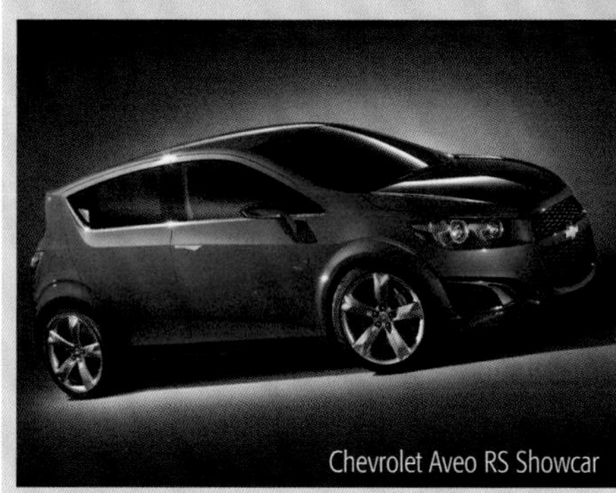

Chevrolet Aveo RS Showcar

DANS LA MÊME CATÉGORIE

Honda Fit, Hyundai Accent, Kia Rio/Rio5, Nissan Versa, Suzuki Swift+, Toyota Yaris

DU NOUVEAU EN 2011

Aucun changement majeur

NOS IMPRESSIONS

Agrément de conduite :	6/10
Fiabilité :	4/10
Sécurité :	6/10
Qualités hivernales :	6/10
Espace intérieur :	6/10
Confort :	6/10

www.gm.ca

Plus d'informations dans la section statistiques en dernière partie du Guide

NE SERAIT-CE QUE POUR LE « SHOW »...

La Chevrolet Camaro, c'est évidemment avec le V8 grondant qu'on l'aime; ainsi qu'avec la boîte manuelle, bien sûr. Cependant, ne boudez pas les autres versions pour autant, parce que plus vous le conduisez, ce coupé deux portes, plus le sourire à votre visage s'élargit. Et pas seulement pour les performances...

Notre premier contact avec l'icône automobile, revenue à la vie après sept ans d'absence, c'est en variante V6 avec boîte automatique que nous l'avons eu. Au départ, nous éprouvons une petite déception. Oui, oui, une déception: où sont les 304 chevaux (recalculés à 312 chevaux cette année) produits par le V6 de 3,6 litres? Avouez que pour traînasser plus ou moins 1700 kg, cette puissance est loin d'être exceptionnelle. Qui plus est, le son qui s'extirpe de l'échappement n'est pas aussi grondant qu'escompté. Un bon point, cependant: sur la grand-route, grâce à l'injection directe, nous avons obtenu du 8,7 L/100 km. C'est plus que les 6,8 L/100 km annoncés (une cote décidément très, très optimiste), mais c'est quand même impressionnant pour un « muscle car ».

En temps normal, on huerait à plein poumons la boîte automatique. Pourtant, on s'y fait vite et bien à cette transmission. Les six rapports sont bien étagés et si ce n'était de l'aiguille des révolutions qui frémit de temps à autre, on n'aurait à peine conscience des passages de rapports. Le mode manuel est possible, mais les palettes au volant ne sont fonctionnelles que si le levier de vitesse est engagé à la bonne position, ce qui est peu pratique dans le feu de l'action.

Parlons suspension maintenant: est-elle si molle que ça? Davantage de type « cruiser » que de type sportive (du moins, les variantes V6), la Camaro est agréablement conciliante avec les aléas de la route, mais c'est au prix d'une souplesse qui fait se déporter l'arrière, avec en prime des répercussions dans le volant. Ce n'est évidemment pas ce que l'on attend d'une propulsion dynamique (rappelons que la Camaro est assemblée sur la plateforme australienne Holden) et l'on prendrait définitivement plus de fermeté.

VIVE LE V8

Pour obtenir gain de cause à ce dernier chapitre, il faut choisir la Camaro V8 et là, on profite d'un bon quart de puissance additionnelle, rugissante à souhait. Il faut quand même y aller doucement avec cette Camaro de 426 chevaux (400 chevaux avec l'automatique). D'abord, la boîte manuelle à six rapports s'inspire de cette ère où il fallait entendre des « clangs » brutaux d'embrayage coriace pour se donner l'illusion d'être le roi de la route. Aussi, la suspension est nettement plus sport et ça vous brasse le camarade, à bord. On a droit à quelques malheureux rebonds et à un arrière qui ne se replace pas toujours de façon prévisible. Par contre, l'impression générale est plus vive qu'avec le V6 – à condition de ne pas hésiter dans les rétrogradations – et ce n'est

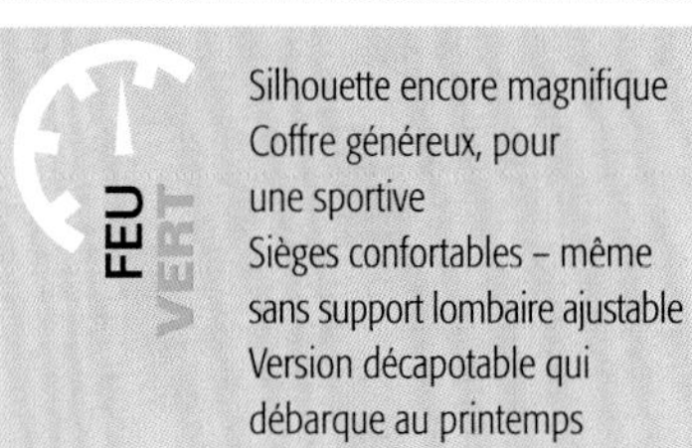

Silhouette encore magnifique
Coffre généreux, pour une sportive
Sièges confortables – même sans support lombaire ajustable
Version décapotable qui débarque au printemps

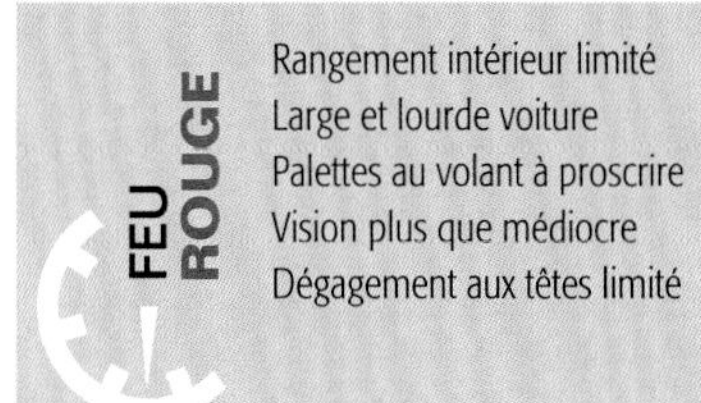

Rangement intérieur limité
Large et lourde voiture
Palettes au volant à proscrire
Vision plus que médiocre
Dégagement aux têtes limité

pas pour nous déplaire ! Même si ça nous expose à du 13,2 L/100 km de consommation moyenne ! Mea culpa, on a eu le pied pesant...

On aime aussi la direction, substantielle et bien connectée, de même que le gros volant qui se prend confortablement en main. Cependant, on déteste férocement la vision : elle est médiocre (le mot est faible) tant à l'avant, à l'arrière, que latéralement. En montée, il faut deviner où se place le long et large capot; avouez que conduire aux chocs, ça ne fait plaisir à personne...

EFFORT DE STYLE DEDANS COMME DEHORS

À première vue, l'habitacle de la Camaro ne fait pas très sérieux et s'apparente davantage à un gros joujou. On a beau vouloir un style rétro, ces cadrans additionnels (en option) au bas de la console empiètent sur un rangement déjà fort peu généreux, tout ça pour indiquer la température du liquide de transmission ou la tension de la batterie.

Ceci dit, l'habitacle de la Camaro est un bel effort de style, rehaussé par cette ligne d'éclairage bleuté qui illumine gentiment la cabine une fois le soir venu. Quelques reproches, bien sûr : les informations ne sont pas très instinctives à consulter, l'ouverture des glaces électriques est difficile à contrôler, les sièges n'offrent pas de support lombaire ajustable et le dégagement aux têtes est limité aux quatre places (non pas aux cinq places, notez bien).

Sinon, que de bons mots : l'insonorisation est dans la très bonne moyenne, les sièges avant ne se font pas sentir même après une dizaine d'heures de route et le coffre, avec sa gueule profonde et ses larges hanches, offre un généreux 320 litres de cargo ; capacité étonnante pour une sportive. On aime également la visualisation à tête haute (une nouveauté cette année) qui reproduit les infos vitales au bas du pare-brise.

Au-delà de ces considérations terre-à-terre, la Camaro gagne les cœurs à coup sûr avec son *look*. Calandre menaçante, silhouette élancée, allure rétro qui mélange la modernité... Le résultat en est un d'enfer et toutes les têtes se tournent encore sur son passage Imaginez maintenant quand sa variante décapotable nous arrivera au printemps prochain...

Nadine Filion

PHOTOS : ALAIN MORIN

Catégorie	Coupé
Échelle de prix	26995$ à 37065$ (2010)
Garanties	3 ans/60000 km, 5 ans/160000 km
Assemblage	Oshawa, Ontario, Canada
Cote d'assurance	n.d.

CHÂSSIS - DONNÉES POUR SS

Emp/lon/lar/haut	2852/4836/1918/1377 mm
Coffre	320 litres
Réservoir	72 litres
Nombre coussins sécurité	6
Antipatinage / contrôle stabilité	oui / oui
Suspension avant	indépendante, jambes de force
Suspension arrière	indépendante, multibras
Freins avant / arrière	disques (ABS) / disques (ABS)
Direction	à crémaillère, ass. variable
Diamètre de braquage	11,5 m
Pneus avant / arrière	P245/45R20 / P275/40R20
Poids	1746 kg
Capacité de remorquage	non recommandé

COMPOSANTES MÉCANIQUES

LS, LT

Cylindrée, soupapes, alim.	V6 3,6 litres 24 s atmos.
Puissance / Couple	312 chevaux / 278 lb-pi
Tr. base (opt) / rouage base (opt)	M6 (A6) / Prop
0-100 / 80-120 / 100-0 km/h	8,4 s / 5,4 s / 39,0 m
Type ess. / ville / autoroute	Ordinaire / 12,3 / 6,8 l/100 km

SS

Cylindrée, soupapes, alim.	V8 6,2 litres 16 s atmos.
Puissance / Couple	426 chevaux / 420 lb-pi
Tr. base (opt) / rouage base (opt)	M6 (A6) / Prop
0-100 / 80-120 / 100-0 km/h	5,3 s / 4,3 s / 35,6 m
Type ess. / ville / autoroute	Super / 13,2 / 8,2 l/100 km

DANS LA MÊME CATÉGORIE

Dodge Challenger, Ford Mustang, Mazda RX-8, Mitsubishi Eclipse, Nissan Z

DU NOUVEAU EN 2011

Version cabriolet

NOS IMPRESSIONS

Agrément de conduite :	8/10
Fiabilité :	7/10
Sécurité :	8/10
Qualités hivernales :	6/10
Espace intérieur :	6/10
Confort :	8/10

www.gm.ca

Plus d'informations dans la section statistiques en dernière partie du Guide

L'EFFET ZR1 DEVIENT CONTAGIEUX

Les membres du groupe Corvette ont abordé le développement de la ZR1 comme un défi et l'ont relevé avec panache. La Corvette la plus puissante et rapide jamais produite a suscité depuis un engouement qui déborde largement le cercle de ses inconditionnels. Sans l'influence qu'elle a sur les autres modèles de la série qui ne s'en portent que mieux. Et quelle sera la suite?

Trois ans après son entrée en scène spectaculaire, la ZR1 alimente un phénomène qui va largement au-delà de sa horde traditionnelle de fanatiques. Par sa puissance et ses performances, elle continue de défier insolemment les sportives et exotiques européennes les plus prestigieuses et huppées à une fraction de leur prix. La vidéo de son tour du Nürburgring en 7:26.4 minutes est devenu un classique sur le site YouTube et ce chrono n'a toujours pas été battu, à la régulière, par une véritable voiture de série plutôt qu'une bête de course avec un peu de rouge à lèvres.

Or, cette notoriété a maintenant un effet bénéfique sur les autres versions de cette grande sportive américaine qui approche d'ailleurs la soixantaine. Et le plus intéressant est de constater que les sœurs de la ZR1 n'empruntent pas seulement les éléments liés à sa présentation mais qu'on les équipe également de certaines des composantes qui font de la ZR1 une sportive d'exception.

CARBONE MAGIQUE

L'exemple le plus probant de ces retombées est la version Carbon de la Z06, disponible en nombre limité. La bonne nouvelle c'est que ce modèle regroupe des éléments inclus à deux groupes optionnels offerts sur toutes les Z06. Le groupe « Z07 Performance » comprend des freins Brembo carbone/céramique semblables à ceux

de la ZR1, des amortisseurs à réglage magnétique et des pneus Michelin Pilot Sport 2 montés sur des jantes d'alliage à vingt rayons. Le groupe « fibre de carbone CFZ » ajoute le becquet, les bas de caisse, le panneau de toit et le mince aileron faits de ce matériau qui donnent fière allure à la ZR1. Les ailes avant de la Z06 étaient déjà en fibre de carbone.

Pour compléter la version Carbon, on ajoute un capot surélevé, toujours en fibre de carbone, un carénage spécial pour le moteur, une sellerie cuir-suède avec surpiqûres assorties à la carrosserie et des éléments graphiques évoquant les 50 ans de la Corvette aux 24 Heures du Mans. Le groupe Corvette présente cette Z06 Carbon comme la meilleure Corvette pour rouler sur un circuit, grâce à son poids inférieur et à l'équilibre des masses favorable que permet son V8 atmosphérique LS7 de 7 litres (le mythique 427 pouces-cube) et 505 chevaux. L'objectif est d'en produire 500, peintes en « bleu supersonique » ou « orange d'enfer ».

IL Y A SPORT ET GRAND SPORT

La Corvette est également offerte en version coupé ou décapotable de son « modèle de base » ou de la Grand Sport, propulsées

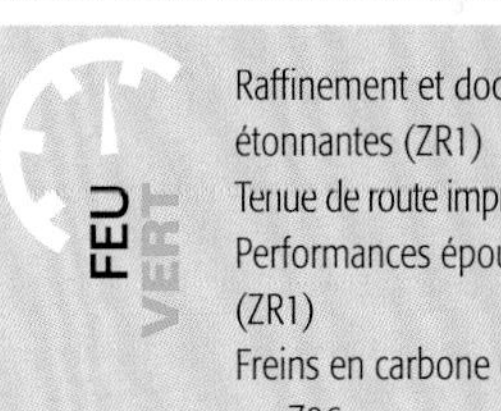

FEU VERT

- Raffinement et docilité étonnantes (ZR1)
- Tenue de route impressionnante
- Performances époustouflantes (ZR1)
- Freins en carbone offerts sur Z06

FEU ROUGE

- Faible maintien latéral des sièges
- Finition intérieure quelconque
- Volant télescopique seulement optionnel
- Levier de vitesses parfois raide
- Fiabilité moyenne

par le V8 LS3 de 6,2 litres et 430 chevaux (436 chevaux avec l'échappement optionnel). Cette dernière a été fort bien accueillie à ses débuts l'an dernier avec ses ailes plus larges, ses becquets, aileron et freins empruntés à la Z06, ses roues et pneus plus larges et des rapports de transmission spéciaux.

La Grand Sport aborde sa deuxième année avec les amortisseurs à réglage magnétique en option et les pneus Goodyear F1 Supercar si on a coché aussi la case de la boîte de vitesses manuelle. Les freins des Corvette « régulières » sont dotés de plus grands rotors et ceux de la Grand Sport sont encore plus costauds et coiffés d'étriers à six pistons à l'avant.

LA ZR1, MISSILE TERRESTRE

La nouvelle reine des Corvette est pratiquement inchangée cette année si ce n'est pour l'ajout d'un port USB et d'une prise d'entrée au système de navigation, de phares et de surpiqûres de couleur contrastée optionnels en plus des deux nouvelles couleurs de carrosserie déjà mentionnées. Son V8 compressé de 638 chevaux est donc intact. Étonnamment doux, souple et silencieux en conduite normale, ce moteur se métamorphose en dragon quand on enfonce l'accélérateur à fond. Son chant mécanique envoûtant est plus ténor que baryton, entre autres parce qu'il fait 6,2 litres en cylindrée plutôt que les 7,0 litres du V8 atmosphérique de la Z06. On entend très peu le sifflement du compresseur de suralimentation Eaton très compact qui niche entre ses deux rangée de cylindres, sous le capot en fibre de carbone percé pour lui d'un hublot en plein centre.

En toute logique, c'est uniquement sur un circuit que la ZR1 peut s'exprimer pleinement, du moins sur notre continent. La mission est d'explorer à la fois le mordant impressionnant des pneus Michelin Pilot Sport 2, surtout au train avant, tout en cherchant le point d'équilibre et la limite d'adhérence des larges pneus arrière, déjà entraînés par les 604 lb-pi de couple que produit le LS8 à 3 800 tr/min. C'est un exercice dont on ne se lasse pas, bien sanglé dans un siège qui devrait maintenir beaucoup mieux dans une sportive aux limites aussi élevées.

De quoi fantasmer une de fois de plus sur ce que devrait être la septième génération de la Corvette dont on ne dit évidemment pas un mot à Détroit ou à Bowling Green où la Corvette est fabriquée et où se trouve le musée Corvette.

Marc Lachapelle

PHOTOS: CHEVROLET

Catégorie	Coupé, *Roadster*
Échelle de prix	67 050 $ à 128 515 $ (2010)
Garanties	3 ans/60 000 km, 5 ans/160 000 km
Assemblage	Bowling Green, Kentucky, É-U
Cote d'assurance	n.d.

CHÂSSIS - DONNÉES POUR Z06 COUPE

Emp/lon/lar/haut	2 685/4 460/1 928/1 245 mm
Coffre	634 litres
Réservoir	68 litres
Nombre coussins sécurité	4
Antipatinage / contrôle stabilité	oui / oui
Suspension avant	indépendante, bras inégaux
Suspension arrière	indépendante, bras inégaux
Freins avant / arrière	disque (ABS) / disque (ABS)
Direction	à crémaillère, ass. variable
Diamètre de braquage	12,0 m
Pneus avant / arrière	P275/35ZR18 / P325/30ZR19
Poids	1 421 kg
Capacité de remorquage	non recommandé

COMPOSANTES MÉCANIQUES

Base, Grand Sport

Cylindrée, soupapes, alim.	V8 6,2 litres 16 s atmos.
Puissance / Couple	430 chevaux / 424 lb-pi
Tr. base (opt) / rouage base (opt)	M6 (A6) / Prop
0-100 / 80-120 / 100-0 km/h	4,8 s / 4,0 s / n.d.
Type ess. / ville / autoroute	Super / 12,9 / 7,7 l/100 km

Z06 Coupe

Cylindrée, soupapes, alim.	V8 7,0 litres 16 s atmos.
Puissance / Couple	505 chevaux / 470 lb-pi
Tr. base (opt) / rouage base (opt)	M6 / Prop
0-100 / 80-120 / 100-0 km/h	4,6 s / 3,0 s / 33,8 m
Type ess. / ville / autoroute	Super / 14,2 / 8,2 l/100 km

ZR1 Coupe

Cylindrée, soupapes, alim.	V8 6,2 litres 16 s surcomp.
Puissance / Couple	638 chevaux / 604 lb-pi
Tr. base (opt) / rouage base (opt)	M6 / Prop
0-100 / 80-120 / 100-0 km/h	3,4 s / n.d. / n.d.
Type ess. / ville / autoroute	Super / 15,5 / 10,2 l/100 km

DANS LA MÊME CATÉGORIE

Aston Martin Vantage, BMW Série 6, Dodge Viper, Jaguar XK, Maserati Gran Turismo, Mercedes-Benz Classe SL, Nissan GT-R, Porsche 911

DU NOUVEAU EN 2011

Groupe performance Z06, ensemble de pièces en fibre de carbone Z06, phares livrables d'une autre couleur que celle de la carrosserie

NOS IMPRESSIONS

Agrément de conduite :	10/10
Fiabilité :	7/10
Sécurité :	10/10
Qualités hivernales :	4/10
Espace intérieur :	5/10
Confort :	7/10

www.gm.ca

Plus d'informations dans la section statistiques en dernière partie du Guide

PARFAITEMENT DANS LA COURSE AU DÉPART

Les petites voitures n'ont jamais été la force de GM en Amérique du Nord mais l'ancien géant américain ne peut plus se permettre de négliger ce segment qui ne cesse de gagner en importance. Chevrolet revient à la charge cette année avec une nouvelle berline compacte drôlement nommée mais plutôt réussie qui pourrait faire oublier les voitures ternes et banales qui l'ont devancée. Que la joute commence.

La Cruze a été développée sur une version de la plateforme de quatrième génération de l'Astra, produite par Opel, la filière et filiale germanique de GM depuis 1929. L'Astra est produite en différentes versions mais Chevrolet ne compte offrir que la berline sur le marché nord-américain. Tant pis pour l'élégante version avec hayon ou la familiale que les Québécois auraient sans doute appréciées.

DES JOUEURS À TOUTES LES POSITIONS

Il y a quatre versions de la Cruze : LS, Eco, LT Turbo et LTZ Turbo. La première nommée est le modèle de base et la seule à être propulsée par un quatre cylindres atmosphérique de 1,8 litre. Les trois autres ont droit plutôt à un nouveau quatre cylindres Ecotec turbocompressé de 1,4 litre. Chevrolet présente même la Cruze Eco comme la compacte qui consomme le moins tout en étant spacieuse comme une intermédiaire.

On lui prédit d'ailleurs une cote de consommation de 5,0 L/100 km sur la route et pour l'espace, la comparaison avec une intermédiaire n'est pas vraiment exagérée. Les places avant des Cruze sont accueillantes et on peut prendre ses aises à l'arrière. Les sièges avant sont bien taillés, faciles à régler et proposent un très bon mélange de confort et de maintien. À l'arrière, les dossiers se replient en deux sections et s'ouvrent sur un coffre aux formes régulières qui étonne surtout par son volume de 415 litres, soit 18 de plus qu'une Honda Accord.

Un groupe optionnel RS, offert sur les LT et LTZ, ajoute des boucliers et bas de caisse plus sculptés, un aileron, des phares d'appoint, des bagues chromées pour les cadrans et un affichage au tableau de bord rétroéclairé par diodes (DEL) bleutées. Les cadrans sont par contre un peu sombres et leur lisibilité affectée par des reflets en plein jour.

L'antidérapage est de série, tout comme l'antipatinage et les freins ABS avec disques à l'avant et tambours derrière. Les LTZ ont quatre freins à disque et de sonars de stationnement. On peut ajouter les disques arrière aux autres modèles en cochant l'option des roues optionnelles de 17 pouces. Le système OnStar est une autre option et Chevrolet a développé une application pour téléphones qui utilise OnStar pour vérifier et faire plein de choses, y compris déverrouiller les portières.

Tous les modèles sont équipés d'une chaîne audio à six haut-parleurs et une chaîne Pioneer à neuf haut-parleurs est en option, tout comme un système de navigation très correct et un port USB pour iPod et autres lecteurs numériques. La connectivité Bluetooth est en option mais devrait être de série chez nous. En sécurité passive, les Cruze proposent dix coussins gonflables soit plus que toutes leurs rivales. Il y en a même pour les genoux.

LE PLUS PETIT MOTEUR N'EST PAS LE MOINDRE

Le moteur de base est le quatre cylindres atmosphérique de la LS, un groupe de 1,8 litre à DACT qui livre 138 chevaux à 6300 tr/min. Le quatre cylindres Ecotec de 1,4 litre des trois autres modèles produit également 138 chevaux mais il y parvient à 4900 tr/min et produit 148 lb-pi de couple à seulement 1850 tr/min grâce à un petit turbocompresseur intégré au collecteur d'échappement pour réduire son poids et son encombrement.

Les Cruze peuvent être dotées d'une boîte manuelle ou d'une automatique, toutes deux à 6 rapports. L'automatique possède un mode manuel classique qu'on invoque en glissant le sélecteur vers la gauche. Il y a en fait deux versions de la boîte manuelle. La première est jumelée au quatre cylindres de 1,8 litre de la LS alors que le quatre cylindres turbo est jumelé à une boite manuelle dont les rapports sont plus espacés.

Un ingénieur ayant participé à la mise au point de cette boîte de vitesses la décrit comme une boîte à « cinq plus un rapport » parce que le sixième, nettement plus long, a été calculé pour réduire le régime-moteur et la consommation au maximum sur autoroute. Le premier rapport est plus démultiplié pour de bons démarrages et les autres sont étagés pour faire le pont vers la sixième. Cette approche est encore plus accentuée dans le modèle Eco.

Le seul véritable agacement au volant d'une Cruze à boîte automatique est une impression d'élasticité et des à-coups qu'on ressent en plein trafic avec ses accélérations et ralentissements incessants. La faute de la boîte de vitesses ou d'un moteur qui accuse un certain temps de réponse malgré son petit turbo ? Chevrolet le sait et promet une solution avant la mise en vente. C'est beaucoup mieux en pleine accélération, toujours avec la boîte automatique. Après des démarrages un peu mous, la Cruze accélère franchement et la boîte passe les rapports de façon plus nette.

CONDUITE STABLE AVANT TOUT

Les Cruze LTZ que nous avons conduites étaient impeccablement solides et à peu près exemptes de bruit de vent. Elles devenaient par contre plus bruyantes sur les chaussées rugueuses, malgré une trentaine de mesures d'insonorisation. Mais puisque c'est le signe d'une carrosserie et d'une structure rigides et solides, on peut facilement vivre avec. Et le confort de roulement en profite, de toute manière.

L'important c'est le résultat. La Cruze se comporte comme une petite berline cossue et axée sur le confort en conduite normale et sur l'autoroute. La direction est un peu inerte au centre et la tenue de cap tout juste correcte. Elle prend vie, par contre, lorsque la route se met à serpenter ou qu'elle devient plus ondulée et bosselée. On découvre alors une direction linéaire et précise à l'effort bien dosé. Le freinage, avec les quatre disques, est d'une puissance très correcte et facile à moduler.

La suspension avant est à roues indépendantes avec jambes de force et barre antiroulis tandis que la suspension arrière

« semi-indépendante » combine un essieu déformable et un « parallélogramme de Watt ». Il s'agit d'un bras central articulé qui limite grandement ou annule carrément tout mouvement latéral de l'essieu arrière en appui ou sur toute déformation.

Cette solution peut sembler moins raffinée qu'une suspension arrière indépendante mais elle nous est apparue très efficace. L'amortissement et la tension des ressorts sont impeccables et la Cruze absorbe les petites irrégularités en souriant et avale les plus grosses avec une facilité étonnante. Surtout ce méchant passage à niveau double en contrebas franchi sans relâcher alors que d'autres voitures se seraient écrasées lourdement. Impressionnant. Cette deuxième LTZ était équipée de la

FEU VERT

- Finition et présentation soignées
- Sièges confortables
- Comportement routier sûr
- Grand coffre

FEU ROUGE

- Hésitation en faible accélération
- Freins arrière à tambour
- Pas de version à hayon
- Performances moyennes

suspension « sport » (code d'option : XJ2) qui se démarque par des ressorts plus ferme de 15 %, des tarages d'amortisseurs spéciaux et une carrosserie abaissée de 5 mm.

DÉCOLLAGE RÉUSSI

Les Cruze ont ce qu'il faut pour bien se débrouiller dès leur lancement et c'est ce qu'elles ont réussi sur d'autres marchés. Ce sont de petites berlines bien construites, équipées, motorisées, spacieuses et sûres. Mais c'est peu dire que la concurrence est féroce chez les compactes où se recrutent depuis longtemps les best-sellers du marché québécois, qui sont maintenant aussi les plus populaires ailleurs au pays et progressent même chez les Américains. Avec de grandes meneuses qui seront bientôt entièrement renouvelées, Chevrolet devra produire des Cruze dont la finition et la fiabilité seront irréprochables et à les vendre à prix imbattable.

Marc Lachapelle

PHOTOS : MARC LACHAPELLE

Catégorie	Berline
Échelle de prix	n.d.
Garanties	3 ans/60 000 km, 5 ans/160 000 km
Assemblage	Lordstown, Ohio, É-U.
Cote d'assurance	n.d.

CHÂSSIS - DONNÉES POUR LT TURBO

Emp/lon/lar/haut	2 685/4 597/1 796/1 476 mm
Coffre	425 litres
Réservoir	57 litres
Nombre coussins sécurité	10
Antipatinage / contrôle stabilité	oui / oui
Suspension avant	indépendante, jambes de force
Suspension arrière	semi-indépendante, multibras
Freins avant / arrière	disque (ABS) / tambour (ABS)
Direction	à crémaillère, ass. variable
Diamètre de braquage	10,9 m
Pneus avant / arrière	P215/60R16 / P215/60R16
Poids	n.d.
Capacité de remorquage	n.d.

COMPOSANTES MÉCANIQUES

LS

Cylindrée, soupapes, alim.	4L 1,8 litre 16 s atmos.
Puissance / Couple	138 chevaux / 125 lb-pi
Tr. base (opt) / rouage base (opt)	M6 (A6) / Tr
0-100 / 80-120 / 100-0 km/h	n.d. / n.d. / n.d.
Type ess. / ville / autoroute	Ordinaire / n.d.

Eco, LT Turbo, LTZ Turbo

Cylindrée, soupapes, alim.	4L 1,4 litre 16 s turbo
Puissance / Couple	138 chevaux / 148 lb-pi
Tr. base (opt) / rouage base (opt)	M6 (A6) / Tr
0-100 / 80-120 / 100-0 km/h	n.d. / n.d. / n.d.
Type ess. / ville / autoroute	Ordinaire / n.d. / 5,0 l/100 km (est)

DANS LA MÊME CATÉGORIE

Dodge Caliber, Ford Focus, Honda Civic, Hyundai Elantra, Kia Forte, Mazda3, Mitsubishi Lancer, Nissan Sentra, Subaru Impreza, Suzuki SX-4, Toyota Corolla, Volkswagen Jetta

DU NOUVEAU EN 2011

Nouveau modèle

NOS IMPRESSIONS

Agrément de conduite :	8/10
Fiabilité :	Nouveau modèle
Sécurité :	9/10
Qualités hivernales :	7/10
Espace intérieur :	8/10
Confort :	8/10

www.gm.ca

Plus d'informations dans la section statistiques en dernière partie du Guide

À MI-CHEMIN ENTRE PETIT ET GRAND

Allez savoir pourquoi : GM mesure son Chevrolet Equinox aux utilitaires compacts, mais lance son GMC Terrain contre les intermédiaires. Pourtant, on a affaire à des jumeaux qui partagent tout, tout, tout...

Pas de vrais jumeaux, cependant. Visuellement, le Chevrolet Equinox est mieux réussi avec ses lignes contemporaines et ce petit quelque chose au flanc qui s'inspire de Cadillac (ou vice-versa ?). Alors, voulez-vous bien me dire pourquoi on est allé ajouter des rapiècements larges et carrés au-dessus des roues du Terrain ? Et qu'est-ce que cette large et béante calandre inutilement chromée ? C'est sans doute pour une allure plus *rough*, mais c'est grossier et raté. En trop essayant de différencier, GM perd au change de l'harmonie avec son Terrain.

Cela dit, les deux utilitaires partagent le reste et tous deux sont assemblés en Ontario. Ils s'installent, comme qui dirait, entre deux chaises : un peu plus gros que les petits, un peu plus petits que les gros... vous me suivez ? Avec 4,7 mètres, le duo vient effectivement se positionner à mi-chemin entre les compacts et les intermédiaires. Malgré tout, GM a résisté à la tentation de la 3e banquette (contrairement aux Rav4 et Outlander), ce qui profite amplement aux jambes des passagers arrière.

MIEUX AVEC LE V6

Si rien ne déçoit à première vue, rien n'excite vraiment non plus. L'Equinox est prévisible, dans le sens ennuyeux du terme. Pas de grandes envolées dithyrambiques, plutôt des reprises que l'on sent circonspectes. En version de base, on a droit à un quatre cylindres (2,4 litres) à la moderne technologie d'injection directe. Son plus grand avantage : sur l'autoroute, nous avons gobé à peine 6,5 l/100 km. Comme pour une voiture ! Par contre, en combiné, notre moyenne s'est élevée à 9,5 l/100 km – presque deux litres de plus qu'annoncé.

Toutefois, les 182 chevaux développés ici ne sont pas suffisants pour déplacer dynamiquement celui qui n'est pas un poids-plume – en moyenne 100 kilos de plus que la concurrence. Ça se perçoit dans des reprises trop timides. Le V6 (3,0 litres) à injection directe de 264 chevaux est nettement mieux adapté. Les accélérations sont plus énergiques et elles le font sentir d'une belle sonorité grondante (quoique avec, en prime, un léger effet de couple). La transmission six rapports (un rapport de plus que la majorité de la compétition) fait son boulot en toute transparence... tant qu'on la laisse en automatique. Car dès qu'on passe le levier en mode manuel (dans une manœuvre trop brutale pour être agréable), on bute sur des passages lents... et une programmation illogique. L'affichage dit maintenir un rapport ? Mensonge ! On entend le moteur révolutionner ou rétrograder, au gré de la pression sur l'accélérateur. Mode manuel, mon œil...

Outre l'ajout de puissance et, par conséquent, une meilleure capacité de remorquage, le V6 est avantagé par un autre

FEU VERT

Volant inclinable et télescopique de série
Tenue de route assurée, même sans AWD
Le plus grand atout: son habitacle
Moteur V6 mieux adapté

FEU ROUGE

Boîte automatique qui défie toute logique
Longue silhouette qui handicape les manœuvres de recul
Sans grande excitation
Large rayon de braquage
Quelques plastiques rêches

élément: sa direction a le bonheur d'être hydraulique, alors qu'elle est électrique pour le quatre cylindres (dans les deux cas, le rayon de braquage est étonnement large). La conduite avec l'hydraulique a plus de caractère et de connexion avec la route. Et c'est une nécessité pour donner de la vie à ces véhicules prévisibles et pour lesquels les éléments suspenseurs misent davantage sur le confort que sur la sportivité. Ceci dit, le freinage est convaincant, la garde au sol fait dans la bonne moyenne et même sans traction intégrale, le comportement est relativement bien assuré.

C'EST EN DEDANS QUE ÇA SE PASSE

Les meilleurs commentaires pour l'Equinox et le Terrain, c'est l'habitacle qui les récolte: celui-ci est beaucoup plus sophistiqué qu'à la génération précédente. Dans les variantes haut de gamme, le revêtement de tissu en alvéoles est d'une résistante qualité et d'un bon chic. La planche, avec ses accents chromés, est plus recherchée que ce qu'il se fait ailleurs et dans l'ensemble, l'assemblage est soigné. C'est à peine si on retrouve encore ici et là ce plastique désagréable au bout des doigts qui, il n'y a pas si longtemps, garnissait plus avant les intérieurs GM.

Malgré les longues silhouettes (vivement l'assistance au recul!), l'espace de chargement n'est pas nécessairement plus abondant qu'ailleurs. On profite plutôt de la générosité des dimensions à la banquette arrière. L'insonorisation est dans la très bonne moyenne, mis à part le bruit persistant des pneus sur la chaussée et... quelques craquements de carrosserie qui se font entendre par petits matins frisquets. On reproche également des portières qui refusent de demeurer en position ouverte (ouch, les mollets!) et des commandes qui exigent un temps d'apprivoisement.

À mi-chemin entre les petits et les gros, les Equinox/Terrain positionnent leur prix d'étiquette d'une façon qui laisse croire qu'ils sont plus chers que la concurrence. Et c'est vrai, d'environ 1000$ en variante de base. Mais l'équipement de série est complet et quelques options intéressantes non disponibles ailleurs sont possibles, tel le hayon électrique. Cependant, il est pas mal plus difficile de faire avaler la pilule des quelque 1500$ supplémentaires que le Terrain exige versus l'Equinox, sans offrir guère davantage qu'une boussole en extra. Ça revient cher la boussole...

Nadine Filion

PHOTOS: ALAIN MORIN

Catégorie	Multisegment
Échelle de prix	25 995 $ à 35 070 $ (2010)
Garanties	3 ans/60 000 km, 5 ans/160 000 km
Assemblage	Ingersoll, Ontario, Canada
Cote d'assurance	n.d.

CHÂSSIS - DONNÉES POUR EQUINOX LTZ TI

Emp/lon/lar/haut	2 857/4 711/1 850/1 684 mm
Coffre	872 à 1 803 litres
Réservoir	71 litres
Nombre coussins sécurité	6
Antipatinage / contrôle stabilité	oui / oui
Suspension avant	indépendante, jambes de force
Suspension arrière	indépendante, multibras
Freins avant / arrière	disque (ABS) / disque (ABS)
Direction	à crémaillère, ass. électrique
Diamètre de braquage	12,2 m
Pneus avant / arrière	P225/65R17 / P225/65R17
Poids	1 801 kg
Capacité de remorquage	680 kg (1 499 lb)

COMPOSANTES MÉCANIQUES

Equinox, Terrain	
Cylindrée, soupapes, alim.	4L 2,4 litres 16 s atmos.
Puissance / Couple	182 chevaux / 172 lb-pi
Tr. base (opt) / rouage base (opt)	A6 / Tr (Int)
0-100 / 80-120 / 100-0 km/h	9,9 s / 6,9 s / 42,0 m
Type ess. / ville / autoroute	Ordinaire / 10,1 / 6,9 l/100 km

Equinox, Terrain	
Cylindrée, soupapes, alim.	V6 3,0 litres 24 s atmos.
Puissance / Couple	264 chevaux / 222 lb-pi
Tr. base (opt) / rouage base (opt)	A6 / Tr (Int)
0-100 / 80-120 / 100-0 km/h	8,0 s / 6,0 s / 42,0 m
Type ess. / ville / autoroute	Ordinaire / 10,1 / 6,9 l/100 km

DANS LA MÊME CATÉGORIE

Dodge Nitro, Ford Escape, Honda CR-V, Hyundai Santa Fe, Jeep Liberty, Mazda Tribute, Mitsubishi Outlander, Subaru Forester, Suzuki Grand Vitara, Toyota RAV4, Volkswagen Tiguan

DU NOUVEAU EN 2011

Aucun changement majeur

NOS IMPRESSIONS

Agrément de conduite:	■■■■■■■□□□	7/10
Fiabilité:	■■■■■■■□□□	7/10
Sécurité:	■■■■■■■■■■	10/10
Qualités hivernales:	■■■■■■■■□□	8/10
Espace intérieur:	■■■■■■■■□□	8/10
Confort:	■■■■■■■□□□	7/10

www.gm.ca

Plus d'informations dans la section statistiques en dernière partie du Guide

LE RÉTRO SERVI À LA MODERNE

General Motors a toujours eu de la difficulté à bien gérer ses nouveaux modèles. Dans bien des cas, on se contentait d'une silhouette anonyme au possible, associée à une mécanique plus ou moins intéressante. Autrement, on avait un concept audacieux et une silhouette hors-norme gâchés ensuite par une exécution bâclée ou des organes mécaniques mal adaptés. Dans le cas du véhicule qui nous concerne, on semble avoir visé juste et c'est tant mieux.

Il faut se rappeler que le HHR fait partie de cette génération de modèles rétro. Il y a eu, bien entendu, la Volkswagen New Beetle ainsi que le Chrysler PT Cruiser et la Mini qui ont créé un engouement pour le genre. D'ailleurs, les lettres HHR signifient *Heritage High Roof* et ce modèle est inspiré de la Chevrolet Suburban des années 40. Heureusement, on a réussi à faire quelque chose de potable.

D'ABORD LE STYLE

Les goûts ne se discutent pas, mais il semble que le caractère quasiment *Hot Rod* de ce modèle a plu à plusieurs personnes, car on en voit beaucoup sur nos routes. Et chose encore plus intéressante, les chiffres de vente sont toujours encourageants, même après quelques années sur le marché. Généralement, ces modèles rétro sont accueillis avec enthousiasme et finissent par perdre de leur popularité au fil du temps. La silhouette intemporelle et passablement nostalgique a été bien exécutée, surtout en avant avec les ailes bombées dégagées du capot.

Les stylistes ont réussi à bien agencer les différentes composantes du tableau de bord. Ils ont ajouté une touche nostalgique avec des cadrans indicateurs cerclés de chrome, comme à la belle époque de l'après-guerre. Pour le reste, c'est sobre avec des buses de ventilation circulaires et un centre de commandes placé dans une console verticale. Les commandes sont simples et faciles d'opération à l'exception sans doute de celle de l'essuie-glace arrière qui aurait avantage à être mieux située. Il faut aussi déplorer la présence de plastiques très durs, un peu plus de raffinement ne ferait pas de tort...

En raison de sa carrosserie de type familiale ou fourgonnette, il est possible de transporter passablement de bagages. De plus, les sièges arrière peuvent s'agencer de multiples façons afin d'adapter la configuration intérieure aux besoins du moment. Malheureusement, à cause des larges piliers de la carrosserie et de la fenestration relativement étroite, la visibilité n'est pas le point fort de ce véhicule. Ce modèle n'est pas aussi songé que le Transit Connect de Ford, ni aussi spacieux, mais il est supérieur au chapitre de la conduite et du confort de la suspension.

SUR LA ROUTE

Une fois derrière le volant, les grandes personnes découvriront que

FEU VERT

- Fiabilité en progrès
- Tenue de route saine
- Habitacle polyvalent
- Silhouette toujours appréciée

FEU ROUGE

- Visibilité à revoir
- Plastiques trop durs
- Places arrière inconfortables
- Moteur 2,2 litres
- Transmission automatique à quatre rapports

la position de conduite pourrait être meilleure car on se sent plutôt à l'étroit. Pour le reste, c'est bien correct. Deux moteurs sont au catalogue. Les modèles plus économiques sont propulsés par un moteur quatre cylindres de 2,2 litres produisant 155 chevaux. Il est associé de série à une boîte manuelle à cinq rapports. Celle-ci est assez bien étagée et c'est tant mieux, car il faut jouer de la boîte de vitesses pour tirer toute la puissance de ce moteur qui s'est révélé un peu juste à maintes occasions. Quant à la boîte automatique à quatre rapports, sa robustesse est son meilleur atout.

Le quatre cylindres de 2,4 litres génère 17 chevaux supplémentaires tandis que son couple est de 167 lb-pi, soit 17 lb-pi de plus que le moteur 2,2 litres. Encore une fois, la transmission de série est une boîte manuelle à cinq rapports et l'automatique est une boîte à quatre vitesses. Pour la conduite de tous les jours, c'est vraiment le moteur idéal. Il ne faut cependant pas croire qu'on va s'assoir au volant d'une voiture sportive en choisissant la boîte manuelle. Celle-ci est purement fonctionnelle, sans plus. Ce qui nous ramène à la boîte automatique à quatre rapports qui fait quand même du bon boulot. Mais un ou deux rapports supplémentaires permettraient de réduire le niveau sonore dans l'habitacle et d'améliorer l'économie de carburant.

Depuis 2008, une nouvelle version s'ajoutait au catalogue. Il s'agissait du modèle SS propulsé par un moteur 2,0 litres turbocompressé d'une puissance de 260 chevaux. Malheureusement pour les amateurs du genre, ce modèle ne sera pas de retour en 2011. Si vous saviez doser la pédale d'accélération, vous étiez en mesure d'obtenir des performances passablement sportives. Naturellement, cette version offrait une suspension plus ferme, de pneumatiques plus larges et une transmission manuelle modifiée, la seule offerte. Sa diffusion a été assez faible, ce qui explique son exclusion de la gamme.

Peu importe le modèle choisi, la tenue de route n'est pas le point faible de ce Chevrolet. En effet, en abordant une courbe à une allure supérieure aux limites affichées, vous serez surpris par la stabilité et la neutralité de ce véhicule à tout faire. Ce n'est pas mal du tout !

Denis Duquet

PHOTOS : CHEVROLET

CHEVROLET HHR

Catégorie	Familiale
Échelle de prix	20 395 $ à 30 955 $ (2010)
Garanties	3 ans/60 000 km, 5 ans/160 000 km
Assemblage	Ramos Arizpe, Mexique
Cote d'assurance	moyenne

CHÂSSIS - DONNÉES POUR LS PANEL

Emp/lon/lar/haut	2 629/4 475/1 755/1 603 mm
Coffre	1 614 litres
Réservoir	65 litres
Nombre coussins sécurité	4
Antipatinage / contrôle stabilité	oui / oui
Suspension avant	indépendante, jambes de force
Suspension arrière	semi-indépendante, poutre de torsion
Freins avant / arrière	disque (ABS) / tambour (ABS)
Direction	à crémaillère, ass. variable électrique
Diamètre de braquage	11,0 m
Pneus avant / arrière	P215/55R16 / P215/55R16
Poids	1 431 kg
Capacité de remorquage	454 kg (1 000 lb)

COMPOSANTES MÉCANIQUES

LS, LT

Cylindrée, soupapes, alim.	4L 2,2 litres 16 s atmos.
Puissance / Couple	155 chevaux / 150 lb-pi
Tr. base (opt) / rouage base (opt)	M5 (A4) / Tr
0-100 / 80-120 / 100-0 km/h	10,0 s / 8,5 s / 43,6 m
Type ess. / ville / autoroute	Ordinaire / 9,2 / 6,1 l/100 km

LT

Cylindrée, soupapes, alim.	4L 2,4 litres 16 s atmos.
Puissance / Couple	172 chevaux / 167 lb-pi
Tr. base (opt) / rouage base (opt)	M5 (A4) / Tr
0-100 / 80-120 / 100-0 km/h	9,0 s / 8,5 s / 43,6 m
Type ess. / ville / autoroute	Ordinaire / 9,5 / 6,6 l/100 km

DANS LA MÊME CATÉGORIE

Dodge Caliber, Jeep Compass, Jeep Patriot, Kia Rondo, Mazda5, Toyota Matrix

DU NOUVEAU EN 2011

Modèles SS et Panel LT abandonnés. Dernière année de production

NOS IMPRESSIONS

Agrément de conduite :	7/10
Fiabilité :	6/10
Sécurité :	8/10
Qualités hivernales :	7/10
Espace intérieur :	7/10
Confort :	7/10

www.gm.ca

Plus d'informations dans la section statistiques en dernière partie du Guide

VESTIGES D'UNE AUTRE ÉPOQUE

Si la compagnie General Motors a connu les affres de la faillite l'an dernier, ce n'est pas uniquement en raison d'une mauvaise conjoncture économique et de généreuses conditions de travail accordées à ses employés. C'est principalement parce que le public n'avait plus confiance en la qualité des produits de ce constructeur. En effet, après avoir dominé le marché et fabriqué des voitures d'une incroyable fiabilité, le tout s'est étiolé au fil des ans. La direction de la compagnie a fait d'importants efforts au cours des récentes années pour produire des véhicules de qualité supérieure ayant un agrément de conduite relevé. Par exemple, la Malibu fait partie de cette génération. Dans cette vaste réorganisation de l'ancien numéro un mondial, certains véhicules représentent les vestiges d'une époque où l'on se contentait de concevoir quelque chose de correct, mais sans plus. L'Impala fait partie de ces modèles.

Cette berline a été dessinée et conçue à une ère où l'on croyait toujours qu'offrir une voiture dans la moyenne à un prix compétitif réussirait à renverser la vapeur. Pour ce faire, les ingénieurs étaient obligés d'utiliser des composantes mécaniques qui ne pouvaient se comparer à la concurrence.

UNE VOITURE FURTIVE

Curieusement, la plupart des berlines Cadillac sont louangées pour leur silhouette agressive et passablement distincte. Les stylistes se sont inspirés des avions de chasse furtifs de l'aviation militaire américaine. Dans le cas de l'Impala, on semble s'être également inspiré d'un avion furtif, mais cela donne des résultats diamétralement opposés à Cadillac. En effet, cette Chevrolet est une voiture furtive car elle se dissimule dans la circulation et on ne la remarque pratiquement pas ! Essayez donc de vous rappeler la dernière fois que vous avez croisé une Chevrolet Impala sur la route… Je suis prêt à parier que vos souvenirs sont assez nébuleux ! Pourtant, les chiffres de vente sont surprenants. Cette grosse Chevy est assez populaire.

Cela ne veut pas dire que la silhouette n'est pas élégante, mais cette élégance est sobre, archi sobre. Et une fois à l'intérieur, on se retrouve face à un tableau de bord qui était jadis populaire auprès des designers de GM grâce à sa grande surface transversale et plane surplombant la nacelle des instruments. Là aussi, c'est générique. Et comme si ce n'était pas assez, on a affublé cette Chevrolet d'un volant à quatre rayons qui semble emprunté à une camionnette ou à un utilitaire sport. Bien entendu, pour faire un peu plus cossu, une garniture en simili-bois ajoute à la banalité de l'ensemble.

Par contre, l'ergonomie des commandes est bonne, la consultation des cadrans indicateurs n'est pas mauvaise et le volant se prend bien en main à défaut d'être élégant. Détail intéressant, sur la version de base il est possible de commander une banquette

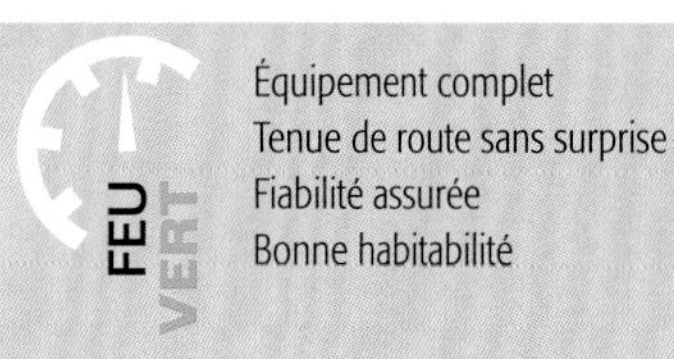

Équipement complet
Tenue de route sans surprise
Fiabilité assurée
Bonne habitabilité

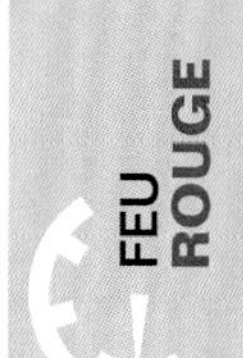

Direction engourdie
Automatique à 4 rapports
Conduite ennuyante
Dépréciation assez forte

pleine largeur à l'avant et le positionnement du levier de vitesses sur la colonne de direction. Cette option s'explique sans doute par l'utilisation commerciale de cette Chevrolet. Mais dans la plupart des modèles, l'Impala est dotée de baquets à l'avant et du levier de sélection des vitesses sur la console au plancher. Autre détail, la même version de base possède un dossier fixe à l'arrière et les modèles plus cossus en ont un de type 60/40 pouvant être rabattus afin de pouvoir transporter des objets plus longs.

MÉCANIQUE NOSTALGIQUE

Pendant que certains modèles fabriqués par ce manufacturier proposent l'injection directe et des turbocompresseurs à débit variable, notre vénérable Impala est toujours équipée de moteurs avec soupapes en tête associés à une transmission automatique à quatre rapports. Il ne faut pas croire pour autant que ces groupes propulseurs soient à dédaigner, mais cette mécanique d'une autre époque n'est pas très efficace en fait de rendement, de consommation de carburant et de silence de roulement. Heureusement, au fil des années, elle s'est beaucoup améliorée au chapitre de la fiabilité.

La version la plus économique est un V6 de 3,5 litres d'une puissance de 207 chevaux tandis que l'autre est un V6 également, mais un 3,9 litres de 230 chevaux. Ce dernier délivre un peu plus de puissance et un couple supérieur alors que la consommation anticipée est moindre pour le moteur de plus petite cylindrée. Mais la différence est tellement peu importante qu'on se demande pourquoi on ne se contente pas du moteur plus puissant.

La conduite est comme le reste du véhicule : dans la moyenne. La direction est bien entendue trop légère, le freinage est correct mais la distance un peu trop longue tandis que la pédale de frein est trop spongieuse pour être rassurante. De plus, le système ABS est moyennement efficace et certainement très bruyant.

Les gens qui préfèrent un équipement relativement complet et à un prix très alléchant n'auront rien à dire de mal sur cette Chevrolet. S'ils ont la bonne idée de suivre les limites de vitesse, cela va bien aller.

Denis Duquet

PHOTOS : CHEVROLET

CHEVROLET IMPALA

Catégorie	Berline
Échelle de prix	27 320 $ à 30 565 $ (2010)
Garanties	3 ans/60 000 km, 5 ans/160 000 km
Assemblage	Oshawa, Ontario, Canada
Cote d'assurance	bonne

CHÂSSIS - DONNÉES POUR LT

Emp/lon/lar/haut	2 807/5 090/1 851/1 491 mm
Coffre	527 litres
Réservoir	64 litres
Nombre coussins sécurité	6
Antipatinage / contrôle stabilité	oui / oui
Suspension avant	indépendante, jambes de force
Suspension arrière	indépendante, jambes de force
Freins avant / arrière	disque (ABS) / disque (ABS)
Direction	à crémaillère, assistée
Diamètre de braquage	11,6 m
Pneus avant / arrière	P225/55R17 / P225/55R17
Poids	1 613 kg
Capacité de remorquage	454 kg (1 000 lb)

COMPOSANTES MÉCANIQUES

LS, LT

Cylindrée, soupapes, alim.	V6 3,5 litres 12 s atmos.
Puissance / Couple	207 chevaux / 215 lb-pi
Tr. base (opt) / rouage base (opt)	A4 / Tr
0-100 / 80-120 / 100-0 km/h	8,6 s / 8,4 s / 47,6 m
Type ess. / ville / autoroute	Ordinaire / 10,8 / 6,7 l/100 km

LTZ

Cylindrée, soupapes, alim.	V6 3,9 litres 12 s atmos.
Puissance / Couple	230 chevaux / 238 lb-pi
Tr. base (opt) / rouage base (opt)	A4 / Tr
0-100 / 80-120 / 100-0 km/h	8,6 s / 7,7 s / 41,0 m
Type ess. / ville / autoroute	Ordinaire / 12,0 / 7,4 l/100 km

DANS LA MÊME CATÉGORIE

Buick Allure, Chrysler 300, Dodge Charger, Ford Taurus, Honda Accord, Hyundai Sonata, Nissan Altima, Toyota Camry

DU NOUVEAU EN 2011

Climatiseur à commande manuelle à une zone de série sur LS, moulures latérales de la couleur de la carrosserie

NOS IMPRESSIONS

Agrément de conduite :	7/10
Fiabilité :	6/10
Sécurité :	8/10
Qualités hivernales :	7/10
Espace intérieur :	8/10
Confort :	8/10

www.gm.ca

Plus d'informations dans la section statistiques en dernière partie du Guide

TROIS ANS PLUS TARD: UNE OMBRE...

C'est fou ce que trois ans peuvent changer les choses ! En 2008, la Chevrolet Malibu remportait le titre nord-américain de Voiture de l'année, devant la Honda Accord. Mais depuis, la concurrence s'est tant affinée que la Malibu n'est plus qu'une ombre.

À sa plus récente réfection, elle s'était pourtant attiré des éloges quant à son habitacle, novateur et dégagé, son insonorisation et ses commandes bien disposées. Certes, la donne n'a pas changé, mais devant le superbe intérieur de la nouvelle Hyundai Sonata ou celui de la Ford Fusion, la Malibu perd des plumes.

SIX, LE CHIFFRE MAGIQUE...

De base, la Malibu propose un quatre cylindres (2,4 litres) qui, s'il n'a pas le mérite de la profondeur, a celui de la douceur. Ne faites pas l'erreur de vous contenter de l'automatique quatre rapports : vous vous demanderez où sont passés les 169 chevaux. Une six rapports moins paresseuse monte à bord pour quelques centaines de dollars de plus et ça vaut la peine, ne serait-ce que pour une réduction moyenne d'un demi-litre aux 100 km. Autre avantage : les palettes au volant, même si on leur reproche de ne pouvoir être actionnées sans engager le levier de vitesses en position M.

De toutes les intermédiaires, la Malibu est sans doute celle dont la suspension est la plus molle. Les amortisseurs s'écrasent en virage et travaillent longuement sur les cahots – et pas toujours en silence ; on entend les « ooomphs »... Le freinage manque de réactivité, mais ne vous y fiez pas : la Malibu s'immobilise de 100 à 0 km/h en 42,5 mètres et c'est dans la très bonne moyenne. De base, la connectivité de la Malibu avec le bitume est anesthésiée par la direction électrique. Qui dit direction électrique, dit généralement bon rayon de braquage, mais pas ici : les 12,3 mètres font

qu'on ne « vire pas sur un dix cents ». Voilà pourquoi la Malibu, c'est avec le moteur V6 (3,6 litres) qu'il faut la choisir. D'abord parce que la direction mise sur la bonne vieille crémaillère, pour une meilleure expérience de conduite. Ensuite, parce que les 252 chevaux sont mieux adaptés à celle qui fait osciller la balance jusqu'à 1 655 kilos – c'est plus lourd que la moyenne, ça. Un peu d'effet de couple se fait sentir en démarrage brusque, mais au moins, la voiture décolle en souplesse.

DIFFICILE DE CONSERVER LA TÊTE

On l'a dit plus haut, la Malibu a impressionné à son lancement avec son habitacle relevé. Encore aujourd'hui, les commandes sont ergonomiques, le dégagement à l'avant est l'un des plus importants de la catégorie et à l'arrière, les passagers ne sont pas à l'étroit. Bravo pour ce double toit ouvrant qui laisse entrer un flot de lumière. Avec ses 428 litres, le coffre de la Malibu accepte moins de choses que celui de la Mazda6, mais tout autant que la nouvelle Hyundai Sonata et plus que la Honda Accord.

On l'oublie, mais GM est le seul à proposer OnStar, à la fois un système de navigation « pas-à-pas », de diagnostics à distance et de

FEU VERT

Beaux habitacles – variantes V6
Boîte automatique six rapports, même pour le «petit» moteur
OnStar

FEU ROUGE

Suspension qui répond trop longuement
Quelques plastiques de mauvaise facture à l'intérieur
Palettes au volant inactives sans positionnement du levier

notification automatique en cas d'accident. Gageons ensemble que si c'était Toyota ou Honda qui avait lancé pareil dispositif, la concurrence se serait empressée de copier...

Cela dit, déplorons le fait que de trouver la bonne position de conduite dans la Malibu tient du défi; l'enjambée des pédales est courte et l'appuie-tête actif est peut-être sécuritaire, mais il est inconfortable. Sinon, les baquets sont enveloppants et s'agencent dans toutes les positions requises. Dans les versions de base, les plastiques de revêtement sont à améliorer et... pourrait-on faire table rase sur ce beige austère aux accents «cheapettes»? Les versions haut de gamme profitent d'intérieurs plus séduisants; pensez ébène-brique...

Un dernier reproche: la visibilité arrière est passable et la faute en revient à ce coffre qui se relève, sans doute pour le style. Parlant style, celui de la Malibu était au départ louangé pour ses lignes classiques et imposantes, mais le design a vieilli et la silhouette se fond désormais dans la masse. Heureusement, sa calandre chromée vient donner une certaine envergure.

À QUAND LE RETOUR DE L'HYBRIDE?

La Malibu n'est pas une mauvaise voiture en soi. Même qu'elle est une bonne routière et elle a le mérite de donner le ton le pas chez GM qui, depuis, nous présente des véhicules plus intéressants.

Si l'on exclut l'actuelle mouture de base qui n'offre toujours pas les sièges chauffants et les commandes audio au volant (pas même en option), toutes les autres versions s'amènent, pour le prix, avec un équipement complet. Ne manque que la clé intelligente – qui devrait au moins être présente sur la variante la mieux nantie, mais ce n'est pas le cas. On peut néanmoins se payer le démarrage à distance, mais les environnementalistes vous diront qu'il n'est pas «vert» que de laisser tourner son moteur au ralenti.

Trois ans; il n'a fallu que trois ans pour que la suprématie accordée à la Malibu de dernière génération pâlisse au firmament. Ce n'est pas que la voiture est «moins», c'est juste que la concurrence est «plus». Comme quoi, en très peu d'années, des pas de géants peuvent être accomplis...

Nadine Filion

PHOTOS: CHEVROLET

Catégorie	Berline
Échelle de prix	23 955 $ à 32 750 $ (2010)
Garanties	3 ans/60 000 km, 5 ans/160 000 km
Assemblage	Kansas City, Kansas, É-U
Cote d'assurance	n.d.

CHÂSSIS - DONNÉES POUR LS

Emp/lon/lar/haut	2 852/4 872/1 786/1 450 mm
Coffre	428 litres
Réservoir	61 litres
Nombre coussins sécurité	6
Antipatinage / contrôle stabilité	oui / oui
Suspension avant	indépendante, jambes de force
Suspension arrière	indépendante, multibras
Freins avant / arrière	disque (ABS) / disque (ABS)
Direction	à crémaillère, assistée
Diamètre de braquage	12,3 m
Pneus avant / arrière	P225/50R17 / P225/50R17
Poids	1 551 kg
Capacité de remorquage	n.d.

COMPOSANTES MÉCANIQUES

LS, LT	
Cylindrée, soupapes, alim.	4L 2,4 litres 16 s atmos.
Puissance / Couple	169 chevaux / 158 lb-pi
Tr. base (opt) / rouage base (opt)	A4 / Tr
0-100 / 80-120 / 100-0 km/h	10,6 s / 9,0 s / 42,5 m
Type ess. / ville / autoroute	Ordinaire / 9,4 / 5,9 l/100 km

LT, LTZ	
Cylindrée, soupapes, alim.	V6 3,6 litres 24 s atmos.
Puissance / Couple	252 chevaux / 251 lb-pi
Tr. base (opt) / rouage base (opt)	A6 / Tr
0-100 / 80-120 / 100-0 km/h	7,8 s / 6,5 s / 42,5 m
Type ess. / ville / autoroute	Ordinaire / 10,8 / 6,7 l/100 km

DANS LA MÊME CATÉGORIE

Buick Allure, Chrysler Sebring, Dodge Avenger, Ford Fusion, Honda Accord, Hyundai Sonata, Kia Magentis, Mazda6, Nissan Altima, Toyota Camry

DU NOUVEAU EN 2011

Boîte automatique à six rapports à commande manuelle au volant de série, nouvelles roues

NOS IMPRESSIONS

Agrément de conduite:	■■■■■■■■□□	8/10
Fiabilité:	■■■■■■■■□□	8/10
Sécurité:	■■■■■■■■□□	8/10
Qualités hivernales:	■■■■■■■□□□	7/10
Espace intérieur:	■■■■■■■■□□	8/10
Confort:	■■■■■■■■□□	8/10

www.gm.ca

Plus d'informations dans la section statistiques en dernière partie du Guide

AVEC DES « SI », ON REFERAIT LE MONDE

Avec des scies aussi ! Sauf que palabrer, c'est bien beau mais ça donne rarement de grands résultats. Tout simplement parce qu'entre la théorie devant un café ou une bière et la réalité, il y a tout un monde. Prenez les immenses VUS commercialisés par General Motors. S'ils sont sur le marché et qu'ils ont survécu à la terrible crise qui a failli faire tomber l'ex-géant de Detroit, c'est sans doute parce qu'ils se vendent... Donc, qu'ils répondent à un besoin, légitime ou non. Quoiqu'en disent les environnementalistes.

Dans son désir d'amadouer, un peu, l'opinion publique, GM a dévoilé, il y a deux ans, une version hybride de ses Tahoe, Yukon et Escalade. Ce système bimode est plus qu'un simple bidule électrique développé uniquement pour pouvoir mettre un logo vert sur la voiture. Le système bimode est très sérieux, autant dans son application que dans ses résultats. En gros, il s'agit d'une transmission qui comporte deux moteurs électriques de 60 kW fournissant 272 livres-pied de couple chacun. Le moteur thermique est un V8 de 6,0 litres. Sous 45 km/h, le véhicule roule à l'électricité seulement tandis qu'au-delà, l'ordinateur de bord décide de l'apport de l'électricité pour appuyer le V8. Bref, ça fonctionne puisque ce système hybride permet de faire économiser au moins 25 % d'essence sans affecter les performances ni les capacités de remorquage (ou si peu). Un match comparatif du *Guide de l'auto 2009* avait démontré que cette motorisation tenait ses promesses.

UNE PLÉTHORE DE MODÈLES

Même si ce texte parle de quatre modèles différents, on pourrait, à la limite, dire qu'il y a deux VUS déclinés en plusieurs versions. Par exemple, les Chevrolet Tahoe, GMC Yukon et Cadillac Escalade sont, à peu de détails près, le même véhicule tandis que les Yukon XL, Suburban et Escalade ESV se réservent la première marche du podium au chapitre des dimensions.

Pourquoi autant de déclinaisons ? Pour rejoindre le plus de gens possible, voyons ! Comme le veut la tradition, les Chevrolet représentent les versions de base tandis que les Cadillac se veulent beaucoup plus luxueuses... Aux États-Unis, la marque GMC connaît beaucoup de succès en se situant entre ces deux extrémités. Il y a même moyen d'opter pour un GMC Yukon Denali, pratiquement aussi impressionnant qu'un Escalade mais à coût moindre. D'ailleurs, les deux se partagent la même mécanique.

Tous les véhicules ont droit à un V8, le plus petit faisant tout de même 310 chevaux. L'Escalade et le Yukon Denali reçoivent un 6,2 litres de 403 chevaux, moteur amplement suffisant pour procurer des accélérations et reprises très énergiques. Ce moulin peut remorquer jusqu'à 8300 livres (Escalade), ce qui n'est pas rien et les autres VUS grand format de GM ne sont pas en reste. Dans tous les cas, la transmission est une automatique à six rapports qui relaie le couple aux roues arrière seulement ou aux quatre roues

Habitacle silencieux et confortable
Moteurs bien adaptés
Hybride bimode sérieux
Comportement routier adéquat
Capacités de remorquage élevées

Dimensions de centre d'achats
Direction trop démultipliée
Consommation élevée
Dépréciation importante

grâce à un rouage à quatre roues motrices. Noblesse oblige, le Cadillac Escalade a plutôt droit à un rouage intégral tout de même très performant.

ESPACE, CONFORT ET PUISSANCE

De toute évidence, on s'achète un VUS grand format pour transporter plusieurs personnes ou beaucoup d'objets. Ceux qui désirent tester les limites en courbe feraient mieux de se tourner vers la Corvette. Pourtant, le comportement routier de ce quatuor est loin d'être mauvais. Certes, lorsque poussés au-delà du raisonnable, ces VUS occasionnent passablement de roulis, gracieuseté d'un centre de gravité élevé et de suspensions qui valorisent le confort mais, dans l'ensemble, on prend un certain plaisir à conduire ces mastodontes. Même que si j'avais à amener ma petite famille jusqu'en Floride, un Yukon, ou mieux un Yukon XL ferait parfaitement mon affaire. Je passerais outre une direction très légère qui ne procure que très peu de sensations malgré sa bonne précision. D'un autre côté, j'apprécierais la puissance, toujours disponible — et ce, peu importe le moteur, la possibilité de changer les rapports manuellement si j'avais une remorque derrière moi et les freins étonnamment puissants pour un véhicule qui avoisine allègrement les 3000 kilos. Bien entendu, les arrêts à la pompe seraient plus stressants qu'avec ma triste Honda Civic mais, encore là, on pourrait s'attendre à bien pire. Si l'économie d'essence est votre priorité, un hybride bimode serait un excellent choix.

Dès qu'on ouvre une portière, c'est le vaste de l'habitacle qui impressionne. Les modèles allongés (Yukon XL, Escalade ESV et Suburban) profitent d'un coffre tout simplement immense. Les sièges avant sont superbement étudiés pour garder leurs occupants frais et dispos même sur de longues distances, tandis que ceux de la deuxième rangée dégagent beaucoup d'espace tout en étant pratiquement aussi confortables. Plusieurs VUS se garnissent d'une troisième rangée de siège utopique mais c'est loin d'être le cas ici, surtout pour les versions allongées.

Il est évident qu'un Cadillac Escalade ou un GMC Yukon XL n'est pas à l'aise dans un centre-ville bondé. Mais ceux qui se procurent un tel véhicule pour les bonnes raisons n'ont vraiment pas à se plaindre. Ce n'est pas pour rien que General Motors domine ce segment.

Alain Morin

GMC Yukon

PHOTOS : ALAIN MORIN

Catégorie	VUS
Échelle de prix	79 575 $ à 94 775 $
Garanties	4 ans/80 000 km, 5 ans/160 000 km
Assemblage	Arlington, Texas, É-U
Cote d'assurance	Moyenne

CHÂSSIS - DONNÉES POUR ESCALADE HYBRIDE

Emp/lon/lar/haut	2 946/5 143/2 007/1 887 mm
Coffre	479 à 3 084 litres
Réservoir	92 litres
Nombre coussins sécurité	6
Antipatinage / contrôle stabilité	oui / oui
Suspension avant	indépendante, bras inégaux
Suspension arrière	indépendante, multibras
Freins avant / arrière	disque (ABS) / disque (ABS)
Direction	à crémaillère, assistée
Diamètre de braquage	11,9 m
Pneus avant / arrière	P285/45R22 / P285/45R22
Poids	2 729 kg
Capacité de remorquage	2 540 kg (5 599 lb)

COMPOSANTES MÉCANIQUES

Suburban

Cylindrée, soupapes, alim.	V8 5,3 litres 16 s atmos.
Puissance / Couple	310 chevaux / 335 lb-pi
Tr. base (opt) / rouage base (opt)	A6 / Prop (Int)
0-100 / 80-120 / 100-0 km/h	9,0 s / 6,8 s / 46,2 m
Type ess. / ville / autoroute	Ordinaire / 14,4 / 9,6 l/100 km

Yukon, Tahoe

Cylindrée, soupapes, alim.	V8 5,3 litres 16 s atmos.
Puissance / Couple	320 chevaux / 335 lb-pi
Tr. base (opt) / rouage base (opt)	A6 / Prop (Int)
0-100 / 80-120 / 100-0 km/h	9,0 s / 6,8 s / 46,2 m
Type ess. / ville / autoroute	Ordinaire / 14,4 / 9,6 l/100 km

Escalade Hybride, Tahoe Hybride

V8 6,0 l, 332 ch, 367 lb-pi - 0-100 : 9,9 s - 9,8 / 9,1 l/100 km

Escalade, Yukon Denali

V8 6,2 l, 403 ch, 417 lb-pi - 0-100 : 7,4 s - 15,3 / 10,1 l/100 km

DANS LA MÊME CATÉGORIE

Infiniti QX, Land Rover Range Rover, Lexus LX, Lincoln Navigator, Mercedes-Benz Classe GL

DU NOUVEAU EN 2011

Système sonore arrière de série (Tahoe, Suburban)

NOS IMPRESSIONS

Agrément de conduite :	7/10
Fiabilité :	6/10
Sécurité :	8/10
Qualités hivernales :	9/10
Espace intérieur :	9/10
Confort :	9/10

www.gm.ca

Plus d'informations dans la section statistiques en dernière partie du Guide

LE PASSÉ ET LE FUTUR RÉUNIS

Au tout début de l'histoire automobile, on ne jurait que par l'électricité. Cependant, le poids des batteries et leur faible autonomie condamnèrent cette forme d'énergie aux milieux urbains. Ferdinand Porsche, le génial ingénieur, se rend compte des limites de ses voitures électriques (à moteurs-roues !). Il trouve donc un moyen de recharger les batteries en cours de route grâce à un moteur à essence qui n'agit pas sur les roues. Il ne sert qu'à recharger les batteries. Cent et quelques années plus tard, on retrouve exactement le même principe sur la Chevrolet Volt…

Au début de 2007, les dirigeants de General Motors profitaient du Salon de l'auto de Détroit pour présenter une future voiture électrique, la Volt. Ce concept était bâti autour de la plate-forme E-Flex, créée pour recevoir un moteur électrique et pouvant facilement être adaptée à différents types de véhicules, allant de la sous-compacte au VUS. Mais ce qui retient le plus l'attention, c'est la possibilité de l'adapter à plusieurs sources d'énergie. Car, on le sait, un moteur électrique tire son énergie d'une batterie et cette dernière demande une source d'énergie pour être rechargée. Outre le branchement à une source électrique domestique, cette source, avec le E-Flex, peut être un moteur à essence diesel ou biodiesel, une pile à combustible (hydrogène), des panneaux solaires, etc.

UNE PLATE-FORME INÉDITE

La première voiture construite sur cette plate-forme révolutionnaire est la Chevrolet Volt. Fidèle à son nom, il s'agit d'une voiture électrique à rayon d'action étendu (extended range). Avant de créer la Volt, les ingénieurs se sont penchés sur le mode de vie des Américains. Ils ont constaté que la moitié des gens parcouraient moins de 30 milles (48 km) par jour et que 78 % ne faisaient même pas 40 milles (64 km). Ils ont donc créé un groupe motopropulseur qui pourrait fonctionner uniquement à l'électricité pendant au moins 40,4 milles (65 km). Cependant, contrairement à une voiture uniquement électrique qui vous laisse en plan lorsque les batteries sont déchargées, la Volt recèle un petit moteur à essence qui permet de ragaillardir les batteries via un générateur, et ainsi de continuer comme si de rien n'était. Génial. En fait, l'autonomie maximale de la Volt (batterie et moteur à essence) est de 640 km. Bien entendu, une foule de facteurs (température, trafic, poids du pied droit, etc.) viendront affecter cette autonomie.

Si une personne ne parcourt qu'une cinquantaine de kilomètres par jour et n'oublie jamais de brancher sa voiture le soir, elle (ou plutôt sa voiture !) n'aura, théoriquement, jamais besoin d'utiliser le moteur à essence. L'élément le plus spectaculaire de la Volt est sa batterie, constituée de 288 cellules de 3,5 volts chacune, fabriquées par LG Chem et assemblées dans une nouvelle usine de GM à Brownstown au Michigan. Ces cellules forment une batterie au lithium-ion d'une capacité de 16 kWh et pesant 180 kilos. Elle fait partie intégrante de la plate-forme et forme un « T » dont la partie allongée sépare l'habitacle en deux, tandis que la partie courte se trouve sous le siège arrière afin d'assurer le plus d'espace possible. Cette batterie peut être rechargée sur une prise domestique de 120 volts en plus ou moins sept heures, tandis qu'un branchement sur une prise de 220 volts la remettra « top shape » en environ trois heures. En admettant qu'un utilisateur parcourt 25 000 km par année, il pourrait sauver jusqu'à 2 150 litres d'essence. Je mets cependant cette affirmation dans la même catégorie que celle du gars du département de l'informatique qui me disait l'autre jour « avec cette nouvelle application, tout va être parfait, inquiète-toi pas mon Alain ! »…

Le moteur à essence est un quatre cylindres Ecotec de 1,4 litre officiant déjà dans certaines voitures européennes (Opel Astra et Corsa entre autres). Ce moteur pourrait, en théorie, ne jamais servir. Cependant, qu'on le veuille ou non, il démarrera tout seul environ tous les deux mois pour éviter que ses pièces ne se grippent. Il y a une autre raison, plus ironique... Puisque la Volt possède un moteur à essence, elle doit se conformer à certaines normes gouvernementales. Et pour prouver aux autorités américaines et canadiennes qu'elle respecte ces normes, il faut que le moteur fonctionne à l'occasion ! Quant au moteur électrique, il émet une puissance équivalente à 150 chevaux et 273 livres-pied de couple. Ce moteur fournit en tout temps 90 kW, mais dans certaines conditions, il peut en donner jusqu'à 110.

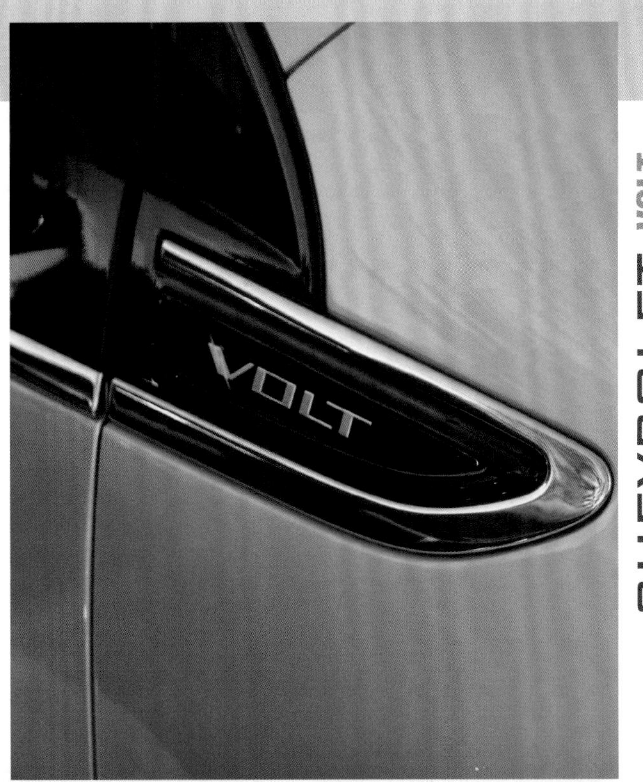

LA SCIENCE-FICTION AU QUOTIDIEN

Durant les Jeux Olympiques d'hiver à Vancouver (si on peut les qualifier d'hivernaux...), nous avons pu faire un essai assez bref d'un prototype de la Volt. Tout d'abord, mentionnons que conduire un tel monument à la technologie n'implique rien de particulier. On démarre le moteur électrique au moyen d'un simple bouton

Start/Stop. L'écran derrière le volant indique alors l'autonomie restante de la pile et affiche d'autres informations. Au centre du tableau de bord, on retrouve un autre écran qui divulgue d'autres informations.

Durant notre parcours, le comportement routier de la Volt ne nous a pas impressionnés outre mesure, mais voilà le cadet de nos soucis, puisqu'il s'agissait d'un prototype. Nous n'avons pas pu faire de tests dynamiques, mais selon GM, la Volt est capable de faire le 0-100 km/h en 9,0 secondes et d'atteindre une vitesse maximale de 160 km/h, ce qui nous semble réaliste… même si on se demande pourquoi quelqu'un s'amuserait à atteindre de tels chiffres au volant d'une voiture dont le but principal est d'être écologique ! Si la motorisation de la Volt relève quasiment de la science-fiction, son architecture est moins ésotérique. À l'avant, on retrouve une suspension à jambes de force, tandis que l'arrière se contente d'un essieu semi-rigide. On ne doit donc pas s'attendre à une voiture très sportive. Cependant, pour un petit « oumph » d'énergie lorsque le besoin se fait sentir, il suffit d'enfoncer le bouton Sport au tableau de bord. En temps normal, le moteur électrique, on l'a vu, développe 90 kWh. Lorsque ce bouton est enfoncé, le moteur expédie 110 kWh, ce qui équivaut à un petit coup de nitro ! Par contre, cela affecte de façon très négative la charge de la batterie. Lorsque cette dernière arrive à 30 % de sa charge, le moteur à essence entre en jeu de façon tout à fait transparente, sauf pour une petite musique qui se fait alors entendre. En faisant bien attention, on note le son du moteur thermique. Mais je suis convaincu qu'après deux journées, on ne le remarque même plus !

Dans l'habitacle, outre un levier de vitesses très stylisé et des touches à effleurement, tout est conforme aux normes actuelles. J'ai trouvé ma position de conduite très rapidement et les sièges m'ont paru confortables, du moins le peu de temps que j'ai conduit. Les deux places arrière aussi sont confortables, même si l'espace est compté. Il est même possible de baisser les dossiers pour agrandir le coffre, déjà d'assez bonnes dimensions, ce que Toyota ne réussit pas encore à faire…

LES TEMPS CHANGENT !

La batterie de la Volt est bonne pour dix ans et coûterait, en dollars 2010, environ 16 000 $ à remplacer. Que ceux qui ressentent soudainement une douleur dans le bras gauche se rassurent.

FEU VERT
- Motorisation réussie
- Autonomie intéressante
- Lignes aérodynamiques
- Conduite sans surprises
- Voiture criante d'écologie

FEU ROUGE
- Prix sans doute corsé
- Quatre places seulement
- Aucune capacité de remorquage
- Valeur de revente à confirmer
- Fiabilité inconnue

Premièrement, la batterie sera garantie pour huit ans ou 240 000 km. Cependant, un marché de la batterie de seconde main est en train de se dessiner d'autant plus que le nombre de véhicules à batterie (hybrides ou pas) commence à proliférer. Par exemple, un fermier qui veut alimenter ses installations grâce à une éolienne aura besoin de batteries pour emmagasiner l'énergie.

La Chevrolet Volt arrivera chez nous l'été prochain. Il s'agira alors de modèles 2012. Même si le prix de base n'a pas encore été dévoilé, il ne faut pas s'attendre à l'aubaine du siècle. Je parie qu'il sera très difficile d'avoir une Volt sous les 40 000 $, ce qui est très cher pour une voiture compacte à quatre places plus petite qu'une Honda Civic. N'oublions pas non plus que cette voiture a beau intéresser tout le monde, bien peu sont assez « verts » pour risquer le coup. Heureusement, la Volt n'a pas encore de compétition directe.

Alain Morin

PHOTOS : ALAIN MORIN

DONNÉES PRÉLIMINAIRES

Catégorie	Berline
Échelle de prix	n.d.
Garanties	n.d.
Assemblage	Armtrack, Michigan
Cote d'assurance	n.d.

CHÂSSIS - DONNÉES POUR VOLT

Emp/lon/lar/haut	2 685/4 404/1 798/1 430 mm
Coffre	301 litres
Réservoir	54 litres
Nombre coussins sécurité	8
Antipatinage / contrôle stabilité	oui / oui
Suspension avant	indépendante, jambes de force
Suspension arrière	semi-indépendante, poutre de torsion
Freins avant / arrière	disque (ABS) / disque (ABS)
Direction	à crémaillère, ass. électrique
Diamètre de braquage	n.d.
Pneus avant / arrière	215/55R17 / 215/55R17
Poids	n.d.
Capacité de remorquage	n.d.

COMPOSANTES MÉCANIQUES

Volt

Cylindrée, soupapes, alim.	3L 1,4 litre atmos.
Puissance / Couple	100 chevaux / 90 lb-pi
Tr. base (opt) / rouage base (opt)	Aucune / Tr
0-100 / 80-120 / 100-0 km/h	9,0 s (const) / 7,0 s (est) / n.d.
Type ess. / ville / autoroute	Ordinaire / consommation nulle pour les premiers 65 km

moteur électrique

Puissance / Couple	150 ch / 273 lb-pi

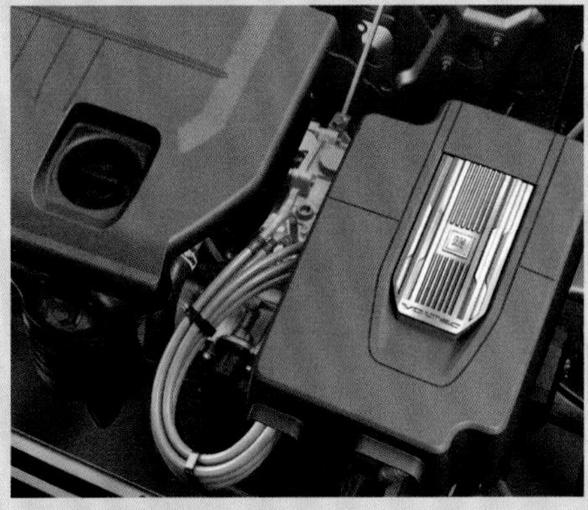

DANS LA MÊME CATÉGORIE

Aucun concurrent

DU NOUVEAU EN 2011

Nouveau modèle sera dévoilé en 2011

NOS IMPRESSIONS

Agrément de conduite :	■■■■■■■□□□ 7/10
Fiabilité :	Nouveau modèle
Sécurité :	Données insuffisantes
Qualités hivernales :	Données insuffisantes
Espace intérieur :	■■■■■■■□□□ 7/10
Confort :	■■■■■■■□□□ 7/10

www.gm.ca

Plus d'informations dans la section statistiques en dernière partie du Guide

LE FUTUR A DÉJÀ BON GOÛT

Ce n'est plus un secret pour personne. Malgré des ventes au détail canadiennes très encourageantes, on ne peut pas dire que Chrysler soit sorti du bois. Et ce, nonobstant l'arrivée de Fiat. L'avenir nous dira, peut-être plus tôt qu'on le pense, ce qu'il réserve à la nouvelle entité américaine. Cet avenir passe, obligatoirement par de nouveaux modèles. Après une trop longue disette, le groupe Chrysler dévoilait, au début de l'été dernier, son tout nouveau Jeep Grand Cherokee. Suivra, d'ici la fin 2010, une flopée de nouveaux modèles. Dont la 300.

Même si cette dernière affiche encore des lignes modernes, force est d'admettre qu'elles n'ont plus le punch d'il y a six ans, alors que la voiture avait été révélée à la presse spécialisée. En effet, à ce moment, tous avaient été foudroyés par son style unique qui lui avait automatiquement octroyé un statut à part. Il était même devenu plus *in* par les vedettes d'Hollywood de se faire voir au volant d'une 300 qu'à celui d'une Rolls-Royce ! La prochaine génération sera-t-elle aussi déterminante ?

Il est bien entendu assez difficile de jouer au devin. Les quelques photos glanées ici et là nous montrent une voiture aux dimensions toujours très imposantes dont le style reprend des éléments de plusieurs marques de prestige. Par exemple, il y a fort à parier que les phares ressemblent à ceux d'une Audi tandis que les feux arrière, allongés, singeraient un peu ceux des Cadillac. Quant au tableau de bord, devenu terne au fil des années, il serait tout en rondeurs. Selon ce qui avait été présenté au Salon de l'auto de New York, il allie style et convivialité.

Cependant, n'oublions pas que nous parlons du futur et que nous jurerons n'avoir jamais écrit ce paragraphe si la 300 de prochaine génération ne possède pas les attributs ci-haut mentionnés. Par contre, il est à peu près certain que la berline aura droit à un meilleur aérodynamisme, à des matériaux de qualité supérieure et au V6 Pentastar qui équipe déjà le nouveau Jeep Grand Cherokee. Dans ce dernier, il s'avère souple, discret et, selon Chrysler, passablement économique malgré une puissance très correcte. Il serait surprenant que sa personnalité change du tout au tout lorsqu'il ira se nicher dans la 300.

UN TIENS VAUT MIEUX QUE DEUX TU L'AURAS

Parler du futur, c'est bien beau mais ça ne change pas grand-chose au présent, du moins dans le cas qui nous concerne. Pour l'instant, la Chrysler 300 2010 poursuit sa route sans modifications, ce qui n'a rien de surprenant ! Cela revient donc à dire que nous avons toujours affaire à une berline aux dimensions plus territoriales que locales. L'habitacle est vaste, très vaste dirais-je, mais l'espace pour la tête est un peu juste, surtout pour les grandes personnes. Le tableau de bord, déjà vu sur les Dodge Charger et Challenger ainsi que sur l'ex Magnum, a beau présenter des jauges d'un style

FEU VERT

- Future version prometteuse
- Habitacle vaste
- Comportement routier solide
- V6 3,5 bien adapté
- Confort certifié

FEU ROUGE

- Direction déconnectée (sauf SRT8)
- Finition encore un peu faible
- Dégagement pour la tête un peu juste
- Modèle en fin de carrière

classique, on n'y croit plus. Vivement du nouveau! Remarquez que ce n'est pas laid du tout. De plus, au fil des années, Chrysler a corrigé plusieurs défauts d'assemblage et la qualité des matériaux n'a pas cessé de s'améliorer.

Les places arrière sont bien dégagées mais pas autant que dans la Ford Taurus, l'éternelle rivale. Aussi, ne laissez pas Jacques Villeneuve conduire une 300 sur une piste de course si vous êtes assis à l'arrière. Le manque de support latéral vous ferait vous péter les deux hanches sur les portières! Villeneuve, lui, au moins, aurait le volant pour se cramponner car son siège n'offre guère plus de support... Quant au coffre, il fait honneur aux dimensions de la carrosserie et il est très grand même si son ouverture est petite.

Les versions les plus basiques proposent un V6 de 3,5 litres. Il s'agit, en fait, du meilleur moteur à associer à la 300. Ses prestations sont très correctes même si elles n'ont pas le punch des autres. Surtout, il consomme passablement moins, une donnée qui vaut son pesant d'or. D'office, on lui a octroyé une transmission automatique à quatre rapports mais la version à rouage intégral, fort désirable, reçoit un rapport supplémentaire, ce qui aide à diminuer la consommation.

Vient ensuite le V8 Hemi de 5,7 litres qui donne pratiquement des ailes à la grosse berline. Aussi souple que peu économe, ce moteur servira particulièrement ceux qui désirent beaucoup de punch sous le pied droit ou qui veulent remorquer davantage (2000 livres contre 1000 pour le 3,5 litres). Sinon, le V6 fait amplement l'affaire.

ÉCOUTEZ LA SRT8

Enfin, on retrouve la fabuleuse 300 SRT8. Cette voiture de course possède un V8 de plus de 400 chevaux ce qui, si l'auteur de ces lignes était le moindrement conséquent, serait vertement décrié. Mais non, l'auteur n'est pas conséquent! Tout simplement parce que la SRT8 n'est pas juste une brute de puissance. Ses suspensions sont passablement plus fermes — sans devenir invivables — et sa direction, plus ou moins précise et offrant peu de retour d'informations dans les autres modèles, montre exactement le contraire. Et une sonorité, une sonorité à vous en émouvoir l'enclume! Il faudrait au moins 30 Honda Civic «tunées» pour en arriver au huitième de la profondeur de ce son...

Alain Morin

PHOTOS: CHRYSLER

DONNÉES 2010

Catégorie	Berline
Échelle de prix	27 745 $ à 49 595 $ (2010)
Garanties	3 ans/60 000 km, 5 ans/100 000 km
Assemblage	Brampton, Ontario, Canada
Cote d'assurance	passable

CHÂSSIS - DONNÉES POUR LIMITED AWD

Emp/lon/lar/haut	3 048/4 999/1 882/1 483 mm
Coffre	442 litres
Réservoir	72 litres
Nombre coussins sécurité	6
Antipatinage / contrôle stabilité	oui / oui
Suspension avant	indépendante, bras inégaux
Suspension arrière	indépendante, multibras
Freins avant / arrière	disque (ABS) / disque (ABS)
Direction	à crémaillère, assistée
Diamètre de braquage	11,9 m
Pneus avant / arrière	P225/6R018 / P225/60R18
Poids	1 829 kg
Capacité de remorquage	907 kg (1999 lb)

COMPOSANTES MÉCANIQUES

Touring, Touring AWD, Limited, Limited AWD

Cylindrée, soupapes, alim.	V6 3,5 litres 24 s atmos.
Puissance / Couple	250 chevaux / 250 lb-pi
Tr. base (opt) / rouage base (opt)	A4 / Prop (Int)
0-100 / 80-120 / 100-0 km/h	9,0 s / 9,2 s / n.d.
Type ess. / ville / autoroute	Ordinaire / 12,6 / 8,6 l/100 km

C, C AWD

Cylindrée, soupapes, alim.	V8 5,7 litres 16 s atmos.
Puissance / Couple	360 chevaux / 389 lb-pi
Tr. base (opt) / rouage base (opt)	A5 / Prop (Int)
0-100 / 80-120 / 100-0 km/h	6,7 s / 5,0 s / 41,2 m
Type ess. / ville / autoroute	Ordinaire / 13,4 / 8,7 l/100 km

SRT8

Cylindrée, soupapes, alim.	V8 6,1 litres 16 s atmos.
Puissance / Couple	425 chevaux / 420 lb-pi
Tr. base (opt) / rouage base (opt)	A5 / Prop
0-100 / 80-120 / 100-0 km/h	4,9 s / 4,0 s / 39,0 m
Type ess. / ville / autoroute	Super / 16,0 / 10,6 l/100 km

DANS LA MÊME CATÉGORIE

Buick Allure, Buick Lucerne, Chevrolet Impala, Dodge Charger, Ford Taurus, Hyundai Genesis, Nissan Maxima, Toyota Avalon

DU NOUVEAU EN 2011

Nouveau modèle sera dévoilé plus tard en 2010

NOS IMPRESSIONS

Agrément de conduite:	8/10
Fiabilité:	6/10
Sécurité:	8/10
Qualités hivernales:	8/10
Espace intérieur:	9/10
Confort:	9/10

www.chrysler.ca

Plus d'informations dans la section statistiques en dernière partie du Guide

ON LUI DIT MERCI ET ADIEU

Une des voitures les plus mal aimées de la planète s'apprête à tirer sa révérence pour de bon. L'aventure Sebring, amorcée en 1995 sous les traits d'un superbe coupé, en duo avec la non moins jolie Dodge Avenger, se termine donc dans l'anonymat le plus complet. Bien des raisons expliquent ce désintérêt du public. Une fiabilité tout juste correcte à ses débuts, un assemblage bâclé et un décalage entre les lignes prometteuses de sportivité et le comportement routier plutôt axé sur le confort ont joué pour beaucoup. D'un autre côté, sa valeur de revente, faible au mieux, conséquence du marché des voitures d'occasion saturé par les retours des agences de location à court terme, n'a pas aidé sa cause.

Pourtant, plusieurs propriétaires rencontrés au fil des ans ont toujours semblé très satisfaits de leur Sebring et ne songeaient pas à la changer. Il faut dire que la voiture possède aussi de belles qualités qui compensent allègrement. Quoiqu'il en soit, le temps est venu pour Chrysler de passer à autre chose.

Sur la remplaçante de la Sebring, nous en savons vraiment très peu. Il est cependant pratiquement assuré que lorsqu'elle sera présentée à la presse spécialisée quelque part vers la fin de 2010, elle changera de nom, faisant table rase du passé. Selon certains sites internet cautionnés par Chrysler, le futur modèle pourrait reprendre les lignes de la superbe Chrysler 200C, vue au Salon de l'auto de Detroit en janvier 2009. On se souviendra que ce concept annonçait une motorisation électrique prometteuse. Une promesse d'ivrogne, semble-t-il! Les dimensions demeureraient très près de celles de la voiture actuelle, mais le châssis, provenant de chez Fiat, le nouveau propriétaire de Chrysler, serait inédit.

Mécaniquement, on parle du V6 de 3,6 litres Pentastar qui officie déjà avec brio dans le nouveau Jeep Grand Cherokee et qui, je le sens, sera utilisé à toutes les sauces chez le groupe Chrysler. La rumeur parle aussi d'un quatre cylindres de conception très moderne. Pourquoi pas le nouveau Multiair de Fiat? Quant à la transmission, le double embrayage serait de mise, toujours selon la même rumeur.

OCCUPONS-NOUS D'ABORD DU PRÉSENT

Mais depuis le début de cet essai, nous ne parlons que du futur. Entretenons-nous du présent plutôt! La Sebring continuera donc d'être vendue, sans aucun doute sous le millésime 2010 jusqu'à son remplacement. Pour l'instant, elle se décline en versions berline et cabriolet. Si plusieurs craquent pour les lignes de la Sebring, il ne faut toutefois pas être trop difficile quant à la finition et à la qualité des matériaux, même dans les versions plus cossues qui amènent un peu plus de chrome et de boiseries. L'habitacle serait confortable si ce n'était de ces sièges avant qui m'horripilent. Mais ça c'est

FEU VERT

Design toujours d'actualité
Toit du cabriolet réussi
Prix correct
Moteur de 2,7 litres bien adapté

FEU ROUGE

Modèle en fin de carrière
Faible valeur de revente
Finition décevante
Sièges plus ou moins confortables
Moteur de 2,4 litres à oublier

moi. Je crois même que ceux à l'arrière sont plus douillets ! Contre toute attente (ou logique), le cabriolet présente deux toits rétractables, un en toile et l'autre, rigide. Ce dernier est l'apanage de la version Limited.

Autant pour la berline que pour le cabriolet, trois moteurs sont proposés. Le quatre cylindres de 2,4 litres fait preuve d'une désolante incapacité et son impopularité est tout à fait compréhensible. Le V6 de 2,7 litres est beaucoup mieux adapté au caractère placide de la voiture. Loin de faire de la Sebring une Viper quatre portes, il a au moins la décence d'offrir des performances correctes tout en consommant avec modération. Quant au V6 de 3,5 litres, il s'avère certes beaucoup plus enjoué, mais malgré les six rapports de la boîte automatique, sa consommation d'essence en conduite urbaine a tôt fait de décourager les accélérations agressives.

ELLE AIME LES GRANDS ESPACES

La Sebring est davantage une boulevardière qu'une dévoreuse d'autoroutes. En raison du débattement un peu trop grand de ses suspensions, la voiture produit inévitablement du roulis dans les courbes. De plus, la direction est très légère, ce qui empêche de la placer de façon très précise. Le châssis est très rigide dans la berline et rigide dans le cabriolet, sans plus. Mais le plus grand problème de la Sebring demeure sans doute sa faible valeur de revente. Alors, imaginez dans quatre ou cinq ans, quand la production de ce modèle aura cessé depuis belle lurette.

L'an prochain, la section consacrée aux produits du groupe Chrysler (Chrysler, Dodge, Jeep et, pourquoi pas Fiat) devrait être passablement différente de celle de cette année. Pour se sortir du pétrin, et pour en sortir son sauveur italien, Chrysler est obligé de présenter des modèles que les gens veulent acheter. Il ne faut pas oublier que si les ventes de Chrysler vont si bien au Canada depuis quelques mois (du moins au moment d'écrire ces lignes, un superbe samedi soir de juillet 2010 alors qu'épouse et enfants profitent de la vie), c'est, en grande partie, grâce aux incitatifs très généreux. Souhaitons au troisième constructeur américain de pouvoir enfin renouer avec le succès légitime. La future Sebring, quel que soit son nom, pourrait très bien y contribuer.

Alain Morin

PHOTOS : CHRYSLER

Catégorie	Berline, Cabriolet
Échelle de prix	21 245 $ à 39 320 $ (2010)
Garanties	3 ans/60 000 km, 5 ans/100 000 km
Assemblage	Sterling Heights, Michigan, É-U
Cote d'assurance	moyenne

CHÂSSIS - DONNÉES POUR LIMITED BERLINE

Emp/lon/lar/haut	2 765/4 842/1 808/1 498 mm
Coffre	385 litres
Réservoir	64 litres
Nombre coussins sécurité	6
Antipatinage / contrôle stabilité	oui / oui
Suspension avant	indépendante, jambes de force
Suspension arrière	indépendante, multibras
Freins avant / arrière	disque (ABS) / disque (ABS)
Direction	à crémaillère, ass. variable
Diamètre de braquage	11,1 m
Pneus avant / arrière	P215/55R18 / P215/55R18
Poids	1 796 kg
Capacité de remorquage	907 kg (1 999 lb)

COMPOSANTES MÉCANIQUES

LX	
Cylindrée, soupapes, alim.	4L 2,4 litres 16 s atmos.
Puissance / Couple	173 chevaux / 166 lb-pi
Tr. base (opt) / rouage base (opt)	A4 / Tr
0-100 / 80-120 / 100-0 km/h	10,0 s / 8,5 s / 46,5 m
Type ess. / ville / autoroute	Ordinaire / 10,3 / 6,9 l/100 km

Touring	
Cylindrée, soupapes, alim.	V6 2,7 litres 24 s atmos.
Puissance / Couple	178 chevaux / 190 lb-pi
Tr. base (opt) / rouage base (opt)	A4 / Tr
0-100 / 80-120 / 100-0 km/h	9,1 s / 7,0 s / 46,5 m
Type ess. / ville / autoroute	Ordinaire / 11,7 / 7,6 l/100 km

Touring, Limited	
Cylindrée, soupapes, alim.	V6 3,5 litres 24 s atmos.
Puissance / Couple	235 chevaux / 232 lb-pi
Tr. base (opt) / rouage base (opt)	A4 (A6) / Tr
0-100 / 80-120 / 100-0 km/h	8,5 s / 7,2 s / 46,5 m
Type ess. / ville / autoroute	Ordinaire / 12,9 / 7,4 l/100 km

DANS LA MÊME CATÉGORIE

Buick Allure, Chevrolet Malibu, Dodge Avenger, Ford Fusion, Honda Accord, Hyundai Sonata, Kia Magentis, Mazda6, Nissan Altima, Toyota Camry, Volkswagen Passat

DU NOUVEAU EN 2011

Nouveau modèle pourrait être dévoilé plus tard en 2010

NOS IMPRESSIONS

Agrément de conduite :	8/10
Fiabilité :	6/10
Sécurité :	10/10
Qualités hivernales :	7/10
Espace intérieur :	7/10
Confort :	8/10

www.chrysler.ca

Plus d'informations dans la section statistiques en dernière partie du Guide

NOM ÉVOCATEUR EXÉCUTION DÉCEVANTE

Si la compagnie Chrysler a connu une année noire en 2009, c'est en partie à cause de chiffres de vente en déclin. Si certains modèles de sa gamme, notamment les camionnettes Ram et la plupart des véhicules Jeep se vendaient bien, plusieurs autres étaient laissés pour compte par les acheteurs. La Dodge Avenger fait partie de ce dernier groupe. En faisant appel à un modèle inspiré du passé, on aurait cru que cette berline aurait pu connaître le même succès que la nouvelle Charger. Mais si cette dernière était bien née, sa petite sœur n'est pas de calibre.

Ces modèles supposément de grande diffusion n'ont donc pas livré la marchandise. Ceci inclut également la Chrysler Sebringqui partage ses organes mécaniques avec la Dodge Avenger. Trop souvent par le passé, et même il n'y a pas si longtemps, les constructeurs américains ont eu la fâcheuse tendance d'utiliser un nom culte et de l'associer à une mécanique qui n'est pas à la hauteur de la concurrence. Il en résulte des modèles qui sont boudés et que l'on doit écouler à coup de promotion et de rabais, et à des taux d'intérêt relativement bas.

BELLE SILHOUETTE !

Pourtant, il est facile de s'emballer pour ce modèle car sa silhouette est tout de même élégante. Les stylistes en ont fait une mini-Charger et l'auto essayée au cours de l'été avait fière allure avec sa carrosserie rouge et ses roues chromées. Elle avait l'air d'une bête prête à bondir. Il serait facile de se laisser tenter par cette intermédiaire. Cependant, dès qu'on s'installe dans l'habitacle, les choses se gâtent très rapidement...

En effet, on est accueilli par des sièges dont l'inconfort est immédiat. Le dossier semble peu rembourré tandis que le siège est très bas. De plus, même si on n'a pas roulé du tout, on sait déjà que le support latéral sera quasiment nul. Et en ajustant le siège, on ne peut s'empêcher de sourire devant les gros boulons qui maintiennent en place l'assise des sièges avant. C'est assez primitif, merci.

Nous jetons un coup d'œil sur la planche de bord qui est dotée de commandes simples et accessibles. Nous avons droit à la classique combinaison des buses de ventilation sur la partie centrale supérieure superposant les commandes de la radio. Ensuite, ce sont les trois gros boutons visant à régler la climatisation. Les cadrans indicateurs à fond blanc sont de consultation aisée et bien disposés avec l'indicateur de vitesse au centre. Bref, jusque-là c'est positif. Mais on constate malheureusement que la qualité des matériaux utilisés pour l'habitacle et le tableau de bord en particulier est vraiment douteuse. Je me demande toujours pourquoi les constructeurs s'entêtent à faire des économies sous les yeux de l'acheteur... On aurait pu ajouter quelques dollars de plus pour nous offrir une planche de bord digne de ce nom et réduire les coûts dans des endroits

Catégorie	Berline
Échelle de prix	20 995 $ à 25 295 $ (2010)
Garanties	3 ans/60 000 km, 5 ans/100 000 km
Assemblage	Sterling Heights, Michigan, É-U
Cote d'assurance	passable

FEU VERT

Silhouette accrocheuse
Prix compétitifs
4 cylindres économique
Équipement de série plus complet

FEU ROUGE

Fiabilité à améliorer
Motricité du train avant
Suspension mal calibrée
Matériaux de l'habitacle

invisibles. Par contre, si la finition n'est pas une priorité pour vous, l'efficacité et l'ergonomie de cette planche de bord vous plairont.

Si les places avant sont assez spacieuses, la banquette arrière est surtout réservée à des personnes de taille moyenne. De plus, avec un faible dégagement pour la tête et une assise de siège relativement basse, vous avez la tête entre les genoux si vous êtes grand.

UN SEUL MOTEUR S'IMPOSE

Si vous lisez la publicité dans les journaux, cette Dodge est offerte à des prix vraiment compétitifs. Mais, en y regardant de plus près, vous constaterez qu'il s'agit des versions propulsées par le moteur quatre cylindres de 2,4 litres associé à une boîte automatique à quatre rapports. Vous avez bien lu, quatre rapports ! Certains ingénieurs de cette compagnie semblent ne pas savoir que nous sommes en 2011. Non seulement ce tandem est peu performant en dépit d'une puissance affichée de 173 chevaux, mais le moteur est rugueux et le passage des rapports saccadé.

Si vous tenez absolument à rouler en Avenger, le modèle R/T mû par le moteur V6 de 3,5 litres produisant 235 chevaux est un bien meilleur choix. Il est en plus associé à une transmission automatique à six rapports, une boîte moderne et efficace. Mais peu importe le groupe propulseur choisi, vous serez déçu par une plate-forme qui manque de rigidité et de raffinement. La suspension n'est pas toujours capable de compenser les trous et les bosses, tandis que la motricité en virage fait penser aux premières tractions avant nord-américaines des années 80. À vrai dire, si vous accélérez à basse vitesse dans un virage, il y a un effet de couple marqué et un manque de motricité de la roue intérieure. C'est à se demander si on n'a pas fait appel au rouage avant des légendaires voitures K.

Une fois de plus, Chrysler a raté le coche en voulant faire des économies relativement mineures mais qui ont d'importants effets négatifs au chapitre du confort, de la tenue de route et de l'agrément de conduite. Tout cela a pour conséquence d'obliger le constructeur à brader ses stocks, ce qui entraîne une valeur de revente catastrophique. Et comme si le portrait n'était pas assez noir, la fiabilité anticipée n'est pas extraordinaire non plus…

Denis Duquet

PHOTOS : DODGE

CHÂSSIS - DONNÉES POUR SE

Emp/lon/lar/haut	2 765/4 849/1 824/1 496 mm
Coffre	368 litres
Réservoir	64 litres
Nombre coussins sécurité	6
Antipatinage / contrôle stabilité	opt / opt
Suspension avant	indépendante, jambes de force
Suspension arrière	indépendante, multibras
Freins avant / arrière	disque (ABS) / disque (ABS)
Direction	à crémaillère, assistée
Diamètre de braquage	11,1 m
Pneus avant / arrière	P215/65R16 / P215/65R16
Poids	1 522 kg
Capacité de remorquage	454 kg (1 000 lb)

COMPOSANTES MÉCANIQUES

SE, SXT	
Cylindrée, soupapes, alim.	4L 2,4 litres 16 s atmos.
Puissance / Couple	173 chevaux / 166 lb-pi
Tr. base (opt) / rouage base (opt)	A4 / Tr
0-100 / 80-120 / 100-0 km/h	11,3 s / 9,0 s / 44,0 m
Type ess. / ville / autoroute	Ordinaire / 9,7 / 6,6 l/100 km

SXT, R/T	
Cylindrée, soupapes, alim.	V6 3,5 litres 24 s atmos.
Puissance / Couple	235 chevaux / 232 lb-pi
Tr. base (opt) / rouage base (opt)	A6 / Tr
0-100 / 80-120 / 100-0 km/h	7,7 s / 6,6 s / 43,5 m
Type ess. / ville / autoroute	Ordinaire / 12,9 / 7,4 l/100 km

DANS LA MÊME CATÉGORIE

Chevrolet Malibu, Ford Fusion, Honda Accord, Hyundai Sonata, Kia Magentis, Mazda6, Nissan Altima, Subaru Legacy, Toyota Camry

DU NOUVEAU EN 2011

Aucun changement majeur

NOS IMPRESSIONS

Agrément de conduite :	7/10
Fiabilité :	5/10
Sécurité :	10/10
Qualités hivernales :	7/10
Espace intérieur :	7/10
Confort :	7/10

www.dodge.ca

Plus d'informations dans la section statistiques en dernière partie du Guide

UN POTENTIEL MAL EXPLOITÉ

Il serait difficile d'accuser la compagnie Chrysler de manquer d'originalité. Nous nous souvenons tous de l'Autobeaucoup qui a connu tellement de popularité qu'elle a incité les autres constructeurs à produire des fourgonnettes à traction avant. Au fil des années, la direction de la compagnie a tenté de réaliser d'autres coups d'éclat semblables qui lui auraient permis de s'imposer dans un nouveau créneau.

La plus récente tentative à ce jour est celle du Dodge Journey, un multisegment qui devait révolutionner le marché. Le public a tardé à réagir ce qui n'empêcha pas ce modèle de connaître une popularité réconfortante pour ce constructeur. Mais une couple d'années auparavant, on avait également tenté un autre coup fumant avec la Caliber. Une fois de plus, on avait essayé de transformer du tout au tout la catégorie des voitures compactes avec un modèle cinq portes qui s'octroyait certains attributs d'un VUS tout en conservant les qualités propresaux compactes.

ORIGINALE ? C'EST CERTAIN !

Quand on veut faire éclater une catégorie avec un nouveau modèle, il ne faut pas avoir peur d'innover. Cette fois-ci, c'est au chapitre de la silhouette puisque ce modèle ressemble à un mélange de fourgonnette, de familiale et de VUS. De plus, la fenestration se rétrécissant vers l'arrière, les passages de roue en relief prononcé ainsi qu'une imposante applique en bas de caisse lui procurent une allure unique. Et on en a rajouté avec la traditionnelle grille de calandre Dodge qui ne fait pas dans la dentelle. Il ne faut pas oublier non plus qu'offrir un seul modèle à hayon est également un pari audacieux puisque le marché américain semble avoir ce type de carrosserie en horreur.

Cette silhouette est une affaire de goût, mais force est d'admettre qu'on n'a pas reculé lorsqu'est venu le temps de prendre des décisions risquées. Dans l'habitacle, on a voulu faire des économies sur la qualité des matériaux et de la finition. Heureusement, l'an dernier, on a révisé tant bien que mal ce tableau de bord qui a été tant critiqué, autant par les clients que par les chroniqueurs spécialisés. Si vous n'êtes pas difficiles, cette planche de bord vous conviendra. Il faut avouer que les trois cadrans indicateurs sont d'une certaine élégance et de consultation aisée. Même chose pour la console centrale qui est d'une simplicité qui sera appréciée par certains et décriée par d'autres. Et même si les matériaux ne sont pas toujours ce qu'il y a de mieux, d'importants progrès ont été réalisés.

En dépit de ses lignes qui nous laissent présager un habitacle plutôt spacieux, l'habitabilité est moyenne, surtout en arrière. Mais ce qui est intéressant, c'est la multitude d'espaces de rangement, notamment une boîte à gants qui est superposée d'un autre espace permettant d'y remiser des breuvages. Il est possible d'y diriger un courant d'air frais afin d'obtenir une boisson légèrement rafraîchie. Il y a également ce plafonnier détachable qui se

FEU VERT
- Consommation de carburant économique
- Habitacle pratique
- Prix compétitif
- Multiples gadgets ingénieux

FEU ROUGE
- Boîte CVT
- Finition sommaire
- Tenue de route sommaire
- Insonorisation perfectible

transforme en lampe de poche ! De plus, il est doté d'une batterie qui se recharge lorsque le véhicule roule.

EXÉCUTION ! EXÉCUTION !

Jusqu'à présent, ce Dodge vendu à prix très compétitif ne s'en tire pas trop mal. Là où ça se gâte, c'est surtout au chapitre du comportement routier et de l'équilibre général. L'an dernier, on a fait le grand ménage dans les groupes propulseurs de sorte qu'un seul moteur est maintenant disponible, soit un quatre cylindres 2,0 litres de 158 chevaux. Pour la petite histoire, on avait auparavant le choix entre un moteur 1,8 litre ou encore un 2,4 litres, ce dernier étant toujours commercialisé aux États-Unis. Par contre, deux transmissions sont au choix. En équipement de base, une transmission manuelle à cinq rapports équipe la Caliber. La transmission CVT est optionnelle.

Et c'est avec cette dernière que les ennuis débutent. Cela ne signifie pas que la fiabilité soit déficiente, mais cette transmission à rapports continuellement variables émet une sonorité vraiment désagréable du moteur. Certaines personnes ont l'impression de conduire un rasoir électrique, s'il faut se fier à leurs dires et le son du moteur est irritant à la longue. Quant à la transmission manuelle, elle ne transforme pas cette Dodge en voiture de sport. C'est plutôt basique comme boîte.

La tenue de route n'est pas mauvaise, mais elle n'est pas extraordinaire non plus. Comme vous pouvez le constater, cette automobile ne fait rien de très mal, mais elle ne fait rien de spectaculaire non plus !. On conduit un moyen de transport qui nous transmet peu d'éléments positifs tant en fait d'agrément de conduite que de performances sur la route ou encore de tenue de route. En plus, l'insonorisation est nettement perfectible : une promenade sur une route de gravillons est accompagnée d'un tintamarre dans l'habitacle.

Si vous voulez une voiture compacte cinq portes, la Caliber a des qualités qui méritent d'être soulignées, notamment un coût d'achat très intéressant et une bonne économie de carburant. Aussi, l'habitacle est très pratique est passablement confortable. Pour plusieurs, ce sera suffisant.

Denis Duquet

PHOTOS : DODGE

Catégorie	*Hatchback*
Échelle de prix	13 995 $ à 17 645 $ (2010)
Garanties	3 ans/60 000 km, 5 ans/100 000 km
Assemblage	Belvidere, Illinois, É-U
Cote d'assurance	n.d.

CHÂSSIS - DONNÉES POUR SXT

Emp/lon/lar/haut	2 635/4 414/1 747/1 533 mm
Coffre	351 à 1 360 litres
Réservoir	51 litres
Nombre coussins sécurité	4
Antipatinage / contrôle stabilité	opt / opt
Suspension avant	indépendante, jambes de force
Suspension arrière	indépendante, multibras
Freins avant / arrière	disque (ABS) / disque (ABS)
Direction	à crémaillère, ass. variable
Diamètre de braquage	11,3 m
Pneus avant / arrière	P215/60R17 / P215/60R17
Poids	1 378 kg
Capacité de remorquage	454 kg (1 000 lb)

COMPOSANTES MÉCANIQUES

Canada Value Package, SE Plus, SXT

Cylindrée, soupapes, alim.	4L 2,0 litres 16 s atmos.
Puissance / Couple	158 chevaux / 141 lb-pi
Tr. base (opt) / rouage base (opt)	M5 (CVT) / Tr
0-100 / 80-120 / 100-0 km/h	9,9 s / 8,6 s / 44,8 m
Type ess. / ville / autoroute	Ordinaire / 9,1 / 6,3 l/100 km

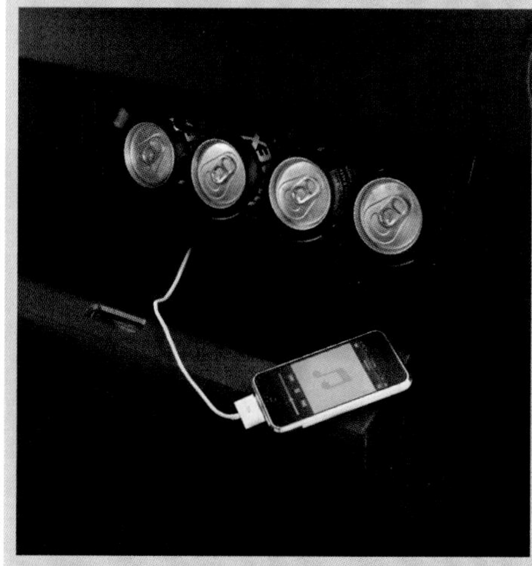

DANS LA MÊME CATÉGORIE

Chevrolet HHR, Hyundai Elantra, Kia Soul, Mazda3, Nissan Cube, Subaru Impreza, Toyota Matrix

DU NOUVEAU EN 2011

Aucun changement majeur

NOS IMPRESSIONS

Agrément de conduite :	8/10
Fiabilité :	8/10
Sécurité :	8/10
Qualités hivernales :	8/10
Espace intérieur :	8/10
Confort :	7/10

www.dodge.ca

Plus d'informations dans la section statistiques en dernière partie du Guide

DESIGN PUR RÉTRO

C'est en s'inspirant de l'inoubliable Challenger des années 1970 et 1971, qui sont de nos jours très recherchées par les collectionneurs, que les stylistes de Dodge ont créé cette version contemporaine de l'un des plus célèbres muscle cars de la belle époque des voitures américaines. Si le style est pur rétro, la technique est résolument moderne puisque la Challenger, comme la Charger d'ailleurs, a été élaborée à partir de la plate-forme LX développée pendant la période de l'alliance entre Mercedes-Benz et Chrysler.

À peu près tous les baby-boomers se souviennent avec nostalgie du film *Vanishing Point* (*Point Limite Zéro* en français) où une Dodge Challenger R/T 1971 blanche tenait le rôle principal, son pilote Kowalski (joué par Barry Newman) étant relégué au second plan. On pourrait facilement qualifier ce film-culte de tout premier *road movie*. Il faut savoir qu'à l'époque, les produits Dodge avaient la cote auprès des amateurs de performances. Non contente de proposer des voitures au style exceptionnel, Dodge leur implantait des mécaniques d'enfer, de gros V8 de 400 et 440 pouces cubes. Il y avait aussi le fabuleux 426 Hemi qui faisait des Challenger, Charger et Plymouth 'Cuda de véritables voitures de « drag » légales.

Un examen attentif des lignes de la Challenger contemporaine nous permet d'apprécier le fait que les designers ne se sont pas simplement contentés de reproduire le modèle des années 1970, mais bien de réinterpréter le concept initial pour le mettre au goût du jour. Le résultat est probant et la nouvelle Challenger respecte la filiation avec l'originale tout en conservant les proportions classiques du modèle. Pour le millésime 2011, la Challenger reçoit une calandre inférieure inversée par rapport à ses prédécesseures. C'est du côté de l'habitacle où le clivage est plus marqué entre les deux modèles, puisque la planche de bord de la voiture d'aujourd'hui est réalisée avec un style inspiré des autres modèles de la marque, mais dont les plastiques ne sont malheureusement pas de grande qualité. En fait, il n'y a que le volant beaucoup trop grand qui rappelle le modèle original. Les sièges avant sont confortables mais pourraient offrir un peu plus de soutien latéral en virage, alors que les passagers s'assoyant à l'arrière devront faire preuve d'une certaine flexibilité pour monter à bord et trouveront l'assise de la banquette un peu courte. Il est également étonnant, considérant la vocation première de cette voiture, que les concepteurs aient pensé à doter la Challenger de dossiers rabattables aux places arrière. Ainsi, le volume de chargement peut être augmenté au besoin. Il faut admettre que cela donne à la voiture un certain côté pratique insoupçonné.

DE 290 À 480 CHEVAUX

La Challenger peut être animée par trois moteurs et la puissance livrée à la route passe presque du simple au double entre le V6 Pentastar et le V8 Hemi de 6,1 litres qui équipe le modèle SRT8 et

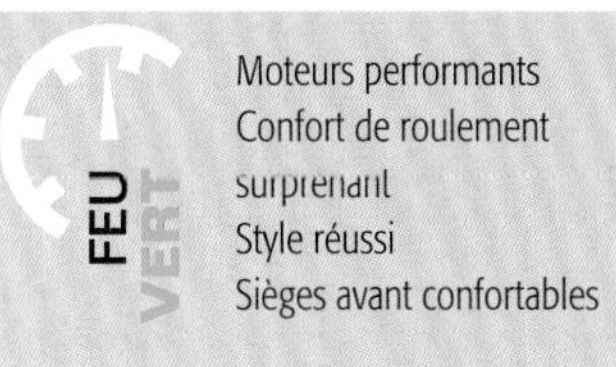

FEU VERT

- Moteurs performants
- Confort de roulement surprenant
- Style réussi
- Sièges avant confortables

FEU ROUGE

- Poids élevé
- Gabarit imposant
- Qualité des matériaux – habitacle
- Visibilité arrière

dont la puissance est portée à 480 chevaux pour le modèle 2011 qui recevra également une boîte automatique à huit rapports développée conjointement par Chrysler et ZF. Entre ces deux extrêmes se trouve le V8 de 5,7 litres du modèle R/T qui déballe 376 chevaux et un étonnant 410 livres-pied de couple.

Conduire la Challenger SRT8 sur la route, c'est un peu comme revivre la belle époque où la puissance faisait foi de tout, mais avec un degré de civilité relevé d'un cran par rapport au modèle original et surtout, une tenue de route qui est à des années-lumière de celle du modèle des années 1970. Le fait que le modèle actuel soit doté d'une suspension indépendante à l'arrière joue pour beaucoup dans le comportement routier de la Challenger dont le facteur limitatif en ce qui a trait à la tenue de route est son poids très élevé de près de deux tonnes, ainsi que sa direction qui ne renvoie pas autant de *feedback* que l'on aurait souhaité. Par contre, une fois bien inscrite en courbe, le sous-virage est limité et il est même possible de faire décrocher le train arrière à l'accélérateur pourvu que l'on ait préalablement désactivé les systèmes électroniques de contrôle de la motricité et de la stabilité. Les liaisons au sol sont assurées par des amortisseurs de marque Bilstein, lesquels font un très bon travail puisque le confort n'est pas trop affecté par les routes dégradées, et les freins surdimensionnés en provenance de chez Brembo se sont avérés très efficaces, ce qui est évidemment souhaitable compte tenu de la puissance livrée par le V8 et le poids élevé de la voiture. Du bon boulot, dans l'ensemble.

Depuis la déroute de Chrysler et sa prise de contrôle par le groupe Fiat, l'avenir de ce modèle marquant de l'histoire de la marque est pour le moins incertain. Néanmoins, ça n'empêche pas les amateurs d'en faire l'acquisition, d'autant plus que la division Mopar ainsi que plusieurs équipementiers proposent toute une série de pièces et d'accessoires permettant de personnaliser la Challenger ou d'en augmenter le niveau de performance. Mais force est d'admettre que dans le merveilleux monde des *muscle cars*, seule la Mustang jouit d'une longévité continue alors que les Challenger et Camaro sont déjà disparues du paysage automobile pour ensuite renaître de leurs cendres. À la lumière des investissements qui sont aujourd'hui commandés par le développement des nouvelles générations de modèles existants, il est loin d'être sûr que la Challenger sera renouvelée après le cycle de vie du modèle actuel.

Gabriel Gélinas

PHOTOS : DODGE

Catégorie	Coupé
Échelle de prix	25 995 $ à 46 995 $ (2010)
Garanties	3 ans/60 000 km, 5 ans/100 000 km
Assemblage	Brampton, Ontario, Canada
Cote d'assurance	passable

CHÂSSIS - DONNÉES POUR R/T MANUELLE

Emp/lon/lar/haut	2 946/5 022/1 923/1 445 mm
Coffre	459 litres
Réservoir	72 litres
Nombre coussins sécurité	4
Antipatinage / contrôle stabilité	oui / oui
Suspension avant	indépendante, bras inégaux
Suspension arrière	indépendante, multibras
Freins avant / arrière	disque (ABS) / disque (ABS)
Direction	à crémaillère, assistée
Diamètre de braquage	11,9 m
Pneus avant / arrière	P235/55R18 / P235/55R18
Poids	1 833 kg
Capacité de remorquage	n.d.

COMPOSANTES MÉCANIQUES

SE, SXT

Cylindrée, soupapes, alim.	V6 3,5 litres 24 s atmos.
Puissance / Couple	250 chevaux / 250 lb-pi
Tr. base (opt) / rouage base (opt)	A5 / Prop
0-100 / 80-120 / 100-0 km/h	8,0 s / 7,0 s / n.d.
Type ess. / ville / autoroute	Ordinaire / 11,8 / 8,0 l/100 km

R/T automatique

Cylindrée, soupapes, alim.	V8 5,7 litres 16 s atmos.
Puissance / Couple	372 chevaux / 401 lb-pi
Tr. base (opt) / rouage base (opt)	A5 / Prop
0-100 / 80-120 / 100-0 km/h	6,5 s / 7,5 s / 40,0 m
Type ess. / ville / autoroute	Ordinaire / 13,5 / 8,0 l/100 km

R/T manuelle

V8 5,7 l, 376 ch, 410 lb-pi - 0-100 : 6,5 s - 13,8 / 8,2 l/100 km

SRT8

V8 6,1 l, 480 ch, n.d. lb-pi - 0-100 : 5,0 s (est) - 16,0 / 10,2 l/100 km

DANS LA MÊME CATÉGORIE

Chevrolet Camaro, Dodge Charger, Ford Mustang

DU NOUVEAU EN 2011

Édition limitée Mopar à venir (changements cosmétiques, moteur Hemi 5,7 litres, suspension Super Track Pack, etc).

NOS IMPRESSIONS

Agrément de conduite :	8/10
Fiabilité :	8/10
Sécurité :	8/10
Qualités hivernales :	6/10
Espace intérieur :	8/10
Confort :	8/10

www.dodge.ca

Plus d'informations dans la section statistiques en dernière partie du Guide

IL N'EST PAS TROP TÔT !

La Dodge Charger est avec nous depuis 2006. Cela fait donc cinq ans que cette berline promène ses lignes intimidantes sur nos routes. Cinq ans, dans le domaine de l'automobile, c'est comme environ un mois dans la vie d'un moustique. C'est très long... D'ici quelques mois, Dodge dévoilera la deuxième génération (ou la 6e si l'on compte les premières générations datant des années 60) de sa populaire Charger. Ce ne sera pas trop tôt !

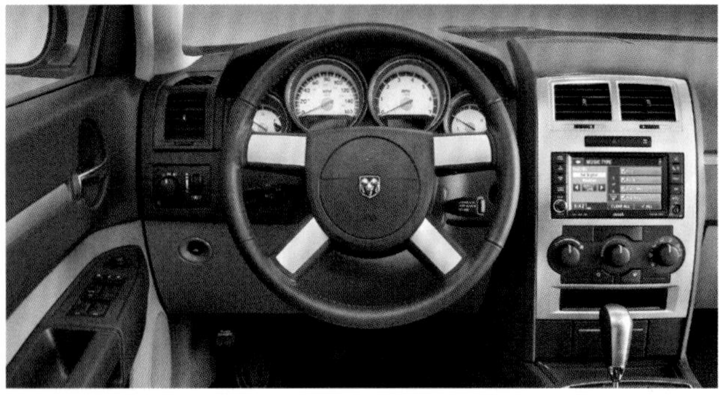

Pour l'instant, nous ne savons que bien peu de choses sur la Charger 2011. Le modèle 2010 poursuit donc son petit bonhomme de chemin sans changements. Ce qui revient à dire que l'influence de la Chrysler 300 continue de se faire sentir, surtout dans l'habitacle alors que le tableau de bord, s'il convient à une berline visant le haut de gamme, figure moins bien dans une voiture aux prétentions sportives. L'habitacle est vaste comme une cathédrale et silencieux comme le Grand Nord une journée sans vent. Le châssis aussi est emprunté à la 300 qui, elle, l'avait obtenu de la Mercedes-Benz Classe E de la génération précédente. C'était à l'époque du mariage de raison entre la noble allemande et la pauvre américaine, mariage qui n'a pas résisté à l'épreuve du budget. Quoi qu'il en soit, cette plate-forme est, sans aucun doute, l'une des meilleures à ne jamais avoir été utilisée par le groupe Chrysler.

ON EN REJOINT DU MONDE !

On ne peut pas dire que la Charger actuelle ne ratisse pas large. Elle peut rejoindre les plus pépères avec son V6 de 2,7 litres et les baby-boomers les plus nostalgiques grâce à sa version SRT8 de 425 chevaux. Le premier moteur n'est sans doute proposé que pour pouvoir offrir une voiture à un prix très abordable. Heureusement, à peu près tout le monde lui préfère le V6 de 3,5 litres, parfaitement adapté à la Charger, suffisamment puissant et assez économique. Ensuite, on retrouve le V8 5,7 Hemi des modèles R/T qui en donne plus que ce que le client demande. Nonobstant une sonorité riche en émotions et des performances allègres, il n'est vraiment utile que pour bien peu de personnes. Et le SRT8, summum de l'inutilité, redonne le goût de vivre à quiconque a connu l'époque bénie des *muscle cars*. Il n'est donc pas si inutile que ça ! Et il ne faudrait pas oublier les Charger Police Vehicle qui veillent constamment sur notre sécurité...

Les modèles de base reçoivent une antédiluvienne transmission automatique à quatre rapports tandis que les autres ont plutôt droit à une automatique à six rapports, infiniment plus moderne. Contrairement à ses principales rivales, la Charger peut être mue par les quatre roues grâce à un rouage intégral qui assure une motricité accrue sur chaussée mouillée ou dans la neige. La SRT8, par contre, demeure toujours une propulsion, un rouage seyant mieux à une sportive performante.

Le comportement routier de la Charger s'améliore au fur et à mesure que l'on monte dans la hiérarchie. De souples, voire

FEU VERT

- Version SRT8 fort désirable
- Confort relevé
- Habitacle vaste et silencieux
- Bon choix de moteurs
- L'avenir promet...

FEU ROUGE

- Consommation SRT8 décourageante
- Tableau de bord terne
- Finition ordinaire
- Visibilité arrière pénible
- Dimensions intimidantes

flasques, dans la version SE de base, les suspensions s'affermissent au point de devenir carrément sportives dans la SRT8. Cependant, jamais elles ne sont inconfortables. La tenue de route suit le même chemin (belle association d'idées ici...), de même que la direction qui gagne en précision à mesure que l'on gagne en sportivité. Mais, excepté pour la SRT8, elle se montre toujours assez peu bavarde sur son travail. Quant aux sièges avant, ils n'éprouvent aucune retenue... sauf, encore une fois, dans la SRT8 où ils ne sont rien moins qu'excellents. Les freins effectuent du bon boulot mais ceux de la SRT8, fabriqués par Brembo, sont nettement plus performants. Il le faut, les performances de cette berline étant beaucoup plus relevées. Mais ce qui fait craquer plusieurs personnes est le style de cette Charger sur les méthamphétamines. Avec ses roues de 20 pouces, sa suspension abaissée et sa prise d'air sur le capot, elle a vraiment belle gueule. Si seulement son tableau de bord n'était pas si générique...

DE QUOI SERA FAIT L'AVENIR?

La prochaine Charger devrait profiter de nombreuses modifications. On chuchote que le châssis demeurerait le même mais qu'il serait sérieusement modifié. Est-ce que les dimensions seront plus imposantes? On ne sait pas. Ce qu'on sait, par contre, c'est que les lignes, tout en restant très Charger, seront passablement modernisées. L'avant, par exemple, vu sur plusieurs sites Internet, sera beaucoup plus agressif... comme s'il ne l'était pas suffisamment avant! Réglera-t-on enfin le problème de la visibilité arrière, franchement mauvaise actuellement? C'est à voir. L'habitacle serait aussi entièrement revampé et serait amené au même niveau que la concurrence. L'intérieur du nouveau Jeep Grand Cherokee nous a d'ailleurs étonnés par sa qualité de fabrication, et si la tendance se maintient, la Charger devrait bénéficier de cet élan de générosité. Il y a fort à parier que la Charger s'éloignera de la 300, sa génitrice qui, elle aussi, connaîtra sa part de changements. Côté moteurs, on parle du nouveau V6 Pentastar et de la transmission à cinq rapports qui équipent le Grand Cherokee. Une boîte à six ou sept rapports serait prévue à moyen terme. Beaucoup de rumeurs font état d'une transmission à huit rapports mais elle serait réservée à la future SRT8. Beaucoup de conditionnel, vous admettrez, mais l'avenir semble passablement plus rose qu'avant pour le groupe Chrysler. Nous vous tiendrons au courant au fur et à mesure que les nouveautés arriveront sur www.guideautoweb.com

Alain Morin

PHOTOS : DODGE

DONNÉES 2010

Catégorie	Berline
Échelle de prix	25 745 $ à 43 195 $ (2010)
Garanties	3 ans/60 000 km, 3 ans/60 000 km
Assemblage	Brampton, Ontario, Canada
Cote d'assurance	passable

CHÂSSIS - DONNÉES POUR SRT8

Emp/lon/lar/haut	3 048/5 082/1 892/1 478 mm
Coffre	458 litres
Réservoir	72 litres
Nombre coussins sécurité	2
Antipatinage / contrôle stabilité	oui / oui
Suspension avant	indépendante, bras inégaux
Suspension arrière	indépendante, multibras
Freins avant / arrière	disque (ABS) / disque (ABS)
Direction	à crémaillère, assistée
Diamètre de braquage	11,8 m
Pneus avant / arrière	P245/45ZR20 / P245/45ZR20
Poids	1 887 kg
Capacité de remorquage	907 kg (1 999 lb)

COMPOSANTES MÉCANIQUES

SE

Cylindrée, soupapes, alim.	V6 2,7 litres 24 s atmos.
Puissance / Couple	178 chevaux / 190 lb-pi
Tr. base (opt) / rouage base (opt)	A4 / Prop
0-100 / 80-120 / 100-0 km/h	9,8 s / 8,5 s / n.d.
Type ess. / ville / autoroute	Ordinaire / 11,3 / 7,7 l/100 km

SE, SXT, SXT AWD

Cylindrée, soupapes, alim.	V6 3,5 litres 24 s atmos.
Puissance / Couple	250 chevaux / 250 lb-pi
Tr. base (opt) / rouage base (opt)	A4 / Prop (Int)
0-100 / 80-120 / 100-0 km/h	8,2 s / 8,0 s / n.d.
Type ess. / ville / autoroute	Ordinaire / 12,6 / 8,6 l/100 km

R/T, R/T AWD

V8 5,7 l, 368 ch, 395 lb-pi - 0-100 : 6,5 s - 13,4 / 8,7 l/100 km

SRT8

V8 6,1 l, 425 ch / 420 lb-pi -0-100 km :
5,3 s - 16,0 / 10,6 l/100 km

DANS LA MÊME CATÉGORIE

Buick LaCrosse, Chrysler 300, Ford Taurus, Nissan Maxima, Toyota Avalon

DU NOUVEAU EN 2011

Nouveau modèle sera dévoilé en cours d'année

NOS IMPRESSIONS

Agrément de conduite :	7/10
Fiabilité :	6/10
Sécurité :	8/10
Qualités hivernales :	7/10
Espace intérieur :	8/10
Confort :	8/10

www.dodge.ca

Plus d'informations dans la section statistiques en dernière partie du Guide

Dodge Grand Caravan

LA POLYVALENCE REFUSE DE LÂCHER PRISE!

Lorsqu'elle fut présentée au public en 1984, la Dodge Caravan fut plus qu'un succès commercial. La minfourgonnette allait redéfinir le statut social américain, rien de moins. Tout le monde voulait être vu au volant de la nouvelle coqueluche. Puis, une dizaine d'années plus tard, les gens se sont tournés massivement vers les nouveaux VUS qui promettaient mer et monde. Aujourd'hui, il faut avoir un multisegment pour être in. Pourtant, aucun véhicule n'a encore approché la polyvalence des fourgonnettes. Comme quoi, le paraître a encore préséance sur l'être...

Les plus perspicaces auront remarqué que le terme aujourd'hui utilisé pour parler de la Grand Caravan et de ses nombreuses cousines est « fourgonnette ». Avec le temps, le préfixe « mini » a disparu, ce qui est parfaitement justifié lorsque l'on constate que l'empattement de la Caravan a gagné, en 27 ans, 23 cm et la longueur totale... 68 ! Le poids, lui, a augmenté de près de 650 kilos. Bref, elle mérite son « Grand ».

DES BRETELLES, CE N'EST PLUS À LA MODE

La dernière refonte des Grand Caravan et Town & Country a été effectuée en 2008 et elle est encore loin de faire l'unanimité. Si la partie avant ne semble pas trop vilipendée, c'est surtout la partie arrière avec ses larges piliers courbés, qui ressemblent à des bretelles, qui est ostracisée. Personnellement, je ne déteste pas du tout. Par contre, la Volkswagen Routan ne présente pas lesdites bretelles. Eh oui, Volks propose une fourgonnette ! On se demande bien pourquoi d'ailleurs. Sans doute dans un élan de nostalgie puisque Volks avait connu beaucoup de succès avec son Type 2 (ou Transporter), une fourgonnette avant le temps, commercialisée entre 1950 et jusque dans les années 80 sur certains marchés. Mais la Routan n'a vraiment rien à voir avec le passé. En fait, il s'agit d'une Chrysler Town & Country dynamisée.

Quoi qu'il en soit, c'est pour la polyvalence de l'habitacle qu'on se procure une fourgonnette et le trio Dodge/Chrysler/Volks nous en donne pour notre argent. L'espace vivable est immense. Sept personnes peuvent s'y assoir sans aucune chance de se toucher, une bénédiction pour les parents. La version de base de la Grand Caravan possède une banquette pour deux personnes qui peut être facilement enlevée. Mais la plupart des gens lui préfèrent le fabuleux Stow'n Go venant de série sur les autres modèles (mais curieusement pas sur la Routan), un ingénieux système qui permet aux sièges capitaines, fort confortables, de se rabattre dans le plancher. Idem pour la banquette arrière qui peut accueillir trois personnes dans un confort relatif. Heureusement, le Stow'n Go fait, là encore, des merveilles. Une fois tous ces sièges enfouis dans le plancher, déménager l'ado dans un CÉGEP le plus loin possible ne sera qu'une balade du dimanche ! Il y a aussi le système Swivel'n Go, offert uniquement sur certaines versions, qui expulse le Stow'n Go mais qui, en revanche, permet aux sièges de la deuxième rangée de

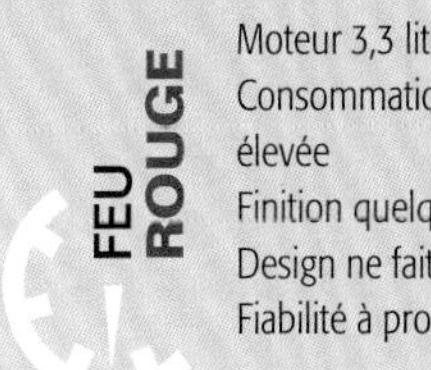

FEU VERT
Polyvalence superlative
Stow'n Go génial
Confort appréciable
Moteur 4,0 litres efficace
Prix bien étudiés
(surtout la Grand Caravan)

FEU ROUGE
Moteur 3,3 litres dépassé
Consommation toujours élevée
Finition quelquefois lâche
Design ne fait pas l'unanimité
Fiabilité à prouver

pivoter vers l'arrière. Une petite table est même prévue et les parties de cartes lors des journées pluvieuses.

Les gens installés à l'avant ne sont vraiment pas à plaindre. Le conducteur est assis haut et profite d'une bonne visibilité tout le tour. Il fait face à un tableau de bord plus fonctionnel qu'esthétique, sauf dans la Volkswagen où il diffère un peu en faisant passer la beauté avant l'ergonomie. Les espaces de rangement pullulent et les traîneux risquent d'y perdre une quantité incroyable d'objets. Si seulement la qualité de certains plastiques n'était pas si moche! Au moins, l'assemblage général est correct. Lors d'un essai hivernal (-33 degrés Celsius, c'est assez hivernal, merci), nous avons été étonnés par la rapidité de chauffage de l'habitacle d'une Routan.

DÉCEPTIONS ET PLAISIRS

La plupart des versions du Grand Caravan reçoivent un V6 de 3,3 litres qui commence d'ailleurs à présenter des rides. Il est associé à une tout aussi ridée transmission automatique à quatre rapports et l'ensemble est loin de faire des miracles. Heureusement, les autres variantes ont droit à un V6 de 4,0 litres nettement plus intéressant (parce que travaillant de pair avec une automatique à six rapports) malgré une consommation d'essence trop élevée. Mais comme elle ne l'est guère plus que celle du 3,3 litres, le choix est facile à faire. Pour bien enfoncer le clou du 3,3, mentionnons que sa capacité de remorquage est de 1 800 livres (818 kilos) tandis que celle du 4,0 est de 3800 livres (1727 kilos)...

La conduite d'un Grand Caravan ou d'un Town & Country n'a rien pour donner des frissons à Michael Schumacher. Plus placide que ça, tu meurs. Pourtant, malgré un bon roulis en courbe et une direction dont la précision et le retour d'informations sont corrects, sans plus, ces deux véhicules pour «*soccer moms*» s'avèrent agréables à conduire sur de longues distances. Cependant, la Routan marque des points à ce chapitre.

Ce trio serait sur le point de connaître quelques changements esthétiques plus ou moins importants. Ces changements pourraient être apportés avant la fin de l'année 2010 et les nouveaux modèles porteront le millésime 2011.

Alain Morin

Volkswagen Routan

PHOTOS: DODGE

DONNÉES 2010

Catégorie	Fourgonnette
Échelle de prix	20945$ à 26295$ (2010)
Garanties	3 ans/60000 km, 5 ans/100000 km
Assemblage	Windsor, Ontario, Canada
Cote d'assurance	moyenne

CHÂSSIS - DONNÉES POUR SE STOW'N GO

Emp/lon/lar/haut	3078/5144/2000/1750 mm
Coffre	920 à 4070 litres
Réservoir	76 litres
Nombre coussins sécurité	6
Antipatinage / contrôle stabilité	oui / oui
Suspension avant	indépendante, jambes de force
Suspension arrière	semi-indépendante, poutre de torsion
Freins avant / arrière	disque (ABS) / disque (ABS)
Direction	à crémaillère, assistée
Diamètre de braquage	11,9 m
Pneus avant / arrière	P225/65R16 / P225/65R16
Poids	1960 kg
Capacité de remorquage	1727 kg (3807 lb)

COMPOSANTES MÉCANIQUES

Grand Caravan	
Cylindrée, soupapes, alim.	V6 3,3 litres 12 s atmos.
Puissance / Couple	175 chevaux / 205 lb-pi
Tr. base (opt) / rouage base (opt)	A4 / Tr
0-100 / 80-120 / 100-0 km/h	12,3 s / 9,9 s / 44,0 m
Type ess. / ville / autoroute	Ordinaire / 12,6 / 8,4 l/100 km

Grand Caravan, Town & Country, Routan	
Cylindrée, soupapes, alim.	V6 4,0 litres 24 s atmos.
Puissance / Couple	251 chevaux / 259 lb-pi
Tr. base (opt) / rouage base (opt)	A6 / Tr
0-100 / 80-120 / 100-0 km/h	8,6 s / 7,6 s / 45,5 m
Type ess. / ville / autoroute	Ordinaire / 12,2 / 7,9 l/100 km

DANS LA MÊME CATÉGORIE

Honda Odyssey, Kia Sedona, Nissan Quest, Toyota Sienna

DU NOUVEAU EN 2011

Nouveau modèle pourrait être dévoilé en cours d'année

NOS IMPRESSIONS

Agrément de conduite:	■■■■■■■□□□	7/10
Fiabilité:	■■■■■□□□□□	5/10
Sécurité:	■■■■■■■■□□	8/10
Qualités hivernales:	■■■■■■■□□□	7/10
Espace intérieur:	■■■■■■■■□□	8/10
Confort:	■■■■■■■■□□	8/10

www.dodge.ca

Plus d'informations dans la section statistiques en dernière partie du Guide

ON RÊVE TOUS D'UNE FERRARI...

Au Salon de l'auto de Montréal, en janvier 2010, un jeune couple s'arrête au kiosque du *Guide de l'auto* pour s'informer sur la Audi Q5. Au fil de la conversation, on en vient à parler du nouveau Chevrolet Equinox et, enfin, du Dodge Journey. Tout à fait par hasard, j'ai rencontré à nouveau ce même couple au Salon de l'auto de Québec, deux mois plus tard. Devinez quoi? Ils s'apprêtaient à faire l'achat d'un Journey! Entre le rêve et la réalité, il y a parfois un décalage...

Remarquez que ce couple, dont la femme était de plus en plus enceinte au fil des Salons, n'a pas fait un mauvais choix. Tout d'abord, la carrosserie n'est pas laide du tout, d'autant plus que les dimensions du véhicule sont tout à fait acceptables. Plus long, plus large et plus haut que les Kia Rondo et Mazda5, tout en étant moins massif qu'un Dodge Grand Caravan, le Journey pourrait, s'il possédait des portes latérales coulissantes, mériter l'appellation de mini fourgonnette.

DU BON... ET DU MOINS BON

L'habitacle, on s'en doute, est passablement grand, suffisamment en tout cas pour offrir trois rangées de sièges. Nous passerons sous silence la piètre qualité de certains plastiques du tableau de bord, les pièces mal alignées et l'allure plutôt ordinaire des sièges, au demeurant confortables. Accéder à ces sièges avant de manière élégante demande une certaine habitude puisqu'ils sont placés assez loin à l'intérieur du véhicule. La position de conduite se trouve facilement et la vision périphérique est excellente... sauf vers l'avant, gracieuseté des piliers très larges du pare-brise. Pour voir en arrière, on peut se fier sur de grands rétroviseurs extérieurs. Les jauges sont facilement lisibles, mais leur design, qui semble emprunté à un Datsun 1979, peut ne pas plaire à toutes les rétines.

S'il est un point où le Journey mérite une étoile dans son cahier, c'est au niveau des espaces de rangement. On ne finit plus d'en découvrir de nouveaux! Deux coffres à gants, un bac sur le dessus du tableau de bord, un autre sous le siège du passager avant de certaines versions, sous le plancher des places arrière, etc. Les sièges de la deuxième rangée offrent beaucoup d'espace et de confort tandis que ceux de la troisième rangée, optionnelle, ne sont pas si mal... pour des sièges de troisième rangée! Quant au coffre, lorsque les dossiers de la troisième rangée sont relevés, l'espace y est forcément réduit mais pas autant que dans celui de la Mazda5 ou de la Kia Rondo, par exemple. Une fois ces dossiers rabattus, de la place, il y en a!

UN MOTEUR OU L'AUTRE, VOUS SAVEZ...

Pour mouvoir le Journey, Dodge fait appel à un quatre cylindres de 2,4 litres qui se tirerait mieux d'affaires si on ne lui avait pas foutu dans les pattes une transmission à quatre rapports qui change rarement de rapports au bon moment. Malgré tout, les performances sont correctes, tout comme la consommation d'essence... lorsque seul le conducteur est inclus! Ajoutez quelques passagers avec bagages et le commentaire sera tout autre! De

Dimensions correctes
Habitacle accueillant
Nombreux espaces de rangement
V6 assez performant
Prix bien étudiés

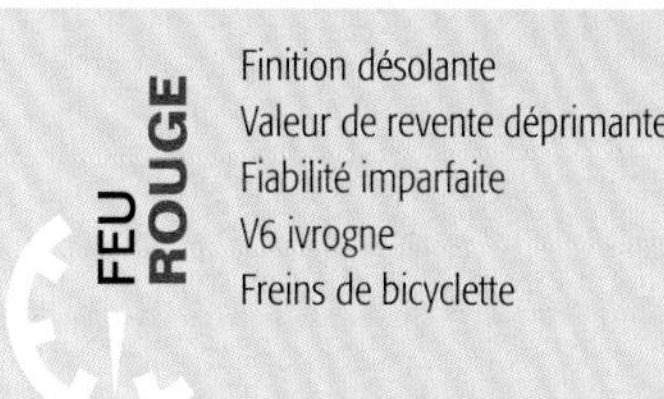

Finition désolante
Valeur de revente déprimante
Fiabilité imparfaite
V6 ivrogne
Freins de bicyclette

son côté, le V6 amène des accélérations plus musclées, mais boit comme s'il n'y avait pas de lendemain ! Au moins, il permet de remorquer davantage (3 500 lbs contre 1 000 pour le 2,4 l). Ce moteur est associé à une transmission automatique à six rapports beaucoup plus compétente que le V4, même si, sur un des modèles essayés, il valait mieux passer les rapports manuellement dans les tronçons de route plus escarpés, l'empêchant ainsi de chasser entre les rapports. Contrairement au Mazda5 et au Rondo, le Journey propose le rouage intégral sur certains modèles, ce qui lui vaut assurément plusieurs ventes.

Le Journey est construit autour du châssis allongé de la Chrysler Sebring et l'on a davantage l'impression de conduire une auto qu'une camionnette. De là à dire qu'il adopte un comportement sportif, il n'y a qu'un pas. Un pas qu'il ne faut surtout pas franchir ! Les suspensions sont invariablement trop souples, même sur le modèle R/T, supposément plus sportif. La direction brille d'imprécision et les freins sont incapables de stopper le véhicule dans des distances correctes. Il faut dire que chausser un véhicule de pneus d'origine qui sont à peine bons pour se retrouver sous une brouette ne peut pas créer de miracle !

Donc, inutile de vouloir jouer les Andrew Ranger au volant du Journey. L'avant veut continuer tout droit et, de toutes façons, le siège du conducteur n'offre aucun soutien, ce qui ralentit aussitôt les ardeurs. Les différents systèmes de contrôle de la traction et de la stabilité latérale interviennent avec l'autorité d'un vieux Frère du Sacré-Cœur, une règle en bois dans les mains. Donc, si vous prévoyez un peu d'excitation lors de vos randonnées, optez plutôt pour une version à quatre cylindres, qui s'avère un peu plus agile, en raison de son poids moins élevé.

Sur le marché depuis déjà trois ans, le Journey est sur le point de connaître plusieurs changements. Malheureusement, ils seront dévoilés beaucoup trop tard pour rencontrer la date d'impression du présent Guide. Les rumeurs les plus sérieuses parlent d'un habitacle tout nouveau (ça ne fera pas de tort...) et de nouveaux moteurs. Le V6 Pentastar qui a déjà trouvé sa place dans le Grand Cherokee ferait très rapidement oublier le triste V6 de 3,5 litres actuel. Et pourquoi pas un nouveau quatre cylindres Multi-air de Fiat? Certains rêveurs parlent même déjà d'un modèle SRT. Ce ne sont pas les idées qui manquent, il y a tant à faire...

Alain Morin

PHOTOS : DODGE

DODGE JOURNEY

DONNÉES 2010

Catégorie	Multisegment
Échelle de prix	18 745 $ à 27 395 $ (2010)
Garanties	3 ans/60 000 km, 5 ans/100 000 km
Assemblage	Toluca, Mexique
Cote d'assurance	n.d.

CHÂSSIS - DONNÉES POUR R/T TI

Emp/lon/lar/haut	2 891/4 887/1 834/1 692 mm
Coffre	1 121 à 1 914 litres
Réservoir	81 litres
Nombre coussins sécurité	6
Antipatinage / contrôle stabilité	oui / oui
Suspension avant	indépendante, jambes de force
Suspension arrière	indépendante, multibras
Freins avant / arrière	disque (ABS) / disque (ABS)
Direction	à crémaillère, assistée
Diamètre de braquage	11,7 m
Pneus avant / arrière	225/55R19 / 225/55R19
Poids	1 923 kg
Capacité de remorquage	454 kg (1 000 lb)

COMPOSANTES MÉCANIQUES

SE, SE Plus

Cylindrée, soupapes, alim.	4L 2,4 litres 16 s atmos.
Puissance / Couple	173 chevaux / 166 lb-pi
Tr. base (opt) / rouage base (opt)	A4 / Tr
0-100 / 80-120 / 100-0 km/h	12,5 s / 10,0 s / 45,6 m
Type ess. / ville / autoroute	Ordinaire / 11,0 / 7,9 l/100 km

SXT, R/T TI

Cylindrée, soupapes, alim.	V6 3,5 litres 24 s atmos.
Puissance / Couple	235 chevaux / 232 lb-pi
Tr. base (opt) / rouage base (opt)	A6 / Tr (Int)
0-100 / 80-120 / 100-0 km/h	9,2 s / 7,9 s / 45,6 m
Type ess. / ville / autoroute	Ordinaire / 13,6 / 8,7 l/100 km

DANS LA MÊME CATÉGORIE

Chevrolet Equinox, Ford Edge, Kia Rondo, Mazda5, Toyota Venza

DU NOUVEAU EN 2011

Nouveau modèle pourrait être dévoilé en cours d'année

NOS IMPRESSIONS

Agrément de conduite :	7/10
Fiabilité :	6/10
Sécurité :	8/10
Qualités hivernales :	8/10
Espace intérieur :	7/10
Confort :	7/10

www.dodge.ca

Plus d'informations dans la section statistiques en dernière partie du Guide

Jeep Liberty

SACRÉ CLOTAIRE!

À la lecture de la fiche technique du duo formé par les Dodge Nitro et Jeep Liberty, il y a de quoi être impressionné : moteur de base de 210 chevaux, 235 livres-pied de couple, 5 000 livres de capacité de remorquage, rouage 4x4 à gamme basse, suspensions indépendantes modernes, pneus de 20 pouces pour le Nitro, etc. Les espoirs les plus fous sont permis...

Cependant, les Nitro et Liberty ont le crayon un peu trop enflammé. Remarquez qu'on ne traite pas ce crayon de menteur. C'est juste que lorsque tous les éléments, à première vue prometteurs, sont assemblés, on se rend compte que quelque chose cloche.

En 2007, la division Dodge accouchait d'un nouveau VUS compact, le Nitro. Superbement carrée, sa silhouette en a fait craquer plus d'un et d'une. Il ne fut pas long que nous découvrîmes un véhicule bien loin de combler les attentes... L'année suivante, dans un geste aussi incompréhensible qu'insensé, Jeep revit de fond en comble son Liberty, qui pourtant connaissait une belle carrière, en lui donnant la plupart des éléments du raté de la famille, le Nitro. Pour scraper un véhicule, les gens de chez Chrysler n'ont quelquefois pas leur pareil! Et on se demande pourquoi cette entreprise vivote aujourd'hui...

BEAUX MAIS INCOMPÉTENTS

La silhouette de nos deux paumés a beau être fort réussie, il ne faut pas s'en approcher de trop près, la qualité de la finition laissant fortement à désirer. D'ailleurs, la peinture est très fière d'avoir remporté le titre de Miss Orange, tellement elle présente d'aspérités... Dans l'habitacle, le tableau de bord de l'un comme de l'autre est esthétiquement réussi, réunissant un mélange de modernité et de robustesse qui sied bien à un 4x4. Mais là s'arrêtent les compliments. L'intérieur n'est pas très grand et les occupants des places avant doivent composer avec un plancher des plus mal foutus qui leur fait toujours chercher une place où mettre les pieds. Le conducteur, lui, n'a même pas droit à un repose-pied. Les sièges sont assez confortables mais n'offrent que très, très peu de soutien latéral et les très grandes personnes pourraient trouver qu'elles n'ont pas suffisamment de dégagement. Mais même une personne normalement constituée doit se résigner à conduire avec des jambes trop rapprochées ou des bras trop tendus, la position de conduite étant probablement un élément jugé non nécessaire par les ingénieurs de Chrysler... Les gens assis à l'arrière, du moins ceux qui auront réussi à s'y rendre, devront faire avec un banc d'église. C'est sans doute la raison pour laquelle, après quelques kilomètres, ils se mettent à prononcer des mots religieux... Le coffre est assez grand et le fait que le dossier des sièges se rabatte à plat ajoute à sa polyvalence. D'ailleurs, il y a un bon bac de rangement sous le plancher mais il ne peut contenir un bidon de lave-glace.

Côté moteur, le Liberty (un nom cher aux Américains et complètement ridiculisé par Jeep) et le Nitro (qu'on aimerait faire sauter)

FEU VERT

Allure sympathique
Bonnes capacités de remorquage
Prix corrects
4x4 sérieux (Jeep Liberty)

FEU ROUGE

Inconfort notoire
Consommation à pleurer
Moteur 3,7 litres exécrable
Finition incompétente
Valeur de revente malsaine

font appel à un V6 de 3,7 litres dont les performances sont nettement plus audibles que véloces. Tenter d'extirper le moindrement de plaisir de ce moteur revient à tenter de déplacer le barrage de Manic 5 avec un tracteur à gazon. En plus, son appétit en carburant est plutôt élevé. Le Nitro, pour tenter de se sortir de cette vie de misère, s'accroche aussi à un V6 de 4,0 litres carrément plus performant et qui consomme à peine plus que l'autre, c'est-à-dire quand même beaucoup. Il faut ici dire merci à la transmission automatique qui, lorsqu'associée au 4,0 litres, comporte cinq rapports, soit un de plus qu'avec le 3,7.

CHOISIR ENTRE : POURRI, LAMENTABLE OU INFECT

Alors, le choix est évident, non ? Et non, il n'est pas évident que le Nitro 4,0 litres est le véhicule à se procurer entre les deux. Si vous aimez les suspensions de Massey Ferguson 1913, par contre, il vous comblera d'aise ! Celles des versions dotées du 3,7 litres, sont, au contraire, tout à fait... (Choisir un des qualificatifs ci-haut mentionnés.) On aura deviné que la conduite de ces mésadaptés est loin d'être celle d'une Porsche Boxster ! La caisse des Liberty et Nitro de base penche indûment à la moindre courbe. Sans parler de comportement sportif, le Nitro 4,0 litres s'avère plus agréable à conduire... sur une route en parfait état. Si, au moins, la direction était correcte ! Je vous laisse le soin de choisir un des deux adjectifs qui reste pour la qualifier. Quant aux freins, ils sont tout simplement... (Choisir.) Les distances d'arrêt ne sont pas beaucoup plus longues que les autres modèles de la même catégorie, mais rarement ai-je vu une pédale aussi mal dosée et mal placée. Bref, les freins sont à l'image du reste...

Le Jeep, comme son nom l'exige, propose un rouage intégral plus performant que celui du Nitro avec sa gamme basse et se mérite même la mention « Trail Rated ». Cependant, la plupart des gens se satisferont parfaitement de l'intégrale du Nitro.

Alors que plusieurs produits du Groupe Chrysler connaîtront des changements assez importants d'ici quelques mois, rien ne semble être prévu pour notre « duo d'humoristes ». On chuchote que le Nitro ne serait disponible qu'avec le 4,0 litres et que ses suspensions seraient nouvelles et sportives (en constatant ce qu'ils ont fait avec l'ancienne, ça fait peur !) Le Liberty, lui, ne connaîtra aucun changement. À suivre... de loin.

Alain Morin

Dodge Nitro

PHOTOS : DODGE

Catégorie	VUS
Échelle de prix	28 495 $ (2010)
Garanties	3 ans/60 000 km, 5 ans/100 000 km
Assemblage	Toledo, Ohio, É-U
Cote d'assurance	passable

CHÂSSIS - DONNÉES POUR NITRO SXT 4X4

Emp/lon/lar/haut	2 763/4 544/1 857/1 775 mm
Coffre	909 à 2 141 litres
Réservoir	74 litres
Nombre coussins sécurité	4
Antipatinage / contrôle stabilité	oui / oui
Suspension avant	indépendante, bras inégaux
Suspension arrière	essieu rigide, multibras
Freins avant / arrière	disque (ABS) / disque (ABS)
Direction	à crémaillère, ass. variable
Diamètre de braquage	11,1 m
Pneus avant / arrière	P235/65R17 / P235/65R17
Poids	1 874 kg
Capacité de remorquage	907 kg (1 999 lb)

COMPOSANTES MÉCANIQUES

Nitro, Liberty

Cylindrée, soupapes, alim.	V6 3,7 litres 12 s atmos.
Puissance / Couple	210 chevaux / 235 lb-pi
Tr. base (opt) / rouage base (opt)	A4 / 4x4
0-100 / 80-120 / 100-0 km/h	9,5 s / 8,3 s / 43,2 m
Type ess. / ville / autoroute	Ordinaire / 14 / 9,7 l/100 km

Nitro

Cylindrée, soupapes, alim.	V6 4,0 litres 24 s atmos.
Puissance / Couple	260 chevaux / 265 lb-pi
Tr. base (opt) / rouage base (opt)	A5 / 4x4
0-100 / 80-120 / 100-0 km/h	7,7 s / 6,7 s / 43,2 m
Type ess. / ville / autoroute	Ordinaire / 14 / 9,7 l/100 km

DANS LA MÊME CATÉGORIE

Chevrolet Equinox, Ford Escape, Hyundai Santa Fe, Kia Sorento, Mazda Tribute, Mitsubishi Outlander, Suzuki Grand Vitara, Toyota RAV4

DU NOUVEAU EN 2011

Aucun changement majeur

NOS IMPRESSIONS

Agrément de conduite :	5/10
Fiabilité :	2/10
Sécurité :	8/10
Qualités hivernales :	8/10
Espace intérieur :	7/10
Confort :	6/10

www.dodge.ca

Plus d'informations dans la section statistiques en dernière partie du Guide

FIN DE CARRIÈRE?

Au moment d'écrire ces lignes, l'avenir de la Viper est pour le moins incertain. À l'époque, pour Chrysler, c'était un moyen d'avoir une voiture phare pour rehausser l'image de la marque Dodge et rivaliser directement avec les versions plus performantes de la Corvette. Aujourd'hui, avec la reprise de Chrysler par le groupe Fiat, le contexte est on ne peut plus différent et rien n'est assuré pour la survie à long terme de cette sportive américaine.

En 2010, Dodge n'aura produit que 500 exemplaires de la Viper, l'usine de Conner Avenue, où elle était construite, ayant cessé ses activités à l'été 2010. Pour l'instant, Dodge ne prévoit pas construire de Viper en 2011, mais une nouvelle version de ce modèle pourrait renaître en 2012, selon un scénario actuellement à l'étude par la haute direction de la marque. De ce côté, il est clair que la Viper jouit de l'appui indéfectible de Ralph Gilles, natif de Montréal, ayant œuvré pendant longtemps au département de design de Chrysler, et qui est présentement le grand patron de la marque Dodge. Qu'à cela ne tienne, les partisans du projet devront faire la démonstration hors de tout doute que le plan de relance de la Viper repose sur des bases solides au plan financier et que le nouveau modèle est en mesure de satisfaire les normes antipollution qui entreront en vigueur au cours des prochaines années, ce qui est loin d'être évident…

L'ÉPREUVE DU CIRCUIT

Conduire la Viper sur un circuit, là où l'on peut exploiter pleinement son potentiel de performance de façon sécuritaire, est un pur délice. Au cours des dernières années, j'ai souvent eu ce privilège en tant que directeur du Challenge Trioomph où la Viper faisait partie de notre flotte de voitures exotiques. Dès la sortie des puits, on sent toute la puissance du moteur qui catapulte littéralement la voiture en avant avec une facilité absolument déconcertante. Ici, l'expression américaine « There's no substitute for cubic inches » prend tout son sens, alors que le V10 monte en régime avec une sonorité plus que présente. De ce côté, il faut préciser qu'il est très facile de faire décoller la Viper qui est dotée d'un embrayage à deux disques, lequel est simple à actionner parce qu'il demande moins d'efforts. De plus, la Viper est équipée d'un différentiel à glissement limité qui joue parfaitement son rôle en permettant que toute la puissance du moteur soit livrée à la route. C'est justement lors de la sortie des virages que l'on apprécie le travail de ce différentiel qui aide le conducteur à bien exploiter les 600 chevaux avec un dosage précis de l'accélérateur.

La Viper étant totalement dépourvue des « anges gardiens » électroniques comme la traction asservie ou le contrôle électronique de la stabilité, il faut donc l'apprivoiser et correctement réchauffer les pneumatiques avant d'aller chercher ses limites; elle fait partie de ces voitures qui sont radicales au point de commander le respect. Au fil des tours, le point faible le plus critique devient rapidement évident, soit la performance au freinage. La Viper est

Puissance moteur
Embrayage progressif
Rapport performances/prix intéressant
Exclusivité assurée

Absence de contrôle de stabilité
Freins un peu justes
Habitacle exigu
Voiture trois saisons

équipée d'un système de freinage mis au point par les experts de Brembo en Italie, et la performance en conduite normale ne pose aucun problème, mais sur circuit, l'efficacité des freins diminuait légèrement tour après tour, ce qui est normal. Néanmoins, il devenait alors difficile de bien sentir l'effort de freinage maximal avant l'intervention du système ABS, la pédale de frein ne donnant pas beaucoup de *feedback*. Il fallait donc appuyer très fermement sur les freins, ce qui provoquait l'entrée en action du système ABS, entraînant automatiquement l'allongement des distances de freinage. Pour le reste, piloter une Viper sur un circuit relève de la jouissance, puisqu'il est relativement facile d'initier de belles glissades en entrée de virage en faisant un transfert de poids vers l'avant pour ensuite compléter la glisse en profitant des 600 chevaux sous le pied droit...

Le mot-clé à retenir pour piloter rapidement une Viper sur le circuit est le mot anglais *smooth*, que l'on peut traduire par progressif, graduel ou fluide. Au volant de la Viper, on n'écrase pas l'accélérateur à fond d'un coup brutal, mais on appuie énergiquement et progressivement sur l'accélérateur, on ne freine pas violemment, mais on trouve le point de friction des freins avant d'appuyer avec force sur la pédale, on ne donne pas de coup de volant brusque, mais on inscrit graduellement la voiture en virage. Ce n'est qu'en conduisant de cette façon que l'on peut atteindre le maximum de ce que la Viper a à offrir. Complétons ce portrait par des statistiques éloquentes: 4,0 secondes pour le sprint de 0 à 100 kilomètres/heure, une vitesse de pointe de 322 kilomètres/heures (200 milles à l'heure) et une accélération latérale de 1,05 G en virage.

Avant d'arriver au circuit, il faut cependant emprunter les routes balisées où la conduite d'une Viper ne présente pas de problèmes majeurs, mais plutôt certains inconvénients, le côté pratique étant loin d'être évident, la visibilité étant limitée et le conducteur devant apprivoiser la bête qui est totalement dépourvue des « anges gardiens » électroniques que l'on retrouve maintenant sur toutes les voitures haut de gamme. De plus, le niveau sonore perçu dans l'habitacle fait en sorte que le confort est relatif, même si le moteur ne tourne qu'à 1 250 tours/minute, soit presque au ralenti, alors que la Viper file à 100 kilomètres/heure en sixième vitesse...

Gabriel Gélinas

PHOTOS: DODGE

DODGE VIPER

Catégorie	Coupé, *Roadster*
Échelle de prix	98 895 $ à 99 895 $ (2010)
Garanties	3 ans/60 000 km, 3 ans/60 000 km
Assemblage	Détroit, Michigan, É-U
Cote d'assurance	n.d.

CHÂSSIS - DONNÉES POUR SRT10 COUPE

Emp/lon/lar/haut	2 510/4 459/1 911/1 210 mm
Coffre	415 litres
Réservoir	70 litres
Nombre coussins sécurité	2
Antipatinage / contrôle stabilité	non / non
Suspension avant	indépendante, bras inégaux
Suspension arrière	indépendante, bras inégaux
Freins avant / arrière	disque (ABS) / disque (ABS)
Direction	à crémaillère
Diamètre de braquage	12,3 m
Pneus avant / arrière	P275/35ZR18 / P345/30ZR19
Poids	1 565 kg
Capacité de remorquage	non recommandé

COMPOSANTES MÉCANIQUES

SRT10	
Cylindrée, soupapes, alim.	V10 8,4 litres 20 s atmos.
Puissance / Couple	600 chevaux / 560 lb-pi
Tr. base (opt) / rouage base (opt)	M6 / Prop
0-100 / 80-120 / 100-0 km/h	4,0 s / 3,6 s / 36,5 m
Type ess. / ville / autoroute	Super / 16,8 / 9,2 l/100 km

DANS LA MÊME CATÉGORIE

Aston Martin Vantage, Audi R8, BMW Série 6, Chevrolet Corvette, Ferrari 458 Italia, Jaguar XK, Lamborghini Gallardo, Maserati Gran Turismo, Mercedes-Benz Classe SL, Nissan GT-R, Porsche 911

DU NOUVEAU EN 2011

Aucun changement majeur. Sans doute la dernière année de production.

NOS IMPRESSIONS

Agrément de conduite:	8/10
Fiabilité:	4/10
Sécurité:	8/10
Qualités hivernales:	nulles
Espace intérieur:	5/10
Confort:	5/10

www.dodge.ca

Plus d'informations dans la section statistiques en dernière partie du Guide

FORZA ITALIA

La plus récente et la plus performante des Ferrari actuelles a été nommée en l'honneur de son pays d'origine, selon la volonté de Luca di Montezemolo, chef de la direction de la marque au cheval cabré. Quant à sa désignation 458, elle évoque la cylindrée (4,5 litres) ainsi que le nombre de cylindres (8) du moteur, tout comme à la belle époque.

Si le respect de la tradition établie demeure une considération de premier plan chez Ferrari, le constructeur italien joue à fond la carte du développement technique lorsque vient le temps de concevoir de nouveaux modèles. En effet, il semble puiser son inspiration dans le développement effréné de ses monoplaces de Formule Un. Elle est peut-être moins élégante que les autres modèles de la marque, mais la 458 Italia a été développée avec une aérodynamique étudiée en soufflerie afin d'optimiser son potentiel de performance, tout comme les F1 actuelles.

C'est pourquoi l'on retrouve toute une série d'éléments aérodynamiques qui sont intégrés, pas toujours très subtilement, à la carrosserie de la voiture, dont le cockpit ressemble davantage au *canopy* d'un avion de chasse. Du nombre, on dénote la présence de très petites ouvertures, pratiquées près des phares, afin de canaliser le flot d'air à haute vitesse et réduire ainsi la portance des ailes avant. À très haute vitesse, les languettes de plastique flexibles intégrées à la partie avant vont se mettre à fléchir de quelques centimètres afin de canaliser le flot d'air sous la voiture plutôt qu'au travers des radiateurs, toujours en vue de réduire la portance.

Également, on retrouve des prises d'air courbées, juste à côté du vitrage latéral. Celles-ci servent à alimenter le moteur et leur design particulier permet justement au V8 de développer 5 chevaux de plus que si elles n'étaient pas fonctionnelles. Stylisée par Pininfarina, la F458 Italia s'approche beaucoup de la super-voiture Enzo, surtout du côté de la partie arrière qui est plus basse que celle de la F430. Le moteur demeure bien visible sous le vitrage de la lunette arrière et on y remarque également la présence de trois tubulures d'échappement localisées au centre de la voiture, tout comme sur la célèbre F40, et les phares s'affichent à la verticale.

UN V8 D'ANTHOLOGIE

Avec le nouveau V8 développé pour la 458 Italia, Ferrari inscrit un nouveau record mondial, soit celui du moteur atmosphérique qui développe le plus de puissance pour sa cylindrée. Avec ses 570 chevaux pour 4,5 litres, le V8 livre presque 125 chevaux par litre, ce qui est tout simplement phénoménal. Pour y arriver, les ingénieurs de Ferrari ont adopté l'injection électronique de carburant, tout comme sur la récente California. Ils ont également amélioré l'entrée d'air et réduit la friction interne, tout en portant le taux de compression à 12.5:1. Le résultat est un moteur capable de tourner jusqu'à 9000 tours/minute, ce qui est prodigieux pour un V8 de 4,5 litres. Le son de ce moteur en haute voltige est tout simplement phénoménal.

FEU VERT

- Performances à couper le souffle
- Aérodynamique très étudiée
- Son fabuleux du moteur
- Boîte à double embrayage très rapide

FEU ROUGE

- Prix stratosphérique
- Délais de livraison
- Utilisation estivale seulement
- Visibilité vers l'arrière

Développée pour la California, la boîte à double embrayage et sept rapports reprend ici du service; elle a été optimisée en fonction de la vocation nettement plus sportive, voire radicale, de la 458 et c'est la seule boîte disponible sur cette voiture, la boîte manuelle qui était disponible sur la F430 ayant été reléguée aux oubliettes. L'une des particularités les plus appréciées de la boîte à double embrayage est la fonction qui permet de rétrograder successivement de plusieurs rapports, lors d'un freinage appuyé à l'approche d'un virage, en maintenant une pression constante sur le palier de commande de gauche. Par ailleurs, puisqu'il est question de freinage, précisons que la 458 Italia reçoit des freins en céramique de carbone en dotation de série, histoire d'optimiser la performance de freinage. Les liaisons au sol sont assurées par une suspension dont les amortisseurs sont pilotés électroniquement, afin d'assurer la meilleure tenue de route possible et de réduire au minimum l'effet de plongée au freinage ou le roulis en virages. La direction s'avère plutôt légère, mais d'une précision remarquable et la 458 Italia s'inscrit en virage comme un véritable scalpel. Malgré son potentiel de performance très élevé, la 458 Italia est relativement facile à conduire et ne demande que très peu d'efforts de la part du conducteur, hormis celui d'apprendre à apprivoiser la nouvelle disposition des commandes au volant.

UN VOLANT *HIGH-TECH*

Tout comme sur une Ferrari de F1, le volant de la 458 Italia regroupe plusieurs fonctions, en plus du bouton de démarrage et du *manettino*, comme sur la F430. En effet, les commandes d'indicateurs de changement de voie se retrouvent sur le volant, ce qui élimine carrément le traditionnel bras de commande. De plus, c'est sur le volant que l'on commande le passage aux phares de route et que l'on actionne les essuie-glaces. Le tachymètre conserve la couleur jaune adoptée sur la F430 ainsi que sa position centrale dans le bloc d'instruments. Il est entouré de deux petits écrans servant à relayer les informations du système de navigation et de la radio en plus d'afficher une reproduction numérique d'un indicateur de vitesse analogique.

Ferrari produit environ 6000 voitures par année, et la 458 Italia devrait représenter environ cinquante pour cent des ventes de la marque de Maranello, tout comme la F430 le faisait précédemment. Il est également à prévoir qu'un modèle cabriolet se pointera à l'horizon prochainement, suivi de versions de type Challenge Stradale ou Scuderia, encore plus performantes.

Gabriel Gélinas

PHOTOS: MARC LACHAPELLE

Catégorie	Coupé
Échelle de prix	290 000 $
Garanties	2 ans/illimité, 2 ans/illimité
Assemblage	Maranello, Italie
Cote d'assurance	n.d.

CHÂSSIS - DONNÉES POUR 458 ITALIA

Emp/lon/lar/haut	2 650/4 527/1 937/1 213 mm
Coffre	230 litres
Réservoir	86 litres
Nombre coussins sécurité	2
Antipatinage / contrôle stabilité	oui / oui
Suspension avant	indépendante, double triangulation
Suspension arrière	indépendante, multibras
Freins avant / arrière	disque (ABS) / disque (ABS)
Direction	à crémaillère
Diamètre de braquage	n.d.
Pneus avant / arrière	235/35ZR20 / 295/35ZR20
Poids	1 485 kg
Capacité de remorquage	non recommandé

COMPOSANTES MÉCANIQUES

458 Italia

Cylindrée, soupapes, alim.	V8 4,5 litres 32 s atmos.
Puissance / Couple	570 chevaux / 398 lb-pi
Tr. base (opt) / rouage base (opt)	seq 7 / Prop
0-100 / 80-120 / 100-0 km/h	3,6 s / n.d. / 32,5 m
Type ess. / ville / autoroute	Super / 16,0 / 11,0 l/100 km (est)

DANS LA MÊME CATÉGORIE

Aston Martin DB9, Audi R8, Dodge Viper, Lamborghini Gallardo, Maserati Gran Turismo, Mercedes-Benz Classe SLR, Nissan GT-R

DU NOUVEAU EN 2011

Nouveau modèle

NOS IMPRESSIONS

Agrément de conduite:	■■■■■■■■■□ 9/10
Fiabilité:	Nouveau modèle
Sécurité:	Données insuffisantes
Qualités hivernales:	nulles
Espace intérieur:	■■■■■■■□□□ 7/10
Confort:	■■■■■■■□□□ 7/10

www.ferrariquebec.com

Plus d'informations dans la section statistiques en dernière partie du Guide

QUELQUES VARIATIONS SPECTACULAIRES

Bien que ce constructeur mythique entre tous ait eu largement recours au moteur central, le cœur mécanique des Ferrari les plus rares et les plus précieuses est encore blotti sous le capot avant. Cette configuration mécanique fait un retour au premier plan au sein de la gamme Ferrari avec la série 599 dont les versions les plus récentes sont parmi les voitures les plus puissantes, rapides et techniquement audacieuses jamais conçues et produites à Maranello.

Notre collègue Gabriel Gélinas a présenté, dans la dernière édition du *Guide de l'auto*, ses impressions de conduite après quelques tours intenses du circuit Mont-Tremblant au volant d'une 599 GTB Fiorano. Il fut carrément émerveillé par la sonorité et la puissance du V12 de 6 litres, mais également par la tenue de route, le freinage et la finition de cette grand tourisme d'exception. Ferrari a pourtant trouvé le moyen d'aller plus loin – dans plusieurs directions – avec cette série qui semble inspirer particulièrement ses ingénieurs.

TROIS LETTRES MAGIQUES ET UN CLASSIQUE ASSURÉ

Gabriel mentionnait l'an dernier la 599XX, une version radicalement sportive de la Fiorano et réservée au pilotage sur circuit. Fabriquée à seulement 25 exemplaires et vendue pour près de deux millions de dollars, la 599XX serait devenue par la suite la première voiture « inspirée de la série » à boucler les 20,8 kilomètres de la boucle nord (Nordschleife) du circuit allemand Nürburgring en moins de 7 minutes.

Ferrari dévoila ensuite la troisième voiture de son histoire à porter la rarissime appellation GTO après la 250 GTO des années 60 et la 288 GTO du début des années 80. Contrairement à ces deux voitures qui furent construites en très petit nombre pour obtenir leur homologation en course (d'où ces initiales qui signifient *Gran Turismo Omologato*) la 599 GTO est un pur modèle de série qui sera construit à exactement... 599 exemplaires d'ailleurs déjà tous vendus.

Version achevée du prototype HGTE (Handling GT Evoluzione), la 599 GTO est plus légère que la 599 GTB de 85 kg et son V12 de 6,0 litres produit 670 chevaux à 8 250 tr/min soit presque 50 de plus que la 599 GTB et un de plus que la légendaire Enzo pour laquelle ce moteur fut développé à l'origine. La nouvelle GTO aurait même bouclé le circuit d'essai de Fiorano en 1 min 24 s soit une pleine seconde de mieux que cette dernière, une pure exotique à coque en fibre de carbone et moteur central. Avec un sprint 0-100 km/h en 3,35 secondes et une vitesse de pointe de 335 km/h, Ferrari présente tout bonnement la GTO comme la voiture de route la plus rapide qu'elle n'ait jamais produite.

Pour y arriver, la 599 GTO reprend plusieurs composantes et technologies utilisées sur la 599XX. Parmi elles, des freins Brembo au carbone inspirés carrément de ceux des F1, avec leurs plateaux

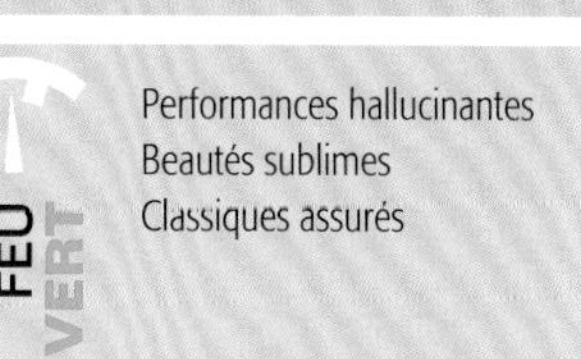

Performances hallucinantes
Beautés sublimes
Classiques assurés

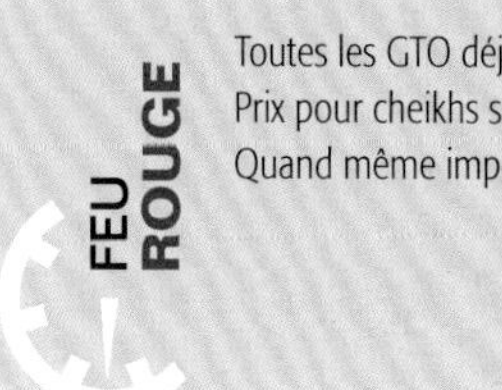

Toutes les GTO déjà vendues
Prix pour cheikhs seulement !
Quand même imposantes

internes qui améliorent le refroidissement, des amortisseurs à variation magnétique de deuxième génération, une direction à crémaillère plus rapide, de nouveaux ressorts, des barres antiroulis plus fermes et de nouveaux pneus Michelin de taille 285/30 à l'avant et 315/35 à l'arrière, montés sur jantes d'alliage de 20 pouces.

Contrairement à la cabine des GTO d'antan qui affichait le dépouillement extrême des voitures de course, l'habitacle de la 599 GTO a droit aux égards que Ferrari avait réservés jusque-là aux versions Scuderia ultrasportives de ses autres séries : sièges plus légers, manettes de sélection plus légères en fibre de carbone pour une boîte de vitesse à double embrayage automatisé plus rapide et volant à segments de fibre de carbone avec diodes pour signaler les changements de rapport en plus du *mannetino* qui permet de choisir entre les divers modes de conduite.

QUAND LE ROUGE PASSE AU VERT

Ferrari n'était pas à court d'idées après avoir complété des sportives extrêmes. Au dernier Salon de Genève, les magiciens de Maranello présentaient ainsi la Hy-KERS, une grande sportive équipée d'un groupe propulseur hybride, rien de moins. Sous une robe d'un vert pâle éclatant, son rouage reprend le système de récupération de l'énergie cinétique (SREC ou KERS en anglais) utilisé par l'équipe de Formule Un durant la saison 2009. D'où ce nom rébarbatif.

Cette mécanique complexe combine des batteries lithium-ion blotties sous le plancher (ce qui abaisse d'ailleurs le centre de gravité de la voiture) et un moteur électrique de 40 kg et 100 chevaux qu'on a couplé directement à un des arbres de la boîte de vitesse à double embrayage. La distribution du couple entre le moteur électrique et le V12 thermique de 612 chevaux se fait ainsi sans à-coups et sans délai.

Ferrari n'a révélé aucune donnée de performance pour la Hy-KERS mais affirme que son groupe hybride émet 35 % moins de gaz carbonique que le V12 seul et peut être adapté à toutes ses voitures. L'intention écologique est noble mais le constructeur italien veut surtout s'assurer que ses étalons soient conformes aux normes d'émissions polluantes plus sévères qui pointent à l'horizon. La survie des Ferrari a de quoi réjouir tous les passionnés.

Marc Lachapelle

PHOTOS : FERRARI

FERRARI 599 / 599 GTO

Catégorie	Coupé
Échelle de prix	403 120 $ (2010) à n.d.
Garanties	2 ans/illimité, 2 ans/illimité
Assemblage	Maranello, Italie
Cote d'assurance	n.d.

CHÂSSIS - DONNÉES POUR GTO

Emp/lon/lar/haut	2 750/4 710/1 962/1 326 mm
Coffre	320 litres
Réservoir	105 litres
Nombre coussins sécurité	2
Antipatinage / contrôle stabilité	oui / oui
Suspension avant	indépendante, bras inégaux
Suspension arrière	indépendante, triangles superposés
Freins avant / arrière	disque (ABS) / disque (ABS)
Direction	à crémaillère, ass. variable
Diamètre de braquage	11,6 m
Pneus avant / arrière	P285/30ZR20 / P315/35ZR20
Poids	1 605 kg
Capacité de remorquage	n.d.

COMPOSANTES MÉCANIQUES

599 GTB Fiorano	
Cylindrée, soupapes, alim.	V12 6,0 litres 48 s atmos.
Puissance / Couple	620 chevaux / 448 lb-pi
Tr. base (opt) / rouage base (opt)	M6 (seq) / Prop
0-100 / 80-120 / 100-0 km/h	3,7 s / 3,0 s / n.d.
Type ess. / ville / autoroute	Super / 19,8 / 13,1 l/100 km

GTO	
Cylindrée, soupapes, alim.	V12 6,0 litres 24 s atmos.
Puissance / Couple	670 chevaux / 457 lb-pi
Tr. base (opt) / rouage base (opt)	M6 / Prop
0-100 / 80-120 / 100-0 km/h	3,4 s / 2,8 s (est) / n.d.
Type ess. / ville / autoroute	Super / n.d. / n.d. l/100 km

DANS LA MÊME CATÉGORIE

Aston Martin One-77, Lamborghini Murciélago, Mercedes-Benz Classe SLS, Porsche 911 Turbo

DU NOUVEAU EN 2011

Modèle GTO, modèle Hy-KERS à venir

NOS IMPRESSIONS

Agrément de conduite :	■■■■■■■■■■	10/10
Fiabilité :	Données insuffisantes	
Sécurité :	■■■■■■■■□□	8/10
Qualités hivernales :	nulles	
Espace intérieur :	■■■■■■□□□□	6/10
Confort :	■■■■■■□□□□	6/10

www.ferrariquebec.com

Plus d'informations dans la section statistiques en dernière partie du Guide

UN V12 POUR QUATRE

Ferrari donne souvent des noms de lieux à ses voitures (Daytona, 360 Modena, etc.), mais à l'occasion elle donne le nom d'individus qui ont marqué l'histoire de la marque. Il en est ainsi avec la 612 Scaglietti, ainsi nommée en hommage à Sergio Scaglietti qui a conçu plusieurs des voitures sport de ce constructeur pendant les années cinquante et soixante. Quant au chiffre de 612, précisons que le chiffre 6 évoque la cylindrée du moteur (5 748 cc arrondi à 6,0) et que le 12, sa configuration à douze cylindres.

La marque de Maranello propose deux voitures de type Gran Turismo à sa clientèle fortunée et si la 599 GTB *Fiorano* n'offre que deux places à bord, la 612 Scaglietti en compte quatre en raison de sa configuration de type 2+2. Ce qui frappe au premier coup d'œil, ce sont les lignes très prononcées qui partent sous la calandre pour remonter sur les phares et se prolonger sur les ailes avant jusqu'à l'arrière de la voiture. La 612 Scaglietti affiche également des flancs incurvés dont le design singulier remonte à la 375MM, un modèle exclusif commandé en 1954 par le réalisateur italien Roberto Rossellini qui en fit cadeau à l'actrice Ingrid Bergman. Même si les proportions de la 612 Scaglietti sont typiques de celle des voitures de cette catégorie et même si la voiture conserve une certaine élégance classique après plusieurs années, le design commence à dater quelque peu.

À l'avant, on se sent tout de suite à l'aise, car la voiture est plutôt large et le pare-brise est relativement éloigné. Dans cette voiture, on respire littéralement le cuir qui recouvre non seulement les sièges, mais plusieurs autres surfaces de l'habitacle. Le charme opère dès les premières minutes passées à son bord, même si prendre place à l'arrière s'avère laborieux, puisque les deux portes de la voiture ne s'ouvrent qu'étroitement. Par ailleurs, les sièges arrière sont très sculptés autour des hanches et il faut placer ses genoux de part et d'autre des sièges avant pour être plus confortable. Même si elle offre quatre places, il y a fort à parier que c'est avec un maximum de deux personnes à bord que la 612 Scaglietti roulera le plus souvent.

GRANDE, MAIS AGILE

Sur le plan technique, la 612 Scaglietti adopte à la fois une structure autoportante de type *space frame* et une carrosserie réalisée entièrement en aluminium, question de réduire le poids de cette GT dont les dimensions sont tout de même imposantes, puisque l'empattement, soit la distance entre l'axe des roues avant et celui des roues arrière, est chiffré à 2 950 millimètres; une longueur égale à l'empattement des VUS de grande taille. Cette longueur d'empattement, ainsi que celle de la voiture elle-même, s'explique par le fait que les concepteurs ont voulu centrer les masses de la voiture en localisant le moteur V12 derrière l'axe des roues avant afin de donner un comportement routier dynamique à la 612 Scaglietti. Le résultat est probant puisque 85 pour cent de la masse de la voiture se trouve localisée

FEU VERT
- Moteur performant
- Tenue de route impeccable
- Exclusivité assurée
- Silhouette classique

FEU ROUGE
- Diffusion limitée
- Piètre visibilité arrière
- Prix exclusif
- Complexité de certaines commandes

entre les trains avant et arrière, ce qui confère une agilité surprenante à la 612 Scaglietti malgré ses grandes dimensions.

UN V12 DÉRIVÉ DE L'ENZO

Le moteur V12 est dérivé de celui de la super-voiture Ferrari Enzo, mais la cylindrée en à été réduite de quelques dixièmes de litre, passant de 6,0 à 5,7 litres, alors que la boîte de vitesse a été localisée près du train arrière, ce qui donne une répartition du poids de 46 pour cent à l'avant et 54 pour cent à l'arrière. Le rapport poids/puissance de la 612 Scaglietti (1 875 kilos/532 chevaux) lui permet d'abattre la marque des 0-100 kilomètres/heure en 4,2 secondes, le quart de mille en 12,3 secondes et la vitesse maximale de 320 kilomètres/heure, selon Ferrari.

Ayant eu l'occasion de boucler quelques tours du circuit Mont Tremblant en plus de rouler sur les routes avoisinantes au volant de la 612 Scaglietti, j'ai été impressionné par sa dynamique. Même s'il s'agit d'une voiture au gabarit imposant pour une sportive, elle m'a toujours donné l'impression d'être moins grande et moins lourde qu'elle ne l'est en réalité, ce qui est le propre des voitures sport qui sont très bien équilibrées. Sur le circuit, il suffisait de régler les amortisseurs à la calibration la plus ferme avant d'attaquer les virages et la voiture faisait ensuite preuve d'un aplomb remarquable. La direction est vive, précise, donne beaucoup de feed-back et le sous-virage n'est pas trop manifeste, malgré le poids élevé de la voiture. Évidemment, il fallait prendre soin d'allonger les distances de freinage par rapport à la F430, mais la 612 Scaglietti m'a tout de même surpris par son endurance au freinage sur circuit, soit l'environnement qui représente la pire torture que l'on puisse infliger à une voiture. Sur la route, le retour aux calibrations plus souples des amortisseurs permettait d'apprécier les qualités dynamiques du véhicule tout en obtenant une conduite plus fluide et moins agressive. C'est justement lors de la conduite plus relaxe que l'on se met à apprécier le confort surprenant de la 612 Scaglietti qui est nettement moins austère que la 599 GTB Fiorano ou la F430.

La 612 Scaglietti représente l'interprétation faite par Ferrari du thème propre aux voitures de type Gran Turismo qui sont capables de performances élevées, mais qui ont comme mission première de parcourir de grandes distances en maintenant le rythme et en assurant un grand confort.

Gabriel Gélinas

PHOTOS : FERRARI

FERRARI 612 SCAGLIETTI

Catégorie	Coupé
Échelle de prix	329 000 $ (2010)
Garanties	2 ans/illimité, 2 ans/illimité
Assemblage	Maranello, Italie
Cote d'assurance	n.d.

CHÂSSIS - DONNÉES POUR 612 SCAGLIETTI

Emp/lon/lar/haut	2 950/4 902/1 957/1 344 mm
Coffre	240 litres
Réservoir	108 litres
Nombre coussins sécurité	4
Antipatinage / contrôle stabilité	oui / oui
Suspension avant	indépendante, multibras
Suspension arrière	indépendante, multibras
Freins avant / arrière	disque (ABS) / disque (ABS)
Direction	à crémaillère, ass. variable
Diamètre de braquage	12,0 m
Pneus avant / arrière	P245/40ZR19 / P285/40ZR19
Poids	1 875 kg
Capacité de remorquage	non recommandé

COMPOSANTES MÉCANIQUES

612 Scaglietti, 612 Scaglietti F1

Cylindrée, soupapes, alim.	V12 5,7 litres 48 s atmos.
Puissance / Couple	532 chevaux / 434 lb-pi
Tr. base (opt) / rouage base (opt)	M6 (seq) / Prop
0-100 / 80-120 / 100-0 km/h	4,2 s / 3,2 s / 32,3 m
Type ess. / ville / autoroute	Super / 22,8 / 12,8 l/100 km

DANS LA MÊME CATÉGORIE

Aston Martin DB9, Bentley Continental, Mercedes-Benz Classe CL65 AMG, Porsche 911 Turbo

DU NOUVEAU EN 2011

Aucun changement majeur

NOS IMPRESSIONS

Agrément de conduite :	8/10
Fiabilité :	8/10
Sécurité :	8/10
Qualités hivernales :	nulles
Espace intérieur :	6/10
Confort :	6/10

www.ferrariquebec.com

Plus d'informations dans la section statistiques en dernière partie du Guide

CALIFORNIA DREAMING...

Nommée ainsi en l'honneur de l'État américain qui représente le plus gros marché pour la marque au cheval cabré, la récente California évoque le modèle 250GT de la fin des années cinquante et la 365 du milieu des années soixante, toutes les deux ayant également été connues sous le nom de California. Elle se distingue aussi en étant la première Ferrari de l'histoire de la marque à adopter la configuration d'un moteur V8 logé à l'avant, la première à être dotée d'un toit rigide-rétractable et la dernière Ferrari stylée par Andrea Pininfarina avant son décès.

Le style est l'un des éléments polarisants de la California, et si la partie avant est généralement considérée comme étant très réussie, la partie arrière essuie son lot de critiques en raison de sa hauteur et de sa largeur, ce qui en fait l'équivalent automobile de la callipyge Beyoncé Knowles. Évidemment, ces formes rondes et galbées à l'arrière sont nécessaires à l'intégration du toit rigide-rétractable qui se range dans le coffre en 15 secondes, faisant alors passer l'espace de chargement de 340 à 240 litres. Vous aurez d'ores et déjà compris que la California vous obligera à voyager léger ou encore à loger certains bagages derrière les sièges avant où l'on retrouve soit l'équivalent de deux strapontins ou un plancher comprenant des sangles d'arrimage, selon la demande de l'acheteur. On remarque tout de même une trappe entre le coffre et les places arrière pour pouvoir loger des skis dans le coffre, ce qui surprend beaucoup sur une Ferrari et qui démontre l'intention du constructeur de vouloir faire de la California une voiture plus conviviale et pratique capable d'être utilisée tous les jours... pourvu que vous rouliez en Californie ou sous d'autres cieux tout aussi cléments.

L'habitacle de ce bolide est plus cossu et luxueux que celui de la F430 ce qui cadre avec sa vocation moins radicale. Mais le volant comporte toujours le *mannetino* permettant de calibrer le degré de sportivité de la voiture en altérant les paramètres de la gestion du moteur, de la boîte de vitesse et de l'intervention des systèmes de contrôle électronique de la stabilité, quoiqu'il n'offre que trois modes sur la California alors qu'il en propose cinq sur la F430.

UNE NOUVELLE BOÎTE À DOUBLE EMBRAYAGE

La California est animée par une version remaniée du moteur de la F430, il s'agit donc d'un V8 de 4,3 litres dont l'alésage a été augmenté alors que sa course a été réduite afin de livrer un peu plus de couple à bas régime. Ce moteur se démarque comme étant le premier de la marque à adopter l'injection directe de carburant, ce qui améliore légèrement le bilan au sujet des émissions de gaz à effet de serre. Malgré le fait que le moteur loge à l'avant, la répartition des masses demeure idéale puisqu'il est localisé derrière l'axe des roues avant, tout comme dans le cas de la 599 GTB Fiorano, et que la boîte de vitesse ainsi que le différentiel sont situés à l'arrière. Jumelée au V8, la présence d'une toute nouvelle boîte à double embrayage à sept rapports, développée par

FERRARI CALIFORNIA

FEU VERT
- Moteur performant
- Exclusivité assurée
- Style distinctif
- Très bonne tenue de route

FEU ROUGE
- Prix stratosphérique
- Diffusion limitée
- Visibilité problématique
- Espace de chargement restreint

l'équipementier Getrag, représente une première pour Ferrari. Cette boîte est une pure merveille avec des changements de rapports en 65 millièmes de seconde en conduite sportive. Aussi, son comportement est plus souple et plus fluide en conduite normale que celle de la F430 lorsque le mode automatique est sélectionné. Une boîte manuelle conventionnelle à six vitesses est également au programme, mais il y a fort à parier que la très grande majorité des acheteurs choisira la boîte à double embrayage.

MOINS RADICALE QU'UNE F430

Lancée à l'attaque en virage, la California fait preuve d'une très bonne tenue de route, malgré les calibrations plus souples de ses suspensions qui font en sorte que l'on ressent un petit effet de plongée vers l'avant lors des freinages intenses de même qu'un certain roulis en courbe qui demeure toutefois bien contrôlé. Ici, le poids plutôt élevé de la voiture est en cause puisqu'elle fait tout de même 1 735 kilos, ce qui est nettement plus que la F430 Spyder. Aussi, la direction est un peu engourdie, pour une Ferrari. Cependant, avec la sélection du mode le plus sportif au moyen du *mannetino* localisé au volant, la California peut même se permettre un comportement légèrement survireur en sortie de courbe, l'électronique autorisant alors une faible glissade bien contrôlée qui fera bien paraître même un conducteur inexpérimenté.

Avec le toit en place, le niveau de confort est excellent, et il faut vraiment atteindre des vitesses largement supérieures à la limite permise avant de percevoir le bruit du vent. Mais le véritable plaisir de conduire se manifeste lorsque la voiture est décapotée, ce qui permet d'apprécier au plus haut point la sonorité du V8, surtout au moment où celui-ci atteint sa limite de révolutions de 8 000 tours/minute. De plus, il faut voir le ballet mécanique du toit qui se rétracte ou se remet en place.

Comme c'est toujours le cas avec les Ferrari, de longs délais sont à prévoir avant de pouvoir obtenir une California, la production étant souvent vendue un an, voire deux, à l'avance dans le cas de certains modèles. Cette production limitée est cependant un gage d'exclusivité qui ne manquera pas d'attirer les automobilistes fortunés qui aiment s'afficher au volant d'une véritable exotique, et pour qui le pouvoir d'attraction de la California est bel et bien réel.

Gabriel Gélinas

PHOTOS : FERRARI

Catégorie	Coupé
Échelle de prix	192 000 $ (2010)
Garanties	2 ans/illimité, 2 ans/illimité
Assemblage	Maranello, Italie
Cote d'assurance	n.d.

CHÂSSIS - DONNÉES POUR CALIFORNIA

Emp/lon/lar/haut	2 670/4 563/1 902/1 308 mm
Coffre	240 à 360 litres
Réservoir	78 litres
Nombre coussins sécurité	4
Antipatinage / contrôle stabilité	oui / oui
Suspension avant	indépendante, double triangulation
Suspension arrière	indépendante, multibras
Freins avant / arrière	disque (ABS) / disque (ABS)
Direction	à crémaillère, ass. variable
Diamètre de braquage	n.d.
Pneus avant / arrière	245/40ZR19 / 285/40ZR19
Poids	1 735 kg
Capacité de remorquage	non recommandé

COMPOSANTES MÉCANIQUES

California

Cylindrée, soupapes, alim.	V8 4,3 litres 32 s atmos.
Puissance / Couple	460 chevaux / 358 lb-pi
Tr. base (opt) / rouage base (opt)	seq (M6) / Prop
0-100 / 80-120 / 100-0 km/h	3,9 s / 2,5 s / 31,0 m
Type ess. / ville / autoroute	Super / 16,9 / 10,6 l/100 km

DANS LA MÊME CATÉGORIE

Aston Martin Vantage, Audi R8, Dodge Viper, Maserati Gran Turismo, Mercedes-Benz Classe SL65 AMG, Nissan GT-R, Porsche 911 Turbo

DU NOUVEAU EN 2011

Aucun changement majeur

NOS IMPRESSIONS

Agrément de conduite :	8/10
Fiabilité :	n.d.
Sécurité :	données insuffisantes
Qualités hivernales :	nulles
Espace intérieur :	6/10
Confort :	6/10

www.ferrariquebec.com

Plus d'informations dans la section statistiques en dernière partie du Guide

LA FILIÈRE ITALIENNE

Si vous n'êtes pas au courant des péripéties financières de la compagnie Chrysler au cours de la dernière année, vous étiez probablement en vacances sur la planète Mars. En effet, après un dépôt de bilan, le constructeur américain a été sauvé de la fermeture et de la liquidation par l'intervention des gouvernements américain, canadien et du constructeur italien Fiat qui en contrôle dorénavant la destinée. Mais contrairement à Daimler qui s'était contenté de développer les voitures Chrysler et Dodge en utilisant certaines composantes des voitures Mercedes-Benz, Fiat a l'intention de commercialiser ses véhicules en Amérique par l'intermédiaire de son propre réseau de concessionnaires.

Toutefois, à part la nouvelle confirmant que la légendaire Fiat 500 sera commercialisée sur notre continent et même fabriquée ici, les détails sont assez nébuleux. Concentrons-nous donc sur la 500.

UN DESIGN EXQUIS

Il faut savoir que cette minivoiture s'inscrit dans la foulée de l'engouement des constructeurs et du public pour la voiture rétro. En effet, au cours des dernières années, on a vu la résurrection de la Mini britannique et de la New Beetle allemande qui ont permis aux nostalgiques et aux BCBG de posséder une version modernisée du passé. En Italie, cette voiture rétro était la fabuleuse 500 dévoilée à la fin des années 50 et qui a été excessivement populaire dans les années 60. L'Italie motorisée à cette époque, c'était la Vespa sur deux roues et la 500 sur quatre. La direction de Fiat a donc ressuscité ce modèle en 2007.

Bien entendu, la nouvelle version est plus grosse que celle qu'elle remplace tout simplement pour répondre à de nouvelles normes de sécurité. Elle demeure une quatre places cependant et elle continue d'offrir la même silhouette. À mon avis, c'est très réussi car elle conserve tout le cachet de sa devancière et ses lignes ont été adaptées avec brio afin d'en faire une voiture moderne. Et c'est la même chose dans l'habitacle alors que la présentation est de notre époque mais avec un sérieux clin d'œil au passé. Contrairement à la première 500 dont la finition se limitait au strict minimum, sa version moderne est un petit bijou de design avec une attention apportée à peu près à tous les éléments. Les places arrière sont par contre beaucoup plus dépouillées de même que le coffre à bagages.

Lors d'un bref essai effectué avec la voiture d'un ami en Europe il y a une couple d'années, j'ai été surpris par l'espace réservé aux occupants des places avant. Quant aux places arrière, comme le dit la documentation de la compagnie, elles ont été dessinées pour accommoder 70 % des tailles adultes. Ce qui signifie en clair que vous avez intérêt à être en bons termes avec la personne assise à côté de vous car c'est un espace de proximité ! Enfin, une version cabriolet est également commercialisée en Europe.

FEU VERT

Silhouette extraordinaire
Habitacle songé
Agréable à conduire
Tenue de route agile
Faible consommation de carburant

FEU ROUGE

Fiabilité inconnue
Réseau de concessionnaires à établir
Places arrière exiguës
Certains détails de finition à revoir
Réputation de la marque à bâtir

ESSENCE ET ÉLECTRICITÉ

Selon toute probabilité, la Fiat 500 sera commercialisée au Canada au cours des 12 prochains mois. Le modèle nord-américain sera doté d'un moteur quatre cylindres de 1,4 litre d'une puissance de 100 chevaux et associé à une boîte manuelle à six rapports. Il sera également possible de commander une boîte robotisée à cinq rapports. Avec la version munie de la boîte manuelle, le 0-100 km/h est bouclé en 10,5 secondes, ce qui devrait être adéquat. Soulignons au passage que sa vitesse de pointe est de 182 km/h. Il faut savoir que ce petit moteur n'est pas rétro du tout avec quatre soupapes par cylindre et le calage continuellement variables des soupapes. Sa consommation de carburant devrait être légèrement inférieure à 5,0 litres aux 100 km.

Et comme la compagnie s'occupe davantage d'exhiber ses voitures que de nous donner des précisions, il n'a pas été confirmé que la version Abarth, plus sportive, sera vendue en Amérique. Mais puisqu'on l'a exhibée au dernier Salon de l'auto de Toronto, on peut conclure qu'elle sera du voyage. Cette fois, le moteur est plus puissant et il permet de boucler le 0-100 km/h en 8,0 secondes en raison de son moteur de 133 chevaux.

Au début de cette année, la direction de la compagnie Chrysler dont le nom officiel est dorénavant Chrysler LLC a annoncé qu'elle allait produire une version électrique de son modèle 500. Vous l'avez deviné, elle sera identifiée comme étant la 500EV. Cette voiture sera construite aux États-Unis à partir de 2012. Au chapitre de la mécanique, elle comportera trois systèmes principaux: un module de motorisation électrique, une batterie ion lithium et une unité de contrôle du courant électrique. Selon les dires du constructeur, la plate-forme de la Fiat 500 est idéale pour la réalisation d'une voiture électrique.

Reste à savoir maintenant si les Américains et les Canadiens accueilleront cette voiture Fiat à bras ouverts. Plusieurs personnes vont se souvenir que cette compagnie a quitté l'Amérique au milieu des années 70 alors que ces voitures connaissaient d'importants problèmes de fiabilité et de rouille alors que son réseau de concessionnaires n'était pas sérieux. D'ailleurs, pour plusieurs, Fiat signifie « Fix it Again Tony » ou en version française « Répare à nouveau, Tony » ! Chez Fiat on espère que les gens ont la mémoire courte…

Denis Duquet

PHOTOS : FIAT

Catégorie	*Hatchback*
Échelle de prix	n.d.
Garanties	n.d.
Assemblage	n.d.
Cote d'assurance	n.d.

CHÂSSIS - DONNÉES POUR FIAT 500

Emp/lon/lar/haut	2 300/3 546/1 627/1 485 mm
Coffre	n.d.
Réservoir	35 litres
Nombre coussins sécurité	7
Antipatinage / contrôle stabilité	oui / oui
Suspension avant	indépendante, jambes de force
Suspension arrière	semi-indépendante, poutre de torsion
Freins avant / arrière	disque (ABS) / disque (ABS)
Direction	à crémaillère, ass. électrique
Diamètre de braquage	10,7 m
Pneus avant / arrière	185/55R15 / 185/55R15
Poids	n.d.
Capacité de remorquage	n.d.

COMPOSANTES MÉCANIQUES

Cylindrée, soupapes, alim.	4L 1,4 litre 16 s
Puissance / Couple	100 chevaux / 97 lb-pi
Tr. base (opt) / rouage base (opt)	M6 (A5) / Tr
0-100 / 80-120 / 100-0 km/h	10,5 s (est) / n.d. / n.d.
Type ess. / ville / autoroute	Ordinaire / n.d.

DANS LA MÊME CATÉGORIE

Scion iQ, smart Fortwo

DU NOUVEAU EN 2011

Nouveau modèle en Amérique

NOS IMPRESSIONS

Agrément de conduite :	n.d.
Fiabilité :	n.d.
Sécurité :	n.d.
Qualités hivernales :	n.d.
Espace intérieur :	n.d.
Confort :	n.d.

www.fiat500.com

Plus d'informations dans la section statistiques en dernière partie du Guide

GROSSE TRANSFORMATION POUR L'EDGE

J'vous dis que Ford en met, des énergies, sur son Edge. Et il serait fou de ne pas le faire: l'utilitaire connaît du grand succès depuis son arrivée en 2007. Pour 2011, on a droit à une transformation significative. On est loin d'une simple évolution, on pourrait même presque parler d'une nouvelle génération. Sauf que... nous n'avons pu conduire ledit véhicule avant d'aller sous presse. Alors, êtes-vous prêt pour le jeu des devinettes?

Première question: est-ce que le style redessiné sera aussi populaire qu'actuellement? Sans doute. Les lignes musclées et dominatrices demeurent et la calandre se fait encore plus massive (qui n'aime pas ça...?). Sinon, la personnalité demeure – Edge un jour, Edge toujours... – et c'est bien tant mieux.

ON PASSE D'UN À TROIS MOTEURS

Pour la première fois de sa jeune carrière, l'utilitaire construit à Oakville en Ontario recevra un moteur quatre cylindres. Vous avez bien lu: un tout petit quatre cylindres de 2,0 litres. Bien sûr, il s'agit d'un Ecoboost (lire: turbo et injection directe), une technologie moderne qui nous promet la puissance d'un V6, pour une consommation 10% moindre. Suspense, suspense, on ne connaît pas encore les détails de performance.

L'idée d'un plus petit moteur turbocompressé est fort intéressante et vrai que les Ecoboost que nous avons conduits jusqu'à présent (des V6, toutefois), étaient fort agréables à ébranler du pied droit. Mais pour une consommation réduite, faudra sans doute repasser. Car toutes nos tentatives jusqu'à ce jour pour en arriver à la cote annoncée par le constructeur ont été vaines. Mea culpa, c'est sûrement de notre faute: nous étions trop impatients de tester le turbo...

Le V6 de 3,5 litres à la puissance contrôlée et mature est toujours au rendez-vous, mais désormais avec la double distribution variable indépendante Ti-VCT, pour une hausse de 20 chevaux (à 285 chevaux). Question de bien distinguer la variante Sport des autres versions, Ford lui accorde nouvellement un V6 de 3,7 litres, pour 305 chevaux (en plus d'une calandre exclusive *noir smoking*...). Vous trouvez que l'écart de puissance n'est pas significatif? C'est que ça se joue plutôt au niveau du couple: 253 lbs-pi pour le premier, 280 lbs-pi pour le second. Ford promet une consommation améliorée bien sûr, mais notons surtout que de l'essence ordinaire suffira pour étancher la soif de ces deux V6 – et on aime ça.

Tout ce beau monde est jumelé à une boîte automatique six rapports avec passage manuel bien sûr – ces derniers monteront même au volant dans la variante Sport, *yéyé*! On dit que la suspension a été revue pour une tenue de route plus stable et plus précise? Eh bien, ça ne fera pas de mal; jusqu'à présent, l'Edge se comportait en bon utilitaire américain, plus confo que dynamo, avec des amortisseurs aux réactions un peu trop molle mais qui, heureusement, se replaçaient bien. Il y avait toutefois un monde

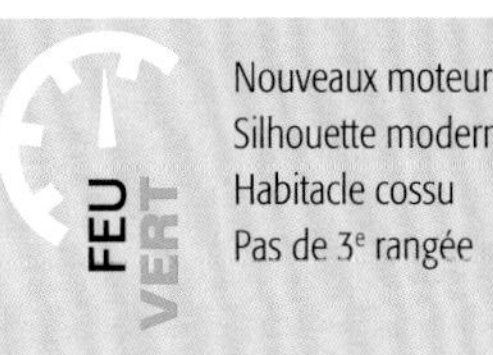

FEU VERT

Nouveaux moteurs
Silhouette modernisée
Habitacle cossu
Pas de 3e rangée

FEU ROUGE

Freinage très moyen
Hayon lourd
Fiabilité à déterminer
Rouage intégral sans verrouillage

de différence avec la sportivité du Mazda CX-7, pourtant assemblé sur la même plateforme. Reste à voir comment se traduiront ces nouveaux ajustements, dans la vie de tous les jours, pour l'Edge. Oh, soulignons que la variante Sport profitera d'une suspension spécialement réglée, qui continuera de rouler sur des roues de 22 pouces, une rareté, sinon une exclusivité dans la catégorie.

Par ailleurs, de nouveaux freins à disques montent à bord. De plus grande dimension, ils utilisent des matériaux améliorés et les rapports de pédale ont été révisés. C'est une bien bonne chose parce que lors de son passage aux tests de l'Association des Journalistes d'Automobiles du Canada (AJAC), l'Edge avait bien mal paru, côté freinage. Il avait mis 48 mètres pour s'immobiliser de 100 à 0 km/h – plus que pour le Chevrolet Tahoe !

Un dernier point « mécanique » : la traction intégrale continue d'être proposée en option, mais elle ne bénéficie toujours pas d'un mode de verrouillage manuel, comme pour le Pilot par exemple. Un jour, peut-être...

C'ÉTAIT DÉJÀ TRÈS BIEN

On dit que l'habitacle a été revu et que les revêtements ont été améliorés. Ah oui ? Ce n'est pas pour faire du lèche-popotin, mais nous affirmons haut et fort que les intérieurs de Ford sont, depuis quelques années, parmi les plus réussis de l'industrie. L'assemblage est de très bonne facture, l'insonorisation est excellente, les designs sont agréables au coup d'œil, les commandes sont ergonomiques...

On ne sait trop ce qui a pu être amélioré pour 2011 mais une chose est sûre, l'Edge a su résister à la tentation d'une 2e banquette et c'est bien tant mieux. Les 6e et 7e passagers auraient été trop à l'étroit – et il y a toujours le Ford Flex pour servir à la tâche...

Nul doute que l'Edge 2011 se distinguera encore par ses bons rangements – la console centrale géante peut se configurer d'une douzaine de façons – et l'un des systèmes de navigation les plus simples à apprivoiser.

Bon, ne reste plus qu'à conduire ce Edge transformé...

Nadine Filion

PHOTOS : FORD

Catégorie	Multisegment
Échelle de prix	26 499 $ à 39 734 $
Garanties	3 ans/60 000 km, 5 ans/100 000 km
Assemblage	Oakville, Ontario, Canada
Cote d'assurance	bonne

CHÂSSIS - DONNÉES POUR SEL TA

Emp/lon/lar/haut	2 824/4 674/2 223/1 702 mm
Coffre	906 à 1 926 litres
Réservoir	68 litres
Nombre coussins sécurité	6
Antipatinage / contrôle stabilité	oui / oui
Suspension avant	indépendante, jambes de force
Suspension arrière	indépendante, multibras
Freins avant / arrière	disque (ABS) / disque (ABS)
Direction	à crémaillère, ass. variable
Diamètre de braquage	11,5 m
Pneus avant / arrière	P245/60R18 / P245/60R18
Poids	1 852 kg
Capacité de remorquage	1 588 kg (3 500 lb)

COMPOSANTES MÉCANIQUES

SE, SEL, LIMITED	
Cylindrée, soupapes, alim.	V6 3,5 litres 24 s atmos.
Puissance / Couple	285 chevaux / 253 lb-pi
Tr. base (opt) / rouage base (opt)	A6 / Tr (Int)
0-100 / 80-120 / 100-0 km/h	7,5 s (est) / 5,5 s (est) / n.d.
Type ess. / ville / autoroute	Ordinaire / 11,8 / 8,1 l/100 km

Sport	
Cylindrée, soupapes, alim.	V6 3,7 litres 24 s atmos.
Puissance / Couple	305 chevaux / 280 lb-pi
Tr. base (opt) / rouage base (opt)	A6 / Tr
0-100 / 80-120 / 100-0 km/h	6,5 s (est) / n.d. / n.d.
Type ess. / ville / autoroute	Ordinaire / n.d.

DANS LA MÊME CATÉGORIE

Hyundai Santa Fe, Mazda CX-7, Mitsubishi Endeavor, Nissan Murano, Subaru Tribeca, Toyota Highlander

DU NOUVEAU EN 2011

Nouveau moteur 3,7 litres, puissance du 3,5 litres augmentée

NOS IMPRESSIONS

Agrément de conduite :	8/10
Fiabilité :	6/10
Sécurité :	10/10
Qualités hivernales :	8/10
Espace intérieur :	7/10
Confort :	8/10

www.ford.ca

Plus d'informations dans la section statistiques en dernière partie du Guide

Mazda Tribute

LE DUO DE LA DERNIÈRE HEURE?

Depuis 2001, le Ford Escape et sa copie le Mazda Tribute promènent leurs jolies bouilles sur nos routes. Sans grands changements, d'ailleurs. On a certes revu l'esthétisme en 2008 (il était temps!) et la mécanique l'année suivante (il était plus que temps!), mais il n'y a pas eu d'évolutions majeures. Aussi, dix ans plus tard, sommes-nous toujours au volant de la première génération. Ce qui est fascinant, c'est de constater que malgré des rides ici et là, ce duo poursuit sa voie sur la route du succès. Pourtant, plusieurs autres véhicules ont été boudés pour bien moins.

C'est dire que l'Escape était bien né. Remarquez que je n'ai pas écrit «l'Escape et le Tribute étaient bien nés» puisque le Tribute n'est qu'un Escape avec un badge Mazda, ce qui implique que les deux sont de petits jumeaux ou presque. D'ailleurs, il suffit de soulever le capot pour y voir quantité de pièces FoMoCo. Ces questions de génétique réglées, soulignons que les lignes commencent à être dépassées, surtout quand on compare l'Escape aux Ford Edge ou Flex. Mais c'est encore plus évident chez Mazda où les CX-7 et CX-9 sont de facture supradynamiques.

BONIFIÉ AVEC L'ÂGE

L'Escape et le Tribute affichent un niveau de finition nettement amélioré depuis quelques années. Nous sommes certes loin du design plus éclaté des tableaux de bord de quelques autres VUS mais celui de notre duo compense par des commandes ergonomiques et simples à comprendre. Pourtant, dans un monde où les manufacturiers investissent annuellement des millions de dollars en recherche sur la sécurité, la simplicité des commandes fait de plus en plus défaut... Mais revenons aux Escape et Tribute qui, eux, ne souffrent pas de cette tare. La visibilité tout le tour est très bonne, gracieuseté d'une position de conduite élevée et d'une fenestration généreuse qui n'a pas été sacrifiée sur l'autel du design, un autre bon point pour les créations plus anciennes! Certains propriétaires se sont plaints de sièges plus ou moins confortables, mais pour ma part, je n'ai jamais eu à me plaindre.

Les sièges arrière, par contre, s'avèrent moins accueillants même si l'espace pour la tête et les jambes est généreux. Aussi, l'accès et la sortie ne sont pas des plus faciles. Le hayon ouvre haut sur un coffre fort logeable. Curieusement, alors que l'Escape présente un bac de rangement sous le plancher dudit coffre, le Tribute n'en a pas. Au moins, dans les deux cas, la vitre ouvre séparément du hayon, une bénédiction si on veut transporter des objets longs comme des madriers.

L'Escape et le Tribute reçoivent d'office un quatre cylindres de 2,5 litres. Sans être une boule de nerfs sur l'ecstasy, ce moteur se tire très bien d'affaire dans la plupart des situations, d'autant plus que sa consommation est fort intéressante. Il y a aussi la possibilité de choisir un V6 de 3,0 litres, certes plus puissant, mais qui

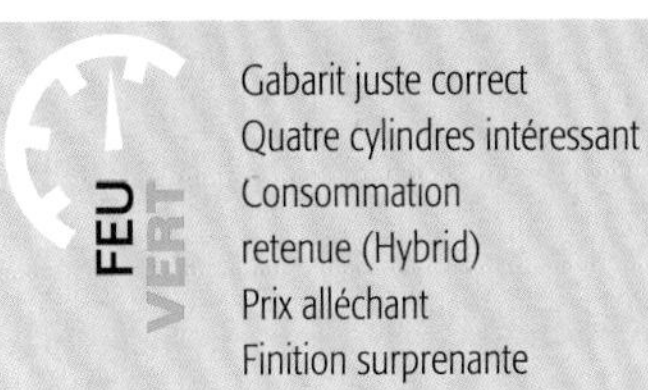

FEU VERT
Gabarit juste correct
Quatre cylindres intéressant
Consommation retenue (Hybrid)
Prix alléchant
Finition surprenante

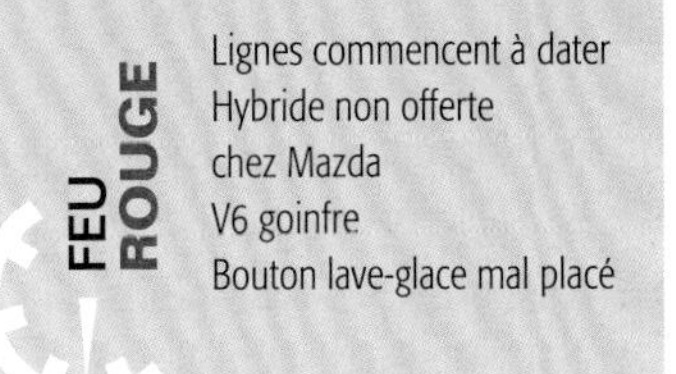

FEU ROUGE
Lignes commencent à dater
Hybride non offerte chez Mazda
V6 goinfre
Bouton lave-glace mal placé

engloutit une quantité effroyable de pétrole à chaque accélération. Il faut dire qu'au moment de sa conception, jadis, la consommation d'essence était le moindre de nos soucis... Quoi qu'il en soit, la seule raison qui pourrait pousser quelqu'un à choisir ce dernier moulin est celle du remorquage. Avec le V6, il est possible de tirer jusqu'à 3500 livres (1588 kilos) tandis que le quatre cylindres n'en remorque que 1500 (680 kilos).

ET L'HYBRID?

L'Escape sait aussi se faire apprécier avec son populaire Hybrid. Ce modèle donne bonne conscience à Ford en plus d'en faire davantage pour son image que n'importe quelle campagne de publicité. Notons qu'il n'est pas proposé sur le Tribute. On a adjoint au quatre cylindres 2,5 litres thermique un moteur électrique suffisamment puissant pour faire plus que de la figuration. Sa batterie nickel-hydrure métallique de 330 volts lui permet de rouler en mode électrique seulement. Mais sur de courtes distances et à une vitesse passablement réduite.

Le 2,5 de base peut être associé à une boîte manuelle à cinq rapports et une transmission automatique à six rapports est optionnelle. Cette dernière, qui travaille généralement avec professionnalisme, est la seule à pouvoir être reliée au V6. Quant à l'hybride, elle reçoit, comme il se doit maintenant avec ce type de motorisation, une transmission à rapports continuellement variables (CVT) qui ne s'attire aucun commentaire négatif... ni positif. Peu importe le moteur choisi, et c'est là la beauté de la chose, l'Escape et le Tribute peuvent être munis de la traction avant ou du rouage intégral que Ford appelle, un peu pompeusement, 4x4. Même si la traction et le quatre cylindres constituent un mariage de raison des plus sérieux, plusieurs personnes lui préfèrent le V6 et les quatre roues motrices. Dommage... Par contre, il ne faut pas condamner ce duo sans procès.

Malgré une sérieuse révision mécanique il y a deux ans, le duo Escape/Tribute n'est pas devenu un sportif à tout crin. On a resserré le ratio de la direction électrique et rendu les suspensions un peu plus fermes, cela a eu un effet bénéfique mais pas drastique. En virage pris à trop vive allure, la caisse penche un peu et la direction manque un tantinet de précision. Mais là, comme partout ailleurs, la modération a bon goût.

Alain Morin

PHOTOS: ALAIN MORIN

Catégorie	VUS
Échelle de prix	24 499$ à 37 299$ (2010)
Garanties	3 ans/60 000 km, 5 ans/100 000 km
Assemblage	Wayne, Michigan, É-U
Cote d'assurance	bonne

CHÂSSIS - DONNÉES POUR LIMITED TI 2,5L

Emp/lon/lar/haut	2 619/4 437/1 806/1 725 mm
Coffre	889 à 1 903 litres
Réservoir	62 litres
Nombre coussins sécurité	6
Antipatinage / contrôle stabilité	oui / oui
Suspension avant	indépendante, jambes de force
Suspension arrière	indépendante, multibras
Freins avant / arrière	disque (ABS) / tambour (ABS)
Direction	à crémaillère, ass. variable
Diamètre de braquage	11,1 m
Pneus avant / arrière	P235/70R16 / P235/70R16
Poids	1 609 kg
Capacité de remorquage	680 kg (1 499 lb)

COMPOSANTES MÉCANIQUES

Escape Hybrid

Cylindrée, soupapes, alim.	4L 2,5 litres 16 s atmos.
Puissance / Couple	153 chevaux / 136 lb-pi
Tr. base (opt) / rouage base (opt)	CVT / Tr (Int)
0-100 / 80-120 / 100-0 km/h	9,9 s / 7,6 s / 45,0 m
Type ess. / ville / autoroute	Ordinaire / 6,6 / 7,3 l/100km

Escape, Tribute

Cylindrée, soupapes, alim.	4L 2,5 litres 16 s atmos.
Puissance / Couple	171 chevaux / 171 lb-pi
Tr. base (opt) / rouage base (opt)	M5 (A6) / Tr (Int)
0-100 / 80-120 / 100-0 km/h	9,4 s / 7,8 s / 43,8 m
Type ess. / ville / autoroute	Ordinaire / 10,4 / 7,6 l/100 km

Escape, Tribute

Cylindrée, soupapes, alim.	V6 3,0 litres 24 s atmos.
Puissance / Couple	240 chevaux / 223 lb-pi
Tr. base (opt) / rouage base (opt)	A6 / Tr (Int)
0-100 / 80-120 / 100-0 km/h	7,8 s / 6,8 s / 44,2 m
Type ess. / ville / autoroute	Ordinaire / 11,6 / 8,8 l/100 km

DANS LA MÊME CATÉGORIE

Chevrolet Equinox, Honda CR-V, Hyundai Tucson, Jeep Compass, Jeep Liberty, Kia Sportage, Mitsubishi Outlander, Nissan Rogue, Subaru Forester, Suzuki Grand Vitara, Toyota RAV4, Volkswagen Tiguan

DU NOUVEAU EN 2011

Aucun changement majeur

NOS IMPRESSIONS

Agrément de conduite:	8/10
Fiabilité:	6/10
Sécurité:	10/10
Qualités hivernales:	8/10
Espace intérieur:	8/10
Confort:	7/10

www.ford.ca

Plus d'informations dans la section statistiques en dernière partie du Guide

Lincoln Navigator

MOINS POPULAIRES MAIS MEILLEURS QUE JAMAIS

Il aura fallu des hausses spectaculaires et répétées du prix de l'essence ainsi que l'une des pires crises économiques de l'histoire pour que la popularité de ces deux mastodontes soit remise en cause. Si au Québec la renommée de ces deux gros VUS était assez partagée, ils connaissaient des heures de gloire sur le marché américain. En effet, après l'époque de la fourgonnette, le public s'est entiché de ces gros véhicules capables de passer partout tout en consommant une quantité assez impressionnante de carburant. De nos jours, la demande est moindre aux quatre coins de notre continent, mais, curieusement, ces véhicules sont plus sophistiqués et plus confortables que jamais.

Ce n'est pas la première fois qu'une telle contradiction se manifeste. Par ailleurs, les personnes qui ont vraiment besoin d'un tel véhicule seront servies tant au chapitre de la solidité que de la tenue de route et de la sécurité. Et dans le cas du Lincoln Navigator, le luxe est au rendez-vous.

L'EXPEDITION D'ABORD

Il est important de préciser que les deux modèles se partagent la même plate-forme et la même mécanique. Ce sont des concurrents directs des gros véhicules tout-terrain dotés d'un châssis autonome et d'un rouage 4X4 à temps partiel. Mais au fil des années, le club des gros 4X4 a perdu des joueurs, et il n'en reste qu'une poignée. Toutefois, ils répondent à des besoins spécifiques et nombreux sont ceux qui ne pourraient s'en passer. Dans le cas du véhicule qui nous concerne, le groupe propulseur est un moteur V8 de 5,4 litres produisant 310 chevaux et capable de remorquer une charge de 9000 livres (4082 kg), ce qui n'est pas une surprise en soi puisque ce duo est dérivé de la camionnette F-150 dont la robustesse n'est plus

à démontrer. Ce moteur est associé à une transmission automatique à six rapports qui fait de l'excellent travail. Malheureusement, déplacer une masse de plus de 3 tonnes exige du carburant. Tant et si bien que la consommation moyenne devrait excéder 17 litres aux 100 km. Accrochez une roulotte à votre Ford ou Lincoln et vous constaterez que la consommation augmente d'au moins 30 %.

Alors que les premiers exemplaires de ces modèles commercialisés il y a maintenant quelques décennies proposaient une tenue de route assez aléatoire et un confort sommaire, les versions actuelles nous gâtent en matière de confort, de tenue de route et même d'agrément de conduite aux yeux des inconditionnels de cette catégorie. Et pour ajouter à la sécurité et à la facilité de conduite, les ingénieurs ont concocté plusieurs aides électroniques à la conduite. L'élément qui me vient en tête en premier est le système de contrôle de stabilité de la remorque qui travaille de concert avec le système de stabilité latérale Advance Trac de Ford et du système anticapotage intégré. Si jamais quelqu'un perd le contrôle de sa remorque au volant d'un Expedition ou d'un Navigator, c'est qu'il aura commis un acte impardonnable derrière le volant. En effet, lorsque les capteurs détectent une possible perte de contrôle, les freins sont appliqués à

FEU VERT

- Moteur bien adapté
- Habitacle spacieux et confortable
- Comportement routier
- Bonne capacité de remorquage
- Équipement complet

FEU ROUGE

- Consommation élevée
- Dimensions encombrantes
- Popularité décroissante
- Marchepieds inutiles

l'une ou l'autre des roues tout en réduisant la puissance du moteur. Et si le pire se produit, le système SOS Post-Crash Alert actionnera automatiquement le klaxon et les clignotants d'urgence après le déploiement des coussins de sécurité. Parmi les autres trouvailles dignes d'intérêt, on oublie toujours de souligner que la compagnie Ford a innové avec un système de ravitaillement en essence sans bouchon. À l'usage, c'est absolument génial, et on peut se demander pourquoi cela ne devient pas la norme dans toute l'industrie.

LE NAVIGATOR

Si le Ford Expedition propose une silhouette relativement anonyme, il en est tout autre du Lincoln Navigator avec son sourire chromé dessiné par la grille de calandre et l'imposante prise d'air sur le pare-chocs avant. Ajoutez à cela des roues chromées et il est impossible de ne pas le remarquer sur nos routes. Mais c'est quand même relatif, puisque les ventes de ce mastodonte sont modérées. Dans l'habitacle, c'est le luxe. Et il est passablement impressionnant de jeter un coup d'œil au tableau de bord en soirée, on se croirait dans un avion de ligne avec tous ces cadrans et toutes ces commandes éclairées. C'est impressionnant!

Cette année, les modifications d'ordre mécanique et esthétique sont pratiquement inexistantes. Par contre, le système de navigation à commande vocale est associé maintenant à une radio HD dont la qualité sonore est supérieure à la moyenne. À ce chapitre, le conducteur n'a rien à faire. Il synchronise ses postes de radio favoris, et si ces postes émettent en mode HD, il bénéficie d'une écoute améliorée. Cette caractéristique est surtout intéressante si vous roulez aux États-Unis où le nombre de postes HD est plus élevé.

Parmi la pléthore d'accessoires et de gadgets, on peut mentionner également des écrans vidéo montés sur la partie supérieure arrière des sièges avant afin que les occupants des places arrière puissent regarder leurs films favoris et les écouter avec des écouteurs sans fil. Il faut également souligner le système MyKey offert aussi sur l'Expedition. Il s'agit d'une clé programmable qui limite la vitesse de pointe, qui empêche de désactiver le système antipatinage, qui limite le volume du système audio à 44 % du maximum et où une sonnerie se fait entendre lorsqu'on atteint les 70, 90 et 105 km/h ! La seule chose que cette clé ne fait pas, c'est de communiquer avec le propriétaire pour l'aviser qu'on « fait des folies » avec son véhicule.

Denis Duquet

Ford Expetition

PHOTOS : FORD

Catégorie	VUS
Échelle de prix	40 709 $ à 56 533 $ (2010)
Garanties	3 ans/60 000 km, 5 ans/100 000 km
Assemblage	Wayne, Michigan, É-U
Cote d'assurance	passable

CHÂSSIS - DONNÉES POUR KING RANCH 4X4

Emp/lon/lar/haut	3 023/5 232/2 311/1 955 mm
Coffre	527 à 3 064 litres
Réservoir	106 litres
Nombre coussins sécurité	6
Antipatinage / contrôle stabilité	oui / oui
Suspension avant	indépendante, double triangulation
Suspension arrière	indépendante, multibras
Freins avant / arrière	disque (ABS) / disque (ABS)
Direction	à crémaillère, ass. variable
Diamètre de braquage	12,4 m
Pneus avant / arrière	P255/70R18 / P255/70R18
Poids	2 652 kg
Capacité de remorquage	4 082 kg (9 000 lb)

COMPOSANTES MÉCANIQUES

Expedition, Expedition Max, Navigator

Cylindrée, soupapes, alim.	V8 5,4 litres 24 s atmos.
Puissance / Couple	310 chevaux / 365 lb-pi
Tr. base (opt) / rouage base (opt)	A6 / 4x4
0-100 / 80-120 / 100-0 km/h	8,9 s / 7,5 s / 45,2 m
Type ess. / ville / autoroute	Ordinaire / 17,3 / 11,6 l/100 km

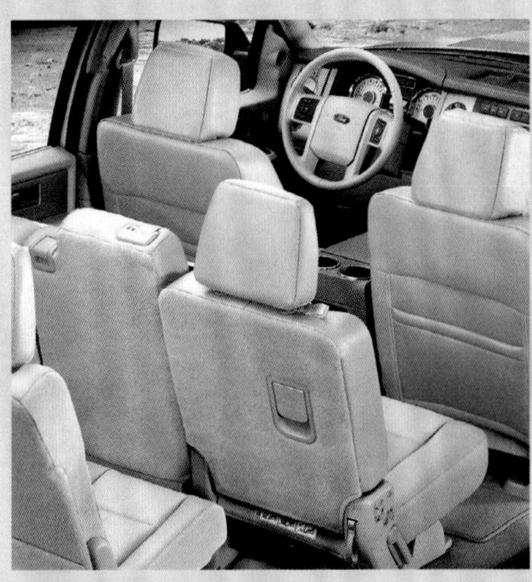

DANS LA MÊME CATÉGORIE

Chevrolet Tahoe, GMC Yukon, Nissan Armada, Toyota Sequoia

DU NOUVEAU EN 2011

Aucun changement majeur

NOS IMPRESSIONS

Agrément de conduite :	8/10
Fiabilité :	6/10
Sécurité :	8/10
Qualités hivernales :	9/10
Espace intérieur :	10/10
Confort :	10/10

www.ford.ca

Plus d'informations dans la section statistiques en dernière partie du Guide

FORD EXPEDITION / LINCOLN NAVIGATOR

LE VAISSEAU TERRESTRE FAMILIAL MODERNISÉ

Il s'en est vendu six millions en vingt ans et les deux tiers roulent encore. Le premier Explorer n'affichait pourtant aucune caractéristique révolutionnaire. Il avait simplement les qualités que recherchait la famille nord-américaine typique. La marque à l'ovale bleu espère que son tout nouvel Explorer touchera encore une fois cette cible en plein cœur. Et cette fois, certains choix techniques sont audacieux, surtout celui d'offrir un quatre cylindres turbocompressé.

Ford croit fermement que les acheteurs ont délaissé les utilitaires classiques pour les multisegments à cause de leur consommation plus raisonnable. Le constructeur est également convaincu que les Nord-américains veulent encore partir à l'aventure à bord du vaisseau terrestre familial même s'il faut escalader un sentier étroit ou traverser une rivière à gué. Le reste du temps, le même vaisseau doit cependant permettre à la famille de se déplacer en tout confort, agrément et sécurité de la maison au bureau ou de l'aréna au centre commercial.

NOUVEAU SQUELETTE ET NOUVELLE PEAU

Pour combler ces objectifs divergents, Ford a d'abord troqué le châssis séparé de l'ancien Explorer pour une coque autoporteuse. L'Explorer 2011 emploie ainsi une version de l'architecture D qui sous-tend déjà le Flex et le Lincoln MKX. La moitié de sa coque est composée d'acier au bore de plus forte résistance. Et pour atteindre des objectifs élevés de qualité, de silence de roulement et d'efficacité aérodynamique, les joints entre les panneaux de carrosserie sont rigoureusement étroits.

Tout ça est enveloppé sous une carrosserie moins anguleuse que celle de l'Explorer d'antan. Plus aérodynamique aussi, avec un coefficient de traînée de 0,35. Seule ressemblance remarquée: une calandre à barres horizontales perforées qui rappelle la Taurus.

NOUVEAUX CŒURS

Le moteur de base de l'Explorer 2011 est un V6 de 3,5 litres. Ford annonce des cotes de 290 chevaux à 6 500 tr/min et 255 lb-pi de couple à 4 000 tr/min mais surtout une consommation réduite de 20 %. Il faut d'ailleurs le V6 pour conduire un Explorer à quatre roues motrices et pour tracter une remorque le moindrement importante. La capacité de remorquage du V6 est effectivement de 2 268 kg alors qu'elle se résume à 907 kg pour le quatre cylindres Ecoboost.

Ce dernier vise en fait l'acheteur qui recherche avant tout la frugalité. Il est d'ailleurs réservé aux modèles à roues avant motrices qui ne vont certainement pas explorer aussi loin que leurs frères. C'est un quatre cylindres turbocompressé de 2,0 litres qui produit 237 chevaux à 5 500 tr/min et livre 250 lb-pi de couple entre 1 700 et 4 000 tr/min. On promet quand même une réduction de consommation substantielle de 30 % par rapport au modèle précédent.

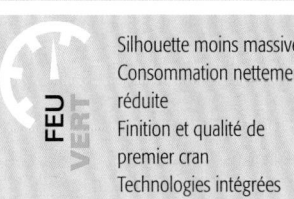

FEU VERT
- Silhouette moins massive
- Consommation nettement réduite
- Finition et qualité de premier cran
- Technologies intégrées et conviviales

FEU ROUGE
- Pas de 4RM avec le moteur Ecoboost
- Troisième rangée peu accueillante
- Fiabilité à démontrer
- Capacité de remorquage limitée (4 cyl.)

CONFORT ET TECHNOLOGIE

La qualité des matériaux et la finition de l'habitacle sont impressionnantes. Les sièges de cuir sont très bien taillés et confortables aux deux premières rangées. Ford innove aussi avec les premières ceintures de sécurité gonflables pour les passagers arrière. Les deux sièges en troisième rangée s'escamotent sous le plancher ou se replient vers l'avant pour plus de rangement.

On le fait en appuyant sur un bouton avec le groupe d'options 1 du modèle Limited qui comprend entre autres aussi un système de navigation à commande vocale avec lecteur de carte SD. Le groupe 2 ajoute le stationnement automatique étonnamment efficace de Ford, un régulateur de vitesse et des essuie-glaces automatiques, des phares au xénon et la surveillance des angles morts. La clarté et la disposition simple du tableau de bord et de la console centrale sont aussi remarquables.

COMPORTEMENT ET CONDUITE TOUT-TERRAIN

Les suspensions avant et arrière du nouvel Explorer sont à roues indépendantes et sa servodirection est électrique. Il est doté de freins à disque antiblocage et d'un système antidérapage et antipatinage complet mais également du système de détection de capotage de Ford et d'un nouveau système baptisé Curve Control qui réduit le couple et applique les freins si on roule trop vite en virage.

Sur les versions à quatre roues motrices, le boîtier de transfert est remplacé par une molette qui permet de choisir un des quatre modes de conduite: boue, neige, sable ou route. Au centre; un bouton pour engager le contrôle de descente en pente. Si ces deux systèmes ressemblent à ce qu'on voit chez Land Rover ce n'est pas une coïncidence: Jim Holland, l'ingénieur-chef du projet Explorer, nous a confirmé que les systèmes ont été développés en parallèle durant les cinq années qu'il a passées chez Land Rover.

Chose certaine, cet Explorer transformé regagnera sans doute le peloton de tête chez les utilitaires. Ce serait toutefois encore mieux avec une ou des versions Ecoboost à quatre roues motrices.

Marc Lachapelle

PHOTOS : FORD

DONNÉES PRÉLIMINAIRES

Catégorie	VUS
Échelle de prix	34 064 $ à 44 888 $ (2010)
Garanties	3 ans/60 000 km, 5 ans/100 000 km
Assemblage	Louisville, KY et St-Louis, MO, É-U
Cote d'assurance	moyenne

CHÂSSIS - DONNÉES POUR V6

Emp/lon/lar/haut	2 860/5 006/2 291/1 803 mm
Coffre	n.d. à 2 285 litres
Réservoir	70 litres
Nombre coussins sécurité	6
Antipatinage / contrôle stabilité	oui / oui
Suspension avant	indépendante, bras inégaux
Suspension arrière	indépendante, multibras
Freins avant / arrière	disque (ABS) / disque (ABS)
Direction	à crémaillère, assistée
Diamètre de braquage	n.d.
Pneus avant / arrière	P245/65R17 / P245/65R17
Poids	n.d.
Capacité de remorquage	2 268 kg (5 000 lb)

COMPOSANTES MÉCANIQUES

Ecoboost	
Cylindrée, soupapes, alim.	4L 2,0 litres 16 s turbo
Puissance / Couple	237 chevaux / 250 lb-pi
Tr. base (opt) / rouage base (opt)	A6 / Tr
0-100 / 80-120 / 100-0 km/h	n.d. / n.d. / n.d.
Type ess. / ville / autoroute	Ordinaire / n.d.

XLT V6 TI	
Cylindrée, soupapes, alim.	V6 3,5 litres 24 s atmos.
Puissance / Couple	290 chevaux / 255 lb-pi
Tr. base (opt) / rouage base (opt)	A6 / Int
0-100 / 80-120 / 100-0 km/h	n.d. / n.d. / n.d.
Type ess. / ville / autoroute	Ordinaire / n.d.

DANS LA MÊME CATÉGORIE

Jeep Commander, Jeep Grand Cherokee, Kia Borrego, Nissan Pathfinder, Toyota 4Runner

DU NOUVEAU EN 2011

Nouveau modèle

NOS IMPRESSIONS

Agrément de conduite:	Données insuffisantes
Fiabilité:	Nouveau modèle
Sécurité:	Données insuffisantes
Qualités hivernales:	Données insuffisantes
Espace intérieur:	Données insuffisantes
Confort:	Données insuffisantes

www.ford.ca

Plus d'informations dans la section statistiques en dernière partie du Guide

UN NOM BIEN CHOISI!

Au cours des cinquante dernières années, les camionnettes, petites et grosses, ont constitué la majeure partie des ventes des manufacturiers américains. Les petites voitures n'étaient proposées que pour répondre aux normes de consommation établies par les gouvernements. Depuis quelques années cependant, à cause des prix pour le moins instables de l'essence et de la crise économique, la tendance s'est radicalement inversée. Les gens demandent de plus en plus de voitures compactes et sous-compactes. Même aux États-Unis, c'est tout dire ! Qui plus est, au moment de la présentation de la Fiesta en avril dernier, Ford avait déjà reçu 4 000 commandes, ce qui n'est pas rien.

Ford, en avance sur General Motors et Chrysler, dévoile cette année sa première sous-compacte depuis des lunes, la Fiesta. En fait, puisqu'elle existait déjà en Europe, Ford n'a eu qu'à effectuer que quelques ajustements pour pouvoir l'offrir sur notre marché. D'ailleurs, l'an dernier, Ford Canada avait anticipé l'arrivée de la sous-compacte en faisant conduire une version européenne à des journalistes canadiens. La voiture nous avait alors impressionnés. Qu'en est-il de la version nord-américaine ?

PRÉSENTATION IMPRESSIONNANTE

Tout d'abord, mentionnons que la Fiesta a beau être une petite voiture, on n'a pas lésiné sur le style. Si la berline affiche un certain dynamisme, le modèle à hayon affiche un dynamisme certain ! Lors de l'essai de la version européenne durant l'été 2009 et au moment de la prise en main de sa contrepartie américaine, plusieurs personnes se sont retournées sur notre passage et j'imagine que ce n'était pas pour admirer le conducteur grisonnant... L'habitacle non plus ne laisse pas de glace. La partie centrale, surtout, épate par sa beauté et sa simplicité. Elle est surmontée d'un écran qui regorge d'informations diverses. Cet écran pourrait très bien diffuser les informations d'un système GPS mais il n'est pas offert, même en option. Cependant, le volant réglable en hauteur et télescopique, les essuie-glaces intermittents à vitesse variable et sept coussins gonflables (une première pour une voiture de cette catégorie) sont proposés de série, peu importe la version. Ceux qui le désireront pourront équiper leur Fiesta comme s'il s'agissait d'une Lincoln (excepté pour le GPS !) : toit ouvrant électrique, garnitures des sièges en cuir, système de sécurité, etc. Les versions SEL de la berline et SES de la *hatchback* sont équivalentes et possèdent, de série, des roues en alliage, des rétroviseurs extérieurs chauffants, un régulateur de vitesse, des sièges avant chauffants, un excellent système SYNC et j'en passe. Notons au passage que les matériaux affichent une belle qualité et leur assemblage est réussi. On est ici à des années-lumière des tristes habitacles des Hyundai Accent et Kia Rio ou des plastiques durs de la Toyota Yaris et de la Nissan Versa. Si la Yaris se démarque par un tableau de bord plus pratique que celui de la Fiesta avec ses nombreux espaces de rangement, l'habitacle de la Versa est plus grand que celui de la nouvelle Ford.

Les sièges avant font preuve de confort, le volant se prend bien en main et la position de conduite, dans mon cas du moins, se trouve très rapidement. La visibilité tout le tour, berline ou *hatchback*, est très bonne. Les gens assis à l'arrière auront sans doute des mots moins nobles concernant les sièges mais, dans l'ensemble, c'est correct... pour deux. Une troisième personne devra s'y faire très, très petite. Les dossiers, autant pour la berline que pour le *hatchback*, s'abaissent de façon 60/40 pour agrandir

un coffre aux dimensions surprenantes compte tenu justement des dimensions extérieures. Cependant, on est encore loin de la modularité d'une Honda Fit, par exemple.

TECHNOLOGIE ET SOUS-COMPACTE

Une présentation raffinée et des formes qui flattent la rétine, c'est bien. Au niveau de la mécanique aussi c'est réussi. Le seul moteur au catalogue est un très moderne quatre cylindres de 1,6 litre de 120 chevaux, un peu faible à bas régime et lors de montées abruptes. Un voyage dans Charlevoix avec quatre adultes à bord et leurs bagages pourrait demander un peu de patience aux véhicules qui suivent... Une vingtaine d'équidés supplémentaires ne seraient pas de refus. Cependant, en conduite normale, ce moteur, bénéficiant de la technologie Twin Independant Variable Camshaft Timing (Ti-VCT) permettant un bon rapport performance/consommation, devrait satisfaire la plupart des conducteurs.

Ce 1,6 litre est épaulé par un excellent duo de transmissions qui transmet le couple aux roues avant. On retrouve tout d'abord une manuelle à cinq rapports très agréable à utiliser. Mais c'est la boîte automatique PowerShift à six rapports (une autre première dans cette catégorie) qui épate. Cette transmission à double embrayage à sec se passe d'une pompe et d'un convertisseur de couple, ce qui réduit le poids et la complexité technique. Franchement impressionnante, bien étagée avec sa première vitesse courte, elle passe ses rapports au bon moment et avec douceur. Sans rendre le moteur plus puissant, elle permet d'en tirer le meilleur parti et nul doute que beaucoup d'acheteurs, auparavant attirés par la manuelle, opteront pour l'automatique même si elle commande environ 1 200$ supplémentaires. D'autant plus que, selon Ford, cette boîte permet au moteur de consommer moins que la manuelle. Dommage qu'elle n'ait pas de mode manuel.

La Fiesta bénéficie d'une direction électrique très sophistiquée appelée EPAS. Elle possède un mécanisme qui permet de compenser les forces latérales, le vent ou des pneus mal gonflés par exemple. Vive et fournit un bon *feedback*, cette direction annule effectivement, jusqu'à un certain point, les forces «occultes» du vent, comme nous avons pu nous en rendre compte par une journée à dépeigner Mad Dog Vachon. Les suspensions effectuent bien leur boulot et offrent un bon compromis entre la tenue de route et le confort. Curieusement, alors que les modèles européens ont toujours été reconnus pour être plus dynamiques sur la route que leurs homologues américains, c'est le cas contraire pour la Fiesta! En effet, le modèle essayé à l'été 2009 nous avait semblé plus «mou».

Peu importe la version, le contrôle de la traction et le système antipatinage sont livrés d'office. Mais le fait de ne pouvoir les désactiver pourrait constituer un élément problématique l'hiver alors que la voiture est enlisée dans un banc de neige. Un ingénieur rencontré lors du lancement nous avait dit que la Fiesta possédait une telle traction dans la neige que désactiver ces systèmes était inutile. Facile à dire...

PARLONS $$$$$

La berline de base (S) sera proposée à prix très, très compétitif mais pour y arriver, il a fallu à Ford couper dans le gras et on se retrouve alors avec une voiture très dépouillée qui ne devrait pas trouver beaucoup de preneurs. Le modèle *hatchback*, lui, débute avec une dotation un peu plus intéressante et un prix plus élevé... Enfin, il est possible de commander une Fiesta pleine aux as mais à un prix qui égale sinon dépasse celui d'une Fusion le moindrement équipée.

Catégorie	Berline, *Hatchback*
Échelle de prix	12 999 $ à 18 899 $
Garanties	3 ans/60 000 km, 5 ans/100 000 km
Assemblage	Cologne, Espagne
Cote d'assurance	n.d.

CHÂSSIS - DONNÉES POUR SE *HATCHBACK*

Emp/lon/lar/haut	2 489/4 067/1 722/1 473 mm
Coffre	n.d.
Réservoir	45 litres
Nombre coussins sécurité	6
Antipatinage / contrôle stabilité	oui / oui
Suspension avant	indépendante, jambes de force
Suspension arrière	essieu rigide, ressorts hélicoïdaux
Freins avant / arrière	disque (ABS) / tambour (ABS)
Direction	à crémaillère, ass. électrique
Diamètre de braquage	10,5 m
Pneus avant / arrière	P185/65R15 / P185/65R15
Poids	1 168 kg
Capacité de remorquage	non recommandé

COMPOSANTES MÉCANIQUES

Fiesta

Cylindrée, soupapes, alim.	4L 1,6 litre 16 s atmos.
Puissance / Couple	120 chevaux / 112 lb-pi
Tr. base (opt) / rouage base (opt)	M5 (A6) / Tr
0-100 / 80-120 / 100-0 km/h	11,2 s / 12,9 s / n.d.
Type ess. / ville / autoroute	Ordinaire / 7,9 / 4,7 l/100 km

FEU VERT

- Lignes éclatantes (*hatchback*)
- Tableau de bord réussi
- Silence de roulement évident
- Boîte automatique compétente
- Consommation retenue

FEU ROUGE

- Puissance un peu juste
- Places arrière serrées
- Désactivation stabilité latérale impossible
- Modèle de base très de base (S)
- Fiabilité inconnue

Dans cette catégorie, le prix demeure le nerf de la guerre. Même si plusieurs seront prêts à dépenser plusieurs dollars pour rouler dans l'énergique Fiesta, la compétition pourrait bien venir de sa cousine, la tout-aussi-nouvelle-pour-nous Mazda2, bâtie sur le même châssis. La mécanique de cette dernière est passablement moins intéressante et la voiture n'est offerte qu'en version *hatchback*, mais les personnes à la recherche d'un moyen de transport entre le point A et le point B, peu sensibles aux innovations ou aux percées technologiques n'en feront pas un plat. Ces personnes pourraient aussi se tourner vers les Hyundai Accent, Kia Rio ou Chevrolet Aveo, beaucoup moins chères mais infiniment moins agréables à conduire et dont la qualité de la construction laisse à désirer, sans compter sur une valeur de revente invariablement basse. Il reste la très réussie Honda Fit et la Toyota Yaris qui commence à prendre de l'âge. Techniquement, la question ne se pose même pas. Ford établit avec sa Fiesta une nouvelle marque, difficile à battre.

Alain Morin

PHOTOS : ALAIN MORIN

DANS LA MÊME CATÉGORIE

Chevrolet Aveo, Honda Fit, Hyundai Accent, Kia Rio/Rio5, Nissan Versa, Suzuki Swift+, Toyota Yaris

DU NOUVEAU EN 2011

Nouveau modèle

NOS IMPRESSIONS

Agrément de conduite :	7/10
Fiabilité :	Nouveau modèle
Sécurité :	8/10
Qualités hivernales :	8/10
Espace intérieur :	8/10
Confort :	8/10

www.ford.ca

Plus d'informations dans la section statistiques en dernière partie du Guide

Y'A DE LA PLACE EN MASSE DANS MON JACUZZI...

Le Flex est une autre preuve que Ford a le vent dans les voiles. Alternative rieuse à la traditionnelle minifourgonnette, le véhicule excelle lorsqu'on l'équipe du V6 biturbo Ecoboost. Même si, pour cela, il faut allonger un tiers de plus en dollars...

N'est-ce pas qu'on s'habitue à ce style radical, à ces rainures de flanc et à ce toit (optionnel) à la couleur distincte du reste de la carrosserie ? On s'habitue, mais le design du Flex reste frappant et se démarque agréablement d'un paysage automobile où, finalement, tous les utilitaires en viennent à se ressembler.

De base (sous les 30 000 $), le Flex est doté d'un V6 de3,5 litres qui développe 262 chevaux. C'est limite pour ce véhicule plutôt lourdaud – il fait osciller la balance d'environ 250 kilos de plus que l'Edge, avec qui il partage sa motorisation. Le 0-100 km/h demande au minimum neuf secondes et les reprises s'essoufflent vite, même avec un seul occupant à bord (imaginez quand la maisonnée est pleine...). La donne aurait pu être facilitée par un passage manuel des vitesses pour redistribuer la puissance à convenance, mais la boîte automatique six rapports n'en propose toujours pas.

Pour ce faire, il faut le moteur Ecoboost et alors seulement, on peut négocier soi-même les six rapports à l'aide de commandes au volant. Ces dernières ne sont pas instinctives (lisez notre texte sur le Lincoln MKT) mais au moins, la possibilité du changement à volonté existe. Cet Ecoboost ajoute au V6 de 3,5 litres non seulement la double (double !) turbocompression, mais aussi l'injection directe, pour des reprises douces et instantanées. Ah, là, tu parles d'une belle modernité... avec, en prime, une belle sonorité grondante ! Sous l'emprise de ces 355 chevaux (et quand même 350 lb-pi de couple), le Flex se démène de 0 à 100 km/h en deux secondes plus vite.

Bon, Ford a beau vanter les mérites écologiques de cet Ecoboost qui, pour 40 % plus de puissance, est censé ne consommer guère plus que le V6 à aspiration naturelle, mais avec cette vigueur sous le pied droit, difficile de s'en tirer avec un combiné sous les 14 l/100 km.

Étrangement, la direction qui se fait électrique avec l'Ecoboost (elle demeure hydraulique avec le V6 de base) est plus intéressante à manier parce qu'on lui sent moins de flou en son centre. En présence d'une aussi looonnngue silhouette (plus de 5 mètres), on ne doit pas s'attendre à une quelconque inspiration des voitures de course. Même que chaussé des optionnelles roues de 20 pouces, notre Flex Ecoboost nous a un peu trop mollement « secoué le canadien » et en virage serré, il faut manifestement faire preuve de prudence. Le freinage est efficace, mais on en est quitte pour un museau qui plonge si on en fait usage brusquement.

C'EST EN DEDANS QU'ON EST BEAU...

Le Flex a tout le côté fonctionnel auquel on est en droit de s'attendre d'un véhicule du genre, avec notamment des banquettes qui se replient facilement (vive la commande automatique !) et de pratiques

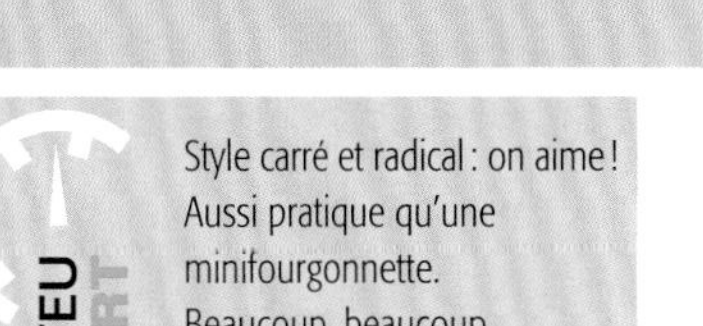

Style carré et radical : on aime !
Aussi pratique qu'une minifourgonnette.
Beaucoup, beaucoup d'espace en 2e rangée
Habitacle bien conçu
Bon niveau d'équipements

Motorisation limite (V6 de base)
Insonorisation moyenne dans les versions de base
Consommation en carburant plus élevée qu'annoncée
Moteur Ecoboost réservé à la variante Limited AWD

et nombreux rangements. Une fois la 3e rangée disparue dans le plancher, on retrouve autant de chargement que dans un utilitaire conventionnel, alors imaginez tout l'espace obtenu en rabattant la seconde banquette... Sans doute préférerez-vous, comme nous, la version six passagers ; les sièges capitaines du centre sont aussi confortables que ceux à l'avant et ils ont le bonheur de s'avancer et se reculer, afin d'accorder encore plus de place aux occupants de la 3e rangée. Ces dernières places du fond ne sont généralement pas les meilleures en ville, mais elles ont ici le mérite d'un dégagement suffisant aux têtes pour que des adultes de taille moyenne y trouvent leur compte.

On aime peu les plastiques rêches et ça, Ford semble l'avoir compris. Voilà pourquoi les quelques revêtements de moyenne facture se retrouvent dans des endroits peu fréquentés par le bout des doigts. Le tout est bien assemblé et la planche de bord, nette et aérée, permet de vitement se familiariser avec les commandes. Les sièges avant sont larges et confortables, bien qu'il leur manque du soutien pour nous empêcher d'en glisser latéralement. Merci aux grandes baies vitrées, de même qu'à l'optionnel toit panoramique (quatre panneaux de verre au toit), l'habitacle tout entier est bien éclairé. On ne reproche qu'un gros pilier B qui vient empirer les angles morts du conducteur.

Depuis l'an dernier, le volant se fait télescopique, ce qui aide à dénicher la bonne position de conduite. Et on est encore plus gâté avec les pédales ajustables, disponibles dans les versions plus luxueuses.

ECOBOOST : ALLÔ LA FACTURE...

De base, le Flex se montre raisonnablement bien équipé pour le prix. Mais la facture grimpe du tiers si on se laisse convaincre par l'Ecoboost. Dommage que cette belle motorisation se réserve exclusivement à la version Limited avec traction intégrale. On a alors évidemment droit à la totale, avec ces *gizmos* qu'on aime bien : cuir, hayon électrique, phares au xénon, radio satellite et stationnement automatisé. Mais si l'on ajoute le toit panoramique, le système de navigation, les sièges chauffants à l'arrière (oui, oui !), la console réfrigérée et les roues de 20 pouces, nous voilà dans les 55 000 $. Nous est donc d'avis qu'une version Ecoboost pourrait s'amener plus rapidement dans l'échelle des options.

Nadine Filion

PHOTOS : DENIS DUQUET

Catégorie	Multisegment
Échelle de prix	28 344 $ à 45 188 $
Garanties	3 ans/60 000 km, 5 ans/100 000 km
Assemblage	Oakville, Ontario, Canada
Cote d'assurance	n.d.

CHÂSSIS - DONNÉES POUR LIMITED TI ECOBOOST

Emp/lon/lar/haut	2 994/5 125/1 927/1 726 mm
Coffre	426 à 2 355 litres
Réservoir	73 litres
Nombre coussins sécurité	6
Antipatinage / contrôle stabilité	oui / oui
Suspension avant	indépendante, jambes de force
Suspension arrière	indépendante, multibras
Freins avant / arrière	disque (ABS) / disque (ABS)
Direction	à crémaillère, assistée
Diamètre de braquage	12,4 m
Pneus avant / arrière	P235/55R19 / P235/55R19
Poids	2 195 kg
Capacité de remorquage	907 kg (1 999 lb)

COMPOSANTES MÉCANIQUES

SE, SEL, Limited	
Cylindrée, soupapes, alim.	V6 3,5 litres 24 s atmos.
Puissance / Couple	262 chevaux / 248 lb-pi
Tr. base (opt) / rouage base (opt)	A6 / Tr (Int)
0-100 / 80-120 / 100-0 km/h	9,0 s / 7,2 s / 40,9 m
Type ess. / ville / autoroute	Ordinaire / 13,4 / 9 l/100 km

Limited EcoBoost, Titanium	
Cylindrée, soupapes, alim.	V6 3,5 litres 24 s turbo
Puissance / Couple	355 chevaux / 350 lb-pi
Tr. base (opt) / rouage base (opt)	A6 / Int
0-100 / 80-120 / 100-0 km/h	7,2 s / 5,9 s (est) / 40,9 m
Type ess. / ville / autoroute	Ordinaire / 13,1 / 9,2 l/100 km

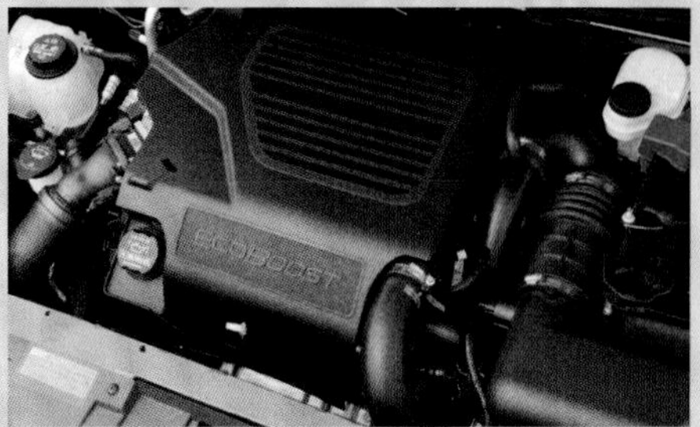

DANS LA MÊME CATÉGORIE

Buick Enclave, Chevrolet Traverse, Honda Pilot, Hyundai Veracruz, Mazda CX-9, Subaru Tribeca, Toyota Highlander

DU NOUVEAU EN 2011

Nouvelle version Titanium, 3e banquette 50/50 à rabattement électrique, chauffe-moteur de série avec Ecoboost

NOS IMPRESSIONS

Agrément de conduite :	8/10
Fiabilité :	6/10
Sécurité :	10/10
Qualités hivernales :	8/10
Espace intérieur :	8/10
Confort :	8/10

www.ford.ca

Plus d'informations dans la section statistiques en dernière partie du Guide

EN ATTENDANT LE FUTUR

Au moment d'écrire ces lignes, la publicité de Ford n'a d'intérêt que pour la nouvelle venue, la sous-compacte Fiesta qui fait son entrée sur notre marché de façon spectaculaire. Les publicités sont multiples, la voiture attrayante et le public emballé si on se fie aux chiffres des ventes préliminaires enregistrées chez les concessionnaires de la province. Puis, au cours des premiers mois de 2011, du moins c'est ce que l'on nous promet, nous allons voir arriver la nouvelle Focus qui sera proposée en version *hatchback* cinq portes et berline. Et la direction de la compagnie semble privilégier la première version puisque c'est ce modèle qui a été dévoilé en grande première au Salon de l'auto de détroit en janvier 2010. La berline n'a eu droit qu'à un modeste rôle secondaire.

Cette nouvelle Focus occupe une place fort importante dans les plans du constructeur de Dearborn. Il s'agit tout d'abord de la première authentique voiture mondiale pour Ford puisque plus de 80 % des composantes seront partagées sur tous les marchés. Par ailleurs, les motorisations seront adaptées en fonction des différents marchés. En plus, la plate-forme de cette voiture de classe C sera utilisée pour l'élaboration de nombreux autres modèles notamment les C-Max et Grand C-Max qui seront les prochains modèles à faire appel à cette plate-forme. Cela signifie aussi que la version actuelle de la Focus sera commercialisée pendant quelques mois encore.

LE PRÉSENT

Il ne faut pas faire l'erreur d'ignorer la version actuelle de la Focus. En effet, lorsqu'un modèle est appelé à être remplacé par

un autre, les derniers modèles commercialisés sont généralement dotés d'un équipement fort relevé et ce à des prix très compétitifs. De plus, puisque la voiture a été fabriquée pendant plusieurs années sans modification importante, cette mécanique est généralement bien rodée et fiable. C'est d'ailleurs le cas de la Focus puisque la dernière génération n'a été qu'un simple recarrossage de la version existante. Ford avait justifié cette décision en soulignant qu'on privilégiait la fiabilité et un prix de vente plus compétitif. Dans cette transition, il y a un modèle qui est éliminé, il s'agit de la version Coupé. Personne ne s'en plaindra parce que cette voiture ne se vendait absolument pas et sa conduite était d'un ennui mortel. On devrait même remercier la direction de la compagnie de l'avoir éliminé de façon prématurée.

La focus 2010 ½ est propulsée par un moteur quatre cylindres de 2,0 litres d'une puissance de 140 chevaux. Elle est équipée de série d'une boîte manuelle à cinq rapports tandis qu'une automatique à quatre vitesses est disponible en option. Il n'y a pas de mauvaises choses à dire sur ce moteur mais pas d'excellentes non plus. Il est correct sans plus. Et c'est la même chose par rapport à ses performances puisque le 0-100 km/h est bouclé en

FEU VERT

(Modèle 2010 1/2)
Mécanique fiable
Équipement complet
Tenue de route correcte
Abandon du coupé
Prix compétitifs

FEU ROUGE

(Modèle 2010 1/2)
Insonorisation perfectible
Système SYNC
parfois récalcitrant
Performances modestes
Boîte automatique
quatre rapports

moins de 10 secondes, mais c'est très juste. Ces chiffres ont été obtenus avec une voiture équipée de boîte manuelle et en conduisant de façon très agressive.

LE FUTUR MAINTENANT

La future Focus a été développée en grande partie au centre de développement des petites voitures de Ford situé à Merkenich en banlieue de Cologne en Allemagne. Les moteurs ont été mis au point au centre technique de ce constructeur à Dunton en Grande-Bretagne en collaboration avec les ingénieurs américains de Dearborn. La production initiale des premières voitures sera effectuée en même temps dans les usines de la compagnie en Allemagne, en Amérique et en Chine. La production doit débuter à la fin de l'année 2010 pour que les véhicules pour faire leur entrée sur notre marché au cours des premiers mois de 2011. Les versions nord-américaines seront propulsées par un tout nouveau moteur 2,0 litres dont la puissance sera approximativement de 160 chevaux. Il sera possible d'associer ce moteur à une toute nouvelle transmission automatique à double embrayage que Ford dit être d'une grande efficacité. De plus, on nous promet une substantielle réduction de la consommation de carburant.

Lors de son dévoilement, la focus 2012 a immédiatement enthousiasmé les personnes présentes en raison de sa silhouette fort élégante. Certains trouvent qu'elle ressemble de trop près à la nouvelle Fiesta, mais c'est quand même mieux que ce que nous propose la version actuelle. Par contre, l'habitacle est totalement différent de celui de la Fiesta. Cette présentation est vraiment unique en son genre. Les stylistes ont refusé d'utiliser à nouveau cette console centrale encadrée par des buses de ventilation insérée dans des triangles pointant vers le bas comme c'est le cas sur bien des modèles.

Chez Ford, on à également dévoilé une version familiale lors du dernier Salon de l'automobile de Genève. On se souvient que la Focus familiale était très populaire sur notre marché avant d'être abandonnée il y a une couple d'années. Il faut espérer que ce modèle ne sera pas confiné aux marchés européens.

Et la direction de Ford nous a promis une version 100 % électrique de la Focus au cours de 2011. Ça promet !

Denis Duquet

PHOTOS : FORD

Catégorie	Berline
Échelle de prix	14 999 $ à 20 399 $ (2010)
Garanties	3 ans/60 000 km, 5 ans/100 000 km
Assemblage	Wayne, Michigan, É-U
Cote d'assurance	moyenne

FORD FOCUS

CHÂSSIS - DONNÉES POUR SEL BERLINE

Emp/lon/lar/haut	2 591/4 445/1 702/1 473 mm
Coffre	368 litres
Réservoir	49 litres
Nombre coussins sécurité	6
Antipatinage / contrôle stabilité	oui / oui
Suspension avant	indépendante, jambes de force
Suspension arrière	indépendante, multibras
Freins avant / arrière	disque (ABS) / tambour (ABS)
Direction	à crémaillère, assistée
Diamètre de braquage	10,4 m
Pneus avant / arrière	P205/50R16 / P205/50R16
Poids	1 190 kg
Capacité de remorquage	454 kg (1 000 lb)

COMPOSANTES MÉCANIQUES

S, SE, SEL, SES

Cylindrée, soupapes, alim.	4L 2,0 litres 16 s atmos.
Puissance / Couple	140 chevaux / 136 lb-pi
Tr. base (opt) / rouage base (opt)	M5 (A4) / Tr
0-100 / 80-120 / 100-0 km/h	9,6 s / 7,9 s / 47,9 m
Type ess. / ville / autoroute	Ordinaire / 8,5 / 5,6 l/100 km

DANS LA MÊME CATÉGORIE

Chevrolet Cruze, Dodge Caliber, Honda Civic, Hyundai Elantra, Kia Forte, Mazda3, Mitsubishi Lancer, Nissan Sentra, Subaru Impreza, Suzuki SX-4, Toyota Corolla, Volkswagen Golf

DU NOUVEAU EN 2011

Version coupé abandonnée. Nouveau modèle sera dévoilé en cours d'année

NOS IMPRESSIONS

Agrément de conduite :	7/10
Fiabilité :	8/10
Sécurité :	8/10
Qualités hivernales :	7/10
Espace intérieur :	8/10
Confort :	7/10

www.ford.ca

Plus d'informations dans la section statistiques en dernière partie du Guide

FIÈRE ET SANS COMPLEXE

Savez-vous pourquoi Ford s'en tire mieux que les deux autres constructeurs américains? Non pas parce que son département de marketing est meilleur qu'un autre, et non plus parce qu'il n'a pas eu recours à du financement gouvernemental. Non, si Ford s'en tire mieux, c'est simplement parce que ses voitures l'ont, l'affaire.

Une des plus récentes démonstrations de ce savoir-faire chez Ford, c'est la Fusion Hybride. Arrivée il y a un peu plus d'un an, la berline «verte» reprenait le meilleur de la voiture lancée trois ans plus tôt, mais l'améliorait d'une nouvelle calandre et lui adjoignait un système hybride performant. Conséquence: cette Fusion Hybride allie le plaisir de conduire à un habitacle joliment aménagé, de même qu'à une puissance qui n'entache pas la frugalité attendue. En prime, le tout s'apprivoise nettement mieux que la Toyota Prius.

La technologie de propulsion essence-électricité est la même que celle qui s'est généralisée au cours de la dernière décennie. Mais surprise: alors que la compétition ne peut rouler plus vite que 40 km/h en mode électrique, la Fusion Hybride accepte de rouler, merci à un convertisseur de tension variable, jusqu'à 75 km/h en mode 100% électrique. C'est majeur comme avancée commercialisée à grande échelle.

Bon, vrai qu'il faut être doux avec l'accélérateur, sinon le moteur à combustion se met vitement de la partie et ç'en est fini, de la balade silencieuse sans émissions. Aussi, seule une courte distance peut être parcourue: quatre ou cinq kilomètres au max.

Mais quatre ou cinq kilomètres par-ci par-là, sans compter la manière dont le moteur à combustion se désengage (sans heurt),

voilà qui accorde une bonne frugalité: 4,3 L/100 km en conduite consciencieuse. Pour les fanas de l'hyperkilométrage, sachez que le 3,0 L/100 km est possible – ça a été réalisé aux États-Unis sur une distance de 2360 kilomètres, mais il a fallu trois nuits et trois jours...

BONNE PUISSANCE POUR UNE HYBRIDE

Il n'y a pas qu'au chapitre de la consommation et de l'autonomie électriques que la Fusion repousse les limites de l'hybride. Elle le fait aussi en vigueur, avec ses 191 chevaux développés en combiné par son quatre cylindres Atkinson de 2,5 litres et son moteur électrique de 70 kW. Voilà de la bonne puissance pour une intermédiaire, avec en prime le 0-100 km/h à 9,2 secondes.

Qu'elle soit hybride ou pas, la Fusion prétend à de belles qualités de routière. Dès son lancement en 2006, elle s'est attiré moult éloges pour son comportement mature et bien planté (mais pas ennuyant pour autant), son contrôle en virage (avec toutefois un zeste de roulis) et ses accélérations linéaires. On ne devrait pas être surpris: la voiture partage sa plate-forme avec la Mazda6 et si elle n'a pas la nervosité de la japonaise (la suspension laisse entrevoir de la mollesse sur les cahots), elle en garde l'équilibre

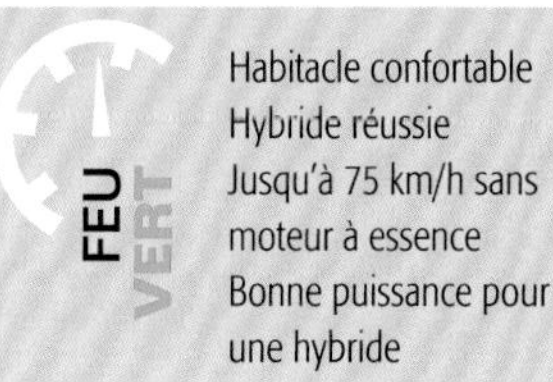

FEU VERT

Habitacle confortable
Hybride réussie
Jusqu'à 75 km/h sans moteur à essence
Bonne puissance pour une hybride

FEU ROUGE

Les batteries handicapent l'espace de chargement
Banquette qui ne se rabat pas (hybride)
Toujours pas de motorisation Ecoboost pour la Fusion
Chère, l'hybride

et l'assurance. Pour l'hybride, tant sa direction électrique (précise et cohérente avec les ordres qu'on lui donne) que sa transmission CVT ne dénaturent pas l'expérience de conduite – avouez, on ne peut en dire autant de toutes les hybrides. Dans ses variantes V6, la Fusion propose la traction intégrale.

PAS DE GÉANT, CÔTÉ INTÉRIEUR

Si vous n'êtes pas montés à bord d'une Ford depuis longtemps, vous ne savez pas que le constructeur américain a développé (et maintenu) tout un talent dans la conception d'habitacles confortables, efficaces et bien assemblés. Les designs sont intéressants, tant pour le coup d'œil que pour leur utilisation, avec des commandes intelligentes et faciles à manipuler.

La cabine de la Fusion, pratique et moderne, nous fait tout de suite nous sentir à la maison. Les sièges avant sont confortables et l'espace aux jambes arrière est fort respectable. Dans les versions plus luxueuses, on a droit à du cuir surpiqué et des appliques laquées, de bel effet. Dans les variantes de base, les plastiques de recouvrement sont caoutchouteux, agréables au toucher et l'insonorisation est de qualité. Bravo pour le volant inclinable et télescopique !

Qui dit hybride, dit généralement complexité d'instrumentation. La Fusion Hybride, tout au contraire, condense les données de consommation et tout le tra-la-la essence/électrique en des tableaux qui n'encombrent pas l'écran. Tout se lit clairement et le conducteur peut même personnaliser la chose, dans une manœuvre simple « once and for all ».

Glissées à l'arrière, les batteries nécessaires au système hybride empêchent évidemment le rabattement de la banquette, en plus de handicaper près du tiers du coffre. Il reste quand même 334 litres pour se débrouiller, côté chargement – la Fusion ordinaire, avec ses 467 litres, offre déjà plus de chargement que la moyenne de sa catégorie.

Mais, et il faut le dire : si la Fusion quatre cylindres débute à un prix de base très intéressant versus la concurrence, la variante écolo fait grimper la facture de plus de 10 000 $. Non seulement la différence est énorme, mais c'est aussi plus cher que la principale concurrente. Dommage.

Nadine Filion

PHOTOS : FORD

Catégorie	Berline
Échelle de prix	20 439 $ à 32 291 $ (2010)
Garanties	3 ans/60 000 km, 5 ans/100 000 km
Assemblage	Hermosillo, Mexique
Cote d'assurance	moyenne

CHÂSSIS - DONNÉES POUR SEL 2.5L

Emp/lon/lar/haut	2 718/4 826/2 032/1 422 mm
Coffre	467 litres
Réservoir	64 litres
Nombre coussins sécurité	6
Antipatinage / contrôle stabilité	oui / oui
Suspension avant	indépendante, bras inégaux
Suspension arrière	indépendante, multibras
Freins avant / arrière	disque (ABS) / disque (ABS)
Direction	à crémaillère, ass. variable électrique
Diamètre de braquage	11,4 m
Pneus avant / arrière	P205/60R16 / P205/60R16
Poids	1 490 kg
Capacité de remorquage	n.d.

COMPOSANTES MÉCANIQUES

Hybride

Cylindrée, soupapes, alim.	4L 2,5 litres 16 s atmos.
Puissance / Couple	156 ch (191 ch net) / 136 lb-pi
Tr. base (opt) / rouage base (opt)	CVT / Tr
0-100 / 80-120 / 100-0 km/h	9.2 s / 6,1 s / 42,3 m
Type ess. / ville / autoroute	Ordinaire / 4,6 / 5,4 l/100 km

S, SE, SEL 2.5L

Cylindrée, soupapes, alim.	4L 2,5 litres 16 s atmos.
Puissance / Couple	175 chevaux / 172 lb-pi
Tr. base (opt) / rouage base (opt)	M6 (A6) / Tr
0-100 / 80-120 / 100-0 km/h	9,9 s / 7,0 s / 46,0 m
Type ess. / ville / autoroute	Ordinaire / 9,4 / 6,4 l/100 km

SEL 3.0L, SEL 3.0L TI

V6 3,0 l, 240 ch, 223 lb-pi - 0-100 : 7,6 s - 11,8 / 7,8 l/100 km

Spor

V6 3,5 l, 263 ch, 249 lb-pi - 0-100 : 7,1 s - 12,6 / 8,3 l/100 km

DANS LA MÊME CATÉGORIE

Chevrolet Malibu, Chrysler Sebring, Dodge Avenger, Honda Accord, Hyundai Sonata, Mazda6, Nissan Altima, Subaru Legacy, Toyota Camry

DU NOUVEAU EN 2011

Aucun changement majeur

NOS IMPRESSIONS

Agrément de conduite :	8/10
Fiabilité :	10/10
Sécurité :	10/10
Qualités hivernales :	8/10
Espace intérieur :	8/10
Confort :	8/10

www.ford.ca

Plus d'informations dans la section statistiques en dernière partie du Guide

LE RETOUR DU 5,0 LITRES !

À l'époque où les coupés sport ont commencé à baisser en intérêt, Ford a décidé de persévérer en continuant d'offrir sa Mustang. À une époque où GM et Chrysler avaient retiré du marché la Camaro et la Challenger, Ford a décidé de persévérer en continuant d'offrir sa Mustang. Est-ce que la persévérance paie? Très souvent! Une décennie plus tard, il faut avouer que Ford a pris le bon pari, puisque la Mustang n'a pas cessé d'avoir du succès.

Proposée sur le marché depuis plus de 45 ans, la Mustang s'est écoulée à pas moins de 9 millions d'exemplaires au cours de ces années. Le plus beau, c'est qu'elle continue de soulever les passions après tout ce temps et qu'on en retrouve toujours bon nombre sur nos routes, tellement que GM et Chrysler ont ravivé leur « Pony car » histoire de profiter de l'engouement. Avec cette nouvelle concurrence, la Mustang a connu une année 2010 plus difficile, surtout en raison de la comparaison au chapitre des chiffres avec ses rivales.

DEUX NOUVEAUX MOTEURS, LE RETOUR DU LÉGENDAIRE 5,0 LITRES !

Histoire de mieux rivaliser en 2011 et surtout d'apporter du nouveau, Ford revoit ses motorisations et propose des puissances à la hausse. La Mustang V6 devient donc pratiquement aussi puissante que l'ancienne GT grâce à son nouveau moteur de 3,7 litres développant 305 chevaux pour un couple de 280 lb pi. À 22 999 $ pour un coupé sport de 305 chevaux, qui dit mieux? Voilà certainement une motorisation qui fera pencher les chiffres de vente vers la Mustang V6, puisque cette dernière devient une voiture drôlement performante, et non une Mustang uniquement abordable.

Par contre, la Mustang GT est loin d'être en reste pour 2011, puisque non seulement elle hérite d'un nouveau moteur, mais Ford en profite au passage pour raviver une appellation issue du passé. Eh oui, pour 2011, vous pourrez commander votre « Mustang 5,0 litres » grâce à l'arrivée d'un tout nouveau V8, de 5,0 litres bien entendu, ce dernier ne développant pas moins de 412 chevaux pour un couple de 390 lb-pi à 7 000 tr/min. Voilà qui permet à la Mustang de mieux rivaliser avec les versions performantes proposées par la compétition. Restons dans le positif puisque malgré cette hausse de puissance, la Mustang GT 2011 offre une consommation de carburant inférieure à l'ancienne grâce notamment à l'incorporation de la technologie de distribution variable indépendante (Ti-VCT) et à l'utilisation de matériaux plus légers dans la conception du moteur.

Histoire d'éclipser la compétition, vous pourrez toujours jeter votre dévolu sur la Mustang Shelby GT500, une véritable bombe dont le moteur V8 suralimenté de 5,4 litres développe un impressionnant 540 chevaux. Voilà une Mustang qui demeure toujours intimidante, sa puissance et son électronique limitée demandant une extrême vigilance.

Nouveaux moteurs plus modernes
Prix compétitif
Insonorisation en hausse
Puissance du V8

Volant non télescopique
Places arrière symboliques
Habitacle trop sobre
Suspension arrière à essieu rigide
Changements stylistiques trop discrets

TOUT SUR LA MÉCANIQUE, PEU POUR LE STYLE !

Du reste, la Mustang 2011 hérite de peu de changements à l'extérieur. On a revu le capot, ce qui lui va à ravir, mais l'arrière demeure fidèle à l'année modèle 2010, donc affligé d'un design que certains déplorent. Disons que les nouvelles motorisations ont de quoi éclipser ces quelques désagréments. Ford propose toutefois de nouvelles jantes qui rehaussent certainement le style de la voiture. Les roues font toujours une différence incroyable et cet élément a souvent été négligé dans le cas de la Mustang. Du reste, difficile de manquer les larges emblèmes 5.0 qu'arborent les flancs de la GT.

Au chapitre des déceptions, on remarque l'absence d'une colonne de direction télescopique, et oui, encore. Les places arrière conservent leur fonction utilitaire étant bien peu confortables.

Sur la route, la Mustang V6 hérite non seulement de performances plus enlevantes, mais les ingénieurs ont revu entièrement la suspension tout en améliorant la rigidité structurelle. On obtient une voiture bien balancée, capable de maîtriser la puissance supplémentaire. Bon point également pour la sonorité améliorée du moteur. Bien entendu, la GT s'avère plus brutale et sa puissance et son couple y sont pour beaucoup. Enfoncez l'accélérateur et vous sentirez le V8 libérer toute sa puissance, le tout avec une riche sonorité. Le seul élément négatif touche son essieu rigide qui, une fois de plus, laisse valser la voiture sur les bosses au lieu qu'on la sente clouée au bitume. Mais pour en revenir à la version à moteur V6, c'est toute une aubaine compte tenu de son prix et de ses performances. Ceci s'applique tout particulièrement à la version cabriolet.

Le freinage est aussi amélioré, mais la voiture est avantagée lorsqu'elle est équipée de l'ensemble Freinage de performance comprenant des freins Brembo. Bon point également pour la visibilité à bord qui demeure très bonne, surtout pour un coupé sport.

Il faut avouer que Ford à su répliquer à la compétition en proposant ces deux nouvelles motorisations, permettant ainsi à la Mustang de revenir à l'avant-plan. Si les gens du marketing chez Ford se sont fait damer le pion par ceux de GM donnant la vedette à la Camaro dans les films Transformer, le retour du 5,0 litres demeure un bon coup !

Sylvain Raymond

PHOTOS : SYLVAIN RAYMOND

Catégorie	Cabriolet, Coupé
Échelle de prix	20 439 $ à 63 699 $
Garanties	3 ans/60 000 km, 5 ans/100 000 km
Assemblage	Dearborn, Michigan, É-U
Cote d'assurance	passable

CHÂSSIS - DONNÉES POUR SHELBY GT500 COUPÉ

Emp/lon/lar/haut	2 720/4 778/1 877/1 438 mm
Coffre	379 litres
Réservoir	61 litres
Nombre coussins sécurité	4
Antipatinage / contrôle stabilité	oui / oui
Suspension avant	indépendante, jambes de force
Suspension arrière	indépendante, multibras
Freins avant / arrière	disque (ABS) / disque (ABS)
Direction	à crémaillère, assistée
Diamètre de braquage	11,6 m
Pneus avant / arrière	P255/40ZR19 / P285/35ZR19
Poids	1 733 kg
Capacité de remorquage	non recommandé

COMPOSANTES MÉCANIQUES

V6

Cylindrée, soupapes, alim.	V6 3,7 litres 24 s atmos.
Puissance / Couple	305 chevaux / 280 lb-pi
Tr. base (opt) / rouage base (opt)	M6 (A6, A5) / Prop
0-100 / 80-120 / 100-0 km/h	6,5 s / 6,0 s (est) / n.d.
Type ess. / ville / autoroute	Ordinaire / 12,4 / 7,6 l/100 km

GT

Cylindrée, soupapes, alim.	V8 5,0 litres 32 s atmos.
Puissance / Couple	412 chevaux / 390 lb-pi
Tr. base (opt) / rouage base (opt)	M5 (A6, A5) / Prop
0-100 / 80-120 / 100-0 km/h	5,1 s (est) / 5,0 s (est) / n.d.
Type ess. / ville / autoroute	Super / 13,8 / 9,0 l/100 km

Shelby GT500

Cylindrée, soupapes, alim.	V8 5,4 litres 32 s surcomp.
Puissance / Couple	540 chevaux / 510 lb-pi
Tr. base (opt) / rouage base (opt)	M6 / Prop
0-100 / 80-120 / 100-0 km/h	4,6 s / 3,3 s / 36,0 m
Type ess. / ville / autoroute	Super / 15,7 / 10,2 l/100 km

DANS LA MÊME CATÉGORIE

Chevrolet Camaro, Dodge Challenger, Hyundai Genesis Coupe, Mazda RX-8, Mitsubishi Eclipse, Volkswagen Eos

DU NOUVEAU EN 2011

Nouveaux moteurs 3,7 litres et 5,0 litres

NOS IMPRESSIONS

Agrément de conduite :	■■■■■■■■■□	9/10
Fiabilité :	■■■■■■□□□□	6/10
Sécurité :	■■■■■■■■□□	8/10
Qualités hivernales :	■■■■■□□□□□	5/10
Espace intérieur :	■■■■■■□□□□	6/10
Confort :	■■■■■■■□□□	7/10

www.ford.ca

Plus d'informations dans la section statistiques en dernière partie du Guide

AVEC OU SANS TURBO: N'IMPORTE QUAND!

La cerise, que cette Ford Taurus SHO de performance? Pour cela, il faudrait que le dessert soit visuellement moins «diète». Mais n'importe quand, je la prendrais comme plat principal. Sa version de base itou, d'ailleurs.

La version SHO de la Taurus n'a pas l'air de ce dont elle est capable. À peine un aileron sur son coffre, des roues de 20 pouces et un double échappement, sans plus. Certes, elle profite d'une suspension raffermie et d'éléments intérieurs qui diffèrent, tels des appliques d'aluminium et du suède aux sièges. Mais dehors, il manque ce «wow» qui lui aurait accordé un air moins débonnaire.

Pourtant, elle en mérite, cette SHO, des signes distinctifs. Je ne sais pas, moi, une calandre qui se démarque, des jupes latérales et, surtout, un son pas mal plus grondant. Après tout, la voiture recèle un V6 de 3,5 litres qui, biturbocompressé (oui, oui, double turbo), dispose de 365 chevaux. C'est beaucoup. C'est même trop, diront certains (mais pas nous, ooooh non!). En troquant un V8 pour ce type de motorisation, Ford vise l'économie d'essence, mais difficile de faire mieux qu'un combiné de 14 l/100 km, avec toute cette puissance sous le pied...

MALGRÉ LE POIDS

Les autres variantes ne sont pas piquées des vers pour autant. Même sans turbo, le V6 (3,5 litres) de 263 chevaux se démène avec une belle aisance. Étonnement, le dynamisme n'est pas entaché par le poids du véhicule, pourtant de plus de deux tonnes métriques. C'est dire à quel point tout est linéaire et bien distribué. Mais vrai qu'avec la SHO, les accélérations sont encore plus... plus! Pas une hésitation des turbos, ce en quoi il faut remercier l'injection directe. On enfonce la pédale et ça décolle,

dans un 0-100 km/h en 6,3 secondes (tests menés par l'AJAC). On ne devrait pas comparer, mais sachez que c'est plus vite que pour les Volks GTi et MazdaSpeed3...

Aussi, difficile de croire que la direction est ici électrique (elle reste hydraulique sur la Taurus de base) tant la connexion avec la route est à la fois solennelle et précise. Le freinage est efficace, progressif et bien dosé. Le châssis est d'une grande solidité, la suspension d'un bel équilibre (j'vous jure, elle n'est pas molle sur nos routes défoncées) et on attaque les virages sans craindre. Même que lorsqu'on les prend à 100 km/h, ces virages, on a l'impression de filer moitié moins vite. La traction intégrale est évidemment de série pour la SHO, ce qui aide à garder le droit chemin. Et dans l'ensemble, la conduite livre une rassurante, mais non ennuyante, impression d'équilibre et de maturité.

Ceci dit, la Taurus, SHO ou pas, demeure une très grande berline. Sa silhouette de 5,2 mètres, jumelée à une mince lunette arrière, handicape les manœuvres de recul et impose l'assistance, sonore ou visuelle. Elle est si grande, la Taurus, que même sans en rabattre la banquette, le coffre dispose de 569 litres – un tiers plus que

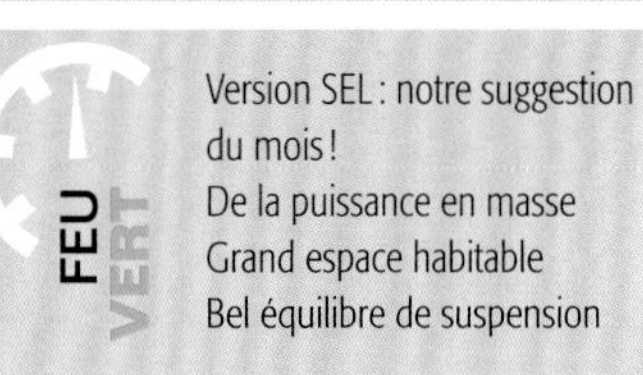

FEU VERT

- Version SEL : notre suggestion du mois !
- De la puissance en masse
- Grand espace habitable
- Bel équilibre de suspension

FEU ROUGE

- Manque de signes pour distinguer la SHO
- V6 biturbo pas si économe que ça…
- Longue silhouette à déplacer
- Absence de boîte manuelle pour la SHO

la moyenne de la catégorie. C'est sans compter un vaste dégagement aux jambes arrière plus que ça et ça tiendrait de la limousine…

Voilà pourquoi il est difficile de considérer la Taurus comme une des sportives de l'heure. Pour ça, il lui faudrait plus qu'une cerise « Ecoboost ». On exagère peut-être, mais… pourquoi pas une boîte manuelle ? Actuellement, si l'automatique six rapports fait du bon boulot lorsqu'on la laisse faire, c'est moins plaisant lorsqu'on décide d'en manier les palettes au volant. Ces petites commandes en plastique (eh oui, du plastique…) sont peu instinctives et exigent qu'on passe le levier en position M. Pour la performance vitement au bout des doigts, on repassera…

RENDONS À CÉSAR…

Il y a des gens pour dire que Ford s'en tire mieux que les autres constructeurs américains car, et je cite : « Ils n'ont rien demandé aux gouvernements ». C'est accorder bien peu de crédit à une entreprise qui a mis les efforts nécessaires pour développer des produits complets. Regardez l'actuelle gamme Ford ; qu'y voyez-vous ? Des bagnoles suffisamment intéressantes pour figurer en tête des listes d'achats.

Une des grandes réussites chez Ford, ce sont ses habitacles et la Taurus en est une autre preuve. Les matériaux sont d'excellente facture, la finition est de qualité – mieux que l'assemblage extérieur qui laisse paraître quelques panneaux mal accolés. Les sièges sont confortables et, en haut de gamme, ils offrent la fonction massage – le paradis… L'instrumentation est moderne et les commandes faciles à apprivoiser. Enfin, l'insonorisation est remarquable : une fois vitres et portières fermées, la cabine est totalement isolée des bruits extérieurs.

Après les fleurs, le pot, vous dites ? Bah, juste un point négatif : la Taurus, surtout SHO, fait tellement monter de gens à bord que c'est à se demander pourquoi les clients se donneraient la peine de magasiner chez Lincoln ! Un dernier mot ? À notre avis, c'est la version SEL qui vaut vraiment le coût. Elle peut s'amener avec la traction intégrale, la climatisation automatique, le démarrage sans clé, les sièges chauffants *ET* réfrigérants. Quand même…

Nadine Filion

PHOTOS : SYLVAIN RAYMOND

Catégorie	Berline
Échelle de prix	26 484 $ à 43 902 $
Garanties	3 ans/60 000 km, 5 ans/100 000 km
Assemblage	Chicago, Illinois, É-U
Cote d'assurance	bonne

CHÂSSIS - DONNÉES POUR SEL TI

Emp/lon/lar/haut	2 868/5 154/1 936/1 542 mm
Coffre	569 litres
Réservoir	72 litres
Nombre coussins sécurité	6
Antipatinage / contrôle stabilité	oui / oui
Suspension avant	indépendante, jambes de force
Suspension arrière	indépendante, multibras
Freins avant / arrière	disques (ABS) / disques (ABS)
Direction	à crémaillère, assistée
Diamètre de braquage	12,2 m
Pneus avant / arrière	P235/55R18 / P235/55R18
Poids	1 916 kg
Capacité de remorquage	454 kg (1 000 lb)

COMPOSANTES MÉCANIQUES

SE, SEL, Limited

Cylindrée, soupapes, alim.	V6 3,5 litres 24 s atmos.
Puissance / Couple	263 chevaux / 249 lb-pi
Tr. base (opt) / rouage base (opt)	A6 / Tr (Int)
0-100 / 80-120 / 100-0 km/h	8,2 s / 5,8 s / 39,8 m
Type ess. / ville / autoroute	Ordinaire / 12,3 / 7,8 l/100 km

SHO

Cylindrée, soupapes, alim.	V6 3,5 litres 24 s turbo
Puissance / Couple	365 chevaux / 350 lb-pi
Tr. base (opt) / rouage base (opt)	A6 / Int
0-100 / 80-120 / 100-0 km/h	6,3 s / 4,3 s / 40,3 m
Type ess. / ville / autoroute	Ordinaire / 12,4 / 8,0 l/100 km

DANS LA MÊME CATÉGORIE

Buick LaCrosse, Chevrolet Impala, Chrysler 300, Dodge Charger, Nissan Maxima, Toyota Avalon

DU NOUVEAU EN 2011

Aucun changement majeur

NOS IMPRESSIONS

Agrément de conduite :	7/10
Fiabilité :	8/10
Sécurité :	8/10
Qualités hivernales :	7/10
Espace intérieur :	9/10
Confort :	8/10

www.ford.ca

Plus d'informations dans la section statistiques en dernière partie du Guide

QUAND L'EUROPE FRAPPE À LA PORTE

Quiconque a déjà mis les pieds en Europe a certainement remarqué nombre de petits véhicules commerciaux. En Amérique, on ne jure que par les Ford de la série E ou les Chevrolet Express / GMC Savana, même dans les centres-villes bondés, mais de l'autre côté du trou d'eau, les différents besoins des gens et, surtout, les rues souvent très étroites, ont mené à la création de véhicules plus petits. L'un d'eux, le Ford Transit Connect, a fait le saut. Il a certes l'air un peu bizarre dans notre jungle automobile mais on s'y fait rapidement.

Le Transit Connect s'adresse à un public beaucoup plus large qu'il n'y paraît de prime abord. Considéré à juste titre comme un véhicule commercial, il est proposé chez nous en trois versions: complètement fermée, fermée avec glaces aux portes arrière et en livrée Tourisme, avec des vitres latérales. Beaucoup de plombiers, d'électriciens ou même de livreurs de petits colis n'ont pas besoin d'un gros véhicule mais plutôt d'un grand espace de chargement.

PAS GROS MAIS MARTEAU

Même s'il est petit, le Transit Connect est un véritable camion. Il est bâti sur une plate-forme autonome et tous ses organes mécaniques sont qualifiés pour le gros ouvrage. Henry Ford, le fondateur, en aurait été fier! Le moteur en est un bel exemple. Ce quatre cylindres de 2,0 litres n'est pas vraiment puissant avec ses 136 chevaux et ses 128 livres-pied de couple. On se demande même comment une si petite écurie pourra mouvoir le véhicule une fois qu'il sera chargé. Cependant, dès les premiers kilomètres, la sonorité et la rugosité de ce moteur donnent à penser qu'il est fait fort et qu'il compensera en durabilité ce qu'il perd en puissance. Les accélérations et dépassements exigent d'ailleurs une certaine planification, même quand la boîte est vide. Même si les moteurs diesel n'ont pas la cote en Amérique (sauf au Québec, société distincte), il est évident que ce type de motorisation est celui qui conviendrait le mieux au Transit Connect, surtout en raison de son couple très élevé, ce qui lui permettrait de transporter des cargaisons encore plus lourdes sans vraiment affecter la consommation. La transmission est une automatique à quatre rapports au comportement sans histoire. Un rapport supplémentaire ferait par contre diminuer le bruit dans l'habitacle. Parce que comme insonorisation, on a déjà fait mieux...

Le Transit Connect est un camion et il se conduit comme tel. Les suspensions tapent plutôt dur mais il faut avouer que durant notre semaine d'essai, nous avons trimballé 3830 litres d'air. Avec une partie arrière le moindrement chargée (maximum de 1600 livres ou 725 kilos), ces suspensions auraient eu moins le loisir de gambader à leur guise. En virage, on dénote, sans surprise, un roulis certain et il faut tenir compte du centre de gravité assez élevé tandis que la direction nous étonne par sa précision.

Dans l'habitacle, les plastiques durs nous rappellent la vocation première du petit véhicule. Le tableau de bord est plus pratique

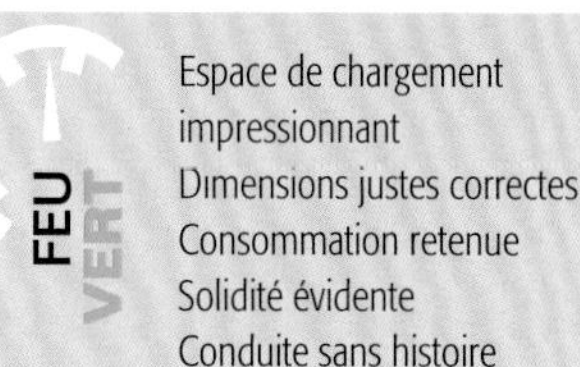

- Espace de chargement impressionnant
- Dimensions justes correctes
- Consommation retenue
- Solidité évidente
- Conduite sans histoire

- Confort très « camion »
- Prix assez élevé
- Puissance juste
- Visibilité arrière problématique
- Facture trop commerciale

qu'esthétique. Heureusement, toutes les commandes et jauges sont là où il le faut et sont faciles à comprendre. Pour sacrer un peu, il faut tenter, par une journée de pluie, d'ouvrir le capot sans au préalable lire le manuel d'instruction… Les sièges, qui ne sont pas chauffants même en option, sont fermes et leur tissu s'avère très résistant. La délicatesse, c'est pour les voitures de tourisme ! Le volant, ajustable en hauteur et télescopique, se prend bien en main et n'est pas trop à l'horizontale comme on serait en droit de s'y attendre. À bord de notre version avec glaces aux portes arrière, la visibilité n'était pas trop mauvaise, étant donné qu'il n'y avait aucune ouverture sur les côtés arrière. Vers l'avant, cependant, aucun problème ! En fait, le seul problème que votre humble serviteur a eu fut de s'habituer à la forte odeur de caoutchouc émanant du tapis recouvrant la boîte.

TOUT UN VIDE !

Une fois les deux portes arrière à charnière ouvertes à 180 degrés, on se retrouve devant une immense caverne dont le seuil est très bas. Je n'ai sans doute pas trouvé comment régler ce problème mais les portes ne restaient pas ouvertes à 180 degrés lorsque le véhicule était stationné dans une pente ascendante. Puisque le Transit Connect est un véhicule commercial, la boîte de chargement est dans un état brut. Oubliez les beaux plastiques recouvrant les parois et cachant les montants. Il faut se souvenir qu'on n'achète pas un Transit Connect pour son confort et son raffinement !

Pour 2011, la gamme du Transit Connect s'enrichit d'un modèle Taxi, disponible avec deux, quatre ou cinq sièges. Parfait pour le transport de gros bagages. On devrait bientôt en voir plusieurs dans les environs des aéroports. Et puis il y a la version électrique, destinée aux entreprises dont les véhicules ne parcourent pas plus de 130 km (80 milles). Le moteur électrique développe l'équivalent de 117 lb-pi de couple. La batterie au lithium-ion possède une capacité de 28 kWh. Enfin, un Transit Connect au gaz naturel, dévoilé au dernier Salon de l'auto de Chicago, pourrait, un jour, être disponible.

Le Transit Connect s'adresse surtout aux flottes de véhicules ou pour une utilisation commerciale. Cependant, il y a fort à parier que ce type de fourgonnette réponde aux besoins de plusieurs personnes, que ce soit pour faire du camping ou tout simplement pour transporter beaucoup, beaucoup de choses.

Alain Morin

PHOTOS : ALAIN MORIN

Catégorie	Fourgonnette
Échelle de prix	26 799 $ (2010)
Garanties	3 ans/60 000 km, 5 ans/100 000 km
Assemblage	Kocaeli, Turquie
Cote d'assurance	n.d.

CHÂSSIS - DONNÉES POUR XLT

Emp/lon/lar/haut	2 895/4 572/2 108/2 006 mm
Coffre	3 830 litres
Réservoir	56 litres
Nombre coussins sécurité	4
Antipatinage / contrôle stabilité	oui / non
Suspension avant	indépendante, jambes de force
Suspension arrière	essieu rigide, ressorts à lames
Freins avant / arrière	disque (ABS) / tambour (ABS)
Direction	à crémaillère, assistée
Diamètre de braquage	11,8 m
Pneus avant / arrière	P205/65R15 / P205/65R15
Poids	1 524 kg
Capacité de remorquage	n.d.

COMPOSANTES MÉCANIQUES

XLT	
Cylindrée, soupapes, alim.	4L 2,0 litres 16 s atmos.
Puissance / Couple	136 chevaux / 128 lb-pi
Tr. base (opt) / rouage base (opt)	A4 / Tr
0-100 / 80-120 / 100-0 km/h	12,8 s / 9,9 s / 45,0 m
Type ess. / ville / autoroute	Ordinaire / 9,5 / 7,9 l/100 km

Électrique	
moteur électrique	300 volts
Couple	117 lb-pi continu, 173 lb-pi max
Transmission	vitesse unique
Batterie	Li-ion, 28 kW/h, 215 à 390 volts
Autonomie	128 km
0-100 km/h	environ 12 secondes

DANS LA MÊME CATÉGORIE

Chevrolet HHR

DU NOUVEAU EN 2011

Nouveau modèle électrique sera disponible en cours d'année
Nouveau modèle taxi

NOS IMPRESSIONS

Agrément de conduite :	7/10
Fiabilité :	n.d.
Sécurité :	7/10
Qualités hivernales :	7/10
Espace intérieur :	10/10
Confort :	7/10

www.ford.ca

Plus d'informations dans la section statistiques en dernière partie du Guide

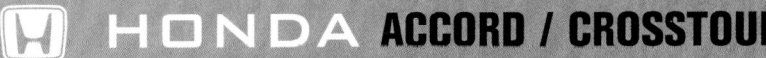

LA NOUVEAUTÉ VIENT LA SAUVER

Depuis sa refonte, la Honda Accord a perdu sa suprématie. On sait tous combien une réputation est aussi difficile à établir qu'elle est rapide à ruiner. Heureusement, la version à hayon, ou familiale, ou encore multisegments (mais appelez-la donc comme vous voulez !) – bref, la CrossTour, vient sauver les meubles.

Il y a trois ans, la Honda Accord s'est payée une 8e génération (quand même), mais ça n'a pas suffit. Cette année-là, l'intermédiaire la plus vendue du continent s'est fait supplanter par la Chevrolet Malibu l'un des Meilleurs véhicules nord-américains. Et *v'lan*, dans les dents.

Cette gifle était-elle méritée ? Sur certains points, non, car la berline (et son coupé) a vraiment pris du galon, côté dimensions. Même qu'on aurait dû lui faire quitter les intermédiaires pour mieux la faire passer chez les grandes, tellement son espace habitable est généreux. Vrai aussi que ses moteurs sont parmi les plus intéressants. Le quatre cylindres (2,4 litres) de 190 chevaux suffit amplement à la tâche et il est si doux qu'on l'entend à peine. Le V6 de 3,5 litres développe ses 271 chevaux sans une once d'effet de couple et si la puissance n'a pas le dynamisme des berlines allemandes, on lui reconnaît une maturité et une souplesse qu'on apprécie encore et toujours.

La direction, une bonne vieille crémaillère, est plaisante à manier de par sa précision que l'on commande du bout des doigts, et le rayon de braquage est étonnement court pour une si grande voiture. L'ensemble repose sur un solide châssis qui assure une tenue de route stable et bien équilibrée, plus agile que ne le laissent deviner ses grandes proportions. On ne reproche qu'une suspension qui travaille beaucoup, mais reste que la balade est conciliante.

Le hic, parce qu'il y en a un, est que la boîte automatique cinq rapports demeure en poste et ce, toujours sans mode manuel (sauf pour le Coupé). Sur ce chapitre, Honda manque carrément le coche dans une industrie où les transmissions se conjuguent désormais en sept, voire huit rapports, avec palettes au bout des doigts, rien de moins. Combien de fois, à bord de l'Accord, l'index monte-il au volant à la recherche des passages pour faire révolutionner le moteur ? Honda répondra qu'une meilleure consommation passe par les moteurs plutôt que par les transmissions et accordons-lui une chose : son V6 désactive la moitié de ses cylindres en puissance réduite, ce qui joue favorablement sur la facture à la station-service.

LA FAMILIALE NOUVEAU-GENRE

Toujours du côté des points faibles, il y a cette histoire de banquette : dans la berline, elle ne se rabat que d'un bloc, ce qui sacrifie toutes les places arrière. Rares sont les voitures d'aujourd'hui qui n'offrent pas le rabattement 60/40. Heureusement, la nouvelle CrossTour ne souffre pas de la même tare, sa banquette se rabattant en deux parties, laissant jusqu'à 1 453 litres de cargo derrière les sièges avant. C'est très bien.

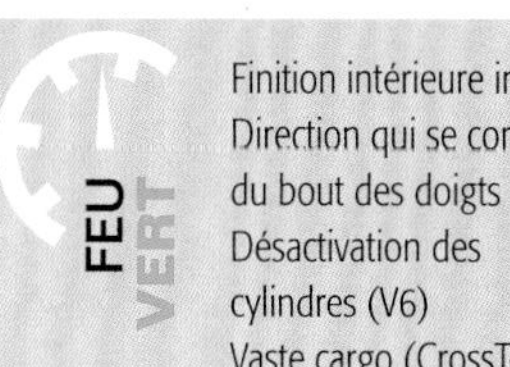

FEU VERT

Finition intérieure impeccable
Direction qui se commande du bout des doigts
Désactivation des cylindres (V6)
Vaste cargo (CrossTour)

FEU ROUGE

Insonorisation déficiente (berline)
Pas de mode manuel à l'automatique
Fourchette de prix arrogante
Banquette qui se rabat d'un seul bloc (berline)

Visuellement, la berline fait preuve d'une belle allure, quoique conservatrice, mais sa silhouette est rompue à l'arrière par un coffre proéminent, un peu comme si ce dernier avait été ajouté à la dernière minute. Encore là, c'est la CrossTour qui sauve la mise : le design fait dans l'étrange à première vue, mais à force de l'admirer, on y voit poindre l'élégance, alliée à un côté pratico-pratique qui fait que ce type de silhouette pourrait bien devenir la familiale nouveau-genre de la décennie.

ENCORE TROP CHÈRE ?

Dans l'habitacle, la finition est impeccable et les versions avec cuir et système de navigation ne jureraient pas chez Acura. Pour la berline, on note cependant une insonorisation moyenne – la faute revient à ce coffre qui, malheureusement, n'est pas tapissé de matériel isolant. Jusqu'à présent, on pestait contre les commandes de climatisation qui, divisées en deux incompréhensibles sections, n'étaient pas intuitives, mais Honda dit avoir procédé à des réaménagements pour 2011 et il faudra voir si cette fois est la bonne.

Les sièges avant sont confortables et sont faits de bons supports pour bien y reposer les cuisses. Le dos est bien soutenu et ne souffre pas, même lors de longs trajets. Bien sûr, la sécurité de série est complète, mais quelques petites gâteries devenues essentielles au fil du temps manquent encore à l'appel : le démarrage sans clé et le toit panoramique, par exemple.

Voilà qui n'empêche pas Honda de pêcher par l'excès côté prix : l'Accord est l'une des berlines les plus chères de sa catégorie et pour le prix d'une voiture moyennement équipée chez Honda, les acheteurs peuvent trouver, chez d'autres marques, une voiture beaucoup mieux pourvue. Certes, l'échelle des versions a été revue pour 2011 avec une variante de base mieux nantie et des équipements de série supplémentaires pour les autres versions.

Si le constructeur nippon restera, cette année du moins, au-dessus de ses affaires, ce sera grâce à la CrossTour. L'allure est distinguée et le concept est fort intelligent, bien que le tout ne soit servi qu'avec le V6. C'est donc au moins 35 000 $ que l'on doit débourser, voire plus, pour la traction intégrale. Pour celle de l'Accord elle-même, on en rêve toujours !

Nadine Filion

PHOTOS : HONDA

Catégorie	Multisegment, Berline, Coupé
Échelle de prix	24 790 $ à 38 900 $ (2010)
Garanties	3 ans/60 000 km, 5 ans/60 000 km
Assemblage	Marysville, Ohio, É-U
Cote d'assurance	passable

CHÂSSIS - DONNÉES POUR CROSSTOUR EX-L TI

Emp/lon/lar/haut	2 797/4 999/1 898/1 670 mm
Coffre	728 à 1 453 litres
Réservoir	70 litres
Nombre coussins sécurité	6
Antipatinage / contrôle stabilité	oui / oui
Suspension avant	indépendante, double triangulation
Suspension arrière	indépendante, multibras
Freins avant / arrière	disque (ABS) / disque (ABS)
Direction	à crémaillère, assistée
Diamètre de braquage	n.d.
Pneus avant / arrière	P225/60R18 / P225/60R18
Poids	1 845 kg
Capacité de remorquage	680 kg (1 499 lb)

COMPOSANTES MÉCANIQUES

Berline

Cylindrée, soupapes, alim.	4L 2,4 litres 16 s atmos.
Puissance / Couple	177 chevaux / 161 lb-pi
Tr. base (opt) / rouage base (opt)	M5 (A5) / Tr
0-100 / 80-120 / 100-0 km/h	9,9 s / 8,4 s / 42,3 m
Type ess. / ville / autoroute	Ordinaire / 9,4 / 6,4 l/100 km

Berline, coupé

Cylindrée, soupapes, alim.	4L 2,4 litres 16 s atmos.
Puissance / Couple	190 chevaux / 162 lb-pi
Tr. base (opt) / rouage base (opt)	M5 (A5) / Tr
0-100 / 80-120 / 100-0 km/h	9,5 s / 8,2 s / 42,3 m
Type ess. / ville / autoroute	Ordinaire / 9,4 / 6,4 l/100 km

Berline, coupé, Crosstour

Cylindrée, soupapes, alim.	V6 3,5 litres 24 s atmos.
Puissance / Couple	271 chevaux / 254 lb-pi
Tr. base (opt) / rouage base (opt)	A5 / Tr (Int)
0-100 / 80-120 / 100-0 km/h	6,6 s / 4,1 s / 42,3 m
Type ess. / ville / autoroute	Super / 12,3 / 8,0 l/100 km

DANS LA MÊME CATÉGORIE

Crosstour : Mazda CX-7, Nissan Murano, Toyota Venza
Berline : Chevrolet Malibu, Ford Fusion, Hyundai Sonata, Mazda6, Nissan Altima, Toyota Camry

DU NOUVEAU EN 2011

Modifications esthétiques apportées à l'avant et à l'arrière

NOS IMPRESSIONS

Agrément de conduite :	8/10
Fiabilité :	8/10
Sécurité :	10/10
Qualités hivernales :	8/10
Espace intérieur :	9/10
Confort :	8/10

www.honda.ca

Plus d'informations dans la section statistiques en dernière partie du Guide

UNE ANNÉE DE PLUS

La Civic demeure la voiture la plus vendue au Canada. Toutefois, la direction de Honda Canada a fait des pieds et des mains ces dernières années, afin de conserver ce précieux titre. Plusieurs d'entre vous doivent se souvenir des dernières semaines de décembre 2009 : on y a vu une succession de promotions et de rabais ciblant les acheteurs de la Civic. En dépit de cette popularité que certains jugent artificielle, plusieurs croyaient que ce modèle serait entièrement transformé pour 2011. Cependant, il faudra être patient et attendre la nouvelle génération.

En effet, les raisons officielles n'ont pas été dévoilées, mais l'arrivée sur le marché de la prochaine Civic a été retardée de plusieurs mois. Qu'à cela ne tienne, l'acheteur n'est pas laissé pour contre, car les modèles disponibles actuellement figurent toujours au sommet des meilleures compactes.

UN BEL ÉQUILIBRE

Même si la silhouette a pris de l'âge, elle continue de faire l'unanimité, ou presque, à son sujet. C'est élégant, bien équilibré et en mesure de plaire à toutes les générations. Il faut cependant souligner que la version coupée est nettement plus raffinée et demeure l'une des plus réussies de sa catégorie. L'habitacle a une belle finition et propose des plastiques de bonne qualité, même si ceux-ci sont parfois durs au toucher. Le pilote doit cependant s'habituer à un tableau de bord à deux étages puisque le compte tours est situé là où se trouve traditionnellement l'indicateur de vitesse tandis que celui-ci, à affichage numérique, se retrouve directement en haut du compte tours. Cette planche de bord est vraiment inhabituelle, donc ne fait pas nécessairement l'unanimité : elle plaît à certains et donne des boutons à d'autres !

Il faut souligner que les places arrière de la berline, qu'elle soit hybride ou traditionnelle, sont suffisamment spacieuses pour une voiture de cette catégorie. Il en est de même du coffre à bagages qui est passablement grand.

Comme toujours, les ingénieurs de Honda sont passés maîtres dans la réalisation de moteurs de petite cylindrée tournant à un assez haut régime et capables de fournir un rendement élevé tout en consommant peu. Le moteur de série est un 4 cylindres de 1,8 litre dont la puissance est de 140 chevaux. Une boîte manuelle à cinq rapports est en équipement de série tandis que l'automatique à cinq rapports est également optionnelle. Ce moteur est renommé pour sa fiabilité et sa durabilité, mais aussi pour son économie d'essence, alors que la moyenne de consommation de carburant observée pour une berline à boîte manuelle est de 7,2 litres au 100 km.

La tenue de route est bonne, la voiture prévisible dans les courbes, tandis que les accélérations sont assez nerveuses. Par contre, l'insonorisation est nettement perfectible et la pédale de frein devient parfois spongieuse. Ces observations, quant au comportement routier, valent pour la berline et le coupé. Il est

FEU VERT
- Consommation réduite
- Moteur ultra fiable
- Choix de modèles
- Version Si
- Fabrication soignée

FEU ROUGE
- Version hybride peu populaire
- Insonorisation perfectible
- Suspension ferme (Si)
- Équipement de base limité

également possible de commander une version à moteur hybride. Bien que cette dernière ne soit plus produite depuis 2009, Honda continue d'écouler les exemplaires restants. Compte tenu de son prix passablement élevé, cette berline ne jouit pas d'une popularité croissante, bien au contraire. Par contre, si vous voulez vraiment rouler au volant d'une voiture hybride fabriquée par Honda, la Civic hybride se révèle un meilleur choix que la Insight.

LA FAMILLE SI

Initialement, c'est le coupé Si qui a été commercialisé sur notre marché. Il remplaçait la version hatchback de la précédente génération qui n'avait pas connu la popularité espérée. Avec son moteur quatre cylindres 2,0 litres d'une puissance de 197 chevaux associé à une boîte manuelle à six rapports, les performances ne manquent pas à l'appel. De plus, cette boîte manuelle, la seule disponible, est un plaisir à manipuler avec des changements de rapports courts et précis. Ajoutez à cela un pédalier en aluminium, des sièges confortables offrants un excellent support latéral, et vous vous retrouvez au volant d'une fusée de poche répondant à vos moindres désirs.

En effet, la tenue de route de la Si est vraiment supérieure à la moyenne de la catégorie, et l'on entend par là les petites compactes sportives dotées d'un moteur plus puissant et d'une suspension modifiée. Bien calé dans le siège sport, c'est avec plaisir que l'on enchaîne les virages serrés tout en jouant du levier de vitesses afin de monter le moteur en régime.

Dorénavant, il est également possible de commander une berline Si avec ce même moteur et ce groupe d'équipement. Ce sera pour plusieurs familles la solution rêvée pour que papa et maman, qui aspirent à une conduite plus sportive, puissent joindre l'utile à l'agréable. Par contre, ils devront supporter une suspension passablement ferme.

Même si un nouveau modèle est prévu d'ici quelques mois, la présente édition des modèles Civic est suffisamment moderne pour répondre aux attentes et aux besoins de la grande majorité. De plus, il faudra surveiller les offres spéciales qui vous permettront d'économiser.

Denis Duquet

PHOTOS: HONDA

Catégorie	Berline, Coupé
Échelle de prix	15990$ à 25880$ (2010)
Garanties	3 ans/60000 km, 5 ans/100000 km
Assemblage	Alliston, Ontario, Canada
Cote d'assurance	n.d.

CHÂSSIS - DONNÉES POUR EX-L COUPÉ

Emp/lon/lar/haut	2650/4457/1751/1396 mm
Coffre	327 litres
Réservoir	50 litres
Nombre coussins sécurité	6
Antipatinage / contrôle stabilité	oui / oui
Suspension avant	indépendante, jambes de force
Suspension arrière	indépendante, double triangulation
Freins avant / arrière	disque (ABS) / disque (ABS)
Direction	à crémaillère, ass. variable électrique
Diamètre de braquage	10,6 m
Pneus avant / arrière	P205/55R16 / P205/55R16
Poids	1230 kg
Capacité de remorquage	454 kg (1000 lb)

COMPOSANTES MÉCANIQUES

Berline, coupé	
Cylindrée, soupapes, alim.	4L 1,8 litre 16 s atmos.
Puissance / Couple	140 chevaux / 128 lb-pi
Tr. base (opt) / rouage base (opt)	M5 (A5) / Tr
0-100 / 80-120 / 100-0 km/h	8,6 s / 7,1 s / 42,8 m
Type ess. / ville / autoroute	Ordinaire / 7,4 / 5,4 l/100 km

Berline Si, coupé Si	
Cylindrée, soupapes, alim.	4L 2,0 litres 16 s atmos.
Puissance / Couple	197 chevaux / 139 lb-pi
Tr. base (opt) / rouage base (opt)	M6 / Tr
0-100 / 80-120 / 100-0 km/h	7,4 s / 5,3 s / 40,8 m
Type ess. / ville / autoroute	Super / 10,2 / 6,8 l/100 km

DANS LA MÊME CATÉGORIE

Chevrolet Cruze, Ford Focus, Hyundai Elantra, Kia Forte, Mazda3, Mitsubishi Lancer, Nissan Sentra, Subaru Impreza, Toyota Corolla, Toyota Prius, Volkswagen Golf

DU NOUVEAU EN 2011

Aucun changement majeur

NOS IMPRESSIONS

Agrément de conduite :	7/10
Fiabilité :	10/10
Sécurité :	10/10
Qualités hivernales :	7/10
Espace intérieur :	7/10
Confort :	7/10

www.honda.ca

Plus d'informations dans la section statistiques en dernière partie du Guide

PRATIQUE CITADINE

Lorsque le premier modèle CR-V est arrivé sur notre marché, il tentait de se faire passer pour un authentique VUS. Il en avait les apparences et il pouvait être doté d'un rouage intégral permettant d'effectuer des randonnées hors route. Cependant, ce rouage intégral était beaucoup mieux adapté aux routes enneigées en hiver ou détrempées l'été. Ceux qui ont tenté de jouer les baroudeurs en circulant sur des routes quasiment impraticables se sont rapidement rendu compte des limites de ce Honda. La seconde génération se voulait plus civilisée et puissante, et on tentait toujours de la faire passer pour un VUS. Ce n'est qu'à la troisième génération qu'on a abandonné cette illusion.

En effet, la présente génération est devenue presque exclusivement une citadine. On a même réduit la garde au sol afin de favoriser son agilité sur la route et abaisser le centre de gravité. En outre, la transmission manuelle n'est plus au catalogue depuis ce lancement. Maintenant, chez Honda, on parle de multisegment et non plus de VUS compact.

UN BEL ÉQUILIBRE

Les stylistes lui ont conféré une silhouette nettement plus citadine et un tantinet sportif. D'ailleurs, il suffit de regarder la fenestration latérale pour se rendre compte de l'effet recherché. Les piliers B et C, de couleur noire, se confondent aux glaces latérales. De plus, la partie arrondie se terminant sur le pilier C ajoute également du dynamisme à cette silhouette. Bien entendu cette configuration accentue l'impression de vitesse, sans compter le hayon arrière incliné vers l'avant. On ne joue plus la carte de la robustesse, mais de l'agilité et de la sportivité. La partie avant est hautement contestée par plusieurs et applaudie par d'autres. Disons que la grille de

calandre a bel et bien des allures de Honda. Par contre, dernier vestige de ses ambitions de jouer le rôle d'un VUS, d'importants boucliers avant et arrière sont toujours présents.

L'habitacle est spacieux pour cette catégorie, et les sièges avant sont confortables, quoique leur support latéral laisse à désirer. Le conducteur a devant lui un tableau de bord relativement simple avec deux cadrans circulaires placés dans un réceptacle protégé des rayons du soleil par un surplomb. L'indicateur de vitesse est à droite et le compte-tours, à gauche. Heureusement pour nous, les ingénieurs de Honda se sont retenus de nous offrir une jungle de boutons et de commandes pour régler la radio et la climatisation. C'est relativement simple et facile d'accès bien que l'absence des trois gros boutons traditionnels pour la climatisation se fasse sentir. Soulignons également que, sur certains modèles, une petite tablette pliable fait le lien entre les deux sièges avant. Une fois cette tablette rabattue, il est alors facile de se rendre aux places arrière. Celles-ci sont spacieuses, mais plusieurs trouveront leur confort plutôt modeste, car les sièges sont très fermes. Comme Honda ne fait pas toujours les choses comme les autres, le dossier de la banquette arrière est de type 40/20/40. Il est donc possible d'accommoder

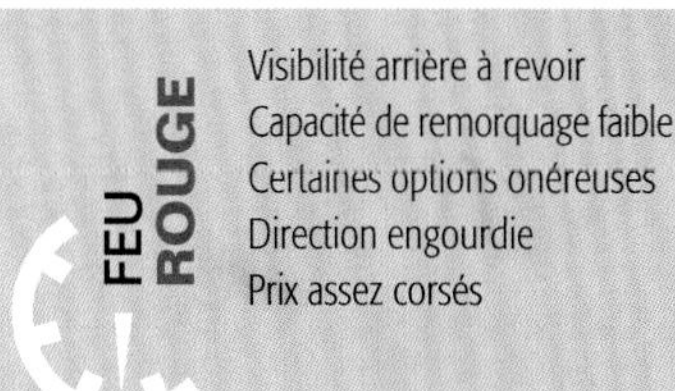

FEU VERT
- Finition sérieuse
- Excellente valeur de revente
- Fiabilité
- Groupe propulseur adéquat
- Tenue de route correcte

FEU ROUGE
- Visibilité arrière à revoir
- Capacité de remorquage faible
- Certaines options onéreuses
- Direction engourdie
- Prix assez corsés

deux occupants aux places arrière et de rabattre la partie centrale afin de transporter un objet long et étroit. Quant à la malle arrière, elle est une des plus spacieuses de sa catégorie et puisque son seuil de chargement est relativement bas, elle est d'autant plus polyvalente.

LA PERFORMANCE, BOF...

Dans cette catégorie de VUS et de multisegments compacts, certains modèles sont propulsés par des moteurs V6 dont la puissance excède aisément les 200 chevaux. Ils possèdent non seulement des performances très intéressantes, mais leur capacité de remorquage peut excéder les 2000 kg. Comme c'est l'habitude chez Honda, on a préféré utiliser un moteur quatre cylindres. Celui-ci est d'une cylindrée de 2,4 litres, alors que sa puissance est de 180 chevaux. Cette cavalerie est associée à une boîte automatique à cinq rapports dotée d'un système de logique de pente qui empêche le chassé-croisé des vitesses lorsqu'on grimpe une côte. Ce rouage d'entraînement est bien adapté et sa consommation est légèrement supérieure à 10 litres au 100 km. De plus, il est possible de commander en option le rouage intégral Real Time AWD. Il s'agit d'un système à temps partiel qui favorise, la plupart du temps, la traction avant, sauf lorsque les roues avant perdent de leur adhérence. Le cas échéant le couple est automatiquement transféré aux roues arrière. Le temps de réponse de ce mécanisme est relativement court et son efficacité est dans la bonne moyenne pour ce genre de système.

Lors de la première prise de contact avec le véhicule, il nous est apparu un peu plus agile que le modèle qu'il remplaçait. Cette impression s'est transformée en certitude, alors que ce petit Honda-à-tout-faire propose une excellente tenue de route avec une bonne neutralité dans les virages et ce, même si on tente de jouer les conducteurs pressés. La transmission accomplit également du bon travail. Par contre, on aurait apprécié une direction un peu moins engourdie, capable de nous transmettre un meilleur feed-back de la route.

Malgré ces quelques réserves, le CR-V se laisse apprécier au fil des kilomètres. La sonorité de son moteur et sa volonté à accepter les régimes plus élevés ajoutent au plaisir de la conduite. Et comme sa consommation de carburant est relativement modeste pour sa catégorie, avec une moyenne légèrement supérieure à 10 litres au 100 km, le CR-V marque encore des points.

Denis Duquet

PHOTOS : HONDA

HONDA CR-V

Catégorie	VUS
Échelle de prix	26 290 $ à 35 590 $ (2010)
Garanties	3 ans/60 000 km, 5 ans/100 000 km
Assemblage	East Liberty, Ohio, É-U et El Salto, Mexique
Cote d'assurance	n.d.

CHÂSSIS - DONNÉES POUR EX-L 4RM

Emp/lon/lar/haut	2 620/4 555/1 820/1 680 mm
Coffre	1 011 à 2 064 litres
Réservoir	58 litres
Nombre coussins sécurité	6
Antipatinage / contrôle stabilité	oui / oui
Suspension avant	indépendante, jambes de force
Suspension arrière	indépendante, multibras
Freins avant / arrière	disque (ABS) / disque (ABS)
Direction	à crémaillère, ass. variable
Diamètre de braquage	10,6 m
Pneus avant / arrière	P225/65R17 / P225/65R17
Poids	1 614 kg
Capacité de remorquage	680 kg (1 499 lb)

COMPOSANTES MÉCANIQUES

CR-V	
Cylindrée, soupapes, alim.	4L 2,4 litres 16 s atmos.
Puissance / Couple	180 chevaux / 161 lb-pi
Tr. base (opt) / rouage base (opt)	A5 / Tr (Int)
0-100 / 80-120 / 100-0 km/h	10,3 s / 8,7 s / 42,5 m
Type ess. / ville / autoroute	Ordinaire / 10,1 / 7,5 l/100 km

DANS LA MÊME CATÉGORIE

Chevrolet Equinox, Ford Escape, Hyundai Tucson, Jeep Compass, Jeep Patriot, Kia Sportage, Mazda Tribute, Mitsubishi Outlander, Nissan Rogue, Subaru Forester, Suzuki Grand Vitara, Toyota RAV4, Volkswagen Tiguan

DU NOUVEAU EN 2011

Aucun changement majeur

NOS IMPRESSIONS

Agrément de conduite :	7/10
Fiabilité :	10/10
Sécurité :	10/10
Qualités hivernales :	7/10
Espace intérieur :	7/10
Confort :	8/10

www.honda.ca

Plus d'informations dans la section statistiques en dernière partie du Guide

SYMPATHIQUE ET FRUGALE MAIS SPORTIVE ?

On attendait avec impatience la version de série du svelte coupé hybride qu'a présenté Honda sous les traits d'une série de prototypes dans les salons ces dernières années. En nommant les plus récents CR-Z, le lien avec le coupé CRX produit de 1984 à 1991 était sans équivoque. Voici donc la CR-Z de série, construite sur une version de l'architecture de l'Insight et de la Fit. S'agit-il alors d'une digne héritière du CRX ou d'une Insight à deux portières en tenue sportive ?

Selon son habitude, le dernier prototype du CR-Z qu'a présenté Honda au Salon de Tokyo fin 2009 était la future version de série à peine déguisée. À l'exception de jantes d'alliage plus grandes et d'un gros écusson posé sur la grille de calandre au lieu du capot, c'était la même voiture. Il était par ailleurs déjà annoncé que le futur coupé CR-Z allait être équipé d'un groupe propulseur hybride tout en jouant la carte sportive.

COUSINES PAR LE MÉTAL

La coque autoporteuse de la CR-Z est composée à 45 % d'acier à haute résistance. Elle est plus courte que l'Insight actuelle de 298 mm et son empattement a été tronqué de 114 mm. Les voies avant et arrière ont par contre été élargies de 20 mm et 25 mm. La CR-Z est plus longue que la dernière CRX produite en 1991 de 307 mm, plus large de 66 mm et plus lourde de 208 kilos. Elle est également plus longue de 140 mm, plus large de 46 mm et plus lourde de 358 kilos que le coupé Insight, première hybride importée en Amérique.

Comme les CRX et le coupé Insight la CR-Z est une deux places. Honda a sagement choisi de remplacer les places arrière pour Lilliputiens offertes dans certains autres marchés par des bacs de rangement. Le faux dossier se replie pour former une surface de rangement plate sous le hayon dont le volume est quand même de 711 litres.

Côté aérodynamique, Honda affirme que le produit du coefficient de traînée et de la surface frontale de la CR-Z est égal à celui de l'Insight, plus longue de 297 mm. Ce serait louable parce qu'il est effectivement difficile de rendre une voiture courte aussi aérodynamique qu'une longue. C'est toutefois du bout des lèvres seulement que Honda révèle que le coefficient de traînée (ou Cx) de la CR-Z est de 0,30 alors que d'autres ont fait mieux. Le Cx de la CRX était par exemple de 0,29 et celui du coupé Insight de seulement 0,25 tout comme la Prius actuelle. Honda a toutefois raison de souligner qu'il n'existe pas de norme universelle pour comparer ces coefficients.

MOTEURS COMPLICES

Le groupe propulseur hybride de la CR-Z est la sixième version de la technologie IMA (pour assistance par moteur intégré) de Honda dont le coupé Insight fut le pionnier. Son cœur est un quatre cylindres de 1,5 litre partagé avec la Fit. Le coupé Insight se contentait d'un tricylindre de 1,0 litre et celui de l'Insight actuelle fait 1,3 litre.

Le moteur thermique de la CR-Z produit à lui seul 113 chevaux et 107 lb-pi de couple tandis que son moteur électrique, qui joue également le rôle de démarreur et de générateur, peut libérer 13 chevaux. Leur puissance combinée est de 122 chevaux. À titre de comparaison toujours, le rouage hybride du coupé Insight produisait 73 chevaux mais son poids nettement plus faible lui permettait de boucler le 0-100 km/h en 11,6 secondes. Nous n'avons pu mesurer les performances de la CR-Z mais elle fera mieux que le 0-100 km/h en 12,0 secondes de la Insight actuelle. Mettons 10 secondes et des poussières.

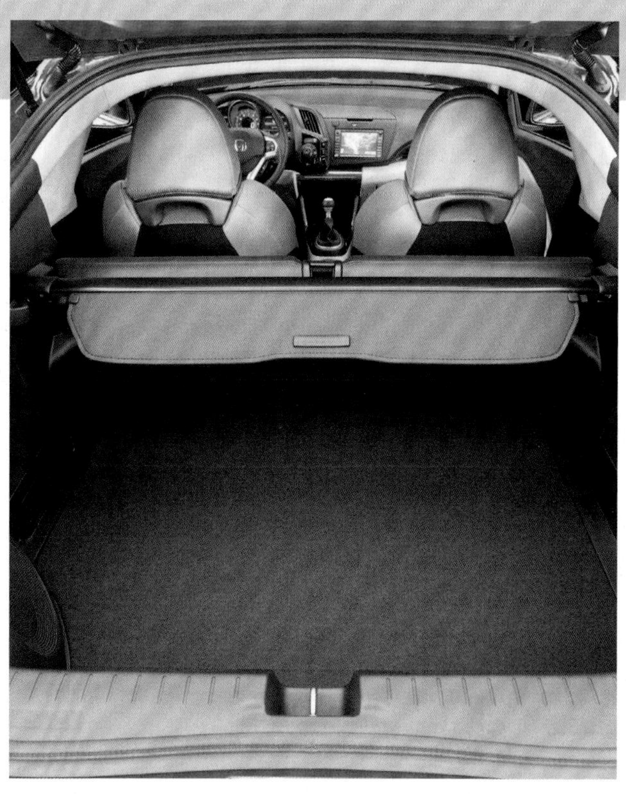

La CR-Z offre trois modes de conduite; Normal, Sport et Econ, qu'on sélectionne par des touches à la gauche du tableau de bord. Si on enclenche le mode Sport en roulant on sent immédiatement une accélération. La servodirection électrique est censée être un peu plus ferme mais c'est peu perceptible. En mode Sport la CR-Z est un peu plus vive mais l'affichage au tableau de bord passe du bleu ou du vert au rouge pour vous rappeler que votre conduite est plus énergivore.

À l'inverse, le bouton «Econ», décoré d'une branche avec ses feuilles sur fond vert, réduit la puissance et le couple de 4% ce qui émousse nettement les accélérations et reprises en plus de limiter le fonctionnement du climatiseur pour sauver quelques gouttes d'essence supplémentaires. Oubliez ça en ville. Le bouton Econ c'est seulement pour les balades tranquilles à la campagne, quand il ne fait pas trop chaud.

CABINE ET CONDUITE

La première sensation qu'on ressent en démarrant au volant de la CR-Z c'est la poussée fluide et constante du moteur électrique qui ajoute son couple à celui du moteur thermique. C'est sa plus belle qualité et celle qu'on appréciera le plus en conduite normale. Il faut dire que le fait que la CR-Z soit éminemment confortable, ergonomique et pratique, grâce à la qualité du design, de l'aménagement et de la finition de son habitacle, est déjà réjouissant.

Les sièges bien sculptés et le tableau de bord moderne sont identiques à ceux du dernier prototype qui a fait la tournée des salons. L'affichage est impeccablement clair, la disposition des commandes sans reproche et on se taille une position de conduite juste sans la moindre peine, avec pédalier d'alliage et bon repose-pied à la clé.

L'équipement comprend tous les accessoires électriques souhaitables, la connectivité Bluetooth et une chaîne audio de 360 watts avec caisson des graves. Les grands rétroviseurs latéraux (chauffants) ne sont pas un luxe parce que la visibilité de trois-quarts arrière est presque nulle, avec le montant arrière large du toit et l'obstruction de l'appuie-tête droit.

Pour le reste, par son comportement et les sensations qu'elle dispense, la CR-Z semble indécise entre les réactions vives d'un coupé sport et les manières douces qu'exige une conduite frugale. En d'autres mots, elle semble souffrir d'une crise d'identité et ne finalement être ni lièvre ni tortue ou alors ni cigale ni fourmi.

Si au moins la CR-Z ne rappelait pas le coupé Insight par certains traits de comportement. La tenue de cap des voitures conduites était vague et leur direction inerte et floue au centre, avec un

rappel trop faible. Elle tend aussi à louvoyer sur les roulières et les ondulations de la chaussée. Or, c'étaient les plus vilains défauts du coupé Insight qui avait au moins l'excuse d'une voie arrière plus étroite de 109 mm et de rouler sur de minces pneus à faible résistance au roulement de taille 165/65R14.

LE RISQUE DES GRANDES ATTENTES

L'ennui c'est que la CR-Z est censée évoquer le coupé vif-argent qu'était le CRX plutôt que le coupé hybride ultra-écolo qui l'a suivi quelques années plus tard. Où sont les réactions vives qu'on imaginait et qu'on pouvait raisonnablement espérer ? En fait les forces du CR-Z ne sont pas dans le registre sportif alors que ses principales lacunes s'y retrouvent entièrement.

Catégorie	Coupé
Échelle de prix	23 490 $
Garanties	3 ans/60 000 km, 5 ans/100 000 km
Assemblage	n.d.
Cote d'assurance	n.d.

CHÂSSIS - DONNÉES POUR BASE

Emp/lon/lar/haut	2 435/4 079/1 740/1 394 mm
Coffre	711 litres
Réservoir	40 litres
Nombre coussins sécurité	6
Antipatinage / contrôle stabilité	oui / oui
Suspension avant	indépendante, jambes de force
Suspension arrière	semi-indépendante, poutre de torsion
Freins avant / arrière	disque (ABS) / disque (ABS)
Direction	à crémaillère, assistée
Diamètre de braquage	n.d.
Pneus avant / arrière	195/55R16 / 195/55R16
Poids	1 205 kg
Capacité de remorquage	non recommandé

COMPOSANTES MÉCANIQUES

Base

Cylindrée, soupapes, alim.	4L 1,5 litre 16 s atmos.
Puissance / Couple	122 chevaux / 128 lb-pi
Tr. base (opt) / rouage base (opt)	M6 (CVT) / Tr
0-100 / 80-120 / 100-0 km/h	10,5 s (est) / n.d. / n.d.
Type ess. / ville / autoroute	Ordinaire / 6,5 / 5,3 l/100 km

FEU VERT

Couple du groupe hybride réjouissant
Habitacle lumineux et accueillant
Excellente boîte de vitesses manuelle
Finition exemplaire
Sièges confortables

FEU ROUGE

Tenue de cap imparfaite
Sensibilité au vent oblique
Performances moyennes
Roulement assez ferme
Roulis en virage rapide

Le coupé CR-Z est une petite voiture agréable, jolie et bien fignolée comme sait les faire Honda. Frugale aussi. Il n'est simplement pas le petit miracle de brio, de verve et d'ingéniosité que nous ont fait espérer les prototypes. Il lui manque cette fabuleuse espièglerie qui faisait la magie unique des CRX.

Nous attendions peut-être trop de cette « renaissance » que suggéraient les initiales des derniers prototypes (Compact Renaissance Zero). En fait, il aurait été plus sage, plus juste et plus exact d'en faire un nouveau coupé Insight. Après tout, c'est exactement ce qu'est la CR-Z: une version courte de l'Insight dotée d'un groupe hybride plus puissant, sous les traits d'un coupé. Dur, dur quand même de succéder à une légende, même toute menue.

Marc Lachapelle

DANS LA MÊME CATÉGORIE

Aucune concurrente

DU NOUVEAU EN 2011

Nouveau modèle

NOS IMPRESSIONS

Agrément de conduite:	■■■■■■■□□□	7/10
Fiabilité:	Nouveau modèle	
Sécurité:	■■■■■■■■□□	8/10
Qualités hivernales:	■■■■■■■□□□	7/10
Espace intérieur:	■■■■■■□□□□	6/10
Confort:	■■■■■■■□□□	7/10

www.honda.ca

Plus d'informations dans la section statistiques en dernière partie du Guide

PHOTOS: HONDA

LA PRATICABILITÉ AU CUBE

Selon la direction de la compagnie Honda, ce véhicule aux formes plutôt déroutantes a été imaginé par deux de ses designers qui assistaient à une compétition de surf sur la côte ouest américaine. Ainsi, ils se sont amusés à dessiner un véhicule ultrapratique capable de transporter le plus de bagages possible et surtout une planche de surf. De retour au travail, ils ont proposé leur concept à leurs supérieurs qui l'ont accepté.

Cela fait plus de huit ans maintenant que cette caisse sur roues sillonne les routes de l'Amérique. L'Element était destiné à de jeunes sportifs qui devaient être insensibles aux formes pour le moins simplifiées de ce monospace très particulier. Mais curieusement, d'autres types d'acheteurs se sont manifestés. En fait, plusieurs papys aux tempes grisonnantes ont craqué pour ce véhicule qui leur permettait de transporter toutes sortes de choses et tout spécialement leurs petits-enfants sur le siège arrière. Bien entendu, beaucoup de cyclistes ont apprécié cette soute à bagages capable d'avaler leurs vélos à la verticale. Ils étaient ainsi mieux protégés des intempéries et des voleurs.

TOUJOURS DANS UNE CLASSE À PART

Cette Honda à tout faire ne se démarque pas uniquement par sa silhouette hors de l'ordinaire. Sa configuration générale est la seule du genre dans la catégorie des véhicules cubiques. En effet, les portières avant sont conventionnelles, mais celles d'en arrière ne le sont absolument pas : il s'agit de panneaux d'accès comme ceux utilisés sur certaines camionnettes compactes. Il faut tout d'abord ouvrir la portière avant pour pouvoir faire de même avec le panneau arrière. L'ouverture ainsi créée permet d'y glisser des objets quand même assez imposants. Par contre, c'est énervant de devoir ouvrir la portière avant chaque fois qu'on veut accéder aux places arrière... Cet inconvénient est un mal pour un bien aux yeux de certains, car cela empêche les enfants d'ouvrir la portière précipitamment et de sortir en toute hâte du véhicule.

Parlons maintenant de ces places arrière. Si en théorie elles sont polyvalentes parce qu'elles s'escamotent facilement ou peuvent se rabattre sur les parois latérales, leurs sièges sont inconfortables en raison d'une assise trop basse : les personnes de grande taille se retrouvent assises la tête entre les genoux ! Les ingénieurs de Honda ont voulu offrir toute la polyvalence voulue en permettant de placer l'un et l'autre de ces sièges individuels le long de la paroi, mais ce n'est pas une tâche facile. En plus de devoir rabattre le dossier et dégoupiller l'ancrage de base du plancher, il faut avoir une poigne assez forte afin d'aller enclencher le mousqueton servant à retenir les sièges à la poignée de rétention placée sur le côté. Ce n'est pas une sinécure. Il est également possible d'enlever complètement ces sièges, mais il faut avoir du muscle et se mettre à genoux dans la soute à bagages pour procéder à cette opération. C'est pourquoi ceux qui n'en avaient pas vraiment besoin ont remisé ces sièges dans le garage et ont fait de l'Element un véhicule deux places.

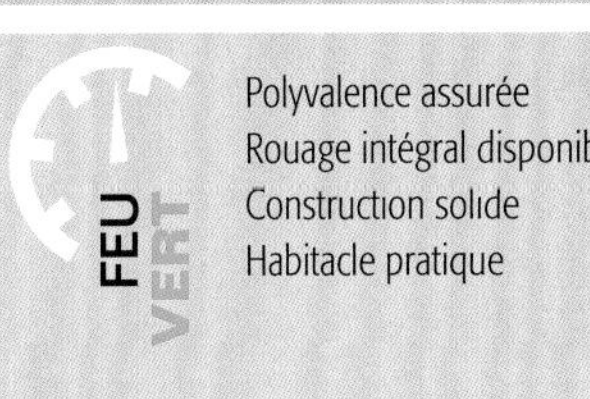

FEU VERT

- Polyvalence assurée
- Rouage intégral disponible
- Construction solide
- Habitacle pratique

FEU ROUGE

- Sensibles aux vents latéraux
- Consommation assez forte
- Visibilité 3/4 arrière
- Accès aux places arrière
- Sièges arrière difficiles à manipuler

Le plancher est recouvert d'un tapis spécial qui se lave à grande eau et qui permet de transporter des objets souillés. Par contre, il semble facile à perforer et il est glissant. Heureusement, des anneaux d'ancrage sont placés un peu partout dans l'espace de chargement.

Parlons un peu des places avant. Celles-ci sont très accessibles, leurs sièges sont confortables et le dossier relativement haut assure un bon support lombaire. N'espérez pas que le support latéral soit aussi impressionnant. Le volant est passablement imposant et possède dans sa périphérie certaines commandes, notamment celle du régulateur de vitesse. Les cadrans indicateurs sont simples à consulter avec l'indicateur de vitesse au centre, le compte-tours à gauche tandis que le thermomètre et la jauge d'essence sont à droite. La climatisation se résume à trois boutons : celui de gauche gère la soufflerie, celui du centre la température et celui de droite les modes d'utilisation. De nombreux espaces de rangement sont placés un peu partout dans l'habitacle et le coffre à gants est superposé d'une tablette de rangement. Bref, c'est simple, pratique, dépouillé et de finition impeccable, comme sur la plupart des véhicules Honda.

PAS POUR LES GYMKHANAS

Il est certain qu'un véhicule à la silhouette verticale n'a pas la même agilité et la même résistance aux vents latéraux qu'une berline Civic. Même si ces deux véhicules se partagent la même plate-forme, la différence s'arrête là. Il faut souligner qu'un seul moteur est disponible, il s'agit d'un quatre cylindres de 2,4 litres dont la puissance de 166 chevaux est adéquate, mais vous avez compris qu'on n'a pas affaire à une sportive. La transmission automatique à cinq rapports fait du bon boulot et son système de logique de pente évite les chassés-croisés des rapports dans les montées. Mais la masse à déplacer est relativement lourde, de sorte que la consommation est supérieure à 10 litres aux 100 km, ce qui est correct mais sans plus. La tenue de route n'a rien d'agile mais c'est très honnête vu la configuration de ce véhicule.

Plus pratique qu'agréable à conduire, l'Element est suffisamment de qualité pour intéresser une clientèle recherchant un véhicule pratique et polyvalent. Si vous voulez plus grand, plus puissant et des portes coulissantes, il y a la fourgonnette Odyssey, mais le prix n'est plus le même.

Denis Duquet

PHOTOS : HONDA

HONDA ELEMENT

Catégorie	Multisegment
Échelle de prix	26 990 $ à 32 090 $ (2010)
Garanties	3 ans/60 000 km, 5 ans/100 000 km
Assemblage	East Liberty, Ohio, É-U
Cote d'assurance	moyenne

CHÂSSIS - DONNÉES POUR EX 4RM

Emp/lon/lar/haut	2 575/4 316/1 819/1 788 mm
Coffre	711 à 2 112 litres
Réservoir	60 litres
Nombre coussins sécurité	6
Antipatinage / contrôle stabilité	oui / oui
Suspension avant	indépendante, jambes de force
Suspension arrière	indépendante, double triangulation
Freins avant / arrière	disque (ABS) / disque (ABS)
Direction	à crémaillère, ass. variable
Diamètre de braquage	11,2 m
Pneus avant / arrière	P215/70R16 / P215/70R16
Poids	1 657 kg
Capacité de remorquage	680 kg (1 499 lb)

COMPOSANTES MÉCANIQUES

LX 2RM, SC 2RM, EX 4RM

Cylindrée, soupapes, alim.	4L 2,4 litres 16 s atmos.
Puissance / Couple	166 chevaux / 161 lb-pi
Tr. base (opt) / rouage base (opt)	A5 / Tr (Int)
0-100 / 80-120 / 100-0 km/h	10,3 s / 9,2 s / 40,0 m
Type ess. / ville / autoroute	Ordinaire / 11,0 / 8,3 l/100km

DANS LA MÊME CATÉGORIE

Chevrolet HHR, Jeep Patriot, Kia Soul, Mazda5, Nissan Cube

DU NOUVEAU EN 2011

Aucun changement majeur

NOS IMPRESSIONS

Agrément de conduite :	7/10
Fiabilité :	10/10
Sécurité :	10/10
Qualités hivernales :	8/10
Espace intérieur :	9/10
Confort :	7/10

www.honda.ca

Plus d'informations dans la section statistiques en dernière partie du Guide

PETITE MERVEILLE

Après un premier bout d'essai prometteur sous les traits d'une série qui avait déjà quelques années au compteur, la Fit a véritablement pris son envol en 2009 lorsque Honda nous en a offert la version fraîchement redessinée. Cette petite voiture vive, moderne, agile et remarquablement pratique est toujours la meilleure sous-compacte en vente chez nous. Le tout est de choisir soigneusement le modèle.

La Fit est au moins aussi vive, frugale et sûre que toute autre petite voiture, tout en donnant l'impression de rouler dans une plus grosse. Remarquablement confortable, spacieuse et pratique pour sa taille, la version actuelle est également assez jolie pour avoir reçu le prix du Design de l'année des journalistes de l'AJAC à son lancement en 2009.

Et cette fabuleuse banquette arrière modulable et repliable à souhait n'a toujours pas d'égale. Le plus étrange est qu'elle n'ait pas encore été copiée par la concurrence comme ce fut le cas pour la troisième banquette escamotable dont Honda fut la pionnière sur ses fourgonnettes Odyssey.

SIMPLE, ERGONOMIQUE ET MODERNE

Le volant des Fit rappelle celui de la Civic et se règle sur les deux axes. On y retrouve des touches impeccables pour le régulateur de vitesse à droite et sa jante est drapée de cuir sur les versions Sport. Les leviers de part et d'autre du volant sont bien taillés, précis et accessibles du bout des doigts. La climatisation est réglée par trois grandes molettes alignées verticalement, à la droite du volant. Juste à côté on trouve les contrôles simples et dégagés de la chaîne audio.

Les cadrans sont également inspirés de ceux de la Civic mais se révèlent un peu trop sombres le jour. Le soir venu, par contre, la finition argent et l'éclairage bleu sont plutôt agréables. Mieux encore, toutes les commandes sont très bien identifiées et rétro-éclairées, sans exception. En l'absence de lampes au plafond à l'avant on doit par contre se contenter de la lumière blafarde du plafonnier pour retrouver ses choses le soir.

La Fit est exceptionnellement spacieuse et pas seulement pour une petite voiture. Le siège du conducteur est bien sculpté et juste assez ferme. L'assise n'est pas réglable et un peu basse mais la position de conduite est néanmoins excellente. Les places arrière sont facilement accessibles par des portières qui s'ouvrent jusqu'à 80 degrés.

On retrouve évidemment à l'arrière ce fabuleux « siège magique » dont on peut relever le coussin ou replier les deux pans du dossier d'une seule main, pour une polyvalence inégalée. Cette solution simple, ingénieuse et remarquablement pratique au casse-tête de la deuxième banquette est du pur Honda. Et puisque le réservoir d'essence est blotti sous les sièges avant, mais à

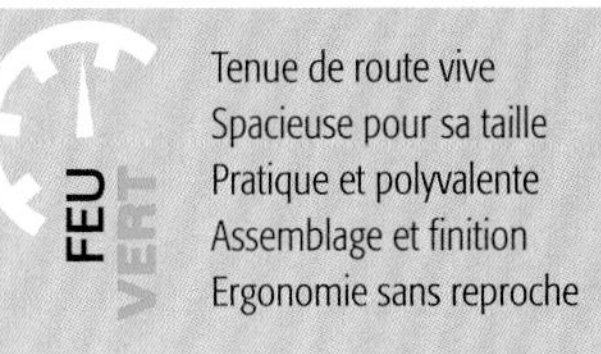

FEU VERT

- Tenue de route vive
- Spacieuse pour sa taille
- Pratique et polyvalente
- Assemblage et finition
- Ergonomie sans reproche

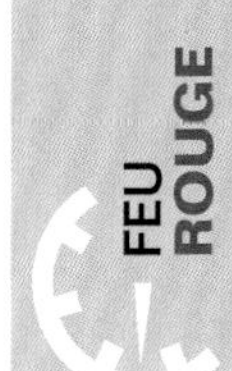

FEU ROUGE

- Plutôt chère avec la moindre option
- Performances ordinaires
- Bruit de roulement
- Suspension plus sèche (Sport)
- Embrayage peu progressif

l'extérieur de l'habitacle, la soute cargo est d'autant plus vaste et accessible avec un seuil de chargement bas et un plancher légèrement abaissé.

LE JUSTE MILIEU

Les Fit DX et LX roulent sur des pneus de taille P175/65 R15 montés sur jantes d'alliage dans le cas de la LX. Cette dernière roule d'ailleurs plus doux que la version Sport qui a tendance à sautiller sur les chaussées ondulées et manifeste bruyamment son déplaisir au passage de fentes ou de saillies. Ses pneus plus larges et bas, de taille P185/55 R16, y sont pour quelque chose mais lui taillent également une tenue de route assez étonnante, de concert avec une barre antiroulis arrière qui lui est exclusive.

La direction de la Sport est effectivement vive, linéaire et son assistance électrique bien dosée. La Sport est même parfaitement réjouissante à piloter sur un circuit ou un tracé d'autocross. Elle est merveilleusement agile et ses réactions sont neutres en virage. La barre antiroulis et les pneus un peu plus larges des modèles Sport y est pour quelque chose.

Les cinq rapports de la boîte des vitesses automatique de la Fit lui permettent de tirer le meilleur d'un couple livré à régime assez élevé puisque les vitesses passent toujours en douceur et vivement. La boîte manuelle est moins convaincante. Son levier est léger mais plutôt relâché et sa course trop longue. De plus, l'embrayage est léger et mord trop sec. Il faut s'appliquer pour conduire celle-là en douceur.

Chose certaine, on n'a aucunement besoin de s'offrir le modèle le plus cher pour profiter des qualités de la Fit. C'est même plutôt le contraire. La version Sport a de la gueule, avec son becquet plus prononcé à l'avant, ses bas de caisse plus sculptés et ses roues d'alliage à rayons de plus grand diamètre. Sa suspension est toutefois trop ferme en conduite de tous les jours et surtout, elle est trop chère. Le modèle LX est aussi bien équipé pour tout ce qui est essentiel et nettement moins cher. C'est le juste milieu et le choix de la raison pour s'offrir celle qui est sans doute la meilleure voiture du moment, kilo pour kilo et toutes catégories confondues.

Marc Lachapelle

PHOTOS : MARC LACHAPELLE

Catégorie	*Hatchback*
Échelle de prix	14 480 $ à 18 780 $ (2010)
Garanties	3 ans/60 000 km, 5 ans/100 000 km
Assemblage	Suzuka, Japon
Cote d'assurance	moyenne

CHÂSSIS - DONNÉES POUR LX

Emp/lon/lar/haut	2 500/4 105/1 695/1 525 mm
Coffre	585 à 1 622 litres
Réservoir	40 litres
Nombre coussins sécurité	6
Antipatinage / contrôle stabilité	non / non
Suspension avant	indépendante, jambes de force
Suspension arrière	essieu rigide, ressorts hélicoïdaux
Freins avant / arrière	disque (ABS) / tambour (ABS)
Direction	à crémaillère, ass. variable électrique
Diamètre de braquage	10,5 m
Pneus avant / arrière	P175/65R15 / P175/65R15
Poids	1 131 kg
Capacité de remorquage	n.d.

COMPOSANTES MÉCANIQUES

DX, DX-A, LX, Sport

Cylindrée, soupapes, alim.	4L 1,5 litre 16 s atmos.
Puissance / Couple	117 chevaux / 106 lb-pi
Tr. base (opt) / rouage base (opt)	M5 (A5) / Tr
0-100 / 80-120 / 100-0 km/h	10,3 s / 9,8 s / 42,0 m
Type ess. / ville / autoroute	Ordinaire / 7,2 / 5,7 l/100 km

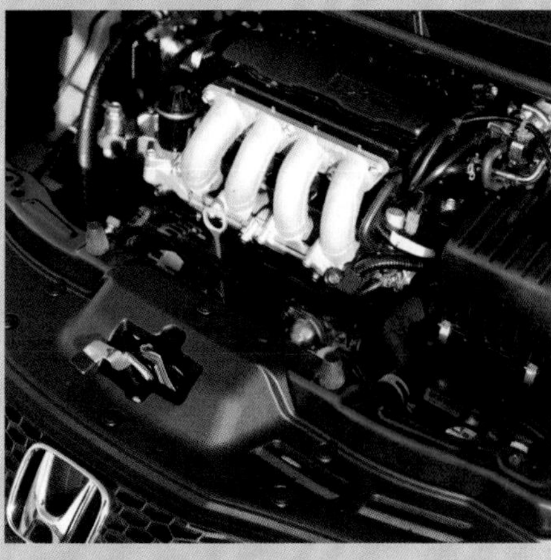

DANS LA MÊME CATÉGORIE

Chevrolet Aveo, Ford Fiesta, Hyundai Accent, Kia Rio/Rio5, Mazda2, Nissan Versa, Suzuki Swift+, Toyota Yaris

DU NOUVEAU EN 2011

Aucun changement majeur

NOS IMPRESSIONS

Agrément de conduite :	8/10
Fiabilité :	8/10
Sécurité :	10/10
Qualités hivernales :	7/10
Espace intérieur :	8/10
Confort :	7/10

www.honda.ca

Plus d'informations dans la section statistiques en dernière partie du Guide

HONDA FIT

ON MANQUE LE BATEAU, CAPITAINE...

Vrai qu'avec son Insight, Honda a concocté l'hybride la plus abordable du marché. Mais à trop vouloir couper, est-ce qu'on n'est pas en train de manquer le bateau ? Eh oui, capitaine, eh oui...

Le prix est sous les 24 000 $, on peut donc dire mission accomplie : l'Insight est l'hybride la moins chère de l'heure. Mais il a fallu faire des compromis. Certes, l'Insight ne joue pas le rôle d'un flash technologique comme la Prius, « l'autre » hybride de qui, d'ailleurs, elle emprunte beaucoup trop de style et d'aérodynamisme pour ne pas y ressembler. On aime quand même l'effet net provoqué par les phares bleus en coin qui accrochent le regard. Donc, l'Insight ne fait pas dans les panneaux solaires, ni le stationnement automatisé et c'est attendu. Mais c'est dommage que ne soient pas au rendez-vous des presque essentiels : sans sièges chauffants, démarrage sans clé et radio satellite, ça fait un peu sec.

L'Insight se conjugue en deux versions, celle de base étant munie du régulateur de vitesse, de la climatisation automatique et du volant télescopique. Mais... pas de système de stabilité, pas même en option. C'est un péché. Dans la EX, on gagne le Bluetooth, les commandes audio et le passage des vitesses au volant.

Dans l'habitacle, on se désole des plastiques rêches et tristounets, mais le bleu des fauteuils et le techno de l'instrumentation apportent de la modernité, à la limite du prototype. Visuellement, le petit volant et l'affichage à deux niveaux sont les pièces de résistance. Aussi, les infos vitales de consommation se lisent bien, merci à de simples commandes au volant qui en actionnent l'affichage clair. L'Insight n'est certainement pas l'hybride la plus complexe et c'est au moins ça de gagné.

Si la vision n'est pas trop gênée par le double hayon vitré, elle l'est cependant par les piliers qui bloquent la vue latérale arrière. Par ailleurs, on tripote souvent la climatisation ; les commandes, en deux parties, ne sont pas intuitives et leur ajustement n'entraîne pas toujours la température souhaitée. L'insonorisation est moyenne et le gravillon se fait distinctement entendre dans les puits de roue ; de l'isolant supplémentaire serait le bienvenu. À la banquette, les grandes têtes et les genoux se sentent à l'étroit. Le rangement est encore plus frugal que la consommation en carburant et les sièges avant, trop minces, manquent rembourrage et de maintien.

Si ces sièges étaient confortables, peut-être qu'on ressentirait moins les cognements de la suspension. Car l'Insight boude l'indépendance et adopte plutôt, en guise de suspension arrière, la poutre de torsion (comme pour la Fit). Jumelée à un châssis étroit, cette architecture rend la tenue de route sèche et bondissante. Sur des cahots plus imposants que d'autres, les amortisseurs font bruyamment la grève. Par contre, le freinage est concluant malgré les tambours arrière et, sous le pied, la pédale ne souffre pas de la rugosité des premières hybrides.

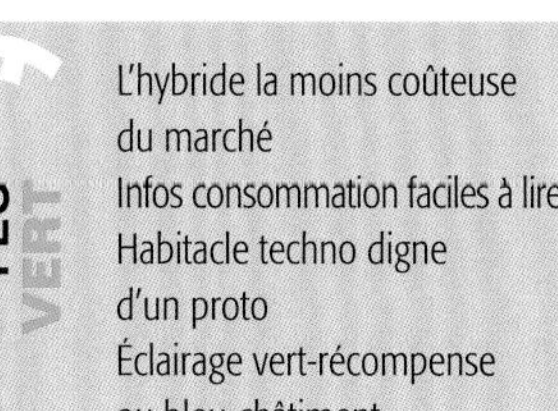

FEU VERT

L'hybride la moins coûteuse du marché
Infos consommation faciles à lire
Habitacle techno digne d'un proto
Éclairage vert-récompense ou bleu-châtiment…

FEU ROUGE

Confort et insonorisation fort moyens
Suspension sèche et bondissante
Sous-motorisée
Plastiques rêches
Pas de sièges chauffants, pas de démarrage sans clé…

MOINS FRUGALE QUE LA – PLUS GROSSE – PRIUS

Côté motorisation, c'est un petit quatre cylindres de 1,3 litre qui produit, avec le moteur électrique de 10 kW, à peine 98 chevaux. La dernière révision de ce duo essence-électrique l'a rendu plus petit, plus léger et plus puissant et Honda soutient que l'Insight gobe un frugal 4,7 L/100 km (en combiné). Hum; c'est non seulement un litre de plus que la Prius, de plus grande dimension, mais c'est également une cote que nous n'avons pu enregistrer… Le mieux que nous avons fait a été du 5,1 l/100 km. C'est que contrairement aux autres hybrides, l'Insight accepte rarement de ne circuler qu'en mode électrique. Relâchez les freins et son moteur se remet tout de suite en marche. Aussi, 98 chevaux, c'est une bien petite puissance pour une compacte dans les 1 235 kg (1 380 kg pour la EX). Sur le marché, seule la Smart est moins puissante, mais elle ne pèse que 750 kilos… Ce manque de fougue, l'Insight s'en ressent en montée par des accélérations superficielles, bruyantes, quasi asthmatiques. En dépassement, l'essoufflement est si marqué qu'on se demande si on réussira sa manœuvre à temps.

Comme pour la majorité des hybrides, l'Insight mise sur une CVT pour négocier ses rapports infinis. En version EX, cette boîte s'enrichit de palettes au volant et simulent 7 rapports virtuels. Certains détestent ces *gizmos* et, malheureusement, on ne peut ici que leur donner raison: leur manipulation se complique de deux modes et ils n'assurent même pas la performance supplémentaire attendue. Au bout de quelques essais, on se lasse une bonne fois pour toutes.

MIEUX VAUT CHOISIR… LA FIT !

Côté comportement, l'Insight rappelle… la précédente génération de Prius (2003). Serait-ce en raison de sa direction (électrique, bien sûr) à l'aise dans les stationnements, mais qui manque de réactivité à grande vitesse? Une chose est sûre, il faut continuellement en corriger le tir, et ça dérange. Qui plus est, quitter la route des yeux un seul instant revient à risquer un séjour illicite dans la voie opposée.

À tout prendre, et au lieu de payer pour l'aventure hybride, mieux vaut miser sur le conventionnel – la Honda Fit, par exemple. Avec son 6,5 l/100 km, la compacte est peu gourmande, pas mal moins chère à l'achat, plus puissante… et d'une centaine de kilos moins lourde. Oh, et merci à son hayon, la Fit accepte son lot de chargement. Plus, même, que l'Insight: 1 662 litres contre 891 litres…

Nadine Filion

PHOTOS: HONDA

Catégorie	*Hatchback*
Échelle de prix	23 900 $ à 27 500 $ (2010)
Garanties	3 ans/60 000 km, 5 ans/100 000 km
Assemblage	Suzuka, Japon
Cote d'assurance	n.d.

CHÂSSIS - DONNÉES POUR LX

Emp/lon/lar/haut	2 550/4 376/1 694/1 427 mm
Coffre	450 à 891 litres
Réservoir	40 litres
Nombre coussins sécurité	6
Antipatinage / contrôle stabilité	non / non
Suspension avant	indépendante, jambes de force
Suspension arrière	semi-indépendante, poutre de torsion
Freins avant / arrière	disque (ABS) / tambour (ABS)
Direction	à crémaillère, ass. variable électrique
Diamètre de braquage	n.d.
Pneus avant / arrière	P175/65R15 / P175/65R15
Poids	1 235 kg
Capacité de remorquage	n.d.

COMPOSANTES MÉCANIQUES

LX, EX

Cylindrée, soupapes, alim.	4L 1,3 litre 16 s atmos.
Puissance / Couple	98 chevaux (total) / 123 lb-pi (total)
Tr. base (opt) / rouage base (opt)	CVT / Tr
0-100 / 80-120 / 100-0 km/h	12,0 s / 11,0 s / 40,0 m
Type ess. / ville / autoroute	Ordinaire / 5,0 / 4,6 l/100 km

DANS LA MÊME CATÉGORIE

Toyota Prius

DU NOUVEAU EN 2011

Aucun changement majeur

NOS IMPRESSIONS

Agrément de conduite:	6/10
Fiabilité:	8/10
Sécurité:	10/10
Qualités hivernales:	6/10
Espace intérieur:	7/10
Confort:	6/10

www.honda.ca

Plus d'informations dans la section statistiques en dernière partie du Guide

TOUTE UNE TRANSFORMATION !

Les constructeurs japonais se livrent une furieuse bataille dans toutes les catégories, et cela même dans le créneau des fourgonnettes. En effet, alors que ce marché est en décroissance, trois constructeurs nippons nous dévoilent des nouveautés. Toyota a pris les devants en dévoilant la Sienna au début de l'été. Suivront probablement dans l'ordre la Honda Odyssey et la Nissan Quest.

De ces trois constructeurs, c'est Honda qui connaît le plus de succès avec sa fourgonnette puisque l'Odyssey domine le marché des États-Unis depuis les deux dernières années. Malgré cette position de tête, les stylistes de Honda n'ont pas eu peur d'innover et de transformer sa silhouette du tout au tout. En effet, chez ses principaux concurrents, on a fait exactement le contraire. Chez Toyota, on s'est contenté de lécher un peu plus la silhouette de la Sienna, tandis que chez Nissan, on a préféré rendre la Quest un peu plus traditionnelle.

PLUS BASSE, PLUS LARGE

Il suffit de jeter un coup d'œil à cette nouvelle venue pour réaliser que les designers ont joué d'audace : elle est plus basse de 4 cm et plus large de 3,5 cm que la version précédente. Ces chiffres ne semblent pas importants, mais ils font toute une différence sur le plan visuel puisque les ajouts et les retraits font paraître la fourgonnette beaucoup plus basse et beaucoup plus large qu'elle ne l'est en réalité. Les stylistes de Honda on nommé ce style « boule de feu ». Avec raison, puisqu'il est certain que plusieurs propriétaires actuels d'Odyssey verront des étincelles en jetant un œil à cette nouvelle venue pour la première fois !

Mais ce ne sont pas les dimensions modifiées qui impressionnent favorablement ou non, ce sont les flancs du véhicule. En effet, la

partie avant est presque identique à celle du modèle actuel. Par contre, c'est complètement transformé sur les côtés avec une ceinture de caisse ascendante jusqu'au pilier C. Par la suite, celle-ci est plus basse, ce qui lui donne une silhouette particulièrement spéciale. Ajoutez à cela un bas de caisse passablement en relief et un léger repli sur la paroi, qui se rend lui aussi jusqu'au pilier C. Par un effet d'optique, cette configuration permet d'affiner les parois, et de rendre le véhicule plus svelte. La partie arrière est beaucoup plus traditionnelle, même si elle comporte un feu rouge traversant le hayon de part en part.

Si les designers ont créé une silhouette destinée à attirer l'attention, c'est dans l'habitacle que les choses sont les plus impressionnantes. En effet, on a voulu faire de cette Honda la fourgonnette la plus confortable, la plus polyvalente et la plus complète que l'on puisse trouver sur le marché. La planche de bord est passablement dérivée du modèle qu'elle remplace, mais c'est mieux agencé. On a toutefois retenu le levier de vitesses placé à même la partie inférieure de la planche de bord, juste à la droite du volant. Le conducteur peut ainsi le manier très facilement. Par contre, on a déplacé les commandes audio entre les deux buses de ventilation

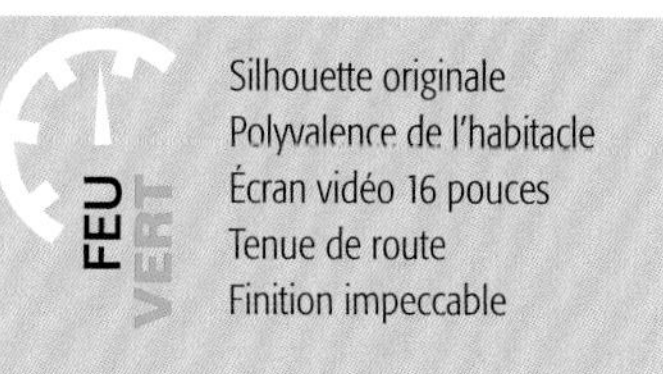

Silhouette originale
Polyvalence de l'habitacle
Écran vidéo 16 pouces
Tenue de route
Finition impeccable

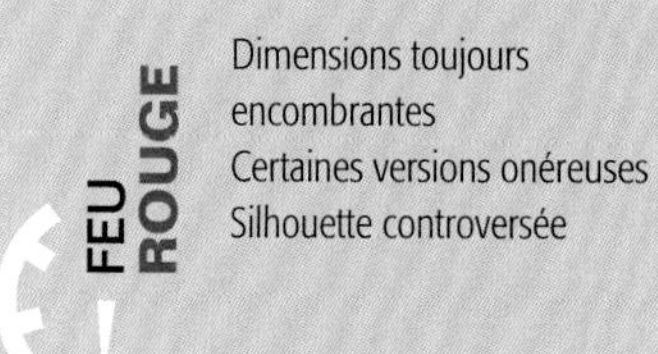

Dimensions toujours encombrantes
Certaines versions onéreuses
Silhouette controversée

situées directement sous l'écran de navigation. La partie centrale de la planche de bord se prolonge vers les deux sièges, et on y retrouve un espace de rangement dans sa partie inférieure. Parlant de console, celle placée entre les deux sièges avant est amovible. Lorsqu'elle est en place, sa partie supérieure peut contenir quatre verres. Bref, par des astuces intéressantes, on semble avoir conservé l'infrastructure mécanique de la planche de bord, mais on a totalement transformé sa présentation. Et, bonne nouvelle, on a résisté à la tentation d'éparpiller des boutons et des commandes un peu partout.

L'HABITACLE GADGET

Sur le plan de la mécanique, les ingénieurs ont de nouveau fait appel au moteur V6 Vi-VTEC de 3,5 litres doté du système de modulation de la cylindrée avec la désactivation d'une partie des cylindres lorsque le moteur n'est pas en charge. Comme il se doit, la tenue de route et l'agrément de conduite de cette Honda n'ont pas régressé, et son centre de gravité plus bas ajoute à la tenue en virage.

Mais le plus spectaculaire chez ce véhicule, c'est la polyvalence de l'habitacle. Non seulement retrouve-t-on des espaces de rangement pratiquement un peu partout, mais la gestion modulaire des sièges est impressionnante. La seconde rangée est constituée de deux sièges capitaines qui peuvent se rapprocher et utiliser une partie centrale pour se transformer en banquette régulière. De plus, ces sièges peuvent se replier à plat facilement tandis que la troisième rangée de sièges se loge en un clin d'œil dans une dépression localisée dans la partie arrière du plancher. Soulignons au passage que c'est Honda qui a inventé ce type de sièges.

Parmi les trouvailles intéressantes, il y a un anneau placé derrière la console centrale et qui se déploie. On peut y insérer un sac-poubelle afin d'y placer tous les détritus. Tandis que la division Dodge a son coffre à gants refroidissant, l'Odyssey possède une mini chambre froide située dans la partie inférieure de la console verticale. Honda souligne que la visibilité avant pour les occupants de la troisième rangée a été améliorée. Ce qui est une bonne nouvelle puisqu'on retrouve sur le pavillon, juste derrière les sièges avant, un écran vidéo horizontal de 16 po ou 40 cm de large. Il est même possible de séparer cet écran en deux images distinctes.

Denis Duquet

PHOTOS : HONDA

HONDA ODYSSEY

Catégorie	Fourgonnette
Échelle de prix	31 690$ à 49 690$ (2010)
Garanties	3 ans/60 000 km, 5 ans/100 000 km
Assemblage	Lincoln, Alabama, É-U
Cote d'assurance	moyenne

CHÂSSIS - DONNÉES POUR DX

Emp/lon/lar/haut	3 000/5 132/1 958/1 748 mm
Coffre	1 087 à 4 147 litres
Réservoir	80 litres
Nombre coussins sécurité	6
Antipatinage / contrôle stabilité	oui / oui
Suspension avant	indépendante, jambes de force
Suspension arrière	indépendante, double triangulation
Freins avant / arrière	disque (ABS) / disque (ABS)
Direction	à crémaillère, ass. variable
Diamètre de braquage	11,2 m
Pneus avant / arrière	P235/65R16 / P235/65R16
Poids	1 990 kg
Capacité de remorquage	1 588 kg (3 500 lb)

COMPOSANTES MÉCANIQUES

Odyssey	
Cylindrée, soupapes, alim.	V6 3,5 litres 24 s atmos.
Puissance / Couple	244 chevaux / 240 lb-pi
Tr. base (opt) / rouage base (opt)	A5 / Tr
0-100 / 80-120 / 100-0 km/h	n.d. / n.d. / n.d.
Type ess. / ville / autoroute	Ordinaire / 14,7 / 10,2 l/100 km

DANS LA MÊME CATÉGORIE

Chrysler Town & Country, Dodge Grand Caravan, Kia Sedona, Nissan Quest, Toyota Sienna, Volkswagen Routan

DU NOUVEAU EN 2011

Nouveau modèle

NOS IMPRESSIONS

Agrément de conduite :	8/10
Fiabilité :	8/10
Sécurité :	10/10
Qualités hivernales :	7/10
Espace intérieur :	8/10
Confort :	9/10

www.honda.ca

Plus d'informations dans la section statistiques en dernière partie du Guide

LE COMPAGNON IDÉAL

Quatre mille kilomètres dans les Maritimes en six jours, et c'est toujours l'amour. L'amour avec le Honda Pilot, qui offre un confort, une polyvalence et une douceur de roulement qui font qu'on l'apprécie comme moyen de transport, mais aussi comme cinéma-maison, voire comme chambre à coucher...

De tous les utilitaires sur le marché, le Honda Pilot est peut-être celui qui, le plus, n'a l'air de rien: silhouette simple et carrée, style masculin très sage... Il a néanmoins le mérite de rapidement se laisser découvrir comme le compagnon idéal de tous les jours. Ses plus grandes qualités? Ses très pratico-pratiques rangements et son habitabilité. En effet, le dégagement est généreux partout, même à la banquette du fond. Vrai que la 8e place exige du passager qu'il soit tout petit ou masochiste — ou les deux à la fois... — mais les 6e et 7e places en sont des vraies. La console centrale est monstre, les vide-poches se multiplient et on trouve toujours un trou pour caser quelque chose. Oh, et imaginez (enfin, pas trop quand même): nous avons casé un matelas King au-dessus des deux banquettes rabattues! C'est dire que le chargement est l'un des plus vastes du segment avec ses 2463 litres derrière les sièges avant.

ATTENTION À LA PÉDALE EN LONG...

Autre vertu du Pilot: sa douce motorisation V6 de 3,5 litres. Les accélérations sont linéaires, la transmission travaille en transparence et sans s'en rendre compte, on dépasse allègrement les limites de vitesse. La consommation se fait alors, elle aussi, fort allègre... Mais si on sait se montrer raisonnable avec la pédale en long, on profite du mode « eco » qui désactive quelques cylindres et procure une bonne frugalité.

Certes, avec ses 250 chevaux, le Pilot n'a pas le dynamisme qu'on lui voudrait en dépassement et il faut patienter avant que la réponse anticipée ne se fasse sentir. On a beau « overdriver », la boîte automatique cinq rapports, un brin paresseuse, nous pousse à chercher un mode séquentiel qui n'existe pas. On aurait pris un 6e rapport, *itou*... Mais pour ça, il faut s'offrir le jumeau de luxe Acura MDX.

En dépit de sa taille, le Pilot se montre agile en stationnement, merci à un rayon de braquage sous les 12 mètres et, lorsqu'il en est équipé, à la caméra de recul. La direction est résistante – plus que pour la moyenne de la catégorie en fait, et on en ressent la gouvernance avec précision. Le freinage est facile à doser malgré un poids qui dépasse les deux tonnes métriques. Petit bémol quant à la suspension: un brin trop molle à l'arrière (des multibras), elle concède des rebonds indus sur les cahots et on aurait manifestement voulu plus de fermeté en attaque de virage. Au lieu de quoi, l'ensemble fait plutôt sentir ses limites d'utilitaire...

La contrepartie est une garde au sol qui se respecte — à 204 mm, ça passe plus souvent que ça casse — et, surtout, un confort inégalé sur les chemins défoncés. Il y a moyen de rejoindre le chalet

FEU VERT

Sièges très confortables
Véhicule très polyvalent
Très douce motorisation
Comportement routier tout en confort
Un 10/10 pour les rangements – grands et nombreux

FEU ROUGE

Puissance limite
À quand le démarrage sans clé?
Suspension arrière trop molle
Transmission sans mode manuel
Commandes audio non offertes sur toutes les versions

perdu dans les bois sans renverser une goutte de son café Tim, à condition évidemment d'opter pour une version munie de la traction intégrale. Ce dernier système a le bonheur de manuellement se verrouiller 50-50.

L'« ÉCŒURANTITE » ? JAMAIS.

À bord de n'importe quel autre véhicule, 4000 kilomètres en six jours pourraient signifier maux de dos, courbatures et « écœurantite aigüe ». Pas avec le Pilot: les sièges avant, très larges et ajustables en tous sens, sont de bon maintien et confortables, même après 12 heures. La position de conduite est plus élevée que la moyenne et la vision périphérique n'est pas handicapée par les grandes dimensions extérieures. On trouve rapidement sa position, merci à un volant inclinable et télescopique, mais aussi à un levier de transmission qui, verticalement accroché à la planche de bord, tombe sous la main. L'insonorisation est *top*, la finition impeccable et pas un « squick » ne trouble l'habitacle, même quand le véhicule s'offre une escapade en *off-road*.

Par contre, même après tout ce temps passé à bord à manipuler les commandes, il faut encore taponner pour trouver ses airs, par exemple pour afficher la température extérieure ou l'autonomie restante. Visuellement, le coup d'œil intérieur impressionne avec tous ces pitons qui foisonnent, mais il faudrait rappeler à Honda que c'est un véhicule qu'on veut conduire, pas un avion, aussi « Pilot » soit-il. Un peu plus de *user friendly* serait apprécié, mais soulignons les excellents services rendus par le système de navigation, facile à comprendre et à utiliser.

La version essayée, Touring, équipée dans les 50000$, proposait le centre de divertissement. Du coup, notre Pilot se transformait, une fois le soir venu, en cinéma-maison avec un remarquable son Surround qui fait résonner les graves jusque dans les pneumatiques. La vitre arrière a le bonheur de s'élever indépendamment du hayon et c'est parfait pour la climatisation du véhicule qui, pour nous, se convertissait avec instantanéité d'un moyen de transport à une chambre à coucher — avec vue sur l'Atlantique, s'il vous plaît.

Quelques regrets, bien sûr: le démarrage sans clé et le toit panoramique ne sont toujours pas offerts. Il serait grand temps que ces petites gâteries honorent la liste d'équipements. Oh, et un dernier point: à quand une version hybride ?

Nadine Filion

PHOTOS : HONDA

Catégorie	VUS
Échelle de prix	34 820$ à 48 420$
Garanties	3 ans/60 000 km, 5 ans/100 000 km
Assemblage	Alliston, Ontario, Canada
Cote d'assurance	moyenne

CHÂSSIS - DONNÉES POUR EX-L RES 4RM

Emp/lon/lar/haut	2775/4850/1995/1846 mm
Coffre	518 à 2464 litres
Réservoir	80 litres
Nombre coussins sécurité	6
Antipatinage / contrôle stabilité	oui / oui
Suspension avant	indépendante, jambes de force
Suspension arrière	indépendante, multibras
Freins avant / arrière	disque (ABS) / disque (ABS)
Direction	à crémaillère, ass. variable
Diamètre de braquage	11,8 m
Pneus avant / arrière	P245/65R17 / P245/65R17
Poids	2058 kg
Capacité de remorquage	2045 kg (4508 lb)

COMPOSANTES MÉCANIQUES

Pilot

Cylindrée, soupapes, alim.	V6 3,5 litres 24 s atmos.
Puissance / Couple	250 chevaux / 253 lb-pi
Tr. base (opt) / rouage base (opt)	A5 / Tr (Int)
0-100 / 80-120 / 100-0 km/h	8,8 s / 7,5 s / 47,1 m
Type ess. / ville / autoroute	Ordinaire / 13,1 / 9,1 l/100 km

DANS LA MÊME CATÉGORIE

Chevrolet Traverse, Ford Flex, GMC Acadia, Hyundai Veracruz, Mitsubishi Endeavor, Nissan Murano, Subaru Tribeca, Toyota Highlander

DU NOUVEAU EN 2011

Aucun changement majeur

NOS IMPRESSIONS

Agrément de conduite :	7/10
Fiabilité :	8/10
Sécurité :	10/10
Qualités hivernales :	8/10
Espace intérieur :	9/10
Confort :	8/10

www.honda.ca

Plus d'informations dans la section statistiques en dernière partie du Guide

EN ATTENDANT LA PROCHAINE GÉNÉRATION

Avec un prix de base inférieur à 10 000 $, l'Accent de Hyundai est la plus abordable des sous-compactes, sans toutefois être la dernière du peloton en termes de conduite. Et même si elle prend un sérieux coup de vieux cette année avec l'arrivée des toutes nouvelles Ford Fiesta et Mazda2, elle n'en demeure pas moins un bon coup compte tenu du prix demandé. Elle offre une bonne qualité de fabrication, un confort correct ainsi que des lignes assez vivantes.

Par contre, avec un prix près de 2 000 $ inférieur à celui de la concurrence, il faut s'attendre à l'absence de quelques éléments, tels les freins ABS et les rideaux gonflables présents seulement dans la version la plus huppée. Peut-être les gens de Hyundai auront-ils corrigé ces quelques manquements à la sécurité sur la nouvelle Accent dont la sortie est prévue pour 2011.

LE LUXE, ÇA COÛTE CHER

L'Accent est actuellement vendue en trois modèles, soit L, GL et GLS. Cette dernière version, offerte uniquement pour la berline, est la seule à proposer une multitude d'options non disponibles sur les autres livrées. Ainsi, on retrouve les sièges chauffants, les coussins gonflables latéraux de même que les freins ABS. La version à hayon GL Sport est par contre la seule à rouler sur des roues de 16 pouces et à posséder une suspension dite « sport »...

Les lignes extérieures de la plus petite des Hyundai n'explorent peut-être pas les sentiers du jamais vu mais arborent plus de dynamisme et de charisme que celles des modèles précédents, spécialement pour la trois portes qui affiche une allure décontractée et jeune alors que la berline tend plus au calme et à la sérénité. Les rares photos publiées de la nouvelle Accent 2011 montrent une calandre se rapprochant de celle de la Sonata.

Là où l'Accent gagne des points, c'est sans aucun doute au niveau de la qualité de son habitacle. L'accès à bord est facile et la position de conduite se trouve sans problème, malgré le volant ajustable uniquement en hauteur. L'appui-bras sur le siège du conducteur ne gêne pas l'accès au levier de vitesses ou au frein à main tel qu'on aurait pu le penser pour un petit habitacle du genre. Les sièges procurent un bon confort même lors d'un long voyage mais apportent peu de soutien latéral en virage. La qualité de la finition ainsi que de l'assemblage est presque parfaite. Je dis presque, car ma voiture personnelle, une Accent Hatchback 2009, qui n'a subi aucun changement en 2010, a connu des problèmes avec son pare-brise. Ce dernier, mal collé, a laissé pénétrer une importante quantité d'eau dans la voiture par une journée particulièrement pluvieuse... Heureusement, le service après-vente de mon concessionnaire a su traiter ce problème rapidement.

Le tableau de bord n'affiche que trois jauges : compte-tours, indicateur de vitesse ainsi que niveau d'essence. La nuit, ledit tableau

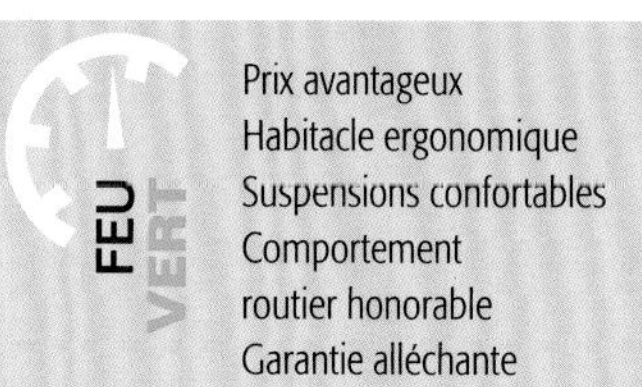

Prix avantageux
Habitacle ergonomique
Suspensions confortables
Comportement routier honorable
Garantie alléchante

Certains éléments de sécurité offerts seulement sur une version
Pneus d'origine à remplacer
Radio de mauvaise qualité
Modèle tout équipé assez dispendieux

est éclairé en bleu, un changement par rapport au modèle 2009 qui avait alors le fameux éclairage « vert malade », fort populaire dans les années 1990. La radio a des commandes limitées, surtout lorsqu'on pense que même la Rio de Kia possède une prise USB et le système Bluetooth dans sa version de base, ce que l'Accent n'a pas. De plus, le son laisse franchement à désirer et incite l'acheteur à se procurer une unité *after-market*.

Toujours dans cet habitacle, on trouve quelques espaces de rangement judicieusement placés mais de capacité limitée. Par exemple, il est difficile de transporter des boitiers de disque compact sans les laisser à la vue de tous. La banquette arrière des deux versions se plie de façon 60/40, mais l'espace de chargement de l'Accent à hayon est supérieur avec une capacité de 450 litres une fois la banquette baissée contre 365 pour la berline.

BIEN DU BRUIT POUR PAS GRAND-CHOSE...

Propulsée par un moteur 1,6 litre de 110 chevaux, l'Accent saura vous mener là où vous le voudrez sans difficulté. Ayez par contre le malheur de lui en demander un peu trop, et elle vous répondra bruyamment sans toutefois livrer des performances proportionnelles au bruit... L'embrayage de la boîte manuelle est mou et le passage des rapports se fait sans effort, malgré le manque de précision du levier de vitesses. Sur l'autoroute, à vitesse constante, la boîte manuelle fait tourner le moteur à un régime supérieur à celui de la boîte automatique, faisant ainsi augmenter la consommation d'essence. Sur la route, hormis le son du moteur, les bruits de vent se font discrets, tout comme les vibrations de la caisse. Ce qui n'est pas le cas des pneus d'origine de piètre qualité qui sont bruyants. La suspension rend la balade rebondissante, surtout sur les routes chaotiques. En virage, le véhicule tangue facilement et porte au sous-virage, les pneumatiques n'aident certainement pas à améliorer les choses. La pédale de frein a beau être spongieuse, les freins travaillent bien.

Même si l'Accent est l'une des seules sous-compactes à être vendue à un prix aussi bas, elle n'en demeure pas moins un achat sensé. Avec une refonte complète en 2011, il serait préférable pour un acheteur — pas trop pressé — d'attendre la sortie du prochain modèle. Malheureusement, très peu d'informations circulent sur cette nouvelle Accent.

Jonathan Morin

PHOTOS : HYUNDAI

Catégorie	Berline, *Hatchback*
Échelle de prix	9 999 $ à 16 995 $ (2010)
Garanties	5 ans/100 000 km, 5 ans/100 000 km
Assemblage	Ulsan, Corée du Sud
Cote d'assurance	moyenne

CHÂSSIS - DONNÉES POUR L *HATCHBACK*

Emp/lon/lar/haut	2 500/4 045/1 695/1 470 mm
Coffre	450 litres
Réservoir	45 litres
Nombre coussins sécurité	2
Antipatinage / contrôle stabilité	non / non
Suspension avant	indépendante, jambes de force
Suspension arrière	indépendante, barres de torsion
Freins avant / arrière	disque / tambour
Direction	à crémaillère, ass. variable
Diamètre de braquage	10,0 m
Pneus avant / arrière	P185/65R14 / P185/65R14
Poids	1 058 kg
Capacité de remorquage	non recommandé

COMPOSANTES MÉCANIQUES

L, GL, GLS, GL Sport

Cylindrée, soupapes, alim.	4L 1,6 litre 16 s atmos.
Puissance / Couple	110 chevaux / 106 lb-pi
Tr. base (opt) / rouage base (opt)	M5 (A4) / Tr
0-100 / 80-120 / 100-0 km/h	10,1 s / 8,3 s / 40,0 m
Type ess. / ville / autoroute	Ordinaire / 7,4 / 6,0 l/100 km

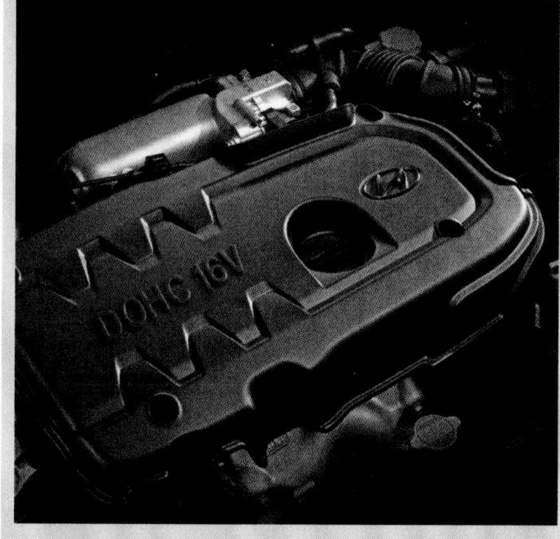

DANS LA MÊME CATÉGORIE

Chevrolet Aveo, Ford Fiesta, Honda Fit, Kia Rio/Rio5, Mazda2, Nissan Versa, Suzuki Swift+, Toyota Yaris

DU NOUVEAU EN 2011

Aucun changement majeur.
Nouveau modèle devrait être dévoilé en cours d'année

NOS IMPRESSIONS

Agrément de conduite :	6/10
Fiabilité :	8/10
Sécurité :	6/10
Qualités hivernales :	6/10
Espace intérieur :	7/10
Confort :	6/10

www.hyundaicanada.com

Plus d'informations dans la section statistiques en dernière partie du Guide

DERNIÈRE ARRIVÉE, PREMIÈRE SERVIE

Curieusement, alors que Hyundai est devenu un incontournable dans la catégorie des sous-compactes, des berlines intermédiaires, des VUS compacts et intermédiaires (Accent, Sonata, Tucson et Santa Fe dans l'ordre), il semble en retrait dans le créneau des berlines compactes avec son Elantra. Pourtant, il s'en est vendu près de 10 000 exemplaires en 2009, au Québec seulement. Étonnamment, il y a quelques années, l'Elantra était proposée en livrées berline et *hatchback*, cette dernière étant, à l'époque, la plus populaire. Encore aujourd'hui, si la berline Elantra passe inaperçue, c'est peut-être à cause d'une autre Elantra *hatchback*, la Touring.

Il faut dire que cette dernière affiche une carrosserie autrement plus dynamique que celle de l'Elantra tout court en plus d'avoir un côté utilitaire plus relevé. La partie avant de la Touring est plus réussie avec des phares qui s'allongent sur les ailes et on a laissé tomber les renflements qui courent un peu bizarrement sur les flancs de la berline. Bien entendu, la partie arrière diffère totalement. Celle de la Touring est franchement réussie. Son hayon ouvre haut sur un espace de chargement étonnamment grand, surtout lorsque les dossiers des sièges arrière sont abaissés. Le seuil de chargement est bas et égal au plancher mais on ne retrouve pas de caoutchouc sur le dessus du pare-chocs, ce qui lui aurait assurément évité quelques égratignures. Le cache-bagage est un charme à utiliser. Or, Hyundai a réussi à mettre en option cet élément pourtant des plus importants dans une familiale… C'est pingre, chiche et pas gentil. Heureusement, on retrouve des bacs de rangement fort utiles sous le tapis. La berline, de son côté, possède un grand coffre dont l'ouverture est imposante.

Le tableau de bord est, à peu de chose près, identique dans les deux voitures, ce qui est une bonne nouvelle. La qualité des matériaux et de leur finition est passablement relevée. Les jauges, la nuit venue, sont éclairées par une jolie lumière bleue. Tous les boutons et commandes sont bien placés, les espaces de rangement sont nombreux mais c'est surtout la générosité de l'habitacle qui nous fait siffler d'admiration. En effet, aussi bien les gens assis à l'avant qu'à l'arrière ont droit à beaucoup d'espace. Les sièges des versions les plus huppées sont chauffants. Bien. Cependant, ils ne possèdent qu'un niveau de chaleur… un niveau de chaleur qui devient vite insoutenable !

ELLES PORTENT POURTANT LE MÊME NOM !

Les deux voitures partagent la même mécanique et un tableau de bord identique. Pourtant, en essayant les deux voitures, on a l'impression de conduire des véhicules provenant de constructeurs distincts ! C'est que le châssis de la Touring est différent et réglé de façon plus sportive. Le moteur est un quatre cylindres de deux litres développant 138 chevaux, une écurie peu douée pour le sport, selon les standards de notre époque. S'il existait un prix pour les moteurs les moins bruyants, il ne le gagnerait assurément pas !

FEU VERT

Lignes intéressantes (Touring)
Coffre très grand
Habitacle spacieux
Comportement agréable (Touring)
Qualité de fabrication relevée

FEU ROUGE

Moteur rugueux
Transmission automatique dépassée
Accélérations de type «bouchon dans les oreilles»
Esthétique banale (berline)
Pneus d'origine désolants

Son manque de raffinement est évident, surtout si on a la mauvaise idée de le marier avec l'automatique à quatre rapports optionnelle qui n'est pas des plus empressée pour passer les rapports. La manuelle est autrement plus agréable à manipuler... dans la Touring. Dans la berline, c'est une autre histoire puisqu'on a droit à un levier imprécis à la course trop longue.

Autre domaine où la familiale est avantagée, la direction. Même si votre journaliste préféré la trouve trop lourde à basse vitesse, elle est un modèle de dynamisme comparativement à celle de la berline. Et si on parlait des suspensions? Encore une fois, la Touring gagne le match haut la main! Bien que les deux voitures présentent une configuration identique (MacPherson à l'avant et multibras à l'arrière), leur comportement diffère royalement. Remarquez que la berline est loin d'être déclassée. Son comportement est certes placide mais il offre un bon compromis entre confort et tenue de route. La Touring, en revanche, possède des suspensions plus sportives sans être inconfortables. Comme toute traction avant qui se respecte, l'Elantra, lorsque poussée dans ses derniers retranchements, sous-vire (l'avant veut continuer tout droit). Le lever du pied droit règle généralement le problème. Et sans doute que si Hyundai équipait ses voitures de pneus d'origine dignes de porter ce nom, la tenue de route et le silence de roulement n'en seraient qu'améliorés.

DU NOUVEAU À VENIR

Cette année, le duo Elantra poursuit sa route sans changements, ce qui est compréhensible dans le cas de la Touring, nouvelle depuis l'année dernière. Et si la berline demeure la même, c'est tout simplement parce qu'une toute nouvelle génération se pointera durant l'hiver, sans doute en tant que modèle 2011, selon Hyundai. Les modèles 2010 continueraient donc à être vendus d'ici là. Quelques photos espions glanées ici et là sur la toujours très pertinente (?) toile Internet nous permettent de découvrir une berline à l'allure beaucoup plus dynamique, qui semble reprendre le nouveau credo «berline coupé», un peu à la Mercedes-Benz CLS. L'habitacle aussi serait complètement revampé. Côté mécanique, je présume qu'il y en aura une...

Malgré le manque de raffinement du moteur actuel, l'Elantra et surtout l'Elantra Touring constituent une excellente affaire. Possédant généralement un bon rapport accessoires/prix, elles jouissent en plus d'une très bonne garantie. En outre, le réseau de concessionnaires est désormais très bien établi. Que demander de plus?

Alain Morin

PHOTOS: HYUNDAI

Catégorie	Berline, Familiale
Échelle de prix	11 999$ à 21 049$ (2010)
Garanties	5 ans/100 000 km, 5 ans/100 000 km
Assemblage	Ulsan, Corée du Sud
Cote d'assurance	bonne

CHÂSSIS - DONNÉES POUR GL BERLINE

Emp/lon/lar/haut	2 650/4 505/1 775/1 480 mm
Coffre	402 litres
Réservoir	53 litres
Nombre coussins sécurité	6
Antipatinage / contrôle stabilité	non / non
Suspension avant	indépendante, jambes de force
Suspension arrière	indépendante, multibras
Freins avant / arrière	disque / disque
Direction	à crémaillère, ass. variable
Diamètre de braquage	10,3 m
Pneus avant / arrière	P195/65R15 / P195/65R15
Poids	1 235 kg
Capacité de remorquage	340 kg (749 lb)

COMPOSANTES MÉCANIQUES

Berline, Touring

Cylindrée, soupapes, alim.	4L 2,0 litres 16 s atmos.
Puissance / Couple	138 chevaux / 136 lb-pi
Tr. base (opt) / rouage base (opt)	M5 (A4) / Tr
0-100 / 80-120 / 100-0 km/h	10,2 s / 7,1 s / 42,5 m
Type ess. / ville / autoroute	Ordinaire / 8,9 / 6,4 l/100 km

DANS LA MÊME CATÉGORIE

Chevrolet Cruze, Dodge Caliber, Ford Focus, Honda Civic, Kia Forte, Mazda3, Mitsubishi Lancer, Nissan Sentra, Subaru Impreza, Toyota Corolla, Toyota Matrix, Volkswagen Golf

DU NOUVEAU EN 2011

Aucun changement majeur. Nouvelle version de la berline sera dévoilée en cours d'année.

NOS IMPRESSIONS

Agrément de conduite:	7/10
Fiabilité:	8/10
Sécurité:	6/10
Qualités hivernales:	8/10
Espace intérieur:	8/10
Confort:	7/10

www.hyundaicanada.com

Plus d'informations dans la section statistiques en dernière partie du Guide

LUXUEUSE, CORÉENNE ET SANS COMPLEXE

Lors de son arrivée sur le marché en 2008, la Hyundai Genesis a créé une forte impression. À tel point qu'elle a remporté les titres de Voiture Nord-Américaine de l'année et Voiture de l'année décernée par l'AJAC. Les journalistes participants à ces choix ont tous été impressionnés par la douceur du moteur V8, ses performances et par la qualité générale de la voiture. Suite à cette spectaculaire arrivée sur notre marché, la direction de Hyundai a décidé de poser un autre geste pour être davantage présent dans le créneau des voitures de luxe : l'Equus. La silhouette de l'Equus est sobre et élégante et la grille de calandre qui détonait a été remplacée par une autre plus seyante dans sa version destinée au marché canadien.

Il s'agit d'une version plus luxueuse de la Genesis avec qui elle partage la mécanique et la plate-forme. Par contre, celle-ci a été allongée et révisée pour mieux répondre aux exigences d'une berline de grand luxe. Les prix définitifs n'avaient pas été dévoilés au moment d'écrire ces lignes, mais ils devraient osciller entre 65000$ et 72000$ selon le modèle et le niveau d'équipement. L'Equus Signature est la version un peu moins chère et elle est en mesure d'accueillir cinq personnes. Le modèle Ultimate est, comme son nom l'indique, le top du top, dans la famille Equus.

QUANT ON DIT TOUTE ÉQUIPÉE !

Si la Genesis a tant impressionné à ses débuts, c'est qu'elle proposait luxe et performance à un prix fort compétitif. L'Equus ne peut la surpasser beaucoup en performances car son moteur ne développe que quelques chevaux de plus, histoire de respecter les lois du *standing*. Mais elle s'impose au chapitre du luxe.

Prenez l'Ultimate, la version quatre places par exemple. Le siège arrière droit se transforme en fauteuil de luxe avec support pour les jambes, dossier inclinable et système de massage doté de multiples réglages. Pour déployer le support pour les jambes, il faut appuyer sur un bouton placé sur la console située entre les deux sièges pour d'abord avancer et incliner le dossier du siège avant droit. Il est alors possible de déployer votre ottoman et de vous faire conduire en toute quiétude en regardant une vidéo sur un écran placé à l'extrémité arrière de la console avant. L'occupant de la place arrière gauche n'a pas droit au repose-jambe mais peut tout de même regarder la vidéo, incliner son dossier et actionner le mode massage.

Mais il n'y a pas qu'à l'arrière que les places sont luxueuses. Les sièges avant sont confortables et réglables à l'infini à l'aide de touches indiquant les principaux points de réglage et affichant une silhouette humaine. Comme l'exige la catégorie, les accessoires de luxe sont fort nombreux. Les sièges avant sont chauffants et climatisés comme ceux à l'arrière tandis que le système audio est de marque Lexicon, le même fournisseur que sur les voitures Rolls Royce. Le volant est chauffant et réglable électriquement en

FEU VERT

- Moteur ultra doux
- Luxe assuré
- Suspension confortable
- Caméra avant
- Modèle exclusif

FEU ROUGE

- Grille de calandre saugrenue
- Distribution limitée
- *Feedback* mitigé
- Valeur de revente inconnue

profondeur et en hauteur. Avec tous ces réglages, il est possible de trouver rapidement une bonne position de conduite.

CONFORT ET ASTUCES

Aussi bien en parler tout de suite, si vous cherchez une berline de luxe aux prétentions sportives, mieux vaut aller ailleurs. Chez Hyundai, avec l'Equus, on cible les personnes désireuses de se payer luxe et confort supérieurs, le tout à un prix compétitif pour la catégorie. Je dis bien pour la catégorie car un prix frôlant les 70 000 $, c'est un peu plus cher qu'une Accent.

Le moteur V8 de 4,6 litres accomplit de l'excellent boulot. Ses 385 chevaux permettent de boucler le traditionnel 0-100 km/h en 6,6 secondes, top chrono. Et si ce genre de statistique vous intéresse, la vitesse de pointe est de 238 km/h. La transmission manumatique à six rapports est d'une grande douceur. Mais ce sont surtout le confort de la suspension, l'insonorisation poussée et les multiples systèmes électroniques d'aide au pilotage qui sont les points marquants de l'Equus. La tenue de route est correcte et sans surprise. De plus, la direction n'est pas trop assistée, mais son système d'assistance électro-hydraulique fait un peu artificiel. Toujours au chapitre des réglages, il est possible de placer la suspension pneumatique en mode Sport ou Régulier tandis qu'on peut élever la garde au sol d'environ 12 cm au toucher d'un bouton.

Toujours au chapitre de la conduite, cette voiture est dotée d'un système anti chevauchement des lignes blanches. Mais il n'est pas activé par défaut et il faut l'engager volontairement, ce qui est excellent. Une fois activé, une légère traction sur la ceinture de sécurité du conducteur et un bip sonore vous avertissent de revenir dans le droit chemin lorsque vous roulez sur une ligne blanche. L'Equus est également dotée d'un gadget unique en son genre, soit une camera affichant l'entourage avant de la voiture lorsque celle-ci est immobilisée ou roule très, très lentement. C'est assez spécial.

Hyundai fait ses premiers pas dans la catégorie des Audi A6, BMW Série 5 et Mercedes-Benz Classe E. Mais le numéro un coréen procède avec prudence et seuls quelques concessionnaires triés sur le volet dans les grandes villes du pays l'offriront à leurs clients.

Denis Duquet

PHOTOS : HYUNDAI

HYUNDAI EQUUS

Catégorie	Berline
Échelle de prix	65 000 $ à 72 000 $ (approx)
Garanties	5 ans / 100 000 km, 5 ans / 100 000 km
Assemblage	Corée du Sude
Cote d'assurance	n.d.

CHÂSSIS - DONNÉES POUR EQUUS

Emp/lon/lar/haut	3 045/5 158/1 889/1 490 mm
Coffre	473 litres
Réservoir	75 litres
Nombre coussins sécurité	6
Antipatinage / contrôle stabilité	oui / oui
Suspension avant	indépendante, multibras
Suspension arrière	indépendante, multibras
Freins avant / arrière	disque (ABS) / disque (ABS)
Direction	à crémaillère, ass. variable électrique
Diamètre de braquage	11,5 m
Pneus avant / arrière	P245/45R19 / P275/40R19
Poids	2 034 kg
Capacité de remorquage	non recommandé

COMPOSANTES MÉCANIQUES

Equus

Cylindrée, soupapes, alim.	V8 4,6 litres 32 s atmos.
Puissance / Couple	385 chevaux / 333 lb-pi
Tr. base (opt) / rouage base (opt)	A6 / Prop
0-100 / 80-120 / 100-0 km/h	6,6 s / n.d. / n.d.
Type ess. / ville / autoroute	Super / n.d.

DANS LA MÊME CATÉGORIE

Audi A6, BMW Série 5, Lexus GS, Mercedes-Benz Classe E

DU NOUVEAU EN 2011

Nouveau modèle

NOS IMPRESSIONS

Agrément de conduite :	8/10
Fiabilité :	Nouveau modèle
Sécurité :	9/10
Qualités hivernales :	7/10
Espace intérieur :	9/10
Confort :	9/10

www.hyundaicanada.com

Plus d'informations dans la section statistiques en dernière partie du Guide

PAS SPORTIVE, MAIS ELLE A LE RESTE TOUT BON

Magasiner une bagnole de plus ou moins 40000$ chez un concessionnaire Hyundai? Ouais, vous avez raison, ça fait tout drôle. Mais reste que la Genesis vaut son pesant d'or – avec, en prime, ab-so-lu-ment rien dans sa présentation extérieure qui révèle qu'elle appartient à la famille coréenne.

Regardez devant, regardez derrière. Que voyez-vous? Une berline mystère dotée d'une grille qui rappelle Mercedes, d'un arrière taillé à la BMW et de touches Lexus ici et là. Et si vous optez pour le sigle optionnel qui, apposé au coffre, ressemble aux ailes de la britannique Jaguar, vous n'aurez aucune indication qu'il s'agisse d'une coréenne Hyundai. L'ensemble est élégant et imposant, bien qu'un peu trop générique en latéral, mais ça a le mérite de marcher: au passage de la Genesis, les sourcils se froncent et se demandent ce que peut bien être cette grande bagnole.

Dedans, si l'on retirait le logo Hyundai posé au centre du volant, on se croirait à bord d'une Lexus. Habitacle accueillant, sièges enveloppants très confortables, cuir de qualité, assemblage qui frise la perfection, insonorisation top, rien à redire. Oh si, peut-être: les sièges arrière ne peuvent être chauffés, pas même en option et le toit ouvrant est très standard – on aurait aimé un panoramique pour éclairer tout le monde à bord. Et si le siège conducteur peut être ventilé, ce n'est pas le cas pour l'occupant tout à côté. Dommage.

Mais sinon, la planche de bord, heureusement non surchargée de commandes, est facile à apprivoiser. Même chose pour le DIS (*Driver information system*), cette réplique du I-drive de BMW qui ne demande pas un baccalauréat avant d'être manipulé. En prime, l'éclairage bleuté de la cabine qui accueille à la nuit tombée est non seulement très efficace, il est aussi du plus bel effet. À l'arrière, les passagers ont droit à de confortables sièges moulés aux extrémités, ainsi qu'à l'espace aux jambes quasiment digne d'une limousine – on ne s'attend pas à moins d'une voiture qui fait presque cinq mètres de long... Un reproche pour le coffre, cependant: s'il est généreux de ses 450 litres bien répartis en largeur et en longueur, il est handicapé d'une banquette qui ne se rabat pas.

Sur la route, c'est la balade douce et linéaire qui attend le conducteur de la Genesis, plus tranquille et mature que vivante et enlevante. Et ce, en dépit de deux puissantes motorisations et de la première architecture à propulsion pour Hyundai – supposée être gage de sportivité, non? À qui la faute? D'abord, à une direction surassistée, maniée d'un volant trop mince qui gagnerait à prendre de l'épaisseur en paume. Dommage, parce que c'est là que le conducteur tire la plus grande part de son enivrement et ici, ça manque de connexion. De plus, la suspension n'est pas calibrée aussi fermement que souhaité. Le tout ne rebondit pas indûment sur les cahots, mais on aurait quand même voulu que l'ajustement manuel des éléments suspenseurs

FEU VERT

- Motorisations douces et puissantes
- Très vaste et très confortable habitacle
- Meilleur rapport qualité-prix de l'heure – et de loin

FEU ROUGE

- Pas de traction intégrale
- Direction qui manque de substance
- Suspension qui gagnerait à se raffermir
- Banquette qui ne se rabat pas

soit possible ou, à tout le moins, qu'une option « sport » vienne mettre un peu plus de liaison dans tout ça.

Au lieu de quoi, on pilote un bolide puissant sans vraiment en sentir toute la vigueur. La boîte automatique fait passer ses six rapports en toute transparence et il faut avoir l'œil sur les révolutions pour savoir à quel moment l'opération s'effectue. Pas de sonorité grondante (dommage...) et ne cherchez pas de palettes au volant, elles ne sont malheureusement pas offertes. Mais vigueur il y a, indéniablement: le V6 de 3,8 litres développe ses 290 chevaux en toute respectabilité et c'est suffisant pour déplacer plus de 1700 kilos de tôle et d'acier dans des accélérations sans coup férir. De fait, voilà qui rend tout à fait inutile le V8 de 4,6 litres – le tout premier V8 de Hyundai, soit dit en passant. À bord de cette dernière variante, les 375 chevaux (368 si on utilise de l'essence régulière) sont anesthésiés par une expérience toute docile. On a peine à croire qu'il se trouve autant de puissance sous le capot.

Loin de la conduite incisive des allemandes, la Genesis se rapproche davantage des Lexus et Cadillac– nous ne dirons pas Lincoln parce que ces dernières ont un p'tit zeste qui les différencie des « bateaux de mon'oncle ». Sur la route, la grande berline coréenne n'est donc pas celle avec laquelle on a envie d'attaquer les virages serrés, mais elle est solide, assurée et bien équilibrée. On ne lui regrette que la traction intégrale – un incontournable, si l'on veut affronter avec sérieux la concurrence des Infiniti M, Mercedes Classe E et BMW Série 5.

Et pendant qu'on est dans les manques, soulignons que la Genesis ne profite pas de *gizmos* technologiques pourtant offerts ailleurs. Le régulateur de vitesse intelligent monte à bord depuis peu, mais le système de précollision et l'avertisseur d'angles morts ne sont toujours pas au rendez-vous. On se console cependant avec une bagnole qui en donne beaucoup, vraiment beaucoup pour le prix. C'est même pratiquement incroyable de voir tous ces équipements sur une version de base qui débute sous les 40 000 $. Faites le test en comparant avec les concurrentes haut de gamme: la Genesis est vendue au prix d'étiquette d'une bonne berline intermédiaire d'entrée de luxe alors qu'elle est nettement « plus-plus-plus » en termes de qualité, de dimensions, de luxe et d'équipements.

Nadine Filion

PHOTOS: HYUNDAI

HYUNDAI GENESIS

Catégorie	Berline
Échelle de prix	38 999 $ à 49 999 $ (2010)
Garanties	5 ans/100 000 km, 5 ans/100 000 km
Assemblage	Ulsan, Corée du Sud
Cote d'assurance	n.d.

CHÂSSIS - DONNÉES POUR 3.8

Emp/lon/lar/haut	2 935/4 975/1 890/1 475 mm
Coffre	450 litres
Réservoir	73 litres
Nombre coussins sécurité	8
Antipatinage / contrôle stabilité	oui / oui
Suspension avant	indépendante, multibras
Suspension arrière	indépendante, multibras
Freins avant / arrière	disque (ABS) / disque (ABS)
Direction	à crémaillère, ass. variable
Diamètre de braquage	11,0 m
Pneus avant / arrière	P225/55R17 / P225/55R17
Poids	1 729 kg
Capacité de remorquage	n.d.

COMPOSANTES MÉCANIQUES

3.8

Cylindrée, soupapes, alim.	V6 3,8 litres 24 s atmos.
Puissance / Couple	290 chevaux / 264 lb-pi
Tr. base (opt) / rouage base (opt)	A6 / Prop
0-100 / 80-120 / 100-0 km/h	7,0 s / 6,1 s / 39,6 m
Type ess. / ville / autoroute	Super / 11,4 / 7,2 l/100 km

4.6

Cylindrée, soupapes, alim.	V8 4,6 litres 32 s atmos.
Puissance / Couple	368 chevaux / 333 lb-pi
Tr. base (opt) / rouage base (opt)	A6 / Prop
0-100 / 80-120 / 100-0 km/h	6,4 s / 5,0 s / 38,6 m
Type ess. / ville / autoroute	Super / 12,6 / 8,1 l/100 km

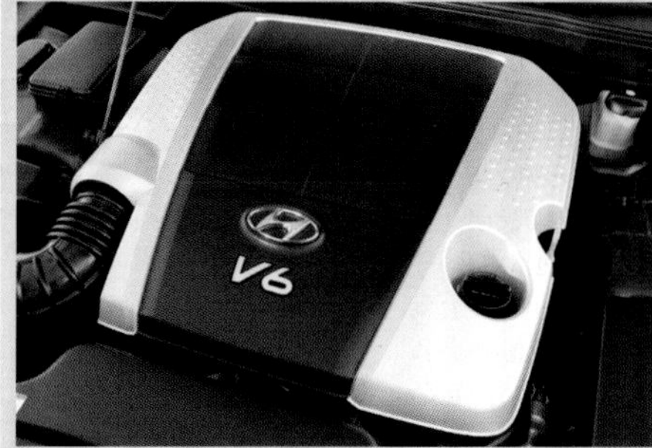

DANS LA MÊME CATÉGORIE

Acura TL, Buick Lucerne, Chrysler 300, Ford Taurus, Lexus ES, Lincoln MKZ, Nissan Maxima, Toyota Avalon

DU NOUVEAU EN 2011

Aucun changement majeur

NOS IMPRESSIONS

Agrément de conduite:	7/10
Fiabilité:	8/10
Sécurité:	10/10
Qualités hivernales:	7/10
Espace intérieur:	8/10
Confort:	8/10

www.hyundaicanada.com

Plus d'informations dans la section statistiques en dernière partie du Guide

L'IMPOSTEUR A UNE GUEULE D'ENFER

Le coupé Genesis a fait une entrée remarquée l'an dernier. Pour sa fine silhouette, surtout, qui en fait une des belles voitures actuelles. Il s'est également débrouillé honnêtement dans le match des sportives de notre édition précédente, même s'il y affrontait des valeurs solidement établies. Tous les ingrédients semblent réunis et pourtant, le coupé Genesis n'a pas le brio de la berline qui porte le même nom. Du moins, pas encore.

Avec une telle gueule, on pouvait raisonnablement attendre plus du coupé que de la berline Genesis dont les lignes sont assurément moins originales. Offert avec le choix d'un quatre cylindres turbo de 2,0 litres ou d'un V6 de 3,8 litres, il n'est jamais parvenu à nous convaincre entièrement de ses qualités sportives. Même en version GT pourvue de freins Brembo, de barres antiroulis plus costaudes, de jambes de force avant renforcées, de tarages plus fermes, d'un différentiel autobloquant Torsen, de phares au xénon, d'un pédalier en aluminium et de roues en alliage de 19 pouces chaussées de pneus de performance.

QUARTIER PAISIBLE

Le dessin du tableau de bord est clair et moderne mais il est d'une froideur plutôt clinique. Les cadrans principaux sont impeccablement clairs et lisibles, en chiffres blancs cerclés d'anneaux bleus. Les commandes sont rétroéclairées de la même couleur. Le résultat est efficace et attrayant pour des commandes à l'ergonomie déjà soignée.

Les sièges avant sont bien taillés, confortables et leurs appuie-tête se règlent en hauteur, bien sûr, mais aussi en profondeur. La protection n'en est que meilleure. Pédalier et repose-pied sont très corrects et la position de conduite très honnête. Les places arrière sont par contre fort limitées. Un adulte de taille moyenne s'y retrouve tête penchée et genoux serrés. Le dossier arrière se replie d'un seul pan et donne sur un coffre assez peu profond dont l'ouverture est courte.

Les feux de croisement au xénon sont clairs et puissants mais les feux de route de type halogène pas mal moins. La visibilité générale est satisfaisante, sauf en marche arrière, avec la ligne fuyante du toit et la hauteur du coffre. Sur les deux coupés que nous avons conduits plus longuement, l'écran du toit ouvrant ne restait jamais complètement fermé. Malgré les nets progrès récents, la qualité de fabrication des Hyundai n'est donc pas encore parfaite.

PLUS DE RIGUEUR

Qu'il s'agisse d'un simple coupé 2.0 ou de la version GT du coupé 3.8, la tenue de cap est flottante et le Genesis tend à louvoyer et suivre ornières et roulières. Il est également sensible au vent latéral. Le silence aérodynamique est louable mais le bruit de roulement monte de quelques crans sur pavage rugueux.

La suspension de la version GT du coupé 3.8 est plus ferme et son aplomb semble meilleur de prime abord. On découvre cependant

- Silhouette magnifique
- Places avant confortables
- Tableau de bord moderne
- Ergonomie des commandes
- Tenue en virage saine

- Moteur 2 litres poussif et peu raffiné
- Tenue de cap imparfaite
- Boîte manuelle quelconque
- Visibilité arrière très pauvre
- Places arrière et coffre limités

vite que ça roule dur, particulièrement sur les fentes transversales. Avec un diamètre de braquage assez long pour sa taille, le coupé 3.8 n'est pas tellement maniable en ville non plus.

À vrai dire, même avec son moteur le plus puissant et les éléments du groupe Sport, le coupé Genesis est nettement plus agréable si on le conduit doucement. Ce qui est en parfaite contradiction avec la nature et la vocation d'un coupé sport dont la conduite devrait se révéler de plus en plus inspirante à mesure qu'on hausse le rythme.

PLUS DE RAFFINEMENT ET DE VERVE

Le quatre cylindres de 2 litres n'a rien de sportif, malgré des deux arbres à cames en tête et son turbocompresseur. Il réagit trop paresseusement à l'accélérateur quand on rétrograde avec la boîte manuelle. Ce moteur est plus agréable à bas régime, même s'il a peu de couple à moins de 3 200 tr/min, chose étrange pour un moteur suralimenté.

La boîte manuelle à 6 rapports est peu plaisante et son levier d'une précision très moyenne. La marche arrière placée à gauche du premier rapport est également une mauvaise idée puisqu'on peut facilement l'engager sans le vouloir à un feu vert. L'avertissement sonore n'est pas suffisant: il faut un butoir plus solide pour bloquer le sillon. Pour ce qui est du V6 de 3,8 litres, il y a peu à dire.

LES MOYENS DE SES AMBITIONS

Le Coupé Genesis n'a pas le comportement souple et rigoureux, non plus que les qualités tactiles et le panache des meilleures en performance. Avec lui, tout est d'abord dans la forme.

Il ne faut pas sous-estimer Hyundai pour autant. Sous une silhouette réussie, l'architecture et la conception de base des coupés Genesis demeurent pleines de promesses. L'empattement est long, les porte-à-faux très réduits et les voies avant et arrière larges. Il leur manque une solide dose de raffinement, dans le registre sportif.

Marc Lachapelle

PHOTOS : ALAIN MORIN

Catégorie	Coupé
Échelle de prix	24 495 $ à 36 995 $ (2010)
Garanties	5 ans/100 000 km, 5 ans/100 000 km
Assemblage	Ulsan, Corée du Sud
Cote d'assurance	n.d.

CHÂSSIS - DONNÉES POUR 3.8

Emp/lon/lar/haut	2 820/4 630/1 865/1 385 mm
Coffre	283 litres
Réservoir	65 litres
Nombre coussins sécurité	6
Antipatinage / contrôle stabilité	oui / oui
Suspension avant	indépendante, jambes de force
Suspension arrière	indépendante, multibras
Freins avant / arrière	disque (ABS) / disque (ABS)
Direction	à crémaillère, ass. variable
Diamètre de braquage	11,4 m
Pneus avant / arrière	P225/45R18 / P245/45R18
Poids	1 543 kg
Capacité de remorquage	n.d.

COMPOSANTES MÉCANIQUES

2.0T

Cylindrée, soupapes, alim.	4L 2,0 litres 16 s turbo
Puissance / Couple	210 chevaux / 223 lb-pi
Tr. base (opt) / rouage base (opt)	M6 (A5) / Prop
0-100 / 80-120 / 100-0 km/h	8,0 s / 5,8 s / 42,5 m
Type ess. / ville / autoroute	Super / 10,1 / 6,6 l/100 km

3.8

Cylindrée, soupapes, alim.	V6 3,8 litres 24 s atmos.
Puissance / Couple	306 chevaux / 266 lb-pi
Tr. base (opt) / rouage base (opt)	M6 (A6) / Prop
0-100 / 80-120 / 100-0 km/h	6,6 s / 5,5 s / 36,7 m
Type ess. / ville / autoroute	Super / 12,0 / 7,6 l/100 km

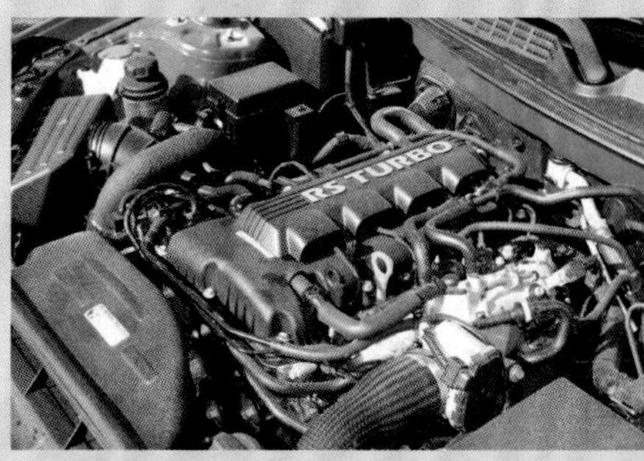

DANS LA MÊME CATÉGORIE

Chevrolet Camaro, Ford Mustang, Mazda RX-8, Mitsubishi Eclipse, Nissan Z, Volkswagen GTI

DU NOUVEAU EN 2011

Aucun changement majeur

NOS IMPRESSIONS

Agrément de conduite :	8/10
Fiabilité :	8/10
Sécurité :	10/10
Qualités hivernales :	6/10
Espace intérieur :	6/10
Confort :	7/10

www.hyundaicanada.com

Plus d'informations dans la section statistiques en dernière partie du Guide

SON ADVERSAIRE EST DANS LA FAMILLE

Les planificateurs des grands constructeurs automobiles se compliquent parfois inutilement la tâche en développant des modèles qui sont presque similaires et qui se font concurrence, tandis qu'une autre version se détache beaucoup trop du reste de la gamme. C'est un peu le cas du Santa Fe qui est plus gros et plus luxueux que le Tucson, mais qui cible les mêmes véhicules multisegments de catégorie compacte. Étant donné qu'il est plus long et plus imposant que le Tucson, il devrait s'attaquer à des compétiteurs de catégorie supérieure, mais il ne fait pas le poids. Cette tâche revient au luxueux Veracruz dont le prix est nettement supérieur au modèle qui nous intéresse.

Bref, on vise la même catégorie avec deux modèles tandis que le Veracruz vient jouer dans les plates-bandes des Ford Flex, GMC Acadia et autres. Et lors du lancement du Veracruz, les représentants de Hyundai ne se gênaient pas pour le comparer à un Lexus RX350, rien de moins. C'est se compliquer inutilement la tâche et celle des acheteurs. Il est certain que le Veracruz est trop gros pour être considéré dans la même catégorie que ses deux « frères », mais il est plus difficile de départager le Santa Fe du Tucson. D'autant plus que ce dernier a été dévoilé avec succès il y a moins d'un an et que sa silhouette est nettement plus moderne que celle du Santa Fe qui, malgré des retouches esthétiques apportées l'an dernier, a l'air d'un véhicule nettement plus vieux.

UNE OFFRE PLUS LOGIQUE

S'il est difficile de distinguer le Santa Fe du Tucson, au moins les ingénieurs ont mis de l'ordre dans la motorisation offerte pour le premier. En effet, le Santa Fe proposait deux V6 qui ne se démarquaient

pas tellement l'un de l'autre, rendant le choix difficile. Depuis quelques mois, c'est beaucoup plus simple puisque le moteur de la version la plus économique est le nouveau quatre cylindres de 2,4 litres produisant 175 chevaux associé à une boîte manuelle à six rapports. Inutile d'aller consulter la fiche du Tucson. Ce modèle est également propulsé par le même moulin. À une différence près, cependant, le Santa Fe à moteur quatre cylindres ne peut être livré qu'avec les roues motrices à l'avant. Si vous voulez bénéficier du rouage intégral qui, soit dit en passant n'est pas mauvais du tout, vous n'avez pas le choix : vous devez cocher le V6 de 3,5 litres d'une puissance de 276 chevaux, qui a gagné en cylindrée et en puissance. Avec ce dernier, uniquement la transmission automatique Shiftronic à six rapports est livrée. Comme la plupart de ces transmissions de type manumatique, le fait de pouvoir passer les vitesses manuellement n'est pas aussi important que les communiqués du constructeur le laissent entendre. C'est parfois utile en certaines circonstances seulement

Donc, pour trancher notre dilemme Tucson / Santa Fe, on pourrait choisir le premier doté du moteur quatre cylindres avec rouage intégral et opter pour le Santa Fe à moteur V6 si on désire plus de

FEU VERT

- Moteurs bien adaptés
- Transmission automatique efficace
- Habitacle confortable
- Bonne tenue de route
- Rouage intégral

FEU ROUGE

- Silhouette un peu rétro
- Pneumatiques moyens
- Pas d'intégrale avec le quatre cylindres
- Compétition du Tucson

puissance et un moteur un peu plus performant. Mais c'est sans doute trop logique pour la majorité.

TOUJOURS COMPÉTITIF

Lorsque Hyundai a revu le Santa Fe de fond en comble au milieu de la dernière décennie, les éloges ont été unanimes. En effet, ce multisegment a impressionné dès son premier tour de roues autant en raison de son équilibre général, de son agrément de conduite que de sa tenue de route. Il était même possible de commander une version avec une troisième rangée de sièges il y quelques années. On a eu la bonne idée d'éliminer cette option, car cette banquette était plus symbolique que pratique.

L'habitacle est toujours d'une finition impeccable et d'une présentation moderne. C'est moins pointu que sur le Tucson, mais personne ne s'en plaindra. Comme le veut la tendance actuelle, toutes les commandes audio et de climatisation sont intégrées dans une console verticale qui abrite également l'écran de navigation disponible sur la version Limited Navigation qui porte bien son nom ! Il faut souligner également que la position de conduite est bonne, que les commandes situées le long du moyeu du volant sont faciles d'accès et de manipulation tandis que les cadrans indicateurs cerclés d'une bande de chrome sont de consultation correcte, à part ce petit écran d'information placé au centre qui est parfois difficile à lire.

Le nouveau moteur quatre cylindres de 2,4 litres est de conception mécanique moderne et il est à la hauteur de la situation. Il faut de plus ajouter que sa consommation de carburant est tout de même intéressante et la possibilité de l'associer à une boîte manuelle à six rapports en influencera certains. Cette transmission est toutefois plus utilitaire que sportive. Par contre, peu importe le moteur choisi, la transmission automatique est excellente.

Le Santa Fe se démarque par une excellente tenue de route, une insonorisation poussée et un habitacle aussi confortable que bien agencé. Il faut également ajouter que la qualité des matériaux est bonne et l'assemblage sérieux.

Denis Duquet

PHOTOS : MARC LACHAPELLE

Catégorie	VUS
Échelle de prix	25 999 $ à 35 799 $ (2010)
Garanties	5 ans/100 000 km, 5 ans/100 000 km
Assemblage	Ulsan, Corée du Sud
Cote d'assurance	excellente

CHÂSSIS - DONNÉES POUR GL 3.5 TI

Emp/lon/lar/haut	2 700/4 676/1 890/1 725 mm
Coffre	968 à 2 214 litres
Réservoir	75 litres
Nombre coussins sécurité	6
Antipatinage / contrôle stabilité	oui / oui
Suspension avant	indépendante, jambes de force
Suspension arrière	indépendante, multibras
Freins avant / arrière	disque (ABS) / disque (ABS)
Direction	à crémaillère, ass. variable
Diamètre de braquage	10,9 m
Pneus avant / arrière	P235/65R17 / P235/65R17
Poids	1 868 kg
Capacité de remorquage	749 kg (1 651 lb)

COMPOSANTES MÉCANIQUES

2.4

Cylindrée, soupapes, alim.	4L 2,4 litres 16 s atmos.
Puissance / Couple	175 chevaux / 169 lb-pi
Tr. base (opt) / rouage base (opt)	M6 (A6) / Tr
0-100 / 80-120 / 100-0 km/h	10,0 s / 8,9 s / 73,9 m
Type ess. / ville / autoroute	Ordinaire / 10,7 / 7,5 l/100 km

3.5

Cylindrée, soupapes, alim.	V6 3,5 litres 24 s atmos.
Puissance / Couple	276 chevaux / 248 lb-pi
Tr. base (opt) / rouage base (opt)	A6 / Tr (Int)
0-100 / 80-120 / 100-0 km/h	9,0 s / 7,6 s / 43,9 m
Type ess. / ville / autoroute	Ordinaire / 10,1 / 7,6 l/100 km

DANS LA MÊME CATÉGORIE

Chevrolet Equinox, Dodge Nitro, Ford Escape, Honda CR-V, Jeep Liberty, Mazda Tribute, Mitsubishi Outlander, Suzuki Grand Vitara, Toyota RAV4

DU NOUVEAU EN 2011

Aucun changement majeur.
Nouvelle version d'entrée de gamme.

NOS IMPRESSIONS

Agrément de conduite :	8/10
Fiabilité :	8/10
Sécurité :	10/10
Qualités hivernales :	8/10
Espace intérieur :	8/10
Confort :	8/10

www.hyundaicanada.com

Plus d'informations dans la section statistiques en dernière partie du Guide

QUI L'AURAIT CRU !

Lorsque la compagnie Hyundai s'est établie dans notre pays, elle n'avait que la Pony à nous offrir. Il s'agissait d'une pâle copie d'une économique de conception britannique fabriquée sous licence. Malgré tout, l'attrait de la nouveauté et un prix sans concurrence ont incité des milliers de gens à acheter une Pony. L'aventure ne faisait que débuter. Les modèles se sont succédé au fil des années, chaque génération apportant de sérieuses améliorations.

Après un quart de siècle, les progrès sont plus que spectaculaires. Non seulement cette nouvelle Sonata possède une silhouette vraiment fort réussie, mais elle se démarque également au chapitre de la mécanique et de l'agrément de conduite. Il est difficile à croire que ce constructeur a commercialisé la Stellar sur notre marché. Et j'allais oublier, la S-Coupe n'était pas piquée des vers en fait de médiocrité. Ce qui rend la Sonata actuelle encore plus impressionnante.

PLACE AU DESIGN

De nos jours, les mots Hyundai et silhouette élégante peuvent être prononcés dans la même phrase sans que votre interlocuteur ne se mettre à rire. La première confirmation de cette situation a eu lieu lors de l'arrivée du nouveau Tucson en décembre 2009. La Sonata a suivi et elle a surpassé le Tucson en élégance. Elle été dessinée au centre de design de Hyundai à Irvine en Californie et sa silhouette adopte le concept de coupé quatre portes initialement lancé par la Mercedes-Benz CLS et repris par Volkswagen avec sa Passat CC. D'ailleurs, plusieurs ne peuvent s'empêcher de retrouver de sérieuses ressemblances avec la Passat CC. La partie avant est la mieux réussie grâce une grille de calandre fort spectaculaire. En plus, son museau plongeant en V procure un excellent coefficient de trainée, un autre élément favorisant une consommation de carburant réduite. La partie arrière est également réussie avec des feux stylisés se prolongeant dans les flancs.

Les stylistes ne se sont pas uniquement intéressés à la carrosserie puisque l'habitacle est tout aussi réussi. En premier, il faut souligner la généreuse habitabilité de ce modèle, sans doute l'un des meilleurs de cette catégorie à ce chapitre. La planche de bord est élégante et bien agencée. Les matériaux sont de qualité. Il faut de plus souligner la présence de surfaces relativement souples sur le tableau de bord. Dans l'ensemble, il est difficile de critiquer cette planche de bord avec sa console centrale en forme de V, sa nacelle des instruments constituée de deux tuyaux, chacun accueillant un cadran indicateur. De plus, une petite casquette en surplomb les abrites des rayons du soleil. Soulignons au passage la commande de direction du flot d'air dans les buses de ventilation à l'aide d'une silhouette humaine, à la Volvo. On peut reprocher cet emprunt, mais c'est simple et efficace. Enfin, la position de conduite est bonne grâce à un volant réglable en hauteur et en profondeur tandis qu'un repose pied fort large se fait apprécier. À l'usage, le dossier arrière de type 60/40 se rabat et deux tirettes

FEU VERT
- Silhouette élégante
- Habitacle spacieux
- Finition sérieuse
- Moteur bien adapté
- Boîte automatique efficace

FEU ROUGE
- Pneumatiques moyens
- Tissus des sièges fait bon marché
- Fiabilité non prouvée
- Dossiers arrière difficiles à rabattre

placées dans le coffre doivent permettre de les abaisser facilement. Mais ce mécanisme s'est avéré peu efficace.

PAS DE V6 !

La Sonata n'est livrée présentement qu'avec un moteur quatre cylindres de 2,4 litres de 198 chevaux et un couple de 184 lb-pi est offert. Il est de conception fort moderne avec l'injection directe d'essence qui améliore les performances et réduit la consommation. Ce moteur peut-être couplé à une boîte manuelle à six rapports dans la livrée de base, et l'automatique à six rapports dans les versions plus cossues.

À la fin de 2010, Hyundai proposera un moteur turbocompressé de 2,0 litres produisant 274 chevaux. C'est toujours un quatre cylindres, mais sa puissance sera identique à celle d'une moteur V6 de cylindrée moyenne. De plus, une version à moteur hybride sera commercialisée au cours des prochain mois.

PLUS QU'UNE BELLE AUTO

La Sonata actuelle se révèle être une berline dotée d'une plate-forme rigide et d'une suspension bien calibrée qui permet de négocier avec aplomb les routes de toutes natures. Qu'il s'agisse de grand-route, d'autoroute ou de route secondaire serpentant dans la nature, la Sonata est en mesure de s'en tirer avec succès. Toutefois, la direction à assistance électrique pourrait offrir un peu plus de *feedback*. Et si vous avez des hésitations, dites-vous que cette mécanique permet de réduire la consommation de carburant.

Avec une puissance de près de 200 chevaux, le moteur demeure bien adapté et le rendement est correct. Il faut souligner que le calage infiniment variable des soupapes permet d'harmoniser les performances à tous les régimes et de réduire les bruits de soupapes lorsque le moteur est en pleine charge à bas régime et avec un rapport supérieur. Jumelé à la boîte automatique à six rapport, l'économie d'essence est environ 8,7 l/100 km sur l'autoroute et de 9,4 l/100 km en ville.

Bref, la nouvelle Sonata est plus qu'une belle silhouette. Il s'agit d'une berline intermédiaire spacieuse, d'une finition sérieuse et dont le comportement routier est équilibré et sans surprise. Il faut maintenait espérer que la cote de fiabilité favorable de la plupart des produits Hyundai continue de se manifester.

Denis Duquet

Photos : Denis Duquet

Catégorie	Berline
Échelle de prix	22 649 $ à 30 999 $
Garanties	5 ans/100 000 km, 5 ans/100 000 km
Assemblage	Montgomery, Alabama, É-U
Cote d'assurance	passable

CHÂSSIS - DONNÉES POUR LIMITED

Emp/lon/lar/haut	2 795/4 820/1 835/1 470 mm
Coffre	464 litres
Réservoir	70 litres
Nombre coussins sécurité	6
Antipatinage / contrôle stabilité	oui / oui
Suspension avant	indépendante, jambes de force
Suspension arrière	indépendante, multibras
Freins avant / arrière	disque (ABS) / disque (ABS)
Direction	à crémaillère, assistée
Diamètre de braquage	10,9 m
Pneus avant / arrière	P215/55R17 / P215/55R17
Poids	1 454 kg
Capacité de remorquage	454 kg (1 000 lb)

COMPOSANTES MÉCANIQUES

Sonata	
Cylindrée, soupapes, alim.	4L 2,4 litres 16 s atmos.
Puissance / Couple	198 chevaux / 184 lb-pi
Tr. base (opt) / rouage base (opt)	M6 (A6) / Tr
0-100 / 80-120 / 100-0 km/h	9,3 s / 7,0 s / 41,0 m (est)
Type ess. / ville / autoroute	Ordinaire / 9,4 / 5,7 l/100 km

DANS LA MÊME CATÉGORIE

Buick LaCrosse, Chevrolet Malibu, Chrysler Sebring, Dodge Avenger, Ford Fusion, Honda Accord, Mazda6, Nissan Altima, Subaru Legacy, Toyota Camry

DU NOUVEAU EN 2011

Nouveau modèle. Version turbocompressée et version hybride seront dévoilées durant l'année.

NOS IMPRESSIONS

Agrément de conduite :	8/10
Fiabilité :	Nouveau modèle
Sécurité :	8/10
Qualités hivernales :	8/10
Espace intérieur :	8/10
Confort :	8/10

www.hyundaicanada.com

Plus d'informations dans la section statistiques en dernière partie du Guide

ÉLÉGANCE ET POLYVALENCE

Introduit en 2004, le Hyundai Tucson a rapidement séduit les acheteurs de VUS compacts en raison de son format pratique et de sa bonne valeur. L'année dernière, le Hyundai nous présentait tardivement la seconde génération du Tucson, le premier lancement d'une longue série de nouveautés pour le constructeur. Malgré la crise, Hyundai a littéralement le vent dans les voiles avec des chiffres de ventes records et le Tucson fait partie des produits qui ont permis d'atteindre ces résultats.

Il faut avouer que les consommateurs ont l'embarras du choix en ce qui a trait aux VUS compacts. Ce créneau est certainement devenu l'un des plus compétitifs. Chez Hyundai, on a droit depuis l'an passé au Tucson de seconde génération. Ce dernier exhibe des lignes beaucoup plus typiques des VUS multisegments. En fait, il se fond maintenant beaucoup plus dans le décor et son style l'apparente à ce que l'on retrouve sur le marché. D'ailleurs, le constructeur a voulu s'assurer que le Tucson serait aux goûts des différents marchés puisqu'il est le premier véhicule dessiné au studio européen de Hyundai à Francfort en Allemagne.

Le Tucson affiche des lignes très réussies qui évoquent celles de son grand frère, le Santa Fe. On perçoit rapidement l'affiliation. Si la partie arrière semble un peu plus commune ou moins distinctive, c'est l'avant qui nous paraît le plus réussi. Comme c'est la mode depuis quelque temps, le Tucson offre une ceinture de caisse très élevée avec des surfaces vitrées réduites à l'arrière. Malgré tout, ce design ne restreint pas à outrance la visibilité arrière qui demeure très bonne. Mon seul reproche touche le bas de caisse et le pare-chocs arrière qui est gris sur toutes les versions. Une question de goût !

Le Tucson a pris du galon avec une longueur supérieure de 7,5 cm (3,3 pouces) et une largeur supérieure de 2,5 cm (1 pouce). Cependant, l'utilisation de matériaux plus légers aura permis à Hyundai d'alléger son Tucson de 27,6 kg, on y gagne donc au change. Voilà qui place le Tucson au même niveau que plusieurs rivaux au chapitre des dimensions. Ça semble être la tendance depuis quelques années, des VUS compacts toujours plus gros !

UN NOUVEAU MOTEUR POUR LA VERSION DE BASE

Lors de son introduction en 2010, le nouveau Tuscon ne proposait qu'un seul moteur quatre cylindres. Alors que la concurrence offrait bien souvent un choix de motorisations, Hyundai avait décidé de ne monter qu'un moteur à bord du Tucson. Le constructeur réajuste le tir pour 2011 avec l'arrivée d'un nouveau quatre cylindres de 2,0 litres, moteur qui équipe la version de base. Toutefois, pas de V6 au catalogue. On comprend que le quatre cylindres génère le plus grand volume de ventes dans ce segment, mais l'option du V6 en attire toujours quelques-uns et ce sont généralement les capacités de remorquage qui sont favorisées par le V6.

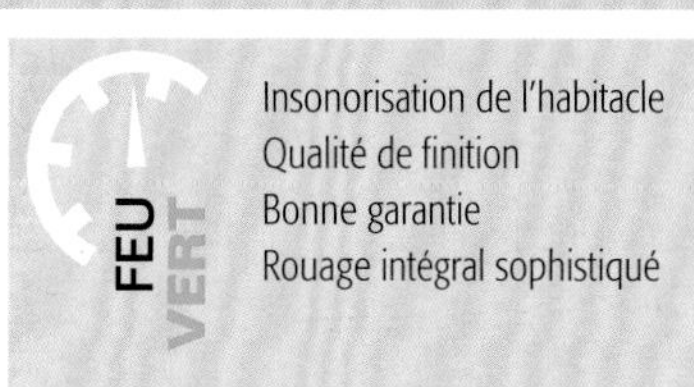

Insonorisation de l'habitacle
Qualité de finition
Bonne garantie
Rouage intégral sophistiqué

Peu de choix de motorisations
Suspension parfois sèche
Boîte manuelle peu agréable

Le moteur recommandé demeure le quatre cylindres de 2,4 litres et 176 chevaux. Outre cette puissance supérieure, c'est son couple de 168 lb-pi développé dès les 4000 tr/min qui lui procure ses meilleurs avantages. Voilà l'élément qui fait la différence et qui assure au Tucson de bonnes performances. Grâce à l'utilisation plus marquée d'un système de calage variable des soupapes, ce moteur s'avère également très économique.

À l'intérieur, on découvre un habitacle qui tranche radicalement d'avec la précédente génération. Le design est beaucoup plus contemporain et le constructeur n'a pas lésiné sur les éléments donnant un sentiment de qualité. Les matériaux sont de bonne facture, leur agencement moderne et leur disposition toute aussi réussie. Ajoutez quelques garnitures au goût du jour et des écrans à cristaux liquides et vous obtenez un bel habitacle. Cinq passagers pourront s'assoir et tous profiteront d'un bon dégagement. Seuls les occupants arrière disposent d'une visibilité moindre en raison des zones vitrées plus restreintes sur les côtés, le tout dû au style du véhicule. L'espace de chargement est généreux alors que la large ouverture du hayon permet d'y loger des objets encombrants.

SUR LA ROUTE

Malgré ses dimensions à la hausse, le Tucson livre de bonnes performances et n'est nullement sous-motorisé avec son quatre cylindres de 2,4 litres. Donc, pas de crainte à ce chapitre. Il dispose d'amplement de puissance pour la plupart des situations tout comme en manœuvre de dépassement. Quant au choix de transmission, il vaut mieux se tourner vers l'automatique. Vous tirerez peu d'avantages de la manuelle, qui est offert dans la version de base, et Hyundai n'est pas réputée pour offrir les meilleures boîtes du genre. Celle du Tucson ne fait pas exception, l'embrayage est haut et n'est pas le plus agréable. L'automatique à six rapports est donc le meilleur choix. L'insonorisation de l'habitacle est sans contredit remarquable. Elle est suffisamment réussie pour qu'on se surprenne à redémarrer le moteur malgré qu'il soit déjà en marche. Sur la route, la suspension offre un bon compromis entre le confort de roulement et la tenue de route. Le constructeur a d'ailleurs adopté une nouvelle configuration de ressorts à l'avant et propose une nouvelle suspension arrière à multibras à l'arrière. Bref, le nouveau Tucson se veut un véhicule de choix qui n'a maintenant rien à envier à la concurrence.

Sylvain Raymond

PHOTOS: SYLVAIN RAYMOND

Catégorie	VUS
Échelle de prix	22 999 $ à 32 449 $
Garanties	5 ans/100 000 km, 5 ans/100 000 km
Assemblage	Ulsan, Corée du Sud
Cote d'assurance	excellente

CHÂSSIS - DONNÉES POUR GLS TI

Emp/lon/lar/haut	2 640/4 400/1 820/1 655 mm
Coffre	728 à 1 580 litres
Réservoir	55 litres
Nombre coussins sécurité	6
Antipatinage / contrôle stabilité	oui / oui
Suspension avant	indépendante, jambes de force
Suspension arrière	semi-indépendante, multibras
Freins avant / arrière	disque (ABS) / disque (ABS)
Direction	à crémaillère, assistée
Diamètre de braquage	10,8 m
Pneus avant / arrière	P225/60R17 / P225/60R17
Poids	1 529 kg
Capacité de remorquage	454 kg (1 000 lb)

COMPOSANTES MÉCANIQUES

L

Cylindrée, soupapes, alim.	4L 2,0 litres 16 s atmos
Puissance / Couple	165 chevaux / 146 lb-pi
Tr. base (opt) / rouage base (opt)	M5 (A6) / Tr
0-100 / 80-120 / 100-0 km/h	9,5 s (est) / 8,0 s (est) / n.d.
Type ess. / ville / autoroute	Ordinaire / 10,1 / 7,4 l/100 km

GL, GLS, Limited

Cylindrée, soupapes, alim.	4L 2,4 litres 16 s atmos.
Puissance / Couple	176 chevaux / 168 lb-pi
Tr. base (opt) / rouage base (opt)	M6 (A6) / Tr (Int)
0-100 / 80-120 / 100-0 km/h	8,0 s (est) / 7,0 s (est) / n.d.
Type ess. / ville / autoroute	Ordinaire / 10,1 / 7,1 l/100 km

DANS LA MÊME CATÉGORIE

Chevrolet Equinox, Ford Escape, Honda CR-V, Jeep Compass, Jeep Patriot, Kia Sportage, Mazda Tribute, Mitsubishi Outlander, Nissan Rogue, Subaru Forester, Suzuki Grand Vitara, Toyota RAV4, Volkswagen Tiguan

DU NOUVEAU EN 2011

Nouveau modèle

NOS IMPRESSIONS

Agrément de conduite :	8/10
Fiabilité :	Nouveau modèle
Sécurité :	8/10
Qualités hivernales :	8/10
Espace intérieur :	8/10
Confort :	8/10

www.hyundaicanada.com

Plus d'informations dans la section statistiques en dernière partie du Guide

LE BON ÉLÈVE S'ASSAGIT ENCORE PLUS

Comme l'élève surdoué de la classe, il a tout bon, ce Hyundai Veracruz. Mais il n'excite pas vraiment non plus. Allure extérieure d'un discret anonymat, motorisation douce mais sans pulsion... L'utilitaire sept passagers se rattrape cependant avec un équipement complet et, pour cette année, une refonte de ses variantes d'entrée de gamme pour un prix de départ encore plus réduit.

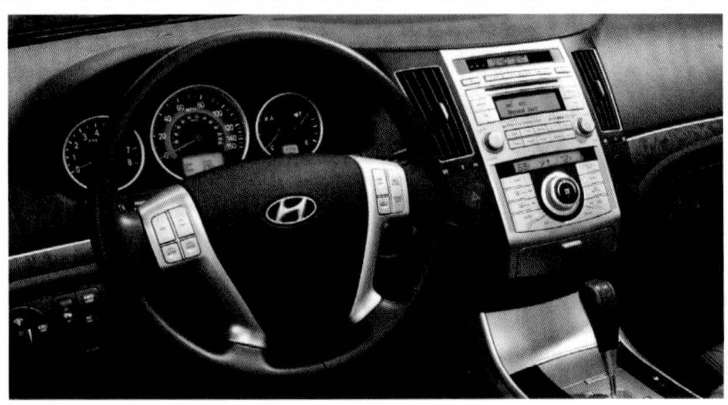

Les lignes fuyantes du Veracruz et la calandre qui n'a rien d'accrocheur ne lui rendent pas justice. Non plus que les bas de caisse en plastique noir qui font bon marché et ces éléments de style qui semblent être tirés d'un peu partout: Lexus RX, Subaru Tribeca...

Sinon, l'esthétisme (trop) intégré et les formes plus replètes que tranchantes ont l'avantage de réduire la taille visuelle de l'utilitaire; dans l'ensemble, le véhicule paraît moins imposant qu'en réalité. Illusion d'optique s'il en est une, parce que le Veracruz est suffisamment d'équerre pour accueillir sept passagers et ceux de la dernière banquette ne souffrent pas démesurément de claustrophobie. Au contraire, ils profitent de l'un des meilleurs dégagements aux jambes et aux hanches de la catégorie – c'est cependant limité aux têtes pour les plus de six pieds...

Si l'extérieur ne mène à rien, l'habitacle montre tout le chemin parcouru par le constructeur coréen ces dernières années. La finition est excellente, les matériaux sont de qualité, agréables au toucher, et le coup d'œil est particulièrement réussi dans la livrée couleur fauve. L'insonorisation est celle d'un cocon (elle n'a d'ailleurs rien à envier aux Lexus, sans doute les champions du thème) et l'ambiance est à la fois conviviale et chaleureuse. On ne cherche pas indument comment manipuler les commandes, qui se font ergonomiques. On aurait pris des compartiments de rangement supplémentaires à l'avant, mais on aime le rétroéclairage bleu qui donne tout aussi bien dans le ton décontracté que sophistiqué.

À l'arrière, c'est la polyvalence qui prime, avec des banquettes qui se rabattent facilement et qui créent un vaste espace de chargement à plat (2458 litres derrière les sièges avant). Et ce, même si la rangée du centre « flip », mais ne « flop » pas. L'espace de chargement est cependant restreint (à peine 184 litres) quand toutes les places sont occupées. Parce qu'elles s'ouvrent toutes grandes, les portières simplifient l'accès à la 2e rangée – cette dernière a le mérite de coulisser pour un meilleur partage de l'espace et de voir ses dossiers s'incliner lorsque vient l'heure de la sieste.

CONDUITE ANESTHÉSIANTE

C'est encore le V6 de 3,8 litres que l'on retrouve sous le capot. À son arrivée sur le marché en 2007, le Veracruz était l'un des plus puissants avec ses 260 chevaux. Depuis, la donne a changé. Le Toyota Highlander a pris du galon (270 chevaux) et le Mazda CX-9 en propose encore plus (273 chevaux). Mais bon, ça reste quand même plus que le Honda Pilot et le Subaru Tribeca. Et cette

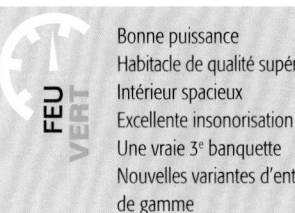

FEU VERT
- Bonne puissance
- Habitacle de qualité supérieure
- Intérieur spacieux
- Excellente insonorisation
- Une vraie 3e banquette
- Nouvelles variantes d'entrée de gamme

FEU ROUGE
- Conduite anesthésiante
- Deuxième rangée qui fait «flip», mais pas «flop»
- Toujours pas de système de navigation
- Design qui n'a rien d'accrocheur

motorisation est jumelée à une boîte automatique six rapports avec passage manuel, ce qui est avant-gardiste comparativement à une partie de la concurrence, qui se contente de cinq rapports – et qui, pour le Pilot par exemple, n'offre pas même le passage manuel.

À bord du Veracruz, les accélérations sont douces et linéaires, mais absolument sans pulsion aucune. La transmission fait si bien son boulot, en toute transparence, qu'on ne sent jamais le besoin de se mêler manuellement de sa course. C'est presque dommage... Ajoutez une suspension qui, sans être spongieuse, mise pas mal trop sur le confort – quoiqu'elle soit un brin trop occupée sur surfaces inégales – de même qu'une direction empesée et bien peu exaltante, et vous obtenez un véhicule accommodant, mais... à la limite de l'anesthésiant.

C'est la plate-forme allongée du Santa Fe qui constitue la base du Veracruz, gage d'un châssis solide – bien qu'un peu de roulis se fasse sentir en virage, comme avec à peu près tous les véhicules du genre. La traction intégrale assure la stabilité avec son dispositif qui transmet la moitié du couple aux roues arrière lors d'une perte d'adhérence, de même qu'en poussée de régime. On aime le fait que cette traction puisse être verrouillée manuellement (50/50) lorsque les conditions se corsent. Mais allez savoir pourquoi, le Veracruz tracte moins (1 588 kilos) que le Toyota Highlander et le Honda Pilot. Spécifions aussi qu'une variante de base s'amène en deux roues motrices.

NOUVELLES VERSIONS DE BASE

Côté équipement, eh bien, c'est à la mode Hyundai : l'offre est pleine de bon sens, avec une liste d'équipements complète pour substantiellement moins cher qu'ailleurs. On ne regrette que l'absence notoire du système de navigation. La version Limited est particulièrement bien nantie avec le démarrage sans clé, les pédales réglables et, gadget que nous, paresseux, encensons régulièrement : le hayon électrique.

Pour 2011, deux nouvelles variantes d'entrée de gamme viennent retrancher quelques gâteries – le toit ouvrant et la climatisation automatique, par exemple. Mais l'exercice a le mérite d'amener le prix de base encore plus bas.

Nadine Filion

PHOTOS : HYUNDAI

Catégorie	Multisegment
Échelle de prix	32 999 $ à 46 999 $
Garanties	5 ans/100 000 km, 5 ans/100 000 km
Assemblage	Ulsan, Corée du Sud
Cote d'assurance	moyenne

CHÂSSIS - DONNÉES POUR LIMITED

Emp/lon/lar/haut	2 805/4 840/1 945/1 807 mm
Coffre	184 à 2 458 litres
Réservoir	78 litres
Nombre coussins sécurité	6
Antipatinage / contrôle stabilité	oui / oui
Suspension avant	indépendante, jambes de force
Suspension arrière	indépendante, multibras
Freins avant / arrière	disque (ABS) / disque (ABS)
Direction	à crémaillère, assistée
Diamètre de braquage	11,2 m
Pneus avant / arrière	P245/60R18 / P245/60R18
Poids	2 010 kg
Capacité de remorquage	1 588 kg (3 500 lb)

COMPOSANTES MÉCANIQUES

GL, Limited, GLS

Cylindrée, soupapes, alim.	V6 3,8 litres 24 s atmos.
Puissance / Couple	260 chevaux / 257 lb-pi
Tr. base (opt) / rouage base (opt)	A6 / Tr (Int)
0-100 / 80-120 / 100-0 km/h	8,4 s / 7,5 s / 44,4 m
Type ess. / ville / autoroute	Ordinaire / 13,2 / 8,9 l/100 km

DANS LA MÊME CATÉGORIE

Buick Enclave, Chevrolet Traverse, Ford Flex, GMC Acadia, Honda Pilot, Mazda CX-9, Mitsubishi Endeavor, Nissan Murano, Subaru Tribeca, Toyota Highlander

DU NOUVEAU EN 2011

Aucun changement majeur

NOS IMPRESSIONS

Agrément de conduite :	8/10
Fiabilité :	6/10
Sécurité :	10/10
Qualités hivernales :	8/10
Espace intérieur :	9/10
Confort :	9/10

www.hyundaicanada.com

Plus d'informations dans la section statistiques en dernière partie du Guide

PLUS SPORTIF QUE LA MOYENNE

De toute l'industrie « normale » de l'automobile, les V6 de Nissan sont parmi les plus aptes à faire frémir –, et ceux qui émettent les plus belles sonorités. Tendez l'oreille au passage d'une G37 et vous ne manquerez pas de reconnaître ce doux roucoulement de performance... Eh bien, dommage: en ce qui a trait à la sonorité, le V6 de 3,5 litres du EX35 se fait trop discret. On ne l'entend guère de l'extérieur et, excellente insonorisation de l'habitacle oblige, on ne l'entend guère de l'intérieur non plus. C'est comme si on avait trop domestiqué la chose, et ça coupe de moitié – bon, juste du quart – l'exaltation de conduite. Sinon, cette motorisation de 297 chevaux est l'une des plus plaisantes à titiller du pied droit, dans des accélérations linéaires et rarement essoufflées.

Mea culpa: nous n'avons pu conduire avant publication le EX35 muni de l'automatique à sept rapports. Cette boîte, nous en avons cependant fait l'essai dans l'Infiniti M, et si l'on se fie à cette expérience, on est en droit de s'attendre à une bonne harmonie entre les deux principaux organes mécaniques du véhicule. On peut aussi prédire que les manœuvres devront s'effectuer en douceur; relâcher l'accélérateur trop rapidement pourrait se traduire, comme pour la M, par un indésirable soubresaut. Un regret, aussi: le passage des vitesses ne monte pas encore au volant, et n'attendez pas que les modes sport, normal et eco soient offerts; l'Infiniti Drive demeure l'apanage de la M.

PLUS SPORTIF QUE LA MOYENNE

Dans un monde – celui du luxe, surtout – où tout va si vite, un véhicule de trois ou quatre ans peut faire figure de vieux « mononcle ».

Pas le EX: le petit (très petit) utilitaire continue d'être l'un des plus intéressants à piloter de sa catégorie. Il faut pour cela remercier la plateforme à propulsion FM qui accueille aussi la G, mais aussi la M et le FX. Gage de solidité sur la route, cette plateforme accorde au EX une tenue de route plus sportive que la moyenne, rehaussée par la traction intégrale (de série), de même qu'une direction très précise et agréable à manier. Pour 2011, les roues de 17 po cèdent la place à des 18 po – des 19 po s'amènent en option.

Le véhicule mise par ailleurs sur une belle fermeté de suspension, ce qui permet d'attaquer avec assurance n'importe quel virage serré. La contrepartie: ça vous brasse pas mal les bourrelets – trop pour la majorité du monde –, mais vous vous en doutez, nous, on aime. Aussi, le freinage est convaincant et dans l'ensemble, on a plus l'impression de piloter une berline cinq portes à hayon qu'un quelconque utilitaire ou « cross-over ».

Cela dit, l'Infiniti EX souffre d'un grand défaut: est-ce qu'on vous l'a déjà dit qu'il est petit, petit, petit? Imaginez: plus court de 25 mm que la G, il est aussi moins large de 49 mm. Ça paraît dans l'habitacle, où les coudes se serrent et où les jambes, à l'arrière,

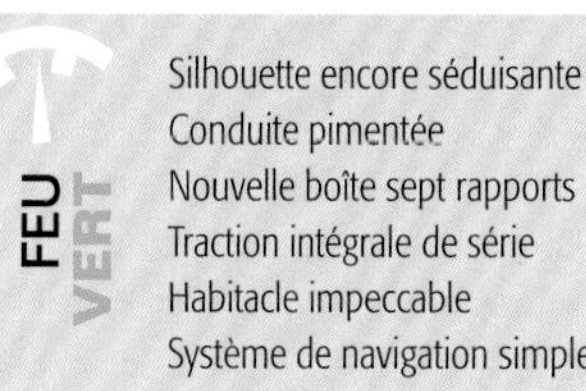

FEU VERT

- Silhouette encore séduisante
- Conduite pimentée
- Nouvelle boîte sept rapports
- Traction intégrale de série
- Habitacle impeccable
- Système de navigation simple à apprivoiser

FEU ROUGE

- Petit, petit, petit...
- Toujours pas de passage des vitesses au volant
- Visibilité arrière limitée
- Peu de rangements
- Suspension trop ferme

ne trouvent pas leur compte. Les rangements sont peu nombreux et... transporter passagers et bagages ? Il faut être optimiste avec ce cargo restreint par une ligne de toit descendante et des éléments suspenseurs qui empiètent... Si l'on risque néanmoins l'aventure du chargement, on est récompensé par l'un des hayons les plus légers à manipuler qui soient.

Pour tout dire, le véhicule est principalement conçu pour le pilote, et à peu près lui seul trouvera son plaisir avec des commandes qui ce manient instinctivement (ce qui n'a pas toujours été le cas chez Nissan, mais le constructeur a fait ses devoirs depuis) et l'un des systèmes de navigation les plus simples à apprivoiser (avec ceux de Ford). L'intérieur « brun chocolat » est de bel effet, agrémenté d'un style qui en met plein la vue et des matériaux de qualité. L'assemblage est évidemment impeccable et si on se plaint à bord de cet Infiniti, c'est qu'on est né pour une Bentley.

POUR L'URBAIN

Le défaut « petitesse » a son bon côté de la médaille : le EX se faufile dans la circulation, même celle dense et urbaine, sans demander son reste. Et il se manœuvre en stationnement aussi aisément que n'importe quelle voiture. Euh... en fait, non, puisque sur ce dernier point, la visibilité arrière est limitée. Vivement le « Bird View » (optionnel) qui retransmet les environs en vue plongeante par le biais de quatre caméras, comme si on était positionné au-dessus du véhicule. C'est fort pratique (et assez psychédélique, merci...).

D'autres gizmos du futur honorent le EX, tel l'avertisseur de changement de voie et celui des angles morts. Mais nous vous parions un p'tit 2$ qu'après une succession de « bips » dans l'habitacle, vous désactiverez rapidement la chose – ce qui se fait d'une simple commande au tableau de bord. Fiou !

Un dernier bon point pour le EX : sa silhouette est encore séduisante, même après plusieurs années sur le marché. Avec son long capot, sa cabine reculée et sa ligne de toit qui fléchit, le véhicule tient davantage du coupé de luxe soufflé aux stéroïdes qu'à l'utilitaire plate et carré. Et ça lui va encore très bien.

Nadine Filion

PHOTOS : INFINITI

INFINITI EX

Catégorie	Multisegment
Échelle de prix	41 250 $ (2010)
Garanties	4 ans/100 000 km, 6 ans/110 000 km
Assemblage	Tochigi, Japon
Cote d'assurance	pauvre

CHÂSSIS - DONNÉES POUR 35

Emp/lon/lar/haut	2 800/4 631/1 803/1 589 mm
Coffre	527 à 1 342 litres
Réservoir	76 litres
Nombre coussins sécurité	6
Antipatinage / contrôle stabilité	oui / oui
Suspension avant	indépendante, double triangulation
Suspension arrière	indépendante, multibras
Freins avant / arrière	disque (ABS) / disque (ABS)
Direction	à crémaillère, ass. variable
Diamètre de braquage	11,0 m
Pneus avant / arrière	P225/60R17 / P225/60R17
Poids	1 739 kg
Capacité de remorquage	n.d.

COMPOSANTES MÉCANIQUES

35

Cylindrée, soupapes, alim.	V6 3,5 litres 24 s atmos.
Puissance / Couple	297 chevaux / 253 lb-pi
Tr. base (opt) / rouage base (opt)	A5 / Int
0-100 / 80-120 / 100-0 km/h	7,4 s / 5,6 s / 39.5 m
Type ess. / ville / autoroute	Super / 12,9 / 8,6 l/100 km

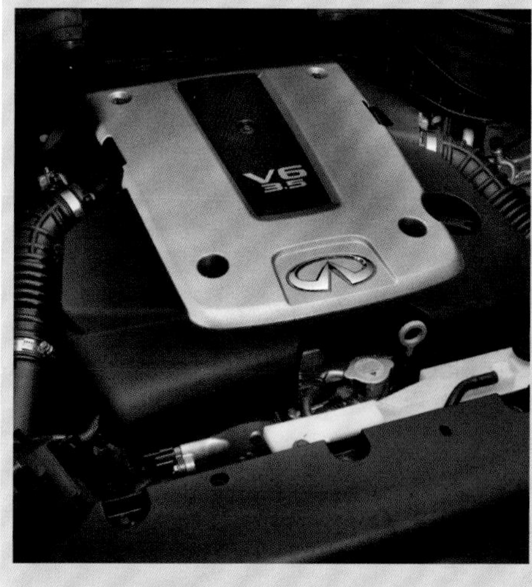

DANS LA MÊME CATÉGORIE

Acura RDX, Audi Q5, BMW X3, Land Rover LR2, Mercedes-Benz Classe GLK, Volvo XC60

DU NOUVEAU EN 2011

Aucun changement majeur

NOS IMPRESSIONS

Agrément de conduite :	8/10
Fiabilité :	10/10
Sécurité :	10/10
Qualités hivernales :	8/10
Espace intérieur :	5/10
Confort :	8/10

www.infiniti.ca

Plus d'informations dans la section statistiques en dernière partie du Guide

SOUS LE SIGNE DES PLUS

Sous l'égide de Carlos Ghosn la division Infiniti a finalement connu du succès, surtout en raison de la présentation de véhicules originaux dont le design était très poussé. Lorsque le FX fut dévoilé en 2003, Monsieur Ghosn l'a décrit comme un guépard bionique, rien de moins. L'auditoire a souri, mais il n'en demeure pas moins qu'avec son capot très long et un arrière écourté, ce modèle donne vraiment l'impression d'un félin prêt à bondir.

Mais il y a les propos ronflants tenus lors des lancements et la réalité lors des essais sur route. Dans le cas de la famille FX, on nous avait promis un multisegment à caractère sportif propulsé par des moteurs nerveux travaillant de concert avec une suspension sport. Ce qui s'est avéré conforme à la réalité. Une seconde génération dévoilée il y a deux ans a permis de raffiner la silhouette et d'améliorer les éléments qui en avaient besoin.

TOUTE UNE SILHOUETTE

Lorsqu'on examine la silhouette des FX 35 et FX50, il est facile de conclure que les stylistes ont eu le feu vert pour donner libre cours à leur imagination et leur créativité. Il est impossible de les accuser de plagiat! Le nez allongé, la section arrière tronquée, la silhouette simulant un coupé, tout cela est vraiment à part et on comprend l'allusion de Carlos Ghosn qui parle d'un félin prêt à bondir. Sur la seconde génération, les designers ont continué dans la même direction en retenant les grandes lignes directrices. Il est certain qu'un design aussi typé ne fait pas l'unanimité. Et c'est tant mieux car on accuse trop souvent les stylistes japonais de manquer d'imagination. Parmi les éléments positifs de la présentation extérieure, il faut souligner le design des roues en alliage, l'extracteur d'air derrière les roues avant ainsi que le motif en relief de la grille de calandre. La partie arrière est également réussie avec ses feux débordants sur les ailes. Par contre, le hayon en cascade accentue peut-être la ligne de la carrosserie mais réduit l'espace de chargement. Une fois encore, les diktats de l'élégance sportive sont responsables de la réduction de la capacité du coffre. Il faut cependant mentionner que les roues et les tours de suspension n'empiètent pas trop dans la soute à bagages, ce qui compense quand même.

Cet élan de créativité s'est poursuivi dans l'habitacle. En fait, cette Infiniti a été l'une des premières à nous offrir une planche de bord similaire à celle d'une berline. Cette planche de bord harmonise fort bien le noir des plastiques avec l'aluminium brossé des multiples commandes. Et comme toute Infiniti qui se respecte, une pendulette analogique trône en plein centre de la planche de bord. Celle-ci est placée juste en dessous d'un écran à affichage par cristaux liquides de dimensions plus grandes que la moyenne et faisant appel à des illustrations de type trois D. Cet écran est également relié à une caméra de recul et à des caméras latérales qui permettent d'avoir une vision périphérique tout autour du véhicule.

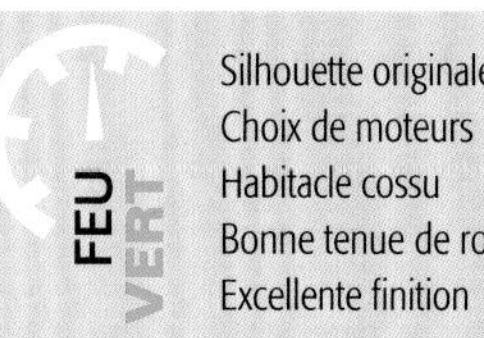

FEU VERT

- Silhouette originale
- Choix de moteurs
- Habitacle cossu
- Bonne tenue de route
- Excellente finition

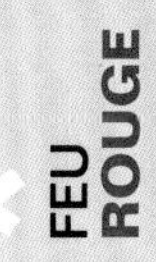

FEU ROUGE

- Techniquement complexe
- Consommation élevée
- Essence super
- Visibilité arrière

Le volant est élégant avec ses appliques en aluminium brossé tandis que le moyeu accueille des commandes multiples visant à régler certaines fonctions du système audio et du régulateur de vitesse. Quant au pilote, il bénéficie d'une position de conduite sans reproche et devant lui il y a des cadrans indicateurs électroluminescents qui sont passablement aisés à consulter. Par contre, je suis persuadé que plusieurs automobilistes pesteront contre certaines commandes audio et contre le gros bouton de commande placé directement sous l'écran d'affichage qui permet d'effectuer de nombreux réglages.

Les places arrière sont assez spacieuses pour la majorité des Nord-Américains, mais l'assise un peu basse des sièges diminue le confort pour les personnes de grande taille.

LE 35 OU LE 50?

La gamme FX se décline en deux versions, le FX35 avec son moteur V6 3,5 litres de 303 chevaux ou encore le FX 50 et son moteur V8 5,0 litres produisant 87 chevaux de plus. Les deux sont couplés à une boîte automatique à sept rapports et à une transmission intégrale ATTESA E-TS à répartition automatique du couple.

D'entrée de jeu, il ne faut pas ignorer le FX 35, ses performances sont plus que correctes et on peut même qualifier sa consommation de raisonnable. En outre, sa tenue de route est plus agile en raison d'un meilleur équilibre des masses par rapport au FX50 dont le gros moteur V8 fait sentir sa présence.

C'est la voix de la raison. Mais si vous faites partie des gens qui veulent toujours ce qui est plus puissant, plus rapide et plus cher, le FX50 risque de vous plaire malgré une consommation frisant continuellement les 15 litres au 100 km... Il est en plus possible de l'équiper de pneus de performance de 21 pouces afin d'optimiser la tenue de route et le système RAS à guidage actif des roues arrière. Ce mécanisme comprend des petits moteurs électriques reliés au système de gestion électronique du véhicule et ces moteurs permettent de bouger les roues arrière de 1 degré afin de faciliter la tenue en virage et la stabilité en ligne droite. Le FX serait le seul de sa catégorie à proposer cette technologie.

Somme toute, le FX, c'est bien plus qu'une silhouette originale!

Denis Duquet

PHOTOS : INFINITI

Catégorie	Multisegment
Échelle de prix	52 300 $ à 64 050 $ (2010)
Garanties	4 ans/100 000 km, 6 ans/110 000 km
Assemblage	Tochigi, Japon
Cote d'assurance	pauvre

CHÂSSIS - DONNÉES POUR FX50

Emp/lon/lar/haut	2 885/4 859/1 928/1 680 mm
Coffre	702 à 1 756 litres
Réservoir	90 litres
Nombre coussins sécurité	6
Antipatinage / contrôle stabilité	oui / oui
Suspension avant	indépendante, double triangulation
Suspension arrière	indépendante, multibras
Freins avant / arrière	disque (ABS) / disque (ABS)
Direction	à crémaillère, ass. variable
Diamètre de braquage	11,2 m
Pneus avant / arrière	265/45R21 / 265/45R21
Poids	2 075 kg
Capacité de remorquage	1 588 kg (3 500 lb)

COMPOSANTES MÉCANIQUES

35

Cylindrée, soupapes, alim.	V6 3,5 litres 24 s atmos.
Puissance / Couple	303 chevaux / 262 lb-pi
Tr. base (opt) / rouage base (opt)	A7 / Int
0-100 / 80-120 / 100-0 km/h	7,5 s / 5,8 s / 40,2 m
Type ess. / ville / autoroute	Super / 13,3 / 9,3 l/100 km

50

Cylindrée, soupapes, alim.	V8 5,0 litres 32 s atmos.
Puissance / Couple	390 chevaux / 369 lb-pi
Tr. base (opt) / rouage base (opt)	A7 / Int
0-100 / 80-120 / 100-0 km/h	5,7 s / 4,6 s / 40,8 m
Type ess. / ville / autoroute	Super / 14,6 / 10,1 l/100 km

DANS LA MÊME CATÉGORIE

Acura ZDX, BMW X5, BMW X6, Cadillac SRX, Land Rover LR4, Lexus RX, Lincoln MKX, Mercedes-Benz Classe M, Volkswagen Touareg, Volvo XC90

DU NOUVEAU EN 2011

Aucun changement majeur

NOS IMPRESSIONS

Agrément de conduite:	8/10
Fiabilité:	8/10
Sécurité:	8/10
Qualités hivernales:	8/10
Espace intérieur:	8/10
Confort:	8/10

www.infiniti.ca

Plus d'informations dans la section statistiques en dernière partie du Guide

PREMIER TRIO

Compte tenu de l'engouement des Québécois pour leur sport national, il est surprenant qu'on ne fasse pas plus souvent d'analogies avec le hockey. Pourquoi ne pas le faire avec la famille de modèles G37 ? Bien souvent, dans les tribunes téléphoniques à la radio, on parle d'un joueur qui est de calibre de premier, de second ou de troisième trio. Dans le cas des trois modèles G37, on peut dire qu'ils ont le potentiel pour constituer un premier trio.

La G37 est offerte en berline mais il ne faut pas oublier que ce modèle est également offert en versions coupé et cabriolet à toit rigide. Les trois se partagent le même groupe propulseur, le même habitacle et la même qualité de finition. Voyons donc ce qu'ils nous proposent.

COUPÉ OU CABRIOLET ?

Pour plusieurs, ce sera un problème difficile à résoudre. Je me suis posé la question et voici comment les départager. En premier lieu, le coupé est sans aucun doute l'un des plus élégants modèles de la gamme Infiniti. La version cabriolet à toit rigide est quasiment similaire, mais sa silhouette de toit est moins épurée. Et on peut d'ailleurs se demander pourquoi proposer un cabriolet à toit rigide qui ressemble à s'y méprendre au coupé. D'autant qu'il est plus lourd, et que sa rigidité structurale est inférieure tandis que le toit rigide une fois remisé occupe toute la place réservée aux bagages. Infiniti aurait pu s'inspirer d'Audi qui se démarque avec ses cabriolets à toit souple plus léger et n'obstruant pas la soute à bagages, déjà petite. Quant au coffre du coupé, il est suffisamment grand pour accommoder deux sacs de golf. On a même pris soin d'apposer une affichette dans le coffre pour expliquer comment y agencer ces sacs. Certains déploreront le fait qu'on ne puisse y loger que deux sacs, mais cela correspond à la charge réelle de cette voiture.

J'ai donc un parti pris pour le coupé qui est également plus performant en fait de tenue de route, même s'il faut nuancer.

UNANIMITÉ POUR L'ÉLÉGANCE

Peu importe le modèle G37 choisi, et cela inclut la berline, on ne se trompe pas en soulignant l'élégance de chaque modèle. Ils se démarquent l'un de l'autre en raison de leur configuration, mais partagent tous cette grille de calandre avec ses lames horizontales tandis que les passages de roues en relief sont juste assez proéminents. Bien entendu, il est facile de s'installer à bord de la berline, mais c'est également le cas du coupé et du cabriolet puisque l'assise des sièges n'est pas trop basse. Ceux-ci sont demeurés confortables même lors de longues randonnées. Il faut dire qu'il est relativement facile d'adopter une bonne position de conduite puisque la nacelle des instruments et le volant se déplacent d'un bloc afin d'optimiser leur positionnement par rapport au conducteur. D'autre part, l'instrumentation est très simple avec les deux cadrans indicateurs avec chiffres blancs sur fond noir qui sont très faciles à consulter. Le

FEU VERT

- Carrosseries élégantes
- Moteur impeccable
- Finition exemplaire
- Prix compétitifs

FEU ROUGE

- Coffre petit (coupé et cabriolet)
- Plate-forme trop souple
- Pneumatiques à revoir
- Visibilité arrière (coupé et cabriolet)

reste de la planche de bord est dépouillé avec une console centrale de couleur aluminium brossé se prolongeant sur la planche de bord elle-même et comprenant l'incontournable pendulette analogique qui est la signature de tous les modèles Infiniti. Cette console comprend aussi un espace de rangement très profond qui permet d'accueillir beaucoup d'objets. Le système de navigation est affiché sur un écran de bonnes dimensions et facile à consulter. Terminons cette visite de l'habitacle en soulignant que les sièges arrière du coupé ne sont pas faciles d'accès, que ceux du cabriolet sont symboliques, et que ceux de la berline sont corrects.

S'il faut se creuser les méninges pour choisir entre le coupé et le cabriolet quand on ne veut pas rouler en berline, le choix du moteur est fort aisé, il n'y en a qu'un seul. Pendant des années, le légendaire V6 de 3,5 litres était incontournable et figurait sur la liste des meilleurs moteurs de la planète. Depuis peu, il a été remplacé par une version évolutive dont la cylindrée a été portée à 3,7 litres. Il est associé à une boîte automatique à sept rapports dotée de la correspondance du régime en rétrogradation qui permet d'adapter le régime moteur de façon automatique lorsqu'on rétrograde. Bien entendu, cette transmission est de type manumatique et actionne les roues arrière puisqu'il s'agit d'une propulsion. Pour démêler le tout, il faut ajouter que les modèles coupé et cabriolet peuvent êtres commandés avec une boîte manuelle à six rapports, et que la transmission intégrale n'est pas offerte sur le cabriolet. La puissance de ce moteur est de 328 chevaux pour la berline, de 325 sur le cabriolet et de 330 sur le coupé.

BOURGEOISE AVANT TOUT

Peu importe le modèle choisi, cette Infiniti se révèle très confortable et très agréable à conduire. La suspension n'est pas trop ferme, la direction est d'une assistance correcte et variable en fonction de la vitesse. Le moteur émet un ronronnement guttural à bas régime, mais la cabine est assez bien insonorisée. Les performances de ce moteur sont très bonnes, car il faut moins de six secondes pour boucler le 0-100 km/h et 6,3 secondes dans le cas du cabriolet. Les reprises sont également vigoureuses. La consommation observée sur les trois versions lors d'essais différents a été d'environ 12 litres aux 100 km en moyenne.

Malgré tout, la G37 sous toutes ses moutures cible plus le confort que le sport. Il suffit d'amorcer un virage à haute vitesse pour s'en convaincre.

Denis Duquet

PHOTOS : MARC LACHAPELLE

Catégorie	Berline, Cabriolet, Coupé
Échelle de prix	38 690 $ à 58 300 $ (2010)
Garanties	4 ans/100 000 km, 6 ans/110 000 km
Assemblage	Tochigi, Japon
Cote d'assurance	passable

CHÂSSIS - DONNÉES POUR G37 CABRIOLET SPORT

Emp/lon/lar/haut	2 851/4 657/1 852/1 453 mm
Coffre	292 litres
Réservoir	76 litres
Nombre coussins sécurité	6
Antipatinage / contrôle stabilité	oui / oui
Suspension avant	indépendante, double triangulation
Suspension arrière	indépendante, multibras
Freins avant / arrière	disque (ABS) / disque (ABS)
Direction	à crémaillère, ass. variable
Diamètre de braquage	11,2 m
Pneus avant / arrière	P225/50R18 / P225/50R18
Poids	1 864 kg
Capacité de remorquage	n.d.

COMPOSANTES MÉCANIQUES

G37 Cabriolet

Cylindrée, soupapes, alim.	V6 3,7 litres 24 s atmos.
Puissance / Couple	325 chevaux / 267 lb-pi
Tr. base (opt) / rouage base (opt)	A7 (M6) / Prop
0-100 / 80-120 / 100-0 km/h	6,3 s / 5,2 s / 41,1 m
Type ess. / ville / autoroute	Super / 12,9 / 8,4 l/100 km

G37 berline

Cylindrée, soupapes, alim.	V6 3,7 litres 24 s atmos.
Puissance / Couple	328 chevaux / 269 lb-pi
Tr. base (opt) / rouage base (opt)	A7 / Prop (Int)
0-100 / 80-120 / 100-0 km/h	5,6 s / 5,4 s / 37,8 m
Type ess. / ville / autoroute	Super / 11,7 / 7,8 l/100 km

G37 coupé

Cylindrée, soupapes, alim.	V6 3,7 litres 24 s atmos.
Puissance / Couple	330 chevaux / 270 lb-pi
Tr. base (opt) / rouage base (opt)	A7 (M6) / Prop (Int)
0-100 / 80-120 / 100-0 km/h	5,8 s / 4,8 s / 38,2 m
Type ess. / ville / autoroute	Super / 12,2 / 7,8 l/100 km

DANS LA MÊME CATÉGORIE

Acura TL, Audi A4, BMW Série 3, Cadillac CTS, Lexus IS, Mercedes-Benz Classe C, Volvo S60

DU NOUVEAU EN 2011

Aucun changement majeur

NOS IMPRESSIONS

Agrément de conduite :	9/10
Fiabilité :	10/10
Sécurité :	8/10
Qualités hivernales :	6/10
Espace intérieur :	7/10
Confort :	7/10

www.infiniti.ca

Plus d'informations dans la section statistiques en dernière partie du Guide

TOUJOURS L'IMAGE!

Il fut une époque où des marques moins prestigieuses réussissaient à obtenir des parts de marché plus que raisonnables chez les berlines de luxe. Les acheteurs accordaient moins d'importance au logo, alors que le produit ou les convictions semblaient primer un peu plus. De nos jours, plus on grimpe dans l'échelle des voitures de luxe, plus le logo, l'image et le prestige associés à une marque s'avèrent des éléments importants pour les acheteurs.

Alors que Infiniti a réussi à s'imposer un peu mieux avec sa gamme G, la M a toujours eu de la difficulté à se tailler une place de choix au royaume des berlines de luxe, face à des voitures comme la Mercedes-Benz de Classe E, la BMW de Série 5 ou la Audi A6. Malgré tout, la M est arrivée à séduire en raison de son style réussi, de ses dimensions généreuses et de sa conduite relativement emballante. C'est sans doute la M35x équipée du rouage intégral qui aura généré la majeure partie des ventes, un véhicule relativement abordable, mais surtout très bien adapté aux goûts des acheteurs.

UNE NOUVELLE GÉNÉRATION

Histoire de revitaliser sa berline porte-étendard, Infiniti nous présente pour 2011 la troisième génération de la M, un nouveau modèle entièrement revu, tant au chapitre mécanique qu'esthétique. Comme c'était le cas avec l'ancienne génération, deux versions sont retenues pour le moment. Le modèle de base M35 fait donc place à la toute nouvelle M37, cette dernière adoptant le nouveau V6 de 3,7 litres greffé à bord de plusieurs nouveaux modèles Nissan et Infiniti. Malgré qu'il n'offre toujours pas l'injection directe, ce moteur s'avère plus qu'intéressant et ses 330 chevaux procurent à la voiture un comportement sportif à souhait. Bien entendu, la M37x, avec son prix majoré d'environ 2500$, est certainement celle qui retiendra le plus l'attention grâce à son rouage intégral, une configuration qui représente, dans le cas de la M, près de 80% des ventes au Canada.

Les amateurs de performances pourront se tourner vers la toute nouvelle M56, cette dernière succédant à la précédente M45 au chapitre des bombes de luxe. Ce V8 de 5,6 litres offrant l'injection directe trouve ici une première application chez le constructeur, qui vient également de le rendre disponible à bord du nouveau Infiniti QX 2010. Léger et moderne, ce moteur développe une puissance de 420 chevaux et un couple de 417 lb-pi, soit une puissance qui permet à la M56 2011 de se frotter aux grosses pointures du créneau en termes de chiffres.

UN BON COUP AU CHAPITRE DU STYLE?

La M 2011 délaisse les lignes un peu plus classiques de la précédente génération pour adopter un style plus fluide et dynamique. En fait, on retrouve plusieurs éléments qui semblent inspirés du FX, le VUS haut de gamme du constructeur. On remarque indéniablement la ceinture de caisse élevée, les parties vitrées plus réduites, mais c'est surtout l'avant avec calandre à arche double, typique de l'Infiniti, qui procure cet effet, tout comme la grille à motif de vagues. Bien entendu, les jantes mettent bien en valeur la sportivité de la voiture et rehausse son style et ce, même à bord de la version de base.

Au chapitre des dimensions, la Infiniti M 2011 fait quelques gains et pertes. Elle conserve le même empattement, mais sa largeur a été augmentée de 55 mm, alors que sa longueur connaît un gain de 16 mm. À l'opposé, sa hauteur est réduite de 10 mm, élément qui contribue à lui donner un style plus trapu, surtout en raison de sa ceinture de caisse élevée. Certains apprécieront ses nouvelles

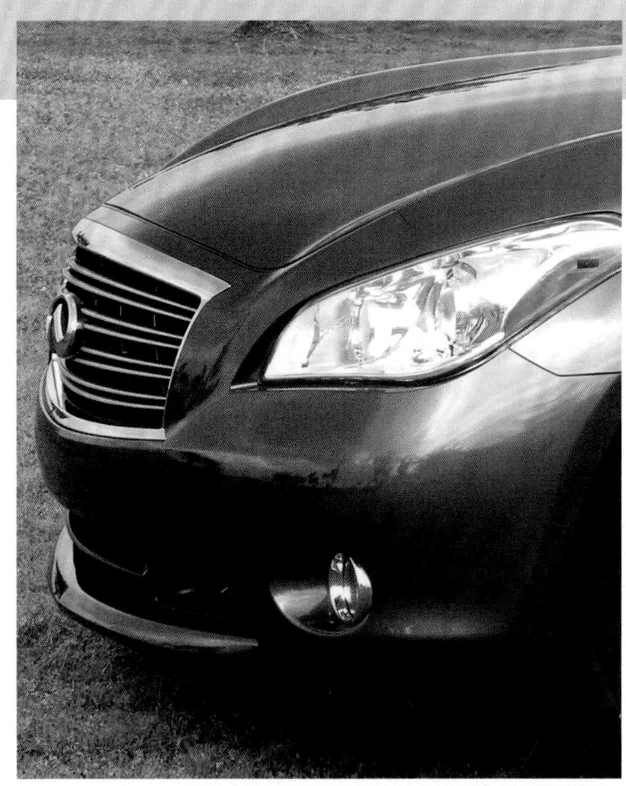

lignes plus modernes, mais d'autres semblent préférer les lignes plus classiques de l'ancienne génération.

À l'intérieur, la nouvelle M propose aussi son lot de modifications, mais on se retrouve aisément puisque l'on reconnaît le style typique du tableau de bord de l'ancienne génération, surtout la partie centrale qui présente les commandes sur deux niveaux, tel un piano. Bon point pour Infiniti qui a décidé d'utiliser des commandes classiques et non pas un système de contrôle multifonctions tel qu'on en retrouve notamment chez BMW et chez Acura. En général, l'intérieur se veut supérieur à celui que l'on retrouvait dans la précédente génération, alors que l'on remarque la richesse des cuirs et des boiseries. Les coutures présentes ici et là rehaussent également l'aspect de l'habitacle et nous donnent réellement le sentiment d'être à bord d'une voiture de luxe.

Sur la route, on apprécie le confort et le silence de roulement de la M. Difficile d'avoir des reproches face à la M37 qui fait office de modèle de base. Ce moteur est l'un des plus intéressants sur le marché et à bord de la M, il offre amplement de puissance et de couple pour procurer une conduite dynamique. Ce moteur transmet sa puissance aux roues arrière via une excellente boîte à sept rapports, cette dernière favorisant également l'économie de carburant. En fait, malgré la puissance supplémentaire apportée par les deux nouveaux moteurs, la M 2011 affiche une consommation de carburant inférieure, soit environ 1,5 l/100 km en moyenne.

Si vous êtes amateurs des suspensions fermes et des directions ultra précises que l'on retrouve normalement chez les constructeurs germaniques, sachez que la M pourrait vous décevoir. Infiniti a préféré miser sur le confort et cet élément peut être compréhensible puisqu'il pourra avantager la M pour certains types d'acheteurs. Par contre, on note l'absence de toute commande ou système permettant de moduler la fermeté de la suspension, ce qui aurait permis d'ajuster les réactions de la voiture en fonction des goûts du conducteur. Voilà un élément offert chez la concurrence.

TROP C'EST TROP!

Histoire de se démarquer de la concurrence, Infiniti semble avoir misé sur les assistants électroniques pour assurer votre sécurité. On peut certes louer l'effort, mais parfois, trop c'est trop. Comme c'est le cas avec plusieurs autres véhicules, on retrouve un système de surveillance de l'angle mort qui vérifie la présence d'un véhicule dans les angles morts, mais dans le cas de la M, ce dernier est jumelé au système d'intervention sur l'angle mort, qui grâce au système de contrôle de traction, pourra faire revenir le véhicule dans sa voie en appliquant légèrement les freins. Ajoutez un système de contrôle de la traction assez intrusif merci et ne pouvant être entièrement désactivé, ainsi que quelques autres systèmes

dont on vous épargne les détails, et vous obtenez en bout de ligne une voiture dont le plaisir de conduite est fortement inhibé.

Difficile dans ce contexte de véritablement profiter de la M56, qui avec ses 420 chevaux devrait rivaliser avec les grandes berlines sport de renom. À sa défense, cette dernière livre tout de même des performances appréciables et c'est surtout l'effet de « punch » une fois l'accélérateur enfoncé qui distingue cette motorisation. Par contre, il faudra être prêt à voir une facture majorée de 14000$ pour obtenir ces quelques chevaux supplémentaires, ce qui nous semble passablement élevé.

Avec une telle débandade de systèmes d'aide à la conduite, il est difficile de comprendre pourquoi le constructeur n'a pas cru bon de

Catégorie	Berline
Échelle de prix	52 400 $ à 68 700 $
Garanties	4 ans/100 000 km, 6 ans/110 000 km
Assemblage	Tochigi, Japon
Cote d'assurance	n.d.

CHÂSSIS - DONNÉES POUR 56X

Emp/lon/lar/haut	2 896/4 928/1 829/1 499 mm
Coffre	422 litres
Réservoir	76 litres
Nombre coussins sécurité	6
Antipatinage / contrôle stabilité	oui / oui
Suspension avant	indépendante, double triangulation
Suspension arrière	indépendante, multibras
Freins avant / arrière	disque (ABS) / disque (ABS)
Direction	à crémaillère, assistée
Diamètre de braquage	11,4 m
Pneus avant / arrière	P245/50R18 / P245/50R18
Poids	1881 kg
Capacité de remorquage	n.d.

COMPOSANTES MÉCANIQUES

37, 37x

Cylindrée, soupapes, alim.	V6 3,7 litres 24 s atmos.
Puissance / Couple	330 chevaux / 270 lb-pi
Tr. base (opt) / rouage base (opt)	A7 / Prop (Int)
0-100 / 80-120 / 100-0 km/h	6,8 s (est) / 6,0 s (est) / n.d.
Type ess. / ville / autoroute	Ordinaire / 12 / 8,3 l/100 km

56, 56x

Cylindrée, soupapes, alim.	V8 5,6 litres 32 s atmos.
Puissance / Couple	420 chevaux / 417 lb-pi
Tr. base (opt) / rouage base (opt)	A7 / Prop (Int)
0-100 / 80-120 / 100-0 km/h	5,6 s (est) / 5,0 (est) / n.d.
Type ess. / ville / autoroute	Ordinaire / 13,4 / 8,5 l/100 km

DANS LA MÊME CATÉGORIE

Acura RL, Audi A6, BMW Série 5, Cadillac STS, Jaguar XF, Lexus GS, Mercedes-Benz Classe E, Volvo S80

DU NOUVEAU EN 2011

Nouveau modèle

NOS IMPRESSIONS

Agrément de conduite :	■■■■■■■□□□ 7/10
Fiabilité :	Nouveau modèle
Sécurité :	■■■■■■■■■■ 10/10
Qualités hivernales :	■■■■■■■■□□ 8/10
Espace intérieur :	■■■■■■■■□□ 8/10
Confort :	■■■■■■■■□□ 8/10

www.infiniti.ca

Plus d'informations dans la section statistiques en dernière partie du Guide

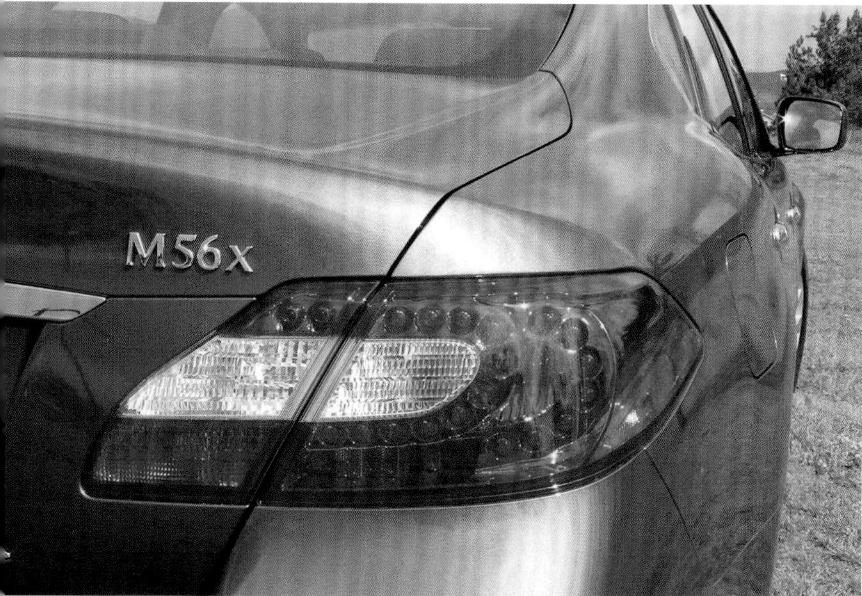

FEU VERT

- Consommation améliorée
- Bon duo de moteurs
- Habitacle soigné et raffiné
- Bonne insonorisation

FEU ROUGE

- Banquette arrière non rabattable
- Systèmes électroniques intrusifs
- Peut devenir coûteuse
- Logo pas aussi prestigieux que d'autres

munir la voiture de systèmes permettant de moduler la suspension, le temps de réponse de l'accélérateur ou bien la courbe de puissance. La seule nouveauté à ce chapitre est l'ajout d'un dispositif permettant de contrôler la transmission selon quatre modes: normal, sport, neige et éco, bien évidemment pour économie. En mode économie, on bénéficie de « l'éco-pédale », un système qui freine les ardeurs en appliquant une résistance sur l'accélérateur, mais il faut avouer que cela devient rapidement irritant et plusieurs décideront simplement de laisser la transmission en mode sport, là où elle semble le plus efficace.

Bien entendu, l'Infiniti M 2011 offre tout de même plusieurs éléments positifs, notamment son espace à bord et son confort sur route. Elle s'avère en général un produit très réussi susceptible de combler ses propriétaires. Par contre, son prix n'est pas des plus compétitifs par rapport à la concurrence et son logo n'a pas le prestige de plusieurs autres.

Sylvain Raymond

PHOTOS : SYLVAIN RAYMOND

UN RETOUR MALGRÉ LA TOURMENTE

Le segment des VUS pleine grandeur a fortement été ébranlé depuis quelques années. Il n'est donc pas étonnant que l'on note la disparition de plusieurs modèles dans ce créneau. Alors que l'on croyait qu'Infiniti ferait de même avec son QX, le constructeur nous surprend en présentant cette année la seconde génération de son grand VUS de luxe. Voilà un pari audacieux mais, avec une concurrence réduite, l'opération devient probablement plus intéressante.

Conscients du marché actuel, les dirigeants d'Infiniti ne se font pas d'illusions. Le QX demeurera un véhicule marginal, surtout au Canada. Cependant, il faut avouer qu'il subsiste tout de même un marché pour ce type de véhicule puisque certains acheteurs ont toujours besoin d'un véhicule spacieux et capable de remorquer de bonnes charges au passage. Si ces derniers disposent en plus d'un portefeuille bien garni, le QX56 pourrait bien répondre à leurs besoins.

LE STYLE ET LE GRAND CONFORT

Avec l'arrivée de cette nouvelle génération, Infiniti veut redorer le blason de son QX en comptant principalement sur deux éléments : le grand confort et le style. Entièrement remanié cette année, le QX56 2011 est maintenant assemblé à partir d'une nouvelle plateforme, celle du Nissan Patrol. Le constructeur a donc mis de côté la plate-forme du Nissan Armada, élément qui élimine en bonne partie toute affiliation avec ce dernier. Voilà qui explique les nouvelles dimensions du QX56, puisqu'il est plus bas (73 mm) et plus large de 28 mm, alors que sa longueur s'est accrue de 35 mm.

Infiniti a également fait du bon boulot au chapitre du style. Si voir le véhicule en photo ne lui rend pas vraiment justice, il faut pouvoir l'admirer de près afin d'apprécier ses lignes. Une chose est certaine, il est difficile de le confondre avec l'ancienne génération. Le nouveau QX hérite d'un style beaucoup plus fluide et dynamique qui lui va à ravir. On reconnaît à l'arrière certains éléments de style empruntés au Cube, mais l'inspiration globale vient du véhicule concept Essence, comme c'est le cas de tous les nouveaux produits chez Infiniti. L'avant hérite de la grille à double arche, alors que le capot, similaire à ceux du FX et de la nouvelle M, reprend un motif à vagues avec ses ailes saillantes. Les prises d'air fonctionnelles, intégrées dans les ailes, ajoutent aussi une belle touche. Par contre, il est certain que cette approche visuelle sera contestée par plusieurs cpmpte tenu de l'allure quelque peu iconoclaste du Qx56.

Quant au choix de la version, le constructeur a décidé de laisser peu de latitude. Le QX est proposé en deux versions, soit 4WD à 7 passagers et 4WD à 8 passagers. Sous le capot, un seul moteur, soit un V8 de 5,6 litres, le même nouveau V8 qui équipe la berline M56. Fort de ses 400 chevaux, ce moteur bénéficie toutefois de réglages différents dans le cas du QX, ce qui explique sa puissance moindre. Cependant, la puissance et son excellent couple de 413 lb-pi sont plus linéaires, ce qui favorise le comportement

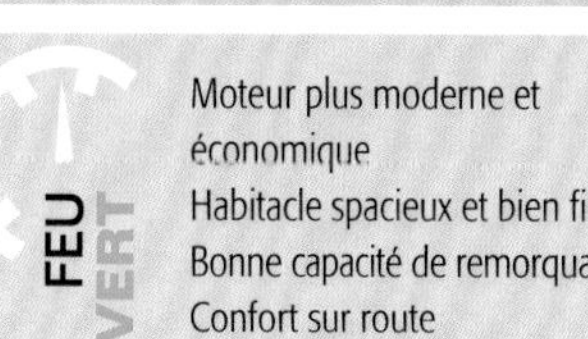

FEU VERT

Moteur plus moderne et économique
Habitacle spacieux et bien fini
Bonne capacité de remorquage
Confort sur route

FEU ROUGE

Électronique trop intrusive
Visibilité arrière difficile
Dimensions encombrantes
Rétroviseurs petits pour remorquage

du véhicule, notamment lors du remorquage. Beaucoup plus moderne que l'ancien V8 de 5,6 litres, ce moteur permet une meilleure économie de carburant, grâce notamment au calage variable des soupapes et à l'injection directe. Ce moteur est marié à une boîte automatique à sept rapports, la seule proposée.

GRAND LUXE À L'INTÉRIEUR

Outre le style et les capacités, l'habitacle est aussi un élément déterminant du nouveau QX. Il reprend le concept d'un jet privé dans lequel on retrouve luxe et espace, le tout pour sept ou huit passagers, selon la configuration choisie. À ce chapitre, vous pourrez opter pour les sièges capitaines de seconde rangée incluant une large console centrale, ou pour la banquette qui permet d'accommoder un passager de plus. Difficile de reprocher quoi que ce soit au chapitre de la qualité et du souci du détail. Le tableau de bord est impeccable et les différentes commandes sont simples à comprendre et à utiliser. L'habitacle transpire le luxe et à ce chapitre, Infiniti a toujours su y faire. Le QX est aussi bien équipé avec notamment un système de navigation de série. Au moins !

Sur la route, le moteur de 5,6 litres offre de bonnes accélérations et profite d'une riche sonorité. Les 400 chevaux suffisent à déplacer avec vigueur le QX56, mais avec un poids de plus de 2600 kg, cette puissance n'est pas superflue. En conduite plus dynamique, on apprécie le travail de la boîte à sept rapports, alors que la direction s'avère relativement précise. On note par contre des transferts de poids assez importants, chose commune pour ce type de véhicule, mais qui pourront être réduits si l'acheteur opte pour un modèle équipé du système HB (Hydraulic Body Motion Control), ce dernier placé dans la suspension et utilisant un système de transfert de fluide qui compense les excès de roulis ou de tangage. On perçoit également la rigidité accrue du véhicule sur la route par rapport à l'ancienne génération.

Offrant une capacité de remorquage de 8500 lb, le QX n'a pas peur des gros travaux. En fait, l'acheteur devra se rabattre vers une camionnette pour trouver mieux. Bon point pour l'attache de remorque qui peut être dissimulée entièrement dernière un panneau, ce qui n'entache pas le style du QX56, mais les rétroviseurs s'avèrent un peu moins adaptés au remorquage. Bref, une fois que l'on convient de la mission du nouveau QX, on découvre un véhicule qui répond certainement aux besoins de l'acheteur type.

Sylvain Raymond

PHOTOS : SYLVAIN RAYMOND

Catégorie	VUS
Échelle de prix	73 000 $
Garanties	4 ans/100 000 km, 6 ans/110 000 km
Assemblage	Canton, Mississipi, É-U
Cote d'assurance	n.d.

CHÂSSIS - DONNÉES POUR QX56 4RM

Emp/lon/lar/haut	3 073/5 283/2 006/1 905 mm
Coffre	566 à 1 606 litres
Réservoir	105 litres
Nombre coussins sécurité	7
Antipatinage / contrôle stabilité	oui / oui
Suspension avant	indépendante, double triangulation
Suspension arrière	indépendante, double triangulation
Freins avant / arrière	disque (ABS) / disque (ABS)
Direction	à crémaillère, ass. variable
Diamètre de braquage	12,4 m
Pneus avant / arrière	P275/60R20 / P275/60R20
Poids	2 682 kg
Capacité de remorquage	3 855 kg (8 500 lb)

COMPOSANTES MÉCANIQUES

56 4RM

Cylindrée, soupapes, alim.	V8 5,6 litres 32 s atmos.
Puissance / Couple	400 chevaux / 413 lb-pi
Tr. base (opt) / rouage base (opt)	A7 / Prop (4x4)
0-100 / 80-120 / 100-0 km/h	6,5 s (est) / 6,0 s (est) / n.d.
Type ess. / ville / autoroute	Ordinaire / 15,7 / 10,3 l/100 km

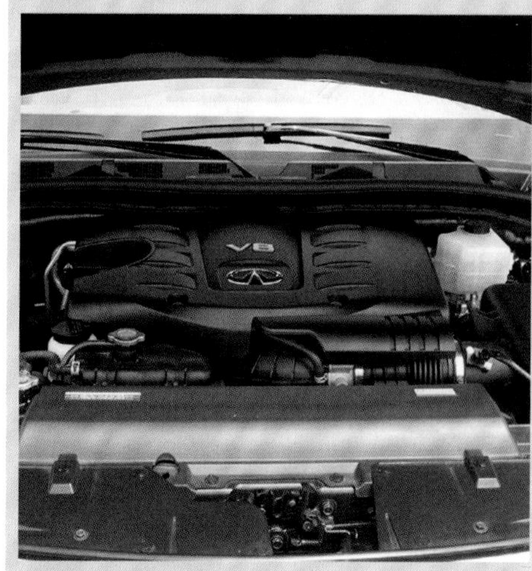

DANS LA MÊME CATÉGORIE

Cadillac Escalade, Land Rover Range Rover, Lexus LX, Lincoln Navigator

DU NOUVEAU EN 2011

Nouveau modèle

NOS IMPRESSIONS

Agrément de conduite :	■■■■■■■□□□ 7/10
Fiabilité :	Nouveau modèle
Sécurité :	■■■■■■■■■■ 10/10
Qualités hivernales :	■■■■■■■■■□ 9/10
Espace intérieur :	■■■■■■■■■□ 9/10
Confort :	■■■■■■■■■□ 9/10

www.infiniti.ca

Plus d'informations dans la section statistiques en dernière partie du Guide

UNE VOITURE DE SON TEMPS

La XF est apparue en 2008. Elle remplaçait la S-Type qui n'avait pas tellement connu de succès. Pourtant, sa silhouette rétro plaisait aux amateurs de la marque tandis que son habitacle proposait toutes les caractéristiques que l'on s'attend à voir dans une Jaguar, soit une présentation traditionnelle, beaucoup de bois et aussi beaucoup de cuir. Mais c'était justement là le problème: le passé glorieux de cette marque ne semblait plus tellement intéresser les acheteurs.

Pour la XF, on a fait fi du passé et concocté cette superbe berline dont la silhouette s'inspire de celle d'un coupé. Il faut souligner que cette voiture a été développée et conçue à une époque où son propriétaire, Ford, tentait désespérément de vendre sa filiale britannique, dont les bilans financiers s'écrivaient à l'encre rouge. Curieusement, la sortie de cette voiture a coïncidé avec l'achat de Jaguar par l'entreprise indienne Tata.

UNE BELLE MODERNITÉ

Il faut rendre hommage aux responsables de cette voiture qui ont accepté le design iconoclaste du styliste maison Ian Callum qui les a convaincus qu'il fallait oublier le passé, et se tourner vers des voitures indéniablement modernes. C'est vraiment réussi sur toute la ligne. Avec sa partie avant allongée, son arrière tronqué et sa silhouette de coupé, cette berline s'impose aussi bien en élégance qu'en sportivité. De plus, on a su trouver une grille de calandre qui est à la fois traditionnelle et moderne. Selon le modèle acheté, vous bénéficierez également de magnifiques jantes en alliage dont le design est réussi, et ce, sur tous les modèles. Quelques petites bandes en aluminium brossé placées ici et là donnent du caractère à la voiture. Et même si c'est une berline, la partie arrière nous laisse croire qu'il s'agit d'un modèle à hayon.

Pendant longtemps, il était impossible de s'asseoir dans une voiture fabriquée par Jaguar sans se retrouver entouré de cuir devant une planche de bord garnie d'appliques en bois exotiques. Naturellement, le volant était en matériau ligneux tandis que le tout semblait dater des années d'avant-guerre ou presque. Cette fois, «au diable le contre-plaqué», il est remplacé par de l'aluminium brossé qui donne une touche de modernité tout comme ce volant qui ne tente pas de ressembler à ce qui était installé dans la Type E de jadis. Mais on ne s'est pas contenté de cela. Un écran de navigation trône en plein centre, encadré par deux buses de ventilation de dimensions fort généreuses. Cet écran sert également à gérer plusieurs commandes de la voiture, et il faut admettre que ce n'est pas toujours heureux. On a beau vouloir jouer la carte de la modernité, cela présente certains inconvénients. Cet écran tactile ne répond pas toujours rapidement, certaines des commandes sont très petites, et il faut avoir du doigté pour atteindre la bonne touche tandis que le soleil oblitère parfois l'image au complet. De plus, plusieurs composantes qui l'entourent sont en aluminium et cela ressemble à certaines chaînes audio des années 70. Vraiment, chez Jaguar on a de la difficulté à oublier le passé. Sur une note quasiment futuriste, on lance le moteur en appuyant sur un gros bouton placé sur la console

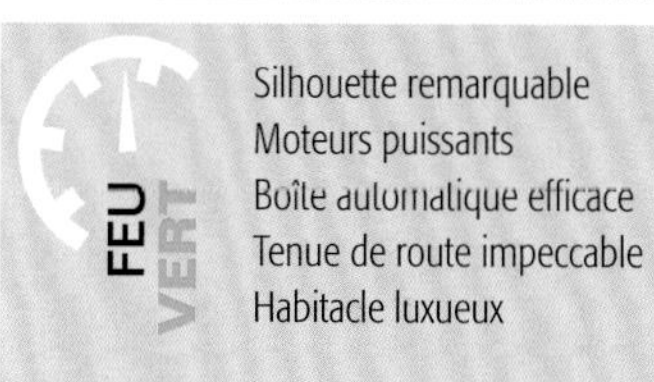

Silhouette remarquable
Moteurs puissants
Boîte automatique efficace
Tenue de route impeccable
Habitacle luxueux

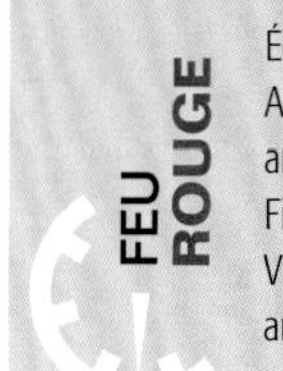

Écran tactile peu convivial
Accès aux places arrière difficiles
Fiabilité problématique
Visibilité de trois quarts arrière pénible

centrale. Juste à côté, on retrouve un plus gros bouton qui se soulève et qui sert de commande pour passer les vitesses. Lorsqu'on lance le moteur, les buses de ventilation s'ouvrent, et elles se referment lorsqu'on le coupe. Cette configuration est intéressante, mais elle m'a toujours inquiété compte tenu de la réputation assez faiblarde de la marque pour tout ce qui est électronique. Et pour passer les vitesses, il y a des palettes montées sur le volant.

DU MOTEUR, MONSIEUR !

Les places avant sont relativement généreuses et le conducteur n'aura pas de difficulté à trouver une bonne position de conduite à l'aide des différents réglages du siège et du volant. Par contre, les places arrière sont un peu plus justes et il faut être passablement agile pour s'y glisser compte tenu de l'inclinaison très forte du toit.

Le moteur offert avec la version de base était un V8 de 4,2 litres qui tire sa révérence pour 2011. Il est remplacé sur la version de base par un moteur V8 de 5,0 litres atmosphérique dont la puissance est de 385 chevaux, ce qui permet de boucler le 0-100 km/h en 5,7 secondes. On retranche ainsi presque une seconde par rapport au modèle XF de l'an dernier. Comme sur tous les modèles de la gamme, il s'agit d'une propulsion qui est activée par une nouvelle boîte ZF à six rapports. Il existe également une version Premium de ce modèle. Comme son nom l'indique, le niveau d'équipement est plus relevé.

Mais il fallait aussi respecter la tradition au chapitre de la motorisation et commercialiser une version R, plus sportive et plus puissante. Le fait de boulonner un compresseur à ce moteur V8 de 5,0 litres a permis de porter la puissance à 510 chevaux. Cette fois, le 0-100 km/h est l'affaire de moins de cinq secondes !

Le plus impressionnant sur ce modèle n'est pas sa vitesse en ligne droite, mais son efficacité en virage, son freinage puissant et la précision de la direction. Par contre, cette suspension plus sportive a une incidence sur le confort.

Mais peu importe le modèle choisi, vous apprécierez cette belle Anglaise à la mode du jour.

Denis Duquet

PHOTOS : JAGUAR

JAGUAR XF

Catégorie	Berline
Échelle de prix	61 800 $ à 85 300 $ (2010)
Garanties	4 ans/80 000 km, 4 ans/80 000 km
Assemblage	Coventry, Angleterre
Cote d'assurance	n.d.

CHÂSSIS - DONNÉES POUR XFR

Emp/lon/lar/haut	2 909/4 961/1 877/1 460 mm
Coffre	500 litres
Réservoir	70 litres
Nombre coussins sécurité	6
Antipatinage / contrôle stabilité	oui / oui
Suspension avant	indépendante, double triangulation
Suspension arrière	indépendante, double triangulation
Freins avant / arrière	disque (ABS) / disque (ABS)
Direction	à crémaillère, ass. variable
Diamètre de braquage	11,5 m
Pneus avant / arrière	255/35ZR20 / 285/30ZR20
Poids	1 891 kg
Capacité de remorquage	non recommandé

COMPOSANTES MÉCANIQUES

Luxury	
Cylindrée, soupapes, alim.	V8 4,2 litres 32 s atmos.
Puissance / Couple	300 chevaux / 310 lb-pi
Tr. base (opt) / rouage base (opt)	A6 / Prop
0-100 / 80-120 / 100-0 km/h	6,5 s / 5,9 s / 37,0 m
Type ess. / ville / autoroute	Super / 13,3 / 8,0 l/100 km

Premium Luxury	
Cylindrée, soupapes, alim.	V8 5,0 litres 32 s atmos.
Puissance / Couple	385 chevaux / 380 lb-pi
Tr. base (opt) / rouage base (opt)	A6 / Prop
0-100 / 80-120 / 100-0 km/h	5,7 s / 4,4 s / 37,0 m
Type ess. / ville / autoroute	Super / 13,1 / 8,2 l/100 km

XFR	
Cylindrée, soupapes, alim.	V8 5,0 litres 32 s surcompressé
Puissance / Couple	510 chevaux / 461 lb-pi
Tr. base (opt) / rouage base (opt)	A6 / Prop
0-100 / 80-120 / 100-0 km/h	4,9 s / 3,9 s / 37,0 m
Type ess. / ville / autoroute	Super / 14,1 / 9,3 l/100 km

DANS LA MÊME CATÉGORIE

Audi A6, BMW Série 5, Cadillac STS, Infiniti M, Lexus GS, Mercedes-Benz Classe E, Volvo S80

DU NOUVEAU EN 2011

Aucun changement majeur

NOS IMPRESSIONS

Agrément de conduite :	9/10
Fiabilité :	5/10
Sécurité :	8/10
Qualités hivernales :	7/10
Espace intérieur :	8/10
Confort :	8/10

www.jaguar.ca

Plus d'informations dans la section statistiques en dernière partie du Guide

RIEN À PERDRE, TOUT À GAGNER

Quand un modèle se vend bien, il est toujours très difficile pour un constructeur de le modifier. Mais quand on a vendu seulement 77 exemplaires de son véhicule le plus prestigieux dans tout le Canada durant toute une année, la décision se prend plus facilement... Dans le cas de la XJ, Jaguar devait repartir à zéro, ou presque.

La XJ 2011 a donc entièrement été revue et, surtout, repensée. Finies les lignes au charme suranné, bienvenue dans le XXIe siècle. Esthétiquement, la XJ reprend certains thèmes déjà vus sur l'à peine moins prestigieuse berline XF, mais la partie arrière diffère totalement. Ce sont surtout la ligne de toit, très allongée, et les feux arrière qui reviennent très haut sur les ailes, un peu à la Citroën C6, qui retiennent l'attention. L'ensemble n'est pas vilain du tout, même si la partie arrière est la plus controversée.

UN MOTEUR, TROIS VERSIONS

La XJ se décline en trois versions: de base (!?!), Supercharged et Supersport, et chacune est proposée en modèle régulier ou à empattement allongé (L). Ce dernier voit ses portes arrière allongées de 125 mm (5 pouces), ce qui ajoute à l'impact visuel de la voiture, surtout de côté. Il y a de bonnes chances que le modèle allongé se mérite les faveurs du public nord-américain tant par son prix relativement abordable (à peine 3000$ de plus que la version régulière) que par l'habitacle aux dimensions accrues qu'il autorise.

C'est plutôt à un autre niveau que la XJ rappelle le passé de Jaguar. Depuis une vingtaine d'années, la marque anglaise s'était éloignée de la tradition en proposant des voitures certes très puissantes, mais surtout confortables et luxueuses. Pourtant, c'est sur les pistes de course que Jaguar avait établi sa réputation. Avec la XJ, c'est un peu ce retour aux sources que Jaguar célèbre. Oui, vous avez bien lu. Confort, luxe et... sportivité dans une berline de prestige! La XJ 2011 n'a rien à voir avec l'ancienne génération. À tel point que Jaguar aurait facilement pu la rebaptiser. S'il s'était agi d'un constructeur américain, on ne se serait même pas posé la question et l'appellation XJ aurait été reléguée rapido presto aux oubliettes.

Tout d'abord, mentionnons que toutes les XJ reçoivent un V8 de 5,0 litres mais de puissance variable. La version «pauvre» se déplace grâce à un moteur atmosphérique d'à peine 385 chevaux, capable tout de même d'abattre le fameux 0-100 km/h en moins de 6,0 secondes. Ce qui n'est pas mal du tout pour une bagnole de près de 1900 kilos. Vient ensuite le Supercharged, qui comme son nom l'indique, reçoit un surcompresseur qui amène la puissance à 470 chevaux. Les accélérations sont excitantes, c'est le moins qu'on puisse dire, et accompagnées par une belle sonorité du V8. Vient ensuite le Supersport avec ses 510 chevaux, de quoi donner des boutons aux radars. Comme la voiture ne pèse pas tout à fait 2000 kilos, le 0-100 est l'affaire de 4,9 petites secondes. Bravo! La consommation d'essence super s'en ressent un peu, remarquez...

Pour transférer la puissance aux roues arrière (la XJ est une propulsion), on retrouve une seule transmission, soit une automatique à six rapports, fabriquée par ZF. Même la XJ de base a droit à des palettes derrière le volant qui la rendent fort agréable à utiliser. Cette boîte, bien qu'elle ne soit pas du type double embrayage, passe ses rapports rapidement et toujours au bon moment. En mode Sport, on la sent encore plus dynamique. Parlant de «dynamique», il est possible, si le conducteur veut se payer une pinte de bonheur, d'enfoncer un bouton sur la console pour activer le mode Dynamic. Là, mes amis, la XJ est à des milliards d'années-lumière (et je n'exagère pas... ou si peu) du modèle qu'elle remplace. Tout d'abord, les ceintures de sécurité se tendent, présage des émotions fortes à venir. Le moteur «tourne» plus rapidement, la transmission maintient ses rapports plus longtemps, l'accélérateur devient plus sensible, le ratio de la direction se resserre et les amortisseurs s'affermissent. En plus, les versions Supercharged et Supersport reçoivent un différentiel actif (Active Differential Control) qui ajuste automatiquement le couple envoyé à chaque roue arrière selon les conditions de la route et la puissance requise. Les courbes les plus raides sont alors passées à des vitesses qui défient quasiment les lois de la physique (pour une berline de grand luxe, s'entend) et on n'a jamais l'impression que la XJ, surtout en versions Supercharged et Supersport, est dépassée par les événements. Et si jamais elle l'était, une panoplie d'aides électroniques à la conduite veillent au grain. Il est toutefois possible de désactiver le contrôle de la traction et de la stabilité latérale pour une utilisation sur une piste de course ou dans un milieu sécurisé. Curieusement, on retrouve seulement six coussins gonflables dans la XJ, ce qui fait un peu pic-pic quand on sait que dans cette catégorie, les chiffres ont souvent préséance sur la logique. Par exemple, Lexus en offre dix dans sa LS !

Mais il n'y a pas que la vitesse en courbes qui compte. Le châssis en aluminium, comme dans la génération précédente, fait preuve

d'une grande rigidité et d'une aussi grande légèreté. Si ça vous intéresse, ses différentes parties sont rivetées et collées en utilisant une technologie originalement développée par l'industrie aéronautique. Les suspensions actives, à bras inégaux à l'avant et à liens multiples à l'arrière, sont montées sur un châssis indépendant. En tout temps, elles préservent le confort tout en autorisant une tenue de route très relevée. La direction, autrefois déficiente, s'avère désormais juste assez ferme et précise tout en « parlant » à la personne qui conduit.

PARLONS DES VRAIES AFFAIRES

Malgré une tenue de route audacieuse et des performances exquises, la plupart des gens qui se procurent une XJ le font pour le prestige de la marque (ils sont bien servis) et, surtout, pour le confort (ils sont bien servis, bis). Comme on est en droit de s'y attendre dans une berline de prestige, l'habitacle mériterait plutôt l'appellation cocon tant il est douillet. En plus, il est différent de tout ce qui se fait présentement! Le tableau de bord, ceinturé dans sa partie supérieure par une bande formant un demi-cercle, recèle des matériaux nobles comme des cuirs agréables au toucher et des boiseries exclusives. L'acheteur devra choisir entre pas moins de dix placages de bois différents (signe des temps, Jaguar offre même un placage de carbone au lieu du traditionnel bois) et dix couleurs de cuir.

Le conducteur fait face à une instrumentation empruntée à Land Rover, entièrement digitale, en HD s.v.p.!, mais qui ressemble à s'y méprendre à une instrumentation analogique. Ce type de graphisme permet au conducteur de personnaliser les données affichées tout en assurant un look traditionnel. Petit détail: lorsque le mode Dynamic est choisi, les jauges se parent d'un rouge du plus bel effet.

Les sièges avant font preuve d'un grand confort et sont chauffants ET climatisés, même dans la plus basique des XJ. La visibilité vers l'avant et les côtés ne pose aucun problème grâce à des piliers de toit que l'utilisation d'aluminium a permis de rendre plus minces tout en respectant les normes de sécurité en cas de renversement. Par contre, la visibilité vers l'arrière est un peu plus problématique à cause de la plage élevée. Les gens prenant place à l'arrière ne manquent pas d'espace pour s'étirer. Sur les versions allongées, on retrouve les petites tablettes de bois, si chères à la tradition Jaguar. Elles sont totalement inutiles, surtout dans une voiture qui se veut en rupture avec son passé. Compte tenu des dimensions généreuses de la voiture, on s'attendrait à un coffre immense. Or, il affiche des dimensions très ordinaires. Et

FEU VERT

- Style réussi... pour certains
- Moteurs en pleine forme
- Tenue de route relevée
- Confort de première classe
- Fiabilité améliorée (selon J.D. Power)

FEU ROUGE

- Entretien qui promet d'être dispendieux
- Confiance à rebâtir
- Dossiers arrière fixes
- Visibilité arrière peu commode
- Consommation assez importante

il est impossible de l'agrandir en abaissant les dossiers des sièges arrière. Il n'y a même pas de trappe pour le transport d'objets longs, comme des skis.

À n'en pas douter, Jaguar vient de frapper un grand coup avec sa nouvelle XJ. La concurrence, déjà bien établie, n'a sans doute pas à craindre à court terme. Il est difficile de prévoir ce que l'avenir réserve à la XJ, mais une version à rouage intégral serait en préparation. Et pourquoi pas une sportive version « R » ? Mais avant de s'exciter le poil des jambes, les gens de Jaguar savent qu'il leur faut regagner la confiance du public, échaudée durant les années 80 et 90 par une fiabilité d'une étonnante nullité. Le fait que le nouveau propriétaire, l'Indien Tata, soit plus à l'écoute de la marque que l'ancien (Ford) devrait sans doute aider beaucoup! Quoiqu'il en soit, la XJ 2011 est une excellente Jaguar et, surtout, une vraie Jaguar.

Alain Morin

PHOTOS : ALAIN MORIN

Catégorie	Berline
Échelle de prix	88 000 $ à 133 500 $
Garanties	4 ans/80 000 km, 4 ans/80 000 km
Assemblage	Coventry, Angleterre
Cote d'assurance	n.d.

CHÂSSIS - DONNÉES POUR XJ L SUPERCHARGED

Emp/lon/lar/haut	3 157/5 247/1 894/1 448 mm
Coffre	520 litres
Réservoir	82 litres
Nombre coussins sécurité	8
Antipatinage / contrôle stabilité	oui / oui
Suspension avant	indépendante, multibras
Suspension arrière	indépendante, multibras
Freins avant / arrière	disque (ABS) / disque (ABS)
Direction	à crémaillère, ass. variable
Diamètre de braquage	12,7 m
Pneus avant / arrière	P275/35ZR20 / P275/35ZR20
Poids	1 961 kg
Capacité de remorquage	non recommandé

COMPOSANTES MÉCANIQUES

XJ, XJ L

Cylindrée, soupapes, alim.	V8 5,0 litres 32 s atmos.
Puissance / Couple	385 chevaux / 380 lb-pi
Tr. base (opt) / rouage base (opt)	A6 / Prop
0-100 / 80-120 / 100-0 km/h	5,7 s (const) / 5,0 s (est) / n.d.
Type ess. / ville / autoroute	Super / 17 / 8,2 l/100 km

XJ Supercharged, XJ L Supercharged

Cylindrée, soupapes, alim.	V8 5,0 litres 32 s surcompressé
Puissance / Couple	470 chevaux / 424 lb-pi
Tr. base (opt) / rouage base (opt)	A6 / Prop
0-100 / 80-120 / 100-0 km/h	5,2 s (const) / 4,5 s (est) / n.d.
Type ess. / ville / autoroute	Super / 18,3 / 8,7 l/100 km

XJ Supersport, XJ L Supersport

Cylindrée, soupapes, alim.	V8 5,0 litres 32 s surcompressé
Puissance / Couple	510 chevaux / 461 lb-pi
Tr. base (opt) / rouage base (opt)	A6 / Prop
0-100 / 80-120 / 100-0 km/h	4,9 s (const) / n.d. / n.d.
Type ess. / ville / autoroute	Super / 18,3 / 8,7 l/100 km

DANS LA MÊME CATÉGORIE

Audi A8, BMW Série 7, Lexus LS, Maserati Quattroporte, Mercedes-Benz Classe CLS, Mercedes-Benz Classe S

DU NOUVEAU EN 2011

Nouveau modèle

NOS IMPRESSIONS

Agrément de conduite :	8/10
Fiabilité :	Nouveau modèle
Sécurité :	8/10
Qualités hivernales :	8/10
Espace intérieur :	7/10
Confort :	8/10

www.jaguar.ca

Plus d'informations dans la section statistiques en dernière partie du Guide

ELLES ONT TOUT POUR ELLES!

Enfin presque... Lors de leur refonte complète en 2006, alors que Jaguar était en pleine tourmente financière, les coupés et cabriolets XK ont été dotés de caractéristiques techniques à la fine pointe et de carrosseries à donner de mauvaises idées au pape. En plus, les ingénieurs et designers ont réussi à les doter d'une personnalité très forte, un élément assez rare dans un monde de rectitude politique. En fait, la seule chose qui manque à la série XK (et à toute Jaguar à bien y penser...), c'est un peu de fiabilité. Nous y reviendrons. Pour le moment, concentrons-nous sur les bons points, car il y en a plusieurs!

La XK se décline en deux modèles, soit coupé et cabriolet. Les deux sont aussi jolies l'une que l'autre (c'est une opinion personnelle que je partage volontiers...) mais le plaisir de rouler à découvert dans une Jaguar influence sans doute plusieurs personnes. Les lignes des versions de «base», si un tel terme peut être utilisé pour une voiture qui frise les 100000$, sont pour le moins attrayantes mais les modèles R, plus sportifs et à l'allure plus agressive sont tout simplement enivrantes. Et on s'est finalement débarrassé de l'antenne de la radio qui semblait tout droit sortie d'une Ford 1963. Parlant de Ford, on trouve encore la trace de cet ancien propriétaire de Jaguar dans la XK. Par exemple, la chambranlante trappe à essence en plastique ou les leviers des clignotants et des essuie-glaces... Des détails me direz-vous mais il vient un moment, dans la hiérarchie automobile où il faut avoir un minimum de standing!

DU SON ET DU BRUIT

Dans l'habitacle, pilote et passager profitent d'un environnement très luxueux et sportif à défaut d'être vaste. Le tableau de bord est pratiquement aussi inspirant que la carrosserie même si quelques

commandes gagneraient à être simplifiées, surtout celles du système audio, à la sonorité au demeurant très correcte. Parlant de sonorité, il faut entendre celle du moteur en pleine accélération... une petite jouissance! Je parle du moteur situé à l'avant. Celui des vitres électriques mène aussi beaucoup de bruit mais c'est nettement moins jouissif...

L'élément le plus distinctif de cet habitacle demeure le bouton rotatif qui commande la transmission automatique. Simple, intuitif et très stylé, ce bouton n'aura besoin que d'un peu de fiabilité pour se faire apprécier... Remarquez qu'il n'a jamais fait défaut dans toutes les Jaguar récentes essayées récemment. Faut dire qu'elles étaient toutes neuves... Autre élément distinctif, les places arrière tout à fait ridicules de petitesse et d'inconfort. Par contre, le coffre est étonnamment logeable et sa finition est plus que correcte. Je parlais du coupé, pas du cabriolet...

L'HÉRITAGE DE LA COURSE AUTOMOBILE

Une Jaguar, c'est peut-être un habitacle cossu mais c'est aussi, et surtout, une mécanique d'enfer. Il ne faut pas oublier que Jaguar a connu énormément de succès en course automobile

FEU VERT
- Lignes racées
- Sonorité des moteurs enivrante
- Moteurs en pleine forme
- Version R appréciée
- Comportement routier sérieux

FEU ROUGE
- Fiabilité très aléatoire
- Places arrière indécentes
- Consommation excessive
- Certaines pièces Ford malvenues

dans les années 50 et 60. Aujourd'hui, cet héritage se traduit par des moteurs pleins de verve et un comportement routier à l'avenant. On retrouve tout d'abord un V8 de 5,0 litres de 385 chevaux qui entraîne la XK avec une facilité déconcertante. Mais pour à peine quelques milliers de dollars supplémentaires, la XK-R propose un V8 de 5,0 litres surcompressé de 510 chevaux. Alors là mes amis, ça déménage ! Les 1 753 kilos d'un coupé R, par exemple, sont amenés à 100 km/h en 5,1 secondes. Faut le faire... Toute cette cavalerie passe aux roues arrière par une transmission automatique à six rapports.

Bien entendu, la version R, autant pour le cabriolet que le coupé, s'avère plus sportive. Grâce à des commandes placées sur la console, il est possible de modifier une foule de paramètres pour obtenir une conduite encore plus dynamique. C'est même le nom choisi pour ce mode, Dynamic. Il permet d'utiliser le plein potentiel de la XK-R, une chose à faire uniquement sur une piste de course. Les versions R peuvent aussi compter sur un différentiel arrière électronique des plus performants.

En usage quotidien, il faut certes être prêt à faire des sacrifices mais malgré tout les choses se passent plutôt bien. La position de conduite est facile à trouver, les sièges (avant est-il besoin de le préciser) sont confortables et la visibilité (vers l'avant est-il besoin de le préciser) est surprenante. Sur les routes en mauvais état (au Québec, ça se trouve...), les suspensions tapent assez dur... à moins que ce ne soient les pneus de 19 pouces à taille basse. La direction est aussi vive que précise mais elle devient anormalement dure lors de changements de voies brusques.

C'est dans les courbes qu'on mesure le potentiel d'une voiture et la XK, surtout en livrée R, remplit ses promesses. La tenue de route est solide, presqu'agile. En mode normal, les divers systèmes de contrôle interviennent assez rapidement mais de façon discrète. Lorsque tous les systèmes sont hors service, il faut y aller mollo avec l'accélérateur en sortie de courbes. Avec un peu de pratique, il est possible d'engendrer de belles dérobades du train arrière... sur un circuit, évidemment. Si jamais l'enthousiasme dépassait les compétences, la XK-R possède des freins très puissants.

Mais s'il est une chose que la XK, et toutes les Jaguar, doivent apprendre, c'est l'art de la fiabilité. Pour l'instant, c'est loin d'être maîtrisé...

Alain Morin

PHOTOS : SYLVAIN RAYMOND

Catégorie	Cabriolet, Coupé
Échelle de prix	96 500 $ à 114 000 $
Garanties	4 ans/80 000 km, 4 ans/80 000 km
Assemblage	Coventry, Angleterre
Cote d'assurance	n.d.

CHÂSSIS - DONNÉES POUR R COUPE

Emp/lon/lar/haut	2 752/4 794/1 892/1 329 mm
Coffre	330 litres
Réservoir	70 litres
Nombre coussins sécurité	4
Antipatinage / contrôle stabilité	oui / oui
Suspension avant	indépendante, double triangulation
Suspension arrière	indépendante, bras inégaux
Freins avant / arrière	disques (ABS) / disques (ABS)
Direction	à crémaillère, ass. variable
Diamètre de braquage	11,0 m
Pneus avant / arrière	P245/40ZR19 / P275/35ZR19
Poids	1 753 kg
Capacité de remorquage	non recommandé

COMPOSANTES MÉCANIQUES

Coupe, Cabriolet	
Cylindrée, soupapes, alim.	V8 5,0 litres 32 s atmos.
Puissance / Couple	385 chevaux / 380 lb-pi
Tr. base (opt) / rouage base (opt)	A6 / Prop
0-100 / 80-120 / 100-0 km/h	5,6 s / n.d. / n.d.
Type ess. / ville / autoroute	Super / 13,3 / 8,4 l/100 km

R Coupe, R Cabriolet	
Cylindrée, soupapes, alim.	V8 5,0 litres 32 s surcompressé
Puissance / Couple	510 chevaux / 461 lb-pi
Tr. base (opt) / rouage base (opt)	A6 / Prop
0-100 / 80-120 / 100-0 km/h	5,1 s / 3,8 s / 37,4 m
Type ess. / ville / autoroute	Super / 14,1 / 9,1 l/100 km

DANS LA MÊME CATÉGORIE

Aston Martin Vantage, BMW Série 6, Chevrolet Corvette, Mercedes-Benz Classe SL, Porsche 911

DU NOUVEAU EN 2011

Aucun changement majeur

NOS IMPRESSIONS

Agrément de conduite :	9/10
Fiabilité :	4/10
Sécurité :	10/10
Qualités hivernales :	6/10
Espace intérieur :	6/10
Confort :	8/10

www.jaguar.ca

Plus d'informations dans la section statistiques en dernière partie du Guide

L'ATTRAIT DE LA MARQUE

Au cours des derniers mois, Chrysler à été dans l'obligation de sabrer plusieurs modèles qui ne jouissaient pas de la popularité nécessaire ou qui coûtaient tout simplement trop cher à produire. Dans cette rationalisation des produits, la plupart des spécialistes s'attendaient à ce que le Jeep Commander soit également abandonné, puisque plusieurs autres VUS chez Chrysler et Dodge avaient été sacrifiés. Contre toute attente, le plus gros modèle chez Jeep est toujours au rendez-vous !

Cela peut surprendre, mais il faut considérer la valeur de la marque Jeep. En effet, lorsque le client est confronté à différents choix incluant un produit Jeep, c'est souvent ce dernier qui est choisi. Cela s'explique en grande partie par la réputation que possède cette marque. En achetant un Jeep et vous devenez automatiquement une personne qui aime l'aventure et qui mène une vie hors de l'ordinaire. C'est du moins l'image que l'on s'en fait.

TAILLÉ AU COUTEAU

Les stylistes qui ont dessiné cette silhouette semblent s'être inspirés du défunt Grand Wagoneer, le plus gros et le plus luxueux véhicule de cette marque à une certaine époque. De ce dernier, on a retenu la grille de calandre chromée, les flancs latéraux très plats de même qu'une partie arrière toute verticale. Cette inspiration rétro cadre assez mal avec les lignes fluides de tous les modèles actuels et du nouveau Grand Cherokee en particulier. On aurait voulu répliquer au Hummer qu'on n'aurait pas fait autrement... Exercice futile aujourd'hui, puisque cette marque n'est plus de ce monde.

Comme il s'agit en fait d'un Grand Cherokee légèrement allongé, l'habitabilité ne fait pas défaut, du moins aux places avant, puisque celles-ci sont spacieuses autant pour le dégagement des jambes que des coudes. Il faut également souligner le confort des sièges, mais comme toujours, le support latéral est pratiquement inexistant, ce qui est un peu agaçant avec les sièges en cuir, puisque cela glisse passablement. Plusieurs ont signalé la trop grande sobriété du tableau de bord. Il faut tout de même admettre que cette sobriété possède un certain chic, entre autres pour la console centrale, très élégante. Notons la multitude de buses de ventilation circulaires qui peuvent être orientées très facilement dans toutes les directions.

Toutefois, si les places avant sont plus que généreuses, on ne peut en dire autant des places arrière, puisqu'on a décidé d'offrir une troisième rangée de sièges. Il en résulte des places médianes plus ou moins accueillantes et une troisième rangée qui est encore plus inconfortable. D'ailleurs, une fois ces sièges arrière déployés, l'espace réservé aux bagages est pratiquement inexistant. C'est à peine si on peut y mettre une simple mallette de travail. Heureusement, lorsque cette banquette est repliée, on bénéficie d'un espace de chargement adéquat pour transporter valises et autres objets nécessaires à quatre personnes.

FEU VERT

- Places avant confortables
- Moteur HEMI puissant
- Bonne capacité de remorquage
- Rouages intégraux efficaces
- Prestige de la marque

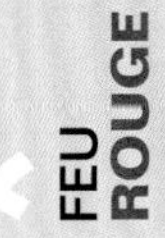

FEU ROUGE

- Silhouette rétro
- Troisième rangée symbolique
- Consommation fort élevée
- Faible valeur de revente
- Suspension peu confortable

FIDÈLE À LA RÉPUTATION

Chez Jeep, on se targue de produire les véhicules tout-terrain les plus efficaces et les plus costauds qui soient et ce, peu importe leur catégorie. Même si on a la possibilité de transporter sept occupants, on n'a pas lésiné sur les moyens pour en faire un authentique tout terrain. Comme il se doit, la plate-forme est solide et possède au surplus des poutres de renforts insérées dans les longerons. De plus, les rouages intégraux Quadra-Trac I et Quadra-Trac II sont parmi les plus efficaces sur le marché.

Le premier est un système à prise permanente. Il est associé de série avec le moteur V6 de 3,7 litres d'une puissance de 210 chevaux et couplé à une boîte automatique à cinq rapports. Ce moteur a fait son temps et son rendement est passable. Ce groupe propulseur peut vous amener assez loin dans la forêt, mais demeure limité. Votre meilleure option est de vous procurer le légendaire moteur HEMI, un V8 de 5,7 litres d'une puissance de 357 chevaux livré avec la boîte automatique à cinq rapports. De plus, le rouage intégral est le Quadra-Trac II, un système actif avec boîte de transfert, dispositif d'assistance au départ en pente et limiteur de vitesse en descente. Si vos ambitions de conduite hors route sont encore plus élevées, vous pouvez commander en option le système Quadra-Drive II avec différentiel autobloquant électronique aux essieux avant et arrière. Par la même occasion, le véhicule sera équipé de plaques de protection pour le réservoir de carburant, la boîte de transfert et la suspension avant.

Malheureusement, le comportement routier de ce mastodonte est passablement moche, surtout sur les routes en piteux état. Sur la grande route, les choses se passent relativement bien, malgré une direction engourdie et des bruits éoliens presque omniprésents. En revanche, dirigez-vous sur une route secondaire mal pavée, c'est-à-dire la quasi totalité des routes du Québec, et vous découvrirez avec horreur un train arrière qui danse la sarabande et qui a de la difficulté à dompter les trous et les bosses. Par contre, dans la circulation urbaine, il se révèle très agile compte tenu de son gabarit.

Bien honnêtement, l'arrivée cette année du nouveau Grand Cherokee risque de lui porter ombrage.

Denis Duquet

PHOTOS : JEEP

Catégorie	VUS
Échelle de prix	36 745 $ à 47 945 $
Garanties	3 ans/60 000 km, 5 ans/100 000 km
Assemblage	Détroit, Michigan, É-U
Cote d'assurance	bonne

CHÂSSIS - DONNÉES POUR SPORT

Emp/lon/lar/haut	2 781/4 788/1 900/1 831 mm
Coffre	212 à 1 028 litres
Réservoir	80 litres
Nombre coussins sécurité	6
Antipatinage / contrôle stabilité	oui / oui
Suspension avant	indépendante, bras inégaux
Suspension arrière	essieu rigide, multibras
Freins avant / arrière	disques (ABS) / disques (ABS)
Direction	à crémaillère, assistée
Diamètre de braquage	11,2 m
Pneus avant / arrière	P245/65R17 / P245/65R17
Poids	1 588 kg
Capacité de remorquage	1 588 kg (3 500 lb)

COMPOSANTES MÉCANIQUES

Sport	
Cylindrée, soupapes, alim.	V6 3,7 litres 12 s atmos.
Puissance / Couple	210 chevaux / 235 lb-pi
Tr. base (opt) / rouage base (opt)	A5 / 4x4
0-100 / 80-120 / 100-0 km/h	n.d. / n.d. / n.d.
Type ess. / ville / autoroute	Ordinaire / 14,6 / 10,6 l/100 km

Sport, Limited	
Cylindrée, soupapes, alim.	V8 5,7 litres 24 s atmos.
Puissance / Couple	357 chevaux / 389 lb-pi
Tr. base (opt) / rouage base (opt)	A5 / 4x4
0-100 / 80-120 / 100-0 km/h	7,9 s / 6,0 s / 41,8 m
Type ess. / ville / autoroute	Ordinaire / 15,7 / 10,6 l/100 km

DANS LA MÊME CATÉGORIE

Ford Explorer, Kia Borrego,Nissan Pathfinder, Toyota 4Runner

DU NOUVEAU EN 2011

Aucun changement majeur

NOS IMPRESSIONS

Agrément de conduite :	7/10
Fiabilité :	2/10
Sécurité :	10/10
Qualités hivernales :	9/10
Espace intérieur :	9/10
Confort :	7/10

www.jeep.ca

Plus d'informations dans la section statistiques en dernière partie du Guide

JEEP COMMANDER

POUR AVENTURIERS URBAINS

Je ne sais pas comment les gens de cette marque s'y prennent, mais ils semblent toujours être capables de commercialiser des modèles qui connaissent une certaine popularité alors que d'autres périclitent. Il n'y a pas si longtemps, le Liberty était un véritable succès malgré une fiabilité problématique. Mais une refonte ratée l'a fait dégringoler du le palmarès des ventes. Heureusement sont arrivés les modèles Compass et Patriot qui connaissent un succès pour le moins surprenant.

En effet, contrairement aux autres véhicules de la marque, ce duo est surtout conçu pour des excursions au centre-ville et sa plate-forme est partagée avec la Dodge Caliber. Pire encore, le rouage de base est une traction, une première pour ce constructeur. Mais on a réalisé un vieux rêve chez Jeep, soit celui de commercialiser des véhicules destinés à des utilisateurs urbains qui n'ont nullement l'intention de s'aventurer dans des sentiers intimidants.

POUR MADAME

Le Compass a été conçu pour satisfaire une clientèle féminine qui apprécie l'aspect aventurier d'un VUS, mais qui ne veut absolument pas des inconvénients attachés à ce genre de véhicule. Dans le cas qui nous concerne, pas besoin de rouage 4X4 réglable, pas besoin d'une suspension archisèche et encore moins de certains éléments exclusifs à la conduite hors route. Avec ses angles arrondis et sa silhouette qui gomme quelque peu les traits anguleux des autres véhicules Jeep, la silhouette du Compass nous donne un bon indice de la clientèle visée. Elle possède bien entendu la fameuse grille de calandre à sept ouvertures verticales, mais pour le reste c'est plus citadin autre chose.

Dans l'habitacle, on a amélioré la présentation du tableau de bord qui était auparavant l'un des pires de l'industrie. Cette fois, les plastiques sont de meilleure qualité, l'esthétique a été également revue à la hausse, mais c'est quand même assez décevant. Il faut toutefois souligner que les sièges sont confortables et que les places arrière sont correctes.

Comme ce modèle est une traction qui peut être commandée avec un rouage intégral optionnel, il n'est pas tellement conseillé d'aller vous promener dans la nature. Le rouage aux quatre roues est surtout destiné à combattre la neige et les chaussées glissantes. Et pour bénéficier de la transmission intégrale, il faut commander le moteur 2,4 litres qui est nettement plus intéressant que celui de base, un 2,0 litres produisant 158 chevaux, soit 14 chevaux de moins. Quant à la tenue de route, elle est satisfaisante, mais il ne faut pas s'énerver au volant.

Les gens qui aiment le Compass ont craqué pour sa silhouette, sa faible consommation de carburant et sa configuration relativement pratique et polyvalente. Mais pour rouler un peu plus loin dans la forêt, le Patriot a des chances de combler vos attentes.

FEU VERT

Prix compétitif
Faible consommation
Prestige de la marque
Rouage intégral
Patriot mieux nanti que le Compass

FEU ROUGE

Agrément de conduite mitigé
Performances modestes
CVT contestée
Hors route léger

UN PEU PLUS MACHO

Marketing, quand tu nous tiens ! Nous en avons le plus bel exemple avec ces véhicules. Alors que le premier cible une clientèle féminine et urbaine, le second a pour mission d'intéresser les gens supposément actifs et plus audacieux.

Le côté un peu plus viril du Patriot est exprimé par sa silhouette plus carrée qui nous fait songer à l'ancien Cherokee, un dur de dur. Les angles plus aigus, la calandre plus droite et la partie arrière plus accentuée sont autant d'éléments visuels qui déterminent le caractère de ce véhicule. Par contre, au chapitre de la motorisation, c'est identique au Compass. Une fois de plus, le choix recommandé est le moteur quatre cylindres 2,4 litres de 172 chevaux. Et même si la transmission CVT n'est pas des plus impressionnantes, elle fait quand même un meilleur travail que la boîte manuelle dont l'embrayage est à revoir sérieusement, de même que la course du levier de vitesses. Ce qui est irritant avec la boîte à rapports continuellement variables, c'est quand elle est en mode automatique : on a l'impression de piloter un véhicule propulsé par un moteur de rasoir électrique tant le bourdonnement provenant de l'avant est incessant. Curieusement, lorsqu'on passe les rapports en mode manuel, cette transmission se fait apprécier.

Ses possibilités de conduite hors route sont meilleures que celles du Compass. Pour ce faire, il faut choisir le rouage intégral Freedom-Drive II. Ce groupe de conduite hors route comprend un système de contrôle de vitesse de descente, des plaques de protection pour le réservoir de carburant, la transmission et le réservoir d'huile, un différentiel pouvant être verrouillé, des crochets de remorquage et un refroidisseur d'huile. Ce n'est pas suffisant pour négocier le légendaire sentier du Rubicon en Californie, mais c'est assez pour afficher la plaque *Trail Rated* sur la carrosserie !

Bien que plusieurs de ses lacunes soient identiques à celle du Compass, le Patriot le devance ce dernier de peu concernant l'agrément de conduite tandis que sa fiabilité est légèrement supérieure. À ce sujet, allez donc savoir pourquoi puisque les éléments mécaniques sont les mêmes…

Denis Duquet

PHOTOS : MARC LACHAPELLE

Catégorie	VUS
Échelle de prix	15 795 $ à 23 395 $
Garanties	3 ans/60 000 km, 5 ans/100 000 km
Assemblage	Belvidere, Illinois, É-U
Cote d'assurance	bonne

CHÂSSIS - DONNÉES POUR COMPASS NORTH 4RM

Emp/lon/lar/haut	2 634/4 404/1 811/1 631 mm
Coffre	643 à 1 518 litres
Réservoir	51 litres
Nombre coussins sécurité	4
Antipatinage / contrôle stabilité	non / oui
Suspension avant	indépendante, jambes de force
Suspension arrière	indépendante, multibras
Freins avant / arrière	disques (ABS) / disques (ABS)
Direction	à crémaillère, assistée
Diamètre de braquage	11,2 m
Pneus avant / arrière	P215/60R17 / P215/60R17
Poids	1 509 kg
Capacité de remorquage	454 kg (1 000 lb)

COMPOSANTES MÉCANIQUES

Compass, Patriot	
Cylindrée, soupapes, alim.	4L 2,0 litres 16 s atmos.
Puissance / Couple	158 chevaux / 141 lb-pi
Tr. base (opt) / rouage base (opt)	M5 (CVT) / Tr
0-100 / 80-120 / 100-0 km/h	11,2 s / 9,8 s / 45,6 m
Type ess. / ville / autoroute	Ordinaire / 8,9 / 6,9 l/100 km

Compass, Patriot	
Cylindrée, soupapes, alim.	4L 2,4 litres 16 s atmos.
Puissance / Couple	172 chevaux / 165 lb-pi
Tr. base (opt) / rouage base (opt)	M5 (CVT) / Tr (Int)
0-100 / 80-120 / 100-0 km/h	10,3 s / 8,8 s / 45,6 m
Type ess. / ville / autoroute	Ordinaire / 9,9 / 8,2 l/100 km

Jeep Compass

DANS LA MÊME CATÉGORIE

Ford Escape, Honda CR-V, Hyundai Tucson, Jeep Patriot, Kia Sportage, Mazda Tribute, Mitsubishi Outlander, Nissan Rogue, Subaru Forester, Suzuki Grand Vitara, Toyota RAV4

DU NOUVEAU EN 2011

Aucun changement majeur

NOS IMPRESSIONS

Agrément de conduite :	7/10
Fiabilité :	6/10
Sécurité :	8/10
Qualités hivernales :	7/10
Espace intérieur :	7/10
Confort :	7/10

www.jeep.ca

Plus d'informations dans la section statistiques en dernière partie du Guide

JEEP COMPASS / PATRIOT

JEEP REPREND LE TERRAIN PERDU

Il y avait déjà quelques années que le Jeep Grand Cherokee était dû pour des changements majeurs, mais les déboires financiers de Chrysler avaient passablement retardé ses projets. Le cahier de charges du futur Grand Cherokee imposait un nouveau V6, un habitacle haut de gamme plus vaste qu'avant, des capacités hors route dignes de Jeep, un niveau de sécurité élevé et un prix attirant. Les ingénieurs et designers allaient-ils remplir leur mandat? En juin dernier, Jeep lançait officiellement son tout nouveau GC...

Extérieurement, on ne peut pas dire que le Jeep Grand Cherokee nouvelle cuvée s'éloigne beaucoup de son ancêtre. La grille avant chromée à sept barres verticales, si chère à Jeep, de même que les angles assez carrés, tout nous rappelle la dernière génération et même, l'avant-dernière. De toute évidence, les designers ont manqué cruellement d'imagination... Remarquez que le Grand Cherokee n'est pas laid, pas du tout en fait. Lors de la présentation, les gens de Jeep ont passé beaucoup de temps à nous expliquer la petite baguette ici, le renflement là, la délicatesse de cette nervure qui amène l'œil vers bla, bla, bla... Par contre, les designers ont réussi à moderniser une ligne classique reconnue par tout le monde sans lui faire perdre son identité et pour cela, félicitations. Par ailleurs, une version Dodge du Grand Cherokee, probablement baptisée Magnum, sera sans doute bientôt proposée. Un autre modèle, celui-là hautement sportif, le SRT8, est déjà prévu. Bon, revenons à nos moutons...

Dans l'habitacle du Grand Cherokee, les changements sont moins subtils et tout à fait bienvenus. La présentation est au goût du jour, de même que la qualité des matériaux et de leur assemblage. On retrouve certes encore quelques plastiques durs, surtout dans la partie inférieure du tableau de bord et des portières, mais les doigts se promènent la plupart du temps sur des surfaces agréables au toucher. Le volant de toutes les versions est ajustable autant en hauteur qu'en profondeur et la plupart des boutons sont placés au bon endroit. Toutefois nous décernons un bonnet d'âne aux jauges, plus ou moins faciles à lire à cause des reflets. L'espace ne manque pas et les sièges, même ceux des versions de base, se révèlent confortables. À l'arrière, à l'exception de la place médiane, les fesses sensibles seront bien traitées et les têtes, même les hautes perchées, ainsi que les jambes démesurées n'auront pas de problème à se loger. Le châssis du nouveau Grand Cherokee est plus long de 135 mm (5,3 pouces) et ce sont les passagers arrière qui en profitent, Jeep répondant ainsi à une des critiques les plus fréquentes concernant l'ancien modèle. Le coffre, pour sa part, est de 19 % plus grand qu'auparavant. Je ne sais pas pour vous, mais 19 % de plus de vide, ça ne me dit pas grand-chose. Disons que cet espace de chargement est, de visu, dans les normes de la catégorie des VUS intermédiaires.

NOUVEAU V6, VIEUX V8

Quatre versions du Jeep Grand Cherokee sont proposées aux clients canadiens. Le Laredo E, comme nous venons de le voir, représente le modèle d'entrée de gamme. Suivent, dans l'ordre, le Laredo X, le Limited et l'Overland. Si l'équipement augmente de façon exponentielle au gré des versions, les différences esthétiques ne sont pas très évidentes, une caractéristique qui pourrait déplaire à certains acheteurs qui préfèreraient que les voisins remarquent, sans équivoque, leur Overland...

Il fut un temps où Chrysler et Mercedes-Benz furent conjoints de fait. De cette union obligée sont nées quelques bonnes voitures, telles les Chrysler 300 et Dodge Charger. On peut aussi mettre le nouveau Grand Cherokee dans cette catégorie, puisque les ingénieurs de Jeep se sont servis du châssis du Mercedes-Benz

Classe ML pour concocter leur nouveau VUS. L'empattement, on l'a vu, gagne de précieux pouces, mais aussi une rigidité et un raffinement encore jamais vus dans un Jeep, même si la génération précédente était loin d'être un monstre d'incivilité.

La fiche technique du GC montre deux moteurs, un V6 et un V8. Les autorités canadiennes de Chrysler croient que, au nord du 45ième parallèle, ces moulins se partageront le marché à part égale. Le V6 Pentastar de 3,6 litres est tout nouveau. Il devrait d'ailleurs se retrouver bientôt dans plusieurs produits Chrysler/Dodge/Jeep. Ses 290 chevaux et 260 livres-pied de couple sont livrés de façon linéaire et ce V6 devrait combler la majorité des besoins du conducteur. Le V8 est un Hemi de 5,7 litres que les amateurs de performance connaissent bien. Curieusement, ses 360 chevaux et 390 livres-pied de couple ne sont pas livrés de façon spectaculaire. Certes, une accélération de 0 à 100 km/h prend une bonne seconde de moins avec ce dernier, mais on ne sent pas une forte poussée comme on pourrait s'y attendre. Sa principale qualité demeure sa capacité accrue de remorquage. Il consomme aussi davantage, le contraire aurait été surprenant. Au Québec, on se désole de

l'absence du moteur diesel qui a été retiré en 2009 après seulement deux années de loyaux services. Selon les autorités de Jeep, ce moteur n'est plus nécessaire, le V6 actuel faisant aussi bonne figure que l'autre en matière d'économie d'essence. Si un jour les Américains se remettent à apprécier les diesels, les mêmes autorités trouveront sûrement une bonne raison de le ramener... Pour la petite histoire, notons que le V6 peut tirer jusqu'à 5000 livres (2269 kilos) tandis que le V8 remorque jusqu'à 7200 livres (3300 kilos). Des chiffres qui parlent d'eux-mêmes.

La transmission est une automatique à cinq rapports, ce qui nous fait penser qu'après avoir acheté un châssis acceptable et créé un nouveau moteur, il restait moins de sous pour cet important organe. Quoiqu'il en soit, cette boîte fonctionne avec douceur et semble bien adaptée aux deux moteurs.

4X4 FORT EFFICACE

Un Jeep qui se respecte est doté d'un rouage 4x4 décent et le Grand Cherokee en est un... Les Laredo E et X reçoivent l'intégral Quadra-Trac I qui ne demande aucune intervention du conducteur et qui peut expédier jusqu'à 50 % du couple aux roues avant si le besoin se fait sentir. La plupart des gens lui préféreront le Quadra-Trac II, beaucoup plus axé vers la conduite hors route. Quant au Quadra-Drive II, il s'agit d'un Quadra-Trac II plus évolué qui sera surtout apprécié par ceux qui font du hors route sérieux.

On retrouve aussi la suspension pneumatique Quadra-Lift qui permet de jouer avec la garde au sol, selon le type de conduite ou de surface. Il y a aussi le nouveau système Selec-Terrain qui comprend cinq types de conduite (Auto, Snow, Sport, Sand/Mud et Rock). Très semblable à ce qu'offrent déjà Land Rover et Toyota/Lexus, il permet au Grand Cherokee de circuler à peu près n'importe où. Une excursion dans une piste assez difficile nous a convaincu de ses capacités hors route. L'angle d'approche est de 34,3 degrés (pour cela, il faut cependant enlever le bas du pare-chocs avant, une opération qui ne prend que quelques minutes), l'angle de départ est de 29,3 degrés, tandis que l'angle ventral (breakover) est de 23,1 degrés. Ces données, obtenues avec la suspension pneumatique à son plus haut niveau, ne sont pas comparables à celles d'un Land Rover LR4, mais à 40000$ de moins, on ne s'en plaindra pas!

ET SUR LA ROUTE?

Là où le Jeep Grand Cherokee a fait des pas de géant, c'est au

Catégorie	VUS
Échelle de prix	37 995 $ à 49 995 $
Garanties	3 ans/60 000 km, 5 ans/100 000 km
Assemblage	Détroit, Michigan, É-U
Cote d'assurance	n.d.

CHÂSSIS - DONNÉES POUR LIMITED

Emp/lon/lar/haut	2 915/4 822/1 938/1 761 mm
Coffre	990 à 1 950 litres
Réservoir	93 litres
Nombre coussins sécurité	6
Antipatinage / contrôle stabilité	oui / oui
Suspension avant	indépendante, leviers triangulés
Suspension arrière	indépendante, multibras
Freins avant / arrière	disque (ABS) / disque (ABS)
Direction	à crémaillère, ass. variable
Diamètre de braquage	11,3 m
Pneus avant / arrière	P265/60R18 / P265/60R18
Poids	2 201 kg
Capacité de remorquage	2 269 kg (5 002 lb)

COMPOSANTES MÉCANIQUES

Laredo E, Laredo X, Limited

Cylindrée, soupapes, alim.	V6 3,6 litres 24 s atmos.
Puissance / Couple	290 chevaux / 260 lb-pi
Tr. base (opt) / rouage base (opt)	A5 / Int (4x4)
0-100 / 80-120 / 100-0 km/h	9,8 s (est) / 7,5 s / n.d.
Type ess. / ville / autoroute	Ordinaire /13,0 / 8,9 l/100 km

Overland

Cylindrée, soupapes, alim.	V8 5,7 litres 16 s atmos.
Puissance / Couple	360 chevaux / 390 lb-pi
Tr. base (opt) / rouage base (opt)	A5 / 4x4
0-100 / 80-120 / 100-0 km/h	8,7 s / 7,0 s / n.d.
Type ess. / ville / autoroute	Ordinaire / 15,7 / 10,6 l/100 km

FEU VERT

Habitacle cossu
Silence de roulement apprécié
Baroudeur infatigable
Bonnes capacités de remorquage
Rapport prix/équipement intéressant

FEU ROUGE

Jauges difficiles à lire
V8 plutôt goinfre
Fiabilité inconnue
Absence de moteur diesel

niveau de la conduite. L'habitacle est silencieux et la tenue de route est saine, le roulis étant fort bien maîtrisé, même sur un modèle de base. D'ailleurs, les suspensions, indépendantes aux quatre roues, une nouveauté pour le GC, accrochées à un châssis des plus rigides, ne sont jamais inconfortables. Reste la direction, dont la précision sur la route n'est pas optimale. Par contre, cela devient une bénédiction en hors route.

Au niveau de la sécurité, on retrouve six coussins gonflables, le minimum requis de nos jours. Bien entendu, on note aussi la présence de plusieurs aides électroniques à la conduite dont le BSM (Blind Sport Monitoring) qui avise le conducteur de la présence d'un véhicule dans son angle mort. Cependant, même si Jeep semble très fière du haut niveau de sécurité de son nouveau Grand Cherokee, il répond simplement aux normes de la catégorie. Quant aux prix, je parlerais plutôt de rapport qualité/prix. À ce niveau, le Jeep Grand Cherokee est imbattable.

Alain Morin

PHOTOS : ALAIN MORIN

DANS LA MÊME CATÉGORIE

Ford Explorer, Jeep Commander, Kia Sorento, Nissan Pathfinder, Toyota 4Runner

DU NOUVEAU EN 2011

Nouveau modèle

NOS IMPRESSIONS

Agrément de conduite :	■■■■■■■■□□	8/10
Fiabilité :	Nouveau modèle	
Sécurité :	■■■■■■■■□□	8/10
Qualités hivernales :	■■■■■■■■■□	9/10
Espace intérieur :	■■■■■■■■■□	9/10
Confort :	■■■■■■■■■□	9/10

www.jeep.ca

Plus d'informations dans la section statistiques en dernière partie du Guide

MAIS JE L'AIIIIIME!

Il consomme, son habitacle est mal insonorisé, sa suspension fait dans le brasse-camarade, bref, le Jeep Wrangler est l'antithèse de ce que la plupart des gens recherchent dans un véhicule. Mais que voulez-vous: je l'aiiiime...

Je l'aimais hier, je l'aime aujourd'hui et je l'aimerai encore demain. Mine de rien, le bon vieux Wrangler est le seul capable de nous promener dans les bois sans coup férir, avec le toit décapoté de surcroît. Feeling « tout est possible » garanti.

Pour certains, le Jeep Wrangler a tous les défauts. Son pire: une consommation qui fait que le passage à la pompe est toujours douloureux. Ça devrait s'améliorer avec l'arrivée (en cours d'année) d'un nouveau V6 Pentastar de 3,6 litres (plus ou moins 290 chevaux). Une chose est sûre: l'actuel V6 de 3,8 litres est dû pour une mise à niveau et on devrait en profiter pour le rendre plus souple. Pour l'heure, la motorisation de 202 chevaux est plutôt rugueuse.

Sans surprise, les reprises sont plus dynamiques avec la manuelle six vitesses qu'avec l'automatique qui, elle aussi, a besoin d'une infusion technologique. Imaginez! Elle n'a que quatre rapports, dans une ère où même les petits véhicules en offrent six, avec mode manuel s'il vous plaît!

Mais bon, boîtes de transmission archaïques ou pas, je l'aiiime...

Cela dit, si vous tenez à ce que vos passagers vous adressent encore la parole, ne leur offrez pas de *lift* en Wrangler; conseillez-leur plutôt de prendre le bus, car dans le Jeep, ça brasse en sapristi! Tous les cahots se répercutent dans la suspension (l'une des rares avec encore l'essieu rigide) et, conséquemment, dans

les colonnes vertébrales. On ne s'en sort pas: rouler en Jeep, c'est rouler cahin-caha, même sur l'autoroute. Ça devient vite énervant, mais c'est le prix à payer pour que le véhicule se comporte comme le Roi de la jungle qu'il est.

L'insonorisation, maintenant : même avec le toit rigide, l'habitacle résonne des bruits de la route, du grondement des pneus et des sifflements au pare-brise. Que voulez-vous, le Jeep Wrangler a l'aérodynamisme d'une brique qui fend le vent et il faut hausser le ton pour se faire entendre des passagers qui ont finalement pris le risque de monter à bord. Et risque il y a aussi en virage! Si on attaque trop sévèrement, c'est la déportation qui nous attend. Le véhicule est haut sur patte, un net avantage dans la brousse, mais sur la grand-route, pas de folie à faire: la tenue de route n'a de tenue... que le nom. La direction est aussi l'une des plus assistées du marché, mais cette crémaillère est réglée pour donner de la latitude en hors-piste et ça fonctionne très bien quand on veut tourner sur un dix cents.

D'AUTRES DÉFAUTS

À tous ces défauts s'ajoute un habitacle très moyen. La planche de bord carrée a beau vouloir faire du style avec de faux

FEU VERT

- Le plus grand virtuose du hors-piste
- Version Unlimited : quatre portes, cinq passagers
- Variante Rubicon
- Boîte manuelle six rapports

FEU ROUGE

- Habitacle bon marché
- Consommation de carburant
- Suspension brasse-camarade
- Boîte automatique quatre rapports archaïque
- Tenue de route… quelle tenue de route ?

appliqués de chrome et un design techno, les matériaux crient le bon marché et ça fait « cheapette ». Les sièges de faux vinyle manquent de soutien latéral et le rangement est minimal. Attention : on peut pester contre le positionnement (au centre) peu intuitif des commandes électriques des fenêtres, mais c'est ce qui permet, pendant la belle saison, de s'affranchir des portières. Soit dit en passant, si vous n'avez jamais roulé en Jeep sans toit ni portières, vous ne savez pas encore ce qu'est la vraie liberté automobile...

Parlant de portières : depuis sa nouvelle génération (2007), le Wrangler s'offre une variante à quatre portières, une première depuis le Jeep Willys 1941. C'est pratique quand on veut concilier famille, amis et bagages – ce Unlimited accueille d'ailleurs une cargaison trois fois plus élevée que le Wrangler dit « régulier ». Personnellement, je trouve que la silhouette est alors trop longue, mais pour avoir testé la chose sur le sentier légendaire Rubicon Trail, je vous confirme que le handicap d'un demi-mètre supplémentaire est négligeable. D'ailleurs, les angles d'approche et de départ sont à un poil près identiques à ceux du Wrangler de base.

RUBICONNEZ-MOI ÇA

Le système Command-Trac fait évidemment l'affaire; dans les tempêtes de neige ou les bois, il permet de se tirer des mauvais pas avec élégance. Ma préférence va cependant au Rock-Track de la version Rubicon. Le ratio à bas régime est plus généreux, les essieux Dana sont plus musclés et, surtout, les différentiels arrière ET avant peuvent être verrouillés. Oh, et la barre antiroulis peut être déconnectée, pour un tiers plus d'amplitude lorsque la situation l'exige. Croyez-moi : à bord d'un Rubicon, impossible de rester coincé quelque part, à moins de vouloir faire le con. Et encore...

D'ailleurs, c'est pour ça qu'on l'aime tant, ce Wrangler. Il est l'un des véhicules les plus aptes, – sinon LE plus apte du marché, en hors-piste. Malgré son âge (70 ans !), il n'a rien perdu de ses aptitudes, et c'est encore et toujours impressionnant de voir ses quatre roues s'articuler au gré des obstacles, puis reprendre de la traction lorsqu'on croit tout perdu. Ce sentiment du « tout est possible » fait totalement oublier les défauts énumérés ci-dessus. Ah, ce que l'amour peut être aveugle !

Nadine Filion

PHOTOS : JEEP

Catégorie	VUS
Échelle de prix	19 095 $ à 29 995 $
Garanties	3 ans/60 000 km, 5 ans/100 000 km
Assemblage	Toledo, Ohio, É-U
Cote d'assurance	moyenne

CHÂSSIS - DONNÉES POUR RUBICON UNLIMITED

Emp/lon/lar/haut	2 946/4 404/1 877/1 801 mm
Coffre	1 314 à 2 458 litres
Réservoir	85 litres
Nombre coussins sécurité	2
Antipatinage / contrôle stabilité	oui / oui
Suspension avant	essieu rigide, multibras
Suspension arrière	essieu rigide, multibras
Freins avant / arrière	disque (ABS) / disque (ABS)
Direction	à crémaillère, ass. variable
Diamètre de braquage	12,6 m
Pneus avant / arrière	LT255/75R17 / LT255/75R17
Poids	1 957 kg
Capacité de remorquage	1 588 kg (3 500 lb)

COMPOSANTES MÉCANIQUES

Wrangler

Cylindrée, soupapes, alim.	V6 3,8 litres 12 s atmos.
Puissance / Couple	202 chevaux / 237 lb-pi
Tr. base (opt) / rouage base (opt)	M6 (A4) / 4x4
0-100 / 80-120 / 100-0 km/h	8,1 s / 10,2 s / 46,8 m
Type ess. / ville / autoroute	Ordinaire / 13,9 / 10,6 l/100 km

DANS LA MÊME CATÉGORIE

Nissan Xterra, Toyota FJ Cruiser

DU NOUVEAU EN 2011

Aucun changement majeur

NOS IMPRESSIONS

Agrément de conduite :	6/10
Fiabilité :	2/10
Sécurité :	8/10
Qualités hivernales :	9/10
Espace intérieur :	7/10
Confort :	6/10

www.jeep.ca

Plus d'informations dans la section statistiques en dernière partie du Guide

CINQ ANS TROP TARD!

Il y a plusieurs années, la mode était aux VUS de type 4X4, des véhicules construits à partir de châssis de camionnettes et capables de vous amener dans les pires sentiers sans encombre. Les constructeurs vantaient à cette époque, à grands coups de publicité, les capacités hors route de leurs véhicules et l'idée semblait pour plusieurs très attirante. Le rationnel a repris le dessus et les acheteurs se sont aperçu qu'ils n'avaient pas réellement besoin de tels véhicules. La mode s'est alors tournée vers des VUS plus compacts et plus civilisés.

C'est à ce moment que Kia a introduit son Borrego, un VUS classique qui n'était pas dépourvu d'attraits, mais qui, malheureusement, ne cadrait déjà plus avec la tendance. Il était à l'époque difficile de concevoir l'arrivée d'un autre VUS sept passagers, proposé avec un moteur V8, surtout que le message marketing qui accompagnait le Borrego avait déjà été abandonné par les autres. Il faut savoir que le Borrego utilise non pas une plate-forme de voiture comme plusieurs petits utilitaires multigements modernes, mais plutôt un châssis à échelle.

UN MARCHÉ DÉLAISSÉ QUI PEUT ÊTRE BÉNÉFIQUE

Alors que ce type de véhicule a été abandonné par plusieurs autres, notamment Dodge avec son Durango, Kia peut toujours profiter des dernières parts de marché qui restent dans ce créneau pour écouler ses unités. En fait, malgré un marché qui s'est déplacé, il reste des gens qui ont besoin de ce type de véhicule et avec une offre réduite, les joueurs qui demeurent en profitent.

Cette année, le Borrego n'offre pratiquement aucun changement par rapport à 2010. Les choix demeurent simplifiés puisqu'uniquement deux versions sont proposées, LX et EX, cette dernière offrant quelques équipements supplémentaires. Par contre, il vous faudra ensuite orienter votre choix sur la motorisation, puisque deux moteurs sont toujours au catalogue. Celui à considérer est sans contredit le V6 de 3,8 litres développant 276 chevaux, ce dernier offrant une meilleure économie de carburant et ce, malgré le poids et la taille du véhicule. Bien entendu, il faudra demeurer poli avec l'accélérateur pour ne pas voir ce chiffre augmenter drastiquement. Certes, ce moteur n'est pas surpuissant, mais il convient à la majeure partie des besoins.

Probablement la seule raison qui devrait vous faire pencher vers le moteur V8 s'avère les capacités de remorquage accrues du véhicule. D'une cylindrée de 4,6 litres, ce V8 développe une puissance de 337 chevaux pour un couple de 323 lb pi. Jumelé à une transmission automatique à six rapports et à un système 4X4 efficace, voilà un modèle qui peut s'avérer très intéressant pour vos loisirs. Il pourra tracter une charge de 7500 lb, alors que le Borrego équipé du moteur V6 doit se contenter d'une charge de 5000 lb. Voilà qui met le doigt sur le principal avantage du Borrego, soit son espace et sa capacité de remorquage. Alors que les VUS compacts modernes

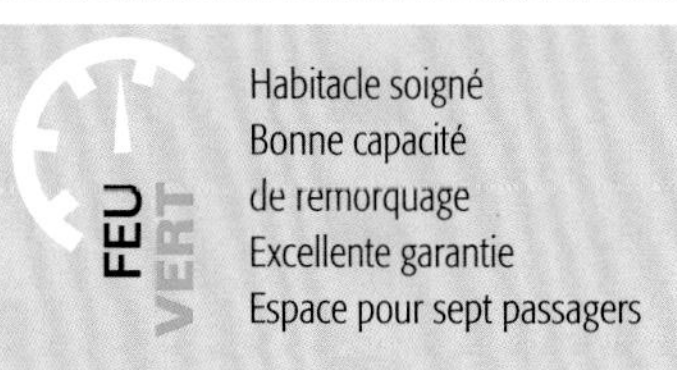

Habitacle soigné
Bonne capacité de remorquage
Excellente garantie
Espace pour sept passagers

Direction lourde
Comportement peu emballant
Moteur V8 gourmand
Marché en baisse

ne peuvent tracter plus que 3500 lb et ce avec leur moteur six cylindres, le Borrego représente ici un choix intéressant pour ceux qui ont des besoins plus importants, surtout considérant que les autres VUS capables de remplir cette mission sont bien souvent plus dispendieux.

Quant au comportement du Borrego, il est fidèle à ce que l'on peut s'attendre de ce type de VUS, soit une conduite moins connectée à la route et sans véritable sensation. Sur la route, on le sent un peu lourdaud et même si son rouage quatre roues motrices l'avantage dans la neige, son poids et son centre de gravité plus élevés l'handicapent au chapitre de la tenue de route. Sa suspension demeure toutefois assez ferme, ce qui améliore un peu le sentiment de contrôle, mais sa direction est un peu trop lourde. On a l'impression de se battre un peu avec le véhicule, surtout à vitesse réduite.

PAS ININTÉRESSANT

Malgré un design qui date, le Borrego offre un style qui demeure agréable. D'ailleurs, il a été entièrement dessiné par les studios de Kia en Californie, histoire de lui procurer des lignes au goût de notre marché et à ce chapitre, c'est assez réussi. Il se présente comme un VUS typique dont les lignes servent à mettre en valeur sa prestance et son caractère. On apprécie son galbe fluide et son style macho, alors que plusieurs éléments rehaussent son caractère.

À bord du Borrego, on découvre un habitacle spacieux qui profite d'un bon souci du détail. Par contre, le tableau de bord demeure on ne peut plus classique comparativement aux nouveaux produits Kia. De par sa taille et son style, le Borrego apporte un espace intérieur très généreux. Aucun problème pour les personnes de grande taille, on retrouve amplement de dégagement pour tous les passagers. Pour ceux qui ont de grands besoins, le Borrego peut aussi accueillir sept passagers grâce à sa troisième banquette. Dans cette configuration, l'espace pour les bagages devient un peu plus réduit, mais somme toute similaire à celui d'une minifourgonnette. Une fois cette troisième banquette divisée à 50/50 rabattue, vous obtenez amplement d'espace pour transporter de plus grands objets.

En conclusion, le Borrego ne cadre plus tellement avec la tendance.

Sylvain Raymond

PHOTOS : KIA

Catégorie	VUS
Échelle de prix	37 395 $ à 44 395 $ (2010)
Garanties	5 ans/100 000 km, 5 ans/100 000 km
Assemblage	Sohari, Corée du Sud
Cote d'assurance	n.d.

CHÂSSIS - DONNÉES POUR 3.8L LX

Emp/lon/lar/haut	2 895/4 880/1 915/1 765 mm
Coffre	350 à 2 765 litres
Réservoir	78 litres
Nombre coussins sécurité	7
Antipatinage / contrôle stabilité	oui / oui
Suspension avant	indépendante, double triangulation
Suspension arrière	indépendante, multibras
Freins avant / arrière	disque (ABS) / disque (ABS)
Direction	à crémaillère, assistée
Diamètre de braquage	n.d.
Pneus avant / arrière	P245/70R17 / P245/70R17
Poids	2 023 kg
Capacité de remorquage	2 268 kg (5 000 lb)

COMPOSANTES MÉCANIQUES

3.8L LX, 3.8L EX

Cylindrée, soupapes, alim.	V6 3,8 litres 24 s atmos.
Puissance / Couple	276 chevaux / 267 lb-pi
Tr. base (opt) / rouage base (opt)	A5 / 4x4
0-100 / 80-120 / 100-0 km/h	7,8 s / 6,9 s / 40,7 m
Type ess. / ville / autoroute	Ordinaire / 12,7 / 9,4 l/100 km

4.6L LX, 4.6L EX

Cylindrée, soupapes, alim.	V8 4,6 litres 32 s atmos.
Puissance / Couple	337 chevaux / 323 lb-pi
Tr. base (opt) / rouage base (opt)	A6 / 4x4
0-100 / 80-120 / 100-0 km/h	7,1 s / 5,8 s / 40,7 m
Type ess. / ville / autoroute	Ordinaire / 13,8 / 9,3 l/100 km

DANS LA MÊME CATÉGORIE

Ford Explorer, Honda Pilot, Jeep Commander, Jeep Grand Cherokee, Nissan Pathfinder, Toyota 4Runner

DU NOUVEAU EN 2011

Aucun changement majeur

NOS IMPRESSIONS

Agrément de conduite :	■■■■■■□□□□	6/10
Fiabilité :	■■■■■■■■□□	8/10
Sécurité :	■■■■■■■■■■	10/10
Qualités hivernales :	■■■■■■■■□□	8/10
Espace intérieur :	■■■■■■■■□□	8/10
Confort :	■■■■■■■■□□	8/10

www.kia.ca

Plus d'informations dans la section statistiques en dernière partie du Guide

OUBLIEZ LE PASSÉ, SONGEZ À L'AVENIR

Le renouvellement des modèles de Kia est pour le moins spectaculaire. Après avoir connu les affres de la faillite et la reprise par Hyundai, le constructeur Kia s'est vu confier une nouvelle mission par son nouveau propriétaire. Celle d'oublier les petites voitures économiques proposant surtout un prix alléchant, pour séduire les acheteurs et produire des modèles aussi compétitifs que ceux fabriqués par Hyundai, mais s'adressant à une clientèle plus jeune et plus active.

Cela explique sans doute pourquoi le numéro deux coréen a commandité de prestigieux tournois de tennis comme les Internationaux d'Australie, et choisi le très populaire Raphaël Nadal comme porte-parole. Plus récemment, au Québec, la marque devenait la voiture officielle des courses de vélo ProTour disputées en septembre dans les villes de Québec et de Montréal. Les meilleurs cyclistes de la planète étaient escortés par des véhicules Kia, ce qui n'est jamais mauvais pour une image de marque !

SEPT ANS PLUS TARD

Parfois, la progression d'un constructeur automobile est fort spectaculaire. Kia en est un bon exemple. Il y a sept ans, je suis allé en Corée pour visiter les installations du constructeur et procéder à l'essai de son modèle de luxe, qui portait le nom d'Opirus. Dévoilée au Salon de l'auto de Genève, cette berline se démarquait par une silhouette quasiment caricaturale.

Mon bref essai s'est déroulé sur une aire d'essai dynamique et s'est poursuivi par quelques tours supplémentaires dans un stationnement d'usine. Ce fut suffisant pour mettre les freins en feu et réaliser que la tenue de route n'était pas le point fort de cette voiture. Puis, elle est arrivée au Canada encore plus équipée que le modèle original. Elle portait dorénavant le nom d'Amanti, mais sa silhouette était toujours aussi excentrique.

QUELLE TRANSFORMATION !

Inutile d'en dire davantage sur l'Amanti. Cette berline à vocation plus luxueuse que tous les autres véhicules Kia de l'époque n'avait pas grand-chose à offrir. Heureusement, on a travaillé à l'améliorer au fil des années. La mécanique a été remplacée, la suspension modifiée, et la finition améliorée de beaucoup. Le produit était presque devenu intéressant, mais sa silhouette faisait fuir les acheteurs.

Cette fois, on repart à neuf avec une nouvelle plate-forme, un moteur plus puissant et surtout une silhouette totalement redessinée. Il faut noter que les stylistes n'avaient pas le choix puisque l'Amanti était nettement en retrait à ce chapitre face à la concurrence.

Curieusement, mon toujours très bref essai au volant de sa remplaçante s'est effectué sur la même aire d'essai dynamique avec un processus quasiment identique. Une élégante berline blanche s'est avancée vers moi, et on m'a invité à prendre le volant alors qu'un ingénieur était assis sur le siège du passager. Son anglais

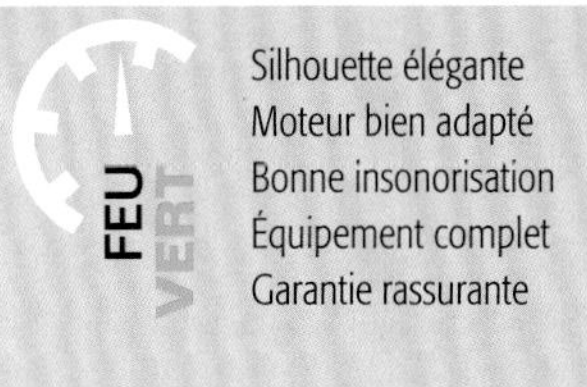

Silhouette élégante
Moteur bien adapté
Bonne insonorisation
Équipement complet
Garantie rassurante

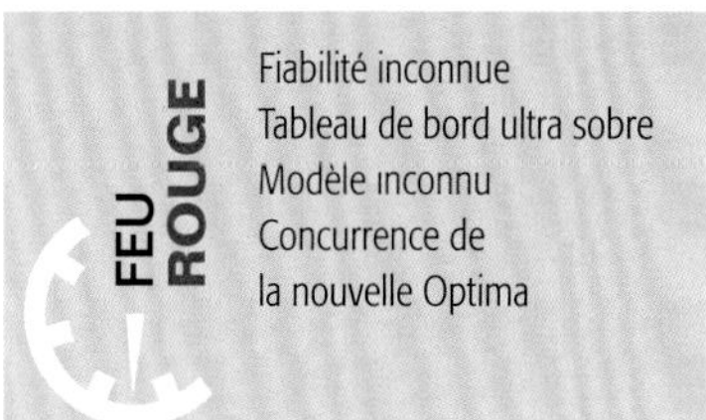

Fiabilité inconnue
Tableau de bord ultra sobre
Modèle inconnu
Concurrence de la nouvelle Optima

était plus que potable, mille fois meilleur que mon coréen, et après m'avoir donné les grandes lignes des composantes mécaniques, il m'a invité à démarrer.

Cette fois, non seulement le nom a changé, mais la silhouette aussi. Cette voiture est élégante et fera oublier sa devancière en un éclair. La grille de calandre est séduisante et dorénavant typique de toutes les Kia. De plus, les lignes de la silhouette sont équilibrées. Toutefois, plusieurs observateurs ont reproché à cette nouvelle venue d'avoir une silhouette trop semblable à celle de la nouvelle Optima.

Il est vrai que les deux se ressemblent, mais quant à savoir laquelle est la plus jolie, c'est une affaire de goût. Il existe pourtant de nombreuses différences visuelles. La grille de calandre de la Cadenza est toujours cintrée en sa partie centrale, mais elle est moins prononcée et plus discrète. Autre différence à souligner: la prise d'air avant n'est plus transversale, mais centrale sur la Cadenza. De plus, l'ampleur des phares avant est moindre que sur l'Optima. Bref, la présentation extérieure est nettement plus conventionnelle et conservatrice.

Dans l'habitacle, c'est sobre. Un peu trop sobre même puisque ça manque certainement d'impact visuel. Au premier coup d'œil, on a l'impression d'être dans une voiture de catégorie beaucoup plus modeste. Par contre, les sièges se sont avérés confortables, du moins lors de notre bref essai. Comme il se doit sur une voiture de cette catégorie, tous les gadgets du genre sont rendez-vous. De plus, pour que cette berline se démarque de l'Optima en matière de prestige, les ingénieurs ont opté pour un moteur V6 de 3,5 litres d'une puissance de 290 chevaux. Monté de manière transversale, il est associé à une transmission de type manumatique à six rapports.

La voiture n'est pas nécessairement sportive, mais ses qualités dynamiques sont à souligner, et la vivacité du moteur également, tandis que la boîte automatique est nerveuse et bien étagée.

Cette nouvelle Cadenza possède donc d'indéniables qualités, mais il est certain qu'on lui reprochera sa ressemblance avec l'Optima, ce qui risque de lui nuire. Les gens préféreront sans doute payer moins cher pour une voiture plus ou moins similaire, tout au moins en fait de silhouette.

Denis Duquet

PHOTOS : DENIS DUQUET

KIA CADENZA

DONNÉES PRÉLIMINAIRES

Catégorie	Berline
Échelle de prix	n.d.
Garanties	n.d.
Assemblage	n.d.
Cote d'assurance	n.d.

CHÂSSIS - DONNÉES POUR BASE

Emp/lon/lar/haut	2 845/4 966/1 849/1 476 mm
Coffre	n.d.
Réservoir	n.d.
Nombre coussins sécurité	n.d.
Antipatinage / contrôle stabilité	oui / oui
Suspension avant	n.d.
Suspension arrière	n.d.
Freins avant / arrière	disque (ABS) / disque (ABS)
Direction	n.d.
Diamètre de braquage	n.d.
Pneus avant / arrière	n.d.
Poids	1 574 kg
Capacité de remorquage	n.d.

COMPOSANTES MÉCANIQUES

Base	
Cylindrée, soupapes, alim.	V6 3,5 litres atmos.
Puissance / Couple	290 chevaux / 248 lb-pi
Tr. base (opt) / rouage base (opt)	A6 / Tr
0-100 / 80-120 / 100-0 km/h	n.d. / n.d. / n.d.
Type ess. / ville / autoroute	Ordinaire / n.d.

DANS LA MÊME CATÉGORIE

Acura TL, Buick LaCrosse, Hyundai Genesis, Lexus ES, Nissan Maxima, Toyota Avalon, Volvo S60

DU NOUVEAU EN 2011

Nouveau modèle remplaçant l'Amanti.
Dévoilement printemps 2011

NOS IMPRESSIONS

Agrément de conduite:	n.d.
Fiabilité:	n.d.
Sécurité:	n.d.
Qualités hivernales:	n.d.
Espace intérieur:	n.d.
Confort:	n.d.

www.kia.ca

Plus d'informations dans la section statistiques en dernière partie du Guide

SOBRE, MAIS COMPÉTENTE

Il n'y a pas si longtemps, Kia était surtout reconnu pour ses petites voitures vendues à bas prix, et dont la silhouette était correcte, mais sans plus. Comme on dit au Québec, c'était le constructeur des « p'tits chars drabes, pas chers et protégés par une excellente garantie. » L'an dernier, le constructeur coréen a dévoilé plusieurs nouveaux modèles tous plus élégants les uns que les autres et cette fois, ils étaient dotés d'une mécanique qui nous faisait oublier les véhicules d'autrefois.

La Forte est une berline compacte qui a été lancée sous un flot d'éloges de la part de nombreux journalistes. Je m'en souviens puisque certains sont revenus très excités du lancement. Plusieurs affirmaient qu'il s'agissait de la voiture de l'année. Ce ne fut pas le cas, ni dans notre pays, ni chez nos voisins du sud, mais il n'empêche que cette berline a beaucoup à offrir.

UNE ÉLÉGANCE DISCRÈTE

Peter Schreyer a été embauché comme designer en chef de Kia. Depuis, cet ancien styliste débauché de chez Audi a réalisé des merveilles. Toutes les voitures lancées depuis son arrivée recueillent des commentaires fort favorables, et la Forte a connu sa part de louanges. Il est vrai que la silhouette n'est pas spectaculaire, mais elle est élégante et bien équilibrée. Sur le plan visuel, le point principal est cette grille de calandre dotée d'un écusson Kia bien en évidence sur la partie centrale. Soulignons en passant que la version coupé (justement appelée Koup) est plus spectaculaire, mais elle ne cible pas la même clientèle. L'acheteur de la berline, ou plutôt l'acheteuse, car plusieurs dames semblent craquer pour ce modèle, sont à la recherche d'une voiture jolie, mais pas nécessairement tape-à-l'œil.

Les deux modèles, coupé et berline, se partagent le même tableau de bord et celui-ci mérite des éloges autant pour sa présentation que pour son ergonomie. Les commandes centrales sont placées dans une console verticale qui est surplombée par un petit tableau indicateur. Juste en dessous de celui-ci se trouve le bouton d'activation des clignotants de secours. Une excellente position, car il faut parfois chercher pour trouver cette foutue commande. Sont ensuite superposées les commandes audio et celles de la climatisation. Comme c'est pratiquement devenu la règle maintenant, les réglages de la climatisation sont constitués de trois gros boutons circulaires, dont le principal est placé en plein centre pour le réglage du flot d'air dans l'habitacle. La console entre les deux sièges avant possède une prise de courant de 12 volts de même que des points d'accès pour les lecteurs iPod et MP3.

Ce n'est pas toujours le cas des voitures de cette catégorie, mais sur les trois branches du volant, on retrouve différentes commandes, que ce soit pour les réglages audio, le commutateur du régulateur de croisière et celui de la téléphonie. Enfin, la qualité des matériaux est bonne et la finition sérieuse pour une voiture de ce prix et de cette catégorie.

- Excellente garantie
- Silhouette élégante
- Tenue de route correcte
- Prix compétitifs
- Finition sérieuse

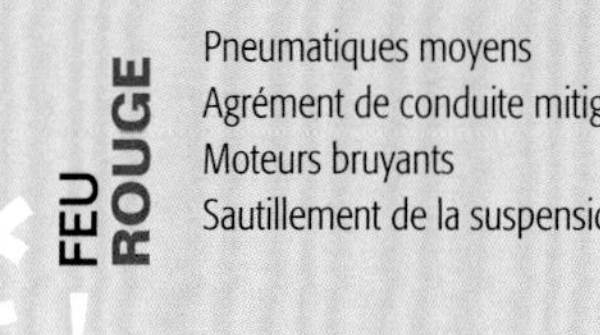

- Pneumatiques moyens
- Agrément de conduite mitigé
- Moteurs bruyants
- Sautillement de la suspension

Par ailleurs, la position de conduite serait meilleure si le volant était réglable en profondeur et pas uniquement à la verticale. Toutefois, compte tenu du prix demandé, il ne faut pas être trop exigeant à ce chapitre. Par ailleurs, on accorde de bonnes notes aux sièges avant qui sont confortables, mais qui, comme toujours, manquent de support latéral. Les places arrière seront surtout appréciées par les personnes de taille moyenne. Un grand de six pieds s'y sentira à l'étroit.

OPINIONS DIVERSES

L'an dernier, à la suite du lancement de ce modèle, la plupart des essayeurs avaient des propos dithyrambiques concernant le comportement routier et la tenue de route de cette voiture. Mes attentes étaient donc fort élevées lorsque je me suis glissé derrière son volant. Compte tenu de la motorisation disponible, je ne m'attendais pas à des performances spectaculaires, mais à un agrément de conduite relevé. Un peu comme cette nouvelle Mazda2 dont le moteur est moyennement puissant, mais qui se démarque par sa tenue de route. Je dois avouer que j'ai été quelque peu déçu au premier contact.

Mais au fil des jours, j'ai appris à découvrir les qualités de cette berline. Ce n'est pas la plus spectaculaire, ni la plus performante, mais elle offre quand même un excellent rapport qualité-prix. Si ce n'est que son comportement routier pourrait être un peu plus relevé, force est d'admettre que pour le reste, c'est plus que correct. Le moteur des versions EX et LX est un quatre cylindres 2,0 litres produisant 156 chevaux et associé de série à une boîte manuelle à cinq rapports. Si vous voulez confier le passage des rapports à une boîte automatique, celle-ci est à quatre vitesses. Ce moteur offre des performances correctes, mais il est bruyant lorsque sollicité. Le modèle SX est pour sa part doté d'un quatre cylindres de 2,4 litres produisant 173 chevaux. La boîte manuelle est à six rapports et l'automatique en possède une de moins. C'est mieux en fait d'accélération et de douceur.

Soulignons en terminant l'arrivée en cours d'année d'une version cinq portes à hayon. Elle se démarquera par une nouvelle grille de calandre et une assise plus basse, et proposera une nouvelle transmission à six rapports. Les moteurs devraient demeurer les mêmes.

Denis Duquet

PHOTOS : MARC LACHAPELLE

Catégorie	Berline
Échelle de prix	17 400 $ à 22 800 $ (2010)
Garanties	5 ans/100 000 km, 5 ans/100 000 km
Assemblage	Sohari, Corée du Sud
Cote d'assurance	n.d.

CHÂSSIS - DONNÉES POUR LX BERLINE

Emp/lon/lar/haut	2 650/4 530/1 775/1 460 mm
Coffre	415 litres
Réservoir	52 litres
Nombre coussins sécurité	6
Antipatinage / contrôle stabilité	oui / oui
Suspension avant	indépendante, jambes de force
Suspension arrière	indépendante, barres de torsion
Freins avant / arrière	disque (ABS) / disque (ABS)
Direction	à crémaillère, assistée
Diamètre de braquage	n.d.
Pneus avant / arrière	P195/65R15 / P195/65R15
Poids	1 228 kg
Capacité de remorquage	n.d.

COMPOSANTES MÉCANIQUES

LX, EX

Cylindrée, soupapes, alim.	4L 2,0 litres 16 s atmos.
Puissance / Couple	156 chevaux / 144 lb-pi
Tr. base (opt) / rouage base (opt)	M5 (A4) / Tr
0-100 / 80-120 / 100-0 km/h	9,3 s / 6,1 s / 43,2 m
Type ess. / ville / autoroute	Ordinaire / 8,3 / 5,8 l/100 km

SX

Cylindrée, soupapes, alim.	4L 2,4 litres 16 s atmos.
Puissance / Couple	173 chevaux / 168 lb-pi
Tr. base (opt) / rouage base (opt)	M6 (A5) / Tr
0-100 / 80-120 / 100-0 km/h	8,7 s / 6,3 s / n.d.
Type ess. / ville / autoroute	Ordinaire / 9,2 / 6,2 l/100 km

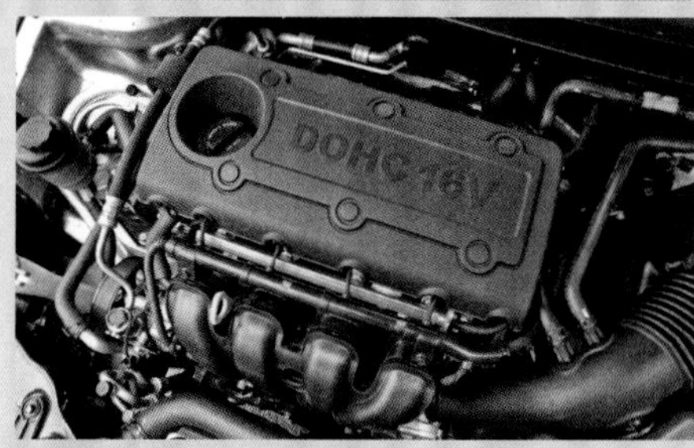

DANS LA MÊME CATÉGORIE

Chevrolet Cruze, Dodge Caliber, Ford Focus, Honda Civic, Hyundai Elantra, Mazda3, Mitsubishi Lancer, Nissan Sentra, Suzuki SX-4, Toyota Corolla

DU NOUVEAU EN 2011

Aucun changement majeur

NOS IMPRESSIONS

Agrément de conduite :	7/10
Fiabilité :	6/10
Sécurité :	8/10
Qualités hivernales :	8/10
Espace intérieur :	7/10
Confort :	8/10

www.kia.ca

Plus d'informations dans la section statistiques en dernière partie du Guide

QUELLE BELLE VOITURE!

Il n'y a pas si longtemps, il était pratiquement impossible de placer les mots Kia et élégance dans la même phrase. En effet, sauf exception, les voitures de ce constructeur coréen possédaient tout au plus une silhouette anonyme. Sans compter qu'il y avait pire, comme l'Amanti par exemple. Cependant, les temps ont changé et les nouveaux modèles dévoilés par Kia sont tous très réussis au chapitre de l'élégance et la Forte Koup n'y fait pas exception.

Cette version deux portes de la berline Forte est l'une des plus réussies de sa catégorie, mais encore faut-il que la mécanique et les performances soient à la hauteur du plumage !

VERDICT UNANIME

Parfois, notre œil est séduit par un modèle en particulier. On trouve ses lignes attrayantes au premier abord, puis l'on se rend compte par la suite être l'une des seules personnes à avoir cette opinion. Ce n'est pas le cas avec ce modèle. Tout au long de la semaine d'essai, les personnes rencontrées émettaient des commentaires flatteurs quant à la silhouette de la voiture. Avec sa ceinture de caisse haute, son toit fuyant, son devant quasiment intimidant grâce à sa grille de calandre noire, sa prise d'air massive également protégée par un grillage noir et les ouvertures béantes des phares antibrouillard, son impact visuel est très fort. Le renflement des ailes avant, le bas de caisse en relief, les roues en alliage avec huit rayons contrastants, voilà autant d'éléments qui viennent renforcer cet effet. Sans oublier une partie arrière bien équilibrée avec un déflecteur intégré dans le couvercle du coffre. Voilà une voiture qui impressionne d'abord par son *look*.

ET L'HABITACLE N'EST PAS VILAIN NON PLUS.

Une fois encore, les stylistes ont réussi à bien harmoniser les couleurs utilisées pour la planche de bord, notamment les éléments contrastants en aluminium. Par contre, le nombre de pièces utilisées pour réaliser le tableau de bord est assez élevé, ce qui risque à long terme d'être une source de bruits. Néanmoins, dans l'ensemble, la qualité des matériaux et de la finition est bonne.

Le conducteur bénéficie d'une position de conduite relativement bonne et le volant, en raison de la grosseur de son boudin, se manipule bien. Les cadrans indicateurs sont très faciles à lire grâce à ses chiffres noirs sur fond blanc. L'indicateur de vitesse trône au centre et est flanqué du compte-tours à gauche et de la jauge de carburant à droite. Une console verticale, dominée sur sa partie supérieure par une montre numérique, accueille les commandes de la climatisation et du système audio. Comme sur toutes les Kia, les prises de raccordement pour lecteurs MP3 et clés USB sont de série.

Les places arrière seront jugées plus ou moins confortables par les occupants de taille moyenne. Ces derniers devront également

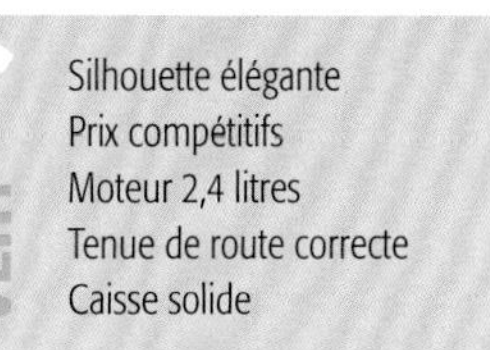

- Silhouette élégante
- Prix compétitifs
- Moteur 2,4 litres
- Tenue de route correcte
- Caisse solide

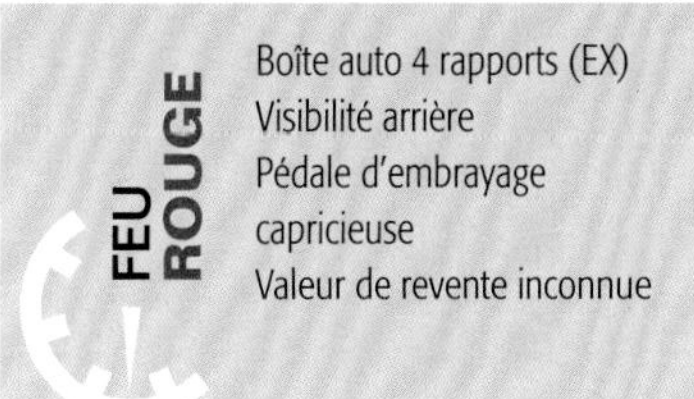

- Boîte auto 4 rapports (EX)
- Visibilité arrière
- Pédale d'embrayage capricieuse
- Valeur de revente inconnue

être agiles pour s'installer, car l'accès à la banquette arrière exige une certaine souplesse.

UN CHOIX LOGIQUE

L'acheteur peut choisir entre deux moteurs. Celui de la version EX, le modèle le plus économique, est un quatre cylindres 2,0 litres produisant 156 chevaux et un couple de 144 lb-pi. Il est associé à une transmission manuelle à cinq rapports, tandis que la boîte automatique à quatre rapports est optionnelle.

Les acheteurs à la recherche de performances un peu plus enlevantes, (notez bien les termes «un peu plus») vont opter pour la SX propulsée par un moteur quatre cylindres de 2,4 litres d'une puissance de 173 chevaux et produisant 168 lb-pi de couple. Ce moteur est couplé de série à une boîte manuelle à six rapports, alors qu'une transmission automatique à cinq rapports est disponible en option. C'est de loin le moteur à choisir. Il est quelque peu rugueux, mais il nous semble rudement solide.

Comme sur presque tous les autres modèles de sa catégorie, la suspension avant est dotée de jambes de force de type MacPherson et la suspension arrière est à essieu rigide maintenu en place par des barres de torsion. Les deux versions sont munies de freins à disques aux quatre roues, mais la direction à crémaillère n'est pas à assistance variable.

La version SX à boîte manuelle en a déçu plusieurs en raison du manque de progressivité de l'embrayage et d'une tringlerie mal calibrée de la pédale d'accélération. Ces deux facteurs nous privent d'un agrément de conduite. Par ailleurs, la boîte automatique à cinq rapports était correcte et nous a permis de mieux apprécier ce petit coupé au comportement routier acceptable. Il ne faut toutefois pas s'attendre à vous retrouver au volant d'une BMW. Il suffit d'ailleurs d'aborder une courbe avec une bonne vitesse pour se rendre compte du caractère sous-vireur de la voiture. Si la route est bosselée, le confort s'en ressent et la voiture a tendance à sautiller. En revanche, la solidité de la caisse est impressionnante.

À part ces quelques irritants, cette voiture propose un rapport qualité/prix élevé, d'autant plus qu'elle est accompagnée d'une généreuse garantie. Pour plusieurs, sa silhouette fort réussie parviendra à faire oublier les quelques points qui sont à améliorer.

Denis Duquet

PHOTOS : MARC LACHAPELLE

Catégorie	Coupé
Échelle de prix	19 995 $ à 22 950 $ (2010)
Garanties	5 ans/100 000 km, 5 ans/100 000 km
Assemblage	Sohari, Corée du Sud
Cote d'assurance	n.d.

CHÂSSIS - DONNÉES POUR SX KOUP

Emp/lon/lar/haut	2 650/4 480/1 765/1 400 mm
Coffre	358 litres
Réservoir	52 litres
Nombre coussins sécurité	6
Antipatinage / contrôle stabilité	oui / oui
Suspension avant	indépendante, jambes de force
Suspension arrière	indépendante, barres de torsion
Freins avant / arrière	disque (ABS) / disque (ABS)
Direction	à crémaillère, assistée
Diamètre de braquage	n.d.
Pneus avant / arrière	P215/45R17 / P215/45R17
Poids	1 297 kg
Capacité de remorquage	n.d.

COMPOSANTES MÉCANIQUES

EX

Cylindrée, soupapes, alim.	4L 2,0 litres 16 s atmos.
Puissance / Couple	156 chevaux / 144 lb-pi
Tr. base (opt) / rouage base (opt)	M5 (A4) / Tr
0-100 / 80-120 / 100-0 km/h	9,3 s / 6,1 s / 43,2 m
Type ess. / ville / autoroute	Ordinaire / 8,3 / 5,8 l/100 km

SX

Cylindrée, soupapes, alim.	4L 2,4 litres 16 s atmos.
Puissance / Couple	173 chevaux / 168 lb-pi
Tr. base (opt) / rouage base (opt)	M6 (A5) / Tr
0-100 / 80-120 / 100-0 km/h	8,7 s / 6,3 s / n.d.
Type ess. / ville / autoroute	Ordinaire / 9,2 / 6,2 l/100 km

DANS LA MÊME CATÉGORIE

Dodge Caliber, Mazda3, Mitsubishi Lancer Sportback, Suzuki SX-4, Volkswagen Golf

DU NOUVEAU EN 2011

Aucun changement majeur

NOS IMPRESSIONS

Agrément de conduite :	8/10
Fiabilité :	6/10
Sécurité :	8/10
Qualités hivernales :	7/10
Espace intérieur :	7/10
Confort :	7/10

www.kia.ca

Plus d'informations dans la section statistiques en dernière partie du Guide

Kia Magentis

NOUVEAU DÉPART, NOUVEAU NOM.

Vous ne connaissez pas la Kia Optima ? En fait, c'est une voiture connue chez nous sous l'appellation Magentis, puisque c'est GM qui possédait les droits d'utilisation du mot « Optima » au Canada. Partout ailleurs sur la planète, c'est l'Optima. Toutefois, c'est chose du passé et comme partout ailleurs, le marché canadien comptera la Kia Optima dans ses rangs. C'est déjà cela de gagné !

Ce nouveau nom vient à point nommé, car il coïncide avec l'arrivée d'une toute nouvelle version, transformée de fond en comble. Comme la Magentis n'était pas un leader du marché, elle cédera tranquillement sa place à cette nouvelle venue qui a tous les atouts pour réussir.

TOUT UN DESIGN !

La nouvelle Optima devrait faire tout un tabac. Si la silhouette de la Magentis est un exemple de discrétion en fait de design automobile, la nouvelle Optima impressionne. Ce modèle réunit tout ce que Kia a fait de bien au chapitre des berlines, et au premier coup d'œil, on pourrait quasiment l'associer à une marque germanique.

Une fois de plus, les stylistes ont utilisé cette calandre si caractéristique qui est cintrée en ses parties centrales inférieures et supérieures. Celle-ci surplombe une prise d'air, dont chaque extrémité abrite un phare antibrouillard. Le capot plongeant doté d'arêtes de chaque côté est une autre source de repérage visuel. Soulignons une prise d'évacuation d'air factice sur la partie supérieure arrière de chaque aile avant, comme le veut la tendance actuelle. La section arrière est un peu puis allégée que l'avant, mais c'est également bien réussi tandis que les roues en alliage de type bâton s'harmonisent fort bien à cette carrosserie.

Dans l'habitacle, le tableau de bord comprend deux éléments, soit la nacelle des instruments avec des cadrans indicateurs séparés par un centre d'information dans l'espace situé entre les deux, et au centre de la planche de bord, un bourrelet qui délimite la section consacrée à l'écran de navigation et aux commandes audio et vidéo. Sur le modèle que nous avons conduit, tout était noir et on a utilisé du plastique laqué de style verni de piano qui est plus ou moins à sa place dans une voiture de cette catégorie.

En conduite, le confort des sièges, la bonne position de conduite, le silence de roulement, les prestations du moteur quatre cylindres de 2,4 litres et les passages rapides et doux des rapports de la transmission manumatique sont autant d'éléments favorables. Par contre, la qualité des plastiques et la disposition des commandes sont moins impressionnantes. Même si cet essai était très limité, on a pu constater que la stabilité directionnelle, l'absence de tangage en freinage et une direction correcte sont autant d'éléments prometteurs qui feront rapidement oublier la Magentis actuelle. Comme sur le Sportage, une transmission manuelle à six rapports et un moteur 2,0 litres turbo seront proposés. Son arrivée sur le marché est prévue pour le début de 2011.

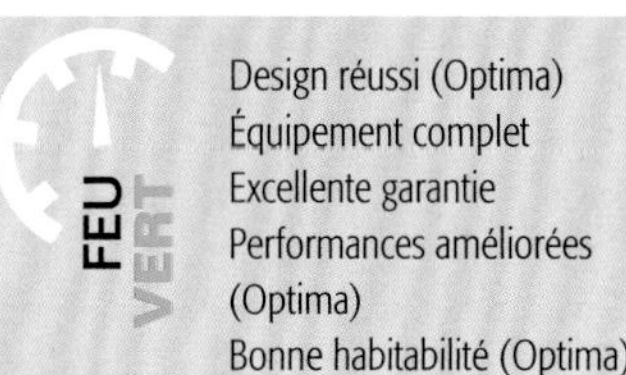

FEU VERT

Design réussi (Optima)
Équipement complet
Excellente garantie
Performances améliorées (Optima)
Bonne habitabilité (Optima)

FEU ROUGE

Silhouette anonyme
Faible valeur de revente
Tableau de bord rétro
Faible diffusion

Bref, autant les ingénieurs que les stylistes semblent s'être surpassés pour réaliser une voiture qui devrait connaître du succès à l'instar de sa sœur ennemie, la Hyundai Sonata qui compte elle aussi sur une belle carrosserie et une mécanique moderne pour convaincre les acheteurs.

EN ATTENDANT L'OPTIMA

La Magentis sera toujours offerte en attendant l'arrivée de son élégante remplaçante. Malgré sa silhouette particulièrement anonyme, cette berline intermédiaire représente tout de même une bonne affaire, car son équipement est complet, son prix plus que compétitif, et il est même possible de commander une version propulsée par un moteur V6. Ce moteur se fait presque damer le pion par le quatre cylindres 2,4 litres offert de série. Ce quatre cylindres produit quand même 175 chevaux, soit seulement 19 de moins que le V6. Il est aussi le seul des deux moteurs à proposer une boîte manuelle. Celle-ci est à cinq rapports. Elle ne transforme pas cette Kia en sportive, mais elle permet d'économiser à l'achat en plus d'offrir une certaine économie de carburant.

Si la position de conduite est bonne, on remarque rapidement que le soutien lombaire du siège est déficient, tout comme le soutien latéral. Mais à part cette lacune, l'habitacle est spacieux et d'une finition correcte tandis que le tableau de bord brille par sa sobriété. Il semble que cette voiture a été créée sous le signe de la simplicité. Il ne faut toutefois pas la snober pour autant. C'est en fait la berline du gros bon sens.

Il est certain que la suspension a été calibrée en fonction du confort, mais personne ne sera pris au dépourvu au volant de cette voiture si elle respecte les limites de vitesse affichées. Par ailleurs, tentez de rouler de façon agressive et vous découvrirez rapidement les limites de la plate-forme et des pneumatiques. Mais la personne qui achète une Magentis pour ce qu'elle est, soit une berline familiale équilibrée, ne sera pas déçue. Mais il est certain qu'il y aura des économies à faire comme c'est le cas avec tous les modèles en fin de carrière.

Malgré les qualités du véhicule, le design d'une autre époque a grandement handicapé les ventes de cette Coréenne qui méritait un meilleur sort. Heureusement, sa remplaçante remettra les pendules à l'heure.

Denis Duquet

Kia Optima

PHOTOS : MARC LACHAPELLE

DONNÉES 2010

Catégorie	Berline
Échelle de prix	23 700 $ à 32 500 $ (2010)
Garanties	5 ans/100 000 km, 5 ans/100 000 km
Assemblage	Hwasung, Corée du Sud
Cote d'assurance	excellente

CHÂSSIS - DONNÉES POUR MAGENTIS LX

Emp/lon/lar/haut	2 720/4 800/1 805/1 480 mm
Coffre	425 litres
Réservoir	62 litres
Nombre coussins sécurité	6
Antipatinage / contrôle stabilité	non / oui
Suspension avant	indépendante, jambes de force
Suspension arrière	indépendante, multibras
Freins avant / arrière	disque (ABS) / disque (ABS)
Direction	à crémaillère, ass. variable
Diamètre de braquage	10,4 m
Pneus avant / arrière	P205/60R16 / P205/60R16
Poids	1 432 kg
Capacité de remorquage	454 kg (1 000 lb)

COMPOSANTES MÉCANIQUES

LX, SX

Cylindrée, soupapes, alim.	4L 2,4 litres 16 s atmos
Puissance / Couple	175 chevaux / 169 lb-pi
Tr. base (opt) / rouage base (opt)	M5 (A5) / Tr
0-100 / 80-120 / 100-0 km/h	10,9 s / 9,3 s / 41,0 m
Type ess. / ville / autoroute	Ordinaire / 9,4 / 6,2 l/100 km

LX-V6, SX-V6

Cylindrée, soupapes, alim.	V6 2,7 litres 24 s atmos
Puissance / Couple	194 chevaux / 184 lb-pi
Tr. base (opt) / rouage base (opt)	A5 / Tr
0-100 / 80-120 / 100-0 km/h	8,4 s / 7,8 s / 41,0 m
Type ess. / ville / autoroute	Ordinaire / 10,5 / 7,0 l/100 km

DANS LA MÊME CATÉGORIE

Chevrolet Malibu, Chrysler Sebring, Dodge Avenger, Ford Fusion, Honda Accord, Hyundai Sonata, Mazda6, Nissan Altima, Toyota Camry

DU NOUVEAU EN 2011

La Magentis sera remplacée par l'Optima en cours d'année

NOS IMPRESSIONS

Agrément de conduite :	7/10
Fiabilité :	8/10
Sécurité :	8/10
Qualités hivernales :	8/10
Espace intérieur :	8/10
Confort :	8/10

www.kia.ca

Plus d'informations dans la section statistiques en dernière partie du Guide

ELLE TIRE DE LA PATTE !

Le créneau des voitures sous-compactes demeure un marché très important, surtout au Québec. Malheureusement, la petite Rio de Kia, qui commence à dater, tire sérieusement de la patte face à une concurrence qui nous propose sans cesse des nouveautés plus qu'intéressantes. Alors que Kia fait bonne figure dans d'autres segments avec notamment sa nouvelle Forte et le Soul, il lui faudra penser rapidement à revamper sa sous-compacte histoire de supporter sa lancée.

C'est encore plus vrai avec l'arrivée cette année de la nouvelle Mazda2 et de la Ford Fiesta, deux véhicules qui risquent fortement de changer la donne chez les sous-compactes. Ne proposant pratiquement aucun changement cette année, la Rio compte donc principalement sur son aspect abordable pour séduire les acheteurs. Voilà une stratégie qui permet à Kia de supporter les ventes en attendant une nouvelle génération, chose qui devrait être prévue pour l'année prochaine. Voilà en fait qui est plus que nécessaire, puisque ce segment est le plus important au Canada et Kia ne peut se permettre de tarder à offrir un produit plus compétitif.

Heureusement, la Rio peut compter sur quelques configurations, ce qui l'avantage par rapport à d'autre rivales. Vous pourrez donc jeter votre dévolu sur la berline quatre portes, ou sur la familiale à cinq portes, baptisée pour la cause : Rio5. On retrouve aussi une version sport réservée à la petite familiale. Cette dernière ajoute quelques artifices à l'intérieur et à l'extérieur, rehaussant le style de la voiture, notamment des jantes de 15 pouces, un aileron, des sièges sport et un pédalier métallisé.

Sous le capot, toutes les Rio reçoivent la même mécanique, soit un moteur quatre cylindres de 1,6 litre, développant 110 chevaux pour un couple similaire. Le tout est marié de série à une boîte manuelle à cinq rapports alors qu'une automatique à quatre rapports s'avère optionnelle. Voilà tout de même une puissance comparable à la majeure partie des rivales que sont la Nissan Versa, la Honda Fit, la Hyundai Accent ou la Toyota Yaris, avec un léger avantage pour la Suzuki SX-4, qui propose un moteur de 2,0 litres développant 150 chevaux. Quant à la boite automatique, avantage à la Honda Fit qui en propose une à cinq rapports, alors que la première étoile ira à la Ford Fiesta avec sa boîte automatique à six rapports. Malgré que le moteur de la Rio ne soit pas dès plus modernes, sa puissance et son rendement permettent à la sous-compacte de continuer à rivaliser correctement dans son créneau. Peu d'inquiétude à ce chapitre.

PLUS JOLIE LA FAMILIALE

Tout demeure toujours une question de goût, mais comme ça semble la tendance chez ses rivales, la Rio est beaucoup plus jolie en version familiale. Cette configuration, en plus d'être plus pratique, apporte un style plus sportif et des lignes moins sévères.

FEU VERT

- Bon niveau d'équipement
- Prix compétitif
- Multiples configurations
- Version Sport attirante

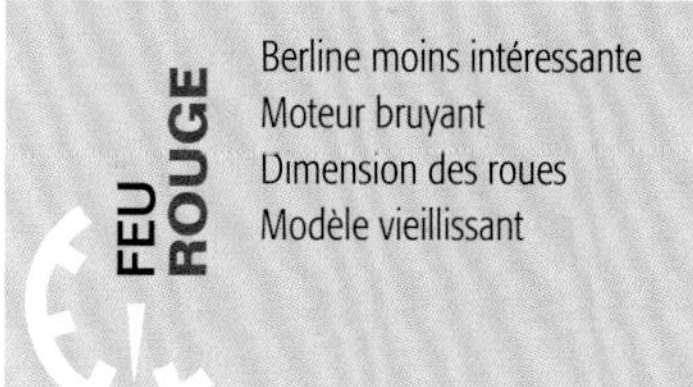

FEU ROUGE

- Berline moins intéressante
- Moteur bruyant
- Dimension des roues
- Modèle vieillissant

On remarque à l'avant la nouvelle calandre, un élément apporté l'année passée et seul véritable changement cosmétique sur la voiture depuis son introduction en 2005. Voilà qui lui donne un air mieux réussi et qui l'harmonise avec les autres produits du constructeur. Disons qu'il lui faudra plus de modernisme.

À bord, l'âge de la Rio se fait aussi sentir par la sobriété, mais surtout, par la disposition des composantes et des commandes. Rien à voir avec les nouveaux produits de Kia. Cependant, on ne peut adresser beaucoup de reproches à la qualité d'assemblage qui demeure plus qu'acceptable. Les quelques changements apportés en 2010 contribuent également à améliorer l'habitacle.

SUR LA ROUTE

Au volant, on découvre une petite voiture agile et somme toute agréable à conduire. Sa direction procure une bonne sensation de la route et se veut communicative. La version sport avec ses roues de 15 pouces offre une meilleure tenue de route, et c'est dommage qu'à l'instar de plusieurs rivales cette dimension de roues n'équipe pas plus de versions. De nos jours, le 15 pouces devrait être un minimum. Quant à la suspension, elle peut sembler ferme de prime abord, mais elle contribue à minimiser les transferts de poids en virage tout en ne réussissant pas à atténuer totalement cet effet au freinage. Parlant de freins, il faut aussi donner un autre avantage à la Rio5 sport qui dispose de freins ABS.

Sans être trop fougueux, le petit quatre cylindres de 1,6 litre se tire bien d'affaire et ce dernier sera avantagé par la boîte manuelle à cinq rapports qui non seulement favorise l'économie de carburant, mais qui permet de mieux tirer profit de la puissance disponible. Le poids assez élevé de la voiture n'aide pas non plus sa cause. En accélération, le moteur devient un peu plus bruyant, même chose lors de reprises. Voilà qui vous évitera sans doute de vous endormir lors de vos manœuvres de dépassement!

À l'aube d'une refonte qui sera la bienvenue, la Rio continue d'être d'une bonne valeur compte tenu de ce qu'elle offre. Un des éléments qui continue de l'avantager s'avère certainement sa garantie de 5 ans / 100000 km, chose inégalée par ses rivales et qui assure une tranquillité d'esprit.

Sylvain Raymond

PHOTOS : KIA

Catégorie	Berline, *Hatchback*
Échelle de prix	13695$ à 18695$ (2010)
Garanties	5 ans/100000 km, 5 ans/100000 km
Assemblage	Sohari, Corée du Sud
Cote d'assurance	bonne

CHÂSSIS - DONNÉES POUR EX BERLINE

Emp/lon/lar/haut	2500/4240/1695/1470 mm
Coffre	337 litres
Réservoir	45 litres
Nombre coussins sécurité	2
Antipatinage / contrôle stabilité	non / non
Suspension avant	indépendante, jambes de force
Suspension arrière	indépendante, barres de torsion
Freins avant / arrière	disque / tambour
Direction	à crémaillère, assistée
Diamètre de braquage	11,8 m
Pneus avant / arrière	P175/70R14 / P175/70R14
Poids	1160 kg
Capacité de remorquage	n.d.

COMPOSANTES MÉCANIQUES

EX, 5 EX, EX Commodite, 5 EX Commodite, 5 Sport

Cylindrée, soupapes, alim.	4L 1,6 litre 16 s atmos.
Puissance / Couple	110 chevaux / 107 lb-pi
Tr. base (opt) / rouage base (opt)	M5 (A4) / Tr
0-100 / 80-120 / 100-0 km/h	10,1 s / 8,3 s / 40,0 m
Type ess. / ville / autoroute	Ordinaire / 7,1 / 5,8 l/100 km

DANS LA MÊME CATÉGORIE

Chevrolet Aveo, Ford Fiesta, Honda Fit, Hyundai Accent, Mazda2, Nissan Versa, Suzuki Swift+, Toyota Yaris

DU NOUVEAU EN 2011

Nouveau modèle sera dévoilé en cours d'année

NOS IMPRESSIONS

Agrément de conduite :	6/10
Fiabilité :	8/10
Sécurité :	6/10
Qualités hivernales :	6/10
Espace intérieur :	7/10
Confort :	6/10

www.kia.ca

Plus d'informations dans la section statistiques en dernière partie du Guide

Modèle 2010

TROP SOUVENT OUBLIÉE

Lorsque vient le temps de se procurer un véhicule polyvalent, la plupart des gens pensent à la Mazda5, à la Toyota Matrix ou, à la limite, aux fourgonnettes que sont les Dodge Grand Caravan ou Honda Odyssey. La marque Kia, on le constate, ne vient pas immédiatement à l'esprit, sauf lorsqu'on recherche une voiture économique. Ce qui est bien dommage, étant donné que Kia propose un véhicule aussi intéressant que polyvalent, le Rondo. Kia offre également une fourgonnette, la Sedona qui fait l'objet d'un essai à part.

Comme nous le disions, on ne pense pas automatiquement au Kia Rondo et c'est dommage. Son gabarit, entre la familiale et la fourgonnette répond parfaitement aux besoins de plusieurs personnes. Cette année, on a enfin revu le museau du Rondo. Il faut dire qu'il n'avait pas changé d'un iota depuis son arrivée en 2006 et qu'il était temps qu'on lui « r'nippe » le nez. On a aussi profité de l'occasion pour revoir la galerie de toit. L'habitacle, on s'en doute, est passablement grand pour une voiture. Car c'est ce qu'est le Rondo, une grosse voiture, sa plate-forme étant dérivée de celle de la berline Magentis. Le tableau de bord, plus fonctionnel que joli, est ergonomique et recouvert de matériaux d'assez bonne qualité. Son assemblage est réussi malgré la plaque recouvrant le coussin gonflable du passager qui est très visible. Comme pour rappeler qu'un événement malheureux peut survenir à tout moment ! Il y a plusieurs espaces de rangement, ce que les traîneux de mon genre adorent. Par contre, comment ne pas souligner la sonorité extraordinairement poche du système audio ? Contrairement à plusieurs de mes collègues, je n'ai pas trouvé les sièges avant en cuir de notre version d'essai tellement confortables. C'est sans doute le prix à payer pour avoir un corps parfait... La position de conduite est élevée et, combinée à une fenestration généreuse, procure une visibilité tout le tour sans faille.

PLUS PETITE QUE LA MAZDA5 ET POURTANT...

Les places arrière sont trop dures pour être vraiment confortables. Et, fait rarement vu dans une automobile, la place centrale m'est apparue plus moelleuse ! Plusieurs versions du Rondo possèdent une troisième banquette. Malgré son inconfort (on y est assis très carré, les genoux dans le front), elle peut servir à l'occasion. D'autant plus que lorsqu'elle est fonction, elle ne bouffe pas tout l'espace du coffre. D'ailleurs, dans les mêmes conditions, il en offre davantage que celui de la Mazda5, la grande rivale, pourtant plus longue. Quand tous les dossiers sont baissés, l'espace de chargement devient franchement épatant. Le seuil de chargement est bas et égal au pare-chocs et sous le plancher on retrouve un intéressant espace de rangement. Sur un des modèles essayés, le hayon craquait indument. Et c'était durant l'été.

Côté mécanique, Kia fait d'abord appel à un quatre cylindres de 2,4 litres qui développe 175 chevaux et 1169 livres-pied de couple,

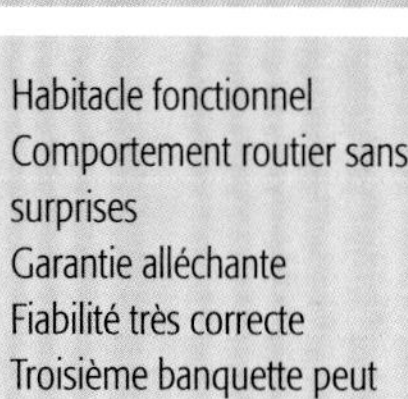

Habitacle fonctionnel
Comportement routier sans surprises
Garantie alléchante
Fiabilité très correcte
Troisième banquette peut dépanner

FEU ROUGE

Réputation de Kia pas encore parfaite
Puissance 2,4 litres un peu juste (si chargé)
Valeur de revente un peu basse
Sonorité de la radio décevante

selon le site humoristique www.kia.ca, du moins au moment d'écrire ces lignes. En fait, on doit soustraire 1 000 livres-pied de couple. Ce n'est certes pas un monstre de puissance néanmoins, il convient la plupart du temps sauf lorsque la voiture est chargée de sept adultes (sept d'après Kia et six si l'on est réaliste...) et de leurs bagages, il peine dans les côtes. Toutefois, sa consommation d'essence est plutôt retenue. L'autre moteur est un petit V6 de 2,7 litres qui, curieusement, ne fournit pas des performances tellement plus relevées même si on remarque son apport dans les côtes. Cependant, il s'avère plus souple et, comme il est associé à une transmission à cinq rapports (on compte un rapport de moins pour celle du quatre cylindres), son comportement est très correct. Il consomme certes un peu plus que le 2,4 litres mais, encore là, la différence n'est pas tellement marquée. Lors d'un essai estival, nous avions obtenu une moyenne de 11,7 litres/100 km, ce qui est un peu élevé mais pas beaucoup plus que celui mené avec une Mazda5 (à quatre cylindres !) dans les mêmes conditions.

LES ÉNERVÉS, ALLEZ VOIR AILLEURS !

Étant donné la vocation familiale du Rondo, on ne sera pas surpris d'apprendre que son comportement routier n'est pas très sportif. Pour s'exciter le poil des jambes, Kia propose la Forte Koup mais avec deux sièges d'enfants, le plaisir passe loin dans les priorités. Quand même, le Rondo tient très bien la route grâce à ses suspensions indépendantes aux quatre roues. Lorsque poussée plus que de raison, elle adopte un comportement sous-vireur (l'avant veut tourner tout droit) tout en affichant un bon roulis (la voiture penche). La direction, peu précise et qui ne présente à peu près aucun retour d'informations, n'aide pas les choses. Quant aux freins, ils sont passablement performants même si la pédale va trop loin, lors d'un arrêt d'urgence par exemple. Heureusement, le système de contrôle de la stabilité latérale, de série sur tous les modèles, intervient très tôt. Six coussins gonflables amortiront le choc si jamais l'improbable se réalisait.

La principale rivale du Rondo, on l'a vu, est la Mazda5. Cette dernière s'avère beaucoup plus agréable à conduire grâce à son dynamisme mais son habitacle n'est pas aussi polyvalent tout en étant plus bruyant. Et puis la garantie de la Mazda est loin d'être aussi intéressante que celle du Rondo. Il faut également considérer la valeur de revente qui est plus élevée dans le cas de la Mazda. Bref, c'est un pensez-y-bien...

Alain Morin

PHOTOS : KIA

Catégorie	Multisegment
Échelle de prix	21 645 $ à 28 445 $ (2010)
Garanties	5 ans/100 000 km, 5 ans/100 000 km
Assemblage	Hwasung, Corée du Sud
Cote d'assurance	bonne

CHÂSSIS - DONNÉES POUR EX V6 5 PLACES

Emp/lon/lar/haut	2 700/4 545/1 820/1 700 mm
Coffre	185 à 2 083 litres
Réservoir	60 litres
Nombre coussins sécurité	6
Antipatinage / contrôle stabilité	oui / oui
Suspension avant	indépendante, jambes de force
Suspension arrière	indépendante, multibras
Freins avant / arrière	disque (ABS) / disque (ABS)
Direction	à crémaillère, assistée
Diamètre de braquage	10,8 m
Pneus avant / arrière	P205/60R16 / P205/60R16
Poids	1 686 kg
Capacité de remorquage	907 kg (1 999 lb)

COMPOSANTES MÉCANIQUES

LX, EX

Cylindrée, soupapes, alim.	4L 2,4 litres 16 s atmos.
Puissance / Couple	175 chevaux / 169 lb-pi
Tr. base (opt) / rouage base (opt)	A4 / Tr
0-100 / 80-120 / 100-0 km/h	10,2 s / 8,8 s / 39,7 m
Type ess. / ville / autoroute	Ordinaire / 10,6 / 7,5 l/100 km

EX-V6

Cylindrée, soupapes, alim.	V6 2,7 litres 24 s atmos.
Puissance / Couple	192 chevaux / 184 lb-pi
Tr. base (opt) / rouage base (opt)	A5 / Tr
0-100 / 80-120 / 100-0 km/h	9,0 s / 7,6 s / 39,7 m
Type ess. / ville / autoroute	Ordinaire / 11,5 / 7,7 l/100 km

DANS LA MÊME CATÉGORIE

Chevrolet HHR, Mazda5, Toyota Matrix

DU NOUVEAU EN 2011

Révisions esthétiques

NOS IMPRESSIONS

Agrément de conduite :	7/10
Fiabilité :	8/10
Sécurité :	7/10
Qualités hivernales :	7/10
Espace intérieur :	8/10
Confort :	7/10

www.kia.ca

Plus d'informations dans la section statistiques en dernière partie du Guide

ENVERS ET CONTRE TOUS

Les temps changent! C'est d'ailleurs on ne peut plus évident dans le secteur de l'automobile. Le marché fluctue au fil des tendances et des goûts du public. Il y a quelques décennies, c'était la rage des fourgonnettes. Toute entreprise qui n'en possédait pas dans sa gamme se dépêchait de combler cette lacune. De nos jours, c'est pratiquement le contraire alors qu'on tente de s'en départir puisque le marché de ces véhicules est en régression. Pourtant, chez Kia, on tient le fort avec la Sedona.

Les raisons qui militent à la faveur du maintien des fourgonnettes de la part de certains constructeurs tiennent davantage de l'espoir que de la réalité, alors que le marché des fourgonnettes a encore fléchi au cours des 12 derniers mois. Ford et GM ont abandonné le navire il y a quelques années maintenant, et il ne reste que Chrysler chez les Américains pour défendre la catégorie. Il faut admettre qu'il le fait avec succès. Une partie des ventes provient de Volkswagen qui propose une version germanisée de la fourgonnette Chrysler. Pourtant, il y a encore de l'espoir, puisque les Honda Odyssey, Nissan Quest et Toyota Sienna ont toutes fait peau neuve pour 2011. Quant à la Sedona, elle s'accroche et elle nous revient inchangée.

UN P'TIT AIR RÉTRO

Force est d'admettre qu'avec toutes les nouveautés, notre fourgonnette d'origine coréenne a quasiment l'air de provenir d'une autre époque. Elle n'est pas laide, pas du tout, mais ses formes nous rappellent celles des modèles qui étaient offerts au début de la dernière décennie. Bref, les nostalgiques apprécieront. La version canadienne n'est commercialisée qu'en empattement long, tandis que le véhicule est également offert en empattement court aux États-Unis. C'est dommage qu'on n'ait pas décidé de faire de même au Canada. Plusieurs personnes n'apprécient pas tellement les véhicules trop longs, et la possibilité de commander une version plus courte, donc plus maniable en ville, est quelque chose qui aurait des chances de faire pencher les acheteurs en faveur de celle-ci. Il faut sans doute croire que la demande infinitésimale pour un tel modèle l'a reléguée aux oubliettes. Les gens ont parfois de curieux comportements: ils se plaignent que les fourgonnettes sont trop encombrantes, mais négligent la version plus agile.

Si la silhouette fait un peu vieux jeu, l'habitacle est nettement plus moderne. L'élément principal est cette impressionnante console qui occupe beaucoup d'espace sur le tableau de bord aussi bien en largeur qu'en hauteur. À sa base, on retrouve le levier de vitesses permettant de contrôler la boîte automatique à cinq rapports. La partie supérieure comprend les commandes du système audio tandis que celles de la climatisation sont immédiatement en dessous. Cette console comprend également des buses de ventilation orientables de chaque côté. Toujours au chapitre des informations, le conducteur ne pourra pas se plaindre de ne pas savoir à quelle vitesse il roule, car l'indicateur de vitesse est

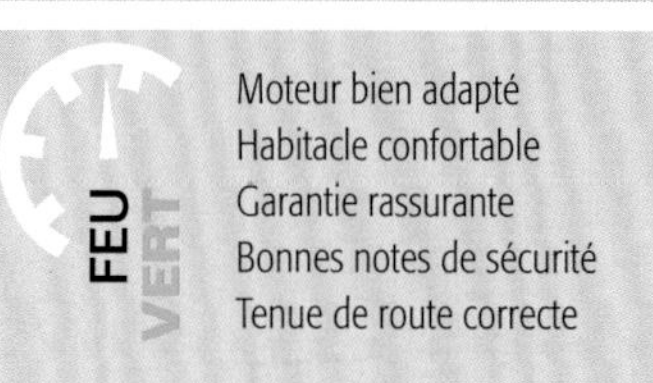

FEU VERT
- Moteur bien adapté
- Habitacle confortable
- Garantie rassurante
- Bonnes notes de sécurité
- Tenue de route correcte

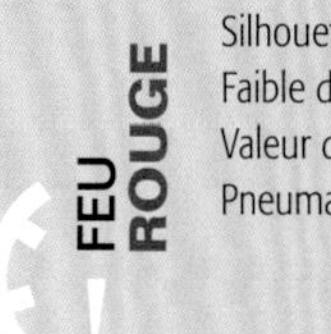

FEU ROUGE
- Silhouette anonyme
- Faible diffusion
- Valeur de revente
- Pneumatiques moyens

vraiment facile à consulter. À sa gauche, on retrouve le compte-tours et à sa droite sont placés la jauge d'essence et le thermomètre.

Toujours dans l'habitacle, il est important de souligner la multitude d'espaces de rangement que l'on a réussi à placer dans ce véhicule, que ce soit dans les portières ou dans les parois latérales arrière. On peut donc se déplacer en transportant tout (ou presque) avec soi. L'espace de chargement est bon une fois la troisième rangée de sièges remisée dans le plancher.

De plus, la finition est impeccable. D'ailleurs, selon plusieurs publications américaines, cette fourgonnette fait partie des véhicules proposant une excellente affaire, mais peu populaires. Dans ce cas, la Sedona est vraiment inconnue du public, car on en rencontre très peu sur nos routes. C'est bien simple, cette faiblesse des ventes s'explique en bonne partie par la vigueur des promotions proposées par la Dodge Grand Caravan qui est bradée à des prix hors compétition. Puisque dans l'esprit des gens Kia rime avec bas prix, la pauvre Sedona est ignorée, car elle est généralement plus chère.

LA SÉCURITÉ

Compte tenu de la vocation familiale de cette catégorie de véhicules, la plupart des acheteurs s'intéressent à la sécurité proposée par un tel véhicule. Chez Kia, on est très fier de souligner que la Sedona a obtenu toutes sortes d'accolades à la suite de tests portant sur la sécurité en cas d'impact. Par contre, il est quelque peu désolant de constater que le système de stabilité latérale et l'antipatinage ne sont offerts de série que sur le modèle le plus huppé, du moins au moment d'écrire ces lignes.

Les ingénieurs ont choisi un moteur V6 de 3,8 litres de 244 chevaux pour propulser cette fourgonnette. C'est quand même impressionnant, car il s'agit de l'un des plus puissants de sa catégorie. Il est associé à une boîte automatique à cinq rapports qui accomplit du bon travail. Quant à la conduite, elle est correcte avec une tenue de route sans surprise pour autant que vous conduisiez en tenant compte des dimensions, du poids et du centre de gravité élevé propres à toute fourgonnette. En terminant, les chefs de famille qui désirent utiliser une remorque ou une tente-roulotte pour leurs vacances seront heureux d'apprendre que la capacité de remorquage est de 1 588 kg (3 500 lb).

Denis Duquet

PHOTOS : KIA

Catégorie	Fourgonnette
Échelle de prix	28 695 $ à 40 845 $ (2010)
Garanties	5 ans/100 000 km, 5 ans/100 000 km
Assemblage	Asan, Corée du Sud
Cote d'assurance	excellente

CHÂSSIS - DONNÉES POUR EX LUXE

Emp/lon/lar/haut	3 020/5 130/1 985/1 820 mm
Coffre	912 à 4 007 litres
Réservoir	80 litres
Nombre coussins sécurité	6
Antipatinage / contrôle stabilité	oui / oui
Suspension avant	indépendante, jambes de force
Suspension arrière	semi-indépendante, multibras
Freins avant / arrière	disque (ABS) / disque (ABS)
Direction	à crémaillère, ass. variable
Diamètre de braquage	12,6 m
Pneus avant / arrière	P235/60R17 / P235/60R17
Poids	2 107 kg
Capacité de remorquage	454 kg (1 000 lb)

COMPOSANTES MÉCANIQUES

LX, LX Commodite, EX, EX Groupe Electrique, EX Luxe

Cylindrée, soupapes, alim.	V6 3,8 litres 24 s atmos.
Puissance / Couple	244 chevaux / 253 lb-pi
Tr. base (opt) / rouage base (opt)	A5 / Tr
0-100 / 80-120 / 100-0 km/h	8,9 s / 6,7 s / 47,0 m
Type ess. / ville / autoroute	Ordinaire / 12,6 / 8,5 l/100 km

DANS LA MÊME CATÉGORIE

Chrysler Town & Country, Dodge Grand Caravan, Honda Odyssey, Nissan Quest, Toyota Sienna, Volkswagen Routan

DU NOUVEAU EN 2011

Aucun changement majeur

NOS IMPRESSIONS

Agrément de conduite :	7/10
Fiabilité :	7/10
Sécurité :	10/10
Qualités hivernales :	7/10
Espace intérieur :	8/10
Confort :	8/10

www.kia.ca

Plus d'informations dans la section statistiques en dernière partie du Guide

UNE HEUREUSE ÉVOLUTION

Tous les constructeurs automobiles doivent, de toute évidence, s'adapter aux fluctuations du marché. Il y a quelques années, le Sorento intéressait les acheteurs à la recherche d'un vrai 4X4 avec un châssis autonome et un rouage intégral traditionnel de type mécanique. Même si certains inconditionnels ne jurent toujours que par cette configuration mécanique, les temps ont changé et les clients potentiels sont à la recherche de plus de raffinement et de confort et veulent pouvoir compter sur un rouage intégral entièrement automatisé à contrôle électronique. Le Sorento en est à sa troisième génération depuis son lancement en 2002 et cette nouvelle cuvée suit la tendance actuelle en fait de configuration mécanique.

Il faut souligner qu'en plus d'avoir subi une transformation complète de sa mécanique, ce Kia tout-terrain est assemblé à la toute nouvelle usine de Kia à West Point en Géorgie. De par ses dimensions, le Sorento rivalise principalement avec les Chevrolet Traverse, Ford Explorer, Jeep Grand Cherokee et Toyota 4Runner Par contre, son prix de détail suggéré le place entre les VUS compacts et les intermédiaires.

MÉCANIQUE MODERNE

La génération précédente du Sorento proposait une configuration mécanique assez traditionnelle avec l'utilisation d'un châssis à échelle. Cette approche permet d'obtenir un véhicule robuste, avec une plus grande capacité de remorquage. Par contre, au niveau de l'insonorisation et du confort, c'est nettement inférieur à une plate-forme monocoque. C'est donc cette dernière que les ingénieurs ont choisie afin d'améliorer la tenue de route et le confort. Ce changement a surtout un effet défavorable sur la capacité de remorquage qui passe de pratiquement 5000 lb à 3500 lb. Par contre, si vous voulez remorquer de plus lourdes charges et demeurer fidèle à ce constructeur coréen, il y a le Borrego dont la capacité de remorquage est de 5000 lb.

La version précédente du Sorento avait bien vieilli sur le plan visuel et le style était dans la bonne moyenne. Mais depuis quelques années maintenant, le design fait partie des priorités de ce constructeur coréen, et les modèles élégants se succèdent. Le nouveau Sorento n'y fait pas exception. Il propose naturellement la nouvelle calandre qui est dorénavant la signature de la marque tandis que les phares antibrouillard, de série, complètent bien la partie inférieure. Les designers ont également réussi à bien agencer les lignes fluides de la caisse et la ceinture de caisse élevée qui s'harmonise assez bien avec une partie arrière plus carrée, accentuant le caractère pratique de ce VUS. Il faut également ajouter que les couleurs pâles rendent davantage justice à cette silhouette.

Le tableau de bord est assez conservateur, mais d'une élégance certaine. Les stylistes ont conservé la console centrale verticale, mais en l'accentuant par la présence de bandes verticales de chaque côté. On y retrouve l'écran de navigation pour les modèles qui en sont dotés. Dans l'ensemble, les commandes sont placées de façon logique tandis qu'un éclairage orangé la nuit assure une bonne lecture des cadrans indicateurs et des différentes touches et commandes. Des appliques noires apposées sur le tableau de bord et dans les portières ajoutent une touche de luxe. Soulignons au passage que la qualité des matériaux est améliorée, tout comme la finition.

L'habitabilité est bonne aux places avant et arrière. Il est possible de commander une troisième banquette optionnelle, mais comme dans la majorité des cas, l'espace convient à de jeunes enfants. Une fois cette troisième rangée en place, l'espace pour les bagages est quasiment symbolique. Heureusement, ces sièges s'escamotent en un tournemain dans le plancher et permettent de bénéficier d'un excellent espace de chargement. Et chez Kia, on s'arrête aux détails. Les dossiers des sièges de la troisième rangée sont dotés d'appuie-tête qui se replient automatiquement lorsqu'on abaisse le dossier. C'est plus astucieux que d'avoir à enlever l'appuie-tête nous-mêmes et de ne plus savoir quoi faire avec par la suite.

L'EMBARRAS DU CHOIX

Afin de pouvoir répondre aux attentes des acheteurs désireux de se procurer ce modèle sans défoncer leur budget, Kia propose une version de base quand même bien équipée, et vendue pratiquement au prix d'un VUS compact. Ce modèle est propulsé par le même quatre cylindres qui équipe certaines versions de la Forte, soit un 2,4 litres développant 175 chevaux et un couple 169 lb-pi. Ce moteur est le seul à pouvoir être jumelé à une transmission manuelle à six rapports. Bien entendu, il est possible de commander en option une transmission automatique Steptronic à six rapports. Cette boîte manumatique est cependant la seule disponible si vous choisissez le rouage intégral, entièrement nouveau et nettement plus sophistiqué que le système 4X4 qu'il remplace. Ce mécanisme à prise constante répartit le couple aux quatre roues selon les besoins du moment, et le différentiel central peut être bloqué. Il est également équipé, de série, du contrôle électronique de stabilité, de l'antipatinage électronique, de l'assistance de démarrage en côte, du contrôle de la motricité en descente, et d'une protection anticapotage. Bref, comme avec le châssis monocoque, Kia a fait un pas de plus vers la modernité.

La transmission manuelle n'apporte pas grand-chose à la conduite et la plupart des acheteurs la choisiront sans doute pour des considérations économiques. Quant au moteur quatre cylindres, il est correct, mais sans plus, et il est à la hauteur si vous roulez avec peu de passagers et de bagages. Par contre, le six cylindres est en mesure de pouvoir affronter toutes les situations avec aplomb.

D'une cylindrée de 3,5 litres, ce moteur V6 développe 276 chevaux et un couple de 248 lb-pi. Il est d'une conception mécanique fort moderne et il ne craint pas les hauts régimes. D'ailleurs, il monte en régime avec beaucoup d'aisance. Les accélérations sont plus vigoureuses tandis que les manœuvres de dépassement sont favorisées par le couple et la puissance plus que suffisants.

DU SOLIDE

La position de conduite est bonne tandis que la visibilité est supérieure à la moyenne de la catégorie bien que le large pilier C

bloque la vision de trois quarts arrière. Notre véhicule d'essai était propulsé par le moteur V6 et le niveau sonore dans l'habitacle était très bas, preuve que la rigidité de la caisse et les produits insonorisants font leur travail. Au volant, on découvre une direction qui est précise, ce qui n'est pas toujours le cas pour un VUS. Cela témoigne d'ailleurs de la vocation plus citadine de ce Kia. Elle est également moins assistée que la plupart des autres VUS intermédiaires, ce qui plaira à certains et déplaira à d'autres. Son *feedback* de la route est par ailleurs légèrement supérieur à la moyenne ce qui est un élément positif aussi bien sur la route qu'en conduite en sentier. Quant à la tenue de route, elle est correcte et sans surprise. Comme tous les autres véhicules de cette catégorie, la suspension n'a pas été dessinée pour faire des tours

FEU VERT
- Silhouette moderne
- Choix de moteurs
- Rouage intégral sophistiqué
- Confort amélioré
- Tenue de route équilibrée

FEU ROUGE
- Suspension ferme
- Troisième rangée peu pratique
- Pneumatiques à revoir
- Fiabilité inconnue

de piste sur un circuit routier, mais la tenue de route est sans histoire. Le seul bémol sérieux est la fermeté de la suspension. C'est assez sec, mais on a l'impression en même temps d'être au volant d'un véhicule très solide. En effet, la suspension est ferme, mais ne nous secoue pas non plus.

Certains puristes regretteront le caractère moins baroudeur et plus sophistiqué de ce nouveau Sorento, mais ce sont les conditions du marché qui l'exigent. Sa silhouette moderne, ses deux moteurs de conception raffinée ainsi qu'un comportement routier sans surprise sont à inscrire dans la colonne des plus. Sur le plan négatif, sa suspension ferme ainsi qu'une troisième rangée de sièges peu pratique sont les éléments les plus fautifs. Toutefois, ce qui saura influencer favorablement la majorité, c'est le prix compétitif et un équipement de série très complet avec comme argument final une garantie de 5 ans/100 000 km.

Denis Duquet

PHOTOS : SYLVAIN RAYMOND

Catégorie	Multisegment
Échelle de prix	25 945 $ à 39 945 $
Garanties	5 ans/100 000 km, 5 ans/100 000 km
Assemblage	Hwasung, Corée du Sud
Cote d'assurance	n.d.

CHÂSSIS - DONNÉES POUR EX V6 LUXE

Emp/lon/lar/haut	2 700/4 670/1 885/1 710 mm
Coffre	258 à 2 052 litres (7 places)
Réservoir	68 litres
Nombre coussins sécurité	6
Antipatinage / contrôle stabilité	oui / oui
Suspension avant	indépendante, jambes de force
Suspension arrière	indépendante, multibras
Freins avant / arrière	disque (ABS) / disque (ABS)
Direction	à crémaillère, assistée
Diamètre de braquage	10,9 m
Pneus avant / arrière	P235/60R18 / P235/60R18
Poids	1 873 kg
Capacité de remorquage	1 588 kg (3 500 lb)

COMPOSANTES MÉCANIQUES

LX, EX

Cylindrée, soupapes, alim.	4L 2,4 litres 16 s atmos.
Puissance / Couple	175 chevaux / 169 lb-pi
Tr. base (opt) / rouage base (opt)	M6 (A6) / Tr (Int)
0-100 / 80-120 / 100-0 km/h	n.d. / n.d. / n.d.
Type ess. / ville / autoroute	Ordinaire / 7,4 / 10,6 l/100 km

LX V6, EX V6, EX V6 Luxe

Cylindrée, soupapes, alim.	V6 3,5 litres 24 s atmos
Puissance / Couple	276 chevaux / 248 lb-pi
Tr. base (opt) / rouage base (opt)	A6 / Tr (Int)
0-100 / 80-120 / 100-0 km/h	n.d. / n.d. / n.d.
Type ess. / ville / autoroute	Ordinaire / 7,7 / 10,3 l/100 km

DANS LA MÊME CATÉGORIE

Ford Explorer, Jeep Grand Cherokee, Mitsubishi Endeavor, Nissan Pathfinder, Subaru Tribeca, Toyota 4Runner

DU NOUVEAU EN 2011

Nouveau modèle

NOS IMPRESSIONS

Agrément de conduite :	■■■■■■■■□□	8/10
Fiabilité :	Nouveau modèle	
Sécurité :	■■■■■■■■□□	8/10
Qualités hivernales :	■■■■■■■■□□	8/10
Espace intérieur :	■■■■■■■■□□	8/10
Confort :	■■■■■■■■□□	8/10

www.kia.ca

Plus d'informations dans la section statistiques en dernière partie du Guide

NE VOUS FIEZ PAS AUX (BELLES) APPARENCES...

À première vue, la Kia Soul propose un design mieux intégré et plus harmonieux que pour le Nissan cube (oui, avec un petit « c » !). Avec, en prime, un prix de départ d'un millier de dollars moins élevé. Mais ne vous laissez pas tromper par les apparences...

Vous avouerez, le style n'a jamais été placé en tête de liste des raisons pour lesquelles on achète du Kia. Mais depuis l'arrivée de la Soul sur le marché, la donne est en train de changer pour le constructeur coréen. Indéniablement, son petit carré sur quatre roues est agréable au coup d'œil, avec sa calandre coquine, ce pavillon de toit qui s'avance avec dynamisme et ces teintes de carrosserie avant-gardistes – pensez Lave, Menthe ou Vanille frappée...

Heureusement, pas de déception une fois dans l'habitacle. La planche de bord exhibe une allure rétro qui fait son effet et, dans les versions plus étoffées, on a droit à des deux tons, des tissus à motifs et des touches originales qui viennent rehausser la note versus tout ce qui se fait d'autre dans la catégorie. Ne vous fiez pas qu'à nous: sachez que la publication américaine *Ward's* a décerné à la Soul en 2009 le titre d'Intérieur le plus *groovy* de l'année.

QUAND ON COMPARE...

Afin de respecter ses tendances qu'elle veut *hip-hop*, la Soul propose un éclairage dans les haut-parleurs qui clignote au rythme de la musique. Vous riez? Vous trouvez ce gadget vain et vaniteux? Peut-être. Mais alors... pourquoi cet intérêt systématique des gens qui montent à bord et qui veulent tous l'essayer?

Au-delà du superflu, la Soul offre des commandes accessibles et intuitives. On aime celles audio au volant, de même que les sièges chauffants et le Bluetooth, de série pour toutes les versions. Vous avez bien lu: de série, même en variante de base, celle-là même qui débute sous les 15800$. Par contre, on regrette le plastique de revêtement qui s'égratigne facilement. Et on critique les sièges avant qui manquent décidément de support, tant latéral que lombaire; les longues randonnées demandent à ce qu'on prenne fréquemment une pause. Notez que dans la version de base, le siège conducteur ne s'ajuste pas en hauteur. Et que malencontreusement, le beige du tableau de bord (certaines versions) se reflète dans le pare-brise, comme si ce dernier était constamment embué.

À l'arrière, l'espace aux jambes est correct, mais contrairement au Nissan, la banquette n'accepte ni de s'avancer ni de se reculer au gré des besoins. Côté chargement, les 1511 litres disponibles sont généreux, même s'ils sont de 10% moindre que dans le cube. Mais une fois la banquette remontée, c'est la Soul qui dégage le plus d'espace (546 litres contre 323).

QUELQUES POINTS EN MOINS

Bon, sur la route, *quossé* ça donne? Une conduite correcte, stable, mais pas aussi intéressante en ville que pour le cube (qui a

FEU VERT

Le style – dedans comme dehors!
Polyvalent, malgré les petites dimensions
Sièges chauffants de série
Commandes accessibles et intuitives

FEU ROUGE

Sièges avant peu confortables
Conduite neutre
Plastiques qui s'égratignent facilement
Boîte manuelle trop lâche pour être précise

pourtant devancé le Kia dans notre match comparatif, l'an dernier). C'est d'abord du bout des lèvres que nous vous parlons de la version de base du Soul. Munie d'un petit quatre cylindres de 1,6 litre qui produit 122 chevaux, cette variante ne vient qu'avec une boîte manuelle – boîte qui souffre de passages trop lâches pour être précise. Combien de fois avons-nous engagé le 3e rapport au lieu du premier? Bonne nouvelle, cependant: cette variante d'entrée de gamme profite de 2011 pour faire amende honorable et ajoute enfin, de série, le système de stabilité.

Toutes les autres variantes de la Soul sont équipées du moteur quatre cylindres de 2,0 litres, pour 20 chevaux de plus (à 142). Si cette nécessaire puissance additionnelle est bien cotée avec la boîte manuelle, elle est néanmoins peu flattée par la transmission automatique. Cette dernière boîte quatre rapports et sans mode manuel n'a pas la modernité de ce qui se fait actuellement sur le marché. Imaginez: même la petite Ford Fiesta propose une automatique six rapports! Du coup, les accélérations sont peu raffinées, bruyantes et tousseuses – la consommation en carburant s'en ressent, d'ailleurs.

La Soul perd encore d'autres points, versus le Nissan cube, pour sa tenue de route. Le petit véhicule coréen n'a décidément pas l'agilité et la légèreté du japonais, même si en général il se comporte plutôt bien. La plus grande différence, on la note au niveau de sa suspension (une poutre de torsion, comme pour le cube), qui bondit plus sèchement sur les cahots. Aussi, pas de direction électrique pour la Soul, ce qui aurait contribué à une réduction de la consommation en carburant; on a donc droit à une traditionnelle architecture à crémaillère assistée, au demeurant d'ajustements un brin trop neutres à notre goût.

Bref, pour vraiment bien s'en tirer avec la Kia Soul, il faut choisir les versions avec moteur 2,0 litres, ce qui fait grimper la facture à plus de 18000$. L'offre demeure intéressante en raison de tous ces équipements de série qui montent à bord (au risque de nous répéter: les sièges chauffants sont de série!), mais versus le cube, la conduite est moins stimulante, la consommation en carburant est plus élevée (versus la CVT du Nissan) et, oh! crime de lèse-majesté, on n'a toujours pas droit au démarrage sans clé. Encore moins à l'assistance en recul et à la climatisation automatique, ce que le cube possède pourtant…

Nadine Filion

PHOTOS: ALAIN MORIN

KIA SOUL

Catégorie	Multisegment
Échelle de prix	15 795 $ à 21 895 $ (2010)
Garanties	5 ans/100 000 km, 5 ans/100 000 km
Assemblage	Sohari, Corée du Sud
Cote d'assurance	n.d.

CHÂSSIS - DONNÉES POUR 2.0 4U BOLIDE

Emp/lon/lar/haut	2 550/4 105/1 785/1 610 mm
Coffre	546 à 1 511 litres
Réservoir	48 litres
Nombre coussins sécurité	6
Antipatinage / contrôle stabilité	oui / oui
Suspension avant	indépendante, jambes de force
Suspension arrière	indépendante, barres de torsion
Freins avant / arrière	disque (ABS) / disque (ABS)
Direction	à crémaillère, assistée
Diamètre de braquage	10,5 m
Pneus avant / arrière	P225/45R18 / P225/45R18
Poids	1 285 kg
Capacité de remorquage	non recommandé

COMPOSANTES MÉCANIQUES

1.6 L

Cylindrée, soupapes, alim.	4L 1,6 litre 16 s atmos.
Puissance / Couple	122 chevaux / 115 lb-pi
Tr. base (opt) / rouage base (opt)	M5 / Tr
0-100 / 80-120 / 100-0 km/h	13,0 s / 10,0 s / n.d.
Type ess. / ville / autoroute	Ordinaire / 7,7 / 6,3 l/100 km

2.0, SX

Cylindrée, soupapes, alim.	4L 2,0 litres 16 s atmos.
Puissance / Couple	142 chevaux / 137 lb-pi
Tr. base (opt) / rouage base (opt)	M5 (A4) / Tr
0-100 / 80-120 / 100-0 km/h	10,7 s / 9,0 s / 42,7 m
Type ess. / ville / autoroute	Ordinaire / 8,6 / 6,5 l/100 km

DANS LA MÊME CATÉGORIE

Chevrolet HHR, Nissan Cube, Suzuki SX-4, Toyota Matrix

DU NOUVEAU EN 2011

Freins ABS et système de stabilité désormais de série, freins à disque aux quatre roues pour toutes les versions, ordinateur de bord maintenant de série

NOS IMPRESSIONS

Agrément de conduite:	8/10
Fiabilité:	8/10
Sécurité:	8/10
Qualités hivernales:	7/10
Espace intérieur:	7/10
Confort:	7/10

www.kia.ca

Plus d'informations dans la section statistiques en dernière partie du Guide

UN AUTRE HIT!

Le constructeur Coréen Kia est sur une lancée au Canada depuis un peu plus d'un an avec de ventes qui sont en hausse constante. L'un des éléments qui explique ce succès s'avère non seulement l'amélioration de la qualité de ses produits, mais le fait que Kia nous propose des véhicules hautement compétitifs dans les créneaux les plus populaires, soit celui des voitures et des VUS compacts. Ces deux segments ne représentent rien de moins que 40% du marché.

Dans le cas des VUS compacts, c'est le Sportage chez Kia qui a la difficile mission de rivaliser avec une ribambelle d'autres modèles tous aussi intéressants les uns que les autres. Fort d'une refonte complète cette année, qu'est-ce que le nouveau Sportage dispose comme arguments susceptibles de vous attirer dans une sale de montre Kia? Bien entendu il offre une excellente valeur pour son prix, l'élément fort de Kia, mais son style et son comportement s'avèrent tout aussi convaincants.

ENFIN UN DESIGN MAISON

Il faut avouer que la nouveau Sportage tranche radicalement d'avec le modèle de la génération précédente. Il affiche un style beaucoup plus moderne et fluide, inspiré du véhicule concept KUE présenté au Salon de l'auto de Détroit en 2007. On retrouve à l'avant la grille de calandre typique des nouveaux produit Kia, soit large et proéminente. De côté, le véhicule offre une fenestration réduite et une ceinture de caisse très élevée, élément commun chez plusieurs nouveaux VUS.

Au chapitre des dimensions, le Sportage de 3e génération voit ses dimensions majorées à tous les points de vue, sauf pour sa hauteur. Il suit la tendance en proposant des dimensions plus généreuses, donc plus d'espace à bord. Sous le capot, tous reçoivent l'unique moteur offert pour le moment, soit un quatre cylindres développant 176 chevaux pour un couple de 168 lb-pi. Ce moteur peut être associé à une boîte manuelle à six rapports dans la version à deux roues motrices, alors que celles qui disposent du rouage intégral adoptent par défaut la boîte automatique à six rapports Avec son prix légèrement majoré, il est difficile de ne pas conseiller la version à rouage intégral, qui justifie principalement l'achat d'un tel véhicule. Sachez toute fois que plus tard cette année, une nouvelle version à vocation plus sportive, recevra un moteur suralimenté de 2,0 litres, mariant économie de carburant et puissance accrue. Aucun V6 n'est donc au catalogue, pour cela il faut se tourner vers le Sorento.

À l'intérieur, le changement est aussi drastique. Cette fois Kia se surpasse encore une fois et nous présente un habitacle qui laisse difficilement imaginer son prix abordable. L'intérieur du Sportage nous donne l'impression d'être à bord d'un véhicule luxueux et même les versions de bases demeurent intéressantes à ce chapitre. Le tableau de bord s'avère très moderne et on apprécie la

FEU VERT

- Style réussi
- Excellente valeur
- Bonne garantie
- Agréable à conduire

FEU ROUGE

- Quelques craquements à bord
- Manque de support des sièges
- Direction électrique un peu lourde
- Fiabilité inconnue

disposition des différentes commandes sur deux niveaux au centre du tableau de bord. Au chapitre des irritants, on note l'assise des sièges qui n'est pas très longue, donc on manque de support pour les cuisses, alors que l'on a noté lors de notre premier contact des craquements dans le tableau de bord, plus marqués dans les versions plus cossues.

SUR LA ROUTE

Au volant, la version de base à traction équipé de la boîte manuelle constitue principalement une solution abordable puisque la boîte manuelle n'a rien d'extraordinaire. Par contre, c'est la version idéale si vous voulez remorquer un Sportage derrière un véhicule récréatif, cette configuration étant la seule à s'y prêter. Pour les autres utilisations, il vaut mieux opter pour l'automatique, tout comme le rouage intégral. Le moteur de 176 chevaux offre des performances suffisantes et c'est son couple développé à bas régime qui le rend aussi efficace. On ne manque jamais de puissance, même en manœuvre de dépassement, le tout bien appuyé par l'excellente boîte automatique à six rapports.

Le Sportage adopte un comportement dynamique qui débute par une bonne position de conduite et une excellente visibilité vers l'avant. On se sent bien en contrôle du véhicule. En virage, les transferts de poids son minimisés et la suspension, maintenant à multibras à l'arrière, offre un bon compromis entre la tenue de route et le confort. En fait, le Sportage offre un comportement beaucoup plus près de celui d'une berline que d'un VUS, et c'est tant mieux. Qui a réellement besoin de franchir les montagnes ?

Avec le nouveau Sportage, Kia prouve à nouveau qu'il a réussi l'exploit de faire de l'achat d'un de ses véhicules, un choix de goût et de plaisir, non pas juste un choix axé sur le budget. Faudra encore quelques temps pour éliminer l'ancienne perception, mais le meilleur moyen pour y arriver demeure les produits et à ce chapitre, Kia livre la marchandise. Le reste devrait suivre !

Sylvain Raymond

PHOTOS : SYLVAIN RAYMOND

KIA SPORTAGE

Catégorie	VUS
Échelle de prix	n.d.
Garanties	5 ans/100 000 km, 5 ans/100 000 km
Assemblage	n.d.
Cote d'assurance	bonne

CHÂSSIS - DONNÉES POUR LX

Emp/lon/lar/haut	2 639/4 440/1 854/1 636 mm
Coffre	739 à 1 546 litres
Réservoir	n.d.
Nombre coussins sécurité	6
Antipatinage / contrôle stabilité	oui / oui
Suspension avant	indépendante, jambes de force
Suspension arrière	indépendante, multibras
Freins avant / arrière	disque (ABS) / disque (ABS)
Direction	à crémaillère, ass. variable
Diamètre de braquage	10,6 m
Pneus avant / arrière	P215/70R16 / P215/70R16
Poids	1 445 kg
Capacité de remorquage	907 kg (1 999 lb)

COMPOSANTES MÉCANIQUES

Base, EX, LX

Cylindrée, soupapes, alim.	4L 2,4 litres 16 s atmos.
Puissance / Couple	176 chevaux / 168 lb-pi
Tr. base (opt) / rouage base (opt)	M6 (A6) / Tr (Int)
0-100 / 80-120 / 100-0 km/h	n.d. / n.d. / n.d.
Type ess. / ville / autoroute	Ordinaire / 11,2 / 8,1 l/100 km

DANS LA MÊME CATÉGORIE

Chevrolet Equinox, Ford Escape, Honda CR-V, Hyundai Tucson, Jeep Compass, Jeep Patriot, Mazda Tribute, Mitsubishi Outlander, Nissan Rogue, Toyota RAV4, Volkswagen Tiguan

DU NOUVEAU EN 2011

Nouveau modèle

NOS IMPRESSIONS

Agrément de conduite :	■■■■■■■■□□ 8/10
Fiabilité :	Nouveau modèle
Sécurité :	■■■■■■■■□□ 8/10
Qualités hivernales :	■■■■■■■■□□ 8/10
Espace intérieur :	■■■■■■■■□□ 8/10
Confort :	■■■■■■■■□□ 8/10

www.kia.ca

Plus d'informations dans la section statistiques en dernière partie du Guide

CELLE QUI A TOUT CHANGÉ PERSISTE

Le jour de la Saint-Jean, l'été dernier, Lamborghini a fièrement annoncé la production d'une 10 000e Gallardo à son usine de Sant'Agata Bolognese. Cette série devenait, du même coup, la plus populaire de l'histoire mouvementée et rocambolesque de cette marque farouchement italienne sauvée et relancée admirablement par Audi dans la galaxie en expansion rapide du géant allemand Volkswagen.

De quelques centaines, la production annuelle de l'usine Lamborghini a franchi le cap du millier dès la première année de fabrication de la Gallardo, en 2003. Depuis, le compte atteint plus de 1 250 voitures chaque année, ce qui est conforme à l'objectif que s'était fixé l'équipe de direction de Lamborghini, en symbiose avec leurs collègues de chez Audi.

Ce mode de fonctionnement ressemble à celui qu'a établi directement le groupe VW avec ses marques Bentley et Bugatti, avec le degré d'indépendance supplémentaire que permet ce lien plus indirect avec Audi. Cet arrangement offre à Lamborghini un accès libre aux ressources techniques d'Audi tout en respectant intégralement sa riche tradition. Ironiquement, on présente souvent la Audi R8 comme une voiture dérivée de la Gallardo, alors que c'est l'Italienne qui a repris la technique *Audi Space Frame* pour la construction de son châssis d'aluminium.

MULTIPLICATION SALUTAIRE

La première Gallardo était un coupé dont le cœur était un V10 de 5,0 litres et 500 chevaux. Sa robe a été dessinée par le jeune styliste belge Luc Donckerwolke, déjà auteur de la spectaculaire Murciélago qui avait succédé à la Diablo l'année précédente. À son lancement, la Gallardo fut immanquablement présentée comme la « petite Lamborghini » aux côtés de la Murciélago. Elle est effectivement plus courte de 405 mm et plus étroite de 158 mm que sa frangine à moteur V12, et elle lui laisse aussi les portières en élytres. Avec son rouage intégral, la Gallardo suivait les traces de la Diablo VT de Lamborghini, deuxième grande sportive à quatre roues motrices après la Porsche 959 qui en fut la pionnière moderne.

Pour que la Gallardo demeure attrayante auprès de la riche clientèle visée, et compétitive face à ses rivales, surtout les ennemies jurées de Maranello, Lamborghini en a créé de nombreuses versions au fil des sept dernières années, y compris des modèles à tirage limité comme la SE (pour *Special Edition*) et la Nera produites à seulement 250 et 185 exemplaires, respectivement. La première comportait des retouches, des ajouts et des modifications qui furent reprises peu après sur toutes les Gallardo. La puissance de son V10 passait également à 522 chevaux et sa boîte de vitesses *e-gear* à embrayage automatisé était dotée d'un mode électronique qui permettait les départs canon en laissant grimper le régime du moteur à 5 000 tr/min.

FEU VERT
Toujours aussi racée
Moteurs puissants et envoûtants
Boîte automatisée *e-gear* rapide
Finition soignée

FEU ROUGE
Direction lourde en virage
Sous-virage sur circuit
Fiabilité inégale
Toujours très chère

La série Gallardo comporte actuellement trois modèles: les LP560-4 et LP570-4 Superleggera sont des coupés, alors que la LP560-4 Spyder est coiffée d'une capote souple. La LP560-4 était la première évolution importante de la Gallardo. Elle a d'abord reçu un nouveau V10 de 5,2 litres à injection directe dont la puissance grimpait à 552 chevaux (SAE). La coque en aluminium a également été redessinée pour augmenter sa rigidité, soigner son esthétique et bonifier l'efficacité aérodynamique de 31 %. Ces améliorations ont permis un sprint de 0 à 100 km/h en 3,7 secondes, une vitesse de pointe de 325 km/h et une réduction de la consommation et des émissions de gaz carbonique de 18 %. La LP560-4 Spyder, lancée peu après, profitait des mêmes avancées, y compris une réduction de poids de 20 kg.

ULTRALÉGÈRE ET PROPULSION

La LP570-4 Superleggera, comme son nom le suggère, est une version encore allégée du coupé. Son poids a été réduit de 70 kg en utilisant la fibre de carbone pour plusieurs éléments de la carrosserie et de l'habitacle, dont la coquille des sièges. Lamborghini utilise la fibre de carbone depuis 1983 et compte y recourir de plus en plus. Les Italiens ont même créé leur propre centre de recherche à Sant'Agata. La LP570-4 Superleggera est plus puissante aussi, son V10 de 5,2 litres étant coté à 570 chevaux (562 SAE).

Notre collègue Gabriel Gélinas a bien connu la Gallardo pour l'avoir maintes fois pilotée sur circuit. Il a louangé la sonorité fabuleuse de son V10 en pleine accélération, la poussée de sa cavalerie et l'excellente motricité du rouage intégral qui achemine 70 % du couple aux roues arrière. Gabriel a par contre souligné la lourdeur relative de la direction, couplée aux roues avant motrices, et un sous-virage. Plus prononcée, à tout le moins, que sur sa rivale d'alors, la Ferrari F430.

Il sera d'ailleurs intéressant de voir quelle réplique Lamborghini compte offrir à sa remplaçante, la F458 Italia. La Gallardo, malgré ses qualités et sa silhouette encore séduisante, en est quand même à sa neuvième année. On y retrouvera sans doute de la fibre de carbone, mais il est question aussi d'un rouage hybride, question de respecter les futures normes antipollution européennes. C'est à suivre.

Marc Lachapelle

PHOTOS : LAMBORGHINI

Catégorie	Coupé, *Roadster*
Échelle de prix	198 000 $ à 221 000 $
Garanties	2 ans/illimité, 2 ans/illimité
Assemblage	Sant'Agata, Italie
Cote d'assurance	n.d.

CHÂSSIS - DONNÉES POUR LP 560-4 SPYDER

Emp/lon/lar/haut	2 560/4 345/1 900/1 184 mm
Coffre	110 litres
Réservoir	80 litres
Nombre coussins sécurité	4
Antipatinage / contrôle stabilité	oui / oui
Suspension avant	indépendante, bras inégaux
Suspension arrière	indépendante, multibras
Freins avant / arrière	disque (ABS) / disque (ABS)
Direction	à crémaillère, ass. variable
Diamètre de braquage	11,5 m
Pneus avant / arrière	P235/35ZR19 / P295/30ZR19
Poids	1 550 kg
Capacité de remorquage	non recommandé

COMPOSANTES MÉCANIQUES

LP 560-4, LP 560-4 Spyder

Cylindrée, soupapes, alim.	V10 5,2 litres atmos.
Puissance / Couple	552 chevaux / 398 lb-pi
Tr. base (opt) / rouage base (opt)	M6 (A6) / Int
0-100 / 80-120 / 100-0 km/h	3,7 s / 3,5 s (est) / n.d.
Type ess. / ville / autoroute	Super / 20,1 / 12,2 l/100 km

LP 570-4 Superleggera

Cylindrée, soupapes, alim.	V10 5,2 litres 40 s atmos.
Puissance / Couple	570 chevaux / 398 lb-pi
Tr. base (opt) / rouage base (opt)	M6 (A6) / Int
0-100 / 80-120 / 100-0 km/h	3,4 s / 3,3 s (est) / n.d.
Type ess. / ville / autoroute	Super / 22,2 / 10,0 l/100 km

DANS LA MÊME CATÉGORIE

Aston Martin DB9, Audi R8, Chevrolet Corvette, Dodge Viper, Ferrari F458 Italia, Lexus LFA, Porsche 911

DU NOUVEAU EN 2011

Introduction de la LP 570-4 Superleggara

NOS IMPRESSIONS

Agrément de conduite :	9/10
Fiabilité :	5/10
Sécurité :	7/10
Qualités hivernales :	3/10
Espace intérieur :	5/10
Confort :	6/10

www.lamborghini.ca

Plus d'informations dans la section statistiques en dernière partie du Guide

LES PARIS SONT OUVERTS

Au moment d'écrire ces lignes, les spéculations vont bon train quand au nom et aux spécifications de la future remplaçante de la Murciélago qui sera dévoilée au Mondial de l'automobile de Paris. S'appellera-t-elle Urus, assurant ainsi la poursuite d'une tradition établie chez Lamborghini de choisir un nom de taureau pour ses modèles, ou s'appellera-t-elle plutôt Jota, du nom d'une danse espagnole ? Là-dessus, comme sur beaucoup d'autres questions, les paris sont ouverts...

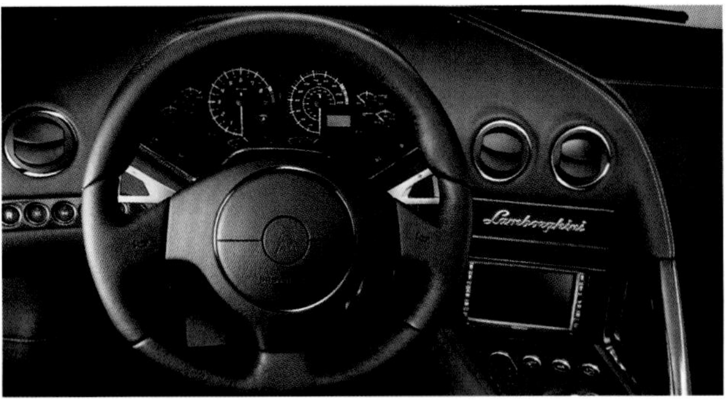

Le mystère plane, donc, sur la nouvelle voiture exotique en cours de développement chez Lamborghini, et comme les rumeurs font état d'une refonte complète plutôt que d'une simple retouche du design actuel, voilà pourquoi un tout nouveau nom serait donné à la plus performante des voitures de la marque au taureau sauvage. De nombreuses photos illégitimes de prototypes à l'essai ont circulées dernièrement, ce qui nous a permis d'entrevoir la nouvelle Lamborghini et d'alimenter les discussions à son sujet.

UN TOUT NOUVEAU V12

Elle a déjà circulé en hiver dans le nord de la Suède, au Portugal et sur plusieurs circuits. La mission de la remplaçante de la Murciélago est de relever la barre d'un cran par rapport au modèle antérieur, histoire de marquer un clivage plus évident avec la « petite » Gallardo, dont les versions plus typées en sont venues à chatouiller sa grande sœur au niveau des performances. C'est pourquoi la nouvelle Lamborghini disposerait toujours d'un V12, qui serait cependant tout nouveau et qui adopterait l'injection directe de carburant. De plus, la cylindrée serait portée à 7,0 litres et la puissance pourrait être chiffrée à plus de 700 chevaux afin de remettre les pendules à l'heure dans la hiérarchie des super exotiques. La transmission intégrale serait encore et toujours au programme, mais la question de la boîte de vitesses n'est pas claire. Lamborghini fera-t-elle appel à une version plus robuste de la boîte DSG développée par Audi ou poursuivra-t-elle dans la même voie avec une boîte manuelle séquentielle ? De plus, comme la Murciélago était également disponible avec une boîte manuelle conventionnelle à levier de vitesses, verra-t-on encore ce type de boîte au catalogue ? Il y a fort à parier que non, car même Ferrari a délaissé la boîte manuelle pour la récente 458 Italia.

Une chose est certaine, le style de la nouvelle Lamborghini sera évocateur des anciens bolides de la marque, tout comme la plus récente Reventon, et la voiture conservera les portières en élytre qui sont le propre de l'actuelle Murciélago. Un examen attentif des premiers clichés saisis sur le vif révèle que la base du pare-brise sera plus avancée et que son angle d'attaque sera plus prononcé. Quant au châssis de la nouvelle bête, il a été question d'adopter la fibre de carbone pour réaliser non seulement la carrosserie, mais également la structure même de la voiture. Cependant, cet ambitieux projet semble avoir été écarté à la faveur d'une structure autoportante réalisée en aluminium et de

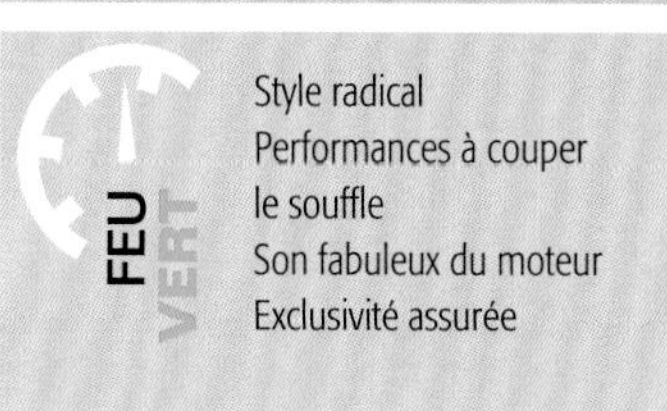

FEU VERT

Style radical
Performances à couper le souffle
Son fabuleux du moteur
Exclusivité assurée

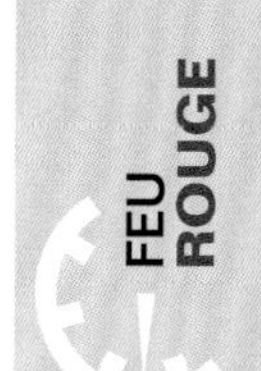

FEU ROUGE

Prix stratosphérique
Délais de livraison
Visibilité vers l'arrière
Fiabilité aléatoire

l'intégration de pièces en composite. De ce côté, il faut préciser que la marque Audi a justement développé une solide expertise pour ce qui est du développement de voitures tout alu et que la marque allemande pourrait en faire profiter la marque italienne, Audi et Lamborghini faisant toutes deux partie du portefeuille Volkswagen. Par ailleurs, cette filiation avec le géant allemand de l'automobile pourrait faire en sorte que l'habitacle de la nouvelle Lamborghini hérite d'éléments empruntés à Audi, comme c'est le cas sur la Gallardo où la clé, le système de chauffage/climatisation et la chaîne audio proviennent directement du constructeur allemand.

L'ÉPREUVE DU CIRCUIT

Ayant eu l'occasion de conduire à la fois la Gallardo et la Murciélago LP 640 sur le circuit du Mont-Tremblant, je peux vous préciser que les Lamborghini sont parmi les voitures les plus « viscérales » à piloter puisqu'elles ont ce don de mettre tous vos sens en éveil dès la sortie des puits de ravitaillement. La sonorité des moteurs est carrément agressive et la tenue de route est superbe, hormis cette tendance plus marquée au sous-virage qui est le propre des sportives à traction intégrale. Au freinage, on sent que le poids de la LP 640 est tout de même élevé (plus de 1 600 kilos), et les freins mis au point par Brembo font leur travail pour ralentir efficacement la voiture. Dès le début de l'accélération en sortie de courbe, le V12 se remet à hurler sa joie et c'est vraiment dans les hauts régimes, vers 8 000 tours/minute, que l'on sent véritablement le surcroît de puissance de la LP 640. L'équilibre des masses demeure bon, car la présence d'éléments du rouage intégral à l'avant de la voiture permet justement de bien les équilibrer.

Par ailleurs, on ne peut passer sous silence la fiabilité plutôt aléatoire des voitures de cette marque, puisque mon expérience personnelle avec la Gallardo m'a fait prendre conscience de certaines lacunes, comparativement à la Ferrari F430 qui, elle, mérite des éloges à cet égard.

La Murciélago est la plus chère, et surtout la plus exclusive des voitures de la marque. Étant donné son prix, qui est presque le double de celui d'une Gallardo, la grande Lamborghini ne représente que dix pour cent des ventes du constructeur italien. Malgré tout, c'est sans conteste ce bolide qui assure le rayonnement de la marque.

Gabriel Gélinas

PHOTOS : LAMBORGHINI

LAMBORGHINI MURCIÉLAGO

Catégorie	Coupé, *Roadster*
Échelle de prix	354 000 $ à 450 000 $
Garanties	2 ans/illimité, 2 ans/illimité
Assemblage	Sant'Agata, Italie
Cote d'assurance	n.d.

CHÂSSIS - DONNÉES POUR LP 640 ROADSTER

Emp/lon/lar/haut	2 665/4 610/2 058/1 135 mm
Coffre	n.d.
Réservoir	100 litres
Nombre coussins sécurité	4
Antipatinage / contrôle stabilité	oui / oui
Suspension avant	indépendante, bras inégaux
Suspension arrière	indépendante, bras inégaux
Freins avant / arrière	disque (ABS) / disque (ABS)
Direction	à crémaillère, assistée
Diamètre de braquage	12,6 m
Pneus avant / arrière	P245/35ZR18 / P335/30ZR18
Poids	1 690 kg
Capacité de remorquage	non recommandé

COMPOSANTES MÉCANIQUES

LP 640, LP 640 Roadster

Cylindrée, soupapes, alim.	V12 6,5 litres 48 s atmos.
Puissance / Couple	640 chevaux / 487 lb-pi
Tr. base (opt) / rouage base (opt)	M6 (A6) / Int
0-100 / 80-120 / 100-0 km/h	3,4 s / n.d. / n.d.
Type ess. / ville / autoroute	Super / 25,9 / 15,8 l/100 km

LP 670-4 SV

Cylindrée, soupapes, alim.	V12 6,5 litres atmos.
Puissance / Couple	670 chevaux / 487 lb-pi
Tr. base (opt) / rouage base (opt)	A6 / Int
0-100 / 80-120 / 100-0 km/h	3,2 s / n.d. / n.d.
Type ess. / ville / autoroute	Super / 29,4 / 18,9 l/100 km

DANS LA MÊME CATÉGORIE

Ferrari 599 GTB Fiorano

DU NOUVEAU EN 2011

Aucun changement majeur

NOS IMPRESSIONS

Agrément de conduite :	8/10
Fiabilité :	5/10
Sécurité :	7/10
Qualités hivernales :	3/10
Espace intérieur :	6/10
Confort :	6/10

www.lamborghini.ca

Plus d'informations dans la section statistiques en dernière partie du Guide

L'ÂME DE L'AVENTURIER ENDORMI

L'ordinateur sur lequel votre journaliste préféré écrit ce texte, un portable d'à peine deux ou trois kilos, est infiniment plus puissant que tous les ordinateurs ayant servi aux premières missions Apollo. Cette comparaison est impressionnante mais comme je ne me sers que d'environ 5 % des capacités de mon ordinateur, qu'est-ce que ça donne ? De la même manière, un ingénieur de Land Rover racontait qu'à peine 5 % des propriétaires de Land Rover neufs roulaient hors route. Pourtant, les produits Land Rover, le LR2 inclus, possèdent des capacités tout-terrain phénoménales. Mais qu'est-ce que ça donne ?

En 2008, Land Rover dévoilait le LR2, autrefois connu sous le nom de Freelander. D'ailleurs, dans plusieurs autres contrées, il porte aujourd'hui le nom de Freelander 2. Toujours est-il qu'en Amérique, le LR2 est le véhicule d'entrée de gamme de Land Rover. Si les plus huppés LR4, Range Rover et Range Rover Sport affichent tous une allure extraordinairement carrée, le LR2, tout comme le futur Range Rover Evoque (voir dans la section « Dernière heure » à la toute fin du présent *Guide de l'auto*), montre plus d'angles arrondis. Malgré tout, il est indéniablement un pur produit Land Rover.

IL Y A UNE VOLVO EN DESSOUS !

En fait, non, ce n'est pas un pur produit Land Rover. On pourrait même dire qu'il s'agit presque d'une Volvo ! Le LR2 a été développé sous l'égide de Ford alors que l'entreprise américaine était aussi propriétaire de Volvo. Pour diminuer les coûts de fabrication, Land Rover a utilisé le châssis et la mécanique de la berline Volvo S80. Bien entendu, cette plate-forme a été sérieusement

revue et rigidifiée et, comme nous le verrons plus loin, c'est réussi. Le moteur, ça, c'est une autre histoire…

Le six cylindres en ligne de 3,2 litres n'est pas le plus récent et, surtout, pas le plus puissant. Ses 230 chevaux et 234 livres-pied de couple ne sont pas impotents, certes, mais le fait qu'ils doivent déplacer près de 2 000 kilos les rend un peu plus engourdis. Un dépassement mal calculé nous le rappelle aussitôt… Aussi, avec une consommation dépassant allègrement les 14 l/100 km en ville, on ne peut pas dire qu'ils se font pardonner leur manque d'enthousiasme…

AMENEZ-MOI LE GRAND CANYON

Ce moteur est associé à une transmission automatique à six rapports et, surtout, à un rouage intégral Haldex qui fait honneur à la réputation de la marque. Même s'il ne s'agit pas d'un système 4x4 aussi performant que dans les autres véhicules Land Rover et qu'il ne possède ni gamme basse (LO) ni suspension ajustable en hauteur, ce rouage s'avère parfaitement adapté au LR2. On lui a même adjoint le système Terrain Response de ses grands frères. Ce système permet au conducteur de choisir le type de sol sur lequel il veut s'engager. Sur la route, donc au moins 95 % du temps pour 95 %

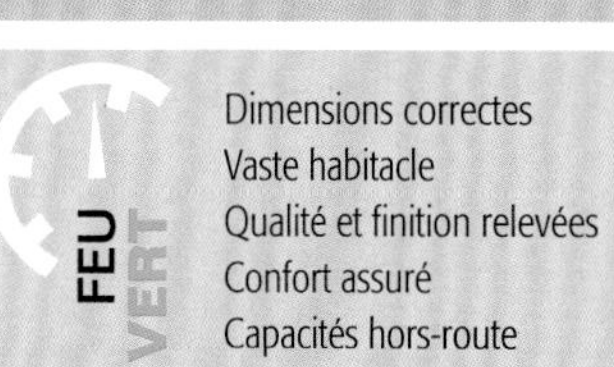

FEU VERT

- Dimensions correctes
- Vaste habitacle
- Qualité et finition relevées
- Confort assuré
- Capacités hors-route impressionnantes

FEU ROUGE

- Moteur très juste
- Consommation élevée
- Fiabilité exécrable
- Dépréciation verticale
- Commandes confuses

des gens, le mode Tarmac (asphalte) est tout indiqué. On retrouve aussi les modes « herbe », « terre », « neige », « boue », « racines » et « sable ». Le *Terrain Response* fait interagir les freins ABS, le système de contrôle de la stabilité, la transmission et l'accélérateur pour offrir le maximum de traction en tout temps. Il y a aussi le système d'aide à la descente qui gère tous les paramètres ci-haut mentionnés pour permettre de descendre des côtes, que dis-je des montagnes, en toute sécurité. Le conducteur n'a qu'à lâcher les freins, ce qui n'est pas évident à faire dans une pente accentuée et recouverte de boue, et le véhicule s'occupe du reste. Bref, n'importe qui peut avoir l'air d'un expert en 4x4 puisque le talent n'est plus nécessaire.

Pourtant, la mécanique et les capacités à franchir le Grand Canyon sont sans doute les éléments les moins recherchés par les acheteurs de Land Rover. Le LR2, même s'il est le plus petit, peut se targuer de posséder un habitacle à la mesure de son nom. La qualité des matériaux, leur présentation et leur finition est très relevée mais le tableau de bord mériterait de recevoir le même traitement fait aux LR4, Range Rover et Range Rover Sport. Ces derniers jouissent d'une planche beaucoup plus moderne et, surtout, moins encombrée de boutons et de commandes, ce qui la rend plus facile à utiliser. Bien entendu, tous les systèmes d'aide au stationnement, de connectivité ou de confort affichent présent. Les sièges sont toujours très confortables et l'espace ne manque pas, même à l'arrière. Et comme tous les autres produits de la marque, l'insonorisation est poussée. On ne peut qualifier le LR2 de sportif même si son comportement routier est très correct. Une courbe prise trop rapidement démontre un roulis considérable.

SI VOUS AIMEZ LES HISTOIRES D'HORREUR...

S'il est un domaine où Land Rover ne peut rivaliser avec qui que ce soit, c'est au niveau de la fiabilité. Aux dernières nouvelles, cette marque croupissait encore, malgré les belles paroles des dirigeants rencontrés l'automne dernier, dans les bas-fonds des sondages de fiabilité générale de la firme J.D. Power, avec Suzuki, Jeep et Volkswagen.

Il y a cependant fort à parier que cela indiffère les propriétaires de Land Rover pour qui il est souvent plus important de placer une belle voiture devant le garage que de s'en servir. D'ailleurs, les plus avisés N'ACHÈTENT PAS un Land Rover, LR2 ou autre. Ils le louent. C'est le seul moyen de s'en débarrasser après quelques années sans avoir à subir une trop importante perte financière.

Alain Morin

PHOTOS : LAND ROVER

Catégorie	VUS
Échelle de prix	44 950 $
Garanties	4 ans/80 000 km, 4 ans/80 000 km
Assemblage	Solihull, Angleterre
Cote d'assurance	n.d.

CHÂSSIS - DONNÉES POUR HSE

Emp/lon/lar/haut	2 660/4 500/1 910/1 740 mm
Coffre	760 à 1 670 litres
Réservoir	70 litres
Nombre coussins sécurité	7
Antipatinage / contrôle stabilité	oui / oui
Suspension avant	indépendante, jambes de force
Suspension arrière	indépendante, jambes de force
Freins avant / arrière	disque (ABS) / disque (ABS)
Direction	à crémaillère, assistée
Diamètre de braquage	11,4 m
Pneus avant / arrière	P235/55R19 / P235/55R19
Poids	1 930 kg
Capacité de remorquage	1 585 kg (3 494 lb)

COMPOSANTES MÉCANIQUES

HSE

Cylindrée, soupapes, alim.	6L 3,2 litres 24 s atmos.
Puissance / Couple	230 chevaux / 234 lb-pi
Tr. base (opt) / rouage base (opt)	A6 / Int
0-100 / 80-120 / 100-0 km/h	9,7 s / 8,3 s / 38,5 m
Type ess. / ville / autoroute	Super / 14,1 / 9,1 l/100 km

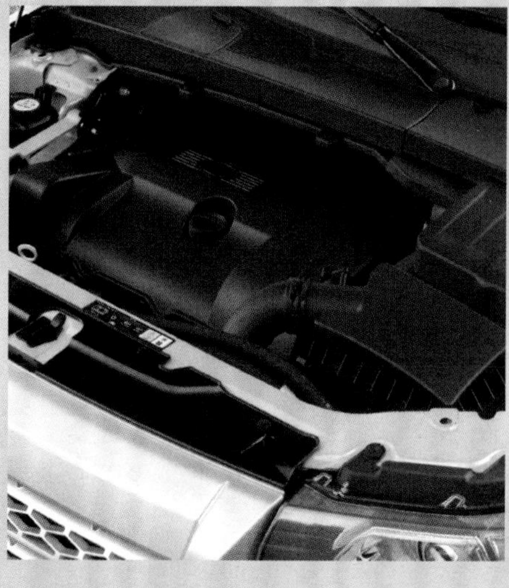

DANS LA MÊME CATÉGORIE

Acura RDX, Audi Q5, BMW X3, Infiniti EX, Mercedes-Benz Classe GLK, Volvo XC60

DU NOUVEAU EN 2011

Aucun changement majeur

NOS IMPRESSIONS

Agrément de conduite :	8/10
Fiabilité :	3/10
Sécurité :	8/10
Qualités hivernales :	9/10
Espace intérieur :	8/10
Confort :	8/10

www.landrover.com

Plus d'informations dans la section statistiques en dernière partie du Guide

EXAGÉRATION AU CARRÉ... OU AU CUBE!

L'an dernier, Land Rover présentait une nouvelle génération de la plupart de ses véhicules. Ceux qui s'attendaient à des changements majeurs ont été déçus... En fait, le LR4 est toujours aussi imposant, aussi carré et aussi raffiné que son prédécesseur, le LR3. Car on a beau être le deuxième plus petit véhicule d'une marque de prestige (le premier étant le LR2), on se doit tout de même de présenter une certaine prestance. Déjà que le fait d'avoir été longtemps associé à Ford est suffisamment humiliant pour la noble marque britannique...

Heureusement, ce temps fordien est révolu. Désormais, Land Rover et Jaguar appartiennent à Tata, un très important manufacturier automobile indien qui aurait, semble-t-il, beaucoup de respect pour ces deux prestigieuses marques. Peut-être que si la nouvelle génération avait été développée sous Tata, les différences seraient-elles plus marquées... Les modifications les plus évidentes ont été apportées à l'habitacle alors que le tableau de bord a été entièrement revu. Malheureusement, certaines commandes rappellent l'époque Ford, comme les leviers des clignotants et des essuie-glaces, les boutons des vitres électriques, etc. Les sièges avant font preuve d'un confort inouï et un petit 600 km en une journée n'a rien de déplaisant.

JAMBES EN L'AIR

Le LR4 est un véhicule haut sur pattes et le fait qu'il n'y ait pas de marchepieds ne facilite pas l'entrée et la sortie du véhicule. Au moins, la position de conduite élevée et une bonne fenestration assurent une bonne visibilité tout le tour et apportent un sentiment d'invulnérabilité et de sécurité qui plaît surtout aux femmes... et à plusieurs hommes qui ne l'avoueront jamais! En passant, soulignons que le pare-brise est strié de très minces bandes chauffantes qui peuvent déranger la vision du conducteur, surtout au début. Mais on s'y fait rapidement. Les matériaux sont de belle qualité et leur assemblage est réussi. Les sièges de la deuxième rangée sont confortables, mais y accéder demande d'avoir la patte légère (à ne pas confondre avec la cuisse légère!). On retrouve aussi une troisième rangée qui demande d'avoir la patte légère ET souple. Mais avant de s'asseoir sur un des deux sièges ma foi fort confortables, il faut d'abord les mettre en place grâce à un mécanisme extraordinairement mal foutu. Il est d'ailleurs difficile de le qualifier autrement que par un mot religieux suivi d'un terme fécal... Comme si ce n'était pas suffisant, lorsque les dossiers de cette troisième rangée sont relevés, l'espace disponible dans le coffre est passablement réduit.

Là où ce « petit » Land Rover a connu des changements l'an dernier, c'est au niveau de la mécanique. Maintenant, un seul moteur est offert, soit un nouveau et fort moderne V8 de 5,0 litres, puissant et souple à souhait, à la sonorité envoûtante lorsqu'il travaille « à fond ». Il est marié à une excellente transmission automatique à six rapports, et elle les passe rapidement. Et au bon moment, ce qui est encore plus important et qui aide à réduire la consommation...

FEU VERT
Lignes carrées inspirant la robustesse
Robustesse confirmée
Habitacle douillet
Puissance adéquate
Bonnes capacités de remorquage

FEU ROUGE
Gabarit intimidant
Consommation décevante
Banquette de 3e rangée mal foutue
Fiabilité encore questionnable
Valeur de revente à pleurer

un peu. En étant fort poli avec l'accélérateur et en conduisant 90 % du temps sur autoroutes à une vitesse constante de 110 km/h, nous avons obtenu une moyenne de 13,8 l/100 km. Quelques feux rouges et hop, le LR4 peut facilement vous monter ça à 15,0, 16,0 ou même 17... Ce qui revient à dire que les 86 litres du réservoir d'essence se vident rapidement et obligent souvent à planifier les trajets en fonction des pompes à essence.

YOUPPI, UNE SORTIE DE ROUTE !

Là où le LR4 fait preuve d'une maestria hors du commun, c'est lorsque la route ne peut plus porter ce nom. Oh my God ! Pour escalader une montagne ou la descendre en toute sécurité (et en tout confort !), rien ne bat un LR. Dans l'habitacle, on retrouve un bouton appelé « Terrain Response » qui permet de sélectionner un paramètre de terrain entre les cinq proposés. Le conducteur peut ensuite choisir la gamme basse et relever la suspension pneumatique. Après ça, il ne reste qu'à tourner le volant, le véhicule s'occupe de tout et on passe pour un pro du 4x4 !

L'équipe du Guide de l'auto a aussi eu la chance d'examiner le dessous d'un LR4. Des différentiels au boîtier de transfert en passant par les longerons du châssis, les suspensions et les freins, tout est gros. Et tout est propre à Land Rover, aucune pièce provenant de Ford. Ce qui implique des coûts d'entretien faramineux. Car le moteur, le réservoir d'essence et le système d'échappement ont beau être bien protégés pour la conduite hors route, n'empêche qu'on reste surpris de constater une couette de fils vulnérable derrière la roue arrière gauche et de fluets bras de suspension active en plastique.

Sur la route, le LR4 étonne par son agilité. La direction n'est pas des plus précises, le roulis en virage est important, mais on se plaît à le conduire, principalement à cause du confort de ses suspensions. Curieusement, cette grosse boîte n'est pas trop sensible aux vents latéraux.

Le LR3 était un véhicule très raffiné. Le LR4 en remet une couche. Malgré ses lignes très carrées, à la limite du classique, nombreux sont les gens qui se retournent sur son passage. Dans le fond, c'est peut-être ce qui impressionne le plus les propriétaires de Land Rover...

Alain Morin

PHOTOS : ALAIN MORIN

Catégorie	VUS
Échelle de prix	59 990 $
Garanties	4 ans/80 000 km, 4 ans/80 000 km
Assemblage	n.d.
Cote d'assurance	moyenne

CHÂSSIS - DONNÉES POUR LR V8

Emp/lon/lar/haut	2 885/4 829/1 915/1 831 mm
Coffre	1 260 à 2 476 litres
Réservoir	86 litres
Nombre coussins sécurité	6
Antipatinage / contrôle stabilité	oui / oui
Suspension avant	indépendante, double triangulation
Suspension arrière	indépendante, double triangulation
Freins avant / arrière	disque (ABS) / disque (ABS)
Direction	à crémaillère, ass. variable
Diamètre de braquage	11,5 m
Pneus avant / arrière	P255/55R19 / P255/55R19
Poids	2 587 kg
Capacité de remorquage	3 500 kg (7 716 lb)

COMPOSANTES MÉCANIQUES

LR V8

Cylindrée, soupapes, alim.	V8 5,0 litres 32 s atmos.
Puissance / Couple	375 chevaux / 375 lb-pi
Tr. base (opt) / rouage base (opt)	A6 / Int
0-100 / 80-120 / 100-0 km/h	8,4 s / 7,0 s / 42 m (est)
Type ess. / ville / autoroute	Super / 17,1 / 11,6 l/100 km

DANS LA MÊME CATÉGORIE

Acura MDX, BMW X5, Infiniti FX, Lexus RX, Mercedes-Benz Classe M, Porsche Cayenne, Volkswagen Touareg, Volvo XC90

DU NOUVEAU EN 2011

Aucun changement majeur

NOS IMPRESSIONS

Agrément de conduite :	8/10
Fiabilité :	4/10
Sécurité :	8/10
Qualités hivernales :	9/10
Espace intérieur :	8/10
Confort :	8/10

www.landrover.com

Plus d'informations dans la section statistiques en dernière partie du Guide

AU-DELÀ DES SENTIERS BATTUS

En 1948, Maurice Wilks, alors à l'emploi de Rover, dessinait à partir d'un châssis de Jeep un premier Land Rover, baptisé à juste titre Série 1. Les Land Rover allaient sans tarder dévoiler de redoutables aptitudes en hors route. Avec les années, ces véhicules britanniques sont devenus de plus en plus luxueux tout en conservant leur robustesse initiale. Aujourd'hui, les produits Land Rover font partie de la noblesse britannique.

Le plus bel exemple de ce mélange réussi de robustesse et de noblesse est le Land Rover Range Rover. Tous les autres Land Rover, bien qu'ils fassent partie intégrante de la prestigieuse famille, doivent leur renommée au Range Rover. Le futur LRX sera sans doute renié haut et fort par les mordus de la marque (et ce, même s'il s'avère réussi !), le LR2 n'est, toujours selon les puristes, qu'un véhicule d'entrée de gamme, le LR4 est un Range Rover en plus petit et le Range Rover Sport une extrapolation pour plaire à une clientèle particulière. Il n'y a pas à en douter, le Range Rover est LE Land Rover par excellence, lui qui a fêté, à l'été 2010, ses 40 ans.

DE 24 À 23 BIÈRES PAR JOUR...

L'an dernier, Land Rover a fait un véritable cadeau à ses fans. De nouveaux moteurs ! Exit les déplorables 4,4 et 4,2 litres surcompressés, goinfres comme un ogre affamé devant un petit chat sans défense. Place au V8 de 5,0 litres, avec ou sans surcompresseur. Pour être bien franc avec vous, les 375 chevaux et 375 livres-pied de couple suffisent amplement la plupart du temps. Ils permettent à cette masse de plus de 2500 kilos de faire le 0-100 km/h en 7,6 secondes et le 80-120 en environ 6,0, le tout dans un superbe grondement du V8 qui fait oublier que chaque accélération demande au moteur la même quantité d'essence qu'un Boeing au décollage... Dire qu'il consomme moins que celui qu'il remplace ! Ceux qui aiment mieux un véhicule qui, à chaque accélération, requiert le débit quotidien des chutes Niagara, sans parler d'un prix d'achat exorbitant, se tourneront vers le 5,0 litres Supercharged de 510 chevaux. Curieusement, il ne permet pas au Range de remorquer une once de plus que la version atmosphérique.

Dans les deux cas, le fonctionnement de la transmission automatique à six rapports est sans reproches et contribue à l'impression de plénitude ressentie au volant. La direction pourrait être plus vive et précise, mais en conduite hors route, ces défauts deviennent des qualités. Et comme le Range est un expert en la matière, nous ne lui en tiendront pas rigueur. Ce dernier possède une multitude d'atouts qui lui permettent de passer n'importe où. Un châssis d'une extraordinaire solidité, une suspension pneumatique permettant de hausser la garde au sol jusqu'à 11,1 pouces (28,2 cm !), un angle d'attaque de 34 degrés et de départ de 26,6, la possibilité de rouler sans problème dans 27 pouces d'eau et des caméras judicieusement placées qui permettent au conducteur de voir tout le tour font partie des qualités du Range Rover en hors route. Le Terrain Response aussi. Ce bouton situé sur la

FEU VERT

- Quintessence du classicisme
- Habitacle supra luxueux
- Moteurs très puissants
- Extraordinaires capacités 4x4
- Capacité de remorquage intéressante

FEU ROUGE

- Prix démentiels
- Consommation outrageuse
- Fiabilité honteuse (mais à la hausse semble-t-il...)
- Coûts d'entretien surréels
- Dépréciation extraordinaire

console centrale permet de choisir entre plusieurs types de terrain. Selon la demande du conducteur, un ordinateur central modifie les paramètres de gestion du moteur, de la transmission, des trois différentiels, des suspensions et des systèmes de contrôle de la traction et de la stabilité latérale. Ouf ! Tout ça c'est bien beau, mais ça fait beaucoup d'électronique et dans le passé, ce constructeur a prouvé hors de tout doute son incompétence en matière de fiabilité de tels systèmes... Contrairement à la plupart des marques produisant des 4x4, beaucoup de gens possédant un Land Rover âgé de plus de dix ans ne se gênent pas pour se servir de leur véhicule pour chasser le lièvre ou la truite. Souhaitons que l'électronique tienne le coup jusque-là...

CHARME SURANNÉ

Les lignes extérieures du Range Rover n'ont guère évolué depuis 1970 et ce ne sont pas les timides retouches apportées l'an dernier qui vont y changer quoi que ce soit. Mais pour les puristes, ce frigo sur roues demeure la quintessence du charme. L'habitacle, quant à lui, ressemble à s'y méprendre à celui de la génération précédente et il faut avoir l'œil pour trouver les différences. Le tableau de bord présente une instrumentation qui paraîtrait veillotte si elle n'était pas entièrement numérique. L'effet est saisissant. Lorsqu'on roule en mode 4x4, l'odomètre se déplace et fait place à des informations pertinentes, surtout quand la situation est corsée. Voilà l'avantage d'une telle technologie.

Dire que l'habitacle du Range est luxueux serait un euphémisme. Les bois sont nobles, les cuirs doivent provenir de vaches royales et les rares pièces de plastique affichent une excellente qualité, de même que les tapis, moelleux à souhait. Les sièges font preuve d'un confort quasiment indécent, or y accéder demande une souplesse certaine. Des marchepieds seraient bienvenus, mais comme ils seraient contraires à la bienséance en conduite hors route, on comprend mieux leur absence. L'habitacle est vaste et d'un silence monacal, même s'il y avait l'explosion d'une bombe à proximité. Les sièges arrière sont aussi très confortables et leur dossier s'abaisse pour agrandir le coffre.

Le Range Rover était, est et demeurera l'authentique VUS grand luxe pour plusieurs années. Mais pour y parvenir, Land Rover devra prévoir des moteurs moins gourmands donc mieux adaptés aux tendances actuelles.

Alain Morin

PHOTOS : LAND ROVER

LAND ROVER RANGE ROVER

Catégorie	VUS
Échelle de prix	93 830 $ à 111 900 $ (2010)
Garanties	4 ans/80 000 km, 4 ans/80 000 km
Assemblage	Solihull, Angleterre
Cote d'assurance	n.d.

CHÂSSIS - DONNÉES POUR LR V8 SUPERCHARGED

Emp/lon/lar/haut	2 880/4 972/1 956/1 877 mm
Coffre	994 à 2 099 litres
Réservoir	104 litres
Nombre coussins sécurité	6
Antipatinage / contrôle stabilité	oui / oui
Suspension avant	indépendante, jambes de force
Suspension arrière	indépendante, double triangulation
Freins avant / arrière	disque (ABS) / disque (ABS)
Direction	à crémaillère, ass. variable
Diamètre de braquage	11,6 m
Pneus avant / arrière	P255/50R20 / P255/50R20
Poids	2 672 kg
Capacité de remorquage	3 500 kg (7 716 lb)

COMPOSANTES MÉCANIQUES

LR V8

Cylindrée, soupapes, alim.	V8 5,0 litres 32 s atmos.
Puissance / Couple	375 chevaux / 375 lb-pi
Tr. base (opt) / rouage base (opt)	A6 / Int
0-100 / 80-120 / 100-0 km/h	7,6 s / n.d. / n.d.
Type ess. / ville / autoroute	Super / 17,5 / 11,6 l/100 km

LR V8 Supercharged

Cylindrée, soupapes, alim.	V8 5,0 litres 32 s surcomp.
Puissance / Couple	510 chevaux / 461 lb-pi
Tr. base (opt) / rouage base (opt)	A6 / Int
0-100 / 80-120 / 100-0 km/h	6,2 s / n.d. / n.d.
Type ess. / ville / autoroute	Super / 18,1 / 11,7 l/100 km

DANS LA MÊME CATÉGORIE

Cadillac Escalade, Infiniti QX, Lexus LX, Lincoln Navigator, Mercedes-Benz Classe G, Mercedes-Benz Classe GL

DU NOUVEAU EN 2011

Aucun changement majeur

NOS IMPRESSIONS

Agrément de conduite :	8/10
Fiabilité :	4/10
Sécurité :	8/10
Qualités hivernales :	9/10
Espace intérieur :	7/10
Confort :	8/10

www.landrover.com

Plus d'informations dans la section statistiques en dernière partie du Guide

PAS DE TATAOUINAGES!

Il y a à peine trois ans, la marque Tata s'était fait connaître grâce à sa Nano, la voiture de production la moins dispendieuse au monde. Rien de vraiment surprenant de la part d'un constructeur indien, un pays où, on le sait, le peuple ne roule pas sur l'or. Donc, c'était entendu, les Tatas allaient demeurer bien tranquilles dans leur coin. Mais, surprise, Tata n'était pas une petite entreprise de rien. Même que c'était un géant de l'automobile... Qui plus est, il s'est porté acquéreur des marques Jaguar et Land Rover, abandonnées par Ford. C'était, ont cru plusieurs à ce moment, la fin de ces deux fleurons britanniques. Après tout, comment être tata et conserver sa noblesse...

Pourtant, à l'aube de 2011, force est d'admettre que Tata, malgré des heures difficiles, semble s'y connaître beaucoup plus en matière de véhicules de grand luxe que Ford. En fait, il ne s'agit sans doute pas, comme dans bien des domaines, de s'y connaître. Il suffit d'un peu de bonne volonté. L'an dernier, Land Rover remaniait une partie de sa gamme. Ainsi, les LR4, Range Rover et Range Rover Sport ont été revus. Le Range Rover Sport (appelons-le RRS, ce sera plus simple), de son côté, a vu ses parties avant et arrière modifiées. Ces changements sont subtils mais assez efficaces. C'est surtout dans l'habitacle que les modifications sont les plus significatives. Le tableau de bord, tout nouveau, affiche un style moderne (un adjectif rarement associé à Land Rover...) et présente moins de boutons que l'ancien et, surtout, ils sont plus gros donc plus facilement manipulables, sauf ceux situés à l'extrême droite, plus difficiles à atteindre sauf pour les joueurs de basket. La console centrale, très imposante, gruge passablement l'espace dévolu aux gens assis à l'avant. Bien

entendu, on retrouve toujours, au centre du tableau de bord, l'horloge analogique ronde qui ajoute à cette mer de prestige.

UN HABITACLE TOUT EN LUXE

Le conducteur s'installe devant un volant au boudin épais qui se prend bien en main. La visibilité tout le tour, sans être exceptionnelle, est pas mal du tout, compte tenu du gabarit imposant du RRS. Inutile de chercher des bibittes du côté de la qualité des matériaux, extraordinairement relevée. Le RRS, curieusement, n'est pas une version sportive du Range Rover. Il possède son propre châssis, plus court. Si l'espace aux places arrière n'est pas touché, préservant ainsi le confort, c'est le coffre qui écope. Malgré tout, il peut contenir passablement même quand les dossiers des sièges sont relevés. Pour les baisser, il faut auparavant relever l'assise, une opération indigne d'un véhicule qui flirte allègrement avec les 75 000 $. Le hayon, comme sur les autres produits de la marque, ouvre en deux parties.

Le « Sport » dans le nom Range Rover Sport n'est pas usurpé même s'il partage les mêmes moteurs que le Range Rover tout court. On retrouve tout d'abord un V8 de 5,0 litres atmosphérique

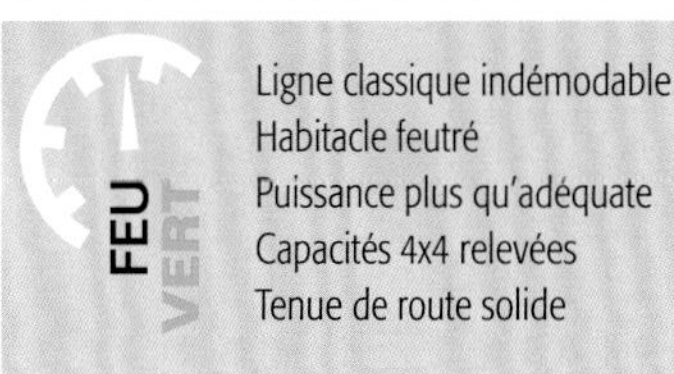

- Ligne classique indémodable
- Habitacle feutré
- Puissance plus qu'adéquate
- Capacités 4x4 relevées
- Tenue de route solide

- Consommation outrageuse
- Dimensions importantes
- Fiabilité d'une connaissance qui vous doit de l'argent
- Dépréciation phénoménale
- Entretien $$$ $$$ $$$ $$$ $$$$

développant 375 chevaux et autant de couple. Les 7,6 secondes qu'il met pour effectuer le 0-100 km/h devraient satisfaire la plupart des gens. Sa consommation déclarée est de 11,2 litres/100 km... sur une autoroute et de 18,4 litres en ville. De super, noblesse oblige... Pour encourager les pauvres pétrolières, il y a aussi le 5,0 litres surcompressé de 510 chevaux. Les performances sont alors époustouflantes, rien de moins. Par contre, ce monument à la consommation ne permet pas de remorquer une once de plus que l'autre V8. Bizarre.

La transmission est une automatique à six rapports fabriquée par ZF. Elle comprend trois modes (Normal, Sport et Manuel) et elle s'acoquine avec un système 4x4 très sophistiqué qu'on retrouve dans les autres Land Rover. Même s'il est plus axé vers le sport que les autres, le RRS peut pratiquement aussi bien faire dans les sentiers les plus difficiles, ses angles d'approche, de départ étant quasi-identiques à ceux du Range Rover (34 et 27 degrés respectivement), mais son angle ventral (*ramp breakover*) est un peu moins élevé (25 degrés contre 30). Grâce à ses suspensions pneumatiques, il est possible d'obtenir avec la version « de base » une garde au sol de 255 mm (10 pouces) à l'avant et de 310 mm (12,2 pouces) à l'arrière.

VRAIMENT SPORTIF

L'équipe du Guide de l'auto a eu la chance de conduire un Range Rover Sport immédiatement après avoir laissé les clés d'un Range Rover. Dès les premiers mètres, on note des suspensions plus fermes, et ce, même sur le mode Normal. En mode Sport, elles sont carrément dures. Cependant, les sièges superbement étudiés et un habitacle tout en onctuosité ne rendent pas les randonnées pénibles. Loin de là ! La direction est vive et précise. Même si les dimensions du véhicule sont intimidantes, on se prend assez vite au plaisir de le conduire rapidement dans les courbes serrées. Le transfert de poids est bien contenu et la caisse ne penche pas indûment. Franchement, j'avais l'impression de conduire un Porsche Cayenne Turbo qui aurait possédé un bel habitacle... Cependant, j'aurais aimé mettre ces deux gros sportifs sur une piste. Je ne suis pas sûr que le RRS ait pu suivre le rythme de l'autre.

Il est cependant un élément sur lequel Tata devra se pencher avec beaucoup d'attentions : la fiabilité. Aux dernières nouvelles, Land Rover croupissait encore dans les bas-fonds du classement de J.D.Powers, une firme spécialisée dans les recherches sur la fiabilité.

Alain Morin

PHOTOS : LAND ROVER

LAND ROVER RANGE ROVER SPORT

Catégorie	VUS
Échelle de prix	73 200$ à 87 400$ (2010)
Garanties	4 ans/80 000 km, 4 ans/80 000 km
Assemblage	Solihull, Angleterre
Cote d'assurance	n.d.

CHÂSSIS - DONNÉES POUR LR V8

Emp/lon/lar/haut	2 745/4 783/1 932/1 789 mm
Coffre	958 à 2 013 litres
Réservoir	88 litres
Nombre coussins sécurité	6
Antipatinage / contrôle stabilité	oui / oui
Suspension avant	indépendante, double triangulation
Suspension arrière	indépendante, double triangulation
Freins avant / arrière	disque (ABS) / disque (ABS)
Direction	à crémaillère, ass. variable
Diamètre de braquage	11,6 m
Pneus avant / arrière	P255/50R19 / P255/50R19
Poids	2 489 kg
Capacité de remorquage	3 500 kg (7 716 lb)

COMPOSANTES MÉCANIQUES

LR V8

Cylindrée, soupapes, alim.	V8 5,0 litres 32 s atmos.
Puissance / Couple	375 chevaux / 375 lb-pi
Tr. base (opt) / rouage base (opt)	A6 / Int
0-100 / 80-120 / 100-0 km/h	7,6 s / n.d. / n.d.
Type ess. / ville / autoroute	Super / 18,4 / 11,2 l/100 km

LR V8 Supercharged

Cylindrée, soupapes, alim.	V8 5,0 litres 32 s surcomp.
Puissance / Couple	510 chevaux / 461 lb-pi
Tr. base (opt) / rouage base (opt)	A6 / Int
0-100 / 80-120 / 100-0 km/h	6,2 s / n.d. / n.d.
Type ess. / ville / autoroute	Super / 18,1 / 11,7 l/100 km

DANS LA MÊME CATÉGORIE

Audi Q7, BMW X5, BMW X6, Infiniti FX, Mercedes-Benz Classe M, Porsche Cayenne, Volvo XC90

DU NOUVEAU EN 2011

Aucun changement majeur

NOS IMPRESSIONS

Agrément de conduite :	8/10
Fiabilité :	4/10
Sécurité :	8/10
Qualités hivernales :	9/10
Espace intérieur :	7/10
Confort :	8/10

www.landrover.com

Plus d'informations dans la section statistiques en dernière partie du Guide

CAMRY *PIMPÉE* OU AUTHENTIQUE LEXUS?

La division Lexus de Toyota jouit d'une excellente réputation à presque tous les égards. Lorsqu'une personne annonce à son entourage qu'elle roule en Lexus, les gens sont généralement impressionnés. Toutefois, il existe une exception: la ES350. En effet, chaque fois qu'un propriétaire de ES350 mentionne qu'il conduit ce modèle Lexus, les gens se regardent, quelque peu gênés. Serait-il possible que ce propriétaire ait payé trop cher pour une Camry arborant un écusson Lexus?

C'est le problème des constructeurs qui produisent une marque plus populiste, notamment la Toyota dans le cas qui nous concerne. En effet, plusieurs modèles Lexus sont établis à partir de plates-formes de véhicules Toyota. De quoi donner raison aux snobs qui lèvent leur nez sur ceux-ci. Chez Mercedes-Benz ou BMW par exemple, il n'existe pas de marque cadette, donc pas de problème d'arbre généalogique automobile trahissant le caractère plébéien de tel ou tel modèle. Pour en revenir à notre Lexus, il est vrai qu'elle est dérivée de la Toyota Camry, mais elle possède quand même sa part d'éléments exclusifs à toutes les Lexus.

LA QUALITÉ, TOUJOURS LA QUALITÉ

La réputation de Toyota et de sa filiale Lexus en a pris pour son rhume au cours des derniers mois avec des rappels en cascade. Sans vouloir diminuer l'importance de la chose, ces rappels ont porté sur des éléments précis et non sur la qualité générale de la fabrication et de l'assemblage des voitures. Et c'est là le point fort de notre modèle d'essai. En effet, la division Lexus est passée maître dans l'application d'une peinture sur la carrosserie pour obtenir un effet lissé et dépourvu de pelure d'orange que presque aucune autre marque ne peut dupliquer. De plus, il faut souligner que la qualité d'assemblage et de fabrication est sans reproche. D'ailleurs, cette marque sert toujours d'étalon dans l'industrie pour évaluer la qualité des produits de marques concurrentes. Quant à la silhouette, elle est générique au possible, et ce, malgré de nombreuses retouches esthétiques effectuées l'an dernier aussi bien à la partie avant qu'à l'arrière. On n'achète certainement pas cette Lexus pour se faire remarquer.

La très grande qualité des matériaux utilisés dans l'habitacle et l'assemblage des composantes est à souligner. D'ailleurs, une fois qu'on monte à bord, on a l'impression d'être vraiment dans une Lexus et non dans une simple Camry qui aurait reçu une sellerie de cuir de meilleure qualité. De plus, avec les appliques en bois, le boudin du volant partiellement en bois, les cadrans indicateurs électroluminescents, les petits détails de finition propres à cette marque, on a l'impression d'en avoir pour notre argent. On aurait par contre dû améliorer la console centrale qui fait quelque peu rétro avec sa partie supérieure arrondie. Cela manque d'élégance et convient assez mal à cette voiture.

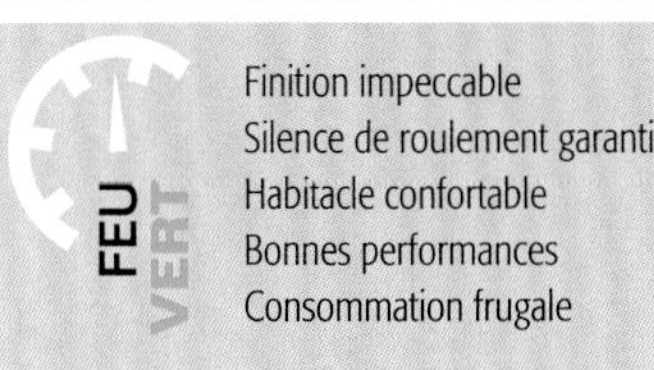

FEU VERT

Finition impeccable
Silence de roulement garanti
Habitacle confortable
Bonnes performances
Consommation frugale

FEU ROUGE

Direction engourdie
Roulis dans les virages
Silhouette anonyme
Gare aux groupes d'options !
Conduite ennuyeuse

L'habitabilité de la voiture est bonne, l'insonorisation parfaite, et même les places arrière permettront aux personnes de grande taille d'être passablement confortables. À ce chapitre donc, on a bien réussi la transformation de Toyota à Lexus.

AIMEZ-VOUS CONDUIRE ?

La plupart des chroniqueurs automobiles critiquent bon nombre de véhicules de cette marque pour leur manque d'agrément de conduite qui provoque parfois des risques d'endormissement au volant. Je fais partie de ce groupe qui se plaint de la direction engourdie, du manque de *feedback* de la route et de cette insonorisation poussée qui nous isole totalement. Il y a certaines rares exceptions dans la gamme Lexus, mais la plupart nous proposent ce type de comportement qui ne privilégie absolument pas l'agrément de conduite. Mais il ne faut pas oublier que pour plusieurs, une voiture intéressante n'est pas nécessairement agréable à conduire.

En effet, j'ai rencontré au cours de ma carrière bien des gens qui recherchent une voiture confortable et fiable, un point c'est tout. Et si leurs ressources financières sont plus élevées, ils se tourneront vers des modèles dont la qualité de fabrication surpasse de loin leur potentiel routier. C'est le cas de la ES. Il ne faut pas en conclure pour autant que c'est une voiture qui ne tient pas la route. Il est vrai que si vous conduisez avec exubérance, vous devrez combattre un important roulis de caisse, et une direction qui ne vous informe pas toujours, et dont l'assistance est trop généreuse. Mais dans l'ensemble, c'est dans la bonne moyenne. D'ailleurs, dans la plupart des cas, les acheteurs de cette berline s'émerveilleront du confort des sièges, de la qualité du cuir, et ne se plaindront même pas une seconde du soutien lombaire et latéral déficient. Ils s'amuseront avec le système de navigation par satellite, et apprécieront la sonorité du système audio et la consommation passablement réduite de ce moteur V6 de 3,5 litres. Mieux encore, ce moteur est silencieux et très doux.

Quoi demander de mieux si vous n'aimez pas conduire et que l'automobile est pour vous un simple moyen de transport ? Cela explique bien entendu la popularité de la ES350 qui est pénalisée au chapitre de l'agrément de conduite, mais qui en retour vous en offre beaucoup en fait de luxe et de confort.

Denis Duquet

PHOTOS : LEXUS

Catégorie	Berline
Échelle de prix	41 950 $ (2010)
Garanties	4 ans/80 000 km, 6 ans/110 000 km
Assemblage	Kyushu, Japon
Cote d'assurance	bonne

CHÂSSIS - DONNÉES POUR 350

Emp/lon/lar/haut	2 775/4 855/1 820/1 450 mm
Coffre	416 litres
Réservoir	70 litres
Nombre coussins sécurité	8
Antipatinage / contrôle stabilité	oui / oui
Suspension avant	indépendante, jambes de force
Suspension arrière	indépendante, jambes de force
Freins avant / arrière	disque (ABS) / disque (ABS)
Direction	à crémaillère, ass. variable
Diamètre de braquage	11,8 m
Pneus avant / arrière	P215/55R17 / P215/55R17
Poids	1 624 kg
Capacité de remorquage	n.d.

COMPOSANTES MÉCANIQUES

350

Cylindrée, soupapes, alim.	V6 3,5 litres 24 s atmos.
Puissance / Couple	272 chevaux / 254 lb-pi
Tr. base (opt) / rouage base (opt)	A6 / Tr
0-100 / 80-120 / 100-0 km/h	6,9 s / 4,7 s / 41,0 m
Type ess. / ville / autoroute	Ordinaire / 10,9 / 7,2 l/100 km

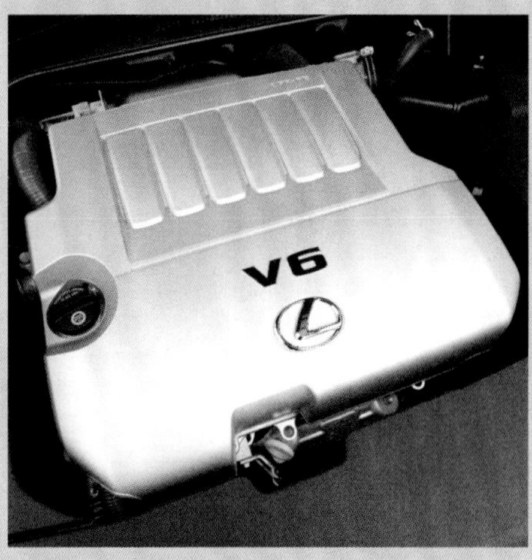

DANS LA MÊME CATÉGORIE

Acura TL, Buick Lucerne, Cadillac CTS, Chrysler 300, Ford Taurus, Hyundai Genesis, Lincoln MKZ, Mercedes-Benz Classe C, Nissan Maxima, Toyota Avalon

DU NOUVEAU EN 2011

Aucun changement majeur

NOS IMPRESSIONS

Agrément de conduite :	6/10
Fiabilité :	8/10
Sécurité :	8/10
Qualités hivernales :	8/10
Espace intérieur :	8/10
Confort :	8/10

www.lexus.ca

Plus d'informations dans la section statistiques en dernière partie du Guide

LES ANNÉES PASSENT ET LA GS DEMEURE

« Les années passent et la GS demeure ». C'est en ces mots que notre collègue et néanmoins ami Marc Lachapelle débutait son texte sur la berline de luxe de Lexus dans le Guide de l'auto 2010. Une année plus tard, la GS demeure encore. Plusieurs personnes prévoyaient son remplacement par une toute nouvelle série en 2011 mais il faudra sans doute attendre l'an prochain. Car, de toute évidence, la GS est sur la voie de desserte. Cette année, la moitié des modèles sont éliminés.

La moitié des modèles, ça veut dire deux. Jusqu'à l'année dernière, on retrouvait la GS350, la GS350 AWD, la GS460 et la GS450h, une hybride surprenante comme nous le verrons plus loin. Désormais, il faut se concentrer sur la GS350 AWD et la GS450h. La décision de Lexus peut s'expliquer assez facilement dans le cas de la GS350 à laquelle les clients préféraient la GS350 AWD avec son rouage intégral. Quant à la très puissante GS460, elle reprenait la mécanique de sa grande sœur, la LS460 tout en étant moins chère, ce qui cannibalisait assurément les ventes de cette dernière. D'un autre côté, la GS460 proposait le même niveau de performance que sa sœur hybride (GS450h) pour un prix similaire mais une image écologique infiniment moins intéressante. Bref, on s'est débarrassé du bois mort.

Les deux voitures qui demeurent s'avèrent intéressantes à plus d'un point de vue. Tout d'abord, leur robe, même après six ans, demeure dans le coup. Remarquez qu'on en voit si peu souvent sur les routes que personne n'a eu le temps de se fatiguer de ces lignes, lignes qui furent les premières à porter le message L-Finesse si cher aux designers de Lexus. Ne me demandez surtout pas d'expliquer cette philosophie, l'art abstrait et moi ayant des rapports tendus depuis plusieurs années. Personnellement, je trouve la voiture belle au point de me battre pour la défendre. Vous ne partagez pas mon avis ? Je suis bien d'accord avec vous…

UN HABITACLE CONVIVIAL… C'EST LE MOINS QU'ON PUISSE DIRE !

Lorsque la portière se referme, conducteur et passagers sont enfermés dans un cocon tout à fait Lexus. Les cuirs, les boiseries, les plastiques et les appliqués de chrome ou d'aluminium sont de belle qualité et pour trouver un défaut dans leur assemblage, bonne chance… Le silence de roulement en devient exaspérant tellement il est soigné, l'équipement est plus que complet et le confort est, on s'en doute, très relevé. En passant, comment terminer ce tour rapide de l'habitacle sans parler de la chaîne audio Mark Levinson, créée tout spécialement pour ravir les oreilles les plus difficiles. Bien des cinéma-maison ne possèdent pas une telle sonorité. Mais il faut bien trouver à redire… le coffre n'est pas très grand avec ses 360 litres (300 pour l'hybride), des données qui sont à peu près les mêmes que celles d'une vulgaire berline Hyundai Accent.

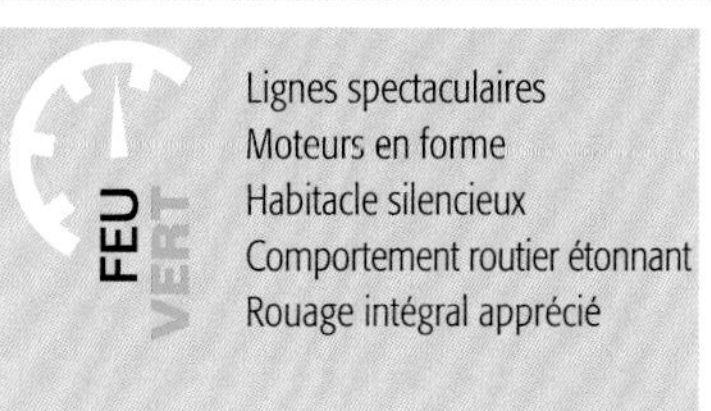

FEU VERT
- Lignes spectaculaires
- Moteurs en forme
- Habitacle silencieux
- Comportement routier étonnant
- Rouage intégral apprécié

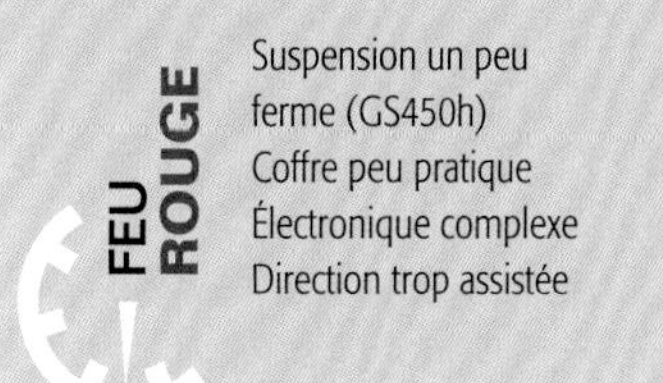

FEU ROUGE
- Suspension un peu ferme (GS450h)
- Coffre peu pratique
- Électronique complexe
- Direction trop assistée

Cette année, comme on l'a vu précédemment, la GS350 reçoit d'office le rouage intégral. Son V6 de 3,5 litres (d'où le 350) développe 303 chevaux et 274 livres-pied de couple, des données qui peuvent sembler bien maigrichonnes compte tenu du statut de la voiture et, surtout, de son poids de près de 1800 kilos. Malgré tout, les accélérations et reprises ne sont pas piquées des vers et la consommation d'essence est retenue. La transmission automatique à six rapports relaie la cavalerie aux quatre roues grâce à un rouage intégral plutôt performant. En utilisation normale, ce dernier fait parvenir le couple aux roues arrière dans une proportion de 70%. Cette répartition peut aller jusqu'à 50/50 lorsque le besoin se fait sentir.

UNE HYBRIDE LÂCHÉE LOUSSE

Mais la vedette de la gamme, c'est la GS450h mue par un moteur à essence de V6 3,5 litres (d'où ne provient pas le suffixe, Lexus estimant que la puissance du moteur à essence et celui du moteur électrique équivalait à celle d'un V8 de 4,5 litres. Vive la constance...) Nous disions donc que le V6 de 3,5 litres développe 253 chevaux et 267 livres-pied de couple. Cependant, lorsqu'il est associé au moteur électrique, l'ensemble donne 340 chevaux et 362 livres-pied de couple ce qui assure des performances de haut niveau. Dans le cas présent, seules les roues arrière sont motrices.

La Lexus GS, hybride ou pas, fait preuve d'un grand confort, on l'a vu, mais aussi d'un dynamisme routier surprenant. La tenue de route impressionne et on ne se rend pas compte qu'on conduit une voiture aussi lourde. Malheureusement, la direction est trop légère et peu portée sur le «feedback». Si vous n'étiez pas des nôtres l'an passé et celui d'avant, sachez que notre Marc Lachapelle préféré (c'est vrai qu'on en connaît juste un...) a piloté une GS450h durant la très éprouvante course Targa Terre-Neuve, une épreuve de 2200 km. La grosse berline s'en est tirée avec brio, surtout la deuxième année alors qu'il s'agissait d'une version avec différentiel autobloquant et que l'échappement était moins restrictif. Mais, surtout, les différents systèmes électroniques d'aide à la conduite avaient été réduits au silence.

Pour l'an prochain, on chuchote que la GS serait renouvelée et qu'elle proposerait un modèle très sportif, la GS-F, de la même trempe que la plus petite IS-F. En regardant ce que les ingénieurs de Lexus ont réussi à faire avec la GS actuelle, on est en droit de s'attendre à toute une bagnole!

Alain Morin

PHOTOS: LEXUS

Catégorie	Berline
Échelle de prix	54650$ à 71750$
Garanties	4 ans/80000 km, 6 ans/110000 km
Assemblage	Tahara, Japon
Cote d'assurance	n.d.

CHÂSSIS - DONNÉES POUR 450H

Emp/lon/lar/haut	2850/4825/1820/1425 mm
Coffre	292 litres
Réservoir	65 litres
Nombre coussins sécurité	8
Antipatinage / contrôle stabilité	oui / oui
Suspension avant	indépendante, double triangulation
Suspension arrière	indépendante, multibras
Freins avant / arrière	disque (ABS) / disque (ABS)
Direction	à crémaillère, ass. variable électrique
Diamètre de braquage	11,2 m
Pneus avant / arrière	P245/40ZR18 / P245/40ZR18
Poids	1875 kg
Capacité de remorquage	n.d.

COMPOSANTES MÉCANIQUES

350 TI

Cylindrée, soupapes, alim.	V6 3,5 litres 24 s atmos.
Puissance / Couple	303 chevaux / 274 lb-pi
Tr. base (opt) / rouage base (opt)	A6 / Int
0-100 / 80-120 / 100-0 km/h	7,2 s / 6,4 s / 37,0 m
Type ess. / ville / autoroute	Ordinaire / 11,6 / 8 l/100 km

450h

Cylindrée, soupapes, alim.	V6 3,5 litres 24 s atmos.
Puissance / Couple	253 ch (340 total) / 267 lb-pi
Tr. base (opt) / rouage base (opt)	CVT / Prop
0-100 / 80-120 / 100-0 km/h	6,0 s / 4,6 s / 39,1 m
Type ess. / ville / autoroute	Ordinaire / 8,7 / 7,8 l/100 km

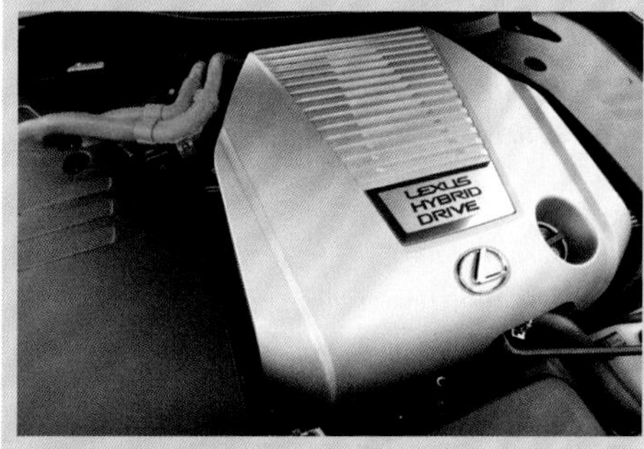

DANS LA MÊME CATÉGORIE

Acura RL, Audi A6, BMW Série 5, Cadillac STS, Infiniti M, Lincoln MKS, Mercedes-Benz Classe E, Volvo S80

DU NOUVEAU EN 2011

Modèles GS350 et GS460 abandonnés

NOS IMPRESSIONS

Agrément de conduite:	8/10
Fiabilité:	10/10
Sécurité:	8/10
Qualités hivernales:	8/10
Espace intérieur:	8/10
Confort:	8/10

www.lexus.ca

Plus d'informations dans la section statistiques en dernière partie du Guide

LES VERTUS DE L'HUMILITÉ

Dans le *Guide de l'auto* de l'an dernier, dans son article sur le Lexus GX470, Denis Duquet nous entretenait de la quête de Toyota/Lexus pour devenir le numéro un mondial de l'automobile. Pour ce faire, l'entreprise nippone se devait de présenter un produit dans chaque créneau, quitte à cannibaliser les produits Toyota pour en faire des Lexus. De plus, monsieur Duquet dénonçait le comportement condescendant de certains dirigeants.

Le temps semble avoir donné raison à notre rédacteur en chef préféré, les malheurs s'abattant sur Toyota/Lexus comme les frais sur un utilisateur de téléphone cellulaire. D'ailleurs, il est assez ironique de constater que la présentation du nouveau GX460 à la presse québécoise a eu lieu en janvier 2010 (en tant que modèle 2010), la veille de l'annonce du premier des problèmes affectant les produits de la marque japonaise, à savoir une pédale d'accélérateur trop zélée. Et, fait assez rare, le GX a perdu environ 2 % de sa dénomination alors que généralement, on cherche à impressionner davantage les consommateurs. Par exemple, un GX480 serait plus puissant qu'un GX470.

QUI PERD GAGNE

Pourtant, ce n'est pas le cas. En passant au V8 de 4,6 litres, on gagne 38 chevaux et 6 livres-pied de couple. Quelquefois, moins c'est mieux! Ce moteur, d'une souplesse et d'une discrétion exemplaire, se veut des plus modernes et j'irais même jusqu'à dire, assez économique. Toyota promet 14,1 litres aux 100 km en ville et 9,8 sur la route, mais l'ordinateur de bord de notre véhicule d'essai indiquait 12,9 après une semaine passée à 80 % sur les routes. Cependant, il ne faut pas oublier que ce moteur doit promener 2 320 kilos, un poids loin d'être plume, tout en assurant des performances relevées. Bien entendu, le nom Lexus réclame de l'essence super...

La transmission est une automatique à six rapports d'une grande douceur. Le rouage 4x4 Torsen à temps plein permet de passer à peu près n'importe où et personne, ou presque, n'exploitera la moitié de ces capacités hors route. Pour ceux que ça intéresserait, la garde au sol est de 20 cm pouces tandis que les angles d'attaque et de départ sont, respectivement, de 28 et 25 degrés. Le GX460 de « base » jouit d'une gamme basse et du contrôle de descente en pente. La version haut de gamme, Ultra Premium, reçoit, en plus, le Sélecteur Tout-Terrain qui permet d'optimiser la traction selon le type de surface sur laquelle on roule. D'ailleurs, on retrouve déjà ce système, à quelques petites nuances près, dans le Toyota 4Runner duquel le GX est intimement dérivé. Cependant, on remarque plusieurs différences entre les deux véhicules, question de respecter les normes plus élevées de Lexus. Par exemple, le 4Runner possède un six cylindres tandis que le GX460 en a deux de plus. La transmission de ce dernier présente un rapport supplémentaire et la capacité de remorquage est plus élevée chez le Lexus (6 500 livres contre 5 000).

FEU VERT

- Luxe et confort omniprésents
- Habitacle silencieux
- Finition monacale
- Très habile en hors route
- Grandes capacités de remorquage

FEU ROUGE

- Dimensions irraisonnables
- Consommation élevée
- Direction déconnectée
- Comportement routier de type « bof »
- Troisième rangée de sièges risible

Si ce n'était des marchepieds intégrés, accéder à l'habitacle du GX460 serait plutôt ardu puisqu'il est haut sur pattes. Une fois monté à bord, on est frappé par le luxe et par la qualité des matériaux. Les sièges sont très confortables et font face à un tableau de bord de belle facture avec ses différents agencements de couleur et ses boiseries de qualité. L'espace, on s'en doute, ne fait pas défaut, tout comme les espaces de rangement. La deuxième rangée de sièges, de type 40/20/40 s'avère tout aussi accueillante malgré sa dureté initiale. Quant à la troisième rangée dont les dossiers s'abaissent à parts égales, permettez-nous d'en rire puisqu'elle est difficile d'accès et n'accueille que des gens sans jambes. Remarquez que plusieurs concurrents ne font guère mieux. Le coffre est superbement fini mais son seuil est très élevé. La porte arrière ouvre grâce à des pentures situées à droite. Plusieurs préféreraient un hayon même si la configuration du GX peut être très utile à l'occasion. La vitre ouvre séparément de la portière, une bénédiction quand vient le temps de transporter des objets longs.

UTILITAIRE SPORT... OÙ ÇA?

Il faudrait être passablement déconnecté de la réalité ou incroyablement naïf pour croire à la partie « sport » dans le terme « utilitaire sport » utilisé par Lexus pour définir son GX460. Dès les premiers tours de roue, la direction, inconsciente du travail des roues avant et imprécise, sert d'avertissement. Une courbe prise à une vitesse le moindrement élevée fait naître un roulis important. De plus, dès que les pneus glissent d'un seul millimètre, une panoplie de systèmes d'aide à la conduite intervient avec un « bip bip bip » plus stressant qu'informatif. D'ailleurs, malgré quelques virages serrés pris rapidement, le GX460 n'avait aucune intention de se retourner sur lui-même (on se souvient que Lexus avait effectué un rappel l'hiver dernier à la suite de plaintes plus ou moins justifiées, selon moi, concernant le risque de capotage). Même à des vitesses supra-illégales, on n'a aucune impression de la vélocité du véhicule. Au moins, la tenue de cap, même sur une route bosselée est excellente.

Par contre, il faut souligner le confort de l'habitacle et le silence de roulement. J'imagine qu'au moins 10 % du poids du GX460 est constitué de matériel isolant. De plus, malgré le roulis de la caisse et le manque de précision de la direction, il s'accroche au bitume avec une belle ténacité. C'est juste qu'à part des journalistes consciencieux, personne n'a intérêt à le pousser.

Alain Morin

PHOTOS : MARC LACHAPELLE

Catégorie	VUS
Échelle de prix	68 500 $ à 77 500 $
Garanties	4 ans/80 000 km, 6 ans/110 000 km
Assemblage	Tahara, Japon
Cote d'assurance	n.d.

CHÂSSIS - DONNÉES POUR 460 ULTRA PREMIUM

Emp/lon/lar/haut	2 790/4 805/1 885/1 875 mm
Coffre	692 à 1 525 litres
Réservoir	87 litres
Nombre coussins sécurité	6
Antipatinage / contrôle stabilité	oui / oui
Suspension avant	indépendante, double triangulation
Suspension arrière	essieu rigide, ressorts elliptiques
Freins avant / arrière	disque (ABS) / disque (ABS)
Direction	à crémaillère, assistée
Diamètre de braquage	11,6 m
Pneus avant / arrière	P265/60R18 / P265/60R18
Poids	2 326 kg
Capacité de remorquage	2 948 kg (6 499 lb)

COMPOSANTES MÉCANIQUES

GX460

Cylindrée, soupapes, alim.	V8 4,6 litres 32 s atmos.
Puissance / Couple	301 chevaux / 329 lb-pi
Tr. base (opt) / rouage base (opt)	A6 / Int
0-100 / 80-120 / 100-0 km/h	9,2 s / 7,1 s / 42,0 m (est)
Type ess. / ville / autoroute	Ordinaire / 14,1 / 9,8 l/100 km

DANS LA MÊME CATÉGORIE

Acura MDX, Audi Q7, BMW X5, Cadillac Escalade, Land Rover LR4, Lincoln Navigator, Mercedes-Benz Classe GL, Volvo XC90

DU NOUVEAU EN 2011

Nouveau modèle

NOS IMPRESSIONS

Agrément de conduite :	6/10
Fiabilité :	8/10
Sécurité :	10/10
Qualités hivernales :	8/10
Espace intérieur :	8/10
Confort :	8/10

www.lexus.ca

Plus d'informations dans la section statistiques en dernière partie du Guide

L'HYBRIDE... LA MOINS HYBRIDE!

Autant la Prius crie: « Hybride ! », autant la Lexus HS250h se fait discrète sur la question. Et autant la première hybride de Toyota se fait un porte-étendard technologique, autant la HS250h se conduit comme n'importe quelle voiture conventionnelle.

Se conduit... encore faut-il avoir l'impression de la conduire, cette voiture! Car malheureusement, on oublie vite qu'on la pilote. Les sensations sont gommées par une direction électrique qui manque de substance et si le volant est agréable en main, il transmet une bien faible connexion avec la route. On aurait aimé des ajustements plus... ajustés.

Aussi, la suspension (double triangulation à l'arrière) mise plus sur le confort que sur la sportivité. C'est de bonne guerre pour une voiture qui clame la petite consommation plutôt que la puissance, mais la balade porte comme sur un nuage aux rebonds moelleux. Certains aiment ces suspensions qui semblent avoir avalé un *smoothie*, mais pas nous... Pour s'en tirer avec un peu plus de communication, il faut la version Premium Sport.

Et puis ne vous fiez pas aux données de performance: la HS250h semble être animée d'un moteur plus puissant que ses 187 chevaux. Ce moteur de cycle Atkinson (2,4 litres) est le tout premier quatre cylindres à se glisser sous le capot d'une Lexus et, de concert avec le moteur électrique, il travaille si souplement que l'on croirait avoir affaire à au moins 250 chevaux. On ne sent jamais la transition entre les deux moteurs. Pour savoir qui fait quoi, il faut consulter l'affichage central. Bref, on oublie vite que l'on conduit « hybride » et personnellement, je ne me suis jamais autant peu souciée de ma consommation lors d'un essai du genre.

C'est naturellement une CVT qui passe les rapports de façon infinie. Pas de mode manuel, encore moins de palettes de changement au volant, mais on ne peut s'en plaindre: cette boîte distribue la puissance de façon limpide et sophistiquée. Pour aider le conducteur à obtenir une toute petite consommation, la HS250h emprunte à la Prius sa sélection trois modes. Pour réussir le 100 % électrique, il ne faut toutefois pas être pressé; une pression indue sur l'accélérateur réanime vitement le moteur à essence. Le « bip-bip » qui déclare que l'électrique n'a plus cours est frustrant. Vivement que les fabricants de batteries en arrivent à une technologie plus permissive – l'avenir des voitures hybrides-électriques en dépend.

Revenons à nos trois modes: les conducteurs capables de maintenir l'éco économiseront à la pompe, mais il leur faut composer avec un accélérateur qui, rôle d'entremetteur oblige, fait de la résistance. Le pied droit n'aime pas ce mode « matante », particulièrement à l'approche d'une pente abrupte ou pour dépasser un escargot roulant. Rapidement, on passe au mode *Power* et l'accélérateur réagit plus dynamiquement. Tant pis pour la consommation... Cependant, en mélangeant un peu tous les modes et, surtout, en ne nous forçant pas plus que de coutume, nous avons terminé notre essai avec une

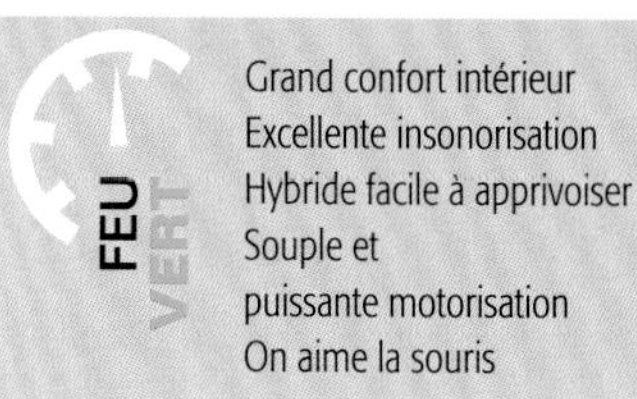

Grand confort intérieur
Excellente insonorisation
Hybride facile à apprivoiser
Souple et puissante motorisation
On aime la souris

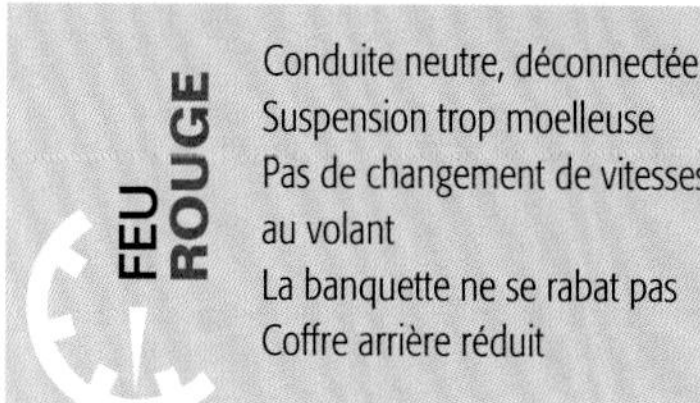

Conduite neutre, déconnectée
Suspension trop moelleuse
Pas de changement de vitesses au volant
La banquette ne se rabat pas
Coffre arrière réduit

moyenne de 6,2 l/100 km. C'est à peine plus que les 5,7 l/100 km annoncés par Lexus et c'est excellent pour une berline intermédiaire.

ON AIME LA SOURIS !

Autant la Prius crie « techno ! » avec ses panneaux solaires et son affichage aussi ésotérique que complexe, autant la Lexus HS250h fait *mainstream* – de luxe, évidemment. Le cuir (de série) est souple, l'assemblage est pile-poil et l'insonorisation nous coupe du monde extérieur. On se glisse dans des sièges hyperconfortables – trop, même, ce qui vient accroître ce sentiment de « salon ». La planche de bord en angle enveloppe les occupants de belle façon et, à portée de main droite du conducteur, se trouve un fantastique gadget : une souris informatique.

Ce *joystick* si amusant à manier fait apparaître à hauteur des yeux non seulement la route, mais aussi la sélection musicale et les ajustements climatiques. On devrait garder les deux mains sur le volant, mais on ne peut résister à l'envie d'empoigner la chose, un surcroît de plaisir résidant dans le mode haptique – qui fait que le curseur rencontre une résistance toute virtuelle, facilitant la navigation d'un menu à l'autre.

TROP PASSE-PARTOUT

Bon, qui dit hybride, dit moins d'espace afin d'accommoder les batteries. Pour la HS250h, cela signifie un coffre nettement moins spacieux. Il est large, l'ouverture est béante, mais la profondeur n'est pas au rendez-vous. On ne se retrouve qu'avec 343 litres, l'équivalent du coffre d'une Corolla. Et comme la banquette ne se rabat pas, eh bien, on pense aux amis ou aux voisins pour transporter sa grande échelle !

Pour ce qui est du prix, on a quand même droit à une voiture qui débute sous les 40 000 $ avec, de série, le cuir, le toit ouvrant, la climatisation bizone et le démarrage sans clé. Installée entre la petite IS et l'intermédiaire ES, la HS se positionne en entrée de gamme de luxe, hybride de surcroît, sans pour autant exiger de compromis côté confort et équipement. C'est bien. Reste qu'en misant sur du tout aussi conventionnel et sur un style combien passe-partout (le design non plus, ne crie pas « hybride ! »), la HS tient à distance ceux qui cherchent davantage de sensations de conduite.

Nadine Filion

PHOTOS : SYLVAIN RAYMOND

Catégorie	Berline
Échelle de prix	39 900 $ à 48 750 $ (2010)
Garanties	4 ans/80 000 km, 6 ans/110 000 km
Assemblage	n.d.
Cote d'assurance	n.d.

CHÂSSIS - DONNÉES POUR HS250H PREMIUM

Emp/lon/lar/haut	2 700/4 695/1 785/1 505 mm
Coffre	343 litres
Réservoir	55 litres
Nombre coussins sécurité	10
Antipatinage / contrôle stabilité	oui / oui
Suspension avant	indépendante, jambes de force
Suspension arrière	indépendante, double triangulation
Freins avant / arrière	disque (ABS) / disque (ABS)
Direction	à crémaillère, assistée
Diamètre de braquage	11,4 m
Pneus avant / arrière	P215/55R17 / P215/55R17
Poids	1 670 kg
Capacité de remorquage	non recommandé

COMPOSANTES MÉCANIQUES

HS250h

Cylindrée, soupapes, alim.	4L 2,4 litres 16 s atmos.
Puissance / Couple	187 chevaux / 138 lb-pi
Tr. base (opt) / rouage base (opt)	CVT / Tr
0-100 / 80-120 / 100-0 km/h	9,7 s / 6,8 s / n.d.
Type ess. / ville / autoroute	Ordinaire / 5,6 / 5,9 l/100 km

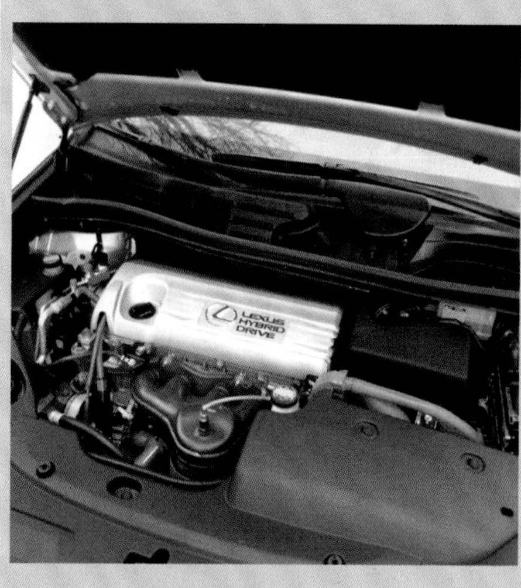

DANS LA MÊME CATÉGORIE

Aucune concurrente directe

DU NOUVEAU EN 2011

Nouveau modèle

NOS IMPRESSIONS

Agrément de conduite :	6/10
Fiabilité :	Nouveau modèle
Sécurité :	8/10
Qualités hivernales :	8/10
Espace intérieur :	8/10
Confort :	8/10

www.lexus.ca

Plus d'informations dans la section statistiques en dernière partie du Guide

BIPOLAIRE

Chez Lexus, la gamme IS fait vraiment bande à part en ajoutant un certain degré de sportivité, à géométrie variable selon les modèles, alors que les autres véhicules de la marque misent presque exclusivement sur le confort et le silence de roulement. Et si la IS peut être qualifiée de bipolaire, c'est que les performances livrées par la IS-F sont nettement supérieures à celle des autres modèles de la gamme, au point où l'on se demande s'il s'agit véritablement d'une Lexus.

Campée sur ses jantes en alliage de 19 pouces, la IS-F est une propulsion qui joue le grand jeu avec ses ailes élargies et surtout son capot bombé sous lequel se trouve son V8 de 5,0 litres et 416 chevaux jumelé à une boîte automatique à huit rapports avec paliers de commande au volant. C'est de loin la plus performante des Lexus, exception faite de la très exotique LFA dont la diffusion est limitée à seulement 500 exemplaires, et le suffixe « F » chez Lexus représente l'appellation désignée pour les modèles de performance, au même titre que les modèles « M » chez BMW ou AMG chez Mercedes-Benz.

MÉTAL HURLANT

Au premier contact, on est tout simplement ébahi par la sonorité évocatrice du V8 dès que le moulin dépasse la barre des 4 000 tours/minute. Ce son est tellement enivrant que je me suis souvent amusé à baisser les vitres en roulant dans le tunnel Ville-Marie pour ensuite rétrograder afin d'entendre le V8 à plein régime... En conduite normale, le fait que la boîte automatique compte huit rapports permet de bonifier la consommation à vitesse d'autoroute et, tant et aussi longtemps que la route est en bon état, on ne se plaint pas de la fermeté des suspensions. Par contre, si le revêtement est dégradé, on obtient une très bonne idée de ce que doit ressentir un gallon de peinture lorsqu'il est brassé dans la machine du quincailler. En fait, le débattement des suspensions semble avoir été calibré afin d'optimiser la tenue de route à tout prix, ce qui a une incidence directe et marquée sur le niveau de confort, à un point tel que ça en devient désagréable à la longue. Mise à l'épreuve sur le circuit du Mont Tremblant, la IS-F s'est montrée d'attaque avec une tenue de route surprenante qui n'a rien à voir avec celle des autres modèles Lexus, et un freinage nettement plus performant. Il faut simplement désactiver le système antidérapage pour pouvoir exploiter pleinement son potentiel de performance.

DE RETOUR À NOTRE PROGRAMMATION RÉGULIÈRE

Si la IS-F est carrément hors-norme dans l'univers typique des Lexus, la conduite d'une IS350 Cabriolet vous ramènera vite à la réalité de ce qui est proposé par la marque de luxe de Toyota. Au programme : une conduite aseptisée qui plaira certainement aux automobilistes pour qui les performances ne sont pas au sommet des priorités. D'abord les fleurs, ensuite le pot...

La IS350 Cabriolet est dotée d'un châssis très rigide qui représente une vaste amélioration par rapport à celui des modèles

FEU VERT

- Style réussi
- Qualité d'assemblage
- Structure de caisse rigide
- Performances relevées (IS-F)
- Très bonne fiabilité

FEU ROUGE

- Intervention trop rapide de l'antidérapage
- Puissance un peu juste (IS 250)
- Prix des options
- Conduite aseptisée

cabriolets antérieurs de Lexus, avec le résultat que l'on perçoit à peine les bruits de caisse. De plus, avec le toit en place, le silence de roulement est à la hauteur des berlines conventionnelles de la marque, la boîte automatique fait tellement bien son travail que les changements de rapports sont très peu perceptibles et le moteur livre sa cavalerie de 306 chevaux avec enthousiasme. Du côté de l'habitacle, les matériaux utilisés pour réaliser la planche de bord sont de première qualité et la finition intérieure est sans reproches.

Par contre, la IS350 Cabriolet n'est pas à la hauteur de la concurrence allemande en ce qui a trait à la dynamique. La direction est vague et surassistée, le freinage est adéquat mais sans plus, et le système antidérapage intervient beaucoup trop tôt ce qui prive le conducteur de toute forme de plaisir en virage, d'autant plus que les sièges avant ne procurent pas assez de soutien latéral. Les places arrière sont carrément symboliques et le volume de chargement est limité au point d'être presque inexistant avec le toit rigide-rétractable replié dans le coffre. Bref, vous aurez compris qu'il est très agréable de rouler en ligne droite et nettement moins en virages au volant de cette voiture !

Quant aux berlines de la gamme IS, précisons que seule la IS250 est livrable avec un rouage intégral offert en option et que la puissance de son moteur est un peu juste compte tenu du poids plus élevé de ce modèle comparativement à la IS250 à simple propulsion. Peu importe le modèle choisi, toutes les IS font preuve d'une très bonne qualité d'assemblage et la finition intérieure est sans reproches. De plus, la marque Lexus obtient d'excellents scores en ce qui a trait à la fiabilité après trois ans d'usage, selon le sondage Vehicle Dependability Study de J.D. Power mesurant le taux de satisfaction de la clientèle à cet égard. En effet, la marque Lexus se classe au quatrième rang sur les 35 marques répertoriées dans le sondage 2010, n'étant devancée que par Porsche (1), Lincoln (2) et Buick (3).

Même si la IS représente la gamme la plus sportive de la marque, il y a encore beaucoup de travail à faire avant de pouvoir faire jeu égal avec BMW ou Audi pour ce qui est de la dynamique, la IS-F étant l'exception à cette règle.

Gabriel Gélinas

PHOTOS : ALAIN MORIN

Catégorie	Berline, Cabriolet
Échelle de prix	34 400 $ à 68 000 $
Garanties	4 ans/80 000 km, 6 ans/110 000 km
Assemblage	Tahara, Japon
Cote d'assurance	moyenne

CHÂSSIS - DONNÉES POUR 350 TI

Emp/lon/lar/haut	2 730/4 580/1 800/1 425 mm
Coffre	378 litres
Réservoir	65 litres
Nombre coussins sécurité	6
Antipatinage / contrôle stabilité	oui / oui
Suspension avant	indépendante, double triangulation
Suspension arrière	indépendante, multibras
Freins avant / arrière	disque (ABS) / disque (ABS)
Direction	à crémaillère, ass. variable
Diamètre de braquage	10,2 m
Pneus avant / arrière	P225/45R17 / P225/45R17
Poids	1 680 kg
Capacité de remorquage	n.d.

COMPOSANTES MÉCANIQUES

IS250, IS250 TI

Cylindrée, soupapes, alim.	V6 2,5 litres 24 s atmos.
Puissance / Couple	204 chevaux / 185 lb-pi
Tr. base (opt) / rouage base (opt)	M6 (A6) / Prop (Int)
0-100 / 80-120 / 100-0 km/h	7,8 s / 6,1 s / n.d.
Type ess. / ville / autoroute	Super / 11,6 / 7,6 l/100 km

IS350, IS350 TI

Cylindrée, soupapes, alim.	V6 3,5 litres 24 s atmos.
Puissance / Couple	306 chevaux / 277 lb-pi
Tr. base (opt) / rouage base (opt)	A6 / Prop (Int)
0-100 / 80-120 / 100-0 km/h	6,5 s / 4,7 s / 40,8 m
Type ess. / ville / autoroute	Super / 11,5 / 7,9 l/100 km

IS-F

Cylindrée, soupapes, alim.	V8 5,0 litres 32 s atmos.
Puissance / Couple	416 chevaux / 371 lb-pi
Tr. base (opt) / rouage base (opt)	A8 / Prop
0-100 / 80-120 / 100-0 km/h	5,5 s / 4,6 s / 37,9 m
Type ess. / ville / autoroute	Super / 13,0 / 8,5 l/100 km

DANS LA MÊME CATÉGORIE

Acura TL, Audi A4, BMW Série 3, Cadillac CTS, Infiniti G, Mercedes-Benz Classe C, Volvo S60

DU NOUVEAU EN 2011

Parties avant et arrière des IS250 et IS350 redessinées, rouage intégral disponible sur IS350, IS350 propulsion reçoit suspension sport, palettes au volant et système de navigation avec disque dur.

NOS IMPRESSIONS

Agrément de conduite :	■■■■■■■■□□	8/10
Fiabilité :	■■■■■■■■■■	10/10
Sécurité :	■■■■■■■■■■	10/10
Qualités hivernales :	■■■■■■■■□□	8/10
Espace intérieur :	■■■■■■■■□□	8/10
Confort :	■■■■■■■■□□	8/10

www.lexus.ca

Plus d'informations dans la section statistiques en dernière partie du Guide

DE LA TRÈS HAUTE TECHNOLOGIE

Le son du V10 qui hurle à 9000 tours/minute alors que je file sur la ligne droite du circuit de Homestead en Floride est tout simplement hallucinant, les ingénieurs de Lexus ayant réussi l'exploit de reproduire la sonorité propre d'un moteur de F1 à un degré que personne n'a été en mesure d'accomplir précédemment... Bienvenue à bord de la Lexus LFA, l'une des supervoitures les plus attendues, et si je me retrouve au volant d'une des deux seules LFA expédiées en Amérique du Nord, c'est que Lexus a décidé de convier un groupe très limité de journalistes d'un peu partout à travers le monde à conduire leur nouveau pur-sang pour une évaluation sur circuit.

Ainsi, seulement quatre journalistes canadiens ont eu la chance de prendre le volant de la LFA et Le Guide de l'Auto est le seul média québécois qui a eu cette opportunité. Le galop d'essai sera court, seulement six tours de piste, mais quels tours... Dès la sortie des puits, la LFA annonce la couleur d'un essai exceptionnel alors que les 552 chevaux s'expriment avec autorité et que le V10 monte rapidement en régime en route vers sa limite de révolutions de 9000 tours/minute avec ce hurlement qui deviendra rapidement la signature propre de la LFA. De ce côté, je dois préciser que j'ai eu l'occasion de conduire la Ferrari F430 ainsi que la 599 GTB Fiorano, la Lamborghini Murcielago LP640 et la récente Audi R8 V10, mais aucune de ces voitures n'arrive à émuler la sonorité d'un moteur de F1 aussi fidèlement que la LFA, les ingénieurs ayant porté une attention particulière à cet aspect en peaufinant le développement du moteur et de l'échappement, mais aussi en intégrant des passages avec membranes entre le compartiment moteur et l'habitacle justement afin de bonifier l'expérience auditive. À 9000 tours/minute, les pistons du V10 de la LFA voyagent à 25 mètres par seconde et les deux pompes à huile assurent un débit de 240 litres par minute ce qui signifie que le réservoir d'huile qui contient 10 litres voit son contenu recyclé 24 fois par tranche de 60 secondes.

UN MOTEUR DÉVELOPPÉ CONJOINTEMENT AVEC YAMAHA

Ce moteur, appelé 1 LR-GUE, à été développé conjointement avec Yamaha spécifiquement pour la LFA, et ce V10 de 4,8 litres, qui opte pour une configuration à 72 degrés, est doté de bielles et de soupapes en titane, du calage variable des soupapes ainsi que d'un carter sec. Même s'il s'agit d'un V10, le moteur de la LFA est plus court, plus étroit, plus léger et est localisé plus bas sous le capot que le V6 de 2,5 litres de la Lexus IS, ainsi que derrière l'axe des roues avant. Autre fait d'armes, ce V10 passe du ralenti à sa limite de révolutions de 9000 tours/minute au neutre en seulement six dixièmes de seconde, et le régime moteur semble chuter presque aussi rapidement. Le résultat, c'est que jouer avec l'accélérateur au neutre produit le même *Wap-Wap-Wap* qu'un véritable moteur de course. La puissance maximale de 552 chevaux est atteinte à 8700 tours/minute et le couple maximal est de 354 livres-pied est obtenu à 6800 tours/minute. Le poids de la Lexus LFA étant de 1480 kilos, celle-ci bénéficie donc d'un meilleur rapport poids-puissance que la Ferrari 599 GTB Fiorano.

La boîte est une Aisin à six vitesses, qui est accolée au différentiel et donc localisée sur le train arrière afin d'obtenir une répartition optimale des masses, et elle est contrôlée électroniquement au moyen de paliers localisés sur la colonne de direction et celui de gauche, qui commande le rétrogradage, requiert un peu plus d'effort que celui de droite qui lui commande le passage au rapport supérieur. Les ingénieurs de Lexus ont jonglé avec l'idée d'adopter une boîte à double embrayage, mais cette configuration n'a pas été retenue, les ingénieurs jugeant qu'une boîte à double embrayage ne permet pas de bien sentir le changement de vitesse. La boîte passe les vitesses en 200 millièmes de seconde, lorsque le mode « sport » est sélectionné, ce qui est un peu lent compte tenu du fait que Ferrari prévoit un temps de passage en 60 millièmes de seconde pour la nouvelle 458 Italia, et c'est là l'un des rares points faibles de la LFA.

Un autre point faible est que la direction à assistance électrique pourrait donner un peu plus de *feed-back*. En effet, avec une répartition des masses de 48 pour cent sur le train avant et de 52 pour cent sur le train arrière, ce qui est remarquable compte tenu du fait que le moteur est en position centrale-avant, l'équilibre du châssis est à ce point réussi que la voiture change de direction très rapidement dans un enchaînement de virages lents, tout en demeurant stable et prévisible dans les rares courbes rapides du circuit routier de Homestead. À part la sonorité plus qu'évocatrice du moteur, l'autre aspect qui impressionne grandement est la performance des freins développés conjointement avec Brembo et dont les disques sont réalisés en composite de céramique. Sur le

circuit routier de Homestead, l'impression générale qui se dégage de la LFA est celle d'une voiture qui est féroce en accélération ainsi qu'en décélération, mais qui demeure facile à conduire rapidement et qui est nettement moins intimidante que d'autres rivales exotiques en raison de la grande facilité que l'on éprouve à la piloter et de l'impressionnante stabilité du châssis à haute vitesse.

UN HABITACLE BIPOLAIRE

L'habitacle de la LFA est un mélange de *high-tech* et des traditionnelles touches de luxe qui font l'apanage de la marque. Ainsi, la LFA n'est pas dotée d'un bloc d'instruments conventionnels, mais plutôt d'un écran qui reproduit en images le tachymètre qui se retrouve ainsi « visualisé » de différentes façons selon la sélection par le conducteur de l'un des quatre modes de conduite, soit automatique, normal, sport et chaussé mouillée. De plus, les baudriers des ceintures de sécurité comportent un coussin gonflable, histoire de réduire les blessures au thorax en cas d'accident à haute vitesse, ce qui représente une première mondiale selon les concepteurs de Lexus. Les sièges sport moulants sont recouverts d'un cuir de très grande qualité et la LFA est également équipée de série d'un système de son performant ainsi que d'un système de navigation.

Sur le plan technique, la LFA est à la fine pointe avec son châssis réalisé à 65 pour cent en fibre de carbone et à 35 pour cent en aluminium, une configuration adoptée en cours de développement, le premier prototype ayant été réalisé sur un châssis tout alu, afin de réduire le poids de la LFA. Cette nouvelle technique de production explique en partie le long délai entre le dévoilement de la voiture-concept LF-A, présentée au Salon de l'Auto de Détroit en 2005, et l'arrivée sur le marché du modèle de série, renommé LFA, en 2011.

Par ailleurs, le choix de la fibre de carbone comme matériau de base pour la réalisation du châssis de la LFA a fait en sorte que Toyota est revenue jusqu'à ses origines... En effet, la marque qui allait un jour devenir un géant de l'automobile sur le plan mondial construisait, à ses débuts, des machines à tisser le textile et les ingénieurs de Toyota ont donc développé une nouvelle machine circulaire pour tisser et tresser la fibre de carbone nécessaire à la confection de nombreux éléments du châssis de la voiture.

L'EXCLUSIVITÉ EST ASSURÉE

En terminant, quelques détails importants à l'intention de l'acheteur potentiel... Seulement 500 exemplaires de la LFA seront produits au cours des années modèle 2011 et 2012 à l'usine de

Catégorie	Coupé
Échelle de prix	375 000 $ (U.S.)
Garanties	n.d.
Assemblage	Motomachi, Japon
Cote d'assurance	n.d.

CHÂSSIS - DONNÉES POUR LFA

Emp/lon/lar/haut	2 605/4 505/1 895/1 220 mm
Coffre	n.d.
Réservoir	73 litres
Nombre coussins sécurité	n.d.
Antipatinage / contrôle stabilité	oui / oui
Suspension avant	indépendante, double triangulation
Suspension arrière	indépendante, multibras
Freins avant / arrière	disque (ABS) / disque (ABS)
Direction	à crémaillère, assistée
Diamètre de braquage	n.d.
Pneus avant / arrière	P265/35ZR20 / P305/30ZR20
Poids	1 480 kg
Capacité de remorquage	non recommandé

COMPOSANTES MÉCANIQUES

LFA

Cylindrée, soupapes, alim.	V10 4,8 litres 40 s atmos.
Puissance / Couple	552 chevaux / 354 lb-pi
Tr. base (opt) / rouage base (opt)	A6 / Prop
0-100 / 80-120 / 100-0 km/h	3,7 s / 3,0 s (est) / n.d.
Type ess. / ville / autoroute	Super / n.d.

FEU VERT

Exclusivité assurée
Performances démentielles
Sonorité absolument spectaculaire

FEU ROUGE

Prix stratosphérique
Design particulier de l'habitacle
La verra-t-on vraiment sur la route?

Motomachi par une équipe de 1 540 techniciens au rythme d'une voiture par jour, et toutes seront construites sur commande aux spécifications de l'acheteur pour ce qui est de la couleur de la carrosserie et de l'habitacle. De ce nombre, dix voitures seront allouées au marché canadien à raison de cinq par année. Le prix à été fixé à 375 000 dollars américains et les acheteurs devront d'abord louer la LFA pendant une période de deux ans avant de pouvoir se prévaloir du droit de l'acheter, histoire de décourager les spéculateurs qui voudraient capitaliser sur l'exclusivité assurée de ce modèle.

Véritable tour de force sur le plan technique, la LFA est une voiture d'anthologie. Son seul problème est son prix stratosphérique, surtout lorsque la LFA est comparée à la GT-R de Nissan dont les performances ne sont pas toutes égales à celles de la Lexus, mais dont le prix est six fois moindre...

Gabriel Gélinas

PHOTOS: LEXUS

DANS LA MÊME CATÉGORIE

Audi R8, Chevrolet Corvette ZR1, Ferrari F458 Italia, Lamborghini Gallardo, Mercedes-Benz Classe SLR, Nissan GT-R, Porsche 911 GT3

DU NOUVEAU EN 2011

Nouveau modèle

NOS IMPRESSIONS

Agrément de conduite :	■■■■■■■■■□ 9/10
Fiabilité :	Nouveau modèle
Sécurité :	Données insuffisantes
Qualités hivernales :	nulles
Espace intérieur :	■■■■■■□□□□ 6/10
Confort :	■■■■■■□□□□ 6/10

www.lexus.ca

Plus d'informations dans la section statistiques en dernière partie du Guide

DISCRÉTION ET ENNUI

Si la division Lexus de Toyota a atteint une réputation aussi enviable, c'est en grande partie grâce à son modèle le plus cher et le plus huppé, soit la LS. Au tout début, cette berline s'est rapidement bâti une grande popularité en raison de sa finition impeccable, de sa fiabilité et du service sans faille que réservaient les concessionnaires aux acheteurs de ce modèle. De plus, à ses débuts, les prix offerts étaient plus que compétitifs. Par contre, rares étaient les commentaires positifs quant à son comportement routier et ses performances.

Si l'on se fie aux LS que l'on croise sur la route, les conducteurs semblent davantage intéressés au confort de la suspension et au luxe de l'habitacle. Le modèle a beau avoir connu une refonte complète en 2007, ces mêmes critères ont prévalu.

RISQUE D'ASSOUPISSEMENT

La silhouette de la LS peut être décrite comme étant sobre, ultra sobre même. Si ce n'était de la grille de calandre, ainsi que des barres de bas de caisse qui sont chromées, on se retrouverait dans l'anonymat le plus total. Certaines mauvaises langues accusent ce design de s'être sérieusement inspiré de celui de la Série 7 de BMW, mais si c'est le cas, il s'agit d'une version très fade de cette dernière. Il en découle quand même une élégance qu'apprécient les gens qui ont les moyens de se procurer une Lexus LS, mais qui ne veulent pas nécessairement l'afficher par l'intermédiaire d'une carrosserie excentrique.

L'habitacle, comme il se doit, respecte lui aussi la tradition de la marque avec ces fameux cadrans électroluminescents que Lexus a offerts dès la première génération de ce modèle. Pour le reste, c'est d'une grande discrétion, avec une console centrale parsemée de boutons placés sous un écran à cristaux liquides. Bien entendu, les sièges sont chauffants et ventilés en plus d'être d'un grand confort, du moins si vos critères sont ceux d'un fauteuil de salon. Les places arrière dorlotent leurs occupants et la version à empattement allongé leur procure encore plus d'espace.

Le moteur utilisé pour propulser la LS460 est un V8 de 4,6 litres produisant 380 chevaux. Il est couplé à une boîte automatique à huit rapports, la première du genre à avoir été commercialisée. Cette transmission est à l'image du reste de la voiture. Les changements de rapports sont imperceptibles et elle effectue son travail avec la plus grande discrétion. Cette cavalerie permet de boucler le 0-100 km/h en 7,3 secondes ce qui n'est pas à dédaigner. À titre de comparaison, une Mercedes-Benz S450 effectue le même exercice en 5,9 secondes.

Cette seule statistique nous dévoile le caractère de cette grosse Lexus. On a quand même amélioré son comportement routier et je défie tout conducteur normal de perdre le contrôle au volant de

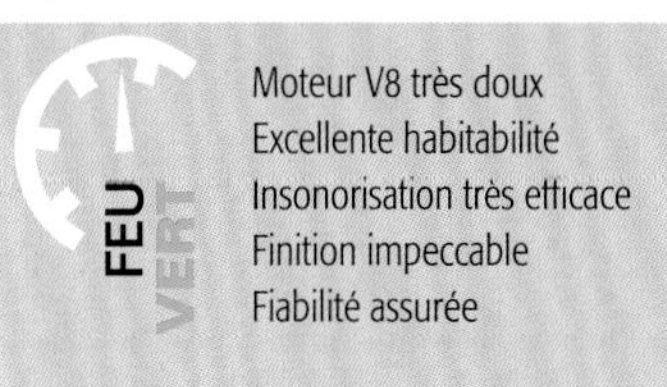

Moteur V8 très doux
Excellente habitabilité
Insonorisation très efficace
Finition impeccable
Fiabilité assurée

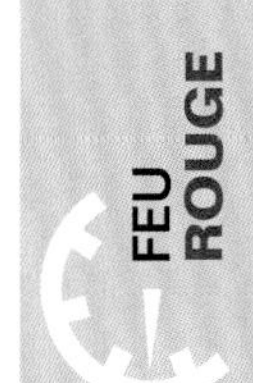

Très faible agrément de conduite
Direction ultra engourdie
Mécanique complexe
Système de stationnement automatique lent
Silhouette anonyme

cette voiture même en prenant des virages relativement serrés à grande vitesse. Le danger avec cette voiture, c'est l'assoupissement. En effet, en raison d'une insonorisation très efficace, d'une direction totalement déconnectée de la route et d'une suspension absorbant pratiquement toutes les imperfections de la chaussée, le conducteur se retrouve au volant d'un cocon géant fait d'acier et de verre.

L'HYBRIDE À LA DÉRIVE

Lorsque Toyota et sa filiale Lexus ont débuté sur le marché, on faisait preuve d'humilité. On affirmait vouloir tenter sa chance dans ce créneau du marché dominé par les grosses berlines allemandes. Puis, devant les succès qui s'accumulaient, on est devenu un peu plus prétentieux et passablement arrogant. D'ailleurs, lorsqu'on a dévoilé la version hybride de la LS, soit la LS600hL, il fallait entendre le présentateur de cette berline. Selon lui, les constructeurs allemands étaient en pleine débâcle et chez Lexus on allait leur montrer comment faire des voitures de luxe.

Toyota a connu beaucoup de succès avec ses versions hybrides au point que certains modèles comme la Prius sont devenus des icônes. Cependant, cette stratégie de marché ne fonctionne pas toujours. Nous en avons la preuve avec la LS600hL qui n'a pas connu le succès escompté. Pourtant, on n'a rien épargné au chapitre de la technologie. En effet, le moteur V8 5,0 litres est associé à un moteur électrique qui porte la puissance totale à 438 chevaux.

Étant davantage luxueux que la version à moteur thermique et équipé d'encore plus de gadgets, ce somptueux hybride n'est pas plus agréable à conduire pour autant. Par contre, au chapitre des accélérations et des reprises, elle est nettement plus rapide. Sans oublier la consommation de carburant qui est d'environ 10 litres au 100 km.

Finalement, lorsque vient le temps de débourser une somme fort substantielle pour ce type véhicule hybride, il semble que les acheteurs se tournent encore vers le prestige des germaniques. Toute impressionnante soit-elle, la première voiture hybride de grand luxe est peu populaire.

Denis Duquet

PHOTOS : MARC LACHAPELLE

Catégorie	Berline
Échelle de prix	82 900 $ à 119 950 $ (2010)
Garanties	4 ans/80 000 km, 6 ans/110 000 km
Assemblage	Tahara, Japon
Cote d'assurance	n.d.

CHÂSSIS - DONNÉES POUR 460 L TI

Emp/lon/lar/haut	3 090/5 150/1 875/1 475 mm
Coffre	510 litres
Réservoir	84 litres
Nombre coussins sécurité	8
Antipatinage / contrôle stabilité	oui / oui
Suspension avant	indépendante, multibras
Suspension arrière	indépendante, multibras
Freins avant / arrière	disques (ABS) / disques (ABS)
Direction	à crémaillère, ass. électrique
Diamètre de braquage	12,1 m
Pneus avant / arrière	P235/50R18 / P235/50R18
Poids	2 150 kg
Capacité de remorquage	n.d.

COMPOSANTES MÉCANIQUES

460 , 460 TI, 460 L TI

Cylindrée, soupapes, alim.	V8 4,6 litres 32 s atmos.
Puissance / Couple	380 chevaux / 367 lb-pi
Tr. base (opt) / rouage base (opt)	A8 / Prop (Int)
0-100 / 80-120 / 100-0 km/h	7,3 s / 5,7 s / 42,6 m
Type ess. / ville / autoroute	Super / 12,9 / 8,2 l/100 km

600h L

Cylindrée, soupapes, alim.	V8 5,0 litres 32 s atmos.
Puissance / Couple	438 chevaux / 385 lb-pi
Tr. base (opt) / rouage base (opt)	CVT / Int
0-100 / 80-120 / 100-0 km/h	6,5 s / 4,7 s / 46,5 m
Type ess. / ville / autoroute	Super / 10,6 / 9,1 l/100 km

DANS LA MÊME CATÉGORIE

Audi A8, BMW Série 7, Jaguar XJ, Mercedes-Benz Classe S

DU NOUVEAU EN 2011

Aucun changement majeur

NOS IMPRESSIONS

Agrément de conduite :	6/10
Fiabilité :	8/10
Sécurité :	8/10
Qualités hivernales :	8/10
Espace intérieur :	9/10
Confort :	10/10

www.lexus.ca

Plus d'informations dans la section statistiques en dernière partie du Guide

LEXUS LS

OBSESSIF, COMPULSIF ET ALCOOLIQUE

Au cours de la dernière année, Lexus, la marque de prestige de Toyota, ne l'a pas eue facile. Malmenée au chapitre des ventes à cause de campagnes de rappel plus ou moins bien gérées, Lexus peut au moins se rabattre sur plusieurs véhicules hybrides pour se refaire une image. Heureusement qu'il y a les hybrides, car si Lexus se fiait uniquement sur ses gros VUS pour assurer sa survie, la mort aurait déjà fait son œuvre !

Le plus imposant véhicule de la gamme Lexus, le LX570, n'a plus sa raison d'être dans un monde où chaque millilitre d'essence économisé pour chaque tranche de 100 kilomètres fait désormais l'objet d'une campagne de publicité monstre. Car le LX570 n'est pas gros, il est immense. Il ne se stationne pas, il accoste. Il n'est pas luxueux, il est luxurieux. Il ne consomme pas d'essence, il l'avale goulument. Bref, on est loin d'une Prius. Cependant, il existe une clientèle pour ce genre de palace, une clientèle qui n'a rien à cirer des revendications des écologistes et qui préconise le luxe et l'opulence. Il faut, bien entendu, avoir les moyens de ses choix et certains les ont !

TECHNIQUEMENT PARLANT

Le moteur est un V8 de 5,7 litres suffisamment puissant pour permettre de laisser en plan beaucoup de berlines bien moins lourdes. Il engloutit facilement une quinzaine de litres d'essence à tous les 100 kilomètres et, avec un minimum de mauvaise volonté de la part du pied droit, il peut vous monter ça à 18 ou 20 litres. De super, bien entendu. Ce moteur se montre d'une douceur incroyable, tout comme la transmission à six rapports. Oh, elle n'est pas très rapide mais qu'est-ce qu'on s'en fout. Elle transmet le couple élevé du moteur à un rouage intégral incroyablement sophistiqué et performant. Les rares personnes qui oseront vraiment explorer

les limites de leur LX570 seront épatées. Les autres s'impressionneront elles-mêmes en traversant quelques mètres de boue ou une congère...

Le LX, à défaut d'afficher de la retenue, est conséquent avec lui-même, préconisant le confort bien avant les qualités dynamiques. En ligne droite, il n'affiche aucun complexe malgré une direction assez floue au centre. Il faut par contre se montrer un peu plus délicat dans les courbes, où il affiche un roulis impressionnant. Curieusement, et heureusement, les distances de freinage sont courtes, moins de 43 mètres (de 100 km/h à zéro). Bien entendu, le transfert de poids est aussi important que les transferts entre mon compte de banque et celui de mon fils, mais, semble-t-il, cela fait partie de la vie... Une foule d'aides électroniques à la conduite veillent toujours au grain et ont le sommeil très léger car ils interviennent à la moindre occasion. Et si jamais le besoin s'en faisait sentir, l'habitacle recèle dix coussins gonflables.

LES CHOSES SÉRIEUSES MAINTENANT

L'habitacle n'est pas seulement vaste, il est aussi superbement fini. Tenter de trouver un plastique retroussé, une couture un peu

FEU VERT

Confort princier
Capacités hors route
Capacités de remorquage élevées
Fiabilité encore parmi les meilleures

FEU ROUGE

Consommation outrancière
Triste valeur de revente
Aménagement du coffre à revoir
Aucunement sportif
Direction floue

croche ou une boiserie le moindrement mal finie relève de la science-fiction, du moins dans les quelques véhicules essayés depuis deux ans. La position de conduite se trouve rapidement et les sièges avant font preuve d'un confort suprême. Le tableau de bord n'émet jamais de craquements, mais il est un peu compliqué à utiliser, surtout au début, à cause de la multitude de boutons qu'il présente. Le conducteur fait face à une instrumentation des plus complètes. Le système audio optionnel Mark Levinson demeure l'un des meilleurs de l'industrie et mes oreilles, formées à un Juliette 1976, ont souri... Comme de raison, un LX570, ça vient d'office avec le climatiseur à quatre zones, le filtre à air, à poussière et à pollen désodorisant SVP, de la moquette ultra épaisse sur le plancher, des marchepieds éclairés et des phares adaptatifs. Le groupe Ultra Premium, pour une petite dizaine de milliers de dollars supplémentaires, ajoute le système DVD pour les places arrière, le régulateur de vitesse adaptatif par radar et autres petites gâteries du genre.

Si les sièges avant font preuve d'un grand confort, on peut en dire autant des places de la deuxième rangée. L'espace dévolu aux trois passagers n'est pas compté et si une de ces trois personnes ose se plaindre de son sort, faites-lui finir le trajet à l'arrière d'une Mitsubishi Eclipse... Petit bonheur, ces sièges avancent et reculent (électriquement, voyons !). Comme tout gros VUS qui se respecte, le LX570 offre une troisième banquette. D'accès plus ou moins facile et conçue pour deux personnes malgré ses trois ceintures, elle ne doit servir que pour dépanner ou pour y loger de jeunes enfants. Ces sièges se replient de chaque côté (électriquement, voyons !) pour agrandir un coffre déjà vaste, le contraire eût été surprenant, mais pas autant qu'on serait porté à le croire au regard des dimensions extérieures. Les sièges de la deuxième rangée ne se replient pas dans le plancher ou de manière à former un fond plat comme dans la plupart des VUS. En lieu et place, ils basculent vers l'avant, volant ainsi de précieux centimètres au coffre qui fait à peine 60 pouces (152 cm) de longueur. Enfin, on ne peut passer sous silence les capacités de remorquage plutôt élevées de 8 500 livres (3 856 kilos).

Toyota a beau se faire un devoir de paraître plus vert qu'un terrain de golf, n'empêche que le LX570 vient jeter une douche froide sur les écologistes. Mais quand on sait qu'il s'en est vendu à peine 41 unités l'an dernier au Québec, ça leur fait moins mal !

Alain Morin

PHOTOS : LEXUS

Catégorie	VUS
Échelle de prix	89 750 $
Garanties	4 ans/80 000 km, 6 ans/110 000 km
Assemblage	Araco, Japon
Cote d'assurance	n.d.

CHÂSSIS - DONNÉES POUR 570

Emp/lon/lar/haut	2 850/4 990/1 970/1 920 mm
Coffre	439 à 2 560 litres
Réservoir	93 litres
Nombre coussins sécurité	10
Antipatinage / contrôle stabilité	oui / oui
Suspension avant	indépendante, double triangulation
Suspension arrière	indépendante, multibras
Freins avant / arrière	disque (ABS) / disque (ABS)
Direction	à crémaillère, ass. variable
Diamètre de braquage	12,8 m
Pneus avant / arrière	P285/50R20 / P285/50R20
Poids	2 660 kg
Capacité de remorquage	3 856 kg (8 501 lb)

COMPOSANTES MÉCANIQUES

570

Cylindrée, soupapes, alim.	V8 5,7 litres 32 s atmos.
Puissance / Couple	383 chevaux / 403 lb-pi
Tr. base (opt) / rouage base (opt)	A6 / Int
0-100 / 80-120 / 100-0 km/h	7,6 s / 5,7 s / 42,6 m
Type ess. / ville / autoroute	Super / 17,0 / 11,4 l/100 km

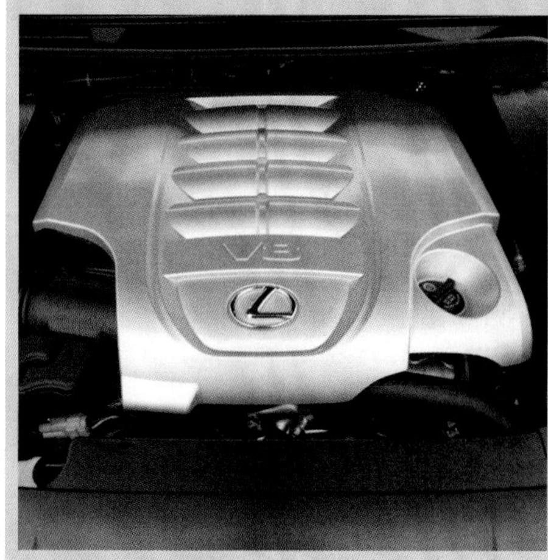

DANS LA MÊME CATÉGORIE

Cadillac Escalade, Infiniti QX, Land Rover Range Rover, Lincoln Navigator, Mercedes-Benz Classe G, Mercedes-Benz Classe GL

DU NOUVEAU EN 2011

Aucun changement majeur

NOS IMPRESSIONS

Agrément de conduite :	6/10
Fiabilité :	8/10
Sécurité :	8/10
Qualités hivernales :	8/10
Espace intérieur :	7/10
Confort :	8/10

www.lexus.ca

Plus d'informations dans la section statistiques en dernière partie du Guide

LE CHARME DISCRET DE LA BOURGEOISIE

Calme, silence et volupté. Voilà le menu proposé par le RX de Lexus, qui a été revu l'an dernier, et qui poursuit sa route en deux déclinaisons, soit le RX350 à motorisation conventionnelle et le RX450h à motorisation hybride. On peut, à juste tritre, qualifier le RX de pionnier puisqu'il devenait, à son lancement en 1999, le premier véritable sport-utilitaire de luxe, alors que l'arrivée du modèle à motorisation hybride en 2005 faisait également figure de première pour la catégorie.

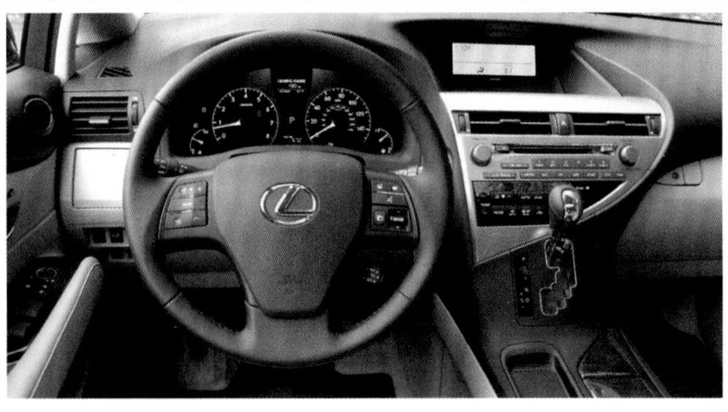

Lors de la dernière refonte, les concepteurs ont choisi de conserver l'allure sobre et relativement discrète du modèle antérieur, alors que la qualité d'assemblage supérieure est également restée au rendez-vous. L'habitacle propose un environnement feutré qui fait preuve de beaucoup de raffinement et la qualité des cuirs utilisés pour les sièges est vraiment exceptionnelle. Le tableau de bord et la console centrale manquent peut-être d'inspiration mais toutes les commandes et indicateurs tombent facilement sous la main. Le RX se distingue également par son contrôleur *Remote Touch* qui fait partie d'un ensemble d'options et qui fonctionne un peu à la manière d'une souris d'ordinateur, permettant d'accéder aux différents menus des systèmes. Pour ce qui est de l'ergonomie, le design de ce contrôleur ne prête pas flanc à la critique, puisqu'il épouse parfaitement la forme de la main droite, mais il est parfois difficile d'amener la flèche sur le bon icône de l'écran central avant de cliquer avec le pouce tout en roulant, ce qui fait que son utilisation n'est pas nécessairement facile au premier contact.

Les places arrière sont confortables et offrent un bon dégagement pour les jambes, le RX étant dépourvu d'un tunnel central malgré le fait qu'il soit équipé d'un rouage intégral. Par ailleurs, le RX marque des points pour sa polyvalence puisqu'il est possible de replier les dossiers des sièges arrière qui sont séparés en trois parties permettant par exemple d'abaisser seulement la partie centrale pour transporter des skis tout en conservant deux places pour les passagers. De plus, le RX est doté de commandes localisées dans le coffre permettant d'abaisser ces dossiers alors que l'on procède au chargement du véhicule, ce qui ajoute au côté pratique.

UNE CONDUITE ASEPTISÉE

Autant vous prévenir tout de suite, si vous êtes à la recherche d'un sport-utilitaire dont la dynamique s'apparente à celle d'une berline sport, regardez ailleurs car ce n'est pas du tout la vocation du RX qui a pour mission de d'isoler conducteur et passagers par une conduite largement aseptisée. Pour ce qui est des accélérations, pas de problèmes, les 275 chevaux du V6 de 3,5 litres répondent présent et la boîte automatique à six rapports est bien adaptée à ce moteur. C'est au freinage et en virages que ça se gâte, avec un direction trop légère, des suspensions dont le calibrage manque un peu de fermeté, ce qui entraîne du roulis en virage, et des pneumatiques qui ont été choisis plus en fonction du confort que de l'adhérence. Ajoutez à cela une intervention

FEU VERT

Grand confort
Silence de roulement
Bonne fiabilité
Qualité de finition

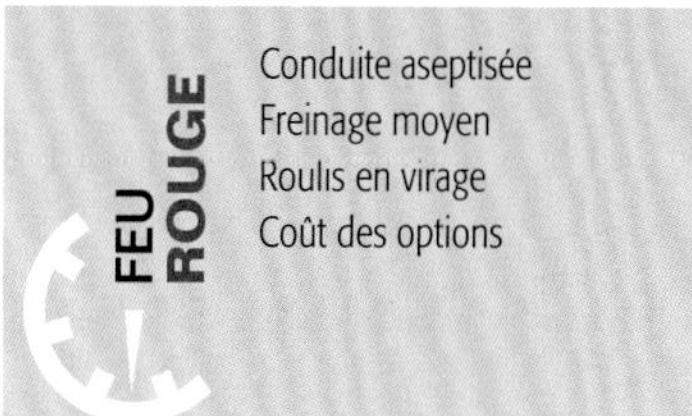

très hâtive du système de contrôle électronique de la stabilité, et tous les ingrédients sont réunis pour assurer une conduite sécuritaire et confortable, mais qui n'enflammera pas du tout les passions. Si la conduite sportive à l'occasion fait partie de vos priorités, allez voir du côté du BMW X5 ou du Porsche Cayenne, et même le ML de Mercedes-Benz ainsi que le Q7 de Audi s'avèreront plus satisfaisant que le RX à cet égard.

L'HYBRIDE : PLUS CHER ET PLUS LOURD

Le modèle hybride 450h est à la fois plus cher et plus lourd que le RX à motorisation conventionnelle ce qui fait que ses performances sont en retrait à tous les niveaux, sauf en ce qui a trait à la consommation qui est bonifiée d'environ 20 pour cent. Sur le RX450h, le V6 est secondé par deux moteurs électriques, soit un pour chaque train de roues. Le premier, qui est d'une puissance équivalente à 167 chevaux, agit sur les roues avant alors que le second, qui est jumelé aux roues arrière, en développe 68 et n'entre en action que lorsque les conditions d'adhérence l'exigent.

Il y a également un troisième moteur électrique, localisé dans la transmission, qui agit au démarrage et pour récupérer l'énergie en décélération, permettant ainsi de recharger les batteries. Ce système permet donc au RX450h de rouler en mode tout électrique lorsque les conditions le permettent, à savoir si le conducteur n'appuie que très légèrement sur l'accélérateur, en conduite urbaine par exemple, et le sentiment que l'on éprouve en circulant tout à fait silencieusement dans un sport-utilitaire de luxe est particulièrement satisfaisant. Toutefois, le prix du RX450h est élevé, tout comme le coût des ensembles d'options d'ailleurs.

On en revient donc à la case départ, soit que le RX, qu'il soit à motorisation conventionnelle ou hybride, fait l'apologie du confort et du silence de roulement au détriment de la conduite dynamique ou sportive, ce qui plaira à une partie de la clientèle et en décevra l'autre. Dans le cas de la marque Lexus, il faut également noter la qualité du service à la clientèle offert par les concessionnaires. Cette approche du client a joué pour beaucoup pour assurer les ventes des véhicules de la division de luxe de Toyota, et a également eu un effet bénéfique pour les clients des marques rivales qui ont été forcés de relever leur jeu d'un cran ou deux à cet égard.

Gabriel Gélinas

PHOTOS : ALAIN MORIN

Catégorie	VUS
Échelle de prix	46 900 $ à 59 500 $ (2010)
Garanties	4 ans/80 000 km, 6 ans/110 000 km
Assemblage	kyushu, Japon
Cote d'assurance	n.d.

CHÂSSIS - DONNÉES POUR 350

Emp/lon/lar/haut	2 740/4 770/1 885/1 720 mm
Coffre	1 132 à 2 273 litres
Réservoir	73 litres
Nombre coussins sécurité	10
Antipatinage / contrôle stabilité	oui / oui
Suspension avant	indépendante, jambes de force
Suspension arrière	indépendante, jambes de force
Freins avant / arrière	disque (ABS) / disque (ABS)
Direction	à crémaillère, ass. électrique
Diamètre de braquage	11,8 m
Pneus avant / arrière	P235/60R18 / P235/60R18
Poids	1 970 kg
Capacité de remorquage	1 587 kg (3 498 lb)

COMPOSANTES MÉCANIQUES

350

Cylindrée, soupapes, alim.	V6 3,5 litres 24 s atmos.
Puissance / Couple	275 chevaux / 257 lb-pi
Tr. base (opt) / rouage base (opt)	A6 / Int
0-100 / 80-120 / 100-0 km/h	8,2 s / 6,2 s / 42,0 m
Type ess. / ville / autoroute	Ordinaire / 11,5 / 8 l/100 km

450h

Cylindrée, soupapes, alim.	V6 3,5 litres 24 s atmos.
Puissance / Couple	295 chevaux / 234 lb-pi
Tr. base (opt) / rouage base (opt)	A6 / Int
0-100 / 80-120 / 100-0 km/h	8,0 s / 6,1 s / 44,1 m
Type ess. / ville / autoroute	Super / 6,6 / 7,2 l/100 km

DANS LA MÊME CATÉGORIE

Acura MDX, Audi Q7, BMW X5, Cadillac SRX, Infiniti FX, Lincoln MKX, Mercedes-Benz Classe M, Volkswagen Touareg, Volvo XC90

DU NOUVEAU EN 2011

Aucun changement majeur

NOS IMPRESSIONS

Agrément de conduite :	■■■■■■■■□□	8/10
Fiabilité :	■■■■■■■■□□	8/10
Sécurité :	■■■■■■■■■□	9/10
Qualités hivernales :	■■■■■■■■□□	8/10
Espace intérieur :	■■■■■■■■□□	8/10
Confort :	■■■■■■■■□□	8/10

www.lexus.ca

Plus d'informations dans la section statistiques en dernière partie du Guide

UNE VIE RÉSUMÉE EN QUELQUES MOTS

L'été dernier, mes parents fêtaient leur 50e anniversaire de mariage. Pour transporter les jubilaires, votre journaliste préféré, à défaut de dénicher un Pontiac 1959 comme « dans l'temps », a trouvé une Lincoln MKS toute noire.

Pour cette occasion, j'aurais pu mettre la main sur une Lexus LS460 ou une Mercedes-Benz Classe S. Pour le quadragénaire que je suis, ces voitures sont plus prestigieuses. Pourtant, il fallait voir les yeux de mon père alors qu'il admirait la MKS, « Une Lincoln, c'est pas rien... », pour être convaincu que mon choix était le bon. Il y a, pour les gens de certains groupes d'âge, quelque chose de rassurant dans les marques américaines Cadillac et Lincoln. J'irais même jusqu'à dire que ces noms, autrefois synonymes de prestige, représentent, encore, une part de rêve. Bien plus que BMW, Lexus ou Mercedes-Benz, inaccessibles.

ÇA, C'T'UN VRAI GROS CHAR...

Si les dimensions de la voiture ont impressionné le paternel, que dire de l'habitacle des plus accueillants ! Il fallait voir Gisèle passer des doigts caressants sur le cuir des sièges et sur le bord du tapis ! Les places arrière, chauffantes dans toutes les versions, sont très confortables — même celle du centre —, et l'espace ne fait pas défaut pour deux adultes. À l'avant, les occupants ne sont pas trop mal non plus même si les sièges, chauffants ET ventilés de série, ne procurent pas tout le support latéral qu'on attend d'eux. Le volant, ajustable en hauteur et en profondeur, se prend bien en main et la plupart des commandes respectent les principes de l'ergonomie. Comme bien des voitures américaines, les espaces de rangement ne sont pas légion et l'on se surprend toujours à tenter d'ouvrir le panneau situé sur la console centrale, tout juste devant le levier de la transmission, pour accéder à un grand espace de rangement. Mais non, il est fixe ! Le coffre est très grand mais il serait plus pratique si son seuil n'était pas si élevé et si son ouverture était d'une grandeur proportionnelle à ses dimensions. La visibilité vers l'arrière est assez problématique et les angles morts sont importants. Toutefois, Ford a eu l'excellente idée de placer des miroirs grand angle dans le coin supérieur de ses rétroviseurs extérieurs, éliminant ainsi la majeure partie des angles morts. Même pas besoin de recourir à une coûteuse technologie !

Le MKS reçoit, d'office, un V6 de 3,7 litres suffisamment puissant pour la plupart des occasions. Ce moteur est souple et, ma foi, fort sobre. Réussir du 11 litres/100 km avec une voiture de près de 1 900 kilos et cachant un moteur de 273 chevaux tient presque du miracle. Nous l'avons pourtant réalisé sans trop nous forcer. Sans doute que la transmission automatique à six rapports y est pour quelque chose. Cette boîte passe ses rapports avec douceur et elle possède un mode manuel qui n'est pas très intéressant à utiliser puisque c'est l'ordinateur qui prend toutes les décisions ! De plus, même si la version à moteur Ecoboost (nous y viendrons) affiche des palettes au volant, on ne peut pas

FEU VERT
- Habitacle silencieux et confortable
- Moteurs bien adaptés
- Équipement de série complet
- Un certain prestige
- Comportement routier relevé

FEU ROUGE
- V6 Ecoboost plus ou moins utile
- Dossiers arrière ne s'abaissent pas
- Poids substantiel
- Mode manuel peu invitant
- Peu d'espaces de rangement

rétrograder à la volée si le levier est sur le « D ». Dommage car il faut parfois rétrograder rapidement pour obtenir un surplus de puissance (*kick down*, en bon français !). La version de base est mue par les roues avant seulement (version TA) tandis que la TI a droit à la traction intégrale. Dans le premier cas, l'effet de couple en accélération vive est certes présent comme sur toutes les tractions puissantes mais il est fort bien maîtrisé. Bien entendu, ce comportement n'existe pas sur la version intégrale.

UN *BOOST* ÉCOLOGIQUE ?

L'autre moteur est un V6 de 3,5 litres Ecoboost, un beau nom qui comprend le mot « eco », ce qui fait bien plaisir au grand public. En fait, ce terme désigne un moteur biturbo. Dans le cas qui nous intéresse, il développe 355 chevaux et 350 livres-pied de couple, des données qu'on retrouvait uniquement dans des voitures très sportives il n'y a pas si longtemps. Elles permettent à Ford de clamer que ce moteur possède la puissance d'un V8 et la consommation d'un V6. À vitesse constante sur autoroute avec un vent de dos, ce simili V8 ne consomme effectivement pas plus qu'un V6 atmosphérique. Mais amenez-lui quelques arrêts obligatoires et une couple d'accélérations musclées et on change de registre! Si, au moins, il permettait de remorquer davantage que le 3,7 litres... Tous les deux peuvent tracter jusqu'à 1 000 livres (454 kilos). Dans le cas de l'Ecoboost, seul le rouage intégral est proposé, ce qui est une excellente chose !

Même s'il est très puissant et qu'il s'accroche avec ténacité au bitume, on ne peut pas qualifier le MKS de sportif. Ses suspensions sont manifestement axées vers le confort et à ce chapitre, c'est parfaitement réussi. La direction est bien dosée et offre un bon retour d'information néanmoins, elle déteste être brusquée. En virage, on dénote un certain roulis. Le contraire serait surprenant mais il faut avouer que les suspensions le maîtrisent passablement bien, compte tenu du poids quand même élevé du véhicule.

La Lincoln MKS a, un peu, contribué à faire de la fête de mes parents un succès. Il s'agissait, à ce moment-là, de la voiture qui répondait le mieux aux besoins et, surtout, à l'image que les jubilés se faisaient d'une voiture de luxe. Et pour ça, ça prend un passé glorieux. Souhaitons que dans cinquante ans, il le soit encore autant...

Alain Morin

PHOTOS : ALAIN MORIN

Catégorie	Berline
Échelle de prix	43 164 $ à 49 654 $
Garanties	4 ans/80 000 km, 6 ans/110 000 km
Assemblage	Chicago, Illinois, É-U
Cote d'assurance	n.d.

CHÂSSIS - DONNÉES POUR TI ECOBOOST

Emp/lon/lar/haut	2 845/5 182/2 159/1 549 mm
Coffre	521 litres
Réservoir	72 litres
Nombre coussins sécurité	6
Antipatinage / contrôle stabilité	oui / oui
Suspension avant	indépendante, jambes de force
Suspension arrière	indépendante, multibras
Freins avant / arrière	disque (ABS) / disque (ABS)
Direction	à crémaillère, assistée
Diamètre de braquage	12,1 m
Pneus avant / arrière	P235/55R18 / P235/55R18
Poids	1 940 kg
Capacité de remorquage	454 kg (1 000 lb)

COMPOSANTES MÉCANIQUES

TA, TI

Cylindrée, soupapes, alim.	V6 3,7 litres 24 s atmos.
Puissance / Couple	273 chevaux / 270 lb-pi
Tr. base (opt) / rouage base (opt)	A6 / Tr (Int)
0-100 / 80-120 / 100-0 km/h	7,4 s / 6,3 s / 40,0 m
Type ess. / ville / autoroute	Ordinaire / 12,8 / 8,8 l/100 km

TI EcoBoost

Cylindrée, soupapes, alim.	V6 3,5 litres 24 s turbo
Puissance / Couple	355 chevaux / 350 lb-pi
Tr. base (opt) / rouage base (opt)	A6 / Int
0-100 / 80-120 / 100-0 km/h	7,0 s / 5,4 s / 40,0 m
Type ess. / ville / autoroute	Ordinaire / 12,3 / 8,0 l/100 km

DANS LA MÊME CATÉGORIE

Acura RL, Audi A6, BMW Série 5, Cadillac DTS, Cadillac STS, Infiniti M, Jaguar XF, Lexus GS, Mercedes-Benz Classe E, Volvo S80

DU NOUVEAU EN 2011

Aucun changement majeur

NOS IMPRESSIONS

Agrément de conduite :	8/10
Fiabilité :	8/10
Sécurité :	10/10
Qualités hivernales :	8/10
Espace intérieur :	8/10
Confort :	8/10

www.lincolncanada.com

Plus d'informations dans la section statistiques en dernière partie du Guide

AMENEZ-EN DES LINCOLN COMME ÇA!

Regardez-le. Regardez-le bien. Vous n'êtes pas sûr d'aimer ce style «corbillard»? Vrai que ça frappe fort, et pas qu'au premier coup d'œil. Mais au moins Ford/Lincoln a-t-il osé avec son MKT. Et personnellement, ça me fait sourire tout grand.

Dans un paysage automobile qui se libéralise, le MKT n'a pas hésité à jouer la carte de la diversité. Sa longue silhouette racée est coiffée d'une mégacalandre chromée au sourire carnassier à une extrémité et, à l'autre, d'un hayon bulbeux. Le design est surprenant et ça prend une grosse semaine d'essai avant de s'y faire. Et c'est pour découvrir que finalement, on ne veut plus s'en départir, de ce MKT. Dans l'habitacle, surtout en variante six passagers (2+2+2), c'est le summum du luxe avec lequel Lincoln sait maintenant y faire.

L'instrumentation est classique, invitante et d'un grand chic. Partout, on sent – que dis-je, on obtient – toutes les preuves qu'un soin particulier a été apporté afin que l'expérience soit accommodante (le mot du jour...) et concluante. On y établit vite ses repères, qu'il s'agisse de la climatisation, des commandes audio ou du système de navigation. L'assemblage est d'excellente qualité, les matériaux sont haut de gamme et l'ensemble n'a absolument rien à envier aux intérieurs germaniques tout en froide techno. On note également des sièges douillets, aux nombreux positionnements. Bravo pour ces sièges chauffants ET ventilés, même en 2e rangée...

L'insonorisation est impressionnante: assis en 3e rangée, tout à l'arrière, les passagers participent aux conversations qui se déroulent à l'avant sans avoir à tendre l'oreille. En contrepartie, ces mêmes personnes doivent composer avec un piètre dégagement en hauteur. S'ils mesurent plus de 5,5 pieds, ils doivent incliner la tête... ou se la faire couper (!). De quoi être jaloux des

occupants en 2e rangée, confortablement installés dans leurs optionnels sièges capitaines: l'espace aux jambes y est si grand qu'on se croirait en classe affaire aérienne. Avec cette console centrale qui s'étire tout du long et qui abrite un réfrigérateur, c'est la grande classe. L'espace de chargement? Un si long véhicule (5,3 mètres) en propose nécessairement un vaste: 2149 litres toutes banquettes rabattues, entre autres parce que celle d'en arrière a la bonne idée de se replier dans le plancher.

L'ECOBOOST FAIT DES PETITS... PUISSANTS

De plus en plus de produits Ford/Lincoln adoptent la sauce Ecoboost et le MKT ne fait pas exception. Outre le V6 de 3,7 litres (268 chevaux) en motorisation de base, il y a le V6 de 3,5 litres biturbo et à injection directe, pour 355 chevaux et un énergique 350 lb-pi de couple. Pas de soin: avec ce dernier Ecoboost, les accélérations sont linéaires, sans tergiversation, pour un 0-100 km/h en sept secondes (données de l'AJAC), et ce, malgré un poids loin d'être plume (2222 kilos, rouage intégral de série compris). De fait, ça déplace tellement d'air qu'on aurait voulu un indicateur de turbo – et, tant qu'à y être, un son plus grondant à l'échappement, question de coller avec cet air menaçant.

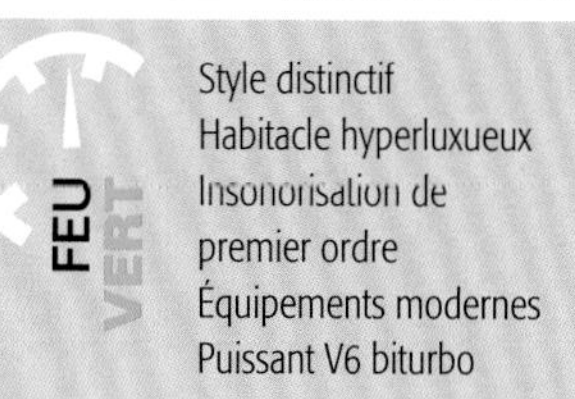

FEU VERT

- Style distinctif
- Habitacle hyperluxueux
- Insonorisation de premier ordre
- Équipements modernes
- Puissant V6 biturbo

FEU ROUGE

- Palettes au volant peu instinctives
- 3e rangée : oubliez votre tête...
- Consommation plus grande qu'annoncée
- 2 222 kilos, c'est lourd...

Les reprises sont athlétiques, jamais essoufflées, même quand on confie à la boîte automatique la tâche de négocier elle-même ses six rapports – ce qu'elle fait en douceur et de bon étagement. Le mode manuel est évidemment offert, mais il l'est par le biais de palettes au volant qui ne sont pas instinctives. Ces petites commandes (en plastique!) sont peu plaisantes à manipuler et elles demandent, à l'opposé de tout instinct, à ce qu'on les pousse pour rétrograder et à ce qu'on les tire pour accélérer. Conséquence : on se tanne vite.

Consommation d'essence? Euh... en théorie, l'Ecoboost cherche à rendre la puissance d'un V8 pour la consommation d'un V6. L'idée est intéressante, mais c'est sans compter qu'avec 355 chevaux sous le pied, on se montre trop enthousiaste. Après une semaine, notre MKT avait enregistré un combiné moyen au-delà des 14 l/100 km... Le MKT partage sa plate-forme d'assemblage avec le Ford Flex, s'étirant cependant de 15 cm supplémentaires. Pour lui, comme pour l'extra-terrestre Flex, on mise sur un comportement plus dynamique qu'attendu : pas de conduite surassistée, pas de roulis au moindre virage, pas d'éléments suspenseurs trop mielleux. Au contraire, la suspension se resserre pour accorder une balade bien équilibrée. La direction est électrique, mais elle a su conserver une bonne liaison avec la route.

APPRIVOISEMENT FACILE

C'est sans complexe que les gadgets de l'heure montent à bord du MKT : avertisseur d'angles morts, régulateur de vitesse intelligent, stationnement automatisé... Tous ont été mis au point de façon à être efficaces et, surtout, pratiques à utiliser. Pas besoin d'en référer au manuel du propriétaire pour comprendre le MyKey ou le Sync ; l'apprivoisement est facile, toujours. Bravo pour cette caméra de recul qui a le bonheur de montrer non seulement les arrières, mais aussi d'avertir du passage perpendiculaire d'un véhicule.

Définitivement, le MKT se montre à la hauteur de sa catégorie, avec un comportement routier intéressant, un luxe moderne et des équipements de pointe. La totale, quoi! Parti comme cela, Lincoln devrait réussir à convaincre les acheteurs de véhicules haut de gamme.

Nadine Filion

PHOTOS : MARC LACHAPELLE

LINCOLN MKT

Catégorie	Multisegment
Échelle de prix	49 950 $ à 53 350 $
Garanties	4 ans/80 000 km, 6 ans/110 000 km
Assemblage	Oakville, Ontario, Canada
Cote d'assurance	n.d.

CHÂSSIS - DONNÉES POUR TI ECOBOOST

Emp/lon/lar/haut	2 972/5 258/2 159/1 702 mm
Coffre	507 à 2 150 litres
Réservoir	68 litres
Nombre coussins sécurité	6
Antipatinage / contrôle stabilité	oui / oui
Suspension avant	indépendante, jambes de force
Suspension arrière	indépendante, multibras
Freins avant / arrière	disque (ABS) / disque (ABS)
Direction	à crémaillère, assistée
Diamètre de braquage	12,4 m
Pneus avant / arrière	P255/45R20 / P255/45R20
Poids	2 222 kg
Capacité de remorquage	2 041 kg (4 499 lb)

COMPOSANTES MÉCANIQUES

TI EcoBoost

Cylindrée, soupapes, alim.	V6 3,5 litres 24 s turbo
Puissance / Couple	355 chevaux / 350 lb-pi
Tr. base (opt) / rouage base (opt)	A6 / Int
0-100 / 80-120 / 100-0 km/h	7,0 s / 5,3 s / 48,0 m
Type ess. / ville / autoroute	Ordinaire / 13,1 / 9,1 l/100 km

TI

Cylindrée, soupapes, alim.	V6 3,7 litres 24 s atmos.
Puissance / Couple	268 chevaux / 267 lb-pi
Tr. base (opt) / rouage base (opt)	A6 / Int
0-100 / 80-120 / 100-0 km/h	7,7 s / 6,1 s / 48,0 m
Type ess. / ville / autoroute	Ordinaire / 13,0 / 9,2 l/100 km

DANS LA MÊME CATÉGORIE

Acura MDX, Audi Q7, BMW X5, Buick Enclave, Land Rover LR3, Mercedes-Benz Classe R, Volvo XC90

DU NOUVEAU EN 2011

3e banquette à rabattement électrique, groupes d'options modifiés

NOS IMPRESSIONS

Agrément de conduite :	8/10
Fiabilité :	8/10
Sécurité :	10/10
Qualités hivernales :	8/10
Espace intérieur :	9/10
Confort :	9/10

www.lincolncanada.com

Plus d'informations dans la section statistiques en dernière partie du Guide

Modèle 2010

LA VOITURE DE BILL GATES?

Je sais, quand on est aussi riche que le fondateur de Microsoft, on peut se payer quelque chose de plus onéreux, une Lincoln MKT par exemple. Mais après tout, comme il s'agit d'un Geek, Monsieur Gates se déplace peut-être en vélo. Mais une chose est certaine, si jamais il conduit cette nouvelle version de la MKX, il va certainement l'apprécier car cette voiture possède une foule de gadgets électroniques en mesure de faire plaisir à toutes ces personnes qui aiment les gadgets semblables. Et, selon les communiqués tonitruants du constructeur, ces mêmes nouveautés technologiques et électroniques nous rendent la tâche plus facile et augmentent le niveau de sécurité du véhicule.

En effet, dans le cadre d'une refonte complète de ce modèle, les ingénieurs de Ford en ont profité pour la doter d'une foule d'innovations technologiques en plus d'insérer un nouveau moteur V6 sous le capot.

LE *LOOK* LINCOLN

Au cours des années précédentes, on reprochait à la MKX de trop ressembler au Ford Edge avec qui elle partageait sa plate-forme et sa mécanique. Cette fois, les stylistes se sont mis à l'œuvre et ont réalisé un multisegment doté de sa propre personnalité visuelle. Pour être plus précis, celui-ci adopte les critères utilisés sur les autres modèles Lincoln, notamment, cette grille de calandre constituée de deux éléments indépendants dans lesquels on a inséré une grille verticale en forme de chutes d'eau. Les parois latérales sont également exclusives à ce modèle tandis que la partie arrière fait appel à des feux horizontaux comme sur la MKT.

Ce n'est pas uniquement la carrosserie qui a été changée, le tableau de bord a également eu droit à une refonte totale. L'élément dominant est cette console verticale placée en plein centre de la planche de bord et dont la surface en aluminium brossé ajoute un heureux contraste avec le reste du tableau de bord qui est noir de jais. La grande nouveauté est l'utilisation de touches sans contact. Vous avez bien lu, un peu comme dans les émissions de science-fiction, on n'a plus besoin d'appuyer sur un bouton ou une touche de commandes, il suffit tout simplement de mettre son doigt vis-à-vis cette commande pour que celle-ci s'exécute. Le secret: un champ électromagnétique qui réagit dès que notre doigt s'y approche. Pour être logique avec cette technologie, l'écran d'affichage est tactile et il suffit d'appuyer sur les touches qui sont affichées pour régler soit la climatisation, soit la navigation ou tout autre élément. Il est même possible de réduire le niveau sonore du système audio à l'aide de ses doigts en touchant des points de contact répartis sur cet écran. En plus, on retrouve bien entendu les systèmes à commande vocale que Ford utilise depuis quelques années maintenant sur plusieurs modèles.

FEU VERT

- Moteur plus puissant
- Transmission automatique SelectShift
- Commandes sans contact
- Cadrans indicateurs originaux
- Finition encore meilleure

FEU ROUGE

- Version hybride en attente
- Fiabilité inconnue de certains accessoires
- Visibilité arrière perfectible
- Bouton-poussoir sur la portière

Et comme tout modèle de cette marque qui se respecte, l'insonorisation a été poussée davantage. Dans ses communiqués, le constructeur souligne que l'utilisation de matières acoustiques très sophistiquées rend la MKX plus silencieuse à l'intérieur qu'un véhicule Lexus ou Audi.

NOUVEAU MOTEUR

Si on avait réalisé une nouvelle version de la MKX très poussée au point de vue des gadgets électroniques mais dont la mécanique serait quelque peu vieillotte, on aurait sérieusement raté le coche. On a également effectué les modifications qui s'imposaient. En tout premier lieu, un nouveau moteur V6 ronronne sous le capot. Il s'agit d'une version 3,7 litres du Duratec. Ce nouveau groupe propulseur est doté d'un nouveau système de calage variable des soupapes. Mais il se démarque puisque les deux arbres à cames sont totalement indépendants l'un de l'autre assurant ainsi une optimisation du rendement et une réduction de la consommation de carburant. C'est ainsi que la puissance a été portée à 305 chevaux alors que l'ancienne version n'en proposait que 265. Malgré cette hausse de puissance, la consommation de carburant serait réduite. Il faudra voir sur le terrain si ce moteur tient ses promesses. Une autre amélioration est la présence d'une boîte automatique à six rapports mais qui est cette fois dotée du système SelectShift qui permet au pilote de passer les vitesses manuellement. Autre détail, l'alimentation en carburant est interrompue momentanément lorsque le système de contrôle du moteur détecte une décélération. Comme sur le modèle précédent, il est possible de commander la transmission intégrale qui est beaucoup plus logique que la simple traction pour un véhicule de ce genre et de cette catégorie.

Lincoln veut faire de sa MKX un modèle de luxe capable de soutenir la comparaison avec la concurrence. Par exemple, on y retrouve un régulateur de croisière adaptative qui permet de maintenir une distance préréglée avec les véhicules qui circulent devant. En plus, le système d'information de présence d'un véhicule dans l'angle mort est également offert, tout comme celui détectant les véhicules venant de chaque côté.

Somme toute, on a équipé ce modèle de façon à le rendre non seulement plus agréable et plus performant, mais offrant certaines exclusivités au niveau des gadgets de l'habitacle, notamment ses boutons sans contact.

Denis Duquet

PHOTOS : LINCOLN

Catégorie	Multisegment
Échelle de prix	41 635 $
Garanties	4 ans/80 000 km, 6 ans/110 000 km
Assemblage	Oakville, Ontario, Canada
Cote d'assurance	passable

CHÂSSIS - DONNÉES POUR V6

Emp/lon/lar/haut	2 824/4 742/1 930/1 709 mm
Coffre	915 à 1 942 litres
Réservoir	76 litres
Nombre coussins sécurité	6
Antipatinage / contrôle stabilité	oui / oui
Suspension avant	indépendante, jambes de force
Suspension arrière	indépendante, double triangulation
Freins avant / arrière	disque (ABS) / disque (ABS)
Direction	à crémaillère, assistée
Diamètre de braquage	12,0 m
Pneus avant / arrière	P245/60R18 / P245/60R18
Poids	2 063 kg
Capacité de remorquage	1 588 kg (3 500 lb)

COMPOSANTES MÉCANIQUES

V6

Cylindrée, soupapes, alim.	V6 3,7 litres 24 s atmos.
Puissance / Couple	305 chevaux / 280 lb-pi
Tr. base (opt) / rouage base (opt)	A6 / Int
0-100 / 80-120 / 100-0 km/h	n.d. / n.d. / n.d.
Type ess. / ville / autoroute	Ordinaire / n.d.

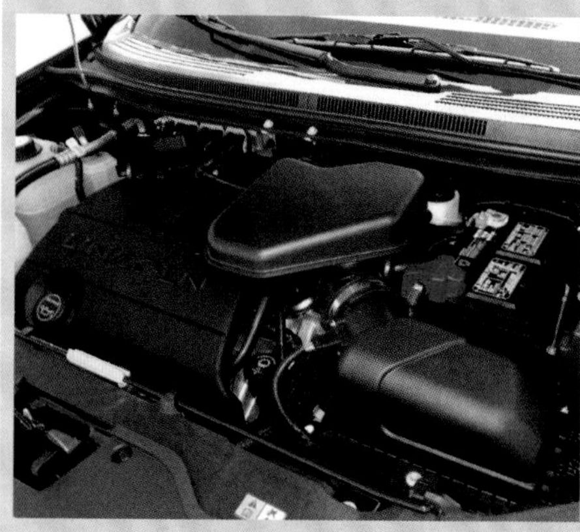

DANS LA MÊME CATÉGORIE

Acura MDX, Audi Q7, BMW X5, Cadillac SRX, Infiniti FX, Land Rover LR4, Lexus RX, Mercedes-Benz Classe M, Volkswagen Touareg, Volvo XC90

DU NOUVEAU EN 2011

Nouveau modèle

NOS IMPRESSIONS

Agrément de conduite :	■■■■■■■□□□ 7/10
Fiabilité :	Nouveau modèle
Sécurité :	■■■■■■■■■■ 10/10
Qualités hivernales :	■■■■■■■■□□ 8/10
Espace intérieur :	■■■■■■■■□□ 8/10
Confort :	■■■■■■■■□□ 8/10

www.lincolncanada.com

Plus d'informations dans la section statistiques en dernière partie du Guide

LA VOITURE DE SISYPHE?

Vous ne connaissez pas Sisyphe? Non, ce n'est pas un joueur de hockey roulant en Lincoln. Ce n'est pas non plus un chanteur rock scandinave! C'est un personnage de la mythologie grecque qui a été condamné jusqu'à la fin des temps à pousser une grosse pierre sur une pente, et à recommencer sans cesse. Eh bien, il semble que jusqu'à maintenant, la MKZ connaît une carrière semblable, car les ingénieurs n'ont jamais cessé de la transformer année après année.

Cette berline intermédiaire a débuté comme Lincoln Zephyr en 2006 pour ensuite devenir la MKZ dès l'année suivante. Des changements divers ont suivi afin que celle-ci puisse être compétitive et en harmonie avec les autres membres de la famille Lincoln. Enfin, l'an dernier, elle a connu d'autres transformations avec une nouvelle partie avant, un arrière redessiné et un nouveau tableau de bord. De plus, l'équipement de série a été amélioré. Après tous ces changements, on semble satisfait chez Lincoln puisque ce modèle revient en 2011 sans aucune modification majeure. Mais s'il n'y a pas de changement important, il y a un ajout de taille: une version hybride!

LUXE ET ENVIRONNEMENT

On ne doit pas être trop heureux chez Lexus de voir la MKZ finalement offerte en version hybride, car elle devient de facto la meilleure voiture hybride d'entrée de gamme parmi les voitures de luxe. Cette Lincoln utilise la plate-forme du Ford Fusion, et elle en emprunte la mécanique, ce qui est une bonne nouvelle. En effet, dans le cadre d'un match réalisé par le *Guide de l'auto 2010*, la Fusion avait surclassé toutes les autres hybrides inscrites à ce match, et de beaucoup.

Comme cette dernière, la MKZ hybride est propulsée par un moteur quatre cylindres de 2,5 litres de cycle Atkinson travaillant en harmonie avec un moteur électrique et produisant une puissance totale de 191 chevaux. Mais le plus important, c'est sa souplesse de fonctionnement. En mode électrique seul, le véhicule peut rouler plus vite et plus loin que ce que propose la Lexus HS250h, sa concurrente directe. Pour le reste, le comportement routier et l'agrément de conduite sont également supérieurs à sa concurrente nippone.

Par ailleurs, la voiture partage la même silhouette et le même habitacle que la version à moteur thermique avec l'addition de cadrans indicateurs appropriés à la conduite d'un véhicule hybride.

UN AIR DE FAMILLE

Si la MKZ a subi cette pléthore de changements au fil des années, ce fut en grande partie pour adapter sa présentation aux autres modèles Lincoln qui étaient commercialisés. Mais c'est souvent une illusion de croire qu'ils sont tous similaires. Ils ont une silhouette généralement semblable, mais les grilles de calandre diffèrent toutes, de même que les phares arrière. On est loin de chez Mercedes-Benz par exemple, alors que la grille de calandre et les

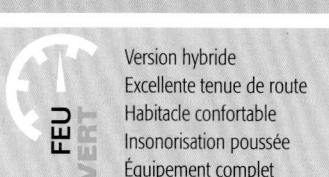

FEU VERT
- Version hybride
- Excellente tenue de route
- Habitacle confortable
- Insonorisation poussée
- Équipement complet

FEU ROUGE
- Image de marque
- Système Sync parfois sourd
- Écusson affreux
- Places arrière moyennes

phares arrière sont quasiment identiques d'une voiture à l'autre. Il semble que les designers nord-américains ne peuvent s'empêcher de finasser d'un modèle à l'autre. Malgré cette tendance au changement, c'est le statu quo cette année sur la Z. On retrouve donc la grille de calandre en forme de chute d'eau tandis que les jantes en alliage ressemblent plus ou moins à ce qui est proposé sur les autres Lincoln. Soulignons que la partie arrière est particulièrement élégante avec ses phares horizontaux placés dans la partie supérieure.

Mais de grâce, pourquoi s'entête-t-on chez Lincoln à conserver cet écusson vertical qui est non seulement anonyme, mais d'une grande laideur? Je plains les stylistes qui doivent tenter de l'incorporer à leur design! Soulignons au passage la qualité de l'habitacle en fait de matériaux et de finition. L'agencement des éléments de la planche de bord, des appliques de bois et des pièces métalliques est réussi. Soulignons au passage que les cadrans indicateurs sont faciles à lire, tandis que l'écran d'affichage central est excellent. Quant au système Sync à commande vocale, il utilise cette année le programme Dragon Naturally Speaking de Nuance afin d'améliorer la reconnaissance vocale et, croyez-moi, ce n'est pas un luxe.

OUBLIEZ LA RÉPUTATION

Quand on souffle le mot « Lincoln » à quelqu'un, il nous regarde souvent insulté et réplique : « Je ne suis pas si vieux et si ringard pour conduire une Lincoln ! Je ne veux pas non plus devenir chauffeur de taxi à l'aéroport ! » Cette réputation, Lincoln n'est pas près de s'en débarrasser. Et la direction de cette division n'a qu'elle à blâmer après des années d'incurie et de modèles minables. C'est dommage puisque la MKZ et tous les autres modèles de cette marque n'ont rien à voir avec les vestiges du passé. Non seulement sa qualité de fabrication est-elle exemplaire, mais elle est capable d'en imposer à la concurrence en raison de son équipement complet, de son luxe, de son silence de roulement et... de sa tenue de route. Et il ne s'agit pas d'une boutade. Je suis sérieux.

Cette voiture est en fait une Ford Fusion « pimpée » en Lincoln. Elle hérite donc des excellentes qualités routières de la Ford, de son agrément de conduite et de son moteur V6 de 3,5 litres bien adapté. Il ne faut pas oublier qu'elle est également offerte en version à transmission intégrale, ce qui est particulièrement apprécié dans certaines parties du pays.

Denis Duquet

PHOTOS : LINCOLN

Catégorie	Berline
Échelle de prix	36 579 $ à 39 029 $ (2010)
Garanties	4 ans/80 000 km, 6 ans/110 000 km
Assemblage	Hermosillo, Stamping, Mexique
Cote d'assurance	n.d.

CHÂSSIS - DONNÉES POUR TI

Emp/lon/lar/haut	2 728/4 841/1 834/1 445 mm
Coffre	447 litres
Réservoir	66 litres
Nombre coussins sécurité	6
Antipatinage / contrôle stabilité	oui / oui
Suspension avant	indépendante, bras inégaux
Suspension arrière	indépendante, multibras
Freins avant / arrière	disque (ABS) / disque (ABS)
Direction	à crémaillère, ass. variable
Diamètre de braquage	12,2 m
Pneus avant / arrière	P225/50R17 / P225/50R17
Poids	1 710 kg
Capacité de remorquage	454 kg (1 000 lb)

COMPOSANTES MÉCANIQUES

Hybride

Cylindrée, soupapes, alim.	4L 2,5 litres 16 s atmos.
Puissance / Couple	156 chevaux / 135 lb-pi
Tr. base (opt) / rouage base (opt)	CVT / Tr
0-100 / 80-120 / 100-0 km/h	n.d. / n.d. / n.d.
Type ess. / ville / autoroute	Ordinaire / 5,7 / 6,5 l/100 km (est)

TA, TI

Cylindrée, soupapes, alim.	V6 3,5 litres 24 s atmos.
Puissance / Couple	236 chevaux / 249 lb-pi
Tr. base (opt) / rouage base (opt)	A6 / Tr (Int)
0-100 / 80-120 / 100-0 km/h	7,8 s / 5,2 s / 41,7 m
Type ess. / ville / autoroute	Ordinaire / 12,6 / 8,3 l/100 km

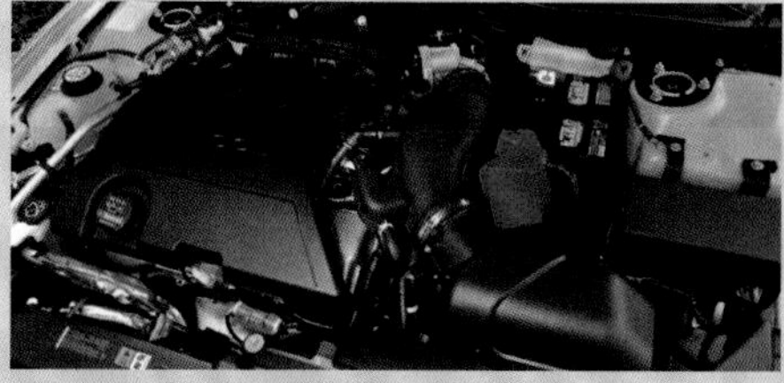

DANS LA MÊME CATÉGORIE

Acura TL, Buick Lucerne, Cadillac CTS, Chrysler 300, Hyundai Genesis, Lexus ES, Mercedes-Benz Classe C, Nissan Maxima, Toyota Avalon, Volvo S60

DU NOUVEAU EN 2011

Aucun changement majeur.
Version hybride sera dévoilée en cours d'année

NOS IMPRESSIONS

Agrément de conduite :	8/10
Fiabilité :	8/10
Sécurité :	8/10
Qualités hivernales :	8/10
Espace intérieur :	8/10
Confort :	8/10

www.lincolncanada.com

Plus d'informations dans la section statistiques en dernière partie du Guide

Lotus Elise

BALLERINES POUR LA ROUTE ET LES CIRCUITS

La première Elise fut lancée seulement en 1996 et la production de ce petit roadster représente pourtant le tiers de toutes les voitures que Lotus a construites en plus de 61 ans d'histoire. Sans parler de ses variantes et de voitures comme la Tesla Roadster électrique qui utilise une version de son châssis d'aluminium ultraléger qui fut dévoilé au Salon de Genève en 1991. Nul besoin d'être grande et lourde pour être géante.

Il était donc tout naturel pour Lotus Cars de choisir le 80e Salon de Genève, au printemps 2010, pour présenter la version rafraîchie de sa chère Elise. Cette toute petite voiture, par sa conception et da tenue de route brillantes, n'a cessé d'entretenir et d'alimenter la réputation de Lotus pour la conception, le développement et le raffinement de systèmes, de voitures complètes ou des technologies les plus novatrices et avancées.

La série Elise comporte trois modèles pour 2011. Le modèle simplement éponyme est propulsé par un tout nouveau moteur de 1,6 litre tandis que l'Elise R est équipée d'un groupe de 1,8 litre et que l'Elise SC profite de la version suralimentée par compresseur (d'où le SC pour *Supercharged*) du même moteur. Dans tous les cas, il s'agit de quatre cylindres à double arbre à cames en tête conçus pour Toyota par Yamaha et adaptés par les ingénieurs de Lotus aux besoins spécifiques des *roadsters* Elise et des coupés Exige qui partagent la même architecture.

Les modestes 134 chevaux du nouveau moteur de l'Elise sont suffisants pour un 0-100 km/h de 6,5 secondes dans ce roadster de 876 kilos mais Lotus est particulièrement fière d'avoir réduit la consommation de 23 % et les émissions de gaz carbonique de 16 % par rapport au modèle précédent, soit seulement 149 grammes par kilomètre. Le CO_2 n'a pas encore la même importance chez nous qu'en Europe mais avec une consommation moyenne de 5,04 l/100 km sur le cycle européen, on comprend immédiatement.

Pour compléter ce portrait de famille, notons que la Elise R boucle le 0-100 km/h en 5,4 secondes, atteint 222 km/h et produit 196 g/km de CO_2 avec son moteur de 190 chevaux. L'Elise SC et son moteur compressé de 217 chevaux abat le même sprint en 4,6 secondes, file à 233 km/h et produit 199 g/km de CO_2, selon les données du constructeur.

FORMES ET FONCTIONS BONIFIÉES

Lotus a également pris soin de rafraîchir la jolie silhouette de l'Elise pour 2011. Sa partie avant et sa calandre ont été redessinées pour accentuer sa présence et son aplomb. À l'arrière, on a créé un carénage à double renflement pour le nouveau moteur et intégré un diffuseur plus accentué au nouveau pare-chocs. Ces modifications ne sont pas uniquement pour la forme. Elles ont effectivement apporté une réduction du coefficient de traînée aérodynamique de l'ordre de 4 %.

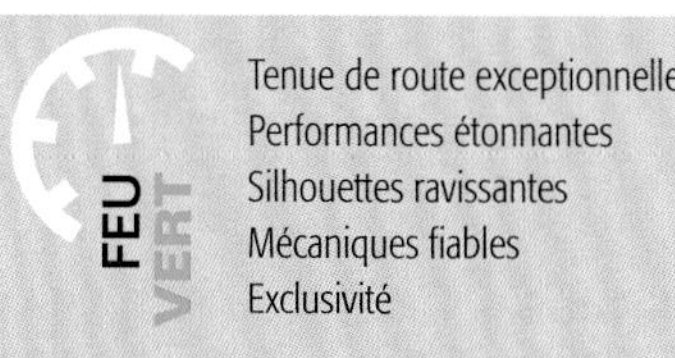

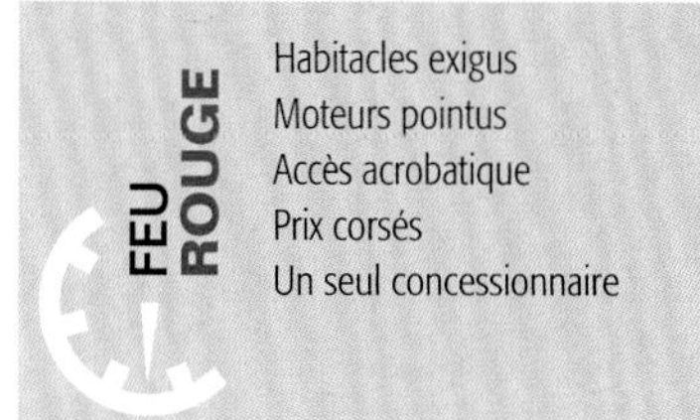

Les nouveaux phares des Elise sont sertis de rangées de diodes électroluminescentes dont certaines jouent le rôle de phares de jour et d'autres de clignotants. De plus, son nouveau capot arrière s'ouvre maintenant de l'intérieur de l'habitacle plutôt qu'avec la télécommande de verrouillage. Les acheteurs de ces Elise soigneusement recarrossées peuvent choisir aussi entre de nouvelles jantes en alliage forgé exceptionnellement légères ou en alliage coulé disponibles en finition argent ou noire. Derrière ces roues on retrouve des freins à disque avec des étriers AP Racing à l'avant et Brembo à l'arrière.

VITESSE OBLIGE

Quelles que soient les qualités dynamiques des roadsters Elise, les passionnés de conduite purs et durs jettent volontiers leur dévolu sur la série Exige. Ces coupés sont construits sur les mêmes bases mais axés encore plus sérieusement sur la performance et le pilotage, entre autres sur circuit. Leur carrosserie est coiffée d'un toit rigide en fibre de verre qui ajoute à la rigidité de la coque et améliore l'aérodynamique tout en générant de la portance pour mieux plaquer la voiture au sol. Une écope sur le toit alimente le refroidisseur du compresseur en air frais.

Les deux modèles sont propulsés par des versions compressées encore plus puissantes du même moteur Toyota/Yamaha de 1,8 litre, doté du calage variable intégral de ses 16 soupapes. Avec ses 240 chevaux et un poids de 942 kilos, la S240 boucle le 0-100 km/h en 4,2 secondes et peut filer à 240 km/h. Elle profite d'un différentiel autobloquant de type Torsen.

L'Exige S260 est encore plus pointue avec sa carrosserie truffée d'éléments en fibre de carbone qui réduisent son poids à 916 kilos, les amortisseurs Bilstein à réservoirs externes et les barre antiroulis réglables de sa suspension, des étriers avant à quatre pistons et des plaquettes plus résistantes pour ses freins italiens et un moteur de 257 chevaux qui permet de retrancher un dixième de seconde au chrono 0-100.

De toute manière, les Elise et Exige sont vouées à offrir une tenue de route et des sensations tactiles inégalées plutôt que des accélérations sidérantes. Leur habitacle exigu, spartiate et difficile d'accès est la rançon exigée pour cette pureté de conduite. Poseurs s'abstenir, surtout au tarif demandé qui atteint 75 000$ US pour l'Exige S260.

Marc Lachapelle

PHOTOS : LOTUS

Catégorie	*Roadster* / Coupé
Échelle de prix	60 750$ à 69 995$ (2010)
Garanties	3 ans/60 000 km, 3 ans/60 000 km
Assemblage	Hethel, Norwich Norfolk, Angleterre
Cote d'assurance	moyenne

CHÂSSIS - DONNÉES POUR ELISE SC

Emp/lon/lar/haut	2 301/3 785/1 720/1 143 mm
Coffre	112 litres
Réservoir	40 litres
Nombre coussins sécurité	2
Antipatinage / contrôle stabilité	opt / non
Suspension avant	indépendante, bras inégaux
Suspension arrière	indépendante, bras inégaux
Freins avant / arrière	disque (ABS) / disque (ABS)
Direction	à crémaillère, ass. variable
Diamètre de braquage	10,0 m
Pneus avant / arrière	P175/55R16 / P225/45R17
Poids	914 kg
Capacité de remorquage	non recommandé

COMPOSANTES MÉCANIQUES

Elise

Cylindrée, soupapes, alim.	4L 1,6 litre 16 s atmos.
Puissance / Couple	134 chevaux / 118 lb-pi
Tr. base (opt) / rouage base (opt)	M6 / Prop
0-100 / 80-120 / 100-0 km/h	6,5 s / 5,0 s (est) / 33,5 m
Type ess. / ville / autoroute	Super / n.d.

Elise R
4L 1,8 l, 190 ch, 133 lb-pi - 0-100 : 5,4 s - 11,2 / 8,7 l/100 km

Elise SC
4L 1,8 l, 218 ch / 156 lb-pi - 0-100 : 4,7 s - 11,9 / 9,0 l/100 km

Exige S240
4L 1,8 l, 240 ch / 170 lb-pi - 0-100 : 4,2 s - 11,8 / 9,0 l/100 km

Exige S260
4L 1,8 l, 257 ch / 174 lb-pi - 0-100 : 4,1 s - 11,8 / 9,0 l/100 km

DANS LA MÊME CATÉGORIE

Audi TT, BMW Z4, Mercedes-Benz Classe SLK, Nissan Z, Porsche Boxster

DU NOUVEAU EN 2011

Modifications esthétiques

NOS IMPRESSIONS

Agrément de conduite :	■■■■■■■■■■ 10/10
Fiabilité :	■■■■■■□□□□ 6/10
Sécurité :	■■■■■■■■□□ 8/10
Qualités hivernales :	nulles
Espace intérieur :	■■■□□□□□□□ 3/10
Confort :	■■■□□□□□□□ 3/10

www.lotuscars.com

Plus d'informations dans la section statistiques en dernière partie du Guide

UNE GRANDE SŒUR POUR ELISE

Les vertus de la légèreté, si chères à la marque Lotus, ont été brillamment défendues et démontrées par le *roadster* Elise et le coupé Exige au fil des quinze dernières années. Lotus vise maintenant plus haut avec la nouvelle Evora, un coupé 2+2 plus grand et plus spacieux qui prend pour cible certaines des meilleures sportives et grand-tourisme de l'heure.

L'Evora est la seule sportive 2+2 à moteur central et la première voiture construite sur le nouveau châssis VVA de Lotus (*Versatile Vehicle Architecture*), composé d'éléments en aluminium rivetés et collés à l'époxy auxquels s'ajoute un toit en matière composite. Plus grande que celle de l'Elise et de l'Exige, la coque de l'Evora est néanmoins deux fois et demie plus rigide.

PLUS D'ESPACE ET DE CONFORT

L'Evora à quatre places est plus longue qu'un coupé Exige biplace de 557 mm, plus large de 129 mm et plus haute de 106 mm. Avec son V6, elle est également plus lourde de 440 kg mais profite encore d'un avantage de 55 kg sur la plus légère des Porsche 911.

Contrairement à l'habitacle dépouillé des Elise et Exige, celui de l'Evora est bien fini et confortable avec sièges Recaro, prises pour iPod et autres bidules numériques, climatiseur de série et volant gainé de cuir, réglable en hauteur et en profondeur. Seule lacune évidente : un régulateur de vitesse qu'on obtient uniquement en choisissant le groupe Technologie optionnel qui rassemble une foule d'accessoires mais coûte environ 3000$.

Avec le groupe Premium, on retrouve du cuir Muirhead partout, même sur les seuils des portières ! Le groupe Sport ajoute un mode qui aiguise l'accélérateur et rehausse le régime maximum, un antipatinage qui permet un peu plus de dérive, un diffuseur arrière, des embouts d'échappement en titane et des disques de frein perforés avec étriers peints en noir.

CABINE TOUTE EN CONTRASTES

L'habitacle de l'Evora est lumineux, ouvert, moderne et original. La qualité des matériaux est louable et la finition très correcte, surtout avec le cuir du groupe Premium. Le confort est très honnête une fois assis cependant, il faut une bonne dose d'agilité pour se glisser à bord en franchissant les larges seuils. Les cadrans sont clairs et les contrôles bien placés, mais certains boutons sont durs et leurs inscriptions rétroéclairées peu visibles le jour et parfois bizarres.

L'accès aux places arrière est réservé aux enfants et aux contorsionnistes ! Elles serviront principalement à ranger des objets. Lotus offre une version deux places un peu moins chère de l'Evora pour les puristes mais prédit que sa valeur de revente sera moindre. Le coffre de 161 litres est isolé de la chaleur du moteur juste devant et même refroidi mais certainement pas immense. Les rangements sont rares à l'intérieur. Il y a un petit coffre à gants et c'est à peu près tout.

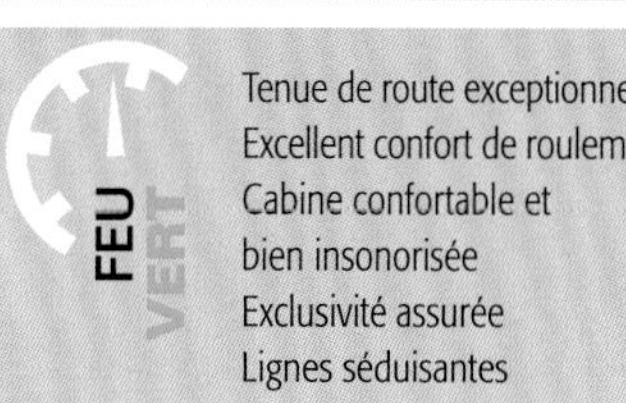

Tenue de route exceptionnelle
Excellent confort de roulement
Cabine confortable et bien insonorisée
Exclusivité assurée
Lignes séduisantes

Pas de repose-pied
Levier de vitesses long et imprécis
Visibilité arrière exécrable
Peu d'espaces de rangement
Dispendieuse avec les options

Il n'y a même pas de repose-pieds à gauche de la pédale d'embrayage ! Le maintien latéral des sièges Recaro est une bénédiction sans appui solide pour la jambe gauche en virage.

PLUS DE MUSCLE JAPONAIS

Le moteur de l'Evora est un V6 Toyota à double arbre à cames en tête de 3,5 litres retouché par Lotus. Il produit 276 chevaux à 6400 tr/min et 258 lb-pi de couple à 4700 tr/min. Il est jumelé à une boîte manuelle à 6 rapports dont on peut obtenir une version dont les rapports 3 à 6 sont plus démultipliés. L'Evora peut atteindre 100 km/h en 5,1 secondes et une vitesse de pointe de 261 km/h, selon Lotus.

Le V6 est flexible et puissant mais il lui manque le caractère vif et la sonorité qui font l'attrait viscéral des Porsche ou Ferrari. Lotus a annoncé que le motoriste Cosworth apportera désormais sa touche unique à tous les moteurs Toyota qu'elle emploiera. Une version compressée du V6 est déjà en préparation.

TENUE DE ROUTE BRILLANTE

Sur la route, la nouvelle Lotus est un modèle d'agilité, de grâce et d'équilibre. Impossible, par contre, d'y explorer les limites de sa tenue de route en toute sécurité. Même en poussant fort, les pneus n'ont jamais émis le moindre crissement lors du lancement californien. Il faudra un circuit pour en savoir plus.

La servodirection hydraulique procure des sensations tactiles exceptionnelles et le freinage est superbement puissant et facile à moduler. Les gros disques Lotus/AP Racing de 350 mm à l'avant et 332 mm à l'arrière sont pincés par des étriers à quatre pistons et perforés avec le groupe Sport. Le seul bémol en conduite, à part le repose-pied manquant, est un levier de vitesses à la course trop longue et imprécise, qui sonne plutôt creux.

Puisque Lotus ne peut construire qu'environ 2000 Evora par année, dont le tiers viendra en Amérique, exclusivité et rareté sont assurées. Silhouette racée et tenue de route d'exception devraient faire le reste, en attendant les variantes plus performantes et pointues, y compris une suite au prototype Evora 414E à rouage hybride essence-électricité dévoilé au dernier Salon de Genève.

Marc Lachapelle

PHOTOS : MARC LACHAPELLE

LOTUS EVORA

Catégorie	Coupé
Échelle de prix	73 200 $
Garanties	3 ans/60 000 km,
Assemblage	Hethel, Angleterre
Cote d'assurance	n.d.

CHÂSSIS - DONNÉES POUR BASE

Emp/lon/lar/haut	2 575/4 342/1 848/1 223 mm
Coffre	170 litres
Réservoir	60 litres
Nombre coussins sécurité	2
Antipatinage / contrôle stabilité	oui / oui
Suspension avant	indépendante, leviers triangulés
Suspension arrière	indépendante, leviers triangulés
Freins avant / arrière	disque (ABS) / disque (ABS)
Direction	à crémaillère, assistée
Diamètre de braquage	10,1 m
Pneus avant / arrière	P225/40ZR18 / P255/35ZR19
Poids	1 382 kg
Capacité de remorquage	non recommandé

COMPOSANTES MÉCANIQUES

Base	
Cylindrée, soupapes, alim.	V6 3,5 litres 24 s atmos.
Puissance / Couple	276 chevaux / 258 lb-pi
Tr. base (opt) / rouage base (opt)	M6 (A6) / Prop
0-100 / 80-120 / 100-0 km/h	5,1 s / 4,0 s / n.d.
Type ess. / ville / autoroute	Super / 12,4 / 6,5 l/100 km

DANS LA MÊME CATÉGORIE

Audi TT, Mercedes-Benz Classe SLK, Porsche Cayman

DU NOUVEAU EN 2011

Nouveau modèle

NOS IMPRESSIONS

Agrément de conduite :	■■■■■■■■■□	9/10
Fiabilité :	Nouveau modèle	
Sécurité :	■■■■■■■■□□	8/10
Qualités hivernales :	■■■■■■□□□□	6/10
Espace intérieur :	■■■■■■□□□□	6/10
Confort :	■■■■■■■■□□	8/10

www.lotuscars.com

Plus d'informations dans la section statistiques en dernière partie du Guide

TROIS BELLES ITALIENNES

Si Maserati est moins connue du public que Ferrari de nos jours, il faut se souvenir qu'elle était l'une des marques les plus prestigieuses de la planète bien avant que celle arborant l'écusson au cheval cabré fasse ses débuts. En effet, la marque au trident a été fondée en 1914 et a connu ses heures de gloire par la suite. Dans les années 50, l'immortel Fangio a savouré de nombreuses victoires au volant d'une Maserati. Par la suite, des propriétaires plus ou moins compétents se sont succédé, et ont pratiquement tué la marque. Heureusement, elle a été acquise en 1993 par Ferrari, son ancien grand rival, avant de faire partie du groupe Fiat en association avec Alfa Romeo.

Cela explique l'arrivée de deux nouveaux modèles au cours des trois dernières années. Le premier, le coupé GranTurismo, a été dévoilé en 2007. Il empruntait la plate-forme de la berline Quattroporte. Puis, les ingénieurs ont repris le coupé pour produire un cabriolet, le GranCabrio, qui a fait ses débuts au cours des derniers mois.

LA GT

La GranTurismo est un coupé dont les formes sont nettement plus élégantes que le modèle qu'elle remplace depuis 2007. En effet, les stylistes ont utilisé avec succès la grille de calandre arborant le célèbre trident sans oublier les célèbres extracteurs d'air placés de chaque côté des ailes avant. La partie arrière est plus large et plus basse, ce qui donne à cette voiture l'allure d'un félin prêt à bondir. Cette élégance se traduit également dans l'habitacle, alors que les cuirs les plus fins, les bois exotiques et un agencement unique en son genre font de cette voiture une automobile

d'exception. Par contre, il y a toujours ces petits détails qui sonnent faux et qui semblent être l'apanage des voitures italiennes vendues à fort prix. Cette fois, c'est raté avec le couvercle du coussin de sécurité du côté passager; même les voitures bas de gamme sont mieux équipées à ce chapitre. Toujours au niveau de l'habitacle, les places arrière sont relativement exiguës.

Ce coupé est offert en trois configurations: GranTurismo, GranTurismo S et sa version automatique. Le premier est propulsé par un moteur V8 de 4,2 litres provenant de chez Ferrari, et il produit dorénavant 405 chevaux. La version S, qu'elle soit à boîte manuelle ou automatique, est propulsée par un moteur V8 de 4,7 litres, et celui-ci a été réalisé par les ingénieurs de chez Alfa Romeo. Sa puissance est de 440 chevaux et ses prestations, tout comme la sonorité de son échappement, sont en mesure de faire rêver les amateurs du genre. Tous ces modèles sont dotés de la suspension à réglage électronique Skyhook. Sur la version avec transmission automatique, cette suspension travaille de concert avec celle-ci afin d'harmoniser les performances et la tenue de route. Cette boîte automatique comprend quatre réglages distincts.

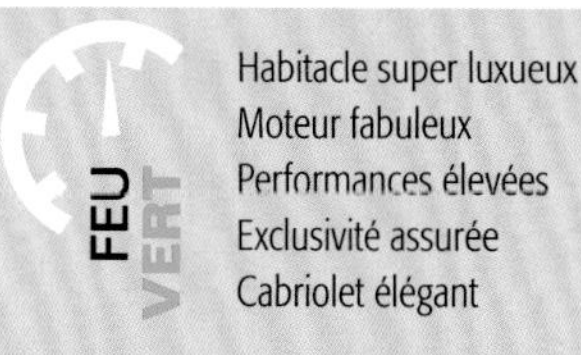

Habitacle super luxueux
Moteur fabuleux
Performances élevées
Exclusivité assurée
Cabriolet élégant

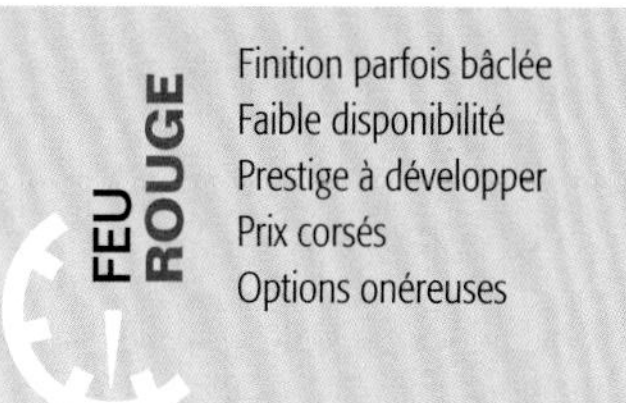

Finition parfois bâclée
Faible disponibilité
Prestige à développer
Prix corsés
Options onéreuses

Avec une telle plate-forme et des moteurs aussi sophistiqués, il est normal que cette voiture soit non seulement agréable à piloter, mais qu'elle propose un comportement routier digne de son héritage. On la retrouve également en course. Il est dommage que sa diffusion au Québec soit si limitée, car c'est une gamme de modèles qui est en mesure de plaire à certains connaisseurs.

LA GC

La rumeur circulait quant à l'arrivée d'une version cabriolet, la GranCabrio, de ce magnifique coupé. Selon des sources bien informées, on nous parlait d'un toit rigide amovible qui se serait replié dans le coffre à bagages comme sur une certaine Mercedes-Benz. Pourtant, lorsque la version définitive de la voiture a été dévoilée, on a pu constater que les ingénieurs avaient opté pour un toit souple, ce qui est une excellente idée. Non seulement réduit-il le poids, mais il permet de conserver l'espace du coffre à bagages une fois remisé. De plus, on peut parler d'un cabriolet quatre places, même si les places arrière sont destinées à des personnes de taille moyenne, sans plus. À 30 km/h maximum, il suffit d'appuyer sur une touche pour transformer la GranCabrio de coupé à cabriolet en 28 secondes seulement.

Un seul moteur est disponible pour l'instant, il s'agit du moteur V8 de 4,7 litres de 440 chevaux associé à une transmission automatique ZF à six rapports. Comme sur le coupé, la suspension à réglage électronique Skyhook est utilisée. Et ce ne sont pas les performances qui font défaut avec une vitesse de pointe de 283 km/h, et un temps de 5,1 secondes pour boucler le 0-100 km/h. Vous admettrez que ça décoiffe !

LA QUATTROPORTE

Cette berline de grand luxe est avec nous depuis quelques années maintenant et elle méritait une grande popularité et une meilleure renommée. Il est vrai que sa silhouette dessinée par Pininfarina est très discrète, mais elle possède cette rare élégance appréciée des gens recherchant un style classique. L'acheteur a d'ailleurs l'embarras du choix en ce qui concerne l'aménagement de l'habitacle avec une vaste sélection de cuirs et autres aménagements qui permettent de rendre cette voiture encore plus exclusive. C'est une expérience sensorielle que de monter à bord d'une Quattroporte. En comparaison, les berlines allemandes de luxe nous donnent la sensation de pénétrer dans un frigo.

Denis Duquet

PHOTOS : MASERATI

Catégorie	Cabriolet, Coupé
Échelle de prix	118 000 $ à 135 800 $
Garanties	4 ans/80 000 km, 4 ans/80 000 km
Assemblage	n.d.
Cote d'assurance	n.d.

CHÂSSIS - DONNÉES POUR GRAN TURISMO S

Emp/lon/lar/haut	2 942/4 881/1 915/1 353 mm
Coffre	260 litres
Réservoir	86 litres
Nombre coussins sécurité	6
Antipatinage / contrôle stabilité	oui / oui
Suspension avant	indépendante, bras inégaux
Suspension arrière	indépendante, double triangulation
Freins avant / arrière	disque (ABS) / disque (ABS)
Direction	à crémaillère, ass. variable
Diamètre de braquage	12,3 m
Pneus avant / arrière	P245/35R20 / P285/35r20
Poids	1 880 kg
Capacité de remorquage	n.d.

COMPOSANTES MÉCANIQUES

Gran Turismo

Cylindrée, soupapes, alim.	V8 4,2 litres 48 s atmos.
Puissance / Couple	405 chevaux / 339 lb-pi
Tr. base (opt) / rouage base (opt)	seq / Prop
0-100 / 80-120 / 100-0 km/h	5,6 s / 4,1 s / 36,0 m
Type ess. / ville / autoroute	Super / 17,8 / 10,4 l/100 km

Gran Turismo S, Gran Turismo Convertible, Quattroporte GTS

Cylindrée, soupapes, alim.	V8 4,7 litres 48 s atmos.
Puissance / Couple	440 chevaux / 361 lb-pi
Tr. base (opt) / rouage base (opt)	seq (A6) / Prop
0-100 / 80-120 / 100-0 km/h	5,1 s / 3,7 s / 35,0 m
Type ess. / ville / autoroute	Super / 18,4 / 10,6 l/100 km

Quattroporte
V8 4,2 l, 400 ch / 339 lb-pi - 0-100 : 5,6 s - 18,1 / 11,5 l/100 km

Quattroporte S
V8 4,7 l, 430 ch / 361 lb-pi - 0-100 : 5,4 s - 18,4 / 10,9 l/100 km

DANS LA MÊME CATÉGORIE

Aston Martin Vantage, Audi R8, BMW Série 6, Chevrolet Corvette, Ferrari F458 Italia, Jaguar XK, Mercedes-Benz Classe CL, Mercedes-Benz Classe SL, Porsche 911

DU NOUVEAU EN 2011

Aucun changement majeur

NOS IMPRESSIONS

Agrément de conduite :	8/10
Fiabilité :	7/10
Sécurité :	6/10
Qualités hivernales :	2/10
Espace intérieur :	6/10
Confort :	8/10

www.maseratiquebec.com

Plus d'informations dans la section statistiques en dernière partie du Guide

Y A-T-IL UN MOTEUR SOUS LE CAPOT?

Bentley et Rolls-Royce jouissent d'une réputation enviable dans le petit monde des voitures très haut de gamme et doivent leur popularité actuelle à leur riche passé. Lorsque Mercedes-Benz a décidé d'investir ce créneau, pour le moins restreint mais tellement lucratif, la marque germanique a choisi de ressortir des boules à mites un nom autrefois prestigieux, Maybach. Or, Maybach a beau être bien connu en Allemagne, c'est loin d'être le cas ailleurs. En fait, seuls quelques maniaques de voitures anciennes savent que la marque Maybach a produit certaines des bagnoles les plus marquantes des années 1920, 30 et 40.

Mais le nom Maybach n'est pas mal choisi pour autant puisque Wilhelm Maybach et Gottlieb Daimler ont collaboré aux prémices de l'automobile en créant, entre autres, le *riding car*, une sorte de motocyclette à moteur monocylindre vertical en 1885. En 1909, Maybach crée sa propre marque de prestige. Il décède le 29 décembre 1929. Voilà pour l'origine du nom, bien choisi mais peu connu.

MAYBACH AUJOURD'HUI

Les Maybach actuelles ne connaissent pas le succès escompté, en grande partie parce que le lien, surtout visuel, avec la Mercedes-Benz Classe S est trop évident. En effet, la Maybach repose sur la plate-forme allongée d'une Classe S. En plus, cette dernière lui fournit son V12, nous y reviendrons. Dans ce monde, les changements sont plutôt évolutifs. Mais cette année, grosse révolution, la partie avant est remaniée: le capot est un peu surélevé, la grille de calandre est différente et la partie inférieure du pare-chocs montre deux rangées de lumières à DEL. Les changements à la partie

arrière sont des plus discrets mais même s'ils avaient été plus prononcés, il en aurait fallu bien plus pour que l'on cesse de confondre une Maybach avec une Classe S « pimpée »

Malgré des ventes très confidentielles, Maybach propose pas moins de cinq modèles. On retrouve tout d'abord la version de base, la 57 (57 représentant la longueur de la voiture – 5734 mm) et la 62 (6171 mm). Ces deux modèles se déclinent en variantes « S », non pour Sport mais pour Spezial, le terme Sport étant sans doute tabou chez les très riches. Il y a aussi la très spécialisée Landaulet, qu'il est permis d'appeler « Landau laitte » tellement ses lignes sont... différentes. En fait, tout comme certains modèles anciens très luxueux, la partie arrière de son toit s'ouvre pour permettre aux occupants de saluer la foule alors que le chauffeur ganté avance lentement dans le défilé protocolaire. Je me demande bien qui, outre un premier ministre ou un pape peut avoir besoin de ce véhicule ? On peut aussi se poser la question à savoir qui a besoin d'une Maybach, peu importe le modèle...

DES VERSIONS POUR MULTIMILLIONNAIRES PAUVRES

La différence de longueur entre les versions 57 et 62 se remarque

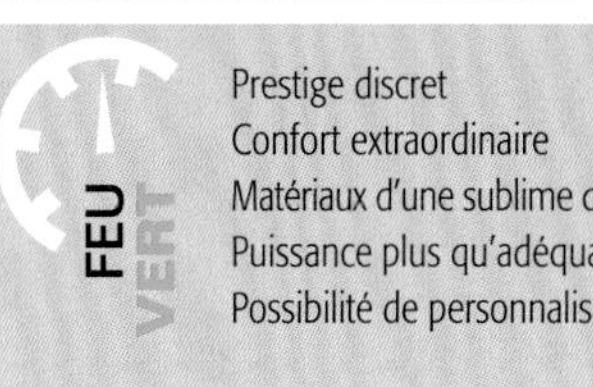

FEU VERT

- Prestige discret
- Confort extraordinaire
- Matériaux d'une sublime qualité
- Puissance plus qu'adéquate
- Possibilité de personnalisation

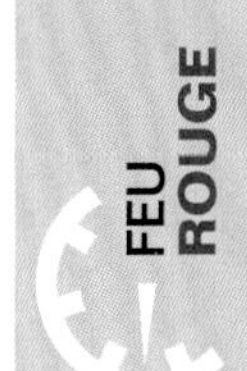

FEU ROUGE

- Image de marque diluée
- Incroyablement gros et lourd
- Consommation éhontée
- Conduite endormante
- Boite automatique à cinq rapports seulement

surtout au niveau des places arrière qui passent d'extraordinairement grandes pour la 57 à « galactiquement » grandes pour la 62. Lors du lancement de la marque en 2002, Maybach parlait d'un habitacle digne d'un jet privé. Et, effectivement, je ne vois pas de meilleure référence. Les matériaux sont d'une qualité rarement égalée et leur assemblage est parfait. Une fois les portières refermées, c'est le silence le plus total. Il faut d'ailleurs voir l'épaisseur des vitres. Un millimètre de plus et on appelle ça du blindage ! Inutile d'insister sur le fait que les sièges sont confortables ou que l'espace n'est pas compté. Les sièges arrière possèdent tous les ajustements imaginables et inimaginables, les coupes de champagne sont spécialement dessinées pour ne pas renverser leur capiteux contenu sur les occupants habillés par Armani (qui aurait l'indécence de s'asseoir dans une Maybach avec des vêtements provenant de chez l'Équipeur ?), la connectivité Bluetooth et toutes les autres technologies sont contrôlées par les passagers arrière, le système DVD est double, ce qui permet à chacun de regarder son film préféré et, enfin, gâterie entre toutes, on retrouve un flacon de parfum branché au système de climatisation arrière...

Le chauffeur, lui, s'ennuie à mourir. Conduire une Maybach, en particulier de base, est d'une navrante platitude. Le moteur des 57 et 62 est un V12 turbo de 5,5 litres dont la puissance limitée à 550 chevaux est quand même suffisante pour des dépassements en toute sécurité. Lorsque des clients ont montré leur intérêt pour une Maybach plus puissante, les dirigeants n'ont surtout pas voulu les offenser (ils en ont tellement peu...). C'est ainsi que les modèles S ont droit à un V12 turbo de 6,0 litres de 630 chevaux, une hausse de 80 par rapport au 5,5 litres. Certes, les S sont très performants mais l'habitacle est si feutré qu'on n'a aucune sensation de vitesse. Sur une autoroute, conserver une vitesse de croisière de 100 km/h sans utiliser le régulateur de vitesse tient du miracle. Les suspensions des modèles Spezial sont un peu plus fermes, ce qui améliore la tenue de route. Si vous étiez sur le point de faire l'achat d'une S, ne craignez rien. Chez Maybach, suspension plus ferme veut quand même dire ultraconfortable. D'un autre côté, les 57 et 62, sans être des bêtes de circuit de course (les prototypes ont assurément été testés sur les autoroutes allemandes plutôt qu'au Nürburgring !) tiennent très bien la route. Après tout, quand une voiture peut atteindre 250 km/h, elle est mieux de bien coller à la route ! Et de très bien coller à la route quand elle peut rouler jusqu'à 278 km/h !

Alain Morin

PHOTOS : MAYBACH

Catégorie	Berline
Échelle de prix	387 000 $ à 1 380 000 $
Garanties	4 ans/illimité, 4 ans/illimité
Assemblage	Sindelfingen, Allemagne
Cote d'assurance	n.d.

CHÂSSIS - DONNÉES POUR 62S

Emp/lon/lar/haut	3 827/6 171/2 151/1 573 mm
Coffre	442 litres
Réservoir	110 litres
Nombre coussins sécurité	7
Antipatinage / contrôle stabilité	oui / oui
Suspension avant	indépendante, double triangulation
Suspension arrière	indépendante, multibras
Freins avant / arrière	disque (ABS) / disque (ABS)
Direction	à billes, assistée
Diamètre de braquage	13,4 m
Pneus avant / arrière	P275/45R20 / P275/45R20
Poids	2 875 kg
Capacité de remorquage	n.d.

COMPOSANTES MÉCANIQUES

57, 62

Cylindrée, soupapes, alim.	V12 5,5 litres 36 s turbo
Puissance / Couple	550 chevaux / 664 lb-pi
Tr. base (opt) / rouage base (opt)	A5 / Prop
0-100 / 80-120 / 100-0 km/h	5,2 s / 3,2 s / 39,2 m
Type ess. / ville / autoroute	Super / 21,1 / 12,9 l/100 km

57S, 62S, Landaulet

Cylindrée, soupapes, alim.	V12 6,0 litres 36 s turbo
Puissance / Couple	630 chevaux / 738 lb-pi
Tr. base (opt) / rouage base (opt)	A5 / Prop
0-100 / 80-120 / 100-0 km/h	5,2 s / 3,2 s / 39,2 m
Type ess. / ville / autoroute	Super / 21,2 / 12,9 l/100 km

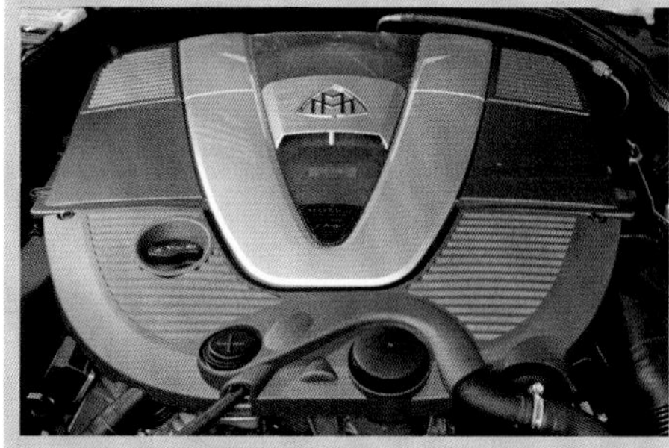

DANS LA MÊME CATÉGORIE

Bentley Mulsanne, Mercedes-Benz Classe S, Rolls-Royce Phantom

DU NOUVEAU EN 2011

Partie avant redessinée

NOS IMPRESSIONS

Agrément de conduite :	6/10
Fiabilité :	10/10
Sécurité :	10/10
Qualités hivernales :	8/10
Espace intérieur :	10/10
Confort :	10/10

www.maybachusa.com

Plus d'informations dans la section statistiques en dernière partie du Guide

DESIGN ET ZOOM ZOOM

De toutes les voitures lancées récemment sur le marché par ce constructeur, la plus récente génération de la Mazda2 est celle qui a reçu le plus d'accolades et d'accessits. Dévoilée en première mondiale au Salon international de l'auto de Genève en 2007, elle a accumulé les succès dans tous les pays où elle a été commercialisée depuis. Elle a d'ailleurs été nommée *Voiture mondiale de l'année en 2008*. Malgré cela, son arrivée sur notre marché se faisait attendre.

Pour cause, la direction de Mazda refusait d'introduire cette sous-compacte dans le marché nord-américain. Les excuses étaient nombreuses, notamment un manque de capacité de production, de même qu'un marché potentiel trop limité. Mazda a heureusement révisé sa position et a finalement décidé d'importer cette petite cinq portes. Il est certain que son arrivée en Amérique du Nord va être fort remarquée, car elle possède plusieurs atouts jouant en sa faveur. Bien évidemment, chacun sait que tous ces titres récoltés à l'étranger ne sont pas le fruit du hasard.

UN AIR DE FAMILLE

Au cours des derniers mois, plusieurs modèles Mazda ont été revus sur le plan esthétique afin de partager les mêmes caractéristiques esthétiques, notamment cette grille de calandre en forme de sourire. Les CX-7 et CX-9, entres autres, ont bénéficié de ces changements. Chez Mazda, on parle de design *Zoom-Zoom* visant à représenter visuellement les caractéristiques sportives de tous leurs véhicules et ce, peu importe leur catégorie. J'ai cru pendant longtemps que le leitmotiv *Zoom-Zoom* de Mazda n'était qu'une tactique commerciale. Je dois faire aujourd'hui mon mea culpa, car au fil des années et des modèles, la plupart des véhicules Mazda ont démontré un caractère plus sportif que la moyenne et un agrément de conduite plus relevé. Bien entendu, le design des voitures doit être également *Zoom-Zoom*.

La Mazda2 adopte donc une silhouette cunéiforme avec son capot plongeant et son arrière relevé. Elle est sportive avec des angles obtus et des porte-à-faux avant et arrière réduits au maximum. Ceci permet d'obtenir un habitacle vraiment spacieux pour sa catégorie, contrairement à plusieurs modèles concurrents qui arborent une silhouette carrée afin d'optimiser l'espace dans l'habitacle. Comme il se doit, les stylistes ont conservé le « sourire Mazda » avec une entrée d'air elliptique placée sous la grille de calandre. Pour donner plus d'élan à ce design, la fenestration est tout de même généreuse à l'avant, pour diminuer à l'arrière en raison d'une ceinture de caisse qui remonte. Cette petite japonaise arbore également des rétroviseurs de très grande dimension, ce qui est apprécié.

À une certaine époque, les acheteurs de voitures économiques et de petit format n'étaient pas tellement choyés par les constructeurs. Les habitacles étaient dépouillés au maximum et la qualité des matériaux était basique tout au plus. Les temps ont changé et ce n'est pas qu'une façon de parler. Les buses de ventilation sont circulaires et la planche de bord est simple et moderne avec deux principaux centres d'attraction. Le premier est l'indicateur de vitesse en forme de demi-lune. Il est situé au centre du module des instruments et la partie supérieure de ce module le protège des rayons du soleil. À sa gauche, on retrouve le compte-tours dont les dimensions sont moindres. Un écran multifonctionnel placé du côté droit permet de nous informer de nombreuses données. Le second est la console centrale abritant les commandes de la radio et de la climatisation. Il est situé quant à lui au centre de la planche de bord et encadré dans sa partie supérieure par deux buses de ventilation. La radio se démarque par son cadran circulaire dont la partie supérieure affiche le poste sélectionné, tandis que la moitié inférieure accueille le bouton marche-arrêt et celui du volume. Le réglage de la climatisation est assuré par trois gros boutons.

Peu importe le type de transmission choisi, le levier de commande est placé sur un module ancré au tableau de bord. Cela donne un petit cachet particulier et est sans doute plus économique à produire. Peu importe le marché où elle est vendue, la Mazda2 est pratiquement identique. Toutefois, pour les versions nord-américaines, la console placée entre les deux sièges avant a été spécialement dessinée afin d'accommoder des contenants de plus grande dimension en usage au Canada et aux États-Unis.

La position de conduite est bonne tandis que le volant se manipule bien. Sur les versions plus équipées, les rayons du volant accueillent les commandes de la radio et du régulateur de vitesse.

Pour donner un peu plus de *Zoom-Zoom* à l'habitacle, le tissu des sièges est texturé au centre et lisse sur les côtés, ces deux zones étant délimitées par une bordure rouge. En plus d'être élégants, ces sièges sont confortables, malgré le support un peu court pour les cuisses. Une randonnée de quelques heures a confirmé cette impression de confort. Les places arrière sont également assez confortables pour une voiture aux dimensions relativement petites. Soulignons au passage qu'il est facile de prendre place à l'arrière. Une fois le siège arrière rabattu, l'espace pour les bagages est acceptable, du moins, davantage que lorsque le dossier est en place.

RÉGIME MINCEUR

Lors du développement de cette Mazda, les ingénieurs se sont attardés à la chasse aux kilogrammes afin d'alléger la voiture le plus possible. Cette philosophie de développement a été inspirée de celle qui a prévalu lors de la création de la première MX-5. Ce roadster n'était pas le plus puissant, mais il offrait un rapport poids/puissance intéressant qui expliquait son agrément de conduite et son agilité. Donc, au lieu d'augmenter la puissance et la cylindrée du moteur, les ingénieurs ont préféré réduire le poids du véhicule pour compenser. Tous les trucs ont été utilisés. Pour la carrosserie pax exemple, de l'acier de haute qualité a été utilisé. Celui-ci est plus rigide et il est également plus léger. On a ainsi réalisé une réduction de poids de 22,68 kg. La suspension a également connu un régime minceur qui a permis une diminution de 12,7 kg. On s'est également intéressé à de multiples éléments mineurs qui ont contribué à un allégement de la masse totale, cela inclut la couette de fils, le système d'ancrage du capot, l'aimant des haut-parleurs des portes avant de même que leur support.

PETIT MOTEUR, FAIBLE CONSOMMATION

L'un des objectifs primordiaux des équipes travaillant au développement d'une voiture sous-compacte est de trouver le juste milieu

entre les performances et la consommation de carburant. Un acheteur de cette catégorie de véhicule aime bien une voiture agréable à conduire, mais pas au détriment de la consommation.

La Mazda2 doit son succès à une mécanique bien adaptée, installée dans une voiture fort légère. Son moteur quatre cylindres de 1,5 litre produisant 100 chevaux n'est pas le plus puissant de sa catégorie, mais sa courbe de puissance et de couple travaillent de concert pour favoriser les accélérations linéaires. La boîte manuelle à cinq rapports est bien étagée et le guidage du levier est très précis. L'élément le plus discutable de la mécanique est sans doute cette transmission automatique à quatre rapports, alors que la plupart des modèles concurrents en offrent

Catégorie	*Hatchback*
Échelle de prix	13 995 $ à 19 280 $
Garanties	3 ans/80 000 km, 5 ans/100 000 km
Assemblage	Hiroshima, Japon
Cote d'assurance	n.d.

CHÂSSIS - DONNÉES POUR GS

Emp/lon/lar/haut	2 489/3 950/1 694/1 476 mm
Coffre	377 à 787 litres
Réservoir	43 litres
Nombre coussins sécurité	4
Antipatinage / contrôle stabilité	oui / oui
Suspension avant	indépendante, jambes de force
Suspension arrière	indépendante, poutre de torsion
Freins avant / arrière	disque (ABS) / tambour (ABS)
Direction	à crémaillère, assistée
Diamètre de braquage	9,8 m
Pneus avant / arrière	185/55R15 / 185/55R15
Poids	1 043 kg
Capacité de remorquage	n.d.

COMPOSANTES MÉCANIQUES

GX, GS, Édition Yozora

Cylindrée, soupapes, alim.	4L 1,5 litre 16 s atmos.
Puissance / Couple	100 chevaux / 98 lb-pi
Tr. base (opt) / rouage base (opt)	M5 (A4) / Tr
0-100 / 80-120 / 100-0 km/h	10,2 s / 9,6 s / n.d.
Type ess. / ville / autoroute	Ordinaire / 7,2 / 5,6 l/100 km

FEU VERT

Bonne tenue de route
Bonne habitabilité
Faible consommation
Plate-forme rigide
Prix compétitif

FEU ROUGE

Boîte auto 4 rapports
Coffre limité
Pneumatiques moyens
Commande de recirculation d'air
Fiabilité inconnue

un cinquième. Chez Mazda, on a expliqué cette décision par le fait qu'on voulait alléger le véhicule et que cette boîte convenait fort bien à la dynamique de cette voiture. Dans l'ensemble, cette transmission automatique à quatre rapports est satisfaisante. Par contre, une personne plus exigeante en la matière va regretter l'absence d'un ou même de deux rapports additionnels.

Pour le reste, ce n'est que du positif. La voiture est silencieuse, sa direction précise et son insonorisation impressionnante. Sur l'autoroute, on n'a pas l'impression de conduire une sous-compacte. Nous avons circulé sur des routes dont le revêtement était fort bosselé et la suspension s'en est sortie avec honneur. Enfin, la tenue de route est très neutre.

La Mazda2 est appelée à connaître beaucoup de succès. L'emballage est excellent et l'agrément de conduite est indéniable.

Denis Duquet

PHOTOS : MAZDA

DANS LA MÊME CATÉGORIE

Chevrolet Aveo, Ford Fiesta, Honda Fit, Hyundai Accent, Kia Rio/Rio5, Nissan Versa, Suzuki Swift+, Toyota Yaris

DU NOUVEAU EN 2011

Nouveau modèle

NOS IMPRESSIONS

Agrément de conduite :	■■■■■■■■□□ 8/10
Fiabilité :	Nouveau modèle
Sécurité :	n.d.
Qualités hivernales :	■■■■■■■■□□ 8/10
Espace intérieur :	■■■■■■■■□□ 8/10
Confort :	■■■■■■■■□□ 8/10

www.mazda.ca

Plus d'informations dans la section statistiques en dernière partie du Guide

DE TOUT POUR TOUS

Elle arbore fièrement une calandre en forme de sourire, qui plaît ou non, selon le regard de l'acheteur, mais c'est indéniablement avec le sourire aux lèvres que l'on conduit la Mazda3 qui est «la plus germanique des nippones» avec sa tenue de route performante et ses motorisations efficaces. Malgré une consommation plus élevée que certaines rivales, la Mazda3 s'impose comme la référence de la catégorie des compactes.

Renouvelée l'an dernier, la Mazda3 n'a mérité rien de moins que le titre de Voiture de l'année du *Guide de l'Auto 2010*. Voilà qui en dit long sur les qualités intrinsèques de cette compacte proposée en version berline conventionnelle ou en modèle à 5 portes plus polyvalent. Une version survitaminée étant également au programme avec la MazdaSpeed3, c'est donc une gamme complète et étendue qui est présentée à l'acheteur par le constructeur japonais.

UN MODÈLE DE BASE MOINS DÉPOUILLÉ

Pour l'année-modèle 2011, Mazda Canada a apporté plusieurs changements en ce qui concerne la dotation de série des modèles de la Mazda3. Ainsi, la version GX, qui méritait vraiment son qualificatif de modèle de base auparavant, s'enrichit des systèmes électroniques de contrôle de la traction et de contrôle de la stabilité. La motorisation demeure inchangée avec le 4 cylindres de 2,0 litres, dont la puissance est adéquate avec ses 148 chevaux et dont la consommation est plus raisonnable que celle des modèles équipés du moteur 4 cylindres de 2,5 litres qui offre plus de puissance, mais qui a également une consommation nettement plus élevée... L'essai d'une berline mue par ce moteur de 2,5 litres nous a valu une consommation moyenne supérieure à 10 litres aux 100 kilomètres, malgré sa boîte manuelle à six rapports.

Précisons de ce côté que le régime moteur était supérieur à 3000 tours/minute en sixième à 120 kilomètres/heure sur l'autoroute, ce qui indique que Mazda aurait intérêt à revoir le rapport de la sixième vitesse afin qu'elle devienne une véritable surmultipliée bonifiant ainsi la consommation.

Le comportement routier de la Mazda3 est tout simplement excellent avec une tenue de route performante ce qui contribue grandement à assurer l'agrément de conduite. De ce côté, la Mazda3 marque des points par rapport à la Civic et la Corolla qui est aussi ennuyante à conduire que peut l'être une journée de pluie... Pour les automobilistes qui aiment conduire, la Mazda3 s'impose comme la référence de la catégorie avec son châssis très rigide et ses suspensions dont le tarage assure une bonne adhérence en virage.

Du côté de l'habitacle, la Mazda3 propose une planche de bord à deux paliers, mais l'écran logeant au palier supérieur et servant soit au système de navigation (pour les modèles qui en sont équipés) ou à la lecture des informations transmises par l'ordinateur de bord est trop petit pour être vraiment efficace. Le modèle à 5 portes, appelé Sport chez Mazda, offre une polyvalence accrue

FEU VERT

Moteurs performants (2,0 et 2,5 litres)
Habitabilité et polyvalence (Mazda 3 Sport)
Excellente tenue de route (MazdaSpeed3)

FEU ROUGE

Consommation élevée
Écran de navigation petit
Prix élevé (MazdaSpeed3)
Coût des assurances (MazdaSpeed3)
Absence de rouage intégral (MazdaSpeed3)

et se démarque de la berline grâce à son volume de chargement plus élevé ainsi que par un accès plus facile à l'espace de chargement, la berline étant pénalisée à cet égard par l'étroitesse de l'ouverture du coffre.

LA MAZDASPEED3 : PERFORMANTE ET CHÈRE

La version dopée aux stéroïdes qu'est la MazdaSpeed3 se distingue par ses performances, son niveau d'équipement et par son prix très élevé si on la compare à ses rivales directes que sont les Subaru Impreza WRX à rouage intégral ainsi qu'à la Volkswagen GTI. En effet, le prix de la MazdaSpeed3 est près des 33000 dollars, ce qui s'explique par le fait que le modèle proposé aux acheteurs canadiens est très fortement équipé avec des sièges en cuir à commande électrique, une chaîne audio Bose à 10 haut-parleurs et un système de navigation (entre autres). Il s'agit là d'éléments qui ne sont pas essentiels pour une voiture à vocation sportive, et il est dommage que Mazda Canada ne soit pas en mesure d'offrir une version moins luxueuse de la MazdaSpeed3 aux acheteurs canadiens alors qu'un tel modèle existe aux États-Unis. Voilà qui permettrait aux amateurs de performances d'obtenir une voiture performante sans avoir à payer pour des équipements dont ils n'ont pas besoin.

Cela étant dit, c'est une véritable petite bombe que cette MazdaSpeed3 qui s'accroche à la route avec une ténacité remarquable sans trop pénaliser le confort. La direction est à la fois vive et précise et c'est un véritable plaisir que de « piloter » la MazdaSpeed3, malgré un effet de couple toujours présent dans le volant qui fait en sorte que la voiture a tendance à louvoyer légèrement en accélération franche. En dépit de ce léger impair, la tenue de route sur pavé sec est carrément impressionnante. Toutefois, la MazdaSpeed3 ne propose pas un rouage intégral, ce qui la rend moins à l'aise en hiver, où une rivale comme la Subaru Impreza WRX excelle. À part le prix élevé, il faut également souligner que les primes d'assurances associées à ce modèle à vocation sportive seront nettement plus élevées que celles des modèles moins typés de la gamme des Mazda3.

Somme toute, la Mazda3 se démarque par son comportement routier exemplaire et le plaisir de conduire qui est au rendez-vous. À mon avis, le modèle Sport (*hatchback*) en version GS s'avère le choix avisé en raison de sa plus grande polyvalence et d'un rapport équipement/prix favorable si l'on demeure raisonnable lors du choix des options.

Gabriel Gélinas

PHOTOS : ALAIN MORIN

Catégorie	Berline, *Hatchback*
Échelle de prix	15 995 $ à 32 995 $ (2010)
Garanties	3 ans/80 000 km, 5 ans/100 000 km
Assemblage	Hiroshima, Japon
Cote d'assurance	passable

CHÂSSIS - DONNÉES POUR GT SPORT

Emp/lon/lar/haut	2 640/4 500/1 755/1 470 mm
Coffre	481 litres
Réservoir	55 litres
Nombre coussins sécurité	6
Antipatinage / contrôle stabilité	oui / oui
Suspension avant	indépendante, jambes de force
Suspension arrière	indépendante, multibras
Freins avant / arrière	disque (ABS) / disque (ABS)
Direction	à crémaillère, assistée
Diamètre de braquage	10,4 m
Pneus avant / arrière	P205/50R17 / P205/50R17
Poids	1 372 kg
Capacité de remorquage	n.d.

COMPOSANTES MÉCANIQUES

GX, GX Sport, GS

Cylindrée, soupapes, alim.	4L 2,0 litres 16 s atmos.
Puissance / Couple	148 chevaux / 135 lb-pi
Tr. base (opt) / rouage base (opt)	M5 (A5) / Tr
0-100 / 80-120 / 100-0 km/h	9,9 s / 7,0 s / 45,7 m
Type ess. / ville / autoroute	Ordinaire / 8,1 / 5,9 l/100 km

GS Sport, GT, GT Sport

Cylindrée, soupapes, alim.	4L 2,5 litres 16 s atmos.
Puissance / Couple	167 chevaux / 168 lb-pi
Tr. base (opt) / rouage base (opt)	M6 (A5) / Tr
0-100 / 80-120 / 100-0 km/h	8,4 s / 7,5 s / 40,5 m
Type ess. / ville / autoroute	Ordinaire / 10,1 / 6,9 l/100 km

MazdaSpeed3

Cylindrée, soupapes, alim.	4L 2,3 litres 16 s turbo
Puissance / Couple	263 chevaux / 280 lb-pi
Tr. base (opt) / rouage base (opt)	M6 / Tr
0-100 / 80-120 / 100-0 km/h	6,9 s / 4,8 s / 38,0 m
Type ess. / ville / autoroute	Super / 11,5 / 8,0 l/100 km

DANS LA MÊME CATÉGORIE

Chevrolet Cruze, Dodge Caliber, Ford Focus, Honda Civic, Hyundai Elantra, Kia Forte, Mitsubishi Lancer, Nissan Sentra, Subaru Impreza, Suzuki SX-4, Toyota Corolla, Toyota Matrix, Volkswagen Golf

DU NOUVEAU EN 2011

Aucun changement majeur

NOS IMPRESSIONS

Agrément de conduite :	9/10
Fiabilité :	8/10
Sécurité :	9/10
Qualités hivernales :	7/10
Espace intérieur :	8/10
Confort :	7/10

www.mazda.ca

Plus d'informations dans la section statistiques en dernière partie du Guide

BIENTÔT TOUT SOURIRE!

Introduite en Amérique du Nord en 2006, la Mazda5 a rapidement séduit les acheteurs, surtout au Québec. Elle a réussi cet exploit non seulement en raison de son caractère unique, mais parce qu'elle offrait une solution de rechange aux acheteurs de fourgonnettes qui désiraient un véhicule différent, et qui ne voulaient pas nécessairement se tourner vers un VUS. Non seulement la Mazda5 répond bien aux besoins des familles, mais elle le fait tout en procurant au conducteur un indéniable agrément de conduite. Voilà sans doute le secret de son succès.

La Mazda dispose de peu de rivales et c'est sans doute la Kia Rondo et la Dodge Journey qui font office de véritables concurrentes. Toutefois, si vous visitez un concessionnaire Mazda cette année, vous ne trouverez pas de Mazda5 2011 en stock. La raison est fort simple, le véhicule est à l'aube d'une refonte complète et dès cet hiver, nous aurons droit à une nouvelle Mazda5, cette dernière offerte comme modèle 2012. D'ici là, vous pourrez toujours vous procurer un modèle 2010 dont la commercialisation sera prolongée pour assurer la transition.

NOUVEAU STYLE, NOUVELLE MOTORISATION

La future Mazda5 a été officiellement présentée au dernier Salon de l'auto de Genève. Il s'agit d'une nette évolution par rapport à la génération courante et le tout semble très réussi. Le changement le plus notable touche son style alors que la petite familiale profite du même traitement visuel que les nouveaux véhicules du constructeur. Elle aussi embrasse maintenant la philosophie de design baptisée «Nagare» qui met l'emphase sur la fluidité. En fait, elle sera le premier véhicule Mazda à intégrer entièrement ce concept de style. À la vue des premières images, il est difficile de ne pas remarquer le museau avant dont le style émule un large sourire, élément typique à la Mazda3. L'arrière bénéficie également de nombreux changements alors que les feux verticaux font place à des feux profilés qui s'étirent loin dans les flancs, élément que l'on retrouve sur la Mazda6. Il semble que Mazda a également réussi l'exploit de bien intégrer les glissières des portes coulissantes puisque ces dernières se fondent entre les feux arrière et un motif à vague encastré tout le long de la carrosserie. Voilà sans doute l'élément le plus réussi de la voiture.

Au chapitre de la motorisation, rien n'est encore confirmé, mais les versions européennes ont droit à un moteur quatre cylindres de 2,0 litres à injection directe, marié à une boîte manuelle à six rapports offerte de série alors qu'une automatique, également à six rapports, est livrable. Voilà sans doute la motorisation à laquelle nous aurons droit, sinon, il y a fort à parier que la version canadienne recevra de série ou en option le moteur quatre cylindres de 2,5 litres en remplacement de l'ancien 2,3 litres. Ce moteur plus puissant développe, dans le cas de la Mazda3, une puissance de 167 chevaux pour un couple similaire, soit une puissance légèrement supérieure à l'actuel 2,3 litres. Bref, cette

FEU VERT

- Conduite agréable
- Espace pour six
- Rigidité du châssis
- Consommation raisonnable

FEU ROUGE

- Nouvelle génération à venir
- Espace cargo limité
- Puissance un peu juste
- Insonorisation perfectible

nouvelle motorisation va sans doute corriger les principaux reproches faits à la génération courante qui, sans être trop sous-motorisée, manquait néanmoins de « pep » à certaines occasions, surtout lorsque la voiture était plus chargée.

Force est de constater que la Kia Rondo et la Dodge Journey continueront d'être les seules à bénéficier de l'avantage d'offrir un moteur V6. Même si cette motorisation n'est pas la plus populaire, elle convient à certaines personnes qui devront alors lever le nez sur la Mazda5. Même constat au chapitre du rouage intégral alors que seule la Journey peut en être équipée, un autre élément qui intéresse plusieurs acheteurs.

On remarque aussi plusieurs changements à bord de la future Mazda5, notamment la disposition des commandes sur le tableau de bord. La grande force de la Mazda5 est sans contredit son habitacle spacieux et confortable qui est capable d'accueillir six personnes, élément très pratique pour les jeunes familles. Cependant, rien n'est parfait puisque l'espace de chargement est plutôt réduit lorsque les sièges arrière sont utilisés. Les deux portes coulissantes facilitent également l'accès à bord, surtout lorsque vous êtes dans un stationnement et que l'espace latéral est restreint. Voilà un autre élément appréciable et qui avantage ce type de véhicule.

UN COMPORTEMENT VROOM VROOM

C'est surtout au chapitre du plaisir que la Mazda5 se distingue. Alors que les minifourgonnettes mettent en avant-plan l'aspect pratique, bien souvent au détriment du plaisir de conduite, la Mazda5 offre un bien meilleur compromis à ce chapitre. Pas étonnant puisqu'elle partage sa plate-forme avec la Mazda3, la plus sportive des voitures compactes. Sans être au même niveau qu'une berline sport, la Mazda5 offre une conduite beaucoup plus dynamique et emballante, recevant tout le vroom vroom des produits du constructeur. On apprécie l'excellente visibilité à bord alors que la direction nous connecte bien avec la route. Voilà sans doute un élément que les ingénieurs auront pris soin de préserver à bord de la prochaine génération et même, de pousser un peu plus.

Sylvain Raymond

PHOTOS : DENIS DUQUET

DONNÉES 2010

Catégorie	Fourgonnette
Échelle de prix	20 495 $ à 24 295 $ (2010)
Garanties	3 ans/80 000 km, 5 ans/100 000 km
Assemblage	Hiroshima, Japon
Cote d'assurance	bonne

CHÂSSIS - DONNÉES POUR GT

Emp/lon/lar/haut	2 750/4 620/1 745/1 630 mm
Coffre	112 à 426 litres
Réservoir	60 litres
Nombre coussins sécurité	6
Antipatinage / contrôle stabilité	oui / oui
Suspension avant	indépendante, jambes de force
Suspension arrière	indépendante, multibras
Freins avant / arrière	disque (ABS) / disque (ABS)
Direction	à crémaillère, ass. variable électrique
Diamètre de braquage	10,6 m
Pneus avant / arrière	P205/50R17 / P205/50R17
Poids	1 557 kg
Capacité de remorquage	non recommandé

COMPOSANTES MÉCANIQUES

GS, GT

Cylindrée, soupapes, alim.	4L 2,3 litres 16 s atmos.
Puissance / Couple	153 chevaux / 148 lb-pi
Tr. base (opt) / rouage base (opt)	M5 (A5) / Tr
0-100 / 80-120 / 100-0 km/h	10,2 s / 9,9 s / 40,2 m
Type ess. / ville / autoroute	Ordinaire / 9,6 / 7,0 l/100 km

DANS LA MÊME CATÉGORIE

Chevrolet HHR, Dodge Journey, Kia Rondo

DU NOUVEAU EN 2011

Aucun changement majeur, nouveau modèle sera dévoilé plus tard en 2010

NOS IMPRESSIONS

Agrément de conduite :	■■■■■■■■□□	8/10
Fiabilité :	■■■■■■□□□□	6/10
Sécurité :	■■■■■■■■□□	8/10
Qualités hivernales :	■■■■■■■□□□	7/10
Espace intérieur :	■■■■■■■□□□	7/10
Confort :	■■■■■■■■□□	8/10

www.mazda.ca

Plus d'informations dans la section statistiques en dernière partie du Guide

MÉCONNUE – ET POURTANT...

Quelle méconnue, que cette Mazda6 ! De toutes les berlines intermédiaires du marché, elle est sans doute la plus pimentée, celle qui transmet la meilleure connexion avec le bitume et qui peut le plus prétendre au titre de sportive. Comment se fait-il qu'on n'en voit pas davantage sur nos routes ?

Si vous avez l'occasion de réunir une dizaine de berlines intermédiaires en un seul endroit et de les piloter les unes après les autres pendant toute une journée, votre coup de cœur, côté conduite dynamique, ira à la Mazda6. Cette dernière hérite de l'une des suspensions les plus fermes – vraiment ferme en variante GT – de toute la catégorie, sans pour autant être une « cogneuse ». Voilà qui lui permet un comportement athlétique, même avec le « petit » quatre cylindres (2,5 litres).

Cette motorisation est particulièrement plaisante à faire réagir avec la transmission manuelle six vitesses – vous savez que les boîtes manuelles de Mazda sont parmi les mieux réussies de toute l'industrie... Les petits 170 chevaux se débrouillent de belle façon pour propulser la voiture sur routes sinueuses, et ce, sans roulis. En piste, la voiture colle exceptionnellement au bitume, au point de faire rougir les autres concurrentes dont les amortisseurs n'ont pas autant de retenue.

LE QUATRE CYLINDRES AVANT TOUT

Ceci dit, la Mazda6 quatre cylindres équipée de la boîte automatique (cinq rapports) donne quelques fils à retordre en démarrage brusque ou lors d'une montée abrupte. Son comportement souffre d'une indésirable petite lenteur et le conducteur est appelé à jouer des passages manuels s'il veut s'en tirer avec les honneurs.

La direction à crémaillère (fiou, on ne fait pas encore dans l'électrique chez Mazda !) est des plus plaisantes à manier et ce n'est pas qu'en raison du volant sportif qui se prend bien en main; la connexion est directe avec la route et son ajustement est de bonne résistance. On encense également le tout petit rayon de braquage (10,8 mètres) qui permet des manœuvres aisées en stationnement.

Versus la première génération lancée en 2004, la Mazda6 dotée du moteur V6 (3,7 litres) est nettement plus docile qu'auparavant, un peu comme si on l'avait... américanisée. Certes, ses 272 chevaux ne manquent pas d'air et les reprises sont dynamiques, transigées par une boîte automatique six rapports avec mode manuel. Même sans traction intégrale (ça aussi, c'était l'apanage de la MazdaSpeed 6...), la voiture se fait rassurante sur une route de gravier tortueuse.

Reste que le « vroum-vroum » est pas mal moins au rendez-vous avec le V6 qu'avec le moteur de base et du coup, le comportement général se fait plus générique. C'est pourquoi notre recommandation va à la version quatre cylindres (GT, de préférence) qui, bien sûr, consomme moins – mais qui le fait quand même un peu plus que la concurrence. Après tout, c'est du Mazda...

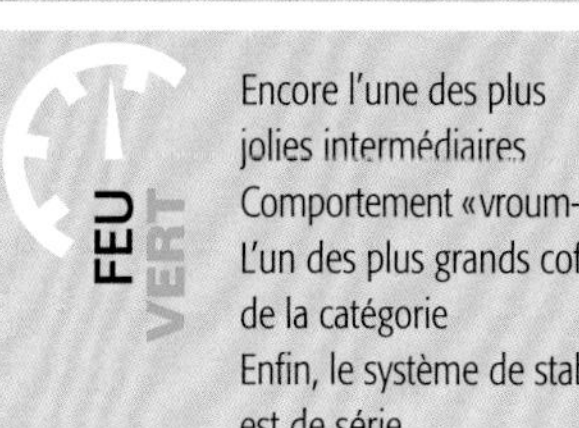

FEU VERT

- Encore l'une des plus jolies intermédiaires
- Comportement « vroum-vroum »
- L'un des plus grands coffres de la catégorie
- Enfin, le système de stabilité est de série

FEU ROUGE

- Variante V6 pas aussi équipée que souhaité
- Toujours pas de MazdaSpeed 6
- Automatique 5 rapports (version quatre cylindres)
- On attend le passage des rapports au volant

ELLE A DU... COFFRE !

Visuellement, la Mazda6 profite d'un design extérieur parmi les plus élancés de la catégorie. La personnalité esthétique tire son inspiration de la sportive RX-8 et de la musclée CX-7, ce qui lui va très bien. Même plus de trois ans après son arrivée, l'intermédiaire à l'allure de culturiste continue de se démarquer dans le paysage automobile. Allez savoir pourquoi, c'est la Mazda6 qui offre l'un des plus vastes coffres: 469 litres, c'est non seulement nez à nez avec la Ford Fusion, mais c'est 10 % plus que pour la Toyota Camry et... presque 20 % de plus que pour la Honda Accord. Au contraire, et curieusement, l'habitacle fait sentir ses occupants à l'étroit.

Quoi qu'il en soit, même si c'est limite pour la tête, les grands de six pieds trouvent néanmoins leur compte sur la banquette arrière. Aussi, un bon mot pour l'instrumentation illuminée de bleu et d'orangé, qui vient traduire à l'intérieur toutes les prétentions sportives affichées à l'extérieur. Lorsque le cuir est choisi, on a droit à un revêtement plus relevé que ce qui se fait généralement dans le segment. Et si l'insonorisation laisse passer quelques bruits de vent au pare-brise, l'ensemble de l'œuvre profite d'une bonne qualité de matériaux et d'assemblage.

TOUJOURS PAS DE MAZDASPEED 6

La génération précédente avait eu droit à sa version Speed, une saprée sportive qu'on aimait beaucoup. Cette Mazdaspeed 6 avait le bonheur de se faire « *Mini-Wheat* », si je puis dire: un côté sucré avec son turbo pour les folies (en circuit fermé, bien sûr!) et un côté sérieux avec la traction intégrale pour quand les choses se corsaient. Malheureusement, toujours pas d'intentions chez Mazda de ramener cette variante de performance au sein de l'actuelle génération. Un jour, peut-être? On le souhaite. En attendant, il serait bien que la Mazda6 de tous les jours pense à emprunter à cette feue MazdaSpeed6 les commandes de vitesse au volant et la traction intégrale, ce qui n'est pas encore le cas. Et pendant qu'on y est, peut-être que la gamme d'intermédiaires pourrait retrouver les versions familiale et à hayon qui, à la génération précédente, la différenciait de la concurrence de bien belle façon. À tout le moins, pour 2011, le système de stabilité est devenu de série pour toutes les variantes. C'est une excellente nouvelle.

Nadine Filion

PHOTOS: MAZDA

Catégorie	Berline
Échelle de prix	23 195 $ à 36 695 $ (2010)
Garanties	3 ans/80 000 km, 5 ans/100 000 km
Assemblage	Flat Rock, Michigan, É-U.
Cote d'assurance	passable

CHÂSSIS - DONNÉES POUR GS V6

Emp/lon/lar/haut	2 790/4 940/1 840/1 470 mm
Coffre	469 litres
Réservoir	70 litres
Nombre coussins sécurité	6
Antipatinage / contrôle stabilité	oui / oui
Suspension avant	indépendante, double triangulation
Suspension arrière	indépendante, multibras
Freins avant / arrière	disque (ABS) / disque (ABS)
Direction	à crémaillère, ass. variable
Diamètre de braquage	10,8 m
Pneus avant / arrière	P215/55R17 / P215/55R17
Poids	1 610 kg
Capacité de remorquage	454 kg (1 000 lb)

COMPOSANTES MÉCANIQUES

GS, GT

Cylindrée, soupapes, alim.	4L 2,5 litres 16 s atmos.
Puissance / Couple	170 chevaux / 167 lb-pi
Tr. base (opt) / rouage base (opt)	M6 (A5) / Tr
0-100 / 80-120 / 100-0 km/h	9,4 s / 8,0 s / 42,3 m
Type ess. / ville / autoroute	Ordinaire / 10,4 / 6,9 l/100 km

GS V6, GT V6

Cylindrée, soupapes, alim.	V6 3,7 litres 24 s atmos.
Puissance / Couple	272 chevaux / 269 lb-pi
Tr. base (opt) / rouage base (opt)	A6 / Tr
0-100 / 80-120 / 100-0 km/h	7,3 s / 5,8 s / 42,3 m
Type ess. / ville / autoroute	Ordinaire / 12,1 / 8,0 l/100 km

DANS LA MÊME CATÉGORIE

Chevrolet Malibu, Chrysler Sebring, Dodge Avenger, Ford Fusion, Honda Accord, Hyundai Sonata, Nissan Altima, Subaru Legacy, Toyota Camry,

DU NOUVEAU EN 2011

Système de contrôle de la stabilité latérale de série

NOS IMPRESSIONS

Agrément de conduite:	8/10
Fiabilité:	8/10
Sécurité:	10/10
Qualités hivernales:	8/10
Espace intérieur:	8/10
Confort:	8/10

www.mazda.ca

Plus d'informations dans la section statistiques en dernière partie du Guide

VROUM, VROUM, TRACTION ET TURBO

La Mazda CX-7 jouit d'une grande popularité sur notre marché depuis son lancement. Les acheteurs ont toujours été attirés par sa belle silhouette sportive tandis que les prestations routières de cette petite nipponne à tout faire réussissaient à les convaincre davantage. L'an dernier toutefois, la direction de la compagnie a ajouté une autre corde à son arc, soit une version à moteur atmosphérique.

Mais avant de parler de mécanique, d'habitabilité et de tenue de route, il faut préciser que la silhouette de ce modèle multisegment a connu un changement assez marquant en sa partie avant. En effet, les stylistes lui ont greffé cette grille de grande ouverture placée dans le pare-chocs avant dont les extrémités accueillent de grands orifices, rendant ainsi la voiture très facile à identifier. Plusieurs parlent du « sourire Mazda ». Les avis sont partagés quant à cette présentation. Soulignons au passage que d'autres petites retouches ont été effectuées à la carrosserie, mais c'est plus discret. Malgré cette chirurgie, la CX-7 demeure l'un des plus élégants VUS sur le marché.

POLYVALENCE ÉCONOMIQUE

À ses débuts, plusieurs ont louangé les caractéristiques sportives de ce modèle en raison de la présence de son moteur turbocompressé de 244 chevaux. Cela permettait à Mazda d'affirmer le côté « vroum vroum » de ce modèle. Mais les fluctuations du marché aidant et le désir de convaincre des acheteurs plus intéressés par le caractère pratique de ce véhicule que par ses performances ont poussé Mazda à concocter une nouvelle version dotée d'un moteur quatre cylindres atmosphérique. Ce moteur de 2,5 litres produit 161 chevaux, soit 83 de moins que le moteur turbo de 2,3 litres. Autre différence, sa transmission automatique de type manumatique est à cinq rapports, soit un de moins que celle qui équipe le turbo. Il est impossible de commander la transmission intégrale sur ce modèle moins puissant.

Vous avez certainement deviné que les intentions de Mazda étaient d'offrir un modèle plus économique aux gens dont les ressources financières sont moins importantes. Le modèle de base propose, cela va de soi, un équipement un peu moins complet. À ce chapitre, je vous fais grâce de l'énumération de l'équipement de série de chaque version, mais sachez que celle à moteur 2,5 litres n'est pas trop pénalisée à ce chapitre. Comme c'est l'habitude chez Mazda, on réussit toujours à concocter des versions plus économiques qui sont quand mêmne bien nanties en fait d'équipement.

Comme tous les modèles CX-7, les lignes sont toujours élégantes et élancées. Ceux qui n'aiment pas les boîtes carrées n'ont que de bons mots pour cette silhouette. Si on veut être négatif, on peut mentionner que le toit fuyant vers l'arrière et le hayon incliné vers l'avant réduisent quelque peu la capacité du coffre, mais c'est quand même suffisant pour la plupart des gens, à moins d'avoir des besoins très particuliers. Soulignons au passage que

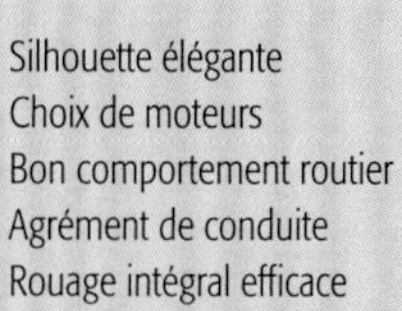

FEU VERT

- Silhouette élégante
- Choix de moteurs
- Bon comportement routier
- Agrément de conduite
- Rouage intégral efficace

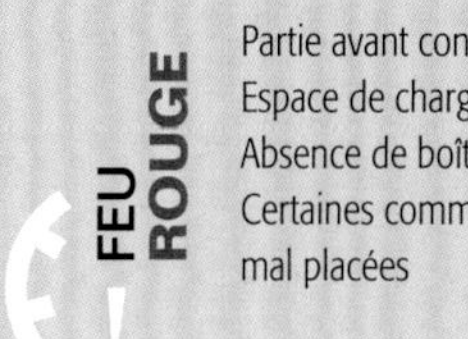

FEU ROUGE

- Partie avant controversée
- Espace de chargement moyen
- Absence de boîte manuelle
- Certaines commandes mal placées

le seuil de chargement de cette soute à bagages est relativement bas, ce qui sera apprécie par tous.

La planche de bord est jolie avec cette console verticale placée en plein centre et qui possède plusieurs commandes relativement simples à manipuler. Le volant est dorénavant télescopique et inclinable et la position de conduite est bonne. Par ailleurs, grâce au grand cadran indicateur du milieu, on sait très facilement à quelle vitesse on roule. De bonnes notes également pour les sièges avant qui sont confortables et fournissent un support latéral correct.

On serait porté à croire qu'une différence de plus de 80 chevaux entre cette version et le modèle plus sportif transformerait cette Mazda atmosphérique en modèle poussif et moins agréable à conduire, mais ce n'est absolument pas le cas. Certes, la nervosité et les reprises sont moins impressionnantes, mais c'est quand même très honnête. De plus, la direction est toujours précise et la suspension bien calibrée, de sorte que le roulis en virage est pratiquement inexistant. Le prix à payer pour cette tenue de route est une suspension un peu plus ferme que la moyenne. Mais à moins d'avoir un arrière-train très sensible, c'est acceptable !

POLYVALENCE SPORTIVE

Lorsqu'on utilise un moteur quatre cylindres turbocompressé d'assez faible cylindrée et doté de l'injection directe dans un véhicule à vocation utilitaire, c'est pour en faire un produit performant et agréable à conduire. C'est le genre de véhicule qui convainc les amateurs de voitures sportives dont les obligations familiales les amènent à se procurer un produit dans cette catégorie. Il faut de plus souligner que c'est le seul modèle CX-7 offert avec la traction intégrale. Et ce rouage d'entraînement est d'une grande efficacité soit dit en passant. Il est rapide, transparent et contribue à l'équilibre général du véhicule.

Il faut également souligner que la consommation de carburant de la version turbocompressée a été fortement critiquée par plusieurs de mes collègues. Ils ont raison, mais en partie seulement. Si l'on conduit vigoureusement, la consommation est élevée, mais en utilisant l'accélérateur avec moins d'enthousiasme, la consommation observée a été d'un peu plus de 12,0 litres aux 100 km.

Denis Duquet

PHOTOS : DENIS DUQUET

Catégorie	Multisegment
Échelle de prix	27 995 $ à 38 990 $ (2010)
Garanties	3 ans/80 000 km, 5 ans/100 000 km
Assemblage	Hiroshima, Japon
Cote d'assurance	passable

CHÂSSIS - DONNÉES POUR GT 4RM

Emp/lon/lar/haut	2 750/4 682/1 872/1 645 mm
Coffre	848 à 1 658 litres
Réservoir	62 litres
Nombre coussins sécurité	6
Antipatinage / contrôle stabilité	oui / oui
Suspension avant	indépendante, jambes de force
Suspension arrière	indépendante, multibras
Freins avant / arrière	disque (ABS) / disque (ABS)
Direction	à crémaillère, ass. variable
Diamètre de braquage	11,4 m
Pneus avant / arrière	P235/55R19 / P235/55R19
Poids	1 818 kg
Capacité de remorquage	907 kg (1 999 lb)

COMPOSANTES MÉCANIQUES

GX 2RM

Cylindrée, soupapes, alim.	4L 2,5 litres 16 s atmos.
Puissance / Couple	161 chevaux / 161 lb-pi
Tr. base (opt) / rouage base (opt)	A5 / Tr
0-100 / 80-120 / 100-0 km/h	11,0 s / 9,8 s / n.d.
Type ess. / ville / autoroute	Ordinaire / 10,4 / 7,2 l/100 km

GS 4RM, GT 4RM

Cylindrée, soupapes, alim.	4L 2,3 litres 16 s turbocompressé
Puissance / Couple	244 chevaux / 258 lb-pi
Tr. base (opt) / rouage base (opt)	A6 / Int
0-100 / 80-120 / 100-0 km/h	8,7 s / 6,8 s / 41,2 m
Type ess. / ville / autoroute	Super / 12,2 / 8,7 l/100 km

DANS LA MÊME CATÉGORIE

Chevrolet Equinox, Dodge Nitro, Ford Edge, Honda CR-V, Hyundai Santa Fe, Jeep Liberty, Mitsubishi Outlander, Toyota RAV4, Volkswagen Tiguan

DU NOUVEAU EN 2011

Aucun changement majeur

NOS IMPRESSIONS

Agrément de conduite :	■■■■■■■■□□	8/10
Fiabilité :	■■■■■■□□□□	6/10
Sécurité :	■■■■■■■■□□	8/10
Qualités hivernales :	■■■■■■■■□□	8/10
Espace intérieur :	■■■■■■■□□□	7/10
Confort :	■■■■■■■■□□	8/10

www.mazda.ca

Plus d'informations dans la section statistiques en dernière partie du Guide

CONFORT À TOUT FAIRE

Les dirigeants de la compagnie Mazda ne sont pas à court d'imagination et d'audace. En fait, ils font rarement les choses comme les autres et cela leur a valu beaucoup de succès, du moins sur notre marché. Pour Hiroshima, Mazdaland c'est le Canada mais surtout le Québec. La raison en est bien simple, la plupart des véhicules produits par ce constructeur offrent un petit quelque chose au niveau de l'agrément de conduite et un peu plus de sportivité que la majorité de la concurrence.

Cela dit, le CX-9 est le véhicule le plus bourgeois dans la gamme de ce constructeur. Ça ne veut pas dire que les ingénieurs ont concocté un multisegment à la suspension guimauve, à la direction entièrement déconnectée de la route et propulsé par un moteur anémique. Non, mais si l'on compare le CX-9 au CX-7, celui-ci est de plus petites dimensions, cela va de soi, mais il est plus nerveux, plus agile et son agrément de conduite est un peu plus relevé. Toutefois, le CX9 ne doit pas être ignoré, bien au contraire.

ESPACE ET CONFORT

Il est certain qu'un véhicule d'une telle dimension ne peut qu'offrir à ses occupants une habitabilité de bon aloi. C'est vrai pour les places avant et celles de la seconde rangée qui sont confortables et faciles d'accès. Mais cette Mazda propose également une troisième rangée de sièges qui est peut-être moins spacieuse que les autres, mais qui est relativement accessible par l'intermédiaire d'un siège médian coulissant qui permet de se hisser aux places arrière. Si le confort de ces dernières est correct, le dégagement pour la tête sera un peu juste pour les personnes de grande taille. Ce siège se replie facilement, dégageant ainsi un espace de chargement passablement spacieux. Ce n'est pas le plus important de la catégorie, mais pas le plus petit non plus.

Il faut souligner la qualité des matériaux et de la finition de ce véhicule. La présentation de la planche de bord est sobre, certains la jugeront même trop sobre. Mais mieux vaut avoir un minimum de commandes et une présentation logique que des boutons à gogo éparpillés un peu partout. Comme le veut la tendance actuelle, les commandes de climatisation sont l'affaire de trois gros boutons faciles à trouver et à opérer. Notre modèle d'essai était doté d'un système de navigation par satellite et donc d'un écran d'affichage passablement grand et simple à consulter. Par contre, à la partie supérieure de la console verticale, on retrouve un petit centre d'information qui est difficile à lire. La position de conduite est bonne et les sièges avant confortables bien que leur support latéral soit moyen.

PARFAIT POUR LES VACANCES

Cette Mazda offre un équipement complet, une présentation luxueuse et est propulsée par un moteur V6 de 3,7 litres dont la

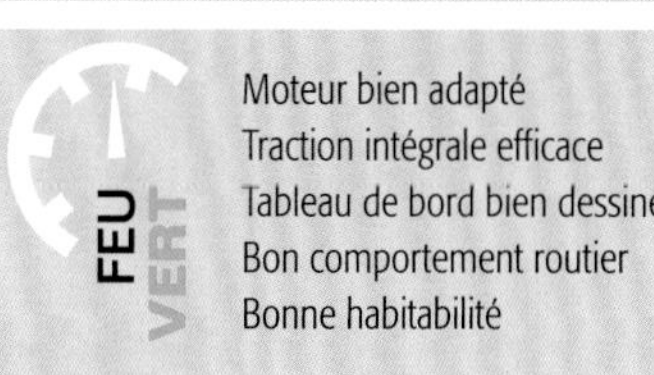

FEU VERT

Moteur bien adapté
Traction intégrale efficace
Tableau de bord bien dessiné
Bon comportement routier
Bonne habitabilité

FEU ROUGE

Dimensions encombrantes
Pédale de freinage un peu molle
Faibles capacités de remorquage
« Museau » avant contesté

puissance est de 273 chevaux. Ce qui est suffisant pour boucler le traditionnel 0-100 km/h en moins de huit secondes. Certains lui reprochent un amour inconsidéré pour les hydrocarbures. Selon plusieurs, la consommation est d'environ 14,0 L/100 km. Cependant, j'ai eu l'occasion d'effectuer un essai long terme de cette même Mazda et la consommation observée a été d'un peu plus de 12,7 L/100 km, ce qui est très correct compte tenu des dimensions et du poids de ce véhicule. Par contre, si vous êtes un conducteur impatient qui aime accélérer à fond, vous allez en payer le prix c'est certain !

Selon les modèles et les options, il est possible de commander la traction intégrale dont l'efficacité est impressionnante. Tout comme la boîte automatique à six rapports qui fonctionne sans à-coup et en douceur. Ce groupe propulseur est donc fort adapté pour la conduite sur de longues distances. L'habitabilité est bonne, le confort excellent et ce moteur est d'une grande douceur et d'une grande souplesse, ce qui facilite les longues randonnées. Soulignons au passage la présence d'un indicateur de véhicules dans l'angle mort. Ce système fonctionne très bien et il est apprécié, surtout dans la circulation dense. On peut également s'en servir pour doubler plus facilement, car il indique si l'on est suffisamment dégagé de la voiture que l'on double pour se rabattre devant celle-ci.

Et il ne faut pas croire qu'il s'agisse uniquement d'un véhicule qui a sa place sur les autoroutes. Au fil de plusieurs essais, j'ai eu l'occasion de rouler sur des routes assez sinueuses et d'adopter une conduite sportive qui n'a nullement déséquilibré ce véhicule. Il n'a pas la même sensibilité et la même rapidité de réaction que le CX-7, mais sa tenue de route est bonne. Par contre, la suspension a paru sèche sur des routes dont le revêtement était fort détérioré. Ce qui est surprenant compte tenu de la vocation plus bourgeoise de la CX-9.

Bien que la catégorie des véhicules multisegment soit encombrée de véhicules fort compétitifs et tous aussi élégants les uns que les autres, la Mazda CX-9 connaît une bonne popularité et ce n'est pas le fruit du hasard. Son niveau d'équipement, sa silhouette, son moteur bien adapté, une tenue de route sans surprise et un bon niveau de confort, voilà autant d'éléments qui prêchent en sa faveur.

Denis Duquet

PHOTOS : MAZDA

Catégorie	Multisegment
Échelle de prix	37 995 $ à 47 450 $ (2010)
Garanties	3 ans/80 000 km, 5 ans/100 000 km
Assemblage	Ujina, Japon
Cote d'assurance	n.d.

CHÂSSIS - DONNÉES POUR GS TI

Emp/lon/lar/haut	2 875/5 101/1 936/1 728 mm
Coffre	487 à 1 371 litres
Réservoir	76 litres
Nombre coussins sécurité	7
Antipatinage / contrôle stabilité	oui / oui
Suspension avant	indépendante, jambes de force
Suspension arrière	indépendante, multibras
Freins avant / arrière	disque (ABS) / disque (ABS)
Direction	à crémaillère, ass. variable
Diamètre de braquage	11,4 m
Pneus avant / arrière	P245/60R18 / P245/60R18
Poids	2 062 kg
Capacité de remorquage	1 588 kg (3 500 lb)

COMPOSANTES MÉCANIQUES

GS TA, GS TI, GT TI

Cylindrée, soupapes, alim.	V6 3,7 litres 24 s atmos.
Puissance / Couple	273 chevaux / 270 lb-pi
Tr. base (opt) / rouage base (opt)	A6 / Tr (Int)
0-100 / 80-120 / 100-0 km/h	7,9 s / 6,8 s / 39,8 m
Type ess. / ville / autoroute	Ordinaire / 14,0 / 9,6 l/100 km

DANS LA MÊME CATÉGORIE

Buick Enclave, Chevrolet Traverse, Ford Flex, GMC Acadia, Honda Pilot, Hyundai Veracruz, Mitsubishi Endeavor, Nissan Murano, Subaru Tribeca, Toyota Highlander

DU NOUVEAU EN 2011

Aucun changement majeur

NOS IMPRESSIONS

Agrément de conduite :	7/10
Fiabilité :	6/10
Sécurité :	8/10
Qualités hivernales :	8/10
Espace intérieur :	8/10
Confort :	9/10

www.mazda.ca

Plus d'informations dans la section statistiques en dernière partie du Guide

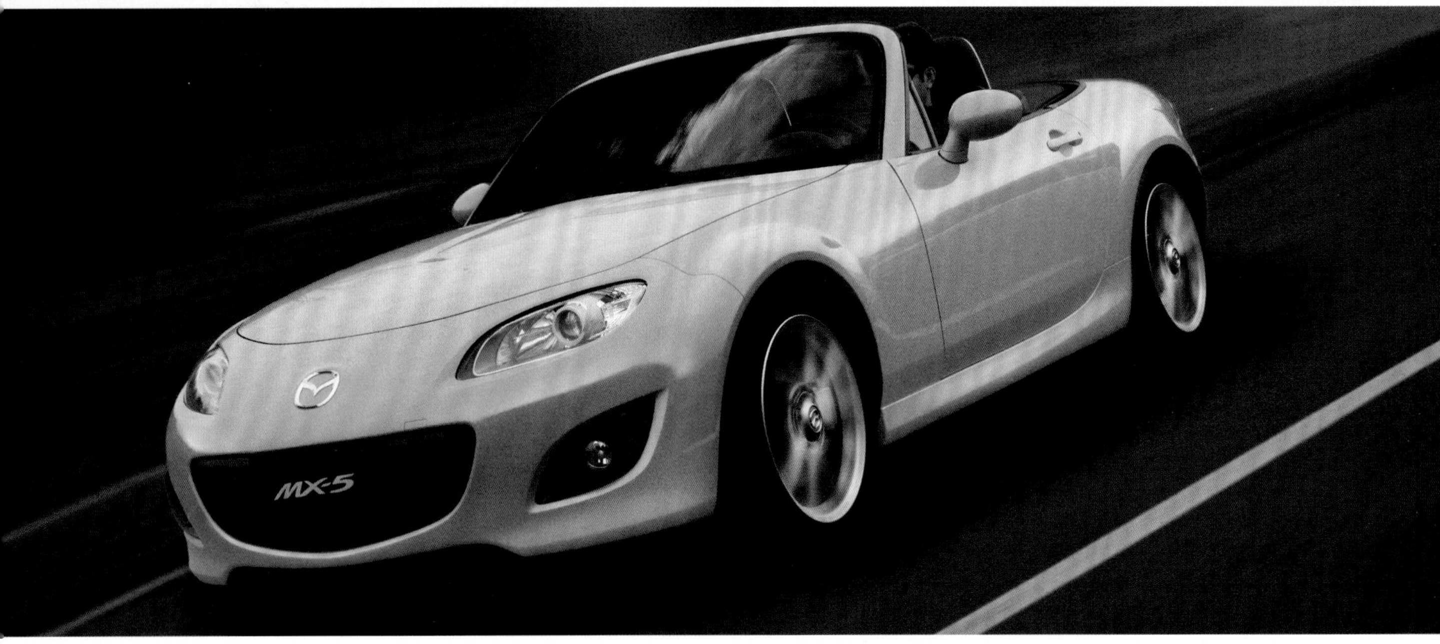

CONTENTE D'ÊTRE UNE FILLE !

Que je suis donc contente d'être une fille ! Je peux m'en donner à cœur joie dans une MX-5 (la Miata, pour les intimes) et en apprécier toutes les facettes sans craindre les qu'en-dira-t-on.

Avouez, Messieurs, que vous avez un p'tit sursaut d'orgueil juste à la pensée d'être vus au volant de ce que vous considérez comme un « char de poulette »... Mais tant pis pour vous si cet orgueil mal placé vous prive d'une belle expérience de conduite. Quoi ? Vous dites que vous avez acheté la MX-5 pour votre femme ? Ben oui, ben oui...

Personnellement, c'est avec les boîtes manuelles que je préfère la MX-5. Les passages en sont rapprochés et, comme pour à peu près toutes les manuelles Mazda, ils se passent sportivement, avec émotion. On sent, sous le pied droit, toute la modulation que l'on peut accorder aux accélérations, tellement la voiture nous va comme un gant. Toutefois, à 120 km/h avec la MX-5 de base, les révolutions à presque 3500 tr/min nous font chercher un rapport supplémentaire qui, fort heureusement, existe sur les versions GS et GT. Notre essai en GT manuelle s'est terminé sur du 8,3 L/100 km, ce qui est plutôt gourmand de la part d'une toute petite et légère décapotable deux places. Le quatre cylindres de 2,0 litres livre ses 167 chevaux (158 chevaux avec l'automatique) dans une belle sonorité et une bonne linéarité. On aurait pris un peu plus que les 140 lb-pi de couple, mais on compense lors des reprises en rétrogradant d'un rapport pour aller chercher davantage de dynamisme. À quand le retour d'une version Speed turbo ? En attendant, il faut résister à l'option du silencieux Speed (875 $) : le son qui s'en extirpe résonne tellement comme un mal de ventre qu'on s'est demandé si, garde au sol très basse oblige, on n'avait pas accroché quelque chose qui aurait percé la canalisation...

ON AIME L'AUTO QUAND MÊME

Malgré toutes les fleurs lancées aux boîtes manuelles, il ne faut pas dénigrer la boîte automatique. Cette dernière fait monter le passage de ses six rapports au volant (GS et GT) et elle a le bonheur de maintenir la sélection choisie tant que la conduite demeure dynamique. C'est le conducteur qui gagne en réactivité et on dirait presque – j'ai bien dit presque – qu'on a affaire à la transmission à double embrayage DSG d'Audi.

Merci à son architecture à propulsion, son châssis très rigide et sa distribution de poids parfaite quand l'habitacle est plein de ses deux occupants, la MX-5 se conduit lestement. Sa suspension (multibras à l'arrière) est ferme et n'eût été des sièges confortables (ceux en cuir enveloppent et sont de maintien supérieur), on trouverait peut-être même les éléments suspenseurs trop fermes. Que non : la balade est athlétique, le tout se replace selon les attentes et la tenue de route est solidement accrochée au bitume. La direction est d'une belle précision, bien sentie, avec juste assez de résistance pour nous mettre en plein contrôle.

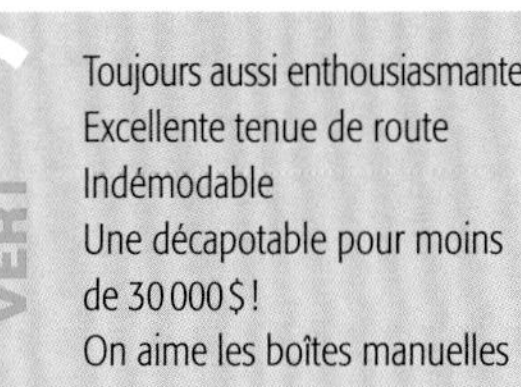

- Toujours aussi enthousiasmante
- Excellente tenue de route
- Indémodable
- Une décapotable pour moins de 30 000 $!
- On aime les boîtes manuelles

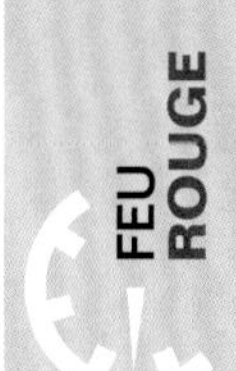

- Petit coffre
- Faut pas être peureux...
- Oubliez le silencieux « Speed »...
- Climatisation en option sur le modèle de base

LA BELLE IMMORTELLE

Extérieurement, la MX-5 conserve une ligne classique, élégante et immortelle. Il y a de ces voitures qui ne se démodent pas et celle qui a célébré son 20e anniversaire en 2009 est de celles-là. Même si elle en est à sa 6e année sur le marché dans sa génération actuelle, elle est toujours d'actualité. Avouez que ça constitue un exploit dans cette industrie automobile qui file plus vite que son ombre.

Elle est jolie, la MX-5, avec son toit souple – au demeurant, fort simple à manipuler. Mais elle a plus d'envergure avec le toit rétractable-rigide, qui accepte de se déshabiller électriquement en moins de 12 secondes. Ce toit, de série pour la GT et optionnel (2 300 $) pour la GS, demande un temps d'apprivoisement; quand ça ne marche pas, c'est que le contact n'est pas mis, que l'embrayage n'est pas engagé, que la boîte manuelle n'est pas au neutre, que le coffre est ouvert, que le frein n'est pas enfoncé... tout autant de raisons pour faire pester. Reste que le toit rigide a l'avantage d'un habitacle clos mieux insonorisé, et ce, sans retrancher quoi que ce soit aux 150 litres de chargement du coffre. Ces 150 litres sont corrects pour quelqu'un qui voyage en solitaire.

Dans l'habitacle, l'instrumentation est sobre mais efficace, avec les bons cadrans lisibles bien placés en évidence. Les commandes sont faciles à apprivoiser et à manipuler. On aime les commandes audio au volant et les sièges chauffants en cinq positions (une option à ne pas dénigrer si on pense se faire des balades décapotées par de fraîches soirées). Aussi, bravo pour ces quatre porte-gobelets qui nous entourent – deux à la console centrale et deux dans les portières. L'espace intérieur est évidemment restreint, mais l'ensemble est maximisé et bien agencé.

Un dernier point : petite, la MX-5, elle est toute petite. On s'y sent parfois bien minus lorsqu'on frôle les gros poids lourds – les roues nous arrivent à hauteur de nez... Il y en a pour régulièrement nous demander si c'est un poil effrayant de rouler en Smart. À ceux-là, je dirais : tentez le coup en MX-5 et vous m'en redonnerez des nouvelles...

Nadine Filion

PHOTOS : MAZDA

Catégorie	*Roadster*
Échelle de prix	28 995 $ à 39 995 $ (2010)
Garanties	3 ans/80 000 km, 5 ans/100 000 km
Assemblage	Hofu, Japon
Cote d'assurance	bonne

CHÂSSIS - DONNÉES POUR GX

Emp/lon/lar/haut	2 330/4 032/1 720/1 245 mm
Coffre	150 litres
Réservoir	48 litres
Nombre coussins sécurité	4
Antipatinage / contrôle stabilité	oui / non
Suspension avant	indépendante, bras inégaux
Suspension arrière	indépendante, multibras
Freins avant / arrière	disque (ABS) / disque (ABS)
Direction	à crémaillère, ass. variable
Diamètre de braquage	9,4 m
Pneus avant / arrière	P205/50R16 / P205/50R16
Poids	1 130 kg
Capacité de remorquage	non recommandé

COMPOSANTES MÉCANIQUES

GX, GS, GT automatique

Cylindrée, soupapes, alim.	4L 2,0 litres 16 s atmos.
Puissance / Couple	158 chevaux / 140 lb-pi
Tr. base (opt) / rouage base (opt)	M5 (A6) / Prop
0-100 / 80-120 / 100-0 km/h	8,3 s / 7,9 s / 37,8 m
Type ess. / ville / autoroute	Ordinaire / 9,7 / 7,1 l/100 km

GX, GS, GT manuelle

Cylindrée, soupapes, alim.	4L 2,0 litres 16 s atmos.
Puissance / Couple	167 chevaux / 140 lb-pi
Tr. base (opt) / rouage base (opt)	M5 (A6) / Prop
0-100 / 80-120 / 100-0 km/h	8,3 s / 7,9 s / 37,8 m
Type ess. / ville / autoroute	Ordinaire / 9,7 / 7,1 l/100 km

DANS LA MÊME CATÉGORIE

MINI Cooper

DU NOUVEAU EN 2011

Aucun changement majeur

NOS IMPRESSIONS

Agrément de conduite :	10/10
Fiabilité :	8/10
Sécurité :	8/10
Qualités hivernales :	4/10
Espace intérieur :	5/10
Confort :	6/10

www.mazda.ca

Plus d'informations dans la section statistiques en dernière partie du Guide

LE CŒUR A SES RAISONS

À sa huitième année sous sa forme actuelle, la RX-8 est toujours unique. C'est le seul coupé sport à quatre places et quatre portières véritablement pratique et la seule voiture à être animée par un moteur rotatif de type Wankel qui la rend à la fois brillante et imparfaite. Mise à jour avec doigté pour 2009, la RX-8 demeure une sportive remarquable à maints égards, pourvu qu'on accepte de vivre avec sa soif immodérée pour les hydrocarbures. Hélas, ses jours sont sans doute comptés !

La Mazda RX-8 est assurément une bête exceptionnelle dans le paysage automobile actuel. À vrai dire, elle est plus exotique que la plus chère des sportives italiennes ou allemandes par le simple fait qu'aucune d'elles ne peut se vanter d'être propulsée par un moteur au cœur duquel tournent les rotors quasi triangulaires d'abord imaginés par Felix Wankel.

PRIX ET TROPHÉES

Exceptionnelle mais pas tellement rare, la RX-8. Mazda en a même produit plus de 200 000 à son usine d'Hiroshima depuis son lancement en 2004. La RX-8 avait pleinement réussi son entrée, décrochant le titre de meilleure nouvelle sportive de l'année chez nous, parmi bien d'autres. Mazda récolta aussi le prix international du moteur de l'année pour son Renesis, évolution importante du rotatif qu'il persiste à raffiner et produire depuis les années 60.

Malgré ces réussites, Mazda n'a toujours pas produit de version plus poussée de la RX-8 dans le moule des Mazdaspeed3 ou Mazdaspeed6. Du moins, pas de modèle à moteur turbocompressé. Ce qui n'empêche aucunement la version R3 actuelle d'être une sportive tout à fait intéressante et réjouissante à conduire. La RX-8 inscrite au match comparatif des sportives publié dans l'édition précédente du *Guide* s'était tirée plus qu'honorablement de l'exercice. Elle y décrocha la troisième place au classement final, même si elle était de loin la plus ancienne et la moins musclée des sept voitures en lice.

En dépit de sa puissance modeste, face aux sportives et aux *muscle cars* américains les plus nouveaux, la RX-8 R3 avait inscrit le troisième meilleur tour chronométré sur un tracé mixte circuit-autocross, tout en affichant la tenue de route la plus agile et la direction la plus fine et précise du groupe. Très bien notée pour son confort et ses qualités pratiques, elle fut évidemment pénalisée par sa consommation relativement élevée. Les opinions et préférences sont également très marquées quant aux caractéristiques et la sonorité uniques du rotatif. Certains adorent, d'autres pas du tout. La RX-8 n'est certainement pas pour tous.

DEUX VERSIONS ÉGALEMENT INTÉRESSANTES

Mazda a ramené la série RX-8 à deux seuls modèles : R3 et GT. Les deux ont profité des mêmes gains notables en solidité, en comportement, en finesse et en esthétique il y a deux ans. La

Comportement routier inspiré
Direction fine et précise
Sonorité et douceur du moteur rotatif
Sportive confortable et pratique

Dépréciation rapide
Consommation élevée
Faible couple en reprise
En fin de cycle

GT mérite entièrement ses initiales, ce qui n'est certes pas toujours le cas. C'est effectivement une vraie grand-tourisme, à la fois agile, performante et confortable. Ses pneus de taille 225/45 R18 sont un peu plus conciliants que les gommes de taille 225/40 R19 que chausse la R3, mais il n'y a rien de mou dans son comportement.

La R3 joue simplement la carte du sport plus ouvertement avec ses sièges Recaro, ses amortisseurs Bilstein et une carrosserie plus typée. La GT offre plutôt des éléments comme un toit ouvrant, la radio satellite et plus de surfaces en cuir. Les performances des deux modèles sont quasi-identiques avec des 0-100 km/h respectifs mesurés de 7,09 et 7,02 secondes avec la boîte manuelle. En conduite, les deux sont un pur plaisir à tout moment et leur moteur rotatif est très souple et docile, malgré son couple modeste. Il faut toutefois rétrograder d'au moins deux rapports pour doubler, mais c'est une sinécure avec une boîte manuelle impeccablement précise, rapide et légère à manier.

Quelques détails finissent par agacer néanmoins, ce sont des banalités comme un pare-soleil qui émet un craquement d'enfer quand on l'extrait de sa pince en plastique pour le tourner vers la glace latérale. De même, on s'ennuie vite de la connectivité Bluetooth pour le téléphone cellulaire alors qu'on en profite, de série, sur certaines des voitures les plus modestes. Pour le reste, la RX-8 est une merveille de finesse en conduite. Elle ne pèse d'ailleurs que 28 kg de plus que la nouvelle Lotus Evora et son châssis tout en aluminium, une légèreté qui contribue autant au confort de roulement qu'aux performances et à la tenue de route.

UN AVENIR EMBRUMÉ

Si seulement Mazda réussissait à rendre son précieux rotatif aussi frugal et performant qu'il est compact et léger. Or, la RX-8 en serait à sa dernière année parce que le moteur Renesis ne pourra se conformer aux prochaines normes d'émissions européennes sous sa forme actuelle. Mazda préparerait plutôt une version moderne de la RX-7 qui serait propulsée par un nouveau rotatif à injection directe de cylindrée légèrement supérieure (1,6 litre au lieu de 1,3) et nettement plus puissant. Espérons que le constructeur d'Hiroshima aura l'intelligence de donner suite à cette sportive remarquable qu'est la RX-8.

Marc Lachapelle

PHOTOS : MARC LACHAPELLE

MAZDA RX-8

Catégorie	Coupé
Échelle de prix	41 995 $ à 43 795 $ (2010)
Garanties	3 ans/80 000 km, 5 ans/100 000 km
Assemblage	Hiroshima, Japon
Cote d'assurance	pauvre

CHÂSSIS - DONNÉES POUR GX

Emp/lon/lar/haut	2 700/4 424/1 770/1 340 mm
Coffre	290 litres
Réservoir	60 litres
Nombre coussins sécurité	6
Antipatinage / contrôle stabilité	oui / oui
Suspension avant	indépendante, double triangulation
Suspension arrière	indépendante, multibras
Freins avant / arrière	disque (ABS) / disque (ABS)
Direction	à crémaillère, ass. variable électronique
Diamètre de braquage	10,6 m
Pneus avant / arrière	P225/40R19 / P225/40R19
Poids	1 389 kg
Capacité de remorquage	non recommandé

COMPOSANTES MÉCANIQUES

GT

Cylindrée, soupapes, alim.	Rotatif 1,3 litre atmos.
Puissance / Couple	212 chevaux / 159 lb-pi
Tr. base (opt) / rouage base (opt)	M6 (A6) / Prop
0-100 / 80-120 / 100-0 km/h	7,3 s / 5,7 s / 37,9 m
Type ess. / ville / autoroute	Super / 12,8 / 9,2 l/100 km

R3, GT

Cylindrée, soupapes, alim.	Rotatif 1,3 litre atmos.
Puissance / Couple	232 chevaux / 159 lb-pi
Tr. base (opt) / rouage base (opt)	M6 (A6) / Prop
0-100 / 80-120 / 100-0 km/h	7,1 s / 5,4 s (est) / 37,9 m
Type ess. / ville / autoroute	Super / 12,8 / 9,2 l/100 km

DANS LA MÊME CATÉGORIE

Audi TT, BMW Série 3, Ford Mustang, Infiniti G, Mitsubishi Eclipse, Nissan Z

DU NOUVEAU EN 2011

Aucun changement majeur

NOS IMPRESSIONS

Agrément de conduite :	9/10
Fiabilité :	6/10
Sécurité :	8/10
Qualités hivernales :	6/10
Espace intérieur :	6/10
Confort :	7/10

www.mazda.ca

Plus d'informations dans la section statistiques en dernière partie du Guide

COMMENT ÉLARGIR SA CLIENTÈLE

Pour assurer sa survie, un constructeur automobile n'a d'autre choix que d'élargir sa clientèle. Pour Mercedes-Benz, cela revient à produire des véhicules qui se vendront moins chers. Mais si cette opération est mal menée ou mal perçue par le public, l'image de l'entreprise pourrait en souffrir. Après tout, la personne qui vient de payer 100 000 $ pour sa Mercedes-Benz Classe S pourrait être bien offensée de voir la célèbre étoile trônant sur la calandre d'une vulgaire voiture de 35 000 $!

La Classe B, débarquée au Canada en 2006 (elle n'est toujours pas offerte aux États-Unis où sa petitesse serait sans aucun doute très mal perçue), présente une ligne qui lui permet d'être différente tout en ne se prenant pas pour une berline ou un VUS typique, déjà offerts par Mercedes.

MERCEDES-BENZ FAIT DES SANDWICHES

Mercedes-Benz est réputé pour le niveau élevé de sécurité de ses véhicules et la Classe B ne fait pas exception à cette règle. Par exemple, son plancher est constitué d'un ensemble de matériaux placés de manière à former un sandwich dans lequel viendrait se loger le moteur en cas d'impact frontal. Si jamais vous montez à bord d'une Classe B, remarquez l'épaisseur impressionnante du plancher. Ce qui lui permet d'offrir une position de conduite élevée, un élément apprécié de plusieurs personnes. En plus, la fenestration généreuse autorise une excellente visibilité tout le tour.

PETITE EN DEHORS, GONFLÉE EN DEDANS!

Si la carrosserie ne réfère pas immédiatement à Mercedes-Benz malgré l'étoile sur la calandre, l'habitacle, lui, est du plus pur Mercedes. Sobre, pour ne pas dire triste, recouvert de plastiques et de matériaux de bonne qualité, il impressionne par son immensité, compte tenu des dimensions de la voiture. Les sièges, malgré leur dureté, font preuve de confort même lors de longs trajets, mais les fesses trop charnues risquent de les trouver étroits. Prendre note qu'il faut débourser plus de 500$ pour les avoir chauffants. Le hayon ouvre haut sur un généreux espace de chargement. Lorsque les dossiers du siège arrière (siège au demeurant confortable) sont relevés, on peut y engouffrer 544 litres. Une fois baissés, ils forment un fond plat et on y entre alors 1 530 litres, soit passablement plus qu'une Toyota Matrix (1 398) mais moins qu'une Kia Rondo (2 083). Il est possible de relever le plancher pour qu'il soit à égalité avec le seuil si on a à déménager un objet lourd, par exemple.

Malgré les apparences, il existe deux Classe B. La régulière (B200) et la Turbo (B200T). La première fait appel à un quatre cylindres de 2,0 litres de 134 chevaux. La B200T, elle, reçoit un moteur de la même cylindrée mais alimenté par turbocompression, ce qui le rend drôlement plus intéressant. Ses 193 chevaux assurent des performances honnêtes tout en permettant une utilisation plus agréable lorsque le véhicule est chargé, ce qui peut arriver à l'occasion avec un hayon !

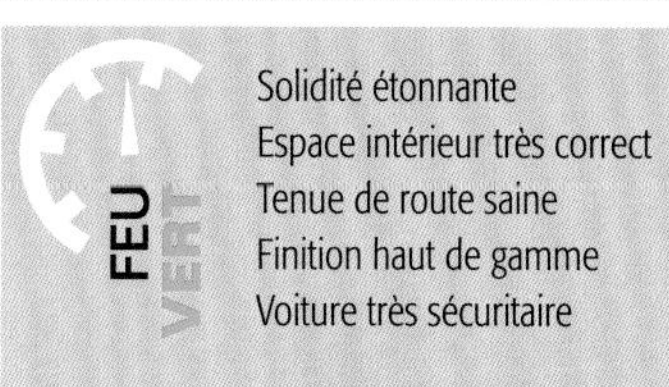

FEU VERT

- Solidité étonnante
- Espace intérieur très correct
- Tenue de route saine
- Finition haut de gamme
- Voiture très sécuritaire

FEU ROUGE

- Pas très sportive
- Version B200 moins intéressante
- Essence super seulement
- Insonorisation déficiente
- Quelques options dispendieuses

Si la transmission CVT à sept rapports virtuels optionnelle est la même pour les deux moteurs, la B200T a droit d'office à une manuelle à six rapports, beaucoup mieux étagée que celle à cinq rapports de la B200. Les six rapports permettent aussi de diminuer l'envahissant bruit du quatre cylindres. La CVT à sept rapports virtuels, peu importe le modèle, demande 1 500$ supplémentaires… mais ils seront récupérés lors de la revente !

La B200T est peut-être plus délurée que la B200, mais cela n'en fait pas une sportive pour autant, ses roues avant motrices ne lui permettent pas de grandes incartades routières. Le châssis se révèle d'une extraordinaire rigidité, les suspensions font un excellent travail autant pour garder le contact entre le véhicule et la route que pour préserver le confort des occupants. La suspension arrière, à poutre déformable, se montre un tantinet moins confortable lorsque la route devient cahoteuse, mais puisqu'elle autorise un grand espace de chargement, nous ne lui en tiendrons pas rigueur. Et puis, lever le pied droit n'a jamais nui dans une telle situatio… Un coin de rue tourné trop rapidement avec une Classe B200 prouve deux choses : A) la caisse penche passablement, B) la conjointe n'apprécie pas, pas du tout… Le même coin de rue tourné trop rapidement avec une Classe B200T prouve deux choses : A) la caisse penche moins que celle de la B200, B) attendre d'être seul est une bonne idée. Comme toute Allemande qui se respecte, la Classe B est très agréable à conduire à haute vitesse alors qu'elle fait preuve d'un aplomb surprenant, autant sur une route en mauvais état que dans les courbes où elle s'accroche avec conviction. La Classe B se montre passablement sensible aux vents latéraux.

Lors de nos différents essais avec la Classe B, surtout lors de son arrivée, les gens avaient peine à croire qu'il s'agissait d'une Mercedes et qu'elle ne coûtait qu'entre 30 000 et 32 500$. Comme c'est devenu l'habitude chez les constructeurs allemands, une mauvaise habitude dont il est sans doute très difficile de se départir, le coût des options frise quelquefois l'hérésie. Mais, à tout prendre, j'aime mieux me priver de sièges chauffants, par exemple, et savoir que le véhicule que je conduis sera encore aussi solide dans dix ans qu'il l'était neuf. C'est ça, une Mercedes, qu'elle soit prestigieuse… ou pas !

Alain Morin

PHOTOS : MERCEDES-BENZ

MERCEDES-BENZ CLASSE B

Catégorie	Familiale
Échelle de prix	29 900 $ à 34 400 $ (2010)
Garanties	4 ans/80 000 km, 4 ans/80 000 km
Assemblage	Rastatt, Allemagne
Cote d'assurance	moyenne

CHÂSSIS - DONNÉES POUR B200 TURBO

Emp/lon/lar/haut	2 778/4 273/1 777/1 604 mm
Coffre	544 à 1 530 litres
Réservoir	54 litres
Nombre coussins sécurité	6
Antipatinage / contrôle stabilité	oui / oui
Suspension avant	indépendante, jambes de force
Suspension arrière	semi-indépendante, essieu parabolique
Freins avant / arrière	disque (ABS) / disque (ABS)
Direction	à crémaillère, ass. variable électrique
Diamètre de braquage	11,9 m
Pneus avant / arrière	P215/45R17 / P215/45R17
Poids	1 395 kg
Capacité de remorquage	non recommandé

COMPOSANTES MÉCANIQUES

B200

Cylindrée, soupapes, alim.	4L 2,0 litres 16 s atmos.
Puissance / Couple	134 chevaux / 136 lb-pi
Tr. base (opt) / rouage base (opt)	M5 (CVT) / Tr
0-100 / 80-120 / 100-0 km/h	10,1 s / 8,4 s / 40,4 m
Type ess. / ville / autoroute	Ordinaire / 9,2 / 6,7 l/100 km

B200 Turbo

Cylindrée, soupapes, alim.	4L 2,0 litres 16 s turbocompressé
Puissance / Couple	193 chevaux / 206 lb-pi
Tr. base (opt) / rouage base (opt)	M6 (CVT) / Tr
0-100 / 80-120 / 100-0 km/h	7,6 s / 5,8 s / 40,4 m
Type ess. / ville / autoroute	Super / 10,3 / 6,9 l/100 km

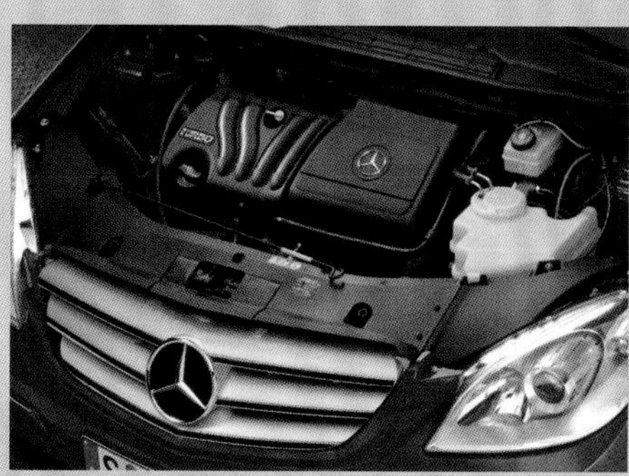

DANS LA MÊME CATÉGORIE

Audi A3, Volkswagen Golf, Volvo V50

DU NOUVEAU EN 2011

Aucun changement majeur

NOS IMPRESSIONS

Agrément de conduite :	7/10
Fiabilité :	6/10
Sécurité :	10/10
Qualités hivernales :	7/10
Espace intérieur :	7/10
Confort :	8/10

www.mercedes-benz.ca

Plus d'informations dans la section statistiques en dernière partie du Guide

LA CLASSE À TOUT FAIRE

Lors de sa dernière révision en 2007, la berline de Classe C a subi une agréable transformation tant au chapitre de son apparence que de ses caractéristiques routières. Auparavant, la silhouette était d'une grande discrétion, alors que plusieurs trouvaient que ses performances routières étaient dans la bonne moyenne, mais pouvaient être nettement améliorées. Il semble que la direction de Stuttgart a acquiescé à ces critiques, car depuis, cette nouvelle génération impressionne, tant au chapitre de la présentation que des performances.

Comme le marché canadien est différent de celui des États-Unis, la gamme de produits Mercedes-Benz dans notre pays n'est pas tout à fait similaire à celle de nos voisins du sud. Si la Classe C est la petite Mercedes aux États-Unis, elle fait quasiment office de grosse voiture au Canada, en comparaison à la Classe B, une voiture qui, en Amérique du Nord, est exclusive au Canada.

DU MORDANT

Tel que mentionné précédemment, l'ancienne génération de la Classe C nous proposait une silhouette bien sage qui se contentait de reprendre les éléments esthétique visuels propres à cette marque. Lors de la refonte, les stylistes ont donné un sérieux coup de crayon à la carrosserie qui est devenue nettement plus sportive et plus dynamique. Les parois latérales et les passages de roues en relief sont sculptés de façon à donner plus de dynamisme à l'ensemble du véhicule. Le devant de la voiture est doté d'une grille de calandre à trois bandes horizontales abritant la célèbre étoile d'argent. De son côté, le renflement du capot permet de donner plus d'émotivité à cette présentation. Bref, on lui a

donné un nouveau souffle plus sportif qui fait toute la différence et qui lui permet d'être autre chose qu'une belle berline de luxe.

L'habitacle a également été revu et c'est assez bien réussi dans l'ensemble. Comme c'est la tradition chez ce constructeur, la planche de bord est très sobre avec pratiquement toutes ses commandes regroupées sous les buses de ventilation centrales. De plus, une commande multifonction est placée sur la console entre les deux sièges. Avec un peu de pratique, il est possible de régler la plupart des paramètres de cette voiture sans trop d'écarts de vocabulaire. Il faut également noter la présence d'un écran d'affichage qui se rétracte dans la planche de bord lorsqu'il n'est pas utilisé.

Les sièges avant sont fermes, mais confortables et leur support latéral, supérieur à la moyenne de la catégorie. Les places arrière sont correctes, la banquette, d'une hauteur respectable, mais l'espace pour les jambes n'est pas tellement généreux. Il faut également ajouter que la qualité des matériaux est à la hauteur de la réputation de la marque et la finition est impeccable. La position de conduite est bonne puisque le volant se règle en

FEU VERT

- Carrosserie très solide
- Choix de moteurs
- Tenue de route impressionnante
- Fiabilité en progrès
- Système 4Matic amélioré

FEU ROUGE

- Commande du régulateur de croisière
- Certaines options onéreuses
- Moteur 2,5 litres un peu juste
- Pneumatiques moyens

hauteur et en profondeur. Malheureusement, nous devons déplorer encore une fois le levier servant à gérer le régulateur de vitesse. Il est mal positionné et on se prend souvent à le confondre avec le levier des clignotants. Comme toute voiture de luxe qui se respecte, la fermeture des portes est suivie d'un bruit sec qui nous porte à croire que la caisse est solide, très solide.

PETIT MOTEUR, SUPER MOTEUR

La personne qui désire s'acheter une voiture de la Classe C a plus que l'embarras du choix. La carrosserie demeure la même, mais il existe de nombreuses variantes en fait de présentation. À ce chapitre, Mercedes-Benz fait appel cette année à des phares de jour constitués de diodes électroluminescentes comme le veut la tendance actuelle. Ces lumières brillent davantage, consomment moins d'énergie et durent très longtemps.

Il y a deux ans, Mercedes-Benz Canada nous proposait une exclusivité mondiale. Il s'agissait de la C230 4Matic. En effet, ce n'est qu'en sol canadien qu'on pouvait se procurer ce modèle à rouage intégral, vendu à un prix plus que compétitif. Il a été remplacé l'an dernier par la C250 qui est proposée en version propulsion ou 4Matic. Mercedes-Benz n'a fait qu'aligner la nomenclature du modèle à la cylindrée du moteur. Celui-ci produit 201 chevaux et il peut être commandé avec une boîte manuelle à six rapports ou l'automatique 7G –Tronic qui, comme son nom l'indique, est une boîte à sept rapports. Au sujet de la boîte manuelle, celle-ci n'est disponible que sur les modèles C250 et C300. Par contre, tous les modèles à traction intégrale 4Matic sont associés à l'automatique. Cette année, le rouage 4Matic a été révisé et allégé. Son temps de réponse est encore plus court et son efficacité améliorée. Il est offert sur tous les modèles à l'exception du C63 AMG.

Cette dernière version est vraiment hors-norme avec son moteur V8 de 6,2 litres produisant 451 chevaux et qui propulse la voiture à 100 km/h en 4,5 secondes. Vous avez compris, qu'il s'agit d'un modèle d'exception. Sur une note plus raisonnable, la version la plus intéressante est sans doute la C350 dont le moteur V6 de 3,5 litres produit 268 chevaux tout en proposant une consommation de carburant quasiment similaire à celle du C300 et son moteur V6 3,0 litres de 228 chevaux. Par contre, ce dernier peut être commandé avec la boîte manuelle à six rapports. Malheureusement, tous les moteurs de la Classe C utilisent de l'essence super.

Denis Duquet

PHOTOS : MERCEDES-BENZ

MERCEDES-BENZ CLASSE C

Catégorie	Berline
Échelle de prix	35 800 $ à 63 500 $ (2010)
Garanties	4 ans/80 000 km, 4 ans/80 000 km
Assemblage	Sindelfingen, Allemagne
Cote d'assurance	moyenne

CHÂSSIS - DONNÉES POUR C300 4MATIC

Emp/lon/lar/haut	2 760/4 625/1 770/1 445 mm
Coffre	354 litres
Réservoir	66 litres
Nombre coussins sécurité	7
Antipatinage / contrôle stabilité	oui / oui
Suspension avant	indépendante, jambes de force
Suspension arrière	indépendante, multibras
Freins avant / arrière	disque (ABS) / disque (ABS)
Direction	à crémaillère, ass. variable
Diamètre de braquage	11,0 m
Pneus avant / arrière	P225/45R17 / P225/45R17
Poids	1 695 kg
Capacité de remorquage	n.d.

COMPOSANTES MÉCANIQUES

C250, C250 4Matic

Cylindrée, soupapes, alim.	V6 2,5 litres 24 s atmos.
Puissance / Couple	201 chevaux / 181 lb-pi
Tr. base (opt) / rouage base (opt)	M6 (A7) / Prop (Int)
0-100 / 80-120 / 100-0 km/h	8,4 s / n.d. / n.d.
Type ess. / ville / autoroute	Super / 11,5 / 7,5 l/100 km

C300, C300 4Matic

Cylindrée, soupapes, alim.	V6 3,0 litres 24 s atmos.
Puissance / Couple	228 chevaux / 221 lb-pi
Tr. base (opt) / rouage base (opt)	M6 (A7) / Prop (Int)
0-100 / 80-120 / 100-0 km/h	7,3 s / n.d. / n.d.
Type ess. / ville / autoroute	Super / 12,0 / 8 l/100 km

C350, C350 4Matic
V6 3,5 l, 268 ch, 258 lb-pi - 0-100 : 6,6 s - 12,5 / 8,2 l/100 km

C63 AMG
V8 6,2 l, 451 ch, 443 lb-pi - 0-100 : 4,5 s - 17,2 / 10,4 l/100 km

DANS LA MÊME CATÉGORIE

Acura TL, Audi A4, BMW Série 3, Cadillac CTS, Infiniti G, Lexus ES, Lexus IS, Lincoln MKZ, Volvo S60

DU NOUVEAU EN 2011

Lumières à DEL dans le bouclier avant

NOS IMPRESSIONS

Agrément de conduite :	8/10
Fiabilité :	6/10
Sécurité :	10/10
Qualités hivernales :	9/10
Espace intérieur :	8/10
Confort :	8/10

www.mercedes-benz.ca

Plus d'informations dans la section statistiques en dernière partie du Guide

LA GRANDE CLASSE

S'il est une catégorie d'exception dans l'univers automobile, c'est bien celle des grands coupés de luxe dont la mission première est d'assurer un confort souverain pour quatre personnes tout en faisant preuve d'un certain style. Le coupé CL de Mercedes-Benz en fait partie au même titre que la Bentley Continental GT ou la Ferrari 612 Scaglietti.

Le nom CL évoque les mots *Comfort Leicht* en allemand, ou confort et légèreté en français, quoique la notion de légèreté soit aujourd'hui largement évacuée compte tenu du fait que ce grand coupé pèse plus de 2000 kilos... Qu'à cela ne tienne, le coupé CL représente en quelque sorte la vitrine technologique du constructeur, au même titre que la berline de Classe S dont il est dérivé. C'est cependant avec un certain retard, par rapport à la Classe S dévoilée au Salon de Shanghai en 2009, que le millésime 2011 du coupé CL a connu son dévoilement en marge du prestigieux Festival of Speed à Goodwood en Angleterre au cours de l'été 2010. Avec le restylage du nouveau modèle, et surtout la mise à jour de sa dotation technologique, le coupé CL rattrape aujourd'hui le terrain perdu par rapport à la berline de luxe de Classe S.

Au premier coup d'œil, les changements apportés à la carrosserie ne sautent pas immédiatement aux yeux et se révèlent plutôt subtilement. Ainsi, la calandre est plus dynamique et les entrées d'air pratiquées dans le bouclier avant sont plus évidentes, alors que les phares de jour, ainsi que les feux arrière, adoptent la technologie DEL. Mais, comme c'est souvent le cas à chaque refonte du coupé CL, on a droit à une véritable avalanche de nouveaux dispositifs de technologie de pointe alors que le constructeur allemand fait la démonstration de son expertise sur le plan technique.

PUISSANCE EN HAUSSE, CONSOMMATION EN BAISSE

Au chapitre de la motorisation, le coupé CL550 à rouage integral 4MATIC évolue avec un nouveau moteur qui livre plus de puissance malgré une cylindrée réduite par rapport au modèle antérieur. Ainsi, on retrouvera désormais sous le capot un V8 biturbo de 4,6 litres capable de livrer 429 chevaux, plutôt que l'ancien V8 de 5,5 litres qui en développait 382. De plus, le couple maximal passe de 391 à 516 livres-pied, soit une augmentation significative de 32 pour cent. Paradoxalement, cette hausse de la puissance et du couple s'accompagne d'une réduction de l'ordre de 10 à 15 pour cent de la consommation de carburant et d'une diminution de 23 pour cent des émissions de gaz à effet de serre, selon Mercedes-Benz. Au sommet de la pyramide, on retrouve encore et toujours l'onctueux V12 biturbo dont la puissance est maintenant chiffrée à 620 chevaux, alors que le CL63 recevra un V8 biturbo de 5,5 litres capable de livrer 536 chevaux.

ELLE PENSE POUR VOUS

Truffé de véritables « cerveaux » électroniques ainsi que d'une armée de capteurs, de caméras et de radars, le coupé CL s'est donné comme mission d'assister le conducteur dans ses tâches,

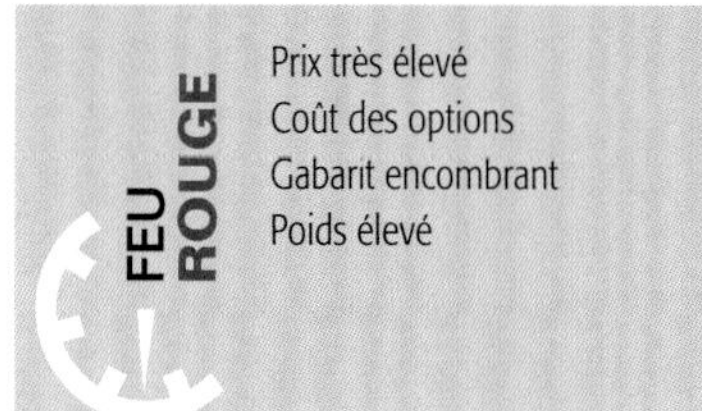

FEU VERT
- Confort souverain
- Très bonne tenue de route
- Véritable quatre places
- Technologie de pointe

FEU ROUGE
- Prix très élevé
- Coût des options
- Gabarit encombrant
- Poids élevé

ce qui en fait l'un des véhicules les plus avancés sur le plan technique. Pour ce qui est des innovations avancées par le modèle 2011, on retrouve le système Active Lane Keeping Assist qui analyse les images retransmises par la caméra montée à l'intérieur de l'habitacle pour ensuite intervenir si la voiture semble vouloir traverser une ligne continue sur la chaussée. Dans un premier temps, le conducteur sentira une vibration dans le volant. S'il ne réagit pas, le système commandera le freinage sélectif des roues opposées à la ligne continue pour ramener la voiture dans sa voie. De plus, le système Active Blind Spot Assist prévoit trois niveaux d'intervention si le conducteur fait un changement de voie alors qu'un autre véhicule se trouve dans l'angle mort. Le système fera d'abord apparaître un symbole rouge dans le rétroviseur extérieur pour ensuite émettre un signal sonore puis finalement commander le freinage sélectif des roues pour éviter qu'il y ait une collision entre les deux véhicules.

La somnolence au volant étant également un facteur de taille comme cause d'accidents, les ingénieurs de Mercedes-Benz ont mis au point le système Attention Assist qui analyse constamment 70 paramètres de façon à cerner le niveau d'alerte du conducteur pour intervenir avant que celui-ci ne s'endorme au volant. Dans leurs recherches sur ce phénomène, les spécialistes du constructeur allemand se sont aperçu qu'un conducteur somnolent fait souvent des erreurs minimes de guidage pour les corriger très rapidement au volant d'une manière caractéristique juste avant de tomber dans la phase du microsommeil. Ce comportement au volant est analysé par le capteur d'angle de la direction et un message d'alerte est transmis au conducteur. Toujours au sujet de la sécurité, le système Active Body Control (ABC), qui contrôle les mouvements de la suspension, a été optimisé afin de compenser l'effet du vent latéral en ajustant les suspensions de la voiture en quelques millièmes de seconde.

Le confort souverain qui est la marque du coupé CL se retrouve bonifié par l'ajout du système SPLITVIEW qui, au moyen d'un prisme, permet au passager avant de regarder un DVD sur l'écran central alors que le conducteur consulte la cartographie du système de navigation sur ce même écran.

Véritable vitrine technologique de la marque, le coupé CL permet de disposer d'une voiture de grand luxe qui est un peu plus expressive côté design.

Gabriel Gélinas

PHOTOS : MERCEDES-BENZ

MERCEDES-BENZ CL

Catégorie	Coupé
Échelle de prix	130 500 $ à 241 000 $ (2010)
Garanties	4 ans/80 000 km, 4 ans/80 000 km
Assemblage	Stuttgart, Allemagne
Cote d'assurance	n.d.

CHÂSSIS - DONNÉES POUR CL600

Emp/lon/lar/haut	2 955/5 095/1 871/1 419 mm
Coffre	490 litres
Réservoir	90 litres
Nombre coussins sécurité	7
Antipatinage / contrôle stabilité	oui / oui
Suspension avant	indépendante, multibras
Suspension arrière	indépendante, multibras
Freins avant / arrière	disque (ABS) / disque (ABS)
Direction	à crémaillère, ass. variable
Diamètre de braquage	11,6 m
Pneus avant / arrière	P255/40R19 / P275/40R19
Poids	2 220 kg
Capacité de remorquage	n.d.

COMPOSANTES MÉCANIQUES

CL550 4Matic

Cylindrée, soupapes, alim.	V8 4,6 litres turbo
Puissance / Couple	429 chevaux / 516 lb-pi
Tr. base (opt) / rouage base (opt)	A7 / Int
0-100 / 80-120 / 100-0 km/h	4,9 s / n.d. / n.d.
Type ess. / ville / autoroute	Super / n.d. / n.d.

CL600

Cylindrée, soupapes, alim.	V12 5,5 litres 36 s turbo
Puissance / Couple	510 chevaux / 612 lb-pi
Tr. base (opt) / rouage base (opt)	A5 / Prop
0-100 / 80-120 / 100-0 km/h	4,6 s / n.d. / n.d.
Type ess. / ville / autoroute	Super / 19,2 / 12 l/100 km

CL63 AMG

V8 5,5 l, 536 ch / 590 lb-pi - 0-100 : 4,5 s - n.d. l/100 km

CL65 AMG

V12 6,0 l, 620 ch / 738 lb-pi - 0-100 : 4,4 s - 19,1 / 11,8 l/100 km

DANS LA MÊME CATÉGORIE

BMW Série 6, Bentley Continental, Jaguar XK

DU NOUVEAU EN 2011

Révisions esthétiques, nouveau V8 4,6 litres (CL550) et V8 6,2 litres (CL63 AMG)

NOS IMPRESSIONS

Agrément de conduite :	8/10
Fiabilité :	8/10
Sécurité :	10/10
Qualités hivernales :	7/10
Espace intérieur :	7/10
Confort :	8/10

www.mercedes-benz.ca

Plus d'informations dans la section statistiques en dernière partie du Guide

LA REINE DE L'ÉLÉGANCE

Par le passé, le stylisme des voitures produites par Mercedes-Benz n'a pas toujours fait l'unanimité. On reprochait à la silhouette de ces Allemandes de manquer d'inspiration et d'être un peu fade. Mais s'il est une voiture qui ne peut être l'objet de ces critiques, c'est bien la CLS. En effet, ce coupé quatre portes figure toujours parmi les plus jolies voitures sur le marché, et ce, bien qu'elle soit commercialisée depuis plus de cinq ans maintenant. Elle fait partie de ces voitures qui sont devenues un classique dès leur apparition dans les salles de démonstration.

Tout élégante soit-elle, son cycle de vie commercial est à la veille de se terminer. En effet, une toute nouvelle version sera commercialisée au début de 2011. Après son lancement au Salon de l'auto de Paris, cette nouvelle génération de la CLS sera présentée en Amérique au début de l'année pour ensuite faire son entrée chez les concessionnaires.

EN ATTENDANT

Cette situation se traduit par une période de transition alors que le nombre de modèles 2011 mis en marché sera peut-être limité tandis qu'on termine la production de l'un et qu'on entame la fabrication de l'autre. Plusieurs personnes préféreront attendre l'arrivée de la nouvelle génération. Les gens aiment toujours se procurer la toute dernière nouveauté. Ce phénomène est de plus en plus populaire dans notre société de consommation et explique pourquoi les gens font la file toute une nuit pour être parmi les premiers à se procurer un téléphone cellulaire iPhone de Apple par exemple. Pourtant, dans les jours, les semaines et les mois qui suivront, ce même téléphone sera offert à gogo.

Les personnes qui s'intéresseront aux modèles toujours en marché bénéficieront d'une voiture d'une excellente maturité sur le plan mécanique. Ce qui signifie que les bogues des premières années de production ont été corrigés, et que la qualité d'assemblage est généralement un peu supérieure à ce qui était proposé au début de la carrière de ce modèle.

En ce qui a trait à la mécanique, le choix est relativement simple puisque seulement deux moteurs et deux versions sont au catalogue. Le modèle de base, si l'on peut s'exprimer ainsi, est doté d'un moteur V8 de 5,5 litres d'une puissance de 382 chevaux et associé à une boîte automatique à sept rapports. J'ai lu dans certaines publications américaines que cette transmission hésitait parfois à rétrograder, et que les passages des rapports étaient parfois saccadés. J'ai eu beau regarder dans mes carnets de notes, je n'ai jamais constaté cela. Cette transmission est efficace, et les passages d'un rapport à l'autre ont toujours été effectués en grande douceur. Mais contrairement à plusieurs modèles de cette marque, la CLS n'est pas offerte avec la transmission intégrale 4Matic. Il faut également préciser que, comme le modèle 2011 en est un de transition, le nombre d'accessoires et d'options est limité.

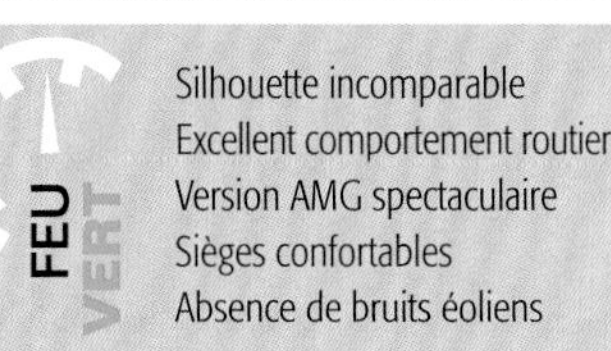

FEU VERT

- Silhouette incomparable
- Excellent comportement routier
- Version AMG spectaculaire
- Sièges confortables
- Absence de bruits éoliens

FEU ROUGE

- Rouage 4Matic non disponible
- Prix élevé
- Visibilité de trois quarts arrière
- Accès difficile aux places arrière
- Options limitées

Cette voiture offre bien entendu un niveau de luxe et de confort que nous propose toute Mercedes-Benz, peu importe sa classe. Comme cette version est basée sur l'ancien modèle de la Classe E, la tenue de route est bonne, le silence aérodynamique est excellent, mais le feedback de la direction pourrait être amélioré. Il faut déplorer toutefois la complexité de certaines commandes et une visibilité de trois quarts arrière assez pénible en raison de la silhouette de la voiture. Cette même silhouette rend difficile l'accès aux places arrière, et il faut se contorsionner quelque peu pour monter à bord. Heureusement, une fois assis, ces places sont confortables.

Vous pouvez également choisir la CLS 63 AMG dont le moteur V8 de 6,2 litres produit la bagatelle de 507 chevaux. Il est associé à une transmission automatique à sept rapports. Elle aussi ne peut être commandée avec le rouage intégral. Ce modèle est particulièrement intéressant, car il permet d'obtenir une voiture dont la silhouette est extraordinaire et qui propose des performances hors-normes. L'exercice du 0-100 km/h est bouclé en moins de cinq secondes tandis que le comportement routier de cette voiture n'est limité que par votre audace et la peur d'être intercepté par les forces policières. Bien entendu, c'est une voiture d'exception qui n'est offerte qu'en petites quantités. Et même s'il s'agit de sa dernière année sur le marché, elle mérite que les gens qui ont les moyens financiers s'y intéressent.

LA NOUVELLE, ALORS !

Au moment d'écrire ces lignes, très peu d'informations ont été divulguées quant à la Classe CLS de la nouvelle génération. Mais comme chez Mercedes-Benz on procède à des développements évolutifs, on peut parier que cette élégante silhouette sera reconduite tout en étant raffinée. Elle sera naturellement plus aérodynamique et dotée d'accessoires et d'éléments visuels partagés avec les autres modèles récemment dévoilés. Le plus important ne sera pas un nouveau moteur révolutionnaire, mais l'ajout à la liste de l'équipement de série et en option d'une multitude d'éléments visant à améliorer la sécurité active et passive de cette voiture. En fait, elle proposera la grande majorité des innovations technologiques et électroniques qui ont été utilisées sur la nouvelle génération des modèles de la Classe E, puisqu'elle partage sa plate-forme et sa mécanique avec celle-ci.

Denis Duquet

PHOTOS : MERCEDES-BENZ

Catégorie	Berline
Échelle de prix	88 500 $ à 121 300 $
Garanties	4 ans/80 000 km, 4 ans/80 000 km
Assemblage	Stuttgart, Allemagne
Cote d'assurance	n.d.

CHÂSSIS - DONNÉES POUR CLS550

Emp/lon/lar/haut	2 854/4 910/1 873/1 414 mm
Coffre	495 litres
Réservoir	80 litres
Nombre coussins sécurité	6
Antipatinage / contrôle stabilité	oui / oui
Suspension avant	indépendante, multibras
Suspension arrière	indépendante, multibras
Freins avant / arrière	disque (ABS) / disque (ABS)
Direction	à crémaillère, assistée
Diamètre de braquage	11,2 m
Pneus avant / arrière	P255/35R19 / P285/30R19
Poids	1 825 kg
Capacité de remorquage	n.d.

COMPOSANTES MÉCANIQUES

CLS550

Cylindrée, soupapes, alim.	V8 5,5 litres 32 s atmos.
Puissance / Couple	382 chevaux / 391 lb-pi
Tr. base (opt) / rouage base (opt)	A7 / Prop
0-100 / 80-120 / 100-0 km/h	5,4 s / 5,3 s / 39,0 m
Type ess. / ville / autoroute	Super / 15,1 / 9,5 l/100 km

CLS63 AMG

Cylindrée, soupapes, alim.	V8 6,2 litres 32 s atmos.
Puissance / Couple	507 chevaux / 465 lb-pi
Tr. base (opt) / rouage base (opt)	A7 / Prop
0-100 / 80-120 / 100-0 km/h	4,8 s / n.d. / n.d.
Type ess. / ville / autoroute	Super / 17,8 / 11,2 l/100 km

DANS LA MÊME CATÉGORIE

Aston Martin Rapide, Audi A8, BMW Série7, Jaguar XJ, Maserati Quattroporte, Porsche Panamera

DU NOUVEAU EN 2011

Aucun changement majeur, groupes d'options remaniés.

NOS IMPRESSIONS

Agrément de conduite :	8/10
Fiabilité :	6/10
Sécurité :	10/10
Qualités hivernales :	8/10
Espace intérieur :	7/10
Confort :	10/10

www.mercedes-benz.ca

Plus d'informations dans la section statistiques en dernière partie du Guide

L'EXCELLENCE DANS LA DIVERSIFICATION

Il est tout aussi difficile d'essayer de résumer la gamme complète des modèles de la Classe E que de tenter de décrire en un seul paragraphe les différentes péripéties du club de hockey les Canadiens au cours de la dernière année. Chez Mercedes-Benz, les différentes variantes de ce modèle constituent l'élément le plus alléchant pour l'acheteur, ce qui explique la multitude des versions offertes ainsi que les spectaculaires innovations sur le plan technologique.

Lancée il y a un peu moins de deux ans, la nouvelle génération de la berline de la Classe E nous dévoilait un véhicule plus homogène, plus élégant et surtout doté d'une multitude d'éléments technologiques visant à améliorer les performances et la sécurité active et passive. Elle a été suivie ensuite de la version coupé deux portes, du cabriolet et finalement de la familiale. Sans oublier, bien entendu, la version AMG de la berline qui permet de combiner luxe et confort à des performances époustouflantes.

TECHNOLOGIE À GOGO

Depuis que les ingénieurs de chez Mercedes-Benz ont adopté l'électronique comme élément destiné à améliorer le rendement, les performances et la sécurité des voitures de la marque, on a eu droit à une véritable avalanche d'innovations toutes aussi raffinées les unes que les autres. Avant de vous faire une énumération non exhaustive de ces éléments, qui sont variables selon les versions et les groupes d'options, soulignons une de ces innovations en particulier, commune à tous les modèles, le système AirCap. Ce dernier permet de faire passer l'air au-dessus de l'habitacle une fois le toit rétracté. Un déflecteur à commande électrique se déploie sur la partie supérieure du pare-brise et dirige l'air directement au-dessus de l'habitacle et des ses occupants. Il faut en plus souligner la présence d'une grille anti turbulence placée entre les appuie-têtes arrière.

Parmi les autres accessoires dignes de mention, il faut signaler le très efficace régulateur de vitesse Distronic qui respecte automatiquement une distance préréglée avec les véhicules qui nous précèdent sur la route. Mercedes-Benz a été l'un des premiers à installer ce système sur ses véhicules et cela s'est révélé fort impressionnant. Une version plus élaborée, appelé Distronic Plus, permet de gérer des réglages plus fins et même d'immobiliser complètement le véhicule. Toujours u chapitre de la sécurité, un mécanisme détecte une conduite erratique de votre part et un témoin lumineux sous la forme d'une tasse de café vous incite à prendre une pause. Par ailleurs, le système d'avertissement de chevauchement des lignes blanches est vraiment plus sophistiqué que ce qui est proposé ailleurs. En effet, au lieu d'avoir un infernal « Beeb Beep », le volant vibre légèrement pour vous avertir de revenir dans le droit chemin. Comme sur plusieurs autres voitures, le détecteur de présence dans l'angle mort est une bénédiction.

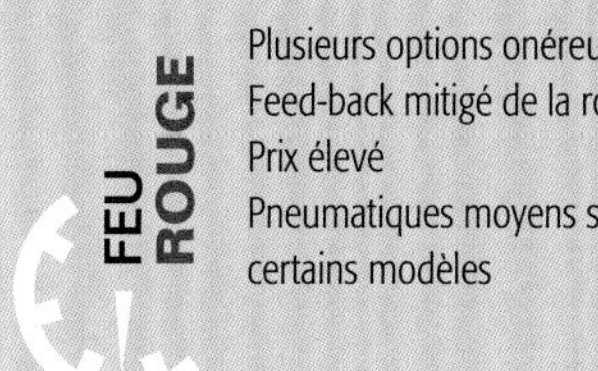

FEU VERT
- Multitude de moteurs
- Assistance électronique au pilotage
- Tenue de route exemplaire
- Habitacle confortable
- Sécurité impressionnante

FEU ROUGE
- Plusieurs options onéreuses
- Feed-back mitigé de la route
- Prix élevé
- Pneumatiques moyens sur certains modèles

La liste est tellement longue qu'il faut en ignorer plusieurs, mais il ne faut surtout pas oublier le système d'éclairage adaptatif AHA qui règle l'intensité lumineuse des phares de croisement selon la densité de la circulation. Il y a également ces phares actifs qui suivent le déroulement de la route.

DIFFÉRENTE MOUTURE, MÊME QUALITÉ

Qu'il s'agisse de la berline, du coupé, du cabriolet ou de la familiale, la plupart de ces modèles sont offerts avec une alternative quant au choix du moteur: un V6 de 3,5 litres donnant 268 chevaux et un V8 de 5,5 litres produisant 382 chevaux. Les deux sont associés à une transmission automatique à sept rapports dont le fonctionnement est impeccable. Cette année, les gens intéressés à se procurer la berline pourront commander une version à moteur diesel BlueTec. Ce moteur V6 3,0 litres produit 210 chevaux et son couple est de 400 lb/pi. Dans un tout autre registre, la berline E63 AMG assure des accélérations et des performances quasiment hors normes avec son moteur V8 de 518 chevaux qui permet de boucler le 0-100 km/h en 4,5 secondes.

Les temps d'accélération varient selon les modèles, mais toutes ces Mercedes partagent plusieurs points en commun, notamment une finition impeccable, des sièges confortables et une multitude d'accessoires visant à améliorer le confort à l'intérieur de l'habitacle.

Avec cette multitude d'éléments pour nous protéger et nous garder dans la bonne voie, on serait presque porté à croire que la tenue de route de ces modèles est déficiente. Bien au contraire! Vous avez l'impression de piloter un véhicule solide comme le roc qui est imperturbable peu importe la vitesse de la voiture. De plus, en raison d'une suspension gérée électroniquement, on bénéficie toujours des réglages optimaux en fonction de la vitesse et du type de conduite. Sans oublier la possibilité de commander la berline et la familiale avec le rouage intégral 4Matic, qui a été révisé et qui est plus efficace que jamais.

Finalement, il semble que Mercedes-Benz ait réussi à améliorer la fiabilité de ses modèles en général et celle des nouveaux arrivants de la Classe E en particulier. C'était à espérer, compte tenu de la complexité technologique de ces belles allemandes.

Denis Duquet

PHOTOS: SYLVAIN RAYMOND

Catégorie	Berline, Familiale
Échelle de prix	58 600 $ à 106 900 $ (2010)
Garanties	4 ans/80 000 km, 4 ans/80 000 km
Assemblage	Stuttgart, Allemagne
Cote d'assurance	moyenne

CHÂSSIS - DONNÉES POUR E550 CABRIOLET

Emp/lon/lar/haut	2 760/4 698/1 786/1 412 mm
Coffre	390 litres
Réservoir	66 litres
Nombre coussins sécurité	6
Antipatinage / contrôle stabilité	oui / oui
Suspension avant	indépendante, multibras
Suspension arrière	indépendante, multibras
Freins avant / arrière	disque (ABS) / disque (ABS)
Direction	à crémaillère, ass. variable
Diamètre de braquage	11,0 m
Pneus avant / arrière	P235/40R18/P255/35R18
Poids	1 840 kg
Capacité de remorquage	n.d.

COMPOSANTES MÉCANIQUES

E350 BlueTEC

Cylindrée, soupapes, alim.	V6 3,0 litres 24 s turbo
Puissance / Couple	210 chevaux / 400 lb-pi
Tr. base (opt) / rouage base (opt)	A7 / Prop
0-100 / 80-120 / 100-0 km/h	7,8 s (est) / 6,2 s (est) / n.d.
Type ess. / ville / autoroute	Diesel / n.d. / n.d.

E350, E350 4Matic

Cylindrée, soupapes, alim.	V6 3,5 litres 24 s atmos.
Puissance / Couple	268 chevaux / 258 lb-pi
Tr. base (opt) / rouage base (opt)	A7 / Prop (Int)
0-100 / 80-120 / 100-0 km/h	7.4 s / 6,0 s / 43,1 m
Type ess. / ville / autoroute	Ordinaire / 12,7 / 8,3 l/100 km

E550, E550 4Matic

V8 5,5 l, 382 ch, 391 lb-pi - 0-100: 5,3 s - 13,8 / 8,6 l/100 km

E63 AMG

V8 6,2 l, 518 ch, 465 lb-pi - 0-100: 4,5 s - 16,5 / 10,2 l/100 km

DANS LA MÊME CATÉGORIE

Acura RL, Audi A6, BMW Série 5, Cadillac STS, Infiniti M, Jaguar XF, Lexus GS, Lincoln MKS Volvo S80

DU NOUVEAU EN 2011

Modèle familial et moteur diesel (E350 BlueTEC)

NOS IMPRESSIONS

Agrément de conduite:	9/10
Fiabilité:	6/10
Sécurité:	10/10
Qualités hivernales:	7/10
Espace intérieur:	7/10
Confort:	7/10

www.mercedes-benz.ca

Plus d'informations dans la section statistiques en dernière partie du Guide

NON À LA SIMPLICITÉ VOLONTAIRE

Dans le but de simplifier sa gamme, Mercedes-Benz a décidé, l'an dernier, de se départir de sa CLK. Celle-ci était proposée en livrées coupé et cabriolet. Et comme on ne laisse pas ce marché restreint mais sans aucun doute lucratif à la toujours très opportuniste compétition, il fallait remplacer la CLK le plus rapidement possible. Ça tombait bien, l'auguste marque allemande venait de lancer sa fort réussie berline Classe E. Elle en a donc tiré un coupé et, ensuite, un cabriolet.

En fait, et aussi bien le dire tout de suite, l'un et l'autre sont des mieux réussis, ce qui implique qu'on a fait beaucoup plus que simplement enlever deux portières et supprimer un toit! Mercedes a d'abord présenté son coupé qui, contrairement aux apparences, ne partage aucun panneau de carrosserie avec la berline Classe E. Depuis le printemps 2010, le cabriolet est offert chez nous. Les deux voitures partagent le tableau de bord de la berline, à quelques détails près. Ce qui revient à dire qu'il est sobre, à la limite de l'austérité, et superbement fini. Bien entendu, comme toute Mercedes qui se respecte, il y a du bois véritable ici et là.

Pour accéder à cet habitacle des plus accueillants, il faut ouvrir des portières très longues et incroyablement lourdes. Première constatation, à l'avant, le dégagement pour la tête est très restreint. Au moins, les sièges avant font preuve d'un confort tout germanique en ce sens où leur dureté initiale n'incommode jamais, même après de longues heures de route. Pour ce qui est des places arrière, c'est une autre paire de manches, surtout à cause du dégagement accordé aux jambes et à la tête, autant pour le coupé que le cabriolet. J'entends déjà certaines personnes très perspicaces aviser que le dégagement pour la tête dans le cabriolet est plus qu'adéquat une fois le toit baissé. Bon point.

À TOILE L'HONNEUR

Contrairement à la tendance, Mercedes a préféré, pour son cabriolet, un toit en toile plutôt qu'un toit rigide-rétractable. Ce choix s'explique par le fait que plusieurs personnes aiment bien montrer à tout le monde qu'elles conduisent un cabriolet, ce qui est moins évident avec un toit rigide. L'autre raison évoquée, et plus importante selon moi, serait qu'un toit en toile prend moins de place dans le coffre. Si l'espace de chargement du coupé est agréablement surprenant avec ses 450 litres, celui du cabriolet s'avère de toute évidence moins intéressant, surtout lorsque le toit est remisé. Il passe ainsi de 390 à 300 litres.

Quand on paie au-delà de 70 000 $ pour avoir le toupet à l'air, il est tout à fait normal qu'il ne se fasse pas trop dépeigner... Pour protéger ceux qui ont le cheveu douillet, Mercedes a concocté l'AIR-CAP, une sorte d'aileron posé sur la partie supérieure du pare-brise du cabriolet et qui vient bloquer les turbulences dans l'habitacle. Cet accessoire m'est apparu beaucoup plus utile pour capturer les insectes qu'à protéger les occupants... Par contre, le AIRSCARF qui envoie un discret jet de chaleur dans le cou m'a beaucoup plus impressionné.

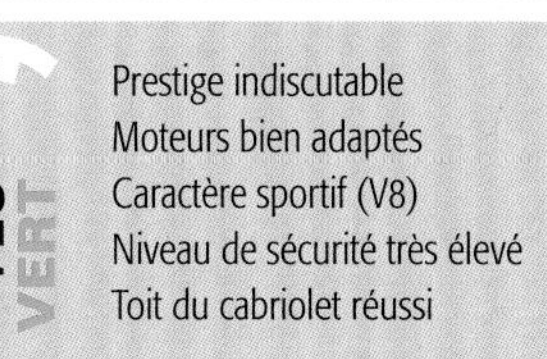

FEU VERT

- Prestige indiscutable
- Moteurs bien adaptés
- Caractère sportif (V8)
- Niveau de sécurité très élevé
- Toit du cabriolet réussi

FEU ROUGE

- Portières très lourdes
- V8 gourmand
- V6 moins sportif
- Coffre réduit (cabriolet)
- GPS assez sommaire

V6 ÉCONOME, V8 SPORTIF

Les deux modèles possèdent à peu de choses près la même fiche technique. Le moteur de base est le V6 de 3,5 litres qui offre des performances décentes et une consommation d'essence très correcte. Même si ce moteur devrait constituer approximativement 70 % des ventes au Canada, c'est le V8 de 5,5 litres qui retient le plus l'attention, autant par ses performances relevées que par sa sonorité envoûtante et sa consommation moins retenue... Sans oublier qu'il commande environ 10 000 $ de plus !

Peu importe le moteur, la transmission automatique à sept rapports fonctionne avec une infinie douceur, passant les rapports toujours au bon moment, rétrogradant rapidement, suffisamment rapidement pour oublier d'utiliser le passage manuel des rapports qui se fait grâce à des palettes derrière le volant. Le couple est ainsi relayé aux roues arrière sans délai. On ne parle pas d'une boîte à double embrayage mais on s'en approche. Compte tenu de la vocation plus sportive du coupé et du cabriolet, seules les roues arrière sont motrices, le rouage intégral 4Matic étant réservé à la berline.

Bien que le châssis, les suspensions et les freins soient empruntés à la berline, il va sans dire qu'ils sont adaptés à une conduite plus dynamique. Dans le cas du cabriolet, des renforts supplémentaires ont été prévus dans les piliers « A » (entre le pare-brise et les vitres latérales) et derrière les portes, ce qui augmente son poids de 70 kilos par rapport au coupé. Mais, pour être bien franc, il faut piloter les deux voitures sur un circuit pour détecter une différence. Peu importe le matériau du toit, on a affaire à une voiture à la tenue de route solide, très solide dans le cas des versions V8 dont les pneus sont plus imposants et les suspensions plus dures. Même si la E350 est de nature à encourager les vitesses élevées en courbe, les amateurs de conduite sportive auront plus de plaisir avec la E550, plus affutée, agile presque.

Il va sans dire qu'avec l'ajout récent du coupé et du cabriolet, la Classe E de Mercedes-Benz commence à être passablement étoffée. On comptera bientôt une familiale et la berline se décline maintenant en version sportive AMG. Tiens, pourquoi pas un coupé AMG 6,3 avec un moteur de plus de 500 chevaux ? Il pourrait facilement s'y prêter...

Alain Morin

PHOTOS : MARC LACHAPELLE

Catégorie	Cabriolet, Coupé
Échelle de prix	58 600 $ à 106 900 $ (2010)
Garanties	4 ans/80 000 km, 4 ans/80 000 km
Assemblage	Stuttgart, Allemagne
Cote d'assurance	moyenne

CHÂSSIS - DONNÉES POUR E550 CABRIOLET

Emp/lon/lar/haut	2 760/4 698/1 786/1 412 mm
Coffre	390 litres
Réservoir	66 litres
Nombre coussins sécurité	6
Antipatinage / contrôle stabilité	oui / oui
Suspension avant	indépendante, multibras
Suspension arrière	indépendante, multibras
Freins avant / arrière	disque (ABS) / disque (ABS)
Direction	à crémaillère, ass. variable
Diamètre de braquage	11,0 m
Pneus avant / arrière	P235/40R18 / P255/35R18
Poids	1 840 kg
Capacité de remorquage	n.d.

COMPOSANTES MÉCANIQUES

E350 Coupé, E350 Cabriolet

Cylindrée, soupapes, alim.	V6 3,5 litres 24 s atmos.
Puissance / Couple	268 chevaux / 258 lb-pi
Tr. base (opt) / rouage base (opt)	A7 / Prop
0-100 / 80-120 / 100-0 km/h	7,5 s / 6,1 s / 43,1 m
Type ess. / ville / autoroute	Ordinaire / 12,3 / 7,9 l/100 km

E550 Coupé, E550 Cabriolet

Cylindrée, soupapes, alim.	V8 5,5 litres 32 s atmos.
Puissance / Couple	382 chevaux / 391 lb-pi
Tr. base (opt) / rouage base (opt)	A7 / Prop
0-100 / 80-120 / 100-0 km/h	5,6 s / 3,7 s / 43,1 m
Type ess. / ville / autoroute	Ordinaire / 14,3 / 9 l/100 km

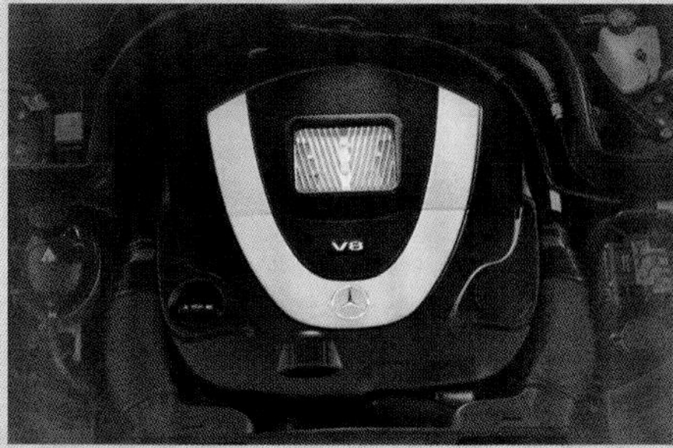

DANS LA MÊME CATÉGORIE

Audi A5, Infiniti G37 cabriolet, Lexus IS-C, Nissan 370Z Roadster, Volvo C70

DU NOUVEAU EN 2011

Cabriolet dévoilé au printemps 2010

NOS IMPRESSIONS

Agrément de conduite :	9/10
Fiabilité :	6/10
Sécurité :	10/10
Qualités hivernales :	7/10
Espace intérieur :	7/10
Confort :	7/10

www.mercedes-benz.ca

Plus d'informations dans la section statistiques en dernière partie du Guide

MACHINE À VOYAGER DANS LE TEMPS

Au cours des dernières années, la compagnie Mercedes-Benz a pratiquement transformé toute sa gamme de modèles, sauf un. En effet, depuis son arrivée sur notre continent, les années se succèdent et les véhicules de la Classe G demeurent inchangés. C'est d'autant plus anachronique qu'il s'agit du plus vieux modèle de cette marque offert sur notre marché. Ce vestige des années 70 se démarque par ses formes ultra carrées, son centre de gravité très élevé et son allure de baroudeur à nul autre pareil.

Malgré ses origines lointaines, ce modèle jouit d'une grande popularité auprès des gens qui ont les moyens de se payer un tel mastodonte. En effet, ce n'est pas tout le monde qui peut débourser 100000$ et plus pour un vestige du passé. Même si le premier modèle appelé Gelandewagon à été conçu il y a plus de trois décennies, il ne faut pas oublier de souligner que des améliorations aux chapitres de l'équipement, des accessoires (visant à améliorer le confort) et des groupes propulseurs (plus modernes) se sont succédés au cours de cette période, afin d'offrir le maximum de confort et de capacité hors route.

COMME JADIS

Il y a toujours des personnes qui ont la nostalgie du passé. Pour eux, la Belle Époque était celle où les produits de consommation et les véhicules moteurs en particulier étaient plus solides, plus pratiques et même plus agréables à conduire. Ces gens ne se souviennent que des éléments positifs et oublient les irritants. L'avantage du véhicule qui nous concerne, est qu'il est possible d'acheter ce vestige du passé avec la technologie d'aujourd'hui. Il s'agit donc d'un véhicule fabriqué sur un châssis autonome, afin d'avoir toute la robustesse nécessaire. Il faut se souvenir que le Gelandewagon a été initialement conçu pour les forces policières argentines et l'armée allemande. Ces origines pour le moins utilitaires expliquent la présence des parois latérales ultra plates, des pentures extérieures visibles et la minceur des portières. Lorsqu'on ferme celle-ci, on entend un bruit sec comme si on fermait une porte de coffre-fort.

Une fois à bord, il est étonnant de constater que l'espace réservé pour les coudes est assez réduit malgré les dimensions extérieures du véhicule. Par contre, aucun problème pour le dégagement de la tête. Bien entendu, comme toute Mercedes-Benz qui se respecte, la qualité des matériaux et de la finition est impeccable. De plus, au fil des années, la présentation intérieure s'est étoffée et s'est raffinée. On y retrouve tout ce qui est nécessaire pour le confort moderne. On ne peut s'empêcher d'imaginer quelles ont été les acrobaties techniques des ingénieurs, afin que soient insérés des éléments ultramodernes dans une carrosserie conçue il y a plus de 30 ans. Soulignons au passage que l'inclinaison du pare-brise est très minime, ce qui explique en partie que le coefficient de pénétration dans l'air n'est absolument pas aérodynamique.

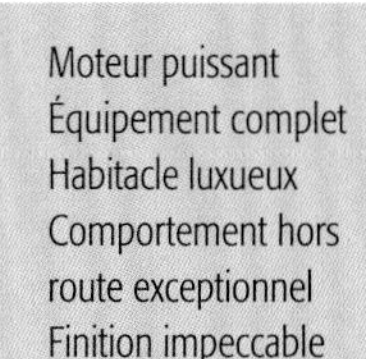

FEU VERT

- Moteur puissant
- Équipement complet
- Habitacle luxueux
- Comportement hors route exceptionnel
- Finition impeccable

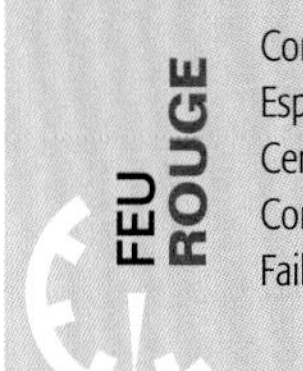

FEU ROUGE

- Consommation hors norme
- Espace limité pour les coudes
- Centre de gravité est élevé
- Conception vétuste
- Faible visibilité arrière

Finalement, bien que les sièges soient très luxueux et que l'habitabilité soit bonne, on a toujours l'impression d'être à bord d'un véhicule converti tant bien que mal à partir de quelque chose de très costaud et de très primitif. Ceci est un tour de force en soi.

RIEN NE L'ARRÊTE

Nul besoin d'insister sur le fait que les acheteurs de ce gros VUS ne l'achètent pas pour ses qualités sportives ou sa vitesse de pointe. Ce sont plutôt pour sa robustesse tous azimut et ses capacités de conduite hors route. En effet, même si les BCBG en ont fait un habitué de Rodeo Drive à Beverley Hills, le « G » est capable de franchir pratiquement n'importe quel obstacle. Son rouage intégral permanent 4Matic n'est pas aussi costaud que celui disponible il y a quelques années, mais son efficacité a été démontrée à plusieurs reprises.

Le modèle de base, même si cette appellation fait sourire, est le G550 propulsé par un moteur V8 de 5,5 litres d'une puissance de 382 chevaux et couplé à une transmission automatique à sept rapports. Cette combinaison permet de boucler le 0-100 km/h en 9,7 secondes, ce qui est impressionnant compte tenu de son poids de 2500 kg !

Pour répondre aux demandes de celles et ceux qui ne peuvent se contenter que du maximum à tous les égards, les ingénieurs ont concocté la 55 AMG avec son moteur V8 de cylindrée quasiment égale, mais produisant 500 chevaux grâce à la suralimentation. Ce monstre de puissance et de couple est offert avec une transmission automatique à cinq rapports, la seule assez robuste chez ce constructeur pour pouvoir gérer cette puissance. Bien entendu, les temps d'accélération sont égaux à ceux d'une voiture sportive de haut niveau, car on atteint 100 km/h, départ arrêté, en 5,5 secondes. Heureusement, on a eu la sagesse chez Mercedes-Benz de limiter la vitesse de pointe à 190 km/h pour la G550 et à 210 km/h pour la 55G.

Même avec toute cette puissance sous le capot, le comportement routier s'apparente davantage à celui d'un camion qu'à celui d'une grande sportive. De plus, la direction n'offre pas vraiment un bon feed-back de la route. Sans oublier, ce centre de gravité élevé que l'on doit toujours avoir en tête lorsqu'on décide d'augmenter la vitesse sur une route parsemée de virages.

Denis Duquet

PHOTOS : MERCEDES-BENZ

MERCEDES-BENZ CLASSE G

Catégorie	VUS
Échelle de prix	111 900$ à 152 450$ (2010)
Garanties	4 ans/80 000 km, 4 ans/80 000 km
Assemblage	Graz, Autriche
Cote d'assurance	n.d.

CHÂSSIS - DONNÉES POUR G550

Emp/lon/lar/haut	2 850/4 662/1 760/1 931 mm
Coffre	480 à 2 250 litres
Réservoir	96 litres
Nombre coussins sécurité	4
Antipatinage / contrôle stabilité	oui / oui
Suspension avant	essieu rigide, ressorts hélicoïdaux
Suspension arrière	essieu rigide, ressorts hélicoïdaux
Freins avant / arrière	disque (ABS) / disque (ABS)
Direction	à billes, assistée
Diamètre de braquage	13,3 m
Pneus avant / arrière	P265/60R18 / P265/60R18
Poids	2 500 kg
Capacité de remorquage	3 175 kg (6 999 lb)

COMPOSANTES MÉCANIQUES

G550

Cylindrée, soupapes, alim.	V8 5,5 litres 24 s atmos.
Puissance / Couple	382 chevaux / 391 lb-pi
Tr. base (opt) / rouage base (opt)	A7 / Int
0-100 / 80-120 / 100-0 km/h	9,7 s / 7,7 s / 47,1 m
Type ess. / ville / autoroute	Super / 18,7 / 13,8 l/100 km

G55 AMG

Cylindrée, soupapes, alim.	V8 5,5 litres 24 s atmos.
Puissance / Couple	500 chevaux / 517 lb-pi
Tr. base (opt) / rouage base (opt)	A5 / Int
0-100 / 80-120 / 100-0 km/h	7,0 s (est) / 5,0 (est) / n.d.
Type ess. / ville / autoroute	Super / 19,8 / 13,4 l/100 km

DANS LA MÊME CATÉGORIE

Cadillac Escalade, Infiniti QX, Land Rover Range Rover, Lexus LX, Lincoln Navigator

DU NOUVEAU EN 2011

Aucun changement majeur

NOS IMPRESSIONS

Agrément de conduite :	6/10
Fiabilité :	6/10
Sécurité :	10/10
Qualités hivernales :	8/10
Espace intérieur :	8/10
Confort :	7/10

www.mercedes-benz.ca

Plus d'informations dans la section statistiques en dernière partie du Guide

ROBUSTESSE ET TENUE DE ROUTE ASSURÉES

Le Mercedes-Benz Classe GL peut sembler superflu de nos jours, alors que la plupart des constructeurs pensent à réduire les dimensions de tous leurs véhicules, mais lors de son entrée en scène en 2006, il était fort logique de proposer un gros VUS de luxe à sept places. En effet, le public demandait ce genre de véhicules et les modèles capables de transporter sept occupants avaient la cote. Puisque la Classe ML ne répondait pas à ces normes, la GL était la solution parfaite. Quoi qu'il en soit, les investissements n'ont pas été trop importants, puisque ce modèle emprunte sa plate-forme à la classe R.

Bien entendu, lorsque Mercedes-Benz s'implique dans une catégorie, il ne fait rien à la légère. La silhouette doit nécessairement s'inspirer de modèles existants, notamment la très populaire ML, tandis que l'habitacle est aussi luxueux que tous les autres modèles de cette catégorie.

LE GRAND CONFORT

Il est certain qu'un véhicule de ces dimensions ne peut que proposer une excellente habitabilité. Toutefois, dans le cas qui nous concerne, cette habitabilité est même impressionnante par rapport au volume extérieur. C'est comme si on réussissait à faire entrer 1,5 litre de liquide dans un contenant d'un litre seulement. Les places avant sont excessivement spacieuses et le passager qui se plaindra d'être à l'étroit doit nécessairement avoir une corpulence hors norme. La seconde rangée de sièges est également confortable et spacieuse bien que la place du centre soit difficilement recommandable. Finalement, la troisième rangée est passablement spacieuse et d'un confort acceptable pour des trajets de courte ou moyenne durée. Par contre, l'accès y est particulièrement difficile.

Cet habitacle est bien entendu réalisé à partir de matériaux de qualité et la finition, de son côté, est à la hauteur de la réputation de cette marque. La planche de bord est très sobre avec une console verticale comprenant bien entendu un écran à cristaux liquides qui permet d'afficher le système de navigation par satellite. Ce dernier est efficace et simple à programmer une fois qu'on s'est familiarisé avec la logique de ses concepteurs.

Enfin, la position de conduite est bonne et la visibilité tous azimut est correcte. Il faut également accorder de bonnes notes au volant qui possède, sur ses rayons, différentes commandes. De plus, ce volant est convenablement réussi sur le plan esthétique.

AVANTAGE DIESEL

Il est certain qu'un véhicule de ces dimensions et de ce poids va consommer passablement de carburant. D'autant plus que son rouage intégral de série ajoute à l'addition. Ceci est vrai si vous optez pour les modèles propulsés par des moteurs à essence. Par contre, si vous cochez l'option du moteur turbo diesel, vous allez obtenir une consommation de carburant vraiment surprenante d'un peu plus de 12 litres au 100 km, ce qui est quand même assez remarquable.

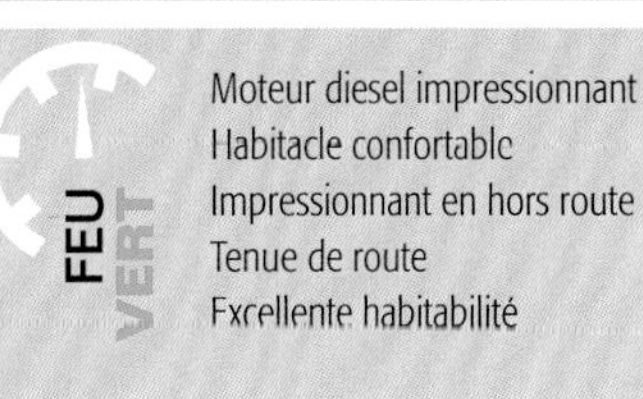

Moteur diesel impressionnant
Habitacle confortable
Impressionnant en hors route
Tenue de route
Excellente habitabilité

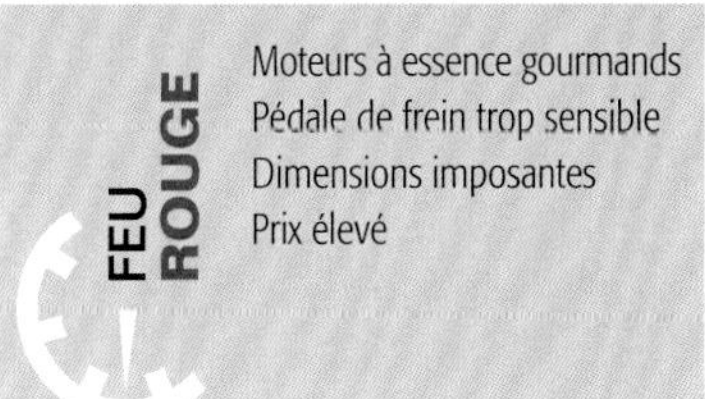

Moteurs à essence gourmands
Pédale de frein trop sensible
Dimensions imposantes
Prix élevé

De plus, vous ne sacrifierez rien au chapitre des performances dans le but d'obtenir une bonne consommation de carburant. Le moteur V6 3,0 litres turbo diesel ne produit que 210 chevaux, ce qui est assez peu pour un véhicule pesant plus de deux tonnes, mais son impressionnant couple de 400 lb-pied compense amplement. Tant et si bien que ce petit V6 nous permet de boucler le 0-100 km/h en moins de 10 secondes et ce n'est pas tout. Ce moteur est également silencieux et se laisse apprécier dans la circulation urbaine, alors que là encore, son merveilleux couple se fait sentir. Ce moteur, comme tous les autres disponibles, est associé à une transmission automatique à sept rapports qui accomplit du bon boulot. Il faut souligner que ce moteur est également très propre au chapitre des émissions en raison du système Ad Blue qui injecte une solution à base d'urée dans le système d'échappement.

Deux autres moteurs sont au catalogue, il s'agit d'un V8 de 4,6 litres de 335 chevaux et d'un autre V8, cette fois-ci d'une cylindrée de 5,5 litres produisant 382 chevaux. Ils équipent respectivement les modèles GL450 et GL550. À notre avis, il y a un modèle de trop dans ce catalogue. On pourrait facilement se passer du GL 550 dont la performance et la consommation sont presque identiques à celles de la GL450 tout en demandant un prix plus élevé. C'est certainement une question de marketing et de prestige, plutôt qu'une affaire de quelques différences mineures d'un modèle à un autre.

À voir ce gros VUS, on serait porté à croire que son comportement routier est l'équivalent de celui d'un pachyderme et que seules ses prestations en conduite hors route valent le prix d'achat. Ce n'est absolument pas le cas. En effet, sur la route, ce costaud nous impressionne par son agilité et sa tenue en virage. Il est d'ailleurs très facile de se laisser piéger par les capacités routières de cette Mercedes-Benz et de dépasser allègrement les limites de vitesse en vigueur sans s'en apercevoir, tant la conduite est facile. Une seule ombre au tableau, il faut quelque temps pour s'habituer à la pédale de frein. Celle-ci nous déconcerte quelque peu au début, car sa course est très courte avant que les freins entrent en action. Pour le reste, c'est impressionnant. Même la conduite hors route est impeccable avec son système de traction intégrale à réglage électronique qui accomplit un travail superlatif vous permettant de franchir bien des obstacles.

Denis Duquet

PHOTOS : MERCEDES-BENZ

Catégorie	VUS
Échelle de prix	69 000 $ à 88 600 $ (2010)
Garanties	4 ans/80 000 km, 4 ans/80 000 km
Assemblage	Tuscaloosa, Alabama, É-U
Cote d'assurance	bonne

CHÂSSIS - DONNÉES POUR GL450 4MATIC

Emp/lon/lar/haut	3 075/5 088/1 920/1 840 mm
Coffre	200 à 2 300 litres
Réservoir	100 litres
Nombre coussins sécurité	8
Antipatinage / contrôle stabilité	oui / oui
Suspension avant	indépendante, double triangulation
Suspension arrière	indépendante, multibras
Freins avant / arrière	disque (ABS) / disque (ABS)
Direction	à crémaillère, ass. variable
Diamètre de braquage	12,1 m
Pneus avant / arrière	P275/50R20 / P275/50R20
Poids	2 425 kg
Capacité de remorquage	3 401 kg (7 497 lb)

COMPOSANTES MÉCANIQUES

GL350 BlueTEC 4Matic	
Cylindrée, soupapes, alim.	V6 3,0 litres 24 s turbo
Puissance / Couple	210 chevaux / 400 lb-pi
Tr. base (opt) / rouage base (opt)	A7 / Int
0-100 / 80-120 / 100-0 km/h	9,5 s / n.d. / n.d.
Type ess. / ville / autoroute	Diesel / 12,3 / 8,7 l/100 km

GL450 4Matic	
Cylindrée, soupapes, alim.	V8 4,6 litres 32 s atmos.
Puissance / Couple	335 chevaux / 339 lb-pi
Tr. base (opt) / rouage base (opt)	A7 / Int
0-100 / 80-120 / 100-0 km/h	6,9 s / 6,1 s / 39,5 m
Type ess. / ville / autoroute	Super / 16,5 / 11,6 l/100 km

GL550 4Matic	
Cylindrée, soupapes, alim.	V8 5,5 litres 32 s atmos.
Puissance / Couple	382 chevaux / 391 lb-pi
Tr. base (opt) / rouage base (opt)	A7 / Int
0-100 / 80-120 / 100-0 km/h	6,5 s / 5,4 s / 39,9 m
Type ess. / ville / autoroute	Super / 17,1 / 11,9 l/100 km

DANS LA MÊME CATÉGORIE

Audi Q7, Cadillac Escalade, Infiniti QX, Land Rover Range Rover, Lexus LX, Lincoln Navigator

DU NOUVEAU EN 2011

Aucun changement majeur

NOS IMPRESSIONS

Agrément de conduite :	9/10
Fiabilité :	6/10
Sécurité :	8/10
Qualités hivernales :	9/10
Espace intérieur :	9/10
Confort :	9/10

www.mercedes-benz.ca

Plus d'informations dans la section statistiques en dernière partie du Guide

UN STYLE DE BAROUDEUR

Dans la catégorie des utilitaires sport de luxe de taille compacte, le GLK se distingue par son allure de baroudeur qui évoque la conduite hors route. Cela dit, vous avez à peu près autant de chance de voir un conducteur de GLK s'aventurer sur des sentiers rocailleux que d'apercevoir les quatre vedettes du film *Sexe à New York* magasiner entre filles dans un marché aux puces...

Depuis son lancement, le GLK s'est avéré un indéniable succès pour Mercedes-Benz en raison, principalement, d'une stratégie de mise en marché très agressive et d'un prix très intéressant. Le fait que le GLK soit doté de lignes très carrées, qui sont en complète opposition à la tendance actuelle, ainsi que de jantes de 20 pouces lui permet également de se démarquer par son aspect robuste et de paraître plus gros qu'il ne l'est en réalité, même s'il est en fait élaboré à partir de la plate-forme de la berline de Série C.

En montant à bord du GLK, les conducteurs qui sont justement familiers avec la Série C du constructeur allemand ne seront pas totalement dépaysés, car les planches de bord des deux véhicules sont très similaires. Tous les cadrans et indicateurs sont bien disposés, exception faite des commandes du système de chauffage/climatisation qui sont localisées à la base de la console centrale. Il faut aussi souligner le fait que l'intérieur n'est pas des plus chaleureux puisqu'on y retrouve beaucoup d'éléments en plastique noir. Comme il s'agit d'un Mercedes-Benz, la sécurité a été sérieusement étudiée par les ingénieurs et c'est pourquoi le GLK cache toute une série de coussins gonflables comprenant même des coussins pour protéger les genoux des occupants des places avant en cas d'impact. Les sièges avant offrent un soutien latéral adéquat en virage et ceux d'en arrière laissent assez de dégagement pour les jambes des passagers adultes. Ces derniers devront cependant faire un peu de gymnastique pour pouvoir y accéder en raison de la relative étroitesse des portes.

UNE TRÈS BONNE TENUE DE ROUTE

Sur la route, le GLK impressionne par la qualité de son comportement routier. La tenue de route est exemplaire grâce en partie à la monte pneumatique de série ainsi qu'à la suspension adaptative Agility Control. Pour ce qui est des pneus, le GLK roule sur des pneus de haute performance de cote 235/45R20, ce qui signifie que la facture sera assez salée lorsque viendra le temps de les remplacer ou d'acheter des pneus d'hiver. Quant à la suspension adaptative, précisons que le tarage des amortisseurs est calibré automatiquement au moyen d'une soupape selon la qualité du revêtement. Essentiellement, quand de légers chocs sont ressentis, l'amortissement est réduit afin de les absorber en douceur, alors que des chocs plus importants entraînent un raffermissement de l'amortissement dans le but de contribuer à stabiliser le véhicule. Toutes ces actions se font automatiquement, sans que le conducteur ait à intervenir d'aucune façon.

FEU VERT
- Très bonne tenue de route
- Bonne habitabilité
- Moteur performant
- Style distinctif

FEU ROUGE
- Coût des options
- Bruits de roulement
- Localisation des commandes de chauffage/climatisation
- Absence du moteur diésel

Le GLK est animé par un V6 de 3,5 litres qui développe 268 chevaux et 258 livres-pied de couple, ce qui lui permet de livrer des accélérations et des reprises tout à fait satisfaisantes, et ce, malgré son poids très élevé qui se chiffre à 1850 kilos. Le groupe motopropulseur est complété par l'excellente boîte automatique qui compte sept rapports, permettant ainsi d'endiguer la consommation sur autoroute en profitant du septième rapport tout en permettant un étagement plus serré des rapports inférieurs, histoire d'améliorer les performances et la vitalité du GLK. En conduite normale, les changements de rapport de la boîte automatique sont à peine perceptibles ce qui contribue au niveau de confort. Au sujet de la consommation, prévoyez une moyenne élevée qui sera supérieure à 13 litres aux 100 kilomètres, poids élevé et rouage intégral de série obligent. Il est toutefois dommage que le moteur diesel, proposé sur le GLK en Europe, ne soit pas au programme pour l'Amérique du Nord.

QUELQUES CHANGEMENTS POUR 2011

Pour l'année-modèle 2011, Mercedes-Benz a apporté quelques modifications au GLK qui est à présent doté de phares de jour à lumières DEL si l'acheteur sélectionne l'option des phares Bi-Xenon. Du côté de l'habitacle, précisons que des appliques en bois noir sont maintenant au programme et que l'image de la caméra de recul est moins déformée qu'auparavant. Pour ce qui est des groupes d'options, le toit ouvrant de type Panorama a été intégré à l'ensemble d'options Premium et un ensemble AMG Sport est désormais au catalogue avec des éléments de carrosserie donnant un style plus sportif, des roues de 20 pouces d'un nouveau design, et des paliers de changement de vitesse au volant. Alors que les constructeurs automobiles proposent souvent en option des roues d'un diamètre plus grand que celui des roues de série, Mercedes-Benz fait exactement le contraire en offrant des roues de 19 pouces en option pour 2011, tandis que celles d'origine sont de 20 pouces. Voilà qui devrait bonifier le confort du GLK sans trop affecter sa très bonne tenue de route.

Somme toute, le GLK mise sur des atouts de taille, soit un équipement complet pour un prix qui demeure intéressant, même si le prix du véhicule est aujourd'hui plus élevé que lors de sa phase de lancement initiale. Il s'agit d'un excellent choix pour cette catégorie, mais le GLK est devancé à la ligne d'arrivée par le plus récent Q5 d'Audi au palmarès des meilleurs choix dans la catégorie des sport-utilitaires de luxe de taille compacte.

Gabriel Gélinas

PHOTOS: ALAIN MORIN

Catégorie	VUS
Échelle de prix	43 500 $ (2010)
Garanties	4 ans/80 000 km, 4 ans/80 000 km
Assemblage	n.d.
Cote d'assurance	n.d.

CHÂSSIS - DONNÉES POUR 350 4MATIC

Emp/lon/lar/haut	2 755/4 525/1 840/1 698 mm
Coffre	450 litres
Réservoir	66 litres
Nombre coussins sécurité	7
Antipatinage / contrôle stabilité	oui / oui
Suspension avant	indépendante, jambes de force
Suspension arrière	indépendante, multibras
Freins avant / arrière	disque (ABS) / disque (ABS)
Direction	à crémaillère, ass. variable
Diamètre de braquage	11,5 m
Pneus avant / arrière	P235/45R20 / P235/45R20
Poids	1 850 kg
Capacité de remorquage	1 588 kg (3 500 lb)

COMPOSANTES MÉCANIQUES

350 4Matic

Cylindrée, soupapes, alim.	V6 3,5 litres 24 s atmos.
Puissance / Couple	268 chevaux / 258 lb-pi
Tr. base (opt) / rouage base (opt)	A7 / Int
0-100 / 80-120 / 100-0 km/h	8,1 s / 6,0 s / 38,9 m
Type ess. / ville / autoroute	Super / 13,3 / 8,7 l/100 km

MERCEDES-BENZ GLK

DANS LA MÊME CATÉGORIE

Acura RDX, Audi Q5, BMW X3, Infiniti EX, Land Rover LR2, Volvo XC60

DU NOUVEAU EN 2011

Aucun changement majeur

NOS IMPRESSIONS

Agrément de conduite :	8/10
Fiabilité :	6/10
Sécurité :	10/10
Qualités hivernales :	9/10
Espace intérieur :	8/10
Confort :	8/10

www.mercedes-benz.ca

Plus d'informations dans la section statistiques en dernière partie du Guide

LE DIESEL EN TÊTE

Il faut rendre à César ce qui lui appartient puisque le Mercedes-Benz ML a été le premier VUS de luxe à circuler sur nos routes il y a plus de 10 ans, alors que le Lexus RX suivait de très peu. Voilà qu'une nouvelle mode était lancée et le constructeur était certainement loin de s'imaginer l'ampleur que ce segment prendrait au fil des années. Malgré une compétition grandissante, le ML a su conserver ses parts de marché en innovant et en s'adaptant aux goûts des acheteurs.

Bien entendu, la mode est maintenant aux VUS de luxe compacts, le nouveau créneau en vogue, mais il y a tout de même plusieurs acheteurs qui ont besoin d'un VUS plus spacieux et pour qui le luxe et le confort demeurent des arguments de taille. Le ML a donc la difficile tâche de rivaliser avec des véhicules aux grandes qualités tels l'Acura MDX, l'Audi Q7, le BMW X5, et le Volvo XC90 pour n'en nommer que quelques-uns.

DES ÉDITIONS PLUS EXCLUSIVES

Profitant de transformations plus marquées l'an passé, le ML 2011 n'a pas beaucoup changé, si ce n'est que les miroirs latéraux ont été revus — ils reprennent le style de ceux des autres véhicules — alors que le capot reçoit un traitement visuel différent et unique au Canada. On note aussi de nouveaux ensembles qui créent des versions plus uniques, par exemple la Grand Edition ou la Designo Edition. Au chapitre du style, le ML continue de séduire avec ses lignes sophistiquées, parfois plus sportives sur certaines versions. Ses larges zones vitrées ajoutent non seulement au style, mais elles procurent une excellente visibilité à bord.

À l'intérieur, on apprécie la qualité des matériaux utilisés et le souci du détail. Difficile de reprocher quoi que ce soit à ce chapitre. Le tout s'avèrera encore plus unique si vous optez pour les nouveaux ensembles mentionnés plus haut. La console centrale regroupe les différentes commandes qui sont relativement simples à assimiler. Si certains rivaux peuvent accommoder sept ou huit passagers, le ML se limite à cinq puisqu'il ne possède pas de troisième rangée de sièges. Il faudra vous rabattre sur le GL pour l'avoir. Cependant, l'habitacle se veut spacieux et tous obtiennent de bons dégagements, surtout à la tête.

LA MOTORISATION DIESEL À FAVORISER

Histoire de combler tous les goûts, ou toutes les bourses selon le cas, le ML est offert sous de multiples déclinaisons. Toutes héritent toutefois du rouage intégral 4MATIC à prise permanente, tout comme d'une boîte automatique à sept rapports. Le ML 350 cache sous le capot un moteur V6 de 3,5 litres régissant 268 chevaux. Cette motorisation pourrait certes être la plus alléchante, mais la seconde l'est encore plus. Alors que normalement la motorisation diesel apporte un déboursé supplémentaire qui en refroidit plus d'un, Mercedes-Benz nous surprend à ce chapitre puisque le

FEU VERT
- Conduite dynamique
- Motorisation diesel
- Version AMG performante
- Habitacle spacieux

FEU ROUGE
- Certains équipements en option
- Nouveau moteur AMG plus efficace à venir
- Coût d'entretien supplémentaire pour le diesel

ML 350 BlueTEC, équipé d'un V6 diesel de 3,0 litres, est offert avec une facture majorée uniquement d'un peu plus de 1000$. Pas étonnant que ce dernier représente pratiquement 70% des ventes du modèle au Canada. Ses 210 chevaux n'ont rien pour écrire à sa mère, mais ses 400 lb-pi de couple développés dès les 1600 tr/min lui procurent des performances plus qu'intéressantes, le tout jumelé à une économie de carburant plus qu'appréciable, soit environ 11 L/100 km au lieu d'un peu plus de 14L/100 km pour la version à essence. Voilà qui rentabilisera assez rapidement votre investissement supplémentaire. Le tout sera encore plus avantagé si vous devez charger le véhicule ou l'utiliser pour remorquer, la motorisation diesel demeurant beaucoup plus efficace dans ce cas et plus économe. À ce chapitre, le ML peut tracter une charge de 3266 kg, soit 7200 lb, ce qui est plus qu'honorable.

Vient ensuite le ML 550 qui livre principalement un peu plus de puissance en raison de son moteur V8 de 382 chevaux. Histoire de rivaliser avec les VUS à vocation plus sportive tel le Porsche Cayenne, le ML est proposé à la sauce AMG. Le ML 63 AMG dispose tout de même d'arguments intéressants grâce à son moteur V8 atmosphérique de 6,2 litres déployant 503 chevaux. Voilà qui transforme ce VUS en véritable bolide, capable de laisser dans son sillage bien des berlines, et ce, même en virage. Par contre, même si ce n'est pas encore officiel, le ML AMG recevra sous peu le nouveau moteur V8 de 5,5, litres biturbo, lequel remplace le 6,2 litres AMG à bord de la Classe S cette année. Ce moteur est non seulement plus puissant, mais il favorise une économie de carburant plus qu'appréciable, élément qui profitera certainement au ML AMG.

Au volant, le ML adopte une conduite inspirante que l'on pourrait même qualifier de dynamique. Plusieurs autres compétiteurs sont beaucoup moins connectés à la route. En fait, son style, son capot qui plonge, sa position de conduite et ses réglages de la suspension et de la direction sont tous des éléments qui dotent le ML d'un comportement plus près de celui d'une voiture que d'un gros VUS et c'est tant mieux. Nous avons également mis à l'essai la version AMG sur piste et il faut avouer que le véhicule s'est comporté admirablement si l'on tient compte de sa vocation.

Le Mercedes-Benz ML 2011 continue d'être un choix à considérer dans son créneau et sa motorisation diesel BlueTEC lui donne un avantage difficile à égaler par la concurrence, surtout au prix proposé.

Sylvain Raymond

PHOTOS : MERCEDES-BENZ

MERCEDES-BENZ CLASSE M

Catégorie	VUS
Échelle de prix	57 400$ à 97 500$ (2010)
Garanties	4 ans/80 000 km, 4 ans/80 000 km
Assemblage	Tuscaloosa, Alabama, É-U
Cote d'assurance	bonne

CHÂSSIS - DONNÉES POUR ML350 4MATIC

Emp/lon/lar/haut	2 915/4 781/1 911/1 815 mm
Coffre	833 à 2 050 litres
Réservoir	95 litres
Nombre coussins sécurité	6
Antipatinage / contrôle stabilité	oui / oui
Suspension avant	indépendante, double triangulation
Suspension arrière	indépendante, multibras
Freins avant / arrière	disque (ABS) / disque (ABS)
Direction	à crémaillère, ass. variable
Diamètre de braquage	12,0 m
Pneus avant / arrière	P255/50R19 / P255/50R19
Poids	2 145 kg
Capacité de remorquage	3 266 kg (7 200 lb)

COMPOSANTES MÉCANIQUES

ML350 BlueTEC 4Matic

Cylindrée, soupapes, alim.	V6 3,0 litres 24 s turbo
Puissance / Couple	210 chevaux / 400 lb-pi
Tr. base (opt) / rouage base (opt)	A7 / Int
0-100 / 80-120 / 100-0 km/h	8,6 s / 7,1 s / 41,3 m
Type ess. / ville / autoroute	Diesel / 11,8 / 8,2 l/100 km

ML350 4Matic

Cylindrée, soupapes, alim.	V6 3,5 litres 24 s atmos.
Puissance / Couple	268 chevaux / 258 lb-pi
Tr. base (opt) / rouage base (opt)	A7 / Int
0-100 / 80-120 / 100-0 km/h	8,4 s / 6,5 s / 39,5 m
Type ess. / ville / autoroute	Super / 14,1 / 10,1 l/100 km

ML550 4Matic

V8 5,5 l, 382 ch / 391 lb-pi - 0-100 : 5,8 s - 16,1 / 11,4 l/100 km

ML63 AMG

V6 6,2 l, 503 ch / 465 lb-pi - 0-100 : 5,0 s - 20,4 / 14,0 l/100 km

DANS LA MÊME CATÉGORIE

Acura MDX, Audi Q7, BMW X5, Cadillac SRX, Infiniti FX, Lexus RX, Lincoln MKX, Porsche Cayenne, Volkswagen Touareg, Volvo XC90

DU NOUVEAU EN 2011

Partie avant redessinée, nouveaux ensembles.

NOS IMPRESSIONS

Agrément de conduite :	8/10
Fiabilité :	6/10
Sécurité :	10/10
Qualités hivernales :	9/10
Espace intérieur :	8/10
Confort :	8/10

www.mercedes-benz.ca

Plus d'informations dans la section statistiques en dernière partie du Guide

TEMPÊTE DANS UN VERRE D'EAU… VIDE

Il y a de ces moments dans la vie où le bonheur des uns, à défaut de rendre les autres heureux, les laisse perplexes. Prenez, par exemple, la toute nouvelle génération du Mercedes-Benz Classe R. Qui dit nouvelle génération, dit nouveau châssis, nouvelle mécanique et lignes inédites. Pourtant, Mercedes-Benz, dans un excès d'enthousiasme incroyable, et surprenant de la part de ce constructeur somme toute sérieux, nous présente sa nouvelle génération de véhicules et celle-ci se résume à une partie avant redessinée (et ma foi bien réussie), des rétroviseurs modernisés, de nouvelles jantes, une partie arrière subtilement remaniée et… et rien d'autre, finalement.

Le Classe R promène sa carrosserie pour le moins différente depuis 2006. On ne peut pas vraiment dire qu'on s'est habitué à ses lignes… car on n'en voit tellement peu sur nos routes ! Il faut dire que son prix, mais aussi son gabarit, n'en n'ont jamais fait un modèle de ventes. Au moins, depuis cette année, on a revu l'esthétisme du véhicule tout en respectant l'approche de Mercedes-Benz, ce qui pourrait lui amener quelques nouveaux propriétaires. À notre avis, au moins deux ou trois…

STATU QUO MÉCANIQUE

À cause, sans doute, des nombreux bouleversements qu'a connus le Classe R cette année, on a eu la bonne idée de ne pas toucher à la mécanique. Ça aurait pu mêler les gens… Donc, on retrouve le R350 mû par un V6 de 3,5 litres dont la puissance est un peu faible pour un véhicule de près de 2 200 kilos appelé à transporter six ou sept adultes selon la version. Nous lui préférons, de loin, le moteur diesel du R350 Bluetec. D'ailleurs, au moins 75 % des Canadiens (et je soupçonne les Québécois d'y

être pour beaucoup!) achètent un diesel quand il est proposé par rapport à un modèle à essence. Malgré le « 350 » de sa dénomination, il s'agit d'un V6 de 3,0 litres. Souple, économe de carburant (il consomme beaucoup moins que son équivalent à essence) et propre, il autorise des performances très correctes. En plus, il possède une meilleure autonomie, ce qui signifie que les arrêts à la pompe seront moins nombreux et, avec un peu de volonté de la part des pétrolières, coûteront moins cher qu'avec de l'essence. Enfin, soulignons que même si les données techniques de ce moteur n'ont pas changé d'une décimale, les ingénieurs ont revu certains paramètres pour diminuer davantage sa consommation.

Une transmission automatique à sept rapports ultra compétente transfère le couple aux quatre roues grâce au système 4Matic, reconnu comme étant l'un des plus performants sur le marché. Tout est donc en place pour obtenir un véhicule aux prétentions sportives ou, à tout le moins, affichant un certain dynamisme. D'autant plus que la Classe R est bâtie sur le châssis, modifié, il va de soi, de la Classe ML. Cependant, la direction trop assistée et vague, ainsi que les suspensions définitivement axées vers le

Habitacle douillet
Matériaux de qualité
Prix plus réaliste qu'avant
Moteur diesel recommandé
Rouage 4Matic compétent

FEU ROUGE

Changements trop peu importants
Ligne encore surprenante
Dimensions de paquebot
Moteur à essence un peu juste
Conduite peu inspirée

confort nous fait rapidement réaliser qu'il n'en n'est rien. Le Classe R est un gros bateau, comme les Américains les aiment !

ESPACE, CONFORT ET LUXE

Ce qui retient surtout l'attention des amateurs du genre se trouve davantage dans l'habitacle que sous le capot. De ce côté, personne ne sera déçu. Dès qu'on ouvre les larges portières, on retrouve l'ambiance, la qualité et le design Mercedes-Benz, c'est-à-dire, du haut de gamme. L'habitacle est aussi vaste qu'une église, ce qui n'a rien de surprenant compte tenu des dimensions extérieures. La position de conduite est haute, ce qui plait toujours à une certaine clientèle, mais la visibilité, surtout vers les trois-quarts arrière n'est pas extraordinaire.

Le confort est garanti, autant par les sièges que par les suspensions. Même les gens prenant place sur la deuxième rangée n'auront pas à se plaindre. Elle est composée de deux baquets et d'un siège central amovible. Comme sur à peu près tous les véhicules offrant trois rangées de sièges, la dernière n'est pas particulièrement invitante. Pourtant, l'espace dévolu aux jambes et à la tête n'est pas mal du tout, même si les trous et les bosses sont nettement plus ressentis qu'à l'avant. Une fois les dossiers des sièges des deux rangées postérieures rabattus, on se retrouve devant une avalanche de litres cubes. Avertissons tout de suite ceux qui seraient intéressés à acheter le Classe R, qu'il serait préférable pour eux de s'évader à l'étranger à l'approche du premier juillet. Sinon, ils seront assaillis de toutes parts par une foule de nouveaux amis ! Bien entendu, Mercedes-Benz rime avec sécurité et le Classe R ne fait pas exception. On retrouve six coussins gonflables, ce qui n'est plus très impressionnant aujourd'hui, surtout de la part d'une Mercedes. Ce véhicule propose une quantité impressionnante d'aides électroniques à la conduite qui ont pour mandat d'éviter un accident. Si toutefois, l'inévitable devait se produire, la solidité du châssis et les nombreux éléments de sécurité passive, jumelés aux six coussins, devraient réduire les dégâts au maximum.

Il serait surprenant que le Mercedes-Benz Classe R connaisse cette année une augmentation exponentielle de ses ventes, puisque les modifications sont trop modestes. Peu importe, ce n'est pas l'Amérique qui intéresse Mercedes. La Chine est, depuis peu, le meilleur marché de la Classe R. Alors ce qu'on en pense, ici, au Québec…

Alain Morin

PHOTOS : ALAIN MORIN

MERCEDES-BENZ CLASSE R

Catégorie	Multisegment
Échelle de prix	54 700 $ à 56 200 $ (2010)
Garanties	4 ans/80 000 km, 4 ans/80 000 km
Assemblage	Tuscaloosa, Alabama, É-U
Cote d'assurance	n.d.

CHÂSSIS - DONNÉES POUR R350 BLUETEC 4MATIC

Emp/lon/lar/haut	3 215/5 173/1 922/1 663 mm
Coffre	314 à 2 385 litres
Réservoir	80 litres
Nombre coussins sécurité	6
Antipatinage / contrôle stabilité	oui / oui
Suspension avant	indépendante, double triangulation
Suspension arrière	indépendante, multibras
Freins avant / arrière	disque (ABS) / disque (ABS)
Direction	à crémaillère, ass. variable
Diamètre de braquage	12,4 m
Pneus avant / arrière	P255/55R18 / P255/55R18
Poids	2 390 kg
Capacité de remorquage	1 588 kg (3 500 lb)

COMPOSANTES MÉCANIQUES

R350 BlueTEC 4Matic	
Cylindrée, soupapes, alim.	V6 3,0 litres 24 s turbo
Puissance / Couple	210 chevaux / 400 lb-pi
Tr. base (opt) / rouage base (opt)	A7 / Int
0-100 / 80-120 / 100-0 km/h	8,8 s / 7,0 s / 40,0 m
Type ess. / ville / autoroute	Diesel / 11,6 / 8,3 l/100 km

R350 4Matic	
Cylindrée, soupapes, alim.	V6 3,5 litres 24 s atmos.
Puissance / Couple	268 chevaux / 258 lb-pi
Tr. base (opt) / rouage base (opt)	A7 / Int
0-100 / 80-120 / 100-0 km/h	8,5 s / 6,9 s / 40,0 m
Type ess. / ville / autoroute	Super / 14,4 / 10,3 l/100 km

DANS LA MÊME CATÉGORIE

Acura MDX, Audi Q7, BMW X5, Buick Enclave, Lincoln MKT, Volvo XC90

DU NOUVEAU EN 2011

Parties avant et arrière légèrement redessinées

NOS IMPRESSIONS

Agrément de conduite :	7/10
Fiabilité :	6/10
Sécurité :	10/10
Qualités hivernales :	8/10
Espace intérieur :	8/10
Confort :	9/10

www.mercedes-benz.ca

Plus d'informations dans la section statistiques en dernière partie du Guide

DU GRAND LUXE À LA SPORTIVITÉ EXTRÊME

Dans le monde des nantis, on recherche une voiture à la hauteur de nos aspirations et lorsque l'on magasine pour une berline de grand luxe, on accorde beaucoup moins d'importance au budget, et beaucoup plus à la voiture. Dans le cas de Mercedes-Benz, c'est la Classe S qui occupe le haut du pavé et cette dernière a la difficile tâche de satisfaire les plus exigeants, tout en offrant des choix susceptibles de répondre à tous les goûts.

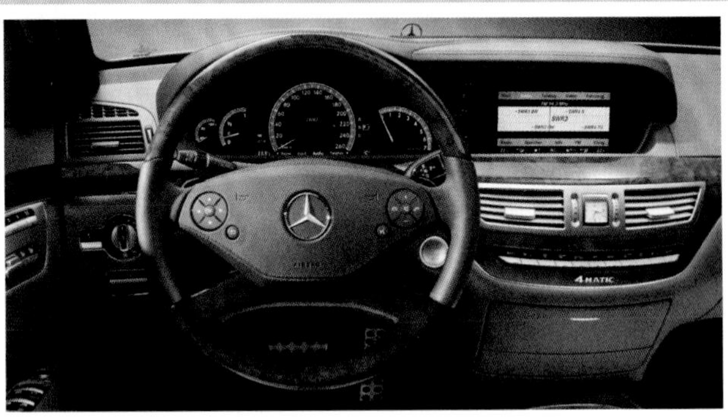

Dans ce segment, le logo et le prestige ont une importance majeure, mais la voiture doit aussi être la plus spacieuse, la plus élégante, la plus sécuritaire, la plus technologique et aussi, la plus puissante. Eh bien, sachez que la Mercedes-Benz de Classe S est tout ça, sans ménagement.

UNE PLÉIADE DE SYSTÈMES DE SÉCURITÉ

Cette dernière se doit de rivaliser avec les principaux rivaux du constructeur que sont BMW, Lexus et Audi, mais elle doit aussi composer avec des marques de prestige. Voilà qui s'avère tout un défi puisqu'il faut constamment innover et épater la galerie pour dominer le marché. Ce que fait Mercedes-Benz en jouant tout d'abord la carte de la sécurité, incorporant à sa classe S une multitude de systèmes de sécurité. Outre tous les systèmes usuels, on en retrouve un de détection de l'angle mort qui vous avertira de la présence d'un véhicule dans l'angle mort, mais qui appliquera aussi légèrement les freins opposés afin de vous ramener dans votre voie si vous deviez vous déporter vers l'autre véhicule. Les mêmes actions sont aussi prises par le *Active Lane Keeping Assist*, un système qui détecte les changements de voies involontaires (sans clignotant ou légère déportation) et qui au passage vous avertira via une vibration dans le volant et un indicateur visuel. Avec une panoplie d'autres systèmes du genre, ce véhicule est capable de vous sortir de bien des embarras.

L'autre élément qui démarque la Classe S est son choix de modèles puisque la gamme ne compte pas moins de six versions, toutes comportant des motorisations distinctes. En premier lieu, il y a les deux versions à rouage intégral, soit la très docile S 450 4MATIC qui possède un moteur V8 de 335 chevaux, suivie de la très populaire S 550 4MATIC qui de son côté hausse la barre au chapitre de la puissance avec son V8 de 382 chevaux.

Vient ensuite la très écologique S 400 HYBRIDE, ironiquement la plus abordable de la gamme, qui vous permettra de mettre en valeur votre fibre écologique grâce à sa consommation de 7,7 l/100 km favorisée par un V6 de 3,5 litres jumelé à un moteur électrique. Un peu perdue dans la gamme se trouve la S 600 qui ne fait pas partie du club sélect AMG, mais qui propose tout de même un moteur V12 développant 510 chevaux et un couple de 612 lb-pi, le tout transmis aux roues arrière par l'unique boîte offerte à travers la gamme : une automatique à sept rapports.

Plusieurs technologies de sécurité
Bon choix de modèles
Versions AMG enivrantes
Confort sur route

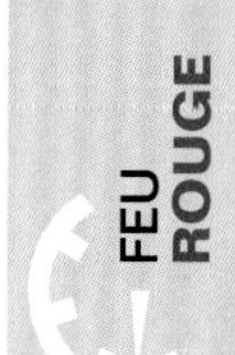

Coût d'entretien
Très dispendieuse
Conduite plus aseptisée (sauf AMG)

UN TOUT NOUVEAU MOTEUR POUR 2011

Si la Classe S met un peu plus en lumière sa grande classe dans les autres versions, elle peut aussi se révéler une véritable sportive et c'est la version AMG qui prend le relais. En fait, au Canada, un grand nombre d'acheteurs choisit les versions AMG (il y en a deux), car de toute manière, au prix de la Classe S, ce n'est pas quelques milliers de dollars supplémentaires qui font la différence. Voilà d'ailleurs la grande nouveauté cette année chez la Classe S puisque la S 63 AMG fait place à la S 63 AMG. Selon la logique des appellations chez Mercedes, elle devrait être rebaptisée S 55 AMG en raison de son nouveau moteur V8 de 5,5 litres qui remplace l'ancien V8 de 6,2 litres atmosphérique. Mais histoire de ne pas créer de confusion avec les autres motorisations et surtout afin de ne pas diminuer l'égo de cette récente mouture, le constructeur a décidé de conserver l'ancienne dénomination. On triche un peu! La principale raison de ce changement est fort simple: ce nouveau moteur suralimenté est l'une des modifications qui permettront à Mercedes de satisfaire les nouvelles normes de consommation et d'émission imposées d'ici 2015.

Ce V8 biturbo a une cylindrée moindre, mais l'utilisation de la surcompression mariée à l'injection directe permet plus de puissance que l'ancien moteur (19 chevaux), soit 536 chevaux et un couple de 590 lb-pi. La consommation de carburant passe d'environ 18 l/100 km à tout juste 10,5 l/100, selon le constructeur. Voilà ce qu'on appelle joindre l'utile à l'agréable! Et si ce n'est pas assez, il vous reste toujours la S 65 AMG qui, pour un prix exorbitant, possède un moteur V12 biturbo de 603 chevaux, rien de moins. Quant au style de ces versions plus sportives, c'est fort réussi. Les versions AMG en offrent juste assez pour que tout soit de bon goût. Elles arborent un magnifique mariage de sophistication et de sportivité. Bref, Mercedes est passé maître dans l'art de bien doser.

L'habitacle de la Classe S ne déçoit pas. On retrouve à bord une qualité de finition exemplaire et le choix des matériaux n'a rien de commun. On se sent dans un environnement riche et unique, élément qui frappe tout non-initié. Ajoutez l'espace d'une limousine pour les passagers et une panoplie de gadgets incluant un nouveau système audio Bang & Olufsen à 15 haut-parleurs et vous venez de transformer les longs trajets en véritable partie de plaisir.

Sylvain Raymond

PHOTOS: MERCEDES-BENZ

MERCEDES-BENZ CLASSE S

Catégorie	Berline
Échelle de prix	105 900 $ à 234 000 $
Garanties	4 ans/80 000 km, 4 ans/80 000 km
Assemblage	Stuttgart, Allemagne
Cote d'assurance	n.d.

CHÂSSIS - DONNÉES POUR S600

Emp/lon/lar/haut	3 165/5 206/1 871/1 473 mm
Coffre	560 litres
Réservoir	90 litres
Nombre coussins sécurité	9
Antipatinage / contrôle stabilité	oui / oui
Suspension avant	indépendante, multibras
Suspension arrière	indépendante, multibras
Freins avant / arrière	disque (ABS) / disque (ABS)
Direction	à crémaillère, ass. variable
Diamètre de braquage	12,2 m
Pneus avant / arrière	P255/40R19 / P275/40R19
Poids	2 250 kg
Capacité de remorquage	n.d.

COMPOSANTES MÉCANIQUES

S400 Hybrid

Cylindrée, soupapes, alim.	V6 3,5 litres 24 s atmos.
Puissance / Couple	295 chevaux / 284 lb-pi
Tr. base (opt) / rouage base (opt)	A7 / Prop
0-100 / 80-120 / 100-0 km/h	8,1 s / 6,0 s / 41,4 m
Type ess. / ville / autoroute	Super / 11,0 / 7,6 l/100 km

S450 4Matic
V8 4,7 l, 335 ch / 339 lb-pi - 0-100 : 5,9 s - 14,2 / 9,0 l/100 km

S550 4Matic
V8 5,5 l, 382 ch / 391 lb-pi - 0-100 : 5,4 s - 14,9 / 9,3 l/100 km

S600
V12 5,5 l, 510 ch / 612 lb-pi - 0-100 : 4,7 s - 18,9 / 11,5 l/100 km

S63 AMG
V8 5,5 l, 536 ch / 590 lb-pi - 0-100 : 4,4 s - n.d. / n.d. l/100 km

S65 AMG
V12 6,0 l, 603 ch / 738 lb-pi - 0-100 : 4,4 s - 19,4 / 12,0 l/100 km

DANS LA MÊME CATÉGORIE

Audi A8, BMW Série 7, Bentley Continental, Jaguar XJ, Lexus LS, Maserati Quattroporte

DU NOUVEAU EN 2011

Nouveau moteur pour la S63 AMG

NOS IMPRESSIONS

Agrément de conduite :	7/10
Fiabilité :	6/10
Sécurité :	10/10
Qualités hivernales :	8/10
Espace intérieur :	9/10
Confort :	10/10

www.mercedes-benz.ca

Plus d'informations dans la section statistiques en dernière partie du Guide

PERFORMANCE ET LUXE À LA CARTE

Avec l'arrivée de la spectaculaire SLS, plusieurs ont affirmé que ce modèle venait remplacer la SL. Ce n'est absolument pas le cas, puisque ce coupé-roadster a sa place dans la gamme des modèles de Mercedes-Benz. En effet, il suffit d'appuyer sur un bouton pour se retrouver au volant d'un cabriolet dont les formes sont toujours fort élégantes. On appuie sur le même bouton, et la voiture se transforme en coupé sport. Que demander de mieux?

Il faut également que ce modèle réponde aux différentes exigences des acheteurs. Selon le groupe propulseur choisi, la SL est une élégante boulevardière ou encore un bolide rugissant capable de spectaculaires accélérations et reprises.

TOUT UN QUATUOR!

Comme il en été fait mention précédemment, choisissez le moteur qui convient à vos aspirations et vous allez obtenir une voiture dont les prestations et le comportement sont différents. Même si c'est presque un sacrilège de parler de modèle d'entrée de gamme en ce qui concerne la SL550, il s'agit quand même de la version la plus économique avec un prix de 126 000 $. Celle-ci est propulsée par le moteur V8 de 5,5 litres d'une puissance de 382 chevaux qui est associé à une boîte automatique à sept rapports. Cette transmission a fait ses preuves et elle est particulièrement efficace même si elle hésite parfois à rétrograder en certaines circonstances.

Si vous trouvez que cette cavalerie manque d'équidés, il y a la SL600 dont le moteur V12 biturbo produit 510 chevaux. Compte tenu du couple élevé de 612 lb-pi de ce moteur, les ingénieurs ont choisi une transmission automatique à cinq rapports, mieux adaptée à cette puissance et à ce couple.

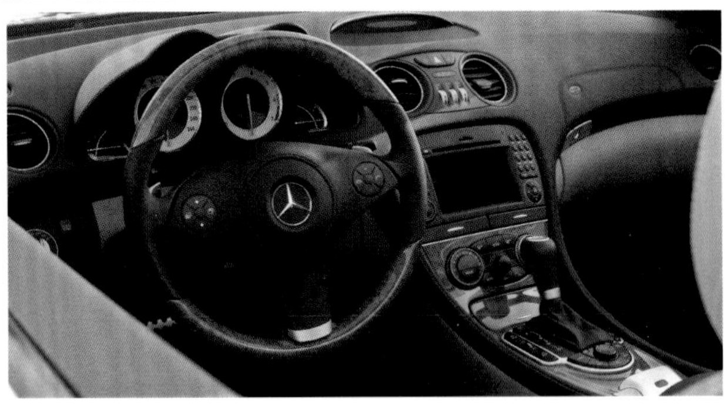

Supposons que vous venez de remporter le gros lot à la loterie et que vous brûlez d'envie de faire une folle dépense. Mercedes-Benz est en mesure de combler vos attentes avec les deux versions AMG de la SL. Une fois de plus, c'est sous le capot que les choses se passent.

Si on procède par ordre de puissance et de prix, la SL63 AMG est pourvue du désormais légendaire moteur V8 de 6,2 litres produisant 518 chevaux. Et pour gérer cette puissance de façon efficace, les ingénieurs d'AMG ont concocté une transmission automatique à sept rapports appelée MCT pour *Multi-Clutch Technology*. Cette transmission possède quatre modes d'opération différents. La commande de ces modes est placée sur la console médiane. Pour circuler en ville et sur les grands boulevards, il y a le mode C, pour confort, qui assure des accélérations correctes et favorisant une meilleure économie de carburant. Si vous en désirez un peu plus en fait de réaction, enclenchez le mode S pour sport.

Ce n'est pas fini, car il y a encore la SL65 AMG avec son moteur V12 biturbo de 603 chevaux associé à une boîte automatique à

- Choix de moteurs
- Version AMG très performante
- Excellente tenue de route
- Habitacle confortable
- Silhouette classique

- Dimensions encombrantes
- Consommation élevée
- Coffre limité (toit remisé)
- Prix prohibitif

cinq rapports. Comme tous les modèles propulsés par un moteur V12, les accélérations sont plus linéaires que spectaculaires même si le résultat final est impressionnant. En effet, il faut 4,2 secondes à ce V12 pour boucler le 0-100 km/h alors qu'il en faut 0,9 de plus pour la SL63 AMG.

BOURGEOISE ET SPORTIVE

Il ne faut pas sous-estimer ce coupé-cabriolet. Avec son habitacle fort confortable doté de tous les accessoires que l'on s'attend à retrouver dans une voiture de ce prix, la SL est fort bien adaptée à des randonnées sur les grands boulevards ou sur la grande route. La suspension à réglage constant est d'ailleurs fort confortable et absorbe relativement bien les trous et les bosses qui parsèment nos routes. De plus, ces gros moteurs sont très dociles et semblent toujours être à la hauteur de la situation.

La polyvalence de ce modèle se prolonge au toit articulé. En effet, une fois en place, nous nous retrouvons au volant d'un coupé confortable, étanche et bien isolé. Une fois ce toit remisé dans le coffre, le châssis ne subit pas trop de flexion et les turbulences de l'air dans l'habitacle sont bien contrôlées. Un bémol cependant, cette capote rigide prend beaucoup de place dans le coffre.

Par contre, si vous désirez pousser davantage, cette Mercedes-Benz demeure à la hauteur de la situation. Il est vrai qu'elle ne possède pas l'agilité d'une Lotus Evora ou d'une Porsche Boxster en raison de ses dimensions et de sa lourdeur, mais sa tenue de route et son freinage sont tout de même impressionnants. Elle est stable dans les virages et très neutre également.

Soulignons cette année, l'arrivée d'un modèle produit à moins de 20 exemplaires pour le Canada. Il s'agit de la « Night Edition » qui comprend, comme son nom l'indique, une peinture de carrosserie noire, du cuir Nappa exclusif pour l'habitacle, des roues spéciales AMG de 19 pouces, des sièges climatisés, un toit panoramique en verre, en plus d'un bois exclusif sur le tableau de bord, de la fermeture électronique du coffre et du système de confort Airscarf permettant de rouler le toit baissé par temps froid.

Denis Duquet

PHOTOS : MERCEDES-BENZ

Catégorie	*Roadster*
Échelle de prix	126 000 $ à 240 100 $
Garanties	4 ans/80 000 km, 4 ans/80 000 km
Assemblage	Bremen, Allemagne
Cote d'assurance	n.d.

CHÂSSIS - DONNÉES POUR SL600

Emp/lon/lar/haut	2 560/4 562/1 820/1 295 mm
Coffre	288 litres
Réservoir	80 litres
Nombre coussins sécurité	4
Antipatinage / contrôle stabilité	oui / oui
Suspension avant	indépendante, multibras
Suspension arrière	indépendante, multibras
Freins avant / arrière	disques (ABS) / disques (ABS)
Direction	à crémaillère, ass. variable électrique
Diamètre de braquage	11,0 m
Pneus avant / arrière	P255/35R19 / P285/30R19
Poids	2 040 kg
Capacité de remorquage	n.d.

COMPOSANTES MÉCANIQUES

SL550

Cylindrée, soupapes, alim.	V8 5,5 litres 32 s atmos.
Puissance / Couple	382 chevaux / 391 lb-pi
Tr. base (opt) / rouage base (opt)	A7 / Prop
0-100 / 80-120 / 100-0 km/h	5,4 s / 5,1 s / 37,0 m
Type ess. / ville / autoroute	Super / 15,8 / 9,4 l/100 km

SL600

Cylindrée, soupapes, alim.	V12 5,5 litres 36 s turbo
Puissance / Couple	510 chevaux / 612 lb-pi
Tr. base (opt) / rouage base (opt)	A5 / Prop
0-100 / 80-120 / 100-0 km/h	4,5 s / n.d. / n.d.
Type ess. / ville / autoroute	Super / 18,5 / 11,4 l/100 km

SL63 AMG

V8 6,2 l, 518 ch / 465 lb-pi - 0-100: 5,1 s - 17,9 / 10,6 l/100 km

SL65 AMG

V12 6,0 l, 603 ch / 738 lb-pi - 0-100: 4,2 s - 18,4 / 11,1 l/100 km

DANS LA MÊME CATÉGORIE

Aston Martin Vantage, BMW Série 6, Bentley Continental, Cadillac XLR, Chevrolet Corvette, Dodge Viper, Ferrari F458 Italia, Jaguar XK, Porsche 911

DU NOUVEAU EN 2011

Aucun changement majeur.
Version SL550 Night Edition (20 unités au Canada)

NOS IMPRESSIONS

Agrément de conduite :	■■■■■■■■■□	9/10
Fiabilité :	■■■■■■□□□□	6/10
Sécurité :	■■■■■■■■■■	10/10
Qualités hivernales :	■■■■■■□□□□	6/10
Espace intérieur :	■■■■■■□□□□	6/10
Confort :	■■■■■■■■□□	8/10

www.mercedes-benz.ca

Plus d'informations dans la section statistiques en dernière partie du Guide

LA NOUVELLE EN 2011

La SLK de Mercedes-Benz sera entièrement renouvelée et sera lancée en cours d'année 2011, possiblement comme un modèle 2012. Au moment d'écrire ces lignes, des rumeurs persistantes faisaient état d'un lancement au Mondial de l'Automobile de Paris à l'automne 2010 pour la nouvelle génération du coupé-cabriolet de Mercedes-Benz.

Les photos-espion saisies sur le vif lors d'essais dynamiques menés par le constructeur allemand sur le circuit du Nürburgring en Allemagne laissent entrevoir une voiture dont le style reprend plusieurs éléments de la plus grande SL, ainsi que de la supervoiture AMG SLS. Ainsi, le design d'inspiration F1 de la partie avant du modèle actuel laissera place à une calandre surdimensionnée beaucoup plus agressive, tout comme sur l'actuelle SL. Le nouveau look adopté pour l'avant permettra également à la voiture de rencontrer les normes européennes visant à réduire les blessures infligées aux piétons en cas d'accident, et il y a fort à parier que la nouvelle SLK fera usage de la technologie DEL pour ses phares de jour. À l'arrière, le volume du coffre sera augmenté de 20 litres par rapport au modèle actuel.

INTÉRIEUR D'INSPIRATION CLASSE E ET AMG SLS

Il faut également s'attendre à ce que l'habitacle de la nouvelle SLK emprunte plusieurs éléments de la Classe E, mais que son design soit résolument plus sportif, à l'image de la AMG SLS. Parmi les équipements qui seront probablement proposés en option ou en groupe d'options, on devrait retrouver le système de navigation, ainsi que toute une panoplie de dispositifs de sécurité active comprenant l'avertissement de la présence d'un véhicule dans l'angle mort des rétroviseurs, entre autres... De plus, la nouvelle génération du coupé-cabriolet devrait être dotée d'une version revue et augmentée du système de télématique COMAND et devrait logiquement reprendre le très efficace dispositif Airscarf qui souffle de l'air chaud à la base du cou des occupants, bonifiant ainsi le confort tout en permettant de prolonger la saison des balades à ciel ouvert.

Tout comme le modèle actuel, la nouvelle génération de la SLK sera élaborée à partir de la plate-forme de la Série C, ce qui signifie que son empattement sera supérieur à celui du modèle actuel. La vocation plus sportive de la SLK lui vaudra certainement de recevoir des suspensions ajustables, des freins surdimensionnés, ainsi qu'une direction active et des jantes sport de 18 pouces. De plus, la boîte automatique 7G-Tronic à sept rapports remplacera la boîte à cinq rapports du modèle actuel, permettant d'améliorer le bilan de la SLK en matière de consommation et d'émissions polluantes. Le moteur V6 de 3,5 litres et 300 chevaux reprendrait du service, et une version AMG serait actuellement en voie de développement et devrait être animée par le très performant V8 de 6,2 litres développant la bagatelle de 502 chevaux. La clientèle européenne bénéficiera également d'une offre diesel pour animer la SLK, mais ce moteur ne sera probablement pas offert en Amérique du Nord.

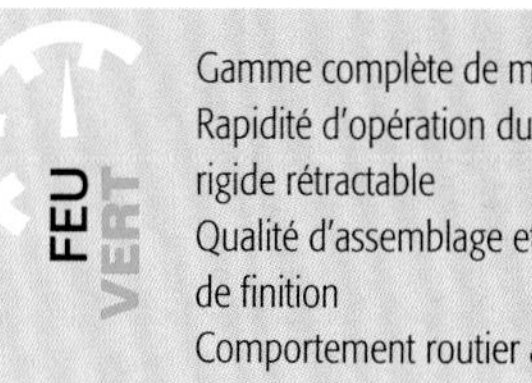

Gamme complète de modèles
Rapidité d'opération du toit rigide rétractable
Qualité d'assemblage et de finition
Comportement routier axé sur le confort

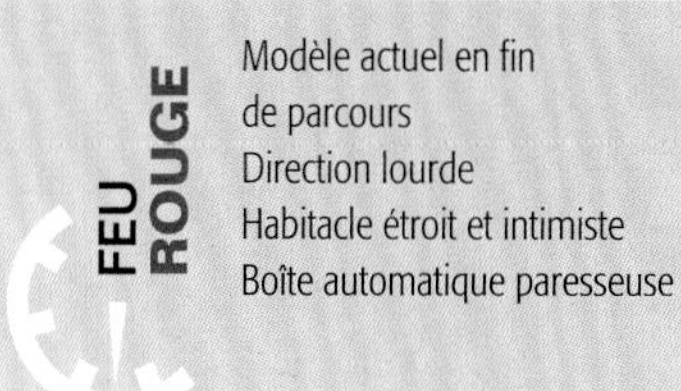

Modèle actuel en fin de parcours
Direction lourde
Habitacle étroit et intimiste
Boîte automatique paresseuse

LA FIN DE LA ROUTE

L'arrivée de la SLK de nouvelle génération signifie que le modèle actuel tirera sa révérence dans l'ombre de la récente BMW Z4 et de l'Audi TT remaniée pour 2011, deux rivales directes qui lui sont largement supérieures pour ce qui est de leurs qualités dynamiques, sans parler de la Porsche Boxster, qui demeure encore et toujours la référence de la catégorie. L'actuelle SLK n'est pas une mauvaise voiture, loin de là, mais les ingénieurs de Mercedes-Benz ont préféré lui donner une vocation plus proche de celle d'une voiture de tourisme plutôt que celle d'une authentique sportive. Ainsi, les calibrations retenues pour les systèmes antipatinage et de contrôle électronique de la stabilité font en sorte que ces systèmes interviennent trop rapidement et trop fortement, privant le conducteur d'une expérience de conduite au dynamisme plus relevé. Il est intéressant de noter que la clientèle de la SLK est majoritairement féminine, exception faite des versions survitaminées proposées par AMG, ce qui amène le problème suivant: lorsqu'une voiture est trop considérée comme «féminine», même les femmes n'en veulent plus... C'est donc là l'une des raisons pour lesquelles la nouvelle génération de cette voiture adoptera un look plus agressif ou plus «masculin», justement afin de renverser la tendance établie.

Bref, la SLK est une belle voiture confortable qui n'aime pas trop se faire brasser, ce qui est parfaitement acceptable dans le cas d'une clientèle qui n'est pas à la recherche de sensations fortes, mais qui désire simplement faire de belles balades à ciel ouvert, tout en profitant de la sécurité et du confort accru d'une voiture dotée d'un toit rigide rétractable, ce qui respecte parfaitement la philosophie du constructeur. Alors que Porsche et BMW mettent l'emphase sur les performances et le dynamisme de la conduite avec leurs Boxster et Z4, Mercedes-Benz mise plutôt sur le confort et l'élégance. Dans ce peloton, l'actuelle SLK est donc carrément larguée par ses rivales sur le plan de la dynamique, une situation que devrait corriger le modèle de nouvelle génération, qui sera également plus spacieux et probablement conforme à la philosophie de la marque en matière de confort. Une chose est certaine, ce modèle sera en mesure d'inquiéter la concurrence et de séduire de nouveaux acheteurs, afin de pouvoir se mettre à nouveau parmi le groupe de tête. En plus, le prestige de la marque est toujours un argument convaincant pour plusieurs.

Gabriel Gélinas

PHOTOS : MERCEDES-BENZ

MERCEDES-BENZ SLK

Catégorie	*Roadster*
Échelle de prix	57 500 $ à 84 800 $ (2010)
Garanties	4 ans/80 000 km, 4 ans/80 000 km
Assemblage	Bremen, Allemagne
Cote d'assurance	passable

CHÂSSIS - DONNÉES POUR SLK350

Emp/lon/lar/haut	2 430/4 103/1 788/1 298 mm
Coffre	300 litres
Réservoir	70 litres
Nombre coussins sécurité	4
Antipatinage / contrôle stabilité	oui / oui
Suspension avant	indépendante, jambes de force
Suspension arrière	indépendante, multibras
Freins avant / arrière	disque (ABS) / disque (ABS)
Direction	à crémaillère, ass. variable
Diamètre de braquage	10,5 m
Pneus avant / arrière	P225/40R18 / P245/35R18
Poids	1 490 kg
Capacité de remorquage	n.d.

COMPOSANTES MÉCANIQUES

SLK300

Cylindrée, soupapes, alim.	V6 3,0 litres 24 s atmos.
Puissance / Couple	228 chevaux / 221 lb-pi
Tr. base (opt) / rouage base (opt)	M6 (A7) / Prop
0-100 / 80-120 / 100-0 km/h	6,3 s / 5,5 s (est) / n.d.
Type ess. / ville / autoroute	Super / 11,5 / 7,3 l/100 km

SLK350

Cylindrée, soupapes, alim.	V6 3,5 litres 24 s atmos.
Puissance / Couple	300 chevaux / 266 lb-pi
Tr. base (opt) / rouage base (opt)	M6 (A7) / Prop
0-100 / 80-120 / 100-0 km/h	5,6 s / 5,0 s / 36,6 m
Type ess. / ville / autoroute	Super / 12,6 / 8,0 l/100 km

SLK55 AMG

Cylindrée, soupapes, alim.	V8 5,5 litres 24 s atmos.
Puissance / Couple	355 chevaux / 376 lb-pi
Tr. base (opt) / rouage base (opt)	A7 / Prop
0-100 / 80-120 / 100-0 km/h	4,9 s / n.d. / n.d.
Type ess. / ville / autoroute	Super / 14,8 / 9,0 l/100 km

DANS LA MÊME CATÉGORIE

Audi TT, BMW Z4, Lotus Elise, Nissan Z, Porsche Boxster

DU NOUVEAU EN 2011

Aucun changement majeur, dernière année de production

NOS IMPRESSIONS

Agrément de conduite :	9/10
Fiabilité :	6/10
Sécurité :	10/10
Qualités hivernales :	6/10
Espace intérieur :	7/10
Confort :	8/10

www.mercedes-benz.ca

Plus d'informations dans la section statistiques en dernière partie du Guide

LA LÉGENDE MODERNISÉE

Si on part du fait que Mercedes-Benz est à l'origine de l'automobile, les chances de retrouver des modèles d'anthologie dans son histoire sont excellentes. L'une des plus célèbres est sans conteste la 300 SL qui a été développée dans les années 50 pour participer à des courses comme la Targa Florio et la Mille Miglia. À cette époque, ces courses disputées sur les voies publiques étaient on ne peut plus populaires. Plusieurs autres voitures y ont brillé, mais aucune n'a eu la popularité de cette Mercedes-Benz.

Cet engouement pour la 300SL s'explique en bonne partie par ses succès en course, mais c'est surtout sa silhouette spectaculaire qui en a fait une légende. Les portières en forme d'aile de mouette qui s'ouvraient verticalement étaient toute une innovation pour l'époque et donnaient à la voiture une allure vraiment particulière. Il est intéressant de savoir que ces portières n'ont pas été dessinées pour des raisons esthétiques, mais purement pratiques. Pour obtenir le plus de rigidité possible, les ingénieurs de l'époque avaient dessiné un bas de caisse très haut et également très large. Cette configuration mécanique empêchant l'utilisation de portières traditionnelles, les portières en aile de mouette étaient la solution la plus logique.

SILHOUETTE CLASSIQUE, HABITACLE SOBRE

Les ingénieurs qui ont procédé au développement de ce modèle nous jurent que leur intention n'était pas de faire une version moderne de la 300SL et que ce n'est que dans le cadre de ce processus que les portes en ailes de mouettes ont été envisagées. Quoiqu'ils en disent, il est certain que la silhouette de la SLS fait songer à la légendaire voiture de course. Force est d'admettre que les stylistes ont effectué du bon boulot et dessiné une voiture à la fois classique et moderne. Si la partie avant est fort réussie, l'arrière est trop arrondi. Ce qui explique pourquoi les versions de course de la SLS doivent être dotées d'un aileron gigantesque. Malgré la sobriété de ses lignes, cette Mercedes-Benz est l'une des voitures les plus spectaculaires qui soit sur la route. Soulignons au passage la présence de buses d'extraction d'air dans les ailes qui ressemblent à celles employées sur la SLR, une voiture qui n'est plus en production depuis plusieurs mois maintenant.

En harmonie avec la silhouette, l'habitacle est sobre et classique. La planche de bord est relativement dépouillée, alors que seules des buses de ventilation circulaires ornent sa partie frontale. Des cadrans indicateurs de bonne dimension, séparés par un centre d'information à affichage numérique, sont regroupés dans un petit module servant à les protéger des rayons parasites et du soleil. Pour rehausser l'apparence du tableau de bord, il est possible de choisir entre deux présentations : l'une avec appliques en fibres de carbone et l'autre, en aluminium brossé. Certaines voitures ultra sportives sont dotées de sièges plus ou moins confortables mettant surtout l'accent sur le support latéral. Les sièges de la SLS ne sont pas en reste à ce chapitre, mais ils sont d'autant plus confortables grâce à un excellent support pour les cuisses et le bas du dos.

La planche de bord de ce modèle est dépouillée parce que plusieurs commandes ont été placées sur la très large console située entre les deux sièges. On y retrouve les boutons servant à commander les modes de passages des rapports, le bouton de démarrage, celui pour actionner le déflecteur arrière, ainsi que le gros bouton central réglant la plupart des fonctions de la radio et du système de navigation. Par contre, la climatisation est gérée par des commandes situées dans la partie inférieure de la planche de bord.

RIGIDITÉ HORS PAIR

Au lieu d'emprunter le châssis de la SL, les ingénieurs ont préféré développer un tout nouveau châssis en aluminium de type *spaceframe*. On fait appel à différents types d'aluminium afin d'obtenir la légèreté nécessaire, ainsi que la rigidité voulue. Il faut préciser qu'en plus du châssis, la plupart des éléments de la carrosserie ont été réalisés à partir de ce même matériau. L'utilisation de la fibre de carbone a été envisagée, mais l'aluminium offrait plus d'avantages, tout en étant presque aussi léger. Les composantes de la suspension en aluminium forgé permettent d'obtenir la rigidité nécessaire.

Le moteur est en position centrale avant, ce qui permet de répartir 47 % du poids à l'avant et 53 % à l'arrière. Le moteur choisi est bien entendu le V8 de 6,2 litres déjà utilisé sur d'autres modèles. Les ingénieurs ont utilisé un carter sec cette fois, afin d'abaisser au maximum le centre de gravité. Développé par AMG, ce V8 a encore été amélioré. Sa puissance est maintenant de 563 chevaux. En raison de la légèreté de la voiture, le rapport poids/puissance est de 2,84 kg/ch, ce qui lui permet de boucler le 0-100 km/h en 3,8 secondes et d'atteindre une vitesse de pointe de 317 km/h (données du constructeur). Ce gros moteur a vu sa puissance augmentée, mais son poids a été diminué. Il pèse 205 kg, ce qui est impressionnant pour une telle mécanique. Puisque ce moteur est monté en position centrale avant, la transmission a été placée à l'arrière. Il s'agit d'une transmission à double embrayage, qui est reliée au moteur par l'entremise d'un tube de couple dans lequel tourne l'arbre de transmission en fibre de carbone. Ceci permet d'obtenir un lien rigide et très léger en même temps. La nouvelle transmission à double embrayage à sept rapports se démarque par des changements de vitesse excessivement rapides : moins de 100 millisecondes en mode Sport. Le conducteur peut choisir quatre types de réglage de la transmission : C pour efficacité contrôlée, S pour sport, S+ pour Sport Plus et enfin M pour le mode manuel. À cela s'ajoute un différentiel autobloquant, des freins en céramique optionnels et un système de contrôle de dérapage latéral pouvant être réglé en trois modes distincts.

La consommation de carburant annoncée par le constructeur est de 13,2 litres aux 100 km en conduite normale. C'est difficile à croire sur une voiture de cette puissance, mais une randonnée en ville et sur les autoroutes nous a exactement donné cette moyenne. Par contre, après cinq tours à fond de train sur le circuit de Laguna Seca en Californie, la moyenne a alors franchi la barre des 20 litres aux 100 km…

ULTRA RAPIDE, ULTRA DOCILE

En raison de ses portières très particulières, il faut trouver la bonne technique pour prendre place à bord et ne pas se heurter la tête lorsqu'on quitte la voiture. Toutefois, après un ou deux

essais, la technique est facilement maîtrisée. Une fois assis, on se rend compte que les sièges sont ajustables de toutes les manières, et que la position de conduite est bonne en raison d'un volant réglable en hauteur et en profondeur.

Le moteur est lancé à l'aide d'un bouton placé sur la console centrale et sa sonorité est gutturale, mais juste ce qu'il faut. Sur la route, la SLS se dirige au doigt et à l'œil. En effet, la suspension est ferme, mais pas excessivement, et la direction n'est pas trop assistée ou trop ferme et ce, à toutes les vitesses. De plus, l'accélérateur est bien dosé. Il est progressif et linéaire ce qui facilite la conduite dans la circulation urbaine. Par contre, la visibilité est perfectible, mais les rétroviseurs extérieurs sont de bonne dimension.

FEU VERT

- Silhouette extraordinaire
- Moteur très musclé
- Freinage puissant
- Tenue de route supérieure
- Habitacle confortable

FEU ROUGE

- Visibilité 3/4 arrière pénible
- Pneumatiques moyens
- Accès à bord difficile
- Partie arrière manque de mordant

Sur la piste, la rigidité de la caisse, ainsi que la puissance du moteur et des freins permettent de réaliser des moyennes impressionnantes. Lors d'essais sur le circuit de Laguna Seca en Californie, la SLS a dominé le parcours. La transmission était réglée en mode S+ et son efficacité était impressionnante, rétrogradant avec le fameux *blip* à chaque passage aux rapports inférieurs. Les voitures en piste étaient équipées de freins en céramique et en carbone, dont la puissance est hors-norme, alors que leur résistance à l'échauffement est elle aussi surprenante. Les pneus Continental se sont bien acquittés de leur tâche, mais l'adhérence en virage aurait été probablement supérieure avec des Pirelli P-Zero.

La SLS excelle en tout: que l'on flâne sur les grands boulevards, que l'on circule à vitesse plus élevée sur les autoroutes ou encore que l'on aborde une route sinueuse, elle est toujours à la hauteur de la tâche. Bref, cette Mercedes-Benz SLS AMG 6.3 est déjà entrée dans la légende.

Denis Duquet

PHOTOS : MERCEDES-BENZ

MERCEDES-BENZ SLS AMG

Catégorie	Coupé
Échelle de prix	198 000 $
Garanties	4 ans/80 000 km, 4 ans/80 000 km
Assemblage	n.d.
Cote d'assurance	n.d.

CHÂSSIS - DONNÉES POUR 6.3 AMG

Emp/lon/lar/haut	2 680/4 638/2 078/1 262 mm
Coffre	176 litres
Réservoir	85 litres
Nombre coussins sécurité	8
Antipatinage / contrôle stabilité	oui / oui
Suspension avant	indépendante, multibras
Suspension arrière	indépendante, multibras
Freins avant / arrière	disque (ABS) / disque (ABS)
Direction	à crémaillère, assistée
Diamètre de braquage	11,9 m
Pneus avant / arrière	265/35R19 / 295/30R20
Poids	1 620 kg
Capacité de remorquage	n.d.

COMPOSANTES MÉCANIQUES

Composantes mécaniques

6.3 AMG

Cylindrée, soupapes, alim.	V8 6,2 litres 32 s atmos.
Puissance / Couple	563 chevaux / 479 lb-pi
Tr. base (opt) / rouage base (opt)	A7 / Prop
0-100 / 80-120 / 100-0 km/h	3,8 s / 3,5 s (est) / n.d.
Type ess. / ville / autoroute	Super / 15,6 / 10,3 l/100 km

DANS LA MÊME CATÉGORIE

Aston Martin DB9, Audi R8, BMW Série 6, Ferrari California, Lamborghini Gallardo, Lexus LFA, Maserati Gran Turismo, Nissan GT-R

DU NOUVEAU EN 2011

Nouveau modèle

NOS IMPRESSIONS

Agrément de conduite :	10/10
Fiabilité :	Données insuffisantes
Sécurité :	10/10
Qualités hivernales :	4/10
Espace intérieur :	8/10
Confort :	8/10

www.mercedes-benz.ca

Plus d'informations dans la section statistiques en dernière partie du Guide

Mini Countryman

QUATRE, COMME LES BEATLES...

Tout comme les Beatles qui étaient quatre, la gamme des Mini s'enrichit en 2011 d'un quatrième modèle appelé Countryman dont l'identité est marquée du chiffre 4. C'est la première Mini qui fait quatre mètres en longueur, la première à être dotée de quatre portières et de quatre sièges baquets, et c'est surtout la première Mini qui offre la traction intégrale en option.

Bien qu'elle soit plus longue, plus large et plus haute que les Cooper et Clubman, le style de la Countryman est «pur Mini», et comme la voiture elle-même demeure plus courte qu'une Volkswagen Golf, cela en fait une Mini plus grande et plus spacieuse, sans toutefois être géante. Alors que l'espace intérieur et le volume de chargement sont de format réduit sur la Cooper, la Countryman peut accueillir quatre adultes confortablement tout en transportant 350 litres de bagages. Les deux sièges arrière, qui sont montés sur des rails, peuvent être avancés ou reculés sur une plage de 13 centimètres et peuvent être repliés afin d'augmenter le volume de chargement à 1 170 litres. La Countryman innove avec son ingénieux rail central qui court entre les sièges de gauche et ceux de droite, et sur lequel plusieurs accessoires comme un iPod ou un boîtier à lunettes peuvent être fixés. De plus, il est possible de commander une chaîne audio de qualité supérieure de même que des interfaces permettant l'intégration complète d'un iPhone ou d'autres téléphones intelligents en option.

L'ATTRAIT DE L'INTÉGRALE

Voilà pour l'allure, mais qu'en est-il de la conduite ? Lors du lancement de cette nouvelle version de la Mini, seuls des modèles Countryman S à traction intégrale étaient disponibles, aussi, nos impressions de conduite se limitent-elles particulièrement à ce modèle. Celui-ci est animé par le moteur 4 cylindres de 1,6 litre dont la puissance est gonflée à 184 chevaux par le turbocompresseur qui comporte deux entrées distinctes (TwinScroll), et par l'adoption de l'injection directe de carburant de même que le calage variable des soupapes d'admission et d'échappement. Au décollage, la Countryman accélère avec aplomb et enthousiasme, mais pas à l'emporte-pièce. Le sprint de 0 à 100 kilomètres/heure se fait en 7,6 secondes, ce qui s'explique par son poids de 1 380 kilos, soit environ 250 de plus que la Cooper de base. Aussi, l'entrée en action du rouage intégral a pour effet d'éliminer tout patinage des roues avant en transférant le couple aux roues arrière, rendant ainsi la voiture plus stable mais moins nerveuse en accélération initiale que la Cooper S à traction avant. En virage, la Countryman fait preuve d'un peu plus de roulis et ses suspensions paraissent plus souples que celles de la Cooper S. La direction semble également plus lente que sur les autres variantes de la Mini. Résulta : la sensation au volant est celle d'une voiture qui fait un peu moins *go-kart* que la Cooper S et qui est plus stable en toutes conditions, mais qui conserve l'agrément de conduite faisant le charme de la Cooper. En conduite hors route pas trop intense sur une surface comme le sable ou la terre,

FEU VERT
- Moteur performant (S)
- Rouage intégral (Countryman S)
- Habitabilité en progrès (Clubman et Countryman)
- Conduite inspirée

FEU ROUGE
- Prix élevés
- Coût des options
- Volume d'espace intérieur (Cooper et Cabriolet)
- Puissance moteur (modèles de base)

il est même possible d'induire un léger survirage en sortie de courbe en accélération franche, pourvu que l'on ait pris soin de désactiver le système de contrôle électronique de la stabilité au préalable.

La Mini Countryman se pointera chez nous au printemps 2011 en trois modèles: la Countryman à traction avant, la Countryman S à traction avant et la Countryman S avec le rouage intégral ALL4 offert en option. Au moment d'écrire ces lignes, aucune information n'était disponible quant à l'échelle de prix de la Countryman qui devrait être plus chère que la Clubman et même se rapprocher de la Cabriolet. Il faut également s'attendre à ce que la liste d'options et de groupes d'options soit aussi longue que celle des autres modèles de la marque, permettant ainsi des possibilités presque illimitées en ce qui a trait à la personnalisation.

Avec le côté pratique rehaussé par la présence de quatre portières et la disponibilité du rouage intégral, il est clair que la Countryman permet de rejoindre plus directement une partie de la clientèle qui a été séduite par le style ravageur de la Mini mais qui n'a pas choisi cette voiture pour des considérations pratiques. La Countryman S à traction intégrale peut donc s'imposer comme une voiture utilisable tous les jours et en toutes saisons, mais le prix sera le facteur clé qui déterminera si la Countryman augmentera ou non les ventes de la marque au Canada.

ET LES AUTRES...

Pour 2011, tous les modèles de la gamme Mini reçoivent un nouveau pare-chocs avant, conçu pour satisfaire les nouvelles normes européennes limitant les blessures infligées aux piétons en cas d'impact. Des changements ont également été apportés aux phares et aux feux, alors que le pare-chocs arrière a lui aussi fait l'objet de retouches. Un nouveau système multimédia appelé MINI Connected sera offert en option et permettra aux utilisateurs de l'iPhone de syntoniser la radio sur Internet et d'utiliser Google, Facebook et Twitter par l'interface de l'écran central, mais pas tout en conduisant, du moins on l'espère...

Parmi les quatre modèles qui composent la gamme des Mini, les Clubman et Countryman s'imposent pour ceux qui recherchent une voiture capable de répondre à tous leurs besoins.

Gabriel Gélinas

PHOTOS : MINI

MINI COOPER

Catégorie	Cabriolet, *Hatchback*, VUS
Échelle de prix	22 800 $ à 42 500 $ (2010)
Garanties	4 ans/80 000 km, 4 ans/80 000 km
Assemblage	Oxford, Angleterre
Cote d'assurance	moyenne

CHÂSSIS - DONNÉES POUR CLUBMAN JOHN COOPER WORKS

Emp/lon/lar/haut	2 547/3 958/1 683/1 432 mm
Coffre	260 à 930 litres
Réservoir	50 litres
Nombre coussins sécurité	4
Antipatinage / contrôle stabilité	oui / oui
Suspension avant	indépendante, jambes de force
Suspension arrière	indépendante, multibras
Freins avant / arrière	disque (ABS) / disque (ABS)
Direction	à crémaillère, assistée
Diamètre de braquage	10,6 m
Pneus avant / arrière	P205/45R17 / P205/45R17
Poids	1 310 kg
Capacité de remorquage	n.d.

COMPOSANTES MÉCANIQUES

Base, Clubman, Cabriolet

Cylindrée, soupapes, alim.	4L 1,6 litre 16 s atmos.
Puissance / Couple	118 chevaux / 114 lb-pi
Tr. base (opt) / rouage base (opt)	M6 (A6) / Tr
0-100 / 80-120 / 100-0 km/h	8,3 s / 10,2 s / 40,2 m
Type ess. / ville / autoroute	Super / 7,1 / 5,3 l/100 km

S, Clubman S, Cabriolet S

Cylindrée, soupapes, alim.	4L 1,6 litre 16 s turbocompressé
Puissance / Couple	172 chevaux / 192 lb-pi
Tr. base (opt) / rouage base (opt)	M6 (A6) / Tr
0-100 / 80-120 / 100-0 km/h	7,1 s / 4,5 s / 37,7 m
Type ess. / ville / autoroute	Super / 7,8 / 5,7 l/100 km

John Cooper Works
4L 1,6 l, 208 ch, 207 lb-pi - 0-100 : 6,8 s - 7,8 / 5,7 l/100 km

Countryman
4L 1,6 l, 122 ch, 118 lb-pi - 0-100 : 10,5 s - consomm : nd

Countryman S
4L 1,6 l, 184 ch, 177 lb-pi - 0-100 : 7,6 s - consomm : nd.

DANS LA MÊME CATÉGORIE

Audi A3, BMW Série 1, Volvo C30

DU NOUVEAU EN 2011

Esthétique légèrement remaniée, ajout du modèle Countryman

NOS IMPRESSIONS

Agrément de conduite :	8/10
Fiabilité :	6/10
Sécurité :	8/10
Qualités hivernales :	7/10
Espace intérieur :	6/10
Confort :	6/10

www.mini.ca

Plus d'informations dans la section statistiques en dernière partie du Guide

L'ENFER, C'EST PAS NOUS AUTRES!

Il y a déjà plusieurs années que Mitsubishi a présenté la plus récente génération de son coupé Eclipse et de son cabriolet Eclipse Spyder. La génération précédente avait été froidement reçue par les amateurs de Mitsubishi qui ne juraient que pas les lignes sensuelles de la première édition. Édition qui, malheureusement, n'a jamais été distribuée au Québec, Mitsubishi n'ayant pas pignon sur rue chez nous à l'époque.

Toujours est-il que l'Eclipse dévoilé en 2006 en avait séduit plusieurs. Encore aujourd'hui, ses lignes râblées attirent encore les regards, une fleur lancée aux designers qui ont vu juste. Dessiner une carrosserie éclatante qui passe le test des années dans une industrie qui vit plus vite que son ombre, c'est tout un exploit! Il faut cependant souligner que le cabriolet se montre un peu moins élégant, surtout lorsque son toit de toile est relevé. Il est certain que des belles lignes, ça se paie quelque part... et ce quelque part, c'est le coffre, petit, aux contours tourmentés, au seuil trop élevé et à l'ouverture bien peu pratique. Au moins, le dossier de la banquette du coupé s'abaisse pour ajouter au volume.

LA ROBE CACHE UN PHYSIQUE BIEN ORDINAIRE...

Si l'extérieur est réussi, l'habitacle fait contrepartie... Tout d'abord, le noir intégral et le tableau de bord massif sont loin de lui donner un soupçon d'apparence de grandeur. Claustrophobes s'abstenir... Le tableau de bord n'est pas très élégant et manque de raffinement malgré des matériaux de qualité. Les espaces de rangements sont peu nombreux et le système audio de base n'excitera aucun tympan. Le système Rockford Fosgate, par contre, offre une sonorité fort appréciée. À noter que le système Bluetooth fait partie d'un groupe d'options dans la version GS alors qu'il est standard dans la GT-P. Les sièges avant sont confortables mais ceux à l'arrière sont à placer dans la catégorie des farces ratées dans le coupé et dans celle de la provocation à la violence pour le cabriolet... Le seul moment où la visibilité vers l'arrière est correcte, c'est lorsque le toit de la Spyder est baissé. Sinon, il faut déjà avoir conduit un camion cube pour comprendre ce que vit un propriétaire d'Eclipse! À tout le moins, une fois le toit du cabriolet relevé, les bruits extérieurs sont bien maîtrisés et son étanchéité ne peut être mise en doute. En plus, il faut souligner que l'ouverture et la fermeture de ce toit s'effectue rapidement même si ces opérations ne sont pas totalement automatisées (il faut «déclipser» deux agrafes avant de baisser le toit et les remettre en place après l'avoir remis en place)

Le coupé et le cabriolet se déclinent en deux modèles: GS et GT-P. Le premier est mû par un quatre cylindres de 2,4 litres qui ne brille pas par ses performances mais, comme nous le verrons plus loin, il est loin d'être à dédaigner. Sa consommation, d'essence régulière, est assez retenue. On lui a assigné une boîte manuelle à cinq rapports qui, comme on dit chez nous, «fa la job». En option, on peut commander une transmission automatique à quatre rapports

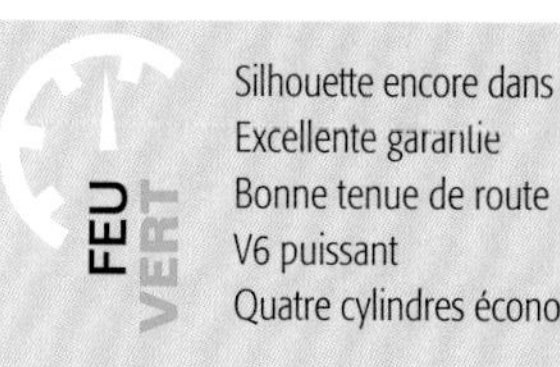

FEU VERT

- Silhouette encore dans le coup
- Excellente garantie
- Bonne tenue de route
- V6 puissant
- Quatre cylindres économique

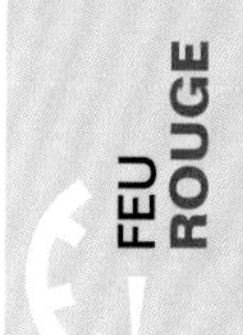

FEU ROUGE

- Solidité du châssis à revoir (Spyder)
- Consommation sans retenue du V6
- Visibilité arrière pénible
- Places arrière pour ennemis seulement

seulement, de l'indigence par les temps qui courent, la plupart des autres manufacturiers offrant, au pire, cinq rapports.

Quant à la GT-P, elle a droit à un V6 de 3,8 litres autrement plus déluré que le quatre cylindres ! Ses 265 chevaux autorisent des accélérations et des reprises franches ce qui n'est pas sans causer un effet de couple dans le volant. Au moins, ils le font avec une belle sonorité. Mais avec une soif assez importante, ce qui réduit l'attrait de ce moteur pour plusieurs personnes. Ce moulin est associé à une manuelle à six rapports au maniement franchement sportif. On retrouve aussi, en option, une automatique à cinq rapports bien étagée.

MOINS C'EST MIEUX

Si on se laisse impressionner par la présentation extérieure de l'Eclipse, on s'imagine facilement au volant d'un bolide capable d'en découdre avec une 911 Turbo S. Mais la réalité est tout autre… L'amateur de performances optera aussitôt pour le V6, plus puissant, mais son poids plus élevé modifie l'équilibre des masses et rend la voiture moins maniable et plus sous-vireuse. De son côté, le quatre cylindres s'avère moins porté sur les contraventions mais il rend la voiture beaucoup plus agréable à piloter sur une route sinueuse. Il faut aussi souligner que le diamètre de braquage est trop grand pour être serviable lorsque l'espace fait défaut.

Comme on est en droit de s'y attendre, la plate-forme du coupé est passablement plus rigide que celle du cabriolet bien que dans ce dernier, le dossier de la banquette arrière est fixe pour ajouter à la rigidité structurelle. Je tiens cependant à souligner qu'aucun des cabriolets essayés au fil des ans ne présentait de bruits inappropriés. Faut dire qu'ils étaient tous neufs… La position de conduite se trouve facilement et s'avère par la suite impeccable et le volant est à la fois précis et bavard sur le travail des roues. Le comportement routier de l'Eclipse est définitivement sous-vireur (l'avant refuse de tourner), surtout, comme on l'a vu, avec le V6. À moins d'entrer beaucoup trop rapidement dans une courbe, le simple levé du pied règle la situation.

Esthétiquement, la Mitsubishi Eclipse est encore dans le coup. Mais son habitacle et son comportement routier ne font pas le poids. Heureusement, il reste la garantie, la meilleure de l'industrie.

Alain Morin

PHOTOS : GILLES OLIVIER

Catégorie	Cabriolet, Coupé
Échelle de prix	24 498 $ à 35 998 $
Garanties	5 ans/100 000 km, 10 ans/160 000 km
Assemblage	Normal, Illinois, É-U
Cote d'assurance	n.d.

CHÂSSIS - DONNÉES POUR GT-P SPYDER

Emp/lon/lar/haut	2 575/4 583/1 835/1 375 mm
Coffre	147 litres
Réservoir	67 litres
Nombre coussins sécurité	4
Antipatinage / contrôle stabilité	oui / oui
Suspension avant	indépendante, jambes de force
Suspension arrière	indépendante, multibras
Freins avant / arrière	disque (ABS) / disque (ABS)
Direction	à crémaillère, ass. variable
Diamètre de braquage	12,2 m
Pneus avant / arrière	P235/45R18 / P235/45R18
Poids	1 675 kg
Capacité de remorquage	n.d.

COMPOSANTES MÉCANIQUES

GS Coupe, GS Spyder	
Cylindrée, soupapes, alim.	4L 2,4 litres 16 s atmos.
Puissance / Couple	162 chevaux / 162 lb-pi
Tr. base (opt) / rouage base (opt)	M5 (A4) / Tr
0-100 / 80-120 / 100-0 km/h	9,0 s / 8,0 s (est) / n.d.
Type ess. / ville / autoroute	Ordinaire / 10,6 / 7,3 l/100 km

GT-P Coupe, GT-P Spyder	
Cylindrée, soupapes, alim.	V6 3,8 litres 24 s atmos.
Puissance / Couple	265 chevaux / 262 lb-pi
Tr. base (opt) / rouage base (opt)	M6 (A5) / Tr
0-100 / 80-120 / 100-0 km/h	6,8 s / 6,3 s / 40,1 m
Type ess. / ville / autoroute	Super / 13,1 / 8,0 l/100 km

DANS LA MÊME CATÉGORIE

Coupé : Dodge Challenger, Ford Mustang, Honda Accord, Nissan Altima, Volkswagen Eos

Cabriolet : Chrysler Sebring, Ford Mustang, Volkswagen Eos

DU NOUVEAU EN 2011

Aucun changement majeur

NOS IMPRESSIONS

Agrément de conduite :	6/10
Fiabilité :	6/10
Sécurité :	8/10
Qualités hivernales :	7/10
Espace intérieur :	7/10
Confort :	7/10

www.mitsubishi-motors.ca

Plus d'informations dans la section statistiques en dernière partie du Guide

SAVOIR RESTER OU NE PAS SAVOIR PARTIR?

Il y a de ces voitures, comme de certains humains, qui ne savent pas partir. Pour le meilleur et pour le pire. Le Mitsubishi Endeavor pourrait donner des cours en la matière tant sa présence sur notre marché, depuis quelques années, nous semble précaire. Pourtant, il revient en 2011, fidèle au poste, prêt au combat. Éric Lapointe ajouterait « les chums, c'est fait pour ça », mais l'Endeavor n'a pas beaucoup d'amis...

Ce n'est pas parce que l'Endeavor est l'un des VUS intermédiaires les plus discrets dans le paysage automobile québécois qu'il n'a pas de qualités. Bien au contraire! Lors de son dévoilement en 2004, il avait même été l'un des coups de cœur du *Guide de l'auto*. Sa silhouette tourmentée et le réseau ténu de Mitsubishi constituaient cependant des bémols majeurs. Depuis, sa carrosserie a été modernisée et Mitsubishi compte maintenant une trentaine de concessionnaires... mais l'Endeavor ne se vend toujours pas!

MAUDIT RAFFINEMENT

Une des raisons principales de cet échec vient plutôt de la concurrence qui a la mauvaise habitude de toujours se raffiner, un élément qui manque cruellement à l'Endeavor. Les lignes ne sont pas laides du tout, mais avouez qu'elles commencent à dater face aux nouveaux Chevrolet Traverse, Kia Sorento ou Mazda CX-9. Et la qualité très, très ordinaire de la peinture de quelques exemplaires vus ici et là ne plaide pas en sa faveur. Dans l'habitacle, vaste, c'est encore plus évident. Le volant, selon votre journaliste préféré, n'est pas très joli mais c'est surtout l'écran central, qui autrefois accueillait le système GPS, qui détonne. Il ne sert plus maintenant qu'à informer sur certains paramètres du véhicule. Posé — foutu serait plus juste — en plein milieu du tableau de bord sans aucune recherche stylistique, il semble toujours prêt à entrer dans son réceptacle. Mais non, il est malheureusement fixe. D'un autre côté, la qualité d'assemblage est très correcte, les diverses commandes sont simples à comprendre et à manipuler et les jauges, bleutées la nuit venue, sont du plus bel effet. Une bonne note également pour le système audio Rockford Acoustic Design. Les sièges sont confortables et une bonne position de conduite se trouve aisément même si le volant n'est pas ajustable en profondeur. Les gens montant à l'arrière ne seront pas en reste avec de l'espace à revendre et une banquette au confort surprenant. Contrairement à la concurrence, Mitsubishi n'offre pas de troisième rangée, ce qui est quasiment une bénédiction quand on voit ce qu'ils ont fait avec celle de l'Outlander... Le coffre est vaste et bien aménagé et la vitre du hayon ouvre séparément, ce qui permet de transporter plus facilement de longs objets.

MOTEUR JUSTE MAIS BON

Côté mécanique, on ne s'est pas trop cassé le coco. On retrouve un seul moteur, une seule transmission et un seul rouage. Le V6 de 3,8 litres n'est pas très puissant mais son couple élevé compense. Comme l'Endeavor pèse près de 1 900 kilos, on serait en droit de

FEU VERT

Lignes originales
Habitacle confortable
Excellente garantie
Comportement routier sans histoire
Performances correctes

FEU ROUGE

Design du tableau de bord controversé
Transmission dépassée
Consommation assez élevée
Valeur de revente dramatique
Véhicule en fin de carrière

s'attendre à des performances diminuées. Pourtant, le 0-100 est parcouru en 9,1 secondes, ce qui n'est pas mal du tout. Lors de telles accélérations, le bruit dans l'habitacle devient passablement élevé. Signe que ce Mitsubishi a de l'âge, sa transmission automatique ne comporte que quatre rapports alors que de nos jours, les boîtes à cinq rapports commencent à être obsolètes... Mais il faut avouer qu'elle travaille fort bien même si son mode manuel n'est utile que lorsqu'on remorque une charge, laquelle ne doit pas dépasser 3500 livres (1588 kilos). Depuis l'année dernière, les versions à traction sont abandonnées. Il reste un rouage intégral assez primitif mais qui, lui aussi, fait bien son boulot. Comme celui de ses principales rivales, il ne possède pas de démultipliée, ce qui empêche l'Endeavor, malgré ses airs costauds, d'affronter l'Everest. Il ne faudrait pas, non plus, croire qu'il est à l'égal de ceux qui équipent les Mitsubishi de course qui ont gagné à peu près tout ce qui peut se gagner en rallye. Bref, un rouage intégral, une transmission à quatre rapports seulement et un véhicule lourd, ça se traduit par une consommation assez élevée, selon les standards actuels.

Le châssis fait preuve d'une belle rigidité et les suspensions privilégient le confort au détriment de la tenue de route. Une conduite le moindrement sportive amène beaucoup de sous-virage tandis que la caisse penche passablement. Cependant, lorsqu'on respecte les limites de l'Endeavor, on découvre un véhicule agréable à conduire malgré une direction un peu trop vague. Ce n'est qu'au passage de bosses ou trous (en nombre équivalent sur notre réseau routier!) que les suspensions indépendantes aux quatre roues semblent perdre de leurs moyens et deviennent alors plus dures. Les freins, de leur côté, n'affichent pas le mordant désiré même si les distances d'arrêt sont très correctes.

L'Endeavor, comme on vient de le voir, n'est pas un vilain véhicule. Certes dépassé en termes de style et de mécanique, il présente tout de même de belles qualités. Mais il est évident que Mitsubishi a soit lancé la serviette, soit s'apprête à dévoiler une deuxième génération. Si cette dernière option est retenue, il est à peu près certain qu'un moteur plus puissant, la transmission très sophistiquée de l'Outlander XLS et un aspect plus moderne — particulièrement dans l'habitacle — seraient à l'ordre du jour. Pour l'instant, l'Endeavor se démarque surtout grâce à des vendeurs motivés à voir leurs quelques exemplaires sortir de leur salle d'exposition!

Alain Morin

PHOTOS: MITSUBISHI

MITSUBISHI ENDEAVOR

Catégorie	VUS
Échelle de prix	39 298 $ (2010)
Garanties	5 ans/100 000 km, 10 ans/160 000 km
Assemblage	Normal, Illinois, É-U
Cote d'assurance	n.d.

CHÂSSIS - DONNÉES POUR SE AWD

Emp/lon/lar/haut	2 750/4 830/1 870/1 769 mm
Coffre	1 152 à 2 163 litres
Réservoir	81 litres
Nombre coussins sécurité	6
Antipatinage / contrôle stabilité	oui / oui
Suspension avant	indépendante, jambes de force
Suspension arrière	indépendante, multibras
Freins avant / arrière	disque (ABS) / disque (ABS)
Direction	à crémaillère, assistée
Diamètre de braquage	11,7 m
Pneus avant / arrière	P235/65R17 / P235/65R17
Poids	1 855 kg
Capacité de remorquage	1 588 kg (3 500 lb)

COMPOSANTES MÉCANIQUES

SE AWD

Cylindrée, soupapes, alim.	V6 3,8 litres 24 s atmos.
Puissance / Couple	225 chevaux / 255 lb-pi
Tr. base (opt) / rouage base (opt)	A4 / Int
0-100 / 80-120 / 100-0 km/h	9,1 s / 7,4 s / 43,0 m
Type ess. / ville / autoroute	Ordinaire / 14,2 / 10,3 l/100 km

DANS LA MÊME CATÉGORIE

Chevrolet Traverse, Ford Edge, GMC Acadia, Honda Pilot, Hyundai Veracruz, Jeep Grand Cherokee, Kia Sorento, Mazda CX-9, Subaru Tribeca, Toyota Highlander

DU NOUVEAU EN 2011

Aucun changement majeur

NOS IMPRESSIONS

Agrément de conduite :	7/10
Fiabilité :	6/10
Sécurité :	8/10
Qualités hivernales :	8/10
Espace intérieur :	8/10
Confort :	8/10

www.mitsubishi-motors.ca

Plus d'informations dans la section statistiques en dernière partie du Guide

LE PILIER DU TEMPLE

Il est inutile de se «faire des à croire», comme dirait mon oncle Ernest; si la Lancer ne faisait pas partie de la gamme de modèles de ce constructeur, Mitsubishi ne serait plus présent sur notre marché. Ce qui explique sans doute pourquoi on l'apprête à toutes les sauces afin d'attirer le plus de clients possible. Il faut également souligner qu'il s'agit d'une voiture dotée d'une excellente plate-forme qui se prête fort bien à la multiplication des modèles.

En effet, on nous propose la Lancer en version régulière, en Sportback cinq portes et la spectaculaire Evolution à rouage intégral et moteur dérivé des courses de rallyes. Et même si ce n'est pas le sujet de cet essai, cette même plate-forme est utilisée avec succès sur l'Outlander.

LA FONDATION

Même si ce constructeur aime à parler de ses modèles un peu plus sophistiqués, il n'en demeure pas moins que le fer de lance de Mitsubishi sur notre marché est la Lancer dans sa version la plus économique. À part quelques fioritures reprises sur les autres versions, on retrouve la même silhouette élégante dont les angles relativement aigus la démarquent des autres compactes de sa catégorie. Notamment, la partie avant très verticale qui confère une allure plus frappante à ce modèle. Soulignons également que la finition extérieure est correcte. Par contre, si le tableau de bord se veut simple et bien agencé, il faut déplorer la qualité des plastiques utilisés. Comme la fourchette de prix varie largement d'un modèle à l'autre, si cette approche est adéquate sur un modèle de base, elle le sera moins sur une version Evo dont le prix frise les 50000$! Toujours au chapitre de l'habitacle, il faut préciser que les commandes sont simples, faciles à opérer et je crois que personne ne s'en plaindra.

Le moteur de série est un quatre cylindres de 2,0 litres d'une puissance de 152 chevaux. Ses prestations sont dans la bonne moyenne, mais il devient assez bruyant à haut régime. Il est associé de série à une boîte manuelle à cinq rapports. Par ailleurs, le modèle GTS est propulsé par un autre quatre cylindres. Il s'agit d'un moteur de 2,4 litres produisant 168 chevaux et il est lui aussi couplé à une boîte manuelle à cinq rapports. Dans les deux cas, une boîte à rapports continuellement variables est offerte en option. Il faut souligner au passage que Mitsubishi maîtrise assez bien cette technologie et cette transmission devrait plaire à une bonne majorité d'acheteurs.

La Lancer se révèle sur la route une voiture bien équilibrée dont la plate-forme très rigide procure une bonne stabilité tant en virage qu'en ligne droite. Et pour plusieurs, une alléchante garantie est l'argument final pour prendre leur décision.

RALLIART ET SPORTBACK

Dans le dédale des modèles proposés par Mitsubishi, on trouve les versions Ralliart qui disposent d'un moteur plus puissant aux performances plus sportives. Il s'agit d'un quatre cylindres de 2,0 litres turbocompressé d'une puissance de 237 chevaux et relayé par une

FEU VERT

Feu vert
Multiplicité de modèles
Excellente garantie
Version Ralliart
Hatchback cinq portes
Bonne tenue de route

FEU ROUGE

Plastiques de l'habitacle à revoir
Consommation élevée (moteurs turbo)
Absence de boîte manuelle à six rapports
Suspension ultra ferme (Evo)

boîte automatique à six rapports. Cette boîte Sportronic à double embrayage est d'ailleurs la seule proposée. Par contre, comme l'ont souligné les essayeurs de notre match des sportives compactes en première partie de cet ouvrage, cette transmission semble dotée d'un temps de réponse assez particulier. En plus, les Ralliart sont offertes avec une transmission intégrale passablement efficace et raffinée. Comme il se doit sur des versions similaires, la suspension est plus sportive, les pneus plus performants tandis que des artifices visuels permettent à votre entourage de savoir que vous avez opté pour le « gros modèle ».

Cette version est disponible sur la berline et également sur la Sportback cinq portes. Il s'agit dans ce cas d'une heureuse combinaison de carrosserie pratique, d'un moteur performant et d'une voiture passablement agréable à conduire. C'est vraiment joindre l'utile à l'agréable. Par ailleurs, si les performances de la Ralliart ne vous intéressent pas, mais que la configuration de la Sportback répond à vos besoins, il est possible de la commander avec le même moteur que celui de la berline GTS, soit un quatre cylindres de 2,4 litres qui est offert de série avec la boîte manuelle à cinq rapports ou la CVT en option.

VIVA L'EVOLUTION

Après avoir été privé de la Lancer Evo pendant des années pour une vague histoire de pare-chocs, le constructeur peut maintenant l'offrir aux conducteurs enthousiastes. Elle est munie d'un moteur de 2,0 litres turbo d'une puissance de 291 chevaux. Une transmission manuelle à cinq rapports est de série tandis qu'il est possible de commander, comme sur la Ralliart, la boîte SST à six rapports et à double embrayage.

Bien entendu, un rouage intégral de haute technicité se charge de transmettre toute cette puissance au bitume. Aussi prestigieuse soit-elle, et malgré des performances en mesure d'inquiéter bien d'autres sportives, le caractère assez radical de cette voiture n'est pas de nature à plaire à tous. Pour plusieurs, les modèles Ralliart sont suffisamment puissants et performants pour intéresser les amateurs de voiture sportive, mais leur suspension moins rigide les rend plus agréables en usage quotidien. Il s'agit là d'une solution de juste milieu.

Denis Duquet

PHOTOS : MITSUBISHI

Catégorie	Berline, *Hatchback*
Échelle de prix	15 998 $ à 51 798 $
Garanties	3 ans/60 000 km, 5 ans/100 000 km
Assemblage	Mizushima, Japon
Cote d'assurance	pauvre

CHÂSSIS - DONNÉES POUR SPORTBACK RALLIART

Emp/lon/lar/haut	2 635/4 585/1 760/1 515 mm
Coffre	390 à 1 492 litres
Réservoir	55 litres
Nombre coussins sécurité	6
Antipatinage / contrôle stabilité	oui / oui
Suspension avant	indépendante, jambes de force
Suspension arrière	indépendante, multibras
Freins avant / arrière	disque (ABS) / disque (ABS)
Direction	à crémaillère, assistée
Diamètre de braquage	10,0 m
Pneus avant / arrière	P215/45R18 / P215/45R18
Poids	1 620 kg
Capacité de remorquage	n.d.

COMPOSANTES MÉCANIQUES

DE, SE

Cylindrée, soupapes, alim.	4L 2,0 litres 16 s atmos.
Puissance / Couple	152 chevaux / 146 lb-pi
Tr. base (opt) / rouage base (opt)	M5 (CVT) / Tr
0-100 / 80-120 / 100-0 km/h	9,1 s / 6,8 s / n.d.
Type ess. / ville / autoroute	Ordinaire / 9,4 / 6,5 l/100 km

GTS, Sportback GTS

Cylindrée, soupapes, alim.	4L 2,4 litres 16 s atmos.
Puissance / Couple	168 chevaux / 167 lb-pi
Tr. base (opt) / rouage base (opt)	M5 (CVT) / Tr
0-100 / 80-120 / 100-0 km/h	8,9 s / 6,8 s / 41,5 m
Type ess. / ville / autoroute	Ordinaire / 10,4 / 7,4 l/100 km

Ralliart, Sportback Ralliart
4L 2,0l, 237 ch, 253 lb-pi - 0-100: 7,8 s - 12,2 / 8,0 l/100 km

Evolution GSR, Evolution MR
4L 2,0 l, 291 ch, 300 lb-pi - 0-100: 5,6 s - 12,9 / 9,0 l/100 km

DANS LA MÊME CATÉGORIE

Acura CSX, Chevrolet Cruze, Dodge Caliber, Ford Focus, Honda Civic, Hyundai Elantra, Kia Forte, Mazda3, Nissan Sentra, Subaru Impreza, Suzuki SX-4, Toyota Corolla, Volkswagen Jetta

DU NOUVEAU EN 2011

Aucun changement majeur

NOS IMPRESSIONS

Agrément de conduite :	8/10
Fiabilité :	8/10
Sécurité :	10/10
Qualités hivernales :	7/10
Espace intérieur :	8/10
Confort :	7/10

www.mitsubishi-motors.ca

Plus d'informations dans la section statistiques en dernière partie du Guide

MITSUBISHI LANCER / SPORTBACK / EVOLUTION

« QUOSSÉ » QU'ON LUI A FAIT?

Le Mitsubishi Outlander est sans doute l'utilitaire compact le plus sportif du marché. Direction précise, suspension plus ferme qu'ailleurs, solide comportement... Bref, on l'aime. On aurait pu penser que la supertraction intégrale de la Lancer Evo allait accroître d'autant le plaisir de conduire. Pas tout à fait.

D'abord, un mot sur cette S-AWC: avec son différentiel actif, sa répartition avant de gauche à droite et son verrouillage 50/50, elle est d'une coche – non, deux coches - plus sophistiquée que ce qui se fait dans la catégorie. D'ailleurs, elle a été nommée Meilleure nouvelle technologie en 2009 par l'AJAC. Dans le Mitsubishi Outlander (version XLS seulement), elle permet encore plus d'assurance en route – spécifions toutefois que le mode « deux roues motrices » n'est alors plus disponible.

Cette supertraction vient néanmoins jouer un drôle de tour aux autres organes de l'Outlander, qu'il a fallu recalibrer. La puissance n'a plus la même pureté que pour l'Outlander V6 (3,0 litres, 230 chevaux) à traction intégrale régulière (et qui, heureusement, demeure au catalogue). On sent de la rugosité sous le pied droit, comme si le moteur se payait un début d'asthme. Ça nous a étonnés au point de soulever le capot et nous assurer qu'il y avait bien un V6 là-dedans, pas un quatre cylindres!

Aussi, la boîte automatique six rapports est plus lente à réagir et les palettes au volant (qui ne montent que dans ce XLS) n'ont plus l'instantanéité qu'on leur connaissait. Encore là, nous nous sommes interrogés à savoir si nous n'avions pas affaire à une CVT... C'est demander beaucoup, mais n'y aurait-il pas eu lieu de choisir la belle boîte à double embrayage Ralliart?

Ceci dit, ne « bitchons » pas trop les CVT. Pour l'Outlander de base (ES), avec le quatre cylindres de 2,4 litres, la CVT fait du bon boulot. Il faudrait mettre juste un peu plus de jus que les actuels 168 chevaux et l'affaire serait ketchup. Le véhicule garde ses bons attributs sportifs et on peut même lui accoler l'AWD. Reste que pour des reprises en profondeur et une boîte automatique qui se comporte... en boîte automatique, il faut le V6 avec traction intégrale « normale ». À notre avis, c'est encore là que l'affaire se passe et on évite, du coup, de faire grimper la facture au-delà des 35 000 $.

PLUS SPORTIF QU'AILLEURS

L'Outlander, qui partage sa plate-forme avec la Lancer, profite d'une suspension plus rigide que la concurrence, sans pour autant être « cogneuse ». Ça se traduit par une bonne tenue de route, même en version de base deux roues motrices. Le fait que le toit, plutôt que le capot, soit en aluminium joue avantageusement sur le centre de gravité. La direction est d'une belle précision, le petit rayon de braquage facilite les manœuvres en stationnement et le freinage est convaincant. Bref, le comportement est agréablement sportif et le véhicule peut fièrement arborer cette calandre en nez de requin empruntée à la Lancer – et qui lui donne une belle allure

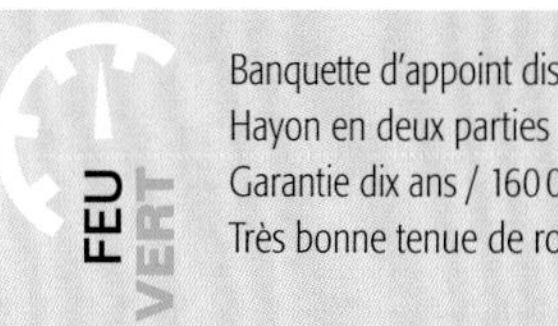

FEU VERT

Banquette d'appoint disponible
Hayon en deux parties
Garantie dix ans / 160 000 km
Très bonne tenue de route

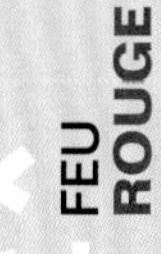

FEU ROUGE

La facture grimpe vite…
Troisième banquette illogique
Intérieur en plastique plutôt commun
« Quossé » qu'on a fait à la variante XLS ?

menaçante. Toutefois, il faudrait repenser ce hayon pas mal tourmenté et peu contemporain (vous aimez ces phares arrière « picotés » ?). Mais bon, c'est le prix à payer pour cette ouverture en deux parties qui simplifie le chargement.

UN SIÈGE D'APPOINT, POINT.

Simpliste, l'habitacle de l'Outlander et ce n'est certes pas ici qu'on se sent perdu. Même que le coup d'œil manque de *punch* en raison de ces commandes peu nombreuses et de ces lignes trop épurées. Mais ça a le mérite d'être convivial et facile à apprivoiser. Sauf… pour ce système audio/navigation ; les petits pitons, difficiles à enfoncer, sont répartis à l'encontre de la plus élémentaire des compréhensions, mon cher Watson. Et en plus, il coûte cher…

Dans l'Outlander de base, les plastiques sont communs et pas toujours de bonne facture. On préfère le raffinement du cuir que viennent enjoliver des surjets blancs, mais on doit souffrir des sièges moins enveloppants. L'insonorisation est dans la bonne moyenne, l'assemblage serré et les rangements, disséminés ici et là, pratiques. La vision est correcte aux quatre coins et l'assistance au recul n'est pas nécessaire.

Côté chargement, c'est généreux, avec plus de 2 000 litres derrière les sièges avant – assez pour qu'on y installe une 3e banquette (V6, uniquement). Chez les utilitaires compacts, seul le Toyota Rav4 a osé. Mais… 3e banquette, il faut ici le dire vite ; parlons plutôt d'un siège d'appoint. Et avant de vous y commettre, demandez-vous si vous aimez vos genoux ; assis presque à niveau du sol, vous les verrez de près…

Vite fait, l'Outlander peut sembler un tantinet plus coûteux que ses concurrents, mais c'est parce qu'il s'amène de série avec les sièges et les rétros chauffants, ainsi que les commandes audio au volant. Là s'arrêtent les bonnes nouvelles ; ensuite, la facture grimpe vite. Traction intégrale, moteur plus puissant, ajoutez toit ouvrant et démarrage sans clé… Au fil des années, les prix ont augmenté alors que l'offre s'est, ailleurs, peaufinée. Des concurrents japonais demandent désormais moins cher (tel le Rav4 : surpris, hein ?). L'Outlander ne devrait pas se montrer aussi gourmand. Une garantie motopropulseur de dix ans, même fort généreuse, n'explique pas tout…

Nadine Filion

PHOTOS : ALAIN MORIN

Catégorie	VUS
Échelle de prix	25 498 $ à 34 498 $ (2010)
Garanties	5 ans/100 000 km, 10 ans/160 000 km
Assemblage	Mizushima, Japon
Cote d'assurance	passable

CHÂSSIS - DONNÉES POUR XLS 4RM

Emp/lon/lar/haut	2 670/4 640/1 800/1 680 mm
Coffre	1 014 à 2 056 litres
Réservoir	60 litres
Nombre coussins sécurité	6
Antipatinage / contrôle stabilité	oui / oui
Suspension avant	indépendante, jambes de force
Suspension arrière	indépendante, multibras
Freins avant / arrière	disque (ABS) / disque (ABS)
Direction	à crémaillère, assistée
Diamètre de braquage	10,6 m
Pneus avant / arrière	P225/55R18 / P225/55R18
Poids	1 715 kg
Capacité de remorquage	1 588 kg (3 500 lb)

COMPOSANTES MÉCANIQUES

ES 2RM

Cylindrée, soupapes, alim.	4L 2,4 litres 16 s atmos.
Puissance / Couple	168 chevaux / 167 lb-pi
Tr. base (opt) / rouage base (opt)	CVT / Tr
0-100 / 80-120 / 100-0 km/h	9,8 s / 7,5 s / 43,0 m
Type ess. / ville / autoroute	Ordinaire / 10,5 / 7,8 l/100 km

LS 4RM

Cylindrée, soupapes, alim.	V6 3,0 litres 24 s atmos.
Puissance / Couple	230 chevaux / 215 lb-pi
Tr. base (opt) / rouage base (opt)	A6 / Int
0-100 / 80-120 / 100-0 km/h	8,8 s / 7,6 s / 40,3 m
Type ess. / ville / autoroute	Ordinaire / 12,0 / 8,2 l/100 km

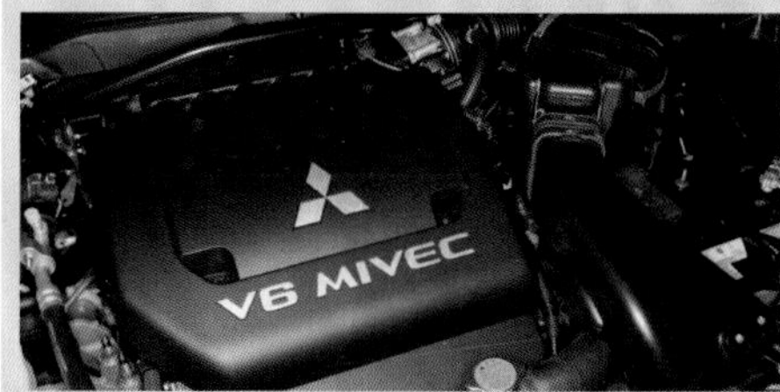

DANS LA MÊME CATÉGORIE

Chevrolet Equinox, Dodge Nitro, Ford Escape, Honda CR-V, Hyundai Santa Fe, Jeep Liberty, Mazda CX-7, Mazda Tribute, Nissan Rogue, Subaru Forester, Suzuki Grand Vitara, Toyota RAV4, Volkswagen Tiguan

DU NOUVEAU EN 2011

Aucun changement majeur

NOS IMPRESSIONS

Agrément de conduite :	8/10
Fiabilité :	8/10
Sécurité :	10/10
Qualités hivernales :	8/10
Espace intérieur :	8/10
Confort :	8/10

www.mitsubishi-motors.ca

Plus d'informations dans la section statistiques en dernière partie du Guide

UNE EFFRONTÉE QUI SE RAFFINE

Nissan a célébré l'an dernier le 40e anniversaire de sa légendaire 240Z en lançant la sixième génération de la série qu'elle a engendrée. La 370Z prenait le relais de la 350Z qui a fait renaître avec succès la Z après une éclipse de sept ans. Plus moderne, plus puissante, mieux équipée et moins chère, elle a plutôt fière allure. Pour l'âme et le cœur, par contre, c'est une autre histoire.

La svelte 240Z a marqué le début d'une nouvelle ère et mis fin du même coup au règne du « sports car » britannique et de ses semblables en 1970. Cette première « Z » se vendait 4000$ au Québec en 1970. Elle était belle, performante bien équipée et les premiers acheteurs furent bientôt ravis de la découvrir également fiable.

La 350Z, une deux places élancée, performante, solide et bien équipée, marqua le retour aux valeurs qui avaient fait le succès de la pionnière. Elle fut couronnée Voiture de l'année, Design de l'année et meilleure nouvelle sportive au pays par l'AJAC en 2003.

EN PLUS RAFFINÉ

La 370Z est venue la remplacer sept ans plus tard. Sa carrosserie un peu plus courte, large et basse est posée sur un empattement abrégé de 100 mm. Ses lignes sont plus fluides mais la nouvelle Z est surtout plus légère que sa devancière de près de 60 kg et moins chère de près de 10000$ malgré un équipement plus complet, une finition plus soignée et un nouveau V6 de 3,7 litres plus puissant et moins assoiffé.

La 370Z était le pivot parfait pour notre match des sportives de l'édition précédente. Elle y a décroché la deuxième place et fait grande impression mais pas toujours pour les bonnes raisons. Au

meilleures notes du groupe pour la silhouette et le freinage s'opposent les pires pour le confort et le silence de roulement, une soute à bagages peu profonde et le peu de rangement dans l'habitacle. Elle fut également de loin la plus rapide dans notre épreuve sur piste à Sanair, s'exécutant avec une brusquerie certaine en exploitant à fond l'adhérence des pneus plus larges du groupe Sport.

Le même groupe Sport ajoute des disques ventilés de plus grand diamètre. Le freinage est d'ailleurs une force de ce modèle. Ses 36,3 mètres en freinage de 100 km/h est une des distances les plus courtes que nous ayons mesurées. Par contre, la pédale est sensible et difficile à moduler en conduite normale.

LA LOI DU COUPLE

Les 332 chevaux du V6 en imposent sur papier mais ne se manifestent qu'à 7000 tr/min et le couple maximum de 270 lb-pi n'est produit à 5200 tr/min. Avec la boîte manuelle à 6 rapports, la Z passe de 0 à 100 km/h en 6,0 secondes. À titre de comparaison, le coupé BMW 135i qui l'a devancée au match de l'an dernier se contentait de 300 chevaux à 5800 tr/min mais son couple maxi de

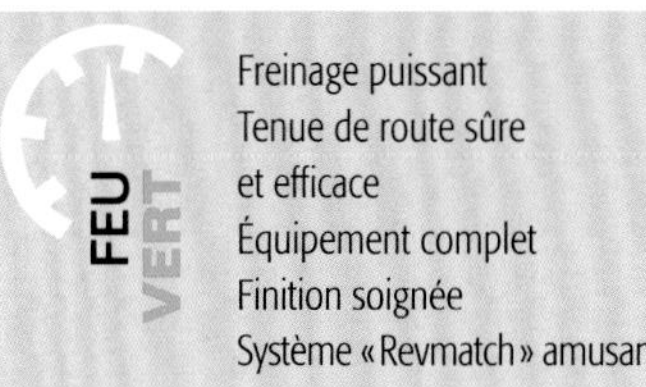

FEU VERT

Freinage puissant
Tenue de route sûre et efficace
Équipement complet
Finition soignée
Système « Revmatch » amusant

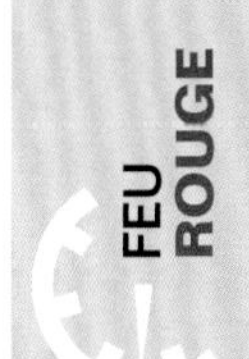

FEU ROUGE

V6 faible en couple et en charisme
Direction peu sensible
Bruit de roulement prononcé
Rétroviseur gauche bloque la vue
Soute à bagages étriquée

317 lb-pi était livré dès 1 400 tr/min. Or, il a bouclé le 0 à 100 km/h en 5,2 secondes malgré ses quelque 40 kilos en plus.

Le V6 de la 370Z a peu de caractère et sa sonorité n'a rien d'inspirant non plus. Cette courbe de couple linéaire atteint son apogée à régime élevé pour un moteur atmosphérique de cette cylindrée. La Z met d'ailleurs 6,45 secondes à passer de 80 à 120 km/h en 3e alors que le coupé 135i s'exécute en 4,24 secondes. Cette souplesse découle d'un couple abondant à bas et moyen régime.

PROGRAMME COMPLET

À défaut d'une mécanique envoûtante, la 370Z propose un équipement moderne qui comprend le démarrage sans clé, la téléphonie Bluetooth, la radio satellite XM, un système de navigation sur disque dur avec écran tactile, un autre disque dur de 9,3 gigaoctet pour les fichiers numériques et un port USB pour iPod et semblables.

La position de conduite est correcte et le volant gainé de cuir impeccable. La boîte de vitesse est dure mais assez précise et rapide. On peut s'amuser en activant le dispositif « SynchroRev Match » qui ajuste le régime du moteur quand on rétrograde. Cette innovation est amusante et efficace mais se désactive heureusement en appuyant sur un bouton.

La 370Z est civilisée en ville mais devient bruyante sur une chaussée le moindrement texturée ou rude. Cet effet de résonance est typique sur une voiture sport dont la coque rigide est gage de tenue de route précise.

Avec un équilibre des masses quasi idéal, la Z s'inscrit en courbe sans hésitation. Elle pivote aussitôt et on ajuste facilement la dérive à l'accélérateur. Elle est très sensible aux transferts de poids, par contre, et l'arrière s'allège et décroche assez facilement si on braque en freinant. Le survirage se contrôle sans peine, par contre.

Dans l'ensemble, la 370Z est assez réussie, malgré son côté tapageur. Ne lui demandez simplement pas d'être un pur sang et une grande sportive avec un tel moteur.

Marc Lachapelle

PHOTOS : MARC LACHAPELLE

NISSAN 370Z

Catégorie	Coupé, *Roadster*
Échelle de prix	40 498 $ à 46 998 $ (2010)
Garanties	3 ans/60 000 km, 5 ans/100 000 km
Assemblage	Tochigi, Japon
Cote d'assurance	passable

CHÂSSIS - DONNÉES POUR 370Z ROADSTER TOURISME

Emp/lon/lar/haut	2 550/4 246/1 845/1 326 mm
Coffre	119 litres
Réservoir	72 litres
Nombre coussins sécurité	6
Antipatinage / contrôle stabilité	oui / oui
Suspension avant	indépendante, double triangulation
Suspension arrière	indépendante, multibras
Freins avant / arrière	disque (ABS) / disque (ABS)
Direction	à crémaillère, ass. variable
Diamètre de braquage	10,8 m
Pneus avant / arrière	P225/50R18 / P245/45R18
Poids	1 573 kg
Capacité de remorquage	n.d.

COMPOSANTES MÉCANIQUES

Coupe, Roadster	
Cylindrée, soupapes, alim.	V6 3,7 litres 24 s atmos.
Puissance / Couple	332 chevaux / 270 lb-pi
Tr. base (opt) / rouage base (opt)	M6 (A7) / Prop
0-100 / 80-120 / 100-0 km/h	6,0 s / 6,4 s / 42,1 m
Type ess. / ville / autoroute	Super / 11,9 / 8,1 l/100 km

DANS LA MÊME CATÉGORIE

Audi TT, BMW Série 3, Ford Mustang, Infiniti G, Lotus Elise, Mazda RX-8, Mercedes-Benz Classe SLK, Porsche Boxster, Porsche Cayman

DU NOUVEAU EN 2011

Aucun changement majeur pour le coupé, nouveau roadster

NOS IMPRESSIONS

Agrément de conduite :	8/10
Fiabilité :	8/10
Sécurité :	8/10
Qualités hivernales :	4/10
Espace intérieur :	6/10
Confort :	6/10

www.nissan.ca

Plus d'informations dans la section statistiques en dernière partie du Guide

UNE BONNE VALEUR

Les constructeurs nippons ne lâchent jamais. Même si leurs véhicules ne sont pas toujours dans le coup, ils ne cessent de les améliorer au fur et à mesure des générations. Nous en avons la preuve avec l'Altima. Cette berline a toujours été très populaire, mais était loin d'être parfaite lors de son arrivée sur le marché. Sa finition, sa suspension arrière manquant de finesse, ainsi que ses matériaux plus ou moins raffinés étaient à porter à la colonne des points négatifs lors de sa première mouture.

Les variantes se sont succédées jusqu'à l'an dernier, alors que de nombreuses modifications l'ont rendue plus homogène.

L'ÉLÉGANCE RAPPORTE

Si l'Altima jouit d'une très forte popularité depuis ses débuts, c'est en grande partie en raison de sa silhouette. En effet, cette berline, suivie du coupé par la suite, est très réussie sur le plan visuel. Elle a été l'une des premières à adopter des phares de route se prolongeant sur les ailes avant pendant qu'à l'arrière, ses feux à lentille cristalline la démarquaient du lot. Toujours dans le but de mettre l'Altima au goût du jour, celle-ci a connu plusieurs modifications esthétiques l'an dernier. La calandre, les phares avant et arrière ainsi que les pare-chocs ont été modifiés. Ce qui lui donne une allure plus moderne sans pour autant perdre cette apparence générale qui lui a valu sa popularité. Il est important de souligner que le coupé est encore mieux réussi sur le plan esthétique. À son volant, vous êtes assurés de faire tourner les têtes.

Enfin, dans l'habitacle, de nombreuses petites retouches, tant au niveau des commandes que dans le choix des différents matériaux, ont permis de corriger l'une des plus importantes lacunes de ces voitures, soit un tableau de bord qui semblait avoir été produit avec des matériaux de qualité inférieure. La situation s'est améliorée à ce chapitre alors que le tableau de bord est beaucoup moins décevant que par le passé. Les commandes sont plus intuitives et celles placées sur le volant tombent bien sous la main. De leur côté, les cadrans indicateurs sont bien placés et très faciles à consulter. Par contre, les commandes audio sont parfois déconcertantes et il est facile de confondre une commande pour une autre. Malgré tout, on a également progressé à ce chapitre.

Notre voiture d'essai était équipée d'une clé intelligente qui permet de déverrouiller les portières sans clé et de lancer le moteur en appuyant sur un bouton. Par contre, il est facile d'oublier la clé intelligente à l'intérieur ou de quitter la voiture sans l'apporter avec nous. Heureusement, un pictogramme nous rappelle que nous ne devons pas partir sans elle.

L'habitabilité est bonne avec des places avant spacieuses et confortables. C'est un peu moins réussi à l'arrière, alors que la

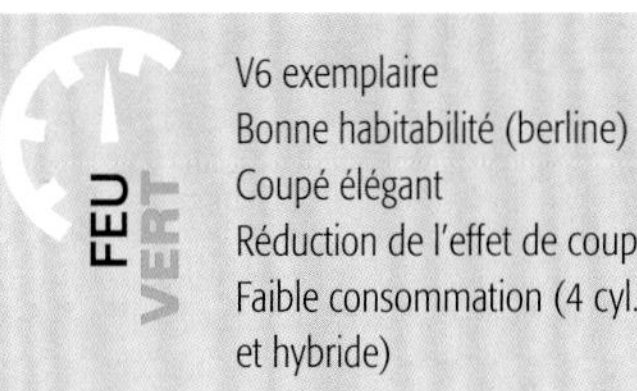

FEU VERT

- V6 exemplaire
- Bonne habitabilité (berline)
- Coupé élégant
- Réduction de l'effet de couple
- Faible consommation (4 cyl. et hybride)

FEU ROUGE

- Version de base dépouillée
- Boîte CVT (pour certains)
- Places arrière (coupé)
- Coffre petit (hybride)

banquette pourrait être plus confortable et offrir une assise légèrement plus haute afin d'accommoder les personnes de grande taille. Malheureusement, c'est beaucoup moins positif en ce qui concerne les places arrière du coupé qui sont difficiles d'accès et pas tellement confortables.

TRIPLE CHOIX

Il y a à peine quelques années encore, l'Altima n'était disponible qu'avec des moteurs thermiques. Chez Nissan on boudait les moteurs hybrides, car Carlos Ghosn, le grand patron, n'y croyait pas. Devant les succès de Toyota dans ce créneau, on s'est finalement révisé chez Nissan en commercialisant une Altima à moteur hybride utilisant, sous licence, la technologie Toyota. Avec son moteur quatre cylindres de 2,5 litres couplé à un moteur électrique et à une transmission CVT, cette Nissan plus écolo peut s'avérer une bonne alternative si la Toyota Camry Hybride ne vous intéresse pas.

En ce qui concerne les autres modèles à moteur thermique, la berline et le coupé offrent les mêmes groupes propulseurs. Le moteur de base est un quatre cylindres de 2,5 litres dont la réputation n'est plus à faire. Il produit 175 chevaux et ses performances sont acceptables. En effet, il permet de boucler le 0-100 kilomètre/heure en 8,6 secondes, alors que sa consommation moyenne enregistrée a été de 10,2 litres aux 100 km et ce, en plein hiver. Une boîte manuelle à six rapports est de série, tandis que l'automatique optionnelle est de type CVT, à rapports continuellement variables. Nissan maîtrise assez bien cette technologie émergente, tant en matière de fiabilité que d'efficacité. Par contre, la sonorité du moteur avec cette boîte en agace toujours plusieurs. Par ailleurs, il est possible de commander cette berline avec un moteur V6 de 3,5 litres, reconnu comme l'un des meilleurs de sa catégorie. Celui-ci n'est offert qu'avec la boîte CVT.

Sur la route, plusieurs améliorations sont à souligner. La suspension arrière, autrefois si revêche, a pris du galon en étant plus efficace pour absorber les trous et les bosses. Ça sautille beaucoup moins qu'avant sur mauvais revêtement. La direction demeure toujours un peu floue, mais reste dans la moyenne.

Denis Duquet

PHOTOS : NISSAN

NISSAN ALTIMA

Catégorie	Berline, Coupé
Échelle de prix	23 798 $ à 34 698 $ (2010)
Garanties	3 ans/60 000 km, 5 ans/100 000 km
Assemblage	Smyrna, Tennessee, É-U
Cote d'assurance	passable

CHÂSSIS - DONNÉES POUR 3.5 S BERLINE

Emp/lon/lar/haut	2 776/4 821/1 796/1 471 mm
Coffre	371 litres
Réservoir	76 litres
Nombre coussins sécurité	6
Antipatinage / contrôle stabilité	oui / oui
Suspension avant	indépendante, jambes de force
Suspension arrière	indépendante, multibras
Freins avant / arrière	disque (ABS) / disque (ABS)
Direction	à crémaillère, ass. variable
Diamètre de braquage	11,8 m
Pneus avant / arrière	P215/60R16 / P215/60R16
Poids	1 526 kg
Capacité de remorquage	454 kg (1 000 lb)

COMPOSANTES MÉCANIQUES

2.5 S Hybride	
Cylindrée, soupapes, alim.	4L 2,5 litres 16 s atmos.
Puissance / Couple	158 chevaux / 162 lb-pi
Tr. base (opt) / rouage base (opt)	CVT / Tr
0-100 / 80-120 / 100-0 km/h	8,0 s / 7,0 s / n.d.
Type ess. / ville / autoroute	Ordinaire / 5,6 / 5,9 l/100 km

2.5 S, 2.5 S Coupe	
Cylindrée, soupapes, alim.	4L 2,5 litres 16 s atmos.
Puissance / Couple	175 chevaux / 180 lb-pi
Tr. base (opt) / rouage base (opt)	M6 (CVT) / Tr
0-100 / 80-120 / 100-0 km/h	8,6 s / 7,1 s / 43,0 m
Type ess. / ville / autoroute	Ordinaire / 9,0 / 6,3 l/100 km

3.5 S, 3.5 SR, 3.5 SR Coupe	
Cylindrée, soupapes, alim.	V6 3,5 litres 24 s atmos.
Puissance / Couple	270 chevaux / 258 lb-pi
Tr. base (opt) / rouage base (opt)	CVT / Tr
0-100 / 80-120 / 100-0 km/h	6,5 s / 4,8 s / 42,0 m
Type ess. / ville / autoroute	Ordinaire / 11,4 / 7,3 l/100 km

DANS LA MÊME CATÉGORIE

Chevrolet Malibu, Dodge Avenger, Ford Fusion, Honda Accord, Hyundai Sonata, Mazda6, Subaru Legacy, Toyota Camry

DU NOUVEAU EN 2011

Aucun changement majeur

NOS IMPRESSIONS

Agrément de conduite :	8/10
Fiabilité :	6/10
Sécurité :	10/10
Qualités hivernales :	7/10
Espace intérieur :	8/10
Confort :	7/10

www.nissan.ca

Plus d'informations dans la section statistiques en dernière partie du Guide

GROSSES DIVERGENCES...

Jusqu'à l'an dernier, le Nissan Armada et l'Infiniti QX56 étaient quasiment des frères jumeaux, le QX étant, en fait, un Armada de luxe. Or, cette année, Infiniti présente un tout nouveau QX, ce qui amenait immédiatement à penser que l'Armada connaîtrait les mêmes changements. Eh non... L'Armada poursuit sa route tout seul (enfin, pas vraiment tout seul puisqu'il est accompagné des Chevrolet Tahoe, GMC Yukon, Ford Expedition et Toyota Sequoia), une route inexorable vers le maximum de litres, sinon sous le capot, du moins dans le coffre...

L'Armada n'est pas gros. Il est très gros. Nissan lui a d'ailleurs octroyé le châssis de la titanesque camionnette Titan, s'assurant ainsi de ne pas mal paraître dans la course vers l'immensité. Et l'entreprise japonaise a réussi au-delà de toutes les attentes. Quand une smart au complet tient dans ton empattement, que tu le veuilles ou non, t'es gros! La smart a beau être petite, il faut savoir regarder la réalité en face! Donc, les centres-villes, ce n'est pas pour l'Armada. Par contre, comme chacun le sait, ce que la nature n'a pas donné ici, elle le rend au centuple là. Et ce «là», c'est l'habitacle dont l'espace vivable tient plus du wagon que de l'automobile. Pour tout dire, il faut quasiment un interphone pour que les gens de la troisième rangée de sièges puissent communiquer avec les passagers avant!

Parlant des passagers avant, mentionnons qu'ils seraient bien mal avisés de se plaindre de leur sort. Leurs sièges sont très corrects et l'espace ne manque pas, que ce soit en avant, en arrière, au-dessus ou de chaque côté. Le conducteur a droit à un tableau de bord complet et bien lisible. Le seul élément offert en option est l'ensemble Technologie qui comprend un système de navigation, un disque dur de 9,3 Go, un système de reconnaissance vocale pour le système audio, la climatisation et j'en passe. La qualité des matériaux n'est pas optimale mais l'assemblage des divers panneaux est réussi.

COMME UN WAL MART VIDE

Les gens s'installant à la deuxième rangée bénéficient d'autant d'espace que s'ils s'assoyaient dans un autobus mais, au moins, le confort est plus relevé. Quant aux places de la troisième rangée, selon Nissan, elles peuvent accueillir trois personnes. Disons deux adultes de taille moyenne et nous serons plus près de la réalité. À la plus récente convention des CCPIUP (Coffres Caverneux des Plus Immenses Utilitaires de la Planète), l'Armada a connu beaucoup de succès avec son incroyable espace de chargement. Il aurait même remporté la chasse au trésor. À la fin de cette chasse, on y aurait retrouvé une smart, une voute du barrage de Manic 5 et un pétrolier. Mais on dit que ce dernier était vide, l'Armada ayant vidé tout son contenu pour se rendre à la convention. Je n'étais pas là mais je me fie à mes sources! Bref, c'est grand en masse, surtout lorsque tous les dossiers des sièges sont abaissés.

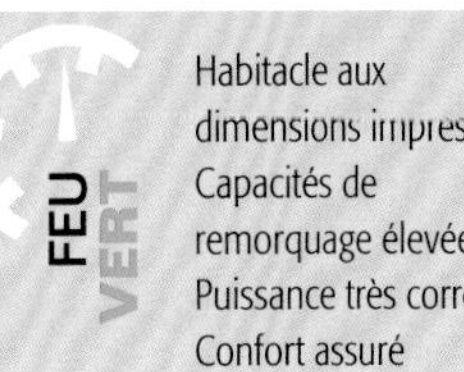

FEU VERT

Habitacle aux dimensions impressionnantes
Capacités de remorquage élevées
Puissance très correcte
Confort assuré
Équipement complet

FEU ROUGE

Nissan doit avoir des parts dans Shell...
Dimensions intimidantes
Diamètre de braquage immense
Quelques plastiques bon marché
Qu'en est-il de l'avenir?

Un véhicule comme l'Armada demande un moteur en conséquence... Nissan lui a donc placé le V8 de 5,6 litres du Titan sous le capot. Curieusement, j'ai peine à croire que ce moteur développe « seulement » 317 chevaux et 385 livres-pied de couple. En pleine accélération, et dans une belle sonorité que seul un gros V8 peut reproduire, on sent une bonne poussée. La transmission fait un peu figure de parent pauvre avec ses cinq rapports dans un monde où les boites à six ou même sept rapports sont de mise. Elle transmet le couple aux quatre roues grâce à un rouage intégral plutôt réussi avec sa gamme basse. L'Armada peut remorquer jusqu'à 4 082 kilos (9 000 livres), de quoi satisfaire bien des gens.

Bien entendu, nous avons ici affaire à un véhicule de plus de 2 600 kilos (5 753 livres !) qui possède un gros moteur, une boîte à cinq rapports seulement et un rouage intégral. En résumé, l'Armada boit au point de vider un pétrolier en moins de deux... Remarquez que sur la route, l'Armada affiche une certaine retenue. Mais un ou deux arrêts lui ouvrent les vannes comme c'est pas possible !

N'EN DEMANDONS PAS TROP, QUAND MÊME...

Sur la route, on se doute bien que l'Armada n'est pas un parangon de sportivité. Malgré son centre de gravité élevé et son poids monstrueux, la caisse ne penche pas trop en virage, selon les standards de la catégorie, s'entend. La direction est passablement précise et offre un retour d'information correct tandis que les freins réalisent de petits miracles lors de chaque arrêt d'urgence. Le véhicule est toutefois assez sensible aux vents latéraux, ce qui n'est pas surprenant compte tenu de ses dimensions. Quant au rayon de braquage, notre pétrolier demanderait à peine moins d'espace pour effectuer un demi-tour. La suspension arrière indépendante, contrairement à celle, rigide, du Titan, procure un confort très relevé, souligné par un silence de roulement de bon aloi. Nous ne sommes certes pas au volant d'une 370Z mais le comportement routier est quand même très satisfaisant.

Est-ce que l'Armada survivra au-delà de 2011? Personne ne le sait. Peut-être sera-t-il revu? Sans doute que Nissan ne voudra pas laisser le morceau aux seuls Américains et à Toyota. Après tout, Nissan vient de se lancer dans l'aventure (risquée) des véhicules commerciaux avec sa gamme NV (Nissan Van) qui utilise, comme l'Armada, le châssis modifié du Titan.

Alain Morin

PHOTOS : NISSAN

Catégorie	VUS
Échelle de prix	55 398 $ (2010)
Garanties	3 ans/60 000 km, 5 ans/100 000 km
Assemblage	Canton, Mississippi, États-Unis
Cote d'assurance	n.d.

CHÂSSIS - DONNÉES POUR PLATINE

Emp/lon/lar/haut	3 130/5 255/2 001/1 998 mm
Coffre	566 à 2 750 litres
Réservoir	105 litres
Nombre coussins sécurité	6
Antipatinage / contrôle stabilité	oui / oui
Suspension avant	indépendante, double triangulation
Suspension arrière	indépendante, double triangulation
Freins avant / arrière	disque (ABS) / disque (ABS)
Direction	à crémaillère, ass. variable
Diamètre de braquage	12,4 m
Pneus avant / arrière	P275/60R20 / P275/60R20
Poids	2 609 kg
Capacité de remorquage	4 082 kg (8 999 lb)

COMPOSANTES MÉCANIQUES

Platine	
Cylindrée, soupapes, alim.	V8 5,6 litres 32 s atmos.
Puissance / Couple	317 chevaux / 385 lb-pi
Tr. base (opt) / rouage base (opt)	A5 / 4x4
0-100 / 80-120 / 100-0 km/h	9,1 s / 8,2 s / 44,3 m
Type ess. / ville / autoroute	Ordinaire / 17,3 / 11,4 l/100 km

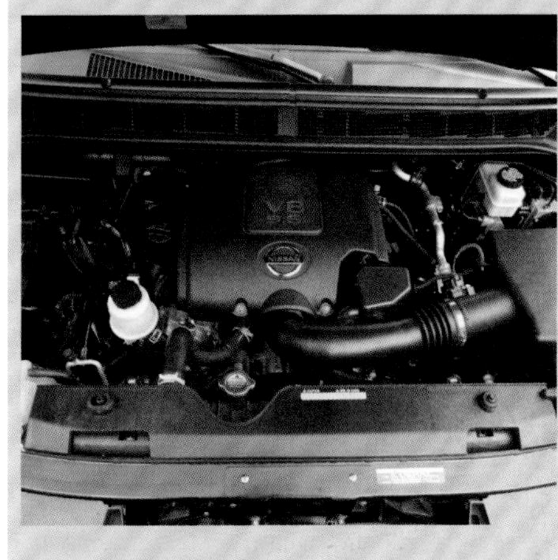

DANS LA MÊME CATÉGORIE

Chevrolet Tahoe, Ford Expedition, GMC Yukon, Toyota Sequoia

DU NOUVEAU EN 2011

Aucun changement majeur

NOS IMPRESSIONS

Agrément de conduite :	8/10
Fiabilité :	7/10
Sécurité :	8/10
Qualités hivernales :	9/10
Espace intérieur :	10/10
Confort :	9/10

www.nissan.ca

Plus d'informations dans la section statistiques en dernière partie du Guide

POURQUOI N'EN VEND-ON PAS PLUS QUE ÇA?

Formes trop quadrilatères? Pas assez d'espace derrière la banquette? Qu'importe la raison, les ventes du Nissan cube (oui, avec un « c » minuscule!) ne sont pas à la hauteur de ce qu'elles devraient être. Après tout, le véhicule est bien équipé, intéressant à conduire et peu cher à l'achat. Mais c'est sans compter la Kia Soul qui lui donne toute une « rince »...

Le cube a roulé au Japon plus d'une décennie et pendant deux générations avant de finalement se pointer sur notre continent. Et honnêtement, à son arrivée, tous les espoirs étaient permis. Non mais, en connaissez-vous beaucoup des véhicules au design original, avec des équipements de série tels le groupe électrique, la climatisation et le régulateur de vitesse, pour un prix d'étiquette aussi petit que 17000$ et des poussières? C'est dur à battre, même pour les voitures compactes les plus généreuses. Voilà pourquoi le cube aurait dû faire un malheur. Mais non: il se vend de trois à quatre fois moins que la Kia Soul, au Canada du moins...

Pourquoi? À première vue, difficile à dire. J'ai eu l'occasion de le conduire à plusieurs reprises et toujours, j'y ai pris beaucoup de plaisir. Bien sûr, tous n'aiment pas son style carré et son hayon asymétrique – voyez comme cette glace arrière s'enroule sur un seul flanc, question de tromper l'œil? Moi, j'aime bien. Et pas juste pour l'esthétique. En effet, cette haute mais peu longue silhouette offre deux avantages: beaucoup, vraiment beaucoup de dégagement aux têtes et des manœuvres aisées en stationnement. Cette dernière qualité est rehaussée par une excellente vision tout autour, attribuable à de grandes baies vitrées, à des piliers de toit presque verticaux et à un capot presque inexistant.

IL PRÉFÈRE LA VILLE

Le cube emprunte sa plate-forme à la petite Versa et on lui reconnaît une distribution de poids presque parfaite (51% à l'avant). La suspension arrière mise sur une poutre de torsion qui, d'habitude, livre une balade moins souple qu'avec une indépendante, mais ici, le résultat est nettement moins sautillant avec, en prime, un freinage très honorable en dépit de tambours (et non des disques) à l'arrière.

Vrai que le quatre cylindres de 1,8 litre (122 chevaux) n'est pas des plus performants. Imaginez: une Toyota Corolla recèle plus que ça! Mais le cube ne pèse pas lourd dans la balance: à peine 1275 kilos. Cela dit, pour tirer le meilleur parti de sa petite puissance, mieux vaut opter pour la boîte manuelle six vitesses (pas cinq, six!). Malgré son levier « agricole », cette manuelle se manipule facilement. Le hic, c'est qu'elle n'équipe que la version de base, donc lorsqu'on la choisit, on doit faire table rase sur la clé intelligente, les commandes audio au volant et la radio satellite. Gros, gros compromis...

On se console avec la CVT qui, en ville, permet d'épargner un litre de carburant aux 100 km versus la manuelle. Les accélérations,

- Très bon niveau d'équipement pour 17 400 $
- Tout petit rayon de braquage
- Grand dégagement intérieur – et 11 porte-gobelets !
- Excellente visibilité tout autour

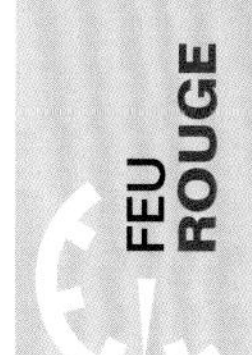

- Direction qui manque de précision sur l'autoroute
- Boîte manuelle qu'en version de base
- Volant non télescopique
- Silhouette asymétrique – tout le monde n'aime pas

comme avec toute bonne CVT, miaulent un brin tant que l'accélérateur demeure enfoncé, ce qui nous fait souhaiter un mode manuel qui aurait de belle façon simulé des rapports virtuels. Mais ça serait sans doute pas mal trop exagérer sur le pain béni...

C'est en situation urbaine que le cube se surpasse, merci à sa plus grande qualité – qui se transforme toutefois en son plus grand défaut sur l'autoroute : sa direction électrique. Cette direction est si légère et si maniable qu'elle permet, en ville, des manœuvres vraiment athlétiques. Considérez qu'avec un petit 10 mètres de rayon de braquage, le cube est parmi les véhicules les plus agiles du marché et il le prouve en se faufilant lestement dans la circulation. Mais à des vitesses plus grandes, on manque indéniablement de relation avec la route. De surcroît, le véhicule a tendance à danser sur les ornières laissées par les véhicules plus lourds – de quoi sérieusement enlever toute envie d'attaquer les virages à grande vitesse ! D'ailleurs, à ce chapitre, le cube a terminé bon dernier à notre match comparatif l'an dernier.

PEUT-ÊTRE QUE...

L'habitacle du cube a beau proposer 11 porte-gobelets (!) et un mégadégagement aux têtes, reste que l'espace de chargement est étroit si les cinq places sont occupées. À l'arrière de la banquette, à peine 323 litres de chargement peuvent tenir, versus les 546 litres de la Kia Soul. Par contre, en s'ouvrant latéralement à la manière d'une porte de frigo, le hayon facilite les manœuvres et l'ouverture est si béante qu'on peut y faire tenir un grand écran télé.

L'intérieur est bien insonorisé et fait appel à des matériaux agréables au toucher – par exemple, ce doux similisuède qui recouvre les sièges. Le tableau de bord, concave vis-à-vis du passager avant, accorde une belle impression d'espace. Les commandes, peu nombreuses, sont pratico-pratiques et faciles d'accès.

Bref, rien pour expliquer qu'on ne s'arrache pas plus de cube que ça. Si ce n'est que la principale concurrente, la Kia Soul, propose... ah bien, ça doit être ça, l'explication : la Soul troque la climatisation de série pour les sièges chauffants, ajoute la connectivité Bluetooth et trouve quand même le tour de demander presque un millier de dollars de moins...

Nadine Filion

PHOTOS : ALAIN MORIN

Catégorie	Multisegment
Échelle de prix	17 398 $ à 23 098 $ (2010)
Garanties	3 ans/60 000 km, 5 ans/100 000 km
Assemblage	n.d.
Cote d'assurance	n.d.

CHÂSSIS - DONNÉES POUR 1.8S KROM EDITION

Emp/lon/lar/haut	2 530/3 980/1 695/1 650 mm
Coffre	323 à 1 645 litres
Réservoir	50 litres
Nombre coussins sécurité	6
Antipatinage / contrôle stabilité	oui / oui
Suspension avant	indépendante, jambes de force
Suspension arrière	semi-indépendante, poutre de torsion
Freins avant / arrière	disque (ABS) / tambour (ABS)
Direction	à crémaillère, ass. variable électrique
Diamètre de braquage	10,0 m
Pneus avant / arrière	P195/55R16 / P195/55R16
Poids	1 289 kg
Capacité de remorquage	non recommandé

COMPOSANTES MÉCANIQUES

1.8 S, 1.8 SL, 1.8S Krom Edition

Cylindrée, soupapes, alim.	4L 1,8 litre 16 s atmos.
Puissance / Couple	122 chevaux / 127 lb-pi
Tr. base (opt) / rouage base (opt)	M6 (CVT) / Tr
0-100 / 80-120 / 100-0 km/h	10,6 s / 8,7 s / 43,0 m
Type ess. / ville / autoroute	Ordinaire / 7,3 / 6,5 l/100 km

DANS LA MÊME CATÉGORIE

Chevrolet HHR, Kia Soul, Toyota Matrix

DU NOUVEAU EN 2011

Aucun changement majeur

NOS IMPRESSIONS

Agrément de conduite :	8/10
Fiabilité :	8/10
Sécurité :	7/10
Qualités hivernales :	7/10
Espace intérieur :	8/10
Confort :	7/10

www.nissan.ca

Plus d'informations dans la section statistiques en dernière partie du Guide

UN MONSTRE SYMPATHIQUE

Godzilla. C'est le surnom donné à la GT-R, cette supervoiture exotique dont les performances sont à couper le souffle et qui est pourtant vendue à un prix d'aubaine quand on tient compte du niveau de ses performances. C'est l'une des sportives les plus attendues de l'histoire récente, avec la nouvelle LF-A de Lexus qui, elle, coûte plus de trois fois le prix d'une GT-R...

La lecture des spécifications techniques de la GT-R donne une idée de la détermination des ingénieurs de la marque à faire la preuve de leur savoir-faire. Un chrono de 3,85 secondes pour le sprint de 0 à 100 kilomètres/heure et un temps canon sur un tour du Nürburgring, l'endroit de prédilection pour établir la hiérarchie des sportives. La GT-R s'y est montrée plus rapide que la Corvette Z06 et la Porsche 911 Turbo. Se mettre à l'aise à bord de la GT-R est très facile à faire, car il n'y a que deux commandes électriques pour ajuster la position du siège et un levier à manipuler pour ajuster la colonne de direction, et c'est là que la simplicité prend fin.

INSTRUMENTS EN MODE JEU VIDÉO

La GT-R est une voiture très complexe et elle fait donc appel à un écran électronique qui peut être configuré au goût du conducteur et permettant d'afficher plus d'information que ledit conducteur ne peut en utiliser lors de la conduite sportive. Plus de 11 instruments peuvent apparaître sur cet écran afin de suivre les signes vitaux de la voiture, tels que pression et température des huiles du moteur et de la transmission, ainsi que la pression du turbo, l'accélération latérale en virage ou même le chronométrage d'un tour de circuit. Et l'on ne fait là qu'effleurer la surface !

L'ÉPREUVE DU CIRCUIT

Sur circuit, avec la boîte séquentielle à double embrayage à six rapports en mode manuel, le passage des vitesses se fait aussi rapidement que l'action d'une carabine semi-automatique, soit en seulement 0,18 seconde, mais surtout sans les chocs qui sont généralement associés à ce type de boîte. Voilà qui est assez surprenant compte tenu du fait que 485 chevaux (5 de plus qu'à la première année du modèle) sont alors livrés aux quatre roues par l'entremise de massifs pneus Bridgestone Potenza. En fait, la livrée de la puissance est tellement constante et linéaire que l'on n'a pas l'impression viscérale d'une accélération à tout casser, mais, faites-moi confiance, ça déménage... Un autre facteur qui atténue quelque peu l'impression de vitesse est le fait que la sonorité du moteur est un tantinet assourdie, ce qui est typique d'un moteur turbocompressé, et ce qui nous prive du cri de guerre strident d'un moteur atmosphérique à pleine charge.

Les freins ventilés Brembo font un travail très efficace en décélération et la direction de la GT-R est juste assez lourde pour éviter que le conducteur ne donne trop d'angle au volant en entrée de courbe. Après une première série de tours, j'étais fin prêt à

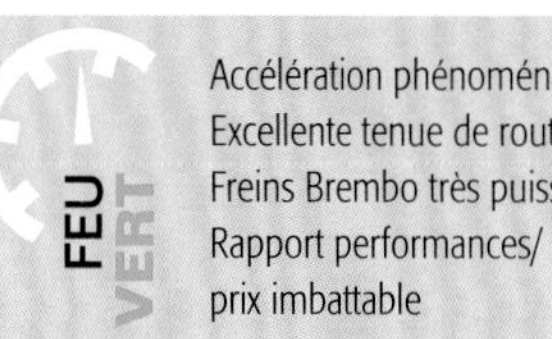

FEU VERT

Accélération phénoménale
Excellente tenue de route
Freins Brembo très puissants
Rapport performances/prix imbattable

FEU ROUGE

Inconfort sur routes dégradées
Places arrière symboliques
Embrayage sec en conduite normale
Bruit de roulement très présent

pousser la voiture un peu plus et c'est à ce moment-là que j'ai senti un peu de sous-virage dans les courbes rapides, ce qui est le propre d'à peu près toutes les voitures de type GT comme notamment la Porsche 911 Turbo. Cela peut être attribué au poids de la GT-R et à la répartition axée vers l'arrière de la motricité, ce qui a pour effet de pousser légèrement les roues avant de la voiture vers l'extérieur de la courbe lors de l'accélération franche en sortie de virage.

Afin de rouler vraiment rapidement avec la GT-R sur circuit, il faut faire preuve de patience à l'accélération ou encore choisir la configuration retenue par Toshio Suzuki, pilote d'essai pour Nissan. En bref, il choisit les réglages « R » pour obtenir la calibration la plus ferme des suspensions de même que la vitesse la plus rapide de passage des rapports de la boîte séquentielle, mais il désactive complètement le système de contrôle de la motricité. De cette façon, il peut conduire de façon plus agressive en faisant littéralement pivoter la voiture en entrée de virage par un mouvement sec sur le volant suivi d'un redressement et d'un usage de la puissance moteur, en essayant de faire glisser la voiture au travers du virage en ajustant faiblement l'angle de braquage du volant de manière à maintenir la trajectoire idéale, alors que les pneus hurlent... C'est une démonstration éloquente de la familiarité qu'il a atteinte avec la GT-R au cours de son développement.

Sur la base de mon expérience au volant de la GT-R, je peux définitivement dire que c'est l'une des sportives les plus accomplies que j'ai eu l'occasion de conduire. Elle est très rapide et fait la preuve de l'expertise technique de la marque, mais malgré les prouesses dont elle est capable, elle n'excite pas l'âme autant qu'une Ferrari sait le faire, et de ce côté, la GT-R est très semblable à la Porsche 911 Turbo. Les deux sont des missiles capables de performances éblouissantes mais qui font presque trop bien les choses avec un degré de précision très élevé, ce qui fait que la conduite est impressionnante mais pas transcendante. Cependant, la GT-R offre un rapport performances-prix absolument démentiel et elle assure une exclusivité certaine à l'acheteur puisque la capacité totale de production de la GT-R tourne au rythme de 1 000 exemplaires par mois.

Toutefois, il semble que l'ardeur des mordus en sa faveur s'est quelque peu estompée depuis son arrivée sur le marché l'an dernier.

Gabriel Gélinas

PHOTOS : NISSAN

NISSAN GT-R

Catégorie	Coupé
Échelle de prix	99 500 $
Garanties	3 ans/60 000 km, 5 ans/100 000 km
Assemblage	Tochigi, Japon
Cote d'assurance	n.d.

CHÂSSIS - DONNÉES POUR BASE

Emp/lon/lar/haut	2 779/4 650/1 902/1 372 mm
Coffre	249 litres
Réservoir	71 litres
Nombre coussins sécurité	6
Antipatinage / contrôle stabilité	oui / oui
Suspension avant	indépendante, double triangulation
Suspension arrière	indépendante, multibras
Freins avant / arrière	disque (ABS) / disque (ABS)
Direction	à crémaillère, ass. variable électronique
Diamètre de braquage	n.d.
Pneus avant / arrière	P255/40R20 / P285/35R20
Poids	1 730 kg
Capacité de remorquage	non recommandé

COMPOSANTES MÉCANIQUES

Base

Cylindrée, soupapes, alim.	V6 3,8 litres 24 s turbocompressé
Puissance / Couple	485 chevaux / 434 lb-pi
Tr. base (opt) / rouage base (opt)	M6 / Int
0-100 / 80-120 / 100-0 km/h	3,9 s / 3,9 s / 37,0 m
Type ess. / ville / autoroute	Super / 13,9 / 9,5 l/100 km

DANS LA MÊME CATÉGORIE

Audi R8, BMW Série 6, Chevrolet Corvette, Dodge Viper, Ferrari California, Lexus LF-A, Porsche 911

DU NOUVEAU EN 2011

Aucun changement majeur

NOS IMPRESSIONS

Agrément de conduite :	8/10
Fiabilité :	6/10
Sécurité :	10/10
Qualités hivernales :	5/10
Espace intérieur :	6/10
Confort :	6/10

www.nissan.ca

Plus d'informations dans la section statistiques en dernière partie du Guide

THE JUKE OF HAZARDS

Nissan titille le hasard, avec son Juke. Si ça marchera? Sans doute. Parce que le tout petit, vraiment tout petit véhicule est une solution pas mal intéressante à la traditionnelle *hatchback* – avec turbo, s'il vous plaît. Un nouveau segment vient-il d'être créé?

Le Nissan Juke nous arrive cet automne. Sur papier, il donne l'illusion d'un véhicule plus grand alors qu'en vrai, il n'est pas plus haut et pas plus long qu'un petit Scion xB. Même que sa silhouette ramassée le fait paraître encore plus petit. Mais quel style, mes amis! Les flancs sont musclés, la ligne de toit plonge athlétiquement vers une mince glace arrière (ce qui réduit la vision arrière, mais bon), les phares arrière tiennent du sourcil froncé et le pare-brise, fortement incliné, donne dans le guépard prêt à s'élancer – un thème cher à Nissan et qui rappelle l'Infiniti EX.

Surtout, la calandre vient distinguer le Juke dans un style farfouilleur mais savamment déséquilibré. Dans les chaumières, on jasera probablement autant de ce grand sourire menaçant qu'on l'a fait pour la nouvelle devanture de la Mazda3... Le pare-chocs est bombé à l'extrême, les phares tout ronds qui y sont intégrés passent pour des antibrouillards et les clignotants se retrouvent dans une enveloppe claire surmontant un capot qui se relève fièrement. Le conducteur doit d'ailleurs compter sur ces «yeux» pour le guider, sinon il n'aperçoit rien de l'extrémité avant de son véhicule.

Le grand mystère, avec ce Juke, c'est: contre qui se mesurera-t-il? Nissan avance la Mazda3 Sport, la Toyota Matrix, la Mini Cooper et la Suzuki SX4. Nous ajoutons: peut-être les Jeep Compass/Patriot, la nouvelle Mini Countryman, le cube (malheureusement pour Nissan...), la Kia Soul et, surtout, le Volkswagen Tiguan. On parie un p'tit 2$?

UN TURBO SOUS LE CAPOT

Le Juke se veut un petit sportif. Pas juste en design extérieur, en conduite aussi. Voilà pourquoi on lui octroie le premier quatre cylindres turbo à injection directe offert par Nissan en Amérique du Nord. Cette motorisation, puisée du giron Versa, hérite de la suralimentation et de la nouvelle technologie «DIG» pour une meilleure réactivité et une plus grande économie d'essence – mais ce dernier point doit être vérifié lors d'un essai à plus long terme. Malgré sa toute petite cylindrée (1,6 litre), ce moteur vient livrer un peu plus de 180 chevaux dans des manœuvres linéaires, sans effet de couple (il n'y a pas assez de vigueur sous le capot pour ça...). Et aussi sans qu'on ait à patienter après le turbo pour ébranler celui qui, somme toute, ne pèse que 1350 kilos.

Pas d'accélérations et de reprises endiablées, cependant. Même qu'il manque à l'expérience turbo une certaine profondeur dont profite, tout au contraire, le Tiguan. S'il était nôtre, ce Juke, on le gratifierait par ailleurs d'un échappement au son pas mal plus guttural. Nul doute que la puissance sèche est attribuable à la transmission CVT (une manuelle six vitesses est proposée en variante de base). Heureusement que cette CVT s'offre avec le mode manuel, mais regrettons quand même qu'il ne se négocie qu'avec le levier de vitesses (au demeurant agréable à manier et positionné «en podium» pour un accès qui tombe sous la main). C'est donc dire qu'on n'a pas droit au passage des vitesses au volant et c'est dommage pour un véhicule avec des prétentions sportives.

AWD D'AVANT-GARDE

De base (ce que nous n'avons pas testé), le Juke s'amène avec la poutre de torsion en guise de suspension arrière. Si l'on se fie à ce type d'architecture, nous sommes d'avis que la balade sera un brin «sautilleuse». En version étoffée, la suspension multibras prend le flambeau, ajustée assez fermement pour bien communiquer avec la

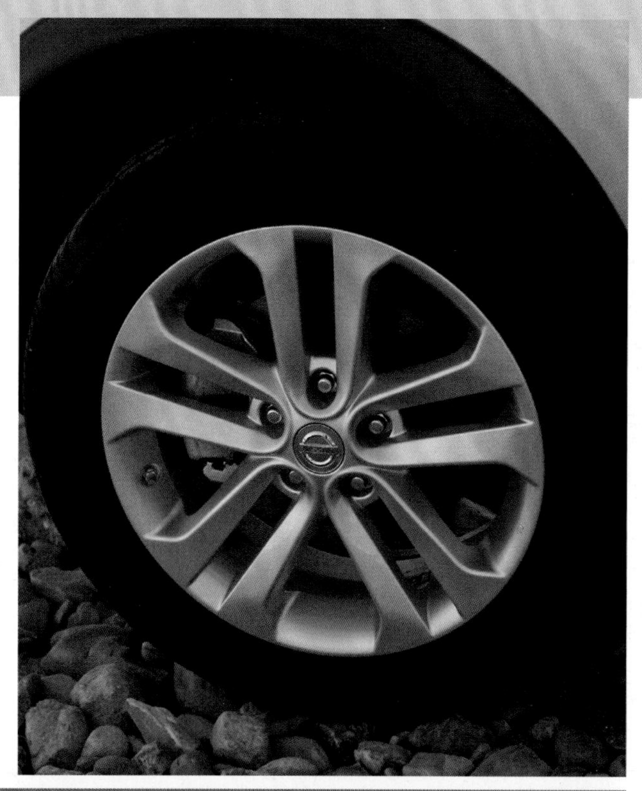

route. Pas de rebonds indus, au contraire on sent très bien les aspérités du bitume. Nous avons lancé la version à traction intégrale dans des virages serrés et les manœuvres ont été d'autant plus assurées que ce AWD électronique (sans différentiel) répartit le couple de gauche à droite à l'arrière (une nouveauté chez Nissan, avec en plus l'heureuse possibilité de verrouiller le couple à 50-50.) Les petites dimensions ont également aidé le véhicule à diligemment se faufiler là où on le pointait, dans un comportement tout à fait prévisible.

INTERFACE I-CON : *COOL* !

Bon, il y en a pour dire que le prochain gadget est aussi farfelu qu'inutile, mais ça retient l'attention : la nouvelle interface I-con. On est loin des I-drive de BMW et autres bidules du genre (une chance !), mais on peut quand même personnaliser sa conduite, possibilité rare dans la catégorie. Trois modes affectent directement la CVT, la direction, de même que la réponse de l'accélérateur. D'un extrême à l'autre, la différence se fait nettement sentir par une direction qui se resserre (agréablement) ou qui se relâche (un peu trop, mais quel bon rayon de braquage !). En mode sport, des rapports virtuels ont été créés pour une rapide escalade automatique qui donne une impression de vitalité. Sous le pied droit, en mode éco, l'accélérateur fait opposition, question de ralentir les ardeurs et de favoriser une meilleure consommation.

On se doute que le mode « entre les deux » sera peu utilisé (le mode sport sera sûrement le plus populaire), mais reste que le Juke s'adapte aux situations selon qu'on le veuille plus sportif ou plus économique (on avance une consommation de 7,2 L/100 km en combiné, mais il faudra vérifier). Aussi, on aime que chaque mode vienne avec ses propres informations, soit l'indicateur de turbo en mode sport ou les étoiles qui récompensent un bel historique de consommation en mode éco.

Le summum : en appuyant sur la touche Climate, on voit les commandes se métamorphoser comme par magie en contrôles de soufflerie et de température. Ça paraît simple, dit comme ça (c'est effectivement très discret), mais ça fait un effet bœuf et ça a le mérite de limiter le nombre de pitons sur la planche de bord. Reprochons cependant que le système audio, qui peut aussi accueillir la navigation et la caméra de recul, soit moins aisé à apprivoiser et qu'il soit difficile à consulter lorsque les rayons du soleil y plongent.

UN FUTUR « MEILLEUR INTÉRIEUR » ?

Visuellement, la pièce maîtresse de l'habitacle est sans conteste la console centrale qui, avec son plastique rouge ou gris aux allures métallisées, vient rappeler… une motocyclette. L'effet, à la fois rétro et branché, est insolite et « ça fesse dans le *dash* » même si, pour cela, il faut sacrifier l'appuie-bras

central. Une prédiction : le Nissan Juke remportera sûrement l'un des prix des Meilleurs intérieurs automobiles au cours de la prochaine année…

Côté dimensions, on le répète : le Juke est pas mal plus petit qu'il en a l'air, avec ses 17 cm plus courts que pour la Versa (!). Les deux passagers avant doivent s'y serrer les coudes et avec la silhouette qui s'incline vers l'arrière (en son point le plus haut, elle arrive… au menton d'une fille de 5'7" !), le dégagement aux têtes n'est pas des plus généreux. Les sièges avant sont peu larges et ne profitent d'aucun ajustement électrique (que du manuel), mais ils offrent un bon confort et, en option, on peut les avoir revêtus de cuir et chauffants.

FEU VERT

- Quel style!
- Premier turbo à injection directe pour Nissan
- AWD sophistiqué
- Petites dimensions qui le rendent agile
- Le i-con!

FEU ROUGE

- Visibilité handicapée à l'avant et à l'arrière
- Pas de passage des vitesses au volant
- Puissance sèche
- Petit habitacle

À l'arrière, l'accès est handicapé par de petites portières qui ouvrent bien peu, mais l'espace pour les jambes est raisonnable. On reproche aux dossiers leur non-inclinaison – ce qui aurait permis une assise moins carrée et un peu plus d'espace pour les têtes.

Côté prix, on s'attend à ce que le Juke demande un peu plus de 20 000 $ en variante de base et qu'il touche les 28 000 $ – après tout, il doit réussir à se caser chez Nissan entre le cube et le Rogue. Parions qu'il fera d'ailleurs de l'ombre dans sa propre salle d'exposition, avec son style et ses avancées technologiques.

Si nous avions à conseiller quoi que ce soit, nous recommanderions au Juke de ne pas se montrer trop gourmand, côté bidous. Avec une échelle de prix raisonnables, il pourrait certainement s'établir en créateur d'une nouvelle et populaire catégorie de véhicules: le *hatchback* qui n'en a pas l'air...

Nadine Filion

PHOTOS : NISSAN

DONNÉES PRÉLIMINAIRES

Catégorie	Multisegment
Échelle de prix	n.d.
Garanties	3 ans/60 000 km, 5 ans/100 000 km
Assemblage	n.d.
Cote d'assurance	n.d.

CHÂSSIS - DONNÉES POUR 4RM

Emp/lon/lar/haut	2 530/4 125/1 765/1 570 mm
Coffre	n.d.
Réservoir	n.d.
Nombre coussins sécurité	6
Antipatinage / contrôle stabilité	oui / oui
Suspension avant	indépendante, jambes de force
Suspension arrière	indépendante, multibras
Freins avant / arrière	disque (ABS) / disque (ABS)
Direction	à crémaillère, ass. électrique
Diamètre de braquage	n.d.
Pneus avant / arrière	215/55R17 / 215/55R17
Poids	1 350 kg
Capacité de remorquage	n.d.

COMPOSANTES MÉCANIQUES

2RM, 4RM

Cylindrée, soupapes, alim.	4L 1,6 litre 16 s turbo
Puissance / Couple	180 chevaux / 170 lb-pi
Tr. base (opt) / rouage base (opt)	M6 (CVT) / Tr (Int)
0-100 / 80-120 / 100-0 km/h	n.d. / n.d. / n.d.
Type ess. / ville / autoroute	Super / 8,2 / 6,5 l/100 km (est)

DANS LA MÊME CATÉGORIE

Kia Soul, Mini Cooper, Nissan cube, Scion tC, Volkswagen Tiguan

DU NOUVEAU EN 2011

Nouveau modèle

NOS IMPRESSIONS

Agrément de conduite:	■■■■■■■■□□ 8/10
Fiabilité:	Nouveau modèle
Sécurité:	Données insuffisantes
Qualités hivernales:	Données insuffisantes
Espace intérieur:	■■■■■■■■□□ 8/10
Confort:	■■■■■■■■□□ 8/10

www.nissan.ca

Plus d'informations dans la section statistiques en dernière partie du Guide

L'AVENTURE ÉLECTRIQUE

Signe des temps, plusieurs constructeurs se lancent à fond dans la nouvelle course vers les technologies vertes, conscients du fait que les premiers à commercialiser des véhicules « zéro émission » seront favorablement récompensés par un public qui semble désormais prêt à faire face au réchauffement planétaire et à adopter de nouvelles technologies en matière de transport. Après un « faux départ », il y a une dizaine d'années, avec General Motors qui a été le premier constructeur à commercialiser la EV-1, un véhicule électrique pour le grand public qui n'a pas connu le succès escompté et qui a été retiré du marché, Nissan fait le pari que les automobilistes sont maintenant prêts à accueillir la Leaf qui sera lancée dès 2010 aux États-Unis, en Europe ainsi qu'en Asie.

Lors du lancement de la tournée de promotion de la Leaf en sol américain à Los Angeles, il a été possible de conduire une Nissan Versa à empattement allongé dotée de la motorisation électrique de la Leaf sur un court circuit aménagé dans le stationnement du Dodgers Stadium. Premier constat, cette voiture n'avait rien d'artisanal, était bien achevée et capable d'une accélération initiale plutôt franche, courtoisie de son couple chiffré à 206 livres-pied, ce qui est largement supérieur à celui d'une Versa à motorisation conventionnelle. Comme c'est le cas pour les véhicules à motorisation hybride, ce prototype (tout comme la Leaf) était équipé d'un système de freinage régénératif servant à recharger la batterie à chaque décélération, mais son entrée en action était tellement subtile que l'on pourrait presque le qualifier d'imperceptible, ce qui n'est pas le cas sur certaines voitures hybrides. Bref, le comportement de ce prototype était en tous points conforme à celui

d'une Versa à motorisation conventionnelle sur ce court circuit, mais son comportement lors d'une utilisation normale sur la route reste à valider.

UN PROJET AMBITIEUX

Le projet de Nissan est à la fois ambitieux et visionnaire puisqu'il consiste non seulement à construire le véhicule électrique lui-même mais également les batteries qui l'alimenteront. L'usine Nissan d'Oppama au Japon a été choisie pour produire la Leaf, une berline à cinq places élaborée sur une toute nouvelle plateforme présentée au dernier Salon de l'auto de Tokyo, alors que les cellules au lithium-ion qui seront la source d'énergie pour son moteur de 80 kilowatts (environ 107 chevaux) seront fabriquées à l'usine de Zama au Japon. L'usine américaine de Nissan à Smyrna au Tennessee servira éventuellement aussi à construire la Leaf et à produire les batteries, augmentant ainsi la capacité totale de production de 150 000 voitures et de 200 000 batteries par année. Selon Carlos Ghosn, président et chef de la direction de Nissan et de Renault, la Leaf sera capable de rouler sur 160 kilomètres, de faire le 0-100 kilomètres/heure en 10 secondes, d'être rechargée à 80 % en moins de trente minutes au moyen d'un chargeur

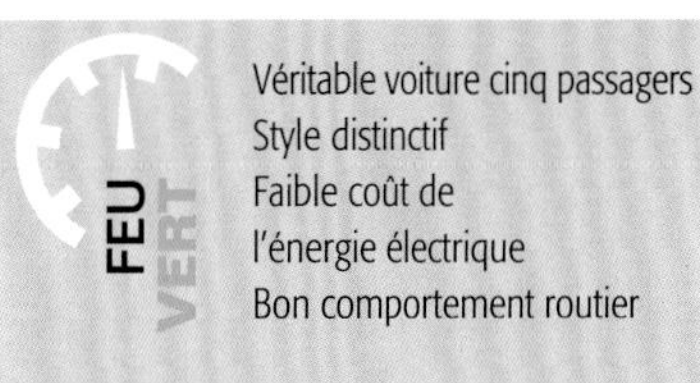

Véritable voiture cinq passagers
Style distinctif
Faible coût de l'énergie électrique
Bon comportement routier

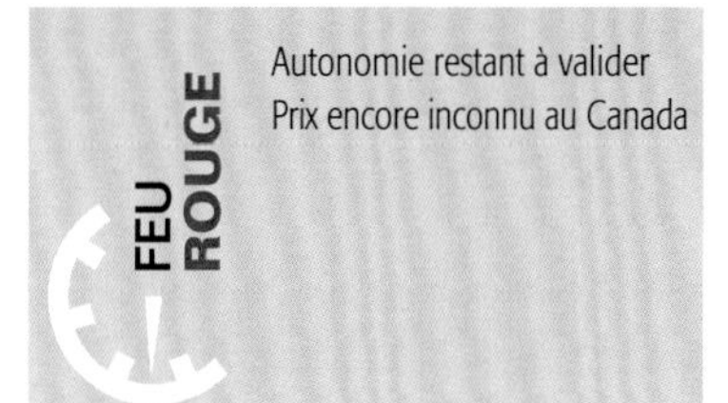

Autonomie restant à valider
Prix encore inconnu au Canada

rapide et d'être complètement rechargée après une période de moins de 8 heures lorsque branchée sur une source de courant conventionnelle de 220 volts.

UN PRIX ENCORE INCONNU POUR LE CANADA

Le prix de la Leaf n'a pas encore été annoncé pour le marché canadien, mais il est déjà connu pour les États-Unis où il a été fixé à 32800 dollars. Évidemment, les acheteurs canadiens pourront se prévaloir des programmes incitatifs mis de l'avant par les différents paliers de gouvernement, ce qui signifie que les acheteurs québécois pourront bénéficier d'un crédit d'impôt et de subventions pouvant totaliser jusqu'à 10000 dollars. L'arrivée de la Leaf en sol canadien est prévue pour l'automne 2011 dans la ville de Vancouver, qui a déjà établi un programme de partenariat avec Nissan, pour ensuite s'étendre au reste du pays en 2012. Chez nous, les abonnés du service d'autopartage Communauto seront parmi les premiers à rouler en mode tout électrique puisque ce service fera l'acquisition de 50 Nissan Leaf qui seront mises à la disposition de la clientèle. De plus, plusieurs municipalités ainsi qu'Hydro-Québec procèdent actuellement à des études portant sur la mise en place d'un réseau de bornes de recharge rapide à des endroits stratégiques.

Toujours selon Carlos Ghosn, les véhicules électriques devraient représenter 10 % du marché en 2020. Cependant, cet essor ne sera possible que si les gouvernements mettent la main à la pâte non seulement en ce qui a trait à la mise en place de programmes incitatifs servant à « survolter » les ventes de véhicules électriques, mais également en développant des réseaux de production d'énergie électrique renouvelable, ce qui n'est pas forcément le cas partout sur la planète, de même qu'un réseau d'alimentation plus efficace qui sera en mesure de composer avec la demande accrue en électricité engendrée par l'arrivée sur nos routes de véhicules électriques comme la Leaf.

Bien que la diffusion de la Leaf, comme celle des autres véhicules électriques éventuellement proposés par Chevrolet et Mitsubishi, sera très limitée au Québec, il n'en demeure pas moins qu'il est encourageant de voir que les premiers tours de roue se feront dans un avenir rapproché.

Gabriel Gélinas

PHOTOS : NISSAN

NISSAN LEAF

DONNÉES PRÉLIMINAIRES

Catégorie	*Hatchback*
Échelle de prix	n.d.
Garanties	n.d.
Assemblage	Oppama, Japon
Cote d'assurance	n.d.

CHÂSSIS - DONNÉES POUR BASE

Emp/lon/lar/haut	2 700/4 445/1 770/1 550 mm
Coffre	n.d.
Réservoir	aucun
Nombre coussins sécurité	6
Antipatinage / contrôle stabilité	oui / oui
Suspension avant	n.d.
Suspension arrière	n.d.
Freins avant / arrière	disque (ABS) / disque (ABS)
Direction	n.d.
Diamètre de braquage	n.d.
Pneus avant / arrière	P205/55R16
Poids	n.d.
Capacité de remorquage	n.d.

COMPOSANTES MÉCANIQUES

Moteur électrique	80 kW (environ 107 ch)
Batterie	Lithium-ion 24 kWh
Chargeur intégré	3,3 kW
Charge rapide	80 % en 30 minutes
0-100 / 80-120 / 100-0 km/h	10,0 s (est) / n.d. / n.d.
Autonomie approximative	160 km

DANS LA MÊME CATÉGORIE

Mitsubishi i-MiEV

DU NOUVEAU EN 2011

Nouveau modèle

NOS IMPRESSIONS

Agrément de conduite :	n.d.
Fiabilité :	n.d.
Sécurité :	n.d.
Qualités hivernales :	n.d.
Espace intérieur :	n.d.
Confort :	n.d.

www.nissan.ca

Plus d'informations dans la section statistiques en dernière partie du Guide

BONNE VOITURE CHERCHE CLIENTÈLE

L'autre jour, j'ai croisé une Nissan Maxima sur la route. J'ai salué le conducteur, croyant fermement qu'il s'agissait d'un confrère conduisant un véhicule de presse. En effet, ce modèle dans sa dernière mouture est tellement peu populaire qu'à chaque fois qu'on en voit un, on s'imagine qu'il s'agit d'un véhicule appartenant à la flotte de presse du manufacturier. C'est dire à quel point les ventes de cette berline ont chuté au cours des dernières années.

Pourtant, il n'y a pas si longtemps, la Maxima était l'une des Nissan les plus populaires sur notre marché. Cette berline intermédiaire offrait un juste équilibre entre un certain niveau de luxe, un comportement routier intéressant et une bonne habitabilité, le tout associé à un prix compétitif. Les choses se sont progressivement dégradées depuis l'arrivée de l'Altima. Cette berline est pratiquement de même dimension, se vend beaucoup moins cher et propose tout de même des prestations intéressantes.

PERSONNALITÉS MULTIPLES

Lorsque l'Altima a commencé à faire des ravages dans les chiffres de vente de la Maxima, la direction de Nissan a décidé de relever le niveau de luxe de cette dernière. Les ingénieurs se sont laissés aller et nous ont même concocté plusieurs variantes à partir du même modèle. C'est ainsi que sont apparus les deux sièges baquets arrière, les puits de lumière longitudinaux en plus d'une multitude d'accessoires électroniques tant pour la conduite que pour le confort.

Malheureusement, toutes ces transformations n'ont pas connu les succès anticipés. On a repris le collier avec une nouvelle version qui est apparue en 2009 et qui ne connaît pas plus de succès. On a tenté dans un premier temps de modifier sa carrosserie afin de la rendre plus typée, notamment en utilisant une grille de calandre moins inclinée vers l'arrière et dotée de quatre bandes transversales au centre desquelles trône l'écusson Nissan. Il y a également les phares de route dont la forme très particulière est unique à ce modèle dans la famille Nissan. Tous ces efforts lui donnent un petit air à part qui n'est pas mal du tout, mais il semble que ce ne soit pas suffisant pour intéresser de nouveaux clients.

Toujours dans le but de donner un sérieux coup de pouce aux ventes par le biais d'un habitacle plus raffiné, les stylistes nous proposent une planche de bord stylisée au maximum. La principale caractéristique qui la distingue est cette nacelle centrale en bas relief qui accueille une buse de ventilation de chaque côté et avec, au centre, un écran à cristaux liquides d'une assez grande surface. Immédiatement à la base de celui-ci, il y a le clavier des commandes et un gros bouton central destiné à gérer les différentes fonctions associées à cet écran, notamment les réglages de la voiture et du système de navigation. Le volant est passablement élégant avec des appliques en aluminium brossé sur les deux rayons horizontaux, lesquels sont dotés également de commandes.

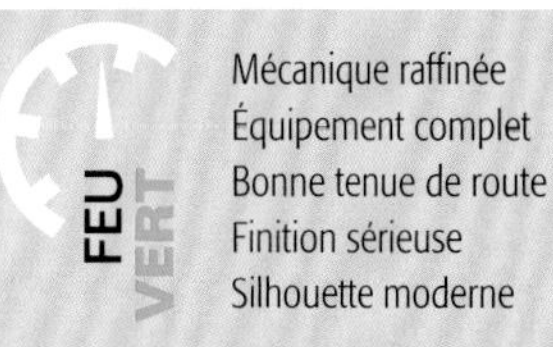

FEU VERT

- Mécanique raffinée
- Équipement complet
- Bonne tenue de route
- Finition sérieuse
- Silhouette moderne

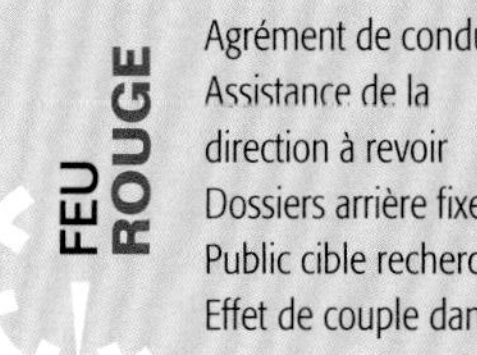

FEU ROUGE

- Agrément de conduite mitigé
- Assistance de la direction à revoir
- Dossiers arrière fixes
- Public cible recherché
- Effet de couple dans le volant

Soulignons la présence de palettes de passages des rapports placés derrière ce volant. Quant au pilote, il jouit d'une position de conduite convenable en raison de multiples réglages du siège et du volant. Si, malencontreusement, le conducteur est arrêté pour excès de vitesse, il ne pourra pas avoir l'excuse de ne pas avoir vu la vitesse à laquelle il roulait, car l'indicateur de vitesse est clair et de grande dimension. Malgré toute cette série d'accessoires, la finition demeure moyenne, au mieux, alors que la qualité des plastiques peut être qualifiée de marginale. Autre détail ennuyant, afin d'obtenir une meilleure rigidité de la caisse, les dossiers arrière ne peuvent être rabattus à plat. On compense par une trappe à skis. Il faut également souligner la grandeur du coffre, insatisfaisante, aussi bien que son ouverture, trop petite. Les tours de suspension y empiètent allègrement.

LA PAGE BLANCHE

Tout journaliste a la frayeur de la page blanche. Vous savez, ce manque d'inspiration qui nous empêche d'écrire quoi que ce soit. Dans le cas de la Maxima, c'est surtout mon carnet de notes qui a des pages blanches. En effet, malgré ces nombreux éléments techniques, ce moteur V6 primé et cette boîte CVT parmi les meilleures disponibles, je n'avais toujours rien noté après plusieurs jours d'essai. Heureusement, Nissan m'a confié une autre Maxima et cette fois, les impressions étaient un peu plus étoffées. Pas de beaucoup par contre…

C'est curieux, cette voiture possède tout pour réussir sur papier. Sa silhouette est élégante, son habitacle confortable, sa mécanique, toute aussi bonne sinon supérieure aux autres, mais on a oublié de lui donner une personnalité. On la conduit, tout simplement, sans l'apprécier nécessairement, sans la détester non plus. Il lui faudrait un peu plus de caractère. Un effet de couple dans le volant et une direction trop légère sont parmi les points négatifs, tandis que les impressions de conduite, qu'elles soient positives ou négatives, sont assez minces. En cherchant un peu plus, il y a cette assistance de la direction qui est inégale. Cette assistance variable est souvent trop légère à basse vitesse pour devenir soudainement trop ferme lorsque la vitesse augmente. Autre bémol, l'accès aux places arrière est assez difficile en raison d'une ligne de toit fuyante.

Bref, les ingénieurs de Nissan ont conçu une bonne voiture, mais ils ont oublié de cibler sa clientèle.

Denis Duquet

PHOTOS : NISSAN

NISSAN MAXIMA

Catégorie	Berline
Échelle de prix	39 450 $ (2010)
Garanties	3 ans/60 000 km, 5 ans/100 000 km
Assemblage	Smyrna, Tennessee, É-U
Cote d'assurance	moyenne

CHÂSSIS - DONNÉES POUR 3.5SV

Emp/lon/lar/haut	2 776/4 841/1 859/1 468 mm
Coffre	402 litres
Réservoir	76 litres
Nombre coussins sécurité	6
Antipatinage / contrôle stabilité	oui / oui
Suspension avant	indépendante, jambes de force
Suspension arrière	indépendante, multibras
Freins avant / arrière	disque (ABS) / disque (ABS)
Direction	à crémaillère, ass. variable
Diamètre de braquage	n.d.
Pneus avant / arrière	P245/45R18 / P245/45R18
Poids	1 621 kg
Capacité de remorquage	n.d.

COMPOSANTES MÉCANIQUES

3.5SV

Cylindrée, soupapes, alim.	V6 3,5 litres 24 s atmos.
Puissance / Couple	290 chevaux / 261 lb-pi
Tr. base (opt) / rouage base (opt)	CVT / Tr
0-100 / 80-120 / 100-0 km/h	6,4 s / 4,6 s / 41,2 m
Type ess. / ville / autoroute	Ordinaire / 10,9 / 7,7 l/100 km

DANS LA MÊME CATÉGORIE

Acura TL, Buick Lucerne, Chevrolet Impala, Chrysler 300, Dodge Charger, Ford Taurus, Hyundai Genesis, Lexus ES, Lincoln MKZ, Toyota Avalon, Volvo S60

DU NOUVEAU EN 2011

Aucun changement majeur

NOS IMPRESSIONS

Agrément de conduite :	8/10
Fiabilité :	6/10
Sécurité :	10/10
Qualités hivernales :	8/10
Espace intérieur :	9/10
Confort :	8/10

www.nissan.ca

Plus d'informations dans la section statistiques en dernière partie du Guide

FIDÈLE À SES ORIGINES

Lorsque la compagnie Nissan a réussi à se sortir du pétrin économique dans lequel elle s'était enlisée, c'était en bonne partie grâce au coup de crayon de ses designers. En effet, ce constructeur a toujours produit des véhicules dont la plate-forme et la mécanique flirtaient avec les meilleurs. Malheureusement, les silhouettes n'étaient pas toujours au goût du jour. Le Murano a fait partie de ce premier contingent de véhicules aux formes spectaculaires et appréciées du public.

En plus de cette apparence audacieuse, ce multi segment a été pratiquement le premier à amalgamer dans un même modèle un comportement routier presque similaire à celui d'une automobile, un habitacle plus que confortable et la capacité de rouler hors route. Le Murano est devenu la référence dans cette catégorie.

FIDÈLE À SON HÉRITAGE

La nouvelle version de ce modèle date maintenant de trois ans, ou presque, et elle est toujours actuelle. Il faut donc donner le crédit aux stylistes qui ont géré sa refonte, puisqu'ils ont réussi à conserver la personnalité de la version originale tout en modernisant ses lignes. Ils ont même accentué l'importance de la calandre avant. Celle-ci est encore plus en évidence avec ses huit barres verticales séparées au centre par l'écusson Nissan. Également, comme le veut la tendance actuelle, les phares de route en forme d'amande se prolongent dans les ailes. En plus, on retrouve sous la calandre une vaste prise d'air qui donne beaucoup de caractère à cette nipponne.

La première génération proposait des porte-à-faux réduits et ils le sont davantage sur cette version, ce qui accentue encore plus le caractère dynamique de la carrosserie. Les passages de roues sont en relief, mais fait de façon assez subtile.

La partie arrière comprend un hayon moins arrondi où les feux chevauchent à la fois l'aile et le hayon. Ce dernier est motorisé, ce qui peut être vraiment pratique en maintes occasions, et possède en sa partie supérieure un déflecteur donnant, encore ici, du caractère à la silhouette et qui du même coup protège la lunette arrière contre les dépôts de saleté.

La première génération du Murano possédait un tableau de bord qui était très design, mais qui manquait un peu de raffinement et qui était doté de matériaux de qualité moyenne. Dans cette nouvelle cuvée, il a été complètement remanié et il ressemble beaucoup à celui de la Maxima. En fait, à quelques exceptions près, on pourrait dire que c'en est pratiquement une copie conforme. C'est élégant, pratique et bien exécuté. L'écran est de bonne dimension et permet d'afficher les réglages de la climatisation, de la chaîne audio ou encore la carte géographique du système de navigation. Un clavier et un gros bouton se chargent de gérer les fonctions de la voiture. C'est quelque peu intuitif, mais on s'y adapte assez

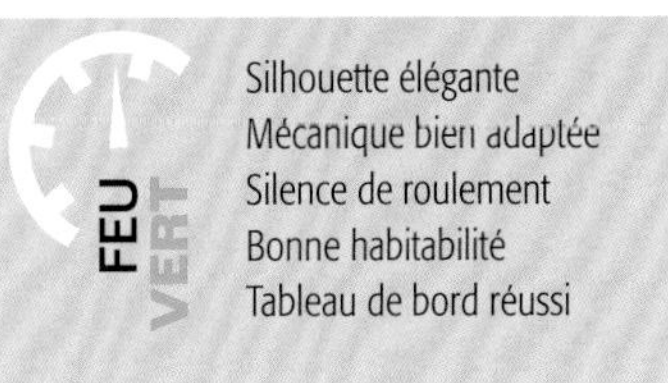

Silhouette élégante
Mécanique bien adaptée
Silence de roulement
Bonne habitabilité
Tableau de bord réussi

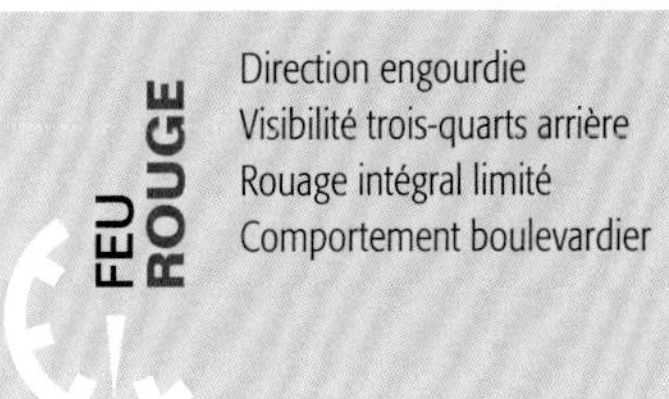

Direction engourdie
Visibilité trois-quarts arrière
Rouage intégral limité
Comportement boulevardier

facilement. Dans tous les cas, c'est nettement plus simple que sur plusieurs modèles concurrents. Après avoir levé la jambe assez haute pour prendre place à bord, on se retrouve assis dans des sièges avant confortables et réglables de multiples façons. Les occupants des places arrière ne sont pas négligés, bien au contraire. Celles-ci sont spacieuses, la banquette est même chauffante et on peut y prendre ses aises. On décerne également de bonnes notes à l'espace de chargement, qui est passablement grand.

QUASIMENT UNE AUTO

Comme d'habitude, le choix des couleurs de la caisse et de l'habitacle peut devenir compliqué en raison de l'abondance de choix. C'est beaucoup plus simple pour la mécanique, car il n'y a qu'un seul moteur et une seule transmission. L'incontournable moteur V6 de 3,5 litres est relié à une transmission CVT. Cette transmission à rapports continuellement variables est l'une des meilleures sur le marché. Son niveau sonore est très faible et on ne perçoit pas ce ronronnement incessant, et agaçant pour bien des gens, de la mécanique qui tourne sous le capot. Toujours pour simplifier les choses, seule la transmission intégrale est au programme. La capacité de remorquage est tout de même digne de mention. En effet, elle est de 1 588 kg ou 3 500 lb.

Pour ne pas être en reste avec ses principaux concurrents, le Murano possède une suspension indépendante aux quatre roues. Cette suspension est plutôt calibrée en fonction du confort et de la tenue de route qu'en fonction d'une utilisation hors route. D'ailleurs, il faudrait être vraiment audacieux ou encore totalement inconscient pour soumettre cette élégante Nissan à la torture d'un parcours hors routes pur et dur. Sa transmission intégrale est de type toutes routes afin d'assurer une bonne traction lorsque la chaussée est mouillée, enneigée ou glacée. Si vous voulez jouer les audacieux, choisissez plutôt le Pathfinder.

Souvent des véhicules nous séduisent par leur allure, pour ensuite nous décevoir en raison d'un manque de confort ou de performance ou parce que l'agrément de conduite n'est pas à la hauteur de nos attentes. Rien de tout cela avec le Murano, qui ne déçoit à aucun niveau. Son comportement routier est sans surprise, son confort, grandement apprécié et les multiples accessoires d'aide à la conduite sont bienvenus.

Denis Duquet

PHOTOS : NISSAN

Catégorie	Multisegment
Échelle de prix	38 298 $ à 47 948 $ (2010)
Garanties	3 ans/60 000 km, 5 ans/100 000 km
Assemblage	Kyushu, Japon
Cote d'assurance	pauvre

CHÂSSIS - DONNÉES POUR SL TI

Emp/lon/lar/haut	2 825/4 788/1 882/1 730 mm
Coffre	895 à 1 812 litres
Réservoir	82 litres
Nombre coussins sécurité	6
Antipatinage / contrôle stabilité	oui / oui
Suspension avant	indépendante, jambes de force
Suspension arrière	indépendante, multibras
Freins avant / arrière	disque (ABS) / disque (ABS)
Direction	à crémaillère, ass. variable
Diamètre de braquage	11,4 m
Pneus avant / arrière	P235/65R18 / P235/65R18
Poids	1 836 kg
Capacité de remorquage	1 588 kg (3 500 lb)

COMPOSANTES MÉCANIQUES

S TI , SL TI, LE TI, LE DVD

Cylindrée, soupapes, alim.	V6 3,5 litres 24 s atmos.
Puissance / Couple	265 chevaux / 248 lb-pi
Tr. base (opt) / rouage base (opt)	CVT / Int
0-100 / 80-120 / 100-0 km/h	8,2 s / 6,5 s / 44,0 m
Type ess. / ville / autoroute	Ordinaire / 11,8 / 8,7 l/100 km

DANS LA MÊME CATÉGORIE

Chevrolet Traverse, Ford Edge, GMC Acadia, Honda Pilot, Hyundai Veracruz, Lincoln MKX, Mazda CX-9, Mitsubishi Endeavor, Subaru Tribeca, Toyota Highlander

DU NOUVEAU EN 2011

Aucun changement majeur

NOS IMPRESSIONS

Agrément de conduite :	■■■■■■■□□□	7/10
Fiabilité :	■■■■■■■■□□	8/10
Sécurité :	■■■■■■■■■■	10/10
Qualités hivernales :	■■■■■■■■□□	8/10
Espace intérieur :	■■■■■■■■□□	8/10
Confort :	■■■■■■■■□□	8/10

www.nissan.ca

Plus d'informations dans la section statistiques en dernière partie du Guide

GRAND-PAPA PAT

Même s'il n'est plus la « saveur du mois » depuis longtemps, il ne faut pas voir le Nissan Pathfinder comme une antiquité. Il faut plutôt le considérer comme un regard sur un passé pas si lointain où les VUS purs et durs avaient la cote. L'Humain, un jour, a enfin compris qu'un confort de camion et des capacités hors route de tank ne lui apportaient pas le bonheur tant attendu. Est donc venue la folie des multisegments, promesse de raffinement et, surtout, d'un monde meilleur car moins pollué. Pas de danger, par contre, que l'Humain cherche le bonheur du côté des compactes ou des sous-compactes, ces indigentes voitures l'éloignant du but ultime...

Curieusement, dans ce monde de raffinement, des véhicules costauds comme le Pathfinder ont toujours leur place. Plusieurs personnes ont besoin de remorquer de lourdes charges, que ce soit pour des exigences familiales ou professionnelles. De plus, lorsqu'elles doivent le faire dans des sentiers plus ou moins passables, il leur faut compter sur un véhicule qui ne s'évanouira pas à la vue du premier trou d'eau. Conclusion, les vieux ont toujours leur place...

QUAND TON PÈRE S'APPELLE TITAN ET TA MÈRE ARMADA...

Puisque le Pathfinder est bâti sur la plate-forme modifiée des immenses Titan et Armada, il ne faut pas être surpris que ses dimensions soient aussi d'une autre époque. Certes, il y a un problème quand vient le temps de se stationner dans un espace réduit, mais c'est une bénédiction pour ceux qui aiment voyager sans côtoyer leur voisin ou la portière. Je n'ai eu aucune

difficulté à trouver une bonne position de conduite même si le volant ne s'ajuste pas en profondeur. Le tableau de bord est simple et bien exécuté, les jauges sont lisibles et tous les boutons et commandes se manipulent aisément. Cependant, la disposition des boutons du système audio est déroutante : celui du volume est placé près du conducteur tandis que celui des stations est situé à l'autre bout du monde. Mais comme défaut, on a déjà vu bien pire. Le gros Pat a beau avoir de l'âge, cela ne l'empêche pas d'être correctement assemblé et de posséder des matériaux généralement de belle facture... pour un VUS datant de quelques années ! En passant, soulignons que les espaces de rangement sont nombreux : au tableau de bord, sous l'assise des sièges de la deuxième rangée et sous le plancher du coffre.

Les sièges avant, de même que ceux de la deuxième rangée, s'avèrent très confortables, mais ceux de la troisième rangée sont aux antipodes et ne doivent être utilisés que pour dépanner. Lorsque les dossiers de cette rangée sont relevés, l'espace de chargement est acceptable mais, bien entendu, il est possible d'obtenir un grand fond plat en abaissant tous les dossiers.

FEU VERT
- V6 bien adapté
- Habitacle accueillant
- Rouage 4x4 professionnel
- Comportement routier correct
- Très bonnes capacités de remorquage

FEU ROUGE
- V6 assoiffé
- Dimensions intimidantes
- Troisième rangée de sièges restreinte
- Version de base très de base
- Freins ordinaires

L'ESSENCISME, VOUS CONNAISSEZ?

Côté moteur, Nissan fait confiance à un V6 de 4,0 litres de 266 chevaux au couple généreux. Souple et agréable à écouter en pleine accélération, ce moteur est atteint d'une bien terrible maladie: l'essencisme, une intoxication par les boissons à essence. Contrairement à l'alcoolisme, ça ne se traite pas. D'autant plus que je n'ai encore jamais vu un Pathfinder reconnaître son problème. En fait, il n'y a qu'une seule façon d'empêcher sa soif, c'est de le laisser le plus souvent possible dans l'entrée... Durant une année environ, Nissan proposait aussi aux Canadiens un V8, rendu encore plus bas dans son essencisme. Il continue de s'enivrer aux États-Unis. Avec son V6, le Pat peut remorquer jusqu'à 6000 livres (2722 kilos), ce qui n'est pas mal du tout. Cependant, le V8, malgré sa consommation de dégénéré, était apprécié de ceux qui devaient tirer jusqu'à 7000 livres (3175 kilos). La transmission est une automatique à cinq rapports avec mode manuel. Les Américains ont droit à une version deux roues motrices mais, au Canada, Nissan a préféré n'offrir que le rouage 4x4 et c'est sans doute une bonne décision. Un bouton au tableau de bord permet de choisir entre les modes 2WD (propulsion), Auto (intégrale sans intervention du conducteur), 4H (quatre roues motrices) ou 4L (quatre roues motrices avec démultiplication). Le Pathfinder n'est peut-être pas aussi agile qu'un Jeep Wrangler dans les situations vraiment corsées mais si toutefois vous restez pris avec, c'est un bulldozer que ça vous aurait pris!

On s'en doute, le gros Pat n'est pas particulièrement sportif. En virage, la caisse penche et on ne se sent pas des plus rassurés. Pourtant, il s'accroche au pavé avec ferveur et la précision de la direction surprend. Les ingénieurs des suspensions ont trouvé le bon calibrage entre confort et tenue de route. Les freins, par contre, nous rappellent que nous avons affaire à un véhicule de plus de 2000 kilos, haut sur pattes en plus.

Au fil des années, et en particulier depuis sa remise à jour en 2008, le Pathfinder a évolué au gré de la concurrence. Ainsi, il présente maintenant six coussins gonflables de série. Au moment d'écrire ces lignes, le prix de l'essence joue entre de 1,03$ et 1,06$ le litre. Dès que les prix augmenteront (ce qui est peut-être fait au moment de mettre sous presse), il y aura plusieurs Pathfinder sur le marché de l'usagé...

Alain Morin

PHOTOS: NISSAN

NISSAN PATHFINDER

Catégorie	VUS
Échelle de prix	37548$ à 47348$ (2010)
Garanties	3 ans/60000 km, 5 ans/100000 km
Assemblage	Kyushu, Japon
Cote d'assurance	passable

CHÂSSIS - DONNÉES POUR LE

Emp/lon/lar/haut	2850/4884/1850/1845 mm
Coffre	467 à 2243 litres
Réservoir	80 litres
Nombre coussins sécurité	6
Antipatinage / contrôle stabilité	oui / oui
Suspension avant	indépendante, double triangulation
Suspension arrière	indépendante, double triangulation
Freins avant / arrière	disque (ABS) / disque (ABS)
Direction	à crémaillère, ass. variable
Diamètre de braquage	11,9 m
Pneus avant / arrière	P265/60R18 / P265/60R18
Poids	2236 kg
Capacité de remorquage	2722 kg (6000 lb)

COMPOSANTES MÉCANIQUES

S, SE, LE

Cylindrée, soupapes, alim.	V6 4,0 litres 24 s atmos.
Puissance / Couple	266 chevaux / 288 lb-pi
Tr. base (opt) / rouage base (opt)	A5 / 4x4
0-100 / 80-120 / 100-0 km/h	7,9 s / 6,5 s / 40,1 m
Type ess. / ville / autoroute	Ordinaire / 14,9 / 10,3 l/100 km

DANS LA MÊME CATÉGORIE

Ford Explorer, Honda Pilot, Jeep Commander, Jeep Grand Cherokee, Kia Borrego, Toyota 4Runner

DU NOUVEAU EN 2011

Aucun changement majeur

NOS IMPRESSIONS

Agrément de conduite:	7/10
Fiabilité:	6/10
Sécurité:	8/10
Qualités hivernales:	8/10
Espace intérieur:	8/10
Confort:	8/10

www.nissan.ca

Plus d'informations dans la section statistiques en dernière partie du Guide

EN QUÊTE DE... DE QUOI, DONC ?

Les décisions de Nissan sont quelquefois bien compliquées à comprendre pour nous, communs et mortels. L'entreprise nipponne peut détruire la carrière d'une voiture comme bien peu savent le faire. La Maxima en est un exemple frappant. À l'inverse, alors qu'elle aurait tout le loisir de se planter, elle réussit à bien faire (la 370Z, pour ne pas la nommer). Nissan se permet même de se lancer dans un créneau extraordinairement difficile puisqu'occupé, du moins chez nous, par les Américains, celui des camions commerciaux avec sa gamme NV. D'un autre côté, elle peut conserver, et même renouveler, un véhicule qui n'a jamais été populaire car trop différent. Nous parlons, bien entendu, de la fourgonnette Quest. La décision est d'autant plus étrange que l'usine dans laquelle était fabriquée la Quest, à Canton au Mississippi, a été reconvertie pour assembler les NV. Plusieurs manufacturiers se seraient départis de l'encombrant véhicule pour bien moins...

Pour la petite histoire, mentionnons qu'il n'y a pas eu de Quest 2010. Les modèles 2009 ont été écoulés jusqu'à épuisement des stocks. Alors que la Quest était déjà oubliée (elle l'était même quand elle était vendue...), voilà que Nissan s'apprête à dévoiler une nouvelle version. Remarquez que ce n'est peut-être pas une si mauvaise décision que ça. Après tout, Dodge, Chrysler, Volkswagen, Honda, Toyota et Kia proposent toutes une fourgonnette. Même Ford, avec son Flex, peut, à la limite, faire partie de ce créneau. Et puis, on ne cesse de le répéter, une fourgonnette est tellement plus polyvalente que les VUS ou la plupart des multisegments, que ce soit pour transporter des gens ou des objets.

SUR PHOTO, C'EST BEAU !

Pour l'instant, nous savons bien peu de choses sur la Quest qui sera offerte aux consommateurs au début de 2011. Les rares photos qui sont parvenues jusqu'à nous avant la ligne de mort (le *deadline* — heure de tombée, en bon français —, une invention diabolique mais nécessaire, sinon aucun journaliste ne livrerait son matériel à temps !), les photos, donc, nous montrent, timidement, un véhicule aux lignes particulières qui ne sont pas sans rappeler, de côté, celles, encore excentriques deux ans après son lancement, du Ford Flex. L'avant est plutôt incliné alors qu'à l'arrière, le hayon est pratiquement vertical. La longue ceinture de caisse (la jonction entre les fenêtres et les glaces) sans courbes semble allonger davantage le véhicule. On retrouve des ondulations sur les flancs, ce qui ajoute au dynamisme de l'ensemble. La partie avant ressemble passablement à celle de plusieurs nouveaux produits Kia et cela semble réussi. La partie arrière reprend le style des feux de la Mazda3 et, de visu, l'ouverture du coffre paraît grande.

IL SERAIT DIFFICILE DE FAIRE PIRE...

Si la carrosserie de la Quest précédente ne faisait pas l'unanimité, que dire du tableau de bord dont elle était affligée à ses débuts?

Données insuffisantes

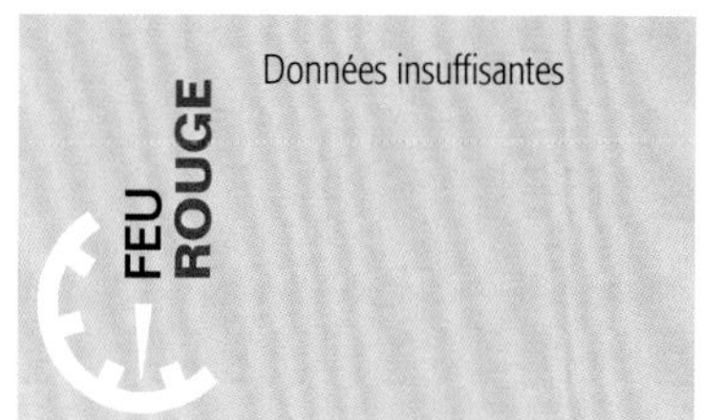

Données insuffisantes

Heureusement, on avait sérieusement revu ce dernier en 2007. Celui de la future Quest nous paraît fort réussi, du moins au vu des photos de presse. Le levier de vitesses est placé au centre du tableau de bord, tout comme celui des nouvelles Honda Odyssey et Toyota Sienna. Dans cette même partie, on retrouve, de haut en bas, l'écran du système GPS qui sert aussi, sans doute, à diffuser les informations de l'ordinateur de bord, le module des boutons et commandes pour lesdits GPS et ordinateur, le système de chauffage et, enfin, les commandes de la radio. Il est difficile de se faire une bonne idée d'après une photo mais il serait surprenant que l'ergonomie soit aussi ratée que dans la Quest de dernière génération... En se fiant à la photo fournie par Nissan, on devine qu'il s'agit d'un modèle haut de gamme.

Sinon, c'est le néant. Côté mécanique, nous verrions bien le V6 de 3,5 litres de la Maxima ou, mieux, le 3,7 litres de la 370Z. De nos jours, une transmission ayant moins de six rapports est considérée comme une indigente. Nous tenons à préciser à Nissan que sa Z en possède une à sept rapports... Pourvu qu'on n'aille pas y foutre une CVT (à rapports continuellement variables). Mais ce serait très étonnant. Remarquez qu'avec Nissan, nous n'en sommes plus à une bizarrerie près! Traction avant ou rouage intégral? L'ancienne ne proposait que le tout à l'avant.

UNE HISTOIRE À SUIVRE...

S'il est un domaine où la précédente Quest pouvait en montrer à plusieurs fourgonnettes, c'est au niveau des dimensions intérieures. Dire que l'habitacle de la Quest était caverneux serait un euphémisme! C'était immense. Non, immensément immense. Il serait surprenant que le modèle 2011 s'ouvre sur moins d'espace, autant pour les personnes que pour le coffre, étant donné qu'un modèle qui en remplace un autre est toujours plus, plus, plus. Lorsque le modèle 2011 sera dévoilé au prochain Salon de Los Angeles, Nissan nous abreuvera de détails techniques. Nous vous tiendrons au courant sur notre site www.guideautoweb.com.

À ses tout débuts, en 2005 (oublions la première génération vendue, sans succès, entre 1994 et 2001), la Quest était affligée d'une plate-forme peu rigide qui était à l'origine de craquements variés. Ajoutez à cela une insonorisation plus que déficiente, une ergonomie irritante, une fiabilité ordinaire et, le comble, un prix assez corsé et vous avez les bons ingrédients pour faire un superbe échec. Il serait surprenant que Nissan se plante avec cette nouvelle génération. Quoique...

Alain Morin

PHOTOS: NISSAN

DONNÉES GÉNÉRATION PRÉCÉDENTE

Catégorie	Fourgonnette
Échelle de prix	29 998 $ à 44 498 $ (2010)
Garanties	3 ans/60 000 km, 5 ans/100 000 km
Assemblage	Canton, Mississipi, É-U
Cote d'assurance	passable

CHÂSSIS - DONNÉES POUR 3.5 SL

Emp/lon/lar/haut	3 150/5 185/1 971/1 826 mm
Coffre	915 à 4 126 litres
Réservoir	76 litres
Nombre coussins sécurité	6
Antipatinage / contrôle stabilité	oui / non
Suspension avant	indépendante, jambes de force
Suspension arrière	indépendante, multibras
Freins avant / arrière	disque (ABS) / disque (ABS)
Direction	à crémaillère, ass. variable
Diamètre de braquage	12,1 m
Pneus avant / arrière	P225/65R16 / P225/65R16
Poids	1 990 kg
Capacité de remorquage	1 588 kg (3 500 lb)

COMPOSANTES MÉCANIQUES

3.5 S, 3.5 SL, 3.5 SE

Cylindrée, soupapes, alim.	V6 3,5 litres 24 s atmos.
Puissance / Couple	235 chevaux / 240 lb-pi
Tr. base (opt) / rouage base (opt)	A5 / Tr
0-100 / 80-120 / 100-0 km/h	9,4 s / 7,2 s / 40,0 m
Type ess. / ville / autoroute	Ordinaire / 12,9 / 8,4 l/100 km

DANS LA MÊME CATÉGORIE

Chrysler Town & Country, Dodge Grand Caravan, Honda Odyssey, Kia Sedona, Toyota Sienna, Volkswagen Routan

DU NOUVEAU EN 2011

Nouveau modèle sera dévoilé en cours d'année

NOS IMPRESSIONS

Agrément de conduite:	8/10
Fiabilité:	8/10
Sécurité:	8/10
Qualités hivernales:	7/10
Espace intérieur:	10/10
Confort:	8/10

www.nissan.ca

Plus d'informations dans la section statistiques en dernière partie du Guide

UN MULTISEGMENT FORT CIVILISÉ

Le Rogue, venu en remplacement du très rustique X-Trail depuis 2008, connaît un succès de vente dépassant sans doute les attentes de son constructeur. Par contre, plusieurs essayeurs n'ont pas été très tendres envers ce nouveau venu. Ils ont raison s'ils le considèrent comme un VUS, ce qu'il n'est pas. En effet, comme plusieurs autres véhicules de cette catégorie, il s'agit davantage d'un multisegment que d'un véhicule capable d'en découdre avec des sentiers quasiment impraticables.

D'ailleurs, comme sa plate-forme est empruntée à la Sentra, une berline compacte pas trop robuste, rien ne permet de croire qu'on pourrait jouer les baroudeurs à son volant. En revanche, sa traction intégrale optionnelle, sa silhouette élégante et ses bonnes manières sur la route en font un véhicule urbain fort apprécié surtout auprès des dames qui recherchent élégance et polyvalence.

ÉLÉGANCE ET CONFORT

Avec son capot plongeant, ses phares en forme d'amande s'étirant sur les ailes et sa calandre elliptique comprenant en son centre le logo Nissan, sans oublier les passages d'aile en relief, le Rogue nous fait songer au Murano, le VUS intermédiaire qui a jumelé pour la première fois caractère pratique et silhouette élégante. Et cette similitude se poursuit dans la fenestration avec une ceinture de caisse relativement haute qui se prolonge en montant vers le pilier C. À cela s'ajoute une partie arrière inclinée vers l'avant afin d'afficher une silhouette sportive et dynamique. Sans oublier, bien entendu, la prise d'air sous le pare-chocs avant qui est encadrée par les phares anti-brouillard ; une présentation esthétique partagée par ces deux modèles. Toutefois, le Murano est plus costaud en raison de ses dimensions extérieures.

Une fois assis dans l'habitacle, le pilote appréciera très rapidement le confort des sièges ainsi que leur support latéral qui est nettement supérieur à la moyenne de cette catégorie. La planche de bord est très stylisée avec ses buses de ventilation rondes cerclées d'un anneau en aluminium brossé qui donne du relief à l'ensemble. Les deux principaux cadrans indicateurs sont également cerclés de métal. Quant aux commandes elles-mêmes, elles sont simples avec les incontournables trois boutons pour la climatisation tandis que le système audio est géré par une double rangée de touches. Par contre, il faudra un certain temps pour s'habituer à la mise en mémoire des postes de radio qui sont affichés en raison de nos préférences et non pas selon les bandes de diffusion. Il faut également ajouter que le volant est réglable en hauteur et en profondeur, ce qui permet à la majorité des gens de trouver la position de conduite qui leur convient.

Les occupants arrière n'auront pas trop à se plaindre à condition de ne pas mesurer six pieds. À l'image de ces places arrière, le coffre à

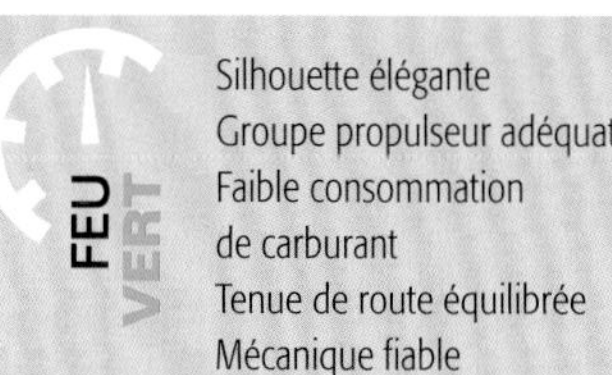

FEU VERT

Silhouette élégante
Groupe propulseur adéquat
Faible consommation de carburant
Tenue de route équilibrée
Mécanique fiable

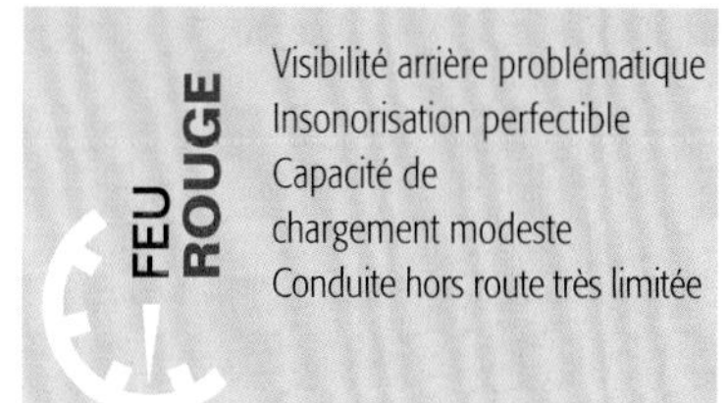

FEU ROUGE

Visibilité arrière problématique
Insonorisation perfectible
Capacité de chargement modeste
Conduite hors route très limitée

bagages est correct, mais sans plus. Pour avoir plus d'espace et déplacer des objets encombrants, il faudra abaisser les dossiers arrière qui sont de type 60/40.

CHOIX SIMPLIFIÉ

Pour des raisons inconnues, plusieurs constructeurs prennent un malin plaisir à offrir deux ou trois groupes propulseurs pour un modèle donné. C'est souvent un effort inutile, car généralement un seul moteur répond aux critères de la majorité des gens. En plus, cela augmente les coûts de fabrication et d'entreposage à l'usine. Nissan a eu la bonne idée de simplifier les choses : seul le moteur quatre cylindres de 2,5 litres de 170 chevaux est offert. Cette simplicité est reprise au chapitre de la boîte de vitesse puisque la transmission à rapports continuellement variables est la seule disponible.

Force est d'admettre que ce groupe propulseur est bien adapté et travaille harmonieusement avec cette transmission CVT qui demeure l'une des plus efficaces dans la catégorie. En outre, s'il faut se fier au sondage réalisé auprès des consommateurs de l'Amérique du Nord, ce tandem est d'une rassurante fiabilité. De toute évidence, les accélérations ne sont pas foudroyantes, mais on peut quand même boucler le 0-100 km/h en moins de 9,0 secondes, ce qui est correct. Et si vous n'aimez pas le ronronnement incessant émis par cette transmission à rapports continuellement variables, on vous laisse le choix de passer manuellement les rapports virtuels.

Les ingénieurs attitrés pour régler la suspension ont réussi un compromis intéressant entre une bonne tenue de route et le confort. Les trous et les bosses sont amortis efficacement tandis que le roulis en virage est très peu prononcé. Le Rogue se veut un véhicule maniable et agile dans la circulation, élément important compte tenu de sa vocation en grande partie urbaine. Par contre, s'il se débrouille fort bien dans la circulation les manœuvres de stationnement sont plus difficiles en raison d'une faible visibilité arrière. On ne peut tout avoir !

Ce modèle arrive de série avec la traction avant, ce qui conviendra à bien des gens. Mais puisqu'une intégrale est offerte, et ce, à prix passablement raisonnable, plusieurs acheteurs choisissent cette option.

Denis Duquet

PHOTOS : NISSAN

Catégorie	VUS
Échelle de prix	23 198 $ à 27 798 $
Garanties	3 ans/60 000 km, 5 ans/100 000 km
Assemblage	Kyushu, Japon
Cote d'assurance	n.d.

CHÂSSIS - DONNÉES POUR SL TI

Emp/lon/lar/haut	2 690/4 645/1 800/1 684 mm
Coffre	818 à 1 639 litres
Réservoir	60 litres
Nombre coussins sécurité	6
Antipatinage / contrôle stabilité	oui / oui
Suspension avant	indépendante, jambes de force
Suspension arrière	indépendante, multibras
Freins avant / arrière	disque (ABS) / disque (ABS)
Direction	à crémaillère, ass. variable électrique
Diamètre de braquage	11,4 m
Pneus avant / arrière	P225/60R17 / P225/60R17
Poids	1 574 kg
Capacité de remorquage	454 kg (1 000 lb)

COMPOSANTES MÉCANIQUES

S TA, SL TA, S TI, SL TI

Cylindrée, soupapes, alim.	4L 2,5 litres 16 s atmos.
Puissance / Couple	170 chevaux / 175 lb-pi
Tr. base (opt) / rouage base (opt)	CVT / Tr (Int)
0-100 / 80-120 / 100-0 km/h	8,9 s / 7,7 s / 40,6 m
Type ess. / ville / autoroute	Ordinaire / 9,4 / 7,7 l/100 km

DANS LA MÊME CATÉGORIE

Chevrolet Equinox, Ford Escape, Honda CR-V, Hyundai Tucson, Jeep Compass, Jeep Patriot, Kia Sportage, Mazda Tribute, Mitsubishi Outlander, Subaru Forester, Suzuki Grand Vitara, Toyota RAV4, Volkswagen Tiguan

DU NOUVEAU EN 2011

Aucun changement majeur

NOS IMPRESSIONS

Agrément de conduite :	7/10
Fiabilité :	8/10
Sécurité :	10/10
Qualités hivernales :	8/10
Espace intérieur :	7/10
Confort :	8/10

www.nissan.ca

Plus d'informations dans la section statistiques en dernière partie du Guide

UNE TROP TIMIDE EN FIN DE PARCOURS

La concurrence des voitures compactes est féroce et qui s'y frotte, s'y pique. Certaines s'y piquent plus que d'autres et c'est le cas de la Nissan Sentra, qui n'a plus le panache des premières années. Vivement sa 7e génération, qui devrait nous arriver d'ici un an ou deux...

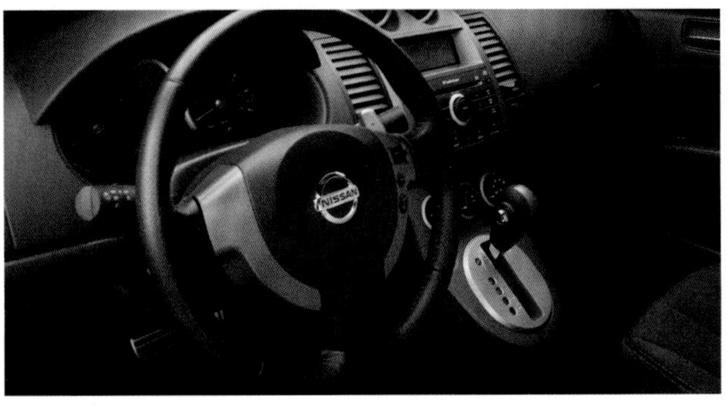

En attendant, la Sentra souffre. Elle souffre versus la compétition, mais elle souffre aussi versus sa consœur la Versa, une petite pas mal plus populaire qui bosse dans la même salle d'exposition. Si vous faites le test et que vous prenez place sur la banquette arrière de l'une comme de l'autre, vous découvrirez que la Versa propose davantage de dégagement aux jambes (à peine 876 mm pour la Sentra...) – et pas à peu près. Qui plus est, la Versa est définitivement plus logeable, côté cargo. Ça fait mal à la doyenne...

RIEN DE FAUX

Ceci dit, la Sentra n'a rien de faux. Vrai que son style extérieur commence à dater et ce qu'on trouvait joli il y a quelques années est devenu à la fois générique et trop timide. Mais reste que l'ensemble est encore honnête. La planche de bord est peut-être simpliste, mais elle demeure fonctionnelle et ergonomique, de sorte qu'on s'y retrouve rapidement. Aussi, on aime que le levier de vitesse soit positionné en hauteur comme pour la Toyota Matrix, à la tombée de la main.

Certes, les versions de base sont... vraiment de base, sans groupe électrique, sans ajustement en hauteur du siège conducteur (une nécessité, sinon les plus grands trouveront trop bas le plafond) et sans contrôle de traction ni système de stabilité (tous deux en option). Mais si l'on y met le prix, on peut quand même équiper la petite avec les sièges de cuir chauffants, les commandes audio au volant, la caméra de recul (!) et le système de navigation, des gâteries qui ne sont pas toujours offertes ailleurs. De fait, la Sentra se trouve tellement en fin de parcours qu'on peut décrocher davantage pour le prix que pas mal d'autres de la catégorie.

Quand même, si l'on s'en tient au minimum, côté facture, on obtient une voiture respectable, avec de bons matériaux qui sont bien assemblés (on aime le doux revêtement de tissu « suédé »), une bonne insonorisation et des sièges relativement confortables. Un seul regret: toujours pas de volant télescopique, mais c'est une lacune que la prochaine génération viendra assurément corriger. Patience...

PENSEZ SE-R SPECV

Côté motorisation, le quatre cylindres de 2,0 litres produit une puissance de 140 chevaux, ce qui est raisonnable lorsque distribué par la boîte manuelle (à six rapports, notez bien). Cette dernière se passe bien, malgré un embrayage assez haut qui force la réflexion plutôt que l'instinct. Par contre, la conduite est ce qu'il y a de plus neutre: la balade est rendue plus bondissante que la moyenne en

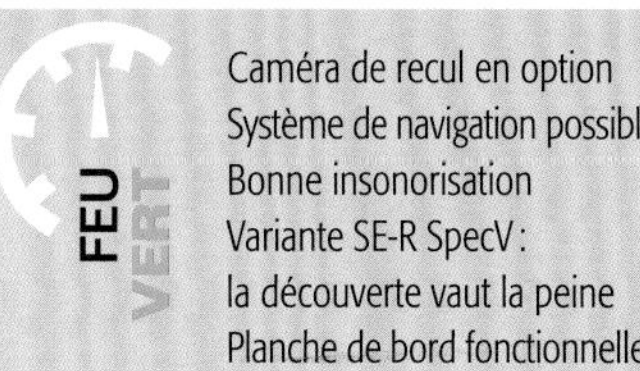

FEU VERT

Caméra de recul en option
Système de navigation possible
Bonne insonorisation
Variante SE-R SpecV : la découverte vaut la peine
Planche de bord fonctionnelle

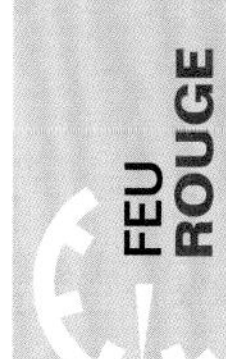

FEU ROUGE

Espace aux jambes arrière : zéro pis une barre…
Pas de volant télescopique
Contrôle de traction en option (version de base)
Direction électrique anesthésiante

raison de la poutre de torsion à la suspension arrière et dans son ensemble, l'expérience est anesthésiée par une direction électrique qui manque de connexion avec la route. C'est comme si la voiture y flottait plutôt que d'y rouler. La boîte à variation continue (CVT) qui, ici, fait office de transmission automatique, retranche encore plus de sensations et il faut s'adapter à ce style d'accélérations qui titille l'oreille sans pour autant se traduire par une vivacité convaincante.

Pour sa fin de parcours, la Sentra est nettement plus intéressante dans sa livrée SE-R SpecV. Au-delà de la soupe à l'alphabet servie par ces acronymes, on se retrouve avec un quatre cylindres de 2,5 litres qui produit 200 chevaux et qui a le bonheur d'être uniquement jumelé avec une belle boîte manuelle à six vitesses rapprochées. La suspension sport surbaissée (de 20 mm) et les pneus de 17 pouces accordent une tenue de route plus dynamique et on s'amuse à transiger les rapports dans des accélérations souples – quoiqu'avec parfois un p'tit effet de couple au volant. Aussi, on aime les sièges sport, les pédales d'aluminium et l'effet visuel qu'aileron et jupes latérales lui procurent.

N'allez toutefois pas croire que la Sentra SE-R SpecV parvient à concurrencer les MazdaSpeed3 et Volks GTi de ce monde. Le zest n'y est pas complètement, la suspension en poutre de torsion n'est pas à la hauteur et, surtout, on ne nous fera pas accroire qu'une « pocket rocket » peut s'en tirer haut la main avec une direction électrique. Aussi, on se rigole des deux cadrans additionnels qui indiquent la pression d'huile et… le nombre de « g » subis, mais longitudinalement ! Faudrait quand même pas exagérer…

Reste que la petite Sentra en livrée sportive est plaisante à manœuvrer et même si elle n'a pas l'envergure ou encore l'aplomb des deux autres, elle montre suffisamment les dents pour qu'on ait envie, encore et encore, de la tester en accélérations et en virages serrés. Bref, la découverte vaut la peine.

Oh, un dernier conseil : oubliez la SE-R tout court. Le moteur de 2,5 litres n'y développe que 177 chevaux et la variante est uniquement livrée avec la transmission CVT. Même le passage des rapports (virtuels, bien sûr) au volant ne parvient pas à mettre assez de piquant là-dedans…

Nadine Filion

PHOTOS : MARC LACHAPELLE

NISSAN SENTRA

Catégorie	Berline
Échelle de prix	15 198 $ à 23 198 $ (2010)
Garanties	3 ans/60 000 km, 5 ans/100 000 km
Assemblage	Aguascalientes, Mexique
Cote d'assurance	moyenne

CHÂSSIS - DONNÉES POUR SE-R

Emp/lon/lar/haut	2 685/4 575/1 791/1 511 mm
Coffre	371 litres
Réservoir	55 litres
Nombre coussins sécurité	6
Antipatinage / contrôle stabilité	oui / oui
Suspension avant	indépendante, jambes de force
Suspension arrière	indépendante, barres de torsion
Freins avant / arrière	disque (ABS) / disque (ABS)
Direction	à crémaillère, ass. variable
Diamètre de braquage	10,6 m
Pneus avant / arrière	P225/45R17 / P225/45R17
Poids	1 397 kg
Capacité de remorquage	454 kg (1 000 lb)

COMPOSANTES MÉCANIQUES

2.0, 2.0 S, 2.0 SL

Cylindrée, soupapes, alim.	4L 2,0 litres 16 s atmos.
Puissance / Couple	140 chevaux / 147 lb-pi
Tr. base (opt) / rouage base (opt)	M6 (CVT) / Tr
0-100 / 80-120 / 100-0 km/h	9,6 s / 8,0 s / 41,6 m
Type ess. / ville / autoroute	Ordinaire / 7,5 / 5,8 l/100 km

SE-R

Cylindrée, soupapes, alim.	4L 2,5 litres 16 s atmos.
Puissance / Couple	177 chevaux / 172 lb-pi
Tr. base (opt) / rouage base (opt)	CVT / Tr
0-100 / 80-120 / 100-0 km/h	8,1 s / n.d. / 40,5 m
Type ess. / ville / autoroute	Ordinaire / 8,7 / 6,5 l/100 km

SE-R Spec V

Cylindrée, soupapes, alim.	4L 2,5 litres 16 s atmos.
Puissance / Couple	200 chevaux / 180 lb-pi
Tr. base (opt) / rouage base (opt)	M6 / Tr
0-100 / 80-120 / 100-0 km/h	7,3 s / n.d. / 40,5 m
Type ess. / ville / autoroute	Ordinaire / 9,8 / 7 l/100 km

DANS LA MÊME CATÉGORIE

Chevrolet Cruze, Ford Focus, Honda Civic, Hyundai Elantra, Kia Forte, Mazda3, Mitsubishi Lancer, Subaru Impreza, Suzuki SX-4, Toyota Corolla, Volkswagen Golf

DU NOUVEAU EN 2011

Système de contrôle de la traction et de la stabilité latérale de série

NOS IMPRESSIONS

Agrément de conduite :	■■■■■■■□□□	7/10
Fiabilité :	■■■■■■□□□□	6/10
Sécurité :	■■■■■■■■■□	9/10
Qualités hivernales :	■■■■■■■■□□	8/10
Espace intérieur :	■■■■■■■□□□	7/10
Confort :	■■■■■■■□□□	7/10

www.nissan.ca

Plus d'informations dans la section statistiques en dernière partie du Guide

ELLE CONTINUE DE SURPRENDRE !

Faisant partie de notre paysage automobile depuis 2007, la sous-compacte de Nissan, la Versa, continue de nous surprendre. À ce moment, seul le modèle à hayon existait et il avait mérité la deuxième place d'un match comparatif mené par le *Guide de l'auto*, la première position allant à son éternelle rivale, la Honda Fit. Depuis, une version berline est apparue, démolissant à coup de bas prix, le peu de crédibilité de sa grande sœur, la Sentra.

Comme nous venons tout juste de le voir, la Versa est proposée en versions *hatchback* et berline. Des deux, le *hatchback* nous apparait comme la plus jolie mais il s'agit d'une question de goût dont nous ne discuterons pas ! Elle s'avère, par contre, indubitablement plus pratique avec son grand coffre même si le hayon n'ouvre pas suffisamment haut pour ne pas scalper les personnes de plus de six pieds, même si les dossiers des sièges, une fois baissés, ne forment pas un fond plat, même si son seuil de chargement est trop élevé et même si le cache-bagages nous semble d'une extrême fragilité. Quant au coffre de la berline, il ne démérite pas pour autant. Son ouverture, tout comme ses dimensions, est étonnamment grande mais son seuil, à lui aussi, est trop élevé.

DU PAREIL AU MÊME

L'habitacle de la berline ou du *hatchback* est identique et très grand. Le tableau de bord est pratique à défaut d'être esthétique et la nuit venue, son éclairage jaunâtre est d'un pathétique rarement vu... Les jauges se consultent aisément cependant, il ne faut pas chercher d'aiguille pour la température du moteur, une omission que l'on retrouve malheureusement dans plus en plus de modèles. Il est certain qu'un miroir derrière un pare-soleil est un accessoire bien plus important... La qualité des plastiques est correcte et les sièges sont très confortables malgré le tissu de la version de base qui ramasse les poils et poussières mieux que n'importe quel préposé au ménage. La position de conduite se trouve facilement et la visibilité tout le tour est très bonne, merci aux petites fenêtres en triangle logées à la base des piliers du pare-brise. La banquette arrière offre beaucoup d'espace et deux adultes n'auront aucun problème à s'y installer pour un long voyage. La place centrale, en revanche, est à éviter à tout prix.

La Versa à hayon reçoit un quatre cylindres de 1,8 litre de 122 chevaux, une écurie adéquate, d'autant plus qu'on n'achète pas une Versa pour faire de l'épate. La transmission de base est une manuelle, à six rapports, s'il vous plait ! La course du levier, par contre, est trop longue pour prétendre à la sportivité. On retrouve, en option sur la version de base, une boîte automatique à quatre rapports dont le seul avantage est de... de... si vous le trouvez, appelez-nous. La livrée SL, plus luxueuse, a droit à une automatique de type CVT, c'est-à-dire à rapports continuellement variables. On peut ne pas aimer cette boîte qui, lors des accélérations, amène le niveau sonore dans l'habitacle près de celui d'un Boeing au

NISSAN VERSA

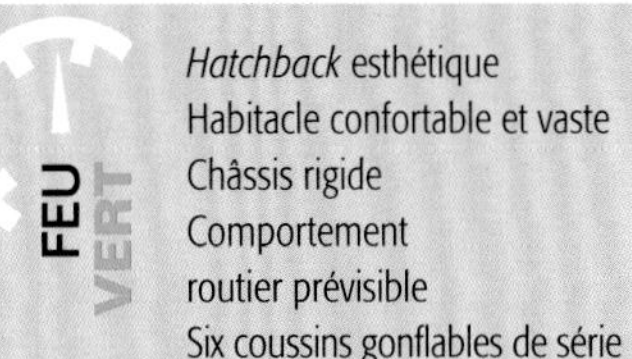

Hatchback esthétique
Habitacle confortable et vaste
Châssis rigide
Comportement routier prévisible
Six coussins gonflables de série

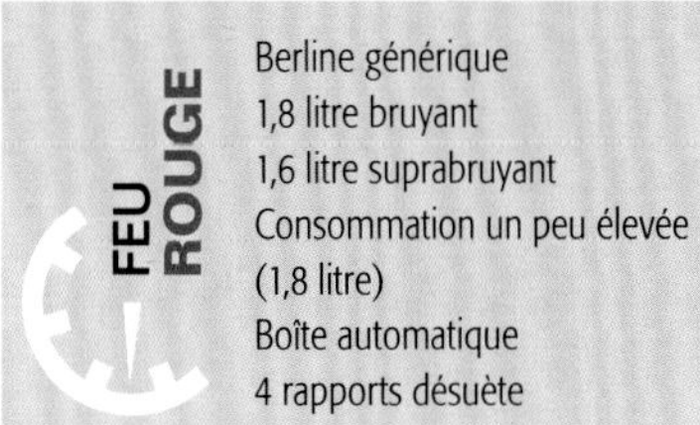

Berline générique
1,8 litre bruyant
1,6 litre suprabruyant
Consommation un peu élevée (1,8 litre)
Boîte automatique 4 rapports désuète

décollage, mais elle permet de garder la consommation d'essence dans les limites du raisonnable, le 1,8 litre se montrant plutôt assoiffé avec les deux autres boîtes.

De son côté, la Versa berline cache sous son capot un quatre cylindres de 1,6 litre de 107 chevaux seulement. Ce moteur, sans faire preuve d'enthousiasme au travail, permet des accélérations et des reprises acceptables, compte tenu du prix de la voiture et de sa vocation. Cependant, il est extraordinairement bruyant dès qu'il fournit le moindre effort. La transmission automatique à quatre rapports passe les rapports de manière peu délicate mais comme elle le fait au bon moment, on ne lui en voudra pas. Une manuelle à cinq rapports, proposée en équipement standard, permet de bien exploiter la puissance du moteur. Curieusement, il n'y a pas une différence énorme entre la prestation des deux moteurs et si le 1,6 était offert pour le *hatchback*, nous n'hésiterions pas à le recommander. Mais bon sang qu'il est bruyant ! Peu importe le moteur, l'effet de couple (les roues avant tirent chacune de leur côté en accélération vive) est très bien contrôlé.

ÉTONNANTE VERSA

Le comportement routier de la Versa, à hayon ou pas, étonne. À tel point qu'on se croirait au volant d'une compacte... ce qu'est la Versa sur plusieurs autres marchés ! Le châssis est très rigide et les suspensions offrent un confort relevé. La direction électrique est passablement précise pourvu qu'on ne la brusque pas. Les freins à disque à l'avant et à tambour à l'arrière, dont l'ABS est de série sur pratiquement tous les modèles, travaillent très fort pour stopper la voiture lors d'un arrêt d'urgence et les distances sont à peine correctes. Même si la Versa affiche un sous-virage prononcé lorsqu'on la pousse trop, son comportement routier général inspire la confiance, pour autant qu'on respecte ses limites. À ce chapitre, cependant, elle se fait royalement damer le pion par la Honda Fit.

Même si ses dimensions en font presque une compacte, la Versa demeure une voiture très abordable, confortable, spacieuse et bien construite. Mais elle doit faire face à la féroce concurrence de la Honda Fit, plus agréable à conduire et mieux aménagée, et de la Toyota Yaris dont la fiabilité et la valeur de revente sont supérieures. Reste les Kia Rio et Hyundai Accent, à l'aube d'une refonte et les nouvelles Ford Fiesta et Mazda2...

Alain Morin

PHOTOS : ALAIN MORIN

Catégorie	Berline, *Hatchback*
Échelle de prix	12 698 $ à 17 398 $ (2010)
Garanties	3 ans/60 000 km, 5 ans/100 000 km
Assemblage	Aguascalientes, Mexique
Cote d'assurance	n.d.

CHÂSSIS - DONNÉES POUR 1.8 S HAYON

Emp/lon/lar/haut	2 600/4 295/1 695/1 535 mm
Coffre	504 à 1 427 litres
Réservoir	50 litres
Nombre coussins sécurité	6
Antipatinage / contrôle stabilité	opt / opt
Suspension avant	indépendante, jambes de force
Suspension arrière	semi-indépendante, barres de torsion
Freins avant / arrière	disque (ABS en option) / tambour (ABS en option)
Direction	à crémaillère, ass. variable électrique
Diamètre de braquage	10,4 m
Pneus avant / arrière	P185/65R15 / P185/65R15
Poids	1 222 kg
Capacité de remorquage	non recommandé

COMPOSANTES MÉCANIQUES

1.6	
Cylindrée, soupapes, alim.	4L 1,6 litre 16 s atmos.
Puissance / Couple	107 chevaux / 111 lb-pi
Tr. base (opt) / rouage base (opt)	M5 (A4) / Tr
0-100 / 80-120 / 100-0 km/h	10,6 s / n.d. / 41,5 m
Type ess. / ville / autoroute	Ordinaire / 8,5 / 6,3 l/100 km

1.8	
Cylindrée, soupapes, alim.	4L 1,8 litre 16 s atmos.
Puissance / Couple	122 chevaux / 127 lb-pi
Tr. base (opt) / rouage base (opt)	M6 (A4, CVT) / Tr
0-100 / 80-120 / 100-0 km/h	9,5 s / 8,3 s / 41,5 m
Type ess. / ville / autoroute	Ordinaire / 8,5 / 6,3 l/100 km

DANS LA MÊME CATÉGORIE

Chevrolet Aveo, Ford Fiesta, Honda Fit, Hyundai Accent, Kia Rio/Rio5, Mazda2, Suzuki Swift+, Toyota Yaris

DU NOUVEAU EN 2011

Aucun changement majeur

NOS IMPRESSIONS

Agrément de conduite :	■■■■■■■□□□	7/10
Fiabilité :	■■■■■■□□□□	6/10
Sécurité :	■■■■■■■■□□	8/10
Qualités hivernales :	■■■■■■■□□□	7/10
Espace intérieur :	■■■■■■■■□□	8/10
Confort :	■■■■■■■□□□	7/10

www.nissan.ca

Plus d'informations dans la section statistiques en dernière partie du Guide

SI L'EVEREST VOUS INTERPELLE

C'était en 1999. Cher obtenait la première place du palmarès avec *Believe, Shakespeare in Love* remportait l'Oscar du meilleur film et Nissan profitait pleinement de la vague déferlante des VUS, en dévoilant son Xterra, un truck plus adapté à l'Everest qu'à l'autoroute 20. En 2006, cet infatigable baroudeur connaissait un second départ après une refonte complète et depuis, plus rien. Nous sommes donc surpris de son retour ! Complètement largué par des multisegments infiniment plus modernes, le Xterra trouve quand même preneur. Il est même surprenant de constater que durant les six premiers mois de 2010, il s'en est vendu 455 exemplaires à travers tout le Canada.

Alors, qui sont donc ces 455 personnes ? On ne peut présumer de rien, mais j'imagine (en fait, j'espère serait plus juste) qu'elles ont vraiment des besoins très particuliers en termes de hors route et des attentes bien peu élevées sur les routes… Il faut dire que Xterra est un camion comme il ne s'en fait à peu près plus. Bâti sur la plate-forme du Nissan Frontier, il est muni d'un essieu rigide à l'arrière, ce qui n'aide pas à rendre la promenade sur le bitume des plus douces. Par contre, dès que la route n'est plus, le Xterra se dévoile. Grâce à ses angles d'attaque et de départ généreux, sa garde au sol élevée, son boîtier de transfert à gamme basse et son couple moteur volontaire, il peut s'attaquer à des sentiers impraticables. Pourtant, on parle ici des versions qui ne sont même pas munies de l'ensemble Tout-Terrain qui comprend un rapport final de différentiel adapté à la conduite hors-route sérieuse, un refroidisseur de la boîte de vitesse, le contrôle de l'adhérence en pente et l'assistance au démarrage en côte. Ainsi équipé, le Xterra ne rougit pas devant les Jeep

Wrangler ou Toyota FJ Cruiser. Ces trois véhicules ne possèdent pas de « Multi Terrain Response » ou autre bidule électronique du genre qui permet à n'importe quel ignare en matière de hors route d'avoir l'air brillant. Avec notre trio, il faut travailler.

Il ne faudrait pas condamner la conduite sur route du Xterra pour autant. On est, bien entendu, loin d'une sportive, mais un aller-retour Montréal-Québec à l'intérieur de la même journée ne nous laisse pas la colonne vertébrale dans un état neurovégétatif. Je dirais même que le Nissan est plus confortable que les Wrangler et FJ Cruiser. La direction, curieusement, est bien dosée et précise. Enfin, pour un 4x4 disons, car en conduite hors route, un certain jeu dans la direction est nettement préférable à une précision de modeleur. Un retour de volant après avoir heurté une roche est si vite arrivée !

MÉCANIQUE SIMPLE

Le moteur V6 de 4,0 litres est suffisamment puissant pour permettre au Xterra de s'arracher de son inertie avec un bel aplomb, dans une sonorité assez intéressante. Certes, on entend le moteur rouspéter un peu, mais une fois parti, plus rien ne semble l'arrêter ! S'il

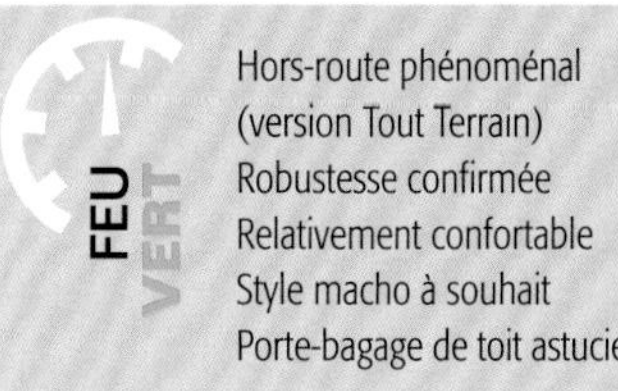

FEU VERT

Hors-route phénoménal (version Tout Terrain)
Robustesse confirmée
Relativement confortable
Style macho à souhait
Porte-bagage de toit astucieux

FEU ROUGE

Consommation à pleurer
Plusieurs plastiques « cheap »
Randonnée assez ferme
Accès à bord plus ou moins facile
Valeur de revente dans 4 ou 5 ans ???

était moins assoiffé, il n'en serait que plus admiré. Deux transmissions sont au programme, soit une manuelle à six rapports, dont le maniement du levier est quasiment un plaisir, et une automatique à cinq vitesses, fort réussie. Un coup de volant trop enthousiaste fait rapidement ressortir un roulis considérable. Par contre, le soutien latéral des sièges est une agréable surprise. C'est une chance, puisqu'ils ne sont pas si confortables !

De l'extérieur, on ne peut pas dire que l'Xterra manque de caractère. Moins caricatural que le FJ Cruiser, il montre tout de même des éléments typiques des 4x4 de brousse. Par exemple, les ailes très saillantes et les nombreuses parties en PVC noir. De son côté, le hayon présente un renflement à sa gauche qui imite un jerrican ou une trousse de premiers soins. Ça tombe bien, c'est justement une trousse que l'on retrouve à l'intérieur du hayon, bien enchâssée dans ce renflement ! Il y a aussi ces feux de conduite hors route, offerts de série sur la version « Tout Terrain », placés bien en évidence sur le toit, juste devant le porte-bagages. Ces deux éléments ajoutent joyeusement au style du véhicule. En fait, le porte-bagages a une fonction aussi esthétique que pratique puisqu'il est suffisamment grand pour camoufler à la fois certains objets et le toit à deux niveaux. Astucieux.

Accéder à l'habitacle demande une certaine souplesse, le plancher étant situé relativement haut. Heureusement, on retrouve des marchepieds en équipement standard, sauf sur la version Tout-Terrain où ces appendices deviendraient un handicap en hors-route. Une fois à l'intérieur, on découvre un habitacle très grand, mais dont la qualité de matériaux n'est plus tout à fait à la mode. En effet, la grande majorité des plastiques sont durs et s'égratignent juste à les regarder. Le tableau de bord est complet et très ergonomique, ce qui fait pardonner son manque d'excentricité. Curieux comment les designers peuvent créer une carrosserie déjantée et un habitacle quelconque... C'est rarement l'inverse, aviez-vous remarqué ? Ce n'est pas parce qu'on est vieux qu'on n'est plus dans le coup, s'est dit le Xterra : il propose, d'office, six coussins gonflables et, bien entendu, les systèmes électroniques du contrôle de la traction et de la stabilité latérale.

L'Xterra n'est pas pour tout le monde, mais si vous êtes un baroudeur actif, il a le potentiel pour vous plaire.

Alain Morin

PHOTOS : NISSAN

Catégorie	VUS
Échelle de prix	33 698 $ à 37 498 $ (2010)
Garanties	3 ans/60 000 km, 5 ans/100 000 km
Assemblage	Smyrna, Tennessee, É-U
Cote d'assurance	moyenne

CHÂSSIS - DONNÉES POUR SE

Emp/lon/lar/haut	2 700/4 540/1 850/1 903 mm
Coffre	991 à 1 869 litres
Réservoir	80 litres
Nombre coussins sécurité	6
Antipatinage / contrôle stabilité	oui / oui
Suspension avant	indépendante, double triangulation
Suspension arrière	essieu rigide, ressorts à lames
Freins avant / arrière	disque (ABS) / disque (ABS)
Direction	à crémaillère, ass. variable
Diamètre de braquage	11,3 m
Pneus avant / arrière	P265/65R17 / P265/65R17
Poids	2 007 kg
Capacité de remorquage	2 268 kg (5 000 lb)

COMPOSANTES MÉCANIQUES

S, Tout Terrain, SE

Cylindrée, soupapes, alim.	V6 4,0 litres 24 s atmos.
Puissance / Couple	261 chevaux / 281 lb-pi
Tr. base (opt) / rouage base (opt)	M6 (A5) / 4x4
0-100 / 80-120 / 100-0 km/h	7,9 s / 6,2 s / 41,8 m
Type ess. / ville / autoroute	Ordinaire / 14,5 / 10,2 l/100km

DANS LA MÊME CATÉGORIE

Dodge Nitro, Jeep Liberty, Jeep Wrangler, Toyota FJ Cruiser

DU NOUVEAU EN 2011

Aucun changement majeur

NOS IMPRESSIONS

Agrément de conduite :	6/10
Fiabilité :	8/10
Sécurité :	8/10
Qualités hivernales :	9/10
Espace intérieur :	8/10
Confort :	6/10

www.nissan.ca

Plus d'informations dans la section statistiques en dernière partie du Guide

DES MACHINES À DÉFIER LE TEMPS

La série 911 est simultanément le passé, le présent et l'avenir du constructeur de Zuffenhausen. Les modèles produits depuis près de soixante maintenant lui ont tissé une histoire et un palmarès fabuleusement riches, sur la route, les circuits et même en plein désert. Les modèles actuels évoluent constamment. À preuve : une nouvelle 911 Turbo plus raffinée que jamais, aux performances carrément stupéfiantes. Et ce n'est certainement pas tout puisque les ingénieurs de Porsche ne cessent de projeter la 911 vers l'avenir.

Dans le cycle continuel de son évolution et de renouvellement des différents modèles de la série 911, c'était d'abord au tour de la Turbo d'être l'objet de toutes les attentions des ingénieurs et développeurs. Cet archétype de la voiture sport en est ressorti avec tellement de modifications, retouches et mises à jour que Porsche la présente comme une deuxième édition de la 997.

Ses dimensions essentielles sont intactes et les changements peu apparents de l'extérieur. L'œil averti détectera de nouveaux blocs optiques à DEL, des prises d'air avant gris titane et des embouts d'échappement plus gros. À l'intérieur, on remarque l'écran de contrôle plus grand et plus clair, mais surtout un nouveau volant sport optionnel enfin doté de grandes manettes en aluminium montées derrière la jante. Elles permettent de passer les 7 rapports de la boîte PDK à double embrayage automatisé, autre nouveauté pour la Turbo. Plus efficace et compacte, elle réduit également le poids de 25 kg par rapport à l'ancienne Tiptronic S.

PERFORMANCES SPECTACULAIRES

La Turbo reçoit également un premier moteur entièrement nouveau en 35 ans. La cylindrée grimpe de 3,6 à 3,8 litres et il profite désormais de l'injection directe et d'une lubrification par carter sec, ce qui le rend plus compact et léger. On lui a greffé une paire de turbos à géométrie variable, dotés d'une turbine d'impulsion plus grande.

La puissance passe de 480 à 500 chevaux à 6000 tr/min et le couple maxi est maintenant de 479 lb-pi, livré entre 1900 et 5000 tr/min, soit 22 lb/pi de mieux. On se régale aussi d'une pointe de couple de 516 lb-pi qui dure dix secondes en pleine accélération, grâce à un mode Surpression (*overboost*) qui se répète à volonté. La consommation est malgré tout réduite de 16 % et les émissions de gaz carbonique de 18 % sur la Turbo avec la PDK !

La boîte PDK comporte un mode de « démarrage assisté » (ou *launch control*) électronique simple et redoutablement efficace. Il suffit d'appuyer sur le bouton Sport Plus, pied gauche sur le frein et accélérateur à fond. Lorsque l'aiguille du compte-tours est à 5000 tr/min et que les mots *Launch Control* s'allument sur le volant, on lâche le frein et la Turbo est catapultée vers l'avant pendant que les ordinateurs de bord modulent le patinage des pneus en jouant sur le blocage des embrayages à disque de la boîte PDK.

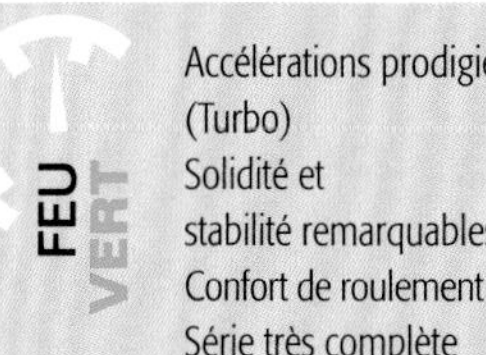

FEU VERT

- Accélérations prodigieuses (Turbo)
- Solidité et stabilité remarquables
- Confort de roulement amélioré
- Série très complète
- Excellente visibilité

FEU ROUGE

- Sonorité du moteur étouffée (Turbo)
- Sous-virage sur circuit (Turbo)
- Volume de chargement limité
- Voitures et options très chères
- Coût d'entretien pharaonique

Résultat: un 0-100 km/h de 3,32 secondes et un quart de mille départ-arrêt en 11,28 secondes, avec une pointe de 204,1 km/h, comme mesuré sur la ligne droite du circuit portugais d'Estoril, lors du lancement. C'est nettement mieux que sa devancière, la plus rapide jusque-là avec des chronos respectifs de 3,55 secondes et 11,75 secondes, avec une pointe de 199,9 km/h.

PERSONNALITÉS MULTIPLES

Sur la route, la nouvelle Turbo est plus raffinée, équilibrée et souple que jamais. Sa direction est d'une finesse sans égale. Le roulement est assez ferme mais plus confortable que sur le modèle précédent. Malgré ses performances exceptionnelles, la Turbo est parfaitement docile sur la route. Comme toutes les 911, elle est superbement compacte et offre une visibilité incomparable.

Sur un circuit comme celui d'Estoril, la Turbo est évidemment rapide, avec de telles accélérations et des freinages mordants. Elle possède, de série, quatre disques de 350 mm avec des étriers à six pistons à l'avant et quatre à l'arrière. On peut l'équiper de freins en céramique qui sont plus légers de 18 kg en tout.

Elle n'est pas tellement enjouée, par contre. Même avec les raffinements apportés à son rouage intégral, le sous-virage à la limite s'accentue si on met les gaz en courbe. Le nouveau système PTV (*Porsche Torque Vectoring*) censé appliquer le frein sur la roue intérieure arrière pour réduire le sous-virage ne semble pas y changer grand-chose en piste.

Pour le pilotage et les sensations pures, il faut plutôt se tourner vers la GT3 ou alors la GT3 RS, offerte à prix quasi égal à la Turbo. Ces deux propulsions sont équipées de versions atmosphériques plus pointues du *boxer* de 3,8 litres qui font 435 et 450 chevaux. Et au sommet, il y a maintenant la GT2 RS, la Porsche de série la plus puissante jamais produite avec son groupe turbo de 620 chevaux.

Porsche a même inscrit une GT3 RS de série aux 24 Heures du Nürburgring. La voiture fut conduite et ramenée du circuit sur la route et a terminé 13e sur les quelque 200 voitures inscrites. Toujours dans cette course, une 911 RS Hybrid dotée d'un volant d'inertie développé par l'écurie de F1 Williams et d'une paire de moteurs électriques de 80 chevaux, couplés aux roues avant, a mené pendant le tiers de la course. La série 911, c'est l'âme de Porsche. La suite ne sera pas ennuyante.

Marc Lachapelle

PHOTOS: MARC LACHAPELLE

Catégorie	Cabriolet, Coupé
Échelle de prix	96 700 $ à 178 400 $
Garanties	4 ans/80 000 km, 4 ans/80 000 km
Assemblage	Stuttgart, Allemagne
Cote d'assurance	n.d.

CHÂSSIS - DONNÉES POUR GT3 RS

Emp/lon/lar/haut	2 355/4 460/1 852/1 280 mm
Coffre	205 litres
Réservoir	67 litres
Nombre coussins sécurité	4
Antipatinage / contrôle stabilité	oui / oui
Suspension avant	indépendante, jambes de force
Suspension arrière	indépendante, multibras
Freins avant / arrière	disque (ABS) / disque (ABS)
Direction	à crémaillère, ass. variable
Diamètre de braquage	n.d.
Pneus avant / arrière	P245/35ZR19 / P325/30ZR19
Poids	1 370 kg
Capacité de remorquage	non recommandé

COMPOSANTES MÉCANIQUES

Carrera
H6 3,6 l, 345 ch, 288 lb-pi - 0-100: 4,8 s - 11,4 / 7,9 l/100 km

Carrera S
H6 3,8 l, 385 ch, 310 lb-pi - 0-100: 4,6 s - 11,8 / 8,0 l/100 km

GT3
H6 3,8 l, 435 ch, 317 lb-pi - 0-100: 4,1 s - 15,2 / 9,7 l/100 km

GT3 RS
H6 3,8 l, 450 ch, 317 lb-pi - 0-100: 4,0 s - 19,4 / 9,6 l/100 km

Turbo
H6 3,8 l, 500 ch, 479 lb-pi - 0-100: 3,6 s - 17,5 / 8,3 l/100 km

Turbo S
H6 3,8 l, 530 ch, 516 lb-pi - 0-100: 3,3 s - 16,7 / 8,2 l/100 km

GT2 RS
H6 3,6 l, 620 ch, 516 lb-pi - 0-100: 3,5 s - 17,9 / 8,7 l/100 km

DANS LA MÊME CATÉGORIE

Aston Martin Vantage, Audi R8, BMW Série 6, Chevrolet Corvette, Dodge Viper, Jaguar XK, Maserati Gran Turismo, Mercedes-Benz Classe SL, Nissan GT-R

DU NOUVEAU EN 2011

Aucun changement majeur, nouvelles couleurs

NOS IMPRESSIONS

Agrément de conduite:	■■■■■■■■■□	9/10
Fiabilité:	■■■■■■□□□□	6/10
Sécurité:	■■■■■■■■■■	10/10
Qualités hivernales:	■■■■■■□□□□	6/10
Espace intérieur:	■■■■■■□□□□	6/10
Confort:	■■■■■■■□□□	7/10

www.porsche.com

Plus d'informations dans la section statistiques en dernière partie du Guide

PLAISIR DES SENS, L'ESSENCE DU PLAISIR

Ayant connu des changements mécaniques d'importance l'an dernier, la Boxster, avec nous depuis 1998, devrait subir des modifications majeures l'an prochain. Il s'agira alors de la troisième génération. N'allez cependant pas croire que la dernière année de la Boxster telle qu'on la connaît se fait sous le signe du statu quo. Ce serait bien mal connaître les gens de chez Porsche !

La grande nouveauté de l'année est l'arrivée de la version Spyder, joyeusement comparée à la première Porsche, la 356 (les nostalgiques se souviennent que Jimmy Dean s'était tué en 1955 dans une 356). Certes, les deux voitures sont destinées aux puristes qui apprécient davantage les qualités dynamiques que le confort. Mais la comparaison, voulue par Porsche, s'arrête là.

POUR PURISTES SEULEMENT

La Spyder reprend le châssis de la Boxster S et la mécanique de la Cayman S, cette dernière seyant mieux au caractère sportif de la nouvelle venue. Le six cylindres à plat de 3,4 litres ne développe pas une puissance extraordinaire (une Nissan 370Z fait mieux !), mais c'est la façon dont cette puissance est délivrée qui fait toute la différence. Les suspensions de la Boxster S ont été abaissées de 20 mm, amenant le centre de gravité de la Spyder plus près du sol. Grâce à une direction d'une précision inouïe qui permet de placer la voiture au millimètre près, on se sent en confiance comme rarement on a pu se sentir en confiance dans une voiture sport. Mais ces éléments ne pourraient se démarquer aussi bien si les ingénieurs de Porsche n'avaient pas travaillé très fort pour réduire le poids de la Boxster S. Le toit, par exemple, et sur lequel nous reviendrons, le couvercle de la partie arrière et les portières en aluminium ont permis d'éliminer 36 kilos. Les sièges, eux, pèsent 12 kilos de moins que ceux de la Boxster S. Bref, on parle, en tout, de 80 kilos de moins que la génitrice. Oh, un petit détail... pour en arriver là, il a aussi fallu supprimer le système de climatisation, la radio, les porte-gobelets et autres inutilités du genre. La Spyder s'adresse aux puristes, on vous l'a dit ! Ces inutilités, de même que le GPS, sont toutefois offertes en option mais le propriétaire d'une Spyder ainsi équipée serait mal avisé de s'introduire dans un club Porsche en prétendant être un « vrai »...

Les deux transmissions qu'on retrouve à bord des Boxster S sont au programme de la Spyder. L'automatique à double embrayage PDK à sept rapports fonctionne avec une machiavélique précision et s'avère même plus rapide sur un circuit que la manuelle à six rapports, pourtant très douée elle aussi. Une ou l'autre se marie parfaitement bien avec le caractère de la voiture, mais plusieurs préféreront le pointe-talon aux boutons sur le volant... d'autant plus que ces boutons qui commandent la PDK ne sont pas des plus intuitifs. Lors d'un essai sur les routes californiennes, notre voiture a maintenu une moyenne de 13,9 L/100 km (16 milles au gallon américain). On ne parle donc pas d'une Prius mais on a déjà vu bien pire sur des voitures moins performantes !

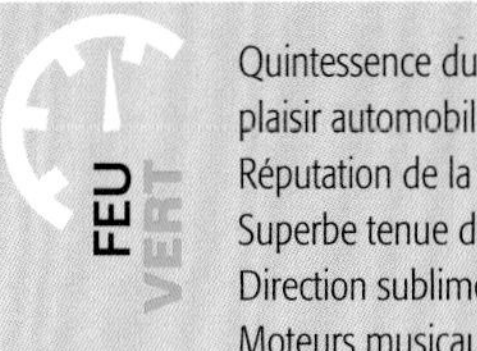

FEU VERT

- Quintessence du plaisir automobile
- Réputation de la marque
- Superbe tenue de route
- Direction sublime
- Moteurs musicaux

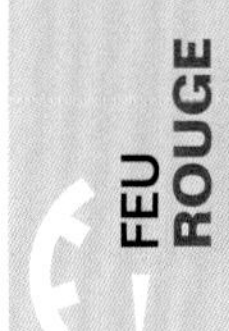

FEU ROUGE

- Habitacle plutôt contraignant
- Prix dramatique de certaines options
- Visibilité arrière problématique (Spyder)
- Boîte PDK peu intuitive
- Coûts d'entretiens faramineux

Les gros Bridgestone Potenza RE050A de 19 pouces de notre voiture d'essai la plaquaient au sol avec une volonté hors du commun, aidés en cela par le différentiel arrière à glissement limité. Les suspensions, certes fermes, font, elles aussi, un boulot exceptionnel, tout comme le PSM (Porsche Stability Management) qui agit avec une autorité quasiment paternelle. Une sortie trop rapide d'une courbe serrée nous a prouvé ses compétences en ramenant la voiture dans le droit chemin sans à-coups ni sans lui faire perdre de la vélocité. Sur une piste, un pilote chevronné aura un plaisir évident à contrôler sa Spyder à l'accélérateur, toute aide électronique désactivée. Et quels freins mes amis !

La Spyder, c'est aussi un toit en toile bizarre. Cette tente de fortune comporte deux éléments faciles à installer malgré les apparences. Une fois en place, les bruits du moteur et de la route ne sont à peu près pas filtrés et la visibilité arrière n'est alors pas meilleure que dans un sous-marin. Avec le toit installé, le passage dans un lave-auto est fortement déconseillé, ainsi que la conduite à plus de 200 km/h, question de pression plus que d'étanchéité ou de solidité. En dépit de son aspect tiers-mondiste, ce toit est plus sérieux qu'il n'y paraît, mais j'ai quand même des doutes sur son utilisation à -20 degrés Celcius.

NOUS ALLIONS OUBLIER LES BOXSTER ET BOXSTER S !

Encore et toujours la référence lorsqu'on parle de voiture sport, la Boxster et la Boxster S demeurent des Porsche pures, sans être dures. Même la version de base fait preuve d'un agrément de conduite bien au-delà de la moyenne tout en ayant une consommation d'essence ma foi très raisonnable... en conduite normale faut-il mentionner. En utilisation sportive, c'est une autre histoire... Par contre, la version S, plus puissante et amenant le plaisir de conduire à un niveau encore supérieur, grâce, entre autres, à des pneus plus imposants et des suspensions plus fermes, ne consomme pas beaucoup plus. Mais il faut être prêt à mettre les 12 000 $ supplémentaires que le « S » amène...

Quoi qu'il en soit, si l'on se fie au passé de Porsche, la prochaine Boxster ne sera pas très différente de la génération actuelle même si elle sera sans doute révisée de fond en comble. Après tout, on ne change pas une recette gagnante !

Alain Morin

PHOTOS : ALAIN MORIN

Catégorie	*Roadster*
Échelle de prix	59 600 $ à 72 900 $
Garanties	4 ans/80 000 km, 4 ans/80 000 km
Assemblage	Stuttgart, Allemagne
Cote d'assurance	n.d.

CHÂSSIS - DONNÉES POUR SPYDER

Emp/lon/lar/haut	2 415/4 342/1 801/1 231 mm
Coffre	130 à 150 litres
Réservoir	54 litres
Nombre coussins sécurité	6
Antipatinage / contrôle stabilité	oui / oui
Suspension avant	indépendante, jambes de force
Suspension arrière	indépendante, jambes de force
Freins avant / arrière	disque (ABS) / disque (ABS)
Direction	à crémaillère, ass. variable
Diamètre de braquage	n.d.
Pneus avant / arrière	235/35ZR19 / 365/35ZR19
Poids	1 275 kg
Capacité de remorquage	non recommandé

COMPOSANTES MÉCANIQUES

Base	
Cylindrée, soupapes, alim.	H6 2,9 litres 16 s atmos.
Puissance / Couple	255 chevaux / 290 lb-pi
Tr. base (opt) / rouage base (opt)	M6 (A7) / Prop
0-100 / 80-120 / 100-0 km/h	5,9 s / 7,6 s / n.d.
Type ess. / ville / autoroute	Super / 11,2 / 7,4 l/100 km

S	
Cylindrée, soupapes, alim.	H6 3,4 litres 16 s atmos.
Puissance / Couple	310 chevaux / 360 lb-pi
Tr. base (opt) / rouage base (opt)	M6 (A7) / Prop
0-100 / 80-120 / 100-0 km/h	5,2 s / 6,4 s / n.d.
Type ess. / ville / autoroute	Super / 11,1 / 7,5 l/100 km

Spyder	
Cylindrée, soupapes, alim.	H6 3,4 litres 16 s atmos.
Puissance / Couple	320 chevaux / 370 lb-pi
Tr. base (opt) / rouage base (opt)	M6 (A7) / Prop
0-100 / 80-120 / 100-0 km/h	5,0 s / 6,1 s / n.d.
Type ess. / ville / autoroute	Super / 14,2 / 7,1 l/100 km

DANS LA MÊME CATÉGORIE

Audi TT, BMW Z4, Lotus Elise, Mercedes-Benz Classe SLK

DU NOUVEAU EN 2011

Modèle Spyder disponible depuis juin 2010

NOS IMPRESSIONS

Agrément de conduite :	10/10
Fiabilité :	7/10
Sécurité :	7/10
Qualités hivernales :	4/10
Espace intérieur :	4/10
Confort :	5/10

www.porsche.ca

Plus d'informations dans la section statistiques en dernière partie du Guide

IL MANQUE LE DIESEL

Même si son entrée en scène a été fortement critiquée, le Porsche Cayenne a été un succès sur toute la ligne. Les ventes ont dépassé les attentes et Porsche a engrangé des profits, ce qui lui a permis de développer la Panamera. À présent, le cycle de vie de ce gros VUS étant complété, voici la seconde génération qui, comme la première, a été développée en collaboration avec le Volkswagen Touareg.

Malgré cette filiation, il serait faux de conclure qu'il s'agit de jumeaux identiques. Chacun de ces deux modèles possède des caractéristiques qui lui sont exclusives de même qu'un comportement routier bien distinct. Cette différence débute avec la silhouette respective de chacun.

UNE ALLURE À PART

Le Cayenne a été accueilli assez froidement en raison de sa silhouette vraiment unique et jugée peu élégante par beaucoup. Au fil des années, de subtiles améliorations ont permis de raffiner son apparence et de la faire accepter par la majorité. Il faut également ajouter que l'on s'est progressivement habitué à cette iconoclaste. Cette fois, la silhouette si particulière a été conservée, mais des changements mineurs ont été apportés afin de poursuivre le travail de raffinement. Évidemment, les ailes avant sont toujours plus hautes que le capot, un design Porsche traditionnel. En fait, les nouveaux blocs optiques sont le changement le plus significatif de cette nouvelle génération et incorporent des LED en tant que phares de jour.

Dans l'habitacle, l'élément qui attire le plus le regard est la console centrale, encadrée de part et d'autre d'une poignée de maintien. Les stylistes ont également placé une poignée semblable dans les

portières. Le support latéral des sièges a été amélioré et les places arrière sont plus généreuses en raison d'un empattement qui a gagné 40 millimètres. La banquette arrière peut être déplacée longitudinalement de 160 millimètres. Par contre, oubliez la place centrale, elle ne servira que pour dépanner.

UNE HYBRIDE ORIGINALE

Chez Porsche, on jette toujours un œil nouveau sur des technologies en place. Dans le cas du moteur hybride, les ingénieurs ont retenu la combinaison moteur thermique/moteur électrique. Le moteur électrique produit 34 kW (47 ch.) et se marie au moteur thermique à compresseur de 333 chevaux. Lorsque les deux fonctionnent, la puissance maximale est de 380 chevaux et les performances correspondent à celles du Cayenne S à moteur V8.

Il est également possible de parcourir quelques kilomètres en mode exclusivement électrique et atteindre une vitesse maximale de 60 km/h. Jusque là, c'est plutôt commun. Là où ce rouage hybride se démarque, c'est dans sa possibilité à rouler « en roue libre ». Lorsque le moteur ne doit pas fournir de puissance et que le conducteur lâche l'accélérateur, le moteur thermique est

FEU VERT

Système hybride raffiné
Excellente tenue de route
Performances assurées
Finition impeccable
Freins ultra puissants

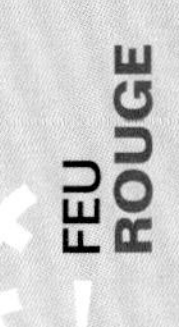

FEU ROUGE

Moteur diesel non disponible
Prix corsés
Options onéreuses
Moteur V6 rugueux

entièrement coupé à des vitesses allant jusqu'à 156 km/h et débrayé du rouage d'entraînement. Cela permet une réduction substantielle de la consommation. La compression du moteur et son effet de freinage sont ainsi annulés lors du fonctionnement « en roue libre ». Il suffit d'appuyer sur l'accélérateur pour relancer le moteur, au quart de tour, sans le moindre à-coup.

UNE TRISTE OMISSION

Dans le cadre de cette seconde génération, les ingénieurs ont révisé tous les groupes propulseurs et développé une nouvelle transmission automatique à huit rapports. Le modèle de base est doté d'un moteur V6 de 3,6 litres dont la puissance est passée à 300 chevaux. Ce moteur consomme 20 pour cent de moins que son prédécesseur, soit 9,9 litres aux 100 kilomètres. Malheureusement, la version à moteur diesel ne sera pas commercialisée sur notre continent, ce qui est fort regrettable, car sa consommation est de 7,4 litres aux 100 kilomètres. De plus, en conduite, il est nettement plus agréable que le V6 à essence qui n'est pas tellement doux.

Le Cayenne S est toujours propulsé par le V8 de 4,8 litres dont la puissance passe de 385 chevaux à 400 chevaux, mais sa consommation est de 10,5 litres aux 100 kilomètres. Le moteur V8 biturbo de 4,8 litres produit toujours 500 chevaux, mais sa consommation est réduite de 23 pour cent par rapport à son devancier tout comme pour la version atmosphérique de ce V8. Ces réductions de consommation s'expliquent en partie par l'utilisation de la nouvelle boîte Tiptronic S à huit rapports, le système arrêt/départ et l'allègement de tous les modèles.

Comme tout véhicule Porsche, le Cayenne a un comportement routier nettement supérieur à sa catégorie. Mieux encore, il réussirait sans doute à surclasser des voitures de sport, tant au chapitre des performances que de la tenue de route. Une suspension bien calibrée et une plate-forme ultra rigide expliquent en grande partie ce brio. Il faut également souligner l'efficacité de la transmission intégrale active.

Le Cayenne offre un agrément de conduite élevé et ses capacités hors route sont impressionnantes. Dommage que le moteur V6 diesel 3,0 litres ne soit pas de la partie.

Denis Duquet

PHOTOS : PORSCHE

Catégorie	VUS
Échelle de prix	56 700 $ à 125 915 $
Garanties	4 ans/80 000 km, 4 ans/80 000 km
Assemblage	Leipzig, Allemagne
Cote d'assurance	moyenne

CHÂSSIS - DONNÉES POUR S

Emp/lon/lar/haut	2 895/4 846/1 939/1 699 mm
Coffre	670 à 1 780 litres
Réservoir	100 litres
Nombre coussins sécurité	6
Antipatinage / contrôle stabilité	oui / oui
Suspension avant	indépendante, double triangulation
Suspension arrière	indépendante, multibras
Freins avant / arrière	disque (ABS) / disque (ABS)
Direction	à crémaillère, assistée
Diamètre de braquage	11,9 m
Pneus avant / arrière	P255/55R18 / P255/55R18
Poids	2 065 kg
Capacité de remorquage	3 500 kg (7 716 lb)

COMPOSANTES MÉCANIQUES

S Hybride

Cylindrée, soupapes, alim.	V6 3,0 litres 24 s atmos.
Puissance / Couple	380 chevaux / 427 lb-pi
Tr. base (opt) / rouage base (opt)	A8 / Int
0-100 / 80-120 / 100-0 km/h	6,1 s / n.d. / n.d.
Type ess. / ville / autoroute	Ordinaire / 8,7 / 7,9 l/100km

Base

Cylindrée, soupapes, alim.	V6 3,6 litres 24 s atmos.
Puissance / Couple	300 chevaux / 295 lb-pi
Tr. base (opt) / rouage base (opt)	M6 (A6) / Int
0-100 / 80-120 / 100-0 km/h	8,1 s / 9,9 s / n.d.
Type ess. / ville / autoroute	Super / 15,4 / 9,8 l/100 km

S

V8 4,8 l, 400 ch, 369 lb-pi - 0-100: 6,8 s - 16,3 / 10,5 l/100 km

Turbo

V8 4,8, 500 ch, 516 lb-pi - 0-100: 5,1 s - 16,2 / 8,8 l/100 km

DANS LA MÊME CATÉGORIE

Acura MDX, Audi Q7, BMW X5, Infiniti FX, Land Rover Range Rover Sport, Lexus RX, Mercedes-Benz Classe M, Volkswagen Touareg, Volvo XC90

DU NOUVEAU EN 2011

Nouveau modèle

NOS IMPRESSIONS

Agrément de conduite :	8/10
Fiabilité :	4/10
Sécurité :	10/10
Qualités hivernales :	8/10
Espace intérieur :	8/10
Confort :	8/10

www.porsche.com

Plus d'informations dans la section statistiques en dernière partie du Guide

UN SECRET BIEN GARDÉ

Dans l'univers Porsche, la Cayman est éclipsée par la mythique 911 Carrera ainsi que par le succès commercial des Boxster et Cayenne, alors que l'arrivée toute récente de la Panamera a pour effet de la rendre encore plus invisible qu'elle l'était précédemment. Pourtant, c'est toute une sportive que ce coupé deux places à moteur central dont l'équilibre est tout simplement parfait.

Côté style, la Cayman évoque le passé glorieux de la marque en sport automobile en adoptant une allure qui rappelle la Porsche 550 Coupé de 1953, avec laquelle la marque allemande remporta à la fois les 24 Heures du Mans et la célèbre Carrera Panamericana, reliant le Mexique du sud au nord. Certaines personnes qualifieront le style de la Cayman S de rétro, mais pour ma part, je trouve que les éléments de design empruntés à la mythique 550 ainsi intégrés au nouveau coupé sont particulièrement réussis. Par ailleurs, il est amusant de constater que les bas de caisse remontent vers l'arrière où la jonction avec les prises d'air ressemble à un étalage de bâtons de hockey...

En se glissant à bord, on retrouve immédiatement cet environnement typique des autres modèles de la gamme, mais la Cayman S séduit également par son côté pratique puisque le volume de chargement est de 410 litres, si on tient compte de la capacité du coffre avant jumelée à celle du volume accessible juste derrière les sièges. Aux fins de comparaison, ce volume de chargement est égal à celui du coffre d'une berline intermédiaire, ce qui est un exploit remarquable compte tenu de la vocation sportive de la Cayman S qui ne manquera pas de charmer ceux et celles qui en feront ainsi leur voiture de tous les jours.

À LA RECHERCHE DU TEMPS PERDU

Pour l'année-modèle 2011, Porsche a choisi de rattraper la parade en ajoutant le système Bluetooth, l'interface audio universelle ainsi que les tapis à la dotation de série de la Cayman, alors qu'il s'agissait auparavant d'équipements offerts en option seulement. De plus, Porsche a choisi d'émuler la concurrence allemande en regroupant certains équipements et accessoires en quatre ensembles d'options. Ainsi, le *Convenience Package* réunit les phares bixenon, le système de chauffage/climatisation automatique et le détecteur de pluie qui commande automatiquement l'entrée en action des essuie-glaces, tandis que le système de navigation est jumelé à une chaîne audio plus performante dans le *Infotainement Package*.

DES PERFORMANCES ÉTINCELANTES

Si, tout comme moi, vous êtes d'avis que la Boxster S est la référence en matière de roadsters, vous serez littéralement estomaqué par les performances en tenue de route de la Cayman S, dont le châssis est deux fois plus rigide que celui de la Boxster S, grâce non seulement au toit fixe mais également à un longeron installé derrière les deux sièges et reliant les deux côtés de la voiture. Conduire une Cayman S sur circuit relève du pur délice, tellement les réactions de

FEU VERT
- Excellente tenue de route
- Freins très puissants (S)
- Excellente boîte manuelle
- Moteur performant (S)

FEU ROUGE
- Coût des options
- Coûts d'utilisation
- Visibilité arrière limitée

la voiture sont à la fois incisives et immédiates. L'osmose entre voiture et conducteur se fait instantanément et permet au conducteur de parfaitement sentir la route au travers de la voiture. En fait, le châssis est si rigide et les suspensions bien calibrées que l'on en vient rapidement à la conclusion que la Cayman S pourrait disposer d'un moteur encore plus puissant sans devoir subir d'importantes modifications, ce qui est le propre d'une excellente voiture.

Le moteur de type « boxer » de la Cayman S livre 320 chevaux à la route par l'entremise d'une superbe boîte manuelle à six vitesses ou de la boîte à double embrayage PDK qui compte sept rapports. Cette boîte exceptionnelle permet des changements de vitesse plus rapide que ceux qu'un conducteur expérimenté est en mesure de le faire avec la boîte manuelle !

Il existe cependant un défaut majeur avec cette boîte PDK, et on le retrouve du côté des commandes localisées au volant sur lesquelles on doit appuyer avec le pouce sur la face recto de l'un ou l'autre des deux commutateurs pour passer au rapport supérieur et actionner la face verso de ces mêmes commutateurs au moyen de l'index pour commander le rétrogradage. C'est loin d'être naturel et fait en sorte que le conducteur peut passer au rapport supérieur en appuyant sans le vouloir sur le bouton de commande tout en négociant un virage serré.

Pour en finir avec cette disposition malhabile des commandes de passage des vitesses au volant, Porsche a finalement décidé de reprendre la configuration classique adoptée par tous les constructeurs automobiles pour le passage des vitesses avec une boîte à double embrayage ou séquentielle, soit avec une disposition de deux paliers de commandes au volant, celui de droite pour la montée des rapports et celui de gauche pour le rétrogradage, mais cet accessoire n'est offert qu'en option au coût de 840 dollars sur toutes les voitures sport de la marque, alors qu'il s'agit d'une option sans frais sur la Panamera et le Cayenne. Trouvez l'erreur…

Même si elle existe dans l'ombre des autres modèles de la marque, la Cayman a de la gueule et elle est capable de livrer des performances enlevantes, ce qui en fait une voiture pour véritables connaisseurs. Et elle sera toujours aussi intègre mécaniquement dans plusieurs années, ce que plusieurs modèles concurrents ne peuvent garantir.

Gabriel Gélinas

PHOTOS : PORSCHE

PORSCHE CAYMAN

Catégorie	Coupé
Échelle de prix	65 300 $ à 77 500 $
Garanties	4 ans/80 000 km, 4 ans/80 000 km
Assemblage	Valmet, Finlande
Cote d'assurance	n.d.

CHÂSSIS - DONNÉES POUR S

Emp/lon/lar/haut	2 415/4 347/1 801/1 304 mm
Coffre	410 litres
Réservoir	64 litres
Nombre coussins sécurité	4
Antipatinage / contrôle stabilité	oui / oui
Suspension avant	indépendante, jambes de force
Suspension arrière	indépendante, jambes de force
Freins avant / arrière	disque (ABS) / disque (ABS)
Direction	à crémaillère, ass. variable
Diamètre de braquage	11,1 m
Pneus avant / arrière	P235/40ZR18 / P265/40ZR18
Poids	1 350 kg
Capacité de remorquage	non recommandé

COMPOSANTES MÉCANIQUES

Base

Cylindrée, soupapes, alim.	H6 2,9 litres 24 s atmos.
Puissance / Couple	265 chevaux / 221 lb-pi
Tr. base (opt) / rouage base (opt)	M6 (A7) / Prop
0-100 / 80-120 / 100-0 km/h	5,8 s / 7,6 s / n.d.
Type ess. / ville / autoroute	Super / 11,2 / 7,4 l/100 km

S

Cylindrée, soupapes, alim.	H6 3,4 litres 24 s atmos.
Puissance / Couple	320 chevaux / 273 lb-pi
Tr. base (opt) / rouage base (opt)	M6 (A7) / Prop
0-100 / 80-120 / 100-0 km/h	5,2 s / 6,5 s / n.d.
Type ess. / ville / autoroute	Super / 11,1 / 7,5 l/100 km

DANS LA MÊME CATÉGORIE

Audi TT, BMW Z4, Lotus Elise, Nissan Z

DU NOUVEAU EN 2011

Aucun changement majeur

NOS IMPRESSIONS

Agrément de conduite :	9/10
Fiabilité :	7/10
Sécurité :	10/10
Qualités hivernales :	5/10
Espace intérieur :	6/10
Confort :	6/10

www.porsche.com

Plus d'informations dans la section statistiques en dernière partie du Guide

QUI A DIT QU'ON AVAIT BESOIN D'UN V8?

L'automne dernier, la Porsche Panamera est arrivée sur notre marché et ses débuts ont été impressionnants. Non seulement les chiffres de ventes ont été à la hauteur des attentes du constructeur de Zuffenhausen, mais les essais routiers à son égard ont été très favorables. En effet, les essayeurs ont louangé non seulement les performances de cette berline cinq portes, mais également sa tenue de route, le confort de son habitacle et le niveau de son équipement. Cette année, il y a encore du nouveau dans la famille Panamera puisqu'un moteur V6 vient s'ajouter à la gamme.

V8 MOINS 2

Avant d'aborder d'autres sujets, il est important de souligner que c'est le premier moteur V6 jamais produit en série par ce constructeur. Il s'agit en fait du V8 développé pour la Panamera et qui a été amputé de deux cylindres. Ce moteur de 3,6 litres a été mis au point conjointement avec la version V8, avec laquelle il partage toutes les caractéristiques techniques, notamment l'injection directe de carburant, le système de calage infiniment variable des soupapes d'admission (VarioCam Plus), un collecteur d'admission à débit variable, un carter sec, une pompe à l'huile fonctionnant sur demande, ainsi que le système arrêt/démarrage.

Il est vrai que si l'on considère les données des deux moteurs V8 offerts lors du lancement, ce V6 affiche une puissance plus modeste puisqu'il produit 300 chevaux. Il concède ainsi 100 chevaux au moteur V8 atmosphérique, tandis que la version turbocompressée de ce même moteur V8 en produit 200 de plus. Toutefois, les données techniques sont d'ordre théorique dans une certaine mesure et c'est sur la route que l'on peut apprécier si ce moteur V6 est à la hauteur des attentes. Sur certains marchés, le Panamera sera offert avec la transmission manuelle à six rapports, tandis que pour le Canada, seule la version dotée de la boîte automatique à double embrayage PDK est disponible. Cette transmission à sept rapports permet non seulement d'avoir des performances plus élevées en accélération, mais elle assure une meilleure économie de carburant en plus d'être davantage écologique. Ce moteur est situé le plus au centre possible afin d'optimiser la répartition du poids.

Comme sur les modèles équipés du moteur V8, ces nouvelles venues sont offertes avec la propulsion aux roues arrière ou la transmission intégrale. Il s'agit dans ce cas de la Panamera 4. Peu importe le modèle choisi, les freins sont naturellement impressionnants de par leur efficacité avec un étrier monobloc abritant six pistons. Il est également possible de commander en option des freins en composite de céramique. À propos d'options et de mécanique, cette Panamera peut être équipé d'une suspension active qui modifie constamment le réglage des amortisseurs. Il est également possible de régler la suspension en trois modes, soit confort, sport et sport plus. Si vous voulez encore plus de performances et d'efficacité de la part de la suspension, il vous est également possible de

FEU VERT
- Carrosserie cinq portes fort pratique
- Rouage intégral
- Sièges confortables
- Choix de moteurs
- Tenue de route exceptionnelle

FEU ROUGE
- Options onéreuses
- Place centrale arrière inconfortable
- Coffre de grandeur moyenne
- Boîte manuelle non disponible

commander la suspension pneumatique de type adaptatif. Poussez le tout à un échelon supérieur et vous obtenez le système PDCC pour Porsche Dynamic Chassis Control qui comprend également le système de gestion de couple. Parmi les raffinements techniques de ces différents systèmes, il faut souligner des barres antiroulis actives dont la fermeté varie en fonction du volant et des forces latérales.

IMPRESSIONNANT !

L'habitacle est similaire à celui des versions plus puissantes et personne ne s'en plaindra. Il est facile de prendre place à bord et on se retrouve assis dans des sièges enveloppants et offrant un excellent support latéral de même qu'un bon support pour les cuisses. Ces sièges sont pratiquement réglables à l'infini. Sur les modèles essayés, ils étaient chauffants et climatisés. Les places arrière sont confortables. Par contre, oubliez la place centrale, elle n'est que symbolique tout au plus.

Le principal élément qui attire l'attention est cette console qui comprend une multitude de commutateurs visant à régler la climatisation et les différents réglages de la suspension. Au premier coup d'œil, ça semble complexe, mais à l'usage, on s'y retrouve en un rien de temps. Mieux encore, la position de ces commandes semble parfaitement logique. Sur une note plus positive, le système de navigation est facile à régler et à utiliser. Bien entendu, la qualité d'assemblage et de fabrication est impeccable. Par contre, je me demande toujours qui a eu la mauvaise idée d'encercler les haut-parleurs, placés en partie supérieure de la planche de bord, d'un cadre en aluminium brossé qui se reflète sur le pare-brise. Finalement, comme il s'agit d'une Porsche, la clé de contact est située à gauche du volant.

Sur la route, bien qu'il doive céder en puissance aux moteurs V8, le 0-100 km/h est l'affaire de 6,3 secondes. Mieux encore, si vous commandez le groupe d'accessoires Sports Chrono et utilisez le mode Launch, vous allez atteindre les 100 km/h en 5,9 secondes. Qui a dit qu'on avait besoin d'un moteur V8 !

Sur la route, la version V6 affiche la même stabilité à haute vitesse, la même neutralité en virage que les modèles V8, en plus d'offrir un agrément de conduite fort relevé. Finalement, si vous conduisez de façon intelligente, vous allez obtenir une consommation de carburant inférieure à 10 litres aux 100 km. Inutile d'en dire plus.

Denis Duquet

PHOTOS : SYLVAIN RAYMOND

Catégorie	Berline
Échelle de prix	77 356 $ à 155 000 $
Garanties	4 ans/80 000 km, 4 ans/80 000 km
Assemblage	Leipzig, Allemagne
Cote d'assurance	n.d.

CHÂSSIS - DONNÉES POUR BASE

Emp/lon/lar/haut	2 920/4 970/1 931/1 418 mm
Coffre	445 à 1 263 litres
Réservoir	100 litres
Nombre coussins sécurité	8
Antipatinage / contrôle stabilité	oui / oui
Suspension avant	indépendante, double triangulation
Suspension arrière	indépendante, multibras
Freins avant / arrière	disque (ABS) / disque (ABS)
Direction	à crémaillère, ass. variable
Diamètre de braquage	12,0 m
Pneus avant / arrière	P245/50R18 / P275/45R18
Poids	1 730 kg
Capacité de remorquage	non recommandé

COMPOSANTES MÉCANIQUES

Base, 4

Cylindrée, soupapes, alim.	V6 3,6 litres atmos.
Puissance / Couple	300 chevaux / 400 lb-pi
Tr. base (opt) / rouage base (opt)	A7 / Prop (Int)
0-100 / 80-120 / 100-0 km/h	5,9 s / 4,4 s / n.d.
Type ess. / ville / autoroute	Super / 13,5 / 7,3 l/100 km

S, 4S

Cylindrée, soupapes, alim.	V8 4,8 litres turbocompressé
Puissance / Couple	400 chevaux / 370 lb-pi
Tr. base (opt) / rouage base (opt)	A7 / Prop (Int)
0-100 / 80-120 / 100-0 km/h	5,0 s / 6,1 s / n.d.
Type ess. / ville / autoroute	Super / 12,9 / 8,3 l/100 km

Turbo

Cylindrée, soupapes, alim.	V8 4,8 litres turbocompressé
Puissance / Couple	500 chevaux / 568 lb-pi
Tr. base (opt) / rouage base (opt)	A7 / Int
0-100 / 80-120 / 100-0 km/h	4,2 s / 5,1 s / n.d.
Type ess. / ville / autoroute	Super / 14,1 / 8,6 l/100 km

DANS LA MÊME CATÉGORIE

Audi A8, BMW Série 7, Jaguar XJ, Maserati Quattroporte, Mercedes-Benz Classe S

DU NOUVEAU EN 2011

Moteur V6

NOS IMPRESSIONS

Agrément de conduite :	9/10
Fiabilité :	8/10
Sécurité :	10/10
Qualités hivernales :	8/10
Espace intérieur :	8/10
Confort :	8/10

www.porsche.com

Plus d'informations dans la section statistiques en dernière partie du Guide

LA FAMILLE ROYALE S'AGRANDIT EN BEAUTÉ

La monumentale Phantom, première Rolls-Royce moderne, a été lancée cinq ans après que BMW ait acquis les droits sur ce nom qui symbolise, plus que tout autre, le luxe automobile ultime. Et puisque cette marque britannique quasi royale a toujours fait de meilleures affaires avec deux séries complémentaires, elle lance maintenant la Ghost, moins imposante et moins chère mais plus performante et maniable. De quoi répliquer enfin à Bentley, marque longtemps jumelle devenue sa plus féroce rivale.

Le développement de cette deuxième série a été annoncé au Mondial de l'Automobile de Paris en 2006, trois ans après le lancement de la Phantom.

UN PEU PLUS MINCE, LÉGÈRE ET SVELTE

Comme sa grande sœur, la Ghost prend les traits d'une berline mais Rolls-Royce en dévoilera bientôt une version décapotable ou *drophead*, selon le jargon de la marque. S'allongeant sur 5,4 mètres, elle est néanmoins plus courte de 434 mm, plus basse de 84 mm et plus étroite de 41 mm que la pharaonique Phantom.

La Ghost est malgré tout un peu plus spacieuse puisque les éléments de sa structure en acier sont plus minces que ceux du châssis en aluminium de la jeune doyenne. Elle est même plus légère de 160 kilos mais fait quand même plus de deux tonnes et demie avec ses 2470 kg. La coque autoporteuse de la Ghost est produite au complexe de Dingolfing en Allemagne où BMW fabrique aussi ses séries 5 et 7. Elle est ensuite transportée par camion spécial à l'usine de Goodwood en Angleterre où la fabrication exige 20 jours de travail presque entièrement fait à la main.

On reconnaît instantanément la Ghost comme une Rolls mais ses lignes sont moins anguleuses, la traditionnelle calandre chromée moins massive et le montant arrière du toit moins large que sur la Phantom. Elle demeure haute et imposante, mais n'est certainement pas aussi intimidante que cette dernière, et son coefficient de traînée aérodynamique de 0,33 est nettement meilleur que le 0,38 de la grande et grosse Phantom.

TECHNOLOGIE DE POINTE ET TRADITION

La Ghost emprunterait environ le cinquième de ses composantes à la Série 7 de BMW. Il est toutefois virtuellement impossible de les reconnaître puisqu'elles ont été méticuleusement adaptées au caractère et aux caractéristiques de la Ghost, une berline plus grande, plus haute et plus lourde.

Le morceau partagé le plus reconnaissable est le large et clair écran de contrôle qui trône au milieu du tableau de bord, sous un élégant volet escamotable en bois vernis. L'arborescence des menus correspond à l'interprétation qu'ont faite les gens de Rolls-Royce de la plus récente version de l'interface iDrive de BMW. Toujours complet mais encore inutilement complexe et pas aussi convivial que le prétendent ses créateurs...

La position de conduite est impeccable. Le volant est dans le style classique de Rolls-Royce avec sa jante plutôt large et mince, enveloppée de cuir anthracite, son moyeu rond et des boutons chromés pour la plupart des contrôles secondaires. Les réglages du siège sont facilement accessibles sur le côté et les boutons de mise en mémoire toujours actifs sur la portière. Droit devant, trois cadrans à fond blanc, dont un qui indique la « réserve d'énergie » du moteur. Un compte-tours, c'est trop banal pour Rolls-Royce. Et au plancher à gauche, un bon repose-pied, large et plat.

Pour le reste, la Ghost regorge des systèmes électroniques les plus pointus et performants, dissimulés derrière un tableau de bord tapissé de boutons chromés ou noirs d'où les chiffres sont presque entièrement absents. On règle la température par la couleur – bleu c'est frais et rouge c'est le contraire – et la vitesse du ventilateur en choisissant entre doux, médium, fort ou maximum.

Parmi les systèmes de sécurité et d'aide à la conduite on compte une caméra de vision nocturne, un excellent affichage de données au pare-brise, des phares au xénon qui s'atténuent d'eux-mêmes et un régulateur de vitesse qui peut stopper et faire redémarrer la Ghost en plein trafic en plus de réduire sa vitesse en virage.

COMME UNE ÉRUPTION CONTRÔLÉE

Sous le long capot de la Ghost se tapit un nouveau V12 de 6,6 litres à double turbo qui produit 563 chevaux à 5 250 tr/min et 575 lb-pi de couple à seulement 1 500 tr/min. Ce qui en fait la voiture la plus puissante depuis la création de la marque il y a plus d'un siècle. Ce moteur est dérivé du V12 de 6 litres de la BMW 760i. On y a installé les pistons plus larges du V8 de 4,4 litres pour augmenter sa cylindrée et il est jumelé à une nouvelle boîte automatique ZF à 8 rapports.

Malgré sa masse, la Ghost pourrait atteindre 100 km/h en 5 secondes et boucler le traditionnel quart de mille en 13,2 secondes, des performances de sportive. Elle en donnait certainement l'impression lors du lancement sur les routes californiennes. Elle accélère sans relâche et sans brusquerie, comme une fusée à propulsion hydraulique, avec la complicité d'une boîte automatique irréprochable. Sauf que sa prestation s'accompagne d'un rugissement feutré absolument réjouissant. Le freinage est puissant et facile à moduler, assuré par les rotors surdimensionnés des Série 7 blindées. Plongée au freinage, tangage et roulis sont maîtrisés par une suspension à ressorts pneumatiques et amortisseurs pilotés, laquelle réagit en 2,5 millièmes de seconde.

La tenue de route est étonnante, sinon remarquable pour une berline de cette taille et de ce poids dont le constructeur est reconnu avant tout pour le confort de roulement moelleux de ses voitures. Or, les masses réparties de façon quasi parfaitement égale entre les essieux avant et arrière et le mordant des grands pneus optionnels de la voiture essayée (taille 255/45R20) gomment pratiquement tout sous-virage. Une direction précise fait le reste, à défaut d'offrir de grandes sensations tactiles.

En conduite normale, la Ghost est un tapis magique, même si la douceur de roulement n'est pas aussi parfaite que dans une Phantom. Les fentes et saillies transversales provoquent effectivement des tremblements minimes, presque rien, surtout avec les flancs plus raides des pneus anticrevaison.

LA MANIÈRE OPULENTE

À l'intérieur, il y a tout l'espace et le confort souhaitables pour en profiter, quels que soient le rythme et la vitesse. Il y a amplement d'espace à l'avant et on se glisse à l'arrière par de grandes portières en accolade qui s'ouvrent presque à angle droit. Les sièges sont moelleux, drapés de cuirs épais et souples. On s'y cale haut comme dans un fauteuil, cependant ils offrent également un maintien latéral surprenant.

CLASSE À PART

La Ghost occupe évidemment l'avant-scène cette année mais Rolls-Royce n'en poursuit pas moins le raffinement et l'expansion de sa série Phantom. À la première berline se sont ajoutés une

Catégorie	Berline, Coupé, Cabriolet
Échelle de prix	245 000 $ à 615 000 $
Garanties	4 ans/illimité, 4 ans/illimité
Assemblage	Goodwood, Angleterre
Cote d'assurance	n.d.

CHÂSSIS - DONNÉES POUR GHOST

Emp/lon/lar/haut	3 295/5 399/1 948/1 550 mm
Coffre	396 litres
Réservoir	82 litres
Nombre coussins sécurité	n.d.
Antipatinage / contrôle stabilité	oui / oui
Suspension avant	indépendante, pneumatique, multibras
Suspension arrière	indépendante, pneumatique, multibras
Freins avant / arrière	disque (ABS) / disque (ABS)
Direction	à crémaillère, assistée
Diamètre de braquage	n.d.
Pneus avant / arrière	P255/50R19 / P255/50R19
Poids	2 470 kg
Capacité de remorquage	n.d.

COMPOSANTES MÉCANIQUES

Ghost	
Cylindrée, soupapes, alim.	V12 6,6 litres 48 s turbo
Puissance / Couple	563 chevaux / 575 lb-pi
Tr. base (opt) / rouage base (opt)	A8 / Prop
0-100 / 80-120 / 100-0 km/h	5,0 s / n.d. / n.d.
Type ess. / ville / autoroute	Super / 16,6 / 10,1 l/100 km

Phantom, Phantom Coupe, Drophead Coupe	
Cylindrée, soupapes, alim.	V12 6,7 litres 48 s atmos
Puissance / Couple	453 chevaux / 531 lb-pi
Tr. base (opt) / rouage base (opt)	A6 / Prop
0-100 / 80-120 / 100-0 km/h	5,8 s / 5,5 s / 40,0 m
Type ess. / ville / autoroute	Super / 18,7 / 11,4 l/100 km

FEU VERT

Comportement routier superbement équilibré
Remarquablement douce et silencieuse
Performances étonnantes
Unique, distinguée et rare

FEU ROUGE

Rétroviseurs gigantesques bloquent la vue
Pas de bouton pour désactiver le régulateur
Menus de contrôle multiples et déroutants
Pour milliardaires seulement

version à empattement allongé, le coupé Phantom et la Drophead Coupé décapotable. Toutes sont animées par le même V12 de 6,7 litres, coté à 453 chevaux et jumelé à une boîte automatique à 6 rapports.

Les Phantom sont effectivement les voitures les plus douces et silencieuses qui soient. On les jurerait propulsées par des moteurs électriques. La finition de leur habitacle est également d'une richesse inouïe. Ça va de soi, pour des voitures qui coûtent près d'un demi-million pièce, si l'on profite le moindrement du service de personnalisation de Rolls-Royce qui offre, par exemple, le choix de 45 000 couleurs de carrosserie différentes. C'est ce que font les trois-quarts des clients. Ceux-là ne s'inquièteront pas outre mesure de la portière électrique récalcitrante de la Phantom Drophead dans laquelle nous avons roulé en Californie. Ils appelleront simplement leur hélicoptère personnel à la rescousse...

Marc Lachapelle

Photos : Marc Lachapelle

DANS LA MÊME CATÉGORIE

Aston Martin Rapide, BMW Série 6, Bentley Continental, Jaguar XJ, Lexus LS, Maserati Quattroporte, Mercedes-Benz Classe S, Porsche Panamera

DU NOUVEAU EN 2011

Nouveau modèle Ghost

NOS IMPRESSIONS

Agrément de conduite :	8/10
Fiabilité :	8/10
Sécurité :	9/10
Qualités hivernales :	6/10
Espace intérieur :	9/10
Confort :	10/10

www.rolls-roycemotorcars.com

Plus d'informations dans la section statistiques en dernière partie du Guide

Saab 9-5

TOUJOURS À PART

Depuis sa création, la compagnie Saab a toujours produit des voitures totalement différentes des autres. La première version était inspirée par les lois de l'aérodynamisme et se contentait de petits moteurs deux temps qui étaient plus que poussifs. Avec cette motorisation aux roues avant et cette silhouette très particulière, les modèles Saab ont toujours intéressé les gens qui n'avaient pas peur de la différence. Mais ces voitures n'étaient pas seulement originales, elles avaient plusieurs qualités fort intéressantes.

Après avoir été acquis par General Motors en 1990, ce constructeur suédois se constituait une intéressante gamme de modèles. De plus, l'incroyable manque de fiabilité propre à la marque a beaucoup diminué. Tant et si bien que certains modèles étaient cotés parmi les plus fiables sur le marché. Mais la situation financière s'est embrouillée, General Motors s'est mis sous la protection des lois de la faillite aux États-Unis, sa filiale Saab a été laissée à elle-même et elle aussi a déposé son bilan. Par la suite, c'est un roman-feuilleton économique. Même si ce petit constructeur suédois possédait quelques modèles intéressants et relativement nouveaux, les acheteurs ne se sont pas bousculés au portillon. Après les plus folles rumeurs et des acheteurs qui ont changé d'idée, c'est la compagnie néerlandaise Spyker qui s'est portée acquéreur de Saab.

C'est vrai que c'est une toute petite compagnie qui ne fabrique chaque année qu'une poignée de voitures sportives de très grand luxe, mais derrière cette enseigne, on retrouve de solides appuis financiers venant de pays ceinturant le golfe Persique. Tant et si bien que la production a redémarré très lentement et les livraisons commencent à s'effectuer dans différents pays. Mais cela n'inclut pas le Canada. Tout simplement parce que cette marque était distribuée par la division Saturn de GM et que celle-ci a cessé ses activités et tous ses concessionnaires ont fermé leurs portes. La marque est toujours vivante, mais elle n'a pas de distributeur dans notre pays. Par contre, l'infrastructure commerciale aux États-Unis est différente et les voitures Saab y sont encore vendues.

Au moment d'écrire ces lignes, un réseau d'une vingtaine de concessionnaires serait en voie de constitution en vue de l'ouverture de points de vente et d'entretien au Canada. Mais ce projet est toujours à l'étude et il est certain que les concessionnaires concernés devront être patients s'ils veulent rentabiliser leur investissement. Mais pour plusieurs adeptes de cette marque, le fait qu'elle ne soit plus dans le giron du grand constructeur américain est un argument plaidant en faveur de Saab.

PEU MAIS BIEN

Les spécialistes de la marque vont nous dire que ce constructeur n'a jamais proposé une gamme de modèles très diversifiée. C'est sous la férule de son maître américain qu'on a tenté toutes sortes de choses afin d'intéresser de nouveaux acheteurs. Cela a donné

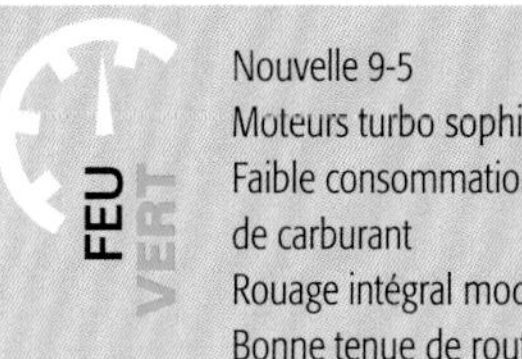

FEU VERT

Nouvelle 9-5
Moteurs turbo sophistiqués
Faible consommation de carburant
Rouage intégral moderne
Bonne tenue de route

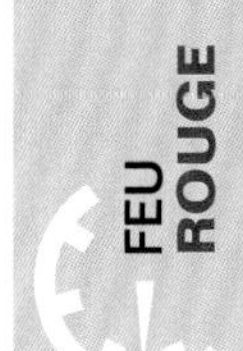

FEU ROUGE

Avenir fort incertain
Réseau de concessionnaires inconnu
Faible valeur de revente
Fiabilité inégale

une Subaru déguisée en Saab, la 9-2X, et une Oldsmobile Bravada transformée en 9-7X. Cette fois ce sera différent si jamais Saab revient dans notre pays.

On retrouvera bien entendu la berline 9-3 qui s'était fait sa part d'inconditionnels aussi bien en raison de son agrément de conduite, de ses performances que de l'économie intéressante de son moteur 2,0 litres. De plus, sa fiabilité s'est améliorée au fil des années. Cette voiture est non seulement d'une bonne habitabilité, mais elle a toujours obtenu des cotes de sécurité impressionnantes.

Mais la voiture la plus spectaculaire sera sans doute la nouvelle 9-5. Cette berline intermédiaire possède une toute nouvelle silhouette qui est à la fois très moderne, très épurée et qui conserve toutes les caractéristiques visuelles qu'on attribue aux véhicules de cette marque. Il y a une élégance certaine et ce petit brin de folie qui est propre à Saab. L'habitacle est confortable et spacieux. La planche de bord conserve les mêmes credo ergonomiques des autres modèles, des commandes intuitives et les cadrans indicateurs sur fond noir. Et on a toujours la possibilité d'éteindre tous les autres cadrans, à l'exception de l'indicateur de vitesse pour la conduite de nuit. Il faut souligner le confort et le support des sièges avant tandis que les places arrière sont généreuses et ses occupants pourront regarder leurs films favoris sur des écrans vidéo articulés. Cette berline est propulsée par un moteur quatre cylindres 2,0 litres turbo produisant 210 chevaux, également offert avec une transmission intégrale fort sophistiquée. Celle-ci est de série sur le modèle doté du moteur V6 2,8 litres de 280 chevaux. Soulignons également le système Drive Sense, qui permet de régler les paramètres de conduite en tournant un simple bouton. Enfin, la troisième voiture serait la 9-3X, un multisegment dérivé de la 9-3 Combi et doté du rouage intégral Haldex de seconde génération. Cette version est légèrement surélevée et se prête davantage à la conduite sur des routes en mauvaise condition. Ce serait notamment une réplique à la Subaru Outback.

Bien entendu, tout ceci n'est que simples supputations au moment d'écrire ces lignes. Mais compte tenu de la qualité relevée de ces modèles et de la nouvelle 9-5 en particulier, ce serait vraiment agréable de constater que cette marque si fascinante soit à nouveau distribuée dans notre pays.

Denis Duquet

Saab 9-3 Sportcombi

PHOTOS : SAAB

SAAB 9-3 / 9-3X / 9-5

Catégorie	Familiale / Berline / Cabriolet
Échelle de prix	36 255 $ à 59 295 $ (2009)
Garanties	4 ans/80 000 km, 5 ans/160 000 km
Assemblage	Trollhättan, Grèce et Graz, Autriche
Cote d'assurance	passable

CHÂSSIS - DONNÉES POUR 9-3 AERO XWD SPORTCOMBI

Emp/lon/lar/haut	2 675/4 647/1 763/1 496 mm
Coffre	841 à 2 047 litres
Réservoir	61 litres
Nombre coussins sécurité	6
Antipatinage / contrôle stabilité	oui / oui
Suspension avant	indépendante, jambes de force
Suspension arrière	indépendante, multibras
Freins avant / arrière	disque (ABS) / disque (ABS)
Direction	à crémaillère, ass. variable
Diamètre de braquage	11,9 m
Pneus avant / arrière	P235/45R18 / P235/45R18
Poids	1 500 kg
Capacité de remorquage	454 kg (1 000 lb)

COMPOSANTES MÉCANIQUES

9-3 Base	
Cylindrée, soupapes, alim.	4L 2,0 litres 16 s turbo
Puissance / Couple	210 chevaux / 221 lb-pi
Tr. base (opt) / rouage base (opt)	M6 (A6) / Int
0-100 / 80-120 / 100-0 km/h	8,5 s / 8,0 s / n.d.
Type ess. / ville / autoroute	Super / 11,1 / 7,3 l/100 km

9-3 Aero	
Cylindrée, soupapes, alim.	V6 2,8 litres 24 s turbo
Puissance / Couple	280 chevaux / 273 lb-pi
Tr. base (opt) / rouage base (opt)	M6 (A6) / Int
0-100 / 80-120 / 100-0 km/h	6,4 s (est) / 6,0 s (est) / n.d.
Type ess. / ville / autoroute	Super / 13,3 / 7,7 l/100 km

9-5	
Cylindrée, soupapes, alim.	4L 2,3 litres 16s turbo
Puissance / Couple	260 chevaux / 258 lb-pi
Tr. base (opt) / rouage base (opt)	M5 (A5) / Tr
0-100 / 80-120 / 100-0 km/h	8,3 s / 6,3 s / 40,0 m
Type ess. / ville / autoroute	Super / 11,6 / 7,2 l/100 km

DANS LA MÊME CATÉGORIE

Acura TL, Acura TSX, Audi A4, BMW Série 3, Cadillac CTS, Infiniti G, Lexus IS, Mercedes-Benz Classe C, Volvo C70, Volvo S40, Volvo V50

DU NOUVEAU EN 2011

Distribution encore non déterminée au Canada.
Modèle 9-3x à venir.

NOS IMPRESSIONS

Agrément de conduite :	8/10
Fiabilité :	6/10
Sécurité :	10/10
Qualités hivernales :	9/10
Espace intérieur :	8/10
Confort :	8/10

www.saab.ca

Plus d'informations dans la section statistiques en dernière partie du Guide

Scion XB

LA PATIENCE EST UNE GRANDE VERTU...

Toyota, on le sait, est réputé pour fabriquer des voitures fiables (malgré les récentes campagnes de rappel) mais bien peu excitantes à conduire. Le genre à stimuler bien plus grand-papa que les petits-enfants rendus à l'âge de conduire. Or, pour fidéliser une clientèle, il est préférable pour un manufacturier de commencer à l'intéresser le plus tôt possible. Pour ce faire, Toyota a créé, en 2003, la marque Scion qui offrait des produits branchés, tranchant radicalement avec les Corolla, Camry et autres RAV4.

Le marché canadien étant différent de celui des États-Unis, c'est là que la marque jeunesse de Toyota débarquait en 2003, en Californie d'abord. Puis, le réseau s'est progressivement implanté au sud du 45ième parallèle. Depuis le début de 2009, la marque Scion promet d'arriver au Canada mais la crise du crédit américaine et les déboires de Toyota ont sans doute mis un frein à cet élan. Toujours est-il qu'en août 2010, Scion n'est toujours pas offerte aux Canadiens. Les rares véhicules Scion à sillonner nos routes sont des unités achetées « d'l'aut' bord des lignes ».

SCION XB

Le xB a été le premier véhicule conçu par Toyota pour rejoindre une clientèle jeune. Cela se passait au Japon (cela ne surprend pas !) en 2000 sous le nom de Toyota bB. Ce petit hatchback aux lignes extraordinairement carrées a rapidement conquis les cœurs et les premiers exemplaires à rouler en Amérique détonnaient dans le paysage routier autant qu'une autruche sur la glace du centre Bell (Il s'agit toutefois d'un mauvais exemple...). Le xB en est rendu à sa deuxième génération. Lorsqu'il est débarqué de notre côté du Pacifique il était le seul à présenter une ligne

aussi carrée. Il doit maintenant affronter le Nissan cube et le Kia Soul, deux marques établies depuis longtemps chez nous. Il pourrait se faire des amis grâce à son coffre plus grand que celui des deux autres. Son quatre cylindres de 2,4 litres provenant de la Camry est aussi le plus puissant avec ses 158 chevaux. Soutenu par une architecture des plus conventionnelles, le xB ne promet pas la sportivité annoncée par ses lignes.

SION XD

Reprenant le châssis de la sous-compacte Yaris, le xD se veut un peu plus long (10 cm), donc un peu plus lourd. Son moteur aussi est plus gros (1,8 litre vs 1,5) mais sa puissance est à peine plus importante. Si quelqu'un affirme effectuer le 0-100 km/h en moins de huit secondes avec un xD de série, nous lui ferons passer un test d'urine... Encore une fois, la fonctionnalité a eu le dessus sur la sportivité. Les mêmes remarques faites au sujet de l'habitacle du xB s'appliquent à celui du xD. Dommage.

SION TC

Cette sous-compacte deux portes à hayon affiche une allure moins typée que ses deux comparses mais elle s'avère la plus

FEU VERT

On va finir par avoir des Scion au Canada
Lignes exclusives
Modèle tC intéressant
Prix devraient être abordables

FEU ROUGE

Fiabilité à prouver
Manque de raffinement général
Insonorisation déficiente
Réseau de concessionnaire ténu (au début)

intéressante ! Jolie (l'auteur lui trouve même des airs de Hyundai Tiburon de la dernière génération) et pratique, elle devrait être la plus populaire des trois. Son habitacle est le mieux fini et le plus invitant. Tous ceux qui ont fait l'essai de la tC louangent ses qualités dynamiques, autant au niveau des performances pures que du comportement routier. Ce qui surprend sans doute même les ingénieurs de Toyota, peu habitués au terme « dynamique ». Curieusement, on parle très peu de la tC sur le site www.scionnation.ca, le site officiel de Scion au Canada.

SCION IQ

Cette microvoiture fera bientôt la vie dure à la smart et à la future Fiat 500 ! Prévue pour être dévoilée en 2011, la iQ (qui a d'ailleurs fait l'objet de la page couverture du clairvoyant Guide de l'auto 2010) ne dévoile pas facilement ses atouts. On sait par contre qu'elle possédera 10 (dix !) coussins gonflables, ce qui devrait bien protéger ses quatre occupants. Et dans un des revirements les plus inattendus dont seule l'industrie automobile est capable, la petite iQ a été revue par… Aston Martin (oui, oui, le manufacturiers de voitures de grand-tourisme !) qui la vend à de richissimes excentriques sous le nom de Aston Martin Cygnet.

Le réseau de concessionnaires canadiens de la marque Scion est maintenant connu. On en retrouvera 17 dans la région métropolitaine. Chacun s'engage à créer un espace spécial dans sa salle de montre pour mettre les produits Scion en vedette. Même l'expérience de vente promet d'être différente. La publicité s'adressera, bien entendu, à un public jeune et fortement branché sur les technologies. Toyota tentera donc de les rejoindre via Internet et les réseaux sociaux plutôt que par les journaux ou la télévision.

La plupart des Scions vues dans les différents Salon de l'auto à travers l'Amérique sont rarement « stock ». Elles sont toutes modifiées, quelquefois à l'extrême, par des « tuners » spécialisés. Certes, ces voitures se prêtent bien à ce type de modifications mais l'intérêt pour le « Tuning » n'est plus ce qu'il était. Et ils sont sans doute rares les jeunes qui s'achèteront une voiture d'environ 20 000 $ pour ensuite investir plus du double pour la personnaliser. C'est à se demander si les Scion ne sont pas tellement ennuyantes qu'il faut maquiller la réalité…

Alain Morin

Scion TC

PHOTOS : SCION

SCION TC / XB / XD

DONNÉES U.S.

Catégorie	Coupé / *Hatchback*
Échelle de prix	n.d.
Garanties	n.d.
Assemblage	n.d.
Cote d'assurance	n.d.

CHÂSSIS - DONNÉES POUR SCION TC

Emp/lon/lar/haut	2 700/4 420/1 795/1 390 mm
Coffre	1 002 litres
Réservoir	55 litres
Nombre coussins sécurité	4
Antipatinage / contrôle stabilité	oui / oui
Suspension avant	indépendante, jambes de force
Suspension arrière	indépendante, double triangulation
Freins avant / arrière	disque (ABS) / disque (ABS)
Direction	à crémaillère, assistée
Diamètre de braquage	11,0 m
Pneus avant / arrière	P215/45R17 / P215/45R17
Poids	1 318 kg
Capacité de remorquage	non recommandé

COMPOSANTES MÉCANIQUES

xD

Cylindrée, soupapes, alim.	4L 1,8 litre 16 s atmos.
Puissance / Couple	128 chevaux / 125 lb-pi
Tr. base (opt) / rouage base (opt)	M5 (A4) / Tr
0-100 / 80-120 / 100-0 km/h	10,0 s / 9,0 s (est) / n.d.
Type ess. / ville / autoroute	Ordinaire / 8,7 / 7,1 l/100 km

xB

Cylindrée, soupapes, alim.	4L 2,4 litres 16 s atmos.
Puissance / Couple	158 chevaux / 162 lb-pi
Tr. base (opt) / rouage base (opt)	M5 (A4) / Tr
0-100 / 80-120 / 100-0 km/h	9,0 s / 8,0 s (est) / n.d.
Type ess. / ville / autoroute	Ordinaire / 10,7 / 8,4 l/100 km

tC

Cylindrée, soupapes, alim.	4L 2,4 litres 16 s atmos.
Puissance / Couple	161 chevaux / 162 lb-pi
Tr. base (opt) / rouage base (opt)	M5 (A4) / Tr
0-100 / 80-120 / 100-0 km/h	n.d. / n.d. / n.d.
Type ess. / ville / autoroute	Ordinaire / 11,8 / 8,7 l/100 km

DANS LA MÊME CATÉGORIE

tC: Honda Civic Coupé, Kia Forte Koup, Suzuki SX-4

DU NOUVEAU EN 2011

La marque Scion sera dévoilée au Canada à l'automne 2010

NOS IMPRESSIONS

Agrément de conduite :	■■■■■□□□□□	5/10
Fiabilité :	n.d.	
Sécurité :	■■■■■■■■□□	8/10
Qualités hivernales :	■■■■■■■□□□	7/10
Espace intérieur :	■■■■■■■■□□	8/10
Confort :	■■■■■□□□□□	5/10

www.scionnation.ca

Plus d'informations dans la section statistiques en dernière partie du Guide

CITADINE UN JOUR, CITADINE TOUJOURS

La plus éclatée des voitures actuellement proposées, la smart, continue son petit bonhomme de chemin en 2011. Elle a cependant droit à un très léger restylage et à un nouveau modèle électrisant, c'est le moins qu'on puisse dire.

La smart (avec un « s » minuscule) est, justement, minuscule. À peine plus longue qu'un vélo tandem, elle se faufile dans la circulation comme aucune autre voiture ne sait le faire. Les gens qui voient son habitacle pour la première fois ne peuvent être qu'étonnés par ses dimensions très généreuses... en comparaison avec la grosseur de la carrosserie. Les sièges coulissent suffisamment pour accommoder la plupart des gabarits et la position de conduite se trouve facilement même si le volant ne s'ajuste pas en hauteur ni en profondeur. Le tableau de bord est ultraminimaliste, ce qui accentue le côté urbain de la mignonne allemande. Lors de la refonte de la smart il y a trois ans, la partie arrière a pris du coffre et il est désormais possible d'y ranger plus qu'une brosse à dents. L'hiver dernier, Mercedes-Benz avait organisé une expédition nordique avec plusieurs smart et les deux occupants de chaque voiture avaient réussi à mettre leurs nombreux et surtout imposants bagages dans le coffre. Bravo !

Notre puce des rues est propulsée (le mot est fort mais puisque ce sont les roues arrière qui sont motrices, le terme propulsé est accepté) par un moteur à trois cylindres de 1,0 litre. Pas vraiment dégourdi, il autorise des accélérations et des reprises tout juste acceptables. Cependant, en conduite urbaine, il n'y a pas vraiment de problèmes. Ce moulin s'avère particulièrement frugal mais monsieur ne consomme que de l'essence super, ce qui lui enlève une partie de son charme. Là où Mercedes-Benz manque une belle occasion de nous faire apprécier davantage la smart, c'est au niveau de la transmission. Cette dernière est une

automatique à cinq vitesses dont le passage des rapports prend une éternité. Il s'ensuit une perte de puissance très sentie qui amène le nouveau conducteur d'une smart à penser que sa voiture va caler. Certains s'y font, d'autres jamais. Il est possible de diminuer un peu cet effet en changeant les rapports manuellement par le biais des palettes situées derrière le volant mais encore faut-il le faire au bon moment. Bref, c'est pas le fun.

À cause de son empattement réduit, les trous et les bosses sont durement ressentis. Mais, encore une fois, on est prêt à pardonner bien des choses à la smart !

UNE SMART ÉLECTRIQUE !

Lorsque la smart est débarquée au Canada en 2005, plusieurs personnes croyaient qu'il s'agissait d'une voiture électrique tant ses dimensions et son style se prêtaient à ce type d'énergie. Quelques années plus tard, c'est fait ! Nous aurons une smart électrique !

Le moteur à essence est remplacé par une unité électromagnétique de 30 kW alimentée par une batterie lithium-ion développée par Tesla et fournissant 16,5 kWh. Elle fournit en tout temps 20 kW

Style toujours d'actualité
Moteur essence très économique
Version électrique agréable à conduire
Espace habitable impressionnant
Niveau de sécurité étonnant

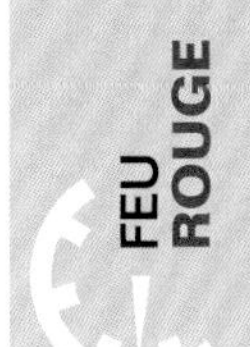

Suspensions sèches
Transmission de clown
Essence super seulement
Diffusion parcimonieuse du modèle électrique
Entretien assez dispendieux

mais lors d'une accélération soudaine qui pourrait s'apparenter à un *kick down*, elle en donne 30. Cette batterie, logée dans le plancher, peut être rechargée sur une prise de courant domestique, par une boîte murale électrique spéciale ou grâce à une station de recharge spéciale. Une batterie pleinement chargée a une autonomie de 135 km mais la température, le climat, la géographie et surtout le conducteur peuvent grandement affecter, à la baisse, ce chiffre.

Esthétiquement, il faudrait être daltonien pour ne pas reconnaître une smart électrique ! Exclusivement blanche avec des éléments de carrosserie verts, elle ne passe pas inaperçue. Même dans l'habitacle, on retrouve du vert partout.

Lors du lancement de la smart Electric Drive, son comportement routier nous est apparu assez près de celui de la smart à essence. Certes, les 140 kilos de plus de cette smart zéro émission n'en font pas une bombe de performance tout en affectant négativement les suspensions, fort dures d'ailleurs. Puisque nous avons roulé la voiture dans les rues de New York, nous n'avons pas pu atteindre la vitesse maximale de 100 km/h, mais nous pouvons affirmer que les accélérations ne sont pas de type canon. Mercedes-Benz annonce un 0-60 km/h en 6,5 secondes, ce qui me semble réaliste. Cependant, l'élément le plus agréable est qu'il n'y a pas de changement de rapports. On oublie donc les pénibles changements de la version ordinaire. Le centre de gravité plus bas à cause de la position de la batterie et les freins plus difficiles à moduler, surtout au début, constituent autant de différences par rapport à l'ordinaire.

Une smart électrique, c'est bien. S'en procurer une, par contre, est une autre histoire. Seulement 45 unités seront disponibles au Canada, et dans certaines villes uniquement. 80 % de ces voitures (36) seront destinées aux entreprises et le peu qu'il restera ira à des particuliers. Les voitures seront louées pour environ 500 $ sur une période de quatre ans, le temps de la garantie.

Après quelques années sur notre marché, la smart connaît, avec sa motorisation électrique, sa deuxième révolution, la première ayant été le passage du moteur diesel à celui à essence. Peut-être qu'un jour, la smart électrique sera la seule proposée. En attendant, la smart à essence fait parfaitement l'affaire des citadins qui ont appris à vivre avec ses petits travers et son immense charme.

Alain Morin

PHOTOS : ALAIN MORIN

Catégorie	Cabriolet, *Hatchback*
Échelle de prix	14 990 $ à 24 900 $ (2010)
Garanties	4 ans/80 000 km, 4 ans/80 000 km
Assemblage	Hambach, France
Cote d'assurance	excellente

CHÂSSIS - DONNÉES POUR PASSION

Emp/lon/lar/haut	1 867/2 695/1 559/1 542 mm
Coffre	340 litres
Réservoir	33 litres
Nombre coussins sécurité	4
Antipatinage / contrôle stabilité	oui / oui
Suspension avant	indépendante, jambes de force
Suspension arrière	indépendante, multibras
Freins avant / arrière	disque (ABS) / tambour (ABS)
Direction	à crémaillère, ass. variable
Diamètre de braquage	8,7 m
Pneus avant / arrière	P155/60R15 / P175/55R15
Poids	820 kg
Capacité de remorquage	non recommandé

COMPOSANTES MÉCANIQUES

smart	
Cylindrée, soupapes, alim.	3L 1,0 litre 12 s atmos.
Puissance / Couple	70 chevaux / 68 lb-pi
Tr. base (opt) / rouage base (opt)	A5 / Prop
0-100 / 80-120 / 100-0 km/h	13,3 s / 13,4 s / 42,0 m
Type ess. / ville / autoroute	Super / 5,9 / 4,8 l/100 km

smart ED	
Puissance / Couple	20 kW (30 kW max) / 88 lb-pi
Batterie	Li-Ion / 16,5 kWh
Autonomie	135 km

DANS LA MÊME CATÉGORIE

Fiat 500

DU NOUVEAU EN 2011

Quelques changements mineurs à la partie avant. Nouveaux équipements. Système de navigation disponible à partir d'octobre 2010. Version électrique.

NOS IMPRESSIONS

Agrément de conduite :	■■■■■■■□□□	7/10
Fiabilité :	■■■■■■■■■■	10/10
Sécurité :	■■■■■■■■□□	8/10
Qualités hivernales :	■■■■□□□□□□	4/10
Espace intérieur :	■■■■■□□□□□	5/10
Confort :	■■■■■■□□□□	6/10

www.thesmart.ca

Plus d'informations dans la section statistiques en dernière partie du Guide

LE VUS DES GENS SENSÉS

Cela peut paraître incroyable à certains, mais plusieurs personnes se procurent des VUS non pas pour les utiliser pour ce qu'ils sont, mais tout simplement pour épater la galerie et afficher leur caractère aventurier. Il en résulte des véhicules dont les lignes sont agressives et la silhouette dessinée pour faire tourner les têtes... Mais, chez Subaru, on s'adresse à une clientèle beaucoup plus équilibrée et qui préfère l'anonymat en matière de silhouette.

Donc, le Forester n'a pas été conçu pour épater la galerie, mais pour répondre à des besoins précis et à une utilisation balancée entre la route et les sentiers impraticables pour une automobile. Avant d'aller plus loin, il est important de préciser que ce Subaru n'est pas un dur de dur. Il s'agit d'un véhicule à la plate-forme monocoque qui est capable d'en prendre, mais qui n'a pas la résistance des modèles plus spécialisés comme les Jeep Wrangler et Toyota FJ Cruiser par exemple.

LA DISCRÉTION

Comme mentionné précédemment, les stylistes se sont appliqués à dessiner une silhouette moderne qui répond au credo esthétique en vogue présentement, mais l'ensemble reste très discret. La première génération du Forester affichait une silhouette quelque peu déséquilibrée, trop en hauteur. Mais cette fois, l'équilibre est meilleur avec une grille de calandre encadrée par des bandes chromées qui donnent un certain relief à la partie avant. Le capot de la version à moteur turbocompressé est facilement reconnaissable puisqu'il exhibe une prise d'air. Parmi les autres éléments de style, notons une autre prise d'air sous le pare-chocs avant, les feux arrière triangulaires débordant sur l'aile et des passages de roue en relief. De plus, les solides jantes en alliage sont dotées de rayons très larges qui donnent un caractère plus macho à ce véhicule.

Dans l'habitacle, la planche de bord est pratique et simple. Si vous aimez le clinquant, ce véhicule vous décevra aussi bien de l'extérieur qu'à l'intérieur. Par contre, les commandes sont simples et faciles d'utilisation, notamment, comme sur bien des véhicules contemporains, les réglages de la climatisation qui se limitent à trois gros boutons placés directement sous les buses de ventilations situées en dessous de l'écran de navigation ou de la radio, selon le modèle choisi. Comme sur toutes les Subaru, les matériaux sont de qualité et l'assemblage précis. Dès le premier coup d'œil, on se rend compte que l'on a affaire à une voiture pratique et durable.

C'est dans cette veine que l'on se réjouit en s'assoyant sur les confortables sièges avant à l'assise suffisamment ferme. Le support latéral pourrait être meilleur, mais compte tenu de la vocation de ce véhicule, il ne faut pas en tenir rigueur. L'espace arrière pour les bagages est très généreux, ce qui coïncide avec la vocation utilitaire de ce véhicule. Une fois les dossiers de la banquette arrière baissés, c'est carrément caverneux !

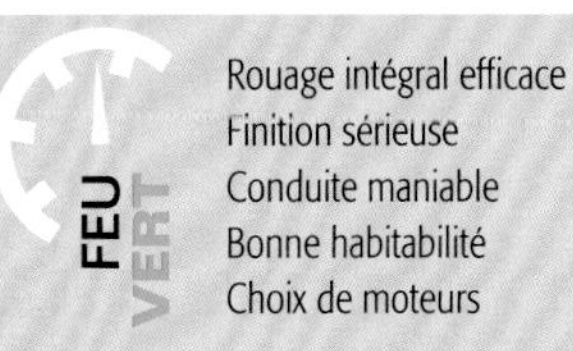

FEU VERT

- Rouage intégral efficace
- Finition sérieuse
- Conduite maniable
- Bonne habitabilité
- Choix de moteurs

FEU ROUGE

- Moteur atmosphérique un peu juste
- Insonorisation perfectible
- Pédale de frein un peu spongieuse
- Boîte automatique rétro

QUATRE CYLINDRES À PLAT ET SOUS-VIRAGE

Année après année, ce constructeur nous propose toujours ces incontournables moteurs à cylindres horizontaux de type boxer qui se sont taillés une enviable réputation au fil des années en fait de fiabilité et de solidité. Le moteur du modèle de base est légèrement modifié cette année alors que sa cylindrée passe de 2457 CC à 2498. La puissance demeure la même tandis que le couple progresse de 4 lb-pi. Une boîte automatique est offerte en option, mais elle ne possède que quatre rapports, ce qui est un peu mince de nos jours. L'autre moteur au catalogue, est une version turbocompressée de ce même moteur boxer. Sa cylindrée est toujours de 2,5 litres, mais sa puissance est de 224 chevaux.

Et c'est là le grand dilemme. Le moteur de base est très bien en utilisation normale, mais il est limité au chapitre des performances lorsqu'on est lourdement chargé ou pour effectuer un dépassement. À ce moment, cette puissance devient un peu juste et il faut planifier ses dépassements. La même remarque s'applique à la conduite hors route pour grimper une côte escarpée. Dans ces circonstances, la puissance supplémentaire du turbo se fait grandement apprécier.

Sachez qu'il est possible de commander une version PZEV dotée d'un moteur moins polluant. Les écologistes peuvent donc choisir une livrée plus verte et bénéficier des autres avantages d'un véhicule Subaru. Par contre, il n'est pas possible d'obtenir ce modèle avec le moteur turbocompressé. Mais peu importe notre choix, la transmission intégrale fait toujours partie de l'équipement de série. Ce rouage intégral est léger, simple et efficace. Il a fait ses preuves au fil des années et sa présence a été appréciée par des centaines de milliers de conducteurs lorsque les conditions routières ou météorologiques se sont manifestées. Par contre, il faut savoir que ce rouage est accompagné d'un sous-virage passablement important. Alors quand il y a une courbe prononcée, au bas d'une côte par exemple, il est nécessaire de réduire sa vitesse afin de ne pas faire un « tout droit » en bas de la côte...

On affectionne donc le Forester pour sa tenue de route généralement sans surprise, sa suspension confortable qui pourrait être un peu plus ferme au goût de certains, sa direction précise et son court diamètre de braquage. Pour le reste, il se fera aimer au fil des kilomètres et des années.

Denis Duquet

PHOTOS : SUBARU

Catégorie	VUS
Échelle de prix	25 995 $ à 35 295 $
Garanties	3 ans/60 000 km, 5 ans/100 000 km
Assemblage	Gunma, Japon
Cote d'assurance	bonne

CHÂSSIS - DONNÉES POUR PZEV

Emp/lon/lar/haut	2 615/4 560/1 780/1 700 mm
Coffre	949 à 1 934 litres
Réservoir	64 litres
Nombre coussins sécurité	6
Antipatinage / contrôle stabilité	oui / oui
Suspension avant	indépendante, jambes de force
Suspension arrière	indépendante, double triangulation
Freins avant / arrière	disque (ABS) / disque (ABS)
Direction	à crémaillère, ass. variable
Diamètre de braquage	n.d.
Pneus avant / arrière	215/65R16 / 215/65R16
Poids	1 480 kg
Capacité de remorquage	1 087 kg (2 396 lb)

COMPOSANTES MÉCANIQUES

2.5X, PZEV

Cylindrée, soupapes, alim.	H4 2,5 litres 16 s atmos.
Puissance / Couple	170 chevaux / 179 lb-pi
Tr. base (opt) / rouage base (opt)	M5 (A4) / Int
0-100 / 80-120 / 100-0 km/h	10,7 s / 9,0 s / 41,5 m
Type ess. / ville / autoroute	Ordinaire / 10,4 / 7,7 l/100km

2.5XT Limited Multimedia, 2.5XT Limited

Cylindrée, soupapes, alim.	H4 2,5 litres 16 s turbo
Puissance / Couple	224 chevaux / 226 lb-pi
Tr. base (opt) / rouage base (opt)	A4 (M5) / Int
0-100 / 80-120 / 100-0 km/h	8,9 s / 8,4 s / 41,5 m
Type ess. / ville / autoroute	Ordinaire / 11 / 8,4 l/100km

DANS LA MÊME CATÉGORIE

Chevrolet Equinox, Ford Escape, Honda CR-V, Hyundai Tucson, Jeep Compass, Jeep Patriot, Kia Sportage, Mazda Tribute, Mitsubishi Outlander, Nissan Rogue, Suzuki Grand Vitara, Toyota RAV4, Volkswagen Tiguan

DU NOUVEAU EN 2011

Nouveau moteur 2,5 litres

NOS IMPRESSIONS

Agrément de conduite :	8/10
Fiabilité :	6/10
Sécurité :	10/10
Qualités hivernales :	8/10
Espace intérieur :	8/10
Confort :	8/10

www.subaru.ca

Plus d'informations dans la section statistiques en dernière partie du Guide

SŒURS TRANSFORMÉES ENCORE RIVALES

Subaru a lancé les dés il y a trois ans en enveloppant l'Impreza d'une silhouette plus arrondie et moderne, en rupture avec le style des modèles précédents. Les versions 2.5i ont été bien reçues, affichant les qualités pragmatiques qui font la réussite de la marque, mais les modèles plus sportifs en ont arraché à cause de performances et d'une tenue de route émoussées, surtout la STI, au sommet de la gamme. Le constructeur y voit cette année avec une carrosserie plus costaude pour la WRX, des retouches sérieuses au comportement de la STI et le retour de la berline pour les deux séries.

L'idée première est de permettre à la WRX de se démarquer plus nettement des autres modèles de la famille Impreza. Solution toute trouvée : construire les WRX avec la même coque autoporteuse que les versions STI, en sommet de gamme. Cette transformation saute aux yeux puisque les ailes bombées couvrent des voies avant et arrière élargies de 35 mm et 40 mm.

Il faut effectivement parler des WRX et STI au pluriel puisque les deux séries sont offertes à nouveau en versions berline ou avec hayon.

AVANTAGES DISCRETS

Avec ces carrosseries communes, les STI et WRX se ressemblent évidemment plus. Les STI profitent toutefois de modifications et raffinements exclusifs mais peu apparents.

La STI est également dotée d'un rouage intégral plus complexe qui combine un différentiel autobloquant avant classique et un

autobloquant arrière de type Torsen avec un différentiel central qui propose trois modes de performance et six réglages manuels comme arbitre. En mode Normal, le différentiel achemine 59 % du couple aux roues arrière pour favoriser l'agilité et réduire le sous-virage typique des Subaru. Cette répartition peut être modifiée du poste de conduite. Le rouage intégral de la WRX, par contraste, est un simple viscocoupleur qui répartit le couple également entre roues avant et roues arrière.

La suspension des STI a été sérieusement modifiée pour la débarrasser de cette mollesse relative pour laquelle on l'a vertement critiquée depuis sa refonte. On a abaissé la carrosserie, installé de nouveaux coussinets à l'avant et de plus rigides à l'arrière, monté des ressorts plus fermes de 15,6 % à l'avant et 53 % derrière pour terminer avec des barres antiroulis de 21 mm à l'avant et 19 mm à l'arrière, un gain d'un millimètre. La barre antiroulis des WRX ne fait que 16 mm en diamètre mais leur suspension arrière profite elle aussi de coussinets plus rigides.

La STI se démarque encore de la WRX au rayon du freinage. Ses disques sont des Brembo (tous ventilés) qui font 326 mm de

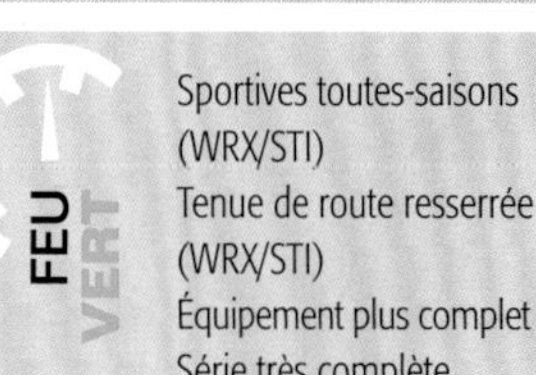

FEU VERT

Sportives toutes-saisons (WRX/STI)
Tenue de route resserrée (WRX/STI)
Équipement plus complet (2.5i)
Série très complète
Finition soignée

FEU ROUGE

Habitacle plutôt austère
Performances modestes (2,5i)
Pneus bruyants (STI)
Performances décevantes (STI)
Embrayage un peu lourd (WRX)

diamètre à l'avant et 316 mm à l'arrière avec des étriers à quatre et deux pistons, respectivement. Les disques des WRX (ventilés à l'avant) font 294 et 286 mm et leurs étriers sont à piston double à l'avant et simple à l'arrière.

De plus, les STI sont dotées de nouvelles jantes d'alliage de 18 pouces plus légères de 8 kg en tout, chaussées de pneus de performance de taille 245/40R18. Les WRX roulent sur des jantes de 17 pouces qui sont plus larges d'un pouce (2,5 cm) et chaussées de pneus de taille 235/45R17 dont la bande de roulement est plus large de 10 mm.

PORTRAIT INACHEVÉ

Objectivement, la STI se débrouillait bien en tenue de route, même sur circuit. Elle n'avait simplement pas les réflexes vifs et les réactions affutées qui faisaient de sa devancière une sportive nerveuse et franchement excitante à conduire. La nouvelle berline STI ramène également l'immense aileron arrière surélevé qui était son signe distinctif alors que la nouvelle berline WRX se contente d'un aileron de taille beaucoup plus modeste.

En fait, c'est sous le capot que le travail est encore inachevé. Les moteurs des WRX et STI ont les mêmes cotes essentielles et une cylindrée identique de 2457 cm^3. Ce sont des quatre cylindres à plat turbocompressés à double arbre à cames qui ne diffèrent essentiellement que par le fait que le calage est variable pour les soupapes d'admission et d'échappement sur la STI et pour l'échappement seulement sur la WRX.

Leurs cotes de puissance et de couple sont inchangées. Elles sont de 265 chevaux à 6000 tr/min et 244 lb-pi de couple à 4000 tr/min pour la WRX et de 305 chevaux et 290 lb-pi de couple aux mêmes régimes pour la STI. L'ennui, c'est que les WRX, même plus baraquées, sont encore plus légères que leurs contreparties STI à quatre ou cinq portières de 80 et 75 kg. Or, la WRX était déjà plus rapide de quelques dixièmes de seconde en accélération. C'était gênant l'an dernier et ce l'est encore, en dépit du raffinement plus poussé et de la tenue de route mieux affutée de la STI. Il lui faut quelques douzaines de chevaux de plus pour qu'elle puisse enfin être à la hauteur de sa propre réputation.

Marc Lachapelle

PHOTOS : SUBARU

Catégorie	Berline, *Hatchback*
Échelle de prix	20995$ à 45995$
Garanties	3 ans/60000 km, 5 ans/100000 km
Assemblage	Gunma et Yajiima, Japon
Cote d'assurance	passable

CHÂSSIS - DONNÉES POUR 2.5I SPORT BERLINE

Emp/lon/lar/haut	2620/4580/1976/1475 mm
Coffre	320 litres
Réservoir	64 litres
Nombre coussins sécurité	6
Antipatinage / contrôle stabilité	oui / oui
Suspension avant	indépendante, jambes de force
Suspension arrière	indépendante, double triangulation
Freins avant / arrière	disque (ABS) / disque (ABS)
Direction	à crémaillère, ass. variable
Diamètre de braquage	10,6 m
Pneus avant / arrière	P205/55R16 / P205/55R16
Poids	1390 kg
Capacité de remorquage	906 kg (1997 lb)

COMPOSANTES MÉCANIQUES

2.5i	
Cylindrée, soupapes, alim.	H4 2,5 litres 16 s atmos.
Puissance / Couple	170 chevaux / 170 lb-pi
Tr. base (opt) / rouage base (opt)	M5 (A4) / Int
0-100 / 80-120 / 100-0 km/h	9.8 s / 9.3 s / 41,0 m
Type ess. / ville / autoroute	Ordinaire / 10,6 / 7,5 l/100 km

WRX	
Cylindrée, soupapes, alim.	H4 2,5 litres 16 s turbo
Puissance / Couple	265 chevaux / 244 lb-pi
Tr. base (opt) / rouage base (opt)	M6 / Int
0-100 / 80-120 / 100-0 km/h	6,1 s / 5,0 s / 39,8 m
Type ess. / ville / autoroute	Super / 11,3 / 8,1 l/100 km

WRX Sti	
Cylindrée, soupapes, alim.	H4 2,5 litres 16 s turbo
Puissance / Couple	305 chevaux / 290 lb-pi
Tr. base (opt) / rouage base (opt)	M6 / Int
0-100 / 80-120 / 100-0 km/h	5,2 s / 4,6 s / 34,9 m
Type ess. / ville / autoroute	Super / 12,4 / 8,9 l/100 km

DANS LA MÊME CATÉGORIE

Chevrolet Cruze, Dodge Caliber, Ford Focus, Honda Civic, Hyundai Elantra, Kia Forte, Mazda3, Mitsubishi Lancer, Nissan Sentra, Suzuki SX-4, Toyota Corolla, Toyota Matrix, Volkswagen Jetta, Volkswagen Golf

DU NOUVEAU EN 2011

Modèle WRX remanié, WRX STi offert en version berline

NOS IMPRESSIONS

Agrément de conduite :	8/10
Fiabilité :	8/10
Sécurité :	9/10
Qualités hivernales :	9/10
Espace intérieur :	8/10
Confort :	8/10

www.subaru.ca

Plus d'informations dans la section statistiques en dernière partie du Guide

Subaru Legacy

CHAMBRE À PART

L'an dernier, l'une des agréables surprises sur la scène automobile a été l'arrivée de ces deux nouveaux modèles complètement remaniés par Subaru. Mieux encore, au lieu de simplement les dépoussiérer puisqu'ils connaissaient quand même des succès intéressants, on a décidé de développer une nouvelle plate-forme et même de les séparer: ils sont désormais des entités autonomes.

Auparavant, la Legacy était disponible en versions berline et familiale tandis que l'Outback était une version un peu plus spécialisée de la Legacy familiale. On a pris la bonne décision en réalisant des véhicules dotés de personnalités différentes, tout en empruntant les mêmes groupes propulseurs.

LA VEDETTE

De ces deux modèles, c'est l'Outback qui a le plus impressionné les rédacteurs du *Guide de l'auto* qui en ont fait le véhicule multisegment de l'année lors de l'édition 2010. Quelle agréable surprise! Dorénavant, pas de solution mitoyenne voulant ménager la chèvre et le chou. Cette fois-ci, ce véhicule possède tous les atouts pour se frotter aux meilleurs de la catégorie et ne sera plus seulement considéré comme une variante de la familiale Legacy. Pour ce faire, l'Outback arbore une silhouette qui lui est particulière. Il suffit d'examiner les grilles de calandre, les blocs optiques et les pare-chocs pour s'en convaincre. De plus, en raison de sa vocation, la garde au sol est maintenant de 220 mm et certains propriétaires vont vouloir profiter du rouage intégral de série de ce modèle pour s'aventurer hors route.

Ne croyez pas que ce modèle est en mesure d'intimider un Jeep Wrangler Unlimited Rubicon, mais dans les mains d'un bon pilote, cette Subaru est capable de passer pratiquement partout.

Réjouissons-nous car le tableau de bord n'est plus aussi morose qu'auparavant, la présentation étant désormais au goût du jour. De plus, on y retrouve toujours la même qualité de finition et les mêmes matériaux supérieurs à la moyenne de cette catégorie. Mais ce qui impressionne carrément, c'est la polyvalence et le caractère vraiment décisif de ce modèle. Sur la route, ce véhicule à tout faire nous épate par la rigidité de sa plate-forme, par sa tenue de route sans surprise et par sa capacité à rouler avec aplomb sur toutes les surfaces ou presque. Le moteur de base est l'incontournable moteur quatre cylindres à plat de 2,5 litres dont les 170 chevaux ont parfois de la difficulté à gérer une pente trop inclinée ou un chargement trop lourd. La boîte de vitesse manuelle à six rapports marque un net progrès comparativement aux versions précédentes. Pour la première fois sur ce modèle, une transmission à rapports continuellement variables a été offerte l'an dernier et elle est de retour cette année. Contrairement à plusieurs autres transmissions de ce genre, celle proposée par Subaru mérite nos éloges.

Mais si vous prévoyez être toujours chargé à bloc ou même tracter une remorque, il est possible d'obtenir un moteur six cylindres

FEU VERT

Finition sérieuse
CVT
Rouage intégral efficace
Bonne tenue de route
Mécanique solide

FEU ROUGE

Insonorisation moyenne
Certains éléments manquants
Performances justes (2,5 litres)
Silhouette effacée (Legacy)

à plat. Ce H6 de 3,5 litres provient du Tribeca et est associé à la transmission automatique à cinq rapports de cette dernière.

PLUS D'ESPACE POUR LA LEGACY

La Legacy a pris du coffre l'an dernier et son habitabilité est meilleure. Et sa plate-forme plus rigide ne fait pas qu'améliorer la tenue de route, elle a aussi un effet positif sur le confort et l'insonorisation. Bien entendu, comme dans le cas de l'Outback, les matériaux de l'habitacle sont de première qualité et la finition est toujours impeccable.

Néanmoins, les améliorations ont été moins spectaculaires que dans le cas de l'Outback. En effet, la Legacy est efficace et sobre tout en proposant une très bonne tenue de route. Mais à mon avis, elle est moins inspirante pour ce qui est de la conduite. Il lui manque cette petite étincelle qui nous fait tant craquer pour l'Outback.

Comme cette dernière, le moteur de base est le quatre cylindres à plat de 2,5 litres de 170 chevaux. Il peut être couplé à une boîte manuelle à six rapports ou encore à une transmission de type CVT. Encore une fois, nous devons préciser que ce moteur est robuste et durable, mais ses prestations sont un peu justes si la voiture est chargée. Sur la berline comme sur la version multisegment, la boîte automatique à rapports continuellement variables est efficace.

Pour les conducteurs un peu plus sportifs, la version GT est animée par une version turbo compressée de ce même moteur 2,5 litres. Mais cette fois, la puissance est de 265 chevaux et seule la boîte manuelle à six rapports est disponible. Cette version est plus nerveuse et plus agréable à conduire, mais il ne faut pas croire que ses performances inquiéteront l'Impreza WRX. De plus, une calibration révisée et certains accessoires supplémentaires accroîtraient l'intérêt pour cette GT. Finalement, la version la plus cossue est propulsée par le moteur 6 cylindres à plat de 3,5 litres et sa transmission automatique à cinq rapports. On y gagne en souplesse et en douceur de roulement.

L'acheteur peut donc choisir, selon ses besoins, entre deux véhicules de qualité mais à la vocation vraiment différente.

Denis Duquet

Subaru Outback

PHOTOS : SYLVAIN RAYMOND

Catégorie	Berline / Familiale
Échelle de prix	23 995 $ à 38 595 $
Garanties	3 ans/60 000 km, 5 ans/100 000 km
Assemblage	n.d.
Cote d'assurance	moyenne

CHÂSSIS - DONNÉES POUR 2.5I SPORT

Emp/lon/lar/haut	2 750/4 735/1 820/1 505 mm
Coffre	415 litres
Réservoir	70 litres
Nombre coussins sécurité	6
Antipatinage / contrôle stabilité	oui / oui
Suspension avant	indépendante, jambes de force
Suspension arrière	indépendante, leviers triangulés
Freins avant / arrière	disque (ABS) / disque (ABS)
Direction	à crémaillère, ass. variable
Diamètre de braquage	n.d.
Pneus avant / arrière	P205/60R16 / P205/60R16
Poids	1 485 kg
Capacité de remorquage	n.d.

COMPOSANTES MÉCANIQUES

2,5i

Cylindrée, soupapes, alim.	H4 2,5 litres 16 s atmos.
Puissance / Couple	170 chevaux / 170 lb-pi
Tr. base (opt) / rouage base (opt)	M6 (CVT) / Int
0-100 / 80-120 / 100-0 km/h	10,0 s / 7,7 s / 45,5 m
Type ess. / ville / autoroute	Ordinaire / 9,2 / 6,5 l/100 km

3.6 R

Cylindrée, soupapes, alim.	H6 3,6 litres 24 s atmos.
Puissance / Couple	256 chevaux / 247 lb-pi
Tr. base (opt) / rouage base (opt)	M6 (A6, A5) / Int
0-100 / 80-120 / 100-0 km/h	9,0 s (est) / n.d. / n.d.
Type ess. / ville / autoroute	Super / 11,5 / 8,0 l/100 km

2.5 GT

Cylindrée, soupapes, alim.	H4 2,5 litres 16 s turbo
Puissance / Couple	265 chevaux / 258 lb-pi
Tr. base (opt) / rouage base (opt)	M6 / Int
0-100 / 80-120 / 100-0 km/h	8,5 s (est) / n.d. / n.d.
Type ess. / ville / autoroute	Super / 9,1 / 6,4 l/100 km

DANS LA MÊME CATÉGORIE

Chevrolet Malibu, Chrysler Sebring, Dodge Avenger, Ford Fusion, Honda Accord, Hyundai Sonata, Mazda6, Nissan Altima, Toyota Camry

DU NOUVEAU EN 2011

Aucun changement majeur.

NOS IMPRESSIONS

Agrément de conduite :	8/10
Fiabilité :	8/10
Sécurité :	10/10
Qualités hivernales :	10/10
Espace intérieur :	9/10
Confort :	8/10

www.subaru.ca

Plus d'informations dans la section statistiques en dernière partie du Guide

MAIS POURQUOI N'EN VOIT-ON PAS PLUS ?

Chez Subaru, il doit y avoir deux départements de marketing et deux de design… Subaru est au Canada depuis 1976 et s'est bâti une réputation crédible grâce à ses voitures solides et surtout utilitaires. Toujours est-il qu'au fil des années, Subaru a produit quelques véhicules délirants, rompant ainsi avec son image de sage constructeur. Qu'on pense à la bizarre XT (1986-1990), la magnifique SVX (1992-1996) ou encore aux camionnettes Brat (1979-1982) et Baja (2003-2006). Nous pouvons quasiment inscrire sur cette liste le Tribeca, baptisé B9 Tribeca lors de son arrivée en 2006.

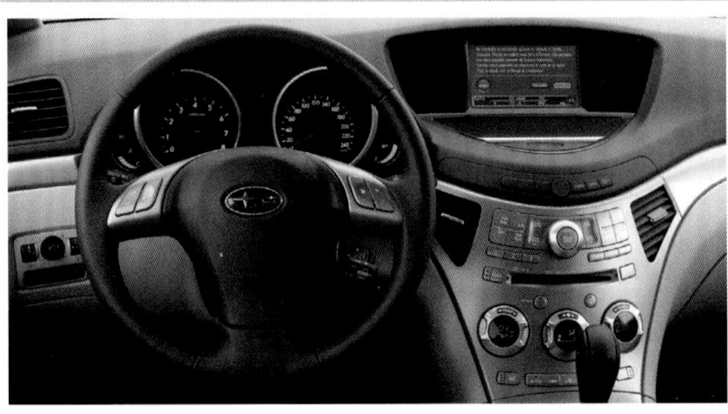

Conçu sans doute pour répondre davantage aux dictats du marketing qui veulent qu'un constructeur présente une voiture dans chaque créneau que pour répondre aux besoins des consommateurs, le Tribeca affichait, durant les deux premières années de sa commercialisation, une carrosserie pour le moins différente… pour être poli ! En 2008, le seul véhicule à sept places proposé par Subaru héritait d'une ligne moins originale, mais plus homogène, qui ne se démarque pas trop dans la jungle automobile.

TABLEAU DE BORD CONTROVERSÉ

L'habitacle, par exemple, n'a pratiquement pas changé et on retrouve toujours ce tableau de bord se prolongeant en son centre pour devenir la console. Les gens qui aiment se sentir enveloppés sont choyés, les autres trouvent cet élément stylistique étouffant. Par contre, il faut avouer qu'en plus d'être originale, cette astuce permet de proposer un tableau de bord ergonomique où tous les boutons sont placés à portée de la main. Et comme ils sont gros, ils sont facilement manipulables même avec des gants d'hiver. Les commandes du système de chauffage sont inédites et franchement intelligentes. En revanche, je n'ai pas aimé que la buse de ventilation située à droite du volant expédie constamment son air sur mes mains ou sur mes cuisses. Cependant, d'autres conducteurs n'ont pas connu ce problème. Curieusement, même sur les versions huppées, le volant n'est pas réglable en profondeur, un manquement sévère à l'étiquette automobile, surtout quand on parle d'un véhicule de plus de 40 000 $. Toutefois, je n'ai eu aucune difficulté à trouver une bonne position de conduite. Une bonne note pour les jauges rétro éclairées faciles à consulter (sauf celles de la température du moteur et de l'essence), le système audio Harman Kardon de 385 watts.

Les sièges de la deuxième rangée pourraient être un peu moins durs mais, au moins, ils s'avèrent beaucoup plus confortables que ceux de la troisième rangée qui, en plus, ne sont pas faciles à atteindre. Aussi, cette troisième rangée ampute une bonne partie du coffre quand elle est relevée. Autrement, l'espace de chargement est passablement grand. Sous le plancher, on retrouve un bac pouvant contenir quelques petits objets. Les plus gros articles doivent demeurer à la vue de tous les mécréants, à moins que vous ayez déboursé pour acheter un cache-bagages optionnel…

Catégorie	VUS
Échelle de prix	40995$ à 49195$ (2010)
Garanties	3 ans/60000 km, 5 ans/100000 km
Assemblage	Lafayette, Indiana, E-U
Cote d'assurance	bonne

FEU VERT
- Silhouette moderne
- Rouage intégral intéressant
- Fiabilité de bon aloi
- Habitacle silencieux
- Véhicule sécuritaire

FEU ROUGE
- Puissance un peu juste
- Consommation élevée
- Troisième rangée de sièges utopique
- Prix assez corsés
- Volant non ajustable en profondeur

MÉCANIQUE TYPIQUE DE SUBARU

Qui dit Subaru, dit moteur à plat et le Tribeca ne fait pas exception. Il reçoit un six cylindres de 3,6 litres suffisamment puissant pour les besoins quotidiens. Rendons grâce aux ingénieurs qui ont réussi à garder ce véhicule sous les 2000 kilos. Cependant, ce moteur pourrait être un peu juste si on installait une remorque de 906 kilos (maximum recommandé par Subaru) à l'arrière. Tout comme il aurait de la difficulté à bien s'exprimer s'il fallait qu'il soit chargé de sept personnes et de leurs bagages ! À ce moment, il doit consommer comme un alcoolique en rechute, si l'on se fie à la consommation moyenne de 13,8 litres/100 km que nous avons obtenue durant une semaine d'essai. Heureusement, il se contente d'essence ordinaire.

Côté transmission, on retrouve une automatique à cinq rapports qui travaille infiniment mieux que celle qui ridiculisait les premiers Tribeca même si son mode manuel n'est guère intéressant. Bien entendu, Subaru fait encore appel à son célèbre rouage intégral symétrique qui permet au Tribeca de facilement passer dans la neige épaisse ou dans la boue. Son châssis, emprunté au duo Legacy/Outback, fait preuve de solidité et les suspensions qu'on lui a accrochées privilégient le confort sans nuire à la tenue de route. Oh, on ne parle pas ici d'un véhicule sport mais le Tribeca s'avère fort agréable à conduire grâce, en grande partie, à sa direction qui fournit un bon retour d'informations tout en étant relativement précise à vitesse de croisière. En conduite, l'habitacle est silencieux, feutré même. La visibilité tout le tour n'est pas si mal, merci aux gros rétroviseurs extérieurs. Les freins font bien leur boulot même si une simulation d'un arrêt d'urgence montre une pédale molle.

Le Subaru Tribeca, comme on le constate, possède de très belles qualités, surtout depuis qu'on s'est débarrassé de ses deux tares initiales, soit sa transmission de clown et sa face de tamanoir qui aurait tenté de vider une fourmilière située entre des rails au moment où le train passait. Pourtant, on voit très peu de Tribeca sur nos routes… Il faut dire qu'avec des prix pouvant facilement aller au-delà de 50000$, on tombe dans une catégorie peuplée de multisegments établis comme les Ford Flex, Honda Pilot et Mazda CX-9. Le Tribeca a beau jouir d'une bonne fiabilité, d'une évidente qualité de fabrication et d'un rouage intégral performant, il en faut aujourd'hui bien davantage pour faire sa place au soleil.

Alain Morin

PHOTOS : ALAIN MORIN

CHÂSSIS - DONNÉES POUR LIMITED

Emp/lon/lar/haut	2749/4865/1878/1720 mm
Coffre	235 à 2106 litres
Réservoir	64 litres
Nombre coussins sécurité	6
Antipatinage / contrôle stabilité	oui / oui
Suspension avant	indépendante, jambes de force
Suspension arrière	indépendante, double triangulation
Freins avant / arrière	disque (ABS) / disque (ABS)
Direction	à crémaillère, ass. variable
Diamètre de braquage	10,8 m
Pneus avant / arrière	P255/55R18 / P255/55R18
Poids	1906 kg
Capacité de remorquage	906 kg (1997 lb)

COMPOSANTES MÉCANIQUES

Base, Limited, Optimum

Cylindrée, soupapes, alim.	H6 3,6 litres 24 s atmos.
Puissance / Couple	256 chevaux / 247 lb-pi
Tr. base (opt) / rouage base (opt)	A5 / Int
0-100 / 80-120 / 100-0 km/h	8,5 s / 7,2 s / 42,0 m
Type ess. / ville / autoroute	Ordinaire / 13,2 / 9,4 l/100 km

DANS LA MÊME CATÉGORIE

Chevrolet Traverse, Ford Edge, Ford Flex, GMC Acadia, Honda Pilot, Hyundai Veracruz, Mazda CX-9, Mitsubishi Endeavor, Nissan Murano, Toyota Highlander

DU NOUVEAU EN 2011

Aucun changement majeur

NOS IMPRESSIONS

Agrément de conduite :	8/10
Fiabilité :	8/10
Sécurité :	10/10
Qualités hivernales :	10/10
Espace intérieur :	9/10
Confort :	8/10

www.subaru.ca

Plus d'informations dans la section statistiques en dernière partie du Guide

À QUELQUES DÉTAILS PRÈS

Suzuki figure parmi les plus importants constructeurs de la planète. Cela en surprend toujours plusieurs quand on constate la timide présence de cette marque sur notre marché. Au fil des années, les modèles se sont succédés avec plus ou moins de succès. Trop souvent, il leur manquait des caractéristiques vitales, qu'elles soient techniques ou esthétiques, pour leur permettre de dominer un segment du marché. Le Grand Vitara ne faisait pas exception à cette règle.

En effet, ce VUS compact a beaucoup à proposer aux acheteurs à la recherche d'un rouage intégral relativement moderne et d'une bonne capacité de remorquage. Par contre, comme vous allez le constater, Suzuki s'est fourvoyé plusieurs fois avec des omissions tout de même flagrantes.

LA MAUDITE PORTE !

Il peut paraître futile d'accorder beaucoup d'importance à une porte arrière à battant. Cette configuration a ses avantages aux yeux de certains et des désavantages aux yeux des autres. Ce type de porte est surtout contraignant si vous stationnez votre Grand Vitara dans une rue à circulation à double sens. Vous devez alors faire un détour avec vos bagages pour contourner cette portière afin de les déposer dans la soute à bagages. Dans un sens unique, toutefois, il se peut que cette portière soit du bon côté !

Donc, le problème n'est pas nécessairement de quel côté la porte ouvre. Selon moi, le problème est plutôt la roue de secours qui y est accrochée. Elle rend la portière lourde, en plus de bloquer en partie la visibilité arrière pour le conducteur.

Bon, assez parlé de cette portière. L'habitacle lui-même est relativement spacieux et les sièges confortables. En plus, les places arrière conviendront à la plupart des occupants. Quant à la planche de bord, elle se démarque par sa sobriété et son ergonomie de bon aloi. Malheureusement, le volant a des allures « bon marché », bien que des commandes, placées sur les rayons horizontaux de celui-ci, soient pratiques. Heureusement, la position de conduite est très bonne, de même que la visibilité en général et ce, malgré la présence de la roue de secours qui obstrue partiellement la lunette arrière.

BONNE NOUVELLE, MAUVAISE NOUVELLE

Il y a plus d'un an maintenant, la direction de Suzuki Canada dévoilait avec beaucoup de fierté son Grand Vitara à moteur quatre cylindres. Ce moteur de 2,4 litres d'une puissance de 166 chevaux devenait le groupe propulseur de base, tandis que le moteur V6 de 3,2 litres équipait les versions plus luxueuses. Avec ses 230 chevaux, il est capable de remorquer quasiment deux tonnes. Au fait, la version à moteur quatre cylindres est capable, elle aussi, de remorquer la même charge, mais avec une sérieuse pénalité au chapitre de la consommation.

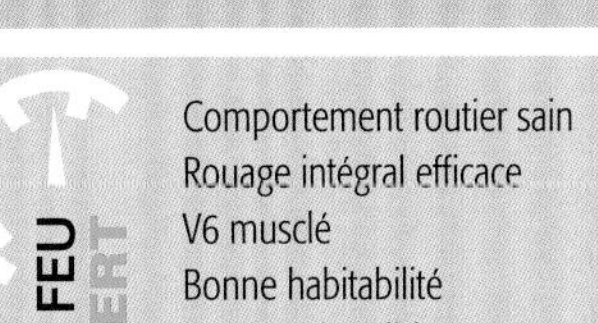

FEU VERT

- Comportement routier sain
- Rouage intégral efficace
- V6 musclé
- Bonne habitabilité
- Carrosserie solide

FEU ROUGE

- Moteur quatre cylindres gourmand
- Boîte automatique 4 rapports (4 cylindres)
- Portière arrière à ouverture latérale
- Faible diffusion

On se félicitait chez Suzuki de pouvoir offrir un moteur quatre cylindres, comme la majorité des modèles concurrents dans cette catégorie. Même si ce moteur offre une performance correcte, on a eu la mauvaise idée de l'associer à une transmission automatique à quatre rapports offerte en option. Il faudrait peut-être envoyer une petite note aux dirigeants de ce constructeur pour leur souligner que nous terminons la première décennie du XXIe millénaire et que des transmissions de la sorte sont chose du passé. Non seulement celle-ci rend la conduite plus ou moins agréable avec des passages de vitesses saccadés, mais il en résulte une consommation de carburant quasiment identique à celle de la version équipée du moteur V6. Vous pourrez obtenir une consommation un peu plus économique en optant pour la boîte manuelle à cinq rapport.

Cette façon de décider et de choisir est typique de ce constructeur. Pourquoi ne pas avoir opté pour une transmission automatique moderne ou, à tout le moins, pour la boîte automatique à cinq rapports livrée avec la version à moteur V6? Poser la question, c'est y répondre. Il faut aussi souligner que, lors de la refonte de ce même moteur V6, on a modifié la tringlerie de la pédale d'accélération, de sorte que la moindre pression sur l'accélérateur se traduit par un bond en avant.

Au chapitre de la conduite, peu importe le moteur choisi, la tenue en virage est bonne, rassurante même. Par contre, la direction pourrait être plus précise bien que plusieurs essayeurs se disent satisfaits de cette dernière. Si vous fréquentez de mauvaises routes, un événement quotidien pour les conducteurs habitant au Québec, la rigidité de la caisse est mise en évidence, bien que la suspension ait parfois de la difficulté à maîtriser les trous et les bosses.

Il ne faut pas oublier de souligner les qualités hivernales de ce véhicule qui est doté d'un système de chauffage puissant, d'essuie-glaces fort efficaces et d'une mécanique qui démarre même par temps très froid. En plus, les ingénieurs de Suzuki ont réussi à développer un rouage intégral qui est performant que ce soit sur la neige, la glace ou même sur les routes en gravier.

Somme toute, il s'agit d'un véhicule bien conçu dans son ensemble, d'une bonne efficacité sur route autant que hors route et d'une construction solide.

Denis Duquet

PHOTOS : SUZUKI

Catégorie	VUS
Échelle de prix	27 995 $ à 33 195 $ (2010)
Garanties	3 ans/60 000 km, 5 ans/100 000 km
Assemblage	Iwata, Japon
Cote d'assurance	passable

CHÂSSIS - DONNÉES POUR JLX-L V6

Emp/lon/lar/haut	2 640/4 500/1 810/1 695 mm
Coffre	680 à 1 930 litres
Réservoir	66 litres
Nombre coussins sécurité	6
Antipatinage / contrôle stabilité	oui / oui
Suspension avant	indépendante, jambes de force
Suspension arrière	indépendante, multibras
Freins avant / arrière	disque (ABS) / disque (ABS)
Direction	à crémaillère, assistée
Diamètre de braquage	11,2 m
Pneus avant / arrière	P225/60R18 / P225/60R18
Poids	1 795 kg
Capacité de remorquage	1 360 kg (2 998 lb)

COMPOSANTES MÉCANIQUES

JX, JLX, JLX-L

Cylindrée, soupapes, alim.	4L 2,4 litres 16 s atmos.
Puissance / Couple	166 chevaux / 162 lb-pi
Tr. base (opt) / rouage base (opt)	A4 / Int
0-100 / 80-120 / 100-0 km/h	n.d. / n.d. / n.d.
Type ess. / ville / autoroute	Ordinaire / 11,2 / 8,6 l/100 km

JLX V6, JLX-L V6

Cylindrée, soupapes, alim.	V6 3,2 litres 24 s atmos.
Puissance / Couple	230 chevaux / 213 lb-pi
Tr. base (opt) / rouage base (opt)	A5 / Int
0-100 / 80-120 / 100-0 km/h	11,5 s / 12,0 s / 41,0 m
Type ess. / ville / autoroute	Ordinaire / 12,5 / 8,6 l/100 km

DANS LA MÊME CATÉGORIE

Chevrolet Equinox, Dodge Nitro, Ford Escape, Honda CR-V, Hyundai Santa Fe, Jeep Liberty, Mazda Tribute, Mitsubishi Outlander, Nissan Rogue, Subaru Forester, Toyota RAV4, Volkswagen Tiguan

DU NOUVEAU EN 2011

Aucun changement majeur

NOS IMPRESSIONS

Agrément de conduite :	■■■■■■■□□□	7/10
Fiabilité :	■■■■■■■■□□	8/10
Sécurité :	■■■■■■■■□□	8/10
Qualités hivernales :	■■■■■■■■□□	8/10
Espace intérieur :	■■■■■■■□□□	7/10
Confort :	■■■■■■■■□□	8/10

www.suzuki.ca

Plus d'informations dans la section statistiques en dernière partie du Guide

SUZUKI GRAND VITARA

LE VERRE À MOITIÉ VIDE

Il est difficile pour nous, Nord-Américains, de concevoir que Suzuki est un très important manufacturier qui distribue ses produits à travers le monde. En 2009, par exemple, l'entreprise japonaise employait pas moins de 14 000 personnes. Suzuki est surtout reconnue pour ses scooters, motos, VTT, moteurs de bateaux, petites voitures et tout aussi petits 4x4. On ignore qu'elle produit aussi des fauteuils roulants motorisés, de l'équipement industriel et, depuis peu, des voitures intermédiaires, dont la nouvelle Kizashi !

La Kizashi se mesure à des vedettes établies telles les Honda Accord, Toyota Camry, Subaru Legacy, Hyundai Sonata et autres Ford Fusion et Chevrolet Malibu. Cependant, ses dimensions plus réduites que celles de ses « amies » la placent plutôt entre les intermédiaires ci-haut mentionnées et les compactes que sont les Honda Civic, Toyota Corolla, Subaru Impreza ou Ford Focus. Mais, comme nous le verrons plus loin, son comportement routier la rapproche effectivement des intermédiaires.

La Kizashi, contrairement à toutes ses rivales, n'est offerte qu'en une seule version, nommée SX. Aucune option n'est même proposée. Très bien équipée, on n'y retrouve toutefois pas de GPS. Selon Suzuki, cet accessoire aurait trop fait augmenter le prix de vente. De plus, les manufacturiers ne peuvent rivaliser, en termes de prix, avec les fournisseurs indépendant que sont les TomTom et Garmin, par exemple. L'idée de n'offrir qu'une seule version « full au bouchon » peut être débattue, mais toujours selon Suzuki, les Canadiens préfèrent les versions ainsi équipées.

ALORS, ÇA S'EN VIENT ?

Au-delà d'un nom bizarre qui, en français, veut dire « quelque chose de grandiose s'en vient », traduction libre de « something great is coming », il faut avouer que la Kizashi affiche une robe dynamique... à défaut d'être très originale. En fait, elle ressemble beaucoup à une Volkswagen Jetta, surtout à l'avant. La partie arrière se montre toutefois plus inédite avec un dessus de coffre arrondi qui fait penser à une queue de canard. Les gens rencontrés lors de nos différents essais menés au volant de cette nouvelle Suzuki ont tous apprécié son look. Un look qui ne devrait pas se démoder demain matin.

L'habitacle, on n'en sera pas surpris, n'est pas des plus vastes. Cependant, les designers de Suzuki ont réussi à créer un milieu qui ne rebute pas les claustrophobes. Pour autant que le noir intégral ne leur donne pas le cafard... Le tableau de bord est réussi, tant au niveau des jauges au design un tantinet rétro, que des boutons et commandes faciles à comprendre et à manipuler, même en hiver. Un bémol par contre pour certaines commandes du système audio Rockford Fosgate, à la sonorité au demeurant fort agréable, qui sont un peu trop éloignées du conducteur. Heureusement, ces commandes sont dupliquées au volant. Les espaces de rangement sont nombreux et le coffre à gants peut contenir plus que des gants, une rareté de nos jours.

Les sièges avant font preuve de confort, celui du conducteur possédant même trois mémoires ! Néanmoins, les très grandes personnes ou celles possédant une enveloppe corporelle exagérée pourraient trouver que le siège du conducteur manque de recul. La position de conduite se trouve en un clin d'œil, mais au fil des kilomètres, j'ai trouvé le repose-pied inconfortable, n'étant pas suffisamment incliné vers le conducteur. Le volant se prend bien en main... Heureusement, car le cuir de son boudin est un peu trop glissant à mon goût, signe d'un cuir de qualité sans doute assez ordinaire, merci. D'ailleurs, le pommeau du levier de vitesses, recouvert du même matériau, était passablement égratigné dans une de nos voitures d'essai qui n'avait même pas 3000 kilomètres. Autrement, la finition intérieure s'avère fort relevée et les matériaux sont de belle qualité.

Les places arrière proposent un espace correct, autant pour les jambes, les coudes que la tête. Le même qualificatif s'applique au confort général de cette banquette dont les dossiers se replient pour agrandir un coffre ma foi fort logeable, compte tenu des dimensions extérieures. Et comble d'anachronisme dans une voiture moderne, son ouverture est suffisamment grande !

UNE PLATE-FORME INÉDITE

La Kizashi est la carte de visite de Suzuki dans le monde des grands. Pour être pris au sérieux, le constructeur a conçu une toute nouvelle plate-forme, très solide. Côté mécanique, Suzuki a passablement moins dépensé... On s'est contenté du quatre cylindres 2,4 litres du Grand Vitara qu'on a légèrement modifié. Sa puissance est correcte malgré un certain manque d'enthousiasme à bas régime, mais comme la voiture est l'une des plus lourdes de sa catégorie, ses performances sont en retrait.

Comme si ce n'était pas suffisant, on a affublé ce moteur d'une transmission à rapports continuellement variables (CVT), qui semble constamment bouffer une trentaine de chevaux. En usage normal, bien des gens ne se rendront même pas compte qu'ils ont affaire à une CVT. Mais en accélération vive, l'augmentation phénoménale du nombre de décibels en amènera plusieurs à lever le pied, par instinct de survie mécanique ! Un peu plus de matériel isolant ne réglerait pas le problème, mais on se rendrait moins compte des limites de cette transmission. Au moins, son mode manuel, activé par des palettes placées derrière le volant, est agréable à utiliser. Une bonne transmission manuelle à six rapports aussi serait agréable à utiliser... La Kizashi est donnée pour 9,3 litres aux cent kilomètres en ville et 6,8 sur la route. Lors d'un essai hebdomadaire, nous avons obtenu une moyenne de 9,4, mais nous devons avouer que nous avons roulé en grande majorité sur autoroutes. Ce qui ne fait pas de la Kizashi un modèle de sobriété. Mais elle n'est pas, non plus, une alcoolique finie. Cependant, le fait que le réservoir d'essence soit plutôt petit (63 litres) entraîne des arrêts plus fréquents à la pompe, ce qui peut induire en erreur les personnes qui calculent leur consommation en termes de temps, genre « Je fais même pas une semaine avec ma *tank* ! ».

Là où cette nouvelle Suzuki se démarque de la concurrence, c'est au niveau de son rouage intégral. Dit « intelligent », il anticipe les pertes de traction. Si nos voisins sous le 45e parallèle ont le choix entre une version traction (roues avant motrices) et une autre AWD (intégrale), nous n'avons droit qu'à cette dernière. En

revanche, un bouton au tableau de bord permet de rouler en mode traction uniquement. Les éléments se déchaînent ? Le conducteur n'a qu'à activer le rouage intégral. Cependant, il faut noter que même en mode traction, le système envoie une infime partie du couple aux roues arrière. Aussi, même en mode intégral, la majeure partie du couple sera expédiée aux roues avant. Dès que le besoin se fait sentir, le couple est envoyé aux roues arrière jusqu'à hauteur de 50 %. Avec une Kizashi, on ne peut pas suivre un Jeep Wrangler, mais une Subaru Legacy, ça oui !

LE BÉNÉFICE DU DOUTE

C'est sur la route que la Kizashi donne sa pleine mesure. Agréable à conduire à défaut d'être agile, douce, feutrée même, cette

Catégorie	Berline
Échelle de prix	29 995 $
Garanties	3 ans/60 000 km, 5 ans/100 000 km
Assemblage	n.d.
Cote d'assurance	n.d.

CHÂSSIS - DONNÉES POUR SX

Emp/lon/lar/haut	2 700/4 650/1 820/1 480 mm
Coffre	378 litres
Réservoir	63 litres
Nombre coussins sécurité	6
Antipatinage / contrôle stabilité	oui / oui
Suspension avant	indépendante, jambes de force
Suspension arrière	indépendante, multibras
Freins avant / arrière	disque (ABS) / disque (ABS)
Direction	à crémaillère, assistée
Diamètre de braquage	11,0 m
Pneus avant / arrière	235/45R18 / 235/45R18
Poids	1 620 kg
Capacité de remorquage	non recommandé

COMPOSANTES MÉCANIQUES

SX

Cylindrée, soupapes, alim.	4L 2,4 litres 16 s atmos.
Puissance / Couple	180 chevaux / 170 lb-pi
Tr. base (opt) / rouage base (opt)	CVT / Int
0-100 / 80-120 / 100-0 km/h	11,6 s / 8,8 s / 40,0 m
Type ess. / ville / autoroute	Ordinaire / 9,3 / 6,8 l/100 km

FEU VERT

Lignes agréables
Habitacle confortable
Rouage intégral décent
Conduite dynamique
Équipement complet

FEU ROUGE

Moteur et transmission dépassés
Valeur de revente sans doute triste
Peinture appliquée avec parcimonie
Réseau de concessionnaires limité

chose grandiose qui s'en vient tient très bien en courbes, même en mode traction, ses suspensions conventionnelles mais bien fignolées assurant à la fois confort et lien avec la route. En virage serré, on dénote un certain roulis, mais ce n'est pas dramatique, d'autant plus que la direction électrique étonne par sa précision. Lorsqu'on pousse la machine, il ne faut pas être surpris par l'action très bruyante du système de contrôle de la traction et de la stabilité latérale, qui heureusement pour des nordiques devant quelquefois se sortir d'un banc de neige, se désactive complètement. Les freins sont suffisamment puissants même si la pédale, lors d'un arrêt d'urgence, est trop molle à mon goût.

Les dirigeants de Suzuki ne s'attendent pas, avec la Kizashi, à révolutionner le marché de la berline intermédiaire. Bien leur en prenne, ils ne seront pas déçus...

Alain Morin

DANS LA MÊME CATÉGORIE

Ford Fusion, Honda Accord, Hyundai Sonata, Mazda6, Nissan Altima, Subaru Legacy, Toyota Camry

DU NOUVEAU EN 2011

Nouveau modèle

NOS IMPRESSIONS

Agrément de conduite :	8/10
Fiabilité :	Nouveau modèle
Sécurité :	n.d.
Qualités hivernales :	8/10
Espace intérieur :	8/10
Confort :	8/10

www.suzuki.ca

Plus d'informations dans la section statistiques en dernière partie du Guide

PHOTOS : ALAIN MORIN

DEUX MODÈLES, UN SEUL CHOIX

Décidément, la compagnie Suzuki peut être considérée comme le Gaston La Gaffe du monde de l'automobile ! Du moins en ce qui concerne notre continent. Année après année, cet important constructeur au niveau mondial nous sort des voitures dont la mise au point n'est pas tout à fait complète ou encore des modèles qui ne sont absolument pas compétitifs. Avec l'arrivée de la SX4, on croyait qu'on avait enfin touché la cible en plein centre.

Non seulement ce petit *hatchback* cinq portes avait une allure d'enfer, mais il était le seul de la catégorie à proposer un rouage intégral. En outre, son prix de vente fort compétitif venait compléter les éléments du succès. Mais c'était sans compter la présence de groupes propulseurs qui semblaient avoir été conçus pour faire mal paraître cette voiture.

VIVE LE *HATCHBACK*!

Il en est résulté des débuts assez médiocres pour cette voiture puisque toutes les personnes qui la conduisaient déploraient le manque de vigueur de son moteur et des transmissions mal adaptées. En fait, c'était surtout la boîte automatique à quatre rapports la principale coupable. Une balade au volant de la SX4 à boîte automatique suffisait pour remarquer un niveau sonore très élevé dans l'habitacle.

L'an dernier, chez Suzuki, on a pris les bonnes décisions en révisant le fonctionnement interne du moteur quatre cylindres 2,0 litres qui a gagné en puissance et en couple grâce à l'utilisation d'un système de calage variable des soupapes. Ce n'est que sept chevaux de plus, mais ils font tout de même sentir leur présence. Et la transmission automatique à quatre rapports a été remplacée par une boîte à rapports constamment variables qui n'est pas la meilleure sur le marché, mais dont le fonctionnement est correct.

Une fois le problème de la motorisation réglé, les acheteurs vont pouvoir s'intéresser aux nombreuses qualités que possède ce modèle, et ce, depuis son lancement. Il y a d'abord cette silhouette qui fait craquer les gens et c'est normal puisque ce véhicule a été développé en collaboration avec Fiat qui a demandé au légendaire styliste Gugiaro de dessiner la carrosserie. C'est élégant et dynamique, bref un succès sur toute la ligne à ce chapitre. Ensuite, il y a l'habitacle qui est passablement spacieux et la qualité d'assemblage est bonne. Quant au tableau de bord, il est dans la moyenne, les stylistes utilisant quelques pièces d'aluminium brossé afin de relever le tout. Il est également important de souligner la présence de commandes sur les rayons du volant, ce qui facilite certaines opérations.

Par ailleurs, sachez que les ingénieurs de Suzuki ont développé un rouage intégral fort sophistiqué pour cette catégorie, puisqu'il propose trois réglages. Il y a le mode traction avant ainsi que le mode intégral automatique. Comme tous les systèmes de ce genre, les

FEU VERT

- Silhouette réussie (*hatchback*)
- Rouage intégral ingénieux
- Prix compétitifs
- Consommation de carburant modeste
- Tenue de route correcte (*hatchback*)

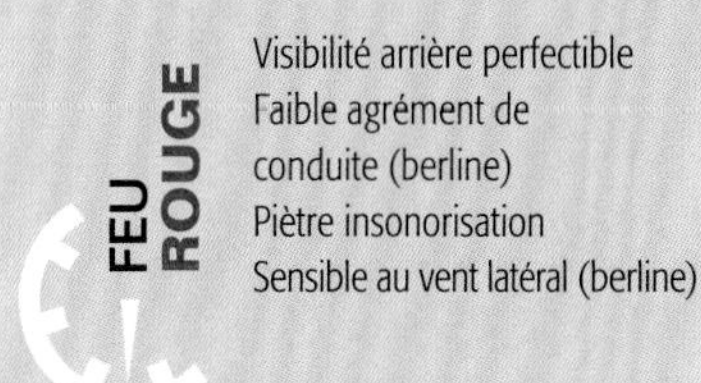

FEU ROUGE

- Visibilité arrière perfectible
- Faible agrément de conduite (berline)
- Piètre insonorisation
- Sensible au vent latéral (berline)

roues avant sont motrices jusqu'à ce qu'elles perdent de la motricité. Une partie de la puissance est alors automatiquement transférée aux roues arrière. Le troisième réglage permet de verrouiller de façon égale le couple aux roues avant et arrière. Cette seule caractéristique devrait inciter bien des gens à s'intéresser à cette Suzuki. Cependant, seule la version *hatchback* offre cette transmission intégrale.

Malgré une puissance accrue, les temps d'accélération sont assez modestes mais quand même satisfaisants. Quant à l'agrément de conduite, il est intéressant. Somme toute, la SX4 *hatchback* demeure l'un des meilleurs produits que Suzuki nous offre, du moins, pour le moment.

HARO SUR LA BERLINE !

Dans le cas de la berline, on serait porté à croire qu'il s'agit d'une variante du modèle cinq portes et qu'elle en possède la plupart des qualités. Ce n'est pas tout à fait le cas. Dans un premier temps, la silhouette est beaucoup moins inspirante que celle du *hatchback* et il semble que les éléments de sa finition intérieure soient de qualité inférieure. L'inconvénient de cette silhouette particulièrement haute, c'est que ça rend la voiture très sensible aux vents latéraux.

Dans un deuxième temps, même si elle bénéficie maintenant du même moteur que le *hatchback*, son agrément de conduite n'est pas amélioré pour autant à cause d'une insonorisation déficiente. Et si jamais vous avez le malheur d'aborder un virage un tantinet plus rapidement que la moyenne, vous découvrirez vite à quel point la plate-forme manque de rigidité.

De toutes les voitures que j'ai essayées au cours des 12 derniers mois, cette Suzuki a été celle que j'ai le plus détestée à conduire. Non seulement la position de conduite est des plus perfectibles, mais le guidage du levier de la boîte de vitesse manuelle était flou comme ce n'est pas possible. J'avais l'impression que le tout était retenu ensemble par de gros élastiques! Quant au moteur, il remplissait l'habitacle de son grondement déplaisant tout en livrant des prestations pour le moins déconcertantes... Rarement ai-je été aussi frustré en conduisant une voiture, et ce, peu importe son prix.

Vive la SX4 *Hatchback* !

Denis Duquet

PHOTOS : SUZUKI

SUZUKI SX4

Catégorie	Berline, *Hatchback*
Échelle de prix	17 695 $ à 24 695 $ (2010)
Garanties	3 ans/60 000 km, 5 ans/100 000 km
Assemblage	Magyar, Esztergom, Hongrie
Cote d'assurance	moyenne

CHÂSSIS - DONNÉES POUR JLX AWD HAYON

Emp/lon/lar/haut	2 500/4 135/1 755/1 605 mm
Coffre	203 à 1 218 litres
Réservoir	45 litres
Nombre coussins sécurité	6
Antipatinage / contrôle stabilité	oui / oui
Suspension avant	indépendante, jambes de force
Suspension arrière	indépendante, barres de torsion
Freins avant / arrière	disque (ABS) / disque (ABS)
Direction	à crémaillère, assistée
Diamètre de braquage	10,6 m
Pneus avant / arrière	P205/60R16 / P205/60R16
Poids	1 357 kg
Capacité de remorquage	n.d.

COMPOSANTES MÉCANIQUES

Base, Base Hayon, Sport, JX Hayon, JX AWD Hayon, Aero, JLX AWD Hayon

Cylindrée, soupapes, alim.	4L 2,0 litres 16 s atmos.
Puissance / Couple	150 chevaux / 140 lb-pi
Tr. base (opt) / rouage base (opt)	M6 (CVT) / Tr (Int)
0-100 / 80-120 / 100-0 km/h	9,3 s / 7,2 s / 41,9 m
Type ess. / ville / autoroute	Ordinaire / 8,9 / 6,9 l/100 km

DANS LA MÊME CATÉGORIE

Chevrolet Cruze, Dodge Caliber, Ford Focus, Honda Civic, Hyundai Elantra, Kia Forte, Mazda3, Mitsubishi Lancer, Nissan Sentra, Subaru Impreza, Toyota Corolla, Toyota Matrix

DU NOUVEAU EN 2011

Aucun changement majeur

NOS IMPRESSIONS

Agrément de conduite :	8/10
Fiabilité :	10/10
Sécurité :	8/10
Qualités hivernales :	8/10
Espace intérieur :	7/10
Confort :	7/10

www.suzuki.ca

Plus d'informations dans la section statistiques en dernière partie du Guide

L'AVENTURE SE POURSUIT ET LA ROADSTER CHANGE

Pour un constructeur qui a fabriqué à peine plus d'un millier de voitures, Tesla Motors occupe une part démesurée de l'espace médiatique sur cette planète. C'est ce qui arrive lorsqu'on devient le premier constructeur de véhicules électriques, surtout s'il s'agit d'un roadster qui peut abattre le sprint 0-100 km/h en quatre secondes. En plus de recevoir l'appui du premier constructeur mondial et de faire son entrée en bourse, Tesla s'est payé une usine, présente une version évoluée de son roadster et prépare le lancement de sa berline S.

Tesla a fièrement présenté au dernier Salon de Détroit. son millième roadster fabriqué. C'est un chiffre infime pour un grand constructeur, mais imaginez la courbe de progression en songeant qu'à peine une année plus tôt Tesla n'avait fabriqué que 150 unités. Or cette jeune entreprise, qui n'a amorcé le développement de sa première voiture qu'en 2004, a déjà livré de ses modèles dans 19 pays, y compris une poignée au Canada et au moins un au Québec. Tesla a déjà dix magasins en Amérique du Nord, dont un à Toronto.

Chose certaine, l'histoire de Tesla est déjà truffée de rebondissements, de coups d'éclat, de contretemps et d'incertitudes. Tel est le lot des grands innovateurs. À bien des égards, l'histoire de Tesla ressemble beaucoup aux sagas des grands pionniers de l'automobile il y a plus d'un siècle. Pour un Henry Ford, un Gottlieb Daimler ou un Soichiro Honda, combien de Preston Tucker et de John DeLorean qui auront sacrifié fortune, santé et quoi encore à ce Klondike sur roues ?

LES HAUTS ET LES BAS DE LA DIVA

Lorsque l'histoire de Tesla Motors sera écrite, on y lira que l'année 2010 aura été celle où Toyota lui aura promis un appui concret et où la compagnie aura enfin fait son entrée à la Bourse de New York. On y découvrira aussi les tribulations d'Elon Musk son PDG, créateur de PayPal, qui aurait déjà englouti plus de 70 millions de dollars de sa poche dans l'entreprise.

Les 226 millions de dollars US recueillis par cette première vente d'actions s'ajoutent au prêt de 465 millions de dollars US consenti par le département des Transports du gouvernement américain. Ces fonds doivent avant tout servir à financer le développement du modèle S, une très jolie berline à propulsion électrique que Tesla compte produire et mettre en vente dès 2012, à un prix d'environ 50 000$ US en comptant la généreuse ristourne de 7 500$ US qui sera consentie par Oncle Sam pour l'achat d'une voiture électrique.

Tesla ferait également l'acquisition de l'usine NUMMI de Fremont en Californie, où GM et Toyota ont longtemps été partenaires, dans laquelle elle fabriquerait la berline S en collaboration avec cette dernière. En attendant de lancer sa berline, Tesla Motors poursuit l'expansion de son réseau et accélère la distribution de son premier modèle, dont la production s'effectue toujours à

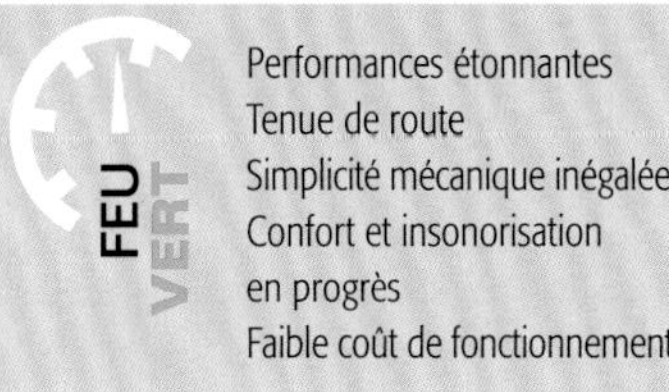

- Performances étonnantes
- Tenue de route
- Simplicité mécanique inégalée
- Confort et insonorisation en progrès
- Faible coût de fonctionnement

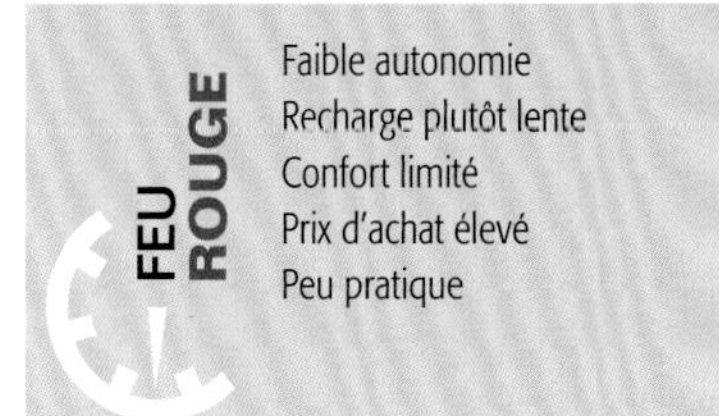

- Faible autonomie
- Recharge plutôt lente
- Confort limité
- Prix d'achat élevé
- Peu pratique

l'usine Lotus de Hethel, en Angleterre. Les coques des voitures destinées au marché nord-américain sont ensuite acheminées à Palo Alto en Californie, au cœur de Silicon Valley, où le groupe propulseur est installé sous la carrosserie entièrement en fibre de carbone.

LA ROADSTER MISE À NIVEAU

Dans le pur style des firmes d'informatique qui entourent son siège social, Tesla Motors a lancé une version rafraîchie de sa Roadster, qu'elle a désignée 2.5 et qui succède à la 2.0 lancée l'an dernier. Les changements les plus visibles ont été apportés à la silhouette, sous la direction du styliste en chef Franz von Holzhausen. Venu de chez Mazda, ce dernier a dessiné les Solstice et Sky alors qu'il était chez GM. Il a l'œil pour les roadsters et avait retouché avec goût la silhouette de la Tesla Roadster Sport à son arrivée. La nouvelle Roadster 2.5 est dans le même moule, avec une calandre et un diffuseur arrière inédits.

La finition de l'habitacle a été soignée tout comme l'insonorisation. Les sièges sont plus sculptés et dotés de nouveaux supports lombaires réglables. La 2.5 peut désormais être équipée d'un système de navigation Alpine avec écran tactile de 7 pouces qui affiche également les images de la caméra de marche arrière. Un écran plus petit, placé vers l'avant de la console centrale, est réservé à l'affichage de données. La jante gainée de cuir du volant sport Momo est impeccablement moulée, mais ce serait bien d'y retrouver les contrôles pour la sono et le régulateur de vitesse auxquels nous ont habitués une majorité de constructeurs.

Peu de changements côté technique, par ailleurs, si ce n'est que les ingénieurs ont modifié le module de contrôle du moteur de propulsion électrique pour améliorer les performances par temps exceptionnellement chaud. À l'autre extrême, les voitures vendues au Canada sont toujours dotées d'un chauffe-batterie qui permet les recharges jusqu'à une température de -20 Celsius.

La Tesla Roadster poursuit donc sa route et joue le rôle de pionnière et d'ouvreuse de piste pour la future berline S. Il se prépare certainement un duel intéressant entre cette dernière et la Nissan Leaf, sans compter la Chevrolet Volt et les variations que prépare Toyota sur les thèmes du rouage hybride et de la propulsion électrique. Une nouvelle ruée vers l'or s'amorce et Tesla est en première ligne.

Marc Lachapelle

PHOTOS : TESLA

Catégorie	*Roadster* / Berline
Échelle de prix	129 000 $ (2010)
Garanties	n.d.
Assemblage	n.d.
Cote d'assurance	n.d.

CHÂSSIS - DONNÉES POUR *ROADSTER*

Emp/lon/lar/haut	2 337/3 937/1 829/1 117 mm
Coffre	n.d.
Réservoir	aucun
Nombre coussins sécurité	2
Antipatinage / contrôle stabilité	oui / non
Suspension avant	indépendante, bras inégaux
Suspension arrière	indépendante, bras inégaux
Freins avant / arrière	disque (ABS) / disque (ABS)
Direction	n.d.
Diamètre de braquage	n.d.
Pneus avant / arrière	P175/55R16 / P225/45R17
Poids	1 235 kg
Capacité de remorquage	n.d.

COMPOSANTES MÉCANIQUES

Roadster

Moteur électrique	375 volt (288 ch, 273 lb-pi)
Batterie	Lithium-ion
0-100 / 80-120 / 100-0 km/h	4,0 s (est) / n.d. / n.d.
Autonomie approximative	395 km

Roadster Sport

Moteur électrique	375 volt (288 ch, 295 lb-pi)
Batterie	Lithium-ion
0-100 / 80-120 / 100-0 km/h	3,9 s (est) / n.d. / n.d.
Autonomie approximative	350 km (est)

DANS LA MÊME CATÉGORIE

Aucune concurrence

DU NOUVEAU EN 2011

Aucun changement majeur

NOS IMPRESSIONS

Agrément de conduite :	■■■■■■■■□□ 8/10
Fiabilité :	Données insuffisantes
Sécurité :	n.d.
Qualités hivernales :	Données insuffisantes
Espace intérieur :	■■■■■■■■■□ 9/10
Confort :	■■■■■■■■□□ 8/10

www.teslamotors.com

Plus d'informations dans la section statistiques en dernière partie du Guide

DANS UNE CLASSE À PART

Ce n'est plus un secret pour personne. Les gros 4x4 purs et durs n'ont plus la cote depuis que les gens ont découvert que les multisegments sont beaucoup plus confortables et consomment moins. Ils s'avèrent certes moins à l'aise dans la boue profonde mais, entre nous, qui fait réellement du hors route sérieusement? Et qui a besoin de remorquer sa maison, ce que réussissaient parfaitement les VUS? Eh bien, il en reste! En effet, certaines personnes ont des besoins spécifiques, et des véhicules comme le 4Runner sont là pour y répondre.

D'ailleurs, on ne peut pas dire que Toyota laisse tomber ces gens puisqu'elle leur offre, en plus du 4Runner et des camionnettes Tacoma et Tundra, le FJ Cruiser et le Sequoia, sans oublier les Lexus GX460 et LX570. Si vous n'y trouvez pas votre compte, c'est que vous êtes difficile! Même si les ventes dans ce créneau ne sont plus ce qu'elles étaient, Toyota a entièrement revu son 4Runner, le faisant ainsi entrer dans sa cinquième génération, la première ayant débuté en 1985. Tout en conservant ses qualités hors route initiales, les ingénieurs devaient améliorer son confort. Ont-ils réussi?

Tout d'abord, mentionnons que lors du lancement du 4Runner, les avis sur sa nouvelle carrosserie étaient très partagés. Presque un an plus tard, certains s'y sont faits, d'autres non. Cependant, on ne peut pas dire que ses angles carrés, ses imposants renflements ici et là et ses dimensions tout aussi imposantes en font un camion efféminé. L'habitacle aussi fait très «truck», autant au niveau des plastiques assez sommaires que des gros boutons qui seront, l'hiver venu, faciles à manipuler avec des gants. En fait,

pas seulement les boutons sont surdimensionnés. Les jauges, les branches du volant, la console et les sièges, confortables, le sont aussi. Ce n'est pas l'espace qui manque et la large console est là pour nous le rappeler. La visibilité tout le tour n'est pas vilaine compte tenu du gabarit pour le moins magistral.

PARTY TIME!

Le Toyota 4Runner se décline en trois versions: SR5, Édition Trail et Limited. Cette dernière variante offre une troisième rangée de sièges difficile d'accès et au confort très relatif. La principale qualité de cette banquette est de se rabattre dans le plancher pour former un grand coffre. Fait à noter, la version Trail, qui ne reçoit pas la troisième banquette, a droit à un plateau de chargement coulissant qui peut supporter jusqu'à 200 kilos (440 livres). Toutes les variantes viennent d'office avec huit coussins gonflables et le mode Party, lequel ne permet pas au conducteur de conduire avec une bière entre les jambes... Il s'agit plutôt de haut-parleurs placés dans le hayon qui, une fois relevé, fait office de petite discothèque. La vitre du hayon s'ouvre séparément, grâce à un bouton placé sur la console centrale. Bravo!

FEU VERT
- Style macho
- Habitacle confortable
- Rouage 4x4 sérieux
- Consommation correcte
- Bon rapport qualité/prix

FEU ROUGE
- V6 un peu juste (si remorquage)
- Capacités de remorquage peu élevées
- Troisième rangée peu confortable
- Sensible aux vents latéraux

EXIT LE V8, VIVE LE V6

Comme le veut la tendance, le moteur du nouveau 4Runner est plus petit que celui qu'il remplace tout en étant plus puissant et plus économique. Donc, exit le V8, bienvenue au V6 de 4,0 litres de 270 chevaux. Cette puissance semble élevée mais, en regard du poids du véhicule (bien au-delà de 2000 kilos), on se rend rapidement compte que tous ces chevaux ne sont pas de trop lorsque le véhicule aura à travailler fort. Ce qui explique sans doute la capacité de remorquage de 5000 livres, plus limitée que celle de ses concurrents. La transmission est une automatique à cinq rapports au fonctionnement sans histoire. Toyota parle de 12,6 litres/100 km en ville, ce qui nous semble un tantinet optimiste. Mais soyons francs, sa consommation est loin d'être aussi excessive qu'auparavant.

Le 4Runner, bâti sur un châssis autonome, peut passer à peu près n'importe où. Toutes les versions ont droit à un rouage 4x4 sérieux, mais c'est surtout lorsqu'on lui adjoint le Sélecteur Multi-Terrain optionnel qu'il tombe dans les ligues majeures. Ce système est calqué sur celui déjà offert depuis quelques années chez Land Rover ou sur le nouveau Jeep Grand Cherokee. Il permet de choisir le type de terrain sur lequel on roule, optimisant ainsi le fonctionnement du système de stabilité latérale, des freins ABS, de la gestion du moteur et de la transmission. L'angle d'attaque est de 33 degrés tandis que celle de départ est de 34 degrés. L'angle ventral est de 24 degrés, des données avantageuses par rapport à celles du Grand Cherokee. La version Trail reçoit des plaques de protection sous le moteur, le boîtier de transfert et le réservoir d'essence.

Sur une route bosselée, le confort est passablement relevé malgré la présence d'un essieu arrière rigide. Je dirais même que les suspensions sont assez molles. Le Limited reçoit une suspension sport nommée X-REAS. Remarquez que le mot sport provient du site de Toyota. Nous n'aurions jamais eu assez d'imagination pour ça... Par contre, malgré le centre de gravité élevé, le 4Runner se comporte décemment. La direction retourne bien peu d'impressions et sa précision est loin d'être parfaite. Le Toyota 4Runner, ainsi que les Jeep Grand Cherokee, Nissan Pathfinder et Ford Explorer, s'adresse à un public averti qui a des besoins particuliers. Il faut croire que ce marché est encore suffisamment lucratif puisque trois de ces quatre véhicules sont tout nouveaux en 2011.

Alain Morin

PHOTOS: TOYOTA

Catégorie	VUS
Échelle de prix	36 800 $ à 49 420 $ (2010)
Garanties	3 ans/60 000 km, 5 ans/100 000 km
Assemblage	Toyota City, Japon
Cote d'assurance	passable

CHÂSSIS - DONNÉES POUR SR5 LIMITED V6

Emp/lon/lar/haut	2 790/4 820/1 925/1 780 mm
Coffre	1 300 à 2 500 litres
Réservoir	80 litres
Nombre coussins sécurité	6
Antipatinage / contrôle stabilité	oui / oui
Suspension avant	indépendante, double triangulation
Suspension arrière	essieu rigide, multibras
Freins avant / arrière	disque (ABS) / disque (ABS)
Direction	à crémaillère, ass. variable
Diamètre de braquage	11,7 m
Pneus avant / arrière	P265/70R17 / P265/70R17
Poids	2 111 kg
Capacité de remorquage	2 268 kg (5 000 lb)

COMPOSANTES MÉCANIQUES

4Runner

Cylindrée, soupapes, alim.	V6 4,0 litres 24 s atmos.
Puissance / Couple	270 chevaux / 278 lb-pi
Tr. base (opt) / rouage base (opt)	A5 / 4x4
0-100 / 80-120 / 100-0 km/h	9,1 s / 6,8 s / 42,0 m (est)
Type ess. / ville / autoroute	Ordinaire / 12,6 / 9,2 l/100 km

DANS LA MÊME CATÉGORIE

Ford Explorer, Jeep Commander, Jeep Grand Cherokee, Nissan Pathfinder

DU NOUVEAU EN 2011

Nouveau modèle

NOS IMPRESSIONS

Agrément de conduite :	7/10
Fiabilité :	10/10
Sécurité :	8/10
Qualités hivernales :	9/10
Espace intérieur :	9/10
Confort :	8/10

www.toyota.ca

Plus d'informations dans la section statistiques en dernière partie du Guide

NOUVELLE ALLURE, PRIX COMPÉTITIF

L'ancienne Toyota Avalon n'avait pas bonne presse auprès des chroniqueurs spécialisés, car elle était considérée comme une voiture soporifique destinée aux papys de la route. Et il semble que ceux-ci ne trouvaient pas ce modèle intéressant non plus, car Toyota Canada en a vendu moins de 300 unités en 2009. Il était devenu évident pour la direction de la compagnie, tant aux États-Unis qu'au Canada, qu'une cure de jeunesse était obligatoire.

DESIGN CALIFORNIEN

La Californie, ce n'est pas exclusivement des surfeurs et des acteurs de cinéma. C'est aussi la Mecque des studios de design des grands constructeurs automobiles et Toyota ne fait pas exception. On a donc demandé aux stylistes du centre Calty Design Research de Newport Beach en Californie de donner un peu plus de punch à la carrosserie de cette grosse Toyota. Pour ce faire, ils ont dessiné une grille de calandre plus imposante et surtout plus visible grâce à l'utilisation du chrome. Ils ont également placé une barre longitudinale chromée sur le bas de la caisse afin d'augmenter le relief lorsque le véhicule est vu de côté. Autre changement majeur, les phares antibrouillard sont maintenant intégrés au pare-chocs avant tandis que les feux de route à multiréflecteurs comprennent des tubes qui créent une apparence distinctive la nuit. Les feux arrière ont été redessinés et comportent les feux d'arrêt, les clignotants et les feux de position latéraux.

TOUJOURS SPACIEUSE, PLUS LUXUEUSE

La première génération de l'Avalon se voulait une concurrente directe des grosses berlines nord-américaines comme la Mercury Grand Marquis. Pareillement à celle-ci, elle proposait une banquette pleine largeur à l'avant afin d'accommoder trois occupants et les places arrière étaient généreuses. La vocation de la plus grosse Toyota a changé, mais l'habitabilité est toujours la même.

Le tableau de bord générique a été remplacé du tout au tout et l'élément principal est le centre d'information central comprenant un écran de sept pouces à affichage par diodes électroluminescentes. Le système de navigation par satellite et la caméra de recul font un bon usage de cet écran tactile. Les cadrans indicateurs de type Optitron emploient un éclairage gradué et des aiguilles blanches.

Mais le plus important est le niveau d'équipement de série. La direction de Toyota Canada a décidé de n'offrir qu'un seul et unique modèle proposant une multitude d'accessoires afin de convaincre les acheteurs qu'une Toyota Avalon, c'est une véritable aubaine ! Toutes les Avalon possèdent donc un équipement « tout compris » et la seule option est une peinture spéciale qui nécessite un déboursé additionnel. Même la sellerie de cuir est de série ! D'ailleurs, chez Toyota, personne ne contestera que cette voiture doit séduire grâce à son confort et son luxe.

FEU VERT
- Finition impeccable
- Silhouette améliorée
- Habitabilité assurée
- Moteur bien adapté
- Tenue de route correcte

FEU ROUGE
- Agrément de conduite mitigé
- Direction trop assistée
- Roulis en virage
- Pneumatiques moyens
- Coffre à gants mal placé

Dans le cadre de cette refonte, les ingénieurs ont refusé de jouer la carte du moteur V8. On a conservé le même groupe propulseur, soit un moteur V6 de 3,5 litres à 24 soupapes et à double arbre à cames en tête qui produit 268 chevaux à 6200 tr/min. Ce moteur est équipé du mécanisme électronique VVT-i double gestion des soupapes qui élargit la bande de puissance. Ce V6 est couplé à une transmission automatique six rapports multimode. Selon le constructeur, sa consommation estimée est de 10,7 L/100 km en ville, de 7,0 L/100 km sur la route et de 9,0 L/100 km combinée.

Au volant de l'Avalon, il ne faut pas s'attendre à retrouver l'impressionnante tenue de route d'une européenne de luxe qui privilégie la tenue de route et les performances. Disons que celui de l'Avalon est honnête à des vitesses légales alors que la suspension n'est pas excessivement molle et absorbe assez bien les imperfections de la route. Par contre, il n'y a aucun tangage, une caractéristique jadis associée aux grosses américaines. Le roulis en virage est assez bien contrôlé tandis que le la direction pourrait être plus précise et moins assistée, mais c'est quand même correct. À la condition que vos exigences ne soient pas trop élevées. Bref, on a réussi à marier confort et tenue de route honnête. Ce n'est certes pas une sportive, mais ce n'est pas non plus un cocon monté sur des guimauves. En fait, il serait intéressant d'installer des pneus plus sportifs et des amortisseurs plus fermes. La voiture serait certainement plus intéressante à conduire. Le groupe propulseur est demeuré inchangé, mais les performances et le rendement du moteur sont adéquats en raison du caractère de cette voiture.

La nouvelle Avalon ne casse rien, mais sa silhouette a été améliorée tandis que l'habitacle est mieux réussi qu'auparavant. Il faut également souligner que la réputation négative de la version antérieure est surfaite car il s'agissait d'une Camry plus spacieuse, plus luxueuse et dotée d'une suspension un tantinet plus souple. Cette refonte permet de mettre plus d'emphase sur un modèle qui mérite un meilleur sort sur notre marché. Même si ce n'est pas la nouvelle clientèle visée par le constructeur, une Avalon, c'est la voiture idéale pour un retraité qui se dirige en Floride pour y passer l'hiver. Mais ce n'est pas sa seule vocation.

Denis Duquet

PHOTOS : DENIS DUQUET

Catégorie	Berline
Échelle de prix	41 100$ (modèle unique)
Garanties	3 ans/60 000 km, 5 ans/100 000 km
Assemblage	Georgetown, Kentucky, É U
Cote d'assurance	moyenne

TOYOTA AVALON

CHÂSSIS - DONNÉES POUR XLS

Emp/lon/lar/haut	2 820/5 020/1 850/1 470 mm
Coffre	408 litres
Réservoir	70 litres
Nombre coussins sécurité	7
Antipatinage / contrôle stabilité	oui / oui
Suspension avant	indépendante, jambes de force
Suspension arrière	indépendante, jambes de force
Freins avant / arrière	freins (ABS) / freins (ABS)
Direction	à crémaillère, ass. variable
Diamètre de braquage	11,5 m
Pneus avant / arrière	P215/55R17 / P215/55R17
Poids	1 618 kg
Capacité de remorquage	454 kg (1 000 lb)

COMPOSANTES MÉCANIQUES

XLS

Cylindrée, soupapes, alim.	V6 3,5 litres 24 s atmos.
Puissance / Couple	268 chevaux / 248 lb-pi
Tr. base (opt) / rouage base (opt)	A6 / Tr
0-100 / 80-120 / 100-0 km/h	7,4 s / 5,3 s / 40,0 m
Type ess. / ville / autoroute	Ordinaire / 10,7 / 7,0 l/100 km

DANS LA MÊME CATÉGORIE

Buick Lucerne, Chevrolet Impala, Chrysler 300, Ford Taurus, Hyundai Genesis, Lexus ES, Lincoln MKZ, Nissan Maxima

DU NOUVEAU EN 2011

Esthétisme revu

NOS IMPRESSIONS

Agrément de conduite :	6/10
Fiabilité :	8/10
Sécurité :	10/10
Qualités hivernales :	7/10
Espace intérieur :	9/10
Confort :	9/10

www.toyota.ca

Plus d'informations dans la section statistiques en dernière partie du Guide

SI TRANQUILLE ET SI DÉNONCÉE

La très populaire Camry a beaucoup fait parler d'elle ces derniers mois... et pas toujours pour les bonnes raisons, ses problèmes d'accélérateurs coincés défrayant les manchettes autant qu'une série Canadiens-Flyers. Toyota a reconnu son erreur (du bout des lèvres, mais elle l'a reconnue quand même) et a corrigé le problème. Quiconque a eu l'air fou au moins une fois dans sa vie sait qu'on peut parfois se rattraper avec beaucoup de volonté...

Outre les pépins ci-haut mentionnés, il faut avouer que la compétition s'est passablement raffinée. Depuis sa refonte en 2007, la Camry fait face à une Honda Accord plus imposante, à une Hyundai Sonata fort réussie, à une Ford Fusion pas piquée des vers et à une Buick Regal toute neuve. Pis, sa qualité de fabrication a quelque peu perdu de son lustre depuis quelques années. Malgré tout, la Camry demeure une valeur sûre.

Depuis cinq ans dans sa robe actuelle, cette voiture n'a pratiquement pas connu de changements esthétiques et c'est tant mieux. Sans être un parangon de stylisme, la Camry propose des lignes dynamiques et équilibrées. On peut en dire autant de l'habitacle, vaste et accueillant. Le tableau de bord non plus ne redéfinit pas les règles de l'art, mais comme les boutons tombent bien sous la main, sont simples à utiliser et suffisamment gros pour être facilement manipulés avec des gants, on ne peut lui en vouloir. Fait à noter, on retrouve de bons espaces de rangement, ce qu'apprécient les traîneux de tout acabit. Les jauges sont facilement lisibles et la qualité des matériaux, si elle n'est plus celle des beaux jours, est encore respectable. La finition de l'ensemble se mérite toujours de belles notes. Les sièges avant s'avèrent confortables, l'espace ne manque pas et le conducteur trouve rapidement une bonne position de conduite.

Les gens prenant place à l'arrière ne seront pas en reste avec des sièges douillets. Cette remarque ne s'applique toutefois pas à la place centrale. L'espace pour les jambes est très correct, mais les plus grands risquent de porter la tonsure après un long voyage... Certaines versions de la Camry proposent un dossier de banquette arrière se rabattant de façon 60/40 ou, mieux pour les plus huppées, 40/20/40. Cependant, certaines autres versions ne proposent pas d'accès au coffre. De l'économie de bout de chandelle qui n'a d'autre effet que de faire suer le propriétaire d'une telle Camry, qui 2x4 en mains un samedi matin de rénovations, se dit qu'il aurait mieux fait d'acheter une vulgaire Corolla. En plus, l'ouverture du coffre n'est pas très grande (une plaie qui affecte de plus en plus de véhicules) et son seuil pourrait être plus bas.

Côté motorisation, Toyota fait appel à un très intéressant quatre cylindres qui est passé à 2,5 litres l'an dernier. Sobre et suffisamment puissant, il devrait satisfaire la plupart des gens, surtout qu'il est associé avec une transmission automatique à six rapports.

FEU VERT

- Style assez plaisant
- Habitacle aussi confortable que vaste
- Consommation réduite
- Fiabilité toujours imposante
- Niveau de sécurité élevé

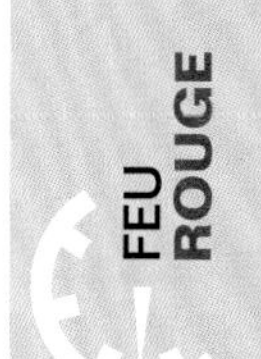

FEU ROUGE

- Nom Toyota moins renommé qu'avant
- Prix assez corsés
- Direction vague
- Coffre réduit (Hybrid)
- Certaines fautes d'équipement

L'autre moteur est un V6 de 3,5 litres utilisé à toutes les sauces chez Toyota. Il est souple, puissant et même s'il consomme plus que le quatre cylindres, certaines personnes préféreront ses performances. Ce moteur aussi reçoit l'aide de l'excellente transmission à six rapports pour passer le couple aux roues avant de manière très transparente. Par contre, avec le V6, on dénote un certain effet de couple.

Peu importe le moteur, la Camry ne doit en aucun cas être considérée comme une sportive. Son châssis a beau être très solide et ses suspensions assurer une tenue de route correcte, la Camry privilégie le confort. Poussée le moindrement, on dénote un peu de roulis et un léger sous-virage, mais conduite dans les règles de l'art, on ne peut pas lui reprocher grand-chose. Cependant, là où cette populaire Toyota perd des points et gagne une réputation de voiture pépère, c'est au niveau de la direction, engourdie et n'offrant à peu près aucun retour d'informations. Mais c'est exactement ce que recherche une certaine clientèle qui privilégie le confort et le silence de roulement.

ET LA CAMRY HYBRID, ELLE?

Dans un désir de toujours en faire plus pour l'environnement, Toyota propose une Camry Hybrid (sans doute pour compenser pour les énergivores Tundra, Sequoia et autres Lexus LX570...). Cette Camry verte se distingue des autres modèles par une calandre distinctive et, ma foi, fort jolie. Elle fait appel à un moteur de 2,4 litres auquel on a greffé un moteur électrique de 105 kilowatts. L'ensemble donne un total de 187 chevaux et 138 ivres-pied de couple. Le moteur électrique est nourri par une batterie nickel-hydrure de métal de 244 volts.

Mais rien n'étant parfait sur notre belle Terre, le prix demandé est assez élevé, compte tenu de sa dépréciation sans doute plus rapide et de coûts d'entretien plus élevés. De plus, le coffre voit ses dimensions amputées à cause de la batterie. Notre gars avec son 2x4 doit se gratter la tête ! D'un autre côté, je préférerais, et de loin, une Camry Hybrid à une Prius certes plus économique et un peu moins chère à l'achat, mais ô combien moins agréable à conduire...

La Camry se fait sérieusement chauffer les fesses par la concurrence tout en n'aidant pas sa cause. Elle demeure cependant parmi les meilleures de sa catégorie, qui surtout, sait rejoindre un large public.

Alain Morin

PHOTOS : TOYOTA

Catégorie	Berline
Échelle de prix	25 310 $ à 36 410 $
Garanties	3 ans / 60 000 km, 5 ans / 100 000 km
Assemblage	Georgetown, Kentucky, É-U
Cote d'assurance	passable

CHÂSSIS - DONNÉES POUR SE V6

Emp/lon/lar/haut	2 775/4 805/1 820/1 470 mm
Coffre	425 litres
Réservoir	70 litres
Nombre coussins sécurité	7
Antipatinage / contrôle stabilité	oui / oui
Suspension avant	indépendante, jambes de force
Suspension arrière	indépendante, jambes de force
Freins avant / arrière	disque (ABS) / disque (ABS)
Direction	à crémaillère, assistée
Diamètre de braquage	11,0 m
Pneus avant / arrière	P215/60R16 / P215/60R16
Poids	1 500 kg
Capacité de remorquage	454 kg (1 000 lb)

COMPOSANTES MÉCANIQUES

Hybride

Cylindrée, soupapes, alim.	4L 2,4 litres 16 s atmos.
Puissance totale / couple total	187 ch / 138 lb-pi
Tr. base (opt) / rouage base (opt)	CVT / Tr
0-100 / 80-120 / 100-0 km/h	8,6 s / 7,9 s / 42,1 m
Type ess. / ville / autoroute	Ordinaire / 5,7 / 5,7 l/100 km

LE, XLE

Cylindrée, soupapes, alim.	4L 2,5 litres 16 s atmos.
Puissance / Couple	169 chevaux / 167 lb-pi
Tr. base (opt) / rouage base (opt)	A6 / Tr
0-100 / 80-120 / 100-0 km/h	9,1 s / 7,8 s / 42,7 m
Type ess. / ville / autoroute	Ordinaire / 9,0 / 6,1 l/100 km

SE

4L 2,5 l, 179 ch, 171 lb-pi - 0-100: n.d. - 9,5 / 6,1 l/100 km

LE V6, SE V6, XLE V6

V6 3,5 l, 268 ch, 248 lb-pi - 0-100: 7,4 s - 10,7 / 7,0 l/100 km

DANS LA MÊME CATÉGORIE

Buick Allure, Chevrolet Malibu, Chrysler Sebring, Dodge Avenger, Ford Fusion, Hyundai Sonata, Mazda6, Nissan Altima, Subaru Legacy

DU NOUVEAU EN 2011

Aucun changement majeur

NOS IMPRESSIONS

Agrément de conduite :	7/10
Fiabilité :	6/10
Sécurité :	8/10
Qualités hivernales :	8/10
Espace intérieur :	8/10
Confort :	8/10

www.toyota.ca

Plus d'informations dans la section statistiques en dernière partie du Guide

PRESQUE PARFAITE, MAIS ENNUYANTE !

La compagnie Toyota n'aurait pas connu le succès qu'elle a obtenu au cours des dernières décennies, sans la grande popularité de sa berline compacte Corolla et ce, sur la plupart des marchés de la planète. Cette petite voiture, qui s'est modernisée récemment, offre un bon compromis entre une qualité d'assemblage supérieure à la moyenne, une consommation de carburant passablement réduite et une fiabilité à long terme rassurante.

Ces chiffres de vente positifs ont été obtenus malgré le fait que cette voiture traîne avec elle la réputation d'être plutôt ennuyante à conduire. Pour trancher le débat une fois pour toutes entre les journalistes qui prétendent que c'est une voiture agréable à piloter et ceux qui la vilipendent, nous allons utiliser le verdict du très respecté *Consumer Reports*, qui lui la qualifie d'assez fade au chapitre de la conduite. Étant donnée que la réputation de cette publication est plutôt d'ignorer l'agrément de conduite au dépend de la qualité de fabrication et de la fiabilité, c'est tout dire.

FABRICATION CANADIENNE

Curieusement, en dépit des différences politiques et culturelles entre les citoyens du Québec et ceux des autres provinces, une voiture portant l'étiquette « Made in Canada » obtient un bon succès auprès des Québécois. Cette tendance remonte à l'ancienne Volvo « Canadienne » qui pouvait en séduire certains, de par ses origines.

Quoi qu'il en soit, ce penchant pour la feuille d'érable n'est pas une mauvaise chose non plus, car cette Toyota compacte, produite en Ontario, est une voiture d'une belle qualité d'assemblage. Par contre, la qualité de la peinture sur certains modèles examinés n'était pas tellement impressionnante, alors que les plastiques utilisés dans l'habitacle pourraient être certainement moins durs et de meilleure facture. Malgré ces quelques bémols, l'habitacle est confortable, les sièges offrent un support adéquat et la planche de bord est toute aussi sobre qu'elle est pratique. Pour aller de pair avec la silhouette de cette voiture, qui s'est modernisée lors de sa dernière refonte il y a maintenant plus de deux ans, on aurait pu faire un effort pour donner un peu plus de mordant à la planche de bord et au volant. Ce dernier semble avoir été emprunté à une voiture destinée au tiers monde. Quant aux commandes générales, elles sont faciles à trouver et à opérer. Comme c'est maintenant la norme, la climatisation est l'affaire de trois gros boutons. Le premier s'occupe du niveau de la température, le second de la soufflerie pendant que le troisième gère la circulation de l'air. Toujours au chapitre de l'ergonomie, la boîte de vitesses automatique est gérée par un levier qui doit serpenter le long d'une ouverture afin de pouvoir passer d'un rapport de vitesse à l'autre. On a voulu s'inspirer de chez Mercedes, mais force est d'admettre que les Allemands ont beaucoup mieux réussi leur coup.

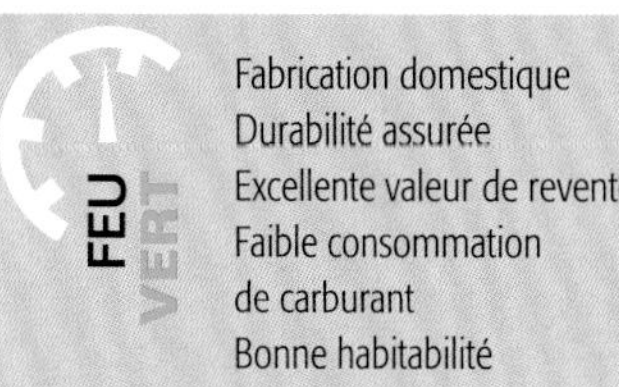

- Fabrication domestique
- Durabilité assurée
- Excellente valeur de revente
- Faible consommation de carburant
- Bonne habitabilité

- Boîte automatique à quatre rapports (1,8 l)
- Suspension arrière moyenne
- Insonorisation perfectible
- Plastiques durs dans l'habitacle

BUZZ, BUZZ

Sur le plan de la mécanique, on a voulu jouer une fois de plus la carte de la fiabilité et de la durabilité. Le moteur choisi pour les modèles les plus populaires de la Corolla est donc l'infatigable quatre cylindres de 1,8 litre, associé à une boîte manuelle à cinq rapports. Ce moteur se démarque surtout par sa faible consommation de carburant. Il s'attire cependant des commentaires négatifs en raison de son bourdonnement constant, car il doit travailler très fort pour propulser cette voiture. Celles et ceux qui n'aiment pas jouer du levier de vitesses vont trouver le temps long. D'autant plus que les deux rapports supérieurs sont démultipliés et qu'il faut souvent rétrograder en troisième vitesse si l'on veut doubler de façon sécuritaire. Pourtant, avec ses 132 chevaux, on s'attendrait à plus de nervosité. Heureusement, une boîte automatique est disponible. Il s'agit pourtant d'une transmission à quatre rapports, ce qui ne fait malheureusement rien pour atténuer le niveau sonore dans l'habitacle, puisque l'insonorisation est plus que perfectible. C'est d'autant plus agaçant que le moteur ne cesse de gronder. Toutefois, même s'il semble toujours travailler fort, la longévité de ce quatre cylindres a été démontrée à maintes reprises. Le seul ennui que cette Corolla a connu lors des désormais célèbres rappels de Toyota, est cette pédale d'accélérateur qui refusait de collaborer.

Si vous désirez plus de puissance et un moteur un peu plus performant, Toyota vous propose un autre quatre cylindres, soit le 2,4 litres. Celui-ci produit 158 chevaux et il est associé une fois de plus à une boîte manuelle à cinq rapports. Par contre, la transmission automatique possède une vitesse de plus. Ce qui est surprenant, c'est que malgré un avantage de 26 équidés, ses performances sont assez moyennes. De plus, ce moteur aime les régimes élevés et sa conduite en milieu urbain n'est pas nécessairement une expérience agréable.

Sur la route, cette petite berline propose un comportement routier honnête, lequel serait fortement amélioré par la présence de pneumatiques de meilleure qualité. Ceux-ci sont durables, doivent certainement favoriser l'économie de carburant, mais sont également plutôt durs par temps froid et leur comportement sur pavé mouillé n'est pas des plus éblouissants. Quant à la suspension, elle est moyennement confortable, puisque son essieu arrière à poutre rigide a parfois de la difficulté à dompter les soubresauts causés par le mauvais revêtement de la chaussée.

Denis Duquet

PHOTOS : TOYOTA

TOYOTA COROLLA

Catégorie	Berline
Échelle de prix	15 460 $ à 22 550 $ (2010)
Garanties	3 ans/60 000 km, 5 ans/100 000 km
Assemblage	Cambridge, Ontario, Canada
Cote d'assurance	passable

CHÂSSIS - DONNÉES POUR LE

Emp/lon/lar/haut	2 600/4 540/1 760/1 465 mm
Coffre	348 litres
Réservoir	50 litres
Nombre coussins sécurité	6
Antipatinage / contrôle stabilité	oui / oui
Suspension avant	indépendante, jambes de force
Suspension arrière	indépendante, barres de torsion
Freins avant / arrière	disque (ABS) / tambour (ABS)
Direction	à crémaillère, ass. variable
Diamètre de braquage	11,3 m
Pneus avant / arrière	P205/55R16 / P205/55R16
Poids	1 275 kg
Capacité de remorquage	680 kg (1 499 lb)

COMPOSANTES MÉCANIQUES

CE, S, LE

Cylindrée, soupapes, alim.	4L 1,8 litre 16 s atmos.
Puissance / Couple	132 chevaux / 128 lb-pi
Tr. base (opt) / rouage base (opt)	M5 (A4) / Tr
0-100 / 80-120 / 100-0 km/h	10,1 s / 8,6 s / 43,1 m
Type ess. / ville / autoroute	Ordinaire / 7,6 / 5,7 l/100 km

XRS

Cylindrée, soupapes, alim.	4L 2,4 litres 16 s atmos.
Puissance / Couple	158 chevaux / 162 lb-pi
Tr. base (opt) / rouage base (opt)	M5 (A5) / Tr
0-100 / 80-120 / 100-0 km/h	9,5 s / 7,8 s / n.d.
Type ess. / ville / autoroute	Ordinaire / 9,5 / 6,7 l/100 km

DANS LA MÊME CATÉGORIE

Chevrolet Cobalt, Ford Focus, Honda Civic, Hyundai Elantra, Kia Forte, Mazda3, Mitsubishi Lancer, Nissan Sentra, Subaru Impreza, Suzuki SX-4, Volkswagen Jetta

DU NOUVEAU EN 2011

Aucun changement majeur

NOS IMPRESSIONS

Agrément de conduite :	6/10
Fiabilité :	8/10
Sécurité :	10/10
Qualités hivernales :	8/10
Espace intérieur :	8/10
Confort :	8/10

www.toyota.ca

Plus d'informations dans la section statistiques en dernière partie du Guide

UN COSTAUD VICTIME DE SON DESIGN

Lorsque Toyota a dévoilé le concept de ce véhicule, tous les intervenants se sont entendus pour dire que : « Non ! Jamais ce constructeur ne va oser produire un tel véhicule en série ! » En effet, avec ses allures de camionnette Tonka, très peu de gens croyaient qu'un jour on pourrait rouler à son volant sur nos routes. Cette silhouette caricaturale étonne, mais il suffit de s'y attarder pour se rendre compte que les stylistes ont effectué beaucoup de compromis sur le plan pratique pour dessiner un véhicule original.

Avec ses couleurs pastel et son toit blanc qui le démarquent facilement dans la circulation, il est certain que ce modèle intéresse les personnes qui aiment se faire remarquer. Mais c'est beaucoup plus qu'un véhicule qui fait tourner les têtes. Il faut souligner que les stylistes se sont inspirés du Toyota FJ40, un costaud s'il en était un parmi une génération de VUS tous aussi élémentaires et primitifs les uns que les autres, mais capables d'en prendre. Le FJ Cruiser est son équivalent moderne.

IL FAUT SOUFFRIR POUR PLAIRE

L'exécution d'une telle carrosserie impressionne les gens et même plusieurs années après son lancement, ce Toyota fait toujours figure d'original. Cela prouve également que lorsqu'ils sont laissés à leurs élans créatifs, les stylistes de ce constructeur sont capables d'innovations. Innover et épater c'est beau, mais cela comporte des inconvénients. En tout premier lieu, le pilier C est d'une telle largeur qu'il handicape fortement la visibilité 3/4 arrière. Et comme si ce n'était pas assez en fait de visibilité, on a accroché le pneu de secours sur la portière arrière. Heureusement que les rétroviseurs extérieurs sont d'assez bonnes dimensions pour afficher une vue arrière décente. En outre, pour accéder aux places arrière, il faut ouvrir la portière avant et ensuite ouvrir un panneau d'accès de type porte inversée afin de pouvoir s'assoir à l'arrière. C'est un peu comme sur plusieurs camionnettes compactes qui utilisent cette configuration pour permettre d'accéder aux strapontins arrière. Dans le cas qui nous intéresse, cela nécessite une certaine flexibilité puisqu'il faut lever la patte relativement haut. Et une fois en place, le siège est moyennement confortable et la visibilité atroce. Avis aux claustrophobes.

Malgré sa vocation de pur et dur des sentiers les plus impraticables, le design a eu préséance sur le caractère pratique. Il est vrai que le trio de cadrans indicateurs placés dans une nacelle posée en plein centre de la planche de bord est censé plaire. Mais côté pratique, c'est plus pour faire de l'épate que pour leur utilité. Il faut également ajouter que la partie centrale est de couleur coordonnée à la carrosserie. C'est peut-être plus stylisé, mais pas tellement inspirant. Un autre bémol pour la console centrale : deux leviers en plus du frein à main occupent beaucoup d'espace et en laissent peu en fait de rangement. C'est comme si on avait voulu donner du style à un véhicule à vocation militaire. On a quand même réussi assez bien avec le Hummer, mais ça me semble moins bien sur le FJ.

FEU VERT

- Construction solide
- Mécanique fiable
- Excellent en conduite hors route
- Prix compétitifs
- Silhouette originale

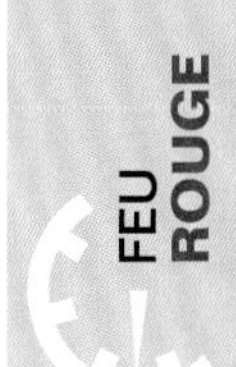

FEU ROUGE

- Visibilité atroce
- Direction imprécise
- Consommation toujours élevée
- Comportement routier très moyen
- Accès aux places arrière difficile

Sur une note plus positive, il faut parler du coffre de grande dimension, du tapis en caoutchouc fort robuste pouvant subir les pires abus et des sièges recouverts d'un matériau qui se lave facilement. De plus, comme tout produit Toyota, la qualité d'assemblage est bonne et les matériaux pas trop mal non plus.

UNE GROSSE POINTURE

C'est vrai que la silhouette est une question de goût. C'est également vrai d'affirmer que l'habitacle pourrait être un tantinet plus pratique et moins tarabiscoté. Et comme mentionné précédemment, la largeur de tous les piliers de ce véhicule limite la visibilité. Pourtant, on nous a toujours dit que la fenestration d'un gros VUS doit être excellente afin d'avoir une bonne vision de l'entourage. Et puisque ce FJ est capable de grandes choses en conduite hors route, cette lacune est d'autant plus regrettable.

Sous ses allures de gros jouet, ce VUS est un authentique passe-partout doté de toute la robustesse nécessaire pour affronter avec aplomb les légendaires sentiers hors route reconnus par la communauté des adeptes du franchissement d'obstacles. L'an dernier, le moteur a gagné en puissance avec l'arrivée de 20 équidés additionnels sous le capot grâce à l'utilisation d'un système de calage variable des soupapes. Outre ce gain de puissance, la consommation de carburant a été réduite. Et c'est la bonne nouvelle, puisque la version précédente de ce moteur V6 4,0 litres avait une soif quasiment inconsidérée pour les hydrocarbures. En bon québécois, il était « dur sul'gaz » !

Chez Toyota, on a aussi déclaré que la suspension et la direction avaient été recalibrées. Il semble que ces modifications aient été relativement modestes, car ce chevalier de la boue et des gros cailloux n'est pas très maniable sur la route. Sa suspension est essentiellement dessinée pour briller dans les sentiers et il faut admettre qu'elle y met le paquet. Mais sur la route, il faudra s'adapter à un comportement routier assez pataud. Même remarque pour la direction qui manque non seulement de précision, mais qui affiche toujours un flou important au centre. Si cette caractéristique est désagréable sur la route, elle est appréciée hors route.

Bref, il ne faut pas se fier uniquement au plumage, vous risquez d'être déçu…

Denis Duquet

PHOTOS : TOYOTA

TOYOTA FJ CRUISER

Catégorie	VUS
Échelle de prix	31 500 $ (2010)
Garanties	3 ans/60 000 km, 5 ans/100 000 km
Assemblage	Hamura, Japon
Cote d'assurance	passable

CHÂSSIS - DONNÉES POUR BASE

Emp/lon/lar/haut	2 690/4 670/1 905/1 830 mm
Coffre	790 à 1 892 litres
Réservoir	72 litres
Nombre coussins sécurité	6
Antipatinage / contrôle stabilité	oui / oui
Suspension avant	indépendante, double triangulation
Suspension arrière	essieu rigide, multibras
Freins avant / arrière	disque (ABS) / disque (ABS)
Direction	à crémaillère, ass. variable
Diamètre de braquage	12,7 m
Pneus avant / arrière	P265/70R17 / P265/70R17
Poids	1 963 kg
Capacité de remorquage	2 268 kg (5 000 lb)

COMPOSANTES MÉCANIQUES

Base

Cylindrée, soupapes, alim.	V6 4,0 litres 24 s atmos.
Puissance / Couple	259 chevaux / 270 lb-pi
Tr. base (opt) / rouage base (opt)	M6 (A5) / 4x4
0-100 / 80-120 / 100-0 km/h	10,1 s / 8,6 s / 44,0 m
Type ess. / ville / autoroute	Ordinaire / 13,7 / 10,3 l/100 km

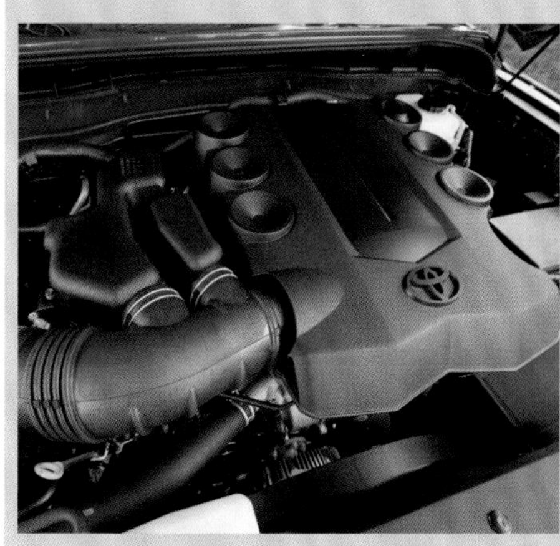

DANS LA MÊME CATÉGORIE

Dodge Nitro, Jeep Liberty, Jeep Wrangler, Nissan Xterra

DU NOUVEAU EN 2011

Aucun changement majeur

NOS IMPRESSIONS

Agrément de conduite :	6/10
Fiabilité :	10/10
Sécurité :	10/10
Qualités hivernales :	10/10
Espace intérieur :	8/10
Confort :	6/10

www.toyota.ca

Plus d'informations dans la section statistiques en dernière partie du Guide

UN PREMIER DE CLASSE TYPIQUE

Le Highlander est à l'image des ces élèves studieux et doués qu'on n'entend jamais et qu'on remarque à peine mais qui récoltent prix, bourses et honneurs en fin d'année. Lancée il y a une décennie et entièrement redessinée pour 2008, cette famille de multisegments sages et discrets a droit cette année une série de retouches et de mises à jour pour le milieu de leur cycle actuel. La version Hybride y gagne même un tout nouveau groupe propulseur.

Lorsque Toyota a voulu créer un premier multisegment pour concurrencer sérieusement le Subaru Outback pour 2001, elle lui a dessiné une silhouette haute et anguleuse d'utilitaire plutôt que d'en faire une familiale surélevée. Ces lignes carrées recelaient essentiellement l'architecture de la berline Camry, best-seller nord-américain de la marque.

UN ALIGNEMENT COMPLET

Le Highlander a gagné nettement en taille et s'est refait une beauté – toujours dans la discrétion – lors de son remodelage complet il y a trois ans. Il pouvait enfin rivaliser plus directement avec les Ford Edge, Honda Pilot, Nissan Murano et autres en termes d'habitabilité et de volume cargo. Chez nous il est même vendu désormais uniquement en version à sept places. Dommage parce que les cinq places étaient moins chers et plus légers, sans compter que ces sièges en troisième rangée sont aussi peu accueillants que pratiquement tous leurs semblables. Heureusement ils s'escamotent entièrement sous le plancher à l'arrière, libérant du coup 1 200 litres de volume cargo. Sinon, on doit se contenter d'un maigre 290 litres.

Trois versions sont offertes cette année : d'abord le Highlander à roues avant motrices propulsé par le quatre cylindres de 2,7 litres et 187 chevaux. Ensuite les quatre roues motrices de base et « Limited », équipées du V6 de 3,5 litres et 270 chevaux. Ironiquement, le « quatre » est jumelé à une boîte automatique à 6 rapports alors que les V6 n'ont encore qu'une boîte à 5 rapports. Le département du marketing chez Toyota Canada a choisi de remplacer le modèle Sport par un groupe Sport optionnel qui comporte un toit ouvrant, des roues de 19 pouces, un climatiseur thermostatique à trois zones et du cuir noir pour les sièges, la jante du volant et le pommeau du levier de vitesses.

La troisième version est le Highlander Hybride qui profite du changement mécanique le plus important cette année en héritant du nouveau groupe propulseur hybride d'abord apparu sur le Lexus RX 450h, son frère de sang en termes de technique. Le cœur de cette version du rouage hybride essence-électricité de Toyota est donc un V6 de 3,5 litres à cycle Atkinson qui produit à lui seul dans le Lexus, 295 chevaux à 6 200 tr/min, ce qui représenterait une hausse de 27 chevaux par rapport au V6 de 3,3 litres du modèle précédent.

Comme sur le RX, de nouveaux systèmes de recirculation des gaz d'échappement et de récupération de leur chaleur perdue aident à

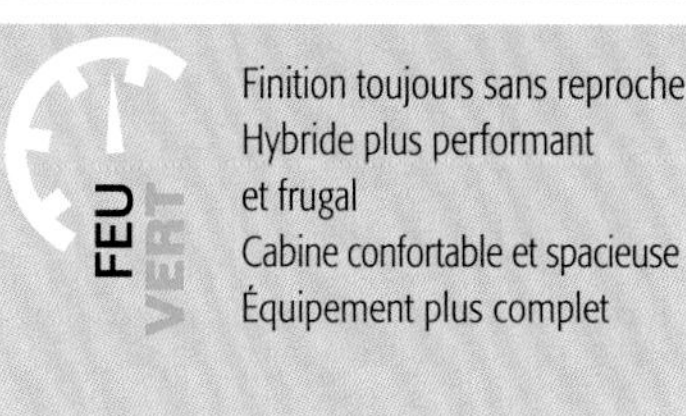

Finition toujours sans reproche
Hybride plus performant et frugal
Cabine confortable et spacieuse
Équipement plus complet

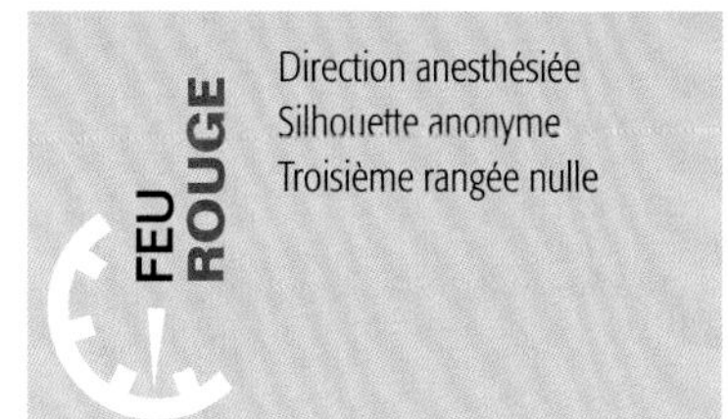

Direction anesthésiée
Silhouette anonyme
Troisième rangée nulle

réduire les émissions polluantes et la consommation. Avec de nouveaux moteurs électriques plus performants – deux pour la propulsion à chaque essieu et le troisième pour le redémarrage et la recharge des accumulateurs – la version hybride devrait pouvoir égaler les cotes de consommation du RX 450h, sinon faire mieux.

De plus, en prenant du coffre, le Highlander Hybride avait également pris environ 106 kilos lors de son dernier remodelage. Sa prestation de 0 à 100 km/h était d'ailleurs passée de 7,25 à 8,65 secondes. La puissance additionnelle du nouveau groupe lui permettra de retrouver sa verve de jadis, en tout ou en partie. Sans compter que cette deuxième génération du Highlander Hybride était nettement plus pataude et engourdie en conduite alors que le premier était plutôt sympathique et, comme on l'a vu, assez performant.

PLUS BRANCHÉ DEHORS COMME DEDANS

On s'intéresse rarement au Highlander pour la pure beauté de sa silhouette mais dans une catégorie aussi populaire, le style est important quand même. Paraître démodé c'est risquer d'être déclassé ou simplement perçu comme tel, ce qui est presque aussi mauvais. C'est pourquoi la carrosserie du Highlander affiche cette année une partie avant redessinée, tout comme ses bas de caisse latéraux et ses blocs optiques et son pare-chocs à l'arrière.

Les versions quatre cylindres et les V6 et Hybride de base roulent également sur de nouvelles jantes d'alliage de 17 pouces chaussées de pneus de taille P245/65. Les modèles V6 et Hybride Limited sont équipés plutôt de pneus de taille P245/55 sur les jantes d'alliage de 19 pouces existantes.

Dans l'habitacle, le tableau de bord et la présentation ont aussi été rafraîchis. Pour que le Highlander demeure attrayant face à ses plus nouvelles rivales, Toyota bonifie son équipement et ajoute les technologies et gadgets les plus récents, selon la pratique consacrée. Tous les modèles ont ainsi droit à une meilleure chaîne audio avec radio satellite XM, des phares automatiques et des réglages pour la climatisation à l'arrière. Les V6 ajoutent un port USB et la connectivité Bluetooth tandis que les Limited y gagnent un changeur pour quatre CD et le système de navigation. À défaut de passionner son conducteur le Highlander devrait arriver à dorloter et distraire ses passagers, en toute fiabilité.

Marc Lachapelle

PHOTOS : TOYOTA

Catégorie	VUS
Échelle de prix	33 250 $ à 55 075 $ (2010)
Garanties	3 ans/60 000 km, 5 ans/100 000 km
Assemblage	Kyushu, Japon
Cote d'assurance	passable

CHÂSSIS - DONNÉES POUR 4RM V6 LIMITED

Emp/lon/lar/haut	2 790/4 785/1 910/1 760 mm
Coffre	290 à 2 700 litres
Réservoir	73 litres
Nombre coussins sécurité	7
Antipatinage / contrôle stabilité	oui / oui
Suspension avant	indépendante, jambes de force
Suspension arrière	indépendante, jambes de force
Freins avant / arrière	disque (ABS) / disque (ABS)
Direction	à crémaillère, ass. électrique
Diamètre de braquage	11,8 m
Pneus avant / arrière	P245/55R19 / P245/55R19
Poids	1 960 kg
Capacité de remorquage	2 268 kg (5 000 lb)

COMPOSANTES MÉCANIQUES

2RM

Cylindrée, soupapes, alim.	4L 2,7 litres 16 s atmos.
Puissance / Couple	187 chevaux / 186 lb-pi
Tr. base (opt) / rouage base (opt)	A6 / Tr
0-100 / 80-120 / 100-0 km/h	10,0 (est) / 9,0 s (est) / n.d.
Type ess. / ville / autoroute	Ordinaire / 10,4 / 7,3 l/100 km

Hybride (données préliminaires)

Cylindrée, soupapes, alim.	V6 3,5 litres 24 s atmos.
Puissance / Couple	295 chevaux / 234 lb-pi
Tr. base (opt) / rouage base (opt)	CVT / Int
0-100 / 80-120 / 100-0 km/h	7,0 s (est) / n.d. / n.d.
Type ess. / ville / autoroute	Ordinaire / 7,4 / 8,0 l/100 km

V6

Cylindrée, soupapes, alim.	V6 3,5 litres 24 s atmos.
Puissance / Couple	270 chevaux / 248 lb-pi
Tr. base (opt) / rouage base (opt)	A5 / Int
0-100 / 80-120 / 100-0 km/h	7,6 s / 7,2 s / 40,0 m
Type ess. / ville / autoroute	Ordinaire / 12,3 / 8,8 l/100 km

DANS LA MÊME CATÉGORIE

Buick Enclave, Chevrolet Traverse, Ford Flex, GMC Acadia, Honda Pilot, Hyundai Veracruz, Mazda CX-9, Mitsubishi Endeavor, Nissan Murano, Subaru Tribeca

DU NOUVEAU EN 2011

Parties avant et arrière redessinées, moteur passe de 3,3 à 3,5 litres (Hybrid), nouvelle banquette 3ième rangée, nouveau système audio.

NOS IMPRESSIONS

Agrément de conduite :	7/10
Fiabilité :	10/10
Sécurité :	8/10
Qualités hivernales :	8/10
Espace intérieur :	9/10
Confort :	9/10

www.toyota.ca

Plus d'informations dans la section statistiques en dernière partie du Guide

TOUJOURS AUSSI PRATICO PRATIQUE

L'an prochain, la Toyota Matrix fêtera dix belles années de ventes. Dix ans pour une voiture à hayon, sur un continent qui n'est pourtant pas très amoureux des *hatchbacks*, ça mérite d'être souligné. Il doit bien y avoir quelque chose qui marche là-dessous...

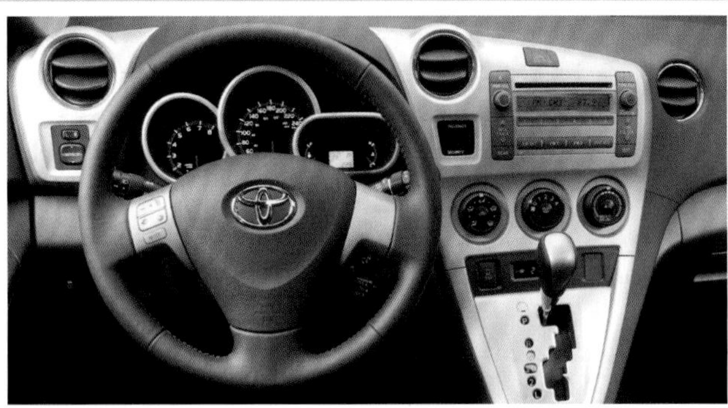

La deuxième génération de la Toyota Matrix – une voiture assemblée à Cambridge en Ontario, rappelons-le – est avec nous depuis 2009. Lors du dernier passage générationnel, on a gratifié la voiture d'une allure moins familiale et plus sportive, voire plus agressive, merci à la collaboration d'une équipe de design établie à Turin. L'ensemble fait plus jeune et depuis la disparition de la marque Pontiac l'an dernier, donc du jumeau Vibe, la Matrix se retrouve doublement en position de force.

Évolution et démocratisation des éléments de sécurité obligent, la Matrix en est venue, au fil des ans, à offrir les freins ABS de série – et c'est une bien bonne chose. Le système de stabilité a aussi le bonheur, désormais, d'être sur toutes les versions, sauf sur celle de base où il est néanmoins proposé en option. On aime. Les six coussins gonflables, eux, sont évidemment de série.

Cet aspect de la sécurité réglé, discourons sur l'habitacle : fonctionnalité et simplicité règnent à bord et c'est ce sympathique côté pratico pratique qui est le plus grand atout de la voiture. Les plastiques de revêtement sont de bonne facture, bien assemblés et le dégagement accordé aux passagers est très correct, même à l'arrière. La banquette se rabat à plat aisément, d'un seul mouvement, et on aime que l'espace cargo soit recouvert d'un plateau amovible et nettoyable. Toutefois, des sangles de retenue sont absolument requises, sinon les objets qui y sont disposés glissent au moindre virage – ce n'est pas beau à voir, des sacs d'épicerie valsant de droite à gauche !

Côté insonorisation, on prendrait davantage de matériel isolant à l'arrière, où les bruits de la route sont amplifiés par l'aire ouverte du hayon. Ça aurait aussi le mérite d'accorder une impression intérieure plus douillette, moins sèche. La planche de bord est dégagée et visuellement agréable au coup d'œil, mais si les commandes sont faciles à apprivoiser, elles demeurent difficiles d'accès.

MÊME AVEC L'AUTOMATIQUE

Rien ne sert de se mettre la tête dans le sable : la Matrix adopte la plupart des organes vitaux de la berline Corolla, gage de respectabilité, de fiabilité et... de conduite peu palpitante par rapport aux concurrentes Mazda3 Sport, Mitsubishi Lancer Sportback et Volkswagen Golf.

Sans surprise, on retrouve sous le capot le bon vieux quatre cylindres de 1,8 litre (pour 132 chevaux) ou le 2,4 litres qui a déjà équipé la Camry (pour 158 chevaux). La seconde motorisation est évidemment plus dynamique, mais si elle est celle que l'on préfère, ce n'est

FEU VERT

- Plateau de cargo amovible et nettoyable
- Bonne sécurité de série
- Motorisation de base très correcte
- Pratico pratique
- Économique à la pompe

FEU ROUGE

- Direction électrique : sans inspiration
- Insonorisation déficiente
- La facture grimpe vite
- Poutre de torsion en guise de suspension (versions de base)

pas en raison de sa puissance additionnelle ; c'est plutôt qu'elle peut venir, en option, avec l'automatique cinq rapports, plus souple et qui offre le passage manuel.

Reste que la motorisation de base n'est pas déplaisante pour autant. Certes, elle s'essouffle plus rapidement et son optionnelle transmission automatique n'a que quatre rapports, de surcroît sans mode manuel, mais la consommation en carburant est toute petite et l'ensemble se démène correctement, en autant que l'on sache se montrer indulgent.

Si, d'habitude, nous préférons les transmissions manuelles, l'automatique est ici suffisamment bien étagée et de bonne douceur pour être considérée. Il faut dire qu'avec la boîte manuelle, le point de friction est plutôt bas, ce qui rend les embrayages de départ moins instinctifs. Dans un cas comme dans l'autre, on aime que les leviers se trouvent en hauteur, à la console centrale, soit à portée de la main.

PLUS INSIPIDE QU'ÉNERGIQUE

Là où le bât blesse, c'est au niveau de la direction. On a droit ici à une direction de type électrique sans grande inspiration, qui ne communique pas beaucoup avec la route et ça se traduit par une expérience de conduite plus insipide qu'énergique. Autre reproche : c'est une poutre de torsion qui fait office de suspension arrière, là où la grande majorité de la compétition mise pourtant sur des éléments indépendants (sauf la SX-4, elle aussi à poutre de torsion). Résultat : la balade est plus sautillante que souple et elle n'assure pas toujours un comportement en douceur, avec parfois quelques résonnances d'amortisseurs dans l'habitacle.

Pour une tenue de route rehaussée, mieux vaut opter pour les variantes haut de gamme de la Matrix : la XRS et celle à transmission intégrale adoptent la double triangulation arrière, une architecture plus stable et plus intéressante à malmener en virage. Par contre, la facture grimpe alors assez vite...

Justement, terminons avec la transmission intégrale : à bord de la Matrix, ce dispositif se débrouille bien dans les conditions hivernales, avec 45 % du couple qui peut être acheminé aux roues arrière lorsque requis. Encore là, cette voiture demande dans les plus ou moins 24 000 $ et à ce prix-là, on serait fou de ne pas reluquer la Subaru Impreza – pour laquelle j'ai une nette préférence...

Nadine Filion

PHOTOS : TOYOTA

DONNÉES 2010

Catégorie	*Hatchback*
Échelle de prix	16 665 $ à 26 275 $ (2010)
Garanties	3 ans/60 000 km, 5 ans/100 000 km
Assemblage	Cambridge, Ontario, Canada
Cote d'assurance	bonne

CHÂSSIS - DONNÉES POUR XR

Emp/lon/lar/haut	2 600/4 365/1 765/1 550 mm
Coffre	561 à 1 398 litres
Réservoir	50 litres
Nombre coussins sécurité	6
Antipatinage / contrôle stabilité	oui / oui
Suspension avant	indépendante, jambes de force
Suspension arrière	indépendante, barres de torsion
Freins avant / arrière	disque (ABS) / disque (ABS)
Direction	à crémaillère, assistée
Diamètre de braquage	11,0 m
Pneus avant / arrière	P205/55R16 / P205/55R16
Poids	1 350 kg
Capacité de remorquage	680 kg (1 499 lb)

COMPOSANTES MÉCANIQUES

Base

Cylindrée, soupapes, alim.	4L 1,8 litre 16 s atmos.
Puissance / Couple	132 chevaux / 128 lb-pi
Tr. base (opt) / rouage base (opt)	M5 (A4) / Tr
0-100 / 80-120 / 100-0 km/h	9,4 s / 8,8 s / 42,6 m
Type ess. / ville / autoroute	Ordinaire / 7,8 / 6,2 l/100 km

XR, AWD, XRS

Cylindrée, soupapes, alim.	4L 2,4 litres 16 s atmos.
Puissance / Couple	158 chevaux / 162 lb-pi
Tr. base (opt) / rouage base (opt)	M5 (A5) / Tr (Int)
0-100 / 80-120 / 100-0 km/h	8,2 s / 8,9 s / 41,0 m
Type ess. / ville / autoroute	Ordinaire / 9,6 / 7,1 l/100 km

DANS LA MÊME CATÉGORIE

Chevrolet HHR, Dodge Caliber, Kia Soul, Mazda3, Mitsubishi Lancer, Nissan Cube, Subaru Impreza, Suzuki SX-4, Volkswagen Rabbit

DU NOUVEAU EN 2011

Nouveau modèle sera dévoilé en cours d'année

NOS IMPRESSIONS

Agrément de conduite :	7/10
Fiabilité :	10/10
Sécurité :	10/10
Qualités hivernales :	8/10
Espace intérieur :	7/10
Confort :	7/10

www.toyota.ca

Plus d'informations dans la section statistiques en dernière partie du Guide

QUAND C'EST TOUT OU RIEN

J'ai un petit faible pour la Toyota Prius. Après tout, n'est-elle pas celle qui mène le bal hybride depuis dix ans (dix ans !) ? Alors, qu'importe si son insonorisation est moyenne, sa motorisation un brin rugueuse et son mode électrique pas aussi persévérant que souhaité.

Bon, vrai que dit comme ça, ces trois insuffisances peuvent sembler monstres. Mais c'est oublier que la Prius, véritable laboratoire sur quatre roues, en offre pas mal plus. On a qu'à penser au stationnement automatisé (repris maintenant chez Ford), au système précollision, au panneau qui recourt à l'énergie solaire ou encore à la possibilité de démarrer la climatisation à distance.

Versus les deux générations précédentes, l'hybride est devenue une meilleure routière, ne serait-ce que parce qu'elle s'est amendée, côté connexion avec la route. Cette fois, sa direction (électrique, bien sûr) n'oublie pas d'entrer en bonne relation avec le parcours, en plus d'être extrêmement maniable. La voiture est plus stable, mieux assise sur le bitume et le freinage est beaucoup plus naturel; il ne livre presque plus ce sentiment rêche des premières Prius. Par contre, la suspension a conservé son architecture à poutre de torsion avec, comme résultat, une balade qui se fait sèche et « balloteuse ». Ça cogne sur nos cahots québécois et, insonorisation moyenne oblige, ça résonne un peu trop dans l'habitacle.

4,2 L/100 KM EN SITUATIONS RÉELLES

Côté motorisation, il serait mal vu de se plaindre; une hybride mise sur l'économie d'essence et la Prius le fait bien. Notre essai d'une semaine, nous l'avons mené plus sur autoroute qu'en situations urbaines et nous l'avons terminé avec une très intéressante moyenne de 4,2 litres/100 km. Toyota déclame plutôt un combiné de 3,8 litres/100 km, mais sachez qu'on peut faire encore mieux: en prenant tooouuut son temps, on réussit du 2,9 litres/100 km... Quand même !

Mais le prix à payer pour cette frugalité est un petit quatre cylindres de 1,8 litre et un moteur électrique de 60 watts qui ne développent, conjointement, que 134 chevaux et 105 lb-pi. C'est peu, pour une berline intermédiaire; ce type de puissance est davantage l'apanage des voitures compactes, plus légères. Résultat: les accélérations sont rugueuses et pas toujours aussi dynamiques qu'escomptées. Mais encore une fois, il est mal vu de se plaindre de l'une des voitures les moins gourmandes du marché...

Toyota a voulu atténuer la chose avec trois modes que le conducteur peut sélectionner selon les besoins: *eco, power* et EV. En mode *power*, on ressent effectivement moins de résistance de la part de l'accélérateur, pour une conduite plus directe. Le mode EV, qui commande la propulsion 100% électrique, souffre du peu de capacité des batteries à fournir à la tâche. Vivement les percées technologiques parce que pour le moment, en plein bouchon montréalais, la Prius n'accepte de rouler qu'un court laps de temps sans son moteur

FEU VERT

Comportement routier amélioré
Frugale: 4,2 L/100 km sans forcer
Démarrage sans clé de série
Technologies d'avant-garde – mais attention à la facture...

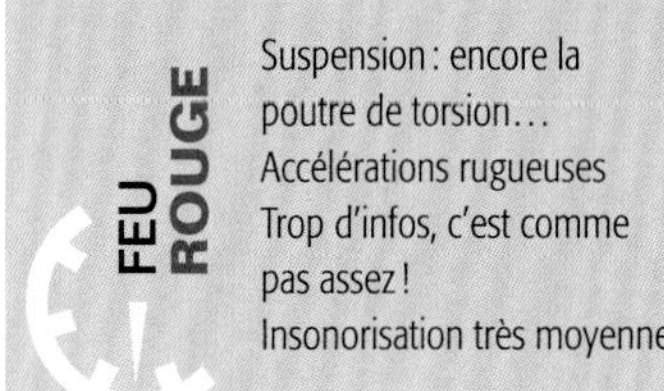

FEU ROUGE

Suspension: encore la poutre de torsion...
Accélérations rugueuses
Trop d'infos, c'est comme pas assez!
Insonorisation très moyenne

thermique. Et encore faut-il y aller doucement avec la pédale d'accélération... il faut y aller avec tellement de douceur que c'est quasiment ridicule.

Évidemment, c'est une transmission CVT qui équipe la Prius, comme pour toute hybride qui se respecte. Cette transmission, ne lui cherchez pas un mode manuel, encore moins de palettes au volant. Au contraire, il faut un certain temps pour s'habituer au levier de vitesse en fourchette. Tout comme il faut du temps pour apprivoiser un tsunami d'informations, réparti entre l'instrumentation devant le conducteur et une mince ligne d'affichage au bas du pare-brise.

Pour naviguer dans tout ça, Toyota a conçu le Touch Tracer qui, dès que l'on effleure les commandes au volant, s'illumine en superposé sur une présentation visuelle déjà fort occupée. C'est hypertechno et ça en fait pas mal à assimiler.

N'OUBLIONS PAS: PRATIQUE

On discoure hybride, consommation, motorisation... mais reste que la Prius, en digne *hatchback* qu'elle est, est une voiture fort pratique. On peut y loger jusqu'à 1 121 litres de marchandises lorsque sa banquette est rabattue. Merci à une ligne de toit qui, au dernier passage générationnel, a reculé d'une dizaine de centimètres, les passagers assis à l'arrière ont gagné en dégagement à la tête. Le coefficient de traînée a aussi été amélioré à 0,25 cx, ce qui fait de la Prius l'une des voitures les plus aérodynamiques du marché.

Dans l'habitacle, le premier coup d'œil est celui d'un véhicule prototype, avec cette console flottante qui a le mérite non seulement de dégager un rangement supplémentaire, mais de rendre les commandes très accessibles. Par contre, mieux vaut ne pas trop promener ses doigts sur ce revêtement en plastique rigide et peu agréable au toucher. Pour une copmpagnie qui se vante d'être la référence en fait de qualité, ce n'est pas fort. Aussi, les longs trajets font ressortir le manque de rembourrage et de soutien aux sièges avant.

Oh, un dernier point: fidèles à la tradition Toyota, les groupes d'options sont conçus pour... faire dépenser le client. Il souhaite les sièges en cuir et chauffants? Il lui faut se payer la totale avec la variante Technologie qui, pour 10 000$ de plus que le prix de base, ajoute tous les *gizmos* possibles. Avec la Prius, vraiment, c'est tout ou rien...

Nadine Filion

PHOTOS: SYLVAIN RAYMOND

Catégorie	*Hatchback*
Échelle de prix	27 800 $
Garanties	3 ans/60 000 km, 5 ans/100 000 km
Assemblage	Toyota City, Japon
Cote d'assurance	bonne

CHÂSSIS - DONNÉES POUR HYBRIDE

Emp/lon/lar/haut	2 700/4 460/1 745/1 480 mm
Coffre	445 à 1 121 litres
Réservoir	45 litres
Nombre coussins sécurité	7
Antipatinage / contrôle stabilité	oui / oui
Suspension avant	indépendante, jambes de force
Suspension arrière	semi-indépendante, poutre de torsion
Freins avant / arrière	disque (ABS) / disque (ABS)
Direction	à crémaillère, ass. variable
Diamètre de braquage	10,4 m
Pneus avant / arrière	P195/65R15 / P195/65R15
Poids	1 380 kg
Capacité de remorquage	n.d.

COMPOSANTES MÉCANIQUES

Hybride

Cylindrée, soupapes, alim.	4L 1,8 litre 16 s atmos.
Puissance / Couple	98 ch (134 ch total) / 105 lb-pi
Tr. base (opt) / rouage base (opt)	CVT / Tr
0-100 / 80-120 / 100-0 km/h	10,8 s / 8,5 s / 43,6 m
Type ess. / ville / autoroute	Ordinaire / 3,7 / 4,0 l/100 km

DANS LA MÊME CATÉGORIE

Honda Insight

DU NOUVEAU EN 2011

Groupe d'options «Premium» avec panneaux solaires

NOS IMPRESSIONS

Agrément de conduite:	6/10
Fiabilité:	8/10
Sécurité:	8/10
Qualités hivernales:	6/10
Espace intérieur:	7/10
Confort:	8/10

www.toyota.ca

Plus d'informations dans la section statistiques en dernière partie du Guide

VOUS AVEZ DIT COMPACTE ?

Le Toyota RAV4 est l'un des plus populaires dans la catégorie des VUS compacts. En effet, les gens apprécient sa grande habitabilité, le choix des moteurs et le rouage intégral optionnel. En plus, malgré les déboires que le constructeur a connus au cours de la dernière année, nombreux sont les acheteurs qui se procurent encore un produit de cette marque en raison de sa fiabilité et de sa durabilité. Il est toutefois important de souligner que si Toyota l'inscrit dans la catégorie des compactes, ses dimensions intérieures et extérieures en font un petit intermédiaire.

Il est tout de même curieux de constater qu'il n'y a pas si longtemps, le RAV4 était le plus petit de sa catégorie et également celui propulsé par le plus petit moteur. À son volant, on avait l'impression de conduire un gros modèle Tonka motorisé. Néanmoins, comme c'est souvent le cas chez les constructeurs nippons, on s'est entêté et, on a réussi à obtenir, quelques générations plus tard, un best-seller.

DE GRANDS ESPACES

L'achat de véhicules utilitaires sport comprend pour plusieurs personnes une bonne part de rêve. On s'imagine circuler dans la forêt boréale au volant de son multisegment, franchir des obstacles impressionnants ou encore dévaler des pentes abruptes parsemées de roches. Dans la quasi-totalité des cas, il s'agit de rêves. La plupart des propriétaires de VUS, qu'ils soient compacts ou intermédiaires, vont surtout utiliser leur véhicule pour leur usage personnel: aller au travail, au centre commercial ou conduire les enfants à une activité quelconque. Certains vont conduire hors route, mais il s'agit d'une minorité.

En effet, à part quelques millimètres ici et là concédés à certaines concurrentes, il s'agit du modèle le plus spacieux de sa catégorie. Sans surprise d'ailleurs, parce qu'il en est le plus long. Cela a permis aux ingénieurs de placer une troisième rangée de sièges, afin de répondre à une demande de plus en plus grande. Inutile de souligner que cette troisième rangée de sièges est essentiellement symbolique et ne pourra accueillir que des passagers de petite taille et ce, pour un trajet de très courte durée. Par contre, l'un des bénéfices de cette configuration est le fait que la rangée secondaire coulisse sur des rails en plus de proposer un dossier inclinable. Cet agencement a été concocté afin de pouvoir accéder à la troisième rangée. Il faut également souligner que le Rav4 est celui qui propose le plus grand espace de chargement de sa catégorie. Pour y accéder, on doit ouvrir une porte à ancrage latéral. Celle-ci s'ouvre de gauche à droite ce qui risque d'être embarrassant lorsqu'on est stationné dans la rue. En outre, la présence de la roue de secours boulonnée sur cette portière rend l'ouverture de celle-ci un peu difficile.

Comme il se doit sur un produit Toyota, la finition et l'assemblage sont impeccables. Même si les plastiques utilisés sont toujours relativement durs, on remarque une nette amélioration par rapport

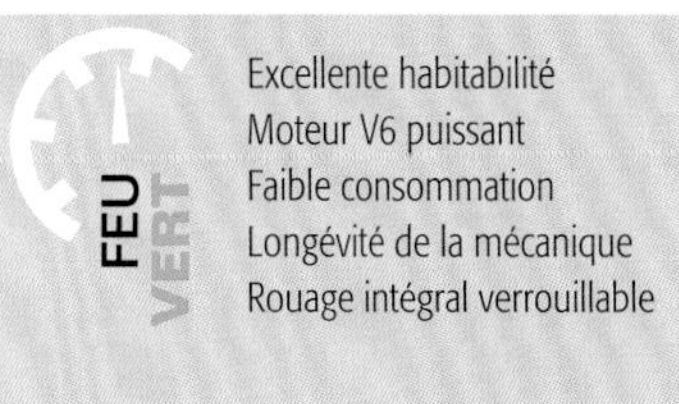

FEU VERT

Excellente habitabilité
Moteur V6 puissant
Faible consommation
Longévité de la mécanique
Rouage intégral verrouillable

FEU ROUGE

Absence de transmission manuelle
Agrément de conduite fort mitigé
Boîte automatique 4 rapports (4 cylindres)

aux versions antérieures. En effet, la première génération avait créé un précédent en fait de matériaux bon marché pour un habitacle. Au fil des modèles et des années, on est revenu à une certaine normalité, mais il reste des progrès à faire.

Ceci dit, la planche de bord se démarque par ses trois cadrans indicateurs, cerclés d'un anneau de couleur contrastante. Les chiffres blancs sur fonds noirs sont de consultation facile.

DE LA PUISSANCE

La première génération du RAV4 était tellement de faible puissance que ce véhicule avait de la difficulté à grimper un raidillon en conduite hors route. Les choses ont grandement évolué puisque ce modèle propose des moteurs qui sont parmi les plus puissants de sa catégorie. Le moteur de base est un quatre cylindres de 2,5 litres dont la puissance est de 179 chevaux, ce qui est plus que suffisant. Seule une boîte automatique à quatre rapports est disponible. Il serait toutefois préférable d'être équipé d'une boîte manuelle afin de ne pas avoir à supporter cette transmission à quatre vitesses carrément rétrograde. Par contre, ce moteur est vigoureux et nerveux et sa consommation de carburant est fort raisonnable car elle est inférieure à 10 litres au 100 km.

Si vous désirez une transmission automatique à cinq rapports, vous devrez opter pour le moteur V6 de 3,5 litres produisant 90 chevaux de plus, c'est-à-dire 269. Cette fois, ce n'est pas la puissance qui fait défaut. D'ailleurs, il ne faut que 6,7 secondes pour boucler le 0-100 km/h. En outre, sa consommation de carburant est fort raisonnable en raison de la puissance et de la cylindrée du moteur.

On pourrait s'attendre à un agrément de conduite intéressant compte tenu de la motorisation de ce véhicule. Malheureusement, comme sur plusieurs produits de cette marque, la conduite nous laisse indifférent. La tenue de route est correcte, mais le *feedback* de la route est quasiment nul, sans doute en raison de la direction à assistance électrique.

Bref, ce modèle est pratique, fiable et sa motorisation est excellente. De plus, le rouage intégral est assez sophistiqué. Nul doute que si l'on pouvait ajouter un peu d'agrément de conduite, ce serait d'autant plus satisfaisant.

Denis Duquet

PHOTOS : TOYOTA

TOYOTA RAV4

Catégorie	VUS
Échelle de prix	24 595 $ à 34 640 $ (2010)
Garanties	3 ans/60 000 km, 5 ans/100 000 km
Assemblage	Cambridge, Ontario, Canada
Cote d'assurance	pauvre

CHÂSSIS - DONNÉES POUR 4RM LIMITED

Emp/lon/lar/haut	2 660/4 620/1 855/1 745 mm
Coffre	1 015 à 2 074 litres
Réservoir	60 litres
Nombre coussins sécurité	6
Antipatinage / contrôle stabilité	oui / oui
Suspension avant	indépendante, jambes de force
Suspension arrière	indépendante, double triangulation
Freins avant / arrière	disque (ABS) / disque (ABS)
Direction	à crémaillère, ass. électrique
Diamètre de braquage	11,4 m
Pneus avant / arrière	P225/65R17 / P225/65R17
Poids	1 615 kg
Capacité de remorquage	680 kg (1 499 lb)

COMPOSANTES MÉCANIQUES

Base, Sport, Limitede

Cylindrée, soupapes, alim.	4L 2,5 litres 16 s atmos.
Puissance / Couple	179 chevaux / 172 lb-pi
Tr. base (opt) / rouage base (opt)	A4 / Tr (Int)
0-100 / 80-120 / 100-0 km/h	9,6 s / n.d. / 41,0 m
Type ess. / ville / autoroute	Ordinaire / 9,7 / 7,2 l/100 km

V6

Cylindrée, soupapes, alim.	V6 3,5 litres 24 s atmos.
Puissance / Couple	269 chevaux / 246 lb-pi
Tr. base (opt) / rouage base (opt)	A5 / Int
0-100 / 80-120 / 100-0 km/h	6,7 s / 5,7 s / 42,0 m
Type ess. / ville / autoroute	Ordinaire / 11,1 / 7,7 l/100 km

DANS LA MÊME CATÉGORIE

Chevrolet Equinox, Dodge Nitro, Ford Escape, Honda CR-V, Hyundai Santa Fe, Jeep Liberty, Mazda Tribute, Mitsubishi Outlander, Nissan Rogue, Subaru Forester, Suzuki Grand Vitara, Volkswagen Tiguan

DU NOUVEAU EN 2011

Aucun changement majeur

NOS IMPRESSIONS

Agrément de conduite :	7/10
Fiabilité :	10/10
Sécurité :	10/10
Qualités hivernales :	9/10
Espace intérieur :	8/10
Confort :	8/10

www.toyota.ca

Plus d'informations dans la section statistiques en dernière partie du Guide

COMME UNE MÉTÉORITE DANS UNE ROSERAIE

Les Japonais ont fait leur renommée en Amérique grâce à leurs petites voitures, tombées pile lorsque le pétrole a fait une crise en 1973. Puis, ils ont commencé à mener le jeu. Puisqu'ils proposaient des véhicules à traction (roues avant motrices), les Américains se sont mis à faire de même. Et lorsque qu'à peu près tous les constructeurs américains ne faisaient plus que des tractions, les Japonais ont commencé à faire des propulsions (roues arrière motrices) ! Et les Américains de retourner à la propulsion. Mais s'il est un domaine où les Japonais ne sont pas en avance sur les Américains, c'est au niveau des grands VUS.

Pourtant, le Sequoia de Toyota est sans doute le véhicule qui se rapproche le plus de ceux de Ford ou de General Motors, Chrysler étant absent de cette catégorie depuis la mise au rancart du Durango en 2009. Aussi imposant que ses compères, le Sequoia n'a pas peur du travail, avec son châssis emprunté à la camionnette Tundra. Sur cette dernière, la partie arrière du châssis n'est pas aussi solide que ce que l'on est en droit d'attendre d'un tel véhicule. Cependant, sous le Sequoia, elle fait des merveilles puisqu'elle a été raccourcie et qu'elle est boulonnée à une carrosserie fermée, contrairement à la camionnette dont la cabine est séparée de la boîte.

VIVE LE GROS MOTEUR!

Pour mouvoir avec une certaine célérité, pour ne pas dire avec une célérité certaine, son immense Sequoia, Toyota fait appel aux moteurs du Tundra. On retrouve donc le V8 de 4,6 litres de 310 chevaux et 327 livres-pied de couple qui devrait satisfaire la plupart des gens. Les accélérations et dépassement sont loin d'être pénibles, sauf quand on traîne une remorque à la limite du poids permis (7 000 livres). Sur la route, à vitesse constante et avec un vent de dos, la consommation est franchement étonnante. Modifiez un tant soi peu un des trois paramètres et cette consommation s'avère franchement étonnante… mais d'une autre manière !

L'autre moteur est un V8 de 5,7 litres de 381 chevaux et de 401 livres-pied de couple, une puissance quasiment inutile. La logique demanderait d'opter pour le 4,6 mais quand on constate que le 5,7 peut remorquer jusqu'à 8 800 livres et qu'il ne consomme pas tellement plus que le 4,6, les avis changent.

Dans les deux cas, on retrouve une transmission automatique à six rapports qui s'avère bien étagée pour… économiser de l'essence ! En effet, à 100 km/h, elle permet au moteur de ne « tourner » qu'à 1 600 tours/minutes (2 000 à 120 km/h). Imaginez la consommation si elle ne comptait que cinq rapports…

Puisque le Sequoia est appelé à se rendre souvent dans des endroits difficiles d'accès comme des chantiers de construction, il fallait à Toyota lui donner les moyens de ses ambitions. Son rouage 4x4 est donc très performant à défaut d'être sophistiqué. Il s'agit

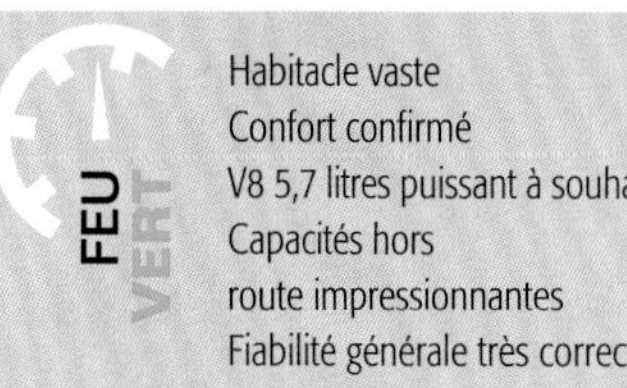

FEU VERT

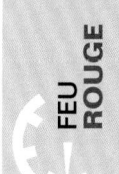

Habitacle vaste
Confort confirmé
V8 5,7 litres puissant à souhait
Capacités hors route impressionnantes
Fiabilité générale très correcte

FEU ROUGE

Consommation d'alcoolique
V8 4,6 litres consomme autant que le 5,7
Direction très peu communicative
Dimensions extravagantes

sans doute d'un détail mais j'aime bien sentir qu'un rouage 4x4 est solide. Dans le Sequoia, le passage entre les modes 2RM (propulsion) et 4RM (4x4) est bien senti. Ça donne confiance ! Lors du dévoilement du Sequoia, nous avions pu le mettre à l'épreuve dans un sentier passablement difficile et il s'en était sorti avec brio.

CONDUIRE UNE PYRAMIDE D'ÉGYPTE

Dire que le Sequoia est gros est un euphémisme. Après tout, on ne porte le nom de l'arbre le plus gros au monde pour rien... Ces dimensions se reflètent dans l'habitacle alors qu'il faut invariablement hausser le ton pour que les gens assis à l'autre bout puissent nous entendre! Même la troisième banquette possède de bons dégagements sans être pourtant très confortable.

Le tableau de bord, à l'image du reste, ne fait pas dans le micro. Les surfaces sont plates, larges et les boutons et diverses commandes sont surdimensionnés, ce qui les rend faciles à manipuler, même avec de gros gants. Les espaces de rangement sont nombreux et de bonnes dimensions. Même les sièges sont larges et confortables, se faisant ainsi apprécier des popotins de tout acabit. Le conducteur fait face à une instrumentation complète, incluant même la charge de la batterie et la pression d'huile, ce qui est plus rare qu'on croit... Le Sequoia peut accueillir six ou sept personnes, selon la version. La plus huppée propose des sièges baquets pour la rangée médiane plutôt qu'une banquette. Peu importe, l'espace ne manque pas, ni le confort. Il y a fort à parier qu'un Sequoia, après avoir trimé dur toute la semaine, amènera la petite famille reconstituée au chalet le week-end.

Avec ses dimensions de pyramide d'Égypte, il ne faut pas se surprendre de constater que le Sequoia n'est pas le plus agile des véhicules. Ses suspensions sont davantage calibrées pour le confort que pour la tenue de route. En virage serré, on dénote un fort roulis, ce qui n'a rien d'étonnant. La direction, qui semble connectée à un nuage, n'est pas très précise. Je profite de l'occasion pour mentionner le court rayon de braquage, un élément des plus appréciés lorsque vient le temps d'effectuer un demi-tour avec un tel édifice. Un freinage d'urgence fait plonger le véhicule au point où on se demande si le dessous du pare-chocs avant ne frottera pas sur l'asphalte. Malgré tout, le Sequoia s'avère plutôt agréable à conduire pour autant qu'on respecte ses limites... une sage remarque qui s'applique à tous les véhicules présentés dans ce *Guide* !

Alain Morin

PHOTOS : TOYOTA

Catégorie	VUS
Échelle de prix	48 820 $ à 65 975 $ (2010)
Garanties	3 ans/60 000 km, 5 ans/100 000 km
Assemblage	Princeton, Indiana, É-U
Cote d'assurance	n.d.

CHÂSSIS - DONNÉES POUR PLATINUM V8 5.7L

Emp/lon/lar/haut	3 100/5 210/2 030/1 955 mm
Coffre	804 à 3 421 litres
Réservoir	100 litres
Nombre coussins sécurité	7
Antipatinage / contrôle stabilité	oui / oui
Suspension avant	indépendante, double triangulation
Suspension arrière	indépendante, double triangulation
Freins avant / arrière	disque (ABS) / disque (ABS)
Direction	à crémaillère, ass. variable
Diamètre de braquage	12,5 m
Pneus avant / arrière	P275/55R20 / P275/55R20
Poids	2 721 kg
Capacité de remorquage	3 990 kg (8 796 lb)

COMPOSANTES MÉCANIQUES

SR5 4.6L

Cylindrée, soupapes, alim.	V8 4,6 litres 32 s atmos.
Puissance / Couple	310 chevaux / 327 lb-pi
Tr. base (opt) / rouage base (opt)	A6 / 4x4
0-100 / 80-120 / 100-0 km/h	n.d. / n.d. / n.d.
Type ess. / ville / autoroute	Ordinaire / 16,0 / 11,1 l/100 km

Limited V8 5.7L, Platinum V8 5.7L

Cylindrée, soupapes, alim.	V8 5,7 litres 32 s atmos.
Puissance / Couple	381 chevaux / 401 lb-pi
Tr. base (opt) / rouage base (opt)	A6 / 4x4
0-100 / 80-120 / 100-0 km/h	7,1 s / 6,1 s / 42,9 m
Type ess. / ville / autoroute	Ordinaire / 16,3 / 11,2 l/100 km

DANS LA MÊME CATÉGORIE

Chevrolet Tahoe, Ford Expedition, GMC Yukon, Nissan Armada

DU NOUVEAU EN 2011

Aucun changement majeur

NOS IMPRESSIONS

Agrément de conduite :	6/10
Fiabilité :	6/10
Sécurité :	8/10
Qualités hivernales :	9/10
Espace intérieur :	10/10
Confort :	9/10

www.toyota.ca

Plus d'informations dans la section statistiques en dernière partie du Guide

PLUS CONFORTABLE NULLEMENT SPORTIVE

La Toyota Sienna s'est surtout fait connaître par son habitabilité, sa fiabilité et son excellente valeur de revente. Mais cette Camry transformée en fourgonnette était fortement déficiente en fait d'agrément de conduite. C'était le véhicule soporifique par excellence. Espérons que la nouvelle Sienna est améliorée à ce niveau.

Plusieurs observateurs croyaient que le constructeur nippon proposerait un véhicule plus léger, plus petit et équipé d'un groupe propulseur hybride. Mais cette nouvelle version a une silhouette qui la fait paraître plus grosse même si ses dimensions sont demeurées sensiblement les mêmes, et il n'y a pas de moteur hybride à l'horizon.

INSPIRÉE DE LA VENZA

Il est certain que la Sienna précédente était d'une esthétique discrète au maximum. C'est comme si on avait voulu faire le véhicule le moins excitant du marché, tant au chapitre de la présentation que de la conduite. Heureusement, les stylistes de ce constructeur démontrent maintenant un peu plus d'imagination. Ils nous ont comblés avec la Venza qui est une réussite en raison de sa belle silhouette et surtout de sa remarquable calandre.

Il ne faut pas être un grand connaisseur en design pour constater que la Sienna partage plusieurs éléments visuels avec la Venza, et c'est tant mieux. La grille de calandre très typée est la pièce maîtresse de cette ressemblance. Toutefois, le capot est plus court et les phares sont nettement plus distinctifs. Malheureusement, malgré les diodes électroluminescentes dans les feux de position et de freinage, la partie arrière est carrément plus sobre. Chez Toyota, on est très fier d'affirmer que le coefficient de pénétration dans l'air est de .036, ce qui

est excellent pour un véhicule de cette catégorie. Parmi les astuces utilisées pour obtenir de tels chiffres, mentionnons un carénage placé sous le véhicule et des rétroviseurs extérieurs plus aérodynamiques.

La planche de bord ressemble à celle de la Venza et c'est réussi. Sur la partie verticale se situe le levier de vitesses. Les commandes de climatisation et de la radio sont simples d'accès et faciles d'opération. Néanmoins, il faut déplorer la qualité des plastiques qui sont durs comme du béton... Chez Toyota, on nous a avoué que la direction tenterait de corriger ce défaut qui apparaît sur plusieurs nouveaux produits Toyota.

Les sièges avant sont confortables mais ce sont les sièges optionnels de la seconde rangée qui volent la vedette. Ils sont non seulement inclinables, mais ils possèdent un support pour les jambes ! Les gens pourront même regarder un vidéo sur un écran de 16 pouces de large. Sur certaines versions, il est possible de commander un siège médian qui se place entre les deux sièges capitaines. Ce siège temporaire peut être remisé sur la paroi gauche arrière sans nécessiter d'outils.

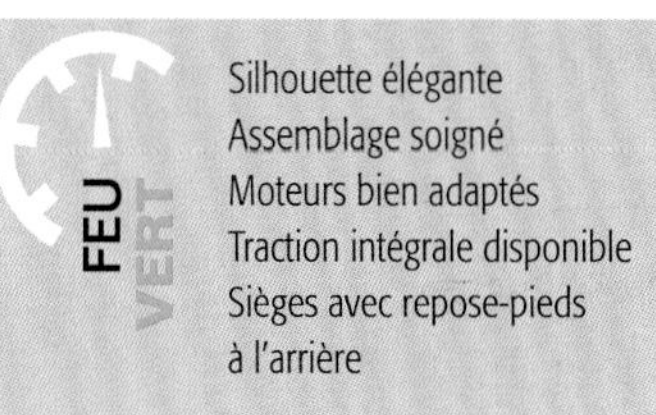

Silhouette élégante
Assemblage soigné
Moteurs bien adaptés
Traction intégrale disponible
Sièges avec repose-pieds à l'arrière

Agrément de conduite mitigé
Plastiques du tableau de bord trop durs
Certaines versions onéreuses
Peinture de qualité moyenne
Roulis en virage

HO LES MOTEURS !

Dans le cadre de la présentation à la presse, dans un élan d'enthousiasme, un dirigeant de Toyota Canada a parlé de fourgonnette sportive. Cette affirmation n'a aucun fondement et il suffit de conduire le véhicule pendant quelques mètres pour s'en convaincre. En fait de motorisation d'ailleurs, on a repris les mêmes moteurs qu'auparavant et ceux-ci sont associés à une transmission manumatique à six rapports. Le moteur de base est un 4 cylindres de 2,7 litres d'une puissance de 187 chevaux et d'un couple de 186 lb-pi. Cela peut sembler un peu juste pour propulser une fourgonnette de cette taille, mais il faut réaliser que ce moulin produit plus de chevaux que certains V6 concurrents. Le moteur V6 de la Sienna est d'une cylindrée de 3,5 litres et d'une puissance de 266 chevaux, ce qui en fait le plus puissant de la catégorie. Il est possible de le relier à une transmission intégrale de type temporaire qui permet de répartir le couple du moteur dans une proportion de 50-50 avant et arrière lorsque la chaussée est glissante. Présentement, cette Toyota est la seule à proposer la traction intégrale sur une fourgonnette. Terminons ce tour de la mécanique en soulignant que la direction est à assistance électronique, tandis que la suspension avant a connu certaines améliorations et révisions. Comme précédemment, la suspension arrière est à poutre déformante, ce qui permet d'offrir un plancher arrière complètement plat.

Si la Sienna a fait d'énormes progrès en fait de tenue de route, d'agrément de conduite, de précision de la direction, ce n'est toujours pas une sportive. C'est tout au plus une fourgonnette plus agréable à conduire que précédemment. D'ailleurs, sur la route, ce véhicule se contente de tout faire dans la moyenne, mais sans plus.

Les modèles équipés de la transmission intégrale semblent avoir un meilleur équilibre dans les virages, probablement en raison d'une meilleure répartition de poids. Pour le reste, il s'agit d'un véhicule sans reproche majeur en fait de comportement routier. Mais, vous n'aurez pas de palpitations en conduisant cette Sienna, même si Toyota aimerait beaucoup que ce soit le cas. Ses dirigeants peuvent toujours rêver, mais ce sera en vain.

En fin de compte, ce n'est pas la sportive annoncée, mais une Sienna améliorée, plus polyvalente que jamais, qui offre un agrément de conduite un peu plus relevé mais pas nécessairement sportif.

Denis Duquet

PHOTOS : TOYOTA

Catégorie	Fourgonnette
Échelle de prix	27 900 $ à 49 100 $
Garanties	3 ans/60 000 km, 5 ans/100 000 km
Assemblage	Georgetown, Kentucky, É-U
Cote d'assurance	passable

CHÂSSIS - DONNÉES POUR LIMITED AWD 7 PLACES

Emp/lon/lar/haut	3 030/5 085/1 985/1 750 mm
Coffre	1 110 à 4 250 litres
Réservoir	79 litres
Nombre coussins sécurité	7
Antipatinage / contrôle stabilité	oui / oui
Suspension avant	indépendante, jambes de force
Suspension arrière	semi-indépendante, poutre de torsion
Freins avant / arrière	disque (ABS) / disque (ABS)
Direction	à crémaillère, ass. électrique
Diamètre de braquage	11,2 m
Pneus avant / arrière	P235/55R18 / P235/55R18
Poids	2 145 kg
Capacité de remorquage	1 585 kg (3 494 lb)

COMPOSANTES MÉCANIQUES

LE 7 Places

Cylindrée, soupapes, alim.	4L 2,7 litres 16 s atmos.
Puissance / Couple	187 chevaux / 186 lb-pi
Tr. base (opt) / rouage base (opt)	A6 / Tr
0-100 / 80-120 / 100-0 km/h	11,5 s (est) / 9,0 s (est) / n.d.
Type ess. / ville / autoroute	Ordinaire / 10,4 / 7,5 l/100 km

V6 7 places, LE 8 Places, LE AWD 7 Places, SE 8 Places, XLE 7 Places, Limited AWD 7 Places

Cylindrée, soupapes, alim.	V6 3,5 litres 24 s atmos.
Puissance / Couple	266 chevaux / 245 lb-pi
Tr. base (opt) / rouage base (opt)	A6 / Tr (Int)
0-100 / 80-120 / 100-0 km/h	8,5 s (est) / (7,5 s (est) / n.d.
Type ess. / ville / autoroute	Ordinaire / 12,8 / 9 l/100 km

DANS LA MÊME CATÉGORIE

Chrysler Town & Country, Dodge Grand Caravan, Honda Odyssey, Kia Sedona, Nissan Quest, Volkswagen Routan

DU NOUVEAU EN 2011

Nouveau modèle

NOS IMPRESSIONS

Agrément de conduite :	■■■■■■■□□□ 7/10
Fiabilité :	nouveau modèle
Sécurité :	■■■■■■■■□□ 8/10
Qualités hivernales :	■■■■■■■■□□ 8/10
Espace intérieur :	■■■■■■■■□□ 8/10
Confort :	■■■■■■■■□□ 8/10

www.toyota.ca

Plus d'informations dans la section statistiques en dernière partie du Guide

ÉLÉGANTE, POLYVALENTE CONFORTABLE

Depuis son lancement à l'automne 2008, la Venza jouit d'une grande popularité auprès du public. D'ailleurs, lors des premiers mois de sa mise en marché, il fallait être très patient pour obtenir le modèle voulu. Dans certains cas, on a parlé d'une liste d'attente. Ce qui est intéressant avec le ce véhicule, c'est qu'il ne s'agit pas de la refonte d'un modèle existant et populaire, mais d'un tout nouveau modèle. La réputation de Toyota en fait de qualité et de fiabilité a certainement joué pour mousser cette popularité, mais le véhicule a des mérites qui lui sont propres.

En effet, les designers se sont sentis plus inspirés que la moyenne et nous ont proposé un véhicule d'une rare élégance, surtout de la part de Toyota. Mieux encore, ces lignes ont servi d'inspiration aux concepteurs de la Sienna. D'ailleurs, lorsqu'on croise une Venza sur la route, on est toujours impressionné par son élégance et ce plus de deux ans après son lancement.

CALANDRE ET LIGNES FUYANTES

Avant de parler du design lui-même, il faut situer la Venza sur le marché. Certains affirment qu'il s'agit d'une version familiale de la Camry tandis que d'autres disent que c'est une variante de la Sienna. Quoi qu'il en soit, elle possède une capacité de chargement presque similaire à une fourgonnette et sa carrosserie l'apparente à une familiale. Généralement, dans les deux cas, la silhouette est passablement anonyme alors que le caractère pratique du véhicule a eu le dessus sur l'élégance des lignes. Cette fois, on a réussi à combiner les deux. En fait, l'élément majeur de cette présentation esthétique est la grille de calandre très large et chromée qui surplombe un pare-chocs assez imposant. Lorsqu'on croise une Venza sur la route, c'est la calandre qu'on remarque immédiatement. Par ailleurs, les lignes fuyantes des parois latérales apportent beaucoup de dynamisme au véhicule dont la partie arrière est inclinée vers l'avant afin de donner un caractère plus sportif. Toutefois, cette coquetterie à l'arrière réduit quelque peu la capacité de chargement. Mais comme on a eu la bonne idée de ne pas inclure une troisième rangée de sièges, l'espace de chargement est très généreux, que la banquette arrière soit repliée ou pas. En fait, si elle avait des portes coulissantes, la Sienna n'aurait aucune raison d'être.

DESIGN, DESIGN, QUAND TU NOUS TIENS !

En effet, après avoir réalisé un extérieur dynamique et moderne, les stylistes ont également visé juste avec la planche de bord. Il est vrai que la console centrale est large et empiète sur l'espace des occupants avant, mais c'est élégant, pratique et innovateur. Un sérieux bémol cependant pour la qualité des plastiques qui sont d'une rare dureté. On se croirait aux pires jours de General Motors! Idem pour le tissu des sièges qui est lui aussi désappointant en raison de sa texture et de ses motifs.

FEU VERT
- Silhouette élégante
- Bon choix de moteurs
- Bonne habitabilité
- Tenue de route moyenne
- Nombreux espaces de rangement

FEU ROUGE
- Plastiques trop durs
- Direction trop engourdie
- Agrément de conduite mitigé
- Roulis en virage
- Certaines options onéreuses

Comme c'est la coutume chez Toyota, les cadrans indicateurs sont de type électroluminescent et leur consultation est très facile. Parlant de simplicité, les commandes de climatisation et du système audio en font la preuve. Par contre, si un écran d'information affiche les images de la caméra de recul lorsqu'on est en marche arrière, ledit écran est tellement petit qu'il est difficile à consulter.

MOTEURS ADÉQUATS

Il est vrai que Toyota ne fabrique pas les véhicules les plus excitants à conduire et que leur tenue de route est souvent dans la moyenne. C'est exactement le cas de la Venza. En revanche, en conduite normale, on peut critiquer la souplesse de la suspension, mais son comportement général est dans la bonne moyenne à défaut d'être enivrant. Néanmoins, avec des pneus de 20 pouces, la suspension est plus ferme mais la tenue de route meilleure.

Cela dit, les moteurs proposés sont non seulement excellents, mais bien adaptés au véhicule. Pour plusieurs, un moteur quatre cylindres n'a pas sa place dans une auto de cette grosseur. Mais il suffit de piloter la Venza propulsée par le quatre cylindres de 2,7 litres développant 182 chevaux pour se convaincre du contraire. Associé à une transmission automatique à six rapports fort efficace, il conviendra dans la plupart des cas. Il est même possible de commander la traction intégrale avec ce groupe propulseur. Donc, pas besoin de commander tout le catalogue des options et le moteur V6 pour obtenir la transmission intégrale. Celle-ci ne fait jamais sentir sa présence et son opération est transparente.

Bien entendu, le V6 de 3,5 litres de 268 chevaux est doux, silencieux et relativement économique en carburant. Il sera choisi par ceux qui doivent rouler avec plusieurs passagers et leurs bagages sur une base très fréquente ou encore pour remorquer une roulotte ne dépassant pas 1 587 kg, la capacité maximale de remorquage.

Sur la grande route, cette Toyota est idéale pour effectuer de longs voyages en famille. Son confort, son silence de roulement et les multiples espaces de rangement dans l'habitacle se feront appréciés au fil des kilomètres. C'est probablement ce que Toyota a réussi de mieux depuis belle lurette.

Denis Duquet

PHOTOS : TOYOTA

Catégorie	Multisegment
Échelle de prix	28 900 $ à 32 050 $ (2010)
Garanties	3 ans/60 000 km, 5 ans/100 000 km
Assemblage	Georgetown, Kentucky, É-U
Cote d'assurance	n.d.

CHÂSSIS - DONNÉES POUR V6 AWD

Emp/lon/lar/haut	2 775/4 800/1 905/1 610 mm
Coffre	870 à 1 990 litres
Réservoir	67 litres
Nombre coussins sécurité	7
Antipatinage / contrôle stabilité	oui / oui
Suspension avant	indépendante, jambes de force
Suspension arrière	indépendante, jambes de force
Freins avant / arrière	disque (ABS) / disque (ABS)
Direction	à crémaillère, assistée
Diamètre de braquage	11,9 m
Pneus avant / arrière	P245/50R20 / P245/50R20
Poids	1 835 kg
Capacité de remorquage	1 587 kg (3 498 lb)

COMPOSANTES MÉCANIQUES

Base, Base AWD	
Cylindrée, soupapes, alim.	4L 2,7 litres 16 s atmos.
Puissance / Couple	182 chevaux / 182 lb-pi
Tr. base (opt) / rouage base (opt)	A6 / Tr (Int)
0-100 / 80-120 / 100-0 km/h	10,5 s / 7,5 s / 42,1 m
Type ess. / ville / autoroute	Ordinaire / 10,2 / 7,1 l/100 km

V6, V6 AWD	
Cylindrée, soupapes, alim.	V6 3,5 litres 24 s atmos.
Puissance / Couple	268 chevaux / 246 lb-pi
Tr. base (opt) / rouage base (opt)	A6 / Tr (Int)
0-100 / 80-120 / 100-0 km/h	8,4 s / 6,8 s / 43 m (est)
Type ess. / ville / autoroute	Ordinaire / 11,5 / 7,9 l/100 km

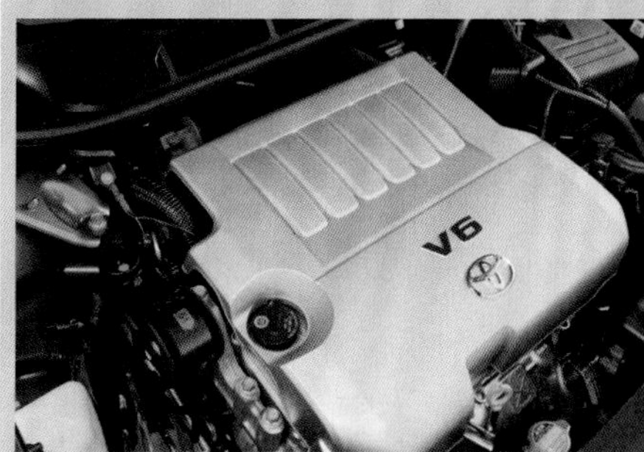

DANS LA MÊME CATÉGORIE

Dodge Journey, Ford Edge, Hyundai Santa Fe, Mazda CX-7, Mitsubishi Endeavor, Nissan Murano

DU NOUVEAU EN 2011

Aucun changement majeur

NOS IMPRESSIONS

Agrément de conduite :	6/10
Fiabilité :	8/10
Sécurité :	10/10
Qualités hivernales :	8/10
Espace intérieur :	8/10
Confort :	8/10

www.toyota.ca

Plus d'informations dans la section statistiques en dernière partie du Guide

SUPRÉMATIE DISPARUE

***Ouch*! Les nouvelles sous-compactes Mazda2 et Ford Fiesta qui s'amènent cette année feront mal à la Toyota Yaris. Celle qui a pratiquement lancé la mode des petites autos il y a cinq ans devra vitement se mettre à la page, tant mécaniquement que technologiquement. Et en attendant sa nouvelle génération, la Yaris perd dramatiquement de sa suprématie.**

L'avantage principal de la Toyota Yaris, c'est ses possibles configurations: berline quatre portes, ainsi qu'à hayon trois et cinq portes. C'est plus élargi versus la nouvelle Mazda2 qui ne vient qu'en *hatchback*, la Hyundai Accent qui ne propose pas de cinq portes, la Nissan Versa qui n'a pas la trois-portes et la Honda Fit qui n'offre pas de berline. Par contre, la Yaris est l'une des plus petites du marché et ça se sent dans sa capacité de chargement réduite. Plusieurs de vos effets personnels ne tiendront pas à bord.

L'UNE DES PLUS PETITES PUISSANCES DE L'HEURE

À part la Smart, c'est la Yaris qui dispose de la moins puissante motorisation du marché et ça se traduit par des accélérations poussives, à la limite du rugueux. Le petit moteur quatre cylindres de 1,5 litre ne développe que 106 chevaux et même si la voiture est un poids-plume (moins de 1 100 kilos en ordre de marche), reste que ça manque vite d'énergie. Si vous le pouvez, privilégiez la boîte manuelle cinq vitesses, elle transige mieux la petite vigueur que l'automatique – à condition de ne pas lésiner sur la rétrogradation. Si le haut levier souffre de tendances agricoles et d'engrenages trop lâches, sa souplesse le rend parfait pour celui ou celle qui fait l'apprentissage « standard ». Si vous ne conduisez que les transmissions automatiques, eh bien, vous en serez quitte pour un essoufflement rapide. Reste que le passage des quatre rapports (la Ford Fiesta en a six...!) s'effectue en douceur et que la consommation en carburant n'est guère plus élevée qu'avec la manuelle.

Question d'économiser encore davantage sur l'essence, la petite Toyota compte sur une direction électrique qui, malheureusement, livre bien peu de connexion avec la route. La manœuvre flotte en son centre et à haute vitesse sur l'autoroute, on cherche ses références. La contrepartie est un excellent rayon de braquage – sans doute le plus petit de toute industrie – et ça facilite les déplacements en stationnement.

Comme à peu près toutes les sous-compactes, la Yaris mise sur une poutre de torsion en guise de suspension arrière, ce qui lui procure une tenue de route un brin sautillante. Rien de bien désagréable, mais on doit quand même y aller mollo, puisque la petite a tendance à se déporter, surtout la variante à hayon— moins longue et d'empattement plus court que la berline.

EN PERTE DE VITESSE

La Yaris aura eu le mérite de nous prouver, à son arrivée sur le marché en 2005, que les petits pots pouvaient effectivement receler les

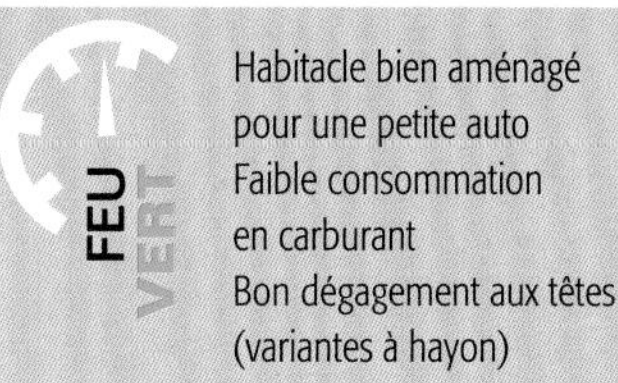

FEU VERT

Habitacle bien aménagé pour une petite auto
Faible consommation en carburant
Bon dégagement aux têtes (variantes à hayon)

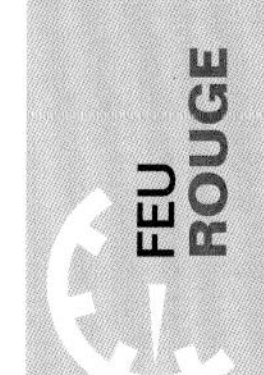

FEU ROUGE

Dégagement aux jambes arrière limité
N'est plus dans le coup
L'une des plus petites puissances du marché
Direction électrique sans substance

meilleurs onguents. Malgré ses petites dimensions, la voiture proposait (et propose encore) un habitacle bien aménagé, parsemé de bons rangements et un généreux dégagement aux têtes (pour les variantes à hayon qui bénéficient d'un pavillon plus haut).

Mais depuis, la concurrence a évolué (et comment!). Et à plusieurs chapitres, la Yaris ne tient plus le haut du pavé, loin de là. Ainsi, les plastiques intérieurs sont bon marché, pas toujours d'assemblage serré et le volant non télescopique donne du fil à retordre dans les tentatives pour dénicher la bonne position de conduite. Les sièges avant, peu enveloppants, manquent de support. L'instrumentation, placée au centre de la planche de bord, ne tombe pas naturellement sous les yeux, mais on s'habitue vite et il faut dire qu'avec à peine deux ou trois commandes (bon, peut-être quatre…) à manipuler, on trouve facilement qu'est-ce qui fait quoi. L'insonorisation est moyenne et les places à la banquette sont limitées pour les moyennes et grandes jambes. À ce sujet, on peut accommoder ses passagers arrière avec la Yaris RS, la seule à proposer la banquette qui s'avance et se recule (les dossiers s'inclinent, aussi).

Parlons un peu de cette variante RS (uniquement à hayon cinq-portes) pour souligner ses autres atouts: elle est la seule à offrir, de série, la climatisation, l'accueil sans clé et les phares antibrouillards. Elle est également plus jolie avec ses éléments visuels sportifs – notez cependant que l'habit ne fait pas le moine, côté motorisation, et qu'aucun cheval-vapeur additionnel n'est malheureusement envisagé.

Cela dit, la RS se détaille à un prix d'étiquette (tout juste sous les 20 000$...) qui fait qu'on a férocement envie de regarder ailleurs. Vous vous dites que la version de base de la Yaris, sous les 14 000$, fera bien l'affaire? *Tut,tut,tut*: cette dernière est particulièrement dépouillée et d'y ajouter la banquette 60/40 et le groupe électrique fait allègrement grimper la facture. Pour la même somme, la Hyundai Accent offre sièges chauffants et toit ouvrant…

Bref, devant une concurrence de plus en plus pimentée et équipée, la Yaris n'est plus la référence et elle devra rapidement s'ajuster, entre autres en rehaussant son expérience de conduite. Parce que pour l'heure, les nouvelles Mazda2 et Ford Fiesta en jettent autrement plus…

Nadine Filion

PHOTOS: TOYOTA

Catégorie	Berline, *Hatchback*
Échelle de prix	13 620$ à 19 555$ (2010)
Garanties	3 ans/60 000 km, 5 ans/100 000 km
Assemblage	Nagakusa, Japon
Cote d'assurance	passable

CHÂSSIS - DONNÉES POUR LE 5 PORTES *HATCHBACK*

Emp/lon/lar/haut	2 460/3 825/1 695/1 525 mm
Coffre	228 à 728 litres
Réservoir	42 litres
Nombre coussins sécurité	2
Antipatinage / contrôle stabilité	oui / oui
Suspension avant	indépendante, jambes de force
Suspension arrière	indépendante, barres de torsion
Freins avant / arrière	disque (ABS) / tambour (ABS)
Direction	à crémaillère, assistée
Diamètre de braquage	9,4 m
Pneus avant / arrière	P185/60R15 / P185/60R15
Poids	1050 kg
Capacité de remorquage	318 kg (701 lb)

COMPOSANTES MÉCANIQUES

CE, LE, RS

Cylindrée, soupapes, alim.	4L 1,5 litre 16 s atmos.
Puissance / Couple	106 chevaux / 103 lb-pi
Tr. base (opt) / rouage base (opt)	M5 (A4) / Tr
0-100 / 80-120 / 100-0 km/h	9,4 s / 7,7 s / 41,8 m
Type ess. / ville / autoroute	Ordinaire / 6,9 / 5,5 l/100 km

DANS LA MÊME CATÉGORIE

Chevrolet Aveo, Ford Fiesta, Honda Fit, Hyundai Accent, Kia Rio/Rio5, Mazda2, Nissan Versa, Suzuki Swift+

DU NOUVEAU EN 2011

Contrôle de la stabilité offert en option sur versions CE (3 portes) et LE (5 portes), régulateur de vitesse de série sur version RS

NOS IMPRESSIONS

Agrément de conduite:	7/10
Fiabilité:	10/10
Sécurité:	8/10
Qualités hivernales:	7/10
Espace intérieur:	7/10
Confort:	6/10

www.toyota.ca

Plus d'informations dans la section statistiques en dernière partie du Guide

UN CABRIOLET AVEC TOIT OUVRANT!

Les ingénieurs allemands ne sont pas des suiveurs. Ils ne se préoccupent pas tellement de ce que fait la concurrence et apportent des solutions techniques et mécaniques originales qui font souvent école. Prenez cette Volkswagen cabriolet par exemple. Depuis des lunes, ce constructeur nous a habitués à des toits souples en toile qui, une fois repliés, prennent beaucoup de place car ils sont isolés est donc très épais. Dans le cas qui nous concerne, on parle d'un toit rigide… rétractable!

Oui, je sais, il existe d'autres modèles semblables avec toit rigide qui se replie dans le coffre. Mais, chez Volkswagen, on a ajouté une petite touche d'exclusivité puisqu'on a installé un toit ouvrant. Ainsi, les amateurs de plein air et de soleil peuvent tout de même se payer un bol d'air lorsque la température extérieure est trop froide pour abaisser le toit. Vous avouerez que c'est une solution passablement songée.

PARI RÉUSSI

Il y a une couple d'années, l'auteur de ces lignes avait fait réagir les relationnistes de la compagnie en soulignant qu'il fallait être passablement effronté pour commercialiser une voiture dotée d'un toit mécanique aussi complexe alors que cela avait pris quelques décennies pour assurer la fiabilité de simples commutateurs de feux de route. Pour me convaincre que la fiabilité pouvait être à nouveau associée à Volkswagen, j'avais eu droit à un essai de quelques semaines non pas d'une Eos mais de la Golf V de l'époque. Et l'essai avait été concluant.

Quoi qu'il en soit, ce toit infiniment complexe n'a pas connu les ennuis que l'on craignait. Il se déploie ou se replie en peu de temps et son mécanisme semble ne pas tellement faillir à la tâche. Mais fut un temps ou l'étanchéité était un problème, toutefois, un essai réalisé récemment m'a permis de sortir du lave-auto sans que l'eau se soit infiltrée dans l'habitacle. Youpi!

Vraiment, les stylistes ont réussi ce qui n'est pas toujours facile avec les cabriolets à toit rigide: assurer une belle silhouette. Celle de l'Eos est toujours jolie, que le toit soit remisé ou en place. Par contre, comme tous les autres modèles de ce genre, la présence de ces panneaux de tôle repliés dans le coffre diminue drôlement la capacité de chargement. On peut facilement compenser en posant les bagages sur les sièges arrière puisque ceux-ci sont assez peu accueillants pour des humains… De plus, si vous installez le déflecteur afin de réduire le tourbillonnement de l'air dans l'habitacle, ces places deviennent carrément inutiles. Cette solution un peu bébête vient compenser pour le côté brillant du toit rigide avec son toit ouvrant en prime. Celles d'en avant sont beaucoup mieux réussies avec des sièges à la fois fermes et confortables. Plusieurs personnes ont de la difficulté à croire que des sièges si fermes puissent être confortables à long terme. C'est pourtant vrai, d'autant plus que le support latéral est

FEU VERT

- Esthétique réussie
- Agrément de conduite
- Moteur performant
- Boîte DSG
- Finition impeccable

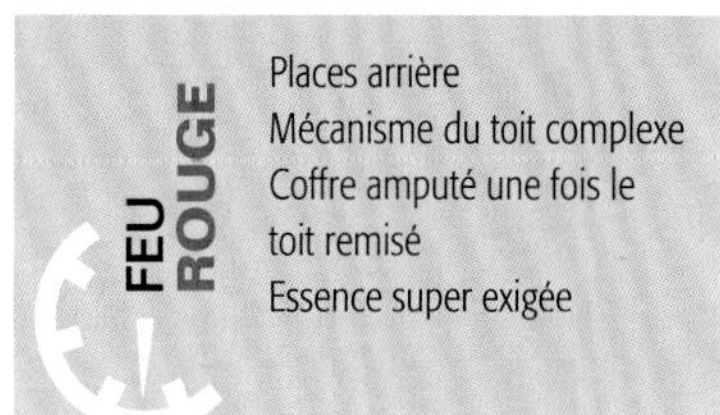

FEU ROUGE

- Places arrière
- Mécanisme du toit complexe
- Coffre amputé une fois le toit remisé
- Essence super exigée

supérieur à la moyenne de cette catégorie. Comme tout produit Volkswagen, la qualité des matériaux et de l'assemblage est à souligner. Comme il se doit, la sobriété est de mise avec un volant à trois branches, très dépouillé. Les deux cadrans indicateurs cerclés de chrome et avec chiffres blancs sur fond noir sont faciles à lire. La console centrale comprend un centre d'information qui permet de régler les différentes fonctions de la voiture, notamment le système audio.

SIMPLICITÉ ET EFFICACITÉ

Souvent, on retrouve des véhicules dotés de trois groupes propulseurs, mais aucun d'entre eux n'est à la hauteur de la tâche. Chez Volkswagen, on préfère n'offrir qu'un seul moteur, mais un bon. Il s'agit de l'incontournable moteur quatre cylindres 2,0 litres turbo d'une puissance de 200 chevaux. Il est livré de série avec une boîte manuelle à six rapports tandis qu'une boîte DSG à double embrayage est optionnelle.

Je ne veux pas faire de peine aux amateurs de transmission manuelle, mais bien que celle de l'Eos soit efficace et bien étagée, question agrément de conduite et efficacité, elle doit s'incliner devant la boîte DSG qui effectue le passage des rapports avec célérité et transparence. De plus, ce moteur ne faillit jamais à la tâche. En effet, le temps de réponse du turbocompresseur est quasiment nul et la ligne de couple est tellement bien étudiée, que le moteur réagit à la moindre sollicitation de l'accélérateur. Vous voulez accélérer, tout simplement? Appuyez sur l'accélérateur et la voiture bondit comme si l'on avait affaire à un moteur plus puissant.

Mais il n'y a pas que le moteur qui soit digne de mention sur ce cabriolet. Puisqu'il s'agit d'une plate-forme empruntée à la Jetta, il n'est pas surprenant de constater que la tenue de route soit de qualité supérieure. Trop souvent, les cabriolets nous déçoivent à ce chapitre en raison d'une plate-forme trop souple qui ne parvient pas à compenser l'amputation du toit. L'utilisation d'un toit fixe aide à la rigidité. Mais même lorsque ce dernier est remisé dans le coffre, cette Volkswagen est capable de faire plaisir aux conducteurs qui apprécient les voitures dynamiques.

Bien entendu, ce petit bijou germanique est accompagné d'une étiquette de prix assez corsée tandis que la fiabilité, même si elle a fait d'énormes progrès au cours des dernières années, n'est pas tout à fait à la hauteur de la concurrence.

Denis Duquet

PHOTOS : VOLKSWAGEN

Catégorie	Cabriolet
Échelle de prix	36 575 $ à 43 375 $
Garanties	4 ans/80 000 km, 5 ans/100 000 km
Assemblage	Setubal, Portugal
Cote d'assurance	bonne

CHÂSSIS - DONNÉES POUR 2.0 TSI HIGHLINE

Emp/lon/lar/haut	2 578/4 410/1 791/1 443 mm
Coffre	187 à 297 litres
Réservoir	55 litres
Nombre coussins sécurité	4
Antipatinage / contrôle stabilité	oui / oui
Suspension avant	indépendante, jambes de force
Suspension arrière	indépendante, multibras
Freins avant / arrière	disque (ABS) / disque (ABS)
Direction	à crémaillère, ass. variable
Diamètre de braquage	10,9 m
Pneus avant / arrière	P235/45R17 / P235/45R17
Poids	1 590 kg
Capacité de remorquage	n.d.

COMPOSANTES MÉCANIQUES

2.0 TSI Comfortline, 2.0 TSI Highline

Cylindrée, soupapes, alim.	4L 2,0 litres 16 s turbocompressé
Puissance / Couple	200 chevaux / 207 lb-pi
Tr. base (opt) / rouage base (opt)	M6 (A6) / Tr
0-100 / 80-120 / 100-0 km/h	7,9 s / 5,8 s / 40,3 m
Type ess. / ville / autoroute	Super / 10,0 / 6,6 l/100 km

DANS LA MÊME CATÉGORIE

BMW Série 1, Chrysler Sebring, Ford Mustang, MINI Cooper, Mitsubishi Eclipse

DU NOUVEAU EN 2011

Nouveau système audio, nouvelles couleurs remplacent certaines anciennes

NOS IMPRESSIONS

Agrément de conduite :	7/10
Fiabilité :	6/10
Sécurité :	10/10
Qualités hivernales :	7/10
Espace intérieur :	7/10
Confort :	7/10

WWW.VW.CA

Plus d'informations dans la section statistiques en dernière partie du Guide

UNE FAMILLE DE SURDOUÉES

Au cours de la dernière année, la Volkswagen Golf a mérité une pléthore de titres prestigieux, notamment celui de la voiture mondiale de l'année. Et pour une fois, ce constructeur semble définitivement être sérieux en ce qui concerne le marché nord-américain. La gamme de modèles est plus étoffée, on s'est débarrassé de l'embarrassante désignation Rabbit et on retrouve même une familiale.

HATCHBACK ET FAMILIALE

Puisque la gamme Golf offerte sur notre marché comporte trois modèles, nous allons décliner notre présentation en deux parties. La première cible surtout la version trois et cinq portes avec le moteur 4 cylindres de 2,5 litres tandis que nous consacrerons une section à part pour la fabuleuse GTi. Peu importe le modèle, la gamme a été entièrement revue au cours des 12 derniers mois. La Rabbit nous a quittés, la Golf est de retour. Comme il se doit, cette nouvelle cuvée est une évolution de la version précédente. Les deux se ressemblent passablement même s'il y a plusieurs modifications concernant l'esthétique et la planche de bord, mais ce qu'il faut retenir, c'est l'excellence de la finition de l'habitacle et la qualité des matériaux. De plus, l'ergonomie de cette allemande est exemplaire avec une disposition logique des commandes, une bonne position de conduite et un repose-pied accueillant. Mais il faut apporter un sérieux bémol pour les commandes du système de ventilation, notamment celles du système équipant les versions moins cossues. Il est très difficile de savoir à quel mode nous avons réglé la climatisation et à quel degré. Ce qui est curieux car les ingénieurs de la marque ont une excellente réputation en fait d'ergonomie et de commandes.

Le moteur à essence de 2,5 litres développe 170 chevaux et il est associé de série à une boîte manuelle à six rapports dont l'étagement est pratiquement sans reproche. Vous pouvez commander en option une boîte automatique à six rapports de type à double embrayage. Cette transmission DSG fait l'unanimité par son efficacité et réussit à convaincre les irréductibles de la boîte manuelle aux charmes de cette automatique surdouée Ce groupe propulseur est un plaisir à utiliser, peu importe la transmission choisie. Comme sur la plupart des Volkswagen, c'est le pilote qui contrôle la voiture et non pas la voiture qui commande. La direction est imprécise et l'assistance fort bien dosée. Quant aux sièges avant, ils fournissent un bon support latéral. Comme le veut la tradition, ils sont également très fermes, mais leur confort est surprenant. Par contre, les places arrière, sont moins confortables et l'espace y est quelque peu limité.

La familiale n'exhibe pas la même silhouette élégante que les modèles trois et cinq portes. C'est sobre, moderne, mais elle ne fait pas tourner les têtes. Le modèle de base propose le même moteur à essence de 2,5 litres que sur les hatchback trois et cinq portes. Et comme ces derniers, il est possible de commander le moteur 2,0 litres TDI. Grâce à son turbocompresseur et l'injection directe, sa puissance est de 140 chevaux mais c'est son

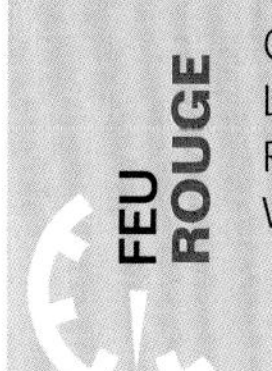

FEU VERT
- Moteurs impressionnants
- Économie du diesel
- Agrément de conduite
- Construction solide
- Tenue de route
- Qualité de fabrication

FEU ROUGE
- Certaines commandes à revoir
- Large console centrale
- Rapports de boîte manuelle
- Versions huppées onéreuses

couple de 236 lb-pi qui fait toute la différence. En effet, les accélérations ont du mordant, les reprises sont impressionnantes et c'est un moteur idéal pour la conduite urbaine. De plus, bonne nouvelle, sa consommation est inférieure à 7 litres/100 km.

LA SUBLIME GTI

Cette voiture est douée comme ce n'est pas possible. En effet, elle a raflé plusieurs titres importants et prestigieux hors du pays, en plus d'être nommée voiture de l'année par l'AJAC (Association des journalistes automobiles du Canada). Bref, rares sont les voitures à caractère sportif qui ont un tel agrément de conduite en plus d'être infiniment pratiques.

Sa plate-forme très rigide et une suspension fort bien calibrée s'associent pour tirer le meilleur parti du moteur quatre cylindres turbo d'une puissance de 200 chevaux travaillant de concert avec une boîte manuelle à six rapports qui est un plaisir à utiliser. Si vous optez pour l'automatique, vous ne serez pas en reste car la transmission DSG en a converti plus d'un aux vertus des boîtes automatiques.

Bien entendu, l'équipement de la GTi est un peu plus étoffé, et le prix demandé est assez élevé aux yeux de certains. Mais il faut relativiser et la comparer aux autres versions plus performantes d'autres modèles compacts pour constater que Volkswagen vend un produit dont le prix est à la mesure de la concurrence.

Le plus important dans ce modèle, c'est sa qualité de conduite, son impressionnante tenue de route en plus du *feedback* de la route. Il est difficile de trouver une voiture de ce prix — et même de prix beaucoup plus élevé — qui permet une pareille communication avec la route et un tel agrément de conduite. Après tout, ces prix et tous ces accessits ne sont pas le fruit du hasard ou d'une vaste campagne promotionnelle de la part du constructeur ! Si la voiture est agréable à conduire, certaines particularités propres à la plupart des Volkswagen auront pour effet d'en irriter plusieurs. Quelques boutons et commandes, un régulateur de vitesse à revoir et même une console centrale qui pourrait être redessinée, voilà autant de petits éléments qui seraient à corriger.

Denis Duquet

PHOTOS : MARC LACHAPELLE

VOLKSWAGEN GOLF

Catégorie	Familiale, *Hatchback*
Échelle de prix	20 175 $ à 30 475 $ (2010)
Garanties	4 ans/80 000 km, 5 ans/100 000 km
Assemblage	Wolfsburg, Allemagne
Cote d'assurance	passable

CHÂSSIS - DONNÉES POUR 2.0 TDI HIGHLINE FAMILIALE

Emp/lon/lar/haut	2 578/4 556/1 781/1 504 mm
Coffre	929 à 1 897 litres
Réservoir	55 litres
Nombre coussins sécurité	6
Antipatinage / contrôle stabilité	oui / oui
Suspension avant	indépendante, jambes de force
Suspension arrière	indépendante, multibras
Freins avant / arrière	disque (ABS) / disque (ABS)
Direction	à crémaillère, ass. variable
Diamètre de braquage	10,9 m
Pneus avant / arrière	P205/55R16 / P205/55R16
Poids	1 484 kg
Capacité de remorquage	n.d.

COMPOSANTES MÉCANIQUES

2.0 TDI

Cylindrée, soupapes, alim.	4L 2,0 litres 16 s turbo
Puissance / Couple	140 chevaux / 236 lb-pi
Tr. base (opt) / rouage base (opt)	M5 (A6) / Tr
0-100 / 80-120 / 100-0 km/h	10,2 s / 7,4 s / 43,0 m
Type ess. / ville / autoroute	Diesel / 6,7 / 4,7 l/100 km

2.5

Cylindrée, soupapes, alim.	5L 2,5 litres 20 s atmos.
Puissance / Couple	170 chevaux / 177 lb-pi
Tr. base (opt) / rouage base (opt)	M5 (A6) / Tr
0-100 / 80-120 / 100-0 km/h	9,2 s / 7,0 s / 43,5 m
Type ess. / ville / autoroute	Ordinaire / 10,4 / 7 l/100 km

GTI

Cylindrée, soupapes, alim.	4L 2,0 litres 16 s turbo
Puissance / Couple	200 chevaux / 207 lb-pi
Tr. base (opt) / rouage base (opt)	M6 (A6) / Tr
0-100 / 80-120 / 100-0 km/h	6,9 s / 4,6 s / 42,8 m
Type ess. / ville / autoroute	Super / 10,0 / 6,6 l/100 km

DANS LA MÊME CATÉGORIE

Chevrolet Cruze, Dodge Caliber, Ford Focus, Honda Civic, Kia Forte, Mazda3, Mitsubishi Lancer, Nissan Sentra, Subaru Impreza, Suzuki SX-4, Toyota Corolla, Toyota Matrix

DU NOUVEAU EN 2011

Nouveau système audio, contrôle de stabilité inclut différentiel verrouillable électronique

NOS IMPRESSIONS

Agrément de conduite :	9/10
Fiabilité :	7/10
Sécurité :	8/10
Qualités hivernales :	8/10
Espace intérieur :	8/10
Confort :	8/10

www.vw.ca

Plus d'informations dans la section statistiques en dernière partie du Guide

REFAIRE SA VIE

Pour beaucoup de gens, la vie n'est pas un long fleuve tranquille et il arrive un moment où il faut prendre des décisions qui auront une incidence pour le reste de leurs jours. Il en va de même pour certaines voitures. La Jetta par exemple. Depuis ses tout débuts, il s'agissait d'une Golf dotée d'un coffre. Elle se positionnait ainsi une toute petite coche au-dessus de la Golf. Mais en dévoilant le modèle 2011, Volkswagen annonce qu'il en sera dorénavant bien autrement…

La marque de Wolfsburg (Allemagne) ne cache pas vouloir devenir le plus important constructeur d'automobiles au monde d'ici 2018. Il y a quelques années, une telle annonce aurait fait s'écrouler de rire la population mais c'est loin d'être le cas aujourd'hui. Après tout, Volkswagen est propriétaire, entre autres, de Seat, Audi et Skoda. Certaines autres marques du groupe Volkswagen (Bentley, Lamborghini, Bugatti et plus récemment Porsche) ne vendent pas beaucoup d'unités annuellement mais elles apportent une expertise technique qui ne peut être ignorée.

Quoiqu'il en soit, pour atteindre son but, Volkswagen doit prendre des décisions dès maintenant, question de mieux se positionner pour le futur. Ces décisions touchent principalement, et pour l'instant, la nouvelle Jetta, créée spécialement pour répondre aux goûts de l'Amérique. Il faut savoir que cette berline n'a jamais connu beaucoup de succès en Europe où la Golf demeure la Volks la plus vendue. En Amérique, c'est le contraire… sauf au Québec mais, on le sait, nous sommes distincts… Donc, pour mieux dissocier la Jetta de la Golf et de créer une voiture pouvant se battre à armes égales avec les compactes que sont les Honda Civic, Hyundai Elantra, Toyota Corolla, Mazda3 et autres, Volkswagen a pris la décision, sans doute difficile, de faire de la Jetta une voiture d'entrée de gamme.

LES CIVIC, MAZDA3 ET COROLLA DANS LA MIRE

Avec un prix de base de 15 875 $, on peut déjà parler de sérieuse concurrence aux valeurs établies mentionnées plus haut. Elle s'avère même moins chère que la Jetta City (qui, de toute évidence, n'est plus proposée) et, surtout, elle est plus abordable que la Golf la moins dispendieuse de plus de 4 000 $. C'est du repositionnement ça, monsieur !

Bien entendu, pour offrir une voiture sous les 16 000 $, Volks a dû couper un peu… Oubliez le climatiseur, le verrouillage central et les sièges chauffants. Cependant, l'équipement demeure quand même intéressant : Banquette arrière rabattable 60/40, six coussins gonflables, vitres électriques et volant télescopique font partie de la dotation de base.

PLUS ÇI, MOINS ÇA…

Cette nouvelle Jetta se permet non seulement d'être moins chère que l'ancienne, elle est aussi plus imposante ! Toutes les dimensions ont gagné en dimensions. Par exemple, l'empattement s'allonge sur 7,3 cm de plus que l'ancien modèle. Puisque la longueur totale a augmenté d'autant, ce sont les places arrière qui en bénéficient le plus.

Les Allemands sont peu réputés pour leur excentricité et ce n'est pas la nouvelle Jetta qui y changera quoi que ce soit! Les lignes sont d'une sobriété toute germanique, à la limite de l'ennui, malgré une classe certaine. La partie arrière pourrait même être facilement prise pour celle d'une A4. Cette ligne élégante devrait bien vieillir.

Une voiture nouvelle, plus grande et mieux équipée pour moins cher. Bravo ! Mais si vous êtes propriétaire d'une Jetta 2009 ou 2010, par exemple, vous perdrez lorsque reviendra le temps de la revente…

Quiconque a déjà monté à bord d'un produit Volkswagen ne sera pas dépaysé en prenant place à bord. Par rapport à la génération précédente, l'espace habitable est plus grand et la qualité des matériaux, même si elle n'est pas optimale, s'avère fort relevée compte tenu du prix demandé. Aussi, il faudrait être de mauvaise foi pour dénigrer la qualité de la fabrication. Les sièges, d'une fermeté toute allemande, sont confortables même après plusieurs heures. La position de conduite se trouve en un clin d'œil, merci au volant inclinable et télescopique et au siège du conducteur ajustable en hauteur de série sur tous les modèles. Les jauges, dans la plus pure tradition Volkswagen, sont faciles à lire mais, comme le veut malheureusement la tendance, on n'y retrouve pas de jauge de température du moteur. Vous me direz que les moteurs d'aujourd'hui ne surchauffent plus et vous avez raison… aujourd'hui. En sera-t-il de même dans cinq ou dix ans quand la voiture aura atteint un âge vénérable ?

S'il est (et a toujours été) un élément impressionnant dans la Jetta, c'est son coffre, qu'il faut décrire en termes cosmologiques plutôt qu'en vulgaires petits litres !

MÉCANIQUE CONNUE

Côté mécanique, on va du désenchantement au rêve. On commence par le sempiternel et désuet quatre cylindres de 2,0 litres de 115 chevaux qui officiait dans les Golf et Jetta City. Nous n'avons pas pu en faire l'essai lors de notre prise en main de la voiture à peine quelques jours avant la date de tombée du Guide 2011 mais d'après nos expériences précédentes, et puisqu'il n'a pas changé d'un iota, nous croyons qu'il s'agit d'un bon moteur de base qui satisfera les gens à la recherche d'un moyen de transport du point A au point B, peut-être même jusqu'à C. Il se marie de série à une manuelle à cinq rapports ou, en option, à une automatique qui en compte autant.

L'autre moteur est le cinq cylindres de 2,5 litres qui, lui aussi, prenait place dans la dernière génération. C'est ce moteur qui équipait toutes les Jetta lors du lancement international. Avec ses 170 chevaux, il est mieux équipé que le 2,0 litres pour affronter la vie et les accélérations intempestives. Néanmoins, sa sonorité en accélération n'est pas des plus réjouissantes. Encore une fois, la manuelle à cinq rapports ou l'automatique à six sont au rendez-vous. Les amateurs de Volkswagen retrouvent donc deux boîtes qu'ils connaissent déjà bien et dont le fonctionnement est irréprochable. Ce moteur consomme certes un peu plus que le 2,0 litres mais la différence n'est pas très marquée.

Lors du lancement de la Jetta, vers la fin septembre 2010, la version TDI sera aussi proposée. Adulée de tous les amateurs

de Volkswagen et de diesel (deux mots qui vont de pair), cette mécanique compte sur un couple très élevé (236 lb-pi) pour se démarquer. Avec une consommation d'à peine 6,7 litres/100 km en ville et de 4,6 sur la route, Volkswagen prévoit une autonomie de plus de 1100 km entre chaque plein. Bien entendu, la plus élémentaire des précautions serait de faire le plein AVANT d'atteindre ce chiffre... Plus tard, Volkswagen proposera une version GLI, plus sportive et luxueuse, qui a toujours connu beaucoup de succès au Québec. Son 2,0 litres turbocompressé de 200 chevaux devrait être satisfaisant...

La direction brille par sa précision et son retour d'informations et le châssis semble d'une solidité à toute épreuve. Par contre, j'ai

Catégorie	Berline
Échelle de prix	15 875 $ à 26 655 $
Garanties	4 ans/80 000 km, 5 ans/100 000 km
Assemblage	Mexique
Cote d'assurance	n.d.

CHÂSSIS - DONNÉES POUR 2.0 TDI

Emp/lon/lar/haut	2 651/4 628/1 778/1 453 mm
Coffre	440 litres
Réservoir	55 litres
Nombre coussins sécurité	6
Antipatinage / contrôle stabilité	oui / oui
Suspension avant	indépendante, jambes de force
Suspension arrière	semi-indépendante, poutre de torsion
Freins avant / arrière	disque (ABS) / disque (ABS)
Direction	à crémaillère, assistée
Diamètre de braquage	n.d.
Pneus avant / arrière	195/65R15 / 195/65R15
Poids	1 434 kg
Capacité de remorquage	n.d.

COMPOSANTES MÉCANIQUES

2.0

Cylindrée, soupapes, alim.	4L 2,0 litres atmos.
Puissance / Couple	115 chevaux / 125 lb-pi
Tr. base (opt) / rouage base (opt)	M5 (A6) / Tr
0-100 / 80-120 / 100-0 km/h	10,1 s / n.d. / n.d.
Type ess. / ville / autoroute	Ordinaire / 9,1 / 6,0 l/100 km

2.0 TDI

Cylindrée, soupapes, alim.	4L 2,0 litres turbocompressé
Puissance / Couple	140 chevaux / 236 lb-pi
Tr. base (opt) / rouage base (opt)	M6 (A6) / Tr
0-100 / 80-120 / 100-0 km/h	9,0 s / n.d. / n.d.
Type ess. / ville / autoroute	Diesel / 6,7 / 4,6 l/100 km

2.5

Cylindrée, soupapes, alim.	5L 2,5 litres atmos.
Puissance / Couple	170 chevaux / 177 lb-pi
Tr. base (opt) / rouage base (opt)	M5 (A6) / Tr
0-100 / 80-120 / 100-0 km/h	8,5 s / n.d. / n.d.
Type ess. / ville / autoroute	Ordinaire / 9,9 / 6,2 l/100 km

DANS LA MÊME CATÉGORIE

Chevrolet Cruze, Ford Focus, Honda Civic, Mazda3, Mitsubishi Lancer, Nissan Sentra, Subaru Impreza, Toyota Corolla

DU NOUVEAU EN 2011

Nouveau modèle

NOS IMPRESSIONS

Agrément de conduite :	■■■■■■■■□□	8/10
Fiabilité :	Nouveau modèle	
Sécurité :	■■■■■■■■□□	8/10
Qualités hivernales :	■■■■■■■■□□	8/10
Espace intérieur :	■■■■■■■■■□	9/10
Confort :	■■■■■■■■□□	8/10

WWW.VW.CA

Plus d'informations dans la section statistiques en dernière partie du Guide

- Habitacle plus grand qu'avant
- Coffre immense
- Comportement routier solide
- Modèle de base abordable
- ADN Volks préservé

- Lignes manquent un peu de punch
- Techniquement moins élaborée
- Moteur 2,0 litres assez juste
- Accélérateur peu progressif

trouvé les suspensions plus dures que dans la génération précédente. Il faut dire que la suspension arrière est à poutre semi-rigide alors que les Européens ont droit à des bras multiples. Les freins de la version de base sont à tambours, un retour en arrière pour Volks qui devait bien couper quelque part pour en arriver à un prix abordable…

Dans les courbes, même les plus sinueuses, la tenue de route est des plus relevées et le roulis très bien maîtrisé. La boîte DSG est un plaisir à utiliser mais elle le serait bien davantage si on pouvait changer les rapports grâce à des palettes derrière le volant. La TDI DSG les offre, ces palettes pourtant! Dans toutes les Jetta essayées, l'accélérateur était difficilement modulable et les départs s'avéraient souvent saccadés, même avec la boîte automatique. Mais s'il faut déplorer quelque chose, c'est l'abandon d'un bouton permettant de désactiver le contrôle de traction et de stabilité latérale. Ça va être le fun dans un banc de neige…

Alain Morin

PHOTOS : ALAIN MORIN

DANS UNE CLASSE À PART

La compagnie Volkswagen est en voie de restructurer toutes ses opérations en Amérique du Nord. Cela signifie également une révision complète des modèles offerts. Par exemple, cette année, la Passat n'est plus au rendez-vous et sera remplacée sous peu par un tout nouveau modèle fabriqué à l'usine de Chattanooga au Tennessee. La seule Passat disponible est la CC, ce coupé quatre portes aux lignes si élégantes. Si ce modèle demeure sur le marché, il fera dorénavant partie d'une famille de modèles différents de la Passat.

Les amateurs de berline intermédiaire Volkswagen devront donc patienter avant de retrouver cette berline super pratique et spacieuse. Par contre, ceux qui seront prêts à débourser un peu plus, pourront se procurer l'une des voitures les plus élégantes et les plus agréables à piloter que l'on retrouve sur le marché.

MÉCANIQUE PERFORMANTE

Lorsqu'on parle de la CC avec des acheteurs éventuels, ceux-ci soulignent immédiatement le coût élevé de cette voiture. Pourtant, en examinant de plus près les prix des modèles disponibles, on doit conclure que ces personnes se sont contentées de regarder le prix du modèle Highline V6 sans se préoccuper des autres modèles. Il est vrai que cette version, propulsée par le moteur V6 de 3,6 litres produisant 280 chevaux et associé à la transmission automatique à six rapports et au rouage intégral, se vend passablement cher. Cependant, il ne faut pas oublier non plus qu'il est possible de commander un modèle propulsé par un moteur quatre cylindres associé de série à une transmission manuelle à six rapports. Cette CC représente une option beaucoup plus économique.

Avec ses 200 chevaux et sa boîte manuelle à six rapports, ce moteur 2,0 litres est performant et ses prestations sont tout de même intéressantes puisque le 0-100 km/h est l'affaire de moins de huit secondes, soit, 1,3 seconde de plus qu'avec la version à moteur V6. Si vous optez plutôt pour la transmission automatique, vous ne serez pas perdant au change, car il s'agit d'une boîte DSG à double embrayage. Si vous n'avez jamais conduit une voiture munie d'une boîte DSG, un bref essai vous convaincra de son efficacité et vous fera même oublier la transmission manuelle.

LOOK D'ENFER

La berline Passat qui nous quitte était élégante, mais d'une grande sobriété. Espérons que les modèles qui vont la remplacer en cours d'année auront un peu plus de mordant sur le plan visuel. Par contre, la CC est un coupé quatre portes qui fait définitivement tourner les têtes. Il s'agit en fait de l'une des plus élégantes voitures sur le marché avec son toit fuyant, sa calandre avant encadrée par des phares longilignes et la présence de roues en alliage dont le design s'harmonise fort bien avec la silhouette.

Comme il faut s'y attendre sur un produit Volkswagen, la finition extérieure est sans faille avec une peinture au fini dépourvu de

FEU VERT

- Silhouette élégante
- Rouage intégral (V6)
- Finition impeccable
- Tenue de route rassurante
- Ergonomie exemplaire

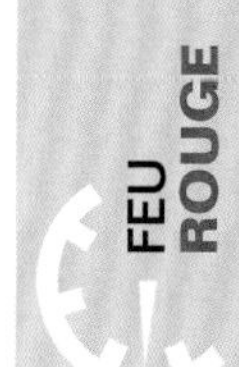

FEU ROUGE

- Certains modèles onéreux
- Quatre places seulement
- Accès aux places arrière ardu
- Transmission Tiptronic avec moteur V6
- Nouvelle berline disponible plus tard

pelure d'orange et une grande attention apportée aux moindres détails. L'habitacle est de même mouture avec des matériaux de qualité et une finition impeccable. Peu importe que vous choisissiez la version économique ou la version plus onéreuse, vous allez retrouver le même tableau de bord pratique et ergonomique. Soulignons que la télécommande d'ouverture des portes agit également en tant que clé de démarrage. Il suffit de la placer dans une fente placée à la gauche de la console de commande audio et d'appuyer sur ce module pour lancer le moteur.

Dans l'habitacle, les places arrière sont confortables, mais il n'est pas facile d'y prendre place en raison d'une ligne de toit fuyante qui oblige à faire preuve de beaucoup de souplesse pour y prendre place. De plus, seulement deux occupants peuvent s'asseoir à l'arrière, puisque le centre du siège abrite un espace de rangement. Le dossier se rabat pour permettre une plus grande capacité du coffre à bagage qui est déjà passablement importante.

VOUS ÊTES LE PATRON

Une fois bien assis dans un siège confortable, le conducteur bénéficie d'une excellente position de conduite avec un volant qui se prend bien en main. Entre les deux cadrans principaux dont la lecture est facile, il y a un centre d'information qui s'avère fort pratique. Soulignons au passage que les sièges en cuir, le toit ouvrant ainsi que les phares au xénon, sont de série sur le modèle Highline. Cette année, le modèle R-Line fait son entrée. Il comprend des roues en alliage de 1 pouces R-Line, des feux arrière teintés, un ensemble extérieur pour la carrosserie R-Line, comprenant le pare-choc avant et des jupes, un volant sport R-Line avec la possibilité de palettes et des écussons extérieurs R-Line.

Toutefois, ce qui impressionne le plus sur cette voiture est son équilibre général, tant sur le chapitre des performances que de la tenue de route. À son volant, vous avez l'impression d'être le patron. La voiture réagit à vos demandes, la tenue de route est vraiment bonne et le freinage, tout aussi impressionnant avec une distance de freinage inférieure à 40 mètres.

Bref, si vous aimez les voitures élégantes et agréables à conduire, cette Passat CC risque de vous intéresser.

Denis Duquet

PHOTOS: VOLKSWAGEN

Catégorie	Berline
Échelle de prix	33 075 $ à 45 875 $ (2010)
Garanties	4 ans/80 000 km, 5 ans/100 000 km
Assemblage	Emden, Allemagne
Cote d'assurance	passable

CHÂSSIS - DONNÉES POUR CC 2.0 TSI SPORTLINE

Emp/lon/lar/haut	2 710/4 796/1 856/1 422 mm
Coffre	402 litres
Réservoir	70 litres
Nombre coussins sécurité	8
Antipatinage / contrôle stabilité	oui / oui
Suspension avant	indépendante, jambes de force
Suspension arrière	indépendante, multibras
Freins avant / arrière	disque (ABS) / disque (ABS)
Direction	à crémaillère, ass. variable
Diamètre de braquage	10,9 m
Pneus avant / arrière	P235/45R17 / P235/45R17
Poids	1 510 kg
Capacité de remorquage	454 kg (1 000 lb)

COMPOSANTES MÉCANIQUES

2.0	
Cylindrée, soupapes, alim.	4L 2,0 litres 16 s turbo
Puissance / Couple	200 chevaux / 207 lb-pi
Tr. base (opt) / rouage base (opt)	M6 (A6) / Tr
0-100 / 80-120 / 100-0 km/h	7.9 s / 5.9 s / 43.1 m
Type ess. / ville / autoroute	Super / 10,0 / 6,6 l/100 km

CC V6 4Motion Highline	
Cylindrée, soupapes, alim.	V6 3,6 litres 24 s atmos.
Puissance / Couple	280 chevaux / 265 lb-pi
Tr. base (opt) / rouage base (opt)	A6 / Int
0-100 / 80-120 / 100-0 km/h	6,6 s / n.d. / n.d.
Type ess. / ville / autoroute	Super / 12,7 / 8,3 l/100 km

DANS LA MÊME CATÉGORIE

Buick Allure, Chevrolet Malibu, Ford Fusion, Honda Accord, Hyundai Sonata, Mazda6, Nissan Altima, Subaru Legacy, Toyota Camry

DU NOUVEAU EN 2011

Version régulière abandonnée

NOS IMPRESSIONS

Agrément de conduite :	7/10
Fiabilité :	6/10
Sécurité :	10/10
Qualités hivernales :	8/10
Espace intérieur :	7/10
Confort :	7/10

WWW.VW.CA

Plus d'informations dans la section statistiques en dernière partie du Guide

LE CŒUR A SES RAISONS

Lorsque le géant allemand nous a enfin offert un utilitaire compact, il n'a pas raté son coup. Dès son entrée en scène il y a trois ans le Tiguan s'est imposé comme le plus chic de la catégorie et assurément un des plus intéressants à conduire. Il s'en pratiquement taillé un créneau dans ce segment en offrant le cachet et le comportement d'un modèle européen huppé à un tarif moins douloureux.

À dire vrai, le Tiguan est le chaînon manquant entre les versions les plus abordables d'utilitaires compacts rationnels comme les Ford Escape et Honda CR-V d'une part et celles de modèles européens comme les Audi Q5 et Mercedes-Benz GLK. Ces derniers font certainement payer cher leur nom et leur écusson prestigieux.

Le Tiguan profite d'abord, sur les premiers, de l'avantage d'une silhouette élégante croisée à un comportement routier de premier cran. Le brio habituel de son quatre cylindres turbo de 2,0 litres et 200 chevaux y est certainement pour quelque chose. Le constructeur ne se gêne d'ailleurs aucunement pour souligner que ses Tiguan et GTI ont le même moteur. Pas de V6 pour lui ce qui est un bienfait puisque ce type de moteur fait généralement piètre figure face au 2,0 litre à injection directe du constructeur allemand, qui collectionne les honneurs.

TROIS PALIERS

Les trois versions du Tiguan sont définies par leur équipement et la richesse de leur présentation plutôt que par d'autres choix mécaniques. Cette année VW offre aussi les roues avant motrices en version Comfortline en plus de Trendline. Cette dernière est la seule à pouvoir combiner la traction et la boîte manuelle à six rapports mais on peut l'équiper aussi de l'automatique seule ou jumelée au rouage 4Motion. Dans le cas du Tiguan, il s'agit d'un rouage automatique Haldex dont l'embrayage central multidisque répartit le couple entre les roues avant et arrière. Comfortline et Highline sont livrés de série avec une boîte automatique à six rapports et le rouage 4Motion.

Les Comfortline et Highline se distinguent ensuite par des touches et accessoires qui rehaussent le niveau de luxe et d'équipement: glaces teintées, toit ouvrant, sièges chauffants, longerons de toit et pneus de taille 235/55 sur roues d'alliage de 17 pouces au lieu de pneus et roues de 16 pouces.

Le Highline a droit à des touches de luxe telles que des rétroviseurs électriques et chauffants avec mise en mémoire, des essuie-glaces automatiques, une boussole numérique et un climatiseur thermostatique à réglages sur deux zones. Cette version est la seule à offrir des sièges de cuir avec réglages entièrement électriques à l'avant. Les sièges avant du Comfortline ont seulement un dossier à réglage électrique et dans le Trendline, vous faites tout à la main.

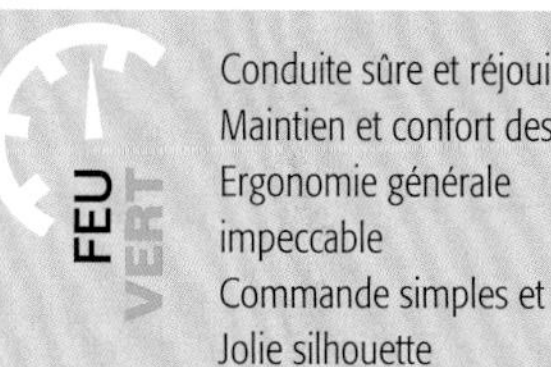

Conduite sûre et réjouissante
Maintien et confort des sièges
Ergonomie générale impeccable
Commande simples et claires
Jolie silhouette

Soute à bagages limitée
Plus cher que ses rivaux
Cadrans peu contrastés
Régulateur de vitesse archaïque
Console centrale encombrante

PAS DE « MAINS-LIBRES » POUR TOUS

Les Comfortline et Highline sont équipées d'une chaîne audio avec écran tactile de 6,5 pouces, changeur de CD à six disques et radio satellite Sirius. On peut y ajouter le groupe « technologie » qui comprend un système de navigation avec un disque dur de 30 Go qui réserve le tiers de son espace aux cartes numérisées et le reste aux fichiers audio. Son lecteur peut jouer les CD, DVD et DVD audio. En prime: une caméra à l'arrière, pour le stationnement. Dommage que la connectivité Bluetooth soit de série seulement sur le Highline, en option sur le Comfortline et pas même disponible sur le Trendline.

UN HÉDONISTE

Le Tiguan est vraiment aux petits soins pour ses occupants. Il est d'abord assez spacieux, ce qui n'est pas la règle dans cette catégorie. Les places avant et les places extérieures arrière, à tout le moins, parce qu'il faut oublier la place centrale arrière qui est étroite et presque inutilisable, comme c'est souvent le cas. Le prix à payer, pour cet espace, est une soute cargo dont le volume est assez faible quand les dossiers de la banquette arrière sont en place. Les rangements sont nombreux et pratiques dans la cabine, par contre.

Les sièges sont bien sculptés et offrent un maintien plus que correct. La position de conduite est juste et les commandes de bonne taille et placées avec logique, selon les meilleurs règles en termes d'ergonomie. Les cadrans sont assez grands mais leurs chiffres illuminés en bleu offrent toujours aussi peu de contraste. Vivement que Volkswagen renonce à ce tic de design qui afflige ses produits depuis une douzaine d'années.

La Tiguan est maniable en ville. Sa direction est nette, précise au centre et assez vive mais plutôt légère et un peu trop assistée à notre goût. Sur la route il affiche beaucoup d'aplomb et il est très silencieux mais plutôt sensible au vent oblique. Le moteur turbo est toujours animé mais se révèle bruyant et rugueux sous le capot du Tiguan, bizarrement. Toutes ses versions ont une capacité de remorquage de 998 kilos mais quelque chose nous dit qu'on ne verra pas tellement de Tiguan tractant une tente-roulotte sur nos routes.

Marc Lachapelle

PHOTOS: GILLES OLIVIER

Catégorie	VUS
Échelle de prix	27 875 $ à 37 775 $ (2010)
Garanties	4 ans/80 000 km, 5 ans/100 000 km
Assemblage	Wolfsburg, Allemagne
Cote d'assurance	n.d.

CHÂSSIS - DONNÉES POUR 4MOTION HIGHLINE

Emp/lon/lar/haut	2 604/4 427/1 809/1 683 mm
Coffre	674 à 1 589 litres
Réservoir	64 litres
Nombre coussins sécurité	6
Antipatinage / contrôle stabilité	oui / oui
Suspension avant	indépendante, jambes de force
Suspension arrière	indépendante, multibras
Freins avant / arrière	disque (ABS) / disque (ABS)
Direction	à crémaillère, assistée
Diamètre de braquage	12,0 m
Pneus avant / arrière	P235/55R17 / P235/55R17
Poids	1 557 kg
Capacité de remorquage	998 kg (2 200 lb)

COMPOSANTES MÉCANIQUES

Tiguan	
Cylindrée, soupapes, alim.	4L 2,0 litres 16 s turbocompressé
Puissance / Couple	200 chevaux / 207 lb-pi
Tr. base (opt) / rouage base (opt)	M6 (A6) / Tr (Int)
0-100 / 80-120 / 100-0 km/h	9,2 s / 7,2 s / 44,3 m
Type ess. / ville / autoroute	Super / 11,6 / 8,3 l/100 km

DANS LA MÊME CATÉGORIE

Chevrolet Equinox, Ford Escape, Honda CR-V, Hyundai Tucson, Jeep Compass, Jeep Patriot, Kia Sportage, Mazda CX-7, Mazda Tribute, Mitsubishi Outlander, Nissan Rogue, Subaru Forester, Suzuki Grand Vitara, Toyota RAV4

DU NOUVEAU EN 2011

Traction avant disponible avec Comfortline et Trendline, nouvelle suspension sport optionnelle sur Comfortline et Highline

NOS IMPRESSIONS

Agrément de conduite :	8/10
Fiabilité :	6/10
Sécurité :	10/10
Qualités hivernales :	8/10
Espace intérieur :	7/10
Confort :	8/10

WWW.VW.CA

Plus d'informations dans la section statistiques en dernière partie du Guide

UN PREMIER VÉHICULE HYBRIDE POUR VW

V6 à essence, V6 diesel, hybride... alouette! Décidément, Volkswagen fait feu de tout bois avec sa nouvelle génération de Touareg. Les deux premières variantes nous arrivent cet automne, mais il faudra patienter au moins une année-modèle avant de recevoir le tout premier véhicule hybride du constructeur « du peuple » allemand.

Bon, qu'on se le dise tout de suite, Volkswagen est n° 1 en Europe, ce qui lui permet un soupçon d'arrogance avec son Touareg. Là-bas, l'utilitaire est bardé de gadgets technologiques avant-gardistes dignes des plus grands constructeurs de luxe. Mais avec à peine 3 % du marché nord-américain, et soucieux de ne pas embarrasser le parent Audi, Volks doit ici se montrer plus raisonnable. Pour nous, donc, pas d'avertisseur de changement de ligne qui fasse vibrer le volant, pas de pédale de frein qui frémisse à l'approche d'un obstacle, pas de régulateur hyperintelligent (comme celui d'Audi qui vous arrête aux bouchons de circulation), pas non plus d'Aera View pour retransmettre les environs sur l'écran de bord.

Mais remettons les privations à plus tard et mettons plutôt l'accent sur le fait qu'en offrant à la fois une motorisation diesel et une hybride, Volkswagen assure une réponse à deux types de clients diamétralement opposés. Le Touareg TDI, avec son V6 turbodiesel (3,0 litres) de 240 chevaux, parle d'une belle frugalité sur autoroute (7,4 L/100 km), alors que le Touareg Hybrid (première manifestation hybride chez Volks) le fait, tout au contraire, en situation urbaine (8,2 L/100 km). Avouez, rares sont les constructeurs qui proposent et le diesel, et l'hybride : tout juste Mercedes, BMW et, maintenant, Volks.

HYBRIDE...

La variante hybride du Touareg, prévue pour l'année-modèle 2012, mise sur un V6 turbo à injection directe de 3,0 litres pour livrer, de concert avec l'unité électrique, quelque 374 chevaux et 428 lb-pi. C'est la puissance d'un V8, mais avec une consommation peu gloutonne pour cette décharge de 0-100 km/h en 6,5 secondes : à peine 8,2 l/100 km (encore que ça reste à être vérifié en conditions réelles). Nous vous reparlerons davantage de l'hybride à temps pour son arrivée – soit l'an prochain, c'est donc un rendez-vous dans le *Guide de l'auto 2012*! Sachez cependant qu'une petite virée urbaine européenne nous a fait constater un échange sans heurt entre les deux motorisations. Aussi, le moteur électrique a accepté de travailler seul jusqu'à 40 km/h (quoique Volkswagen prétende à du 50 km/h), mais c'était à condition d'être tout doux et tout gentil avec l'accélérateur. En fait, un peu trop de pression sur l'accélérateur et voilà que le moteur à essence se mettait de la partie. De même, le freinage était si réactif qu'on avait de la difficulté à le doser équitablement. Il faudra penser à assouplir cette pédale de frein.

Le Touareg hybride deviendra donc, pour nous Nord-américains, le *top of the line* de la gamme. Normes antipollution obligent, il nous faut malheureusement faire sans la fantastique machine de guerre Touareg V8 TDI, offerte chez nos amis européens (les chanceux...). Je ne voudrais pas tourner le fer dans la plaie, mais sachez que ce V8 est absolument phénoménal en termes de puissance – imaginez le 0-100 km/h en 5,8 secondes...

... MAIS DIESEL D'ABORD

Ceci dit, le V6 TDI de 3,0 litres, ses 240 chevaux et, surtout, ses 406 lb-pi de couple sont pas mal – que dis-je, ils sont plus que bien ! Le tout déménage sans demander son reste, sans temps mort et dans une conduite dynamique rehaussée d'une solide

tenue de route – après tout, la plateforme d'assemblage de l'utilitaire n'est-elle pas celle du nouveau Porsche Cayenne ?

La puissance est livrée linéairement, voire même de façon gutturale avec, en prime, un beau grondement qui s'extirpe des tuyaux d'échappement. C'est une transmission à huit rapports qui régit le tout – la vitesse maximale est atteinte au 6e rapport, alors que les 7e et 8e vitesses assurent une diminution du régime-moteur, pour une meilleure consommation en carburant. Bien étagée, cette boîte livre la puissance sans qu'on ait besoin de se mêler de sa course – ce qui est quand même possible à même le levier. Les commandes au volant ne sont cependant pas au rendez-vous. Dommage...

Fidèle à la tradition germanique, la direction est un bonheur de précision, de légèreté et on aime définitivement la fermeté de la suspension (qui n'est plus à multibras à l'arrière, mais désormais à double triangulation). On regrette toutefois que le dispositif à air ne traverse pas l'Atlantique jusqu'à nous. Avec ses trois ajustements, cette suspension optionnelle accorde une bien belle sportivité à l'expérience de conduite, mais il paraît que nous n'en voudrons pas...

PLUS UN VRAI 4X4 – POUR NOUS, DU MOINS.

Autre élément d'importance qui ne vient pas jusqu'à nous: le 4xMotion qui assure les mêmes capacités hors route qu'à la première génération. Question de sauver sur le poids et les pièces, et donc sur le carburant, le Touareg nous est désormais livré avec un différentiel à glissement limité Torsen, pour une traction intégrale permanente. Pour plus *rock'n roll* que ça, il faudra... déménager en Europe et se payer le Terrain Tech avec sa boîte de transfert, sa gamme à bas régime, de même que ses différentiels central et arrière verrouillés.

Volkswagen Canada prévoit écouler la presque totalité de ses Touareg en motorisation TDI – après tout, la première génération s'est targuée, depuis l'arrivée du V6 TDI à mi-2009, de s'écouler à 96 % en TDI. Cela dit, le modèle d'entrée de gamme du Touareg demeure celui doté du moteur V6 à essence (3,6 litres) à injection directe qui, malheureusement pour lui, est le plus gourmand du lot, V8 TDI compris. Heureusement que le ridicule ne tue pas... À 9,9 l/100 km, c'est 20 % de moins qu'auparavant, mais nous avons senti la puissance (280 chevaux) plutôt limite avec quatre grands adultes à bord. Reste qu'on promet un 0-100 km/h en 7,8 secondes (c'est nez à nez avec le V6 TDI), ainsi qu'une impressionnante capacité maximale de remorquage de 3 500 kilos.

Oh, avant d'oublier: sachez que d'ici un an, et si tout va bien, toutes les versions V6 du Touareg, hybride ou pas, recevront le « start-go ». Vous savez, ce dispositif qui fait s'assoupir le moteur aux arrêts? Voilà qui contribuera d'une autre belle façon à la réduction de la consommation en carburant. Il faut dire que si le Touareg a perdu quelque 200 kilos au change générationnel (notamment au niveau du châssis et du matériel insonorisant), l'utilitaire fait quand même osciller la balance à plus de deux tonnes métriques.

TOUAREG UN JOUR...

Visuellement, le Touareg garde l'allure... d'un Touareg. *Fiou*, l'hérédité est sauvée! Les portières ont gagné une concavité extérieure qui accroche la lumière, les phares avant (lorsque bixénon) se distinguent par leur éclairage au DEL.

Côté longueur, largeur et empattement, la nouvelle mouture de Touareg gagne quelques centimètres, ce qui avantage de près du double les genoux arrière (les mauvaises langues vous diront que c'était bien nécessaire...), de même que l'espace de

FEU VERT

Habitacle digne des constructeurs de luxe
Moteur V6 TDI qui fait 406 lb-pi de couple…
Tenue de route toute germanique
Plus d'espace aux jambes arrière

FEU ROUGE

Fiabilité « sous la moyenne » pour la première génération
Beaucoup de « gadgets » qui ne viennent pas jusqu'à nous
V6 de base plus gourmand que tous les autres…

chargement avec une petite augmentation de 5 % (sauf pour l'hybride qui, batteries obligent, perd 25 % au change).

L'habitacle a le mérite de s'être simplifié, avec moitié moins de commandes qui sont, au demeurant, beaucoup plus instinctives qu'auparavant. Par contre, le système d'information est d'une complexité qui nous enlève toute envie d'y recourir.

Les sièges, redessinés, sont sans doute les plus confortables de toute la famille Volkswagen, merci à leurs multiples ajustements. Question de rehausser le confort arrière, la banquette accepte désormais de s'avancer et de se reculer et ses dossiers s'inclinent en trois positions. Le hayon à ouverture électrique est évidemment de mise.

Nadine Filion

PHOTOS : VOLKSWAGEN

DONNÉES PRÉLIMINAIRES

Catégorie	VUS
Échelle de prix	45 300 $ à 58 300 $ (2010)
Garanties	4 ans/80 000 km, 5 ans/100 000 km
Assemblage	Bratislava, Slovaquie
Cote d'assurance	n.d.

CHÂSSIS - DONNÉES POUR V6 HIGHLINE

Emp/lon/lar/haut	2 895/4 795/1 940/1 710 mm
Coffre	n.d.
Réservoir	100 litres
Nombre coussins sécurité	n.d.
Antipatinage / contrôle stabilité	oui / oui
Suspension avant	indépendante, jambes de force
Suspension arrière	indépendante, multibras
Freins avant / arrière	disque (ABS) / disque (ABS)
Direction	à crémaillère, assistée
Diamètre de braquage	11,9 m
Pneus avant / arrière	P255/55R18 / P255/55R18
Poids	2 100 kg
Capacité de remorquage	n.d.

COMPOSANTES MÉCANIQUES

V6 TDI

Cylindrée, soupapes, alim.	V6 3,0 litres 24 s turbo
Puissance / Couple	240 chevaux / 406 lb-pi
Tr. base (opt) / rouage base (opt)	A8 / Int
0-100 / 80-120 / 100-0 km/h	9,1 s / 6,7 s / 40,8 m
Type ess. / ville / autoroute	Diesel / n.d. / 7,4 l/100 km

V6 essence

Cylindrée, soupapes, alim.	V6 3,6 litres 24 s atmos.
Puissance / Couple	280 chevaux / 265 lb-pi
Tr. base (opt) / rouage base (opt)	A8 / Int
0-100 / 80-120 / 100-0 km/h	7,6 s (const) / n.d. / n.d.
Type ess. / ville / autoroute	Super / n.d. / n.d. l/100 km

V6 hybride

Cylindrée, soupapes, alim.	V6 3,0 litres turbo
Puissance / Couple	374 chevaux / 428 lb-pi
Tr. base (opt) / rouage base (opt)	A8 / Int
0-100 / 80-120 / 100-0 km/h	6,5 s (const) / n.d. / n.d.
Type ess. / ville / autoroute	Ordinaire / 8,2 / n.d. l/100 km

DANS LA MÊME CATÉGORIE

Acura MDX, Audi Q7, BMW X5, Cadillac SRX, Infiniti FX, Land Rover LR3, Lexus RX, Lincoln MKX, Mercedes-Benz Classe M, Porsche Cayenne, Volvo XC90

DU NOUVEAU EN 2011

Nouveau modèle

NOS IMPRESSIONS

Agrément de conduite :	8/10
Fiabilité :	Nouveau modèle
Sécurité :	8/10
Qualités hivernales :	Données insufisantes
Espace intérieur :	8/10
Confort :	8/10

WWW.VW.CA

Plus d'informations dans la section statistiques en dernière partie du Guide

DANS LES PETITS POTS...

Lorsque ce modèle a été dévoilé en 2007, nombreuses ont été les personnes qui ont été attirées par le prix élevé de cette petite suédoise. Pourtant, ces gens n'avaient pas attentivement regardé la gamme de prix. Elles se sont contentées de jeter un coup d'œil à la version la plus onéreuse pour ensuite critiquer. Il faut cependant savoir que la C30 est disponible en plusieurs versions et que le modèle d'entrée de gamme est tout de même de prix fort compétitif.

En outre, il existe un dicton dans la langue de Shakespeare qui affirme qu'il ne faut pas juger un livre par sa couverture. C'est un peu la même chose avec cette Volvo ! Il est vrai qu'il s'agit d'une très petite voiture puisqu'elle est 22 cm plus courte que la berline S40 du même constructeur. Ce qui amène plusieurs personnes à conclure que si c'est petit, cela doit être bon marché. Étant donné que de plus en plus de modèles de format réduit, mais de haute qualité, seront dévoilés sur notre marché au cours des années à venir, mieux vaut cesser d'associer dimensions et prix réduits ! Cette Volvo se vend un peu plus cher que la moyenne et même relativement cher dans sa version la mieux équipée et la plus puissante, mais on en a pour notre argent.

QUELLE SILHOUETTE !

Ce petit *hatchback* trois portes dessiné par le Québécois Simon Lamarre fait l'unanimité par son élégance. La partie avant est toute en rondeurs, ce qui est assez exceptionnel pour une Volvo. On retrouve également la même grille rectangulaire traversée de haut en bas par cette barre si typique sur laquelle est greffé en son centre l'écusson Volvo. Ce museau sert de point d'ancrage aux lignes fuyantes qui se dirigent vers l'arrière. On a même conservé la ceinture de caisse en relief, propre à toutes les Volvo. Mais c'est la partie arrière qui est la plus spectaculaire avec son hayon constitué d'une très grande vitre encadrée par les traditionnels feux arrière verticaux dotés d'une base très large. Ces feux sont la signature visuelle de la voiture et contribuent à la sécurité en étant très visibles dans la circulation et la nuit, évidemment.

Cette voiture s'ouvre sur un habitacle fortement élégant. S'inspirant des credos du design scandinave, la planche de bord est très dépouillée et comprend de vastes espaces dénudés de tout artifice ou commande. Certains aiment, d'autres non. Quoi qu'il en soit, il faut reconnaître que c'est efficace avec les deux cadrans indicateurs placés dans le champ de vision du pilote. Celui-ci bénéficie d'un volant dont le boudin de bonne grosseur se prend bien en main. Toutes les autres commandes ou presque sont situées dans une console verticale de type flottant qui se détache du tableau de bord. Ça aussi, c'est élégant et pratique. Et même si les touches de contrôle sont nombreuses, elles sont faciles à localiser et à utiliser. Comme il se doit sur une Volvo, les sièges avant sont très confortables et apportent un excellent support à tous points de vue.

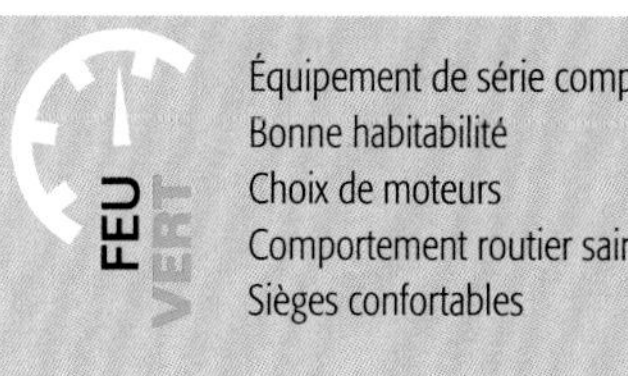

- Équipement de série complet
- Bonne habitabilité
- Choix de moteurs
- Comportement routier sain
- Sièges confortables

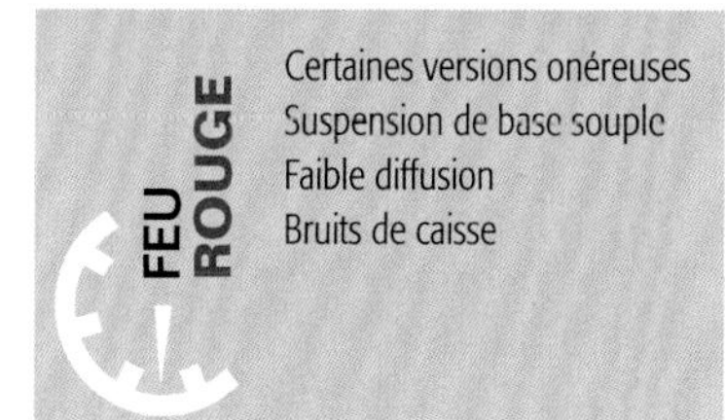

- Certaines versions onéreuses
- Suspension de base souple
- Faible diffusion
- Bruits de caisse

Il va sans dire que les places arrière sont également confortables, et ce, même pour des personnes de grande taille. Ce qui est tout de même impressionnant pour une voiture de cette dimension. En effet, deux grands adultes pourront douillettement s'asseoir dans les deux sièges baquets situés à l'arrière. De plus, leurs dossiers se rabattent pour offrir un vaste espace de chargement. On n'a pas non plus lésiné sur la qualité des matériaux et la finition est bonne. Enfin, si ce genre de détails vous intéresse, le système de climatisation est muni d'un filtre à pollen.

SAVOIR CHOISIR
Comme mentionné précédemment, la C30 peut se révéler fort onéreuse lorsqu'on considère le modèle T5 R-Design et son moteur turbocompressé de 2,5 litres d'une puissance de 227 chevaux. À ce moment, la facture dépasse les 40 000 $. Il est vrai par contre qu'on se retrouve au volant d'une voiture bouclant le 0-100 km/h en moins de sept secondes et qu'on bénéficie de tout le confort et le luxe d'une voiture de catégorie Premium.

Il y avait d'autres alternatives qui vous permettaient d'acquérir ce modèle et de jouir tout de même d'une voiture de qualité et agréable à conduire. Ainsi, le modèle 2,4i se vendait pour moins de 30 000 $ et son équipement était assez complet tant au chapitre de la sécurité que du confort. Il était propulsé par un moteur cinq cylindres de 2,4 litres d'une puissance de 168 chevaux. Cela peut sembler assez mince aux yeux de certains, mais le rapport poids/puissance était correct. Quoi qu'il en soit, ce modèle plus abordable bouclait le 0-100 km/h en moins de neuf secondes, ce qui n'était pas mal. Malheureusement dans sa sagesse, Volvo l'a éliminé.

Sur la route, cette voiture est agile, et dotée d'un diamètre de braquage relativement court qui la fait apprécier en conduite urbaine. D'ailleurs, lors de son développement, dans le cahier des charges, il était mentionné d'en faire une petite citadine pour des gens voulant une voiture au design spectaculaire et munie d'un système audio impressionnant. On peut dire que c'est mission accomplie. En fait, le cahier des charges a été largement dépassé !

Denis Duquet

PHOTOS : VOLVO

Catégorie	Coupé
Échelle de prix	33 995 $ à 39 995 $
Garanties	4 ans/80 000 km, 4 ans/80 000 km
Assemblage	Gand, Belgique
Cote d'assurance	n.d.

CHÂSSIS - DONNÉES POUR T5

Emp/lon/lar/haut	2 640/4 266/2 039/1 447 mm
Coffre	433 à 1 542 litres
Réservoir	62 litres
Nombre coussins sécurité	6
Antipatinage / contrôle stabilité	oui / oui
Suspension avant	indépendante, jambes de force
Suspension arrière	indépendante, multibras
Freins avant / arrière	disque (ABS) / disque (ABS)
Direction	à crémaillère, ass. variable
Diamètre de braquage	10,6 m
Pneus avant / arrière	205/50R17 / 205/50R17
Poids	1 424 kg
Capacité de remorquage	700 kg (1 543 lb)

COMPOSANTES MÉCANIQUES

T5, T5 R-Design

Cylindrée, soupapes, alim.	5L 2,5 litres 20 s turbo
Puissance / Couple	227 chevaux / 236 lb-pi
Tr. base (opt) / rouage base (opt)	M6 (A5) / Tr
0-100 / 80-120 / 100-0 km/h	6,9 s / 5,4 s / 42,4 m
Type ess. / ville / autoroute	Super / 10,2 / 6,8 l/100 km

DANS LA MÊME CATÉGORIE
Audi A3, BMW Série 1, MINI Cooper, Volkswagen GTI

DU NOUVEAU EN 2011
Partie avant redessinée, châssis R-Design plus rigide, abandon du 2,4 litres

NOS IMPRESSIONS

Agrément de conduite :	8/10
Fiabilité :	9/10
Sécurité :	10/10
Qualités hivernales :	7/10
Espace intérieur :	7/10
Confort :	7/10

www.volvocanada.com

Plus d'informations dans la section statistiques en dernière partie du Guide

LA SUÉDOISE ENLÈVE LE HAUT

À l'image d'une starlette vieillissante, la Volvo C70 se paye un *lifting*, histoire de s'offrir une seconde jeunesse, mais également d'entrer en phase avec le nouveau style Volvo développé pour la récente XC60 ainsi que la toute nouvelle S60. C'est fou comme le temps passe... Lancée en 2006, la C70 faisait alors figure de pionnière en devenant le premier coupé-cabriolet à quatre places doté d'un toit rigide-rétractable, une configuration adoptée depuis par BMW pour la Série 3 Cabriolet ainsi que par Volkswagen avec l'EOS, entre autres.

La mise à jour toute récente de la C70 n'affecte en rien la conception ou le fonctionnement de l'ingénieux toit développé conjointement avec Pininfarina et Webasto ou encore son châssis ou sa motorisation, puisqu'elle se limite essentiellement à un restylage de la partie avant qui intègre désormais le nouveau design des phares adopté par la S60 ainsi qu'une calandre légèrement arrondie, et à l'adoption de feux arrière à technologie DEL. Du côté de l'habitacle, le design de la planche de bord a été revu, de même que certains matériaux afin de donner une touche de luxe plus soutenue à l'intérieur.

DE COUPÉ À CABRIOLET EN 30 SECONDES

Le secret de l'élégance de la C70 réside dans le fait que cette voiture a d'abord été conçue comme un coupé, les ingénieurs trouvant par la suite une solution aussi fonctionnelle qu'élégante permettant de replier son toit rigide. Ce toit se distingue grâce à ses trois sections qui se replient dans le coffre en s'empilent l'une sur l'autre dans un véritable ballet mécanique commandé par la seule pression d'un bouton par le conducteur. Trente secondes et le tour est joué ! Le coffre autorise alors un chargement de bagages limité à 170 litres, chargement qui demeure cependant accessible une fois le toit replié, puisqu'un bouton de commande électrique permet justement de soulever légèrement les panneaux du toit afin que l'on puisse accéder au contenu du coffre. Il faut toutefois tenir compte du fait que le volume du coffre est sérieusement limité avec le toit replié, et que le volume complet du coffre avec ledit toit en place est de 362 litres, donc à peu près égal à celui d'une Toyota Corolla. Aussi vous faudra-t-il voyager léger en mode cabriolet ou partir avec armes et bagages en mode coupé. Mentionnons néanmoins que la structure de la C70 manque de rigidité lorsque le toit est replié et que la voiture peut alors être affligée de sérieux bruits de caisse, courtoisie du triste état de notre réseau routier...

UNE CONDUITE DÉCONTRACTÉE

La C70 fait appel à un moteur 5 cylindres à 20 soupapes et doubles arbres à cames en tête d'une cylindrée de 2,5 litres et qui reçoit l'aide d'un turbocompresseur ainsi que d'un échangeur de chaleur afin de porter la puissance à 227 chevaux. Autant vous prévenir tout de suite, la présence d'un turbo n'est pas gage d'accélérations à l'emporte-pièce ou de reprises fulgurantes, la C70 affichant un poids très élevé de plus de 1 745 kilos. Bref, vous aurez compris que la C70 est carrément larguée par la BMW Série 3 Cabriolet et

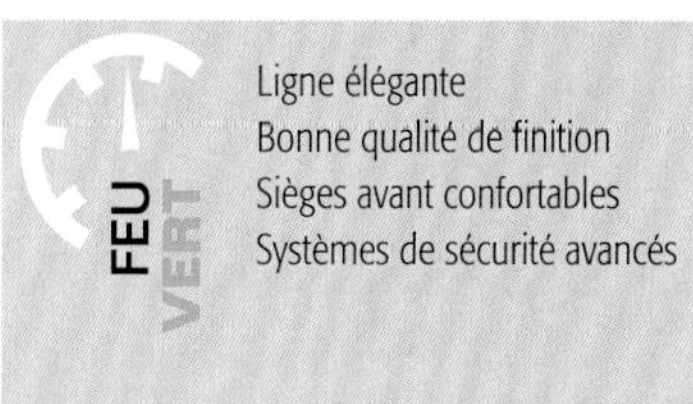

Ligne élégante
Bonne qualité de finition
Sièges avant confortables
Systèmes de sécurité avancés

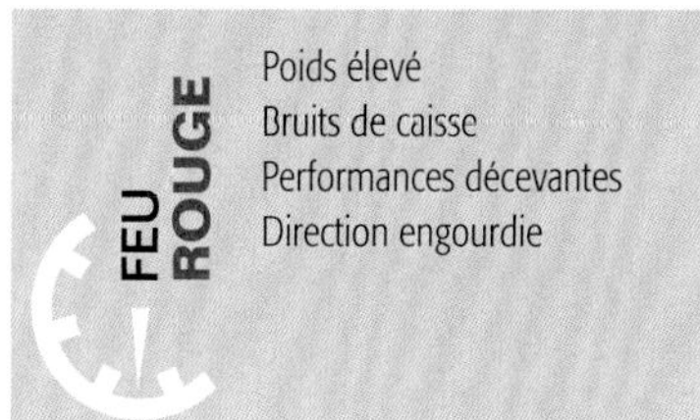

Poids élevé
Bruits de caisse
Performances décevantes
Direction engourdie

par plusieurs rivales directes au chapitre des performances. Par conséquent, il faut plutôt la considérer comme une voiture de tourisme plutôt qu'une voiture à vocation sportive.

De plus, le comportement routier de la C70 varie selon que le toit est en place ou qu'il soit replié dans le coffre, le poids de toute cette quincaillerie ayant une incidence directe sur la répartition des masses d'après sa localisation. La tenue de route n'est pas mauvaise, mais elle n'est pas impressionnante, et la direction plutôt engourdie manque de précision, ce qui n'aide pas la cause de la C70 avec laquelle il faut également composer avec un rayon de braquage important.

Les sièges des véhicules Volvo sont parmi les plus confortables de l'industrie automobile et ceux des places avant sont à la hauteur des attentes à cet égard, en plus d'être dotés du système de sécurité WHIPS conçu pour réduire le risque de blessures graves à la nuque en cas d'impact à l'arrière. Quant aux places arrière, précisons que les dossiers enveloppent bien le corps mais que le dégagement pour les jambes demeure limité pour deux adultes.

Côté sécurité, la C70 le nouveau coupé-cabriolet possède un coussin latéral qui se déploie vers le haut à partir des portières afin de protéger la tête des occupants. Généralement, ce type de coussin se déploie à partir du toit, mais la C70 étant à la fois un coupé et un cabriolet, les ingénieurs ont dû adapter ce dispositif de façon à ce que les coussins se déploient à partir des portières. Cela représentait une première dans l'industrie automobile pour un coupé-cabriolet lors du lancement de la C70 en 2006.

Jusqu'à tout récemment, Volvo faisait partie du portefeuille des marques de luxe de Ford, au même titre que Jaguar et Land Rover. Dans un premier temps, Ford a vendu ses deux marques britanniques au constructeur indien Tata, pour ensuite vendre Volvo au constructeur chinois Geely pour la somme de 1,8 milliard de dollars. Bien que les intentions annoncées par Geely pour Volvo fassent état de leur désir pour que la marque suédoise conserve son identité propre au sein du nouveau groupe, cette prise de contrôle par des intérêts chinois aura certainement une incidence sur la valeur de revente des modèles de la marque et sur l'avenir à moyen terme de Volvo...

Gabriel Gélinas

PHOTOS : VOLVO

VOLVO C70

Catégorie	Cabriolet
Échelle de prix	54 495 $
Garanties	4 ans/80 000 km, 4 ans/80 000 km
Assemblage	Gothenburg, Suède
Cote d'assurance	n.d.

CHÂSSIS - DONNÉES POUR T5

Emp/lon/lar/haut	2 640/4 615/1 836/1 400 mm
Coffre	170 à 362 litres
Réservoir	62 litres
Nombre coussins sécurité	6
Antipatinage / contrôle stabilité	oui / oui
Suspension avant	indépendante, jambes de force
Suspension arrière	indépendante, multibras
Freins avant / arrière	disque (ABS) / disque (ABS)
Direction	à crémaillère, assistée
Diamètre de braquage	12,7 m
Pneus avant / arrière	P235/45R17 / P235/45R17
Poids	1 745 kg
Capacité de remorquage	750 kg (1 653 lb)

COMPOSANTES MÉCANIQUES

T5	
Cylindrée, soupapes, alim.	5L 2,5 litres 20 s turbo
Puissance / Couple	227 chevaux / 174 lb-pi
Tr. base (opt) / rouage base (opt)	A6 / Tr
0-100 / 80-120 / 100-0 km/h	8,6 s / 7,5 s / 39,3 m
Type ess. / ville / autoroute	Super / 10,8 / 7,2 l/100 km

DANS LA MÊME CATÉGORIE

Audi A5, BMW Série 3, Infiniti G, Lexus IS

DU NOUVEAU EN 2011

Partie avant redessinée

NOS IMPRESSIONS

Agrément de conduite :	7/10
Fiabilité :	6/10
Sécurité :	10/10
Qualités hivernales :	7/10
Espace intérieur :	7/10
Confort :	7/10

www.volvocanada.com

Plus d'informations dans la section statistiques en dernière partie du Guide

COINCÉES ENTRE L'ARBRE ET L'ÉCORCE

Élégantes et modernes, la berline S40 et la familiale V50 ont incontestablement rajeuni la gamme de Volvo et permis au constructeur suédois d'offrir à nouveau des modèles plus compacts et compétitifs lorsqu'elles furent lancées. C'était il y a sept ans cependant et elles n'ont guère changé depuis. Toujours jolies, elles ont de plus en plus de mal à s'imposer dans une catégorie où évoluent certaines des meilleures voitures de l'heure, toutes catégories confondues. En attendant un remodelage complet, elles misent tout sur leur version T5 à moteur turbo et roues avant motrices.

Les S40 et V50 actuelles sont construites sur la première version de l'architecture C1 qu'ont développée conjointement Ford, Mazda et Volvo au début des années 2000. Chez Volvo, la plate-forme porte le code P1 et sous-tend également les modèles C70 et C30. On peut s'attendre au dévoilement imminent de versions renouvelées des S40 et V50 qui seront vraisemblablement élaborées sur la deuxième version de l'architecture C1 qui fait ses débuts avec la nouvelle Ford Focus « mondiale ». Rien d'officiel encore.

La mince console centrale « flottante » dont Volvo a d'ailleurs fait grand cas lors du lancement des S40 et V50 est effectivement très design et attrayante en termes purement esthétiques. Suspendue ainsi à plusieurs centimètres du tableau de bord, c'est loin d'être une réussite complète pour ce qui est de la commodité quotidienne, surtout parce que l'espace de rangement aménagé juste en dessous est pratiquement inaccessible des places avant. Assez frustrant, merci ! De plus, les boutons pour la climatisation, les sièges chauffants et le dégivrage sont trop petits et trop rapprochés. On se surprend, par exemple, à couper

l'alimentation en air frais alors qu'on voulait activer les sièges chauffants... Un détail, certes, qui peut devenir sérieusement agaçant en plein hiver.

En revanche, les quatre grandes molettes qui permettent de régler la climatisation et la chaîne audio sont très efficaces. Ainsi, il est possible de syntoniser rapidement un poste de radio au dixième de fréquence près, ce qui est assez rare de nos jours. Une fois maîtrisée, la technique de mise en mémoire propre à Volvo se révèle rudement pratique.

Au sujet du volume de chargement, la berline S40 et la familiale V50 sont plutôt à l'opposé l'une de l'autre face à leurs rivales directes. Le coffre de la première est nettement plus petit que celui des Audi A4 et Série 3, par exemple, tandis que celui de la V50 est carrément avantagé comparé à celui des modèles correspondants. Il faut évidemment reconnaître que ces deux dernières sont essentiellement des familiales « sportives » qui privilégient le style alors que la V50 est fidèle à la longue tradition des familiales Volvo, même si sa silhouette n'a rien à envier à ces bavaroises en termes de finesse et d'allure sportive.

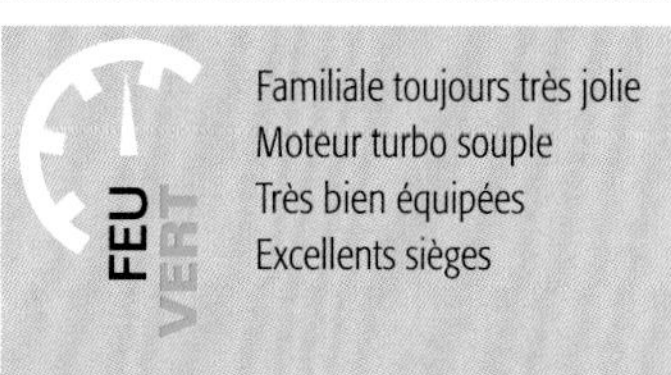

Familiale toujours très jolie
Moteur turbo souple
Très bien équipées
Excellents sièges

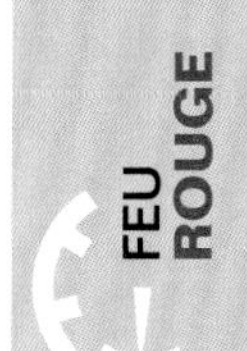

Roulement ferme
Console centrale peu commode
Banquette arrière juste
Direction légère

La direction légère et surassistée de la V50 trahit également une réaction de couple assez nette en accélération. Malgré ces défauts, on peut aisément prendre un plaisir grandissant à la conduire au fil des kilomètres, pour peu qu'on apprécie la sonorité unique de son cinq cylindres en ligne, un type de moteur qui n'est pas au goût de tous, surtout en terre nord-américaine. C'est le turbo qui fait la différence pour le couple abondant qu'il permet à ce groupe de 2,5 litres de produire, même à faible régime, et la souplesse qu'il confère à la conduite.

La boîte manuelle à 6 rapports est correcte aussi. Une pédale d'embrayage légère et peu progressive, combinée à la faible inertie du volant-moteur, impose une adaptation. La chose est d'autant plus vraie maintenant que les S40 et V50 ne sont disponibles qu'avec le moteur T5 turbo jumelé aux seules roues avant motrices. Fini le rouage Haldex à quatre roues motrices qui ajoutait à la polyvalence des deux séries mais gonflait leur prix !

Le roulement est ferme, sinon sec, quand on file sur une chaussée le moindrement bosselée ou craquelée. Comme avec plusieurs Volvo, la maîtrise des mouvements de caisse n'a simplement pas la même rigueur et précision que sur les meilleures. La conduite demeure malgré tout agréable, grâce au couple et à la souplesse du moteur turbo. Par contre, le freinage est plutôt sec en amorce et difficile à moduler si on aime conduire en douceur.

À la panoplie complète de systèmes de sécurité passive qu'on retrouve chez Volvo s'ajoutent des phares orientables au faisceau puissant et bien découpé qui bonifient quant à eux la sécurité active. Toujours au rayon de la visibilité, les Volvo méritent une très bonne note pour les essuie-glaces à lame monobranche souples qu'on peut également soulever sans peine pour nettoyer le pare-brise. L'adaptation à l'hiver est assez irréprochable chez Volvo, mais on doit s'interroger sur la sagesse de n'offrir que la version traction de la T5 turbocompressée alors que ce moteur n'était jumelé qu'au rouage à quatre roues motrices l'an dernier.

Sûres, bien équipées et confortables, les S40 et V50 se contentent de tenir le fort en attendant qu'arrivent de nouvelles recrues. Entre-temps, elles risquent de n'intéresser désormais que les inconditionnels de la marque de Göteborg.

Marc Lachapelle

PHOTOS : VOLVO

Catégorie	Berline, Familiale
Échelle de prix	28 995 $ à 30 495 $
Garanties	4 ans/80 000 km, 4 ans/80 000 km
Assemblage	Gand, Suède
Cote d'assurance	moyenne

VOLVO S40 / V50

CHÂSSIS - DONNÉES POUR S40 T5

Emp/lon/lar/haut	2 640/4 476/2 022/1 454 mm
Coffre	357 litres
Réservoir	60 litres
Nombre coussins sécurité	6
Antipatinage / contrôle stabilité	oui / oui
Suspension avant	indépendante, jambes de force
Suspension arrière	indépendante, multibras
Freins avant / arrière	disque (ABS) / disque (ABS)
Direction	à crémaillère, ass. variable
Diamètre de braquage	10,6 m
Pneus avant / arrière	P205/55R16 / P205/55R16
Poids	1 504 kg
Capacité de remorquage	900 kg (1 984 lb)

COMPOSANTES MÉCANIQUES

T5

Cylindrée, soupapes, alim.	5L 2,5 litres 20 s turbo
Puissance / Couple	227 chevaux / 236 lb-pi
Tr. base (opt) / rouage base (opt)	M6 (A5) / Tr
0-100 / 80-120 / 100-0 km/h	6,8 s / 5,4 s / 38,0 m
Type ess. / ville / autoroute	Super / 10,2 / 6,8 l/100 km

DANS LA MÊME CATÉGORIE

Acura TSX, Audi A3, Audi A4, BMW Série 3, Lexus IS, Mercedes-Benz Classe C

DU NOUVEAU EN 2011

Abandon du moteur 2,4 litres

NOS IMPRESSIONS

Agrément de conduite :	7/10
Fiabilité :	6/10
Sécurité :	8/10
Qualités hivernales :	8/10
Espace intérieur :	7/10
Confort :	8/10

www.volvocanada.com

Plus d'informations dans la section statistiques en dernière partie du Guide

ENFIN DU NOUVEAU !

Il faut avouer que la Volvo S60 était sur la voie de desserte depuis les dernières années si on regarde les chiffres de vente par rapport à ses rivales, alors le temps commençait à faire inévitablement son effet. Il faut aussi comprendre que cette génération a connu un cycle de vie extrêmement long, soit dix ans, élément n'aidant pas sa cause. Quoi qu'il en soit, 2011 nous apporte du sang neuf chez Volvo avec l'apparition d'une toute nouvelle S60 qui, à première vue, devrait certainement raviver l'intérêt des consommateurs.

Il faut avouer que le constructeur n'a pas eu toute l'attention méritée au cours des dernières années alors que Ford vivait une période plus que difficile. D'ailleurs, la plus récente S60 nous arrive pendant que le constructeur suédois se retrouve en période de transition avec son passage de Ford vers ses nouveaux propriétaires chinois, Geely. Voilà un autre élément qui explique en bonne partie le ralentissement des activités de Volvo.

Du reste, la Volvo S60 a la difficile mission de rivaliser dans le segment des berlines de luxe d'entrée de gamme aux côtés de véhicules telles la BMW de Série3, l'Audi A4, la Mercedes-Classe C, ainsi que Lexus avec la IS et Infiniti avec la G. C'est tout un défi dans un contexte où les ténors germaniques se livrent une bataille sans merci, sans oublier que chez les voitures de luxe, le prestige du logo joue bien souvent un rôle important. Après dix ans de « gestation », on se serait attendu à une nouvelle S60 plus que peaufinée et susceptible de changer la donne dans son segment, mais on constate que certains éléments ou décisions ne lui faciliteront pas la vie chez nous...

UNE SEULE VERSION OFFERTE

Tout d'abord, tandis que la concurrence exhibe des gammes étendues incluant diverses configurations (coupé, cabriolet, familiale) et motorisations, la Volvo S60 n'est offerte que sous la forme d'une berline quatre portes. Qui plus est, une seule motorisation est retenue pour le Canada alors que plusieurs moteurs existent ailleurs. Volvo a décidé de proposer un seul modèle, censé correspondre aux goûts des Canadiens.

Nous avons donc droit à la Volvo S60 T6, équipée d'un moteur turbocompressé six cylindres de 3,0 litres développant 300 chevaux pour un couple de 325 lb-pi. En fait, il s'agit d'une évolution de l'ancien moteur T6, le même qui se niche dans la S80 et le XC60, mais engendrant dans le cas de la S60 quelques 20 chevaux de plus. Ce moteur est jumelé à une excellente boîte automatique à six rapports, la seule au menu, alors que le rouage intégral fait aussi partie de l'équipement de série. Dans le cas de ce dernier, voilà une décision que l'on ne peut critiquer puisque ce type de rouage s'avère très populaire chez nous.

La S60 dispose de nombreux équipements de série, notamment un toit ouvrant, un climatiseur automatique à deux zones, des sièges en cuir et chauffants en plus d'un excellent système de sonorisation. De quoi rendre le modèle très intéressant, mais le tout se traduit par une voiture un peu plus haut de gamme, donc le prix de base s'en reflète. La disponibilité d'autres versions, dont une plus abordable, aurait sans doute été très bénéfique. À ce chapitre, Volvo aurait pu nous proposer, comme c'est le cas ailleurs, une S60 équipée du tout nouveau quatre cylindres de 2,0 litres suralimenté et à injection directe, très moderne et qui, selon les dires de quelques collègues, s'avère très intéressant. Quant aux amateurs de performance, rien n'est encore confirmé, mais Volvo pourrait bien faire revivre dans le futur la S60R, histoire de rivaliser avec les bombes du créneau.

AGRÉABLE À REGARDER!

Au chapitre du style, la dernière génération tranche radicalement de la précédente. Si le design est très réussi, c'est grâce à Peter Horbury, le même qui a opéré la relance de Volvo dans les années 90 et qui est de retour chez le constructeur suédois après avoir été responsable du design chez Ford pendant plusieurs années.

On apprécie les lignes fluides qui donnent à la S60 l'allure d'un coupé, spécialement en raison des piliers C qui s'étirent jusqu'aux feux arrière. Voilà la nouvelle tendance: transformer les berlines en coupés. À l'avant, la calandre plongeante et plus imposante arbore la grille typique à Volvo avec sa barre diagonale. Cette silhouette améliore non seulement le coefficient de traînée, mais elle procure une excellente visibilité. Si les jantes de 17 pouces offertes de série s'avèrent réussies, celles de 18 pouces venant en option rehaussent encore plus le caractère de la voiture. Bon point également pour le choix de coloris dont certains font beaucoup plus « extraverti ». Bref, pour ce qui est du style, cette voiture se veut beaucoup plus concurrentielle.

À l'intérieur, peu de reproches à faire. Volvo n'est pas le dernier venu en matière d'habitacle et on se doit encore une fois de souligner le confort exemplaire des sièges, même lors de longues randonnées. L'autre élément qui assure une position de conduite idéale, c'est la colonne de direction télescopique qui ne se contente pas que de s'ajuster de quelques centimètres. Ajoutez-y un volant sport offrant une bonne prise en main et vous obtenez un véhicule confortable à tous les points.

Le tableau de bord est identique à ce que le constructeur propose dans ses nouveaux produits depuis quelque temps, notamment la console centrale flottante. En fait, tous les intérieurs de Volvo sont très similaires. On n'a pas souvent fait de reproches à Volvo au sujet de l'ergonomie, mais cette fois, le tout n'est pas sans tache... La partie centrale s'orne d'un écran de bonne dimension, ce dernier affichant toutes les informations vitales, mais plusieurs fonctions sont contrôlées par un seul bouton dont l'utilisation demande une certaine adaptation afin d'en comprendre toutes les subtilités. On a déjà vu plus intuitif. Malgré certains défauts, vive les écrans tactiles !

TOUJOURS LA SÉCURITÉ

La sécurité a toujours été la marque de commerce de Volvo, mais plusieurs autres constructeurs se sont emparés du même message marketing. Les voitures modernes disposent d'une panoplie d'éléments et de système destinés à assurer notre sécurité. Difficile alors pour Volvo d'être l'unique porteur du message. Quoi qu'il en soit, le constructeur innove encore en nous proposant à bord de la S60 la seconde génération de son système City Safety. La première génération permettait de détecter les obstacles et de freiner le véhicule lorsque l'on circulait à basse vitesse en ville, mais cette fois, on a poussé l'idée plus loin avec l'ajout d'un dispositif utilisant une caméra qui pourra détecter un piéton ou un cycliste et ira jusqu'à freiner automatiquement le véhicule si vous circulez sous les 35 km/h.

Sur la route, la nouvelle S60 s'est avérée très agréable à conduire. On la sent solide et rigide, alors que la suspension offre un bon compromis en confort et tenue de route. On note une excellente visibilité à bord et cet élément maximise le sentiment de sécurité et de contrôle. Avec ses 300 chevaux, le moteur délivre amplement de puissance et la boîte automatique tire bien profit du couple et de la puissance disponible. Enfoncez l'accélérateur et le

Catégorie	Berline
Échelle de prix	37 700 $
Garanties	4 ans/80 000 km, 4 ans/80 000 km
Assemblage	Gand, Suède
Cote d'assurance	n.d.

CHÂSSIS - DONNÉES POUR T6 AWD

Emp/lon/lar/haut	2 776/4 628/1 564/1 484 mm
Coffre	340 litres
Réservoir	68 litres
Nombre coussins sécurité	6
Antipatinage / contrôle stabilité	oui / oui
Suspension avant	indépendante, jambes de force
Suspension arrière	indépendante, multibras
Freins avant / arrière	disque (ABS) / disque (ABS)
Direction	à crémaillère, assistée
Diamètre de braquage	15,0 m
Pneus avant / arrière	235/40R18 / 235/40R18
Poids	1 769 kg
Capacité de remorquage	1 500 kg (3 306 lb)

COMPOSANTES MÉCANIQUES

T6 AWD

Cylindrée, soupapes, alim.	6L 3,0 litres 24 s turbo
Puissance / Couple	300 chevaux / 325 lb-pi
Tr. base (opt) / rouage base (opt)	A6 / Int
0-100 / 80-120 / 100-0 km/h	6,5 s / n.d. / n.d.
Type ess. / ville / autoroute	Super / 13,1 / 9 l/100 km

FEU VERT

Habitacle spacieux
Sièges très confortables
Moteur puissant
Nombreux systèmes de sécurité

FEU ROUGE

Une seule version offerte
Peut devenir onéreuse avec les options
Certains contrôles moins intuitifs
Image de marque... chinoise

moteur six cylindres répond promptement, sans aucun délai. On a peut-être droit qu'à une seule motorisation, mais on ne peut lui reprocher de ne pas être efficace.

La nouvelle S60 ne déçoit pas, mais on se demande ce qu'elle a véritablement comme argument-choc face à la concurrence, mis à part quelques éléments. Elle réussira sans doute à faire mieux dans d'autres marchés, mais elle aura certainement plus de difficulté à se tailler une place de choix ici, au Canada. Pour le moment, il faut être un fervent de la marque afin de succomber aux plaisirs de la nouvelle S60.

Sylvain Raymond

DANS LA MÊME CATÉGORIE

Acura TL, Audi A4, BMW Série 3, Cadillac CTS, Infiniti G, Lexus IS, Mercedes-Benz Classe C

DU NOUVEAU EN 2011

Nouveau modèle

NOS IMPRESSIONS

Agrément de conduite :	8/10
Fiabilité :	Nouveau modèle
Sécurité :	10/10
Qualités hivernales :	9/10
Espace intérieur :	8/10
Confort :	8/10

www.volvocanada.com

Plus d'informations dans la section statistiques en dernière partie du Guide

PHOTOS : VOLVO

LA MORT D'UNE ÉTOILE

Lorsque Volvo a présenté une nouvelle S80 en 2007, tous les espoirs étaient permis. Après tout, cette voiture était, et est toujours, la plus luxueuse de la prestigieuse marque suédoise. Même si cette berline haut de gamme en a séduit plus d'un lors de son lancement, force est d'admettre que quatre années plus tard, elle se retrouve sur une pente descendante...

Et quand on se mesure à des Audi A6, BMW Série 5, Mercedes-Benz Classe E et autres Lincoln MKS, vaut mieux être bien armé pour se défendre. En matière de style (et dans le domaine de l'automobile, le style fait souvent foi de tout), cette grosse Volvo fait preuve d'une sobriété et d'un raffinement rarement vus. De la grande classe, quoi. Mais il s'agit d'une question de goût et certains la trouvent, justement, trop sobre malgré les subtils changements apportés l'an dernier.

MAIS QUEL HABITACLE !

Dans l'habitacle, par contre, il faudrait être de mauvaise foi pour trouver à redire. Le tableau de bord demeure l'un des plus fonctionnels de l'industrie avec une ergonomie exemplaire (les commandes de la climatisation/chauffage représentées par un bonhomme assis est un trait de génie, rien de moins), des matériaux de superbe qualité et un assemblage digne d'une Lexus. La console flottante, un élément de style à ne pas négliger, est plus jolie que fonctionnelle même si elle amène les commandes à portée de la main droite du conducteur. Partir à la conquête d'objets laissés dans l'espace de rangement qu'elle dégage conduit à une inévitable torsion du poignet. Par contre, pour les sièges, mes amis, c'est réussi. Extraordinaires, je vous le jure. L'habitacle est passablement vaste et la banquette arrière fait preuve d'un très bon confort, incluant la place centrale, un exploit dont peu de berlines, même haut de gamme, peuvent se vanter. Les dossiers s'abaissent de façon 60/40 pour agrandir un coffre déjà de bonnes dimensions. Cependant, son ouverture est trop petite pour pouvoir y loger de gros objets.

Bien entendu, qui dit Volvo dit sécurité et la S80 ne déroge pas à la tradition. L'habitacle regorge de huit coussins gonflables et de plusieurs systèmes électroniques tels le BLIS (*Blind Spot Information System*) qui avise le conducteur qu'une voiture se trouve dans son angle mort, le CWAB (*Collision Warning with Auto Brake*) qui anticipe, via un radar, les risques de collision et applique les freins le cas échéant ou, enfin, le IDIS (*Intelligent Driver Information System*) qui empêche le conducteur d'être distrait en retardant la sonnerie du téléphone cellulaire, par exemple, tout en ne camouflant pas les informations nécessaires. Bref, tout plein de belles technologies mieux maîtrisées que chez certains manufacturiers, Nissan et Infiniti, pour ne pas les nommer.

AU DIABLE LE V8

Cette année, la S80 perd un moteur. En effet, le V8 de 4,4 litres fait ses adieux mais il n'y a personne sur le parvis qui sort un

FEU VERT

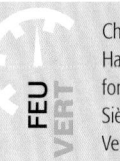

Charme discret
Habitacle esthétique et fonctionnel
Sièges supraconfortables
Version T6 AWD agréable
Niveau de sécurité élevé

FEU ROUGE

Prestige qui s'étiole
Moteur de base style «bof»
Consommation assez importante
Petite ouverture du coffre
Entretien dispendieux

mouchoir. Certes très performant, il affectait négativement le comportement de la voiture, trop lourd qu'il était. Il reste donc le six cylindres en ligne turbocompressé de 3,0 litres de la T6 AWD et l'inutile six cylindres en ligne atmosphérique de 3,2 litres. Ce dernier n'est pas suffisamment puissant pour les 1 740 kilos de la voiture et, surtout, il n'a pas le punch recherché dans une voiture se prétendant luxueuse. En fait, le moteur le mieux adapté à la S80 demeure le 3,0 litres qui permet des accélérations vives, encore plus vives cette année puisque sa puissance a gagné 19 chevaux. Il consomme passablement, toutefois on lui pardonne mieux ses écarts que le moins puissant et pratiquement aussi assoiffé. L'autre avantage du 3,0 litres est qu'il est livré d'office avec le rouage intégral alors que le 3,2 ne donne vie qu'aux roues avant, ce qui ne fait pas très noble, convenez-en. Un rouage intégral est certes plus dispendieux à l'achat mais en plus d'assurer une bien meilleure traction dans la neige, il autorise une meilleure valeur de revente. Peu importe le moteur, une seule transmission est proposée, soit une automatique à six rapports qu'on peut difficilement prendre en défaut.

Le comportement routier de la S80 se veut des plus placides. La direction n'est pas très vive et dès qu'on pousse le moindrement la machine, les différents systèmes électroniques de contrôle prennent le dessus. La version de base affiche un sous-virage marqué tandis que la T6 AWD se veut plus enjouée. Elle est dotée du Four-C Active Chassis, un système permettant de choisir entre différents réglages de suspension. S'il faut se concentrer comme un chat qui reluque un oiseau pour sentir la différence entre les différents réglages de suspension de plusieurs autres voitures, celui de Volvo fonctionne sans questionnement. On passe pratiquement d'une mollesse duveteuse à une dureté favorisant la tenue de route, selon le réglage choisi. Par contre, même le réglage extrême ne fait pas de la S80 un modèle de sportivité et ne peut lui apporter la personnalité qui lui manque. BMW et Audi, par exemple, sont encore loin devant.

En fait, si Volvo n'avait jamais offert que la T6 AWD, sans doute que son image de luxe serait encore intacte. Ou serait moins en déficit. La sobriété de sa carrosserie peut aussi lui jouer des tours dans un monde où l'on cherche souvent à paraître plus qu'à être... Cependant, le nom Volvo rime encore avec confort et sécurité et, à ce chapitre, la S80 est une Volvo pure et dure.

Alain Morin

PHOTOS : VOLVO

Catégorie	Berline
Échelle de prix	46 995 $ à 59 995 $ (2010)
Garanties	4 ans/80 000 km, 4 ans/80 000 km
Assemblage	Torslanda, Suède
Cote d'assurance	n.d.

CHÂSSIS - DONNÉES POUR T6 AWD

Emp/lon/lar/haut	2 835/4 851/1 861/1 493 mm
Coffre	480 litres
Réservoir	70 litres
Nombre coussins sécurité	8
Antipatinage / contrôle stabilité	oui / oui
Suspension avant	indépendante, jambes de force
Suspension arrière	indépendante, multibras
Freins avant / arrière	disque (ABS) / disque (ABS)
Direction	à crémaillère, assistée
Diamètre de braquage	12,2 m
Pneus avant / arrière	P245/40R18 / P245/40R18
Poids	1 740 kg
Capacité de remorquage	750 kg (1 653 lb)

COMPOSANTES MÉCANIQUES

3.2

Cylindrée, soupapes, alim.	6L 3,2 litres 24 s atmos.
Puissance / Couple	235 chevaux / 236 lb-pi
Tr. base (opt) / rouage base (opt)	A6 / Tr
0-100 / 80-120 / 100-0 km/h	8,2 s / n.d. / 39,5 m
Type ess. / ville / autoroute	Super / 12,2 / 7,6 l/100 km

T6 AWD

Cylindrée, soupapes, alim.	6L 3,0 litres 24 s turbo
Puissance / Couple	300 chevaux / 0 lb-pi
Tr. base (opt) / rouage base (opt)	A6 / Int
0-100 / 80-120 / 100-0 km/h	6,9 s / n.d. / 39,5 m
Type ess. / ville / autoroute	Super / 13,3 / 8,6 l/100 km

DANS LA MÊME CATÉGORIE

Acura RL, Audi A6, BMW Série 5, Cadillac STS, Infiniti M, Jaguar XF, Lexus GS, Mercedes-Benz Classe E

DU NOUVEAU EN 2011

V8 abandonné, modèle T6 plus puissant

NOS IMPRESSIONS

Agrément de conduite :	8/10
Fiabilité :	8/10
Sécurité :	10/10
Qualités hivernales :	8/10
Espace intérieur :	8/10
Confort :	9/10

www.volvocanada.com

Plus d'informations dans la section statistiques en dernière partie du Guide

ABONNÉES AU SUCCÈS

Tout le monde le sait, depuis des décennies, les familiales Volvo connaissent une bonne cote de popularité. Même que pour plusieurs, elles permettent à leur propriétaire d'afficher son rang social. En effet, si vous conduisez une V70 ou, encore mieux, une XC70, cela veut dire que vous avez des moyens financiers supérieurs à la moyenne et que vous êtes une personne pratique qui apprécie les voitures sophistiquées.

Au fil des années, le prix de ces belles suédoises n'a cessé de grimper. Malgré tout, les Volvo familiales de la série 70 sont toujours aussi populaires. Il semble y avoir une association entre les gens qui aiment les qualités de la marque et la configuration qu'apporte une familiale. À ce sujet, il faut savoir qu'une voiture de cette catégorie est non seulement éminemment commode, mais qu'elle permet également de profiter d'un comportement routier beaucoup plus intéressant que ce que nous proposent les fourgonnettes et les multisegments. Quant à l'offre de Volvo en la matière, elle se divise ainsi : ordinaire avec laV70,ou extra avec la XC70.

Cette année cependant, la V70 tire sa révérence et la XC70 est la seule familiale Volvo offerte. Mais puisque les inventaires des concessionnaires ont encore plusieurs V70 en stock, nous allons quand même l'évaluer, histoire de vous donner l'heure juste si vous voulez profiter de modèles bradés pour fin de production.

AU REVOIR !

Certains trouvent que la silhouette de la défunte V70 est trop sobre et trop discrète. On lui reproche son manque de punch, d'effets visuels et que sais-je encore. C'est sans doute vrai qu'elle pourrait être un peu plus dynamique sur le plan visuel, mais force est d'admettre que sa silhouette est classique et que les feux arrière verticaux le long du pilier D viennent épicer quelque peu la présentation.

La qualité des matériaux et de la finition est remarquable tandis que la présentation de la planche de bord est classique. Bien entendu, comme toute Volvo qui se respecte, les sièges avant sont excellents car ils procurent un bon support lombaire, latéral et pour les cuisses.

Quant à la planche de bord, elle est sobre et ses commandes sont faciles d'accès et de manipulation. Sur la partie centrale de la console verticale, on retrouve la silhouette d'un corps humain, accompagnée de boutons qui servent à diriger l'air vers le secteur désiré. La position de conduite est satisfaisante de même que la prise du volant. Une bonne note également pour le coffre dont la finition est impeccable et l'espace supérieur à la moyenne. Enfin, le dossier du siège arrière est de type 40/20/40, ce qui facilitera la cohabitation occupants/bagages.

Dans leurs essais, plusieurs chroniqueurs se font un point d'honneur à critiquer le moteur six cylindres en ligne de 3,2 litres,

Assemblage impeccable
Rouage intégral efficace
Suspension Four-C
Tenue de route
Sécurité intégrée

Fiabilité perfectible
Nombreuses options
Prix corsés
Habitabilité moyenne (arrière)
Long diamètre de braquage

soulignant que ses performances sont en dessous de la moyenne. C'est peut-être vrai qu'il est un peu juste en certaines circonstances mais, pour la majorité des gens, ses performances sont correctes. Quant à sa consommation, elle est plus ou moins similaire à celle du moteur T6 3,0 litres turbo produisant 36 chevaux de plus et uniquement disponible sur la XC70.

Le comportement routier de cette suédoise tout usage qu'est la V70 s'avère supérieur à la moyenne et permet de ressentir un certain agrément de conduite, ce qui n'est pas toujours le cas pour une familiale. Précisons que ce modèle n'est offert qu'avec les roues motrices avant.

PLUS ! PLUS !

Le XC70 est un peu comme cet ancien confrère de classe, vous en connaissez sûrement vous-même, qui voulait constamment dépasser tous les autres : nombreuses conquêtes féminines, exploits sportifs ou encore meilleures notes aux examens. Le XC70 me fait penser à ce *winner*. Ce modèle à rouage intégral possède une silhouette plus agressive en raison de ses boucliers avant et arrière et de ces cercles en aluminium mettant en évidence les phares antibrouillards. Il se démarque aussi par une suspension surélevée, la suspension intelligente Four- C qui est fabuleuse ainsi que le système de contrôle de pente.

Le moteur six cylindres turbo et le rouage intégral Haldex font du bon travail aussi bien sur le pavé sec que sur les routes détrempées, glacées ou enneigées. Et puisque la garde au sol du XC70 est plus élevée que la moyenne, sa conduite sur une route peu carrossable ou enneigée est rassurante. L'agrément de conduite de ce modèle est plus relevé grâce à la puissance accrue de son moteur.

Les deux privilégient également la sécurité active et passive. Selon le modèle et le niveau d'équipement, votre familiale peut être dotée d'un système de détection de présence latérale, d'un régulateur de vitesse progressif, d'un système de navigation par satellite, d'éléments de rangement pour le coffre à bagages, d'écrans vidéo au dos des appuie-tête avant, d'un hayon motorisé et j'en passe. Malheureusement, plusieurs de ces accessoires magiques sont optionnels et leur coût est passablement élevé. Ceci dit, ce ne sont pas non plus des gadgets ou des babioles, mais des éléments technologiquement raffinés et efficaces.

Denis Duquet

PHOTOS : VOLVO

WWW.GUIDEAUTOWEB.COM/VOLVO/XC70/

VOLVO XC70

Catégorie	Multisegment
Échelle de prix	43 995 $ à 55 995 $ (2010)
Garanties	4 ans/80 000 km, 4 ans/80 000 km
Assemblage	Torslanda, Suède
Cote d'assurance	n.d.

CHÂSSIS - DONNÉES POUR T6 AWD

Emp/lon/lar/haut	2 815/4 838/2 119/1 604 mm
Coffre	944 à 2 042 litres
Réservoir	70 litres
Nombre coussins sécurité	6
Antipatinage / contrôle stabilité	oui / oui
Suspension avant	indépendante, jambes de force
Suspension arrière	indépendante, multibras
Freins avant / arrière	disque (ABS) / disque (ABS)
Direction	à crémaillère, ass. variable
Diamètre de braquage	10,6 m
Pneus avant / arrière	P215/65R16 / P215/65R16
Poids	1 887 kg
Capacité de remorquage	1 500 kg (3 306 lb)

COMPOSANTES MÉCANIQUES

3.2 AWD

Cylindrée, soupapes, alim.	6L 3,2 litres 24 s atmos.
Puissance / Couple	235 chevaux / 236 lb-pi
Tr. base (opt) / rouage base (opt)	A6 / Int
0-100 / 80-120 / 100-0 km/h	9,2 s / 8,5 s / 39,7 m
Type ess. / ville / autoroute	Super / 13,7 / 8,8 l/100 km

T6 AWD

Cylindrée, soupapes, alim.	6L 3,0 litres 24 s turbo
Puissance / Couple	281 chevaux / 295 lb-pi
Tr. base (opt) / rouage base (opt)	A6 / Int
0-100 / 80-120 / 100-0 km/h	7,8 s / 7,3 s / 39,7 m
Type ess. / ville / autoroute	Super / 13,7 / 9,0 l/100 km

DANS LA MÊME CATÉGORIE

Subaru Outback

DU NOUVEAU EN 2011

Modèle V70 abandonné

NOS IMPRESSIONS

Agrément de conduite :	8/10
Fiabilité :	6/10
Sécurité :	10/10
Qualités hivernales :	9/10
Espace intérieur :	8/10
Confort :	8/10

www.volvocanada.com

Plus d'informations dans la section statistiques en dernière partie du Guide

ÉLÉGANCE, POLYVALENCE ET SÉCURITÉ

Les temps ont beaucoup changé pour la compagnie Volvo. Jadis exclusivement suédoise, elle a ensuite été acquise par le constructeur américain Ford avant que le Chinois Geely en devienne propriétaire. De plus, au fil des années, les véhicules Volvo ont connu une escalade des prix et une montée de catégorie. Autrefois un peu plus chers qu'une berline intermédiaire d'origine nord-américaine, les produits suédois sont venus s'attaquer au marché réservé à des marques telles Audi, BMW et Mercedes-Benz.

ÉQUILIBRE VISUEL

Pour ce faire, les voitures Volvo doivent également proposer une silhouette qui fait tourner les têtes et un habitacle aussi confortable qu'élégant. Les formes carrées ont disparu, mais on a conservé la traditionnelle calandre rectangulaire traversée en diagonale par une barre chromée supportant l'écusson Volvo. Cette fois ledit écusson est davantage en évidence. Cette calandre, qui surplombe une prise d'air d'assez bonnes dimensions, est encadrée par des blocs optiques en forme d'amande servant de point de départ à l'épaulement de la paroi latérale, propre à toutes les Volvo.

Depuis quelques années maintenant, les véhicules utilitaires Volvo se démarquent du lot par des feux arrière verticaux placés de chaque côté de la lunette arrière. Leur partie inférieure est nettement plus large et, dans le cas de la XC60, celle-ci déborde sur la paroi latérale.

Dans l'habitacle, les sièges sont plus stylisés, avec des pièces en cuir de couleur contrastante, mais ils demeurent toujours aussi confortables et parmi les meilleurs sur le marché.

CONFORT SCANDINAVE

Pendant des années, alors que l'on vilipendait la silhouette, on se confondait en louanges pour les sièges de tous les véhicules de la marque. Ceux-ci ci étaient reconnus pour leur confort, leurs multiples réglages et leur support latéral bien supérieur à la moyenne. Les passagers des places avant ne se plaindront jamais du manque d'espace ou d'être mal assis et les places arrière sont assez bien nanties à ce chapitre. Les occupants de ces dernières aimeront la banquette chauffante et le flot d'air réglable de la buse latérale placée derrière le pilier B. Le toit ouvrant est très grand et le coffre est de bonne taille et relativement haut. Autant d'éléments qui viennent consolider la polyvalence de cette belle suédoise.

Chez Volvo, les concepteurs du tableau de bord ne cessent de parler de design scandinave et de sobriété dans la présentation. Ce modèle ne fait pas exception à ce credo esthétique. La planche de bord est simple et dégagée tandis qu'une petite nacelle dans la partie supérieure centrale affiche les réglages choisis, la température de la climatisation, etc. Ce centre d'information aurait pu être escamotable et personne ne s'en serait plaint. Mais cela aurait certainement coûté plus cher et augmenté la

FEU VERT

- Silhouette élégante
- Bonne tenue de route
- Sécurité active et passive fort relevée
- Habitacle confortable
- Rouage intégral efficace

FEU ROUGE

- Moteur turbo gourmand
- Nombreuses options onéreuses
- Diamètre de braquage important
- Véhicule lourd
- Orientation de la marque : inconnue

complexité avec une mécanique en charge du retrait et du déploiement. Par ailleurs, les réglages de la climatisation sont très intuitifs grâce au pictogramme illustrant une silhouette : il suffit d'appuyer sur la partie de l'anatomie que l'on veut réchauffer ou refroidir et c'est tout !

SÉCURITÉ ET AGRÉMENT DE CONDUITE

Pendant longtemps, Volvo a été l'une des rares compagnies à vouloir améliorer la sécurité des véhicules moteurs. De nos jours, toutes les voitures, peu importe leur logo ou leur pays d'origine, sont sécuritaires et Volvo doit trouver des solutions de plus en plus sophistiquées à ce chapitre. C'est dans cette optique que le système City Safety est proposé. Il vise à éradiquer les collisions pouvant survenir à moins de 30 km/h. Un radar détecte la présence d'un objet métallique sur notre route et immobilise la voiture complètement. Toujours au chapitre de la sécurité, ce modèle est doté d'un régulateur de vitesse de proximité, du système Bliss de détection de véhicule dans l'angle mort, d'un détecteur de franchissement de la ligne blanche, d'un radar de recul et d'un mécanisme qui détecte l'endormissement au volant. Avec tout cet attirail, il est impossible de nier le côté sécuritaire de la Volvo !

Pour plusieurs, une Volvo doit être pratique et polyvalente. L'agencement de l'habitacle, le rouage intégral et un coffre à bagages facile d'accès et spacieux satisfont à ces critères. C'est également une voiture qui propose un agrément de conduite fort intéressant. Le moteur 3,0 litres turbo de 281 chevaux est suffisamment nerveux pour répondre aux attentes des conducteurs sportifs tandis que le 3,0 litres, un autre six cylindre en ligne, assure des prestations correctes.

Il est difficile de trouver à redire quant au comportement routier. La tenue de route est relativement neutre et le roulis en virage est presque inexistant. Si l'on pousse davantage, le train avant ne coopère pas et un léger sous-virage se manifeste, mais rien de bien sérieux. De plus, la puissance du moteur est bien adaptée à ce style de conduite, malgré un léger temps de réponse du turbo. Par contre, le diamètre de braquage est trop important et la direction trop assistée, mais pour le reste, ce n'est que du positif. Il faut également souligner une bonne insonorisation, une excellente visibilité pour la catégorie et un agrément de conduite assez relevé pour un multisegment.

Denis Duquet

PHOTOS : MARC LACHAPELLE

Catégorie	VUS
Échelle de prix	39 995 $ à 53 495 $ (2010)
Garanties	4 ans/80 000 km, 4 ans/80 000 km
Assemblage	Gand, Belgique
Cote d'assurance	n.d.

CHÂSSIS - DONNÉES POUR T6 AWD

Emp/lon/lar/haut	2 774/4 628/2 142/1 713 mm
Coffre	873 à 1 907 litres
Réservoir	70 litres
Nombre coussins sécurité	6
Antipatinage / contrôle stabilité	oui / oui
Suspension avant	indépendante, jambes de force
Suspension arrière	indépendante, multibras
Freins avant / arrière	disque (ABS) / disque (ABS)
Direction	à crémaillère, ass. variable
Diamètre de braquage	11,9 m
Pneus avant / arrière	235/60R18 / 235/60R18
Poids	1 928 kg
Capacité de remorquage	500 kg (1 102 lb)

COMPOSANTES MÉCANIQUES

3.2, 3.2 AWD

Cylindrée, soupapes, alim.	6L 3,2 litres atmos.
Puissance / Couple	235 chevaux / 236 lb-pi
Tr. base (opt) / rouage base (opt)	A6 / Tr (Int)
0-100 / 80-120 / 100-0 km/h	9,7 s / 6,6 s / 41,9 m
Type ess. / ville / autoroute	Super / 13,0 / 9,0 l/100 km

T6 AWD, T6 AWD R-Design

Cylindrée, soupapes, alim.	6L 3,0 litres 24 s turbo
Puissance / Couple	281 chevaux / 295 lb-pi
Tr. base (opt) / rouage base (opt)	A6 / Int
0-100 / 80-120 / 100-0 km/h	8,9 s / 6,8 s / 41,0 m
Type ess. / ville / autoroute	Ordinaire / 13,5 / 9,1 l/100 km

DANS LA MÊME CATÉGORIE

Acura RDX, Audi Q5, BMW X3, Infiniti EX, Land Rover LR2, Mercedes-Benz Classe GLK

DU NOUVEAU EN 2011

Aucun changement majeur

NOS IMPRESSIONS

Agrément de conduite :	■■■■■■■■□□	8/10
Fiabilité :	■■■■■■□□□□	6/10
Sécurité :	■■■■■■■■■□	9/10
Qualités hivernales :	■■■■■■■■■□	9/10
Espace intérieur :	■■■■■■■■■□	9/10
Confort :	■■■■■■■■■□	9/10

www.volvocanada.com

Plus d'informations dans la section statistiques en dernière partie du Guide

MÊME HEURE, MÊME POSTE...

Lancé sur le marché en 2002, le XC90 de Volvo n'a pas connu beaucoup de changements majeurs au cours de sa carrière, si ce n'est un léger restylage en 2007 et quelques modifications au chapitre des motorisations qui comprennent aujourd'hui un six cylindres en ligne ainsi qu'un V8 développé par Yamaha. Pour 2011, le XC90 poursuit sa route sans modifications, tout en continuant de se distinguer comme étant le véhicule le plus vendu à l'échelle mondiale chez Volvo.

Fidèle à la tradition établie chez le constructeur suédois, le XC90 met l'accent sur la sécurité. Ainsi, il a été le premier véhicule sport-utilitaire au monde à recevoir un système anticapotage qui commande le freinage sélectif des roues pour éviter que le véhicule ne se retourne lors de brusques changements de direction. Et si un accident majeur devait survenir, le XC90 renferme des rideaux gonflables, couvrant l'entière surface latérale du véhicule, qui demeureront gonflés pendant sept secondes afin d'absorber les chocs à répétition qui se produisent pendant un capotage. De plus, certaines parties du toit sont réalisées en acier au bore, un alliage dont la résistance est de quatre à cinq fois supérieure à celle de l'acier ordinaire.

L'aspect sécurité est également rehaussé par plusieurs détails de conception avancée. Du nombre, on relève le fait que le XC90 est équipé d'une traverse localisée derrière et sous le pare-chocs avant, c'est-à-dire à la même hauteur que le pare-chocs d'une voiture conventionelle, et qui sert précisément à activer les coussins gonflables du véhicule avec lequel le XC90 entre en collision, tout en empêchant le Volvo de monter par-dessus le pare-chocs de cet autre véhicule. La présence de cet élément démontre une certaine attention au fait que les collisions entre véhicules de taille différente se soldent toujours par des blessures plus graves infligées aux passagers du plus petit des véhicules impliqués. Mais il faut noter que cette innovation n'en est pas une de Volvo, mais bien de Ford qui l'a développée pour ses véhicules, Volvo ayant simplement choisi de l'intégrer au XC90.

UNE CONDUITE DE GRAND CONFORT

Au départ, le XC90 n'a pas été conçu en priorisant la conduite hors route mais plutôt la circulation sur routes asphaltées. À ce titre, il n'est donc pas équipé d'une boîte de transfert et ses aptitudes en conduite hors route sont par conséquent limitées. En choisissant un rouage intégral de type Haldex, qui peut varier la répartition de la motricité jusqu'à diriger 95 pour cent de celle-ci vers les roues qui ont le plus d'adhérence, les concepteurs du XC90 ont choisi d'opter pour un système qui s'avère efficace pour la plupart des situations et qui ne nécessite aucune intervention de la part du conducteur.

Deux moteurs sont au programme, dont le six cylindres en ligne de 3,2 litres avec une puissance de 235 chevaux est un peu juste compte tenu de la masse à déplacer. Quant au V8 de 4,4 litres, on

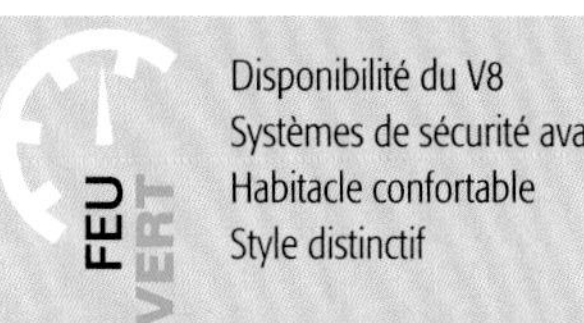

FEU VERT

- Disponibilité du V8
- Systèmes de sécurité avancés
- Habitacle confortable
- Style distinctif

FEU ROUGE

- Roulis en virage
- Fiabilité aléatoire
- Rayon de braquage élevé
- Consommation élevée (V8)

note que la puissance passe à 311 chevaux et que ce moteur autorise une capacité de remorquage de 4 960 livres, soit environ 1 000 livres de mieux que celle du moteur six cylindres. La consommation de carburant demeure élevée avec le V8, elle est acceptable avec le six cylindres, et ces deux moteurs sont jumelés à une boîte automatique à six rapports.

Sur le plan des performances et de la dynamique, le XC90 n'est pas en mesure de soutenir la comparaison avec les modèles concurrents que sont les Volkswagen Touareg et BMW X5 pour ne nommer que ceux-là. Aussi, le montage transversal du moteur six cylindres en ligne fait en sorte que le rayon de braquage du XC90 est très grand, l'espace étant limité pour le mouvement des roues avant, compliquant ainsi les manœuvres de stationnement. De plus, la pédale de frein est un peu molle, ce qui fait que la course de la pédale est longue avant que l'on sente les freins entrer en action. Les freins sont très efficaces et le XC90 stoppe avec autorité, il faut simplement apprivoiser la sensation de la pédale de frein au préalable. Sur autoroute, on note le silence de roulement et on apprécie au plus haut point le confort inégalé des sièges avant qui est devenu l'une des marques de commerce de Volvo.

L'habitacle est réalisé avec soin et les matériaux sont de qualité supérieure, mais le design simpliste de la planche de bord et de la console centrale commence à dater un peu, bien que l'aspect fonctionnel soit encore et toujours au rendez-vous. Comme c'est souvent le cas, les sièges de la troisième rangée ne conviendront qu'à des enfants, et le volume de chargement, avec les sièges de la troisième rangée repliés, est très convenable. Tout comme le X5, le XC90 se distingue avec son hayon en deux parties, ce qui évite les chutes de contenu à l'ouverture, les colis étant retenus à bord par la partie inférieure du hayon.

Le choix d'un XC90 s'avère valable pourvu que l'agrément de conduite ne soit pas au sommet des priorités, car le Volvo met plus l'accent sur le confort que les performances. Par ailleurs, le dossier fiabilité de la marque n'est pas sans tache et le plus récent sondage J.D. Power portant sur la fiabilité des véhicules après trois ans d'usage place Volvo au vingtième rang sur trente-cinq marques, ce qui indique clairement qu'il y a place à amélioration.

Gabriel Gélinas

PHOTOS : VOLVO

VOLVO XC90

Catégorie	VUS
Échelle de prix	51 995 $ à 69 995 $ (2010)
Garanties	4 ans/80 000 km, 4 ans/80 000 km
Assemblage	Iorslanda, Suède
Cote d'assurance	moyenne

CHÂSSIS - DONNÉES POUR 3.2 AWD LUXURY

Emp/lon/lar/haut	2 857/4 807/1 898/1 784 mm
Coffre	249 à 2410 litres
Réservoir	80 litres
Nombre coussins sécurité	8
Antipatinage / contrôle stabilité	oui / oui
Suspension avant	indépendante, jambes de force
Suspension arrière	indépendante, multibras
Freins avant / arrière	disque (ABS) / disque (ABS)
Direction	à crémaillère, ass. variable
Diamètre de braquage	12,5 m
Pneus avant / arrière	P255/60R18 / P235/60R18
Poids	2 132 kg
Capacité de remorquage	2 250 kg (4 960 lb)

COMPOSANTES MÉCANIQUES

3.2 AWD

Cylindrée, soupapes, alim.	6L 3,2 litres 24 s atmos.
Puissance / Couple	235 chevaux / 236 lb-pi
Tr. base (opt) / rouage base (opt)	A6 / Int
0-100 / 80-120 / 100-0 km/h	9,7 s / 7,8 s / 42,2 m
Type ess. / ville / autoroute	Super / 15 ,0/ 10,0 l/100 km

V8 AWD Executive

Cylindrée, soupapes, alim.	V8 4,4 litres 32 s atmos.
Puissance / Couple	311 chevaux / 325 lb-pi
Tr. base (opt) / rouage base (opt)	A6 / Int
0-100 / 80-120 / 100-0 km/h	7,6 s / 7,1 s / 42,9 m
Type ess. / ville / autoroute	Super / 16,2 / 10,6 l/100 km

DANS LA MÊME CATÉGORIE

Acura MDX, Audi Q7, BMW X5, Cadillac SRX, Infiniti FX, Lexus RX, Lincoln MKX, Mercedes-Benz Classe M, Porsche Cayenne, Volkswagen Touareg

DU NOUVEAU EN 2011

Aucun changement majeur

NOS IMPRESSIONS

Agrément de conduite :	8/10
Fiabilité :	6/10
Sécurité :	10/10
Qualités hivernales :	9/10
Espace intérieur :	8/10
Confort :	9/10

www.volvocanada.com

Plus d'informations dans la section statistiques en dernière partie du Guide

CAMIONNETTES

Cadillac / Chevrolet / Dodge / Ford / GMC / Honda / Nissan / Suzuki / Toyota

Chevrolet Avalanche

SI LA POLYVALENCE VOUS INTÉRESSE

Il faut bien admettre que l'équipe responsable de la mise au point de l'Avalanche a réussi à développer et produire un véhicule très original tout en demeurant pratique. Il s'agit d'une camionnette dotée d'une boîte de chargement relativement courte (1,6 m) qui peut quand même transporter des objets d'une longueur de 2,3 m grâce à un ingénieux système.

En fait, qu'il s'agisse du Chevrolet Avalanche ou de la Cadillac EXT, les deux possèdent l'impressionnant système MidGate qui permet de rabattre dans l'habitacle la cloison avant de la caisse. Il est de plus passablement précis et facile à manipuler. Qui plus est, les bruits de caisse et cliquetis que l'on pourrait craindre avec un tel mécanisme ne sont pas de la partie. Bien entendu, les places arrière deviennent inutilisables, mais c'est quand même un compromis intéressant. Une fois la cloison refermée et les dossiers relevés, ces camionnettes proposent des places arrière confortables et spacieuses.

L'AVALANCHE D'ABORD

Bien que la marque Cadillac soit plus prestigieuse que Chevrolet, c'est la division au nœud papillon qui a conçu et développé cette camionnette. En plus du système MidGate, les ingénieurs ont pensé à des espaces de rangement dans les parois de la caisse, une initiative qui a été copiée par la suite sur les camionnettes Ram par exemple. En plus, la caisse peut être recouverte de trois panneaux amovibles qui se manipulent bien et qui peuvent aisément se remiser. En outre, des appuis pour les pieds et des poignées sont placés de chaque côté de la caisse arrière afin de faciliter la montée. Bref, on ne s'est pas contenté de concocter un produit original, l'exécution est réussie.

Malgré le caractère brillant de l'Avalanche, la crise économique et les conditions difficiles qu'a connues General Motors au cours des derniers mois ont obligé quelques réductions des effectifs. En premier lieu, un seul moteur est disponible depuis l'an dernier, il s'agit de l'incontournable moteur V8 de 5,3 litres dont les 310 chevaux sont suffisants dans la plupart des cas. Il est associé à une boîte automatique à six rapports dont le fonctionnement est sans reproche. L'acheteur peut choisir entre la propulsion ou encore un rouage intégral entièrement automatique. Ce système ne comprend toutefois qu'une seule vitesse. Si vous voulez une démultipliée, vous devrez la commander par l'entremise du catalogue des options.

L'habitacle est relativement spacieux bien que la console centrale occupe beaucoup d'espace. La planche de bord est simple avec des commandes accessibles et la position de conduite sera jugée bonne par la plupart des conducteurs. Sur la route, la première chose que l'on remarque est le confort relatif de cette camionnette transformable. En effet, les ingénieurs ont prévu que les acheteurs utiliseraient ce modèle surtout pour des besoins familiaux et ils ont donc remplacé les ressorts elliptiques par des ressorts hélicoïdaux assurant ainsi un meilleur confort.

FEU VERT
Système MidGate
Suspension confortable
Bon comportement routier
Utilisation multiple
Excellents moteurs
Transmission six rapports

FEU ROUGE
Consommation élevée
Direction engourdie
Dimensions gargantuesques
Avenir incertain
Absence de version hybride

Sur la grande route, il faut faire attention et surveiller l'indicateur de vitesse, car une bonne insonorisation et un moteur tournant à bas régime nous font rouler bien au-dessus des limites de vitesse affichées sans que nous nous en rendions compte, ce qui pourrait avoir de fâcheuses conséquences... Malgré tout, ce modèle demeure une camionnette avec des dimensions encombrantes, un poids élevé et une consommation en conséquence.

POUR *GENTLEMAN-FARMER* FORTUNÉ

Pourquoi la division Cadillac propose-t-elle sa propre version de l'Avalanche, soit l'Escalade EXT ? Tout simplement parce qu'on a flairé un très bon marché. En effet, nombreuses sont les personnes ayant les moyens d'acheter un véhicule à ce prix et qui ont besoin d'une camionnette offrant le confort d'un gros VUS tout en possédant une caisse de chargement à l'arrière. Il y avait bien le Hummer SUT, mais cela faisait un peu trop militaire aux yeux de plusieurs riches Américains et Canadiens.

Donc, pour aller à votre club de chasse ou de pêche ou encore pour traverser votre ranch, un tel véhicule vous permet de circuler hors route dans un confort très substantiel. Et il ne faut pas oublier également l'attrait du système MidGate ! Cela dit, on ne pouvait se contenter d'appliquer des écussons Cadillac sur une camionnette Chevrolet. On a quand même conservé la carrosserie en majeure partie, mais on retrouve sur la EXT les feux de route verticaux typique des autres Cadillac, des rétroviseurs chromés ainsi que des roues en alliage exclusives à Cadillac. Dans l'habitacle, c'est le luxe absolu avec des sièges en cuir de série, des appliques en bois ainsi que de nombreux accessoires, notamment un système audio de meilleure qualité et un climatiseur plus sophistiqué.

Toujours au chapitre de l'exclusivité, cette « Caddy » des routes et des champs est propulsée par un moteur Cadillac de 6,2 litres produisant 403 chevaux et couplé à une transmission automatique à six rapports. Cette fois, seul le rouage intégral est proposé. Ceci assure des performances impressionnantes avec un temps de 7,4 secondes pour franchir le 0-100 km/h. Mais le prix à payer pour cela est une consommation de plus de 17 litres au 100 km...

Denis Duquet

Cadillac Escalade EXT

PHOTOS : CHEVROLET

WWW.GUIDEAUTOWEB.COM/CHEVROLET/AVALANCHE/

CHEVROLET AVALANCHE / CADILLAC ESCALADE EXT

Catégorie	Camionnette
Échelle de prix	42 235 $ à 78 535 $ (2010)
Garanties	3 ans/60 000 km, 5 ans/160 000 km
Assemblage	Silao, Mexique
Cote d'assurance	passable

CHÂSSIS - DONNÉES POUR AVALANCHE LT 4X4

Emp/lon/lar/haut	3 302/5 621/2 009/1 946 mm
Longueur de boîte	6 091 mm (63.3 pouces)
Réservoir	117 litres
Nombre coussins sécurité	6
Antipatinage / contrôle stabilité	oui / oui
Suspension avant	indépendante, bras inégaux
Suspension arrière	essieu rigide, ressorts à lames
Freins avant / arrière	disque (ABS) / disque (ABS)
Direction	à crémaillère, assistée
Diamètre de braquage	13,1 m
Pneus avant / arrière	P265/70R17 / P265/70R17
Poids	2 560 kg
Capacité de remorquage	3 764 kg (8 100 lb)

COMPOSANTES MÉCANIQUES

LS, LT, LTZ

Cylindrée, soupapes, alim.	V8 5,3 litres 16 s atmos.
Puissance / Couple	310 chevaux / 335 lb-pi
Tr. base (opt) / rouage base (opt)	A6 / Prop (4x4)
0-100 / 80-120 / 100-0 km/h	11,3 s / 7,6 s / 45,1 m
Type ess. / ville / autoroute	Ordinaire / 14,4 / 9,6 l/100 km

Cadillac EXT

Cylindrée, soupapes, alim.	V8 6,2 litres 16 s atmos.
Puissance / Couple	403 chevaux / 417 lb-pi
Tr. base (opt) / rouage base (opt)	A6 / Int
0-100 / 80-120 / 100-0 km/h	7,4 s / 5,6 s / 45,8 m
Type ess. / ville / autoroute	Ordinaire / 15,3 / 10,1 l/100 km

DANS LA MÊME CATÉGORIE

Chevrolet Silverado, RAM 1500, Ford F-150, GMC Sierra, Nissan Titan, Toyota Tundra

DU NOUVEAU EN 2011

Chevrolet Avalanche : Sièges baquets à l'avant, console au plancher, longerons pour porte-bagages et centraux, connexion Bluetooth de série.
Cadillac Escalade EXT : Aucun changement majeur

NOS IMPRESSIONS

Agrément de conduite :	7/10
Fiabilité :	7/10
Sécurité :	8/10
Qualités hivernales :	7/10
Espace intérieur :	8/10
Confort :	8/10

www.gm.ca

Plus d'informations dans la section statistiques en dernière partie du Guide

GMC Canyon

UN DUO MODERNE

La famille des camionnettes compactes s'amenuise chaque année. Cette année, c'est Mazda qui quitte la catégorie faute de pouvoir convaincre les acheteurs que son *pick-up* Série B est mieux qu'un Ford Ranger, son jumeau sur le plan mécanique et esthétique.

Les gens leur préfèrent des intermédiaires plus grosses et plus puissantes que sont les Dodge Dakota, Nissan Frontier et Toyota Tacoma. Malgré tout, le duo proposé par GM est quasiment le seul à tenir tête au Ford Ranger, le plus populaire de ce créneau.

Le Chevrolet Colorado et le GMC Canyon sont de conception beaucoup plus récente que leur concurrent direct en provenance de Dearborn. Mais tant dans la réalisation générale que dans la motorisation, les ingénieurs de l'ancien numéro un mondial ont une fois de plus tourné les coins un peu trop ronds.

POURQUOI TROIS MOTEURS?

Ces deux camionnettes proposent pas moins de trois groupes propulseurs, ce qui est assez exceptionnel pour cette catégorie. Le moteur de la version la plus économique est un quatre cylindres de 2,9 litres d'une puissance de 185 chevaux associé de série à une boîte manuelle à cinq rapports. Il est bruyant et manque de raffinement, mais sa puissance est correcte et son économie de carburant se situe dans la bonne moyenne. Jusqu'à l'an dernier, le seul autre moteur offert était un cinq cylindres en ligne de 3,7 litres produisant 242 chevaux. Il s'agit, certains d'entre vous l'auront sans doute deviné, du moulin qui propulsait les Chevrolet Trailblazer et GMC Envoy. Si l'on se fie à sa description technique, on serait en droit de s'attendre à des performances relevées et à une bonne économie de carburant. Avec ses arbres à cames en tête, le calage variable des soupapes et l'injection de carburant séquentiel, ce cinq cylindres est intéressant sur papier. Mais, comme sur les VUS qu'il propulsait autrefois, les performances sont moyennes et la consommation de carburant pourrait être meilleure. Cette fois, pas de boîte manuelle, juste une transmission automatique à quatre rapports. On peut bien croire que l'utilisation anticipée de ces camionnettes peut justifier une telle transmission, mais deux rapports additionnels amélioreraient non seulement le rendement, mais diminueraient le niveau sonore en plus de réduire la consommation de carburant.

Par contre, l'an dernier, on a voulu mettre un peu plus de crème sur le gâteau, et on a donné la possibilité de retrouver un moteur V8 sous le capot. Ce V8 de 300 chevaux offre également un couple de beaucoup supérieur au moteur cinq cylindres. Ses accélérations et reprises sont nettement plus performantes, mais si vous croyez pouvoir remorquer une grosse roulotte, vous constaterez que sa capacité de remorquage est quasiment similaire à celle du moteur cinq cylindres. En revanche, vous allez vous assoir au volant d'une camionnette qui consomme davantage et dont la tenue de route est affectée par un certain déséquilibre en raison d'un moteur plus lourd

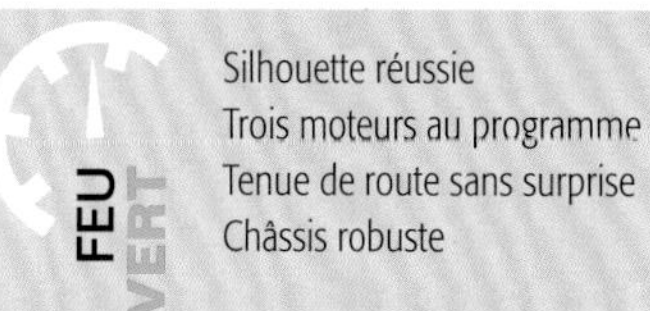

FEU VERT

- Silhouette réussie
- Trois moteurs au programme
- Tenue de route sans surprise
- Châssis robuste

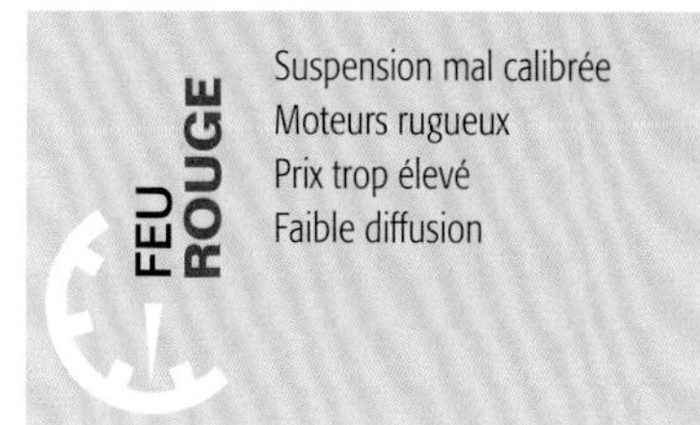

FEU ROUGE

- Suspension mal calibrée
- Moteurs rugueux
- Prix trop élevé
- Faible diffusion

à l'avant. Et malgré toute cette puissance, même la version avec moteur V8 est dotée de freins arrière à tambour, une idée qui n'est pas des plus réjouissantes.

SILHOUETTE MODERNE

Si les ingénieurs semblent avoir fait leur travail à moitié, les stylistes ont quand même accompli du bon boulot. La silhouette moderne et les passages de roue bombés donnent un peu plus de caractère à cette camionnette compacte. Et le fait d'offrir une version à cabine double ajoute à l'élégance. L'habitacle est sobre, pratique et les matériaux ont l'air d'avoir été surtout choisis en fonction d'un usage presque exclusivement utilitaire.

Dans cet habitacle, tout est simple et à portée de la main. Les commandes de ventilation, de climatisation et du système audio sont faciles à décoder et à utiliser. Le volant à quatre branches est passablement bien stylisé, mais il est d'une sobriété tout industrielle qui risque d'en décourager certains. En passant, la position de conduite est bonne, les sièges moyennement confortables et, comme il faut s'y attendre sur une camionnette, leur support latéral fait défaut. Les propriétaires de ce modèle quatre portes pourront accommoder deux adultes de taille moyenne avec un certain niveau de confort à l'arrière. Mais les grands ados vont se sentir à l'étroit. Et peu importe votre taille, l'inclinaison du dossier est trop verticale.

Sur la route, le châssis et la suspension ont beaucoup de difficultés à maîtriser les irrégularités de la chaussée. Le véhicule semble sautiller constamment et on se demande pourquoi les amortisseurs sont aussi souples. Pourtant, lorsqu'on franchit un trou, il y a un tel choc qu'on réalise que la suspension n'est pas si souple que cela. En ville, ses dimensions relativement compactes lui permettent de se faufiler dans la circulation sans trop de problèmes. Malheureusement, un diamètre de braquage quasiment hors-norme rend les manœuvres de stationnement assez pénibles.

Somme toute, il suffirait d'un groupe propulseur un peu plus incisif associé à une transmission automatique à six rapports et à une suspension révisée pour que ce tandem soit grandement amélioré. Et il faudrait également que les responsables de la mise en marché se décident à réduire considérablement le prix.

Denis Duquet

GMC Canyon

PHOTOS : GMC

Catégorie	Camionnette
Échelle de prix	23 860 $ à 36 475 $ (2010)
Garanties	3 ans/60 000 km, 5 ans/160 000 km
Assemblage	Shreveport, Louisiane, É-U
Cote d'assurance	moyenne

CHÂSSIS - DONNÉES POUR COLORADO LT 4X4 CABINE MULTIPLACE

Emp/lon/lar/haut	3 200/5 260/1 742/1 725 mm
Longueur de boîte	1 551 mm (61,1 pouces)
Réservoir	74 litres
Nombre coussins sécurité	6
Antipatinage / contrôle stabilité	oui / oui
Suspension avant	indépendante, barres de torsion
Suspension arrière	essieu rigide, ressorts à lames
Freins avant / arrière	disque (ABS) / tambour (ABS)
Direction	à crémaillère, assistée
Diamètre de braquage	12,0 m
Pneus avant / arrière	P235/75R16 / P235/75R16
Poids	1 846 kg
Capacité de remorquage	2 495 kg (5 500 lb)

COMPOSANTES MÉCANIQUES

Cabine simple, allongée	
Cylindrée, soupapes, alim.	4L 2,9 litres 16 s atmos.
Puissance / Couple	185 chevaux / 190 lb-pi
Tr. base (opt) / rouage base (opt)	M5 (A4) / Prop (4x4)
0-100 / 80-120 / 100-0 km/h	n.d. / n.d. / n.d.
Type ess. / ville / autoroute	Ordinaire / 11,3 / 7,8 l/100 km

Cabine multiplaces	
Cylindrée, soupapes, alim.	5L 3,7 litres 16 s atmos.
Puissance / Couple	242 chevaux / 242 lb-pi
Tr. base (opt) / rouage base (opt)	M5 (A4) / Prop (4x4)
0-100 / 80-120 / 100-0 km/h	8,7 s / n.d. / 41,0 m
Type ess. / ville / autoroute	Ordinaire / 12,5 / 8,7 l/100 km

Optionnel	
Cylindrée, soupapes, alim.	V8 5,3 litres 16 s atmos.
Puissance / Couple	300 chevaux / 320 lb-pi
Tr. base (opt) / rouage base (opt)	M5 (A4) / Prop (4x4)
0-100 / 80-120 / 100-0 km/h	7,0 s (est) / n.d. / 41,0 m
Type ess. / ville / autoroute	Ordinaire 14,4 / 9,9 l/100 km

DANS LA MÊME CATÉGORIE

RAM Dakota, Ford Ranger, Nissan Frontier, Suzuki Equator, Toyota Tacoma

DU NOUVEAU EN 2011

Aucun changement majeur

NOS IMPRESSIONS

Agrément de conduite :	6/10
Fiabilité :	4/10
Sécurité :	8/10
Qualités hivernales :	7/10
Espace intérieur :	6/10
Confort :	7/10

www.gm.ca

Plus d'informations dans la section statistiques en dernière partie du Guide

Chevrolet Silverado

À L'AUBE D'UNE REFONTE

C'est à l'automne 2006 que GM nous présentait la nouvelle génération de son tandem Silverado et Sierra, une camionnette qui, à l'époque, innovait à plusieurs chapitres, et qui a reçu plusieurs honneurs bien mérités. Quatre ans plus tard, force est d'admettre que la compétition féroce qui sévit dans ce créneau commence à désavantager GM face à une concurrence rafraîchie. Alors que GM nous présente sa nouvelle gamme de modèles HD en 2011, la refonte de la camionnette légère devrait suivre l'an prochain.

Tout d'abord, il faut avouer que, dans le segment des camionnettes, il existe une loyauté peu commune à un logo. Peu importe les avantages d'un véhicule par rapport à l'autre, chaque marque possède son lot d'irréductibles prêts à défendre haut et fort les vertus de sa camionnette. Voilà un élément bien apprécié des constructeurs, sauf qu'à l'opposé, il devient plus difficile de voler des ventes à la concurrence. Malgré l'âge de cette génération, GM a su conserver sa compétitivité en apportant quelques changements à ses véhicules au fil des ans. Il n'est pas évident de rivaliser avec le Ford F-150, le ténor du segment en matière de ventes, ni avec le Dodge Ram, deux camionnettes qui ont profité d'une refonte complète il y a peu de temps.

UN STYLE MOINS MACHO

Outre le logo, le style est certainement l'un des éléments qui influencent le plus l'achat d'une camionnette. Si le Ram offre des lignes très sportives, le F-150 de son côté mise sur la robustesse avec son style imposant. Quant à GM, sa camionnette propose un style un peu plus classique et sophistiqué. D'ailleurs, ce style change au gré des versions et des équipements que vous choisissez, ce qui transforme une camionnette au design peu emballant, en un véhicule beaucoup plus agréable à l'œil. L'élément sans doute le plus distinctif de cette camionnette est la caisse avec ses passages de roue en relief, apportant un peu plus de sportivité. Si l'on se fie à l'évolution de la version HD au chapitre du style, le Sierra et le Silverado devraient conserver passablement le même style, avec peut-être des accents plus robustes.

Difficile de décrire les multiples déclinaisons, mais tout comme la concurrence, le Sierra/Silverado propose un choix de trois cabines (Classique, Allongée et Multiplace), jumelées à trois longueurs de caisse. Il faut ici faire un choix: plus d'espace dans la cabine ou plus d'espace dans la caisse. Voilà qui déterminera la combinaison idéale pour vous.

BIEN CHOISIR SON MOTEUR

Vient ensuite le moteur. Voilà sans doute le principal élément à considérer puisqu'il détermine principalement les capacités de la camionnette. Dans le cas de GM, on retrouve un choix de moteurs plus qu'exhaustif: pas moins de cinq motorisations sont proposées. Le V6 de 4,3 litres est offert avec quelques versions de base

FEU VERT

Bon choix de moteur
Comportement agréable
Choix de modèles impressionnant

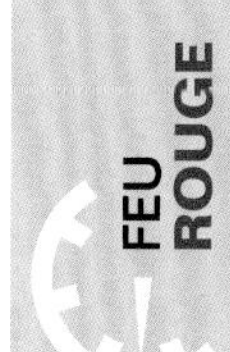

FEU ROUGE

Modèle de nouvelle génération à venir
Version hybride peu intéressante
Boîte automatique à quatre rapports
Freins à tambour à l'arrière

à deux roues motrices. Vient ensuite le V8 de 4,8 litres qui équipe la majeure partie des versions et qui développe une puissance de 302 chevaux. Optionnel à bord de plusieurs versions et de série sur la version plus cossue, le V8 de 5,3 litres nous semble le plus intéressant du lot. Ce n'est pas ses quelque douze chevaux supplémentaires qui le rendent aussi intéressant, mais plutôt le fait qu'il est marié à une boîte automatique à six rapports, plutôt qu'à quatre rapports. En fait, en plus d'offrir des chiffres plus éloquents, ce moteur comporte une meilleure économie de carburant que le V8 de 4,8 litres, soit près de 1,0 l/100 km de moins en moyenne.

Au sommet de la gamme trône le V8 de 6,2 litres qui développe 403 chevaux. Jumelé à la boîte automatique à six rapports, il offre les capacités maximales de remorquage du véhicule, soit 10400 lb dans la version à quatre roues motrices. Cette mesure passe à 9600 lb en présence du moteur de 5,3 litres. Le dernier V8 du lot, celui de 6,0 litres, est réservé à la version hybride, une motorisation unique à GM dans le segment. Ce moteur à essence se voit couplé à un moteur électrique de 300 volts qui entraîne une consommation de carburant sous la barre des 10 l/100 km. Cependant, il faut composer avec des capacités de chargement et de remorquage bien moindre.

À bord, on remarque un peu plus l'âge de cette génération. Le tableau de bord est beaucoup moins moderne que ce que l'on retrouve dans les nouveaux véhicules du constructeur qui, de plus, disposent des derniers gadgets et accessoires de connectivité. Il faut avouer qu'au chapitre de l'habitacle, la barre a été rehaussée avec les nouveaux produits de Ford et Chrysler, surtout dans le cas du Ram qui remporte la palme à ce chapitre. Étonnant de la part de Dodge qui n'est pas réputé pour ses habitacles !

Du reste, le Sierra/Silverado adopte sur la route un comportement très confortable qui nous fait rapidement oublier que l'on est à bord d'une camionnette. Sa suspension inhibe bien les défaits de la route, tout en réagissant avec aplomb en virage. Au chapitre des dernières déceptions, on note, contrairement à la concurrence, l'utilisation de freins à tambour à l'arrière, moins efficaces que des freins à disques. Seules la version Denali et celles équipées de l'ensemble Remorquage Max bénéficient de quatre freins à disques.

Sylvain Raymond

GMC Sierra

PHOTOS : DENIS DUQUET

Catégorie	Camionnette
Échelle de prix	26260$ à 51655$ (2010)
Garanties	3 ans/60000 km, 5 ans/160000 km
Assemblage	Oshawa, Ontario, Canada
Cote d'assurance	passable

CHÂSSIS - DONNÉES POUR SILVERADO LS 4X2 CABINE ALLONGÉE

Emp/lon/lar/haut	3645/5847/2029/1877 mm
Longueur de boîte	2483 mm (97,7 pouces)
Réservoir	128 litres
Nombre coussins sécurité	6
Antipatinage / contrôle stabilité	oui / oui
Suspension avant	indépendante, bras inégaux
Suspension arrière	essieu rigide, ressorts à lames
Freins avant / arrière	disque (ABS) / disque (ABS)
Direction	à crémaillère, assistée
Diamètre de braquage	13,6 m
Pneus avant / arrière	P245/70R17 / P245/70R17
Poids	2388 kg
Capacité de remorquage	4536 kg (10000 lb)

COMPOSANTES MÉCANIQUES

Silverado, Sierra	V6 4,3 litres, 195 ch / 260 lb-pi
Tr. base (opt) / rouage base (opt)	A4 / Prop (4x4)
Type ess. / ville / autoroute	Ordinaire / 14,1 / 10,0 l/100 km
Silverado, Sierra	V8 4,8 litres, 302 ch / 305 lb-pi
Tr. base (opt) / rouage base (opt)	A4 (A6) / Prop (4x4)
Type ess. / ville / autoroute	Ordinaire / 15,9 / 11,4 l/100 km
Silverado, Sierra	V8 5,3 litres, 315 ch / 338 lb-pi
Tr. base (opt) / rouage base (opt)	A4 (A6) / Prop (4x4)
Type ess. / ville / autoroute	Ordinaire / 14,4 / 9,5 l/100 km
Silverado Hybrid, Sierra Hybrid	V8 6,0 litres, 332 ch / 367 lb-pi
Tr. base (opt) / rouage base (opt)	A4 / Prop (4x4)
Type ess. / ville / autoroute	Ordinaire / 9,8 / 9,1 l/100 km

Silverado, Sierra Denali
V8 6,2 l, 403 ch / 417 lb-pi, 17,0 / 10,6 l/100 km

DANS LA MÊME CATÉGORIE

RAM 1500, Ford F-150, Nissan Titan, Toyota Tundra

DU NOUVEAU EN 2011

Aucun changement majeur

NOS IMPRESSIONS

Agrément de conduite :	8/10
Fiabilité :	6/10
Sécurité :	6/10
Qualités hivernales :	7/10
Espace intérieur :	8/10
Confort :	8/10

www.gm.ca

Plus d'informations dans la section statistiques en dernière partie du Guide

REMANIEMENT COMPLET DES MOTEURS!

Lorsque vient le temps de se procurer une camionnette pleine grandeur, il est difficile de ne pas considérer sérieusement le F-150. Ford est loin d'être le dernier venu dans le créneau et chaque génération du F-150 profite d'un investissement colossal de la part du constructeur qui ne veut rien concéder à la concurrence. Trois ans à peine après l'arrivée de la nouvelle génération, voilà que le F-150 propose cette année pas moins de quatre nouveaux moteurs, une autre preuve que le F-150 demeure l'un des plus importants produits chez Ford.

LA RECETTE DU SUCCÈS

Outre le fait que chaque marque comporte son lot de fidèles, trois éléments attirent principalement les acheteurs, soit le style, les fonctionnalités et les capacités. Voilà trois choses que Ford maitrise très bien, ce qui explique en bonne partie le succès de la Série F.

Fort d'une refonte complète en 2009, le F-150 séduit en raison de ses lignes musclées et trapues. Sa ceinture de caisse élevée, sa grille avant imposante et son capot surélevé procurent au véhicule un sentiment de robustesse, ce que plusieurs apprécient. Ajoutez divers ensembles (XTR, King Ranch, Platinum et Harley-Davidson), un peu plus de chrome ou quelques éléments distinctifs et vous obtenez une camionnette toute aussi belle à l'œil qu'une voiture sport. En fait, dans certains cas, c'est peut-être même un peu trop poussé.

Si la version Supercrew avec ses quatre portes ajoute un côté pratique, plusieurs se laisseront tenter par les lignes plus sportives de la version à cabine double. À ce chapitre, diverses options s'offrent

à vous car le F-150 peut être commandé avec trois types de cabine (Classique, Double, *Supercrew*) et trois longueurs de plateau, soit 5,5, 6,5 et 6,0 pieds. Cependant, sachez que la plus longue des cabines, Supercrew, ne peut-être jumelée à la plus longue des caisses (8,0 pieds). Il faut donc choisir, plus d'espace dans l'habitacle ou une caisse aux dimensions supérieures.

À l'intérieur, on aime la finition et l'excellente ergonomie. Tout est bien pensé et placé au bon endroit. Les commandes tombent bien en main, sont simples à comprendre et bien en vue. Le système de navigation avec son écran tactile embellit le tableau de bord tout en facilitant le contrôle de nombreux équipements, mais son prix le rend malheureusement moins accessible. C'est surtout l'affichage de la caméra de recul que l'on apprécie puisqu'en l'absence d'un tel système, l'image est projetée dans le rétroviseur, dans un format beaucoup plus petit.

Le F-150 dispose d'une panoplie de rangements pratiques tant à l'avant qu'à l'arrière. Les versions de base pourront accueillir six passagers en raison d'une banquette à l'avant. Aussi, les versions FX4 et supérieures héritent d'une large console qui intègre le

FEU VERT

- Nouveaux choix de moteurs
- Capacités exemplaires
- Style réussi
- Transmission six rapports efficace

FEU ROUGE

- Certains équipements uniques aux versions cossues
- Cuir des sièges qui craque
- Toujours pas de motorisation diesel

sélecteur de vitesse. Bien entendu, les divers ensembles mentionnés plus haut dans le texte peuvent rendre l'habitacle aussi luxueux que celui de plusieurs grandes berlines. Bon point également pour la banquette arrière qui peut être relevée afin d'augmenter l'espace de chargement.

DU NOUVEAU DANS LES MOTORISATIONS

Le F-150 domine le segment au chapitre de la capacité de remorquage (11 300 lb) et de chargement. Cet élément est apporté par l'utilisation de lames de suspension de dimensions supérieures, même chose pour les longerons du châssis. Ajoutez une rigidité exemplaire et vous obtenez une camionnette prête pour les gros travaux. Cependant, le talon d'Achille du F-150 était son moteur de 5,4 litres dont les performances n'étaient pas très éloquentes. Voilà que le Ford corrige le tir avec l'arrivée de quatre nouveaux moteurs, tous jumelés à une nouvelle boîte automatique à six rapports, le seul constructeur à proposer six rapports pour toutes les versions. Ce sont là les changements les plus drastiques en plus de 62 ans. Au moment d'aller sous presse, voici les quelques informations que nous avons réussi à arracher aux gens de Ford...

Tout d'abord, pour les travaux légers, il y a un moteur V6 de 3,7 litres développant 291 chevaux et apportant une économie de carburant appréciable grâce à l'utilisation de la technologie de calage variable des soupapes. On verra ultérieurement l'arrivée d'un moteur V6 EcoBoost de 3,5 litres qui, via la turbocompression, livre la puissance d'un V8 et l'économie d'un six cylindres. C'est la toute première fois que l'on retrouve un moteur turbo à bord du F-150. Vient ensuite le V8 de 5,0 litres, dérivé de celui de la Mustang mais ayant reçu nombre de modifications, histoire de maximiser ses applications à bord d'une camionnette. Eh oui, nous avons maintenant le F-150 5,0 litres ! Ce moteur génère une puissance de 360 chevaux pour un couple de 380 lb-pi. Ce qui est supérieur aux 320 chevaux déployés par l'ancien V8.

Finalement au sommet de la gamme trône le V8 de 6,2 litres, le même moulin proposé de série à bord des versions Super Duty 2500/3500. Ce moteur, qui équipe de série le F-150 SVT Raptor, commande 411 chevaux pour un couple de 434 lb-pi. Voilà qui fait du F-150 la plus puissante des camionnettes d'une demie tonne offertes cette année.

Sylvain Raymond

PHOTOS : SYLVAIN RAYMOND

FORD F-150

Catégorie	Camionnette
Échelle de prix	23 415 $ à 51 799 $ (2010)
Garanties	3 ans/60 000 km, 5 ans/100 000 km
Assemblage	Oakville, Ontario, Canada
Cote d'assurance	moyenne

CHÂSSIS - DONNÉES POUR LARIAT 4X4 CABINE DOUBLE

Emp/lon/lar/haut	3 683/5 885/2 004/1 816 mm
Longueur de boîte	1 981 mm (78,0 pouces)
Réservoir	136 litres
Nombre coussins sécurité	6
Antipatinage / contrôle stabilité	oui / oui
Suspension avant	indépendante, double triangulation
Suspension arrière	essieu rigide, ressorts à lames
Freins avant / arrière	disque (ABS) / disque (ABS)
Direction	à crémaillère, assistée
Diamètre de braquage	13,0 m
Pneus avant / arrière	P275/65R18 / P275/65R18
Poids	2 475 kg
Capacité de remorquage	4 400 kg (9 700 lb)

COMPOSANTES MÉCANIQUES (DONNÉES 2010)

	V8 4,6 l 248 ch / 294 lb-pi
Tr. base (opt) / rouage base (opt)	A4 / Prop (4x4)
Type ess. / ville / autoroute	Ordinaire / 14,4 / 10,4 l/100 km
	V8 4,6 l 292 ch / 320 lb-pi
Tr. base (opt) / rouage base (opt)	A6 / Prop (4x4)
Type ess. / ville / autoroute	Ordinaire / 14,9 / 10,2 l/100 km
	V8 5,4 l 320 ch / 390 lb-pi
Tr. base (opt) / rouage base (opt)	A6 / Prop (4x4)
Type ess. / ville / autoroute	Ordinaire / 15,9 / 11,3 l/100 km
SVT Raptor	
Cylindrée, soupapes, alim.	V8 6,2 l 411 ch / 434 lb-pi
Tr. base (opt) / rouage base (opt)	A6 / Prop
0-100 / 80-120 / 100-0 km/h	6,5 s (est) / n.d. / n.d.
Type ess. / ville / autoroute	18,0 / 14,0 l/100 km (est)

DANS LA MÊME CATÉGORIE

Chevrolet Silverado, Ram 1500, GMC Sierra, Nissan Titan, Toyota Tundra

DU NOUVEAU EN 2011

Nouveaux moteurs

NOS IMPRESSIONS

Agrément de conduite :	8/10
Fiabilité :	6/10
Sécurité :	10/10
Qualités hivernales :	7/10
Espace intérieur :	8/10
Confort :	8/10

www.ford.ca

Plus d'informations dans la section statistiques en dernière partie du Guide

TOUTE BONNE CHOSE A UNE FIN

Le Ford Ranger promène sa bouille de sympathique macho depuis déjà plus de 28 ans. Il a donc pleinement mérité sa retraite ! Durant l'année, Ford cessera sa production, après plus de 7 millions d'unités. Nous parlons ici du Ranger nord-américain, ce nom étant repris ailleurs sur le globe pour d'autres camionnettes Ford, souvent beaucoup plus modernes. Toujours est-il qu'on parle du départ de notre Ranger depuis quelques années, mais des ventes plus qu'intéressantes ont amené les dirigeants de Ford à revoir leur stratégie. Qui sait s'il n'y aura pas un Ranger 2012 inchangé !!! Mazda, de son côté, proposait le Série B, un clone du Ranger, sans jamais connaître autant de succès. Cette année, Mazda abandonne ce marché.

Pour la petite histoire, mentionnons que lors de sa présentation en 1983, le moteur de 2,0 litres du Ranger développait un gros 75 chevaux. Aujourd'hui, le plus petit moteur du Ranger, le 2,3 litres, fait tout de même 143 chevaux, presque le double. Mais comme le poids a sérieusement augmenté, équipement de sécurité oblige, cette petite camionnette n'est toujours pas une bombe !

Ce 2,3 litres provenant de chez Mazda peut convenir pour les petits travaux. Il consomme peu, mais ses capacités de remorquage sont limitées à 1016 kilos (2240 livres). De plus, son manque d'enthousiasme lorsque vient le temps de dépasser un véhicule plus lent (s'il s'en trouve...) ne plaide pas en sa faveur. Et comme le nombre de versions est très restreint, on passe rapidement au V6 4,0 litres. Plus puissant, suffisamment en tout cas pour procurer au Ranger des accélérations décentes, il consomme effrontément, nous

rappelant ainsi qu'on a affaire à un moteur développé il y a plus de deux décennies. Cependant, il permet de remorquer jusqu'à 2658 kilos (5860 livres) selon le rapport de différentiel retenu. En option, il est possible d'obtenir une attache de remorque de classe III/IV. La charge maximale (le payload en bon français) est de 572 kilos (1260 livres), peu importe la version.

MÉCANIQUE RAFFINÉE... IL Y A LONGTEMPS !

Contrairement aux grosses camionnettes qui demandent un doctorat en mathématiques pour bien comprendre leurs nombreuses déclinaisons, le Ranger ne s'en fait pas avec la vie. Deux moteurs, deux transmissions (automatique quatre rapports et manuelle cinq rapports), deux rouages (propulsion et 4x4, selon le modèle), deux cabines (simple et double, cette dernière appellation étant très pompeuse puisqu'il s'agit simplement d'une cabine allongée), une longueur de boîte, cé toutte comme disent les serbo-ougandais. Autant les moteurs, les transmissions que les rouages nous ramènent aux belles années du disco. C'est primitif, aucunement raffiné, mais au moins, la fiabilité est au rendez-vous. En même temps, n'importe quel mécanicien qui a fait ses études en 1955 peut réparer le Ranger sans se gratter la tête devant un

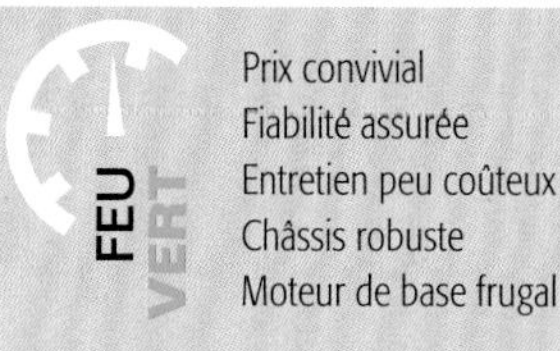

FEU VERT

- Prix convivial
- Fiabilité assurée
- Entretien peu coûteux
- Châssis robuste
- Moteur de base frugal

FEU ROUGE

- Conception ancestrale
- Confort d'une autre époque
- Suspension arrière rétive
- Consommation effarante (V6)
- Modèle en fin de carrière

problème technologique. Et puis, sept millions de véhicules depuis 28 ans, ça vous donne un marché des pièces usagées rarement égalé, donc pas chères.

Même la conduite d'un Ranger nous rappelle le bon vieux temps ! Imaginez qu'un F 150, beaucoup plus imposant, se montre incroyablement plus raffiné. Si le train avant du Ranger se comporte d'une façon des plus décentes, il en va autrement pour l'archaïque suspension arrière qui sautille au moindre trou. Sur une belle route, le Ranger étonne par son confort. Pour une camionnette, la tenue de route est correcte, surtout si « tenue de route correcte » ne veut pas dire « sportive »... Une courbe prise le moindrement au-delà des limites donne du roulis au véhicule, qui en même temps, veut continuer tout droit. Mais si quelqu'un achète un Ranger pour impressionner les copines, il a de meilleures chances d'impressionner un psychiatre. La direction n'est pas des plus dégourdies, les freins non plus. L'odomètre a beau être gradué à 200 km/h, il est fortement déconseillé de tenter d'atteindre cette marque ! Les versions 4x4 sont plus populaires, avec raison. Plus faciles à revendre malgré leur consommation d'essence plus élevée, elles sont aussi plus faciles à conduire en hiver.

SIMPLICITÉ INVOLONTAIRE

L'habitacle est du même acabit. Le design, la position de conduite, l'ergonomie, les matériaux et la finition nous ramènent aux standards d'il y a trente ans. Les boutons sont posés ici et là, au gré de l'espace disponible ou de l'humeur du designer du moment. Les sièges sont plutôt confortables malgré un manque évident de support latéral. La version à cabine allongée a droit à des strapontins peu invitants placés face à face. La boîte de chargement de six pieds est fermée par une porte battante très lourde et deux types de recouvrements de plateau sont proposés en option.

Oui, le Ranger est dépassé. Cependant, si on mettait un Ranger 1983 et un 2011 côte à côte, nous verrions une grosse différence. Ford a quand même su adapter sa petite camionnette aux besoins du moment. Grâce à une politique de prix serrée et de nombreux incitatifs (et une providentielle augmentation des prix de l'essence), le Ranger a toujours connu de bonnes ventes. Comme quoi le prix fait pardonner bien des défauts. Il y a toujours les Chevrolet Colorado/GMC Canyon, plus modernes, mais leur prix plus élevé joue en leur défaveur.

Alain Morin

PHOTOS : FORD

Catégorie	Camionnette
Échelle de prix	17 799 $ à 26 699 $ (2010)
Garanties	3 ans/60 000 km, 5 ans/100 000 km
Assemblage	Louisville, Kentucky, É-U
Cote d'assurance	moyenne

CHÂSSIS - DONNÉES POUR XL 4X2 CABINE SIMPLE

Emp/lon/lar/haut	2 819/4 800/1 752/1 676 mm
Longueur de boîte	1 836 mm (72,3 pouces)
Réservoir	64 litres
Nombre coussins sécurité	4
Antipatinage / contrôle stabilité	oui / oui
Suspension avant	indépendante, bras inégaux
Suspension arrière	essieu rigide, ressorts à lames
Freins avant / arrière	disques (ABS) / tambours (ABS)
Direction	à crémaillère, assistée
Diamètre de braquage	13,2 m
Pneus avant / arrière	P225/70R15 / P225/70R15
Poids	1 392 kg
Capacité de remorquage	699 kg (1 541 lb)

COMPOSANTES MÉCANIQUES

Ranger

Cylindrée, soupapes, alim.	4L 2,3 litres 16 s atmos.
Puissance / Couple	143 chevaux / 154 lb-pi
Tr. base (opt) / rouage base (opt)	M5 (A5) / Prop
0-100 / 80-120 / 100-0 km/h	11,2 s / n.d. / 44,0 m
Type ess. / ville / autoroute	Ordinaire / 9,5 / 7,3 l/100 km

Ranger

Cylindrée, soupapes, alim.	V6 4,0 litres 12 s atmos.
Puissance / Couple	207 chevaux / 238 lb-pi
Tr. base (opt) / rouage base (opt)	M5 (A5) / Prop (4x4)
0-100 / 80-120 / 100-0 km/h	9,2 s / 8,4 s / 44,0 m
Type ess. / ville / autoroute	Ordinaire / 13,4 / 9,7 l/100 km

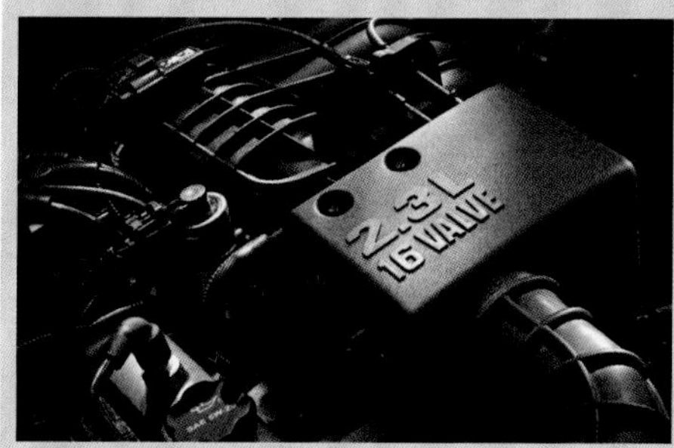

DANS LA MÊME CATÉGORIE

Chevrolet Colorado, RAM Dakota, GMC Canyon, Nissan Frontier, Toyota Tacoma

DU NOUVEAU EN 2011

Aucun changement majeur. Mazda Série B abandonné

NOS IMPRESSIONS

Agrément de conduite :	6/10
Fiabilité :	6/10
Sécurité :	6/10
Qualités hivernales :	7/10
Espace intérieur :	6/10
Confort :	6/10

www.ford.ca

Plus d'informations dans la section statistiques en dernière partie du Guide

TOUJOURS ORIGINALE TOUJOURS PRATIQUE

La compagnie Honda a la réputation de ne pas faire les choses comme les autres que ce soit sur le plan du design ou de la mécanique. Par exemple, ce constructeur a toujours préconisé des moteurs de plus petites cylindrées tournant à un régime plus élevé que la moyenne. En outre, ses concepteurs ne se gênent pas pour nous proposer des designs à nul autre pareil. Le Ridgeline en est un bel exemple

En effet, la majorité des constructeurs, lorsque le temps est venu de se lancer sur le marché des camionnettes intermédiaires ou pleine grandeur, se sont contentés d'analyser ce que les meilleurs de la catégorie produisaient et de tenter de faire mieux. Dans le cas qui nous concerne, on a essayé d'améliorer le véhicule sans pour autant respecter les lois de la catégorie. Et vous savez, les résultats ont été surprenants.

UNE STRUCTURE D'AUTOMOBILE

Il n'est pas une camionnette qui se respecte qui ne possède pas un châssis autonome de type échelle afin d'offrir robustesse et rigidité. Pourtant, le Ridgeline se démarque avec un châssis intégré sur une structure autoporteuse. Un peu comme dans le cas du Jeep Grand Cherokee, on a intégré les longerons longitudinaux et transversaux sur une plate-forme monocoque pour obtenir le maximum de rigidité tant en flexion qu'en torsion. C'est d'une grande simplicité, mais encore fallait-il y penser. Cette approche technique a permis de réaliser un véhicule rigide et léger en plus de donner l'opportunité aux stylistes de concevoir une carrosserie unique en son genre. En effet, contrairement à toutes les autres camionnettes, la boîte arrière n'est pas simplement boulonnée sur les longerons du châssis, elle fait partie d'un ensemble complet. C'est ce qui donne sans doute cette silhouette si particulière que plusieurs trouvent iconoclaste et que d'autres trouvent très intéressante.

Mais ce n'est pas tout! Le véhicule est doté d'une suspension indépendante aussi bien à l'avant qu'à l'arrière, une autre approche technique qui diffère totalement des solutions adoptées pour les autres camionnettes. Cette suspension arrière indépendante assure bien entendu une meilleure tenue de route et un confort supérieur, mais elle a également permis de placer un coffre de rangement pouvant être verrouillé sous le plancher de la caisse. Le panneau arrière peut se rabatte horizontalement comme sur toutes les camionnettes ou encore s'ouvrir vers le côté comme une grande portière. Cette caisse de chargement possède aussi des encoches permettant de transporter une motocyclette ou un VTT. Pour les chargements plus longs, un système d'extension de caisse intégré est de série.Chez Honda, on a pratiquement réinventé la camionnette!

COMME UNE AUTOMOBILE?

Pour décrire le Ridgeline, on peut quasiment dire qu'il s'agit d'une camionnette pour les personnes qui n'ont pas besoin d'une vraie camionnette. Je m'explique. Ce véhicule s'adresse aux personnes

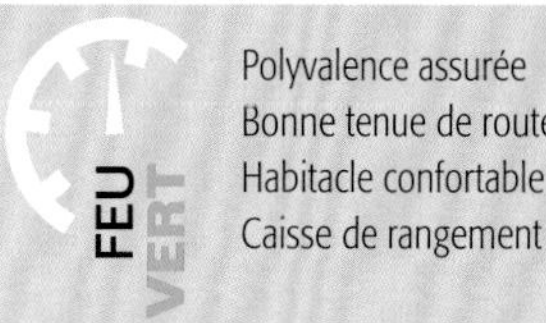

FEU VERT

- Polyvalence assurée
- Bonne tenue de route
- Habitacle confortable
- Caisse de rangement

FEU ROUGE

- Silhouette controversée
- Capacité de remorquage un peu faible
- Caisse relativement courte
- Consommation de carburant moyenne

qui ont besoin de temps à autre d'une caisse de chargement de capacité moyenne, d'une capacité de remorquage correcte et qui propose en plus un comportement routier tout au moins égal à celui d'un VUS. Bien entendu, l'habitacle doit être confortable et spacieux. Toutes ces caractéristiques, le Ridgeline les possède.

Et pour conclure sur cette originalité, le moteur V6 de 3,5 litres d'une puissance de 250 chevaux est en position transversale, une autre exception à la règle. De fait, ce rouage intégral est en mode de traction la plupart du temps, tandis que le couple est dirigé vers les roues arrière lorsque le système détecte une certaine perte d'adhérence des roues avant. Une seule transmission est au catalogue, il s'agit d'une boîte automatique à cinq rapports.

La position de conduite est bonne, le volant au moyeu triangulaire se prend bien en main et les cadrans indicateurs sont de lecture facile avec les chiffres blancs sur fond noir. Et ce n'est pas l'espace qui fait défaut aussi bien à l'avant qu'aux places arrière. On accède à celles-ci par une portière de bonne largeur et une fois en assis, c'est douillet. En fait, comparé à une Honda Accord, le Ridgeline possède de meilleures places arrière.

Donc, nous nous retrouvons au volant d'un véhicule polyvalent et confortable. Mais le plus intéressant dans tout ça, c'est la conduite de ce véhicule qui est vraiment supérieure à la moyenne de la catégorie. Tout d'abord, la suspension est bien calibrée et ne sautille pas sur mauvaise route, une caractéristique que l'on retrouve souvent sur les camionnettes lorsque celles-ci ne sont pas chargées. Ce n'est pas vraiment le cas du Ridgeline. Et en plus, la tenue de route est sans surprise. Finalement, le moteur est suffisamment puissant tandis que sa consommation de carburant est correcte, étant d'environ 14,1 litres aux 100 km.

Bref, le Ridgeline est différent, mais d'un bel équilibre. Son seul défaut majeur, et encore faut-il pondérer, est sa silhouette différente qui a sa part de détracteurs, mais également une forte proportion d'admirateurs. Par ailleurs, plusieurs personnes qui ne trouvaient rien de positif à dire quant à la silhouette ont été conquises après avoir conduit le véhicule.

Denis Duquet

PHOTOS : HONDA

Catégorie	Camionnette
Échelle de prix	34 990 $ à 3 690 $ (2010)
Garanties	3 ans/60 000 km, 5 ans/100 000 km
Assemblage	Alliston, Ontario, Canada
Cote d'assurance	moyenne

CHÂSSIS - DONNÉES POUR EX-L

Emp/lon/lar/haut	3 100/5 255/1 976/1 808 mm
Coffre	241 litres
Longueur de boîte	1 524 mm (60,0 pouces)
Réservoir	83 litres
Nombre coussins sécurité	6
Antipatinage / contrôle stabilité	oui / oui
Suspension avant	indépendante, jambes de force
Suspension arrière	indépendante, multibras
Freins avant / arrière	disque (ABS) / disque (ABS)
Direction	à crémaillère, ass. variable
Diamètre de braquage	12,9 m
Pneus avant / arrière	P245/60R18 / P245/60R18
Poids	2 065 kg
Capacité de remorquage	2 268 kg (5 000 lb)

COMPOSANTES MÉCANIQUES

DX, VP, EX-L

Cylindrée, soupapes, alim.	V6 3,5 litres 24 s atmos.
Puissance / Couple	250 chevaux / 247 lb-pi
Tr. base (opt) / rouage base (opt)	A5 / Int
0-100 / 80-120 / 100-0 km/h	9,4 s / 8,4 s / 42,0 m
Type ess. / ville / autoroute	Ordinaire / 14,1 / 9,8 l/100 km

DANS LA MÊME CATÉGORIE

RAM Dakota, Nissan Frontier, Suzuki Equator, Toyota Tacoma

DU NOUVEAU EN 2011

Aucun changement majeur

NOS IMPRESSIONS

Agrément de conduite :	7/10
Fiabilité :	10/10
Sécurité :	10/10
Qualités hivernales :	9/10
Espace intérieur :	8/10
Confort :	8/10

www.honda.ca

Plus d'informations dans la section statistiques en dernière partie du Guide

Nissan Frontier

SÉPARÉS À LA NAISSANCE

Les associations entre constructeurs pour partager un modèle ou un autre ont parfois de curieuses ramifications. Prenez le cas du Suzuki Equator qui n'est rien d'autre qu'un Nissan Frontier arborant un écusson différent. Le plus cocasse dans cette situation, c'est que Suzuki est associé au groupe Volkswagen tandis que Nissan appartient à Renault qui vient tout juste de signer une entente avec Mercedes-Benz. Mais peu importe les alliances, il est certain que l'Equator ne cassera rien sur le marché.

Nous sommes même en droit de nous demander qui a eu l'idée d'un modèle aussi farfelu que cette camionnette roulant sous un nom d'emprunt!

COMME LE SAINT-ESPRIT

Cette camionnette Suzuki est un peu comme le Saint-Esprit. Les catholiques savent qu'il existe, mais sans jamais être capable de le représenter si ce n'est sous la forme d'une colombe. Eh bien l'Equator, est un peu comme ça. On sait qu'il existe, mais ses apparitions sont fort rares aussi bien sur nos routes que dans les salles de démonstration des concessionnaires. En fait, chaque concessionnaire a le choix d'en offrir ou pas. Et compte tenu des faibles chiffres de ventes de cette camionnette depuis son arrivée sur le marché, on peut conclure que la plupart n'en veulent pas...

Ce n'est pas parce que le produit n'est pas de qualité, mais pourquoi acheter sa camionnette Frontier chez Suzuki alors qu'on peut le faire pour trois bonnes raisons chez Nissan? La première: le choix proposé par Suzuki est assez mince aussi bien en fait de type de carrosserie et d'équipements que de couleurs. La deuxième: les concessionnaires Nissan ont une bien meilleure connaissance de ce produit au chapitre des réparations et de l'entretien. Et la troisième: il est certain que la valeur du Frontier sera supérieure.

Une fois de plus, les grands penseurs de Suzuki ont trouvé le moyen de commercialiser un véhicule qui n'a pas beaucoup de chances de réussir. Et puis, dites-moi, avez-vous déjà vu une publicité de Suzuki vantant les mérites de cette camionnette?

POURQUOI?

Si Suzuki ne dépense rien pour la publicité de cette camionnette Frontier roulant sous un nom d'emprunt, on ne peut pas dire non plus que Nissan ait cassé sa tirelire en fait de marketing pour ce produit. Pourtant, le Frontier n'est pas dépourvu de qualités et il est capable de soutenir la comparaison avec les meilleurs de la catégorie. C'est un des nombreux mystères chez ce constructeur.

Laissons le marketing de côté pour revenir au produit. En tout premier lieu, la plate-forme est excellente. Elle est partagée avec le Pathfinder et le Xterra, et il s'agit d'une version à plus petite échelle du châssis du gros camion Titan. Et même si sa silhouette commence à démontrer des signes de vieillesse, elle est toujours

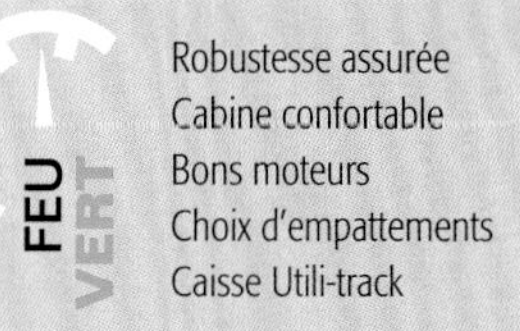

FEU VERT

- Robustesse assurée
- Cabine confortable
- Bons moteurs
- Choix d'empattements
- Caisse Utili-track

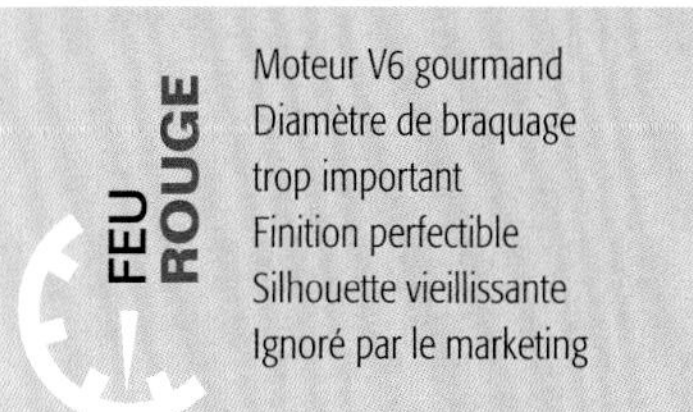

FEU ROUGE

- Moteur V6 gourmand
- Diamètre de braquage trop important
- Finition perfectible
- Silhouette vieillissante
- Ignoré par le marketing

au goût du jour. Soulignons au passage que seuls les modèles à cabine allongée (*King Cab*) et double (*Crew Cab*) sont commercialisés. De plus, les places arrière de ce dernier modèle sont assez limitées par rapport à ce que les Ram Dakota et Toyota Tacoma proposent.

Le pilote est assis dans un siège confortable et a devant lui deux cadrans de lecture facile, avec chiffres blancs sur fond noir. Les branches horizontales du volant accueillent les commandes de la téléphonie mains libres, du système audio et du régulateur de vitesse. Il faut toutefois déplorer la qualité des matériaux et de la finition qui est décevante pour un produit Nissan.

Le moteur équipant les modèles moins cossus est un quatre cylindres de 2,5 litres dont la réputation n'est plus à faire. Robuste et frugal, il est couplé à une boîte manuelle à cinq rapports tandis que l'automatique à cinq rapports est optionnelle. Celle-ci est la seule disponible si vous commandez le moteur V6 4,0 litres de 261 chevaux. La transmission intégrale ne peut être commandée qu'avec ce moteur. Si le rendement et les performances de ce V6 sont supérieurs à la moyenne pour cette cylindrée, sa consommation l'est aussi... Il devient alors plus logique de choisir une camionnette d'une autre marque propulsée par un moteur V8 plus puissant et moins gourmand.

Étant donné que son châssis est dérivé de celui du Titan, on n'a pas à craindre en fait de robustesse et de rigidité. L'acheteur a le choix entre une multitude de variantes qu'il s'agisse du *King Cab* à cabine allongée ou du *Crew Cab* quatre portes. Et si la caisse est dotée d'un battant outrageusement lourd, il est possible de recouvrir le fond de la caisse d'un enduit protecteur.

Sur la route, le Frontier est agile est relativement agréable à conduire. Par contre, sa suspension sera jugée ferme par plusieurs tandis que son diamètre de braquage démesurément long remet les virages en trois points au goût du jour. Quant au rouage 4X4, il est à temps partiel et se règle par un bouton rotatif. Sont également disponibles les systèmes de contrôle de descente et de démarrage de pente, lesquels sont activés par le conducteur.

Somme toute, le Frontier mérite un meilleur sort que celui qui lui est réservé par son constructeur.

Denis Duquet

Suzuki Equator

PHOTOS : NISSAN

NISSAN FRONTIER / SUZUKI EQUATOR

Catégorie	Camionnette
Échelle de prix	24 098 $ à 41 098 $ (2010)
Garanties	3 ans/60 000 km, 5 ans/100 000 km
Assemblage	Smyrna, Tennessee, É-U
Cote d'assurance	moyenne

CHÂSSIS - DONNÉES POUR SE 4X2 KING CAB

Emp/lon/lar/haut	3 200/5 220/1 850/1 770 mm
Longueur de boîte	1 560 mm (61,4 pouces)
Réservoir	80 litres
Nombre coussins sécurité	6
Antipatinage / contrôle stabilité	oui / oui
Suspension avant	indépendante, double triangulation
Suspension arrière	essieu rigide, ressorts à lames
Freins avant / arrière	disque (ABS) / disque (ABS)
Direction	à crémaillère, ass. variable
Diamètre de braquage	12,4 m
Pneus avant / arrière	P265/70R16 / P265/70R16
Poids	1 876 kg
Capacité de remorquage	1 588 kg (3 500 lb)

COMPOSANTES MÉCANIQUES

Frontier

Cylindrée, soupapes, alim.	4L 2,5 litres 16 s atmos.
Puissance / Couple	152 chevaux / 171 lb-pi
Tr. base (opt) / rouage base (opt)	M5 (A5) / Prop
0-100 / 80-120 / 100-0 km/h	11,2 s / 8,5 s / n.d.
Type ess. / ville / autoroute	Ordinaire / 10,7 / 8,7 l/100 km

Frontier, Equator

Cylindrée, soupapes, alim.	V6 4,0 litres 24 s atmos.
Puissance / Couple	261 chevaux / 281 lb-pi
Tr. base (opt) / rouage base (opt)	A5 / Prop (4x4)
0-100 / 80-120 / 100-0 km/h	9,0 s / 7,4 s / 41,0 m
Type ess. / ville / autoroute	Ordinaire / 14,7 / 10,4 l/100 km

DANS LA MÊME CATÉGORIE

Chevrolet Colorado, RAM Dakota, Ford Ranger, GMC Canyon, Honda Ridgeline, Toyota Tacoma

DU NOUVEAU EN 2011

Aucun changement majeur

NOS IMPRESSIONS

Agrément de conduite :	7/10
Fiabilité :	8/10
Sécurité :	8/10
Qualités hivernales :	9/10
Espace intérieur :	7/10
Confort :	8/10

www.nissan.ca

Plus d'informations dans la section statistiques en dernière partie du Guide

UN RÔLE DE FIGURATION

Pas facile de se tailler une place au royaume des camionnettes pleine grandeur. Les constructeurs américains n'ont jamais rien concédé à la concurrence, se livrant eux-mêmes une bataille plus que féroce. Lancé en 2003 sous modèle 2004, le Nissan Titan n'a jamais réussi à réellement s'imposer dans son créneau et l'âge plus que vénérable de cette génération n'aidera certainement pas sa cause cette année. En fait, le Titan est la plus vieille des camionnettes actuellement sur le marché et les choses ne risquent pas de changer d'ici peu.

Malgré une incursion de la part de Toyota et Nissan dans ce segment, ce sont toujours les trois constructeurs américains qui dominent les ventes. La Série F s'est écoulée à près de 82 000 unités l'an passé au Canada, 74 000 unités pour le combo GMC Sierra et Chevrolet Silverado et finalement, un peu moins de 31 000 dans le cas du Dodge Ram. Toyota avec son Tundra suit avec des ventes d'un peu plus de 7 500 unités alors que Nissan ferme le bal avec des ventes inférieures à 1 400 unités. Voilà qui met les choses en perspective.

UNE ENTENTE AVORTÉE

En fait, nous aurions pu dès cette année voir arriver une nouvelle génération du Nissan Titan puisque le constructeur avait conclu une entente avec Chrysler pour le développement et la production de sa nouvelle camionnette. Cependant, vu la situation financière de Chrysler et sa vente récente, l'entente a avorté. Nissan devra donc assumer seul la production du prochain Titan et la génération courante risque de s'étirer jusqu'en 2014, selon certains. Alors que Nissan vient de lancer une division commerciale, il serait étonnant que le constructeur cesse simplement la production du Titan. D'ailleurs, la prochaine génération devrait certainement profiter des éléments de cette nouvelle division.

Quoi qu'il en soit, le Titan nous revient et demeure pratiquement inchangé. Sans offrir autant de possibilités que la concurrence, le Titan prend tout de même forme sous plusieurs variantes intéressantes et surtout, populaires. Deux types de cabines sont proposés, Double et *King Cab*, alors qu'il existe trois longueurs de caisses. Comme plusieurs versions se distinguent par leur niveau d'équipement, on obtient un choix relativement complet.

GLOUTON, LE MOTEUR

Sous le capot niche un seul moteur. C'est sans doute ici l'un des principaux éléments reprochés au Titan, le manque de choix au chapitre des motorisations. Il faut donc se rabattre sur le V8 de 5,6 litres, ce dernier développant une puissance de 317 chevaux pour un couple de 385 lb-pi. À l'époque, ce moulin livrait une puissance plus qu'intéressante, mais depuis, la concurrence a su se rattraper et déployer plus de puissance. Le constructeur aurait pu apporter un peu de nouveau en proposant son récent V8 de 5,6 litres, moteur que l'on retrouve à bord de l'Infiniti QX et qui offre une puissance de

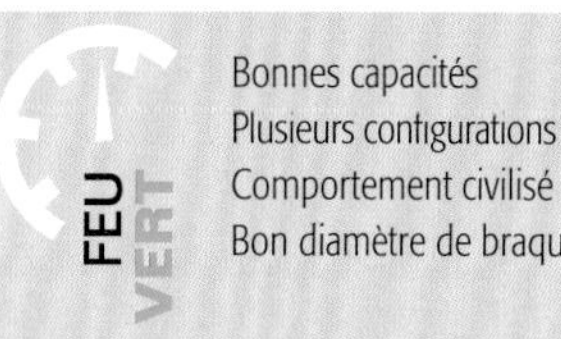

FEU VERT

- Bonnes capacités
- Plusieurs configurations offertes
- Comportement civilisé
- Bon diamètre de braquage

FEU ROUGE

- Un seul moteur au menu
- Consommation gargantuesque
- Génération vieillissante

400 chevaux pour un couple 413 lb-pi. Non seulement ce moteur est beaucoup plus moderne, mais il permet une meilleure économie de carburant grâce, notamment, au calage variable des soupapes et à l'injection directe. Voilà qui aurait été plus que bienvenu dans le cas du Titan car le moteur V8 actuel affiche une consommation titanesque. Difficile d'être sous les 16,0 L/100 km et ce chiffre est encore moins favorable lorsque le véhicule est chargé. La concurrence fait maintenant beaucoup mieux à ce chapitre. Le fait que le Titan dispose d'une boîte automatique à cinq rapports, au lieu de six, contribue aussi à cette consommation plus élevée.

Le Titan s'avère un outil de travail efficace. Son châssis à échelle entièrement cloisonné lui procure une excellente rigidité et sur ce point, il est supérieur au Toyota Tundra. On apprécie dans la caisse l'ensemble de rails, optionnel, permettant de bien arrimer les objets. Cependant, la concurrence a su innover au cours des dernières années en nous offrant plus de fonctionnalité.

Pour ce qui est des capacités, le Titan fait bonne figure puisqu'il pourra tirer une charge de 9 500 livres dans le cas de la version *King Cab* et de 9 300 livres pour la version à cabine double, ce qui se situe dans la moyenne. Le Ford F-150 continue de dominer dans ce domaine avec une capacité de 11 300 lb.

Lors de son introduction, Nissan a voulu attirer les acheteurs en misant sur la puissance et surtout, le style. Le Titan est massif et à sa vue, on le sent capable. Sa ceinture de caisse élevée, ses jantes de 18 pouces ou de 20 pouces, selon la version sélectionnée, ainsi que l'utilisation massive du chrome contribuent à donner au Titan une stature imposante. À l'intérieur, le véhicule profite du même traitement qu'à l'extérieur, alors que plusieurs éléments mettent bien en valeur sa robustesse. Que ce soit les larges appuie-bras, le tableau de bord ou la console centrale, tout y est pour donner un sentiment de puissance.

Force est d'admettre que le Titan demeure relégué à un rôle de figuration, du moins jusqu'à ce que Nissan nous présente une nouvelle génération. Des rumeurs veulent aussi que Nissan nous propose une gamme de type *Heavy Duty*, ce qui permettrait d'étendre la portée de sa camionnette et ainsi, rentabiliser encore plus l'opération. Une chose est certaine, il n'est pas facile de rivaliser avec les Américains dans ce segment.

Sylvain Raymond

PHOTOS : NISSAN

NISSAN TITAN

Catégorie	Camionnette
Échelle de prix	33 448 $ à 50 148 $ (2010)
Garanties	3 ans/60 000 km, 5 ans/100 000 km
Assemblage	Canton, Mississipi, É-U
Cote d'assurance	passable

CHÂSSIS - DONNÉES POUR SE 4X4 CABINE DOUBLE

Emp/lon/lar/haut	3 550/5 704/2 019/1 937 mm
Longueur de boîte	1 710 mm (67,3 pouces)
Réservoir	106 litres
Nombre coussins sécurité	6
Antipatinage / contrôle stabilité	oui / oui
Suspension avant	indépendante, double triangulation
Suspension arrière	essieu rigide, ressorts à lames
Freins avant / arrière	disque (ABS) / disque (ABS)
Direction	à crémaillère, ass. variable
Diamètre de braquage	14,0 m
Pneus avant / arrière	P265/70R18 / P265/70R18
Poids	2 487 kg
Capacité de remorquage	4 218 kg (9 299 lb)

COMPOSANTES MÉCANIQUES

Titan

Cylindrée, soupapes, alim.	V8 5,6 litres 32 s atmos.
Puissance / Couple	317 chevaux / 385 lb-pi
Tr. base (opt) / rouage base (opt)	A5 / Prop (4x4)
0-100 / 80-120 / 100-0 km/h	7.8 s / 6,2 s / 44,2 m
Type ess. / ville / autoroute	Ordinaire / 17,7 / 12,0 l/100 km

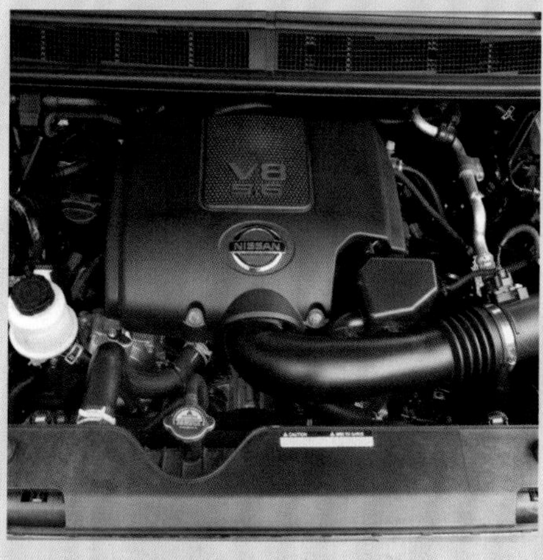

DANS LA MÊME CATÉGORIE

Chevrolet Silverado, RAM 1500, Ford F-150, GMC Sierra, Toyota Tundra

DU NOUVEAU EN 2011

Aucun changement majeur

NOS IMPRESSIONS

Agrément de conduite :	8/10
Fiabilité :	6/10
Sécurité :	6/10
Qualités hivernales :	7/10
Espace intérieur :	9/10
Confort :	8/10

www.nissan.ca

Plus d'informations dans la section statistiques en dernière partie du Guide

UN SUCCÈS QUI S'EXPLIQUE

Les gens craignent pour la survie de la compagnie Chrysler. En effet, sa gamme d'automobiles n'a pas présenté de nouveautés depuis plusieurs mois. Il en résulte des chiffres de vente qui sont assez décevants un peu partout en Amérique. Toutefois, le marché canadien et le marché québécois en particulier sont très encourageants pour Chrysler. En effet, mois après mois, les ventes domestiques battent des records. Du moins au moment d'écrire ces lignes. Et il est important de souligner que les camionnettes Ram sont très demandées.

Il ne faut pas croire que ces ventes s'expliquent uniquement par des prix cassés et des campagnes de promotion assaisonnées de taux d'intérêt intéressants. Les améliorations apportées à cette camionnette en 2009 ont permis de la mettre au niveau de la concurrence et de surpasser plusieurs marques pourtant respectées. Comme dans tous les autres secteurs du marché, les derniers arrivés sont souvent les plus compétitifs et les plus homogènes.

SILHOUETTE CONNUE, HABITACLE COSSU

Depuis des années maintenant, le Ram se démarque par une silhouette très agressive qui s'inspire de celle des tracteurs de semi-remorque. Avec son long nez se terminant par une calandre proéminente surplombant un pare-chocs très imposant, il est impossible de se méprendre : c'est un Ram, c'est certain ! On peut trouver que l'écusson permettant de l'identifier — une tête de mouflon— est un peu trop important, mais il semble que cela plaise aux amateurs du genre. Comme il existe plusieurs variantes de présentation extérieure, la grille de calandre peut être chromée ou harmonisée avec la couleur de la carrosserie. Il en est de même pour le pare-chocs qui est soit chromé ou monochrome. Dans la récente mouture, les stylistes ont affiné la silhouette, la rendant plus sophistiquée et plus aérodynamique, sans toutefois déroger du credo esthétique de cette camionnette. Celle-ci est livrée en versions à cabine ordinaire, à cabine double ou encore avec la cabine Megacab qui comprend également quatre portières mais offre plus d'espace pour les places arrière. Vous ne pourrez vous plaindre de ne pas avoir l'embarras du choix.

Avec cette dernière option, cependant, vous bénéficierez d'une caisse très courte, soit d'une longueur de 5,7 pieds. C'est souvent le choix des personnes qui veulent utiliser la camionnette pour remorquer une roulotte à bec de cygne nécessitant la présence d'une cinquième roue dans la boîte. Toujours au chapitre du rangement, il est possible de commander les Ram Box placées de chaque côté de la caisse. Ces boîtes sont à l'épreuve de l'eau et se verrouillent. Leur capacité de rangement est assez bonne. Par contre, elles empiètent quelque peu sur la largeur de la boîte.

Mais le gros changement se situe dans l'habitacle. Alors qu'auparavant le tableau de bord était d'une désolante simplicité et que les

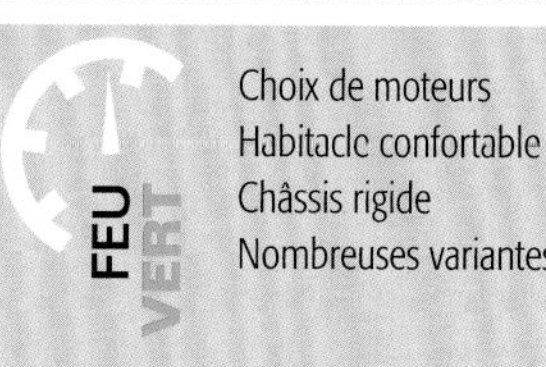

FEU VERT

- Choix de moteurs
- Habitacle confortable
- Châssis rigide
- Nombreuses variantes

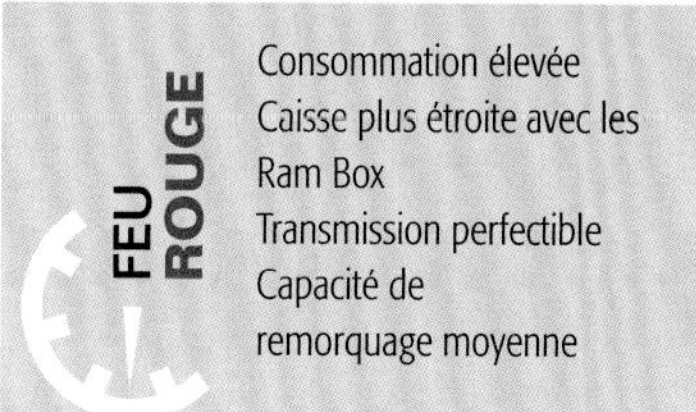

FEU ROUGE

- Consommation élevée
- Caisse plus étroite avec les Ram Box
- Transmission perfectible
- Capacité de remorquage moyenne

matériaux étaient nettement à revoir, le design de la nouvelle mouture nous en met plein la vue. Aussi, la qualité des matériaux et de l'assemblage est encourageante. Tout dans cet habitacle est destiné à être pratique et cela comprend une très vaste console de rangement à deux niveaux qui peut avaler beaucoup de choses.

Sur la version que nous avons essayée, le pédalier était réglable et les commandes électriques des glaces étaient automatiques. Détail intéressant, les sièges de notre modèle étaient chauffants et ventilés. Quant aux places arrière, elles étaient très confortables et le fait de pouvoir relever la banquette permet de transporter des objets tout de même assez encombrants.

LE HEMI ET LES AUTRES

Comme sur toute grosse camionnette, l'acheteur a le choix entre plusieurs moteurs. Si vous ne prévoyez pas transporter de lourds objets, il est possible de commander le moteur V6 de 3,7 litres dont les 215 chevaux ne devraient être appréciés que si vous roulez toujours allège. De plus, la boîte automatique à quatre rapports est passablement vétuste. Une solution intérimaire serait de choisir un moteur V8 de 4,7 litres dont les 310 chevaux font sentir leur présence et vous permettent de tracter les charges intermédiaires. En outre, il est associé à une boîte automatique à cinq rapports qui est nettement plus intéressante. Les passages de rapport sont imperceptibles et l'étagement des vitesses est sans reproche. Mais si vous êtes du genre à vouloir ce qu'il y a de mieux ou de plus puissant, un choix s'impose: le moteur Hemi. Ce V8 de 5,7 litres déballe 390 chevaux et a une capacité de remorquage de 9100 livres, bien que celle-ci puisse varier selon le modèle — deux ou quatre roues motrices. Mais puisque la consommation entre le Hemi et le moteur V8 de 4,7 litres est quasiment semblable, pourquoi se priver du meilleur? Cette similitude de consommation s'explique par le dispositif de désactivation des cylindres et du calage variable des soupapes dont jouit le Hemi.

La puissance est au rendez-vous et il faut maintenant prendre la route. Malgré le fait que nous conduisions une version 4X4 dotée d'une suspension plus ferme, nous n'avons pas tellement été secoués. Sans doute parce que les ressorts hélicoïdaux à l'essieu rigide arrière ont fait leur boulot.

Pour un usage familial, cette camionnette Dodge offre plusieurs avantages en plus de sa motorisation légendaire. Sa cabine est confortable et raffinée.

Denis Duquet

PHOTOS: SYLVAIN RAYMOND

RAM 1500

Catégorie	Camionnette
Échelle de prix	20545$ à 39440$
Garanties	3 ans/60000 km, 5 ans/100000 km
Assemblage	St-Louis MO et Dodge City, Warren MI, É-U
Cote d'assurance	passable

CHÂSSIS - DONNÉES POUR LARAMIE 4X4 CABINE QUAD

Emp/lon/lar/haut	3556/5817/2017/1900 mm
Longueur de boîte	1939 mm (76,3 pouces)
Réservoir	98 litres
Nombre coussins sécurité	4
Antipatinage / contrôle stabilité	oui / oui
Suspension avant	indépendante, bras inégaux
Suspension arrière	essieu rigide, multibras
Freins avant / arrière	disque (ABS) / disque (ABS)
Direction	à crémaillère, assistée
Diamètre de braquage	13,7 m
Pneus avant / arrière	P275/60R20 / P275/60R20
Poids	2489 kg
Capacité de remorquage	3765 kg (8300 lb)

COMPOSANTES MÉCANIQUES

STD pour propulsion	
Cylindrée, soupapes, alim.	V6 3,7 litres 12 s atmos.
Puissance / Couple	215 chevaux / 235 lb-pi
Tr. base (opt) / rouage base (opt)	A4 / Prop
Type ess. / ville / autoroute	Ordinaire / 14,8 / 10,0 l/100 km

STD pour 4x4	
Cylindrée, soupapes, alim.	V8 4,7 litres 16 s atmos.
Puissance / Couple	310 chevaux / 330 lb-pi
Tr. base (opt) / rouage base (opt)	A5 / Prop (4x4)
Type ess. / ville / autoroute	Ordinaire / 16,7 / 11,4 l/100 km

STD pour Sport et Laramie	
Cylindrée, soupapes, alim.	V8 5,7 litres 16 s atmos.
Puissance / Couple	390 chevaux / 407 lb-pi
Tr. base (opt) / rouage base (opt)	A5 / Prop (4x4)
Type ess. / ville / autoroute	Ordinaire / 15,4 / 10,2 l/100 km

DANS LA MÊME CATÉGORIE

Chevrolet Silverado, Ford F-150, GMC Sierra, Nissan Titan, Toyota Tundra

DU NOUVEAU EN 2011

Aucun changement majeur. La division camion de Dodge est devenue Ram durant l'année modèle 2010

NOS IMPRESSIONS

Agrément de conduite:	8/10
Fiabilité:	6/10
Sécurité:	7/10
Qualités hivernales:	7/10
Espace intérieur:	8/10
Confort:	8/10

www.ramtrucks.com

Plus d'informations dans la section statistiques en dernière partie du Guide

DANS L'OMBRE DU BÉLIER

Les sauveurs actuels de Chrysler ont vite reconnu la force du nom Ram dans le monde des camionnettes et en ont presque aussitôt fait une marque. On retrouve désormais à cette enseigne la descendante directe de la première camionnette de format moyen. Mais ce brave Dakota aurait besoin des mêmes attentions et moyens que ses grands frères pour se démarquer et se débrouiller aussi bien qu'eux.

Chrysler a tout bonnement inventé la camionnette de taille moyenne il y a un quart de siècle en lançant le premier Dakota. C'était tout juste après le lancement de ses premières fourgonnettes et la compagnie entière était portée par ce miracle encore en pleine accélération à l'époque. Le Dakota était la réponse originale et inédite de Chrysler aux camionnettes compactes de ses grandes rivales, elles-mêmes créées pour donne la réplique aux compactes japonaises.

Le premier Dakota était un peu plus spacieux et costaud que les Chevrolet S-10 ou Ford Ranger et d'autant plus pratique. En théorie, du moins. À l'inverse, il était nettement moins lourd et encombrant que les grandes camionnettes. Surtout les Ram du moment qui étaient particulièrement archaïques. On était encore loin de cet autre miracle que fut la camionnette Ram de 1993 et sa fabuleuse calandre de Freightliner en colère.

Ce premier Dakota était donc apparu comme une très bonne idée à l'équipe du *Guide de l'auto* édition 1987. Sa motorisation était trop modeste mais on pouvait en dire autant des premières « Autobeaucoup ». L'essentiel était de constater qu'il était solide, bien conçu et mieux fini que plusieurs de ses contemporains chez Chrysler. Il a poursuivi sa progression au fil des années.

Une première version à quatre roues motrices s'est ajoutée à la série pour la première année complète en 1987 et les modèles à cabine allongée trois ans plus tard. Il s'est écoulé une décennie avant le lancement d'un Dakota de deuxième génération, entièrement redessiné, pour l'année 1997. Cette série adoptait une calandre qui évoquait celle de la nouvelle Ram pour profiter de sa grande popularité mais surtout un habitacle plus moderne et une motorisation solide. Elle fut remplacée à son tour par la troisième génération de la série Dakota en 2005.

La série actuelle en est donc déjà à sa septième année. Le dernier moteur à quatre cylindres a été largué en 2003 et la cabine régulière abandonnée avec la dernière refonte complète. Le Dakota est offert avec le choix d'une cabine allongée ou d'une cabine complète à quatre portières. Ils s'appelaient Club Cab et Quad Cab en 2005 mais le marketing les présente maintenant comme les Extended Cab et Crew Cab.

Les Dakota sont propulsés par un V6 de 3,7 litres ou un V8 de 4,7 litres depuis leur refonte. Le V6 a été mis à jour au fil des années mais sa puissance s'est maintenant à 210 chevaux. Celle

FEU VERT

- Motorisation solide avec le V8
- Bon comportement routier
- Cabines spacieuses
- Longue plate-forme
- Grands rétroviseurs

FEU ROUGE

- Finition intérieure quelconque
- Freinage médiocre
- Dossiers avant bombés
- Coffre à gants minuscule
- Fiabilité moyenne

du V8 optionnel de 4,7 litres est par contre passée de 230 à 302 chevaux avec la version revampée qui est apparue sous les capots des Dakota en 2008. Ce moteur est également moins glouton, plus écolo et plus raffiné que l'ancien tout en étant le seul moteur autre que le V8 « Hemi » de 5,7 litres chez Chrysler à être équipé d'une paire de bougies pour chacun de ses cylindres.

Ce gain de puissance avait permis d'améliorer le temps d'accélération sur le quart de mille de 16,8 secondes à exactement 16,0 secondes, à configuration égale. Il est toutefois plus important de noter que ses 329 lb-pi de couple procurent au Dakota une capacité de remorquage de 7 500 livres (3 400 kg), la meilleure de la catégorie. La caisse de 2,0 mètres des versions à cabine allongée est également nettement plus longue que celle de la Toyota Tacoma, sa plus proche rivale, qui fait 1,87 mètre.

Le châssis à longerons hydroformés du Dakota est un gage de solidité et de rigidité. Une telle robustesse est essentielle pour le travail dur et pour porter ou tracter des charges lourdes mais également pour la conduite normale, sans presque de charge, qui est le lot quotidien d'une forte proportion de ces camionnettes. Or le Dakota propose un comportement routier solide, stable et accuse peu de roulis en virage. Son confort de roulement est supérieur à celui de son grand rival, le Toyota Tacoma.

Le Dakota est également la plus spacieux de la catégorie mais la finition de son habitacle et la qualité des matériaux qu'on y trouve sont par contre encore nettement inférieurs à ce qu'on trouve dans le Tacoma ou le Honda Ridgeline. Il lui manque aussi le repose-pied solide et plat de ces derniers et il n'y a qu'un seul levier, à la gauche du volant, pour contrôler les clignotants et les essuie-glaces. On peut lui reprocher aussi des commandes et contrôles trop complexes et confuses pour le régulateur de vitesse sur le volant qui ne sont pas éclairées non plus en conduite nocturne. Les boutons pour la chaîne audio derrière le volant sont par contre impeccables et on apprécie constamment les grands rétroviseurs extérieurs.

Il serait bien que le Dakota soit l'objet des mêmes attentions que le grand Ram qui lui fait toujours de l'ombre. Ce sera cependant difficile si l'on songe que ses ventes avaient fondu de près de 80 % au premier trimestre alors que celles du Ram avaient plus que doublé.

Marc Lachapelle

PHOTOS : RAM

Catégorie	Camionnette
Échelle de prix	19 545 $ à 29 545 $
Garanties	3 ans/60 000 km, 5 ans/100 000 km
Assemblage	Warren, Michigan, É-U
Cote d'assurance	moyenne

CHÂSSIS - DONNÉES POUR ST 4X2 CABINE ALLONGÉE

Emp/lon/lar/haut	3 335/5 550/1 822/1 743 mm
Longueur de boîte	2 002 mm (78,8 pouces)
Réservoir	83 litres
Nombre coussins sécurité	2
Antipatinage / contrôle stabilité	non / non
Suspension avant	indépendante, bras inégaux
Suspension arrière	ressorts à lames
Freins avant / arrière	disque (ABS) / tambour (ABS)
Direction	à crémaillère, assistée
Diamètre de braquage	13,4 m
Pneus avant / arrière	P245/70R16 / P245/70R16
Poids	2 121 kg
Capacité de remorquage	2 563 kg (5 650 lb)

COMPOSANTES MÉCANIQUES

Cylindrée, soupapes, alim.	V6 3,7 litres 16 s atmos.
Puissance / Couple	210 chevaux / 235 lb-pi
Tr. base (opt) / rouage base (opt)	A4 / Prop (4x4)
Type ess. / ville / autoroute	Ordinaire / 14,4 / 9,8 l/100 km

Cylindrée, soupapes, alim.	V8 4,7 litres 16 s atmos.
Puissance / Couple	302 chevaux / 329 lb-pi
Tr. base (opt) / rouage base (opt)	A5 / Prop (4x4)
Type ess. / ville / autoroute	Ordinaire / 15,0 / 10,7 l/100 km

DANS LA MÊME CATÉGORIE

Chevrolet Colorado, Ford Ranger, GMC Canyon, Honda Ridgeline, Nissan Frontier, Suzuki Equator, Toyota Tacoma

DU NOUVEAU EN 2011

Aucun changement majeur. La division camion de Dodge est devenue Ram durant l'année modèle 2010

NOS IMPRESSIONS

Agrément de conduite :	7/10
Fiabilité :	5/10
Sécurité :	6/10
Qualités hivernales :	8/10
Espace intérieur :	8/10
Confort :	8/10

www.ramtrucks.com

Plus d'informations dans la section statistiques en dernière partie du Guide

SAVOIR GARDER LA TÊTE HAUTE

Inutile de se le cacher. Les *pick-up* Toyota ne jouissent pas de la même aura que celles des constructeurs américains. Pourtant, le Tacoma a réussi à s'imposer dans ce marché, pour le moins exclusif, grâce à ses qualités et au fait… qu'il rencontre bien peu de concurrence!

En effet, cette camionnette intermédiaire, plus grosse que les Ford Ranger et Chevrolet Colorado, se permet même de battre le Ram Dakota, pourtant le pionnier de la camionnette semi-intermédiaire, si on peut dire. Ce dernier ne se vend pratiquement pas, victime de ses dimensions qui ne satisfont à peu près personne. Le Tacoma, lui, se rapproche des camionnettes grand format que sont les Ford F-150, Chevrolet Silverado et Ram 1500. Pour ne pas créer de confusion dans sa gamme, Toyota a décidé, il y a quelques années, de grossir son déjà gros Tundra.

ON S'ASSUME!

Même s'il n'a pas la gueule de macho d'un Ford Ranger, on ne peut pas dire qu'il manque de charisme. On remarque surtout son imposante grille avant, des passages de roues en relief, ainsi que des bas de caisse soulignés à grand coup de moulures. La caisse de 6 pieds (ou de 5 pieds pour un des modèles) est recouverte d'un matériau composite destiné à protéger ses parois et le fond des coups durs de la vie. Chacune de ces boîtes reçoit quatre crochets de fixation. La porte à battant, la *tailgate* en bon français, n'est pas très lourde, une bénédiction pour plusieurs personnes. Toutefois, si Toyota avait la brillante idée d'installer une lumière pour éclairer la boîte, je ne crois pas que quiconque leur intenterait une poursuite…

Si l'extérieur fait plutôt «truck», l'habitacle ne donne pas sa place non plus. Étant assez haut sur pattes, il impose une certaine gymnastique à ses passagers pour accéder aux sièges. Heureusement, il est possible de choisir des marchepieds parmi les accessoires proposés. Alors que la tendance veut maintenant des camionnettes qui ont des allures d'automobiles, le Tacoma est un camion qui s'assume. Les plastiques durs et les gros boutons faciles à manipuler ont de moins en moins leur place, mais ils assurent un côté à la fois «rough» et raffiné qui plait. Ne cherchez pas, de sièges cuir, de glace arrière coulissante électriquement ou de système GPS, même dans la liste des options. En lieu et place de ces gadgets, on retrouve un volant ajustable en hauteur et en profondeur, un système audio (assez quelconque, j'en conviens) avec prise auxiliaire et pré-câblage pour la radio satellite et plusieurs espaces de rangement. Les sièges avant sont passablement confortables, mais après quelques heures coincé dans le trafic montréalais (c'est à ce moment qu'on comprend que ville et *pick-up* ne vont pas nécessairement de pair), je commençais à avoir le dos fatigué. Les places arrière des modèles à cabine double ne sont pas à dédaigner, surtout si la personne devant a la bonne idée d'avancer un peu son siège. De toute évidence, les sièges arrière des modèles à cabine Accès sont destinés à des voyages courts.

- Gabarit juste correct
- Fiabilité reconnue
- Un quatre cylindres peu gourmand
- Tenue de route prévisible
- Habitacle accueillant

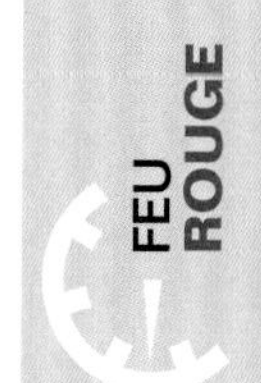

- Suspensions assez fermes
- V6 aime bien les pompes à essence
- Pas de lumière pour éclairer la boîte
- Sonorité radio ordinaire
- Certains modèles dispendieux

QUATRE OU SIX CYLINDRES?

Deux moteurs sont proposés. Le premier est un quatre cylindres de 2,7 litres. Même s'il n'est pas très puissant, la possibilité de l'associer à une boîte manuelle à cinq rapports de vitesse le rend intéressant. Grâce à celle-ci, il propose une consommation d'essence fort réjouissante, mais il ne peut travailler très dur même s'il est possible de le marier à un rouage 4x4. Pour ce faire, il faut plutôt regarder du côté du V6 de 4,0 litres, plus puissant, mais surtout, offrant un couple plus imposant. Ce moteur est invariablement apparié aux quatre roues motrices. Davantage de chevaux, tous les écuyers vous le diront, ça veut dire davantage de foin et le V6 ne fait pas exception. Les cotes de Transport Canada vont de 10,1 l/100 km à 13,5 (route, ville) pour une version munie de l'automatique à cinq rapports. Une semaine d'essai, passée à 80 % sur les routes, nous donne une moyenne de 12,0 l/100 km.

La transmission automatique à cinq rapports de notre véhicule d'essai fonctionnait généralement très bien, sauf à l'occasion, lors des passages entre la première et la deuxième, où le temps de passage était plus long que la normale. Cette boîte avait pour mission de relayer le couple du moteur aux quatre roues grâce à un système 4x4 pas nécessairement sophistiqué, mais très efficace. Possédant une gamme basse, il permet de se sortir d'à peu près toutes les impasses, aidé en cela par une garde au sol généreuse et des pneus passablement agressifs. Les pneus Dunlop AT20 Grandtrek se sont montrés fort silencieux tout au long de notre essai.

Si les randonnées routières ne sont pas trop pénibles, c'est en grande partie à grâce aux sièges, car les suspensions font généralement fi des occupants et les brassent passablement. Si le confort est correct sur une surface lisse comme un billard, il en va autrement quand la chaussée se gâte et l'arrière, surtout, à tendance à danser.

Le Toyota Tacoma n'est certainement pas à dédaigner. Dans bien des cas, les gens le préfèrent à l'immense et peu estimé Tundra. De plus, il faut souligner que le Tacoma n'a pratiquement pas été incommodé par les nombreux rappels dont ont souffert plusieurs produits Toyota depuis un an. Il s'ensuit une confiance réitérée qui n'est pas usurpée.

Alain Morin

PHOTOS : ALAIN MORIN

TOYOTA TACOMA

Catégorie	Camionnette
Échelle de prix	21 895 $ à 32 645 $
Garanties	3 ans/60 000 km, 5 ans/100 000 km
Assemblage	Georgetown Ky., Fremont CA., É-U
Cote d'assurance	passable

CHÂSSIS - DONNÉES POUR 4X4 V6 CABINE DOUBLE

Emp/lon/lar/haut	3 246/5 286/1 895/1 781 mm
Longueur de boîte	1 531 mm (60,3 pouces)
Réservoir	80 litres
Nombre coussins sécurité	6
Antipatinage / contrôle stabilité	oui / oui
Suspension avant	indépendante, double triangulation
Suspension arrière	essieu rigide, ressorts à lames
Freins avant / arrière	disque (ABS) / tambour (ABS)
Direction	à crémaillère, assistée
Diamètre de braquage	14,2 m
Pneus avant / arrière	P245/75R16 / P245/75R16
Poids	1 873 kg
Capacité de remorquage	2 903 kg (6 400 lb)

COMPOSANTES MÉCANIQUES

Cylindrée, soupapes, alim.	4L 2,7 litres 16 s atmos.
Puissance / Couple	159 chevaux / 180 lb-pi
Tr. base (opt) / rouage base (opt)	M5 (A4) / Prop (4x4)
0-100 / 80-120 / 100-0 km/h	n.d. / n.d. / n.d.
Type ess. / ville / autoroute	Ordinaire / 10,5 / 7,8 l/100 km

Cylindrée, soupapes, alim.	V6 4,0 litres 24 s atmos.
Puissance / Couple	236 chevaux / 266 lb-pi
Tr. base (opt) / rouage base (opt)	M6 (A5) / 4x4
0-100 / 80-120 / 100-0 km/h	7,3 s / 6,2 s / 40,3 m
Type ess. / ville / autoroute	Ordinaire / 13,5 / 10,1 l/100 km

DANS LA MÊME CATÉGORIE

Chevrolet Colorado, RAM Dakota, Ford Ranger, GMC Canyon, Honda Ridgeline, Nissan Frontier, Suzuki Equator

DU NOUVEAU EN 2011

Aucun changement majeur

NOS IMPRESSIONS

Agrément de conduite :	■■■■■■■□□□	7/10
Fiabilité :	■■■■■■■■□□	8/10
Sécurité :	■■■■■■■■□□	8/10
Qualités hivernales :	■■■■■■■□□□	7/10
Espace intérieur :	■■■■■■■□□□	7/10
Confort :	■■■■■■■□□□	7/10

www.toyota.ca

Plus d'informations dans la section statistiques en dernière partie du Guide

LA GRENOUILLE ET LE BŒUF

À défaut d'être le véhicule le plus vendu de Toyota, le Tundra est, en revanche, le plus gros. À ses côtés, un Sequoia a quasiment l'air d'une Yaris. D'ailleurs, le châssis du Tundra partage plusieurs éléments de celui du Sequoia, dont la partie avant. Bref, on est dans les grosses pointures. Cependant, comme l'oncle Martin qui est bâti comme une armoire à glace et qui attrape le moindre rhume, le Tundra n'est pas nécessairement aussi solide que son physique le laisse supposer. Voyons-y de plus près.

Tant qu'à donner dans le gigantisme, Toyota n'a pas été dans la dentelle. La grille avant, immense, droite et résolument dominatrice donne le ton. Les pneus de généreuses dimensions, les gros phares, les larges portières supportant de bons rétroviseurs, les piliers des vitres imposants et la garde au sol qui demande à la patte de se lever bien haut pour accéder à l'habitacle, tout en impose. La boîte de chargement est du même acabit et elle est recouverte, en option, d'une doublure faite de copolymère polyéthylène haute densité. Du pvc, sans doute... Petite fleur mignonne dans un champ de roche, la porte de cette benne bascule avec douceur et se relève facilement. En passant, soulignons que cette boîte mesure 8 ou 5 pieds six pouces selon le modèle choisi.

SUBTILITÉ DE GARS DE CHANTIER

Rendu à l'intérieur, c'est tout aussi intimidant. Le tableau de bord s'allonge comme pour mieux montrer ses grandes jauges et ses boutons et commandes démesurés. Le revers, c'est que les boutons situés à l'extrême droite sont difficiles à rejoindre pour quiconque ne possède pas un bras droit de plus 18 pieds de longueur. Comme sur la plupart des camionnettes, le tableau de bord du Tundra est très complet et toute l'information dont le conducteur pourrait avoir besoin est là, bien présentée. Les espaces de rangement ne font pas défaut et la console centrale, à elle seule, peut avaler deux ou trois Yaris. Passons outre le fait que la plupart des plastiques sont assez « cheaps » merci et que la visibilité est réduite par des piliers très larges et attardons-nous sur l'espace vivable. Si vous espérez toucher le bras d'une jolie personne pour lui faire subtilement part de vos sentiments et/ou désirs, le Tundra n'est vraiment pas le véhicule indiqué. Même en hiver avec de bons manteaux, il n'y aucune chance pour frôler l'autre. Les sièges avant offrent un confort correct même si les modèles dotés de la banquette sont moins nantis à ce sujet. Au risque de se répéter, l'accès à bord est pénible et des marchepieds, offerts dans la liste des accessoires, pourraient être une solution à envisager.

Deux moteurs se disputent le capot du Tundra. On retrouve tout d'abord un V8 de 4,6 litres qui répond parfaitement lorsque les travaux ne sont pas trop durs. Qu'on s'entende bien, pas trop dur, pour un Tundra, veut quand même dire passablement dur... Il est d'ailleurs utilisé dans la majorité des Tundra. Ce moteur consomme de manière modérée, pour une grande camionnette.

Participez GRATUITEMENT
au concours
Le Guide de l'auto 2011* sur
Guideautoweb.com
ABONNEZ-VOUS
DÈS MAINTENANT
au magazine d'automobile
#1 au Québec
4 façons simples et rapides de s'abonner:
Poste: complétez le coupon ci-dessous
Internet: www.guideautoweb.com
Téléphone: 1 866 522.5656
Télécopieur: 450 464.8271
[PAS BESOIN DE SLOGAN, VOUS ÊTES DÉJÀ
CONVAINCUS]
*Tous les détails sur le site.

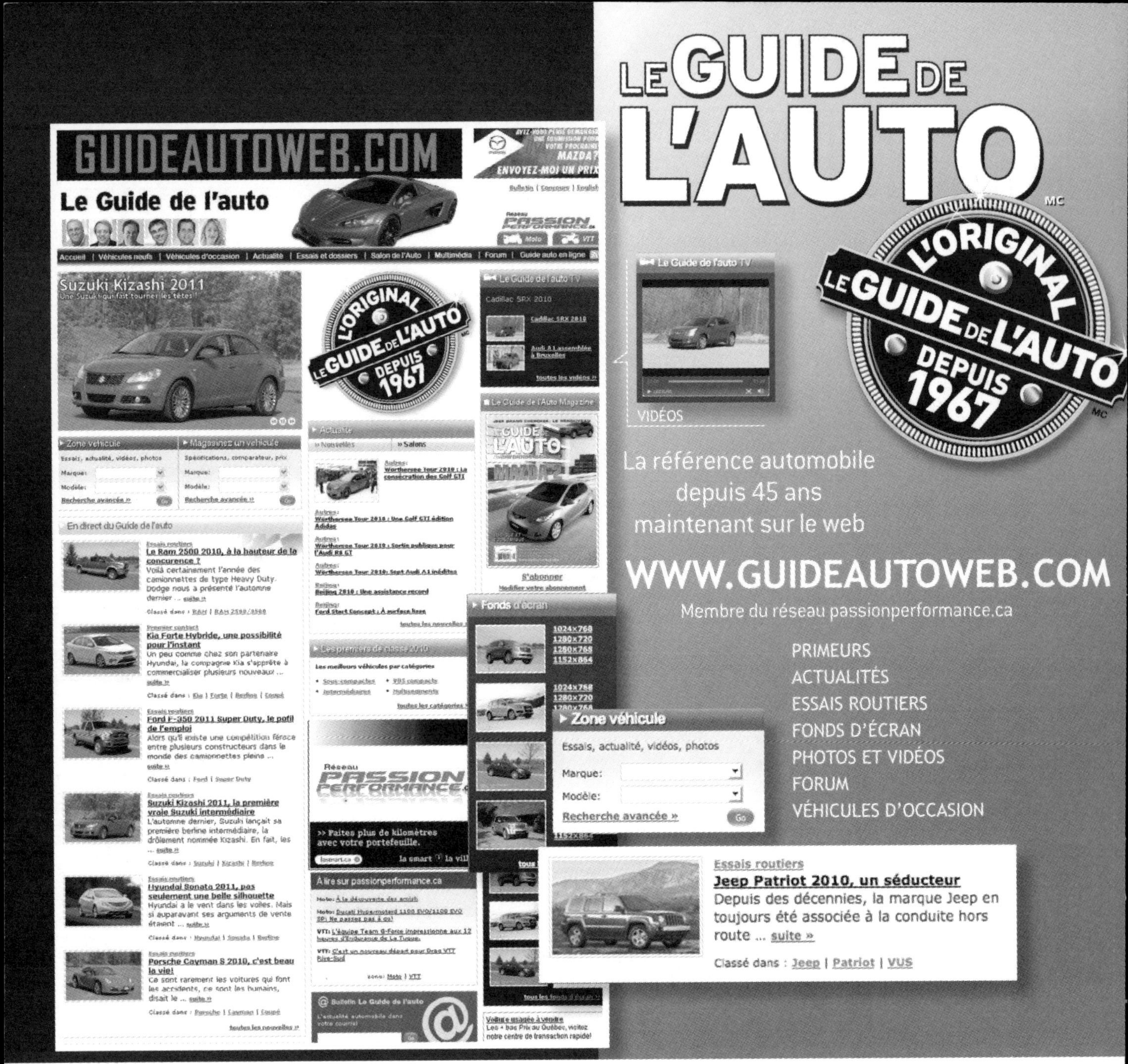

1000069868-J3G4S5-CR01

LC MÉDIA INC
200-1895 RUE DE L'INDUSTRIE RR1
SAINT-MATHIEU-DE-BELOEIL QC J3G 9Z9

FEU VERT

Style macho qui plait
Vaste habitacle
Confort très correct
Moteur 4,6 litres assez économe
Moteur 5,7 litres très puissant

FEU ROUGE

Dimensions trop, simplement trop
Capacité de chargement maigrichonne
Direction floue
Plate-forme manquant de rigidité
5,7 litres goinfre au possible

Cependant, pour plus de *punch*, autant lors des accélérations que pour les capacités de remorquage, le V8 de 5,7 litres est indubitablement le moteur à privilégier. Il permet au véhicule de se déplacer aussi rapidement que bien des voitures sport puisqu'il a la souplesse et la sonorité requise. Aussi, il peut remorquer jusqu'à 10 800 livres (4 895 kilos) selon la version. Le 4,6 litres, lui, peut tirer « seulement » 8 900 livres (4 035 livres) encore une fois selon la version. De bien bons mots pour ce 5,7, non? Il y a par contre un petit hic... sa soif démesurée. Bon sang qu'il boit! Sur la grand-route, malgré les prétentions de Toyota, n'espérez pas faire mieux que 14 ou 15 litres aux cent kilomètres. En ville, 18 ou 19 seraient plus appropriés. À ce chapitre, seul le Titan de Nissan peut lui tenir tête...

IL PERD DES POINTS À L'ARRIÈRE

Les modèles de base sont mus par les roues arrière tandis que les autres ont droit à un système 4x4 très efficace. Sur la route, le Tundra se comporte passablement bien. Il faut oublier les prestations sportives malgré la puissance du 5,7 litres pour mieux se concentrer sur sa suspension arrière, peu sautillante sur mauvaise route même lorsque la boîte est vide. Mais cette suspension arrière est aussi le point faible du Tundra. Les ressorts à lame sont trop petits pour être pris au sérieux, tout comme les freins. C'est peut-être la raison pour laquelle la capacité de charge (*payload*) est l'une des plus faibles parmi les grandes camionnettes. Ce qui étonne vu les dimensions pachydermiques du Tundra. Au moins l'avant est soutenu par une suspension plus solide. Cependant, quand on affronte des valeurs établies comme les Ford F-150, Chevrolet Silverado et même le Dodge Ram à suspension arrière à ressorts hélicoïdaux, il ne faut pas fafiner sur les détails comme la capacité de charge. Et comme Le Guide de l'auto le rapportait l'an dernier, un test extrême sur chaussée bosselée mené avec la grande camionnette des constructeurs américains et celle de Toyota a prouvé que la rigidité structurelle de ce dernier laissait à désirer. Ce qui prouve que les concepteurs de Toyota ont peut-être compris que leur camion devait être le plus gros mais ils ont oublié qu'il devait aussi être le plus fort pour espérer faire sa place au soleil en Amérique...

Alain Morin

PHOTOS : SYLVAIN RAYMOND

Catégorie	Camionnette
Échelle de prix	28 975 $ à 52 020 $ (2010)
Garanties	3 ans/60 000 km, 5 ans/100 000 km
Assemblage	Princeton IN, San Antonio TX, É-U
Cote d'assurance	passable

CHÂSSIS - DONNÉES POUR 4X4 LIMITED 5.7L CREWMAX

Emp/lon/lar/haut	3 700/5 810/2 030/1 940 mm
Longueur de bo[ite	1 695 mm (66,7 pouces)
Réservoir	100 litres
Nombre coussins sécurité	6
Antipatinage / contrôle stabilité	oui / oui
Suspension avant	indépendante, double triangulation
Suspension arrière	essieu rigide, ressorts à lames
Freins avant / arrière	disque (ABS) / disque (ABS)
Direction	à crémaillère, assistée
Diamètre de braquage	13,4 m
Pneus avant / arrière	P275/55R20 / P275/55R20
Poids	2 561 kg
Capacité de remorquage	4 580 kg (10 097 lb)

COMPOSANTES MÉCANIQUES

Cylindrée, soupapes, alim.	V8 4,6 litres 32 s atmos.
Puissance / Couple	310 chevaux / 327 lb-pi
Tr. base (opt) / rouage base (opt)	A6 / Prop (4x4)
0-100 / 80-120 / 100-0 km/h	n.d. / n.d. / n.d.
Type ess. / ville / autoroute	Ordinaire / 14,9 / 10,5 l/100 km

Cylindrée, soupapes, alim.	V8 5,7 litres 32 s atmos.
Puissance / Couple	381 chevaux / 401 lb-pi
Tr. base (opt) / rouage base (opt)	A6 / Prop (4x4)
0-100 / 80-120 / 100-0 km/h	6,9 s / 5,2 s / 45,9 m
Type ess. / ville / autoroute	Ordinaire / 16,8 / 11,8 l/100 km

DANS LA MÊME CATÉGORIE

Chevrolet Silverado, Dodge RAM, Ford F-150, GMC Sierra, Nissan Titan

DU NOUVEAU EN 2011

Aucun changement majeur

NOS IMPRESSIONS

Agrément de conduite :	7/10
Fiabilité :	7/10
Sécurité :	8/10
Qualités hivernales :	7/10
Espace intérieur :	9/10
Confort :	7/10

www.toyota.ca

Plus d'informations dans la section statistiques en dernière partie du Guide

DC 145XN

TABLEAU DE CONSOMMATION

LES HAUTS ET LES BAS DE L'ÉCONOMIE DE CARBURANT

Voiture économique

Comme pour les années passées, la présente édition du Guide de l'auto vous informe des voitures les plus économiques en fait de consommation de carburant et les plus énergivores également. Ces données ne sont pas inventées mais issues de la brochure Énerguide publiée par Ressources naturelles du Canada. Afin de vous proposer des chiffres qui collent davantage à la réalité, nous prenons les chiffres de consommation « ville » qui sont moins optimistes et plus réalistes que la consommation « route ». En plus, les chiffres sont pour les modèles dotés de la boîte manuelle quand c'est possible. Vous serez donc en mesure de comparer les données de consommation de façon plus équitable.

Nous avons utilisé, comme pour l'an dernier, le logo vert « Voiture économique » pour identifier toute voiture consommant moins de 9,0 litres aux cent kilomètres.

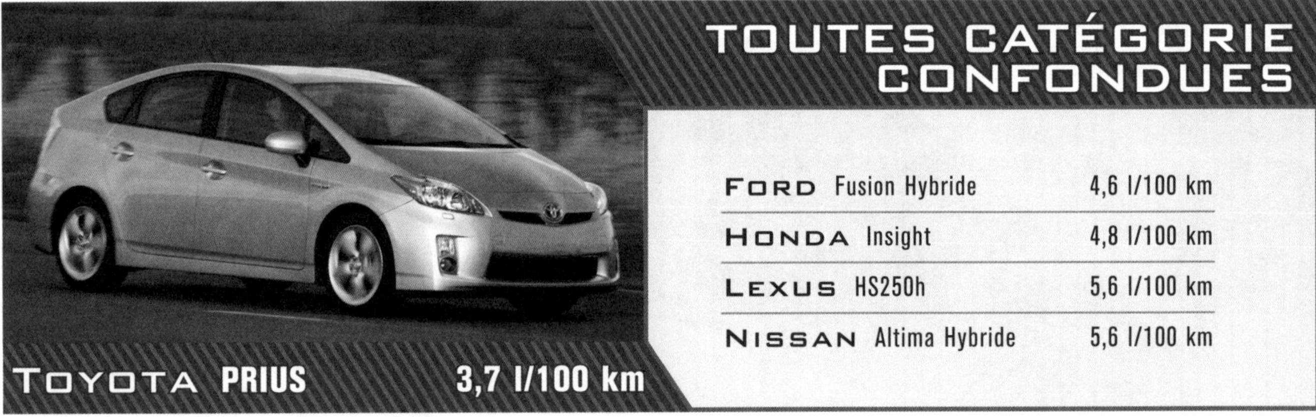

TOUTES CATÉGORIE CONFONDUES

TOYOTA PRIUS 3,7 l/100 km

FORD Fusion Hybride	4,6 l/100 km
HONDA Insight	4,8 l/100 km
LEXUS HS250h	5,6 l/100 km
NISSAN Altima Hybride	5,6 l/100 km

SOUS-COMPACTES

TOYOTA Yaris	6,9 l/100 km
KIA Rio	7,1 l/100 km
MINI Cooper	7,1 l/100 km
HONDA Fit	7,2 l/100 km
MAZDA2	7,2 l/100 km

SMART FORTWO 5,9 l/100 km

COMPACTES

TOYOTA PRIUS 3,7 l/100 km

HONDA Insight	4,8 l/100 km
HONDA CR-Z	6,5 l/100 km
AUDI A3 TDI	6,7 l/100 km
VOLKSWAGEN Jetta TDI	6,7 l/100 km

INTERMÉDIAIRES

FORD FUSION HYBRID 4,6 l/100 km

LEXUS HS250h	5,6 l/100 km
NISSAN Altima Hybrid	5,6 l/100 km
TOYOTA Camry Hybrid	5,7 l/100 km
NISSAN Altima 2,5	8,8 l/100 km

VUS COMPACTS

JEEP Patriot	8,8 l/100 km
JEEP Compass	8,9 l/100 km
NISSAN Rogue	9,1 l/100 km
CHEVROLET Equinox	9,2 l/100 km

FORD ESCAPE HYBRID 5,8 l/100 km

CABRIOLETS ET *ROADSTERS*

SMART FORTWO ROADSTER5,9 l/100 km

MINI Cooper cabrio	7,1 l/100 km
MAZDA MX-5	9,2 l/100 km
AUDI TT	9,5 l/100 km
VOLKSWAGEN Eos	10,0 l/100 km

ET LES PIRES !

BENTLEY Continental Flying Spur Speed	25,31 l/100 km
BENTLEY Continental Supersports Convertible	25,5 l/100 km
LAMBORGHINI Murciélago LP 640	25,9 l/100 km
BENTLEY Mulsanne	26,3 l/100 km

LAMBORGHINI MURCIÉLAGO LP 670-4 SV 29,44 l/100 km

ACURA

Modèle	Prix	
CSX Technologie	27490$	x
CSX Type S	29990$	x
MDX	51990$	x
MDX Technologie	57290$	x
MDX Elite	61990$	x
RL	63900$	x
RL Elite	69500$	x
RDX	39990$	x
RDX Technologie	42990$	x
TL	39990$	x
TL Technologie	43490$	x
TL SH-AWD	44990$	x
TL SH-AWD Technologie	48490$	x
TL A-Spec	51290$	x
TSX man	32990$	x
TSX Premium man	36290$	x
TSX Technologie man	39290$	x
TSX V-6	39790$	x
TSX V-6 Technologie	42790$	x
ZDX	55990$	x
ZDX Technologie	59590$	x

ASTON MARTIN

Modèle	Prix	
DB9 Coupe	206795$	
DB9 Volante	224465$	
DBS Coupe	306495$	
DBS Volante	323195$	
Rapide	215000$	
V8 Vantage	137495$	
V8 Vantage N420	150000$	
V8 Vantage Roadster	152795$	
V8 Vantage Roadster N420	165300$	
V12 Vantage	183000$	
V12 Vantage Carbon	197000$	

AUDI

Modèle	Prix	
A3 Sportback 2.0T man	32300$	
A3 Sportback 2.0T quattro DSG	36900$	x
A3 Sportback 2.0 TDI DSG	35300$	
A4 Berline 2.0T FWD man	37800$	
A4 Berline 2.0T quattro man	39700$	x
A4 Avant 2.0T quattro	42800$	
A5 Coupé 2.0T quattro man	44100$	x
A5 Coupé 3.2 quattro	53350$	x
A5 Cabriolet 2.0T quattro	56300$	x
A6 Berline 3.2 FWD	52900$	x
A6 Berline 3.0T quattro	63300$	x
A6 Berline 4.2 quattro	75900$	x
A6 Avant 3.0T quattro	66700$	x
A8 4.2 quattro	95000$	x
A8L 4.2 quattro	100000$	x
Q5 2.0T quattro	41200$	
Q5 3.2 quattro	43500$	x
Q5 3.2 quattro Premium	48600$	x
Q7 3.0T quattro	53900$	
Q7 3.0 TDI quattro	57700$	x
R8 4.2 quattro man	144000$	
R8 5.2 quattro man	173000$	x
R8 Spyder 5.2 quattro	n.d.	
S4 Berline 3.0T quattro man	52500$	
S5 Coupé 4.2 quattro man	65900$	x
S5 Cabriolet 3.0T quattro	68300$	x
S6 5.2 quattro	99500$	x
TT Coupé 2.0T quattro	49350$	x
TTS Coupé 2.0T quattro	57900$	
TT Roadster 2.0T quattro	52350$	x
TTS Roadster 2.0T quattro	62200$	

BENTLEY

Modèle	Prix	
Continental GT	201100$	x
Continental GT Speed	228500$	x
Continental Flying Spur	199300$	
Continental Flying Spur Speed	227300$	
Continental GTC	226200$	
Continental GTC Speed	259700$	
Continental Supersports Coupe	293700$	
Continental Supersports Cabriolet	308400$	
Mulsanne	325000$	

BMW

Modèle	Prix	
M3 Berline	69900$	
M3 Coupé	71300$	
M3 Cabriolet	81900$	
M5 Berline	106900$	x
M6 Coupé	121300$	x
M6 Coupé Competition	139400$	x
M6 Cabriolet	131300$	x
Série 1 Coupé 128i	35800$	
Série 1 Coupé 135i	43000$	
Série 1 Cabriolet 128i	41200$	
Série 1 Cabriolet 135i	48500$	
Série 3 Berline 323i	34900$	
Série 3 Berline 325i Coupe	46800$	
Série 3 Berline 328i	41100$	
Série 3 Berline 328i xDrive	44100$	
Série 3 Berline 335i	51400$	
Série 3 Berline 335i xDrive	52100$	
Série 3 Berline 335d	49900$	
Série 3 Coupé 328i	44300$	
Série 3 Coupé 335i	53400$	
Série 3 Coupé 335i xDrive	54100$	
Série 3 Coupé 335is	58100$	
Série 3 Cabriolet 328i	57300$	
Serie 3 Cabriolet 335i	68900$	
Serie 3 Cabriolet 335is	74300$	
Série 3 Touring 328i xDrive	45700$	
Série 5 Berline 528i	53900$	
Série 5 Berline 535i	62300$	
Série 5 Berline 550i	73300$	
Série 6 Coupé 650i	95500$	x
Série 6 Cabriolet 650i	105500$	x
Série 7 750i xDrive	108600$	
Série 7 750Li xDrive	116600$	
Série 7 ActiveHybrid	132300$	
X3 2.8i xDrive	39900$	x
X3 3.0i xDrive	45900$	x
X5 3.0i xDrive	59990$	
X5 3.5d xDrive	62800$	
X5 5.0i xDrive	74300$	
X5 M	97900$	
X6 3.5i xDrive	65700$	
X6 5.0i xDrive	81000$	
X6 ActiveHybrid	99900$	
X6 M	99900$	
Z4 Roadster 3.0i	54300$	
Z4 Roadster 3.5i	63900$	
Z4 Roadster 3.5is	77900$	

BUGATTI

Modèle	Prix	
Veyron 16.4	1400000$	
Veyron Grand Sport	1700000$	
Veyron Super Sport	2400000$	

BUICK

Modèle	Prix	
Enclave CX	43520$	
Enclave CXL	46520$	
Enclave CX (TI)	48490$	
Enclave CXL (TI)	51490$	
LaCrosse CX	31645$	
LaCrosse CXL	34795$	
LaCrosse CXL (TI)	38870$	
LaCrosse CXS	41870$	
Lucerne CX	33870$	
Lucerne CXL	36610$	
Lucerne Super	55150$	
Regal CXL	31990$	

CADILLAC

Modèle	Prix	
CTS 3.0L	40455$	
CTS 3.6L	48785$	
CTS 3.0L AWD	44480$	
CTS 3.6L AWD	51410$	
CTS-V	72565$	
CTS Coupe	47450$	
CTS Coupe 3.6 AWD	50080$	
CTS-V Coupe	71250$	
CTS Familiale sport 3.0L	44130$	
CTS Familiale sport 3.6L	50760$	
CTS Familiale sport 3.0L AWD	46755$	
CTS Familiale sport 3.6L AWD	53795$	
CTS-V Familiale sport	n.d.	
DTS	56540$	
DTS Platinum	74680$	
Escalade	84645$	
Escalade Hybride	94790$	
Escalade ESV	88345$	
Escalade EXT	79645$	
SRX	41780$	
SRX AWD	45080$	
SRX Performance	56590$	
SRX Premium Turbo AWD	62775$	
STS V6	61135$	

CHEVROLET CAMIONS

Modèle	Prix	
Avalanche LS (2RM)	42310$	
Avalanche LT (2RM)	43835$	
Avalanche LS (4RM)	45555$	
Avalanche LT (4RM)	47080$	
Avalanche LTZ (4RM)	58320$	
Colorado LS à cabine classique (2RM)	23875$	
Colorado LT à cabine classique (2RM)	24915$	
Colorado LS à cabine classique (4RM)	27680$	
Colorado LT à cabine classique (4RM)	28610$	
Colorado LS à cabine allongée (2RM)	25945$	
Colorado LT à cabine allongée (2RM)	27040$	
Colorado LS à cabine allongée (4RM)	29750$	
Colorado LT à cabine allongée (4RM)	30735$	
Colorado LT à cabine multiplace (2RM)	31490$	
Colorado LT à cabine multiplace (4RM)	36490$	
Equinox LS	25995$	
Equinox LS (TI)	27605$	
Equinox 1LT	27725$	
Equinox 1LT (TI)	29335$	
Equinox LTZ	33650$	
Equinox LTZ (TI)	35260$	
HHR LS	20395$	
HHR LT	22040$	
Silverado 1500, à cabine classique caisse régulière (2RM)	26260$	
Silverado 1500, à cabine multiplace caisse longue (4RM)	35695$	
Silverado 1500 LTZ, à cabine allongée caisse régulière (4RM)	46800$	
Silverado 1500, à cabine multiplace caisse longue (4RM) Hybride	51655$	
Suburban 1500 LS	52015$	
Suburban 1500 LS (4RM)	55465$	
Suburban 1500 LT	57515$	
Suburban 1500 LT (4RM)	60965$	
Suburban 1500 LTZ (4RM)	72275$	
Tahoe LS	49365$	
Tahoe LS (4RM)	53825$	
Tahoe LT	54370$	
Tahoe LT (4RM)	58825$	
Tahoe Hybride bimode	68625$	
Tahoe Hybride bimode (4RM)	71610$	
Tahoe LTZ (4RM)	69175$	
Traverse LS	35715$	
Traverse LT	38375$	
Traverse LS (TI)	38715$	
Traverse LT (TI)	41375$	
Traverse LTZ	47540$	
Traverse LTZ (TI)	50540$	

CHEVROLET

Modèle	Prix	
Aveo berline LS	14150$	
Aveo berline LT	16850$	
Aveo 5 portes LS	13950$	
Aveo 5 portes LT	16650$	
Camaro LS	26995$	
Camaro 1LT	28065$	
Camaro 2LT	32505$	
Camaro 1SS	37065$	
Camaro 2SS	41905$	
Corvette Coupé	67135$	
Corvette Cabriolet	77040$	
Corvette Coupé Grand Sport	74960$	
Corvette Cabriolet Grand Sport	83740$	
Corvette Z06	95705$	
Corvette ZR1	128600$	
Cruze Eco	n.d.	
Cruze LS	14995$	
Cruze LT Turbo	19495$	
Cruze LTZ Turbo	24780$	
Impala LS	27235$	
Impala LT	28215$	
Impala LTZ	30565$	
Malibu LS	23995$	
Malibu LT	26135$	
Malibu LT Platinum	27895$	
Malibu LTZ	32750$	
Volt	40000$	
Environ		

CHRYSLER

Modèle	Prix	
300 Touring	32995$	x
300 Touring (TI)	37295$	x
300 Limited	36995$	x
300 Limited (TI)	41295$	x
300C	46745$	x
300C (TI)	50295$	x
300C SRT8	54845$	x
Sebring LX	23995$	x
Sebring Touring	26995$	x
Sebring Limited	28295$	x
Sebring Cabriolet LX	30665$	x
Sebring Cabriolet Touring	35465$	x
Sebring Cabriolet Limited	44070$	x
Town & Country Touring	37845$	x
Town & Country Limited	43845$	x

DODGE

Modèle	Prix	
Avenger SE	20995$	x
Avenger SXT	22795$	x
Avenger R/T	25295$	x
Caliber Canada	13995$	x
Caliber SE Plus	15795$	x
Caliber SXT	17645$	x
Caliber HEAT	20495$	x
Caliber Uptown	21995$	x
Challenger SE	25995$	x
Challenger SXT	27695$	x
Challenger R/T	35395$	x
Challenger SRT8	46995$	x
Charger SE	25745$	x
Charger SXT	27595$	x
Charger R/T	36345$	x
Charger SRT8	43195$	x
Grand Caravan SE	20945$	x
Grand Caravan SXT	26295$	x
Journey SE	18745$	x
Journey SE Plus	20745$	x
Journey SXT	23295$	x
Journey R/T	27395$	x
Nitro SXT 4X4	28495$	x

Viper SRT10 Coupe	99 895$	x
Viper SRT10 Roadster	98 895$	x

FERRARI

599 GTB Fiorano F1	425 600$	x
612 Scaglietti F1	390 570$	x
California	262 000$	x
F458 Italia Coupe	290 000$	
F458 Italia Spyder	n.d.	

FIAT

500	n.d.	

FORD

Edge SE	27 999$	
Edge SEL	33 999$	
Edge SEL (TI)	35 999$	
Edge Limited	37 799$	
Edge Limited (TI)	39 799$	
Edge Sport (TI)	43 499$	
Escape XLT 2.5L man.	19 999$	
Escape XLT 3.0L	27 199$	
Escape XLT 2.5L (4RM)	27 999$	
Escape XLT 3.0L (4RM)	29 599$	
Escape Limited 2.5L (4RM)	33 549$	
Escape Limited 3.0L (4RM)	35 149$	
Escape Hybride	38 399$	
Escape Hybrid (4RM)	40 799$	
Escape Hybrid Limited	43 399$	
Escape Hybrid Limited (4RM)	45 799$	
Expedition XLT	46 999$	
Expedition Limited	58 499$	
Expedition Max Limited	60 999$	
Explorer XLT V6 4X4	37 499$	x
Explorer XLT V6 Sport (TI)	38 799$	x
Explorer XLT V8 4X4	38 999$	x
Explorer XLT V8 Sport (TI)	40 299$	x
Explorer Eddie Bauer V6	43 899$	x
Explorer Eddie Bauer V8	45 399$	x
Explorer Limited V8	49 799$	x
Explorer Sport Trac XLT 4.0L 4X4	35 699$	x
Explorer Sport Trac XLT 4.6L 4X4	37 199$	x
Explorer Sport Trac Limited 4.6L 4X4	42 299$	x
Explorer Sport Trac Adrenalin (TI)	43 199$	x
F150 XL Cabine régulière 4X2 126 po	24 599$	x
F150 XLT Cabine régulière 4X2 126 po	28 699$	x
F150 XL SuperCab 4X4 145 po	35 499$	x
F150 XLT SuperCrew 4X4 145 po	39 299$	x
F150 Lariat SuperCrew 4X2 157 po	44 099$	x
F150 FX4 SuperCrew 4X4 145 po	44 299$	x
F150 Lariat King Ranch SuperCrew 4X4 157 po	52 499$	x
F150 Lariat Platinum SuperCrew 4X4 157 po	56 799$	x
Fiesta berline S	12 999$	
Fiesta berline SE	16 099$	
Fiesta berline SEL	18 199$	
Fiesta hatchback SE	16 799$	
Fiesta hatchback SES	18 999$	
Flex SE	29 999$	
Flex SEL	35 999$	
Flex SEL (TI)	37 999$	
Flex Limited	41 199$	
Flex Limited (TI)	43 199$	
Flex Limited (TI) EcoBoost	46 599$	
Flex Titanium (TI)	49 599$	
Focus Berline S	13 999$	
Focus Berline SE	17 999$	
Focus Berline SES	20 499$	
Focus Berline SEL	20 999$	
Fusion S I4	19 999$	
Fusion SE I4	23 199$	
Fusion SEL I4	26 199$	
Fusion SEL V6	29 199$	
Fusion SEL V6 (TI)	31 199$	
Fusion Sport V6 (TI)	35 299$	
Fusion Hybride	34 199$	
Mustang Coupé V6 Value	22 999$	
Mustang Coupé V6	26 999$	
Mustang GT Coupé	38 499$	
Mustang Cabriolet V6	31 399$	
Mustang GT Cabriolet	42 899$	
Ranger XL 2.3L 4X2	11 199$	
Ranger XL 4X2	13 999$	
Ranger XL Supercab 4X2	14 999$	
Ranger Sport Supercab	19 999$	
Ranger Sport Supercab 4X4	24 199$	
Ranger XLT Supercab 4X4	26 699$	
Shelby GT500 Coupe	58 999$	
Shelby GT500 Convertible	63 699$	
Taurus SE	27 999$	
Taurus SEL	32 499$	
Taurus SEL (TI)	34 999$	
Taurus Limited (TI)	40 999$	
Taurus SHO (TI)	48 199$	
Transit Connect Utilitaire XLT	26 799$	
Transit Connect Tourisme XLT	28 499$	

GMC

Acadia SLE	37 945$	
Acadia SLT	46 200$	
Acadia SLE (TI)	40 945$	
Acadia SLT (TI)	49 200$	
Canyon SL à cabine classique (2RM)	23 875$	
Canyon SLE à cabine classique (2RM)	24 915$	
Canyon SLE à cabine classique (4RM)	27 680$	
Canyon SLE à cabine allongée (2RM)	25 945$	
Canyon SLE à cabine allongée (4RM)	30 735$	
Canyon SLE à cabine multiplace (2RM)	31 490$	
Canyon SLE à cabine multiplace (4RM)	36 490$	
Sierra 1500 SLE, à cabine classique, caisse standard (2RM)	30 225$	
Sierra 1500 SLE, à cabine classique, caisse longue (4RM)	34 675$	
Sierra 1500 SLT, à cabine allongée, caisse longue (4RM)	46 800$	
Sierra 1500 Denali, à cabine multiplace, caisse courte (4RM)	56 605$	
Terrain SLE-1	27 465$	
Terrain SLE-2	29 815$	
Terrain SLT-1	31 440$	
Terrain SLT-2	34 400$	
Yukon SLE (2RM)	49 365$	
Yukon SLE (4RM)	53 825$	
Yukon SLT (2RM)	54 370$	
Yukon SLT (4RM)	58 825$	
Yukon SLT Hybride bimode (2RM)	68 625$	
Yukon SLT Hybride bimode (4RM)	71 610$	
Yukon Denali	72 610$	
Yukon Denali Hybride bimode (4RM)	80 300$	
Yukon XL SLE (2RM)	52 015$	
Yukon XL SLT (2RM)	57 515$	
Yukon XL SLE (4RM)	55 465$	
Yukon XL SLT (4RM)	60 965$	
Yukon XL Denali (TI)	76 295$	

HONDA

Accord Coupé EX	27 790$	x
Accord Coupé EX-L	30 090$	x
Accord Coupé V6 EX-L	34 890$	x
Accord LX	24 790$	x
Accord EX	28 490$	x
Accord EX-L	30 790$	x
Accord V6 EX	31 190$	x
Accord V6 EX-L	34 390$	x
Accord Crosstour EX-L	34 900$	x
Accord Crosstour EX-L AWD	36 900$	x
Civic Berline DX	15 990$	x
Civic Berline DX-G	18 580$	x
Civic Berline Sport	20 780$	x
Civic Berline EXL	22 680$	x
Civic Berline SI	25 880$	x
Civic Coupé DX	16 190$	x
Civic Coupé DX-G	18 880$	x
Civic Coupé LX	20 780$	x
Civic Coupé EXL	22 980$	x
Civic Coupé SI	25 880$	x
CR-V LX	26 290$	x
CR-V LX (4RM)	28 290$	x
CR-V EX	29 490$	x
CR-V EX (4RM)	31 490$	x
CR-V EX-L	33 490$	x
CR-Z	23 490$	
Element LX	26 990$	x
Element SC	31 690$	x
Element EX (4RM)	32 090$	x
Fit DX man	14 480$	x
Fit LX man	16 880$	x
Fit Sport man	18 780$	x
Insight LX	23 900$	x
Insight EX	27 500$	x
Odyssey DX	31 690$	x
Odyssey SE	37 790$	x
Odyssey EX-L	41 390$	x
Odyssey Touring	49 690$	x
Pilot LX (2RM)	34 820$	
Pilot LX (4RM)	37 820$	
Pilot EX (4RM)	40 720$	
Pilot EX-L (4RM)	43 020$	
Pilot EX-L RES (4RM)	44 620$	
Pilot Touring	48 420$	
Ridgeline DX	34 990$	x
Ridgeline VP	36 690$	x
Ridgeline EX-L	41 490$	x

HYUNDAI

Accent 3 portes L man	13 599$	x
Accent 3 portes GL man	15 299$	x
Accent 3 portes GL Sport man	16 999$	x
Accent Berline L man	14 299$	x
Accent Berline GL man	15 749$	x
Accent Berline GLS	18 999$	x
Elantra Berline L man	15 849$	x
Elantra Berline GL man	18 099$	x
Elantra Berline GLS	20 999$	x
Elantra Berline GL Sport man	21 499$	x
Elantra Berline Limited	23 799$	x
Elantra Touring L	14 999$	
Elantra Touring GL	17 399$	
Elantra Touring GLS	19 799$	
Elantra Touring GLS Sport	22 049$	
Equus	n.d.	
Genesis 3.8	38 999$	
Genesis 3.8 Premium	42 999$	
Genesis 3.8 Technologie	46 499$	
Genesis 4.6 Technologie	49 999$	
Genesis Coupe 2.0T man	24 495$	x
Genesis Coupe 2.0T Premium man	27 495$	x
Genesis Coupe 2.0 GT	30 745$	x
Genesis Coupe 3.8 man	32 995$	x
Genesis Coupe 3.8 GT man	36 495$	x
Santa Fe 2.4 GL FWD man	25 999$	x
Santa Fe 3.5 GL V6 FWD	28 999$	x
Santa Fe 3.5 GL V6 AWD	30 999$	x
Santa Fe 3.5 GL Sport V6 FWD	31 299$	x
Santa Fe 3.5 GL Sport V6 AWD	33 299$	x
Santa Fe 3.5 Limited V6 AWD	35 799$	x
Sonata GL man	22 649$	
Sonata GLS	26 249$	
Sonata Limited	28 999$	
Tucson L FWD man	20 999$	
Tucson GL FWD man	22 999$	
Tucson GL AWD	26 299$	
Tucson GLS	26 799$	
Tucson GLS AWD	28 799$	
Tucson Limited	32 249$	
Veracruz GL	36 999$	x
Veracruz GLS	40 999$	x
Veracruz Limited	47 299$	x

INFINITI

EX35	41 250$	x
FX37	52 300$	x
FX50	64 050$	x
G37	38 690$	x
G37x	42 550$	x
G37 Sport	45 640$	x
G37x Sport	47 640$	x
G37 Coupé	46 300$	x
G37 Coupé Sport	48 800$	x
G37x Coupé	48 800$	x
G37 Cabriolet M6	58 300$	x
G37 Cabriolet Premium	61 600$	x
M37	52 400$	
M37 Sport	63 400$	
M37x	54 900$	
M56 Premium	66 200$	
M56 Sport	73 400$	
M56x	68 700$	
QX56	73 000$	

JAGUAR

XF	62 800$	
XF Premium	68 300$	
XF R	85 300$	
XJ	88 000$	
XJL	95 500$	
XJ Supercharged	104 000$	
XJL Supercharged	107 000$	
XJ Supersport	128 000$	
XJL Supersport	131 000$	
XK Coupé	96 500$	
XK Cabriolet	103 200$	
XK R Coupé	107 000$	
XK R Cabriolet	114 000$	
XK R Coupé 175 Limited Edition	115 500$	

JEEP

Commander Sport	43 495$	x
Commander Limited	54 695$	x
Compass Sport	18 795$	x
Compass Sport (4X4)	20 995$	x
Compass North Edition	21 795$	x
Compass North Edition (4X4)	23 995$	x
Compass Limited	24 195$	x
Compass Limited (4X4)	26 395$	x
Grand Cherokee Laredo	37 995$	
Grand Cherokee Limited	46 995$	
Grand Cherokee Overland	49 995$	
Liberty Sport	29 795$	x
Liberty Rocky Mountain	31 795$	x
Liberty Renegade	32 795$	x
Liberty Limited	33 795$	x
Patriot Sport	17 795$	x
Patriot North	20 795$	x
Patriot Limited	23 795$	x
Wrangler Sport	20 595$	x
Wrangler Unlimited Sport	25 995$	x
Wrangler Islander	24 990$	x
Wrangler Unlimited Islander	26 990$	x
Wrangler Mountain	25 690$	x
Wrangler Unlimited Mountain	27 690$	x
Wrangler Sahara	27 495$	x
Wrangler Unlimited Sahara	29 495$	x
Wrangler Rubicon	30 495$	x
Wrangler Unlimited Rubicon	32 495$	x

KIA

Borrego V6 LX	38 895 $	
Borrego V6 EX	43 495 $	
Borrego V8 LX	41 295 $	
Borrego V8 EX	46 095 $	
Forte LX man	15 695 $	x
Forte EX man	17 995 $	x
Forte SX man	20 995 $	x
Forte Koupe 2.0 EX man	18 495 $	x
Forte Koupe 2.4 SX man	21 495 $	x
Magentis LX	21 995 $	x
Magentis LX V6	24 295 $	x
Magentis SX	29 495 $	x
Magentis SX V6	30 795 $	x
Rio EX man	13 695 $	
Rio EX Convenience man	15 895 $	
Rio5 EX man	14 095 $	
Rio5 EX Convenience man	16 495 $	
Rio5 EX Sport man	18 795 $	
Rondo LX	19 995 $	
Rondo EX	22 795 $	
Rondo EX V6	23 895 $	
Rondo EX Premium	25 095 $	
Rondo EX V6	27 195 $	
Sedona LX	27 995 $	
Sedona EX	34 195 $	
Sedona EX Luxe	39 995 $	
Sorento LX man	23 995 $	
Sorento LX AWD	28 495 $	
Sorento LX V6	29 095 $	
Sorento EX	29 795 $	
Sorento LX V6 AWD	30 995 $	
Sorento EX V6 AWD	33 695 $	
Sorento EX V6 Luxe AWD	39 395 $	
Soul 1.6	15 795 $	x
Soul 2.0 2u man	18 295 $	x
Soul 2.0 4u man	20 295 $	x
Soul 2.0 4u Retro	20 995 $	x
Soul 2.0 4u Burner	21 295 $	x
Soul 2.0 4u SX man	21 895 $	x
Sportage LX man	21 995 $	
Sportage LX AWD	26 695 $	
Sportage EX	26 995 $	
Sportage EX AWD	29 395 $	
Sportage EX Luxe	32 895 $	

LAMBORGHINI

Gallardo LP560-4	198 000 $	
Gallardo LP550-2 Valentino	219 800 $	
Gallardo LP560-4 Spyder	221 000 $	
Murciélago LP640 Coupe	354 000 $	
Murcielago LP640 Roadster	382 400 $	
Murciélago LP670-4	450 000 $	
Murcielago LP650-4	525 000 $	

LAND ROVER

LR2	44 950 $	
LR4 V8	59 990 $	
Range Rover HSE	94 290 $	
Range Rover Supercharged	112 280 $	
Range Rover Sport HSE	73 200 $	
Range Rover Sport Supercharged	88 980 $	

LEXUS

CT 200h	n.d.	
ES 350	41 950 $	x
GS 350 RWD	52 500 $	x
GS 350 AWD	54 500 $	x
GS 460 RWD	67 100 $	x
GS 450h	71 900 $	x
GX 470 Premium	68 500 $	x
GX 470 Ultra Premium	77 500 $	x
HS 250h Premium	39 900 $	x
HS 250h Premium Luxe	45 300 $	x
IS 250 RWD man	34 400 $	x
IS 250 AWD	40 550 $	x
IS 250C man	52 100 $	x
IS 350	45 900 $	x
IS 350C	60 400 $	x
IS-F	68 000 $	x
LF-A	375 000 $ U.S.	
LS 460	82 900 $	x
LS 460 (TI)	88 000 $	x
LS 460 L (TI)	103 150 $	x
LS 600h L	119 950 $	x
LX 570	89 750 $	x
RX 350	46 900 $	x
RX 450h	59 500 $	x

LINCOLN

MKS	47 400 $	
MKS (TI)	49 600 $	
MKS EcoBoost	53 000 $	
MKT (TI)	49 950 $	
MKT EcoBoost (TI)	53 350 $	
MKX (TI)	46 500 $	
MKZ	38 400 $	
MKZ (TI)	42 200 $	
Navigator	73 100 $	
Navigator L	76 100 $	

LOTUS

Elise	60 750 $	x
Elise SC	69 995 $	x
Evora	85 880 $	x
Exige S 240	80 500 $	x
Exige S 260	91 795 $	x

MASERATI

GranTurismo	118 500 $	
GranTurismo S	122 500 $	
GranTurismo Cabriolet	135 800 $	
Quattroporte	125 150 $	
Quattroporte S	126 750 $	
Quattroporte Sport GT S	134 700 $	

MAYBACH

57	n.d.	
57S	387 500 $	x
62	399 000 $	x
62S	438 000 $	x
Landaulet	1 380 000 $	x

MAZDA

CX-7 GX FWD	27 995 $	x
CX-7 GS (4RM)	32 295 $	x
CX-7 GT (4RM)	38 990 $	x
CX-9 GS	37 995 $	x
CX-9 GS (TI)	39 995 $	x
CX-9 GT (TI)	47 450 $	x
Mazda2 GX man	13 995 $	
Mazda2 GS man	18 195 $	
Mazda3 berline GX man	15 995 $	x
Mazda3 berline GS man	19 395 $	x
Mazda3 berline GT man	22 995 $	x
Mazda3 Sport GX man	16 995 $	x
Mazda3 Sport GS man	20 895 $	x
Mazda3 Sport GT man	23 995 $	x
MazdaSpeed3	32 995 $	x
Mazda5 GS man	20 495 $	x
Mazda5 GT man	24 295 $	x
Mazda6 GS-I4 man	23 195 $	x
Mazda6 GT-I4 man	28 695 $	x
Mazda6 GS-V6	30 195 $	x
Mazda6 GT-V6	36 695 $	x
MX-5 GX man	28 995 $	x
MX-5 GS man	33 495 $	x
MX-5 GT man	39 995 $	x
RX-8 R3	41 995 $	x
RX-8 GT man	43 795 $	x
Tribute GX man	23 450 $	x
Tribute GX V6	26 345 $	x
Tribute GS V6	27 900 $	x
Tribute GT V6 (TI)	34 995 $	x

MERCEDES-BENZ

B200	29 900 $	x
B200 Turbo	32 400 $	x
C250	35 800 $	x
C250 4MATIC	39 500 $	x
C300	41 200 $	x
C300 4MATIC	44 900 $	x
C350	48 200 $	x
C350 4MATIC	50 400 $	x
C63 AMG	63 500 $	x
CL550	130 500 $	x
CL600	189 500 $	x
CL63 AMG	159 000 $	x
CL65 AMG	241 000 $	x
CLS550	91 200 $	
CLS63 AMG	126 700 $	
E350 Berline 4MATIC	62 900 $	
E550 Berline 4MATIC	73 200 $	
E63 AMG	106 900 $	
E350 Familiale 4MATIC	66 900 $	
E350 Coupe	58 600 $	
E550 Coupe	68 200 $	
E350 Cabriolet	67 900 $	
E550 Cabriolet	77 500 $	
G550	114 400 $	x
G55 AMG	154 950 $	x
GL350 BlueTEC	69 000 $	x
GL450	79 900 $	x
GL550	88 600 $	x
GLK350	42 900 $	x
ML350	57 400 $	x
ML350 BlueTEC	58 900 $	x
ML550	69 700 $	x
ML63 AMG	97 500 $	x
R350	54 700 $	x
R350 BlueTEC	56 200 $	x
S400 Hybrid	105 900 $	x
S450 4MATIC	108 000 $	x
S550 4MATIC	123 500 $	x
S600	187 000 $	x
S63 AMG	150 000 $	x
S65 AMG	234 000 $	x
SL550	126 000 $	
SL600	176 300 $	
SL63 AMG	152 600 $	
SL65 AMG	240 100 $	
SLK300	59 900 $	
SLK350	66 500 $	
SLK55 AMG	84 800 $	x
SLS AMG	198 000 $	
Sprinter 2500	42 900 $	x
Sprinter 3500	48 800 $	x

MINI

Cooper Classique	22 800 $	x
Cooper	24 900 $	x
Cooper S	29 900 $	x
Cooper John Cooper Works	36 600 $	x
Cooper Cabriolet	29 950 $	x
Cooper S Cabriolet	36 350 $	x
Cooper John Cooper Works Cabriolet	42 500 $	x
Cooper Clubman	26 500 $	x
Cooper S Clubman	31 500 $	x
Cooper John Cooper Works Clubman	38 400 $	x

MITSUBISHI

Eclipse GS man	24 498 $	
Eclipse GT-P man	33 298 $	
Eclipse Spyder GS man	30 498 $	
Eclipse Spyder GT-P man	35 998 $	
Endeavor SE (TI)	36 998 $	x
Lancer DE man	16 998 $	x
Lancer SE man	20 298 $	x
Lancer GTS man	23 598 $	x
Lancer Ralliart	33 198 $	x
Lancer Evolution GSR	41 998 $	x
Lancer Evolution MR	51 798 $	x
Lancer Sportback GTS man	24 098 $	x
Lancer Sportback Ralliart	33 698 $	x
Outlander ES (2RM)	25 498 $	x
Outlander ES (4RM)	27 998 $	x
Outlander LS (4RM)	29 498 $	x
Outlander XLS (4RM)	34 498 $	x

NISSAN

370Z Coupé Touring M6	40 498 $	x
370Z Roadster Touring M6	46 998 $	x
Altima Berline 2.5 S man	23 798 $	x
Altima Berline 3.5 S	28 298 $	x
Altima Berline 3.5 SR	31 898 $	x
Altima Berline Hybrid 2.5 S	33 398 $	x
Altima Coupé 2.5 S man	27 348 $	x
Altima Coupé 3.5 SR man	34 698 $	x
Armada Platinum	55 398 $	x
Cube 1.8 S	17 398 $	x
Cube 1.8 SL	20 898 $	x
Cube 1.8 Krom	23 098 $	x
Frontier King Cab XE 4X2 man	24 098 $	x
Frontier King Cab SE 4X2	28 048 $	x
Frontier King Cab SE 4X4 man	30 048 $	x
Frontier King Cab PRO-4X 4X4	32 998 $	x
Frontier Cabine double SE 4X2	31 848 $	x
Frontier Cabine double SE 4X4	33 848 $	x
Frontier Cabine double PRO-4X 4X4	34 548 $	x
Frontier Cabine double LE 4X4	41 098 $	x
GT-R GR6	99 500 $	
Juke	n.d.	
Leaf	n.d.	
Maxima 3.5 SV	39 450 $	x
Murano S (TI)	38 298 $	x
Murano SL (TI)	39 998 $	x
Murano LE (TI)	47 948 $	x
Pathfinder S	37 548 $	x
Pathfinder SE	41 948 $	x
Pathfinder LE	47 348 $	x
Quest	n.d.	
Rogue S	23 198 $	x
Rogue S (TI)	25 998 $	x
Rogue SL	25 798 $	x
Rogue SL (TI)	27 798 $	x
Sentra 2.0 man	15 198 $	x
Sentra 2.0 S man	18 198 $	x
Sentra 2.0 SL	23 098 $	x
Sentra SE-R	21 798 $	x
Sentra SE-R Spec V	23 198 $	x
Titan King Cab XE 4X2	33 448 $	x
Titan King Cab SE 4X2	37 048 $	x
Titan King Cab SE 4X4	40 448 $	x
Titan King Cab PRO-4X 4X4	42 448 $	x
Titan King Cab LE 4X4	46 148 $	x
Titan Cabine double XE 4X4	39 448 $	x
Titan Cabine double SE 4X4	43 148 $	x
Titan Cabine double PRO-4X 4X4	45 148 $	x
Titan Cabine double LE 4X4	49 848 $	x
Versa Berline 1.6 S man	12 698 $	x
Versa Hatchback 1.8 S man	14 198 $	x
Versa Hatchback 1.8 SL man	17 398 $	x
Xterra S man	33 698 $	x
Xterra Off-Road man	36 198 $	x
Xterra SE	37 498 $	x

PORSCHE

Modèle	Prix	
911 Carrera Coupe	94 100 $	
911 Carrera Cabriolet	107 300 $	
911 Carrera 4 Coupe	101 400 $	
911 Carrera 4 Cabriolet	114 700 $	
911 Carrera S Coupe	109 300 $	
911 Carrera S Cabriolet	122 300 $	
911 Carrera 4S Coupe	116 800 $	
911 Carrera 4S Cabriolet	129 900 $	
911 Targa 4	111 100 $	
911 Targa 4S	126 400 $	
911 GT3	142 400 $	
911 GT3 RS	166 300 $	
911 Turbo Coupe	167 900 $	
911 Turbo Cabriolet	181 500 $	
911 Turbo S Coupe	200 000 $	
911 Turbo S Cabriolet	213 200 $	
Boxster	58 000 $	
Boxster S	70 600 $	
Boxster Spyder	72 900 $	
Cayenne V6	58 200 $	
Cayenne S	76 000 $	
Cayenne S Hybrid	80 800 $	
Cayenne Turbo	123 900 $	
Cayman	62 800 $	
Cayman S	75 000 $	
Panamera	88 000 $	
Panamera 4	92 800 $	
Panamera S	115 100 $	
Panamera 4S	120 300 $	
Panamera Turbo	155 000 $	

RAM

Modèle	Prix	
1500 ST Cabine régulière 4X2	26 495 $	x
1500 SLT Cabine régulière 4X2	29 395 $	x
1500 ST Cabine double 4X2	30 795 $	x
1500 SLT Cabine double 4X2	33 695 $	x
1500 Laramie Cabine double 4X4	45 195 $	x
Dakota Cabine allongée ST 4X2	27 795 $	x
Dakota Cabine allongée SXT 4X2	28 995 $	x
Dakota Cabine allongée ST 4X4	31 395 $	x
Dakota Cabine allongée SXT 4X4	32 595 $	x
Dakota Crew cab SXT 4X2	31 495 $	x
Dakota Crew cab SLT 4X2	34 095 $	x
Dakota Crew cab SXT 4X4	35 195 $	x
Dakota Crew cab SLT 4X4	37 795 $	x

ROLLS-ROYCE

Modèle	Prix	
Ghost	n.d.	
Phantom	380 000 $	x
Phantom Coupé	408 000 $	x
Phantom Drophead Coupé	443 000 $	x

SCION

Modèle	Prix	
Xb	n.d.	
Xd	n.d.	
Tc	n.d.	
iQ	n.d.	

SMART

Modèle	Prix	
Fortwo Coupé Pure	14 990 $	x
Fortwo Coupé Passion	18 250 $	x
Fortwo Coupé Brabus	21 900 $	x
Fortwo Cabriolet Passion	21 250 $	x
Fortwo Cabriolet Brabus	24 900 $	x

SUBARU

Modèle	Prix	
Forester 2.5X man	25 995 $	x
Forester 2.5 PZEV	28 095 $	x
Forester 2.5X Sport man	28 695 $	x
Forester 2.5X Limited	32 795 $	x
Forester 2.5XT Limited	35 295 $	x
Impreza berline 2.5i	20 995 $	
Impreza berline 2.5i Commodité	21 995 $	
Impreza berline 2.5i Sport	24 695 $	
Impreza berline 2.5i Limited	26 695 $	
Impreza berline WRX	32 495 $	x
Impreza berline WRX Limited	35 495 $	x
Impreza 5 portes 2.5i	21 895 $	
Impreza 5 portes 2.5i Commodité	22 895 $	
Impreza 5 portes 2.5i Sport	25 595 $	
Impreza 5 portes 2.5i Limited	27 595 $	
Impreza 5 portes WRX	33 395 $	x
Impreza 5 portes WRX Limited	36 395 $	x
Legacy berline 2.5i man	23 995 $	
Legacy berline 2.5i PZEV	27 095 $	
Legacy berline 2.5i Sport man	27 995 $	
Legacy berline 2.5i Limited	31 995 $	
Legacy berline 2.5GT	38 595 $	
Legacy berline 3.6R	31 895 $	
Legacy berline 3.6R Limited	34 695 $	
Outback 2.5i man	28 995 $	
Outback 2.5i PZEV	30 895 $	
Outback 2.5i Sport man	31 795 $	
Outback 2.5i Limited	35 795 $	
Outback 3.6R	35 695 $	
Outback 3.6R Limited	38 495 $	
Tribeca	40 995 $	x
Tribeca Limited	46 495 $	x
Tribeca Premier	49 195 $	x
WRX STI	39 995 $	x
WRX STI Sport-Tech	45 995 $	x

SUZUKI

Modèle	Prix	
Equator JX V6	34 995 $	x
Grand Vitara JX	27 995 $	x
Grand Vitara JLX	29 495 $	x
Grand Vitara JLX-L	30 495 $	x
Grand Vitara V6 JLX	32 195 $	x
Grand Vitara V6 JLX-L	33 195 $	x
Kizashi SX AWD	29 995 $	
SX4 5 portes man	17 695 $	x
SX4 5 portes JX CVT	20 295 $	x
SX4 5 portes JX (TI) man	21 595 $	x
SX4 5 portes JLX (TI) CT	24 695 $	x
SX4 Berline man	17 695 $	x
SX4 Berline Sport man	19 695 $	x

TESLA

Modèle	Prix	
Roadster	125 000 $	
Roadster Sport	147 300 $	

TOYOTA

Modèle	Prix	
4Runner SR5 V6	36 800 $	x
Avalon XLS	41 100 $	
Camry LE	25 310 $	
Camry SE	27 755 $	
Camry XLE	31 235 $	
Camry LE V6	29 020 $	
Camry SE V6	34 255 $	
Camry XLE V6	36 410 $	
Camry Hybride	31 310 $	
Corolla CE man	15 460 $	x
Corolla S man	20 285 $	x
Corolla LE	20 425 $	x
Corolla XRS man	22 550 $	x
FJ Cruiser V6 man	31 900 $	x
Highlander 4L FWD	33 250 $	x
Highlander V6 (4WD)	37 870 $	x
Highlander V6 Sport (4WD)	42 810 $	x
Highlander V6 Limited (4WD)	46 510 $	x
Highlander Hybrid	43 025 $	x
Highlander Hybrid Limited	55 075 $	x
Matrix man	16 665 $	x
Matrix XR man	20 575 $	x
Matrix (TI)	23 695 $	x
Matrix XRS man	26 275 $	x
Matrix XRS auto	27 825 $	x
Prius	27 800 $	x
RAV4	24 595 $	x
RAV4 Sport	28 345 $	x
RAV4 Limited	30 185 $	x
RAV4 (4RM)	27 230 $	x
RAV4 Sport (4RM)	30 540 $	x
RAV4 Limited (4RM)	32 385 $	x
RAV4 V6 Sport	30 100 $	x
RAV4 V6 Limited	32 440 $	x
RAV4 V6 (4RM)	29 845 $	x
RAV4 V6 Sport (4RM)	32 295 $	x
RAV4 V6 Limited (4RM)	34 640 $	x
Sequoia SR5 V8 4.6l	48 820 $	x
Sequoia Limited V8 5.7l	57 735 $	x
Sequoia Platinum V8 5.7l	65 975 $	x
Sienna LE 7 places	27 900 $	
Sienna V6 7 places	28 900 $	
Sienna V6 LE 8 places	32 500 $	
Sienna V6 LE AWD 7 places	35 350 $	
Sienna V6 SE 8 places	36 600 $	
Sienna V6 XLE 7 places	38 700 $	
Sienna V6 Limited AWD 7 places	49 100 $	
Tacoma Access Cab 4X2 man	21 355 $	x
Tacoma Access Cab 4X4 man	25 995 $	x
Tacoma Access Cab V6 4X4 man	28 380 $	x
Tacoma Double Cab V6 4X4	31 845 $	x
Tundra Cab régulière 4X2 4,6 litres	25 310 $	x
Tundra Cab régulière 4X2 5,7 litres	28 975 $	x
Tundra Cab double 4X2 4,6 litres	32 040 $	x
Tundra Cab double 4X2 5,7 litres	36 015 $	x
Tundra CrewMax SR5 4X2 5,7 litres	37 630 $	x
Tundra Cab régulière 4X4 4,6 litres	28 795 $	x
Tundra Cab régulière 4X4 5,7 litres	29 895 $	x
Tundra Cab double SR5 4X4 4,6 litres	36 105 $	x
Tundra Cab double SR5 4X4 5,7 litres	40 080 $	x
Tundra CrewMax SR5 4X4 5,7 litres	41 745 $	x
Tundra Cab double Limited 4X4 5,7 litres	48 275 $	x
Tundra CrewMax Platinum 4X4 5,7 litres	52 070 $	x
Venza 4L	29 310 $	x
Venza 4L (TI)	30 760 $	x
Venza V6	30 800 $	x
Venza V6 (TI)	32 250 $	x
Yaris Hatchback 3 portes CE man	13 905 $	x
Yaris Hatchback 5 portes LE man	15 195 $	x
Yaris Hatchback 5 portes RS man	19 555 $	x
Yaris Berline man	14 990 $	x

VOLKSWAGEN

Modèle	Prix	
Eos 2.0T Comfortline man	36 975 $	
Eos 2.0T Highline man	43 775 $	
Golf 2.5L man Trendline	20 475 $	
Golf 2.5L man Comfortline	22 875 $	
Golf 2.5L man Sportline	23 900 $	
Golf 2.5L man Highline	26 475 $	
Golf 2.0L man Comfortline	25 275 $	
Golf 2.0L man Highline	28 775 $	
Golf Familiale 2.5L man Trendline	22 975 $	
Golf Familiale 2.5L man Comfortline	24 075 $	
Golf Familiale 2.0 TDI man Comfortline	26 875 $	
Golf Familiale 2.0 TDI man Highline	30 775 $	
GTI 2.0T 3 portes man	28 875 $	
GTI 2.0T 5 portes man	29 875 $	
Jetta 2.0L man Trendline	15 875 $	
Jetta 2.0L man Comfortline	19 075 $	
Jetta 2.5L man Comfortline	21 175 $	
Jetta 2.5L man Sportline	23 300 $	
Jetta 2.5L man Highline	23 980 $	
Jetta 2.0 TDI man Comfortline	23 875 $	
Jetta 2.0 TDI man Highline	26 655 $	
New Beetle 2.5L Comfortline man	24 175 $	x
New Beetle Cabriolet 2.5L Comfortline man	29 175 $	x
Passat Berline 2.0T Trendline man	27 775 $	x
Passat Berline 2.0T Comfortline man	31 075 $	x
Passat Berline 2.0T Highline man	36 775 $	x
Passat Familiale 2.0T Trendline man	29 275 $	x
Passat Familiale 2.0T Comfortline man	32 575 $	x
Passat Familiale 2.0T Highline man	38 275 $	x
Passat Familiale 3.6 Highline 4Motion	52 100 $	x
Passat CC 2.0T Sportline man	33 375 $	
Passat CC 2.0T Highline man	39 275 $	
Passat CC 3.6 Highline 4Motion	46 375 $	
Routan Trendline	28 075 $	x
Routan Comfortline	34 375 $	x
Routan Highline	40 575 $	x
Routan Execline	50 575 $	x
Tiguan 2.0T Trendline man	27 875 $	
Tiguan 2.0T Trendline 4Motion	31 275 $	
Tiguan 2.0T Comfortline man	31 275 $	
Tiguan 2.0T Comfortline 4Motion	34 875 $	
Tiguan 2.0T Highline 4Motion	37 775 $	
Touareg 3.6L Comfortline	45 300 $	x
Touareg 3.6L Highline	54 300 $	x
Touareg 3.0L TDI Comfortline	49 300 $	x
Touareg 3.0L TDI Highline	58 300 $	x

VOLVO

Modèle	Prix	
C30 T5 man	30 995 $	
C30 T5 R-design man	39 995 $	
C70 T5	54 495 $	
S40 2.4i man	28 995 $	x
S40 2.4i Premium man	35 995 $	x
S40 2.4i R-Design man	40 495 $	x
S40 T5 AWD man	42 995 $	x
S40 T5 AWD R-Design man	46 695 $	x
S60 T6 AWD	45 450 $	
S80 3.2	46 995 $	x
S80 T6 (TI)	59 995 $	x
S80 V8 (TI)	69 995 $	x
V50 2.4i man	30 495 $	x
V50 2.4i Premium man	37 495 $	x
V50 2.4i R-Design man	41 995 $	x
V50 T5 AWD man	44 495 $	x
V50 T5 AWD R-Design man	49 695 $	x
V70 3.2	42 495 $	x
V70 3.2 Premium	48 495 $	x
V70 3.2 R-Design	52 495 $	x
XC60 3.2 (TA)	39 995 $	x
XC60 3.2 (TI)	44 495 $	x
XC60 T6 (TI)	49 995 $	x
XC70 3.2 (TI)	43 995 $	x
XC70 3.2 (TI) Premium	49 995 $	x
XC70 T6 (TI)	55 995 $	x
XC90 3.2	51 995 $	x
XC90 3.2 Luxe	58 995 $	x
XC90 3.2 R-Design	61 995 $	x
XC90 V8	69 995 $	x

NOTE : les prix identifiés avec un x sont les prix des modèles 2010.
Il ne s'agit pas d'une liste exhaustive.
Pour plus de renseignements, veuillez contacter le concessionnaire.

Afin de mieux comprendre les informations chiffrées qui accompagnent chaque essai, voici quelques explications supplémentaires.

En première partie, on retrouve des informations générales sur la voiture à l'essai. Parmi celles-ci notons les garanties. La première représente la garantie de base, dite « pare-chocs à pare-chocs » pour un maximum d'années et un maximum de kilométrage. Elle se termine à la première des deux limites atteintes. La seconde couvre le groupe motopropulseur : le moteur et les autres éléments des rouages d'entraînement.

Nous désirons aussi attirer votre attention sur la cote d'assurance. Puisque rien n'est plus aléatoire que le calcul d'une prime, nous avons préféré nous en tenir à une cote générale qui reflète le bilan du véhicule analysé et non celui d'un conducteur fictif. Cette cote est « pauvre », « passable », « moyenne », « bonne » ou « excellente ». En fait, nous avons utilisé les données du BAC (Bureau d'Assurances du Canada) et établi une moyenne pour les quatre dernières années disponibles (2005-2006-2007-2008). Donc, meilleure est la cote, moins la voiture devrait coûter cher à assurer. Il faut cependant noter que ce n'est pas parce qu'une voiture s'est méritée une note « excellente » qu'elle efface un mauvais dossier de conduite tout comme une note « pauvre » ne reflète pas nécessairement une prime très élevée mais les chances sont plus grandes ! Car en plus de la cote de la voiture, il y a celle de la région et, surtout, celle du conducteur... et ça, nous n'y pouvons rien ! Pour plus d'informations, allez sur www.ibc.ca/assurance autos/ vous songez à acheter une voiture / différence entre les voitures

La deuxième partie de nos fiches techniques fait état des données de base d'un des modèles de la gamme parmi les plus populaires.

DIMENSIONS

On y retrouve les dimensions extérieures, la capacité du coffre et du réservoir d'essence et le nombre de coussins de sécurité.

SUSPENSIONS

Les suspensions les plus souvent employées par les manufacturiers sont à jambes de force à l'avant et multibras à l'arrière. Jambes de force est un terme pour désigner, tout simplement, MacPherson, du nom de son concepteur. Un autre type de suspension souvent utilisé est double triangulation ou, pour les initiés *double wishbone*. Il s'agit d'une variante du système Macpherson et utilisée surtout pour des voitures performantes.

À l'arrière, on utilise de plus en plus la suspension multibras (*multi-link*). Il s'agit de plusieurs bras (habituellement cinq) qui agissent chacun de façon différente pour permettre le meilleur compromis possible entre tenue de route et confort. Les voitures plus économiques reçoivent plutôt un essieu semi-rigide à poutre de torsion. Générant moins de confort, ce type de suspension requiert toutefois moins d'espace dans le coffre, un grand avantage lorsque l'espace est compté.

FREINS

Avancer c'est bien beau disait le sage mais s'arrêter à temps est encore mieux ! Cette ligne vous renseigne sur le type de freins dont est munie la voiture dont nous publions les données. Il s'agit encore ici d'une donnée redondante puisqu'à peu près tous les véhicules sont munis de freins à disque aux quatre roues et de l'ABS. Par contre, on note une certaine tendance au retour vers des freins arrière à tambour, moins coûteux d'entretien et particulièrement bien adaptés aux petites voitures.

POIDS

Le poids, en kilos, du modèle essayé. Il s'agit du poids brut du véhicule (*curb weight*), ce qui correspond au poids du véhicule en ordre de marche (incluant un plein d'essence, l'huile à moteur, le lave-glace, l'antigel, etc)

CAPACITÉ DE REMORQUAGE

Cette donnée est fort importante pour quiconque désire accrocher une remorque à son véhicule. Cependant, cette donnée varie passablement selon le moteur, la transmission, le nombre de roues motrices et l'équipement du véhicule. Il faut aussi prendre en considération le fait que la remorque soit équipée ou non de freins. On ne doit jamais se fier uniquement à la donnée inscrite dans la fiche technique et il faut IMPÉRATIVEMENT vérifier avec son concessionnaire avant de faire installer un mécanisme de remorquage.

MOTEUR !

La quatrième partie est réservée aux différents moteurs qui se retrouvent sous le capot de la voiture analysée. On y dévoile, en gros :

La configuration du moteur (en V, en ligne (L), rotatif (R) et même en W !), sa cylindrée, le nombre total de soupapes et son alimentation (atmosphérique, turbocompressée ou surcompressée). La ligne suivante dévoile le nombre de chevaux développés par le moteur ainsi que le couple (en livres-pied). Règle générale, plus ces deux chiffres sont élevés, plus la voiture est performante... et plus elle engloutit d'essence !

Sous les chevaux et les livres-pied, on retrouve la transmission de base et, entre parenthèse, la ou les transmission (s) optionnelle (s) ainsi que le rouage de base et, entre parenthèse, le ou les rouage(s) optionnel (s). Pour les transmissions, elles sont « A » pour automatique, « M » pour manuelle, « CVT » quand elles sont à rapports continuellement variables ou « séq » pour séquentielle. Quant aux rouages, il s'agit : « Tr » pour traction (roues avant motrices), « Pr » pour propulsion (roues arrière motrices), « Int » pour intégrale (deux / quatre roues motrices sans l'action du conducteur) et, enfin, « 4x4 » (quatre roues motrices)

Les données de performance, c'est-à-dire le temps qu'il faut à la voiture pour effectuer le 0 à 100 km/ h et, plus important, pour passer de 80 à 120 km/h, lors d'un dépassement par exemple. La dernière donnée indique la distance requise au véhicule pour passer de 100 km/h à un arrêt complet. Dans quelques cas, nous avons estimé ces temps ou distance (est). La plupart des données proviennent de l'AJAC (Association des Journalistes Automobiles du Canada) dont font partie tous les journalistes du *Guide de l'auto*, de nos essais ou des constructeurs.

LES DONNÉES DE CONSOMMATION

Cette ligne d'informations débute par le type d'essence (Ordinaire – Indice d'octane 87, Super – indice d'octane 92 et diesel) À l'éternelle question de savoir si vous pouvez mettre de l'essence ordinaire dans une voiture réclamant du super, la réponse est... noui ! En fait, votre concessionnaire est le mieux placé pour répondre à cette épineuse question. La donnée suivante est celle de la consommation en ville puis sur la route. Pour d'évidentes raisons de constance, nous utilisons les données du *Guide de consommation de carburant* publié par Ressources naturelles Canada et disponible gratuitement chez les concessionnaires ou dans les Salons de l'auto.

À cause de ce satané manque d'espace qui caractérise le domaine de l'édition (et sans doute depuis Gutenberg !), nous avons quelquefois dû couper un peu sur les informations de certains moteurs. Dans ces cas, nous avons simplement noté la configuration du moteur, sa cylindrée, le nombre de chevaux et de livres-pied, le 0-100 km/h et, enfin, la consommation. C'est quand même pas mal pour une seule ligne !

ENSUITE... DANS LA MÊME CATÉGORIE

Ce paragraphe énumère tous les autres véhicules qui pourraient aussi intéresser le consommateur. Sont pris en considération, la configuration, les dimensions, la motorisation et le prix des autres véhicules. Vous magasinez une Nissan Altima ? Vous pourriez aussi être intéressé par une Ford Fusion, une Chevrolet Malibu, une Honda Accord ou une Hyundai Sonata !

DU NOUVEAU EN 2011

Même si beaucoup de modèles ne changent pratiquement pas d'une année à l'autre, certains autres connaissent des améliorations notables ou sont carrément redessinés. C'est dans ces quelques lignes que vous le saurez ! Notez que nous n'avons indiqué que les changements les plus importants.

Dans la section « Impressions », nous utilisons désormais les données publiques de *Consumer Reports* pour déterminer la fiabilité et la sécurité. Pour bien utiliser les données de la catégorie « Impressions », il faut toujours comparer un véhicule avec un autre de la même catégorie.

Cette année, nous avons ajouté, au tout début de chaque fiche technique, le lien pour accéder à notre site internet www.guideautoweb.com et à la voiture convoitée. Vous y retrouverez plusieurs autres essais et diverses informations complémentaires. À la toute fin de la fiche, nous vous donnons le site internet du manufacturier où vous retrouverez plusieurs informations et des prix constamment mis à jour.

Enfin, les maniaques de statistiques seront ravis de constater que cette section devenue incontournable depuis le *Guide de l'auto 2009* regorge de... statistiques complémentaires !

Les plus perspicaces auront remarqué la présence, cette année, d'icônes dans la bande supérieure. Chaque véhicule s'est vu octroyer entre un et trois icônes, selon ses « compétences ». On retrouve :

Plein air

Sport

Familial

Hors route

Ville

Luxe

Travail

L'équipe du *Guide de l'auto* veut ainsi faciliter la tâche aux lecteurs qui recherchent un véhicule pour des besoins particuliers. Il faut toutefois noter que ce classement n'est pas exclusif. Ce n'est pas parce que l'essai d'un véhicule est coiffé des icônes et qu'il ne peut pas emmener la famille et tout son équipement à la plage ou en camping !

Dans le but d'alléger les différents textes du *Guide de l'auto*, seul le masculin est utilisé et englobe le féminin.

CAPACITÉ DE REMORQUAGE

Plusieurs personnes ne tiennent pas compte de la capacité de remorquage de leur véhicule et ils ont parfois de drôles de surprises. Afin d'éviter ces inconvénients, voici les capacités de remorquage des voitures, camions, VUS et multisegments sur le marché. Plusieurs de ces données sont valables pour les versions équipées d'un ensemble remorquage. Vérifiez auprès du concessionnaire.

	kg	lbs
Toyota Yaris	318	701
Hyundai Elantra	340	750
Acura TSX	450	992
Acura RL	454	1001
Buick LaCrosse	454	1001
Buick Lucerne	454	1001
Buick Regal	454	1001
Cadillac CTS	454	1001
Cadillac DTS	454	1001
Cadillac STS	454	1001
Chevrolet Impala	454	1001
Chevrolet Malibu	454	1001
Chrysler Sebring	454	1001
Dodge Avenger	454	1001
Dodge Caliber	454	1001
Dodge Charger	454	1001
Dodge Journey	454	1001
Ford Escape	454	1001
Ford Focus	454	1001
Ford Mustang	454	1001
Ford Taurus	454	1001
Honda Accord	454	1001
Honda Civic	454	1001
Hyundai Sonata	454	1001
Hyundai Tucson	454	1001
Jeep Compass	454	1001
Jeep Patriot	454	1001
Jeep Wrangler	454	1001
Kia Rondo	454	1001
Kia Sedona	454	1001
Kia Sportage	454	1001
Lincoln MKS	454	1001
Lincoln MKZ	454	1001
Mazda Mazda6	454	1001
Mitsubishi Lancer	454	1001
Nissan Altima	454	1001
Nissan Rogue	454	1001
Nissan Sentra	454	1001
Toyota Avalon	454	1001
Toyota Camry	454	1001
Volkswagen Passat	454	1001
BMW Série 3	480	1058
Volvo XC60	500	1102
Ford Ranger	599	1321
Acura ZDX	680	1499
Chevrolet Equinox	680	1499
Chrysler Sebring	680	1499
Ford Escape	680	1499
GMC Terrain	680	1499
Honda Accord Crosstour	680	1499
Honda CR-V	680	1499
Honda Element	680	1499
Mazda CX-7	680	1499
Mazda Tribute	680	1499
Mitsubishi Outlander	680	1499
Toyota Corolla	680	1499
Toyota Matrix	680	1499
Toyota RAV4	680	1499
Acura RDX	681	1501
Ford Ranger	699	1541
Volvo C30	700	1543
Kia Sorento	748	1649
Hyundai Santa Fe	749	1651
BMW Série 5	750	1653
Jaguar XF	750	1653
Volvo C70	750	1653
Volvo S80	750	1653
Chevrolet Colorado	861	1898
GMC Canyon	861	1898
Volvo S40	900	1984
Volvo V50	900	1984
Subaru Impreza	906	1997
Subaru Tribeca	906	1997
Buick Enclave	907	2000
Chevrolet Traverse	907	2000
Chrysler 300	907	2000
Chrysler Sebring	907	2000
Dodge Avenger	907	2000
Dodge Charger	907	2000
Dodge Nitro	907	2000
Ford Escape	907	2000
Ford Flex	907	2000
Infiniti FX	907	2000
Jeep Wrangler	907	2000
Kia Rondo	907	2000
Kia Sportage	907	2000
Mazda CX-7	907	2000
Chevrolet Colorado	953	2101
GMC Canyon	953	2101
Chevrolet Colorado	998	2200
GMC Canyon	998	2200
Volkswagen Tiguan	998	2200
Subaru Forester	1087	2396
Chevrolet Colorado	1089	2401
GMC Canyon	1089	2401
Toyota Venza	1134	2500
Cadillac SRX	1136	2504
Suzuki Grand Vitara	1360	2998
Chevrolet Colorado	1361	3000
GMC Canyon	1361	3000
Ford Ranger	1388	3060
Volvo S60	1500	3307
Volvo XC70	1500	3307
RAM 1500	1542	3400
Land Rover LR2	1585	3494
Toyota Sienna	1585	3494
Lexus RX	1587	3499
Toyota Highlander	1587	3499
Toyota RAV4	1587	3499
Toyota Tacoma	1587	3499
Toyota Venza	1587	3499
Ford Edge	1588	3501
Honda Odyssey	1588	3501
Hyundai Veracruz	1588	3501
Infiniti FX	1588	3501
Jeep Commander	1588	3501
Jeep Wrangler	1588	3501
Kia Sorento	1588	3501
Lincoln MKX	1588	3501
Mazda CX-9	1588	3501
Mazda Tribute	1588	3501
Mercedes-Benz Classe GLK	1588	3501
Mercedes-Benz Classe R	1588	3501
Mitsubishi Endeavor	1588	3501
Mitsubishi Outlander	1588	3501
Nissan Frontier	1588	3501
Nissan Murano	1588	3501
Nissan Quest	1588	3501
Honda Pilot	1590	3505
Chrysler Town & Country	1633	3600
Dodge Grand Caravan	1633	3600
BMW X3	1700	3748
RAM 1500	1724	3801
Dodge Grand Caravan	1727	3807
Chevrolet Silverado	1996	4400
GMC Sierra	1996	4400
Audi Q5	2000	4409
Lincoln MKT	2041	4500
RAM Dakota	2041	4500
Honda Pilot	2045	4508
RAM Dakota	2109	4650
Chevrolet Silverado	2132	4700
GMC Sierra	2132	4700
RAM Dakota	2155	4751
Chevrolet Silverado	2177	4799
RAM Dakota	2177	4799
GMC Sierra	2223	4901
Volvo XC90	2250	4960
Chevrolet Avalanche	2268	5000
Ford Explorer	2268	5000
Honda Ridgeline	2268	5000
Jeep Liberty	2268	5000
Kia Borrego	2268	5000
Nissan Xterra	2268	5000
Toyota 4Runner	2268	5000
Toyota FJ Cruiser	2268	5000
Toyota Highlander	2268	5000
Toyota Tacoma	2268	5000
Acura MDX	2269	5002
Jeep Grand Cherokee	2269	5002
Chevrolet Avalanche	2313	5099
Chevrolet Silverado	2313	5099
Chevrolet Suburban	2313	5099
GMC Sierra	2313	5099
GMC Acadia	2359	5201
Chevrolet Avalanche	2449	5399
Chevrolet Suburban	2449	5399
Chevrolet Tahoe	2449	5399
RAM 1500	2472	5450
Audi Q7	2495	5501
Chevrolet Colorado	2495	5501
Chevrolet Silverado	2495	5501
GMC Canyon	2495	5501
GMC Sierra	2495	5501
RAM 1500	2517	5549
Cadillac Escalade	2540	5600
RAM Dakota	2563	5650
GMC Sierra	2585	5699
Chevrolet Tahoe	2586	5701
Chevrolet Silverado	2676	5900
GMC Sierra	2676	5900
BMW X5	2722	6001
BMW X6	2722	6001
Chevrolet Silverado	2722	6001
Chevrolet Tahoe	2722	6001
GMC Sierra	2722	6001
GMC Sierra	2722	6001
Nissan Pathfinder	2722	6001
RAM 1500	2744	6049
Chevrolet Silverado	2767	6100
GMC Sierra	2767	6100
Nissan Frontier	2767	6100
RAM 1500	2767	6100
Suzuki Equator	2767	6100
RAM 1500	2790	6151
Chevrolet Tahoe	2812	6199
RAM 1500	2812	6199
Nissan Frontier	2858	6301
Toyota Tacoma	2903	6400
RAM 1500	2926	6451
Lexus GX	2948	6499
Nissan Titan	2948	6499
RAM 1500	2948	6499
Nissan Frontier	2950	6504
BMW X6	3000	6614
RAM 1500	3016	6649
Chevrolet Silverado	3039	6700
Mercedes-Benz Classe G	3175	7000
Toyota Sequoia	3175	7000
Jeep Commander	3266	7200
Mercedes-Benz Classe M	3266	7200
Mercedes-Benz Classe GL	3401	7498
Cadillac Escalade	3402	7500
GMC Sierra	3402	7500
Kia Borrego	3402	7500
BMW X5	3500	7716
Land Rover LR4	3500	7716
Land Rover Range Rover	3500	7716
Land Rover Range Rover Sport	3500	7716
Porsche Cayenne	3500	7716
Volkswagen Touareg	3500	7716
Cadillac Escalade	3538	7800
Toyota Tundra	3760	8289
RAM 1500	3765	8300
Infiniti QX	3855	8499
Lexus LX	3856	8501
Lincoln Navigator	3856	8501
Toyota Tundra	3900	8598
Ford Expedition	3946	8699
Lincoln Navigator	3946	8699
Toyota Sequoia	3990	8796
Ford Expedition	4037	8900
Nissan Armada	4082	8999
Toyota Sequoia	4125	9094
Nissan Titan	4128	9101
Chevrolet Suburban	4218	9299
GMC Sierra	4218	9299
Nissan Titan	4218	9299
Chevrolet Suburban	4354	9599
RAM 1500	4513	9949
Toyota Tundra	4580	10097
Ford F-150	5080	11199

Les fluctuations parfois sauvages des prix de l'essence ainsi que les intentions des dirigeants politiques de resserrer les normes antipollution sensibilisent de plus en plus les consommateurs à s'informer de la consommation de carburant de leur véhicule actuel et de celui qu'ils ont l'intention de se procurer. Dans les essais individuels du *Guide*, nous vous indiquons la consommation de carburant en ville et sur la route. Afin de dresser un tableau plus complet, voici les cotes de consommation en ordre de grandeur.

CONSOMMATION EN VILLE	l/100 km
Toyota Prius	3,7
Ford Fusion Hybride	4,6
Honda Insight	4,8
Lexus HS250h	5,6
Nissan Altima Hybride	5,6
Toyota Camry Hybride	5,7
Ford Escape Hybride	5,8
smart Fortwo	5,9
Honda CR-Z	6,5
Lexus RX450h	6,6
Audi A3 TDI	6,7
Volkswagen Golf 2,0 TDI	6,7
Volkswagen Jetta 2,0 TDI	6,7
Toyota Yaris	6,9
Kia Rio/Rio5	7,1
MINI Cooper	7,1
Honda Fit	7,2
Mazda Mazda2	7,2
Mazda Mazda2	7,2
Honda Civic	7,4
Hyundai Accent	7,4
Kia Sorento	7,4
Toyota Highlander Hybride	7,4
Chevrolet Aveo	7,5
Nissan Sentra	7,5
Toyota Corolla	7,5
Kia Sorento V6	7,7
Kia Soul 1,6	7,7
MINI Cooper S	7,8
Toyota Matrix	7,8
Ford Fiesta	7,9
Suzuki Swift+	7,9
Mazda Mazda3 2,0	8,1
Kia Forte 2,0	8,3
Nissan Cube	8,3
Hyundai Elantra	8,4
Ford Focus	8,5
Nissan Versa 1,6	8,5
Nissan Versa 1,8	8,5
Kia Soul 2,0	8,6
Acura CSX	8,7
Lexus GS450h	8,7
Nissan Sentra SE-R	8,7
Porsche Cayenne S Hybride	8,7
Nissan Altima 2,5	8,8
Suzuki SX-4	8,8
Hyundai Elantra Touring	8,9
Jeep Patriot 2RM	8,9
Kia Forte 2,4	9,0
Toyota Camry	9,0
Dodge Caliber	9,1
Jeep Compass	9,1
Jeep Patriot 4RM	9,1
Nissan Rogue TA	9,1
Volkswagen Jetta	9,1
Chevrolet Equinox TA	9,2
Chevrolet HHR	9,2
GMC Terrain TA	9,2
Mazda MX-5	9,2
Mercedes-Benz Classe B200	9,2
Subaru Legacy	9,2
Suzuki Kizashi	9,3
Suzuki SX-4 AWD	9,3
Audi A5 2.0T	9,4
Chevrolet Malibu	9,4
Ford Fusion 2,5	9,4
Hyundai Sonata	9,4
Mitsubishi Lancer	9,4
Nissan Rogue TI	9,4
Toyota RAV4	9,4
Audi TT 2.0T	9,5
Ford Transit Connect	9,5
Scion xB	9,5
Toyota Corolla XRS	9,5
Hyundai Tucson TA	9,6
Mazda Mazda5	9,6
Chevrolet Silverado Hybride	9,7
Chevrolet Tahoe Hybride	9,7
Dodge Avenger	9,7
Toyota RAV4 4RM	9,7
GMC Sierra Hybride	9,8
Hyundai Tucson TI	9,8
Nissan Sentra SE-R Spec V	9,8
Honda Accord	9,9
Volkswagen Jetta	9,9
Toyota Venza	10,0
Volkswagen Eos	10,0
Volkswagen GTI	10,0
Volkswagen Passat CC	10,0
Chevrolet Equinox TI	10,1
GMC Terrain TI	10,1
Honda CR-V 4RM	10,1
Hyundai Genesis Coupe 2,0T	10,1
Hyundai Santa Fe TI 3,5	10,1
Mazda Mazda3 2,5	10,1
Honda Civic Si	10,2
Mitsubishi Lancer GTS	10,2
Nissan Altima 3,5	10,2
Toyota Venza AWD	10,2
Volvo C30 T5	10,2
Volvo S40 T5	10,2
Mercedes-Benz Classe B200T	10,3
Toyota Matrix AWD	10,3
Audi A3 2.0T	10,4
Mazda CX-7 2RM	10,4
Mazda Mazda6	10,4
Subaru Forester	10,4
Toyota Sienna	10,4
Volkswagen Golf	10,4
Mitsubishi Outlander 2RM	10,5
Kia Rondo	10,6
Lexus LS600h L	10,6
Mitsubishi Eclipse	10,6
Subaru Impreza	10,6
BMW X5 35d	10,7
Hyundai Santa Fe TA 2,4	10,7
Nissan Frontier 4x2	10,7
Toyota Avalon	10,7
Toyota Camry V6	10,7
Volvo V50 T5	10,7
BMW 128i	10,8
BMW Z4 30i	10,8
Buick Regal	10,8
Volvo C70 T5	10,8
Lexus ES350	10,9
Lexus IS350	10,9
Mazda Tribute 2RM	10,9
Nissan Maxima	10,9
Honda Accord V6	11,0
Honda Element 4RM	11,0
Mercedes-Benz Classe S400 Hybrid	11,0
Subaru Forester XT	11,0
Toyota Venza V6	11,0
Ford Fusion 3,0	11,1
Porsche Boxster S	11,1
Porsche Cayman S	11,1
Toyota RAV4 4RM V6	11,1
Infiniti G37	11,2
Kia Sportage	11,2
Lotus Elise	11,2
Porsche Boxster	11,2
Porsche Cayman	11,2
Suzuki Grand Vitara	11,2
Acura TSX V6	11,3
Porsche 911 Carrera	11,3
Subaru Impreza WRX	11,3
Audi A6 3.2	11,4
Cadillac STS	11,4
Hyundai Genesis 3,8	11,4
Lexus IS250	11,4
Mazda Tribute 4RM	11,4
Audi Q5 3.2	11,5
Cadillac SRX	11,5
Honda Accord Crosstour TA	11,5
Kia Rondo V6	11,5
Lexus RX350	11,5
Mazda MazdaSpeed3	11,5
Mercedes-Benz Classe C250 4Matic	11,5
Mercedes-Benz Classe SLK300	11,5
Subaru Legacy GT	11,5
Toyota Venza V6 AWD	11,5
Acura TL	11,6
Audi A5 3.2	11,6
BMW 135i	11,6
BMW Z4 35i	11,6
Ford Escape	11,6
Lexus GS350 AWD	11,6
Mercedes-Benz Classe R350 BlueTEC 4Matic	11,6
Porsche 911 Carrera S	11,6
Volkswagen Tiguan	11,6
Cadillac CTS 3.6	11,7
Chrysler Sebring	11,7
Infiniti G37x	11,7
Lincoln MKZ TA	11,7
Lotus Exige S 240	11,8
Mercedes-Benz Classe ML350 BlueTEC 4Matic	11,8
Nissan Murano	11,8
Porsche 911 Carrera 4S	11,8
Scion tC	11,8
Subaru Legacy 3.6R	11,8
Lotus Elise SC	11,9
Nissan Z	11,9
Volkswagen Touareg TDI	11,9
Audi A6 3.0T	12,0
Buick Lucerne	12,0
Chevrolet Impala	12,0
Hyundai Genesis Coupe 3,8	12,0
Infiniti M37x	12,0
Mercedes-Benz Classe C300 4Matic	12,0
Mitsubishi Outlander 4RM	12,0
Audi S4	12,1
Mazda Mazda6 V6	12,1
BMW X3 28i	12,2
Buick LaCrosse	12,2
Chrysler Town & Country	12,2
Mazda CX-7 4RM	12,2
Mitsubishi Lancer Ralliart	12,2
Volvo S80 3.2	12,2
Volvo XC60 3.2	12,2
BMW 328xDrive	12,3
BMW 335i	12,3
BMW 528 xDrive	12,3
Chevrolet Camaro	12,3
Dodge Grand Caravan	12,3
Ford Taurus SHO	12,3
Honda Accord Crosstour TI	12,3
Lincoln MKS TI Ecoboost	12,3
Mercedes-Benz Classe GL350 BlueTEC 4 Matic	12,3
Toyota Highlander V6	12,3
Lotus Evora	12,4
Subaru Impreza WRX Sti	12,4
BMW X3 30i	12,5
Lincoln MKS TA	12,5
Mercedes-Benz Classe C350 4Matic	12,5
Suzuki Grand Vitara V6	12,5
Ford Fusion 3,5	12,6
Hyundai Genesis 4,6	12,6
Kia Sedona	12,6
Lincoln MKZ TI	12,6
Mercedes-Benz Classe SLK350	12,6
Toyota 4Runner	12,6
Acura ZDX	12,7
Buick Enclave	12,7
Chevrolet Traverse TA	12,7
GMC Acadia TA	12,7
Kia Borrego 3,8	12,7
Mercedes-Benz Classe E350 4Matic	12,7
Lincoln MKS TI	12,8
Mazda RX-8 R3	12,8
Audi S5	12,9
Chevrolet Corvette	12,9
Infiniti EX35	12,9
Lexus LS460	12,9
Mitsubishi Lancer Evolution GSR	12,9
Mitsubishi Lancer Evolution MR	12,9
Porsche Panamera 4S	12,9
Porsche Panamera S	12,9
Jeep Grand Cherokee	13,0
Lexus IS-F	13,0
Lincoln MKT TI	13,0
Volvo XC60 3.2 AWD	13,0
Acura RL	13,1
Audi A6 4.2	13,1
Audi A8 4.2	13,1

	l/100 km
Cadillac CTS 3.0	13,1
Chevrolet Traverse TI	13,1
Ford Flex TI Ecoboost	13,1
GMC Acadia TI	13,1
Honda Pilot	13,1
Lincoln MKT TI Ecoboost	13,1
Mitsubishi Eclipse V6	13,1
Volvo S60 T6 AWD	13,1
Acura MDX	13,2
Audi Q7 TDI	13,2
BMW X5 35i	13,2
Hyundai Veracruz	13,2
Subaru Tribeca	13,2
Chevrolet Colorado	13,3
GMC Canyon 4x4	13,3
Infiniti FX35	13,3
Jaguar XF	13,3
Mercedes-Benz Classe GLK350 4Matic	13,3
Volvo S80 T6 AWD	13,3
Ford Flex TI	13,4
Ford Ranger 4x2	13,4
Infiniti M56x	13,4
Mazda CX-9 TA	13,4
Chrysler 300C	13,5
Dodge Challenger	13,5
Dodge Charger	13,5
Porsche Panamera 4	13,5
Toyota Tacoma 4x4	13,5
Volvo XC60 T6 AWD	13,5
Dodge Journey	13,6
Toyota FJ Cruiser	13,7
Volvo XC70 3.2 AWD	13,7
Volvo XC70 T6 AWD	13,7
Acura RDX	13,8
Buick Lucerne Super	13,8
Cadillac DTS	13,8
Kia Borrego 4,6	13,8
Mercedes-Benz Classe E350 4Matic	13,8
BMW 650i	13,9
Jeep Wrangler	13,9
Nissan GT-R	13,9
Dodge Nitro	14,0
Jeep Liberty	14,0
Mazda CX-9 TI	14,0
Toyota Tundra 4x2 4,6	14,0
Honda Ridgeline	14,1
Jaguar XF R	14,1
Jaguar XK R	14,1
Land Rover LR2	14,1
Lexus GX460	14,1
Mercedes-Benz Classe ML350 4Matic	14,1
Porsche Panamera Turbo	14,1
Chevrolet Corvette Z06	14,2
Mercedes-Benz Classe S450 4Matic	14,2
Mitsubishi Endeavor	14,2
Porsche Boxster Spyder	14,2
BMW X6 35i	14,4
Chevrolet Avalanche	14,4
Chevrolet Avalanche 4x4	14,4
Chevrolet Suburban 4x2	14,4
Chevrolet Tahoe	14,4
Mercedes-Benz Classe R3504Matic	14,4
RAM Dakota 4x2	14,4
Suzuki Equator	14,4
Nissan Xterra	14,5
Infiniti FX50	14,6
Honda Odyssey	14,7
Ford Mustang Shelby	14,8
Mercedes-Benz Classe SLK55 AMG	14,8
Volkswagen Touareg V6	14,8
Cadillac CTS-V	14,9
Mercedes-Benz Classe S550 4Matic	14,9

	l/100 km
Nissan Pathfinder	14,9
Volvo XC90 3.2 AWD	15,0
Mercedes-Benz Classe CLS550	15,1
Audi S6	15,2
BMW M3	15,3
Cadillac Escalade	15,3
Toyota Tundra 4x2	15,3
Aston Martin Vantage V8	15,4
Porsche Cayenne	15,4
Chevrolet Corvette ZR1	15,5
Ford F-150 4x4	15,6
Mercedes-Benz SLS 6.3 AMG	15,6
RAM RAM 1500 4x2	15,6
Infiniti QX56	15,7
Jeep Commander	15,7
Jeep Grand Cherokee	15,7
Mercedes-Benz Classe SL550	15,8
Chevrolet Silverado 4x4	15,9
Chrysler 300 SRT8	16,0
Dodge Challenger SRT8	16,0
Dodge Charger SRT8	16,0
Toyota Sequoia 4,6	16,0
Audi Q7 3.0T	16,1
Mercedes-Benz Classe ML550 4Matic	16,1
Aston Martin Vantage V12	16,2
Porsche Cayenne Turbo	16,2
Volvo XC90 V8 AWD	16,2
Porsche Cayenne S	16,3
Toyota Sequoia 5,7	16,3
BMW 750Li xDrive	16,4
Mercedes-Benz Classe E63 AMG	16,5
Mercedes-Benz Classe GL450 4Matic	16,5
Porsche 911 Turbo S	16,5
Rolls-Royce Ghost	16,6
RAM RAM 1500 4x4	16,7
Dodge Viper	16,8
Ferrari California	16,9
BMW X5M	17,0
Jaguar XJ	17,0
Lexus LX570	17,0
Audi R8 4.2	17,1
BMW X6 50i	17,1
Land Rover LR4	17,1
Mercedes-Benz Classe GL550 4Matic	17,1
Porsche Panamera	17,1
Mercedes-Benz Classe C63 AMG	17,2
Ford Expedition	17,3
Nissan Armada	17,3
Porsche 911 Turbo	17,3
BMW X5 50i	17,5
GMC Sierra Denali	17,5
Nissan Titan 4x4	17,7
Maserati Gran Turismo	17,8
Mercedes-Benz Classe CLS63 AMG	17,8
Mercedes-Benz Classe SL63 AMG	17,9
Porsche 911 GT2 RS	17,9
Aston Martin DBS	18,1
Land Rover Range Rover Sport Supercharged	18,1
Land Rover Range Rover Supercharged	18,1
Jaguar XJ Supercharged	18,3
Jaguar XJ Supersport	18,3
Land Rover Range Rover Sport	18,4
Mercedes-Benz Classe SL65 AMG	18,4
Mercedes-Benz Classe SL600	18,5
Lamborghini Gallardo LP 560-4	18,7
Mercedes-Benz Classe CL63 AMG	18,7
Mercedes-Benz Classe G550	18,7
Rolls-Royce Phantom	18,7
Mercedes-Benz Classe S63 AMG	18,8
Aston Martin DB9	18,9
Mercedes-Benz Classe S600	18,9
Audi R8 5.2	19,1

	l/100 km
Mercedes-Benz Classe CL65 AMG	19,1
Mercedes-Benz Classe CL600	19,2
BMW X6M	19,3
Mercedes-Benz Classe S65 AMG	19,4
Porsche 911 GT3 RS	19,4
Ferrari 599	19,8
Mercedes-Benz Classe G55 AMG	19,8
BMW M6	19,9
Mercedes-Benz Classe ML63 AMG	20,4
Bentley Continental Flying Spur	20,9
Maybach 57	21,1
Maserati Quattroporte	22,0
Ferrari 612 Scaglietti	22,8
Maserati Quattroporte GT S	24,0
Bentley Continental Flying Spur Speed	25,3
Bentley Continental Supersports Convertible	25,5
Lamborghini Murciélago LP 640	25,9
Bentley Mulsanne	26,3
Lamborghini Murciélago LP 670-4 SV	29,4

CONSOMMATION ROUTE

	l/100 km
Toyota Prius	4,0
Honda Insight	4,5
Audi A3 TDI	4,6
Volkswagen Jetta 2,0 TDI	4,6
Ford Fiesta	4,7
Volkswagen Golf 2,0 TDI	4,7
smart Fortwo	4,8
Honda CR-Z	5,3
MINI Cooper	5,3
Ford Fusion Hybride	5,4
Honda Civic	5,4
Toyota Yaris	5,5
Ford Focus	5,6
Mazda Mazda2	5,6
Mazda Mazda2	5,6
Toyota Corolla	5,6
Chevrolet Aveo	5,7
Honda Fit	5,7
Hyundai Sonata	5,7
MINI Cooper S	5,7
Suzuki Swift+	5,7
Toyota Camry Hybride	5,7
Kia Forte 2,0	5,8
Kia Rio/Rio5	5,8
Nissan Sentra	5,8
Chevrolet Malibu	5,9
Lexus HS250h	5,9
Mazda Mazda3 2,0	5,9
Nissan Altima Hybride	5,9
Hyundai Accent	6,0
Hyundai Elantra	6,0
Volkswagen Jetta	6,0
Chevrolet Equinox TA	6,1
Chevrolet HHR	6,1
GMC Terrain TA	6,1
Toyota Camry	6,1
Nissan Altima 2,5	6,2
Toyota Matrix	6,2
Volkswagen Jetta	6,2
Dodge Caliber	6,3
Kia Forte 2,4	6,3
Kia Soul 1,6	6,3
Nissan Versa 1,6	6,3
Nissan Versa 1,8	6,3
Acura CSX	6,4
Ford Fusion 2,5	6,4
Hyundai Elantra Touring	6,4
Audi A5 2.0T	6,5
Buick Regal	6,5
Ford Escape Hybride	6,5
Honda Accord	6,5

	l/100 km
Kia Soul 2,0	6,5
Lotus Evora	6,5
Mitsubishi Lancer	6,5
Nissan Sentra SE-R	6,5
Subaru Legacy	6,5
Dodge Avenger	6,6
Hyundai Genesis Coupe 2,0T	6,6
Nissan Cube	6,6
Suzuki SX-4 AWD	6,6
Volkswagen Eos	6,6
Volkswagen GTI	6,6
Volkswagen Passat CC	6,6
Audi A3 2.0T	6,7
Honda Accord V6	6,7
Hyundai Tucson TA	6,7
Mercedes-Benz Classe B200	6,7
Suzuki SX-4	6,7
Toyota Corolla XRS	6,7
Chevrolet Camaro	6,8
Honda Civic Si	6,8
Suzuki Kizashi	6,8
Toyota Venza	6,8
Volvo C30 T5	6,8
Volvo S40 T5	6,8
BMW 128i	6,9
BMW Z4 30i	6,9
Cadillac STS	6,9
Chevrolet Equinox TI	6,9
GMC Terrain TI	6,9
Mazda Mazda3 2,5	6,9
Mazda Mazda6	6,9
Mercedes-Benz Classe B200T	6,9
Toyota RAV4	6,9
Audi TT 2.0T	7,0
Mazda Mazda5	7,0
Nissan Sentra SE-R Spec V	7,0
Toyota Avalon	7,0
Toyota Camry V6	7,0
Volkswagen Golf	7,0
Volvo V50 T5	7,0
Hyundai Tucson TI	7,1
Jeep Patriot 2RM	7,1
Mazda MX-5	7,1
Porsche Boxster Spyder	7,1
Toyota Venza AWD	7,1
Honda Accord Crosstour TA	7,2
Hyundai Genesis 3,8	7,2
Jeep Compass	7,2
Jeep Patriot 4RM	7,2
Lexus ES350	7,2
Lexus RX450h	7,2
Mazda CX-7 2RM	7,2
Nissan Altima 3,5	7,2
Nissan Rogue TA	7,2
Scion xB	7,2
Toyota RAV4 4RM	7,2
Volvo C70 T5	7,2
Buick LaCrosse	7,3
Ford Fusion 3,0	7,3
Mercedes-Benz Classe SLK300	7,3
Mitsubishi Eclipse	7,3
Mitsubishi Lancer GTS	7,3
Porsche Panamera 4	7,3
Acura TSX V6	7,4
Audi A6 3.2	7,4
Buick Lucerne	7,4
Cadillac CTS 3.6	7,4
Chevrolet Impala	7,4
Lincoln MKZ TA	7,4
Porsche Boxster	7,4
Porsche Cayman	7,4
Acura TL	7,5

	l/100 km
BMW X5 35d	7,5
Honda CR-V 4RM	7,5
Hyundai Santa Fe TA 2,4	7,5
Infiniti G37	7,5
Kia Rondo	7,5
Lexus IS250	7,5
Mercedes-Benz Classe C250 4Matic	7,5
Porsche Boxster S	7,5
Porsche Cayman S	7,5
Subaru Impreza	7,5
Toyota Sienna	7,5
Audi A5 3.2	7,6
BMW 328xDrive	7,6
BMW 335i	7,6
BMW 528 xDrive	7,6
Chrysler Sebring	7,6
Hyundai Genesis Coupe 3,8	7,6
Hyundai Santa Fe TI 3,5	7,6
Mercedes-Benz Classe S400 Hybrid	7,6
Toyota Venza V6	7,6
Volvo S80 3.2	7,6
Volvo XC60 3.2	7,6
BMW 135i	7,7
BMW Z4 35i	7,7
Cadillac CTS 3.0	7,7
Chevrolet Corvette	7,7
Kia Rondo V6	7,7
Nissan Maxima	7,7
Nissan Rogue TI	7,7
Subaru Forester	7,7
Toyota Matrix AWD	7,7
Toyota RAV4 4RM V6	7,7
Infiniti G37x	7,8
Lexus GS450h	7,8
Lexus IS350	7,8
Mitsubishi Outlander 2RM	7,8
Porsche 911 Carrera S	7,8
Audi S4	7,9
Chrysler Town & Country	7,9
Ford Transit Connect	7,9
Mitsubishi Lancer Ralliart	7,9
Porsche 911 Carrera	7,9
Porsche Cayenne S Hybride	7,9
Porsche Panamera	7,9
Toyota Venza V6 AWD	7,9
Audi A6 3.0T	8,0
Cadillac SRX	8,0
Chrysler 300C	8,0
Dodge Challenger	8,0
Dodge Charger	8,0
Ford Taurus SHO	8,0
Honda Accord Crosstour TI	8,0
Jaguar XF	8,0
Lexus GS350 AWD	8,0
Lexus RX350	8,0
Lincoln MKS TI Ecoboost	8,0
Mazda Mazda6 V6	8,0
Mazda MazdaSpeed3	8,0
Mazda Tribute 2RM	8,0
Mercedes-Benz Classe C300 4Matic	8,0
Mercedes-Benz Classe SLK350	8,0
Mitsubishi Eclipse V6	8,0
Porsche 911 Carrera 4S	8,0
Subaru Legacy GT	8,0
Toyota Highlander Hybride	8,0
Volkswagen Touareg TDI	8,0
Audi S5	8,1
Hyundai Genesis 4,6	8,1
Kia Sportage	8,1
Nissan Z	8,1
Porsche 911 Turbo S	8,1
Subaru Impreza WRX	8,1

	l/100 km
BMW X3 30i	8,2
Chevrolet Corvette Z06	8,2
Jaguar XJ	8,2
Lexus LS460	8,2
Mercedes-Benz Classe C350 4Matic	8,2
Mercedes-Benz Classe ML350 BlueTEC 4Matic	8,2
Mitsubishi Outlander 4RM	8,2
Subaru Legacy 3.6R	8,2
Audi Q7 TDI	8,3
BMW X3 28i	8,3
BMW X5 35i	8,3
Dodge Grand Caravan	8,3
Ford Fusion 3,5	8,3
Honda Element 4RM	8,3
Infiniti M37x	8,3
Lincoln MKZ TI	8,3
Mercedes-Benz Classe E350 4Matic	8,3
Mercedes-Benz Classe R350 BlueTEC 4Matic	8,3
Porsche 911 Turbo	8,3
Porsche Panamera 4S	8,3
Porsche Panamera S	8,3
Volkswagen Tiguan	8,3
Buick Enclave	8,4
Chevrolet Traverse TA	8,4
GMC Acadia TA	8,4
Lincoln MKS TA	8,4
Subaru Forester XT	8,4
BMW 750Li xDrive	8,5
Infiniti M56x	8,5
Kia Sedona	8,5
Lexus IS-F	8,5
Infiniti EX35	8,6
Mazda Tribute 4RM	8,6
Mercedes-Benz Classe E350 4Matic	8,6
Porsche Panamera Turbo	8,6
Suzuki Grand Vitara	8,6
Suzuki Grand Vitara V6	8,6
Volvo S80 T6 AWD	8,6
Audi A8 4.2	8,7
Buick Lucerne Super	8,7
Cadillac DTS	8,7
Dodge Journey	8,7
Jaguar XJ Supercharged	8,7
Jaguar XJ Supersport	8,7
Lotus Elise	8,7
Mazda CX-7 4RM	8,7
Mercedes-Benz Classe GL350 BlueTEC 4 Matic	8,7
Mercedes-Benz Classe GLK350 4Matic	8,7
Nissan Frontier 4x2	8,7
Nissan Murano	8,7
Porsche 911 GT2 RS	8,7
Scion tC	8,7
Acura ZDX	8,8
Audi A6 4.2	8,8
Chevrolet Traverse TI	8,8
Ford Escape	8,8
GMC Acadia TI	8,8
Lincoln MKS TI	8,8
Porsche Cayenne Turbo	8,8
Toyota Highlander V6	8,8
Volvo XC70 3.2 AWD	8,8
Volvo XC70 T6 AWD	8,8
Hyundai Veracruz	8,9
Jeep Grand Cherokee	8,9
Subaru Impreza WRX Sti	8,9
Acura RL	9,0
Audi Q5 3.2	9,0
Ford Flex TI	9,0
Lotus Elise SC	9,0
Lotus Exige S 240	9,0
Mercedes-Benz Classe S450 4Matic	9,0
Mercedes-Benz Classe SLK55 AMG	9,0

	l/100 km
Mitsubishi Lancer Evolution GSR	9,0
Mitsubishi Lancer Evolution MR	9,0
Volvo S60 T6 AWD	9,0
Volvo XC60 3.2 AWD	9,0
Chevrolet Silverado Hybride	9,1
Chevrolet Tahoe Hybride	9,1
Ford Mustang Shelby	9,1
GMC Sierra Hybride	9,1
Honda Pilot	9,1
Jaguar XK R	9,1
Land Rover LR2	9,1
Lexus LS600h L	9,1
Lincoln MKT TI Ecoboost	9,1
Mazda CX-9 TA	9,1
Volvo XC60 T6 AWD	9,1
Dodge Viper	9,2
Ford Flex TI Ecoboost	9,2
Lincoln MKT TI	9,2
Mazda RX-8 R3	9,2
Toyota 4Runner	9,2
Chevrolet Colorado	9,3
GMC Canyon 4x4	9,3
Infiniti FX35	9,3
Jaguar XF R	9,3
Kia Borrego 4,6	9,3
Mercedes-Benz Classe S550 4Matic	9,3
Kia Borrego 3,8	9,4
Mercedes-Benz Classe SL550	9,4
Subaru Tribeca	9,4
Chevrolet Tahoe	9,5
Mercedes-Benz Classe CLS550	9,5
Nissan GT-R	9,5
Acura MDX	9,6
BMW 650i	9,6
BMW X5 50i	9,6
Chevrolet Avalanche	9,6
Chevrolet Avalanche 4x4	9,6
Chevrolet Suburban 4x2	9,6
Mazda CX-9 TI	9,6
Porsche 911 GT3 RS	9,6
BMW M3	9,7
Dodge Nitro	9,7
Ford Ranger 4x2	9,7
Jeep Liberty	9,7
Honda Ridgeline	9,8
Lexus GX460	9,8
Porsche Cayenne	9,8
RAM Dakota 4x2	9,8
Aston Martin Vantage V8	9,9
Toyota Tundra 4x2 4,6	9,9
BMW X6 35i	10,0
Volvo XC90 3.2 AWD	10,0
Aston Martin Vantage V12	10,1
Cadillac Escalade	10,1
Infiniti FX50	10,1
Mercedes-Benz Classe ML350 4Matic	10,1
Rolls-Royce Ghost	10,1
Toyota Tacoma 4x4	10,1
Chevrolet Corvette ZR1	10,2
Dodge Challenger SRT8	10,2
Honda Odyssey	10,2
Mercedes-Benz Classe E63 AMG	10,2
Nissan Xterra	10,2
Audi R8 4.2	10,3
Infiniti QX56	10,3
Kia Sorento V6	10,3
Mercedes-Benz Classe R3504Matic	10,3
Mercedes-Benz SLS 6.3 AMG	10,3
Mitsubishi Endeavor	10,3
Nissan Pathfinder	10,3
Toyota FJ Cruiser	10,3
Audi S6	10,4

	l/100 km
Maserati Gran Turismo	10,4
Mercedes-Benz Classe C63 AMG	10,4
Suzuki Equator	10,4
Volkswagen Touareg V6	10,4
Cadillac CTS-V	10,5
Maserati Quattroporte	10,5
Porsche Cayenne S	10,5
Chrysler 300 SRT8	10,6
Dodge Charger SRT8	10,6
Ferrari California	10,6
Jeep Commander	10,6
Jeep Grand Cherokee	10,6
Jeep Wrangler	10,6
Kia Sorento	10,6
Mercedes-Benz Classe SL63 AMG	10,6
Volvo XC90 V8 AWD	10,6
Acura RDX	10,7
GMC Sierra Denali	10,7
BMW X6M	10,8
RAM RAM 1500 4x2	10,8
Toyota Tundra 4x2	10,9
BMW X6 50i	11,0
Maserati Quattroporte GT S	11,0
Mercedes-Benz Classe SL65 AMG	11,1
Toyota Sequoia 4,6	11,1
Aston Martin DBS	11,2
Audi Q7 3.0T	11,2
Ford F-150 4x4	11,2
Land Rover Range Rover Sport	11,2
Mercedes-Benz Classe CL63 AMG	11,2
Mercedes-Benz Classe CLS63 AMG	11,2
Mercedes-Benz Classe S63 AMG	11,2
Toyota Sequoia 5,7	11,2
Chevrolet Silverado 4x4	11,4
Lexus LX570	11,4
Mercedes-Benz Classe ML550 4Matic	11,4
Mercedes-Benz Classe SL600	11,4
Nissan Armada	11,4
RAM RAM 1500 4x4	11,4
Rolls-Royce Phantom	11,4
Bentley Mulsanne	11,5
Lamborghini Gallardo LP 560-4	11,5
Mercedes-Benz Classe S600	11,5
Audi R8 5.2	11,6
Bentley Continental Flying Spur Speed	11,6
Bentley Continental Supersports Convertible	11,6
Ford Expedition	11,6
Land Rover LR4	11,6
Mercedes-Benz Classe GL450 4Matic	11,6
Aston Martin DB9	11,7
Land Rover Range Rover Sport Supercharged	11,7
Land Rover Range Rover Supercharged	11,7
Mercedes-Benz Classe GL550 4Matic	11,7
Mercedes-Benz Classe CL65 AMG	11,8
Bentley Continental Flying Spur	11,9
BMW M6	11,9
BMW X5M	11,9
Mercedes-Benz Classe CL600	12,0
Mercedes-Benz Classe S65 AMG	12,0
Nissan Titan 4x4	12,0
Ferrari 612 Scaglietti	12,8
Maybach 57	12,9
Ferrari 599	13,1
Ferrari F458 Italia	13,3
Mercedes-Benz Classe G55 AMG	13,4
Mercedes-Benz Classe G550	13,8
Mercedes-Benz Classe ML63 AMG	14,0
Lamborghini Murciélago LP 640	15,8
Lamborghini Murciélago LP 670-4 SV	18,9

On en parle de plus en plus mais on ne peut pas dire qu'ils arrivent en grand nombre, les véhicules à motorisation hybride, diesel ou électrique. Même que l'offre est passablement la même que celle de l'année dernière malgré quelques ajouts intéressants. L'an prochain, si les promesses des manufacturiers sont tenues, cette section devrait compter passablement plus de voiture. On s'en reparle dans douze mois !

HYBRIDES

Audi A8 (à venir)
Audi Q5 (à venir ?)
BMW Série 7 ActiveHybrid (à venir)
BMW X6 ActiveHybrid (à venir)
Cadillac Escalade
Chevrolet Silverado
Chevrolet Tahoe
Ford Escape
Ford Fusion
GMC Sierra
GMC Yukon
Honda CR-Z
Honda Insight
Hyundai Sonata (à venir)
Lexus GS450h
Lexus HS250h
Lexus LS600h L
Lexus RX450h
Lincoln MKZ (à venir)
Mercedes-Benz Classe S400 Hybrid
Nissan Altima
Porsche Cayenne (à venir)
Toyota Camry
Toyota Highlander
Toyota Prius
Volkswagen Touareg (à venir)

DIESEL

Audi A3 TDI
Audi Q7 TDI
BMW 335d
BMW X5 xDrive35d
Mercedes-Benz Clase GL350 BlueTEC
Mercedes-Benz Classe E350 BlueTEC
Mercedes-Benz Classe ML350 BlueTEC
Mercedes-Benz Classe R350 BlueTEC
Volkswagen Golf TDI
Volkswagen Jetta TDI
Volkswagen Touareg TDI

ÉLECTRIQUES

Chevrolet Volt
Ford Focus (à venir)
Ford Transit Connect (à venir)
Nissan Leaf
Smart ED (à venir)
Tesla
Volvo C30E (à venir?)

VITESSE MAXIMALE

Même si la Sureté du Québec et les corps policiers de partout au Québec et d'ailleurs désapprouvent les personnes qui atteignent la vitesse maximale au volant de leur véhicule, il est toujours intéressant de connaître le potentiel de sa voiture. Voici donc en ordre alphabétique et en ordre croissant les vitesses de pointe de plusieurs véhicules commercialisés au Québec.

VITESSE MAXIMALE EN ORDRE ALPHABÉTIQUE	km/h
Acura MDX	198
Acura RDX	198
Acura RL	225
Acura TL	225
Acura TSX	210
Aston Martin DB9	306
Aston Martin DBS	307
Aston Martin One-77	323
Aston Martin Vantage V12	305
Aston Martin Vantage V8	290
Audi A3 2.0 TDI	200
Audi A3 2.0T	209
Audi A5 2.0T	250
Audi A6 3.0T	209
Audi A8 4.2	250
Audi Q5 3.2	210
Audi Q7 3.0T	222
Audi Q7 TDI	215
Audi R8 4.2	300
Audi R8 5.2	315
Audi S4	250
Audi S60 T6	250
Audi TT 2.0T	245
Audi TT RS	280
Audi TTS	250
Bentley Continental Flying Spur	312
Bentley Continental Flying Spur Speed	322
Bentley Continental GT Speed	326
Bentley Continental GTC	314
Bentley Continental GTC	318
Bentley Continental Supersports	325
BMW 328i	210
BMW M3	250
BMW X3 xDrive 28i	209
BMW X5 xDrive 35i	235
BMW X5 xDrive 50i	240
BMW X6 ActiveHybrid	240
BMW X6 xDrive35i	210
BMW X6M	250
BMW Z4 sDrive30i	250
Buick Enclave	200
Buick Lucerne	190
Cadillac DTS	210
Cadillac STS	225
Chevrolet Impala	210
Chevrolet Volt	160
Chrysler 300 SRT8	250
Chrysler 300C	210
Chrysler Sebring	180
Dodge Avenger	210
Dodge Challenger R/T	250
Dodge Nitro	190
Dodge Viper	322
Ferrari 599	335
Ferrari 612 Scaglietti	320
Ferrari California	310
Ferrari F458 Italia	325
Fiat 500	200
Ford Focus	175
Ford Mustang Shelby GT500	270
Ford Mustang V6	190
Ford Taurus SHO	215
Honda Accord V6	225
Honda Civic	180
Honda Civic Si	200
Honda Element	190
Honda Pilot	175
Hyundai Accent	175
Hyundai Elantra	190
Hyundai Equus	238
Hyundai Santa Fe	190
Hyundai Veracruz	195
Jaguar XF	195
Jaguar XF R	250
Jaguar XJ	195
Jaguar XJ L Supercharged	250
Jaguar XK R	250
Jeep Commander	200

	km/h
Kia Rio/Rio5	180
Kia Rondo	185
Kia Sedona	180
Lamborghini Gallardo LP 560-4	325
Lamborghini Murciélago LP 640 Coupé	340
Lamborghini Murciélago LP 640 Roadster	330
Lamborghini Murciélago LP 670-4 SV	342
Land Rover LR2	207
Land Rover LR4	195
Land Rover Range Rover	210
Land Rover Range Rover	225
Land Rover Range Rover Sport	209
Lexus ES350	220
Lexus IS350	250
Lexus LFA	325
Lexus LS600h L	250
Lincoln MKZ	210
Lotus Elise SC	240
Lotus Evora	261
Lotus Exige S240	240
Maserati Gran Turismo	285
Maserati Quattroporte	270
Maserati Quattroporte GT S	285
Maserati Quattroporte S	280
Maybach 57	250
Maybach 57S	278
Mazda 6	214
Mazda CX-7	210
Mazda CX-9	225
Mazda Mazda5	192
Mazda MX-5	206
Mazda RX-8	235
Mercedes-Benz Classe B200	196
Mercedes-Benz Classe B200T	210
Mercedes-Benz Classe C250	210
Mercedes-Benz Classe C63 AMG	250
Mercedes-Benz Classe CLS550	250
Mercedes-Benz Classe E550	210
Mercedes-Benz Classe E63 AMG	250
Mercedes-Benz Classe G55 AMG	210
Mercedes-Benz Classe G550	190
Mercedes-Benz Classe GL350 BlueTEC 4Matic	210
Mercedes-Benz Classe S600	210
Mercedes-Benz Classe S65 AMG	250
Mercedes-Benz Classe SL550	210
Mercedes-Benz Classe SL600	210
Mercedes-Benz Classe SL63 AMG	250
Mercedes-Benz SLS 6.3 AMG	317
MINI Cooper	198
MINI Cooper	203
MINI Cooper	236
MINI Cooper S	223
MINI Countryman	190
MINI Countryman S	215
Mitsubishi Endeavor	195
Nissan Altima 3.5	225
Nissan GT-R	311
Nissan LEAF	140
Nissan Murano	195
Nissan Pathfinder	195
Nissan Quest	185
Nissan Rogue	195
Nissan Sentra	185
Nissan Versa 1.8	175
Porsche 911	288
Porsche 911 Carrera 4	284
Porsche 911 Carrera S	302
Porsche 911 GT2 RS	330
Porsche 911 GT3	312
Porsche 911 GT3 RS	310
Porsche 911 Targa 4S	297
Porsche 911 Turbo S	315
Porsche Boxster	263
Porsche Boxster S	274
Porsche Boxster Spyder	267
Porsche Cayenne	227
Porsche Cayenne S Hybrid	242
Porsche Cayenne S Hybrid	250
Porsche Cayenne Turbo	278
Porsche Cayman	265
Porsche Cayman S	277
Porsche Panamera Turbo	303
Porsche Panamera	261
Porsche Panamera 4	257
Porsche Panamera 4S	282
Porsche Panamera S	283
Rolls-Royce Ghost	250
Rolls-Royce Phantom	240
smart Fortwo Brabus	145
Suzuki Grand Vitara V6	182
Toyota Avalon	220
Toyota Prius	170
Volkswagen Eos	232
Volkswagen Golf 2.0 TDI	209
Volkswagen GTI	209
Volkswagen Jetta	195
Volkswagen Jetta 2.0 TDI	209
Volkswagen Touareg TDI	218
Volvo C30 T5	240
Volvo C70 T5	235
Volvo S40 T5	235
Volvo S60 T6	210
Volvo S80 3.2	240
Volvo S80 T6 AWD	250
Volvo V50 T5	240

VITESSE MAXIMALE EN ORDRE CROISSANT

	km/h
Nissan LEAF	140
smart Fortwo Brabus	145
Chevrolet Volt	160
Toyota Prius	170
Ford Focus	175
Honda Pilot	175
Hyundai Accent	175
Nissan Versa 1.8	175
Chrysler Sebring	180
Honda Civic	180
Kia Rio/Rio5	180
Kia Sedona	180
Suzuki Grand Vitara V6	182
Kia Rondo	185
Nissan Quest	185
Nissan Sentra	185
Buick Lucerne	190
Dodge Nitro	190
Ford Mustang V6	190
Honda Element	190
Hyundai Elantra	190
Hyundai Santa Fe	190
Mercedes-Benz Classe G550	190
MINI Countryman	190
Mazda Mazda5	192
Hyundai Veracruz	195
Jaguar XF	195
Jaguar XJ	195
Land Rover LR4	195
Mitsubishi Endeavor	195
Nissan Murano	195
Nissan Pathfinder	195
Nissan Rogue	195
Volkswagen Jetta	195
Mercedes-Benz Classe B200	196
Acura MDX	198
Acura RDX	198
MINI Cooper	198
Audi A3 2.0 TDI	200
Buick Enclave	200
Fiat 500	200
Honda Civic Si	200
Jeep Commander	200
MINI Cooper	203
Mazda MX-5	206
Land Rover LR2	207
Audi A3 2.0T	209
Audi A6 3.0T	209
BMW X3 xDrive 28i	209
Land Rover Range Rover Sport	209
Volkswagen Golf 2.0 TDI	209
Volkswagen GTI	209
Volkswagen Jetta 2.0 TDI	209
Acura TSX	210
Audi Q5 3.2	210
BMW 328i	210
BMW X6 xDrive35i	210
Cadillac DTS	210
Chevrolet Impala	210
Chrysler 300C	210
Dodge Avenger	210
Land Rover Range Rover	210
Lincoln MKZ	210
Mazda CX-7	210
Mercedes-Benz Classe B200T	210
Mercedes-Benz Classe C250	210
Mercedes-Benz Classe E550	210
Mercedes-Benz Classe G55 AMG	210
Mercedes-Benz Classe GL350 BlueTEC 4Matic	210
Mercedes-Benz Classe S600	210
Mercedes-Benz Classe SL550	210
Mercedes-Benz Classe SL600	210
Volvo S60 T6	210
Mazda 6	214
Audi Q7 TDI	215
Ford Taurus SHO	215
MINI Countryman S	215
Volkswagen Touareg TDI	218
Lexus ES350	220
Toyota Avalon	220
Audi Q7 3.0T	222
MINI Cooper S	223
Acura RL	225
Acura TL	225
Cadillac STS	225
Honda Accord V6	225
Land Rover Range Rover	225
Mazda CX-9	225
Nissan Altima 3.5	225
Porsche Cayenne	227
Volkswagen Eos	232
BMW X5 xDrive 35i	235
Mazda RX-8	235
Volvo C70 T5	235
Volvo S40 T5	235
MINI Cooper	236
Hyundai Equus	238
BMW X5 xDrive 50i	240
BMW X6 ActiveHybrid	240
Lotus Elise SC	240
Lotus Exige S240	240
Rolls-Royce Phantom	240
Volvo C30 T5	240
Volvo S80 3.2	240
Volvo V50 T5	240
Porsche Cayenne S Hybrid	242
Audi TT 2.0T	245
Audi S4	250
Audi A5 2.0T	250
Audi S60 T6	250
Audi A8 4.2	250
Audi TTS	250
BMW M3	250
BMW X6M	250
BMW Z4 sDrive30i	250
Chrysler 300 SRT8	250
Dodge Challenger R/T	250
Jaguar XF R	250
Jaguar XJ L Supercharged	250
Jaguar XK R	250
Lexus IS350	250
Lexus LS600h L	250
Maybach 57	250
Mercedes-Benz Classe C63 AMG	250
Mercedes-Benz Classe CLS550	250
Mercedes-Benz Classe E63 AMG	250
Mercedes-Benz Classe S65 AMG	250
Mercedes-Benz Classe SL63 AMG	250
Porsche Cayenne S Hybrid	250
Rolls-Royce Ghost	250
Volvo S80 T6 AWD	250
Porsche Panamera 4	257
Lotus Evora	261
Porsche Panamera	261
Porsche Boxster	263
Porsche Cayman	265
Porsche Boxster Spyder	267
Ford Mustang Shelby GT500	270
Maserati Quattroporte	270
Porsche Boxster S	274
Porsche Cayman S	277
Maybach 57S	278
Porsche Cayenne Turbo	278
Audi TT RS	280
Maserati Quattroporte S	280
Porsche Panamera 4S	282
Porsche Panamera S	283
Porsche 911 Carrera 4	284
Maserati Gran Turismo	285
Maserati Quattroporte GT S	285
Porsche 911	288
Aston Martin Vantage V8	290
Porsche 911 Targa 4S	297
Audi R8 4.2	300
Porsche 911 Carrera S	302
Porsche Panamer a Turbo	303
Aston Martin Vantage V12	305
Aston Martin DB9	306
Aston Martin DBS	307
Ferrari California	310
Porsche 911 GT3 RS	310
Nissan GT-R	311
Bentley Continental Flying Spur	312
Porsche 911 GT3	312
Bentley Continental GTC	314
Audi R8 5.2	315
Porsche 911 Turbo S	315
Mercedes-Benz SLS 6.3 AMG	317
Bentley Continental GTC	318
Ferrari 612 Scaglietti	320
Bentley Continental Flying Spur Speed	322
Dodge Viper	322
Aston Martin One-77	323
Bentley Continental Supersports	325
Ferrari F458 Italia	325
Lamborghini Gallardo LP 560-4	325
Lexus LFA	325
Bentley Continental GT Speed	326
Lamborghini Murciélago LP 640 Roadster	330
Porsche 911 GT2 RS	330
Ferrari 599	335
Lamborghini Murciélago LP 640 Coupé	340
Lamborghini Murciélago LP 670-4 SV	342

MOTEURS

Pas de voiture sans moteur. Histoire de vous permettre de comparer la puissance respective des véhicules d'une catégorie ou tout simplement pour conclure une discussion entre amis, voici quel moteur tourne sous le capot de quelle voiture et sa puissance. Et nous ne faisons pas se ségrégation, qu'ils soient à essence, diesel, hybride ou autres, nous les avons tous mis par ordre alphabétique et croissant ! Rien de moins.

MOTEURS EN ORDRE ALPHABÉTIQUE	cyl.		ch	lb-pi
Acura CSX	4L	2,0	155	139
Acura MDX	V6	3,7	300	270
Acura RDX	4L	2,3	240	260
Acura RL	V6	3,7	300	271
Acura TL	V6	3,5	280	254
Acura TL	V6	3,7	305	273
Acura TSX	4L	2,4	201	172
Acura TSX	V6	3,5	280	254
Acura ZDX	V6	3,7	300	270
Aston Martin DB9	V12	6,0	470	443
Aston Martin DBS	V12	6,0	510	420
Aston Martin One-77	V12	7,3	700	n.d.
Aston Martin Rapide	V12	6,0	470	443
Aston Martin Vantage	V8	4,3	420	346
Aston Martin Vantage	V12	6,0	510	420
Audi A3	4L	2,0	140	236
Audi A3	4L	2,0	200	207
Audi A4	V6	3,0	333	325
Audi A5	4L	2,0	211	258
Audi A5	V6	3,2	265	243
Audi A5	V6	3,0	333	325
Audi A5	V8	4,2	450	317
Audi A6	V6	3,2	265	243
Audi A6	V6	3,0	300	310
Audi A6	V8	4,2	350	325
Audi A6	V10	5,2	435	398
Audi A8	V8	4,2	372	325
Audi Q5	4L	2,0	211	n.d.
Audi Q5	V6	3,2	270	243
Audi Q7	V6	3,0	225	406
Audi Q7	V6	3,0	272	266
Audi Q7	V6	3,0	333	325
Audi R8	V8	4,2	420	317
Audi R8	V10	5,2	525	390
Audi TT	4L	2,0	211	258
Audi TT	4L	2,0	272	258
Audi TT	5L	2,5	340	332
Bentley Continental	W12	6,0	552	479
Bentley Continental	W12	6,0	600	553
Bentley Continental	W12	6,0	621	590
Bentley Mulsanne	V8	6,8	505	752
BMW Série 1	6L	3,0	230	200
BMW Série 1	6L	3,0	300	300
BMW Série 3	6L	2,5	200	180
BMW Série 3	6L	3,0	230	200
BMW Série 3	6L	3,0	265	425
BMW Série 3	6L	3,0	300	300
BMW Série 3	V8	4,0	414	295
BMW Série 6	V8	4,8	360	360
BMW Série 6	V10	5,0	500	383
BMW Série 7	V8	4,4	400	450
BMW Série 7	V8	4,4	455	515
BMW X3	6L	3,0	215	185
BMW X3	6L	3,0	260	225
BMW X5	6L	3,0	265	425
BMW X5	6L	3,0	306	295
BMW X5	V8	4,4	407	442
BMW X5	V8	4,4	555	500
BMW X6	6L	3,0	300	300
BMW X6	V8	4,4	400	450

	cyl.		ch	lb-pi
BMW X6	V8	4,4	555	500
BMW Z4	6L	3,0	255	220
BMW Z4	6L	3,0	300	300
Buick Enclave	V6	3,6	288	270
Buick LaCrosse	4L	2,4	182	172
Buick LaCrosse	V6	3,6	280	259
Buick Lucerne	V6	3,9	227	237
Buick Lucerne	V8	4,6	292	288
Buick Regal	4L	2,4	182	172
Buick Regal	4L	2,0	220	258
Cadillac CTS	V6	3,0	270	223
Cadillac CTS	V6	3,6	304	273
Cadillac CTS	V8	6,2	556	551
Cadillac DTS	V8	4,6	275	295
Cadillac DTS	V8	4,6	292	288
Cadillac Escalade	V8	5,3	320	335
Cadillac Escalade	V8	6,0	332	367
Cadillac Escalade	V8	6,0	332	367
Cadillac Escalade	V8	6,2	403	417
Cadillac SRX	V6	3,0	265	223
Cadillac SRX	V6	2,8	300	295
Cadillac STS	V6	3,6	302	272
Chevrolet Avalanche	V8	5,3	310	335
Chevrolet Avalanche	V8	6,2	395	417
Chevrolet Avalanche	V8	6,2	403	417
Chevrolet Aveo	4L	1,6	108	105
Chevrolet Camaro	V6	3,6	312	278
Chevrolet Camaro	V8	6,2	426	420
Chevrolet Colorado	4L	2,9	185	190
Chevrolet Colorado	5L	3,7	242	242
Chevrolet Colorado	V8	5,3	300	320
Chevrolet Corvette	V8	6,2	430	424
Chevrolet Corvette	V8	7,0	505	470
Chevrolet Corvette	V8	6,2	638	604
Chevrolet Cruze	4L	1,8	138	125
Chevrolet Cruze	4L	1,4	138	148
Chevrolet Equinox	4L	2,4	182	172
Chevrolet Equinox	V6	3,0	264	222
Chevrolet HHR	4L	2,2	155	150
Chevrolet HHR	4L	2,4	172	167
Chevrolet HHR	4L	2,0	260	260
Chevrolet Impala	V6	3,5	207	215
Chevrolet Impala	V6	3,9	230	238
Chevrolet Malibu	4L	2,4	170	158
Chevrolet Malibu	V6	3,6	252	251
Chevrolet Silverado	V6	4,3	195	260
Chevrolet Silverado	V8	4,8	302	305
Chevrolet Silverado	V8	5,3	315	338
Chevrolet Silverado	V8	6,0	332	367
Chevrolet Silverado	V8	6,2	403	417
Chevrolet Suburban	V8	5,3	320	335
Chevrolet Tahoe	V8	5,3	320	335
Chevrolet Tahoe	V8	6,0	332	367
Chevrolet Traverse	V6	3,6	281	266
Chevrolet Traverse	V6	3,6	288	270
Chevrolet Volt	3L	1,4	100	90
Chrysler 300	V6	3,5	250	250
Chrysler 300	V8	5,7	360	389
Chrysler 300	V8	6,1	425	420
Chrysler Sebring	4L	2,4	173	166
Chrysler Sebring	V6	2,7	178	190
Chrysler Sebring	V6	3,5	235	232

	cyl.		ch	lb-pi
Chrysler Town & Country	V6	4,0	251	259
Dodge Avenger	4L	2,4	173	166
Dodge Avenger	V6	3,5	235	232
Dodge Caliber	4L	2,0	158	141
Dodge Challenger	V6	3,5	250	250
Dodge Challenger	V8	5,7	372	401
Dodge Challenger	V8	5,7	376	410
Dodge Challenger	V8	6,1	425	420
Dodge Charger	V6	2,7	178	190
Dodge Charger	V6	3,5	250	250
Dodge Charger	V8	5,7	368	395
Dodge Charger	V8	6,1	425	420
Dodge Grand Caravan	V6	3,3	175	205
Dodge Grand Caravan	V6	4,0	251	259
Dodge Journey	4L	2,4	173	166
Dodge Journey	V6	3,5	235	232
Dodge Nitro	V6	3,7	210	235
Dodge Nitro	V6	4,0	260	265
Dodge Viper	V10	8,4	600	560
Ferrari 599	V12	6,0	620	448
Ferrari 599	V12	6,0	670	457
Ferrari 612 Scaglietti	V12	5,7	532	434
Ferrari California	V8	4,3	460	358
Ferrari F458 Italia	V8	4,5	570	398
Fiat 500	4L	1,4	100	97
Ford Edge	V6	3,5	285	253
Ford Edge	V6	3,7	305	280
Ford Escape	4L	2,5	153	136
Ford Escape	4L	2,5	171	171
Ford Escape	V6	3,0	240	223
Ford Expedition	V8	5,4	310	365
Ford Explorer	4L	2,0	237	250
Ford Explorer	V6	3,5	290	255
Ford F-150	V8	4,6	248	294
Ford F-150	V8	4,6	292	320
Ford F-150	V8	5,4	320	390
Ford F-150	V8	5,4	320	390
Ford Fiesta	4L	1,6	120	112
Ford Flex	V6	3,5	262	248
Ford Flex	V6	3,5	355	350
Ford Focus	4L	2,0	140	136
Ford Fusion	4L	2,5	156	136
Ford Fusion	4L	2,5	175	172
Ford Fusion	V6	3,0	240	223
Ford Fusion	V6	3,5	263	249
Ford Mustang	V6	3,7	305	280
Ford Mustang	V8	5,0	412	390
Ford Mustang	V8	5,4	550	510
Ford Ranger	4L	2,3	143	154
Ford Ranger	V6	4,0	207	238
Ford Taurus	V6	3,5	263	249
Ford Taurus	V6	3,5	365	350
Ford Transit Connect	4L	2,0	136	128
GMC Acadia	V6	3,6	288	270
GMC Canyon	4L	2,9	185	190
GMC Canyon	5L	3,7	242	242
GMC Canyon	V8	5,3	320	320
GMC Sierra	V6	4,3	195	260
GMC Sierra	V8	4,8	302	305
GMC Sierra	V8	5,3	315	338
GMC Sierra	V8	6,0	332	367
GMC Sierra	V8	6,2	403	417

	cyl.		ch	lb-pi
GMC Terrain	4L	2,4	182	172
GMC Terrain	V6	3,0	264	222
Honda Accord	4L	2,4	177	161
Honda Accord	4L	2,4	190	162
Honda Accord	V6	3,5	271	254
Honda Accord Crosstour	V6	3,5	271	254
Honda Civic	4L	1,8	140	128
Honda Civic	4L	2,0	197	139
Honda CR-V	4L	2,4	180	161
Honda CR-Z	4L	1,5	122	128
Honda Element	4L	2,4	166	161
Honda Fit	4L	1,5	117	106
Honda Insight	4L	1,3	88	88
Honda Odyssey	V6	3,5	244	240
Honda Pilot	V6	3,5	250	253
Honda Ridgeline	V6	3,5	250	247
Hyundai Accent	4L	1,6	110	106
Hyundai Elantra	4L	2,0	138	136
Hyundai Equus	V8	4,6	385	333
Hyundai Genesis	V6	3,8	290	264
Hyundai Genesis	V8	4,6	368	333
Hyundai Genesis Coupe	4L	2,0	210	223
Hyundai Genesis Coupe	V6	3,8	306	266
Hyundai Santa Fe	4L	2,4	175	169
Hyundai Santa Fe	V6	3,5	276	248
Hyundai Sonata	4L	2,4	198	184
Hyundai Tucson	4L	2,4	176	168
Hyundai Veracruz	V6	3,8	260	257
Infiniti EX	V6	3,5	297	253
Infiniti FX	V6	3,5	303	262
Infiniti FX	V8	5,0	390	369
Infiniti G	V6	3,7	325	267
Infiniti G	V6	3,7	328	269
Infiniti G	V6	3,7	330	270
Infiniti M	V6	3,7	330	270
Infiniti M	V8	5,6	420	417
Infiniti QX	V8	5,6	400	413
Jaguar XF	V8	4,2	300	310
Jaguar XF	V8	5,0	385	380
Jaguar XF	V8	5,0	510	461
Jaguar XJ	V8	5,0	385	380
Jaguar XJ	V8	5,0	470	424
Jaguar XJ	V8	5,0	510	461
Jaguar XK	V8	5,0	385	380
Jaguar XK	V8	5,0	510	461
Jeep Commander	V6	3,7	210	235
Jeep Commander	V8	5,7	357	389
Jeep Compass	4L	2,0	158	141
Jeep Compass	4L	2,4	172	165
Jeep Grand Cherokee	V6	3,6	290	260
Jeep Grand Cherokee	V8	5,7	360	390
Jeep Liberty	V6	3,7	210	235
Jeep Patriot	4L	2,0	158	141
Jeep Patriot	4L	2,4	172	165
Jeep Wrangler	V6	3,8	202	237
Kia Borrego	V6	3,8	276	267
Kia Borrego	V8	4,6	337	323
Kia Cadenza	V6	3,5	290	248
Kia Forte	4L	2,0	156	144
Kia Forte	4L	2,4	173	168
Kia Rio/Rio5	4L	1,6	110	107
Kia Rondo	4L	2,4	175	169

		cyl.	ch	lb-pi
Kia Rondo	V6	2,7	192	184
Kia Sedona	V6	3,8	244	253
Kia Sorento	4L	2,4	175	169
Kia Sorento	V6	3,5	276	248
Kia Soul	4L	1,6	122	115
Kia Soul	4L	2,0	142	137
Kia Sportage	4L	2,4	176	168
Lamborghini Gallardo	V10	5,2	552	398
Lamborghini Gallardo	V10	5,2	570	398
Lamborghini Murciélago	V12	6,5	640	487
Lamborghini Murciélago	V12	6,5	670	487
Land Rover LR2	6L	3,2	230	234
Land Rover LR4	V8	5,0	375	375
Land Rover Range Rover	V8	5,0	375	375
Land Rover Range Rover	V8	5,0	510	461
Land Rover Range Rover Sport	V8	5,0	375	375
Land Rover Range Rover Sport	V8	5,0	510	461
Lexus ES	V6	3,5	272	254
Lexus GS	V6	3,5	303	274
Lexus GS	V6	3,5	340	267
Lexus GX	V8	4,6	301	329
Lexus HS	4L	2,4	187	138
Lexus IS	V6	2,5	204	185
Lexus IS	V6	3,5	306	277
Lexus IS	V8	5,0	416	371
Lexus LFA	V10	4,8	552	354
Lexus LS	V8	4,6	380	367
Lexus LS	V8	5,0	438	385
Lexus LX	V8	5,7	383	403
Lexus RX	V6	3,5	275	257
Lexus RX	V6	3,5	295	234
Lincoln MKS	V6	3,7	273	270
Lincoln MKS	V6	3,5	355	350
Lincoln MKT	V6	3,7	268	267
Lincoln MKT	V6	3,5	355	350
Lincoln MKX	V6	3,7	305	280
Lincoln MKZ	4L	2,5	156	135
Lincoln MKZ	V6	3,5	236	249
Lincoln Navigator	V8	5,4	300	365
Lotus Elise	4L	1,8	190	133
Lotus Elise	4L	1,8	218	156
Lotus Evora	V6	3,5	276	258
Lotus Exige	4L	1,8	240	170
Lotus Exige	4L	1,8	257	174
Maserati Gran Turismo	V8	4,2	405	339
Maserati Gran Turismo	V8	4,7	440	361
Maserati Quattroporte	V8	4,2	400	339
Maserati Quattroporte	V8	4,7	430	361
Maserati Quattroporte	V8	4,7	440	362
Maybach 57 - 62	V12	5,5	550	664
Maybach 57 - 62	V12	6,0	630	738
Mazda CX-7	4L	2,5	161	161
Mazda CX-7	4L	2,3	244	258
Mazda CX-9	V6	3,7	273	270
Mazda2	4L	1,5	100	98
Mazda3	4L	2,0	148	135
Mazda3	4L	2,5	167	168
Mazda3	4L	2,3	263	280
Mazda5	4L	2,3	153	148
Mazda6	4L	2,5	170	167
Mazda6	V6	3,7	272	269
Mazda MX-5	4L	2,0	158	140
Mazda MX-5	4L	2,0	167	140
Mazda RX-8	Rotatif	1,3	212	159
Mazda RX-8	Rotatif	1,3	232	159
Mazda Tribute	4L	2,5	171	171
Mazda Tribute	V6	3,0	240	223
Mercedes-Benz Classe B	4L	2,0	134	136
Mercedes-Benz Classe B	4L	2,0	193	206
Mercedes-Benz Classe C	V6	2,5	201	181
Mercedes-Benz Classe C	V6	3,0	228	221
Mercedes-Benz Classe C	V6	3,5	268	258
Mercedes-Benz Classe C	V8	6,2	451	443

		cyl.	ch	lb-pi
Mercedes-Benz Classe CL	V8	4,6	429	516
Mercedes-Benz Classe CL	V12	5,5	510	612
Mercedes-Benz Classe CL	V8	5,5	536	590
Mercedes-Benz Classe CL	V12	6,0	603	738
Mercedes-Benz Classe CLS	V8	5,5	382	391
Mercedes-Benz Classe CLS	V8	6,2	507	465
Mercedes-Benz Classe E	V6	3,0	210	400
Mercedes-Benz Classe E	V6	3,5	268	258
Mercedes-Benz Classe E	V8	5,5	382	391
Mercedes-Benz Classe E	V8	6,2	518	465
Mercedes-Benz Classe G	V8	5,5	382	391
Mercedes-Benz Classe G	V8	5,5	500	517
Mercedes-Benz Classe GL	V6	3,0	210	400
Mercedes-Benz Classe GL	V8	4,6	335	339
Mercedes-Benz Classe GL	V8	5,5	382	391
Mercedes-Benz Classe GLK	V6	3,5	268	258
Mercedes-Benz Classe M	V6	3,0	210	400
Mercedes-Benz Classe M	V6	3,5	268	258
Mercedes-Benz Classe M	V8	5,5	382	391
Mercedes-Benz Classe M	V8	6,2	503	465
Mercedes-Benz Classe R	V6	3,0	210	400
Mercedes-Benz Classe R	V6	3,5	268	258
Mercedes-Benz Classe S	V6	3,5	295	284
Mercedes-Benz Classe S	V8	4,7	335	339
Mercedes-Benz Classe S	V8	5,5	382	391
Mercedes-Benz Classe S	V12	5,5	510	612
Mercedes-Benz Classe S	V8	5,5	536	590
Mercedes-Benz Classe S	V12	6,0	603	738
Mercedes-Benz Classe SL	V8	5,5	382	391
Mercedes-Benz Classe SL	V12	5,5	510	612
Mercedes-Benz Classe SL	V8	6,2	518	465
Mercedes-Benz Classe SL	V12	6,0	603	738
Mercedes-Benz Classe SLK	V6	3,0	228	221
Mercedes-Benz Classe SLK	V6	3,5	300	266
Mercedes-Benz Classe SLK	V8	5,5	355	376
Mercedes-Benz SLS	V8	6,3	563	479
MINI Cooper	4L	1,6	118	114
MINI Cooper	4L	1,6	172	192
MINI Cooper	4L	1,6	208	207
MINI Countryman	4L	1,6	122	118
MINI Countryman	4L	1,6	184	177
Mitsubishi Eclipse	4L	2,4	162	162
Mitsubishi Eclipse	V6	3,8	265	262
Mitsubishi Endeavor	V6	3,8	225	255
Mitsubishi Lancer	4L	2,0	152	146
Mitsubishi Lancer	4L	2,4	168	167
Mitsubishi Lancer	4L	2,0	237	253
Mitsubishi Lancer	4L	2,0	291	300
Mitsubishi Outlander	4L	2,4	168	167
Mitsubishi Outlander	V6	3,0	230	215
Nissan Altima	4L	2,5	158	162
Nissan Altima	4L	2,5	175	180
Nissan Altima	V6	3,5	270	258
Nissan Armada	V8	5,6	317	385
Nissan Cube	4L	1,8	122	127
Nissan Frontier	4L	2,5	152	171
Nissan Frontier	V6	4,0	261	281
Nissan GT-R	V6	3,8	485	434
Nissan Juke	4L	1,6	180	170
Nissan Maxima	V6	3,5	290	261
Nissan Murano	V6	3,5	265	248
Nissan Pathfinder	V6	4,0	266	288
Nissan Quest	V6	3,5	235	240
Nissan Rogue	4L	2,5	170	175
Nissan Sentra	4L	2,0	140	147
Nissan Sentra	4L	2,5	177	172
Nissan Sentra	4L	2,5	200	180
Nissan Titan	V8	5,6	317	385
Nissan Versa	4L	1,6	107	111
Nissan Versa	4L	1,8	122	127
Nissan Xterra	V6	4,0	261	281
Nissan Z	V6	3,7	332	270
Porsche 911	H6	3,6	345	288

		cyl.	ch	lb-pi
Porsche 911	H6	3,8	385	310
Porsche 911	H6	3,8	435	317
Porsche 911	H6	3,8	450	317
Porsche 911	H6	3,8	500	650
Porsche 911	H6	3,8	530	700
Porsche 911	H6	3,6	620	700
Porsche Boxster	H6	2,9	255	290
Porsche Boxster	H6	3,4	310	360
Porsche Boxster	H6	3,4	320	370
Porsche Cayenne	V6	3,6	300	295
Porsche Cayenne	V6	3,0	380	427
Porsche Cayenne	V8	4,8	400	369
Porsche Cayenne	V8	4,8	500	516
Porsche Cayman	H6	2,9	265	221
Porsche Cayman	H6	3,4	320	273
Porsche Panamera	V6	3,6	300	400
Porsche Panamera	V8	4,8	400	370
Porsche Panamera	V8	4,8	500	568
RAM Dakota	V6	3,7	210	235
RAM Dakota	V8	4,7	302	329
RAM 1500	V6	3,7	215	235
RAM 1500	V8	4,7	310	330
RAM 1500	V8	5,7	390	407
Rolls-Royce Ghost	V12	6,6	563	575
Rolls-Royce Phantom	V12	6,7	453	531
Saab 9-3	4L	2,0	210	221
Saab 9-3	V6	2,8	280	273
Scion tC	4L	2,4	161	162
Scion xB	4L	2,4	158	162
Scion xD	4L	1,8	128	125
smart Fortwo	3L	1,0	70	68
Subaru Forester	H4	2,5	170	174
Subaru Forester	H4	2,5	224	226
Subaru Impreza	H4	2,5	170	170
Subaru Impreza	H4	2,5	265	244
Subaru Impreza	H4	2,5	305	290
Subaru Legacy	H4	2,5	170	170
Subaru Legacy	H6	3,6	256	247
Subaru Legacy	H4	2,5	265	258
Subaru Tribeca	H6	3,6	256	247
Suzuki Equator	V6	4,0	261	281
Suzuki Grand Vitara	4L	2,4	166	162
Suzuki Grand Vitara	V6	3,2	230	213
Suzuki Kizashi	4L	2,4	180	170
Suzuki Swift+	4L	1,6	108	105
Suzuki SX-4	4L	2,0	150	140
Toyota 4Runner	V6	4,0	270	278
Toyota Avalon	V6	3,5	268	248
Toyota Camry	4L	2,4	147	138
Toyota Camry	4L	2,5	169	167
Toyota Camry	4L	2,5	179	171
Toyota Camry	V6	3,5	268	248
Toyota Corolla	4L	1,8	132	128
Toyota Corolla	4L	2,4	158	162
Toyota FJ Cruiser	V6	4,0	259	270
Toyota Highlander	4L	2,7	187	186
Toyota Highlander	V6	3,5	270	248
Toyota Matrix	4L	1,8	132	128
Toyota Matrix	4L	2,4	158	162
Toyota Prius	4L	1,8	98	105
Toyota RAV4	4L	2,5	179	172
Toyota RAV4	V6	3,5	269	246
Toyota Sequoia	V8	4,6	310	327
Toyota Sequoia	V8	5,7	381	401
Toyota Sienna	4L	2,7	187	186
Toyota Sienna	V6	3,5	266	245
Toyota Tacoma	4L	2,7	159	180
Toyota Tacoma	V6	4,0	236	266
Toyota Tundra	V8	4,6	310	327
Toyota Tundra	V8	5,7	381	401
Toyota Venza	4L	2,7	182	182
Toyota Venza	V6	3,5	268	246
Toyota Yaris	4L	1,5	106	103

		cyl.	ch	lb-pi
Volkswagen Eos	4L	2,0	200	207
Volkswagen Golf	4L	2,0	140	236
Volkswagen Golf	5L	2,5	170	177
Volkswagen GTI	4L	2,0	200	207
Volkswagen Jetta	4L	2,0	115	125
Volkswagen Jetta	4L	2,0	140	236
Volkswagen Jetta	5L	2,5	170	177
Volkswagen Passat	4L	2,0	200	207
Volkswagen Passat	V6	3,6	280	265
Volkswagen Tiguan	4L	2,0	200	207
Volkswagen Touareg	V6	3,0	240	406
Volkswagen Touareg	V6	3,6	280	265
Volkswagen Touareg	V6	3,0	374	428
Volvo C30	5L	2,5	227	236
Volvo C70	5L	2,5	227	174
Volvo S40	5L	2,5	227	236
Volvo S60	6L	3,0	300	325
Volvo S80	6L	3,2	235	236
Volvo V50	5L	2,5	227	236
Volvo XC60	6L	3,2	235	236
Volvo XC60	6L	3,0	281	295
Volvo XC70	6L	3,2	235	236
Volvo XC70	6L	3,0	281	295
Volvo XC90	6L	3,2	235	236
Volvo XC90	V8	4,4	311	325

MOTEURS EN ORDRE CROISSANT

		cyl.	ch	lb-pi
smart Fortwo	3L	1,0	70	68
Honda Insight	4L	1,3	88	88
Toyota Prius	4L	1,8	98	105
Chevrolet Volt	3L	1,4	100	90
Fiat 500	4L	1,4	100	97
Mazda2	4L	1,5	100	98
Toyota Yaris	4L	1,5	106	103
Nissan Versa	4L	1,6	107	111
Chevrolet Aveo	4L	1,6	108	105
Suzuki Swift+	4L	1,6	108	105
Hyundai Accent	4L	1,6	110	106
Kia Rio/Rio5	4L	1,6	110	107
Volkswagen Jetta	4L	2,0	115	125
Honda Fit	4L	1,5	117	106
MINI Cooper	4L	1,6	118	114
Ford Fiesta	4L	1,6	120	112
Kia Soul	4L	1,6	122	115
MINI Countryman	4L	1,6	122	118
Nissan Cube	4L	1,8	122	127
Nissan Versa	4L	1,8	122	127
Honda CR-Z	4L	1,5	122	128
Scion xD	4L	1,8	128	125
Toyota Corolla	4L	1,8	132	128
Toyota Matrix	4L	1,8	132	128
Mercedes-Benz Classe B	4L	2,0	134	136
Ford Transit Connect	4L	2,0	136	128
Chevrolet Cruze	4L	1,8	138	125
Hyundai Elantra	4L	2,0	138	136
Chevrolet Cruze	4L	1,4	138	148
Honda Civic	4L	1,8	140	128
Ford Focus	4L	2,0	140	136
Nissan Sentra	4L	2,0	140	147
Audi A3	4L	2,0	140	236
Volkswagen Golf	4L	2,0	140	236
Volkswagen Jetta	4L	2,0	140	236
Kia Soul	4L	2,0	142	137
Ford Ranger	4L	2,3	143	154
Toyota Camry	4L	2,4	147	138
Mazda3	4L	2,0	148	135
Suzuki SX-4	4L	2,0	150	140
Mitsubishi Lancer	4L	2,0	152	146
Nissan Frontier	4L	2,5	152	171
Ford Escape	4L	2,5	153	136
Mazda5	4L	2,3	153	148
Acura CSX	4L	2,0	155	139
Chevrolet HHR	4L	2,2	155	150

	cyl.		ch	lb-pi
Lincoln MKZ	4L	2,5	156	135
Ford Fusion	4L	2,5	156	136
Kia Forte	4L	2,0	156	144
Mazda MX-5	4L	2,0	158	140
Dodge Caliber	4L	2,0	158	141
Jeep Compass	4L	2,0	158	141
Jeep Patriot	4L	2,0	158	141
Nissan Altima	4L	2,5	158	162
Scion xB	4L	2,4	158	162
Toyota Corolla	4L	2,4	158	162
Toyota Matrix	4L	2,4	158	162
Toyota Tacoma	4L	2,7	159	180
Mazda CX-7	4L	2,5	161	161
Scion tC	4L	2,4	161	162
Mitsubishi Eclipse	4L	2,4	162	162
Honda Element	4L	2,4	166	161
Suzuki Grand Vitara	4L	2,4	166	162
Mazda MX-5	4L	2,0	167	140
Mazda3	4L	2,5	167	168
Mitsubishi Lancer	4L	2,4	168	167
Mitsubishi Outlander	4L	2,4	168	167
Toyota Camry	4L	2,5	169	167
Chevrolet Malibu	4L	2,4	170	158
Mazda6	4L	2,5	170	167
Subaru Impreza	H4	2,5	170	170
Subaru Legacy	H4	2,5	170	170
Subaru Forester	H4	2,5	170	174
Nissan Rogue	4L	2,5	170	175
Volkswagen Golf	5L	2,5	170	177
Volkswagen Jetta	5L	2,5	170	177
Ford Escape	4L	2,5	171	171
Mazda Tribute	4L	2,5	171	171
Jeep Compass	4L	2,4	172	165
Jeep Patriot	4L	2,4	172	165
Chevrolet HHR	4L	2,4	172	167
MINI Cooper	4L	1,6	172	192
Chrysler Sebring	4L	2,4	173	166
Dodge Avenger	4L	2,4	173	166
Dodge Journey	4L	2,4	173	166
Kia Forte	4L	2,4	173	168
Hyundai Santa Fe	4L	2,4	175	169
Kia Rondo	4L	2,4	175	169
Kia Sorento	4L	2,4	175	169
Ford Fusion	4L	2,5	175	172
Nissan Altima	4L	2,5	175	180
Dodge Grand Caravan	V6	3,3	175	205
Hyundai Tucson	4L	2,4	176	168
Kia Sportage	4L	2,4	176	168
Honda Accord	4L	2,4	177	161
Nissan Sentra	4L	2,5	177	172
Chrysler Sebring	V6	2,7	178	190
Dodge Charger	V6	2,7	178	190
Toyota Camry	4L	2,5	179	171
Toyota RAV4	4L	2,5	179	172
Honda CR-V	4L	2,4	180	161
Nissan Juke	4L	1,6	180	170
Suzuki Kizashi	4L	2,4	180	170
Buick LaCrosse	4L	2,4	182	172
Buick Regal	4L	2,4	182	172
Chevrolet Equinox	4L	2,4	182	172
GMC Terrain	4L	2,4	182	172
Toyota Venza	4L	2,7	182	182
MINI Countryman	4L	1,6	184	177
Chevrolet Colorado	4L	2,9	185	190
GMC Canyon	4L	2,9	185	190
Lexus HS	4L	2,4	187	138
Toyota Highlander	4L	2,7	187	186
Toyota Sienna	4L	2,7	187	186
Lotus Elise	4L	1,8	190	133
Honda Accord	4L	2,4	190	162
Kia Rondo	V6	2,7	192	184
Mercedes-Benz Classe B	4L	2,0	193	206
Chevrolet Silverado	V6	4,3	195	260

	cyl.		ch	lb-pi
GMC Sierra	V6	4,3	195	260
Acura CSX	4L	2,0	197	139
Honda Civic	4L	2,0	197	139
Hyundai Sonata	4L	2,4	198	184
BMW Série 3	6L	2,5	200	180
Nissan Sentra	4L	2,5	200	180
Audi A3	4L	2,0	200	207
Volkswagen Eos	4L	2,0	200	207
Volkswagen GTI	4L	2,0	200	207
Volkswagen Passat	4L	2,0	200	207
Volkswagen Tiguan	4L	2,0	200	207
Acura TSX	4L	2,4	201	172
Mercedes-Benz Classe C	V6	2,5	201	181
Jeep Wrangler	V6	3,8	202	237
Lexus IS	V6	2,5	204	185
Chevrolet Impala	V6	3,5	207	215
Ford Ranger	V6	4,0	207	238
MINI Cooper	4L	1,6	208	207
Saab 9-3	4L	2,0	210	221
Hyundai Genesis Coupe	4L	2,0	210	223
Dodge Nitro	V6	3,7	210	235
Jeep Commander	V6	3,7	210	235
Jeep Liberty	V6	3,7	210	235
RAM Dakota	V6	3,7	210	235
Mercedes-Benz Classe E	V6	3,0	210	400
Mercedes-Benz Classe GL	V6	3,0	210	400
Mercedes-Benz Classe M	V6	3,0	210	400
Mercedes-Benz Classe R	V6	3,0	210	400
Audi A5	4L	2,0	211	258
Audi TT	4L	2,0	211	258
Audi Q5	4L	2,0	211	n.d.
Mazda RX-8	Rotatif	1,3	212	159
BMW X3	6L	3,0	215	185
RAM 1500	V6	3,7	215	235
Lotus Elise	4L	1,8	218	156
Buick Regal	4L	2,0	220	258
Subaru Forester	H4	2,5	224	226
Mitsubishi Endeavor	V6	3,8	225	255
Audi Q7	V6	3,0	225	406
Volvo C70	5L	2,5	227	174
Volvo C30	5L	2,5	227	236
Volvo S40	5L	2,5	227	236
Volvo V50	5L	2,5	227	236
Buick Lucerne	V6	3,9	227	237
Mercedes-Benz Classe C	V6	3,0	228	221
Mercedes-Benz Classe SLK	V6	3,0	228	221
BMW Série 1	6L	3,0	230	200
BMW Série 3	6L	3,0	230	200
Suzuki Grand Vitara	V6	3,2	230	213
Mitsubishi Outlander	V6	3,0	230	215
Land Rover LR2	6L	3,2	230	234
Chevrolet Impala	V6	3,9	230	238
Mazda RX-8	Rotatif	1,3	232	159
Chrysler Sebring	V6	3,5	235	232
Dodge Avenger	V6	3,5	235	232
Dodge Journey	V6	3,5	235	232
Volvo S80	6L	3,2	235	236
Volvo XC60	6L	3,2	235	236
Volvo XC70	6L	3,2	235	236
Volvo XC90	6L	3,2	235	236
Nissan Quest	V6	3,5	235	240
Lincoln MKZ	V6	3,5	236	249
Toyota Tacoma	V6	4,0	236	266
Ford Explorer	4L	2,0	237	250
Mitsubishi Lancer	4L	2,0	237	253
Lotus Exige	4L	1,8	240	170
Ford Escape	V6	3,0	240	223
Ford Fusion	V6	3,0	240	223
Mazda Tribute	V6	3,0	240	223
Acura RDX	4L	2,3	240	260
Volkswagen Touareg	V6	3,0	240	406
Chevrolet Colorado	5L	3,7	242	242
GMC Canyon	5L	3,7	242	242

	cyl.		ch	lb-pi
Honda Odyssey	V6	3,5	244	240
Kia Sedona	V6	3,8	244	253
Mazda CX-7	4L	2,3	244	258
Ford F-150	V8	4,6	248	294
Honda Ridgeline	V6	3,5	250	247
Chrysler 300	V6	3,5	250	250
Dodge Challenger	V6	3,5	250	250
Dodge Charger	V6	3,5	250	250
Honda Pilot	V6	3,5	250	253
Chrysler Town & Country	V6	4,0	251	259
Dodge Grand Caravan	V6	4,0	251	259
Chevrolet Malibu	V6	3,6	252	251
BMW Z4	6L	3,0	255	220
Porsche Boxster	H6	2,9	255	290
Subaru Legacy	H6	3,6	256	247
Subaru Tribeca	H6	3,6	256	247
Lotus Exige	4L	1,8	257	174
Toyota FJ Cruiser	V6	4,0	259	270
BMW X3	6L	3,0	260	225
Hyundai Veracruz	V6	3,8	260	257
Chevrolet HHR	4L	2,0	260	260
Dodge Nitro	V6	4,0	260	265
Nissan Frontier	V6	4,0	261	281
Nissan Xterra	V6	4,0	261	281
Suzuki Equator	V6	4,0	261	281
Ford Flex	V6	3,5	262	248
Ford Fusion	V6	3,5	263	249
Ford Taurus	V6	3,5	263	249
Mazda3	4L	2,3	263	280
Chevrolet Equinox	V6	3,0	264	222
GMC Terrain	V6	3,0	264	222
Porsche Cayman	H6	2,9	265	221
Cadillac SRX	V6	3,0	265	223
Audi A5	V6	3,2	265	243
Audi A6	V6	3,2	265	243
Subaru Impreza	H4	2,5	265	244
Nissan Murano	V6	3,5	265	248
Subaru Legacy	H4	2,5	265	258
Mitsubishi Eclipse	V6	3,8	265	262
BMW Série 3	6L	3,0	265	425
BMW X5	6L	3,0	265	425
Toyota Sienna	V6	3,5	266	245
Nissan Pathfinder	V6	4,0	266	288
Toyota Venza	V6	3,5	268	246
Toyota Avalon	V6	3,5	268	248
Toyota Camry	V6	3,5	268	248
Mercedes-Benz Classe C	V6	3,5	268	258
Mercedes-Benz Classe E	V6	3,5	268	258
Mercedes-Benz Classe GLK	V6	3,5	268	258
Mercedes-Benz Classe M	V6	3,5	268	258
Mercedes-Benz Classe R	V6	3,5	268	258
Lincoln MKT	V6	3,7	268	267
Toyota RAV4	V6	3,5	269	246
Cadillac CTS	V6	3,0	270	223
Audi Q5	V6	3,2	270	243
Toyota Highlander	V6	3,5	270	248
Nissan Altima	V6	3,5	270	258
Toyota 4Runner	V6	4,0	270	278
Honda Accord	V6	3,5	271	254
Honda Accord Crosstour	V6	3,5	271	254
Lexus ES	V6	3,5	272	254
Audi TT	4L	2,0	272	258
Audi Q7	V6	3,0	272	266
Mazda6	V6	3,7	272	269
Lincoln MKS	V6	3,7	273	270
Mazda CX-9	V6	3,7	273	270
Lexus RX	V6	3,5	275	257
Cadillac DTS	V8	4,6	275	295
Hyundai Santa Fe	V6	3,5	276	248
Kia Sorento	V6	3,5	276	248
Lotus Evora	V6	3,5	276	258
Kia Borrego	V6	3,8	276	267
Acura TL	V6	3,5	280	254

	cyl.		ch	lb-pi
Acura TSX	V6	3,5	280	254
Buick LaCrosse	V6	3,6	280	259
Volkswagen Passat	V6	3,6	280	265
Volkswagen Touareg	V6	3,6	280	265
Saab 9-3	V6	2,8	280	273
Chevrolet Traverse	V6	3,6	281	266
Volvo XC60	6L	3,0	281	295
Volvo XC70	6L	3,0	281	295
Ford Edge	V6	3,5	285	253
Buick Enclave	V6	3,6	288	270
Chevrolet Traverse	V6	3,6	288	270
GMC Acadia	V6	3,6	288	270
Kia Cadenza	V6	3,5	290	248
Ford Explorer	V6	3,5	290	255
Jeep Grand Cherokee	V6	3,6	290	260
Nissan Maxima	V6	3,5	290	261
Hyundai Genesis	V6	3,8	290	264
Mitsubishi Lancer	4L	2,0	291	300
Buick Lucerne	V8	4,6	292	288
Cadillac DTS	V8	4,6	292	288
Ford F-150	V8	4,6	292	320
Lexus RX	V6	3,5	295	234
Mercedes-Benz Classe S	V6	3,5	295	284
Infiniti EX	V6	3,5	297	253
Mercedes-Benz Classe SLK	V6	3,5	300	266
Acura MDX	V6	3,7	300	270
Acura ZDX	V6	3,7	300	270
Acura RL	V6	3,7	300	271
Cadillac SRX	V6	2,8	300	295
Porsche Cayenne	V6	3,6	300	295
BMW Série 1	6L	3,0	300	300
BMW Série 3	6L	3,0	300	300
BMW X6	6L	3,0	300	300
BMW Z4	6L	3,0	300	300
Audi A6	V6	3,0	300	310
Jaguar XF	V8	4,2	300	310
Chevrolet Colorado	V8	5,3	300	320
Volvo S60	6L	3,0	300	325
Lincoln Navigator	V8	5,4	300	365
Porsche Panamera	V6	3,6	300	400
Lexus GX	V8	4,6	301	329
Cadillac STS	V6	3,6	302	272
Chevrolet Silverado	V8	4,8	302	305
GMC Sierra	V8	4,8	302	305
RAM Dakota	V8	4,7	302	329
Infiniti FX	V6	3,5	303	262
Lexus GS	V6	3,5	303	274
Cadillac CTS	V6	3,6	304	273
Acura TL	V6	3,7	305	273
Ford Edge	V6	3,7	305	280
Ford Mustang	V6	3,7	305	280
Lincoln MKX	V6	3,7	305	280
Subaru Impreza	H4	2,5	305	290
Hyundai Genesis Coupe	V6	3,8	306	266
Lexus IS	V6	3,5	306	277
BMW X5	6L	3,0	306	295
Toyota Sequoia	V8	4,6	310	327
Toyota Tundra	V8	4,6	310	327
RAM 1500	V8	4,7	310	330
Chevrolet Avalanche	V8	5,3	310	335
Porsche Boxster	H6	3,4	310	360
Ford Expedition	V8	5,4	310	365
Volvo XC90	V8	4,4	311	325
Chevrolet Camaro	V6	3,6	312	278
Chevrolet Silverado	V8	5,3	315	338
GMC Sierra	V8	5,3	315	338
Nissan Armada	V8	5,6	317	385
Nissan Titan	V8	5,6	317	385
Porsche Cayman	H6	3,4	320	273
GMC Canyon	V8	5,3	320	320
Cadillac Escalade	V8	5,3	320	335
Chevrolet Suburban	V8	5,3	320	335
Chevrolet Tahoe	V8	5,3	320	335

		cyl.	ch	lb-pi
Porsche Boxster	H6	3,4	320	370
Ford F-150	V8	5,4	320	390
Ford F-150	V8	5,4	320	390
Infiniti G	V6	3,7	325	267
Infiniti G	V6	3,7	328	269
Infiniti G	V6	3,7	330	270
Infiniti M	V6	3,7	330	270
Nissan Z	V6	3,7	332	270
Cadillac Escalade	V8	6,0	332	367
Cadillac Escalade	V8	6,0	332	367
Chevrolet Silverado	V8	6,0	332	367
Chevrolet Tahoe	V8	6,0	332	367
GMC Sierra	V8	6,0	332	367
Audi A4	V6	3,0	333	325
Audi A5	V6	3,0	333	325
Audi Q7	V6	3,0	333	325
Mercedes-Benz Classe GL	V8	4,6	335	339
Mercedes-Benz Classe S	V8	4,7	335	339
Kia Borrego	V8	4,6	337	323
Lexus GS	V6	3,5	340	267
Audi TT	5L	2,5	340	332
Porsche 911	H6	3,6	345	288
Audi A6	V8	4,2	350	325
Ford Flex	V6	3,5	355	350
Lincoln MKS	V6	3,5	355	350
Lincoln MKT	V6	3,5	355	350
Mercedes-Benz Classe SLK	V8	5,5	355	376
Jeep Commander	V8	5,7	357	389
BMW Série 6	V8	4,8	360	360
Chrysler 300	V8	5,7	360	389
Jeep Grand Cherokee	V8	5,7	360	390
Ford Taurus	V6	3,5	365	350
Hyundai Genesis	V8	4,6	368	333
Dodge Charger	V8	5,7	368	395
Audi A8	V8	4,2	372	325
Dodge Challenger	V8	5,7	372	401
Volkswagen Touareg	V6	3,0	374	428
Land Rover LR4	V8	5,0	375	375
Land Rover Range Rover	V8	5,0	375	375
Land Rover Range Rover Sport	V8	5,0	375	375
Dodge Challenger	V8	5,7	376	410
Lexus LS	V8	4,6	380	367
Porsche Cayenne	V6	3,0	380	427
Toyota Sequoia	V8	5,7	381	401
Toyota Tundra	V8	5,7	381	401
Mercedes-Benz Classe CLS	V8	5,5	382	391
Mercedes-Benz Classe E	V8	5,5	382	391
Mercedes-Benz Classe G	V8	5,5	382	391
Mercedes-Benz Classe GL	V8	5,5	382	391
Mercedes-Benz Classe M	V8	5,5	382	391
Mercedes-Benz Classe S	V8	5,5	382	391
Mercedes-Benz Classe SL	V8	5,5	382	391
Lexus LX	V8	5,7	383	403
Porsche 911	H6	3,8	385	310
Hyundai Equus	V8	4,6	385	333
Jaguar XF	V8	5,0	385	380
Jaguar XJ	V8	5,0	385	380
Jaguar XK	V8	5,0	385	380
Infiniti FX	V8	5,0	390	369
RAM 1500	V8	5,7	390	407
Chevrolet Avalanche	V8	6,2	395	417
Maserati Quattroporte	V8	4,2	400	339
Porsche Cayenne	V8	4,8	400	369
Porsche Panamera	V8	4,8	400	370
Infiniti QX	V8	5,6	400	413
BMW Série 7	V8	4,4	400	450
BMW X6	V8	4,4	400	450
Cadillac Escalade	V8	6,2	403	417
Chevrolet Avalanche	V8	6,2	403	417
Chevrolet Silverado	V8	6,2	403	417
GMC Sierra	V8	6,2	403	417
Maserati Gran Turismo	V8	4,2	405	339
BMW X5	V8	4,4	407	442
Ford Mustang	V8	5,0	412	390
BMW Série 3	V8	4,0	414	295
Lexus IS	V8	5,0	416	371
Audi R8	V8	4,2	420	317
Aston Martin Vantage	V8	4,3	420	346
Infiniti M	V8	5,6	420	417
Chrysler 300	V8	6,1	425	420
Dodge Challenger	V8	6,1	425	420
Dodge Charger	V8	6,1	425	420
Chevrolet Camaro	V8	6,2	426	420
Mercedes-Benz Classe CL	V8	4,6	429	516
Maserati Quattroporte	V8	4,7	430	361
Chevrolet Corvette	V8	6,2	430	424
Porsche 911	H6	3,8	435	317
Audi A6	V10	5,2	435	398
Lexus LS	V8	5,0	438	385
Maserati Gran Turismo	V8	4,7	440	361
Maserati Quattroporte	V8	4,7	440	362
Audi A5	V8	4,2	450	317
Porsche 911	H6	3,8	450	317
Mercedes-Benz Classe C	V8	6,2	451	443
Rolls-Royce Phantom	V12	6,7	453	531
BMW Série 7	V8	4,4	455	515
Ferrari California	V8	4,3	460	358
Jaguar XJ	V8	5,0	470	424
Aston Martin DB9	V12	6,0	470	443
Aston Martin Rapide	V12	6,0	470	443
Nissan GT-R	V6	3,8	485	434
BMW Série 6	V10	5,0	500	383
Porsche Cayenne	V8	4,8	500	516
Mercedes-Benz Classe G	V8	5,5	500	517
Porsche Panamera	V8	4,8	500	568
Porsche 911	H6	3,8	500	650
Mercedes-Benz Classe M	V8	6,2	503	465
Chevrolet Corvette	V8	7,0	505	470
Bentley Mulsanne	V8	6,8	505	752
Mercedes-Benz Classe CLS	V8	6,2	507	465
Aston Martin DBS	V12	6,0	510	420
Aston Martin Vantage	V12	6,0	510	420
Jaguar XF	V8	5,0	510	461
Jaguar XJ	V8	5,0	510	461
Jaguar XK	V8	5,0	510	461
Land Rover Range Rover	V8	5,0	510	461
Land Rover Range Rover Sport	V8	5,0	510	461
Mercedes-Benz Classe CL	V12	5,5	510	612
Mercedes-Benz Classe S	V12	5,5	510	612
Mercedes-Benz Classe SL	V12	5,5	510	612
Mercedes-Benz Classe E	V8	6,2	518	465
Mercedes-Benz Classe SL	V8	6,2	518	465
Audi R8	V10	5,2	525	390
Porsche 911	H6	3,8	530	700
Ferrari 612 Scaglietti	V12	5,7	532	434
Mercedes-Benz Classe CL	V8	5,5	536	590
Mercedes-Benz Classe S	V8	5,5	536	590
Ford Mustang	V8	5,4	550	510
Maybach 57 - 62	V12	5,5	550	664
Lexus LFA	V10	4,8	552	354
Lamborghini Gallardo	V10	5,2	552	398
Bentley Continental	W12	6,0	552	479
BMW X5	V8	4,4	555	500
BMW X6	V8	4,4	555	500
Cadillac CTS	V8	6,2	556	551
Mercedes-Benz SLS	V8	6,3	563	479
Rolls-Royce Ghost	V12	6,6	563	575
Ferrari F458 Italia	V8	4,5	570	398
Lamborghini Gallardo	V10	5,2	570	398
Bentley Continental	W12	6,0	600	553
Dodge Viper	V10	8,4	600	560
Mercedes-Benz Classe CL	V12	6,0	603	738
Mercedes-Benz Classe S	V12	6,0	603	738
Mercedes-Benz Classe SL	V12	6,0	603	738
Ferrari 599	V12	6,0	620	448
Porsche 911	H6	3,6	620	700
Bentley Continental	W12	6,0	621	590
Maybach 57 - 62	V12	6,0	630	738
Chevrolet Corvette	V8	6,2	638	604
Lamborghini Murciélago	V12	6,5	640	487
Ferrari 599	V12	6,0	670	457
Lamborghini Murciélago	V12	6,5	670	487
Aston Martin One-77	V12	7,3	700	n.d.

PRIX

Chaque fiche technique du Guide présente les prix de la gamme du véhicule à l'essai. Outre une liste de prix complète ailleurs dans cet ouvrage, voici les prix en ordre croissant. Veuillez noter que cette liste n'est pas exhaustive et que les prix suivis d'un « X » sont des prix 2010.

Ford Ranger XL 2.3L 4X2	11 199$	
Nissan Versa Berline 1.6 S man	12 698$	x
Ford Fiesta berline S	12 999$	
Hyundai Accent 3 portes L man	13 599$	x
Kia Rio EX man	13 695$	
Toyota Yaris Hatchback 3 portes CE man	13 905$	x
Chevrolet Aveo 5 portes LS	13 950$	
Dodge Caliber Canada	13 995$	x
Mazda 2 GX man	13 995$	
Ford Focus Berline S	13 999$	
Ford Ranger XL 4X2	13 999$	
Kia Rio5 EX man	14 095$	
Chevrolet Aveo berline LS	14 150$	
Nissan Versa Hatchback 1.8 S man	14 198$	x
Hyundai Accent Berline L man	14 299$	x
Honda Fit DX man	14 480$	x
smart Fortwo Coupé Pure	14 990$	x
Toyota Yaris Berline man	14 990$	x
Chevrolet Cruze LS	14 995$	
Ford Ranger XL Supercab 4X2	14 999$	
Hyundai Elantra Touring L	14 999$	
Toyota Yaris Hatchback 5 portes LE man	15 195$	x
Nissan Sentra 2.0 man	15 198$	x
Hyundai Accent 3 portes GL man	15 299$	x
Toyota Corolla CE man	15 460$	x
Kia Forte LX man	15 695$	x
Hyundai Accent Berline GL man	15 749$	x
Dodge Caliber SE Plus	15 795$	x
Kia Soul 1.6	15 795$	x
Hyundai Elantra Berline L man	15 849$	x
Volkswagen Jetta 2.0L man Trendline	15 875$	
Kia Rio EX Convenience man	15 895$	
Honda Civic Berline DX	15 990$	x
Mazda 3 berline GX man	15 995$	x
Ford Fiesta berline SE	16 099$	
Honda Civic Coupé DX	16 190$	x
Kia Rio5 EX Convenience man	16 495$	
Chevrolet Aveo 5 portes LT	16 650$	
Toyota Matrix man	16 665$	x
Ford Fiesta hatchback SE	16 799$	
Chevrolet Aveo berline LT	16 850$	
Honda Fit LX man	16 880$	x
Mazda Sport GX man	16 995$	x
Mitsubishi Lancer DE man	16 998$	x
Hyundai Accent 3 portes GL Sport man	16 999$	x
Nissan Cube 1.8 S	17 398$	x
Nissan Versa Hatchback 1.8 SL man	17 398$	x
Hyundai Elantra Touring GL	17 399$	
Dodge Caliber SXT	17 645$	x
Suzuki SX4 5 portes man	17 695$	x
Suzuki SX4 Berline man	17 695$	x
Jeep Patriot Sport	17 795$	x
Kia Forte EX man	17 995$	x
Ford Focus Berline SE	17 999$	
Hyundai Elantra Berline GL man	18 099$	x
Mazda 2 GS man	18 195$	
Nissan Sentra 2.0 S man	18 198$	x
Ford Fiesta berline SEL	18 199$	
smart Fortwo Coupé Passion	18 250$	x
Kia Soul 2.0 2u man	18 295$	x
Kia Forte Koupe 2.0 EX man	18 495$	x
Honda Civic Berline DX-G	18 580$	x
Dodge Journey SE	18 745$	x
Honda Fit Sport man	18 780$	x
Jeep Compass Sport	18 795$	x
Kia Rio5 EX Sport man	18 795$	
Honda Civic Coupé DX-G	18 880$	x
Ford Fiesta hatchback SES	18 999$	
Hyundai Accent Berline GLS	18 999$	x
Volkswagen Jetta 2.0L man Comfortline	19 075$	
Mazda 3 berline GS man	19 395$	x
Chevrolet Cruze LT Turbo	19 495$	
Toyota Yaris Hatchback 5 portes RS man	19 555$	x
Suzuki SX4 Berline Sport man	19 695$	x
Hyundai Elantra Touring GLS	19 799$	
Kia Rondo LX	19 995$	
Ford Escape XLT 2.5L man.	19 999$	
Ford Fusion S I4	19 999$	
Ford Ranger Sport Supercab	19 999$	
Toyota Corolla S man	20 285$	x
Kia Soul 2.0 4u man	20 295$	x
Suzuki SX4 5 portes JX CVT	20 295$	x
Mitsubishi Lancer SE man	20 298$	x
Chevrolet HHR LS	20 395$	

TENIR FERMEMENT VOTRE 24H EN **POSITION 10H10.**

Section Autonet tous les mercredis.

www.24heures.ca

Toyota Corolla LE	20425$	x
Volkswagen Golf 2.5L man Trendline	20475$	
Dodge Caliber HEAT	20495$	x
Mazda 5 GS man	20495$	x
Ford Focus Berline SES	20499$	
Toyota Matrix XR man	20575$	x
Jeep Wrangler Sport	20595$	x
Dodge Journey SE Plus	20745$	x
Honda Civic Berline Sport	20780$	x
Honda Civic Coupé LX	20780$	x
Jeep Patriot North	20795$	x
Mazda 3 Sport GS man	20895$	x
Nissan Cube 1.8 SL	20898$	x
Dodge Grand Caravan SE	20945$	x
Dodge Avenger SE	20995$	x
Jeep Compass Sport (4X4)	20995$	x
Kia Forte SX man	20995$	x
Kia Soul 2.0 4u Retro	20995$	x
Subaru Impreza berline 2.5i	20995$	
Ford Focus Berline SEL	20999$	
Hyundai Elantra Berline GLS	20999$	x
Hyundai Tucson L FWD man	20999$	
Volkswagen Jetta 2.5L man Comfortline	21175$	
smart Fortwo Cabriolet Passion	21250$	x
Kia Soul 2.0 4u Burner	21295$	x
Toyota Tacoma Access Cab 4X2 man	21355$	x
Kia Forte Koupe 2.4 SX man	21495$	x
Hyundai Elantra Berline GL Sport man	21499$	x
Suzuki SX4 5 portes JX (TI) man	21595$	x
Jeep Compass North Edition	21795$	x
Nissan Sentra SE-R	21798$	x
Kia Soul 2.0 4u SX man	21895$	x
Subaru Impreza 5 portes 2.5i	21895$	
smart Fortwo Coupé Brabus	21900$	x
Dodge Caliber Uptown	21995$	x
Kia Magentis LX	21995$	x
Kia Sportage LX man	21995$	
Subaru Impreza berline 2.5i Commodité	21995$	
Chevrolet HHR LT	22040$	
Hyundai Elantra Touring GLS Sport	22049$	
Toyota Corolla XRS man	22550$	x
Hyundai Sonata GL man	22649$	
Honda Civic Berline EXL	22680$	x
Dodge Avenger SXT	22795$	x
Kia Rondo EX	22795$	
Mini Cooper Classique	22800$	x
Volkswagen Golf 2.5L man Comfortline	22875$	
Subaru Impreza 5 portes 2.5i Commodité	22895$	
Volkswagen Golf Familiale 2.5L man Trendline	22975$	
Honda Civic Coupé EXL	22980$	x
Mazda 3 berline GT man	22995$	x
Ford Mustang Coupé V6 Value	22999$	
Hyundai Tucson GL FWD man	22999$	
Nissan Cube 1.8 Krom	23098$	x
Nissan Sentra 2.0 SL	23098$	x
Mazda 6 GS-I4 man	23195$	x
Nissan Rogue S	23198$	x
Nissan Sentra SE-R Spec V	23198$	x
Ford Fusion SE I4	23199$	
Dodge Journey SXT	23295$	x
Volkswagen Jetta 2.5L man Sportline	23300$	
Mazda Tribute GX man	23450$	x
Honda CR-Z	23490$	
Mitsubishi Lancer GTS man	23598$	x
Toyota Matrix (TI)	23695$	x
Jeep Patriot Limited	23795$	x
Nissan Altima Berline 2.5 S man	23798$	x
Hyundai Elantra Berline Limited	23799$	x
Chevrolet Colorado LS à cabine classique (2RM)	23875$	
GMC Canyon SL à cabine classique (2RM)	23875$	
Volkswagen Jetta 2.0 TDI man Comfortline	23875$	
Kia Rondo EX V6	23895$	
Honda Insight LX	23900$	x
Volkswagen Golf 2.5L man Sportline	23900$	
Volkswagen Jetta 2.5L man Highline	23980$	
Chevrolet Malibu LS	23995$	
Chrysler Sebring LX	23995$	x
Jeep Compass North Edition (4X4)	23995$	x
Kia Sorento LX man	23995$	
Mazda 3 Sport GT man	23995$	x
Subaru Legacy berline 2.5i man	23995$	
Volkswagen Golf Familiale 2.5L man Comfortline	24075$	
Mitsubishi Lancer Sportback GTS man	24098$	x
Nissan Frontier King Cab XE 4X2 man	24098$	x
Volkswagen New Beetle 2.5L Comfortline man	24175$	x
Jeep Compass Limited	24195$	x
Ford Ranger Sport Supercab 4X4	24199$	
Kia Magentis LX V6	24295$	x
Mazda 5 GT man	24295$	x
Hyundai Genesis Coupe 2.0T man	24495$	x
Mitsubishi Eclipse GS man	24498$	
Toyota RAV4	24595$	x
Ford F150 XL Cabine régulière 4X2 126 po	24599$	x
Subaru Impreza berline 2.5i Sport	24695$	
Suzuki SX4 5 portes JLX (TI) CT	24695$	x
Chevrolet Cruze LTZ Turbo	24780$	
Honda Accord LX	24790$	x
Mini Cooper	24900$	x
smart Fortwo Cabriolet Brabus	24900$	x
Chevrolet Colorado LT à cabine classique (2RM)	24915$	
GMC Canyon SLE à cabine classique (2RM)	24915$	
Jeep Wrangler Islander	24990$	x
Kia Rondo EX Premium	25095$	
Volkswagen Golf 2.0L man Comfortline	25275$	
Dodge Avenger R/T	25295$	x
Toyota Camry LE	25310$	
Toyota Tundra Cab régulière 4X2 4,6 litres	25310$	x
Mitsubishi Outlander ES (2RM)	25498$	x
Subaru Impreza 5 portes 2.5i Sport	25595$	
Jeep Wrangler Mountain	25690$	x
Dodge Charger SE	25745$	x
Nissan Rogue SL	25798$	x
Honda Civic Berline SI	25880$	x
Honda Civic Coupé SI	25880$	x
Chevrolet Colorado LS à cabine allongée (2RM)	25945$	
GMC Canyon SLE à cabine allongée (2RM)	25945$	
Chevrolet Equinox LS	25995$	
Dodge Challenger SE	25995$	x
Jeep Wrangler Unlimited Sport	25995$	x
Subaru Forester 2.5X man	25995$	x
Toyota Tacoma Access Cab 4X4 man	25995$	x
Nissan Rogue S (TI)	25998$	x
Hyundai Santa Fe 2.4 GL FWD man	25999$	x
Chevrolet Malibu LT	26135$	
Ford Fusion SEL I4	26199$	
Hyundai Sonata GLS	26249$	
Chevrolet caisse régulière (2RM)	26260$	
Toyota Matrix XRS man	26275$	x
Honda CR-V LX	26290$	x
Dodge Grand Caravan SXT	26295$	x
Hyundai Tucson GL AWD	26299$	
Mazda Tribute GX V6	26345$	x
Jeep Compass Limited (4X4)	26395$	x
Volkswagen Golf 2.5L man Highline	26475$	
RAM 1500 ST Cabine régulière 4X2	26495$	x
Mini Cooper Clubman	26500$	x
Volkswagen Jetta 2.0 TDI man Highline	26655$	
Kia Sportage LX AWD	26695$	
Subaru Impreza berline 2.5i Limited	26695$	
Ford Ranger XLT Supercab 4X4	26699$	
Ford Transit Connect Utilitaire XLT	26799$	
Hyundai Tucson GLS	26799$	
Volkswagen Golf Familiale 2.0 TDI man Comfortline	26875$	
Honda Element LX	26990$	x
Jeep Wrangler Unlimited Islander	26990$	x
Chevrolet Camaro LS	26995$	
Chrysler Sebring Touring	26995$	x
Kia Sportage EX	26995$	
Ford Mustang Coupé V6	26999$	
Chevrolet Colorado LT à cabine allongée (2RM)	27040$	
Subaru Legacy berline 2.5i PZEV	27095$	
Kia Rondo EX V6	27195$	
Ford Escape XLT 3.0L	27199$	
Toyota RAV4 (4RM)	27230$	x
Chevrolet Impala LS	27235$	
Nissan Altima Coupé 2.5 S man	27348$	x
Dodge Journey R/T	27395$	x
GMC Terrain SLE-1	27465$	
Acura CSX Technologie	27490$	x
Hyundai Genesis Coupe 2.0T Premium man	27495$	x
Jeep Wrangler Sahara	27495$	x
Honda Insight EX	27500$	x
Dodge Charger SXT	27595$	x
Subaru Impreza 5 portes 2.5i Limited	27595$	
Chevrolet Equinox LS (TI)	27605$	
Chevrolet Colorado LS à cabine classique (4RM)	27680$	
GMC Canyon SLE à cabine classique (4RM)	27680$	
Jeep Wrangler Unlimited Mountain	27690$	x
Dodge Challenger SXT	27695$	x
Chevrolet Equinox 1LT	27725$	
Toyota Camry SE	27755$	
Volkswagen Passat Berline 2.0T Trendline man	27775$	x
Honda Accord Coupé EX	27790$	x
RAM Dakota Cabine allongée ST 4X2	27795$	x
Nissan Rogue SL (TI)	27798$	x
Toyota Prius	27800$	x
Toyota Matrix XRS auto	27825$	x
Volkswagen Tiguan 2.0T Trendline man	27875$	
Chevrolet Malibu LT Platinum	27895$	
Mazda Tribute GS V6	27900$	x
Toyota Sienna LE 7 places	27900$	
Kia Sedona LX	27995$	
Mazda CX-7 GX FWD	27995$	x
Subaru Legacy berline 2.5i Sport man	27995$	
Suzuki Grand Vitara JX	27995$	x
Mitsubishi Outlander ES (4RM)	27998$	x
Ford Edge SE	27999$	
Ford Escape XLT 2.5L (4RM)	27999$	
Ford Taurus SE	27999$	
Nissan Frontier King Cab SE 4X2	28048$	x
Chevrolet Camaro 1LT	28065$	
Volkswagen Routan Trendline	28075$	x
Subaru Forester 2.5 PZEV	28095$	x
Chevrolet Impala LT	28215$	
Honda CR-V LX (4RM)	28290$	x
Chrysler Sebring Limited	28295$	x
Nissan Altima Berline 3.5 S	28298$	x
Toyota RAV4 Sport	28345$	x
Toyota Tacoma Access Cab V6 4X4 man	28380$	x
Honda Accord EX	28490$	x
Dodge Nitro SXT 4X4	28495$	x
Kia Sorento LX AWD	28495$	
Ford Transit Connect Tourisme XLT	28499$	
Chevrolet Colorado LT à cabine classique (4RM)	28610$	
Mazda 6 GT-I4 man	28695$	x
Subaru Forester 2.5X Sport man	28695$	x
Ford F150 XLT Cabine régulière 4X2 126 po	28699$	x
Volkswagen Golf 2.0L man Highline	28775$	
Toyota Tundra Cab régulière 4X4 4,6 litres	28795$	x
Hyundai Tucson GLS AWD	28799$	
Volkswagen GTI 2.0T 3 portes man	28875$	
Toyota Sienna V6 7 places	28900$	
Toyota Tundra Cab régulière 4X2 5,7 litres	28975$	x
Mazda MX-5 GX man	28995$	x
RAM Dakota Cabine allongée SXT 4X2	28995$	x
Subaru Outback 2.5i man	28995$	
Volvo S40 2.4i man	28995$	x
Hyundai Santa Fe 3.5 GL V6 FWD	28999$	x
Hyundai Sonata Limited	28999$	
Toyota Camry LE V6	29020$	
Kia Sorento LX V6	29095$	
Volkswagen New Beetle Cabriolet 2.5L Comfortline man	29175$	x
Ford Fusion SEL V6	29199$	
Volkswagen Passat Familiale 2.0T Trendline man	29275$	x
Toyota Venza 4L	29310$	x
Chevrolet Equinox 1LT (TI)	29335$	
Kia Sportage EX AWD	29395$	
RAM 1500 SLT Cabine régulière 4X2	29395$	x
Honda CR-V EX	29490$	x
Jeep Wrangler Unlimited Sahara	29495$	x
Kia Magentis SX	29495$	x
Suzuki Grand Vitara JLX	29495$	x
Mitsubishi Outlander LS (4RM)	29498$	x
Ford Escape XLT 3.0L (4RM)	29599$	
Chevrolet Colorado LS à cabine allongée (4RM)	29750$	
Jeep Liberty Sport	29795$	x
Kia Sorento EX	29795$	
GMC Terrain SLE-2	29815$	
Toyota RAV4 V6 (4RM)	29845$	x
Volkswagen GTI 2.0T 5 portes man	29875$	
Toyota Tundra Cab régulière 4X4 5,7 litres	29895$	x
Mercedes-Benz B200	29900$	x
Mini Cooper S	29900$	x
Mini Cooper Cabriolet	29950$	x
Acura CSX Type S	29990$	x
Suzuki Kizashi SX AWD	29995$	
Ford Flex SE	29999$	
Nissan Frontier King Cab SE 4X4 man	30048$	x
Honda Accord Coupé EX-L	30090$	x
Toyota RAV4 V6 Sport	30100$	x
Toyota RAV4 Limited	30185$	x
Mazda 6 GS-V6	30195$	x
GMC caisse standard (2RM)	30225$	
Jeep Wrangler Rubicon	30495$	x
Suzuki Grand Vitara JLX-L	30495$	x
Volvo V50 2.4i man	30495$	x
Mitsubishi Eclipse Spyder GS man	30498$	
Toyota RAV4 Sport (4RM)	30540$	x
Chevrolet Impala LTZ	30565$	
Chrysler Sebring Cabriolet LX	30665$	x
Chevrolet Colorado LT à cabine allongée (4RM)	30735$	
GMC Canyon SLE à cabine allongée (4RM)	30735$	
Hyundai Genesis Coupe 2.0 GT	30745$	x
Toyota Venza 4L (TI)	30760$	x
Volkswagen Golf Familiale 2.0 TDI man Highline	30775$	
Honda Accord EX-L	30790$	x
Kia Magentis SX V6	30795$	x
RAM 1500 ST Cabine double 4X2	30795$	x

Toyota Venza V6	30 800 $	x
Subaru Outback 2.5i PZEV	30 895 $	
Kia Sorento LX V6 AWD	30 995 $	
Volvo C30 T5 man	30 995 $	
Hyundai Santa Fe 3.5 GL V6 AWD	30 999 $	x
Volkswagen Passat Berline 2.0T Comfortline man	31 075 $	x
Honda Accord V6 EX	31 190 $	x
Ford Fusion SEL V6 (TI)	31 199 $	
Toyota Camry XLE	31 235 $	
Volkswagen Tiguan 2.0T Comfortline man	31 275 $	
Volkswagen Tiguan 2.0T Trendline 4Motion	31 275 $	
Hyundai Santa Fe 3.5 GL Sport V6 FWD	31 299 $	x
Toyota Camry Hybride	31 310 $	
RAM Dakota Cabine allongée ST 4X4	31 395 $	x
Ford Mustang Cabriolet V6	31 399 $	
GMC Terrain SLT-1	31 440 $	
Chevrolet Colorado LT à cabine multiplace (2RM)	31 490 $	
GMC Canyon SLE à cabine multiplace (2RM)	31 490 $	
Honda CR-V EX (4RM)	31 490 $	x
RAM Dakota Crew cab SXT 4X2	31 495 $	x
Mini Cooper S Clubman	31 500 $	x
Buick LaCrosse CX	31 645 $	
Honda Element SC	31 690 $	x
Honda Odyssey DX	31 690 $	x
Jeep Liberty Rocky Mountain	31 795 $	x
Subaru Outback 2.5i Sport man	31 795 $	
Toyota Tacoma Double Cab V6 4X4	31 845 $	x
Nissan Frontier Cabine double SE 4X2	31 848 $	x
Subaru Legacy berline 3.6R	31 895 $	
Nissan Altima Berline 3.5 SR	31 898 $	x
Toyota FJ Cruiser V6 man	31 900 $	x
Buick Regal CXL	31 990 $	
Subaru Legacy berline 2.5i Limited	31 995 $	
Toyota Tundra Cab double 4X2 4,6 litres	32 040 $	x
Honda Element EX (4RM)	32 090 $	x
Suzuki Grand Vitara V6 JLX	32 195 $	x
Hyundai Tucson Limited	32 249 $	
Toyota Venza V6 (TI)	32 250 $	x
Mazda CX-7 GS (4RM)	32 295 $	x
Toyota RAV4 V6 Sport (4RM)	32 295 $	x
Audi A3 Sportback 2.0T man	32 300 $	
Toyota RAV4 Limited (4RM)	32 385 $	x
Mercedes-Benz B200 Turbo	32 400 $	x
Toyota RAV4 V6 Limited	32 440 $	x
Jeep Wrangler Unlimited Rubicon	32 495 $	x
Subaru Impreza berline WRX	32 495 $	x
Ford Taurus SEL	32 499 $	
Toyota Sienna V6 LE 8 places	32 500 $	
Chevrolet Camaro 2LT	32 505 $	
Volkswagen Passat Familiale 2.0T Comfortline man	32 575 $	x
RAM Dakota Cabine allongée SXT 4X4	32 595 $	x
Chevrolet Malibu LTZ	32 750 $	
Jeep Liberty Renegade	32 795 $	x
Subaru Forester 2.5X Limited	32 795 $	x
Kia Sportage EX Luxe	32 895 $	
Acura TSX man	32 990 $	x
Chrysler 300 Touring	32 995 $	x
Hyundai Genesis Coupe 3.8 man	32 995 $	x
Mazda Speed3	32 995 $	x
Nissan Frontier King Cab PRO-4X 4X4	32 998 $	x
Suzuki Grand Vitara V6 JLX-L	33 195 $	x
Mitsubishi Lancer Ralliart	33 198 $	x
Toyota Highlander 4L FWD	33 250 $	x
Mitsubishi Eclipse GT-P man	33 298 $	
Hyundai Santa Fe 3.5 GL Sport V6 AWD	33 299 $	x
Volkswagen Passat CC 2.0T Sportline man	33 375 $	
Subaru Impreza 5 portes WRX	33 395 $	x
Nissan Altima Berline Hybrid 2.5 S	33 398 $	x
Nissan Titan King Cab XE 4X2	33 448 $	x
Honda CR-V EX-L	33 490 $	x
Mazda MX-5 GS man	33 495 $	x
Ford Escape Limited 2.5L (4RM)	33 549 $	
Chevrolet Equinox LTZ	33 650 $	
Kia Sorento EX V6 AWD	33 695 $	
RAM 1500 SLT Cabine double 4X2	33 695 $	x
Mitsubishi Lancer Sportback Ralliart	33 698 $	x
Nissan Xterra S man	33 698 $	x
Jeep Liberty Limited	33 795 $	x
Nissan Frontier Cabine double SE 4X4	33 848 $	x
Buick Lucerne CX	33 870 $	
Ford Edge SEL	33 999 $	
RAM Dakota Crew cab SLT 4X2	34 095 $	x
Kia Sedona EX	34 195 $	
Ford Fusion Hybride	34 199 $	
Toyota Camry SE V6	34 255 $	
Volkswagen Routan Comfortline	34 375 $	x
Honda Accord V6 EX-L	34 390 $	x
GMC Terrain SLT-2	34 400 $	
Lexus IS 250 RWD man	34 400 $	x
Mitsubishi Outlander XLS (4RM)	34 498 $	x
Nissan Frontier Cabine double PRO-4X 4X4	34 548 $	x
Toyota RAV4 V6 Limited (4RM)	34 640 $	x
GMC caisse longue (4RM)	34 675 $	
Subaru Legacy berline 3.6R Limited	34 695 $	
Nissan Altima Coupé 3.5 SR man	34 698 $	x
Buick LaCrosse CXL	34 795 $	
Honda Pilot LX (2RM)	34 820 $	
Volkswagen Tiguan 2.0T Comfortline 4Motion	34 875 $	
Honda Accord Coupé V6 EX-L	34 890 $	x
BMW Série 3 Berline 323i	34 900 $	
Honda Accord Crosstour EX-L	34 900 $	x
Honda Ridgeline DX	34 990 $	x
Mazda Tribute GT V6 (TI)	34 995 $	x
Suzuki Equator JX V6	34 995 $	x
Ford Taurus SEL (TI)	34 999 $	
Ford Escape Limited 3.0L (4RM)	35 149 $	
RAM Dakota Crew cab SXT 4X4	35 195 $	x
Chevrolet Equinox LTZ (TI)	35 260 $	
Subaru Forester 2.5XT Limited	35 295 $	x
Ford Fusion Sport V6 (TI)	35 299 $	
Audi A3 Sportback 2.0 TDI DSG	35 300 $	
Toyota Sienna V6 LE AWD 7 places	35 350 $	
Dodge Challenger R/T	35 395 $	x
Chrysler Sebring Cabriolet Touring	35 465 $	x
Subaru Impreza berline WRX Limited	35 495 $	x
Ford F150 XL SuperCab 4X4 145 po	35 499 $	x
Chevrolet caisse longue (4RM)	35 695 $	
Subaru Outback 3.6R	35 695 $	
Ford Explorer Sport Trac XLT 4.0L 4X4	35 699 $	x
Chevrolet Traverse LS	35 715 $	
Subaru Outback 2.5i Limited	35 795 $	
Hyundai Santa Fe 3.5 Limited V6 AWD	35 799 $	x
BMW Série 1 Coupé 128i	35 800 $	
Mercedes-Benz C250	35 800 $	x
Volvo S40 2.4i Premium man	35 995 $	x
Mitsubishi Eclipse Spyder GT-P man	35 998 $	
Ford Edge SEL (TI)	35 999 $	
Ford Flex SEL	35 999 $	
Toyota Tundra Cab double 4X2 5,7 litres	36 015 $	x
Toyota Tundra Cab double SR5 4X4 4,6 litres	36 105 $	x
Nissan Xterra Off-Road man	36 198 $	x
Acura TSX Premium man	36 290 $	x
Dodge Charger R/T	36 345 $	x
Mini Cooper S Cabriolet	36 350 $	x
Subaru Impreza 5 portes WRX Limited	36 395 $	x
Toyota Camry XLE V6	36 410 $	
Chevrolet Colorado LT à cabine multiplace (4RM)	36 490 $	
GMC Canyon SLE à cabine multiplace (4RM)	36 490 $	
Hyundai Genesis Coupe 3.8 GT man	36 495 $	x
Mini Cooper John Cooper Works	36 600 $	x
Toyota Sienna V6 SE 8 places	36 600 $	
Buick Lucerne CXL	36 610 $	
Honda Ridgeline VP	36 690 $	x
Mazda 6 GT-V6	36 695 $	x
Volkswagen Passat Berline 2.0T Highline man	36 775 $	x
Toyota 4Runner SR5 V6	36 800 $	x
Audi A3 Sportback 2.0T quattro DSG	36 900 $	x
Honda Accord Crosstour EX-L AWD	36 900 $	x
Volkswagen Eos 2.0T Comfortline man	36 975 $	
Chrysler 300 Limited	36 995 $	x
Mitsubishi Endeavor SE (TI)	36 998 $	x
Hyundai Veracruz GL	36 999 $	x
Nissan Titan King Cab SE 4X2	37 048 $	x
Chevrolet Camaro 1SS	37 065 $	
Ford Explorer Sport Trac XLT 4.6L 4X4	37 199 $	x
Chrysler 300 Touring (TI)	37 295 $	x
Volvo V50 2.4i Premium man	37 495 $	x
Nissan Xterra SE	37 498 $	x
Ford Explorer XLT V6 4X4	37 499 $	x
Nissan Pathfinder S	37 548 $	x
Toyota Tundra CrewMax SR5 4X2 5,7 litres	37 630 $	x
Volkswagen Tiguan 2.0T Highline 4Motion	37 775 $	
Honda Odyssey SE	37 790 $	x
RAM Dakota Crew cab SLT 4X4	37 795 $	x
Ford Edge Limited	37 799 $	
Audi A4 Berline 2.0T FWD man	37 800 $	
Honda Pilot LX (4RM)	37 820 $	
Chrysler Town & Country Touring	37 845 $	x
Toyota Highlander V6 (4WD)	37 870 $	x
GMC Acadia SLE	37 945 $	
Jeep Grand Cherokee Laredo	37 995 $	
Mazda CX-9 GS	37 995 $	x
Ford Flex SEL (TI)	37 999 $	
Volkswagen Passat Familiale 2.0T Highline man	38 275 $	x
Nissan Murano S (TI)	38 298 $	x
Chevrolet Traverse LT	38 375 $	
Ford Escape Hybride	38 399 $	
Lincoln MKZ	38 400 $	
Mini Cooper John Cooper Works Clubman	38 400 $	x
Subaru Outback 3.6R Limited	38 495 $	
Ford Mustang GT Coupé	38 499 $	
Subaru Legacy berline 2.5GT	38 595 $	
Infiniti G37	38 690 $	x
Toyota Sienna V6 XLE 7 places	38 700 $	
Chevrolet Traverse LS (TI)	38 715 $	
Ford Explorer XLT V6 Sport (TI)	38 799 $	x
Buick LaCrosse CXL (TI)	38 870 $	
Kia Borrego V6 LX	38 895 $	
Mazda CX-7 GT (4RM)	38 990 $	x
Ford Explorer XLT V8 4X4	38 999 $	x
Hyundai Genesis 3.8	38 999 $	
Volkswagen Passat CC 2.0T Highline man	39 275 $	
Acura TSX Technologie man	39 290 $	x
Ford F150 XLT SuperCrew 4X4 145 po	39 299 $	x
Kia Sorento EX V6 Luxe AWD	39 395 $	
Nissan Titan Cabine double XE 4X4	39 448 $	x
Nissan Maxima 3.5 SV	39 450 $	x
Mercedes-Benz C250 4MATIC	39 500 $	x
Audi A4 Berline 2.0T quattro man	39 700 $	x
Acura TSX V-6	39 790 $	x
Ford Edge Limited (TI)	39 799 $	
BMW X3 2.8i xDrive	39 900 $	x
Lexus HS 250h Premium	39 900 $	x
Acura RDX	39 990 $	x
Acura TL	39 990 $	x
Kia Sedona EX Luxe	39 995 $	
Mazda CX-9 GS (TI)	39 995 $	x
Mazda MX-5 GT man	39 995 $	x
Subaru WRX STI	39 995 $	x
Volvo C30 T5 R-design man	39 995 $	
Volvo XC60 3.2 (TA)	39 995 $	x
Nissan Murano SL (TI)	39 998 $	x
Chevrolet Volt	40 000 $	Environ
Toyota Tundra Cab double SR5 4X4 5,7 litres	40 080 $	x
Ford Explorer XLT V8 Sport (TI)	40 299 $	x
Nissan Titan King Cab SE 4X4	40 448 $	x
Cadillac CTS 3.0L	40 455 $	
Volvo S40 2.4i R-Design man	40 495 $	x
Nissan 370Z Coupé Touring M6	40 498 $	x
Lexus IS 250 AWD	40 550 $	x
Volkswagen Routan Highline	40 575 $	x
Honda Pilot EX (4RM)	40 720 $	
Ford Escape Hybrid (4RM)	40 799 $	
GMC Acadia SLE (TI)	40 945 $	
Subaru Tribeca	40 995 $	x
Ford Taurus Limited (TI)	40 999 $	
Hyundai Veracruz GLS	40 999 $	x
Nissan Frontier Cabine double LE 4X4	41 098 $	x
BMW Série 3 Berline 328i	41 100 $	
Toyota Avalon XLS	41 100 $	
Ford Flex Limited	41 199 $	
Audi Q5 2.0T quattro	41 200 $	
BMW Série 1 Cabriolet 128i	41 200 $	
Mercedes-Benz C300	41 200 $	x
Infiniti EX35	41 250 $	x
Chrysler 300 Limited (TI)	41 295 $	x
Kia Borrego V8 LX	41 295 $	
Chevrolet Traverse LT (TI)	41 375 $	
Honda Odyssey EX-L	41 390 $	x
Honda Ridgeline EX-L	41 490 $	x
Toyota Tundra CrewMax SR5 4X4 5,7 litres	41 745 $	x
Cadillac SRX	41 780 $	
Buick LaCrosse CXS	41 870 $	
Chevrolet Camaro 2SS	41 905 $	
Nissan Pathfinder SE	41 948 $	x
Lexus ES 350	41 950 $	x
Mazda RX-8 R3	41 995 $	x
Volvo V50 2.4i R-Design man	41 995 $	x
Mitsubishi Lancer Evolution GSR	41 998 $	x
Lincoln MKZ (TI)	42 200 $	
Ford Explorer Sport Trac Limited 4.6L 4X4	42 299 $	x
Chevrolet Avalanche LS (2RM)	42 310 $	
Nissan Titan King Cab PRO-4X 4X4	42 448 $	x
Volvo V70 3.2	42 495 $	x
Mini Cooper John Cooper Works Cabriolet	42 500 $	x
Infiniti G37x	42 550 $	x
Acura TSX V-6 Technologie	42 790 $	x
Audi A4 Avant 2.0T quattro	42 800 $	
Toyota Highlander V6 Sport (4WD)	42 810 $	x
Ford Mustang GT Cabriolet	42 899 $	
Mercedes-Benz GLK350	42 900 $	x
Mercedes-Benz Sprinter 2500	42 900 $	x
Acura RDX Technologie	42 990 $	x
Volvo S40 T5 AWD man	42 995 $	x
Hyundai Genesis 3.8 Premium	42 999 $	
BMW Série 1 Coupé 135i	43 000 $	
Honda Pilot EX-L (4RM)	43 020 $	
Toyota Highlander Hybrid	43 025 $	x
Nissan Titan Cabine double SE 4X4	43 148 $	x
Dodge Charger SRT8	43 195 $	x
Ford Explorer Sport Trac Adrenalin (TI)	43 199 $	x
Ford Flex Limited (TI)	43 199 $	
Ford Escape Hybrid Limited	43 399 $	
Acura TL Technologie	43 490 $	x
Jeep Commander Sport	43 495 $	x
Kia Borrego V6 EX	43 495 $	
Ford Edge Sport (TI)	43 499 $	
Audi Q5 3.2 quattro	43 500 $	x
Buick Enclave CX	43 520 $	
Volkswagen Eos 2.0T Highline man	43 775 $	
Mazda RX-8 GT man	43 795 $	x
Chevrolet Avalanche LT (2RM)	43 835 $	
Chrysler Town & Country Limited	43 845 $	x
Ford Explorer Eddie Bauer V6	43 899 $	x
Volvo XC70 3.2 (TI)	43 995 $	x
Chrysler Sebring Cabriolet Limited	44 070 $	x
Ford F150 Lariat SuperCrew 4X2 157 po	44 099 $	x

Audi A5 Coupé 2.0T quattro man	44 100$	x
BMW Série 3 Berline 328i xDrive	44 100$	
Cadillac CTS Familiale sport 3.0L	44 130$	
Ford F150 FX4 SuperCrew 4X4 145 po	44 299$	x
BMW Série 3 Coupé 328i	44 300$	
Cadillac CTS 3.0L AWD	44 480$	
Volvo V50 T5 AWD man	44 495$	x
Volvo XC60 3.2 (TI)	44 495$	x
Honda Pilot EX-L RES (4RM)	44 620$	
Mercedes-Benz C300 4MATIC	44 900$	x
Land Rover LR2	44 950$	
Acura TL SH-AWD	44 990$	x
Cadillac SRX AWD	45 080$	
Nissan Titan Cabine double PRO-4X 4X4	45 148$	x
RAM 1500 Laramie Cabine double 4X4	45 195$	x
Lexus HS 250h Premium Luxe	45 300$	x
Volkswagen Touareg 3.6L Comfortline	45 300$	x
Ford Explorer Eddie Bauer V8	45 399$	x
Volvo S60 T6 AWD	45 450$	
Chevrolet Avalanche LS (4RM)	45 555$	
Infiniti G37 Sport	45 640$	x
BMW Série 3 Touring 328i xDrive	45 700$	
Ford Escape Hybrid Limited (4RM)	45 799$	
BMW X3 3.0i xDrive	45 900$	x
Lexus IS 350	45 900$	x
Subaru WRX STI Sport-Tech	45 995$	x
Kia Borrego V8 EX	46 095$	
Nissan Titan King Cab LE 4X4	46 148$	x
GMC Acadia SLT	46 200$	
Infiniti G37 Coupé	46 300$	x
Volkswagen Passat CC 3.6 Highline 4Motion	46 375$	
Subaru Tribeca Limited	46 495$	x
Hyundai Genesis 3.8 Technologie	46 499$	
Lincoln MKX (TI)	46 500$	
Toyota Highlander V6 Limited (4WD)	46 510$	x
Buick Enclave CXL	46 520$	
Ford Flex Limited (TI) EcoBoost	46 599$	
Volvo S40 T5 AWD R-Design man	46 695$	x
Chrysler 300C	46 745$	x
Cadillac CTS Familiale sport 3.6L AWD	46 755$	
BMW Série 3 Berline 325i Coupe	46 800$	
Chevrolet caisse régulière (4RM)	46 800$	
GMC caisse longue (4RM)	46 800$	
Lexus RX 350	46 900$	x
Dodge Challenger SRT8	46 995$	x
Jeep Grand Cherokee Limited	46 995$	
Volvo S80 3.2	46 995$	x
Nissan 370Z Roadster Touring M6	46 998$	x
Ford Expedition XLT	46 999$	
Chevrolet Avalanche LT (4RM)	47 080$	
Hyundai Veracruz Limited	47 299$	x
Nissan Pathfinder LE	47 348$	x
Lincoln MKS	47 400$	
Cadillac CTS Coupe	47 450$	
Mazda CX-9 GT (TI)	47 450$	x
Chevrolet Traverse LTZ	47 540$	
Infiniti G37x Sport	47 640$	x
Nissan Murano LE (TI)	47 948$	x
Ford Taurus SHO (TI)	48 199$	
Mercedes-Benz C350	48 200$	x
Toyota Tundra Cab double Limited 4X4 5,7 litres	48 275$	x
Honda Pilot Touring	48 420$	
Acura TL SH-AWD Technologie	48 490$	x
Buick Enclave CX (TI)	48 490$	
Volvo V70 3.2 Premium	48 495$	x
BMW Série 1 Cabriolet 135i	48 500$	
Audi Q5 3.2 quattro Premium	48 600$	x
Cadillac CTS 3.6L	48 785$	
Infiniti G37 Coupé Sport	48 800$	x
Infiniti G37x Coupé	48 800$	x
Mercedes-Benz Sprinter 3500	48 800$	x
Toyota Sequoia SR5 V8 4.6l	48 820$	x
Toyota Sienna V6 Limited AWD 7 places	49 100$	
Subaru Tribeca Premier	49 195$	x
GMC Acadia SLT (TI)	49 200$	
Volkswagen Touareg 3.0L TDI Comfortline	49 300$	x
Audi TT Coupé 2.0T quattro	49 350$	x
Chevrolet Tahoe LS	49 365$	
GMC Yukon SLE (2RM)	49 365$	
Ford Flex Titanium (TI)	49 599$	
Lincoln MKS (TI)	49 600$	
Honda Odyssey Touring	49 690$	x
Volvo V50 T5 AWD R-Design man	49 695$	x
Ford Explorer Limited V8	49 799$	x
Nissan Titan Cabine double LE 4X4	49 848$	x
BMW Série 3 Berline 335d	49 900$	
Lincoln MKT (TI)	49 950$	
Jeep Grand Cherokee Overland	49 995$	
Volvo XC60 T6 (TI)	49 995$	x
Volvo XC70 3.2 (TI) Premium	49 995$	x
Hyundai Genesis 4.6 Technologie	49 999$	
Cadillac CTS Coupe 3.6 AWD	50 080$	
Chrysler 300C (TI)	50 295$	x
Mercedes-Benz C350 4MATIC	50 400$	x
Chevrolet Traverse LTZ (TI)	50 540$	
Volkswagen Routan Execline	50 575$	x
Cadillac CTS Familiale sport 3.6L	50 760$	
Acura TL A-Spec	51 290$	x
BMW Série 3 Berline 335i	51 400$	
Cadillac CTS 3.6L AWD	51 410$	
Buick Enclave CXL (TI)	51 490$	
Chevrolet caisse longue (4RM) Hybride	51 655$	
Mitsubishi Lancer Evolution MR	51 798$	x
Acura MDX	51 990$	x
Volvo XC90 3.2	51 995$	x
Chevrolet Suburban 1500 LS	52 015$	
GMC Yukon XL SLE (2RM)	52 015$	
Toyota Tundra CrewMax Platinum 4X4 5,7 litres	52 070$	x
BMW Série 3 Berline 335i xDrive	52 100$	
Lexus IS 250C man	52 100$	x
Volkswagen Passat Familiale 3.6 Highline 4Motion	52 100$	x
InfinitiFX37	52 300$	x
Audi TT Roadster 2.0T quattro	52 350$	x
Infiniti M37	52 400$	
Volvo V70 3.2 R-Design	52 495$	x
Ford F150 Lariat King Ranch SuperCrew 4X4 157 po	52 499$	x
Audi S4 Berline 3.0T quattro man	52 500$	
Lexus GS 350 RWD	52 500$	x
Audi A6 Berline 3.2 FWD	52 900$	x
Lincoln MKS EcoBoost	53 000$	
Audi A5 Coupé 3.2 quattro	53 350$	x
Lincoln MKT EcoBoost (TI)	53 350$	
BMW Série 3 Coupé 335i	53 400$	
Cadillac CTS Familiale sport 3.6L AWD	53 795$	
Chevrolet Tahoe LS (4RM)	53 825$	
GMC Yukon SLE (4RM)	53 825$	
Audi Q7 3.0T quattro	53 900$	
BMW Série 5 Berline 528i	53 900$	
BMW Série 3 Coupé 335i xDrive	54 100$	
BMW Z4 Roadster 3.0i	54 300$	
Volkswagen Touareg 3.6L Highline	54 300$	x
Chevrolet Tahoe LT	54 370$	
GMC Yukon SLT (2RM)	54 370$	
Volvo C70 T5	54 495$	
Lexus GS 350 AWD	54 500$	x
Jeep Commander Limited	54 695$	x
Mercedes-Benz R350	54 700$	x
Chrysler 300C SRT8	54 845$	x
Infiniti M37x	54 900$	
Toyota Highlander Hybrid Limited	55 075$	x
Buick Lucerne Super	55 150$	
Nissan Armada Platinum	55 398$	x
Chevrolet Suburban 1500 LS (4RM)	55 465$	
GMC Yukon XL SLE (4RM)	55 465$	
Acura ZDX	55 990$	x
Volvo XC70 T6 (TI)	55 995$	x
Mercedes-Benz R350 BlueTEC	56 200$	x
Audi A5 Cabriolet 2.0T quattro	56 300$	x
Cadillac DTS	56 540$	
Cadillac SRX Performance	56 590$	
GMC caisse courte (4RM)	56 605$	
Ford F150 Lariat Platinum SuperCrew 4X4 157 po	56 799$	x
Acura MDX Technologie	57 290$	x
BMW Série 3 Cabriolet 328i	57 300$	
Mercedes-Benz ML350	57 400$	x
Chevrolet Suburban 1500 LT	57 515$	
GMC Yukon XL SLT (2RM)	57 515$	
Audi Q7 3.0 TDI quattro	57 700$	x
Toyota Sequoia Limited V8		
TTS Coupé 2.0T quattro	57 900$	
Porsche Boxster	58 000$	
BMW Série 3 Coupé 335is	58 100$	
Porsche Cayenne V6	58 200$	
Infiniti G37 Cabriolet M6	58 300$	x
Volkswagen Touareg 3.0L TDI Highline	58 300$	x
Chevrolet Avalanche LTZ (4RM)	58 320$	
Ford Expedition Limited	58 499$	
Mercedes-Benz E350 Coupe	58 600$	
Chevrolet Tahoe LT (4RM)	58 825$	
GMC Yukon SLT (4RM)	58 825$	
Mercedes-Benz ML350 BlueTEC	58 900$	x
Volvo XC90 3.2 Luxe	58 995$	x
Ford Shelby GT500 Coupe	58 999$	
Lexus RX 450h	59 500$	x
Acura ZDX Technologie	59 590$	x
Mercedes-Benz SLK300	59 900$	
BMW X5 3.0i xDrive	59 990$	
Land Rover LR4 V8	59 990$	
Volvo S80 T6 (TI)	59 995$	x
Lexus IS 350C	60 400$	x
Lotus Elise	60 750$	x
Chevrolet Suburban 1500 LT (4RM)	60 965$	
GMC Yukon XL SLT (4RM)	60 965$	
Ford Expedition Max Limited	60 999$	
Cadillac STS V6	61 135$	
Infiniti G37 Cabriolet Premium	61 600$	x
Acura MDX Elite	61 990$	x
Volvo XC90 3.2 R-Design	61 995$	x
Audi TTS Roadster 2.0T quattro	62 200$	
BMW Série 5 Berline 535i	62 300$	
Cadillac SRX Premium Turbo AWD	62 775$	
BMW X5 3.5d xDrive	62 800$	
Jaguar XF	62 800$	
Porsche Cayman	62 800$	
Mercedes-Benz E350 Berline 4MATIC	62 900$	
Audi A6 Berline 3.0T quattro	63 300$	x
Infiniti M37 Sport	63 400$	
Mercedes-Benz C63 AMG	63 500$	x
Ford Shelby GT500 Convertible	63 699$	
Acura RL	63 900$	x
BMW Z4 Roadster 3.5i	63 900$	
Infiniti FX50	64 050$	x
BMW X6 3.5i xDrive	65 700$	
Audi S5 Coupé 4.2 quattro man	65 900$	x
Toyota Sequoia Platinum V8 5.7l	65 975$	x
Infiniti M56 Premium	66 200$	
Mercedes-Benz SLK350	66 500$	
Audi A6 Avant 3.0T quattro	66 700$	x
Mercedes-Benz E350 Familiale 4MATIC	66 900$	
Lexus GS 460 RWD	67 100$	x
Chevrolet Corvette Coupé	67 135$	
Mercedes-Benz E350 Cabriolet	67 900$	
Lexus IS-F	68 000$	x
Mercedes-Benz E550 Coupe	68 200$	
Audi S5 Cabriolet 3.0T quattro	68 300$	x
Jaguar XF Premium	68 300$	
Lexus GX 470 Premium	68 500$	x
Chevrolet Tahoe Hybride bimode	68 625$	
GMC Yukon SLT Hybride bimode (2RM)	68 625$	
Infiniti M56x	68 700$	
BMW Serie 3 Cabriolet 335i	68 900$	
Mercedes-Benz GL350 BlueTEC	69 000$	x
Chevrolet Tahoe LTZ (4RM)	69 175$	
Acura RL Elite	69 500$	x
Mercedes-Benz ML550	69 700$	x
BMW M3 Berline	69 900$	
Lotus Elise SC	69 995$	x
Volvo S80 V8 (TI)	69 995$	x
Volvo XC90 V8	69 995$	x
Porsche Boxster S	70 600$	
Cadillac CTS-V Coupe	71 250$	
BMW M3 Coupé	71 300$	
Chevrolet Tahoe Hybride bimode (4RM)	71 610$	
GMC Yukon SLT Hybride bimode (4RM)	71 610$	
Lexus GS 450h	71 900$	x
Chevrolet Suburban 1500 LTZ (4RM)	72 275$	
Cadillac CTS-V	72 565$	
GMC Yukon Denali	72 610$	
Porsche Boxster Spyder	72 900$	
Infiniti QX56	73 000$	
Lincoln Navigator	73 100$	
Land Rover Range Rover Sport HSE	73 200$	
Mercedes-Benz E550 Berline 4MATIC	73 200$	
BMW Série 5 Berline 550i	73 300$	
Infiniti M56 Sport	73 400$	
BMW Serie 3 Cabriolet 335is	74 300$	
BMW X5 5.0i xDrive	74 300$	
Cadillac DTS Platinum	74 680$	
Chevrolet Corvette Coupé Grand Sport	74 960$	
Porsche Cayman S	75 000$	
Audi A6 Berline 4.2 quattro	75 900$	x
Porsche Cayenne S	76 000$	
Lincoln Navigator L	76 100$	
GMC Yukon XL Denali (TI)	76 295$	
Chevrolet Corvette Cabriolet	77 040$	
Lexus GX 470 Ultra Premium	77 500$	x
Mercedes-Benz E550 Cabriolet	77 500$	
BMW Z4 Roadster 3.5is	77 900$	
Cadillac Escalade EXT	79 645$	
Mercedes-Benz GL450	79 900$	x
GMC Yukon Denali Hybride bimode (4RM)	80 300$	
Lotus Exige S 240	80 500$	x
Porsche Cayenne S Hybrid	80 800$	
BMW X6 5.0i xDrive	81 000$	
BMW M3 Cabriolet	81 900$	
Lexus LS 460	82 900$	x
Chevrolet Corvette Cabriolet Grand Sport	83 740$	
Cadillac Escalade	84 645$	
Mercedes-Benz SLK55 AMG	84 800$	x
Jaguar XF R	85 300$	
Lotus Evora	85 880$	x
Jaguar XJ	88 000$	
Lexus LS 460 (TI)	88 000$	x
Porsche Panamera	88 000$	
Cadillac Escalade ESV	88 345$	
Mercedes-Benz GL550	88 600$	x
Land Rover Range Rover Sport Supercharged	88 980$	
Lexus LX 570	89 750$	x
Mercedes-Benz CLS550	91 200$	
Lotus Exige S 260	91 795$	x
Porsche Panamera 4	92 800$	
Porsche 911 Carrera Coupe	94 100$	
Land Rover Range Rover HSE	94 290$	
Cadillac Escalade Hybride	94 790$	
Audi A8 4.2 quattro	95 000$	x
BMW Série 6 Coupé 650i	95 500$	x
Jaguar XJL	95 500$	
Chevrolet Corvette Z06	95 705$	
Jaguar XK Coupé	96 500$	
Mercedes-Benz ML63 AMG	97 500$	x
BMW X5 M	97 900$	

Modèle	Prix	
Dodge Viper SRT10 Roadster	98 895$	x
Audi S6 5.2 quattro	99 500$	x
Nissan GT-R GR6	99 500$	
Dodge Viper SRT10 Coupe	99 895$	x
BMW X6 ActiveHybrid	99 900$	
BMW X6 M	99 900$	
Audi A8L 4.2 quattro	100 000$	x
Porsche 911 Carrera 4 Coupe	101 400$	
Lexus LS 460 L (TI)	103 150$	x
Jaguar XK Cabriolet	103 200$	
Jaguar XJ Supercharged	104 000$	
BMW Série 6 Cabriolet 650i	105 500$	x
Mercedes-Benz S400 Hybrid	105 900$	x
BMW M5 Berline	106 900$	x
Mercedes-Benz E63 AMG	106 900$	
Jaguar XJL Supercharged	107 000$	
Jaguar XK R Coupé	107 000$	
Porsche 911 Carrera Cabriolet	107 300$	
Mercedes-Benz S450 4MATIC	108 000$	x
BMW Série 7 750i xDrive	108 600$	
Porsche 911 Carrera S Coupe	109 300$	
Porsche 911 Targa 4	111 100$	
Land Rover Range Rover Supercharged	112 280$	
Jaguar XK R Cabriolet	114 000$	
Mercedes-Benz G550	114 400$	x
Porsche 911 Carrera 4 Cabriolet	114 700$	
Porsche Panamera S	115 100$	
Jaguar XK R Coupé 175 Limited Edition	115 500$	
BMW Série 7 750Li xDrive	116 600$	
Porsche 911 Carrera 4S Coupe	116 800$	
Maserati GranTurismo	118 500$	
Lexus LS 600h L	119 950$	x
Porsche Panamera 4S	120 300$	
BMW M6 Coupé	121 300$	x
Porsche 911 Carrera S Cabriolet	122 300$	
Maserati GranTurismo S	122 500$	
Mercedes-Benz S550 4MATIC	123 500$	x
Porsche Cayenne Turbo	123 900$	
Tesla Roadster	125 000$	
Maserati Quattroporte	125 150$	
Mercedes-Benz SL550	126 000$	
Porsche 911 Targa 4S	126 400$	
Mercedes-Benz CLS63 AMG	126 700$	
Maserati Quattroporte S	126 750$	
Jaguar XJ Supersport	128 000$	
Chevrolet Corvette ZR1	128 600$	
Porsche 911 Carrera 4S Cabriolet	129 900$	
Mercedes-Benz CL550	130 500$	x
Jaguar XJL Supersport	131 000$	
BMW M6 Cabriolet	131 300$	x
BMW Série 7 ActiveHybrid	132 300$	
Maserati Quattroporte Sport GT S	134 700$	
Maserati GranTurismo Cabriolet	135 800$	
Aston Martin V8 Vantage	137 495$	
BMW M6 Coupé Competition	139 400$	x
Porsche 911 GT3	142 400$	
Audi R8 4.2 quattro man	144 000$	
Tesla Roadster Sport	147 300$	
Aston Martin V8 Vantage N420	150 000$	
Mercedes-Benz S63 AMG	150 000$	x
Mercedes-Benz SL63 AMG	152 600$	
Aston Martin V8 Vantage Roadster	152 795$	
Mercedes-Benz G55 AMG	154 950$	x
Porsche Panamera Turbo	155 000$	
Mercedes-Benz CL63 AMG	159 000$	x
Aston Martin V8 Vantage Roadster N420	165 300$	
Porsche 911 GT3 RS	166 300$	
Porsche 911 Turbo Coupe	167 900$	
Audi R8 5.2 quattro man	173 000$	x
Mercedes-Benz SL600	176 300$	
Porsche 911 Turbo Cabriolet	181 500$	
Aston Martin V12 Vantage	183 000$	
Mercedes-Benz S600	187 000$	x
Mercedes-Benz CL600	189 500$	x
Aston Martin V12 Vantage Carbon	197 000$	
Lamborghini Gallardo LP560-4	198 000$	
Mercedes-Benz SLS AMG	198 000$	
Bentley Continental Flying Spur	199 300$	
Porsche 911 Turbo S Coupe	200 000$	
Bentley Continental GT	201 100$	x
Aston Martin DB9 Coupe	206 795$	
Porsche 911 Turbo S Cabriolet	213 200$	
Aston Martin Rapide	215 000$	
Lamborghini Gallardo LP550-2 Valentino	219 800$	
Lamborghini Gallardo LP560-4 Spyder	221 000$	
Aston Martin DB9 Volante	224 465$	
Bentley Continental GTC	226 200$	
Bentley Continental Flying Spur Speed	227 300$	
Bentley Continental GT Speed	228 500$	x
Mercedes-Benz S65 AMG	234 000$	x
Mercedes-Benz SL65 AMG	240 100$	
Mercedes-Benz CL65 AMG	241 000$	x
Bentley Continental GTC Speed	259 700$	
Ferrari California	262 000$	x
Ferrari F458 Italia Coupe	290 000$	
Bentley Continental Supersports Coupe	293 700$	
Aston Martin DBS Coupe	306 495$	
Bentley Continental Supersports Cabriolet	308 400$	
Aston Martin DBS Volante	323 195$	
Bentley Mulsanne	325 000$	
Lamborghini Murciélago LP640 Coupe	354 000$	
Lexus LF-A	375 000$ U.S.	
Rolls Royce Phantom	380 000$	x
Lamborghini Murcielago LP640 Roadster	382 400$	
Maybach 57S	387 500$	x
Ferrari 612 Scaglietti F1	390 570$	x
Maybach 62	399 000$	x
Rolls Royce Phantom Coupé	408 000$	x
Ferrari 599 GTB Fiorano F1	425 600$	x
Maybach 62S	438 000$	x
Rolls Royce Phantom Drophead Coupé	443 000$	x
Lamborghini Murciélago LP670-4	450 000$	
Lamborghini Murcielago LP650-4	525 000$	
Maybach Landaulet	1 380 000$	x
Bugatti Veyron 16.4	1 400 000$	
Bugatti Veyron Grand Sport	1 700 000$	
Bugatti Veyron Super Sport	2 400 000$	

NOTE : les prix identifiés avec un x sont les prix des modèles 2010.
Il ne s'agit pas d'une liste exhaustive.
Pour plus de renseignements, veuillez contacter le concessionnaire.

VOIE AVANT, VOIE ARRIÈRE

Voie avant, voie arrière? En fait, il s'agit de la distance, sur un même essieu, entre les pneus qu'ils soient avant ou arrière. Plus la voie est large, meilleure est la tenue de route. Il arrive souvent que les voies avant et arrière diffèrent. Une voie avant plus large qu'à l'arrière rend le véhicule plus facile à manier en virages. Par contre, une voie arrière élargie par rapport à l'avant amène une plus grande stabilité du train arrière.

	av. (mm)	ar. (mm)
Acura CSX	1499	1528
Acura MDX	1720	1715
Acura RDX	1572	1590
Acura RL	1576	1585
Acura TL	1605	1620
Acura TSX	1581	1582
Acura ZDX	1720	1719
Aston Martin DB9	1570	1560
Aston Martin Vantage	1570	1560
Audi A3	1534	1507
Audi S4	1564	1551
Audi A5	1590	1577
Audi A6	1612	1618
Audi A8	1625	1600
Audi Q5	1617	1613
Audi Q7	1651	1676
Audi R8	1638	1595
Audi TT	1572	1558
Bentley Continental Supersports	1623	1657
Bentley Mulsanne	1615	1652
BMW Série 1	1474	1507
BMW Série 3	1506	1535
BMW M3	1540	1539
BMW Série 6	1558	1596
BMW M6	1567	1584
BMW Série 7	1620	1633
BMW X3	1524	1542

	av. (mm)	ar. (mm)
BMW X5M	1660	1672
BMW X5	1644	1650
BMW X6	1644	1706
BMW Z4	1511	1559
Buick Enclave	1709	1704
Buick LaCrosse	1567	1576
Buick Lucerne	1591	1577
Buick Regal	1585	1587
Cadillac CTS	1575	1577
Cadillac CTS-V	1575	1577
Cadillac DTS	1588	1567
Cadillac Escalade	1732	1702
Cadillac SRX	1626	1620
Cadillac STS	1570	1582
Chevrolet Avalanche	1732	1702
Chevrolet Aveo	1450	1430
Chevrolet Camaro	1618	1628
Chevrolet Colorado	1461	1461
Chevrolet Corvette ZR1	1613	1588
Chevrolet Cruze	1544	1558
Chevrolet Equinox	1587	1570
Chevrolet HHR	1491	1491
Chevrolet Impala	1585	1562
Chevrolet Malibu	1514	1524
Chevrolet Silverado	1730	1702
Chevrolet Suburban	1732	1702
Chevrolet Tahoe	1732	1702

	av. (mm)	ar. (mm)
Chevrolet Traverse	1721	1711
Chrysler 300	1600	1602
Chrysler Sebring	1570	1570
Chrysler Town & Country	1664	1646
Dodge Avenger	1570	1570
Dodge Caliber	1520	1520
Dodge Challenger	1626	1603
Dodge Charger	1600	1603
Dodge Grand Caravan	1664	1646
Dodge Journey	1570	1582
Dodge Nitro	1549	1549
Dodge Viper	1565	1547
Ferrari 599	1701	1618
Ferrari 612 Scaglietti	1688	1641
Ferrari California	1630	1605
Ferrari F458 Italia	1672	1606
Ford Edge	1661	1651
Ford Escape	1552	1534
Ford Expedition	1702	1702
Ford Explorer	1702	1702
Ford Fiesta	1466	1466
Ford Flex	1651	1651
Ford Focus	1473	1473
Ford Fusion	1549	1549
Ford Mustang	1575	1575
Ford Mustang Shelby	1572	1588
Ford Ranger	1473	1455

	av. (mm)	ar. (mm)
Ford Taurus	1658	1664
Ford Transit Connect	1498	1549
GMC Acadia	1704	1704
GMC Canyon	1514	1519
GMC Sierra	1730	1702
GMC Terrain	1598	1578
Honda Accord	1580	1580
Honda Accord Crosstour	1648	1648
Honda Civic	1499	1528
Honda CR-V	1565	1565
Honda CR-Z	1515	1500
Honda Element	1577	1582
Honda Fit	1492	1475
Honda Insight	1492	1475
Honda Odyssey	1694	1697
Honda Pilot	1720	1715
Honda Ridgeline	1705	1700
Hyundai Accent	1470	1460
Hyundai Elantra	1546	1544
Hyundai Equus	1620	1628
Hyundai Genesis	1620	1636
Hyundai Genesis Coupe	1599	1615
Hyundai Santa Fe	1615	1620
Hyundai Sonata	1591	1591
Hyundai Tucson	1591	1592
Hyundai Veracruz	1670	1670
Infiniti EX	1593	1641

	av. (mm)	ar. (mm)
Infiniti FX	1635	1640
Infiniti G	1519	1529
Jaguar XFR	1559	1571
Jaguar XJ	1626	1604
Jaguar XKR	1504	1499
Jeep Commander	1590	1590
Jeep Compass	1519	1519
Jeep Grand Cherokee	1623	1627
Jeep Liberty	1549	1549
Jeep Patriot	1519	1519
Jeep Wrangler	1572	1572
Kia Borrego	1615	1625
Kia Forte Koup	1542	1546
Kia Magentis	1563	1552
Kia Rio/Rio5	1470	1460
Kia Rondo	1575	1570
Kia Sedona	1685	1685
Kia Sorento	1618	1621
Kia Soul	1570	1575
Kia Sportage	1613	1615
Lamborghini Murciélago	1635	1695
Land Rover LR2	1601	1614
Land Rover LR4	1605	1613
Land Rover Range Rover	1629	1625
Land Rover Range Rover Sport	1605	1612
Lexus ES	1575	1565
Lexus GS	1535	1540
Lexus GX	1585	1585
Lexus HS	1535	1530
Lexus IS	1535	1535
Lexus IS-F	1560	1515
Lexus LFA	1580	1570
Lexus LS	1610	1615
Lexus LX	1640	1635
Lexus RX	1630	1620
Lincoln MKS	1626	1651

	av. (mm)	ar. (mm)
Lincoln MKT	1651	1651
Lincoln MKX	1661	1656
Lincoln MKZ	1557	1549
Lincoln Navigator	1702	1707
Maserati Quattroporte	1582	1592
Maybach 57 - 62	1675	1695
Mazda CX-7	1617	1612
Mazda CX-9	1654	1644
Mazda Mazda3	1535	1525
Mazda Mazda5	1530	1515
Mazda Mazda6	1585	1585
Mazda MX-5	1490	1495
Mazda RX-8	1500	1505
Mazda Tribute	1542	1530
Mercedes-Benz Classe B	1552	1547
Mercedes-Benz Classe C	1541	1544
Mercedes-Benz Classe CL	1601	1607
Mercedes-Benz Classe CLS	1587	1570
Mercedes-Benz Classe E	1580	1599
Mercedes-Benz Classe G	1501	1501
Mercedes-Benz Classe GL	1645	1648
Mercedes-Benz Classe GLK	1567	1588
Mercedes-Benz Classe M	1619	1621
Mercedes-Benz Classe R	1643	1636
Mercedes-Benz Classe S	1600	1606
Mercedes-Benz Classe SL	1559	1537
Mercedes-Benz Classe SLK	1530	1549
Mercedes-Benz SLS	1682	1653
MINI Cooper	1459	1467
Mitsubishi Eclipse	1570	1570
Mitsubishi Endeavor	1600	1600
Mitsubishi Lancer	1530	1530
Mitsubishi Outlander	1540	1540
Nissan Altima	1549	1544
Nissan Armada	1715	1715
Nissan Cube	1475	1480

	av. (mm)	ar. (mm)
Nissan Frontier	1570	1570
Nissan GT-R	1590	1600
Nissan Maxima	1585	1585
Nissan Murano	1609	1610
Nissan Pathfinder	1570	1570
Nissan Quest	1709	1709
Nissan Rogue	1540	1550
Nissan Sentra	1519	1544
Nissan Titan	1715	1715
Nissan Versa	1480	1485
Nissan Xterra	1570	1570
Nissan Z	1550	1595
Porsche 911 GT2 RS	1515	1550
Porsche 911	1488	1548
Porsche Boxster	1486	1528
Porsche Cayenne	1643	1657
Porsche Cayman	1490	1534
Porsche Panamera	1656	1646
RAM Dakota	1595	1598
RAM RAM 1500	1730	1715
Rolls-Royce Ghost	1622	1660
Rolls-Royce Phantom	1687	1671
Saab 9-3	1524	1506
Scion tC	1506	1506
Scion xB	1525	1520
Scion xD	1485	1490
smart Fortwo	1283	1385
Subaru Forester	1530	1530
Subaru Impreza	1495	1495
Subaru Impreza WRX STi	1530	1540
Subaru Legacy	1565	1570
Subaru Tribeca	1580	1578
Suzuki Equator	1570	1570
Suzuki Grand Vitara	1540	1560
Suzuki Kizashi	1565	1565
Suzuki Swift+	1450	1410

	av. (mm)	ar. (mm)
Suzuki SX-4	1500	1495
Tesla Roadster	1448	1499
Toyota 4Runner	1605	1605
Toyota Avalon	1580	1565
Toyota Camry	1575	1565
Toyota Corolla	1518	1522
Toyota FJ Cruiser	1605	1605
Toyota Highlander	1625	1630
Toyota Matrix	1519	1522
Toyota Prius	1525	1520
Toyota RAV4	1560	1560
Toyota Sequoia	1725	1755
Toyota Sienna	1720	1720
Toyota Tacoma	1600	1610
Toyota Tundra	1725	1725
Toyota Venza	1640	1635
Toyota Yaris	1470	1460
Volkswagen Eos	1545	1553
Volkswagen Golf	1541	1514
Volkswagen GTI	1533	1514
Volkswagen Jetta	1541	1538
Volkswagen Passat	1553	1557
Volkswagen Tiguan	1570	1571
Volkswagen Touareg	1650	1670
Volvo C30	1535	1531
Volvo C70	1550	1560
Volvo S40	1535	1531
Volvo S60	1583	1580
Volvo S80	1578	1575
Volvo V50	1548	1544
Volvo XC60	1632	1586
Volvo XC70	1604	1570
Volvo XC90	1634	1624

DISTRIBUTION DU POIDS

La distribution du poids joue énormément sur le comportement d'une voiture. Il y a certes d'autres facteurs tout aussi importants mais, en général, plus le poids est placé à l'avant, plus la voiture aura tendance à sous-virer (l'avant veut continuer tout droit dans les courbes). À l'inverse, un poids trop imposant placé à l'arrière entraînera un survirage (l'arrière a tendance à vouloir passer devant dans une courbe). Donc, en théorie, lorsqu'une voiture possède une distribution parfaite, sa tenue de route est optimale. Et non, vous n'avez pas mal lu. Le Lincoln Navigator affiche un équilibre parfait. Entre la théorie et la pratique, vous savez…

	% av.	% ar.
Acura CSX	60	40
Acura MDX	56	44
Acura RDX	57	43
Acura RL	58	42
Acura TL	59	41
Acura TL	60	40
Acura TSX	60	40
Audi A3	61	39
Audi A4	60	40
Audi A6	60	40
Audi A8	53	47
Audi Q7	52	48
Audi R8	44	56
Audi R8 5.2	44	56
Audi R8 5.2 Spyder	44	56
Audi S4	60	40
Audi TT	60	40
BMW M3	50,5	49,5
BMW Série 3	50,5	49,5
BMW Série 5	49,7	50,3

	% av.	% ar.
BMW Série 6	52,6	47,4
BMW Série 7	49,9	50,1
BMW X3	50,8	49,2
BMW X5	50,2	49,8
BMW X5	51,7	48,3
BMW X5	52,9	47,1
BMW Z4	50	50
Cadillac CTS	51	49
Cadillac Escalade	52	48
Cadillac Escalade Hybrid	46	54
Chevrolet Avalanche	52	48
Chevrolet Impala	61	39
Chevrolet Suburban	51	49
Chevrolet Tahoe	52	48
Chrysler 300	53	47
Chrysler Town & Country	56	44
Dodge Caliber	58	42
Dodge Challenger	55	45
Dodge Charger	54	46
Dodge Grand Caravan	56	44

	% av.	% ar.
Dodge Viper	49,5	50,5
Dodge Viper Roadster	49,5	50,5
Ferrari 599	47	53
Ferrari 612 Scaglietti	46	54
Ferrari California	47	53
Ferrari F458 Italia	42	58
Ford Edge	60	40
Ford Expedition	49,6	50,4
Ford Fusion	59	41
Ford Mustang	55	45
Ford Mustang	56	44
GMC Terrain	58	42
Honda Accord	60	40
Honda Civic	61	39
Honda CR-V	57	43
Honda Element	57	43
Honda Fit	62	38
Honda Odyssey	55	45
Honda Ridgeline	58	42
InfinitiEX	53	47

	% av.	% ar.
Infiniti FX	54	46
Infiniti G	52	48
Infiniti QX	51	49
Jeep Compass	56	44
Jeep Grand Cherokee	53	47
Jeep Liberty	44	56
Jeep Patriot	57	43
Kia Rio/Rio5	61	39
Kia Sedona	58	42
Kia Soul	60	40
Lamborghini Gallardo LP 560-4	43	57
Lamborghini Gallardo LP 570-4 Superleggara	43	57
Lamborghini Murciélago LP 640	42	58
Lamborghini Murciélago LP 670-4 SV	42	58
Lexus LFA	48	52
Lincoln MKX	60	40
Lincoln MKZ	61	39
Lincoln Navigator	50	50
Lotus Elise	38	62
Lotus Elise SC	38	62

	% av.	% ar.
Maserati Gran Turismo	49	51
Maserati Quattroporte	49	51
Mercedes-Benz Classe CL	51	49
Mercedes-Benz Classe E	48	52
Mercedes-Benz Classe G	52	48
Mercedes-Benz Classe GL	53	47
Mercedes-Benz Classe M	54	46
Mercedes-Benz Classe R	52	48
Mercedes-Benz Classe S	52	48
Mercedes-Benz Classe SL	52	48
Mercedes-Benz Classe SLK	52	48
Mercedes-Benz SLS	47	53
Mitsubishi Eclipse	59	41
Mitsubishi Endeavor	57	43
Mitsubishi Lancer	56,7	43,3
Mitsubishi Lancer Evolution	57,4	42,6
Mitsubishi Lancer Sportback	58	42
Mitsubishi Outlander	55	45
Nissan Altima	62	38
Nissan Cube	51	49
Nissan Frontier	54	46
Nissan GT-R	53	47
Nissan Murano	59	41
Nissan Pathfinder	51	49
Nissan Quest	60	40
Nissan Rogue	60	40
Nissan Sentra	62	38
Nissan Versa	53	47
Nissan Z	53	47
Porsche Boxster	50	50
Saab 9-3	60	40

DISTRIBUTION DU POIDS EN ORDRE CROISSANT

	% av.	% ar.
Lotus Elise	38	62
Lotus Elise SC	38	62
Ferrari F458 Italia	42	58
Lamborghini Murciélago LP 640	42	58
Lamborghini Murciélago LP 670-4 SV	42	58
Lamborghini Gallardo LP 560-4	43	57
Lamborghini Gallardo LP 570-4 Superleggara	43	57
Audi R8	44	56
Audi R8 5.2	44	56
Audi R8 5.2 Spyder	44	56
Jeep Liberty	44	56
Cadillac Escalade Hybrid	46	54
Ferrari 612 Scaglietti	46	54
Ferrari 599	47	53
Ferrari California	47	53
Mercedes-Benz SLS	47	53
Lexus LFA	48	52
Mercedes-Benz Classe E	48	52
Maserati Gran Turismo	49	51
Maserati Quattroporte	49	51
Dodge Viper	49,5	50,5
Dodge Viper Roadster	49,5	50,5
Ford Expedition	49,6	50,4
BMW Série 5	49,7	50,3
BMW Série 7	49,9	50,1
BMW Z4	50	50
Lincoln Navigator	50	50
Porsche Boxster	50	50
BMW X5	50,2	49,8
BMW Série 3	50,5	49,5
BMW M3	50,5	49,5
BMW X3	50,8	49,2
Cadillac CTS	51	49
Chevrolet Suburban	51	49
Ford Expedition	51	49
Infiniti QX	51	49
Mercedes-Benz Classe CL	51	49
Nissan Cube	51	49
Nissan Pathfinder	51	49
BMW X5	51,7	48,3
Audi Q7	52	48
Cadillac Escalade	52	48
Chevrolet Avalanche	52	48
Chevrolet Tahoe	52	48
Infiniti G	52	48
Mercedes-Benz Classe E	52	48
Mercedes-Benz Classe G	52	48
Mercedes-Benz Classe R	52	48
Mercedes-Benz Classe S	52	48
Mercedes-Benz Classe SL	52	48
Mercedes-Benz Classe SLK	52	48
BMW Série 6	52,6	47,4
BMW X5	52,9	47,1
Audi A8	53	47
Chrysler 300	53	47
Infiniti EX	53	47
Infiniti G	53	47
Jeep Grand Cherokee	53	47
Mercedes-Benz Classe E	53	47
Mercedes-Benz Classe GL	53	47
Mercedes-Benz Classe S	53	47
Nissan GT-R	53	47
Nissan Versa	53	47
Nissan Z	53	47
Dodge Charger	54	46
Infiniti FX	54	46
Infiniti G	54	46
Mercedes-Benz Classe E	54	46
Mercedes-Benz Classe M	54	46
Mercedes-Benz Classe S	54	46
Nissan Frontier	54	46
Dodge Challenger	55	45
Dodge Charger	55	45
Ford Mustang	55	45
Honda Odyssey	55	45
Infiniti G	55	45
Mitsubishi Outlander	55	45
Acura MDX	56	44
Chrysler Town & Country	56	44
Dodge Grand Caravan	56	44
Ford Mustang	56	44
Infiniti G	56	44
Jeep Compass	56	44
Mercedes-Benz Classe M	56	44
Mitsubishi Lancer	56,7	43,3
Acura RDX	57	43
Honda CR-V	57	43
Honda Element	57	43
Jeep Patriot	57	43
Mitsubishi Endeavor	57	43
Mitsubishi Lancer Evolution	57,4	42,6
Acura RL	58	42
Dodge Caliber	58	42
GMC Terrain	58	42
Honda Ridgeline	58	42
Kia Sedona	58	42
Mitsubishi Lancer Sportback	58	42
Acura TL	59	41
Ford Fusion	59	41
Mitsubishi Eclipse	59	41
Nissan Murano	59	41
Acura CSX	60	40
Acura TL	60	40
Acura TSX	60	40
Audi A4	60	40
Audi S4	60	40
Audi A6	60	40
Audi TT	60	40
Ford Edge	60	40
Honda Accord	60	40
Kia Soul	60	40
Lincoln MKX	60	40
Mitsubishi Lancer	60	40
Nissan Quest	60	40
Nissan Rogue	60	40
Saab 38962	60	40
Audi A3	61	39
Chevrolet Impala	61	39
Ford Fusion	61	39
Honda Civic	61	39
Kia Rio/Rio5	61	39
Lincoln MKZ	61	39
Honda Fit	62	38
Nissan Altima	62	38
Nissan Sentra	62	38

RAYON DE BRAQUAGE

Une voiture tourne-t-elle sur un « dix cennes » ou sur un deux piastres ? Pour plusieurs personnes qui doivent se stationner souvent dans des endroits restreints, le rayon de braquage d'une voiture est un élément très important. C'est pourquoi le *Guide de l'auto* vous donne les meilleures à ce chapitre, en ordre croissant.

	(m)
smart Fortwo	8,7
Mazda MX-5	9,4
Toyota Yaris	9,4
Mazda2	9,8
Acura CSX	10,0
Hyundai Accent	10,0
Lotus Elise	10,0
Lotus Exige	10,0
Mitsubishi Lancer	10,0
Nissan Cube	10,0
Chevrolet Aveo	10,1
Lotus Evora	10,1
Suzuki Swift+	10,1
Ford Mustang	10,2
Lexus IS	10,2
Hyundai Elantra	10,3
Cadillac CTS	10,4
Ford Focus	10,4
Kia Magentis	10,4
Mazda3	10,4
Nissan Versa	10,4
Toyota Prius	10,4
Toyota Yaris	10,4
Honda Fit	10,5
Kia Soul	10,5
Mercedes-Benz Classe SLK	10,5
Honda Civic Sport	10,6
Honda CR-V	10,6
Kia Sportage	10,6
Mazda5	10,6
Mazda RX-8	10,6
MINI Cooper	10,6
Mitsubishi Outlander	10,6
Nissan Sentra	10,6
Subaru Impreza	10,6
Suzuki SX-4	10,6
Volvo C30	10,6
Volvo S40	10,6
Volvo V50	10,6
Volvo XC70	10,6
Audi A3	10,7
BMW Série 1	10,7
BMW Z4	10,7
Fiat 500	10,7
Maserati Gran Turismo	10,7
Hyundai Tucson	10,8
Jeep Liberty	10,8
Jeep Patriot	10,8
Kia Rondo	10,8
Kia Sportage	10,8
Mazda6	10,8
Nissan Z	10,8
Subaru Tribeca	10,8
Chevrolet Cruze	10,9
Hyundai Genesis	10,9
Hyundai Santa Fe	10,9
Hyundai Sonata	10,9
Kia Sorento	10,9
Lexus IS	10,9
Porsche 911	10,9
Volkswagen Eos	10,9
Volkswagen Golf	10,9
Volkswagen GTI	10,9
Volkswagen Passat	10,9
Audi TT	11,0
BMW Série 3	11,0
Cadillac CTS	11,0
Chevrolet HHR	11,0
Hyundai Genesis	11,0
Infiniti EX	11,0
Jaguar XK	11,0
Lexus IS	11,0
Lexus LS	11,0
Mazda3	11,0
Mercedes-Benz Classe C	11,0
Mercedes-Benz Classe E	11,0
Porsche Boxster	11,0
Scion tC	11,0
Suzuki Kizashi	11,0
Toyota Camry	11,0
Mercedes-Benz Classe SL	11,0
Aston Martin Vantage	11,1
Audi A4	11,1
Chrysler Sebring	11,1
Dodge Avenger	11,1
Dodge Nitro	11,1
Ford Escape	11,1
Porsche Cayman	11,1
Honda Element	11,2
Honda Odyssey	11,2
Hyundai Veracruz	11,2
Infiniti FX	11,2

FordFocus
GG YG 229

DERNIÈRE HEURE

Audi / BMW / Chevrolet / Ford / Kia / Lexus / Mazda / Mitsubishi / Scion

AUDI A7 SPORTBACK

Chez Mercedes-Benz, on a choisi le style coupé à quatre portières pour le modèle CLS. Aujourd'hui, cette voiture qui, jusqu'à présent était toute seule sur son orbite, s'apprête à accueillir des rivales qui ont plutôt opté pour la carrosserie de style coupé *hatchback* à cinq portières. Parmi ces prétendantes, nous retrouvons la toute nouvelle Audi A7 Sportback dont la silhouette ressemble à s'y méprendre à celle du Concept Sportback dévoilé à Détroit en 2009. Elle vient se positionner entre les Audi A6 et A8. D'entrée de jeu, elle dispose d'un nouveau moteur V6 TFSI de 300 chevaux. On parle déjà de versions S et RS en développement.

BMW X1 XDRIVE 30I

Cette année, le BMW X1 a fait son apparition sur les marchés européens et sous peu, il sera des nôtres en Amérique. Chez BMW, on le considère en tant que SAV (*Sport Activity Vehicule*) conçu autour des principaux éléments de la BMW de Série1. Sur le Vieux Continent, il bénéficie de motorisations essence et diesel, mais chez nous, un seul moteur est offert, soit l'increvable six cylindres en ligne de 3,0 litres de 255 chevaux accouplé à une boîte Steptronic à six rapports. De dimensions à peine inférieures à celles du modèle X3, il viendra affronter en Amérique, les Acura RDX, Cadillac SRX, Infiniti EX et Land Rover LR2.

CHEVROLET AVEO RS ET SPARK

Chevrolet Spark

Difficile de parler de l'un sans parler de l'autre puisqu'ils sont très complémentaires. Esthétiquement, ils se ressemblent à s'y méprendre sauf que le Spark est le plus petit des deux et que le modèle Aveo prend ici du galon. De son côté, le Spark nous parviendra des usines sud-coréennes de GM tandis que la 2e mouture de l'Aveo sera assemblée chez nos voisins du Sud. Dans les deux cas, on a prévu des moteurs quatre cylindres de petites cylindrées qui se veulent à la fois suffisamment puissants et très économiques. Ils seront tous les deux en concession au cours de l'année 2011.

FORD FOCUS

Les ingénieurs de Ford USA et Ford Europe ont fait de grands efforts pour que cette mouture de la Focus à diffusion mondiale soit une grande réussite, et ce, à tous les niveaux. Son allure n'est pas sans rappeler celle de la Fiesta, mais de gabarit supérieur, notamment dans sa version *hatchback* laquelle est secondée par une élégante berline. Sous son capot, on lui a assigné un nouveau moteur quatre cylindres de 2,0 litres à injection directe avec calage variable des soupapes qui développe 155 chevaux. Le tout accouplé à des boîtes manuelle ou automatique à six rapports.

KIA FORTE *HATCHBACK*

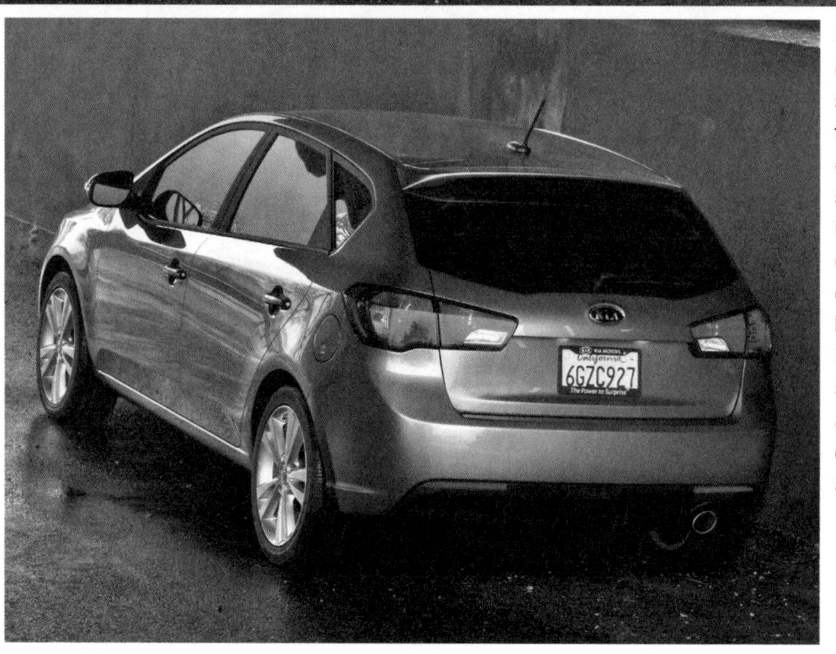

Chez Kia, la famille Forte ne cesse de s'agrandir. Ainsi, après la berline et le Koup voici que s'annonce une version *hatchback* à cinq portières. Une nouvelle déclinaison qui pourra offrir un peu plus de versatilité au niveau de ses différents espaces de chargement. À l'instar des autres membres de cette famille, elle donne le choix entre deux motorisations quatre cylindres de 2,0 et 2,4 litres qui développent respectivement 156 et 173 chevaux. Des transmissions, manuelle et automatique à six rapports, sont au programme. Elle peut accueillir aisément quatre passagers, lesquels bénéficient de généreux dégagements aux places arrière.

LEXUS CT 200H

Avec cette nouvelle venue, Lexus présentera pour la première fois une voiture de catégorie compacte de luxe. Elle sera vendue au début de 2011 et deviendra la seule voiture de sa catégorie à profiter d'une motorisation hybride. Sa technologie hybride est équivalente ou presque à celle de la légendaire Prius, sauf, qu'elle dispose de deux systèmes générateurs qui, ensemble, lui permettront d'acquérir une autonomie plus généreuse. Malgré ses dimensions compactes, cette berline *hatchback* à cinq portières à traction avant peut tout de même accueillir jusqu'à cinq occupants. À l'intérieur, ils bénéficieront d'un luxe, d'un confort et de gâteries dignes d'une Lexus.

MAZDA5

La récente — et surtout très attendue — Mazda5 dévoilée en grande première mondiale au Salon de Genève ne se contente pas d'arborer le museau « sourire » de la marque. Elle a aussi profité de multiples changements en profondeur. Avec ce nouvel avant et ses dimensions ragaillardies, elle présente un style plus mature et des plus aboutis, voire à incidence sportive. Demeurant fidèle à ses portières coulissantes, elle peut désormais accueillir jusqu'à sept passagers. Son nouveau moteur quatre cylindres à injection directe annonce une réduction des émanations de CO_2 à hauteur de 15 %.

MITSUBISHI RVR

Le premier VUS compact de Mitsubishi est passé à un cheveu de porter le nom Outlander Sport au Canada, mais fort heureusement, on a décidé de l'appeler RVR. Esthétiquement, il a l'air d'un clone de son grand frère Outlander, mais en fait, ses dimensions sont équivalentes à celles du Volkswagen Tiguan. Offert à compter de la mi-octobre, il est propulsé par un moteur écoénergétique à quatre cylindres, marié à une boîte manuelle à 5 vitesses de série, ou, en option, à une boîte Sportronic CVT à 6 vitesses, contrôlée par des palettes de changement de vitesse en alliage de magnésium.

RANGE ROVER EVOQUE

La marque britannique Range Rover célèbre cette année son 40e anniversaire de naissance et ses dirigeants profitent de l'occasion pour nous présenter un tout nouveau modèle appelé Range Rover Evoque. Ce dernier quitte radicalement le style conventionnel aux formes très angulaires des véhicules de la marque pour adopter la silhouette d'un coupé sport utilitaire des plus séduisants. Offert en versions à deux ou quatre roues motrices, il sera et de loin le véhicule le plus compact, le plus léger et par conséquent le plus économique jamais produit par cette marque. Il sera offert dans plus de 160 pays à compter de l'été prochain.

SCION IQ

Les Scion tC, xD et xB arriveront au Canada dès cet automne et la lilliputienne iQ suivra quelques mois plus tard. Cette microvoiture, contrairement à sa rivale Smart, peut accueillir presque quatre passagers ou si vous préférez trois adultes plus un enfant (ou un animal de compagnie !). Sous son tout petit capot se cache un moteur quatre cylindres de 1,3 litre qui produit 90 chevaux. Ce bloc-moteur est accouplé à une boîte CVT. Aux fins de sécurité, la structure et la cage ont été renforcies tandis que l'habitacle renferme 10 coussins gonflables de série.

SUZUKI SWIFT

Avec l'arrivée en grand nombre de petites voitures sous-compactes en Amérique du Nord, telles les Ford Fiesta, Honda Fit, Mazda2 et bien d'autres, il est indéniable que le constructeur Suzuki devra répondre à cette nouvelle demande et le retour chez nous de la vraie Suzuki Swift ne serait que bénéfique. Avec une longueur hors tout de 3850 mm, elle viendrait ainsi se positionner côté dimensions entre la Toyota Yaris et la Honda Fit. En Europe, elle est offerte en versions *hatchback* à trois ou cinq portières. Un moteur de 1,5 litre d'un peu plus de 100 chevaux devrait faire l'affaire en Amérique.

Une page couverture signée Bill Petro

Cette année, pour réaliser la photo de notre page couverture, le *Guide de l'auto* a eu la chance de bénéficier des services du photographe Bill Petro dont la réputation n'est plus à faire. En effet, au fil des années, le photographe torontois s'est spécialisé dans la photographie de véhicules motorisés qu'il s'agisse d'automobiles, de motos et de VTT. D'ailleurs, son studio est spécialement équipé pour photographier des motos ou des VTT. En plus, pendant des années, Bill a été le photographe attitré au chapitre des produits d'un important constructeur automobile japonais. Son expertise en la matière explique l'excellence des photos de la Pléthore que l'on retrouve sur les couvertures avant et arrière de cette 45e édition du *Guide de l'auto*. Il faut également ajouter qu'il collabore de façon régulière aux publications *Cycle Canada* et *Moto Journal*.

La séance photo s'est déroulée pendant deux jours. La première journée a été essentiellement consacrée aux photos d'action de la Pléthore. Il faut préciser que la photo de la page couverture n'est pas un montage ou un trucage photo réalisé avec Photoshop, mais une authentique photo d'action réalisée à l'aide d'un appareil photo numérique Canon 1D sur lequel on avait installé un gyroscope. Cela a permis d'utiliser une très faible vitesse d'obturation et une grande stabilité de l'image. L'utilisation d'un gyroscope explique en plus la netteté de la voiture et le filé du sol et du ciel. Pour capter ces images, Bill s'est installé dans la soute à bagages d'une Volvo familiale qui précédait la Pléthore. Le *supercar* québécois était piloté par son concepteur Luc Chartrand qui a pris beaucoup de plaisir à l'exercice. La seconde journée a été consacrée aux photos de détail de la voiture qui ont été utilisées dans le texte de Marc Lachapelle portant sur la voiture.

Sur le plan technique, Bill n'utilise que des appareils Canon 1D de différentes moutures et les objectifs professionnels de la marque allant du zoom grand angulaire et télé de moyen amplitude à des super téléobjectifs de 500 et 600 mm de 2,8F d'ouverture. Toutes les photos sont captées en mode Raw avant d'être transformées dans un format final.

Achevé d'imprimer à Scott, Canada
sur les presses d'Imprimerie Solisco Inc. en août 2010